Provided By:
Family Nurse Practitioner Program
OU College of Nursing

THE PROCESS OF HUMAN DEVELOPMENT

THIRD EDITION

A Holistic Life-Span Approach

THE PROCESS OF HUMAN DEVELOPMENT

THIRD EDITION

A Holistic Life-Span Approach

CLARA SHAW SCHUSTER, Ph.D., R.N.

Formerly Assistant Professor of Nursing
Kent State University
Kent, Ohio
Child and Family Development Specialist
Developmental/Educational Consultant

SHIRLEY SMITH ASHBURN, M.S., R.N.

Professor of Nursing
Cypress College
Cypress, California

J. B. LIPPINCOTT COMPANY   *Philadelphia*

New York   London   Hagerstown

Sponsoring Editor: Barbara Nelson Cullen
Project Editor: Amy P. Jirsa
Indexer: Anne Cope
Design Coordinator: Kathy Kelley-Luedtke
Cover and Interior Design: Susan Blaker
Production Manager: Helen Ewan
Production Coordinator: Nannette Winski
Compositor: Circle Graphics
Printer/Binder: Courier-Westford

3rd Edition

6   5   4   3   2

Library of Congress Cataloging-in-Publication Data

Schuster, Clara Shaw.
    The process of human development: a holistic life-span
approach / Clara Shaw Schuster, Shirley Smith Ashburn. — 3rd ed.
        p.   cm.
    Includes bibliographical references and index.
    ISBN 0-397-54881-8
    1. Developmental psychology.   2. Life cycle, Human.
  3. Developmental biology.   I. Ashburn, Shirley
Smith.   II. Title.
    BF713.S36   1992
    155 — dc20   91-21236
                                                          CIP

Any procedure or practice described in this book should be
applied by the health-care practitioner under appropriate
supervision in accordance with professional standards of care
used with regard to the unique circumstances that apply in each
practice situation. Care has been taken to confirm the accuracy of
information presented and to describe generally accepted
practices. However, the authors, editors, and publisher cannot
accept any responsibility for errors or omissions or for any
consequences from application of the information in this book
and make no warranty, express or implied, with respect to the
contents of the book.

Every effort has been made to ensure drug selections and
dosages are in accordance with current recommendations and
practice. Because of ongoing research, changes in government
regulations and the constant flow of information on drug therapy,
reactions and interactions, the reader is cautioned to check the
package insert for each drug for indications, dosages, warnings
and precautions, particularly if the drug is new or infrequently
used.

Photo credit information appears after the Appendices

Our thanks and praise to the Lord for providing:
  resources,
  wisdom,
  strength,
  endurance,
beyond our natural endowments

For their inspiration,
  patience,
  love,
  support,
  encouragement,
in thanks, we dedicate this book to:
  our mentors,
  our students,
  our family members:
    Richard,
    Elizabeth,
    Jodi

Dr. Clara Shaw Schuster unexpectedly passed away on August 29, 1991.

This edition is a tribute to Dr. Schuster's rigorous scholarship, and is a living gift from her to all the students, practitioners, parents, and others who will benefit from the information presented.

Richard Schuster

I was a young and relatively inexperienced educator when I first began working with Clara Schuster in 1972. She encouraged me to engage in independent critical thinking, and taught me more efficient ways to organize data. Clara Schuster was one of the most creative and productive individuals with whom I have ever shared a project. Her neverending perseverance and commitment to perfection remains unsurpassed.

Shirley Smith Ashburn

CONTRIBUTING AUTHORS

> *To know someone here or there with whom you feel there is understanding in spite of distances or thoughts unexpressed—that can make of this earth a garden.*
>
> —JOHANN WOLFGANG VON GOETHE

James R. Abel, M.D.
Chapter 20
Coordinator, Pediatric Department; Senior Staff Physician, University Health Services, University of Massachusetts, Amherst, Massachusetts

Lois G. Andreas, M.S.N., R.N.
Chapter 36
Assistant Professor of Nursing, Kent State University—Tuscarawas, New Philadelphia, Ohio; Nursing Consultant/Educator

Shirley Smith Ashburn, M.S., R.N.
Chapters 6, 8, 9, 10, 11, 26, 35, and Appendix B
Professor of Nursing, Cypress College, Cypress, California

Robert Bornstein, Ph.D.
Chapters 27 and 38
Associate Professor of Psychology; Fellow of the Scripps Gerontological Center, Miami University, Oxford, Ohio

Helen Bray-Garretson, Ph.D.
Chapter 22
Clinical Psychologist, Hillcrest Educational Center, Pittsfield, Massachusetts

Carol M. Cariglio, B.S., P.T.
Chapter 6
Physical Therapist, Mansfield, Ohio

Kaye V. Cook, Ph.D.
Chapter 22
Associate Professor of Psychology, Gordon College, Wenham, Massachusetts; Staff Psychologist,

Children's Hospital, Harvard Medical School, Boston, Massachusetts

Pearl Slavik Cowen, Ph.D., R.N.
Chapter 33
Assistant Professor, University of Iowa, Iowa City, Iowa

Randy L. Cronk, Ph.D.
Chapters 24 and 25
Assistant Professor of Psychology, Mount Vernon Nazarene College, Mount Vernon, Ohio

M. Patricia Donahue, Ph.D., R.N.
Chapter 19
Associate Professor of Nursing, University of Iowa, Iowa City, Iowa

Jarrell W. Garsee, Ph.D.
Chapter 16
Adjunct Professor of Psychology, Southern Nazarene University, Bethany, Oklahoma; Senior Pastor, Anaheim First Church of the Nazarene, Anaheim, California

Keith A. Holly, Ph.D.
Chapter 21
Professor of Psychology, Point Loma Nazarene College, San Diego, California

Carol A. Miller, M.S.N., R.N.,C.
Chapter 37
Lecturer, Cleveland State University; Clinical Instructor, Frances Payne Bolton School of Nursing, Case Western Reserve University, Cleveland, Ohio

Cecil R. Paul, Ph.D.
Chapter 28
President, Eastern Nazarene College, Wollaston,
    Massachusetts

F. Wayne Reno, Ed.D.
Chapter 25
Professor of Psychology, Mount Vernon Nazarene
    College, Mount Vernon, Ohio

Debra A. Ronk, B.S., O.T.R./L.
Chapter 9
Occupational Therapist, Mansfield, Ohio

Clara Shaw Schuster, Ph.D., R.N.
*Chapters 1, 2, 3, 4, 5, 7, 8, 10, 11, 13, 14, 15, 16,
17, 18, 20, 21, 23, 25, 27, 29, 30, 31, 32, 34, 39,
Appendix A, C, G, and I*
Assistant Professor of Nursing, Kent State University,
    Kent, Ohio; Child and Family Development
    Specialist; Developmental/Educational Consultant

Linda M. Smolak, Ph.D.
Chapter 12
Associate Professor of Psychology, Kenyon College,
    Gambier, Ohio

PREFACE

The process of human development is at once both simple and complex: simple when we observe the orderly, uncomplicated evolution of an individual as described by the theoretical frameworks of Erikson, Piaget, or Maslow; complicated when we consider all the unpredictable variations in human development created by the interaction of the developing individual with the environment.

Each of us is unique. Differences in inherited potentials, interests, and background experiences of individuals can both enrich and frustrate relationships. When our interests and experiences are similar to those of another person, we are more likely to feel comfortable with that person and seek frequent contact. When life's experiences are widely divergent, we may find ourselves disliking or even avoiding those whom we do not understand. We are uncomfortable when forced into closer contact with them as co-workers or in a practitioner-client relationship. Understanding can lead to the ability to accept and to work with other people more objectively, less judgmentally, with more compassion, and with greater effectiveness.

The Process of Human Development is designed to explore comprehensively (holistically) the human experience, particularly in Western cultures. It is the study of our own development and potential futures. Information is considered relevant when it facilitates the answering of questions and offers opportunity for better understanding of both ourselves and others.

This text focuses on the functioning of healthy individuals—persons developing their potentials in spite of limitations—not just persons free of illness or stressors. Five major domains (biophysical, cognitive, affective, social, and spiritual) are discussed from a pragmatic perspective in an attempt to meet the overlapping needs of professionals in people-oriented occupations. An attempt is made to identify the major factors that affect the development of these domains—factors which inspire the beauty and diversity of humanity. Also discussed are conceptual, situational, or developmental crises and the common variations in development that may be exceptional but are not considered pathological.

This book is dedicated to opening the mind of the reader rather than merely filling it. The reader is challenged to analyze the empirical data and theories presented in the text and to synthesize these with their own experiences and observations. The underlying goal is to facilitate the reader's ability to assess individuals and families, and to create and evaluate intervention strategies designed to maximize the potentials of individual clients in all five domains. This book presents the most significant observations and theories from multiple disciplines and our own experience. The information covered is not meant to be final or complete; it represents an attempt to introduce some order and integration into the increasing bulk of available knowledge. The one overriding criterion for inclusion was relevance to life in technologically oriented societies. We have avoided focusing on developmental research per se in favor of a practical approach to understanding human behaviors in today's world as explained by research, concepts, and theories. Inclusion of observations, concepts, and concerns from various disciplines provides an interdisciplinary approach to development throughout the life span. Developmental changes that are significant to parents, teachers, nurses, social workers, and other human services practitioners are targeted.

To facilitate study, four of the domains are presented separately and chronologically from conception through old age. The fifth (spiritual) is integrated as appropriate throughout. Each chapter provides a verbal picture of the "how," "what," and "why" of behavior at each age. The authors emphasize, however, that **each individual must be approached as a total, unique entity, not as a stereotyped representative of a particular domain, age group, or social environment.**

The rapidity of change is a significant factor in deciding the amount of space allotted to each developmental level. During the first days of life, hours are significant; during the first weeks of life, days are significant; during the first months of life, weeks are significant; during the first years of life, months are significant. Gradually, years become adequate guides for study, and during the adult years, phases offer sufficient parameters.

THE AUTHORS' PERSPECTIVE ON HUMAN DEVELOPMENT

Everyone has his or her own perspective and ideas about the nature of humanity. The authors—each one in this text—also have theirs. It colors the research they cite, and the examples they share. Although we have attempted to present many other views objectively—even those we disagree with—in fairness to the reader, we share the biases of the primary authors. Our own backgrounds, experiences, and education, and the unique blending of these factors are bound to be reflected in both the content and the emphasis rendered.

We believe that **people are holistic organisms** who can be understood only when all relevant factors are considered. All behavior must be seen in context and appreciated for its meaning to the individual. Any intervention must consider the impact *of* and *on* the other domains.

We believe that **human potentials are biologically determined,** but that the environment can facilitate or hinder the realization of those potentials. The functioning of the individual, therefore, is subject to the unique blending of his or her biological potentials, maturation, opportunities, and experiences.

We believe that **individuals play a crucial role in their own destiny.** Even the infant seeks new stimuli and attempts to control events that directly impact him or her. With increased maturity in all five domains, we are able to create our own attitudes, goals, and meanings in life. Within the sphere of our influence and resources, we also are able to create our own environments. Thus, we are not at the mercy of heredity and environment, but of our own conscious and unconscious will to find meaning and satisfaction in life.

We believe that a person's current behavior is the result of a unique integration of knowledge and past experiences blended with the anticipation of future events. As such, **behavior is an integrated function of all five domains.** Early experiences are significant because they must be integrated into all future experiences. A critical experience can continue to influence later behavior, or it can be overruled if a person has several contradicting experiences later in life. From this perspective, development is not complete at age 21; **humans continue to construct and change themselves throughout their entire life span.** Those who settle into ruts of behavior or fail to find life-giving goals and meanings, "die" before their bodies do. They survive, but live without verve or direction.

The family system is crucial to the continued development of its members—both children and adults. The primary caregiver (whether mother, father, or other adult) is the most significant component in the early biophysical, cognitive, affective, social, and spiritual developmental of the child. This person structures the environment to provide the challenges and reciprocity that comprise early education. Children, in turn, offer challenges which provide opportunities for continued social, emotional, and spiritual development of the adults.

We believe that **the major responsibility of parenthood is to prepare the child for adulthood.** Successful adulthood is the ability to cope with the demands of one's culture flexibly and independently. The skills for successful coping are most naturally learned during childhood. These skills are most easily learned when the parents (1) offer good role models; (2) moderate guidance according to the child's developmental level; (3) are consistent in their expectations; and (4) love both themselves and their children enough to enjoy a warm, respectful, and affirming relationship.

We believe that **all people have the right to maximize their potentials.** We believe that every person wants to be his or her best, and that most individuals are capable of higher levels of functioning. Even severely disabled persons have the potential for continued development with every experience, and therefore, for gaining satisfaction from the dynamic process of self-realization. Individuals who are deficient in one or more areas still possess potentials that can be developed for fuller living; many individuals only need the opportunity, encouragement, or both, to express their talents and potentials.

We observe that each reference group defines what is "normal" for its members, and therefore that a wide range of "normal" not only exists, but is a subjective criterion. In other words, **"normal" people are not all alike.** This variation in people provides challenge, interest, and allows for interdependent cooperation for a better world.

We believe that **adult maturity is discovered when one gives of one's self to meet the needs of another,** when one finds the balance between personal rights and societal responsibilities, when one masters life's challenges, and when one is comfortable with oneself. When a person is sure of his or her own identity, there can be self-respect and true respect (versus fear) for others.

In order **to reach maximal levels of functioning, each person must be offered opportunities and encouragement** by family members and other significant persons. The key to offering support is a belief in, and a commitment to, the value of the other person. For some, this means love; for others it is intimate caring. However this commitment is shared or conveyed, it requires the valuing of the other person as strongly as one values oneself. This is an intangible element, but most of us are intuitively aware of whether the other person **really** cares. It is this commitment to others that we hope you will find in your relationships with family and friends and carry with you into professional contacts. We hope that by exploring the process of human development, you will increase your appreciation of holistic human development.

A frost pattern on a winter window beautifully captures the authors' view of human development. Each pattern, like each one of us, is unique. The potential for growth is always present. The form, direction, and expressions of both are influenced by environmental conditions. Although each entity is unique in itself, there are commonalities and explanations for the patterns and behaviors displayed (even though we may not be able to identify them). The beauty of both is in the eye of the beholder; none is inherently good, bad, or deformed. Each time we look, we see a new feature or develop a renewed appreciation for the uniqueness and value of the patterns and the person.

This text presents a transdisciplinary approach to the study of the human life span. It is hoped that from this study you will better understand both yourself and others. We hope that you will find professional satisfaction by helping others to maximize their potentials, for in so doing, you will begin to maximize your own potentials and find richer meaning in life.

With these thoughts in mind, we challenge you to a richer, more meaningful relationship with yourself and others as you begin a holistic study of the process of human development through the life span.

Let each become all that he was created, capable of being: expand, if possible, to his full growth, and show himself at length in his own shape and stature, be these what they may.

Thomas Carlyle
C.S.S.
S.S.A.

ACKNOWLEDGMENTS

> *It is one of the most beautiful compensations of this life that no man can sincerely try to help another without helping himself.*
>
> —RALPH WALDO EMERSON

There are many people over the course of the years who have contributed directly or indirectly to the content, the scope, and the approach of this book. Only a few can be formally recognized, but without their expertise and advice, the quality of the text would have been greatly diluted. We particularly express our thanks to the following persons for reviewing parts of the manuscript in process or providing valuable insight and information; their input has contributed to a more comprehensive and comprehensible text:

Carol M. Cariglio, B.S., P.T.
Jennifer Young Carroll, M.A., CCC-SLP
Thomas Clifford, Ph.D.
Kay Cubie, B.A.
Lora Donoho, Ph.D.
Eula Gould, M.A., R.N.
Ruth Hackman, B.A.
R. Michael Jenkins, Ph.D., R.D., L.D.
Carol Liles, M.Ed.
Paul Madtes, Ph.D.
Jeanette McConnell, R.N.
Douglas McLeod, D.D.S.
Carolyn Peugh, R.D.M.S./R.T.
Helena Piano, M.L.S.
Artie Sue Pisanelli, M.S.N., R.N.
Elaine Popewiny, R.N.
Rhonda Kiser Riddle, M.A.
Debra Romas, M.A., CCC-SLP
Debra A. Ronk, B.S., O.T.R./L.

Lincoln Stevens, M.Litt.
Laura Tappan, B.A.
Mary Tiedeman, Ph.D., R.N.
Alex Varughese, Ph.D.
Jon Williams, Ph.D.
Kathy Wukela, R.N.
William Youngman, D.Min.

Other people have offered invaluable advocacy and support—providing meaningful encouragement and assistance through difficult times:

Mary Steed Ewell
Eileen Hains
Vi Wells Maxwell
Robert McLaughlin
Alan Reed
Alan Schronk
James Skon
Ann West
Students, friends, and colleagues

One person deserves special recognition for his commitment to a quality book—Richard Schuster. He typed most of this book, assiduously relinquishing evenings, weekends, holidays, and vacation time—typing away even when tired or ill, while maintaining a fulltime career as a college librarian. Thank you, Richard, for the tangible evidence of your love and support.

CONTENTS

INTRODUCTION FOR THE PROFESSOR

The third edition of *The Process of Human Development: A Holistic Approach* introduces some major new concepts and developmental tasks as well as revised and updated material. Some content has been consolidated (e.g., cognitive development during the adult years), while new information has been added to reflect increased understanding of development in each of the five domains (biophysical, cognitive, affective, social, and spiritual).

This book is not focused toward any one discipline; the material has been written for any person who has chosen a service-oriented career. Because the text is geared toward students who are preparing for professions in applied settings, empirical data are the base for the text, but clinical applicability is the focus.

Practitioners already in the field, such as social workers, counselors, teachers, nurses, rehabilitation therapists, physicians, lawyers, and ministers have found this book to be a valuable resource. Many public libraries and parents have purchased the book as a permanent reference because of its completeness and readability.

As a text, *The Process of Human Development* is intended to lay a broad foundation for understanding the ontogenetic process of human development; to explain and describe behaviors, not just theories. The book may be used as a text for students who do not plan to take additional courses in human development, but it is anticipated that the student will acquire more knowledge in those areas germane to his or her chosen profession.

Use of *The Process of Human Development* has been much broader than initially anticipated. It has been used by senior students enrolled in seminars designed to integrate and apply information studied in isolated courses, as well as by undergraduate students enrolled in "Human Growth and Development" courses. Some doctoral programs have assigned the text as a foundation for a holistic approach to further professional development. *The Process of Human Development* has been recommended as a resource for persons preparing for the psychology licensing examination. Bookstores and students indicate that a greater than usual number of students opt to keep the book for later reference because of the clarity of explanations, the inclusion of difficult-to-find information, and the detail of the index which makes topics easy to locate.

Over the years, we have discovered that before we can treat or teach a **person as a patient**, we must greet and reach the **patient as a person**. This requires understanding and acceptance of the client's actions, reactions, and interactions on the basis of developmental levels and the person's perceived needs. The patient's priorities often are different from the practitioner's priorities even though the end goal may be the same. The client's perceived needs must be met before he or she is able to attend or commit to what the practitioner may identify as more critical matters.

Often, the client's perceived needs and concerns fall outside the traditional focus of the profession. Thus, it is essential to have a comprehensive knowledge of normal development and its variations to understand and to meet the needs of those with whom we work. The professional person's knowledge about human growth and development must go beyond the confines of a specific professional data base to encompass information from many disciplines before one can obtain a truly holistic view.

A broad data base is fundamental for accurate interpretation of behaviors and the development of appropriate intervention approaches. For example, a husband may develop headaches or nausea during his wife's pregnancy, a newborn many develop jaundice, a 2-year-old may bite a new baby, or a 15-year-old girl may not yet be menstruating. Are these signs of pathology or merely variations of the normal? The difference between platitudes and reassurance lies in the practitioner's knowledge of "normal" and its variations.

As practitioners, it helps to understand our own biases, needs, and development. Inadequate self-awareness may prevent sensitivity to the client's needs and cause us to focus on our own agenda, thus decreasing our effectiveness on the client's behalf.

The primary authors are of the opinion that no single authority or discipline could adequately cover an area as complex or multidisciplinary as normal human development. Consequently, this volume combines the knowledge and observations of contributing authors from diverse disciplines. The professor may wish to selectively emphasize particular chapters, identifying those areas that the students of a particular discipline need to explore in greater depth. Finding the balance between covering too much or too little has been difficult at times. There is always opportunity for expansion of data in the classroom or through special assignments. Some topics have been covered in more depth because of the relative scarcity of data or the difficulty in collecting pertinent resources.

This book is not intended to replace a text in general psychology, sociology, or physiology. Students who have had courses in one or more of these areas may find some topics easier to understand, but the authors have endeavored to present enough information to facilitate comprehension by even the most naïve student.

The third edition is organized into 12 developmentally sequenced units. Unit I may be considered the introduction to the text, and Unit XII, the conclusion. In most units, the first two or three chapters cover normal biophysical, cognitive, and psychosocial development of that phase of the life span. Unit V covers critical concepts and common factors that transcend more than one phase of the life span.

The family provides the major environment through which society transmits its values and influences the individual's development. Events that affect the family will also affect the development of the individual and vice versa. Unit IX presents the family—its formation, development, maintenance, and problems.

We suggest that the chapters be read in sequence. However, unique situations and professorial preferences may call for longitudinal study of one domain. Because a holistic approach necessitates integration of domains, the chapters dealing with critical concepts (e.g., death) and special issues (e.g., uniqueness) may touch on several domains. At the same time, a specific experience (e.g., childbirth) or construct (e.g., turn-taking) may be approached from different aspects in as many chapters. Most concepts (e.g, attachment) or theories (e.g, Information Processing) are presented but once, in the most pertinent chapter, even though they may apply to multiple age groups. The index is purposefully detailed to facilitate finding material of interest to the reader.

An **Instructor's Manual** with **Test Bank** is available. Included in the Instructor's Manual section are Objectives, Terminology, Teaching-Learning Activities, and Discussion Questions. The Test Bank provides objective-type test questions for each chapter of the text.

We hope that this book will facilitate your teaching of human growth and development. We also hope that you will feel comfortable recommending the book to practitioners already in the field to refresh their knowledge of human development and to serve as a reference on normal development. We would appreciate your comments and recommendations on content.

Clara S. Schuster

INTRODUCTION FOR THE STUDENT

It has been suggested that the real title of this book should be *What You Always Wanted to Know About What Makes People Tick But Didn't Know Where to Look or Who to Ask.* Even with such an impressive title, however, the book is not an encyclopedia of human behavior; rather, it is an **overview** of human development from conception through old age. We have attempted to focus on the priorities of data from many disciplines and to offer explanations of how and why people of various ages and circumstances function as they do. People are different—that is what makes them so interesting to study and to know, and at times, it is also what makes them so frustrating.

Sometimes you will recognize yourself or someone you know in the descriptions of development. You may recall your own examples from past experiences. You may laugh; you may even cry. At other times you may become angry or even argue with the data or theories presented, wondering how any rational person could ever propose such a theory or think and behave in such a manner. You may not always agree with each view offered, neither do we, but our professional experience has proved to us that knowledge of many views is essential in assessing and planning intervention strategies. This is considered an eclectic approach. Throughout this book, you will consciously and unconsciously begin to evaluate and develop your own theories (a process we hope you will continue throughout your life span).

As you study how you have developed and will continue to develop and learn how others have developed through life experiences quite different from your own, it is hoped that you will discover new facets of your own potentials, and that you will find many of your stereotypes beginning to mellow

and your appreciation for the experiences and needs of others increasing. The study of individuals who possess common traits (e.g., age, gender, disability, living circumstances) is helpful in understanding trends, but **each individual must be viewed in light of his or her unique combination of traits, potentials, and needs.**

Because professionals need to be aware of what data are available to the lay public through literature and other forms of mass media, you are encouraged to listen critically to radio and television broadcasts, and to read and review articles written in the lay literature. Such sources often generate questions or requests for help from your clients. Many of the articles are authoritative and well written. At times you may find it helpful to refer clients to a particular article. Pertinent resources are listed throughout the text. You may wish to begin your own file of additional agencies and organizations to which you may refer clients in the future. No professional person has all the answers to a client's questions, but a good practitioner will help the client to find pertinent resources where answers, support, equipment, or assistance are available.

We hope that you enjoy this book. We have included what we wished we had known or understood earlier in our own professional and personal lives. We have attempted to present you with comprehensible material that is relatively free of professional jargon, yet comprehensive in scope. Most importantly, we hope this text will help you to lay a solid foundation on which you can and will build in the years ahead of you as a practitioner—that it will enable you to be more empathic in all your relationships, realistic in your expectations, and supportive in your approaches.

THE PROCESS OF HUMAN DEVELOPMENT

THIRD EDITION

A Holistic Life-Span Approach

I PROLOGUE

Changes are both inevitable and necessary as a person travels through the life span. Each developmental phase presents its own unique and predictable challenges as one faces (1) biophysical, (2) environmental, and (3) personal pressures for change.

The infant begins life as a highly dependent, undisciplined, self-centered, demanding person. Gradually, over the years, as the person faces and masters the challenges of life, changes occur, and a mature, highly independent, self-disciplined, allocentric, generative person emerges. However, high-level health and maturity are not automatically achieved. Much depends on the interface between the unique needs and abilities of the individual and the environmental opportunities and pressures. Stereotyped expectations based on age, gender, or any other factor can be repressive. The environment must recognize and encourage individual uniqueness in all five domains of development (physical, intellectual, social, emotional, and spiritual) to maximize the potentials of each person as well as of society as a whole.

The most significant factor precipitating change is the growth and development of the neurological, skeletal, muscular, and reproductive systems, which present the person with differing challenges and opportunities at each phase of the life span. These changes provide biologically mediated challenges for higher level goals and a gradual unfolding of the person's potentials.

As family and society provide and coordinate the environment, they set specific expectations and exert pressures for the growing person to assume more mature functioning. They also provide the guidance and contingencies (rewards and punishments) that help a person to channel changes in the culturally approved direction. The social environment facilitates or sets limits on the extent to which a person is able to maximize his or her potentials.

The third major factor influencing development is a person's willingness to actively seek and uniquely create meaning from interactions with the environment. Self-generated change initially emerges from curiosity and the need for affiliation. However, as the individual matures, he or she consciously strives to master increasingly complex skills, imitates the behavior of others, and eventually adopts or creates goals and values that guide behaviors and contribute to individuality. Self-generated changes require increasing self-discipline as the person internalizes specific values and pursues individualized goals.

With this edition of *The Process of Human Development: A Holistic Life-Span Approach*, Clara Schuster introduces a new set of developmental tasks. These tasks reflect the collective wisdom of others such as Erikson, Piaget, Mahler, Duvall, Curran, Brazelton, Maslow, and Kohlberg. Their ideas served as springboards for this holistic set of developmental tasks for the life span.

Schuster has found that despite differences in financial, political, or biophysical circumstances, some tasks emerge that are common to the healthy growth and development of individuals. Mastery of these tasks is essential for self-confidence, self-esteem, the maximization of potentials, and successful adaptation to the exigencies of life. These developmental tasks are presented for their heuristic as well as their descriptive value. The individual who is maturing in a healthy fashion will work on the designated tasks throughout the indicated phase of life. Mastery should be complete by the end of that phase. However, individuals may begin to work on some tasks before the designated period, and many will continue to work on the tasks beyond the time period specified.

These developmental tasks are not seen as inclusive or exclusive, but rather to identify crucial issues leading toward maturity, regardless of the cultural context. They can serve as a general basis for assessment and for the development of holistic intervention strategies appropriate to the individual, family, or culture. Not every task is equally significant to later development. Those tasks deemed most crucial to continued maturation are marked with an asterisk.

Each unit is introduced by its corresponding developmental tasks. The epilogue lists 5 factors which the family and society need to provide to its members to ensure high-level wellness and mastery of the developmental tasks. All the tasks are presented for review in Appendix C.

Study of the Human Life Span

Clara S. Schuster

The process of human development is influenced by three interacting forces: biophysical endowment, psychosocial environment, and self-creation. The first two factors affect our lives even before we are born. Each individual receives a unique genetic makeup at the moment of conception that establishes the substrata of biophysical potentials, cognitive abilities, special talents, and, some believe, temperament that thus sets a ceiling on ultimate levels of development. However, the existence of biological propensities does not imply that behavior is reflexive, predetermined, or immutable.[8]

Our psycho-sociocultural heritage is just as powerful an influence as our biological heritage. Actualization of genetic potentials, or self-fulfillment, depends on the nurturing and opportunities available for expressing and developing one's potentials. Variables such as the neighborhood in which our family lives (urban or rural, suburban or ghetto), economic level, basic attitude of our parents toward us (i.e., were we wanted, understood, loved?), religious orientation, educational and cultural opportunities, size of our family, and availability of medical care all influence the formation of our attitudes, personality, and skill repertoire. Even the political climate, cultural philosophies, geographic location, and ethnic affiliation have their impact.

Each person is a unique expression of the total combination of hereditary and environmental factors that touch his or her life, not the sum of each, but the result of their interactions. This does not mean, however, that we are at the mercy of heredity and environment, only that these two factors provide the raw materials out of which we uniquely create our self, our approaches, and our responses to life. Each of us chooses what to attend to from the multiple stimuli in the environment, and we create our own unique understanding of events. Each person chooses where to focus one's energies and how to approach life's challenges. Thus, we actively construct our knowledge of the world and ourselves (Fig. 1-1).

The process of human development has almost as many interpretations and theories as there are people to give their views. Our own life history influences our response to the behavior and values of others and our understanding of human development. Remember the proverb about the six blind men who each gave a different description of the elephant they examined by touch (one felt the tail, one an ear, another the trunk, a fourth felt a leg, the fifth a tusk, and the last the side)? Each of us tends to explain human nature, the sequences of development, and cause-effect relationships on the basis of our own experiences and observations. Each profession, likewise, tends to investigate selectively those attributes of the individual that are considered relevant to that particular discipline. These differing orientations frequently appear to offer incompatible or conflicting concepts. However, when humans are viewed from a holistic perspective, integration of varying concepts is essential and compatible. It would be difficult to explain how an elephant ate with a tail or moved from one place to another with an ear. One must have some broader theory or knowledge to understand the pattern and meaning of what is observed. Without this

FIGURE 1–1.
Even twins develop different personalities and concepts of their world as they experience each event differently by their selective attention to different stimuli.

knowledge, events are viewed from a narrow, biased perspective. Knowledge functions as a filter and an organizer to help interpret the environment.[12]

An understanding of qualitative differences in functioning based on age or developmental level is relatively recent. The following review of history, research methodology, and theories of human nature offers a foundation for the remainder of the text.

HISTORICAL PERSPECTIVE

Everyday life continues to be influenced by the history of the human race. "The history of childhood is a nightmare from which we have only recently begun to awaken. The further back in history one goes, the lower the level of child care, and the more likely children are to be killed, abandoned, beaten, terrorized, and sexually abused."[16] Few people raised in such dehumanizing environments ever reach their full potentials,[30] and few are able to develop the maturity essential to nurture their own children toward maturity. In previous centuries, parents may have loved their children, but love was generally contingent on the child's ability to please the parent. Parent-child relationships are unhealthy unless the parents are able to "regress to the psychic age of their children [able to empathize] and work through the anxieties of that age in a better manner the second time they encounter them than they did during their own childhood."[16]

Even though Solon spoke to *The Ten Ages of Man* in his ancient Greek poem, and Shakespeare identified seven stages in his famous soliloquy by Jaques in *As You Like It,* neither they nor their cultures indicated an appreciation for the qualitative intellectual or emotional differences of individuals through the life span. Throughout history, appreciation of one's humanness has hinged on the person's contribution to society through wealth or power. Consequently, those with no power (e.g., women, slaves, handicapped, children) were seen as *subhuman,* not entitled to all the rights, respect, and privileges of those who were deemed to be fully human. As such, they were relegated to the status of a possession, work animal, or pet and treated accordingly. This attitude removed any sense of guilt, remorse, or responsibility for the results of abuse, killing, or selling of a chattel. It was the right of the owner to do as he pleased. Unowned people were viewed as stray animals and treated accordingly.

Gradually, each generation has reared its children marginally better than the previous generation.[12] Consequently, over the centuries, our appreciation and understanding of the rights and value of others has blossomed into a national policy of equal rights and freedom to maximize potentials. The recognition of "humanness" has broadened to include all people regardless of age (though many still struggle with the issue of the unborn), ethnic origin, financial status, racial characteristics, or disabling condition.

Psychogenic evolution has proceeded at different rates in different families and cultural groups. Many people are still "stuck" in earlier historical modes.[16] Consequently, as we work and live with others, we discover remnants of earlier attitudes toward children, women, handicapped, and other minority groups that continue to influence relationships and behaviors in individual families and in many cultures and subcultures today. A review of history may help us appreciate our own perspective and that of others more fully.

Ancient Eras

Before the Middle Ages, life was so uncertain that adults lived mainly for immediate gratification. Only males of the upper classes were viewed as fully human. All others were viewed as subhuman or in a transitional state. Even the heir was not considered fully human. Consequently, severe corporeal punishments or even death penalties for infractions of the "master's" wish or pleasure were expected. Human sacrifice was common, gladiator fights were seen as high sport, and male infants were frequently castrated. The male-female ratio is estimated to have been as high as 4 to 1, because infanticide, especially for females, was justified for economic, familial, and societal survival. Even though laws against infanticide emerged as early as 374 AD, evidence proves that infanticide was still prevalent in Europe as late as 1890. Infanticide was defended on the basis that infants were not yet human and therefore would not be counted as "sinners" if they died.[16]

Those who were allowed to live were so tightly swaddled that movement was impossible and circulation was frequently impaired. The arms were bound for as long as 4 months, and the legs for up to 9 months. Many babies were underfed and became withdrawn and passive. Motor development was markedly delayed. Intellectual and emotional retardation were common because of the poor child-rearing practices.[16]

Beatings, mutilation, and whippings were used routinely to extract "the evil" from a child. Sexual abuse of both boys and girls was rampant, especially in ancient Athens and Rome. Such "play" with children was an expected part of leisure activity well into the Middle Ages.[3] Psychohistorians identify such behavior as ambisexual rather than homosexual in nature, because, in such poor child-rearing environments, adults never reached the oedipal level (5–6 years) of psychic development and integration.[16] Jewish and Christian priests, playing an advocacy role, had some influence in reducing physical punishment, but many parents, even into the 18th and 19th centuries, merely switched to locking the children in closets or drawers for hours or even days.[16]

Middle Ages

For the average person, life continued to be difficult during the Middle Ages. Causes of disease were not understood, and hygiene measures were unknown. "The density of society left no room for the [nuclear] family."[3] Living quarters were small and communal family living was common. The family consisted of everyone, including servants and apprentices, living under the same roof and responsible to the same head of household for guidance and protection.[48] Social responsibilities were viewed as more important than an individual's need for privacy, which was uncommon, even on the wedding night. In some communities, entire villages functioned as a

family in establishing and enforcing moral codes, protecting orphans, and distributing wealth.[20] The concept of family as "kinsfolk living together" did not formally emerge until 1869.[20]

The philosophy of the day appears to have been "eat, drink, and be merry, for tomorrow you die." There was no time or place for childhood; one had to live life before it ended. The life span was short, pleasures were few, and death was certain. The advent of pregnancy and birth were necessary evils. Infant and child mortality rates were high—10% to 30% in the first year of life, and 50% or more before age 20[20]—a factor which discouraged emotional, social, and educational investment by the parents in their offspring. One expected to have many children in order to keep a few. This attitude is consistent with the technology existing at that time; without methods for improving the quality of life, the quantity of life (number of children) became important and valued by the culture and its institutions.

Society felt that children younger than age 7 were in a transitional period between eternity and life. It was believed that young children had no mental activities, so their death was no real loss. Childhood death was seen as a necessary waste, and the child was buried as we bury a pet today.[3] Few records were kept of childhood mortality, since childhood was viewed as such an insignificant phase of life.

Little time was devoted to, or available for, forming warm family relationships. Middle and upper class parents, concerned with their own pleasures, hired wet nurses to care for the infants for the first 2 years so that the woman would be freely available for sexual relationships and to prevent disfiguration of the woman's body by the process of nursing. Wet nurses frequently assumed the care of more children than they could nourish to earn extra money, only to lose 65% or more of the babies because of lack of adequate nourishment and attention.[20]

Many doctors, recognizing the adverse effect on the infants, enticed mothers to nurse their own babies because it would give the mother "a thousand delights" by cooing, smiling, and fondling her; that is, the baby would meet the *mother's* sensual needs, would parent *her*. "The child's facility in mothering adults was often its salvation."[16] A reversal of roles was common. Many parents dressed the child (even the boys) in costumes of the style worn by their own biological mother and literally as well as symbolically made a parent out of their own child. The parents lacked the emotional maturity essential to see the child as a separate individual.

When women discovered that breast feeding offered some birth control protection, it further encouraged them to keep the infant at home.[61] Nevertheless, child care was considered a bother and not one of the joys of life. Children were encouraged to make a rapid transition from the nursing infant to the weaned adult. Only two phases of life were recognized, infancy and adulthood. The concept of childhood was unknown in this society. As soon as children were weaned and able to separate from their mothers, were able to walk and to use language, the youngsters were on their own; they entered the world of adulthood, often competing with adults to meet the basic necessities of life, such as food or a sleeping spot. By 3 or 4 years of age, children had already joined in adult leisure and recreational activities and had participated actively in the rowdiness and sexual play of that era.

The commoner's children were rarely coddled and often ignored.[3] If a male child survived to age 7, he was sent to live with a craftsman as an apprentice; the child thus entered the adult work force, assuming responsibilities alongside grown men and women. The 7 year old was not seen as qualitatively different from adults, only as quantitatively different. Children were viewed as miniature adults. In medieval works of art, the children are portrayed with adult faces and bodies even shortly after birth. Clothing is a miniature version of adult attire (Fig. 1-2).[3]

Royal families tried to insulate their children from death by surrounding them with servants (In 1454, 1-year-old Prince Edward had his staff *cut* to 38!) and by maintaining a resident physician and surgeon.[48] Even royal children, however, were sent to live with other families around the age of 7 because parents believed that children would be raised better by disinterested people than by indulgent parents.[48]

Parents often arranged the marriage of their children

FIGURE 1-2.
Children are treated as miniature adults when people fail to recognize the qualitative differences between children and adults.

during infancy and consummated it at 12 to 14 years of age to protect the child's future in case of the untimely death of the parent.[48]

Sixteenth and Seventeenth Centuries

Although families began to celebrate the birth of a new child, many continued to be underfed and neglected by mothers or nurses who distrusted the infant's primitive survival behaviors and saw them as "demanding and dangerous little animals."[61] The idea that children had special and legitimate needs evolved gradually. Much of this new sensitivity appears to be related to the influence of Gerson, a 15th-century religious teacher.[3] Because children were thought to be unaware of or indifferent to sex before the age of puberty, playing with a child's genitalia and sharing the same bed were common practices. Gerson was appalled by the amount of open talk, coarse jokes, gestures, and sexual exposure that was considered normal and acceptable in front of children. Gerson preached that masturbation and causing erections in children represented "pollution and sodomy," that is, premature sexuality.[3]

Under Gerson's teaching, Western European society of the era of Enlightenment and Romanticism began to protect children. At the end of the 16th century, sexual references began to be removed from books used for educating children. During the 17th century, society began to accept the idea of the innocence of childhood and the pendulum of sexual expression in public began to swing in the opposite direction. Modesty became the rule; bodies were scrupulously concealed even from family members and people of the same gender. Some even went so far as to view it as a sin to love one's wife too dearly and condemned intercourse with one's wife as adultery if it was performed for pleasure rather than for procreation.[20]

In Europe, the emergence of a new, commercial middle class in the latter part of the 17th century had great impact on the value and roles of children through changes in both social and family structures. Although the lower classes continued to prefer the communal family or collective society of the Middle Ages, the middle class began to separate itself in disgust from the lower classes and in contempt from the upper classes of society. These smaller middle class family units began to realize that children were not ready to face the rigors of adult life. Children were seen as weak and innocent and therefore in need of education and discipline. As trades and craftsmanship assumed more importance, the need for high levels of skill, combined with Gerson's teachings, impressed the middle class family that it was responsible for the academic and moral training of children as well as for the transmission of name and inheritance.

Portraits painted during the 16th and 17th centuries indicate that the childhood phase of life began to have more value. Separation of adulthood and childhood was indicated by differences in costuming. Children began to wear clothing reminiscent of styles worn 100 years earlier. Although males profited first from the emergence of the concept of childhood innocence and the need for education, females also began to receive better treatment in some circles by the end of the 17th century.[3] The poor continued to make little change or distinction based on age or gender.

At the end of the 17th century, John Locke, an English philosopher, proposed the theory that the infant's mind was a blank slate, or **tabula rasa,** and that parents need to educate children from "their very cradles."[42] The significance he attached to environmental influences put much responsibility on the home and family. He observed that the self-centeredness of indulged children became more pronounced with age and that children could not suddenly restrain themselves at the age of 7, 14, or 21. He instructed parents to teach obedience to rules and restraints early. "The difference lies not in the having or not having of appetites, but in the power to govern, and deny ourselves in them. He that is not used to submit his will to the reason of others, when he is young, will scarce harken or submit to his own reason, when he is of an age to make use of it. And what kind of a man such a one is like to prove, is easy to foresee."[43] He also advocated balancing firm punishment with praise, love, respect, and reverence for the child's personage.

In Europe, many parents still maintained some emotional distance from their children to insulate themselves from the pain of an untimely death. Many parents did not even attend the funeral services for their child.

Even under the best of conditions in the American colonies, 10% to 30% of the children died before their second birthday, and in some homes, 50% were buried before that age.[60] Although parents "maintained a degree of aloofness and detachment," they were not indifferent, only resigned.[72] Religion permeated every aspect of life, and an "other-world" attitude was consciously fostered in children as the rigid Puritans sought early spiritual conversion as preparation for untimely death.

Eighteenth Century

The Industrial Revolution created significant changes in social structure by forcing nuclear family units to leave rural areas, changing the economic basis of society and increasing the sense of isolation. Although the population density was actually increased in urban areas, psychological isolation was intensified with separation from extended family members. Consequently, the nuclear family drew closer and spent more time together.[17] The authority of parents was weakened as individual rights became stronger and young people began to choose their own marital partners. Marked differences were observed in the status and value of children depending on the socioeconomic level and religious orientation of the family. They were welcomed as future laborers and security for the parents in later life.[72]

In Europe, poor children were forced to work long, hard hours in mills and coal mines under inhumane conditions.

Parents could not meet expenses on their combined salaries, consequently, 4- to 5-year-old children worked 12-hour shifts, and adolescents were relieved only for brief naps, often sleeping in their clothes. Conditions were more brutal than those faced by slaves in the Colonies.[12]

As families entered the middle class, more time was available for leisure, and money was available to support children for a longer period of time before they had to work to help meet the financial obligations of the family. Increases in technology emphasized the need for more education. Age-graded schools emerged under the influence and direction of the church. Society encouraged the refinement of manners for the upper class and the value of responsibility and hard work for the lower class.

Older people were no longer considered useful or worthy of respect in the industrialized society and often were left to fend for themselves in a socially hostile environment without the social support systems known today. In Europe, four phases of life emerged during the 18th century: infancy (birth through age 5), childhood (ages 6 through 14), adulthood (postpuberty), and old age.

In America, a person was not considered to be an adult until marriage, and marriage was not allowed until a man owned his own land and proved himself to be economically independent, whether it be at age 21 or 40.[7] Consequently, when obtained, a man's house became his castle, and privacy was valued. To assure that a home ran smoothly, roles became age-graded and gender-related. Women were treated as minors and considered to be unsuited to vote and physically and mentally inferior, even though they worked beside their husbands in farming and homesteading.[46] More than 50% could not sign their own names because of lack of education. Yet those who could indicate that they faced the same problems of their predecessors and of women today: concerns about child bearing and parenting, marital conflict, courting, death, chastity, adultery, family violence, adoption, and divorce.[58] The issues of family relations, budgeting, child rearing, social status, and survival are human issues with which everyone struggles, regardless of financial status, geographical location, or historical era.[62]

The "Protestant work ethic" (i.e., evil can be overcome by hard work) evolved from this era. A pert child was thought to be bewitched, and amusement or childish mischief was interpreted as sinful.[9] Time and talents were to be focused toward an eternal end. Fear and repression were predominant forms of discipline.[38] Children were subjected to rigid rules to "make them pure" and "keep them in their place." Often they were fed separately, and frequently they were not allowed to enjoy adult luxuries, such as spiced foods or adequate bed covers for warmth. Children in this era were to be seen, but not heard.

Gradually, the philosophy that children were naturally evil changed to the philosophy that they were naturally good. This change in outlook was fostered by the French philosopher Jean-Jacques Rousseau, who felt that children would instinctively know right from wrong (the idea of the **noble**

savage) if allowed to develop with less parental interference.[57] As happiness became more significant than the issue of sin, theological dogma was exchanged for rules of good conduct (e.g., honesty, industry, sobriety) as the basis for child guidance in the home. Increased affluence, especially in the Colonies, allowed more time for both education and leisure during childhood. The availability of primitive birth control methods allowed the married couple more control over family size.

The American Revolution marked not only the beginning of freedom for the American people but also the emancipation of the child.[38] Parents began to realize that they could improve child welfare and prevent diseases through improved hygiene, diet, clothing, and education. Juvenile literature began to change from theological philosophies to more instructive and humorous material. Printer John Newbery began to print books especially for children in 1744,[38] a welcome relief from the former stark readers. Many of our classic poems (Mother Goose) and fairy tales (Cinderella, Sleeping Beauty, Puss-in-Boots, Red Riding Hood) originated in the latter half of the 18th century.

Nineteenth Century

In the 19th century, the status of the American child continued to advance. Unfortunately, many families of European descent were so busy clearing and settling the land that little time was available for education. Others were caught up in surviving the urban industrial revolution. Nevertheless, respect for childhood had been established, and children were seen as the hope for the future of the new nation. Childhood and motherhood both began to be idealized by the middle class.[29] A couple without children was to be pitied.

In the post-Victorian era, society began to denounce the artificial standards fostered by the puritanical heritage; yet, great concern existed about the future of the United States and people wanted to realize "the millennium" in this new world by activating high moral standards.[70]

A spirit of humanitarianism encouraged improvement in social conditions. The newly industrialized society recognized that lives could be improved through technology and education. Equality before the law included the right to education.[53] Public schools and compulsory education laws were adopted in almost every state. Massachusetts led the way with the first free public high school in 1821 and the first compulsory school attendance law in 1852.

Each geographic area and class had its own way of teaching children how to work and to perpetuate its values. Northern families tended to embrace Locke's philosophy (the child is passively molded by the environment) and thus perpetuated harsh discipline practices, even starving children into obedience[30] when they combined his view with the position of innate depravity. Fortunately, after 1830, concepts of individuality, self-discipline, habit, and initiative were more prominent.[55] White Southern families with more liberal religious commitments adopted Rousseau's view (children

merely need a supportive environment) and consequently tended to indulge and enjoy their children more.[61] By 1850, most families began to modify their stance with a better balance between discipline and indulgence. The pre-Civil War era was viewed as a "golden age of virtue and innocence"; the South was a "Greek democracy," and the North, an "agrarian republic."[70]

As industry began to require more skilled workers, young children were no longer employable. Even adolescents became economically useless to an urban middle class family. Fortunately, businesses began to pay men a "family wage," which enabled the head of household to support a wife and dependent family. As middle class women had time to concentrate on home management and personal talents, the "cult of true womanhood" emerged.[67] Although the patriarchical family was still the rule, much responsibility was placed on the mother for socialization and religious education of the children. As she assumed chores formerly assigned to the children, they had more time for play, education, and idle leisure.

Children assumed more importance within the family because of their contribution to the woman's role within the family.[72] Teaching the values and characteristics deemed by society to give life purpose and meaning became her career. As society became more child-centered, classes in child care were offered[38] and popular literature was flooded with information on child care, parenting, and education.[70] Parents no longer passively attributed childhood accidents to the "will of God" as punishment for their own sins. They took an active part in promoting health and in accident prevention[16] and even began to purchase life insurance for children[72] since childhood death was no longer an expectation of parents.

Baby diaries and biographies, like those of Charles Darwin, began to appear. Although these diaries added little in the way of concrete data, they did focus attention on the qualitative differences between children and adults. Writers like Mark Twain helped people to see childhood pranks as funny and natural, rather than sinful. Parents began to encourage play activities both for merriment and to facilitate the use of the body. During this era, the generation gaps narrowed as parents began to make friends with their children, and older people were again respected and appreciated for their social contribution to the family.

The experience of minority children differed greatly from that of white children during the 18th and 19th centuries. Slaves were deprived of their African culture, yet were not permitted to engage in the neo-European culture.[56] Consequently, they created their own unique culture independent of white values and resisted assimilation into the white culture.[69] The conditions under which slaves lived varied considerably, depending on the location and size of the plantation as well as the personality of the owner of their physical bodies and time. However, their spirit was not owned and they "recognized each other as a distinctive society with a common historical experience."[69] They formed "a vibrant group of individuals who created an energetic slave quarter community characterized by black solidarity not hopeless dependency."[69] Courage and resourcefulness were fostered in the face of poverty and oppression.[66]

The African-American instinctively realized that "heavy-handed patronization could suffocate human autonomy as easily as heavy-handed lashings."[56] Though they could not control the events, they could control their response to them, and they maintained self-dignity by refusing to be patronized. The parents socialized their children for the world they knew, teaching them survival under slavery and how to passively resist without seeming to resist.[56]

Many slaves were not allowed to marry, they were merely seen as "breeding stock" for the owner. The strength of the infant-mother bond forced masters to respect this relationship, thus leading to a matriarchal society. This relationship was a child's only source of continuity. The mother was often forced to return to the field a month after delivery, leaving the infant in the care of other children except when she returned three or four times each day to nurse her child.[66]

Slave children usually did not work at hard chores until puberty and consequently spent much time playing with and caring for each other. Most of their time was involved in cooperative games. Few combative games and no elimination-of-player games existed.[69] The prolonged period of childhood play facilitated healthy social-emotional development and the opportunity to discover their personal identity.[69] Social cooperation, not work, became the basis for evaluating personal integrity and character.

In the 1800s, slave treatment gradually improved as owners recognized that "work animals" last longer and give better service with gentler treatment. Owners who began to realize the humanness of slaves started to emancipate them. By the beginning of the Civil War, about 11% were already freemen.[52] However, the fact that they were free does not mean that they had equal rights. Social patterns were slow to change; after the war, some former owners continued to use indentureships and apprenticeships of children to retain the substance of slavery for blacks who could find no other source of income in a world ruled by white power and finances.[59] Childhood became as difficult for these children as for the factory and mining children of England a hundred years earlier.

Although marriage was allowed, it was the woman who was forced to support the family when jobs were unavailable for black men. Much bitterness, despair, and feelings of futility accompanied the role overload of women and lack of employment for men.[66] Marital and personal instability and disorganization occurred frequently because of the "social and psychological consequences of unemployment and unrest."[66] However, many became stronger as they were forced to find ways to face society and survive.

Twentieth Century

New inventions occurred in rapid succession during the late 19th and early 20th centuries, changing both employment opportunities and the quality of life. Washing machines, telephones, electric lights, and automobiles revolutionized the way people lived. Most children were raised in two-parent families with a strong father image who was increasingly involved in the lives of his children. Over the last century, as higher levels of education became essential for employment, the length of time a child remained in the home increased. Each generation looked forward to an improved lifestyle, as technological advances and finances accumulated.

Not everyone, however, enjoyed the benefits of life in an idealized "Norman Rockwell" America. The "tired and poor," those "yearning to be free," did indeed teem to America's shores or escape from the bondage of Southern repression[26] only to get caught up in the squalor and new bondage of the crowded flats and sweat houses in the inner cities.[31, 58] Poor mothers, forced to work for survival, left their babies in the care of strangers or older children. In the absence of playgrounds and parks, the children usurped and played on the streets, forming social alliances or gangs to protect their turf.[47] If parents could not afford to feed their children, the children were sent to live in other households by 10 to 11 years of age to work as maids, houseboys, or apprentices.[47] Those lucky enough to find a factory job remained at home. With increased mechanization, however, it became more prudent for industry to hire newly immigrated men for the same salaries they paid children.[47] Children left school by age 14 to secure work,[64] and families took in boarders to help meet the demands of greedy landlords.[47] Social as well as physical conditions for urban dwellers of the early 1900s were strongly reminiscent of the Middle Ages with its extended community family. Everyone felt a sense of responsibility for children and helped them as needed.[28, 47] Although the majority of inner city immigrant and African American families were double-headed households,[26] contact with the men in the community provided role models for those without fathers.[28]

Although parents realized that education was the ticket out of poverty, many were too poor to afford that luxury. It was also difficult to convince young people to stay with a boring curriculum when a job served as the "rite of passage" to adulthood. In 1920, only 27% of 16 and 17 year olds remained in school.[64] An entertainment industry began to emerge as young people, no longer in school, looked for activities to keep them occupied during nonworking hours.

Native Americans also suffered oppression, poverty, and dehumanization. In 1900, more than 17,000 Indian children were placed in boarding schools in spite of strong parental and tribal objections.[63] Conditions were deplorable. The Meriam Report of 1928 states that food, clothing, teachers, dormitory facilities, and medical care were insufficient to meet the needs of developing children. Mandatory student labor was used to maintain the facilities; military discipline and a "lock up" system were used to maintain control.[63] When the adolescents returned to their reservations, they did not know the language or possess the skills necessary to function within or perpetuate their culture. With the poor quality education, they discovered that they were unprepared to live successfully in either the Native American or Anglo world. Not only was the parent-child relationship disrupted, but the individual-culture relationship was disrupted as well. The Kennedy Report of 1969 stated that 75% of the population had "severe social and emotional problems" because of their experiences.[63] Many Native American individuals and families today still suffer from the effects of forced assimilation, and aspects of their cultures may never be recaptured.

During the second half of the 20th century, technology has continued to advance rapidly. Medical sciences have improved both the quality and length of life. Child mortality rates have dropped so dramatically that, by 1970, many death insurance policies were rewritten as education insurance policies.[72] Improved employment conditions, transportation systems, and financial status allow most families to spend more money on leisure and luxuries. No longer must every penny be allocated toward pure survival. Contraceptive methods and infertility treatment have become so effective that couples can plan both family size and spacing.

The status of women and children has improved markedly since World War II. Women demanded the right to work so that they could survive widowhood.[37] During the 1950s, home and motherhood were again idealized, but during the '60s women began to demand equal employment opportunities. The employment status and opportunities have improved over the years; however, many women still face discrimination issues both at home and at work as they attempt to find creative ways to balance reproduction and family life with career and talent development.[37] Men find their personal lives enriched as they spend more time with family pursuits. Both roles and child-rearing practices are changing rapidly as women face more years in the work force than in child rearing.

Although affluence and poverty live side by side in the world today, their cultures are worlds apart. Each person continues to be influenced by the history of his or her own family, ethnic group, and culture. Individuals in poverty still struggle for survival for even the bare necessities of food and shelter. Twenty percent of American children are raised in poverty.[41] Poor parents do not love their children any less than those of middle or upper classes, but the struggles for existence can eclipse their ability to empathize with the child's needs. Children raised in an emotional environment of earlier eras may bear the scars of reduced psychic development as they reach adulthood, a factor that can threaten the stability of society.[41]

Many middle class parents are concerned about the effects of "too much" material comfort and pleasure on their child's ability to become a responsible, independent, hard-working, allocentric adult. The truly affluent family also tries to pass its tastes, ideals, traditions, and social characteristics on to its children. Responsible wealthy parents are concerned about the sense of "entitlement" that frequently is associated with people endowed with money and power. Many humbly recognize the **responsibilities** of privilege, which include

the ability to empathize with the needs of others. If the power of entitlement "goes to one's head," then a narcissistic orientation undermines all relationships, eventually leading the person into the emptiness of emotional isolation.[13] These parents realize that an individual finds pleasure and happiness in life through dedicated service to others and by the responsible use of money or power.

Both parents and professionals today recognize distinct qualitative differences in functioning through the life span. First, childhood was divided into two distinct phases, **school-ager** and **adolescence**; then the period of infancy was subdivided into true **infancy** and early childhood. The period of early childhood was then subdivided into **toddlers** and **pre-schoolers.** In the 1960s, the preadolescent phase **pubes-cence** was differentiated by Fritz Redl[54], and **youth** as a late-adolescent–preadult phase was described by Kenneth Keniston[36]. In the early 1970s, the **neonate** (first 28 days of life) became differentiated from infancy. During the late '70s and '80s, developmental characteristics of the adult years have attracted research. The concept of **middlescence** has emerged as a phase of life that separates the **early adult** years from **senescence,** or the **late adult** years.

The authors recognize 10 basic phases of the human life span, as described in Table 1-1. However, many of these phases have distinct subphases, as indicated. Specific ages are attached to the phases, not to indicate discrete stages, but to give the reader the **approximate ages** of individuals in each phase. These age ranges are of particular importance in the biophysical domain; much greater variance is seen in the other domains. **Developmental phases should be recog-**

TABLE 1–1. PHASES OF THE LIFE SPAN

Phase	Ages
Fetus	Conception to birth
Neonate	0–28 days
Infant	0–15 months
Toddler	16–30 months
Preschooler	2½–5 years
Schoolager	
Early	6–8 years
Middle	8–10 years
Pubescent	10–12 years
Adolescent	
Early	13–15 years
Middle	16–17 years
Late/Youth	18–20 years
Early adult	20–40 years
Middle adult (middlescence)	40–60 years
Late adult (senescence)	
Early	60–75 years
Middle	75–90 years
Late	90 + years

nized as part of a continuous process and not as a set of discrete stages.

RESEARCH IN HUMAN DEVELOPMENT

As people began to appreciate and value children, they realized that a better understanding of childhood and human development would (1) contribute to the development of theories of human behavior that could be used both to interpret and to predict behaviors and (2) that this knowledge could contribute in a practical way to improving the quality of life on both the individual and societal levels. The earliest research efforts were directed toward describing and differentiating age-related behaviors to develop theories and establish norms. **Norms** are the behaviors, skills, and parameters considered to be descriptive or normal for a defined age group based on observations or assessments of large populations. Norms can serve as guidelines for assessing developmental progress and for identifying variations and deviations. Norms can provide guides for anticipating and facilitating the emergence of skills and behaviors.

That which is considered normal is influenced by the individual's reference group (e.g., family, peers, ethnic group inheritance); therefore, normal growth patterns or behaviors in one group may be atypical or unacceptable in another. Few people are "normal" in every area. Parents are sometimes guilty of thinking that norms in one area of development or domain will predict norms in others. Although highly interrelated, each domain evolves at its own pace. The infant who walks at 8 months is not automatically assured the position of valedictorian of the high school class.

Psychologists and parents soon realized that norms did not explain why variations and deviations occurred, nor did they necessarily provide a guideline for optimal development. Consequently, researchers began to look for antecedent-consequence relationships. Since a good theory should have both explanatory and heuristic power, approaches to toilet training, weaning, maternal employment, and other specific factors were evaluated for their potential effects on child and adult personality. Although some correlations were identified, it was discovered that too many other factors were involved to predict adult personality and behaviors accurately from a childhood experience. To say that one event *caused* a later characteristic was impossible.

The state of the art is still more descriptive than predictive. However, as more refined measurement techniques and analysis procedures become available, more relationships between antecedents and consequences are being identified that have implications both for theory building and for clinical application.

Sources of Knowledge

Each individual develops hypotheses about human behavior. The major source of knowledge is **experience.** Because people have observed or participated in an event, they hold tenaciously to their own views. Unfortunately, this source of knowledge is severely limited and biased. What people fail to consider is that every other person who observed or participated in the same or similar event also formulated a hypothesis and is equally convinced of its truth. Because events are uncontrolled, like the experience of the blind men and the elephant, their theories may bear little, if any, resemblance to "The Truth." The contribution of experience should not be underestimated, but knowledge gained through experience must be validated before it can be accepted without question.

A more reliable source of knowledge is the opinion or the experience of an **expert** in the field. Identifying with the name or theory of a respected researcher offers more credence to personal observations or theories. However, even the most astute authority is not infallible.

A third source of insight is through the **a priori** or intellectual approach, which states that a theory is developed through reasoning. One proceeds logically from a known fact to an assumed effect. A theory may be developed through **deductive reasoning,** in which a specific idea is extracted from a general concept through logical reasoning. In **inductive reasoning,** specific observations are logically combined to develop a more general theory or viewpoint. These methods are useful, but they are not always reliable. Two qualified people may come to equally supportable but opposite viewpoints. The history of science reveals that the understanding of phenomena has frequently been impeded by the acceptance of "obvious" assumptions that are not true.

The most valid and reliable knowledge is obtained through the use of a **scientific approach** to explaining phenomena, described here in four steps. First, as an individual interacts with the environment, he or she becomes aware of a problem. Over a period of time, the **problem becomes more clearly identified,** and critical factors are delineated. Second, through inductive reasoning, the individual **formulates these factors into a theory,** a statement that explains and predicts. Theories are developed to cover the greatest number of facts as simply as possible. Third, further observations or experiments are performed to **test the hypotheses** that are derived from the theory (deductive reasoning). Fourth, **the data are evaluated** for the degree to which the research supports each hypothesis. If the data collected do not support the hypothesis, then the theory must be reevaluated. The scientific approach, when used properly, is a continuous process with self-corrective mechanisms.

Descriptive Research

Critical to the effective use of a scientific approach is the adequate identification of the problem with its parameters and variables. This identification necessitates adequate attention to data gathering through observations.

Observations

The first systematic recording of child behavior was done by Tiedemann for the first $2\frac{1}{2}$ years after his son's birth in

1787.[32] In 1877, Charles Darwin, in his efforts to identify the place of humans in the evolutionary chain, also used **natural observation** to describe his son's "natural" development within the context of the family. His interest in childhood spurred further interest and research in the area. However, neither he nor anyone since has been able to prove that humans are a direct descendant of animals (the **phylogenetic** approach to the study of humanity) in the evolutionary chain. This book is restricted to the study of developmental events of the human species (the **ontogenetic** approach).

The person who is planning to systematically observe children or adults in a natural setting needs to approach the assignment thoughtfully and thoroughly. Nancy Carbonara offers the following suggestions for naturalistic observation:[10]

1. The observer is a passive member of the environment. He should not disrupt normal activities and interactions.
2. The process of observation requires extreme concentration, empathy, and sensitivity to clues. All antecedent and subsequent behaviors must be noted. The observer must also be aware of his own biases.
3. Observations should be very thorough and specific.
    a. Observe the entire setting, people and objects present, time of day, overview of activities, and any significant antecedent events.
    b. Focus attention on one activity or one individual for at least 10 to 15 minutes.
    c. Record all objective and subjective observations—behaviors, verbal and nonverbal communication efforts, responses to others, and so forth.
4. Be objective and descriptive, using adjectives and adverbs freely in order to capture the client's individuality.
5. Write a rough draft as soon as possible after note taking, or minor details will be forgotten.
6. Interpret the behaviors in light of known theories as well as suspected intent of the person.

Contrived observations can be made by placing and observing individuals in restricted environments or by posing specific problems to elicit a response. Piaget used (and most assessment tools today use) this method to evaluate cognitive and physical skills of young children.

Surveys
In 1891, G. Stanley Hall pioneered the technique of systematic study of large groups of children by the use of a questionnaire[27]. This method was an example of a **cross-sectional** research design (many individuals of differing ages are evaluated for differences between age groups and for the identification of norms for each age group). In a **longitudinal** design, the same individuals are evaluated several times to identify changes that occur with maturation or aging.

Ex Post Facto Studies
Many problems in education, medicine, and human development do not lend themselves to experimental research. Con-

sequently, relationships between variables must be identified through careful history taking. **Case studies** fall into this category. Because the researcher has no control over the variables, no correlation between factors can be offered as absolute proof of a cause-effect relationship.

Correlational Research
When a large number of variables have been identified as potentially related to a problem, a researcher, through detailed study and high-level statistical evaluation, may attempt to identify the degree to which two or more factors are related to each other. Like the ex post facto design, this method offers no proof of causal relationships, only a description of the strength of the relatedness. Both factors may actually be under the influence of an as yet unknown third variable.

Experimental Research

The four research designs just discussed can identify significant relationships that the researcher may weave into a theory. Experimental designs test the ability of a theory to generate hypotheses that can predict a result. As such, they can assess the possible existence of a causal relationship.

The true experimental design is identified by two criteria. First, the experimenter must have **control** over the variables that are significant to the research. Environmental consistency is essential for the interpretation of the results. Second, there must be **randomization** in (1) selection of subjects (for external validity), (2) assignment of the subjects to groups (for internal validity), and (3) assignment of treatment to the group. Each group is offered a different condition on one factor (independent variable) while the target behavior (dependent variable) is measured for differences between groups. Single-subject research designs can also prove powerful cause-effect relationships even though the second criteria cannot be met.

Ethics in Research

Much human research remains in the descriptive category because of the technical and humane problems inherent in experimenting with humans. One cannot deliberately subject a pregnant woman to severe stress to see if it will cause birth defects in the offspring; neither does one deliberately avoid all talking to infants to discover "natural" language (an experiment that was performed in the 1200s [see Chap. 8]). If an experiment might cause severe or permanent psychological or physical damage, the researcher must locate a population of subjects which experiences an alteration in a significant variable because of naturally occurring events. Although this method means more detective work for the researcher and fewer conclusive results, the rights of clients to full participation in life are protected.

The right to privacy and informed consent have become critical issues. Awareness of the atrocities committed in the concentration camps by Nazi Germans in the name of medical science prompted the U.N. General Assembly to adopt the Nuremberg Code in 1946.[24] These standards require researchers to keep subjects informed of the purpose, nature, and potential side effects of research projects and to obtain signed consent from the participants. In the case of children, parents or legal guardians must give permission, but the child must also be informed as much as possible about the research design. Such information may change the behavior of those involved as they give deeper thought to the critical issues, however, and many of those whose lives may give the richest data may refuse to participate.[24]

Many hypotheses that cannot be adequately tested in humans because of ethical and financial problems or the constraints of time may be successfully tested in animals.[15] Animal research has increased our understanding of theories of learning, biophysical growth, medical issues, and socialization. Because of the expense, complexity of humans, and restraints of research approaches, much of our knowledge is still in the theory rather than fact stage.

THEORIES OF HUMAN DEVELOPMENT

No one theory has yet been created to encompass all aspects of human development. At best, we have partial theories that are age-specific or domain-specific; therefore, we work with what we know until new knowledge and theories are available to enable us to interpret the behavioral variability we observe. Theorists go one step beyond description by attempting to identify meaningful relationships. Complex behaviors are reduced to simple frames by the identification of core problems, tasks, or developmental foci for each phase of life.

Theories reflect the culture and the life experiences of those who develop them. Two respected theories may be diametrically opposed. People tend to lean toward a particular theory because it helps them to understand their own past experiences or it blends with their philosophy of life.

One of the tasks of science is to transform observable data into theoretical constructs that facilitate understanding, prediction, and control of phenomena. Because of the difficulty in identifying, measuring, or manipulating variables with humans, many theories are developed through inductive reasoning. These theories or concepts are often so broad and abstract (e.g., self-esteem, inferiority, superego) that measurement by empirical research methods is difficult, if not impossible. When these broad concepts are broken down into smaller, researchable hypotheses, they become too narrow, artificial, or sterile to have practical application. Models developed from narrow perspectives do not lend themselves to life-span developmental theories. Consequently, many theories of development still have a poor empirical foundation.

Another crucial point about theories is that they do not and cannot explain all behaviors, only "the average expected behavior." Non-normative factors such as untimely family death, disability, the Holocaust, or national catastrophe can influence an individual or a whole segment of a population in unpredictable ways.

Despite this state of the art, theories are as important as facts in the study of human development. A theoretical framework interprets and orders facts so than an integrated view emerges. Theory imparts meaning to facts, providing a frame of reference in which to consider and apply information.[33] The theorists of human development differ in two major ways. First, they differ in their position on the origin of behavior; thus, Rousseau's and Locke's views still provoke controversy in theory development and child-rearing practices today. Should nature be allowed to take its course, or should adults actively shape a child's development? A third view on the origin of behavior involves the issue of self-generativity.[4] Do heredity and environment shape us, or do we shape ourselves in the context of hereditary and environmental factors? Is the individual a passive or an active learner?

Developmental theories attempt to explain both change and consistency over time. The second major area of controversy concerns how the theorists explain the nature of changes. Although all theories recognize orderly, sequential changes from simple to more complex behaviors, some theories characterize these changes as smooth and continuous. **Continuity** views focus on **quantitative** changes that occur gradually over time until the target behavior is achieved (successive approximations). By **development,** immature skills are strengthened or modified into more complex skills.

Discontinuity views focus on abrupt changes in behavior patterns. The organization of behavior becomes **qualitatively** different from one period of the life span to the next through **growth.** Many behaviors may change simultaneously, heralding the entrance to a new level of functioning. Each new stage integrates past and present experience into new, more complex response patterns. The behavior patterns for each stage can be described and interrelated around a core problem or tasks. Incomplete resolution of the problem or tasks interferes with the quality of growth at the next stage. During transition periods, an individual may exhibit behaviors of two successive stages. The stages are sequentially arranged so that the order cannot be changed, nor can a stage be skipped if the final level is to be reached. However, it is acknowledged that the speed of passing through various stages may be accelerated or delayed as a result of genetic or environmental factors, and the person may "revisit" a stage under stress or voluntarily for more effective resolution.

Theories generally focus on the growth (addition of new skills) or development (expansion of old skills) of a person; however, a dynamic and continuous interplay is found between both gains and losses as one traverses the life span.[5] Differentiation during cellular growth precludes the ability of a cell to develop along an alternative course. Commitment to one marital partner or career precludes simultaneous commitment to another. Assumption of advanced cognitive operations can repress some perceptual skills.[11] Life provides balances (e.g., the adaptive capacities of elderly people can compensate for some of the biological losses)[5]; consequently, each stage of life has its own privileges and pleasures.

Psychodynamic View

The psychodynamic view of human development emerged during the late 19th century, when artificial social standards and puritanical prudery prevailed in the late Victorian upper- and middle-class European circles. It was in this context that Sigmund Freud, a physician and neurologist, began to encourage his clients to reiterate their childhood experiences in search of antecedents to "phobias" and "hysterias." He felt that all behavior was determined by earlier events. Repressed ideas and experiences became part of the unconscious and therefore could not be controlled, but took on a life of their own.[23] Freud combined the data gathered from these interviews with his own life experiences and intuitive inductive reasoning to develop the first major theory on personality development. Many other theorists have used his theory as a point of departure for developing their own.

Psychodynamic theories view people as basically affective (emotional) and irrational. The energy to act and react originates in genetically or biologically determined passions and impulses (instincts). Even the infant's growth is motivated by unconscious, pleasure-seeking urges.[23] Only gradually, under the influence of societal restrictions, does the child begin to control these impulses and passions. People are portrayed in a constant state of conflict between natural instinctual impulses and unnatural societal mores.[22] According to the psychodynamic views of human development, we are neither active nor passive in shaping our personalities; we merely attempt to balance the internal and external forces in such a way that we can live adaptively with them. This dynamic process of balancing or maintaining homeostasis continues throughout life on the unconscious level.[25] The adjustment process helps to change personality structures so that the person interacts differently with the environment in the future. Through this constant process of disequilibrium and homeostasis, identity is formed.

Psychodynamic theories put heavy emphasis on the importance of the mother-infant relationship for development of the basic psychic structures, which "provide the template for later relationships."[23] Pathologies of the adult years are believed to be remnants of inadequately resolved early tensions due to a poor mother-child relationship.[22] Healing comes through insight into the unconscious motives (Fig. 1-3).[25]

Theory of Freud

Sigmund Freud postulated that, as the child matures, his or her instinctual sexual-sensual energy (libido) is sequentially invested in biologically predetermined areas of the body. In each stage, one body organ dominates the mode of interaction with other people. First the mouth, then the anus, and finally the genital organs become the primary focus (investment) for stimulation, input, output, and control. Over- or under-indulgence of a child interferes with adequate resolution, causing a child to "fixate" at that stage; evidence of fixation would become manifest during the adult years. According to Freud,

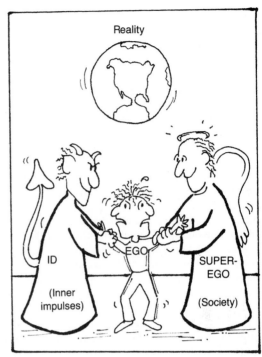

FIGURE 1–3.
According to psychodynamic theory, the self, or ego, must balance the impulses of the id with the constraints of the superego to meet the realities of everyday life.

oral fixations (infancy) are characterized by obsessive eating, talking, or smoking, alcoholism, and unrealistic self-confidence or depression. **Anal** fixations (toddler) are exhibited through obstinacy, compulsiveness, autocratic dogmatism, extravagance, passive resistance, possessiveness, and aggression. **Phallic** fixations (preschooler) are characterized during the adult years by homosexuality, narcissism, arrogance, flamboyance, and chauvinism.[22]

According to Freud, the major tasks of personality development were completed by about age 6 with the resolution of the oedipal complex (see Chap. 14). The school years were labeled **latency,** since he felt that all sexual curiosity and activity was submerged during that period. During adolescence, the **genital stage,** the conflicts of early childhood were revived. If these conflicts had been handled well in earlier stages, the individual entered into normal heterosexual relationships. From Freud came the belief that personality development is set by school-age years and is complete by the end of adolescence. For further information on Freud, see Appendix B.

Theory of Erikson

Eric Erikson extended Freud's theory to embrace his observations on the contributions of the socialization process to development.[25] Whereas Freud looked for the origin of pathology, Erikson looked for components that were conducive to healthy development. Erikson identified eight stages of development[18] and suggests that there may be a ninth that deals with "premonition of immortality."[19] Each stage consists of two opposing dispositions (positive and negative) that must be balanced, yet they work together to form the basic strengths of life (Table 1-2). As the person confronts new social and biological pressures, each stage surrenders its dominance to the next stage, even if it is inadequately resolved. "The fact that one quality at a time dominates implies that all eight qualities are present during each stage."[65] However, each disposition or task assumes a different form and is reworked in the service of the targeted crisis.[19] He proposed a basic virtue that emerges with successful resolution of each stage.[18]

According to Erikson, the infant is faced with the task of learning to **trust** life, and from this basic trust springs hope. Inadequate resolution can lead to mistrust of others, of the environment, even of the self. In the face of inadequate hope, the child dies,[19] a point upheld by research on infant neglect studies. The toddler strives for **autonomy** and expression of the will: "Me do!" Too many restrictions on this newfound independence lead the toddler to feelings of shame and doubt about his or her own skills and value. The preschooler begins to take **initiative** and to show directed purpose in activities. If intentions are not recognized or accepted, feelings of guilt result. The school-age child develops competence through **industry** or attention focused toward task accomplishment. If the child cannot master desirable goals, feelings of inferiority arise.

The central task of life occurs during adolescence. One's unique **identity** is actively forged from previously recognized competencies and the choice of one's life goals and value systems. Role confusion results when the person avoids this "identity homework" process (see Chap. 25). The process for people of genius is frequently painful and prolonged as they identify more options and struggle with deeper issues of life.[25] Mentors are particularly valuable during this period as the young person searches for something worth committing one's life to.[25] Once an identity has been firmly established, the young adult can intimately share values, ideologies,

dreams, and fears. Even if others disagree, self-identity is stable enough not to shatter under criticism. The ideologies chosen during this period are "fleshed out" as life progresses and as one begins to stand up for or against an issue. Those with strong identities are frequently in the midst of controversy because they dare to "march to a different drummer." Identity is reassessed throughout life as confrontations arise, resulting in a renewal of the youthful struggle and energy as the person remains true to the inner self.

The **intimate** person selectively learns to share love in its many forms: parent love, spouse love, child love, friend love, spiritual love. Those who are unable to express their unique self become emotionally isolated. If one's identity is not clear, then it interferes with intimacy because one plays the game of "chameleon" to gain acceptance. "Isolated" people do not know who they really are because of avoidance of the process of "identity homework." They play a socially accepted role, but they do not truly express themselves in life.

During the middle years, people who have learned to accept themselves find it easier to accept others and to extend themselves to help others enjoy a fuller life. Erikson calls this **generativity,** the creation of others. This activity is not accomplished through the biological bearing of children but through the psychological giving of self, through parenting, teaching, artistic endeavors, and so forth.[18, 19] People who are unable to find creative, productive outlets begin to stagnate ("couch potatoes"). In the last phase, **ego integrity,** the individual looks back on life realistically and says, "It's been good." Although errors are recognized, individuals can live with the idea that they did their best under the circumstances. A new wisdom emerges. As the infant learned to trust life, now the older adult learns to trust death. Those who cannot trust the idea of death experience despair, feeling that life was not worth it. They are afraid of the next step. For more information on Erikson, see Appendix B.

Theory of Adler
Alfred Adler spent 9 years studying with Freud but finally left him because he was unable to accept the concept of infantile sexuality. Adler believed that the **desire for power** offers

---

TABLE 1–2. ERIK H. ERIKSON'S PSYCHOSOCIAL DEVELOPMENTAL LEVELS

Developmental Level	Basic Task	Negative Counterpart	Basic Virtues
1. Infant	Basic trust	Basic mistrust	Drive and hope
2. Toddler	Autonomy	Shame and doubt	Self-control and will power
3. Preschooler	Initiative	Guilt	Direction and purpose
4. Schoolager	Industry	Inferiority	Method and competence
5. Adolescent	Identity	Role confusion	Devotion and fidelity
6. Young adult	Intimacy	Isolation	Affiliation and love
7. Middlescent	Generativity	Stagnation	Production and care
8. Older adult	Ego-integrity	Despair	Renunciation and wisdom

(Erikson, E. H. (1963). Childhood and Society (2nd ed.). New York: Norton.)

impetus for growth;[1] likewise, **feelings of inferiority** offer the impetus to strive to improve one's skills and behaviors. Although one is engaged in continuous, interpersonal competition throughout life, the basic foundations of personality structure are formed by age 6. Adler believed that feelings of inferiority originate from real or perceived organic deficiencies (malformation or immaturity), spoiling (overprotectiveness that prevents growth), or neglect (children are forced to be responsible for themselves before prerequisite skills are developed).[1]

Theory of Sullivan

Harry Stack Sullivan, a neo-Freudian, retained Freud's idea of developmental levels and the significance of the maternal relationship in personality development. He felt that **security,** rather than Adler's need for superiority, is a major goal in life. Security is achieved through satisfying social relationships. The anxiety that arises from perceived or real distance in relationships serves to motivate the individual to new, growth-producing, adaptive behaviors. (See Chap. 8 for further discussion.)

Behaviorist View

The theories of the behaviorists were developed in direct rebellion against the global, intangible theories presented by the psychodynamic theorists. Mental activity and unconscious motivations were dismissed as being outside the scientific realm. How can one observe, measure, and validate trust, inferiority, anxiety, or other mental processes and instincts? they asked. Their objective approach restricted attention to behaviors that could be directly observed and measured.[35] Today, these behaviors include physiological responses such as blood values and brain waves as well as specific social behaviors, psychomotor skills, and academic tasks. Historically, cognitive and affective (mental) processes have been ignored since they cannot be objectified and measured.

The behaviorist, adopting Locke's "passive man," tabula rasa philosophy, assert that the infant starts life with a "blank slate" and that innate tendencies are strengthened, shaped, and modified by experiences offered by the environment. The basic theory is quite simple: all behavior is under the control of environmental contingencies. The antecedent (stimulus or need) sets the occasion for behavior. Behaviors are maintained by the consequences (contingencies) supplied by the environment when the behavior is performed (Fig. 1-4). A basic presupposition of behaviorist theory is that people are pleasure-seeking creatures and behave in ways that result in pleasant consequences. If the consequence is seen as desirable, then the behavior is increased in frequency or intensity. If the environment does not respond or if the behavior results in unpleasant consequences, then the behavior gradually decreases until it becomes extinguished.

The behaviorists offer no comprehensive framework of human development except that knowledge of an individual's responses in past situations can be used to predict responses in the future. Heredity and physical maturation are under-

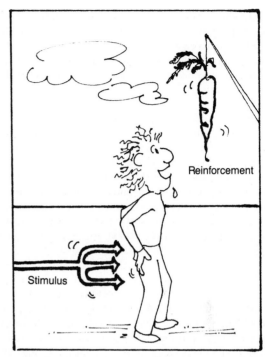

FIGURE 1–4.
According to behaviorist theory, a person emits a certain behavior because of the reinforcement received after performing that behavior.

emphasized, primarily because they are uncontrollable. The behaviorists are more concerned with systematic research to discover the mechanics (how and why) of learning than with a description of evolving phases (what or when). They attempt to identify long- and short-term causal relationships. Their carefully designed research methodology has proved to be extremely valuable in developing scientific, effective teaching and parenting strategies.

Behavior continues to change during the entire life span as a result of adding new behaviors, modifying old behaviors, and losing other behaviors. "Social conditions dictate the existence of developmental phases"[44] by differentially responding to age-dependent skills, roles, and responsibilities. The environmental reinforcement of successive approximations to the final desired behaviors is responsible for much of the shaping or the modification that occurs in behavior over time. Growth occurs as limited response elements are gradually organized by association into larger, more complex response patterns that can be transferred or generalized to new situations. The theoretical aim of behaviorists concerned with developmental profiles is to identify how earlier events are associated with and effect responses to environmental stimuli later in life, through the organization of behaviors and habit formation to provide a more accurate prediction and control of behavior.[39] This view obviously assumes that all behavior has an antecedent and leaves little room for spontaneous actions, will, or creativity on the part of the individual. Individual differences are seen to be the result of differing experiences or genetic influences. The mature individual has internalized the antecedents and consequences of behavior to become self-regulating and less dependent on concrete environmental events. In other words, eventually the individual internally reinforces his or her behavior.

Theory of Watson

J. B. Watson is considered the "father of American behaviorism" because of his clarification and formalization of the theory around 1915.[39] He completely rejected the concepts of mind and consciousness; he demonstrated that both emotions and motor responses could be "taught" through environmental experiences by pairing a furry animal with a loud noise in the presence of infants. The infants soon exhibited fear when they saw the furry animal. Watson also felt that language development was the product of conditioning.

Theory of Skinner

B. F. Skinner is probably the most famous name in behaviorism because of his mid–20th-century discovery and application of behaviorist learning principles to systematically change behavior. Critics feel that the data from his animal experiments should not be applied to human learning. Advocates of his research state that elementary learning principles are the same regardless of the animal species; therefore, generalization to human learning is by implication. It must be noted that every behaviorist principle has been demonstrated at all levels of phylogeny: fish, rats, pigeons, apes, and humans.

Theory of Bandura

In the 1960s, Albert Bandura observed that all learning did not occur in isolation or through trial and error, with the individual struggling to learn the significant relationships and contingencies. He proposed that much learning occurred through observation of other individuals and replication of the model's behaviors.[6] Bandura recognized the joint influence of social modeling and cognitive processes on behavior patterns and postulated an internal representation to guide behaviors. Expectations of the consequence serve as a self-restraint or a motivator. Bandura's social learning theory has marked implications for the effects of family life and television on the development of aggression and affection, prosocial and antisocial behaviors, gender roles, and self-discipline.

Organic Maturation Views

The maturationalist postulates that there is an autogenetic, species-typical path (creod or canalization) that all members of a species follow given a "normal, expected environment." Individuals have strong self-righting tendencies if the environment is atypical. Biological maturation serves as the impetus for the emergence of social and cognitive skills. Functionalists study structure and activities from a biological perspective and focus on adaptation. Cognitivists concentrate on information processing and cognitive structuring (Fig. 1-5).[39]

FIGURE 1–5.
According to the organic maturation views, individuals proceed through a series of increasingly complex skills as body systems mature and opportunities become available to practice these skills.

Individuals (consciously and unconsciously) internally organize, integrate, and transform themselves to maintain meaningful, adaptive interaction with the environment. The individual actively guides his or her own growth and development through (1) possession of genetically endowed sensitivities or skills for initial interactions with the environment, (2) determining one's own orientation to both self and the world and thereby constructing one's own experiences, (3) organizing one's inner world to interact meaningfully with the outer world, and (4) actively seeking experiences to actualize genetic potentials.[40] Mastery of skills is seen as self-generative toward higher levels of achievement.

Although discontinuous developmental stages are identified, personal continuity is maintained as each new stage emerges. One subview, **orthogenesis,** sees development as progressive hierarchical integration or "nesting" of skills and associations, with the result that more highly developed systems regulate less highly developed skills. A second subview, **equilibration,** postulates that periods of disequilibrium are experienced by an individual as new skills are being mastered. The temporary instability accompanying the transition period is healthy since it represents and facilitates progress toward stability. Periods of disequilibrium occur less frequently as the individual matures physically, socially, cognitively, spiritually, and emotionally.

Theory of Piaget

Jean Piaget's theory of cognitive development assumes that an individual's basic goal in life is to learn to master the environment (both external and internal).[21] The pleasure received from mastery spurs increased curiosity, problem solving, imitation, practice, and play activities.[51] His assumption is that human nature is essentially rational and that human knowledge is self-created.

Piaget proposes four major cognitive processes: (1) a **schema,** which is a unit or category of thought, a mental classification for an object or an action (see Chap. 7); (2) **assimilation,** the process whereby stimuli are recognized and integrated into an already existing schema; (3) **accommodation,** the creation of a new schema or the modification of an old one to account for newly recognized differences in a behavior or stimulus; and (4) **equilibration,** the balance a person maintains between assimilation and accommodation. Equilibration is a self-regulating process which prevents overloading or underloading of a system by the search for, or avoidance of, novel experiences.

In Piaget's theory, cognitive development is divided into four developmental levels, each of which is characterized by specific interaction patterns with the environment.[49] During the **sensorimotor** stage (birth to age 2), understanding proceeds from the reflexive activities of the neonate through sensorimotor solutions to problems. The child in the **preoperational** stage (2–7 years) solves simple motor problems internally through the use of symbols and language. The **concrete operational** child (7–11 years) is able to provide logical solutions to specific, practical, concrete problems. Between 11 and 15 years, the child develops the ability to think scientifically about complex and abstract issues. Once **formal operations** (mature thought processes) are developed, quantitative, but not qualitative, changes in intellectual functioning occur.[50]

Havighurst's Developmental Tasks

Robert Havighurst, an educator, proposed that at each life phase the individual is presented with a set of core tasks to master. These tasks are both organically and socially determined.[29] Accomplishment of lower-level tasks prepares one for higher-level skills. His tasks reflect the middle class ideals of the 1960s. Havighurst's tasks can be helpful in developing educational programs (see Appendix C).

Theory of Gesell

Arnold Gesell made detailed longitudinal observations of infant and child development. From these observations, he proposed that maturation of the neuromuscular system allows for progressive organization of behaviors and age-specific norms. He felt that his description of the cyclic emergence of periods of psychosocial equilibrium and disequilibrium was useful in predicting intrapersonal and interpersonal relationships.[34] Like the other two organic maturationalists discussed, Gesell felt that the environment influences many of an individual's modes of expression, but that the emergence of behavior patterns is basically determined from within. The evolution of every type of behavior (physical, social, cognitive, and emotional) exhibits remarkably predictable stages. From Gesell comes the concept that "the child is just going through a stage; he'll outgrow it." Gesell recognized the influence of individual temperament as a critical variable in the amount of fluctuation observed between periods of equilibrium versus those of disequilibrium. He also proposed that the cycle begins at birth and continues during the adult years. This cycle is discussed further in Chapter 2. (See Table 2-6).

Humanistic View

The humanistic view of development (the "Third Force") emerged during the mid-20th century as a reaction against both the psychodynamic and behaviorist models. Humanistically oriented psychologists could not accept the theory that people were in constant conflict between societal mores and inner impulses, nor could they accept the view that individuals responded mechanically to environmental contingencies. Psychodynamic views originated from interviews with individuals who exhibited pathological behaviors in adaptation to life; consequently, the concept of "constant conflict" was quite valid on the basis of the populations studied, that is, mentally disturbed people.

Humanists looked for normal, healthy subjects to interview and analyze in developing their theory of the healthy, self-actualizing individual who is constantly growing toward successively higher levels of personal integration. They contend that the "will to health" or the incentive toward growth is innate. The basic drive is to grow, to find meaning in life, unity in experiences, and to actualize one's innate potentials. The humanist contends that behavior is ambiguous or confusing unless its meaning and intent are understood from the point of view of the particular individual. For example, one person may cry as an expression of intense joy, another, as an expression of pity, pain, fear, or relief. Attempts to describe and analyze behavior apart from feelings, beliefs, values, thoughts, and aspirations artificially bisect the individual and insult the integrity of the person as a holistic unit (Fig. 1-6).[14]

Humanistically oriented psychologists emphasize the distinctively human characteristics of choice, will, creativity, values, and self-realization. The uniqueness of each individual, rather than the norm, is a primary focus. Each individual is endowed with "value" and "dignity." From the humanistic viewpoint, each individual, regardless of the degree of innate potential, has the right to develop his or her potentials to the maximum. Human development is never complete, and growth experiences may be painful. Humans are constantly assessing and organizing experiences to construct their own growth. Happiness does not become a goal in life but is a by-product of proactive, self-actualizing activity.[2] One can enjoy or appreciate his or her current self while at the same time evolving or becoming a more authentic self. It should be noted that humanistic theories have little predictive value and are difficult to subject to empirical verification.

In contrast to the maturationalists' concept of canaliza-

FIGURE 1–6.
According to the humanistic view, potentials for growth are always present and need only a nurturing environment to develop.

tion, humanistic psychologists generally believe, as Maslow says, that "our inner nature is not strong, like instincts in animals, rather it is subtle, delicate, and in many ways weak. It is easily drowned out by learning, by cultural expectations, by fear, by disapproval, etc."[45] Maslow is the only representative of the humanistic position who has identified sequential developmental changes. Other humanistic psychologists present a core unifying goal, which guides interactions with the environment. Robert White's focal organizer is the quest for competence.[68] Arthur Combs describes the person as striving to maintain and enhance the production of a more adequate self.[14] The more adequate the self, the broader the field of awareness (the perceptual field) and the wider the range of available responses.

Theory of Allport

Gordon Allport was one of the first to develop a theory of "becoming," the conscious striving toward adaptive realization of self within the culture. He felt that one could intentionally create one's own lifestyle. He stressed the development of proactive coping behaviors, in contrast to Freud's reactive defense mechanisms. In other words, the problems that block life's pathway become stepping stones to further growth with Allport's coping, but become stumbling blocks if one accepts Freud's defense mechanisms. (These concepts are discussed in more depth in Chapters 36 and 39.)

Theory of Maslow

Abraham Maslow is generally acknowledged as the founder of the "Third Force." After the birth of his first child, he could no longer accept the behaviorist view of development. He stressed the need to provide children with physical comfort and nurturing, protection, love, acceptance, a feeling of belonging, and a sense of personal value or esteem. Maslow felt that children should be allowed and encouraged to make choices in a supportive environment. In this framework, children are allowed to grow, to become individuals, and to maximize potentials.[45]

Maslow offers a five-level hierarchy of needs that serve as motivators for behavior (see Chap. 39 and Appendixes B and C). As the needs of each level are met, the individual is able to advance to the next level. Lower-level needs are always present, but they require minimal attention once they are adequately met. Maslow recognizes that the environment can stifle the full expression of an individual's potentials. One may return to focusing on lower-level needs given negative changes in the environment. Once a person stops looking to the future with conscious planning and anticipation of events, stagnation occurs. Maslow estimates that only about 1% of those in the Western culture ever reach complete self-actualization or full maximization of potentials.[45]

Holistic Developmental View

The tasks cited at the beginning of each unit were developed by the author, Clara Schuster, a developmentalist with backgrounds in nursing, education, exceptional children, and developmental psychology. In her work with children of varying disabilities and social backgrounds, she found the developmental tasks of other theorists to be useful but not always relevant to children with multifaceted needs. For instance, the developmental tasks of Havighurst are too specific to use with some disabled children. The specific skill schedules of the developmental assessments are often too mechanistic. Using a pragmatic, eclectic approach derived from her own observations, other disciplines, and the concepts of theorists from the maturational, psychoanalytic, and humanistic persuasions, Schuster developed a set of generic, culture-free tasks to provide a more holistic description of developmental phases. Failure to master these crucial tasks was observed to interfere with healthy development in multiple domains. These tasks prove to be useful for both assessment and intervention. Specific objectives are formulated according to the unique characteristics or context of the person's life and are limited only by the creativity of the practitioner.

Like the maturationalists, Schuster recognizes the role of neuromuscular development in setting the stage for skill emergence, especially in the early years. However, she observes that the stimuli, opportunities, and contingencies of the environment are crucial to helping the young child organize adaptive responses. She believes that biophysical, psychosociocultural, and self-generating factors all play significant roles in growth and development. However, the self-generating skills of the young child are weak and need a synchronized, nurturing, contingent environment to maximize potentials. Age-relevant tasks are presented at the opening of each unit and again in Appendix A.

CONCLUSION

The concept that qualitative differences in cognitive, biological, and psychological functioning accompany various stages of the life span is a relatively recent discovery. This recognition has been facilitated by advances in technology and medicine that have resulted in reduced attention to survival needs and greater attention to the needs for security, self-esteem, and self-actualization. However, many adults in today's Western society still view children and minority groups in ways that are reminiscent of earlier eras. Many families, caught in the cycles of poverty, are disadvantaged by both their cultural and financial heritage. These attitudes must be identified and acknowledged if professionals hope to maximize both their own potentials and those of their clients. Western cultures, under the humanistic view, are beginning to appreciate the individuality of each person and to stress the need for approaches by both family and society that maximize the individual's potentials without violating the rights of others.

An individual's or society's concept of humanness (that is, who is or is not entitled to the full benefits of protection, respect, education, medical care, affection, and opportunities) is more significant than political system, financial status, or geographic location in determining the quality of life, the ability of persons to cooperate, and the ability of individuals and cultures to maximize potentials.

Research with human subjects is difficult because of the researchers' inability to identify and control all the critical variables as well as the potential for violation of human or individual rights. Although not all theories and views can be supported by empirical studies, they do offer frameworks for understanding, explaining, or predicting human behavior.

The four theoretical umbrellas, or "grand theories," all originated before 1930 and continue to influence our understanding of development today.[32] No one theory has a corner on the truth. Knowledge of each view is essential to obtain a holistic view of human nature and functioning. At this point, we echo Piaget, who says, "clearly, though the modest facts assembled in this work may have permitted us to answer a few minor outstanding questions, they continue to pose a host of problems. This may well perturb even the most patient of readers, but does not daunt the research worker to whom new problems are often more important than the accepted solutions."[51] We must work with what we know—or think we know—until research or another great theoretician can explain development better. In spite of a host of both positive and negative data, no research has "provided sufficiently serious challenge to any given theory to necessitate theory revision or theory generation."[32] Although the four main views contain many contradictory points, they can be used in

tandem to explain behavior or to plan individualized approaches.

Appendix B gives a brief history and expands on some of the psychological theories of personality development. Appendix C provides a quick reference to the basic theoretical frameworks of theorists, offering a sequential stage approach to development.

REFERENCES

1. Adler, A. (1956). *The individual psychology of Alfred Adler: A systematic presentation in selections from his writings* (Ed. and annotated by H. L. Ansbacher and R. R. Ansbacher). New York: Harper & Row.
2. Allport, G. W. (1955). *Becoming: Basic considerations for a psychology of personality.* New Haven, CT: Yale University Press.
3. Ariès, P. (1962). *Centuries of childhood: A social history of family life* (R. Baldick, Trans.). New York: Vintage Books.
4. Aronoff, J., Rabin, A. I., & Zucker, R. A. (1987). The emergence of personality. In J. Aronoff, A. I. Rabin, & R. A. Zucker (Eds.), *The emergence of personality* (pp. 1–12). New York: Springer Publishing Company.
5. Baltes, P. B. (1987). Theoretical propositions of life-span developmental psychology: On the dynamics between growth and decline. *Developmental Psychology, 23,* 611–626.
6. Bandura, A. (1977). *Social learning theory.* Englewood Cliffs, NJ: Prentice-Hall.
7. Beale, R. W., Jr. (1985). In search of the historical child: Minature adulthood and youth in colonial New England. In N. R. Hiner & J. M. Hawes (Eds.), *Growing up in America: Children in historical perspective* (pp. 7–24). Urbana, IL: University of Illinois Press.
8. Block, J. H. (1982). Psychological development of female children and adolescents. In P. W. Berman & E. R. Ramey (Eds.), *Women: A developmental perspective* (pp. 107–121). Bethesda, MD: U.S. Dept. of Health & Human Services. (NIH Publication No. 82-2298)
9. Calhoun, A. W. (1973). *A social history of the American family from colonial times to the present.* New York: Arno Press.
10. Carbonara, N. T. (1961). *Techniques for observing normal child behavior.* Pittsburgh, PA: University of Pittsburgh Press.
11. Chapman, M. (1988). *Constructive evolution: Origins and development of Piaget's thought.* Cambridge, UK: Cambridge University Press.
12. Cleverley, J., & Phillips, D. C. (1986). *Visions of childhood: Influential models from Locke to Spock* (rev. ed.). New York: Teachers College Press.
13. Coles, R. (1981). How the other half lives: Children of the rich. In M. Albin & D. Cavallo (Eds.), *Family life in America, 1620–2000* (pp. 49–61). St. James, NY: Revisionary Press.
14. Combs, A. W., Richards, A. C., & Richards, F. (1989). *Perceptual psychology: A humanistic approach to the study of persons* (rev. ed.). Lanham, MD: University Presses of America.
15. Council on Scientific Affairs of A.M.A. (1989). Animals in research. *Journal of the American Medical Association, 261,* 3602–3606.
16. deMause, L. (1974). The evolution of childhood: History of childhood in the west. In L. deMause (Ed.), *The history of childhood* (pp. 1–73). New York: The Psychohistory Press.
17. Demos, J., & Boocock, S. S. (Eds.). (1978). *Turning points:*

Historical and sociological essays on the family. Chicago: University of Chicago Press.

18. Erikson, E. H. (1963). *Childhood and society,* 2nd edition. New York: W.W. Norton.

19. Erikson, E.H., Erikson, J. M., & Kivnick, H. Q. (1986). *Vital involvement in old age.* New York: W. W. Norton.

20. Flandrin, J. L. (1979). *Families in former times: Kinship, household and sexuality* (R. Southern, Trans.). New York: Cambridge University Press.

21. Flavell, J. H. (1968). *The developmental psychology of Jean Piaget.* Princeton, NJ: Van Nostrand.

22. Freud, S. (1935). *A general introduction to psycho-analysis* (authorized English translation of the revised edition by J. Riviere). New York: Liveright.

23. Frosh, S. (1987). *The politics of psychoanalysis: An introduction to Freudian and post-Freudian theory.* New Haven, CT: Yale University Press.

24. Greenberg, J., & Folger, R. (1988). *Controversial issues in social research methods.* New York: Springer-Verlag.

25. Gross, F. J., Jr. (1987). *Introducing Erik Erikson: An invitation to his thinking.* Lanham, MD: University Press of America.

26. Gutman, H. G. (1976). *The Black family in slavery and freedom, 1750–1925.* New York: Pantheon Books.

27. Hall, G. S. (1891). The contents of children's minds on entering school. *Pedagogical Seminary* 1: 139–173.

28. Hannerz, U. (1981). Growing up male in a black ghetto. In M. Albin & D. Cavallo (Eds.), *Family life in America, 1620–2000* (pp. 220–233). St. James, NY: Revisionary Press.

29. Havighurst, R. J. (1972). *Developmental tasks and education* (3rd ed.). New York: David McKay.

30. Hiner, N. R., & Hawes, J. M. (Eds.). (1985). *Growing up in America: Children in historical perspective.* Urbana, IL: University of Illinois Press.

31. Hoglund, A. W. (1986). *Immigrants and their children in the United States: A bibliography of doctoral dissertations, 1885–1982.* New York: Garland Publishers.

32. Horowitz, F. D. (1987). *Exploring developmental theories: Toward a structural/behavioral model of development.* Hillsdale, NJ: Lawrence Erlbaum Associates.

33. Horrocks, J. E. (1976). *The psychology of adolescence* (4th ed.). Boston: Houghton Mifflin.

34. Ilg, F. L., Ames, L. B., & Baker, S. M. (1981). *Child behavior* (rev. ed.). New York: Barnes and Noble.

35. Kendler, H. H. (1985). Behaviorism and Psychology: An uneasy alliance. In S. Koch & D. E. Leary (Eds.), *A century of psychology as science* (pp. 121–134). New York: McGraw-Hill.

36. Keniston, K. (1970). *The uncommitted: Alien youth in American society.* New York: Dell.

37. Kessler-Harris, A. (1986). Independence and virtue in the lives of wage-earning women: The United States, 1870–1930. In J. Friedlander, B. W. Cook, A. Kessler-Harris, & C. Smith-Rosenberg (Eds.), *Women in culture and politics: A century of change* (pp. 3–17). Bloomington, IN: Indiana University Press.

38. Kiefer, M. M. (1948). *American children through their books, 1700–1835.* Philadelphia: University of Pennsylvania Press.

39. Kleinginna, P. R., Jr., & Kleinginna, A. M. (1988). Current trends toward convergence of the behavioristic, functional, and cognitive perspectives in experimental psychology. *The Psychological Record, 38,* 369–392.

40. Langer, J. (1969). *Theories of development.* New York: Holt, Rinehart & Winston.

41. Levitan, S. A., Belous, R. S., & Gallo, F. (1988). *What's happening to the American family? Tensions, hopes, realities* (rev. ed.). Baltimore: Johns Hopkins University Press.

42. Locke, J. (1964). Some thoughts concerning education (abridged). In P. Gay (Ed.), *John Locke on education.* New York: Bureau of Publications, Teacher's College, Columbia University.

43. Locke, J. (1973). Some thoughts concerning education (1690). In the Works of John Locke, in nine volumes (9th ed.: London, 1794) Vol. VIII, pp. 26–43, 93–97, 102–104. In P. J. Greven (Ed.), *Child-rearing concepts, 1628–1861: Historical sources* (pp. 20–33). Itasca, IL: F. E. Peacock Publishers.

44. Maier, H. W. (1988). *Three theories of child development,* 3rd edition. Lanham, MD: University Press of America.

45. Maslow, A. H. (1968). *Toward a psychology of being,* 2nd edition. New York: Van Nostrand.

46. Merriam, E. (Ed.). (1971). *Growing up female in America: Ten lives.* Garden City, NJ: Doubleday.

47. Nasaw, D. (1985). *Children of the city: At work and at play.* Garden City, NJ: Doubleday.

48. Orme, N. (1984). *From childhood to chivalry: The education of the English kings and aristocracy 1066–1530.* New York: Methuen.

49. Piaget, J. (1962). *Play, dreams and imitation in childhood* (C. Gattegno & F. M. Hodgson, Trans.). New York: W. W. Norton.

50. Piaget, J. (1966). *The psychology of intelligence* (M. Piercy & D. E. Berlyne, Trans.). Totowa, NJ: Littlefield, Adams.

51. Piaget, J. (1978). *Success and understanding* (A. J. Pomerans, Trans.). Cambridge, MA: Harvard University Press.

52. Ploski, H. A., & Marr, W. (Eds.) (1989). *The negro almanac: A reference work on the Afro American* (5th ed.). New York: Bellwether Company.

53. Power, E. J. (1970). *Main currents in the history of education* (2nd ed.). New York: McGraw-Hill.

54. Redl, F. (1974). *Pre-adolescents—What makes them tick?* New York: Child Study Association of America.

55. Rodgers, D. T. (1985). Socializing middle-class children: Institutions, fables, and work values in nineteenth-century America. In N. R. Hiner & J. M. Hawes (Eds.), *Growing up in America: Children in historical perspective* (pp. 119–132). Urbana, IL: University of Illinois Press.

56. Rose, W. L., & W. W. Freehling (Ed.) (1982). *Slavery and freedom.* New York: Oxford University Press.

57. Rousseau, J. J. (1962). *Émile* (W. Boyd, Trans.). In W. Boyd (Ed.), *The Émile of Jean Jacques Rousseau.* New York: Bureau of Publications, Teachers College, Columbia University.

58. Scott, D. M., & Wishy, B. (Eds.). (1982). *America's families: A documentary history.* New York: Harper and Row.

59. Scott, R. J. (1985). The battle over the child: Child apprenticeship and the Freedmen's Bureau in North Carolina. In N. R. Hiner & J. M. Hawes (Eds.), *Growing up in America: Children in historical perspective* (pp. 193–207). Urbana, IL: University of Illinois Press.

60. Slater, P. G. (1985). From the cradle to the coffin: Parental bereavement and the shadow of infant damnation in Puritan society. In N. R. Hiner & J. M. Hawes (Eds.), *Growing up in America: Children in historical perspective* (pp. 227-243). Urbana, IL: University of Illinois Press.

61. Smith, D. B. (1985). Autonomy and affection: Parents and children in eighteenth-century Chesapeake families. In N. R. Hiner & J. M. Hawes (Eds.), *Growing up in America: Children in historical perspective* (pp. 45–58). Urbana, IL: University of Illinois Press.

62. Soliday, G. L. (Ed.). (1980). *History of the family and kinship:*

A select international bibliography. Millwood, NY: Kraus-International Publications.

63. Szasz, M. C. (1985). Federal boarding schools and the Indian child: 1920–1960. In N. R. Hiner & J. M. Hawes (Eds.), *Growing up in America: Children in historical perspective* (pp. 209–218). Urbana, IL: University of Illinois Press.

64. Tentler, L. W. (1981). The working-class daughter 1900–1930. In M Albin & D. Cavallo (Eds.), *Family life in America, 1620–2000* (pp. 184–203). St. James, NY: Revisionary Press.

65. van Geert, P. (1987). The structure of Erikson's model of the eight ages: A generative approach. *Human Development, 30,* 236–254.

66. Washington, V. (1988). The black mother in the United States: History, theory, research and issues. In B. Birns & D. F. Hay (Eds.), *The different faces of motherhood* (pp. 185–213). New York: Plenum Press.

67. Welter, B. (1983). The cult of true womanhood: 1820–1860. In M.

Gordon (Ed.), *The American family in social-historical perspective* (pp. 372–392). New York: St. Martin's Press.

68. White, R. W. (1959). Motivation reconsidered: The concept of competence. *Psychological Review, 66,* 297–333.

69. Wiggins, D. K. (1985). The play of slave children in the plantation communities of the Old South, 1820–1860. In N. R. Hiner & J. M. Hawes (Eds.), *Growing up in America: Children in historical perspective* (pp. 173–190). Urbana, IL: University of Illinois Press.

70. Wishy, B. W. (1968). *The child and the republic: The dawn of modern American child nurture.* Philadelphia: University of Pennsylvania Press.

71. Zelizer, V. A. (1981). The price and value of children: The case of children's insurance. *American Journal of Sociology, 86,* 1036–1056.

72. Zelizer, V. A. (1985). *Pricing the priceless child: The changing social value of children.* New York: Basic Books.

The Holistic Approach

Clara S. Schuster

Every individual is a unique entity, functioning as a total unit. At any given moment, our behavior is influenced by a cumulative repertoire of skills and experiences, current physiological state, goals, values, and the cultural milieu as well as our perception of the immediate environment. "The phenomena and processes of [human] development are a magnitude of complexity that has no parallel in any other science."[36]

To understand and maximize human functioning, each discipline examines a separate aspect of development. The educator looks at cognitive development; the medical practitioner, at biophysical development; the social worker, at social development; the psychologist, at affective and cognitive development; and the clergyman, at spiritual development. These focused approaches are deemed essential for effective, efficient **intervention** (supportive or therapeutic) strategies. However, there is an inherent danger to this segmentation: When a person exhibits a **variation** (alternative predictable behavior) or a **deviation** (unpredictable or pathological behavior) from the norm, the **practitioner** (professionally trained person) of a specific discipline may concentrate so heavily on that one aspect of the life of the **client** (person who needs assistance) that the other normal aspects may be ignored. In other words, the practitioner may fail to appreciate the client's strengths, to see a behavior in context, to assess behavior from a developmental perspective while trying to remedy the weaknesses, or to work with the person's developmental level or strengths. In extreme cases, several practitioners, concurrently working with a client, may use counteracting therapies because, in their myopic molecular approach, they have failed to see the client as a total person, or they have failed to cooperate with each other. The client may actually "get lost in the shuffle."

A holistic approach is essential to prevent compartmentalized study and treatment of clients. The **holistic approach** recognizes the person as an indivisible totality and considers the interdependent functioning of the affective, biophysical, cognitive, social, and spiritual domains, the client's developmental level, and the context or **umwelt** (total internal and external environment) as vital elements for assessment and intervention. **Holism,** a term coined in 1926,[61] is a philosophy that supports the need to be concerned with all aspects of a person's life. The individual's family, history, environment, goals, and roles are all considered significant. This integrated approach to understanding the individual also addresses concepts such as self, value, meaning, purpose, and intention.

Each one of us is like *all* other people in some aspects, like *some* other people in other aspects, and like *no* other person in still other aspects. Only through a holistic approach can **inter**individual (among or between people) similarities and differences be identified, and one's uniqueness be respected and appreciated. The holistic approach also recognizes that most people experience **intra**individual (within a person) discrepancies; that is, we approach the norms in some aspects of our lives but exhibit variations and deviations in others. Development among domains may be uneven, a factor which creates stress for all of us.

For study purposes, the various domains can be reviewed separately for developmental stages, behavioral manifestations, and significant influencing factors. However, whether dealing with others or ourselves, we must appreciate the integration of these domains and respect each person's humanness in the midst of life's dramas and problems.

THE HOLISTIC APPROACH TO CLIENT CARE

Most people who go into "helping professions" care about the welfare of other people and want in some way to ease the pain and problems associated with "being human." However, we learn early in our careers that caring is not enough; *caring must be coupled with knowledge,* a large body of knowledge that must be systematically applied to offer effective and efficient care. This knowledge has to go beyond the confines of our specific discipline and embrace the whole realm of developmental changes, lest we create further stressors for individuals by failing to recognize the normalcy (or pathology) of a behavior in context. At times, even those armed with adequate knowledge may fail to integrate essential information because of their professional orientation and perceived role.

Perspectives on Assessment and Intervention

Models

Practitioners trained in an **orthodox model** (medical or disease model) approach their profession as detectives. "I am responsible for determining the pathology, the cause, the treatment, and the cure." The practitioner approaches the client with a single-discipline "repair-shop" mentality, while encouraging a passive stance on the part of the client.[9, 14] "I will do something to or for you to make you better." This controlling molecular approach dehumanizes the client, as the clinician concentrates on the one issue that demands attention. The orthodox model tends to focus on curing illness rather than on maintaining or supporting health or growth and development.[14] This autocratic approach assumes that the practitioner knows the "one best way."[9]

Clinicians who use a **systems model** (holistic model) approach their professions as consultants. "What do you see as the problem, and how can I help you to deal with it?" The client maintains control over the decision-making processes. The client is viewed as the custodian of his or her own life; consequently, the practitioner and the client work together to assess strengths and weaknesses and to identify optimal ways to use internal and external resources. Assessment and treatment follow a comprehensive multidimensional approach.[14] The focus is on maintaining and facilitating health. The practitioner may serve as an assessor, teacher, coordinator, consultant, advocate, or provider of care as the client expresses need. This **gestalt** approach (total person in context) considers all aspects of the person's life and thus "exceeds the capabilities of the disease model"[24] by helping to mobilize the client's resources, recognizing the client's contribution to the quality of his or her own life, and respecting the client as a competent decision maker. Even the infant makes better progress in a therapy program if muscle movement is initiated voluntarily rather than forced by the practitioner. Holistic models facilitate effective functioning of all five domains and the successful integration of those components.[14] The holistic approach requires an empathetic practitioner who understands and respects the client as a person in the context of his or her family, developmental level, responsibilities, and concerns.[9]

Definitions

Definitions of terms change with one's orientation. For instance, the orthodox model sees **disease** as a pathological process, whereas the systems model defines it as a symptom of imbalance in functioning. **Health** is the absence of disease for the orthodox professional,[70] but it is the state of balance or equilibrium of an organism for the holistic practitioner, who views the state of health as a dynamic process, changing and accommodating to fluctuations in both the internal and external environments.[70] The natural righting properties of the person are observed to compensate for temporary imbalances in one domain (Table 2-1).

The orthodox model, using an interindividual perspective, defines **high-level wellness** as the ability to function at or above expected norms in one or more areas of life. The teacher looks for giftedness; the ophthalmologist, high visual acuity and accommodation; the sociologist, leadership qualities; and the physician, resistance to diseases or high cardiac reserve. The systems model, on the other hand, never compares one person to another but looks at the ability of an individual to use potentials optimally to meet the demands of the realities of everyday life (intraindividual perspective). This perspective accommodates for temporary or permanent disability or chronic disease as well as developmental levels because it is a proactive definition that implies optimal use of *current* potentials and appreciates the dynamic character of accommodation. Therefore, it acknowledges individual uniquenesses in skills, needs, and circumstances when determining the level of wellness. Thus, a person with diabetes, severe cerebral palsy, or mental retardation or even a person who has had a stroke can still have high-level wellness when all the factors are considered. The client activates the

TABLE 2–1. COMPARISON OF THE ORTHODOX AND HOLISTIC MODELS

	Orthodox Model	*Holistic Model*
Perspective	Interindividual differences	Intraindividual functioning
Disease	Pathological process	Symptom of imbalance
Health	Absence of disease	State of balance
High-level wellness	Functioning at or above the norms	Optimal use of current potentials
Stressor	Hazard to optimal functioning	Opportunity for growth and development

strengths of another domain to compensate for the domain with impaired functioning.

All persons face **stressors** throughout the life span. They may be in the form of interpersonal conflict, environmental change, illness, or even the aging process. The orthodox practitioner encourages avoiding, submerging, or extricating stressors because of their degenerative effects on functioning. The holistic model, however, views each stressor as a challenge, an opportunity for learning and personal development. When faced well, stressors encourage stretching and change and thus are essential to higher levels of understanding, integration, and functioning. From a holistic view, even the most gruelling stressors can have their growth points.

Holistic Health or Medicine Versus Holistic Approach

Because of the similarity in terminology, holistic health and medicine are sometimes thought to be synonymous with the holistic approach. They are quite different on all fronts.

Holistic Health or Medicine

Holistic health or medicine is heavily influenced by religious definitions of the nature of man.[57] People are described as a composition of either two or three domains. The **dichotomy** view defines people as having two divisions: Physical (mortal, material self) and Spiritual (immortal, nonmaterial self). The **trichotomy** view designates three divisions: Body (physical, the tool or house for the mind and spirit), Mind (one's temporal, conscious being), and Spirit (the eternal self) (Fig. 2-1). The focus of holistic health or medicine is the effect of the psyche (mind and spirit) on the soma (body). Consequently, the practice emphasizes the psychosomatic aspects of health and illness and uses traditional (non-Western) approaches to preventing and treating illness, including self-awareness, nutrition, stress reduction, hypnosis, meditation, biofeedback,[70] energy fields, therapeutic touch,[40] acupressure, and acupuncture.[30] The goals of holistic health are personal peace and high-level physical wellness through high-level nonphysical wellness. This approach is used mainly by spiritual leaders and lay healers for postadolescent people. It is also increasingly recognized by many orthodox health practitioners as a valuable adjunct in treating stress-induced dysfunctions.[15] Ho-

listic medicine requires a high degree of personal involvement and commitment.

Holistic Approach

The holistic approach is influenced by the fields of general systems theory[68] and developmental psychology. Five domains are recognized: **biophysical, cognitive, affective, social,** and **spiritual*.** The focus of the holistic approach is the interdependence of the domains in maintaining a person's state of health. Consequently, the approach emphasizes that, because an individual is an indivisible totality, other domains can help compensate for decreased functioning in a

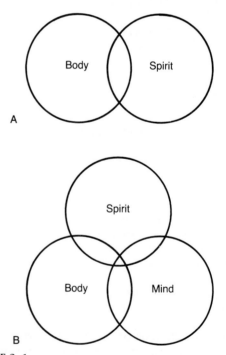

FIGURE 2–1.
Holistic concepts of the human organism: (A) dichotomy view; (B) trichotomy view.

---

*It is interesting to note that factors mentioned in Mark 12:29–31 parallel the five domains.

TABLE 2–2. COMPARISON OF HOLISTIC HEALTH AND HOLISTIC APPROACH

	Holistic Health	*Holistic Approach*
Domains	2–3	5
Emphasis	Psychosomatic issues of physical health	Interdependence of domains for total health
Treatment	Traditional medicine	Orthodox model for crisis, but otherwise mobilize strengths of total person
Goals	Personal peace, high-level physical wellness	Personal independence, maximization of potentials
Practitioners	Spiritual leaders, lay leaders	Practitioners of any discipline, parents

single domain. However, one potential or domain cannot be maximized at the expense of the others. Therefore, any intervention must consider the total person and incorporate all domains in any health maintenance or restabilization plans. This theory does not rule out orthodox focused attention to crisis dysfunction, but the holistic approach is resumed as quickly as possible, using family members as necessary to aid in decision making when the client is unable to make decisions for himself or herself. The goals are client independence and maximization of potentials through capitalizing on strengths. The holistic approach can be used equally effectively by teachers, parents, physicians, psychologists, nurses, occupational therapists, or social workers for either children or adults (Table 2-2).

THE FIVE DOMAINS

Focusing attention on five major domains does not rule out the potential for the existence of other domains, major or minor. However, the study of these five domains appears to organize and capture what is known and observed about the way humans function. The practitioner must be cognizant of the developmental changes expected in each of these areas if a truly holistic approach is to be assumed in meeting client needs and helping clients maximize potentials. This multidomain approach to working with clients enables the clinician to appreciate and work with the intraindividual differences exhibited by people. Table 2-3 presents an overview of each domain.

Definitions

Growth refers to the addition of new components or skills. In the biophysical domain, growth means an increase in body size by the *addition* of new cells (*hyperplastic growth*). **Development** is the refinement, the improvement, or the expansion of an existing component or skill. In the biophysical domain, development means an increase in body size by *enlargement* of cells already present (*hypertrophic growth*). **Maturation,** a concept similar to development, is the process

of achieving full or *optimal development* of a component or a skill. In the biophysical domain, maturation means the final differentiation or refinement in the functioning of cells, tissues, and organs and the establishment of cooperation among the components of the body. *At maturity,* or in high-level wellness, *minimal energy is expended to maintain optimal functioning.*

Throughout the text, there is reference to the term **maximization of potentials.** This concept does not imply that one must function at maximal capacity in all domains at all times; the organism would soon "burn out." The top athlete may run a mile in less than 4 minutes, but the same pace cannot be maintained in a 26-mile marathon. Maximization of potentials refers to uninhibited judicious use of one's innate talents and abilities or external resources.

Biophysical Domain

The biophysical domain encompasses all the tangible aspects of self—the body. It includes every aspect of the physical self, from conception until death; from the fertilized egg through fetal development, infancy, childhood, adulthood, and the

TABLE 2–3. OVERVIEW OF THE FIVE DOMAINS

Domain	*Description*
Biophysical	Concrete, physical reality of the self-system; the tool through which the other four domains express themselves
Cognitive	Interpreter, processor, and organizer of stimuli; one's "knowing system"; the conscious problem solver and decision maker for the system
Affective	**Internal** responses to events; one's intrapersonal relationships, self-concept, emotions
Social	**External** responses to events; one's interpersonal relationships, social skills
Spiritual	Life force, soul, consciousness of existence; one's transcendental relationships

aging processes. It includes how we inherit characteristics from our parents and how these characteristics in turn are transmitted to our offspring. Study of the biophysical domain is concerned not only with what happens, but with why and how a factor affects the physical functioning of the individual, and how to use this knowledge to maintain high-level physical wellness.

From a philosophical viewpoint, the body is seen as a tool for the expression of the other domains. Though a precise understanding of the interdependence with other domains is not yet clear, it is obvious that growth and development of the other four domains is heavily dependent on the adequacy of the relevant biophysical substrata. A holistic view recognizes that the other domains do not develop in isolation from the biophysical domain. Intact sensory **modalities** (e.g., visual, auditory, haptic, gustatory, and olfactory) are prerequisites for perception of the environment and subsequent cognitive organization of the information. The inadequately nourished child frequently has inadequate energy to attend to stimuli; thus, perception or organization of information by the cognitive domain may be altered. Inadequate awareness of stimuli also alters the person's motivation to interact with the environment (see Chaps. 7, 13, and 37).

Patterns of Growth

Physical growth appears to be governed by genetically determined, harmoniously channeled time schedules. Although the sequence of growth and development appears to be the same for all people, the rate of development and the end product are individual. Because of variations in nutrition, heredity, and environmental factors, the **biological age** (stage of physical growth and development achieved) is not always identical with the **chronological age** (time since birth). Obviously, the individual requires adequate nutrition, exercise, and stimuli to develop and maintain optimal biophysical functioning. Some practitioners indicate that, if appropriate stimuli are not given at the time the individual is biophysically programmed or ready to receive and use particular types of challenges for the development of a specific psychomotor skill, the skill becomes more difficult or impossible to learn later in the developmental sequence (critical period theory).[3, 5, 32, 33, 56] Examples might include three-dimensional vision, language acquisition, learning to eat solids, to jump, to use scissors, or to ride a bicycle. However, since the learning of each of these skills is also heavily influenced by sociocultural factors, it is difficult to negate psychological factors that may inhibit or motivate the acquisition of a specific skill at a later date (a more holistic approach). Knowledge of expected skill sequences can help the parent or clinician support optimal physical development by providing realistic goals and encouraging appropriate experiences to support the emergence of new skills.

The acquisition of skills, especially for young children, is heavily determined by neurological development. Since the nervous system develops from the brain toward the feet (**cephalocaudal**), infants raise their heads before they can

sit, and they must sit before they can crawl or walk. The nervous system also develops from the spinal cord toward the extremities (**proximodistal**). Consequently, **gross motor** (large muscle) activities precede **fine motor** (small muscle) activities. Children grasp an object with the palm (palmar grasp) before they grasp it with the finger and the thumb (pincer grip); they catch a ball with their arms before they can catch it with their hands.

Increase in body size, especially during the fetal and infancy periods, is primarily through **hyperplasia** (increase in the number of cells). Gradually, hyperplastic growth is replaced by **hypertrophic** growth (increase in the size of cells). After the adolescent years, increase in body size is a result of hypertrophic growth only. Each body organ has its own optimal periods of growth. These growth periods are discussed throughout the text; it is sufficient to indicate here that body tissues are most sensitive to permanent damage during periods of the most rapid hyperplastic growth.

Intraindividual differences in the developmental maturity of various organ systems can lead to temporary functional imbalances, such as the hormonal imbalances experienced during the pubertal years or the "growing pains" of the school-age years (see Chap. 20).

The aging process actually begins with the formation of each new cell. However, the cumulative effects of aging usually do not become apparent until the middlescent years, when the individual may begin to recognize changes in energy level, appearance, and functioning. The longer one lives, the greater is the chance of living beyond the average life expectancy. In 1988 in the United States, a newborn male could expect 71.5 years of life, and the female, 78.3 years.[74] However, a 70-year-old man can expect to live about 11 more years, and a woman of 70 can expect to have about 14 more years of life[65] (Table 2-4). Good health care and the avoidance of illness and

TABLE 2-4. EXPECTED REMAINING YEARS OF LIFE FOR GIVEN AGES IN THE UNITED STATES IN 1985

| Age (years) | Expected Remaining Years | | | |
| | White | | Black | |
	Male	Female	Male	Female
5	67.8	74.5	61.9	70.0
10	62.9	69.6	57.0	65.1
20	53.3	59.8	47.4	55.3
30	44.0	50.1	38.5	45.8
40	34.7	40.4	30.2	36.6
50	25.8	31.1	22.5	27.9
60	18.0	27.6	16.0	20.3
70	11.6	15.0	10.8	13.8
80	6.8	8.7	6.8	8.6
85	5.1	6.4	5.7	6.9

(U.S. Bureau of the Census. (1987). Statistical Abstract of the United States: 1988 (108th ed.). Washington, DC: U.S. Government Printing Office.)

accidents can increase the life span, but these measures cannot postpone death indefinitely. With increased longevity, maintenance of high-level wellness in all five domains becomes a challenge. The other four domains may exert as much influence as genetics on the physical domain at this point in life. The key appears to be maintaining a vital involvement in one's environment[19] and continuing to actively participate in the activities of daily living. A person without goals or an orientation toward the future "dies" before the body does. Because of the interdependence of domains, biophysical functioning may be depressed when one loses meaning in life or the will to live.

Physiological Parameters

Some **physiological parameters** (range of normal measurements), such as the acidity or the concentration of oxygen in the blood, remain fairly stable throughout the life span. Other parameters, such as the body temperature, exhibit minor changes under the influences of age, gender, hormonal balance, and time of day. Other parameters change markedly during one's lifetime. Changes in body surface area and organ size or maturity cause corresponding changes in pulse rate and fluid intake. The unique **metabolic** (growth, maintenance, and repair) needs of each growth period determine the caloric, calcium, and protein requirements of each developmental phase. Physiological parameters are given in Appendix E; the reader is advised to consult them as necessary while reading the text and for clinical practice.

The patterns for physical growth and development, especially in the areas of height and weight, can be predicted both for the "average" person and for individual children (see Appendixes D, E, and F). Height and weight charts are helpful primarily for quick reference and identification of gross abnormalities. Since "normal" ranges are wide, the practitioner should focus on the person, not on the norms. Particularly in the areas of height and weight, a child must serve as his or her own guide to normalcy. Hereditary factors set a pattern that can be readily distinguished by 3 years of age. By plotting changes on a height-weight grid, the clinician can identify otherwise nonapparent deviant (pathological) changes in a child's growth pattern. Any child who changes his or her growth pattern by 10% or who places outside the 10th or 90th percentile should receive an in-depth evaluation for potential health problems.

Biological Rhythms

The rising and the setting of the sun or moon, work schedules, the seasons, and other periodically recurring events help to establish a rhythm to physiological functioning. Blood pressure, temperature, electrolyte excretion, blood values, pulse rate, and even rapid eye movement (REM) sleep patterns, alertness, cognition, and psychomotor efficiency have all demonstrated patterned fluctuations during a 24-hour day.[10, 12] Therefore, the "normal" parameters must provide enough leeway to accept these variations. Although biological rhythms appear to be endogenous (internally mediated), they

are influenced by exogenous (externally imposed) factors.[49] An internal or "living" clock somehow signals the time for the onset of physiological activities, such as sleep. A monosynaptic pathway that leads from the retina to the suprachiasmatic nucleus of the hypothalamus appears to coordinate component rhythms and maintain synchrony of the body rhythms with the external environment.[12] In free-running time experiments (e.g., living in a cave without light, schedules, or clocks),[50] the suprachiasmatic nucleus maintains a "natural" endogenous circadian oscillation of about 25 hours (same as two moon rotations).[49, 73]

A primary exogenous factor that affects this temporal pacesetter is bright light.[11] Light appears to stimulate the pineal gland to secrete melatonin, which effects circadian oscillations.[73] Many sighted people, and one half of all blind people, find it difficult to "reset" their endogenous clock to the 24-hour day and thus fight sleepiness and insomnia at inappropriate times.[73]

The most commonly studied rhythm is the 24-hour day, the **circadian** rhythm (*circa,* about; *dies,* day). This internal clock signals when it is time to eat, to rest, and to sleep; it may even tell a person when to wake up. The circadian pacemaker begins to function by the 28th week of fetal life,[1] and by birth it is coordinated with the daily light-dark cycles.[54] Regular sleep-wake cycles begin to emerge around 3 weeks of age. By the 18th week, a 24-hour periodicity is well established, and adultlike fluctuations in body functions are achieved by the ninth month of extrauterine life.[52]

Studies indicate a positive correlation between body temperature and variations in mood or performance. For instance, the body temperature of "larks" (morning people) rises and declines earlier in the day than that of "owls" (night people). One's best performance also correlates with the peaks of temperature.[50] For most people, this peak occurs in the middle of the waking period. The body excretes more epinephrine during these periods of high alertness.[42] Studies with children indicate that 98% achieve a higher score when teaching periods are synchronized with their preferred or "best" time for learning.[17]

These rhythms are easily disrupted. Those who have experienced jet lag are acutely aware of the dyssynchrony between the internal clock and the external stimuli. When the clocks are set forward or back 1 hour in the spring or fall, it takes 2 days for the blood pressure to make the shift and 5 days for the body temperature to reestablish its rhythm.[64] The more dramatic and abrupt changes of jet lag or shift work may require 4 to 10 days for a resetting of the biological clock and rhythms.[60] "Re-entrainment" is necessary when the sleep period is modified or changed.[27] Sixty percent of people who work rotating shifts experience serious symptoms of dyssynchrony: fatigue, depression, anorexia, nervousness, hunger and sleepiness at inappropriate times, tension, decreased mental alertness, delayed reaction time, and even increased medical problems such as ulcers and heart attacks.[59] A marked increase in industrial accidents is also found. Both the Chernobyl and the Three Mile Island nuclear reactor accidents occurred in the early morning hours with "shift" employees.[35, 59] When shift changes occur every 3 weeks on a forward rotation, workers adjust 50% faster, experience a 20% increase in productivity, have a lower turnover rate, and experience fewer accidents than when they are rotated on a backward rotation.[35, 59] Employers should consider the implications of mandatory shift work versus monetary incentives for regular employment at the less desirable hours. People who experience jet lag, depression, insomnia, or other problems precipitated by circadian dysfunctional disorders can "reset" their suprachiasmatic nucleus by systematic exposure to bright light each morning.[12, 44]

Many people experience energy dips at midmorning, after lunch, and in the early evening. These decreases in energy appear to be part of a basic rest-activity cycle;[42] they appear at approximately 90-minute cycles, even during sleep, after the eighth month of fetal life.[2] The assessment of rhythms can help a person identify and use points of high energy to promote optimal adaptive behaviors and thus increase independence by matching cognitive and social activities to one's internal clock. For example, a person can work with these natural rest-activity rhythms to enhance study efficiency. Taking a 10- to 15-minute break from studies every 1½ to 2 hours is more productive than studying for 4 hours straight.

(Studying for 30-minute periods usually does not allow sufficient time for integration and continuity.) Human growth hormone secretion in infants is highest during REM sleep and depends on rhythmic recurrences of sleep. Fifty percent of infant sleep, 25% of adolescent sleep, and 20% of adult sleep is spent in active REM sleep.[69]

Some biological rhythms are repeated at periods greater than 24 hours. Some energy cycles are repeated on a weekly basis or every 3 to 4 days; the menstrual cycle repeats itself about every 4 weeks. The reader may wish to keep a record to discover his or her own high and low energy cycle. People are most efficient when they can work with rather than in spite of their cycles (Fig. 2-2).

Cognitive Domain

The cognitive domain encompasses all those processes involved in interpreting, organizing, storing, coordinating, retrieving, and using stimuli received from the internal and external environments. It also includes problem solving and the creative activities involved in forming new combinations of information to adapt to the unique needs of a new situation. In short, the cognitive domain is concerned with processes of thinking and memory—our intellectual processes.

FIGURE 2–2.
Different people may find their natural pace or temperament more suited to one environment than another. The environment has definite effects on development of all five domains. Attitudes and lifestyle are greatly affected by the community in which the individual lives.

Patterns of Growth

The growth of the cognitive domain appears to depend heavily on the development of the central nervous system as well as on individual experiences. As in the biophysical domain, growth appears to be governed by a genetically determined time schedule. The sequence of growth and development appears to be the same for all people, but the rate of development and the end product are individual. Current views hold that cognitive potential is genetically determined, but the functioning level one achieves is environmentally mediated. One cannot progress beyond the biologically determined levels, but the individual can function maximally within those levels if the environment is optimally supportive. It should be noted that the affective domain strongly effects the energy available to activate the cognitive functions. For many adults, success in a career depends more on factors such as attention to task and perseverance (self-discipline factors) than to intelligence per se.

Knowledge, or "one's theory of the environment,"[28] is "progressively scaffolded in response to challenging environmental pressures."[28] Simple skills are gradually incorporated into more complex skills. To the behaviorist, these earlier skills are known as prerequisite skills, because the end skill cannot be achieved unless the earlier skills have been mastered. For example, teachers find that a child must be able to match similar stimuli (**recognition knowledge**) before differentiating a target stimulus from a group of stimuli on request (**receptive knowledge**). This skill precedes the ability to name or replicate a stimulus without the presence of the model (**expressive knowledge**). Algebra skills are predicated on basic arithmetic skills. The child cannot understand the concept of subtracting 3 from 5 before being able to rote count 5 objects, understand the meaning of 5, add numbers to 5, subtract 1 from 5, and subtract 2 from 5. This process of step-by-step advancement from lower-level to higher-level skills is known as **successive approximations**; each skill takes the individual one step closer to the targeted skill. By breaking a goal down into smaller steps (task analysis), both the child and the adult can experience success, and progress toward the goal becomes more obvious. This principle holds true for any teaching–learning situation, whether it is directed by a social worker, dietitian, nurse, occupational therapist, parent, or teacher.

Cognitive changes proceed from concrete sensory experiences to abstract thought processes. Benjamin Bloom observes that the maturing individual progresses through six increasingly complex skills for interpreting information: **knowledge, comprehension, application, analysis, synthesis,** and **evaluation.**[4]

Piaget offers the best explanation of emerging cognitive operational structures. He emphasizes that each of us plays an active role in the growth and development of our own cognitive domain. His four-stage theory begins with knowledge based on sensory input and problem solving dependent on motor manipulation of the environment. Stage two knowledge is dominated by perceptual qualities of objects and egocentric distortion of stimuli. Problem solving is influenced by concepts of magical interpretation of cause–effect relationships. The knowledge base of stage three expands rapidly as the child is able to include the concrete experiences of others along with personal experiences to structure an understanding of the factual world to which one is exposed. Simple deductive reasoning is used to solve objective, concrete problems. The fourth stage is mastered when the person is able to structure comprehensive understandings through integration of discrete pieces of information, to use inductive reasoning and abstract thought for problem solving, and to create and consider multiple hypothetical options simultaneously. Piaget's theory is covered in depth in Chapters 7, 10, 21, and 24.

Factors That Affect Growth

The environment has the greatest effect on the individual during periods of rapid change. Thus, the challenges, synchrony, and support offered during the early months and years of life are critical to the long-range development of the individual. Throughout life, environmental change must be frequent enough to maintain interest and to provide challenge but not so rapid as to prevent comprehension of events. Ideally, novel experiences are paced to the individual's needs.

Learning does not consist merely of a successive accumulation of bits of knowledge, and cognitive processes cannot be accelerated merely by enriching the environment. What is learned and how it is learned depend both on the environment and on the cognitive structuring processes available to the individual. A person's internal representations and thought processes change consciously or unconsciously only when he or she recognizes that a discrepancy exists between current knowledge and environmental input. Studies repeatedly indicate that an individual cannot incorporate the reasoning involved in stages that are beyond the person's current level of cognitive development. Interactions between the environment and the individual are observable and measurable. However, the individual's mental organization and representation of the environment can only be inferred from observable behaviors.

Adults can facilitate a child's concept formation by providing the child with a wide variety of experiences and information and helping the child to assess the validity of a concept in relation to personal experiences and knowledge. In short, the child needs to be taught *how,* not *what,* to think. As the child becomes aware of discrepancies in his or her thought processes, the child strives to reorganize and reintegrate current structures or to create new ones that ensure greater flexibility and restore equilibrium.

Chronological age and cognitive age are not always synonymous. This discrepancy is the basis of intellectual testing (see Chap. 21). Intraindividual discrepancies are readily observable in the infant or the young child who experiences advanced cognitive age. The child knows what needs to be done to achieve a goal but cannot manipulate the body adequately to perform the required psychomotor task. An infant may pick up two pop beads yet not be able to snap them together. The toddler attempts unsuccessfully to tie shoes, and the preschooler creates a lopsided drawing. Each knows what is wrong but cannot adequately command the body to perform as desired. The resulting frustration of unachieved goals may precipitate anger or passivity, depending on other environmental and personality factors. It is important for the adult to help the child to achieve success through appropriate supportive assistance (see Chap. 13).

Adequate nutrition and challenges are as essential to cognitive growth as they are to biophysical growth. During the early years, a child needs adequate opportunities to explore objects and the environment to test reality and to develop sufficient concrete mental images to lay a foundation for internal manipulation of objects and events. Children (and adults) also must have sufficient emotional security to allow them freedom to explore novel experiences. Repetition of experiences is essential to learning because it allows one to accurately predict an outcome. The ability to predict an outcome is as basic to emotional security and proactive interaction with the environment as it is to effective problem solving (Table 2-5).

Affective Domain

The affective domain encompasses all the subjective or emotional aspects of the self: feelings, longings, motivations, aspirations, frustrations, restraints, self-esteem, and identifications. In short, the affective domain is concerned with internal responses to external events, other people, and self—one's basic attitude toward life.

Regardless of a person's genetic potentials for development in the biophysical and cognitive domains, most individuals should be able to achieve high-level wellness in the affective domain. Nevertheless, in spite of the fact that known genetically imposed limitations on emotional growth are few, personality theorists, mental health clinics, formal research, and personal observations all indicate that a large percentage of people function at much lower levels of affective development than chronological age or potentials in other domains would predict. During the early years, the health of the affective domain is highly reflective of the understanding and support of the caregiver.[5, 20, 28] This relationship is so crucial that it can set the tone for life unless another point of reference and self-generative skills supersede the original relationship.[28]

The Mind-Body Continuum

Although the human organism is separated into five major divisions for study purposes, it would be both foolish and detrimental to use this approach when working with clients. The body and the mind cannot be so readily separated in our everyday interactions. Body configuration, mediated by sociocultural valuations, often affects how an individual feels about

TABLE 2–5. SELECTED COMPONENTS OF THE FIVE DOMAINS

BIOPHYSICAL DOMAIN

Body systems	Organ development
Gross motor skills	Fine motor skills
Sensory skills	Vital signs
Physiological parameters	Height and weight
Genetics	Organ functioning

COGNITIVE DOMAIN

Perception	Memory
Analyzing	Problem solving
Thinking	Creativity
Language	Moral decisions

AFFECTIVE DOMAIN

Self-other differentiation	
Feelings	Emotions
Response to frustration	Identity
Self-esteem	Self-confidence
Self-discipline skills	

SOCIAL DOMAIN

Affiliations	Communication
Peer relations	Negotiation skills
Play behaviors	Social adaptation
Enculturation	Roles
Status	Social identity

SPIRITUAL DOMAIN

Commitments	Purpose/drive in life
Verve/resiliency	Allocentrism
Ethics	Integrity
Survival instincts	Meaning of life
Faith	Hope
Ability to love and be loved	Will

the self as a person (see Chap. 17). When a person is physically ill, it is common to become discouraged, even depressed. Energies are invested back into the self; perceptions and cognitive thought processes may be altered and attention span shortened. When a person is severely depressed or upset emotionally, this state of mind can affect biological functioning. Many illnesses, such as asthma, ulcers, cardiac disease, and allergies, are known to be heavily influenced by and may even be caused by emotional stress (see Chaps. 35 and 36).

Cognitive processes are also heavily affected by one's emotional state. For example, it is difficult to take an examination the day of a major confrontation with a roommate or after breaking up with a loved one. Likewise, more household and automobile accidents occur following personal confrontations. Concentration on maintaining internal integrity appears to limit attention to external events and to delay cognitive processing.

Patterns of Growth

Although the growth of the affective domain has received attention by psychologists for more than 100 years, normalcy and the factors that affect healthy development are still poorly understood. This lack of understanding is caused by four factors:

1. Affective development is a personal matter. As an internal event, it cannot be directly measured and therefore must be inferred.
2. External behaviors are culturally influenced and therefore may not match one's internal state. A person may specifically "hide" or deny expression of true feelings and may even express the opposite feelings.
3. The same external behaviors may be mediated by entirely different internal forces; thus, obedience may be motivated by either love or fear, tears by joy or sorrow.
4. The subjective emotional state and developmental level of the observer tend to bias the interpretation of behavior, thus thwarting objectivity.

This last point is particularly true if the individual under study is functioning at a higher level of emotional maturity than the observer. Just as Piaget indicates that a person cannot completely understand or appreciate reasoning processes beyond the current level of functioning, theorists such as Maslow, Kohlberg, and Erikson indicate that a person cannot truly understand or appreciate the motivations or affective processes involved in stages beyond the current level of affective development.

Although the terms "feelings" and "emotions" commonly are used interchangeably, they are not synonymous. **Feelings** are one's innate response to a specific stimulus based on the meaning of the event, item, or person to the individual. They are private, uncontrollable, and normal. The cognitive domain functions in the service of the affective domain at this point since it perceives and processes the symbolic value of the stimulus.

Emotions are closely related in that feelings precipitate physiological responses that release energy and find expres-

sion in species-specific behavior patterns.[39] Research indicates that emotions such as joy, sadness, anger, shame, fear, guilt, jealousy, pride, contempt, surprise, sorrow, relief, envy, and so forth tend to emerge on schedule.[39] The functional mechanisms for most of the fundamental emotions are in place by the 10th month of life, and the rest by the 18th month.[39] The complexity of feelings and an understanding of one's own and others' emotions increase with maturation. By 3 years of age, children begin to understand the relationship between events and emotions[46] with beginning attempts to control their own emotional expressions (see Chap. 11). However, children cannot grasp the causal relationships of emotions until about 7 years of age.[46] These biological responses become "civilized" or "socialized" through the processes of enculturation and the learning of self-discipline. As one matures, feelings are still acknowledged, but the accompanying emotions are selectively expressed.

Attitude, or one's position for interpreting events, is consciously or unconsciously *chosen* by the individual. One's attitude (e.g., positive or negative) acts as a filter for rendering meaning to events and thus influences one's feelings and emotions. People tend to have social or emotional problems when a single feeling (e.g., anger, sadness, excitement) is allowed to become an attitude or is sought through artificial means for its physiological effects.

Researchers at the Gesell Institute observed that children exhibit cycles of psychosocial behavior that are reflective of the internal state of adaptation to the environment. Each cycle becomes progressively longer as the individual matures. This cyclical developmental pattern may continue into the adult years (e.g., midlife crisis, retirement); however, no one has continued this investigation beyond age 16. The cycle consists of six phases. The child begins the cycle in **good equilibrium**; behavior is smooth and consolidated. This phase is followed by a period of **marked disequilibrium** between the self and the environment. A period of **relative equilibrium** is then followed by a **pronounced withdrawal** or inward introspection; this period is characterized by marked touchiness and sensitivity to events, emotional lability, and pessimism, a phase that is followed by periods of **extreme expansiveness,** even to the point of endangering one's life. The child then goes through another period of **neurotic disequilibrium** before returning to good equilibrium (Table 2-6).[38]

TABLE 2–6. GESELL INSTITUTE'S CYCLES OF BEHAVIOR

4 weeks	4 months	10 months	2 yrs	5 yrs	10 yrs	Good equilibrium
5 weeks	5 months	11 months	2½ yrs	5½–6 yrs	11 yrs	Marked disequilibrium
6 weeks	6 months	12 months	3 yrs	6½ yrs	12 yrs	Relative equilibrium
8 weeks	7 months	15 months	3½ yrs	7 yrs	13 yrs	Pronounced withdrawal
10 weeks	8 months	18 months	4 yrs	8 yrs	14 yrs	Extreme expansiveness
12 weeks	9 months	21 months	4½ yrs	9 yrs	15 yrs	Neurotic disequilibrium

Based on systematic research by the Gesell Institute. (Ilg, F. L., Ames, L. B., & Baker, S. M. (1981). Child Behavior (rev. ed.). New York: Barnes & Noble.)

Because growth of the affective domain mediates the energies available for cognitive processes, growth of the spiritual domain, and the tone of social relationships, inadequate growth can leave one full of tensions and disquietude; adequate growth can lead toward a joy in living, a sense of stability, emotional "highs," and a clarity of thought unobtainable by artificial means.

As one becomes socialized, feelings (what one feels) and emotions (what one symbolizes or expresses) become more independent. As the cognitive domain matures, understands, and internalizes the social "display rules" of the culture, the individual is able to "short-circuit" the elicitation of a particular emotion.[6] **Personality** is the set of emotional systems one typically uses to interact with the environment.[39] It is unique to each person since it includes one's typical energy level, emotions, value system, attitudes, motivations, and social adaptive behaviors.

Social Domain

The social domain encompasses those aspects that identify a person's "niche" or relationship with society or the culture: attachments, roles, affiliations, communication styles, adaptive behaviors, social skills, expressions of internal responses, self-discipline, interactional patterns, and the expression of emotions, ideas, and needs. In short, the social domain is concerned with the individual's external response to events, other people, and self—one's interpersonal relationships. One's personality provides the unique blending of the intrapersonal and interpersonal selves.

Mores and taboos are the culture's collective rules that govern interpersonal relationships. The individual's ability to respond appropriately or according to socially sanctioned behaviors depends on the **enculturation** process (training in the culture's rules) as well as the level of affective development and the state of tension at the time.

A person's ability to relate openly with others depends on the security of his or her own identity (Erikson's fifth crisis). During earlier levels of development, the child finds identity through attachment to a strong, significant person. However, with normal development, the person begins to differentiate and appreciate a separate identity. Thus, the insecure person (functioning at a lower level) exhibits the need to quote other people frequently or to express only those behaviors or opinions that are accepted by the current peer group. The person who has mastered the self-identity crisis is not afraid to express and support opinions even though others may disagree vehemently. This individual is able to maintain personal integrity by consciously separating the value of the personal (spiritual or affective) self from publicly expressed ideas, goals, philosophies, or creative endeavors. These people make good role models and leaders because of their ability to face social pressures without loss of personal appreciation. Social behaviors become an expression of one's inner integrity rather than a crutch for one's identity. The level of development in the social domain, then, closely reflects the intrapersonal relationships of the affective

domain. Erikson's theory reflects this duality. This text combines discussion of these two domains under the term **psychosocial development.**

Patterns of Growth

Growth in the social domain also develops from simple to complex and from proximal to distal relationships. The young infant's world is **autistic** (totally self-centered). The infant attends only to the self and to those external events that directly impinge on the senses or meet needs. The emotional response of the primary caregiver to the infant influences the quality of the infant's attachment to the adult and all future relationships.[8] An intense symbiotic relationship develops between the young infant and primary caregiver.[45] This simple one-to-one relationship gradually extends to other family members during the toddler and preschool years. During the school-age years, relationships are extended to peers in the school and neighborhood settings. The ability to travel independently and the diversification of skills and interests lead the adolescent into the larger community to seek satisfying relationships and experiences. During the adult years, the individual is free to leave home and community to extend his or her relationships or social horizons around the world if finances and interests permit (Fig. 2-3).

The individual learns to separate from the family of origin and to appreciate the ability to depend on one's own strengths by experiencing brief separations that begin during infancy. Staying with a baby-sitter or attending preschool helps to prepare the younger child for formal school experiences. Overnight stays (e.g., summer camp experiences) gradually prepare the older child for college or a separate apartment.

A person's reciprocal experiences with the external world can significantly affect self-concept and thus establish a framework for later social interactions. As one has successful interactions, self-confidence and anticipation of social successes are increased. If one experiences negative relationships, the tendency to withdraw from potentially growth-producing social experiences is found. Figure 2-4 illustrates the concept of cycles of competence and incompetence. These conceptual frameworks also embody the **epigenetic principle** that one's past experiences or levels of development heavily influence the anticipation of future events and goals and thus modify current perceptions and behaviors.

Parents often attempt to transmit their roles, values, customs, skills, and goals to their children intact. However, relationships and responsibilities change so rapidly in our technological society that the roles and values of the parents may be grossly inadequate to meet the relationships and responsibilities faced by the children.[63] To cope with a rapidly changing world, children need experiences that are developmentally sequenced to support (1) the formation of a positive self-identity, (2) the development of a sensitivity to the needs of others, (3) the establishment of meaningful relationships, (4) the ability to solve novel problems creatively, (5) the acquisition of social skills that enable retention of personal identity while fostering the capacity for growth, and (6) the

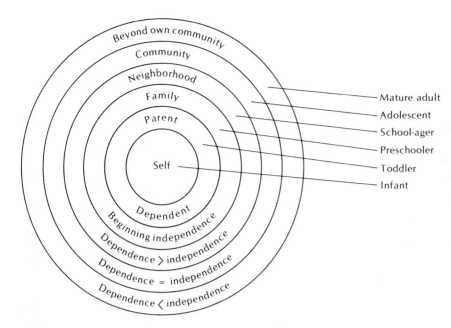

FIGURE 2–3.
Sociological horizons of the life span. Horizons expand with each developmental level. (Adapted from Rines, A. R., & Montag, M. L. (1976). Nursing concepts and nursing care. *New York: Wiley.) With permission.*

development of values that transcend cultural and technological changes. These competencies are most effectively learned within a warm, supportive, respecting family system that provides both strong role models and consistent, loving guidance and challenges.

The Interdependence Continuum
The developing individual gradually progresses from dependence to independence while approaching maturity. However, no one is ever completely dependent on other people except during a critical illness, and few if any people are completely independent in all domains. The dependence-

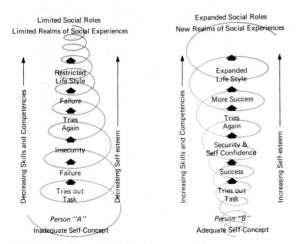

FIGURE 2–4.
"Vicious" and "benign" cycles involved in the development of social competence and incompetence. (Lugo, J. O., & Hershey, G. L. (1979). Human development: A psychological, biological and sociological approach to the life span *(2nd ed.). New York: Macmillan.) With permission.*

independence concept is a relative one that is embodied within the framework of the interdependence continuum. The term **interdependence** describes the reciprocity of interaction between two or more people. Since it is recognized that both partners in a relationship may not assume the same degree of responsibility or need for maintaining the relationship, the polar ends of the continuum are designated as **dependence** and **independence.**

Not even the neonate is completely dependent on others. The neonate's ability to capture attention through crying, eye contact, mouthing behaviors, suckling, and vocalizations allows the infant to be an active participant in a social interaction. In fact, evidence is accumulating to indicate that a mother may lose interest in a baby who is unable to give her adequate feedback for her caregiving efforts (see Chap. 13).

Not even millionaires are completely independent; they depend on other people to help manage financial affairs, maintain a home, cook meals, or type letters. Even if they can handle these affairs alone, the banker must handle the money, the farmer must produce the food, and the service station attendant sells the gasoline to run the car. Every interaction requires some dependency. Perhaps the person who comes closest to complete independence is the hermit who lives alone in the desert or forest; yet even the hermit is dependent on local and federal security personnel to keep a domain free from intrusion by land theft or war. The real value of the concept of interdependence is revealed in the section "General Systems Theory."

Spiritual Domain

The spiritual domain encompasses all the transcendental aspects of our self. It is the center of awareness or consciousness of our own existence. It is the hope, the life-force within us that clings to and pursues temporal life in the face of adversity. It is the soul that strains for union with something or someone higher than ourself to provide goals, direction, stability, and meaning to life. It is the very core of our personhood, the essence of our humanness—that which separates us as unique in the animal world.[34, 62, 68] Most religious doctrines identify the spirit as that part of each of us that lives beyond the death of the biophysical domain. It is the ultimate factor of our personhood that is held responsible for the choices and course of our lives.

Interdependence of Domains

"Consciousness is wholly outside the realm of matter and energy, although at the same time it is coextensive with the whole of it."[72] The spiritual domain is highly interdependent with the other four domains, especially the affective and cognitive domains. It is through them that the spiritual domain is awakened during those early months of life; it is through them that one develops discernment, establishes values worth living for, and activates one's moral code. However, it is the spiritual domain which, in turn, provides them energy to face challenges, the motivation to seek continued involvement in the exigencies of life, and the drive toward continued growth and development.

The spiritual domain is the first domain to begin to emerge as a separate system in the undifferentiated world of the newborn. Birth memories elicited via LSD or hypnosis have revealed that the neonate possesses sufficient maturity of the consciousness to record and remember feelings of fear for self and *empathy for the mother.*[7] In an unsupportive social matrix, the young infant may experience failure-to-thrive (see Chap. 8), may fail to be drawn out of the primary narcissism of the neonate (autism) (see Chaps. 8 and 31), or may even die (see Chap. 8). The sense of hope or faith that emerges from these early months "orients us toward centers of power [which refuel our emotional reserves] and values which promise to sustain our lives and to guarantee 'more-being.' "[23] In the absence of hope, there is no life force to propel the child toward more complex and satisfying interactions with the environment. Without hope, life loses meaning, value, and its future. At best, one merely exists; at worst, one physically dies. Erik Erikson identifies hope as the ontological basis of faith that attaches first to the mother and is "climaxed by . . . the ultimate other in a belief system maintained by faith."[19]

However, even though the spiritual domain must begin to emerge during those early months of life, it is the last domain to reach full maturity, if it ever does. People in their 50s, 70s, or 90s admit to working on attaining higher levels of sensitivity and development of this domain. It is interesting to note that the basic virtues (**hope, will, purpose, competence, fidelity, love, care, wisdom**) that emerge from successful resolution of Erikson's tasks are all components of the spiritual domain (see Table 1-2 or Appendixes B and C). Erikson indicates the possibility of a ninth stage of development, or a final maturity, that results in "an existential identity," or "the spiritual personality" that transcends time-bound identities.[19]

The literature offers minimal concrete data or theories on the growth of the spiritual domain,[34] even though several people have attempted to describe different levels or types of spiritual functioning.[25, 26, 31, 47] Religious leaders assume its existence and build from there into religious dogma, concentrating on the latter. They presume the presence of a God (or gods) and construct with varying degrees of elaborateness a set of rules and rituals for pleasing, appeasing, or achieving union with the embodiment of their concept of The Higher Order. Individuals are expected to subject themselves to these criteria to find salvation from the terrors and sins of temporal life or to ensure eternal life. Religion is a universal experience of humankind,[29] which includes belief in transcendental reality, a sense of "God's rich nearness," prayer, and a belief that a harmonious relationship with God is the true goal of life.[25] Religion is influenced by culture and vice versa.

Psychologists, on the other hand, have highly mixed reactions to acknowledging a spiritual domain. More than one-third deny the existence of God.[51] Literal translation of the word "psychology" means the study of the soul, and so it started out. However, the elusiveness of such a concept and the pressures for objectivity in academia have forced most psychologists to avoid the topic. The spiritual domain provides no way to be objectified or quantitatively measured. The close interdependence with the affective and cognitive domains tends to eclipse its unique qualities. Yet, the lack of adequate methods to describe or measure it is hardly reason to negate its existence.

Patterns of Growth

James Fowler, a theologian who became deeply involved with the theories of Piaget, Kohlberg, and Erikson, has identified seven stages of faith that provide some insight into the growth and development of the spiritual domain.[22] One must differentiate between faith as a psychological construct of trust versus a religious construct of beliefs or doctrinal creed. The choice of a religion differs from and may or may not facilitate spiritual growth or a personal experience with God (one may need to get beyond the confines of the religion).[25] Fowler's concept of faith is a self-constructed "discernment-system" that strives to extract guidance and meaning from the significant relationships or "centers of power" in one's life. The affective, cognitive, and social domains are employed in the service of the spiritual domain to construct an "ultimate environment" that provides the individual with orientation, direction, patterns, meaning, unity, and identity. Faith growth, from his perspective, is a universal process that is not necessarily religious in orientation. It is an integral part of daily life, which "serves to organize the totality of our lives and gives rise to our most comprehensive frames of meaning."[23] It involves our ego, conscious and unconscious thought, emotions, reasoning, perceptions, and identity.

Fowler's stages of faith parallel Piaget's stages of intellectual growth. However, although mastery of Piaget's levels is essential for growth in the "faith-knowing system," their mastery is not sufficient for progression through the faith levels.

Fowler's faith evolution theory provides a scaffold for both process and content as the individual's faith system progressively integrates broader and more abstract issues in the search for values by which to live. At each successive stage, one develops a reliance on or an attachment or commitment to what the individual considers to be the new center of power, whether person, symbol, or philosophy. The concept of a loving, protecting God sometimes can become an essential substitute when the lack of a loving parent prevented advancement beyond the narcissistic primal faith stage.[43] In the dynamic relationship of the self to a "significant other," a set of supraordinate self-transcending values becomes the rules that govern not only this self-transcending relationship but also one's relationship with other people, organizations, philosophies, and events of life. One's identity is intimately bound to the locus of control of this relationship, in other words what or who identifies the value system. One's self-esteem is intimately related to the integration of one's behaviors with the chosen value system. The closer the match, the higher the individual's esteem and confidence.

The affective and cognitive structuring represents the processes of Fowler's theory. The center of power, what one "rests the heart on," represents the content. In Fowler's theory, a specific religion or creed may become the content for any stage. One relates to religious doctrine in a different way at each level. His research indicates that most middle class American churches and synagogues foster functioning at stage 3 or a little beyond.[22] It is difficult to achieve stages 5 or 6 without a concept of an Ultimate Being or God.[22]

An individual begins life in an undifferentiated state with a lack of clarity not only among the five domains but also in the ability to differentiate between (1) the self; (2) the significant other; (3) and the supraordinate values that govern the relationship. As each stage emerges, the domains and the three basic elements of one's faith-knowing system become more clearly differentiated and then are gradually reintegrated, with the last stage representing a highly integrated unity of the five domains, the self, Significant Other, and motivating values. Regardless of the culture or religious belief system, people who master the last stage closely resemble each other in both structure and content of faith.[19,21]

Fowler has found that most people appreciate the opportunity to discuss their faith-knowing system and that just talking about it seems to help to spur them toward higher integration.[23] However, perhaps partly for the lack of opportunity to discuss such intimate issues in depth, he finds that only a small percentage of people ever achieve the highest stages.[22] Fortunately, "each stage has a potential for wholeness, grace, and integrity."[23]

Stage 0: Primal or Undifferentiated Faith (0–2 Years)

One's social awareness is limited to one's egocentric perceptions and needs. Relationships are based on the interactional rituals with the parent. The synchrony and contingency of responses is the infant's essential source of meaning.[28] From this relationship, the child draws strength to face life and a

growing awareness of self as a separate person.[46] Almost every theory of human development speaks in some way to the primacy of this initial relationship to the development of a basic attachment to and trust in life and others, because of its life-giving potential and the establishment of a pattern for self–other relationships. Fowler proposes that the quality of mutuality determines the strength of trust or undermines hope. Consequently, the quality of resolution of this stage effects the quality of all later faith development.

Stage 1: Intuitive-Projective Faith (2–6 Years)

At this stage, conscious attempts are made to give meaning to one's experiences and relationships. "Children combine fragments of stories and images given by their cultures into their own clusters of significant associations dealing with God and the sacred."[22] Because of so much information about God through language, television, holidays, and so forth, few children in Western culture reach school age without some concept of God, even without formal religious instruction.[55] The magical thought processes typical of the preschooler create powerful fantasy-filled concepts of supernatural events from the narratives of the culture. The "ultimate environment" is construed in terms of visible signs of power, which are significant adults or concrete images. The examples, attitudes, behaviors, taboos, and moral expectations provided at this time supply the life-governing values and can produce long-lasting images and feelings (positive or negative).

Stage 2: Mythical-Literal Faith (6–12 Years)

The school-ager "begins to take on for him- or herself the stories, beliefs and observances that symbolize belonging to his or her community. Beliefs are appropriated with literal interpretations, as are moral rules and attitudes. Symbols are taken as one-dimensional and literal in meaning."[22] The person now relates to "those like us." A conscious attempt to interpret and shape meaning from experiences based on concrete facts and symbols is found. This person relies heavily on issues of order, fairness, and goodness. Rituals, stories, and symbols of one's cultural tradition and religious heritage are critical in creating order out of chaos. Values are accepted as decreed by the traditions of one's culture or religious leaders. The rituals and symbols have meaning in themselves.

Stage 3: Synthetic-Conventional Faith (12 and Beyond)

The individual gradually begins to find a need for a "more personal relationship with the unifying power of the ultimate environment,"[22] and thus begins to evaluate the self through the guidelines and "eyes" of others (friend, religious codes of conduct). Active measures are taken to try to change one's self, to bring one's will under the subjection of or to meet the approval of the significant other. The beliefs and values are largely unexamined, but symbols and rituals provide roles on which one can base his or her identity. The person accepts that the other (person, cultural pressure, God) knows what is best. Symbols and rituals are seen as sources of strength and power in their own right to face life since the symbol and meaning are bound up together. The transcendent is reached through the symbol; therefore, any attempt to separate the meaning from the person, emblem, or ritual (demythologization) is seen as a threat to the meaning. A danger of this stage is that "the expectations and evaluations of others can be so compellingly internalized (and sacralized) that later autonomy of judgment and action can be jeopardized."[22]

Stage 4: Individuative-Reflective Faith (Early Adulthood and Beyond)

At this stage, one begins to examine the value system, to break reliance on an external source of authority, and to assume a "qualitatively new authority and responsibility for oneself."[23] One's identity becomes regrounded as one revels in the ability to assume responsibility for value orientation and choices. Roles and relationships now become expressions of, not crutches for, identity. The person is able to separate the symbol from its meaning. This stage is "vulnerable to the self-deception that forgets mystery, including the mystery of its own unconsciousness."[23] In the process, one may lose the sense of community and traditions as one relinquishes symbols and rituals in search of meaning created from one's own power and control. The person also can develop "excessive confidence in conscious mind and in critical thought and a kind of second narcissism in which the now clearly bounded, reflective self over-assimilates 'reality' and the perspective of others into its own world view."[22] It is easy to make a neat little package—simple, clear distinctions and abstract concepts to explain the world—that becomes flat and sterile, a world of black and white, with explanations that become an end in themselves, devoid of meaning. Many radical leaders have reached this level, constructing their own philosophy, "religion," political dogma, or social cause. Disillusionment with earlier philosophies, religious dogma, or familial and social relationships can lead to expressions of anger, hostility, and self-aggrandizement as seen in leaders such as Hitler and Stalin. Such an approach effectively prevents progression to the next two stages and causes reversion to level 0, where one's own needs and impulses become the values that guide behaviors and relationships.

However, this stage also has the potential to create a coherent life-enhancing construct of the ultimate environment through critical analysis and unique reworking of the faith of others. Although one may end up with the same explicit system of meanings, they are now personally restructured and not merely the extension of a parent's or the culture's faith-knowing system.

Stage 5: Conjunctive Faith (Midlife and Beyond)

Conjunctive faith moves beyond the narrow, dichotomizing, sterile logic of stage 4 because of increased ability or willingness to see many sides of an issue simultaneously. Rather than trying to fit insights and "facts" into one's construct (assimilation), this person now tries to see the total structure before categorizing (accommodation). The person lets the truth of a

message or Scripture speak for itself. Symbols and rituals are once again appreciated for their ability to *represent* the internalized verities of an ever more complex internalized value system (although they are seen as a pale representation of anything honored). People in stage 5 can appreciate symbols, myths, and rituals (both their own and others') because they have been grasped, in some measure, by the depth of the reality to which these symbols refer. The person "develops a second or willed naïveté, and an epistemological humility in face of the intricacy and richness of mystery."[23] Awe of the Holy and a reverence for paradox emerges as the Ultimate Environment is seen to transcend temporal constraints or human creations as one realizes that all questions cannot be answered by a human's finite mind. One moves beyond the "norms" of a reference group to the "truth" of other traditions. This level of maturity does not mean a lack of commitment to one's own traditions but an openness to correct or expand truth. Whereas people in stage 4 equate self with one's own conscious awareness, those in stage 5 come to terms with their own unconscious, aware that the "conscious ego is not master of its own home."[22] This person has the capacity to understand a group's "most powerful meanings while simultaneously recognizing that they are relative, partial and inevitably distorting apprehensions of transcendent reality."[22] This person may be caught between "an untransformed world and a transforming vision and loyalties."[22] Because of the complexity of this faith level, Fowler observes that few reach it before middlescence.

Stage 6: Universalizing Faith (Midlife and Beyond)

Universalizing faith, the final mature form of faith, is rare. The ultimate environment for this person goes beyond finite centers of value and power to an identification with all the human species and a transnarcissistic love of being. "Identification with or participation in the Ultimate brings a transformation in which one begins to love and value from a centering located in the Ultimate."[23] One assumes a "spiritual stance of pure conscientiousness where the subject makes his goal the simple doing of his duty as he sees it, without worrying about its relationships to the natural or supernatural order."[21] These persons engage in "spending and being spent for the transformation of present reality in the direction of a transcendent actuality."[22] Their involvement in the life and concerns of others is heedless of their own needs or self-preservation. Every community has such a person, but he or she frequently goes unrecognized. Sometimes, the events of history place these people in the forefront of political unrest or social injustice. These are the ones who, like Ghandi and King, become martyrs for their "symbolic construct of God and the world."[67] They do not plan to become subversives or to create national discord. They, like Mother Teresa, are living by a vision greater than themselves. "They learn to radically live the kingdom of God as a means of overcoming division, oppression, and brutality,"[16] and draw others to them by the truth of their commission (Table 2-7).

Fowler believes that each successive stage "represents

TABLE 2–7. FOWLER'S FAITH-KNOWING SYSTEM

Stage	Center of Power (Content)	Processes	Value
0	Symbiotic relationship with parent	Egocentric perceptions	Own needs
1	Caregiving adult	Magical thought	Appeasement
2	Cultural and religious rules and traditions	Rituals and rules	Order, rituals, fairness
3	Peers, cultural or religious leader	Symbols provide meaning	Approval
4	Self	Construct own symbols	Own meaning
5	Truth	Verities expressed through symbols, awe	Openness to others, humility
6	The Ultimate God	Relationship expressed through life lived	Love, others' needs

genuine growth toward a wider and more accurate response to God, and toward more consistently humane care for other human beings."

> The restlessness which so characterizes our frenzied lives of work and consumption has a source deeper than can be cured by our ambitious activities. The search for intimacy and sensation in contemporary cultures bespeaks a loneliness deeper than even our closest ties of friendship and love can overcome. Faith development theory, for all its technical language and abstract concepts, is an expression of the story of our search for communication with Saint Augustine's, "Thou." . . . Our restlessness for divine companionship, if denied, ignored, or distorted, dehumanizes us and we destroy each other. Recognized and nurtured, it brings us into that companionship with God which frees us for genuine partnership with our sisters and brothers, and for friendship with creation.[23]

GENERAL SYSTEMS THEORY

A holistic approach to the study of human growth and development requires an understanding of general systems theory, since one cannot obtain a realistic perspective of human functioning by examining only one component. If one part of the body is ill, the functioning of other aspects is affected. A headache decreases the appetite and the desire for body movement, socialization, or study. If one approaches the study of human development from a family context, then each family member both affects and is affected by the behaviors of the others, and all members are critical to the functioning of the total family as a separate system within society. A **system** is any entity of two or more interacting components that function independently, yet in interaction as a single unit to meet previously specified objectives. The unit takes on a life of its own separate from its parts because of the unique qualities that emerge from the relationship of the parts.[13]

General systems theory is not a separate discipline but rather is a way of thinking about, organizing, or approaching complex organizations. Ludwig von Bertalanffy first introduced the theory in 1932 as a theoretical, conceptual approach to analyzing organized entities and to facilitate communication and cooperation among practitioners of the applied sciences.[68] He developed the theory as he became aware of the isomorphic structures within different fields of study and realized that parts and processes must be studied in context as well as in isolation.[68] He observed that scientific disciplines had been dissecting nonlinear, multi-level, complex entities to analyze them, to find the minute significant elements of these entities. He particularly despised the dehumanizing approach of the behaviorists.[41,66] He did not deny the importance of this process but felt that the clinical sciences, especially psychology,[13,53,66] must think in terms of the total entity (systems in mutual interaction) if they were to be effective in understanding why changes occur and in helping any system maximize its potentials. He felt that the structural relationships among system components were more important in determining system behavior than the individual components themselves. Von Bertalanffy viewed the human as the "ultimate expression of organized complexity, as a system with uniquely emergent qualities of human creativity."[13]

Characteristics of an Open System

Von Bertalanffy identified two types of systems. The **closed system** is an entity that is isolated from its environment. Once the components are in the system, no new components are added from the environment. A chemical experiment performed within a test tube is a good example; the final product depends on the initial composition. The elements within the system tend to become equally distributed over time.

Living organisms, such as humans or social systems, are classified as **open systems** because they are continually exchanging energy, matter, and information with the environment to evolve into higher levels of heterogeneity, organization, and order (**negentropy**). The environment influences but does not determine the final state. The final products tend to resemble each other (**equifinality**) even though they began with different initial components because of the dynamic interaction of the system with the environment and the ability for self-direction and monitoring.[66]

The components of an open system are hierarchically arranged into **subsystems.** The environment, or **suprasystem,** consists of those people, things, resources, and systems outside the target system that affect the system and are in turn affected by it. The designations of subsystems and suprasystem are arbitrary; thus, it is important to identify clearly the **parameters** (boundaries) of the target system under discussion. A specific component may be the subsystem of one target system but the suprasystem for another. Therefore, one must identify the level of analysis and the component parts to discuss meaningfully and clearly the relationships between the components. Higher levels of organization become increasingly complex because they incorporate all the systems below them (Table 2-8).

Open systems have semipermeable boundaries that allow for dynamic, selective exchange with the environment. When matter, energy, or information is brought into the system (**input**), it must be processed (**throughput**) by the components to create a product (**output**) that is consistent with the goals of the system. A sensitive **feedback** mechanism allows the system to monitor the exchanges to maintain a fairly steady state by preventing overload or underload to the system (see Fig. 2-5). Open systems are characterized by importing more energy, information, or matter than is essential to maintain the status quo. This process allows for evolutionary self-directed growth and for storage of energy for emergency use.

Each subsystem is assigned specific tasks, which are critical to the maintenance of the total organism. The roles of the subsystems gradually become better defined as the system evolves. Each subsystem is responsible for carrying out its task independent from, yet in concert with, the functioning of the other subsystems. Because of the interdependence, a change in the functional ability of one component affects the balance of interdependence within the system and the functioning of other subsystems to meet the goals of the system. A schematic representation of the five major subsystems of a person is given in Figure 2-6. Efficiency of the target system

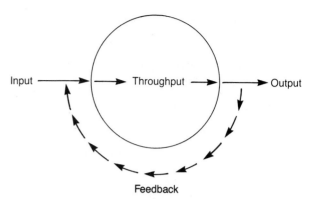

FIGURE 2–5.
Schematic representation of an open system.

depends on the degree of communication the subsystems maintain with each other. The job of delegating tasks or decision making usually is relegated to one "master" subsystem to facilitate system functioning by minimizing energy expenditure for goal achievement.

The purpose or goal of a system determines its work and, therefore, its stability or ability to adapt to the environment (suprasystem). An open system attempts to maintain a steady state or equilibrium, which enables it to maximize its potentials into productive work. This steady state can be achieved only when management is clearly delineated and when (1) the system remains oriented and focused toward the same goal regardless of changes in the environment, (2) progress is maintained toward the goal, (3) the capacities of the system are matched with the demands of the environment, (4) the resources of the environment provide adequate input to meet the needs of the system, and (5) the subsystems are committed to the goals of the system yet maintain sufficient autonomy to function independently.[18]

Disequilibrium occurs when the needs and resources of the suprasystem are not synchronized with the needs or skills of the system or do not allow the system time to enhance,

TABLE 2–8. EXAMPLES OF LEVELS OF SYSTEM ANALYSIS

Physical Realm	*Social Realm*
Cell	Self-other awareness
Tissue	Self-control, self-discipline
Organ	Social skill
Physiological system	Social domain
Biophysical domain	Human as an organism
Human as an organism	Family
Family	Community
Clan	Culture
Race	Nation
Humanity	World

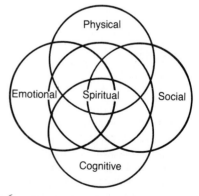

FIGURE 2–6.
Schematic representation of the interdependence of the five domains of humans.

elaborate, or reorganize its subsystems to achieve a new steady state. Disequilibrium in reasonable amounts can challenge the system to new levels of maturity.

Because the system creates its own meanings from input, its response to the environment is unique to the needs and interpretation of the system. A system thus can be highly adaptive, and success can be built on failures. A systems approach is concerned with relationships as well as components; consequently, understanding the total person in context is crucial to effective intervention. General systems theory offers a positive view of human development and recognizes the value of alternative intervention strategies to achieve the system's goals within the constraints of the environment.

Evaluation of System Functioning

A system cannot be understood without evaluating all the forces that influence it. Therefore, to understand a system (person or family), the practitioner needs to specify the following:

1. The components of the system and the specific boundaries
2. The suprasystem, environment, resources, and constraints of the system
3. The relationship between the components and the efficiency of the communication system
4. The objectives or goals of the total system
5. The roles or responsibilities of the component subsystems
6. The efficiency or maturity level with which the subsystems carry out their responsibilities
7. The management component of the system
8. The feedback or regulating mechanism for the system
9. The history or time perspective of the system

When these aspects have been identified, the practitioner can work with the person or family to identify ways to improve (1) the efficiency of a subsystem (or subsystems); (2) the degree of differentiation among subsystems; (3) the interaction or communication between subsystems; (4) the use of internal and environmental resources; (5) or the sensitivity to the feedback mechanism. In addition to this task-oriented approach, one can evaluate a system in terms of maturity level or health (Fig. 2-7).

System Maturity

Heinz Werner, a psychologist who studied the developmental aspects of systems, used the **orthogenetic principle** to explain the evolution of systems from an initial state of "relative globality and lack of differentiation to a state of increasing differentiation, articulation, and hierarchical integration."[71] The orthogenetic principle may be easily applied to biological development by following the development of the fetus; how-

ever, it may also be applied to the development of social relationships (e.g., Mahler's theory), cognitive development (e.g., Piaget's theory), or even to perceptual or language development (if one chooses to conceptualize perception or language as a separate system). Werner identified six continuums along which the developmental or **maturity level** of a system can be objectively evaluated.

Undifferentiated-differentiated: As the system matures, subsystems become more clearly identified and independent in their functioning.

Interfused-subordinated: As the system matures, the components assume hierarchical relationships designed to maximize efficiency while reducing duplication of activity and unnecessary energy expenditure.

Diffuse-articulated: As the system matures, the efficiency of communication and cooperation increases between the subsystems.

Syncretic-discrete: As the system matures, external and internal stimuli are more clearly differentiated and separately processed (input issue).

Rigid-flexible: As the system matures, it is able to create alternative routes for goal achievement. The means become a way to the end goal rather than an end in themselves (throughput issue).

Labile-stable: As the system matures, it becomes more independent of the suprasystem in goal setting, and energies are more specifically harnessed and focused toward goal achievement because of increased resistance to distracters (output issue).

System Health

The state of the **health** of a system can be identified by determining (1) the degree of differentiation among component parts, (2) the ability of each subsystem to perform the roles assigned to it, (3) the ability of the subsystems to communicate essential information with each other, (4) their ability to function cooperatively to meet system goals, (5) the system's efficiency in using internal and external resources for meeting goals, (6) its adaptability to the constraints of the environment, and (7) how closely the output meets the goals of the system.

Growth is the central goal of living systems. When the system finds that its usual adaptation mechanisms or responses fail, then it can (1) alter itself through creative use of resources, (2) import additional material, information, or energy, (3) alter the environment, (4) withdraw from the environment, or (5) alter its purpose, goal, or concept of desirable state.

The Systems Approach to Human Development

Practitioners are confronted with both individuals and families as systems in their practice. Both must be acknowledged for effective intervention.

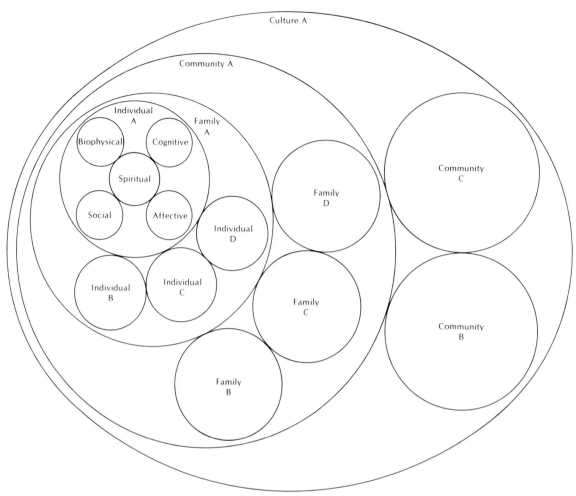

FIGURE 2–7.
Hierarchy of social systems. When working with an individual, the practitioner must clearly identify the significant supra-systems and subsystems that affect the behavior of the system.

The Individual

The first step in the holistic approach requires the identification of the components of the system. The first level of subsystem for the human would be the five domains. Each of them can be further subdivided into relevant subsystems. The relevant suprasystems would depend on the targeted subsystems of the moment.

Humans, as systems, have a limited range for absorption, processing, and retention of stimuli. A systems overload (e.g., cognitive overstimulation) leads to an increased need for decision making. Ignoring, denying, avoiding, or distorting stimuli (assimilation) are adaptive responses to maintain equilibrium even though such behaviors may appear to be maladaptive to the onlooker. A gross overloading (flooding) can lead to the inability to process the stimuli with resultant blockage (refusal to acknowledge or accept input) or gross disorganization of behavioral output.

A systems underload, or deprivation, is also detrimental to efficient functioning because a person cannot draw on reserves forever. A gross underload may lead to self-stimulatory behaviors designed to create controlled diversionary input for the individual.

Either extreme can lead to a breakdown of the system or to low-level wellness. Von Bertalanffy says that, "perception and experience categories need not mirror the 'real' world, they must, however, be isomorphic with it to such a degree as to allow orientation and thus survival. . . . The answer to whether an individual is mentally sound or not is ultimately determined by whether he has *an integrated universe consistent within the given cultural framework.*"[68] No behavior can be evaluated in isolation from history, context, culture, or its individualized meaning to the performer.

In humans, the major physiological tasks of the system are carried out by the body systems, which are well differentiated and well organized. The integumentary system provides the physiological boundaries and limited permeability. The gastrointestinal system is organized both to receive input (nourishment) and to excrete output (feces). The neurological system also is organized to receive input (stimuli and information) and to discharge a product (language, movement). Each body system can be analyzed in terms of its contribution to the total functioning of the body. When one subsystem fails to perform its assigned task, the health professional is challenged to work with the client to identify appropriate goals and to creatively formulate alternative approaches to achieving these goals.

In the nonphysical aspects of life, Herman Witkin observed that the more specialized and clearly delineated the subsystems (cognitive, affective, and social domains, in particular), the more efficiently the system is able to respond to the environment. Individuals with a low degree of differentiation are more dependent on other people for decision making and task accomplishment. Highly differentiated subjects are able to identify their own boundaries and resources and thus can function more effectively.

A word of caution is in order: It is difficult to be objective when studying human functioning and personality because one's own experiences predispose one to subjective biases. Any practitioner becomes a part of the client's suprasystem and is affected by and affects the client. The practitioner must be careful, therefore, to become a resource and a power for the client rather than a stressor or a load. This position requires a broad data base and a sensitivity to the feedback from the client; it also requires that the practitioner attempt to view the environment or suprasystem from the client's perspective to help the client to reestablish equilibrium with it. Since it is the client who has continuity with himself or herself and must live with the consequences of decisions, any actions that foster dependency on the practitioner for decision making or goal achievement are counterproductive to a holistic approach directed toward client growth. The practitioner must foster the client growth by identifying resources or alternative routes to goal achievement. This approach often requires attention to the client's immediate suprasystem, the family.

The Family

The general systems approach broadens the practitioner's definition of client and provides a rationale for interest in and use of the other family members. Since the family generally provides the supportive, protective milieu for its members, a healthy family can help its members achieve maximal health. Families have many different ways of organizing time, space, roles, and values. Many of these combinations are compatible with the healthy development of its members, but some are more appealing or more adaptive to the suprasystem (culture) than others.[48]

The family is a special kind of social system, comprised of two or more interdependent persons, that remains united over time and serves as a mediator between the needs of its members and the forces, demands, and obligations of society.[37] This definition goes beyond the traditional or the legal definition of family (marriage, blood, or adoption) and includes how people view themselves as a family. Family-type relationships also may be achieved through economic obligations, a code of rights and responsibilities (roles), religious values, or any commitment based on dynamic social interactions. This definition is not meant to be loose or all-inclusive but is meant to alert the practitioner to the fact that, in today's world, a client's family bonds may not be those traditionally recognized by society. The client should be allowed and encouraged to identify his or her own family and support systems; thus, a client's roommate or religious group members may be of more support during an illness or crisis than a sibling or parent.

When a person is ill or in crisis, the practitioner must approach the person as a part of a family and intervene at one or several points of the system. Frequently, especially for social or affective dysfunction, the intervention may not focus on the person at all but may be geared toward strengthening the entire system (often seen in alcohol or drug abuse therapies). Too narrow an intervention can actually fractionalize the system, "creating damage in the name of protection";[48] this damage occurs frequently in cases of child neglect or failure-to-thrive. The child may be removed temporarily from the family setting; unless the total system is strengthened and supported, however, the events frequently reoccur.

When one thinks of the subsystems of a family, one usually identifies the number of persons in the family and designates each as a separate subsystem. However, subsystems can also be composed of interactional patterns between these individuals. Thus, one may work with the following relational subsystems as the targeted system:[49]

Spouse Subsystem: Its members exhibit interaction for cooperation, expressing affection, handling stress, decisions on obtaining and releasing of members, and use of resources.

Parent-Child Subsystem: An intergenerational subsystem of unequal power for the purpose of control and guidance.

Sibling Subsystem: A peer relationship that provides competition, cooperation, negotiation opportunities, friends (and enemies) for the developing child.

Blood Relation Subsystems: These may emerge in the blended family as the mother and her children pair off against the father and his children. In some cases, the family of origin or "clan" may continue to provide a stronger bond of affiliation and power than the spousal relationship. The system boundaries and goals have never been clearly established in these family systems.

Each subsystem within a family provides a different learning experience in interdependence. The same individual may be a participant in more than one subsystem; thus, the boundaries and responsibilities must be clear, or role confusion emerges and system dysfunction can occur. The parent generally makes it clear that the child does not possess equal power if the child attempts to become too bossy or independent within the home: "As long as you live under *this* roof...." The child generally does not tolerate a sibling who assumes a parental role: "You are *not* my mother!"

Each subsystem must be free to function without interference from other subsystems; thus, siblings usually should be allowed to settle their own disputes without parental domination. Lines of authority and responsibility must be especially clear if a stepparent, grandparent, or other adult is in the home.

Families whose subsystems are so enmeshed that boundaries are no longer identifiable function poorly as a system. The members are too dependent to execute their tasks efficiently or effectively. Conflict may stem from "seniority" rights or even "juniority" rights. On the other hand, if boundaries are too rigid, family members may become too independent and disengage (decrease commitment) from the family system. Chapter 32 discusses the maintenance of a healthy family relationship, and Chapter 33 explores factors that lead to fractionalized families. Stress is experienced each time a member is admitted to or lost from the system because of the need to restructure, reassign tasks, reassess goals, and maintain continuity.

IMPLICATIONS

The holistic approach takes the clinician beyond the traditional confines of one's profession and focuses on the person rather than the pathology, on the client's perceptions rather than the professional's problem. Such an approach provides respect to the client and fosters growth even in the face of the most difficult of situations. "A general systems perspective presents a humanistic view of man as a holistic, goal-directed, self-maintaining, self-creating individual of intrinsic worth, capable of self-reflection upon his own uniqueness."[60]

Many factors mediate a client's understanding and response to identifying and dealing with problems. Some of these are due to past experience. More are due to one's current levels of development. Cognitive, affective, social, or spiritual developmental levels do not necessarily reflect chronological age. One is more likely to acknowledge immature functioning levels in children, but many adults still function at immature levels in one or more domains. These must be recognized and approached accordingly if intervention strategies are to be effective.

When working with clients, the clinician must assume an ecological or systems approach that includes a concern for the total family as the supportive system. To assume that a practitioner, no matter how skilled, has all the answers or is the magical cure for the client is as naïve and irresponsible on the part of the practitioner as it is for the client. The professional's goal, like that of the professor or the parent, is to foster increasing independence on the part of those who seek or need assistance. True satisfaction is found in the service of helping others grow; for it is in serving that we find our own strength.

REFERENCES

1. Arduini, D., Rizzo, G., Giorlandino, C., Valensise, H., Dell'acqua, S., & Romanini, C. (1986). The development of fetal behavioral states: A longitudinal study. *Prenatal Diagnosis, 6,* 117–124.
2. Bassler, S. F. (1976). The origins and development of biological rhythms. *Nursing Clinics of North America, 11,* 575.
3. Bateson, P. (1983). The interpretation of sensitive periods. In A. Oliverio & M. Zappella (Eds.), *The behavior of human infants.* New York: Plenum Press.
4. Bloom, B. S. (Ed.). (1984). *Taxonomy of educational objectives: The classification of educational goals. Handbook 1. Cognitive domain.* New York: Longman.
5. Bowlby, J. (1965). *Child care and growth of love* (2nd ed.). Baltimore: Penguin.
6. Campos, J. J., & Barrett, K. C. (1984). Toward a new understanding of emotions and their development. In C. E. Izard, J. Kagan, & R. B. Zajonc (Eds.), *Emotions, cognition and behavior* (pp. 229–263). Cambridge, UK: Cambridge University Press.
7. Chamberlain, D. B. (1987). Consciousness at birth: The range of empirical evidence. In T. R. Verny (Ed.), *Pre-and perinatal psychology: An introduction* (pp. 69–90). New York: Human Sciences Press.
8. Cicchetti, D., & Schneider-Rosen, K. (1984). Theoretical and empirical considerations in the investigation of the relationship between affect and cognition in atypical populations of infants. In C. E. Izard, J. Kagan, & R. B. Zajonc (Eds.), *Emotions, cognition and behavior* (pp. 366–406). Cambridge, UK: Cambridge University Press.
9. Cogswell, B. E. (1988). The walking patient and the revolt of the client: Impetus to develop new models of physician-patient roles. In S. K. Steinmetz (Ed.), *Family and support systems across the life span* (pp. 243–256). New York: Plenum Press.
10. Czeisler, C. A., & Allan, J. S. (1987). Acute circadian phase reversal in man via bright light exposure: Application to jet-lag. *Sleep Research, 16,* 605.
11. Czeisler, C. A., Allan, J. S., Strogatz, S. H., Ronda, J. M., Sánchez, R., Ríos, C. D., Freitag, W. O., Richardson, G. S., & Kronauer, R. E. (1986). Bright light resets the human circadian pacemaker independent of the timing of the sleep-wake cycle. *Science, 233*(4764), 667–671.
12. Czeisler, C. A., Kronauer, R. E., Mooney, J. J., Anderson, J. L., & Allan, J. S. (1987). Biological rhythm disorders, depression, and phototherapy: A new hypothesis. *The Psychiatric Clinics of North America, 10*(4), 687–709.
13. Davidson, M. (1983). *Uncommon sense: The life and thought of Ludwig von Bertalanffy (1901–1972), father of general systems theory.* Los Angeles: J. P. Tarcher.
14. Dolph, C. D. (1985). Holistic health and therapy. In D. G. Benner (Ed.), *Baker encyclopedia of Psychology* (pp. 516–518). Grand Rapids, MI: Baker Book House.
15. Dossey, B. M., Keegan, L., Guzzetta, C. E., & Kolkmeier, L. G. (1988). *Holistic nursing: A handbook for practice.* Rockville, MD: Aspen.
16. Downs, P. G. (1986). Is faith staged? *Christianity Today, 30*(15), 29–30.

17. Dunn, R., Dunn, K., Primavera, L., Sinatra, R., & Virostko, J. (1987). A timely solution: Effects of chronobiology on achievement and behavior. *Clearing House, 61*(1), 5–8.
18. Emery, F. E. (Ed.). (1981). *Systems thinking: Selected readings* (rev. ed.). Harmondsworth: Penguin.
19. Erikson, E. H., Erikson, J. M., & Kivnick, H. Q. (1986). *Vital involvement in old age.* New York: W. W. Norton.
20. Erikson, J. M. (1988). *Wisdom and the senses.* New York: W. W. Norton.
21. Findlay, J. N. (1977). Forward and analysis of text. In G. W. F. Hegel (Ed.), *Phenomenology of the spirit* (A. V. Miller, Trans., pp. v–xxvi). Oxford, UK: Oxford University Press. (Original work published in 1807)
22. Fowler, J. W. (1981). *Stages of faith: The psychology of human development and the quest for meaning.* San Francisco: Harper and Row.
23. Fowler, J. W. (1986). Faith and the structuring of meaning. In C. Dykstra & S. Parks (Eds.), *Faith development and Fowler* (pp. 15–42). Birmingham, AL: Religious Education Press.
24. Galland, L. D. (1986). Common sense models of health and disease. *New England Journal of Medicine, 314,* 652.
25. Gillespie, V. B. (1988). *The experience of faith.* Birmingham, AL: Religious Education Press.
26. Goldman, R. (1968). *Religious thinking from childhood to adolescence.* New York: Seabury.
27. Graeber, R. C. (1988). Jet lag and sleep disruption. In M. H. Kryger, T. Roth, & W. C. Dement (Eds.), *Principles and practice of sleep medicine* (pp. 324–331). Philadelphia: W. B. Saunders.
28. Guidano, V. F. (1987). *Complexity of the self: A developmental approach to psychopathology and therapy.* New York: The Guilford Press.
29. Hardy, A. (1979). *The spiritual nature of man.* Oxford, UK: Clarendon Press.
30. Hare, M. L. (1988). Shiatsu acupressure in nursing practice. *Holistic Nursing Practice, 2*(3), 68–74.
31. Harms, F. (1944). The development of religious experience in children. *American Journal of Sociology, 50,* 1q12–122.
32. Havighurst, R. J. (1972). *Developmental tasks and education* (3rd ed.). New York: McKay.
33. Hebb, D. O. (1949). *The organization of behavior.* New York: John Wiley and Sons.
34. Helminiak, D. A. (1987). *Spiritual development: An interdisciplinary study.* Chicago: Loyola University Press.
35. Herbert, W. (1982). Punching the biological timeclock. *Science News, 122*(5), 69.
36. Horowitz, F. D. (1987). *Exploring developmental theories: Toward a structural/behavioral model of development.* Hillsdale, NJ: Lawrence Erlbaum Associates.
37. Horton, T. E. (1977). Conceptual basis for nursing intervention with human systems: Families. In J. E. Hall & B. R. Weaver (Eds.), *Distributive nursing practice: A systems approach to community health.* Philadelphia: J. B. Lippincott.
38. Ilg, F. L., Ames, L. B., & Baker, S. M. (1981). *Child Behavior* (rev. ed.). New York: Barnes and Noble.
39. Izard, C. E. (1984). Emotion-cognition relationships and human development. In C. E. Izard, J. Kagan, & R. B. Zajonc (Eds.), *Emotions, cognition and behavior* (pp. 17–37). Cambridge, UK: Cambridge University Press.
40. Jurgens, A., Meehan, T. C., & Wilson, H. L. (1987). Therapeutic touch as a nursing intervention. *Holistic Nursing Practice, 2*(1), 1–13.
41. Kendler, H. H. (1985). Behaviorism and psychology: An uneasy alliance. In S. Koch & D. E. Leary (Eds.), *A century of psychology as science* (pp. 121–134). New York: McGraw-Hill.
42. Lanuza, D. M. (1976). Circadian rhythms of mental efficiency and performance. *Nursing Clinics of North America, 11,* 583.
43. Lawrence, C. (1987). An integrated spiritual and psychological growth model in the treatment of narcissism. *Journal of Psychology and Theology, 15*(3), 205–213.
44. Lewy, A. J., Sack, R. L., Miller, L. S., & Hoban, T. M. (1987). Antidepressant and circadian phase-shifting effects of light. *Science, 235*(4786), 352.
45. Mahler, M. S., Pine, F., & Bergman, A. (1975). *The psychological birth of the human infant: Symbiosis and individuation.* New York: Basic Books.
46. Masters, J. C., & Carlson, C. R. (1984). Children's and adult's understanding of the causes and consequences of emotional states. In C. E. Izard, J. Kagan, & R. B. Zajonc (Eds.), *Emotions, cognition and behavior* (pp. 438–463). Cambridge, UK: Cambridge University Press.
47. Meadow, M. J., & Kahol, R. D. (1984). *Psychology of religion.* New York: Harper and Row.
48. Minuchin, S., & Minuchin, P. (1976). The child in context. In N. B. Talbot (Ed.), *Raising children in modern American: Problems and prospective solutions.* Boston: Little, Brown.
49. Mistlberger, R., & Rusak, B. (1989). Mechanisms and models of the circadian timekeeping system. In M. H. Kryger, T. Roth, & W. C. Demand (Eds.), *Principles and practice of sleep medicine* (pp. 141–152). Philadelphia: W. B. Saunders.
50. Monk, T. H. (1989). Circadian rhythms in subjective activation, mood, and performance efficiency. In M. H. Kryger, T. Roth, & W. C. Dement (Eds.), *Principles and practice of sleep medicine* (pp. 163–172). Philadelphia: W. B. Saunders.
51. Myers, D. G., & Jeeves, M. A. (1987). *Psychology through the eyes of faith.* San Francisco: Harper and Row.
52. Palmer, J. D. (1976). *An introduction to biological rhythms.* New York: Academic Press.
53. Rapoport, A. (1986). *General system theory: Essential concepts and applications.* Tunbridge Wells, Kent, UK: Abacus Press.
54. Reppert, S. M., Duncan, M. J., & Weaver, D. R. (1987). Maternal influences on the developing circadian system. In N. A. Krasnegor, E. M. Blass, M. A. Hofer, & W. P. Smotherman (Eds.), *Perinatal development: A psychobiological perspective* (pp. 343–356). Orlando, FL: Academic Press.
55. Rizzuto, A. M. (1979). *The birth of the living God.* Chicago: University of Chicago Press.
56. Rutter, M. (1980). The long-term effects of early experience. *Developmental Medicine and Child Neurology, 22,* 800–815.
57. Siegel, B. S., & Siegel, B. H. (1985). Spiritual aspects of the healing arts. *Journal of Holistic Medicine, 7*(1), 73–83.
58. Sills, G. M., & Hall, J. E. (1977). A general systems perspective for nursing. In J. E. Hall & B. R. Weaver (Eds.), *Distributive nursing practice: A systems approach to community health.* Philadelphia: J. B. Lippincott.
59. Siwolop, S., Therrien, L., Oneal, M., & Ivey, M. (1986, December 8). Helping workers stay awake at the switch. *Business Week, 2976,* p. 108.
60. Smolensky, M. H., & D'Alonzo, G. E. (1988). Biological rhythms and medicine. *The American Journal of Medicine, 85*(Suppl. 1B), 34–46.
61. Smuts, J. C. (1926). *Holism and evolution.* New York: Macmillan.
62. Swinburne, R. (1986). *The evolution of the soul.* Oxford, UK: Clarendon Press/Oxford University Press.
63. Toffler, A. (1970). *Future shock.* New York: Random House.

64. Tom, C. K. (1976). Nursing assessment of biological rhythms. *Nursing Clinics of North America, 11*, 621.

65. U.S. Bureau of the Census. (1987). *Statistical abstract of the United States: 1988* (108th ed.). Washington, DC: U. S. Government Printing Office.

66. von Bertalanffy, L. (1968). *General systems theory: Foundations, development, applications*. New York: George Braziller.

67. von Bertalanffy, L. (1968). *Organismic psychology and systems theory*. Barre, MA: Clark University Press.

68. von Bertalanffy, L. (1981). *A systems view of man* (P. A LaViolette, Ed.). Boulder, CO: Westview Press.

69. Webb, W. B. (1982). Sleep and biological rhythms. In W. B. Webb (Ed.), *Biological rhythms, sleep, and performance* (pp. 87–110). New York: John Wiley and Sons.

70. Weil, A. (1983). *Health and healing: Understanding conventional and alternative medicine*. Boston: Houghton Mifflin.

71. Werner, H. (1957). The concept of development from a comparative and organismic point of view. In D. B. Harris (Ed.), *The concept of development*. Minneapolis: University of Minnesota.

72. White, J. (1987). Consciousness and substance: The primal forms of God. *Journal of Near-Death Studies, 6*(2), 73–78.

73. Winfree, A. T. (1987). *The timing of biological clocks*. New York: Scientific American Library.

74. World Almanac. (1989). *World almanac and book of facts: 1990*. New York: World Almanac.

II IN THE BEGINNING

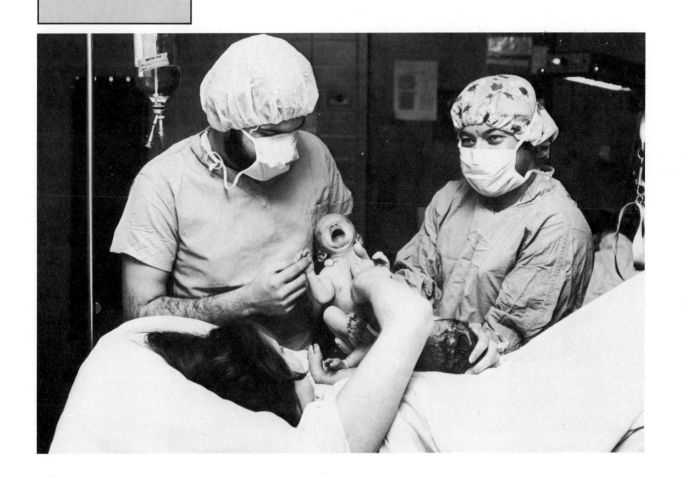

Nature provides each person with a highly protective, nurturing, and supportive environment for the first 9 months of life. The mother's uterus is uniquely created to enable the single-celled conceptus to receive the oxygen, nutrients, warmth, and stimuli essential to form the biological substraits that will enable the baby to survive extrauterine life.

Even before birth, each infant is unique in activity level and response to touch and sounds. After its birth, the baby's ability to respond to stimuli as well as to seek it out helps to establish the initial parent–child relationship.

Developmental Tasks of the Pre-, Peri-, and Postnatal Periods

*1. Develop body systems sufficiently to maintain extra-uterine life, e.g.:
- respiratory system
- gastrointestinal system
- cardiovascular system
- neurological system
- coordination of sucking and swallowing reflexes

*2. Develop awareness of and contingently respond to environmental stimuli:
- tactile
- auditory
- visual
- kinesthetic and vestibular movement
- thermal

*3. Adopt techniques for controlling the state of alertness:
- pay attention to desirable stimuli
- shut out undesirable stimuli
- calm self
- initiate and maintain sleep state when desired

---

* Tasks deemed most crucial to continued maturation are marked with an asterisk.

Antenatal Development

Clara S. Schuster

3 *For no king had any other first beginning; But all men have one entrance into life, And a like departure....*
—THE WISDOM OF SOLOMON, *THE APOCRYPHA*

Every living organism begins life as a single cell. In just 9 months, the single-cell fertilized ovum is transformed into a complex system of about **15 trillion** (15,000,000,000,000) cells,[82] which possesses a synchrony of function capable of sustaining life outside the uterus. It takes about 44 geometrically progressive divisions (2^{44}) of the original cell to transform it into an infant mature enough to sustain life outside the mother's uterus, and only four more divisions to transform the newborn into an adult. It is estimated that the adult body is composed of about 100 quadrillion (10^{14}) cells.[44, 48] If the process has proceeded normally, the genetic material of the nucleus of each of these cells is an exact duplicate of the original cell, but the cytoplasm and cell membranes differentiate so that each cell, tissue, organ, and system of the body is uniquely constructed to carry out a specific function for the entire organism. Each cell works in harmony with other body cells to meet both its own needs and the needs of the total system.

The study of the process of human development, to be complete, must begin with those events that occur before conception: the preparation of a suitable environment, the formation of the parent cells from which the new individual is created, and the hereditary mechanisms that regulate and influence the individual's potentials for growth and development for the rest of the life span.

Growth of the body occurs through the process of **mitosis**: a somatic (body) cell with its cytoplasm and the nucleus with its contents are exactly duplicated, forming two new "daughter cells." However, during fetal development, the cytoplasm may take different forms depending on the ultimate responsibility of that cell within the body (e.g., bone, blood cell, heart muscle, liver cell, skin). It is through the mitotic process that the single cell of conception becomes the complex individual capable of extrauterine survival. It is through mitosis that the organism grows in size, repairs itself when injured, and replaces cells that suffer from wear and tear.

REPRODUCTION

Cell division by the process of **meiosis** prepares a haploid cell (one half of the chromosomes in a somatic cell) for the purpose of reproducing the entire organism. Gametes, or haploids, are formed by the reproductive system through specialized processes of cell division and chromosome reduction known as **gametogenesis.** Each individual begins life as a single cell that is formed by the union of the nuclear material of two gametes, a sperm and an ovum (egg).

Gametogenesis

All normal human body cells have 46 chromosomes contained within the nucleus. The chromosomes are divided into 22 pairs of autosomes and one pair of sex chromosomes.[79] Each member of a pair is similar in size and shape to its sister chromosome, except for the sex chromosomes (the "X" chromosome is *much* larger than the "Y"). Because chromosomes are invisible to the naked eye, special staining and microphotography techniques are used to record the chromosomes of a single cell during the process of cell division. After enlargement, individual chromosomes can be cut from the photograph, matched in pairs, and mounted on another paper; they are then grouped and labeled according to the Denver Karyotype Classification System (Fig. 3-1). The size and shape as well as the unique position of the centromere, a constricted area on each chromosome, are used to sort and identify individual chromosomes. A karyotype is invaluable to the geneticist who is looking for possible causes of hereditary defects. Karyotypes can be used to identify a person's biological gender (e.g., if genital defects make the child's gender ambiguous, or if any question exists about a contestant's eligibility for athletic competition). The individual who has 22 pairs of autosomes and two X chromosomes is a biological female; the individual with 22 pairs of autosomes and one X and one Y chromosome is a biological male.

Production of both the sperm and the ovum is accomplished by the same basic maturational stages, the two-step meiotic process. Immature (primary) germ cells contain 46 chromosomes. During the second meiotic division, the chromatid pairs are divided equally between the two new cells. The original germ cell produces one ovum and three nonfunctional "polar bodies" in the female and four viable sperm in the male (Fig. 3-2).

Female Reproductive System

Anatomy
The female reproductive system consists of four major organs:

1. The **ovaries,** which produce the ovum or egg and the female hormones estrogen and progesterone.

2. The **fallopian tubes,** which transport the mature ovum from the ovary to the uterus.

3. The **uterus,** which protects and nourishes the developing fetus from conception to birth. The three major divisions of the uterus—the fundus (top), body, and cervix (neck)—become most significant during the childbirth process.

4. The **vagina,** which provides an access route for the sperm and exit route for the baby (Fig. 3-3).

The Ovarian Cycle
The ovarian cycle is regulated by a complex series of changes in the hormones secreted by the ovary and the hypothalmic-pituitary axis (in the brain).[41] Changes in the hormonal balance (generally repeated at 21- to 35-day intervals) create changes in the ovaries and uterus for the purpose of reproduction. The cycle consists of two phases, which are distinctly separated by the phenomena of ovulation and menstruation.

PREFOLLICULAR PHASE. Before the onset of the ovarian cycle (at puberty), the woman has already laid the foundation for the process of reproduction. Before she is even born—in fact, by the fifth month of fetal life—she already has 7 million immature ova.[59] Most of these regress so that by birth only about 2 million primary oocytes (immature ova) remain.[55] The 7-year-old girl has about 200,000,[59] and by puberty only about 40,000 remain.[55] These primary oocytes remain dormant until puberty when, with each cycle, 5 to 12 primary oocytes begin to complete the meiotic process under the influence of the hormonal changes.[55] However, usually only one matures sufficiently for reproduction. The others degenerate and are absorbed by the body. Depending on the number of anovulatory cycles (due to pregnancy, illness, breast feeding, or oral

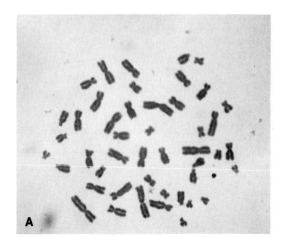

FIGURE 3–1.
A karyotype. (A) Chromosomes during mitosis. (B) Matched, sorted, and labeled chromosomes from (A). Is this karyotype from a male or a female? Answer page 79. (Courtesy Dr. Stella Kontras.)

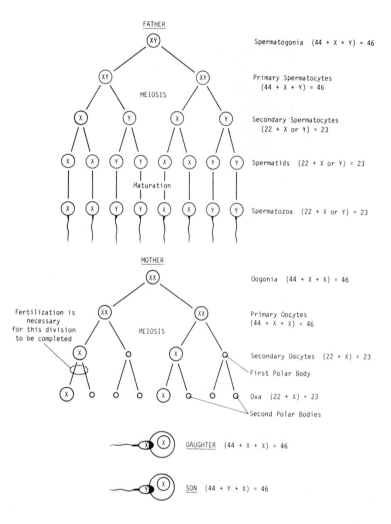

FIGURE 3–2.
Gametogenesis. (Snell, R. S. (1983). Clinical embryology for medical students, 3rd ed. Boston: Little, Brown.) With permission.

contraceptives), only about 400 reach the stage where fertilization is possible.[55]

It is significant to note that an immature ovum may be present in the body for 20, 30, or 40 years before it matures, thus it may be subject to many misfortunes in the meantime (e.g., toxins, x-rays). Consequently, the older the ovum (or maternal age), the greater the chances of producing a defective mature ovum. This fact is shown clearly in the increasing rate of Down syndrome babies (caused by chromosomal abnormality) to older mothers (Table 3-1).[39, 55]

FOLLICULAR PHASE. The follicular phase (also known as the proliferative phase because the lining of the uterus grows profusely during this time) is under the control of follicle-stimulating hormone (FSH), which is produced by the anterior pituitary cells under the influence of gonadatropin-releasing hormone (GnRH) from the hypothalamus.[41] The pituitary gland is a small reddish body located in the brain just behind the root of the nose. The anterior or frontal section of this gland secretes its hormones directly into the bloodstream. Under the influence of FSH, several **primary follicles** (primary ovum with its surrounding cells) begin to

mature in the ovaries, but, by some mechanism that is not yet understood, only one of the follicles becomes a mature **graafian follicle** (small secretory sac that contains the developing ovum).

The graafian follicle enlarges as it fills with follicular fluid and gradually moves toward the surface of the ovary. The layer of cells that surrounds the ovum thickens by developing several layers. The inner layer of cells, known as the **theca**

TABLE 3–1. INCIDENCE OF DOWN SYNDROME ACCORDING TO MATERNAL AGE

Maternal Age	Incidence
20–24	1:1,550
30	1:855
35	1:350
39	1:150
41	1:85
45	1:32
49	1:12

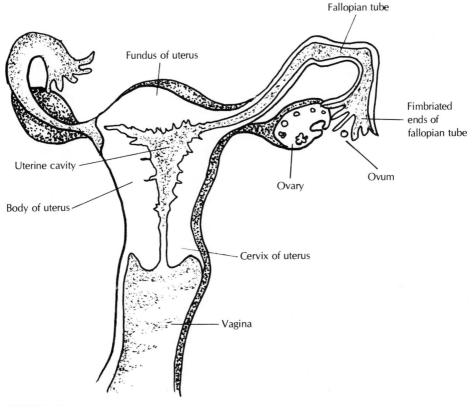

FIGURE 3–3.
The female reproductive system.

interna, secretes the hormone estrogen into the follicular fluid.[41] The immature ovum, which initiated its first meiotic division during fetal life, resumes its maturation process at this time.

Estrogen is absorbed by the bloodstream and enters the general body circulation. It causes thickening and vascularization of the **endometrium** (the lining of the uterus). Another major target organ of estrogen is the anterior pituitary; estrogen suppresses the production of FSH. At the same time, it stimulates the anterior pituitary to produce luteinizing hormone (LH). This process is only one example of the delicate feedback mechanisms that occur among many organs of the body to maintain **homeostasis,** normal rhythmic function of the total body (Fig. 3-4).

Ovulation. The walls of the graafian follicle thin as it continues to expand in size and move toward the surface of the ovary (Fig. 3-5). At full maturity, the follicle may reach ½ inch in diameter as it swells with follicular fluid.[84] In response to the increased amounts of estrogen produced by the follicle, the anterior pituitary releases a large surge of LH. This LH surge appears to stimulate rapid follicular growth and a decrease in the tensile strength of the follicular wall,[25] thus facilitating **ovulation** (follicular rupture with extrusion or release of the ovum) 10 to 16 hours later.[28]

Ovulation may be accompanied by **mittelschmerz** in some women.[55] This momentary midpain can be mild or quite sharp; it may pass unnoticed, or it may cause enough discomfort to awaken the woman from sleep or cause her to gasp and double over momentarily in spontaneous response to the unexpected discomfort. Some women experience vaginal spotting or a dull lower abdominal aching due to a small amount of bleeding that may accompany the rupture of the follicle.

The increase in estrogen levels causes changes in the vaginal secretions and in the mucous plug that blocks the cervix.[22] At ovulation, when estrogen levels are highest, these secretions become thinner, clearer, more copious, and more elastic. Viscosity and pH also change, making the environment receptive to penetration by the sperm and facilitating their entrance into the female reproductive system.

After the ovum is extruded from the graafian follicle, it is at the mercy of the unique structure of the reproductive system. Since it has no means of locomotion, it must depend on the fallopian tubes to propel it to the uterus. The fingerlike projections on the end of the tubes move and appear to set up a current that draws the ovum to it. The cilia move like the oars of a scull boat or like wind blowing over a field of grain. The peristaltic movements, or muscular contractions, move

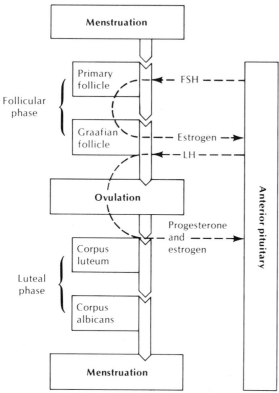

FIGURE 3–4.
The ovarian cycle. Hormonal relationship between the ovary and the anterior pituitary gland.

the ovum in waves down the tube, like an ostrich swallowing a golf ball or a snake swallowing a mouse.

Basal Body Temperature. Basal body temperature elevates after ovulation.[84] If a large group of women are asked how many of them feel cold in a room (temperature about 70°F) and how many feel warm, almost all those who feel cold will be in the follicular phase of the ovarian cycle; those who feel warm will probably be in the postovulatory or luteal phase of the ovarian cycle. Basal body temperature change is caused by the presence of progesterone, a hormone secreted during the luteal phase. Changes in body temperature as related to hormonal balance are discussed in greater detail in Chapter 30 in the section on contraception.

LUTEAL PHASE. After the extrusion of the ovum, the graafian follicle collapses under the influence of LH and becomes a yellow-colored, solid tissue mass known as the **corpus luteum.** The production of FSH ceases (Fig. 3-6). The corpus luteum continues to produce some estrogen but primarily produces progesterone, which stimulates the epithelium to thicken and secrete fluid rich in glycogen (giving this phase a second name, the secretory phase).

The corpus luteum has a life span of 8 to 10 days, after which it begins to deteriorate and is replaced by white con-

nective tissue known as the **corpus albicans,** which is unable to produce hormones. The production of LH ceases in direct response to termination of the secretion of estrogen and progesterone. Decreased levels of progesterone also effect a drop in basal body temperature. If the ovum is fertilized and pregnancy established, the corpus luteum survives and continues to secrete estrogen and progesterone for 3 to 4 months.

Menstruation. One of the major functions of progesterone is to prepare the uterus to receive and to nourish a fertilized ovum. When production ceases, the endometrial lining begins to degenerate and slough off. This phenomenon is known as menstruation (see Chap. 23). At this point, the entire cycle begins to repeat itself. The anterior pituitary resumes production of FSH until the estrogen levels are once again elevated.

Length of Cycle. The length of the follicular phase (first day of menstruation to ovulation) cannot be predicted except to make an estimation based on the history of the individual woman. Although it would be helpful to know exactly when ovulation will occur, many increases in family size bear testimony to the fact that someone's calculations were in error. The luteal phase (ovulation to menstruation), on the other hand, is predictable because of the life span of the corpus luteum. The luteal phase is 12 to 14 days in length.[84] Because of the variation in the length of the follicular phase, the total cycle varies in length with each woman. Most women start a new cycle every 28 days, plus or minus 7 days. The day of ovulation can be estimated by subtracting 12 to 14 days from the day menstruation is expected to begin. If a woman normally has a 24-day cycle, then ovulation would probably occur between days 10 and 12 of the cycle. A woman who has a 32-day cycle would most likely ovulate between days 18 and 20 of the cycle.

Oogenesis

Through meiosis, one ovum and two or three polar bodies are produced with each ovarian cycle. The ovum is the only one of the four resultant haploid (half) cells that is capable of fertilization. It has received not only an equal division of the chromosomes but also a majority of the cytoplasm and nourishment contained in the original germ cell.

Male Reproductive System

Anatomy

The male reproductive system consists of five major parts and several accessory organs.

1.   The **testes,** which produce spermatozoa and the male hormone, testosterone
     a.   The seminiferous tubules, which produce the sperm
     b.   Leydig cells, which produce testosterone
     c.   The epididymis, which stores sperm until maturation is complete and the sperm become mobile

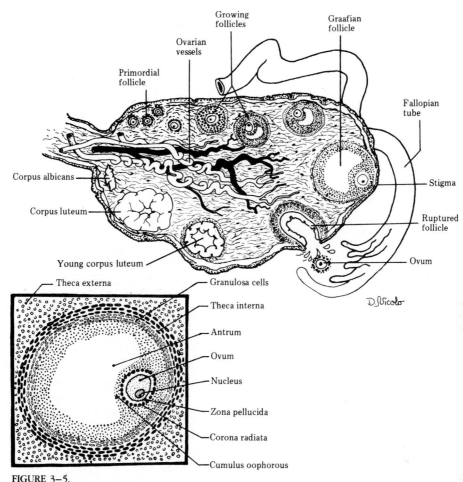

FIGURE 3–5.
Ovarian changes during the ovarian cycle. (Miller, M. A., & Brooten, D. A. [1983]. The childbearing family: A nursing perspective, *2nd ed. Boston: Little, Brown.) With permission.*

2. The **vas deferens,** which is the excretory duct and storage area for mature sperm
3. The **seminal vesicles,** which discharge a fluid at the time of ejaculation of sperm that facilitates mobility and provides nutrition for the sperm
4. The **ejaculatory duct,** which is the excretory tube that allows passage of the sperm to the urethra
5. The **penis,** which is the male organ for urinary excretion and copulation
   a. The urethra, which provides an exit route for the sperm and urine
   b. Erectile tissue, which, on distention of its large sinuses with blood, causes the penis to become firm and erect

Accessory organs that add fluids to the semen include the prostate gland and the bulbourethral (Cowper's) glands (Fig. 3-7).

Spermatogenesis

Beginning at puberty, millions of sperm are continuously in various stages of maturation. Spermatogenesis occurs in the seminiferous tubules of the testes. The inner surfaces of these tubules are lined with both spermatogonia (primary germ cells) and Sertoli's cells. As they mature, the spermatogonium cells gradually move toward the lumen of the tubules, the first and second meiotic divisions occurring as they migrate toward the surface. The spermatids produced by the second meiotic division become embedded in the outer surface of a Sertoli's cell (a process that takes about 25 days from spermatogonium to spermatid) (Fig. 3-8). Here they undergo metamorphic changes that transform them into spermatozoa. The cytoplasmic material gradually dissipates, and a flagellum, or tail, grows at one end. The nucleus of the sperm remains located in its head portion. The anterior portion is covered by the acrosome cap. On completion of this stage of the maturational process (about 22 days), the sperm are

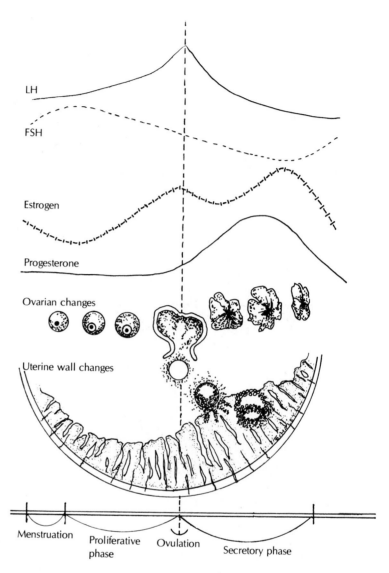

LH

FSH

Estrogen

Progesterone

Ovarian changes

Uterine wall changes

Menstruation   Proliferative   Ovulation   Secretory phase
phase

FIGURE 3–6.
Endometrial and ovarian changes related to hormonal levels.

released into the lumen of the epididymis for storage and final maturation. It takes another 12 to 26 days for sperm to pass through the epididymis and enter the ejaculate after leaving the testes.[8] The ejaculate contents, therefore, represent events initiated 3 months earlier.

Hormonal Control

As in the female, the anterior pituitary of the male also produces FSH and LH. In both the male and the female, FSH stimulates maturation of the gamete; LH stimulates production of the appropriate gender-associated hormone by the gonad. Luteinizing hormone stimulates Leydig's cells of the testes to produce testosterone, and FSH stimulates the production of spermatozoa. Each of these gonadotropic hormones potentiates the action of the other.

Conception

The ovum is viable, or capable of joining with the sperm, for about 10 to 24 hours after ovulation. Once the sperm has entered the female reproductive tract, it generally is viable for 48 to 72 hours. However, under optimal conditions, sperm may survive in the cervical folds for up to 7 days after deposit.[22] Although some women may believe as a result of their personal experience that conception can occur at any point during the ovarian cycle, there are actually only about 90 hours per cycle when intercourse can result in conception. Other points of time during the ovarian cycle are "safe." However, as mentioned earlier, crucial factors include pinpointing when ovulation occurs as well as considering the possibility of sperm that have found safe harbor in the cervical folds.

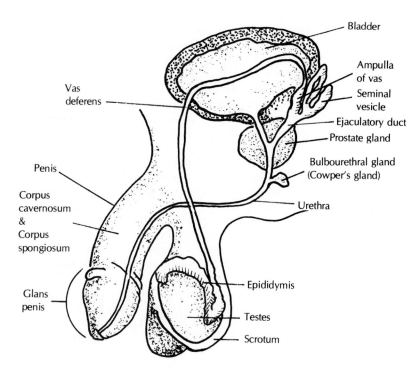

FIGURE 3–7.
The male reproductive system.

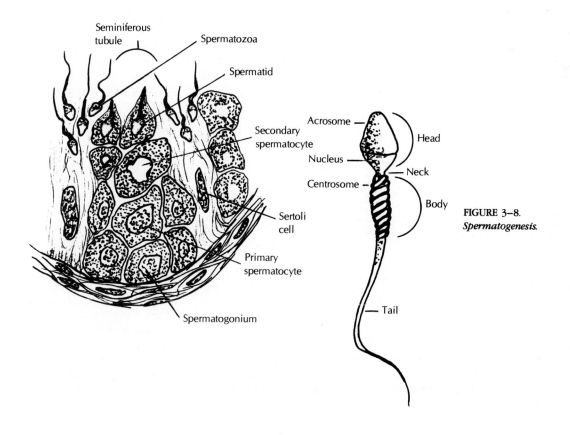

FIGURE 3–8.
Spermatogenesis.

After extrusion from the ovary, the ovum slowly starts its journey through the fallopian tube toward the uterus. Since fertilization generally occurs in the outer one-third of the fallopian tube,[51] the sperm must swim up through the cervix, uterus, and fallopian tube to reach the ovum. During this journey, they are bathed in the secretions of the female genital tract, a factor essential for the removal of the glycoproteins from the surface of the acrosome (or cap) of the sperm (a process known as **capacitation**), as freshly ejaculated sperm are unable to fertilize the ovum.[27] The acrosome is then able to release an enzyme, hyaluronidase, which digests the protective coat of the ovum to gain entrance. Many spermatozoa may enter the outer coat (zona pellucida); however, only one is allowed entrance through the cell membrane (Fig. 3-9). Once this entrance has occurred, all other sperm are rejected. The ovum completes the second meiotic division under the influence of chemicals from the sperm; the nuclei merge, the chromosomes are paired, the gender of the new individual is determined, and a new life begins. Shortly after conception, an immunosuppressant protein, known as the **early pregnancy factor** appears in the mother's blood and becomes the basis for pregnancy tests during the first week of development.[55]

The fertilized ovum becomes known as the conceptus or zygote. After a brief rest, the new cell begins the mitotic process. This is the only whole cell capable of division that will produce a separate individual. Through the process of mitosis, this single cell becomes a moving, breathing, crying newborn infant and, eventually, a biologically mature adult capable of repeating the process of reproduction.

Inheritance

The blueprint for all inherited traits is contained within the chromosomes. The independent random division of the 46 chromosomes from each parent during meiotic division offers at the time of union of the gametes a possibility of 8,388,608 (2^{23}) × 8,388,608 (2^{23}) different chromosomal combinations. At the moment of conception, the individual is endowed with a complex set of biological potentials that may involve factors as divergent as height and skin color to temperament, disease entities, or musical talent. At conception, there are potentially 70,368,744,180,000,000,000,000 or ($8,388,608)^2$ different genetic "me's." Each combination provides a different biological base for future development. Only identical twins (formed from the same fertilized ovum) have the exact same karyotype (combination of chromosomes). This process of chromosomal division, transmission, and mixing accounts for both the continuity and the variations in characteristics found in families and in the human race.

Because of this random selection of chromosomes from the parents and the differences in physical traits exhibited by the parents, the question arises: What happens when parents display different characteristics for the same factor? It is evident that some rules must govern which characteristics the offspring exhibit. Characteristics are inherited according to specific laws, and the possibility of their occurrence in a new individual can be predicted.

Gender Determination

The female can only produce ova that contain 22 autosomes and the X sex chromosome. Males, because of the XY chromosome configuration, produce sperm with 22 autosomes and either the X or the Y chromosome. It is the sperm, therefore, that determines the gender of the new individual. Since half of the sperm contain the male chromosome, it would be expected that 50% of babies would be male; however, for unknown reasons, 105 males are born for every 100 females.[55] No valid, reliable method of controlling gender at the time of conception is available. A higher male infant and childhood

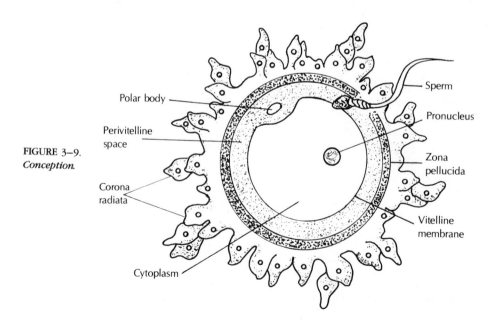

FIGURE 3–9.
Conception.

Polar body

Perivitelline space

Corona radiata

Cytoplasm

Sperm

Pronucleus

Zona pellucida

Vitelline membrane

mortality rate results in a greater number of women than men in the world.

Mendelian Laws

During the 1850s, Gregor Mendel (1822–1884), an Austrian monk, discovered the basic laws of inheritance by working with pea plants. He noted that certain characteristics were transmitted to the offspring in an orderly, predictable manner. Mendel published his findings in an obscure source in 1866, where they were rediscovered at the turn of the century. Although the intricacies of the process of inheritance are not yet completely understood, Mendel's basic laws of inheritance still form the foundation for the study of genetics today.

Gene Theory

Gene is the name given to the section of a chromosome that is responsible for the formation of a specific protein.[79] It is composed of deoxyribonucleic acid (DNA), which is the building block of all life. A single gene may be composed of more than 1000 nucleotides.[39] The growth and functioning of cells are the direct or indirect result of protein formation and enzymatic action; consequently, every hereditary trait is under the influence of one or more of the estimated 100,000 genes.[53] The genetic code that is responsible for a given trait occupies a unique position or locus on the chromosomes of a pair of matching chromosomes. Evidence shows that the mitochondria, organelles found in the cytoplasm of the cell, also carry codes for specific factors. They are passed from the mother through the ova to the offspring and can be used as a tracer for anthropological studies of racial heritage.[79] Re-

searchers have been able to map the location of more than 4300 specific traits through special techniques.[52] With new electronic equipment, information in this area is doubling every 2 to 3 years.[53] Genes that produce alternative characteristics for a specific trait are known as **alleles**. Alleles affect the same target organ, tissue, or cell.

Genotype Versus Phenotype

Alleles become paired when the chromosomes of the gametes join (**genotype,** or genetic blueprint). Although the target tissue is the same, the genetic code held by one member of the pair may not be the same as the blueprint held by the other allele. When the offspring receives the same genetic code from each parent for a specific trait, he or she is said to have a **homozygous** (matching) genotype. The trait exhibited by the individual (**phenotype**) matches the trait carried by the matching genes.

When the offspring receives a different genetic code from each parent for a specific trait, he or she is said to have a **heterozygous** (mixed) genotype. Only one of the characteristics can be expressed. The one that is exhibited (phenotype) is said to be **dominant** (Fig. 3-10). The gene that is not displayed is said to be **recessive**.

Factors other than clear-cut recessiveness or dominance of a gene may affect the phenotype of an individual. The spectrum of characteristics for a trait may be wide, with various levels of dominance in relation to each other. Traits under the influence of several allele pairs are known as polygenic; skin, hair, and eye color are good examples. A blending of traits rather than clear-cut dominance is exhibited.

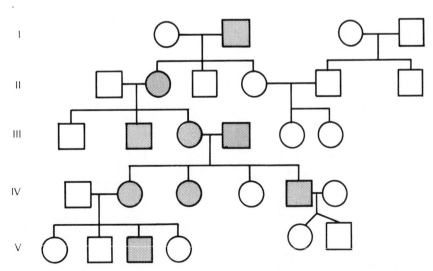

FIGURE 3–10.

Hypothetical model of inheritance of a dominant characteristic, such as polydactyly (extra fingers). Small squares designate males; circles designate females. Horizontal lines that connect a square and a circle indicate matings. Vertical lines indicate offspring. Twins are indicated by an inverted V. Roman numerals along the left-hand side are used to indicate generation. Individuals who exhibit the phenotype are indicated by filled in circles or squares. Only people who exhibit the trait can have children with the trait.

RH FACTOR. If an individual receives two genes for Rh positive (Rh +) blood (homozygous), he or she will have an Rh positive phenotype:

Rh positive (P) + Rh positive (P) = Rh positive (PP)
(genotype)   (phenotype)

What happens, however, if the offspring receives a gene for Rh+ from one parent and Rh negative (Rh−) from the other (heterozygous)? Mendel discovered that dominant characteristics always show if a person carries the gene for that characteristic.

Rh positive (P) + Rh negative (n) = Rh positive (Pn)

This person would have Rh + blood. The individual does not even know that he or she is carrying the gene for Rh− blood. A recessive characteristic exhibits its presence only if both genes are identical for that trait (homozygous).

Rh negative (n) + Rh negative (n) = Rh negative (nn)

The Rh− parent is obviously homozygous for Rh-negative blood and therefore can only give a gene for Rh− blood to any offspring. If the other parent is homozygous for Rh+, then he or she can only give the child genes for Rh+ blood. All the children therefore will carry a heterozygous genotype but exhibit the dominant trait, Rh+. If a heterozygous Rh+

person and Rh− person have a child, it has a 50% chance of expressing the recessive characteristic:

	Rh pos (P)	Rh neg (n)
Rh neg (n)	Pn	nn
Rh neg (n)	Pn	nn

Can two Rh + parents have an Rh − child? Yes, if they are both heterozygous for the trait. Twenty-five percent of the children may have Rh − blood:

	Rh Pos (P)	Rh neg (n)
Rh pos (P)	PP	nP
Rh neg (n)	Pn	nn

It is significant to note that a recessive characteristic for a trait may pass from generation to generation without ever exhibiting itself and then suddenly appear "out of nowhere." If such a trait is undesirable, one might like to think that it came from "the other side of the family." However, since a person must possess two genes for a recessive characteristic before it is exhibited in phenotype, one gene must come from each parent. This fact is the major reason why consanguineous (related by blood) marriages are illegal. Many hereditary diseases are passed by recessive genes (Fig. 3-11).

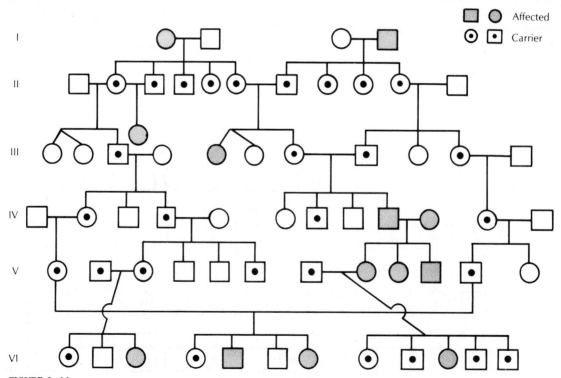

FIGURE 3–11.
Hypothetical model of inheritance of a recessive trait, such as albinism.

Can two Rh − parents have a Rh + child? (See page 79 for answer.)

MUTATIONS. Occasionally, mutations occur. A **mutation** is a random but permanent change in the code of a specific gene and, as such, is transmissible to offspring. Many of these changes are relatively insignificant and may account for the occasional situation in which an unexplainable trait or a dominant characteristic appears in the offspring of parents who express a recessive phenotype. Mutations can account for many minor variations of phenotype. Other mutations, however, can lead to diseases and malformations. A change in just one condon (code word) of a gene may change the corresponding amino acid added to the forming protein chain and thus can produce abnormalities in many organs or even result in the death of an individual. It is estimated that 10% of congenital malformations are a result of gene mutation. Phenotype depends on the genes affected.

INCOMPLETE DOMINANCE. Some genes may show incomplete dominance. Sickle cell anemia is an excellent example in which both genes express themselves fully so that both normal and abnormal hemoglobin are produced. This special case of incomplete dominance is known as codominance. Fifty thousand to 100,000 African Americans in the United States are homozygous for this trait. One out of 10 are heterozygous (or carriers) of the trait.[59] The red blood cells of people who are homozygous for the characteristic exhibit sickling when exposed to lower oxygen tensions. People who are heterozygous for this characteristic may exhibit mild symptoms (sickle cell trait) or no symptoms at all. As a result of incomplete dominance of the characteristic, heterozygous people usually have some red blood cells that are affected by the characteristic. Blood testing procedures have been developed that allow for identification of carriers.

SEX-LINKED CHARACTERISTICS. Recessive characteristics carried on the X or Y chromosomes are known as sex-linked characteristics. X-linked characteristics usually show up only in male offspring because no dominant gene masks the effect of the recessive gene for the trait. Red–green color blindness, muscular dystrophy, and baldness are probably the best known examples, although more than 310 have been described.[52] All female offspring of an affected male are carriers of the trait; the heterozygous genotype of the female masks the fact that she is a carrier of the characteristic. The royal families of Europe were plagued for years with X-linked hemophilia. The female offspring of an affected male may also exhibit the trait if the mother is a carrier (Fig. 3-12).

Sex-linked traits carried on the Y chromosome are passed directly from the father to all male offspring but never to a daughter. Suspected Y-linked traits are rare and have not yet been proved.

BLOOD TYPE. Codominance is observed with some genotypes; blood typing is probably the best example. Four major blood type groupings are known: A, B, O, and AB. Type O is recessive to both A and B, whereas A and B are equally dominant. When genes for both A and B are received, the blood of the offspring contains both A and B antigens:

	A	O		A	A		O	O
B	AB	OB	B	AB	AB	O	OO	OO
O	AO	OO	O	AO	AO	O	OO	OO

	A	O		A	A		A	B
B	AB	OB	B	AB	AB	A	AA	BA
B	AB	OB	B	AB	AB	B	AB	BB

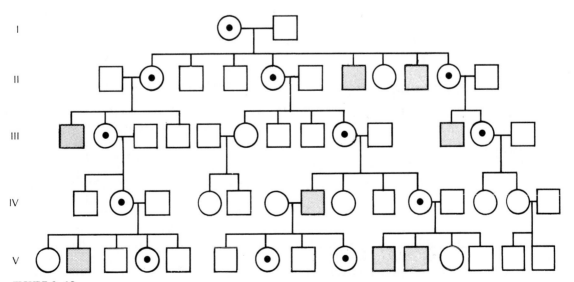

FIGURE 3–12.
Hypothetical model of inheritance of an X-linked trait, such as hemophilia.

Blood typing cannot be used to prove parentage, but it can be used to rule out parentage, a useful piece of knowledge in a court of law.

Chromosomal Alterations

Inheritance, as discussed so far, has dealt with the transmission of a single gene, the genetic code for a specific trait as mediated through protein formation. Changes in the genetic code (mutations) can occur without affecting the overall structure of the chromosome. However, structural changes of the chromosome itself may occur when the chromosomes are "shuffled" during the process of meiosis.[55] Many chemicals that enter the body through environmental pollution or by ingestion are known to alter the meiotic and mitotic processes or to initiate mutations and chromosomal alterations. Such changes are particularly significant, because they can be responsible for severe congenital malformations or birth defects (such as when chromosomes fail to divide properly, with all or part of one chromosome clinging to another and resulting in too much or too little chromosome material in the nucleus of the new cell). Some changes in chromosome configuration can create such severe disruptions in protein formation as to be incompatible with life. Twenty-five percent to 40% of conceptions are lost before they are perceived as a pregnancy by the woman, and another 15% after pregnancy is clinically recognized. Fifty percent to 60% of these spontaneous abortions are caused by chromosomal abnormalities.[27, 55]

Because of the independent nature of meiotic chromosomal division, the inheritance of any characteristic is based on random probability. People who seek a source for genetic counseling may contact their state department of health (Division of Maternal-Child Health) or either of the following for information:

The March of Dimes Birth Defects Foundation, 1275 Mamaroneck Avenue, White Plains, NY 10605 (914-428-7100)

The National Genetics Foundation, P. O. Box 1374, New York, NY 10101 (212-586-5800)

DEVELOPMENT OF THE CONCEPTUS

Growth of the biophysical domain is accomplished through two major processes:

Hyperplasia. Through the mitotic process, the number of cells increases. The size of the cells remains small.

Hypertrophy. The number of cells remains constant, but the cytoplasmic portion of the cell increases in size.

During the early days and weeks of intrauterine life, hyperplastic growth predominates. Mitosis allows for an increase in body mass, while the genetic code guides the differentiation of cellular structure. Hypertrophic growth begins to predominate during the later days and weeks of intrauterine

life. Hyperplastic and hypertrophic growth continue throughout life. Hyperplastic growth during later years allows for replacement and repair of cells rather than body growth.

The 9-month gestational period is divided into three 3-month segments known as **trimesters.** During the first trimester (conception to 12 weeks), the new individual undergoes rapid growth in both number and configuration of cells as cells differentiate into systems and organs. All the basic structures for body systems and the biological foundations for life are established. By 4 weeks after conception, the embryo, though tiny, has a head, back bone, limb buds, and a functional heart; by 8 weeks, it has a distinctly human appearance.[60] Because of this rapid growth and differentiation of cells, the organism is extremely sensitive to insults that can stop or alter the growth pattern.

During the second trimester (13–24 weeks), the fetus experiences continued growth and further tissue differentiation. The functional abilities of all body structures and systems gradually increase. The growth in length is rapid, but body mass remains relatively small. At the end of this trimester, the fetus may be able to sustain extrauterine life if provided with intensive medical and nursing intervention.

During the third trimester (25 weeks to birth), the systems and organs continue to develop to a stage where they can function adaptively outside the uterus. Body weight increases more rapidly than body length. The fetus begins to store up fat, iron, and other minerals in preparation for birth and independent living.

Zygote Stage

For the first week after conception, the conceptus is identified as a **zygote.** About 30 hours after fertilization, the first division or cleavage occurs. Since the two daughter cells are smaller than the original parent cell, the entire organism does not increase in size. The four-cell stage is reached at about 40 hours (Fig. 3-13), the 12- to 16-cell stage at about 60 hours.[42] The entire solid mass, now known as a **morula,** still has not changed in total size; also, no differentiation in cells appears at this point.[60] The cells have merely decreased in size with each cleavage. This fact is significant because the morula must pass through the narrow lumen of the fallopian tube. If the morula were to increase in size, it could easily become wedged in the narrow lumen and never reach the uterine cavity. If this occurs, the conceptus continues to grow for 6 to 8 weeks within the fallopian tube (ectopic pregnancy). Since the tube is unable to expand adequately to accommodate the growing embryo, rupture of the tube usually means death for the embryo. (It may also mean death for the mother because of hemorrhage.)

About 4 days after conception, the morula reaches the uterine cavity. The mitotic process continues at a rapid pace. A cavity forms in the center, and the morula begins to increase in size, as it absorbs fluids from the endometrial lining. The conceptus is now known as a **blastocyst.**

The 4½-day conceptus consists of 107 cells[60] (see Fig.

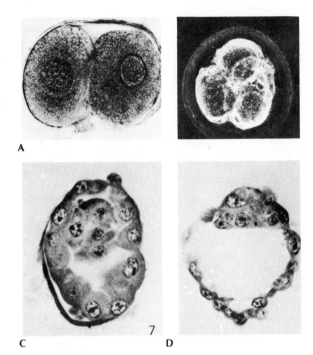

FIGURE 3–13.
Early development of the zygote. (A) Intact two-cell conceptus, showing zona pellucida and two polar bodies. (B) Intact four-cell conceptus. The granular zona pellucida can be distinguished. (C) Section through a 58-cell blastocyst. The zona pellucida is visible on the lower left-hand side, where a polar body can also be seen. Peripheral cells are trophoblastic. (D) Section through a 107-cell blastocyst. The blastula cavity is not quite large. The embryonic disc is in the upper portion. Peripheral cells are trophoblastic. (Courtesy Carnegie Institute of Washington.)

3-13D). A cross section shows a ring shape with a cell mass on one side. Eight of the cells (**embryoblast**) of the inner mass become the embryo (or baby). The other 99 cells (**trophoblast**) form the support structures (e.g., placenta).

Between 5½ and 6 days, a slight thickening is noted in the cells closest to the uterine wall,[42] and the conceptus begins to attach itself to the endometrium (Fig. 3-14). Secretion of proteolytic enzymes by the trophoblast cells allows the conceptus to erode and thus invade the epithelial cells of the endometrium. The uterine mucosa, however, appears to promote production of the enzyme, thus evidencing an interdependent action.[42] By the seventh day, the zygote shows a distinct division between the body cell mass, called the embryonic disc, and the trophoblast.

Nidation

If pregnancy is achieved, the zygote begins to secrete human chorionic gonadotropin (HCG), which stimulates the corpus luteum to remain viable and to continue to secrete pro-

gesterone for another 12 to 16 weeks, at which time the placenta is able to assume the responsibility. The increased levels of progesterone reduce or prevent contractions of the uterus and thus are essential to allow for **nidation,** the implantation of the conceptus, as well as to maintain the pregnancy. The presence of high levels of progesterone explains why most pregnant women complain of feeling too warm throughout pregnancy. A decrease in progesterone toward the end of pregnancy, as the placenta ages, is one of several explanations postulated for the initiation of labor. The mother and fetus have achieved a symbiotic hormonal relationship before the new individual is even 2 weeks old.

Minute amounts of HCG can be detected in the blood and urine samples of a pregnant woman as early as 6 to 8 days after conception (1 week before the menses is due).[17] In-home early pregnancy test kits report high accuracy rates with urine samples obtained 9 days after the menses was due, but they should be confirmed later for accuracy. Many professionals believe that HCG may be one of the major causes of "morning sickness," since women are more likely to experience this reaction when HCG levels are highest.

Nidation occurs 6 to 7 days after conception. The outer cells of the zygote digest their way into the endometrium and begin to obtain nourishment from its rich blood and glycogen supply (Fig. 3-15). The zygote usually implants itself in the upper portion of the uterus. Infants attached to the lower portions of the uterus frequently experience difficulty before or during the birth process because the placenta may partially or completely block the infant's exit from the uterus.

Embryonic Stage

During the second through seventh weeks of life, the embryo firmly establishes its home within the uterus and undergoes a rapid cellular differentiation that changes its appearance from that of a flat, solid mass of cells to an organism that has distinctly human characteristics (Fig. 3-16). This differentiation of cells appears to be the result of several factors:

1. Genetic Regulation. DNA strands contain regulatory genes that have the ability to regulate the activity of other genes.[30]
   a. Some regulatory genes are programmed to activate or inhibit the production of enzymes based on the concentration of specific cellular substances under their control. This sensitive feedback system can function on an intracellular, intratissue, or intraorganism level.
   b. Other regulatory genes appear to be programmed to activate or to inhibit the production of enzymes based on the time since conception. This theory explains why cellular division does not continue where it left off if the conceptus is traumatized.

2. Enzyme Regulation. Inhibition and production of enzymes may be directly or indirectly controlled by other chemical substances or enzymes.

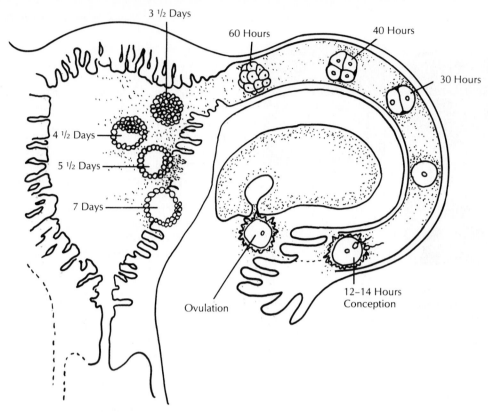

FIGURE 3–14.
First week of life.

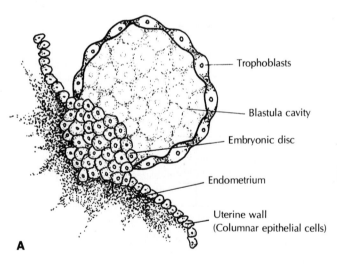

A

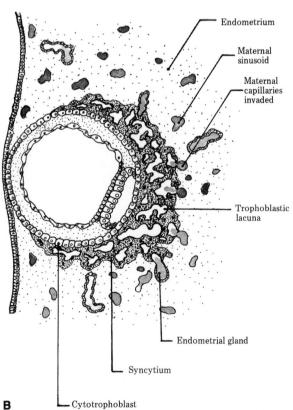

B

FIGURE 3–15A, 3–15B
(A) Seven-day-old zygote invading the endometrium.
(B) Blastocyst embedded in the endometrium approximately 12 days after fertilization. (From Miller, M. A., & Brooten, D. A. [1983]. The child bearing family, 2nd ed. Boston: Little, Brown, p. 121.)

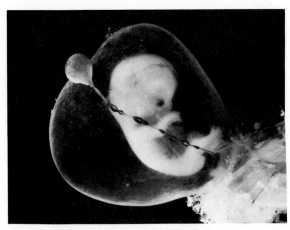

FIGURE 3–16.
The embryo at 40 days' gestation (6¹/₂ weeks, when the second menstrual period would be due). Note the remnant of yolk sac at the upper left. Copyright Roberts Rugh. With permission.

a. Many of the chemical substances formed in the cell have a direct feedback effect on the enzyme that synthesized it.[30] When a threshold level of the substance is achieved, the enzyme is inactivated and synthesis of the product or growth ceases. This effect may explain why, when more than half of the liver is surgically removed, it replaces itself to its original size but no larger.[70]

b. Many body tissues depend on the availability of a

product that is the result of an earlier enzyme reaction or is produced by adjacent cells. The genetic code is responsible for the initial enzyme, but subsequent enzyme formation depends on a specific sequencing of events. It is the sequencing or the chaining of events that is responsible for continued growth. If the enzyme is not present at the critical time, growth of the targeted cells is arrested, as is growth of any further cells that depend on the sensitive chaining of events.

Support Structures

The structures that support the life of the baby in utero develop mainly from the external portions of the blastocyst (trophoblast), which has assumed a shaggy, hairy appearance (villi) (Fig. 3-17).

Placenta

The villi that are closest to the uterine wall enlarge rapidly and invade the deeper layers of the endometrium during implantation. By the 11th to 12th day, placental circulation is evidenced. Tiny blood vessels develop in each of the villi and continue to grow and branch in a treelike fashion. Each **cotyledon** (branch of the placenta) continues to be immersed in a pool of maternal blood. With all the convolutions caused by the branching, it is estimated that the total surface area of a full-term placenta is almost 15 square yards.[56] At term, the placenta measures about 8 inches in diameter and weighs about 1¹/₄ lb (Fig. 3-18). The placenta is the organ of nutrient, oxygen, and waste exchanges between mother and

FIGURE 3–17.
Origin of embryo and support structures.

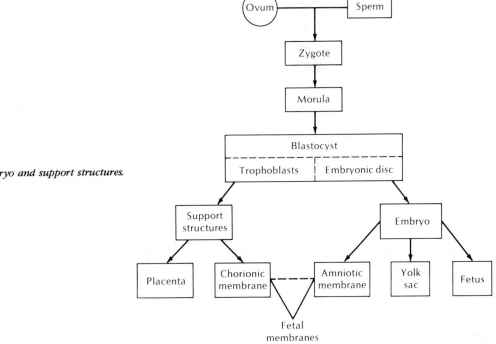

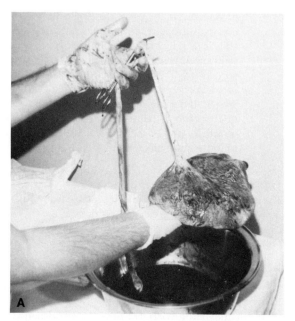

FIGURE 3–18.

Two views of the full-term placenta. (A) Fetal surface and umbilical cord. Because of the presence of the amniotic membrane, the side of the placenta that faces the infant is smooth and shiny. The umbilical cord usually enters the center of the rounded placental disc, and vessels can be seen radiating out to the cotyledons or branches of the placenta. (B) The maternal surface, which resembles a piece of liver, is dull and extremely convoluted where the cotyledons have branched and massed together to conserve space and to use maximally the maternal pools of blood.

baby. Contrary to popular belief, *the baby and mother do not share the same blood supply*; they maintain completely independent circulatory systems. A series of thin membranes between the two systems allows for selective admittance and filtering of substances that pass between the two. This selective processing is known as the blood-placental barrier.

"Bag of Waters"

The villi farthest away from the uterine wall degenerate and leave a membrane, known as the chorion, which envelops the developing baby. The amnion, a smooth membrane that arises from the ectoderm (see next section), lies adjacent to the chorionic membrane. Together, these membranes form the "bag of waters" and help to protect the baby from bacterial invasion. The amnion secretes the amniotic fluid, which provides a medium for movement, protects the infant from injury, and helps to regulate the temperature for the fetus. The amniotic fluid also contains urine from the immature urinary tract. The baby swallows this amniotic fluid throughout gestation and then is able to excrete waste products through the placenta. Toward the end of gestation, the amniotic fluid is completely exchanged every 3 hours.[70]

Yolk Sac

Humans have a yolk sac during early embryologic development, which, among other things, provides early blood cells and the primordial germ cells.[60]

Embryonic Disc

The major event of the second week of life is the development of the embryonic disc, which enlarges and forms two basic layers: the endoderm and the ectoderm. By the 15th and 16th days, when the first menstrual period would be due, the cranial end of this disc has thickened, creating a pear shape, and a third primary germ layer, the mesoderm, appears between the other two. The differentiation process now begins in earnest and becomes increasingly complex as the embryo develops. By the 22nd day, the heart begins to beat, circulating primitive blood components through the placenta and body.[60]

All future body organs can be traced back to one of the three germ layers as indicated in Table 3-2. It is significant to note that one system may have organs or tissues that arise from more than one germ layer (e.g., the urinary system). Synchronization of growth is essential for proper linkage of these organs that arise from different germ layers. Some congenital anomalies are the result of failure to obtain fusion or linkage during the early periods of growth.

Fetal Stage

The foundations or primary organ rudiments for all internal and external structures are present by the 15th day of life. The basic structures of more than 90% of the more than 4500 structures of the adult body have been established by the beginning of the eighth week of life;[60] consequently, the

TABLE 3–2. ORIGIN OF BODY TISSUES AND ORGANS

Ectoderm (Outer Layer)	Mesoderm (Middle Layer)	Endoderm (Inner Layer)
Sensory, epithelia of ear, eye	Connective tissue	Lining of urethra and ear
Epidermis	Dermis	Gastrointestinal tract
Hair, nails	Bones, cartilage	Liver, pancreas
Central nervous system	Gonads, uterus	Tonsils
Cranial nerves	Muscles	Thyroid
Urethra	Kidneys, ureters	Urinary bladder
Upper pharynx and nasal passages	Heart	Pharynx
Enamel of teeth	Dentine of teeth	Trachea and lungs
Peripheral nervous system	Spleen, blood	Parathyroid

remainder of the intrauterine period is spent in growth and refinement of body tissues and organs (Fig. 3-19). Although weighing barely 1 g ($^1/_{30}$ oz) and measuring just more than 1 inch in length, the 8-week fetus has distinctly human characteristics. The rapid growth of the brain creates a top-heavy appearance; at this stage of development, the head accounts for about 50% of the total length of the fetus.[66] The stubby tail at the end of the spinal cord that made its appearance about the 26th day has now disappeared. The heart is pumping

blood through the body at the rate of 40 to 80 beats per minute.[66] A thin pink skin covers the body. Sufficient skeletal, muscular, and neurological development has occurred to allow primitive movement by the fetus.

During the fetal stage (after the eighth week), the body begins to lengthen rapidly. By the 12th week, the head accounts for about one-third of the total body length; by birth, it is about one-fourth of the total length. Although the mother is not usually aware of it, the baby can now move easily and

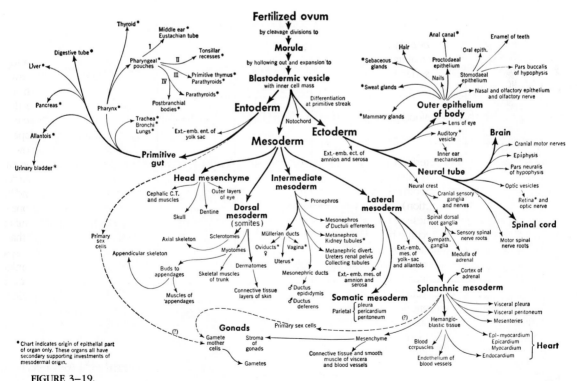

FIGURE 3–19.
Derivation of the various organs and tissues of the body by progressive differentiation and divergent specialization. Note especially how the origin of all the organs can be traced back to the three primary germ layers. (Carlson, B. M., [1981]. **Pattern's foundations of embryology,** *4th ed. New York: McGraw-Hill. With permission).*

frequently. At the end of the first trimester, the limbs and facial features are so refined that the fetus now gives the appearance of a delicate 3½-inch bisque-colored doll (Figs. 3-20 to 3-22).

The list given below summarizes the development of the fetus by the **lunar month.** The weights given are approximate, since authorities vary in their estimates.

First month (0–4 weeks after conception)

Conception, rapid growth
Nidation, symbiotic relationship established
Rudimentary body parts formed
Upper and lower limb buds are present
Cardiovascular system functioning

Second month (5–8 weeks)

Formation of head and facial features
Rapid cell differentiation and growth
Beginning of all major external and internal structures
Skeleton is visible (Fig. 3-23)
Eyes formed and open
Some movement by limbs
Weight: 1 g

Third month (9–12 weeks)

Teeth begin to appear
Kidneys begin to function
Some respiratory-like movements exhibited
Begins to swallow amniotic fluid
Grasp, sucking, blinking, and withdrawal reflexes present
Moves easily (not felt by mother)
Gender easily distinguished
Weight: 30 g (1 oz)

Fourth month (13–16 weeks)

Much spontaneous movement (may be felt by mother)
Moro reflex present
Rapid skeletal development
Meconium present
Downy hair (lanugo) appears on body
Weight 120 g (4 oz)

Fifth month (17–20 weeks)

Mother usually feels movement for first time (quickening)

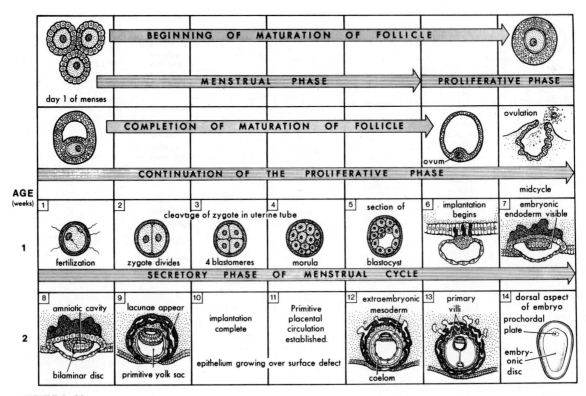

FIGURE 3–20.
Timetable of human prenatal development, 0 to 2 weeks. (Moore, K. L. [1974]. Before we are born: Basic embryology and birth defects. *Philadelphia: WB Saunders. With permission.)*

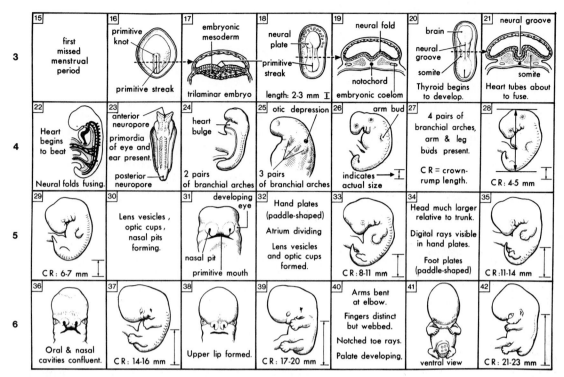

FIGURE 3–21.

Timetable of human prenatal development, 3 to 6 weeks. (Moore, K. L. [1974]. Before we are born: Basic embryology and birth defects. *Philadelphia: WB Saunders. With permission.)*

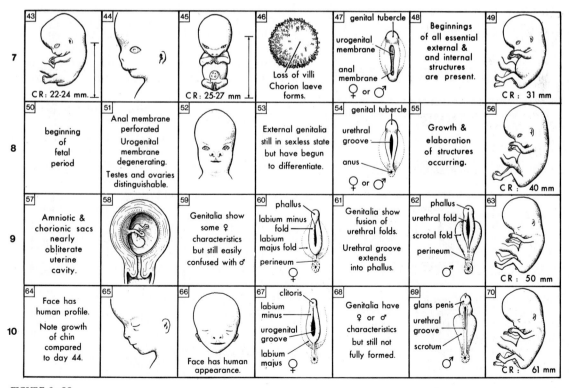

FIGURE 3–22.

Timetable of human prenatal development, 7 to 10 weeks. (Moore, K. L. [1974]. Before we are born: Basic embryology and birth defects. *Philadelphia: WB Saunders. With permission.)*

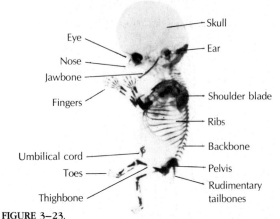

FIGURE 3–23.
Two-month-old-fetal skeleton. (Rugh, R. & Shettles, L. B. [1971]. From conception to birth. New York: Harper and Row. With permission.)

Vernix caseosa (waxy covering) appears
Eyebrows and hair appear
Strong grasp reflex present
Skeleton begins to harden
Permanent teeth buds appear
Brown fat is formed
Heart sounds can be heard with a stethoscope (electronic equipment can pick up the sounds much earlier)
Weight: 360 g (12 oz)

Sixth month (21–24 weeks)

"Miniature baby"
Extra uterine life possible
Begins to produce surfactant
Skin has red wrinkled appearance
Alternates periods of sleep and activity
May respond to external sounds
May try to find "comfortable" position
Weight: 720 g (1½ lb)

Seventh month (25–28 weeks)

Respiratory and central nervous system sufficiently developed; if born may survive with excellent intensive care
Eye lids open and close spontaneously
Assumes head-down position in uterus
Weight: 1200 g (2½ lb)

Eighth month (29–32 weeks)

Begins to store fat and minerals
Testes descend into scrotal sac
Lanugo begins to disappear from face
Skin begins to lose reddish color
Can be conditioned to environmental sounds
Exhibits good reflex development

Good chance of survival if born
Weight: 2000 g (4 lb)

Ninth month (33–36 weeks)

Body begins to round out
Increased iron storage by liver
Increased development of lungs
May become more or less active due to space tightness
Lanugo begins to disappear from body
Excellent chance of survival if born
Weight: 2800 g (6 lb)

Tenth month (37–40 weeks)

Lanugo and vernix caseosa both begin to disappear
High absorption of maternal hormones
Skin becomes smooth, plump
Continued storage of fat and minerals
Ready for birth
Weight: 3200 to 3400 g (7–7½ lb)

Fetal Circulation

During intrauterine life, all nutrients and oxygen are obtained and all waste products are excreted through the placenta.[55] The circulatory system is constructed in such a way that with minimal change, the neonate's body can obtain oxygen from the lungs and nutrients from the gastrointestinal tract (Fig. 3-24). In tracing the course of fetal blood, it is easiest to speak of oxygenated and unoxygenated blood, although the blood circulating through the fetus is never completely oxygenated. Some authorities indicate that the oxygen saturation of fetal blood is as low as 60% to 80% (in extrauterine life, the oxygen saturation of aortic blood should be 95%–100%).[4,33] To compensate for the low oxygen saturation, the fetus produces more red blood cells to carry oxygen to the rapidly growing body. Consequently, the fetus and the neonate have high red blood cell counts. Note that the organs that have first access to the oxygen and nutrient-rich blood are the key organs of the body: the brain, heart, and liver.

Immediately after birth, the ductus venosus and hypogastric arteries cease to carry blood because of the severing of the umbilical cord. The two other cardinal features of fetal circulation, the foramen ovale (opening between the right and left atria) and the ductus arteriosus (vessel that connects the pulmonary artery and the aorta) permanently close at about 3 and 14 days respectively because of the changed pressures within the cardiac chambers.

Estimating the Due Date

When a woman becomes pregnant, both she and the physician want to know when the baby is due to be born. Rough estimates of fetal age can be achieved through a history of the last menstrual period (LMP). The gestational period, the length of time from conception to birth, is about 266 days.[55]

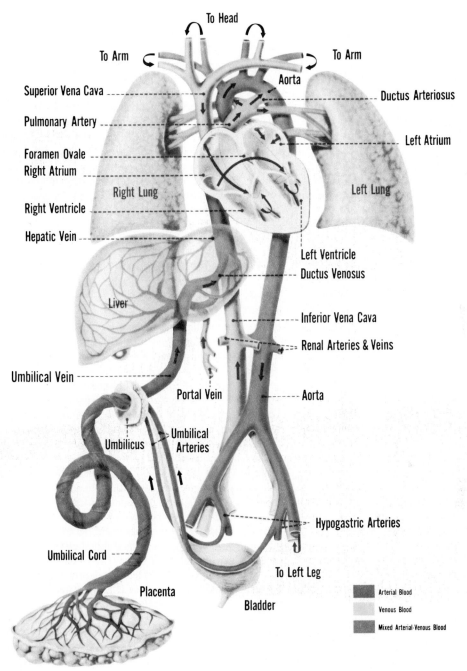

FIGURE 3–24.
Fetal circulation. (Ross Clinical Educational Aid No. 1. Courtesy of Ross Laboratories.)

Medical personnel frequently use lunar months (28 days) for calculation. The length of pregnancy is 280 days, 40 weeks, or 10 lunar months when calculated from the first day of the LMP (assuming a 28-day cycle).

The expected date of delivery is calculated by Naegele's rule: To the first day of the LMP add 7 days, subtract 3 months, and then adjust the calendar year. If the last menstrual period began on November 8 (11th month of the year), the formula indicates that the infant would be due August 15 of the following year:

8th day	11th month	1992
+ 7 days	− 3 months	
15th day	8th month	1993

If the LMP were February 18, then the infant would be

due November 25 of the same year. Fifty percent of deliveries occur within 5 days of the date obtained by Naegele's rule. However, this method is not completely accurate. A woman's menstrual history may be irregular, making the time of ovulation difficult to determine. Occasionally, a woman experiences enough breakthrough bleeding when the first menstrual period after conception is due that the pregnancy is not suspected; as a result, the calculations may be inaccurate by a full month.

Ultrasonography, the use of ultrasound waves to obtain a picture of the fetus, can indicate fetal size, position, and configuration. Gender, some anomalies, and fetal age can be evaluated. Fetal maturity can be estimated within 4 days of gestational age during the first trimester, within 7 days during the second trimester, and within 14 days during the third trimester.

Psychosocial Development of the Fetus

It is not yet known how much the physical and maternal psychosocial events that occur during intrauterine life directly affect the psychosocial development of the fetus. Gesell postulated that biophysical development, movement, and responses in utero lay a foundation for reflexive and voluntary movements or responses after birth.[24] These behaviors lay the foundation for social interaction and skill competence and, thus, emotional development. Through the use of ultrasound, researchers have probed the secret universe of the prenatal world to discover that some psychosocial behaviors (such as sensuality or withdrawal) show continuity from the 12th week of gestation through the preschool years.[62] Some would contend that "the mother's state of mind before birth can affect the child and can go on doing so into adult life."[64] Questions remain, however: (1) What is genetic and what is environmental? (2) Do hormones from the mother affect the fetus' development? (3) Is there some mechanism by which the mother's attitude is transmitted to the developing child, preparing it to adapt to the postnatal environment of acceptance, hostility, sensuality, or neglect?

Systematic studies of psychological interactions between mother and fetus are difficult to design, let alone to assess the effect of such interaction on the development of the fetus. Available studies are limited to those parameters that can be measured objectively, biological and sensory events. Consequently, studies of infant behavior—particularly in the affective domain—are primarily limited to the moment of birth as the point of departure. However, a few pioneers are looking at how prenatal events may help to mold affective, cognitive, and language development.

It has been shown that a woman's emotional state can influence fetal motility and that fetal hyperactivity is related to neonatal hyperactivity.[64] Infants born to stressed mothers during World War II were noted to exhibit disturbed affective behaviors and hyperactivity.[74] Seventy-five percent of the offspring of mothers who experience critical stress during pregnancy suffered from a serious illness at some time during the first 3 years of life; only 28% of infants of nonstressed mothers experienced similar serious illness.[74] Brazelton notes that infants who suffer from intrauterine growth retardation seem to have more difficulty organizing neuromuscular responses and are frequently labeled as "colicky" by mothers.[11] Babies of stressed mothers tend to be more active before birth and tend to have increased irritability, hyperactivity, frequent stools, and feeding problems after birth.

The fetus evidences a wide range of activity patterns. Mothers often indicate that a high correlation can be found between the amount of intrauterine and extrauterine activity. Some fetuses move almost constantly; others establish daily patterns that consist of both peak activity and rest periods; others may be quiet or exhibit inconsistent sleep-activity periods. Many behaviors can be specifically elicited from the fetus by presenting it with specific stimuli.

Visual Responses

Beginning with the 16th week of life, a light placed directly on the mother's abdomen startles the fetus or causes it to move away.[7, 10, 78] By 29 weeks, the fetus searches for the source of the light by turning its head and opening its eyes.[15] This response becomes the basis for the "flashlight game" between parents and their unborn child. (The parents entice the child to move toward the source of light when placed against different parts of the mother's abdominal wall.)

Many mothers complain that the baby seems to enjoy the gentle sway of the mother's body motion but becomes active (or agitated?) when she lies down to sleep at night: "He wakes up just as I am ready to go to sleep." Further questioning often reveals that the baby does not exhibit increased motion during the day when the mother lies down on the couch for a nap. At night, when the mother lies down, she pulls the covers over herself and turns out the room light. This action also makes the environment dark for the baby! It is hypothesized that the baby sees environmental light as a rosy glow through the mother's clothing and abdomen (much like placing the flashlight behind your hand in the dark). When the light source is eliminated, the fetus is deprived of the desirable stimulus. Mothers who place a flashlight under the covers report fewer fetal movements at night.

Auditory Responses

The ability to hear may occur as early as the 16th week of fetal life.[9] Changes in the fetal heart rate indicate that the fetus can discriminate between sounds and habituate to a sound.[12] Decreased kicking and movement, indicators of attention in the fetus, suggest that a fetus appears to favor high-pitched sounds, the human voice, and complicated, classical pieces (such as Vivaldi) over Beethoven or the drum rhythms of rock 'n' roll.[78]

If a man and a woman talk simultaneously to a neonate from opposite sides of the room, the infant turns toward the female voice.[18] Is this reaction an innate preference for higher-pitched sounds or the result of intrauterine familiarity with the mother's voice? The infant also prefers the mother's voice to that of other women.[18, 20] Research to date indicates that the neonate shows no preference for the father's voice even if he or she had explicit prenatal experience with his voice.[19] Perhaps the buffering effect of the uterine conditions on perception of environmental sounds changes the auditory qualities sufficiently to prevent postnatal recognition. However, many actively involved fathers indicate that the neonate turns and quiets to their voice in preference to other voices, even in the delivery room. Research is incomplete in this area. Babies of mute mothers rarely cry "as if they missed their speech lesson in utero."[77] Since crying is a precursor of speech as well as an outlet for expressing emotions, the child may be at risk for communication and social-emotional delays.

Another more recent discovery is that the infant exhibits the ability to remember acoustic cues presented in utero. When neonates were presented with three short stories, one of which had been read by their mother twice daily during the third trimester, the babies showed a definite preference for the familiar story over the other two, regardless of whether their mother or another woman read the story.[20] Does listening to the mother's voice and speech patterns help entrain or prepare the child to decipher and learn to speak the mother's language?

Many mothers who sang or played a musical instrument during pregnancy report that their infants evidenced differential responses to different types of sounds and music before birth and showed a preference for the same mother-produced music after birth.[45] The infant's preference for the specific music as evidenced by discriminative responses has been reported to occur even with a 3- to 5-month lapse in presentation of the same auditory stimulus after birth and to persist for several years.[35, 45] Boris Brott, conductor of the Hamilton (Ontario) Philharmonic Symphony, described in an interview how he "knew" some music before sight reading, especially the cello part. After talking with his mother, he discovered that they were the same pieces she had played on the cello while she was pregnant with him![64]

Other Prenatal Activities

Fetal activity can represent a form of parent-baby communication[11] that helps the parents to become attached to the new family member. Some adoptive parents express a feeling of loss at not having shared this time with the new family member.

By the 7th week of gestation, the fetus has sufficient cutaneous receptors to respond to the touch of a hair around its mouth. Touch receptors spread to the rest of the face, the palms, and the soles by the 11th week, the trunk by the 15th week, and all surfaces by the 20th week of gestation.[2] Brain stem and thalamus pain pathways are completely myelinated by 30 weeks.[2] During the third trimester, some fetuses may arch their backs against the side of the uterus when the mother's abdomen is gently rubbed. Many parents tap the abdomen at the spot of the baby's kicking. Over time, they report that the baby begins to kick back when they tap and to seek the point of the tapping.

Fetal hiccups are a common phenomenon easily felt by the mother. Some mothers state that their infant experiences crying movements and may even emit sound while in utero. This rare phenomenon is known as **vagitus uterinus.**[75]

One study has found that babies who exhibit rapid habituation to sound and vibration before birth score higher on orientation items of the Brazelton Neonatal Assessment Scale and in responses to environmental stimuli on the Mental Development Index.[50] However, whether these responses were learned or are a measurement of a child's underlying sensory integrity is not known. Nevertheless, professional people are encouraged to teach prospective parents about the fetus' perceptual skills and communication potentials to enhance the attachment process[7] or even to begin teaching the infant before birth. (For more information, contact Dr. Van de Carr, Prenatal University, 27225 Calagoga Avenue, Hayward, CA 94545). The effect of conditioning is real but has been inadequately studied.

FACTORS THAT AFFECT DEVELOPMENT

Many factors can cause congenital anomalies or death of the developing baby. Because of the irreversible effects of early influences on development, concerned professionals attempt to promote a high level of health through preventive health education of parents and prospective parents. Two major categories of factors affect fetal development: the genetic or chromosomal makeup, the hereditary factors; and events that occur after conception, the environmental or developmental factors (e.g., virus, poison, inadequate oxygen).

Chromosomal Factors

To date, little if anything can be done to prevent anomalies caused by chromosomal abnormalities except to avoid, when possible, situations that lead to higher incidents of anomalies. Women are encouraged to avoid all exposure of the pelvic area to x-rays before and during pregnancy, especially during the first trimester. Mothers younger than age 18 or older than age 35 have higher incidents of malformed infants.[55] One explanation given for the increased incidence found among younger mothers is that the primary germ cells are not yet ready to successfully complete the meiotic process; another reason is the inadequate nutritional intake of many adolescent mothers. The germ cells of older mothers have been exposed to the potential damaging effects of the environment for a longer period of time, and the meiotic process is more likely to be defective.

About 3% of neonates have a congenital anomaly that requires medical intervention; one-third of these are life-threatening.[67] One half of the children in hospitals have a prenatally acquired defect. When a baby is born with an anomaly, one may not be able to say with certainty that it is related to chromosomal, genetic, or developmental causes. Identical malformations may have either a genetic or a developmental origin. A careful history, including pedigree and karyotyping studies, should be taken to try to determine the causative factor. Potential parents often want to know whether a defect in a family member is hereditary before conceiving children. Unfortunately, even with careful studies undertaken by competent professionals, the etiology remains unknown in about 65% of the children.[47] Anomalies caused by developmental factors are not inheritable.

Developmental Factors

The developing fetus depends on the environment provided by the mother, both positively and negatively. Even the most conscientious mother may unknowingly be exposed to factors that can negatively influence the development of the baby. Many substances are known to pass through the placental barrier to retard or arrest the infant's development.

Teratogens

Substances or factors that are known to cause congenital malformations are called **teratogens.** Some may cause alterations in the configurations or structure of chromosomes, thus disturbing the genetic code. Other substances can prevent transfer of adequate nutrients or oxygen to vital areas or interfere with essential enzymatic or catalytic actions and cause an arrest in cellular division for a brief period of time. Since timing is so critical in early fetal development, and a single step may be part of a chain of reactions, the ability of a substance to interfere with a single step in mitosis, cellular differentiation, or movement and linkage with other cells can result in either minor or gross anomalies of the individual, depending on the stage of growth when the insult occurs and the target reactions arrested. Some arrests are incompatible with continued life of the fetus.

Each organ or tissue has its own timetable for maximal growth. Since several organ systems or tissues are developing simultaneously, some defects are frequently found to be paired with defects in other organs that were also at critical points of development when the teratogen was introduced. Thus, ear anomalies are frequently associated with kidney anomalies. Other teratogens appear to have an affinity for specific tissues or organs. Most teratogens exhibit immediate effects by causing growth retardation or organ deformity. However, some teratogens have a delayed action, and their influences are not apparent until age 7 or even 20 years of age or more, during the final stages of the maturation of a tissue.

Because specific birth defects are relatively rare, and potential teratogens are unique in their effect depending on gestational age, dosage, and individual sensitivity, it often requires years of painstaking detective work to associate the two. A cause–effect relationship is often implied by association rather than by clinical proof. No humane researcher would deliberately expose a fetus to a suspected teratogen. Occasionally, experiments on animals (e.g., thalidomide) do not indicate teratogenic effects because of a difference in the genetic code of animals versus humans. Most agents are not 100% teratogenic. Although thalidomide and rubella have high anomaly-producing rates, many infants may still escape damage after exposure. Other teratogens may avoid detection because they are dose related; effects may not be seen unless the agent reaches a particular threshold. The effects of lower dosages may be so subtle as to go undetected or are not recognized as part of a continuum of effects (e.g., alcohol consumption). Table 3-3 lists potential teratogens and their effects on the fetus.

Researchers are beginning to look at the father's contribution. Recent research has disclosed an association between the father's alcohol consumption in the month before conception and a decreased birth weight in the offspring.[46] It is suspected that alcohol also may effect male fertility and that some drugs also may effect the welfare of the fetus, though evidence is still weak.[73]

The zygote, not yet dependent on the environment for nutrients, usually is not susceptible to teratogens; the chemical either completely destroys it or has no effect.[55] **The embryo is highly sensitive to teratogens** because of the rapid differentiation and growth of new cells, tissues, and organs. Multiple malformations may occur because many body systems are emerging simultaneously. One teratogen may affect several body systems if it arrests all chemical reactions and mitotic divisions at that point. **Arrested development does not resume at a later time**; if a reaction does not occur as scheduled, it is skipped. There are no pauses. If development cannot occur around the missed processes, the fetus dies. If development can continue in spite of the skipped reactions, life continues; the thalidomide babies are a good example of this process. Thalidomide, a tranquilizer, was prescribed for thousands of mothers during the first and second trimester of pregnancy. A high percentage of their babies were born with abnormal limb formation.

Maternal Environment

The infant is affected directly and indirectly by the mother's state of health and nutritional intake.

Nutrition

The amount of caloric and nutritional elements essential to growth and development increase with fetal size, requiring increased maternal intake to meet the needs of both. The embryo makes minimal nutritional demands on the mother. Maternal nutritional intake during the last 4 months of pregnancy, however, appears to be especially critical to optimal fetal development. During World War II, food supplies were cut off to major cities of the Netherlands during the winter of 1944 to 1945. As a result, thousands of pregnant women were exposed to near-starvation conditions for more than 6 months. Birth weights dropped by more than 10%, and an increase in congenital anomalies was noted.[69]

Research indicates that inadequate intake of protein and calories during the last trimester can permanently reduce the number of brain cells by as much as 40%.[81] Improved nutrition after a period of inadequate hyperplastic brain growth does not increase the number of cells. Thus, an individual's

TABLE 3–3. TERATOGENIC AGENTS

Agent	Effect on Fetus
DRUGS	
Accutane (vitamin A)	Hydrocephalus, microcephaly, nerve blindness, ear anomalies, craniofacial defects, heart defects, thymus abnormalities, spontaneous abortion, high infant death rate, increased intracranial pressure, growth retardation, smaller adult brain microphthalmia
Alcohol	Neonatal addiction, IUGR,* cleft palate, cardiac anomalies, microcephaly, postnatal growth retardation, cognitive deficiencies, fine motor dysfunction, increased fetal and perinatal death rate, hyperactivity, learning disabilities
Antihistamines	Fetal death, anomalies
Aspirin	Neonatal bleeding
Barbiturates	Neonatal addiction, neonatal bleeding, neurological impairments
Caffeine	IUGR,* premature delivery, skeletal anomalies
Cigarette smoke	Prematurity, IUGR,* anomalies, spontaneous abortion, delayed cognitive skills, neonatal irritability
Corticosteroids	Anomalies, cleft lip, IUGR*
Dilantin	Cleft lip and palate, abnormal genitalia
DES	Reproductive system anomalies, cancer of reproductive system during late teen and early adult years in both males and females
Ergot	Fetal death
Heroine	Small for gestational age, chromosomal abnormalities, neonatal addiction
Hormones	Masculinization of female infant; feminization of male infant
Insulin (shock)	Fetal death
LSD	Chromosomal damage, anomalies, spontaneous abortion
Marijuana	Chromosomal damage
Morphine and opiates	Neonatal addiction, anomalies
Streptomycin	Damage to 8th cranial nerve, deafness
Sulfonamides	Hyperbilirubinemia
Tetracycline	Discoloration of permanent teeth, inhibited bone growth, syndactyly
RADIATION	Anomalies, microcephaly, chromosomal damage, leukemia
MATERNAL DISEASES	
Cytomegalic inclusion disease	Blood dyscrasia, microcephaly, IUGR,* mental retardation
Diabetes	Large birth weight, stillborn, anomalies, low blood sugar after birth
Gonorrhea	Blindness
Hepatitis	Neonatal hepatitis
Herpes virus	Neonatal infection, neonatal death, microcephaly, retinal dysplasia
Influenza	Abortion, cardiac defects
Rubella	Abortion, cardiac defects, deafness, blindness, mental retardation, IUGR,* infected neonate
Syphilis	Fetal death, anomalies, congenital syphilis, prematurity
Toxoplasmosis (carried by infected cat feces)	Blindness, mental retardation, fetal death, heart problems
OTHER	
Lead	Fetal death, anemia, hemorrhage
Smallpox vaccination	Fetal vaccinia, fetal death

*IUGR = Intrauterine growth retardation.

intellectual functioning for a lifetime can be affected by the nutritional status of the mother. Inadequate caloric intake during fetal and early infant development is associated with a child's later passivity, dependency, and anxious behavior irrespective of cognitive effects.[5] Women, Infants, and Children (WIC) and other prenatal health programs emphasize the importance of nutrition and help mothers obtain an adequate diet.

Pica

Occasionally, a mother develops pica, an abnormal craving for nonedible materials.[16] The craving may be for clay, unprocessed flour, dirt, laundry starch, wood, or many other unusual ingestants. These products may harm the baby because of some teratogenic ingredient or because the mother may actually eat so much of the substance that she fails to have an adequate nutritional intake. Some studies reveal communities in which as many as 55% of women exhibit pica during pregnancy.[49] Pica is frequently culturally influenced but often has no apparent rationale behind the inordinate appetite. Women express the idea that they believe these substances will relieve nausea, prevent vomiting, relieve dizziness, or cure swollen legs and headaches; that they are necessary for the baby's development; or that they will ensure a beautiful baby. Refusal to satisfy a craving may even be thought to cause birthmarks.[49] Pica is frequently associated with iron-deficiency anemia, and in some cases it appears to be resolved by iron therapy.[16]

Maternal Disease

Chronic maternal diseases may contribute to congenital anomalies. The incidence of birth defects is about 10 times greater in mothers with diabetes.[48] These babies tend to gain excessive amounts of weight before birth and tend to become critically hypoglycemic (low blood sugar) after birth. Evidence suggests that mothers with cardiac disease or anemia may not be able to supply the infant with enough oxygen to meet its developmental needs or to support the infant through the birth process. These infants are more likely to experience intrauterine growth retardation and anomalies. The babies of mothers with metabolic diseases may develop hypertrophy of the corresponding affected maternal gland, creating metabolic disturbances that can threaten the life of the baby after birth.

Stress

Severe maternal stressors (e.g., illness or the death of a family member, marital discord, war) are known to be potential teratogens. The incidence of malformations in babies of mothers with critical stress during the first trimester is high compared to those of nonstressed mothers.[74] The biochemical responses associated with maternal emotional reactions to stress (increased corticotropin, corticosteroids, norepinephrine, dopamine, and brain catecholamines) can create changes in the neuroanatomical and biochemical organization of the brain of the fetus as early as 8 weeks after conception. Abnormal changes in the electrical activity of the fetal brain correlate highly with low Apgar scores, neonatal problems, neurological abnormalities,[11] failure to thrive, hyperactivity, developmental delays, and behavior problems.[31] Some researchers indicate that the "prenatal stress syndrome" is associated with feminization and demasculinization of male offspring and may account for reproductive dysfunctions of females (decreased fertility, increased spontaneous abortion and increased neonatal mortality).[31]

An increased number of anomalies were noted during and after World War II in offspring of mothers who experienced emotional stress even before the nutritional deprivation occurred. Central nervous system anomalies were frequent. A survey of 55 German hospitals showed a 400% increase in anomalies from 1930 to 1950.[74] Babies also can be born with peptic ulcers attributed to stress.[31]

Several processes appear to be activated by stress. Stress creates changes in the sympathetic nervous system that in turn may cause reduced blood flow to the uterus and hormonal changes. Reduced uterine blood flow would limit the amount of nutrients and oxygen available for fetal growth. When the mother suffers severe emotional stress, the fetus is known to change activity patterns or to exhibit strong fetal movements in a manner similar to the activity observed in oxygen-deficient fetuses.[74] Both adrenaline and cortisone levels are elevated during stress (Table 3-4). Adrenaline increases fetal activity; cortisone is known to be teratogenic to

TABLE 3–4. RELATIONSHIP OF MATERNAL STRESS TO ELEVATED ADRENALINE AND CORTISONE LEVELS IN FETUS

STRESS
activates
HYPOTHALAMUS
which regulates
AUTONOMIC NERVOUS SYSTEM
to stimulate
ADRENAL MEDULLA
to release
ADRENALINE
which stimulates
ANTERIOR LOBE OF PITUITARY
to produce
CORTICOTROPIN
which activates
ADRENAL CORTEX
to release
CORTISONE
which enters
MATERNAL BLOODSTREAM
passes through
PLACENTAL BARRIER
enters
FETAL BLOODSTREAM

body organs, especially to the developing reproductive system.

For some women, working during the third trimester may serve as a stressor, creating reduced birth weight in the infant.[57] However, 95% of pregnant women and their babies are able to adjust to continued working without experiencing serious side effects.[83]

Drugs

The average woman takes 4 to 10 drugs per pregnancy.[47] The effect of a drug on a fetus depends on the kind of drug, the dosage, the gestational age, and the specific sensitivity of an organ. The fetus may not be able to metabolize and excrete the chemical before it builds up to a toxic level.[54]

Mothers should take no drugs during pregnancy unless they are prescribed by the physician. Occasionally, even drugs thought to be safe have unexpected side effects later in life. The antibiotic tetracycline, when taken by a mother during pregnancy, inhibits bone growth and causes brown stains to appear on the permanent teeth of the child during the school years. Diethylstilbestrol (DES), given to mothers with threatened spontaneous abortions during the late 1930s through the 1950s, was discovered in 1970 to be related to cancer of the reproductive system in postpubertal young women.[65] Male offspring exposed to DES were discovered to have an increased incidence of reproductive system anomalies and cancer.[26] The drug also appears to cause a change in sexual orientation in some people.[54] Most recently, a drug prescribed to treat severe acne (Accutane, a derivative of vitamin A) has been discovered to have devastating teratogenic effects, including hydrocephalus and brain, heart, facial, and glandular abnormalities.[76]

Women are more susceptible to colds during pregnancy.[58] Some medications, such as Dimetapp, can increase birth defects by 300%.[58] Just one tablet of aspirin increases the bleeding time of both mothers and infants exposed to the drug within 1 week of birth. The caffeine in two cups of coffee is sufficient to increase epinephrine concentrations and to reduce placental blood flow. Although no teratogenic effects have been found, an increased incidence of intrauterine growth retardation, miscarriage, premature births, and still births has been found *in mothers with high caffeine intake and of fathers who had a high caffeine intake in the month before conception.*[36] Neurological sensitivity is also seen in the neonate, since maternal caffeine tends to accumulate in the fetal brain and has a long half-life for excretion.[54]

Cigarette smoking, an activity that decreases the oxygen supply (and increases the carbon dioxide, cyanide, nicotine, and over 2000 other chemicals in the blood), is known to increase the risk of spontaneous abortion, intrauterine growth retardation, congenital anomalies, abnormal auditory responses, premature birth, perinatal mortality, and sudden infant death syndrome (SIDS).[6, 40, 54, 68] By 7 to 11 years of age, the children of mothers who smoked heavily during pregnancy exhibit reduced growth patterns, shortened attention spans, hyperactivity, decreased general I.Q. ability, and a 3- to

5-month delay in reading and math skills.[6] In spite of these statistics, more than 30% of pregnant women smoke.[40]

The affects of alcohol on offspring was first recognized in 1973.[37, 38] *Alcohol is the leading known teratogen in the Western world.*[1] Nine percent of pregnant women drink heavily.[34] The frequency and amount of alcohol consumed appear to correlate to the severity and frequency of congenital anomalies, regardless of the maternal nutritional status.[61] Fetal alcohol effects include growth retardation, neurobehavioral impairment, and minor physical anomalies. Fetal alcohol syndrome includes the former plus severe intrauterine growth retardation, specific cranio-facial anomalies, fine motor dysfunctions, and moderate to severe central nervous system dysfunctions, including mental retardation and hearing disorders.[1, 14, 34] The syndrome is found more frequently in North America than in Europe.[1] The fetus appears to be sensitive to the effects of alcohol throughout gestation, but the brain appears to be most sensitive between 18 and 20 weeks of gestation.[63] The National Council on Alcoholism and the National Institute of Alcohol Abuse and Alcoholism (under the federal Department of Health and Human Services) have issued a warning that just two drinks of hard liquor per day may cause congenital defects. It is strongly recommended that all alcohol be avoided during pregnancy.

Street drugs are of particular concern. Lysergic acid diethylamide (LSD) is known to cause chromosomal abnormalities. Marijuana use by the father can cause abnormal and reduced sperm production, sometimes leading to infertility. Marijuana use by the pregnant woman is associated with an increased incidence of congenital anomalies and reduced birth weights.[43, 72, 85] Cocaine increases the risk for spontaneous abortions and IUGR.[34, 85] After birth, infants exhibit tremors, chronic irritability, diarrhea, poor tolerance of oral feedings, poor state regulation, reduced visual following, and depressed interactive behaviors. Several congenital anomalies are suspected but not yet confirmed. The risk of SIDS is increased.[13, 34, 71]

Any infant born to a mother who is addicted to a narcotic or a barbiturate will also be addicted to the drug. These infants frequently are born prematurely, may have seizures, feed poorly, and show increased susceptibility to infections. The babies go through a withdrawal period and often require intensive hospital care to maintain life.[13] The negative effects of drugs may be potentiated by poor nutritional intake. Although I.Q. appears to be minimally affected, there may be delays in sensory processing, which may account for academic delays. Offspring of methadone-addicted mothers may not exhibit symptoms of restlessness, tremor, irritability, or sleep disturbances until 2 to 4 weeks after birth. When the neonate's capacity for state regulation (see Chap. 4) and attention are decreased, then the parent–child relationship is compromised, especially if the parents are caught up in their own immaturity and drug needs rather than needs of the infant.[32, 80] Long-range effects may include inability to concentrate, poor memory and abstract reasoning, attention deficit disorders, sensory-motor deficits, impulsiveness, social–

emotional immaturity, inability to deal with stress, tantrums, and violent acting out.[29,34] The infants of crack-using mothers have even more serious problems, including multiple physical defects. The medical, social, and educational implications are overwhelming. Increased pathology in the mother-child interaction after birth places the child at risk for attachment disorders, academic and behavior problems, and later use of drugs; however, these factors are independent of the infant's original drug dependence.[13,32]

Biological Teratogens

Viruses and bacteria can also have severe teratogenic effects on the fetus. Rubella (German measles) virus is devastating to the embryo, causing severe eye, ear, brain, and heart anomalies. The affected infant may continue to be a reservoir of the rubella virus to other people for as long as a year after birth. Rubella vaccine is now available, and most school systems require all children to have the rubella vaccination along with other immunizations. The vaccine is usually contraindicated for women of childbearing age for fear that it may cause fetal anomalies if the woman becomes pregnant within 3 months after receiving the vaccine.

Syphilis can be transmitted to the infant after the 18th to 20th week of gestation. It can cause serious congenital anomalies, prematurity, or even intrauterine death. Treatment given the mother is also effective for the fetus. Gonorrhea is not transmitted to the fetus during pregnancy but may be transmitted to the baby's eyes during the birth process, causing blindness. An active case of maternal herpes may also be transferred to the baby during the birth process.

Evidence suggests that 50% of babies born to mothers infected with AIDS are infected.[21] Most of these infants do not live as long as their second birthday.

Fetal Factors

Occasionally, the chromosomal configuration and the environment provided by the mother are optimal for the growth and the development of the fetus, but the site chosen for implantation may present a serious threat to survival. Ectopic pregnancy and low implantation of the blastocyst can both result in death of the fetus.

The presence of more than one fetus may also present a threat to maximal development or survival. Twins occur in about 1 out of every 90 pregnancies, or 1 out of every 250 live births, and triplets occur once every 9000 pregnancies.[17] Identical twins account for about one third of twin conceptions; these monozygous twins are formed by the union of one sperm and one ovum. A complete split occurs during one of the early cleavages or by early subdivision of the inner cell mass of the blastocyst, allowing the freed cells to continue development independently (Fig. 3-25).[55] Siamese twins are caused by incomplete separation of the inner cell mass; the twins can be attached to each other at any point of the body. (Most do not survive.) Fraternal, or nonidentical, twins are created by the release of two ova, both of which are fertilized

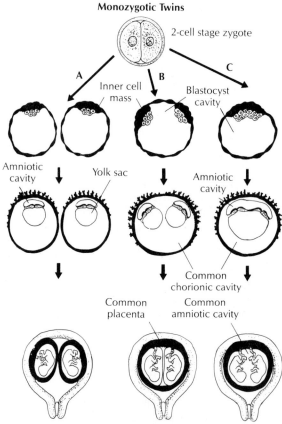

FIGURE 3–25.
The possible relationships of the fetal membranes in monozygotic twins. (A) Splitting occurs at the two-cell stage, and each embryo has its own placenta, amniotic cavity, and chorionic cavity. (B) Splitting of the inner cell mass in two completely separated groups. The two embryos have a common placenta and chorionic sac but separate amniotic cavities. (C) Splitting of the inner cell mass at a late stage of development. The embryos have a common placenta, a common amniotic cavity, and a common chorionic cavity. (Langman, J. [1981]. Medical embryology, *4th ed. Baltimore: Williams & Wilkins. With permission.)*

by separate spermatozoa. These polyzygous twins are no more alike than any other two siblings.

Twins face problems that singletons do not. Because of the limited intrauterine space, the incidence of prematurity is higher. Twins have a perinatal death rate two to three times higher than that of singletons. The second-born twin is especially prone to problems that decrease oxygen supplies during the birth process.[3] Twins also have an increased incidence of congenital anomalies, perhaps because of the same factor that originally caused the abnormal division in the blastocyst, or perhaps because of inadequate oxygen and food. Some monozygotic twins experience the fetal transfusion syndrome: The twins share the same placenta, and an extra blood vessel connects the two fetuses. Under this arrangement, blood is shunted from one twin to the other. At birth, the donor twin shows marked signs of undernourishment; it is pale and anemic and shows signs of severe intrauterine growth retardation. The recipient twin is fat and red, often weighing twice as much as the donor twin. Both twins are considered to be high risk: the one because of inadequate blood supply and shock, the other because of too much blood and possible heart failure.

IMPLICATIONS

"Human development is a continuous process that begins when an ovum from a female is fertilized by a sperm from the male. Birth is merely a dramatic event during development resulting in a change in environment."[55] Never again does change occur so rapidly nor is the environment so critical as during those first nine months of life. The miracle of creation is awesome when we consider even a fraction of what is understood about prenatal development. The parents face an incredible responsibility to provide a positive environment, for it will affect the life of the new individual for the next 80 plus years.

Health care of the infant, therefore, needs to begin even before birth by both the mother and the father through good nutrition and avoidance of drugs and x-rays. Maximal efforts should be directed toward creating an intrauterine environment that is conducive to optimal growth and development of the potentials present at the moment of conception. With 2 million children per year being abused in the United States, it is prudent to develop prophylactic educational and social approaches to decreasing the incidence.[23] Although evidence is still not conclusive, one positive approach appears to include establishing a social-play relationship and personalized affective bond with the baby even before it is born. Health care practitioners are in a unique position to facilitate this relationship through education about the fetus' unique interactional and receptive learning skills.[23]

Answer to question in Figure 3-1: The sex chromosomes are markedly different in size; therefore, this is an XY configuration. The karyotype indicates a male genetic makeup.

Answer to question on inheritance: Can two Rh − parents have a Rh + child? No.

REFERENCES

1. Abel, E. L., & Sokol, R. J. (1988). Alcohol use in pregnancy. In J. R. Niebyl (Ed.), *Drug use in pregnancy* (2nd ed., pp. 193–202). Philadelphia: Lea and Febiger.
2. Anand, K. J. S., Phil, D., & Hickey, P. R. (1987). Pain and its effects in the human neonate and fetus. *New England Journal of Medicine, 317,* 1321–1329.
3. Arnold, C., McLean, F. H., Kramer, M. S., & Usher, R. H. (1987). Respiratory distress syndrome in second-born versus first-born twins: A matched case-control analysis. *New England Journal of Medicine, 317,* 1121–1125.
4. Artal, R. M., & Wiswell, R. A. (Eds.). (1986). *Exercise in pregnancy.* Baltimore: Williams and Wilkins.
5. Barrett, D. E., Radke-Yarrow, M., & Klein, R. E. (1982). Chronic malnutrition and child behavior: Effects of early caloric supplementation on social and emotional functioning at school age. *Developmental Psychology, 18,* 541.
6. Berkowitz, G. S. (1988). Smoking and pregnancy. In J. R. Niebyl (Ed.), *Drug use in pregnancy* (2nd ed., pp. 173–192). Philadelphia: Lea and Febiger.
7. Bernhardt, J. (1987). Sensory capabilities of the fetus. *Maternal Child Nursing, 12,* 44–46.
8. Bernstein, G. S. (1986). Male factor in infertility. In D. R. Mischell, Jr. & V. Davajan (Eds.), *Infertility, contraception and reproductive endocrinology* (2nd ed., pp. 423–447). Oradell, NJ: Medical Economics Books.
9. Birnholz, J. C., & Benacerraf, B. R. (1983). The development of fetal hearing. *Science, 222,* 516–518.
10. Brazelton, T. B. (1986). *On becoming a family: The growth of attachment.* New York: Delacorte Press.
11. Brazelton, T. B., Parker, W. B., & Zuckerman, B. (1976). Importance of behavioral assessment of the neonate. *Current Problems in Pediatrics, 7*(2), 1.
12. Busnel, M. C., & Granier-Deferre, C. (1983). And what of fetal audition? In A. Oliveiro & M. Zapula (Eds.), *The behavior of human infants* (pp. 92–126). New York: Plenum.
13. Chasnoff, I. J. (1986). Perinatal addiction: Consequences of intrauterine exposure to opiate and nonopiate drugs. In I. J. Chasnoff (Ed.), *Drug use in pregnancy: Mother and child* (pp. 52–63). Boston: MTP Press Limited.
14. Church, M. W., & Gerkin, K. P. (1988). Hearing disorders in children with fetal alcohol syndrome: Findings from case reports. *Pediatrics, 82,* 147–153.
15. Comparetti, A. M. (1980). Patterns of analysis of normal and abnormal development: The fetus, the newborn, the child. In D. S. Slaton (Ed.), *Development of movement in infancy* (pp. 1–37). Chapel Hill, NC: University of North Carolina at Chapel Hill.
16. Creasy, R. K., & Resnik, R. (1989). *Maternal-fetal medicine: Principles and practice* (2nd ed.). Philadelphia: W. B. Saunders.
17. Cunningham, F. G., McDonald, P. C., & Grant, N. F. (1989). *Williams obstetrics* (18th ed.). Norwalk, CT: Appleton and Lange.
18. DeCasper, A. J., & Fifer, W. P. (1980). Of human bonding: Newborns prefer their mother's voices. *Science, 208,* 1174.
19. DeCasper, A. J., & Prescott, P. A. (1984). Human newborn's perception of male voices: Preference, discrimination and reinforcing value. *Developmental Psychology, 17,* 481–491.
20. Decasper, A. J., & Spence, M. J. (1986). Prenatal maternal speech influences newborns' perception of speech sounds. *Infant Behavior and Development, 9,* 133–150.
21. Falloon, J., Eddy, J., Wiener, L., & Pizzo, P. (1989). Human immunodeficiency virus infection in children. *Journal of Pediatrics, 114,* 1–30.
22. Flynn, A. M. (1989). Natural family planning. In M. Filshie & J. Guillebaud (Eds.), *Contraception: Science and practice* (pp. 203–223). Boston: Butterworths.
23. Gaffney, K. F. (1988). Prenatal maternal attachment. *IMAGE: Journal of Nursing Scholarship, 20*(2), 106–109.
24. Gesell, A. L. (1945). *The embryology of behavior: The beginnings of the human mind.* New York: Harper and Brothers.
25. Gibbons, W. E., Battin, D. A., & diZerega, G. S. (1986). Mechanisms of action of reproductive hormones. In D. R. Mishell, Jr. & V. Davajan (Eds.), *Infertility, contraception and reproductive*

endocrimology (2nd ed., pp. 31–44). Oradell, NJ: Medical Economics Books.

26. Gill, W. B. (1988). Effects on human males of *in utero* exposure to exogenous sex hormones. In T. Mori & H. Nagasawa (Eds.), *Toxicity of hormones in perinatal life* (pp. 161–177). Baca Roca, FL: CRC Press.

27. Glass, R. H. (1989). Sperm and egg transport, fertilization and implantation. In R. K. Creasy & R. Resnik (Eds.), *Maternal-fetal medicine: Principles and practice* (2nd ed., pp. 108–115). Philadelphia: W. B. Saunders.

28. Goebelsman, U. (1986). The menstrual cycle. In D. R. Mischell, Jr. & V. Davjan (Eds.), *Infertility, contraception and reproduction endocrinology* (2nd ed., pp. 69–89). Oradell, NJ: Medical Economics Books.

29. Greer, J. V. (1990). The drug babies. *Exceptional Children, 56,* 382–384.

30. Guyton, A. C. (1987). *Human physiology and mechanisms of disease* (4th ed.). Philadelphia: W. B. Saunders.

31. Herrenkohl, L. R. (1988). The impact of prenatal stress on the developing fetus and child. In R. L. Cohen (Ed.), *Psychiatric consultation in childbirth settings: Parent- and child-oriented approaches* (pp. 21–35). New York: Plenum Medical Book.

32. Howard, J., Beckwith, L., Rodning, C., & Kropenske, V. (1989). The development of young children of substance-abusing parents: Insights from seven years of intervention and research. *Zero to Three, 9*(5), 8–12. (Bulletin of the National Center for Clinical Infant Programs)

33. Hubbell, K. M., & Webster, H. F. (1986). Respiratory management of the neonate. In N. S. Streeter (Ed.), *High-risk neonatal care* (pp. 107–141). Rockville, MD: Aspen.

34. Hutchings, D. E. (1987). Drug abuse during pregnancy: Embryopathic and neurobehavioral effects. In M. C. Braude & A. M. Zimmerman (Eds.), *Genetic and perinatal effects of abused substances* (pp. 131–151). Orlando, FL: Academic Press.

35. Jackson, K. H. (1978). Music and the fetus. *Child Today, 7*(6), 37.

36. Johnson, T. R. B., & Niebyl, J. R. (1988). Caffeine in pregnancy. In J. R. Niebyl (Ed.), *Drug use in pregnancy* (2nd ed., pp. 231–233). Philadelphia: Lea and Febiger.

37. Jones, K. L., & Smith, D. W. (1973). Recognition of the fetal alcohol syndrome in early infancy. *Lancet, 2,* 999.

38. Jones, K. L., Smith, D. W., & Streissguth, A. P., et al. (1973). Patterns of malformation in offspring of chronic alcoholic women. *Lancet, 1,* 1267.

39. Jones, O. W. (1989). Basic genetics and patterns of inheritance. In R. K. Creasy & R. Resnik (Eds.), *Maternal-fetal medicine: Principles and practice* (2nd ed., pp. 3–77). Philadelphia: W. B. Saunders.

40. Kanwit, E., & Brunel, L. E. (1987). Prenatal care. In K. R. Niswander (Ed.), *Manual of obstetrics: Diagnosis and therapy* (3rd ed., pp. 28–37). Boston: Little, Brown.

41. Kletzky, O. A., & Lobo, R. A. (1986). Reproductive endocrinology. In D. R. Mishell, Jr. & V. Davjan (Eds.), *Infertility, contraception and reproductive endocrinology* (2nd ed., pp. 3–29). Oradell, NJ: Medical Economics Books.

42. Langman, J. (1990). *Langman's medical embryology* (6th ed.). Baltimore: Williams and Wilkins.

43. Legator, M. S., & Au, W. W. (1987). Need to reassess the genetic toxicology of drugs of abuse. In M. C. Braude & A. M. Zimmerman (Eds.), *Genetic and perinatal effects of abused substances* (pp. 3–26). Orlando, FL: Academic Press.

44. Levitan, M. (1988). *Textbook of human genetics* (3rd ed.). New York: Oxford University Press.

45. Lind, J., & Hardgrove, C. (1978). Lullabies. *Child Today, 7*(4), 7.

46. Little, R. E., & Sing, C. F. (1986). Association of father's drinking and the infant's birth weight. *New England Journal of Medicine, 314*(25), 1644.

47. LoBue, C. C. (1987). Effects of drugs on the fetus. In K. R. Niswander (Ed.), *Manual of obstetrics: Diagnosis and therapy* (3rd ed., pp. 278–300). Boston: Little, Brown.

48. Lowery, G. H. (1978). *Growth and development of children* (7th ed.). Chicago: Year Book Medical Publishers.

49. Luke, B. (1977). Understanding pica in pregnant women. *American Journal of Maternal Child Nursing, 2,* 97.

50. Madison, L. S., Madison, J. K., & Adubato, S. A. (1986). Infant behavior and development in relation to fetal movement and habituation. *Child Development, 57,* 1475–1482.

51. Marrs, R. P., & Vargyas, J. M. (1986). Human in vitro fertilization: State of the art. In D. R. Mishell, Jr. & V. Davajan (Eds.), *Infertility, contraception and reproductive endocrinology* (2nd ed., pp. 565–580). Oradell, NJ: Medical Economics Books.

52. McKusick, V. A. (1988). *Mendelian inheritance in man: Catalogs of autosomal dominant, autosomal recessive, and X-linked phenotypes* (8th ed.). Baltimore: John Hopkins University Press.

53. Merz, B. (1989). 700 genes mapped at world workshop. *Journal of the American Medical Association, 262,* 175.

54. Miriran, M., & DeBoer, S. (1988). Long-term effects of chemicals on developing brain and behavior. In V. K. Meyers (Ed.), *Teratogens: Chemicals that cause birth defects* (pp. 271–314). New York: Elsevier.

55. Moore, K. L. (1988). *The developing human: Clinically oriented embryology* (4th ed.). Philadelphia: W. B. Saunders.

56. Moore, M. L. (1981). *The newborn family and nurse.* Philadelphia: W. B. Saunders.

57. Naeye, R. L., & Peters, E. C. (1982). Working during pregnancy: Effects on the fetus. *Pediatrics, 69,* 724.

58. Niebyl, J. R., & Repke, J. T. (1988). Treatment of the common cold in pregnancy. In J. R. Niebyl (Ed.), *Drug use in pregnancy* (2nd ed., pp. 235–238). Philadelphia: Lea and Febiger.

59. Novitski, E. (1982). *Human genetics* (2nd ed.). New York: Macmillan.

60. O'Rahilly, R., & Müller, F. (1987). *Developmental stages in human embryos.* Washington, DC: Carnegie Institution of Washington. (Publication 637)

61. Oulette, E., et al. (1977). Adverse effects on offspring of maternal alcohol abuse during pregnancy. *New England Journal of Medicine, 297,* 528.

62. Piontelli, A. (1987). Infant observation from before birth. *International Journal of Psycho-Analysis, 68,* 453–463.

63. Renwick, J. H., & Asker, R. L. (1983). Ethanol-sensitive times for the human conceptus. *Early Human Development, 8,* 99.

64. Ridgway, R. (1987). *The unborn child: How to recognize and overcome pre-natal trauma.* Aldershot, Hants UK: Wildwood House Limited.

65. Rotmensch, J., Frey, K., & Herbst, A. L. (1988). Effects on female offspring and mothers after exposure to diethystilbestrol. In T. Mori & H. Nagasawa (Eds.), *Toxicity of hormones in perinatal life* (pp. 143–160). Baca Roca, FL: CRC Press.

66. Rugh, R., & Shettles, L. B. (1971). *From conception to birth: The drama of life's beginnings.* New York: Harper and Row.

67. Shepard, T. H. (1989). *Catalog of teratogenic agents* (6th ed.). Baltimore: John Hopkins University Press.

68. Shiono, P. H., Klebanoff, M. A., & Rhodes, G. G. (1986). Smoking and drinking during pregnancy: Their effects on preterm birth. *Journal of the American Medical Association, 255,* 82–84.

69. Smith, C. A. (1947). Effects of maternal undernutrition upon the newborn infant in Holland (1944–1945). *Journal of Pediatrics, 30,* 229.

70. Smith, D. W., Bierman, E. L., & Robinson, N. M. (1978). *The biological ages of man: From conception through old age* (2nd ed.). Philadelphia: W. B. Saunders.

71. Smith, J. (1988). The dangers of prenatal cocaine use. *The American Journal of Maternal/Child Nursing, 13,* 174–179.

72. Smith, R. G., & Holmes, S. D. (1987). Biochemical aspects of marijuana on male reproduction. In M. C. Braude & A. M. Zimmerman (Eds.), *Genetic and perinatal effects of abused substances* (pp. 153–175). Orlando, FL: Academic Press.

73. Soyka, L. F., & Joffe, J. M. (1980). Male mediated drug effects on offspring. In R. H. Schwarz & S. J. Yaffe (Eds.), *Drugs and chemical risks to the fetus and newborn* (pp. 49–66). New York: Alan R. Liss.

74. Stott, D. H. (1971). The child's hazards in utero. In J. G. Howells (Ed.), *Modern perspectives in international child psychiatry.* New York: Brunner/Mazel.

75. Thiery, M., Yo Le Sian, A., Vrijens, M., & Janssens, D. (1973). Vagitus uterinus. *Journal of Obstetrics and Gynecology of the British Commonwealth, 80,* 183–185.

76. Thompson, E. J., & Cordero, J. F. (1989). The new teratogens: Accutane and other vitamin-A analogs. *American Journal of Maternal/Child Nursing, 14,* 244–251.

77. Truby, H. M., & Lind, J. (Eds.). (1965). Cry sounds of the newborn infant. *Acta Paediatrica Scandinavica* (Suppl. 163)

78. Verny, T. (1982). *The secret life of the unborn child.* New York: Dell.

79. Vogel, F. (1986). *Human genetics: Problems and approaches* (2nd ed.). New York: Springer-Verlag.

80. Weston, D. R., Ivins, B., Zuckerman, B., Jones, C., & Lopez, R. (1989). Drug exposed babies: Research and clinical issues. *Zero to Three, 9*(5), 1–7. (Bulletin of the National Center for Clinical Infant Programs)

81. Winick, M. (1971). Cellular growth during early malnutrition. *Pediatrics, 47,* 969.

82. Woollam, D. H. M. (1964). The effect of environmental factors on the foetus. *Journal of the College of General Practitioners, 8*(Suppl. 2), 35.

83. Working in pregnancy. (1980). Working in pregnancy: How long? How hard? What's your role? *Contemporary Ob/Gyn, 16,* 154.

84. Ziegel, E., & Cranley, M. S. (1984). *Obstetric nursing* (8th ed.). New York: Macmillan.

85. Zuckerman, B., Frank, D. A., Hingson, R., Amaro, H., Levenson, S. M., Kayne, H., Parker, S., Vinci, R., Aboagye, K., Fried, L. E., Cabrai, H., Timperi, R., & Bauchner, H. (1989). Effects of maternal marijuana and cocaine use on fetal growth. *New England Journal of Medicine, 320,* 762–8.

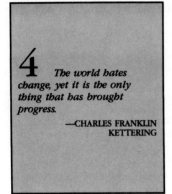

4 *The world hates change, yet it is the only thing that has brought progress.*
—CHARLES FRANKLIN KETTERING

Transition to Extrauterine Life

Clara S. Schuster

The 24 hours surrounding birth are the most tenuous and critical in a person's life. Events that occur during this time can affect the quality of life 7, 18, or even 40 years later. An infant experiences a greater risk of death during the first 7 days than during the next 65 years of extrauterine life.[3] Of the 3.7 million babies born alive each year in the United States, about 1% die within the first 24 hours, 1% die within the first week, and another 1% die in the first year of life.[9]

The leading causes of neonatal death are associated with prematurity.[9] Infants who are born before their body systems and organs are mature enough to maintain life independent of the mother require intensive medical intervention. Other major causes of neonatal deaths include asphyxia, congenital malformations (2%–3% of neonates have identifiable congenital anomalies at birth),[28] birth injuries, pneumonia, problems of the placenta, and infection. Many of these deaths could be prevented with proper health care. According to statistics compiled by the U. S. Bureau of the Census,[43] in 1987 the United States had a **neonatal** (under 28 days of life) death rate of 10.7 per 1000 live births. It is an embarrassment to the United States that it is not first or even second in the world in terms of survival of newborns (one of the indicators of the quality of a country's health care), rather it is 17th![39] Sweden, which ranks first in infant survival, reports only 7.3 neonatal deaths per 1000 live births.[47]

Many of the preventable deaths are associated with inadequate prenatal care, a factor that should spur all practitioners, regardless of their discipline, to encourage every pregnant woman to seek adequate health care to reduce the incidence of prematurity, birth complications, and neonatal deaths. Some high-risk populations in major United States cities have a mortality rate of 20.0 per 1000. The neonatal and infant mortality rate for African American babies is almost twice that of those with European ancestry.[43]

Even with the best of care, the process of transition to extrauterine life, which includes both the birth process and the adjustment of the newborn to physiological independence, is potentially traumatic and precarious. This chapter discusses the major stressors that face the infant and some of the factors that commonly affect the adjustment process.

THE BIRTH PROCESS

For 10 lunar months, the infant has been cradled, protected, nurtured, and nourished within the controlled environment of the mother's uterus. Stimuli have been limited and attenuated; nothing has been demanded of the fetus but to grow. Most fetuses experience no discomfort or pain, only a little cramping of space, yet even this seems to afford security (Fig. 4-1).

Toward the end of the gestational period, the irregular, periodic, uterine contractions (Braxton Hicks contractions) that have been present throughout the entire preg-

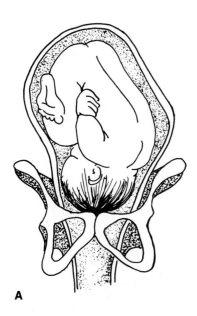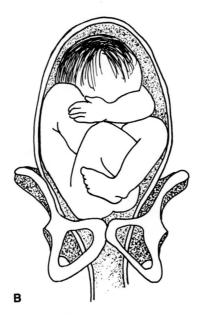

FIGURE 4–1.
Position of fetus at term: (A) cephalic presentation; (B) breech presentation.

A   **B**

nancy become strong enough to be noticeable by both the mother and the infant (as evidenced by increased fetal movement). At some point, these contractions suddenly become regular and strong enough to begin dilatation and effacement (thinning) of the cervix, signaling that labor has begun (see Chap. 31). The intermittent uterine contractions of true labor gradually propel the infant through the mother's pelvic canal and into the world (Fig. 4-2). This chapter concentrates on the **infant's** response to the expulsion from intrauterine life. Chapter 31 covers the mother's response to the birthing process.

Stages of Labor

The birth process is divided into three stages. During the first (and usually the longest) stage, the cervix must thin, and the aperture must open sufficiently to allow the infant to pass through. The presenting part of the infant (usually the head) acts as the dilator of the cervix. Pressure against this presenting part frequently causes bruising and swelling of the infant's tissues. On rare occasions, the baby may actually be injured. Such injuries, which are discussed further in Chapter 5, are usually minor.

Once the cervix is completely dilated, the infant begins to traverse the pelvic passageway. This second stage is not an easy process for the infant, since the pelvic passage is not a straight, wide tube. The narrow, changing diameters and directions of the pelvic passage force the infant to twist, turn, bend, and stretch to negotiate the canal successfully (Fig. 4-3). The head, as the largest part of the infant, must accommodate itself to the widest diameters of the pelvis. The infant is by no means a passive traveler through the passage. Pressure placed against an infant's head after birth elicits a stretching, crawling

response. This same behavior may be elicited during the birth process by the contracting uterus and thus may cause the infant to help push himself or herself out of the uterine cavity.

The chorionic and amniotic membranes frequently rupture during the first stage of labor. If the membranes have not ruptured spontaneously, the physician or nurse in charge of the delivery ruptures them (a painless procedure) at some point during labor or immediately on the birth of the presenting part of the infant. After the head passes between the muscles of the perineal floor, usually a brief pause occurs before the shoulders and then the body emerge from the mother's vagina into the waiting hands of the mother, midwife, or physician.

Even though the infant is safely delivered, all the products of conception must be expelled before the mother can begin the involutional process, the return of the reproductive organs to their nonpregnant stage. During this third stage, the placenta and membranes are expelled.

The length of the birth process is influenced by many factors. A small pelvis or an exceptionally large baby may slow it markedly. If the discrepancy is too great, the baby may not be able to traverse the pelvic passageway; in this situation, the baby can be safely delivered by cesarean section. Unusual position of the head or breech presentation also slows the birth process. One of the factors that influences the length of labor is the number of previous vaginal deliveries experienced by the mother. It usually takes the first baby about 12 hours to traverse the birth passage. Subsequent babies experience substantially shorter labor; the second and third infants of a mother generally are born after about 4 to 8 hours of labor. Other factors known to increase the length of labor include maternal medication, poor maternal health, and a lapse of more than 7 years since the last pregnancy. The length

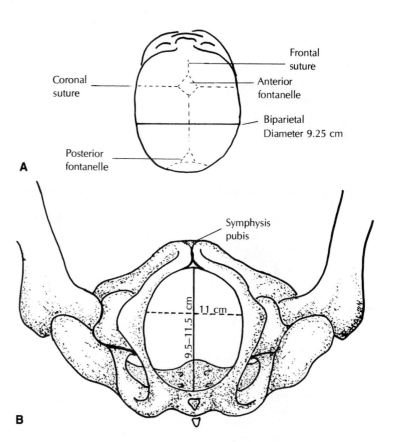

FIGURE 4–2.
Head diameter versus pelvic diameter dimensions:
(A) coronal view of head; (B) pelvic outlet seen
from outlet position.

of labor usually does not have a significant effect on the infant's health unless it is accompanied by a decrease in fetal oxygen level.

Fetal Response to Labor

The infant depends heavily on its environment for both extrusion and survival. The events that occur during the birth process may present stressors that can leave the infant poorly equipped to make the adjustments essential to successful extrauterine survival. One of the major stressors faced by infants is an irregular oxygen supply. Because of the anatomical structure of the uterus, contractions of the uterine muscles cause a decrease in blood flow within the uterus. Subsequently, the amount of blood that fills the intervillous spaces is decreased during contractions, making less oxygen available to the baby. Fortunately, contractions rarely last longer than 60 to 90 seconds. Nature thus provides for a replenishing of oxygen supplies during the 2- to 10-minute rest periods between contractions.

Occasionally, the cord is compressed between the baby and the birth passage. This situation can cause a decrease in the oxygen available to the infant. Infants who experience inadequate oxygen in utero may evacuate meconium (fetal bowel movement) into the amniotic fluid, causing yellow, green, or brown coloration of the otherwise clear fluid. Low-

ered fetal oxygen levels during labor can be identified by monitoring the rate of the fetal heart. The normal fetal heart rate ranges from 120 to 160 beats per minute. The fetal heart can be externally monitored by a special stethoscope or through electronic microphones, which pick up the sound of the baby's heartbeat through the abdominal wall and magnify it for medical personnel, the mother, and the coach.

Internal monitoring of the fetal heart rate provides a more sensitive and reliable method. A tiny electrode is attached to the presenting part of the infant. The fetal heart sounds are amplified if desired, but they are also recorded on a continuous graph paper for identification of patterns of heart rate as compared to the onset and intensity of uterine contractions. A moderate dip in the fetal heart rate with the onset of contractions is a normal phenomenon that accompanies compression of the baby's head as it presses against the cervix (Fig. 4-4).

Most medications given to the mother during labor pass through the placental barrier to the infant (fetus). In utero, the infant discharges the medication back through the placenta for the mother's body to detoxify and excrete. After birth, the baby's immature liver and excretory systems experience difficulty excreting the maternal medications and anesthesia. The infant may be drowsy and difficult to alert at birth if too much medication is given too close to delivery. A baby who is sedated has decreased responses to environmental stimuli.

Engagement,
Descent,
Flexion

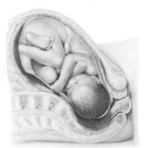 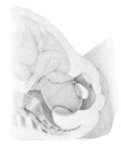

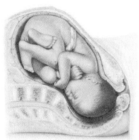

Internal Rotation

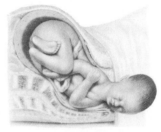

External Rotation (Restitution)

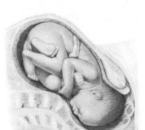

Extension Beginning (Rotation Complete)

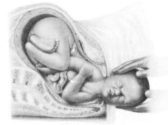

External Rotation (Shoulder Rotation)

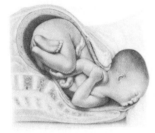

Extension Complete

Expulsion

FIGURE 4–3.
Mechanisms of normal labor. (Ross Clinical Education Aid No. 13. Courtesy Ross Laboratories.)

The infant may require more vigorous stimulation and assistance to begin breathing and may even need occasional reminding to continue breathing efforts for as long as 2 days after birth. The postnatal effects of maternal medications are strongest during the first 2 days and gradually decrease over the next 5 to 10 days.[5, 29] These infants are also sleepier and less responsive to their parents than infants who receive no medication during labor. An under-responsive baby is known to affect the parent–infant relationship negatively, a factor that can have long-range implications (see Chap. 31).

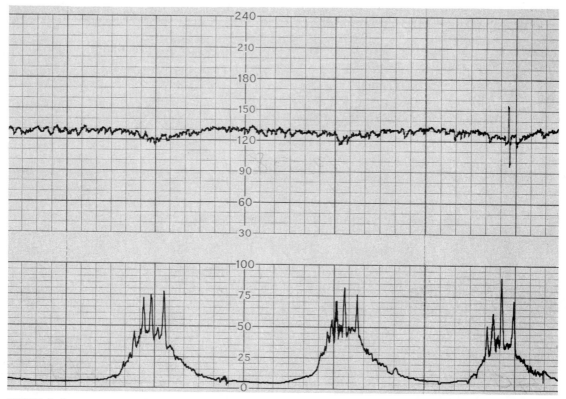

FIGURE 4–4.
Monitor strip from internal monitor. Lower reading is the uterine pressure. Spikes during contractions indicate the mother was pushing down to assist with the descent of the baby. Slight dipping in the fetal heart rate (upper line) is normal during contractions.

Alternative Approaches to the Birthing Process

LeBoyer's Method of Childbirth

In 1929 Otto Rank, a psychoanalyst, identified the experience of birth as a major contributor to an individual's view of the world as either friendly or hostile. He hypothesized that birth trauma could significantly interfere with an individual's ability to cope with stressors later in life.[33] In the early 1970s, Frederick LeBoyer,[22] a French obstetrician, developed a method for handling the newborn during the first 15 to 30 minutes after birth; he felt this method reduced the trauma inherent in the birth experience. According to LeBoyer, medical personnel need to pay greater attention to the newborn as an individual in the minutes after birth. He suggests minimizing stressors for the neonate by reducing the intensity of new stimuli, such as light, gravity, and coolness. He recommends eliminating all but essential talking, turning down all lights, and placing the baby on the mother's abdomen until the cord ceases pulsating (3 to 5 minutes). During this time, the doctor or parent gently massages the baby's back to simulate the uterine contractions. After the cord has been cut, the infant is placed in a warm water bath for 10 to 15 minutes and then

wrapped in a warm blanket and placed at the mother's breast for nursing. LeBoyer proposes that his method of introducing the neonate to the world is less traumatic and, consequently, emotionally safer than the current practice of placing the naked infant in a crib under bright lights. He contends that infants treated by his method experience less crying and are more alert during the first hour of life.

Practitioner observations indicate that gentler treatment of the newborn during this first 15 minutes of extrauterine life does result in quieter, more alert infants during the next few days of life. However, pediatricians T. Berry Brazelton and Marshall Klaus disagree with LeBoyer's rationale for providing a water bath, stating that the increased quiet alertness (Wolff's state 4) found during the first 30 minutes of life is present in any infant who is free of depressant maternal medications and who is kept warm. These doctors claim that the new stimuli, especially mild temperature changes, are essential to maintain respiratory efforts. Brazelton and Klaus offer as evidence an experiment in which three normal 2-hour-old infants stopped breathing completely when they were placed in a water bath that approximated the mother's temperature.[44] Although infants born by the LeBoyer method tend to have higher scores on the Brazelton Neonatal Assessment (see Chap. 5), no observable differences in development or temperament are found by 8 months of age.[30] Additional observations are needed to identify the critical positive components of LeBoyer's method and the long-range as well as the short-range effects.

Underwater Birth

Another approach to gentle childbirth has been proposed by Igor Charkovsky of Russia.[41] The mother is placed in a warm water bath for her labor and delivery. She is attended by her spouse or partner, a birthing specialist, a "baby's advocate," and any others that the mother chooses (physician, midwife, friends) who she believes are able to be supportive and can send out positive thoughts to her and the transitioning child.[24] Advocates of this approach to childbirth believe that the prepared mother is able to relax and release birthing fears, enabling her to communicate with her body and baby. They also believe that the birth can be a pleasant rather than traumatic experience for the child.[10] The infant is able to move from the tight, gravity-free water environment of the uterus through a relaxed birth canal into the freedom of the water bath, unfolding gradually and releasing the tensions of birth before assuming the activities of breathing and moving the muscles against gravity. Because the baby is still attached to the mother through the functioning placenta, he or she does not need to breathe. The infant may remain underwater for 5 to 20 minutes or more (depending on the time that elapses between the birth of the baby and the separation of the placenta from the uterine wall), surfacing occasionally to "taste" the breathing experience gradually.[10]

Couples who have used this approach report that the labor is markedly shorter (a couple of hours), pain is markedly reduced, if not eliminated, the couple experiences a deeper bonding with each other and the child than with other methods of childbirth, and they experience a new understanding of, or relationship with, their own personage.[10] Advocates of this method of childbirth claim that "water-trained babies appear to be more intelligent, healthier, and better motor-coordinated than babies raised in a conventional manner."[10]

Many medical personnel and psychologists are uncomfortable with this approach since the claims are not yet substantiated. Since the first documented underwater birth in the United States occurred in October 1980, enough underwater births have not taken place to develop systematic research.

STAGES IN THE TRANSITIONAL PROCESS

The infant faces several critical stressors once the birth process is initiated. Each stage of labor has unique stressors, as do the periods after birth. Any decrease in oxygen supply during the birth process is treated as a medical emergency, requiring immediate intervention and possible cesarean section to maintain the life of the baby.

The infant's skull is composed of eight freely moving flat plates (bones) separated by membranous spaces known as sutures (see Figs. 4-2*A* and 5-8). During the compression of the birth process, these cranial bones move, slide, and overlap each other at the edges, decreasing the diameter of the cranial vault. The amount of molding that can occur depends on fetal age and size and on the duration and the intensity of intrauterine pressures as well as the size of the pelvic passage. The skull molding and brain edema (swelling) that may accompany the trauma of birth are both normal and temporary. Rarely, an infant may experience intracranial bleeding as a result of the pressures associated with birth; this bleeding can cause temporary or permanent brain damage. The problem occurs more frequently in the premature than in the full-term infant because of greater fragility of the blood vessels.

The First 30 Minutes

Every person who is privileged to witness the entrance of a new life into the world experiences an indescribable thrill. As the head is delivered, each witness instinctively takes a breath, tightens, and waits in anticipatory silence for the newcomer to take the first breath. The skin color ranges from ashen white to a deep bluish gray. The clock slowly measures off time. Each second seems an eternity, as everyone seems to be silently telling the child to breathe, to take a breath, to live. Suddenly, that first gasp is drawn, and the baby's skin begins to flush bright pink. The tension is broken, and everyone breathes. Talking resumes in the delivery room; smiles return to faces. The baby's face, however, does not have a smile. For the first time, the baby is facing light, gravity, and cold air. The newcomer cries and protests vigorously, much to everyone's delight. Now is not a time for sleep!

Activation of the Respiratory System

The newborn consumes 6 mL of oxygen per kilogram per minute, twice that of an adult.[17] Consequently, as placental respiration ends, establishment of effective lung respiratory efforts is essential. Respiratory-like movements of the lungs have been present since the third month of gestation.[17] Although the stimulus for initiating respiratory efforts is not clear, decreasing oxygen levels and increasing carbon dioxide levels of the blood make pulmonary air exchange essential within 1 minute after birth. Theories about respiratory initiators include the physical stimulation of the birth process, the sudden release of pressure from the thoracic cavity, and the decrease in blood oxygen levels.[17] Because it is not unusual for an infant to take the first breath and cry before the birth process is completed (especially if minimal or no medications are given to the mother), the last theory appears to be invalidated. The sudden change in the baby's environment, the exposure to firm touch, and the cooling effect of air have more support as initiators of respiratory efforts (Fig. 4-5).

Clara cells of the lungs begin to mature sufficiently by 24 to 25 weeks of gestational age to produce the lipoprotein **surfactant.** This fluid forms a thin film over the inner lining of the lung. Surfactant is essential to reduce the surface tension of the alveoli, thus allowing them to expand and prevent-

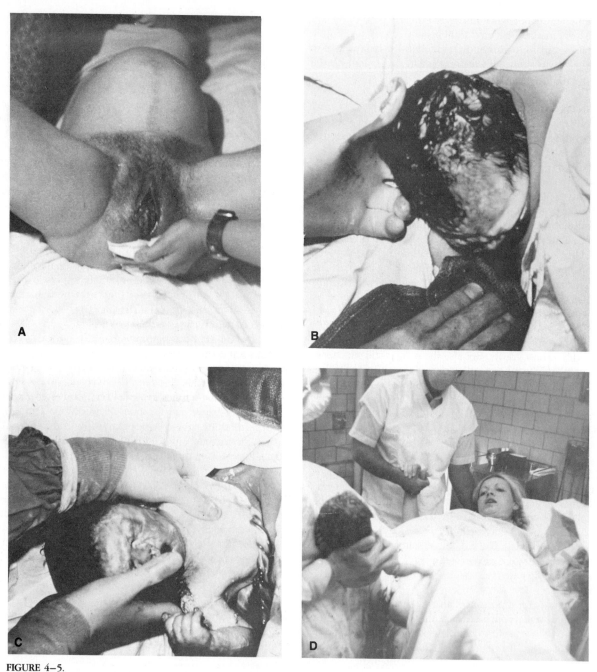

FIGURE 4–5.
Birth of the baby. (A) Crowning. (B) Birth of the head. (C) Birth of the body. (Note that the baby is already crying. Note also the size of the umbilical cord and the white, cheesy substance [vernix caseosa] on the face, right shoulder, and arm). (D) Birth process completed; the baby is shown to the mother and the father. (Photographs B and C used with permission of Sandy Eckstrom, Manchester Monitrice Association, Manchester, Connecticut.)

ing their collapse.[17] Premature infants and infants who experience oxygen deprivation or cold stress experience difficulty producing adequate surfactant. Consequently, the infant may not be able to expand the alveoli sufficiently for exchange of air, a factor that leads to **respiratory distress syndrome (RDS),** also known as hyaline membrane disease. The ability

of the neonate to produce surfactant can be predicted from a sample of amniotic fluid. The ratio of lecithin to sphingomyelin (L–S ratio) in the fluid indicates the ability of the lungs to produce sufficient surfactant to sustain lung expansion after birth. Fortunately, respiratory distress syndrome is a self-terminating disease that is specific to the newborn during the first 4 days of life. Those infants (usually premature) who survive the first 72 hours generally begin to produce surfactant spontaneously. Some may be left with residual lung problems if symptoms were severe.

The pressure exerted on the lungs during crying helps to expand the alveolar (air) sacs. The newborn frequently cries a total of 1 to 2 hours out of every 24. Respiratory rate may range from 50 to 80 breaths per minute during the first 24 hours. After the first 24 hours, respirations average 40 per minute but may range from 30 to 60 per minute. The chest and abdominal wall frequently rise and fall together. Both respiratory rhythm and depth of breaths may be irregular. Short, rapid, shallow breaths are frequently followed by a 5- to 10-second pause in breathing. A frequent interspersing of slow deep respirations may lead the casual observer to believe that the infant is gasping for breath. The occurrence of mild **retractions,** a drawing in of the soft tissues that surround the thoracic cavity during inspiration and crying, is not unusual until the alveoli are fully expanded.

Circulatory System Changes

The placenta of the full-term infant contains about 125 to 150 mL of blood, the umbilical vessels about 75 to 125 mL of blood.[35] The blood volume of the newborn depends heavily on both the timing and the position of the baby in relation to the placenta when the cord is clamped. One fourth to one half of the placental volume is transfused to the infant between 15 and 30 seconds after birth. If the infant is held below the level of the placenta, gravity facilitates the flow of even more blood to the baby.[35] Consequently, the neonate's blood volume may range from 80 to 100 mL/kg of body weight.[35] Some birthing specialists believe that extra blood gives the baby a physiological "head start." However, infants who receive too much blood before the cord is clamped may have excessive red blood cells (polycythemia), a condition that leads to hyperbilirubinemia, or excessive blood volume (hypervolemia), a condition that leads to pulmonary or cardiac overload.[35] Consequently, other practitioners clamp the cord as soon as possible after birth.

When the infant takes the first breath, amniotic fluid in the fetal lungs is replaced by air, alveoli are expanded, and blood vessels experience pressure changes that initiate marked changes in the circulatory system. Blood that was diverted from the lungs through the foramen ovale and ductus arteriosus is now sucked into the pulmonary vessels, where it begins to exchange oxygen and carbon dioxide. The flow of blood through the pulmonary artery increases the pressure within the left atrium, which in turn causes functional closure of a flap valve over the foramen ovale. Transient heart murmurs that last for several days because of leakage of blood through the foramen ovale do not have pathological significance. The four special structures associated with fetal circulation (see Chap. 3) are gradually obliterated during the next few weeks and months.[25] The ductus arteriosus closes in about 14 days.

The pulse rate after the first 24 hours is variable but usually rapid, 120 to 150 beats per minute. It is affected by activity, commonly rising to 170 or 180 when the infant is crying, and dropping as low as 90 during deep sleep. Blood pressure is difficult to obtain in the neonate and is highly subject to the instruments used to measure the pressure as well as to the skill of the practitioner. Birth weight is also a critical factor. The average blood pressure of a full-term baby ranges from 50/30 to 70/40.[25] Vasoconstriction of peripheral vessels during the first few days of life accounts for the blue or white coloration of hands and feet known as **acrocyanosis.**

Apgar Score

At 1 minute and again at 5 minutes after birth, health personnel assess the infant's adaptation to extrauterine life by use of the Apgar newborn scoring system developed by Dr. Virginia Apgar in 1953 (Table 4-1). The five factors evaluated are color, heart rate, reflex irritability, muscle tone, and respiratory effort. Each factor is rated as 0, 1, or 2 according to objective criteria. A delay in "pinking" often prevents a perfect score of 10. The Apgar score alerts health care personnel to infants who need assistance with the transition process (e.g., help with breathing).

TABLE 4–1. APGAR NEWBORN SCORING SYSTEM

Sign		Score		
		0	*1*	*2*
Appearance	Color*	Pale	Blue extremities	Pink
Pulse	Heart rate	Not detectable	Below 100	Above 100
Grimace	Reflex irritability	No response	Grimace	Vigorous cry
Activity	Muscle tone	Flaccid	Some flexion of extremities	Active motion
Respiration	Respiratory effort	Absent	Slow, irregular	Good (crying)

* Alternative measures of circulatory adequacy may be used for assessing nonwhite children (such as color of mucous membranes or color of lips, palms, nail beds, and soles of feet).
(Modified from Apgar, V, (1958). Evaluation of the newborn infant: Second report. Journal of the American Medical Association, 168, 1988.)

Evaluation of the Apgar score is as follows: A score of 7 to 10 is considered good; 5 to 7 is poor: these infants may need assistance to maintain life and have a higher mortality rate; 0 to 4 is very poor: these infants need immediate cardiac and respiratory assistance. Statistically significant correlations have been identified between mortality and low Apgar scores at 1 minute of life; even more significant correlations are found with low 5-minute scores. Surviving infants in the latter category have a high incidence of neurological defects.[28]

Heat Control

The baby, at birth, is the same temperature as the mother (98°–100°F or 36°–38°C). The temperature of the delivery room is usually 20° to 30°F less than the maternal temperature; consequently, heat control becomes a critical factor. Infants are more likely to lose heat in a cold room than adults because of the greater proportion of body surface to body weight. They also have less subcutaneous fat (insulation) than older children or adults. At the same time, the infant is limited in the ways to conserve and to produce heat.[40, 42] It is normal, not pathological, for the infant's temperature to drop 1° to 2°F immediately after birth. In a protected environment, the temperature begins to rise spontaneously and returns to normal by 8 hours of age. Nevertheless, prevention of excessive heat loss, especially during the first 15 minutes of life, is extremely significant to the infant's ability to make a successful transition to extrauterine life.

The body has four major mechanisms for heat loss:

Evaporation: The chill that one feels when stepping out of a shower or a swimming pool is caused by the evaporation of water from the body into the air. Body heat is used to transform the liquid into water vapor. The newborn is covered with amniotic fluid; thus, vigorous efforts to dry the infant are essential to prevent heat loss by evaporation.

Conduction: Body heat is lost to cooler objects that are in direct contact with the skin. Most of us shiver at the thought of putting on a jacket that is kept on the back porch in the winter or jumping between cold bed sheets in the evening. The preheating of blankets, towels, diapers, and cribs can help prevent massive heat loss by this mechanism.

Convection: Cool air that passes over the body also tends to rob it of heat. Specially heated cribs and infant warmers can heat the surrounding air and block air currents that could add unnecessary stress to the newborn.

Radiation: Heat can also be transferred through the air to other cooler objects and to the walls of the room. Have you ever noticed how much cooler 70°F rooms feel during the winter months than during the summer months? It is not a psychological phenomenon; your body is actually helping to maintain the environmental temperature by radiating heat to the walls, which are in contact with the cold outside air.

Well-insulated houses feel much warmer at 70°F than do poorly insulated ones. Protection against radiation loss cannot be ensured except to insulate the room and to block the loss of heat through layers of clothing. Wrapping the newborn securely in blankets helps to reduce heat loss from radiation.

From the moment of birth, the neonate should be provided with a neutral thermal environment, a room temperature at which oxygen consumption and caloric expenditure for heat production is minimized.[40]

Methods for conserving or producing heat are limited in the neonate. The heat control mechanism of the neonate's brain is as yet poorly developed.[40, 42] Few newborns are able to shiver adequately to produce much heat. However, newborns do experience a mild increase in metabolic rate in response to cold, allowing them to produce additional body heat to offset some of the heat loss. Three other mechanisms of heat conservation and production are available to the normal full-term infant:

Constriction of Blood Vessels: By constricting the blood vessels to the body surface areas, the infant can retain heat in the inner parts of the body. Two common side effects are mottled skin and acrocyanosis (bluish-colored hands and feet).

Positional Changes: By flexing the extremities and back, the infant can bring the body closer to itself, thus decreasing the total amount of exposed skin surface (as in Paul Chabas' painting "September Morn"). Since the immature neurologic system of premature infants does not yet allow this defensive behavior, they are at high risk for pathological heat loss.

Metabolism of Brown Fat: During the last month of intrauterine life, the newborn has been storing (in the upper portions of the body) a unique type of adipose (fat) tissue, which can produce heat rapidly under the stress of cooling. Brown fat comprises about 2% to 6% of the neonate's body weight.[46] The rich nerve and blood supply of these special cells gives brown fat both its color and its ability to be metabolized and disseminated quickly as heat when needed.

It is estimated that the wet newborn can lose up to 200 calories of heat per kilogram per minute.[28] When one considers that the adult at full compensation can produce only 90 calories of heat per kilogram per minute, the stress of cooling can be put into a new perspective. An increase in metabolism causes an increase in the consumption of both glucose (sugar) and brown fat and in turn increases the need for oxygen, a factor which increases stress on the lungs.

The impact of the stress of excessive cooling at birth can continue to exhibit its effects through a higher metabolic rate for as long as 7 to 10 days after birth.[51] Energy used for heat maintenance cannot be used to aid in the other adjustments to extrauterine life or for body growth. Moreover, babies who have lost excessive amounts of heat are unable to produce surfactant well. Consequently, even though infants need increased amounts of oxygen to meet the demands of increased metabolism, they may not be able to obtain sufficient oxygen because of respiratory distress syndrome, the result of decreased pulmonary surfactant.

The First 3 Days

During the first 3 to 4 days of life, the newborn continues to take giant steps toward independent physiological functioning. The stomach, the intestines, and the liver must begin to accept and metabolize food for the body. The kidneys and the bowel must begin to function as systems for eliminating wastes. Neurological tissues must recover and begin to assume responsibility for controlling respiratory efforts, heat control, and protective reflexes. Most of these physiological changes are discussed in Chapter 5. The factors discussed here represent normal phenomena in the neonate but offer potential threats to survival if they are not adequately anticipated or monitored.

Behavior Patterns

The first 12 hours after birth are usually marked by two periods of intense activity followed by periods of rest. Most babies then begin to fall into a relatively stable pattern of sleeping versus waking behaviors that coincide with feeding times.

The first period of activity immediately follows birth. The infant may experience vigorous, intense activity characterized by outbursts of intense crying and hyperreflexive reactions. The majority of the first period of activity is spent in the quiet alert state if the infant is kept warm and with the mother.[19] The neonate is generally alert and responsive during this time. He or she seeks eye contact with others and even begins to engage in social or vocal "turntaking" if appropriately stimulated. As mentioned earlier, activity and alertness during the first 2 hours can be greatly depressed if the mother has received medication during labor.

The respiratory rate may be as high as 82 breaths per minute during the first hour of life; this rate gradually decreases to 45 to 55 breaths per minute as the lungs expand and adequate ventilation is achieved. The intense stress of the birth process and the adjustment to independent procurement of oxygen also cause a rapid increase in pulse rate. The pulse rate is commonly 180 beats per minute during the first hour of life but gradually decreases as the physical stressors diminish and emotional comfort is offered, stabilizing between 120 and 160 beats per minute.

The newborn usually remains alert and active until the period of the first extrauterine sleep, which occurs in the nonsedated baby about 1 to 2 hours after birth. After 2 to 4 hours of sleep, the newborn enters a second period of wakefulness. The baby is temporarily hyperactive to all stimuli and experiences swift color changes, quickly flushing red when crying. Many infants secrete excessive amounts of mucus during this time as a normal protective response to the drying effect of air on the tender lungs. After 1 to 2 hours of wakefulness, the neonate enters the second extrauterine sleep, which may be deep and punctuated by apnea periods (periods in which the infant forgets to breathe). During this sleep period, the neonate continues to have excessive mucus. Most infants achieve relative stability with a decrease in hypersensitivity to the environment by 12 hours of age.

States of Consciousness

Wolff objectively categorizes the activity-sleep behaviors of the neonate into six specific states:[50]

State 1 **Quiet Sleep**	Regular respiratory rhythm, frequent Moro reflex, no grimacing or eye movement
State 2 **Active Sleep**	Erratic respiratory rhythm, decreased Moro reflex, increased limb and body movement; grimacing, smiling, and mouthing; frequent rapid eye movements (REM)
State 3 **Drowsiness**	Irregular respiratory rhythm, opening and closing of eyes, less Moro reflex than in quiet sleep but more than in active sleep; activity greater than in quiet sleep, less than in active sleep
State 4 **Quiet Alert**	Fairly regular respiration; eyes wide open, appearing to focus; increased moisture on eyeballs gives "bright" appearance; attends quickly to auditory and visual stimuli
State 5 **Active Awake**	Irregular respirations, nonfocused, dull eye movements; frequent spurts of diffuse activity, grunting, groaning, or fussiness
State 6 **Crying**	Irregular, forceful respirations; diffuse physical activity

These states are well developed by the 38th week of gestation and continue to be exhibited throughout infancy, especially the first 3 months. Behaviors are less clearly differentiated in gestationally younger babies.[11,31] All six states of consciousness are observable in the first 24 hours. The activity periods include expressions of states 4, 5, and 6. The quiet, alert babies described by physicians Kennell, Klaus, Brazelton, and LeBoyer are experiencing state 4, the normal activity state of the 5- to 60-minute-old neonate who is kept warm and secure. State 4 is especially significant to parent-infant interaction and to early childhood education because, in this state, the infant is alert and able to attend, respond to, and seek environmental stimuli.

Common Problems of the Transitional Period

Two rather common but transient problems face the newborn during this transitional period. Because breathing is a new experience to the infant and the respiratory center of the brain may not yet be fully operative, some infants may literally forget to breathe (apnea). Medicated and premature infants in particular can have this problem. Gently hitting the crib or shaking the baby's leg is usually sufficient to rouse the infant from the "too-comfortable" state and reinitiate respiratory efforts. More aggressive interventions are occasionally necessary if these measures are inadequate.

Excessive amounts of thick oral mucus can block the respiratory passages. This hypersecretion is apparently a compensatory effort by the body to keep the lung membranes moist and to prevent entrance of foreign material. The presence of excessive mucous coupled with the typically poor coordination of the sucking and swallowing reflexes can lead to difficulty during the first few feedings. Tipping the baby's face down and gently patting the back facilitates the escape of the mucus through the mouth.

Early Physiological Changes

Changes in the Cord

The bluish white, gelatinous (Wharton's jelly) cord is usually cut 1½ to 3 inches away from its juncture with the abdominal wall. The 1½-inch diameter decreases sharply with the collapse of the umbilical vessels. Because of the high water content, the stump of the cord dries and shrinks rapidly, losing its flexibility by 24 hours after birth. By the second day, it is a hard yellow (dehydrated Wharton's jelly) or black (blood) tag on the skin. Slight oozing where the cord joins the abdominal wall is common and offers an excellent medium for bacterial growth. Parents are encouraged to clean the area with cotton balls and alcohol or another antiseptic solution, several times daily until the cord has dropped off (6–14 days). This frequent cleansing should be continued until the area is completely healed (2–3 days after the cord falls off).

Physiological Jaundice

Fifty percent of all full-term newborn infants exhibit some degree of jaundice (yellow coloration) on the second through the sixth day of life.[26] People who are not familiar with this normal phenomenon of adjustment to extrauterine life—especially new parents—frequently fear that the child's life is in jeopardy because of a disease, such as hepatitis. An explanation can relieve much anxiety.

Because of the low oxygen concentration experienced during intrauterine life, the fetus produces many immature red blood cells to carry the available oxygen to vital areas of the developing body. After birth, when oxygen concentrations increase, this number of red blood cells is unnecessary; consequently, the body begins to hemolyze, or destroy, the excessive and immature red blood cells. The breakdown products circulate in the blood until they are stored, excreted, or metabolized.

Red blood cells break down into heme and globin (Fig. 4-6). Globin, which is a protein, is stored to be recycled by the body for later growth needs. Heme undergoes further breakdown into iron and **indirect bilirubin.** The iron is stored in the liver to be recycled later; the waste product bilirubin, however, is fat soluble and thus cannot be excreted through the kidneys. The enzyme **glucuronyl transferase,** produced by the liver, functions as a catalyst to transform the

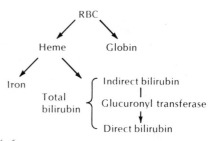

FIGURE 4–6.
Hemolysis of red blood cells. Indirect bilirubin cannot be excreted by the kidneys and will accumulate in the baby's body until it is converted into direct bilirubin.

indirect bilirubin into a water-soluble form, **direct bilirubin,** which can be excreted in the urine.[12]

During the first few days of life, when indirect bilirubin excretion needs are high, the newborn's capacity to convert indirect bilirubin is only 1% to 2% of that of the adult.[21] Consequently, excessive indirect bilirubin builds up in the blood and is deposited in body cells, causing the skin and eyes to become a yellow color. Fortunately, this condition is self-correcting. As the liver gradually mobilizes its resources, the bilirubin is converted and excreted. The jaundice usually disappears without treatment between the 7th and 14th days of life.

Jaundice is three to six times more common in breast-fed than bottle-fed babies.[37] Twenty percent to 25% of breast-fed babies experience hyperbilirubinemia (bilirubin level over 11 mg/dL) during the first week of life.[18] Multiple factors are at play. The breast-fed infant often does not get as much fluid as the formula-fed baby. Breast milk also inhibits the production of glucuronyl transferase.[3, 49] Breast-milk jaundice may appear by the third day and may remain elevated through the first 2 months of life, slowly returning to normal.[37] Mothers are generally asked to substitute bottle feedings for a few days to give the baby's body a chance to correct itself.[49]

It should be noted that jaundice that appears during the first 36 hours of life is considered pathological. All babies who exhibit jaundice should be observed carefully and given appropriate treatment if the blood level of indirect bilirubin becomes too high. Abnormally high concentrations of indirect bilirubin (over 20 mg) can lead to deposits of the bilirubin in the brain (kernicterus), where it can cause brain damage and even death. Moderately high levels (15–20 mg) may be associated with hyperactivity, learning disabilities, and neurological and behavioral problems if small amounts have been deposited in the brain. Early evacuation of **meconium** (fetal bowel movement), which is high in indirect bilirubin content, good hydration through frequent feeding, and exposure to sunlight appear to decrease the bilirubin levels.[49]

Transitory Coagulation Defects

The ability of the liver to produce substances essential to coagulation of the blood is delayed until the intestine is able to synthesize vitamin K. Consequently, bleeding problems may be experienced between the second and fifth days of life (e.g., cephalhematoma). Most health care agencies give all infants an injection of vitamin K shortly after birth as a prophylactic agent to prevent bleeding problems. Once normal intestinal flora are established, the baby is able to synthesize its own vitamin K and produce the essential clotting factors. Adult concentrations of the most significant clotting factors are reached in about 2 weeks. Other blood clotting factors do not reach adult levels until 9 months of age.[35]

FACTORS THAT AFFECT TRANSITION

One of the major factors that affect the newborn's ability to adjust to extrauterine life is gestational age. The length of time spent in the uterus directly correlates with the maturity of the organs and their subsequent ability to function independently of the mother's support. Just as individuals grow at different rates after birth, the same is true during intrauterine development.

Infants who weigh more than the 90th percentile of the norm for gestational age are considered large; those less than the 10th percentile of the norm are considered small. Babies who are large or small for gestational age are known to be at risk. Traditionally, any baby who weighed less than 2500 g (5½ lb) at birth was considered to be premature. However, the terms **premature** and **small for gestational age** are not synonymous. Intrauterine growth may also be affected by hereditary factors. Infants of physically small parents are more likely to be smaller than the average baby. Nevertheless, weight under 2500 g at the time of birth is considered to be suboptimal regardless of the cause. The World Health Organization gives the following definitions based on 40-weeks gestation from the last menstrual period (LMP):[21]

> **Low birth weight:** (LMP) Less than 2500 g
> **Premature:** Born before the end of the 37th week
> **Full term:** Born between the 38th and 41st weeks
> **Postmature:** Born after the beginning of the 42nd week

Assessment of Gestational Age

Because the due date as calculated by the last menstrual period is not always accurate, gestational maturity is often assessed by external signs of physical and neurological maturity. Since gestational age is usually more significant than body weight as an indicator of the problems the infant may experience during the transitional period, assessment of external characteristics is essential for anticipating and planning intervention strategies. Figure 4-7 gives one example of a set of charts used to determine gestational age. The major factors that change with increased gestational age are skin color and translucency, body weight, and neuromuscular functioning. Mature functioning of the central nervous system is exhibited by increased muscle tone and coordinated reflexes.

Prematurity

About 7% of infants may be classified as premature at birth in the United States.[4, 16] This figure includes babies less than 38 weeks gestational age whether heavier or lighter than 2500 g. Babies of diabetic mothers frequently are large for gestational age but still may be premature by birth. Multiple-birth pregnancy increases the frequency of prematurity. African American babies have twice the mortality rate of white babies, primarily because of the higher incidence of small premature babies.[2]

The head of the premature infant characteristically appears to be too large for its body, although this feature depends on the degree of prematurity. Blood vessels can be seen through the delicate, translucent, wrinkled skin. The thin arms and legs frequently lie flat on the mattress; this characteristic is in sharp contrast to the healthy full-term infant, who keeps the extremities flexed (Fig. 4-8). Reflex movements and crying are spasmodic and weak in the premature baby. The eyes and abdomen are prominent and the genitalia small. The fingernails are thin, and the hair is fine and fuzzy. **Lanugo** (downy hair over body) and **vernix** (waxy protective covering on skin at birth) still cover the body. Many of these infants need vigilant observation because of periods of apnea (they "forget" to breathe). The shorter the gestational time, the greater the likelihood that respiratory distress syndrome will develop because of the infant's inability to produce surfactant. This condition is a leading cause of death.

Immediate Problems

The problems and prognosis of the premature infant correlate highly with the degree of immaturity. With excellent aggressive care, 67% of infants who weigh 750 to 999 g (1 lb 10 oz–2 lb 3 oz), and 20% to 44% of infants who weigh 500 to 749 g (1 lb 2 oz–1 lb 10 oz) may survive. However, more than one third of these infants end up with disabilities.[13] Survival of infants who weigh less than 500 g (about 20 gestational weeks) is rare. Scattered literature reports the survival of a 15-oz (440 g),[8, 32] 12-oz (340 g),[1] and even a 10-oz (280 g) infant with very intensive care! Essentially normal premature babies who survive the first 72 hours of life usually have a good chance of continued healthy growth and development.

During the second week of life, a critical but avoidable threat to survival of the premature infant may occur: the danger of infection. The immune system of the premature infant is immature. Even the full-term infant is poorly protected physiologically from bacteria because antibodies are not yet developed to ward off infection. Although the mother does transfer some antibodies to the infant during pregnancy, every effort must be made by all people who have contact with the newborn to avoid transfer of potentially harmful bacteria. Some bacteria that are normally present on the adult body can be controlled and tolerated because of the adult's mature immune system; the same bacteria can cause death in the young infant.

(*Text continues on page 96*)

GESTATIONAL AGE ASSESSMENT (Ballard)

NAME _____ DATE/TIME OF BIRTH _____ BIRTH WEIGHT _____

HOSPITAL NO. _____ DATE/TIME OF EXAM _____ LENGTH _____

  AGE WHEN EXAMINED _____ HEAD CIRC. _____

RACE _____ SEX _____ EXAMINER _____

APGAR SCORE: 1 MINUTE _____ 5 MINUTES _____

NEUROMUSCULAR MATURITY

NEUROMUSCULAR MATURITY SIGN	SCORE						RECORD SCORE HERE
	0	1	2	3	4	5	
POSTURE							
SQUARE WINDOW (WRIST)	90°	60°	45°	30°	0°		
ARM RECOIL	180°		100°-180°	90°-100°	<90°		
POPLITEAL ANGLE	180°	160°	130°	110°	90°	<90°	
SCARF SIGN							
HEEL TO EAR							

TOTAL NEUROMUSCULAR MATURITY SCORE

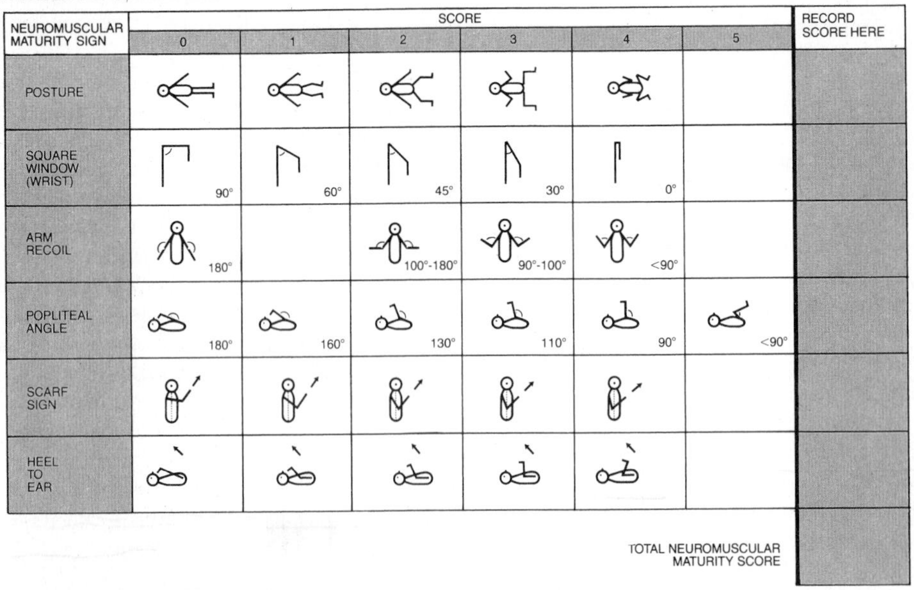

SCORE

Neuromuscular _____

Physical _____

Total _____

MATURITY RATING

TOTAL MATURITY SCORE	GESTATIONAL AGE (WEEKS)
5	26
10	28
15	30
20	32
25	34
30	36
35	38
40	40
45	42
50	44

PHYSICAL MATURITY

PHYSICAL MATURITY SIGN	SCORE						RECORD SCORE HERE
	0	1	2	3	4	5	
SKIN	gelatinous red, transparent	smooth pink, visible veins	superficial peeling, &/or rash few veins	cracking pale area rare veins	parchment deep cracking no vessels	leathery cracked wrinkled	
LANUGO	none	abundant	thinning	bald areas	mostly bald		
PLANTAR CREASES	no crease	faint red marks	anterior transverse crease only	creases ant. 2/3	creases cover entire sole		
BREAST	barely percept.	flat areola no bud	stippled areola, 1-2mm bud	raised areola, 3-4mm bud	full areola 5-10mm bud		
EAR	pinna flat, stays folded	sl. curved pinna; soft with slow recoil	well-curv. pinna; soft but ready recoil	formed & firm with instant recoil	thick cartilage ear stiff		
GENITALS (Male)	scrotum empty no rugae		testes descending, few rugae	testes down good rugae	testes pendulous deep rugae		
GENITALS (Female)	prominent clitoris & labia minora		majora & minora equally prominent	majora large, minora small	clitoris & minora completely covered		

TOTAL PHYSICAL MATURITY SCORE

GESTATIONAL AGE (weeks)

By dates _____

By ultrasound _____

By score _____

A

FIGURE 4–7.

(A) Clinical estimation of gestational age. (Ballard, J. L., Novak, K. K., & Driver, M. (1979). A simplified score for assessment of fetal maturation of newly born infants. Journal of Pediatrics, 95, 769–771.) *With permission.*

CLASSIFICATION OF NEWBORNS (BOTH SEXES) BY INTRAUTERINE GROWTH AND GESTATIONAL AGE[1,2]

NAME _____ DATE OF BIRTH _____ BIRTH WEIGHT _____

HOSPITAL NO. _____ DATE OF EXAM _____ LENGTH _____

RACE _____ SEX _____ HEAD CIRC. _____

GESTATIONAL AGE _____

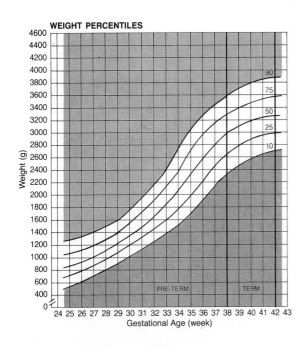

WEIGHT PERCENTILES

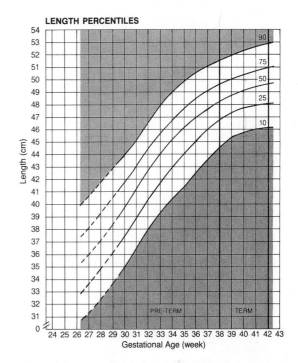

LENGTH PERCENTILES

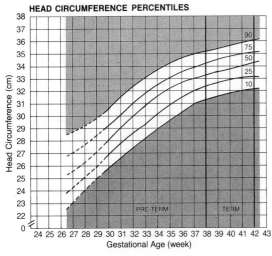

HEAD CIRCUMFERENCE PERCENTILES

CLASSIFICATION OF INFANT*	Weight	Length	Head Circ.
Large for Gestational Age (LGA) (>90th percentile)			
Appropriate for Gestational Age (AGA) (10th to 90th percentile)			
Small for Gestational Age (SGA) (<10th percentile)			

*Place an "X" in the appropriate box (LGA, AGA or SGA) for weight, for length and for head circumference.

References
1. Battaglia FC, Lubchenco LO: A practical classification of newborn infants by weight and gestational age. *J Pediatr* 71:159-163, 1967.
2. Lubchenco LO, Hansman C, Boyd E: Intrauterine growth in length and head circumference as estimated from live births at gestational ages from 26 to 42 weeks. *Pediatrics* 37:403-408, 1966.

Reprinted by permission from Dr Battaglia, Dr Lubchenco, *Journal of Pediatrics* and *Pediatrics*.

B M119/APRIL 1984

ROSS LABORATORIES
COLUMBUS, OHIO 43216
Division of Abbott Laboratories, USA

LITHO IN USA

FIGURE 4—7.

(B) Classification of newborns by intrauterine growth and gestational age. (Battaglia, F. C., & Lubchenco, L. O. (1967). A practical classification of newborn infants by weight and gestational age. Journal of Pediatrics, 71, *159–163; Lubchenco, L. O., Hansman, C., Boyd, E. (1966). Intrauterine growth in length and head circumference as estimated from live births at gestational ages from 26 to 42 weeks.* Pediatrics, 37, *403–408.)*

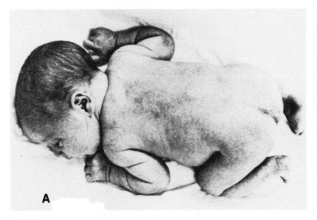 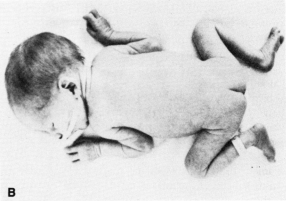

A   **B**

FIGURE 4–8.
Body positions of newborn infants. (A) Full-term infant; muscle tonus is good. The infant keeps the extremities close to the body. (B) Premature infant; body tonus is poor. The hips and shoulder joints exhibit marked extension. (Courtesy Mead-Johnson Laboratories.)

Many premature babies are weak and find it difficult or impossible to suck at a nipple. Consequently, the infant may be tube fed. Medical staff traditionally discouraged breast feeding, assuming that it was more stressful for the infant and that it also potentially exposed the infant to more bacteria. However, research indicates that breast feeding of premature babies, even in the earliest days, is less stressful physiologically than bottle feeding.[27] Babies also appear to have fewer problems with infection when colonized by their mother's bacteria.

Many premature infants who successfully survive the first 2 weeks of life are again threatened during the third month of life.[4] The breakdown of red blood cells after birth, combined with the lack of opportunity to store up sufficient reserves of iron because of the shortened intrauterine period, can lead to **anemia,** a deficiency in hemoglobin and red blood cells. This anemia of the third month of life that results from inadequate iron reserves can be avoided by consistently adding iron to the infant's diet.

Long-Range Problems

Prematurely born children exhibit a higher incidence of mental retardation, abnormal neurologic entities (e.g., cerebral palsy, hypotonia or hypertonia, convulsive disorders, and learning disabilities), lung weakness (e.g., increased respiratory problems, pneumonia, bronchitis), sensory impairment (blindness or deafness), and developmental delays (e.g., language, motor, self-help skills and cognition). However, many of the long-range effects of prematurity are difficult to differentiate from associated prenatal or postnatal complications or even separation from the mother during the early weeks or months of life.[38]

During the 1940s and the 1950s, blindness, specifically retrolental fibroplasia (RLF), now known as retinopathy of prematurity, was a frequent sequela of prematurity. In 1951, it was discovered that high concentrations of oxygen, given to maintain the life of a premature infant and to prevent brain damage, caused pathological changes in the blood vessels of the eye.[6] Hyperoxygenation results in constriction of the retinal vessels, which leads to architectural changes of the retina, causing the retina to become detached and scarred 1 to 2 months after oxygen therapy is terminated. The result in many cases is total irreparable blindness. Careful monitoring of the oxygen concentrations of the arterial blood has caused a marked reduction in retinopathy of prematurity. Nevertheless, the line between too much and too little oxygen is thin for the critically ill premature infant; some newborns still sustain either brain or retinal damage despite the best of medical care. Other visual problems associated with prematurity include strabismus (crossed eyes) and myopia or hyperopia.[4]

The other potentially critical effect of prematurity is maladaptive emotional adjustment. Studies in the area of touch and mother-infant separation in the premature baby are still in the early stages. However, studies show that the premature baby who is gently rocked and caressed and given tactile, kinesthetic, and vestibular stimuli is calmer, gains weight more quickly, spends more time awake and alert, and shows more mature orientation, habituation, and motor responses than the infant who is cared for with a "hands-off" policy.[7, 20, 36]

Parents who have limited contact with their new baby who is ill may feel more like strangers than excited, loving mothers and fathers. Fears of losing the baby, mental retardation, and a myriad of indefinable unknowns coupled with minimal contact and other factors (such as financial concerns and family pressure) may prevent the parents from becoming emotionally attached to their new family member. The parents may express this attitude by either spending minimal time with the baby or by becoming overprotective as a way of denying to themselves and to others how they really feel. An abnormal parent-child relationship is a critical factor in maladaptive behavior.

The parents' inability to interpret or respond to the infant appropriately, and weak, limited behavioral cues or responses from the premature infant may discourage or strain parental interaction with the baby, thus predisposing the baby to the risk of neglect or abuse.[16] Studies by Klaus and Kennell indicate that parental acceptance of the premature infant and the child's long-range affective and cognitive adjustments are enhanced when health personnel encourage and support early parent-child contact.[19] Irritable neonatal temperament, resistance to soothing, or maladaptive emotional adjustment are not inherent characteristics of prematurity,[34] but they may be secondary to maladaptive interactional patterns with the parents. Parents need to be informed of their baby's special physical and interactive needs. They also need to be referred to their local health department or Early Intervention Program for follow-up services (see Chaps. 5, 8, 13, 17, and 31).

Premature infants experience a lag in growth and development. Parents frequently put high emphasis on the first recognized social behavior, the responsive smile. When the sustained responsive smile fails to occur at the expected age, it may confirm parental fears that the child is retarded and may cause them to further separate themselves emotionally from the new baby. Parents should be helped to realize that most of the early developmental milestones, besides being individually determined, are primarily determined by the child's developmental age since *conception* rather than *birth*. To obtain a more accurate idea of when certain skills might be achieved, one should use the expected, not the actual, date of birth as the baseline. With appropriate care and stimulation, most premature infants "catch up" with full-term infants in physical, neurological, and social skills by 2 to 3 years of age (depending on the degree of prematurity). The most critical factor appears to be sensitive, reciprocal, maternal involvement with the infant as expressed through sensory stimulation, language stimulation, positive affect, and environmental enrichment.[15, 38, 48] Synchronized responses to the infant's behaviors are essential to facilitate development of the baby's skills.

Postmaturity

About 9% of babies are born after the 41st week of gestation.[14] The characteristics of these infants depend both on the length of gestation and the efficiency of placental circulation. When a pregnancy lasts longer than expected, there is concern about the safety of the baby. As the placenta approaches 38 weeks, its functional capacity begins to decrease, as calcified areas appear and replace placental tissue. The fetus subsequently may not be able to obtain sufficient nutrients and oxygen to meet continued growth needs; thus, the fetus may begin to depend on fat stores to meet energy needs while in utero. If placental efficiency has deteriorated markedly, it may not be able to provide enough oxygen through labor.

Seventy-five percent to 85% of the deaths of postmature babies occur during the birth process because of insufficient oxygen;[21] other postmature infants may suffer brain damage because of low oxygen availability. A 24-hour maternal urine sample for estriol levels can be used to evaluate placental efficiency. Low levels indicate inadequate functioning of the placenta and the need for cesarean section to prevent fetal problems during birth. Another way to determine the status of the fetus is through amniocentesis. A small amount of amniotic fluid is withdrawn for analysis. Changes in color (usually because of release of meconium) may indicate that the baby is having difficulty.

At birth, the postmature baby may show evidence of recent weight loss. The baggy skin dries, cracks, and peels off quickly after birth because of the loss of the protective vernix caseosa several weeks earlier. Scalp hair is often thick and long. The fingernails are well developed and may require clipping to prevent facial scratches. The postmature baby is long and thin and often has an alert, wide-eyed appearance (Fig. 4-9). Because of this increased maturity, a strong responsive smile can sometimes be elicited from attentive postmature babies, much to the delight of their parents, who may be convinced they have a gifted infant.

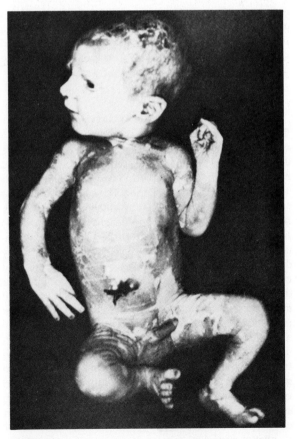

FIGURE 4–9.
Postmature infant. (Clifford, S. H. (1957). Postmaturity. In S. Z. Levine (Ed.), Advances in pediatrics, *Vol. 9. Chicago: Year Book. With permission.)*

Intrauterine Growth Retardation

Some of the causes of intrauterine growth retardation are discussed in Chapter 3. Insults that occur during the embryonic and hyperplastic stages of development can considerably reduce the number of body cells. As a result of interference with mitotic processes, fewer new cells are formed, causing organs to be small and thereby reducing body weight. Insults that occur during the later gestational period (during the hypertrophic stages of development) do not appear to affect the number of cells but rather the amount of cytoplasm present in each cell. Reduced weight is caused by the decrease in cellular weight rather than number of cells.

Studies of the effects of maternal nutrition and fetal malnutrition have been conducted for the last 40 years. The results indicate that the last few months of gestation and the first few months of extrauterine life are the most critical periods for hyperplastic brain growth. Severe or continuous malnutrition during these periods may irrevocably reduce cellular quantity and thus permanently impair intellectual capacity. Autopsies on chronically malnourished infants who died during the first few months of life showed a 60% reduction in the expected number of brain cells, whereas infants whose malnutrition was confined to the postnatal period exhibited a 15% to 20% reduction in the expected number of brain cells for their age.[21] A number of studies have found a significantly higher incidence of brain-wave changes and learning disabilities in children who were small for their age but were full-term infants.[45]

CONCLUSION

The transition from the relative passivity of intrauterine life to the assertiveness that is essential to survival in extrauterine life is a pivotal period of the life span. It cannot be assumed that the infant who appears to be normal and healthy at birth will easily pass through this period. The length of time spent in utero affects the infant's ability to draw on his or her coping skills and to maintain life independently of the mother's protective environment. An appropriate assessment of gestational age and a knowledge of the common problems faced by the newborn can alert health care personnel to potential problems. Many infants experience some type of illness or difficulty during the transitional period; most of these conditions are self-limiting in nature and cause no permanent effects if appropriate treatment is given immediately.

Infants with intrauterine growth retardation,[23] prematurity, or postmaturity tend to give lower scores on the Brazelton Neonatal Behavioral Assessment. Neurological insults or immaturity change the infant's ability to respond to and interact with environmental stimuli. Parents need help understanding and learning how to respond to their infant's unique interactional cues.

When rendering care to the fetus and the newborn, health care practitioners must be concerned with more than survival. Through the provision of a supportive environment, we must also ensure the new citizen's right to maximize his or her potentials and to function as an intelligent, independent, contributing member of family and society.

REFERENCES

1. Anonymous. (1989). Untitled. *People Weekly, 314*(9), 134.
2. Behrman, R. E. (1987). Premature births among black women. *New England Journal of Medicine, 317,* 763–765.
3. Behrman, R. E., & Kliegman, J. M. (1983). Jaundice and hyperbilirubinemia in the newborn. In R. E. Behrman, V. C. Vaughan, III, & W. E. Nelson (Eds.), *Nelson textbook of pediatrics* (12th ed., pp. 378–381). Philadelphia: W. B. Saunders.
4. Blackburn, S. (1987). Health concerns of preterm infants following hospital discharge. *NCAST National News, 3*(2), 1–2.
5. Brazelton, T. B. (1981). Behavioral competence of the newborn infant. In G. B. Avery (Ed.), *Neonatology: Pathophysiology and management of the newborn* (2nd ed.). Philadelphia: J. B. Lippincott.
6. Campbell, K. (1951). Intensive oxygen therapy as a possible cause of retrolental fibroplasia: A clinical approach. *Medical Journal of Australia, 2*(2), 48–50.
7. Chaze, B. A., & Ludington-Hoe, S. M. (1984). Sensory stimulation in the NICU. *American Journal of Nursing, 84,* 68.
8. Cunningham, F. G., MacDonald, P. C., & Grant, N. F. (1989). *Williams obstetrics* (18th ed.). Norwalk, CT: Appleton and Lange.
9. Danforth, D. N., & Ueland, K. (1986). Physiology of uterine action. In D. N. Danforth & J. R. Scott (Eds.), *Obstetrics and gynecology* (5th ed., pp. 582–628). Philadelphia: J. B. Lippincott.
10. Dansby, B. A. (1987). Underwater birth: The ultimate alternative. In T. R. Verny (Ed.), *Pre- and perinatal psychology: An introduction* (pp. 158–166). New York: Human Sciences Press.
11. Dierker, L. J., et al. (1982). Active and quiet periods in the preterm and term fetus. *Obstetrics and Gynecology, 60,* 154.
12. Gannon, R. B., & Pickett, K. (1983). Jaundice. *American Journal of Nursing, 83,* 404.
13. Hack, M., & Fanaroff, A. A. (1986). Changes in the delivery room care of the extremely small infant (<750 g): Effects on morbidity and outcome. *New England Journal of Medicine, 314,* 660–664.
14. Haesslein, H. C. (1987). Diseases of fetal growth. In K. R. Niswander (Ed.), *Manual of obstetrics: Diagnosis and therapy* (3rd ed., pp. 259–265). Boston: Little, Brown.
15. Hayes, J. S. (1980). Premature infant development. *Pediatric Nursing, 6,* 33.
16. Hedlund, R. (1989). Fostering positive social interactions between parents and infants. *Teaching Exceptional Children, 21*(4), 45–48.
17. Hubbell, K. M., & Webster, H. F. (1986). Respiratory management of the neonate. In N. S. Streeter (Ed.), *High-risk neonatal care* (pp. 107–141). Rockville, MD: Aspen.
18. Kivlahan, C., & James, E. J. (1984). The natural history of neonatal jaundice. *Pediatrics, 74,* 364–370.
19. Klaus, M. H., & Kennell, J. H. (1976). *Maternal-infant bonding: The impact of early separation or loss on family development.* St. Louis: C. V. Mosby.
20. Korner, A. (1978). Maternal rhythms and waterbeds: A form of intervention with premature infants. In E. B. Thoman & S. Trotter (Eds.), *Social responsiveness of infants.* New Brunswick, NJ: Johnson & Johnson.
21. Korones, S. B. (1986). *High-risk newborn infants: The basis for intensive nursing care* (4th ed.). St. Louis: C. V. Mosby.

22. LeBoyer, F. (1975). *Childbirth without violence*. New York: Knopf.

23. Lester, B. M., Garcia-Coll, C., Valcarcel, M., Hoffman, J., & Brazelton, T. B. (1986). Effects of atypical patterns of fetal growth on newborn (NBAS) behavior. *Child Development, 57,* 11–19.

24. Liedloff, J. (1986). *The continuum concept* (rev. ed.). London: Arkana.

25. Lynch, T. M. (1986). Cardiovascular conditions in the newborn. In N. S. Streeter (Ed,), *High-risk neonatal care* (pp. 163–228). Rockville, MD: Aspen.

26. Maisels, M. J. (1982). Jaundice in the newborn. *Pediatric Review, 3,* 305–319.

27. Meier, P. (1989). Nursing management of breastfeeding for preterm infants. *Reflections, 15*(2), 9.

28. Moore, M. L. (1981). *The newborn family and nurse* (2nd ed.). Philadelphia: W. B. Saunders.

29. Murray, A. D., Dolby, R. M., Nation, R. L. & Thomas, D. B. (1981). Effects of epidural anesthesia on newborns and their mothers. *Child Development, 52,* 71.

30. Nelson, N. M. (1981). The onset of respiration. In G. B. Avery (Ed.), *Neonatology: Pathophysiology and management of the newborn* (2nd ed.). Philadelphia: J. B. Lippincott.

31. Nijhuis, J. G., et al. (1982). Are there behavioral states in the human fetus? *Early Human Development, 6,* 177.

32. Pleasure, J. R., Dhand, M., & Kaar, M. (1984). What is the lower limit of viability? Intact survival of a 440 g infant. *American Journal of Diseases in Children, 138,* 783–785.

33. Rank, O. (1973). *The trauma of birth*. New York: Harper and Row.

34. Riese, M. L. (1987, August). *Size for gestational age and neonatal temperament*. Paper presented at the Annual Convention of the American Psychological Association, New York.

35. Ryan, R. (1986). Hematological conditions. In N. S. Streeter (Ed.), *High-risk neonatal care* (pp. 409–449). Rockville, MD: Aspen.

36. Schanberg, S. M., & Field, T. M. (1987). Sensory deprivation stress and supplemental stimulation in the rat, pup, and preterm human neonates. *Child Development, 58,* 1431–1447.

37. Schneider, A. P., II. (1986). Breast milk jaundice in the newborn. *Journal of the American Medical Association, 255,* 3270–3274.

38. Schraeder, B. D., Rappaport, J., & Courtwright, L. (1987). Preschool development of very low birthweight infants. *Image: Journal of Nursing Scholarship, 19*(4), 174–178.

39. Schwarz, R. H. (1989). Infant mortality and access to care. *Obstetrics and Gynecology, 73*(1), 123–124.

40. Scopes, J. W. (1981). Thermoregulation in the newborn. In G. B. Avery (Ed.), *Neonatology: Pathophysiology and management of the new born* (2nd ed., pp. 171–181). Philadelphia: J. B. Lippincott.

41. Sidenbladh, E. (Ed.). (1982). *Water babies*. New York: St. Martins Press.

42. Streeter, N. S. (1986). Thermoregulation. In N. S. Streeter (Ed.), *High-risk neonatal care* (pp. 87–106). Rockville, MD: Aspen.

43. U. S. Bureau of the Census. (1988). *Statistical abstract of the United States: 1988* (108th ed.). Washington, DC: U.S. Government Printing Office.

44. Vaughan, V. C., & Brazelton, T. B. (Eds.). (1976). *The family—Can it be saved?* Chicago: Year Book.

45. Walzer, S., & Richmond, J. B. (1973). The epidemiology of learning disorders. *Pediatric Clinics of North America, 20,* 549.

46. Washington, S. (1978). Temperature control of the neonate. *Nursing Clinics of North America, 13,* 23.

47. Wegman, M. E. (1981). Annual summary of vital statistics: 1980. *Pediatrics, 68,* 755.

48. Werner, E. E., et al. (1967). Cumulative effect of perinatal complications and deprived environment on physical, intellectual and social development of preschool children. *Pediatrics, 39,* 490.

49. Wilkerson, N. N. (1988). A comprehensive look at hyperbilirubinemia. *MCN: The American Journal of Maternal/Child Nursing, 13,* 360–364.

50. Wolff, P. H. (1973). The classification of states. In L. J. Stone, H. T. Smith, & L. B. Murphy (Eds.), *The competent infant: Research and commentary*. New York: Basic Books.

51. Ziegel, E., & Cranley, M. S. (1984). *Obstetric nursing* (8th ed.). New York: Macmillan.

The Normal Newborn

Clara S. Schuster

Ababy is a baby is a baby. Not so! Look through the window of a newborn nursery and you begin to see almost as much variation in the characteristics of these initiates to life as among your peers. Ask any new parent; they can (and will) readily share with you all the superior characteristics that individualize their new family member from the other residents of the nursery. Even at this early age, both physiological and affective differences are apparent. Even with the infant's individuality, however, the **neonate** (birth to 28 days of life) shares more common characteristics with peers than at any other stage of extrauterine life. This chapter identifies the normal characteristics of the newborn and some of the reasons for variations in those characteristics.

PHYSIOLOGICAL PARAMETERS

At birth, the newborn is usually covered with some blood and **vernix caseosa,** the thick cheesy coating that protects the skin from the amniotic fluid. Many health care practitioners wash the infant shortly after birth to remove these substances; others prefer to allow the vernix to remain on the skin as a protection against bacteria and as a natural lubricant to prevent drying and cracking during the first 3 to 4 days of life.

Weight

Usually the first question the new parent asks is, "Is it a boy or a girl?" After the gender is established, the second question inevitably is, "Is my baby OK?" or "Is my baby normal?" After a few ooh's and ah's and comments on fingers and toes, color and cry, the third big question is, "How much does he (she) weigh?"

Ninety percent of full-term infants weigh between 5½ and 9½ lb (2500–4300 g). The average weight for males is 7½ lb (3400 g); for females, 7 lb (3200 g). Size is influenced by many factors, including placental efficiency, maternal nutrition, size of the parents, racial characteristics, and environment. Caucasian babies tend to be heavier than Asian, African-American, or Hispanic babies.[47] Mothers who have diabetes during pregnancy tend to have much larger babies. Birth weight decreases as altitude increases because of reduced oxygen availability.[52]

Most infants lose 5% to 10% of their birth weight during the first few days of life. This weight loss is attributed to the relatively low fluid and food intake combined with the loss of body fluids (urine, stool, and physiological edema) after birth.[38] The weight usually stabilizes on the third or fourth day and then begins to increase. Most infants regain birth weight between the 8th and 14th days of life. The average infant continues to gain at a rate of about 1 oz (30 g) per day, or 2 lb (900 g) per month, during the first 3 months of life.[30]

Length

Ninety percent of full-term infants are between 18 and 22 inches in length at birth (46–56 cm); the average length is 20 inches (50 cm).[30] Birth length does not correlate sufficiently with adult height to use this factor as a predictor. By the time a child has reached 3 years of age, however, one can begin to predict adult height.[30]

The neonate's head appears large compared to the diameter of the thorax (chest) and pelvis (hips); it accounts for about one-fourth of the total body length. The adult's head is only one-seventh to one-eighth of the total body length. Relatively large organ size combined with rather weak musculature causes the abdominal wall to protrude. The relatively short arms and legs are kept in a flexed or semiflexed position, making the infant appear even shorter. The short legs place the midpoint of the body at the umbilicus rather than at the symphysis pubis, as in the adult (see Fig. 20-2).

Characteristics of the Head

The newborn's face is typically round and puffy in appearance. The eyes are closed much of the time, even when the baby is awake, a characteristic that may be frustrating to the parents, who feel they have not really been introduced to their baby until the neonate's eyes open and look back at them. Most neonates have eyes of a slate blue color. Some, especially those who will have dark brown or black eyes as adults, may start out with dark blue or gray-black eyes. True eye color usually does not begin to emerge until about 6 weeks of age. Permanent coloration is generally present by 6 months but may not be established until around 12 months of age. Swelling of the eyelids is common in newborns; the most common cause is a temporary reaction to a medication (such as silver nitrate) instilled to prevent blindness from gonorrhea. Only about 20% of neonates produce tears when crying.[55] Many exhibit **strabismus** (crossed eyes) and **nystagmus** (wandering eye movements) because of immaturity of the nervous system and the resultant difficulty in controlling the eye muscles voluntarily.

The newborn has a flat pug nose and a receding chin. These characteristics help the infant to nurse more easily; a protruding nose and chin would get in the way. The fat cheeks of the infant are created by cheek pads, which consist of solid round tissue (1–1½ inches in diameter) that prevents the cheeks from collapsing with the suction required for nursing.

Circumference

The size of the head increases rapidly during infancy. Measurements taken during infancy and early childhood are compared to the baseline head circumference taken shortly after birth and are used to evaluate whether the head is growing too rapidly or too slowly. Early identification of either of these conditions is essential to offer intervention to prevent brain damage or even death from increased intracranial pressure. Ninety-five percent of heads measure between 13 and 14.5 inches (33–36.5 cm) at birth; the average head circumference is 13.5 inches (35 cm). The head should measure about 1 inch (2.5 cm) larger than the chest at birth. Eighty percent of children with a head circumference below the second percentile experience some degree of mental retardation.[30]

Fontanelles

Two fontanelles, the anterior (diamond-shaped area, 2–3 cm wide by 3–4 cm long on the top of the skull) and the posterior (triangular-shaped area, 1 cm, at back of skull), are formed where the bony plates of the head meet (see Figs. 4-2A and 5-8D). Mothers frequently avoid washing the scalp over the anterior fontanelle for fear of injuring the infant's brain; this precaution is unnecessary These "soft spots" are covered by a tough membrane that helps to prevent damage to the soft brain tissue underneath. The gradual addition of bone to the perimeters of the cranial plates causes closure of the posterior fontanelle during the third month of life and of the anterior fontanelle by 18 months (14–21 months).

The fontanelles are considered nature's safety valve because they allow for the rapid growth of the brain, accommodate for the birth process, and reduce undue pressure on the brain if fluid is retained. It is normal for the anterior fontanelle to pulsate with the heartbeat; it also becomes tense during crying. A tense bulging anterior fontanelle during periods of relaxation is indicative of increased intracranial pressure and requires immediate medical evaluation. A depressed fontanelle may indicate a state of dehydration.

CHARACTERISTIC FUNCTIONING OF THE MAJOR SYSTEMS

Every system of the body undergoes some adjustment to extrauterine life. Transitory phenomena (e.g., acrocyanosis and mild retractions during crying) are characteristic during the transitional period but would be considered pathological in the same baby at 1 month of age. Changes that occur in the respiratory and circulatory systems are discussed in Chapter 4; other changes are covered here.

Gastrointestinal System

The gastrointestinal system includes the body's entire alimentary tract, from lips to anus. Although the newborn has been swallowing amniotic fluid during intrauterine life, the introduction to and ingestion of milk and the passage of the first stool are major milestones.

Intake

The infant's mouth is equipped with a shallow, rigid, hard, flat palate and a large tongue for easy grasping and compression of the nipple. During and after nursing, the area around the lips may turn white or even bluish from the effort of sucking. This phenomenon, known as **perioral cyanosis,** is considered normal when nursing. The lips may also be slightly puffy or swollen after nursing. A large white blister in the middle of the upper lip, known as a **labial tubercle,** or sucking callus, may be found for about one-half hour after each nursing until about 6 months of age.

The boat-shaped stomach stretches easily, causing some babies to overeat. The ready emptying of stomach contents into the duodenum may cause the baby to cry from perceived hunger about 2 hours after eating. Most pediatricians recommend waiting at least 3 hours before refeeding the infant to allow for complete emptying of the stomach. However, breast-fed babies may need more frequent feedings than bottle-fed babies because of the easier digestibility of breast milk as opposed to cow's milk.[28] The intestine, which is proportionally longer than in the adult, is poorly equipped with muscular or elastic tissue. Nervous system control is also inadequate. Some digestive enzymes are present, but the infant can digest only simple foods, not complex starches or proteins.

Practitioners generally encourage the breast-feeding mother to nurse the infant immediately after birth, during the first period of activity when the infant is in state 4 (see Chapter 4). Early-fed infants appear to experience less weight loss. The infant receives **colostrum** (precursor to milk), and the early suckling stimulates earlier production of milk by the mother.[28] Close contact with the mother's normal bacteria and factors in the milk, such as antibodies, help to impart immunity to the infant.[22] Another significant advantage of this approach is the responsiveness of the infant to the mother at this early time, which helps to foster a more positive mother-infant relationship. Therefore, long-range as well as short-range effects may be noted by fostering early contact and breast feeding.[27,40] The nutritional needs of premature babies differ from those of full-term babies in terms of protein and caloric content of milk. The milk of mothers who deliver early has a greater concentration of the essential ingredients, making breast milk the feeding of choice for premature infants.[38] Research indicates that even very small premature babies (under 1400 g) fare better when breast fed than when bottle fed.[37] They seem to experience less feeding stress, coordinate suck-swallow behaviors, and participate in reciprocal social exchanges with their mother.

Some health care practitioners recommend waiting about 2 hours before bottle feeding the infant for the first time to allow the infant to adjust to extrauterine life and to begin stabilizing critical functions. Glucose (sugar) water or sterile water is usually the fluid of choice for this first bottle feeding.

The full-term infant needs 140 to 160 mL of fluid per kilogram per day.[38] The new baby often plays with the nipple (breast or bottle) and seldom takes more than 1/2 oz (15 mL) of fluid. Often this fact distresses the mother, who may interpret the baby's difficulty with feeding as a rejection of her. If feeding problems continue, she may feel she is an incompetent mother.[49] After the infant is able to coordinate sucking and swallowing, milk is offered. The total intake may be only 45 to 90 mL during the first 24 hours. The amount taken with each subsequent feeding varies greatly with the child's state of alertness and hunger. By the end of the third day, most infants are consuming 75 to 120 mL per feeding.

Babies who are not breast-fed are usually placed on a cow's milk formula. The manufacturers try to replicate the constituents of human milk as closely as possible; however, some significant differences are as yet unavoidable and warrant brief discussion. Cow's milk contains twice as much protein as human milk. Since it is not as easily digested by the infant, water is added to dilute the protein and to aid in the excretion of waste products. The extra water reduces the number of calories per ounce, requiring the addition of some form of sugar to elevate the caloric value to 20 calories per ounce, the same as breast milk. However, the amount of sugar must be carefully regulated, because too much sugar in a formula can cause loose stools and too little may lead to constipation. By the second week of life, the full term neonate needs 110 to 150 kcal/kg daily to meet the maintenance and growth needs.[38]

Many mothers question the wisdom of giving an infant extra water, which supplies no calories for energy and growth. Some babies may need extra fluid, especially if the baby experiences physiological jaundice. Because of the low fluid intake of both bottle-fed and breast-fed infants, many experience a transitory fever between the second and third days of life. The temperature may rise to 100° or 101°F. Other symptoms of dehydration may be present, such as dry skin, flushing, marked weight loss, sunken fontanelles, and decreased urine output. These symptoms are readily remedied by increasing the fluid intake.

Output

The newborn frequently voids reflexively at birth when the body comes in contact with the cool air. This reaction persists for several months (to the frustration of the person who just changed a wet diaper!). Failure to void within 12 hours after birth calls for closer observation. An infant who fails to void within 24 hours should be checked carefully for congenital malformations or a health problem.

Stool Cycle

During fetal life, the infant swallows amniotic fluid. The water is absorbed into the infant's bloodstream, while the solid particles and nonabsorbable wastes are passed through the intestines. The swallowed fluid with its lanugo, skin cells, and vernix combines with the mucus, digestive secretions, indirect bilirubin, and bile pigments to form an odorless, dark green, thick, bowel movement known as **meconium.** The fetus routinely releases meconium into the amniotic fluid for the first 16 weeks. After 20 weeks, release of meconium would be considered pathological, occurring only when the fetus experiences physiological stress, such as hypoxia (inadequate oxygen).[1] Babies born in the breech position (buttocks first) or those who experience some distress during labor may pass meconium stool before or during the birth process. Most babies begin excretion of this bowel filler during the first 24 hours after birth. Occasionally, the first sticky movement is accompanied by a 2- to 5-cm, capsule-shaped, rubbery mass that is white or white and green in color, called a **meconium plug.**

Between 36 and 72 hours of life, the stool changes character as the meconium mixes with the milk. This **transitional stool** is lighter green, sticky, and rather watery and contains curds of undigested milk. Its passage is frequently accompanied by the explosive sounds of **flatus** (bowel gas).

After the first 3 to 4 days, the color and character of the stools depend on the type of milk the infant is fed. The yellow or golden stools of breast-fed babies have a slightly sour (generally nonoffensive) odor. At first, the breast-fed infant may have six to eight soft or loose stools per day because of the laxative effects of **colostrum,** the precursor to human milk. By 4 weeks of age, the breast-fed baby generally has only one or two stools per day; some breast-fed infants only defecate every other day.

The bottle-fed baby usually has lighter yellow stools, which are more formed than those of the breast-fed baby in spite of adequate fluid intake. The young formula-fed infant has about four to six (foul-smelling) stools per day. It is normal for the infant to flush, and strain or push, during a bowel movement. The infant should be evaluated for constipation if there is excessive effort and evidence of discomfort or passage of very dry, hard stools.

Regurgitation

Regurgitation, or spitting up milk, is a frequent occurrence in young infants. Almost all babies gag and vomit at least once during the first 36 hours because of mucus. Regurgitation frequently accompanies a burp or an air bubble released from the stomach. Even breast-fed babies swallow air while nursing and need to be "bubbled" well during and after each nursing. The baby should be held in an upright position and patted or rubbed *gently* on the back to facilitate relaxation of the cardiac sphincter of the stomach, which allows escape of the swallowed air (Fig. 5-1). Babies with weak cardiac sphincters tend to "spit up" between as well as after feedings.

Other common causes of regurgitation are over feeding, too much physical activity after feeding, or placement of the head lower than the stomach during or after feeding. The baby should be placed on the abdomen or right side after feeding to reduce the possibility of aspiration (inhalation) of the regurgitated milk. The infant who frequently vomits large amounts immediately after feedings should be medically evaluated even in the absence of other symptoms.

Genitourinary System

As mentioned previously, the stimulation of cold air frequently causes the infant to void. Urine output is only 1 to 4 mL/h during the first 24 hours, for a total of about 15 to 60 mL.[31] The output gradually increases to 8 or 10 voidings per 24 hours, amounting to a daily output of about 100 to 400 mL by 3 days of life. In the neonate, the bladder is an abdominal organ, since the pelvis is still too small to hold it. Occasionally, **uric acid crystals** found in concentrated urine may cause a

 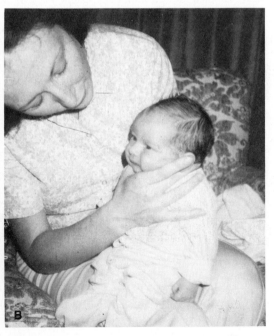

FIGURE 5–1.
Burping position. Elevating the baby's head off the shoulder facilitates release of air bubbles from the stomach after eating. (A) This baby is held over his grandmother's shoulder, a comfortable position for going to sleep. The baby's weight is supported at the buttocks, which frees the other hand to pat his back. (B) The lap position allows the mother to talk to the baby and to observe his responses during burping. The baby's weight is supported under the chin, with the heel of the hand on the baby's chest. The mother's other hand is used to pat or rub the baby's back.

rusty stain on the diaper during the first 2 days of life; these have no known significance.

The vaginal area of female babies is covered with a thin, bluish white mucus known as **smegma.** This mucus offers a protective coating for the tissues, which helps to prevent fungal and bacterial infections.

Testicles

The testes descend into the scrotum during the last months of fetal life. Therefore, the testes are palpable in the scrotal sac of 90% of full-term male infants, but only 70% of premature infants.[30] When the perineal area is cold, however, the scrotum wrinkles and becomes smaller because of muscular contractions. The testes may be drawn back and up into the inguinal canal. Testes that have not descended at birth usually descend within the next 3 months. If they have not descended by 1 year of age, the infant may need surgical assistance. Testicles that remain undescended until the pubertal years are incapable of producing viable sperm and experience an increased risk of cancer. Surgery is usually performed during the toddler years, because critical emotional overtones may arise when genital surgery is performed during the preschool or early school-age years.

Circumcision

Many parents choose to have their male infants circumcised. **Circumcision** (removal of the foreskin of the penis) has special religious significance to some parents.[24] Other parents have adopted the custom for its hygienic value to help prevent infections or to avoid the stigma of being different later in life, since most American parents in today's culture have their boys circumcised. Some parents look on it as a sign of manhood and want the child to "look like his daddy."[24] Many parents never really think about it, they just assume it is protocol for male infants. In 1975, the American Academy of Pediatrics found that *circumcision has no proven medical rationale* and, consequently, no longer endorses the practice.

Neuromuscular System

The integrity of the neurological system is generally evaluated in terms of its effect on the muscular activity of an infant; thus, the two are frequently approached as one system. The nervous and muscular systems of the newborn are extremely immature. As a result, the movements of the neonate appear to be uncoordinated and weak. Tremors of the extremities or the chin are normal at this stage of life and have no pathological significance; they merely reflect immature myelinization. Because the **myelin sheath** (which acts as insulation around nerves) is not yet complete, it is not unusual for the newborn to "short-circuit"; for instance, a touch on the foot may elicit a total body response; or opening of the eyes to better see an object may trigger opening of the mouth or even a yawn when the infant cannot voluntarily stop the opening process!

At birth, the brain is only one-fourth of its adult size.[30] The brain continues rapid hyperplastic as well as hypertrophic growth during the first 5 months of extrauterine life.

However, many more years elapse before the anatomical and physiological growth of the system is complete. There are marked differences in maturational rates between the genders. Neurologically, the female neonate is about 4 to 6 weeks more mature than the male. The maturational gap widens with age, females reaching terminal neurological and physical maturation at about 21 years and males at 24 years.[4] On the average, black infants have greater biological maturity at birth than white neonates.[48]

The normal full-term infant maintains some flexion in all four extremities. When held, the newborn should mold comfortably into the adult's arms or body contours. Movements should exhibit bilaterally equal strength and range of motion. A very tense or very flaccid baby should be evaluated for neurological problems.

Reflexes

Much of the newborn's physical behavior appears to be reflexive in nature. As the nervous system matures, these reflexes disappear and are replaced by more purposeful, directed, voluntary, and coordinated movements. The presence or the absence of these early reflexes is used to evaluate the health and developmental progress of an infant.

Moro Reflex

Moro reflex (also known as the **startle reflex**) is probably the most significant reflex in terms of evaluating the baby's neurological status. This reflex can be elicited in response to any sudden internal or external stimulus; it is also common during periods of sleep. The Moro reflex is characterized by a sudden stiffening of the body and legs accompanied by an outward thrust of the arms, followed by a rapid inward movement of the arms as if to embrace. The thumb and forefinger form the shape of a "C" (Fig. 5-2). The Moro response fre-

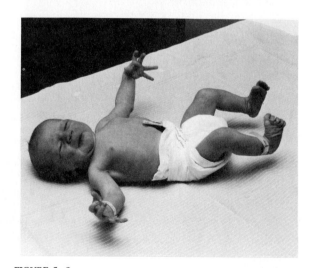

FIGURE 5–2.
The Moro reflex. The infant appears to be reaching outward as if to hook onto something to break a fall. Even legs, feet, and toes appear to be embracing. Note the clamped umbilical cord on this 15-hour-old baby.

quently is followed by crying. Absence of this reflex in the first 24 hours may be due to brain edema caused by the birth process and has no known clinical significance.[46] A lack of symmetry or a persistent absence of the Moro reflex is indicative of pathology and the need for medical evaluation. This reflex usually disappears by 5 months of age.[30]

Asymmetrical Tonic Neck Reflex (Fencing Position)
Turning of the head to the side while lying on the back causes the arm and leg on that side to straighten and stiffen and the opposite arm and leg to bend, causing the baby to assume a "fencing" position. If this reflex does not resolve by 4 months of age, motor coordination will be delayed (see Chap. 6).

Rooting Reflex
The rooting reflex was so named because the infant's behavior resembles that of a piglet hunting for roots. *When hungry, the baby moves the mouth or head in the direction of the cheek that is touched.* The baby often breathes rapidly and makes sucking noises with the lips. Mothers frequently push against the opposite cheek in an attempt to direct the baby's mouth toward the nipple; this behavior only counteracts the natural reflex of the infant and causes the infant to struggle to take hold of the mother's fingers with the mouth. This reflex can be made to work for the caregiver if one merely touches the cheek on the side to which the baby needs to turn. The rooting response may persist during sleep until 7 or 8 months of age.[25]

Sucking, swallowing, and gag reflexes are poorly coordinated at birth. Babies who are fed immediately after birth seem to catch on more quickly and have fewer coordination problems during the next 48 hours.

Palmar Grasp and Hand-to-Mouth Reflexes
The full-term newborn curls the fingers tightly around any small object placed in the palm of the hand. (The baby also curls the toes around an object, **planter grasp**). The **palmar grasp** is tight enough and can be held long enough to actually support the baby's body weight briefly (Fig. 5-3). This palmar grasp reflex is often combined with the **hand-to-mouth reflex,** which causes the baby to direct a curled-up hand to the mouth. When the infant's hand or an object touches the mouth, the rooting reflex is elicited; this in turn elicits the sucking reflex. This sequence of events can be seen even in the delivery room. It does not take long for the infant to perfect this sequence (or schema, to use Piaget's terminology). This pattern of behavior facilitates both learning and self-comforting. By the third day of life, the infant may have established a preference for sucking of thumb versus knuckle versus index or index and middle finger. Evidence indicates that thumb- and finger-sucking also occur in utero.[45]

Stepping and Crawling Reflexes
Whether held upright or lying on a flat surface, the baby makes **walking** movements when the soles of the feet touch an object (Fig. 5-4). This reflex disappears by 2 months of age

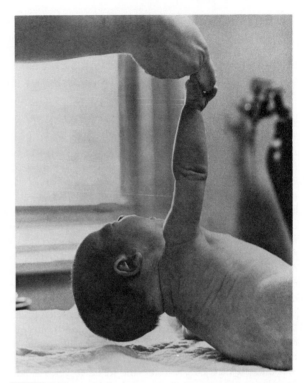
FIGURE 5–3.
Palmar grasp reflex.

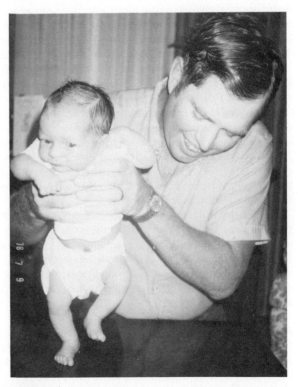
FIGURE 5–4.
Stepping reflex. Note the stump of the umbilical cord, which is still intact on this 7-day-old baby.

and reappears as purposeful, directed movement several months later. **Crawling** movements may be present when the baby is placed on the abdomen. These movements can actually propel the infant forward or backward and should be considered a safety hazard when the baby is placed on a flat surface.

Protective Reflexes

The newborn also has a wealth of protective reflexes. Initially the whole body may react (e.g., when the foot is pricked with a pin) because the nervous system cannot yet isolate the exact source of the irritant. The normal newborn soon conserves energy, however, and withdraws only the touched extremity if the procedure is repeated several times.[6] Bright lights, an object that zooms in, or a quick tap on the forehead causes the neonate to **blink** or shut the eyes tightly (**Glabellar** reflex). A firm touch on the eyelid causes the baby to squeeze the eyelids shut so tightly that it is almost impossible to force them open. If the head is face down and the airway is occluded, the healthy neonate turns the head to the side. Some experiments indicate that newborns hold their breath briefly if placed under water. A small cloth placed over the infant's face elicits batting motions of the hands and the fists to remove the offending object.[6]

Sudden bright lights cause the infant to release fluid from the tear ducts to protect the eyeball. The immature body does not yet know how much to release and consequently excretes more fluid than is necessary. The extra fluid trickles down the nasal passage where it may elicit the **sneeze reflex. Sneezing,** a method of clearing the nasal passages, is also elicited by attempts to look at an object and as such is not symptomatic of upper respiratory complications. Extra fluid on the eyeball helps the young infant to bring objects into focus (therefore, the infant in state 4 gives a bright, sparkly eyed appearance).

Yawning may be triggered when the infant cannot stop the process of mouth opening and opens its mouth too widely. **Hiccups** appear to be a reflection of an incompetent cardiac sphincter and immaturity of innervation to the diaphragm. Many mothers indicate that their babies experienced hiccuping even before birth. Giving the neonate a nipple to suck on frequently stops the symptoms.

The **baby doll reflex** is another phenomenon of neonates. In states 3, 4, and 5 (see Chap. 4), the infant often closes the eyes when horizontal and opens them when raised to a 30° vertical position. This reflex appears to be mediated by the vestibular response to positional change.[6] If this reflex persists beyond 3 months, however, it may indicate brain damage.[10]

Pain

Newborns frequently are not given an analgesic or anesthetic agent for circumcision or other invasive procedures, including surgery,[3] because it has been assumed that premature and newborn infants feel minimal or no pain,[16] or it was theorized that a high threshold to painful stimuli protected the infant from pain perception.[5] After observing the vigorous withdrawals and anguished cries of neonates to a simple heel stick or circumcision, some psychologists became concerned about the subconscious but potentially long-lasting negative impact of a circumcision or other painful procedure initiated to save the life of a high-risk neonate.[41]

Regardless of one's philosophical stance on consciousness in the neonate, it is increasingly evident that nociception (pain perception) is functional in the neonate. The density of nociceptive nerve endings is similar to or greater than that found in adult skin.[20] Nociceptive nerve tracts of the spinal cord, brain stem, central nervous system, and thalamus are completely myelinated (insulated) by the 30th week of gestation.[19] Plasma cortisol levels,[23] heart rates,[54] blood pressure,[33,35] and intracranial pressure[44] are all elevated when painful, invasive procedures are performed on premature or term infants without analgesia or anesthesia. Stress responses to pain are three to five times greater in the neonate than in the adult, even if the duration is short.[2] Neonates who have been circumcised without an analgesic show lower Brazelton Neonatal Behavioral Assessment scores for more than 22 hours[33] and greater irritability, reduced orientation, and reduced attention for 2 days.[12] Administration of an analgesic or anesthetic eliminates or reduces the physiological effects. "The evidence that nociceptive activity constitutes a physiologic stress in newborns is so overwhelming that physicians can no longer act as if infants were indifferent to pain."[16] Thus, "humane considerations should apply as forcefully to the care of neonates and young, nonverbal infants as they do to children and adults in similar painful and stressful situations."[2]

Awareness of the Environment

The neonate, far from being passive or unresponsive to the environment, is amazingly alert to a wide variety of stimuli. The alert, discerning professional can objectively identify and use for evaluative purposes many of these subtle but specific responses. The healthy newborn shows strong preference for specific stimuli and quickly adapts to new stimuli. The infant responds differentially to prolong contact with a pleasant stimulus or to avoid contact with an unpleasant stimulus.

Vision

Because of the neonate's aversion to bright lights and the presence of nystagmus, professionals thought for many years that newborns were essentially blind, except to distinguish light from dark. However, many mothers would say, even on the first day of life, that "the baby stares at me as if he knows I am the mother." These mothers were right, at least about the focusing of attention. The neonate is able to **fixate,** to zero in on an object visually. The infant consistently prefers complex patterns to simple patterns and curved lines to straight lines.[14] Sharply contrasting colors, black-white contrasts, and medium-bright lighted objects are also appealing to the neonate and elicit a prolonged fixation behavior.[13] The young infant often exhibits strabismus when trying to look at objects. If this condition persists through 3 months of age, the infant should

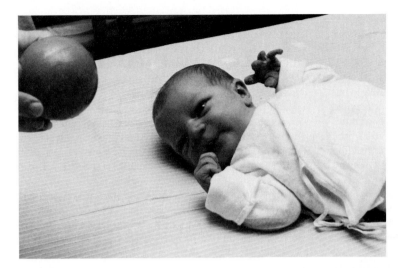

FIGURE 5–5.
Fixation. This 1-hour-old infant is able to look at and follow with her eyes and head movements the course of a small red ball held 7 to 10 inches away from her face.

be seen by a pediatric ophthalmologist, since the resulting double visual image may interfere with binocular vision, image making, depth perception, and optic system development.[43]

Within 5 minutes after birth, the quiet infant can see and visually follows a brightly colored object with his or her eyes. The infant even turns the head to track an object moved in a slow 180° arc 7 to 10 inches from the eyes (Fig. 5-5).[6,17] A narrow visual field (15° in infants as compared to 90° in adults, see Chap. 7)[51] and limited voluntary ocular movement ability forces the infant to turn its head to see objects and events.[34,43] Visual acuity is about 20/150 for objects 7 to 12 inches away, an amount adequate to perceive both form and color.[17] However, the infant's eyes are unable to accommodate well for distance, since most infants have a fixed focal length of about 19 cm (7½ inches).[7] Up to 10 weeks of age, distance vision is about 20/800; at 3 months, 20/200; by 1 year, 20/50.[43]

The infant prefers and visually follows the human face more readily than other stimuli. Even 7 to 10 minutes after birth, neonates who have never seen a human face (doctors and examiners were masked) consistently fixated and visually followed a pattern of a normal human face significantly more than scrambled facial patterns or a blank card.[21] These results indicate that visual discrimination is present at an early age, fixation and following is an unlearned ability, and there is an unlearned responsiveness to or innate bias toward the design of the human face. The infant also shows a marked preference for the unique pattern of the human face in the **en face position** (the position in which the adult's and infant's eyes are parallel to each other) (Fig. 5-6). In this position, the neonate maintains interest longer than when the adult's head is turned sideways to the infant. The adult's eyes appear to offer contrast points. Perhaps this preference is the reason why so many mothers instinctively assume the en face position when holding the newborn; the greater focusing attention elicited from the baby encourages the mother to maintain and repeat her behavior. When fixating, the infant stops or

reduces sucking, and quiets body movement, and elevates the eyelids, giving an alert, bright-eyed appearance. At birth, vision is not only a sensory system but a perceptual system as well.

Some neonates are noted to be able to imitate tongue protrusion or mouth opening when exhibited by an attentive adult.[26] The infant must be in state 4. The mechanisms by which this action occurs are not yet explained, since cognitive skills to process and imitate behavior are not believed to be accessible to the infant until about 8 months.[42]

Hearing

Elicitation of the Moro reflex or turning of the head in response to loud sounds indicates that the infant is able to hear within an hour after birth.[6,55] In states 2 and 3, the infant changes breathing patterns, grimaces, sucks the lips, or twitches an eyelid, which indicates an acute awareness of sounds in the environment. Infants show distinct preference for particular sounds. The sound of the human heart has a quieting effect (perhaps because of familiarity with a sound

FIGURE 5–6.
En face position. The mother aligns her face with the plane of the baby's face so that their eyes are parallel.

associated with intrauterine life). The neonate also appears to be predisposed to respond selectively to auditory stimuli (pattern, pitch, volume) that are embodied in human caregivers, especially females.[11] The newborn prefers and distinguishes higher-pitched sounds more readily than lower-pitched ones.[17] If one listens to a mother talk alternately to her baby and then to an older child or another adult, it is noted that the mother instinctively slows her speech, exaggerates her words, and elevates her vocal pitch when addressing the baby. In the middle of a sentence, she may turn to an adult in the room and, without a breath, suddenly drop her voice to a normal pitch; just as rapidly, she can reverse the sequence.

Many parents appear to have an insatiable desire to talk to their babies, especially to repeat the baby's name frequently, as if to connect the two, to reassure themselves of the reality of this new life in their care, to confirm the miracle. In state 4, the infant changes breathing patterns, widens the eyes, moves the mouth, and may even try to make vocal sounds. These subtle facial changes encourage parents to continue talking to their baby. Studies indicate that by 3 to 8 days of life the newborn responds differentially to the mother's voice repeating his or her name as opposed to other words or other voices repeating the name.[53] The crying infant is often soothed by the calm, directed human voice. Crying stops, and attempts are made to locate the source of comfort by turning the head and opening the eyes, another strong reinforcement to the caregiver to vocalize with the newborn.

Condon and Sander have discovered that neonates as young as 12 hours of age exhibit precise and sustained segments of movement that are synchronized with the adult's articulation of words and sentences.[9] Frame-by-frame microanalysis of audio-visual recordings of the infant's response (in state 4) to both taped and live adult vocalizations indicates an amazing correlation of the rhythm of the extremities, the eyes, and the mouth with the speed and the pitch of the adult's speech. Disconnected vowel sounds fail to show the same degree of correspondence that is elicited by natural rhythmic speech. Although the synchrony is often too subtle to pick up by merely observing the parent-child interaction, it is apparently this phenomenon that accounts for the mother's comment, "He acts as if he knows what I'm saying." Interactional synchrony may be evaluated in the future as a method of early identification of children with aphasia, autism, schizophrenia, and learning disabilities.

Taste and Smell

The neonate is able to differentiate among sweet, sour, and bitter tastes at birth.[34] The newborn shows a distinct preference for sugar water rather than plain water and for milk rather than sugar water. Studies indicate that breast-fed newborns are able to distinguish the odor of their mother's milk by the sixth day of life.[32] Breast-fed infants often respond differentially to the mother with an increased number of snuggling and rooting behaviors directed toward the mother versus other people, yet another reinforcement to the mother.

Touch

The newborn is sensitive to tactile stimulation. In fact, adequate physical contact is essential to optimal growth. A gentle, soothing touch helps the baby to relax, which leaves more energy available for growth purposes. Unpleasant stimuli, such as pain, cold, or a wet diaper, increase activity and energy expenditure, depleting the calories available for growth. Newborns are uncomfortable on a flat surface without support. Wrapping the baby comfortably in a blanket or turning the infant onto the abdomen (a position that gives more surface contact) appears to increase the feeling of security. The cuddled, touched, caressed infant usually responds by relaxation and snuggling behaviors. The lips appear to be particularly sensitive to touch, responding by smacking or sucking movements when touched. These behaviors usually cause the caregivers to repeat the touching activity.

Neonatal Assessment

Dr. T. Berry Brazelton has been a pioneer in recognizing the individuality of infants. He postulates that the neonate is not a *tabula rasa* at birth but, rather, a unique individual already possessing specific unlearned skills that are significant to fostering and shaping the parent-infant interaction.[39] To Dr. Brazelton, the infant's skill in organizing and controlling reflexes and reactions to both internal and external environments is as significant as the integrity of the nervous system. He evaluates the neonate's ability to quiet himself or herself when distressed, as well as the neonate's need for and attention to stimulation. The Brazelton Neonatal Behavioral Assessment Scale (BNBAS), reflecting a range of behavioral capacities of the normal full-term neonate, is based on a competency rather than a neurological deficit approach to assessment. The assessment evaluates the neonate's capacity to (1) organize his or her level of consciousness; (2) habituate his or her response to disturbing events; (3) attend to and process both simple and complex environmental stimuli; (4) control motor tone and activity while attending to stimuli; and (5) perform integrated motor behaviors.[6] The evaluation is relatively simple and quick to perform by both medical and nonmedical personnel trained in the assessment skills.

Brazelton postulates that the neonate's ability to selectively use different states of consciousness to maintain control of reactions is a reflection of the integrity of the central nervous system and of the infant's potential for self-organization. As such, this ability is a predictor of individual temperament and measures the baby's potential for response to the environment.

The baby's responses to visual, auditory, and tactile stimuli are "tools" for interacting with the environment. The infant uses crying, quieting behavior, gaze aversion, and searching behavior to indicate a need for more or less of the stimulus. The clearness and readability of these cues is important for a parent's response to the baby.[15] If a baby is fussy or has difficulty with state control, it may exert a negative influence and contribute to parent–infant stress. If the infant's cues are not read correctly, the parent may not be able to establish contingently responsive interactions with the baby.[15] The parent and infant may thus unilaterally or mutually fail to support the continuing development of the other.[50]

The Brazelton scale is a valuable parent teaching tool as well as an infant assessment tool.[18] It can be used to familiarize parents with their infant's unique qualities, facilitate synchronized communication, and relieve parents of the total responsibility for the interaction. If the baby is difficult to care for, this assessment tool, properly used, can provide insight into the baby's abilities, thus offering guidance for the parents, enabling them to interact positively with the child despite poor or weak infant communication skills.

COMMON VARIATIONS

Some characteristics are peculiar to the newborn period of life. If parents are unprepared for these unique but common variations, they may become unduly concerned about the infant's health in terms of both present survival and future functioning. The mother's perception of her infant's health can be intimately intertwined with her concept of personal adequacy both as a woman and as a mother. Parents who fear that the child will die or will be retarded may not be able to express joy and spontaneity in interacting with the baby. They may withdraw to protect themselves from the pain of loss they are sure will come. A simple explanation is often all that is needed to help them to experience the joy of parenthood that is rightfully theirs.

One mother of healthy premature twins refused to visit the nursery and spent hours crying in her hospital room. A concerned student nurse helped her to express what she was feeling and the reason for her behavior. To everyone's amazement, the mother believed that all premature babies were retarded—and that now she had two retarded children! Within half an hour she was smiling, asking to see her babies, and helping to feed them. Knowledge of the normalcy of common characteristics of newborns can allay many parental anxieties and thus enhance the parent-infant relationship.

Birth Traumas

Some characteristics are a direct result of the stressors experienced during birth. Swelling of the presenting part due to **edema** (fluid in the tissues) and **bruises** (resulting from breakage of the fine blood vessels) are to be expected.

Caput succedaneum is a swelling of the soft tissues of the scalp. The scalp becomes a soft, boggy mass that causes an elongated appearance of the head. The swelling is not limited to the suture lines. Tissue fluid that is present at birth or shortly thereafter is absorbed by 1 to 3 days of age (Fig. 5-7A).

Molding, or the reshaping of the infant's head, occurs as the head accommodates to the size of the birth passage during stage 2 of labor. The repositioning and overriding of the bony plates of the cranium cause a temporary asymmetry of the infant's head (Fig. 5-8). A normal round shape is usually regained within 72 hours, although overriding may occasionally be found in a 2-week-old baby. Molding does not cause brain damage.

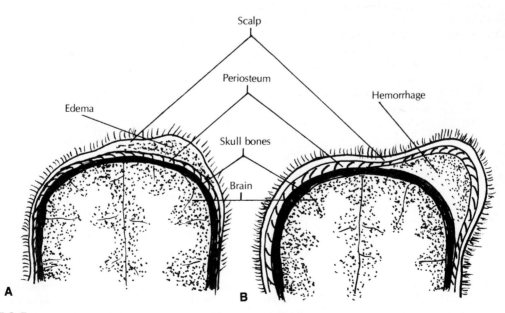

FIGURE 5–7.
(A) Caput succedaneum: swelling of the soft tissues of the scalp. (B) Cephalhematoma: bleeding under the periosteum, causing it to separate from the bony plate.

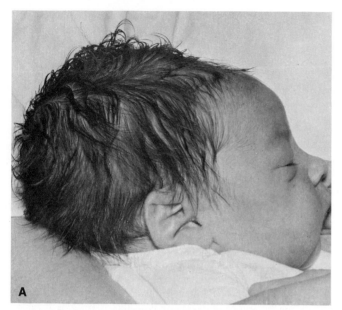

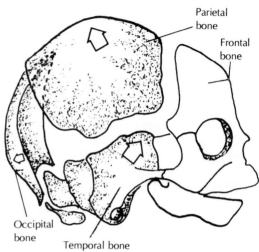

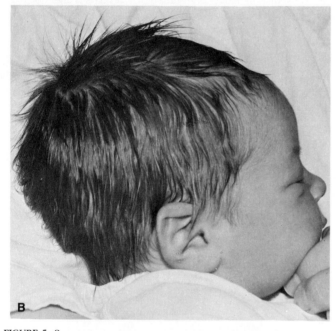

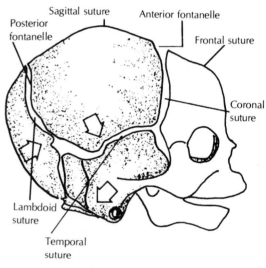

FIGURE 5–8.

Molding. (A) Elongation of the head immediately after birth due to the pressures of the birth process. (B) The same baby 24 hours later; the elongation has receded considerably, and the head has assumed a more rounded shape. (Ziegel, E., & Cranley, M.S. (1978). Obstetric nursing *(7th ed.). New York: Macmillan. With permission.) (C) Overlapping and movement of the cranial bones during molding. (D) Return of the bony plates to normal positions.*

Bruising and **abrasions** are frequently seen on the head and the cheeks. They may be associated with the use of forceps but also may be caused by tightness of the birth passage.

Petechiae (small, nonraised, irregular, round, purplish red hemorrhage spots) are frequently found on the face or

scalp (or on the buttocks of breech-born babies). These spots are caused by breakage of the tiny skin vessels when the cervix tightens around the presenting part. Petechiae usually disappear between 3 and 7 days of life.

Subconjunctival hemorrhage may be found in both the mother (as a result of straining during labor) and the infant. The crescent-shaped red patches in the sclera adjacent to the iris are caused by the breakage of vessels on the surface of the eye due to the pressure of the birth process. These hemorrhagic areas may turn brown or yellow before being absorbed spontaneously about 3 weeks after birth. This phenomenon has no clinical significance, and parents can be assured that it does not cause blindness or other visual problems.

Cephalhematoma, which occurs in about 1% to 2% of deliveries,[32] is often not apparent until several hours to several days after birth. The pressure of the head against the bony parts of the birth passage can cause a loosening of the periosteum (membrane that covers a bone) from one of the bony plates of the cranial vault. This separation causes a breakage of the capillaries with subsequent bleeding. The blood collects between the bony plate and the periosteum, causing a gradually increasing bulge on the scalp. The bleeding is limited to the surface of the specific bone (or bones) involved; therefore, the swelling does not cross the suture line. Since the bleeding is on the outer surface of the bony plate, no pressure is placed on the infant's brain. Most of these "blood blisters" are gradually absorbed without treatment by 6 weeks of age; in rare instances, they may calcify and become a small but permanent nodule under the scalp. Mothers should be encouraged not to touch the area unnecessarily and to protect it from further injury (see Fig. 5-7B).

Hormonal Influences

During intrauterine life, maternal hormones cross the placental barrier and influence the infant's development. After birth, their presence and withdrawal can cause transient symptoms that are not clinically significant.

Engorgement of the breasts may be found in both male and female infants (Fig. 5-9). This enlargement, caused by maternal estrogen, may last several weeks. During the first weeks of life, babies of both genders have a small amount of

fluid in the breast, known as **witch's milk.**[8] Eighty percent of these infants may actually secrete some of the fluid.[30] Gentle, regular body cleaning is all the care that is needed. Attempts to extract the fluid can cause infection.

Genital hypertrophy is found in both sexes, but especially in female babies. It may be particularly pronounced when combined with the edema that accompanies a breech birth. This swelling also recedes in a few weeks.

During fetal life, high estrogen levels cause hypertrophy of the endometrial lining of the female infant's uterus. At birth, a decline in estrogen levels causes disintegration of the endometrial tissue, simulating the process found in mature females. This **pseudomenstruation** causes small to moderate amounts of blood to stain the smegma between the third and fifth days of life. Parents of female infants should be advised of this phenomenon.

Skin Markings

History and folklore offer many stories surrounding the presence or appearance of birthmarks; tales are told of inheritances and kingdoms won or lost on the basis of a skin marking. Some marks do appear to be genetically determined, but most are merely quirks of nature.

The common **birthmark** (pigmented nevus) is usually a single small brown area. It may be slightly elevated and may even have tufts of hair. Since it is a permanent marking and may appear on any body surface, the parents may wish to have the nevus removed for cosmetic purposes; otherwise it has no clinical significance.

Freckles—multiple, small, flat patches of darker-colored skin—are rarely found on infants. Most tend to appear later in life, especially after exposure to sunlight, a factor which darkens skin pigments.

Mongolian spots are nonelevated blue colorations found over the buttocks and occasionally on the back and outer surfaces of the legs, arms, hands, or feet of babies with Indian, Mediterranean, Oriental, Spanish, or Negroid ancestry. Since the appearance is similar to that of severe bruises, it is essential to tell the parents about this birthmark. Difficult situations have arisen from fathers who have accused mothers (or vice versa) of child abuse because of the coloration. Mongolian spots, even when severe, generally disappear by the time the child is 5 years old.

Capillary hemangiomas are caused by hyperplastic development of blood vessels; they may be apparent at birth or may appear several months later. Except for the true nevus flammeus, they disappear spontaneously with age. Four types of hemangiomas are commonly found in infants:

1. A **stork bite** (pseudo nevus flammeus) is a flat, pinkish purple coloration found on the midline of the face, usually on the nasal bridge, the upper lip, or the eyelids. Many infants also have stork bite marks on the back of the neck just above the hair line. This mark becomes brightly colored when the infant cries. Mothers and fathers are

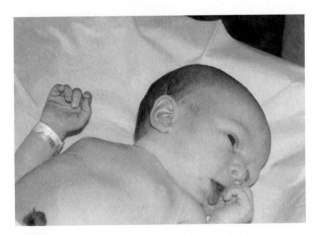

FIGURE 5—9.
Engorgement of the breasts of a two-day old infant.

reassured to know that the marks (except those on the nape of the neck) tend to fade after 8 months of age.

2. A **port-wine stain** (true nevus flammeus) is a flat, irregularly shaped, red to deep purple mark found unilaterally on the face or other parts of the body. The mature nature of the capillaries prevents blanching of the skin when pressed, and spontaneous disappearance does not occur with age. The area covered remains stable as the child ages. The parents may be so upset by the infant's appearance that a normal parent–child relationship may be difficult; they can be assured that cosmetic preparations and surgery are available. Argon laser beam surgery is also successful in reducing the skin color.[29]

3. A **strawberry mark** (nevus vasculosus) may or may not be present at birth. The immature capillaries usually become apparent by 4 weeks of age. Any surface of the body may be affected, although the face and neck are the most common targets. Strawberry marks begin to enlarge rapidly once they appear. They are named for their red elevated appearance. Nevi vasculosi continue to increase in size and color for about 8 to 10 months, leading some parents to fear the child has a skin cancer. They begin to recede spontaneously around the age of 1 year; most disappear by 3 years of age (Fig. 5-10). More extensive strawberry marks, however, may take 5 to 8 or even 10 years to resolve completely. Treatment is unnecessary unless the growth interferes with vital functioning (e.g., if it presses against the trachea).

4. **Cavernous hemangioma** is a rare phenomenon that consists of a meshwork of vessels located in the subcutaneous tissue. A large sinus within the birthmark causes the area to become enlarged and boggy. The skin surface may be neutral or red, depending on the presence or absence of an overlying strawberry nevus or port-wine stain. Extremely rapid growth or bleeding occasionally necessitates surgical removal; otherwise, spontaneous gradual involution can be expected after 8 months of age.

Other Variations

Erythema toxicum neonatorum (newborn rash) mimics the symptoms of a skin infection or allergy. Small red blotches, often with hivelike centers, spread rapidly over the body, and just as rapidly disappear. The cause of this rash is not known; some feel it may be the result of contact of the tender, sensitive skin with the harsh fabrics of clothing and bedding. Symptoms may continue to appear during the first month of life.

    Milia pinpoint white spots across the infant's nose, chin, and forehead, are caused by retention of secretions in the ducts of immature sebaceous glands. It is imperative not to squeeze them. Milia disappear spontaneously in 2 to 4 weeks as the glands mature.

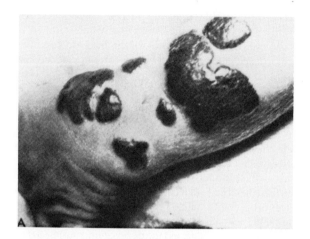

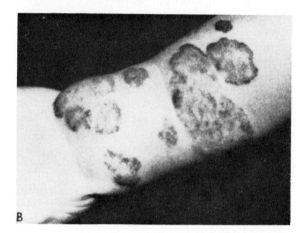

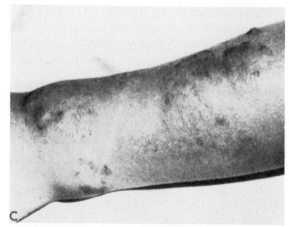

FIGURE 5–10.
The spontaneous progressive involution of a severe strawberry hemangioma. Some mild cavernous hemangioma may be seen. (A) age 6 weeks; (B) age 8 months; (C) age 2 years. (Burgoon, C. F., Jr. (1975). The skin. In V. C. Vaughan & R. J. McKay (Eds.), Nelson textbook of pediatrics (10th ed.). Philadelphia: WB Saunders. With permission.

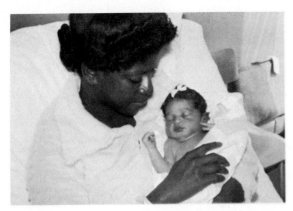

FIGURE 5-11.
This mother and daughter exemplify the pigmentation differences that are evident in newborns of dark-skinned parents.

Epstein's pearls, hard accumulations of epithelial cells on the gum line or over the posterior portion of the hard palate, are present in about 50% of newborns. They disappear spontaneously within a few weeks of birth.

Hymenal tags are frequently found on female infants. They are of no clinical significance and usually fall off by 1 month of age.[36]

Intrauterine molding is the result of prenatal positioning. Pressure of body parts against each other prevents the accumulation of body fat, creating misshapen body parts (face, arms, legs). Although the appearance may resemble a congenital defect, the form corrects itself within the first 4 to 6 months of life.

Babies of dark-skinned parents are usually born with light **skin color**; the pigmentation then darkens over the next 2 to 6 days and continues to darken gradually over the next year. The darker skin found around the navel, genitalia, nail beds, and ear lobes gives some indication of future coloration during childhood and adult years (Fig. 5-11).

CONCLUSION

Newborn infants share many common physiological characteristics. However, variations in both physical appearance and ability to attend to the environment make each newborn unique from the start. Many phenomena, although transient in nature, may mimic serious congenital defects. A thorough understanding of the causes and courses of particular characteristics can allay the practitioner's or parents' anxiety.

The newborn is far from a passive piece of clay to be molded by the environment. During the newborn period, temperamental and interactional differences are clearly apparent. Although the five domains are primitive at this point, the infant is able to skillfully intertwine his or her biological, emotional, social, spiritual, and cognitive domains into behaviors that enhance interaction with the caregiver.

Students who are interested in further exploration of this period of life are encouraged to take a course in neonatology.

REFERENCES

1. Abramovich, D. R., & Gray, E. S. (1982). Physiologic fetal defecation in midpregnancy. *Obstetrics and Gynecology, 60,* 294.
2. Anand, K. J. S. (1986). Hormonal and metabolic functions of neonates and infants undergoing surgery. *Current Opinions in Cardiology, 1,* 681–689.
3. Anand, K. J. S., Phil, D., & Hickey, P. R. (1987). Pain and its effects in the human neonate and fetus. *New England Journal of Medicine, 317,* 1321–1329.
4. Arganian, M. (1973). Sex differences in early development. In J. C. Westman (Ed.), *Individual differences in children.* New York: Wiley.
5. Bondy, A. S. (1980). Infancy. In S. Gabel & M. T. Erikson (Eds.), *Child development and developmental disabilities* (pp. 3–19). Boston: Little, Brown.
6. Brazelton, T. B. (1973). Neonatal Behavioral Assessment Scale. In *Clinics in Developmental Medicine,* No. 50. Philadelphia: J. B. Lippincott.
7. Brazelton, T. B. (1981). Behavioral competence of the newborn infant. In G. B. Avery (Ed.), *Neonatology: Pathophysiology and management of the newborn* (2nd ed.). Philadelphia: J. B. Lippincott.
8. Buehring, G. C. (1982). Witch's milk: Potential for neonatal diagnosis. *Pediatric Research, 16,* 460.
9. Condon, W. S., & Sander, L. W. (1974). Neonate movement is synchronized with adult speech: Interactional participation and language acquisition. *Science, 183*(4120), 99.
10. Cratty, B. J. (1986). *Perceptual and motor development in infants and children* (3rd ed.). Englewood Cliffs, NJ: Prentice-Hall.
11. D'apolito, K. (1984). The neonate's response to pain. *MCN: The American Journal of Maternal/Child Nursing, 9,* 256.
12. Dixon, S., Snyder, J., Holve, R., & Bromberger, P. (1984). Behavioral effects of circumcision with and without anesthesia. *Journal of Developmental Behavior in Pediatrics, 5,* 246–250.
13. Eisenberg, R. B. (1978). Stimulus significance as a determinant of infant responses to sound. In E. B. Thoman & S. Trotter (Eds.), *Social responsiveness of infants.* New Brunswick, NJ: Johnson & Johnson Baby Products Company.
14. Fantz, R. L. (1958). Pattern vision in young infants. *Psychological Record, 8,* 43.
15. Field, T. M. (1979). Interactional patterns of pre-term and term infants. In T. M. Field (Ed.), *Infants born at risk: Behavior and development.* New York: S.P. Medical and Scientific Books.
16. Fletcher, A. B. (1987). Pain in the neonate. *New England Journal of Medicine, 317,* 1347–1348.
17. Freedman, D. G. (1974). *Human Infancy: An evolutionary perspective.* New York: Halsted Press.
18. Gibes, R. M. (1981). Clinical uses of the Brazelton Neonatal Behavioral Assessment Scale in nursing practice. *Pediatric Nursing, 7*(3), 23.
19. Gillies, F. J., Shankle, W., & Dooling, E. C. (1983). Myelinated tracts: Growth patterns. In F. H. Gilles, A. Leviton, & E. C. Dooling (Eds), *The developing human brain: Growth and epidemiologic neuropathology* (pp. 117–183). Boston: John Wright.
20. Gleiss, J. (1970). Morphologic and functional development of the skin. In U. Stave (Ed.), *Physiology of the perinatal period* (vol. 2;, pp. 889–906). New York: Appleton-Century-Crofts.
21. Goren, C. C., et al. (1975). Visual following and pattern discrimination of face-like stimuli by newborn infants. *Pediatrics, 56,* 544.

22. Grams, K. E. (1978). Breast-feeding: A means of imparting immunity. *MCN: The American Journal of Maternal/Child Nursing, 3,* 340.

23. Gunnar, M. R., Fisch, R. O., Korsvik, S., & Donhowe, J. M. (1981). The effects of circumcision on serum cortisol and behavior. *Psychoneuroendocrinology, 6,* 269–275.

24. Harris, C. C. (1986). Cultural values and the decision to circumcise. *Image: Journal of Nursing Scholarship, 18*(3), 98–104.

25. Haynes, U. (1967). *A development approach to casefinding, with special reference to cerebral palsy, mental retardation, and related disorders.* Washington, DC: U.S. Department of Health, Education and Welfare, Children Bureau.

26. Heimann, M., & Schaller, J. (1985). Imitative reactions among 14–21 day old infants. *Infant Mental Health, 6*(1), 31–39.

27. Klaus, M. H., & Kennell, J. H. (1976). *Maternal-infant bonding: The impact of early separation or loss on family development.* St. Louis: C. V. Mosby.

28. La Lache League International. (1987). *The womanly art of breastfeeding* (4th rev. ed.). Franklin Park, IL: La Lache League International.

29. Larrow, L., & Noe, J. M. (1982). Port wine stain hemangiomas. *American Journal of Nursing, 82,* 786.

30. Lowrey, G. H. (1986). *Growth and development of children* (8th ed.). Chicago: Year Book.

31. Lynch, T. M. (1986). Cardiovascular conditions in the newborn. In N. S. Streeter (Ed.), *High-risk neonatal care* (pp. 163–227). Rockville, MD: Aspen.

32. MacFarland, A. (1975). Olfaction in the development of social preferences in the human neonate. In *Ciba Foundation Symposium (New Series) 33: Parent-Infant Interaction.* New York: *Elsevier.*

33. Marshall, T. A., Deeder, R., Pai, S., Berkowitz, G. P., & Austin, T. L. (1984). Physiologic changes associated with endotracheal intubation in preterm infants. *Critical Care Medicine, 12,* 501–503.

34. Maurer, D., & Maurer, C. (1988). *The world of the newborn.* New York: Basic Books.

35. Maxwell, L. G., Yaster, M., & Wetzel, R. C. (1986). Penile nerve block reduces the physiologic stress of new born circumcision. *Anesthesiology, 65,* A432.

36. McKilligin, H. R. (1970). *The first day of life: Principles of neonatal nursing.* New York: Springer Publishing Co.

37. Meier, P., & Anderson, G. C. (1987). Responses of small preterm infants to bottle- and breast-feeding. *MCN: The American Journal of Maternal/Child Nursing, 12,* 97–105.

38. Moyer-Mileur, L. J. (1986). Nutrition. In N. S. Streeter (Ed.), *High-risk neonatal care* (pp. 263–295). Rockville, MD: Aspen.

39. Nugent, J. K. (1981). The Brazelton Neonatal Behavioral Assessment Scale: Implications for intervention. *Pediatric Nursing, 7*(3), 118.

40. Ogra, P. L., & Greene, H. L. (1982). Human milk and breast feeding: An update on the state of the art. *Pediatric Research, 16,* 266.

41. Owens, M. E. (1984). Pain in infancy: Conceptual and methodological issues. *Pain, 20,* 213–230.

42. Piaget, J. (1962). *Play, dreams and imitation in childhood* (C. Gattengo & F. M. Hodgson, Trans.). New York: Norton.

43. Pushkar, R. G. (1988, March). What baby sees. *Parents Magazine,* pp. 90–94.

44. Raju, T. N. K., Vidyasagar, D., Torres, C., Grundy, D., & Bennett, E. J. (1980). Intracranial pressure during intubation and anesthesia in infants. *Journal of Pediatrics, 96,* 860–862.

45. Rugh, R., & Shettles, L. B. (1971). *From conception to birth: The drama of life's beginnings.* New York: Harper and Row.

46. Scipien, G. M., Barnard, M. V., Chard, M. A., Howe, J., & Phillips, P. J. (Eds.). (1986). *Comprehensive pediatric nursing* (3rd ed.). New York: McGraw-Hill.

47. Shiono, P. H., Klebanoff, M. A., Graubard, B. I., Berendes, H. W., & Rhoads, G. G. (1986). Birth weight among women of different ethnic groups. *Journal of the American Medical Association, 255,* 48–52.

48. Tanner, J. M. (1989). *Foetus into man: Physical growth from conception to maturity* (rev. ed.). Ware, Herts, UK: Castlemead.

49. Taylor, L. S. (1981). Newborn feeding behaviors and attaching. *MCN: The American Journal of Maternal/Child Nursing, 6,* 201.

50. Thoman, E. B. (1979). *Disruption and asynchrony in early parent-infant interactions.* Storrs, CT: University of Connecticut. (ERIC Document Reproduction Service No. ED 180 140).

51. Tronick, E. (1972). Stimulus control and the growth of the infant's effective visual field. *Perception and Psychophysics, 11,* 373–376.

52. Unger, C., Weiser, J. K., McCullough, R. E., Keefer, S., & Moore, L. G. (1988). Altitude, low birth weight, and infant mortality in Colorado. *Journal of the American Medical Association, 259, 3427–3432.*

53. Vaughan, V. C., & Brazelton, T. B. (Eds.). (1976). *The family: Can it be saved?* Chicago: Year Book.

54. Williamson, P. S., & Williamson, M. L. (1983). Physiological stress reduction by a local anesthetic during newborn circumcision. *Pediatrics, 71,* 36–40.

55. Wolff, P. H. (1973). Observations on newborn infants. In L. J. Stone, H. T. Smith, & L. B. Murphy (Eds.), *The competent infant: Research and commentary.* New York: Basic Books, 257–268.

III INFANCY

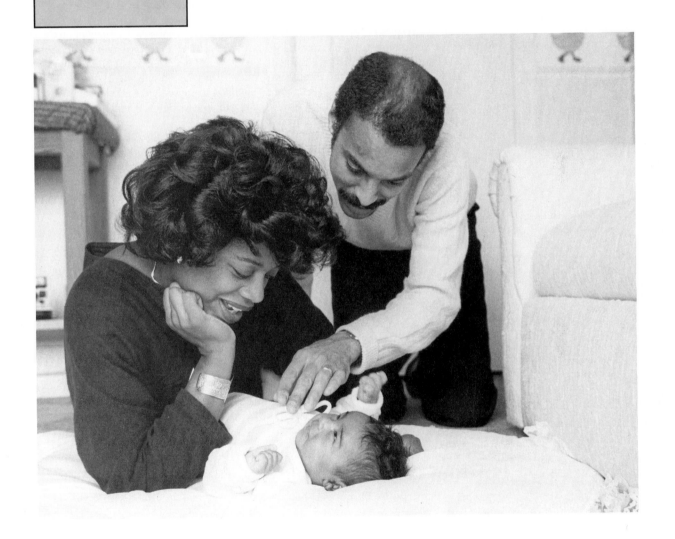

The 12 to 15 months of infancy have a charm unmatched by other periods of life. However, these months are more than a "holding period," waiting for the child to mature sufficiently to become a "little person." The skills learned during these few months are critical to later development. The infant is far from dependent. Even the young infant is able to signal to the caregiver the need for food and feelings of discomfort, interest, and delight. These behaviors influence the behaviors of the caregiver, and thus help to establish the milieu essential for emotional, intellectual, and social growth.

Although the neonate is well-equipped to attend to and influence the environment, continued growth and development are dependent on the caregiver's consistent ability to respond contingently to the infant's cues. This consistency engenders trust in the environment and enables the infant to predict that a response will occur. From this synchronized interaction emerge three important developments: (1) the child's ability to "fall in love" with the parent (comfort with the person who is positive, supportive, and predictable), (2) heightened attention to cause–effect relationships (attempts to make an event happen at will, and simple experiments), and (3) initiation of attempts to communicate with others.

On these three factors rests the quality of development throughout life. Although multiple factors intervene between infancy and adulthood, it is very difficult to correct serious deficits incurred during this period of life, especially if the first three tasks are not adequately mastered.

Developmental Tasks of Infancy

*1. Establish a meaningful emotional/social relationship:
    recognize primary caregivers
    develop trust in caregivers
    develop attachment behaviors
    evolve refueling skills

*2. Learn how to learn:
    orient to objects and stimuli
    activate curiosity
    evolve exploration skills
    attend to details
    predict and practice obtaining responses from
        the environment (animate and inanimate)
    synthesize/integrate input from modalities/senses

*3. Develop social communication skills:
    develop vocalization skills
    recognize social signals of others
    participate in synchronized vocal reciprocity and
        social turntaking activities/games
    initiate interactions with others
    develop nonverbal forms of communication
    imitate simple vocal and social behaviors of
        others

4. Develop voluntary control of neuromuscular systems:
    antigravitational skills
    eye–hand coordination
    object manipulation
    balance responses
    mobility

5. Establish rhythms for activities of daily living:
    eating
    sleeping
    elimination

6. Recognize self as a person, physically separate from attachment person:
    engage in physical exploration and comparison
    experiment with separation and reunion experiences
    begin to understand and trust own sensations
    begin to see self as capable of meeting own
        needs, e.g.:
        positioning comfort
        self-comforting skills
        obtaining objects
        feeding self

---

*Tasks deemed most crucial to continued maturation are marked with an asterisk.

6

...I look upon your creation in amazement For we are indeed fearfully and wonderfully made All its secret, silent machinery— the meshing and churning— what a miracle of design.

—ALTON OCHSNER

Biophysical Development During Infancy

Shirley S. Ashburn

Parents rarely need reminding to take pictures of their fast-growing babies, especially during the first 15 months, when so many physical changes are apparent. The average baby grows about 1 inch per month in length for the first 6 months and increases in length by about 50% by the end of the first year.[27] Weight gain is usually considered to be an indication of satisfactory growth progress and is probably the best index of nutrition and growth. The average baby gains almost 2 pounds per month, or nearly 1 ounce per day for the first 3 months of life.[27] Caregivers should not weigh their babies daily because minimal fluctuations in the baby's weight may cause them to falsely perceive a health problem. Most babies double their birth weight by 5 months. After 6 months, the baby's weight gain decreases to about 1 pound per month. Birth weight often triples by the end of the first year. Parents may become overly concerned during the second year when the monthly increment slows to $1/2$ pound.[27]

Growth charts indicate **average** physiological parameters (see Appendices D and E), but **individual** children should be evaluated in terms of health, race, gender, genetic, and environmental factors. Premature infants, for example, generally weigh less than the norms for their age because they are actually younger than the full-term infants on whom the norms are based. Children born prematurely, without significant health problems, usually catch up in height and weight to their age peers by the time they enter school.[13, 27, 36] Weight measurements for an individual baby usually fall within the same percentile group at sequential ages or change only gradually from one period to another. Although a baby's height and weight often differ in their actual percentile positions, they tend to keep the same general relationships over time. Babies and children whose height and weight measurements fall close to, or outside of, the 5th and 95th percentiles should be seen by a health professional to rule out growth abnormalities.

SOMATIC DEVELOPMENT

The tissues that compose the muscular and skeletal systems provide structure and allow movement of the infant's rapidly growing body.

Skeletal System

Bone development follows well-defined steps. In general, connective tissue becomes cartilage and then gradually is replaced by bone.[27] Ossification (bone formation) is explained in more detail in Chapter 20, but it is important to emphasize here that except for the bones of the face, cranium, and the shaft centers of long bones (which are ossified during fetal life), all other bony structures undergo gradual hardening *after* birth.[27] If this immature soft bone is subjected to trauma, "greenstick" or incomplete fractures may result. Fortunately, rapidly growing bones heal quickly. While ossification is occurring, bones continue to grow in length and width and consequently change in shape. Racial and gender variations are apparent. Black children show more rapid maturation than white children; the bones of girls usually grow and mature faster than those of boys.[27, 42]

Muscular System

During infancy, muscular growth is due mainly to hypertrophic growth of the already formed muscle fibers, although some hyperplastic growth continues. Of the three types of muscle tissue—voluntary (striated), involuntary (smooth), and cardiac (heart)—the voluntary muscles comprise the bulk of body weight at birth. The growth rate of muscle is about twice as fast as that of bone during the period of time from 5 months to 3 years. During these early years, pituitary growth hormone, thyroid hormones, and insulin all play a role in the growth of muscle tissue. As a muscle grows in size, its strength should increase if adequately exercised. Play activities are critical for developing the potentials of the baby's motor functioning (Fig. 6-1). Table 6-1 summarizes the average age at which major gross motor (large muscle) and fine motor (small muscle) activities are attained by infants. The speed of an individual baby's development may differ slightly from the average yet still be healthy. Although cross-cultural studies illustrate variability of motor development in young children, it is difficult to determine which differences are primarily related to environmental factors (e.g., nutrition, child-rearing practices) and which are due to genetic factors.[15, 20] The sequence of motor skill development is more critical than the specific age of its emergence. Children who "skip a stage" frequently experience motor refinement prob-

FIGURE 6–1.
Toy gyms encourage reaching, stretching, and the development of eye–hand coordination in young babies.

lems later in development. For example, babies need a prolonged crawling experience to strengthen the shoulder girdle muscles. Children frequently experience difficulty with fine motor development (e.g., ball throwing accuracy and writing skills) if the muscles are not strong enough to stabilize the shoulder joint when using the arm. Therefore, *parents should encourage the baby to crawl as long as possible* rather than encourage early walking.

Neurological System

The human nervous system consists of two major components: the **central nervous system** (CNS) and the **peripheral nervous system.** The CNS, composed of the brain and the spinal cord, orchestrates control of all body functions. The peripheral nervous system consists of the *autonomic (involuntary)* and *somatic (voluntary) nervous systems,* both of which carry impulses to and from the CNS. Nerve impulses transmitted by the autonomic nervous system control the smooth muscles of the body's internal organs (e.g., heart, liver, kidneys) without conscious control. The somatic nervous system transmits impulses to and from the brain through the spinal cord to the voluntary muscles of the body. *Afferent (or sensory) nerves,* carry information (e.g., vision, pressure, taste, pain) to the CNS, and *efferent (or motor) nerves,* carry movement message impulses from the CNS to muscle groups.

Nearly one-half of the brain's postnatal growth is achieved by the end of the first year.[27] Most of the growth in size occurs in the *cerebral cortex* (the outer layer of the cerebrum), which is associated with sensory perception, motor functioning, speech, and cognitive activities (such as processing, organizing, storing, and retrieving information). The *brain stem,* located at the base of the brain, is relatively well developed at birth compared to the other structures of the CNS. The brain stem primarily controls survival functions (such as temperature control, respiration, digestion, and heart rate) and the other activities of the autonomic nervous system. These vital functions continue to be irregular through the early months of infancy, indicating that brain stem development is incomplete. The *cerebellum,* located behind the brain stem, shows an increase in weight throughout the first decade.[27] The cerebellum coordinates movement and equilibrium.

Head Circumference

During infancy the head grows at a relatively rapid rate. Skull growth closely parallels brain growth. The measurement of head circumference and the assessment of fontanelle status are ways to monitor this growth. The head circumference increases from an average of 34 cm (approximately 13 1/2 inches) at birth to 44 cm by 6 months, and to 47 cm by 1 year.[6] The posterior fontanelle closes during the third month of extrauterine life. The anterior fontanelle may increase in size until the baby is 6 months old; then it begins to diminish and is closed by 18 months.

TABLE 6-1. NEUROMOTOR DEVELOPMENT DURING INFANCY

	Gross Motor Skills	*Fine Motor Skills*
1 MONTH	Head lags when baby is pulled from a supine to a sitting position. When prone, baby may lift head occasionally, but unsteadily. Will turn head from side to side. Will make crawling movements when prone. Is able to push feet against a bare surface to propel self forward. Assymetrical tonic neck reflex (ATNR) present. Moves arms asymmetrically. Dancing or stepping reflex when held upright. Symmetrical Moro reflex.	Hands are held predominantly in fists. Demonstrates a tight reflex grasp. Head and eyes move together. Rooting and sucking reflexes present. Follows persons with eyes and head.
2 MONTHS	Head righting reactions emerging (tonic labyrinthine reaction) but not strong enough to keep head upright in sitting position. When prone, can lift head and chest off firm surfaces to 45°. Kicks feet alternately. Rolls from side to back.	Hands begin to open. May hold a toy placed in hand for a brief time. Uses *primitive palmar grasp* (ie, grasps objects with finger and palm of hand, with no thumb opposition). Hand to mouth activity. Good visual regard. Follows movements of objects with eyes from side to midline. Social smiling in response to various stimuli.
3 MONTHS	When prone, lifts head to 90° when propped on forearms. Stepping and crawling reflexes absent. When supported, sits with rounded back and flexed knees, leaning forward. Holds head at midline. May roll from front to back. ATNR reflex disappearing as the STNR reflex appears.	Brings hands to midline. Bats at and reaches toward bright objects with one arm, but will obtain them only by chance. Is able to carry an object from hand to mouth. When supine, moves eyes and turns head 180° to follow moving object or person. Follows with eyes past midline. Looks from one object to another. Grasping, rooting, and sucking reflexes begin to fade.
4 MONTHS	Symmetrical arm and leg movements and posture. Hands to knees. Head midline. Strong head-righting reactions. Rolls from back to side. Bears weight briefly when held upright. Will sit upright if supported at hips. No head lag when pulled to sit. Moro reflex disappearing.	Hands held predominantly open. Spreads fingers to grasp. Fingers and plays with own hands at midline. Reaches for objects with both hands in supine position and will briefly hold on to and shake small objects. Uses *ulnar–palmar grasp* (object held against palm with little and ring finger). Will bring hands to midline and watch them for prolonged periods of time.
5 MONTHS	Will hold back straight with no head lag when pulled to sitting position. Reaches for objects in supported sitting. Rolls from back to side, and front to back. Feet to mouth.	Brings toys to mouth to explore. Able to grasp objects voluntarily. Follows objects with eyes without head movement. Uses "mitten grasp" (ie, grasps with whole hand. All fingers except thumb hold object against palm) or *palmar grasp*. Reaches for objects with both hands, symmetrical movement. Can transfer small object from hand to hand.
6 MONTHS	Pushes up onto extended arms, with chest and abdomen cleared of floor. May pull self up to a sitting position. Sits independently propped on hands or with arms in high guard position to facilitate trunk stability. Forward protective responses appear. Can turn completely over in either direction. Pivots in prone. Some babies may hitch (propel self backward in a sitting position, using arms and legs to move body). When held in standing position, bears almost all of weight.	Can hold two objects at once. Bangs objects on table surface (see Fig. 6-6). Will unconsciously release one object to reach for and grasp another object. Uses *radial–palmar grasp* (all four fingers in opposition to base of the thumb) for grasping. Uses raking motion to scoop up a raisin with hand. Much mirroring or overflow behaviors seen in opposite hand/arm. May grasp feet and suck on toes.
7 MONTHS	Lifts head as if attempting to sit up when supine. Sits well. Pushes up onto hands and knees and rocks. Bears full weight on feet. Enjoys bouncing when sitting or held in a standing position. Moves from sitting position to prone or quadruped (hands and knees). Protective sideways responses appear.	Reaches for toy with straight elbow and grasps with one hand. Uses *radial–digital grasp* (the tips of all fingers against the thumb) to hold a small object. Will bring feet to midline and watch them for prolonged periods of time.
8 MONTHS	May stand while holding on. Raises one foot while standing. Moves from prone to quadruped to sit (see Fig. 6-2). Crawls backward and forward (abdomen on floor, body propelled with arm movement, legs dragging).	Uses *inferior pincer grasp* (index and middle fingers in opposition to the thumb). Spontaneously releases objects. Bangs two blocks together at midline. Pulls large pegs from pegboard. Holds bottle and places nipple in mouth as wanted.

continued

TABLE 6-1. NEUROMOTOR DEVELOPMENT DURING INFANCY (*Continued*)

	Gross Motor Skills	*Fine Motor Skills*
9 MONTHS	May creep (trunk is above and parallel to floor, with both hands and knees used in locomotion; see Fig. 6-3). Pulls self to stand holding on to something for support. Stepping movements but may not move from spot.	Complete thumb opposition. Uses *lateral grasp* (thumb and side of index finger) for small objects. Manipulates objects by pushing, pulling, sliding, squeezing. Purposefully releases objects (if the skill of creeping has developed). Takes objects out of containers.
10 MONTHS	Stands briefly independently. Can cruise, or walk sideways holding on to something (see Fig. 6-4). May cry when unable to sit down without assistance. Sits by falling down. Walks with hands held. Protective backward responses appear. Pivots in sitting position.	Uses isolated index finger to poke at objects. Feeds self finger foods (eg, crackers). Can bring hands together and play "pat-a-cake" and "peek-a-boo." Enjoys throwing and dropping objects. Releases objects into larger containers.
11 MONTHS	Can stand erect while holding on to some form of support with one hand. Creeps rapidly. Will walk holding on to adult hand. Lowers self to floor while holding on. May take one-two steps independently with arms in high guard position.	Picks up tiny objects, such as raisins, with *neat pincer grasp* (very precise opposition of thumb and tip of index finger). Can hold marker (to make a mark on paper). Releases objects into small-mouthed container. Supinates (rotates) forearm.
12 MONTHS	Stands alone well. May walk alone (some before 1 year; some after). May sit down from standing without assistance or holding on. Kneels. (See Fig. 6-5.)	Begins to use objects as tools, such as spoon, cup, comb. Gives toy on request. Removes lids from containers. Can turn pages in a book, several at a time. Can drink holding cup, but needs assistance.
13 MONTHS	Walks without support. Climbs stairs well on hands and knees. Throws ball while seated, whole body in motion. Stoops to pick up an object. Climbs onto sofa, chairs.	Holds adult's hand while being spoon-fed. Will position body to assist with dressing. Places large pegs in peg board. Builds 2 block tower.
14 MONTHS	Steps off one step well with help. Creeps down steps. Walks backwards.	Pats picture in books. Holds spoon to feed, but needs assistance. Inverts a container to get block. Drinks independently from cup with occasional spills. Points with index finger.
15 MONTHS	Creeps up stairs. May not be able to walk around corners or stop suddenly without losing balance. Walks sideways. Fast walk–run. Gets up to standing from middle of floor. Bends over to look through legs. Pulls toy behind self while walking.	Builds a tower of 3 to 4 blocks. Opens most boxes, pokes fingers into holes and playdough (clay). Scribbles spontaneously.

Myelinization

The structural unit of the nervous system is a highly specialized cell, a *neuron,* which is designed to receive a stimulus and conduct it via electrical impulse and chemical transmitters either to another nerve cell or to the target muscle cell. These nerve cells have long, thin processes known as *axons* which stretch from one nerve cell to another. A fatty substance called **myelin** grows around each axon of the nervous system. This myelin sheath, which began to appear around sensory nerve fibers during the fourth month of intrauterine life,[33] functions much like the insulation on an electric wire; it prevents loss of the nerve impulses and helps to ensure that they reach the targeted muscle cell. As the myelin sheath becomes thicker and more complete, the efficiency of the neuromuscular system improves. The appearance, disappearance, and coordination of selected reflexes and motor skills are correlated with the growth of the myelin sheath.

All of the cranial nerves and most of the afferent nerves are myelinated before birth. This does not mean, however, that the neonate will react to a sensation (e.g., pain) in the same way as a neurologically mature individual. Most of the infant's efferent nerves and the brain are insufficiently myelinated to enable coordinated voluntary movements.[33] Reflexive behavior is thus normal during early infancy but slowly begins to fade as voluntary efferent pathways mature. The myelinization of these efferent nerve fibers follows the cephalocaudal and proximodistal principles discussed in Chapter 2. Myelinization explains why the infant first acquires neurological control of head and neck and then trunk, arms, hands, pelvic girdle, legs, bowel, bladder, and so forth (Fig. 6-2). Some nerve tracts are not myelinated until several years after birth. Even after they are covered, the myelin sheath will continue to thicken for several years. The fibers of the higher centers of the brain (e.g., cerebral cortex, thalamus) are the last to be myelinized.[27]

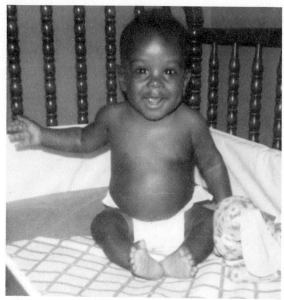

FIGURE 6–2.
Most 8-month-old babies are able to sit steadily unassisted, which frees their hands to engage in other activities. Infants should use both hands equally. If one hand is used almost exclusively for play and grasping, motor and neurological development should be evaluated.

Postural Reactions

This section by Carol M. Cariglio

The *primitive reflexes* described in Chapter 5 provide a basis for movement in the very young infant. These reflexes gradually disappear within the first six months of life with neuron development and myelinization. New reflexes and motor responses appear which serve as stepping stones to more mature, voluntary motor movements. For example, the *symmetrical tonic neck reflex (STNR)* gradually replaces the asymmetrical tonic neck reflex (ATNR) of the neonatal period. The STNR is triggered by the position of the head. When the head is extended (tipped backward), both arms straighten while the legs assume a flexed position as in quadruped (creeping) position. When the head is flexed (bent forward), the arms flex and the legs extend. The STNR begins to emerge at about 3 months of age and assists in breaking up the strong extensor patterning (all 4 extremities are in extension at the same time) of the 6-month-old (as in the Landau reflex). The STNR enables the infant to assume and maintain the hands and knees position which would be impossible if the ATNR or Landau reflexes predominated. While the STNR is strong, the infant exhibits "mirroring" behaviors—that is, whatever one side of the body does is reflected in an overflow of energy to the opposite side. Consequently, the infant will bat at objects with both hands, or kick the feet in unison. The STNR reflex must be integrated by 8 to 10 months of age to allow reciprocal creeping (Fig. 6-3).[3] Some children will continue to exhibit

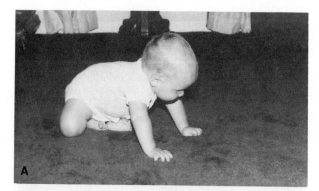

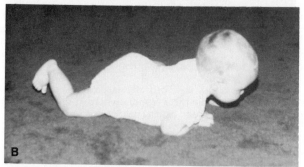

FIGURE 6–3.
Infants use different ways for moving from one place to another. These skills tend to progress from rolling through hitching, crawling, and then creeping. (A) Hitching: The baby moves backward in a modified sitting position by using arms and hands to push. (B) Crawling: While prone with the abdomen touching the floor, the weight of the upper body is borne on the elbows. The baby pulls the body and drags the legs as the arms move. (C) Creeping: While the trunk is carried above the floor and parallel to it, the baby uses reciprocal action of the hands and knees to move forward.

some mirroring behaviors during their preschool years when engaged in activities such as brushing their teeth or painting at an easel.

A series of *automatic postural reactions* gradually come into play which provide a foundation from which all voluntary movement is accomplished, such as moving from one posi-

FIGURE 6–4.
Before balance skills are adequately developed, the child "cruises" by holding onto walls and furniture. The sideways walk is typical of this stage.

tion to another (e.g., sit to stand), walking, and later learning to ride a bicycle. It is through automatic postural reactions that muscle skills are strengthened and coordinated to allow *anti-gravity positions* such as unsupported sitting, quadruped position, and standing to be maintained (Fig. 6-4). The ultimate function of these *balance responses* is to allow the individual to maintain an upright position even when one is accidentally knocked off balance, one's foot slips on the ice, or one rounds a corner while seated in a car. The automatic postural responses are generally divided into two groups, **righting reactions** and **equilibrium reactions.**

Righting reactions serve to maintain the head in vertical alignment with the body and in an upright position in space (perpendicular to the ground). This allows the individual to maintain orientation to his or her own body and to the environment for optimal processing of incoming information. It should also be noted that the baby is more alert when the head is in an upright position. Various righting reactions are discussed below.[3, 14]

1. *Labyrinthine righting reflex.* When sitting, standing, or in any unsupported position, if the body tips forward, backward, or sideways, the infant brings the head into an upright position with eyes facing forward and ears level. Since the stimulus is vestibular, the infant will do this even with the eyes closed. This reflex appears at about 2 months.

2. *Neck righting reflex.* When the head is rotated, stretching the neck muscles, the infant will bring the shoulders, trunk, and hips into midline alignment with the head. This reflex appears at about 2 months.

3. *Body-on-head righting reflex.* Pressure on the body from a supporting surface gives sensory cues which help the baby to orient to gravity. This will cause the baby to attempt to move the head into an upright position (perpendicular to gravity). It facilitates strengthening of the muscles of the upper body and prepares the baby to sit up. This reflex appears at about 2 months.

4. *Body-on-body righting reflex.* If the hips and shoulders are rotated in opposite directions, the body will de-rotate to align the shoulders with the pelvis. Reflex appears at about 4 months.

5. *Optical righting reflex.* The baby will orient the head into an upright position based on visual cues, starting at about 2 months.

6. *Landau reflex ("airplaning").* This reaction represents the combined effects of the labyrinthine head righting, optical righting, and body-on-head righting reflexes. When suspended in prone position, the infant lifts the head, arches the back, and extends the hips and legs (the entire body is arched upward, away from gravity) (see Fig. 6-5A). Some babies will even do this when laying on

FIGURE 6–5.
(A) *Airplaning reflex.* (B) *Parachuting reflex.*

their abdomen on a flat surface. This reaction first appears at about 3 months and begins to break up the predominately flexed posture of the very young infant. The Landau reflex matures at about 6 months of age, thus facilitating the infant's ability to prop on arms and pivot while prone. This reaction disappears by 24 months of age, and its persistence may be an indication of neurological damage.[3, 14]

The second group of postural responses is the *equilibrium reactions*. They develop in a predictable pattern, beginning in prone, then supine, sitting, quadruped and standing positions, in accordance with the normal developmental sequence. These reactions include the following:[3]

1. *Tilting reactions,* closely related to righting reactions, attempt to maintain the body's center of gravity over the base of support (e.g., when the balance is upset backward, the body curls forward to regain stability). Sitting tilt appears about 8 to 9 months.

2. *Postural fixation reactions* "fix" or prepare the body for an outside force by tensing appropriate musculature. For example, the body stiffens and leans slightly into the wind when a gust is encountered. A similar "tensing" reaction occurs when you are handed a heavy object. These reactions are considered higher level equilibrium responses as they require cognitive evaluation as well as maturation of the nervous system, particularly the extrapyramidal system, the vestibular system, and the cerebellum.

3. *Primitive protective reactions* are called into play when the higher level responses are not successful in maintaining or regaining balance or equilibrium. When the body moves off the center of gravity, threatening a fall, the baby's arm(s) or leg(s) reach out to catch the fall and prevent injury to the head.
   a. *Arm extension reactions* are called into action when the body tips in any direction off the center of gravity. The arms extend in the direction of the fall to regain balance or to break the fall. They emerge in sequence:
      Downward, about 4 months
      Forward, about 6 months
      Sideways, about 7 months
      Backward, about 10 months
   b. *Parachuting reaction* is elicited when the child is suspended in a position vertical to the floor. The baby will extend the legs, and pull up the foot so that the heel would hit the floor first. The arms are extended toward the floor and hands open as if trying to "catch" as much air as possible to slow the fall. This action appears at about 4 months (Fig. 6-5B).
   c. *Staggering and stepping reactions* are also placed in the category of primitive protective reactions. If the balance of a standing person is upset enough that other equilibrium responses are not effective, one

will take several steps in an attempt to place the feet directly under the center of gravity or to brace the body against further movement in an unwanted direction. These reactions appear at about 15 months.

The development of righting and equilibrium reactions are prerequisites for active mobilization (e.g., reaching, walking and running) within the environment, but also for more passive activities such as sitting or riding (Fig. 6-6). Although these postural reactions emerge during infancy, they remain with us for the rest of our lives. They appear so naturally and are so well integrated into everyday activities that most of us are unaware of their continued significance. Some persons with cerebral palsy never develop one or more of these balance responses.

Sensory Organ Development

The sensory organs bring the baby information about the external world. Development of the perceptual systems are discussed in Chapter 7.

THE EYE. The shape of the eyeball changes throughout life. In the beginning, the eye is short, which causes light rays to focus behind the retina (see Chap. 20). The ability of the lens of the eye to accommodate (adjust to different distances) increases rapidly during the first few months of infancy. By 5 months of age, most babies can fixate on a 1-inch cube brought within 1 to 2 feet of their eyes.[23] Because of the immaturity of the eye

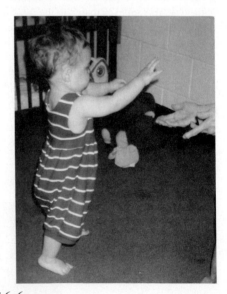

FIGURE 6–6.
Mastery of the righting and equilibrium reflexes is essential to allow antigravitational positions and to maintain balance. The child is not able to walk or run well until these automatic postural reflexes are strengthened and coordinated. Note how high the shoulders and arms are held by this child taking his first steps, a position known as "high guard" that helps to keep the back stiff and to maintain balance.

muscles of the young infant, the eyes may not be able to fixate consistently on an object or may not always appear to be fixating together. The baby who has persistent crossing of one or both eyes should be evaluated by an ophthalmologist by 6 months of age.[33]

THE EAR. The cartilage that gives the external earlobe its shape does not reach full maturation until late infancy; consequently, it tends to temporarily assume the shape of whatever is pressed against it. The eardrum (tympanic membrane) separates the middle and outer ear. The middle ear is almost adult size at birth, and the three small bones that conduct sound vibrations from the eardrum to the inner ear are well developed at birth. The inner ear contains the vestibular system, which facilitates postural equilibrium, and the cochlea, which transmits auditory sensations to the brain (see Fig. 6-7). Both are well developed at birth.

TASTE BUDS. The taste buds, which are present at birth, are more widely distributed about the tongue in the infant and the child than they are in the adult.[39] Infants prefer sweet-tasting substances.

THE NOSE. The nose is an important organ for filtration, temperature control, and humidification of inspired air. The olfactory membrane, lying in the upper part of the back of the nose, is almost adult-size at birth.[27, 39] The sense of smell in humans does not develop to the same extent that it does in many other animals. Nevertheless, from birth, the infant begins to learn about the world through the use of smell. Breast-fed infants are able to smell breast milk and will cry for their

mothers when the breasts are engorged and leaking. Infants are also able to differentiate the breast milk from their mothers or from other females by the smell, thus contributing to mother-child attachment.[28, 35]

Integumentary System

The integumentary system includes the nails, hair, skin, and selected glands that pass through the skin.

Skin

In addition to its cosmetic function, the skin aids in protecting the body from extreme temperatures, excess humidity, bacterial invasion, and other harmful agents. The outer layer of skin, or **epidermis,** gives protection against such elements. During infancy, the epidermis is loosely connected to the layer of skin beneath it, the **dermis.** Because both layers are relatively thin, the infant has an increased susceptibility to blistering and chafing (or *rub burns*). Melanocytes in the skin produce pigmentation (melanin) that protects the body from harmful sun rays. However, the infant's ability to produce pigmentation is limited, with a resulting sensitivity to the sun. Infants under 6 months of age should not be placed in direct sunlight or sunlight filtered through a window during the hottest part of the day. Older infants should have waterproof sunblock with a skin protection factor (SPF) of 27 applied every 2 hours.[40] The sunblock should be PABA-free because many babies have an allergic reaction to PABA. Sunblock should also be applied under the baby's clothing because sun filters through lightweight clothing. The baby's head should be protected with a cap or bonnet because the infant's head represents a large proportion of body surface. The infant should initially be placed in the sunlight for only 2 minutes, with exposure increased gradually. Dark-skinned babies have no more melanocytes than fair-skinned babies.

Body Surface Area

The infant's *body surface area* (BSA), the ratio of surface area to body mass, is approximately 2 to 3 times greater than that of an adult.[27] Because BSA correlates closely with biophysical functions (e.g., cardiac output, total oxygen consumption, insensible water loss, caloric requirements), medicine dosages based on BSA are usually the most accurate. To determine an individual's BSA, one must know the current weight and height and compute BSA using a graph called a *nomogram.* Body surface area is measured in square meters (m^2).

Dermatoglyphics

Each individual has a distinct set of handprints, fingerprints, and footprints created by epidermal creases and ridges.[18] Many of these patterns, or *dermatoglyphics,* are formed in the third fetal month. Other explicit wrinkles develop throughout the individual's life span. These patterns, unique to each individual, provide cues to possible chromosomal abnormalities as well as clues to personal identification.

FIGURE 6–7.
Active play stimulates the vestibular system, increases sensitivity to position changes, and strengthens the muscles essential for mastery of the righting and balancing reflexes.

Glands

During adulthood, the two types of sweat glands (eccrine and apocrine) secrete perspiration in response to emotional stimuli. The eccrine glands, which produce sweat in response to both thermal and emotional stimuli, are present but are not fully functional during early infancy. This may be one way the baby is able to conserve water to meet the relatively high need for fluid. Apocrine sweat glands (responsible for what is commonly called *body odor*) are fully developed at birth but do not begin to function until the prepubertal years.[27]

The sebaceous glands, which help to produce the vernix caseosa of the newborn, are distributed all over the infant's body except on the palms and the soles of the feet. These glands actively secrete sebum during early infancy and thus lubricate the baby's skin. The sebaceous glands decrease in activity during childhood and are reactivated during the pubertal period (see Chap. 23). Because of this decrease in active production of sebum, older infants and children may have relatively dry skin in cold and low-humidity environments.

Even though the epidermis and the glands work together to prevent bacterial invasion, infection can still occur because of the extreme sensitivity of the skin to rubbing, heat, or trauma. Routine cleansing and drying of all the body areas are the best deterrents to bacterial growth.

Hair

The development of the baby's scalp hair often provides a topic for lively discussion among relatives. Some babies are born with a full head of hair, and others are bald. Genetic factors affect the appearance of the hair. The texture and color of the hair at birth may be quite unlike the hair the same individual will possess later on. Scalp hair tends to be very fine and thin during infancy and may even fall out and reappear with a different texture, color, or both.

Nails

Full-term babies are born with fingernails and toenails. Although the nails are very thin, they grow fast and need to be kept clean and neatly trimmed.

Cardiovascular System

The blood and the vessels that transport it, as well as the heart that pumps it, comprise the cardiovascular system. This system carries nutrients to, and waste products from, every cell of the body.

Heart

The heart of the infant will double its weight by the first birthday.[27] It lies in an almost horizontal position at birth. As the baby grows older, the heart will gradually shift to a permanent, more vertical position. The heart in the infant and the child is situated higher in the chest than it is in the adult. For this reason, the external cardiac compressions of cardiopulmonary resuscitation (CPR) are performed just below an imaginary line between the nipples on the chest of a baby, but are performed much lower on the chest of older individuals.

At birth the left and right lower chambers of the heart (ventricles) are approximately the same size. By 2 months of age, the muscular walls of the left ventricle will become thicker than those of the right ventricle.[33] This differentiation in size is critical because the left ventricle is responsible for pumping blood to the entire body, while the right ventricle pumps blood to the lungs. The strength of the left ventricle contraction is reflected in the numerator of the blood pressure fraction (systolic pressure). As the heart grows larger, the heartbeat will slow and the blood pressure will rise (see Appendix E). Heart murmurs produced by vibrations within the heart chambers or in the major arteries from the back-and-forth flow of the blood are common and are not necessarily pathological in infancy.

Blood Vessels

Under the influence of the involuntary nervous system and hormones, the small capillaries in the infant's body contract to conserve body heat and expand to cause heat loss. These abilities, which are essentially absent in the neonate, gradually begin to develop after the first few weeks of extrauterine life.

Blood Values

The blood values of the infant reflect information such as the oxygen-carrying capacity of the red blood cells and the defense abilities of the white blood cells (see Appendix E). During early infancy, the hemoglobin can drop as low as 10 g/dL. This *physiological anemia* reflects the body's need to decrease the number of immature red blood cells (and thus the attached hemoglobin) because of the relative overproduction during the fetal period. Under normal circumstances, the baby will not be endangered because the lowered hemoglobin will stimulate the bone marrow to produce more red blood cells. Lymphoid tissue (a part of which exists in the blood as lymphocytes) grows rapidly during infancy and provides some protection against illness. Lymphocytes are active in the formation of antibodies (see Chap. 9).

Respiratory System

Although the neonate's initial respiratory efforts expand most of the alveoli, not all are expanded until a few days or even a few weeks after birth. These alveoli increase in numbers and complexity at a relatively rapid rate during infancy.[32] The weight of the lungs is doubled by 6 months and tripled by 1 year.[27]

The infant's relatively more rapid respiratory rate is due in part to the large amount of *dead air space,* or that portion of the airway where air passes but gases are not exchanged. This anatomical situation combined with the high metabolic rate requires that proportionately more air enter and exit the lungs per minute. The baby is predominantly a nose breather during the first few months of life, and then gradually learns to breathe through the mouth by the third or fourth month. Blocked nostrils (e.g., a cold) will make nursing and swallowing very difficult and will require more time for feeding.[45]

Gastrointestinal System

At birth, the gastrointestinal system of the infant is mature enough to digest breast milk or its equivalent. With further growth and development of the child, it is capable of digesting a wide variety of different types and textures of foods.

Mouth

Salivation is adequate at birth to maintain moisture in the baby's mouth. However, maturation of many of the salivary glands does not occur until the third month of life. At this time, the baby is just beginning to learn to swallow voluntarily. The result is a marked increase in the baby's drooling. Swallowing, sucking, and respiratory reflexes must be brought under voluntary control and coordination to prevent aspiration of solid foods during feeding. Many babies experience a temporary increase in gagging, spitting, and coughing behaviors around 5 to 6 months when they are learning how to voluntarily control the tongue, jaw, and swallowing behaviors needed for eating solids.

Dentition

The teeth begin to grow during the prenatal months. The first *baby teeth* to erupt are called *primary* or *deciduous teeth;* the teeth that a person develops later in life are referred to as *permanent teeth*. There is wide variation in what is considered a normal time for the emergence of the first tooth. The first and second teeth (usually a lower tooth [the primary mandibular central incisor]) cut through the gums at about 6 to 7 months of age. The time of emergence depends on health, heredity, prenatal and postnatal nutrition, race, gender, and other factors; for example, females usually cut their first tooth earlier than males. There are a total of 20 deciduous teeth that appear at a rate of about 1 per month after the first tooth emerges until the child is 1 year of age. It is the sequence of these eruptions that is far more important than the age of eruption. An irregularity in the sequence of eruption can cause misalignment of the teeth and result in poor alignment of the jaws (malocclusion), even affecting the position of the permanent teeth.

By 1 year of age, the four upper maxillary incisors are usually present. A few months may pass before more teeth appear, then in relatively rapid succession, the two remaining lower mandibular incisors and all four first molars emerge. The rest of the deciduous teeth emerge during toddlerhood, and the set is usually complete by 2½ years of age.

Esophagus and Stomach

The muscle tone of the lower esophageal sphincter is poor, accounting for the frequent spitting up of foods. The first 3 months of life constitute the most rapid growth period for the stomach. The capacity of the stomach varies among individuals. By the age of 1 month, the stomach's capacity is generally 90 to 150 mL (3 to 5 oz); at 1 year of age, the capacity is 210 to 360 mL (7 to 12 oz).[27] The rate of gastric (stomach) emptying also varies among individual infants. Digestion in the stomach occurs primarily as a result of the secretion of hydrochloric acid and pepsin, both of which aid in the breakdown of protein. This ability, however, is relatively limited throughout infancy. Consequently, many pediatricians advise delay of the introduction of solids until the second half of the first year of life.

Small Intestine

Most of the digestion and absorption of foodstuffs occurs in the small intestine, which increases its length by 50% during the first year. Pancreatic secretions composed of three enzymes (trypsin, lipase, and pancreatic amylase) are released into the small intestine. Neonatal levels of trypsin, which further break down the partially digested proteins that travel from the stomach, are equal in amount to adult levels.

Pancreatic amylase, which digests starch, is secreted at adult levels by 3 months. Lipase, which breaks down fats, also reaches adult level at 3 months, although this does not mean that the infant is capable of digesting all fats by this age.[37] Lipase needs mature bile (secreted from the liver and stored in the gallbladder) to aid in digestion of fat. By the time the infant is 1 year of age, the lipase and bile are working together well enough to approximate adult fat digestion. Polyunsaturated fatty acids (found in breast milk and in infant formulas) are more easily absorbed than saturated fats during the first years of life.[37]

Large Intestine

Although some water is absorbed in the small intestine, more is absorbed into the bloodstream, along with electrolytes, by the walls of the large intestine. Since the intestinal contents move rapidly through the gastrointestinal tract and the large intestine is initially immature in water absorption, the infant's stools during the first year of life contain relatively more water and are consequently looser. This biophysical fact combined with the environmental factors of more adult foods being added to the infant's diet contribute to the stools becoming more formed and solid in consistency at approximately 1 year of age. While the newborn may have a bowel movement after each feeding, during later infancy the frequency may range from 3 to 6 stools per day.[19]

The large intestine also plays an important role in the production of vitamin K, an essential precursor for the synthesis of prothrombin, which is necessary for normal blood clotting (coagulation). After birth, especially, when the newborn begins to ingest milk or formula, bacteria (i.e., *Escherichia coli*) are introduced to the intestinal tract, which are necessary for the synthesis of vitamin K. Inadequate vitamin K, especially during the first week of life, may lead to bleeding disorders.[46]

Genitourinary System

Genitals and Reproductive Organs

The baby's genitals and reproductive organs remain relatively immature during infancy. However, the internal reproductive organs do increase in weight in preparation for later functioning. A discussion of the development of these organs is deferred until Chapter 23.

Excretory System

The excretory organs (kidneys, ureters, bladder, and urethra) constitute the genitourinary system. The kidneys are responsible for filtering wastes from the blood and maintaining fluid and electrolyte balance; they function in an immature way during the first few weeks of extrauterine life. The ability to form urine involves many factors: among these are the reabsorption and secretion powers of the kidney tubules and the filtering capacity of the kidney epithelium. The tubules, short and narrow at birth, closely approximate adult size by 6 months.[30] At the time of birth, some kidney epithelium is very thick and is therefore less efficient in filtration; it gradually becomes thinner throughout infancy. Thus the young infant's ability to concentrate urine (reabsorb urinary filtrates for body use) gradually improves. Since more urine must pass through the kidneys to excrete wastes, the infant's fluid needs, which are based on body weight, are relatively greater than the adult's. However, if an infant is given an overload of fluid, the kidneys are unable to respond adequately by increasing urinary output.[27] Consequently, a baby can become over hydrated if given too much fluid. A baby needs approximately 2 ounces per pound, or 120 to 160 mL/kg, in a 24-hour period (or a comparable amount over a smaller increment of time).[4]

Fluid and Electrolyte Balance

Body fluid consists mostly of water and dissolved substances. Those substances whose atoms possess an electrical charge (i.e., in ionic form) are called *electrolytes*. Water and electrolytes transport nutrients and other substances to and from body cells, maintain the blood volume, dilute the products of metabolism, and regulate the pressure of all body fluids (including blood) as well as the acid-base balance and the conductibility of neurological impulses.

WATER. Water is more essential to the body than food; it is second only to oxygen in importance for physical survival. Water comprises the major portion of body structures, serves as a solvent for minerals and other compounds, aids in the transport of food and wastes to and from the cells, facilitates mobility of joints, and helps to maintain body temperature.

The newborn's body is approximately 75% water. By 1 year of age, the total body water content has decreased to 64%. *Extracellular water* refers to the water in plasma (the liquid fraction of the blood), and between cells. During infancy, extracellular water comprises a greater proportion of total body water than in older children and adults.[30] Because of the relatively greater proportions of total body water and extracellular water, the infant must consume more water per unit of body weight than adults. The infant is also more susceptible to dehydration than is an adult because the kidneys do not yet conserve water well. *Intracellular water*, the fluid contained within body cells, is less subject to problems of fluid imbalance, but these problems are more serious when they do occur.

Water is lost from the body through several routes; its excretion in urine is obvious. The gastrointestinal tract, sometimes considered to be an extension of body surface area, is also relatively larger in infancy and is a source of proportionately greater fluid loss (especially during diarrhea). Perspiration, water excreted with feces, and water "blown off" from the lungs during normal breathing all comprise the rather difficult-to-measure *insensible water loss (IWL)*. The level of IWL is relatively greater in infancy than in adulthood, owing in part to the infant's proportionately greater area of body surface, increased respiratory rate, and looser bowel movements. Evaporative water loss is estimated to be approximately 210 mL/day at 1 month of age and 500 mL/day at 1 year of age.[29, 30]

Relatively more fluid is required to rinse the body of products left by the infant's high metabolic rate. The term *renal solute load* refers to those solutes that must be excreted by the kidneys; this load is affected by the amount of protein and salts in the diet. Infants who are fed formulas receive a slightly higher renal solute load than do breast-fed infants. The renal solute load is generally not a major concern unless the infant receives excessive amounts of protein through improper formula preparation or through overuse of solids at an early age. Infants are particularly vulnerable to water imbalances during illness. Any condition such as infection that increases metabolism causes a rise in heat production and fever, with concomitant increased IWL and an increasing need for water excretion in order to flush out the increased metabolic wastes. Vomiting and diarrhea can markedly increase fluid losses. Therefore, extra attention must be paid to the fluid requirements of the infant during illness or when fluid intake is poor.

ELECTROLYTES. Sodium and chloride are the primary electrolytes found in extracellular fluids; potassium is concentrated within the cells. A proper balance of electrolytes is essential for the functioning of all the cells of the infant's body. Imbalances in electrolytes become a major concern when losses are increased through gastrointestinal routes (e.g., vomiting, diarrhea), particularly when fluid losses are replaced only by nonelectrolyte fluids, such as water or diluted tea. Boiled milk contains an excess of protein and electrolytes because of water evaporation. Homemade electrolyte solutions are risky if they are incorrectly prepared. The World Health Organization recommends (for young children in underdeveloped countries without adequate medical services) 8 teaspoons of sugar and 1 teaspoon of salt per one liter of boiled and cooled water for *temporary* fluid and electrolyte replacement.[17] When possible, health professionals should ascertain the specific type of dehydration an infant is experiencing to individualize fluid and electrolyte replacement.

Endocrine System

The endocrine system is composed of glandular structures found throughout the body. These glands secrete hormones directly into the bloodstream to affect the functioning of organs in other parts of the body. The immaturity of this system at birth becomes a disadvantage if for some reason the infant must adjust to wide fluctuations in fluid balance, electrolyte levels, glucose (simple sugar), or amino acids (building blocks for proteins). Mature hormonal control of physiological functions by the endocrine system is not achieved during infancy.

Glandular Structures

The pituitary gland (hypophysis), which lies at the base of the brain, produces several hormones. The most important hormone produced during infancy is the pituitary growth hormone (PGH). This hormone, produced by the anterior lobe of the pituitary, aids in the control of skeletal growth as well as the metabolism of proteins, fats, and carbohydrates. After the infant reaches 1 year of age, PGH becomes a major factor in growth control.[12, 27]

Adrenocorticotropic hormone (ACTH) is secreted by the anterior pituitary. Antidiuretic hormone (ADH), also referred to as *vasopressin,* is produced by the posterior pituitary. The functions of both these hormones are limited during infancy. Adrenocorticotropic hormone stimulates the adrenal glands to produce hormones affecting the metabolism of glucose, protein, and fat. Antidiuretic hormone acts on the kidneys, so that water excretion through urine is diminished when the body needs to conserve water (e.g., in a baby with fever). Unfortunately, the infant's kidneys do not respond well to ADH. Furthermore, it is suspected that the pituitary's ability to produce ADH is limited during the first few months of infancy.[27]

The thyroid gland, located in the lower neck in front of the trachea, stores and secretes the thyroid hormones that are responsible for tissue respiration rate and other important metabolic processes at the cellular level. The thyroid function is mature from birth. If the thyroid gland produces too much hormone (hyperthyroidism), the individual will demonstrate symptoms of a rapid metabolism (e.g., extreme nervousness, weight loss). When the thyroid gland produces too little hormone (hypothyroidism), skeletal maturation and central nervous system development are adversely affected. Mental retardation (e.g., cretinism) may result if hormonal therapy is not started by 3 months of age.

The parathyroid glands, located in the lower neck near the thyroid, produce a hormone that acts with vitamin D to regulate calcium and phosphorus metabolism, which is vital to the growth and the development of bones.

The adrenal glands, which are located on top of the kidneys, are quite limited in function at birth. The inner part of each adrenal gland (called the *adrenal medulla*) secretes epinephrine (adrenalin) and norepinephrine (noradrenalin). In a situation perceived as threatening, both of these hormones work to decrease blood flow to tissues such as the gastrointestinal tract (which is not needed in emergency situations), and to increase blood flow to tissues such as the heart and the skeletal muscle, which are usually needed to meet a sudden challenge. These same hormones also aid in the use of fat, increase the basal metabolic rate, and elevate the level of blood sugar. The hormones secreted by the adrenal cortex mediate the metabolism of water, sodium, potassium, protein, fat, and carbohydrate. During infancy, however, the efforts of the adrenal cortex are immature.

The islets of Langerhans of the pancreas manufacture insulin and glucagon, both of which facilitate glucose metabolism. Blood sugar levels may fluctuate widely throughout infancy and childhood. When the child's blood sugar level is too low, he or she will tire easily, become irritable, and interact less effectively with the environment. Too much refined sugar may lead to hyperactivity in some children.

The liver, located behind the ribs in the upper right portion of the abdomen, is relatively large at birth. It performs several metabolic functions: converting the blood sugar into glycogen, storing the glycogen, and converting the stored glycogen into glucose to be released into the bloodstream as needed. The liver also synthesizes and oxidizes fats, stores some vitamins and minerals, manufactures some blood proteins, and removes toxic substances (e.g., drugs and alcohol) from the blood. Because its functioning remains immature throughout infancy, babies born addicted to drugs and alcohol are not only placed in a life-threatening situation when they experience withdrawal, but may already be suffering from the toxic effects of drugs and alcohol before they leave the womb.

Basal Metabolism

The basal metabolic rate (BMR) is highest during periods of rapid growth, particularly during the first 2 years of life. Basal metabolism is the minimum amount of heat produced by the body in a fasting state while one is awake but at rest. It indicates the amount of energy needed to maintain life processes. The rate of metabolism in infancy is significantly higher than in adulthood because of the larger body surface area in relation to the mass of active tissue. The BMR is affected by other factors, including gender, age, weight, endocrine activity, and general state of nutrition. Basal metabolic requirements decline gradually during adulthood.

Energy requirements are stated in kilocalories (kcal) per kilogram (kg) or pound of body weight. A kcal is the amount of energy required to raise 1 kg of water 1°C. Total energy requirements are based on metabolic rates, rate of growth, body size and surface area, and physical activity. The recommended energy intake for children of various ages is given in Appendix E.

MAINTAINING HIGH-LEVEL WELLNESS

Nutrition

Initial Feedings

Two primary sources are available to meet the nutritional needs of the neonate: human breast milk and commercially prepared infant formulas. The formulas have vegetable oils, carbohydrates, vitamins, and minerals added. Breast milk and the majority of commercially prepared formulas contain approximately 20 calories per ounce. When provided in sufficient volume, both breast milk and commercially prepared formulas are adequate to meet the protein, caloric, and vitamin needs of the infant during the first 4 to 6 months of life. Breast milk offers, in addition, antibodies and enzymes that may protect the infant against infections.[2] Cow's milk, whether whole, 2% fat, or skimmed, is not adequate to meet the nutritional needs of the young infant. It is deficient in iron, fluoride, and vitamins A, C, and D. The protein of whole cow's milk has caused bleeding into the gastrointestinal tract of some infants that in turn has led to iron-deficiency anemia.[7,16] Neither low fat nor nonfat milk is recommended for infants less than 1 year of age, and nonfat milk is not recommended before 2 years of age. These milks are frequently fortified with nonfat milk solids that increase the renal solute load on the young child's maturing kidneys. The infant or young toddler who drinks either nonfat or low fat milk will not derive enough calories because of low carbohydrate content.[34] Although breast milk and infant formulas are recommended for infant feeding, the American Academy of Pediatrics Committee on Nutrition has approved the use of whole cow's milk after infants reach 6 months of age provided that they are consuming one-third of their calories (and adequate iron and vitamin C) from supplemental food.[10]

Babies cannot remain healthy with milk as the only source of nutrients throughout infancy. Healthy full-term infants have sufficient body stores of iron to meet their needs until 5 or 6 months of age. Low-birth-weight infants (often born this way owing to an unhealthy prenatal environment) exhaust their iron stores at an earlier age (2 to 3 months) because of lower stores and more rapid postnatal growth.[10] Supplemental iron in formula or vitamin preparations will help maintain adequate levels and prevent iron-deficiency anemia. Iron-deficiency anemia has detrimental effects on growth, immune factors, energy capacity, and learning abilities of young children. It is controversial whether the iron available in breast milk is well-absorbed and sufficient to meet the infant's requirements. A number of pediatricians recommend addition of an iron supplement to the diet of the young breast-fed infant (see Chap. 31 for further discussion of breast-feeding).

For the first few years of childhood, many pediatricians recommend multivitamin preparations that contain B vitamins as well as vitamins A, C, and D. Orange juice, although a good source of vitamin C, should not be introduced until 6 months of age, since many younger infants demonstrate an allergic response to it. During the second half of the first year,

the baby's skin (especially the palms, the ear lobes, and the soles of the feet) may exhibit a yellow sheen. This condition, called *carotenemia,* is due to an excess of carotene (a precursor of vitamin A) circulating in the blood. Since it is usually caused by the ingestion of yellow vegetables, it will disappear as carotene sources are reduced. Carotenemia may be differentiated from jaundice (from increased bilirubin levels) by looking at the sclerae (the firm outer coatings of the eyes), which do not turn yellow with carotenemia as they do with jaundice.[33]

Introduction to Solids

Much confusion and misinformation exists regarding the introduction of solid foods to the infant's diet. The addition of solid foods to a baby's diet is a highly individual matter. Most infants will *tolerate* cereals and other solids even when introduced in the first weeks of life; however, the fact that the foods are tolerated does not mean that it is desirable to offer them at such an early age. In fact, a number of potential problems may result from the too early introduction of solids.

Initially, all foods placed in the infant's mouth are manipulated in the same way that the infant suckles the nipple. This forward-thrusting movement of the tongue (extrusion reflex) may be misinterpreted by many parents as a dislike for solid foods; it is a reflex that begins to fade at about 4 months. Thus, it is better for the baby to be fed solid foods later, after the extrusion reflex has disappeared. The baby must learn to voluntarily coordinate tongue, chewing and lip movements. It is much easier for a baby to chew after 6 months of age, when the jaw muscles mature.

The addition of solids at a very early age may result in an inadequate intake of milk, with insufficient or inappropriate vitamin and protein intakes as well as insufficient fluid intake. The addition of solids to an adequate intake of milk may result in overfeeding and obesity. The introduction of certain solids before the infant is 6 months of age also increases the risk of developing certain food allergies; wheat cereals, citrus juices, and egg whites are the most frequent causes of allergic reactions. A noticeable increase in appetite often indicates that a baby is ready for foods to supplement breast milk or formula. If the baby breast-feeds more frequently than every 3 hours or consumes more than 1 quart of formula per day, a need for additional food may be indicated.

The first food introduced is generally rice cereal, since few babies are allergic to this grain. The infant should be started on 1 or 2 small spoonfuls of dry cereal mixed with water, breast milk, or formula; this amount can be gradually increased to 2 to 4 tablespoonfuls twice a day. Preparing the cereal with strained citrus juices or vitamin C-fortified juices will increase the bioavailability (the amount absorbed into the bloodstream) of the iron in the cereal.[11] Once the infant has accepted and tolerated cereal, mashed banana and other strained fruits or vegetables may be added. Some physicians recommend that vegetables be added before fruits, since the sweet flavor of fruits often interferes with the baby's desire to eat the more bland vegetables. Strained meats are generally added last.

New foods should be introduced one at a time, initially in small amounts and allowing several days to elapse between each addition of new food. When eggs are introduced, the yolk is commonly fed to the infant first because it is a good source of iron and because babies are more often allergic to the egg white. If at any time the infant appears to develop a reaction such as vomiting, rash, or diarrhea, a food should be withdrawn and reintroduced several weeks later. Any new food will cause some alteration in the color and the consistency of the stool; these minor changes do not necessarily indicate an intolerance of the food.

Parents who elect to use commercially prepared baby food should be advised to read the labels carefully. Mixed-food dinners sometimes contain foodstuffs and additives that could cause allergic reactions in some babies. The food contents are listed on the label in descending order from highest to lowest weight. Foods that have unnecessary additives of salt, sugar, and starches should be avoided.

Feeding Schedules

For most infants, a semi-flexible demand feeding schedule is preferable to a rigid feeding schedule. If the infant is fed when hungry, the tendency to underfeed or to overfeed is minimized. For most infants, a demand schedule may start with as many as 8 feedings per day at irregular intervals, but with time the infant generally establishes a 3½- to 4-hour feeding schedule. In the first 3 months of life, the bottle-fed infant requires from 5 to 7 feedings per day because of the smaller capacity of the stomach and the high metabolic needs in relation to body size. By 4 or 5 months of age, the number of feedings generally decreases to 4 per day. Babies may be ready for three main feedings per day any time between the ages of 4 and 10 months. However, additional fluids and snacks will need to be offered between meals. Many variations exist to these guidelines; Dr. Benjamin Spock's sensible discussion of the matter in his *Baby and Child Care* is recommended.[40] One safety point is critical: *Bottles should **never** be propped.* The danger of a baby choking or inhaling the contents of a propped bottle is very real.

It is important that the caregiver recognize the infant's cues of satiation as well as for readiness to feed. The young infant indicates satisfaction by slowing the sucking activity, falling asleep, turning the head away, or allowing milk to run from the mouth. Cues of satiety provided by the older infant are more direct: The child may clamp down on the nipple rather than sucking, push the spoon or cup away with the hand, or draw the head back. The parent or caregiver should not try to coax the infant to finish solids or formula, since this can lead to overfeeding, discomfort, and obesity.

The baby's rate of growth begins to slow down at the end of the first year of life. At this time many parents become concerned that their child is not eating enough. This is a normal phenomenon and should not be a cause for concern as long as the child continues to make expected weight gains (see Appendix D).

Most babies are eating mashed or junior food preparations by 8 to 9 months. Self-feeding can be initiated by providing small pieces of toast, teething crackers, bananas, cooked vegetables, meat, and cheese sticks. The use of finger foods allows the infant to explore different shapes and textures. Wieners, raw carrots, nuts, raisins, grapes, small candies, and popcorn are difficult for the older infant (and toddler and young preschooler) to chew and can cause choking and aspiration.[10] The child who is beginning to self-feed should not be left alone, because he or she has a tendency to "bite off more than he can chew," and may choke (Fig. 6-8).

At approximately 9 months of age, a training cup can be introduced. The infant will be awkward and messy with the cup at first, but it is important that the opportunity be given to try it. Some parents allow the child to play with cups in the bathtub in order to provide opportunities to practice pouring and drinking.

Weaning an infant from the bottle or breast to a cup should be a gradual process. The cup can be introduced during meals, with the bottle being reserved for nap and bedtime. Weaning is generally accomplished by 12 to 14 months of age, although some children will continue to need a bedtime bottle or the breast for a short time longer. Adult foods can be gradually added as tolerated. Individual families and cultures vary widely in their perception of an infant's readiness to be weaned and the manner of introducing new foods and textures.

Overfeeding

In recent years the long-term effects of infant overfeeding and obesity have become a concern. A fat baby has a high chance of becoming an obese child. Longitudinal and retrospective studies have demonstrated that most overweight children become overweight adults.[5, 25] Studies of the number and the size of adipose (fat) cells in obese and nonobese children and adults suggest that there may be two subgroups of obese

FIGURE 6–8.
During midinfancy, babies enjoy manipulating objects by pushing, pulling, sliding, banging, and squeezing them. They make use of these skills as they attempt to feed themselves.

children: The group with increased numbers of adipose cells are apt to remain obese while the other group will outgrow their baby fat. Genetic predisposition and family eating patterns also influence the development of childhood obesity. There is some evidence that overfeeding of babies may induce an excessive number of fat cells to be produced during this sensitive growth period.[41]

However, early restriction of cholesterol and saturated fats in infant diets is not healthy for children. Modifying dietary fat intake in infants involves restricting dairy products and meat. These foods provide essential nutrients such as calcium, iron, and protein. In addition, dietary fat is needed for the growing brain and nervous system. Inadequate fat intake also affects absorption of essential vitamins. While excessive intake of fats is not advised for infants and children because fats may depress the appetite for other foods, it is also important to make sure the child of this age is not on such a fat-restrictive diet that the child's growth suffers.

Sleep

The infant's rapidly growing body needs adequate rest for optimal growth, since pituitary growth hormone is excreted mainly during periods of sleep.[27] New babies tend to be noisy sleepers; they gurgle, cough, sneeze, sigh, and make other sounds that only a baby can produce. As the baby's nervous system develops and matures, periods of deep sleep and alertness become longer. Every infant has a unique sleep pattern. As he or she learns how to sleep and how to stay awake, the patterns of sleep will change (see Chap. 26 for further discussion of sleep) (Fig. 6-9).

By 2 months of age, most babies are beginning to sleep through the night feeding; by 3 months, most babies will sleep most of the night. At 6 months of age, the baby is probably taking two or three naps per day and sleeping a total of 16 to 18 hours out of 24. The baby may again begin episodes of frequent night awakenings at approximately 7 to 9 months.[44] Although some babies wake up because they are teething, many do so because they have not yet learned family sleep (when dark) versus wake (when light) patterns, have had a period of illness with waking for legitimate needs (and liked the nighttime attention), or are learning how to awaken and fall asleep voluntarily. At about 10 months, they usually sleep 10 to 12 hours at night and take two naps during the day. By 1 year of age, most babies sleep 11 to 12 hours at night and 3 or more hours during the day in one or two naps.

Dental Care

The health of teeth and gums is affected not only by the baby's current diet, but also by the prenatal nutritional environment. Fluoride strengthens the enamel of the teeth and increases their resistance to decay. It is especially effective when it is incorporated in the tooth during the formation of enamel (which occurs prenatally and before the tooth has erupted). Prenatal fluoride preparations are available for pregnant women. Infants and children who drink water containing

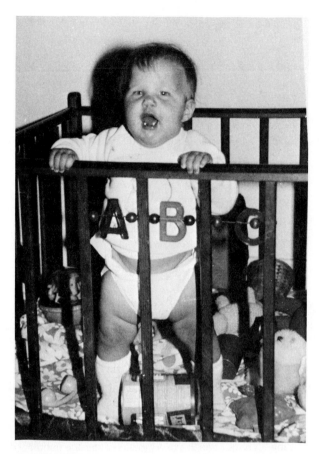

FIGURE 6–9.
Once a baby is able to stand, side rails must *be kept in high position to prevent falls. Once toddlers can climb, the crib should be replaced with a low bed or cot.*

approximately 1 part per million (ppm) fluoride throughout the period when their teeth are forming have a decrease in tooth decay (caries).[8, 21] Children who do not have access to fluoridated drinking water should receive fluoride supplements through the adolescent years (see Table 6-2).

During the early postnatal months, adequate oral hygiene consists of cleaning the baby's mouth with sips of clear water after feedings. The baby may enjoy having the gums massaged with a moist, clean gauze pad. Massaging the gums removes plaque (patches of bacteria). Tooth brushing should begin when the baby's first tooth has erupted. Proper care of the deciduous teeth is essential to prevent tooth decay and tooth loss; the deciduous teeth maintain spaces for the later permanent teeth and assist in developing correct speech habits. A soft-bristled brush for the infant and the young child is recommended. By the beginning of the second year, the baby will be helping to hold the toothbrush, but is in no way capable of efficiently brushing the teeth without assistance. Tooth powders are not recommended because babies may inhale or choke on them.

TABLE 6-2. SUPPLEMENTAL FLUORIDE DOSAGE SCHEDULE (MG/DAY)*

Age	Concentration of Fluoride in Drinking Water (ppm)		
	<0.3	0.3–0.7	>0.7
2 weeks to 2 years	0.25	0	0
2 years to 3 years†	0.50	0.25	0
3 years to 14 years	1.00	0.50	0

*2.2 mg sodium fluoride contains 1 mg of fluoride.

† Because breast milk contains only trace amounts of fluoride and fully breast-fed infants consume little or no water, a fluoride supplement of 0.25 mg/day should be prescribed for the infant who is breast-fed exclusively more than 6 months.

(Adapted from the Committee on Nutrition, American Academy of Pediatrics (1986). Fluoride supplementation. Pediatrics, 77, 758–761.)

Because children less than 3 years of age are apt to swallow much of the toothpaste used in brushing their teeth, and because there may be 1 mg of fluoride per gram of fluoridated toothpaste, only the smallest amount of dentifrice (i.e., no larger than the size of a small pea) should be used each time. Some dentists recommend that nonfluoridated toothpaste be used in the early years. Because most children under the age of 4 years swallow 40% or more of mouth rinses, those containing fluoride are not recommended for young children.[38] An excess of ingested fluoride will cause tooth discoloration.[22]

Teething

Infants vary in their response to teething. One baby may gnaw on objects, drool excessively, and fret for 3 or 4 weeks before a tooth emerges. Another baby's mother may discover a new tooth without warning when she hears it click against the feeding spoon. Teething sometimes interferes with a baby's sleep patterns or appetite.

During teething, the baby is at the height of incorporating and learning about the environment by way of the mouth. Oral gratification is necessary; providing the baby with a safely made teething ring may prove refreshing to teething gums, especially if it has been cooled in the refrigerator. Increased fluid consumption at this time is encouraged. Many caregivers unwisely use products that contain drugs or alcohol, allegedly to ease the baby's teething pain. A rise in body temperature, loose stools, increased salivation, and a rash around the mouth can occur during teething; however, other illnesses that have these same symptoms should be ruled out. The stress of teething may increase susceptibility to illness by lowering resistance.

Dental Caries

Dental caries (tooth decay), which may begin any time after the first tooth has erupted, occur when the normal bacteria (flora) of the mouth digest carbohydrates (sugars) and leave an acid that erodes tooth enamel. The production of this acid begins as soon as sugar in any form (e.g., milk, formula, or juice) is placed in the mouth. Teeth should be brushed after eating sticky foods (e.g., peanut butter, cheese) that allow the acid to remain in contact with the teeth. If no toothbrush is available, a water rinse will help.

At least 5% of children less than 1 year of age and 10% of children less than 2 years of age develop dental caries.[31] The baby's teeth need to be inspected regularly for a general assessment and to check for caries. Children should be seen by a dentist for the first time during their first year if they are considered to be at high risk for dental disease (i.e., a history of development disability, nonexposure to fluoride, a high carbohydrate diet, not performing daily preventative techniques, or a family history of dental disease).

One form of tooth decay that is very difficult to treat but relatively easy to prevent is known as **baby bottle mouth** or **nursing bottle mouth syndrome.** During the toddler or early preschool years, the upper and lower front and side teeth are discovered to be blackened, severely decayed, and may be broken off. Inevitably, the parents admit to putting the baby to bed for naps and at night with a bottle. The baby nurses slowly at these times or the liquid (e.g., milk, formula, juice) continues to drip from the nipple to coat the front and side teeth for long periods of time. The coated teeth literally begin to be digested by the acid. Because of these problems, many pedodontists recommend that children be offered a bottle with water for mouth rinsing after feeding, that children be weaned from the night bottle feeding by at least 1 year of age, and that they not be allowed to remain at the breast or bottle after they have fallen asleep. A pacifier can replace the bottle if the child's sucking needs exceed nutritional needs, but **a pacifier should never be used to replace essential human contact.**

Immunizations

Immunity involves the ability of the body to defend itself against substances (e.g., bacteria, viruses) that can cause physical disequilibrium or illness. The purpose of immunization or vaccination is to protect a child from disease by causing the body to produce antibodies for use against these substances (see Chap. 9 for a further discussion of immune system development).

In most cases, the newborn has a temporary, naturally acquired immunity (3 to 6 months) to the following diseases: measles (rubeola), German measles (rubella), mumps, poliomyelitis, diphtheria, and scarlet fever. The infant is not protected from chickenpox, tetanus, whooping cough (pertussis), streptococcal infections, and the common cold. Giving the newborn immunizations will not help since the infant's immature immune system is unable to produce effective antibodies. Table 6-3 gives a recommended immunization schedule for normal infants and children. Research is ongoing to find new immunizations to combat diseases which as yet have

TABLE 6-3. RECOMMENDED SCHEDULE FOR ACTIVE IMMUNIZATION OF NORMAL INFANTS AND CHILDREN

Recommended Age*	Vaccine(s)†	Comments
2 months	DTP-1[a], OPV-1[b]	Can be given earlier in areas of high endemicity
4 months	DTP-2, OPV-2	6-week to 2-month interval desired between OPV doses to avoid interference
6 months	DTP-3	Additional dose of OPV at this time optional in areas with a high risk of polio exposure
15 months[c]	MMR**, DTP-4, OPV-3	Completion of primary series of DTP and OPV
18 months	HbCV[d]	Conjugate preferred over polysaccharide vaccine***
4–6 years††	DTP-5, OPV-4	Preferably at or before school entry
11–13 years	MMR	Second dose of a 2-dose schedule
14–16 years	Td§§	Repeat every 10 years throughout life

*These recommended ages should not be construed as absolute: that is, at exactly 2 months of age.

†For all products used, consult manufacturer's package enclosure for instructions for storage, handling, and administration. Immunobiologics prepared by different manufacturers may vary, and those of the same manufacturer may change from time to time. The package insert should be followed for a specific product.

[a] DTP—diptheria and tetanus toxoids and pertussis vaccine.

[b] OPV—attenuated oral poliovirus vaccine contains poliovirus types 1, 2, and 3.

[c] Simultaneous administration of MMR, DTP, and OPV is appropriate so long as 6 months have elapsed since DTP-3 or, if fewer than 3 doses, 2 DTP have been received, 6 weeks since the previous dose of DTP or OPV. MMR at 15 months and DTP-4, OPV-3 at 18 months is acceptable.

** Live measles, mumps, and rubella viruses in a combined vaccine. Vaccination at 12 months is recommended for children living in high-risk areas, followed by revaccination at 15 months and at entrance to middle school or junior high (American Academy of Pediatrics, 1989).

[d] Hemophilius b conjugate vaccine.

*** If HbCV is not available, give polysaccharide vaccine (HbPV) at age 24 months or older. Children at risk (day care settings) may receive HbPV at 18 months and revaccination at 24 months. Children less than 5 years of age and previously vaccinated with HbPV between 18 and 23 months of age should be revaccinated with a single dose of HbCV if 2 months have elapsed since receiving HbPV.

†† Up to the seventh birthday.

§§ Adult tetanus toxoid and diptheria toxoid in combination, which contains the same dose of tetanus toxoid as DTP or DT and a reduced dose of diptheria toxoid.

(Recommendations of the Immunization practices advisory committee [ACIP]. [1989, Apr. 7]. Morbidity and Mortality Weekly Report, 38(13), 205–214.)

no Federal Drug Administration-approved vaccines (e.g., chickenpox, scarlet fever).

Under normal circumstances, the adequately immunized adolescent of 14 or 15 years of age would receive an adult tetanus and diphtheria booster (Td) and would be due for another one at 24 or 25 years of age, provided a serious major wound has not been sustained.

Tuberculin skin tests (Tbc) are not immunizations, but they are recommended at 1 year of age. The individual's reaction to Tbc indicates whether or not there has been exposure to the tubercle bacillus, which causes tuberculosis. A positive test requires follow-up investigation by a physician. Local health departments provide immunizations and Tbc testing for infants and young children for free or low costs (see Figure 6-10). They also provide selected immunizations free of charge to individuals in late adulthood.

Health Assessment

Most neonates are examined several times during their hospital stay and then are scheduled for a follow-up physical examination between 3 and 6 weeks of age. Following the first official checkup, the baby should be scheduled for visits according to the guidelines in Table 6-4.

In newborns, vision is tested mainly by checking for reaction to light. A light is shined into the eyes and responses are noted, such as pupillary constriction, blinking, following the light to midline, increased alertness, or refusal to open the eyes after exposure to the light. Special tests are available during infancy to check for blindness.

If a baby's hearing ability is questioned (e.g., the infant does not appear to be soothed by the parent's voice in early infancy), a hearing test should be arranged. Special tests can

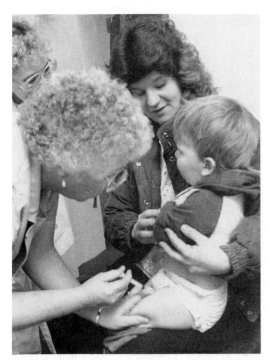

FIGURE 6–10.
Immunizations are an essential part of health care for young children.

document hearing loss in young infants. Poor hearing due to an accumulation of ear wax (cerumen) can be prevented by proper ear cleaning. A health professional should be consulted as to how it should be removed.

Parent Education

New parents usually have many questions. In addition to being concerned with the common variations discussed in Chapter 5, they may have various practical questions; for example, they may want to know how to take a baby's temperature. Most health professionals recommend taking it under the baby's armpit (axillary method).

Although there is an abundance of well-written baby care literature, such books and pamphlets should not replace the consultation of a health professional who can individualize the baby's care. Information about infant health care and safety is often provided by the local health department or clinic. Parents can learn how to care for their infants and children more effectively by attending the classes provided by the local chapter of the American Red Cross, the extension service of their state's Department of Agriculture, the Children's Service Division of the Department of Health and Human Services, or Adult Education programs. Numerous federal programs have been created to support healthy infants and children. The local Health Department will provide or coordinate developmental assessments for young children.

COMMON CONCERNS WITH INFANTS

Some of the concerns that precipitate anxiety in caregivers, especially those who have the responsibility for the first time, have already been mentioned. Three additional topics have been selected for brief discussion.

Spitting Up and Regurgitation

The return of small amounts of food during or after a feeding is common during infancy. It should not be confused with vomiting or other more serious feeding problems. The following terms are defined for clarification:

> *Spitting up:* Dribbling of unswallowed formula from the infant's mouth immediately after a feeding.
> *Regurgitation:* The *involuntary* return of undigested food from the stomach, usually accompanying burping.
> *Vomiting:* The forcible *involuntary* ejection of stomach contents, often accompanied by nausea.
> *Rumination:* The *voluntary* return of swallowed food to the mouth. The food is then rechewed, reswallowed, or expelled. Rumination is often caused by the same factors that precipitate nonorganic failure-to-thrive syndrome (see Chap. 8).

Regurgitation generally resolves spontaneously around 2 to 3 months of age as the sphincter muscle tone of the lower esophagus tightens. In the interim, caregivers can help many infants with this problem by placing them in an infant seat after feedings to keep their heads higher than their stomachs, or by instituting minor changes in feeding routines, such as more frequent, gentle burping during feedings (Fig. 6-11).

FIGURE 6–11.
Many parents place the infant carrier on a table, chair, or counter so that the child can be talked to more easily and can see more of the room. However, if the child becomes active or the weight shifts, the carrier and infant can fall, leading to serious injuries.

TABLE 6–4. AAP GUIDELINES FOR HEALTH SUPERVISION

AGE[2]	Infancy						Early Childhood					Late Childhood					Adolescence[1]			
	By 1 mo.	2 mos.	4 mos.	6 mos.	9 mos.	12 mos.	15 mos.	18 mos.	24 mos.	3 yrs.	4 yrs.	5 yrs.	6 yrs.	8 yrs.	10 yrs.	12 yrs.	14 yrs.	16 yrs.	18 yrs.	20+ yrs.
HISTORY																				
Initial/interval	●	●	●	●	●	●	●	●	●	●	●	●	●	●	●	●	●	●	●	●
MEASUREMENTS																				
Height and Weight	●	●	●	●	●	●	●	●	●	●	●	●	●	●	●	●	●	●	●	●
Head Circumference	●	●	●	●	●	●														
Blood Pressure										●	●	●	●	●	●	●	●	●	●	●
SENSORY SCREENING																				
Vision	S	S	S	S	S	S	S	S	S	S	O	O	O	O	S	O	O	S	O	O
Hearing	S	S	S	S	S	S	S	S	S	S	O	O	S[3]	S[3]	S[3]	O	S	S	O	S
DEVEL./BEHAV. ASSESSMENT[4]	●	●	●	●	●	●	●	●	●	●	●	●	●	●	●	●	●	●	●	●
PHYSICAL EXAMINATION[5]	●	●	●	●	●	●	●	●	●	●	●	●	●	●	●	●	●	●	●	●
PROCEDURES[6]																				
Hereditary/metabolic Screening[7]	●																			
Immunization[8]		●	●	●		●	●	●				●					●			
Tuberculin Test[9]						●														
Hematocrit or Hemoglobin[10]					●				●					●					●	
Urinalysis[11]									●					●					●	●

136

ANTICIPATORY GUIDANCE[12]

INITIAL DENTAL REFERRAL[13]

[1] Adolescent related issues (e.g., psychosocial, emotional, substance usage, and reproductive health) may necessitate more frequent health supervision.

[2] If a child comes under care for the first time at any point on the schedule, or if any items are not accomplished at the suggested age, the schedule should be brought up to date at the earliest possible time.

[3] At these points, history may suffice; if problem suggested, a standard testing method should be employed.

[4] By history and appropriate physical examination: if suspicious, by specific objective developmental testing.

[5] At each visit, a complete physical examination is essential, with infant totally unclothed, older child undressed and suitably draped.

[6] These may be modified, depending upon entry point into schedule and individual need.

[7] Metabolic screening (e.g., thyroid, PKU, galactosemia) should be done according to state law.

[8] Schedule(s) per Report of Committee on Infectious Disease, 1986 Red Book.

[9] For low risk groups, the Committee on Infectious Diseases recommends the following options: (1) no routine testing or (2) testing at three times—infancy, preschool, and adolescence. For high risk groups, annual TB skin testing is recommended.

[10] Present medical evidence suggests the need for reevaluation of the frequency and timing of hemoglobin or hematocrit tests. One determination is therefore suggested during each time period. Performance of additional tests is left to the individual practice experience.

[11] Present medical evidence suggests the need for reevaluation of the frequency and time of urinalysis. One determination is therefore suggested during each time period. Performance of additional tests is left to the individual practice experience.

[12] Appropriate discussion and counselling should be an integral part of each visit for care.

[13] Subsequent examinations as prescribed by dentist.

N.B.: Special chemical, immunologic, and endocrine testing are usually carried out upon specific indications. Testing other than newborn (e.g., inborn errors of metabolism, sickle disease, lead) are discretionary with the physician.

Key: ● = to be performed; S = subjective, by history; o = objective, by a standard testing method.

(Adapted from American Academy of Pediatrics Guidelines for Health Supervision II [1988]. Elk Grove Village, IL: American Academy of Pediatrics.)

Some babies regurgitate if they are rocked too vigorously during or after the feeding. A preferred position after feeding an infant is to place the baby on the right side to permit the feeding to flow toward the lower end of the stomach and to allow any swallowed air to rise above the fluid and exit through the esophagus. Keeping the corners of the infant's mouth dry of formula will decrease the chance of a rash. Persistent regurgitation at any age should be referred for medical evaluation.

Colic

Many infants are assumed to have colic, or severe, gripping abdominal pain. The colicky infant may express abdominal pain by extending the legs and body in a rigid manner or by drawing the knees up to the abdomen. The persistent crying may sometimes last for several hours, regardless of soothing efforts. Some pass large amounts of flatus (gas). The cause of true colic, which commonly begins when the baby is 2 to 6 weeks old, is still subject to debate.

Colicky behavior may be a symptom of an underlying problem such as food allergy, malabsorption, inadequate caloric intake, dehydration, or central nervous system immaturity. Infants with "difficult" temperaments are more likely to be colicky (see Chap. 8).[43] Sometimes a nervous caregiver may be the cause of a baby's display of colicky behavior. Meeting the needs of an anxious caregiver may alleviate much of the problem. Colic may be a sign of a sensitivity to cow's milk. Thus the elimination of cow's milk products from the diet of the baby or lactating mother may reduce the symptoms.[26] Unless an underlying disease is found, parents can be reassured that the infant is not ill and will probably outgrow the colic at about 3 months of age. A few babies have colic until they are 6 months old. Despite the indications of colic pain, the baby gains weight.

Treatments for colic vary. Colicky babies usually appear most comfortable when lying on their abdomens. It is suggested that the caregiver place the infant across the lap, over the shoulder, or even lie down with the baby's abdomen against the adult's. Decreasing environmental stimuli (e.g., turning down the volume of the telephone, closing the blinds, feeding the baby in a quiet area of the house) may soothe the sensitive, colicky baby. Some babies seem to fare better with a pacifier. Placing a hot water bottle on the baby's abdomen is **not** recommended. They are dangerous even if padded with towels, since they may leak or burn. Over-the-counter medication rarely helps if the baby has true colic, and even prescription medications should never be given just to keep the baby quiet. Medication may decrease the infant's ability to attend adequately to the environment, and thus may affect cognitive and socioaffective development. If the colicky behavior is caused by thirst (especially in warm weather), a bottle of water may relieve the behaviors. Colicky behavior may interfere with the establishment of a positive parent–child relationship. Parents should not feel that the infant's behavior is a result of their inadequacies. Parents can be

shown how to read their infant's subtle interaction cues, thus facilitating more effective communication with the infant. Tense parents can decrease their anxiety by learning how to understand, play with, and physically care for the infant. As the colicky behavior decreases, the parents and the baby will be able to synchronize their responses to each other more quickly.

Respiratory Infections

Some anatomical features predispose the infant to respiratory difficulties. A short, wide, horizontal eustachian tube connects the middle ear to the nasopharynx and facilitates the traffic of organisms that cause middle-ear infection. Mucous membranes lining the airway are loosely attached, increasing the risk for airway swelling. The infant's trachea (airway to the lungs) is relatively small in diameter and is surrounded by soft (as opposed to rigid and more supporting) cartilaginous rings. Both of these factors contribute to blockage of air if inflammation or swelling are present.

The major path to the right lung (the right main bronchus) is larger than the left main bronchus, as well as being more in line with, and at less of an angle to, the trachea. Thus aspirated foreign bodies more often enter the right bronchus and cause obstruction or infection. Relatively large tonsils and adenoids may also cause obstruction, even though their purpose is to aid the body in fighting infection.

The chest muscles are immaturely innervated, with the result that the infant depends primarily on abdominal muscles and the diaphragm to breathe. The relatively large abdominal organs may also impede vital breathing. The infant's small thoracic cavity is cylindrical with horizontal ribs, a factor which limits expansion potentials. All these factors, coupled with a tongue that is not well supported, make the infant's cough less effective and cause fatigue much more rapidly. To compensate, the infant must breathe faster to get the much-needed oxygen. The infant who is breathing faster than usual can upset the body's delicate acid–base balance through increased water loss.

Acute infection of the respiratory tract is the most common cause of illness in infants and young children.[24] Dressing the baby properly and assuring adequate housing, temperature, humidity, nutrition, hydration, and ventilation promote high-level wellness. Babies should not be exposed to tobacco smoke. Studies have proved the increased risk of healthy infants contracting bronchitis or pneumonia in such environments. Tobacco smoke aggravates the condition of the child with asthma or other respiratory difficulties.[1]

CONCLUSION

Each part of the infant's body grows and develops at its own rate. The infant's motor skills become more complex with the maturation of the musculoskeletal and neurological systems, and the opportunity to exercise them. Most of the baby's senses are well developed at birth, allowing input from the world. Many changes occur in the cardiovascular system that aid in transporting life-giving blood. The gastrointestinal, genitourinary, and endocrine systems meet the needs of the healthy baby in terms of ingestion, digestion, secretion, excretion, and general homeostasis. Under normal conditions, the infant's respiratory system adequately supplies oxygen and removes the necessary amount of carbon dioxide. The baby's delicate skin is adequate for protecting the body.

As the infant's baby teeth emerge and erupt, and as the body systems continue to grow and mature, feeding habits change. Proper nutrition and feeding schedules are important to provide the necessary ingredients to support the baby's biophysical growth. From the very beginning, feeding becomes the vehicle to survival, not only by supplying essential biophysical nutrients, but also by laying the foundation for interpersonal relationships (see Chap. 8).

For a few months after birth, the baby retains antibodies received from the mother, providing limited immunity to several diseases. However, the importance of prophylactic health measures and of immunizations according to schedule cannot be overemphasized. Regular health assessment can help maintain high-level wellness. This assessment should include not only the baby, but also the family and the community in which they live. Intervention, which includes parent education and referrals for community involvement, should be identified and offered. The infant's biophysical systems are well-equipped to meet the requirements of everyday living. Under stress, however, the infant may need additional assistance from the parents or health professionals.

REFERENCES

1. American Lung Association. (1989, Dec.). *Tobacco smoke emissions: Fact Sheet.* Santa Ana, CA: American Lung Association of Orange County.
2. Anholm, P. C. H. (1986). Breastfeeding: A preventive approach to health care in infancy. *Issues in Comprehensive Pediatric Nursing, 9*(1), 1–10.
3. Barnes, M. L., Crutchfield, C., & Heriza, C. (1984). *The neurophysiological basis for patient treatment: Vol. II. Reflexes in motor development.* Atlanta, GA: Stokesville.
4. Barness, L. A. (1983). Nutrition and nutritional disorders. In V. C. Vaughan, et al. (Ed.), *Nelson textbook of pediatrics* (12th ed.). Philadelphia: W.B. Saunders.
5. Beaton, G. H. (1985). Nutritional needs during the first year of life: Some concepts and perspectives. *Pediatric Clinics of North America, 32*(2), 275–288.
6. Behrman, R. E., & Vaughan, V. C. (1987). *Nelson textbook of pediatrics* (13th ed.). W.E. Nelson, Senior Editor. Philadelphia: W. B. Saunders.
7. Committee on Nutrition, American Academy of Pediatrics. (1983). The use of whole cow's milk in infancy. *Pediatrics, 72,* 253.
8. Committee on Nutrition, American Academy of Pediatrics. (1986). Fluoride supplementation. *Pediatrics, 77,* 758–761.
9. Committee on Nutrition, American Academy of Pediatrics. (1986). Prudent life-style for children: Dietary fat and cholesterol. *Pediatrics, 78,* 521–525.
10. Committee on Nutrition, American Academy of Pediatrics. (1985). *Pediatric nutrition handbook* (2nd ed.). Elk Grove Village, IL: American Academy of Pediatrics.
11. Dallman, P. R., et al. (1980). Iron deficiency in infancy and childhood. *American Journal of Clinical Nutrition, 33,* 86.
12. Davidson, M. B. (1987). Effect of growth hormone on carbohydrate and lipid metabolism. *Endocrine Reviews, 8*(2), 115–131.
13. Davis, D. H., & Thoman, E. B. (1988). Behavioral states of premature infants: Implications for neural and behavioral development. *Developmental Psychobiology, 20,* 25–38.
14. Downie, P. (1986). *Cash's textbook of neurology for physiotherapists* (4th ed.). Philadelphia: Faber and Faber.
15. Eckert, H. M. (1987). *Motor development* (3rd ed.). Indianapolis, IN: Benchmark Press.
16. Fomon, S. J., et al. (1977). Human milk and the small premature infant. *American Journal of Diseases of Children, 131,* 463.
17. Grant, J. P. (1985). *The state of the world's children, 1986.* New York: Oxford University Press for UNICEF.
18. Green, M. (1986). *Pediatric diagnosis: Interpretations of symptoms and signs in different age periods* (4th ed.). Philadelphia: W.B. Saunders.
19. Gryboski, J., & Walker, W. (1983). *Gastrointestinal problems in the infant* (2nd ed.). Philadelphia: W. B. Saunders.
20. Haywood, K. M. (1986). *Life span motor development.* Champaign, IL: Human Kinetics.
21. Horowitz, H. S. (1981). Community water fluoridation. In D. J. Forrester, M. L. Wagner, & J. Fleming (Eds.), *Pediatric dental medicine.* Philadelphia: Lea & Febiger.
22. Jorgensen, R. J., & Yost, C. (1988). Etiology and enamel dysplasias. *Journal of Pedodontics, 12,* 315–328.
23. Kempe, C. H., et al (Ed.). (1987). *Current pediatric diagnosis and treatment* (9th ed.). Los Altos, CA: Appleton & Lange Medical Publications.
24. Kendig, E. L., & Chernick, V. (Eds.). (1983). *Disorders of the respiratory tract in children.* Philadelphia: W. B. Saunders.
25. Knittle, J. (1972). Obesity in childhood: A problem in adipose tissue cellular development. *Journal of Pediatrics, 81,* 1048.
26. Lothe, L., et al. (1982). Cow's milk formula as a cause of infantile colic: A double-blind study. *Pediatrics, 70*(1), 7.
27. Lowrey, G. H. (1986). *Growth and development of children* (8th ed.). Chicago: Year Book.
28. MacFarlane, A. (1977). *The psychology of childbirth.* Cambridge, MA: Harvard University Press.
29. Maffly, R. H. (1981). The body fluids: Volume, composition and physical chemistry. In B. M. Brenner & F. Rector (Eds.), *The Kidney.* Philadelphia: W. B. Saunders.
30. Masiak, M. J., Naylor, M. D., & Hayman, L. L. (1985). *Fluids and electrolytes through the life cycle.* Norwalk, CT: Appleton, Century-Crofts.
31. Matthewson, R. J., et al. (1982). *Fundamentals of dentistry for children. Vol. 1. A complete guide to comprehensive dental care for the child and adolescent.* Chicago: Quintessence.
32. Murray, J. F. (1986). *The normal lung: The basis for diagnosis and treatment of pulmonary disease* (2nd ed.). Philadelphia: W. B. Saunders.
33. Pillitteri, A. (1987). *Child health nursing: Care of the growing family* (3rd ed.). Boston: Little, Brown.
34. Pipes, P. L. (Ed.). (1989). *Nutrition in infancy and childhood* (4th ed.). St. Louis: C. V. Mosby.

35. Porter, R., Cernock, J., & Perry, S. (1983). The importance of odors in mother-infant interactions. *Maternal-Child Nursing Journal, 12*(3), 147–154.

36. Scott, D. T. (1987). Premature infants in later childhood: Some recent follow results. *Seminars in Perinatology, 11,* 191–199.

37. Silverman, A., & Roy, C. (1983). *Pediatric clinical gastroenterology* (3rd ed.). St. Louis: C. V. Mosby.

38. Simard, P. L., et al. (1989). The ingestion of fluoride dentifrice by young children. *Journal of Dentistry for Children, 56,* 177–181.

39. Spence, A. P. (1989). *Biology of human aging.* Englewood Cliffs, NJ: Prentice-Hall.

40. Spock, B., & Rothenberg, M. B. (1985). *Baby and child care* (rev. ed.). New York: E. P. Dutton.

41. Stunkard, A. J., & Stellar, E. (Eds.). (1984). *Eating and its disorders.* New York: Raven Press.

42. Tanner, J. M. (1989). *Foetus into man: Physical growth from conception to maturity* (rev. & enl.). Cambridge, MA: Harvard University Press.

43. Weissbluth, M., Christoffel, K. K., & Davis, A. T. (1984). Treatment of infantile colic with dicyclomine hydrochloride. *Journal of Pediatrics, 104*(6), 951–955.

44. Wenner, W., & Barnard, K. (1979). The changing infant: Sleep and activity patterns during the first months of life. In K. Barnard (Ed.), *The nursing child assessment sleep/activity record.* Seattle: University of Washington.

45. Winikoff, B., et al. (1986). Dynamics of infant feeding. *Pediatrics, 77,* 357.

46. Ziai, M. (Ed.). (1975). *Pediatrics.* Boston, MA: Little, Brown.

7

IT IS A RARE PRIVILEGE TO WATCH THE BIRTH, GROWTH, AND FIRST FEEBLE STRUGGLE OF A LIVING MIND.

—ANNIE SULLIVAN

Cognitive Development During Infancy

Clara S. Schuster

The task of *learning how to learn* is probably the most significant task of infancy. Indeed, almost every other task of infancy and of the life span itself is founded upon this one skill. The infant cannot develop a meaningful relationship with a significant other unless he or she has learned to differentiate that person from all others.

Sensitive parents become acutely aware of how much this initiate to life has to learn during the first few months and years of life: from how to shake a rattle to how to play peek-a-boo; from how to feed one's self to how to find a hidden object; from how to attract attention to how to talk. All these activities are built upon the ability to see relationships and to predict an outcome. The infant must learn how to attend to relevant cues and how to explore and gain more information. The major elements of the learning process appear during the first 6 months of life.[58]

Provision of stimulation is not sufficient for infant learning. The young child must have control and repetitive experiences in "making things happen" in order to be able to associate action with a response (**cause–effect relationship**). Such associations, once recognized, provide motivation to practice "making it happen again." Repetitive experiences at controlling environmental events leads to the anticipation of finding new events that can come under one's control. Gradually, the infant begins to consciously explore objects and events in the environment to identify how they work or can be made to work.

Mastery of the tasks of learning, attachment, and communication are initially dependent on the contingency and predictability provided by the social environment. Consistency helps the infant to develop trust in the environment, in people, and in him or herself. "Infant mental potentialities only become actualized through [the] parents' efforts to support and extend their infant's activities. Thus, development in all spheres is socially mediated; infants do not develop on their own, but rather through a combination of their own efforts and those of their parents."[15] AuQ. 1

The five domains and their development are very difficult to differentiate during the infancy period. Although all five domains are involved in the infant's learning processes, the biophysical and cognitive domains are the primary participants. The sensory organs of the nervous system receive input from the environment and transmit the sensations to the brain. The cognitive domain must then assign meaning to the information and decide how to respond to the stimulus.

Piaget has helped us to understand the different cognitive levels people use to process and organize information (from the sensorimotor understanding of infancy to the abstract understanding of adolescent and adult years).[55, 56, 57] **Learning** is a dynamic process of concept formation that leads to a change in understanding and behavior. Learning does not necessarily follow immediately after the reception of input, but occurs when insight or new meaning is attached to experiences. Differences in the social environment, the infant's temperament, and the degree of neurologic maturity can produce early individual differences in learning.

Initially, much of an infant's behavior appears to be facilitated by a broad repertoire of reflexive responses, stimulus preferences, and innate social skills that lay a foundation for responding to and seeking interaction with the environment. Gradually, as others respond to and reinforce the infant's use of primitive interactional tools, the infant becomes aware of a cause–effect relationship between his or her own behavior and events in the environment. The infant, even in the first weeks of life, begins to anticipate events and to show behavioral change in the presence of specific stimuli (e.g., infant brightens and alters breathing patterns in anticipation of being picked up when a parent comes to the bedside). Gradually, the infant tries to purposefully make the event happen again (e.g., cries out experimentally to see if the parent will come).

DEVELOPMENT OF PERCEPTION

Perception is the process of receiving and analyzing sensory information. It includes transmitting stimulation from the sensory end organs to the central processes of cognition in order to organize a response to the stimulation. Initially, the infant's attention appears to be "captured" by specific stimuli. With experience and maturity, the child learns to voluntarily focus on or ignore specific stimuli. Some hypothesize an innate releasing mechanism activated in the presence of specific stimuli, since many of the early responses are found in all neurologically normal neonates (e.g., rooting reflex, tongue-protrusion imitation, or turning toward sound).[49, 52]

D. O. Hebb,[41] an experimental psychologist, postulated the concept of *cell assemblies* or neurological building blocks of the brain. He reported that animals reared in the dark experience marked visual disabilities and suggested that the lack of early experience may be related to perceptual disabilities. Hebb maintained that development of the cell assemblies depends on adequate exposure to sensory experiences during biologically determined critical periods and that the neural network remains unconnected if inadequate sensory experience is provided. Infants with cataracts, severe strabismus, or other conditions reducing visual acuity are noted to experience permanent visual perceptual difficulties if corrective interventions are delayed too long. However, the relationship of adequate stimulation to the development of the other modalities (senses) is less clear.[40] Infants with inadequate exposure to different textures are noted to become tactually defensive as they become toddlers, but this can be corrected with appropriate intervention.

Sensory Capabilities

The sensory receptors are divided into three categories:

> **Exteroceptors** (distance senses):
> Vision
> Hearing

> **Proprioceptors** (near senses):
> Cutaneous (skin) senses
> Touch/pressure
> Pain
> Temperature
> Taste
> Smell
> **Interoceptors** (deep senses):
> Kinesthetic sense–detects changes in the position of the body and motions of the muscles, tendons, and joints.
> Vestibular sense–detects changes related to maintaining one's balance and position in space (includes awareness of gravitational pull, acceleration, and direction change).

The integrity of the sensory system is a critical factor to cognition and learning in the early years of life, since inadequate or distorted sensations present a different world to the child than to others. The lack of one functioning sensory system may be compensated to a degree by the interpretation of information from the other senses (e.g., a change in the subtle wind currents against the skin as well as a change in the sound patterns encountered when walking through a building allow a blind person to be aware of doorways, barriers, and even room size). However, one system cannot assume the responsibilities of another. Each sensory organ is energy-specific (uniquely designed to respond to the specific qualities of a stimulus—color, tone, texture, odor, taste, and so forth). Therefore, if a stimulus is received by the wrong sensory organ, it will transmit a different message (e.g., blowing on the ear will produce sound, and pressing on the eyeball will present the brain with a confusion of colors). If two or more systems are functioning below normally expected levels, or if the cognitive system is not yet able to adequately integrate the information from the other senses, then the baby usually experiences delays in adaptation to the environment. Table 7-1 lists characteristics of the five major senses.

Vision

Vision appears to be the dominant modality (sensory system) for learning about the environment.[59] Eighty to ninety percent of all learning occurs through the visual mode. Not only does vision bring us information about the distant environment, the activities of other people, and the presence of potential dangers, but vision also enables the interpretation of information received from the other senses. Perhaps this is why the visual and auditory senses are already coordinated at birth as evidenced by the neonate's propensity to turn to sound.[13]

By determining how long a reflected image of a stimulus appeared in the baby's pupil, Fantz discovered that 1-week-old infants are capable of differentiating between patterns (such as horizontal stripes, a bull's-eye, a checkerboard, and a

TABLE 7-1. CHARACTERISTICS OF THE FIVE MAJOR SENSES

Sense	Stimulus	Receptors	Minimum Stimulus	Equivalent Stimulus
Vision	Electromagnetic energy, photons	Rods and cones in the retina	1 photon absorbed by one rod	Candle flame viewed from a distance of 48 km (30 miles)
Hearing	Sound pressure waves	Hair cells on basilar membrane of the inner ear	0.0002 dynes/cm	Ticking of a watch in a quiet room 6 m (20 ft) away
Taste	Chemical substances dissolved in saliva	Taste buds on the tongue	Several molecules (depending on the substance)	1 tsp of sugar dissolved in 2 gal of distilled water (1 part in 2,000)
Smell	Chemical substances in the air	Receptor cells in the upper nasal cavity	Several molecules (depending on the substance)	1 drop of perfume in a three-room house (1 part in 500,000,000)
Touch	Mechanical displacement of the skin	Nerve endings in the skin*	0.1 μ (0.00000001 mm) (depending on the part of the body)	The wing of a bee falling on your cheek from a distance of 1 cm (0.39 in)

*Yield sensations of warmth, cold, touch, pain.
(Bourne, L. E. and Ekstrand, B. R. (1985). Psychology: Principles and meaning [5th ed.]. New York: Holt, Rinehart & Winston, p. 76. Used with permission.)

gray patch) and selecting the one of interest to them.[29] Visual acuity is discussed in Chapters 5 and 20.

The infant has a visual field of only 15° to 20° at 2 weeks of age.[74] Ocular movement is also limited, so the infant typically moves its head to see or follow object movement. When the infant's vision is captured by a moving object or series of objects moving rapidly across the visual field, the eyes follow the object(s) in the direction of the movement, then snap back into the opposite direction to lock onto a new object (optokinetic nystagmus). This is a normal behavior, and its absence indicates a neurological problem. By moving stripes of varying widths across the infant's visual path, researchers are able to determine the smallest width the infant can see, and thus can estimate a baby's visual acuity.

The very young infant's sense of depth and distance is limited by *acuity* and *fusion* issues. The neonate has no ability to accommodate (change the shape of) the lens for distance. There is a fixed visual distance of about 19 cm, which gradually extends with age. By 2 weeks, babies appear to have some appreciation of distance through the *looming reflex*. If an object is moved toward an infant's face rapidly, the baby will show apprehension, blink, pull its head back, and even shield its face with the hands. The behaviors subside as the object is moved further away.[10, 87] The mechanisms of the infant's interpretation of visual approach is not clear.

Both foveas will fixate on the same point (*bifoveal vision*) by three months of age. The brain gradually learns to integrate the two retinal images (*fusion*) into a single perceived object. If the brain cannot fuse the images, double vision occurs. *Stereopsis* (depth perception) is based on the disparity between the two images. The median age for the onset of binocular disparity is 16 weeks.[42] Girls appear to develop depth perception earlier than boys.[86]

Color vision appears to be present from birth. Infants less than 1 week old can discriminate red and yellow from gray;[2] by three months, they clearly differentiate between red, blue, yellow, and green[8, 48] and indicate preference in the order presented.

Hearing

Many neonates can detect the difference between tones of 200 and 250 cycles per second, which is approximately equivalent to one step in a musical scale.[16] By 5 to 6 months of age most babies will turn expectantly toward a person who says their name. Long before the end of the first year, the infant is sensitive to minute differences between combinations of sounds and will show recognition of frequently used, meaningful words. Young infants are more perceptive of subtle inflection or sound differences than adults. Yet, by 12 months, the ability to discriminate between subtle differences not found in the infant's natural language environment has already begun to decrease.[78] Children thus gradually become attuned to the nuances of their own language.

Touch

The sense of touch (discussed further in Chap. 8) is an important perceptual tool. At birth, the skin's receptors are capable of receiving sensations of touch, pain, pressure, and temperature although individual differences in sensitivity are observed. Immaturity of the cerebral components that interpret and organize responses to tactile sensations accounts for the differences in infant versus adult responses (see Chap. 5 for a discussion of pain in the infant). In general, the sensorimotor aspects of a child's behavior develop earlier than the cognitive and conative aspects (conscious, planned response). Localization of pain or touch is established well before the child achieves integration of the various neural centers that permit an appropriate response.

The infant uses its hands for touching, holding, transferring, and transforming objects. Consequently, it is difficult to determine if an infant is manipulating an object for tactile information or just to change the stimulus for the eyes to see. By 5 months, the infant's attention will be held to a haptic (touch) stimulus three times longer than to a visual stimulus, indicating that touch has become a significant perceptual system.[73] It also appears that it takes the infant longer to process haptic than visual information (a significant factor to keep in mind when working with blind persons).

Taste

At birth, babies perceive differences between widely varying tastes such as sugar and salt. By 2 weeks of age, babies will suck when given sugar water and grimace when citric acid (contained in orange juice) is placed on their tongues (Fig. 7-1). They also stop sucking when salty solutions or quinine water are placed on their tongues.

Infants are born with many taste buds, enabling them to savor the natural flavor of foods. Hence, adding sugar or salt to a baby's food is unnecessary. During the first 5 years of life, the number of taste buds gradually decreases. Taste preferences are influenced by individual cultures. The Eskimo child learns to ask for whale blubber, the Hawaiian youngster craves poi, and the Japanese child develops an appreciation for sushi (raw fish). A number of young children, especially blind children, are noted to touch their tongue to the skin of a person as if using taste and smell as a part of their identification system.

Smell

The newborn will turn the head away when exposed to unpleasant olfactory stimuli such as ammonia or acetic acid. However, they are generally nonreactive to stimuli that older children and adults find disgusting (such as flatus or sulfur) because they have not yet associated cultural stigma with such odors. Breast-fed babies can smell their mother's milk and often refuse formula. Locating the source of odors is not very precise in humans, and appears to vary greatly from one individual to another. Nevertheless, the infant's sense of smell can be a valuable tool for learning (Fig. 7-2). Many babies, even young infants, are noted to become fussy during the time when the odors of a meal are strong in the air even if they have eaten recently.

The Perceptual Process

The perceptual process involves an intimate interplay of the biophysical and cognitive domains as information is received and interpreted. Although insight into an abstract idea is a form of perception, that level of perception is only found in more mature persons. Therefore, we will deal only with *sensorimotor perception*. The perceptual process, for our discussion, will include three major steps: **detection, analysis,** and **response** to a stimulus. Some basic assumptions about perception are given in Table 7-2.

Detection of Stimulus Energy

Detection of stimulus energy is based on two primary factors: the characteristics of the infant and the characteristics of the stimulus.

FIGURE 7–1.
Even though the initial physical reaction to a piece of lemon or sour pickle may be strong, many young babies will continue to suck on the tidbit until the flavor is gone and may even cry if it is taken away. Such exposure to new experiences helps children to increase their awareness of the world and their own bodies.

FIGURE 7–2.
Imitation is a form of learning that originates during infancy. This mother's encouragement to sniff the flowers is helping the baby to use the sense of smell to gain more information about the environment.

TABLE 7–2. ASSUMPTIONS ABOUT PERCEPTION

Statement	Explanation/Example
1. Perception includes both the sensing of input and the interpretation of that input.	1. Someone slams a door, and a baby hears the noise (detects an auditory stimulus) and perceives it as uncomfortable (interpretation of the input).
2. Perception is each individual's representation or image of reality.	2. Different people attach different values to different stimuli.
3. Perception is selective.	3. Individuals do not perceive accurately, but selectively, choosing to complete the perceptual process by interpreting some input and disregarding other input.
4. Psychosocial as well as neurophysiological factors affect perceptual processes.	4. Physical fatigue as well as emotional stress can affect what a person perceives as a stimulus.
5. Perceptions differ according to past experiences, self-concept, socioeconomic group, biological inheritance, and educational background.	5. Preferences for foodstuffs vary according to culture and geographical location: Orientals find raw fish a delicacy but may at first shun the traditional American fried chicken.
6. Perceptual processes are important to learning and interacting.	6. Perception serves as a selective filter. Through perception, potentially significant events are brought into meaningful focus.
7. Perceptual skills gradually become more refined, stable, and integrated.	7. Individuals are able to differentiate and articulate input at increasingly more complex levels with maturation and experience.
8. Perception is a dynamic process, which becomes increasingly adaptive with development.	8. Perceptual input is synthesized and becomes more complex and richly patterned with experience.
9. An individual who is unable to receive sensory input from one modality can learn to depend more heavily on alternative sensory input.	9. An individual who does not have vision can learn to rely heavily on the senses of touch, taste, smell, and hearing.
10. The use of alternative sources for sensory input may affect interpretation and thus perception of the environment.	10. An individual who has partially lost the abilities to taste and smell may prefer foods more highly seasoned than an individual who has normal olfactory senses.

Human Factors

Preattentional State. A critical factor in the detection of stimulus energy is the person's **preattentional state.** A baby in state 4 (the quiet, alert state; see Chap. 4) will be looking for and is generally ready to process and respond to a stimulus. In states 1 and 2 (sleep states) or state 6 (crying state), the child's level of consciousness obviously is not conducive to receiving and organizing an adaptive response to a stimulus. An infant who is intensely involved with or "hooked" by another stimulus may also fail to become aware of the presence of a new stimulus (much like an adolescent involved in reading a book may fail to respond to the parent's call). Thus, to obtain optimal responses from an infant (or anyone), close attention must be paid to the child's preattentional state. If the child is in state 3 or 5, then the adult must entice the baby into state 4 before expecting an appropriate response.

Scanning Ability. A person's **scanning ability** also affects one's response to a stimulus. Our senses are barraged by a wide range of stimuli, each calling for attention at the same time. Our eyes pick up information from the many objects, colors, and words before us. Simultaneously, our ears pick up the buzz of a light bulb, the whir of a fan, air conditioner, or furnace. Motor vehicles in the street, noises from people around us, birds chirping outside, a squeaky chair, and music from the radio all vie for our attention. We also are receiving messages from our skin, mouth, and inner body. We feel the

pencil in our hand, the chair on which we sit, our heart beating, and an itch on our back. Yet, we can only attend to one or two of these stimuli at one time.

Perception thus is subdivided into *central perception*—the ability to focus attention on a specific stimulus, and *peripheral perception*—the ability to monitor but not attend or respond to non-meaningful stimuli. Scanning ability involves the cognitive processes that subconsciously evaluate all stimuli which come to the attention of the peripheral perceptual system, filtering and prioritizing them for transmission to the central perceptual system.

Alerting. When a stimulus is read as meaningful (e.g., the parent says, " . . . and I mean NOW!" and suddenly a book plot is not quite so important), there is an arousal of attention. The person is **alerted** to the need to change the focus of attention to the new stimulus. **Alerting** prepares the person to analyze the input on a conscious level and to organize a specific response. Some believe that the infant's poor visual abilities limit what must be processed.[74] Innate preferences for specific stimuli (for example, the 1–4 month old infant has a definite preference for normal facial configurations over other patterns[28]) serve as a natural filtering process. These compensate for immature scanning ability, thus preventing sensory overload and facilitating the "tuning in" to significant stimulation.[21]

The amount of time between presentation of the stimulus

and the individual's response is known as *latency*. Latency, or *reaction time,* decreases with maturation of the central nervous system because of increased speed and efficiency in organizing information.[61] The speed of reaction time in 9-month-old babies is noted to predict response time at 3½ years.[61] Thus, an affective or intelligence factor may also underlie the speed of alerting.

Orienting. Once a person is alerted to the presence of a potentially meaningful stimulus, he or she must **orient** toward the stimulus. This means that the stimulus must be localized before it can become the focus of attention. Localization involves the coordination of modalities. Even as early as 3 to 10 minutes after birth, the baby is able to move the eyes and head in the direction of a sound.[80] This orienting reflex provides the infant with more information about the environment and sets the stage for bimodal integration. Neonates will turn with fair accuracy toward a sound presented at 90° or 45° from midline and will then search with their eyes for the source.[51] By 4½ months, they can turn directly to a 30° displacement, and within 5° of a 60° displacement. The 6-month-old can detect horizontal sound displacements of 19°. By 18 months, sound displacement detection reaches adult levels (1–2° displacement detection).[3] The increasing circumference of the head leads to increased differences in sound arrival time. This, combined with experience, facilitates auditory localization. Reduced hearing in one ear will affect orientation responses (Fig. 7-3).

The young infant orients every part of the body toward a stimulus to obtain maximal information. Many of these early orienting responses appear to be as reflexive as the rooting or

FIGURE 7–3.
The alert infant is ready to make optimal use of learning opportunities in the environment.

tonic neck reflexes. Physical maturity and experience gradually allow the infant to selectively alert, orient, and concentrate attention on a stimulus of choice. By 4 months, the infant evidences an ability to coordinate stimuli from two modalities. For example, when shown a split-screen movie with a woman saying "peek-a-boo" on one side and a stick rhythmically beating a piece of wood on the other, the baby will selectively spend more time looking at the picture which matches the experimenter-manipulated sound track.[5, 72]

STIMULUS FACTORS. The **attention-drawing** properties of stimuli appear to be fairly constant throughout life (e.g., a bright light or a loud sound will generally cause one to alert), but the **attention-holding** factors change with development of the cognitive domain and experience.[71]

Context. The context surrounding a stimulus is a critical factor influencing its attention-drawing ability. Other stimuli in the environment can mask the value of a stimulus or can interfere with a person's ability to detect the presence of the stimulus. For example, at a party, we may find that it becomes difficult, if not impossible to hear and understand our partner in a conversation. We have to work very hard to draw the relevant factors into our central perceptual processing system. Our peripheral perceptual system is working overtime, and we frequently find that the environment tires us. We know that our scanning system is working, because in the midst of all the noise, we suddenly become aware that someone across the room is saying our name.

The infant and young child may likewise find it difficult to sort out relevant and irrelevant stimuli and organize an adaptive response. Even the very young infant makes attempts to regulate the amount of stimuli that must be processed by visually seeking more stimuli when in underload and by tuning out when in sensory overload. Too many stimuli presented at once, such as a noisy, chaotic household or an overenthusiastic greeting by a grandparent, may force the infant or young child to retreat in self-defense. Even the very young infant will close the eyes or avert the head when stimulation becomes intrusive and overwhelms the immature perceptual and cognitive systems. Thus, *an overstimulating environment may actually interfere with, rather than facilitate intellectual development.*

Contrast. The contrast (intensity, strength, or size) of a stimulus is probably the major factor influencing its alerting ability. Each stimulus, whether visual, auditory, or tactile, must be strong enough to break through the sensory system's discrimination thresholds in order to alert the person that there is something to attend to. Young infants, because of neurological immaturity, have very high thresholds in all modalities except hearing. Consequently, they experience difficulty distinguishing visual or tactile patterns if the contrast is poor (e.g., shades of gray on white, blending of hues of the same color family, or two smooth objects). Marked contrasts in stimulus intensity (e.g., black/white visual designs, fuzzy/smooth tactile toys) are essential to facilitate initial detection and discrimination activities.

Contour. Contour, or shape of a stimulus can affect the infant's response. Visually, infants appear to prefer the most complex pattern they can currently see.[71] They prefer curved lines to straight lines, symmetrical to asymmetrical patterns, and multi-part patterns to simple designs.[29, 30, 45]

Contingency. The attention-drawing properties (what happens *before* the child is aware of the stimulus) of a stimulus will alert the infant to its presence, but the attention-holding properties (what happens *after* the child is aware of the stimulus) are determined by its meaningfulness to the child. The most critical factor in determining meaningfulness of a stimulus to the young child is its temporal relationship to the child's behavior. When the action of a stimulus is contingent on the child's action, it will hold the child's attention for a longer period of time. A delay of more than 3 seconds interrupts contingency learning by the 6-month-old infant.[50]

Personal observations indicate that by 3 months, the visual behavior of infants varies greatly depending on their experience with contingent reciprocity in the environment. Those infants who have had very responsive parents appear to be more alert and assume a very active role in scanning the environment. They seem to be actively looking for interesting things to capture their attention. Their facial expressions indicate that they *expect* a response from their environment and are looking for the next source of activity. They attend to movements and people with intense curiosity and interest, even after any reciprocal interaction has ceased. They will call out with their voice and reach with their hands as if "wooing" the person, or willing the event to recur. Those infants with minimally responsive parents are noted to become alert when a stimulus is presented to them, but interest is maintained for shorter periods of time and only while the attention-drawing characteristic is still dominant. Most babies with short attention spans begin to increase interest as they mature, but are often less alert or assertive about interacting with the environment than those infants who learned how to learn during the first few months.

Closure. Initially, an infant must have tactile contact or interaction with an object for it to have meaning (e.g., the nipple must be placed in the infant's mouth to elicit a sucking behavior). As visual memory develops, the infant is able to recognize an object when it appears. Consequently, the infant will begin to show sucking movements of the mouth when the bottle or nipple comes into view. Gradually, the infant's memory is able to fill in what is not seen. Thus, if the bottle (or other object) is partially hidden under a cloth, the infant still recognizes it as the desired bottle, making sucking mouth movements or attempts to retrieve the object. Around 8 to 9 months, the infant develops what Piaget refers to as **object permanence.** The infant is now able to remember that an object or stimulus exists and to seek it independently of an attention-drawing property. Memory is no longer tied to the presence of the object, or **recognition memory.** Memory is reorganized into an expressive mode, motivating the infant to seek what is not immediately perceived. Thus, an object completely hidden under a cloth in the presence of the infant will elicit search efforts if the object is desired. If the infant is not able to search for the object, but must watch someone else retrieve it, the infant will express surprise if the object is retrieved from a location different from where the infant saw the object hidden.[6] As the child's memory matures, he or she will remember and seek a specific object at greater temporal distances from the original stimulus. **Closure** (the filling in by the mind what the senses do not fully receive) thus represents a blending of child and stimulus characteristics. We use closure in different settings as we mature (e.g., to fill in missed sounds or words in a spoken sentence) (Fig. 7-4).

Analysis

The detection of a stimulus is basically the responsibility of the sensory organs. The analysis, however, is the responsibility of the cognitive domain. Once a stimulus (full or partial) has entered the central perceptual system, the person must analyze and make a conscious or unconscious (i.e., automatic) decision on what to do with the information.

ATTENDING. A person cannot analyze information without giving full attention to the stimulus. Looking at an object does not equal meaningful attention. Attending assumes an **encoding process**—the stimulus is actively received and more information is sought so that it can be meaningfully interpreted. In other words, attending is an active process.[36] The infant must be in state 4 to attend to a stimulus. At 7 months, only 25% of a child's "looking time" is spent in active attention; by 12 months, this has only increased to 38%.[19] Research indicates that infants who are efficient visual and auditory encoders

FIGURE 7–4.
The baby who has developed object permanence will hunt for a hidden object.

tend to be more proficient on intelligence and language assessments during childhood.[9]

Data Gathering. Information is received from several modalities simultaneously. The infant selectively attends to each piece of information, and then gradually learns to coordinate the information to "know" an object from more than one modality.[36] The data-gathering process appears to go through a developmental sequence. Initially, the infant will *randomly manipulate* objects held in the hand. As the infant begins to learn how to learn, he or she will begin to *grossly explore* objects, using the mouth and tongue, sucking on objects, holding them out to look at them, and beginning to turn them around in the hand(s). Infants as young as 2 months will continue to explore objects tactually and visually as long as interesting and contingent responses result.[36] As cognitive and motor skills develop, the infant begins to *minutely examine* objects both visually and tactually. The child's eyes intensely examine the details of a face or object, and the fingers begin to explore the crevices and curves and to scratch at or feel the texture and surface of objects. The infant's behaviors indicate that he or she is trying to extract maximal information from the object.[73] The child discovers what an object or person can do and begins to *practice* making the event happen again at will. Multiple repetitions of an event seal in the child's mind the relationships between cause and effect and the permanency or stability of the data gathered.

As the child becomes more confident of the characteristics of a stimulus, he or she begins to *experiment* with it. What else can this object do? Can I use it in another way? Can I make the same event happen through another approach? Obviously, the cognitive domain becomes very critical in guiding the data-gathering process of the perceptual system. Another step in this data-gathering sequence is to put the information to *use*. *Analysis* of its effectiveness in meeting a goal is an ongoing process, but at this point, the infant or child is confident enough of the information to be able to use it as a base for exploring new horizons.

Differentiating. Integral to data gathering is the ability to extract the distinctive features of an object or event. This process shows remarkable changes with maturation of cognitive and perceptual skills (see section on "Emergence of Discrimination Skills"). The infant gradually learns to differentiate the relevant from the irrelevant features and how to filter out the irrelevant. The infant also learns how to differentiate between similar objects to choose the desired one. For example, almost all faces have two eyes, a nose, a mouth, and hair. The infant learns to differentiate between familiar and unfamiliar faces through attention to the minor variations between them. A 5- to 10-month-old baby will go to someone who looks like Mommy more readily than someone who does not. The infant's ability to differentiate between two objects is assessed by the baby's tendency to attend to one object or event longer than the other when both are presented simultaneously (visual or tactile stimuli) or sequentially (e.g., auditory stimuli). In this way, researchers can also identify a child's preferences. By 5 months, the infant indicates the ability to tactually differentiate between a square block and a square block with a hole in it; or between a six-pointed star and a six-petaled flower.[73] Discrimination ability improves with maturation of the cognitive skills and practice.

JUDGMENT. Once the child has given sufficient attention to extract the relevant data, he or she must decide whether or not to continue to attend to the stimulus. This involves both memory and volition.

Memory. **Memory,** or the storage of information by cognitive processes is assessed by the infant's response to the introduction of stimulation. When new information comes to our attention, one of the first cognitive acts is to *compare* it to that which is already stored in our memory banks. The stimulus is then identified as *novel* or *familiar*. Presumably because of the very short memory span of infants, most stimuli are initially responded to as a novel stimulus. As the infant is alerted, the pulse rate and respirations will increase; however, breathing and heart rate will slow, and body movements will be greatly reduced, as the infant focuses energies toward maximal exposure toward a stimulus. If a nipple is in the baby's mouth, sucking will stop. The attention of a young infant is complete.

Familiarity or pattern recognition is examined by assessing two factors: **Perceptual memory** and **stimulus constancy.** Perceptual memory is exhibited through the phenomenon of **habituation.** Initially, the infant spends much time looking at, examining, or listening to the target stimulus. Examining represents focused attention and active intake of information. With a visual stimulus, a baby will avert the eyes or turn the body and head away for a brief period and then come back for more looking. This cyclic attention to a stimulus provides maximal exposure without overloading the infant's immature sensory and cognitive skills.[14] The infant thus controls how much and how quickly information will be processed. Sensitive adults respect this natural cycling, interacting when the child is attending and withholding extra stimulation when the baby retreats. When the infant is able to identify the order and invariance of a stimulus, the baby becomes satiated.[36] The baby has extracted as much information as the cognitive system maturity will allow, becomes bored, and ceases to attend to the stimulus (**habituated**). At this point, a second, novel stimulus, is introduced. The infant now proceeds to attend to the second stimulus with as much energy as expended on the first. Experiments involving the habituation phenomenon prove the infant's ability to discriminate between novel and familiar stimuli and the existence of perceptual memory.

The very young infant also exhibits functioning of the short- and long-term memory systems. However, they are limited in scope and are perceptually based. The issue of **stimulus constancy** assumes that the baby has internalized a stable impression of a stimulus, which is used as a comparison point to assess the familiarity of incoming stimuli. One example is the neonate's ability to differentiate its mother's voice from that of other women (see Chap. 3).[23] Subtle signs of visual recognition of people emerge during the first 2 to 3 weeks of life.[14] When a person comes to the bedside, the baby initially will reach out with the extremities, eyes, mouth, and head as alerting occurs. If the person is the mother, the movements, especially of the hands, become smooth and cyclic as if expecting a reciprocal, soothing response. When the father appears, a different pattern emerges. The infant gives a more wide-eyed, playful, and bright-faced response, and the hands and fingers extend in bursts of movement as if anticipating a period of exciting play. Some "parent constancy" has occurred. Strangers elicit longer periods of "hooked" attention, as much as given to any other novel object.[14]

Avoidance of unfamiliar people through turning away, signs of apprehension, and clinging to a familiar person is frequently observed around 20 weeks (stranger anxiety). All these responses indicate the presence of stimulus constancy or memory. Observation of pupillary response also can be used to assess the pleasantness or unpleasantness of a specific stimulus for even the youngest or most profoundly retarded individual. The pupils will dilate with the recognition of pleasant stimuli or a familiar person and constrict in the presence of an unfamiliar person or an abrasive stimulus.[18]

Obviously, the young infant has limited use of the scanning mechanism of the memory bank. The infant also possesses a relatively small amount of data. It has been stressed that those experiences the young infant does have are not yet tied together through a symbol system such as language. Language helps to "cluster memories together so they can be retrieved as a single bundle, rather than one at a time."[34]

Elkind identifies two levels of memory.[24] The elementary, or *sensorimotor memory* is most prominent in infancy and early childhood. It involves the retention of sensorimotor coordinations that are learned as the individual adapts to the immediate environment. It is this type of learning that includes the retention of motor coordinations practiced in infancy and childhood (e.g., swimming, dancing, bike riding). The memory traces left by such sensorimotor activities facilitate relearning of the same unpracticed coordinations years later. When a person gives directions, the eyes are frequently closed to picture the route, the body position is redirected, the arms are used to indicate turns, and so forth; this represents adult functioning at a sensorimotor level.

Representative memory, or memory involving the retention of certain means–end relationships, makes its debut in mid-infancy. An excellent example of this type of memory is demonstrated when the infant seeks an object that is hidden from view. An adult may see a flower or a unique color or hear a song that is reminiscent of an earlier event; an object or symbol is used to represent a part of an earlier experience. Sensorimotor and representative memory are refined through experience and maturation of cognitive structures.

"The processes involved in early recognition memory and attention are important to later outcome."[60] The visual recognition and memory of novelty scores achieved by 7-month-old infants show a substantial relationship to intel-

ligence scores during the toddler and preschool years. Rapid sustained attention is associated with higher IQ scores.[60] Processes of discrimination, attention, encoding, storage, and retrieval are all involved.

Through assessment of the signs of recognition, attention, and habituation, infants are observed to have developed color constancy by about 20 weeks.[22] The infants are shown the same color until they lose interest in it; then that color is brought back later along with an entirely new color. The rationale is that if the babies have forgotten the first color, they will find both colors equally fascinating. Selective attention to the new color indicates the ability to both discriminate and to remember the previous color.

Use of the habituation paradigm indicates that even premature babies possess some visual perceptual memory.[79] Two-month-old infants show preference for a new visual shape as long as 2 weeks after habituation to a specific visual shape.[30] Similar behaviors are also observed with tactile constancy.

Crossmodal Transfer. Curiosity is a major motivator of behavior from birth onward.[37] By manipulating, mouthing, listening, and looking, the infant discovers the properties of objects and events. Presenting a stimulus simultaneously to two or more modalities helps to increase its stimulus value and increases its relevancy to the young child. Thus, adding sound and movement to a visual object such as a rattle helps to attract and maintain attention (Fig. 7-5).

Through multiple modality contacts with objects, the infant gradually begins to realize that an object can be known and identified by more than one modality. By 1 month, infants

FIGURE 7–5.
The normally developing infant wants to know an object from every angle and modality.

exhibit the ability to visually recognize the shape, texture, and substance of objects formerly explored only by mouth.[39] More concrete evidence of an ability to synthesize and integrate input from the senses is present as early as 5 months of age. If an infant is allowed to explore an object tactually, without being able to see it, when that object is presented visually along with a new, but similar object (e.g., six-pointed star versus six-petaled flower) the infant will spend more time visually exploring the novel shape. The same phenomenon is seen when the visual presentation precedes the tactile presentation.[73]

Before 4 months, the infant tends to bring everything to the mouth for exploration; after 4 months, the infant begins to replace mouthing with visual exploration and fingering.[58] By 7 months, the compulsory oral inspection of objects begins to disappear as the baby begins to trust the alternative modalities for interpretation of the environment.[58] Between 6 and 12 months, there is a marked increase in fine motor coordination through fingering, rotating, banging, and so forth. These activities facilitate coordination of visual, haptic, auditory, and oral sensory input.

Infantile Amnesia. Since infants evidence memory so early in life, many adults wonder why they are unable to retrieve memories from this period of life. Two-year-olds are able to remember singular events that occurred the previous year,[53] and middlescents are able to recognize the pictures in their high school yearbook up to 35 years later.[4] Consequently, passage of time is an insufficient explanation for infantile amnesia. Two possible explanations are the reorganization and the encoding theories.[71] The first hypothesizes that memory stores are reorganized with maturation of the central nervous system and qualitative differences in thinking; therefore, the material becomes inaccessible. The second theory postulates that retrieval of information is based on the person's ability to reconstruct the perspective from which the original material was encoded.[75] Since environmental cues are viewed differently by an infant during the encoding and storage process than by an adult or child attempting to revive the memory, the incompatibilities appear to interfere with retrieval.

Response

Once a stimulus is attended to, the person must assign meaning and priority for continued attention. Even ignoring a stimulus can be a conscious choice. The infant's response to a stimulus is generally immediately observable, allowing the adult to make sensitive changes in the stimuli offered in order to prevent overloading or underloading the baby's perceptual system. Understanding issues of attention/retreat and novelty/habituation can facilitate maintaining the baby's attention, extending the baby's attention span, and establishing a reciprocal or turntaking interaction—all critical factors in the process of learning how to learn. As the baby matures, the effects of experience and practice begin to play more predominate roles in peripheral attention, seeking of stimuli, and maintenance of attention to a specific stimulus.

Emergence of Discrimination Skills

Perceptions of any type of stimulus follow a general pattern of emergence. The tasks that comprise this process are overlapping and to some degree go on forever—a person does not just master each task once and then forget it. Every time a person is confronted with a stimulus, at least part of the process is repeated. The more novel the stimulus, the further back (and thus closer to the first tasks) the person must go to conceptualize what is being interpreted. Initially, sensory attention appears to be **innately determined,** whereas experiential and cognitive factors contribute increasingly important effects as higher levels of the perceptual tasks are mastered.

Sensory attention is **hooked** in the neonate, or "caught and held by one or another dominant aspect of the perceptual field."[26] To a certain degree, this hooking continues throughout infancy. Because of the strong tendency to **centrate (concentrate) on a specific stimulus,** the infant, rather than seeing the whole picture or object, may concentrate on one aspect—a bright color, the eye of an animal, a hole in the toy. This focus on details may prevent recognition of the whole object or picture.

Gradually, the specific characteristics of a stimulus appear to release an **innately determined pattern of searching behaviors** in infants. For example, 1-month-old infants presented with a simple visual design such as a triangle inside of a square, tend to *scan the outer edges and corners* of the square, but rarely scan the inner triangle. When examining a face, they tend to look at the outer edges of the face and the eyes of the person.[62] By 2 months, infants *scan the inner triangle,* and also visually explore the eyes and mouth more than the perimeter of the head.[62] Attention to the inner pattern and detail of designs generally continues through 4 years of age.[21] The child gradually extracts more information and isolates more of the details.

During the early months, the child is working on **identifying objects through their form.** This task involves recognizing similarities in contour and differentiating those essential to the concept. The child must **develop stimulus or object constancy** in order to recognize the object the next time there is contact. This means that the infant recognizes that the same object can be viewed from several different positions (watch an infant explore a bottle or his own fingers by turning them over and over to see them from different angles). The infant begins to realize that the object is identical regardless of where it is explored or seen—in the bedroom, the car, the kitchen, or the grocery store. It appears that young infants perceive an object as a different object when it is moved to a new location. Bower used mirrors to create the illusion that there were three of the baby's own mother in the room with the baby.[10] He found that 3-month-old babies reacted with pleasure to three mothers, whereas 4-month-old babies tended to cry and to exhibit disturbed behaviors. From this experiment, he suggested that babies less than 4 months old may think that they have many identical mothers. Piaget's theory of **cognitive object constancy** means that the infant has internalized the concept that even though an object (or mother) may be viewed from many different angles and in many different places, it is still the same. Mother-from-a-side-view is the same as mother-from-a-front-view (Fig. 7-6).

Around 5 months, the infant is noted to do a lot of visual checking between the familiar and unfamiliar, especially comparing the mother to other persons in the environment. The concept of *cognitive object constancy* (which emerges around 4–5 months) is to be distinguished from Piaget's concept of *object permanence* (emerges around 8–9 months), which entails remembering an object or a person when the child is no longer in direct contact (usually visual) with that object or person. The first is an example of *receptive* memory, the second is *expressive* memory.

Piaget's concept of object constancy (cognitive domain) is to be distinguished from Mahler's theory of object constancy (affective domain) which is covered in Chapter 11. The skill of cognitive object constancy develops from the need to conserve cognitive effort in the overpopulated world of objects. As the child begins to remember more objects, people, and events, information overload occurs. The ability to categorize is crucial to continued cognitive development. Object constancy is one of the first categorizing skills to emerge. This grouping, or structuring, of information facilitates generalization and encourages further differentiations through attention to details.[44] Some children with learning disabilities continue to have difficulty with object constancy, categorization, and differentiation skills all their lives.

Cross-modal transfer or *sensory integration* is another critical perceptual/discrimination skill. The older infant will be seen to touch the tongue and lips to a picture in an effort to taste it (or perhaps to evaluate the two-dimensional quality of a three-dimensional object), or to reach to a shadow to grab hold of it. With increased experience and maturation of the cognitive skills, the child will begin to drop some modes of exploration and will be able to evaluate a stimulus with an alternate modality. For instance, an infant learns to discriminate furry texture from smooth texture by vision (the child will move the hands as if touching fur).

Gradually, the infant is able to **respond to the pattern as a whole** rather than just to the attention-drawing stimulus. This means that the infant begins to take in as many aspects of the stimulus as possible so that increased information is gained. The baby will pat the whole picture and say the appropriate label ("Mama" or "kitty," and so forth).

If individual objects such as pieces of fruit are used to make a picture of a bird, a happy face, or other common design, the 3- to 4-year-old child will continue to focus on the identity of the individual items comprising the larger picture because of the tendency to centrate and concentrate on the inner patterns. By 5 years of age, the child will begin to do more visual exploration of the external boundaries, but still will only identify the specific objects in the picture, not the pattern. By 6 to 7 years, the child will *see both the parts and the pattern.* But it is not until the child is 8 to 9 that he or she is able to *see that the pattern is made up of other parts.*[27]

The ability to **distinguish a form from its background** also emerges gradually. The person must learn to select a pattern, to treat it as a separate entity, and hold it against the tendency for some other stimulus to occlude the pattern. The child is gradually able to identify one person, animal, or object in a picture of many people or objects. The child must differentiate one sound from many in the environment and respond differentially to it. By 2 to 2½ months, the infant can recognize and locate the mother's voice in a noisy room.[77] During school-age years, children delight in identifying the individual instruments playing in an orchestra.

Infants initially have difficulty with pictures that contain multiple details, animals, or people. Gradually, the child is able to see and identify *individual objects* if they are separated by space from other objects in the picture. Clearly differentiated entities are easier to identify than pictures of objects or people that overlap or have merging colors or ambiguous shapes. Eventually, the child begins to pick out *embedded forms* that share *common boundaries* with other objects in a picture (e.g., "find the hidden picture" activities). After infancy, there are minimal changes in sensory reception, yet there continue to be major changes in awareness and interpretation of visual, auditory, and tactile forms within the environment. Perception continually changes because of experience. "Our perception of the world is more a product of our experiences, expectations, and mental processes than of the stimuli reaching our senses."[21]

The healthy infant also begins to develop a sense of **spatial relationships.** The mastery of this task is critical for the individual's orientation to the environment and mobility within it. Blind persons experience much difficulty mastering this task.[68] Our spatial perception enables us to make assumptions about the world. We can judge distance by picking up cues from texture, brightness, clarity, shadows, relative sizes, and sound echoes, as well as binocular disparity.

One facet of spatial relationships is the development of a *body-space concept.* The individual forms a mental picture of

FIGURE 7–6.
Joint looking into a mirror helps the baby to begin to differentiate between self and others, to recognize self, and to identify contingent movement in the mirror.

his own body that becomes a stable reference point from which to view and to relate all the experiences and observed phenomena of life. Opportunities for the development of gross and fine motor skills are essential to aid the child in developing body image and spatial awareness. As the child moves, he or she begins to identify the self as a separate entity, developing a sense of individual physical potentials, boundaries, and relationships to other objects. The very young infant has to learn how to move the eyes and the hands at will. When a neonate visually fixates on an interesting object, his hands, mouth, arms, and eyes will all open wide as if to engulf the object. While children are learning a new skill, they must consciously think about which parts of the body to move and how to restrict movement to the nonpertinent muscle groups. There will be much overshooting and undershooting of reaching behaviors as the child learns how much energy to put into the activity to reach the exact spot of a desired object. Body concept and awareness continues to change, especially during childhood. Perceptions of the self and the world change dramatically as the child successively advances from a supine position to sitting, standing, walking, running, jumping, riding, and so forth.

The idea of space emerges gradually—first, the *space between oneself and various objects,* and, later, the *space between objects.* The first primitive concept of space is called the *action–space concept* because the baby is aware only of the area being experienced at a particular moment. Several spaces exist for the infant under 4 months of age (e.g., visual space, auditory space). Gradually, the baby begins to cognitively map (mentally organize) various spaces into a more holistic environment or gestalt. There is a reaching space and a crawling space as the child begins to coordinate the size and abilities of his or her body to the realities of the environment (e.g., too small, too far).

The most dramatic evidence of the infant's awareness of distance is found in the *visual cliff* phenomenon. This is traditionally assessed by placing the infant on a clear glass table which has checkered linoleum secured immediately under the glass on one side, and 3 to 4 feet below the glass on the other side. The infant is allowed to move freely on the table top. After 7 months, the infant will only move on the table surface that has the linoleum secured immediately under the glass.[38, 63] Infants must have had some crawling experience before they will refuse to get too close to the "cliff." The noncrawler who is placed on the deep side of the table apparently does not experience fear but does perceive some difference, because the infant's heart rate will decrease markedly (one of the signs of intense attention).[17]

Infant Tools

The infant is an active seeker of the stimulation that is so vital to cognitive development.[36] Babies are able to subordinate their affective and social domains to their cognitive domain to initiate and control parental reactions. Cries, smiles, and other forms of deliberate social communication are observed in babies as young as 2 months of age.[65] Babies give even more subtle cues of social interaction soon after birth (e.g., they pause and stop sucking during feeding, and turn the head away from the nipple).[47] Parents tend to interpret these minute interactional skills as intentional communication.[15] Consequently, initial skills are strengthened within the parent–infant dyad and become the foundation for learning about the environment as the infant notes their effect on the parent and begins to consciously use them to produce a desired effect ("the game").

The quality of the early caregiver–infant relationship is critical to optimal development of the cognitive domain.[70] Early interaction between babies and their primary caregivers is facilitated through the use of innate tools. When they are functioning optimally, the reciprocal use of these tools leads to and reinforces an intense, mutually satisfying relationship that facilitates the development of the cognitive domain (see Chap. 8 as well as the section on parent–infant bonding in Chap. 31).

Infants use both the senses and sensorimotor development as tools to make social contact with others. Although infants have a variety of expressive behaviors, those mentioned in the following section appear to be the most critical in facilitating a positive response from caregivers.[66]

Smiling

Smiling, in Western cultures, is indicative of happiness, relaxation, and acceptance of others; thus it becomes an essential tool in positive interactions. Mothers have been telling us for years that their babies smile during the first week of life. Research now identifies two distinct kinds of neonatal smiles that may occur as early as the seventh month of fetal life. The *gas-bubble smile* is accompanied by tensing of the body and grimacing, indicating that the baby has intestinal discomfort. Another, more relaxed type of neonatal smiling is *eyes-closed smiling.*[33] At first, the neonate tends to turn up the corners of the mouth fleetingly, with no involvement of the muscles of the eyes. Wolff[82] categorizes smiling as either (1) spontaneous, which occurs without known external causes, or (2) elicited, which appears to be caused by external stimulation (e.g., high-pitched voices, tickling, bright lights). The state of consciousness is a critical factor in the elicitation of smiling (Fig. 7-7).

John Bowlby, a noted child psychologist, has offered observations on elicited smiling:[12]

1. The motor pattern of a smile is instinctive.
2. Smiles can be elicited by many types of stimuli, but because the human organism is biased from the first, some stimuli are more effective than others.
3. The most satisfying stimuli are associated with people, often the human voice and face.
4. Effective stimuli are presented more frequently by the mother figure (or primary caregiver) than by anyone or anything else.

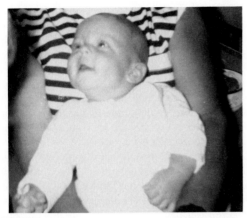

FIGURE 7–7.
The infant learns early in life that smiling and laughing will "capture" the caregiver and prolong interaction time.

5. With satisfying experiences, smiles are elicited more promptly and more intensely by a familiar voice. It does not take the baby long to figure out that parental attention—a reinforcer to the baby—can be retained through continuing to smile in the parents' presence.

Although facial postures and their meanings vary from culture to culture, infants soon learn that smiles are the rudimentary aspects of interpersonal relations. When infants combine smiles with vocalization, they have an effective tool for social control of the environment.

Volitional, sustained smiling is a significant developmental milestone. Parents appear to need to see the smile as an affirmation of their own efforts to be "good parents." Full-term babies who do not demonstrate a social smile by the age of 2 months warrant a neurodevelopmental examination. If infant smiling is delayed, the parents may need to provide a different approach to child care (see Chap. 8 for further information on smiling).

Crying

All babies cry. When a baby cries, all heads turn and each person (externally or internally) reaches out to shut off the cry—whether altruistically motivated to decrease the infant's distress or because the sound is an unpleasant stimulus. When the infant cries, the adult is motivated to perform activities such as holding and rocking. Almost always, the crying then ceases and the caregiver is reinforced; the infant's tension is decreased and the infant also is reinforced for making sound.

Gradually, the infant learns to control the environment through crying (or vocalization with greater maturation). This is a very positive developmental step because it is the foundation for intentional efforts to communicate.

It takes time for novice parents to differentiate among the various types of cries of their child. "Hunger" and "pain" cries are unique for each child. Infants differ in breathing patterns during pain cries. Some sound as if they try to squeeze the

very last bit of air out of the lungs before daring to take another breath. Others seem to panic, packing as many short, high-pitched cries into a minute of crying as they can. As the infant ages, patterns for sorrow, anger, discomfort, frustration, and fear all take different forms.

Many factors can precipitate crying: fatigue, overexcitement, or difficulty relaxing and falling to sleep. Even quiet music or rocking may seem to irritate the little one. Some babies get lonely and want company; others find it difficult to soothe themselves and tend to be more irritable than their peers. Some babies become quite distressed at a wet or dirty diaper, others become upset when too warm, too cold, or when some other external factor makes them uncomfortable. Interpretation of cries is not always easy, but it is the baby's only form of active communication.

Most babies have unexplained episodes of crying, even healthy infants—not just infants of an "irritable nature." The crying may continue even after the caregivers have exhausted their efforts in making the environment pleasant or comforting (e.g., position change, offering a new toy or a bottle). This type of crying, unless it becomes a pattern or occurs for extensive periods of time, does not hurt the baby. In most cases, it should be considered a healthy outlet and is just another form of cathartic exercise. It is not unusual for a baby to have one to two hours of "fussy time" daily during the early months—especially in the early evening (Fig. 7-8).

Wolff found that after 5 weeks, even a fussy baby may stop crying upon hearing a voice or seeing a face.[83] This finding has implications for quieting a crying baby, since speaking to a mildly crying baby at this age may arrest the crying as long as the baby can see the face belonging to the voice. Other babies need a gentle, warm hand placed on their back or chest in addition to the soothing voice. Infectious crying may be observed in babies; when one baby starts crying, others are observed to become apprehensive and join in the chorus.

Babies learn that crying or sound-making brings atten-

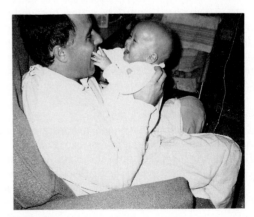

FIGURE 7–8.
Some babies have difficulty relaxing and falling asleep. When all other approaches fail, sometimes the best way to handle a crying baby is to let him or her cry it out.

tion and begin to repeat the behavior purposefully. Around 6 to 7 months, many infants are observed to experiment with crying to see if the parent will come on demand. Rapid adult response to an infant's initial and more subtle calls for attention encourages prosocial communication. Delays in adult response or waiting until the baby *demands* attention tends to reinforce more negative communication behaviors.

Looking

The infant's ability to look directly at a face is a tool highly prized by parents. Mothers frequently say that they have not seen their baby until he or she opens the eyes and looks back at them. The state 4 alertness that is present during the first hour after birth is an optimal time for parent–infant introduction. The sleepy baby who does not meet his parents until 6 or even 12 hours after delivery often does not appear interested—a factor which can be a detriment to the relationship. An alert baby elicits adult attention.

Fixation, the ability to visually zero in on an object, is a form of looking that is deemed very special by parents. Since the infant shows a marked preference for the unique pattern of the human face (especially when the head is held on the same plane as the infant's), the baby's fixating on the caregiver's eyes can be a great thrill, both for the parent, who usually exclaims, "He (or she) is looking at **me**!" and for the baby, who is reinforced by the adult's apparent excitement. When fixating, the infant will also stop or reduce sucking, will elevate the eyebrows, and may stop other body movements. This adds to the import of the episode because all these behaviors give the baby an alert, bright-eyed appearance that makes many caregivers feel they are truly the object of the baby's affection. This kind of feedback may be critical for maintaining quality interaction between a parent and an infant.

Hearing

The infant's ability to hear is another effective tool for learning and establishing interpersonal relationships. The infant's tendency to turn the head toward the source of sound as the parent enters the room or speaks can be most endearing. The synchronous response of the baby's body movement to the articulation, pitch, and speed of the caregiver's voice[20] accounts for the comment, "He acts as if he understands what I say to him!"

Selected Reflexes

The *palmar grasp* and *hand-to-mouth reflexes* provide mechanisms for learning and also endear the baby to caregivers, as in "He's holding my hand," or "She already knows how to suck her thumb." Interpreting these behaviors as infant trust and intelligence, parents may begin to stimulate the infant further and thus augment the baby's opportunities for learning.

The psychoanalytical school places high emphasis on the *sucking reflex,* stating that the infant equates food with the mother and that the mother in turn equates the infant's acceptance of food or feeding as an acceptance of herself. New parents (especially breast-feeding mothers and adoptive parents) express great anxiety if the neonate nurses poorly and elation when the baby eats vigorously. These verbal expressions indicate a dual concern; that the infant may not get enough to eat, and that the infant does not like the parents. The infant who nurses well helps the parents to relax, to smile, and to enjoy feeding time. If the mother is breast-feeding, this relaxation helps the "letdown" of milk—another reinforcer for good sucking.

Initially, the infant uses the sucking mode for investigating and exploring all new objects. However, as the infant begins to realize that the other modalities also give reliable information about an object, a new approach emerges—the infant merely touches the object to the lips and tip of tongue as if to check, but no longer tries to suck the object. This indicates that the infant has developed a rudimentary categorization skill, distinguishing things to suck versus things not to suck.

General physical appearance should not be ignored as a tool for enhancing interaction and learning. The "cute" baby elicits more interactional behaviors from the primary caregivers and other adults. The general appearance of an infant seems to elicit universal responses, but sustained attention is related to the adult's interpretation of the infant's cuteness.[43] Characteristics such as a large head, rounded cheeks, pleasing coloration, fuzzy hair, and petite proportions appear to elicit adult attention in the form of touching, caressing, holding, and talking to the child—all critical ways for the baby to begin learning about the world. Variations in infant appearance influence adult expectations and can therefore result in differential treatment.[1, 43] If the infant is premature or malformed in some way, the parents may experience difficulty in establishing positive feelings toward the child, a factor that may lead to behavioral and personality disorders in later childhood.[43] Acquaintances and strangers also tend to interact more frequently and more positively with a cute baby—a reinforcement to both the infant and the parents.

Significance of Tools

The primary caregiver (usually the mother) also possesses critical tools that facilitate adult–infant social and cognitive interaction (see Chap. 31 for a discussion of parental tools). As the baby uses a tool, the caregiver ideally reciprocates with a reinforcing tool that encourages the infant to repeat the behavior or to continue the interaction.

If the child's innate tools are weak or missing, it can interfere with the parent–child bond and the quality of interaction with the infant.[67, 70] The quality of the home environment or the ability of the parent to draw out the "weaker" infant can change the outcome for the infant. Those infants whose developmental functioning places them at risk for continued delays will often exhibit normal functioning at 2 years of age if they are offered an appropriately stimulating home environment.[70] Early intervention programs have positive long-range results, in part because children and their parents establish early healthy patterns of interaction that resist change.[25]

As children learn to control a particular behavior, they identify its effect on the environment. Behaviors that produce the desired outcome are strengthened; behaviors that cannot be associated with an outcome or that produce an unpleasant or less desirable result are weakened. Infants begin to anticipate a result from their actions; thus they will kick their feet to cause the crib mobile to move, smile at their mother to get her to speak, or let go of a toy to watch it drop to the floor. Chapters 11 and 13 discuss the effect on child development when there is no response to the infant's tools and when there is an absence of manipulative, stimulating toys.

DEVELOPMENT OF COGNITION

Concept Formation

We structure reality and deal with the world by forming concepts. Concepts start out very broad because of limited experience and understanding. Stimuli tend to be grouped and categorized together, with any response developed for one stimulus in the category being generalized and applied to all objects in the category. With experience and intellectual growth, these concepts are gradually refined. Associations may be made on the basis of some arbitrary characteristic of a stimulus (e.g., if I can hold it, I can eat/suck it) or on the common elements possessed by several stimuli (e.g., marbles, oranges, balloons, and circles are all round; therefore, they are all balls).

According to maturationalist theory, the psychological structures that support perceptual and intellectual skills emerge with neurological maturation, regardless of the quality of the environment or the child's interaction with it. Piaget, however, maintained that even in the first 18 months of life, people actively participate in creating or constructing their cognitive structures by developing and coordinating actions into an organized *schemata of action* (or sensorimotor schemata).

Piaget's Sensorimotor Stage

The attention-holding value of stimuli change as the child's familiarity with the environment expands and understanding deepens. The young child does not use the same discriminators as those used by older children or adults to categorize their world. During Piaget's sensorimotor stage (birth to 24 months), the infant experiences the world only as it interacts with the senses and understands it only as far as he or she is able to exert control of events. Gradually, the infant changes from operating primarily at a reflex level to consciously organizing sensorimotor activities to understand and to exert control on the environment. Piaget observes that the baby's activities progress from organized reflex action to trial-and-error learning. The baby gradually becomes goal-oriented and begins to experiment with ways to get what is wanted.

A brief review of Piaget's definitions and assumptions (see Chap. 1 and Appendixes B and C) may be helpful to the reader before proceeding to the following sections concerning the substages of Piaget's sensorimotor stage.

Substage I: Reflex Activity (Birth to 1 Month)

Piaget hypothesizes that the neonate exists in a state of complete egocentrism, unaware that any other viewpoints exist.[57] When the neonate is stimulated, innate reflexes mediate responses. When an object is put into the neonate's mouth, it is sucked; when an object is placed on the palm, it is grasped; when another human cry is heard, the baby joins the chorus. The infant in this substage cannot differentiate between objects or stimuli. In fact, even sounds will elicit the sucking response. Thus it would seem that most activity during this first month is *assimilated* or incorporated into the primitive schemata of ready-made reflexes. Because reflexive behavior can enable the neonate to survive, it is adaptive. Piaget believes that these reflexes constitute the foundation of all subsequent sensorimotor and intellectual development, because the repetitive nature of the reflexes is the beginning of associations between an act and a contingent response.

Substage II: Primary Circular Reactions (1 to 4 Months)

During substage II, the reflexes begin to be modified as a function of experience and neurological maturation. The infant reproduces behaviors that were previously achieved by chance (through random activity). Building on reflexive sucking action, an infant discovers that inserting the thumb in the mouth brings pleasure and comfort, so it is repeated again and again. The baby will suck on almost anything if it provides sucking pleasure. Thus, the young baby assimilates each object into the sucking schema.

The baby begins to show recognition of objects, or *object concept.* For instance, when the breast or feeding bottle is presented, there will be signs of eager anticipation. During substage II, the infant will immediately and purposefully repeat his or her own behaviors that bring sensual pleasure (such as kicking), or a vocal sound (especially if an adult mimics the baby's vocalizations). However, the baby will not imitate a behavior or sound introduced by the adult even if it is within his or her repertoire of skills.

Substage III: Secondary Circular Reactions (4 to 8 Months)

During substage III, the infant's behaviors become increasingly oriented toward objects and events in the environment. Previously, the infant's behavior was directed primarily toward the self and what physically felt good or pleased the senses. Five-month-olds begin to learn to control their environments by making use of visually directed reaching (sighting an object, reaching for it, and making contact with it)—a skill the infant could not accomplish neurologically until this stage.

Piaget says that actions during this period are secondary because they are *intentional,* that is, the behavior is initiated to create an effect on another object (e.g., crying to get mother). The infant now develops new goals for motor responses that already exist. The baby now will kick vigorously to activate a crib mobile. In this substage, a behavior is repeated and prolonged for the response that results. Behaviors begin to be expanded or combined under cognitive control. Thus grasping and holding now become shaking and banging.

Play is noted to become differentiated according to the type of toy during this stage (e.g., a cradle gym is to hit, a rubber toy is to squeeze or press, a teething ring is to bite).[54, 58] During substage III, the infant will imitate the behavior of others if the skill is already within the infant's repertoire (e.g., coughing or kissing sounds, table patting, or head shaking).

Substage IV: Coordination of Secondary Schemata and Their Application to New Situations (8 to 12 Months)

The entrance into substage IV is heralded by the emergence of **object permanence,** or the knowledge that an object exists independently of one's current perceptions. This is the first evidence of expressive memory. During the later part of substage III, the goal (desired toy) must be at least partly visible behind the obstacle before the infant will seek it. Babies as young as 20 days appear to know that an object still exists when it is hidden, but short memory and attention span prevent search efforts for the hidden object.[10]

The baby in substage II will continue to look briefly at the place where an object disappeared, but will not actively seek it. During substage III, the baby begins to anticipate where a moving object will reappear if it goes behind a barrier, but still will not actively attempt to find it. The baby who is 8 to 10 months old will not only protest the disappearance of a desired object, but will search for the object. Thus, if a desired toy is hidden under a blanket or cup while the baby is watching, the baby will easily retrieve the toy by reaching under the barrier. The baby now demonstrates an awareness that objects still exist when they disappear from view. Some would claim that search and reach behaviors do not appear earlier because the infant is physically unable to engage in the activity, or is bored with the object.[71] However, if the object is hidden under a transparent cup, even a 5-month-old is able to retrieve it. If it is hidden under an opaque cup, the infant loses the perceptual cue and (without expressive memory) the motivation to retrieve it.[11]

Once object permanence emerges, it is a fragile skill. If the desired object is moved from one hiding place to another (e.g., under another cup, pillow, or blanket), the infant of this age does not always search for objects where they disappeared, but where they were found the last time. This is known as *stage IV error.* The original hiding place assumes an independent status as "hiding place".[71] This is one reason why it becomes critical to provide the child of this age with physical and temporal order. The baby is actively trying to learn

associations. The infant is able to predict and control events, to cooperate, and to be more independent if a particular sleeping place, box for toys, and sleeping, eating, and bathing schedules are provided.

By this substage, changes have occurred in how the baby approaches the solving of a problem. Earlier, the baby would simply run through a repertoire of schemata, in any order, whether or not they were appropriate. By the end of this substage, the baby uses primarily those actions that worked in previous situations. This suggests that the baby possesses memory and is beginning to do some mental processing of problems before acting. By using responses that have been previously mastered, the infant can now solve simple problems and begins to use the behaviors to achieve more complex goals. An unwanted toy, for example, will be moved out of the way to reach a more desirable one.

The infant shows clear signs of anticipation of specific events as particular signs are associated with them. Thus, the 9- or 10-month-old infant may cry when Mother picks up her pocketbook, when Daddy rattles the keys in his pocket, or when another person comes into the home (all interpreted as, "My mother (or father) is going to leave me").

During this substage, the infant begins to show awareness that objects (besides the self) can cause activity. An 8-month-old baby may laugh gleefully as mother winds up a musical swing. When the swing begins to slow and come to a standstill, the baby may try to reach for the winding crank, realizing that the crank starts the fun all over again. During substage IV, the infant modifies and extends skills and will imitate the behaviors of others if the skill is similar to skills already mastered. For example, the baby learns to wave bye-bye, clap hands, or will imitate hitting a spoon on a dish or a stick on a xylophone.

Substage V: Tertiary Circular Reactions—The Discovery of New Means Through Active Experimentation (12 to 18 Months)

During substage V, the infant actively attempts to discover and understand cause–event relationships. One of the more common scenarios involves a minor trauma. The toddling child will accidentally fall, hitting his or her head on a chair or door frame, creating a novel sound. The child will look surprised, cautiously and purposefully hit the head against the same spot to recreate the same effect, look pleased (at having discovered the relationship), and then will often look around for the parent before emitting a cry of feigned pain. For the moment, curiosity eclipsed the emotional response to the discomfort. Once a cause–effect relationship is discovered, the infant will attempt to apply the new information to find another solution to an old problem. Active experimentation is also observed as variations of an old response pattern are developed to accommodate to the needs of a new problem or object. The infant of this age is a very active, self-directed learner.

During this substage, stage IV error disappears and the infant begins to search for objects in the area of the last visible displacement. If a toy originally hidden in place A is now hidden in place B while the baby is watching, the baby searches for the toy in place B. However, the ability to search for objects that are hidden while the child is not looking (*invisible displacements*) does not occur until substage VI, which is considered to be well into toddlerhood in this text (see Chap. 10).

Piaget contends that the infant's behaviors first become "intelligent" during substage VI because the child begins to manipulate events mentally and anticipate the result before acting.[55] The infant in substage V will physically manipulate events to test their effect, but does not evidence the ability to mentally manipulate the event before it happens. This is especially evident in the child's ability to place puzzle pieces. There is much guessing, trial–error, slipping and sliding of pieces, and attempts to force pieces into slots.

The infant in substage V realizes that objects and people not only respond to one's behavior, but that they can be the cause of other events. They will begin to look for cause–effect events in the environment (e.g., what made the light come on,

or the shadow cross my path?) and then attempt to make the event happen over and over again in the joy of the discovery and personal control (e.g., playing with light switches and television buttons, or dropping toys from the high chair). They make use of their knowledge that other people can make things happen by looking to the adult to fetch a remote object for them, or demanding to go for a car ride. In previous substages, the infant was learning how sensations and movements interrelated, but tended to focus on just those two entities; at this point, the infant is capable of noticing the relationship between objects in different spaces and the different ways that modalities can be used to obtain or send information about the objects. Thus, pointing and grunting begin to give way to language (see Chap. 12). During substage V, the infant will actively attempt to imitate novel behaviors exhibited by others—a significant factor in the teaching and enculturation processes of children.

A summary of Piaget's stage I with examples of infant behavior in each of the six substages is found in Table 7-3.

TABLE 7–3. SUMMARY OF PIAGET'S SENSORIMOTOR STAGE

Substage	Approximate Age	Developmental Unit	Behavioral Example
I	0–1 month	Exercising ready-made sensorimotor schemata	Baby improves efficiency of neurological reflexes (e.g., rooting, sucking, swallowing) by beginning to initiate some at will (e.g., thumb suck)
II	1–4 months	Primary circular reactions	Baby repeats own behavior for sensual pleasure (e.g., repetitive kicking, fingering of an object placed in or near hand, sucking for a long period of time); begins to modify a reflex (e.g., adjusts swallow to different textures of food). Early coordination of selected reflexes (e.g., sucking and swallowing, reaching and grasping),
III	4–8 months	Secondary circular reactions	Behavior becomes "intentional." Baby repeats behaviors that produce novel, pleasing, and interesting effects on the environment (e.g., to elicit laughter from caregiver or sound from a musical toy). Increased voluntary coordination of motor skills enables exploration (e.g., mouthing objects in environment by combining grasping and sucking). Imitates skills already in repertoire. Early understanding of cause–effect relationships. **Cognitive object constancy** appears at about 5 months.
IV	8–12 months	Coordination of secondary reactions (schemata) and applications to new situations	Infant consciously uses an action that is a means to an end (e.g., uses reaching ability to obtain many new and interesting objects); begins to solve simple problems. **Object permanence** appears at about 8 months. Imitates simple behaviors of others. Active search for cause–effect relationships. Repetitive explorations.
V	12–18 months	Tertiary circular reactions	Infant shows early experimental approaches to knowledge gathering and problem solving by varying approaches to an old situation or applying old approaches to new problems. Much trial and error learning. Must physically solve a problem to understand cause–effect relationship. Imitates simple novel behaviors.
VI	18–24 months	Invention of new means through mental combinations	Child first shows "intelligent behavior" by manipulating objects mentally before acting. Begins to predict events and results. Much trial and error problem solving. Can solve detour problems; can predict effects from observing causes, and can also infer a cause when only the effect is seen; is able to follow an invisible displacement. Early symbolic play. Both immediate and deferred (delayed) imitation of actions and words noted.

Assessment of Development

Cognitive Assessments

GESELL. Many developmental assessments lean heavily on the work of Arnold Gesell and his original Gesell Developmental Schedules.[35,69] The updated version of his scales evaluates the child from 4 weeks to 5 years of age in four areas: motor, adaptive, language, and personal–social.[46] Information is obtained through observing the baby's responses to objects and events (e.g., does the baby merely stare at the bottle and pellet or does the baby attempt to do something with them?), as well as through reports from the infant's parent about what the baby usually does at home.

A raw score is extracted and then converted into a percentile for each of the areas evaluated. A fifth, overall score, the **developmental quotient** (DQ) is calculated. This is **not** synonymous with the **intelligence quotient** (IQ), which measures intellectual behavior in older children and adults. The DQ and IQ are two separate entities and should not be confused with each other (IQ is discussed in Chap. 21).

BAYLEY. The Bayley Scale of Infant Development is designed to evaluate children between the ages of one month and 30 months in three areas: mental, psychomotor, and behavioral development.[7] Each scale is composed of tasks that are similar to the pioneer work of Gesell. Multiple factors are tested: postural development, motor development, perception, attention span to objects and humans, receptive language, expressive language, object manipulation, and problem solving. The widely used Bayley Scale provides a raw score, which is converted to an estimated mental age. The Bayley Scale of Infant Development has been standardized for most sociocultural populations of the United States.

THE INFANT PSYCHOLOGICAL DEVELOPMENT SCALES. The Gesell and Bayley assessments are based on the quantitative accretion of skills accompanying neurological maturation. Uzgiris and Hunt, greatly influenced by Piaget, devised the Infant Psychological Development Scales (IPDS) that evaluate the qualitative differences in the levels of cognitive organization of children 1 month to 2 years.[76] The six ordinal-based scales evaluate changes in object awareness, problem solving, imitation, causality, spatial relations, and use of objects.

Even though these three assessments have been carefully developed and extensively validated, they have only minimal to moderate correlation with intellectual assessments designed for older children and adults.[85] This may be caused by uneven intellectual growth, the lack of a stable factor in intelligence, early mental plasticity, the influences of the environment, or the measurement of differing factors. These early tests tend to evaluate IQ through sensorimotor skills (reaching, grasping, orienting, manipulating), not through cognitive factors per se.[9] Such findings do not negate the value of early childhood evaluations, but they do rule out the temptation to make long-range predictions of competency based on these assessments. Neither does the lack of strong

association invalidate the value of the tests for the period of life for which they are constructed. Apparently, the qualitative differences in symbolization, categorization, and generalization of events account for much of the discrepancy in early childhood versus later childhood scores. When researchers begin to look at information-processing skills such as habituation speed, decrement and recovery of attention, response to novelty, attention span, and so forth, then moderate but significant levels of continuity of cognitive competence begin to emerge.[9,61] Longer attention spans, rapid habituation, and preference for novelty during infancy are associated with more efficient information-processing as the child ages. Early childhood educators and intervention specialists tend to lean toward general developmental assessments rather than intellectual scales because of the greater specificity of a child's practical abilities and interactions with the everyday world.

Developmental Assessments

Early childhood professionals began to realize that the physical, emotional, and social domains were just as critical to developmental progress as was the intellectual domain, and that delays in one of the other domains could cause delays in cognitive development. They were also disenchanted with an assessment which gave one or more developmental quotients but no practical information that could pinpoint a specific need or be used to develop an intervention program. Consequently, multiple developmental assessments have been developed in the past 15 years to fill this need. These assessments are especially valuable for professionals working in Early Intervention Programs (family-centered programs for disabled and delayed children birth to 36 months of age). The assessor needs to be familiar with infant characteristics to elicit the baby's *best* performance. Parental input is valuable to evaluate representativeness of the child's performance.[69] Correction for age should be made for children who were prematurely born. Parental observation of assessments becomes an intervention in itself, since parents can gain insight and understanding of their child's behavior and can observe effective approaches. It also opens the door for parent–professional communication.[69]

DENVER DEVELOPMENTAL SCREENING TEST. Professionals working with young children need a quick method for checking a child's developmental progress to evaluate whether or not an in-depth assessment may be necessary to determine a need for special services. One of the most widely used screening tools is the Denver Developmental Screening Test (DDST) (Figs. 7-9 and 7-10).[31] The test is divided into four scales: personal-social, fine motor-adaptive, language, and gross motor skills. It is applicable for children from birth through 6 years of age. On the score sheet, each task to be tested is represented by a horizontal bar; various points on these bars represent the ages at which 25%, 50%, 75%, and 90% of children master the task. An abbreviated form of the DDST is available for practitioners who need to save time and to save the child from any more testing than necessary.[32] If all items are passed, the child receives no further testing at that time.

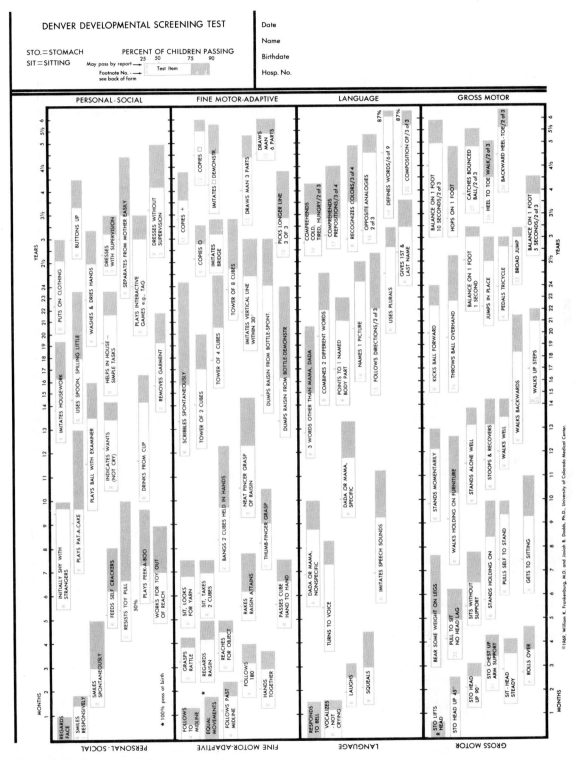

FIGURE 7–9.
The Denver Development Screening Test (DDST). (Courtesy of W. K. Frankenburg, MD, and J. B. Dodds, PhD, University of Colorado Medical Center, 1969)

1. Try to get child to smile by smiling, talking or waving to him. Do not touch him.
2. When child is playing with toy, pull it away from him. Pass if he resists.
3. Child does not have to be able to tie shoes or button in the back.
4. Move yarn slowly in an arc from one side to the other, about 6" above child's face.
    Pass if eyes follow 90° to midline. (Past midline; 180°)
5. Pass if child grasps rattle when it is touched to the backs or tips of fingers.
6. Pass if child continues to look where yarn disappeared or tries to see where it went. Yarn
    should be dropped quickly from sight from tester's hand without arm movement.
7. Pass if child picks up raisin with any part of thumb and a finger.
8. Pass if child picks up raisin with the ends of thumb and index finger using an over hand
    approach.

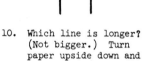

9. Pass any en-
    closed form.
    Fail continuous
    round motions.
10. Which line is longer?
    (Not bigger.) Turn
    paper upside down and
    repeat. (3/3 or 5/6)
11. Pass any
    crossing
    lines.
12. Have child copy
    first. If failed,
    demonstrate

When giving items 9, 11 and 12, do not name the forms. Do not demonstrate 9 and 11.

13. When scoring, each pair (2 arms, 2 legs, etc.) counts as one part.
14. Point to picture and have child name it. (No credit is given for sounds only.)

15. Tell child to: Give block to Mommie; put block on table; put block on floor. Pass 2 of 3.
    (Do not help child by pointing, moving head or eyes.)
16. Ask child: What do you do when you are cold? ..hungry? ..tired? Pass 2 of 3.
17. Tell child to: Put block on table; under table; in front of chair, behind chair.
    Pass 3 of 4. (Do not help child by pointing, moving head or eyes.)
18. Ask child: If fire is hot, ice is ?; Mother is a woman, Dad is a ?; a horse is big, a
    mouse is ?. Pass 2 of 3.
19. Ask child: What is a ball? ..lake? ..desk? ..house? ..banana? ..curtain? ..ceiling?
    ..hedge? ..pavement? Pass if defined in terms of use, shape, what it is made of or general
    category (such as banana is fruit, not just yellow). Pass 6 of 9.
20. Ask child: What is a spoon made of? ..a shoe made of? ..a door made of? (No other objects
    may be substituted.) Pass 3 of 3.
21. When placed on stomach, child lifts chest off table with support of forearms and/or hands.
22. When child is on back, grasp his hands and pull him to sitting. Pass if head does not hang back.
23. Child may use wall or rail only, not person. May not crawl.
24. Child must throw ball overhand 3 feet to within arm's reach of tester.
25. Child must perform standing broad jump over width of test sheet. (8-1/2 inches)
26. Tell child to walk forward, heel within 1 inch of toe.
    Tester may demonstrate. Child must walk 4 consecutive steps, 2 out of 3 trials.
27. Bounce ball to child who should stand 3 feet away from tester. Child must catch ball with
    hands, not arms, 2 out of 3 trials.
28. Tell child to walk backward,  toe within 1 inch of heel.
    Tester may demonstrate. Child must walk 4 consecutive steps, 2 out of 3 trials.

DATE AND BEHAVIORAL OBSERVATIONS (how child feels at time of test, relation to tester, attention
span, verbal behavior, self-confidence, etc,):

FIGURE 7–10.

*The DDST score sheet offers simple guidelines on how to administer portions of the assessment. (Courtesy of W. F.
Frankenburg, MD, and J. B. Dodds, PhD, University of Colorado Medical Center, 1969)*

However, if one or more items are failed or refused, the full, nonabbreviated DDST is administered.

A person who wants to use the DDST for screening should receive training and be checked for reliability before administering the test routinely. (Forms and instruction manuals for DDST are available from LADOCA Publishing Founda-tion, East 51st Ave. and Lincoln St., Denver, CO 80216.) It is important for the child's parents to understand that the DDST is not an IQ test, but rather is a way to identify areas potentially needing an in-depth assessment.

Once a lag is suggested by the screening, arrangements should be made for additional, more specific assessment of the child and for consultation for the family. Multiple childhood assessments are available. Only a few representative ones can be mentioned. Each assessment represents a different philosophical approach and can be used for different purposes. A practitioner needs to identify the purpose and potential goals of an assessment before choosing which tool is most appropriate for the particular child or setting.

DEVELOPMENTAL PROGRAMMING FOR INFANTS AND YOUNG CHILDREN. The Developmental Programming for Infants and Young Children assessment includes 6 areas: cognition, perceptual/fine motor, gross motor, language, social/emotional, and self care. Although it is a competency-based assessment, the developers claim it has high correlation with the standardized instruments discussed previously. Each test item is accompanied by a brief description on how to present the materials or to elicit the skill, with specific directions for a disabled child. Skills are grouped into 3-month categories, a factor that prevents assessment precision in the early months. However, it is concise and easy to use (more information is available from the University of Michigan Press, Ann Arbor, MI).

EARLY LEARNING ACCOMPLISHMENT PROFILE. The Early Learning Accomplishment Profile (E-LAP) is another criterion-referenced assessment developed for children functioning in the birth through 36-month range. It provides assessment of six developmental skill areas and can be used with normally developing children as well as disabled children. Multiple teacher preparation materials are available (more information is available from Chapel Hill Training-Outreach Project, Lincoln Center, Merritt Mill Road, Chapel Hill, NC 27514).

HAWAII EARLY LEARNING PROFILE. The Hawaii Early Learning Profile (HELP) is one of the newest "kids on the block," but also is the most complete. It is specifically developed for working with young or handicapped infants. The assessment is divided into 6 areas: cognitive/receptive language, expressive language, fine motor, gross motor, social, and self help. Specific observable skills are developmentally sequenced with identification of the usual age of emergence. An extensive set of manuals, charts, and activity guides makes this interdisciplinary assessment practical and functional for even a novice professional. Teaching materials and booklets are available for facilitating parental understanding of child development, premature infant behaviors, and intervention approaches. There are even manuals available to teach a Spanish-speaking or disabled parent how to help the infant to develop a specific skill (more information is available from VORT Corporation, P.O. Box 60880, Palo Alto, CA 44306).

ECO SCALES ASSESSMENT MODEL. Professionals concerned about the communication, social, and cognitive processes may wish to use the ECO (Ecological) assessment manual. Though cumbersome, it provides extensive insight into the reciprocal nature of communication and the value of turntak-

ing or contingent responsivity to learning by the young child. Parental input is essential and use of the materials enhances parental understanding of their interaction with the child. Because ECO is process-oriented, it does not yield a communication developmental age (more information is available from James D. MacDonald, Ph.D., Nisonger Center, Ohio State University, Columbus, OH 43210; or from Special Press, 11230 West Ave., Suite 3205, San Antonio, TX 78213).

NURSING CHILD ASSESSMENT SATELLITE TRAINING. The Nursing Child Assessment Satellite Training (N-CAST) is actually a battery of assessment tools collected or developed to assess the social/emotional functioning and environment of the young child. Several of the tools require intensive training for the practitioner to achieve reliability in using the materials. However, once mastered, the practitioner is sensitized to the nuances of the infant–parent interaction and can use this information for parental support and teaching. Because of its precision, the N-CAST information is also valuable as a part of the assessment of a failure-to-thrive child and for child protection hearings. Assessments include evaluations of sleeping patterns, responsivity of the child, responsivity of the parent, and adequacy of the home environment to the needs of a developing infant (more information is available from Kathryn Barnard, Ph.D., N-CAST, WJ-10, University of Washington, Seattle, WA 98195).

MAXIMIZING THE COGNITIVE POTENTIALS OF THE INFANT

How important is good parenting to the development of a child's intelligence? What helps (or hinders) a child to develop full learning potential? Questions such as these led to an extensive research project by psychologist Burton L. White.[81] The research method of his Harvard Preschool Project is described in Chapter 13, but the results of his study merit emphasis here: The period in a child's life that is most decisive for the development of intellectual potentials appears to be the time from birth to 10 months—in other words, infancy. This conclusion is not meant to imply that stimulation and interaction after this period are insignificant; what it does emphasize is that the factors contributing to effective learning are established before the child is a toddler and are very strongly influenced by the infant–caregiver interaction.

Infant Stimulation

Crucial to a baby's successful learning, as well as ultimately to successful living, is a climate in which the baby receives synchronized stimulation and contingent responses. Contingent adult responses, mutual focusing of attention and interests, and shaping of language input to the understanding level of the infant facilitate attention span, language learning, social skills, communication, and knowledge acquisition.[84] Noncontingent stimulation may cause the child to "tune out," thus limiting learning rather than enhancing it. A delay of only three seconds interrupts contingency learning in 6-month-old infants.[50] The infant must learn the contingencies before he or she can predict and then control the outcomes. This is the basic foundation of learning how to learn! In the early years, diversity needs to be kept within logical limits to prevent overload and bewilderment. New stimulations and experiences are offered as the child becomes familiar with or habituates to old ones. Thus, promptness, consistency, appropriateness, and pacing are critical factors in infant stimulation.[64]

Parents are cautioned that environments with too many attention-drawing stimuli and inadequate contingent responses (e.g., blinking Christmas lights strung up around the room; loud, confusing noises coming from many different people simultaneously, but with minimal response or attention to the presence or needs of the infant) can overwhelm the baby and may precipitate frustration, fatigue, and withdrawal. On the other hand, environments offering inadequate stimulation fail to challenge the baby's emerging cognitive potentials. Most parents seem to offer an adequate environment as a natural consequence of the mutual use of interactional tools to seek and respond to each other.

The goals of infant stimulation programs should be based on two major assumptions: (1) that services to enhance a child's development should be available as early in the child's life as possible, especially if the child is disabled in any way; and (2) that services should be offered to caregivers to enable them to guide their child's growth effectively. The best Early Intervention Programs offer interdisciplinary professional consultation to parents and base suggestions on normal developmental sequences, keeping a holistic view of the child in mind so that one domain is not overemphasized at the expense of the other domains. Activities should aid the infant to mentally coordinate different sensory impressions of the biophysical and socioaffective world.

Teaching

Because of the infant's limited physical, cognitive, and emotional skills, the adult must be careful not to overstimulate the child. It is critical that the adult attend to the infant's energy pacing to maintain interest and attention span. This requires high emotional investment and very sensitive synchrony on the part of the adult. The adult must be aware of the cutting edge of the child's burgeoning skills in order to find the balance between familiarity and novelty and to provide appropriate challenges. Both words and actions should be used to show the child how to solve a task or how to play with a new toy. However, the adult should not persist with teaching the new skill for more than five minutes, nor require more than three attempts to perform the new task. All efforts to attempt new skills should be recognized and support offered to ensure success. When the infant is unsuccessful, comments such as, "good try" and, "you almost did it! We can try again later" are supportive of the child's efforts. Once insight is gained into the performance of a skill, the child needs multiple

opportunities to practice the activity in order to master the skill and make it a part of a working repertoire of abilities (schema) to call upon for facing new problems. Emerging skills are unstable in their appearance, explaining why a child will be unable to perform for "Grandma" or in any other situation which increases the child's stress.

Safety

Regardless of how much cognitive prowess we attribute to the infant, we must be constantly aware of the infant's need to be placed in a safe environment (Fig. 7-11). The infant is not capable of predicting outcomes in a potentially dangerous situation or of exerting self-discipline. Even when the parent is positive that the child understands that she is not to touch an object or go past a certain point, the adult must still think for the baby, who lacks experience, memory, problem-solving skills, and self-discipline.

Accidents are a principal cause of injury and death to infants. Even neonates placed on the abdomen in a crib will be found minutes later in a different part of the crib. A newborn can roll and fall from an unguarded table, bed, or couch. It is therefore of paramount importance that safety precautions be instituted immediately after birth. The use of an infant car seat—from birth—is now mandatory in all states. Consistent use will establish the habit of using seat belts while riding in a vehicle and will make it easier for the parents to restrain the active toddler or preschooler (Fig. 7-12).

The 4-month-old baby will attempt to reach out for things and practice the palmar grasp. Consequently, the infant should not be placed close to heat sources, shiny and bright (but hot) water faucets, or anything with a flame. Since young infants will try to place almost anything into the mouth, small toys, diaper pins, loose buttons, coins, sharp-edged objects,

FIGURE 7–11.
The young child's increasing repertoire of motor skills, insatiable curiosity, and lack of self-discipline make it imperative that poisons, electrical sockets, and other potentially harmful items are made inaccessible by parents and caretakers.

FIGURE 7–12.
Safety is an integral part of maintaining biological integrity. Establishing an attitude of safety early in life can foster maximization of potentials.

poisonous plants, and other toxic or inhalable materials must be kept away from the infant's "action space." As the baby becomes more mobile, opportunities to explore (and to get into danger) increase. The knowledge of what the baby can do today and might do tomorrow are important aspects of baby-proofing an environment. Curiosity must be redirected as biophysical skills outstrip cognitive reasoning and self-discipline.

Older infants begin to learn caution and self-discipline from the guidance offered by caregivers. Babies frequently check the expression on a caregiver's face when confronted with a stranger, a novel object, or new experience. A frown or grimace serves as a damper to curiosity, whereas a smile may encourage continued exploration. Many helpful pamphlets and supplementary literature are provided free of cost by the U.S. Consumer Product Safety Commission (Washington, DC 20207). Local chapters of the American Red Cross are involved in child safety programs.

CONCLUSION

Those who are involved in an intimate, long-term relationship with one or more children become acutely aware of how much information we as adults take for granted. These little ones have a lot to learn in a very short period of time. At this point, the keys to maximizing the intellectual potentials of an infant appear to be: (1) *a warm, secure caregiver relationship* that frees the child to attend to external stimuli; (2) adequate *sensory stimulation,* to enable the child to develop neural networks, appreciation of various perceptual modalities, and the motor meaning of events; (3) a sensitive, *contingently responsive environment* and persons who can help the child to experience control of some events; (4) sufficient *consis-*

tency of experiences to allow the child to see relationships and to predict the outcome of his or her own behaviors as well as the behaviors of others; and (5) a *joint focusing of attention* on mutually satisfying topics for joyful play and information exchange (turntaking). "It is this sensitivity to the child's current level of functioning that enables the adult to help the child progress to further developmental levels".[64] It is in this environment that the infant "learns how to learn."

REFERENCES

1. Adams, G. R. (1977). Physical attractiveness research: Toward a developmental social psychology of beauty. *Human Development, 20,* 217.

2. Adams, R. J., & Maurer, D. (1984). *The use of habituation to study newborn's color vision.* New York: Paper Presented at the 4th International Conference on Infant Studies.

3. Ashmead, D. H., Clifton, R. K., & Perris, E. E. (1987). Precision of auditory localization in human infants. *Developmental Psychology, 23*(5), 641–647.

4. Bahrick, H. P., Bahrick, P. O., & Wittlinger, R. P. (1975). Fifty years of memory for names and faces: A cross-sectional approach. *Journal of Experimental Psychology, 104,* 54–75.

5. Bahrick, L. E. (1988). Intermodel learning in infancy: learning on the basis of two kinds of invariant relations in audible and visual events. *Child Development, 59,* 197–209.

6. Baillargeon, R., & Graber, M. (1988). Evidence of location memory in 8-month-old infants in a nonsearch A B task. *Developmental Psychology, 24,* 502–511.

7. Bayley, N. (1969). *Bayley Scales of Infant Development.* New York: Psychological Corporation.

8. Bornstein, M. H. (1978). Chromatic vision in infancy. In H. W. Reese & L. P. Lipsett (Eds.), *Advances in child development and care.* New York: Academic Press.

9. Bornstein, M. H., & Sigman, M. D. (1986). Continuity in mental development from infancy. *Child Development, 57,* 251–274.

10. Bower, T. G. R. (1971). The object in the world of the infant. *Scientific American, 225,* 30.

11. Bower, T. G. R., & Wishart, J. G. (1972). The effects of motor skill on object permanence. *Cognition, 1,* 165–172.

12. Bowlby, J. (1969). *Attachment and loss, Vol. 1: Attachment.* New York: Basic Books.

13. Brazelton, T. B. (1973). Neonatal Behavioral Assessment Scale. *Clinics in Developmental Medicine, No. 50* (Philadelphia), Lippincott.

14. Brazelton, T. B. (1976). Early parent–infant reciprocity. In V. C. Vaughn & T. B. Brazelton (Eds.), *The family—can it be saved?* (pp. 133–141). Chicago: Year Book Medical Publishers.

15. Bremner, J. G. (1988). *Infancy.* New York: Basil Blackwell.

16. Bridger, W. H. (1961). Sensory habituation and discrimination in the human neonate. *American Journal of Psychiatry, 117,* 991.

17. Campos, J., Langer, A., & Krowitz, A. (1970). Cardiac responses on the visual cliff in prelocomotor human infants. *Science, 170,* 196.

18. Chaney, R. H., Givens, C. A., Aoki, M. F., & Gombiner, M. L. (1989). Pupillary responses in recognizing awareness in persons with profound mental retardation. *Perceptual and Motor Skills, 69,* 523–528.

19. Cohen, L. B. (1972). Attention-getting and attention-holding processes of infant visual preferences. *Child Development, 43,* 869–879.

20. Condon, W. S., & Sander, L. W. (1974). Neonatal movement is synchronized with adult speech: Interactional participation in language acquisition. *Science, 183,* 99.

21. Coren, S., & Ward, L. M. (1989). *Sensation and Perception* (3rd ed.). San Diego, CA: Harcourt Brace Jovanovich.

22. Dannemiller, J. L. (1989). A test of color constancy in 9- and 20-week-old human infants following simulated illuminant changes. *Developmental Psychology, 25*(2), 171–184.

23. DeCasper, A. J., & Spence, M. J. (1986). Prenatal maternal speech influences newborns' perception of speech sounds. *Infant Behavior and Development, 9,* 133–150.

24. Elkind, D. (1967). Cognition in infancy and early childhood. In Y. Brackbill (Ed.), *Infancy and early childhood: A handbook and guide to human development.* New York: Free Press.

25. Elkind, D. (1976). Cognitive frames and family interactions. In V. C. Vaghan & T. B. Brazelton (Eds.), *The family—can it be saved?* Chicago: Year Book.

26. Elkind, D. (1978). *The child's reality: Three developmental themes.* Hillsdale, NJ: Lawrence Erlbaum.

27. Elkind, D., Koegler, R., & Goh, E. (1964). Studies in perceptual development II: Part-whole perception. *Child Development, 56,* 892–898.

28. Fantz, R. H. (1965). Visual perception from birth as shown by pattern selectivity. *Annals of the New York Academy of Sciences, 118,* 793–814.

29. Fantz, R. L. (1958). Pattern vision in young infants. *Psychological Record, 8,* 43–47.

30. Fantz, R. L., Fagan, J. F., & Miranda, S. B. (1975). Early perceptual development as shown by visual discrimination, selectivity, and memory with varying stimulus and population parameters. In L. B. Cohen & P. Salapatek (Eds.), *Infant Perception: From sensation to cognition.* New York: Academic Press.

31. Frankenburg, W. K., & Dodds, J. B. (1967). The Denver Developmental Screening Test. *Journal of Pediatrics, 71,* 181–191.

32. Frankenburg, W. K., et al: (1981). The newly abbreviated and revised Denver Developmental Screening Test. *Journal of Pediatrics, 99,* 995.

33. Freidman, S., & Vietz, P. (1972). The competent infant. *Peabody Journal of Education, 49,* 314.

34. Gallagher, J. J. (1975). Perception. In J. J. Gallagher (Ed.), *The application of child development research to exceptional children.* Reston, VA: Council for Exceptional Children.

35. Gesell, A. (1925). *The mental growth of the preschool child.* New York: Macmillan.

36. Gibson, E. J. (1987). Introductory essay: What does infant perception tell us about theories of perception? *Journal of Experimental Psychology: Human Perception and Performance, 13,* 515–523.

37. Gibson, E. J., & Spelke, E. S. (1983). The development of perception. In P. H. Mussen (Ed.), *Handbook of child psychology* (Vol. 3, pp. 1–76). New York: Wiley.

38. Gibson, E. J., & Walk, R. D. (1960). The visual cliff. *Scientific American, 202,* 64.

39. Gibson, E. J., & Walker, A. S. (1984). Development of knowledge of visual-tactual affordances of substances. *Child Development, 55,* 453–461.

40. Gottlieb, G., & Krasnegor, N. A. (Eds.). (1985). *Measurement of audition and vision in the first years of postnatal life: a methodological overview.* Norwood, NJ: Ablex.

41. Hebb, D. O. (1958). The motivation effects of exteroceptive stimulation. *American Psychologist, 13,* 109.

42. Held, R., Birch, E., & Gwiazda, J. (1980). Stereoacuity in human infants. *Proceedings of the National Academy of Sciences, USA, 77,* 5572–5574.

43. Hildebrandt, K. A., & Fitzgerald, H. E. (1983). The infant's physical attractiveness: Its effect on bonding and attachment. *Infant Mental Health Journal, 4,* 3.

44. Hupp, S. C., & Mervis, C. B. (1982). Acquisition of basic object categories by severely handicapped children. *Child Development, 53,* 760.

45. Karmel, B. Z., & Maisel, F. B. (1975). A neuronal activity model for infant visual attention. In L. B. Cohen & P. Salapatek (Eds.), *Infant perception: From sensation to cognition, Vol. 1 Basic visual processes* (pp. 78–133). New York: Academic Press.

46. Knobloch, H., & Pasamanick, B. (1974). *Gesell and Amatruda's developmental diagnosis: the evaluation and management of normal and abnormal neuropsychologic development in infancy and early childhood* (3rd ed.). New York: Harper & Row.

47. Korner, A. F. (1973). Individual differences at birth: Implications for early experiences and later development. In J. C. Westman (Ed.), *Individual differences in children.* New York: Wiley.

48. Lamb, M. E., & Campos, J. J. (1982). *Development in infancy: An introduction.* New York: Random House.

49. Meltzoff, A. N., & Moore, M. K. (1989). Imitation in newborn infants: Exploring the range of gestures imitated and the underlying mechanisms. *Developmental Psychology, 25,* 954–962.

50. Millar, W. S. (Ed.). (1972). A study of operant conditioning under delayed reinforcement in early infancy. *Monograph of the Society for Research in Child Development, 37*(2, Whole No. 147).

51. Muir, D., & Clifton, R. K. (1985). Infants' orientation to the location of sound sources. In G. Gottlieb & N. Krasnegor (Eds.), *Measurement of audition and vision in the first year of postnatal life: A methodological overview* (pp. 171–194). Norwood, NJ: Ablex.

52. Muir, D., & Field, J. (1979). Newborn infants orient to sounds. *Child Development, 50,* 431–436.

53. Nelson, K., & Ross, G. (1980). The generalities and specifics of

long term memory in infants and young children. In M. Perlmutter (Ed.), *New directions for child development: Children's memory.* San Francisco: Jossey-Bass.

54. Palmer, C. F. (1989). The discriminating nature of infants' exploratory actions. *Developmental Psychology, 25,* 885–893.

55. Piaget, J. (1952). *The origins of intelligence in children* (M. Cook, Trans.). New York: International Universities Press.

56. Piaget, J. (1969). *The language and thought of the child* (M. Gabain, Trans.). New York: Meridian Books.

57. Piaget, J., & Inhelder, B. (1969). *The psychology of the child* (H. Weaver, Trans.). New York: Basic Books.

58. Rochat, P. (1989). Object manipulation and exploration in 2- to 5-month-old infants. *Developmental Psychology, 25,* 871–884.

59. Rock, I. (1975). *An introduction to perception.* New York: Macmillan Publishing.

60. Rose, S. A., Feldman, J. F., Wallace, I. F., & McCarton, C. (1989). Infant visual attention: Relation to birth status and developmental outcome during the first five years. *Developmental Psychology, 25,* 560–576.

61. Ruff, H. A. (1986). Components of attention during infants' manipulative exploration. *Child Development, 57,* 105–114.

62. Salapatek, P. (1975). Pattern perception in early infancy. In L. B. Cohen & P. Salapatek (Eds.), *Infant perception: From sensation to cognition.* New York: Academic Press.

63. Scarr, S., & Salapatek, P. (1970). Patterns of fear development during infancy. *Merrill-Palmer Quarterly, 16,* 53.

64. Schaffer, H. R., & Collis, G. M. (1986). Parental responsiveness and child behavior. In W. Sluckin & M. Herbert (Eds.), *Parental behavior* (pp. 283–315). New York: Basil Blackwell.

65. Schaffer, H. R., & Emerson, P. E. (1973). Patterns of response to physical contact in early human development. In L. J. Stone, H. T. Smith, & L. B. Murphy (Eds.), *The competent infant: Research and commentary.* New York: Basic Books.

66. Schuster, C. S. (1977). *The relationship of neonatal characteristics to specific learning disabilities and behavioral disorders of early childhood.* (Unpublished paper).

67. Schuster, C. S. (1981). *The relationship of prenatal and perinatal factors to the mother's perception of her one-month-old infant.* (Doctoral Dissertation: The Ohio State University)

68. Schuster, C. S. (Ed.). (In Press). *Orientation and mobility training for visually impaired infants and toddlers.*

69. Shelton, T. L. (1989). The assessment of cognition/intelligence in infancy. *Infants and Young Children, 1*(3), 10–25.

70. Siegel, L. S. (1981). Infant tests as predictors of cognitive and language development at two years. *Child Development, 52,* 545.

71. Siegler, R. S. (1986). *Children's thinking.* Englewood Cliffs, NJ: Prentice-Hall.

72. Spelke, E. (1976). Infant's intermodal perception of events. *Cognitive Psychology, 8,* 553–560.

73. Streri, A., & Pêcheux, M. G. (1986). Tactual habituation and discrimination of form in infancy: A comparison with vision. *Child development, 57,* 100–104.

74. Tronick, E. (1972). Stimulus control and the growth of the infant's effective visual field. *Perception and Psychophysics, 11,* 373–376.

75. Tulving, E. (1983). *Elements of episodic memory.* New York: Oxford University Press.

76. Uzgiris, I. C., & Hunt, J. M. (1989). *Assessment in infancy: Ordinal scales of psychological development.* Urbana, IL: University of Illinois Press.

77. Valadian, I., & Porter, D. (1977). *Physical growth and development: From conception to maturity.* Boston: Little, Brown.

78. Werker, J. F., Gilbert, J. H., Humphrey, K., & Tees, R. C. (1981). Developmental aspects of cross-language speech perception. *Child Development, 52,* 349–355.

79. Werner, J. S., & Siqueland, E. R. (1978). Visual recognition memory in the preterm infant. *Infant Behavior and Development, 1,* 79–94.

80. Wertheimer, M. (1961). Psychomotor coordination of auditory and visual space at birth. *Science, 134,* 1692.

81. White, B. L. (1985). *The first three years of life* (rev. ed.). New York: Prentice-Hall.

82. Wolff, P. H. (1963). Observations on the early development of smiling. In B. M. Foss (Ed.), *Determinants of infant behavior, IV.* New York: Wiley.

83. Wolff, P. H. (1973). The natural history of crying and other vocalizations in early infancy. In L. J. Stone, H. T. Smith, & L. B. Murphy (Eds.), *The competent infant: Research and commentary* (pp. 1185–1198). New York: Basic Books.

84. Wood, D. (1988). *How children think and learn.* New York: Basil Blackwell.

85. Yang, R. K. (1979). Early infant assessment: An overview. In J. D. Osofsky (Ed.), *Handbook of infant development.* New York: John Wiley and Sons.

86. Yonas, A., Arterberry, M. E., & Granrud, C. E. (1987). Four-month-old infants' sensitivity to binocular and kinetic information for three-dimensional-object shape. *Child Development, 58,* 910–917.

87. Yonas, A. (1981). Infants' responses to optical information for collision. In R. N. Aslin, J. R. Alberts, & M. R. Peterson (Eds.), *Development of perception: Psychological perspectives* (Vol. 2: The visual system, pp. 313–334). New York: Academic Press.

Psychosocial Development During Infancy

Clara S. Schuster and Shirley S. Ashburn

King Frederick II, a 13th-century monarch of Sicily, was curious about the "natural" language of mankind.[63] To find out more about innate human language, he set up a special nursery for a group of babies where all physical needs were to be met, but where the foster mothers were forbidden to talk to or around the children. Play with the children was also forbidden lest the infants learn the nonverbal elements of communication. They were to interact only with each other so that innate language forms could emerge. The king's question was never answered because all the babies died. Some stimulus necessary to sustain life was missing. We now know that it was the absence of synchronized, meaningful responses from the caregivers.

Most theories of emotional and social development contend that the early mother–child relationship is pivotal to the quality of social relationships and emotional maturity in the adult years. The infant begins life as an asocial being. The parent facilitates development by orchestrating a social context that supports the infant's potentials and efforts.[18] Through mutual focusing on interactions that capture the infant's attention and interest, the infant gradually begins to establish a meaningful relationship with the primary caregiver, to develop social communication skills, and to learn how to learn. This puts a lot of responsibility on the parent(s) for the successful development of their infant. Through mutual cueing and responding, the dyad establishes a synchronized communication "dance" where each is reinforced to continue the satisfying interaction, and where each learns to know the other and to predict responses.

The infant is a gregarious person from the moment of birth. Inadequate attention to the affective and social needs of the young infant can have serious consequences. The biophysically normal infant who suffers even minor deprivation or inadequate synchronization of the social environment may experience negative cognitive, physical, and social consequences.

The infant is an active and reactive participant in the social process, sometimes the recipient of an interaction and at other times the initiator. Individual differences in infant activity level and temperament can be observed at birth, before environmental factors have had time to produce any effect.[17,23,24] These differences elicit qualitatively and quantitatively different responses from the parents. The baby's ability to accept and to use comforting to control his state of consciousness will frequently influence the mood and quality of care administered by the baby's principal caregiver. The quality, quantity, and consistency of the caregiver's reactions to the baby's crying will in turn help to mold their relationship and will affect, in part, the way the baby interacts in social environments.[4,64,69] Both the baby's and the parents' behaviors change rapidly over the course of the infancy period as they accommodate to one another.[18]

The biological mother of the child may not always assume the traditional mothering role; therefore, the terms **mother, parent,** and **caregiver** are used interchangeably to indicate the primary person whose actions and interactions are associated with the nurturing role.

THE PROCESS OF ATTACHMENT

For centuries artists have attempted to capture on canvas the essence of the mother–infant relationship. During the past century, psychologists and social scientists have attempted to describe and to explain this relationship through theory and research. **Attachment,** a term coined by Bowlby in 1958, refers to the selective emotional ties that one person (in this case the infant) has for another person or persons, for a pet, or even for objects.[64] This focused relationship develops over time as the child experiences repeated contacts. **Attachment behaviors** are those activities that serve to obtain or to maintain contact or proximity with the attachment object (e.g., visual tracking, grasping, reaching, smiling, babbling, clinging, crying).

Attachment persists over time even during periods of absence. This selective relationship generally is present by 6 months.[29, 64] Attachment gives the child a security base, which at first provides a source of strength and identity and later provides a point of differentiation or separation. Most infants form multiple attachments. Although attachments are similar in quality, they differ in intensity and are not freely interchangeable.[64] When the child is under stress, a hierarchy of relationships appears as the child seeks comfort and security from the person nearest the top of this pyramid.

The establishment of a meaningful emotional/social relationship is seen as the cornerstone of all future development because early attachment facilitates the following:

1. Differentiation between self and others
2. Exploration of the environment
3. Development of a conscience
4. Harnessing of energies
5. Development of self-discipline
6. Emergence of empathy
7. Coping with stress and frustration
8. Development of self-reliance
9. Reduction of fear and anxiety
10. Dissipation of jealousies and rivalries
11. Development of autonomy
12. Attainment of self-confidence
13. Development of self-acceptance
14. Development of later social and emotional relationships
15. Sense of caring for the self

Sensitive Period

Farmers and researchers have observed that ducks, geese, and goats selectively attach to the first moving object they see after birth. In one experiment, Konrad Lorenz became the attachment object of incubator-hatched geese who saw him before seeing an avian mother.[46] The little birds followed him about with great vigor. They ran toward Lorenz for comfort when frightened, even if their biological mother was present. As the goslings matured, they demonstrated courting behaviors toward him. This phenomenon, dubbed *imprinting,* occurs only during the critical period following birth. No evidence supports the phenomenon of imprinting in humans. However, infants more than 5 months of age who change caregivers (e.g., because of maternal illness, return to work, or adoption) evidence extreme stress.[29, 64] This behavior indicates that selective attachment has been established during the first 6 months of life. Even though disruption of a relationship is traumatic, once a child has learned to trust and attach to one person, it is easier to attach to a second person. Children who have never attached to another person experience great difficulty with this process (Fig. 8-1).[29, 64]

Need Satisfaction

Early theories emphasized physiological need satisfaction as the basis for the infant's development of attachment to, and meaningful relationships with, others. In 1958 Harry and Margaret Harlow proved that there is more to attachment behavior than just being fed adequately.[32] They raised infant monkeys in cages with two very different surrogate mothers. One "mother" was covered with soft terry cloth; the other was composed of hard wire mesh and had a feeding apparatus. The baby monkeys did not spend much time with the wire

FIGURE 8–1.
The best start for a neonate is two parents who genuinely care.

surrogate mother that fed them, but clung to the cloth surrogate that did not feed them. The need theory was shattered; the provision of food was not the basis for attachment. Comforting potential was a much stronger basis.

When the infant monkeys in Harlow's experiment reached adulthood, they demonstrated marked social difficulties and sexual maladjustment.[32] Research with well-cared-for institutionalized children who experienced as many as 50 to 80 caregivers indicates that inadequate attachment experiences in infancy lead to excessive attention-seeking and indiscriminate friendliness by 4 years of age[83] and to impaired relationships with peers and adults during school years.[82] Inadequate, inconsistent, or nonresponsive attachment objects in infancy prevent adequate socialization.

Communication Development

Socialization depends on the ability of the adult and infant to establish meaningful communication. From this communication dyad emerges emotional security, cognitive skills, and the foundations for language development. Emerging cognitive and physical skills also affect the form communication takes. Schaffer describes five stages of communicative development which unfold during the first two years of life.[70]

STAGE 1: THE IMMEDIATE POSTBIRTH PERIOD. Interactions focus on establishing rhythm in biological patterns of eating and sleeping. Mother and infant begin to predict the other's behaviors. Synchronization of adult responses to the infant's behavior are pivotal. Parents learn how to "read" the baby's state and to bring the baby to state 4.

STAGE 2: TWO TO FOUR MONTHS. The infant seeks out face-to-face interactions with others. Much "wooing" and vocal turntaking occurs. The infant is most interested in people stimuli. The baby begins to learn the rules of nonverbal communication.

STAGE 3: FIVE TO SEVEN MONTHS. As physical manipulation abilities increase, interest switches to objects and cause–effect actions. Adult and infant engage in **topic sharing.** The parent focuses communication and activity on the object that has captured the infant's interest. This type of turntaking is the foundation for cooperative work/play.

STAGE 4: EIGHT TO 16 MONTHS. The infant begins to understand that vocal and nonverbal behaviors serve to convey messages to others. They begin to modify and refine their behaviors based on feedback. The baby begins to actively try to predict and control outcome and events. More equal balance in the communication relationship emerges, but the interpretation of infant cues and signs still weighs heavily on the more mature communicator of the dyad. Behaviors become intentional as communicative power is realized.

STAGE 5: 18 MONTHS ONWARD. The child begins to realize that words stand for things and actions. Thus, he or she consciously learns and experiments with language for communication. Generalized behaviors and nonverbal forms of communication are gradually eliminated as language competency increases.

Theories of Attachment

Infants become attached to caregivers who provide a source of consistent, intimate interaction. Several theorists offer explanations of the process. Freud based his theory of attachment on instinctual drives, viewing the infant as a narcissistic organism who attaches to people who can reduce tensions and meet his or her needs.

Mary Ainsworth observed that 12- to 18-month-old infants could be classified as securely or insecurely attached based on their behavior in an unfamiliar setting.[1] The child is first left with a stranger for three minutes and is later left completely alone in an unfamiliar room. *Securely attached* infants are noted to cry with mild intensity following maternal departure, to greet the mother's return eagerly, and to be easily soothed upon her return. Insecurely attached babies exhibit two patterns of behavior. *Anxious avoidant* infants show little stress when mother leaves and do not greet her when she returns. *Anxious ambivalent* babies show extreme stress when she leaves, and are not easily soothed at her return. Research bears out Ainsworth's hypothesis that the security of the attachment is correlated with the sensitivity of maternal feedback to the young infant's behaviors.[1, 8, 73] Recent research also indicates that the security of attachment at 1 year is predictive of security at 6 years of age.[50] Boys who showed extreme distress in the *stranger situation* at 1 year are more likely to be withdrawn at 6 years, whereas girls are more likely to exhibit aggression.[45]

Jacob Gewirtz, a behavioral learning theorist, suggests that differential reinforcement leads to attachment.[30, 31] He hypothesizes that attachment is a specific pattern of response that evolves as a result of the infant and caregiver learning to exert control over one another's behavior (a positive stimulus and reinforcer). However, even in the face of severe maltreatment and severe punishment, attachment behaviors may be exhibited by infants and young children.[64]

Robert Sears, a developmental learning theorist, equates attachment with dependence. He calls attachment a *secondary drive,* arising from association with primary drives. The mother acquires a positive value as she meets the primary drives or needs of the infant: hunger, thirst, discomfort, and so forth. At the same time, the parent becomes a secondary general reinforcer; therefore, the desire for the caregiver's nearness as a dispenser of primary reinforcers results in attachment.[49]

Although each theorist offers a different explanation, the scenario is the same: Infants who receive warm, consistent, synchronized responses from a primary person appear to develop a specific attachment to that person. **The paradox is that the more securely an infant is attached, the easier it is for the child to separate, to move outward to explore the environment, enjoy new experiences, and associate with other people.**

Bowlby's Theory of Attachment

John Bowlby, a child psychiatrist, postulates that attachment is the result of interaction between adaptive predispositions in the infant and behaviors of the parent. He believes that certain types of stimulation elicit certain types of behavior in the infant, and that infant behaviors elicit particular behaviors in the adult. For example, a mother may speak more frequently and lovingly to a baby who smiles or babbles in response to her efforts. Since the mother and baby feel good about this, they repeat the act and begin to form a meaningful relationship. Bowlby asserts that infants use attachment behaviors such as sucking, clinging, following, crying, and smiling to elicit parental caregiving. He believes that feeding plays only a minor role in the development of attachment.[15] Sensitive social reciprocity is a more critical component. Attachment occurs as the infant learns to "distinguish the familiar from the strange".[14]

Bowlby differentiates between the terms **dependence** and **attachment,** which are considered synonymous by some theorists (see Table 8-1). Dependence is the extent to which one individual relies on another to meet needs. Dependent behaviors may be exhibited toward anyone. Two categories are identified: *instrumental* (seeking help or assistance) and *emotional* (seeking attention or approval). Both types of dependence are maximal at birth and gradually diminish over time. In fact, dependent behaviors are considered a sign of immaturity if they persist.

Attachment is absent at birth, and increases over time. Bowlby discusses four overlapping phases in the normal development of attachment. He labels phase 1 as *orientation and signals without discrimination of figure.* He believes that the infant's ability to discriminate one person from another either is absent or is extremely limited from birth until 2 or 3 months. However, Brazelton has observed that infants begin to respond discriminately to mother versus father versus stranger by 3 weeks of age.[16] Unfavorable conditions (e.g., inconsistency of care, neglect, abuse) may extend this phase. Bowlby acknowledges that the baby elicits responses in others during this time by using the infant tools (see Chap. 7) of communication and gradually learns specific behaviors which prolong interactions with others.

The infant begins nonselective social smiling between 2 and 4 weeks. This response is characteristically elicited by both stationary and moving visual stimuli (even the pendulum of a clock). Other stimuli (e.g., auditory, tactile) may also be used in conjunction with visual stimuli to elicit the smile. Smiling occurs whether the stimulating face is familiar or unfamiliar.

During phase 2 (3 to 6 months), *orientation and signals directed toward one or more discriminated figures,* the infant begins to behave toward the mother figure "in more marked fashion" than toward others. During this phase, the various components of full facial smiling become integrated. Massive, total body activity also emerges around this age.

Selective social smiling usually emerges before 20 weeks and overlaps with nonselective smiling. Between 4 and 6 months, the securely attached infant will visually explore the face of a stranger and then visually check the parent's face, as if comparing and analyzing the similarities and differences between the two. This visual-checking behavior is usually continued during the first 18 to 24 months. Selective social smiling coincides with the baby's increasing fear of, or caution with, strangers and anxiety when separated from primary caregivers. Around five months, many babies display sobriety or cry at a friendly smile if the stranger gets too close or makes attempts to hold them. Some babies will deliberately avoid eye contact with strangers.

Scary situations (e.g., encountering Halloween masks) and alterations of the human face (e.g., sunglasses or beard) usually will not evoke crying in an infant until the end of the sixth month. If a *familiar* face becomes altered, however, crying may occur in an even younger baby (Fig. 8-2). One 4-month-old baby girl began to cry in terror when she first saw her mother wearing a turban towel wrapped around her

TABLE 8-1. BOWLBY'S VIEW OF ATTACHMENT VERSUS DEPENDENCY

Factor	Attachment	Dependency
Specificity	1 person	Anyone
Duration	Over time	Transient
Developmental level	All ages	Immature only
Affect	Strong, intrinsic passion	Minimal or no emotional involvement
Proximity-seeking	Focused toward specific person	Contact with anyone who can meet/relieve need
Acquisition	Learned; becomes stronger with time	Unlearned; maximal at birth; should diminish over time

FIGURE 8–2.
Fear of a distorted face indicates that the baby has internalized an expectation of what a face should look like.

FIGURE 8–3.
Infant carriers allow the baby to remain in close proximity to the parent, while allowing the parent to complete other tasks. This closeness provides opportunities for conversations, demonstrations, and sampling (if parent is cooking).

just-washed hair. However, not all distortions of the familiar face will provoke an adverse response. For instance, the removal of glasses from the mother's face when the baby is accustomed to seeing her with glasses might provoke crying, but the addition of glasses to a mother's face that is usually seen without glasses may not.[88]

During Bowlby's third phase of attachment formation (7 to 36 months), *maintenance of proximity to a discriminated figure by means of locomotion as well as signals,* the infant demonstrates extreme discrimination between the mother figure and others. The infant tends to become less friendly to others, except for a select few, and often demands constant contact with, or close proximity to, the mother figure—a situation some mothers find difficult while fulfilling their other responsibilities (Fig. 8-3). Some infants who have had little contact with a stable mother figure may not begin this phase until after 12 months of age.

Around the first birthday, the child begins to understand that the mother figure is an independent person who tends to behave in predictable ways. This is the beginning of Bowlby's fourth phase, called *formation of a goal-directed partnership.* Under healthy circumstances, this newfound but vacillating security lays a foundation for the child and the mother to develop a more complex, interdependent relationship.[13, 15]

THE SEPARATION-INDIVIDUATION PROCESS

The psychological birth of the human infant, unlike the readily observable biological birth, is a slowly unfolding intrapsychic process.[47, 48] During the first 2½ to 3 years of life, the young child gradually becomes more aware of the biological and psychological separateness of self from significant others. This awareness leads to the development of a body image, a sense of self, and a rudimentary understanding of object relationships (relationships with significant others) and the reality of the external environment. The development of cognitive object constancy and object permanence appear to be prerequisites for developing a sense of self (see Chap. 7). It is

possible to think of oneself as a coherent and lasting entity only when one is aware that both self and others are entities that remain in essentially the same form (*cognitive object constancy*) and continue to exist, although not seen all the time (*object permanence*).

Mahler's Psychological Birth of the Infant

Margaret Mahler, a psychoanalyst, theorizes that every individual gradually establishes an awareness of a relationship to, yet a sense of separateness from, the world of reality.[48] This process involves recognition of the separateness of one's own body and will from that of the primary love object (person) (see Table 8-2).

Mahler postulates that the major achievements of this process are accomplished between the 4th or 5th month to the 30th or 36th month of life. Although the processes of separation and individuation are closely related and intertwined, they are not identical. **Separation** is the recognition of *biological distinctness* and consists of the child's emergence from a symbiotic dependency relationship with the mother. **Individuation** is the recognition of *affective* and *social distinctness* and consists of the child's awareness of differences in will, viewpoint, needs, goals, and reactions. Both processes deal with the infant's gradual emancipation from a "mass," or "fused," ego identity, a process that may continue throughout life in other relationships if inadequately resolved during early childhood (see Chap. 29).[12, 48] With mastery of the processes, the person gradually assumes

TABLE 8-2. MAHLER'S INTRAPSYCHIC SEPARATION-INDIVIDUATION PROCESS

Phase	Age	Characteristics of Child
FORERUNNERS OF PROCESS		
Normal autism	Birth–1 month	"Absolute primary narcissism." Lack of awareness of mothering agent. Unaware of self–other differentiation. "Primitive hallucinatory disorientation." Physiological rather than psychological processes dominate behaviors. Energies focused toward physiological need satisfaction and maintenance of homeostasis. Minimal response to external events.
Normal symbiosis	1–5 months	"Sociobiological interdependence." Primary narcissism now includes mothering agent. Sees mother as a part of self—a dual unity with a common boundary. Dimly aware that he cannot meet his own needs. Beginning to be aware of and attend to external events, but unable to distinguish between internal and external experiences.
SUBPHASES OF PROCESS		
Differentiation	5–9 months	"Lap baby." Specific bond between the infant and his primary caregiver emerges. Explores her face and body. Begins to distinguish and differentiate between own and mother's body, self–nonself, and mother–not mother. Molds to body of caregiver. Begins to alter behavior in response to mother's cues. Curiosity and wonderment with novel experiences. Much visual inspection of both people and the environment.

Practicing
  Early (crawling)
  Late (walking)
	9–14 months	Elated investment in his own burgeoning physical autonomy. Begins to move away from mother physically. Becomes absorbed in own activities, but mother needs to be present as an anchor for safe exploration of the environment. Many "emotional refueling" behaviors. May have a transitional toy or object.

Rapprochement	14–24 months	Uses mother as an extension of self. Recognizes own physiological separateness from mother. Wants to share each new accomplishment with her. Shadowing and darting away behaviors. Stranger shyness and adverse reactions to separations may be due to a growing sense of vulnerability. Increased "emotional refueling" behaviors.
Consolidation	24–36 months	Establishment of *affective object constancy*—ability to separate from mother without extreme anxiety. Emergence of core gender-identity. Play becomes more purposeful and constructive. Symbolic play emerges. Able to wait for need gratification.

(Mahler, M. S., Pine, F., & Bergman, A. (1975). The psychological birth of the human infant: Symbiosis and individuation. New York: Basic Books.)

more responsibility for an independent identity and self-revitalizing activities.

Antecedents of the Separation-Individuation Process

Before the infant can begin to differentiate between self–nonself and good–not good, psychosocial equilibrium must be attained. This equilibrium depends on the ability of the mother and infant to establish communication. A mutual cueing begins, with the parent focusing on the infant's needs and responses. Over a period of several months, the situation evolves to a more balanced sharing of feelings and needs between the parent and the child.

NORMAL AUTISM. According to Mahler, the early weeks of life are characterized by absolute primary narcissism. The infant is unaware of the role of the mothering agent in satisfying needs. The mother protects the neonate from extremes of stimulation to facilitate physiological growth. Since the infant's natural tendency is to spend considerable periods of time in Wolff's states 1, 2, or 3 (see Chap. 4), the mother's ministrations not only help to maintain physiological homeostasis but also help to increase the neonate's "sensory awareness of and contact with the environment" by helping the infant to spend more time in state 4.[48]

The neonate gradually develops an awareness that needs cannot be satisfied without assistance. Innate skills and reflexes begin to be used as tools to obtain wished-for pleasures and to achieve homeostatic equilibrium. Movement to the symbiotic phase is facilitated by the increased responsiveness to external stimuli found in state 4 (if the caregiver has previously responded consistently and in synchrony with the baby's needs and behaviors).

NORMAL SYMBIOSIS. According to Mahler, from the second month of life until the fourth or fifth month, the infant develops a "dim awareness of the need-satisfying object." The infant no longer responds only to physiological needs and perceptions but begins to exhibit conscious attempts to control stimuli in the environment. During this time, the infant perceives the self and the mother figure as "a dual unity with one common boundary." Self–nonself is not yet differentiated. The infant appears to experiment with obtaining and maintaining the appearance of mother's face, touch, and voice in much the same way as the infant experiments with the movements of his or her own body to create a desired effect.

This observation is consistent with Piaget's description of the infant in substage II (see Chap. 7).

Symbiosis is optimal when enfolding, caressing, and en face behaviors are freely used by the caregiver, and when the caregiver responds contingently to the infant. As the parent allows the infant time to respond with cooing, body movements, and smiles (*turntaking*), the infant begins to attach to the caregiver. This ability to invest oneself emotionally in another person lays the foundation for all subsequent human relationships.[15, 48]

Mahler's Separation-Individuation Period

DIFFERENTIATION. Differentiation, the first subphase of the separation-individuation period, begins at the peak of normal symbiosis (7 to 8 months). The infant's more alert state enables more learning about the external world through increased use of the senses. Visual and tactile exploration of faces, watches, eyeglasses, and so forth aid in gaining information about objects and lay the foundation for the ability to compare objects never before seen with familiar objects. Children of this age spend much time in close contact with the mother. Touching the mother's face and other parts of her body allows the infant to make comparisons with the corresponding parts of the infant's own body and the bodies of other people. Naming the parts of the body as the baby touches them fosters language development. "Pat-a-cake," "itsy-bitsy-spider," and other games foster reciprocal and cooperative interaction. This **lap-baby period** may be critical to the ability to engage comfortably in intimate physical relationships later in the life span.

PRACTICING. The differentiation period is overlapped by the **practicing** subphase. This subphase is characterized by the infant's attempts to move away physically from the caregiver (e.g., crawling, climbing, running). Exploration of the environment and inanimate objects is a hallmark of this subphase; the baby can be seen fingering, tasting, shaking, and smelling objects. Three important skills are gained: The infant (1) increases familiarity with, and knowledge about, the world, (2) begins perceiving, recognizing, and enjoying the mothering person from a greater distance,[48] and (3) begins synthesizing sensory input.

Emotional refueling is evidenced by a baby during this phase and continues into the toddler and preschool years (and beyond). It takes great courage and emotional energy for the newly separating infant to venture forth to explore the environment independently. Consequently, the infant makes frequent physical and visual contact with the mother before continuing exploratory and play activities. The baby who crawls across the room from the mother may find it necessary to travel back to her side and lean against her briefly before again venturing forth. In new or strange situations, the child will cling to the mother or hide behind her legs. The baby "refuels." The physical contact gives the baby the security and the emotional power to go out into the world again (even if it

means only traveling to the other couch, or waving "bye-bye" to a departing visitor).

Mahler's third and fourth subphases, which normally occur during the toddler and preschool years, are discussed in Chapter 11.

Erikson's Basic Trust Versus Basic Mistrust

Erik Erikson's theory of infant psychosocial development is complementary to Mahler's model.[27] Erikson states that the degree to which the infant develops self-trust as well as trust in other people and the world in general depends on the quality of care the infant receives during the early months. He asserts that the most significant developmental task of infancy is to resolve a crisis between a *sense of basic trust* and a *sense of basic mistrust*. The consistency and quality of parent–infant interaction have a direct impact on the development of the infant's ego-identity, or self-concept. Erikson views trust as the foundation of healthy psychosocial development. The well-developing child acquires a sense of hope, which permeates the entire life span.

The neonate has come from a warm, protective intrauterine environment in which all needs were met and no demands were made. Birth presents a new world where comfort and protection are no longer guaranteed. The baby needs feeding, sucking pleasure, warmth, comfort, sensory stimulation, and many other ministrations to develop the sense of security. The consistency with which needs are met enables the infant to begin to predict responses and to develop trust in and love for (or attachment to) the parents. Erikson is quick to point out that the degree of trust "does not seem to depend on absolute quantities of food or demonstrations of love, but rather on the **quality** of the [parental] relationship."[27] It is the manner (not necessarily the technical skill) in which these needs are met that is fundamental.

If care of the infant is inconsistent, inadequate, or rejecting over a period of time, a sense of mistrust develops. This mistrust, according to Erikson, imparts an attitude of suspicion and fear toward oneself, other people, and the world in general. A sense of mistrust will prevent or delay cognitive development and the achievement of other stages of psychosocial development.

Early Incorporative Stage
Erikson views the infant's first 6 months of extrauterine life as a time when the infant "takes in" the external world. Erikson goes beyond Freud's emphasis on the mouth to include the infant's visual abilities to explore and incorporate the "world." He calls this first stage the "incorporative mode," when the infant visually and orally explores everything offered.[28] Erikson emphasizes that the primary caregiver must coordinate and offer stimulation in appropriate degrees of intensity at the right time (*synchronized interactional exchange*), lest the infant's willingness to accept be converted to either a defensive schema or lethargy.[28] Too much stimulation will be overwhelming, causing the infant to tune out stimuli as a defense

against the environment. Integration of the experiences for cognitive and affective growth becomes impossible. The consistency of synchronized, positive sensory stimulation helps the infant to trust the environment as well as his or her own abilities to predict and begin to control outcomes of behavior.

The infant begins to associate the primary caregivers with relief, comfort, and the pleasurable sensations of being picked up, caressed, rocked, and fed. Erikson recognizes the coordination of the psychosocial and biophysical domains when he concludes: "The first demonstration of social trust in the baby is the ease of his feeding, the depth of his sleep, the relaxation of his bowels."[27] One research study indicates that the regularity of sleep patterns may be predictive of cognitive and social development at 2½ years.[80]

Advanced Incorporative Stage

The second stage of Erikson's incorporative mode emerges about the time the first teeth erupt. The infant has now learned to control the environment to some extent. The infant discovers that the mouth can be used to learn about the texture, size, and temperature of an object, and that biting can relieve some of the pain that accompanies teething. The baby begins to coordinate oral, olfactory, visual, auditory, and motor skills with neuromuscular maturation and experience. The older infant gradually coordinates touching and grasping with visual, auditory, and tactile stimuli to learn more about the environment (Fig. 8-4).

During infancy the individual needs to learn that the world is a safe, happy place that will meet basic needs and provide sufficient novelty to stimulate interest beyond self. The infant needs protection and emotional support while attempting new skills, exploring new objects, or making a new acquaintance. Each situation helps to produce expectations of the ability to face new experiences. Situations eliciting mistrust should also occur. The infant also needs to learn to trust feelings of mistrust—fear of heights and strangers can be healthy.

The problem of basic trust versus mistrust is not resolved once and for all during infancy, but must be resolved in a new way at each successive stage of development. Each new relationship goes through a period of trust evaluation. If the basically trusting child is lied to by someone, a sense of mistrust can develop. On the other hand, a very suspicious child or adult who becomes part of a meaningful relationship may eventually be led to experience a sense of trust. An overview of Erikson's theory is given in Appendixes B and C.

Sullivan's Need-Anxiety-Satisfaction

Harry Stack Sullivan emphasizes the importance of interactions between people. Like Mahler and Erikson, he believes that the nature of early social relationships between the infant and the mother are critical in the child's personality development. Sullivan hypothesizes that people are constantly trying to reduce tensions that are the result of biological needs and

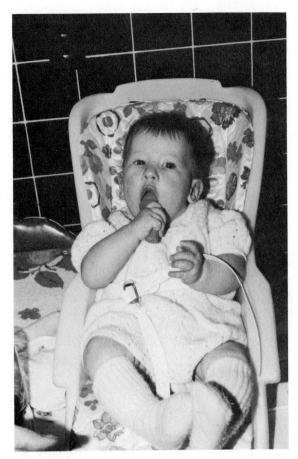

FIGURE 8–4.
During Erikson's advanced incorporative stage, the baby's mouth, instead of sucking in a relaxed way, may be found clamped onto many different types of objects. It is the satisfaction of such needs that gives the baby a sense of the world as a good, stable, pleasant, and somewhat predictable place—all of which is necessary for the formation of basic trust.

social insecurity. When a biological need (e.g., food, water, rest) is met, Sullivan postulates that satisfaction is achieved. As long as basic needs are met, the infant is in a state of *euphoria* or well-being: if they are not met, *anxiety* or a fearlike state occurs. Sullivan believes that an infant may display increased anxiety by difficulty with sleeping or feeding and by excessive crying.

Sullivan indicates that anxiety may be felt on a continuum of levels. Mild anxiety serves as an incentive or "power motive" for action. The infant soon discovers the tools (e.g., crying) for gaining attention and relief. Sullivan observes that infants are extremely sensitive to the attitudes of others. He believes that a mother consciously and unconsciously communicates her emotional mood (positive or negative) while meeting the infant's physical needs. Children understand the feelings before the content of a message.

Sullivan's Modes of Experience

Sullivan identifies three ways of experiencing the world. The **prototaxic** mode focuses on feelings and sensations. Since the young infant is unable to differentiate or categorize various experiences, each experience is responded to as it occurs and as a separate, isolated, unrelated event. The infant responds nondiscriminately and globally to all stimuli.

When memory and the ability to discriminate emerge (by organizing and drawing meaning from experiences), the infant experiences life from the **parataxic** mode. Visual and auditory cues help the infant to understand relationships and to predict the next event (e.g., "Milk follows the sight of the bottle," "Daddy is smiling, so he's going to pick me up and hug me"). The baby begins to distinguish between "me" and "not me," and to use some language.

During this mode, the infant's mental images of the mother are not realistic but are often perceptions of the interactions experienced between the two. Sullivan postulates that the young infant thinks of mother as a "nipple" because of her nurturing role. In later infancy the baby perceives the mother as a person who is sometimes good (or tender and approving) and sometimes bad (or disapproving and anxiety-provoking). Although the child still cannot connect experiences logically, as adults do, the more consistent the baby's environment and the sequences of life events, the easier it is for the infant to form a secure view of the world and the self. Sullivan contends that the child experiences events primarily through the parataxic mode during the second year of life and that this form of experience continues to occur throughout life.[55]

In Sullivan's third and highest type of experience, the **syntaxic** mode, the child learns the meanings and use of the symbols (i.e., gestures, words) that are collectively shared by others in the environment. This enables the child to test subjective perceptions against those of others. Since a child usually begins the syntaxic experience as a toddler, this concept is discussed more fully in Chapter 11.

Sullivan's Personifications

Sullivan believes that one's self-image emerges from the infant's interpretation of the original mother–infant relationship. Two personifications, the **good-me** and the **bad-me,** arises from this relationship and eventually fuse to form the "essential self." Good-me feelings occur when the baby senses acceptance; bad-me feelings are aroused when the baby experiences anxiety. The fusion of good-me and bad-me occurs at approximately 18 months of age.[55] Which "me" is dominant can change with each situational or maturational crisis. Excessive anxiety can lead to a basic perception of self as bad, to depression, and to feelings of inferiority. The essential self is highly resistant to change.

A third personification, **not-me,** may develop in the presence of prolonged, intense anxiety; it represents the individual's attempt to escape the negative feelings evolving from intense or continuous bad-me perceptions. The anxiety or bad behavior is projected onto another person or object in an attempt to distance one's self from the anxiety. In self protection, the child separates from, ignores, or tries to deny true feelings. Much of Sullivan's not-me concept pertains to later schizophrenic tendencies, and multiple personalities. Sullivan proposes that an infant who suffers intense anxiety over a period of time may drop into an apathetic, sleeplike state called *somnolent detachment*. If somnolent detachment is used frequently or for long periods of time, Sullivan predicts that permanent physical, psychological, and cognitive impairment can occur. These children may be clingy but do not necessarily attach to their caregiver.

Caregiver Role

The parental role is to help the child achieve a state of contentment. This does *not* mean that the parent protects the child from all discomfort or meets the child's needs before they exist (e.g., continuously offering food before the child is hungry). A sense of trust emerges from the child's ability to discern the cycle of arousal/relaxation (need-displeasure-action-satisfaction-quiescence-recurrence of need). The consistent relief of the unpleasant state by the caregiver is the key to feelings of trust, security, and attachment.[29] All through life, a person must confront challenges head-on in order to refine discriminations and responses. Successful encounters with challenges foster self-confidence and self-respect. The consistency of the caregiver's response is critical to the development of trust and self-confidence. The cycle of need-satisfaction is as follows:

1. Need exists
2. Infant gives generalized behavior
3. Caregiver responds
4. Need satisfied
5. Need recurs
6. Infant predicts caregiver response
7. Infant repeats previous behavior
8. Caregiver's response consistent
9. Need satisfied
10. Infant trusts caregiver
11. Need recurs
12. Infant confident that behavior will elicit appropriate caregiving
13. Infant refines behavior

Anxiety in the Infant

All infants experience some insecurity and anxiety. During the second month of life, some babies appear to experience a feeling of "being left" and cry when a meaningful object (mother figure) can no longer be seen. However, they usually will not cry as long as another person is present. If that person leaves, however, the baby will frequently cry as hard as when left alone by the parent. This suggests that the infant is beginning to recognize a dependence on adult ministrations but shows nonspecific attachment to people.

The terms **separation anxiety** and **stranger anxiety** are often used interchangeably, but they are not synonymous. Separation anxiety is the insecurity experienced by a young child when removed from a familiar person, object, or environment. Regardless of the culture or ethnic group studied, the majority of children 10 to 24 months of age will begin to cry when separated from a significant caregiver.[57] Stranger anxiety is the tension felt by the young child when introduced to an unfamiliar person. The child may display the same behaviors (e.g., crying, attempting to withdraw, refusing to cooperate) when experiencing either of these forms of anxiety.

Although stranger anxiety has been reported to occur as early as 3 months,[21] most researchers indicate that wariness of strangers begins at approximately 5 to 6 months, peaks about 12 to 18 months, and then gradually decreases. Because many babies begin to exhibit negative responses to strangers a few months after specific attachments have begun, this behavior has been termed **8-month anxiety.** This anxiety is demonstrated in various ways by individual babies, including sober examination of a new face, cessation of smiling, or physical withdrawal and crying.

Learning theorists observe that each mother–infant dyad establishes a unique communication system. Both mother and infant make significant contributions to the relationship by mutually eliciting and reinforcing behaviors. Social interaction is dependent on the infant's ability to identify cues, to form schemata, and to respond discriminatingly. The infant may not be able to predict a stranger's responses. The novel stimulus of a stranger becomes a source of anxiety; the infant is not yet able to generalize discriminatory cues or response behaviors with the new person.

Cognitivists such as Yarrow believe that attachment is based on the infant's ability to structure perception of the environment and to respond discriminatingly.[89] Attachment occurs because the child develops a schema for "mother" and prefers stimuli that are only mildly discrepant from known stimuli or schemata. Other persons provide different stimuli that do not fit into the child's "people-behavior schema," thereby eliciting stranger anxiety. Some infants may develop stranger anxiety or wariness toward their fathers during the second half of the first year; this is especially likely to occur if minimal time is spent with one another because of the father's work schedule and the baby's sleep schedule. Babies in daycare environments may become attached to the surrogate caregiver and respond with anxiety when picked up at the end of the day by their parents.

The infant becomes most securely attached to the person whose behavior or responses can be predicted, that is, a parent or a permanent parent substitute. Separation anxiety peaks when the child is beginning to feel secure in the ability to predict events (approximately 8 to 10 months) and again when the child begins to realize the ability to control some events (18 to 24 months). When children are separated from known persons, toys, environments, or routines, they can no longer predict events, a factor that increases the amount of energy that must be expended to process stimulus input. Thus a move to a new home or child care center may elicit symptoms of intense anxiety and insecurity.

When separation occurs, the baby's communication partner is lost. We can equate the experience to travel in a foreign country with a limited knowledge of the language. The child is unable to generalize the communication system or to anticipate the contingencies about a second person until there have been more experiences with persons other than the primary caregiver to facilitate generalization.[85] The number of adults with whom a baby is familiar influences the baby's degree of anxiety with strangers. Infants with limited contact with persons outside the home may have anxiety intensified or prolonged.[72] The degree of trust developed in the primary caregiver also influences the baby's ability to generalize trust to other people.

The appearance of stranger anxiety and separation anxiety in the baby reflects an emerging awareness of differentiation of self from others and an awareness of the need for a significant other. It is also a clear demonstration that the baby is able to discriminate among people and to **identify to whom he or she belongs**—all positive steps in psychosocial development (Fig. 8-5).[87] However, if anxiety reactions are severe and prolonged, professional intervention is appropriate.

What are the practical implications of this anxiety toward strangers and fear of separation? First, a baby should not be separated from the mother for extended periods of time. When a person first approaches a baby, it is wise to keep a safe distance, as *defined by the baby's behaviors.* Giving the baby a chance to "look you over" reduces anxiety and facilitates positive interaction. Since primary caregivers are sometimes absent necessarily, it is helpful to build other attachments. The baby should be introduced gradually to new situations so that sudden stimulus changes are minimal, and their novelty can be fun. Separations should be avoided if anxiety is acute or when anxiety reactions are at their peak. Hospitalization of either the infant or the primary caregiver should be post-

FIGURE 8–5.
Eight-month-old babies typically experience much anxiety when separated from their primary caregiver.

poned during such times if possible, or else the dyad should be allowed to remain together in the hospital. If separation must occur during peaks of anxiety, the baby can be provided with a favorite toy or a personal possession of the person to whom the child is attached. Fostering attachment to a transitional object (e.g., Linus's security blanket) can facilitate the child's separation from mother and serve as a source of emotional refueling in her absence. Although we have referred consistently to mothers, the fathers, siblings, grandparents, or permanent baby sitters are also recognized as significant contributors to the infant's early development. Anxiety can be greatly reduced if one of them is present for comfort and refueling.

FACTORS INFLUENCING PSYCHOSOCIAL DEVELOPMENT OF THE INFANT

There has been a gradual shift in the concept of parenting from doing things **for** the baby (e.g., diapering, feeding, bathing, etc.) to parenting as a process of reciprocal **interaction** (e.g, communicating, teaching, enjoying). Sensitive responsiveness appears to be the one factor most likely to foster secure attachment. A secure reciprocal relationship will change in balance and characteristics as the child matures.

Multiple Caregivers

Attachment theories initially assumed that the only person essential for the infant's mental health was the mother. Recent research indicates that this view is too narrow; however, in most cases, it is the mother who is the primary caregiver/attachment object.

Multiple Mothers

Margaret Mead, a well-known anthropologist, was one of the first to question the prevailing view that care by a single, continuous mother figure was a necessary condition for healthy personality development.[52] She studied arrangements that appeared to be successful in other cultures and suggested that children who grow up "mothered" by many women in the tribe are more secure than those who have had an exclusive, intense relationship with only one woman. She observed that the loss of an individual mother is less traumatic when the child can easily and comfortably turn to someone else. In cultures where multiple mothering is an accepted practice, the children are happy and thrive and behave in a socially acceptable way for the culture.

Day-Care Centers

Although cross-cultural studies suggest no harmful effect of multiple mothering, critics have questioned whether these findings can be generalized to the infant in a day-care center in the United States. Several studies have found no significant differences (physically, cognitively, emotionally) between infants in competent day-care centers and those from psychologically intact homes.[19, 40, 66] When the home environment is poor, there is documented evidence that **good** early day-care experiences increase cognitive competency and social skills,[19, 62] and may compensate for insecure maternal attachments.[37] However, Burton L. White notes that until adequate outcome criteria are identified, research indicating no significant difference may be misleading.[86] He strongly contends that children get a better start in life when they spend the majority of their waking hours with one or both parents, since most parents are more intensely involved and responsive to the child's burgeoning skills.

Almost 60% of mothers of firstborn children return to work during the infant's first year. By the year 2000, this figure may reach 80%.[39] There is much concern among developmentalists about the effects of this separation upon the psychosocial development of the infant and the potential long-range effects. Recent research indicates that infants of mothers employed full-time tend to exhibit insecure attachments and avoidant behaviors when compared to infants of mothers employed part-time or to infants who remained with their mothers throughout the first year, even when substitute care was offered in the home setting of low-risk, middle-income families.[3, 6, 7, 25] Although separation from significant others does place the infant at risk for social-emotional problems, over half of the infants of full-time employed mothers still show secure attachments.[37] Concern is expressed that children in day care will develop a less involved attitude toward life and thus limit development of potentials in all domains.[6]

It is of primary importance in child-care arrangements that infants be cared for by a consistent person with whom they are comfortable and can form an alternative attachment. Infants who change child care arrangements tend to appear less socially competent as toddlers, preschoolers, and first graders.[35, 36] Ideally, the infant's caregivers, whether at home or at a day-care center, should subscribe to the same principles that the parents deem important in guiding a child to maturity. Day-care centers need to provide individualized, synchronized attention and not just child watchers who keep the children safe and out of mischief.[58]

Fathers

In Western cultures, infants form attachments to both parents even if the father spends relatively little time with the child.[26, 43] However, these relationships differ in quality, and under stress, the infant preferentially seeks the mother for comfort.[26, 40, 43] Most mothers and fathers interact quite differently with infants. Fathers tend to play vigorously with the infant, whereas mothers engage in more caregiving, soothing, and containing modes of play.[5, 41] Studies indicate, however, that the father can be as sensitive to infant cues as is the mother (Fig. 8-6).[10, 43]

The characteristic, culturally influenced differences between maternal and paternal interactional styles ensure that mothers and fathers will have distinct and independent yet interdependent influences on their infant's development.[43] Differentiated paternal responses appear to be a major influence in sex-role socialization.[42, 43] The indirect effects of

FIGURE 8–6.
This father is providing sensory as well as affective and social stimulation for his infant.

fathers can include financial support, which frees the mother to devote herself to child rearing, and emotional support, which provides a warm, nurturing relationship with the mother and the child.[43] The most sociable infants are the ones who are securely attached to both parents. Fathering is as crucial a factor in a child's development as mothering (the concept of fathering is further explored in Chap. 31).

Interactional Styles

Interactional styles are heavily influenced by individual temperament, memory traces of earlier life events, the immediate stimulus of the external and internal environment, hierarchical family relationships, level of emotional development, cognitive functioning level, and culture. Consequently, each relationship is unique even within the same family. Since most studies to date have assumed that it is usually the mother who creates the milieu for the first social interactions, an analysis of the mother–infant dyad is presented here. The reader is reminded that the actual primary nurturing caregiver is not always the child's biological mother.

The Mother–Infant Dyad

The individual differences of temperament in mothers rather than in infants may actually be the major contributor to infant temperament.[68] Mothers who are subjectively rated by researchers as loving, skillful, attentive, and involved tend to have babies who reciprocate with accelerated mental and motor maturity. These mothers, in turn, are described as being emotionally involved with their infants. On the other

hand, mothers who tend to be abrupt in their movements involving the baby, who respond indifferently to the child's distress, delay responses, and who are assessed as having a somewhat low level of affective involvement, tend to have infants who display "hostile demandingness," a factor that appears to reinforce a negative picture of low maternal self-esteem.[78]

Louis Sander's research indicates that the early mother–infant relationship is a sequence of adaptations focused around specific interactional tasks. At each level, the child's burgeoning skills demand an adjustment in the mother's responses in order to maintain synchrony. If the pair experiences difficulty coordinating responses at one level, it subsequently interferes with comfortable adjustment at the next. Sander's epigenesis of interaction involves five stages[69]:

1. *Initial Adaptation* (Birth to 3 Months): This stage centers around achieving stability of regulation of biological processes (eating, sleeping, elimination.) Mother learns to read infant's cues, and infant gives some sign of preferential responsivity to mother.

2. *Establishing Reciprocal Exchanges* (4 to 6 Months): Reciprocal play activities develop around spontaneous smiling. Infant begins to participate more in feeding and diapering.

3. *Early Directed Activity* (7 to 9 Months): Baby begins to initiate bids for attention, play, exploration, and to indicate preferences. Mother facilitates success or provides interferences that helps to shape direction of baby's behavior.

4. *Focalization* (10 to 13 Months): Locomotion skills enable child to seek own entertainment and maintain desired amount of proximity to mother. Previous maternal availability and consistency determines child's confidence in exploring versus clinging behaviors.

5. *Self-Assertion* (14 to 20 Months): The child assumes increasing initiative to determine own activity and amount of contact with mother. Reciprocity of interaction with mother increasingly balanced with environmental interaction.

Mothers who encourage the child to assume more initiative in determining the direction of energy expenditure (toward or away from her) find that the child gradually uses her more as a resource for knowledge, direction, and reinforcement. Mothers who continue to maintain full responsibility for the direction of the child's energy expenditure or who ignore the child's cues will experience increasing frustration with parenting as the child either withdraws from initiating activities, clings to her, or aggressively asserts autonomy without regard for her directions.[69] Sensitive reciprocity is the key to effective parenting and healthy early psychosocial development.

SPOILING. Contrary to popular belief, picking up the infant and giving attention to his or her needs (especially the crying infant) will not spoil the child. Bell and Ainsworth found that a mother's prompt response to the crying infant with close, comforting, physical contact is associated with fewer and shorter bouts of crying in the baby's first year.[4] Using Mahler's theory, mutual focusing on the infant's needs lays a foundation for later individuation. Therefore, spoiling is impossible in the first few months. However, continuation of the intensely focused, infant-directed relationship into the late symbiotic and separation-individuation phases delays the child's ability to differentiate between self and others, and interferes with progression toward a realistic perception of the external world. Thus minor delays in the meeting of needs and mild frustrations as the infant grows older aid the infant in learning how to differentiate between self and nonself, encourage the meeting of personal needs, and force the infant to recognize the needs of others.

FEEDING. The child's degree of adjustment during the feeding process may have a larger impact on the developing personality than any other human experience.[11] Sylvia Brody, who extensively researched patterns of mothering, found feeding to be a rich source for data collection.[20] She postulated that the success of the feeding process (both psychosocially to mother and baby and biophysically to the infant) was more a product of the mother's attitude than of the infant's neuromuscular skill. This is an excellent time to observe the abilities of the mother and infant to "read" each other's cues.

TACTILE STIMULATION. Around 1920, the infant mortality rate in foundling institutions throughout the United States was nearly 100%.[54] When Dr. Fritz Talbot was visiting the Children's Clinic in Dusseldorf, Germany, he noticed a "fat old woman, named 'Old Anna,'" who apparently made the babies very happy by carrying them around on her hip as she went about her duties. Whenever the clinical personnel felt everything had been done for a baby medically, and the child still failed to thrive, the infant was turned over to her. "Old Anna" was reported to have always been successful, that is, she always "pulled the child through."[54] When foundling hospitals encouraged staff to hold and play with the babies, the mortality rate declined. Babies need tactile stimulation to mediate physical and psychological growth.

Some babies tend to cuddle more than others. Yarrow emphasizes that the quantity of parental physical contact is not as important as its quality.[89] He found that an appropriate, flexible, and consistent response on the part of the parents to their baby's communications (whether in the form of crying or cooing) was more important than the amount of physical contact they had with the child. Mahler observed that children separated easily or with difficulty from their mothers, depending on how each child perceived the mother's holding on to them both physically and emotionally.[48]

These observations have implications for a caregiver who does not feel well or who is subject to a prolonged amount of stress. Having someone else help with housework or child care on a short-term basis or decreasing whatever is causing the severe anxiety (or both) can influence the direction of the parent–child relationship.

Socioeconomic and Cultural Differences

The attitudes toward parent–child relationships, child-rearing goals, discipline, and life in general vary among families, socioeconomic classes, and cultures. An important determinant of how the young child will be handled is the parents' belief about the basic nature of children and their personal theory of how one shapes a child into the ideal adult. These differences affect the personal development of each individual. One example is holding an infant. In some families, the parents hold the infant frequently, whereas others limit their caregiving primarily to meeting basic needs. In many non-Western cultures, babies are maintained in almost constant contact with their mothers, which often includes sleeping with them during the night. Babies may be strapped to cradleboards and kept vertical or horizontal most of the time. Even the process of bathing varies greatly; it may involve submersion in a tub, bathing with one or more persons in the same vessel, or never being placed in a container of water. With different methods of stimulation, it is presumed that different norms of behavior and development will evolve.

Expressions of Individuality

Temperament

To better understand the individuality of personality, researchers have studied the concept of **temperament,** the style of behavior that a child or person habitually uses to cope with the demands and the expectations of the environment. Thomas and Chess identified nine temperament variables present in infants:[81]

1. *Activity level:* the amount of motor movement and energy expenditure
2. *Rhythmicity:* regularity/predictability of eating, sleeping, bowel movement schedules
3. *Approach–Withdrawal:* the infant's initial response to a new stimulus
4. *Adaptability:* how easily the infant adapts or adjusts a routine to fit a new situation
5. *Intensity:* the degree to which the infant expresses self
6. *Threshold:* how much stimulus is required before the infant reacts to a given situation
7. *Mood:* the amount of happy versus unhappy behavior
8. *Attention—persistence:* the length of time a given activity is pursued by the infant and continuation of an activity in spite of obstacles
9. *Distractibility:* how easily the infant's behavior or attention can be diverted

Thomas and Chess further observed several temperament patterns that appeared to remain fairly stable over the first 5 years of life.[81] They hypothesized that the traits were innate. The most common were the following:

1. *Easy-child pattern:* High rhythmicity, positive mood, positive approach, high adaptability, high intensity
2. *Difficult-child pattern:* Low rhythmicity, negative mood, withdrawal, low adaptability, high intensity
3. *Slow-to-warm pattern:* Low activity, withdrawal, low adaptability, negative mood, low intensity

Being placed in a particular category does not make a child good or bad. Rather, it is the degree of fit between the infant's temperament and the caregiver's ability to respond and positively adapt to it that determines if the parent–infant relationship is at risk (Fig. 8-7). There is question as to whether basic temperament is innately or environmentally determined.

Maternal anxiety during the early months may cause her interactions to be uncertain, inappropriate or noncontingent. The baby, in response, develops irregular feeding and sleeping patterns and delays in attention span, focused attention, and contingent responses, giving the appearance of a difficult temperament. A difficult temperament decreases the mother's pleasure; consequently, she spends less time with

FIGURE 8–7.
From the moment of birth, babies vary immensely in temperament. Parents can better adapt to meeting their child's individual needs and adjusting to their own new roles if they recognize and accept these differences.

the child. "By interacting less with the child, and especially speaking less, the mother may be diminishing the child's chances of developing the language skills necessary to pass preschool language tests."[67] The development of communication and social skills essential for comfortable interaction with others may also be diminished, thus perpetuating the appearance of a difficult temperament. The mother's initial anxiety may be caused by her difficulty in adjusting to the responsibilities of parenthood, a difficult delivery, neonatal complications, congenital disabilities, anxiety about returning to work, maternal immaturity due to her age or her own inadequate upbringing, current social problems unrelated to childbirth, or any number of stressors.[51,61,67] The results are the same: insecure attachment, temperamental difficulties, and developmental delays.[75]

Brazelton's Differences in Interactional Styles

From the very moment of birth, and perhaps before, differences in infant behaviors become apparent (e.g., some babies kick more than others *in utero*). Brazelton indicates that a baby tends to adopt the characteristics of one of three interactional styles. In his book, *Infants and Mothers: Differences in Development,* he describes the antics, trials, and tribulations of "average" Louis, "active" Daniel, and "quiet" Laura from the moment they are formally introduced to their mothers in the delivery room through their first 12 months of life.[17] They all laugh, cry, sleep, and eat in very different ways. The temperament of these three babies dramatically affects the tenor of parental response and the foundation on which further relationships will be built. Some infants have reactions that are scattered in all three categories. Brazelton's observations are supportive in helping parents to recognize the strengths of their individual babies.

Tensional Outlets of Infancy

Crying is only one way in which the infant releases tension. Each baby has a unique way of "letting off steam," as well as receiving a sense of security from various comforting behaviors. These self-stimulatory behaviors include hair twisting, pre-sleep rocking in the crib, thumbsucking, or even masturbation in older infants and young children.

Around 6 months of age, infants begin to decrease reliance on the parents by increasing reliance on comforters.[77] A **comforter** is any object or behavior that recreates a physical stimulus that was psychosocially nurturing during early infancy. This increase for the need of comforters is concurrent with the emerging separation process. Transitional objects such as security blankets may be thought of as comforters, although they serve more as parent substitutes to facilitate extension of self into the environment. Thumbsucking, an oral comforter, is a response by infants as young as 2 months of age to distress caused by psychological factors, especially by being left alone.[88] Thumbsucking is most likely to begin around 3 or 4 months of age. The baby may seek continued oral pleasure by sucking the thumb immediately after a feeding. Later the urge spreads to other times of the day and night. Babies who do not suck their thumbs probably have their sucking needs satisfied during feedings. It is important to note that babies who suck their thumbs and those who do not may be equally normal, healthy, and loved.

Thumbsucking often reaches a peak around 7 months of age, since the infant is enthralled with hand-mouth behaviors at that time. After this period, much variation in the amount and type of thumbsucking occurs. Many resort to finger sucking, lip pulling, or thumbsmelling. It will often recur during toodlerhood and may remain a precious comforter through the preschool years.

The long-range effects of thumbsucking are still controversial. It may assist the baby to get through teething more easily than the baby who does not thumbsuck. Prolonged sucking of the thumb may push the upper front baby teeth forward and the lower teeth back, marring the shape of the mouth and facial features (see Fig. 15-5A). The American Academy of Pediatrics suggests that if a thumbsucking habit persists beyond age 4 the parent should consult a pedodontist or general dentist for advice. Misalignment of the baby teeth can change the child's mouth movements and lead to articulation problems. Variables such as how often and in what position the thumb is held, as well as the general structure of the child's mouth, may be additional significant factors. Thumbsucking after the permanent teeth emerge can permanently alter the child's appearance.

Most specialists in child behavior advise that the least traumatizing way for parents to intervene if they are disturbed by the thumbsucking is to substitute another object for the thumb rather than to pull the thumb directly out of the mouth; this could be done by encouraging the young child to hold a toy or to suck on a pacifier. Pacifiers are given up more easily than the thumb.[77] An intervention during the peak of a thumbsucking period (or during a crisis, such as the birth of a new sibling) will be least effective and perhaps traumatizing to both the child who wants some form of comforting and to the parents who want peace and quiet (Fig. 8-8).

Another mode of intervention is to modify the length and nature of each infant feeding. The adult should make sure that bottle feedings last at least 15 to 20 minutes, even if it means changing the nipple so that the bottle contents flow more slowly (one must remember that the baby *needs* to suck). Breast-fed babies should also be kept at the breast for the same amount of time. When satiated, the infant may be switched back to the empty breast for sucking satisfaction. It is not just the length of feedings, but also the frequency that may be significant to a particular infant for adequate sucking. Young babies fed every 3 hours do not suck their thumbs as much as babies who are fed every 4 hours.[77]

PSYCHOSOCIAL DEPRIVATION DURING INFANCY

The infant's need for a primary caregiver is absolute. However, the primary caregiver's need for the infant is relative.[48] The validity of these statements becomes apparent when for

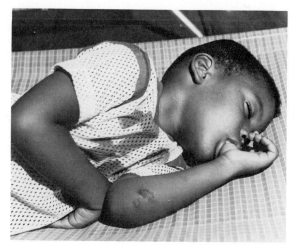

FIGURE 8–8.
This youngster, revealed in all his innocence, is still very much a baby. Many children continue to suck their thumbs through their toddler and preschool years.

some reason the parent does not or cannot provide the physical or psychosocial nurturing the infant needs. When basic physical needs are not met, the infant perceives that the environment is hostile and may learn to distrust those around him or her. When the infant's attachment behaviors are not consistently responded to and encouraged, they are eventually extinguished. The child begins to consume large amounts of energy meeting self-needs; weight loss and developmental delays may be the result.

Two interrelated yet different terms are used in speaking of psychosocial deprivation. **Psychosocial separation** refers to the physical loss of the maternal figure—the love object. It does not necessarily imply a loss of mothering or a loss of physical care, since this can be provided by the father, a sibling, a surrogate parent, or another person. The term **psychosocial deprivation** is reserved for the emotional loss of a warm, synchronized relationship. It may not mean loss of the physical presence of the maternal figure, but it frequently is accompanied by loss of adequate physical care.[65] It is difficult to study the effects of these two conditions separately because they often occur together and are combined with many variables.

Factors Affecting Infant Response to Prolonged Separation from the Primary Caregiver

The **age** of the child when the separation occurs is a significant variable, affecting the infant's response to separation or deprivation. Before differentiation of a specific mother figure occurs, any caregiver may be readily substituted, although the lack of consistency in response to the infant's interactional cues may cause delays in the cognitive and psychosocial processes. For instance, the institutionalized infant may show developmental delays as early as 2 months of age.[65] Regular attendance at a day-care center before the first birthday also increases the risk of insecure attachment relationships.[7] Most babies over 6 to 8 months exhibit some anxiety and protest when the mother leaves, and show anxiety or behavior changes if the separation is longer than the child's emotional energy stores.

The **gender** of the infant as a significant variable needs more study. Current studies indicate that the male infant is more vulnerable to separation experiences than the female.[65] Boys are more likely to develop insecure attachment to both parents, but especially to fathers.[22] Girls who experience nonmaternal care exhibit more maternal proximity-attaining behaviors than boys.[33]

Infant **temperament** affects how the baby will react to separation. Active infants will usually not become as developmentally retarded as their passive peers when placed in a depriving environment; they will demand attention.

If the **previous mother–child relationship** has been a comfortable one, short-term separation does not appear to cause undue infant stress. Babies whose parents work and who are therefore accustomed to another caregiver in their absence may adapt to new caregivers better than those babies who are used to only one primary figure.

To say that **previous separation experiences** make successive ones easier is not necessarily true. Closely related to how well a child adjusts to separation experiences are how well the child adjusted to earlier ones, how long the separation lasted, and how intensely the separation was perceived.

The other **people** who are **present** at the time of the separation may be a significant variable. Familiar people, such as siblings, can help to reduce stress in children placed in a strange environment.[79] If the infant is consistently left with an alternative caregiver, that person may become the primary attachment figure or an alternative attachment person for the child, thus reducing separation anxiety. In fact, a study of kibbutz children found that the quality of attachment to the alternative caregiver to be more predictive of later social and emotional development than the quality of attachment to either parent.[59] The **approval and caregiving style of the surrogate mother** may also be a decisive factor in the child's adaptation to separation. A warm, nurturing **person who knows how and when to respond to the infant's cues** can facilitate the child's perception of and adaptation to separation.

Failure-to-Thrive Syndrome

The term **failure-to-thrive** (FTT) is used to describe infants and children whose weight (and sometimes height) fall below the fifth percentile for their ages (see Appendix D). These children are characterized by inadequate physical growth, malnutrition, and retardation of motor and social development. Failure-to-thrive is divided into two categories: organic FTT, which is caused primarily by a physical factor, and nonorganic FTT, which is frequently associated with disturbances of parenting and of family organization.[34] The mothers generally are less affectionate, initiate fewer positive interactions,

use physical punishment readily, and hold negative feelings toward their children.[90] The mothers do not read the infant's interactional cues and have noticeably failed to establish a synchronized relationship with their child.

The mechanism linking emotional deprivation with failure-to-thrive is unclear. It appears that the increased tensions arising from unmet psychosocial (and physical) needs interfere with sleep patterns. Abnormal sleep patterns may inhibit secretion of growth hormone from the anterior pituitary, thus decreasing hyperplastic cellular growth. The potential for long-range effects is obvious.

Increased tension levels may also correlate with increased vomiting and diarrhea. Ingested calories are not retained, and weight loss results. Restlessness in the form of rocking or spasticity reduces the calories available for growth. Many tense infants experience anorexia—an aversion to food. This behavior may continue into the adult years when some individuals will find it difficult to eat when under stress (others will use food to cope with stress). These children begin to show developmental delays, apathy, irritability, and even self-destructive behaviors.[90]

Therapy for children with FTT must include the mother figure.[53] The best programs offer in-home programming or live-in facilities for the infant–mother dyad. The mother figure is taught how and when to respond to her infant's cues for interaction. An effective program results in weight gain for the baby and a more satisfying relationship for both mother and child.[38]

The Effects of Separation or Deprivation on Development

Two classic studies have been carried out on infants separated from their mothers. The effects of separation on the child were greatly influenced both by age and by the previous mother–infant relationship. Both studies were performed in institutions where separation of the infant from the mother was the rule. Because of the results of these studies, marked changes have been made in the institutional care of infants.

Separation During the First 6 Months

During World War II, John Bowlby studied children in orphanages who had experienced no contact with their natural mothers and had received little nurturing from the multiple caregivers available.[13] He noted that the infants exhibited four behaviors directed toward the caregivers: visual following, smiling, clinging, and crying. When these attachment behaviors were unrewarded, severe psychological and physiological results occurred.

By 3 months of age, these children no longer made attempts to communicate (e.g., neither cooing nor babbling). They did not adapt or mold their posture to the caregivers when held. Although their joints were movable, they remained stiff and unresponsive. Gradually these infants began to refuse contact and lost interest in the environment. Smiles were rare; facial features became unresponsive or rigid. Motor development was retarded, and symptoms of FTT were present. The babies suffered from insomnia and restlessness and exhibited poor resistance to infections. Many became so severely depressed both physically and psychosocially that death ensued. Many of the survivors never fully recovered from the effects of the deprivation; they continued to show delays in social, cognitive, and language development, even though their environment was altered.

Separation During the Second 6 Months

René Spitz, a psychoanalyst who studied under Sigmund Freud, discovered an institution housing young women and their babies.[76] The infants received both physical and psychosocial nurturance from their own mothers for the first 6 months of life. The infants all exhibited happy, outgoing behaviors. Six months later, the mothers left the institution, leaving the infants to be cared for by other residents and staff while they reestablished themselves in the community. Although the babies received adequate care, they exhibited depression through crying and withdrawal. Spitz observed that this **anaclitic depression** followed a predictable pattern. It is of interest that infants who had previously had a poor relationship with their mothers experienced milder symptoms.

The first month was characterized by weepy, demanding, and clinging behaviors—an attempt to regain mothering by force, and by maximal use of attachment behaviors. During the second month, the infants exhibited intense grief that was evidenced by inconsolable wailing, weight loss, and arrests in cognitive and psychosocial development. During the third month of the separation, the infants lost hope and the desire to reinvest themselves in others. They refused human contact and would lie wide-awake for hours in a prone position. They refused food, developmental delays became more pronounced, and illness was common. After the third month of separation, lethargy and apathy became the dominant mode of interaction, but the children no longer refused adult attention, and whimpering replaced weeping. The rigidity of their faces and their lack of affective responses indicated that the infants had developed a defensive shell against outside intrusion and reinvestment.

Spitz observed that if the mother was restored after 3 months but before 5 months of separation, the child experienced marked recovery. However, Spitz felt that the recovery was never complete, and emotional scars were left. Those who remained separated 5 months or more exhibited increasingly serious deterioration with irreversible damage to the psyche. These children became severely retarded, participating in bizarre posturing and finger movements. Like King Frederick's infants, many of the long-term institutionalized infants in Spitz's study died.

Implications

When an infant must be separated from the mother figure, either temporarily or permanently, the child's care should be assumed by one person insofar as this is possible. Adoption or placement in a foster home is preferable to a group setting.

FIGURE 8–9.
Most hospitals encourage parents to stay with hospitalized infants in order to maintain the parent-infant bond and to facilitate emotional coping.

Maintaining similar routines and known foods can help to reduce stress. The surrogate parent should be warm and sensitive to the infant's unique communication style and flexible enough to allow the infant to set the pace of their interaction.

If an infant is hospitalized, it is important to include the significant parent in the child's care. Many hospitals have a rooming-in program that allows the parent to stay with the infant or the infant with the ill parent. This arrangement can greatly reduce the infant's anxiety, facilitate recovery, and strengthen the parent–infant relationship (Fig. 8-9).

CONCLUSION

During the first 6 months of life, the parent and child are getting to know one another. They begin to establish a primitive communication system. The infant tries to communicate long before he or she has the use of language.[91] Consistent, sensitive responsivity on the parents' part is critical to the child's ability to develop a sense of trust in the environment and to be able to anticipate the adults' responses. This is the foundation of secure attachment and learning. Babies are noted to "woo" their parents into social interaction. If the parent is too responsive, the infant withdraws. However, if the parent keeps an immobile face and does not respond, "wooing" behaviors will initially increase and then, in frustration, the baby will withdraw, cry, and show other signs of stress. If the parent remains under-responsive over time, the baby's social-emotional development is negatively impacted.[44, 56] Consequently, parents need to synchronize their responses to the baby's pace and intensity.

The young child usually develops several attachments, but these are not equal in strength, nor are they freely interchangeable. Fathers, siblings, grandparents, and nonfamily caregivers may all be included as attachment figures. Under stress, the child will seek the comfort of the closest attachment figure.

Attachment bonds persist over time, even when there is no contact with the specific attachment person. The child may undergo a dramatic grief process if separation is prolonged. Once a child has formed a healthy attachment to at least one person, it is easier to transfer that attachment to a second person or to form additional attachments.

Research indicates that as poorly attached children mature beyond infancy, cognitive development is impeded, logical thinking is constricted, ability to cope with frustration and stress is reduced, conscience development is impaired, and social behaviors are disrupted. The mother's presence is not sufficient to foster attachment or to serve as a security base. The mother must be **emotionally available** to respond to the cues of the child for help or encouragement before the child has the permission or the strength to explore the opportunities offered by the environment.[74] The parent must be empathetic to the child's developmental needs and abilities to understand the day-to-day interactions, to validate the baby's inner state, and to foster growth.[60]

The apparent purpose of attachment is to facilitate one's identity as a separate, valued individual and to serve as a foundation for exploring one's capabilities and the environment. This early love bond teaches us that we are lovable and how to love in return. The process of attachment teaches us how to be human.[84] It is a paradox that the most securely attached children are those who separate the most easily from their parents to explore the environment, enjoy the company of peers, and interact more comfortably with strangers. They have learned to trust. This trust dissipates fear, and extends to a general trust in new situations: "When our first connections are unreliable or broken or impaired, we may transfer that experience, and our responses to that experience, onto what we expect from our children, our friends, our marriage partner, even our business partner."[84] The underlying mistrust defends the ego from disappointment by clinging dependency or angry rejection (e.g., "I don't need you" or "I don't care").

Although much research indicates that the infant contributes highly to the quality of the interaction by the strength, consistency, and clarity of signals of need and feeling, a heavy burden still falls on the parents to read the child's cues and orchestrate meaningful environmental responses.[69] Thus, the parents of an atypical baby (i.e., premature, postmature, or disabled) will carry more of the burden for establishing a synchronous interaction.[2] Sensitivity to the child's current level of functioning "enables the adult to help the child progress to further developmental levels."[71]

Fortunately, when provided with a normal expected environment, most babies and parents are eventually able to establish a mutually nurturing relationship. Even when the parents and the baby get off to a difficult start, the marvelous resiliency of the infant will usually act as a buffer against any long-range detrimental consequences of a single traumatic episode or a poor interaction during the first few months of life.[2]

"The mother needs to be secure enough within her own self to be able to 'lose' herself in the process of achieving empathy and intimacy with her infant."[9] As the mother balances empathy (the child's experience) with objectivity (her experience), she becomes flexibly available to provide both support and the gentle push necessary to help the child adapt to the outside world. "A mother who unnecessarily retaliates by becoming unavailable, aloof, or uninterested or a mother who continues to draw the child back into her own orbit does not provide the optimal environment for the unfolding of the child's separate self."[9] Parents must recognize the child's motivations for behavior. When behavior is misunderstood (seen from the adult's perspective) or ignored, the child frequently becomes demanding or physically aggressive, and negative interactions ensue. Repeated negative experiences color the parent–child relationship. When parents age, they may become "targets for their grown children's unconscious need to revenge themselves for past hurts by becoming withholding and unresponsive to them."[60] Conversely, a warm, positive relationship during these first months and years of life sets the stage for a lifetime of positive, meaningful relationships.

REFERENCES

1. Ainsworth, M. D. S., Blehar, M. C., Waters, E., & Wall, S. (1978). *Patterns of attachment: A psychological study of the strange situation.* Hillsdale, NJ: Erlbaum.

2. Bakemann, R., & Brown, J. V. (1980). Early intervention consequences for social and mental development at three years. *Child Development, 51,* 437.

3. Barglow, P., Vaughn, B. E., & Molitor, N. (1987). Effects of maternal absence due to employment on the quality of infant-mother attachment in a low-risk sample. *Child Development, 58,* 945–954.

4. Bell. S. M., & Ainsworth, M. D. S. (1972). Infant crying and maternal responsiveness. *Child Development, 43,* 1171.

5. Belsky, J. (1979). Mother-father-infant interactions: A naturalistic observational study. *Developmental Psychology, 15,* 601.

6. Belsky, J. (1988). The "effect" of infant day care reconsidered. *Early Childhood Research Quarterly, 3,* 235–273.

7. Belsky, J., & Rovine, M. (1988). Nonmaternal care in the first year of life and security of infant-parent attachment. *Child Development, 59,* 157–167.

8. Benn, R. K. (1986). Factors promoting secure attachment relationships between employed mothers and their sons. *Child Development, 57,* 1224–1231.

9. Bergman, A. (1985). The mother's experience during the earliest phases of infant development. In E. J. Anthony & G. H. Pollock (Eds.), *Parental influences: In health and disease* (pp. 165–181). Boston: Little, Brown.

10. Berman, P. W. (1981). Are women more responsive than men to the young? A review of developmental and situational variables. In S. Chess & A. Thomas (Eds.), *Annual progress in child psychiatry and child development.* New York: Brunner/Mazel.

11. Bettelheim, B. (1971). *Dialogue with mothers.* New York: Avon Books.

12. Bowen, M. (1985). *Family therapy in clinical practice.* New York: Jason Aronson.

13. Bowlby, J. M. (1966). *Maternal care and mental health.* New York: Schocken.

14. Bowlby, J. M. (1977). The making and breaking of affectional bonds: Aetiology and psychopathology in the light of attachment theory. *British Journal of Psychiatry, 130,* 201–210.

15. Bowlby, J. M. (1982). *Attachment and loss, Vol. 1: Attachment* (2nd ed.). New York: Basic Books.

16. Brazelton, T. B. (1976). Early parent-infant reciprocity. In V. C. Vaughan & T. B. Brazelton (Eds.), *The family—can it be saved?* Chicago: Year Book.

17. Brazelton, T. B. (1983). *Infants and mothers: Differences in development* (rev. ed.). New York: Delta.

18. Bremner, J. G. (1988). *Infancy.* New York: Basil Blackwell.

19. Brock, W. M. (1980). *The effects of day care: A review of the literature.* Los Alamitos, CA: Southwest Regional Laboratory for Educational Research and Development. (ERIC Document Ed. 195–348).

20. Brody, S. (1956). *Patterns of mothering: maternal influence during infancy.* New York: International Universities Press.

21. Bronson, G. W. (1973). Infants' reactions to an unfamiliar person. In L. J. Stone, H. T. Smith, & L. b. Murphy (Eds.), *The competent infant: Research and commentary* (pp. 1139–1149). New York: Basic Books.

22. Chase-Lansdale, P. L., & Owen, M. T. (1987). Maternal employment in a family context: Effects on infant-mother and infant-father attachments. *Child Development, 58,* 1505–1512.

23. Chess, S., & Thomas, A. (1973). Temperament in the normal infant. In J. C. Westman (Ed.), *Individual differences in children.* New York: Wiley.

24. Chess, S., Thomas, A., & Birch, H. (1976). *Your child is a person: A psychological approach to parenthood without guilt.* New York: Penguin.

25. Clarke-Stewart, A. (1988). "The 'effects' of infant day care reconsidered," reconsidered. *Early Childhood Research Quarterly, 3,* 293–318.

26. Cohen, L. J., & Campos, J. J. (1974). Father, mother, and stranger as elicitors of attachment behavior in infancy. *Developmental Psychology, 10,* 146.

27. Erikson, E. H. (1963). *Childhood and society* (2nd ed., rev. and enl.). New York: Norton.

28. Erikson, E. H. (1968). *Identity: Youth and crisis.* New York: Norton.

29. Fahlberg, V. (1979). *Attachment and separation.* Lansing, MI: Michigan Dept. of Social Services.

30. Gewirtz, J. L. (1961). A learning analysis of the effects of normal stimulation, prevention, and deprivation on the acquisition of social motivation and attachment. In B. M. Foss (Ed.), *Determinants of infant behavior.* London: Methuen.

31. Gewirtz, J. L. (Ed.). (1972). *Attachment and dependency.* Washington, DC: V. H. Winston.

32. Harlow, H. F., & Harlow, M. (1970). Learning to love. In P. H. Mussen, J. J. Conger, & J. Kagan (Eds.), *Readings in child development and personality* (2nd ed.). New York: Harper & Row.

33. Hock, E., & Clinger, J. B. (1980). Behavior toward mother and stranger of infants who have experienced group day care, individual care, or exclusive maternal care. *Genetic Psychology, 137,* 49.

34. Homer, C., & Ludwig, S. (1981). Categorization of etiology of failure to thrive. *American Journal of Diseases of Children, 135,* 848.

35. Howes, C. (Ed.). (1988). Peer interaction of young children. *Monographs of the Society for Research in Child Development, 53*(1, Serial No. 217).

36. Howes, C. (1988). Relationship between child care and schooling. *Developmental Psychology, 24,* 53–57.

37. Howes, C. (1989). Infant child care. *Young Children, 44*(2), 24–28.

38. Hufton, I., & Oates, K. (1977). Nonorganic failure to thrive: A long term follow up. *Pediatrics, 59*(1), 73.

39. Hymes, J. L., Jr. (1987). *Early childhood education: the year in review. A look at 1986.* Carmel, CA: Hacienda Press.

40. Kagan, J., Kearsley, R. B., & Zelago, P. R. (1976). *The effects of infant day-care on psychological development.* Paper presented at a symposium on "The Effect of Early Experience on Child Development," American Association for the Advancement of Science, Boston, Feb. 19, 1976.

41. Lamb, M. E. (1976). Interactions between eight-month-old children and their fathers and mothers. In M. E. Lamb (Ed.), *The role of the father in child development.* New York: Wiley.

42. Lamb, M. E. (1977). The development of parental preferences in the first two years of life. *Sex roles, 3,* 495.

43. Lamb, M. E. (1982). Paternal influences on early socio-emotional development. *Journal of Child Psychology and Psychiatry, 23,* 185.

44. Lamb, M. E., Morrison, D. C., & Malkin, C. M. (1987). The development of infant social expectations in face to face interaction: A longitudinal study. *Merrill-Palmer Quarterly of Behavior and Development, 33,* 241–254.

45. Lewis, M., Feiring, C., McGuffog, C., & Jaskir, J. (1984). Predicting psychopathology in six-year-olds from early social relations. *Child Development, 55,* 123–136.

46. Lorenz, K. (1957). Companionship in bird life. In C. Schiller (Ed.), *Instinctive behavior.* New York: International Universities Press.

47. Mahler, M. S. (1972). On the first three subphases of the separation-individuation process. *International Journal of Psychoanalysis, 53*(Part 3), 333.

48. Mahler, M. S., Pine, F., & Bergman, A. (1975). *The psychological birth of the human infant: Symbiosis and individuation.* New York: Basic Books.

49. Maier, H. W. (1988). *Three theories of child development* (3rd ed.). Lanham, MD: University Press of America.

50. Main, M., & Cassidy, J. (1988). Categories of response to reunion with the parent at age 6: Predictable from infant attachment classifications and stable over a 1-month period. *Developmental Psychology, 24,* 415–426.

51. McBride, S., & Belsky, J. (1988). Characteristics, determinants, and consequences of maternal separation anxiety. *Developmental Psychology, 24,* 407–414.

52. Mead, M., & MacGregor, F. C. (1951). *Growth and culture: A photographic study of Balinese childhood.* New York: Putnam.

53. Mira, M., & Cairns, G. (1981). Intervention with interaction of a mother and child with nonorganic failure to thrive. *Pediatric Nursing, 7*(2), 41.

54. Montagu, A. (1978). *Touching: The human significance of the skin* (2nd ed.). New York: Harper & Row.

55. Mullahy, P. (1970). *Psychoanalysis and interpersonal psychiatry: The contributions of Harry Stack Sullivan.* New York: Science House.

56. Murray, L., & Trevarthen, C. (1985). Emotional regulation of interactions between two-month-olds and their mothers. In T. M. Field & N. A. Fox (Eds.), *Social perception in infants.* Norwood, NJ: Ablex.

57. Mussen, P. H., et al. (1979). *Psychological development: A life-span approach.* New York: Harper & Row.

58. National Association for the Education of Young Children. (1983). How to choose a good early childhood program. *Young Children, 39*(1), 28.

59. Oppenheim, D., Sagei, A., & Lamb, M. E. (1988). Infant-adult attachments on the kibbutz and their relation to socioemotional development four years later. *Developmental Psychology, 24,* 427–433.

60. Ornstein, A., & Ornstein, P. H. (1985). Parenting as a function of the adult self: A psychoanalytic developmental perspective. In E. J. Anthony & G. H. Pollock (Eds.), *Parental influences: In health and disease* (pp. 183–232). Boston: Little, Brown.

61. Osofsky, J. D., Osofsky, H. J., & Diamond, M. O. (1988). The transition to parenthood: Special tasks and risk factors for adolescent parents. In G. Y. Michaels & W. A. Goldberg (Eds.), *The transition to parenthood: Current theory and research* (pp. 209–232). New York: Cambridge University Press.

62. Ramey, C. T., Farron, D. C., & Campbell, F. A. (1979). Predicting I.Q. from mother-infant interactions. *Child Development, 50,* 804.

63. Robertson, J., & Robertson, J. (1982). *A baby in the family: Loving and being loved.* New York: Penguin Books.

64. Rutter, M. (1979). Maternal deprivation, 1972–1978: New findings, new concepts, new approaches. *Child Development, 50,* 283.

65. Rutter, M. (1981). *Maternal deprivation reassessed* (2nd ed.). New York: Penguin Books.

66. Rutter, M. (1981). Social-emotional consequences of day care for preschool children. *American Journal of Orthopsychiatry, 51*(1), 4.

67. Sameroff, A. J., & Fiese, B. H. (1988). The context of language development. In R. L. Schiefelbush & L. L. Lloyd (Eds.), *Language perspectives: Acquisition, retardation, and intervention* (2nd ed., pp. 3–20). Austin, TX: Pro-ed.

68. Sameroff, A. J., Seifer, R., & Elias, P. K. (1982). Sociocultural variability in infant temperament ratings. *Child Development, 53,* 164.

69. Sander, L. W. (1969). The longitudinal course of early mother-child interaction: Cross-case comparison in a sample of mother-child pairs. In B. M. Foss (Ed.), *Determinants of infant behavior IV.* London: Methuen.

70. Schaffer, H. R. (1984). *The child's entry into a social world.* London: Academic Press.

71. Schaffer, H. R., & Collis, G. M. (1986). Parental responsiveness and child behavior. In W. Sluckin & M. Herbert (Eds.), *Parental behavior.* (pp. 283–315). New York: Basil Blackwell.

72. Schaffer, H. R., & Emerson, P. E. (1973). Patterns of response to physical contact in early human development. In L. J. Stone, H. T. Smith, & L. B. Murphy (Eds.), *The competent infant; Research and commentary* (pp. 64–70). New York: Basic Books.

73. Smith, P. B., & Pederson, D. R. (1988). Maternal sensitivity and patterns of infant-mother attachment. *Child Development, 59,* 1097–1101.

74. Sorce, J. F., & Emde, R. N. (1981). Mother's presence is not enough: Effect of emotional availability on infant's exploration. *Developmental Psychology., 17,* 737.

75. Spieker, S. J. (1986). Patterns of very insecure attachment found in samples of high-risk infants and toddlers. *TECSE, 6*(3), 37–53.

76. Spitz, R. A., & Wolf, K. M. (1946). Anaclitic depression: An inquiry into the genesis of psychiatric conditions in early childhood. In R. A. Spitz & K. M. Wolf (Eds.), *The psychoanalytic study of the child* (Vol. II). New York: International Universities Press.

77. Spock, B., & Rothenberg, M. B. (1985). *Baby and child care* (rev. and updated ed.). New York: E. P. Dutton.

78. Stern, G. G., et al. (1969). A factor analytic study of the mother-infant dyad. *Child Development, 40*(1), 163.

79. Stewart, R. B. (1983). Sibling attachment relationships: Child-infant interaction in the strange situation. *Developmental Psychology, 19,* 192–199.

80. Thoman, E. B., et al. (1981). State organization in neonates; Developmental inconsistencies indicates risk for developmental dysfunction. *Neuropediatrics, 12,* 45–54.

81. Thomas, A., & Chess, S. (1977). *Temperament and development* New York: Brunner/Mazel.

82. Tizard, B., & Hodges, J. (1978). The effect of early institutional rearing on the development of eight-year-old children. *Journal of Child Psychology and Psychiatry, 19,* 99.

83. Tizard, B., & Rees, J. (1975). The effect of early institutional rearing on the behavior problems and affectional relationships of four-year-old children. *Journal of Child Psychology and Psychiatry, 16,* 61.

84. Viorst, J. (1986). *Necessary losses.* New York: Simon and Schuster.

85. Watson, J. (1978). Perception of contingency as a determinant of social responsiveness. In E. B. Thoman & S. Trotter (Eds.), *Social responsiveness of infants: A round table.* New Brunswick, NJ: Johnson & Johnson Baby Products.

86. White, B. L. (1980). Should you stay home with your baby? *Educational Horizons, 59*(1), 22.

87. White, B. L. (1985). *The first three years of life* (rev. ed.). New York: Prentice-Hall.

88. Wolff, P. H. (1973). The natural history of crying and other vocalizations in early infancy. In L. J. Stone, H. T. Smith, & L. B. Murphy (Eds.), *The competent infant; Research and commentary* (pp. 1185–1198). New York: Basic Books.

89. Yarrow, L. J. (1972). Attachment and dependency: A developmental perspective. In J. L. Gewirtz (Ed.), *attachment and dependency.* Washington, DC: Winston.

90. Yoos, L. (1984). Taking another look at failure-to-thrive. *MCN: American Journal of Maternal/Child Nursing, 9,* 32.

91. Ziajak, A. (1981). *Prelinguistic communication in infancy.* New York: Praeger.

IV

THE TODDLER AND THE PRESCHOOLER

Curiosity is given wings once the child learns that events can be controlled. Now the child must harness energies to try to figure out the relationships between events and their causes. Naïveté and a very narrow perceptual focus lead the child to make erroneous connections, which often lead to superstitious fears and ritualistic behaviors. Ignorance and lack of self-control lead the child to explore and examine *everything* in the physical world.

The egocentric, intrusive, selfish, and demanding behaviors of the young child soon run into conflict with the needs and comforts of others or violate the accepted behavior codes of the parents and culture. Clashes of will and goals occur as the parents try to direct the child toward more acceptable behaviors. These confrontations temporarily increase the child's sense of vulnerability as he or she begins to recognize psychological separateness from the "love object." The desire to please the parent provides incentive to obey, to imitate adults, and to learn expected behaviors.

Gradually, as the adults orchestrate appropriate learning opportunities and provide assistance, the child learns to use the body efficiently, to function independently in the activities of daily living, to communicate ideas and needs effectively, and to observe the basic social skills of the culture. As parents provide guidance in and opportunities for decision making and expression of emotions, the child learns self-discipline, how to plan ahead, and how to live with the consequences of one's own decisions and behaviors.

The self-centered love relationships of infancy gradually expand to an appreciation of other people and the basic values of the family and culture. Within this frame, the child finds a confident love of self as a respected and valued member of the family and community. This knowledge of self, family, community, and culture will be expanded and refined during the school-age years.

Developmental Tasks of the Toddler/Preschooler

*1. Recognize self as a person, psychologically separate from attachment person:
  tolerate separation from attachment person
  recognize and express own ideas, feelings, needs, and will
  develop self-entertainment skills
  reinvest separation anxiety energies

*2. Learn how to harness and focus energies:
  identify short-range goals
  invest in activity at hand
  increase attention span
  persist at tasks
  resist distractors
  listen actively

*3. Learn prosocial behaviors (to be socialized):
  imitate and practice roles, responsibilities, and relationships observed in the family and culture
  share attention
  begin to postpone own gratification in deference to the needs of others
  respect rights of others
  work and play cooperatively with others
  observe basic social skills
  develop and express empathy/sympathy for others

*4. Adopt collective communication skills:
  develop receptive comprehension skills
  develop expressive communication skills
  use a language for sharing ideas, feelings, observations

*5. Develop basic self-control skills:
  evolve awareness of feeling states
  learn culturally acceptable ways to express feelings, frustration, and anger
  cooperate with adult guidance
  obey simple rules without adult reminding
  develop safety awareness and self-protection behaviors

*6. Learn to live with consequences of own choices:
  recognize simple cause–effect relationships
  make simple decisions regarding activities of daily living
  project decisions into the near future

7. Coordinate body movements for skill mastery:
  develop awareness of body-space relationships
  achieve independent mobility within the immediate environment
  manipulate objects and tools meaningfully
  refine gross- and fine-motor skills

8. Learn basic values and mores of the family and culture:
  deference
  etiquette
  roles
  cultural myths and identities

9. Function independently in basic activities of daily living:
  eating
  dressing
  toileting
  simple chore mastery

10. Seek information and understanding:
  ask questions
  experiment with events
  verify knowledge and understanding
  practice skills

---

*Tasks deemed most crucial to continued maturation are marked with an asterisk.

Biophysical Development During the Toddler and Preschool Years

Shirley S. Ashburn

It is exciting to watch the transformation of the infant into a toddler. One of the most significant biophysical changes of this period is that the horizontal infant becomes a vertical toddler. Both gross motor and fine motor skills become more refined in all areas. The enthusiasm of the toddling child facilitates learning about the world. Every experience is accompanied by wide-eyed wonder and abandon. Biophysically, toddlerhood encompasses the period from 16 through 30 months; preschoolerhood evolves from this period and continues until the child's sixth birthday, although these age demarcations are only arbitrary. Biophysical growth during these years is relatively slow compared to the infancy period.

The alterations of the child's body proportions create striking changes in appearance. In the beginning, the toddling baby has a top-heavy appearance that is accentuated by a relatively long trunk and perhaps a bulky diaper that causes the buttocks to appear to be closer to the floor than they really are. As the child begins the second year, the legs begin to grow much faster than the trunk. As the toddler learns to walk, a compensating convex lumbar curve (in the small of the back) begins to develop. These changes, coupled with erect posture, make the child resemble, in some ways, a miniature adult.

The abdominal musculature is not as well developed in the toddler as in the child of 4 years or more, and this contributes to a "potbelly" appearance. The potbelly disappears as the child's muscles strengthen, allowing the pelvis to assume a more neutral position rather than the forward tip of the young toddler. The feet may appear flat until muscles strengthen to form arches.

From the child's first birthday to the sixth, height will progress from an average of 30 inches to approximately 46 inches. More than two-thirds of all children will stay within 1½ to 2 inches of the average height for their ages. By age 4, the preschooler will double his or her birth length.[21] Gender differences in height during this time are minimal, although males are generally slightly taller than females of the same age (see Appendixes D and E).

After the child's second birthday, the rate of weight gain will average about 5 pounds yearly until the 9th or 10th birthday. This means that beginning with the second year, the child may gain only one-half pound per month, with many plateaus interspersed throughout this span of time.[21] The accumulation of adipose tissue declines greatly during the preschool years; it begins to increase again at approximately 6 years of age. Most black children have less subcutaneous fat than white children, but they are taller and heavier by 2 years of age.[21] Many of the changing body proportions are the direct result of growth of the child's musculoskeletal system.

SOMATIC DEVELOPMENT

Skeletal System

Ossification slows after infancy but continues until early adulthood. From infancy to 4 years of age, the child's long-shafted bones contain red marrow, which is capable of blood cell production. From 4 to 7 years, this active marrow is gradually replaced by fatty tissue, eventually leaving red marrow only in pelvic bones, the sternum (breastbone), vertebrae, and some skull and short-shafted bones (Fig. 9-1).[21]

Chest

The child's chest has become less cylindrical by 1 year of age and approximates the adult thoracic shape by the sixth birthday.[21] This change greatly aids the child's ability to expand the lungs fully when taking deep breaths.

Legs and Feet

The legs and feet of toddlers and preschoolers grow more rapidly than their trunks. Babies who walk before 1 year of age have a bowed appearance of the legs during the early months because (1) hyperextension of the knees is necessary to in-

FIGURE 9–1.
The progress of balanced reflexes and motor control are apparent when one compares (A) the young toddler resting on a mini-cycle and (B) the older preschooler steering a bicycle. Note that this child still has training wheels. (C) Once the skills are mastered, they are further refined and become a tool for socialization. (D) Refined further, the skills become unique talents that create personal enjoyment as well as pleasure for others.

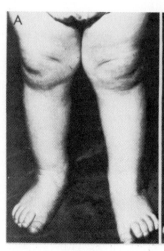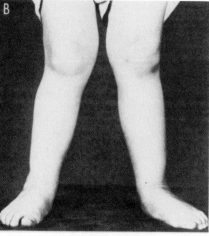

FIGURE 9–2.
(A) *These feet and legs belong to a healthy 13-month-old who is just learning to walk. It is often difficult to assess whether abnormal growth is occurring because of the infant's early stances.* (B) *With simple flatfoot, the whole foot is rotated outward, the longitudinal arch is not present, and the legs take on a "knock-kneed" appearance.* (Lowrey, G. H. Growth and Development of Children, 6th ed. Copyright 1973 by Year Book Medical Publishers, Inc., Chicago, IL. Used with permission)

crease stability during walking; (2) anteversion of the femur in the hip joint gives a greater angle of the femoral neck the first 18 months; and (3) uneven development of the musculature causes the lateral side of the legs to appear fuller than the medial side.[6,16] With skeletal and musculature maturation, this bowed appearance will disappear. During the second year, the small-shafted bones rotate and gradually straighten the appearance of the toddler's legs.[2] Babies and young walkers typically separate their feet (broad walking base), turn them outward, and rest on the medial sides of the feet until the muscles are refined and strong enough to maintain balance with a narrower distance between the feet (Fig. 9-2).

Flat-foot is normal during the early months. There is some evidence that indicates the wearing of shoes is unnecessary until the baby is walking.[39] Walking barefoot during these early years can help to develop the foot arch.[21] Even after a child is walking, Spock states that there is real value in leaving the child barefoot much of the time when the weather is warm and the walking surfaces are safe.[36]

Properly fitting footwear is essential to aid growth and development of the child's lower extremities, posture, and walking habits (Fig. 9-3). Socks, booties, and shoes should extend at least ¹/₂ inch beyond the toes. There should also be ¹/₄ inch between the edge of the little toe and the lateral edge of the shoe when the heel is snug against the back of the shoe. Infants and very young children ordinarily need no heel lift; it is usually not until school age that the child requires a ¹/₂-inch heel.[7] High-top shoes are not necessary to support the walking child's ankles and may in some cases actually impede the child's mobility. In some cases, however, they may be desirable because they help keep the foot in the shoe.

The American Foot Care Institute recommends that the sock and shoe sizes of a child who is 2 to 6 years old be checked carefully every 1 to 2 months.[7] Since one foot is often larger than the other, both feet should be measured. The rapid growth of the child's feet may require the purchase of new shoes every 3 to 4 months. The presence of reddened skin or curled toes when shoes are removed indicates the need for a larger size.[40]

Knee varus is common in children up to 18 months of age, causing the toes to turn inward and to give a bow-legged appearance. The upper long-shafted bone (femur) may still be internally rotated after the age of 15 months. Thus, toeing-in may be the result of internal torsion of the same bones that cause bowing.[2] Orthopedic consultation is needed for most cases of toeing-in or "pigeon-toeing." As the lower ends of the

FIGURE 9–3.
A wide-walking base is gradually closed, enabling the child to walk on progressively narrower surfaces. The preschooler loves to challenge the ability to maintain balance and to refine heel–toe placement skills by walking on top of walls, fences, and balance beams.

short-shafted bones or ankle joints (malleoli) rotate externally to give the child a wider base, the knees are brought nearer together, and developmental knock-knee (genu valgum) may result (Fig. 9-2). Knock-knee is common between 3 and 6 years of age with a peak incidence between 3 and 3½ years of age, which can lead to frequent stumbling and falling. Maturation of the hip, knee, and ankle joints reverses this rotation during the fourth and fifth years. Spontaneous correction is seen in most children between the ages of 5 and 7 years.[2]

Most babies learn to walk during the first half of the second year. Children who have not begun to walk unaided by the age of 15 months should be assessed by a team of health professionals. Walking encourages the child's sense of autonomy and expands the opportunities to learn about the environment.[37]

Muscular System

Muscles grow faster than bones during the toddler and preschool years. Actual muscle strength (the amount of force exerted by a contracting muscle) is directly correlated with the amount of muscle tissue (mass). Genetic inheritance, nutritional intake, and the opportunity to use the muscles all play a role in how strong a child will be.

Motor Functioning

Although walking is a major developmental milestone, it is only one of the many motor functions acquired during the toddler and preschool years. Table 9-1 gives examples of the normal sequence of various gross and fine motor skills. The sequencing of development is critical for the mastery of basic skills, which are later integrated into more complex behaviors. Thus, the acquisition of correct muscular movements is more salient than the age of their emergence. "Maturation provides a young child with the ability to perform a specific movement skill at a very low level of performance. It is only with continuous practice and instruction that a child's level of performance will increase."[28] However, research indicates that because of inadequate exercise today's preschoolers are weaker in the areas of cardiovascular endurance, muscular strength, and body leanness than they were 20 years ago.[11] Children need more than opportunity; they also need guided assistance in learning and perfecting more mature, challenging or complex motor skills.[28]

By 3 years of age, the motor patterns for walking have become so automatic that the child is able to walk comfortably even on uneven surfaces. The gait and length of step are well established. By 4 years of age, the child achieves an adult ease and smoothness for transfer of weight, body swing, rhythmical stride, and ability to turn sharp corners.[8] Running uses the same movements as walking, but requires more strength and better balance skills as the child propels the body quickly enough and with sufficient energy to suspend momentarily in space. The toddler's running is uneven and jarring. The shoulders are held high and the arms swing widely to help maintain balance (Fig. 9-4).[42] Toddlers frequently stumble over feet which have not been raised high enough to clear the ground. By 5 to 6 years of age, the child swings the arms and raises the feet in an adult manner.[8] The child can now use running to achieve other goals (Table 9-2).

Handedness

Whether a child's hand preference (handedness) is hereditary or the result of training and social conditioning has been debated for many generations. Scientists are still trying to piece together the relationship among handedness, cerebral dominance, and the ability of the individual to write and to speak. Does a right-handed person have an advantage in these areas? If so, why? Why are so many people right-handed

A

B

FIGURE 9–4.
(A) *Running form of a 15-month-old child.* (B) *A 5-year-old boy demonstrating more advanced arm and leg movements. (Wickstrom, R. L. Fundamental Motor Patterns, 3rd ed. Philadelphia: Lea & Febiger, 1983. By permission of the publisher.)*

TABLE 9-1. NEUROMOTOR DEVELOPMENT DURING THE TODDLER AND PRESCHOOL YEARS

Gross Motor Skills	*Fine Motor Skills*

18 MONTHS

Runs with less falling; climbs; pulls toys and large objects, followed soon by pushing them; throws small balls forward; walks up or down stairs with adult holding hand; sits self in small chair; squats fully and stands again without falling; carries large toy while walking.

Puts blocks in large holes, rings on peg, or beads into bottle; scribbles and may attempt horizontal lines; can drink from a cup without much spilling; still has frequent spills in getting spoon contents properly inserted into mouth; unties bow by pulling string; builds a tower of 4 to 5 blocks; can take off socks and other easy-to-manipulate clothing.

2 YEARS

Jumps in place and from low step; can walk up and down stairs nonreciprocally holding on to handrail or using wall for support; throws large ball with both hands without falling; kicks ball; propels riding toys (without pedals).

Can line blocks horizontally to make a train; can turn reachable doorknobs; can imitate a stroke while scribbling; can drink from a small cup using only one hand; still spills liquids (e.g., soup, milk) from spoon when eating; turns pages of a book one at a time; zips and unzips large zipper; unbuttons large button; likes to dress and take off clothes; builds tower of 6 to 7 blocks; can use straw to drink; may brush teeth with help; pulls on coat with assistance.

2¹/₂ YEARS

Can stand on one foot alone for at least 1 second; can throw a large ball about 5 feet; can walk on tiptoe; gets down from adult chair without assistance; catches soft object with both arms and body.

Is able to make a tower of 9 large blocks; still likes to fill containers with objects; will disassemble objects; puts on coat and large, simple clothes independently; snaps large snap; buttons large button; moves fingers and thumb separately in imitation games; twists lids off jars; places simple shapes in correct holes; uses fork, but is held with fist; may use toilet, but needs assistance.

3 YEARS

Pedals a tricycle; jumps from 12-inch height; can walk a straight line, walks with heel-to-toe pattern and reciprocal arm swing; can go to toilet unaided; can get undressed in most situations; can go up stairs using alternating feet without holding on; throws large ball with one hand; can put on own coat without assistance; catches soft object with both arms.

Begins to use blunt scissors by snipping paper; strings large beads on shoelace; can copy a circle; can help with simple household tasks (dusting, picking up); can wash and dry hands with some wetting of clothes; can brush teeth, but not adequately; drinks from water fountain; can imitate a bridge made of three blocks; can pull pants up and down for toileting without assistance; puts shoes on feet.

3¹/₂ YEARS

Rides tricycle without bumping into objects; skips on one foot; hops forward on both feet; runs well without falling; kicks large ball; twists upper body while holding feet in one place; walks down stairs with alternating feet; jumps forward; rises to stand through mature, half-kneel pattern; catches soft object with both hands; catches large ball with arms.

Can cut straight lines with scissors without tearing paper; manipulates pieces into position for simple puzzles; builds 9–10 block tower; can weave yarn randomly through a card; places small pegs in pegboard; unbuttons small buttons; puts socks on independently; can eat from spoon without spilling; eats with fork, holding with fingers and thumbs.

4 YEARS

Jumps well; hops forward on one foot; climbs ladders and playground equipment, walks on wide balance beam; stands on one foot for 6 seconds; gallops; catches soft object with one hand; catches small ball with arms; swings.

Cuts on curved line with scissors; can copy a square; can button small buttons; dresses independently; may bathe self, with assistance; uses toilet independently; can wash and dry hands without supervision; folds napkin into a triangle or a rectangle; outlines a picture with yarn; strings small beads; serves self from large bowl.

5 YEARS

Can jump rope; can walk on balance beam; runs lightly on toes; alternates feet to skip; roller skates; can imitate dance steps (if motivated to do so); gets up without using hands; catches small ball with two hands; walks down steps carrying an object; swings self on swing; walks forwards and backwards on balance beam.

May be able to print own name; copies a triangle; dresses without assistance; opens lock with key; may be able to lace shoes; can put toys away neatly; bathes self; needs help with hair; threads small beads on a string; still needs assistance with tooth brushing and flossing; pours from small pitcher; spreads butter with knife; cuts out simple shapes with scissors.

TABLE 9–2. SUMMARY OF MOTOR SKILL DEVELOPMENT

Skill	2–3 years	3–4 years	4–5 years	5–6 years
Walking	Rocker action of foot. Step pattern smoother. Walk backwards easily. Walk with 1 foot on balance board. Walk on tiptoe.	Well-coordinated walk. Walk along line without stepping off. Alternate feet part way on balance board.	Stabilized gait pattern. Walk length of balance board. Walk along circle without stepping off.	Stand on tiptoe for 10 sec. Balance on 1 foot 4–6 sec. Increase speed of walk on balance board.
Running	Jerky action: changing from full sole to rocker action.	Can run smoother and on toes.	More control and power. Increased length of stride and nonsupport period.	Control turn and stop. Use run effectively in games.
Hopping Galloping Skipping	Balance on 1 foot. Jump off floor with both feet.	Consecutive jumps off floor with 2 feet. Early gallop by varying beat of run.	Hop on foot. Master gallop beat. Skip on 1 foot.	Hop with better form for 10 or more hops on 1 foot. Hop on either foot. Good galloping skill. Alternate foot skip.
Climbing	Walk upstairs alone: mark time.	Walk upstairs alone: alternate feet. Descend stairs with help, alternate feet.	Descend stairs alone: alternate feet. Ascend ladders: mark time.	Ascend short ladder: alternate feet. Descend ladders: mark time.
Jumping	Jump from 12″ height one foot ahead. Rudimentary jump and reach.	Jump from 12″ height feet together. Jump rope lower than 20 cm. Distance jump: 10–35 cm. Arms used as stabilizer. Better jump and reach form.	Increased distance jump, height in jump and reach and over obstacle. Better form with arms used to augment action.	Continued increase in height jumped and distance jumped. Continued improvement in form.
Kicking	Contacts ball during "walk."	Contacts ball directly in front. Little leg backswing or follow through.	Adjusts to ball. More backswing and follow-through.	Full backswing; forward body lean. Better foot contact.
Throwing	Some force in anterior-posterior hand release.	Anterior-posterior throwing action of arm and trunk. Feet stationary.	Horizontal arm. Some trunk rotation. Ipsilateral step forward.	Horizontal arm action and trunk rotation. Ipsilateral step but also some alternate step during throw.
Catching	Extended parallel arm with no or little action to trap ball (large).	Scooping action with parallel arms with large ball.	Smaller ball catch with vice grip and elbows in front of body.	Large ball catch with vice grip and elbows in front of body.
Ball bouncing	Bounce small ball with one hand 1–3 ft. Tapping action of hand.	Bounce larger ball with both hands.	Bounce smaller ball further distance. Use chasing action of hand.	Bounce larger ball with one hand 1–3 ft.

(Eckert, H. M. (1987). Motor development [3rd ed.]. pp. 230–231. Indianapolis: Benchmark Press. With permission.)

today? A recent study found no correlation between handedness and reading ability, or between handedness and general intelligence.[24] Before 3½ years of age, many children demonstrate bilaterality in the use of their hands. Unilateral function of the body (which includes handedness) is usually established by about 4 years of age. For an unknown reason, left-handers show a stronger preference for their left hand than right-handers for their right.[24] Left-handed children need to have appropriate tools available for their use, especially scissors. Children should be encouraged to use their dominant side, since coordination is usually better. Children also need to develop the motor coordination pathways (motor habits or schemata) during preschool years so that they can concentrate on the end product rather than the use of the hands per se.

Neurologic System

The gradual maturation of the nervous system accounts for many of the behavioral changes observed in toddlers and preschoolers. Electroencephalograms (EEG), which record brain activity and can help to measure the maturation of its different areas, demonstrate that rhythms associated with the mature adult brain begin to emerge during these years.[21] These changes suggest a complex pattern of maturation, which facilitates an increased attention span (needed later for formal schooling) as well as increased motor skills. It is during this time that neural control becomes more integrated so that the child is capable of independent, self-help activities (e.g., taking off a coat, getting under the covers, asking for mittens).

The Brain

The brain continues to grow during the toddler and preschool years, but not as rapidly as it did during infancy. By the time the child has reached 2 years of age, the brain is two thirds of its adult size; by 3 years of age, it is three quarters of its adult size.[21] The increasing maturation of the brain, combined with opportunities to experience more of the world, greatly contributes to the child's emerging cognitive abilities. Because so much growth has already taken place, head circumference is not routinely measured at physical assessments on children over 2 years of age.

The temperature-regulating center in the brain is becoming more mature, so that the child is less subject to the temperature fluctuations that were common in infancy. As the child's neurological system matures, it is better able to read the messages of "cold" and "warm" sent to the brain stem. The capillaries (small blood vessels) also respond more efficiently to messages from the brain stem. Consequently, they now constrict rapidly in response to cold and dilate in response to heat. Shivering is also more effective in producing body heat than it was during early infancy.

Various areas of the cerebrum develop at different rates. Because the young toddler's immature nervous system cannot handle more than one incoming stimulus at a time, the introduction of a second stimulus will intensify and prolong the action that has resulted from a first stimulus. For example, when the hand of a 16-month old is slapped for touching a forbidden object, the child's grasp (a result of the first stimulus) momentarily tightens, or is prolonged, instead of releasing the object. The child's inability to respond immediately to the parent's command is, in part, physiological, not just a refusal to cooperate.[29]

Myelinization

Although most of the nerve fibers are myelinated by 2 years of age, the myelin sheaths continue to thicken, and the number and the size of nerve endings within and between cortical areas continue to grow at least until adolescence.[21] By 2 years of age, one of the toddler's major motor pathways, the corticospinal tract, is myelinated enough to allow the child to gain voluntary control over elimination and to refine movement of the lower extremities. By 4 years of age, the fibers that connect the cerebellum to the cerebral cortex are mature enough to allow refined voluntary hand and finger move-

ments for drawing pictures and reproducing simple shapes. Further refinement of these movements will occur with increased myelinization, cognitive development, and appropriate experiences.

Vestibular Stimulation

This section by Debra A. Ronk

The vestibular organ is located in the inner ear. It is the sensory organ that detects motion of acceleration, deceleration, and gravitational pull. This sensory information is then used to coordinate reflexes of the eye, neck, and body for maintaining equilibrium, in accordance with one's posture and movement.[22]

Quick, rapid motion such as gentle roughhousing and running is excitory to the vestibular system and results in improved motoric responses. Slow, rhythmical, passive motion such as rocking and bouncing tends to slow or depress movement. This is frequently used by mothers to calm and lull their child to sleep. Research is also being done in this area to determine its effect on psychosocial development.[3]

Vestibular stimulation through swinging, rocking, roughhousing, and so forth, affects the child in three major ways (Fig. 9-5). One way is to increase input to the muscles that straighten or extend the trunk and limbs, thus supporting

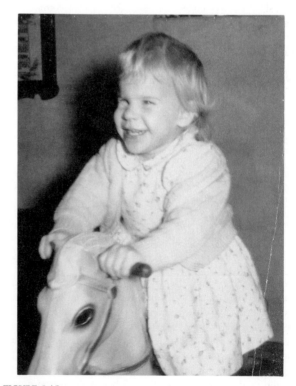

FIGURE 9–5.
The hobby horse is an excellent indoor activity that uses up surplus energy while providing vestibular stimulation.

the ability to assume and maintain antigravity positions, such as propping in prone, standing, and walking.[3, 22] The second way vestibular information influences the body is in providing sensory input so that the child can learn what position he or she occupies in space (i.e., lying, sitting, standing) and whether the position is stable or unstable. It is this sensory information, along with kinematic and proprioceptive input, that initiates head and trunk righting responses to keep the head in an upright position, protective responses to break a fall, and equilibrium responses to maintain balance (see Chap. 6).[3, 22] The third way vestibular stimulation influences the body is through the eyes. This stimulation helps the eye muscles in the young infant work together to focus on an object. The older child uses this information to develop the visual perceptual skills that determine if the object is tilted, the child's head is tilted, or whether the supporting surface and the child are both tilted when looking at an object.[3, 22]

The growing child will continually seek out vestibular stimulation through somersaults, running, climbing, swinging, and twirling in circles, in order to learn to coordinate the body in different positions and to challenge the ability to maintain balance. Such practice sharpens the ability of the vestibular system to discern and discriminate sensory information and of the motor system to coordinate an appropriate response. Such stimulation continues in the older child through sports and amusement park rides. Children without adequate vestibular stimulation find it difficult to ride a bicycle, since balance coordination has not been adequately mastered. Adults become increasingly sensitive to vestibular stimulation, skipping the amusement park rides of earlier years, and even becoming excessively dizzy on a swing ride.

Sensory Organ Development

The concomitant factors of an increased attention span and improved cognitive discrimination skills heighten the child's ability to select and to study details and to coordinate schemata (see Chap. 10) (Fig. 9-6).

THE EYE. The specific biophysical development of the eye is covered in Chapter 20. Depth perception continues to improve throughout preschoolerhood, but because of the child's immature neurological system and poor motor coordination, there may be overshooting and undershooting of extremities and poor eye–hand coordination. This in turn leads to many spills, poor art work, or even falls from furniture or climbing equipment.

Functional amblyopia ("lazy eye") is usually the result of not using an eye (neural inhibition in the visual pathways in the brain) to avoid the discomfort of double vision that is often caused by imbalanced eye muscles (strabismus). The exact cause of functional amblyopia is unknown. The child with amblyopia has no way of knowing that he or she is not seeing properly, but the vision is decreased by the fact that the child is allowing one eye to do most of the work. Treatment may include patching the stronger eye (often for several months) to encourage use of the affected eye, wearing glasses,

FIGURE 9–6.
Family values, esthetic appreciation, and cultural traditions are established as parents offer experiences that help develop the child's sensory discrimination skills.

or doing eye exercises. Occasionally, eye-muscle surgery may be necessary. The younger the child when treatment is begun, the greater the possibility of the success of treatment. Strabismus will interfere with depth perception, and thus may affect eye–hand coordination, participation in sports, and even learning to read.

It is important that adults be aware of the signs of possible eye problems in the young child. Some of these behaviors include rubbing the eyes, blinking excessively, squinting, appearing irritable when playing games that require good distance vision, shutting or covering one eye, tearing, headaches, and tilting the head or thrusting it forward when looking at something. If any of these behaviors are present, the child should be examined by a pediatric ophthalmologist.

THE EAR. The external ear canal in the child who is less than 3 years of age approaches the internal canal at an oblique upward angle. (For this reason, when ear drops are instilled in a child this age, the pinna should be held down and back to straighten the external canal and thus facilitate the flow of the medication.) Sometimes the middle-ear becomes filled with a serous fluid. This is caused by blockage of the eustachian tube and consequent negative pressure in the middle-ear cavity. In most cases, decongestants prescribed by a physician will aid in resolving the condition. When a middle-ear infection has been caused by pathologic bacteria (usually traveling through the short, wide eustachian tube after causing an upper respiratory infection), the doctor may prescribe an antibiotic. When a middle-ear infection or inflammation occurs, it must be treated immediately because it can cause reduced hearing or, in some cases, permanent deafness. If the condition persists, the tympanic membrane (eardrum) may need to be surgically incised to facilitate drainage of the fluid. When drainage is insufficient, polyethylene tubes are inserted through the membrane to aid the drainage and facilitate healing. These tubes remain in place for several weeks; then, at the discretion of the pediatrician, they may be removed or allowed to fall out spontaneously (usually 6–24 months later).

THE TASTE BUDS. The taste buds become more sensitive to the natural flavors of foods during these years. Cognitive processes aid in discrimination of various flavors. By toddlerhood, children are already learning which foods they prefer and which tastes are preferred by those whose culture they share. Preschoolers soon volunteer their advice (and thus assert their initiative) by asking for something that tastes "yummy" and requesting that something else be totally removed from their presence because it tastes "yucky".

THE NOSE. The capacity to smell, which is closely linked to taste, is also influenced by voluntary control, cultural attitudes, and cognitive development. Usually young children do not mind and may even like body odors. Gradually, they assume the attitudes of the family and the culture toward these odors. Some cultures find body odors quite acceptable, while others consider them to be unpleasant or even offensive. Older preschoolers and school-agers often respond to odors in an uninhibited manner as they learn the taboos, but not the social graces, for handling the situation. They may make faces, laugh, tease, act sick, hold their nose, or rebuke the offender (to the embarrassment of any adult in the situation).

THE SKIN. The skin, as a sensory and a protective organ, continues to develop during the toddler and preschool years.

Adequate contact with varying textures is essential during these years to facilitate sensory integration. The child instinctively knows this and seems unable to resist touching everything to learn about the world. Children enjoy closing their eyes and identifying different objects by their various shapes and textures (stereognosis) (see Fig. 10-11). Contact with different textures, positions, and temperatures all help the child to become more aware of body shape and body space. Most toddlers and preschoolers still like to be near to, and hugged by, significant others if they are in the mood, and especially when they need to "refuel" (see Chaps. 8 and 11). Rubbing the child's body with lotion and drawing simple shapes on the child's back with a finger can help with perceptual discrimination.

Integumentary System

The child's skin is not as soft as it was during infancy because the epidermis and dermis are more tightly bound together. This increases resistance to infection and irritation. It also forms a more effective barrier against fluid loss. The frequency of skin rashes and eruptions due to contact irritants (e.g., harsh detergents) decline during toddlerhood.

The eccrine glands are functional during toddler/preschool years and react to changes in temperature; they still produce relatively minimal perspiration, however. A minimal amount of sebum is secreted during these years, making the skin rather dry. Baby lotion may help maintain the integrity of the skin when it is exposed to drying weather conditions. On the other hand, the skin is better protected from the harsh rays of the sun during the preschool years because the production of the melanin-forming cells has increased (Fig. 9-7). The child should still wear a sunscreen with a high skin protection factor (SPF) and (as with any other individuals) should especially avoid the sun between 10 A.M. and 3 P.M.. During the preschool years, the scalp hair grows thicker and may lose some curliness, and it often darkens. Fine hair appears on the lower arms and legs.

Respiratory System

As the lungs grow in size, their volume, and thus the capacity for oxygenation, increases. The respiratory rate decreases because the lungs are relatively more efficient than they were in infancy. Respirations remain primarily diaphragmatic until the child's fifth or sixth year.[21] The bifurcation of the trachea (airway) into the smaller bronchi (branches of the airway) is situated farther down in the chest, so that choking on food particles that could potentially lodge in this part of the airway while eating is less likely to occur. The epiglottis, a flaplike, cartilaginous structure that closes over the opening to the trachea when the child is swallowing, also slowly descends after infancy. The epiglottis is so high in the chest during infancy that it can be seen through the baby's open mouth. The tonsils and adenoids increase in size but do not need to be removed so long as they are functional (protecting the

FIGURE 9–7.
Young children love water. Swimming facilitates learning how to use the body effectively. Adults must offer close supervision to prevent sunburning as well as drowning. (Photograph by Candy Schults)

child from serious infections) and are not causing obstruction or pressure.

With the increased size of the respiratory tract and associated structures, there is increased resistance to respiratory infections. The toddler and preschooler are still candidates for several respiratory infections, however.

Cardiovascular System

The Heart
By the time the child is 5 years old, the heart has increased its weight fourfold.[21] The decrease in heart rate (pulse) that normally occurs during early childhood is generally thought to be due to the increase in the size of the heart. The larger heart can pump blood with more and more efficiency than it could when the child was younger. As the pulse decreases, the blood pressure rises (see Appendix E). Through all these maturational changes, both toddlers and especially the preschoolers increase their capacity for more sustained and strenuous physical exercise. By 5 years of age, early signs of arteriosclerosis may already be present. Aerobic exercise and medically directed dietary measures can slow this disease process.[15]

Blood Values
As long as the child consumes adequate dietary iron during the toddler and preschool years, healthy levels of hemoglobin will be maintained. The hemoglobin and red blood cell count increase during these years. Conversely, the number of white

blood cells needed has decreased because their quality has improved. Therefore, the child's natural ability to fight infection and disease is increased.

Immune System

To understand how resistance develops, it is helpful to review the normal functioning and development of the immune system. The immune system must first recognize *self* from *nonself* and then initiate responses to eliminate the nonself (antigens or foreign substances) from the body. Antigens are usually protein in nature and are viewed by the body as an attacking force. When the body is attacked by antigens (e.g., bacteria, viruses, substances that elicit allergic responses), it has three ways of defending itself: the phagocytic immune response, the humoral (antibody) immune response, and the cellular immune response.

The first line of defense, the **phagocytic immune response,** involves the white blood cells, which have the ability to ingest and digest foreign particles. These phagocytes can move to the point of attack to destroy the foreign agents. This form of immunity is often called a nonspecific immune defense because the phagocytes are activated on exposure to any foreign substance. The other two mechanisms of defense are specific immune responses because they have the ability to recognize specific antigens and respond selectively.

Humoral immunity, which is the major protective defense mechanism of the body, is involved with antibody production. The primary cell involved in antibody production is the B-lymphocyte. The exact site of B-lymphocyte production in humans is unknown, although some evidence suggests that it is in the bone marrow. B-lymphocytes, when challenged by antigen, produce and secrete large quantities of antibodies specific to the antigen. When an antibody reacts with an antigen, they bind and form an antigen–antibody complex, a compound that is more readily destroyed by phagocytes. Five types of antibodies, or immunoglobulins, have been identified: IgG (Gamma G), IgM, IgA, IgD, and IgE.

When initially exposed to an antigen, the B-lymphocyte system begins to produce antibodies, predominantly IgM, which appear in 2 to 3 days. This process is called the *primary antibody response.*

With subsequent exposure to the same antigen, a *secondary antibody response* occurs. The immune system can recognize the same antigen for months, years, or indefinitely. Thus, antibodies, chiefly IgG, are produced in much greater quantities within 1 to 2 days. IgG is the only class of immunoglobulin capable of crossing the placental barrier and does so at an increased rate toward the end of gestation. IgA is the predominant immunoglobulin in colostrum and breast milk.

A third protective response, the *cellular immune response,* is a function of the T-lymphocyte, so named because it is produced in thymus gland. In contrast to humoral immunity, which can be transferred from one person to another by plasma transfusions, cellular immunity depends on the presence of immune cells.

The cellular immune response is initiated when a T-lymphocyte is sensitized by an antigen. In response to this contact, the T-lymphocyte releases lymphokines, which eventually kill the antigen. One type of lymphokine, interferon, is currently being researched and used as a treatment for selected types of cancer.

The defense mechanisms of the toddler and preschooler, especially the phagocytes, are much more efficient than they were in the infant. IgG reaches adult levels by the time the child is 2 years old. IgM attains adult levels during late infancy. Levels of IgA, IgD, and IgE gradually increase, reaching adult values in later childhood.[21]

Gastrointestinal System

Dentition

When the child is between the ages of 18 months and 2 years, the sharp-pointed canine teeth (cuspids) erupt. The last four deciduous teeth to appear are usually the second molars, and they do so shortly after the second birthday. Their appearance completes the set of 20 deciduous teeth. Teeth are like icebergs: much goes on underneath the surface—in this case, under the gums. The mere emergence of a tooth does not mean that its development is complete. The root of the tooth is still growing and developing for several months after its emergence.

At the end of the preschool years, the deciduous teeth begin to loosen and fall out; the central incisors are usually the first to go. Premature loss of deciduous teeth may affect the alignment of permanent teeth; therefore, dental consultation should be sought.

Salivary Glands

By the end of the second year, the child's salivary glands are adult-sized and have reached functional maturity. The child is capable of chewing food, so that it stays longer in the mouth, and the salivary enzymes have an opportunity to begin breaking down the food. The saliva also covers the teeth with a protective film that helps prevent decay.[17] The drooling that began in infancy should no longer be present after 2 years; by this time the toddler should have learned to swallow saliva and keep the lips closed when not speaking or eating.

Stomach

The secretion of hydrochloric acid continues to increase during early childhood, raising the acidity of the child's gastric juices, but adult levels are not present until puberty.[21] The acidity of the stomach contents has a protective function in that it destroys many types of bacteria. The child's stomach is able to hold approximately 500 mL (almost 17 oz) by 2 years of age and 750 to 900 mL (25 to 30 oz) in later childhood.[21] These increases allow the child to assume a schedule of three meals a day. However, between-meal snacks are very important to prevent low blood sugar, fatigue, and the resulting irritability, noncompliance, or inattentiveness.

Intestines

Sometime during the child's second year, the child becomes physically ready to control the eliminative functions of the bowel and the bladder. This physical readiness for toilet training is discussed later in this chapter.

Genitourinary System

Genitals

The genital organs continue to increase in size but not in function during the early childhood years. If the testes have not descended into the scrotum (cryptochidism) by one year of age, they are generally corrected surgically during the toddler years, but must be descended before the fifth birthday to prevent potential damage to sperm production.[4] Sterility will result if they remain within the abdominal cavity. The seminiferous tubules of the testes develop their passageways (lumens) and increase in size during childhood. Immature sperm are also experiencing both hyperplastic and hypertrophic growth during these years.[21]

It is not uncommon for girls between the ages of 2 and 6 years to have skin adhesions between the inner lips of the vagina (labia minora). These adhesions may be caused by irritation, mild infection, or a nonpathological delay in hormonal influence. Consistent, thorough cleansing and perhaps an occasional separating of the labia minora (usually by the parent) may resolve the problem. If it continues to form or causes pain when the caregiver attempts to separate the labia, a health professional should be consulted.

A bubble bath can serve as an irritant to the urethra of the young female, causing inflammation that may quickly lead to an infection. It is not uncommon for females under 5 years of age to complain of itching and burning in the genitourinary area when urinating if this infection is present. In such cases the child should be seen and evaluated by a doctor, especially since the infection can spread to the rest of the urinary tract as well as to the vagina.

Kidneys

By the child's second birthday, the kidneys are able to conserve water under normal conditions and to concentrate urine on a level that approximates adult capabilities.[21] This efficiency is caused in part by the filtering membranes of the kidneys, which have become thinner and are therefore more mature. The kidneys are now capable of adequately responding to antidiuretic hormone (ADH) and are producing a more concentrated urine.[21] Since the urine composition does not change significantly once the child becomes a toddler, and because it reflects kidney functioning (among other things), a urinalysis (chemical examination of the urine) should be initiated at this time and repeated periodically through the lifetime.

Bladder

The capacity of the bladder to hold urine increases during toddlerhood. At 2½ years of age, the average bladder will hold approximately 85 mL (3 oz).[13] The child will experience and respond to a feeling of bladder fullness. The ability of the child to remain dry for at least 2 hours during the day and to wake up dry from a nap indicates readiness for the toilet-training process. A further discussion of toilet training can be found later in this chapter. Occasional accidents still occur after toilet training is complete because the child, engrossed in play, is not aware of the signs of a full bladder until it is too late.

Urethra

Bacteria can ascend the urethra and cause an infection in any portion of the urinary tract. In males, the length of the urethra usually proves to be effective in preventing such infections. In females, however, the urethra is less than 2 cm in length, and it opens directly into an area that predisposes it to be easily contaminated by poor hygiene practices.[34] Females of all ages should wipe themselves from front to back, toward the rectum. Education to prevent contamination is essential. Diapers (even the disposables) and panties (including any soiled clothing) should be changed when wet. Swimming or playing in heated pools and hot tubs for prolonged periods of time may precipitate irritation or infection in young females. Cleanliness and prompt drying of the genital area decrease the incidence of infection. Panties with a cotton crotch aid the circulation of air to this area and thus decrease the susceptibility to infection.

Endocrine System

Glandular Secretion

The endocrine system continues to mature during the early childhood years. The secretions of the pancreas and the liver, which aid in the digestive process, are functioning at an adult level.[21] Variations in blood sugar still occur because of the labile production of insulin and glucagon. As the child grows, the ability to cope biophysically with stress is increased by more effective adrenal medullar secretions of norepinephrine and epinephrine (see Chap. 35 for a discussion of stress).

Several hormones are vital to normal growth and development during these years; among these are the thyroid hormones and pituitary growth hormone (PGH). The production of hormones, especially aldosterone, by the adrenal cortex remains relatively limited. The adrenal cortex, however, does increase production enough to give the toddler and preschooler more protection against fluid and electrolyte imbalance than during infancy.

Fluid and Electrolyte Balance

By the end of the second year, the total body water of the child is approximately 60% of body weight.[26] Although this figure approximates the adult percentage, the distribution of intracellular and extracellular fluids is different. During toddlerhood, about 34% of this water is contained within the cells and about 26% is outside the cells (compared to 47% and 19%,

respectively, in the adult).[23, 26] The toddler is still vulnerable to fluid volume deficits because of the relatively greater extracellular fluid to exchange. The high metabolic rate results in large amounts of wastes to be excreted, and the endocrine system is still not functioning at maximal capacity. The child, therefore, requires more fluid per unit of body weight in a 24-hour period than does an adult. By the time the child is 5 years old, the electrolyte blood concentrations are essentially equal to those of an adult.[23]

MAINTAINING HIGH-LEVEL WELLNESS

Nutrition

Recommended Intake

The total caloric intake of toddlers and preschoolers when compared to adult norms is relatively low. Approximately 1300 calories per day are needed by the toddler, and 1800 calories are required by the preschooler.[43] The actual amount of calories needed per unit of body weight decreases during these years because toddlers and preschoolers are growing less rapidly than they did as infants. However, since several systems of the body, such as the muscles, are still growing quite rapidly, protein needs remain high. Toddlers and preschoolers require 1.2 g of protein per kg of body weight per day.[10] One-half of this protein should be of animal origin to ensure adequate intake of amino acids, B-complex vitamins, vitamin D, iron, and calcium.

Calcium recommendations for these growing children are 800 mg per day.[10] Both calcium and phosphorus are important for this age group, owing to the increased mineralization taking place within their teeth and bones. Although milk is also a good source of protein, phosphorus, and calcium, too much milk will decrease the child's appetite for other foods and can thus lead to anemia.

The actual portion sizes of foods that a child this age should consume daily do not directly correspond to the popular adult servings of the basic four food groups. Table 9-3 lists realistic portions of food needed by toddlers and preschoolers to promote nutritional high-level wellness during early childhood. Food habits vary from one child (and one family) to another. Few children conform to eating 3 meals per day; preschool children eat an average of 5 to 7 times per day.[27]

Pediatricians and other health professionals vary in their opinions as to whether toddlers and preschoolers should take daily vitamins. The child who is not consuming an adequate daily diet should certainly take them, but a vitamin pill should not be an excuse to replace good eating habits. Some doctors believe that a child should remain on a daily vitamin pill (often with iron or fluoride supplementation) until completion of the "too-busy-to-eat" preschool years (Fig. 9-8).

The child's liver has been capable of storing fat-soluble vitamins (e.g., vitamins A and D) since infancy. Consequently, excess quantities may lead to toxicity or poisoning; therefore, multiple doses of vitamins should not be given to a child even

TABLE 9-3. AVERAGE FOOD INTAKE FOR YOUNG CHILDREN[a]

Food	Portion Size	Number of Portions Advised	
		2–4 yrs	4–6 yrs
Milk and dairy products			
Milk[b]	4 oz	3–6	3–4
Cheese	1/2–3/4 oz	May be substituted for 1 portion of liquid milk	
Yogurt	1/4–1/2 cup	May be substituted for 1 portion of liquid milk	
Meat and meat equivalents			
Meat,[c] fish,[d] poultry	1–2 oz	2	2
Egg	1	1	1
Peanut butter	1–2 tbsp		
Legumes (dried peas and beans)	1/4–1/3 cup cooked		
Vegetables and fruits			
Vegetables[e]		4–5, including 1 green leafy or yellow	
Cooked	2–4 tbsp		
Raw	Few pieces		
Fruit		1 citrus fruit or other vegetable or fruit rich in vitamin C	
Canned	4–8 tbsp		
Raw	1/2–1 small		
Fruit juice	3–4 oz		
Bread and cereal grains			
Whole grain or enriched white bread	1/2–1 slice	3	3
Cooked cereal	1/4–1/2 cup	May be substituted for 1 serving of bread	
Ready-to-serve dry cereals	1/2–1 cup		
Spaghetti, macaroni, noddles, rice	1/4–1/2 cup		
Crackers	2–3		
Fat			
Bacon	1 slice	Not to be substituted for meat	
Butter or vitamin A-fortified margarine	1 tsp	3	3–4
Desserts	1/4–1/2 cup	As demanded by caloric needs	
Sugars	1/2–1 tsp	2	2

[a] Diets should also be monitored for adequacy of iron and vitamin D intake.

[b] Approximately 2/3 cup can easily be incorporated in a child's food during cooking.

[c] Liver once a week can be served as liver sausage or cooked liver.

[d] Should be served once or twice per week to substitute for meat.

[e] If a child's preferences are limited, use double portions of preferred vegetables until appetite for other vegetables develops.

Source: Adapted from P. L. Pipes, Nutrition in Infancy and Childhood. St. Louis: Mosby, 1985

if the child is a picky eater. Water-soluble vitamins (B vitamins and vitamin C) are not stored in excess in the body. It is thought that large amounts of water-soluble vitamins are merely passed from the body, primarily in the urine.[27]

Vitamin supplements come in tasty chewable forms and as fruit-flavored liquids, but should be treated like all other forms of medicine: Bottles should have childproof caps and should be placed out of the reach of climbing, curious children. Some hyperactive children have been noted to experience adverse effects (such as increased motor activity, more aggressive and noncompliant behaviors, more incorrect answers on simple tests) when they ingest sugar food that is not preceded by a protein food.[20] Food allergies are discussed in Chapter 20.

Feeding and Eating Habits

Most parents worry if their child does not appear to eat much. Some adults are concerned about the nutritional content of the foods that the child consumes, while others emphasize a concern for developing appropriate eating habits. All of these concerns, when combined with the normal decrease in appetite and food intake of the developing child, can potentially precipitate both situational and maturational crises. A situational crisis can arise if caregivers force foods and eating habits on a nonconforming child. This situation, in turn, if handled inappropriately over a period of time, can stifle and distort the child's desire for independence and assertiveness. An understanding of the normal sequence of a child's growth and development can aid immensely in assisting the parents

FIGURE 9–8.
Fluoride is essential for strong tooth enamel. When communities do not include fluoride in their water supply, supplements are available to ensure that the child has sufficient fluoride.

to help the child to establish acceptable eating habits. Parental education, positive role modeling, patience, and time are all that usually are needed to prevent major crises.

STRATEGIES THAT ENCOURAGE NUTRITIOUS EATING. Eating can become an excellent medium through which the child tests the boundaries of what is deemed acceptable behavior. A knowledge of normal growth and development can be used to optimize food intake by the toddler and preschooler. For example, the child who is walking is capable of seeking his or her own food, which has implications for the caregivers. It means that food must be kept locked up or in inaccessible places for the youngster lest she or he find it, eat it, and then have no desire to eat healthy food at the next scheduled meal. In addition, young children frequently choke on food and should never be allowed to assume responsibility to eat without adult supervision (see Chap. 10 for safety discussion).

Giving the child a cup or glass that is half full will lessen the probability of spilling (and thus the possibility of a feeling of shame in the child). Pieces of meat should be relatively moist (not extremely well done, since this makes the meat tougher to chew) because the deciduous teeth (or lack of them) are not as capable of grinding as are the permanent teeth. Some 4-year-olds begin to develop the skill of cutting their food into bite-sized pieces, but they still need assistance for a period of time.[27] Sandwiches cut into quarters are popular with children. Soup can be drunk from a cup or thickened

for spooning to make eating a more positive, autonomous experience for the child.

Most children are more likely to eat foods with which they are familiar; it is therefore advisable to introduce new foods one at a time in small portions. Gradual introduction to a wide variety of foods during toddler years helps to prevent "picky" eating as the child grows older. A parental attitude of expectation that the child will eat and like the food is a significant factor in acceptance of new foods.

Children, like adults, enjoy a variety of foods, including varieties of texture, flavor, and color. Simple pieces of raw vegetables are easier to manipulate in the beginning than salads with drippy dressings. Natural fruit juices (as well as fresh water) should be offered to the child rather than sweetened, colored, and artificially flavored drinks.

PATTERNS OF EATING. Idiosyncratic eating patterns or "food jags" are common throughout early childhood. In learning to be more independent, a child may indicate a dislike for a food he or she appeared to relish yesterday. Adult attempts to alter the child's refusals are usually met with more resistance. It is better, therefore, to accept the food jags and offer other foods in small portions that may compensate for nutritional value. When the child is ready to eat, she or he will eat the healthy food on the plate. Rituals which instill security often become a part of mealtime routines. For example, one special bowl may be preferred by the child when eating a certain brand of cereal. Having his or her own dishes, drinking utensils, and tableware also seems to enhance individuality.

Both the toddler and the preschooler frequently eat differing amounts of food at each meal. The child may eat virtually nothing (in the parents' estimation) during one meal. It is important for adults to remember that toddlers and preschoolers need less food per unit of body weight than they did during infancy. Because of this decreased nutritional need, around 18 months of age, many children develop *physiological anorexia,* a lack of interest in eating. A general guideline to serving size is for the young child to have one tablespoon of each solid food per year of age.[31]

The length of intervals between meals varies from one child to the next. Most growing children need a nutritious snack to tide them over between meals. However, it is not wise to allow a child to eat a heavy snack when a regular meal is scheduled within the next hour. An earlier feeding time might be more appropriate when children (toddlers eat more frequently than adults) are not able to wait as long as adults until a meal is served. When the child does eat with other adults and family, the social atmosphere should be pleasant but not boisterous. Since the social aspects of mealtime proves distracting for many young children, they will eat better after active play if they are given 10 or 15 minutes to calm down before they begin eating. Young children, especially toddlers, tend to dawdle during their eating. As a result, they should be allowed at least 30 to 40 minutes to consume a meal, no matter what time of the day it is (or in how much of a hurry the parents are).

Dental Care

Since infants and young children do not have the manual dexterity necessary to clean their teeth thoroughly, their parents must assume responsibility for their oral hygiene. The task of cleaning the oral cavity can be divided into four steps: staining, brushing, flossing, and inspection.[17]

STAINING. A disclosing agent is helpful in identifying those areas of the teeth where plaque accumulates. It also helps to motivate children to clean their teeth when plaque locations can be seen.

BRUSHING. It is important to encourage the child to become involved with personal oral hygiene early. The child less than 6 to 8 years of age should be given the opportunity to practice using the toothbrush, but the parent should inspect and provide additional cleaning where needed. During the period when both primary and permanent teeth are present, the child may hesitate to clean the teeth thoroughly because of the discomfort associated with cleaning the spaces created by lost teeth. Brushing after every meal is ideal. It is best to brush each time the child is given liquid medication since most of these preparations contain large quantities of sugar to make them more palatable.[38]

FLOSSING. Careful brushing will not clean the areas where the teeth are in contact with one another; these areas can only be reached with dental floss. Again, parents must assist young children with this procedure.[18] It should begin as soon as two teeth are side-by-side. Some dentists claim that unwaxed floss cleans most effectively because its fibers separate to spread over a larger surface and there is no danger of depositing wax during the flossing procedure.

INSPECTION. Inspecting the teeth is the final step performed (usually by a parent) to ensure that all plaque has been removed. Good lighting is essential.

Sleep and Rest

Sleep Needs

Toddlers and preschoolers expend a great deal of energy in growing, learning, and just acting their age; thus, adequate rest and sleep are essential for high-level wellness. The toddler requires an average of 12 hours of sleep each night in addition to a daytime nap. Preschoolers need 11 to 12 hours of sleep in a 24-hour period. It is important for parents to realize that preschool children vary widely in the amount of sleep they require. Some children function well without naps during the preschool years, but many still need to nap.[9]

The preschooler may not want to sleep during nap time, especially if the child slept well the previous night. Many need a quiet period of rest, however, to give them the necessary energy to carry out their daily activities. This period of rest might include the child's lying quietly and listening to favorite music or reading a preschool book. Without adequate rest periods during the day, the child can readily become fatigued, which may lead to irritability, poor resistance to infection, and restless nighttime sleep.

Sleep Routines

Establishing healthy sleeping patterns in the toddler and preschooler becomes a major concern for many parents. The young child is reluctant to give up an exciting day's activities and to depart from loved ones to go off to a darkened room and do nothing but lie down and remain still. To help develop realistic sleeping routines, the family must not only assess the child as an individual, but also their own schedules. Parental work schedules can interfere with the child's bedtime and awakening time if not carefully planned. The sound and excitement from the television set can keep the child awake at night.

Many toddlers are ready to graduate out of a crib and into a youth bed or regular bed with side rails or some other device for protection. Moving the child to a larger, more grownup bed is usually preferable to making the child sleep in an unwanted crib. The child needs to understand that sleeping in a bigger bed does not give license to get up and roam around at night. A folding gate placed across the bedroom door often serves as a helpful reminder.

Suggestions for encouraging sleep in the toddler include reducing stimulation prior to naptime and bedtime, providing quiet toys for bedtime use, and not using bed as punishment. As with feeding routines, the toddler's love of ritual can be used to establish sleeping routines which help the child assimilate a predictable chain of events that culminate in going to bed. After-dinner bathing, selecting and helping dress oneself in pajamas, saying good-night to family members, choosing a favorite bed toy, hearing a prespecified number of bedtime stories in bed, saying a prayer, turning on one's own night light, and taking a trip to the bathroom are possible rituals that can be adapted to the individual child. A special music or story record often helps to keep the child in bed and lulls the child to sleep.

Many of these ideas also work well in getting the preschooler to bed. Caregivers should ascertain that the child is truly tired (he may have slept at the baby sitter's or at the preschool, and thus may not yet be ready for sleep). Preschoolers need an established bedtime that is the same every night, avoidance of excitement a half-hour before bedtime, and a satisfying meal, but no high carbonate snacks immediately before bedtime. However, even with quiet time preparation, the child may not fall asleep immediately after going to bed. A bedroom door left slightly ajar will often help decrease the night fears of many imaginative preschoolers. The topic of early childhood fears is discussed in Chap. 10.

Children with sleeping problems resistant to these approaches might benefit from a neuromuscular relaxation program. Helping such children learn head-to-toe relaxation may facilitate their falling asleep at bedtime and may decrease night time wakefulness.[19, 32, 33] Children usually respond to parental firmness that is consistent, and soon learn that they must go to sleep. Spock and Rothenberg offer hints for helping youngsters to go to sleep.[36] Brazelton's *Toddlers and Parents* also provides enjoyable and informative reading about this topic.[5]

Exercise, Practice, and Instruction

The emergence of many of the child's motor skills are largely a matter of growth and development, but the child needs the opportunity, the environment, and the encouragement to engage in sufficient gross motor and fine motor activities to learn how the body works and what can be done with it. Children without this experience have a poor concept of body boundaries, body space, or spatial relationships. Many simple movements (e.g., jumping and running) require little instruction or coaching.

Other more complicated motor skills (e.g., skipping, swimming, skating, gymnastics, dancing, model building, self-help skills, or picture painting) require more formal instruction (Fig. 9-9). Many older preschoolers are enrolled in such activities. Although early exposure to, and practice of, these more complicated skills may give children an advantage in their performance, it is important for parents to remember some concepts about the child's motor skills, feelings, and interests that are essential for the child's biopsychosocial wellness:

1. The child must have achieved a minimal physical size and neurological maturity.

2. The child should be interested in the activity. The parents should not be reliving their childhood days or trying to realize their own unfulfilled dreams.

3. The child must possess enough motivation and self-discipline to "stick with it," and should not be forced or frequently bribed to participate.

4. The child should be given frequent periods of rest if the activity requires intense performance, whether physical, cognitive, or psychosocial in nature.

5. The parents should be familiar with the health and safety policies of the program.

6. The parents should ascertain the goals and the qualifica-

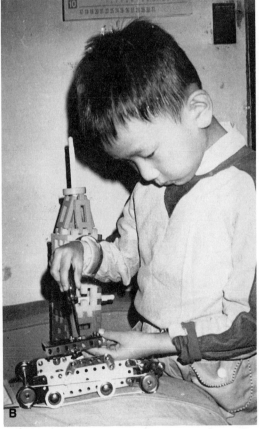

FIGURE 9–9.
Preschoolers develop their fine motor and eye–hand coordination skills as they work on intricate toys, puzzles, and self-help skills such as zipping, buttoning, dressing, and hair combing.

tions of the adults in the program.[35] It is helpful to observe the behavior of these adults with the children: how they reward behavior, give guidance, and interact with the children in general.

Health Assessment

Periodic health assessments are a necessity for young children. The child from 18 to 30 months of age should visit a health professional every 6 months. Checkups at least every 12 months are usually sufficient during the preschool years (see Table 6-4).[36] The child's ability to hear should be tested during these sessions; testing methods vary from technical audiometric methods to whispering to ascertain how well the child hears.

Visual Checkups

The Snellen charts with letters of different sizes are used to determine visual acuity. **Visual acuity** refers to the ability to see near and far objects clearly. The Snellen charts consist of six to thirteen lines of letters in decreasing sizes. Each line is given a value corresponding to the distance from which a person with normal vision is able to see that size print. One line has a value of 20. The individual to be tested stands 20 feet from the chart to try to read each line. If the 20 foot line can be read, then the person has 20/20 vision, the accepted standard for normal acuity. If only the 100 line can be read, the person has 20/100 vision. At the 20 foot distance, this individual can see only what the individual with 20/20 vision can see from 100 feet. Younger children may simply be asked to indicate which direction the three legs of the letter E are pointing (using the Snellen illiterate E chart). The National Society for the Prevention of Blindness recommends the following criteria for referring children for an ophthalmologic examination when using the Snellen chart:[41]

1. Three-year-old children with vision in either eye of 20/50 or less (inability to read the 40 foot line)
2. Children 4 years of age and older with vision in either eye of 20/40 or less
3. Children with a one-line difference or more between the two eyes, even if visual acuity is within passing standards
4. All children who consistently show any of the signs of possible visual disturbances regardless of visual acuity

Many young preschoolers can see the E clearly, but become confused in identifying the direction of the E. Because of this, the Blackbird Vision Screening System was devised. It is a modified E that resembles a bird and a story about a Blackbird that helps hold the child attention.[30] The Rader Visual Acuity Screening Chart uses "happy face" and "sad face" to assess the visual acuity of the younger preschool child.

Physical Integrity

Motor functioning and reflex performance are also tested during health visits. One of the reflexes is the popular knee jerk, which is elicited by tapping the knee with a medical hammer. The child's pupils should constrict when a flashlight is beamed into the eyes.[25] Several other neurological assessments are performed on the child, since every human function—biophysical, cognitive, and psychosocial—is controlled by neural impulses.

Every child 3 years of age and older should have the blood pressure taken at least annually.[1] In the United States, high blood pressure is being diagnosed in children of all ages with an increasing frequency. The problems that lead to high blood pressure may be prevented by teaching the child and counseling the parents on stress reduction, weight control, salt intake, and exercise. The American Academy of Pediatrics recommends blood tests to determine cholesterol levels in children over 2 years of age in families with a history of hyperlipidemia or early myocardial infarction (heart attack).[12] Children of black and Mediterranean ancestry should be evaluated for **sickle cell disease,** a blood illness in which there is a tendency for blood to thicken so much that it is unable to flow to various parts of the body.

Dental Visits

The child should visit the dentist when all 20 deciduous teeth have emerged. It is best that the child meet the dentist and see the dental equipment while the child is feeling no pain. The child should receive a simple explanation from parents on what to expect before this visit and each subsequent dental checkup. There are several colorful picture-story books written especially for children that describe what to expect when they go to the dentist. The early visits are a time for an assessment of the oral hygiene practices followed at home. Dental visits are encouraged every 6 months after the initial checkup. There are dentists who specialize in the care of young children (pedodontists); other dentists may be highly recommended to parents as being able to work well with children (Fig. 9-10).

TOILET TRAINING: A COORDINATION OF DOMAINS

Parents in different cultures vary widely in their concept of when and how to teach children to control body functions. The reason for this variance is ascribed to different attitudes regarding cleanliness, self-control, and the question of who should teach the child. The variety in timing and methods of toilet training found among cultures is also present among individual families in different subcultures. Some socioeconomic classes in the United States think that a child should be completely trained by the second birthday—a most difficult expectation for many children to meet. As with any other type of learning, the biophysical, socioaffective, and cognitive domains of development must all have matured enough in the individual child to allow mastery of the new behavior. When these interdependent domains have reached adequate levels of maturity, they are capable of aiding the child in meeting both short-term goals (e.g., not wetting the pants, telling

FIGURE 9–10.
Regular health checkups are essential during the toddler and preschool years. A gentle, individualized approach engenders trust and cooperation.

mother he or she has to "go") and may influence long-range behaviors (e.g., the degree of self-assertion in future, social relationships of giving and receiving).

The child's mastery of total training occurs over a period of time. Bowel control is usually achieved first, gradually followed by daytime bladder control, with nighttime bladder control being last. Daytime bladder control rarely occurs with much success before the age of 2 years.[14] As in other areas of development, normal children express a wide variety of individual behaviors. Some children may take longer than others to become "totally" trained; some may experience relapses in the process due to their concentration on other issues when the bladder or bowel happen to be full.

Physical Readiness for Toilet Training

In our culture, some method of toilet training is expected to be initiated by the time the child has reached late toddlerhood. The child should want to assume some responsibility for toileting; he or she should also know what the need to go to the bathroom feels like and what to do about this feeling. Neurological maturity is essential before the child can feel the sensations that indicate a full bladder or bowel and can volun-

tarily control the muscles that retain or release the contents. These physical signs of readiness, however, do not necessarily imply that the child is ready for toilet training in the other domains. To maximize individual potential, the child must be prepared in all domains.

Parents should not begin toilet training until the child is mature enough physically, cognitively, and emotionally to cooperate in the social skill of controlling the time and the location of elimination of body wastes. No two children are ready for toilet training at exactly the same time.

For the child to be ready for toilet training, the nerves and muscles that control the urinary and anal sphincters must be mature. These sphincters operate at a reflex level until there is sufficient myelinization of the neural pathways to allow voluntary control (which includes both contraction to "hold in" and relaxation to "let go"). This control is not *physically* possible until *after* the child is walking. In every other neuromuscular skill the child has mastered he or she has learned how to *contract* the specific muscles which create the desired body action. However, for bowel or bladder emptying, the child must learn how to *relax* the specific muscle—a much more difficult task. Because of this difference, many toddlers will try hard to evacuate (unsuccessfully) only to release the contents 2 to 5 minutes *after* leaving the toilet!

The gross motor skills of walking, perhaps climbing, sitting, and squatting, and the fine motor skills to remove clothing also are necessary for toilet training. Boys may begin toilet training in either the standing or sitting position (imitating other males during the toddler/preschool years is a powerful motivator for standing).

Signs of Cognitive and Psychosocial Readiness

The average toddler is not *cognitively* or *psychologically* ready to begin toilet training until 18 to 24 months of age. As the toddler becomes aware first that the bowel needs emptying, and then later that the bladder is full, he or she learns to indicate this knowledge by pulling at the diapers, grasping the genital area, squatting on the spot where he or she is standing, and eventually repeating a word or phrase that has come to be associated with the feelings being experienced. Many children have learned the difference between "wet" and "dry" if the caregiver has encouraged such fundamental symbolic thought in caring for the child previous to toilet training (e.g., "Your diaper is wet, let's change it and make it dry" or "Your diaper is still dry").

Anyone who has cared for a toddler will recall that before toilet training, the child eliminates regardless of where he or she is, what time it is, or who is holding the child. Gradually, the child learns that this behavior is socially unacceptable and that it makes the parent happy when he or she makes use of facilities expressly made for such purposes. The child learns to accept these values best through gentle and consistent reinforcement. In addition, around 2 years of age the toddler's desire to please significant others emerges, and the child begins to learn that sometimes it is more beneficial to please the parent by "holding on," rather than by satisfying oneself by "letting go."

Signs of Parental Readiness for Toilet Training

There are times when the family is not ready for the child to initiate such learning. Crises such as illness of the caregiver, a new baby or a child joining the family, the death of a family member, or a family move from one location to another warrant the delay of actual toilet training until the family stressors are reduced. The caregiver must recognize the child's level of readiness and be willing to invest the time required for toilet training.

How To Begin

Developing Bowel Control

Many children move their bowels at approximately the same time each day. Since eating stimulates bowel action, evacuation frequently occurs shortly after a meal. Therefore, the training process is facilitated if the caregiver observes the child's habits and places the child on the potty at the time a movement is expected. This action accustoms the toddler to sitting on the potty to evacuate the bowels. Sometimes, after a few weeks of this form of conditioning, an infant or young toddler may discover the ability to "push" and learn to evacuate the bowels whenever he or she is placed on and feels the potty. This ability does *not,* however, indicate that the young toddler is trained. The child has not indicated to anyone a desire to "go"; he or she has not gone to the potty alone or pulled the pants down. It indicates that the primary caregiver has been successful in "catching" the child when he or she had to "go." Some perfectly normal babies do not move their bowels daily. The use of enemas or any other form of medication without the guidance of a pediatrician is potentially dangerous both physically and psychologically.

When toddlers are placed on the potty, they should be told in a positive manner why they have been placed there. They should not be required to sit there until they eliminate lest they experience feelings of frustration, shame, or doubt because of their inability to please someone they love very much. After approximately 5 minutes, the child should be removed, wiped, and if successful, rewarded with praise. If the child was not successful, praise can still be given for any cooperative efforts that were made (such as sitting relatively still and not trying to get off).

Giving toys while the child sits on the potty may only divert attention from the task at hand. Initially, the adult should sit with the child (as long as the experience does not become an expected social occasion). This strategy may prove especially helpful with the child who is somewhat anxious because of what a movement feels like. Sitting with the child who is starting toilet training may also help if the child is

apprehensive about the toilet itself. In such a situation, it is especially useful to use a less threatening child-size potty chair or a toilet that allows the child to sit comfortably and more securely with the feet on the floor or a footstool. Having the feet on the floor also gives the child better control in "pushing" and thus in evacuating the bowels. Because many young children are afraid of the sound of a toilet flushing and because some do not understand why the adult wants to discard immediately the much-wanted product from their bodies, it may be better initially to empty the potty and flush the toilet **after** the child is either off the large toilet (if it was used) or out of the bathroom completely.

Sometimes reading a book to the child written for children about toilet training contributes to motivation and aids the learning process. These illustrated books usually reinforce the process by praising the child who acts like a "big girl" or a "big boy." Changing from diapers to training pants makes some children feel more responsible in assuming some control of their elimination. If the child does not respond to, or thoroughly protests against, any of these training tips, he or she may not be ready for bowel training, and all attempts at training should be discontinued for several weeks.

Toddlers, by nature, like to explore and "mess." Playing with and smearing of feces, however, must be restricted because it is unsanitary and causes arousal of disgust in others that might be interpreted by the toddler as self-deprecating. The best way to handle such activity is to direct the child in a consistent and nonpunitive way to a more constructive form of activity (e.g., self-wiping or indulging in fingerpainting, squeezing clay, or even crayoning) without calling much attention to the initial socially unacceptable action. However, the opportunity to explore the "product" once or twice under supervision may satisfy the child's curiosity and thus the tendency to explore feces at a less opportune time and in a less opportune fashion when the parent is not present.

Developing Bladder Control

Many of the strategies used in promoting effective bowel training also apply to helping a child establish bladder control. Bladder training, although it indirectly begins at the same time as bowel training, usually takes much longer to achieve. Even when the child's bladder is physically capable of holding urine for more than a 2-hour period, the average child may still not be ready cognitively or psychosocially for bladder training. It is often around the age of 12 to 18 months that the child notifies the primary caregiver *after* he or she has already wet. Gradually the child begins to recognize the feeling of the full bladder as a signal that he or she needs to "go," and will then gradually learn to inform the adult before the act has occurred. But even at this point, there may not be time to get to the toilet. The child may be too busy to notice a full bladder and will have accidents. As a matter of fact, many children up to 5 years of age sometimes have to be reminded to take a trip to the bathroom.

Little boys vary in their wish to sit or to stand when urinating (usually they can master going to the bathroom alone and stand to urinate by 3½ years of age). Little girls who have had the opportunity to observe members of the opposite gender void may try to imitate this behavior by standing over the potty; this generally proves to be a frustrating experience that quickly extinguishes itself. An understanding adult is essential. To the child, learning about bladder control is a very serious experience.

Nighttime control of the bladder usually comes after daytime control has been established. Children vary in the age at which they are able to stay dry for the duration of the night. In most cases, the establishment of such control occurs simply because the child's bladder has matured sufficiently to hold a larger amount. Girls tend to gain such control earlier than boys; relaxed children tend to stay dry throughout the night at an earlier age than high-strung children.[36]

Doctors and researchers do not always agree on the age at which **enuresis** (bed-wetting) becomes abnormal. Limiting fluids in the evening and getting the child up to go to the bathroom before the parents retire for the night are two supportive measures. If a child continues to wet the bed when most of his or her peers are remaining dry, the caregivers should seek the advice of a health professional. It may be that the child is experiencing anxiety in some dimension of life (e.g., too rigid toilet training, inability to make friends, inadequate private time with parents, arrival of a new baby in the family). Such anxiety needs to be identified and dealt with. The child delay in remaining dry throughout the night may also be due to a physiological factor or minor infection.

No matter when an individual child's total toilet training is considered to be complete, there will be times when relapses or accidents occur. When this happens, the adult should handle the situation in a manner that promotes healthy toilet training. Lack of parental empathy coupled with harsh discipline are felt by some to foster an obsessive, meticulous, rigid personality. It is the caregiver's calm and patient reassurance that helps the child to establish pride in this new responsibility, instead of shame and doubt about the ability to function in an independent, acceptable manner.

CONCLUSION

Many factors facilitate increased complexity of the motor functioning of young children: increased muscle size, continued myelinization of the neural pathways, and the opportunity to practice a skill. As the various components of the nervous system grow and develop and as the muscular and skeletal systems become more mature, the young child's movements come under greater conscious control and allow for more refined movements. Stronger bones and a tougher skin help to protect the child from serious injury when experiencing the many tumbles and spills associated with learning and perfecting new skills. Curious toddlers and preschoolers must be observed carefully and taught not to place foreign bodies into the various orifices (e.g., nose, ear, vagina) of their often self-examined, growing bodies.

The toddler's and preschooler's internal physical systems mature sufficiently to allow the child to maintain physiological homeostasis. Under stress, however, they function in a less adaptive manner. Active, systematic stimulation of the senses allows the child to become more aware of the environment and his or her place within it.

A child is not *biophysically* ready to begin toilet training until late toddlerhood. The child must also be ready in the cognitive and psychosocial domains before toilet training is initiated. Some children are too enthralled by or involved with the environment and its potentials to pay attention to the sensations and activities of their own bodies. Parental patience is essential as they help the child to become aware of social expectations.

The toddler and preschooler years are critical periods in which parents can help the child to establish good eating habits: The child can be encouraged to consume nutritious foods and snacks instead of eating junk foods that contain high levels of saturated fats, salt, and sugar. These early years are also the optimal time for establishing habits of oral hygiene. Similarly, the way in which parents guide the child's sleep routines can have a profound effect on physical, socioaffective, and cognitive realms of development. Adequate sleep, rest, and exercise optimize healthy development of all domains of the toddler and preschooler. Clothes and shoes should fit so that the child can comfortably engage in physical activity and have room to grow.

Regular medical checkups are essential. The young child's developing immune system is greatly assisted in fighting infection if he or she is receiving immunizations according to the recommended schedule.

REFERENCES

1. American Academy of Pediatrics. (1988). *American Academy of Pediatrics guidelines for health supervision*. Elk Grove Village, IL: American Academy of Pediatrics.
2. Asher, C. (1975). *Postural variations in childhood*. Boston: Butterworth.
3. Ayres, A. J. (1972). *Sensory integration and learning disorders*. Los Angeles, CA: Western Psychological Services.
4. Behrman, S. J., & Patton, G. W. (1988). Evaluation of infertility in the 1980s. In S. J. Berman, R. W. Kistner, & G. W. Patton (Eds.), *Progress in infertility* (3rd ed., pp. 1–22). Boston: Little, Brown.
5. Brazelton, T. B. (1989). *Toddlers and parents: A declaration of independence* (rev. ed.). New York: Delacorte Press/Seymour Lawrence.
6. Conner, F. P., Williamson, G. G., & Seip, J. M. (1978). *Program guide for infants and toddlers with neuromotor and developmental disabilities*. New York: Teachers College Press.
7. Damerel, P. (1976). How to choose shoes that fit your kid's feet. *Family Health/Today's Health, Aug. 1976, 36*.
8. Eckert, H. M. (1987). *Motor development* (3rd ed.). Indianapolis: Benchmark Press.
9. Esslinger, P. N. (1982). The preschooler. In M. J. Smith, et al. (Ed.), *Child and family: Concepts of nursing practice*. New York: McGraw-Hill.
10. Food and Nutrition Board, National Academy of Sciences-Na-

tional Research Council. (1989). *Recommended dietary allowances* (10th ed.). Washington, DC: The Academy Press.

11. Gallahue, D. (1990). Cited in: Poest, C.A., Williams, J. R., Witt, D. W., & Atwood, M. E., Challenge me to move: Large muscle development in young children. *Young Children, 1990:45*(45), 4–10.

12. Gates, D. M., & McClure, M. J. (1989). Forestalling the progress of heart disease. *MCN: American Journal of Maternal Child Nursing, 14,* 174–178.

13. Horner, M. M. E., & McClellan, M. A. (1981). Toilet training: Ready or not? *Pediatric Nursing, 7*(1), 17.

14. Ilg, F. L., Ames, L. B., & Baker, S. M. (1982). *Child behavior* (rev. ed.). New York: Barnes & Noble.

15. Institute for Aerobic Research. (1987). *Get fit.* Dallas, TX: Institute for Aerobic Research.

16. Kendall, H. O., Kendall, F. P., & Boynton, D. A. (1981). *Posture and Pain.* Malabar, FL: Robert E. Krieger.

17. Kilmon, C., & Helpin, M. L. (1981). Update on dentistry for children. *Pediatric Nursing, 7*(5), 41.

18. Kronmiller, J. E., & Nirschl, R. F. (1985). Preventive dentistry for children. *Pediatric Nursing, 11,* 446–49.

19. Lamontagne, L. L., Mason, K. R., & Hepworth, J. T. (1985). Effects of relaxation on anxiety in children: Implications for coping with stress. *Nursing Research, 34,* 289–292.

20. Lipsitt, L. P. (1987). Breakfast and sugar: Are there effects on children's behavior? *Brown University Child Behavior and Development Letter, 3*(12), 5–6.

21. Lowrey, G. H. (1986). *Growth and development of children* (8th ed.). Chicago: Year Book.

22. Manter, J. T. (1987). *Manter and Gantz's essentials of clinical neuroanatomy and neurophysiology* (7th ed.). Philadelphia: F. A. Davis.

23. Masiak, M. J., et al. (1985). *Fluids and electrolytes through the life cycle.* Norwalk, CT: Appleton-Century-Crofts.

24. McManus, I. C., Sik, G., Cole, D. R., Mellon, A. F., Wong, J., & Kloss, J. (1988). The development of handedness in children. *British Journal of Development Psychology, 6,* 257–273.

25. Meier, E. M. (1983). Evaluating head trauma in infants and children. *MCN: American Journal of Maternal Child Nursing, 8,* 54–57.

26. Metheny, N. M., & Snively, W. D. (1983). *Nurses' handbook of fluid balance* (4th ed.). Philadelphia: J. B. Lippincott.

27. Pipes, P. L. (1989). *Nutrition in infancy and childhood* (4th ed.) St. Louis: Times Mirror/Mosby College Pub.

28. Poest, C. A., Williams, J. R., Witt, D. W., & Atwood, M. E. (1990). Challenge me to move: Large muscle development in young children. *Young Children, 45*(5), 4–10.

29. Ramsey, N. L., & Haugan, B. (1982). The toddler. In M. J. Smith, et al (Ed.), *Child and Family: Concepts of nursing practice.* New York: McGraw-Hill.

30. Sato-Viacrucsis, K. (1985, Spring). The evolution of the Snellen E to the Blackbird. *School Nurse,* pp. 18–19.

31. Satter, E. (1984). Developmental guidelines for feeding infants and young children. *Food and Nutrition News, 56*(4), 21–26.

32. Scandrett, S., & Vecker, S. (1985). Relaxation training. In G. M. Bulechek & J. C. McCloskey (Eds.), *Nursing interventions: Treatments for nursing diagnoses.* Philadelphia: W. B. Saunders.

33. Schumann, M. J. (1981). Neuromuscular relaxation: A method for inducing sleep in young children. *Pediatric Nursing, 7*(5), 9.

34. Scipien, G. M., et al. (1990). *Pediatric nursing care.* St Louis: C. V. Mosby.

35. Smith, N. J. (1981). Medical issues in sports medicine. *Pediatrics in Review, 2*(8), 229.

36. Spock, B., & Rothenberg, M. B. (1985). *Baby and child care* (rev. and updated ed.). New York: Pocket Books.

37. Starfield, B. (1985). Giant steps and baby steps: Toward child health. *American Journal of Public Health, 75,* 599.

38. Wei, S. H. (1981). Nutrition, diet, fluoride, and dental health. *Pediatric Basics, 30,* 4.

39. Weiss, J., et al. (1981). Purchasing infant shoes: Attitudes of parents, pediatricians, and store manager. *Pediatrics, 67*(5), 718–720.

40. Wenger, D. R. (1983). Baby needs shoes. *Foot Ankle, 3,* 207.

41. Whaley, L. F., & Wong, D. L. (1987). *Nursing care of infants and children* (3rd ed.). St. Louis: C. V. Mosby.

42. Wickstrom, R. L. (1983). *Fundamental motor patterns* (3rd ed.). Philadelphia: Lea & Febiger.

43. Williams, S. R. (1990). *Essentials of nutrition and diet therapy* (5th ed.). St. Louis: Times Mirror/Mosby College Publishing.

10

The mind... is so constituted that it cannot remain content with the mere observation of facts but always attempts to penetrate into the inner reason of things.

—GEORGES SOREL

Cognitive Development of the Toddler and the Preschooler

Clara S. Schuster and Shirley S. Ashburn

The child's insatiable curiosity and quest for new experiences are probably greater during toddlerhood than in any other period of life.[15] Burton White views this time as "the second half of the most important period" for educating a child.[30] The boundless inquisitiveness and indefatigable energy set the stage for conflict with the social environment while increasing knowledge.

This inquisitive behavior is carried over into the preschool years when knowledge acquisition is greatly facilitated by the increased refinement and coordination of neuromuscular and neuroperceptual skills. A child will shake, sniff, and visually examine an unfamiliar object to determine its qualities and functions. Every sensory modality may be called upon to enable the child to "know" an object or person completely. By harnessing and focusing energies, the child continues the process of learning how to learn and becomes a teacher of self through thorough explorations (Fig. 10-1).

The cognitive ability to differentiate, synthesize, and interpret stimulus input is not yet fully perfected, nor does the child have the linguistic skill to precisely verbalize observations. Nevertheless, most are able to share their observations quite adequately. One 5-year-old (informing his father about his brother's encounter with a skunk) exhibited a classic mixing of the senses when he said, "You ought to see Jimmy—he smells so bad you can hear him!" Other socioaffective sensations (e.g., pleasure, discomfort, anger) and the meanings they have for individual children are also subject to various interpretations (for example, "I'm so mad my hand wants to hit you!" or "I'm so happy that I taste like chocolate cake!"). The complex mechanisms that enable an individual to identify and to control emotions effectively are not fully developed during these years, but a foundation is laid. As children become more verbal, they are better able to share the volume and complexity of thoughts entering their very active minds.

COGNITION

Piaget's Substage VI of Sensorimotor Intelligence

The last subphase of the sensorimotor period of cognition (Piaget's substage VI: *the invention of new means through mental combinations*) extends to the toddler years. It is during this stage (18–24 months) that the toddler makes the transition from the sensorimotor level of intelligence to **representational intelligence** (the ability to picture an event in the mind). Mental representations enable the child to play out in the mind a sequence of behaviors without actually having to participate in the event physically or to manipulate the physical aspects of the event. In substage V (see Chap. 7), the infant attained new means for solutions to problems through laborious trial and error experimentation. In substage VI, because many solutions can be tried out in

FIGURE 10–1.
The best preparation for school and adult-hood is parents who capitalize on the child's curiosity by pointing out and explaining phenomenon in the world around the child.

the mind, the child is capable of inventing new means much more quickly. Furthermore, the child also can remember the actions of others no longer present and imitate them (delayed imitation).

This new cognitive accomplishment is reflected in the child's advanced concept of objects. He or she can now find an object hidden by invisible displacement (i.e., searching for and finding objects that the child has not observed being hidden). The child knows that objects are permanent and that they (as well as significant people) exist even though they cannot be seen. The child can recall some previous hiding places and will search them first, doing his or her best to hunt for the object until it is found.

Through the use of this new capacity for mental representations, the toddler can begin to predict many cause–effect relationships accurately. For example, the child begins to have an awareness that some situations may cause physical injury (climbing too high, running down a hill too fast, touching a hot surface) and will withdraw from the danger. Subsequent intellectual development continues primarily within the symbolic realm, as opposed to working through sensorimotor experiences. Sensorimotor experiences continue to be important, but thoughts and actions are dominated by representational activities.

Piaget's Semiotic (Symbolic) Function

When the child is approximately 1½ years old, a cognitive process appears that is fundamental to the development of language, mental imagery, and symbolic gestures. This process, called the **semiotic** (or symbolic) function, consists of the ability to represent something (a *signified* something: object, event, conceptual schema, and so forth) by means of a *signifier,* which is differentiated from other objects and serves a representative purpose (Fig. 10-2).[26]

Piaget says that although true mental representations do not exist in the early sensorimotor substages, young babies do begin to recognize **significates**—the actual object, event, action, or behavior.[26] Receptive (or recognition) intelligence is dependent on memory of previous contact or experience. The essential difference between a child who is in the sensorimotor stage and one who is at a representational level of cognition is the latter's increased ability to mentally manipulate symbols that represent the environment.[18] The foundations of symbolic activity are laid during the sensorimotor stage.

The baby may identify some salient feature or part of the significate as an indicator (index or signal) that the schema is present. An **index** or signal is usually undifferentiated from its significate (or that which is signified), so a young baby who sees an orange ball (the significate I) and focuses on the color (the signal) may immediately perceive that it is orange juice (the significate II). The baby's specific-to-specific association that all orange objects are orange juice is an example of transductive reasoning, which is more fully described later in this chapter.

Motor meaning develops in substage III, when the infant begins to imitate an object by reproducing a simple action that is associated with its presence. For example, making sucking movements of the mouth when seeing the nipple, or moving the fingers when seeing a cat (as if recreating the tickle sensation of touching the fur). In substage IV, *symbolic meaning* takes place when the child associates an object or action (the glass, the keys) with its symbolic meaning (milk, mother's departure). During substage V, the infant will begin to imitate some simple behaviors while the adult is exhibiting the same behavior, for example, dusting the furniture or pretending to eat.

Piaget does not believe, however, that the child is thinking in truly representative fashion until he or she can inter-

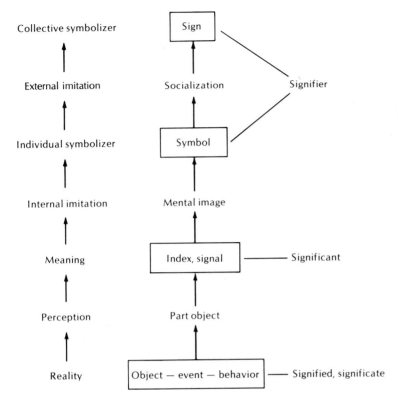

Collective symbolizer	Sign	
↑	↑	
External imitation	Socialization	Signifier
↑	↑	
Individual symbolizer	Symbol	
↑	↑	
Internal imitation	Mental image	
↑	↑	
Meaning	Index, signal	Significant
↑	↑	
Perception	Part object	
↑	↑	
Reality	Object — event — behavior	Signified, significate

FIGURE 10–2.
Differentiation between signified and signifier (semiotic function). A system of ready-made collective signs is inadequate and hard for the young child to master; consequently these signs are acquired over a period of many years. In the early months, only concrete, time-limited reality has any meaning to the child. Gradually the child recognizes a significant part of the phenomenon as an indication that the significate is present or is soon to be present. Marked advance in cognitive structuring is evidenced when the child is able to retain or to recall a mental image of the significate. Eventually, this idiosyncratic, personal significant is accommodated to the culturally accepted gestural (e.g., sign language) or verbal symbolizer. It is not until the child as a fairly good concept of verbal or gestural collective symbolizers that he or she is able to comprehend and to accept the even more abstract concept of written collective symbolizers.

nally evoke some word or image in the mind *without* some form of external cue. Piaget observes that during the last substage of the sensorimotor period, the child begins to imitate a schema when it is absent (e.g., pretend dusting the furniture or driving a car). This delayed imitation is proof that the child can internally represent or form a mental image. The most common example of representative thought is the use of language (or collective signs) to represent an object that is not immediately present (this can lead to confusion if the child is still at a level where the meaning of the word used is still very personal or is not known to the person with whom the child is conversing!). When a child learns to write, he or she learns that written signs in addition to verbal signs can represent objects, events, or concepts. Each level of symbolic representation is one step more abstract than the previous level. It also becomes obvious that the steps are sequential, since they build on each other. Therefore, inadequate sensorimotor experience may delay or prevent formation of adequate indexes and thus the ability to develop more abstract representation of an object.

Semiotic functioning expands and becomes stabilized between 2 and 4 years of age. In addition to changing mental symbols into words to communicate with others, the child also consciously uses one object to represent another in "make-believe" or symbolic play (object substitution) because the two objects have some common feature that is used as an index for both. The child distorts reality by taking into account only the characteristics of the object that meets imme-

diate needs (assimilative process). The index may be shape, color, movement, or any other salient feature of the object. Consequently, a shell may become a cup, a cap, or a fan with equal facility; it may also be a boat, a flower, or even a telephone, depending on the child's skill at specific-to-specific association, which is essential to conscious representational thought and symbolic play (Fig. 10-3).

Piaget's Preoperational Stage

During Piaget's preoperational stage (2 to 6 or 7 years of age), new cognitive processes allow the child to use mental symbols to think about events of the past, to anticipate the future, and to think about what might be going on somewhere else at the present moment. In the beginning, the child will probably call every night in the past "last night" and every day in the future "tomorrow" and will love to ask if other boys and girls are getting up to eat breakfast just as he or she is preparing to do.

The preoperational stage is divided into two substages: preconceptional thought and intuitive thought. Because toddlers base their thinking heavily on the concrete perceptions and actions of their immediate environment, Piaget labels their thinking *preconceptional*.[25] Until a child is halfway through the preschool years, he or she is unable to form true concepts. Up to that time, the child inconsistently assigns one word to several rather similar actions instead of using one word to identify just one class of objects (for example,

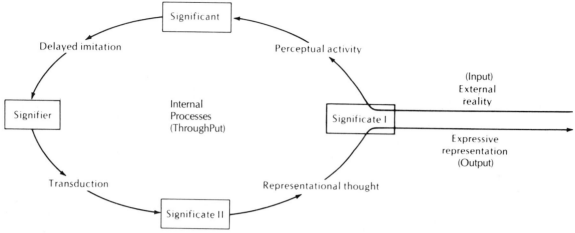

FIGURE 10–3.

Operational dynamism of representational thought, symbolic function, or symbolic play. Significate I is the actual object or event (which becomes representative for Significate II through representational or symbolic thought). Significate II is the signified object or event. "As long as egocentric assimilation of reality to the subject's own action prevails, the child will require symbols; hence symbolic play or imaginative play, the purest form of egocentric and symbolic thought, the assimilation of reality to the subject's own interest and the expression of reality through the use of images fashioned by himself."[25] Perceptual activity is the incomplete accommodation of present significate (e.g., egocentric distorting or receptive assimilation), in which the child zeros in on just one feature. This significate is placed in the category with all other objects/experiences using the same index. In delayed imitation, the association with the category enables the child to trigger memories of other objects/experiences within that category with the choice of one of them (signifier) as an alternate to reality. Transduction is representative assimilation. Centration on significant specific-to-specific association enables the child to pretend the other features commonly associated with the chosen signifier and to ignore reality, thus using one object/experience to represent another. Representational thought includes (1) ludic (play) symbol—expressive assimilation, symbolic play; (2) conceptual activity—representative imitation; and (3) the beginning of representative adaptation, which is early cognitive representation leading to conceptual representation or primitive conceptual framework.

"Daddy" describes any male voice on the telephone; "Nanny" may be any woman with white hair and glasses).

Intuitive thinking (4 to 7 years of age) emerges as the child begins to realize the ability of words to truly represent objects, events and actions, thoughts, fears, and feelings. The intuitive child can more efficiently differentiate between signifiers (mother getting her pocketbook) and significates (mother going out to the car), realizing that the pocketbook does not necessarily have to be associated with mother leaving or going for a ride. During the intuitive substage, the child begins to be able to give reasons for beliefs and a rationale for actions. The logic, however, remains biased and immature or illogical by adult standards. Intuitive thinking enables the child to internally represent, relive, and reshape events. Early preoperational thought is dominated by seven conceptual schemes.[9] These characteristics often serve as obstacles to what is commonly referred to as *adult logic:*

Egocentrism
Centration
Focus on states
Illogical thought
Action rather than abstraction
Irreversibility
Transductive reasoning

Egocentrism

The thoughts of the toddler and the preschooler continue to be greatly influenced by what is seen, heard, or otherwise experienced at a given moment. Although social interaction and empathy increase, the older preoperational child still is not able to see the viewpoint of another person. The only thought in mind is, "This is how the world looks to me." As a result, the preoperational child never questions his or her own subjective perceptions or viewpoints because they are, as far as the child is concerned, the only thoughts possible and consequently must be correct. Since the egocentric child can only think about things in terms of the subjective meanings attached to them, he or she cannot understand and will become angry when others do not understand his or her concrete, idiosyncratic speech and thoughts.

Cognitive egocentrism prevents the child from understanding another's experience, feelings or viewpoint. If asked to point to the picture that replicates object positions on a table, the preoperational child will choose the picture that shows objects in the same spatial relationship that he or she sees. However, if asked to choose a picture that represents how a person in another position at the table would see the same objects, the child is unable to do so with accuracy. Piaget says that it is not until the child's thoughts and those of peers conflict in verbal exchange (usually around 6 or 7 years) that the child begins to accommodate to others; egocentric thought may give way under social pressures at this time.

Centration

Another characteristic of preoperational thinking is evidenced by the child's tendency to *center,* or focus on only one aspect of an experience, neglecting to process information from other aspects of the same situation. This reduced environmental awareness facilitates symbolic play (see Fig. 10-3), but at the same time often limits the preoperational child's ability to solve what adults would consider the most simple of problems. When solving a puzzle, the child may concentrate on only one detail of the piece, trying to force that segment into any similar space, ignoring other relevant cues such as color or overall contour. Consequently, multiple piece puzzles, and especially directional puzzles are difficult to solve, especially during the preconceptional substage. The child also finds it difficult to follow more than one direction at a time, a frustration to parents that often precipitates conflict or unwarranted punishment. But, initially, the child is unable to *decenter.* If he or she does, then the first thought may be eclipsed by the intensity of concentrating on the second issue. The ability to follow two directions in sequence or to attend to two or more critical factors simultaneously emerges gradually during the intuitive substage (Fig. 10-4).

Focus on States

The preoperational child who is observing a sequence of changes or successive states does not understand how an object is transformed from one state to another. If a preschooler is given a series of 4 or 5 pictures of an apple being eaten, the child will be unable to reconstruct the series of events in terms of a beginning-to-end relationship. The child may choose the picture of the whole apple (the initial state) and an apple core (the transformed state), but is confused as to what to do with the pictures of partially eaten apples.

Action Rather Than Abstraction

The preoperational child simply "runs through" the symbols or mental representations for an event as if actually participating in the event itself. This concreteness is ever-present during the preoperational stage (as opposed to the analyzing and synthesizing of adults). Even the activities of others are viewed vicariously. One often can observe body movements of the child—especially the hands, which mimic those of the person whom the child is watching.

Illogical Thought

Because the preoperational child is unable to order all the sequences of an event realistically, he or she will exhibit a lack of consistent direction in thinking. Some successive conclusions will contradict one another (for example, "Only mommies can have babies" or "Men can have babies if they are married"). The child throughout these early years feels no need to justify a rationale (and even if an attempt is made, the

FIGURE 10–4.

In guiding preschoolers through a new learning experience, it is usually beneficial to assign one task at a time. A short attention span is optimally used when directed toward the mastery of individual, sequential steps—especially when mastery of these short-term tasks results in immediate and desirable products.

child would cognitively be unable to reconstruct the steps that led to the conclusions).

Adult:	Tommy, what happens when it rains?
Child:	The sky cries.
Adult:	How does it happen?
Child:	Because we cry.
Adult:	What makes it rain?
Child:	Because we have tears.

The fact that raindrops precipitate from above and that tears fall from our eyes is sufficient reason, Tommy believes, to make the statements he does. In addition, the child at this cognitive level attributes life and feeling to inanimate objects and believes that natural phenomena (e.g., lightning) have a mind and will of their own (see Chap. 18).[24]

Irreversibility

Since the child cannot hold on to two or more relevant or sequential thoughts simultaneously, neither is he or she able to reverse thoughts or follow a line of reasoning back to its beginnings. Because every logical or mathematical statement is reversible, toddlers and preschoolers often become confused or frustrated when older children or adults try to use reasoning with them. One example to illustrate the irreversibility of thought is to ask a 5-year-old if he or she has a brother. The child will answer, "Yes" (assuming the child does indeed have a brother), but when asked if that brother has a brother (or sister), the child will answer, "No." Over half of all children are able to solve this kind of problem correctly by age 7.[19] If a child takes a toy apart, he is unable to remember the sequences for putting it back together. If a child is taken on a walk, he is unable to retrace his steps and return to the original point.

Transductive Reasoning

Piaget sees transductive reasoning as a transition between the reasoning of sensorimotor causality and adult reasoning.[26] Transductive reasoning is synonymous with "specific-to-specific" thinking. Thinking "moves from particular-to-particular, regardless of contradictions, because it is ignorant of the logic of relations" and is unable to seek information systematically.[26] If two things are alike or related in one aspect, the child reasons that they are alike in all aspects; and the child assimilates the real world to his or her subjective experiences. Thus, symbolic play is facilitated. Although there may be no relationship between events, the child will act upon his or her inferences about a causal relationship. However, with transductive reasoning, the child fails to differentiate between *causal* and *casual* relationships.

Cognitive Uniqueness of Early Childhood

As children's language matures, adults tend to believe that the young child imparts words with the same meaning as used by adults. Consequently, adults tend to overestimate the young child's knowledge and understanding. Toddlers and preschoolers still exhibit marked limitations in understanding language meanings and the world around them.

Classification

Children in the preoperational stage tend to group objects and experiences on a perceptual or sensorimotor basis rather than by abstract qualities. Expressive classification activities evolve gradually, first by **matching** identical objects. Gradually, the child is able to match two objects based on one common quality, such as color, shape, name, or use. Eventually, a transitional classification activity, called **chaining**, emerges. The child lines up several objects that bear some relationship to one another (e.g., beads of the same color or shape). However, the index used to match A and B may be different from that used to match B and C, since only one dimension is considered at a time and each matching is

independent of the previous matching (e.g., A and B may be matched by color, but B and C by shape). The child cannot keep the single index in mind through multiple experiences. When the child is able to maintain a constant index for a large group of objects, he or she will then be able to **sort** objects into separate piles or make a long chain of matching items based on a prespecified index. Gradually, the child is able to coordinate two indices at the same time, such as color and shape, thus refining the piles or the chain.

Early classifications are based on concrete indices, such as color. In time, the child is able to make more refined distinctions and to use more abstract qualities, such as use. More abstract classification indices (weight, size, tonal pitch) appear later as the child begins to make quantitative comparisons of the same index. Objects can then be placed in order according to height, tonal quality (musical scale), color shade, and so forth in the process known as **seriation.** (This skill generally does not appear until the concrete operational stage.)

Conservation

During the preoperational stage, children usually cannot **conserve,** or hold one dimension invariant, when changes occur in the other dimensions of a schema. For example, if a row of six pennies is suddenly altered in such a way that the spaces between the pennies are made larger, there are still six pennies; that is, the *number* of pennies does not change when an alteration is made in another irrelevant dimension (the length of the row in this case). However, the early preoperational child believes the number of pennies does change in this situation because the child is incapable of conserving the concept of number. By the end of the preoperational period, some forms of conservation (there are several) develop. A continuing discussion of conservation is found in Chapter 21.

Animism

Toddlers and preschoolers, because of their limited experience and knowledge, tend to believe that inert objects are alive, that is, they possess consciousness and can think and function with intent. Thus, when these children fall and injure themselves, it is the rock or the door frame that "hurt me on purpose. That is a bad rock (or door frame)." They may afterward treat the injuring object as an enemy. Other objects can assume a positive valance by their presence during a positive event.

One of the most comprehensive and well-known studies of animistic thinking was made by Piaget, who concluded that children's animistic thinking evolves through four stages.[21]

Stage I: Child believes that all objects, whether animate or inanimate, are alive.
Stage II: Child believes that everything that moves (e.g., wagon, car, pendulum clock) has life.

Stage III: Child believes that objects that can move on their own accord (e.g., sun, wind) are alive.

Stage IV: Child believes that both plants and animals, or maybe just animals, possess life (for further discussion, see Chap. 18).

Time

Young children do not have an adult concept of time (e.g., springtime, afternoon, Wednesday, 9 o'clock). Toddlers relate to the predictable concrete activities of their ritualistic everyday schedule ("We will go shopping *after* your nap"). During the preschool years, time words begin to be associated with weekly and seasonal events. Many 5-year-olds know the days of the week; some begin to recognize that time is measured by the placement of the big and little hands on the clock. As with all concepts, experience with the concept of time and reinforcements to the child's interpretation of time will aid in a correct understanding.

Magical Thought

Young children, observing that adults make things happen with ease, often miss the action that caused the event. They attribute the result to magical powers—thoughts and wishes alone can make it happen. Most parents, having already learned the sequence of events, or knowing the cause–effect relationships, warn a child what will happen. Some parents, anticipating the child's needs, meet them before the child expresses them. These events lend credence to the concept that parents can read minds or have magical powers of thought. The preoperational child begins to believe that magic, that is, personal wishes, and thoughts command the universe—one only needs to learn the right secrets to have "the power." The child stands midway between two worlds: the egocentric world of magic and the world of reality (Fig. 10-5).[10]

Throughout the preoperational period, the child believes that the magical power of thought is the cause of many events and believes that wishing something will make it so. Toddlers and many preschoolers may feel supremely powerful or responsible for happenings, but are also vulnerable to feelings of shame, self-doubt, and guilt. Sometimes a child believes that personal wishes actually caused some tragic event (e.g., the death of an unliked relative, birth of a disabled sibling, or the loss of a parent by divorce) and will need assistance to understand that wishes do not cause events.

Fantasy

Through the use of fantasy or mental play, the child can adapt to the tensions, the anxieties, and the fears experienced about self and the surrounding world.

Fairy Tales

Stories help children to begin the quest toward self-identity and the resolution of developmental tasks. They stimulate imagination, help develop intellect, clarify emotions, reflect anxieties and aspirations, deal with frustrations, and offer guidelines for behavior or potential solutions to the problems that perturb the child.[5, 12]

Fairy tales, constructed by adults who want to pass on some moral, often contain key values of the culture. For example, in Japan, where politeness takes priority over feelings of anger, fear, or individuality, children learn the story of a child, lost in the woods, who meets a child-eating *Kappa*. Overcoming fear, the child bows to the Kappa, who dies when returning the bow, because vital fluid spills from the shallow bowl on the top of its head. In America and Western Europe, where ingenuity and independence are cherished, children learn about *Hansel and Gretel*, two children who escape the child-eating witch of the woods by their use of intelligence.

FIGURE 10–5.
Young children possess a remarkable curiosity that observes and searches for causes. "Hands on' experiences facilitate learning about the world and helps reduce the need to use magical powers of thought.

Both stories are meant to scare children into obedience of parents and to prevent wandering, but each also presents a contingency plan in case curiosity and wanderlust are stronger than experience and obedience, and embraces the basic values of the culture.

Fairy tales and their meaning, like other forms of art, will be interpreted differently by each individual and by the same child at various times in life.[5] Depending on the concerns and needs of a given moment, a child may extract from the story of *Three Billy Goats Gruff, Cinderella,* or *The Three Little Pigs* the idea that the smallest, weakest person is really the smartest—giving support to the child's growing awareness of vulnerability. The child may return to a fairy tale at a later time, searching to enlarge on the same meaning or literally to reconstruct it (e.g., "If I confront the hard realities of life I can find a way to solve them successfully," or "All people have fears; that does not make them a baby!"). The healthy child will extract only those parts of a fairy tale that can be handled and will not be frightened to the point of hysteria (as adults sometimes think) when the witch threatens to eat Hansel and Gretel. Play-acting fairy tales enables children to explore their developing inner selves, to take risks, and to exercise imagination and creativity while facilitating cooperative group activities.[12] Each child puts a unique stamp on the role and develops strengths to face real life as he or she enacts pretend people.

Beliefs

SANTA CLAUS AND FRIENDS. Most American families promote belief in Santa Claus, the Easter Bunny, or the Tooth Fairy; most toddlers and preschoolers accept such beliefs with enthusiasm. Magical thought and inability to reason logically lend to complete acceptance of these legends. Three- and four-year-olds love to hear stories and every detail about Santa (especially the part about the gifts!). Five- and six-year-old children possess an unshakable and dedicated belief in Santa (when magical thought is at its peak).[13] The 6-year-old delights in printing requests to Santa and will deny any suggestion that Santa is not "real." This loyalty and magical thought usually reaches a peak just before the child's seventh birthday and is slowly replaced by a growing skepticism that parallels the child's ability to use more logical thought processes in analyzing the world. First, the belief that Santa travels over the *entire* world may be questioned; then the child may ask how *all* those toys could fit into one sack, or how he gets into a house without a fireplace. This process continues until around 8 or 9 years of age, when the child accepts the concept of Santa Claus as a symbol of love and sharing rather than an actual physical entity. Most parents feel that the joy children derive from an early belief in Santa Claus is worth the minimal disillusionment that may occur later "when they find out the truth."[13]

BELIEF IN A DEITY. Throughout these early years, the child's overall religious beliefs will be a reflection of the kind and amount of religious teaching received in the home environment. How the parents live their beliefs is as important as what they tell the child. Unless the parents' concept of God embodies a belief in a personal relationship, this concept, like the belief in Santa Claus or the Easter Bunny, will begin to fade into an intellectual exercise or cultural myth along with the other traditions of the culture and the family. It will become merely the *symbol* of interpersonal love.

One kind of religious concept that exists in the young preschooler is what Piaget calls the "religion of the parents." Because the small child sees parents as all-knowing, all-powerful, and living forever, the child may equate them with a Supreme Being. It is not unusual for adolescents and adults to continue to depict God as loving or punitive based on the model presented by their own parents.

Ilg and Ames have studied many aspects of the factual (as opposed to the reverential or subjective) side of a child's concept of a deity.[13] They found that it is usually around the age of 4 (when the child seems to begin every other sentence with "Why?" "Who?" "Where?") that a religious sense is first evidenced. Some parents of deep religious persuasion share that their children are sensitive to concepts of God and to their basic belief about a transcendental relationship to God as early as the fourth and fifth years of life. Church school attendance augments but cannot replace the values taught by parents. Children learn best from that which they see and are encouraged to live in everyday life.

Toddlers love music and the rhythm of simple poetry or Scriptures. They also begin to join the family in short mealtime and bedtime prayers. By 3 years of age they love stories. The tales from Scripture and short stories of religious significance can lay a foundation for later spiritual interpretation. Both 4- and 5-year-olds can memorize short prayers and Scriptures, although they can not attribute the same meanings to their recitations as can older children or adults. By age 5, the child's concepts of God and religious affiliation are still nebulous.[3,8] Concepts of God need to be related to the child's egocentric, concrete, everyday life,[4] for example: "God made the rain so the flowers can grow;" "I'm so glad God gave you to me to take care of;" "We obey God because He gave us rules to help us have a happy life;" and "God loves you, even more than I do." Thus, all of life becomes a school when God is related to the totality of experience.[3] Interestingly, Ilg and Ames found many 5-year-olds critical of what they deemed "God's mistakes" (e.g., "Give me one good reason why He made a mosquito").[13]

The 6-year-old may become extremely interested in hearing about the adventures of God (as well as the activities of an opposite entity—the Devil). Many deeply religious family members may become distraught if this enthusiasm later turns to skepticism. It may be of some comfort to know that this skepticism is, in part, a healthy questioning that feeds into a fundamental sense of affiliation and identity.

Those families who do not adhere to a traditional religious affiliation may be frustrated by their 6-year-old's avid interest in God. Piaget says that this interest may be inspired by the child's discovery that the capacity of humans is limited;[23] the child thus attributes the quality of omnipotence to a Supreme Being and begins to see the vulnerability of self and others—especially the parents (see Chap. 18). An invisible God also provides a logical explanation for events not understood.[22] Awareness of a Supreme Being or of something higher than self is also introduced in multiple ways through mass media. It behooves parents to become aware of cultural influences and to provide the religious ideals and training they feel to be important to successful life while the child is still young.

Untruthful Fantasies ("White Lies")

The toddler and the preschooler often appear to have little regard for the truth itself. They may recognize it as something that appears to make their parents happy; nevertheless, many "white lies" are told by children during these years. The young child's white lie is not intended to deceive others; children share what they **want** to be the truth and actually believe what they are saying (e.g., "Kitty tell me she break glass, Mommy"). Other white lies stem from daydreaming, when children review things they would like to be doing in real life. "I fly airplane yesterday, Daddy." The frequency of white lies tends to peak around 4 to 5 years, and decreases in frequency as the child makes cognitive advances. Some children will tell a white lie as a means of trying to justify an event, because they think it is what the adult wants to hear, or because it will make the adult feel better. They may even feel they are protecting a cherished adult. They may repeat what they have heard another say or the white lie may be the externalization of a fantasy. Because they do not realize the inconsistencies or implications, further problems may arise. The point is that the child still has great difficulty distinguishing between reality and fantasy, the magical power of what they want to be true versus causal realities.

The way in which others react to a white lie can affect its extinction as well as the child's self-concept. Acting overly amused (e.g.,"How cute! Say that again for Aunt Mary!") will only serve to reinforce such behavior. This reaction does not help the child begin to understand the value of telling the truth or to perceive the world as it really exists. On the other hand, to assume that the child is maliciously lying and to punish him or her may only make the child feel guilty and ashamed of inner wishes. This reaction will not help the child to form a positive self-concept and may decrease the desire to be creative. A child will benefit most when the reaction consists of acceptance followed by guidance to ascertain what, why, and how something really occurred:

Mother: So, Kitty said she broke the glass?
Child: Uh-huh.
Mother: How did she tell you that?
Child: She open her mouth and say 'Meow'!
Mother: And you think that means she broke the glass?
Child: Kitty say 'Meow.' I think she broke glass.

Mother: Maybe Kitty meant she was sorry **you** broke the glass.
Child: I sorry, mama.
Mother: I know you are, honey. I'm glad you told me the truth. Now, let's clean it up before Kitty hurts her paw on it.

During the period of conscience development, children are most sensitive to the behavior and examples set by adults. They therefore need to live (and love) in an environment where trust and truth are a mutual basis for interpersonal relationships.

Daydreaming

Daydreaming, a form of mental fantasy, differs from regular make-believe or dramatic play. The child engaged in dramatic play is more likely to play out activities and concerns related to daily living, whereas the child who is daydreaming is more often pretending to be either a hero or a martyr (depending on the child's adjustment in the socioaffective domain) and is often startled when the daydreaming is interrupted. Well-adjusted children tend to daydream more about becoming very important people in real life (e.g., an expert in some field or endeavor). On the other hand, if a child is adjusting poorly, daydreams may predominantly revolve around being a misunderstood martyr or a long-suffering invalid. Without doubt, the daydreams of all children, regardless of their psychosocial adjustment, may be influenced by the mass media. Daydreaming, or mental play, may begin during the preschool years and reach a peak during early adolescence. Daydreaming is a way to attain omnipotence by warding off feelings of vulnerability. Daydreaming also offers a way to anticipate and solve real-life problems before they actually occur. Thus, it can be a very positive, adaptive response, especially at this stage of development and again during adolescence.

Too little daydreaming may be as detrimental to a child's (or any individual's) socioaffective development as too much of this form of retreat and entertainment.[27] The healthy child will usually resort to daydreaming when bored or unable to participate in some other form of play. The poorly adjusting child, on the other hand, may frequently substitute daydreaming for other forms of age-appropriate play. Any adult who observes a child consistently daydreaming as a form of avoiding play with other children or in the presence of symptoms of potential abuse, should refer the child and the family for professional guidance. Daydreaming can be a constructive activity when used to expand and understand one's world, but it may become very destructive when used to retreat from the realities of life.

Imaginary Playmates

"Mommy, you shut the car door on Kristin's fingers!" cried Kara as her mother walked toward the house. In actuality, no such person was still sitting in the car experiencing excruciating pain. But as a companion and confidante, Kristin did very much exist (and therefore her fingers were turning blue) in the creative mind of 4-year-old Kara.

Similar experiences are common with children 3 to 6 years of age. Imaginary playmates are invisible to the adult, but their creation has special significance to the child. An adult can often infer the presence of an imaginary playmate by listening to the child's "discussions" with a newfound friend. Imaginary playmates have been known to replace a next-door friend who moved away, an older sibling who started going to school, or a significant other who died. In some instances, imaginary playmates have been "born" as a prop to help the developing child to separate from the parent or when the child needs an outlet for a creative mind. Preschoolers may use imaginary friends to talk to so they can express their innermost feelings and find out more about themselves. Imaginary playmates also take the blame for a misdemeanor, such as spilled milk or clothes put on the wrong way. Imaginary playmates also serve as a forum for dealing with all the new things the child is learning about life, culture, and coping. The child is in control of what happens in the fantasy world, and therefore can begin to deal with reality in bits and pieces, and at his or her own pace.

Imaginary friends are created more often by the child with an above-average intellectual potential. Constructing an imaginary companion involves increased mental activities and energy. Bright children, even in a stimulating environment, may be lonely and thus may have the time as well as the motivation to conceive such a fantasy. One normal and healthy gifted child created a whole community of imaginary friends, who married, gave birth, built houses, gave plays, and even died as part of a fantasy that extended over a 3-year period. (This same child, at the age of 12, wrote a delightful six-chapter fantasy tale, and at 16, a whole novel!) Most imaginary playmates, however, are not adults, but may possess the adult characteristics of power, strength, knowledge, or authority.

A child who is experiencing a fractionalized relationship within the family (e.g., newborn brother or sister, hospitalized parent, or actual child abuse) also has a tendency to construct an imaginary character. The Sullivan school of thought maintains that children who cannot, for some reason, obtain "cooperation" from the significant others in their lives are likely to "multiply the imaginary personifications that fill their minds and influence their behavior."[16] Therefore, imaginary friends can be a sign of pathology.

It is important to emphasize that happy children who are successfully mastering their developmental tasks still envision imaginary playmates during the preschool years. Imaginary friends constitute a normal, creative phenomenon of early childhood. However, not all children share their imagination with adults.

Since having an imaginary friend can, if continued over a lengthy period, alienate the child from other children and encourage an exaggerated egocentrism, adults need to accept the fantasy while trying to work through and decrease the need for its existence. When the child's needs are met, it is not uncommon for the child to announce, for example, that "Kristin went to live somewhere else and isn't coming back." The child who needs professional intervention is the one who would rather stay in a fantasy world than play with peers or engage in activities that would help master the environment at increasingly complex levels.

Fears

Fear is a normal, and often necessary, phenomenon. It is a way of alerting one that danger is present and that something may need to be done to protect oneself. Therefore, there are some fears that a child should have, but they should exist only to the point of aiding the child in averting absolute trauma. A child, for example, should be cautious with a strange dog because of the possibility of harm, but this prudence should not become an immobilizing threat every time the child sees a dog or views a picture of one.

The toddler and the preschooler, in their naïveté often misinterpret situations. It takes time, experience, cognitive growth, and loving guidance for the young child to understand that a screeching siren means someone is receiving help or that the dark makes it easier to sleep. Because children of this age readily absorb the fears held by significant others in their lives, it is appropriate for these other persons to work through their own fears and recognize the attitudes they may be passing on to the child.

Since every child is unique, so will be the child's fears and the way they are formed. One young child may have been handled roughly during an x-ray and thus is afraid of sitting still to have her picture taken. Another child may be afraid of Grandma because he accidentally fell and hit his head as she came through the front door. Vivid imaginations become more active when children are left alone at night. Shadows on the wall take on strange forms; the rustle of leaves outside a window suddenly become mysterious footsteps. Some children will adjust to their fears more quickly than others; nevertheless, some fears tend to be characteristic of certain age levels, for example: fear of loud, sudden noises at age 2; fear of animals at ages 3 and 4; fear of the dark at ages 4 and 5; and fear of the dark and being lost at age 6.

Children demonstrate fear in many ways. They may not always be capable of verbalizing their fears. They may regress (e.g., by resuming thumbsucking, whining, wetting their pants) in the presence or the expectation of the feared object or situation. Other tension outlets (see Chap. 11) may also begin to appear: The child may become cruel (both physically and verbally) toward other people, animals, or toys; or he may be restless or irritable. Although such behaviors can be symptomatic of other things besides fear, they warrant investigation.

A child will frequently attempt to play out fears. For example, a 4-year-old who tries to put a bandage on the family dog may actually be working out how he feels about receiving an immunization in the doctor's office earlier in the day. This action is a way of making the situation more familiar through dramatic play and thus serves as a strategy for handling fear. Therapeutic play, or adult-guided and structured play can be used by practitioners to help children to face fears, stressors, and feelings.[17] However, these approaches do not replace guidance from a child psychologist for a severely disturbed child.

After a young child has been in a fearful situation, he or she may want to have close contact with the parent. The child may also want the adult to listen over and over again to his or her perception of what happened. Recognizing that each child is an individual, and that any general advice is sometimes of limited value, Ilg and Ames have composed a list of "dos" and "don'ts" for assisting the child who is afraid[13]:

Don't make fun of the child's fears.
Don't humiliate him or her in front of others because the child has a fear.
Don't force the child to confront the fear (an unknowing parent may throw a hysterical child into a swimming pool to "get him (or her) over fear of the water").
Don't call the child a "baby" because he or she has a certain fear.
Do realize that with time the child will outgrow the majority of his or her fears.
Do allow the child a respected period of withdrawal from the object or situation that evokes fear before gradual attempts to adjust to it are made. For example, if the child is afraid of cars, first allow the child to sit with you in a car that is not moving.
Do try within reason to avoid situations that scare the child so much that he or she cannot cope.
Do be familiar with the common fears that children naturally experience at various ages.

With a gradual introduction to potentially frightening situations, the young child will begin to learn how to master new situations by small steps instead of withdrawing from them.

Dreams

Just when dreams first appear is open to question. However, Piaget reports that he and his associates have been unable to "find evidence of authentic dreams" until the child is able to symbolize and mentally manipulate events (substage VI). Piaget goes on to say that the youngest age at which he observed definite proof of dreaming was between 21 and 24 months. These children talked in their sleep and gave an account of their dreams when they awoke.[20] Many parents report, however, that their children begin waking up at night around 18 months with crying and expressions of confusion as if they were awakened by a dream (Fig. 10-6).

Piaget was less interested in when dreams first occur, however, and more interested in the type of symbolism present in childhood dreams. The question he asked was whether or not the manifestations of symbolic thought in childhood dreams became more complex as the child developed cog-

DENNIS the MENACE

" HOW COME YOU DON'T REMEMBER MY DREAM? YOU WAS **IN** IT ENOUGH !"

FIGURE 10–6.

This Dennis the Menace cartoon illustrates the preschooler's difficulty distinguishing dreams from reality. (Reprinted courtesy of Dennis the Menace. Copyright by Field Newspaper Syndicate, T.M.®).

nitively. He found that indeed they did become more complicated, although the construction of play is much more "deliberately controlled" than that of dreams, which contain schemata from the unconscious.[20]

The frequency of dreams as well as their content tends to change from one phase of development to the next. The younger 3-year-old may be awakened by a dream, for example, but may not appear to be very disturbed by it. In contrast, the older 3-year-old who experiences a nightmare may require some comforting after calling out in the night that he or she is frightened. If the child's dreams are frightening, they often have a theme related to the fears the child experiences when awake. Dreaming appears to increase in quantity when the child approaches 5 years of age. He or she may have considerable difficulty in going back to sleep after a nightmare and needs the caregiver's calm and reassuring presence until falling asleep again. Parents may help children who have trouble waking from a frightening dream by carrying them into another room or washing their faces gently with cool water.[13]

Preschoolers are learning to distinguish fantasy from

reality and may still be confused about the reality of a dream. Frightening experiences of the day may be blown out of proportion, causing the child to wake up feeling that something terrible is about to happen. Another possibility is that some of the common fears of early childhood take control while the child is sleeping. Not all childhood dreams are unpleasant, however; on the contrary, many children report having a "fun time" while dreaming.

Pleasant dreams occur more often as preschoolers grow older. In his studies, Piaget categorized different dreams according to their content: wish fulfillment, painful experience recalled but given a happy ending, real nightmares, punishment or autopunishment, and dreams that are a "straightforward symbolic translation of an immediate organic stimulus" (e.g., a child with a stomachache may dream of eating a pebble).[20] It might be noted that Freudian psychology places heavy significance on the content and meaning of dreams, theorizing that dreams are an essential part of coping with life. The symbolism of dreams is used by psychoanalysts to help individuals understand problem areas in their lives.

Whatever the true significance of dreaming to a child, it is important to realize that dreams are probably related to unconscious symbolic thought and are soon forgotten by the child who experiences them.

Body Concept

Throughout childhood (and throughout life), the image of one's body and the affective significance of that image are in a state of continual change. In infancy, the child's clearest concepts of self as an entity are based on stimuli from the body. Arms and legs, hands and feet, skin, and gastrointestinal tract all continue to provide sensations that help the child to construct a body image.[29] Despite having lived in the body for 2 or more years, the toddler is unaware of the whole body and its functioning, and might even consider feet or other distal parts as something only peripherally related to self. Some are unaware of the body's position in the amount of space it occupies—a factor leading to clumsiness and running into objects.

Around 3 or 4 years of age, the child's attempts to draw a human figure become recognizable to most adults. These illustrations usually consist of the head (with features such as eyes, nose, ears, and so on being added as the child grows older) and the arms and the legs (drawn as four or more lines issuing from the head). As the child engages in systematic and repetitive gross motor activities (somersaults, climbing, running, obstacle course negotiation, animal pretending), he or she becomes more aware of body parts, body movement, body space, and spatial relationships. By the end of the preschool years, the child should be able to name and move separately all major body parts and be able to move through a room without hitting stationary objects with hips, shoes, arms, and so forth.

A concept of inner body is also emerging during these

years. A study of hospitalized children found that, contrary to traditional belief, even 4-year-olds could name appropriate items contained within their bodies. They tend to conceive that their inner bodies contain elements, such as food, beverages, bowel movements, urine, and blood. Some children also become aware of components, such as bones, heart, nerves, and stomach.[11] By 4 years of age, some children are even aware that the brain is an internal body part associated with an array of distinctly mental acts.[14]

Body Integrity

As preschoolers become more aware of themselves as individuals, they become more concerned about body integrity and intactness (Fig. 10-7). The sense of vulnerability that accompanies growing self-awareness is often manifested in their specific fears or anxieties and in increased awareness of the potential dangers in the environment. The child's fears may or may not be realistic, since they are often related to the child's difficulty in distinguishing fact from fantasy.

The more conscious the child becomes of self as a separate person, an "I," the more he or she appears to fear physical

FIGURE 10–7.
The preschooler's concept of body is constantly changing in accordance with daily experiences. Preschool children are well-known for their conscientious concern about the intactness of their bodies—every scratch and scrape is a crisis.

injury and seeks assistance and consolation when injured. The child's "wholeness" as a personality seems to be closely related to the completeness and integrity with which he or she views the body. Emotionally impaired preschoolers may show no or minimal reactions to pain or injury.

The child values the body because within it is the source of feelings of self (the psychic "I") and of pleasure (the physical "I"). It is understandable, then, that during late toddlerhood or the early preschool years (around age 3), children begin to show greater concern for the safety and intactness of their bodies. During this time, many children exhibit concern about minor cuts and scratches. For the 2- to 3-year-old, a box of adhesive bandages is a treasured gift. The child who is extremely upset by a minor bruise or scratch is frequently "restored" with a Band-Aid and feels "whole" again.[10]

DEVELOPMENT OF COGNITIVE SKILLS

Cognitive skills unfold very rapidly during the toddler and preschool period. The normal child's curiosity combined with the unending energy level force the adults to maintain a constant state of vigilance both for teaching and safety purposes. Some of the cognitive behaviors of typical toddlers and preschoolers are listed in Table 10-1.

Attention

One of the most critical tasks of the toddler and preschool years is to learn how to harness and focus energies. Focused attention is fundamental to learning. Unless a child attends to the stimulus, he or she will be unable to isolate the properties or indexes that differentiate one stimulus from another. Once a child learns to attend to the relevant features of a stimulus, he or she can learn to **generalize,** or transfer the knowledge learned, to other more difficult tasks.

The skills of harnessing and focusing energies build off of the infancy skill of "learning how to learn" and lay the foundation for the school-agers' task of "learning how to work." Harnessing and focusing energies includes the abilities to invest oneself in the targeted activity, to resist distractors (although environmental scanning continues), to persevere at a task (note that there is a big difference between perseverance and perseveration [meaningless repetition of an activity]), and maintain attention to a task long enough to master the challenge or at least to recognize one's limitations or alternatives.

Attention span depends on the nature of the materials as well as on the intellectual level and self-confidence of the individual child. The responsivity of the materials becomes a critical factor. Highly responsive materials tend to draw and capture the young child's attention, making it easy for the child to identify cause–effect relationships. The child becomes excited and energized as he or she is able to exert conscious control over the results. Materials from this category are identified as *fluid materials,* since they respond very rapidly, and in many ways.[31] Fluid materials require minimal physical or intellectual energy to respond to the child's efforts. One of the reasons why children *love* water and sand so much is because of the highly responsive nature of the materials (Fig. 10-8).

Structured materials are those that require precise physical and intellectual skills to make them respond in a positive way.[31] Because of their minimally responsive nature, they drain emotional energy from the young child. By their nature, the child can exert control only by first figuring out the relevant discriminators and then forcing the self to accommodate to the requirements of the materials. Puzzles and learning to tie one's shoes fall into this category.

Materials can be placed on a responsivity continuum in terms of the degree of cognitive/physical effort necessary to interact successfully with the materials (Fig. 10-9). Fluid materials are a critical component of the environment for infants and children or for adults who are physically, emotionally, or cognitively limited. The highly responsive nature of fluid materials draws attention and maintains attention through multiple successful reactions. Children learn how to learn through the use of these materials. The sense of voluntary control of the results energizes the child to repeat the activity.

Awareness of this continuum can be valuable to both parents and professionals. The child is challenged to attend and learn by presenting materials at the child's highest level of functioning, or what is commonly known as the "growing edge" of development. However, highly structured materials can be used only by persons who have a high reserve of energy or for short periods of time because the thought processes involved in identifying the cause–effect relationships and the routes to successful use drain energy. The child "begins to run on empty," and will become restless or disruptive from the tension which ensues. Energy tends to accumulate, however, when playing with materials which require minimal energy to create an effect, and may result in emotional "flooding" if the child remains with the activity too long.[31] The child then begins to lose control of his or her own social behaviors. Consequently, the wise adult alternately offers fluid and structured activities to capitalize on energy fluctuations and to help the child to increase his or her attention span by remaining in control of the energy level and the materials.

Memory

Information gained through selective attention to the environment is placed in the child's long-term memory. Each child, because of experiences and cultural context will have a different repertoire of information and memories.

Representative memory, which involves retaining a mental image of a perceptual quality appears with the emergence of substage VI of Piaget's sensorimotor stage. It is aided by verbal mediation as words begin to serve as symbols to repre-

TABLE 10-1. COGNITIVE SKILLS OF EARLY CHILDHOOD

Average Age	*Expected Behaviors*
18 months	Begins many questions with "what"
	Uses some words and many gestures to indicate needs
	Imitates anyone and anything in the environment
	Is beginning to understand that something else besides the present exists
	Understands space only from the activity of moving through it
	Begins to follow simple, one-part directions
	Begins to use "magical" power of thought
	Will infer causes from observing effects
	Will explore extensively
	May indicate wet pants
2 years	Is beginning to learn about time sequences (e.g., "after lunch")
	Will attempt new solutions to old problems
	Increases use of "magical" power of thought
	May arrange several words together in grammatically incorrect two- and three-word sentences
	May demonstrate a beginning cooperation in toilet training by anticipating a need to "go"
	Matches simple shapes and colors
	Names three body parts on request
2½ years	Is beginning to understand "tomorrow" and "yesterday"
	Often talks by abbreviating grammatical adult speech (e.g., "Mommy eat")
	Tends to talk in monologue (as though not expecting listener feedback)
	Is beginning to think about the consequences of behavior
	May sort objects (blocks, dolls) and pretend they are members of a family (e.g., big block is head of the family)
	Names six body parts on request
	Undertands 2 to 3 prepositions
3 years	Asks many "Why" questions
	Talks in sentences using four or more words
	May talk about fears
	Can give first and last name
	May explore environment outside the home if given the chance
	"Chains" objects using subjective attribute for categorizing (e.g., red block next to yellow block next to yellow crayon)
	May retain urine through a night's sleep and wake up dry
	May use profane language if older children or adults heard using it
	Counts to three
4 years	Begins many questions with "Where"
	May talk with imaginary playmate
	May threaten to "run away from home"
	Can count to 5 and is learning number concepts
	Can name color of three objects
	Can give opposite of up (down), and hot (cold)
	Can associate familiar holidays with the season in which they occur
	Completes 8- to 10-piece puzzle
	Understands 4 to 6 prepositions
	"Magical" power of thought at a peak
5 years	May begin many questions with "How"
	Asks the meaning of words
	Knows days of the week
	Can count to 10
	Talks "constantly"
	Can identify coins correctly
	May need to be reminded to eat and to go to bathroom because attention is so externally focused, may not recognize subtle internal cues
	Can follow a three-step direction in proper order
	Capable of memorizing own address

FIGURE 10–8.
Fluid materials such as sand are responsive to the child's actions. Even though these children are motivated to experiment with the sand by pouring it into containers of assorted shapes and sizes, none of them will be able to conserve a given quantity of it until the school-age years.

sent objects and actions. Initially, it is difficult for the child to separate words from the object or action they represent. Gradually, with the transition to intuitive thought, the child (around age 4) begins to realize that words can substitute for actions or feelings, recreate events, evoke common memories, and be used to convey an idea to the minds of others.

Initially, the child exhibits rote memory. Thus the child may be able to count to 10 or 20 but cannot tell you how many blocks are on the table. Sentences or words are repeated verbatim without regard to format. Toddlers will use the second person pronoun or even use a question format when expressing a need, since they repeat what they have heard (e.g., "Do you need to go potty?" meaning, "I have to go potty"). Initially, these repetitions immediately follow the adult's statement, and later will appear randomly as the child is playing as if he or she is remembering and practicing previously heard statements. Eventually, the child will exhibit **delayed echolalia**—the rote repetition of previously heard statements in the presence of need. This is a normal phenomenon in the process of learning language. As the child becomes more skilled in the ability to analyze grammar and to associate specific meaning to the individual words, he or she is able to use language creatively to express more precise ideas (see Chap. 12 for a discussion of language development).

Assessment of Developmental Level

Because of PL 99-457 (see Chap. 17), there has been a heightened interest in the assessment of preschool children to identify those at risk for academic failure and to provide

Structure

Shape puzzle

Sorting

Matching

Book pictures

Lite–brite

Hard blocks

Work bench

Etch–a–sketch

Crayons/paper

Bristle blocks

Chalk board

Paint/paper

Play dough

Responsivity Continuum

Blowing bubbles

Empty–fill toy

Xylophone

Sand toys

Magic markers

Finger paints

Car/truck

Hobby horse

Busy box

Squeeker

Rattle

Crackle paper

Tub toys

Mirror

Bells

Fluid   Water

FIGURE 10–9.
Responsivity continuum. Each activity requires increased attention to the environment and increased motor or cognitive skill. (Adapted from model proposed by C. H. Wolfgang.)

enrichment or early intervention programs designed to ameliorate the effects of disability or environment.

Intelligence Testing

Many persons continue to be apprehensive about assessing the intellectual functioning of preschoolers, even though there is a high correlation between the measures of intellectual performance in the preschool years and academic progress later. The correlation is frequently due to genuine differences in intellectual potential, but it may also be due to differences in language comprehension, social environment, testing environment, disability, or the way adults approach the child based on their understanding of the child's potentials. Parents are concerned that their child will be labeled as "retarded" and segregated into a special class before he or she ever has a chance to participate in the activities offered to other children. This is a realistic fear based on the experience of many families, especially those from lower socioeconomic groups and ethnic affiliations. It behooves all professionals to use the data gained from such tests judiciously and to provide each child with experiences which will maximize potentials in every domain.

The most common test of intelligence in the United States is the Stanford-Binet, which measures intelligence (i.e., what the person has learned). This test includes several verbal and performance items. The child may be asked to name pictures that illustrate a variety of common objects, to name objects from memory, to discriminate between geometric forms, or to define words.

Another common intelligence test used with preschool-aged children is the Wechsler Preschool-Primary Scale of Intelligence (WPPSI), which also has verbal and performance scales. There is a high correlation between intelligence quotients (IQ) derived from the Stanford-Binet and from the WPPSI, even though there are differences in the test items given and the methods of computing the IQ scores.

Developmental Assessment

Many of the assessments listed in Chapter 7 also have scales for toddlers and preschoolers. The Denver Developmental Screening Test (DDST) continues to be an effective screening tool to identify potential delays. The Developmental Programming for Infants and Young Children, Learning Accomplishment Profile (LAP), and Hawaii Early Learning Profile (HELP) assessment tools have excellent, easy to use checklists that have been developed to assist in determining the abilities (e.g., cognitive, motor, self-help, social, and communication skills) of preschool-aged children and to assist practitioners in setting age-appropriate, practical objectives.

The *Portage Guide to Early Education* is another major assessment tool used by many preschool and Head Start programs to evaluate a child's developmental progress. This criterion-referenced assessment provides checklists for the five areas mentioned above. Age categories are divided into yearly rather than more specific monthly divisions, making

only general evaluation of progress possible. However, it is very practical and acceptable to parents and serves as a guideline for intervention strategies (more information is available from The Portage Project, CESA 12, Box 564, Portage, WI 53901).

The Gesell Preschool Test measures four aspects of early development: motor, adaptive (self-help), language, and personal-social.[2] The assessment makes use of a variety of common play materials to assess factors such as eye–hand coordination, direction following, visual perception, language comprehension, spatial concepts, short-term memory, practical problem solving, adaptability, and attention span. This assessment for 2½- to 6-year-old children claims to be "culture-free" and "culture-fair."

MAXIMIZING THE COGNITIVE POTENTIALS OF THE TODDLER AND PRESCHOOLER

Since no two children have precisely the same cognitive potentials or exactly the same opportunities to learn, no two children will have identical concepts. However, children experiencing similar training and living in situations where there is an adherence to similar values will have similar concepts. The question often arises as to whether or not children can be taught selected concepts (e.g., conservation, classification) before actually discovering them for themselves. The child who is experiencing a transitional cognitive period at the time such training is introduced may be accelerated; however, the actual benefit of such acceleration remains to be proved. **As with the infant, it is more important that the environment keep pace with the child than to force the child to keep pace with the environment.** The child's interests and motivations should always be kept in mind in providing social interaction, offering play materials, or presenting guidelines for social behavior or safety (Fig. 10-10).

Play

Play is an essential ingredient in a child's cognitive development. Through activities which adults view as play, the child learns how to control and refine both gross and fine motor movements and how to approach and solve problems. Play is a *child's work*. The child learns and practices new skills through play which are or will be essential to the activities of daily living.

When a child is first learning a new skill, much emotional and intellectual energy is invested in the activity, whether it be learning how to walk, how to button, how to cut with scissors, or how to put a puzzle together. Observation of the demeanor of the child's face alerts the adult to the seriousness of the activity to the child. Intense concentration must be invested in the task to master it. Piaget incorporates this initial work activity into his theory of cognitive development as an **ac-**

FIGURE 10–10.
Young children are sensory-oriented in their learning. They love a "Feely box," which challenges them to refine their perceptual discrimination skills.

commodation activity.[20] The child is actively changing his or her approach and is consciously creating new schemata to be successful at the skill.

Once a child figures out the cause–effect relationships or physical movements necessary to master a task, the skill is replicated multiple times and in different settings or with alternative materials. Thus, the child may walk all over the house or on and off the sidewalk; may button and unbutton his or her own clothes and those of others; may cut paper, hair, clothes, or the curtains; and may try to put puzzles and any other shapes together. This practicing phase is essential for assuring the child that he or she is able to control events and to develop the physical and intellectual skills to the point where the activity no longer requires concentrated thought and has become a habit firmly entrenched in the child's repertoire of skills. During this practicing phase, the skill will be unstable in its appearance as the child continues to work at accommodation.

Once the child has mastered a skill, the activity becomes easy and fun to perform. Piaget says that at this point **assimilation** is the cognitive activity involved.[20] The child's relaxed face and approach are external indicators of the decreased concentration required for success. The activity is no longer an end in itself, but becomes a tool for mastering the next task or to meet new challenges—to get to a specific place as quickly as possible, to dress oneself for the day, to cut out a specific shape for an art project, or to fit objects together in as small an area as possible (e.g., packing a suitcase). Thus, adults may identify all of a child's activities as play because they would be easy, relaxing, or fun for the adult. But, the activity is work for the child during the learning process, and does not become play until it can be accomplished easily by the child. All the play activities help the child gain the skills that will be needed for school and general adaptation to life (for further discussion of play, see Chap. 15).

Safety

More than one half of all childhood deaths are caused by accidents. Many of these involve motor vehicles. However, three out of four nonfatal accidents to young children occur in the home or in areas nearby.[28] Of these accidents, 90% have been estimated to be preventable. Prevention must take the form of continued supervision as well as education. No matter how much learning adults may think has transpired, nothing should be taken for granted. By toddlerhood the child is cognitively ready to understand the meaning of "hot," "sharp," "hurt," and "no" (although such words must be consistently repeated from one situation to another). However, **the toddler's insatiable curiosity easily overrides self-discipline** and parental admonitions about "not getting into things." For that reason, all potential poisons (including cosmetics) should be kept out of the reach of ingenious youngsters who have learned how to pull drawers out, use them as steps, and climb (Fig. 10-11). Young children should be warned about appliances that burn, and they should never be left alone when such equipment is in operation. Matches are a temptation to many toddlers; young children **must** be taught the dangers of playing with matches or fire of any source. Guns and sharp-edged objects, such as razor blades or scissors, are a potential hazard to anyone and should be stored in safe places. No sharp object should be carelessly tossed aside into a wastebasket where a young child may discover and examine it. Any babysitter should be informed of all the precautions and safety rules of the household so that the rules can be enforced when the primary caregivers are not present.

Children are not as safe in their own yard as is often thought. Poisonous plants that look "good enough to eat" should be removed. In addition to "childproofing" the yard, the caregiver should make sure that the child understands the boundaries of the play area and should provide constant supervision or check frequently to make sure the child remembers. Children should be taught to use caution with all animals, no matter how gentle the animal has been in the past.

Even before preschoolers are old enough to cross the street alone, they should be taught how to do so and what will happen if they do not cross carefully. Caregivers can illustrate this safely and graphically with toy trucks (Fig. 10-12). Parents need to be highly vigilant of children around any moving vehicle. The impulsive nature of young children causes them to dart out into traffic or to play in unsafe areas. Their small

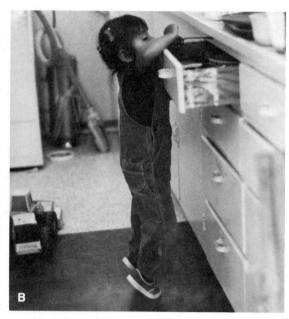

FIGURE 10–11.
(A) *The inquisitive toddler must be carefully watched by caregivers as he or she examines the beautiful but potentially dangerous decorations of Christmas and other busy holidays.* (B) *The curiosity of the preschooler may prompt the opening of many containers that should remain safely closed and untouched by little hands.*

size makes them difficult to see. A major cause of pedestrian fatality in children under five is to be backed over in the home driveway by the family car, van, or light truck.[7]

The safest place for any child riding in an automobile is usually in the back seat; the child is **least** safe when held in the arms of a person in the front seat of a car or sitting in the back of a station wagon. Equipment specially devised to protect the child who weighs less than 40 pounds (e.g., car seats, harnesses) can be purchased. Instructions on how these safety devices should be used accompany the product or can be obtained from the manufacturer. Most children who weigh over 40 pounds are able to use a standard seat belt. Car doors should always be locked and the windows rolled up to a safe height. Children should **never** be left alone in a car—not even for a few minutes. They need to be protected not only from their own curiosity but also from vulnerability to strangers. These rules should be enforced from the beginning. Riding in a car can be fun for children who are taught activities, such as naming the things they see, identifying their colors, counting them, and so forth.

Preschoolers can be taught their name, address, and telephone number, as well as how to use the telephone to obtain help in an emergency. Some persons recommend that children wear identification tags in case of injury.[6]

Most young children love water and for this reason may be given swimming lessons very early. Even after children have learned to swim, they must have constant adult supervi-

sion (and that adult should be an accomplished swimmer). Sprinklers are safer than pools for young children. A full forward fall into just 3 inches of water may so frighten a young child that he or she may not be able to raise the head out of the water for air.

Why do young children sometimes disobey the rules? A variety of factors interplay: Perhaps they become too busy and forget; perhaps they have a greater need to assert self-will; perhaps they are confused about the caregiver's expectations in the first place. Frequently a child has to see if the adults really mean what they say. More often, curiosity outweighs self-discipline, or naïveté leads to poor judgments.

CONCLUSION

Selma Fraiberg has dubbed the toddler-preschool period as the "magical years."[10] And indeed they are for both children and their parents. Children are enchanted by the world around them. Each new object and event has a magical drawing power on the child, who stares in wide-eyed wonderment at events as simple as a chicken pecking at grains in the gravel or as complex as Mardi Gras or the Rose Bowl parade. Each new object is explored and re-explored with all the senses and from every angle. Even emerging motor skills become events to explore and to repeat ad infinitum until the novelty wears off, mastery is assured, and the skill is incorporated into

FIGURE 10–12.
The preschool years are an excellent time to start teaching vehicular safety rules.

the repertoire of tools used by the child for further exploration of the environment. Through all these experiences, children are refining and expanding their schemata or bases of knowledge.

When the parents are equally caught up in the child's joy of learning, they provide new experiences and challenges and are rewarded by the child's obvious infatuation with, and enthusiasm for, the event. They are amused by their child's observations, questions, and conclusions, often recalling comparable experiences from their own early years. This can be a thrilling, enriching period of family life as the parents share the culture and its rules, values, and accoutrements with the child.

A major theme of these years is the discovery of cause–effect relationships. Toddlers and preschoolers do not possess the same concepts of these relationships as do adults. Their processing of information is rarely logical and may lead them to false or unsafe conclusions. Their observations of the ease with which adults make things happen may lead them to believe that all adults have magical powers—events occur because of the power of thought. Consequently, they may

express as "truth" those events they would like to have happen, and they may feel responsible when a catastrophic event occurs during a period when they were angry or "feeling bad thoughts."

Gradually the child begins to differentiate between internal feelings and external behaviors and to separate internal images from external events. The increased ability to use symbols and signs facilitates both the child's internal thought processes and communication with others.

Children become fascinated by their own learning processes. They actively seek new information and try to identify relationships during these years. Children learned how to learn during infancy, but during toddler and preschool years children learn how to teach themselves through trial and error, repetition, and experimentation.

Young children learn by doing. Sometimes a mistake can be a way of learning; the adult can encourage the child to feel that it is all right to attempt a realistic goal, and that failure does not make the child "bad." A negative result is not a "failure" but an opportunity for another learning experience.

Provided with a relaxed environment that includes love

and sharing, friendly and interested people, books, creative materials and toys, and pleasant trips and excursions with significant others, the healthy child will "learn as naturally as he grows and breathes."[1]

REFERENCES

1. Ames, L. B., & Ilag, F. L. (1980). *Your four-year-old: Wild and wonderful.* New York: Delacorte Press.
2. Ames, L. B., et al. (1980). *The Gesell Institute's child from one to six: Evaluating the behavior of the preschool child.* London: Hamish Hamilton.
3. Ballard, S. N. (1988). Religious concept development. In D. G. Benner (Ed.), *Psychology and religion* (pp. 100–107). Grand Rapids, MI: Baker Book House.
4. Beers, V. G. (1975). Teaching theological concepts to children. In R. B. Zuck & R. E. Clark (Eds.), *Childhood education in the church.* Chicago: Moody Press.
5. Bettelheim, B. (1976). *The uses of enchantment: The meaning and importance of fairy tales.* New York: Knopf.
6. Blyskal, J., & Hodge, M. (1986). Have you tagged your kids today? *Reader's Digest, 129*(772), 80–83.
7. Brison, R. J., Wicklund, K., & Mueller, B. A. (1988). Fatal pedestrian injuries to young children: A different pattern of injury. *American Journal of Public Health, 78,* 793–795.
8. Elkind, D. (1978). *The child's reality: Three developmental themes.* Hillsdale, NJ: Lawrence Erlbaum Assoc.
9. Flavell, J. H. (1968). *The developmental psychology of Jean Piaget.* Princeton, NJ: Van Nostrand.
10. Fraiberg, S. H. (1968). *The magic years: Understanding and handling the problems of early childhood.* London: Methuen.
11. Gellert, E. (1962). Children's conceptions of the content and functions of the human body. *Genetic Psychology Monographs, 65,* 293.
12. Howarth, M. (1989). Rediscovering the power of fairy tales: They help children understand their lives. *Young Children, 45*(1), 58–65.
13. Ilg, F. L., Ames, L. B., & Baker, S. M. (1982). *Child behavior* (rev. ed.). New York: Barnes & Noble.
14. Johnson, C. N., & Wellman, H. M. (1982). Children's developing conceptions of the mind and brain. *Child Development, 53*(1), 222.
15. Missildine, W. (1976). The toddler and motivation. *Feelings and Their Medical Significance, 18*(4), 19.
16. Mullahy, P. (1970). *Psychoanalysis and interpersonal psychiatry: The contributions of Harry Stack Sullivan.* New York: Science House.
17. Petrillo, M., & Sanger, S. (1980). *Emotional care of hospitalized children: An environmental approach* (2nd ed.). Philadelphia: J. B. Lippincott.
18. Phillips, J. L. (1975). *The origin of intellect: Piaget's theory* (2nd ed.). San Francisco: Freeman.
19. Piaget, J. (1928). *Judgment and reasoning in the child.* New York: Harcourt, Brace.
20. Piaget, J. (1982). *Play, dreams and imitation in childhood* (C. Gattengo and F. M. Hodgson, Trans.). New York: Norton.
21. Piaget, J. (1968). *Six psychological studies* (A. Tenzer, Trans.). New York: Vintage Books.
22. Piaget, J. (1969). *The child's conception of physical causality* (M. Gabain, Trans.). Totowa, NJ: Littlefield, Adams.
23. Piaget, J. (1969). *The child's conception of the world* (J. Tomlinson and A. Tomlinson, Trans.). Totowa, NJ: Littlefield, Adams.
24. Piaget, J. (1972). *The child's concept of physical causality* (M. Gabain, Trans.). Totowa, NJ: Littlefield, Adams.
25. Piaget, J. (1976). *The psychology of intelligence* (M. Piercy and D. E. Berlyne, Trans.). Totowa, NJ: Littlefield, Adams.
26. Piaget, J., & Inhelder, B. (1969). *The psychology of the child* (H. Weaver, Trans.). New York: Basic Books.
27. Segal, J. (1975). The gentle art of daydreaming. *Family Health, 7*(3), 22.
28. Wegman, M. E. (1981). Annual summary of vital statistics—1980. *Pediatrics, 68*(6), 755.
29. Wenar, C. (1971). *Personality development from infancy to adulthood.* Boston: Houghton Mifflin.
30. White, B. L. (1985). *The First Three Years of Life* (rev. ed.). New York: Prentice Hall.
31. Wolfgang, C. H. (1977). *Helping aggressive and passive preschoolers through play.* Columbus, OH: Charles E. Merrill Publishing.

11 *Along with the
sober anxiety which brings
us face to face with our
individualized potentiality-
for-being, there goes an
unshakable joy in this
possibility.*

—MARTIN HEIDEGGER,
BEING AND TIME

Psychosocial Development During the Toddler and Preschool Years

Shirley S. Ashburn and Clara S. Schuster

The ability to walk presents the child with new challenges in all domains. The world and its relationships take on new perspectives and meaning. As experience broadens, children become more aware of self and family with a larger social context. Children are confronted with increasingly complex conflicts, challenges, and fears as they struggle to identify themselves and their individual potentials, roles, and responsibilities in their ever-expanding world.

The establishment of independence is a major theme of toddlerhood. During the toddler years, primitive self-knowledge and self-image emerge as the child progressively differentiates self from the environment. As children begin to think and act on their own, they increasingly are able and want to regulate their own behavior. Those with a supportive home environment begin to become aware of and incorporate the basic prosocial rules of the family and culture.

Weaning from a relatively great dependency on the mother and other family members is well under way at this age. Once the child is established as a separate, autonomous individual, the ability to interact with others is enhanced. As contacts with other children increase during the preschool years, elementary lessons of give and take are learned in preparation for the social adjustments that are essential to school and to life outside the family. The beginnings of cooperative behavior emerge as the child's concentration on his or her wishes and impulses is gradually superseded by concern about social relationships. The child begins to assume responsibility for both the self and the world.

The establishment of a personal and social identity is highly complex. Interrelated aspects during early childhood include (1) dependence/independence; (2) autonomy/shame or doubt; (3) initiative/guilt; (4) aggression/cooperation; (5) curiosity/self-discipline; and (6) gender-role identity. Each aspect exerts a modifying or regulating influence on the child's personality and lays a foundation for future development.

At the beginning of this unit, ten developmental tasks were identified for the toddler/preschool period. These tasks accommodate both individual needs and societal demands and are fundamental to the child's successful adaptation to both the current and future demands of life. They assume an active learner within a responsive, supportive social environment. Some tasks arise mainly from physical maturation (e.g., coordination of body movements for motor skill mastery); others arise primarily from cultural pressures, such as learning prosocial behaviors and developing basic self-control skills. A third source of developmental tasks is the personal values and the aspirations of the individual. Early childhood examples arising from this source include seeking information and understanding or learning to live with the consequences of one's own choices.

These tasks clearly demonstrate four major principles: (1) all areas of growth and development are interrelated; (2) the environment plays a critical role in stimulating and supporting the direction of task mastery; (3) the child plays an active role in forging his or her own development; and (4) the process of development, while similar for all children, is also unique for each child. The child who feels a sense of accomplishment in mastering these tasks will experience a sense of independence, individuality, initiative, and early identity.

PSYCHOSOCIAL DEVELOPMENT DURING THE TODDLER YEARS

As the wills of the toddler and the caregiver come into conflict, the child becomes aware of psychological separateness—a factor that is both exciting and frightening. Insatiable curiosity and the drive to "test one's wings" bring the child into confrontations with social prohibitions and inabilities as well as new doors and horizons. This creates an increased need for supportive adult contact at a time when the drive for independence seems so strong.

Mahler's Rapprochement Subphase

The separation-individuation process described by Margaret Mahler continues throughout early childhood as the child establishes psychological separateness from the mother and significant others (see Table 8-2).[19] The toddler years roughly correspond to Mahler's third subphase, the early phase of individuation, or *rapprochement,* that extends from about 15 to 24 months. Her fourth and final subphase, *consolidation,* represents the second half of individuation, which occurs primarily during the third year of life (24 to 36 months). Although the process of identifying and drawing on one's own characteristics and reserves continues throughout life, it is during this period that the child recognizes the ongoing reality of self and others and begins to realize that he or she can function adaptively without the constant presence of the primary caregiver.

With the increase in locomotion, cognition, and language skills, the stage is set for the child to emerge as a separate, autonomous person. Mahler postulates that with the advent of independent locomotion, the child becomes more aware of physical separateness from the mother.[19] This new freedom to move away from her freely creates both a pleasure in mastery and an awareness of vulnerability. As the toddler becomes more aware of a growing ability to move away, he or she seems to develop a heightened desire and need for the primary caregiver to share every new experience and skill that is acquired. Consequently, the child begins to become more concerned about the mother's whereabouts when they are separated.

As the child becomes more aware of physical separateness, he or she practices controlling the amount of contact with or absence from this source of security by alternately moving away from and toward the mother. The contact with novel experiences, objects, and events appears to require

more energy than the toddler has to expend. Thus, the child must emotionally "**refuel**" by physically approaching or making eye contact with the primary caregiver before returning to the world with renewed vigor (Fig. 11-1). The toddler's growing awareness of personal vulnerability heightens the need to seek protection and to control the environment through eliciting the mother's attention and assistance at times of anxiety. The child's degree of pleasure in independent functioning and desire to venture into an expanding environment seem to be proportionate to the ease of eliciting the caregiver's continued interest and participation.

The child's need for the mother as a "love object" is essential to security and mental health.[19] The sensitivity of the "object's" love and attention are critical to continued security and mental health. The child actively approaches the mother figure each time a stressor arises. The increased awareness of

FIGURE 11–1.
The phenomenon of "refueling" continues for several years when novel situations arise and may be displayed in various ways by the individual child. It provides the child with the necessary affective energy for independent exploration of, and interaction with, the environment, or to face an anxiety-provoking situation (in this case, a stranger with a camera).

vulnerability and the continued need for adult assistance lead many children to panic when the mother or caregiver leaves their sight. The factor that is most critical appears to be whether or not the child feels in control of the adult's physical or attentional withdrawal. Thus the child can leave the mother with confidence if she remains in a constant place and free access is assured. However, anxiety arises if the child feels that free access is or will be denied. Many toddlers become jealous of anyone or anything (even the telephone!) that competes with them for the mother's attention. Many mothers fear that they will never be able to retreat to the bathroom in privacy again.

The child's calm acceptance of knocks and falls begins to disappear. Signs of directed aggression begin to emerge, along with a growing possessiveness and ambivalence, as the child's awareness of physical and psychological separateness increases. The toddler appears to become more easily frustrated and demands more assistance, especially from the mother, when faced with frustration. During this period, the toddler's need is specifically for the mother (or primary caregiver); substitutes are not easily accepted, particularly for physical or comforting contact.

Sometime between the ages of 18 and 24 months, the rapprochement struggle reaches a peak in what Mahler terms the **rapprochement crisis.**[19] The child's clamoring for omnipotent control, the extreme expressions of separation anxiety, and the ambivalent demands for both closeness and autonomy become intensified. Life is difficult for everyone. The child appears to use the mother as an extension of self, yet demands separateness from her. Gradually, as individuation proceeds, this crisis becomes integrated and resolved. The child begins to find an optimal distance from the mother, a physical and psychological distance at which he or she can function well without the necessity of the mother's constant physical presence.

At first, physical contact is essential for refueling, but gradually eye contact becomes sufficient. Some children eventually will be satisfied with carrying an object around with them that belongs to or represents the mother (*transitional object*). Others prefer to carry a photo of her. With the resolution of this stage of the "hatching process," the toddler reaches a first level of identity, that of being a separate entity. The words "me," "mine," and "I" appear in the child's language. A "self" is established.[19]

Erikson's Autonomy versus Shame or Doubt

Once the infant learns to predict some events and cause-effect relationships, he or she begins to experiment with the repetition of events to discover which and how many events can be controlled. One of the major goals of toddlerhood, therefore, is to discover how much one can control. The most prominent statements of children this age are "Me do!" and "No!" The child is ensuring and asserting psychological separateness

even if the results are disastrous. Toddlers insist that they be allowed to explore and to do things for themselves (or at least to try). Allowing safe activities is critical to the emergence of a sense of autonomy.

The mastery of basic cognitive, motor, and language skill, allows the child to differentiate self, both physically and emotionally, from the primary caregiver and the environment. Two psychological processes seem to be related to this enhanced self-awareness. As the child meets and masters problems, there is a feeling of being competent and "good." Awareness also comes from the child's expanding ability to recognize other people's reactions to what he or she does. Thus, if mother is proud of the toddler's accomplishments, the toddler takes pride as well. However, if the caregiver provides many restrictions and criticisms of the child's curiosity and mistakes, the child begins to doubt self-feelings and the ability to control events. Shame follows botched efforts, and the child retreats to the role of passive observer, which results in decreased learning and self-esteem. Throughout toddlerhood, then, much of the energy of healthy children centers on asserting that they are human beings with minds and wills of their own.

As the child discovers his or her separate will, the potential for conflict with others increases. Parental management of these conflicts is critical to positive resolution. When the child is allowed and encouraged to be independent and to make simple decisions, confidence emerges. However, if in the process of curbing energy, intrusiveness, impulsivity, and so forth, the parents squelch the child's individuality too harshly, a sense of shame and doubt about self may emerge. The child learns to expect defeat in any battle of wills with those who are bigger and stronger. As they develop a secure sense of autonomy—the feeling that they are independent human beings—healthy toddlers become more comfortable in seeking and using the help of others. They are no longer fearful of being engulfed by the personality and strength of the more competent adult.

The toddler experiences an irrepressible urge to express will and satisfy curiosity while simultaneously feeling apprehension about facing new experiences. Erikson considers these conflicting pulls—to assert the self and to hold back—as major themes during this phase; the child struggles between the need for help and the urge to acquire independence. The child attempts to establish a sense of self and self-control without loss of self-esteem. This means that parents need to provide protection from physical and emotional harm while allowing the child as much independent activity and as many choices as possible. The parents can maintain control, yet provide choices by predetermining the alternatives for meeting a goal, for example, by saying, "You may hold either my hand or your grandmother's hand when we cross the street" or by giving the child a choice between white milk and chocolate milk. Unfair criticism, lack of opportunity, or the child's inability to master tasks that foster a sense of autonomy can result in feelings of shame in the child and a lasting sense of doubt about self and others.[8] Erikson believes that this stage is decisive in determining the individual's capacity for, or balance between, love and hate, cooperation and willfulness, and the freedom of self-expression or its suppression.

Erikson agrees with Freud in that the ego is based on the reality principle and struggles with the id, which operates on the pleasure principle. The ego emerges victor as the child learns to tolerate delayed gratification. Erikson also states that the child's superego, or conscience, has a rudimentary beginning as he begins to incorporate sociocultural mores of the immediate environment (see Chap. 16 for discussion of Freud's theory).

Erikson considers the stage of autonomy extremely important because "in it is played out the first emancipation, namely from the mother." The child's desire for autonomy may find expression in negativism toward the mother and others. In situations where the mother has been the primary caregiver, the father assumes increasing significance as the child's world expands and he or she begins to explore and to develop more meaningful relationships with others in the family. Self-control and willpower emerge as the child successfully achieves a sense of autonomy.[7]

Sullivan's Syntaxic Mode

Harry Sullivan postulates that when a child is capable of using words that convey the same meaning to the child as to others, the highest form of relating to others (the syntaxic mode) is reached (between the 12th and 18th months).[24] From this time onward, the child is able to *consensually validate,* or to check messages sent and received. Language distinguishes syntaxic operations from the prototaxic or parataxic ones discussed in Chapter 8. The ability to consensually validate thoughts and actions clarifies communication with others and facilitates interpersonal relationships throughout the life span. As the young child recognizes the signs of approval or disapproval of behavior and as he or she experiments with how much the behavior of others can be manipulated, the child learns more about the ability to control personal desires and behaviors. If there is an excess of parental disapproval during these years, the child may come to view the world and even the self in negative and hostile terms.[24]

As the child's command of language increases, so does the opportunity to experience the syntaxic mode. Since true communication is a two-way process, adults must be mindful to validate their communications with the child. "Do it because I say so," or the use of words in an explanation that the child does not understand creates problems. Since the child is still learning what words and gestures symbolize and perceives the world at a different cognitive level than adults, caregivers should be sure the child understands what is said and find out exactly what a child is trying to say and **what it means to the child.** Successful communication through the spoken word and body language supports the child's developing sense of autonomy and lays a foundation for initiating experiences. It takes an empathetic adult to understand and respond to the child's point of view and intentions in order to encourage positive development of the emerging ego.

Living With a Toddler

Expressions of Autonomy

The words "I," "me," and "mine" begin to have great affective significance as the child's sense of self deepens and the knowledge of physical structures and boundaries progresses. The use of these words appears to parallel the child's emerging awareness of individuation from the parents and other people. The toddler is able to point to facial features and major body parts on request, understanding "your" versus "my."

Toddlers try vigorously to use their bodies and mobility to do everything on their own: to feed themselves, to climb, to open and shut things, and to dress (or, more often, undress) themselves. The body becomes a tool for experimentation. The young "researcher" attacks anything that appears interesting, such as cereal, mud, the cat box, or his own feces, although afterward he or she is likely to demand clean fingers.

Because the body is a proud possession, the toddler may resist handling from adults, particularly if held in a passive position, (e.g., for dressing or diapering). The toddler may not like to be hugged or kissed at times. Throughout this process of separating the self from the primary caregiver and identifying the self as an independent entity capable of asserting some control over self and the environment, three classic autonomy struggles emerge: negativism, ritualism, and ambivalence.

NEGATIVISM. One of the most dramatic manifestations of developing autonomy is negativism. The toddler's negativism is expressed in a variety of ways. Verbal expressions of "No," total body rigidity, kicking, biting, hitting, throwing, breath-holding, and severe temper tantrums are characteristic of most children at some time during toddlerhood. This behavior is so universal that the toddler period is frequently referred to as the *terrible twos.* Negative behavior indicates, however, a major step in the child's progress from the passivity and dependency of infancy to the assertion of an autonomous will.

The child appears to say "No" verbally or behaviorally to almost every suggestion which comes from others. The need to be in control or to be self-directed is so strong that to cooperate with others, or to let them cooperate with him or her, seems to be a loss of individuality, independence, and control. The child feels smothered and engulfed by the symbiotic nature of the cooperative experience. Consequently, the toddler may refuse to put boots on and then will refuse to accept help in putting on the boots, insisting that he or she will do it by him- or herself. After several minutes of unsuccessful trying, the child may cry in frustration, but still refuse parental help. This requires much patience from caregivers. The child does not yet know how to balance the dependence/independence issue. Even when the child is offered a positive choice (e.g., "Do you want some ice cream?"), the toddler may still say, "No!" even though he or she may very much want the ice cream. When the parent respects the toddler's "no" and puts the ice cream away, the child may begin to cry and exhibit distressed behavior—the stage is set for additional conflict when exasperated parents try to reason with the child about the communication and negativism. "Well, if you want it, SAY SO!"

According to Mahler, the child *must* say "no." Unable to distinguish between valid choices and directives, the child says "no" as a way of resisting feelings of being an extension of the parent's will. It is as if the child reasons: "If I say 'yes,' if I agree, then I lose my own free will. I *must* say 'no' even when I really want something" (Fig. 11-2). With guidance and assistance, the child gradually learns how to balance dependence and cooperation. Negativism reaches a peak sometime during the second or third year and then gradually declines throughout the preschool years as the child learns how to control behavior and realizes that to cooperate with others is mutually advantageous. Parental patience, humor, and rewording of guidance can help the child to pass through this phase with minimal trauma.

The toddler becomes easily frustrated when adult authority prevents the pursuing of an urgent need or a wish, requests that the child change an activity, or suggests a novel experience. Toddlers perceive most activity as being urgent; postponement of such urgent wishes (activities) requires so much exertion that they have to summon all their energy reserves to oppose the wish. Usually a 2-year-old cannot summon enough strength when urges are very strong; the adult must help the child with redirection and self-control.

Negative behavior in the context of how children learn to deal with frustration is discussed in more detail later in this chapter in the section on the development of self-control.

RITUALISM. When cause–effect relationships are poorly understood, causal and casual relationships are not distinguished. Consequently, many positive and negative superstitious beliefs are spawned. The child's emergent autonomy is tied to the ability to predict and control events. Therefore, the toddler and young preschooler will insist on uniformity and exactness of events to ensure cognitive and affective comfort (e.g., "I was able to go to sleep after three stories"). Therefore, great distress is experienced if those same three stories are not read the next night (or if milk is poured into the wrong glass, the child is asked to sit in the "wrong" chair, or sleep in a strange bed). A set number of stuffed toys *must* be hugged because the child is convinced that the secret of going to sleep is somehow tied to pre-sleep rituals. Failure of significant adults to recognize and accept the importance of these rituals to the child's mental health and sense of control will increase the stress of the event. The increased flexibility in cognitive processing that comes with maturation will enable the child to release these rituals spontaneously. The child gradually begins to find other, more effective, ways to cause the same event to happen at will. Adult attempts to pre-

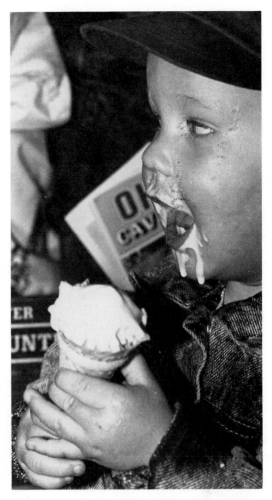

FIGURE 11–2.
Many toddlers will say "No!" when asked if they want ice cream, either because they have not yet learned the word "Yes!" or because to say "Yes!" evokes feelings reminiscent of the symbiotic phase of individuation. The need for autonomy eclipses the desire for the ice cream.

maturely abort the ritualistic behaviors will increase stress and insecurity, and will usually prolong the need for the behaviors. It may even prevent the ability to develop a comfortable sense of autonomy.

AMBIVALENCE. Ambivalence, or finding something simultaneously attractive and repulsive, is characteristic of the child's struggle to achieve autonomy. The toddler must learn to coordinate a number of highly conflicting action patterns characterized by "holding on" and "letting go."[8] Play behaviors often reflect these patterns. Activities such as hoarding and piling up rather than putting things away become pronounced. Ambivalence can be clearly seen in the child's attempts to hold on and to let go with the eyes, mouth, hands, and eventually the sphincters. Psychoanalytical theorists hypothesize that the anal zone is extremely important in the child's expression of the conflicting desire for dependence and autonomy. Experiences during bowel and bladder training provide a major test for the child's growing concept of self-regulation or self-control versus control by others (see Chap. 9).[20]

As the child becomes more aware of separateness, he or she begins to employ numerous mechanisms that deny the actual separateness. Mahler describes the toddler's behavior of "shadowing" the mother versus darting away in the expectation of being chased and swept into her arms.[19] The term **shadowing** refers to the child's incessant watching and following every move of the caregiver. The toddler experiences rapidly alternating desires to push the parent away and to cling to her—to hold on and to let go. When on a walk, the toddler may plunge off in pursuit of an interesting animal or activity only to stop short and come hurtling back into the parent's arms. The child may strike out alone and then burst into tears with the discovery of being surrounded by strangers. Every mother has experienced how a toddler will snuggle close to her one minute and ruthlessly push her away the next. Just when children are vigorously asserting autonomy, they may suddenly want to be helped, carried, babied, or cuddled.

The toddler's ambivalent behavior becomes compounded if the parents are also ambivalent about the growing autonomy. Most parents take pride in each new step forward and yet may lament the child's increasing independence and separateness. Parents may feel unsure of how much to admire the child's developing competence, when to keep hands off, and when to intervene. The child's insistence on autonomy may be aggravating to the parents. "A moment ago you did not want me to help. OK! Do it yourself!" may be the adult's response. Parental support and tolerance of ambivalence are extremely important to assist the child in meeting the demands of burgeoning autonomy without creating a feeling of shame or doubt.

Separation Anxiety

The rapprochement phase is characterized by the toddler's renewed sensitivity to the parents' whereabouts. Thus, separation anxiety (insecurity experienced when removed from someone or something familiar) begins to peak again. The child's intense desire to function independently occurs at the point in development when the child's own feelings and wishes versus those of the parents are still poorly differentiated. The toddler's wish to be autonomous—to let go and to leave the mother—means that mother might also wish to leave. This fear may be compounded when the mother scolds the child for following her to the bathroom or for interrupting her on the phone, or when talking to others. Thus one finds a powerful resurgence of stranger anxiety (discomfort experienced when in the presence of an unfamiliar person), even toward people who earlier may have been regarded as friends.

Difficulties with leave-taking itself begin to emerge, and

the child may desperately cling to the mother and cry if she attempts to leave. The toddler may enjoy darting away, but does not like to be passively left behind.[19] Separations can be well-tolerated if the child initiates them, but the child may "fall apart" when the parent initiates them. The toddler is particularly vulnerable to separation, if the separation is prolonged.

It is important to apprise children about imminent separations and reunions, even though the child may protest vigorously. It is best to tell a toddler about the separation just before it occurs lest he become overstimulated or confused. Thus, the child is able to predict even though he or she cannot control the event; the trust relationship with adults is enhanced, and the child is offered the opportunity to develop elementary coping strategies.[13] Toddlers experience separation anxiety because they know who they belong to and want to remain close to persons they need and love.[19] Activities such as peek-a-boo, disappearance-and-return games, and the shadowing and darting-away behavior described by Mahler assist children to overcome the anxiety experienced with separation. By repeating disappearance-and-return games under conditions they can control, children are helped to overcome the anxiety that accompanies separation. Children thus learn to manage small amounts of discomfort and frustration. Toddlers usually demonstrate less fear of strangers than infants if their parents are present, but are very fearful and angry when the parents leave. A toddler who experiences separation anxiety needs to be provided with copious positive, affectionate attention when reunited with the primary caregiver. Immediate emotional refueling is critical to regain security and confidence. If the parents make the reunion a joyful, unhurried refueling time, the child seems to make a better adjustment to separation experiences.

Interpersonal Relationships

Living with a toddler can be simultaneously entertaining, challenging, exciting, endearing, and exasperating (Fig. 11-3). The beauty and frustration of living with a child who is discovering the limits of autonomy are sensitively described by Fraiberg:[9]

> Everyone complains about the two-year-old. His parents complain about his willfulness, his stubbornness. His older sister complains about his peer group integration. "He won't share. He wants everything for himself!" If there is a younger brother or sister, an infant, he adds his lamentations to the chorus. In rare moments . . . when silence descends upon the household, the intuitive mother tenses herself in expectation of a shriek of pain which will certainly come in a moment from the direction of the baby's room. Everyone complains. But the family dog does not complain. When the two-year-old comes after him with playful cries, this sensible beast takes off to his sanctuary under the couch.
>
> But miraculously, out of these ominous beginnings, a civilized being begins to emerge. For we have painted a dark picture, the two-year-old as his worrying parents see him. There is another side of the two-year-old which holds the real promise for the future.
>
> He loves, deeply, tenderly, extravagantly, and he holds the

FIGURE 11–3.
Sometimes toddlers fear that whatever is harming a crying baby may also harm them. To reduce the possibility of danger to themselves, they will attempt to comfort the baby, thus reflecting poorly differentiated boundaries between the baby's feelings and their own.

love of his parents more dearly than anything in the world. To be fair about it, he also loves himself very, very much, and this conflict between self-love and love of others is the source of his difficulty at this age. But when put to the test, it is love for his parents which wins out . . . He wants to be good so he can win their love and approval; he wants to be good so that he can love himself.

PSYCHOSOCIAL DEVELOPMENT DURING THE PRESCHOOL YEARS

Mahler's Consolidation Subphase

As the toddler moves into the preschool years, the process of separation should be well-established; however, the process of individuation continues. Mahler's fourth subphase, *consolidation of individuality and beginning of emotional constancy,* centers around a twofold task: (1) the beginning of a lifelong search for individuality or self-identity, and (2) the attainment of emotional object constancy.[19] As used by Mahler, **affective object constancy** describes the "gradual internalization of a positively cathected, inner image of mother."[19] Affective object constancy is founded on *cognitive object constancy,* which appeared around 5 months, and *object permanence,* which appeared around 8 months (see Chap. 7). Maturation of these two concepts during infancy

facilitated attachment to the primary caregiver and a gradual awareness that she was still present somewhere, even though she could not be seen. As memory processes mature, the child is able to retrieve thoughts of mother as desired or needed. Thus, the 3- to 4-year-old child is able to maintain a mental representation of the loved one and *can periodically "refuel" from positive emotions engendered by her mental image* (affective object constancy). A photograph can help some children to bridge the gap between physical presence and mental image.

When the preschooler develops this ability to remember the "object" (the mother), and recognizes that needs can be satisfied even though the mother may not be present, the child becomes able to accept separation once again. This ability leads to a greater tolerance of temporary separation experiences and appears to signal the point of readiness for preschool. Thus the preschool child begins the slow transition from the ambivalent love characteristic of toddlers, which exists only as long as needs are satisfied, toward the more mature, mutual, give-and-take relationships seen in healthy school-age children and adults.[19]

Mahler postulates that during the fourth subphase (24 to 36 months) a stable sense of self-boundaries (emotional constancy) is attained, along with consolidation of gender identity. Verbal communication, which began during the third subphase, develops rapidly and replaces other modes of communication, although gestural language may still be used. Play becomes much more purposeful and constructive with a beginning of fantasy play, role-playing, and make-believe. Observations about the real world become more detailed and are included as a predominant theme in the child's play. There is an increasing interest in playmates and other adults. The child's rapidly expanding cognitive capacity also assists him or her to tolerate greater delays in gratification.

The fourth subphase, then, is enhanced by the unfolding of complex cognitive functions. Individuation proceeds rapidly. This subphase is not a subphase in the same sense as the first three; Mahler describes the process as "open-ended." As the child learns to recognize and deal with physical and emotional separateness from the parent, a new level of self-awareness is attained. Although Mahler's separation-individuation process is essentially mastered when the child is able to refuel from the internalized mental image, remnants of the processes and behaviors are still evident years later when we face new or traumatic situations. The tears of the child entering school or homesickness during a camping trip, entering the military or going away to college are good examples. We long for the concrete reassurances that we can face the challenges of life. Letters and telephone calls now take the place of eye contact and hugs. Even people in their 50s or older express satisfaction in the opportunity to share joys, accomplishments, and sorrows with the primary caregivers of their childhood. With maturation, the person goes beyond refueling from the image of the parent and is now able to refuel from the memories of positive experiences, support, and confidence others have bestowed. The healthy adult develops ways to "refuel" and refresh or renew one's self in the face of life's exigencies and disappointments.

Personal style becomes evident during the preschool years. Some styles can be defined in terms of orientation, such as leader, follower, participant, or onlooker. Other dimensions such as bold versus timid, hostile versus friendly, and independent versus dependent, become more individually characteristic. Children even exhibit type-A behaviors such as competitiveness, aggression, and impatience as early as the preschool years (see Chap. 35).[27]

Erikson's Initiative versus Guilt

As the child learns to function independently and make events happen through his or her own actions, he or she begins to go beyond imitation to creatively explore new materials and experiences. The child may identify ways to "help" another person. Unfortunately, although the intent may be admirable, these forages into new territory often lack sufficient physical skill or cognitive understanding of the context, contingencies, or side effects of an action. Consequently, failure, chaos, unexpected problems, disasters, and parental censorship frequently follow attempts to initiate events. For example, the child may "help" pick up the art corner, but fail to put the lid on the glue tube, thus squeezing the glue across the table or room; another may "help" mother to make the "house smell nice for Grandma" by sprinkling bath powder through every room of a freshly cleaned house. Adult handling is critical to mental health. Feelings of anxiety and guilt may emerge if the child assumes a conviction that he or she is clumsy, dumb, or bad.

Both Erikson and Mahler credit the child's psychosocial development on increased facility of motor, language, and cognitive skills. First, as the child masters skills such as buttoning, running, or eye-hand coordination, the child begins to concentrate on constructive goals, or on what can be done with these skills. Second, increased facility in the use of language allows for finer discrimination among, and expression of, ideas. The child begins to question everything and everyone incessantly and likes to predict or to control the answers. Third, increased cognitive skills permit children to expand fields of imagination. They may even frighten themselves with some of their ideas. They feel and fear, "I am what I can imagine I will be."[7, 19] Separation of reality and fantasy may be difficult for the young preschooler.

The ability to remain focused on a goal gradually increases during these years. At 15 months, the child "plays for the sake of playing." There is no obvious goal. Manipulation and exploration of materials are sufficient goals in themselves. By 20 months the child will "work persistently toward a goal," but becomes perseverative in the activity once a sense of mastery is felt. The child seems to find pleasure in proving to the self and others that the skill (e.g., block building or somersault) can be repeated at will. Most 26-month-old children can "complete a simple task," such as an adult request to imitate a 2- or 3-block pattern. They do not "correct their

mistakes" until around 32 months.[2] The stage now is set for the active, self-directed goals of the preschool years. The child begins to harness and focus energies and to evaluate actions. Consequently, preschoolers can now begin to assume some responsibility for self and others (e.g., their bodies, their toys, their pets, other children). Healthy preschoolers begin to show initiative in play and social activities.

Preschoolers begin to search for and create fantasies about the kind of person they would like to become. They begin to pretend "grownup" roles, to try to comprehend possible future careers, and to try out various role responsibilities (Fig. 11-4). Role models become critical to this process. The joyful spontaneity and characterizations of adult life can be delightful and sometimes painful to observe.

Naïveté about social rules and immature self-discipline results in behaviors which "intrude" into the spheres of others in an attempt to understand other people and events.

FIGURE 11–4.
Toddlers and preschoolers, in their striving for independence and competence, need to feel that their efforts are appreciated. Imitation of adult behaviors is very common during these years. Parents can set limits as to how much the child can help.

This behavior includes: (1) intrusion into space by vigorous locomotion; (2) intrusion into other people's minds with questions; (3) intrusion into other's social relationships by using the aggressive voice; (4) intrusion into the unknown by consuming curiosity; (5) intrusion upon or into other bodies by actual physical attack; (6) intrusion into other people's work spaces; and (7) intrusion upon other people's time by requests for a play companion or assistance with a task. These behaviors can result in feelings of discomfort and guilt because they reopen conflicts of dependence/independence and because a growing awareness of social rules warns the child that such behaviors are unacceptable. But curiosity is stronger than self-discipline.

During this period, the conscience (superego) begins to function as an inner censor of behavior (see Chap. 16). Erikson refers to the conscience as the "great governor of initiative." The child begins the slow process of becoming a "parent" to the self (internalizing controls that have previously been external). The first step in becoming a parent involves the preschooler's ability to begin to monitor the self in the place of the parents. The child hears the "inner voice" of self-observation, self-guidance, and self-punishment and increasingly assumes the supporting and controlling functions of significant adults in the environment. The child's emerging conscience can be primitive, cruel, and uncompromising as it conflicts with curiosity, creativity, initiative, and spontaneity. The crisis, then, according to Erikson, is to test one's will without an overwhelming sense of guilt about one's actions.

Actions, such as using words instead of fists, asking instead of demanding, completing a task, or waiting for one's turn, need to be reinforced frequently. When a behavior is critical to safety, the child's goal should be acknowledged as desirable, but the dangers should be explained in such a way as to maintain self-esteem and to minimize guilt. The positive outcome is a sound sense of initiative that is guided and modified by a growing sense of conscience and reality.[7, 20]

Early Identity

Many writers, including Erikson, have spoken of the preschool years as a "first adolescence."[7] It is a time for the first identity formation, as the child prepares to move away from the family into the world of school, peers, and practical achievement. The child invests a great deal of energy in refining muscular activity, accuracy of perception, assessment of roles, and communication skills. The healthy preschooler is an eager learner who begins to direct effort toward defining a sense of self.

It is difficult for the child to learn to respect limits without feeling guilty for bad wishes. Behavior and feelings/thoughts are not yet well-differentiated. The child needs to be assured that feelings of anger and disappointment are normal and to be given words and behaviors appropriate for expression of those feelings. Parents can help the child in two ways. First, they can view the child's frustration, fury, and fear sympathetically. Second, at the same time they can convey silently the reassuring message, "I will protect you from your fearful wishes." This attitude is very important to the preschool child because primitive thinking still dominates some areas of his or her life, and the child may fear that "terrible wishes" will come true. Such "magical power of thought," or believing that "whatever I wish will be" is characteristic of preschool thinking. During the preschool years, then, the child moves from being the center of the universe to assuming a modest place in human society; he or she achieves what Erikson has called a "realization of purpose."

Major sources of fear during the preschool years include fears about the body and body mutilation, fears about death, and fears associated with loss of self-control. These specific sources of anxiety are related to the child's growing identity, concern for the body, and awareness of vulnerability. The reader is referred to Chapter 10 for a discussion of other fears encountered during this period of development.

Gender Identity

Freudian theory proposes that the child has no clear concept of "boy" or "girl" until he or she makes the first observations of genital differences between self and others. For most children, this observation occurs sometime during the third or fourth year of life, depending, of course, on the child's contact with parents, siblings, other children, and animals. Observations of small children indicates that the discovery of genital differences may produce reactions of surprise or shock and may be disturbing and painful. There is evidence that the discovery may lead to infantile fantasies of body damage and mutilation. Freudians state that as parents provide the necessary support and information to correct primitive thought, the little boy begins to recognize that nothing has been taken away from the little girl, and that nothing will be taken away from him (see Chap. 14). Gradually the child begins to take pride in his or her own gender because the child is made like a beloved parent and will play a unique role as an adult.[10]

The preschool child's increasing interest in sex, body functioning, and body configurations is simply an extension of curiosity about all aspects of living. This vivacious little person, not yet cognizant of the feelings of others, is actively interested in toilet activities and innocently unaware of adult standards of modesty (although many young preschoolers sporadically display episodes of false modesty). Preschoolers want to watch others use the toilet, are full of "bathroom humor," and want to look at and touch breasts and bottoms (both their own and those of others).

The young child's interest and curiosity in sexual differences is expressed in many ways. The child begins to question, "Where did I (and other babies) come from?" and "How did I get there?" The little boy or girl may be observed to stuff a teddy bear under a T-shirt to simulate the "big tummy" of pregnancy (Fig. 11-5). Some children may ask to bathe with the parents or to touch their bodies; others may innocently burst into the bathroom or bedroom when parents or siblings are attempting to maintain privacy.

FIGURE 11–5.
This young man is envisioning himself as a woman—complete with dress, long-haired wig, and "extra room for the breasts!"

The child begins to learn how cultural concepts of gender influence feelings and behavior in relation to others.[20] Preschoolers consciously begin to learn and to practice their roles as male or female in an expanding social realm.

"Sex play" with other children often occurs in the form of assuming social-play roles (e.g., mother-father, doctor-patient). Parents are often concerned about how to handle sex play, masturbation, and the preschooler's consuming curiosity related to gender differences. Parents must respect the child's curiosity and actions as being normal without judging the child or the activity as wrong or bad. At the same time, parents must decide on limits of privacy for themselves and others. This is the age to help the child begin to learn about "public" self and "private" self. Masturbation and toileting are natural activities involving the "private" self. Such clarification sets limits without criticism, thereby reducing the potentially damaging emotional undertones. Such clarification also lays a foundation for prevention of sexual abuse.

When parents discover their child involved in sex play with other children, the children can be reminded about "the private self" and then be asked to dress and find something else to do. The parents of both children can talk privately with them about the incident at a later time. Talking privately helps each child to maintain a sense of dignity. Children are often

ashamed or worried about their games, even though they cannot control their curiosity; excessive shame or anxiety connected with the genitals can seriously disturb the child's personality development and adult sexual functioning. At times children appear to arrange the situation so the adults can "find out." In talking with the child, it is important to point out (1) that interest in how boys and girls are made is natural, but (2) the child cannot get all the answers to questions by looking or playing games, and (3) that the child can ask mother or father anything he or she wants to know. In this way, the child is not made to feel ashamed or frightened. Curiosity can be satisfied within the context of the parents' moral philosophy while helping the child to set more socially acceptable limits on behavior. The issue of sexual curiosity may be discussed along with discipline if the child is cared for by another person in the parents' absence (i.e., if both parents work).

All questions should be answered simply and truthfully without elaborate explanations. Preschoolers can accept straightforward answers, even though they may not understand them completely. Children should learn the correct terms for body parts. They gradually learn the basic anatomical structures and functions of their own body and those of the opposite gender as well as simple facts about conception, pregnancy, and the birth process. Preschool children can be told that a baby grows for several months in a special place inside the mother and that there is a special place for the baby to come out when it is ready to be born. Information must be modified according to the child's cognitive development. Numerous books are available to assist parents in teaching their children.

Most families in the United States believe that the young child must realize and accept the fact that parents have a private life from which he or she is excluded. The parents' bedroom can become a symbol of such privacy. Many parents exclude the child from the dressing, toileting, and bathing of the parent of the opposite gender. Other parents do not feel strongly about this, or may feel strongly about **not** hiding everyday activities of personal hygiene. If the child does happen to walk into the room with a nude parent or when they are involved in lovemaking, the parents should handle the situation as naturally as possible, without embarrassment or excitement, redirecting the child's attention to other issues or environmental concerns. In any case, the child should learn very early that mother and father belong to each other and that the quality of their love for each other is different from, but does not eclipse, the quality of their love for the child.

FACTORS AFFECTING PSYCHOSOCIAL DEVELOPMENT

Significant Relationships

The role of the family, especially the parents, is discussed either directly or indirectly in almost every chapter of this text. Family relationships lay the foundation for all future interactions. Family experiences provide the opportunities for a child to become aware of the emotions of others as well as of his or her own, to appreciate individual differences, and how to negotiate. During toddlerhood, the child is capable of experiencing sympathy toward family members, although this is partly an imitation of the attention and ministrations offered to the child at times of stress. (Paradoxically, a young child who has been the victim of abuse may attempt to soothe a frustrated abuser when sensing that there is again a danger of being harmed.)

Relationships with Siblings

Siblings offer constant challenges to the development of interpersonal relationships. Firstborn children are most likely to experience the arrival of a sibling during the toddler or preschool years. Limited intellectual maturity makes it difficult to understand that a parent can love two or more children at the same time. Sibling rivalry arises when the child fears that the new arrival has stolen, or will steal, the parents' affections and attentions. Poorly identified feelings and language skills set the stage for aggression and negative social behaviors. When unresolved, such rivalries can mar the child's developing personality and can even continue into the adult years. Yet, when childhood rivalries are resolved successfully, the sibling bond can become one of support and companionship for a lifetime.

The single most critical factor for parents to remember is to recognize and affirm each child's individuality. Comparisons of abilities, behaviors, characteristics, or interests tend to exacerbate feelings of tension. Special days and accomplishments can be recognized without a need to "compensate" the other child—his or her time will come. Now is a time to teach the children how to be proud of each other. Attempts to "be fair" seem "unfair" to one of the children. Planned, uninterrupted private time which focuses on the child's choice of activity is one of the best ways to recognize and affirm individuality. Preschoolers need at least 30 minutes daily. Adolescents need at least one 2- to 3-hour period per week of planned private time with a parent. Each child should be allowed to have some toys and friends that do not have to be shared.

Obviously, not all children experience positive feelings toward their siblings all the time; such thinking would be contrary to human nature and especially to the egocentrism of the normal preschooler. Younger children tend to grab toys and knock down "constructive masterpieces." These scenarios offer opportunities to teach patience and humor. The older child can be helped to see his or her own developmental progress and to participate in becoming a helper or teacher of the younger sibling. Parents can laugh at the inconveniences and give an extra hug for good measure. Wise parents also provide fun activities that children can enjoy together such as water play, bubble blowing, and finger or pudding painting.

Young children may be "allowed" to play with older siblings, but are not always happy with the roles they are assigned (e.g., "baby" when playing house). Other young children do not seem to mind what roles they play as long as they are included; they willingly become the sibling's servant in exchange for the privilege of participation.

Relationships with Grandparents

The influence of grandparents on the developing child varies with the personality structure of the persons involved as well as the social structure of which they are a part (see Chap. 36). When grandparents engage in a mutually fun-seeking relationship, the child usually looks forward to their times together (although the grandparents may be a threat to the parents' rules of discipline in such situations). The grandparent who is in some way aloof when he or she interacts with the child may teach the child that material goods serve as tokens of recognition or as substitutes for more meaningful relationships. Separation or infrequent visitation need not be synonymous with apathy if the quality of relationship is rich and meaningful to both when they are together. Cards, letters, and telephone calls can help maintain a meaningful relationship.

Those grandparents who serve as surrogate parents may affect the child's development as strongly as if they were the child's real parents (Fig. 11-6). If the grandparents live in the home with the parents and child, the three-way relationship may become very complex, since discipline and values may be sources of conflict. Many families still reside within extended family groups where any member may hold the reins of power. In some Native American cultures, for example, the grandmother, not the parent, has authority over the grand-

FIGURE 11–6.
Grandparents can play a significant role in transmitting cultural and family values to young children.

children (to the point of being consulted if the child needs a consent form signed for surgery). The lines of authority and responsibility must be clearly defined in each multi-generation family to prevent frictions resulting from role confusion (see Chap. 29).

Relationship with Age-Mates

Toward the middle of the second year, children become curious about the behaviors and play activities of their peers. At first, there is no understanding of the other child's humanness, and consequently other babies and toddlers are treated as inanimate objects or pets. Only gradually does the child become aware that other children are human and have feelings like his or her own. During the preschool years, "buddies" and "best friends" begin to appear, which is manifested by ensuring that the other child's rights are protected.

The older toddler's first reaction to the distress of an age-mate (other than a sibling) usually takes the form of bursting into tears. This is probably a display of "sympathetic participation" rather than actual empathy, and such behavior probably reflects poorly differentiated boundaries between the child's feelings and those expressed by others. True empathy, which in the beginning is sporadically displayed for sometimes questionable reasons (e.g., guilt or wanting to be in charge), begins to appear in the late preschool years. Relationships with peers tend to reflect relationships observed or experienced in the home.

Relationships with Pets

Many adults have fond memories of their childhood pets. Having a pet who loves a child unconditionally gives the child a sense of self-worth. With guidance, young children can learn the facts of life and death, gentleness, compassion, caring, and sharing by having animals in the environment. An only child may value a pet both as a playmate and as a prized possession to "show off" when others come to visit. Being introduced to various animals by an understanding adult can help a child to overcome fears of certain animals, or to learn how to approach an unfamiliar animal. Children without pets can learn to appreciate the lives and purposes of other living beings when a thoughtful teacher brings an animal to school.

Many parents believe that a pet will teach the youngster to be responsible. Such parents are likely to be disappointed. A sense of responsibility cannot be acquired overnight; it develops gradually, and must be modeled, taught, and reinforced by caregivers. In choosing an animal for children, the parent or teacher should consider the temperament and habits of the animal as well as its compatibility with the family and their lifestyle. Responsibilities should be determined beforehand (e.g., schedule and type of feedings required, walking the animal, cleaning up accidents, grooming the pet, and doctor's visits). Veterinarians and the library are valuable sources of information. Above all, a family with both a young child and a pet must continuously assess their ability to live safely in each other's presence.

Stress and the Young Child

Some children are able to maximize their potentials **because of** their families; others, it seems, do the same **in spite of** their families. Young children may be presented with additional stressors or tasks because of family events. The child of divorced parents, for example, must often adjust to a new home environment, deal with anxiety of separation from a parent, and a new substitute caregiver if the custodial parent works outside the home. Because of the child's immature cognitive structures, he or she may perceive stress in situations that adults or older children take for granted, and may use different coping strategies to face the event.[16,17] The preschooler may need to be helped to overcome guilt that he or she is being punished for misbehavior or has caused the divorce.

Regression to earlier levels of social and emotional adaptation may be seen to some degree in all children who are under stress from illness, separation from parents, birth of a sibling, or any other factor. Inept parenting practices, presence of a handicapped sibling, child abuse and neglect, new teachers, hostile social environments, family conflict, community overcrowding, poverty, parental absence, mental illness of parent, threat of war, or death of a family member all serve as stressors to young children.[16,17] Because of the lack of refined verbal skills, the young child's adaptation to stress must be assessed through nonverbal behavior responses. The child may express stress through increased crying and temper tantrums; self-criticism and self-punishment (e.g., head-banging, self-slapping and name-calling); changes in patterns of eating, sleeping, and toileting; restlessness, hyperirritability, hyperactivity, and aggression; stereotyped, perseverative play activities; withdrawal, mobilization, and depression; clinging or regression to infantile behaviors; signs of tensions such as teeth grinding, rigidity, refusal of touching, trembling, or stuttering; and increased use of primitive gratification (thumbsucking, rocking, masturbation).[17] Although these behaviors may be "normal" for a child during an acute crisis, they are not positive adaptive responses in a developmental sense unless they are used only temporarily as the child mobilizes the strength to deal with the stressor in a better way.[1,16]

Tensional Outlets

Some degree of anxiety is both normal and necessary for growth. Stress is a normal part of life and living.[16] It functions as an energizer—an impetus for problem solving, decision making, or skill performance. When tension becomes marked, the excessive energies may be released through physical activities (motor discharge). Many parents discover that their toddler or preschooler develops what appear to be bad habits, such as body-rocking, head-banging, masturbation, or thumbsucking. These behaviors may simply reflect the child's way of dealing with tension by providing a predictable, soothing form of self-stimulation. Most children outgrow the need to resort to these behaviors unless they become a way to procure coveted parental attention.

Some behaviors may persist through the early years and into the school age period of development. Children of $2\frac{1}{2}$, $3\frac{1}{2}$, and $5\frac{1}{2}$ to 6 years appear to harbor more tension than other ages.[18] Many parents may be able to accept these behaviors during infancy but may consider them to be signs of insecurity, unhappiness, immaturity, or maladjustment as the child grows older, reasoning that "normal children don't behave this way." A parental attitude of calmness, relaxation, and acceptance will help to reduce tension and thus will benefit the child.

These behaviors may also be used by the child simply because they provide pleasurable sensations. Thumbsucking as a form of tension relief often reaches a peak during late infancy or early toddlerhood. This form of behavior, along with practical suggestions for dealing with it, is discussed in Chapter 8.

SECURITY OBJECTS. The use of security objects or transitional objects is common during toddlerhood. The toddler begins to use inanimate objects provided by the parents, such as car keys, a piece of silky material, a stuffed toy, or a baby bottle, to face the insecurity experienced when separated from the parent. Separation from the mother may seem less intense to the young child who is able to cling to an object identified with her.[13] Some toddlers may carry a blanket with them at all times; others may use a "security blanket" only at bedtime when they separate from the activities of a busy day, or when they are unusually distressed. Security objects are often used in conjunction with thumbsucking or other forms of tensional outlets. The specific object and use of that object is unique for each child.

ROCKING. Around 25 weeks of age, an infant gets up on the hands and knees and begins to rock. This developmentally normal rocking generally subsides once the child is able to creep; however, once started, this behavior may persist for several years as a form of vestibular stimulation and self-soothing. Rocking behavior often reaches a peak around $2\frac{1}{2}$ to $3\frac{1}{2}$ years and then gradually fades away. Although rocking is essentially harmless to the child, it may be troublesome for the parents. Since rocking during toddlerhood occurs primarily at bedtime, parents may try several things to minimize the behavior and the noise such behaviors may create: cribs can be padded and tightly screwed together, and a rug can be placed under the crib. These measures will reduce noise and movement, so that the rocking behavior may not be as reinforcing for the child. Sometimes a prolonged bedtime routine that involves pleasurable, quiet activity may reduce tension and minimize auto-rocking. Some children may spontaneously release this form of relaxer when they are moved to a larger bed.

HEAD-BANGING. Head-banging is similar to rocking, but is more frightening for parents, since it may result in actual bumps or welts on the child's forehead. The child simply selects a hard surface (e.g., bed frame, wall, stove) and bumps the head (usually the forehead) against it. This form of tensional outlet usually begins to disappear around 3 years of age as language skills increase.

Head-banging is common enough to be listed as a variation of development; this view can be reassuring for parents. Except for welts and bruises, it is uncommon for the head banger to do any real damage. Parents can assist the head banger by picking the child up and comforting him or her, but without drawing attention to the behavior. Distraction with music, a toy, or some other device is also helpful. As a rule, scolding and punishing are completely ineffective. Assessment of the environment from the child's perspective may identify stressors that could be eliminated. A more responsive, appropriately stimulating environment may also help to reduce the behavior.

Head-banging and rocking are considered normal when they (1) begin in late infancy, (2) occur at naptime, bedtime, or when the child is ill, and (3) last for less than 1 hour at a time. These tensional outlets, once commenced, become hard to break habits, and even though stressors are reduced, may not fully extinguish for months or years. Pre-bedtime rocking from the parent may reduce the need to rock or head-bang after being placed in the crib.

MASTURBATION. Masturbation is another tensional outlet of early childhood. It does not have the same social or sexual connotations to the young child that it does to adults. Young children may masturbate before they sleep, or when they are fatigued or bored. Masturbation serves the child as a form of self-love when lonely, self-employment when bored, and self-consolation when upset.

Late in the first year, the male infant may discover genital sensations; the genitals, however, do not become an important focus of pleasurable sensations until the third year or later. At this time, one can observe an increased interest in, and more frequent handling of the genitals by the child. Children $2\frac{1}{2}$ to 3 years old are often very casual in the way they handle themselves. When his or her hands stray to the genitals, the young child is not self-conscious about the presence of others. As the child grows older, he or she begins to internalize adult standards and thus tends to masturbate only when alone.

Although masturbation may comfort the child, it can cause conflicts for many parents. The manner in which parents respond to this behavior can significantly affect the child's developing awareness of his or her own sexuality and feelings about the self. If a parent strongly forbids this behavior, a child may feel extreme guilt or shame when, for example, half asleep, he cannot keep himself from doing what is forbidden.

Experts differ in suggestions for dealing with masturbation. A realistic and objective assessment of how much masturbation is occurring is essential. The occasional or before bedtime variety is usually considered normal, but persistent masturbation to the exclusion of other activities needs intervention. Many psychologists feel that excessive parental efforts to prevent masturbation may be psychologically harmful and suggest ignoring the behavior when it occurs.[18] They suggest that parents may exert mild pressure to eliminate the behavior, but the emphasis should be to assess and to improve the child's life in general so that the child will feel less tension or will find other means of satisfaction. Personal achievements and relationships should be the child's main source of satisfaction. Redirection of attention to other activities, especially those that involve both hands, appears to be a comfortable and productive way to deal with masturbation.

Frequent and open masturbation by the school-age child does not have the same meaning as the casual touching characteristic of toddlers. Persistence of masturbation in older children may indicate unresolved anxieties; it may become a "too ready consolation" for mishaps, failures, or feelings of discomfort. In fact, a child who touches the genitals repeatedly throughout the day, usually derives no pleasure from this behavior; it restricts the ability to become fully involved in more productive behaviors, it begins to interfere with social relationships, and it may interfere with sexual relationships later in life. Parents may want professional assistance in evaluating or handling such behavior in a child.

SLEEP DISTURBANCES. Sleep disturbances are common during the toddler and preschool years. During toddlerhood, when the separation-individuation struggle is at its peak, falling asleep may represent another separation. Mild sleep disturbances of a transitory nature are a normal phenomenon in children 15 to 30 months of age. The sleep disturbances may be related to an anxiety dream in which a frightening experience of waking life (particularly a separation experience) is reexperienced. The child will awaken with frightened cries, both as a reaction to the dream and a summons to the parents.

The toddler may resist sleep even if the parents come to comfort him or her. In early childhood, a dream is considered a real event; it is not until the middle or late preschool years that a child knows that dreaming is not a real event (Fig. 11-7). Before then, the child is convinced that there really was "a car about to hit me," or "a tiger under the bed." (A more detailed discussion of fears and dreams is found in Chapter 10.)

When preschoolers have older siblings who stay up later, they may rebel at bedtime and not sleep well because they exaggerate what they may be missing. Sleep disturbances may be legitimately triggered or intensified by illness, moving to a new home, the arrival of a new baby, a prolonged separation from the parents, staying up to watch television, or overstimulating movies. Busy parents may not realize that overscheduled lifestyles may breed sleep problems in their children. Even waking up to find a strange baby-sitter may be traumatic enough to disturb a toddler's or a preschooler's sleep for several weeks. A consistent bedtime ritual is helpful.

The child who suffers from sleep disturbances or awakens in the middle of the night with anxious, fearful cries should, of course, be reassured by the mother or father. The parents should try to reassure the child in the child's own bed. If the parents offer the child too many special satisfac-

FIGURE 11–7.
Young children have difficulty separating reality from fantasy. Consequently, pretend animals and people can provide positive suggestions and role models, as well as frightening experiences.

tions and pleasures, such as prolonged rocking, a bottle, toys, or the opportunity to come into bed with them, they may inadvertently provide another motive for waking—the motive of pleasure gain. The parents should go to the child in an unhurried manner and talk in a quiet voice. The diaper should be checked and changed if necessary. If very young and unduly upset, the child may be held for a few minutes, but then should be put back to bed again, even though still awake. An older child can be patted and talked to reassuringly. After the child has had time to awaken fully and to absorb the reassurance, he or she will usually go back to sleep. Some parents find that children who have developed the habit of awakening in the middle of the night may have to "cry it out" for several nights before they realize that the previous reinforcers of their waking-up behaviors are no longer available. Other parents feel that this solution is too punitive and prefer to live with the situation until it resolves itself (which may be 6–12 months!). Another alternative is for the parent to sleep in the child's room for a few nights, on a cot or a floor pad. After the child is asleep, the parent can leave for the more comfortable bed.

The child who has severe anxiety at bedtime, wakes up several times at night, and clings desperately to the mother or the father in panic (to be differentiated from anger) needs more support. This type of severe sleep disturbance indicates an excessive reaction to separation or fears that the child has developed. Parents may need to seek professional assistance in determining the source of the child's anxiety and in modifying daily routines to reduce the child's anxieties. If the child has been recently hospitalized or otherwise separated from the parents, extra attention before bedtime may be helpful. The parent may put the child to bed but stay with the child to read or to sew, thus providing additional reassurance. A night light and listening to gentle music or story records frequently prove beneficial to children.

Development of Self-Control

Learning self-control—how to handle frustration and aggression—is one of the more critical tasks of the toddler and preschool years. Frustration of goals or will elicits a surge of adrenalin, which creates excessive energy within the child. The normal response is to discharge this energy through aggressive behavior toward the source of frustration. However, the child must learn to control and to use aggressive impulses constructively to avoid infringing upon others or depriving them of their rights.

When children fail to learn how to control the expression of their emotions, explosive, negative, manipulative behavior may become a lifetime pattern for social relationships. Many of these children terminate their education prematurely and experience socio-economic problems during the adult years (e.g., few military promotions, low-status jobs, erratic work trajectory, higher divorce rate, parenting difficulty).[4]

Socialization, the acquisition of culturally acceptable standards of behavior (which includes restricting some forms of impulses, wishes, and aggressive behavior), is achieved through the laws of learning theory. The child acquires self-control as the parents model appropriate responses and set and enforce limits. **Patterns of parental control during these early years serve as patterns of self-control in later years.**[14] The toddler's ability to modulate aggression is highly correlated with the parents' ability to promote a warm, positive, emotionally responsive relationship with the child and with each other.[15]

Spitz observed a developmental sequencing of four behavior patterns in response to the frustration of self-will.[23] The infant's response to limits is usually **passivity.** For example, when a toy is removed from an infant or the infant is told "No" when touching the television knob, the child generally retreats and cooperates. As the child matures, memory, goals, and will become stronger. The phase of passivity soon changes into active **physical aggression** or resistance. The young toddler frequently strikes out at the adult or the object seen as the source of frustration (Fig. 11-8). This form of behavior is a natural expression of the child's progress from relative dependence toward increasing autonomy, self-assur-

FIGURE 11–8.
Healthy children express their egocentrism, aggression, and unwillingness to share in many ways. Thsoe who have not yet become sufficiently socialized to adopt culturally approved ways of discharging their affective energy will physically attack other children, adults, or objects. Constructive direction by an adult may be needed.

ance, and initiative. It is the child's way of expressing autonomy of thinking, of negotiating the individuation process.[30]

Temper tantrums are an example of active physical aggression. The child may aggressively resist, but at the same time he or she may want to do what the beloved parents want. It is not uncommon for toddlers to utter parental prohibitions to themselves. For example, a toddler may walk over to a stove or an electric outlet, knowing it is out of bounds, and begin to play with the forbidden object while mumbling, "No, no, hurt, no" to himself. The prohibition is remembered, but self-discipline is inadequate to prevent the behavior—**curiosity is stronger than self discipline.** This process of incorporating parental inhibitions to attain self-control requires several years.[9]

With increased cognitive maturity and language skills, the child's physical aggression gradually gives way to a somewhat more sophisticated form of frustration management—**verbal aggression**—particularly four letter words, bathroom language, or "I don't like you!" The child's increased mental flexibility allows the symbols (words) to stand in for physical aggression. The child "hits" the other person with words and ideas instead of fists and toys. Verbal aggression expands during the preschool years (as physical aggression decreases) into name-calling and verbal rejection (i.e., "I don't want you to be my Mommy," "I hate you," or "I wish you were dead").

With adult assistance, the young child begins to move toward **acceptance** of limits and more socialized forms of impulse control and frustration. The preschooler who yells, "You're a poopy pants" to a peer who has "stolen" a toy may not appear to be any more mature than the preschooler who retaliates with outward physical attack. However, this child's initial use of language will lead to the more socialized response, "That's mine. Give it back," and eventually, "That's mine, but I'll share it with you if you share with me."[30] It is important to note that the child's transition is not smooth. Children will fluctuate in their ability to control themselves for many years, and it is not uncommon to see the preschooler physically attack a peer, even though the child has the ability to use words instead.

Schuster has observed that each of Spitz's four stages of response to frustration is comprised of three or four overlapping substages, which appear to emerge sequentially (Table 11-1). These substages, especially physical aggression toward self, generally are resolved quickly by the normally developing child, but may be extended or even fixated by emotionally or behaviorally disturbed children, thus requiring adult guidance. Adults who insist on obedience and use stern approaches to child discipline are generally effective at extinguishing the undesirable behaviors and eliciting **compliance.** However, when the adult is absent, the negative behaviors tend to reappear because the child has developed fear of punishment in the presence of the adult rather than a desire to **cooperate.** When adults show respect and help the child to see alternative approaches and tensional outlets, self-discipline and prosocial behaviors emerge which are used even when no adult is present to enforce "rules." Cooperation retains the self-respect, the self-control, and the autonomy of the child. Compliance extinguishes them, even though on the surface the adult may obtain the same behavior. Cooperation is growth-inducing; compliance is growth-inhibiting.

The child who is taught how to control events through alternative means or goals or through bargaining eventually develops internally mediated, mutually cooperative behaviors

TABLE 11-1. PRESCHOOLER RESPONSES TO FRUSTRATION

I. Passive Acceptance
   A. Naïveté
   B. Bewilderment
   C. Protest
   D. Noncompliance

II. Physical Aggression
   A. Toward others (bite, hit, pinch, kick)
   B. Toward self (grab hands, bite arm)
   C. Toward inanimate objects (throw, hit)
   D. Generalized energy expression (run, foot-stomp)

III. Verbal Aggression
   A. Overt toward people
   B. Overt toward inanimate
   C. Overt to self
   D. Covert to self

IV. Socially Acceptable Behavior
   A. Alternative means
   B. Bargaining
   C. Alternative goal

V. Cooperation

(Developed by Clara Schuster, based on work of R. A. Spitz.)

with other persons. However, the child who is unable to use alternative strategies for dealing with frustration may comply with externally enforced behaviors without developing alternative means or goals for dealing with frustrations. Many persons continue to use physical aggression (e.g., kick car tire or abuse spouse) or verbal aggression (e.g., swear or name-call) throughout life because of inadequate learning of how to deal with angry feelings during early childhood.

Parents, through the limits they set, play a major role in the child's ability to learn self-control. Limit setting for young children should not be considered as punitive but rather as a vehicle for enabling the child to balance maturing capabilities with an expanding world and an awareness of the feelings and needs of others. The setting of firm limits helps to develop self-control, character, orderliness, and efficiency.

It is not advisable for parents to respond to the blows or bites of the physically aggressive child by striking or hitting back. This may serve only to reinforce the child's physical behaviors. The parents should stop or restrain the behavior while acknowledging the feelings and identifying other ways in which to express anger. If parents deny their child the right to express feelings in any way, the child may infer that the emotions themselves are unacceptable and may begin to repress and deny quite normal feelings. This child may grow up believing that any anger or other strong feeling will result in alienation, and consequently may concentrate on behavior rather than feelings, even in intimate relationships.

Parents need to acknowledge the feelings which elicit the child's aggressive behavior. The feelings are normal and healthy in context. Children who are given permission to have the feelings are in a better position to understand themselves, to separate their feelings from their behavior, and to choose a more socially acceptable way of expressing frustration (Table 11-2).

Once the six principles of Table 11-2 are incorporated into the parent–child relationship, they can frequently be telescoped, putting more of the responsibility on the child. The following scenario was overheard in the women's fashion section of a department store between a Daddy (holding a 10-month-old baby) and his increasingly restless 3-year-old:

Daddy: "You're bored, aren't you, because Mommy is taking so long?"

Son: (face brightening) "Uh-huh."

Daddy: "What do we do when we're bored?"

Son: (after some hesitation) "Find something fun."

Daddy: "That's right! Do you think you can find something fun to do?"

Son: (looking around) "A mirror!"

The toddler found the three-way mirror and entertained himself contentedly for 20 minutes. A potentially difficult parent–child situation was defused and redirected toward the child's psychosocial growth. Everyone was a winner!

The child's education in self-control takes many years. Although improved control can be expected by the end of the third year, the child is still a pleasure-loving little person, and

TABLE 11-2. STEPS TO HELPING THE CHILD (OF ANY AGE) TO UNDERSTAND SOCIALLY ACCEPTABLE BEHAVIORS

1. **Acknowledge the child's feelings:** "You are angry because . . . disappointed when . . . sad because . . ."

2. **State why the child is upset:** "Because Sister took your toy . . . you want to go bye-bye with Grandma . . . the toy won't work."

3. **Set a limit on the behavior:** "But I can't let you bite Mommy . . . Sister, that hurts."

4. **Assure the child of your love and protection:** "I love you. I won't let Sister hurt you, and I can't let you bite Sister."

5. **Give the child an alternative behavior:** "Use your words. Say 'Help, Daddy,' or, 'My toy.'" Sometimes it also helps to give the child an object that she can bite or to suggest a pillow, toy, or piece of furniture that is O.K. to hit to get rid of the anger energy. Some children like to "run off" or "scream off" the extra energy generated by anger or frustration. Identify a place in the house or yard where that behavior is O.K.

6. **Help the child to experience success when he uses the alternative behavior:** Have Daddy "help" or encourage Sister to return the toy.

lapses in control are frequent. Without consistent parental discipline, a child is inclined to remain on a more primitive discharge level because it is easier. Without limits, the child will experience heightened anxiety, tension, and ambivalence during this critical stage of social development.

Response to Illness and Hospitalization

Children 1 to 3 years of age average 8 to 9 illnesses per year; 4- to 10-year-olds average 4 to 6 per year; for the rest of life, people average 4 illnesses per year.[21] Illness is a threat to the young child's burgeoning autonomy and to the separation-individuation process.

Hospitalization may present one of childhood's most fearful experiences, particularly for children under 6 years of age. When a child is hospitalized, the energy normally used to attack and to master the activities of daily living and tasks of development must be reinvested by the child in efforts to cope with the added physiological and psychological stresses inherent in the hospital setting. The hospitalized child experiences separation from significant others, familiar environment, and everyday routine; unconscious perception of threat to life or body integrity; regard of illness as punishment; painful procedures; fears of mutilation or disfigurement; and loss of independent activity. In addition, the anxiety of parents or other caregiving adults often is communicated to the child. One or more of these stressors, when associated with hospitalization, may be sufficient to produce a significant degree of anxiety or tension. The age of the child and the child's relationship with the parent may be crucial variables in determining the extent to which the child can successfully cope with these stress-producing situations.[29] The toddler and the young preschooler are particularly sensitive to separation

from parents during hospitalization (see Chap. 18 for discussion of protest, despair, and detachment/denial).

Parents play a major role in promoting the young child's adjustment and psychological health both during and after hospitalization. The mere presence of parents offers support as the child attempts to cope with stress (unless they are so anxious that they communicate their anxiety to the child). Children who make the most successful adjustments to the stressors involved in hospitalization are those who have the most secure relationships with their parents.

A child normally draws on the strength of the parents to cope with stress and anxiety.[21] The fundamental basis for personality development is the sense of trust that results from parent–child interactions. This sense of trust may be jeopardized by the child's hospitalization. In the child's mind, the parents may have allowed or caused the traumatic events to occur. Resultant changes in the child's behaviors and responses may lead the parents to feel that they are dealing with a different child. Thus, the parent–child relationship may need to be renegotiated. The interactions may positively or negatively affect the child's physical recovery and future mental health. If positive, supportive parent–child interaction can be maintained while the child is hospitalized, the relationship and the child's emotional health can be strengthened. If the parents cannot be present during much of the child's hospitalization, alternative measures must be taken by the hospital staff to preserve the child's sense of security as well as autonomy and initiative (Fig. 11-9). Assigning the child to a small group of the same people to administer care may help the child to maintain a trust in people, to predict events and responses, and to express feelings.

However, childhood illness is not all negative. Illnesses "provide many opportunities for children to increase their knowledge of self, others, prosocial behavior, and empathy, as well as a realistic understanding of the sick role."[21] The physical and emotional changes accompanying illness provide opportunities for the child to begin to cognitively recognize the different domains of self. The experiences with recovery of self or others helps the child to begin to appreciate stressors in context, engendering hope for a "better tomorrow," rather than seeing illness as a permanent or terminal condition.

Young children tend to confuse "feeling bad" with bad behavior, as punishment for a transgression, or parental punishment.[21] Thus, the opportunity is offered for parents to help the child to separate the physical self from the emotional and social selves. The child can begin to realize unseen causes of events and to develop empathy for others who are ill. Illness can also offer an opportunity to learn how to balance dependence and independence.

Child Abuse

Child abuse is a comprehensive term that includes intentional or unintentional physical abuse or neglect, emotional abuse or neglect, and sexual abuse. Three major factors appear to be necessary for a child to become a victim: specific abuser traits, categorical environmental conditions, and selected child

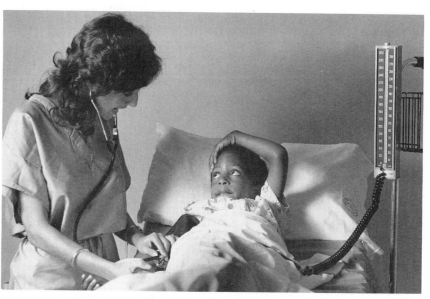

FIGURE 11–9.
Holistic care of the hospitalized child includes a consideration of developmental needs, understandings, and fears. Effective approaches can facilitate continued positive social-emotional development.

characteristics which are viewed negatively by the potential abuser.

Individuals who have the potential to abuse show one common characteristic: a low tolerance for frustration. The abuser has little emotional energy to cope with the usual tasks of child rearing, sees the child as an extension of his or her self, and is extremely vulnerable to additional crises of any nature. The person strikes out at the child as the source of or scapegoat for frustration and anxiety (Spitz, level two). Often the precipitating factor for the abuse is something that would not upset an emotionally stable adult who is familiar with normal childhood growth and development. Abusers usually have high, self-oriented, inappropriate expectations, which the child cannot fulfill. The person with the potential to abuse often cannot cope with the ordinary daily tasks of child rearing (from caring for the totally dependent infant to guiding the child in self-help skills, speech development, toilet training, and so forth).

The high-risk environment typically includes high-stress factors such as long-term illness or disability, interactional discord, financial deficit, unemployment, and alcohol or drug addiction. Thus, the abuser's emotional reserves may already be depleted.

Several factors predispose a child to be the victim of abuse, including temperament (such as a high or low activity level that is not in synchrony with that of the potential abuser), dependency (especially additional physical needs), and insensitivity to parental interests or needs. When considering the characteristics of the normal toddler and preschooler—the quests for autonomy and initiative, lack of self-control, intrusive behaviors, and temper tantrums—it is easy to understand why they comprise the most highly abused age group.

The separation-individuation process is seriously impaired as a result of the abusive parent–child relationship. Abuse may instill the belief that no person or event can be trusted, a feeling that is characteristic of both the abuser and the abused.

The incidence of child abuse and neglect is increasing. Every person in every community must be concerned with protecting all children. Health professionals, teachers, social service persons, and law enforcement officials are taught how to identify abusive situations, and many receive training in how to help the abuser to cope positively with stress. To fully address the issue of child abuse and how the vicious cycle of abuse can be broken (abused children often become abusers) is beyond the scope of this book. The effect of abuse on the family is discussed in Chapter 33.

Play During Toddler and Preschool Years

Play assumes special significance during early childhood. It provides a "safe island" for learning the skills necessary to function autonomously or to deal with stressors. The activities of eating, dressing, bathing, locomotion, and active exploration can all become forums for play. Even periods of negativism often have a playful quality. It is during the toddler years that the beginnings of dramatic play are seen—the imitation or acting out of scenes and events of everyday life. Through dramatic play, the child tries out roles and begins to identify with the adult models he or she is exposed to. In other words, as the child mirrors and imitates, he or she begins to identify with the other person.

Simple imitative play becomes more elaborate and imaginative as the child grows into preschoolerhood. Preschoolers especially enjoy associative play, such as groups reenacting the activities of cooking, shopping, cleaning, and so forth, in preparation for actual involvement in these activities with the parents in late preschool and school age years (see Chap. 15 for further discussion of play).

Day-Care Center Experience

It is estimated that 57% to 70% of mothers of preschoolers in the United States work outside the home.[3, 11] In Europe, the percentage of working mothers runs from 75% in Italy to 97% in France.[3] Almost 25% of the children of working American mothers are in a day-care or preschool setting. Others are cared for in their own or another's home by a relative (40%) or non-relative (29%).[11]

Working parents frequently express concern about the effect of day care on their child's long-term social-emotional health, and on the parent–child relationship. Separation from the parents, the home, and the routines of family life are viewed as potentially detrimental to the child's sense of security, emotional development, and family relationships. Some studies show no negative effects;[31] others indicate that boys show more stress than girls.[12] Another study suggests that toddlers of working mothers are more peer-oriented and self-sufficient, whereas toddlers of non-working mothers have higher IQs.[22] Therefore, although some concern may be valid, the day-care experience potentially has beneficial effects on children.

Many factors interact to influence the effect of the experience: (1) the quality of the program as indicated by equipment, space, curriculum, staff-child ratio, staff knowledge of child development, and staff sensitivity to the child's needs and communication;[25] (2) parental involvement in the program and communication with the teachers; (3) the previous and ongoing parent–child relationship; (4) the maturity or readiness of the child for the separation experience; and (5) the amount of time the child is away from the parents.

Because of immature intrapsychic structures, the day-care experience is a greater stressor to the infant than to the toddler, and to the toddler than to the preschooler.[16, 28] Toddlers of mothers who do not work outside the home tend to be more cooperative and more independent in self-help, to whine less, to cope with stress more effectively, to be more enthusiastic in attacking new materials and situations, and to approach problems with a greater sense of control and structure than toddlers of working mothers.[26] Most young children learn to adapt to the separation experience and appear to do well when quality substitute care is provided.

Separation serves as a stressor. Until emotional object constancy is well-established, the child may experience difficulty tolerating the separation while simultaneously remaining comfortably attached to the parents. Some psychologists are concerned that the prematurely separated child may form many semi-exchangeable relationships rather than the secure, identity-facilitating, energy-renewing relationship parents provide.[6, 19, 28] Children who attach to their peer group rather than to their parents may develop more impersonal relationships with parents—a factor which may erode family ties and foster the acceptance of a group-imposed value system.[6] Other parents are concerned that the child's intellectual and skill development as well as social-emotional development will be delayed because of inadequate one-to-one atten-

tion. Because of these concerns, a family may choose to tighten the budget and allow one parent to remain at home.[5]

Some of these concerns can be minimized by careful selection of a child care option. The attitude of the caregiver is significant to the child's emerging self image, confidence, and values since the alternate caregiver may actually spend more time with the child than the parents themselves. Consequently, the parents should choose a person or a program which shares their value system.[5]

Children enrolled in high quality day-care programs tend to be more advanced psychosocially and cognitively (more informed about their environment, more considerate, more friendly, more socially competent, more achievement-oriented) than children attending low quality day-care programs.[25] Children also appear to be socially well-adjusted if their parents communicate frequently and positively with day-care center staff. The children of involved parents play well together (more sharing, turntaking, and laughing with each other) and take more initiative (especially in conversing with adults) than those children whose parents rarely or infrequently interact with day-care center staff.

When parents have had an open, trusting relationship with the child, it provides a secure departure point for interacting with the larger world. The child knows from experience that the parents will return at the end of the day. If the parents continue to offer private time to the child and to allow the child to "refuel" at the end of the working day, before going to the car, fixing supper, or becoming involved with other "necessities," the child seems to be able to adapt to the separation more easily and with less sense of loss.

Children have differing views as to *why* they are attending a child-care center, and these views may color their adaptation to the center as well as to life. Some may feel that the parents are banishing them as a form of punishment. One child thought that she was put out of the house "because she was too big."[13] A child who starts "school" when a new child enters the family may feel "replaced." Children who make the best adjustments are those who are able to refuel from a mental image, and whose parents are honest about their need to work, provide warm reassurances of continued love, and continue to take an active interest and part in the child's burgeoning skills.

CONCLUSION

The toddler and preschool years are pivotal to the individual's mental health. Parents can either foster or squelch the child's emerging sense of competence and self-esteem by the emotional climate they establish in the home. The natural curiosity and impulsiveness of the young child can be directed toward knowledge acquisition, competence, and self-discipline, or they can be thwarted, repressed, and stigmatized. When parents respond warmly and freely to dependence and the need to "refuel," they provide an emotional springboard for the child's independence. When a child is confident that the parent will be available if needed, it provides the security necessary to explore new horizons.

The well-developing child's curiosity and expressions of will set the stage for confrontations. However, when adults see these scenarios as opportunities for teaching, the outcome can be positive even though the experience may be difficult for the adult.

Many parents find limit setting very difficult; they may be afraid that they will not be liked by the child if they exercise control. However, discipline, periodic physical separation, and opportunities for independent functioning are just as important for the child's mental health as are love and security. The child cannot experience the pride of mastery unless there is a challenge to overcome. This is as true in the social domain as in the physical domain.

It is psychologically healthy to say "no" to children of all ages. Judicious use of limits is mandatory for helping children develop a sense of inner control, responsibility, and social competence. However, guidance must go beyond saying "no" to include value training and the identification of alternative ways to express feelings, satisfy curiosity, or meet needs.

Parental wisdom in the conduct of feeding, toilet training, sex education, and discipline can support the child's self-esteem by promoting love and confidence in the parents and by strengthening the child's own ability to regulate body needs and impulses. However, even the most ideal early environment does not eliminate all anxiety or remove the hazards that exist in the child's world. One cannot help the child avoid all fears and frustrations—nor is this desirable. There is no growth without challenge or frustration.

The ways in which young children are helped to manage frustrations determines the course of their socio-affective development. The ultimate outcome of achieving a sense of autonomy is the attainment of self-control and willpower; the eventual goal of achieving a sense of initiative is to acquire inspiration for direction and purpose.

REFERENCES

1. Bowlby, J. (1960). Grief and mourning in infancy and early childhood. *Psychoanalytical Study of the Child, 15,* 9.
2. Bullock, M., & Lutkenhaus, P. (1988). The development of volitional behavior in the toddler years. *Child Development, 59,* 664–674.
3. Cadden, V., & Kamerman, S. (1990). Where in the world is child care better? *Working Mother, September,* 62–68.
4. Caspi, A. (1987). Personality in the life course. *Journal of Personality and Social Psychology, 53,* 1203–1213.
5. Chandler, M. L. (1988). New Concerns about Child Care. *Christian Parent Today, 1,* 50–53.
6. Elkind, D. (1988). *The hurried child* (rev.ed.). Reading, MA: Addison-Wesley.
7. Erikson, E. (1968). *Identity: Youth and crisis.* New York: Norton.
8. Erikson, E. (1978). *Childhood and society* (rev.ed.). St. Albans, Eng.: Triad/Paladin.
9. Fraiberg, S. H. (1968). *The magic years: Understanding and handling the problems of early childhood.* London: Methuen.
10. Freud, S. (1935). *A general introduction to psychoanalysis* (Authorized English translation of the revised edition by J. Riviere). New York: Liveright.
11. Garland, S. B. (1989). America's child-care crisis: The first tiny steps toward solutions. *Business Week, 3114,* 64–68.
12. Gold, D., & Andres, D. (1978). Developmental comparisons between 10-year-old children with employed and non-employed mothers. *Child Development, 50*(2), 306–318.
13. Gottschall, S. (1989). Understanding and accepting separation feelings. *Young Children, 44*(6), 11–15.
14. Hammer, D., & Drabman, R. J. (1981). Child discipline: What we know and what we can recommend. *Pediatric Nursing, 7*(3), 31.
15. Heinicke, C. M., Diskin, S. D., Ramsey-Klee, D. M., & Oates, D. S. (1986). Pre- and post-birth antecedents of 2-year-old attention, capacity for relationships, and verbal expressiveness. *Developmental Psychology, 22,* 777–787.
16. Honig, A. S. (1986). Stress and coping in children (Part 1). *Young Children, 41*(4), 50–63.
17. Honig, A. S. (1986). Stress and coping in children (Part 2) Interpersonal family relationships. *Young Children, 41*(5), 47–59.
18. Ilg, F. L., Ames, L. B., & Baker, S. M. (1981). *Child behavior* (rev. ed.). New York: Barnes & Noble.
19. Mahler, M. S., Pine, F., & Bergman, A. (1975). *The psychological birth of the human infant: Symbiosis and individuation.* New York: Basic Books.
20. Maier, H. W. (1978). *Three theories of child development* (3rd ed.). New York: Harper & Row.
21. Parmelee, A. H. (1986). Children's illnesses: Their beneficial effects on behavior development. *Child Development, 57,* 1–10.
22. Schacter, F. F. (1981). Toddlers with employed mothers. *Child Development, 52,* 958–964.
23. Spitz, R. A. (1966). *No and yes: On the genesis of human communication.* New York: International Universities Press.
24. Sullivan, H. S. (1953). *The interpersonal theory of psychiatry.* New York: Norton.
25. Vandell, D. L., Henderson, V. K., & Wilson, K. S. (1988). A longitudinal study of children with day-care experiences of varying quality. *Child Development, 59,* 1286–1292.
26. Vaughan, B. E., Dean, K. E., & Waters, E. (1985). The impact of out-of-home care on child-mother attachment quality: Another look at some enduring questions. In I. Bretherton & E. Waters (Eds.), *Growing points of attachment theory and research. Monographs of the Society for Research in Child Development, 50* (1–2). Serial No.: 209.
27. Vega-Lahr, N., & Field, T. M. (1986). Type A behavior in preschool children. *Child Development, 57,* 1333–1348.
28. White, B. L. (1975). *The first three years of life.* Englewood Cliffs, NJ: Prentice-Hall.
29. Wolff, S. (1981). *Children under stress* (2nd ed.). Harmondsworth, Eng.: Penguin.
30. Wolfgang, C. H. (1977). *Helping aggressive and passive preschoolers through play.* Columbus, OH: Merrill.
31. Yarrow, M. R., Scott, P., deLeeuw, L., & Heinig, C. (1978). Child-rearing families of working and non-working mothers. In H. Bee (Ed.), *Social issues in developmental psychology* (2nd ed). New York: Harper and Row.

V LIFE-SPAN DEVELOPMENTAL CONCEPTS

Some developmental tasks (e.g., develop a philosophy for dealing with own mortality) stretch through several developmental phases. In fact, mega-concepts such as communication, death, sexuality, self-discipline, and play extend over a lifetime. The prerequisite skills for mastery of these tasks appear during the developmental years in a predictable, orderly manner as the cognitive, affective, and social domains mature. During the adult years, the concepts continue to be refined as family, cultural experiences, and self-initiated searches provide new horizons and meanings to life. Knowledge of expected developmental sequences and their manifestations can help adults to understand behaviors unique to specific age groups or circumstances, and to orchestrate experiences conducive to healthy mastery of a concept or task.

Some tasks arise from the need to master the basic skills valued by the society (e.g., develop expertise in career). Most cultures provide formal schooling opportunities to enable individuals to gain the essential skills. However, technical skills alone are insufficient preparation for adulthood. A holistic approach must be assumed to optimize development of all five domains. Many factors, not just the curricula offered, affect the success of task mastery. These factors need to be understood by professionals and parents to ensure adequate challenges and opportunities to practice the skills that lay the foundation for successful adaptation to school and, eventually, to adulthood.

Issues such as abuse, inadequate or inappropriate discipline, disability, or premature confrontation with death can place additional strain on an individual and interfere with mastery of age-appropriate developmental tasks. However, an understanding and appreciation of the unique stressors faced by individuals can spur understanding and creative approaches to task mastery. Warm, responsive relationships facilitate healthy development of persons, regardless of the unique situations they face in life.

Development of Communication and Language

Linda Smolak

Language is crucial to virtually every aspect of human life. It facilitates thought and may even be a prerequisite for the most advanced forms of thought.[97] It is integral to our social interactions and is partially responsible for cultural continuity. Indeed, it is probably the primary means of socialization, in that parents talk to children more for the purpose of teaching them how to behave than specifically to teach them language.[18] Language may also be used to express individual creativity. In fact, human language has "infinite generativity," the ability to produce (generate) an infinite number of meaningful utterances (sentences) from a finite group of symbols (namely, vocabulary words).[21]

Language requires certain brain structures and vocal apparatus (such as the tongue, lips, vocal cords, larnyx). But, physiology alone will not explain language. There are perceptual and cognitive skills that must develop. The social milieu must provide verbal stimulation and input as well as opportunities and support for speech. Even temperament may play a role in the early stages. [11, 113]

Language also affects the cognitive, affective, and social domains. For example, when people hear "he," even when it is used in the generic sense, they tend to think of a male.[62, 71, 85] Language may also help to guide our problem solving. This is a primary purpose of talking to ourselves, whether we do it aloud or internally.[37, 123] Language facilitates both expression and regulation of emotions. We know how to "count to 10" to quell anger. Finally, language is the core of social interactions, as we communicate our needs, desires, and interests to others and are able to understand their communications. Children suffering from speech delays are often rejected by their peers. Even when they get the opportunity to participate they often fail because they cannot play by the rules of social interaction.[129]

THE DEVELOPMENT OF COMMUNICATION SKILLS

Definitions

Language and communication are not synonymous. **Communication** is the broader term, referring to the ability to convey information. Preverbal infants can communicate using, for example, cries and reaching behaviors. Adults can send messages through nonverbal modes such as pictures, gestures, and facial expressions. **Language** is a system of socially defined symbols (or in Piaget's terminology, signs), organized phonologically, semantically, and syntactically for communication and representation. It includes the sign languages used by persons who are deaf as well as sound or verbal utterances.

Speech is the oral form of language. People use their lips, teeth, and tongue to form language sounds. Fluency, pitch, regulating volume, and pausing between words are all part of the speech system. These skills are learned but they also require the physical abilities to control breathing (including how much air is released) and to hear pitch and tone. Very young infants are unable to produce the breathing patterns needed for language because of rib and larynx position.[68]

Principles of Communication

Formal Features of Language

Three elements determine an utterance's form. The first, **phonology,** defines which sounds are included in the language and their combinatorial rules. The smallest units of sound in a language (which when strung together form words) are called **phonemes.** Phonological systems vary across languages. Japanese, for example, does not have an *l* sound similar to ours, and we do not roll our *r*s as Scots do. Adults usually have difficulty producing sounds not appearing in their own language.

The smallest units of meaning are known as **morphemes.** These may be entire words or **free morphemes.** For example, the word *cola* cannot be broken down into smaller units of meaning. **Bound morphemes,** by comparison, cannot stand alone. They are attached, as prefixes or suffixes, to free morphemes. Adding the bound morpheme *-s* to the free morpheme *cola* marks the word as referring to more than one cola. First words are free morphemes. Bound morphemes, including their governing rules, are acquired later, during the preschool years. **Semantics** is the meaning system of the language. It includes both the definitions of specific words and the interrelationships among words. The semantic system contains the information that allows us to recognize synonyms and antonyms. This system also identifies the roles words can play. For example, words can identify actors in a sentence, signify action, or indicate location.

Syntax refers to the rules of grammar that guide the creation of phrases and sentences from morphemes. These rules include how to make subject and verb "agree," when to make morphological changes (such as indicators for plural or tense), and, in some languages, how to apply the rules for gender markers. How people learn the specific rules used in their native language is unclear. Some theorists argue that the general principles are innate,[21] others believe they reflect cognitive development,[2, 108] and some argue they are learned through the differential reinforcement of the environment.

Language learning begins early. Even children under 2 years of age have rudimentary knowledge of phonology, semantics, and syntax. Without it, they could not produce utterances that are comprehensible to other people.

Functional Features of Language

One function of language is to transmit information among people. Language may be used to control other people's behavior, share feelings, provide information, sustain social rituals, solve problems, or imaginatively interpret reality.[127] With practice, people become adept at conveying specific messages accurately, even if their content involves absent objects, past events, or abstract concepts.

The second function of language is representation. There are many forms of representation. Some, such as miming, drawing, or pretending, are defined by the individual rather than society. These are called symbols. Others, including language, are socially defined and are called signs (see Fig. 10-2).[98] Words "stand in for" real objects, people, and events. They allow us to talk about absent or past things or even possibilities rather than reality. Words also facilitate thinking about objects or situations and are necessary for abstract thought.[37, 44, 98] This representational function is one of the features that distinguishes words from the prelinguistic infant's gestures.[96]

Language, then, is a form of communication and a type of representation. While other forms of communication and representation are available, language is the most common and most powerful form of each.

Communication Model

Components

There are at least four elements in any communication.[127] There are the *participants,* the people involved in the communication. We can freeze the communication at any moment and identify one participant as the transmitter or speaker and the other as the receiver or listener. The transmitter encodes the message, translating thoughts into words and intonation patterns and combining the words with gestures and facial expressions for emphasis. The receiver decodes the message, trying to interpret not only the individual words but also the overall intent or gist of the message.

It might appear that the participants operate independently. In fact, however, they are intertwined in an interaction where one's behavior affects the other's.[127] Even prelinguistic infants can affect their mother's speech.[87] Children must learn how to appropriately participate in conversations instead of interjecting irrelevant statements.[33] One must learn to monitor one's own statements for clarity and impact. Part of this, of course, will be based on the reaction of the other participant. Thus, the two are in a feedback loop. If the two do function independently, so that one's statements are not dependent on the other's, we consider the interaction to be a **collective monologue** rather than a **dialogue.**

The second element is the *setting* of the conversation, its time and place.[127] This includes the presence of other people. The setting affects both the phrasing and the interpretation of a message. Context is particularly important in interpreting children's early nonverbal and verbal communications. Adults rely on context to interpret crying, gestures, and language efforts.[52] For example, the phrase "Mommy sock" might be a possessive statement in one situation (as in "That is Mommy's sock") but a request in yet another (as in "Put on my sock, Mommy").

The third component is the *topic* or subject matter of the message.[127] This includes the information we wish to convey and can range from an object's name, to a desire or a fantasy. Messages include subjective as well as objective content, and information about the speaker's attitudes towards the listener. Intonation and word choice are critical components of the message.

Finally, there is the *goal* of the communication. One's purpose may be to persuade, comfort, amuse, or inform. This will affect the chosen presentation style as well as the content of the message.

The Communication Process

All four components contribute to the nature and structure of the communicative attempt. An effective, competent communicator will be able to evaluate all of these factors to maximize the likelihood of being understood. Figure 12-1 outlines the communication process as the message structure is determined and encoded, then transmitted, received, and decoded.

Nonverbal Communication

There are three broad categories of nonverbal communication.[127] First is **kinesics,** more popularly known as "body language." This includes gestures, movements, body positions, and facial expressions which convey information. Some of these movements are voluntary and controllable. Others, such as pupil dilation when one is excited, occur reflexively and cannot be controlled. The meaning of body language is largely culturally determined.[127] However, certain facial expressions, such as smiles and grimaces, have universal meaning.

The second type of nonverbal communication is **pros-**

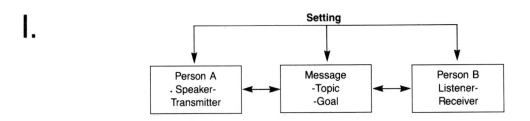

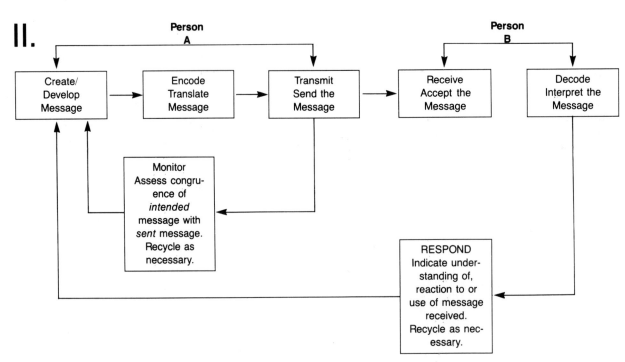

FIGURE 12–1.
The process of communication. I. General communication model. II. A "frozen moment" of communication.

ody. These nonverbal elements of speech include pitch, loudness, and pausing. Again, culture assigns the meaning to these cues. There are also biological constraints; for example, females have one more pitch register than males.[63]

Finally, there is **proxemics,** or the study of how we use space. How close together we stand when addressing someone can convey trust, liking, and status. There are cultural differences in how close to stand when speaking to another. Our failure to recognize these differences can interfere with effective communication.

Gestures, facial expression, and voice tone add important information to adult verbalizations and can even convey a message without words. For the language-learning child, nonverbal communication is important in understanding others' behavior. Five-month-olds react negatively to angry faces but smile at happy faces.[17] Nine-months-olds will look in the appropriate direction when adults point at an object. Children whose parents point while labelling objects develop language more quickly.[3]

Children's earliest communicative attempts also rely heavily on nonverbal cues. Their preverbal and single word utterances are almost uninterpretable without accompanying gestures.[127] Children use three types of gestures.[127] The first, **deictic gestures,** are used to point to objects or places. **Pantomimic gestures** copy components of objects or events so that the child "acts out" what happened. These gestures typically occur with an object present and so are not considered representational.[96] Finally, **semantic and relational gestures** add information about object characteristics (e.g., shape or size) or feelings (e.g., anger or cautiousness). As children gain verbal facility, deictic and pantomimic gestures decrease while semantic and relational gestures increase.[127]

Prerequisites to Language Acquisition

Physical Skills
Figure 12-2 shows the main speech organs. Before a child can speak, control of the lips and tongue must be mastered. Sounds are partially determined by the shape and placement of the lips and tongue. So, for example, the difference between the sounds [i] (as in beat) and [u] (as in boot) is that in [i] the tongue is raised near the front of the roof of the mouth while in [u] it is raised near the back. Lip and tongue muscles are more highly developed in humans than in other animals. Control develops gradually, which is one reason young children cannot pronounce all sounds. Most children will gain sufficient control simply through practice. Abnormalities in the oral apparatus, such as cleft palate or partial attachment of the tongue (tongue tie), will cause problems in articulatory development.

The language user must also regulate breathing and swallowing. The air intake during speech is much greater and faster than during "normal" breathing. Similarly, the outflow of air is quite different since it is primarily through the mouth rather than the nose and so involves different

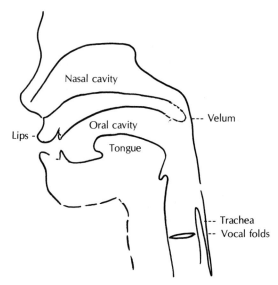

FIGURE 12–2.
Model of the vocal mechanism. Articulators within the oral cavity as well as in proximity to it (e.g., sinuses) contribute to the uniqueness of each voice.

muscles. Persons with cerebral palsy frequently experience difficulty with breath coordination.

Babies are well-prepared to receive social stimulation, particularly in the form of language. There is both neurological and behavioral evidence that babies can distinguish between various language sounds.[35,83] Language is processed in the brain differently than are other sounds.[28] Babies seem to prefer human voices to other sounds and will work particularly hard to hear their mothers' voices. The preference for mother's voice is apparent even in newborns.[29]

Hearing is prerequisite for normal speech development and can be tested even in infants. Many language delays and articulatory problems can be traced to treatable hearing impairments. For example, ear infections may lead to clogged eustachian tubes and hearing loss. Inserting tubes in the ear to open up the passage can result in improved pronunciation, pitch, and volume.

Auditory perception is also important. Even very young infants can distinguish speech from other sounds and can differentiate among some language sounds.[84] Eventually, the language learner must be able to recognize a sequence of sounds and compare it to other stored sequences in order to interpret it (i.e., a meaning must be assigned to it).[36] In normal children, the skills will emerge naturally from social experiences (such as feeding) and cognitive growth.[4,6]

Social Skills
Since language is a tool for, and is rooted in, social interaction, it is important to consider the interactional capabilities of the young infant. Infants develop three critical skills in early interactions. First, they learn about the rhythms of language

and conversation. Second, they learn that their behavior influences the behavior of others. This influence is one of the main reasons why we speak. Finally, infants learn about the structure of conversation, that is, **turntaking.**

Early research suggested that babies naturally move in synchrony with their mother's language. This seemed to indicate that language rhythms are innate. More recent work, however, suggests this synchrony is unusual, if it occurs at all.[32] The infant may learn more from the dis-synchrony of behaviors than from the synchrony.[122] When the mother is *not* interacting, the baby must do something to gain her attention. Indeed, even 3-month-olds will work to recapture an interaction (as when the mother's face goes "blank"). This teaches the baby that she influences the behavior of others.[122] Parental reactions to crying and gesturing also encourage the baby to repeat communication efforts.[86,96] Thus, reciprocity rather than absolute synchrony is the critical factor.

The ability to take turns is crucial for effective communication. Rudiments of turntaking appear early.[65,119] This is evident in the feeding situation. Initially, the mother jiggles the nipple when the baby pauses in his nursing. This speeds up the renewal of sucking. In fact, the baby often starts sucking before the jiggling stops. After 2 weeks, though, the pattern changes. The pause in sucking is still followed by jiggling, but now the jiggling stops before the sucking is reinstituted. Although the mother is probably doing most of the adapting here, turntaking patterns are being developed. By 2 or 3 months, turntaking is also evident in vocal and kinesic interactions between mothers and babies.[9,75] The baby may need more cues from the parent to "take his turn" than adults regularly need, indicating that there is much refinement needed in turntaking skills.[75]

Although the baby influences the nature of the interaction, adults do more of the adapting and accommodating in adult–infant interactions than do babies or other adults in an adult–adult interaction.[9] Mothers and babies are about equally likely to initiate interactions;[25] however, the baby is more likely to end an interaction and the mother is more likely to modify her behavior (e.g., stop or start vocalizing) based on the baby's behavior.[9,24] This is especially true during the first 6 months or so.[119]

Cognitive Skills

Many cognitive skills are needed for learning and maintaining the language system as well as for conversation. One such skill is memory. This is painfully clear in adults with Alzheimer's disease; their memory impairment prevents them from remembering the previous utterance or even the beginning of their current sentence. While researchers have not evaluated young infants' recognition memory for verbal stimuli, it is evident that they can recognize familiar sounds from an early age. It is more difficult to ascertain recall skills of young infants. One way is to see if they can imitate a new behavior after a time delay. This is called *deferred imitation*.[98] Babies as young as 9 months old can do this.[80]

Imitation itself is an important skill for language development.[116] Newborns can imitate simple mouth movements.[81]

When children match mouth movements to sounds, it allows them to imitate mouth movements to articulate specific sounds.[67] Children parrot adults and older children to learn structures of phrases and sentences. Some children adopt this approach more than others.[47] Most toddlers go through a phase of repeating adults' utterances (*developmental echolalia*). At first it may be just the last word of a sentence and then the final phrase. It may facilitate processing the sentence content or may facilitate learning phonemic and grammatical rules. Many children will exhibit *delayed imitation* before the rules for grammatical transformations are understood. Thus, a 30-month-old child may say, "You want to go outside?" (repetition of the parent's phrase) when meaning, "I want to go outside." Some children rely on imitation of adult utterances, in at least some situations, to communicate.[117] Similarly, adults acquiring a second language often imitate social phrases in order to interact.[53] In both situations, the individual words in the imitated utterance are initially probably unanalyzed and poorly understood by the speaker. However, they serve as the basis for interactions in which more information can be gained about language. They also provide important practice in language use, especially in syntax.

Other specific cognitive skills are important. Babies need to understand means–ends relationships before they will intentionally communicate.[58,59] In other words, they need to know that one thing (such as their vocalizations) can affect another (such as an adult's behavior). They also appear to need some form of nonlinguistic representational thought (such as pretend play) before language will develop (Fig. 12-3).[112]

Babies also form categories that enable them to recognize various exemplars of a particular class (e.g., two different dogs). These categories can then be labeled. However, a category is not always formed before its name is learned. Indeed, it is probably common for a category to be only partially formed at the time its name is acquired.[100]

THE PROCESS OF LANGUAGE ACQUISITION

Theories of Language Acquisition

Given the complexity of language, it is not surprising that there is little agreement about how it develops. Some theories focus on only one component of language, whereas others try to be more comprehensive. There are three general schools of thought concerning the roots of language. Within each of these, there are several different theories. What follows is a sampling of those broader models.

Nativist Positions

No other species has language as complex as ours. Even the most sophisticated interactive computer software is a linguistic lightweight compared to a kindergartner. Experts cannot describe language in enough detail to program a computer to use it "naturally."

Yet, healthy children all over the world learn language with very little apparent effort or direct training. In fact, not all

FIGURE 12–3.
The adult who wishes to communicate effectively with a young child must understand the child's cognitive abilities. It is also helpful and less threatening to the child if the interaction occurs at eye level.

cultures believe it is appropriate to talk to infants.[18, 64] Nevertheless, the rate and sequence of language development is similar across cultures.[110] This uniformity is not surprising since languages share many features. For example, they all have categories to express grammatical relations such as subject, predicate, and object. These similarities are known as linguistic universals.

Nativists have cited the uniqueness, ease of acquisition, and universality of linguistic elements as evidence of a species-specific, innate predisposition for language. One could argue that this predisposition is physical in that the human cerebral cortex and vocal musculature give us abilities that other animals do not have. However, such physiological explanations are not the core of most nativist theories.

More commonly, nativists follow the lead of Noam Chomsky. Chomsky argued that syntax is innate, based in a hypothetical structure called the Language Acquisition Device (LAD).[20–22] The LAD is mental rather than physical. In other words, you cannot point to a specific area of the brain as the location of the LAD. Some theorists argue that the LAD contains the actual rules of human language and a person simply learns how to express the rules in a specific language. Others have argued that the LAD acts as a filter, allowing children to focus on important aspects of syntax.[82] In either case, the LAD is functioning at or shortly after birth, enabling the child to understand and gradually use syntax.

The nativist position has made us aware of the universals of language and the probability of an innate substrate to language development and use. However, this native aspect is inadequate to explain language. It does not tell us how specific syntactic structures are acquired. Furthermore, Chomsky never even intended that this explanation include semantic or pragmatic aspects of language.

Cognitive Explanations

Many people were dissatisfied with the argument that linguistic universals were based in an innate mental structure.[15, 108]

How could you test for these structures? Furthermore, if the structures are present from birth, why does language, especially syntax, develop so slowly?

Piaget's theory of cognitive development offered a possible solution. Piaget argued that cognitive structures, gradually constructed by the child in interaction with the environment (see Chaps. 2, 7, and 10), provided forms of thought that were systematic though not adultlike. He hypothesized that language reflected cognitive growth and development.[26, 42, 98, 108]

However, it has been difficult to link cognition and language. Some researchers looked at general forms of cognitive functioning (such as stage VI sensorimotor functioning) and tried to relate it to specific forms of language (e.g., the use of representation in language).[128] Others tried to link specific cognitive forms (such as different levels of symbolic play) to general language acquisition.[78, 114] Still others have tried to show relationships between specific cognitive accomplishments (e.g., object permanence development) to specific language developments (e.g., the use of disappearance words).[50]

The evidence seems to indicate that syntactic development does not simply mirror cognition.[27] Indeed, it may be a uniquely linguistic skill. Semantic development, on the other hand, may be dependent on cognitive development.[27] Theorists have also suggested that the experiences, interactions, and situations that contribute to cognitive development may simultaneously contribute to language development. Thus, the two may develop from the same roots.[4, 6, 100]

Social Interactionist Perspectives

Nativists and cognitive-developmentalists agree that linguistic interaction is necessary for language development. However, they argue that the specific structure of the interaction is less important than its presence.

Interactionists argue that social interaction is *the key* to language development.[16] Why? Let us assume that the primary purpose of language is to enable communication and that the formal systems of language—syntax, phonology, and semantics—are designed to make communication simpler and easier. Communication needs would then influence the organization and acquisition of the formal systems. This implies that language development is rooted in communicative functions. Since communication is really a form of social interaction, knowledge about and information from social interactions is critical to language development.

The argument is that adults, most commonly parents, do *something* that enables language. Research and theory have focused on three possible "somethings": simplified or specialized speech registers, scaffolding, and reinforcement.

SPECIALIZED SPEECH REGISTERS. Developmentalists have known for over 15 years that mothers talk differently to their language-learning children than to adults. This speech has been dubbed "motherese." Fathers, too, use a special form, or *register,* of speech in addressing young children. Registers are specialized forms of speech and include vocabulary, vocal tones, and communication patterns. Special registers are found among professionals (e.g., doctors or computer experts) as well as between persons of different age and gender. Even children use the "baby talk" register when talking to their younger siblings. This register is not simply the cute euphemisms for body parts, food, or toileting that are commonly used in addressing infants. Rather, it reflects significant structural shifts from the language used in talking to adults so that young children hear simpler speech with fewer words than typical adult speech. More specifically, statements directed to children are shorter (containing fewer verbs and modifiers), have fewer embedded and subordinate clauses, and are more fluent and intelligible. Adults are also more likely to repeat themselves when talking to children.

Motherese is not unique to American mothers. Similar patterns have been found among Latvian, Polish, Lithuanian, Russian, Arabic, Comanche, Greek, Japanese, Maltese, and Spanish mothers.[39] It is not used in addressing very young babies (less than about 7 months) and its specifics change as the baby gets older. This seems to indicate that its function is related to the language learning task per se rather than simply a way to talk to any baby.

SCAFFOLDING. A second aspect of social interaction that has been related to language acquisition is *scaffolding.*[16] The more competent communicator provides the "scaffold," or activity and linguistic environment, for the less mature communicator.[104] Caregivers tailor a situation to fit the baby's abilities and interests. This structure, known as a format, puts constraints on what the baby is asked to attend to and process. It also improves the adult's ability to interpret the baby's actions. This makes the baby's communicative attempts more effective, thereby encouraging more communication.[104, 117] Since formats are repeated over and over again, the baby can use them to learn the communicative functions of language as well as vocabulary.

The basic mechanism at work in these formats is joint attention. When mother and baby focus on the same object or

event, the mother can "teach" the baby how to talk about that object. She may use motherese, shortening her statements, perhaps even using only the object name paired with the object.[120] Through repetitions of this process the baby, when cognitively ready, comes to associate a name with an object. *Language learning is more likely if the mother "tunes in" to what the baby is attending to rather than calling the child's attention to things.*[120] Indeed, the achievement of parent–infant joint attention is primarily the responsibility of the adult (Fig. 12-4).[104, 117]

REINFORCEMENT. It has been argued that the "something" that adults do is to **reinforce** language. B.F. Skinner argued that all language development is a function of reinforcement contingencies.[109] The process begins when the baby babbles a phoneme, such as "da," which sounds like a rudimentary word form. The parents react positively. The baby repeats the sound to regain (or maintain) the parents' reaction. Eventually, the sound only gets a positive response if it sounds more like the target word. So, the parents may reinforce "dada" but not "da." Using this reinforcement procedure, the parents *shape* the baby's *successive approximations* of the word from a sound to the real word.

Skinner's approach is too simplistic to explain all of normal language development. Planned reinforcement and shaping of successive approximations are, however, useful in teaching language to children with disabilities.[70] If we think of language as a series of specific skills to be learned, rather than a complex entity that is acquired all at once, a learning theory approach may be more plausible than the nativists thought.[82]

Reinforcement does affect language. Children who are reinforced for using certain words learn them faster than children who are not.[125] Grammatical structures may also be reinforced, at least indirectly.[13, 30, 95] Adults also help to "model" the proper forms to the child.[82] For example, parents are likely to *expand* (and, thereby, correct) ungrammatical utterances, but simply proceed with the topic if the child's statement is well-formed. Adults are also more likely to ask a child to clarify a statement if the utterance is not grammatically correct. These parental responses alert a child to grammatical errors thereby strengthening the correct form while weakening the incorrect one.[12]

A Final Word About the Theories

Quite simply there is no universally accepted theory of language acquisition. We are a long way from understanding the specific components, much less their interrelationships.

The various explanations may not be as mutually exclusive as they first seem. For example, both cognition (in the form of understanding intention or means-ends relationship) and social interactions may be crucial in language development. Motherese may facilitate the work of any innate Language Acquisition Device.

It is not yet clear what *facilitates* language development versus what is *required* for language development.[12, 117] No *single form* of the social interactional behaviors just described

FIGURE 12–4.
The most mundane activities of daily living provide a scaffolding for warm, focused, meaningful interactions between parent and child.

is necessary for the child to learn words. Despite diverse parental behaviors, children in all cultures learn language.[51, 64, 103, 105] Some form of social interactional facilitation occurs in every culture, though we may not have identified all the possible variations that might occur.[117] Similarly, understanding cognitive development alone will not explain language. Something allows cognitive or even native concepts to be translated into actual language. That "something" remains undefined.

Sequence of Language Acquisition

The Prelinguistic Period

During the first 6 months of life, babies' communication is not goal directed.[68, 86, 118, 119] This means that they do not think about what idea they wish to convey and then try to express it in a particular way to a specific individual. Nonetheless, communication does occur. First, the baby does produce different sounds, facial expressions, and gestures under different circumstances. Second, adults ascribe meaning to these sounds and gestures and thus respond to them.[96] This increases the baby's sense of efficacy and is probably critical in motivating the infant's communicative development.

CRYING. Initially, cries are the primary form of vocal communication. There are different types of cries, signaling, for example, pain versus hunger. These differ primarily in terms of how they start. The pain cry begins with a sharp inspiration of air while other types of cries begin more gradually.[126] After the first few seconds, all cries revert to a similar pattern. This means that it is easier for adults to identify the cause of a cry if they hear it from the beginning rather than if they come in

after the child has been crying for several seconds.[52] Context is also significant for interpretation.

Crying is intended to signal distress. It is probably a graded signal, demonstrating different levels rather than specific types of distress.[52] Adults with caregiving experience are better able to assess the amount of distress a baby is experiencing.[52] Experience may also cause a person to find crying less aversive and thereby more sympathy provoking. This may be one reason why women tend to report infant cries as less annoying than men.[86] If crying is too aversive, the adult may respond by leaving or by abusing the baby.[43, 86]

As development proceeds, crying may be used to make specific requests.[52] The context of the situation will help the adult interpret the request. In fact, crying may eventually be used simply to initiate contact even in the absence of real distress. Concurrently, the child may begin to direct crying towards a particular person. All of this, occurring in the second half of the first year, indicates goal-directed communication and may be an important step toward language.[4, 52]

COOING AND BABBLING. Crying is not the only sound available to prelinguistic infants (see Table 12–1). *Cooing,* vowel-like sounds such as aah or ooo, appears around 3 weeks of age, although, because of physiological constraints, it does not become strong and regular until the child is about 2 months old.[126] A few consonant-like sounds may also appear.[118] These are affected by gravity. When the young infant is on his back, guttural sounds are heard; on the abdomen, labial sounds. During the first 2 or 3 months, the baby will make random sounds including sucking and comfort sounds. Parents interpret these sounds as if they were communicative, but there is no evidence that the babies are aware of the sounds' communicative value. *Chuckling* and *laughing* also emerge during

TABLE 12-1. THE DEVELOPMENT OF EXPRESSIVE LANGUAGE SKILLS

Age	Skill
0–2 months	Vocalizations become more differentiated as cries become recognizably different. Fussing and vegetative sounds also present. Some random sounds, occasionally in "response" to adult vocalizations.
2–4 months	Shows more control over sounds as cooing (single vowel sounds) appears. Vowels are also sometimes combined with other sounds to create trills. Chuckling and laughing also are evident.
5–6 months	Lolling (chains of vowel sounds) appears. Pitch intonations appear. Babbling begins although only marginally. Single consonant sounds appear.
7–9 months	True babbling (consonant-vowel combinations) is evident. Reduplicated babbling evident. Can imitate familiar sound patterns. Baby can "yell."
10–12 months	Sound patterns become more complex. Nonreduplicated babbling. Intentional communication, first in the form of protolanguage, appears. First words, most commonly single nouns, may appear.
12–18 months	Slow vocabulary growth. At 18 months, the average vocabulary is about 30 words. Some normal children will not yet be talking.
18–24 months	More rapid vocabulary growth. Some children will experience a sudden "vocabulary spurt." Normal vocabulary ranges from 50–400 words at 24 months. Children will begin combining words into sentences, with 2 and 3 word sentences usually appearing between 18 and 24 months.
2–4 years	Production becomes increasingly sophisticated as grammatical morphemes (e.g., plural forms) begin to appear, vocabulary grows (to an average of about 1500 words at age 4), and syntax becomes more complex. There are still many miscommunications, however, due to the child's egocentrism and limited understanding of the precise meaning of words. Pronunciation is still noticeably immature.
Over 4 years	Pronunciation problems continue into school years. Language becomes more adult-like although not all forms (e.g., metaphors and irony) will be used and understood until late school age or adolescence. Specialized language, including slang, usually does not appear until early adolescence.

(Based on data from Brandstadter-Palmer, G. [1982]. Ontogenetic growth chart. In C. Kopp & J. Krakow [Eds.], The Child. Reading, MA: Addison-Wesley; and from Stark, R. [1989]. Early language intervention: When, why, how? Infants and Young Children, 1, *44–53.)*

the second quarter, adding to the pleasantness of interacting with the baby.

Sounds become more differentiated during the second half of the first year. The baby begins to *babble,* combining consonant and vowel sounds as in ba, goo, or da. These sounds become increasingly speechlike. The baby can imitate first familiar, and later, new sounds. Babies also enjoy repeating their own sounds, a process Piaget called *functional assimilation.* These imitative and practicing games provide important feedback and experience as the baby learns to control phonological production.

The baby also makes chains of consonant-vowel sounds. Some of these are reduplicated sounds, that is, repetitions of one sound ("dadadadada") while others are simple nonreduplicated series ("bawa"). Once the baby starts producing reduplicated sequences, he or she has the necessary phonetic base for producing words. During the fourth quarter of the first year, the child usually produces the first word. However, most of the baby's "language" during the first half of the second year is still *jargon,* intonated strings that sound as if the baby is trying to tell you something.

Infants babble many different sounds, but they do not produce all sounds used in all languages. There does appear to be a core of babbled sounds, at least among American children.[69] Cross-cultural research shows similar, though not identical, patterns. This suggests that babbling may be guided by innate rules or physiological constraints. However, children must hear vocalizations in order to produce them on time and to move towards more language-like sounds.

GESTURES. Prelinguistic infants use gestures, by themselves or in conjunction with vocalizations, to communicate. As is true with vocalizations, the success of these communicative attempts relies heavily on the attentiveness and interpretative abilities of the adults in the environment.

By about 9 months, children begin to use the pointed index finger to indicate a desired object. There can be no doubt that these gestures are goal-directed and communicative. However, unlike words, they cannot be effectively used in the absence of an object and therefore are not representational in nature.

Other manual gestures appear simultaneously. These include reaching, waving, throwing, and, most commonly, the open-close gesture.[96] These gestures are not representational and they do not have one particular referent. In other words, they tend to be used in a variety of situations to convey many different meanings. Indeed, the child seems to realize only that the gestures can elicit a reaction. This means that the interpretation of the gesture is heavily determined by context so that a parent will understand the same gesture to mean different things at various times.[96] For example, the open-close hand gesture may mean, "I want," "bye-bye," or some other idiosyncratic message.

At about 1 year, two new types of gestures appear.[96] First, the child begins to gesture with objects, as in drinking from an empty cup or stirring in an empty bowl. Some theorists interpret these gestures as early forms of naming.[5] Thus, they argue that the child seems to be communicating something about the object. Other theorists treat these gestures primarily as part of play and learning about objects because the children do not seem to be directing them towards anyone.[96]

The second form of gesture has a clear communicative value. These instrumental empty-handed gestures include raising the arms to be picked up. As with earlier gestures, these cannot be considered representational since they are linked to the context. Nonetheless, they do represent an advance over earlier gestures in that they have a meaning that is maintained across situations.[96]

At about 16 months, *iconic* gestures appear. These gestures appear to be representational and communicative. Thus, a child might signal opening a jar by a twisting motion even without the jar in hand. These gestures are not very frequent and are typically used in conjunction with a word.[96] They differ from words in that they are not arbitrary signs.

Receptive Language

Parents routinely believe that their babies understand more than they can say. The parents are right. Language comprehension, or receptive language, begins to develop before speech appears (see Table 12-2). Receptive language also develops more quickly than does speech, at least during the early stages of acquisition.

Most children start to understand single words around 10 months of age.[10, 61] Thus, they can respond to a word without any gestural cues (such as mother staring at the object she's requesting) and can retrieve a requested object that is out of sight.

Early comprehension differs from production in several important ways. First, comprehension vocabulary growth is much faster. The children in one study[10] understood 50 words by about 13.5 months of age; and 100 or more words by 16 months. But, these same children did not, on the average, produce 50 words until just past 18 months. Furthermore, it took these children about 2.7 months to expand their comprehension vocabulary from 10 to 50 words but about 4.8 months to do the same in the production mode. This difference may seem like a trivial point, but it was one of the first clues that production did not simply mirror comprehension. Instead, production requires new skills and advances.

Furthermore, the actual content of production and comprehension vocabularies differs. While nouns are very common in both, comprehension has a much higher percentage of action words (e.g., *give, kiss*). Production has a higher percentage of modifiers (e.g., *pretty, hot*) and personal-social words (e.g., *hi, yes*).[10]

Finally, comprehension and production seem to have different relationships to cognitive development. Researchers have had more difficulty linking cognitive development to language comprehension than to production.[8, 19, 111]

Expressive Language

PROTOLANGUAGE. By 8 to 10 months, babies are aware of both the idea they are trying to convey and the individual who will receive the message. This, in combination with babbling, is

TABLE 12-2. THE DEVELOPMENT OF RECEPTIVE LANGUAGE SKILLS

Age	Skill
0–3 months	Preferences for human voice, especially mother's, and language. Innate neurological and perceptual skills allow differential processing of language.
3–6 months	Develops expectations about interpersonal communication including that faces have expressions and that voices match facial movements.
7–9 months	Begins to recognize "communications" from others in the form of facial expressions and pointing. May respond to object names if the object is present.
10–12 months	Clearly understands names of objects even when they are absent.
12–18 months	Comprehension vocabulary grows dramatically—typically to over 100 words by about 16 months. Will show comprehension of simple sentences even before starting to produce word combinations. Will understand many more words, especially action words, than produced.
2–4 years	Comprehension continues to range ahead of production. Can understand more complex syntax. Can understand adult references to events the child has not personally experienced.
Over 4 years	Gap between comprehension and production gradually closes. Will even sometimes say things without full comprehension of them as a way of "adding" new vocabulary. Comprehension becomes increasingly complex and adultlike.

the basis for *protolanguage*.[56, 57] Protolanguage, like regular language, expresses meaning but it has no *socially* defined vocabulary or grammatical rules. The child uses specific sounds, typically combined with gestures, to convey a particular meaning. One child, for example, used the sound *na* to mean "I want that."[56] Protolanguage indicates that the child has learned that vocalizations can be used to express feelings and desires to others. Some of the communicative intents frequently displayed in protolanguage are listed in Table 12-3. Some theorists view this as the beginning of the pragmatic function (knowledge of the communicative uses of language) and, therefore, the onset of true language acquisition.

EARLY VOCABULARY. Early vocabulary growth is usually slow. The *average* 18-month-old has a productive vocabulary of 10 to 20 words. By 24 months, vocabulary ranges from 50 to 250 words.[129] Almost every parent of a 2-year-old with a 50-word vocabulary knows a child with a 200+ word vocabulary, sometimes leading them to mistakenly conclude that their child is developmentally delayed. It is important to recognize that language is a series of skills that are acquired at different rates by different children.

Typically, nouns dominate the early vocabulary. These

TABLE 12-3. PRAGMATIC FUNCTIONS IN PROTOLANGUAGE IN APPROXIMATE ORDER OF APPEARANCE

Pragmatic Function	*Description*
Personal	The child is trying to convey something about his own attitude or interests. Statements of pleasure (the equivalent of I like) and interest are included here.
Instrumental	A demand for a specific object or service. The requests may involve objects but are person-mediated. The statement is addressed to a particular person with the goal of obtaining that person's assistance.
Regulatory	A demand designed to regulate a person's behavior. No object is involved. The child might, for example, want a person to repeat an act (such as picking up the dog or making a funny face).
Interactional	An utterance intended to encourage social interaction. For example, the child may respond to his name being called or, may ask a parent to look at or play with something together. This category includes greetings.
Heuristics	This develops later than the previous four functions. It serves to organize experience by asking for labels for objects, people, and so forth.

(Based on examples from Halliday, M. [1979]. One child's protolanguage. In M. Bullowa [Ed.], Before speech: The beginning of interpersonal communication. *London: Cambridge University Press; order of appearance from Stark, R. [1989].* Early language intervention: When, why, how? Infants and Young Children, 1, *44–53.)*

nouns commonly name family members (including the word *baby* to refer to themselves), food items (most popularly *juice, milk, cookie,* and *water*), animals (especially *dog* and *cat*), toys (most likely *ball, block, book,* and *doll*), and body parts (particularly parts of the face).[23]

Two points need to be made about these early object names. First, children often use some variant of the common word. So, a dog may be a *bow-wow.* This effect is intensified by the children's limited pronunciation skills. Children find it difficult to string sounds together (that's why those reduplicated babbles, noted earlier, are so important). Young children may, therefore, drop part of a word. So, *bow-wow* may be reduced to *wow.*

Second, it is not unusual for a child's word meanings to differ from adults'. For example, the word *daddy* may be applied to all adult men (overextension), while the word *dog* might be applied only to the child's own pet (underextension). This is probably due to a mismatch between the child's concept and the socially agreed upon concept underlying the word although in some cases the child is simply trying to extend a limited vocabulary as far as it will go.

In the earliest stages of language development, underextension may mean something slightly different than an ill-defined concept. The child is not yet using the word represen-

tationally. Rather than having the word "stand in" for the object, *the child sees the word as part of the object.* Before a child achieves true language, the word must be detached from the context within which it was first learned. This process, called **decontextualization,** is rooted in cognitive development according to Piagetians. Decontextualizaton partially explains why a child who says *dog* so nicely while petting her own dog is silent when asked to show off her naming skills with Gramma's dog.

Sometime after 18 months, many, but not all, children will go through a vocabulary spurt, a rapid and sudden growth in vocabulary. The spurt occurs in both comprehension and production. It is made possible by the newfound ability to "fast map" new meanings [100]. Fast-mapping involves using a word after quickly forming a partial meaning for it and then refining the understanding of the word by using it. Many children will rely heavily upon imitation in this process and, indeed, will seem to imitate everything. Cognitive development, specifically in terms of categorization skills, may underlie this spurt. However, environment and language-learning style will mediate the impact of the cognitive advance so that not all children will "spurt" even after categorization skills have developed.[46]

Since naming objects is the major use of language for most children, nouns are the dominant speech form in early vocabulary (Fig. 12-5). However, some children use their

FIGURE 12–5.
Although reading to a young child helps to model the rules underlying language, the very young child's main interest is in the pictures and the unstructured exchanges about what is on the pages.

language primarily for social interactions, learning small phrases, or social formulas, rather than lots of nouns. Thus, phrases such as *stop it, come here, let me, I wanna see,* and *I don't want to* dominate their vocabulary. While all children learn some nouns and some social phrases, some children focus on one or the other. Children who concentrate on labels are termed *referential* while those who are more socially oriented are known as *expressive.*[7, 76, 89]

Expressive children will often appear to be slower in their language development for two reasons. First, there are fewer social formulas than names. Second, expressive children typically run all the words within a phrase together. This makes them very difficult to understand and may lead to an underestimation of their vocabulary. They typically will not have a dramatic vocabulary spurt.[46]

EARLY SYNTAX. Theorists used to argue that even the single-word utterances of young children reflected a knowledge of syntax. They called single-word utterances *holophrases,* meaning that single words stood in for entire phrases or sentences. But if children really understand the concept of sentence, what keeps them from combining the single words into sentences? Certainly, their memory spans, vocabulary, and attention are sufficient to allow them to use sentences earlier than they do. Theorists now believe that single-word utterances do not encode syntactic relations, although they do, in combination with gestures and intonation, communicate more than simply the meaning of the individual word.[31]

Children begin combining words into phrases or sentences at about 18 to 24 months, often around the time of their vocabulary spurt. The first combinations are typically two words long. Referential children are particularly likely to follow this pattern, since expressive children speak in (formulaic) phrases from the beginning.

Two-word combinations are formulated so as to best capture the gist of the child's intended meaning. Conjunctions, articles, and other "fine points" are omitted, giving the speech a telegraphic quality. Children use semantic relationships to organize these utterances; they organize and order words based on what the words mean in that particular situation rather than on grammatical roles (e.g., subject-object).[73] Table 12-4 illustrates the semantic relations commonly found in early multiword utterances.

The rules of how to create sentences (syntax) are one component of grammar. The other major component is how to make morphological changes. These are the rules for adding suffixes and prefixes that mark plurals, past tense, negation (*un-*), possessive, and so forth. Children do not usually use these before age 2 and are still refining their use into the early school years. For example, early in morphological acquisition, the child often uses forms correctly (including irregular plural forms such as *feet* or *mice*). But it is soon evident that the child had only memorized or imitated those words because he begins overgeneralizing the rules to produce non-adult forms such as *foots* and *mouses* or *feet* and *mices.* It is not until 7 or 8 years that rule usage is completely adultlike.

Variations in Early Language Acquisition

Stuttering
Preschoolers often stutter, especially when they are upset, excited, or angry. "Developmental stuttering" differs from "problem stuttering" in that it will occur with a variety of sounds and even entire phrases. It does not usually begin until language development is well under way (age 2–3) and diminishes with time. Developmental stuttering probably reflects the child's difficulties in accessing and integrating newly acquired phonological, syntactic, and semantic rules. If a child is still stuttering frequently at age 5 or if the stuttering seems to be restricted to a few sounds (e.g., *d* or *b*) and appears regularly, the child should be evaluated. Such evaluations are routinely available in public health or school systems.

Parental criticism can aggravate any form of stuttering.

TABLE 12-4. SOME SEMANTIC RELATIONS ENCODED IN EARLY TWO-WORD UTTERANCES

Semantic Relation	Definition	Example
Agent-Action	Encodes the "cause" of the action and the action itself	Car go; Mommy push
Action-Object	Encodes the action and the person who "receives" that action.	Hit Mommy; Push Billy
Entity-Locative	Encodes an object (or person) and its location.	Lady home; Baby car
Possessor-Possession	Encodes "owner" and owner's possession.	Daddy chair; Mama shoe
Entity-Attribute	Describes a characteristic of a thing.	Little dog; Hot soup
Demonstrative-Entity	Specifies which particular thing is being discussed.	That chair; This dog

(Brown, R. [1973]. A first language: The early stages. Cambridge, MA: Harvard University Press.)

Similarly, speaking for the child, whether out of impatience or concern, can reduce his motivation for speech. In either case, the child may become self-conscious about speech and, in extreme situations, may even stop talking.

Deaf Children

Auditory evaluation of infants is possible, but not routine. Because of this, many deaf and hard-of-hearing children are not diagnosed until the toddler years or later when a speech defect or language delay is noted.

Unusual babbling may be the first indicator that an infant is deaf. Children who are able to hear nothing may coo and lall appropriately but will stop the normal progression (see Table 12-1) around 5 months. Even those who have been fitted with a hearing aid and receive considerable stimulation start babbling late. Deaf children also produce a smaller percentage of reduplicated syllables ("mamama") in their babbling, making their babbling sound less language-like.[94]

Once a hearing problem has been identified, deaf children can learn sign language. The developmental progression in sign language is remarkably similar to verbal language. The children will "babble" in sign language.[96] Signs will be spontaneously combined into short sentences.[48,49] This relatively normal pattern of acquisition is found only in the children's sign language. Acquisition of spoken language lags behind in deaf children, even with hearing amplification and intense linguistic stimulation.[94]

Educators used to argue that deaf children should not learn sign language, contending that the children would "fit in" better if they learned to speak. The appeal of this argument to frustrated, disappointed parents is evident. *Learning signs does not interfere with acquiring spoken language.* In fact, signing children are somewhat *more* likely than other deaf children to learn to speak.[74] Deaf parents generally are able to accept their child's deafness and are more willing to teach their children to use sign language.[66] Children who learn sign language first often have better language skills, higher educational attainment, and better personal adjustment than deaf children restricted to oral methods (lip reading and sound amplification).[74]

The biggest barrier to language learning among deaf children does not seem to be an inherent language disability but the parents' inability to accept the child's deafness or to use sign language. If the adults do not sign, the deaf child is raised in a language impoverished environment—a factor known to lead to developmental delays even in hearing children. The key to language development in deaf children is the introduction of a manually based language. If signing is used, language training is no more necessary than with hearing children. In fact, deaf babies with signing parents are observed to babble with their hands.

Language Development

During their first 3 to 4 years, children acquire the components of the linguistic system sufficient to carry on a more or less comprehensible conversation. Nevertheless, language development is a life-span process. There are considerable refinements and expansions of language abilities throughout childhood and adulthood.

Developmental Years

PHONOLOGICAL DEVELOPMENT. Many children continue to have problems producing many sounds at school-age or later. Consonant omissions and substitutions are common. Articulation is not 90% intelligible until about age 5, and even then 10% of the speech may be hard to understand (Table 12-5).

School-aged children may mispronounce consonant combinations such as *tw* or *thr.* They also still have difficulty combining sounds, particularly in words with several consonant combinations. Commonly mispronounced words include *s'getti* or *p'sghetti* (for spaghetti) and *lumnun* (for aluminum). Sometimes the sounds within a word are transposed. For example, temperature might be pronounced *tentuper.*

SYNTAX. Many syntactic forms do not appear until age 3 or later. Consider the relatively simple *wh* questions: what, who, where, when, why, and how. Children first begin to use these around age three. The fully mature forms may not appear until school age. Forms using *what,* such as "whatsit" or "whatsat," come first. Some children, especially those using the expressive acquisition strategy, use these during the first year. The most mature forms use not only the *wh* word but also auxiliary and inverted forms. Where a younger child might say "What that girl want?" or "Why you can't play?" an older one will say "What does that girl want?" and "Why can't you play?"

Children also need to learn other interrogative forms, passive voice, and embedded clauses. Table 12-6 provides some examples of the syntactic forms developing during the preschool and school years. The precise order and mechanisms for syntactic development are unknown. However, the child must start with some kind of information.[73] Although some of this is probably cognitive, some is specifically linguistic and may even be innate.[27] In addition, although children

TABLE 12-5. PHONOLOGICAL ACQUISITION IN CHILDHOOD

English Sounds	Not Commonly Well Articulated Until Age
p, b, m, h, w, n, ng	3.5 years
k, j, g, f, d	4.5 years
t, r, sh, v, l, s, th	5.5 years
tw, dw, bl, kl, fl, gl, pl, sl, br, kr, dr, fr, gr, pr, tr, thr, sk, sm, sn, st, kw, z	Still occasional errors at 8.5 years

(Adapted from Zelazo, P., Kearsley, R., & Ungerer, J. [1984]. Learning to speak: A manual for parents. Hillsdale, NJ: Lawrence Erlbaum; and from Eisenson, J. [1984]. Aphasia and related disorders in children [2nd ed.]. New York: Harper & Row.)

**TABLE 12-6. THE DEVELOPMENT OF SYNTAX
IN CHILDHOOD**

Age*	Syntactic Skills	Examples
3–3.5 years	Auxiliary verbs	I am walking. I do like you.
	Negative particles	I didn't do it. This isn't ice cream.
	Yes/No questions	Will I go? Do you want it?
3.5–4 years	Sentence clauses	You think I can do it. I see what you made.
4–5 years	Conjunctions of two sentences	You think I can, but I can't. Mary and I are going.
+5 years	Reversible passive	The truck was chased by the car.
	Connectives	I am going to go but I don't want to.
	Indirect object and direct object con- structions	The man showed the boy his friend
	Pronominalization	He knew that John was going to win the race.

*All ages are rough approximations and represent the average time of appear-
ance for each structure. Individual variation is great. A syntactic structure may
not be used in adult form routinely for some time after its appearance.
(Adapted from Whitehurst, G., (1982) Language development. In B. Wolman
(Ed.) Handbook of developmental psychology (367–386). Englewood Cliffs,
NJ: Prentice-Hall.*

hear simplified, low error syntax (in motherese), there is little
evidence that the form of input is crucial to syntax development.[45] Most of the work of syntax construction seems to fall to
the child.[73] Children build categories and relationships from
specific examples of syntactic structures. This process is slow
with many errors.

SEMANTICS. Vocabulary growth during childhood is dramatic.
The average 3-year-old's production vocabulary is about 850
words, a 6-year-old's is about 1500 words, and a 13- to 14-year-
old's has over 50,000 words.[14] From 1½ to 6 years, children
add about 9 new words a day to comprehension vocabulary
for a total of over 14,000 new items.[101]

The child's understanding of individual words and their
interrelationships also changes. For example, as children's
classification skills improve (see Chap. 10) they better understand the relationships between animals, mammals, dogs, and
collies and can express them linguistically. Word use becomes
more adultlike as underextensions and overextensions fade.
Word definitions shift from being action-based to relating
several semantic properties. Whereas a 6-year-old might define a bird as "something that flies in the sky" (action-based), a
12-year-old's definition might be "warm-blooded animals that
use their wings to fly."[127] These changes in definitional so-

phistication parallel the move from preoperational to formal
operational thought (see Chaps. 2, 10, 21, and 24).

Similarly, the meanings that young children associate
with words are usually quite concrete. They associate only
one meaning with a word. Older school-age children realize
that words can have more than one meaning and that, if
phrased in a certain manner, the word or sentence's meaning
is ambiguous. This enables the child to tell and appreciate
jokes that are based on ambiguity and the violation of expectations. Preschoolers cannot appreciate puns and "knock,
knock" jokes because they do not recognize the violation that
is occurring. A young child would find the following equally
funny:[106]

> "Order, order in the court!
> Ham and cheese on rye, your honor."
> or
> "Silence, silence in the court!
> Ham and cheese on rye, your honor."

An older child, however, would recognize that it is only in
the first joke that the expectations associated with "order,
order in the court" are violated and so would find only the
first joke funny.

Jokes based on the ambiguity of a single word are the
easiest to comprehend. Children cannot appreciate ironic
humor until adolescence. In irony and sarcasm, the meaning of the statement is the opposite of what it appears to be.
The listener must detach the meaning from the concrete
context and look for more subtle clues to the true meaning
of the statement. Several cognitive advances are necessary
for this skill. The child must, for example, understand that
logic can be violated rather than only appreciating illogical
absurdities as jokes. The illogical sequence in the "order,
order" joke makes it funny. But, in sarcasm or irony, the
statements *sound* logical. When a teenager asks, "Where
are my shoes?" and her mother replies, "Gee, I don't remember where I put them," the daughter recognizes the
sarcasm because she knows that her mother did not put the
shoes anywhere. Her mother's message is that the shoes are
the daughter's responsibility.

Changes in understanding word definitions also affect
metaphor comprehension. Metaphors require that the child
detach the words from their literal concrete meaning. For
example, words such as "sour," "cold," and "sweet" can describe both people and objects. By the early school years
children know that the words can be used both ways, but they
often cannot explain how the uses are related. By 9 or 10,
children interpret even unfamiliar metaphors fairly routinely.
The ability to appreciate abstract metaphors increases during
adolescence and adulthood.

The concreteness of early word meaning also makes it
difficult for children to appreciate proverbs and euphemisms.
An example is the following dialogue between a mother and
the young son she picked up from his first music lesson.

Mother: Do you like your teacher?
Boy: Yes, but I don't think you'll like her.

Mother:	Why not?
Boy:	Because she kills birds.
Mother:	What do you mean?
Boy:	Well, she said she was going to kill two birds with one stone.

Because children cannot always appreciate all levels of meaning, adults must be careful when talking to young children (Fig. 12-6). They should avoid using figurative language; the child will try to interpret it literally. Young children also will not recognize humorous sarcasm or irony. Their feelings will be hurt or they may be frightened.

In the same vein, young children will have difficulty with abstract words such as responsibility, freedom, or democracy. They need to develop the ability to think logically and abstractly in order to appreciate the complexity of the definitions of such words. Abstract thought enables a person to plan and monitor both spoken and written language. It also makes it possible for teenagers to better discern a word's meaning from the way it is used. Thus, the teenager is better at achieving certain goals or conveying specific messages than is the school-ager.

DENNIS the MENACE

"SOME OF THE KIDS' MOTHERS WAS WONDERIN' WHERE YOU GET SOME OF THE EXPRESSIONS I USE."

FIGURE 12–6.
Reprinted courtesy of Dennis the Menace. *Copyright Field Newspaper Syndicate, T.M.®*

PRAGMATICS. Both social experience and cognitive development improve the clarity of communication. Preschoolers often omit important details in describing an experience. They do not fully appreciate what information the listener does or does not have. Older children and adults occasionally do this, too, but not as frequently.

The preschooler's cognitive egocentrism can make it difficult to carry on a true dialogue. The preschooler often seems more interested in his own turn than in what his conversational partner is saying. Piaget described collective monologues in which preschoolers appeared to be conversing (i.e., they were taking turns talking) but their statements had nothing to do with each other.[97] So, one child might be describing his painting while the other talked about a new dog. No communication occurred. Piaget probably overestimated how often children do this. Those of us who talk about one section of the Sunday paper while another adult is describing a story in a different section realize that the phenomenon is not limited to children. Nonetheless, with cognitive development, we are better able to monitor our own conversations so as to improve the likelihood of reciprocal communication.

Young children also seem to talk to themselves more than adults do. This speech is not meant to be communicative but instead is used to solve a problem or narrate fantasy play.[123] It is similar to the inner speech (or private speech) that adults often use when working on a problem. Very young children have not internalized this private speech. By the early school years, the shift is typically well underway although even adults sometimes "think out loud."

LEARNING NEW CODES. Sometime between the age of 2 and 4, children discover the flexibility of linguistic rules. They begin to play with language both phonologically and semantically.[1, 40] Some of this is pure play. The child may change one or two sounds in a word as in "wake up, hake ut, bake ut, bake up."[40] This play is often done at a higher than normal pitch and is usually accompanied by laughter. Children are especially amused when they stumble on a "real" word while playing. Other language play is really language practice where the child is trying to perfect a certain sound. In either case, the play expands the child's understanding of the rules of phonology, including what combinations are acceptable.[40]

Language play also occurs in older children in the form of play languages such as pig latin. Play languages are usually derived from ordinary language although sometimes special material is added.[40] Their primary purpose is to mark group membership. Friends who have a secret or play language can communicate without their peers, parents, or teachers knowing what they are discussing. This may explain why play languages are especially popular among adolescents of many cultures.[40] Foreign or sign languages, Morse code, and Braille can serve a similar function and so are also of interest to school-agers and adolescents. Children can only create play languages, however, once they appreciate most of the functions and rules of their own language (Fig. 12-7).

FIGURE 12–7.
The amount and the content of the conversation that takes place between a child and parent will affect the child's vocabulary size, fluency, and language style, as well as self-esteem, problem solving, knowledge, and cultural identification.

Bilingualism

It is estimated that 45% to 50% of the world's population is **bilingual** (able to speak two languages).[99] Some 17% of U.S. citizens and 24% of Canadian citizens are bilingual.[99] Some people, the **simultaneous bilinguals,** learn two languages at the same time, with exposure to both beginning virtually at birth. Usually, each of their parents has a different native language and each uses his or her own language in addressing the child. A child can learn to distinguish between the two languages before 24 months of age if each language is restricted to a specific setting or person.[99] The child will progress in both languages at the same acquisition rate as monolinguals. If the languages are mixed, however, it can delay separation of the language codes until the child is 3 or 4 years of age.[99]

Other bilinguals, initially monolinguals, acquire a second language after proficiency in the first has been established. These people are known as **successive bilinguals.** This may happen if their first language is a minority language in their country. For example, children of Mexican immigrants often hear only Spanish in the home, but when they go to school, they learn English. Others elect to learn a second language to make travel easier, to increase their chances of getting a job, or because of a personal interest.

Simultaneous bilinguals acquire both languages as "first languages." This is particularly true if the child hears both languages equally often. Such children are usually balanced bilinguals, who are equally competent in both languages. If the child hears one of the languages only occasionally, then the other is likely to become dominant. Many simultaneous bilingual children appear to have language impairment during the toddler years, before the individual codes are separated.[99] Consequently, sentences may contain phonemic or grammatical structures from both languages.

Successive bilinguals routinely borrow information from their first language in acquiring their second. At the very least, they understand something about grammar, communication rules, and pragmatic functions. They may start by repeating social phrases in specific contexts rather than concentrating on object names as infants do. This allows them to interact socially, facilitating the interaction they need to acquire the new language.[41]

More specific information (e.g., expression of syntax or phonology) is only occasionally transferable. Indeed, the first language may sometimes interfere with learning the second, especially in terms of phonology. This interference may make successive acquisition more difficult than simultaneous. Nonetheless, successive bilinguals can become proficient at both languages regardless of age at the acquisition of the second language although people usually speak the second language with an accent. Children between 3 and 7 learn a second language very quickly (often less than 1 year) when moving to an area with a different language.[99] Whether a child or an adult, the first language will be forgotten if it is not used on a regular basis. Even college students studying in a foreign country can lose the ability to converse comfortably in their native language if it is not spoken regularly.[99]

People often wonder if exposing a child to two languages will confuse the child and result in linguistic and cognitive impairments. These fears are unfounded.[55] Simultaneous bilinguals become as competent as monolinguals in each of their languages. Acquisition in one language may be a bit later than in the other, especially if a particular syntactic construction is more difficult in one. Table 12-7 outlines the stages of simultaneous bilingual development. Early on, there may be some intermixing of the words from each language. Such problems are short-lived. In fact, bilingualism may facilitate cognitive and linguistic development by improving the child's

TABLE 12-7. STAGES OF SIMULTANEOUS BILINGUAL DEVELOPMENT

Age*	Description of Abilities
0–2 years	Children do not distinguish between the two languages. They are treated as one forming language system. Therefore, the children readily intermix the vocabulary from both languages.
2–4 years	Children begin to discriminate the two languages. They first separate vocabulary and later syntax. They usually use only one language in an utterance, although they may sometimes insert an item from the other language if they cannot find the right term. This is especially likely if one language is dominant. The children show some ability to translate from one language into the other. If children are removed from the bilingual situation at this point, they typically become monolingual.
4+ years	Bilingualism becomes stable. The two languages are treated and used as separate systems. Intermixing is rare. One language may still be stronger than the other or may be preferred in certain settings.

*Ages given are only rough approximations and will vary considerably with circumstances.

(Elliot, A. J. [1981]. Child language. *Cambridge: Cambridge University Press.*)

abstract understanding of language's structure (e.g., the arbitrariness of the name assigned to a particular object).[54,55]

By the year 2000, there are expected to be about 5 million school-age children in the United States whose families do not speak English as their primary language.[55] Hispanic children comprise the single largest group of non-English speakers. Spanish is their first language. Frequently, no one in their families or immediate neighborhood speaks English fluently. This places them at a disadvantage when they enter school and are expected to begin learning reading skills when they do not know the English language.

Some black children, primarily those coming from the lower class, urban environments, have learned Black English (Ebonics) as their first language. Some people have argued that Black English (BE) is not really a separate language from Standard English (STE), claiming instead that BE is just a dialect form of STE. Black English and STE are quite similar linguistically, but there are enough syntactic, semantic, and phonological differences to consider them separate language codes.[107] Thus, the BE monolingual going to a STE school becomes a BE/STE bilingual. As with the Hispanic children, BE speakers may live in an environment where only Black English is routinely spoken. In fact, these differences may contribute to some of the academic problems poor black children face. For example, American schools routinely use phonetically based reading programs. The BE speaker pronounces sounds differently and so is unlikely to accurately recognize STE phonetics. Furthermore, the approaches and

emphases of the classroom may be at odds with the child's home experience.[60]

It is important to note that not all Hispanics are Spanish monolinguals. Some are simultaneous Spanish/English bilinguals; some are English monolinguals. Similarly, not all blacks, even among the lower social classes, are BE speakers, either monolingually or bilingually.

When children are monolingual in a language other than Standard American English, two educational issues arise. The first is how to teach them STE. The second is how much to encourage or discourage the use of their native language. One of the best ways to teach any second language is to give the learner a reason to learn it. For many people, being able to interact easily and effectively with the majority is sufficient motivation. However, teachers may need to make an extra effort to ensure this as a source of motivation. Blacks and whites do not always have high levels of interaction despite desegregation. Similarly, Hispanic and Anglo children do not always immediately accept each other. Teachers can design activities to facilitate interaction, thereby increasing the minority language speaker's motivation to learn the majority language. Later academic progress and career opportunities frequently are affected by the person's facility in STE.

But should the interactions be designed only to encourage the minority language speakers to learn the majority language? And how exclusively should the teacher use the majority language for instruction, counseling, and social interaction with the minority speaker? Right now, most American schools operate as if the minority language ought to be displaced and, perhaps, lost. Supporters of this perspective argue that if the children are to succeed, they need to know STE. Although this is generally true, the acquisition of STE does not need to be at the expense of BE or Spanish. Indeed, use of "rap" games and other forms of BE word play might make language learning more fun for all students.[60]

There are several problems in the exclusive use of STE for instruction in bilingual classrooms. First, the Spanish or BE speakers may miss some of the curriculum because of comprehension and production difficulties. Some will acquire STE quickly; others will be quite slow. Temperament, language habits, and motivation all affect rate of acquisition. A slower learner may become frustrated or withdrawn, further slowing acquisition.

Secondly, the exclusive use of STE gives it a privileged status, telling the child that his native tongue is inferior or unacceptable. Yet, this may be the language of everyone the child knows. Furthermore, the child may identify himself as Hispanic or black and may not wish to lose that identity. There are many linguistic, cognitive, and social advantages to bilingualism. Given this, it may be better to encourage *additive* bilingualism rather than *subtractive* monolingualism.

Adulthood

Language continues to develop throughout adulthood, most obviously in terms of vocabulary. Some of these are new additions to the language itself. New technology, discoveries, slang, and inventions all add new words to the language. Additionally, as more adults enroll in college courses, they will acquire the technical language of their chosen fields such as economics or psychology.

Older people (especially those over 70) may have some difficulty retrieving the exact word they want. Consequently, they tend to use elaborate, somewhat circumventing language or generalized word substitutes. This makes them score more poorly than young adults on vocabulary tests that emphasize single word synonyms as answers.[93] There may also be some losses in the ability to comprehend some complex syntactic structures.[92] However, neither of these changes is severe enough to seriously impair communication.[91–93]

The major linguistic changes in adulthood concern learning to use the appropriate language for the situation (refinement). For example, a child development professional may use one vocabulary in addressing a convention of colleagues, another in lecturing to a college class, and yet another when talking to a parents' group. Even her syntax may vary. Yet, the topic may be similar in all of the settings and all of the audiences are adults. Imagine the shift in conversational style and vocabulary when one is speaking to one's children, spouse, or a stranger, about topics ranging from directions to politics.

We have different registers (special styles of speaking) for various types of social interactions (remember the baby register?). Some registers, such as those associated with gender roles, are widely used.[77] Other registers are expressed only by persons within a specialized profession such as the jargon of veterinarians, nurses, or computer programmers.

No one knows how adults acquire these registers. Exposure to a register may be sufficient for at least comprehension to develop. Hearing the register spoken in an appropriate context is probably more effective than reading or hearing about it. Some practice is probably necessary for most people to use a register fluently. The ability of adults to monitor and revise their own utterances probably makes acquisition easier for them than it is for children.[91]

MAXIMIZING COMMUNICATION POTENTIALS

Infants and Toddlers

Historical and cross-cultural studies demonstrate that not all parents treat infants in the same way. There are variations in the amount of interaction and exposure to language. Nonetheless, children must hear language to acquire it, and the more parents talk to children, the quicker the children acquire language. But parents should not completely dominate conversation. It is important to engage the child in turntaking conversation.[79] The relatedness of the parents' statements to the child's is critical; parents who recast, expand, and repeat their children's utterances have faster developing children.[117] Such parental behavior provides an adequate model of language while maintaining the child's interest and participation in the conversation.

Adults need to provide a good model of language by using "real" words in talking to the baby. Parents should not scold children for incorrect pronunciations. Such errors are part of normal development. But parents should not encourage mispronunciations by adopting the child's "word" in place of the appropriate one.

Middle-class Americans have long assumed that reading to a child facilitates language development. However, research indicates that not all reading is equally effective. Parents should encourage the child to talk about the book, should repeat or expand the child's statements, and should provide positive feedback to the child during the reading session. These are the same parental speech characteristics associated with faster language development. For toddlers, looking at and talking about the pictures is more important than reading the specific words on the page. Thus, reading per se is not important for spoken language to develop, but it does provide an excellent context for parents to interact with their children.

There are also nonlinguistic factors that affect language development. For example, although older children may learn vocabulary from television,[102] younger children's language development may be slowed by TV viewing. Viewing Sesame Street is associated with vocabulary increases in 3- to 5-year-olds.[101] However, many parents routinely sit their 1-year-olds in front of the TV to watch Sesame Street, apparently thinking it will give their children a head start on numbers, letters, and so forth. Instead, it appears to slow their language acquisition, since it is a passive experience and does not allow for reciprocal responses or sensorimotor experiences.[88]

Experiences outside of the home also seem to encourage language development.[88] Outings provide additional social interactions that allow babies to practice their growing language skills. They also give the parents and child more to talk about.

The presence of older siblings seems to slow language development.[89] Perhaps parents do not have as much time to interact with later-borns as with a first-born, or the older children talk for the younger ones. Parents can mediate these effects by providing one-on-one interactions with the younger children. They can also monitor siblings to ensure that the younger ones have the chance to talk (Fig. 12-8).

Preschoolers and Early School-Agers

By age 3, most children will be able to carry on a conversation. A 3-year-old who is not talking or cannot be understood by a non-family member should be evaluated for hearing loss and language functioning by a speech pathologist. Pediatricians, preschool teachers, health departments, and public schools can provide recommendations about such testing as well as information about treatment programs.

Once children learn to talk, parents' concern about language development usually wanes, although questions about enunciation may persist. Parents should continue to model and encourage proper pronunciation. Evaluations and speech

FIGURE 12–8.
The older child experiences many opportunities to practice language skills with younger siblings.

therapy are available in public school systems, even to preschoolers.

As schooling begins, written language may become a concern. Increasingly, children are expected to acquire some minimal reading and writing skills in kindergarten. Some parents even purchase reading programs for their preschoolers. The value of such programs is unproven. Reading requires the coordination of a variety of skills, and many children, especially boys, are not capable of such coordination until 6 or 7 years of age. Parents should not panic if their child cannot read in kindergarten or has some difficulty with reading in first grade. If, however, the child falls a year or more below grade level in reading, evaluation for learning disabilities may be warranted. These problems are treatable, and the child and his family can be spared much frustration if the treatment is started early.

Parents can plan activities that encourage reading. Since children love to imitate, it is valuable for a parent to model reading. Parents who value reading have children who value reading. This does not require buying books. Trips to the library can provide books as well as an enjoyable family activity (Fig. 12-9). Newspapers and periodicals also count as reading. Street and store signs provide a spontaneous medium. Reading should be seen as an extension of the spoken word to a permanent form. Children can be encouraged to "tell their own story" through drawing pictures and writing words to share the message or experience with family and friends.

Reading to a child will not *cause* the child to learn to read, much less to be an early reader. Reading the same book over and over (which children often demand) may be helpful since it helps the child "memorize" the words in the story and, perhaps, associate sounds with the memorized words on the page.

Adolescents

As children get older, reading can be encouraged if adults can find topics and writing styles adolescents enjoy reading. In general, children and adolescents prefer real-life themes, especially if they can relate them to their own lives. Some books can actually help them to deal with fears, special stressors, and the unknown.

Family interactions may encourage the development of more advanced linguistic and communication skills. Parents should be aware and tolerant of the adolescents' growing ability to offer adultlike opinions on a range of subjects. The adolescents' views should be carefully considered. Conversations and word games can help adolescents to expand their vocabularies and to refine the use of words to their more precise meanings. Parents should also encourage their teenagers to participate in opportunities (such as a language or computer club) that will expand their understanding of language structures and use.

Adults

The crucial issue here is maximizing the potential of older adults. Ageist myths have left many of us with the mistaken impression that skills will be lost as a part of normal aging. This is generally not true in spoken or written language.

Physical disabilities can interfere with language skills. Hearing and eyesight should be checked regularly and corrected as necessary. If a person's hearing is failing and an aid

FIGURE 12–9.
Public libraries offer language stimulation for people of all ages. Regular visits as a young child can help instill the love of books and the habit of life-long reading and language development.

is not workable, face the listener directly and speak more slowly. Rooms can also be arranged to reduce extraneous noises and echos during a conversation.

Sometimes memory is a problem. The older person may lose a train of thought or have difficulty finding a word. A certain amount of this is normal and even occurs with young adults. Memory loss should not be so substantial that it creates constant frustration for the speaker or listener. Nor should it render normal conversation impossible. If it does, a physical should be scheduled. Memory problems may be due to drug interaction effects (the elderly often take multiple medications). Depression may also be the culprit. Both are treatable.

CONCLUSION

Language is primarily a social tool acquired in a social setting for use in interpersonal exchanges. It is a code that unites a society or a subculture. Indeed, one way to make someone an "insider" is to teach them the nuances of the group's language.

We have a cultural bias in favor of Standard English. This is evident in our educational programs and policies as well as in the research on language acquisition. This bias is detrimental to all children as well as to our understanding of the universal aspects of language development and use.

Few things frighten parents more than the idea that their child will never talk. Parents of deaf children sometimes go to

great lengths to try to help their children into the speaking world. Immigrant parents may deny their own language to help their children become enculturated by the new language. Certainly, a major goal of education is to teach better control of both oral and written language. We work hard to maximize the likelihood that our children will be able to use language effectively. However, in all situations, if one keeps in mind that language is the tool for communication, then the doors are opened to be more flexible and thus use more effective language teaching approaches.

Many people do, however, have problems with language. Among children, we must recognize the difference between "normal" development and delays. Contrary to popular belief, language development is not completed in the first few years of life. We need to be sensitive to the child's limitations while helping with the acquisition of more advanced levels of functioning. Developmental readiness is a relevant concept here. Forcing children into reading or writing too early only leads to frustration.

Adults can also acquire new language skills. There is no evidence that it is ever too late to learn a second language or, in the case of illiterate adults, to learn to read (see Chap. 27). Elderly adults who are experiencing significant communication difficulties should be evaluated. Many of their problems can be remediated.

REFERENCES

1. Ames, L., Gillespie, C., Haines, J., & Ilg, F. (1979). *The Gesell Institute's child from one to six: Evaluating the behavior of the preschool child.* New York: Harper & Row.
2. Anisfeld, M. (1984). *Language development from birth to three.* Hillsdale, NJ: Erlbaum.
3. Baldwin, D., & Markham, E. (1989). Establishing word-object relations: A first step. *Child Development, 60,* 381–398.
4. Bates, E., Benigni, L., Bretherton, I., Camaioni, L., & Volteraa, V. (1979). *The emergence of symbols: Cognition and communication in infancy.* New York: Academic.
5. Bates, E., Bretherton, I., Shore, C., & McNew, S. (1983). Names, gestures, and objects: The role of context in the emergence of symbols. In K. Nelson (Ed.), *Children's language* (Vol. 4) (pp. 59–123). Hillsdale, NJ: Erlbaum.
6. Bates, E., Bretherton, I., & Snyder, L. (1988). *From first words to grammar: Individual differences and dissociable mechanisms.* Cambridge: Cambridge University Press.
7. Bates, E., O'Connell, B., & Shore, C. (1987). Language and communication in infancy. In D. Osofsky (Ed.), *Handbook of infant development* (2nd ed.). New York: Wiley.
8. Bates, E., Snyder, L. (1987). The cognitive hypothesis in language development. In I. Uzgiris & J. M. Hunt (Eds.), *Infant performance and experience: New findings with the ordinal scales.* Urbana, IL: University of Chicago Press.
9. Beebe, B., Jaffe, J., Feldstein, S., Mays, K., & Alson, D. (1985). Interpersonal timing: The application of an adult dialogue model to mother-infant vocal and kinesic interactions. In T. Field & N. Fox (Eds.), *Social perception in infants* (pp. 217–248). Norwood, NJ: Ablex.
10. Benedict, H. (1979). Early lexical development: Comprehension and production. *Journal of Child Language, 6,* 183–200.

11. Bloom, L., & Capatides, J. (1987). Expression of affect and the emergence of language. *Child Development. 58,* 1513–1522.

12. Bohannon, J., MacWhinney, B., & Snow, C. (1990). No negative evidence revisited: Beyond learnability or who has to prove what to whom. *Developmental Psychology, 26,* 221–226.

13. Bohannon, J., & Stanowicz, L. (1988). The issue of negative evidence: Adult responses to children's language errors. *Developmental Psychology, 24,* 684–689.

14. Branstadter-Palmer, G. (1982). Ontogenetic growth chart. In C. Kopp & J. Krakow (Eds.). *The child.* Reading, MA: Addison-Wesley.

15. Brown, R. (1973). *A first language: The early stages.* Cambridge, MA: Harvard University Press.

16. Bruner, J. (1983). *Child's talk: Learning to use language.* New York: Norton.

17. Campos, J., Barrett, K., Lamb, M., Goldsmith, H., & Stenberg, C. (1983). Socio-emotional development. In P. Mussen (Ed.), *Handbook of child psychology* (4th ed.) (Vol. 2). New York: Wiley.

18. Cazden, C. (1988). Environmental assistance revisited: Variation and functional equivalence. In F. Kessel (Ed.), *The development of language and language researchers: Essays in honor of Roger Brown* (pp. 281–298). Hillsdale, NJ: Erlbaum.

19. Chapman, R. (1981). Cognitive development and language comprehension in 10- to 21-month-olds. In R. Stark (Ed.). *Language behavior in infancy and early childhood.* New York: Elsevier.

20. Chomsky, N. (1975). *Syntactic structure.* The Hague: Mouton.

21. Chomsky, N. (1975). *Reflections on language.* New York: Pantheon.

22. Chomsky, N. (1980). *Aspects of the theory of syntax.* Cambridge, MA: M.I.T. Press.

23. Clark, E. (1983). Meanings and concepts. In P. Mussen (Ed.), *Handbook of child psychology* (4th ed.) (Vol 3.). New York: Wiley.

24. Cohn, J., & Tronick, E. (1987). Mother-infant face-to-face interaction: The sequence of dyadic states at 3, 6, and 9 months. *Developmental Psychology, 23,* 68–77.

25. Cohn, J., & Tronick, E. (1988). Mother-infant face-to-face interaction: Influence is bidirectional and unrelated to periodic cycles in either partner's behavior. *Developmental Psychology, 24,* 386–392.

26. Corrigan, R. (1979). Cognitive correlates of language: Differential criteria yield differential results. *Child Development, 50,* 617–631.

27. Cromer, R. (1988). The cognition hypothesis revisited. In F. Kessel (Ed.), *The development of language and language researchers: Essays in honor of Roger Brown* (pp. 223–228). Hillsdale, NJ: Erlbaum.

28. Davis, A., & Wada, J. (1977). Hemispheric asymmetries in human infants: Spectral analysis of flash and click evoked potentials. *Brain and Language, 4,* 23–31.

29. DeCasper, A., & Fifer, W. (1980). Of human bonding: Newborns prefer their mothers' voices. *Science, 208,* 1174–1176.

30. Demetras, M., Post, K., & Snow, C. (1986). Feedback to first language learners: The role of repetitions and clarification questions. *Journal of Child Language, 13,* 275–292.

31. Dore, J. (1975). A pragmatic description of early language development. *Journal of Psycholinguistic Research, 3,* 343–350.

32. Dowd, J., & Tronick, E. (1986). Temporal coordination of arm movements in early infancy: Do infants move in synchrony with adult speech? *Child Development, 57,* 762–776.

33. Dunn, J., & Shatz, M. (1989). Becoming a conversationalist despite (or because of) having an older sibling. *Child Development, 60,* 399–410.

34. Edwards, D. (1973). Sensory-motor intelligence and semantic relations in early child grammar. *Cognition, 2,* 395–434.

35. Eimas, P., Siqueland, E., Jusczyk, P., & Vigorito, J. (1971). Speech perception in infants. *Science, 171,* 303–306.

36. Eisenson, J. (1984). *Aphasia and related disorders in children* (2nd ed.). New York: Harper & Row.

37. Elliot, A. J. (1981). *Child language.* Cambridge, Eng.: Cambridge University Press.

38. Fagan, J. (1982). Infant memory. In T. Field, A. Huston, H. Quay, L Troll, & G. Finely (Eds.), *Review of human development.* New York: Wiley.

39. Ferguson, C. (1977). Baby talk as a simplified register. In C. Snow & C. Ferguson (Eds.), *Talking to children: Language input and acquisition.* Cambridge: Cambridge University Press.

40. Ferguson, C., & Macken, M. (1983). The role of play in phonological development. In K. E. Nelson (Ed.), *Children's language* (Vol. 4). Hillsdale, NJ: Erlbaum.

41. Fillmore, L. (1985). Individual differences in second language acquisition. In C. Fillmore, D. Kempler, & W. Wang (Eds.), *Individual differences in language ability and behavior.* New York: Academic.

42. Fischer, K., & Corrigan, R. (1981). A skill approach to language development. In R. Stark (Ed.), *Language behavior in infancy and childhood.* Amsterdam: Elsevier North-Holland.

43. Frodi, A. (1985). When emphathy fails: Aversive infant crying and child abuse. In B. Lester & C. F. Z. Boukydis (Eds.), *Infant crying: Theoretical and research perspectives* (pp. 263–278). New York: Plenum.

44. Furth, H. G. (1966). *Thinking without language: Psychological implications of deafness.* New York: Free Press.

45. Gleitman, L., Newport, E., & Gleitman, H. (1984). The current status of the motherese hypothesis. *Journal of Child Language, 11,* 43–80.

46. Goldfield, B., & Reznick, J. S. (1990). Early lexical acquisition: Rate, content, and the vocabulary spurt. *Journal of Child Language, 17,* 171–184.

47. Goldfield, B., & Snow, C. (1985). Individual differences in language acquisition. In J. Gleason (Ed.), *The development of language.* Columbus, OH: Merrill.

48. Goldin-Meadow, S., & Feldman, H. (1977). The development of language-like communication without a model. *Science, 197,* 401–403.

49. Goldin-Meadow, S., & Mylander, C. (Eds.). (1984). Gestural communication in deaf children: The effects and non-effects of parental input on early language development. *Monographs of the Society for Research in Child Development.* (Ser. No. 207).

50. Gopnik, A., & Meltzoff, A. (1986). Relations between semantic and cognitive development in the one-word stage: The specificity hypothesis. *Child Development, 57,* 1040–1053.

51. Gordon, P. (1990). Learnability and feedback. *Developmental Psychology, 26,* 217–220.

52. Gustafson, G., & Harris, K. (1990). Women's responses to young infants' cries. *Developmental Psychology, 26,* 144–152.

53. Hakuta, K. (1988). Why bilinguals? In F. Kessel (Ed.), *The*

development of language and language researchers: Essays in honor of Roger Brown (pp. 299–318). Hillsdale, NJ: Erlbaum.

54. Hakuta, K., & Dias, R. (1985). The relationship between degree of bilingualism and cognitive ability: A critical discussion and some new longitudinal data. In K. E. Nelson (Ed.), *Children's Language* (Vol. 5). Hillsdale, NJ: Lawrence Erlbaum.

55. Hakuta, K., & Garcia, E. (1989). Bilingualism and education. *American Psychologist, 44,* 374–379.

56. Halliday, M. (1975). *Learning how to mean: Explorations in the development of language.* London: Edward Arnold.

57. Halliday, M. (1979). One child's protolanguage. In M. Bullowa (Ed.), *Before speech: The beginning of interpersonal communication.* London: Cambridge University Press.

58. Harding, C. (1983). Setting the stage for language acquisition: Communication development in the first year. In R. Golinkoff (Ed.), *The transition from prelinguistic to linguistic communication.* Hillsdale, NJ: Erlbaum.

59. Harding, C., & Golinkoff, R. (1979). The origins of intentional vocalizations in prelinguistic infants. *Child Development, 50,* 33–40.

60. Heath, S. (1989). Oral and literate traditions among Black Americans living in poverty. *American Psychologist, 44,* 367–373.

61. Huttenlocher, J. (1974). The origins of language comprehension. In R. Solso (Ed.), *Theories of cognitive psychology: The Loyola Symposium.* Hillsdale, NJ: Erlbaum.

62. Hyde, J. (1984). Children's understanding of sexist language. *Developmental Psychology, 20,* 697–706.

63. Hyde, J. (1985). *Half the human experience: The psychology of women* (3rd ed.). Lexington, MA: Health.

64. Ingram, D. (1989). *First language acquisition: Method, description and explanation.* New York: Cambridge University Press.

65. Kaye, K. (1979). Thickening thin data: The maternal role in developing communication and language. In M. Bullowa (Ed.), *Before speech: The beginning of interpersonal communication.* London: Cambridge University Press.

66. Kopp, C. B., & Krakow, J. B., et al. (1982). *The child, Development in a social context.* Reading, MA: Addison-Wesley.

67. Kuhl, P., & Meltzoff, A. (1988). Speech as an intermodal object of perception. In A. Yonas (Ed.), *Minnesota Symposium on Child Psychology: Perceptual development in infancy.* Hillsdale, NJ: Erlbaum.

68. Lieberman, P. (1985). The physiology of the cry and speech in relation to linguistic behavior. In B. Lester & C. F. Z. Boukydis (Eds.), *Infant crying: Theoretical and research perspectives.* New York: Plenum.

69. Locke, J. (1983). *Phonological acquisition and change.* New York: Academic.

70. Lovaas, O. I. (1980). *The autistic child: Language development through behavior modification.* New York: Irvington.

71. Mackay, D. (1980). Psychology, prescriptive grammar, and the pronoun problem. *American Psychologist, 35,* 444–449.

72. Mahler, M. S., Pine, F., & Bergram, A. (1975). *The psychological birth of the human infant.* New York: Basic Books.

73. Marastsos, M. (1983). Some current issues in the study of the acquisition of grammar. In P. Mussen (Ed.), *Handbook of child psychology* (4th ed.) (Vol. 3). New York: Wiley.

74. Maxwell, M. (1983). Language acquisition in a deaf child of deaf parents: Speech, sign variations, and print variations. In K. E. Nelson (Ed.), *Children's language* (Vol. 4). Hillsdale, NJ: Erlbaum.

75. Mayer, N., & Tronick, E. (1985). Mothers' turn-giving signals and infant turn-taking in mother-infant interaction. In T. Field & N. Fox (Eds.), *Social perception in infancy* (pp. 199–216). Norwood, NJ: Ablex.

76. McCabe, A. (1989). Differential language learning styles in young children: The importance of context. *Developmental Review, 9,* 1–20.

77. McCloskey, L. (1987). Gender and conversation: Mixing and matching styles. In D. B. Carter (Ed.), *Current conceptions of sex roles and typing: Theory and research.* New York: Praeger.

78. McCune-Nicholich, L. (1981). Toward symbolic functioning: Structure of early pretend games and potential parallels with language. *Child Development, 52,* 785–797.

79. McDonald, L., & Pien, D. (1982). Mother conversational behavior as a function of interactional intent. *Journal of Child Language, 9,* 337–358.

80. Meltzoff, A. (1988). Infant imitation and memory: Nine-month-olds in immediate and deferred tests. *Child Development, 59,* 217–225.

81. Meltzoff, A., & Moore, K. (1983). The origins of imitation in infancy: Paradigm, phenomena, and theories. In L. Lipsitt & C. Rovee-Collier (Eds.), *Advances in infancy research* (Vol. 2). Norwood, NJ: Ablex.

82. Moerk, E. (1989). The LAD was a lady and the tasks were ill-defined. *Developmental Review, 9,* 21–57.

83. Molfese, D., & Molfese, V. (1979). VOT distinctions in infants: Learned or innate? In H. Whitaker (Ed.), *Studies in neuro-linguistics* (Vol. 4). New York: Academic.

84. Morse, P., & Cowan, N. (1982). Infant auditory and speech perception. In T. Field, A. Houston, H. Quay, L. Troll, & G. Finley (Eds.), *Review of human development.* New York: Wiley.

85. Moulton, J., Robinson, G., & Elias, C. (1978). Psychology in action: Sex bias in language use: "Neutral" pronouns that aren't. *American Psychologist, 33,* 1032–1036.

86. Murray, A. (1985). Aversiveness is in the mind of the beholder: Perception of infant crying by adults. In B. Lester & C. F. Z. Boukydis (Eds.), *Infant crying: Theoretical and research perspectives* (pp. 217–240). New York: Plenum.

87. Murray, L., & Trevarthen, C. (1986). The infant's role in mother-infant communication. *Journal of Child Language, 13,* 15–30.

88. Nelson, K. (Ed.). (1973). Structure and strategy in learning to talk. *Monographs of the Society for Research in Child Development, 38.* (Ser. No. 149).

89. Nelson, K. (1981). Individual differences in language development: Implications for development and language. *Developmental Psychology, 17,* 170–187.

90. Newport, E., Gleitman, H., & Gleitman, L. (1977). Mother, I'd rather do it myself: Some effects and non-effects of maternal speech style. In C. Snow & C. Ferguson (Eds.), *Talking to children: Language input and acquisition.* Cambridge, Eng.: Cambridge University Press.

91. Obler, L. (1985). Language through the life-span. In J. B. Gleason (Ed.), *The development of language.* Columbus, OH: Merrill.

92. Obler, L. (1989). Language beyond childhood. In J. B. Gleason (Ed.), *The development of language* (2nd ed.). Columbus, OH: Merrill.

93. Obler, L., & Albert, M. (1985). Language skills across adulthood. In J. Birren & K. Schaie (Eds.), *Handbook of the psychology of aging* (2nd ed.). New York: Van Nostrand Reinhold.

94. Oller, & Eilers, R. (1988). The role of audition in infant babbling. *Child Development, 59,* 441–449.

95. Penner, S. (1987). Parental responses to grammatical and ungrammatical child utterances. *Child Development, 58,* 376–384.

96. Pettito, L. (1988). "Language" in the prelinguistic child. In F. Kessel (Ed.), *The development of language and language researchers: Essays in honor of Roger Brown* (pp. 187–222). Hillsdale, NJ: Erlbaum.

97. Piaget, J. (1959). *The language and thought of the child* (3rd ed., rev. & enl.). London: Routledge & Kegan Paul.

98. Piaget, J. (1962). *Play, dreams, and imitation in childhood* (C. Gattengo & F. M. Hodgson, Trans.). London: Routledge & Kegan Paul.

99. Reich, P. A. (1986). *Language development.* Englewood Cliffs, NJ: Prentice-Hall.

100. Rice, M. (1989). Children's language acquisition. *American Psychologist, 44,* 149–156.

101. Rice, M., Huston, A., Truglio, R., & Wright, J. (1990). Words from "Sesame Street": Learning vocabulary while viewing. *Developmental Psychology, 26,* 421–428.

102. Rice, M., & Woodsmall, L. (1988). Lessons from television: Children's word learning when viewing. *Child Development, 59,* 420–429.

103. Richman, A., Levine, R., New, R., Howrigan, G., Welles-Nystrom, B., & LeVine, S. (1988). Maternal behavior to infants in five cultures. In R. LeVine, P. Miller, & M. West (Eds.), *Parental behavior in diverse societies.* San Francisco: Jossey-Bass.

104. Sameroff, A. J., & Fiese, B. H. (1988). The context of language development. In R. L. Schiefelbusch & L. L. Lloyd (Eds.). *Language perspectives: Acquisition, retardation, and intervention* (2nd ed., pp. 3–20). Austin, TX: Proed.

105. Schiefflelin, B., & Ochs, E. (1983). A cultural perspective on the transition from prelinguistic to linguistic communication. In R. Golinkoff (Ed.), *The transition from prelinguistic to linguistic communication.* Hillsdale, NJ: Erlbaum.

106. Schultz, T. (1976). A cognitive-developmental analysis of humor. In A. Chapman & H. Foot (Eds.), *Humor and laughter: Theory, research and applications.* London: Wiley.

107. Sinclair, E. (1983). Important issues in the language development of the Black child. In G. J. Powell, et al. (Ed.), *The psychosocial development of minority group children* (pp. 490–498). New York: Bruner/Mazel.

108. Sinclair de Zwart, H. (1973). Language acquisition and cognitive development. In T. Moore (Ed.), *Cognitive development and the acquisition of language.* New York: Academic.

109. Skinner, B. F. (1957). *Verbal behavior.* New York: Appleton-Century-Crofts.

110. Slobin, D. I. (1985). Cross-linguistic evidence for language making capacity. In D. I. Slobin (Ed.), *The cross-linguistic study of language acquisition* (Vol. 2). Hillsdale, NJ: Erlbaum.

111. Smolak, L. (1982). Cognitive precursors of receptive vs. expressive language. *Journal of Child Language, 9,* 13–22.

112. Smolak, L. (1986). *Infancy.* Englewood Cliffs, NJ: Prentice-Hall.

113. Smolak, L. (1987). Child characteristics and maternal speech. *Journal of Child Language, 14,* 481–492.

114. Smolak, L., & Levine, M. (1984). The effects of differential criteria on the assessment of cognitive-linguistic relationships. *Child Development, 55,* 973–980.

115. Smolak, L., & Weinraub, M. (1983). Maternal speech: Strategy or response? *Journal of Child Language, 10,* 369–380.

116. Snow, C. (1981). The uses of imitation. *Journal of Child Language, 8,* 205–212.

117. Snow, C. (1989). Understanding social interaction and language acquisition: Sentences are not enough. In M. Bornstein & J. Bruner (Eds.), *Interaction in human development.* Hillsdale, NJ: Erlbaum.

118. Stark, R. (1989). Early language intervention: When, why, how? *Infants and Young Children, 1,* 44–53.

119. Stern, D. (1985). *The interpersonal world of the infant.* New York: Basic Books.

120. Tomasello, M., & Farrar, M. (1986). Joint attention and early language. *Child Development, 57,* 1454–1463.

121. Trevarthen, C. (1979). Communication and cooperation in early infancy. In M. Bullowa (Ed.), *Before speech: The beginning of interpersonal communication.* Cambridge: Cambridge University Press.

122. Tronick, E., & Cohn, J. (1989). Infant-mother face-to-face interaction: Age and gender differences in coordination and the occurrence of miscoordination. *Child Development, 60,* 85–92.

123. Vygotsky, L. S. (1986). *Thought and language* (rev. ed.) (A. Kozulin, Trans.). Cambridge, MA: MIT Press.

124. Whitehurst, G. (1982). Language development. In B. Wolman (Ed.), *Handbook of developmental psychology* (pp. 367–387). Englewood Cliffs, NJ: Prentice-Hall.

125. Whitehurst, G., & Valdez-Menchaca, M. (1988). What is the role of reinforcement in early language acquisition? *Child Development, 59,* 430–440.

126. Wolff, P. H. (1973). The natural history of crying and other vocalizations in infancy. In L. J. Stone, H. T. Smith, & L. B. Murphy (Eds.), *The competent infant* (pp. 1185–1198). New York: Basic Books.

127. Wood, B. (1981). *Children and communication: Verbal and nonverbal language development.* Englewood Cliffs, NJ: Prentice-Hall.

128. Zachry, W. (1978). Ordinality and interdependence of representation and language development in infancy. *Child Development, 49,* 681–689.

129. Zelazo, P., Kearsley, R., & Ungerer, J. (1984). *Learning to speak: A manual for parents.* Hillsdale, NJ: Lawrence Erlbaum.

13 *Imitation is natural to man from childhood, one of his advantages over the lower animals being this, that he is the most imitative creature in the world, and learns at first by imitation.*

—ARISTOTLE,
POETICS

Preparation for School

Clara S. Schuster

Entrance into the first grade constitutes a major change in a child's lifestyle. He or she is introduced to (or confronted with, depending on the child's developmental readiness) new friends, new experiences, and new goals and responsibilities. The greater part of the day is now spent away from home; thus the child experiences a change or broadening of orientation to the environment and the culture. The teacher becomes a significant role model, and peers begin to influence the child's perceived desires and needs as well as behavior patterns. As the child is introduced to other lifestyles and becomes more independent of the parents, he or she may begin to question family rules and regulations, standards, and goals. The child also frequently begins to challenge parental authority.

The child who is progressing normally is ready to tackle Erikson's next core problem—industry versus inferiority. Success in mastering this task is dependent not only on the experiences and support offered during the school years, but also on how well the child has been prepared for school by past experiences.

An enormous amount of learning must occur before the child ever enters school. Preparation for school begins the day an infant is born. Its foundation for success is the parent–child relationship. It all seems very simple to adults looking back from their college years, but it was not simple at the time; each new schema took effort to form. Sensitivity and responsiveness on the part of the parents toward the child's developmental level are essential to facilitate the child's cognitive growth from the basically reflexive activities of the neonate to the sensorimotor thought of the toddler and then to the prelogical thought processes of the preschooler. As the parents structure the environment, they must alternately provide enough security, challenges, frustrations, and successes, so that the child begins to make discriminations, to see relationships, to explore independently, and to master cognitive, affective, social, and physical skills.

EXPECTATIONS OF THE FIRST-GRADE TEACHER

The 6-year-old has learned much since birth, but it is only a beginning. The child is not yet ready to face the world alone. Formal education is geared toward helping children to gain the skills essential to cope with adult responsibilities. Although it is recognized that many children may not possess all of the following skills when they enter first grade, success in school is greatly facilitated if they have developed the competencies discussed in the following sections. Neurologically and developmentally, 6-year-old boys tend to lag behind girls by about 6 months, a factor that is frequently to their academic disadvantage.

277

Academic Skills

Some skills are prerequisites for learning to read and to write because they involve the child's ability to use language symbols to represent concrete objects, actions, or events. Reading takes the child one step farther away from concrete reality, thus requiring higher levels of representational thought. The skills discussed in the following sections indicate that lower-level concepts and representational thought have been mastered.

Knowledge

Progress in the first grade is facilitated if the child knows the alphabet before beginning school; this includes knowing the sequence of the letters and the ability to recognize each letter. Teachers frequently find that children know the alphabet song but are unable to identify the corresponding letter. The child who can print the letters and identify the major sound (phoneme) associated with the letter is at a great advantage in beginning to read, especially by the phonetic approach. This ability also involves auditory discrimination skills. Some children are able to recognize the letters and their major sounds but are not able to recreate that symbol on paper. Being able to print a letter has little to do with phonics; it is a reflection rather of the child's visual-motor coordination skills.

Children who are able to write and to recognize their own name in print have already been introduced to the concept that a written sign represents a verbal symbol, which in turn represents a concrete object—"me." The ability to recognize one's own name among several other names or words fosters discrimination skills, supports a sense of mastery, and encourages recognition of individuality and self-identity.

Most 6-year-olds are able to count to 10. They should also be able to recognize the written sign for the numbers, but more importantly, they should know the meaning of the number (i.e., the child should be able to identify "3" pencils or "5" stars). This skill is a prerequisite for early mathematics—both addition and subtraction. An understanding of concepts such as "more" and "less" is also basic to first-grade mathematics (Fig. 13-1).

The ability to recognize the colors of the rainbow or the colors in a basic crayon box is also very helpful. Color is frequently used in the early grades to identify a specific book or as part of the directions for an assignment.

Understanding

One of the basic concepts the first-grader should know is the concept of direction, especially the ability to distinguish right from left. Children who experience difficulty with this skill frequently have difficulty in reading from left to right and may show word or letter reversals.

The ability to understand position words is also essential to comprehending directions. Words, such as _above/below, on/beside, under/over,_ and _inside/outside_ are common in directions given to the first-grader. Direction words are more abstract than words representing concrete objects and thus may present more difficulty to some children, especially those with learning disabilities.

Activities involving classification skills comprise a large proportion of first-grade work: Is the child able to identify things that are alike and things that are different? Differences in size and basic shapes (triangle, square, rectangle, and circle) are usually learned during the preschool years. Discrimination or comparative activities require the child to identify which object is largest, smallest, shortest, or longest. Higher levels of classification require the child to match objects that have similar usage. Discrimination and classification skills are also challenged by asking the child to match pictures with rhyming words (Fig. 13-2). Although to adults these activities seem simple and fun, to the first-grader they may present major challenges to emerging skills and a sense of mastery. The inadequately prepared child may experience repeated failures.

Physical Skills

Specific physical skills are helpful, if not essential, in helping the child to maintain a feeling of independence, personal integrity, and a positive self-concept in the classroom. Some of these skills are critical to independent self-care; others are indirectly related to competence in completing assignments.

Personal Care

The teacher obviously cannot provide personal care for 30 or 35 children. The children should be able to feed themselves, attend to their own toileting needs, and wash their hands independently. Occasionally first-graders need assistance with buttoning clothing or putting on coats or boots. In these instances, the children can be encouraged to help and teach each other, which is a relief for the teacher, a source of pride to the helper, and a peer role model and thus a stimulus for the child who is helped.

Coordination

Coordination of gross motor skills is evidenced by the ability to hop on both one foot and two feet, to do a jumping jack, to skip, and to walk unassisted on a balance board. Many teachers indicate that children who are unable to perform these skills frequently cannot write well. It appears that lack of adequate gross-motor experience correlates highly with inadequate development of the fine-motor skills necessary for writing. The prerequisite motor pathways have not been adequately strengthened or established.

Children should be able to hold a pencil properly;[12] the position is identical to that for holding tableware properly for eating. They should also be able to turn individual pages, a skill that is usually developed during the third year of life. Many children may still have some difficulty with scissors, but some skill in their use is essential to success in classroom assignments. The child should have enough fine motor coordination to be able to draw simple shapes (circle, square),

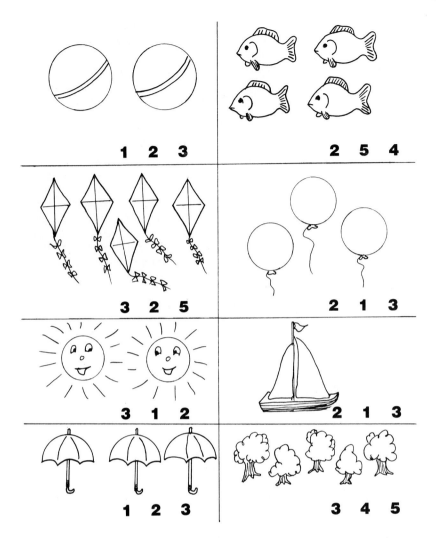

1   2   3   **2   5   4**

3   2   5   **2   1   3**

3   1   2   **2   1   3**

1   2   3   **3   4   5**

FIGURE 13–1.
Typical counting exercise for first graders.

write alphabet letters, and stay within lines when coloring. The abilities to match a tapped-out rhythm and to draw a picture of a person correlate highly with the reading and spelling skill achieved at the end of second grade.[12]

Psychosocial Skills

Most children are very excited and eager to start school; it represents a big step in "growing up." The child entering school will need to be able to tolerate separation from mother. Some children have not adequately resolved the separation-individuation process and thus find that they still need copious amounts of emotional refueling in order to face the world.[26] Erikson theorizes that a deep sense of inadequacy "may be caused by an insufficient solution of the preceding conflict [initiative]; he may still want his mummy more than knowledge. He may still rather be the baby at home than the big boy in school."[16] The child who is unable to tolerate separation from mother may have inadequate energy levels or

inadequate motivation to master school assignments (Fig. 13-3).

The first-grader needs to know how to share with peers; this includes the sharing not only of objects but also of the teacher's attention and time. An only child may have particular difficulty in this area. Self-reliance, self-entertainment, patience, empathy, and the ability to tolerate frustration of one's goals are all subskills for this area of competence.

Although attention span appears to be affected both by age and by experience, the ability to listen effectively is a skill that is reinforced or extinguished by experiences. The parent–child relationship is a critical factor in this area; parents who ignore the child's attempts to communicate will often find that the child, in turn, will ignore them. Reciprocity of communication is mutually reinforcing. The first-grader must be able to listen to two- or three-part instructions and then follow directions accordingly. This skill is obviously closely related to the child's comprehension of language symbols but is also related to the motivation to attend, to remember, and

FIGURE 13—2.
Typical rhyming-word exercise for first graders.

FIGURE 13—3.
The child who is entering school must be able to tolerate separation from the parent before adequate affective energy is available to invest in cognitive and social activities.

then to follow directions—a point to be explored further in the section on learned helplessness.

Children listen to guidance and respond most positively when they respect, but do not fear, authority. Fear may cause them to listen, but it may also immobilize them for action. On the other hand, lack of respect leads to chaos in the classroom and academic confusion because of inattentiveness.

Children who are most likely to do well in the primary grades are those who have learned how to harness, organize, and focus their energies toward a goal. They are self-confident, participate actively with the environment, enjoy mastery for its own sake, and seem to have an advanced state of ego organization.[12] An increasing number of children today, especially from low-income and ethnic populations, do not have the background experiences essential for success in school.[7]

The mature first-grader has enough self-discipline to modify his or her goals to the rules of the classroom or to the desires of others. The child is able to sit still long enough to attend to assignments and complete them and to restrict talking to appropriate times. Most 5- to 6-year-olds want to "be first," but the combination of burgeoning self-discipline, sharing skills, and the knowledge of social protocols encourages them to begin to take turns and to learn politeness and respect for the rights, feelings, and human dignity of others.

General Knowledge

Thus far, three major skill areas have been discussed: academic, physical, and psychosocial skills. The child should develop specific competencies in these skills before entrance into first grade to facilitate mastery of the curriculum and the social environment at school. Although these skills are critical to adjustment, a *good* teacher can still help the child who is weak in one or more skills to achieve mastery and progress successfully in school. Although it appears that there may be critical times for learning some skills, the skills still can be learned at a later time with an individualized program. However, children who are weak in the area of general knowledge may be so handicapped that they cannot be successful in a regular classroom unless extensive remedial assistance is given.

A family who accepted a 5½-year-old girl and an 8-year-old girl as foster daughters is illustrative of this point. Before coming to their foster parents, the girls had apparently spent much time without adult supervision in a small house trailer devoid of running water and electricity. The single bed was shared with their mother. The transient nature of residence in various locations prevented both the establishment of familial attachment and provision of supportive services to the family. The girls were removed from the home as an emergency measure when they failed to attend school and the mother was critically ill. The paucity of their general knowledge, the shortness of their attention span, their inability to remember, their lack of curiosity, and the absence of play activities were astounding. The normal curiosity that begins during the toddler years had literally been extinguished. The girls could not identify the food on their plate or give common names of zoo animals. They did not understand simple commands (e.g., "Sit down," "Open the door," "Pass the potatoes, please"). They did not know the alphabet, nor could they count to 10. The younger girl could not remember three letters in succession.

Since it was summer, the foster parents immediately began an enrichment program. A jungle gym was purchased, and the nearby school playground offered opportunity for gross motor activities. The girls were encouraged to assist in cooking and housekeeping chores. Much guidance, encouragement, and praise was offered for small tasks—jobs they could see they had done. Musical records appropriate for toddlers were played during quiet time and at bedtime. A picture dictionary expanded the world to objects and events the family could not provide in the home or by day trips. The major enrichment technique was communication. The foster parents talked about what they were going to do, what they were doing, and what they had done; they attempted to give the girls a sense of time, planning, and involvement. Each girl was given her own bed, her own toys, her own responsibilities—and her own private time with both the mother and the father.

At the beginning of first grade (the 8-year-old had never attended school), the girls were given assignments, such as those in Figures 13-1, 13-2, and 13-4. But when general knowledge is so weak, how can one be successful at rhyming or identifying initial consonant sounds? These girls, like many others from disadvantaged environments, did not possess the prerequisite skills.

Sara Smilansky's research indicates that severely disadvantaged children tend to experience repeated failure in grade school, despite extensive enrichment and remedial assistance at school.[43] However, when changes are made in the family environment, they are reflected in the academic progress of the children. Intensive, specific support services offered to high-risk or low IQ mothers can result in significant improvement in the behavior and school success of children.[14] If children from deprived early environments are provided with a new enriched environment, they evidence increased IQ scores and social and emotional advances.[8, 13, 19, 22, 42] In this case, after 2 years both of these girls were able to work at their proper grade level. The key difference between Smilansky's research and this situation was the dramatic change that occurred in the girls' home environment. Even though school and peers are very important to the development of the school-ager, the family still remains the key influence in the child's life.

These girls were returned to their natural mother after marked improvements were evidenced in their original home environment. They continued to function at grade level—with enthusiasm—into their high school years, and adapted successfully to the responsibilities of adulthood. The cycle of perceived inadequacy had been broken.

FIGURE 13–4.
Typical initial consonant exercise for first graders (for "f" and "r" sounds).

THE INADEQUATELY PREPARED CHILD

The previous example was presented so that this chapter might be read with the realization that even though the family environment is critical to fostering maximal development of the child's potentials, a child who receives a difficult start in life is not necessarily on a failure course. Children exhibit much plasticity and resiliency.[8] Many factors can change; intervention later in life can help the individual to grow to higher levels of cognitive, social, and emotional maturity. However, the younger the child, the more susceptible he or she is to both permanent damage from overwhelming negative factors and successful remediation by synchronized positive factors.

The Significance of the Parent

Human behavior is so complex and is exposed to so many different variables during the developmental years that the identification of a single correlating variable between early and later development is extremely unlikely. Consequently, it is very significant when found. Research is still in the early stages, but evidence is beginning to accumulate that indicates that the child's primary caregiver is the key to the child's approach to, and mastery of, the environment. Most of the research has centered on the mother–infant/child relationship. However, the gender or the legal relationship of the caregiver is insignificant. The consistency and quality of the interaction are the determining factors (Fig. 13-5).

The Harvard Preschool Project, headed by Burton L. White, identified competency characteristics of "A" (high adaptability or flexibility to function well in a variety of living conditions) and "C" (low adaptability) children 3 to 5 years of age.[33, 48] White discovered that the distinguishing characteristics of the two groups were already clearly identifiable by the age of 3 years. White and his associates then went into the homes of infants and toddlers to track down the point at which the paths of "A" and "C" children began to diverge. They discovered that at 18 months of age the path was already predictable. It was not until they studied children as young as 10 months that the behaviors identified as significant discriminators began to merge. Based on their intensive and extensive observations within the home setting, they concluded that the critical variable in the child's development was the mother's approach to the interaction.[33]

The research team discovered that mothers of "A" children seldom gave their babies undivided attention for more than 10% of the waking day and did not engage in preplanned formal teaching—quite the opposite of what the lay person (and even the researchers) would predict.

The "A" mother was discovered to be superbly effective in two ways: (1) indirectly, as an organizer and designer of the child's environment, and (2) directly, as a consultant to a busy, exploring, curious, active child. She encouraged and reinforced the child's exploration and independence in a safe environment. When the child met an obstacle, frustration, problem, or novel object or experience, she would verbalize the phenomenon, give directions for resolving the discrepancy with the skills available to the child, or teach him or her new skills. Sometimes the mother "set the stage" for problem solving, but at the child's level of development. She supported and shared the joy of discovery and self-accomplishment, offering assistance merely as a backup support system. Thus through these 10- to 20-second episodes scattered throughout the day, the child learned both independence and how to use the adult as a resource—prerequisites for Erikson's autonomy and initiative stages. This kind of intervention is synchronized intervention because it is responsive to **the child's** needs and offered at the **child's pace.**

The "C" mothers, on the other hand, "protected" their children by restricting their freedom to explore. Although they were gentle and loving, gave good physical care, and were patient, these mothers failed to "tune in" to the child's world. They did not share the child's excitement of discovery or verbalize events. They failed to transform the routine diaper change or bath into an intellectually stimulating game of peek-a-boo or water play. White's research indicated that fewer than 10% of the children were provided with an environment that would provide maximal opportunities to develop their potentials or to get a really good start in life.[48]

Sylvia Krown, doing research in Israel, similarly identified very marked differences in the social and cognitive skills of "advantaged" versus "disadvantaged" 3-year-old children. The characteristics found in these two groups of children are summarized in Table 13-1. Krown found that although the mothers of deprived children were interested in their children's progress and showed much physical affection, they did not understand their child's unique communication system.

FIGURE 13–5.
Many activities are available to parents and children that can be mutually enjoyed while increasing the child's general knowledge about the world.

TABLE 13-1. CHARACTERISTICS OF DISADVANTAGED VERSUS ADVANTAGED 3-YEAR-OLDS

Category	Disadvantaged Children	Advantaged Children
	Characteristics	
Physical factors	Clothing about same as advantaged children	Sloppy to new clothes
	Often sent to school ill, with fever	Kept home if ill
	Open, neglected sores; runny noses	Good hygiene
	No breakfast	Fed before school
	Tense posture; guarded movements	Moves with ease and abandon
	Depressed, angry eyes	Alive, alert eyes
	Rigid, unsmiling facial expression	Head up, smiles easily
	Bears pain in silence	Demands attention when hurt
Activity	Constant motion; short attention span	Directed enthusiasm
	Haphazard activity; touches everything	Purposeful activity
	Lacks enthusiasm for exploring	Interested in new experiences
	Disinterested, aimless, wandering	Inquisitive about environment
	Repetitive, stereotyped play	Creative play
	Needs prodding into activity	Exhibits initiative
	Unaware of danger	Avoids hurting self
Mode of thinking	Afraid to tackle new tasks	Interested in new things and information
	Confused sense of time, place, order	Classifies many items
	"In a fog"	Fascinated by surrounding world
	Difficulty remembering concrete events	Talks about events freely
	Does not know how to discriminate	Enthusiastic, curious
	Difficulty with cause-effect relations	Experiments with things around him or her
	Difficulty with sequencing	Follows directions easily
Relationships with people	Withdrawn, shy, suspicious	Friendly, open, outgoing, trusting
	Frequently does not respond	Expresses feelings
	Uneasy with adults	Uneasy when teacher is not near
	Does not address teacher	Seeks attention of adults
	Is a "loner"	Aware of other children
Frustration tolerance	Physical aggression	Controlled, directed behavior
	Impulsive behaviors	Predictable emotional reactions
	Gives up quickly	Seeks teacher's help
Language	Uses isolated words and phrases	Tells stories
	Unable to identify colors, body parts, familiar objects, animals	Rich, expressive vocabulary
	Unable to listen to whole story	Loves story time
	Phonation and enunciation problems	Enjoys speaking and sharing

(Krown, S. [1974]. Three and fours go to school. Englewood Cliffs, NJ: Prentice-Hall.)

These mothers were themselves very disorganized and basically passive, and they seemed to lack faith in their ability to control their own world.[23] The mothers were frequently so concerned with their own needs or roles that they failed to communicate to their child a sense of being a separate, special, protected individual. Krown observes that as a result, the children were unable to predict what would happen from one event to the next, had minimal knowledge of language, had difficulty remembering events, and had a greatly decreased curiosity about the world.[23] Competent parents treat their young child as a capable, resourceful person. They are warm, positive, and consistent in their interactions while assisting the child with problem solving.[28]

Krown developed a very comprehensive preschool program for these children, which included parent training. At the end of 2 years, there was a marked decrease in the contrast between the two groups, but residual effects, especially in the area of socialization, were still evident.

Both Krown and White found that the child's skills correlated highly with the interactional milieu provided by the mother. White looked for factors facilitating competence, whereas Krown was looking for factors causing incompetence, but their observations support each other. The most significant finding of the Harvard Preschool Project was that differences in later academic competence could be predicted by 10 months of age.

T. Berry Brazelton has made numerous analyses of mother–infant interactions during the first month of life. He has discovered that the infant's responsiveness to the mother is determined by the infant's ability to organize the stimuli offered by the mother (see Neonatal Assessment, Chap. 5). True reciprocity of interaction is established only if the mother is able to read the infant's cues for boredom or overstimulation.[6] When the mother does not offer the infant enough stimuli, the infant may temporarily seek more attention, turn attention to other things, or "tune out." If the mother offers too much stimuli, the infant becomes "flooded" and retreats in self-defense until he or she is once more able to organize the stimuli and respond. The infant may become so overwhelmed or flooded by the attention that the child begins to behave very irritably or to cry vehemently. The mother who is sensitive to the infant's initial cues can establish a synchrony of interaction that can sustain the infant in state 4 for prolonged periods of time. Learning is most effective in state 4, since interaction with the environment is at its peak during this state.

Research indicates that synchronized parental responsiveness reduces crying in neonates and young infants. According to Bell and Ainsworth, "spoiled infants" are those whose mothers ignored their cries or delayed in responding to them. The child feels forced to demand attention to meet emotional needs. Maternal responsiveness in the early months promotes confidence in the environment and fosters greater independence by the end of the first year of life.[4] This decrease in crying behavior can also be empirically identified by the third day of life. Infants who are picked up and talked to each time they cry during the first 3 days of life cry less and are more alert at the end of 3 days than infants who are allowed to cry for prolonged periods (a common practice in some hospital nurseries).[45]

Some extremely interesting data have been collected by Marshall Klaus and John Kennell and their associates. Their research indicates that when infants are kept with their mothers during the first 1 to 2 hours of life, and for 15 extra hours during the first 3 days of life, there are significant differences in maternal behaviors at 1 month and 1 year after birth.[20, 21] These mothers were more attentive and responsive and exhibited greater synchrony of responses (ability to read infant cues) than mothers who experienced standard hospital exposure to their infants (introduction 6 to 12 hours after birth and exposure for 30 minutes every 4 hours for feeding). At 1 year, the early-contact infants exhibited more curiosity and less stranger anxiety than the delayed-contact infants. Follow-up research on the same infants at 2 years and 5 years indicated that the children of early-contact mothers had statistically significant higher IQs and more advanced scores on two language tests.[36, 37] The implications of these studies are that significant preparation for school may actually begin during the first hours of life by sensitizing the mother to the infant's cueing skills.

Whether one takes a Piagetian view of cognitive development (in which intellectual skills change from one stage to the next through reorganization or internal structural changes that incorporate lower-level skills) or a behaviorist view (in which cognitive skills evolve through successive approximations, or shaping, to higher-level skills) is insignificant at this point. The skills of children evolve as the environment gives them the opportunity to "try their wings," or the skills may be elicited by an enticing environment. The fact remains that the skills of the neonate are not the same as those of the young school-ager; the skills of the child have evolved sequentially under the combined influence of innate potentials, environmental influences or opportunities, and the individual child's efforts to interpret and control events. White suggests that during the first 8 months of life, the child's progress is assured by nature as long as he or she is provided with a normal amount of love, attention, and care.[48]

Research with twins and adopted children indicates that heredity is very important in determining IQ.[18, 40] However, it is not a fixed entity. Obviously, potentials are limited by neurological maturity, but skills mastered are those that are encouraged, allowed, or supported by the environment. Intelligence quotients can be influenced by motivation, exposure, and experience. J. McVicker-Hunt postulates that any one individual could have a difference (range) of 75 IQ points, depending on the environment experienced during the early years of life.[17, 34] (Consider the pseudoretardation that stems from severely deprived environments versus the high skill levels that emerge from highly synchronized environments.) It is the unique combination of heredity and environment that determines the child's proficiency; it is the parents who structure the environment, and therefore contribute to either maximizing the child's potentials or hindering them.

Learned Helplessness

Research by Martin Seligman has opened a new door for viewing incompetence in early childhood. His theory is based on a behaviorist approach to mastery of the environment but also includes the psychoanalytical concept of inferiority and the humanistic concept of motivation. Seligman's basic theory is that inadequacy is the result of **learned helplessness.**[40] As discussed previously, the behaviorist view of learning basically states that an individual will increase or strengthen those behaviors that elicit a desired response from the environment. Behavior, therefore, is elicited, controlled, or molded by the contingent response of the environment. Expectation of a certain response is the basis of motivational, cognitive, and emotional deliberation to perform a behavior ("I act because I will be rewarded"). When an individual believes or learns that behavior and outcome are independent of one another or that events are uncontrollable, the psychological state of **helplessness** results.[40] If a person believes that his or her actions will not affect the environment, the likelihood of a voluntary response decreases ("Why bother? It won't make any difference.").

Learned helplessness is characterized by both cognitive and affective disturbances. If the child learns early in life that outcomes are independent of responses, cause-effect relationships are not learned. It becomes more difficult to learn later in life that response can produce an outcome. Helplessness becomes a self-perpetuating phenomenon; the perceived independence of events interferes with the learning of the interdependence of behavior-outcome contingencies. The need to control or master the environment appears to be a basic drive of life. Anxiety, frustration, or fear is induced, therefore, when the individual realizes an inability to control events.[40] For most people, these emotional responses can be useful, since they maintain the search for alternative responses. However, if a person believes that the outcome or trauma cannot be controlled, Seligman postulates that fear is replaced by depression. Learned helplessness, therefore, undermines a person's motivation to respond, retards the ability to perceive success and to learn that responding works, and results in heightened emotionality caused by anxiety and depression.

According to Seligman, "Notions of ego strength and competence are related to mastery over events."[40] Motivation and emotion are heavily influenced by the environment. Lack of environmental contingencies can create a child who believes he or she is helpless and cannot succeed. Children who believe that they are helpless will perform inadequately, regardless of IQ. The result can be a falsely low IQ score (pseudoretardation) due to inadequate effort. Seligman observes that children who believe in their own competence "can outperform a more talented peer who lacks such a belief."[40] Unfortunately, helplessness learned in one situation is frequently generalized to other settings. Learned helplessness in essence is failure to master the task of learning how to learn.

The **helplessness syndrome** is characterized by the symptoms given below. The first three symptoms are universal; the last three are found only as the depth of perceived helplessness increases.

1. Reduced initiation of voluntary responses—psychomotor retardation.

2. Negative cognitive set—difficulty learning or accepting that responses will or can produce the desired outcomes.

3. Aggression is attenuated; passivity is exhibited.

4. The effects of helplessness following a single uncontrolled crisis will dissipate with time, but these effects may persist after multiple uncontrollable events.

5. Depressed appetite for food, sex, and socialization; avoidance of self-care or stimulus input, especially if expenditure of energy is required.

6. Physiological change—weight loss, hormonal imbalances, and norepinephrine depletion.

A person may exhibit mild to severe symptoms of the helplessness syndrome, depending on age, the quality of previously developed coping skills, the number of other stressors the person faces, and the significance of the uncontrollable events.

According to Seligman, "A child's or an adult's attitude toward his own helplessness or mastery has its roots in infant development. When an infant has a rich supply of powerful synchronies between his actions and outcomes, a sense of mastery develops. Responsive mothering is fundamental to learning mastery."[40] Each new challenge requires that the child predict an outcome, and outcome is inferred from experience. Seligman believes that at every opportunity the infant analyzes (on a primitive level) the relationship between his or her behaviors and their outcomes. If a high correlation exists, then the child will alter behavior (use of tools for communication) toward obtaining or maintaining the desired environment. If a correlation is not identifiable, the helplessness syndrome results.[40] Therefore, the earlier a child experiences control or lack of control, the more critical and longlasting is the effect of such experience. Stern observes that the maternal responses must occur within 3 seconds after the neonate's behavior to serve as a reinforcer.[44] Helplessness is disastrous to the infant who is laying the structural foundation for cognitive, affective, and motivational development. The baby may never learn how to learn!

The helplessness syndrome can result from stimulus deprivation or from nonresponsive parenting. The failure-to-thrive syndrome and the children of Bowlby's and Spitz's studies (see Chap. 8) are classic examples of severe helplessness syndrome during infancy.

Increased anxiety around strangers is observed when parents fail to warn the young child that they are leaving him or her with a baby-sitter. If the parents do not give the child adequate cues or warning signals about their impending departure, the child becomes extremely anxious at inappropriate times. The child cannot predict what will happen and therefore experiences helplessness. The same may occur with the dispensing of medication in the doctor's office, at the hospital, or even at home. The child's excessive fear is frequently the result of inadequate communication or signals from the parents. The child needs to know that the parents can be trusted—that a situation is safe if the parents say so. This view blends with Erikson's concept of basic trust. The child learns to recognize environmental cues. Parental honesty and consistency are essential to learning this trust and thus mastery. Cues are consistent with events; therefore, the child learns to predict and thus to master his or her internal environment. Children can deal with unpleasant events (e.g., the parents are leaving, the injection will hurt) better in the long run if they are given a warning and an honest explanation.

Through the alternating use of maternal and infant tools, the mother and infant inaugurate a synchronized ballet of interaction. Through this mutually reinforcing interchange, the infant strengthens reflexive responses into preplanned, voluntary behaviors. The infant learns to master the self and to obtain the desired pleasure from the environment—the mother's response. The infant whose mother is nonresponsive is thereby deprived of control over stimulation. On the other hand, the mother who is overresponsive to the infant and does not balance the intensity or frequency of her responses to those emitted by the infant is also out of synchrony. Lack of contingent responsiveness leads to helplessness. The key to the infant's mastery, then, is the sensitive, synchronized response of the mother; this is the same conclusion drawn by

White, Krown, Kennell, Klaus, Brazelton, and many others studying the behavior of the neonate. The children in Krown's study were suffering from rather marked cases of helplessness syndrome, whereas White's "C" infants exhibited mild cases. The mothers of the "A" infants were able to read the infants' cues, and responded appropriately to them. They did not intrude when uninvited or ignore the child's communication efforts. Consequently, "A" infants exhibited mastery of the environment—high level cognitive and affectional functioning that spilled over to the social and biological domains as well.

FOSTERING POTENTIALS

By now the author's position is quite clear: The child is born with cognitive and motor potentials that are determined by heredity; the environment will determine how much of the individual's potential will be realized.

Infant Stimulation

Much concern has arisen in recent years about providing adequate stimulation to young infants to help them maximize their potentials at an early age. Detailed manuals have been written for both professionals and parents on activities and stimuli that will facilitate the development of the growing infant. Most of the programs are highly geared to (1) increasing sensory stimuli through the provision of appropriate toys, and (2) facilitating neuromuscular development through active and passive physical exercises that are specifically geared to the infant's skill level (Fig. 13-6).

Many parents and some professionals hope that early stimulation of this type will increase the child's adaptive and cognitive functioning levels. Seligman's theory may explain the value of early stimulation programs. If the infant learns to have an effect on the environment, this sense of control may increase the child's resiliency when minor setbacks or frustrations occur. The increased motivation that accompanies mas-

FIGURE 13–6.
"Fluid" activities, such as painting, offer an immediate response to the child's efforts. These activities along with a warm, attentive audience can heighten the child's sense of control and self-esteem—an effective immunization against the helplessness syndrome later in life.

tery may help the child to persist at a task longer or to try alternative approaches until a new skill is mastered. The child's attitude toward the environment and learning may make a significant difference in achievement later in life.

It should be noted that sensory stimuli and physical exercises are *not* the critical factors in infant stimulation programs. As stated before, the critical factor is the **synchrony** of communication established between the parent and the child. If interaction is asynchronous, then extra stimuli and physical exercises still may not prevent the helplessness syndrome. However, most parents who attend infant stimulation classes and participate in the suggested activities also begin to assess the infant's skill level and communication style fairly realistically to individualize their approach and establish a mutually satisfying relationship. Synchronized infant stimulation can maximize developmental potentials of intellectually or physically impaired infants, increasing their functional independence. However, it will *not* create a "gifted" child even if early development is accelerated.

Role of the Parents

Parents are the most significant persons in the developing child's life. They structure and organize the environment, establish the contingencies, and offer the opportunities for development. Parents also serve as role models. The young child is frequently compared to a videotape—recording all that is seen, heard, and felt about the environment. Observed behaviors are emulated in later episodes, either in play or in work. Parents who provide encouragement and foster close-

ness, perseverance, mastery, and independence have children with functionally higher intelligence.[9]

Reading Readiness

Parents can help to prepare children for reading activities. The most basic activity is to provide them with a wide variety of experiences that will increase their general knowledge about the world. The more concrete, first-hand experiences children have the greater the number of schemata they will have to draw upon for both verbalization activities and reading (Fig. 13-7). New experiences are easier to assimilate and accommodate if a closely related schema is already present in the child's cognitive structures. The more first-hand experiences children have had, the more indexes they will be able to call upon and to use in more abstract or representational thought processes (see Chap. 10). The child needs opportunities for both large and small motor activity. Running, climbing, throwing, working with clay, building with blocks, coloring, and constructing puzzles all give the child an opportunity to see what his or her own body can do and to gain a sense of independence and satisfaction in mastery.

Reading readiness starts with simple verbal synchrony games with the infant. The reciprocal cooing and babbling is the very beginning of identifying cause-effect relationships and the foundation for social communication. Word-object relationship comprehension can be facilitated by presenting the word and object together and restricting the name used to one word: "pocket-book," for instance, may also be handbag, clutch, wallet, or purse. Multiple names should not be used until the first is clearly associated with the object; then a

FIGURE 13–7.
First-hand experiences help the child to build up a repertoire of knowledge that serves as a foundation for concepts taught at school.

second term can be added in tandem to the first until both are associated with the object.

Communication efforts gradually become more sophisticated and may include simple nursery rhymes and stories with frequent repetition of phrases, such as "The Three Little Pigs" or "The Three Bears." Very young children love these stories because they can predict what will come next. Brief pauses before key words or sentences encourage the child to participate in telling the story. Songs are usually next in the hierarchy of skills and can be performed entirely by the child. Picture books and short stories that can be read aloud or "self-told" also help to prepare the child for reading. The child is becoming interested in what books have to share. Some educators encourage parents of preschoolers to have the children draw pictures and make up their own stories about these pictures; the parent can write the words on each picture and then tie them together as a book. This technique gives the child the idea that what one experiences or thinks can be put into words and shared, and that words in turn can be put into signs and shared again. Written signs begin to have meaning as a form of communication. This activity also helps to encourage the child's growing need for initiative. Sharing, listening, discussing, and experiencing are all significant factors in preparation for reading.

Adequate opportunity for activities that allow dramatic play is also a prerequisite for reading readiness.[43] Through dramatic play, the child is able to use representational thought and to explore alternatives for symbol usage or problem solving. Exposure to educational television is also a very valuable preparatory activity. However, teachers report that children who watch too much television may be bored by school; the child may feel a need to be entertained rather than to participate in activities. This passive approach to life may also be caused by a lack of adequate opportunity for dramatic and sociodramatic play if television absorbs too much of the waking time activity.

Parents frequently ask whether or not the child should be taught to read before starting school. There are many opinions on each side. The most important factor is the child's attitude toward reading. If the child really wants to learn to read and is already beginning to pick up some words, the opportunity should not be denied. However, a child should not be forced to learn to read before school or belittled when errors are made. All teaching should be done in a warm, supportive environment. Those children who do know how to read may create some difficulty in the classroom if they feel the skill makes them superior to the other children. The child who reads early should be treated as if this skill were a natural event. The teacher can give the child extra reading and can either concentrate on other activities in which the child may be less skilled or have the child read to other children.

Discipline

Although discipline is covered later (see Chap. 16), a brief discussion is in order here because of teachers' concerns. It was mentioned earlier that children need to respect, but not fear, authority; this means, in part, that the child knows the meaning of "No." Many children of permissive or inconsistent parents have not learned the meaning of "No" prior to first grade; consequently school becomes more difficult for both the child and the teacher. Children learn self-discipline from learning to obey externally enforced discipline.

Children also need to know how to assume responsibility, which calls for a measure of self-discipline. If the child has not learned how to follow through with responsibilities at home, this will often carry over into the school setting and affect the ability to function independently. The child's lack of self-confidence prevents him or her from working by and for the self. White[48] and Seligman[40] both offer the idea that parents need to provide resolvable frustration and conflict experiences for the developing child. Such experiences help the child to gradually learn to cope with anxiety and frustrations with an increased sense of effectiveness and self-discipline.

Nursery Schools

Many parents choose to send their 3- to 5-year-old children to nursery school. Nursery schools usually meet for 2 to 3 hours, 3 to 5 times a week. They supplement, but do not replace, the home. The major goal of such schools is to offer children peer experiences to help them learn to share attention. Exposure to peers offers opportunity for sociodramatic play, competition, comparison, and cooperation, all of which are essential to development. Nursery school also allows the child to relate to someone besides the parents—an aid to the separation-individuation process and to the resolution of Erikson's task of autonomy (Fig. 13-8).

Head Start Programs

In the early 1960s, the United States government recognized that children who grow up in Level 1 and Level II families (very disorganized, helpless families; see Chap. 33) tend to do poorly in school. This finding has been supported by Krown's and Smilansky's research, and Seligman's theory of learned helplessness now helps to explain this phenomenon. Parents who experience the helplessness syndrome transmit the same attitude to their children by a lack of responsiveness to their children's behaviors; they mutually extinguish one another's proactive behaviors. Although the parents may be concerned about their children's welfare and may display affection toward them, the attitude of hopelessness toward life's events fosters detachment from the environment, which in turn decreases attentiveness and learning. The children enter school with a weak general knowledge and are unprepared to master either the internal or external environments.

Regardless of background, children start school expecting to get good grades. This may be the first time the children have been placed in a competitive situation with peers. When the expectations are not matched and they once again feel out of control, the self-preservation response is to discredit the

FIGURE 13–8.
Young children enjoy learning about their heritage and the crafts or skills of their forebears.

grades. A pattern of failure is established, and the cycles of helplessness and poverty are perpetuated for another generation.

Project Head Start, a federally sponsored preschool education program for children 3 to 5 years of age, was started in 1965 as a massive social experiment to break the cycle of poverty. The program is jointly funded by federal and local sources. Services are offered to children free of charge. The major goal is to help each enrolled child to develop a good self-image and the ego-strength to face school tasks successfully. Although Project Head Start served over 7.5 million children and their families during the first 15 years, this represents only 20% of those who were eligible.[46] Funding is still inadequate to enroll all eligible children.

Components of Head Start Programs

Although the curriculum of Head Start programs has become more structured since its inception, the basic components have remained unchanged.

Health

Children who are reared in poverty frequently experience suboptimal health status because of inadequate money to provide care and proper nutrition or because the helplessness syndrome prevents the parents from seeking care and providing proper nutrition even if money is available. Recognizing that poor health can interfere with learning, the program provides a complete medical examination to every child. The medical checkup is occasionally the first one the

child has had since discharge from the hospital as a neonate, even though free child health clinics are available in most communities. Each child is given visual and hearing tests and dental examinations. Follow-up services are offered in the form of immunizations and referrals when needed.

Nutrition

The hungry child cannot learn; low energy reserves prevent participation in physical activities and shorten the attention span for other activities. The half-day programs provide one snack and one hot meal per day. Many programs also offer the parents an opportunity to learn how to purchase and prepare well-balanced meals.

Education

The educational component is structured (1) to introduce the child to her- or himself, and (2) to introduce the child to the surrounding world. Individualized guidance and group experiences encourage the child to learn how to control and to use physical and social skills adaptively. Self-reliance, self-confidence, and self-esteem are fostered through experiences with toys, games, and special equipment. Teachers help each child to identify, to label, and to express in a socially acceptable way the feelings evoked by experiences. Special visitors, field trips, and special activities at the school encourage the children to expand their general knowledge. Circle times are used to discuss nutrition, safety, health care, social relationships, and avoidance of or handling of abuse.

Parent Involvement

The planners of Head Start recognized that they could not help the child in isolation from the family; therefore, all programs are required to involve parents in the planning and the operation of the centers. Parents are offered opportunities to serve in nonprofessional positions (both paid and volunteer) and are welcomed into the classroom at all times. They are encouraged to share goals for their children and to observe what children can do. Classes are provided for parents in areas such as child care, child development, home improvement, language arts, and first aid. Since each Head Start center is autonomous, the local policy council can determine the programs that best meet the needs of its families.

Many programs offer a home-based program where the teachers go to the home of the family and teach the parent how to teach the child specific self-help, motor, language and cognitive skills. The parent is actively involved in monitoring the child's progress. Teaching the parent has a ripple effect in that other children in the family begin to benefit from the parent's newly learned skills, and many parents share their new insights with neighbors and friends, thus benefiting their children also. Many parents are noted to override former helplessness symptoms as they begin to realize their importance and effectiveness as teachers. Many Head Start mothers become motivated to study for and pass the high school equivalency exam and to pursue further studies resulting in the assumption of a career trajectory.[27]

Social Services

Because of the number of families functioning at Level I and Level II, Head Start provides referral and counseling services as needed. They assist trouble-ridden families to obtain services, such as housing, financial assistance through ADC (Aid to Dependent Children), clothing, medical care, counseling, education, and food stamps from local agencies.

Curriculum

Each Head Start center is free to develop and to implement its own curriculum. Consequently, there is a wide range in the scope and the depth of programs offered. Schools are encouraged to individualize the program to the needs of the community and its ethnic heritage, while fostering the development of the gross-motor, fine-motor, self-help, language, cognitive, and social skills of the individual child. Staff members are provided with preservice and inservice training that helps them to understand child development and to learn how to develop effective classroom strategies for groups or individual children. In 1986, 30% of U.S. children represented ethnic groups (16% black, 10% Hispanic, 3% Asian and Pacific Islanders, 1% American Indians).[11] Yet, in Head Start programs, which target the nation's most disadvantaged children,[25] the enrollment is 68% ethnic representation.[2] Ten percent of enrollment opportunities are reserved for physically handicapped children; consequently, intensive, individualized programming is essential (Fig. 13-9).

Although each center's curriculum varies slightly from the next, some common components can be identified. Language skills are encouraged through listening activities with records, at story time, and through expression with puppets, flannel boards, books, and the relating of events. Curiosity is stimulated through questions and simple experiments. Gross- and fine-motor activities are encouraged to refine physical skills. Children also learn to assume and to share responsibilities through cleanup activities, care of toys, and serving food. A major component of the program is to recognize and express inner feelings appropriately; this is encouraged through social modeling, painting, and singing as well as dramatic play with dolls, blocks, kitchen equipment, and dress-up clothes. Children are encouraged to empathize and sympathize with others. All children are offered an opportunity to develop the cognitive skills involved in differentiation and classification. Older children are assisted in learning the alphabet and number concepts.

Although the program usually matches the academic year provided by the local school district, some centers also offer an 8-week summer program for children starting school in the fall.

Studies indicate that both the children and their families benefit from a well-designed early intervention program. The greatest success is realized when parents are actively involved in the child's education. Although IQ scores are increased,[30] the major change appears to be one of motivation.[49] The children exhibit higher self-esteem, and there is an increase in the vocational aspirations of the mothers for their children.[24] Reading[38, 39] and math[24] skills are higher during the primary grades, children are more likely to be promoted with their age-peers,[24] fewer are placed in special education classes, and a larger percentage graduate from high school.[10, 27] Since poor school performance is correlated with adult crime and welfare dependence, this prophylactic approach is considered to be cost-effective.[10, 39] It appears that early success in mastering the environment can serve to immunize the individual against helplessness later in life (Fig. 13-10).

Television

Studies show that by the time most children enter school, they may have spent more than 4000 hours watching television—more hours than they will spend attending the first six grades

FIGURE 13–9
Preschoolers are introduced to community helpers, such as firefighters or police officers, to help them understand the protective, cooperative role of local agencies.

FIGURE 13–10.
Head Start programs make an effort to involve community leaders in their programs. It enables families, children, the local government and business people to be more aware of each other's needs and interests.

of elementary school.[41] By the time a child graduates from high school, he or she will have spent 11,000 hours in school and 22,000 hours watching television! Children 2 to 5 years of age average over 28 hours a week watching television.[3] "Television impedes children's normal development by giving them no chance to respond actively and creatively to the stimuli imposed on them, no opportunity to exercise their imaginations, think their own thoughts, or play their own games."[32] The active manipulation of, and experimentation with, materials and the repetition of experiences and stimuli that are presented at the child's pace are essential for children to make the transformations in cognitive structures and to coordinate sensory input. Children with inadequate "hands-on" experiences may thus demonstrate difficulty with eye-hand coordination, perceptual integration, problem-solving skills, and other reading readiness skills. These children may establish a passive-onlooker rather than active-participant mentality.

Commercial television programs are designed to sell the sponsors' products; they are not designed to provide education. The vast majority of commercial television programs have little or no real educational value; what is learned is only incidental. The television programmer's first allegiance is to the commercial producer who is paying to have the product advertised; faithfulness to reality and truthfulness in presenting real-life situations and solutions are low on the list of the programmer's priorities. Older and more mature viewers are able to discern what is true to life and what is not, but young children cannot do this. Their limited cognitive skills and their inexperience in separating fact from fantasy can lead them to accept as reality whatever they see on television even by third grade.[8, 29] Children 2 to 11 years of age spend only 11% of their viewing time watching children's programs, and 89% of their time watching programs developed for adults.[1, 8] Children's cartoons average more than 26 violent scenes per hour.

Common stereotypes are perpetuated on television. The white American male is the most visible figure; he is usually young, middle-class, and unmarried. Nurses are frequently shown as cold, impersonal, and totally dominated by the male doctors with whom they work; librarians are seen as quiet, unmarried women; policemen are shown as clever and unfeeling; husbands and fathers are often seen as weak and insecure. The presentation of relationships between men and women is superficial and exaggerated. Sex between unmarried adults is portrayed as a positive and expected part of all male-female relationships. Even crime may be glorified. Children want and need to know about normal, healthy patterns of adult relationships.

Educators and many other adults are concerned about the amount of sex and violence that children see on television. Many developmentalists believe that watching violence and crime on television tends to blunt the child's sensitivities to suffering and injustice in real life. Children are led to believe that violence is to be laughed at and not to be taken seriously, that it is better to be sadistically clever than to be sensitive or compassionate. Studies repeatedly indicate a high correlation between aggressive behaviors and viewing of television violence and aggression.[29] In 1972 Surgeon General Steinfeld stated before a Senate hearing that "my interpretation is that there is a causative relationship between televised violence and subsequent antisocial behavior, and that the evidence is strong enough that it requires some action on the part of responsible authorities, the television industry, the government, and the citizens."[47] Several court cases in the late 1970s involved the effect of television on eliciting juvenile crime or offering models for it. But the conflict between television producers and their sponsors, versus parents and their values continues with only sporadic, token successes on the side of protecting children.

As educators became aware of the potential positive uses of television as well as its negative aspects, they began to consider production of television programs specifically for the education of younger viewers. Educators were also concerned about helping the culturally or socially disadvantaged child to be more successful when he or she enters the educational system. In response to this need, the Children's Television Workshop was created in 1968 to produce a series of daily, hour-long television programs that would provide a useful preschool educational experience for 3- to 5-year-old children, paying special attention to the needs of disadvantaged urban children.[15] The program produced in this experiment in educational television is "Sesame Street." Since it was already known that young children enjoy the style of television commercials, the program was patterned in this manner; that is, the scenes were brief, lively, and to the point.

The major behavioral goals of "Sesame Street" are to promote the intellectual, social, and cultural growth of preschool and kindergarten children. This includes an understanding of (1) symbolic representation (letters, numbers, geometric forms); (2) cognitive organization (perceptual discrimination and organization, relational concepts, classification); (3) reasoning and problem solving (problem sensitivity and attitudes toward inquiry, inferences and causality, generating and evaluating explanations and solutions); and (4) children and their world (self, social units, social interactions, the human-made environment, and the natural environment).[15]

A study of children who had viewed "Sesame Street" for 1 year indicated that these children were more familiar with numbers than with letters. More than one-half of the 4-year-old children showed receptive comprehension of the numbers 1 through 5 as well as the ability to name numerals on presentation. In addition, many children were able to count out objects when the amount totaled less than 5.[35]

The goals of "Sesame Street" have been expanded to include sight vocabulary, addition, and subtraction. With these additions, the program endeavors to teach basic facts, problem solving, and relationships that lay a foundation for the development of concrete operational cognitive skills.[5] Children who view "Sesame Street" for more than one year do not appear to be significantly improved in school readiness, since the programs are repetitious.[15]

"Sesame Street" also helps to reduce cultural and racial prejudices because it includes Spanish- as well as English-language episodes. It helps children to see that others can be different from them and their families but still can be OK people.

Children usually are not tested on what they see and learn through television, but parents and teachers are aware that today's children know more about the world outside of their immediate community than their parents did at the same age. Television has a great potential for educating children, but most of the programs that are broadcast for, and viewed by, children today are of entertainment value only. Parental guidance and concern for what children are watching and discussions of programs with children help to explain or to reinforce any television message. The parents' group, Ac-

tion for Children's Television (ACT), is trying to improve the quality of the programs available for children.

Kindergarten

Kindergarten is required in many states and is optional in others. Although children are taught the basic academic skills mentioned earlier in the chapter, the major goals are to help them learn how to cooperate with peers, to develop good work habits, and to like school. Kindergarten helps the child to develop listening skills, to play and to work independently, and to refine gross- and fine-motor skills. Most teachers feel that kindergarten is essential preparation for a successful first-grade experience. Children's perceptual, motor, and language development should be assessed during kindergarten to determine readiness for first grade. Those who exhibit maturational lags should be offered a "transitional class" program, which can match the educational approach and content to the specific needs of the child. Such extra help for a few weeks to a full year can help the child get off to a good educational start and can avert the need for remedial measures later as well as the emotional frustrations that accompany repeated failure.[12] In 1802 Johann Pestalozzi astutely observed that "to instruct men is nothing more than to help human nature to develop in its own way, and the art of instruction depends primarily on harmonizing our messages and the demands we make upon the child with his powers at the moment."[31]

CONCLUSION

Preparation for school begins with the earliest interactions between parent and neonate. The early establishment of synchronized interaction lays the foundation for cognitive and social structuring. The child who is not offered a synchronized or contingently responsive environment does not learn how to predict and then to control or master the environment—a situation that leads to learned helplessness. Children who feel that behaviors and responses are unrelated are not motivated to learn cause-effect relationships; they begin to withdraw cognitive and affective investment in both people and the external environment. Although intellectual potential is not decreased, marked functional retardation may be observed in cognitive, affective, social, and physical adaptation. Prematurely born children frequently exhibit affective, perceptual, and motor delays in kindergarten.[12] These may be caused by inadequate synchronized stimulation in early infancy, neurological immaturity, minimal brain damage, or by another, as yet unknown, factor.

Infant stimulation programs need to concentrate on the significance of timing and the intensity of interaction as well as appropriate sensory input and physical exercise. Nursery schools can supplement the developmental opportunities offered at home. Head Start offers intensive remedial and supportive services both to the child and to the family, helping them to realize and to actualize their potentials. Kindergarten helps children to prepare academically and socially for first grade.

Although many resources are available to assist in the preparation of a child for school, the single most critical factor, in the author's opinion, is the interaction between the parent and the child. This point should be emphasized in parent education classes and in high school classes on preparation for family living. Parenthood is an awesome but exciting opportunity for the sensitive, prepared adult.

REFERENCES

1. Abelman, R. (1987). TV literacy II: Amplifying the affective level effect of television's prosocial fare through curriculum intervention. *Journal of Research and Development in Education, 20,* 40–49.

2. Administration for Children, Youth and Families. (1987). *Project Head Start statistical fact sheet.* Washington, DC: U.S. Dept. of Health and Human Services, Office of Human Development Services.

3. American Academy of Pediatrics, Task Force on Children and Television. (1990). *Children, adolescents and television.* Elk Grove Village IL: American Academy of Pediatrics.

4. Bell, S. M., & Ainsworth, M. D. S. (1972). Infant crying and maternal responsiveness. *Child Development, 43,* 1171.

5. Bogatz, G. A., & Ball, S. (1971). Some things you've wanted to know about "Sesame Street." *Education, 7*(3), 11.

6. Brazelton, T. B., Koslowski, B., & Main, M. (1974). The origins of reciprocity: The early mother-infant interaction. In M. Lewis & L. A. Rosenblum (Eds.), *The effect of the infant on its caregiver.* New York: Wiley.

7. Charlesworth, R. (1989). "Behind" before they start? Deciding how to deal with the risk of kindergarten "failure." *Young Children, 44*(3), 5–13.

8. Clapp, G. (1988). *Child study research: Current perspectives and applications.* Lexington, MA: Lexington Books.

9. Cohler, B. J., et al. (1980). Child-care attitudes and development of young children of mentally ill and well mothers. *Psychological Reports, 46,* 31.

10. Comptroller General of the United States. (1979). *Early childhood and family development programs improve the quality of life for low-income families* (HRD-79-40). Washington, DC: U.S. Government Printing Office.

11. DBS Corporation. (1987, December). *1986 Elementary and secondary school civil rights survey, national summaries.* Washington, DC: Office of Civil Rights, U.S. Department of Education.

12. De Hirsch, K., Jansky, J. J., & Langford, W. S. (1966). *Predicting reading failure: A preliminary study of reading, writing, and spelling disabilities in preschool children.* New York: Harper & Row.

13. Dennis, W., & Najarian, P. (Eds.). (1957). Infant development under environmental handicap. *Psychological Monographs, 71*(7).

14. Garber, H. L. (1988). *The Milwaukee Project: Preventing mental retardation in children at risk.* Washington, DC: American Association on Mental Retardation.

15. Gibbon, S. Y., Jr., & Palmer, E. L. (1970). *Pre-Reading on Sesame Street. Final Report. Volume V of V Volumes.* New York: Children's Television Workshop.

16. Hauser, S. T., & Kasendorf, E. (1983). *Black and white identity formation: Studies of the psychosocial development of lower socioeconomic class adolescent boys* (2nd ed.). Malabar, FL: R. E. Krieger.

17. Hunt, J. M. (1976). The psychological development of orphanage reared infants: Interventions with outcomes (Teheran). *Genetic Psychology Monographs, 94,* 177.

18. Intelligence. (1975). Intelligence: Genes or environment? *Intellect, 103,* 442.

19. Kadushin, A. (1976). Adopting older children: summary and implications. In A. M. Clarke & A. D. B. Clarke (Eds.), *Early experience: Myth and evidence.* New York: Free Press.

20. Kennell, J. H., Jerauld, R., Wolfe, H., Chester, D., Kreger, N. C., McAlpine, W., Steffa, M., and Klaus, M. H. (1974). Maternal behavior one year after early and extended post-partum contact. *Developmental Medicine and Child Neurology, 16,* 172.

21. Klaus, M. H., Jerauld, R., Kreger, N., McAlpine, W., Steffa, M., and Kennell, J. H. (1972). Maternal attachment: The importance of the first post-partum days. *New England Journal of Medicine, 286,* 460–463.

22. Koluchova, J. (1976). A report on the further development of twins after severe and prolonged deprivation. In A. M. Clarke & A. D. B. Clarke (Eds.), *Early experience: Myth and evidence.* New York: Free Press.

23. Krown, S. (1974). *Three and fours go to school.* Englewood Cliffs, NJ: Prentice-Hall.

24. Lazar, I., & Darlington, R. (1982). Lasting effects of early education: A report from The Consortium for Longitudinal Studies. *Monographs of the Society for Research in Child Development, 47,* 2–3. (Serial No. 195).

25. Lee, V. E., Brooks-Gunn, J., & Schnur, E. (1988). Does Head Start Work? A 1-year follow up comparison of disadvantaged children attending Head Start, no preschool, and other preschool programs. *Developmental Psychology, 24,* 210–222.

26. Mahler, M. S., Pine, F., & Bergman, A. (1975). *The psychological birth of the human infant: Symbiosis and individuation.* New York: Basic Books.

27. McKey, R. H., Condelli, L., Granson, H., Barrett, B., McConkey, C., & Platz, M. (1985). *The impact of Head Start on children, families and communities [Final report of the Head Start evaluation, synthesis and utilization project].* Washington, DC: CSR.

28. Mondell, S., & Tyler, F. B. (1981). Parental competence and styles of problem-solving/play behavior with children. *Developmental Psychology, 17,* 73.

29. National Association of Education of Young Children. (1990). NAEYC position statement on media violence in children's lives. *Young Children, 45*(5), 18–21.

30. Palmer, F. H., & Anderson, L. W. (1979). Long-term gains from early intervention: Findings from longitudinal studies. In E. Zigler & J. Valentine (Eds.), *Project Head Start: A legacy of the war on poverty.* New York: Free Press.

31. Pestalozzi, J. H. (1969). *Education of man, aphorisms.* New York: Greenwood Press.

32. Piers, M. W., & Landau, G. M. (1980). *The gift of play: and why young children cannot thrive without it.* New York: Walker.

33. Pines, M. (1971). A child's mind is shaped before age 2. *Life, 71*(25), 63.

34. Pines, M. (1979). Head start in the nursery. *Psychology Today, 13*(14), 56.

35. Reeves, B. F. (1970). *The first year of Sesame Street: The formative research, Final Report, Vol II of V volumes.* New York: Children's Television Workshop.

36. Ringler, N. M., Trause, M. A., & Klaus, M. (1976). Mother's speech to her two-year-old: Its effect on speech and language comprehension at 5 years. *Pediatrics Research, 10,* 307.

37. Ringler, N. M., Kennell, J. H., Jaruella, R., Navojosky, B. J., and Klaus, M. H. (1975), Mother-to-child speech at 2 years—Effect of early postnatal contact. *Journal of Pediatrics, 86*(1), 141.

38. Rosenberg, L. A., & Adcock, E. P. (1979). *The effectiveness of early childhood education: Third grade reading level interim report, Dec. 1979, ESEA Title IV C longitudinal evaluation program for selected early childhood education programs.* Baltimore, MD: Maryland State Department of Education.

39. Schweinhart, L. J., & Weikart, D. P. (1980). *Young children grow up: The effects of the Perry Preschool Program on youths through age 15.* Ypsilanti, MI: High/Scope Press.

40. Seligman, M. E. P. (1975). *Helplessness: On depression, development, and death.* San Francisco: Freeman.

41. Sesame Street. (1970). Sesame Street asks: Can television really teach? *Nation's Schools, 85,* 58.

42. Skeels, H. M. (1966). Adult status of children with contrasting early life experiences: A followup study. *Monographs of the Study for Research in Child Development, 31*(3). (Serial No. 105).

43. Smilansky, S. (1968). *The effects of sociodramatic play on disadvantaged preschool children.* New York: John Wiley.

44. Stern, D. (1978). Rhythms of maternal behavior during play. In E. B. Thoman & S. Trotter (Eds.), *Social responsiveness of infants.* New Brunswick, NJ: Johnson & Johnson Baby Products.

45. Thoman, E. B., Korner, A. F., & Beason-Williams, L. (1977). Modification of the responsiveness to maternal vocalization in the neonate. *Child Development, 48,* 563.

46. U. S. Department of Health and Human Services. Office of Human Development Services. Administration for Children, Youth and Families. (1980, September). *Head Start in the 1980's: Review and recommendations.* Washington, DC: Head Start Bureau. (HHS-393).

47. U. S. Congress. Senate. (1972, March). *Hearings before the Subcommittee on Communications of the Committee on Commerce.* Washington, DC: U. S. Congress, Senate.

48. White, B. L. (1975). *The first 3 years of life.* Englewood Cliffs, NJ: Prentice-Hall.

49. Zigler, E., Abelson, W. D., Trickett, P. K., and Seitz, V. (1982). Is an intervention program necessary in order to improve economically disadvantaged children's I. Q. scores? *Child Development, 53,* 340.

Development of a Concept of Sexuality

Clara S. Schuster

Sexuality is a critical aspect of each of our lives. Regardless of how egalitarian or nonsexist a person or family may try to be, subtle influences from our earliest years and the cultural or personal biases of other persons still tend to make an impact on our behavior, dress, and self-image.

Each culture establishes its own criteria for gender roles, and the persons within that culture tend to transmit the male or female scripts to the younger generation.[42, 63] From the moment of an infant's birth, people tend to respond to the infant based on their perceptions of gender-appropriate behaviors. As children grow and develop, these gender scripts become a part of their core identity, self-esteem, and personality and thus influence their relationships with other persons at all levels of contact.

PERSPECTIVES ON SEXUALITY

Sexuality has many different definitions. The narrowest definitions incorporate those physical characteristics and behaviors of an individual that lead to, or can lead to, copulatory behaviors. Slightly broader definitions include all behaviors and tendencies associated with sexual-social interactions. Both of these definitions appear to be too narrow, since sexuality is a macroconcept, pervading all five major domains. It is a very complex and personal construct comprised of many subcomponents.

Sexuality is the totality of an individual's attitudes, values, goals, and behaviors (both internal and external) based on, or determined by, perception of gender. A person's concept of sexuality influences many aspects of life, including priorities, aspirations, preferences, social contacts, interpersonal relationships, self-evaluation, expression (or even acknowledgment) of emotions, career, and expressions of friendship. This is not meant to sound like a potpourri, but it must be recognized that one's concept of sexuality is so pervasive that it touches nearly every aspect of self-knowledge, self-expression, and self-ideal. The development or expression of one's concept of sexuality is also closely related to physical, cognitive, and moral development. The total significance of sexuality can be understood only in relation to one's adjustment to life, family, and society and not just in relation to activities engaged in for sensual pleasure or procreation.[56] It is essential to break down the concept of sexuality before synthesizing and applying the concept.

Components of Sexuality

One's concept of sexuality generally becomes more abstract, refined, and stable with age. The individual's gender-expression and gender-preference are usually compatible with a core gender-identity.

CORE GENDER-IDENTITY. The identification of oneself as male or female is a cognitive categorization that occurs early in life and is the foundation on which all other aspects of sexuality are based. It is the basic category a child assigns to her- or himself, and the only one that remains fixed throughout life.[31]

GENDER-ROLE. Clusters of behaviors or characteristics are associated with one gender more frequently than the other; gender-role is an organized set of prescriptions and prohibitions on activities established by the culture.[23] The individual may choose among those behaviors deemed gender-appropriate to foster a unique identity acceptable within the cultural age and historical confines.

GENDER-IDENTITY. This is the conviction that the individual has about his or her gender and its associated role. It is a subjectively determined concept of one's degree of masculinity or femininity,[32] or the private experience of one's gender-role.[51]

GENDER-TYPING. This is the developmental process by which culturally assigned behavior patterns deemed appropriate to each gender are taught and reinforced.[53]

GENDER-EXPRESSION. Gender-expression is the behavior of an individual that reflects his or her concept of gender-appropriate roles. These behaviors are usually compatible with gender-identity but are more likely to be compatible with cultural expectations.

GENDER-ORIENTATION. Gender-orientation is a stable, subjective sense of comfort and linkage with one gender rather than the other for social/sexual relationships.

GENDER-PREFERENCE. The gender-role an individual finds most desirable regardless of compatibility with a personal core gender-identity is his or her gender-preference.

MASCULINITY AND FEMININITY. These are very complex, abstract qualities of personality that are assigned individually and collectively by the culture on the basis of gender. Boundaries are imprecise. It is very difficult to construct operational definitions of masculinity and femininity, as will be seen in the next section.

Gender-Role Stereotypes

In earlier and more primitive cultures, roles were assigned on the basis of physical characteristics that were necessary to carry out tasks essential to the survival of the family or the culture. The childbearing and nursing abilities of a woman relegated her to the raising of children, a task that kept her close to home and frequently involved her in the more agrarian activities. The greater muscular and skeletal strength of the male was essential to hunting, warfare, and protection of the family.

Over time, many gender-related activities and occupational choices developed out of the woman's need to breast-feed the young and to stay near the children. Today, however, when alternative methods are available for infant feeding and contraceptive methods are readily available, many people are beginning to question the value of roles based on gender, and a renewed interest is being directed toward the detection of "real" versus imposed gender differences.

Gender-role stereotypes are culturally assigned clusters of behaviors or attributes covering everything from play activities and personal traits to physical appearance, dress, and vocational activities. Stereotypical personality characteristics popularly associated with gender in Western cultures are included in Table 14-1.

There is mounting evidence that core gender-identity and gender-appropriate roles are learned early in life.[63] Gender-related differences in play behaviors are evidenced as early as 13 months.[20] Boys are generally more aggressive in their play and problem-solving activities, whereas girls exhibit more "refueling" behaviors. Early experiences are apparently so critical to one's core gender-identity that children who experience gender reassignment after the age of 2 years are high-risk candidates for psychotic disorders.[45]

Brown devised a test for evaluating a young child's perception of gender-roles.[8] The child is asked to choose an activity or an object depicted on cards for a stick doll called an "It." The "It" doll test shows conflicting results, but the trend indicates that 3- to 4-year-old children make gender-appropriate choices according to Western stereotypes.[14] Three- to five-year-old boys appear to be more concerned about gender-appropriate play activities than are girls,[52] and by 6 years, boys exhibit extremely stereotyped behaviors.[31] Adolescent boys also appear to be more conscious of gender-roles than do girls.[3] A cross-sectional study of seventh grade, twelfth grade, and adult males and females identified a positive correlation between chronological age and endorsement of gender-desirable traits. Adolescents were particularly rigid.[61] The presence of same-gender siblings also tends to increase preference to adopt gender-role stereotypes.[34]

TABLE 14-1. CULTURAL STEREOTYPES ASSOCIATED WITH GENDER

Male	Female
Aggressive	Passive
Controlling	Submissive
Independent	Dependent
Problem-solving	Nurturant
Exhibitionary	Self-abasive
Stoical	Expressive
Self-confident	Deferential
Dominant	Succoring
Instrumental	Affiliative

Because of culturally imposed roles, many myths have grown up regarding gender-related differences, mainly to justify role stereotyping. In actuality, only a few gender-related differences have been identified through research:[35, 60, 63]

1. Females have greater verbal ability.
2. Males have better visual-spatial skills.
3. Females are more sensitive to sensory input.
4. Males are more aggressive.
5. Females have greater fine motor dexterity and coordination.
6. Males show greater field-independence of visual stimuli.
7. Females are six times more likely to sing in tune.
8. Males are more sensitive to light.

Even the physiological responses to sensual stimulation have been discovered to parallel each other in the two sexes, with four clearly identifiable phases that incorporate nearly identical somatic and genital responses (see Chap. 26).[40]

Nevertheless, gender-role stereotypes persist. Individuals frequently govern or check their own behavior and judge or react to the behaviors of others based on these stereotypes. Males and females experience differential pressure to conform to gender-role stereotypes.[38] Both males and females object to a gender-role that forces them into roles they deem undesirable, forces them to deny or relinquish a valued or desired aspect of self, or prevents them from expressing their perceived attitudes, values, and potentials. Males may object to restrictions on expressing tenderness or nurturant behaviors; females frequently object to restrictions of social and occupational aspirations. Both object to the stigmatization that frequently accompanies violation of cultural stereotypes. Fortunately, recognition of the universality of human characteristics and of the nonequation of physical and cognitive strength has fostered a more egalitarian approach to gender-roles. Research indicates that individuals with a dynamic, flexible orientation toward life have the most positive adjustment to life.[39] This androgynous identity enables the individual to tap both masculine and feminine elements as needed.

Despite the shortcomings associated with rigid gender-roles, these stereotypes also have some positive benefits for both the young child and the adolescent. Stereotypes are a very helpful mechanism for coding, categorizing, organizing, and remembering data; they reduce the number of schemata one has to deal with.[42] This aspect is particularly helpful to the young child with limited categorizing ability. Stereotypes may facilitate personality organization by "allowing the ego to emerge out of chaos and to order its experience."[54] Stereotyping may also help to reduce anxiety arising from recognition of gender differences and may aid in the process of psychic separation from one's parents. Stereotypes provide an external guide to behaviors until the child's gender-identity is sufficiently consolidated to provide internal guidance cohesive with other identities (e.g., body image, moral identity, cognitive skill identity). Stereotypes, then, can provide structure and facilitate development as well as potentially restrict development if they are too rigid or incompatible with a person's potentials.

THEORIES ON THE ORIGIN OF ONE'S CONCEPT OF SEXUALITY

It is very difficult to identify and document etiological factors in gender-role differences, even though the existence of such differences is broadly acknowledged.[5] The question is whether these differences are real or imagined or whether they are innate or environmentally induced. Major personality theorists place different emphases on the role of the sensual aspects of sexuality in personality development. To Freud, sexual-sensual pleasure was the focal point, or organizer, for the developing personality; to Maslow, it became an expendable primary need. We find the same divergence of attitudes in individual lives. Some make sensual pleasure the primary goal of their lives, whereas others all but deny its existence. These attitudes can be explained in part, but not entirely, by the different theories on child development. There are four major theories on the origin of gender-role differences.

Psychoanalytical View

Sigmund Freud postulated that one's sexual drive is biologically based and mandated.[17] The psychosexual energy or libido becomes the energizer and organizer of one's perception of life experiences. He postulated a direct link between libido or sexual energies and emergent behaviors and motives for behaviors. He believed that all contact with or stimulus of a critical organ has protosexual meaning or influence (i.e., early sensual behaviors influence later behaviors). Since an individual is basically a sensual, sexual, pleasure-seeking being, culture (in the form of parents) must channel and control these primitive behaviors to prevent outbreaks of undesirable sexual activity.[18] Freud believed that the first 5 years of life were particularly critical to psychosexual adequacy.

Psychosexual Phases

Freud postulated that individuals experience sexual-sensual pleasure from earliest infancy. Rather than seeing sensuality as synonymous with sinfulness, Freud recognized that sensuality helps the child to become aware of the concreteness of the body and to grow to appreciate the everyday experiences life has to offer (Fig. 14-1). During infancy the individual learns some of the body's capacities for pleasure and comfort. Freud believed it was only when culture denied the reality and beauty of sensuous experiences that neurotic behaviors emerged. He identified three erogenous zones, which, when manipulated, would afford sensual pleasure much as scratching relieves an itch.[22] Research on the vertical and horizontal organizations of the human brain and the response to sensual stimuli indicates that Freud's theory may be supportable.[58]

 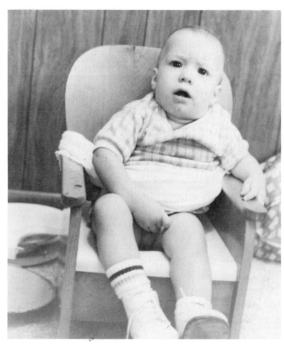

FIGURE 14–1.
Discovery of one's anatomical structures may evoke many different reactions from the young child. It is only one step in the development of gender identity.

However, the process is extremely complex and as yet is not clearly understood.

THE ORAL PHASE. During early infancy, activity centers around the mouth for eating activity, play, vocalization, and exploration. Neurological development renders it one of the most mature and sensitive tactile receptors of the body. Freud felt that the extent of satisfaction or dissatisfaction with the feeding experience would help to establish early attitudes about dependence and aggression;[22] Erikson later expanded this concept to one of learning to trust or to distrust events or persons in the environment.[13] Pleasure is derived both from tactile stimulation and from incorporating into the mouth those objects that satisfy sucking and hunger needs. The mouth has four major modes of relating to objects in addition to incorporating them: (1) holding on to, (2) biting, (3) spitting out, or (4) shutting out. Freud indicated that the need to overuse any one mode can lead to personality problems later on. The normally developing infant will incorporate or embrace objects and experiences not only with the mouth but also with the eyes, the attention, and as much of the body as the infant is able to involve. Later the individual may incorporate love, money, power, knowledge, or material possessions.[22]

THE ANAL PHASE. During the second year of life, myelinization of the nervous system allows the child greater awareness and control of the lower parts of the body. Consequently, the child begins to be aware of pressure created by fecal matter on the lower rectal wall and the anal sphincter. This pressure may be perceived as pleasant or painful, depending on the degree of tension caused by tissue stretching and spasms. Parents usually encourage the child to control the location of evacuation. Evacuation usually brings relief of tension and increased pleasure. Many authorities, including Freud, believe that the attitude of the parents toward evacuation, feces, and toilet training influences later personality characteristics. Freud believed that the child's desire to please the mother through the gift of a bowel movement exhibits itself later in life through generosity and philanthropic activities. On the other hand, if the child feels forced to give up something valued, he or she may subsequently become very frugal, even possessive or stingy. The child also may have an aversion to dirty disorder or messiness if the caregivers indicate excessive distress at soiling.

THE PHALLIC PHASE. During the preschool years, the child becomes aware of genital differences. The child finds that stroking and manipulation of the genitalia (penis or vagina) produces sensual pleasure and consequently may engage in masturbatory activities. This tendency can be augmented by curiosity and boredom. Masturbatory activities have a very different meaning for the preschooler than they do for the adult; however, parents observing the activity frequently execute strong, immediate restrictions. Freud believed that negative parental attitudes could cause the child to believe that the genital area was dirty or sinful, leading to problems in sexual adjustment later in life. On the other hand, it is obvious that children who engage in masturbatory activity to the exclusion of other valuable experiences may be restricting their social and emotional growth.

Freud hypothesized that awareness of genital differences leads to castration anxiety by boys and to penis envy by girls. These phenomena will be discussed further in the section on identification and the Oedipal complex.

THE LATENCY PHASE. At approximately 6 years of age (after the resolution of the Oedipal complex), Freud hypothesized that the child enters a fairly neutral period in the development of sexuality. The child gradually integrates previous sexual experiences and reactions. Most relationships are with peers of the same gender. According to Freud, the child suppresses or even denies sensual needs during this phase, while through the identification process he or she gradually incorporates more gender-appropriate behaviors. "Latency represents a repression of infantile sexuality and is inspired by the child's fear of punishment for his erotic interest in his same-sexed parent."[29] Anna Freud postulates that there is a "transfer of libido from the parental figures to contemporaries, community groups, teachers, leaders."[15] More contemporary psychoanalysts hypothesize that libidinal energies may be redirected to the cognitive and social domains, thus, psychosexual behaviors *appear* to be latent.

THE GENITAL PHASE. With the onset of puberty, the child experiences new emotions and new sexual direction. The desire to derive pleasure from the erogenous zones is increased. Freud felt that the three earlier phases must be relived and resolved before adult genital sexuality can be attained. The pregenital period (birth through 5 years) was characterized by primary narcissism, a self-love arising from pleasurable, and sensual self-stimulation (self-cathexes). During adolescence, the individual seeks other persons to love. Sensual stimulation is exchanged as part of the social and mating process. Freud felt that "the displacements, sublimations, and other transformations of the pregenital cathexes become a part of the permanent character structure."[22] During adolescence, one must identify and consolidate previous sexual experiences, gender commitments, and the identities learned during the pregenital period. Research indicates that adolescent girls are more likely to experience a crisis in this area than boys because of greater cultural restrictions on expression of their full potentials;[62] this observation is consistent with Erikson's theory. Adoption of cross-gender roles is associated with low peer acceptance. However, a balance of both male and female traits (androgyny) is associated with high peer acceptance.[39]

Freud's psychosexual stages attest to his belief that biological processes and impulses are the foundation for affective and social adjustment. A secondary process, identification, is responsible for refinement of the affective and social orientation.

Identification Process

Freud felt that sexuality in its broad sense is learned along with other behaviors in the socialization process. The major process through which social learning occurs is the identification process. **Identification** is a complex process through which the individual emulates the behaviors, attitudes, and emotions of a second, valued person. Identification allows the child to enjoy vicariously the values, powers, and experiences of the other. Freud postulated that the child sequentially experiences two types of identification.[42]

ANACLITIC IDENTIFICATION. Mahler and Piaget both indicate that the young infant is unable to differentiate self from environment.[36,49] All experiences, therefore, are interpreted in terms of effect on the self. According to psychoanalytical thought, the child gradually begins to differentiate between self and others and to become intensely attached to those who meet his or her needs. This attachment becomes more specific as the caregiver is differentiated from other persons and as the child recognizes the dependence on the caregiver (mother) for comfort, pleasure, or even survival. When the mother exhibits warmth and nurturance, the infant cathects his libido to her (anaclitic identification). When mother and infant are separated, anger and frustration are experienced by the infant. Brief separations can be tolerated, but Spitz's classic studies on anaclitic depression indicate that the child's physical survival may depend on this love relationship (see Chap. 8). Both male and female infants appear to develop along the same pattern during the first 3 years; the mother is usually their first love and object of identification.

CROSS-GENDER PARENTAL LOVE. At about 3 years of age, the separation-individuation process is essentially complete.[36] The child realizes that the mother is beginning to move away, and attempts are made to recapture her. At the same time (according to psychoanalytical thought), the child becomes aware of genital differences and feels that the difference is critical in the relationship with the mother. At this time, the child develops both a love and an anger or a jealousy toward the parents.

One of the central postulates of Freud's theory is that the preschool-age boy falls in love with his mother. The sexual impulses of the young boy toward his mother become very strong; as a result, he becomes very possessive of her and jealous of the father's relationship with her (Oedipal complex). The child feels that he is in competition with the father for the mother's love. Since the father is bigger and stronger, he fears that his father will cut off his genitalia in retaliation (castration anxiety); he wonders if this is what happened to little girls, since he cannot imagine anyone without his most prized possession.[16] Gradually the boy learns to repress his sensuous desires, and the possession of a penis becomes a central focus of the relationship.

Freud also hypothesized that the preschool girl falls in love with her father (Electra complex) and attempts to make herself desirable to him. The young girl blames her mother for the lack of a penis and rejects her in favor of the father, who possesses the coveted appendage (penis envy). She becomes jealous of her mother because of the mother's relationship with the father. Freud believed that young girls pass through a masculine stage before reidentifying with the mother. According to Freud, both boys and girls develop love, jealousy, and rivalry with the parent of the same sex because of the possession of, or the lack of possession of, a penis. They may even deny their own gender-roles as they attempt to emulate the parent of the opposite sex. Karen Horney, however, denies this aspect of psychoanalytical psychology, stating that girls exhibit distinctly feminine traits between 2 and 5 years of age.[28]

IDENTIFICATION WITH THE PARENT OF THE SAME SEX. Freud indicates that when the boy realizes he cannot recapture his mother because of the possession of, and sharing of, the penis, or when the girl realizes she cannot attain a penis through favors to the father, each comes to accept his or her own gender and to identify with the parent of the same sex in order to possess the strength and the attributes deemed valuable in "capturing" persons of the opposite gender. It is the control of impulses and the resolution of the Oedipal complex or the Electra complex that helps to develop the conscience or superego and that assure appropriate gender-role identification. Freud believed that inappropriate resolution of this crisis leads to homosexuality later in life. Other theorists disagree with Freud's theory of castration fear and penis envy, stating that it is only one aspect of the development of one's concept of sexuality and not its origin.[59]

Identification with the parent of the same sex helps to establish an ego ideal (Fig. 14-2). Some psychologists observe that boys have a more difficult time consolidating a gender-identity because they must transfer their identification from the mother (during anaclitic identification) to the father at the resolution of the Oedipal complex. This may be a factor leading to a less emotional, more impersonal approach to interpersonal relationships on the part of males, since the transference may be difficult and traumatic.[35]

Psychoanalytical theory, then, holds that the sexual impulses are the core energizer and organizer of life experiences, but that gender-roles are culturally and socially mediated.

Biogenetic-Hormonal View

In contrast to the psychoanalytical view, which holds that one's sexuality is neutral at birth and is subsequently imposed by experiences with the culture, there are some who believe that sexuality is genetically determined and thus is incapable of modification. Social and cognitive behavioral differences come from the physiological makeup. Some believe that the infant is biased at birth in a way that facilitates learning gender-appropriate behaviors and resisting gender-inappropriate behaviors. This view holds that prenatal genetic

FIGURE 14–2.
Identification with an adult of the same gender helps to establish an ego ideal. The best relationship is established with an adult who is comfortable with his or her own body and gender and their expressions.

and hormonal influences predispose gender-orientation; behavior and role have an initial direction at birth, which is only partially modified by experience. "Life experiences most likely act to differentiate and direct a flexible sexual disposition and to mold the prenatal organization until an environmentally (socially and culturally) acceptable gender-role is formulated and established."[9]

Supporting Evidence

The effects of early socialization make it very difficult to identify and to separate the effects of biological predispositions. Although female infants are about 4 to 6 weeks more mature neurologically at birth than male infants,[4] this is hardly evidence of a foundation for gender-identity differences, and cross-cultural studies offer little support since they indicate wide variation in gender-related traits.[41] Most evidence supporting biogenetic predispositions comes from studies of primates. Harlow found a differentiation of nonsexual behaviors in rhesus monkeys raised by inanimate surrogate mothers. Males exhibited higher levels of gross-motor activity when engaged in free-play activities and more frequent and intense threat responses to intruders, whereas females exhibited more passivity and anxiety and more grooming behaviors.[26] He concluded that such differences were unlearned because no models were present.

In another study, Goy injected pregnant rhesus monkeys with testosterone. He postulated that prenatal hormones had a masculinizing effect on the developing brain, since genetically female offspring exhibited malelike behaviors.[21] Similar results have been found in genetically female human infants whose mothers had received large amounts of androgen during pregnancy. Even after corrective hormonal therapy, their psychosexual orientation remained essentially male.[10, 11, 44] One research study indicates that homosexual women tend to have higher plasma testosterone levels than heterosexual women, but the amount of overlap in subjects makes definitive conclusions impossible.[19]

Negating Evidence

John Hampson identifies seven significant variables that potentially influence gender-identity:[25]

1. Biophysical factors
   a. Chromosomal configuration (XX or XY)
   b. Gonad endowment (ovaries versus testes)
   c. Internal reproductive structures (uterus versus prostate)
   d. External genitalia (vagina versus penis)
   e. Hormonal balance (estrogen versus androgen)
2. Psychosocial factors
   a. Gender assigned at birth
   b. Response of the parent to the child's assigned gender

Hampson studied 113 individuals whose biophysical gender was not congruent with their assigned gender because of hermaphroditic incongruity. All of the 19 individuals reared opposite their chromosomal configurations exhibited a gender identity for the gender assigned; of 30 individuals reared opposite their gonadal endowments, 27 fully accepted the assigned gender-role; of 25 individuals reared opposite their internal reproductive structures, 22 accepted the assigned gender-role; of 25 individuals reared opposite their external genitalia, 23 accepted the assigned gender-role; and of 31 individuals reared opposite their sex hormone balances and secondary sexual characteristics, 26 accepted the ambiguity and the assigned gender-role. Hampson indicates that those individuals who were ambivalent about gender-role either had parents who were ambivalent about the child's assigned gender or had experienced gender reassignment after 5 years of age.[25]

A number of authors indicate that the period from birth to 3 years of age appears to be a critical period in the development of core gender-identity. Persons who experience assigned gender change after this point exhibit poor psychological adjustment.[24, 25, 46]

Most evidence indicates that gender-role and gender-identity are not innate. The individual is psychosexually neutral at birth; sexuality and gender-orientation are shaped by experiences. Although hormones definitely influence primary and secondary physical characteristics, there is little evidence that they also influence social behaviors. This leads one to look at environmental factors that influence acquisition of gender-consistent behaviors.

Social Learning View

The social learning or behaviorist view of the acquisition of gender-consistent behaviors is based on the assumption that parents respond differentially to the assigned gender of the child and proceed to elicit and to reinforce what they assess to be gender-appropriate behaviors and traits while using various methods (e.g., punishment, withholding reinforcement, reinforcing incompatible behavior) to extinguish behaviors deemed gender-inappropriate. Although parents appear to treat children similarly across a wide variety of behaviors, they tend to expend more energy extinguishing feminine behaviors in boys.[35] The adoption of gender-roles appears to be influenced by two clusters of environmental variables: (1) the specific behaviors that the parents associate with the target gender, and (2) the effectiveness of the parent as a teacher.[1]

Early Learning

Much of the parent's behavior toward the child is unconscious. However, gender-related differences are noted in the vigor of play, the frequency of parent-child interaction, and parental tolerance of aggression in very young children.[18] Whether these differences are governed by the parent's cognitive set based on gender-identity, subtle differences in the response of the infant and young child to interaction, or a combination of both factors is unclear. Moss did find that male neonates function less effectively and are more poorly organized than females, which may be due to the delay in neurological maturity in males.[48] Boys are more irritable, are more prone to physical distress, and appear to learn social cues less quickly than female infants. This could account for some of the differential behavior observed in mothers; for instance, during the first 6 months, parents hold, soothe, and attend more often to boys, and they talk more to girls.[60] The cumulative effects of the mutual reinforcement patterns may lead to the measurable differences in attachment and play (touching and proximity) behaviors observed in girls at the end of the first year.[33]

Parents have different dreams, or goals, for their sons as opposed to their daughters (e.g., boys should be tough, confident, protecting, have career potential; girls should be soft, sweet, protectable, have marriage potential). These feelings and attitudes may be directly or indirectly translated into differential behaviors.[35] Parents subtly give the children different messages. Toys may differ; the colors the child is exposed to may differ. In our culture, the room and accoutrements of girls are more likely to be pink or yellow, whereas boys are exposed to blues and greens. Opposite-sex twins are usually dressed differently—the girl in a dress, the boy in pants.[33] The girl's clothing is generally pink, red, or yellow, and the boy twin is dressed in blue, brown, or green. These differences are subtle yet measurable. Many other differences have not yet been identified, or in some instances, measuring devices are not sufficiently refined to note differences.

Early learning is believed to occur on a stimulus-response model. Behavior that is compatible with the parent's conception of role-appropriate behavior is reinforced. Since children want approval, they emit those behaviors that were previously reinforced and omit those behaviors that were ignored or punished.

Later Learning

Differential reinforcement must be combined with imitation to obtain the rate and breadth of gender-role acquisition observed. Such behavioral clusters are too broad for everything to be taught.

The social learning theorist believes that as children get older, they observe the behaviors of others, attend to details of behavioral differences, rehearse these behaviors mentally, and socially imitate what they see, independent of external reinforcements of behavior.[42] The elaborate attitudinal and behavioral characteristics and qualities associated with gender are absorbed early and become highly resistant to modification.[35] Parents are most likely to be imitated because of their availability. Children are also observed to imitate more readily those models who are nurturant or similar to themselves or who possess desirable characteristics, such as power or a particular skill.[42, 53] Children are influenced by siblings as well as the parents. As the child becomes older and is exposed to a wider range of potential models, he or she may choose a teacher, a popular hero, a historical character, or any other individual believed to possess desirable characteristics or skills. The process of imitation is similar to the process of identification presented by the psychoanalysts in that the child reproduces the actions, attitudes, and emotional responses of the adult. Freud believed that identification causes imitation, whereas the social learning theorists such as Bandura, Sears, Bijou, and Baer believe that imitation leads to identification.[42] The social learning theorists would interpret the sociodramatic play of the preschooler as preparatory for the assumption of appropriate gender-role behaviors in the adolescent and adult years. The psychoanalytical school would indicate that children engage in such activity to help them to cope with and to integrate roles already accepted as integral parts of their gender-identity (Fig. 14-3).

Cognitive-Developmental View

According to the cognitive-developmental view, "The main difference among the theories does not reside in the specific manner in which the sex role behaviors are adopted or taught, but in the **motive** for modeling, adopting, or identifying with an adult figure."[2] Lawrence Kohlberg presents us with still another motive: He feels that one adopts gender-consistent behaviors or roles to reduce cognitive dissonance—not to gain power or to capture a love object. As such, the emergence of behaviors and identifications is dependent on the cognitive organization of gender-identity and cultural stereotypes. Kohlberg states, "Sexuality constitutes the most significant area of interaction between biological givens and cultural values in human emotional life."[30] As a child categorizes the self as male or female, he or she "actively seeks out knowledge of how to be a boy or a girl. As understanding increases, children become even more attentive to same-sex models and committed to all that is sex-appropriate."[57] He believes that children identify with the parent of the same sex because they recognize that parent as belonging to the same category. Children will identify with and imitate those whom they perceive to be similar to themselves or have characteristics they deem to be desirable.

During the first 2 to 3 years of life, the child is developing a core gender-identity, which becomes the bedrock of later sexual and gender-role attitudes. Kohlberg observes that gender conservation follows a developmental sequence and parallels object conservation in other areas as well as the emergence of concrete operational thought.[31] Prior to age 3, the child is able to label the self correctly and can identify the gender of others with partial accuracy. By 4 years of age, the child can label others correctly and becomes aware that one cannot change

FIGURE 14–3.
The nonsexist emphasis of today's culture allows children more freedom to enjoy joint activities without regard to gender-role stereotypes.

one's gender. At approximately 4½ years, the child begins to associate gender during childhood with adult gender-identity and roles. During the late preschool and early school years, curiosity about gender differences is at a peak. Nurse-doctor and "peeking" games are common during this period, before social taboos become internalized. Experimentation with changes of clothing in sociodramatic play helps the child to test the reality of a budding hypothesis regarding gender constancy. Around 6 to 7 years of age, the child becomes sure that gender is related to genital differences.

One's self-categorization begins to determine the value placed on objects and experiences. Since children want to like and to understand themselves, they seek out others like themselves (both adults and peers) to emulate. Children must see an objective basis for similarity between themselves and their models. This identification is usually made on the basis of gender, but it may take other criteria. Identification allows the child to exaggerate and concretize self-characteristics and to "structure and adapt oneself to physical-social reality, and to preserve a stable and positive self-image."[30] The child avoids what cannot be a part of the self. Consequently, we see increased association with peers of the same gender during the school years and increased antagonism or even hostility toward the opposite gender as a means for reducing cognitive dissonance and maintaining integrity. The child learns to control behavior in order to conform to the cultural standards associated with his or her gender until such behaviors become well-established, internalized sets or patterns.

The adolescent is concerned not only with gender-role, but also with his or her place in society and with moral aspects. There is a very complex interaction between cognitive development, social tendencies, and social experiences as one sorts out and organizes the attitudes toward self, love, work, and parenthood.[31] During the adolescent years, young persons develop a more unified construct of what they want to be, based on a "need for mutuality and equality of individuals in sexual relationships."[31] The cognitive dissonance resulting when a person discovers a preference for same-gender relationships can be devastating, requiring sensitive handling and counseling by empathetic, knowledgeable adults.[7]

Masculinity or femininity, according to Kohlberg, is achieved by the child's desire to achieve cognitive consistency by adopting cultural behavioral standards associated with gender-identity. These behaviors include everything from the way a person positions the legs when sitting, to the holding of a teacup, the tilt of a head, the response to other people, the tone of voice, or even the colors worn. Kohlberg does not rule out the role of early reinforcement experiences, but he emphasizes the child's choice of a role because of its ability to reduce internal cognitive dissonance. The child learns the organized rules deducted from observation, experience, and guidance. These views may be over-simplified, exaggerated, stereotyped, or even distorted, but nevertheless they are adopted because they are deemed desirable by the child (Fig. 14-4). On developing formal operational thought, the adolescent is able to generalize, abstract, and develop many personalized standards; however, for social and emotional reasons, he or she may remain rigid in some behaviors to retain peer group approval.

DENNIS the MENACE

"NO KIDDIN'...UNDER A CABBAGE LEAF, HUH?"

"TELL ME AGAIN WHERE I CAME FROM, I BEEN HEARIN' SOME WEIRD STORIES."

FIGURE 14-4.
Reprinted courtesy of Dennis the Menace. *Copyright Field Newspaper Syndicate, T.M.*®

SEXUALITY IN FOUR OF THE DOMAINS DURING ADOLESCENCE

From the foregoing discussion, it becomes obvious that one's sexual identity does not begin at puberty but develops concomitantly with other cognitive and social skills. However, the primary and secondary sexual changes that accompany puberty appear to highlight one's attention to gender differences, erotic sensations, peer relationships, and future adult roles.

Biophysical Domain

The pubertal period—the period of maturation of the reproductive system—includes all the primary and secondary sexual developments that accompany the endocrine changes in an individual. These changes draw attention to the fact that one is no longer a child. The dramatic change in body configuration demands a change in one's body image, and hence in one's physical, sexual, and social identities. The individual usually becomes very interested in bodily development, is frequently confused by it, and is curious as to the final outcome. Variations in growth may cause concern over the normalcy of one's body, sexuality, ability to compete in athletics, and social and peer relationships. At a time when peer acceptance is so critical, variations in biophysical maturity can create major hurdles. In short, the physical changes of adolescence constitute a major developmental crisis for the individual. The inability to control the changes may precipitate symptoms of the helplessness syndrome.[55] At no point in life is it more important to emphasize the concept of individuality than during the period of early adolescence, although if an emphasis on individuality has not been a priority throughout the earlier years, parental efforts during the pubertal period are unlikely to be convincing.

Those who mature early are frequently at a great advantage with their peers, since they appear to have left the world of childhood and to stand on the threshold of adulthood. The early-maturing male is at a particular advantage because he is usually able to compete in athletics more effectively. This advantage brings admiration and a concomitant elevation in value both to the self and others, which increases self-esteem. However, early-maturing females may find themselves in a social world of dating that they are not yet emotionally mature enough to handle, thus leading to increased stress and even to lowered self-esteem. Late-maturing individuals may become quite anxious about their eventual body configurations, their acceptability, and even their eventual ability to become parents.

It is not unusual for adolescents to tease one another about physical changes and to place a high sensual value on various attributes. The emphasis on "sex appeal" in television advertising and in books and magazines serves to accentuate the significance of possessing the right amount of a target physical characteristic. The adolescent, concerned about acceptance on a concrete, physical level, may experience great concern or great pride over his or her new body and appearance. In either case, much time may be spent at the gymnasium, at the clothing store, or in front of a mirror, to make the most of what one has and to fit the adolescent's concept of physical gender-identity. Plastic surgery is increasingly popular among teens to "correct" body parts that do not meet their attractiveness criteria.

Cognitive Domain

There is no evidence of real IQ differences between men and women, although there may be marked differences in performance because of motivational factors. Each culture places priorities on different characteristics for males and females. When a culture values physical strength over cognitive skills in males, a young boy may feel that his sexuality is in jeopardy if he does well in school and exhibits superior cognitive skills. Consequently, adolescent girls in such a culture may receive better grades in school because they are not exposed to the same pressure. On the other hand, if a girl's concept of sexuality is to marry and to have children, she may not value educational pursuits either. One's concept of sexuality, then, will not affect the IQ but may prevent an individual from maximizing cognitive potentials if cognitive skills are seen as secondary to physical attributes. This observation is consistent with Kohlberg's cognitive dissonance theory: young persons choose to expand or repress those attributes that they view as consistent or inconsistent with their concept of sexuality.

Affective Domain

If the discrepancy between the gender-ideal and the real or recognized potential is too great, the adolescent may experience affective disequilibrium because of the inability to achieve cognitive consistency; he or she may achieve external conformity at the expense of internal conflict. Affective conflict may touch on any aspect of life. The emergent young person may discover interests or skills that are seen as inappropriate for his or her gender. Since the adolescent is actively preparing for adult roles, this discovery may present a conflict. For example, a young man may find himself interested in women's hair styles or home decorating, or a girl may find herself skilled at auto mechanics or politics. If occupations using these skills are incompatible with the individual's concept of gender-appropriate roles, he or she may experience considerable conflict in the consolidation of a cohesive identity. Discrepant interests or skills will have to be denied, repressed, or rechanneled into more gender-consistent outlets.

In other words, during adolescence the normally developing individual attempts to come to grips with various self-perceptions, ideals, and realities of life, to assess their compatibility, and to modify those perceptions or ideals that are incompatible with reality. Two major tasks are involved in this process. First, the adolescent is forced to review gender-identity, gender-role, gender-orientation, and gender-preference for consistency. In the process, he or she may evaluate his or her degree of masculinity and femininity. The adolescent may also question and decide on a homosexual versus a heterosexual expression of the sensual aspect of sexuality. Those who discover a homosexual orientation may experience alienation and a truncated development because of the repression of a significant part of their identity as well as peer rejection and the cultural sanctions on developing intimate homosexual relationships.[37] Self-repulsion and confusion may result if the gap between the ideal and the real cannot be bridged. Second, the adolescent may choose new models with whom to identify, models who possess physical, cognitive, affective, or social characteristics that are deemed valuable. These characteristics may or may not be directly related to the adolescent's concept of sexuality but are generally compatible with it. The homosexual adolescent may have to wait until after his or her high school years to find acceptable role models. It is interesting to note the cumulative effect of parental influence during the adolescent years. As hard as the young person may try to deny parental standards or characteristics, the outside observer can usually note marked similarity of an adolescent's responses to stress and social situations with those of the parents.

It is during the period of adolescence that an individual is able to construct formally an ideal person or an ideal self, which can serve as a goal to stimulate and guide further affective and social growth. This ideal is usually a compilation of attributes extracted from qualities exhibited by parents, friends, teachers, cultural stereotypes, heroes, and other persons deemed to have valued characteristics by the adolescent. This "ideal" self is frequently at variance with the "real" or perceived self. This assumption automatically presents the adolescent with three major tasks:

1. Coming to grips with the discrepancy (or discrepancies) between the real self and the ideal self.

2. Recognizing and integrating the many identities developed during earlier years (e.g., honest scholar, optimistic musician, athlete) into a more cohesive view.

3. Integrating the experiences or identities of the past into an identity of the present in order to achieve the ideal identity of the future (epigenetic principle).

In actuality, these tasks are not limited to adolescence. There is evidence much earlier of striving to reach ideals, and the process, it is hoped, continues throughout one's lifetime; however, adolescence appears to be a critical time for the integration of identities into a fairly cohesive, stable, heuristic model of self that allows maximization of self-potentials while minimizing energy expenditure to do so.

Maslow indicates that adolescence is a period of life when behaviors are motivated by the need for esteem and self-respect.[38] These needs are met as the individual bridges the gap between the real and the ideal by successfully mastering tasks imposed by the self or others. Self-esteem is heavily influenced by the feed-back one receives from others. Incongruity between self-evaluation and evaluation from others can seriously undermine self-esteem. However, the individual who has developed a high degree of self-worth because of congruity of inner identities (or a small gap between ideal and real self) may be only minimally affected by external-internal incongruity. This is possible because such an individual is able to separate the projected identity from the inner self; the individual is able to look at the projected identity objectively without its reflecting on self-worth or self-value. If this individual has not reached the ideal self yet, he or she is able to see the self as a "person in progress." Many individuals are unable to differentiate between the two and consequently suffer identity diffusion, because their inner identities are not sufficiently identified and correlated to withstand incongruent feedback from peers, parents, or culture. The individual who has consolidated identities is able to be inner-directed, whereas the individual who is unable to identify and to coordinate identities is generally outer-directed and is much more dependent on feedback from others to maintain levels of self-esteem conducive to optimal or even adaptive

functioning. These concepts are consistent with Witkin's theory of field-independent versus field-dependent persons.[64] Dependence on external feedback for identity formation or self-worth is normal in earlier stages of development, but continued reliance on the environment may indicate delayed development of identity consolidation.

Erikson notes that the individual who is unable to identify and to achieve compatibility among the various facets of his internal identities becomes "identity-diffuse." Witkin indicates such a person may remain field-dependent. Both indicate that the individual remains dependent on external input or circumstances for guidance or an identity for the moment, rather than developing an internally consistent identity that is independent of circumstances, events, feedback, or time. Events may modify external behaviors of a field-independent person, but not internal identity or feelings of self-worth.[29] If the individual achieves compatibility among his or her concepts of self-potentials, gender-identity, gender-orientation, gender-preference, gender-role, and opportunities, a feeling of security results, which may enable the pursuit of an occupation outside the culture-bound, stereotyped gender-roles without violating one's concept of gender-role or the concept of his or her degree of masculinity or femininity.

Robert Havighurst identifies critical tasks for the adolescent years (see Appendix C).[27] It is interesting to note that tasks 1, 2, 3, and 5 are intimately related to one's concept of sexuality. If a broad definition of sexuality is used, then all eight tasks are directly related to both the development and the expression of one's concept of sexuality.

Social Domain

During the school-age years and early adolescence, the individual generally spends much time with peers of the same sex (homosociality) (Fig. 14-5). This behavior appears to fit Kohlberg's theory that one attempts to spend time with those perceived as being similar to the self. As mentioned earlier, there is much comparison during adolescence between self and others in the effort to assess one's normalcy within the peer group. Those who exhibit characteristics different from oneself (e.g., differences in race or gender, social or cognitive differences, or even differences in residential area or school) may be rejected, even declared to be enemies, to assure one's own integrity or superiority. Since these criteria are very arbitrary, they can be distressing to the "liberated" adult who is attempting to instill concepts of human dignity and equal value. However, intolerance for differences is an essential defense against identity diffusion during the school-age years and early adolescence.[12]

Gender discrimination in relationships continues during the early adolescent years. With the advent of puberty, however, most adolescents begin to extend themselves toward heterosocial relationships.[29] Increased interest is shown in clothing, hair styles, scents, makeup, social behaviors, flirting skills, and physical attributes that are believed to encourage interest from the opposite sex.

FIGURE 14–5.
Gender roles are heavily mediated by the environment and the culture.

Two issues become critical to gender expression during these years; the first is homosexuality. Ten to fifteen percent of adolescents have one homosexual experience.[47,63] Perhaps this experience is part of the continued need to compare oneself with those deemed similar to self, or it may be seen as a "safe" environment for one's first extrafamilial attachment or love affair. However, the critical factor is whether or not the individual continues to maintain a homosexual orientation. According to the theories presented earlier, there is no evidence to support the hypothesis that homosexuality is biologically based.[50] Freud believed homosexuality to be related to an overendowed anal zone or an incomplete resolution of the Oedipal complex. The behaviorist believes that homosexuality is related to environmental contingencies that lead the individual to find contact with persons of the same gender more reinforcing or less stressful than contact with the opposite gender. Kohlberg's theory would indicate either that the individual is unable to achieve cognitive consistency or that cognitive consistency is achieved but is not compatible with the norms for the culture. Even though one's gender orientation is established by adolescence, extensive research has not yet been able to identify the etiology of a homosexual versus a heterosexual orientation.[5] Some research indicates that the father plays a significant role. He tends to be aloof, cold, unaffectionate, detached, rejecting, and hostile in the parent-child relationship.[50] As a result, both male and female homosexuals may harbor feelings of anger, fear, bitterness, and even hate toward their fathers—factors which can affect more than just sexual orientation. "Many gay men and women are the unfortunate victims of parental absence, abuse, and neglect."[50] However, because heterosexuals face the same issues, no conclusions can be made, and the etiology of homosexuality may never be fully understood. Nevertheless, it is clear that individuals must be able to achieve a cohesiveness of

gender-identity, gender-orientation, and gender-preference if they are to be truly secure and happy with their gender-expressions and total self-identity. Counseling is frequently needed to achieve this goal.

The second issue is one's role in the sexual erotic relationship. Premarital chastity has been the ideal for centuries, especially for women. The necessity was enforced by the possibility of pregnancy or venereal disease. As a result of advances in medical science, however, the threat of this outcome is reduced, although not eliminated. Many young people see adulthood as having more privileges than childhood, and sexual intimacy is seen as one of these privileges. Consequently, coitus may be engaged in as a symbol of one's emerging adulthood. For some it may represent an imitation of adulthood or even "avocational play," rather than "sex play" as it may be labeled by some adults.[18] Coitus may also be engaged in as a reassurance of one's gender-identity and sexual attractiveness, as an exchange commodity out of curiosity, or even as an opiate.

The obvious danger is that an individual may use sexuality to achieve nonsexual goals and gratifications rather than concentrating on the internal state. Erikson's sixth developmental crisis is intimacy. However, physical intimacy is only one aspect of the task. Psychosocial intimacy, which builds from the ability to explore, to know, and then to share one's inner self with others, is the more critical component. When there is physical intimacy before internal identity is secure, it may increase the sense of identity-diffusion instead of helping to consolidate identity. Premature engagement in sexual intimacies, then, may create further cognitive dissonance and affective stress, rather than assuring one's sexuality. The externally controlled individual may experience a temporary reassurance regarding his or her sexuality and self-worth, but the internally controlled individual may experience a sense of disappointment, especially if a personal moral code is violated in the process.

The individual's concept of sexuality and its expression will continue to change over a lifetime. Mass media, cultural changes, the normal processes of maturation, and unique personal experiences all influence a person's value system, personality, and behaviors. Individuals who are comfortable with their personal concept of sexuality and who have found ways to express that orientation that are compatible with their value system are more likely to actualize their potentials in other domains (Fig. 14-6).

CONCLUSION

A survey of the literature indicates that environmental factors are more significant than biological factors in determining one's gender-identity, gender-orientation, and gender-preference. Gender-role stereotypes appear to be culturally produced and perpetuated. Advances in medicine and technology have reduced the need for gender-specific roles in the division of labor. Consequently, there exists today a greater concern for the unique needs of the individual than for the collective needs of society. The dichotomy of sexuality concepts implies inherent differences in the cognitive, affective, and social domains of individuals based on physiological

FIGURE 14—6.
A person's concept of sexuality continues to influence his or her relationships for a lifetime. When coupled with intimate affective and social sharing, sexuality can enhance one's enjoyment of life and can help problems seem less oppressive.

composition, but this is not borne out in empirical research. Concerned scholars today are encouraging individuals to recognize both their strengths and their weaknesses realistically and to allow their human qualities to emerge regardless of gender so that both men and women can become more fully human and can actualize their potentials without ridicule or rejection.[6]

Sears recommends rearing children in a warm, accepting, nurturant, supportive home environment.[53] Learner indicates that when parents are comfortable with their own gender-identity, gender-role stereotypes can be discarded without confusing the child.[32] The Sex Information and Education Council of the United States (SIECUS) suggests that sex education should include the following:[56]

1. Knowledge about biophysical functioning
2. Information to decrease fears and anxieties associated with the rapid changes accompanying puberty
3. Assistance in developing an objective, positive attitude toward one's body and its functions
4. Insight into relationships with others
5. Appreciation of the positive satisfactions emanating from a wholesome relationship
6. Guidance on the relationship of moral values and rational decision making
7. Prophylactic information on the misuses of erotic love experiences

Gagnon and Simon observe that men are committed to erotic love expressions and are untrained in romantic love.[18] Women, on the other hand, are committed to romantic love and untrained in erotic love. They suggest that the dating and courtship periods are essential to train the peers of the opposite gender in the meaning and content of their respective commitments.

Child-rearing techniques should help the child to learn to appreciate all his or her potentials and identities without restrictions based on stereotyped, culture-bound gender-roles. Parents who have helped the child to appreciate the pleasures, comforts, and skills of the body during earlier developmental years should continue to be nurturant and supportive of the child's efforts to consolidate identity and other potentials. The body is the house of the spirit, the tool for its expression; it should not be a prison or a shackle. Only when the body is fully appreciated will sexuality become liberating and enjoyable.

REFERENCES

1. Anastasiow, N. J. (1970). *A model for predicting the behavioral aspects of boys' sex-roles.* Bloomington, IN: Indiana University, Institute for Child Study.
2. Anastasiow, N. J., & Homes, M. L. (1975). Identification and sex role. In J. J. Gallagher (Ed.), *The application of child development research to exceptional children.* Reston, VA: Council for Exceptional Children.

3. Angrist, S. S., Mickelson, R., & Penna, A. N. (1977). Sex differences in sex-role conceptions and family orientation of high school students. *Youth and Adolescence, 6,* 179.

4. Argarian, M. (1973). Sex differences in early development. In J. C. Westman (Ed.), *Individual differences in children*. New York: Wiley.

5. Bell, A. P., Weinberg, M. S., & Hammersmith, S. K. (1981). *Sexual preference: Its development in men and women*. Bloomington: Indiana University Press.

6. Boston Women's Health Book Collective. (1984). *The new our bodies, ourselves* (rev. ed.). New York: Simon & Schuster.

7. Brink, P. J. (1987). Cultural aspects of sexuality. *Holistic Nursing Practice, 1*(4), 12–20.

8. Brown, D. G. (1956). Sex-role preference in young children. *Psychological Monographs, 70,* 14.

9. Diamond, M. (1965). A critical evaluation of the ontogeny of human sexual behavior. *Quarterly Review of Biology, 40,* 147.

10. Ehrhardt, A. A., & Baker, S. W. (1974). Fetal androgens, human central nervous system differentiation, and behavior sex differences. In R. C. Friedman, et al. (Ed.), *Sex differences in behavior: A conference*. New York: Wiley.

11. Ehrhardt, A. A., Epstein, R., & Money, J. (1968). Fetal androgens and female gender identity in the early treated adrenogenital syndrome. *Johns Hopkins Medical Journal, 122,* 160.

12. Erikson, E. H. (1970). Identity vs. identity diffusion. In P. H. Mussen, J. J. Conger, & J. Kagen (Eds.), *Readings in child development and personality* (2nd ed.). New York: Harper & Row.

13. Erikson, E. H. (1978). *Childhood and society* (2nd ed.). New York: Norton.

14. Fling, S., & Manosevitz, M. (1972). Sex typing in nursery school children's play interests. *Developmental Psychology, 7,* 146.

15. Freud, A. (1965). *Normality and pathology in childhood*. New York: International Universities Press.

16. Freud, S. (1935). *A general introduction to psychoanalysis* (J. Riviere, Trans.). New York: Liveright.

17. Freud, S. (1962). *Three essays on the theory of sexuality* (J. Strachey, Trans.). New York: Basic Books.

18. Gagnon, J. H., & Simon, W. (1973). *Sexual conduct: The social sources of human sexuality*. Chicago: Aldine.

19. Gartrell, N. K., Loriaux, D. L., & Chase, T. N. (1977). Plasma testosterone in homosexual and heterosexual women. *American Journal of Psychiatry, 134,* 1117.

20. Goldberg, S., & Lewis, M. (1969). Play behavior in the year-old infant: Early sex differences. *Child Development, 40,* 21.

21. Goy, R. (1968). Organizing effects of androgen on the behavior of the Rhesus monkey. In R. P. Michael (Ed.), *Endocrinology and human behavior*. New York: Oxford University Press.

22. Hall, C. S. (1979). *Primer of Freudian psychology* (25th Anniv. Ed.). New York: New American Library.

23. Hamburg, B. A. (1974). The psychobiology of sex differences: An evolutionary perspective. In R. C. Friedman, R. M. Richart, & R. L. Vande Wiele (Eds.), *Sex differences in behavior: A conference*. New York: Wiley.

24. Hamburg, D. A., & Lunde, D. T. (1966). Sex hormones in the development of sex differences in human behavior. In E. E. Maccoby (Ed.), *The development of sex differences*. Stanford, CA: Stanford University Press.

25. Hampson, J. L. (1965). Determinants of psychosexual orientation. In F. A. Beach (Ed.), *Sex and behavior*. New York: Wiley.

26. Harlow, H. (1965). Sexual behavior of the Rhesus monkey. In F. A. Beach (Ed.), *Sex and behavior*. New York: Wiley.

27. Havighurst, R. J. (1972). *Developmental tasks and education* (3rd ed.). New York: David McKay.

28. Horney, K. (1966). The denial of the vagina. In H. M. Ruitenbeek (Ed.), *Psychoanalysis and female sexuality*. New Haven, CT: College and University Press.

29. Horrocks, J. E. (1976). *The psychology of adolescence* (4th ed.). Boston: Houghton Mifflin.

30. Kohlberg, L. A. (1966). A cognitive-developmental analysis of children's sex-role concepts and attitudes. In E. E. Maccoby (Ed.), *The development of sex differences*. Stanford, CA: Stanford University Press.

31. Kohlberg, L. A., & Ullian, D. Z. (1974). Stages in the development of psychosexual concepts and attitudes. In R. C. Friedman, R. M. Richart, & R. L. Vande Wiele (Eds.), *Sex differences in behavior: A conference*. New York: Wiley.

32. Lerner, H. E. (1978). Adaptive and pathogenic aspects of sex-role stereotypes: Implications for parenting and psychotherapy. *American Journal of Psychiatry, 135,* 48.

33. Lewis, M., & Weintraub, M. (1974). Sex of parent and sex of child: Socioemotional development. In R. C. Friedman, R. M. Richart, & R. L. Vande Wiele (Eds.), *Sex differences in behavior: A conference*. New York: Wiley.

34. Logan, L. A. (1988). *Gender, family composition and sex-role stereotyping by young children*. Manhattan, KS: Kansas State University, Farrell Library. (microfiche) (ED 290 564).

35. Maccoby, E. E., & Jacklin, C. N. (1978). *The psychology of sex differences*. Stanford, CA: Stanford University Press.

36. Mahler, M. S., Pine, F., & Bergman, A. (1975). *The psychological birth of the human infant: Symbiosis and individuation*. New York: Basic Books.

37. Malyon, A. K. (1981). The homosexual adolescent: Developmental issues and social bias. *Child Welfare, 60,* 321.

38. Maslow, A. H. (1987). *Motivation and personality* (3rd ed.). New York: Harper & Row.

39. Massad, C. M. (1981). Sex role identity and adjustment during adolescence. *Child Development, 52,* 1290.

40. Masters, W. H., & Johnson, V. E. (1965). The sexual response cycles of the human male and female: Comparative anatomy and physiology. In F. A. Beach (Ed.), *Sex and behavior*. New York: Wiley.

41. Mead, M. (1961). Cultural determinants of sexual behavior. In W. C. Young (Ed.), *Sex and internal secretions* (Vol. 3) (3rd ed.). Baltimore: Williams & Wilkins.

42. Mead, M. (1977). *Sex and temperament in three primitive societies*. London: Routledge and Kegan Paul.

43. Mischel, W. (1970). Sex-typing and socialization. In P. H. Mussen (Ed.), *Carmichael's manual of child psychology* (Vol. 2) (3rd. ed.). New York: Wiley.

44. Money, J. (1970). Sexual dimorphism and homosexual gender identity. *Psychological Bulletin, 74,* 425.

45. Money, J., & Ehrhardt, A. A. (1972). *Man and woman, boy and girl: Differentiation and dimorphism of gender identity from conception to maturity*. Baltimore: Johns Hopkins University Press.

46. Money, J., & Hampson, J. (1957). Imprinting and the establishment of gender role. *AMA Archives of Neurology and Psychology, 77,* 333.

47. Money, J. W., & Tucker, P. (1975). *Sexual signatures: On being a man or a woman*. Boston: Little, Brown.

48. Moss, H. A. (1974). Early sex differences and mother-infant interaction. In R. C. Friedman, R. M. Richart, & R. L. Vande Wiele

(Eds.), *Sex differences in behavior: A conference*. New York: Wiley.

49. Piaget, J. (1962). *Play, dreams and imitation in childhood* (C. Gattengo and F. M. Hodgson, Trans.). New York: Norton.

50. Rekers, G. (1987). Research on homosexuality. *Family Research Today, 3*(3), 1–2.

51. Rosen, A. C., & Rekers, G. A. (1980). Toward a taxonomic framework for variables of sex and gender. *Genetic Psychology Monographs, 102,* 191.

52. Ross, S. A. (1971). A test of generality of the effects of deviant preschool models. *Developmental Psychology, 4,* 262.

53. Sears, R. R. (1965). Development of gender role. In F. A. Beach (Ed.), *Sex and behavior*. New York: Wiley.

54. Segal, H. (1973). *Introduction to the work of Melanie Klein* (New enl. ed.). London: Hogarth.

55. Seligman, M. E. P. (1975). *Helplessness: On depression, development and death*. San Francisco: Freeman.

56. SIECUS (Sex Information and Education Council of the U.S.). (1965, Oct.). *Discussion Guide #1*. New York: SIECUS.

57. Sigelman, C. K., & Singleton, L. C. (1986). Stigmatization in childhood: A survey of developmental trends and issues. In S. C. Ainlay, G. Becker, & L. M. Coleman (Eds.), *The dilemma of difference: A multidisciplinary view of stigma* (pp. 185–208). New York: Plenum Press.

58. Stephens,, G. J. (1978). Creative contraries: A theory of sexuality. *American Journal of Nursing, 78,* 70.

59. Stoller, R. J. (1990). *Sex and gender*. London: Karnac.

60. Thomas, J. (1977). Adam and Eve revisited: The making of a myth or the reflection of reality? *Human Development, 20*(6), 326.

61. Urberg, K. A., & Labouvie-Vief, G. (1976). Conceptualizations of sex roles: A life span developmental study. *Developmental Psychology, 12,* 15.

62. Waterman, C. K., & Navid, J. S. (1977). Sex differences in the resolution of the identity crisis. *Journal of Youth and Adolescence, 6,* 337.

63. Whicker, M. L., & Kronenfeld, J. J. (1986). *Sex role change: Technology, politics, and policy*. New York: Praeger.

64. Witkin, H. A., et al. (1974). *Psychological differentiation: Studies of development*. New York: Wiley.

Developmental Concepts of Play

Clara S. Schuster

Although play is an essential element in the development of healthy individuals, it is a highly abstract, elusive concept. Defining play presents an enigma to the psychologist or educator; although each of us intuitively knows what play is (or is not)—at least for ourselves—a precise definition is virtually impossible. Even Webster's unabridged dictionary, after two full columns of fine print, is forced to reduce the definition of "play" to a series of synonyms rather than a precise, observable, measurable definition. The only common element to be found among the various attempts to define this construct is that play is an **activity voluntarily engaged in for pleasure.**

Theorists offer differing views on the significance of play. In 1975, Schiller defined play as a form of art because of its creative, imaginative quality.[23] Herbert Spencer believed that play serves merely to drain off surplus energy (Fig. 15-1). Spencer, who did not view play as constructive, could not explain why a child continues to play even though he or she is exhausted. Stanley Hall looked on human play as a recapitulation of the activities of ancestral primates, since the sensorimotor play of young children has elements in common with the play of higher-order mammals.[14] In 1915, Karl Groos proposed that play provides early training for adult life. However, Groos did not believe play to be a constructive end in itself but thought that it was merely instinctual. He did not recognize that a child's level of competence in all domains affects the type of play in which the child participates.[17]

THEORIES OF PLAY

Play Versus Work

To help put play into perspective, one must first look at the differences between the definitions of play and work. It is commonly felt that work is the antithesis of play. However, the same activity can be either work or play, according to the meaning of the activity to the individual; one person's play may be another's work, and vice versa. Tending a garden, sewing, or even engaging in sports may be viewed as being in either category. Harlow speculates that play involves work because it requires both thinking and use of energy. Elizabeth Hurlock[8] and Brian Sutton-Smith[24] propose that when the end takes supremacy over the means, the activity leans toward work, but when the means is more important than the end product, the activity may be categorized as play. Piaget takes issue with this point, indicating that the activity itself may be an end product to the child so engaged, since the same activity may be work at one stage of a person's life and play at another stage.

Learning any new activity, such as riding a bicycle, knitting, reading, pouring from one container to another, or picking up a small object with the pincer grasp, requires concentrated effort. Once the activity has been learned, the individual tends to

FIGURE 15–1.
Play activities may serve to use up surplus energy. Play also allows a child to repeat a behavior and to experience the joy of mastery, which leads to proficiency.

repeat it frequently for the pure joy of mastery. It must be kept in mind that both external and internal environmental conditions can change an individual's motivation or ability to participate in a formerly pleasant or play activity, so that the activity may once more become work. Health deterioration, time limitations, or incompatible social or emotional circumstances (e.g., extreme competition) can limit or prevent an activity from being perceived as play per se.

Anna Freud indicates that the ability to work evolves gradually through an individual's developing pleasure in achievement through play activities.[5] Individuals are able to work when the ego acquires the ability to (1) control, inhibit, or modify id impulses; (2) delay gratification; (3) carry out preconceived plans, even when frustrations intervene; (4) neutralize the energy of instinctual drives through sublimated pleasures; and (5) be governed by the reality principle rather than the pleasure principle. Piaget also observed that there is a decrease in play activity as the child "progressively subordinates the ego to reality."[20]

Definitions

The psychoanalytical school, represented here by Anna Freud, Lili Peller, and Erik Erikson, defines play as the ego's attempt to deal with the pain of reality.[19] Their major attitude toward play appears to be consistent with the basic presupposition of Freudian psychoanalytical theory—that the unattractive id impulses must be socialized and brought under control by the ego. Play serves as the vehicle through which the child learns to deal with the pains caused by frustration of the unexpressed or ungratified id. The fragile ego, as the

moderator between the id and society, finds ways to inhibit or sublimate these impulses through voluntary play. Anna Freud suggests that fantasies (pretend play and daydreams) are essential for resolution of anxieties.

Play activities synchronize the bodily impulses with social expectations and experiences, putting the ego in active control of behaviors (Fig. 15-2).[3] These ego expressions are all under the governance of the pleasure principle. When a behavior becomes governed primarily by the reality principle, the activity is no longer play but is work.[5] Peller indicates that play behavior may also confirm one's control and power over life's experiences, or repeat a gratifying experience.[19] The ego engages in action that attains or restores a compatible, gratifying balance between self, society, and the requirements of the superego. In succinct form, then, "play is the sublimated expression of the child's various instincts."[23]

Smilansky, with her interest in the sociodramatic play of the preschooler, defines play as "pretended behavior," that is, behavior imitative of life around the child.[23]

Hurlock feels that any voluntary activity engaged in for the purpose of enjoyment may be classified as play.[8] Such classification is based on the individual's attitude toward the activity rather than the activity per se. Hurlock recognized both active and passive expressions of play, corresponding respectively to neuromuscular versus predominantly cognitive activities. Vicarious experiences, such as reading, watching television, and attending sports events, would fall into the latter category.

Piaget offers the simplest, most holistic, and yet most complex definition of play. It forms an integral part of his theory of cognitive development. In fact, he states that play and cognitive development are inseparable and include both overt behaviors and daydreams. According to Piaget, the cog-

FIGURE 15–2.
Play activities may enable the child to learn to deal with reality and to direct impulses into socially acceptable behaviors. This girl is proud of her "baby's" toilet-training success.

nitive domain develops through the two processes of assimilation and accommodation (see Appendix B). *Assimilation* occurs when perception of stimuli is distorted to fit what the individual already knows or can do (schema). *Accommodation,* on the other hand, is imitation of reality or the changing of one's schema or behaviors to adapt to reality. Play, then, is defined quite simply as pure assimilation—the repetition of a behavior or exercise of a schema solely for the pleasure of feeling virtuosity or power over the skill.[20] With this specific definition of play, the accommodation behaviors preceding mastery are classified as work rather than play, even though casual observation may record the same activity. Piaget often used the child's facial expression to distinguish between work and play: The child still involved with accommodating activity furrowed the forehead and eyebrows and maintained body tension, whereas the child engaged in assimilatory behaviors (ludic behaviors) would smile and have a more relaxed facial and body tension level (Fig. 15-3).

Play in some form occurs throughout the life span. This chapter will focus on the play of children; adult play and recreation will be discussed in the chapters dealing with psychosocial development during the adult years.

FUNCTIONS OF PLAY

The functions of play have been hinted at and even stated in the definitions. Because of a particular bias, each theorist

FIGURE 15–3.
The serious face and tense body tone of these children indicate that they find pouring milk to be work rather than play. They are still working on mastery rather than proficiency of the skill.

views play from a different perspective. However, neither the definitions nor the identified functions of play can be removed from the cultural or subcultural context. The family and educational systems with which the child has the most intimate contact provide the models for behavior, goals and values, tools, time-space perspectives, opportunities, reinforcement systems, and so forth.

Enculturation

Culture is transmitted through the imitating and adapting by each succeeding generation of the skills and particular values held by the preceding generation. Play activities allow children to practice the behavior patterns associated with significant roles in their culture and to add their own variations to the scenarios. Games with rules provide socially acceptable "arenas within which to address issues of love and hate (teammates vs. opponents), cooperation and conflict, and symbolically, life and death."[29]

Cultural Differences

Sutton-Smith has observed that the different types of games are systematically related to cultural variables. Games of strategy appear in cultures that have a hierarchical structure, emphasize diplomacy, or engage in warfare. When survival conditions are tenuous, games of chance are more pronounced. Industrialized societies stress product-oriented play. American culture is designated a capitalistic society; perhaps our enjoyment of "Monopoly" and "Trivial Pursuit" supports Sutton-Smith's theory that "the primary function of play is the enjoyment of a commitment to one's own experience."[24]

Cultural systems that include parents who are "adult-oriented," or "work ethic-oriented," usually view play as being a waste of time for both children and adults.[25] Some examples of adult attitudes in such societies are, "Children are to be seen and not heard," and "Individuals must prove their worth through a productive contribution to society." Children are given substantial responsibility early in life, even during the preschool years; little time or energy is left for leisure-time play.

As Western culture has become more technological and less product-oriented and as the standard of living and health care have improved, there has been less need for children to assume a responsible role in maintaining the viability of the family system. More time, energy, and money are generally available for the pursuit of leisure activities, and parents have time to become more child-oriented.

Many researchers have noted that socially deprived children do not follow the same developmental play patterns as more privileged children. Lacking reinforcement for spontaneous play activity in the home setting, these deprived children may actually need to be taught how to play.[11, 18, 25, 28] In the same sense, the product-oriented parent may be very supportive of academically oriented preschool activities, such as learning to recognize letters and to count, but may only tolerate or may even be resistant to activities such as block play, singing, or dressing up.[21, 24] Professionals intervening in such situations may initially find these children to be hostile, fearful, or apathetic toward more creative or child-specific activities, especially when group participation is expected.

Adult Roles

The years of childhood are spent in preparation for the years of adulthood. Play, especially in early childhood, is the most significant medium through which the developing child learns to adapt to the realities of life in his or her culture. It was probably someone from a work-ethic framework who coined the phrase, "Play is a child's work"; nevertheless, it is true. Through play, children are afforded the opportunity to explore, to master, and to strengthen competencies in all five domains at their own pace and free from most outside constraints.

A child is not transformed into an adult socially, cognitively, physically, or emotionally by one giant step or with the onset of the 18th or 21st birthday. Each theorist expresses in some way that play is the medium through which the child learns how to cope with the realities of the culture. Through play activities, the child gradually adopts and adapts to more mature ways of functioning.

The preschool years are seen as being particularly critical in the development of social skills and the preparation for adult roles.[21] Through sociodramatic play (strongest from 3 to 6 years of age) the child "tries on" many hats, acting out both family and career roles. Through play activities that mix both fantasy and reality in the child's own formula, the preschooler is able to enter the exciting world of adults.[23]

Effect of Play on the Development of the Individual

Play is both the product and the pattern of humanity's biological heritage and culture-creating capacity.[6, 29] Play specifically aids in the development of all five domains, as discussed in the following sections.

Biophysical Development

Almost every imaginable play activity involves the biophysical domain in some way. Play aids in the development of both gross- and fine-motor activity (Fig. 15-4). Piaget, Freud, Erikson, and many others identify the first signs of play as the repetition of pleasurable body movements purely for the joy of repeating an event and for self-control. For instance, sounds are repeated for the auditory feedback, but the child is also learning fine motor control of lips, tongue, vocal cords, and diaphragm movements for emission of the exact vibration, pitch, or volume—all precursors to talking.

The coordination and refinement of neuromuscular movements achieved by hitting out at a dangling noisemaker, shaking a crib toy, or repeating a verbal sound after the mother, give pleasure to the baby and make replication of these activities easier at a later date. The joy of gross-motor activity in the infant is obvious. Once the child has learned to perform a physical skill, it will be repeated over and over (to some adults' annoyance) for the joy of mastery until saturation is reached or a new skill emerges for practice. Once crawling, walking, or running has been mastered, there is no backtracking—the child is constantly moving purely for the joy of moving. He or she will run from one spot to another for

FIGURE 15–4.
Gross motor skills are refined during the preschool years and strengthened during the school-age years. When combined with the cognitive ability to remember and to use rules, they become the basis of many competitive games.

no other purpose than to run, frequently looking to the significant adult for approval and encouragement at the end of each episode (refueling).

As children continue to learn what their bodies can do through play, they gradually incorporate more and more complicated skills. Children move from scribbling to marking, then to coloring, then to drawing and tracing, and finally to the writing of alphabet letters and numerals. Art forms become more refined and reality-oriented (in some cases) through an increased experience in the use of art materials and the refinement of fine-motor skills. Even the child's attempts to "color inside the lines" is a self-initiated attempt to refine and control the muscles involved in precise, smooth finger movements.

Gross-motor skills practiced individually during the preschool years become the basis for the group competitive games of the school years, such as tag, Red Rover, baseball, and relay races (see Fig. 15-4). Throwing a ball, swimming, and riding a bicycle all involve the same principles of learning body control at a more complex level. The use of the body for progressively more complex activities, such as crawling, running, jumping, climbing, tumbling, and swinging, can eventually lead to extremely refined movement, such as that found in Mary Lou Retton, Peggy Fleming, Joe Montana, Jackie Joyner-Kersee, or Rudolf Nureyev. Through play, children learn what the body can do and what they enjoy doing. The gross-motor skills in the four athletes and dancer mentioned were first identified through play and then maximally refined through concentrated practice (which could be classified as either work or play, depending on the intrinsic meaning to the individual involved). Through play, then, children learn to master a skill, to practice the skill until it becomes a natural part of their repertoire, and then to refine the skill so that it can be used purposefully to accomplish a given goal. Physical activities can also help to use up the excess energy of children, thus freeing their minds to concentrate on academic pursuits. Throughout life, the chemicals and enzymes released during physical activity help to maintain high-level physical, cognitive, and affective wellness.

Although the reader is undoubtedly aware of this phenomenon, it bears repeating at this point: unused muscles will waste (atrophy) and eventually cease to function. Emphasis on physical-fitness programs attests to the fact that development of the physical domain through exercise (and play) has become a critical national concern. Physical exercise can help to maintain high-level biophysical functioning and health throughout life.

Cognitive Development

Piaget is very explicit in his viewpoint that play activities are essential to cognitive development. He notes that the type of play activities engaged in are closely related to the child's level of cognitive development. Once accommodation of a schema has occurred, further experience with the schema becomes assimilive. Through continued reenactment of the schema—

whether motoric, verbal, or symbolic—the event or object can assume new and stable relationships to other schemata (Fig. 15-5). The child learns spatial and temporal relationships, creates classification systems, and develops facility in inductive and deductive reasoning. Through play activities, the child can learn internal manipulation of external objects or events. Play becomes critical in balancing subjective conceptions of reality with the objective quality of reality. Representational thought is enacted through dramatic, symbolic play; one object is used in the place of another. "Pretend" activities strengthen symbolic or representational thinking (see Chap. 10).

Representational or fantasy play moves through four stages during the preschool years as the pretending gradually becomes less dependent on the immediate stimulation:[4]

1. Reality Play: Object is used for intended purpose.
2. Object Fantasy: Entirely new identity attributed to object.
3. Person Fantasy: People qualities are actively represented.
4. Announced Fantasy: Theme is announced before acting out.

The child is able to produce novel combinations, to learn to solve problems spontaneously, and to be creatively flexible through play activities.[25] In today's expanding, rapidly changing world, these adaptive skills are highly desirable. Studies show that children with deficient play experiences are not prepared to cope with the demands of a formal academic curriculum and consequently may experience failure despite the concentrated efforts of the teaching staff and the concern of parents.[23] It appears that these children are programmed for failure before they ever start going to school (see Chap. 13). Perceptual skills can be heightened through play. Maria Montessori developed a number of play activities for increasing discrimination skills for all five senses.[16]

The value of play in the development of language cannot be overestimated. Once language has been acquired, children can begin to form stable concepts that are shared with others in the culture.[23] Through play, children can test these concepts against those of others—thus organizing their interior language. Through language, children can communicate their needs and reconstruct or create an experience. Play, especially the sociodramatic play of the preschool years, motivates children to organize their thoughts in order to communicate them to others. This type of play also helps to enhance social relationship skills.

The corrective influence of the concrete experiences offered in play activities leads the child to acquire a broader and more accurate concept of the environment and his or her role in controlling the environment. A young child is often seen repeating an experience in an attempt to comprehend it fully or to establish a cause–effect relationship. Young children will walk alternately on a sidewalk and on grass to test the effect on ease of mobility and balance; they will mix two and then three or more colors of paint to see the result; they

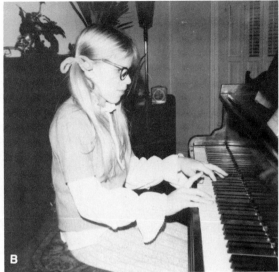

FIGURE 15–5.
Imitative play activities (A) *gradually become the foundation for systematic work* (B). *In play, the child assimilates schemata; in work, the child accommodates.* (A) *During the early years (age 3 years here), the child concentrates on sensorimotor stimuli.* (B) *In later years (age 11 years here), the child concentrates on cognitive stimulation. Note the marked difference in fine motor control and facial seriousness.* (C) *During adolescent and adult years, these skills are further refined and serve as tools for high-level cognitive and social skills.*

will push a bicycle bell with various degrees of strength to assess the effect on tone quality. A child may spend long periods of time grouping and regrouping objects for the pure fun of classification. Table games aid the child in preplanning strategies and their alternatives to achieve a desired end; thus play aids in the development of abstract thought processes. Through play, then, the child's world gradually expands from concrete, *self-centered* thought and activities to symbolic, *object-centered* activities and finally to abstract, *concept-centered activities.* Play helps the child to "comprehend and control the world in which he lives and to distinguish between reality and fantasy."[8]

Affective Development

It is difficult to separate clearly the social and affective domains of development, since they are reflective of each other and are frequently merely expressions of the same phenomenon—the social aspects being external, the emotional ones being internal.

Through play activities, the infant learns to trust both the constancy and the continuity of the external environment (mother, textures, schedules, primitive causal relationships) and the internal environment (awareness of urges, ability to remember and to predict). The consistency and continuity of inner and outer worlds allow the infant to begin to correlate and predict events, which provides a sense of trust and a rudimentary sense of ego identity.[3, 18]

As children mature physically and emotionally, they begin to desire more control over their inner and outer worlds. They begin to experiment with correlations and predictions they have learned to trust. (Can these inner urges and outer events be made to occur at will?) For example, "If I pretend to cry, will my parent come?" At the same time, social restrictions try to modify some of these experiments. Parents differentiate between false and true cries and respond only to "the real thing." If children are provided with appropriate play materials, they can enjoy autonomy without fear of reprisal or feelings of shame regarding their behavior. Anna Freud observes that the toddler period involves actions with play materials that symbolically represent the actions of body cavities, such as filling-emptying, opening-shutting, filling-removing, and messing.[5] Activities involving mobility (e.g., push toys, small cars) and construction-destruction activities (blocks) also allow for symbolic autonomy of action. The child thus learns self-control without loss of self-esteem.

The play activities of the preschool years enable children to set and to work out goals as they assume various roles. Both Piaget and the theorists of the psychoanalytical school stress the importance of play as an outlet for ego expression. Through play, children can express emotions forbidden in normal social situations without fear of reprisal, and they can learn to cope with the environment without repercussions of reality if errors are made. This is especially true of dramatic and sociodramatic play, in which children can reenact events that were confusing or traumatic and can "make" people and events. When children are confronted with a stressful situation in real life, they can use dramatic play to (1) change the roles, (2) change the outcome, or (3) become an active rather than a passive participant in the dramas of life.[19] Dramatic play allows the child to take the stress in small doses without loss of control or self-esteem.

During play, the child can relive an experience at his or her own pace or change the outcome to one that can be accepted. The child can also change roles and become the aggressor instead of the aggressed upon or passive observer. The planning of strategies for resolution of the event can help the child to adapt successfully to similar situations in the future. As children gain mastery over different situations, they develop the ego strength and the self-confidence that enable them to participate more freely and fully in real life; thus the ego integrates individual emotionality and social reality through play activities.

Through play activities, the child can learn to control frustrations, which arise when impulsive behaviors or wish fulfillment are blocked (see Spitz-Schuster, Chap. 11). The child who exhibits an arrest or delay in impulse control can be assisted through guided play activities that afford the child the opportunity to gain mastery over the self through gaining mastery over the activity.[32] Ego identity, ego development, and ego strength are thus facilitated through play.

During the school years, the normally developing child begins to become more concerned with reality and a product rather than the expression of physical and social skills for pure pleasure.[3] The child learns to work by engaging in activities that require more diligence to complete. During this period, one finds children engaging in activities that are halfway between work and play, such as hobbies, competitive

sports, and the development of special interests and talents.[5] These "play" activities can lead to a feeling of increased self-esteem and ego identity (or, if success is not achieved or respected, to feelings of inferiority or ego deterioration).

According to Erikson, successful accomplishment of each of these psychosocial stages is essential for the child to emerge from the childhood years with sufficient self-confidence and ego identity to face the responsibilities and social relationships of the adolescent and adult years. Through play, the child learns, experiments with, coordinates, and applies confidently the "rules" of the external and internal worlds. According to Erikson, "Child's play is the infantile form of the human ability to deal with experience by creating model situations and to master reality by experiment and planning."[3]

Social Development

Infants and young children are, by nature and necessity, very self-centered, or narcissistic. The young child begins life unable to distinguish between self and others.[5, 18, 20] Gradually, through play, the child begins to relate to others—first as an extension of self, then as inanimate objects. Other people are gradually viewed by the child as assistants to aid in completion of a task, and finally they are seen as true and equal partners to be trusted, respected, and afforded human dignities.[5] Through play, then, children learn how to interact with other people, how to get their needs met, and how to meet the needs of others. They learn to find a balance between sharing, giving, and taking.

Parten identifies six sequentially emergent stages of social involvement and awareness as exhibited through the play activities of children up to 6 years of age (Fig. 15-6);[18]

1. In **unoccupied behavior,** the child spends time primarily in autostimulatory behavior and restless, random movements and activities or wanderings while looking sporadically at others. Primarily infancy.

2. **Solitary play** is characterized by engrossed, independent play with toys. Minimal attention or regard is given to the proximity or play activities of others. Primarily toddlerhood.

3. In **onlooker behavior,** the child will closely observe the activities of peers and may even communicate through questions and suggestions with the play participants but will not actively join the activity. Primarily early preschool years.

4. Children imitate each other in **parallel play.** Two or more children are seen to play with toys or to engage in activities similar to those of nearby peers. Occasional interaction may occur. Although the children are compatible, they are essentially still in solitary play and are not cooperative in activities. Begins in middle preschool years.

5. The next level, **associative play,** finds the child still centered on his or her own interests, but within a group. Much borrowing and lending of toys may occur, but no

FIGURE 15–6.
Toddlers and preschoolers exhibit many levels of social involvement and awareness through their play activities. How many levels can you identify in this picture?

group goals are established. Begins in middle to late preschool years.

6. In the final stage, **cooperative play,** highly organized activities are centered around group goals. There are usually one or two leaders. Begins late preschool years.

Through cooperative play activities, the child can learn to cooperate when appropriate, to compete subtly, to sacrifice for peers, to become sensitized to the moods and the feelings of others, to develop friendships, and to control aggression. The preschooler may alternately exhibit four or more of these social involvement skills in a group play setting, depending on the particular goals of the child at the moment. Social play activities allow the child to practice and learn the art of leadership and the skill of following without compliance. One learns diplomacy, cooperation, negotiation, compromise, discussion, and linguistic skills through social play.[27] Through play, then, the autocentric infant gradually develops social competencies that enable him or her to be reciprocally responsive to others in the environment. Flexibility is essential for the establishment of compatible, successful social relationships. Social play activities allow the child to gain this adaptive capacity for varied behaviors.[25]

Hurlock and the theorists of the psychoanalytical school feel that children also learn gender-appropriate roles and behaviors in keeping with cultural expectations through play before kindergarten. These gender-role behaviors are learned through observation, practice, and reinforcement. There is evidence that gender differences are observable in play activities as early as the first year of life.[8] However, whether the propensity of boys for gross-motor activity and that of girls for fine-motor activity is biologically or socioculturally determined is not yet clearly established by empirical research. One might theorize that it is a combination of the two—genetic endowment and the unique, subtly influencing quality and quantity of parent–child interaction.

Spiritual Development

Through play, children gradually develop a sense of moral responsibility, insight into adult roles, and concern for others.[3] They learn to submerge anger and to work cooperatively. Identification with significant adults "permits the dream of early childhood to be attached to the goals of an active adult life."[3] Play activities provide a medium for transcending the immediate environment, its needs and demands. Play takes the child beyond his or her limitations to events and persons stronger, braver, more exciting than current realities. One reason why young boys may choose strong heroic roles to imitate (e.g., firefighter, police officer) is because they do not know enough about their own fathers' careers to imitate them in a play setting.[21] Inadequate contact with parents (i.e., because of their work schedules), grandparents (i.e., because of distance), and significant adults in the community may hinder the child's identification with traditional roles or cultural values and the desire to emulate them.[13] Play, then, is the key to successful adjustments during the childhood years and also serves as a foundation for adult functioning within the culture.

CLASSIFICATIONS OF PLAY

Gender, culture, health, available materials, and environment influence the type of play engaged in by children. Theorists have attempted to identify a core thread that supersedes all of these factors; age is seen as being the most significant factor. By applying a basic theory of play to the activities of children of various ages, each theorist offers a developmental sequencing of play behaviors. The core threads can be further consolidated under theories that emphasize the theme, content, or structure of play. Although approximate ages are shared by some theorists for the emergence and the duration of particular play behaviors, all the ages are flexible and the emergence of play behaviors is heavily influenced by environmental factors.

Themes of Play

Theorists from the psychoanalytical school focus on the theme of play (see Table 15–1). As mentioned earlier, play serves as a mechanism for the ego to gain mastery over the id and reality. The psychoanalytical school views all behaviors as libidinal or sexual in origin. The particular expression of sexuality is sequentially dependent on biological maturity as well as experiences with reality.

The Theory of Anna Freud
Anna Freud divides the oral period (birth to 15 months) into three stages.[5] During stage 1, the infant is completely egocentric and views the self as a biological unity with the mother. There is no awareness of separateness. This constitutes a narcissistic milieu (meeting the mother's needs as well as the infant's). Mahler terms this stage autistic.[15] All stimuli are perceived as being a part of, or for, the enhancement of self. Play activities are autoerotic; any activity yielding erotic pleasure is participated in as play. The infant's own body, then, is the focus of play activity. This is evidenced by the infant's obvious fascination with the hands during this stage. Self-stimulatory behaviors may continue in many forms (lip licking, nail biting, hair twisting, foot swinging, humming) when the environment is inadequately synchronized to the young child's needs or interests.

During stage 2 the child begins to distinguish between self and mother or other objects. Mahler states this is a symbiotic (mutually dependent) relationship. Gradually the infant begins to play with the mother's body as if it were a part of the infant's body; but at first there is no distinction between the two (a dual unity). Some children continue to be physically intrusive if their play has been blocked earlier.

During stage 3 the infant develops object permanence; when the mother is not seen, she is still remembered. The child will frequently play with and be comforted by, a soft, cuddly toy as a substitute for play with the mother. This toy may be given the same love as given to the mother in her absence. Piaget sees object notion as essential before the bodies of others become realities that children can recognize as being comparable to, but not identical with, their own.[20] Transfer of play behaviors extends to other soft toys. People may also be treated as toys, with pinching, biting, tasting, or pushing behaviors. Mahler[15] theorizes that this stage is significant in the separation-individuation process of the mother–child relationship. Peek-a-boo is a common game that aids the child in the separation process. Since the child often equates food with the mother, feeding play as well as feeding difficulties can give clues to the mother–child relationship.[5]

Stage 4 is synonymous with the **pre-Oedipal**—or **anal**—period (16 months through 30 to 36 months) and corresponds to toddlerhood. Cuddly toys gradually begin to disappear except at bedtime, or as transitional objects during separations from mother. Manipulative toys and toys that can be used symbolically to represent body cavities predominate in play activities. Others, especially peers, are still seen as inanimate objects but are gradually incorporated into play activities—if they can help accomplish a task the child wants to accomplish. According to Anna Freud, "Play material serves ego activities and the functions underlying them."[5] Finger painting has been viewed by those adhering to the psychoanalytical school as a desire to smear one's feces.

Stage 5, corresponding to the **phallic** period, incorporates the preschool years (2½ to 3 through 5 years of age). This period is also known as the **object-centered**—or **Oedipal**—stage. During this stage, love for self, which had begun to include the mother, now becomes centered on winning the love of the parent of the opposite gender. Play materials and activities come to be used as expressions of libidinal energy or sexuality either in solitary play or for exhibition to the Oedipal object.[5] This orientation combined with greater contact with peers leads to group play in which themes can be expressed through imaginative play. Others become partners in play and can aid in sublimating Oedipal impulses. Gymnastic activities of this period are also viewed as expressions of sexuality (especially masculine) and symbolic enjoyment of phallic activities.[5]

Stage 6 includes the primary school years (6 through 10 years) and is referred to as the **latency**—or **post-Oedipal**—period. Children in this stage demonstrate an increased mutual respect toward peers. Sexual drives are latent, with pleasure in finished products taking supremacy over object rela-

TABLE 15-1. EVOLUTION OF PLAY BEHAVIORS—THEME OF PLAY

	Birth	4 mo	8 mo	15 mo	2 yr	3 yr	6 yr	7 yr	10 yr	13 yr
Psychoanalytical period	Oral			Anal		Phallic		Latency		Genital
Anna Freud	Stage I: Biological Unity	Stage II: Part Object	Stage III: Object permanence	Stage IV: Pre-Oedipal		Stage V: Oedipal		Stage VI: Post-Oedipal	Stage VII: Pre-adolescent	Stage VIII: Adolescent
Margaret Mahler	Autistic	Symbiotic	Separation-individuation							
	Own body	Mother's body	Toys			Play with peers		Work		
Erik Erikson	Basic trust vs. mistrust			Autonomy vs. shame		Initiative vs. guilt		Industry vs. inferiority		Identity vs. role confusion
		Autocosmic exploration		Microsphere			Macrosphere			
		Self	Others	Small toys			Other people			
Lili Peller		Group 1		Group II		Group III		Group IV		
		Anxieties about body		Fear of maternal loss		Oedipal conflicts		Post-Oedipal play		Continues into adult years
		Solitary play		Play with mother, toys		Co-play, shared fantasies		Organized, competitive play, games		

tions. Play includes hobbies and other constructive behaviors leaning toward work.

Stages 7 and 8, the preadolescent and adolescent years (age 11 and older), include activities that can be defined, according to Freud, more as work than play, even though these activities may be voluntary and occupy leisure time.

To summarize the theory of Anna Freud, play activities are used to transform autoerotic love into constructive work activities through the medium of toys.

The Theory of Erik Erikson

Erik Erikson concentrates more heavily on the sequencing of psychosocial development than the evolution of play. He discusses play as a sequential unfolding of psychosocial relationships.[3]

In stage 1, Erikson's **autocosmic stage,** infants center on their own bodies. Stage 1 is subdivided into two phases. In phase 1, the self is the center of exploration. Vocalizations are repeated, and the child attempts to repeat or to recapture kinesthetic sensations and sensual perceptions. In phase 2, the exploration extends to other people and objects. The infant's focus is still on sensual pleasure. Different vocalizations and cries may be attempted in order to ascertain the effect on the mother's appearance (perhaps a variation of peek-a-boo, or Freud's stage 3).

In Erikson's stage 2, the **microsphere stage** (which corresponds to Freud's stage 4), the toddler uses small toys and objects to work out themes. He or she learns to manipulate and to master the world on a micro level (Fig. 15-7).

Gradually the child enters the **macrosphere stage** of nursery school age (stage 3), in which the world is shared with others. At first other children may be related to as objects, inspected, or even treated as toys, but gradually with time and experience this attitude expands to more cooperative role playing.

To Erikson, play is the vehicle for transforming the egocentric individual into a socialized, other-centered person.

The Theory of Lili Peller

Lili Peller theorizes that play is instigated by the ego in an attempt to compensate for anxieties and frustrations.[19] She centers her theory on object relationships. Her group I and group II play themes overlap in chronological unfolding, but the focus differs.

In group I play, children are concerned with their bodies, feeling that they cannot control them or perform a desired action. Play enables the child to fantasize and to gain control of desired actions. According to Peller, the child is frequently forced by society to substitute tools and materials for body play or use (such as clay versus feces or shovel in place of hand). Functional pleasure is achieved with increased body skill and mastery of tools.

Group II play behaviors evolve from the child's relationship to and anxiety about the mother. Fantasies and games involving control of loss and retrieval aid the child in gaining emotional mastery of the fear of loss. Although other children

FIGURE 15–7.

Microsphere play activities offer the child the opportunity to manipulate and to master the world on the microlevel. Play therapists frequently use microsphere play as a tool for reaching and understanding the young child and helping him or her to deal with stressors.

may occasionally participate in play with the child, the primary focus is toward the mother. Play with dolls is a symbolic exchange of roles between child and mother.

In group III, new anxieties arise in the child with the appearance of the Oedipal period. Children recognize differences between their own world and the adult world and devalue themselves because of this perceived inability to compete for, and win the affection of, the parent of the opposite gender; they fear losing that love. Play, then, serves as a medium for the child to adapt to, and fantasize about, adult roles and relationships. In many homes today, little boys are encouraged to play with dolls in the hope that they will master the tenderness as well as the logistics associated with the mothering role. Colorful, imaginative fantasies emerge as dramatic make-believe play; some complex fantasies require cooperative play with peers who are equally caught up in the drama of their own fantasies.

In Group IV, with entrance to school, the child becomes more reality-oriented and looks to group attachments rather than the Oedipal focus of the previous period. New and intense relationships are formed with peers, including secret clubs. Collecting and hobbies are viewed by Peller as being anal sublimations of a higher order. Group affiliation offers protection from unknown assailants; adherence to group rules, orders, and roles also offers protection against anxieties arising from the superego. Competition exists on an equal footing, in contrast to the previous two levels, where the competition was either unknown or unequally matched. The child learns loyalty to the group through peer relationships.

Peller's view, then, indicates that play activities enable the child gradually to expand relationships and to transfer libidinal energies from self to mother, to other family members, and then to peers—all preparing the way for mature adult relationships in later life.

Content of Play

Some theorists categorize play activities according to the type of activities focused on during each stage of development. These classifications are more descriptive than theoretical, but they can offer some insight into the play behaviors of children (Table 15-2).

The Theory of Hurlock
Elizabeth Hurlock offers very loose descriptive categories.[8] Stage 1, the **exploratory stage,** is divided into two substages. From birth to 3 months the child explores through the visual mode and through random movements. Once voluntary control of the upper extremities is attained, children are able to coordinate movements for a more thorough exploration of their own bodies and of objects.

Stage 2, the **toy stage,** begins somewhere around 1 year of age and extends into the school-age years, peaking at about 7 to 8 years of age. During the toddler years, the child anthropomorphizes objects with the dramatic use of toys. This dramatic make-believe play will continue into the early school years, peaking around 5½ years of age. Constructive use of toys begins about age 3, with gradually increasing complexity and preplanning of activity that eventually leads to productive constructions through hobbies. Collecting also begins at about 3 years of age; anything and everything is brought home—and forgotten. The toddler wants *all* the sand, stuffed animals, blocks, and so forth. They are stuffed into a bag, piled in the middle of the floor, or carried busily to a chair. The goal is to collect as many as possible, not to actually play with the objects. Sharing is very difficult. The child's collections gradually become more refined and discriminating. During the school years, collections can serve as socializing agents and status tokens.

Stage 3, the **play stage** of the school-ager, overlaps stages 2 and 4. Toy play continues here in the more refined form of productive constructions and hobbies. Games with rules and sports replace the spontaneous muscular activity of earlier years. Reading skills learned in school are used for pleasure, especially by bright children.

In stage 4, a decrease in gross-motor activities accompanies the rapid growth and subsequent decline of energy and the increase in body changes accompanying the pubertal period. The **daydreaming** that replaced make-believe play at about 7 years of age now reaches its peak. Daydreaming provides quiet rest for the growing body while allowing integration of past and future, fantasy and reality. Reading becomes a favorite pastime for the same reasons.

According to Hurlock, play allows the child to meet personal needs while adjusting to the demands of the social milieu.

The Theory of Smilansky
Sara Smilansky defines four stages of play. Because of their descriptive nature, these stages may overlap or run parallel to each other or may even continue into adulthood.[23] However, one stage appears to dominate the others at any given point in time. Smilansky's most significant contribution is to the understanding of sociodramatic play.

Functional play includes all simple muscular activities, both behavioral and verbal, that are engaged in for the purpose of manipulation of form. Children try new actions, imitating themselves and others. Play allows them to learn their own physical capabilities, to explore, and to experience the immediate environment.

In **constructive play,** children rejoice in the creation of form. By learning to use materials, they see themselves as the creators of events.

Dramatic play, beginning at about 2 years of age, is symbolic play used to display physical prowess, creative ability, and social skills. By combining reality with magic to fulfill wishes and needs, children are able to connect their own world and the adult world. The two main elements of dramatic play are (1) imitation of an adult (reality), and (2) imaginative or make-believe play (nonreality).

The highest form of dramatic play is **sociodramatic play,** which generally emerges at about 4 years of age. This voluntary social-play activity involves at least one other child. The target child pretends to be someone else by imitating their speech and actions. This make-believe element of sociodramatic play relies heavily on verbalization and provides for richer reproductions of real life. Words are used to (1) declare a role, (2) identify an object's imaginary identity, (3) substitute for an action, and (4) describe the situation. Thus sociodramatic play encourages verbalization in order to (1) interpret an activity, (2) plan and develop a plot, (3) maintain cooperation, (4) solve problems, and (5) bridge the gap to reality (Fig. 15-8).[23]

Sociodramatic play has six elements: (1) imitation of a role, (2) use of make-believe objects, (3) use of make-believe actions and situations, (4) persistence for at least 10 minutes, (5) interaction between two or more children, and (6) use of verbal communication related to the plot. Elements 1 through 4 are components of dramatic play; the addition of 5 and 6 is essential for sociodramatic play. Research indicates that participation in sociodramatic play is critical to cognitive development.[7, 23]

Smilansky's fourth stage, which begins during the school years and continues through adulthood, involves the playing of **games with rules.** An individual must be able to control behavior, actions, and reactions to participate effectively in group games.

Smilansky's theory states that play activities are essential to adequate preparation for life. If the child does not partici-

TABLE 15-2. EVOLUTION OF PLAY BEHAVIORS—CONTENT AND STRUCTURE OF PLAY

	1 mo	4 mo	8 mo	12 mo	18 mo	2 yr	3 yr	7 yr	11 yr
Elizabeth Hurlock	Exploratory		Voluntary			Toy ←→	Anthropomorphizing Dramatic play	Play ←→ Games Sports Hobbies	Daydream
Sara Smilansky		Functional				Constructive	Dramatic play Socio-dramatic Symbolic, group solitary	Games with rules	
Brian Sutton-Smith			Imitative →	Exploratory physical and verbal →		Testing → Dramatic play →	Model building →	Approach and avoidance games → Games with rules →	
Jean Piaget	Practice games → Stage I 0–1 mo	Stage II 1–4 mo	Stage III 4–8 mo	Stage IV 8–12 mo	Symbolic games → Stage V 12–18 mo	Stage VI 18–24 mo	Symbolic games Imaginary friends, symbolic combinations		
	Sensorimotor period 0–2 yr						Preoperational 2–7 yr	Operational 7–11 yr	Formal 11–15 yr

several hours or days to a time when it is more convenient to repeat a behavior. During the third year, the deferred imitation extends to copying the total person—pretending to be that other person through role playing. During the fourth year, role playing begins to be blended with imagination for imaginative sociodramatic play. Roles and leadership positions are exchanged and shared by the group members.

EXPLORATORY PLAY. Exploration activities (systematic manipulation of materials for discovery of their sensory value and action potentials) are seen as serious activities for learning. Exploratory play, to observers, may seem to be identical to exploration activities. However, since learning about the object or skill has already transpired, the same activity is engaged in purely for the pleasure of contact with the stimulus, and to discover new ways the object can be used (Fig. 15-9). Attention is focused toward active involvement in the materials or toys and does not degenerate into random, perseverative activity. Exploratory play may begin as early as 6 months, with the tongue and fingers being used as tools. During the second and third years, the activity increases and becomes

FIGURE 15–8.
Sociodramatic play activities (macrosphere play) carry over to the school-age years but assume a more reality-based, pre-planned character.

pate in all levels of play, it will seriously impede his or her social and cognitive development. Sociodramatic play is especially critical to coordinating experiences and forming workable concepts during the preschool years.

The Theory of Sutton-Smith

Brian Sutton-Smith offers a third approach to categorizing play activities according to content.[24,25] He draws heavily from the theories of others while combining cross-cultural studies to develop his own unique approach to describing play activities. He identifies six major types of play: exploration, self-testing, imitation, construction, contesting, and sociodramatic.[25] He has found the first three types to be universal; the second three, however, are greatly influenced by cultural differences. Since he sees play as the medium through which children gain experience in various behaviors, children may need to be taught how to participate in all six types of play in order to protect them from adaptive deficits in western cultures.[25]

Sutton-Smith consolidates his identified types of play into four categories, which overlap heavily. All four types are found concurrently in the 4-year-old child.

IMITATIVE PLAY. During the first year, the child will repeat what he or she can already do. Perceptual and cognitive skills enable the child to imitate other people during the second year. By 18 months the child may delay the imitation for

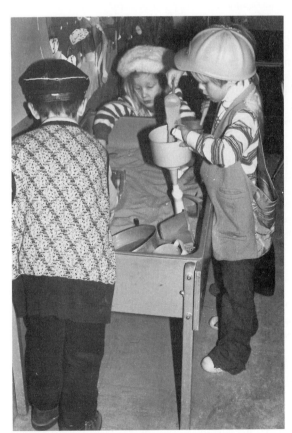

FIGURE 15–9.
Young children must explore the properties and characteristics of materials thoroughly before they can begin to use them constructively.

more complex. Novel verbal combinations used for sound effect and elicitation of responses from others fall under this category. Verbal exploration continues into the school-age years, with jokes, riddles, and exploration of homonyms.

TESTING PLAY. Testing play includes self-assessment of both physical and social prowess. During the second year, children concentrate on gross-motor skills. Increased physical skill and social opportunity lead to complex approach-avoidance games during the school years, such as hide-and-seek, dodge ball, or the video game Space Invaders. Through such activities the child learns and strengthens physical social skills. He or she increases self-awareness through observation and attention to sensations but also learns to control both memory and impulses.

MODEL-BUILDING PLAY. Model-building play begins at about 4 years of age, with the child imaginatively creating houses, cities, parties, and so on for the purpose of play, often to accompany dramatic or sociodramatic activity. Sutton-Smith comments that observations indicating that today's children spend less time in constructive activities than children of the past may reflect the lack of creative adult examples rather than an increased number of realistic toys.[24]

The types of activities that children engage in are unequivocally determined both by innate interests and skills and by environmental opportunities. Sutton-Smith's theory emphasizes that children's participation in play is essential to learning how to enjoy life. "Without the ability to enjoy life, the long years of adulthood can be dull and wearisome."[24]

Structure of Play

A third approach to the categorization of play activities is through the structure of play. Piaget, while recognizing both the themes and the content of play, focuses on the increasing cognitive complexity of play activities beginning with the elementary sensorimotor games and extending to advanced social games.[20] Although there is overlap of these play activities, they are sequentially emergent with very clear delineations among them (Table 15-3).

Practice games are the first to appear. They include any skills that are exercised for the pure pleasure of functioning—whether repeating a vowel sound or jumping a narrow stream. These games, described in the outline below, first appear in stage 2 of the sensorimotor level of cognitive development.

1. Pure sensorimotor practice
   a. Mere practice
   b. Fortuitous or "accidentally produced" combinations (includes destruction of object)
   c. Intentional combinations
2. Mental exercise
   a. Mere practice (e.g., "Why?")
   b. Fortuitous combinations (putting words together)
   c. Intentional combinations (making up stories)

Symbolic games first appear in substage 6 of sensorimotor development. The transition from practice games is very subtle, and externally they may appear to be identical. However, in symbolic games the element of make-believe is added. Elements of absent objects or characteristics of objects or persons are represented by distorting reality. The child subjectively links a "signifier" with the "signified" (see Figs. 10–2 and 10–3). Thus a small stick may become a car, or an old curtain a wedding gown; an empty chair may be a throne, a prison, or mommy's arms.

As the child engages in more social contacts, the practice and symbolic categories of play can appear singly or together in **games with rules.** The content may be identical with the previous stages, but the addition of rules complicates mental organization and operations. Games with rules are games with sensorimotor or intellectual combinations in which there is competition between individuals, regulated by either a temporary agreement or a code handed down from earlier generations.[20]

A fourth category is identified by Piaget, although he specifies that it does not rightfully occupy its own space. **Constructional games** are found in all three structural types but occupy a position "half-way between play and intelligent work, or between play and imitation" (e.g., hobbies, competition, dramatic presentations).[20]

To Piaget, play and cognitive development are inseparable and interdependent; each supports the growth of the other. Any time a new skill is acquired and the individual practices the skill purely for the sake of practice accompanied by pleasure at mastery, play is the result. Table 15-3 describes Piaget's view of the sequential growth of play activities according to the child's cognitive level of development.

FACTORS AFFECTING THE QUALITY AND QUANTITY OF PLAY

Since play is an essential element in the healthy development of individuals, it is important to look closely at the factors influencing its emergence.

Parent–Child Interaction

The infant's caregiver, usually the mother, is extremely important in the structuring of an environment that encourages and facilitates play activities. Such encouragement begins in the minutes and hours after birth as the parent touches, talks to, and looks at the baby. Play activities with the neonate help alert the infant to the environment and encourage him or her to begin discriminating among stimuli present in the environment.[18] Infants of parents who offer consistent auditory, visual, and tactile contact are able to identify and respond discriminatingly to the mother through voice by 5 days of life, through smell by 7 days of life, and through vision by 2 to 3 weeks of life.[1] The parent who talks to, holds, and rocks the infant will maintain the infant in an alert state (which facilitates visual scanning and learning) for longer periods of time

TABLE 15-3. PIAGET'S VIEW OF THE EVOLUTION OF PLAY ACTIVITIES

Types of Games	Average Age Range	Activities
Practice games		
Substage I Pure reflex adaptations	0–1 mo	No differentiation between assimilation and accommodation. Exercising reflex schemata does not constitute "real play"
Substage II Primary circular reactions	1–4 mo	Slight differentiation between assimilation and accommodation. Repetition of schemata and self-imitation, especially vocal and visual
Substage III Secondary circular reactions	4–8 mo	Differentiation between assimilation and accommodation, both still overlap. Repeating action on things to prolong an interesting spectacle.
Substage IV Coordination of secondary schemata	8–12 mo	Clear differentiation between assimilation and accommodation. Application of known schema to new situation. Schemata follow one another without apparent aim. Ritualism of activity for play—the means becomes an end in itself.
Substage V Tertiary circular reactions	12–18 mo	Ritualistic repetition of chance schema combinations. Accentuating and elaborating rituals, experimenting to see the result
Substage VI Invention of new means through mental combinations	18–24 mo	Beginning of pretense by application of schema to inadequate object. A symbol is mentally evoked and imitated in make-believe. Reproduction of behavior—primitive symbolic play. Symbolic schema is reproduced outside of context; transition between practice play and symbolic play proper
Symbolic games		
Stage I	2–4 yr	
Type I		Generalizing symbolic schemata (isolated imitations of schemata)
Subtype A		Projection of symbolic schemata onto new objects
Subtype B		Projection of imitative schemata onto new objects
Type II Subtype A		Symbolic games (assimilation of one schema to another) Simple identification of one object with another
Subtype B		Identification of the child's body with that of other people or with things
Type III	3–4 yr	Symbolic combinations (construction of whole scenes)
Subtype A		Simple combinations (includes imaginary friends). Reconstruction combined with imaginary elements
Subtype B		Compensatory combinations (materializing fears). Reconstruction with compensatory transpositions
Subtype C		Liquidating combinations (intensifying powers, subordinate threat) in pure reconstruction of situations
Subtype D		Anticipatory symbolic combinations (questioning, orders, and advice). Reproduction of reality with exaggerated anticipation of consequences
Stage II	4–7 yr	Increased orderliness; more exact imitation of reality; use of collective symbolism
Stage III	7–12 yr	Decline in symbolism; rise in games with rules and symbolic constructions
Games with rules		
Stage I	2–4 yr	Rare
Stage II	4–7 yr	Some
Stage III	7–11 yr	Peak
Adulthood		Continue to develop
Constructional games	2 yr–adulthood	Imitation of reality or new combinations. Gradually become more complex and unique to the individual

than the infant who receives minimal attention.[10] The cumulative effects of parental attention become clearly distinguishable by the time the child is 10 months old.[31] The author is able to objectively identify differences in quality of parental attention by 4 weeks of age through assessment with the Brazelton Neonatal Behavioral Assessment Scale. When parents have engaged in turntaking with the neonate, he or she is much more alert to and expectant toward the environment. By 3 months, these infants actively seek response from others. Infants whose parents have played with them in the course of everyday events (e.g., playing peek-a-boo during diaper changing, or using bathtime for water play and retrieval of floating objects) can be objectively identified as more alert, responsive, and interactive with the environment throughout infancy.

Play is so significant to the very young infant that inadequate play experiences or ineffectual interaction with the parent can lead to physical failure-to-thrive and even to death (see Chap. 8). The dynamics of this phenomenon are unclear; one explanation is that anxiety and stress levels are increased to the point where energies for growth become depleted; anxiety may also decrease the amount of REM sleep during which growth occurs. Here, the social, emotional, and physical domains become closely intertwined in the phenomenon of play. It might be noted that infants with failure-to-thrive syndrome also exhibit cognitive delays.

The interactional framework established with the parents in the early years continues to influence the child's perception of the freedom to explore and to manipulate and the ability to control the environment, as well as the child's responsiveness to events and objects. A disorganized home environment is correlated with a decrease in organized, satisfying play activities in preschool children.[11, 18, 23, 31] Sears reports that the degree of maternal warmth, as evidenced through acceptance, nurturance, and supportive responses, is directly related to the child's desire to emulate adult roles through play activities.[22] Smilansky reports that children who fail to participate in sociodramatic play activities (mainly enactment of adult roles) have extreme difficulty with both the social and academic requirements of formal schooling.[23] Schaefer and Bayley coined the word *circumplex* to describe the complex, circular interaction between mother and child that leads to the child's positive or negative adaptational patterns to life. Variances in the child's behaviors do not appear to be related to socioeconomic status but to the interactional framework offered by the parents.[28]

Other Cultural Influences

A multistimulatory approach is especially critical during infancy to encourage alertness and responsive interaction with the environment. As children become older, they appear to prefer accoutrements from the adult world instead of specially designed toys. Thus the box and wrappings become more interesting than the doll; kitchen pots and pans hold more interest than the pull toy. Preschoolers and school-agers become even more creative in their imaginative use of raw materials to suit their own ends. Play with these samples of the adult world serves to introduce the child to the tools and equipment of the culture.

Marked cultural differences are found in construction activities, competition games, and the quality and the quantity of sociodramatic play.[12, 25] These play activities are highly dependent on what the parents model, allow, or encourage, which in turn is strongly influenced by the values and mores of the given culture.

MAXIMIZING INDIVIDUAL POTENTIALS THROUGH PLAY

Even though each theorist approaches the concept of play differently, certain core ideas emerge. Play activities are unanimously viewed as behaviors engaged in for pleasure. All theorists also acknowledge that play activities prepare children for successful adult living in their culture.

Although Smilansky develops her thesis more extensively than the other theorists around the significance of sociodramatic play, they all acknowledge its value. Piaget and the theorists of the psychoanalytical school—two views of human development that on the surface appear to be most opposed to each other—are strikingly compatible at this point. Piaget expresses the idea that fear can be neutralized through play by "doing in play what one would not dare to do in reality." He states that the function of symbolic play is to assimilate and consolidate the whole of reality to the ego, while "freeing the ego from the demands of accommodation."[20] The two views are indeed well-blended here.

Preparation for School

Unlike other animals, humans rely more on learning than on instincts for survival.[13] Much of the behavior that contributes to our well-being depends on learning.

Smilansky and Krown noted that children who had inadequate play activities during the preschool years experienced difficulty with academic subjects. This difficulty was noted particularly in children who had not participated in sociodramatic play (a symbolic reenactment of adult roles). It appears that this lack of experience in representational thinking or using symbolic processes, hinders the development of the more abstract forms of thought essential to the use of the verbal and written signs of language. This would agree with Piaget's ladder of representational thought, which leads from concrete to abstract thought experiences (see Fig. 10–2). Montessori,[16] Krown,[11] and Weikart[30] all offer preschool curricula that are structured to facilitate cognitive development; structured, guided play activities are the focus of these methods. Through play as work, the child can learn to attend, to discriminate, to manipulate, to classify, and to symbolize— all essential prerequisites for formal schooling.

Preparation for Adult Responsibilities

The sociodramatic play of the preschool years finds children imitating adult roles. Through sociodramatic play, the child can "try on" the role of a parent, a policeman, a paper girl, a television character, or an animal. "What does it 'feel like' to be a . . . ?" Although many roles may be tried, preschool-age children tend to identify with and thereby emulate the behaviors of adults within the home or the behaviors associated with "what I want to be when I grow up." Identification with and enactment of these behaviors gives children a feeling of mastery or power.[9] Brian Sutton-Smith observes that even in our "role-enlightened" era, preschool-age children tend to stick to stereotypical gender-role activities during the preschool years.[24]

A significant ramification of play is its potential for preparation for life, particularly in the present technological world. With the rapidly moving technology of today, the environment—in terms of expectations, resources, numbers of persons one has contact with, skills needed, and so forth—is expanding at an astronomical rate. Toffler states that we are living in a world that is becoming rapidly obsolete—a throwaway society.[26] What the new generation needs is not product-oriented skills, but process-oriented skills. It has been interesting to note the explosion in the number of computerized games available for children, even for preschoolers. Some kindergarten programs are finding that computers can help to bridge the gap between play and study.[2] Children can learn flexibility through play activities, in particular through sociodramatic play in which many roles can be attempted and each role can have many alternative approaches. Group games, whether table games or sports, also lead to the development of alternative strategies. Individuals who have learned alternative ways of approaching problems adjust to unique experiences more easily than persons with limited experience in problem solving and strategy development. A wide variety of play experiences during childhood, particularly sociodramatic play and games of strategy, facilitates adult adjustment to novel experiences and expectations.

Maintenance of Mental Health

If, as the psychoanalytical school believes, play is the outlet for ego tensions, then play becomes essential in maintaining affective equilibrium or positive mental health in both the child and the adult. This hypothesis is the basis for play therapy programs.[1] Children who are experiencing emotional conflict with parents, peers, or others are given the opportunity to express these fears and hostilities through play experiences in the microcosmic sphere, using dolls and other accoutrements. Under the guidance of a trained specialist, children can express and resolve conflicts in this microworld, releasing energies for more successful adaptation or coping in the real world. Many hospitals have play programs that help children not only to fill their time during hospitalization, but

also to understand how equipment works, to project anger onto representative and appropriate play objects (e.g., doll figures, punching bags, modeling clay), and to reenact what is happening to themselves. By providing an accepting, secure environment, the play therapist offers children the license to explore toys, self, and relationships as fully as possible in order to gain the necessary tools and the confidence to understand, to accept, and to realize their own potentials for maturity, independence, control, and self-direction.[1] Effective use of such programs can make any experience one of personal growth rather than trauma and regression for the child.

Parent Teaching

If play is indeed essential to the development of all five domains and to adaptive living in a rapidly changing society, then parents need to provide opportunities for children to have adequate experiences in play. Descriptions of play activities for each age are insufficient; parents need to know how and why each play activity facilitates development. They also need to know how to assess their child's individual needs and interests. Classes on child development should be included in all high school curricula, and students should be made aware of the necessity of play in maintaining mental health at all ages. If potential parents are not reached during the high school years, they are often missed entirely, since the ones who need parenting information the most usually do not attend the parenting classes offered by the American Red Cross or other community agencies. Parents who expect the child to meet their needs rather than encouraging and assisting the child up to master his or her own needs are setting the child up for potential adjustment problems in adult life—if not before. Children should be seen *and* heard. Children need parents who play with them from infancy on; they need private time to explore and to express their feelings and moods without interference or reprisals; and they need peer experiences to learn social skills and realistic goals. Parents also need to take time to play with their children. This requires one to slow down to the child's pace and offers a temporary escape from the concerns of the adult world. It also offers an opportunity to relive all those activities one enjoyed the most during childhood, and the opportunity to experience activities that were missed.

Children have the right to engage in safe play. Since they are not always aware of the hazards of some types of play or play materials, parental guidance in some form is essential to ensure emotional and social safety as well as physical safety.

Adult Play

Opportunities for play continue to be critical for maintenance of mental health throughout the life span. Although activities considered to be play may vary from person to person and from culture to culture, the goal remains constant: Play provides relief and release from the humdrum, drudgery, or intensity of everyday living. It acts as an oasis for the refreshment and the renewal of affective and cognitive energies. Hobbies, whether constructing models, refinishing furniture, raising horses, or creating handcrafts, serve to break the monotony of life's responsibilities and to provide a source of pride and accomplishment. Play, whether physical or mental, provides a pressure valve, or an energy reserve, for both individuals and for groups of persons or families. The members of families who regularly enjoy mutually satisfying experiences together (e.g., car washing, swimming, vacations, table games, hobbies, sports) are provided with a buffer against more difficult mutual experiences (e.g., death, illness, disability, unemployment). The communication patterns and friendly feelings generated during times that are not stressful facilitate communication and feelings of optimism during periods of high stress.

CONCLUSION

The complexity of the play process and the fact that it is difficult to formulate concrete definitions for the term **play** create discrepancies among theorists as to when play activities actually begin and which activities can be classified as play. The core definition of play includes any activity engaged in for pure pleasure.

The main type of play activity characteristic of each age changes over time:

Early Infancy: Self-centered, self-exploratory, learning to control own body and vocalizations.

Middle Infancy: Beginning to reach out into the environment to explore parent. Imitates self.

Late Infancy: Beginning to reach out into the environment to compare self and parent, to explore toys and objects. Imitates others.

Early Toddler: Learning to manipulate small toys, to control gross- and fine-motor activity.

Late Toddler: Beginning microsphere symbolic solitary play.

Early Preschool: Beginning macrosphere symbolic play (parallel to other children).

Late Preschool: Sociodramatic symbolic play with other children.

Early School Age: Continued gross-motor and linguistic development. Games with simple rules.

Middle School Age: Rules become more complex; hobbies are added.

Late School Age: Much complex diversity—gross-motor sports, reading, hobbies, table games.

Early Adolescence: Continues preferred medium of play expression with addition of day-dreaming.

Late Adolescence and Adulthood: Wide diversity, but usually continues to offer a challenge to at least one domain with a sense of pleasure coming from mastery.

From a cultural perspective, "play has two faces: a social-public one, which addresses social-emotional needs and helps the individual to become assimilated into the protective social network; and a personal-interiorized one, which is more closely associated with ideational needs and is primarily responsible for the generation of new direction in thought and behavior."[29] Through play, the child learns to manipulate and to master body, mind, emotions, and relationships. Such mastery is essential to cognitive development, strong ego development, and good mental health. The flexibility and the optimism that develops through creating alternative approaches to problems in play is essential to the effective adaptation of the individual to the rapid changes of a technological society.

REFERENCES

1. Axline, V. M. (1989). *Play therapy.* New York: Churchill-Livingstone.
2. Burg, K. (1984). The microcomputer in the kindergarten: A magical, useful, expensive toy. *Young Children, 39*(3), 28.
3. Erikson, E. H. (1963). *Childhood and society* (rev. ed.). New York: Norton.
4. Field, T., DeStefano, L., & Koewler, J. H. (1982). Fantasy play of toddlers and preschoolers. *Developmental Psychology, 18,* 503.
5. Freud, A. (1965). The concept of developmental lines. In A. Freud (Ed.), *Normality and pathology in childhood: Assessment of development.* New York: International Universities Press.
6. Garvey, C. G. (1990). *Play* (enl. ed.). Cambridge, MA: Harvard University Press.
7. Golomb, C., & Brandt-Cornelius, C. (1977). Symbolic play and its cognitive significance. *Developmental Psychology, 13,* 246.
8. Hurlock, E. B. (1978). *Child development* (6th ed.). New York: McGraw-Hill.
9. Isaacs, S. S. F. (1979). *Social development in young children.* New York: A.M.S. Press.
10. Korner, A. F., & Thoman, E. B. (1973). Visual alertness in neonates as evoked by maternal care. In L. J. Stone, H. T. Smith, & L. B. Murphy (Eds.), *The competent infant.* New York: Basic Books.
11. Krown, S. (1974). *Threes and fours go to school.* Englewood Cliffs, NJ: Prentice-Hall.
12. Leacock, E. (1976). At play in African villages. In J. S. Bruner, A. Jolly, & K. Sylva (Eds.), *Play—Its role in development and evolution.* New York: Basic Books.
13. Lorenz, K. (1972). The enmity between generations and its probable ethological causes. In M. W. Piers (Ed.), *Play and development: A symposium.* New York: Norton.
14. Lowenfeld, M. (1967). *Play in childhood.* New York: Wiley.
15. Mahler, M. S., Pine, F., & Bergman, A. (1975). *The psychological birth of the human infant: Symbiosis and individuation.* New York: Basic Books.
16. Montessori, M. (1965). *Dr. Montessori's own handbook.* New York: Schocken Books.
17. Munsinger, H. (1975). *Fundamentals of child development* (2nd ed.). New York: Holt, Rinehart & Winston.
18. Parten, M. B., & Newhall, S. (1943). Social behavior of preschool children. In R. G. Barker (Ed.), *Child behavior and development.* New York: McGraw-Hill.
19. Peller, L. E. (1954). Libidinal phases, ego development and play.

In *Psychoanalytic study of the child* (Vol. 9). New York: International Universities Press.

20. Piaget, J. (1962). *Play, dreams and imitation in childhood* (C. Gattengo and F. M. Hodgson, Trans.). New York: Norton.

21. Piers, M. W., & Landau, G. M. (1980). *The gift of play: And why young children cannot thrive without it.* New York: Walker.

22. Sears, R. R., Maccoby, E. E., & Levin, H. (1976). *Patterns of child rearing.* Stanford, CA: Stanford University Press.

23. Smilansky, S. (1968). *The effects of sociodramatic play on disadvantaged preschool children.* New York: Wiley.

24. Sutton-Smith, B. (1971). Children at play. *Natural History, 80*(10), 54.

25. Sutton-Smith, B. (1975). The useless made useful: Play as variability training. *School Review, 83,* 196.

26. Toffler, A. (1970). *Future shock.* New York: Random House.

27. Trawick-Smith, J. (1988). Let's say you're the baby, OK? Play leadership and following behavior in young children. *Young Children, 43*(5), 51–59.

28. Udwin, O., & Shmukler, D. (1981). The influence of sociocultural, economic, and home background factors on children's ability to engage in imaginative play. *Developmental Psychology, 17,* 66.

29. Vandenberg, B. (1981). Play: Dormant issues and new perspectives. *Human Development, 24,* 357.

30. Weikart, D. P., et al. (Ed.). (1971). *The cognitively oriented curriculum: A framework for preschool teachers* (an ERIC-NAEYC publication in early childhood education). Washington, DC: National Association for the Education of Young Children.

31. White, B. L. (1975). *The first 3 years of life.* Englewood Cliffs, NJ: Prentice-Hall.

32. Wolfgang, C. H. (1977). *Helping aggressive and passive preschoolers through play.* Columbus, OH: C. E. Merrill.

Moral Development

Jarrell W. Garsee and Clara S. Schuster

Trusted government officials and esteemed religious leaders fall from their pedestals, loudly proclaiming exemption from the ethics that guide the behaviors of others. The increased crime rates, rejection of traditional values, and degradation of the beauty of humanness found in contemporary social climate raise genuine concern about the way in which we foster the moral development of children and for the future of our democratic society. Even Dr. Ruth Westheimer, notable T.V. "sexpert," now asks the plaintive question, "Who is teaching our children the difference between right and wrong?"

Morality, a dynamic process extending over a lifetime, calls primarily upon the cognitive and affective domains for decisions regarding "right" and "wrong" behavior. However, the moral aspects of life involve a unique interface of all five domains of human experience. Moral decisions are influenced by familial and cultural values, by one's understanding of and sensitivity to the implications of one's behavior on the personage or rights of others, and on one's levels of personal maturity and self-discipline. The crises and chaos of a generation of devalued living have precipitated a new concern for the ultimate questions (and answers) of morality and of life's meaning.

Moral development is one of the dimensions of the "identity crisis" as elaborated by Erikson.[16] According to Erikson, seeking inspiration from others and seeking help from "something higher than self" are activities essential to the establishment of an ideology.

TYPES OF MORALITY

Moral behaviors are the responses that individuals make throughout life to ethical pressures. If these responses are consistent with societal standards of "good," they are regarded as moral; if they contradict those expectations, they are considered immoral. Experiences of rejection, neglect, or abuse during developmental years can create an attitude of detachment from objects and people, and a total disregard for commonly accepted values. One result is the **immoral** person, who is aware of cultural codes of right and wrong, but willingly chooses to violate or ignore many of the values of society to meet his or her own needs and impulses. Immoral behavior often has a component of hostility and disregard for negative consequences on others. A less common outcome of early rejection, neglect, or abuse is an attitude of **amorality.** The person has been so badly damaged during early emotional development that he appears to have no conscience, and no awareness of the rightness or wrongness of an attitude or action. Such a person is not reached by appeals to reason or emotion to abide by commonly accepted standards of behavior. *No social agents provide a source of identification for this person, consequently there is no value-referent to serve as a motivator or guide for moral behavior or attitudes.*

Morality, a willingness to abide by standards of behavior held to be in keeping with the common good, is founded on identification with some source of authority, and characterized by concern about the welfare of others. Because conflict with society is minimal, psychic energy can be expended in creatively developing the potentials of one's own life and those of others. Consequently, acceptance of a culture's moral code generally results in a higher degree of mental health and happiness.

Religious Beliefs Versus Morality and Moral Development

People tend to associate morality with religious beliefs and issues of sin. However, they are separate dimensions of development. Although religion may influence standards for moral behavior within a culture (and vice versa), it is not feasible to equate religion and culture or morality. Formal religions provide a set of rules to guide behavior in the direction believed to endear or appease an ultimate source of authority. Religious doctrines establish external **guidelines** for behavior. Morality is concerned with the **internal criteria** a person uses to guide behavior. These criteria may be based on religious principles or humanitarian concerns. Although the external guidelines and internal motivators of behavior are not synonymous, many people do attribute their ability to live moral lives to supernatural assistance from a divine source, to an adherence to religious beliefs, or to fellowship with other "believers." Obviously, people use different internal criteria or understanding to guide behavior. These criteria are influenced by intellectual development, cultural values, and family teaching, as well as religious affiliation. Moral development refers to the systematic changes that occur over time in one's moral decision-making process. This process is independent of religious doctrine (Fig. 16-1).

Goals of Moral Codes

The survival of the human species and the thriving of the individual within a culture depends in great measure on the ability of the society to impart commonly beneficial values, and on each person's ability to develop sufficient self-control to abide by those values. There is a delicate tension between the individual's desire to express personal attitudes and needs, and the actions that may impinge upon another's survival, welfare, or thinking.

The concept of integrity is a spiritual and moral issue as well as a component of psychosocial maturity, but it is not necessarily a religious issue. The person of integrity:

Exhibits consistency *within self* from one occasion to another, from one point of time to another, and in interactions from one person to another.
Maintains consistency between internal values and exter-

FIGURE 16–1.
Celebration of life passages such as marriage is often a blend of religious beliefs and cultural traditions.

nal behavior: This involves a positive correspondence between what a person says and what a person does.
Is committed to a value system even when faced with difficulties and the painful exigencies of life. There is a driving force to remain true to the values, regardless of the cost, even when others give in to expediencies (the easy solution of the moment).
Is committed to these values over a lifetime, using them as dynamic guides in each new developmental phase, integrating them into each new challenge of changing years, abilities, and opportunities.

Thus, a person of integrity can be depended on to be consistently "moral" in each of life's situations; will maintain self-control in the face of all exigencies, and will, in most cases, bring positive outcomes to personal and social situations.

THEORIES OF MORAL DEVELOPMENT

A number of theorists have attempted to shed light on the complex process by which values are formed, modified by experience, and translated into behavior.

Freud's Theory

Sigmund Freud has had continuing impact on our understanding of human development, emphasizing stages of development and the dynamic interaction of the internal systems.[19, 20]

Personality

Freud described personality as being comprised of three systems: The id, the ego, and the superego. The **id** includes the basic biological, genetically determined characteristics of the individual, including the instincts and the survival needs. Together, the various properties of the id are referred to as the *libido,* an organized, organizing, motivating source of energy. This energy is primarily survival- and pleasure-oriented. Freud emphasized the sexual nature of the libido, although for him this included all sensual and sensate pleasurable experiences (even eating, running and sweating, touching and being touched) and not just reproductive or genital experiences. Impulsiveness and impatient gratification of needs are attributes of the id, since it operates on the pleasure principle. The id is operative at birth.

The **ego** includes many complicated processes, such as learning, perception, memory, and rationality. It functions both as a problem solver and as an ongoing repository of a person's self-perceptions. It is the ego that is responsive to the expectations and realities of both the physical and the social environment. Since it is sensitive to and operates on the reality principle, conflict between the id and the ego often develops. The ego begins to operate during the toddler years.

The **superego** regulates and provides feedback to the individual regarding how closely one's behavior conforms to the accepted value system. The superego is shaped by the primary socializing agents (parents, teachers, strong peers, group leaders) in the environment whose values and social expectations have become an integral part of the perceptual-emotional-volitional process of the personality. Once it emerges (late preschool years), it continually monitors the individual's behaviors and motivations. Discipline by significant adults sensitizes the child's superego.

There are two separate parts of the superego: the **conscience,** which discourages the expression of undesirable behavior; and the **ego-ideal,** which encourages behavior toward desirable goals.

Identification and Internalization

Freud hypothesized that children incorporate parental values and a moral code through the processes of identification and internalization. **Identification** occurs when one consciously or unconsciously incorporates attributes, motives, characteristics, and affective behaviors of a model into one's psychological organization.[35, 59] Generally, children want to become like their parents. Since parents dispense rewards and punishments, they appear to the children to be powerful. Children also observe that the adults in their lives appear to exert control over events and to receive approval from others.

Consequently, children want to emulate the behaviors of parents and other significant adults whom they admire and respect, so that they might obtain this same strength. Amoral behavior occurs when persons have not made an adequate significant identification.

Parental values are internalized as children use them to guide behavior. This whole-hearted acceptance of another's values as one's own is unquestioned in childhood and results in a conforming behavior. The sense of personal responsibility for actions is proportionate to the degree of internalization of adult and cultural values. As children grow into adolescence, they begin to struggle with the discontinuities between parental and peer values. As adolescence continues, they must decide which values to permanently adopt or drop in order to forge their own personal behavioral codes. All this is part of the normal identity crisis and the ensuing identity homework. Living by the values of one's parents, culture, or religion is an issue of compliance and external motivation. When one has gone beyond internalization to the point of evaluation, creation, and integration, there is a new freedom in expression and life. The values become uniquely one's own and support the issue of integrity discussed earlier.

Piaget's Theory

Jean Piaget's theory of intellectual reasoning has contributed much to our understanding of moral reasoning ability.[55] Piaget identifies two distinct stages in a child's understanding of and attitudes toward rules, justice, morality, and punishment. The earlier stage (lasting from approximately age 3 to 11) Piaget calls a **morality of restraint.** Rules are sacred to the child, evidently because they are handed down to him by dominant and omnipotent adults. During this stage, the child progresses from *imitation* of the rules of older children to *cooperation* and *competition.* Morality is imposed primarily by outside forces, and punishment is viewed as either vengeful or compensatory. An 8-year-old child playing a game typically demands that everyone play by the rules, conforms and cooperates himself, and requires immediate reversal of any falsely gained advantage. Restraint has been internalized to a degree, but it is very rigid and inflexible. Because self-esteem is still vulnerable, losing can be devastating to a young child. Consequently, a child may insist on changing the rules for his own advantage to ensure winning a game while still obeying the rules.

A **morality of reciprocity** characterizes the older child (12 and above) for Piaget. The ability to engage in abstract thought and operations enables the young person to extract a cohesive, socially sensitive codification of the rules, to create new rules, and to internally monitor value responses in the cause of mutually advantageous rules and behaviors. Thus two adolescents may consent to change the rules of a game they are playing as an aid to adventure and new experiences.

According to Piaget, in the earlier stages, intentionality has no bearing on the punishment deemed proper by a child. The child judges any behavior in terms of physical consequences, not in terms of motivation or intention. A child is an "eye-for-an-eye" judge; retribution is the mode of moral perceptivity. In the later stage, a child may develop the ability to be more forgiving, or at least to take extenuating factors into consideration before rendering a verdict; reconciliation becomes a goal of justice.

Kohlberg's Theory

Lawrence Kohlberg, one of the leading theorists in moral development, recognized the contribution of cognitive structuring to moral development.[40, 41] He recognized, however, that although moral development is influenced by cognitive structures, it does not parallel cognitive development.

Stages of Moral Development

Kohlberg proposes eight stages of moral development (see Table 16-1).[42, 43] Moral decisions become increasingly differentiated, integrated, and universalized at each successive stage. Justice is the goal of moral judgment. The individual seeks equilibrium at progressively higher stages as cognitive and affective domains mature.

PRECONVENTIONAL LEVEL (PREMORAL LEVEL). The first three stages are characterized by cognitively limited and very biased egocentric thinking.

Stage 0 (0–2 years): Naïveté and Egocentrism. During the first 24 months of life, there is no moral sensitivity. Decisions are made on the basis of egocentric judgment of what the child likes and helps him or her, or what displeases and hurts him or her. Right is what pleases **me.** A child may react to hurt with anger and to pleasure with love. There is no awareness of the impact of his or her behavior on the welfare of others. Self-discipline is nonexistent.

Stage 1 (2–3 years): Punishment and Obedience Orientation. Right or wrong is determined by the physical conse-

quence. Obedience is given in fear of the authority's power. "Might makes right." "If I will be caught and punished for doing it, it is wrong; if I am not seen and will not be punished, it must be right."

Stage 2 (4–7 years): Naïve Instrumental Hedonism. If the consequences are personally advantageous, it is right. There is an early sense of reciprocity in moral judgments. Children in this stage conform to rules out of self-interest or in relation to what others can do in return. "I'll do this for you, if you'll do that for me." But, "if you do something bad to me, I am justified to do something bad back to you." An "eye for an eye" orientation guides behavior.

CONVENTIONAL LEVEL (EXTERNALLY MEDIATED MORAL GUIDELINES). Socially mediated moral reasoning becomes possible as concrete operational thought emerges. The new social sensitivities of the school-age child increase awareness of others' feelings. Maintaining expectations is valuable/crucial regardless of the consequences.

Stage 3 (7–10 years): Good-Boy Orientation. Morality is based on avoiding disapproval. One tries to avoid disturbing the conscience. Consensus is so important that social expediency takes precedence over personal integrity in moral decisions. The maintenance of good relations with one's teacher, family, and friends is the epitome of "right"; broken relationships are "wrong." There is a budding awareness of intentionality.

Stage 4 (Begins at about 10–12 years): Law and Order Orientation. Many religious groups place the "age of accountability" at approximately 12. In this period, right takes on a metaphysical, and usually religious, aura. The authorities of school, church, and home begin to be seen as "shadows of a Higher Authority." It is during this stage that the individual is concerned with doing his duty, showing respect for authority and maintaining social order, as evidenced, for example, by performing on the school safety patrol. Fear-motivated condi-

TABLE 16-1. KOHLBERG'S LEVELS OF MORAL DEVELOPMENT

Level	Stage	Age	Underlying Principles
PRECONVENTIONAL (PREMORAL LEVEL)			
	0	0–2	Do what pleases me
	1	2–3	Avoid punishment
	2	4–7	Do what benefits me
CONVENTIONAL (MAINTAIN EXPECTATIONS OF OTHERS)			
	3	7–10	Avoid disapproval
	4	10–12	Do duty, obey laws
POSTCONVENTIONAL (MAINTAIN INTERNAL PRINCIPLES)			
	5	13–	Maintain respect of others
	6	15–	Implement personal principles
	7	18–	Live by eternal, universal principles

tioning at this point can produce rigid but very "religious" individuals, who are legalistically bound to law and order. You "do your duty" or "obey the law" purely because it *is* the law and it facilitates a harmonious society.

POSTCONVENTIONAL LEVEL (INTERNALLY MEDIATED MORAL GUIDELINES). The last three stages represent morality based on inner principles and reasoning rather than external pressure or emotions. Many people never realize these stages, or may acquire them late in life. One must employ Piaget's formal operational thought to master these stages.

Stage 5: Social Contract Orientation. One must creatively balance personal principles with culturally appropriate values in mutually beneficial social attitudes and behaviors. Right action is defined in terms of what is best for the majority. Although the welfare of the group is important, exceptions must be made if a person's rights or welfare are violated. The end no longer justifies the means. This person gains respect of peers while avoiding loss of self-respect. The "moral" adolescent will not expect to get something for nothing, to take and not to give, or to belong without producing. Laws are for mutual good, mutual cooperation, and mutual development (Fig. 16-2).

Stage 6: Personal Principles. This stage requires self-evaluation, self-motivation, and self-regulation, and thus is found only in the morally mature individual. This person does what he as an individual thinks is right, regardless of legal restrictions, the opinion of others, or the cost to one's self. One concentrates on meeting the expectations of the ego ideal. This person respects life so much that he would never undertake an action that would purposefully harm himself or another person. He acts in accordance with internalized standards (e.g., a strong stance on the abortion issue), knowing he would "condemn" himself if he did not. Integrity takes precedence over expediency. Few people achieve this level of moral development or the proposed next level.

Stage 7: Universal Principles. In this stage, the person transcends the limits of human frailties and fallacies to assume a stance based on cosmic perspective and eternity's values, an awareness of the "reason for existence" for the individual. The individual internalizes principles that go beyond the teachings of an organized religion to a consideration of the self as a part of the cosmic order.[62] Persons in stage 6 may be willing to *die* for their principles, but persons in stage 7 are willing to *live* for their beliefs—a much more difficult task. Only the rare individual achieves this level. Socrates, Joan of Arc, Ghandi, Martin Luther King, Jr., and Mother Teresa of Calcutta represent a few such individuals.

Through these stages, children first show an orientation toward conformity to the requirements of social approval and maintenance of authority, then an orientation toward contractual obligation and the welfare of others, and finally an orientation toward the intrinsic rightness or wrongness of an act.[2] There is no guarantee that an individual will automatically arrive at any stage simply because he reaches a certain age or cognitive functioning level. Many adults still function in preconventional or conventional stages of morality.

Comparisons and Critique

There are close similarities between the theories of Piaget and Kohlberg. Both theorists share the assumption that there are a fixed number and order of potential stages in the development of moral reasoning, that the stages are entered in invariable sequence (although the timing for arrival at the next stage is flexible), and that development through the stages is irreversible. They believe that movement from one stage to the next can be encouraged (1) through creating cognitive disequilibrium by challenging a child with moral problems for which his stage of thinking provides no easy answer, or (2) by presenting the child with moral responses that are one stage higher than his own.[27] Both theorists also believe that social interaction and social experience are major determinants of progression from one stage to another.

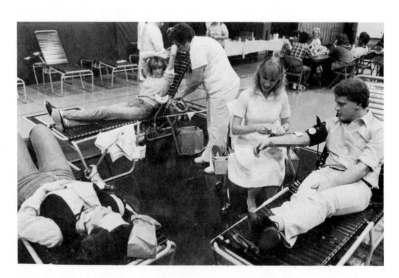

FIGURE 16-2.
The American Red Cross Bloodmobile offers young people the opportunity to translate their inner values into active concern for others.

Both theorists used the same technique in all their research inquiries; that is, eliciting the child's verbalized rationale for the judgment of specific acts in hypothetical situations. This technique creates some difficulty since there is often a discrepancy between what a child can verbalize as being right and what he would actually do in a similar value-choice situation.

Other criticisms relate to the need for greater emphasis on the role of affect.[2,3] Empathy is viewed by some as the primary motivator for moral judgment.[24, 25, 30, 31, 41] The feelings involved in empathy—guilt, remorse, compassion—are vital components of ethical conduct, and have their roots in a sense of altruism, which in itself depends on an empathetic response to the experience of others.

Kohlberg's theory of moral development does not acknowledge gender differences. Carol Gilligan contends that when Kohlberg's model and assessment methods are used, the female's pronounced orientation toward empathy and caring tends to place her at a less advanced stage of moral reasoning.[24, 25] Specifically, females tend to be concerned with relationships and responsibilities, whereas males typically center their responses on rights and rules.

Kohlberg constructed a classic moral dilemma for his research: Heinz's wife was sick and facing certain death. The local druggist was charging an exorbitant price for a cure he had discovered. Kohlberg asked his subjects whether or not they would steal the drug, and **why,** if they were Heinz in this situation. Gilligan concludes that because men and women experience attachment and separation in different ways, each perceives a danger that the other does not see—men in connection, women in separation. Thus, women construct the moral problem as an issue of "care and responsibilities in relationships rather than as one of rights and rules."[24]

Because Kohlberg's stages of moral development are primarily structured on the basis of rules, Gilligan contends that females often fail to reach the zenith of his criteria for moral functioning. Gilligan believes that the different parameters used by men and women for making moral decisions should not be regarded as the basis for judging one moral development system superior to another, but must be acknowledged as a true difference. Although the validity of this statement is not denied, when comparative studies are made of moral development of males and females, no statistically significant differences are found.[22, 67, 69] Gender difference studies indicate that Gilligan's description represents effective psychological functioning for males as well as females.[1, 64] However, females express more empathic usage differences within stages,[22] that dilemma content affects moral reasoning orientation more than gender,[56] educational level is more significant than gender differences,[67–69] people use both orientations depending on the nature of situation conflict,[70] and age but not gender has a significant bearing in a cross-cultural setting.[66] Non-violence and the value of life emerged as principles of an East Indian culture. These fit into Kohlberg's view of justice which embodies respect for human life, personality, and dignity.[66]

Kohlberg and his associates are now exploring the field of meta-ethics and normative moral behavior. The idea of ethical ideality, or moral courage (i.e., the will to take a solitary stand) is gaining interest.[23] Kohlberg is also investigating nine meta-ethical assumptions—a step into the spiritual domain.[46]

Other Theories of Moral Development

Social Learning Theory

Both the psychoanalytic theory and the social learning theory focus on the role of identification in conscience development.[5, 21, 33] The social learning theory, however, places primary emphasis on the power of social models and differential reinforcement. As children begin to imitate adult behavior, they do so to please the parents and to avoid disapproval and punishment for misconduct. Later they realize that good conduct is rewarding in itself, and they find intrinsic pleasure in obedience. Thus, their consciences begin to reward them with high self-esteem for good conduct and with shame and guilt for bad conduct. Gradually, they progress from externally-controlled to internally-directed moral behaviors.

One might ask, "Why does the child choose a particular person as a model?" Identification is more likely to occur when the subject (S) and the model (M) have frequent contact, and the model has the power to reward S for behaving in approved ways. The more direct the contact between M and S, the stronger will be the identification.[35] Since the home and family situation provide the most consistent contact between M and S, the parents play a critical role in the conscience and moral development of children.[26] However, other persons (e.g., teacher, media personality, older sibling, or athlete) may also serve as role models.

Peck's Theory

Robert Peck found a strong correlation between cognitive developmental periods and the predominant characteristics of the various levels of moral behavior.[54] He presents 5 levels of moral development, which closely parallel Kohlberg's stages except that the last stage incorporates all 3 of Kohlberg's postconventional stages.

AMORAL. The amoral level is typical of infancy. At this early stage, the infant has neither the knowledge nor the self-direction to respond to any motivation but that of meeting immediate personal needs and desires. Behavior is impulsive and expressed without regard for its effect on others or its degree of conformity to societal expectations. The individuals who become arrested at this level are called *sociopathic,* that is, they have no internalized moral principles. They are egocentric in their interpersonal relationships and have no sense of remorse or guilt when they behave in ways that violate societal expectations. The individuals are blind to the moral implications of their behavior and its impact on others.

EXPEDIENT. The expedient level of moral behavior is characteristic of early childhood. At this stage, children behave in ways that are mostly self-serving, which will gain for them perceived advantages. These advantages may be in the punishments avoided (by being obedient) or the rewards distributed for compliance to an authority figure's demands. In fact, these children are still very ego-centered but are willing to forgo short-term advantages. They see other persons as primarily the means by which they can satisfy their present, pressing wants and needs. These children behave in subtle ways that manipulate others for their own selfish ends. In the absence of external authority, they do what they want to do. Their behavior is characterized by an overall self-centeredness.

As adults, expedient persons have no internalized set of moral behavior codes. They manipulate their interpersonal relationships and give as little of themselves to others as possible. They see other persons only as objects to be used to satisfy their impulsive wants and not as persons of intrinsic worth.

CONFORMING. The conforming level of moral development is characteristic of the school-age years. Children conform to the group's demands on them. They take their behavioral cues from other persons and groups. When the peer group expects specific social or religious behaviors, the individual will behave consistently with these expectations. When the peer group rewards immoral or socially nonconforming behavior, the individual will do what the crowd expects, even if such behavior violates earlier training. The basic rule is, "When in Rome, do as the Romans do." Ethics are based on the situation rather than a core set of principles. Behavior is externally mediated. This level of moral development helps to explain the "wilding" behavior of inner-city adolescents who go on crime sprees, even gang rape and murder of innocent victims. Conforming adults may be faithful to their marriage commitments and church vows when at home, but when they attend a convention in a distant city, they may ignore those commitments. The attitude is that a behavior is O.K. if you don't get caught.

Conforming individuals have internalized few principles of moral responsibility on which to build their characters. They feel little guilt whenever they break a rule. They may experience shame in some cases because they are quite concerned about what others think of them, but will feel no guilt for violating principles of honesty, loyalty, or truthfulness.

IRRATIONAL-CONSCIENTIOUS. The irrational-conscientious level of moral development characterizes individuals in later childhood or early adolescence. These individuals have an internalized code of moral behavior to which they rigidly adhere, applying this code to themselves and to others almost without exception. The rules must be upheld and enforced; the penalty must be imposed without mercy or amelioration, and there is no consideration of extenuating circumstances or motives.

They are as demanding of themselves as they are of others. Because of such high personal expectations and their intolerance of individual failure, these individuals are often besieged with deep feelings of guilt and shame when failing to act in a morally acceptable manner. In severe instances, such persons may need psychotherapy to help free them from the bonds of irrational guilt.

On the positive side, irrational-conscientious persons try very hard to behave morally and to uphold the moral expectations of their religious code and society. They become deeply involved in social issues, thus improving the quality of life in their communities or the world.

RATIONAL-ALTRUISTIC. Peck's rational-altruistic level of moral development includes adolescents and adults who have moved beyond merely fulfilling legal rules to implementing internalized principles. They have not altogether abandoned articulated rules, but they only use them as guides for individualized moral behaviors. They have adopted the "good-of-others" principle as their operational value system. They constantly seek to direct their behavior in all societal interactions and relationships in ways that implement their basic principles. Thus they choose courses of action based on reason rather than impulse as much as possible. They seek to enhance the welfare of others as much as their own, even if they must curtail the satisfaction of their own needs to do so.

At this level, persons seek to work with others in constructive ways. They enjoy life, and they are not afraid to express their emotional reactions in appropriate ways. They are authentic persons because their conceptual and operational values are closely correlated. They are well-adjusted and not defensive about their actions. They admit their errors; they feel guilt and shame at times, but seek earnestly to rectify their mistakes, make amends, and restore the damaged egos of others. In short, they are fully developed moral persons, who try to behave conscientiously and morally because it is the right thing to do, and not merely to escape a guilty conscience or societal censure.

The Whole Person

As adults, few individuals will fit into any one particular stage all the time. Different social situations and complex moral dilemmas may evoke different behaviors. Thus some persons may adopt the expedient response in one situation and a universal principled response in another. The businessman who gives generously of his time and money in community activities may be afraid to protest his company's discrimination against women because it is an unpopular cause. The "whole person" is realistic, free from debilitating internal tension, appreciative of self-worth, capable of accepting consequences, responsible, and sensitive to the needs of others. Thus the "whole person" is one who develops optimally in each of the five domains, who experiences and expresses awareness of meaningful interaction between the domains, who is moving gradually toward greater preoccupation with the world of *invisible realities* (e.g., values such as honesty, love, faith, trust, hope, dignity, purpose, character) and whose inner responses and external actions place a premium upon the nonmaterial essentials aspects of a positive LIFE.

THE DYNAMICS OF MORAL DEVELOPMENT

Developmental Observations

The ability to look outside oneself for power and direction is a major catalyst of human development. During infancy, it is the mothering person who gives meaning and direction to the child's life. Those infants without such an external organizer may fail to thrive or may even die (see Chap. 8). As one grows older, the perceived "power person" shifts as new identifications are made. Most people extract values and priorities from the common values and concerns of the social matrix, and in the process find efficient, effective ways of living together in social interaction.

Development of Conscience

From studies on moral development and the evolution of conscience, several conclusions can be drawn. First, conscience is inferred because humans experience feelings of guilt and shame if they violate its expectations. Second, the capacity for a conscience is present at birth. Third, conscience develops through discernible, describable stages. Fourth, different moral structures operate at each level of development. Fifth, each stage is influenced differently by environmental events (Fig. 16-3).

    A *need for approval* is partly innate and partly learned. This inner "voice," conditioned to respond to situations involving choices with negative, neutral, or positive feelings, is often called the **conscience.** The training in obedience that each child receives contributes to the strength of this inner reinforcer. The development and the training of the conscience is the avowed intent of all conscientious religious subcultures, and the unconscious purpose, as well, of all socializing agents. The conscience serves to guide behavior in the absence of an external authority figure.

    Parents, teachers, and other authority figures face varying degrees of individual and collective resistance on the part of the younger generation—especially during the toddler and adolescent years. This resistance is intensified by authoritarian rigidity, inconsistency, unrealistic expectations, or emphasis on conformity at any cost. When the values of the older generation appear to be arbitrary, empty, and meaningless, members of the younger generation respond with negative and hostile reactions, thus precipitating confrontations and cultural change.

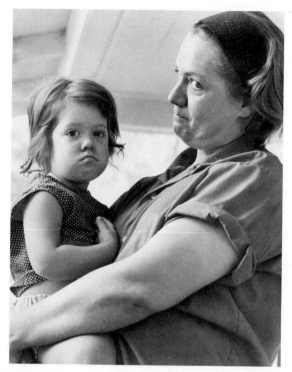

FIGURE 16–3.
Discipline is difficult for both the adult and the child because the goals of each appear to be temporarily thwarted. However, when respect for the individual is maintained, even difficult situations can prove to be growth-producing for both.

The Concept of Deity

The conceptualization of a deity, or a supernatural authority "higher than the self" represents one of the few universal human attributes. The tendency to congregate (gregariousness), the tendency to imitate, and the desire to appeal to persons or superhuman agencies stronger than ourselves when our own resources fail are nearly universal social phenomena (see "Spiritual Development," Chap. 2).[17]

    In philosophy, there has been a continual and difficult circular argument regarding the concept of deity: Did God make men and women, or did humans "make up" God? As it relates to ideology, does God give moral guidance to humans, or do humans use the God they created to sanction their own conceptualizations? Little is usually gained by such contentions, since most people approach the dispute from the standpoint of faith, with a predisposition to believe in one side or the other. Some believe that "truth" is received by revelation; others believe that all "reality" is based on experience.

    For the purpose of understanding this chapter, it is important to recognize that (1) people do appeal to higher authorities; (2) people often anthropomorphize their deity ("making God in their own image"); (3) one's deity is sometimes invoked to produce a fear that conditions the conscience; and (4) a Higher Authority may have had a major part in man's existence. If this is so, instructions for the proper use of man's potentials may also have been provided through holy writ (e.g., the Ten Commandments or the Eight Fold Path), innate conscience, or both.

Facts of Moral Development

Empathy and Role-Taking
Role-taking is the ability to cognitively put oneself in another's place, to understand the context of and reenact a scenario, and to assess the other's behavior on that basis. Because of egocentrism, young children project their own motives and understandings when making moral judgements about another's actions. Therefore, role-taking cannot occur until cognitive decentering skills emerge. **Empathy** is the ability to understand the other's emotional response to circumstances, to feel their pain, or anticipate their feelings. Empathy and role-taking enable one to deal with the questions, "What should I do?" and "What is fair, just, and equitable for all concerned?."[31]

Differential opportunities for role-taking among cultures or among individuals within a given culture can have a significant impact on the rate of moral development. The fewer opportunities the individual has to participate in peer groups and egalitarian family structures, the slower will be the rate of moral reasoning and conscience development.[62]

Altruism
Altruism is the conscious or unconscious effort to consider others with equal or greater concern than one's own self.[12,37] This willingness to give up more than one gains requires an awareness of another's need, as well as self-control and voluntary self-sacrifice or deprivation. Altruism is clearly in the service of another person's welfare and involves going out of one's way to help others even though one has not been responsible for their plight.[30] Western cultures, emphasizing the value of the individual, tend to perpetuate egocentric and even narcissistic concerns. Several Oriental cultures, on the other hand, condition individuals to seek the higher good of others, especially members of the extended family, even those not yet born.

Guilt and Shame
The intrapersonal communication system of the superego is guilt and shame versus self-approval. When one violates accepted moral principles, guilt is felt. When one acts in ways that are not socially approved, shame is felt. If an individual's behavior is consistent with a self-concept and value system, or ego ideal, the individual will feel self-approval. To avoid the negative feelings associated with activation of the conscience, the individual will attempt either to withstand temptation or to perform his or her duty. Inner positive self-approval reinforces and enhances self-direction.

Delayed Gratification
Self-control, or specifically the inhibition of the id (impulse to satisfy one's needs), is a vital part of moral development. Delay of gratification is not part of an individual's natural repertoire of attitudes or behaviors. The ability to delay gratification depends in part on a child's ability to "bind time" into past, present, and future segments. A typical 3-year-old who wants an ice cream cone is incapable of accepting a maternal explanation that he can "have one later." Time for him is divided into two parts: **now,** or **not now.** Now is good (instant gratification); and not now is bad!

Effective moral training enables the individual to gain control of desires, tempering or subjecting them to an awareness of long-term needs or the needs of others. Instant gratification often destroys the possibility of meeting more critical needs (e.g., sleeping with a stranger on an out-of-town trip may damage the respect, trust, and commitment necessary to build a mutually satisfactory lifetime spousal relationship, or spending income on many little "needs" may prevent one from paying for a needed car, home, or medical bill).

Factors Affecting Moral Development

Parents
Transmitting the best of one's personal principles, cultural values, and religious tenets to children (the next generation) is a full-time job. One cannot teach the difference between right and wrong by *talking* about moral values. Parents must live their values and show the children the benefits of self-restraint. An adolescent listening to a lecture on respecting the law gets conflicting signals if his father is speeding at the same time and has asked him to look out for the police. Values must be "grown" into the personality the way the grain grows into a tree—one ring at a time. Parents provide the growing environment with input that nourishes and aids in the growth process.

The parents must be consistent in their expectations of the child, in rewards for the child, and in the relationship between their verbalized instructions and their obvious personal actions in order for the child to learn respect, confidence, and obedience. Self-discipline must be learned through obedience to external rules before a person can formulate and obey his or her own rules.

Peers
Early adolescents become ever more sensitive to the evaluations of their own peers, both because of the need to develop more independence from their parents and because of the desire to develop stronger relationships with the culture through age-mates. The peer group becomes, and remains, dominant in the crystallization and internalization of values *only* if parents have already rejected the child, defaulted on their responsibility, or overreacted to peer pressures. An adolescent child whose deep emotional needs are not met at home, who has an "inner need vacuum," is especially subject

to age-group influences.[11] It is a fortunate child whose parents continue to provide support, love, and realistic discipline without overreacting to the "far-out" behaviors that the adolescent is "trying on for size." Overreaction on the part of the parents begins a negative spiral of growing hostility, anger, and defensive behavior that puts an emotional distance between the adolescent and the parent and literally drives the child into closer, more dependent peer-group involvement. A "negative self-identity" results when pride on both sides, and the need for autonomy on the part of the developing adolescent make negotiation, mutually beneficial interdependence, and change almost impossible.

Mass Media

The ebb and flow of social currents—the "new morality," the mode of dress and personal appearance, artistic "realism," increasing frankness in media presentations—affect the moral development of young people. Curiosity and the "need to belong" deeply affect choices. Information that comes through reading, listening, television, and films not only makes people aware of options, but also indicates what is "the *in* thing to do." Choices are made sometimes simply to experience something new or to fit in; those choices may become patterns of behavior, depending on the sense of internal satisfaction or external approval.

The pervasiveness of television in our society has created serious challenges for those concerned about moral development. The average American home is invaded by 7 hours of heavily value-laden material each day, and some of that content is offensive. One study looked at the young viewers' (grades six through ten) perceptions of and responses to television.[44] About 75% of these young adolescents saw television as "entertainer," almost one half as "informer." Other perceptions were: "educator" (nearly half), "specialized information service" (21%), "stress reducer" (less than 10%), "source of consumer information" (less than 5%), and "social companion" (less than 5%). About one half of those who mentioned negative functions of television say it displaced more constructive or worthwhile activities, and that the passive activity often produced intensified lethargy. Only about 10% of the students felt that television distorted the real world (e.g., in advertising, news coverage, and entertainment programming). Nearly half of the students noted that television emphasizes negative, antisocial behaviors, especially in areas of violence, drug use, and sexual conduct. An extremely unique result of this study was that these young people (predominantly 11 to 15 years of age) did not believe that they themselves were influenced by this content, but were deeply concerned by the fear that it would have a negative impact on younger children's values and behavior.

The students' responses suggest that they are not merely naïve consumers of this pervasive medium, but do in fact make discriminatory judgments. They realize that much of the content presented runs counter to the values and instruction they have received from other sources, and they appear to have their defenses up in response to such content.

Media presentations seem to have a much greater impact on those whose inner emotional needs for warmth, appreciation, acceptance, and affection have not been met in more primary ways and groups. There is concern that the subliminal messages may have an extended latent period, affecting the person's behavior in the young adult years even more than during the adolescent years.

Religious Training

Adolescents tend to be both literal and idealistic. Situations appear to be black or white, and religion provides a touchstone for self-judgment or judgment of others. The naïve acceptance of religious beliefs by the pubescent loses much of its certainty and piety during the intense social and intellectual interchange of later adolescence. A *healthy* belief or faith system gradually moves from an external locus of authority to an internal one, with much less literalistic, judgmental responses (see "Faith Development," Chap. 2). Although moral development and faith development are related, they are not synonymous.

It is only natural that values will have greater internal strength if they represent standards of behavior that have also been consistently taught, rewarded, and acted on by the parents. Formal religious training, either at home or in the church, gives both social and ecclesiastical sanction and support to self-control, concern for others, moderate lifestyle, and positive interaction with others. Not many teenagers are subject to consistent and systematic religious training. Many whose parents "sent them to church" during earlier years use the church as a point of asserting new adolescent independence, and therefore stop going. Relatively few families are concerned about family religious training, either at home or in the church setting. As a result, many young people today seem to be seeking private, personal spiritual insights and meaning apart from traditional religious institutions.

Another way religious belief systems impact upon moral development, both conceptually and behaviorally, is their appeal to a higher authority. This may predispose a person to pride (special status in the eyes of the supernatural), fear (apprehension about divine disapproval), rebellion (personal decision to operate autonomously), or integrity (a combination of cooperation and integration of positive motivations).

Many people have discovered that life is most worth living when it is used in pursuit of a value higher and greater than self. This value may be political, social, or spiritual (nonmaterial). Religious beliefs affect behavior in the moral area by imposing supernatural sanctions, or by encouraging unselfish actions in the interest of securing rewards "beyond this life." All cultures have people who have self-actualized to the extent that they literally "gave their lives" for causes higher than self and their own interests.

FACILITATING HEALTHY MORAL DEVELOPMENT

Much can be done to facilitate healthy moral development throughout the life span.

Parental Guidance

As indicated earlier, the atmosphere created by the parents is a critical factor in a child's personality and moral development. Children truly learn what they live (Fig. 16-4).

Transmission of Values

Parenting is an awesome but exciting challenge. The parents who can balance the five Ls (love, limits, learning, liberty, liability) discover that they themselves continue to grow and to develop as individuals.[21] Discipline's goals of self-direction, self-actualization, and socialization are further refined by the parents as well as established by the children (Fig. 16-5).

1. Every child has the right to be *loved* unconditionally. Not loved "if" or loved "when"—rather, each child should be accepted with unconditional positive regard, including care, concern, contact, communication, cuddling, caring, caressing (so many words begin with "care"). The child should never have to worry or wonder if he or she is loved. Unconditional love is a lifetime need.

2. Every child needs *limits*—physically, emotionally, mentally, socially, morally, and spiritually. Limits may be provided for the convenience of the parent but always for the safety of the child and for his or her proper development. Limits must be realistic, consistent, and flexible (capable of being changed at different need levels).

3. Every child needs an environment conducive to appro-

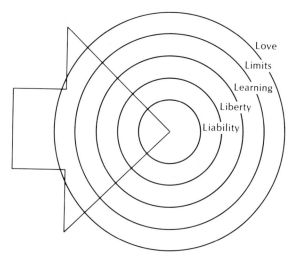

FIGURE 16–5.
Child rearing on target. (Adapted by Jarrell W. Garsee from a model proposed by Jerome Folkman.)

priate *learning,* a process that includes good modeling and the following:
   a. Telling a child what is expected.
   b. Explaining why it is expected.
   c. Defining the consequences if something is not done.
   d. Showing a child how to do what is expected.
   e. Sharing the task with the child; doing it together.
   f. Watching the child perform the task.
   g. Evaluating the results.
   h. Rewarding positively the appropriate response.
   i. Ignoring or responding negatively to an inappropriate response. Discipline ("discipling") is a vital part of learning and teaching.

4. Every child needs *liberty* to make appropriate choices within the limits set by the adults. By beginning with small decisions during the toddler years, the child gradually begins to differentiate among bad, good, better, and best decisions.

5. Every child needs to assume the *liability* for the consequences of behavior and choices. Self-discipline, planning, and responsibility hinge on this principle.[61]

These five factors must be kept in relative balance—not too much or too little of any one of them—if child development is to proceed optimally. The factors, like concentric circles, must gradually expand toward increased individual responsibility until, in early adulthood, there is a common perimeter. Disruptions in parent–child communication can often be diagnosed by identifying which of these factors is not in proper proportion to a child's particular level of development. When the individual bears all liability, has optimal liberty, imposes an environment for self-learning, sets limits

CHILDREN LEARN WHAT THEY LIVE

If a child lives with criticism, He learns to condemn.
If a child lives with hostility, He learns to fight.
If a child lives with ridicule, He learns to be shy.
If a child lives with shame, He learns to feel guilty.
If a child lives with tolerance, He learns to be patient.
If a child lives with encouragement, He learns confidence.
If a child lives with praise, He learns to appreciate.
If a child lives with fairness, He learns justice.
If a child lives with security, He learns to have faith.
If a child lives with approval, He learns to like himself.
If a child lives with acceptance and friendship,
He learns to find love in the world.

FIGURE 16–4.
"Children Learn What They Live." (Courtesy of Dorothy Law Nolte and Ross Laboratories.)

for the self, and is capable of unselfish, reciprocal love, that individual is ready to begin an independent life, establish a home, build a marriage, and guide the next generation.[21]

Self-discipline continues to develop and strengthen over a lifetime as the individual considers alternatives, establishes goals, commits the self to action, delays immediate gratification, and considers the effects of behavior on others besides the self.

Disciplinary Practices and Parameters

Discipline has different meanings. To some, it means guiding children to self-actualization and self-discipline; to others, it means harsh, punitive control of another person's behavior. In the context of this discussion, **discipline** includes all the approaches used to teach children acceptable societal behavior patterns and prepare them for successful adulthood. Discipline should be a conscious and continuous effort to assist children to develop their capacities and potentials.

Research has shown some correlation between the patterns of discipline used by the family and the development of personality patterns in children.[6, 57, 58, 63]

PARAMETERS. Parental behaviors and disciplinary practices can be described using the axes of empathy, authority, and emotionality.

Empathy: Love Versus Hostility. Loving parents see life through their children's eyes. The ability to empathize enables the parent to accept uniqueness, respect freedoms and rights, affirm intrinsic worth, teach rules, and provide frequent, positive rewards. Parents characterized as hostile are unable to empathize. They see only their own, adult-centered views and goals. They tend to use physical punishment or other harsh restraints, coupled with anger and rejecting attitudes.

Authority: Autonomy Versus Control. Indulgent, lenient parents allow the children to usurp authority and allow developmentally premature children the freedom to make decisions. Few demands are made on the children and personal expectations are imposed only when the children appear to be unable to cope successfully or safely with specific environmental demands. More structured parents impose expectations on the children. Some parents do so to help the child focus needs and development toward self-direction and self-actualization, others to meet the needs, convenience, or comfort of the parents. Most parents increase freedom as children gain the required skills.

Parents on the autonomy end of the axis are generally more tolerant and accepting of young children's behaviors, such as sexual exploration, immodesty, a noisy atmosphere, and verbal and physical aggression toward others. Controlling, restrictive parents will be much less tolerant and may structure their expectations for their children to be more consistent with adult behaviors. Some may find it difficult to release that control to the child as he or she matures.

Emotionality: Anxious-Involved Versus Calm-Detached. Parents invest differing degrees of emotionality in the career of rearing children. One set of parents may allow their children a high degree of autonomy and freedom, but they do so in a calm and detached manner. Another set of parents may allow the same degree of freedom, but with an attitude of anxiety and emotional involvement. This difference in emotional tone will color interactions and the child's response. When all the factors are considered in their possible combinations, several potential outcomes of these variables can be plotted on the model shown in Figure 16-6.

EFFECTS ON PERSONALITY DEVELOPMENT. The various combinations of parental disciplinary practices used in rearing children have differing short-term and long-term effects on the children's personality development.

Hostile-Controlling (Quadrant A of Figure 16–6). Parents with restrictive-rejecting attitudes toward child discipline tend to be autocratic and dictatorial or demanding and antagonistic. These parents are classic examples of all that child-rearing experts deplore. Because they view the child as a possession or an extension of themselves, they exercise rigid control and impose arbitrary rules on their children. Punishment, rather than teaching, is used to shape the child's behavior. Because these parents are adult-centered, they cannot empathize with the problems the child faces or see issues from the child's point of view. The difference between the autocratic and the demanding parent is the degree of emotional involvement. Autocratic, dictatorial parents tend to be detached from the child's emotional needs and responses.

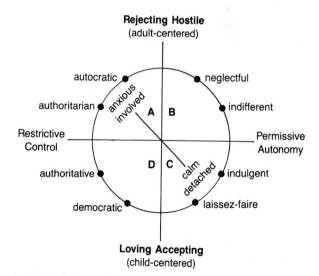

FIGURE 16–6.
Parental approaches to child discipline are outlined in this hypothetical three-dimensional model of parent behaviors and attitudes toward the child (emotionality is the arm of the third dimension).

Children tend to see these parents as cruel and uncaring. As a result, they feel left without a support system and are forced to meet their own emotional needs before they are emotionally mature enough to do so. These children tend to be more neurotic than other children.[38, 57, 58] Children tend to become aggressive, rivalrous, and unaffectionate toward siblings. Since they cannot express their hostility openly toward the parent, they tend to repress and internalize the parental attitude toward themselves and feel a strong need to punish themselves for minor misdeeds, have more suicidal tendencies, and are more accident-prone than other children. They are also more introverted, more socially inept and unresponsive, less motivated, shyer, and more immature than other children.[6, 36]

These individuals frequently do not move beyond Kohlberg's second stage of moral development. As young children, they conform to parental demands as long as they expect to get caught and punished for their misbehavior. As adolescents, they conform to peer group pressures. When the situation is free of pressure to conform, or they think they will not get caught, they disregard the rules.[55] Many of these children become delinquent as they act out anger toward parents on society.[36, 48] Others may be very obedient and exemplary citizens until leaving for college, where they may become involved in an activity (e.g., shoplifting or cheating) which is atypical of his or her lifestyle at home. Why? In the past this person has merely conformed to parental and peer pressure without internalizing the underlying values or developing a self-discipline system. Some adolescents and adults transfer their fear of parental retribution to a fear of God's punishment, continuing to conform to external religious rules throughout life.

Some people internalize the autocratic parent as a part of their personality. They may become strict, legalistic adults who strongly enforce rules regardless of appropriateness or effect on another's physical or psychological well-being. The authoritarian parent may consider the child's needs, but still find it difficult to allow the child to make independent decisions, even at the appropriate age.

Hostile-Permissive (Quadrant B). The permissive-rejecting parent tends to be neglectful or indifferent depending on the degree of parental self-centeredness. These parents tend to be minimally involved in guiding their child's development. Periodically, the child will do something that irritates or interferes with the parent's wishes and, without warning, the parent will impulsively administer some form of punishment. The unpredictability of such restrictions on the child's behavior interferes with learning social rules. The child sees the parents as self-centered and uncaring. Children reared in this environment are confused about their own intrinsic worth as a result of this lack of love and structure; they equate such detachment with their own worthlessness and inadequacy. They have a poor self-concept, and are hostile or rejecting toward their parents.[9] They are also more likely to be impulsive, aggressive, unaffectionate toward their siblings and other persons.[6, 28] The lack of love and predictability

forms a very unstable environment which may lead to mental illness later in life.[10] They may seek affiliation and approval of peers to provide some stability. They may find it difficult to move beyond Kohlberg's stage 3 of moral development.

Loving-Permissive (Quadrant C). Parents who are accepting and permissive are regarded by some psychologists as the "ideal" parents. They bathe children in love, allowing them freedom to take initiative, to make choices, and to be themselves, even when behaviors appear to be undesirable by adult standards. Positive reinforcement rather than punishment is used to shape the child's behavior. Some do not try to shape the child's behavior at all, looking for Rousseau's "noble savage" to emerge triumphant from the throes of childhood. Some parents "go overboard" with this approach, indulging the child's every whim, ignoring behaviors that infringe on the rights of others, and smiling at indiscretions. The child is treated as if he or she is able to reason, to identify behavioral options, and use self-discipline on an adult level even during toddler and preschool years. The parents want the child to see them as loving, supportive parents and to remember their childhood as a happy, utopian period of life. However, *overindulged children have too much responsibility placed on them for limit-setting and decision-making.* Without adult guidelines to provide challenges, they may not strive toward more socially mature and allocentric behaviors. They may emerge from the childhood years as lazy, undisciplined, egocentric, and self-serving persons, expecting the rest of the world to cater to their whims as their parents did. They may experience great difficulty developing sensitivity to the needs of others. As they look back on childhood, they may view their parents as "wimps" rather than friends since the parents never helped make decisions, but always went along with what the child wanted. As adults, these persons are more likely to behave on the basis of their feelings, rather than cognitive self-direction. They generally become highly sociable, highly motivated individuals and may attain Kohlberg's stage 5 of moral development.

As the loving parent moves closer to the middle of the permissive-controlling axes, he or she assumes more responsibility for guiding the child toward socially approved behaviors and in helping the child to become aware of the needs of others. However, the child may still be given as much permission as the parents to express ideas and will, and to make decisions (regardless of age). Outsiders may see such children as disrespectful toward adults, dominating and aggressive toward peers, and at times, disobedient at home. As adults, these persons are more likely to be successful than the overindulged child.

Loving-Controlling (Quadrant D). These parents may have an attitude of possessiveness, as the parent in quadrant A, but focus on the **child's** needs and development rather than their own perspective. Parents in this quadrant consciously seek to understand the child's view and do not impose authority because of their inherent rights as parents to do so.

Overly protective parents are more anxious and emotionally involved with their children. They impose strict controls because they want to shield their children from the harsh realities of life. The effect of inappropriate restrictiveness varies with the age of the child.[36] Early overrestrictiveness (before 3 years) produces dependence and immaturity, whereas in older children (4 to 10 years) it results in hostility and aggressiveness toward the parents, especially the mother. They resent the controls and the smothering, solicitous attitudes of their parents. They may not become autonomous, self-actualized individuals because they were denied the opportunities to set their own goals, to solve their own problems, and to experience the success or the failure of their own decisions.

Most parents vary the degree of restrictiveness with the developmental age of the child, using authoritative approaches (providing rules and guidance) when the child is young, and more democratic approaches as the child matures and is able to become involved in establishing goals, identifying alternatives, and making choices. As the children mature, freedom is increased, and rules are established by cooperation and the consent of family members. Such parents tend to have children who adopt socially desirable adult roles,[45] and who are responsible, considerate, extroverted, active, autonomous, creative, and happy.[6, 11, 39, 47, 63] They earn higher grades during adolescence regardless of gender, age, parental education, ethnic affiliation or family structure,[13] have a positive self-concept,[9] and are highly motivated, self-actualizing, and self-directing individuals. Thus, loving-controlling parents actually are the most ideal parents because they provide sufficient challenges and guidance to encourage growth, as well as sufficient room for initiative and self-direction. In all families, whether single-parent, co-parent, step-parent, or foster-parent, those children raised by authoritative parents have the fewest behavior problems and the greatest appreciation for the rights of others.[11, 28, 39] The principles of the five Ls are

activated. Children tend to see these parents as caring, understanding, supportive, wise friends. Because they are challenged to think through their options and feelings and to consider the needs of others as well as their own, they are more likely to be able to achieve Kohlberg's higher stages of moral development (Fig. 16-7).

Rules are the medium connecting children with their social environment. They aid the child in developing appropriate responses to situations involving moral decisions.[52] If the parents provide warmth and caring, and are both highly supportive and controlling, they tend to have children whose values are similar to their own. Permissive parents (high in support, low in control) and authoritarian parents (high in control, low in support) tend to have children with values different from their own.[8]

Process of Discipline

Parents with a healthy, positive self-concept feel more confident in their parental role. They are more likely to perceive their children as unique individuals who are partners in the teaching–learning enterprise of family living. Parents with a poor self-concept tend to be afraid of their own children's judgment and thus provide minimal guidance, or view their children as extensions of themselves and try to force their children to achieve their own previously unfulfilled goals rather than allowing the children to strive for goals of their own choosing. By imposing their own goals on their children, parents generate hostility and friction.

Parents tend to duplicate the disciplinary patterns they experienced from their own parents. To the extent that parental discipline affects personality development, discipline approaches becomes self-perpetuating. If the model was harsh and punitive, it is likely to be imitated.[5] Since spanking frequently involves more emotion and less reason on the part of

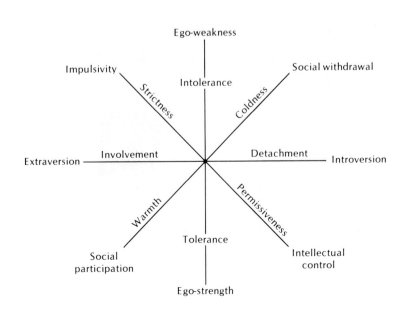

FIGURE 16–7.
Relationship between personality and perceived parental behavior. (Slater, P. E. (1962). Parental behavior and personality of the child. Journal of Genetic Psychology *101:65.)*

parents than other types of discipline, it is easily perpetuated in succeeding generations. Many parents who batter their children were themselves the victims of abuse as children.

Discipline is meted out by parents and other adults to direct a child's behavior in a desired direction. Some adults exert discipline to make life easier for themselves. Others view discipline as the way adults help children to prepare for their own adulthood.

POSITIVE PRACTICES. Positive discipline approaches are based on the principles of behavior management. The adult concentrates on teaching and rewarding acceptable, mature behaviors. A behavior-management program must identify goals and the contingencies before implementation.

First, the parents must decide and agree on the type of behavior they want their children to learn or which behaviors they want to change. They then discuss the behavior with the children and agree on the expectations and rewards to be given for successful accomplishment of a specific task. A chart of the desired behavior and progress toward reaching it may be kept. Older children find that self-monitoring and recording of successes provide motivation for them to maintain the desired behavior. Obviously, parental expectations must be compatible with the developmental level of the child.

Rewards must be chosen carefully; they are effective only when they are meaningful to the child. Rewards may be either unexpected or contracted. Parents can use television viewing, allowing an overnight guest, adding a new pet, spending private time with the parent, or even doing a chore together as rewards. Sometimes, tokens may be earned and saved toward a specific reinforcer. In any case, the parents must have total control of the consequences. The children must not be able to circumvent the requirements and still receive the reward; otherwise, the behavior management system breaks down and the children learn how to manage the system rather than their own behavior.

Extrinsic rewards cannot replace social rewards. Children want to be loved and appreciated by their parents and other adults; compliments and verbal approval are essential to self-esteem. Statements such as, "I'm glad you remembered," or "I appreciate your help with the dishes," help maintain motivation toward more mature behavior. If adults have set a contingency, then they must follow through. If the child is given a choice, then the adults *must* allow the child to live with the consequences of that choice. Adults must be careful to keep their end of a bargain when children have fulfilled theirs. Once the reward has been promised it must be given. To be trusted as a parent by an adolescent, one must have built a foundation of trust throughout the child's earlier years.

When children are treated with respect, and not as objects to be manipulated by adult power, they become inner-directed persons. They learn that they are involved in what happens to them and gradually assume the responsibility for their own behavior; this is the best preparation for any "Just Say No!" program. They also learn to respect the individuality,

rights, and freedoms of other children and adults. In short, positive methods of behavior-shaping help children to attain the goal of discipline: self-discipline (Fig. 16-8).

PUNITIVE MEASURES. Unfortunately, too many parents equate discipline with punishment. Punishment may take either of two forms. The parent may actively inflict pain on the child by spanking, or the parent may withhold a positive reward or temporarily curtail the child's freedom because of the misbehavior. Of the two forms, the second is the most desirable and effective. If the child disobeys by going outside after being told to stay in, the parent may require the child to sit on a chair for a brief period of time. (Rule of thumb: *Do not impose more than one minute of "time out" for each year of the child's age.*)

Inappropriate use of spanking is an ineffective way of redirecting a child's behavior. The child may obey only as long as the parent is present to observe and to enforce the rule (compliance). Should the child think a behavior will not be noticed, the child will disregard the parental admonition (Kohlberg, stage 1). When children are given inadequate positive attention, they may purposefully disobey rules or pester a parent, even though it results in corporal punishment. The spanking is perceived as better than no attention or physical touching at all!

A serious consequence of spanking is the possibility of

DENNIS the MENACE

"AM I HAVIN' A UNHAPPY CHILDHOOD?"

FIGURE 16–8.

Reprinted courtesy of Dennis the Menace. *Copyright Field Newspaper Syndicate. T.M.®*

escalating its severity. When adults give vent to strong emotions, the level of anger may increase uncontrollably. As a result, the child may suffer injuries or even death. Teaching, reasoning, and loss of privileges are more effective, especially for children over 6 years. Adequate positive attention and redirection have positive long-term effects while avoiding the need for punitive approaches.

COUNTERPRODUCTIVE MEASURES. Whenever parents or caregivers fail to carry through with the threatened consequences of disobedience, make unreasonable demands on children, or use punitive measures too harshly or too frequently, the disciplinary measures become counterproductive to developing self-discipline. Conformity (compliance) and passivity, or rebellion and self-assertiveness (aggression) may become the dominant behavioral patterns. In adulthood, the person may become antisocial. Cooperation, not compliance, should be the goal of parent–child interactions. Table 16-2 offers some basic principles of discipline.

Style of Parental Intervention

The style of parental intervention also has a vital bearing on the process of moral development.[29] **Power-assertion,** including physical punishment, deprivation of material objects or privileges, direct application of force, or the threat of any of these, is the parental effort to control the child through superior adult strength and resources. The child fears injury. In **love-withdrawal,** the parent expresses anger or disapproval by ignoring the child, refusing to speak to him, turning his back on him, verbalizing a dislike for the child, isolating, or threatening to leave the child. Such behavior sensitizes the conscience, producing conformity without communication. The child fears abandonment.

The method of **induction** includes techniques in which the parent gives explanations or reasons for the child to change his behavior. This method enlists the child's own inner abilities to accept responsibility for causing distress when provided in a nonthreatening environment.

The story of a boy named John and his experience with a frog offers an excellent example. When he was 6½ years old, John came across the road from a friend's house, excitedly holding a cottage cheese carton with a frog in it. "Isn't this a neat frog, Dad?" he asked. Dad affirmed that it was one of the "neater" frogs he had ever seen, and they were still examining it when Jan, John's sister, who was almost a year older said, "Daddy, John's friend Danny is crying!" When Dad inquired as to the reason for his unhappiness, she said, "Because John took his frog." Dad's first impulse was to pronounce to John, in loud and self-righteous tones: "Son, take this frog back to Danny, immediately!" *(power-assertion)*. Dad's next impulse was just to forget it, since it was no big thing *(noninterventive permissiveness)*. Dad was also tempted to treat John coldly *(love-withdrawal)* in the hope that he would see how he was hurting Danny. Somewhere in there, at a deep level, Dad's religious training and his own moral authority begged him to hit the kid *(extreme power-assertion mixed with frustration)*, either physically, or even better, with the accusation that "God doesn't love a thief!" *(appeal to higher authority plus power-assertion plus frustration plus moral superiority feelings)*. But Dad's professionally trained mind finally overcame all the stored memories of childhood mismanagement, and he determined to use *facets of induction* to deal with the problem. Dad asked John *(enlisting the aid of the child)* what he based his claim to ownership on. "Well, I got it, don't I?" Then Dad asked enough questions *(fact-finding)* to determine that (1) the cottage cheese carton belonged to Danny's mother—one for Danny; (2) the frog was first seen in Danny's yard—one more for Danny; (3) Danny saw it first—another one for Danny; (4) John picked it up—finally, one for his side; and (5) possession remained with John—a questionable call, since he

TABLE 16-2. BASIC PRINCIPLES OF DISCIPLINE

Principle	*Description*
Consistency	Rules are applied as uniformly as possible
Follow-through	Reasonable consequences are carried out; no escape for the child
Pacing	Expectations are consistently based on justice and freedoms, but adapted to the child's developmental level
Modeling	Adults and parents monitor their own behavior so children learn approved behavior by imitating and identifying with them
Immediate feedback	Consequences of behavior are felt as soon as possible after it occurs, or just before it takes place
Truthfulness	Parents are truthful about their reasons for their expectations
Trust	Adults verbally express trust and act trustingly toward their children until such trust is broken by the children
Logical outcomes	Consequences of behavior are logical results of the behavior
Self-disclosure	Parents are not afraid to disclose their own feelings and mistakes to children
Genuine love	The key to all effective discipline is genuine love

was older, stronger, and faster. Next, Dad asked John if he would want the results reversed if the facts were reversed *(role reversal)*; that is, would he have wanted Danny to take the frog to his house if it had been found in his yard. He answered quickly, "No way!"

Endeavoring to *secure empathy,* Dad talked to him about Danny's hurt feelings, but that did not seem to make much of an impression. An effort to *place responsibility* by asking "Who is responsible for Danny's hurt?" received only a noncommittal, "Man, how should I know?" Only two things were left to do at this point, *value education* and *extending autonomy.* Dad endeavored to accomplish the first by saying something like this: "John, your Dad has lived six times as long as you have, and there's one thing I've noticed in my lifetime. It's simply this: It has always been easier to find frogs than it is to make friends." The second objective was attempted by this verbalization: "Now, John, it's time to decide what to do about that frog and that friend. It will be completely your decision. I will never question you about what you do about it, or why you do it. There will be no punishment, no matter what you do. You will also, however, be totally responsible for the results of both your decision and your action. The consequences will be yours to live with. It's decision time! Which is more important—the frog or the friend?" Dad stood up and went into the house, and to this day, 20 years later, neither Dad nor John has mentioned that frog to the other. His sister has a tattletale spirit, though, so it was less than 10 minutes before she came and told Dad that John took the frog and gave it to Danny. Dad still believes that the moral development resulting from the "episode of the frog" was well worth the time and effort.

Conflict Between Conscious and Unconscious Motivation

A common human experience is to realize that one prizes one value more than another at a conscious, verbal level, but fails to activate it when placed in the crisis of choice. In fact, the prized value may have minimal impact on one's actual behavior under the pressure of the circumstances.[49] Knowing and verbalizing rules and expectations does not ensure that action will be consistent with the stated awareness. Moral feelings are often set aside in the heat of conflict.[32, 51]

Why does a person do the thing he should not do? Why does he leave undone the things he should do? Why does the "best me" lose so often in the battle of values? Obviously, there is a deep effort on the part of such individuals to satisfy other primary, unconscious motives whose existence is too ego-painful to allow into conscious thought. The tragedy of "unconscious valuing" is that it is often extremely counterproductive to the best interests of the individual. Freud's theory seems to be borne out by observing the seemingly self-destructive behavior exhibited by many persons whose consciously verbalized motivation is at variance with their actions.

To be human is to make moral choices. Therefore, education must be grounded in morality. It need not teach a narrow, prescriptive value set; however, it must work at promoting the belief that "part (perhaps the essence) of our humanity is being a morally conscious being,"[50] and to willingly accept some restraints from this perspective. Because of the concern for separation of church and state, public schools traditionally have assumed a stance of neutrality regarding the promotion of morals and values, thus creating a vacuum for dealing with serious moral and social issues.[53]

Religious doctrine and value education are not synonymous. The purpose of value education and clarification is to give people an opportunity to talk about hypothetical real-life situations in a way that enables them to become consciously aware of ethical conflicts, to sensitize them to cultural and peer group needs, ideas, and expectations, to facilitate identity homework, to explore issues that affect attitudes in decision making, and to develop greater ability to exercise autonomy and initiative in implementing value choices.

Many public schools are reviewing their position on teaching of values, and some are now mandating instruction in "manners and morals" (e.g., California Education Code, Section 44806).[7] Two key issues remain, however: how to teach values and which values to address. Moral educators often choose to concentrate on strengthening the will, because willpower involves stamina and endurance. A strong will does not guarantee a moral life; however, a weak will can severely limit moral conduct. Willpower (or "won't-power," as one child called it) helps overcome difficult times, but its real test comes when we face our routine, somewhat bland, moral decisions and continue to choose the moral path.[4]

A child without "won't-power" is unable to follow through with the "Just say No!" programs (Fig. 16-9). The greater the internalization of moral principles, the greater the field independence and the higher the stage of moral development. This translates into greater moral courage.

FIGURE 16–9.
Support from adults and approval by peers help young people to commit themselves to a value system or personal goal. However, unless they have high self-esteem and have developed good self-discipline strategies, they may still succumb under pressure of the moment.

Moral Development During Adult Years

Political orientation, socioeconomic class, and section of the country all bring subtle but real social-cognitive pressures to bear on the continuing process of moral development in the adult. There is an overlapping of social context and moral reasoning.[14, 65] One's value system continues to evolve over a lifetime in dynamic interaction with the circumstances and crises one faces. Life's situations—positive, neutral, or negative—have a way of modifying both attitudes and actions. As one senior adult says, however, "the only problem with this kind of learning is that the test always comes before the lesson."

IMPLICATIONS

Moral development peaks as the individual consciously works on the refinement of values and identity through the process of identity homework (see Chap. 25). Environmental circumstances and opportunities as well as religious experiences can also challenge the person toward higher levels of moral functioning. Human beings are "built with moral hardware already installed, but it can be activated only to the moral reasoning level necessary to support the complexity of the ethical dilemmas that present themselves in the prevailing culture."[34]

Cross-cultural studies reveal (1) that there are striking differences between urban and folk cultures on progression among the stages and the upper limits reached, (2) that moral reasoning is motivated by self-interest, (3) that there are no gender differences, and (4) that *the first four Kohlbergian stages are culturally universal.*[64, 66] However, Kohlberg's higher stages are not necessarily reflected in collective moral responsibility or principles of communal well-being.

The need for the ability to direct one's behavior is a lifetime need. The foundations for this ability are laid in childhood, but profoundly affect the person through adolescence and adulthood. Some attention needs to be given to this aspect of self-direction.

Childhood

Moral development and conscience are profoundly affected by childhood experiences and the impact of parents, teachers, and other significant adults. Adults can maximize their positive impact by facilitating the development of the basic skills essential to self-direction. Adults are encouraged to talk to their children about real moral dilemmas rather than hypothetical ones, especially those dilemmas facing the parents, friends, or peers that can help children to perceive how a behavior can hurt another individual.[31] To the extent that empathetic encounters are used, children will be assisted in internalizing their own codes for appropriate behavior. Parents should confront children for failing to act morally in a specific situation, but in order to help them understand the dynamics of the situation, not to humiliate them.

Should the cashier at the supermarket give the parents 50 cents too much in change, the adult sets a good example when he or she takes it back and discusses the reasons for doing so with the child. An adult who goes through a stop sign can discuss intentional versus accidental actions and the reality of living with the consequences regardless of the cause. A child who sees the human frailties of parents will be better able to understand and to accept his or her own shortcomings. Hoffman points out that parents can enhance moral development and self-discipline by showing empathy to their children when they fail.[31]

Parents can also assist children to develop self-direction and communal responsibility by assigning specific tasks to them.[60] The major way in which the parents foster mastery of Erikson's task of industry is by gradually increasing children's responsibilities. They can be responsible for setting the table before meals, picking up the clutter in their rooms, feeding the pets, or mowing the lawn. Assigned chores contribute to the sense of well-being of children by helping them to feel like important, contributing members of their family system. The mastery of relatively simple tasks lays the foundation for mastery of the more complex tasks and the responsibilities to be assumed during the adolescent and adult years. Parents rob children of essential opportunities to learn concern for the welfare of others, responsibility, perseverance, and self-discipline when they absorb all the household tasks or are too lenient in standards of task performance. Families, irrespective of socioeconomic level, can provide children with these opportunities (Fig. 16-10).

Adolescence

The transition from childhood to adolescence increases the need for self-direction. As teenagers move from the close scrutiny of their behavior by their parents, they assume more responsibility for their own choices and behaviors. Individuals who have not learned obedience (cooperation for the benefit of self and others) to external sources of guidance during the earlier years, will find it increasingly difficult to develop a moral value system that considers the needs of others or to discipline the self when immediate gratification of desires is pleasant but the long-range effects of the behavior are potentially harmful (e.g., adolescent sexuality, drugs, alcohol, delinquency, reckless driving, overeating). The "Just Say No!" campaign must begin with the child's confidence that the parents and society seek the person's best welfare, an ability to delay gratification, and a realization that the self—not peers—must live with the consequences of a behavior. To the degree that children escape bearing the brunt of the consequences of their choices, they fail to learn self-discipline.[61]

Adolescents need to decide what value system they will internalize. Will they accept as their own the system modeled and taught by their parents, will they adopt that of another person or the church, or will they uniquely forge their own? Whichever the choice, adolescents need the skill to see the alternatives and to weigh the possible outcomes of each.

FIGURE 16–10.
Moral behaviors are learned through association with community programs such as scouting, as well as through church, school, and family.

Some young people go through a period of trying out other lifestyles, such as joining a cult or becoming a "street person." Their behavior can be an exercise in trying to decide for themselves how they want to express their lives. Unfortunately, these and some other options (e.g., drugs) can preclude clear evaluation of the effects.

Adulthood

The ultimate test of self-direction is faced in adulthood when individuals achieve relative independence and freedom. They make choices and commitments to marriage partners, careers, jobs, and families. If individuals have achieved satisfactory development of the conscience and ego-ideal, and have acquired the skills of self-monitoring and self-instruction along with a healthy self-concept, they will be able to assume and fulfill their commitments and responsibilities with little outside coercion. These individuals will reinforce self-direction as they realize the inner satisfaction and peace that self-direction brings to them.

The person that "goes beyond" existence to a fulfilled life must grapple with the problem of evil and sin. There must be a willingness to seek answers and solutions, rather than "doing the ostrich imitation." The person who "goes beyond" will develop a masterful interaction and interweaving of four major components of moral development:

1. Moral sensitivity—the ability to interpret a situation and its effect on people.
2. Moral judgment—the ability to make a decision about which course of action is morally right (just, good, fair).
3. Moral prioritization—the ability to compare and place values in hierarchical relationships (distinguishing among good, better, and best).
4. Moral courage—the ability and willingness to execute chosen values regardless of the opinion of others. This must of necessity involve commitment, perseverance, and ego strength.

The person who "goes beyond" will be able to talk to others, to cry with others, to get and give hugs, to encourage those who are discouraged, to comfort those who are uncomfortable, to give hope to those who have none.[18] The person who "goes beyond" will learn, through pain, that every crisis can arouse within us a fresh awareness of the transcendent source of and goal for every human life, and that precisely in the trauma which every crisis brings, we are given the opportunity to reassess the principles by which we have lived, in order to proceed in the direction of a more encompassing and adequate set of values, and a deeper faith.[32]

The survival of the human species depends on our willingness and ability to become "good neighbors" for those around us, and in our world. This may be the highest expression of our humanness.

REFERENCES

1. Archer, S. L., & Waterman, A. S. (1988). Psychological individualization: Gender difference or gender neutrality? *Human Development, 31*(2), 65–81.
2. Aronfreed, J. (1968). *Conduct and conscience.* New York: Academic.
3. Aronfreed, J. (1969). The concept of internalization. In D. A. Goslin (Ed.), *Handbook of socialization theory and research.* Chicago: Rand McNally.
4. Atherton, J. M. (1989). One-legged arguments: Virtue advocates debate claims of indoctrination. *Educational Horizons, 67*(3), 55–57.
5. Bandura, A. M. (1973). The role of the modeling processes in personality development. In A. M. Snadowsky (Ed.), *Child and adolescent development.* New York: Free Press.
6. Becker, W. C. (1964). Consequences of different kinds of parental discipline. In M. L. Hoffman & L. W. Hoffman (Eds.), *Review of child development research* (Vol. 1). New York: Russell Sage Foundation.
7. Berger, P. (1989). Reforging the historic intellectual-moral connection. *Educational Horizons, 67*(3), 59–61.
8. Clark, C. A., Worthington, E. L., Jr., & Danser, D. B. (1988). The

transmission of religious beliefs and practice from parents to firstborn early adolescent sons. *Journal of Marriage and Family, 50*(2), 463.

9. Coopersmith, S. (1981). *The antecedents of self-esteem.* Palo Alto, CA: Consulting Psychologists Press.

10. Cox, A. D. (1988). Maternal depression and impact on children's development. *Archives of Disease in Childhood, 63,* 90–95.

11. Curran, D. D. (1985). *Stress and the healthy family.* Minneapolis: Winston Press.

12. Damon, W. (1988). *The moral child.* New York: Free Press.

13. Dornbusch, S.M., Ritter, P. L., Leiderman, P. H., Roberts, D. F., & Fraleigh, M. J. (1987). The relation of parenting style to adolescent preschool performance. *Child Development, 58,* 1244–1257.

14. Emler, N., Renuvisk, S., & Malone, B. (1983). The relationship between moral reasoning and political orientation. *Journal of Personality and Social Psychology, 45,* 1073–1080.

15. Erikson, E. H. (1962). *Young man Luther: A study in psychoanalysis and history.* New York: Norton.

16. Erikson, E. H. (1968). *Identity: Youth and crisis.* New York: Norton.

17. Fernald, L. D., & Fernald, P. S. (1985). *Basic psychology* (5th ed.). Dubuque, IA: W. C. Brown.

18. Ferszt, G. G., & Taylor, P. B. (1988). When your patient needs spiritual comfort. *Nursing 88, 18*(4), 48–49.

19. Freud, S. (1933). *New introductory lectures on psycho-analysis* (J. Strachey, Trans.). New York: Norton.

20. Freud, S. (1938). *The basic writings of Sigmund Freud* (Brill, A. A., Ed. & Trans.). New York: Random House.

21. Garsee, J. W. (1977). *Unpublished material.*

22. Gibbs, J. C., Arnold, K. D., & Burkhart, J. E. (1984). Sex differences in the expression of moral judgment. *Child Development, 55*(3), 1040–1043.

23. Gibbs, J.C., Clark, P. M., Joseph, J. A., Green, J. L., Goodrick, T. S., & Makowski, D. G. (1986). Relations between moral judgment, moral courage, and field independence. *Child Development, 57,* 185–193.

24. Gilligan, C. (1984). *In a different voice.* Cambridge, MA: Harvard University Press.

25. Gilligan, C. (1987). Remapping the moral domain. In T. C. Keller, et al, (Ed.), *Reconstructing individualism: Autonomy, individuality, and the self in Western thought.* Stanford, CA: Stanford University Press.

26. Gordon, T. (1975). *Parent effectiveness training.* New York: New American Library.

27. Hall, R. T., & Davis, J. V. (1975). *Moral education in theory and practice.* Buffalo, NY: Prometheus.

28. Heatherington, E. M. (1988). Parents, children and siblings: six years after divorce. In R. A. Hinde & J. Stevenson-Hinde (Eds.), *Relationships within families: Mutual influences* (pp. 311–331). New York: Oxford University Press.

29. Hoffman, M. L. (1970). Moral development. In P. H. Mussen (Ed.), *Carmichael's manual of child psychology* (3rd ed., Vol. 2). New York: Wiley.

30. Hoffman, M. L. (1976). Empathy, role-taking, guilt and development of altruistic motives. In T. Lockonona (Eds.), *Moral development and behavior.* New York: Holt, Rinehart & Winston.

31. Hoffman, M. L. (1984). Interaction of affect and cognition in empathy. In C. E. Izard, Kagan, J., & Zajone, R. B. (Eds.), *Emotions, cognition, and behavior.* Cambridge, UK: Cambridge University Press.

32. Johnson, D. F., & Goldman, S. R. (1987). Children's recognition and use of rules of moral conduct in stories. *American Journal of Psychology, 100*(2), 205–224.

33. Jourard, S. M. (1967). *Personal adjustment* (2nd ed.). New York: Macmillan.

34. Joy, D. M. (1988). *Parents, kids, and sexual integrity.* Waco, TX: Word.

35. Kagan, J. (1970). The concept of identification. In P. H. Mussen, Conger, J. J., & Kagan, J. (Eds.), *Readings in child development and personality* (2nd ed.). New York: Harper & Row.

36. Kagan, J., & Lamb, S. (1987). *The emergence of morality in young children.* Chicago: University of Chicago Press.

37. Katz, L. G. (1982). Beginner's ethics. *Parents Magazine, 57*(9), 94.

38. Kessler, J. W. (1988). *Psychopathology of childhood* (2nd ed.). Englewood Cliffs: Prentice-Hall.

39. Kimball, G. (1988). *50-50 parenting: Sharing family rewards and responsibilities.* Lexington, MA: Lexington Books.

40. Kohlberg, L. (1963). The development of children's orientations toward a moral order: I. Sequence in the development of moral thought. *Vita Humana, 6,* 11.

41. Kohlberg, L. (1964). Development of moral character and moral ideology. In M. L. Hoffman & L. W. Hoffman (Eds.), *Review of child development research* (Vol. 1, p. 383). New York: Russell Sage Foundation.

42. Kohlberg, L. (1981). *The philosophy of moral development.* San Francisco: Harper & Row.

43. Kohlberg, L., & Gilligan, C. (Fall, 1971). Daedalus. *Daedalus, 100,* 1072.

44. Krendl, K. A., Lasky, K., & Dawson, R. (1989). How television affects adolescents: Their own perceptions. *Educational Horizons, 67*(3), 88–91.

45. Lever, J. (1978). Sex differences in the complexity of children's play and games. *American Sociological Review, 43,* 471–83.

46. Levine, C., Kohlberg, L., & Hewer, A. (1985). The current formulation of Kohlberg's theory and a response to critics. *Human Development, 28*(2), 94–100.

47. McCord, W., McCord, J., & Howard, A. (1961). Familial correlates of aggression in non-delinquent male children. *Journal of Abnormal Social Psychology, 62,* 72.

48. Meyers, C. E. (Ed.). (1944). The effects of conflicting authority on the child. University of Iowa study. *Child Welfare, 409.*

49. Milgram, S. (1974). *Obedience to authority: an experimental view.* New York: Harper & Row.

50. Murray, J. P. (1989). Toward a philosophy of education. *Educational Horizons, 67*(3), 75.

51. Nunner-Winkler, G., & Sodian, B. (1988). Children's understanding of moral emotions. *Child Development, 59*(5), 1323–1338.

52. Onuf, N. G. (1987). Rules in moral development. *Human Development, 30*(5), 257–267.

53. Ornstein, A. C. (1989). The growing nonpublic school movement. *Educational Horizons, 67*(3), 71–74.

54. Peck, R. F., & Hauighurst, R. J. (1960). *The psychology of character development.* New York: Wiley.

55. Piaget, J. P. (1965). *The moral judgment of the child.* New York: Free Press.

56. Pratt, M. W., et al. (1988). Sex differences in adult moral orientations. *Journal of Psychology, 56*(2), 373–391.

57. Rosenthal, J. E., et al. (1959). A study of mother-child relationships in the emotional disorders of children. *Genetic Psychology Monograph, 60,* 65.

58. Rosenthal, J. E., et al. (1962). Father-child relationships and children's problems. *Archives of General Psychiatry, 7,* 360.

59. Schafer, R. (1968). *Aspects of internalization.* New York: International University Press.

60. Schell, R. E. (1983). *Developmental psychology today* (4th ed.). New York: Random House.

61. Schuster, C. S. (in press). Just say "No!". *Christian Parenting Today.*

62. Skolnick, A. (1978). The myth of the vulnerable child. *Psychology Today, 11*(9), 56.

63. Slater, P. E. (1962). Parental behavior and the personality of the child. *Journal of Genetic Psychology, 101,* 53.

64. Snarey, J. (1987). A question of morality (Research on the universality of moral development). *Psychology Today, 21,* 6–7.

65. Sparks, P., & Durkin, K. (1987). Moral reasoning and political orientation: The context sensitivity of individual rights and democratic principles. *Journal of Personality and Social Psychology, 52*(5), 931–936.

66. Vasuden, J., & Hummel, R. C. (1987). Moral stage sequence and principled reasoning in an Indian sample. *Human Development, 30*(2), 105–118.

67. Walker, L. J. (1984). Sex differences in the development of a moral reasoning: A critical review. *Child Development, 55,* 677–691.

68. Walker, L. J. (1986). Experiential and cognitive sources of moral development in adulthood. *Human Development, 29*(2), 113–124.

69. Walker, L. J. (1986). Sex differences in the development of moral reasoning. *Child Development, 57*(2), 522–526.

70. Walker, L. J., DeVries, B., & Trevethan, S. D. (1987). Moral stages and moral orientations in real-life and hypothetical dilemmas. *Child Development, 58,* 842–858.

17 Adaptation to Uniqueness

After crosses and losses, men grow humbler and wiser.
—BENJAMIN FRANKLIN

Clara S. Schuster

Each of us harbors some attribute that distinguishes us from the "norm" of our culture or social group. Skin color, extremes of body height, or unusual hair color may identify one as different from the majority of one's peers. Other people may achieve minority status because of high IQ, ethnic affiliation, physical disability, or religious practices. Interindividual differences, especially those based on physical characteristics, readily become an index by which people can identify, categorize, label, stereotype, or stigmatize others.

Information about interindividual differences can be valuable when used objectively for guiding our interactions. Awareness of diabetes, food allergies, or the religious codes of a guest influences one's menu. Sensitive people avoid initiating a business transaction on a day recognized as the Sabbath or a high holy day for another individual. Thus, individuality is respected and interpersonal relationships are enhanced.

However, many people are deprived of potentially rich relationships and experiences because of lack of knowledge, misunderstandings, or the failure to see beyond uniqueness to appreciate the interindividual similarities.[53] Disabled people, people of ethnic minorities, and poor people are often approached as if they were less intelligent or, at least, less educated than the average person.[83] Some people may label unfriendly and consequently avoid a blind person who does not initiate interactions or respond to a greeting on the street, when, in fact, the visually impaired person did not hear the speaker's voice above the traffic noises or did not realize to whom the salutation was directed. Many exceptional people are refused opportunities for peer contacts, employment, advancements, independent living, or talent development because of the negative judgments of people in decision-making positions. When individuals assert their rights, labels such as "emotionally disturbed" or "troublemaker" may further limit opportunities and relationships. They are accused of "biting the hand that feeds them."[83]

As we go through life, we find that we are not carbon copies of our peers. It is the rare person who does not confront personal uniqueness at least once during the life span. If we are able to accept these differences objectively and positively, then affective energy is available to invest in social relationships and cognitive development. However, if these differences are translated into a negative self-identity, then affective energies may need to be used to protect the developing self, thus limiting the amount of energy available for creative endeavors.

The need to be an accepted part of the subculture is especially strong during the school-age years, compelling children to go to extremes to maintain their homogeneity. Clothing and hair styles frequently become critical issues for confrontation between parents and children as the child tries to seek group identity through conformity to its values. Clubs or gangs are formed with arbitrarily designated criteria (e.g., gender, residence, grade) and are established to bring some children into and to force others out of the group. The child who is different is often teased and rejected by peers; names such as "four eyes," "carrot top," and "honky" may be used to stigmatize the offender of the norm. The child may come to hate a part of self because of this ridicule. Children who belong to a religious sect that has explicit behavioral codes or religious observances may find themselves caught between parental and peer expectations. Strict clothing styles, restricted participation in school social activities, or observance of religious ritual (e.g., Ash Wednesday by the Catholic child) may precipitate embarrassment or internal conflict.

Even adults seek out others who have similar interests, characteristics, problems, or goals. Some individuals seek a total affiliation with others similar to themselves through adopting a communal lifestyle, whereas others establish more casual, yet equally significant, affiliations with social, recreational, or religious groups. Since we are more comfortable with people who we feel are sympathetic to or in agreement with our own uniqueness, values, and lifestyle, we tend to choose friends who share common social values or educational levels. When our uniqueness is shared by others, then other attributes can be more fully recognized, appreciated, and developed. Our humanness is enhanced. *Whatever may constitute our uniqueness, it needs to be accepted as an integral part of our whole personhood, not the hallmark of it.*

We speak of America as the "melting pot of the nations." True, our customs, goals, and values reflect the multiple nationalities of our immigrant forefathers as well as the homogenizing influence of mass media. However, we also find enclaves in our cities and throughout the country where individuals with common ethnic backgrounds or interests have established minicommunities within the larger populace (e.g., Chinatown, Puerto Rican, Polish, or Italian districts, Amish or deaf communities, reservations for Native Americans, and religious communes). These individuals effectively retain their lifestyle and cultural identity by affiliating with others of similar background or value system. In such environments, one's uniqueness from the dominant culture is minimized (Fig. 17-1). Isolation provides for continuity of cultural traditions, values, and communication partners (since language differences frequently constitute a major barrier to integration into the dominant culture). Exclusive affiliations facilitate positive ego-identity for some but can become restrictive for others.

Just as the beauty of an artistic masterpiece is achieved through the subtle blending as well as contrasting of colors and textures, the blending and contrasting of different subcultures within our country has given it a unique beauty. Each minority group and each person with a unique attribute has a special contribution to make at each level of involvement.

PSYCHOLOGY OF EXCEPTIONALITY

Most of us instinctually realize that our true identities come from within, that external features are inadequate criteria for defining our potentials or our value. From a holistic view-

FIGURE 17–1.
For subcultures that want to perpetuate their values and goals, isolation from the mainstream of the culture serves to prevent dilution of their lifestyle.

point, even in the presence of a major distinguishing attribute, most of us are more like other people than different from them. All of us want to believe that we are like the others, that we are acceptable and accepted. This need for belonging and affiliation appears to be critical in the formation of an individual's identity and ego strength, especially during the school-age and adolescent years, since our affiliations serve both to stimulate and to reflect our value in the social matrix.

Living with Stigma

Common values and biases are integral parts of the fabric of a culture. Issues of economics, history, the natural environment, current events, genetics, and so forth affect the development of "norms" and desirable attributes or behaviors for each group. "Each society creates hierarchies of desirable and undesirable attributes and sets rules for the management of such attributes."[3] Depending on the uniqueness and its social and religious meaning to society and family members, people have been killed, revered, or accepted within their cultural-historical context.[74,75,80]

People who possess a desirable or undesirable characteristic tend to be categorized and related to on the basis of that single factor (stereotyped). Other unique talents, abilities, or even deficits of the person tend to be eclipsed in the presence of the dominant characteristic. Which attributes are denigrated depends entirely on the context. However, the results are the same: the person is stigmatized and treated as if one's moral fabric were tainted.[10,48]

Three views on the origin of stereotyping and stigma are prevalent. The **psychodynamic view** hypothesizes that prejudice originates from inadequate maturation of the personality structures or "personality development gone astray."[78] Inner conflicts, inadequacies, and hostilities are expressed through "safe" scapegoating onto people with less social power and value. The **social learning view** holds that discriminatory attitudes and behaviors are learned subtly and overtly as a part of the enculturation process. Consequently, the person finds a sense of power, control, belonging, and approval through imitating the behaviors modeled or reinforced by others. The **cognitive developmental view** holds that stigmatization of people and peers is rooted in the universals of the maturational process.[78] As a child is able to differentiate and categorize specific characteristics, there is a tendency to cherish those factors that are "like me" or that are seen as desirable. One of the developmental tasks of the school-ager is to "derive a sense of belonging from associations with others." This task can translate into an active avoiding and stigmatizing of all that is "not like me." It is not until one can appreciate his or her own uniqueness (adolescent task) that this quest for homogeneity is released for an appreciation of the other's uniquenesses. All three views appear to contribute to the complex process of stigmatization, each playing a role at different points in development.

Stigmatized people are viewed as "less than fully human"[34] and treated accordingly.[2, 32, 79] Consequently, growing up with stigma can profoundly affect one's perception of self and one's identity formation.[4] The person, whether because of skin color, disability, or illness must constantly develop strategies for dealing with the negative, devalued, minority status.[10, 33] The stigma may be rejected as society's problem, integrated into one's identity as a focal issue (negative), or seen as a nonintrusive aspect of self (positive).[10]

A major issue in belonging to a minority group (whether ethnic, racial, or disabled) during the developmental years is that *one is forced to face his or her differences before gaining security in one's similarities* to the peer group. Unless a child is offered sensitive support from caring, knowledgeable adults and contact with accepting peers, permanent negative scars can be left on the emerging personality.[33] The psychological pain of rejection can be as real as the physical pain that accompanies physical injury as one develops heightened sensitivity to the nuances of words and interpersonal relationships.[79] However, what may precipitate a low self-esteem or self-concept for some can serve as the catalyst for the emergence of a new vibrant self in others.[3]

Living with Uniqueness

The ability to transcend stigma depends on many factors,[3] including one's understanding of and attitude toward the stigmatizing factor. Confrontation with depreciation forces one to identify and prioritize one's value system (see "Identity Homework" in Chap. 25). The end result can be the recognition of new horizons and meanings of existence that are not apparent until the artificial standards of society are faced and evaluated. Thus, growth can occur through this value reassessment.[79]

Uniqueness or a Handicap?

Uniqueness, impairment, disability, and handicap are not synonymous terms. It is generally assumed that an impairment causes a disability and that any uniqueness is a handicap, but these lay definitions are not necessarily valid. **Uniqueness** refers to any characteristic (positive or negative) that distinguishes the individual from his or her reference group. Thus, an attribute that is devalued in one group, may be common to all in a second, and highly prized in a third social system (e.g., assertiveness in a woman, high creativity in a school-ager).

Impairment is an identifiable flaw in body structure or appearance, a defect in the biophysical domain. A **disability,** on the other hand, is an inability to execute a specific skill, a defect in functional performance.[90] Impairments and disabilities can be objectively identified, and the degree of disability can be measured. However, not all impairments are disabling. A large nose does not prevent one from smelling, nor does a facial birthmark or acne hamper the ability to smile. Neither are all disabilities the result of impairments. They can result from the helplessness syndrome (see Chap. 13) or from the absence of a desired physical ability. Only a few individuals can run a 4-minute mile, span 10 notes on the piano with one hand, or hit high F when vocalizing. Thus, a person may be physically normal but still be unable to perform a culturally desirable skill.

Uniqueness, impairments, and disabilities tend to create anxieties in other people, leading to changes in interactional behaviors. In a society that places extraordinary stress on external appearance and attractiveness, *aesthetic anxieties* are evoked when a person does not present the socially acceptable physique or behavior.[36] An underlying assumption expects that everyone will master a basic set of skills deemed essential for survival or functioning within the society. *Existential anxiety* arises when a person identifies with another's lack of "functional capacities deemed necessary to the pursuit of a satisfactory life."[36] These two anxieties tend to create prejudicial attitudes and discriminatory behaviors designed to reduce contact with the anxiety-producing factor. Consequently, possession of a "deeply discrediting" attribute can result in a different social environment for the developing child or for the adult who confronts the attribute later in life because of the anxieties of others.

A **handicap** refers to "the disadvantages experienced by the individual as a result of impairments and disabilities."[90] It constitutes a defect in the interaction and adaptation of the individual to the sociocultural environment. Thus, *the fundamental problems experienced by a representative of a minority group tend to be environmentally induced rather than innate to the uniqueness per se.* Many of the problems faced by people with impairments tend to be related to their minority status rather than to the limitations of their disability.[27, 36] A recent Harris Survey reports that 45% of Americans with disabilities believe that they experience minority group status in the same sense as African Americans and Spanish Americans.[38] Healthy relationships and maximization of potentials are based on providing equal opportunity for and interaction with each person based on *who* they are, not *what* they own or look like.

Reaction to One's Own Uniqueness

When a person becomes aware of a deviation (his or her exceptionality) from the norm of the community, one of three reactions may occur:

1. **Intense Pride** ("I am Superior"): The possession of a prized characteristic (money, body build, physical skill, attractiveness, skin color, intelligence) may be equated with increased personal worth, even though the trait is one that was acquired through heredity rather than achieved through personal efforts. As a person changes peer-group affiliation, status criterion may change. One group may value musical talent, another, the distance of one's "wheels" from the road surface, and a third, one's grade-point average.

    The person who takes pride in a difference may be tempted to cheat or to lie to maintain a perceived superiority. When children or adults use these superficial status symbols for group affiliation, scapegoating frequently occurs to maintain superiority by keeping others "where they belong." Human dignity is lost in such a situation.

2. **Intense Shame** ("I am Inferior"): Too often, one's concept of "normal" or even "acceptable" is actually an ideal that few ever reach. Consequently, the person may feel inadequate, unacceptable, or bad. The person may withdraw from social interactions to reduce the risk of discovery or may try to deny or hide the uniqueness to increase acceptability. The person may accept the discriminatory limitations imposed by others or reject oneself for the imperfections, becoming passive or even dependent or subservient in relationships with others to decrease tensions. A person may find that a characteristic valued by one group is subjected to ridicule in a second. For instance, parents and teachers may value a child's academic achievements while peers may value group solidarity, conformity, femininity, or physical prowess. Gifted young people caught between conflicting value systems may consciously repress maximizing cognitive potentials to remain acceptable to the peer group.[56]

3. **Realistic Acceptance** ("I am **me**"): These individuals view their "imperfection" or "gift" as but one aspect of the total self. They are comfortable with themselves and can see both assets and deficiencies realistically, without stigmatizing value. They can proceed to identify their own limits rather than accepting those posed by sociocultural stereotypes. The development of this attitude requires a great deal of personal maturity and support from significant others. The person must set his or her own goals and establish a role based on personal interests and potentials.

Emotional Handicaps

A **sociocultural handicap** is any factor that is deemed undesirable by the social group and consequently affects the quantity or quality of interpersonal relationships. Examples may include an Italian in a Polish community, a hearing person in a deaf community, a light-skinned African American in a black community, or a woman in a political or business world. An **emotional handicap** is the intrapersonal psychological disequilibrium or behavioral maladjustment expressed by the person who perceives the self as undesirable or stigmatized. The altered affective state can inhibit realistic, positive ego-identity as well as learning and social growth, especially during childhood. Gifted, disabled, and minority group children experience more mental illness, behavioral, and social problems than their counterparts.[17,22,31,54,57,60,66,69,72,91,94,97]

The relationship between sociocultural handicaps and emotional handicaps follows this sequence:

1. The person lacks a skill or possesses an undesirable characteristic.
2. Other people devalue the characteristic.
3. The individual is aware of the alteration from the norm or desirable state.
4. The person accepts the judgment of others (or makes own) that the characteristic is undesirable.
5. The person devalues himself or herself.

This sequence of events is a unit. If 1 and 2 do not occur, then 3 and 4 will not occur. If 4 and 5 do not occur, then no emotional handicap has developed. This concept is perhaps the central focus of the entire chapter.

Deviance is an arbitrary socially defined phenomenon that has no valid correlation with an individual's worth as a person. *It is the acceptance of these arbitrary values and subsequent devaluation of self that leads to the development of emotional handicaps and social maladjustment.* The most critical times for development of emotional handicaps are during the school-age years when similarity to peers is so important and again during the young adult years when one's identity is solidifying. Interruption of the chain through appreciation of one's similarities and abilities can prevent maladjustment and facilitate maximization of potentials in all domains.

Prevention or Amelioration of Emotional Handicaps

Emotional handicaps can be prevented or ameliorated by reducing the stress load (liabilities) and increasing the powers (assets) of the individual. When a person is presented with a new situation, he or she generally engages in trial-and-error behaviors to identify a potential solution. This behavior requires high amounts of emotional energy to cope with the accompanying anxiety. The person is placed in conflict ("should I attempt to reach this new goal, or should I retreat to the safety of what I know?''). Each new adventure brings a new challenge and the potential threat of failure: this experience is a source of frustration and emotional disequilibrium.

For most adults, the number of new elements in novel situations is reduced by the gradual assumption of new roles and experiences during the developmental years. An example of a novel situation is a person's first week at college. Although separation from family, introduction to new friends, responsibility for total care of one's room and clothing, and assumption of intensive studies are difficult, most people have had adequate preliminary experiences to help them to make a successful adjustment. However, when a person's repertoire of experiences has been limited because of lifestyle, ethnic affiliation, over-protection, spoiling, or physical disability, the adjustment becomes even more difficult. Seven factors can help to prevent or to ameliorate emotional handicaps.

Acceptance of One's Difference

The most critical factor in adjustment to new challenges is the realistic acceptance of one's difference or disability. Incorporated into this concept is the ability to establish realistic goals in light of both personal and environmental limitations (including the attitudes of others). It includes the ability to tolerate frustration when a goal is not immediately realized and the ability to stick to a task until it is mastered.[30] Realistic establishment of goals also includes the ability to set priorities. For example, a severely disabled person, because of time limitations versus ultimate goals, may need to choose between dressing and feeding self. Putting too much time and energy into nonessential activities may reduce one's ability to deal with essentials.[43] Thus, the physically disabled person may need to balance the stress of the need for independence against the stress of the need for dependence to ensure both psychological and physiological safety. (Fig. 17-2) Stress must be adequate to challenge but not to overwhelm the individual.

Mastery of Basic Skills

The second factor that can facilitate adaptation to new situations is the learning of essential skills and behaviors that ensure goal achievement. This concept includes possession of the skills essential for independence in the activities of daily living (ADL), the ability to communicate freely in the dominant language code, the knowledge of how to get along with other people, and an understanding of culturally defined etiquette nuances. A person does not suddenly know how to live independently on graduating from high school or on marrying; growth-facilitating experiences must be offered during the developmental years. Children need to learn how to handle money through an allowance, a job, and self-planned shopping and budgeting. Individuals who have been deprived of the challenges that lead to competence may develop the helplessness syndrome (see Chap. 13) because they have not learned how to control the environment.[77] Permissive, indulgent child-rearing practices create insecurity in children. As children and adults, they must always rely on someone else rather than on their own talents and abilities; therefore, they are never secure in their own competencies and identities. The overprotected child, whether able-bodied or disabled, learns to be helpless. Family members who absorb all frustrations, pressures, and problems stifle the person's attainment of competence. Mastery of smaller tasks lays the foundation for handling more complex tasks later in life. Disabled adults repeatedly state that a challenging parent, sibling, or teacher was the best preparation they could have had for adulthood.[63]

When a person does not possess the physical skill for performing a specific task, an alternative approach must be used to achieve the goal. Consequently, deaf people learn sign language and lip reading; blind people learn Braille or use talking books; and some physically disabled individuals use animals for guidance or retrieval of objects. (Fig. 17-3) The two most important skills for a person to learn are (1) how to

FIGURE 17-2.
Disabled people need to weigh the effort of accomplishing a task against the benefits received and request assistance as necessary so that available energies can be focused toward maximal goal achievement. (Reprinted courtesy of Garfield. *Copyright 1983 United Feature Syndicate, Inc.)*

FIGURE 17–3.
This young boy obviously has an impairment; he lost his arms in a farm accident at the age of 2. However, he is not necessarily disabled, since he has learned to do many things with his feet, including holding a pencil or a paintbrush between his toes. Here he is painting horseshoes for a family game. (Photograph by Carl Subitch.)

solve problems or to make decisions—that is, to think independently—and (2) self-discipline. The physically disabled person in particular needs to know how to generate viable alternatives to master tasks. All children can be taught, when caught in a novel social situation, to observe the behavior of other people and then follow suit (provided it is not illegal, immoral, or dangerous).

Exposure to the Broad Culture

Young people, regardless of ethnic background or disabling condition, need to be exposed to new experiences as they develop. The wider the exposure to other lifestyles, cultures, environments, and ideas, the more understanding and flexible an individual can be when dealing with others or when solving problems. People raised in restricted environments find it more difficult to predict and adapt to life in the broader more complex culture and work worlds. Integration opportunities for children (e.g., busing and mainstreaming) help to ensure broader contact with the culture (Fig. 17-4).

Nurturing Support

One of the greatest challenges of family members is to balance a person's abilities against the limitations in such a way as to provide support or gradually to guide the person toward confident more independent functioning. This task requires a sensitivity to the individual's developmental level to provide sufficient stress to motivate but not so much as to paralyze the person with fear of failure.

Children need support for their normal developmental needs as well as to face their uniqueness. The first criterion for

FIGURE 17–4.
Pride in one's cultural heritage can be fostered by giving the child an opportunity to share native costumes and customs with teacher and peers. This practice also benefits the child's peers who are from different backgrounds by exposing them to different cultural traditions.

offering support is that *parents must know their own values and goals* well enough to offer stability and consistency in role modeling. They must have come to terms with the uniqueness for themselves (see Chap. 34) before they can convey to the child that **the uniqueness does not define one's value as a person.**

The second criterion is that the parents *share an experience with their children,* not do it *for* them, allowing the children to do as much for themselves as possible even if it takes a little longer. Thus, the father allows the 26-month-old child with cerebral palsy to use her walker, rather than carrying her to the car; the mother places her hands over those of the toddler or preschooler who is attempting to snap together some pop beads or to crack open an egg; and the babysitter allows the 7-year-old stutterer to tell Grandma the story by himself (Fig. 17-5).

When a problem arises at school, it may be more helpful if the parent, rather than handling the situation alone, allows the child to participate in the conference with the teacher. The parent may also engage in role playing with the child in the home setting, practicing teacher-pupil conferences, child-peer interactions, and how to deal with teasing or discriminatory behaviors. This approach can have incredible short- and long-range results by developing frustration management skills, problem-solving skills, interpersonal relationship skills, negotiation skills, understanding of other people (and self), and developing self-confidence. The key is that the parent provides a nurturing milieu that conveys the attitude, "I love you; you are valued; you can do it; I have confidence in you; you can count on my support." Such a parental attitude makes a key difference in whether children from ghetto areas, for example, become successfully adapted to the broader culture as adults.[98]

The third criterion for offering nurturing support is *honesty.* Children and adults who face their uniqueness want to know the truth. Fear of the unknown can be disorganizing and immobilizing. It is difficult to predict the behaviors and reactions of others or to plan the future if one does not know all the factors to be considered in making a decision. Information is both armor and ammunition. Adults seem especially reluctant to talk with children about their disability. One study revealed that only 25% of disabled children 6 to 16 years of age had openly discussed their disability with their parents and only one third of high school students knew the cause of their disability.[51] Such secrecy tends to increase the sense of stigmatization, worry, and depression experienced by disabled children. The news of the permanency of a disability or the pervasiveness of a bias may be disarming, even painful to face, but the information, given with loving support, can enable one to face cultural values and come out on top! It is easier to know that one "will have to be better prepared than the average worker to get the same job" from the beginning than to face multiple rejections for unknown reasons.

Avoidance of Traumatic Situations

Another way to reduce stress that leads to emotional handicaps is to avoid situations that are potentially too traumatic; this approach is related to the realistic acceptance of one's uniqueness or limitations. A person who stutters or slurs speech (e.g., after a stroke) may be able to communicate adequately at home, but giving a speech in a school assembly or for a social gathering might represent a marked threat to self-confidence and self-esteem. This concept does not imply avoidance of growth-producing experiences, but avoidance of growth-threatening experiences (a thin line at times). To remove all challenge because of potential failure or teasing may signify to the individual a lack of worthiness or confidence that can be more devastating than the public exposure. *When one is fully accepted and supported, the process (attempt) becomes more important than the product.*

Education of the Public

Individuals need to see themselves as whole and good people. Since a person's attitude toward self is frequently a reflection of the attitude of others, major cultural attitudes toward ethnic and disabled minority groups need to be changed. School textbooks are already reflecting such changes, and mass media are beginning to give wider exposure to minorities. However, stigmatization is still an individual matter. Each of us must reevaluate our own values and attitudes toward those who are different from ourselves. It is hoped that, in so doing, we will begin to accept people for who they really are, not according to preconceived, stereotyped prejudices or a superficial value system. Minority representatives or physically disabled people themselves can frequently help to change stereotyped public opinions by their own attitudes and unique competent approach to meeting life's responsibilities.[105] Minority and disabled children should be prepared to recognize and handle the embarrassment or discomfort of others and to hold up their own end of an interaction.[7] Role-playing experiences in religious, scout, and social groups can help to sensitize people to the unique barriers and needs of minority and disabled people.

FIGURE 17–5.
When a child has an impairment (blindness in this case), it is important that the parents start early to help the child gain the appropriate skills for the culture. Lack of these tools for effective functioning constitutes a disability, which, in turn, becomes a handicap.

Individualization

Disabled people rightfully complain that the environment and the attitudes of others, even well-meaning professionals, create more handicaps for them than their disability. Individuals can become who others think they are, especially if the other person is significant to them (the Rosenthal effect), because of the opportunities and experiences offered or denied them. For others to help people maximize potentials, the individuals must be seen in context, with a fair acknowledgement of their abilities and limitations. Norms must be set aside and the person's current abilities appreciated for what they are. Keeping good records of a gifted, disabled, "normal," or delayed child's or adult's progress can serve to spur more growth, since the person is competing against his or her own successes. Emotional disequilibrium does not accompany earned and acknowledged success.

The rest of this chapter focuses on the person with physical impairment or disability.

ADAPTATION TO DISABILITY

Forty-three million people (about 20% of the population) in the United States of America have one or more physical or mental disabilities.[67] Fifty percent of people older than age 65 report a chronic disabling condition. Ten percent of people younger than age 21 experience a birth defect, injury, or disease process that results in a chronic disability.[90, 91] In the United States, 350,000 automobile accident victims per year are left with permanent impairments.[19]

The Development Years

Little research has been done in the area of how **congenitally disabled** (born with the impairment) children adapt to their exceptionality or even what it is like to grow up with a disability from the child's point of view.[51] It is frequently assumed that because these children have never experienced a "normal" life, they do not miss it and automatically adjust to living with their disabilities. This assumption simply is not so. Each stage of life has its own unique stressors for the disabled child (Fig. 17-6).

As observational and cognitive processes develop, the child begins to realize that he or she is different from peers and adults. Even the blind child may become aware of his or her difference during the second year of life. Adaptation to disability occurs gradually as the child's cognitive and affective structures emerge (Table 17-1). The intensity and expressions of a child's response are mediated by the child's temperament, cognitive skills, and social supports. Some children appear to sail through childhood with minimal stress. Others, however, may appear to be constantly fighting the disability. Discussions with parents indicate that all children struggle to

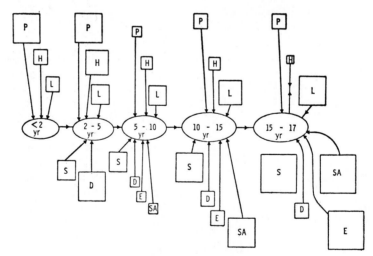

P . . . Stress arising from parents' reaction to child's handicap.

H . . . Stress arising from hospital visits, hospitalization physiotherapy, and operation.

L . . . Stress arising from limitations of activity.

S . . . Stress arising from social limitations and difficulties in social relationships.

D . . . Stress arising from dependence on others.

E . . . Stress arising from educational or employment demands.

SA . . . Stress arising from self-awareness. Realization of own handicap.

FIGURE 17–6.

Hypothetical model of stressors for children with disabilities. The pattern and the intensity of stress in a child's life vary with age as well as with the type of disabling condition. (From Reynell, J. [1973]. Children with physical handicaps. In V.P. Varma [Ed.], Stresses in children. London: University of London Press. With permission.)

TABLE 17-1. ADAPTATION TO PHYSICAL DISABILITY

Stage	Cognitive	Affective	Manifestations
1	Naïve	Naïve	Unaware of difference
2	Awareness	Naïve	Curiosity
3	Rebellion	Awareness	Uncooperative with treatments
4	Adaptation	Rebellion	Social acting out
5	Acceptance	Adaptation	Disability prominent
6	Acceptance	Acceptance	Holistic appreciation

some degree with trying to find the reason for and the meaning of the disability. However, children are more likely to show stress covertly, through behavior, than to identify it and talk it out.[13] As a result, adults must infer the struggle from the child's behaviors. Gradually, the child's understanding of the disability and its cause become an integral part of the child's self-image and personality.[31] Some people who face ethnic discrimination may experience similar stages in the process of integration with the dominant culture.

Cognitive and Affective Naïveté
Because of cognitive and affective immaturity, the infant is completely unaware of the nature or meaning of a disability. The child's behavior, emotions, and needs are the same as those of any other baby except as the disability may specifically limit functioning. The disability may change behavior because of differing ability to interpret or interact with the environment. The greatest threat to healthy development is the inability of the parents to respond contingently to the child because of their own grief processes (see Chap. 34). This lack immediately places the child in a qualitatively different world from that of the "normal" newborn. Many of the social-emotional difficulties of children with birth defects are rooted in dysfunctions of this primary relationship.

Cognitive Awareness, Affective Naïveté
During the toddler and preschool years, the child gradually becomes aware of his or her difference from other people. This dawning depends on the degree and type of disability, cognitive processes, peer contact, and parental management. Although aware of one's own "inability" earlier, the child may not perceive himself or herself as "different" or "disabled" until 4 to 5 years of age.[60] However, the child is unaware of the long-term implications of the disability. Since young children are unable to do many of the things other people accomplish with ease, the disabled child assumes that the skill will appear with age. The child may feel frustration from the inability to master a skill or to be independent, but "being different" per se usually does not create affective stress for the child at this point. Frustration is particularly evident when cognitive skills greatly outstrip physical skills (including highly gifted children), and the child is unable to achieve goals. It is during this period that the child develops early attitudes of work, such as

persistence versus helplessness and dependency. Consequently, parental attitude and approach are critical to healthy development. Parental overprotectiveness can cause more damage than the disability itself.[83]

The magical thought processes of young children can cause them to invent interesting theories or to blame themselves for the disability. Curiosity about how others accomplish skills and why they cannot perform the skill is normal for all children and offers a natural opportunity for parents to discuss openly and honestly the nature, cause, and course of the disability. Appreciation for and development of the child's positive points can help mitigate but cannot prevent the anger of the next stage.

Cognitive Rebellion, Affective Awareness
The attainment of concrete operational skills and formal entrance into the peer world force the child to confront the reality of uniqueness or disability. Gradually, the child becomes aware of the social significance of the uniqueness and begins to suspect that it may be a permanent condition.[24,60] However, ego-identity is still so weak that passive acceptance of the self "as is" with its stigmatizing value is impossible for the emotionally healthy child. The child's need to be "like other people" and acceptable is overpowering. Anger and other forms of cognitive rejection of the "flawed self" are natural consequences. The child may lie about himself or herself to increase social value. Both adults and children may feel like prisoners within their own bodies at this stage.[20]

The child tries hard to gain control of his or her own life through fantasizing normalcy or refusal to cooperate with activities specific to the disability. Lack of contact with disabled adults leads many children to believe that only children are disabled, therefore, special services are not needed.[72,83] It is common for children to feel that they don't need to wear glasses, attend special education classes, do exercises, have an operation, learn Braille, wear a hearing aid, or use a brace. The child may defy reality by cheating on a diet, skipping medications, refusing therapy, or engaging in a forbidden activity. Each of the activities is a reminder to the child of the disability, a symbol of deviation from the normal. This reality-defying behavior is similar to that of children who are dealing with the concept of death: "If I'm brave enough, strong enough, determined enough, I can win" (see Chap. 18). "No minority ever goes from second-class status to first-class status without passing through a zone of hostility. In fact, properly viewed, the hostility is an indication of progress."[41]

Fifty percent of chronically ill and disabled children experience acute distress and depression by 10 years of age as the reality of the permanency begins to dawn and they mourn the loss of normalcy, unattainable skills and goals, or anticipated failures and death.[58,70,72,76] Unrealistic career goals[72] or refusal to talk about the "official secret"[51] are part of the active denial process.

Parents may feel frustrated as they try to help the child adjust to a world limited in peer contacts (the child may not be physically able to participate in activities, may attend segregated classes, or may be rejected by peers) at a time when peers are so critical to healthy psychosocial development, or as they try to maximize the child's potentials when the child is too full of hopelessness or anger to care or to think rationally. Cognitive immaturity prevents long-range perspectives or abstract thought processes; consequently, the disability may assume paramount importance in the child's life. The disability may be blamed for all problems and failures; it may also be used as a weapon to elicit sympathy (attention-getting) or to get one's own way (controlling the environment). Parents and professionals need to initiate open, honest discussions about the disability to facilitate healthy adaptation and realistic future planning.[51, 83]

Some children try to gain control through alliance with someone stronger than the self. They become the "perfect angels" who seem to be unbothered by the disability and do whatever they are told. By "appeasing the gods," by being "good enough," it will go away, they believe: "*They* will not need or want to punish me any more."

Cognitive Adaptation, Affective Rebellion

Gradually, the person becomes aware of the permanence of the disability.[72] When neither fighting nor joining has changed the situation, disillusionment, fear, and loneliness set in. "The person may experience intense anger or guilt as a means of fixing responsibility for the loss either to others or to himself."[60] The child experiences a grieving process as he or she tries to adapt to the external and internal meaning of the loss of normalcy.[60] He or she experiences a sense of being cheated out of the basic tools with which to be successful in adult life. At a time when one is normally critical of the emerging adult body, the disability can loom as an insurmountable barrier to acceptability in a world that seems to worship idealized physical attributes.

During the late school-age, pubescent, and early adolescent years, identify is still heavily based on the concrete, physical self and one's power or skill. Before one's identity is clearly established, it is difficult to separate the physical self from one's personal value. "If my body is no good, then I am no good." One tends to accept the negative views of society as a part of one's identity. Anger and a negative self-identity may emerge.[8] The denial, depression, and anger of this stage may continue to interfere with adaptation and rehabilitation efforts.[60] Some young people may even become pregnant to prove their "normalcy."[72]

As the young person begins to realize that life is "not fair," he or she may have an overwhelming premonition that the rest of life will be unfulfilling. Anger may be expressed through acting out and socially unacceptable behaviors. Parental and societal rules may be continually challenged. "Why should I obey your rules? I tried to be good and you can see where it got me. It doesn't matter what I do, life will never be good for me anyway." The young person may receive inadequate feedback on the effect of behaviors on the quality of interpersonal relationships,[91] and they may fail to learn nego-

tiation and cooperation skills, factors that tend to perpetuate the problem. The parents and peers may feel that the disabled person has fewer emotional resources than most people and therefore may try to protect him or her from the hurts and the ups and downs of life. When the child is thus insulated from the normal issues of growing up (e.g., male-female relationships, disappointments), then the young person continues in his or her immaturity. Thus, the parents continue to shelter and protect because the child is less mature than his or her peers; it becomes a vicious cycle.[83]

Many young people go through a profound depression before coming to terms with the disability.[72] Depression and a sense of helplessness are expressed by isolation from peers and withdrawal from the very activities that could help them to gain the social and work skills necessary for success in later stages of life. Feelings of low self-worth may lead to substance abuse, promiscuity, or even suicide.

Some refuse to accept the limitations of the disability or the stigmatization of society but yet seem to base all relationships in some way on their impairment. They may try to force others to accept their participation in social groups through accusations of discrimination or use the uniqueness as a wedge for obtaining a job. Although this behavior is developmentally normal, without loving support, many individuals get stuck in this phase or the next. Even when they become involved in advocacy groups, it tends to be from an angry, militant deficiency viewpoint that attempts to force integration, rather than from an abundance approach that attempts to elicit cooperation from others based on positive attributes and mutual contribution to a goal.

Cognitive Acceptance, Affective Adaptation

During the middle and late adolescent years, one's identity is still fragile and not yet clearly defined. At this point, the person accepts the permanence of the uniqueness but sees the disability or difference as the central factor that defines oneself.[81] I am a DISABLED person. The disability is so big within their own mind that they play down their positive attributes. With this mentality, they expect the world to see the disability before their personage. They do what they have to do to accommodate to the limitations of the impairment, but they face life without enthusiasm. They frequently have a negative outlook on the future in terms of marriage or career. Some may try to convince themselves that if they try to "act normal" and do not mention the disability, other people will not notice the impairment and will relate to them as a person instead of as a HANDICAPPED person. Although they may no longer devalue themselves, they feel the stigmatization of society.

Most people adapt quite well within this stage. With time and maturing, the sting of life's unfairness abates, especially if they are able to find a comfortable niche within society socially, occupationally, and financially. But the disability always remains as a sore reminder of what might have been. Perhaps Olshansky's concept of *chronic sorrow* is applicable to disabled people as well as their parents.[62]

Cognitive and Affective Acceptance

As the person with a uniqueness masters his or her "identity homework" (see Chap. 25), a holistic view of self begins to emerge. The physical and psychic aspects of the self are separated, and one is able to identify, accept, and concentrate on positive attributes. The disability is seen as but one aspect of the total self. It is an inconvenience, sometimes a severely limiting factor, but it is *not* the essence of one's value. This person transcends the biases of the society.

From this perspective, one is able to make realistic, concrete life plans based on abilities, taking the disability and societal attitudes into consideration. The person is able to discuss the impairment and share limits unself-consciously with others, indicating and accepting assistance as needed. Unfortunately, "transcendence is a goal that most people [disabled or able-bodied] will not experience in their lifetime."[1]

The hallmark of this stage is the comfort one finds within oneself. The person no longer sees the self and the disability as synonymous and no longer resents the intrusion of the disability on the quality of life. He or she is able to recognize and appreciate the growth points offered by living with a disability. Joy is found in living, in exploiting one's abilities, in the challenges faced, and in the lessons learned about life (Fig. 17–7).

The Adult Years

Although presented here in the context of development, observations indicate that **adventitiously** (impairment occurs after birth) disabled children and adults go through the same

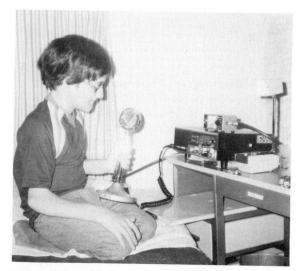

FIGURE 17–7.
Full acceptance of a disability can open new doors. This home-bound adolescent has found great enjoyment and increased social contacts through the use of a C.B. radio.

stages as the child born with a disability, although the time span differs depending on personality structure, coping skills, cognitive awareness, peer networking, and severity of the impairment.[31] The newly injured adult is naïve about the extent of a disability, assuming that, "I just had the wind knocked out of me," or that, "functioning will return with time and healing."

Newly disabled adults must gradually adjust to an impaired image of the self. Some people with newly diagnosed visual alterations resist wearing glasses because they feel it makes them ugly. A person who experiences a serious injury, such as extensive burns, an amputation because of bone cancer, or a spinal injury from an auto accident, is forced to face the reality of body change. People with spinal cord injuries take 1 to 2 years longer to move through the third stage than people with other injuries.[19] Such a person may experience marked grief or anger over loss of the known physical self and may also feel that the events represent a punishment.

The older the person at the time of onset, "the more established is his sense of self and his network of relationships and social roles" to draw on.[60] Although the newly disabled adult feels like the same person (and indeed, he or she is!), the person carries with him or her all the premorbidity biases.[24] People may "now greet him with avoidance, derision, guilt, and oversolicitousness."[24] The loss of independence, chronic illness, or mutilation of the body by accident or surgery may stimulate a complete reevaluation of one's value and priority system before self-acceptance and positive adaptation can be achieved.[6] This re-evaluation involves a period of grief over the loss of the person and potentials known before the current situation occurred (see Chap. 19). Until resolved, this normal and essential grief may hinder full acceptance of the new physical self. Financial problems, family issues, residential barriers, lack of support systems, and other problems of aging may also compound the process of adaptation.

THE PHYSICALLY IMPAIRED CHILD

Disability involves more than just having a physical defect; it is a psychosocial reality that can "breed extensive and serious problems for the disabled person, far beyond those resulting from the physical impairment itself."[16] Awareness of some of the unique challenges faced by disabled people can help family members and professionals facilitate **normalization** (opportunities to experience the "normal rhythms" of the day, week, year, and life span)[81] in relationships, environments, and experiences.

Barriers to Healthy Psychosocial Development

A paradox for many disabled children and their families is that the very approach (e.g., hours of therapy) that would maintain life, ensure adequate stimulation, or facilitate success may at the same time stifle healthy psychosocial development. Although each child is unique, some common experiences emerge.

Attachment and Separation–Individuation Issues

Multiple caregivers and inadequate contact with parents during the early weeks and months of life because of hospitalization can interfere with the infant's attachment process. Some babies experience difficulty attaching to the parents because of lack of adequate reciprocity. Parents immersed in their own grief (see Chap. 34) may be under-responsive to the child's efforts to interact (see Chap. 7). The child's efforts may be misinterpreted if they do not match expected behaviors. Thus, the parents of a 4-month-old child with cerebral palsy may interpret the child's crooked smile as a grimace of pain or the 8-month-old child's attempts to touch its face as aggression. In both situations, interactions may be reduced with the child.

Many severely disabled children and their parents experience difficulty mastering Mahler's tasks of separation and individuation (see Chaps. 8 and 11) because of the need for close and frequent contact.[52] With life-threatening conditions such as heart disease, severe seizures, or respiratory problems, the parent may try to reduce all stressors for the child to avoid a medical emergency. In the process, the parent becomes an extension of the child, prolonging the normal symbiotic phase. The parent may continue this posture long after the child needs such close attention. The parent may be unable or unwilling to leave the child with a babysitter. Some parents may never leave the child alone in a room, giving the child the impression that he or she is not allowed to be separated from the parent. In the press to make life "easy" or safe for the child, growth-inducing challenges are absorbed, and the child is infantilized (treated as a younger person), factors that precipitate delays in all domains.

To reduce stress, the parent may become overcontrolling, failing to ask the child to participate in offering ideas or to assist with problem solving. On the other hand, some parents become too permissive, allowing demanding, demeaning behaviors that perpetuate dependence and the "servant" role of the parent. Even within the confines of severe dependency, the parents must approach the handicapped child with respect and expect the child to respond with equal respect, and in a mature manner.[29]

The orthopedically impaired child may not be able to follow the mother into the next room for refueling, and the visually or auditorily impaired child may be unable to refuel from a distance, thus increasing the sense of vulnerability to the environment. Increased separation experiences due to hospitalization and therapy sessions may also increase the child's feelings of vulnerability and need for refueling.

As the child approaches school-age and adolescent years, separation experiences that facilitate the individuation process and prepare one for the adult years may be lacking. Many severely disabled children are never left alone. Someone is always at home or school who is responsible to "watch over me." Children need some time alone to learn to tolerate separation and to learn how to entertain themselves.[52, 72] The child may not be permitted to experience overnighters at a friend's home, weekends with grandparents, or a week at camp.

The child has reduced opportunities to develop self-esteem based on recognition of individuality, value, and ideas.

Dependence–Independence Continuum

Disabled people may need assistance with mobility, self-care, ADL, and even leisure activities. Inability to toilet independently, to join peers in a game of ball, to manipulate game pieces, or to communicate with a stranger increase stress. Although a plethora of technological aids is available to compensate for the most severe of disabilities at any age level (see Appendix G), expense and lack of awareness of their availability limit distribution and use. The public tends to increase dependence and depersonalization by using the disabled person's companion as a mediator for ordering food in restaurants or even in inquiring about the disabled person's state of health. Medical and educational problems are often handled by the parents instead of arranging for joint conferences or preparing the child to handle the situation independently through preparatory role-playing experiences. Again, the disabled person may be unnecessarily infantilized by a family and a society that fails to appreciate and develop the child's abilities. Indulgence and overprotection remove the challenges essential for growth.[8] The disabled person should be encouraged to handle his or her own business even if it does take longer; options should be available, and opinions should be respected (Fig. 17-8).

The child has reduced opportunities to develop self-esteem based on recognition of one's competence and ability to predict and control situations.

Altered Psychosocial Experiences

People with obvious deviations from culturally desired norms, whether these deviations are due to ethnic background or physical differences, share many common psychological experiences. The physically impaired child, however, faces even greater barriers to positive ego-identity and healthy adaptation to the deviation. The physically impaired child is *always* different, even in the earliest social affiliations with the mother and the family. Ethnic characteristics, on the other hand, usually do not pose difficulties until the child leaves the home for increased peer associations during the school-age years. The physically disabled child faces numerous potential sources of devaluation from the first day of life, the most critical of which are the parents. In light of all the barriers to high level mental health, it is amazing that so many disabled people adjust as well as they do to life in the larger society. Most see themselves as "ordinary people," not as "disabled people."[63]

FIGURE 17–8.
These mentally retarded children are enjoying competition with peers in preparation for the Special Olympics. Such experiences facilitate affective and social growth in spite of disabilities in other domains.

The physically disabled child frequently has reduced opportunities to feel and to share a full range of emotional experiences. Parents may be so overwhelmed by their own grief that the variety of emotions modeled may be dulled, and they may be unable to share the excitement of living with the infant through gentle tickling, tummy kisses, and face blow-ing. They may fail to engage in activities that stimulate the vestibular system such as roughhousing, twirling, bouncing, and tumbling for fear of negative physical effects on the young child (Fig. 17-9). Limited mobility and peer contacts may reduce opportunities for sociodramatic play (see Chap. 15) and make-believe.

Because of expense, the hassle, or the concern over too much excitement, the child may be provided with fewer social experiences such as shopping, visiting a theme park, camping, or traveling (Fig. 7-10). Reduced ability to process stimuli may limit the child's ability to thrill to the sound of music, the beauty of a sunset, the excitement of a thunderstorm, or the reassurance of a caress. The person may never feel the wind blowing through one's hair while racing down a hill or galloping on a horse. The person may never experience the tension preceding a plunge off the high dive, the first date, the first solo drive, or performing in the school play. The sense of "I faced fear and won!" may come only from quelling the fright that accompanies medical treatments and operations. Facing fear internal to oneself and stemming from normal developmental challenges is proactive and growth producing in nature because it concentrates on one's strengths, one's abundance. Facing fears external to oneself elicits self-protective, survival-oriented approaches to life that focus on one's deficiencies.

The child has reduced opportunities to develop self-esteem based on recognition of one's ability to experience and yet control a full range of emotions and to competently cope with the "real world."

FIGURE 17–9.
Gentle roughhousing has social, emotional, and physical benefits.

FIGURE 17–10.
The severely disabled child requires more time from the parent. It is difficult to help the child develop affective and social autonomy when he or she is physically dependent. Some parents curtail normal family activities because they feel that the increased work and exposure to outsiders are too traumatic.

Altered Peer Relationships

Children who differ from the norm tend to spend less time with peers and have fewer friends.[83] The parents may end up serving as companions and the major provider of social relationships when peers are really needed.[51,60] The relative isolation experienced by many severely disabled children makes it difficult to develop caring and intimate relationships.[29] Removal from the "normal" activities of peers and the community offers them a different perception of the world and themselves and profoundly affects their sense of identity.[10,82] The social isolation that accompanies impairments and disabilities can decrease opportunities to observe the natural banter, courtship, pairing, and bonding of peers.[72] Their concept of "appropriate behavior" may be limited to what is learned through television and books. Thus, they may develop "grossly unrealistic ideas about human behavior" and "may adopt extremely moral and censorious attitudes toward anything sexual" as a "form of self-defense."[72]

The school-age child is constantly forced to face his or her differences at a time when blending in is so critical to ego development. More than 50% of disabled children report that they are teased or socially rejected.[51] Some children may be overtly rejected because of their poor social skills and aggressive behaviors rather than the disability per se;[51,85] others may be rejected because of peer discomfort with or misunderstanding of poorly controlled body movements. Peers and siblings may be embarrassed to be seen with someone who drools or is incontinent. Flailing arms may be perceived as aggression rather than a friendly overture, and rocking or grimacing may be seen as "weird" rather than naïve or unavoidable. At a time when the child is working on bringing behavior under control, it is disconcerting for the nondisabled child to deal with the uncontrolled behaviors of the disabled person.

The child may be unable to participate in peer activities because of mobility and accessibility issues. When children cannot freely participate in activities, then they may choose to develop expertise in a socially desirable skill that allows them to take part in an activity or to bring others to them; for instance, an individual may become the timekeeper at the basketball games or the typist for the school newspaper. Parents can invite a child's peers to a party, or they may even arrange to "borrow" a friend to accompany the family on a mini-vacation, short trip, or a picnic.[8]

The child has reduced opportunities to develop self-esteem based on recognition of one's acceptability and sense of belonging to the peer group.

Medical and Habilitative Therapy

Medical and habilitative therapy, though designed to sustain life and maximize potentials, may disrupt relationships through separation of the child from peers and family members. Educational processes may be interrupted, and social activities may be missed. The child, in a crunch for time, may have to decide between the benefits of a therapy session or studying for an exam or writing a paper. Bracing may require prolonged periods of bed rest, and therapy time may preclude joining scouts, taking music lessons, or spending time socializing with friends. Surgery may evoke fear of castration, mutilation, abuse, or even death. The child may see other children wrapped in bandages or wearing casts or may hear screams from the treatment room and envision torture or anticipate excruciating pain. Even a hypodermic needle may be interpreted as a lethal weapon. The whir of the electric cast cutter can frighten a child, even though no pain is involved. Children need careful, honest explanations of what is happening and why. This explanation should include preparation for the pain involved, the projected time schedules, and the anticipated outcome. Even the older infant's or young toddler's cooperation can be effectively elicited and trauma reduced when the explanation is geared to their level of comprehension. For example, after she had been given an explanation of what was happening, the author's 10-month-old daughter remained flat in bed without crying or attempting to get up for more than 48 hours following eye surgery. (Although this child had exceptional language skills, the basic principle is still applicable to all children.)

A child can be so stressed during physical or occupational therapy sessions that he or she is unable to benefit from them. It is important, then, in any therapy situation that the therapist make friends with the child, be honest with the child, and, if possible, make a game out of the therapy to encourage the child's positive, active participation (Fig. 17-11).

Placement in special education classes may provide for special assistance with balancing therapeutic and academic needs, but the isolation from peers may establish artificial social barriers. At the same time, integrated schooling may actually increase one's sense of uniqueness and isolation from peers. Other children may avoid initiating a relationship with a "different" child because they do not understand the nature of the disability, may fear transfer of the impairment to their own bodies, are too wrapped up in their own interests to see the needs of another, fear the ridicule of peers for associating with someone who is "abnormal," or may not know alternative ways of relating to the exceptional child or how to overcome the communication barriers. Children are involved in the concrete here and now, in what they can see. Children usually need help in relating to the *person* who has a disability, rather than to the *disabled* person. When given information, ideas, and modeling, most school-agers are excited about or feel it is a privilege and responsibility to interact positively with exceptional peers.

The disabled child has reduced opportunities to develop self-esteem based on recognition of one's ability to orchestrate and participate in the wider world of peer relationships and to control one's destiny.

Mastery of Developmental Tasks

Disabled children face the same developmental tasks as non-handicapped children, but they encounter more stressors simultaneously.[29] Because of the issues discussed, children with disabilities may experience difficulty acquiring basic life skills and mastering developmental tasks.[82] Since there is a sequential relationship among tasks of each stage, attention to earlier tasks helps to avoid later problems. Schuster's tasks are as applicable to the disabled as to the "normal" population. There is no shame in using an alternative approach or an assistive device for mastery.[102] For example, deaf children who learn sign language during preschool years usually exhibit better command of language concepts and achieve higher academic skills than deaf children who are confined to lip-reading during preschool years (sign language symbols are illustrated in Figure 17-12).[93] Regardless of a person's uniqueness, social-emotional needs remain unchanged. If sensitive adults are available to help impaired children, most of them should be able to master Erikson's tasks (see Chap. 1).

Trust Versus Mistrust

If the infant's parents have not yet resolved their own shock and grief over their child's impairment, they may be inconsistent or inappropriate in their responses. Blind or deaf infants may be startled if picked up without auditory or visual warning of the contact. Lack of the ability to predict events may interfere with trust formation. Adults need to ensure that the

FIGURE 17–11.
A positive relationship with the adult motivates a child to participate effectively in therapy.

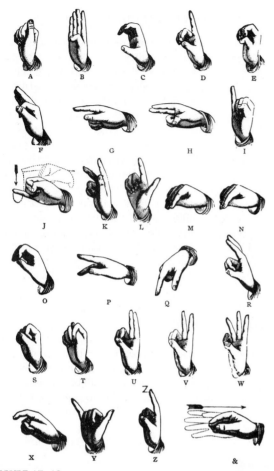

FIGURE 17–12.
Manual alphabet for the deaf. Deaf people also have a manual language with its own codes for words and syntactic structure for sentences. Some individuals use cued speech, a system of 32 hand signals that represent phonemes and accompany lip reading. (Courtesy Ohio School for the Deaf.)

FIGURE 17–13.
Toddlers need the opportunity to manipulate toys independently. Even the toddler with severe cerebral palsy can be provided with meaningful, independent play activities by a creative parent.

infant is able to communicate needs and to predict events to facilitate development of trust in self and the environment.

The visually or auditorily impaired adult may develop mistrust of the environment or people because of inadequate cues to interpret the environment. Inaccessibility and discrimination issues also interfere with trust of society or the environment.

Autonomy Versus Shame and Doubt
During the toddler stage, children normally learn to get things for themselves, to control the bowel and bladder, to walk, run, and talk. The inability of disabled children to make their bodies do what they want them to do can be an acute source of frustration, requiring sensitive parental assistance (Fig. 17-13). Children with neurological disorders may have particular conflict if they are unable to learn to control elim-

ination. They may still need to wear diapers at age 6, even though their cognitive functioning levels are normal.

Disabled adults also express considerable shame and dismay about lack of control of body movements or processes. Inability to express ideas or to remember names can be especially distressing to people after a stroke or with the onset of Alzheimer's disease. Understanding friends with a sense of humor and patience can be invaluable sources of support for maintaining autonomy and dignity.

Initiative Versus Guilt
It is difficult for some children with specific health problems to exert initiative in selecting activities when their choice results in adverse physical effects. When cognitive processes have not yet sufficiently developed to allow the child to understand the reasons for or the mechanics of physical limitations, confusion and guilt may result when a diabetic crisis, seizure, or respiratory difficulty follows the child's attempts to set personal limits. It is difficult for the child to achieve independence from the parents and to set personal goals or limits when so many limits have already been set by the physical disability or when others are always setting the goals for the child. Parents need to balance sensitively the opportunity to make choices (offering two or three safe alternatives) and provide the necessary teaching, with protective restrictions, until the child is able to self-govern behaviors within safe limits.

The blind adult who must ask for assistance in locating landmarks or objects and the neurologically impaired adult who needs assistance with mobility or personal care may experience guilt feelings about the forced dependence on others. Joni Eareckson Tada, paralyzed by a diving accident during late adolescence, resolved this crisis by realizing that it was still she who did the planning and orchestrating of personal care and other activities. She merely used other people's hands and feet to carry out her plans.[84]

Industry Versus Inferiority

The school-ager develops a positive self-identity through the mastery of valued skills. The disabled child of this age needs support in setting appropriate goals and in learning alternative approaches that lead to mastery. Most critical is the need to learn to develop persistence, to stick to a task until it is mastered or completed.[30] The school-ager needs to begin to identify his or her unique interests and talents. Pursuing a socially desirable skill (e.g., musical instrument, ham radio, pet raising, gymnastics) may also increase the child's value in the eyes of peers.

The disabled adult who is unable to secure compatible, challenging employment or to pursue a hobby of interest may develop feelings of inferiority.

Identity Versus Role Confusion

The disabled adolescent may experience great conflict in attempts to blend one's interests, abilities, experiences, and the disability into a positive role identity. Questions about career and marriage may remain nebulous. Anxiety may increase as graduation from the semiprotected educational environment draws closer. ("Will I be able to get a job?" "Can I compete with nondisabled people?" "Is there a niche for me?") If a person's abilities are carefully weighed against the skills needed to perform a job, success can be anticipated. It must be noted, however, that even if the tools and skills are matched well, the job may not be retained if interpersonal relationship skills have not been adequately developed (Fig. 17-14).

Education

It is estimated that 10% to 12% of people under the age of 21 are handicapped. In 1974, the Bureau of Education of the Handicapped discovered that 50% of our nation's 8 million educationally handicapped children had inadequate educational programs and that more than 1 million children between the ages of 6 and 16 had no educational program at all.[68] This situation was felt to be a gross violation of the civil rights of these children. The United States Constitution states that all men are created equal; this statement does not mean that they all have equal potential, but that they all have the legal right to equal opportunity to develop their potentials.[44,87] Each child has the right to receive an education geared to helping him or her learn and maximize potentials to live life to the fullest capacity.

Public Law 94-142

In 1975, the 94th Congress passed Public Law (PL) 94-142, the Education for All Handicapped Children Act of 1975. It man-

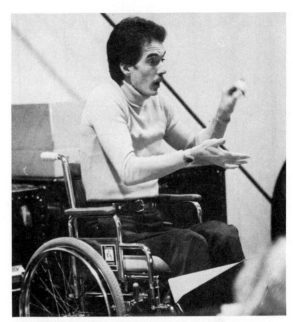

FIGURE 17–14.
Physically disabled people have talents and abilities that can enrich community life. Many obtain superior educations to compensate for motor disabilities and thus make outstanding employees.

dates that *all* children 5 through 21 years of age, regardless of type or degree of disability, *must* be provided a free, appropriate public education. This law embodies a holistic approach to education, which can include adaptive functioning and self-help skills as well as academic skills. Section 10 of the Education Act of 1974 provides similar safeguards in England.[89] The major provisions of PL 94-142 include the following topics.

LEAST RESTRICTIVE ALTERNATIVE. The law stipulates that, to the maximum extent possible, educationally handicapped children are to be educated with ("mainstreamed") children who are not handicapped. Removal is to occur "only when the nature or severity of the handicap is such that education in regular classes with the use of supplementary aids and services cannot be achieved satisfactorily."[68] A hierarchy of educational programs is available to meet the unique needs of the child (Fig. 17-15). One starts with the assumption of normalcy and alters the environment only as necessary, to meet the needs of the *child,* not the needs of the school system.

Although mainstreamed children may be subjected to teasing and bullying and experience more isolation than the nondisabled child, the majority of those who are integrated exhibit higher self-esteem, less passivity, and greater involvement in life.[51,83] They are more likely than segregated children to have a realistic idea of future career options, true abilities, marriage, and adult responsibilities.[51]

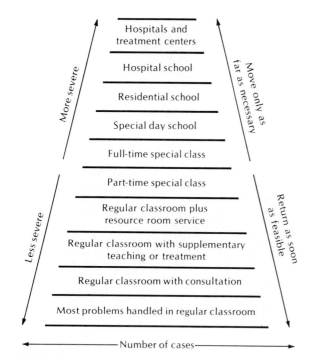

FIGURE 17–15.
Hierarchy of services for special education programs. (From Reynolds, M. C. [1962]. A framework for considering some issues in special education. Exceptional Children, *28, 368. With permission.)*

MULTIFACTORED, NONDISCRIMINATORY EVALUATION. A single IQ test can no longer be used as the basis for educational placement. Assessments must evaluate the needs of the *total* child and must be given in the child's native language or mode of communication if necessary. Testing may be used to identity functional skills but cannot be used to discriminate against the child.

PLACEMENT TEAM. After the assessment is completed, no *one* person can decide on appropriate placement or programming for a child. The team must include representatives of both the home and the school. After an individual evaluation, the child must be placed in the program that is most advantageous to his or her total development. Whatever the team agrees on is considered appropriate.

INDIVIDUALIZED EDUCATIONAL PROGRAM (IEP). The real value of PL 94-142 centers on the fact that each child must be provided with a written statement that specifies the child's needs and the program to be offered. This provision promotes recognition of the intraindividual differences and allows individualization of educational approaches according to the child's unique developmental levels. When unique, alternative approaches are used, frustration can be lowered, successes earned, self-esteem elevated, and social-emotional adaptation problems prevented.

FULL SERVICES. The law stipulates that all education and supportive services be offered at no cost to the family. These services include transportation, private tutoring, special equipment, physical and speech therapies, parent counseling, and even room and board if the child is placed in a residential setting at the recommendation of the placement team.[25] Some schools offer classes in the child's native language (especially Spanish and the Indian languages), and some school systems provide portable schools for children of migrant farm workers. Many schools are making more concerted efforts to honor and extend value to subcultures by including study of native arts and crafts or courses designed to meet the value systems of specific ethnic groups.

DUE PROCESS. Occasionally, the team cannot agree on an appropriate placement or program. In this case, the family is entitled to examine all records and request an impartial hearing. They may even go to court if necessary. However, the law was developed to open up communication, not to create adversaries. Suits are usually the result of inadequate communication and poor individualized planning.

Public Law 99-457

Recognizing that early educational intervention for children with special needs can have life-long positive results as well as reduced costs for special education during the formal school-age years, the 99th Congress passed PL 99-457, the 1986 Amendments to the Education of the Handicapped Act.[96] This law mandates that the local educational agency extend special educational services to children beginning on their third birthday.

This law also encourages states to provide free special educational services to families with disabled and high-risk children during the first 36 months of life. Early Intervention Programs offer therapy services to the children, but they also offer information and support to the parents to help them to understand their own feelings and needs, to understand and meet the unique needs of their young child, and to develop a close and satisfying relationship with the child. The parents and professionals work as a team to assess and meet the child's needs. Community programs can be accessed through the local health or education systems.

THE DISABLED ADULT

As the disabled person grows up, he or she is no longer the cute "poster" child who elicits feelings of benevolence from society.[81] Disabled adults, like all other adults, have emotional needs for friendship and family ties, needs for a useful occupation, and desires to make a contribution to society. They have sexual feelings and need opportunities for recreational and leisure time activities. However, inadequate preparation during the formative years, reduced emotional resources, and the discriminatory practices of society can inhibit their ability to make reciprocal contributions to society.[83]

Transition to Adulthood

At a time when most young people are thinking about leaving the family, the disabled person's need for assistance in ADL may preclude thoughts of independent living. The parents themselves may experience difficulty releasing the child, seeing themselves as indispensable to the young adult's quality of life. Thus, the separation-individuation issue, if not adequately resolved earlier in life, can stifle the continued development of both the parents and the young adult at this critical transition point. Transition is a family affair that begins early in life if the individual is to experience maximal independence and maximize potentials.[15] Mastering the Braille alphabet early in life, for instance, can give the blind adult the confidence needed to pursue a variety of career options (the Braille alphabet is illustrated in Figure 17-16). Transitions for people with mental retardation are often delayed or may never be completed.[45]

Living Arrangements

About 80% of those with developmental disabilities (e.g., mental retardation, autism, cerebral palsy) live at home.[12, 15] Many people with disabilities find it difficult to locate a residence that is accessible or convenient to public transportation. It is also difficult to locate competent, reliable home care attendants or a residence designed to facilitate independent living for people with severe physical or cognitive limitations.[23]

The least restrictive alternative is just as critical for defining appropriate living conditions as it is for education. There is a difference between living with a family (natural, foster, or adoptive) and being placed in a "homelike facility."[86] Not only does institutionalization perpetuate custodianship, dependency, boredom, and loss of meaning in life, but it is also the most expensive way for a community to provide care for those who need assistance with ADL.[11] Communities are beginning to offer a range of services for people with special needs. These may include the following:[86]

Own home with:
    Transportation assistance

Architectural modifications of the home
Homemaker services for cleaning and meals
In-home attendant assistance with ADL
Part-time supervision and assistance with budgeting, health assessment, time management, and so on
Independent living facility with:
    Special technological equipment to ensure ADL
    On-call ADL or emergency assistance
    Part-time attendant assistance
Group home with 24-hour supervision and:
    Assistance as necessary
    Nursing care as needed
Nursing home
Residential institution

A major objective for placement options is to facilitate integration into the community. Observations indicate that when disabled people are accepted and interact freely with the community, their behaviors become more independent and socially appropriate.[14] Multiple adaptations can be made and equipment is available to help people with even severe disabilities live independently and successfully.[40, 99, 101, 103, 104]

Employment

It is estimated that only 21% of the 650,000 disabled children who leave or graduate from school annually find employment![65] People who benefited from PL 94-142 have nowhere to go. In spite of Section 504 of PL 93-112 (The Rehabilitation Act of 1973), employer discrimination on the basis of disability is still a fact with which disabled people live. The U.S. Commission on Civil Rights estimates unemployment to be between 50% and 75% for people with disabilities.[95] Of those who are employed, more than half are underemployed, underpaid, or are unable to secure full-time employment.[12, 42, 90]

Disabled people face discrimination in employment, housing, public accommodations, transportation, communication, recreation, and health services, as well as in the social arena. In short, disabled people can face discrimination in every area of their lives. Public Law 101-336 (The Americans with Disabilities Act of 1990) was passed to eliminate public

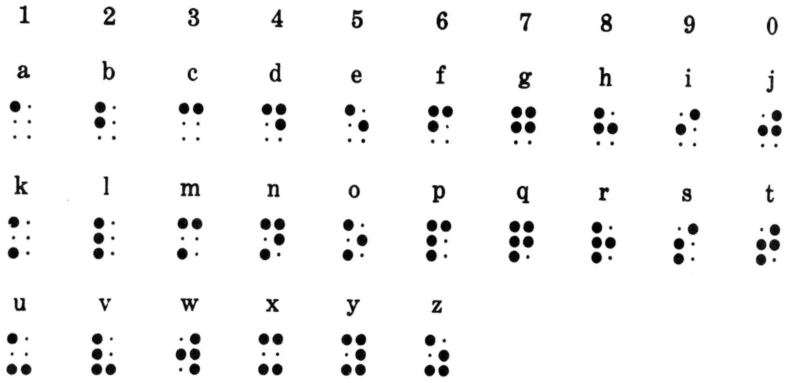

FIGURE 17–16.
The Braille alphabet is developed around the six positions of a cell. The position of the raised dot indicates to the reader the letter represented. Variations of raised dots on this same six-position cell indicate punctuation, letter combinations, or whole words. Even mathematics and music have been translated into this six-position cell code. (From Dorf, M. B., & Scharry, E. R. [1973]. Instruction manual for Braille transcribing. Washington, DC: Library of Congress. With permission.)

and employment discrimination. Employers can no longer discriminate in hiring, compensating, and promoting on the basis of disability. They are required to make reasonable accommodations for disabled employees, including accessibility, communication assistance, and modification of equipment.[67]

Disabled people who are successfully employed tend to have completed an appropriate education, including high school, express that they received much support from school, friends, and family, exhibit a sense of self-determination and desire for independence, and possess good social skills.[39] Unfortunately, many people with congenital disabilities are immature, lack self-discipline, or have inadequate interpersonal relationship skills,[72, 73] factors that interfere with the ability to secure or retain employment even in the presence of adequate technical skills. Lack of employment, whether for reasons of inadequate education, travel or transportation difficulties, lack of opportunities in the community, chronic illness, poor social skills, or discrimination, can have devastating effects on the individual's sense of self-worth and identity as well as one's financial situation. Bitterness, depression, and helplessness are common outcomes.

Many disabled people live at poverty level because of decreased employment options.[12, 16] Most severely disabled individuals are unable to support themselves on the salaries they receive when they have to pay others to help them to dress and go to the bathroom, clean house, or cook a meal. Consequently, they are forced to accept placement in a nursing home at a high cost to themselves and the welfare system instead of remaining employed, using the skills they do have, and contributing to the welfare of others. A subsidized income or accessible, independent-living homes would enable these individuals to remain employed and independent.[63]

Fortunately, most disabled adults and some children are eligible for Social Security assistance. This source of income can be augmented with food stamps and Medicaid assistance for medical care. Many communities also offer housing, heating, and other forms of extended assistance as needed.

Living in Two Worlds

Because of the impact of first impressions, those with visible impairments or disabilities and communication problems generally experience more stress in interpersonal relationships than those with nonvisible impairments.[73] By relating to the disability rather than to the person, the nondisabled individual prevents normal opportunities for the disabled person and forces him or her to adopt a "disabled" role. Disabled people are often an object of curiosity, alternately or simultaneously pitied, sympathized with, helped, patronized, or exhibited. When a disabled person "makes it" in spite of disability, he or she may be praised for spunk or may be criticized for "overcompensating" or being *too* independent.[83] The disabled person continues to be seen primarily as a *disabled* person rather than as an *able person* who also happens to have a disability.

Socialization with similarly disabled or unique peers (racial, ethnic, and linguistic groups face the same issue)

provides a safe, comfortable environment in which individual abilities, interests, and goals receive more attention. The person is more likely to be accepted for his or her true self. When experiences with the larger culture and general knowledge are weak, many normal daily events in the mainstream of the culture are stressful for the person. Whether by choice or default, life within the disabled world provides a small, safe though restricted life space. Depending on the exceptionality, the individual may join a social club or live in a "disabled ghetto," seeking minimal overlap with the dominant culture.[73] This arrangement allows the person to draw on the shared strength of the community.[83] Goals are confined to those situations in which the individual can function with equal or superior advantage.

A second disabled person may reject the disabled world and aspire to function totally in the normal world as if no disability existed. They do not necessarily deny the disability, but they try to avoid the categorization and stigmatization that accompanies *disability*.[83] These people may be successful, but it can be a lonely independence, and many problems may be encountered along the way. The gains may take more effort than they are really worth. These individuals are living in an unreal world, always pretending that their disabilities do not exist and fearing that someone will challenge them. This feeling increases tension levels and precipitates much status-anxiety.[87] "This kind of independence is no independence at all, because it consists of living one's life on terms that are dictated by the able-bodied and despising one's body rather than taking pride in oneself as a person with a disability."[83]

With the greater exposure of the public to the needs and rights of the disabled through education, mass media, and legislation, many persons with disabilities are now able to negotiate their own employment and social worlds.[73] They see the disability as only one aspect of life and participate in the normal world as realistically as possible, using adaptive and alternative skills for achieving goals. The individual views the self as "physically challenged" rather than "physically handicapped" and is able to enjoy association with disabled peers as well as normal people. These people do not accept the stereotyped role established by others in the culture; they establish their own roles, know their own strengths and weaknesses, and work cooperatively with them to find challenge and joy in life. They see and feel the stigma that others associate with their disabilities but do not dwell on it. These individuals educate others through their own joy of living and their ease with their own limitations and potentials (Fig. 17-17).

The disabled person does not achieve this realistic approach to life without help. He or she needs at least one other significant person who believes in and challenges his or her potentials during both the developmental and young adult years.

Living with Disability

Disabled children become aware of their limitations by what is *not* said as well as by what *is* said. Many parents do not talk

FIGURE 17–17.
Many disabled people are able to use animals to assist with orientation to the environment or for hearing, fetching, protection, and mobility. Although a close relationship develops between the disabled person and the dog, it is considered a working animal and not a pet. Thus, friendly overtures toward the dog from strangers are not encouraged.

with the disabled child about life as a married person or a parent, let alone leaving home.[83] These unduly low expectations can place a pall over the adult years.

Mastery of Developmental Tasks
Disabled people have the same developmental tasks as the nondisabled if they are to face adulthood successfully. "The unique aspects and different situations created by disablement are of secondary importance . . . growth relates to such tasks as achieving self-actualization, maximizing human potential, and developing total mind-body-spirit health."[92] Erikson's tasks offer guidelines to high-level mental health during these years.

Intimacy Versus Isolation
Many disabled people, because of unresolved pain that stems from earlier interpersonal relationships and experiences,

prefer to isolate themselves emotionally rather than face the risk of repeated social rejection. If the person has been the center of the family's energies, and repeated concessions have been made to accommodate to the child's needs, then the young person may not have developed a sensitivity to the perspective and needs of others, another factor that can interfere with intimate relationships. Some people accept any quality relationship in an effort to avoid loneliness. Others may substitute sex for emotional intimacy as a way to "prove" desirability.[73] The person who has been supported throughout the periods of intense "identity homework" can find satisfying emotional intimacy in any relationship and does not see marriage as the only true badge of social success. When marriage does occur, it is based on what each can contribute to the growth of the other person.

Generativity Versus Stagnation
Disabled people who are emotionally healthy and cognitively alert are "acutely aware of the need to fulfill a culturally valued role and strive to do so."[48] Physical limitations may restrict the options available to expand a career or to enjoy hobbies, precipitating boredom with life unless aggressive, creative approaches are taken to expand career and social horizons. Any adult who has not developed respect for and a positive concept of self, will experience difficulty with the task of facilitating the development of other people. Even the most severely disabled person has the potential ability to offer ideas, encouragement, and a philosophy of life that can foster the development of other people. Accepting and allowing oneself to be appropriately dependent can enable others to experience their own strength through generativity.

Ego Integrity Versus Despair
People who are unable to integrate their disabilities, impairments, and cultural ideals within a positive framework experience difficulty in achieving a sense of satisfaction or personal value in their later years. They may feel that the negative aspects outweigh the positive experiences and draw the conclusion that life was "not worth the trip." Conversely, impaired people who have met and resolved each challenge as it emerged develop a sense of confidence in themselves and others. They recognize that everyone must face challenges during a lifetime and that their challenges are merely more obvious, not necessarily more difficult.

Sexuality
"Denial of a person's sexuality is perhaps one of the most dehumanizing violations of the human spirit."[28] Yet, regardless of the disability, disabled people tend to be approached as if they are asexual.[9, 21, 28, 55, 71, 72] Handicapped children may develop a "clinical detachment" from their defective body to cope with being treated as "public property over the years in hospital outpatient departments,"[72] and to create a positive sense of self. Any dysfunction may be seen as "a 'mechanical breakdown' requiring objective treatment. This strategy may be more comfortable and less damaging emotionally than allowing feelings through, but it may then become very hard

for the child to switch to a more sensual and emotional approach to the human body."[72] Because of fears of exploitation, embarrassing behaviors, unwanted pregnancy, or lack of fulfillment of desires, many parents avoid discussing sexuality issues.[9, 28] Disabled people need opportunities to develop their sexual-social identity through appropriate social experiences and information on alternate techniques for a satisfying physical relationship.[21, 55, 71]

Marriage and Parenting

Although more disabled people are marrying today,[50] many disabled people do not marry because of immaturity, illness, or lack of self-care skills.[72] Those who do marry indicate a definite preference for the marital state and appear to cope better than those who live alone.[50] Financial, social, emotional, and genetic implications need to be thoroughly discussed. Disabled people need to be able to assume responsibility for their lives, not find a parent model in a spouse.[72] Self-care and home-management skills are best learned during the developmental years from a supportive parent.[63]

Those that feel inferior or unworthy may prefer to marry other disabled people because they are "equals." In some situations, these marriages work out well; however, a couple may withdraw further into the disabled world if they find that frustration in coping with their disability is the focus of their relationship rather than mutual respect and love. If both people are disabled, it may be difficult for them to find privacy.[72]

Many parents and even professional people discourage childbearing for disabled people, especially if they have cognitive deficits.[9, 46, 50] Although the risk of passing genetic disabilities to offspring is increased, no relationship exists between disability and one's success as a parent.[50] Mentally retarded parents often need supervision and assistance to meet the daily demands and developmental needs of young children.[49] Those with genetic disabilities may decide to adopt, providing they can find an agency willing to place a child in their homes. Although the tasks involved in caregiving may be inconvenient, disabled people can learn alternative techniques for stimulating their child's development.[5, 18, 37, 46, 64, 100] Children ask questions about a parent's disability before the third birthday and accept it as a part of the parent's identity by age 5.[46] Most parents feel a sense of fulfillment in childbearing and an increased sense of self-esteem and self-confidence in child rearing as well as an increased sense of normalcy.[46] The children frequently are more mature socially and emotionally because of their experiences in awareness of the needs of another.[9]

The Late Adult Years

People disabled in their adult years have more experiences and resources to draw on than younger people. Previous coping behaviors become influential in how one copes with the illness.[6] Social support remains critical. Although problems may be experienced in physical care, pain, surgery, special equipment, bowel and bladder management, perpet-

ual paralysis, finances, alternative living arrangements, depression, prognosis, adaptation, and isolation,[35] the major issues center on interpersonal relationships that foster independence.[61, 88] Independence can be accomplished by encouraging active participation in decision making, involvement in the community, and meaningful leisure time activities.[88] Infantilization by others may encourage dependency. It is easy to trivialize the emotional and existential aspects of chronic illness and disability, but these may become more painful than the disabilities per se.[47] Younger adults may feel cheated out of an anticipated career and family life. Older adults may feel cheated out of earned retirement years. Older adults with developmental disabilities face the same problems during retirement years as the nondisabled: financial concerns, use of leisure time, need to find meaning in life's activities, and a continued need for contact with extended family members.[26]

IMPLICATIONS

Many people face discrimination through their lifetime because of possession of a factor devalued by their reference group. When the distinguishing factor is present during the childhood years, the child is forced to identify his or her differences from the significant values and characteristics of the culture before identifying sufficient similarities and, thus, may feel alienated. Sensitive guidance and support from a significant adult can help to prevent emotional handicaps and can facilitate maximization of potentials.

Isolation from the mainstream of life can aid or hinder the child's ability to adjust to adolescent and adult living. If one plans to remain within the confines of a subculture, the isolation serves to perpetuate select cultural standards and goals (e.g., religious or ethnic values). However, if the child must or wants to eventually blend into the mainstream of the culture, isolation during the developmental years because of overprotective parents, residential schooling, or inadequate opportunities can present barriers to integration throughout one's life span.

"Being disabled in this society is a complex social/psychological/political reality that breeds extensive and serious problems for the disabled person, far beyond those resulting from the physical impairment itself."[16] Societal attitudes, resistance, and policies create discrimination and handicaps far more difficult to transcend than the limitations of the disability per se. Many disabling conditions do not have to be handicapping if the individual can work with them realistically and set appropriate goals.

Interactions based on stereotyped concepts of individuals limit the potentials of everyone involved. "The deprivation of any man's right to fulfillment diminishes each of us, for we, as well as he, have lost what he has been deprived of, for we are all involved in each other."[59] Although it may take more effort to include a disabled or culturally different person in an educational program, place of employment, or social group, the benefits can far outweigh any inconveniences.

RESOURCES

A truly holistic approach to disabled individuals is not limited to the home or the school. Disabled people need adequate technological devices, information, and social experiences that expand or offer an outlet for their interests and provide for peer contacts. Local agencies such as the American Red Cross, scouts, and YMCA are able to provide sensitive, individualized peer interactions and assistance. The local public library is also a rich source of resources and services. Other sources of information or referral are included in Appendix G.

REFERENCES

1. Abood, D. A., & Burkhead, E. J. (1988). Wellness: A valuable resource for people with disabilities. *Health Education, 19*(2), 21–25.
2. Ainlay, S. C., Becker, G., & Coleman, L. M. (Eds.). (1986). *The dilemma of difference: A multidisciplinary view of stigma.* New York: Plenum Press.
3. Ainlay, S. C., Coleman, L. M., & Becker, G. (1986). Stigma reconsidered. In S. C. Ainlay, G. Becker, & L. M. Coleman (Eds.), *The dilemma of difference: A multidisciplinary view of stigma* (pp. 1–13). New York: Plenum Press.
4. Allen, L., & Majidi-Ahi, S. (1989). Black American children. In J. T. Gibbs & L. N. Huang (Eds.), *Children of color: Psychological interventions with minority youth.* San Francisco: Jossey-Bass.
5. Anderson, H. (1981). *The disabled homemaker.* Springfield, IL: C. C. Thomas.
6. Anderson, M. P. (1988). Stress management for chronic disease: An overview. In M. L. Russell (Ed.), *Stress management for chronic disease* (pp. 3–13). New York: Pergamon Press.
7. Ayrault, E. W. (1974). *Helping the handicapped teenager mature.* New York: Public Affairs Committee.
8. Baird, D. I. (1987). *Dorothee, the silent teacher: A family forgives disaster.* Kansas City, MO: Beacon Hill Press of Kansas City.
9. Baskin, B. H., & Riggs, E. P. (1988). Mothers who are disabled. In B. Birns & D. F. Hay (Eds.), *The different faces of motherhood.* New York: Plenum Press.
10. Becker G., & Arnold, R. (1986). Stigma as a social and cultural construct. In S. C. Ainlay, G. Becker, & L. M. Coleman (Eds.), *The dilemma of difference: A multidisciplinary view of stigma* (pp. 39–57). New York: Plenum Press.
11. Biklen, D., & Knoll, J. (1987). The disabled minority. In S. J. Taylor, D. Biken, & J. Knoll (Eds.), *Community integration for people with severe disabilities* (pp. 3–24). New York: Teacher's College Press.
12. Blalock, G. (1988). Transitions across the lifespan. In B. L. Ludlow, A. P. Turnbull, & R. Luckasson (Eds.), *Transitions to adult life for people with mental retardation: Principles and practices* (pp. 3–20). Baltimore: Paul H. Brookes.
13. Blom, G. E., Cheney, B. D., & Snoddy, J. E. (1986). *Stress in childhood: An intervention model for teachers and other professionals.* New York: Teachers College Press.
14. Bogdan, R., & Taylor, S. J. (1987). Conclusion: The next wave. In S. J. Taylor, D. Biken, & J. Knoll (Eds.), *Community integration for people with severe disabilities* (pp. 209–213). New York: Teacher's College Press.
15. Brotherson, M. J., Backus, L. H., Summers, J. A., & Turnbull, A. P (1986). Transition to adulthood. In J. A. Summers (Ed.), *The right to grow up: An introduction to adults with developmental disabilities* (pp. 17–44). Baltimore: Paul H. Brookes.
16. Cleland, M. (1982). Forward. In M. G. Eisenberg, C. Griggins, & R. J. Duval (Eds.), *Disabled people as second-class citizens* (pp. vii–xvii). New York: Springer Publishing Company.
17. Coleman, D. (1980, February). 1528 little geniuses and how they grew. *Psychology Today,* pp. 28–43.
18. Conine, T., et al. (1988). *Aids and adaptations for parents with physical or sensory disabilities* (2nd ed.). Vancouver, BC: School of Rehabilitation Medicine, University of British Columbia.
19. Coombs, J. (1984). *Living with the disabled: You can help.* New York: Sterling Publishing.
20. Corbin, J. M., & Strauss, A. (1988). *Unending work and care: Managing chronic illness at home.* San Francisco: Jossey-Bass.
21. Cornelius, D. A., Chipouras, S., Makas E., & Daniels, S. M. (1982). *Who cares? A handbook on sex education and counseling services for disabled people* (2nd ed.). Baltimore: University Park Press.
22. Cross, T. L. (1986). *Gathering and sharing: An exploratory study of service delivery to emotionally handicapped Indian children.* Bethesda, MD: National Institute of Mental Health. (Resources in Education, 1988, ED 289 267)
23. Directory of Residential Centers. (1989). *Directory of residential centers for adults with developmental disabilities.* Phoenix: Oryx.
24. Eisenberg, M. G. (1982). Disability as stigma. In M. G. Eisenberg, C. Griggins, & R. J. Duval (Eds.), *Disabled people as second-class citizens* (pp. 3–12). New York: Springer Publishing Company.
25. Esterson, M. M., & Bluth, L. F. (Eds.). (1987). *Related services for handicapped children.* Boston: College-Hill Press.
26. Factor, A. R. (1989, May/June). How I feel about growing older: Conversations with older people with developmental disabilities. *Advantage, a newsletter about aging and developmental disabilities,* pp. 3.
27. Fine, M., & Asch, A. (1988). Disability beyond stigma: Social interaction, discrimination, and activism. *Journal of Social Issues, 44*(1), 3–21.
28. Gardner, N. E. S. (1986). Sexuality. In J. A. Summers, (Ed.), *The right to grow up: An introduction to adults with developmental disabilities* (pp. 45–66). Baltimore: Paul H. Brookes.
29. Gerring, J. P. (1988). Behavioral and emotional conditions of handicapped adolescents. In J. P. Gerring & L. P. McCarthy (Eds.), *The psychiatry of handicapped children and adolescents* (pp. 73–99). Boston: Little, Brown.
30. Gerring, J. P. (1988). Describing and diagnosing psychiatric conditions in handicapped children. In J. P. Gerring & L. P. McCarthy (Eds.), *The psychiatry of handicapped children and adolescents* (pp. 33–71). Boston: Little, Brown.
31. Gerring, J. P., & McCarthy, L. P. (1988). An overview of handicapping conditions and the multidisciplinary team approach to care of handicapped children. In J. P. Gerring & L. P. McCarthy (Eds.), *The Psychiatry of handicapped children and adolescents* (pp. 1–32). Boston: Little, Brown
32. Gerring, J. P., & McCarthy, L. P. (Eds.). (1988). *The psychiatry of handicapped children and adolescents.* Boston: Little, Brown.
33. Gibbs, J. T., & Huang, L. N. (Eds.). (1989). *Children of color: Psychological interventions with minority youth.* San Francisco: Jossey-Bass.
34. Goffman, E. (1963). *Stigma: Notes on the management of a spoiled identity.* Englewood Cliffs, NJ: Prentice-Hall.

35. Goldiamond, B. (1982). Families of the disabled: Sometimes insiders in rehabilitation, always outsiders in policy planning. In M. G. Eisenberg, C. Griggins, & R. J. Duval (Eds.), *Disabled people as second-class citizens* (pp. 152–170). New York: Springer Publishing Company.

36. Hahn, H. (1988). The politics of physical differences: Disability and discrimination. *Journal of Social Issues, 44*(1), 39–47.

37. Hale, G. (Ed.). (1979). *The source book for the disabled: An illustrated guide to easier and more independent living for physically disabled people, their families and friends.* Philadelphia: W. B. Saunders.

38. Hill, N., Mehnert, T., Taylor, T., Kagey, M., & Leizhenko, S. (1986). *The ICD survey of disabled Americans: Bringing disabled Americans into the mainstream.* New York: International Center for the Disabled.

39. Hudson, P. J., Schwartz, S. E., Sealander, K. A., Campbell, P., & Hensel, J. W. (1988). Successfully employed adults with handicaps: Characteristics and transition strategies. *Career Development for Exceptional Individuals, 11*(1), 7–14.

40. Illustrated Directory. (1990). *The illustrated directory of handicapped products.* 497 Cameron Way, Boffalo Grove, IL 60089 (312-253-9426).

41. Jernigan, K. (1989, April/May). Note from the editor. *The Braille Monitor,* p. 267.

42. Jones, R. (Ed.) (1983). *Reflections on growing up disabled.* Reston, VA: National Institute of Education.

43. Kershaw, J. D. (1973). Handicapped children in the ordinary school. In V. P. Varma (Ed.), *Stresses in children.* London: University of London Press.

44. Kirk, S. A., & Gallagher, J. J. (1989). *Educating exceptional children* (6th ed.). Boston: Houghton Mifflin.

45. Knowlton, H. E., Turnbull, A. P., Backus, L., & Turnbull, H. R. (1988). Letting go: Consent and the "Yes, but . . . " problem in transition. In B. L. Ludlow, A. P. Turnbull, & R. Luckasson (Eds.), *Transitions to adult life for people with mental retardation: Principles and practice* (pp. 45–66). Baltimore: Paul H. Brookes.

46. Kopala, B. (1989). Mothers with impaired mobility speak out. *MCN, The American Journal of Maternal/Child Nursing, 14,* 115–119.

47. Lazarus, R. S. (1985). The trivialization of distress. In J. Rosen & L. Solomon (Eds.), *Prevention in healthy psychology.* Hanover, NH: University Press of New England.

48. Levy, J. M. (1988). Family response and adaptation to a handicap. In J. P. Gerring & L. P. McCarthy (Eds.), *The psychiatry of handicapped children and adolescents* (pp. 215–246). Boston: Little, Brown.

49. Lynch, E. W., & Bakley, S. (1989). Serving young children whose parents are mentally retarded. *Infants and Young Children, 1*(3), 26–38.

50. Maavik, S. (1986). Marriage and parenthood. In J. A. Summers (Ed.), *The right to grow up: An introduction to adults with developmental disabilities* (pp. 67–90). Baltimore: Paul H. Brookes.

51. Madge, N., & Fassam, M. (1982). *Ask the children: Experiences of physical disability in the school years.* London: Batsford Academic and Educational Limited.

52. Mahler, M. S., Pine, F., & Bergman, A. (1975). *The psychological birth of the human infant: Symbiosis and individuation.* New York: Basic books.

53. Makas, E. (1988). Positive attitudes toward disabled people: Disabled and nondisabled persons' perspectives. *Journal of Social Issues, 44*(1), 49–61.

54. Mallis, J. (1983). *Diamonds in the dust.* Austin, TX: Multimedia Arts.

55. McKown, J. M. (1986). Disabled teenagers: Sexual identification and sexuality counseling. *Sexuality and Disability, 7*(1/2), 17–27.

56. McMann, N., & Oliver, R. (1988). Problems in families with gifted children: Implications for counselors. *Journal of Counseling and Development, 66,* 275–278.

57. Meyers, M. F., & King, L. M. (1983). Mental health issues in the development of the black American child. In G. J. Powell (Ed.), *The psychosocial development of minority group children* (pp. 275–306). New York: Brunner/Mazel.

58. Minde, K., et al. (1972). How they grew up: Forty-one physically handicapped children and their families. *American Journal of Psychiatry, 128,* 1554.

59. Montagu, A. (1974). *Culture and human development: Insights into growing human.* Englewood Cliffs, NJ: Prentice-Hall.

60. Murphy, A., & Crocker, A. C. (1987). Impact of handicapping conditions on the child and family. In H. M. Wallace, R. F. Biehl, L. Taft, & A. C. Oglesby (Eds.), *Handicapped children and youth: A comprehensive community and clinical approach* (pp. 26–41). New York: Human Services Press.

61. Murphy, C. (1988). *Day to day: Spiritual help when someone you love has Alzheimer's.* Philadelphia: The Westminster Press.

62. Olshansky, S. (1962). Chronic sorrow: A response to having a mentally defective child. *Social Casework, 43,* 190.

63. Orlansky, M. D., & Heward, W. L. (1981). *Voices: Interviews with handicapped people.* Columbus, OH: Charles E. Merrill.

64. Parks, S. (Ed.). (1984). *HELP: When the parent is handicapped.* Palo Alto, CA: VORT Corporation.

65. Patton, S. L. (1985). Introduction [Special issue on transitional employment]. *Journal of Job Placement, 1*(2), iv–vi.

66. Powell, G. J. (1983). America's minority group children: The underserved. In G. J. Powell (Ed.), *The psychosocial development of minority group children* (pp. 3–9). New York: Brunner/Mazel.

67. Public Law 101–336. (1990). *Americans with Disabilities Act of 1990. HR 2273.* Washington, DC: U. S. Congress.

68. Public Law 94–142. (1975). *Education for All Handicapped Children Act of 1975.* Washington, DC: U. S. Congress.

69. Ramirez, B. A. (1988). Culturally and linguistically diverse children. *Teaching Exceptional Children, 20*(4), 45–46.

70. Rodgers, B. M., Hilemeier, M. M., O'Neill, E., & Slonim, M. B. (1981). Depression in the chronically ill or handicapped school-aged child. *MCN: The American Journal of Maternal Child Nursing, 6,* 266–273.

71. Romano, M. D. (1982). Sex and disability: Are they mutually exclusive? In M. G. Eisenberg, C. Griggins, & R. J. Duval (Eds.), *Disabled people as second-class citizens* (pp. 64–78). New York: Springer Publishing Company.

72. Russell, P. (1985). *The wheelchair child: How handicapped children can enjoy life to its fullest.* Englewood Cliffs, NJ: Prentice-Hall.

73. Safilios-Rothschild, C. (1982). Social and psychological parameters of friendship and intimacy for disabled people. In M. G. Eisenberg, C. Griggins, & R. J. Duval (Eds.), *Disabled people as second-class citizens* (pp. 40–51). New York: Springer Publishing Company.

74. Sarason, S. B. (1986). And what is the public interest? *American Psychologist, 41,* 899–906.

75. Scheer, J., & Groce, N. (1988). Impairment as a human constant: Cross-cultural and historical perspectives on variation. *Journal of Social Issues, 44*(1), 23–37.

76. Schowalter, J. E. (1979). The chronically ill child. In J. D. Noshpitz (Ed.), *Basic handbook of child psychiatry.* New York: Basic Books.

77. Seligman, M. E. P. (1975). *Helplessness: On depression, development, and death.* San Francisco: Freeman.

78. Sigelman, C. K., & Singleton, L. C. (1986). Stigmatization in childhood: A survey of developmental trends and issues. In S. C. Ainlay, G. Becker, & L. M. Coleman (Eds.), *The dilemma of difference: A multidisciplinary view of stigma* (pp. 185–208). New York: Plenum Press.

79. Slaby, A., & Glicksman, A. S. (1985). *Adapting to life-threatening illness.* New York: Praeger.

80. Sparks, R. C. (1988). *To treat or not to treat: Bioethics and the handicapped newborn.* Mahwah, NJ: Paulist Press.

81. Summers, J. A. (1986). Introduction. In J. A. Summers (Ed.), *The right to grow up: An introduction to adults with developmental disabilities* (pp. xi–xiii). Baltimore: Paul H. Brookes.

82. Summers, J. A. (1986). Who are developmentally disabled adults? A closer look at the definition of developmental disabilities. In J. A. Summers (Ed.), *The right to grow up: An introduction to adults with developmental disabilities* (pp. 3–16). Baltimore: Paul H Brookes.

83. Sutherland, A. T. (1981). *Disabled we stand.* London: Souvenir Press.

84. Tada, J. E. (1986). *Choices, changes.* Grand Rapids, MI: Zondervan Books.

85. Taylor, A. R., Asher, S. R., & Williams, G. A. (1987). The social adaptation of mainstreamed mildly retarded children. *Child Development, 58,* 1321–1334.

86. Taylor, S. J., Racino, J., Knoll, J., & Lutfiyya, Z. (1987). Down home: Community integration for people with the most severe disabilities. In S. J. Taylor, D. Biken, & J. Knoll (Eds.), *Community integration for people with severe disabilities* (pp. 36–63). New York: Teacher's College Press.

87. Telford, C. W., & Sawrey, J. M. (1981). *The exceptional individual* (4th ed.). Englewood Cliffs, NJ: Prentice-Hall.

88. Thurman, E. (1986). Maintaining dignity in later years. In J. A. Summers (Ed.), *The right to grow up: An introduction to adults with developmental disabilities* (pp. 91–115). Baltimore: Paul H. Brookes.

89. Topliss, E. (1982). *Social responses to handicap.* New York: Longnam.

90. United Nations. (1986). *Disability: Solution, strategies and policies: United Nations decade of disabled people, 1983–1992.* New York: Department of International Economic and Social Affairs.

91. VanHasselt, V. B., & Hersen, M. (1987). Physical and developmental disabilities: An overview. In V. B. VanHasselt & M. Hersen (Eds.), *Psychological evaluation of the developmentally and physically disabled* (pp. 3–15). New York: Plenum Press.

92. Vash, C. L. (1981). *The Psychology of disability.* New York: Springer Publishing Company.

93. Vernon, M., & Koh, S. D. (1970). Early manual communication and deaf children's achievement. *American Annals of the Deaf, 116,* 527.

94. Webb, J. T., Meckstroth, E. A., & Tolan, S. S. (1982). *Guiding the gifted child.* Columbus, OH: Ohio Psychology Publishing Co.

95. Wehman, P., Kregel, J., & Barcus, J. M. (1985). From school to work: A vocational transition model for handicapped students. *Exceptional Children, 53,* 25–37.

96. Weiner, R., & Koppelman, J. (1987). *From birth to 5: Serving the youngest handicapped children.* Alexandria, VA: Education Research Group/Capitol Publications. (ERIC Document Reproduction Service No. ED 288 278)

97. Whitmore, J. R. (1988). Gifted children at risk for learning difficulties. *Teaching Exceptional Children, 20*(Summer), 10–14.

98. Williams, T. M., & Kornblum, W. (1985). *Growing up poor.* Lexington, MA: Lexington Books.

99. Wilshere, E. R. (1983). *Leisure and gardening.* Oxford, UK: Oxfordshire Health Authority.

100. Wilshere, E. R. (1984). *Disabled mother* (5th ed.). Oxford, UK: Oxfordshire Health Authority.

101. Wilshere, E. R. (1985). *Personal care* (5th ed.). Oxford, UK: Oxfordshire Health Authority.

102. Wilshere, E. R. (1986). *Disabled child* (5th ed.). Oxford, UK: Oxfordshire Health Authority.

103. Wilshere, E. R. (1986). *Housing and furniture* (5th ed.). Oxford, UK: Oxfordshire Health Authority.

104. Wilshere, E. R. (1987). *Home management* (6th ed.). Oxford, UK: Oxfordshire Health Authority.

105. Zuckerman, J. (1989, April/May). Fighting blind: Bonnie Peterson challenges stereotypes about the "visually impaired." *Braille Monitor,* pp. 267–272.

Development of a Concept of Death

Clara S. Schuster

An individual's concept of death is a major organizer of the personality. All five domains are embodied in this single complex macro-concept as one attempts to integrate personal concepts of past, present, and future. A mature and healthy concept of life necessarily incorporates a mature and healthy concept of death.[13] The uniqueness of humanity, human dignity, and, in fact, the value and meaning of life itself are all bound up in one's concept of death. Eventually, we all must face our own mortality.

The most dramatic changes in one's concept of death occur during the first decade of life, paralleling changes in cognitive functioning and ego development. Initially, the infant has no awareness of death. Gradually, the young child moves from an awareness of the concrete realities of death to grappling with the more abstract issues involved in facing personal mortality. One's concept of death tends to be modified and refined until physical death ends temporal life.

The words "I will die" have a different meaning to the child than to the adult because of the child's weak ego-strength and inability to think abstractly. A mature understanding of "I will die" presupposes an understanding of the following subconcepts:[37, 83, 85]

1. A difference exists between living and nonliving objects—I am alive.
2. All living things age and will eventually die of old age—death is a part of life.
3. Living things cannot evade all causes of death—death is inevitable.
4. The body becomes nonfunctional at death—all physiological, sensing, and feeling processes cease.
5. Death is irreversible—a permanent end to temporal life.
6. Death is universal—this concept includes me.

The last three elements appear to be most critical in a mature concept of death.[85] Each subconcept develops separately yet in tandem with the others. The last, *universality,* appears to be directly related to a person's level of cognitive development; however, the others are subject to affective elements, experience, and the processes of socialization.[7]

The concept of life and the concept of death appear to develop concurrently, but they are not necessarily correlated.[6] Young children do not see life and death as flip sides of a coin and thus may not clearly distinguish between the two.[69] Death may be seen as another phase or state of life. Young children also lack both the mental operations and the affective strength to integrate these concepts into a single concept of personal mortality.

Although the development of a concept of death is unique and personal to each individual, it has some universal qualities. To appreciate the qualitative changes that occur in the development of one's concepts of life and death, we must examine the values and beliefs of the culture as well as experiences and cognitive development.[65] Understanding of a child's developmental levels is critical in offering sensitive support during a time of loss if the crisis is to be a maturational rather than a destructive experience.

FACTORS THAT AFFECT CONCEPT FORMATION

In past eras, aging and death were integral parts of family life.[4] When several generations live in the same home, or in close proximity, children are able to witness aging and death as parts of the life span.[90] Children were exposed to the process of dying, not just to death itself. In the past, when a loved one died, all the family members participated in the viewing, memorial, and burying events. Although the children might be too young to comprehend the significance of all the events, they were introduced to the fact of permanent separation and grief. The common sharing of grief supported the value of human life, allowed for a therapeutic milieu for expression of sorrow and frustration, and offered experience for further integration and growth of the psyche.

Today, 70% of deaths occur to people older than 65 years of age.[96] A child's emotional bonds with the grandparents may be weak because of distance or infrequency of contacts. Consequently, the child is denied the opportunities to participate in the aging process or to experience the challenges of working through a meaningful grief experience.

Advances in medical care have raised new and troubling questions about life and death. Death is no longer viewed as a natural event in our culture but as a failure of parental supervision or medical technology.[90] Only 4% of deaths are to children younger than 15 years of age.[96] Whereas death used to be seen as an inevitable part of family life before the turn of the century, now it is often seen as the result of personal negligence or a tragic accident. Some people may even be angry that death cannot be permanently avoided or abolished by technology.[95]

Denial and rituals are frequently used to distort or to disguise death as a meaningful part of life.[4] Discussion of death is a taboo subject in many homes,[65] just as discussions of sex and pregnancy were avoided in the Victorian era. Eighty percent of parents are uncomfortable discussing death with children, and 70% avoid discussing it with another adult.[48] When questions are asked, the parent frequently evades the issue or admonishes the child: "Don't talk about awful things like that!" Euphemisms such as "sleep," "pass away," or "rest" are often used to soften the reality of the finality of death; other euphemisms such as "shuffle off" or "croak" attempt to add humor as a form of denial of the reality.

Death is also removed as far as possible from the family setting. Seventy percent of deaths occur in a hospital or other nonhome setting.[96] The wake and the memorial service are at the funeral parlor—no longer in the home. When a family member dies, the parents may attempt to hide the fact from young children, thinking that the child is unaware of what is happening or that the information is detrimental to development (Fig. 18-1).[96] However, the child does not remain blissfully ignorant; subtle changes in parental attitudes, affect, and approach indicate to the child that something is wrong. Lack of information tends to increase rather than to decrease the child's anxiety. The child may even suspect that he or she is somehow responsible for the event. The results of this belief can adversely affect the person's emotional development for the rest of his or her life. Total exclusion from the event may have a damaging effect on the child's personality by depriving the child of a sense of belonging, sharing, and personal respect. Participation in family grief with explanations appropriate to the child's comprehension level can help to avoid potential long-range negative effects.[73]

No child is protected from the discovery of death. It is all around us. Leaves change color, die, and fall in the autumn; a

FIGURE 18–1.
When children are left without answers to their questions of separation, disappearance, or death, their minds are left to the fantasies of magical thought, vulnerabilities, and fears.

dead animal lies beside the highway; a fly is swatted; a pet dies. Each of these events provides experience with loss and offers an opportunity for the discussion of death. Television programs, including cartoons, "cops and robbers" programs, and the evening news all offer examples of death and destruction. Eighty percent of television programs portray death as violent, accidental, or otherwise unnatural.[94] Popular adolescent rock music deals with violent themes of distorted sexuality, pornography, murder, suicide, war, drugs, Satanism, dismemberment, and the grotesque.[64,96]

Many social and personal factors appear to impact on the development of one's concepts of life, death, and personal mortality. Preschoolers are more likely to understand the irreversibility of death and a dead person's inability to hear, see, and think after an experience with the death of a family member.[83] In fact, bereaved children as young as 24 months have been observed to understand the finality of a significant relationship.[21]

The effect of serious or terminal illness on young children is inconclusive. It appears that most children younger than age 6 are more disturbed by the issues of separation, treatments, and hospitalization than the fact of impending death.[88] Terminally ill school-age children demonstrate greater anxiety and concern over personal death than children hospitalized for chronic or serious nonfatal illnesses.[87,92] Terminally ill adolescents are concerned about protecting and facilitating the adaptation of friends and family members to their death as well as the facing of the issue of identity homework and the value of one's life.[60]

The child who faces a protracted terminal illness with cycles of remissions and relapses and multiple hospitalizations begins to understand death as a final and irreversible process early in life. Five stages have been identified in the adaptation of children to the changes in their health status and comprehension of personal mortality:[10]

1. I am seriously ill.
2. I am seriously ill but will get better.
3. I am always ill but I will get better.
4. I am always ill and will never get better.
5. I am dying.

As the child becomes aware of the terminal nature of his or her illness, the affective and social support of others becomes increasingly important. Art, play therapy, and other creative or affective outlets can help the child to work through the process and facilitate living life more fully as long as it lasts.[5]

Socioeconomic status with its attendant stressors and support systems also influence one's concept of death. The children of more highly educated parents tend to have more highly defined concepts of death, especially during the preschool years, than those of less-educated parents.[83] School-age children from middle and upper socioeconomic levels tend to see old age and disease (internal causes) as primary causes of death; whereas, those from lower socioeconomic

groups are more likely to identify aggression (external causes), such as accidents, war, violence, and suicide.[47]

DISCOVERY AND ACCEPTANCE OF DEATH AS A PART OF LIFE

The child's discovery of death is closely related to cognitive developmental levels. As the child strives to understand limits, causality, reversibility, separation, finality, and intention, concepts of life and death begin to emerge. The discovery of death becomes a private experience of great magnitude.[62] The child gradually differentiates between animate and inanimate, loses egocentric thinking that magically connects life and death to one's own thought processes, and develops the ability to deal with the more abstract philosophical issues engendered by the awareness of the universality of death.

Affectively, the child must develop sufficient ego-strength to face the concept of "nonbeing." Facing the reality of personal mortality is a big step beyond facing death as an abstract notion. This task is difficult when one is just beginning to recognize and to appreciate one's separateness and uniqueness. The ego of the young child is vulnerable. Facing this reality before adequate ego-strength and coping skills have been developed can have serious long-range effects.

Stages in the Development of a Concept of Death

Death acceptance involves two dimensions: **cognitive confrontation** and **affective integration.**[39,88] A mature concept of death includes a positive acceptance (affective domain) of the consequences of one's understanding (cognitive domain) of the facts of death. The cognitive and affective domains are intimately related, but not synchronous, in the development of a concept of death. Each domain appears to go through a gradual progression of five phases: **naïveté, awareness, rebellion, adaptation,** and **acceptance.** The cognitive domain appears to precede the affective domain as the two attempt to come to grips with personal mortality.

Although the stages appear to be universal, social factors mentioned earlier and cognitive developmental level influence the age at which the stages are mastered. The ages offered in Table 18-1 reflect comprehension and behaviors from multiple descriptive research studies. Affective changes are not as easy to assess as cognitive changes. Some people may get "stuck" in a phase and continue with cognitive or affective rebellion through part or all of their adult years. Perhaps the quest to be frozen in liquid nitrogen (with hopes of revival at a later time when medical technology is more advanced for treating a specific illness or old age) is an adult form of continued affective rebellion at the universality or irreversibility of death.

Thoughts about death are most frequent and have the greatest affective impact during the times when the ego is least stable: between 5 and 8 years of age, when the superego is emerging and logical or causality thinking is being estab-

TABLE 18-1. QUALITATIVE CHANGES IN ONE'S CONCEPT OF DEATH

Stage	Approximate Age	Cognitive Domain	Affective Domain	Concept of Life	Concept of Death
1	0–2	Naïveté	Naïveté	Universal life	Separation analogous to death; Unaware of own mortality
2	2–4	Awareness	Naïveté	All things active or useful	Dead means "less alive"; Fear injury, not own death
3	5–6	Rebellion	Awareness	Anything that moves	Movement stops, but thinking continues; Associate death with punishment
4	7–9	Adaptation	Rebellion	Anything that moves spontaneously	Death is caused by external forces; My parents will die; I can outwit "Mr. Death"
5	10–12	Acceptance	Adaptation	Plants and animals	Death is a biological finality; I will die—someday
6	Adolescent and adult	Acceptance	Acceptance	Consciousness restricted to people and animals	I can die at any time; Search for life meaning and spiritual continuity

lished; and between 13 and 16 years, when a reorganization of the self-concept occurs through the search for identity and meaningful ideologies. Several studies have found a complete denial of cessation of body functions in people of these age groups, even though younger children indicate an understanding of the concept.[88] Thoughts of death may be intensified at any point of the life span when the individual is experiencing radical personal changes (e.g., marriage, birth of a child, illness, job change, menopause, retirement). Major concerns of each age related to a concept of death are listed in Table 18-2.

Cognitive and Affective Naïveté (Birth to 2 Years)

Concept of Life

A concept of death presupposes a concept of life; a concept of life presupposes a concept of *animism* (the endowment of life, soul, or personality independent of matter). According to Piaget, the child starts life with a primary assumption of universal life.[63] The child gradually refines his or her concept of animate or alive through a process of differentiation, thus

TABLE 18-2. MAJOR CONCERNS OF EACH AGE RELATED TO A CONCEPT OF DEATH

Age	Concerns
Infant and toddler	Separation and deprivation
Preschooler	Biological integrity
School-ager	Psychological integrity
Pubescent	Social integrity
Adolescent	Philosophical and theological integrity
Adult	Life role and goals

eventually distinguishing between animate and inanimate or dead and alive. Piaget believes that the infant begins life with the concept of a continuum between the self and the environment and is aware only of need gratification, not of separateness. Awareness of separateness is a gradual process of differentiation in the biological, social, and affective realms.[44, 63] The infant must begin to develop a concept of self before comprehending me–not me or alive–not alive.

Concept of Death

Although many disagree with him, Otto Rank, a psychoanalyst, states that the child's first experience with death is birth itself.[66] One would not deny the presence of an instinct for physical survival as exhibited by the frantic gasping for air by the neonate who suffers temporary oxygen deprivation; however, this and other protective reflexive behaviors hardly fit into the complex integration of concepts discussed earlier as comprising a mature concept of death.

Although the infant cannot conceptualize death, the baby is aware of a lack of completeness or discomfort. The earliest precursors to a cognitive awareness of death are awarenesses of object loss and separation anxiety, which are first evidenced between 5 and 10 months of age. The infant exhibits distress when a toy disappears and becomes aware that the parent can come and go at will. Losing sight of the parent is responded to as if it were a threat to the child's own survival. As the child's cognitive skills mature, he or she is increasingly aware of separateness and vulnerability consequently, for the infant, *separation is synonymous with death;*[3] it is a form of deprivation, a loss of possession, of affection, of nurturing; it is the loss of all that is essential to security and sense of self. The primary caregiver (or love object) is the source of tension reduction and pleasure gratification and as such is life-sustaining through the process of emotional refueling (see Chap. 11).

Coping With Grief

Infants around 10 months of age typically respond with panic at the loss of the parent. This behavior may resurface periodically through the early years as the child becomes aware of his or her vulnerability.[44] Parents need to differentiate cries of panic from those of sadness or anger and respond appropriately with support as needed to facilitate ego development. Infants gradually learn to control the anxiety associated with separation; they gain primitive skills for dealing with separation through games such as peek-a-boo. An infant engaged in this game with a parent alternately experiences panic and delight; the body tenses, extremities flail, eyes widen, breath quickens, and, finally, the infant begins to cry if the parent disappears behind the cloth or hand too long. Immediate joy is exhibited when the parent reappears. Peek-a-boo is an old English term that means "life or death." Another activity that facilitates acceptance of finality or loss is the concept of "all gone," which is experienced while eating food or blowing away dandelion seeds, for example.

When one is learning to trust the environment, to predict events, and to invest oneself in others, loss of a significant adult may have permanent residual effects on attachment formation (see Chap. 8). When a child is in the process of learning to love and to be loved, it is critical that the process continue uninterrupted. Even nap times can be interpreted as a loss of the love object by the child. Temporary separations can often be facilitated by offering the older baby some object that belongs to the parent or transferring security to a "lovey" (any soft meaningful toy or object that becomes a transitional substitute for mother). If a permanent interruption does occur through death, illness, or other cause, a warm, affectionate, permanent substitute should be located as soon as possible.[11]

Cognitive Awareness, Affective Naïveté (2 to 4 Years)

Concept of Life

According to Piaget, the young child's universe is governed by the idea of purpose; consequently, all things that are active or useful are endowed with life and consciousness (ability to know, to think, to plan).[63] Egocentric thought leads children to believe that all things think, feel, plan, and experience as they do. The child insists that the bed sheet wrapped itself around a foot on purpose, the oven or rocks are alive because they can hurt, or a swinging pendent necklace hit one on the side of the head because it was jealous of the child's talking to the adult. The child, not yet clear on cause–effect relationships, and enmeshed in magical thought, thinks that objects possess a separate will to act in obedience or disobedience to a person's thoughts or wishes.[63] Anthropomorphic thought leads the 3- to 4-year-old to think that a toy feels pain when it is broken or that it hurts to sew the ear back onto a stuffed dog. The child of this age also believes in the omnipotence of his or her own thoughts, insisting that the sun and moon follow one's activities or provide light "because I want them to."[63]

Concept of Death

The toddler gradually becomes aware that some things have an end, and sadness may be felt at the separation from a desired object. He or she continues to learn to cope with the concept of "all gone" as a final separation. The earliest dependable record of cognitive awareness of a finality to life, or a death discovery, is reported by Kastenbaum, who tells of a 16-month-old boy who said "no more" with a depressed, resigned manner after seeing an adult step on a caterpillar.[38] To the astute observer, there are many examples of cognitive accommodation of the concepts of "dead" and "alive" during this period as the child tries to resolve issues of causality and finality. Janssen found many examples as he followed one child's discoveries from 21 to 36 months of age.[33] Some developmentalists suggest that anxiety associated with toilet training and feces disposal may be due to newly acquired concepts of death rather than to castration anxiety or anxiety over the loss of a body part as postulated by Freud.[33]

Although young children are cognizant that some things have an end to their existence,[10] they are still ignorant of the meaning of death. Since the child does not see the concepts of life and death as mutually exclusive, the person can be "dead" and "alive" at the same time.[86] "Dead" appears to mean "less alive" or another state of living. The dead continue to grow, to get hungry, to walk about, to think, and to continue all vital functions.[11,33,54] The possibility of a return to life exists if corrective measures are taken.[88] Their inner mental structures are not flexible enough to understand the cessation of life.[62]

Although toddlers may begin to have an awareness that others die, they are ignorant of the fact that they too will die. Yet, apprehensions about swimming, safety precautions, or even reluctance to sleep alone indicate that toddlers have begun to develop a vague awareness that what has been seen to happen to animals or people could also happen to them.[83] It is also evidence of the child's increasing awareness of separateness from the parents and an accompanying sense of vulnerability to the unknowns of the environment.[44] Children of this age see parents as omnipotent, a source of strength and power. When parents cannot "fix" or "make better" something that has broken, it can make the child insecure.

Coping With Grief

Separation from one's source of omnipotence is difficult to face. The toddler typically fears being left alone and separated from the love object; consequently, death, divorce, and hospitalization can be synonymous for the young child. Even being left with a babysitter or at a day care center can be traumatic to the child with vague concepts of time or duration. The loss of a toy or a security blanket may be as significant to the toddler as the death of a friend to an adult. The toddler has lost something invested with a part of the self. Inadequate coping skills can prevent substitution of supportive alternatives for the loss. Transfer of affectional ties may be difficult, and thus deep depression may continue over time.[11] The child may also express grief through misbehavior.

When loss of a loved person or object does occur, the grief reaction takes much longer for the toddler to resolve than for the adult, partly because the child needs time to mature to understand what has happened. Trust has been disrupted by the inability to predict or control events. It takes time to rebuild the trust relationship, and the child's psychic structures are too fragile to deal with grief all at once. Consequently, in this and later stages, the child mourns in a piecemeal fashion until a new equilibrium is reached.[2] However, *incomplete resolution does not imply pathology.*[2] Some feel that the child should completely let go of the image of the parent or love object (decathexis) to get on with the realities of current life. However, resolution does not mean forgetting or submerging but positively assimilating the memories of the deceased into one's meaning of life. As the child has the opportunity to discuss the deceased parent or loved one in the years after the loss, he or she is enabled to develop a more complete picture of the deceased, of the relationship with the deceased, and consequently of one's own identity.[2] Lack of understanding can distort reality and lead to severe emotional problems later in life.[2] Since the young child believes in the power of his or her own thoughts (and all children get angry at their parent or sibling at some point), the child may feel that a death, separation, divorce, or even a family tragedy is due to his or her own negative thoughts. Self-imposed guilt can continue into the adult years, influencing later relationships and interfering with adult commitments (Fig. 18-2).

James Robertson, a British physician, studied the emotional responses of toddlers to hospitalization and separation (the parents were only allowed one brief visit daily).[72] He discovered that the separation from parents was more traumatic than the hospital procedures themselves. On hospitalization, the children experienced loss of love, fear of the unknown, and fear of punishment. Robertson believed that the children were too young to understand the reason for the separation and lacked sufficient internal resources to cope with it. He noted three specific phases in response to prolonged separation from the parents:

Protest: The children became grief stricken and panicky, calling for the parent and rejecting other people who offered assistance or comfort. They were hostile, uncooperative, and very active. All energies were extended to "recapture" the parent. Sleep came only from sheer exhaustion.

Despair: The children became withdrawn, apathetic, and anorexic. They attempted to "mother" themselves through self-comfort measures such as thumb-sucking, body rocking, attachment to a "security blanket," or by assuming a fetal position. Toddlers continued to watch anxiously for the parent. Mourning became so great that, when the mother did visit, the child could not get enough contact to "refuel," and consequently the pain of loss was exacerbated by the brief visits. The visit also increased the sense of helplessness, since the child

FIGURE 18–2.
There are many opportunities to include young children in the death rituals of the culture.

had no control over the disappearance or retrieval of the parent. Some children were even noted to reject the parent when he or she came to visit. Robertson hypothesized that this behavior was used as a way to punish the parent and gain some control over the situation. Frequently, the child exhibited marked regression to earlier behaviors of soiling and infantile speech; these actions may be ways of letting others know that "I still need to be taken care of," or they may indicate inadequate affective energies available to meet the needs of the social *and* physical domains. The care of a mother substitute was no longer rejected but passively accepted.

Denial and Detachment: The children no longer acted depressed. They began to show interest in the environment and to accept attention in a detached way from anyone who gave it. Feelings for the parent were repressed. Parents were often ignored when they arrived for visits, and no distress was shown when they left. No attempts were made to make the parents stay. The child accepted the fact that he or she had lost ability to control the environment: the helplessness syndrome appeared (Fig. 18-3) (see Chap. 13).

It is significant to note at this point that these three stages can be prevented or attenuated. Hospitals today have liberalized visiting policies and most offer rooming-in for parents. When parents cannot be present, attentive personnel can help reduce the child's emotional trauma by encouraging trusting attachment to one or two staff members.

After separation and return to the home, Robertson's children became "clingy" and wanted to go everywhere with the parent. They did not want to lose sight of the parent again; the abandonment was too terrifying. Other behaviors such as sleep problems, crying, and continued infantile behaviors indicated that the child feared a second separation.

Although Robertson's studies specifically involved a hospital setting, many similar behaviors are exhibited by children of this age in any setting when they are separated from a parent. Even prolonged separation of the father from the home for travel or military service can precipitate mourning behaviors. Separation is a form of death to children of this age. Physical refueling activities with the parents are still essential to autonomy and continued ego development.[2, 44] Loss of this source of strength can be devastating unless adequate support and substitutes are provided. On reunion, the parent needs to offer full and uninterrupted attention to the child for several minutes, or until the *child* is willing to separate voluntarily from the joyful (or desperate) contact with the parent.

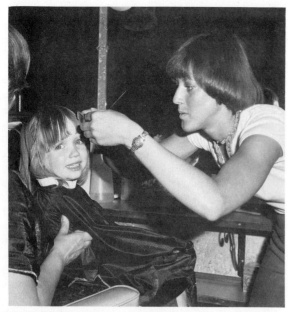

FIGURE 18–3.
Hair cuts are a traumatic experience for young children. Loss of body integrity and fear of physical mutilation are major fears during the toddler and preschool years.

Cognitive Rebellion, Affective Awareness (5 to 6 Years)

Concept of Life

Piaget observes that children of this age use movement as their main criterion for "alive."[63] They are not able to differentiate between spontaneous movement, internally mediated movement, and movement due to external forces. A table, sheet, or rock may no longer be defined as "alive," but they may still be endowed with awareness of when they are moved or damaged. However, the sun, the wind, a stream of water, a clock, or a bicycle may be endowed with life and consciousness. Despite all the questions and searching for answers, life and death are still inexplicable mysteries to the child mainly because causality and finality are not understood.[62]

Children are beginning to identify characteristics of life, but few of them can identify characteristics of death. Thirty-two percent of children younger than 7 years of age are able to give adequate criteria for "alive," but only 6% are able to give an adequate criterion for "dead."[19] As more stable concepts of life and death emerge, virtually all 5 and 6 year olds are able to correctly indicate that animals are alive and can die.[6] However, judgments about inanimate objects are still unstable and are highly influenced by the situation.

Linguistic limitations may account for some of the difficulty.[63, 88] "Alive" may not yet be mapped into the child's concept of life.[6] As Piaget observed, the child may be distinguishing between moving–not moving rather than animate–inanimate. Dead may mean never alive, no longer functional, or formerly alive. A child's concepts consequently may need to be inferred from behaviors rather than from definitions, since the words may have a different meaning from the meaning they have for an adult.

Concept of Death

The child in this phase accepts the fact of death as a cessation of movement but fantasizes that the dead person continues to experience emotion and biological processes in the grave, even though the person does not move. Maria Nagy notes that many primitive people continue to conceptualize death on this level, as evidenced by the custom of putting food, drink, artifacts, and even servants and wives in the tomb with the deceased.[54] The child frequently feels that death is a reversible process—if one is good.

According to Kastenbaum, 75% of adults think that children never or seldom think about death.[37] However, one study indicates that 80% of the young child's fears are associated with death, dying, mutilation, or the death of a family member.[67] Sylvia Anthony reports that 50% to 60% of children 5 to 12 years of age refer to or speak of death in some form when completing stories.[3] Much spontaneous death-related talk and activity can be observed in play experiences: "Bang, bang! There, I killed you," or "I will die, but you fix me and make me alive again," or "You can't move, you're dead."[9] Play activities indicate that children know about death, and they try to control the idea through magical thought processes or "curative" actions (Fig. 18-4). As with many other anxiety-arousing events (getting lost, doctor visits, going to the hospital, visiting a cemetery, or attending a funeral), the child tries to master the concept through play activities.[70] Cartoons that involve violence, death, and revitalization may serve to perpetuate the child's confusion, since many kindergartners still have difficulty distinguishing fact from fantasy. For others, cartoons may offer another vehicle for working through their developing concept and dealing with loss in small doses.

Death is not yet conceptualized as a natural end of life. It is easier to conceive of death that results from violence than death that occurs through disease or natural processes. One study revealed that only 11% of 4 year olds, 20% of 5 year olds, and 22% of 6 year olds admit to the universality of death.[14] Even though one third of the 4 year olds acknowledge the irreversibility of death, not one of the 6 or 7 year olds was able to admit this belief; their emerging egos were still too fragile to acknowledge the probability of personal nonexistence or a permanent cessation of being. They know too much too early and feel forced to repress the knowledge until the ego is stronger.[88, 99] Smilansky discovered that 85% of 4- to 5-year-old children with well-educated parents understood irreversibility, but less than 50% of those from poorly educated families understood the issue of the finality of death.[83] These findings support the role of socialization in the development of one's concept of death.

Children this age frequently associate death with retaliation or punishment;[3] consequently, they may greatly fear the anger or the aggression of others, especially adults. This fear may partially explain the child's attempts to please adults—a common characteristic of this age—as a way to avoid death.[93]

The child begins to suspect that his or her own death is possible but not probable in a loving environment. Affective factors protect them against acceptance of their own deaths.

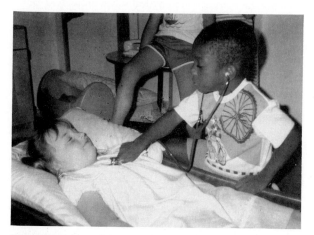

FIGURE 18–4.
The preschooler uses sociodramatic play to cope with a growing awareness of death. Death concepts can be handled in small doses, at their own pace, and with a happy outcome.

The ego, which is just beginning to recognize the self as a separate entity, is overwhelmed by the idea of nonbeing.

Coping With Grief

The greatest fear of this age group is still separation and loss of love and security. If a parent dies during this phase, children may feel resentful, angry, and abandoned. They may believe the parent chose to die, since they still perceive parents as being all-powerful and all-wise. Like the toddler and preschooler, the child may also feel like a secret slayer of the parent because he or she had once wished that the parent were dead.[93] The child who believes that the parent can read thoughts may feel that the death—permanent abandonment—is punishment for a bad thought or behavior. At the same time, the death proves to the child the impotence of his or her own love impulses and magical thought powers to restore the love object.[93]

The loss of a parent through divorce may precipitate analogous responses. Losing one parent heightens the child's awareness of the possibility of losing two parents. Children often worry in silence with an imagination that works overtime. Knowing that many people love them and will take care of them "just in case" can be supportive.

The death of a pet may be almost as significant to the young child as the death of a parent. To replace the pet too quickly is to teach the child not to invest self in others, that things are expendable and relationships are exchangeable.[91] Research with adults indicates that they cannot mourn the loss of a significant other and simultaneously form an attachment to a new family member.[18] The child is placed in an analogous situation when the pet is replaced too soon; one of the processes is submerged. To deny the child an opportunity to mourn is to deny love and attachment and may thus prevent or hinder the growth of future loves.[2] The child's expressions of grief should be encouraged and facilitated through the ceremony of burying, flowers, or whatever is deemed appropriate or meaningful (Fig. 18-5).[43] Discussions with the child about concepts of memory, love, sharing, and significant others can facilitate the grieving process while fostering personal integrity and maintenance of psychosocial security. Explanations must be concrete and should be in terms of personal experiences because children still find it difficult to draw from the experiences of others.[70]

When loss does occur, it is difficult to sustain grief for long periods of time. The child *must* forget, or rather repress, thoughts of the event for periods of time to survive psychologically. The child may be frightened by his or her feelings and thus inhibit their expression. Others, focusing on socially accepted behaviors, may inhibit expressions of grief if they feel that it is infantile, effeminate, or inappropriate. "Crying is a human and dignified response to grief,"[80] and should be allowed and encouraged for both genders at all ages.

Frequently, the child's mood may revert to the opposite emotion, that of laughing or acting excited. This response may be due to inexperience in interpreting and expressing feelings or a form of denial and coping, but it is confusing to the

FIGURE 18–5.
A funeral and burial for an animal facilitate respect for life as well as an emerging concept of death.

adults who are dealing with the grieving child. Acceptance is gradual; true grief may be shown much later as the child's concept of death matures and new crises or special days are faced.

Cognitive Adaptation, Affective Rebellion (7 to 9 Years)

Concept of Life

According to Piaget's observations, during this phase of life, any object that moves spontaneously is categorized as being alive.[63] These objects include the sun and the wind but exclude a bicycle or a tree. The child may realize that the sun does not move for the child's benefit but may state that the rays follow him or her.[63] School-agers assign life to people, animals, and usually plants, but they continue to have difficulty understanding the status of inanimate objects. Although the child may not assign life to an inanimate object, he or she may still assign consciousness to it (e.g., a tree may be able to hear what you say, or a bicycle may throw you off). They may continue to assign consciousness (ability to see, hear, feel, think) to the corpse.

Concept of Death

By 7 years of age, most children understand the inevitability of death for all living things, but they may exempt family and self as an ego defense.[85] Sixty-one percent of 7 year olds, 75% of 8

year olds, and 100% of 9 year olds were able to acknowledge the universality of death in one study. Twenty-five percent of 8 year olds, 30% of 9 year olds, and 63% of 10 year olds admitted to the irreversibility of death.[14]

The school-ager frequently takes a compromise stand that death is real, but it is external to the self. It is associated with old age or an external agent such as an accident or murder.[36] Even illness may be due to external factors.[8] This position enables the child to assert that death can be avoided.[54] Efforts are extended toward achieving a biological understanding of illness and death in the hope of learning how to control and to prevent or at least delay the inevitable. To learn specific ways of controlling the event, children ask many questions, draw on the experiences of others, discuss the matter as openly and freely as others allow, and, at times, seem to focus on the grotesque. In short, school-agers are fascinated with the idea of death as a part of living, but they do not want to stop existing, not while they feel the richness of life and living (Fig. 18-6). Perhaps the striving for competence is partially explained as the effort to overcome a sense of powerlessness in the face of death.

Children begin to realize that significant others can die without warning and that the future offers many uncertainties. They may devise elaborate procedures to distort or deny the fact of universal death; sidewalk cracks are avoided, one's breath is held while passing a cemetery, and contact with dead people and funeral homes is avoided whenever possible. School-agers begin to recognize the human fallibility of their parents and the need for other sources of strength. It is during this period that they frequently ask if they were adopted and also exhibit concern over who would care for them if the parents were to die. They begin to reach out to other adults and peers, extending their attachments and meaningful relationships. Realizing that death can occur to the young as well as to the elderly can have disquieting effects.

Research indicates that children begin to distinguish between the spiritual and physical selves around 9 years of age,[26] giving rise to beliefs in unseen spirits and continued life after death. Maria Nagy found that many children of this age think of death in terms of personification.[54] "Mr. Death" is an invisible bad spirit who can think, plan, and stalk a victim. He comes at night to take one's soul away. Mr. Death may be personified as a skeleton, ghost, black cat, bogeyman, goblin, monster, or other form. If one is smart and quick enough, one can outwit or outrun Mr. Death or other spirits. Doors are locked, dark rooms are avoided, heads are hidden under the covers; children run extra fast through a particular alley, vacant lot, or wooded area. When death is seen as an external aggressor, it can be avoided through logic, strength, and trickery.

Television violence may serve to perpetuate this concept by showing how to outwit death. Peer associations also facilitate working through one's death concept. Games such as "tag," "king of the mountain," and "cops and robbers" allow expression of mastery over danger, fear, or an "enemy." Unfortunately, peer approval may be so important in proving

FIGURE 18–6.
Participation in community expressions of grief, memory, honor, and pride help school-agers integrate the reality of death into a positive concept of life.

who is bravest that children of this age frequently disregard real dangers in games of "I dare you." Fantasy and daydreams also allow the child to try on roles and gain emotional and intellectual mastery.

Coping With Grief

When death of a significant other does occur, cognitive-affective dissonance in accepting reality may inhibit emotional response and grief expression. In fact, some children, on first hearing the news of a significant death, may immediately return to their play activities as if there were no crisis at all. The child no longer feels responsibility for the death of others—an idea that characterized the last stage—and gives up ideas of magical thought to logic and reason. However, the child may feel responsible if he or she believes that action on his or her part could have prevented the death.[24, 45] The child is generally more upset than the parents or teachers realize.[34]

When children do not yet recognize, understand, or know how to express their feelings, they tend to act them out through aggression, decreased attention span, nervousness, poor school work, enuresis, sleep disturbances, attention seeking, nightmares, reduced resiliency, and general sadness.[12, 24, 75] The child may respond with jokes, crassness, or indifference to ward off the impact of the grief. Eighty-five percent of bereaved children have marked symptoms for 12 to 18 months after the loss.[75] It is important to be supportive. Hassling can increase emotional confusion.[12] Some children may not express grief at all but may mourn heavily at a later time. The child frequently finds it easier to mourn at a distance, for example, in writing or in art, rather than in open discussion.

The school-ager may experience a great emptiness after mourning because release of sadness may be equated with release of the love object. They may resist falling in love with or even appreciating the qualities of a new parent or pet because it feels as if they are betraying the original relationship. Much sensitive support is needed to allow children to express their feelings at their own pace, in their own way. It is especially important that a surviving parent offer support to the grieving child to prevent permanent emotional scars. Unfortunately, only 25% of grieving parents are able to actively support the child's bereavement. The others are too immersed in their own grief.[75] The child, consequently, loses two parents.

Cognitive Acceptance, Affective Adaptation (10 to 12 Years)

Concept of Life

Piaget's observations indicate that the child of 10 recognizes that life is a quality possessed by and restricted to members of the plant and animal family. Things that are alive are born, grow, and die. Consequently, inanimate objects do not possess life. However, since the concept of life precedes the concept of consciousness, some young people of this age still continue to attribute consciousness to objects that they know do not have life. Only after attainment of formal operational thought are they able to restrict consciousness to humans and animals.[63] Cognitive processes are sophisticated enough at this point to realize that the sun only *appears* to follow as one changes position.

Concept of Death

By the process of differentiation and default, the young person is now able to form a concept of death similar to that possessed by adults. Death is understood in relation to natural laws and no longer merely the result of aggression or trauma.[3, 54, 63] Illness, age, and dysfunction are recognized as causative agents.[8] Death is acknowledged as originating from within us rather than being external to us and something that can be outsmarted. The individual now accepts the biological finality of death; no longer does the dead person continue to live and feel in the grave. Death is accepted cognitively as being **universal, inevitable,** and **irreversible.**[3, 42, 54]

Focus now shifts to the social "rituals and ceremonies surrounding death, such as what occurs in hospitals, at funerals, and at the grave site."[88]

Because personal mortality is still an uncomfortable concept, research results are somewhat confusing. Many adolescents continue to protect their fragile egos through denial tactics of the previous stage in spite of cognitive understanding of the facts of death. One research study indicates that 50% of pubescents refuse to admit that death is final and absolute.[97] Another indicates that only 20% of young adolescents acknowledge total cessation of body functions.[47] The discrepancy in research may result from how questions are posed to the young person and which trait under scrutiny. Other emerging concepts can also confound research. For example, denial of cessation of body functions increases as belief in spiritual continuation of life after death increases.[47]

Adolescents who are coming to grips with life may devote much conscious and unconscious thought to death as they explore options and alternatives in life. By putting death into the category of a "remote, distant possibility," the adolescent's sense of invulnerability is enhanced.[96] However, the more completely they resolve the issue of their own mortality,

the stronger their own identities become. As adolescents become more secure in their ideologies, they experience greater resilience and coping skills when faced with a life-threatening crisis.

Kastenbaum indicates that "brighter" adolescents and more "psychologically alive" adults devote much thought to the issues of death and continue to modify their orientation toward death throughout life.[37] Contemplation of personal mortality tends to prompt reevaluation of one's sources of identity (see Chap. 25), commitments, and goals.[41] One may experience marked psychological disequilibrium as old values and current concerns are released for their lack of relevance or significance in light of personal mortality. One may also experience a decline in the sense of meaning and purpose of life.[41] Even traditional religious values may be released for increased emphasis on spiritual development and closer interpersonal relationships. Concentration on affective responses while reflecting intensely on personal mortality is a difficult, painful process, but it facilitates continued identity homework and psychological growth (Fig. 18-7).[41] Because of the intensity of thought required, or the insecurity and the pain experienced with confrontations of the less desirable self, or thoughts of mortality, many adults continue to deny or give little thought to death throughout much of

FIGURE 18–7.
On the threshold of their adult years, adolescents begin to think about their vulnerabilities. These thoughts can provide an excuse to "experience all of life's privileges" before it's too late or a sense of responsibility for the life that is uniquely theirs.

their lives.[27] However, willingness to face the issue of mortality is essential for mastery of the final stage: cognitive and affective acceptance.

Coping With Grief

Although cognitive and affective acceptance of death as a part of life is generally mastered during adolescence, young people still have difficulty coping with the feelings evoked and with using socially approved outlets for grief. The heightened awareness of their own vulnerability increases tension and engenders a profound sense of powerlessness.[15] Some adolescents withdraw from family and friends as they try to cope with these intense feelings for the first time.[45] Others tell "sick jokes" as a way of discharging energy.[15] Understanding and acceptance of death is more advanced than their ability to understand, accept, and control their emotional and social behaviors. Counseling is highly advised.[29, 45]

The death of a parent during adolescence is traumatic socially as well as affectively. Some adolescents may feel a deep need to support and protect the surviving parent, and thus they postpone their own grieving.[96] Some feel stigmatized by the situation. At a time when peer support and companionship are so important, who is there to share this event as a common experience? The bereaved adolescent feels different, singled out. The adolescent may also feel the need to replace a lost family member by assuming their responsibilities or even their mannerisms. If financial burdens are intensified by death, the young person may have to change educational and career goals. Resentment and a sense of having been cheated are not uncommon feelings. Reintegration of past, present, and future, one's concept of God, and one's philosophies of life and death may be a difficult task after the death of a loved one. One's own mortality cannot be denied, and the search for a meaning in death may be painful.

Search for the Meaning of Death

The search for the meaning of death cannot occur until the sixth stage: cognitive and affective acceptance. With the acceptance of physical death, most adolescents and adults believe in psychic immortality. A multinational Gallup survey conducted in 16 western countries revealed belief in continued life after death to range from 38% to 84%.[31] Seventy percent of people in the United States believe in life after death.[25] This belief may be a protective coping mechanism perpetuated by the culture to help to control the behavior of the masses, or it may have been developed by theologians because the concept of nonexistence is difficult to accept even for the person capable of abstract thought, or it may be a truth discovered and shared with us through generations by people who are more sensitive to out-of-body experiences, those who have had deep religious experiences, or those who have had near-death experiences.

Healthy adolescents and adults expend considerable energy reviewing their experiences to integrate past, present, and future into a philosophy of life. The adolescent must come to terms with death as a prerequisite for building a philosophy of life.[32] Adolescents begin to realize that growth comes with caring deeply about others[16] and that death stops that growth. As they become more aware of the life-producing potentials of their own bodies and lives, they begin to view death as an enemy, a thief that can deprive them of life's plans, dreams, and goals. They think it unfair to have invested so much in the process of growing up only to have life snatched away before achieving some sense of fulfillment or tasting some of the adult pleasures and privileges. This belief is one reason why some young people resist and object to involvement in war; they do not want to die without the opportunity to live as adults. Others, still caught in the stage of affective rebellion, may accept the challenge of war as a way to tempt fate and prove their ability to outsmart "Mr. Death." Some young people enjoy attaining mastery over fear; they enjoy the "high" received when adrenaline levels are elevated during and after a fast ride in the car, on a roller coaster, or on water skis. The adolescent fears death and yet is fascinated by it.

A major task of each individual, especially during late adolescence and early adulthood, is to find meaning in life—to establish values, goals, and priorities, to find something to live for. This task requires a recognition and an integration of a concept of death into a philosophy of life.[98] "Death asks us for our identity."[20] The high suicide rates among adolescents and college students may be partially explained by the anxiety felt by these individuals in acknowledging the fact of death and trying to find a meaning in life.[76] The attempt to integrate the two and to bring this new concept into focus is sought at the price of self-destruction. "We live our dying according to the meaning we have learned."[52] As the person begins to come to grips with the purpose and meaning of life, then a reflection is seen in identifying the purpose and meaning of death (or is it vice versa? the two cannot be easily separated).[93]

Many religious leaders believe that a deep religious experience can give life and circumstances meaning by bringing the two into focus and giving a person the motivation to live. They believe that the issue is not the circumstances we face but our attitude toward them. Difficult experiences can give a person a realistic confirmation of the value of life and living (Fig. 18-8).[32] In this context, the meaning of life can only be understood within the framework of a sacred doctrine. Death is seen as a personal matter between God and self.[20] The self is seen as a spiritual person living in a physical body.

Life After Death

This view of life, the union of the physical self with a spiritual self (soul or psyche), has been given more concrete support in the last 20 years by the research of Elisabeth Kübler-Ross and Raymond Moody.[40, 50] Kübler-Ross, a psychiatrist, became convinced that psychic life exists after death during conversations with critically ill and dying clients whom she interviewed to try to determine how they could be assisted with the process of dying. Moody, a philosopher and physician, began a systematic investigation of reports of out-of-body experiences related by individuals who had had "near-death

FIGURE 18–8.
Elderly people often wonder why they have been singled out to live longer than peers, spouse, or other family members. Cultural ceremonies revive sensitive memories and help them face their mortality and their life one more time.

experiences" (NDE) or who had been "clinically dead" and then revived. After collecting data from about 150 cases, he noted striking similarities in the relation of the experiences, which included psychic disengagement from the physical body, a heightened awareness of environmental activities, an ability to move through space and to think, hear, and see, and the meeting with spirits of previously deceased friends and relatives. Almost every individual reported an encounter with a bright light, which was identified as a spiritual being with a definite personality. They indicated that this "Being of light" flooded them with warmth, acceptance, and love beyond description while asking one question, variously translated as "Are you ready to die?" or "What have you done with your life that is sufficient?" People also experienced a rapid, detailed, vivid review of their lives. This "being of light" appeared to stress two factors in each life: learning to love other people and acquiring knowledge.

After this encounter, almost all the individuals reported that they did not want to return to life. Most were hesitant to reveal their experiences to others after their return but were frequently profoundly changed by the experience. Moody's research indicates that his observations are almost identical to the experiences of death or dying reported in diverse civilizations, cultures, and eras.

Considerable effort has been made over the past 15 years to validate, refute, or explain Moody's research findings. Surveys of the general population report that 14% to 32% admit to having an out-of-body experience.[56] Many of these are reported to occur during a near-death experience or during surgery but may occur while the person is fully awake, under stress, or during relaxation.[56] About 40% of people who have had a near-death experience report having a "core experi-

ence," or out-of-body experience.[71, 74] Even young children and babies report (when they are old enough to relate the event) experiences almost identical to adult near-death experiences except that they tend to lack a life review.[23, 74, 77] Many people do not relate their out-of-body experience or near-death experience to either professional or family members because of fear that no one will believe them or that they will be identified as emotionally disturbed, yet they welcome the chance to discuss the events when doors of communication are opened.[58, 74]

Kenneth Ring conducted more than 100 interviews in the late 1970s to identify the phenomena reported by Moody and to identify any potential correlates to explain the phenomena.[71] Ring discovered that there appear to be five distinct stages to the core experience of those who have had a near-death experience:

Euphoria: A sense of total peace and well-being is present. All experience of bodily discomfort is gone. Sixty percent to 70% of people express experiencing this stage even if they do not go on to the later stages.

Separation From Body: Thirty-seven percent of interviewees report an out-of-body experience. Most express that they are looking down on their bodies and viewing environmental events with increased sensitivity to visual and auditory cues. Some even report traveling to different locations and are later able to report, in detail, events they observed and conversations overheard. They report that spirits of people who have already died are present "to help with the transition."

Entering the Darkness: Twenty-three percent of people report entering or moving rapidly through a dark tunnel.

Seeing the Light: Sixteen percent of people who have had near-death experiences report seeing and being drawn to a brilliant, unearthly light. This light was variously translated as the embodiment of God and the beginning of a new life.

Entering the Light: Ten percent of these people express entering an environment of intense light and beauty that is described as a lush pastoral field with a stream running down the middle. Some people report that they were asked if they wanted to return to their former life. Others were told that they must return. They had a sense that if they crossed the stream they would not return.

Return to the Body: Return to the body was sudden and without ceremony. In some experiences, the people were immediately conscious; in others, they had to wait until physiological processes were stabilized. Like Moody, Ring found an increased belief in life after death, a loss of fear of death, and an increase in spiritual sensitivity after the core experience.

Ring and others have tried to explain the phenomena through: psychological processes such as depersonalization, wishful thinking, dreams and hallucinations, or subconscious fabrications; pharmacological responses such as anesthesia or mood-altering drug reactions; physiological or neurological explanations such as temporal lobe seizures, endorphin response, or cerebral anoxia.[23, 71, 74, 77, 78] Each of the explanations is contradicted by other evidence, however. All that can be said with surety is that the person is experiencing an altered state of consciousness. An interesting explanation has emerged from Poland. Janusz Slawinski reports that all living organisms continually emit low-intensity light.[82]

> At the time of death, that radiation is 10 to 1000 times stronger than that emitted under normal conditions. This "deathflash" is independent of the cause of death, and reflects in intensity and duration the rate of dying. The vision of intense light reported in near-death experiences may be related to this deathflash, which may hold an immense amount of information. The electromagnetic field produced by necrotic radiation, containing energy, internal structure, and information, may permit continuation of consciousness beyond the death of the body.[82]

Slawinski tries to correlate life with consciousness, consciousness with energy, and energy with light.[82] Like Ring, he proposes the possibility of a holographic theory or paradigm to explain the spiritual domain and life after death. Obviously, the data collected offer no proof of life after temporal life; however, the continual compilation of data makes the possibility impossible to deny.

Those who have experienced an NDE with a core experience are emotionally and socially shaken by what has transpired. One becomes acutely aware that the "old self" is inadequate in light of the new self-awareness. The alteration in consciousness "erodes culturally induced ego control," fosters transcendence of the ego, and promotes transformation and regeneration of the self.[61] This experience may be disconcerting, since one finds oneself "out of step" with the values, views, and even interests of family and peers. Initially, the person may experience bouts of crying, inappropriate anger, and withdrawal from primary relationships as he or she tries to assimilate what has happened. A new frame of reference and world view may cause routine role functions to seem insignificant or superfluous in light of the new values and priorities. "The NDEr is a member of a cultural minority, whose beliefs, values, and attitudes conflict with those of the majority culture."[22]

Thus, a person's adjustment after an NDE falls into a normal and fairly predictable pattern similar to that experienced by those with "culture shock,"[1] beginning with excitement and euphoria at the new experience; going through confusion, disorientation, and disillusionment; protecting the old self and habits; beginning to understand and appreciate the new values and priorities; and finally accepting the similarities and differences between the two cultures. Since these two "cultures" are within the person, considerable stress can accompany the adjustment process.[89] When one cannot or

does not share what has happened, it is a lonely, difficult process. Near-death experience support groups can be found through: Nancy Evans Bush, IANDS, Box U-20, University of Connecticut, Storrs, CT 06268.

In addition to those who see, hear, and feel the presence of another spirit while undergoing an NDE, some claim to see spirits while fully awake. Ring reports the observations of people who have watched the "spirit body" leave the physical body.[71] Erik and Joan Erikson report that, during their interviews with older people, a number of widows reported "visits" from their former spouses.[17] They insist that they were awake, not dreaming. They could see, touch, hold, and hear them. National and international surveys indicate that about 50% of both widows and widowers report seeing their dead spouses while in a clearly awake state.[28, 30, 31, 68, 79] Surveys of the general population indicate that apparition sightings are reported by a quarter of the population,[46] with some subcultures reporting sightings by more than 50% of their population.[35] Since some of these sightings were observed by more than one person, or the people were not known to be dead at the time of the sighting, and they occurred in full daylight, they are thought to be more than just hallucinations.[31, 78] Many doctors and nurses report that people within 24 hours of death joyfully talk of seeing deceased relatives and friends who have come to "take them away."[57] Though we cannot explain it, the preponderance of evidence makes these experiences impossible to deny.

The Role of Religion

Theology attempts to link temporal life with the hereafter and to deal with issues of being–not being, the purpose of life, the nature of humanity, and development of the spiritual domain. Religious beliefs, rituals, and ceremonies for the dead are an expression of both cultural influences and doctrine.[3, 65, 93] As such, they socialize a person's attitude toward death, humanity, and a Supreme Being and reinforce social bonds and values.[20]

Religious beliefs cover a wide continuum of views regarding the purpose of life, the nature of the human being, and the existence of God or a Supreme Being. At one end of the continuum are those who believe only in the concrete reality of the **now** experience. Adherents of this position see no ultimate purpose to life, describe the human as a biological entity able to think and master part of the environment. The idea that the human may be an integration of physical and spiritual components is untenable to them; the concept of the existence of God is too abstract and metaphysical even to entertain. Death represents total annihilation of the self.

At the other end of the continuum are those who believe that the individual's ultimate purpose in life is to worship God; the physical component of existence is secondary to the spiritual component and is merely a vehicle or tool through which the spirit (the true self) can express itself; and that God is the Supreme Ruler of the universe, directly or indirectly orchestrating the activities within it.

Most cultures and religions believe that death and decay

of the body are not synonymous with dissolution of the personality. They also presuppose the existence of God and the spiritual nature of man as basic tenets of their beliefs. Some propose that the spirit or the soul enters another physical life when the present body dies (reincarnation). Other religions—particularly the Catholic and Protestant theological positions—believe that the soul has only one chance to live in the world we know as the planet Earth. They feel that if death is indeed the end of man, then life is empty and without meaning. To them, life on earth is a preparatory process for another life after death. To them, the concept of God gives meaning both to current life and eternal life. Concepts of heaven and hell assure continuity of self and also serve as a guide or check on temporal behavior as a contingency for future reward or punishment—the ultimate cause–effect relationship, the ultimate modifier of behavior.

Children from religiously oriented homes tend to have more specific concepts of death, especially on issues such as heaven versus hell, good versus bad, and temporal versus eternal values.[47] One six-year-old child from a deeply religious home shared her feelings about death with the author. (Note: A 30-year-old man in her church had been killed in a bad fall the previous month.)

> People get sad when someone in their family dies. It is good for them to die, but people don't want them to die. But they have to, it is a part of life. When you die, you will not come back to Earth anymore. You will be with Jesus all the time. There will be no sickness, fights, stealing; no hurt. It will be a wonderful place. I think I will die—when I get to be old. Sometimes people die when they are young by a car accident, fall, or crack their head open. I think there will be happiness when I die. I don't think about it much. I just wonder how old I will be and what it will be like. I would feel sad if I thought I was going to die now. I would miss everybody.

This child's religious background (and cognitive functioning level) has obviously advanced her concept of death beyond that expected for her chronological age. She indicates that she has accepted the universality of death but still sees it as due mainly to external factors. She also maintains some of the preschool concern about separation. Nevertheless, she is able to talk easily and freely about her feelings.

A ten-year-old girl from a similar religious background, who has been blind since birth, presents an interesting view on fulfilling one's purpose in life, even after death.

> Death is not scary because I know I will go to Heaven. That's all I really care about death, and I'm ready to die. I don't want to now. I have too much to do and fulfill. My ghost would come back by its own choice to fulfill my task, and then return to Heaven. In death your spirit merely goes on to another life, an eternal life. The meaning of life is to fulfill the purpose God made us for. You find out that purpose through prayer. In a subtle way, I look forward to death, because I'll be able to see again, be perfect.

The striking point in both of these girls' discussions of death is their attitude of acceptance. Death was a reality with which they lived, were prepared for, and did not fear. Life was an interlude in existence, a preparation for another existence.

Death represented both an end and a beginning. They had learned to trust this life. The quality of this life for which they were already assuming responsibility would determine their future, and they were at peace with that idea. Thus, fear of death is not universal. In fact, fear of death (fact) and fear of dying (process) are two separate entities.[27] One may fear the physical discomforts of the dying process without fearing death itself. Fear of death tends to decrease with age, although heightened anxiety may be present during middle age when the degenerative processes act as a reminder that "time-left-to-live" is running out.[27, 55] Many people in the late adult years wonder why they have lived so long and express that they wish they would hurry up and die, that they have completed their purpose for living and are now just a burden to their families or are merely treading water waiting for their new life. This view is not depression but merely an honest expression of feelings. The elderly are also more accepting of the possibility of life after death than either young or middle-age adults.[27]

HELPING THE CHILD TO UNDERSTAND LOSS AND DEATH

The best preparation for facing both life and death is an environment that fosters self-understanding and healthy interpersonal relationships. Self-actualized people are not only more comfortable with life but also with the issue of personal mortality and loss.[55]

Preparation for coping with death and life begins in infancy by learning to cope with separation. The simple game of peek-a-boo was mentioned earlier as a significant activity for learning to cope with the temporary loss of contact with a significant other. The father's participation in child care helps the infant to accommodate to more than one approach of interaction. Gradual introduction of other caregivers and brief separations help the infant learn gradually that existence can continue without direct maternal contact. Inadequate contact or overt rejection of the child can increase anxiety levels, however. A healthy balance between contact and separation must be based on the individual child's developmental level and tolerance of separation.

During the toddler years, a parent can begin to use flowers, insects, and pets to help the child develop a concept of death as a part of the life span. It is especially important not to equate death with sleep, since children may begin to fear sleep and going to bed and may exhibit marked disturbance of sleep patterns and nightmares.

The preschooler is ready for a simple, direct discussion of death. Smilansky, in her work with Israeli children who daily faced the threat of war and loss of family members and close friends, discovered that under such circumstances the finality of death could be explained clearly to children as young as 2 to 3 years of age.[83] Death is best discussed during nonstressful times in a matter-of-fact, honest, but sensitive manner. As with other stressful subjects, the information needs to be presented in many ways, using different experiences as examples, so that children can begin to remember and to integrate the information into their repertoire of knowledge.[34] Even childhood and parental illnesses can help a child to increase knowledge of self, others, prosocial behaviors, and empathy, as well as illness versus death.[59] Many books offer a forum for adults and children to share the emotions of love and sorrow and to explore feelings about death (Fig. 18-9).[51] The adult needs to be alert to grotesque and unnatural deaths or events that surround the child and to take appropriate action (e.g., turn off the TV, talk about feelings). Encouraging stereotyped "stiff upper lip" responses for boys and tearfulness for girls robs the children of the ability to identify and express true feelings.[51]

Natural events and phenomena are excellent props to explain the life cycle: fallen leaves in autumn, butterflies, a bird found dead in the yard, or the death of a classroom pet.[43] Religious beliefs may help a child accept the fact of death (as in the previous two examples). However, these beliefs should only be expressed if they are a *real* part of the parents' life; otherwise, they tend to increase anxiety. The child is able to sense when parents are not honest or sincere and may believe the religious interpretation to be another fairy tale.

The love relationship should be stressed. When a loss does occur, the child should be assured that it was not his or her fault; that the deceased did not die on purpose; that no one will replace the deceased's unique relationship, but that new relationships are developed throughout life; and that the child will never forget the loved one; our memory can keep them with us whenever we want.[93]

Even a young child should be told about the death of a person who is significant to the child.[49,83] When a loved one just "disappears," it is traumatic—more traumatic than the

FIGURE 18–9.
The discussion of death requires an adult who is sensitive to the child's burgeoning curiosity and affective vulnerability. Such discussions help to lay the foundation for the identity homework of the adolescent years.

truth.[2] One explanation that can be given the young child is that the body is the house where the "me" lives while on Earth. Death is when the "me" has left a body that no longer works right. The body is worn out or cannot be fixed.[67] Children may have a great deal of difficulty developing a positive concept of God if they are told that God "wanted" the person who died.[53]

School-agers often ask if the parents will die. They need to be told honestly, "Yes, I will die. But I don't expect to die for a long time." The underlying concern is generally, "Who will take care of me if my parents die?" Parents should assure children of the arrangements for child care in case of untimely illness or death.

One question that parents face is whether or not to allow the child to attend a wake (viewing) or a funeral. Observing the child's response to death of a pet or other separation experiences can give some clues as to readiness. No child should be forced but each should be included as much as possible.[83,84] Exclusion from all activities gives a sense of unreality and detachment to the event. Moderate sharing of grief by other mourners can help the child feel less alone in the crisis and may help in the personal expression of grief. Some children in the 7- to 9-years-old age group are terrified by the prospect of a funeral. The author's adult daughter remembers with great tenderness saying "good-bye" to her grandmother at the funeral, even though she was only 3½ years old at the time.

When a death occurs in the family, the parents are often so consumed by their own grief that they are unable to observe the needs of the children or to appreciate the contributions of the children (especially adolescents) to the prevention or handling of problems during this time.[29] Children and adolescents need information and extra support during the hospitalization of a family member. Adaptation to the loss of a family member is greatly facilitated by sensitive counseling geared to the child's developmental level and the specific circumstances. Some children may feel that they have lost not only the deceased but also the parents or other significant persons, because the survivors are so caught up in their own grief they are unable to support the continued, let alone special, needs of the child. No child should be placed in a position where he or she feels emotionally abandoned at this time.

Other forms of grief expression and resolution for young children include talking about the deceased and accompanying negative and positive feelings, art, poetry, music, cemetery visits, extra time with surviving parent, and letter writing to the deceased.[84] Acceptance of the child's feelings is critical for positive growth through the experience.[93]

Religious beliefs may or may not offer support at this time, especially to the adolescent. Such support depends on the unique blending of the three major subconcepts (the purpose of life, the nature of human beings, and the existence of God), as well as the degree to which the individual has resolved his or her own mortality into a concept of life, and the depth to which this belief or concept of life has been translated into values, goals, and actions.

CONCLUSION

Concern is expressed that in our modern throwaway society children may be thwarted in the art of becoming attached, investing of oneself in another.[91] Divorce interrupts the primary attachments, desensitizing the child to the security and joy found in the depths of love and commitment and the value of the human bond to our and other's lives. The rapid replacement of pets and toys interferes with normal grieving and the development of the concept that death is inevitable, universal, and irreversible. The violence portrayed in mass media may undermine the valuing of human life and perpetuate the myth that death is the result of external aggression and, therefore, is avoidable.

Adults need to help children face death and loss when they are less personally involved to help them prepare for close contacts with death.[83] Natural opportunities help prepare the child to mobilize coping strategies and to immunize themselves against severe maladaptation later.

The cognitive and affective domains are interdependent in the development of a concept of death (see Table 18-2). To the infant, who has relatively no concept of time or the meaning of death, separation from a significant caregiver, even for nap and sleep times, may be analogous to a death experience. To the egocentric toddler, death is separation from a love object seen as essential to his or her existence. The preschooler, still not understanding cause–effect relationships, is unsure both of the cause of death or ways to "revive" the person or animal that has died. Since death is seen as another form of life, there is much concern about meeting life functions in the grave. The young school-ager feels that death is a form of punishment that can be avoided by "being good." The scary tales of school-agers and the interest they show in Halloween, ghost stories, exhibitions of omnipotence, and strivings for physical prowess may all be partially explained by the concept that death can be outwitted if one is wise enough, brave enough, or strong enough. Bereaved and terminally ill children tend to have more mature concepts of death than age mates.

When the fact of personal mortality is cognitively accepted, it still must be worked into a philosophy of life that includes defining a purpose for life, a concept of God, and the potential for existence of the spiritual self beyond the life of the physical self. Many adults repress thoughts of personal death until times of critical life-change events. Incomplete resolution of the issue before the crisis can increase anxiety levels and interfere with the implementation of constructive coping skills.

Adults who have completely accepted and integrated their own feelings toward life and death are the best resources for facilitating the development of a positive concept of life and death by the maturing child. Parents who feel that they do not have the strength or the security to explain death to their children should seek professional assistance from the clergy, their pediatrician, or a child psychologist.

One's concept of death continues to be modified throughout the adult years as the quality of life changes, crisis experiences are faced, and as a result of identity homework and religious experiences. Erikson shares, "No matter how long one's life expectancy is, one must face oneself as one who shares an all-human existential identity, as creatively given form in the world religions."[17] "Whereas biology describes life, it does not define it, and although psychology illuminates life of the psyche, it does not confine it."[93] Facing one's personal mortality can be an enriching rather than a frightening experience.

> A gift is gotten from the encounter with death that cannot be purchased for any other price. This is an awareness of what one values and does not value, of what one has and does not have, and of what one would want should he or she be given the opportunity to live.[81]

He who does not know how to live is also not capable of dying; and he who fears death is really terrified of life.
—Maria Nagy

REFERENCES

1. Adler, P. (1975). The translation experience: An alternative view of culture shock. *Journal of Humanistic Psychology, 15*(4), 13–23.
2. Altschul, S. (1988). Summary and conclusions. In S. Altschul (Ed.), *Childhood bereavement and its aftermath* (pp. 421–428). Madison, CT: International Universities Press.
3. Anthony, H. S. (1971). *The discovery of death in childhood and after*. London: Penguin Press.
4. Ariés, P. (1981). *The hour of our death* (H. Weaver, Trans.). New York: Alfred A. Knopf.
5. Bertoia, J., & Allan, J. (1988, February). Counseling seriously ill children: Use of spontaneous drawings. *Elementary School Guidance and Counseling*, pp. 206–221.
6. Berzonsky, M. D. (1987). A preliminary investigation of children's conceptions of life and death. *Merrill-Palmer Quarterly, 33*, 505–513.
7. Betz, C. L. (1987). Death, dying and bereavement: A review of literature, 1970–1985. In T. Krulik, B. Holaday, & I. M. Martinson (Eds.), *The child and family facing life-threatening illness* (pp. 32–49). Philadelphia: J. B. Lippincott.
8. Bibace, R., & Walsh, M. E. (1980). Development of children's conceptions of illness. *Pediatrics, 66*, 912–917.
9. Bluebond-Langer, M. (1977). The meanings of death to children. In H. Feifel (Ed.), *New meanings of death* (pp. 47–66). New York: McGraw-Hill.
10. Bluebond-Langner, M. (1978). *The private worlds of dying children*. Princeton, NJ: Princeton University Press.
11. Bowlby, J., & Parkes, C. M. (1970). Separation and loss within the family. In E. J. Anthony & C. Koupernick (Eds.), *The child in his family* (Vol. 1). New York: Wiley-Interscience.
12. Braaten, S., & Braaten, B. (1988). Responding to death and grief in a school. *The Pointer, 32*(4), 27–31.
13. Carr, A. C. (1987). Prologue: Principles of thanatology. In A. H. Kutscher, A. C. Carr, & L. G. Kutscher (Eds.), *Principles of thanatology* (pp. 6–28). New York: Columbia University Press.
14. Childers, P., & Wimmer, M. (1971). The concept of death in early childhood. *Child Development, 42*, 1299–1301.

15. Comer, J. P. (1987). Learning to cope with death. *Parents, 62*(4), 210.
16. Easson, W. M. (1981). *The dying child* (2nd ed.). Springfield, IL: Thomas.
17. Erikson, E. H., Erikson, J. M., & Kivnick, H. Q. (1986). *Vital involvement in old age*. New York: W. W. Norton.
18. Evans, S., Reinhart, J., & Succop, P. (1972). Failure to thrive: A study of 45 children and their families. *Journal of the American Academy of Child Psychiatry, 11*, 440.
19. Formanek, R. (1974). When children ask about death. *Elementary School Journal, 75*(2), 92.
20. Fulton, R. L., & Bendiksen, R. (1976). *Death and identity* (rev. ed.). Bowie, MD: Charles Press.
21. Furman, E. (1974). *A child's parent dies: Studies in childhood bereavement*. New Haven, CT: Yale University Press.
22. Furn, B. G. (1987). Adjustment and the near-death experience: A conceptual and therapeutic model. *Journal of Near-Death Studies, 6*(1), 4–27.
23. Gabbard, G. O., & Twemlow, S. W. (1984). *With the eyes of the mind: An empirical analysis of out-of-body states*. New York: Praeger.
24. Gaffney, D. A. (1988). Death in the classroom: A lesson in life. *Holistic Nursing Practice, 2*(2), 20–27.
25. Gallup. (1985, May). *Religion in America: 50 years 1935–1985* (Report No. 236). Princeton, NJ: The Gallup Report.
26. Gartley, W., & Bernasconi, M. (1967). The concept of death in children. *Journal of Genetic Psychology, 110*, 71–85.
27. Gesser, G., Wong, P. T. P., & Reker, G. T. (1987). Death attitudes across the life-span: The development and validation of the death attitude profile (DAP). *Omega, 18*(2), 113–128.
28. Greeley, A. M. (1975). *The sociology of the paranormal: A reconnaissance*. Beverly Hills: Sage Publications.
29. Grogan, L. B. (1990). Grief of an adolescent when a sibling dies. *MCN: American Journal of Maternal Child Nursing, 15*, 24–24.
30. Haraldsson, E. (1985). Representative national surveys of psychic phenomena: Iceland, Great Britain, Sweden, USA and Gallup's multinational survey. *Journal of the Society for Psychical Research, 53*(801), 145–158.
31. Haraldsson, E. (1988). Survey of claimed encounters with the dead. *Omega, 19*(2), 103–113.
32. Jackson, E. N. (1967). The theological, psychological, and philosophical dimensions of death in Protestantism. In E. A. Grollman (Ed.), *Explaining death to children*. Boston: Beacon Press.
33. Janssen, Y. G. (1983). Early awareness of death in normal child development. *Infant Mental Health Journal, 4*, 95.
34. Johnson, P. A. (1982). After a child's parent has died. *Child Psychiatry and Human development, 12*(3), 160.
35. Kalish, R. A., & Reynolds, D. K. (1973). Phenomenological reality and post-death contract. *Journal for Scientific Study of Religion, 20*, 209–221.
36. Kane, B. (1979). Children's concepts of death. *Journal of Genetic Psychology, 134*, 141–153.
37. Kastenbaum, R. (1967). The child's understanding of death: How does it develop? In E. A. Grollman (Ed.), *Explaining death to children*. Boston: Beacon Press.
38. Kastenbaum, R. (1974). Childhood: The kingdom where creatures die. *Journal of Clinical Child Psychology, 3*(2), 11.
39. Klug, L., Sinha, A. (1987). Death acceptance: A two-component formulation and scale. *Omega, 18*, 229–235.
40. Kübler-Ross, E. (1976). *Questions and answers on death and dying*. New York: Macmillan.
41. Kuiken, D., & Madison, G. (1987). The effects of death contemplation on meaning and purpose in life. *Omega, 18*(2), 103–112.
42. Lonetto, R. (1980). *Children's conceptions of death*. New York: Springer.
43. MacIsaac, P., & King, S. (1989). What did you do with Sophie, teacher? *Young Children, 44*(2), 37–38.
44. Mahler, M. S., Pine, F., Bergman, A. (1975). *The psychological birth of the human infant: Symbiosis and individuation*. New York: Basic books.
45. Marks, J. (1987). We have a problem. *Parents, 62*(6), 70–75.
46. McCready, W. C., & Greeley, A. M. (1976). *The ultimate values of the American population*. Beverly Hills, CA: Sage Publications.
47. McIntire, M. S., Angle, C. R., & Struempler, L. J. (1972). The concept of death in Midwestern children and youth. *American Journal of Diseases of Children, 123*, 527–532.
48. McNeil, J. N. (1984). Death education in the home: Parents talk with their children. In H. Wass & C. A. Carr (Eds.), *Childhood and death* (pp. 293–313). Washington, DC: Hemisphere.
49. Miller, H. L. (1987). Helping kindergartners deal with death. *Childhood Education, 64*(1), 31–32.
50. Moody, R. A. (1977). *Life after life: The investigation of a phenomenon—survival of bodily death*. Harrisburg, PA: Stackpole Books.
51. Moore, T. E., & Mae, R. (1987). Who dies and who cries: Death and bereavement in children's literature. *Journal of Communication, 37*(4), 52–64.
52. Morgan, J. D. (1987). Living our dying: Social and cultural considerations. In H. Wass, F. M. Berardo, & R. A. Neimeyer (Eds.), *Dying: Facing the facts* (2nd ed., pp. 13–27). Washington, DC: Hemisphere.
53. Moss, S. A. (1987). Children's concept of God, death, and life after death. In J. E. Schowalter, P. Buschman, P. R. Patterson, A. H. Kutscher, M. Tallmer, & R. G. Stevenson (Eds.), *Children and death: Perspectives from birth through adolescence* (pp. 11–17). New York: Praeger.
54. Nagy, M. (1948). The child's theories concerning death. *Journal of Genetic Psychology, 73*, 3.
55. Neimeyer, R. A. (1987). Death anxiety. In H. Wass, F. M. Berardo, & R. A. Neimeyer (Eds.), *Dying: Facing the facts* (2nd ed., pp. 97–136). Washington, DC: Hemisphere.
56. Olson, M. (1988). The incidence of out-of-body experiences in hospitalized patients. *Journal of Near-Death Studies, 6*(3), 169–174.
57. Osis, K., & Haraldsson, E. (1986). *At the hour of death* (rev. ed.). New York: Hastings House.
58. Papowitz, L. (1986). Life, death, life. *American Journal of Nursing, 86*, 416–418.
59. Parmelee, A. H. (1986). Children's illnesses: Their beneficial effects on behavioral development. *Child Development, 57*, 1–10.
60. Pazola, K. J., & Gerberg, A. K. (1990). Privileged communication: Talking with a dying adolescent. *MCN: American Journal of Maternal Child Nursing, 15*(1), 16–21.
61. Pennachio, J. (1988). Near-death experiences and self-transformation. *Journal of Near-Death Studies, 6*(3), 162–168.
62. Piaget, J. (1955). *The language and thought of the child* (M. Gabain, Trans.). New York: Meridian Books.
63. Piaget, J. (1969). *The child's conception of the world* (J. Tomlinson & A. Tomlinson, Trans.). Totowa, NJ: Littlefield, Adams.
64. Pielke, R. G. (1986). *You say you want a revolution: Rock music in the American culture*. Chicago: Nelson Hall.
65. Pine, V. R. (1987). A healthy outlook on life necessarily compre-

hends death. In A. H. Kutscher, A. C. Carr, & L. G. Kutscher (Eds.), *Principles of thanatology* (pp. 1–5). New York: Columbia University Press.

66. Rank, O. (1973). *The trauma of birth.* New York: Harper and Row.

67. Reed, E. L. (1970). *Helping children with the mystery of death.* Nashville: Abingdon Press.

68. Rees, W. D. (1971). The hallucinations of widowhood. *British Medical Journal, 4,* 37–41.

69. Richards, D. D., & Seigler, R. S. (1984). The effects of task requirements on children's life judgments. *Child Development, 55,* 1687–1696.

70. Riley, S. S. (1989). Pilgrimage to Elmwood Cemetery. *Young Children, 44*(2), 33–36.

71. Ring, K. (1980). *Life at death: A scientific investigation of the near-death experience.* New York: Coward, McCann and Geoghegan.

72. Robertson, J. (1970). *Young children in hospital* (2nd ed.). London: Tavistock Publications.

73. Rubenstein, J. S. (1982). Preparing a child for a good-bye visit to a dying loved one. *Journal of the American Medical Association, 247,* 2571.

74. Sabom, M. B. (1982). *Recollections of death: A medical investigation.* New York: Harper and Row.

75. Samuels, A. (1988). Parental death in childhood. In S. Altschul (Ed.), *Childhood bereavement and its aftermath* (pp. 19–36). Madison, CT: International Universities Press.

76. Schowalter, J. E. (1987). Adolescents' concepts of death and how these can kill them. In J. E. Schowalter, M. Buschman, & R. G. Stevenson (Eds.), *Children and death: Perspectives from birth through adolescence* (pp. 3–9). New York: Praeger.

77. Serdahely, W. J. (1987). The near-death experience: Is the presence always the higher self? *Omega, 18*(2), 129–134.

78. Siegel, R. K. (1980). The psychology of life after death. *American Psychologist, 35*(10), 911–931.

79. Simon-Buller, S., Christopherson, V. A., & Jones, R. A. (1988). Correlates of sensing the presence of a deceased spouse. *Omega, 19*(1), 21–30.

80. Simpson, E. (1988, May). A death in the family. *Working Mother,* pp. 105–109.

81. Slaby, A. E., & Glicksman, A. S. (1985). *Adapting to life-threatening illness.* New York: Praeger.

82. Slawinski, J. (1987). Electromagnetic radiation and the afterlife. *Journal of Near-Death Studies, 6*(2), 79–94.

83. Smilansky, S. (1987). *On death: Helping children understand and cope.* New York: Peter Lang.

84. Sourkes, B. M. (1987). Siblings of the child with a life-threatening illness. *Journal of Children in Contemporary Society, 19*(3/4), 159–184.

85. Speece, M. W., & Brent, S. B. (1987). Children's understanding of death: A review of three components of a death concept. In T. Krulik, B. Holaday, & I. M. Martinson (Eds.), *The child and family facing life-threatening illness* (pp. 74–96). Philadelphia: J. B. Lippincott.

86. Speece, M. W., & Brent, S. B. (1987). Irreversibility, nonfunctionality, and universality: Children's understanding of three components of a death concept. In J. E. Schowalter, P. Buschman, P. R. Patterson, A. H. Kutscher, M. Tallmer, & R. G. Stevenson (Eds.), *Children and death: Perspectives from birth through adolescence* (pp. 19–29). New York: Praeger.

87. Spinetta, J. J. (1974). The dying child's awareness of death: A review. *Psychological Bulletin, 81,* 256–260.

88. Stambrook, M., & Parker, K. C. H. (1987). The development of the concept of death in childhood: A review of the literature. *Merrill-Palmer Quarterly, 33*(2), 133–157.

89. Strom-Paikin, J. (1986). Studying the NDE phenomenon. *American Journal of Nursing, 86,* 420–421.

90. Tallmer, M. (1987). Preface. In J. E. Schowalter, P. Buschman, P. R. Patterson, A. H. Kutscher, M. Tallmer, & R. G. Stevenson (Eds.), *Children and death: Perspectives from birth through adolescence* (pp. ix–xiii). New York: Praeger.

91. Toffler, A. (1970). *Future shock.* New York: Random House.

92. Waechter, E. H. (1987). Children's awareness of fatal illness. In T. Krulik, B. Holaday, & I. M. Martinson (Eds.), *The child and family facing life-threatening illness* (pp. 101–107). Philadelphia: J. B. Lippincott.

93. Waechter, E. H. (1987). Death, dying and bereavement: A review of the literature. In T. Krulik, B. Holaday, & I. M. Martinson (Eds.), *The child and family facing life-threatening illness* (pp. 3–31). Philadelphia: J. B. Lippincott.

94. Wass, H. (1985). Depiction of death, grief and funerals on national television. *Research Record, 2,* 81–92.

95. Wass, H., Neimeyer, R. A., & Berardo, F. M. (1987). An overview of the facts. In H. Wass, F. M. Berardo, & R. A. Neimeyer (Eds.), *Dying: Facing the facts* (2nd ed., pp. 3–10). Washington, DC: Hemisphere.

96. Wass, H., & Stillion, J. M. (1987). Death in the lives of children and adolescents. In H. Wass, F. M. Berardo, & R. A. Neimeyer (Eds.), *Dying: Facing the facts* (2nd ed., pp. 201–228). Washington, DC: Hemisphere.

97. White, E., Elsom, B., & Prawat, R. (1978). Children's conceptions of death. *Child Development, 49,* 307–310.

98. Woods, B. W. (1982). *Christians in pain: Perspectives on suffering.* Grand Rapids, MI: Baker Book House.

99. Yalom, I. D. (1980). *Existential psychotherapy.* New York: Basic Books.

19

Grieving is as natural as crying when you hurt sleeping when you are tired eating when you are hungry or sneezing when your nose itches.
It is nature's way of healing a broken heart.

—DOUG MANNING
DON'T TAKE MY GRIEF AWAY FROM ME

Concepts of Loss and Grieving

M. Patricia Donahue

*D*EATH—the inescapable fate of every individual human being is often viewed as inconceivable, as a profound mystery, as incomprehensible, as an exceptional experience. Consequently, it is confronted with ambivalence, fear, or total lack of acceptance. However, one's concept of death can affect perceptions of life in many beneficial ways, since the meaning of one's life is closely interwoven with one's concept of death.

It is apparent that the subjects of "death and dying" and "loss and grieving" have become extremely popular, a fact that may potentially diminish the importance of the topics. "Since the late 1960's the number of publications which focus on various aspects of death and dying, care of the dying patient, loss and grief, bereavement, children and death, and a host of related topics have steadily increased."[19] In addition, with the increase in excellent literature, literature of poor quality has also appeared, creating particular difficulty for the lay person who must decide what is indeed credible. Popular writers as well as scholars are addressing these crucial issues, and it is the popular books that have the greatest impact on those individuals searching for answers to questions about death, loss, and grieving. In reality, many people who are attempting to cope with losses of any type are doing so alone or with the assistance of self-help or support groups.

One's concept of death surfaces whenever an individual faces a condition of crisis in life. Death and loss present extremely personal and lonely experiences that can be of positive or negative value. The manner in which the individual learns to cope with losses in childhood (e.g., the loss of a toy, a parent leaving for the evening, moving to a new neighborhood), facilitates or hinders coping with the losses of adulthood, such as death of a spouse, body disfigurement, and bankruptcy. Coping with death and loss is a complex process that involves the concepts of self and personal identity. Consideration of the five major domains (biophysical, cognitive, affective, social, and spiritual) of normal human development and behavior is important to an adequate understanding of the process of loss and grieving. Each of these domains is affected in a variety of uniquely different ways as individuals must encounter, cope with, and successfully overcome the myriad of lifetime losses that occur.

CONFRONTATIONS WITH LOSS

Loss is a natural part of existence that is repeatedly encountered in every individual's life.[62, 65] Loss is complex, for it reaches to the heart of what it means to be human and what it means to have a relationship. Few experiences in life have greater emotional impact than personal loss and the endeavors that are made for the resolution of the accompanying grief. While the death of a loved one or the impending death of self are usually the most difficult losses an individual must face, any loss can produce profound consequences. The concept of loss, therefore, cannot and should not be confined to the loss of a person, nor to a loss that results from death.

Loss has been defined as a "state of being deprived of or being without something one has had."[58] Thus, a deprivation of some kind is always the result of loss.[65] As such, an individual's values, self-esteem, and lifestyle can be threatened by loss experiences to a greater or a lesser degree.[72] Losses may cause changes in a person's life and thus require some type of adaptation. This adaptation or process of grieving can become complicated and result in psychopathology if the process is blocked in some way. Individual response to a loss is thus influenced by the nature of the loss itself (degree of injury to the system), the characteristics of the person who is experiencing the loss (health status of the system), and the social environment in which the loss occurs (support from the suprasystem.) "How someone copes with the challenge of change in their life will determine not only their view of the world but their view of themselves" (Fig. 19-1).[54]

Middlescence appears to be a stage in an individual's life during which losses appear to compound and thus may have greater meaning and impact. For the first time, the individual may face a "profound" loss (e.g., the loss of one's parents). Each loss prompts one to reexamine value systems and discover new sources of meaning and purpose in life. In addition, physiological changes such as menopause and the climacteric may create sufficient loss of body image to precipitate a grieving process. Despite the distresses, however, losses can also lead to growth. Positive outcomes from loss and accompanying grief include an increased capacity for intimacy and empathy, a greater valuing of interpersonal relationships, the recognition of personal adaptive potential, and the recognition of personal strength and survivability.[78]

One of the most beneficial attributes for facing personal loss is the ability to assume a life-cycle perspective.[21, 78] From such a perspective, " . . . death can be viewed as a transactional process involving the deceased and the survivors in a shared life cycle that acknowledges both the finality of death and the continuity of life."[78] The loss of a family member disrupts the family equilibrium and in turn requires both immediate and long-term reorganization, mandating family reorganization and presenting new adaptational challenges or family tasks of mourning that can be identified just as individual tasks have been.[21, 42]

No one can fully understand what another individual is experiencing when a loss occurs. No one can *totally* understand the significance of the lost object or the impact that results.

Universal and Inevitable

Loss and grieving are universal and inevitable parts of human life. Both are processes that begin at birth and continue

FIGURE 19-1.
Entrance into school represents a loss of known environment, routines, and relationships as well as an introduction to multiple unknowns. As such, it may precipitate feelings of grief as well as fear.

throughout the life cycle. Both occur within every stage of life and impact all five domains. It is, however, loss or impending loss that triggers the grieving process and gives rise to a symbiotic relationship between the two. Grief, which may precede (anticipatory grief) or follow a significant loss, is the mechanism through which the biophysical, cognitive, affective, social, and spiritual equilibrium of the individual or the family can be reestablished (resolution).

It is important to understand that some losses are predictable, necessary components of growth and development; others are haphazard and unpredictable. A variety of ways by which to categorize types of losses has emerged through the years. Losses can be classified as physical or symbolic.[62, 65] **Physical losses** are those that are easily recognized, are tangible, or can be touched (such as the death of a friend or the theft or a car). **Symbolic losses,** on the other hand, are psychosocial in nature, are abstract, and cannot be seen or touched. Consequently, a symbolic loss such as divorce or loss of status due to job demotion may not be recognized. It nonetheless elicits a grief response. Other symbolic losses include **developmental losses,** which occur in response to human development and normal change and growth (e.g., weaning, retirement, deteriorating eyesight); **competency-based losses** that result in the loss of striving (college graduation) (Fig. 19-2). **Secondary losses** (physical or symbolic) result from a primary loss, such as the death of a parent or loss of a body part.[62,65]

Losses may also be viewed as maturational and situational. **Maturational losses** are those associated with the natural process of growth and development. They are, for the most part, anticipated, predictable, and desired. Through the acquisition of new skills and roles, the individual is forced to relinquish earlier methods of attaining gratification and ways of perceiving himself or herself. Examples of such losses include birth itself, entry into school, puberty, marriage, and pregnancy. **Situational losses** are those associated with a significant relationship, a possession, or the self (body part, body function, ideals, self-esteem). They are, for the most part, unpredictable, unanticipated, and undesirable. Examples may include the death of a loved one, birth of a sibling, loss of job, divorce, and loss of hearing, vision, or a body part.

Unfortunately, losses tend to be regarded as primarily detrimental to a person's well-being. However, "the saddening aftermath of loss which results from the effects of personal deprivation has obscured the fact that losses, real or otherwise, by serving as catalysts of change and forcing substitution and sublimation, play a critical role in psychic development, and especially in that most exalted of human qualities, creativity."[69] Loss does become an agent for change; *loss forces a reexamination of current value systems in order to discover new meaning and purpose in life.* In turn, feelings of strength and security can be gained as a result of struggling with the loss experience. Loss, then, often does have the potential for enrichment of life, for the development of greater strength and sensitivity, and for opportunities to achieve new and satisfying alternatives. In addition, loss is highly personal and must be dealt with in a highly individualized manner.

> Loss or separation will stimulate individual reactions in a unique way. Nobody's grief will ever be like mine. My loss of dentures can be more painful to me than your loss of a friend to you. Animal lovers sometimes grieve the death of a poodle with more intensity than a brother's death in war. There are similarities in our feelings and reactions, but human grief like all human pain is highly personal and distinctive.[39]

Grief

Grief is a response to a loss of any type; the length and intensity of the grief depends on the value of the lost object. Grief is a normal and healthy process, yet it may lead to physiological and psychological disturbances of a psychopathological nature. People who are grieving may be extremely vulnerable. Although opinions among investigators vary, some general characteristics have been found to exist by which one may determine whether an individual who has experienced a loss is overcoming the agonizing pain associated with grief and is thereby moving toward resolution, or if he or she has a delayed or prolonged grief that is blocking movement toward resolution. Adults and children alike must be enabled to achieve the resolution of loss so that normal functioning and reestablishment of relationships can occur.

Specific stages of grieving through which an individual may progress have been identified by numerous authors and researchers. A continuing controversy, however, exists as to whether grief follows a predictable pattern. Brown and Stoudemire's analysis supports the thesis that the process of uncomplicated grief follows a relatively predictable pattern (Fig. 19-3).[10] They propose that " . . . the process of uncomplicated grief is pictured as an interwoven pattern of changing emotional states, somatic symptoms, thoughts, and motivational stages. The phases overlap, as do each of the components within the phases."[10]

Amenta and Bohnet also propose a three-stage model, summarized in Table 19-1, that identifies both somatic and psychic characteristics.[2]

Many other paradigms can be found to demonstrate stages or phases of uncomplicated grief work. These project a seemingly predictable course of grieving that is followed by individuals who are able to resolve their loss. Joyce proposes that there is no strict timetable for grieving and that grief does not follow a predictable pattern.[34] He draws on the work of mental-health professionals who are reexamining the "rules" of bereavement and grief. He concludes that reactions to grief " . . . cannot be neatly plotted in a series of well-defined stages, nor is the progression from the time of death to the resolution

FIGURE 19–2.
Times of greatest excitement, joy, and achievement, such as graduation, marriage, or the birth of a child, are also times of grief. Life will never be the same again.

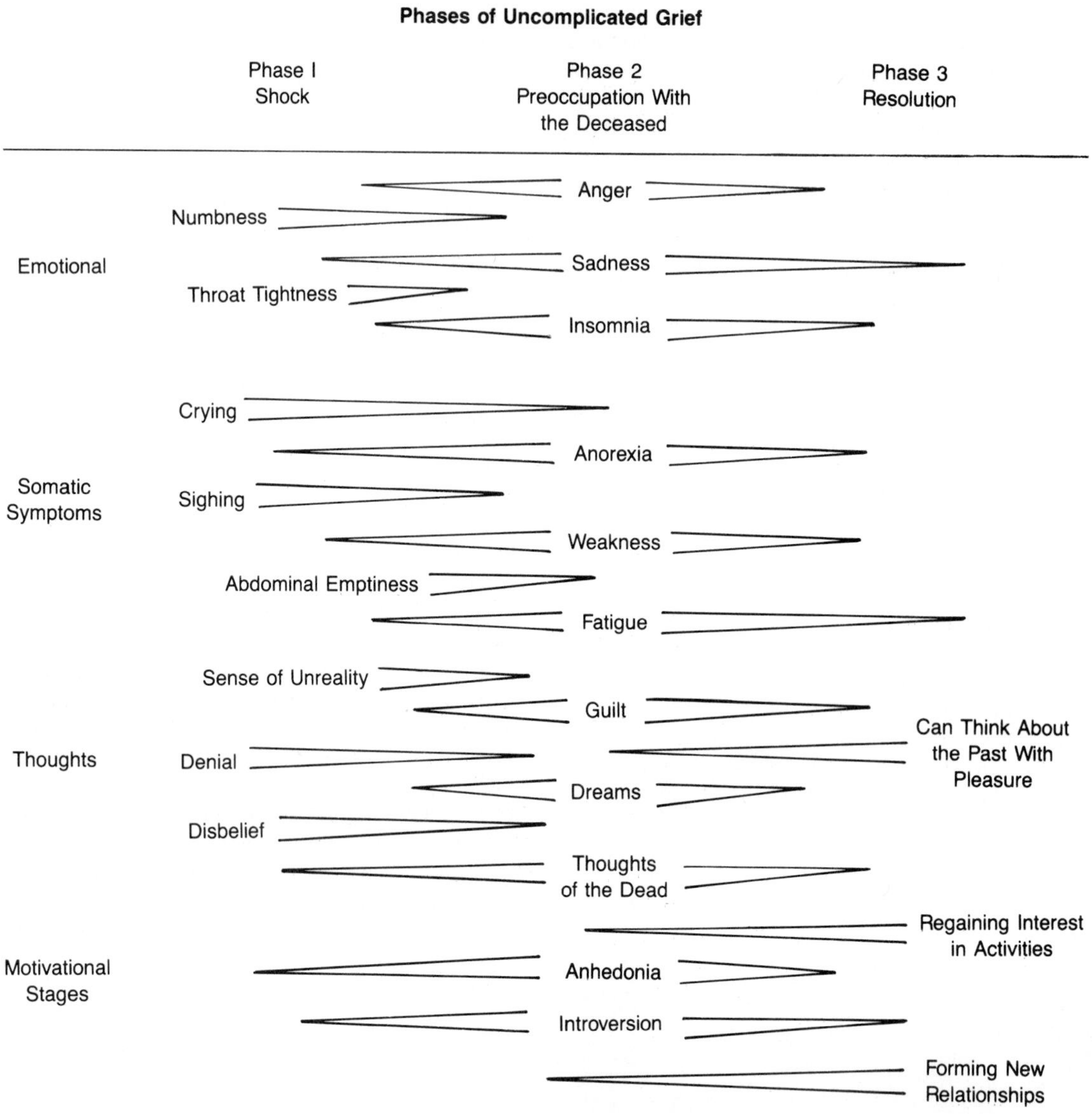

Phases of Uncomplicated Grief

Phase 1 Shock	Phase 2 Preoccupation With the Deceased	Phase 3 Resolution

Emotional
- Anger
- Numbness
- Sadness
- Throat Tightness
- Insomnia

Somatic Symptoms
- Crying
- Anorexia
- Sighing
- Weakness
- Abdominal Emptiness
- Fatigue

Thoughts
- Sense of Unreality
- Guilt
- Denial — Can Think About the Past With Pleasure
- Dreams
- Disbelief
- Thoughts of the Dead

Motivational Stages
- Regaining Interest in Activities
- Anhedonia
- Introversion
- Forming New Relationships

FIGURE 19–3.
Phases of uncomplicated grief. (From Brown, J. T., & Stoudemire G. A. [1983]. Normal and pathological grief. Journal of the American Medical Association, 250, 378. With permission.)

of bereavement likely to be in a straight line. There are a number of psychological, social and biological processes that interact and make it difficult to define a normal reaction to bereavement."[34]

One must be careful, therefore, not to categorize or stereotype an individual's response but rather to consider each experience of loss and grieving as a unique situation. The distinguishing factor between adult and childhood grief is the stage of development of the cognitive and affective domains. At what point the process emerges from its infantile forms is a matter of speculation. One cannot really predict what a child's or adult's reaction to loss will be. Thus, the grieving individual, rather than the stages, phases, or theories, must always remain the primary focus. The identified stages should serve merely as guidelines to evaluate the problem and to provide a framework for intervention.

TABLE 19-1. EMOTIONAL AND SOMATIC REACTIONS TO BEREAVEMENT

	Shock	*Pain*	*Resolution*
Feelings	Helplessness Numbness	Anger Sadness Guilt Loneliness Yearning Anxiety Depression	Emancipation Reintegration
Physical sensations	Dry mouth Tight throat Tight chest	Weakness Fatigue	Return to predeath state
Behaviors	Crying Sighing	Insomnia Overeating Undereating Absentmindedness Social withdrawal Hyperactivity	Social interactions Developing new relations
Cognitions	Disbelief Sense of presence	Preoccupation Hallucinations Confusion	Realistic remembrance of deceased

(From Amenta, M., & Bohnet, N. [1986]. Nursing care of the terminally ill [p. 250]. Boston: Little, Brown.)

General Considerations

No person is immune to the infinite variety of losses that may occur during any stage of the life span. Unfortunately, in many instances, society tends to place all mourners into the same category; they are stereotyped and observed to see if they follow the typical pattern of reaction to loss that has been predetermined. Although many similarities can be documented, many differences are also found among individuals' reactions to loss. These differences usually depend on the significance of the loss itself, the physiological and psychological makeup of the individual, and the sociocultural environment. Frequently, age, gender, and economic factors also have an impact on the process. Thus, it is difficult to provide a concise portrayal of loss and grief in any one developmental stage. Likewise, any loss may trigger responses in all five domains.

Social and Cultural Variations and Death

Crucial to the success of "grief work" is the provision of optimal conditions for healing. Of particular importance is the availability of support systems that will remain intact for the duration of the grieving process. It is not enough for support to be offered for 24 hours or even a 6-month period; grieving may take as long as a year or more. Consideration must also be given to religious beliefs and rituals, as well as to societal and cultural factors that affect the outcome of bereavement. For example, the prevailing attitude of a society or culture about death, loss, and grief can dramatically influence an individual's ability or inability to achieve either partial or complete resolution or prolong the mourning process. This fact was vividly evident with Vietnam casualty survivors who

were faced with conflict because of a discrepancy between personal feelings and beliefs and public ideology.[40] Because the Vietnam War was *unsanctioned,* the survivors had to deal with *stigmatized* losses. At least one study has suggested that "... the circumstances of the death, the lack of concrete evidence, the inadequate support available, and the conflicted social environment all contributed to the prolonged early grief phases and the struggle experienced by these family members to resolve their loss."[61] For several years after the war ended, political and intellectual battles continued and significantly interfered with the survivors' needed support.[80] The "... dedication of the national monument symbolized a turning point in the grief process for the subjects. Acknowledgement, validation and removal of stigmatized feelings from the grieving process were related to the building of this monument."[61] Thus, it is apparent that the mourning process requires permission to grieve; permission, in this instance, was required from the nation.[83]

Viewing the grief process as a social construct further enhances the role of the social and cultural milieu in loss and grieving. "A social construct is an invention which is created among social members and continues to be useful because it explains that which is not readily understood." As such, it "helps link grief and the mourning of survivors, ... sets both a public and private course for the bereaved, ... [and] encompasses public expectations that can influence the grief experience of bereaved."[79] The concept of a grief process was created to explain how survivors responded to the loss of a loved one. A relationship between grief and its public expression is thus presumed as one keeps in mind that **grief** *focuses on the internal reactions to loss* while **mourning** *focuses on the external or public expressions of loss.*[37] This relationship is more readily identifiable when mourning customs are evident and followed routinely by society members. In the United States, with its multiethnic heritage, scientific emphasis, and transient relationships, mourning customs tend to become ambiguous with resultant criticism that funeral practices contribute to the "deritulization of grief."[22]

Both historical and anthropological studies point out that each and every society or culture has customs or practices that deal with mourning and are geared to the preservation of social stability and growth. These customs are usually governed by religious beliefs that also dictate specific practices.[59] Consequently, those who are confronting the issues of loss and grieving must become aware of the need to understand ethnic and cultural differences in values, attitudes, expectations, rituals, and customs.

Caregivers and others have a strong tendency to develop philosophies, policies, and interventions that are based on their own backgrounds and experiences rather than on those of the grieving person.[31] A vivid example is the time allowed for bereavement in the work place (1–3 days), which severely interferes with retention of traditional attitudes and practices among certain cultural groups.

Values regarding bereavement vary significantly among cultures. It is therefore important to learn and appreciate specific beliefs about forms of mourning and to learn what a family and its members believe about death, its required rituals, and the afterlife. The following are examples of such differences:

> In certain Mediterranean cultures, such as Greek and Italian, a woman traditionally was supposed to mourn, and wear the outward signs of mourning, from the time of her husband's death through the rest of her life. At the opposite extreme, Americans of British ancestry tend to value a rational handling of death that involves "no mess, no fuss," with minimal expression of feeling, carried out in the most pragmatic way . . . For other ethnic groups, to die away from the family, which provides support in one's own environment, is a double tragedy. Italians, Greeks, Indians and many other groups consider human inter-

dependence to be natural to life and would consider it unnatural and a deprivation not to care for a family member in time of need.[78]

Social, cultural, and religious traditions and values supply crucial guidelines for the grieving process of the mourners and for those who assist them. A comparison of mourning in 80 different cultures " . . . showed that there are no exceptions to the rule that crying is a necessary part of mourning."[53,70] This "rule" lends support to the view that grief is a psychological process that transcends cultural influences, though culture may influence how grief is expressed (Fig. 19-4).[53]

REACTIONS TO LOSS

A trend seems to exist that emphasizes an individualistic approach to mourning and death rather than a systematic family approach. This trend may ultimately present problems, since important elements of modern family life affect one's adjustment to dying and death. These elements include the following:

1. Adults and children may live for years before a death in the immediate family (current emphasis on health).
2. The phenomenon of dying has changed; with improved medical services, death is often expected and occurs after a prolonged period of illness.
3. The role of religious and sociocultural institutions in bereavement has been diminishing and is being replaced partially by mental health clinics.[26]

Although it is true that death and loss affect each individual differently, the entire family system is also influenced. Thus, some are concerned that the family is not being considered adequately:[32]

> Societal, familial, and intrapsychic processes all operate to promote the isolation of dying. Our society, in keeping with its massive denial of death, has created "death specialists" for

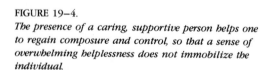
FIGURE 19–4.
The presence of a caring, supportive person helps one to regain composure and control, so that a sense of overwhelming helplessness does not immobilize the individual.

dealing with all aspects of the dying . . . With all of these individuals handling death, the family has gotten increasingly distant from the dying person.

Theories of Loss and Grief

Theories of loss and grief attempt to explain the human response to losses. They may be directed either to the *loss of self* or to the *loss of a significant other*; they may focus on the *process of dying* or on the *grieving process*. Theories cover a wide range of approaches for viewing these complex phenomena, as can be observed from the multitude of books and articles on the subject. For example, Raphael's survey of the entire field of bereavement lists more than 400 references to published works.[66] The historical roots for investigation lie in the early work of Freud, who viewed grief as a normal process that runs a definite and limited course.[24]

Loss of a Significant Other

Numerous authors and investigators have examined reactions to the loss of significant others. Their approaches are many and varied and, at times, focus on specific age groups, delayed reactions, or the nature of death. In Bowlby's work[7,8] with children, he found that children who have been separated from their mothers exhibit a pattern of behavior that is practically indistinguishable from adult grief; he describes this behavior with the terms **protest, despair,** and **detachment.**[8] He defines bereavement as three overlapping stages: (1) urge to recover the lost object—attempt to deny the loss; (2) disorganization—reluctant acceptance of death as a fact; and (3) reorganization—detachment from the loss and integration of the mourning experience. Children's disturbed reactions to the death of a sibling are reported by Cain and colleagues.[11] Delayed reactions to grief are described by Helene Deutsch,[17] while Weisman renders a comprehensive discussion of bereavement associated with untimely death.[82]

Erich Lindemann

Family crises in the form of bereavement and grief were first studied by Lindemann when he interviewed the relatives of the victims of the Cocoanut Grove nightclub fire, which occurred in Boston in 1942.[44] Lindemann observed several stages of "normal," acute grieving through which people progressed as they recovered from personal loss. These manifestations included: (1) somatic distress, a marked tendency to sighing respiration, complaints about lack of strength and exhaustion, and digestive symptoms; (2) preoccupation with the image of the deceased; (3) guilt, leading to a search for failure to do right by the lost one; (4) hostile reactions toward others; and (5) loss of patterns of conduct, especially the habits of social interaction. A sixth aspect, the appearance of traits or voluntary assumption of responsibilities of the deceased in the behavior of the bereaved, would probably be demonstrated by people bordering on psychopathological reactions.

According to Lindemann, the duration of a grief reaction depended on emancipation from bondage to the deceased, readjustment to an environment without the deceased, and the formation of new relationships. Overreaction or underreaction might occur in the process; these reactions represent distortions of normal grief and could result in failure to resolve a loss. Pathological grief then would be characterized by a longer duration and greater intensity of symptoms, giving rise to a serious threat to health. Lindemann's classic observations have provided the major themes of symptomatology that have penetrated subsequent literature on grieving.

George Engel

Engel also provides a framework for the response to loss. He contends that successful grieving follows predictable steps about which a judgment can be made that healing is taking place.[20] He is quick to note, however, that the normal healing processes of grieving cannot be accelerated. Both the theory and the practical problems of grief are evident in his approach; he cautions that it is important not only to recognize that a sequence of events characterizes grief but also to understand the meaning of each event. The healing process can be blocked by unsound interventions, suboptimal conditions for healing, or a lack of individual coping resources. Engel described the normal sequence of grief as the following:[20]

Shock and Disbelief: The overwhelming stress may be dealt with by denial or development of numbness. The bereaved seeks to reduce the impact of loss by admitting reality a little at a time.

Developing Awareness: Anger, despair, and crying become evident. The intensity of the reaction is dictated primarily by cultural mores.

Restitution: The work of mourning is done in this stage with cultural rituals and social support.

Resolving the Loss: The bereaved attempts to deal with the void and may become more dependent on the family. Thoughts are concentrated on the deceased; the bereaved finds it necessary to talk about memories of the dead person.

Idealization: Months are required for this process in which the survivor's preoccupation with the dead person progressively lessens. Abandonment of dependence on the deceased occurs, and interest in new relationships begins. In essence, the continuation of life is initiated.

Colin Murray Parkes

Based on his numerous studies of widows, Parkes proposes four stages of bereavement: **numbness** with denial and the inability to accept the loss; **yearning** to recover the lost one; **despairing disorganization**; and **behavioral reorganization.**[55,56] In addition, he speaks of two additional factors that play a part in determining overall reaction to bereavement: stigma and deprivation.[54] The term **stigma** is used to indicate a change in attitude that takes place in society when a person dies. The bereaved person may feel "tainted" and alone, deserted by people who were previously friendly, receiving only hollow offers of help. **Deprivation** indicates the absence of those essentials previously provided by the lost person. Parkes speaks of these essentials as the psychological equivalents of food and drink.

Loss of Self

In Elisabeth Kübler-Ross's classic work *On Death and Dying,* the dying patient became the teacher, a technique not often observed in the world of health care professionals.[42] Her pioneering studies on the psychological response to the process of dying (loss of self) are regarded as milestones in the grieving literature and clearly demonstrate the close parallel that exists between the processes of grieving and dying. After months of interviews and seminars to determine what dying patients were experiencing, Kübler-Ross concluded that most terminally ill people, in their anticipation of death, pass through the following stages:[42]

Denial and Isolation: This stage occurs with the initial awareness of illness when there is an inability or unwillingness to accept reality.

Anger: Further denial is impossible since the progression of the disease is apparent. The anger may be directed at anyone.

Bargaining: Pleas are made to postpone death through promises to God, the physician, to anyone.

Depression: The individual experiences a period of increasing depression; he or she literally grieves for the self. This grief is a sign that impending death is acknowledged and faced.

Acceptance: The individual is aware of the prognosis, is ready to let go of life, and is planning and preparing for it.

These stages also have been used to identify the grief of individuals after any loss, but they were not intended for that purpose. Not all dying patients progress through the stages at the same pace or in the same order. Vacillation may occur among the stages; some stages may not be resolved before death occurs. The stages can be independent of one another yet may overlap at times. It is evident, however, that these stages do not replace each other.

Interrelationship of Theories

Many theoretical positions on loss and grieving can be identified in the literature. In the final analysis, however, definite similarities can be observed in the various approaches: grief and mourning serve to facilitate an individual's acceptance of loss; the behavior patterns of grieving people are influenced by the social, psychological, spiritual, and cultural orientations of the particular society; the duration of the process is variable; grief may be strong or weak, brief or prolonged, immediate or delayed. The primary difference is the specific terminology that is used; *only the labels differ.* Whether these theories have different names or focus on different topics,

they all encompass loss and grieving. Their importance lies in the provision of *guidelines* to assist with the identification of commonalties or differences and of approaches that support bereaved individuals to facilitate their resolution of *any type* of loss. Thus, care must be exercised to prevent the placement of bereaved individuals into categories from which they are not allowed to escape.

Variations in the Grief Experience

A multitude of factors (a combination of interrelating psychological, sociocultural, spiritual, and biophysiological factors) influence the unique course that grieving will take. What may be true for one individual who is grieving a loss may not be true for another. What may be true for adults may not be applicable to the young. Knowledge of the person's developmental age, emotional and social history, family relationships, bond to the deceased, cultural and ethnic affiliation, personality, and the events that surround the death can help the practitioner understand and predict the course of grief.[54]

Grief must be approached as a part of life rather than as something to be avoided. Parkes believes that the personality or maturity level of the bereaved person and the quality of his or her relationship with the dead person are probably the most critical determinants of the outcome. However, it is not yet clear how much weight can be attributed to each individual factor in predicting the course or outcome of grief.

Religion is one of the variables about which much ambivalence exists. Opinions vary on the value of religion as a supportive factor during bereavement versus the detrimental effects of religion on the bereaved. The relationship between religion and resolution of loss is not simple. While some studies indicate that religious beliefs can offer effective coping mechanisms, others report the reverse. The specific rituals connected with particular religions can provide needed outlets for grief. In most cultures, the management of loss and grief has been one of the main concerns of these ceremonies. Perhaps the issue should not center on whether a particular religion provides for a favorable outcome, but rather one should consider the individual's stage of faith development (see Chap. 2) and the meaning of life and death. Basically, nearly everyone has a potential of hope or a potential of faith that can be worked with, tapped, and used to help with the expression of grief.

Normal Coping Responses

Under normal circumstances, grieving typically follows the course described previously. Each person proceeds through stages or phases in a highly individualistic manner, through a process that runs a definite and limited course. The individual's normal coping behaviors, personality, and mental health contribute to the grief response as they contribute to all other responses in life. It is important to understand the individual's *typical coping responses* to life events and crises, since the majority of people cope with grief using these familiar responses. If a person has consistently coped with crises by emotional denial or running away, the same behavior will probably occur in the grief situation. Such mechanisms may be used consciously or unconsciously as efforts to deal with the pain of loss and to protect oneself from the potentially overwhelming effect of the loss. Thus, an assessment of past coping behaviors is crucial to support those who are healthy and offer alternatives to those who are not.

Anticipatory Grief

Anticipatory grief is given special attention in the literature because of its potential effects on the mourning process.[26] It is considered to be a form of normal grief that encompasses many of the symptoms and processes of grief that normally follow a loss. Research findings are contradictory about the adaptational value and effects of advanced warning and the opportunity to experience grief before a death.[63,64] The primary reasons for these discrepancies is that anticipatory grief is an extremely complex phenomenon in a time of stress. "The truly therapeutic experience of anticipatory grief mandates a delicate balance among the mutually conflicting demands of simultaneously holding onto, letting go of, and drawing closer to the dying patient."[63] Anticipatory grief may be seen as "... a misnomer because 'anticipatory' suggests that one is grieving solely for anticipated, as opposed to past and current, losses, and because 'grief' implies the necessity of complete decathexis from the dying person."[64]

Anticipatory grief provides opportunity for preparation for a loss as well as for the expression of ambivalent and possibly hostile feelings. It also allows for the recognition of the reality of the loss gradually over time, the completion of unfinished business with the dying, and a heightened sensitivity to the needs of the terminally ill. The process of anticipatory grief can be a healthy adaptation to a person's illness because it can serve to cushion the bereaved against the massive and disorganizing impact of a loved one's death. By the time of actual death, some detachment *may have* occurred but it does *not* mean that sadness is absent or there is a lack of love or concern.

Anticipatory grief **does not** have to evolve into premature decathexis from the dying; it has the potential for continued support and stimulation with the dying person. *When anticipatory grief is focused only on one's own loss, support is withdrawn from the dying person,* and the individual may feel an increased sense of isolation in the dying process. The dying person may even experience hostility from the bereaved. Anticipatory grief can also occur before such events as an amputation, "empty nest," graduation, or even the cessation of breast feeding.

Adaptive and Maladaptive Grief Responses

Depending on one's viewpoint, grief may be adaptive or maladaptive, healthy or unhealthy, complicated or uncomplicated, normal or abnormal. Adaptive forms exhibit certain grief characteristics, run a predictable course (self-limiting), are intense and limited in time, and result in a successful conclusion or resolution. Maladaptive forms, on the other hand, exhibit exaggerated or atypical grief characteristics, run an unpredictable course, are prolonged and recurrent, or fail to reach a resolution. It is the maladaptive forms of grief that need professional intervention.

The types of grief that tend to be labeled as maladaptive or atypical follow one of three general forms:

Delayed Grief: In this type, the loss may be denied for months or years; grief occurs later, inappropriately associated with a reminder of the loss. Delayed grief is normal for children who most frequently postpone serious grieving until the psychic structures are mature enough to face the trauma.

Inhibited Grief: This type occurs in individuals in whom mourning is suppressed or consciously subdued. It is frequently longer lasting and associated with disturbed behavior or physical symptoms. Men and adolescents are most likely to experience this form of grief if they feel that acknowledging and expressing intense feelings are immature, unacceptable, or not masculine.

Chronic Grief: This type occurs with a prolonged and intensified normal grief process. Final resolution may never occur. The person may experience "chronic sorrow" or an underlying depression. The loss continues to color response to all experiences and relationships.

Individuals who have sustained a loss may have extreme difficulty with its resolution and may suffer severe psychological and physiological strain. Consequently, the provision of optimal conditions for healing or resolution must be the primary consideration in attempting to deal with any aspect of loss and grieving. Accompanying this provision must be a reevaluation of society's attitude toward grief. Cultural attitudes can complicate the process of grieving, since grief may be viewed as a sign of weakness or self-indulgence. Grief may also be regarded as morbid, unhealthy, degrading, and something that must be repressed. This attitude represents a callousness toward human needs. *Grieving represents one of the deepest of human needs and, as such, cannot and should not be denied or ignored.*

VARIATIONS IN THE LOSS EXPERIENCE

Personal Loss

Most people identify that the loss of a family member is the single most upsetting and feared event in the life of an individual.[35] Grief, in this instance, may give rise to volatile emotions, fear, helplessness, hopelessness, and physiological disturbances. Few individuals, if any, escape such effects, which stem from the intensity of the emotional attachments that have been built up over the years. To lose someone who is special to us is to lose a part of ourselves. It is the final, irretrievable stage in the separation–individuation process (see Chaps. 8 and 11). The refueling source is no longer available. The replacement of a person whose existence has been bound closely with our own is impossible.

Grief implies *caring,* caring so deeply that the depth of one's own feelings and emotions is experienced. The realization that nothing is forever can result in a greater understanding and appreciation of all that an individual still has. Personal loss, therefore, may and can have positive as well as negative effects.

Spouse

Death

The loss of a spouse has been identified as one of the most severe forms of psychological stress for individuals of any age. After the death of a spouse, widows and widowers experience a considerably greater mortality risk than married people of the same age, especially during the first 2 years after bereavement (particularly in the first 6 months, when the rise in the expected mortality rate is about 40%).[46, 52, 54, 56] Allusions to death on the anniversary of the death of one's spouse, death from self-neglect, and death by suicide are prevalent in the literature, as well as the possible existence of the phenomenon of "dying from a broken heart."[67] In addition, the emotional stress of a personal loss may lower the body's resistance to disease and may even affect a person's will to live.

It is apparent that many factors contribute to the ultimate outcome of conjugal bereavement particularly in the elderly population, who may be especially vulnerable due to limited social resources. Thus, loss may be not only psychological and physical but also social and economic and can lead to the phenomenon known as "bereavement overload,"[38] that is, overload by grief that results from the increased number of losses during this stage of life. Health may be lost, occupations may be lost through retirement or disability, socioeconomic status may be lost, and few loved ones may remain. Aged individuals often follow a pattern of inhibited or chronic grief, and they exhibit their grief most commonly through overt somatic pain and distress.[29] Consequently, the process of grieving for a lost spouse among the elderly is likely to be significantly different from that displayed in younger populations.[18]

The crucial element in conjugal bereavement lies with the support that is available to the spouse left behind, who becomes a person at risk, a person who may be helplessly alone. If the help available during the crisis is unsatisfactory, the bereavement may have an unfavorable outcome. The bereavement may be so severe as to be considered a life-threatening illness. It is essential that resources be available not just at the time of the death but continually for as long as it takes. Many widowed spouses feel the stress most acutely 2 to 4 months after the death, when reorganization of one's life without the spouse is most intense. Loneliness as well as the need to assume new responsibilities may be overwhelming. External support in the form of Widow-to-Widow programs or other types of programs may help to expand resources so that coping can be more effective during the different stages of grief. The risk of death during bereavement may thus be reduced through preventive measures.

Divorce

Loss and grieving related to divorce are particularly complicated, since society for a long time has denied the concept of divorce and thereby the idea that a person can be as traumatized through divorce as through death. Society usually does not acknowledge formally the lost relationship. The present divorce rate, the changes in family structure and roles, the women's movement, and various other sociocultural changes are, however, forcing society into a broader understanding of the ramifications of this type of loss.

There is a similarity between grieving due to death and grieving due to divorce. With divorce "... we may label, define, or reframe grief as being normal, healthy, and necessary for recovery, acceptance, and the business of reconstructing one's future."[13] In fact, individuals point out that the stages of loss of self identified by Kübler-Ross are similar to those experienced by the divorced. The primary difference in the processes is the *decision factor* almost always present in divorce but much less present in death.[14]

Interventions for grief resolution similar to those used for widows and widowers are appropriate for the divorce situation. Frequently, a sense of social failure and feelings of guilt become apparent as the process is initiated. External support groups such as *Parents Without Partners, Divorced and Widowed,* and *Solo Parents* include the divorced spouse, since a person may require a positive ongoing relationship to facilitate resolution of the loss and maintenance of high self-esteem.

Parent

All children experience grief in some form during their formative years. Loss of objects or pets most often precipitates grief, which may be intense and prolonged depending on the circumstances and avenues leading to resolution (Fig. 19-5). Homes "broken" by divorce or seriously "bent" by marital strife may elicit the same short-range and long-range effects as the death of a parent.[38] These situations may prove to be more difficult and complex to resolve, because each contact with the noncustodial parent rekindles feelings of attachment, frequently making the next separation a fresh wound. In spite of this pain, developmentalists recommend that children of separated and divorced parents maintain open relationships with *both* parents; these relationships are essential to the formation of their own ego identity and emotional security. The fracturing of the "love bond" is more detrimental than the physical separation. When children have free access by telephone or visits, their feelings of loss are decreased.

Like the adult, the child has a need to work through grief and anxieties. The first step in helping children to accept their loss is to allow them to express fully their fears, fantasies, and feelings—to understand and accept the permanent loss of the parent. Considerations of space prevent a more comprehensive discussion of childhood grief: suffice it to say that a variety parental authority or domination; conflicting feelings of guilt and liberation can be aroused; the middle-age adult may cling tenaciously to other people, often the spouse and children; the threat of personal death becomes a renewed reality and a challenge. In essence, a seemingly mature adult may experience as much difficulty as a child with the expression of grief and resolution after the loss of a parent.

Child

The loss of a child has become a relatively uncommon event with the advent of modern drugs and advanced technology.[41] However, the loss of a child appears to have become the most distressing and long-lasting of griefs. Several factors have contributed to this change of attitude: (1) the structure of the family has changed, with parents having fewer children; (2) parents are unprepared for such losses, since childhood deaths are relatively uncommon; (3) neonates can be kept alive even when born prematurely or with severe physical defects; (4) society, in general, is youth oriented. It is difficult to explain the logic of the death of a child, who has not had time to enjoy life or add significantly to society's welfare and who has not performed a deed that should result in such dire consequences.

Illness

Throughout the course of a prolonged illness followed by death, the family faces continual challenges to identity, goals, standard of living, and values. The emotional strain on the family is great. The family may go through the same five stages faced by a dying adult: denial, anger, bargaining, depression, and acceptance. Parental behavior may be characterized by shock, disbelief, hostility, outbursts of grief, guilt, and anger. Each parent may react differently because of their unique preillness relationships with the child. Mothers may experience the "empty-mother syndrome,"[85] while less-involved fathers may be more accepting of the crisis. "Shadow grief" is used to describe the lingering grief felt by some parents who have lost a child.[57] A particularly poignant statement perhaps explains it all: "When your parent dies, you lose your past; when your child dies, you lose the future."[41]

As with any crisis, the opportunity for personal and family growth is available. Yet, the terminal illness of a child appears to be particularly lethal to the family system if adequate support is not available. Divorce rates as high as 80% are frequently reported for bereaved parents.[16,36,71,75] It is apparent that, unless parents are assisted in their expressions of grief, serious consequences can result not only to themselves but to the family as a whole. Regardless of how stable the marital relationship was before the diagnosis, it is tested to the limit in the course of the illness and during the postdeath period.[30] Frequently, grandparents are unable to offer support and may be less accepting of the diagnosis than the parents themselves.[25]

It is generally assumed that each of the parents can support the other. This assumption is indeed a fallacy, because the parents may not even be able to communicate with each

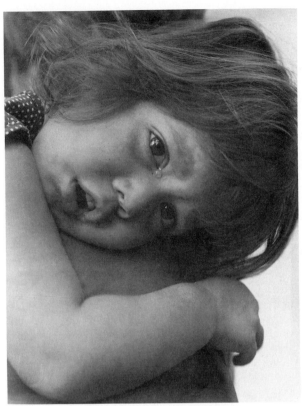

FIGURE 19–5.
Losses occur throughout life. The support and comfort received during earlier losses affect the quality and resolution of grief during adult years.

of reactions to the loss of a parent may occur, and they are related to the intellectual development of the child and the ability to comprehend the meaning of the word *death* (see Chap. 18). The expression of grief and the resolution of loss, in this instance, depend on the development of the cognitive and affective domains of the child or individual. Children should not be forced through the stages of grief, nor should they be expected to exhibit feelings that are unreal to them. At any level of development, simple, concrete, honest, and realistic explanations should be given to the child, along with emotional support and understanding. The child, like the adult, must not be categorized or stereotyped but rather should be considered as a unique individual being.

Considerable attention has been given to the effect of parental bereavement on young children. However, middle-age people also lose parents, and this loss may be very significant to them, although society might expect such a death to be taken in stride. "In general, our society does not encourage either an intense display of grief or a prolonged period of mourning. This seems to be especially the case when the deceased is 'only' an old person whose 'time had come' anyway."[38] Kastenbaum indicates that reactions vary: A middle-age person might still view himself or herself as subject to other; each may be experiencing a different stage of the grieving process, may blame the other for the death of the child, or may be guilt-ridden about the fate of the child. Since men have frequently been socialized to hide or to deny their negative feelings, the father may become quiet or withdrawn and refuse to discuss the situation. Consequently, the mother may experience the "isolated wife syndrome."[23]

In other families, the illness may become the focal point of all interaction. A bereaved mother commented, "When our son died, there was nothing left for us to talk about. Our entire family had revolved around our ill child for $7\frac{1}{2}$ years, and there was nothing left to hold us together. It was as though each of us had died, along with our marriage, and were buried with our son." Although other children may be left, a great void is still present. Many parents wish to have another child soon after the death. However, *it is difficult to bond to a new child while grieving the loss of another.* Each parent must be encouraged to complete the grief process in his or her own unique way and needs to be supported emotionally through that period.

Guilt feelings are normal in parents who are searching for answers or for causes. Guilt may be related to the fact that, if the child had not been conceived, no death could have occurred. Guilt may also be related to feelings of incompetence, punishment, inadequate care and preventive measures, or transmission of the malady. It is much easier to deal with a specific cause for death than continually to face the unknown. One father expressed this idea quite clearly: "If they could only tell us what caused his illness and death, I could handle it." It is difficult to resolve a loss when no specific answers are available. Parents may become overprotective or overindulgent to alleviate their feelings of guilt;[47] they may be unable to treat the extremely ill child in a "normal" manner for the time remaining because of their self-blame.

Several behaviors characterize parents' relationships with dying children. Fatigue is a key factor, since the increased work load of caring for ill children at home or in the hospital is energy demanding. A fear of separation is evidenced by clinging to the child.[50, 51] Some parents attempt to shield the child from the knowledge of the outcome of the terminal illness. However, research indicates that, like dying adults, *dying children are aware of the finality of their illness.*[74, 77] The dying child's reaction to the illness is influenced by developmental stage as well as parental support. For some children and their families, the fear of separation, traumatic procedures, and death can be decreased by the practice of home care.[48]

The maturity level and the coping skills of the individual parents affect their response to the dying child and to each other. In some cases, a strained marital relationship may be strengthened by a shared response to terminal illness; however, the chronic illness is more likely to provide merely a temporary moratorium to an already fractionated relationship.[81] The quality of the parent–child relationship may also influence the experience and the resolution of grief. One

thing remains clear: parents must be able to feel that they did everything possible for their child, that no stone was left unturned. Only then can complete resolution occur.

Accident

Many deaths in childhood are sudden, the result of violent accidents on the highway or elsewhere. These deaths are sharp and sudden tragedies for which the parents or significant others are totally unprepared; thus, available resources have not been mobilized, and a more acute and prolonged grief reaction may be experienced. No time is allowed for anticipatory grief or preparatory mourning. This situation may also occur with an acute short-term illness.

It is important to understand the differences that may exist between parental reactions to sudden death and reactions to a lengthy terminal illness. A fatal illness with a prolonged course provides a period in which anticipatory grief may be experienced before the ultimate death. The symptoms of grief are weakened over time and vary in intensity during the course of the illness. Some people cannot face the stress of the perpetual mourning that accompanies chronic illness associated with a terminal process; consequently, they may withdraw emotionally from the dying child or person in an attempt to escape the mounting pressure and to renew their coping strategies.[30] The process of anticipatory grief is a healthy adaptation to a person's illness, which allows continuation of more normal functioning and attention to other responsibilities during the illness and serves to cushion the bereaved against the massive and disorganizing impact of a loved one's death.[81] It is very difficult to watch a loved one die. It is easier to have it done with. Often, after a lingering illness, the parents may feel only relief. They may have mourned for months or even years; no more tears are left.

A child's sudden death through accident can initiate a greater sense of helplessness, threat, traumatic effects, and potentially difficult bereavements. In the majority of instances, accidental deaths are regarded as senseless and unnecessary; they are considered to be unfair and unjust. Thus, these deaths usually prompt enormous efforts to determine who is at blame, to find meaning in the death, and to regain a sense of control.[65] The potential legal and insurance proceedings that may evolve can act as a positive or negative force in the resolution of loss.

Sudden Infant Death Syndrome (SIDS)

Sudden infant death syndrome (SIDS) is the leading cause of death of infants between 1 week and 1 year of age in the United States. It occurs most frequently during the sleeping hours of a young infant in apparent good health. A number of hypothetical causes have been proposed for this syndrome; none as yet has been proven absolutely correct. About 1 out of every 500 babies born (10,000 to 15,000 occurring per year) die of SIDS in the United States.

Loss of a well cared for, healthy baby initiates the most painful grief reaction and causes a major crisis for the bereaved family. Resulting parental guilt and the effects of this type of infant death go far beyond the mortality itself.[5,15] Because of its distinctive suddenness, the parents are absolutely unprepared to deal with the death; no time has been available for anticipatory grief. Frequent incidents of divorce, psychological disturbance, and other forms of pathology have been reported in families in which crib death has occurred.[60] These reactions tend to be related to excessive parental guilt reactions. In addition, when children die from unexplained causes, society shows a strong tendency to assign blame or infer neglect, a stressor the parents may not be able to face.

Social support groups are available for victims of SIDS. *The National Foundation for Sudden Infant Death, SHARE,* and other organizations provide opportunities for those who have experienced this tragic loss to communicate with others in similar circumstances. Technical support in the form of monitors for apnea (absence of breathing) is also available for use at home with succeeding infants.

Sibling

Loss of a sibling may have immediate or long-term consequences for the surviving child. Children may be affected more by the characteristics of their parents' mourning than by their own grief. The parents may forbid discussion of the recently deceased offspring or discussions of the child's feelings of loss and grief. Therefore, children may feel excluded and isolated and may be potentially unable to resolve the loss. Instead of being "spared," they often become quite confused about the concepts of illness and death and their interrelationship. Their reactions may be heavily guilt-laden, with little or no opportunity for sharing their burden. The living child may be compared to the dead child, thereby providing a threat to the living child's unique identity. Some literature goes so far as to suggest that the loss of a sibling is a *double loss*; the parents, involved in their own grieving, withdraw and are also lost. Disturbed behavior patterns and pathological disturbances can thus arise (Fig. 19-6).[11]

The grief reactions of siblings depend, to a large extent, on age, developmental level, family structure, relationship to the dead sibling, parental mourning, and the availability of open and honest communication. Resolution of the loss can occur only when it is recognized that the dead child's siblings, as well as the grieving parents, must be given assistance. Siblings need to feel that they are important and valued by their parents. Potential problems can be prevented if they are able to participate in the responsibilities and affairs of the family as it faces the crisis and if they are given respect for their own unique responses to grief.

Death of Self

Imminent Death

Most terminally ill people realize that they are dying whether or not they have been told. Human beings accept evidence of approaching death in different ways, through interpretation of symptoms, comparison of their own illness with general knowledge of serious diseases, intuitive feelings, and interpretation of verbal and nonverbal cues of family members or health care workers. The attitude of the individual toward death is tempered by many factors, including religion, culture, education, and personal perspectives on life and living. The most significant factor is that *dying people do not fear*

FIGURE 19-6.
Children are often forgotten as adults try to cope with their own grief. In the process, the child may feel abandoned by both the deceased and the living.

death per se but the anticipated pain of the dying process and abandonment of any type.

Dying is a lonely process. As the dying prepare for their own death, they must face the possibilities of emotional pain, grief, and indignity; and many face these alone. Frequently, they are avoided by loved ones and are separated from the living by physical and communication barriers; thus, they feel rejected or isolated. They must grieve the loss of all their friends and relatives as well as the loss of self. Much of the knowledge about the self-grieving process comes from the efforts of Kübler-Ross.[42] She discovered that, given enough time and adequate support, each person who faces imminent death eventually passes through the five classic and well-defined stages.

No two people face death in identical ways. It might even be said that people die as they have lived. Therefore, channels must be available for the honest expression of feelings without threat of castigation. Without open communication, effective coping on the part of both the living and the dying is impossible. It is important that the dying person, when able, be included in significant personal and family decisions. It is absolutely crucial to remember that **individuals who are dying are not just dying; they are also living.**

Body Functioning

Our bodies are a vital part of our self-image. The loss of body parts, disfiguration, or bodily deterioration results not only in a loss of function but also in a loss of self-image and self-esteem. This fact is particularly true in our culture, which puts great emphasis (overemphasis) on beauty, attractiveness, and youth. Consequently, all of the manifestations of grief can be experienced when one is faced with an insult to any part of the body or psychic systems. One may experience shame, inadequacy, and guilt, along with feelings of being unloved and unwanted.[62] The intensity and length of the response vary with the importance of the loss to the individual, the individual's personality and coping abilities, age, the type of disability, and the support or resources available.

Social and Career Identity

When an individual is confronted with the threat of death and dissolution, attempts are made to retain self-respect, social integrity, and dignity in the process.[62] Social losses can occur at any point in the life span for a variety of reasons, such as a move to a new community, graduation from college, marriage of a friend, or retirement. Each social loss can prompt grief reactions. The loss of or change in a job can affect self-identity and worth, thus leading to grieving. For some, a career is as important as marriage, a family, or a home. Consequently, when an interference of any sort interrupts or prevents the continuation or escalation of the career, grieving can occur; one is forced to redefine the center of one's values. Three major factors appear to influence grief related to job or career loss: personal understanding of why the loss occurred, the effectiveness of available support systems, and personal cop-

ing ability.[33] Ultimately, such losses mandate the recognition of the reality of the situation and the integration of that reality within the self-system.

Catastrophes

Personal and Community

Many personal and community catastrophes result in multiple losses as well as deaths of individuals. The subject of sudden or untimely death is frequently discussed along with its potentially devastating outcomes. The question might be raised, however, if any such thing as a timely death really exists. A case can be made that few deaths arrive in a timely way. One needs only to pick up a daily newspaper to be reminded of the frequency of murders, accidents, suicides, and cardiac arrests as well as of community or national disasters such as tornados, hurricanes, fires, and floods. Untimeliness carries the element of shock and disbelief. The survivors have had no time to deal with the death and no time for anticipatory grieving or reality testing. In addition, they have not been able to say good-bye to the deceased person, express their feelings of love, or resolve petty conflicts.

Three forms of untimely death are identified:[82]

Premature Death: The demise not of a newborn but of a child or adult in the earlier phases of human development.

Unexpected Death: This type occurs at any age, among the healthy or the ill; it is sudden, unpredicted, and conspicuous and includes examples such as death from a heart attack or a car accident.

Calamitous Death: This type is not only unpredicted but is violent, destructive, demeaning, and even degrading; examples include murder, suicide, and disaster.

Each of these types may require a different method of management for resolution to occur; each has different meanings and varying intensities that affect the impact and eventual outcome of the situation. How the survivors cope is determined by religious influences, cultural expectations, societal values, and community practices. Grieving that results from an unexpected loss or a catastrophe in most instances follows a similar pattern to that produced by any other type of loss. It may, however, be more intense and prolonged because a sense of unreality is usually present. An attempt is made to comprehend meaning through a re-creation of the events that led up to the death. Many catastrophes or tragedies, because of shared grieving, allow for increased community or national bonding (the Challenger tragedy is a prime example).[27] Whether the catastrophe is "natural" or "manmade" as a result of human error seems to make a difference. Those who lose loved ones from natural disasters do better than those who have lost loved ones to human error.[65] The primary issues here are *blame* and *responsibility*.

FACILITATING CONFRONTATIONS WITH LOSS

Contemporary Dilemmas

Based on the previous discussions, it would seem that the survivors rather than the dying often have more difficulty in coping with the situation. Is this fact the underlying issue concerning the right to die and death with dignity? Have dying individuals become the projection of society's hopes of cure, treatment, or prolongation of life? Miracle drugs and modern technology have had a profound effect on the treatment of the dying. New medical knowledge and skills have often curtailed one freedom, the freedom to determine the circumstances of our own demise. The fear of being kept alive without consideration of human dignity is becoming more prevalent. "Karen Quinlan" cases are becoming more a rule than an exception. Individuals are being strongly encouraged (some would say, coerced) to donate the vital organs of their loved ones who are dying. Noncompliance to the medical regimen or to societal expectations is met with ostracism, outrage, and legal battles. As a result, "right to die" groups have been established, and their memberships have steadily grown. States have considered and enacted bills that deal with "death with dignity." Individuals are hoping to bypass this problem through the use of a "Living Will" (Fig. 19-7). In the final analysis, the debate seems to center on universal needs versus personal needs, or society versus the individual.

With the *medicalization of dying*,[1] death is viewed as a technological failure rather than as a natural part of life and living. As such, inevitable death is frequently postponed, exacting grave physiological, psychological, and economic hardships for the patient and the family. It is no wonder that the period from the mid-19th century to the present is referred to as the period of *forbidden death*.[3, 49] "Medical practice and technology have increased the problems of adaptation by removing death from everyday reality while at the same time confronting families with unprecedented decisions to prolong or to end life."[78] Consequently, numerous legal and ethical implications and situations have arisen for which no concrete answers exist. Even more startling in this society that demands that no stone be left unturned is the increasing necessity to allocate scarce resources to support continuation of life, often disregarding the quality of that life.

Community Support Systems

Death Education

Death education should be a vital aspect of a child's socialization process.[43] Death education is as important as other types of education, such as those related to health, sex, drug abuse, and safety. It is needed to foster realistic and positive attitudes toward death, facilitate understanding of the dying and the grieving processes, help individuals express emotions, assist in the preparation of one's own mortality, and potentially improve the quality of living. It should be available throughout the entire life span to people of all ages and walks of life. Death education should be offered in both formal and informal settings, should encourage spontaneous group discussions of the topic, and should provide content constructed at the appropriate cognitive levels (Fig. 19-8). Contrary to what most people think, professionals such as physicians, nurses, and social workers are not the only ones to benefit from information and courses offered on dying, death, and bereavement; the lay person can benefit as well. Fortunately, more and more community agencies are offering support groups and courses that consider death as a part of life.

Educational initiatives must be planned with care and sensitivity. An approach that focuses on the development of a knowledge base, prevention and coping strategies, the development and use of grief support groups, and crises intervention should be encouraged. A comprehensive national curriculum for the public schools of the 1990s is being strongly recommended through the cooperative efforts of such national organizations as the American School Health Association, Association for the Advancement of Health Education, and the Society for Public Health Education.[12] According to various sources, this curriculum is needed to systematically and sequentially address issues related to death and dying as well as to general death-related phenomena (e.g., AIDS, homicide, suicide, catastrophes, tragedies).

Hospice Programs

The hospice movement has provided interesting and important options for home care of the dying. These options are particularly important since the cost of caring for the dying continues to increase, resources for third-party payment become increasingly limited, and hospitals and nursing homes have to cope with stringent guidelines for care, such as diagnostic related groups (DRGs). The hospice movement has embraced a philosophy of care that focuses on care of the dying in the home environment when possible. This care permits both patients and family members to face death with dignity as well as to participate in decision making that allows for the maintenance of control over a critical life experience. Together, the dying person and supporting family members are able to proceed through the process in an optimal, caring environment. Essentially, hospice programs permit and promote a refreshing focus on palliation (instead of cure), physical relief through control of symptoms, and psychosocial support to facilitate "... attainment of the most satisfactory possible quality of remaining time together for the patient and the family."[2] The program continues to offer support to family members after the person has died.

Organizations

Various organizations and support groups assist and facilitate the experience of loss and grieving.[86] These local, regional, or national groups are made up of people with similar problems and encourage mutual sharing, support, and self-help. Profes-

TO MY FAMILY, MY PHYSICIAN, MY LAWYER, MY CLERGYMAN
TO ANY MEDICAL FACILITY IN WHOSE CARE I HAPPEN TO BE
TO ANY INDIVIDUAL WHO MAY BECOME RESPONSIBLE FOR MY HEALTH, WELFARE OR
AFFAIRS

Death is as much a reality as birth, growth, maturity and old age—it is the one certainty of life. If the time comes when I, _____, can no longer take part in decisions for my own future, let this statement stand as an expression of my wishes, while I am still of sound mind.

If the situation should arise in which there is no reasonable expectation of my recovery from physical or mental disability, I request that I be allowed to die and not be kept alive by artificial means or "heroic measures." I do not fear death itself as much as the indignities of deterioration, dependence and hopeless pain. I, therefore, ask that medication be mercifully administered to me to alleviate suffering even though this may hasten the moment of death.

This request is made after careful consideration. I hope you who care for me will feel morally bound to follow its mandate. I recognize that this appears to place a heavy responsibility upon you, but it is with the intention of relieving you of such responsibility and of placing it upon myself in accordance with my strong convictions, that this statement is made.

Signed _____

Date _____

Witness _____

Witness _____

Copies of this request have been given to _____

_____

_____

_____

FIGURE 19–7.
The Living Will

To Make the Best Use of Your Living Will

1. Sign and date the Living Will before two witnesses. (This is to ensure that you signed of your own free will and not under any pressure.)

2. If you have a physician, give him a copy for your medical file and discuss it with him to make sure he is in agreement. Give copies to those most likely to be concerned. "if the time comes when you can no longer take part in decisions for your own future." Enter their names on the bottom line of the Living Will. Keep the original nearby, easily and readily available.

*3. Above all, discuss your intentions with those closest to you, **now**.*

4. It is a good idea to look over your Living Will once a year and then to redate it and initial the new date to make it clear that your wishes are unchanged. (Reprinted with the permission of the Euthanasia Education Council, 250 West Fifty-Seventh Street, New York, NY 10019. Copies available on request.)

sionally trained personnel may lead the group, but this leadership does not seem to be a necessity. Support groups have rapidly escalated in number perhaps because of the fact that Americans have felt the inadequacy of traditional institutions in situations that warrant assistance.[73] Support groups are generally free, open-ended (participation is not limited to a certain number of meetings), and unstructured or semistructured to allow for dealing with the attenders' needs and concerns.

Bereavement support groups, both religious and secular, exist throughout the United States.[86] Some are modeled after the Widow-to-Widow program, some are included as part of a

FIGURE 19–8.
Death education activities have maximal benefit when separated from periods of loss or grief.

hospice program, while others are sponsored by churches or different types of organizations. They have been met with widespread acceptance. The list of organizations is impressive (Table 19-2).

Spiritual Support

The spiritual dimension must be considered in any holistic approach to health care. It is especially significant when confronting loss and grieving. The spiritual dimension must be treated broadly and liberally as an equal component of care that allows for the consideration of differing views and values, not just within the context of conventional religions and religious practices. The spiritual domain " . . . is that part of the individual which longs for ultimate awareness, meaning, value, purpose, beauty, dignity, relatedness, and integrity. The spiritual 'is the source of all faith, hope, and courage.' "[2]

Spiritual support can be offered in a variety of ways. What is important is the willingness to accept dying people and families on their terms, recognizing that they may have a different understanding of or meaning for God. Spiritual assessments can and should be done whenever possible to discover pertinent information, such as beliefs and spiritual practices important to the patient and family, the type of spiritual or religious support they desire, and the role established religions will play.[2] This information can be used effectively to facilitate interventions in this area. The special significance of the spiritual dimension to the dying and the bereaved cannot be denied. Clergy, if desired, can be supportive at this time.

Funerals

Specific rituals connected with particular religions can provide needed outlets for grief. Three functions can be performed by rituals: " . . . (1) support in the expression of grief at the loss; (2) approval of the renunciation of what was lost; (3) guidance in redefinition and reinvestment of self."[68] Funerals have typically been the primary ritual used to express the cultural, social, and spiritual aspects of grief. Despite the trend in America to discourage funerals and the accompanying rituals, the view that funeral customs facilitate the grieving process still exists.[4, 6, 28, 49]

> Ritual makes sense of death by placing it in the context of a world view . . . As the distance from one's own death increases and the right to mourn is taken away, the ability to "make sense" of death breaks down and there is growing dissatisfaction with the ritual that supports that rationalization.[84]

Although many criticisms of funerals exist, the fact remains that no acceptable alternatives to this method for coping with death have been found. Perhaps the more significant factor is that Americans do not have nationally or culturally common mourning rituals. Consequently, consensus or approval of appropriate mourning behavior is lacking.[6] The funeral provides an opportunity for friends and family to come to closure on a person's life, to share significant memories, and to support each other in the grief process.

CONCLUSION

Life-Death-Living-Dying. These elusive mysteries have prompted human beings to search for their meanings since time eternal. The search for meaning continues. What remains clear is that all who live will also die. No one can escape this universal and inevitable fate. Yet, the modern, scientific, and technical society constantly attempts to thwart this fate through a variety of means to prolong life at any cost. It is time to finally put this scenario in proper perspective, to comprehend and internalize that life and death are at the very core of human existence. It is time to accept that death is a part of life

TABLE 19-2. ORGANIZATIONS AND SUPPORT GROUPS FOR INDIVIDUALS WHO EXPERIENCE LOSS

Group	Focus
American Association of Suicidology 2459 South Ash Street Denver, Colorado 80222	General information—clearinghouse for survivors of suicide
Candlelighters Childhood Cancer Foundation 1312 18th St NW Suite 200 Washington, D.C. 20036 202-659-5136	Parents with childen with cancer
The Compassionate Friends P.O. Box 3696 Oak Brook, Illinois 60522 312-323-5010	Parents whose children have died
Concern for Dying 250 West 57th Street New York, New York 10107	General information—issues related to health care and dying
The Elisabeth Kübler-Ross Center South Route 616 Head Waters, Virginia 24442	General information—educational services and audiovisual materials
Make Today Count P.O. Box 303 Burlington, Iowa 52601	Terminal illness
Mothers Against Drunk Driving Suite 310 669 Airport Freeway Hurst, Texas 76053	Victims, families, and friends
National Hospice Organization Suite 307 1901 North Fort Myer Drive Arlington, Virginia 22209	General information—provides names of hospices and related service organizations
National Organization for Victim Assistance 717 D. Street, NW Washington, D.C. 20004	National advocacy for victims' rights and crime victims
National Self-Help Referral 1600 Dodge Avenue, Suite S-122 Evanston, Illinois 60201	Information referral service for self-help groups
National SIDS Foundation 10500 Little Patuxent Parkway Suite 420 Columbia, MD 21044 800-221-7437	Families who have lost a child to SIDS
Parents of Murdered Children 100 East Eighth Street Room B41 Cincinnati, Ohio 45202	Families whose children have been murdered
Parents Without Partners, Inc. 8807 Colesville Road Silver Spring, Maryland 20910	Welfare of single parents and their children
SHARE St. John's Hospital 800 East Carpenter Springfield, Illinois 62769	Parents with miscarriages, stillbirths, or neonatal deaths
THEOS (They Help Each Other Spiritually) 1301 Clark Boulevard 717 Liberty Avenue Pittsburgh, Pennsylvania 15222	Widowed and their families
Widowed Persons Service American Association of Retired Persons 1909 K Street, NW Washington, D.C. 20049	Programs and information to the newly widowed

and living. Acceptance can help individuals to forgive, hope, and love.

> The confrontation with death ... makes everything look so precious, so sacred, so beautiful that I feel more strongly than ever the impulse to live it, to embrace it, and to let myself be overwhelmed by it. My river has never looked so beautiful. ... Death, and its ever present possibility makes love, passionate love, more possible. I wonder if we could love passionately, if ecstasy would be possible at all, if we knew we'd never die.—Abraham Maslow

Loss-Grieving. These processes are inextricably bonded to living and dying. They too are inevitable experiences in life that are not totally understood. However, serenity, peace, and joy can be the outcome of loss and grieving as the really important aspects of life are at last understood. The prevailing attitude of society, that grief is a sign of weakness, hinders the acceptance of this position that grief can be positive. If one views the grieving process as an effective means for the resolution of loss and a method of coping with stress, it cannot be anything but positive.

The naturally occurring phenomenon of bereavement is just beginning to be understood, explained, and predicted.[45] Bereavement is a complex and multidimensional experience that deals with the past, the present, and the future experiences of the bereaved. A crucial element is that grieving is highly individualized, and the ultimate course is determined by numerous variables. No one can fully understand what another individual is experiencing when a loss occurs. We can never *totally* understand the significance of the lost object or the impact that results, but we can be available to render assistance on a regular basis. Effective and meaningful intervention in the process thus mandates a careful assessment of the individual that considers the five domains. In the final analysis, however, the following quotation applies:

> Love is the ultimate therapy. For when we love we are transformed. And then we move into a region beyond science. It can be called the spiritual world, the psychic universe, the inner spirit. But call it what you want, it is a world that knows no fear. And harbors no grudge.[76]

REFERENCES

1. Allan, J. D., & Hall, B. A. (1988). Between diagnosis and death: The case for studying grief before death. *Archives of Psychiatric Nursing, 2,* 30–34.
2. Amenta, M. O., & Bohnet, N. L. (1986). *Nursing care of the terminally ill.* Boston: Little, Brown.
3. Aries, P. (1974). *Western attitudes toward death.* (P. M. Ranum, Trans.) Baltimore, MD: Johns Hopkins University Press.
4. Barrett, C. J. (1977). Signs. *Journal of Women in Culture and Society, 2,* 858.
5. Bergman, A. B., et al. (1974). The psychiatric toll of the sudden infant death syndrome. In J. Ellard, V. Volkan, & N. L. Paul, *Normal and pathological responses to bereavement* (pp. 141–153). New York: MSS Information Corp.
6. Bolton, C., & Camp, D. J. (1986–87). Funeral rituals and the facilitation of grief work. *Omega, 17,* 343–352.
7. Bowlby, J. (1961). Process of mourning. *International Journal of Psychoanalysis, 42,* 317.
8. Bowlby, J. (1960). Grief and mourning in infancy and early childhood. *Psychoanalytic Study of the Child, 15,* 9.
9. Broden, A. R. (1970). Reactions to loss in the aged. In B. Schoenberg, Carr, A.C., Peretz, D., & Kutscher, A.H., (Eds.), *Loss and grief: Psychological management in medical practice* (pp. 199–217). New York: Columbia University Press.
10. Brown, J. T., & Stoudemire, G. A. (1983). Normal and pathological grief. *Journal of the American Medical Association, 250*(3), 378.
11. Cain, A. C., Fast, I., & Erickson, M. (1964). Children's disturbed reactions to the death of a sibling. *American Journal of Orthopsychiatry, 34,* 741.
12. Crase, D., & Hamrick, M. H. (1989). The imperative for a national initiative in death-related phenomena. *Journal of School Health, 59,* 79–80.
13. Crosby, J. F., Lybarger, S. K., & Mason, R. L. (1986). The grief resolution process in divorce: Phase II. *Journal of Divorce, 10,* 17–40.
14. Crosby, J. F., Gage, B., & Raymond, M. (1983). The grief resolution process in divorce. *Journal of Divorce, 7,* 3–18.
15. DeFrain, J. D., Taylor, J., & Ernst, L. (1982). *Coping with sudden infant death.* Lexington, MA: Lexington Books.
16. Dempsey, D. K. (1975). *The way we die.* New York: McGraw-Hill.
17. Deutsch, H. (1937). Absence of grief. *Psychoanalytical Annual, 6,* 12.
18. Dimond, M., Lund, D. A., & Caserta, M. S. (1987). The role of social support in the first two years of bereavement in an elderly sample. *Gerontologist, 27,* 599–604.
19. Donahue, M. P. (1986). Review of *Nursing care of the terminally ill. Image: The Journal of Nursing Scholarship, 18,* 188–189.
20. Engel, G. L. (1964). Grief and grieving. *American Journal of Nursing, 64*(9), 93.
21. Falicov, C. J. (Ed.). (1988). *Family transitions: Continuity and change over the life cycle.* New York: Guilford Press.
22. Feifel, H. (Ed.). (1977). *New meanings of death.* New York: McGraw-Hill.
23. Fowler, J. (1980). Moral stages and the development of faith. In B. Munsey (Ed.), *Moral development, moral education, and Kohlberg.* Birmingham, AL: Religious Education Press.
24. Freud, S. (1950). Mourning and melancholia. In S. Freud, *Collected papers* (Vol. 4, pp. 152–170). (Authorized translation under the supervision of Joan Riviere.) London: Hogarth Press.
25. Friedman, S., Chodoff, P., Mason, J., & Hamburg, D. (1963). Behavioral observation on parents anticipating the death of a child. *Pediatrics, 32,* 610.
26. Gelcer, E. (1983). Mourning is a family affair. *Family Process, 22,* 501–516.
27. Goldzwig, S., & Dionisopoulos, G. N. (1986). Explaining it to ourselves: The phases of national mourning in space tragedy. *Central States Speech Journal, 37,* 180–192.
28. Gorer, G. (1965). *Death, grief, and mourning in contemporary Britain.* New York: Doubleday.
29. Gramlich, E. P. (1974). Recognition and management of grief in elderly patients. In J. Ellard, Volkan, V., & Paul, N.L., (Eds.), *Normal and pathological responses to bereavement* (pp. 65–70). New York: MSS Information Corp.
30. Gyulay, J. E. (1978). *The dying child.* New York: McGraw-Hill.
31. Hayes, C., & Kalish, R. A. (1987–88). Death-related experiences and funerary practices of the Hmong refugee in the United States. *Omega, 18,* 63–70.

32. Herz, F. (1980). The impact of death and serious illness on the family life cycle. In E. A. Carter & M. McGoldrick (Eds.), *The family life cycle: A framework for family therapy* (p. 223). New York: Gardner.

33. Jones, W. (1979). Grief and involuntary career change: Its implications for counseling. *Vocational Guidance Quarterly, 27,* 196.

34. Joyce, C. (1984). A time for grieving. *Psychology Today,* 18(11) 42–46.

35. Kalish, R. A. (1977). Dying and preparing for death: A view of families. In H. Feifel (Ed.), *New meanings of death* (pp. 215–231). New York: McGraw-Hill.

36. Kaplan, D., Grobstein, R., & Smith, A. (1976). Predicting the impact of severe illness in families. *Health and Social Work, 71,* 13–18.

37. Kastenbaum, R. J. (1986). *Death, society, and human experience* (2nd ed.). Columbus, OH: C. F. Merrill.

38. Kastenbaum, R. (1977). Death and development through the lifespan. In H. Feifel (Ed.), *New meanings of death* (pp. 18–45). New York: McGraw-Hill.

39. Kavanaugh, R. E. (1972). *Facing death.* Baltimore: Penguin.

40. Kendall, P. (1954). *Conflict and mood: Factors affecting stability of response.* Glencoe, IL: Free Press.

41. Klass, D. (1984–85). Bereaved parents and the compassionate friends: Affiliation and healing. *Omega, 15,* 353–373.

42. Kübler-Ross, E. (1969). *On death and dying.* New York: Macmillan.

43. Leming, M. R., & Dickinson, G. E. (1985). *Understanding dying, death, and bereavement.* New York: Holt, Rinehart and Winston.

44. Lindemann, E. (1944). Symptomatology and management of acute grief. *American Journal of Psychiatry, 101,* 141.

45. Lund, D. A., Caserta, M. S., & Dimond, M. F. (1986). Gender differences through two years of bereavement among the elderly. *Gerontologist, 26,* 314–320.

46. Maddison, D. (1974). The consequences of conjugal bereavement. In J. Ellard, V. Volkan, & N. L. Paul (Eds.), *Normal and pathological responses to bereavement* (pp. 72–77). New York: MSS Information Corp.

47. Mann, S. (1974). Coping with a child's fatal illness. *Nursing Clinics of North America, 2,* 81.

48. Martinson, I. M., et al. (1978). Home care for children dying of cancer. *Pediatrics, 62,* 106.

49. Mitford, J. (1978). *The American way of death.* New York: Touchstone Books.

50. Natterson, J. M., & Knudson, A. G. (1960). Observations concerning fear of death in fatally ill children and their mothers. *Psychosomatic Medicine, 22,* 456.

51. Orbach, C., et al. (1955). Psychological impact of cancer and its treatment: III. The adaptation of mothers to the threatened loss of their children through leukemia: ii. *Cancer, 8,* 20.

52. Osterweis, M., Solomon, F., & Green, M. (Eds.). (1984). *Bereavement: Reactions, consequences and care.* Washington DC: National Academy Press.

53. Parkes, C. M. (1987–88). Research: Bereavement. *Omega, 18,* 365–377.

54. Parkes, C. M. (1986). *Bereavement studies of grief in adult life* (2nd ed.). London: Tavistock Publications.

55. Parkes, C. M. (1970). Seeking and finding a lost object: Evidence from recent studies of the reaction to bereavement. *Social Science and Medicine, 4,* 187.

56. Parkes, C. M., & Weiss, R. (1983). *Recovery from bereavement.* New York: Basic Books.

57. Peppers, L. G., & Knapp, R. J. (1980). *Motherhood and mourning: Perinatal death.* New York: Praeger.

58. Peretz, D. (1970). Development, object-relationships, and loss. In B. Schoenberg, Carr, A.C., Peretz, D., & Kutscher, A.H., (Eds.), *Loss and grief: Psychological management in medical practice* (pp. 3–19). New York: Columbia University Press.

59. Pollock, G. H. (1972). On mourning and anniversaries: The relationship of culturally constituted defensive systems to intrapsychic adaptive processes. *Israel Annals of Psychiatric Related Disciplines, 10,* 9.

60. Pomeroy, M. (1969). Sudden death syndrome. *American Journal of Nursing, 69,* 1886.

61. Provost, P. K. (1989). Vietnam: Resolving the death of a loved one. *Archives of Psychiatric Nursing, 3,* 29–33.

62. Rando, T. A. (1984). *Grief, dying, and death: Clinical interventions for caregivers.* Champaign, IL: Research Press.

63. Rando, T. A. (Ed.). (1986). *Loss and anticipatory grief.* Lexington, MA: D. C. Heath.

64. Rando, T. A. (1988). Anticipatory grief: The term is a misnomer but the phenomenon exists. *Journal of Palliative Care, 4,* 70–73.

65. Rando, T. A. (1988). *Grieving: How to go on living when someone you love dies.* Lexington, MA: D. C. Heath.

66. Raphael, B. (1983). *Anatomy of bereavement.* New York: Basic Books.

67. Rees, W. D., & Lutkins, S. G. (1967). Mortality of bereavement. *British Medical Journal, 5570,* 13.

68. Reeves, R. B. (1970). The hospital chaplain looks at grief. In B. Schoenberg, Carr, A.C., Peretz, D., & Kutscher, A.H., (Eds.), *Loss and grief: Psychological management in medical practice* (pp. 362–372). New York: Columbia University Press.

69. Rochlin, G. (1965). *Griefs and discontents: The forces of change.* Boston: Little, Brown.

70. Rosenblatt, P. C., Walsh, R. P., & Jackson, D. A. (1976). *Grief and mourning in cross-cultural perspective.* New Haven, CT: H. R. A. F. Press.

71. Schiff, H. S. (1977). *The bereaved parent.* New York: Penguin Books.

72. Simos, B. G. (1979). *A time to grieve: Loss as a universal human experience.* New York: Family Service Association of America.

73. Sklar, F., & Huneke, K. D. (1987–88). Bereavement, ministerial attitudes, and the future of church-sponsored bereavement support groups. *Omega, 18,* 89–102.

74. Spinetta, J. J., Rigler, D., & Karon, M. (1974). Personal space as a measure of a dying child's sense of isolation. *Journal of Consulting and Clinical Psychology, 42,* 751.

75. Strauss, A.L., et al. (1984). *Chronic illness and the quality of life* (2nd ed.). St. Louis: C. V. Mosby.

76. Veninga, R. (1985). *A gift of hope: How we survive our tragedies.* Boston: Little, Brown.

77. Waechter, E. (1971). Children's awareness of fatal illness. *American Journal of Nursing, 71,* 1167.

78. Walsh, F., & McGoldrick, M. (1988). Loss and the family life cycle. In C. J. Falicov (Ed.), *Family transitions: Continuity and change over the life cycle* (pp. 311–335). New York: Guilford Press.

79. Wambach, J. A. (1985–86). The grief process as a social construct. *Omega, 16,* 201–211.

80. Webb, J. (1985, April 6). Viet vets didn't kill babies and they aren't suicidal. *The Washington Post,* Section C, pp. 1, 2.

81. Weiner, J. M. (1970). Reaction of the family to the fatal illness of a child. In B. Schoenberg, Carr, A.C., Peretz, D., & Kutscher, A.H.,

(Eds.), *Loss and grief: Psychological management in medical practice* (pp. 87–101). New York: Columbia University Press.

82. Weisman, A. D. (1973). Coping with untimely death. *Psychiatry, 36,* 366.

83. Weizman, S., & Kamm, P. (1985). *About mourning: Support and guidance for the bereaved.* New York: Human Sciences.

84. Wilcox, S. G., & Sutton, M. (Eds). (1977). *Understanding death and dying: An interdisciplinary approach* (3rd ed.). Palo Alto, CA: Mayfield.

85. Wong, D. (1980). Bereavement: The empty mother syndrome. *American Journal of Maternal-Child Nursing, 5,* 385.

86. Worden, J. W. (1982). *Grief counseling and grief therapy.* New York: Springer.

VI

THE SCHOOL-AGER

Now that the child has learned how to harness and focus energies, attention can be directed toward systematic information gathering and mastery of intricate new skills. The healthy child begins to assume increasing responsibility for setting goals in all five domains, and begins disciplining the self to achieve them. As skills are mastered, the child is able to assume greater independence from the parents in self-guidance, self-care, and self-motivation.

On entering school, the child carries separation-individuation from the family one step further. Peers are brought into the circle of significant others as the child seeks other sources of self-evaluation, support, and refueling to assuage feelings of vulnerability that accompany increased awareness of separateness and mortality. Peers provide opportunities for competition and cooperation on many levels. They offer realistic models for comparison, challenges to become more sensitive to the needs and feelings of others, reassurance of acceptability, and sounding boards for solving problems. Association with people like one's self (e.g., same gender, same ethnic group) reduces the need to face personal uniqueness and frees energies to consciously concentrate on how to be an acceptable part of that group.

The school-age years are a crucial period in the social development of individuals. With the emergence of new cognitive powers and the introduction to formal schooling, the child begins to explore his or her relationship to the broader worlds of peers, community, nation, and world. The child moves beyond the egocentric thought of the preschooler to actively seek the perceptions, views, knowledge, and traditions of others. The young person consciously accommodates to the expanded understanding of roles, skills, and responsibilities valued by the culture.

These are the primary years for the enculturation processes—those activities that teach and help to bond the individual to the ethnic group or culture. Engaging in the activities and traditions of the family and culture, association with others like one's self, development of skills, and expansion of one's understanding of roles all help the child to find a niche within **the society of contact.** A sense of belongingness, bonding, and commitment emerges as the individual explores the nuances of social relationships that lend to cultural identity.

Developmental Tasks of School-agers

*1. Derive a sense of belonging from associations with others:
>   participate in family activities and responsibilities
>   socialize with small group of peers (clubs, same gender)
>   identify similarities to peers and significant others
>   identify and build relationship with a special friend
>   develop a sense of contributing to a social community

*2. Learn how to work:
>   commit self to mastering a skill or project
>   organize own schedule/activities
>   sacrifice leisure in service of goals
>   persevere until goals realized
>   evaluate own products
>   correct own errors
>   find pleasure in process as well as product

*3. Establish a conscience:
>   recognize the importance of rules for society
>   differentiate between right and wrong
>   develop a sense of respect for parents, authority figures
>   develop an awareness of the rights and needs of others
>   learn to be charitable
>   modify behaviors according to own moral code
>   practice self-discipline
>   delay gratification

4. Master the basic skills valued by the society (e.g., hunting, reading, crafts, social skills, computer skills).

5. Develop competence in selected areas:
>   interests
>   talents
>   hobbies

6. Develop appreciation of socially and culturally generated roles:
>   gender roles
>   recognition and practice of differing roles/relationships in varying situations
>   appreciation of uniqueness of own culture
>   awareness of other cultures

7. Participate in and identify with cultural traditions:
>   holidays
>   religious ceremonies
>   family celebrations
>   vacations
>   community events

8. Balance the issues of dependence, independence, and interdependence:
>   appreciate self as a "person in process"
>   function independently as able
>   identify own limitations realistically
>   seek help and information as necessary
>   balance issues of competition and cooperation
>   participate as a team member
>   extract safety and social rules from rules and experience

9. Refine communication skills (e.g., grammar, vocabulary, humor, new codes).

10. Refine motor strength and coordination:
>   gross-motor
>   fine-motor

---

*Tasks deemed most crucial to continued maturation are marked with an asterisk.

20 *Childhood shows the man, As morning shows the day.*

—JOHN MILTON, *PARADISE LOST*

Biophysical Development of the School-Ager and the Pubescent

Clara S. Schuster

The biophysical growth and development of the child during the school-age years are singularly unremarkable. From 6 to 10 years of age, most children experience a relative plateau in growth, a lull between the rapid growth of early childhood and that which they will once more experience during the prepubertal years (ages 10–13 years in girls, 12–15 years in boys). The changes that do occur are gradual and relatively subtle. The body appears to be undergoing a period of refinement, of hypertrophic development, rather than the hyperplastic growth that predominated in the earlier years. Differences in body contour between boys and girls are minimal until the late school years.

The individuality of children as influenced by both heredity and environment becomes more obvious. Although growth from child to child has many similarities, each child has his or her own growth pattern and timetable.

After age 6, an individual's general relationship to height and weight norms usually does not change. Consequently, one can begin to estimate whether a child is going to be tall, petite, or stocky. A child's adult height can be predicted from the average height of the parents and grandparents (Fig. 20-1). Although repeated measurements can give an indication of the child's health status, it is the pattern of progress that becomes the critical factor. Great variations in height and weight may still be considered normal when all the contributing factors are considered.

Growth patterns are more significant than single measurements; therefore, standardized charts should be used as reference points only, as tools to reinforce and improve clinical judgment (see Appendices D and E). Periodic measurements of height and weight are imperative for evaluating the growth pattern of individual children and for identifying potential deviation. However, deviations in growth accompany or follow, not herald, a disorder. Accurate height and weight measurements are especially important with hospital admissions because body surface area is calculated from these two measurements. Dosages of many medications and fluid replacements are calculated on the basis of body surface area rather than by chronological age, height, or body weight alone.

The body proportions of the school-ager are quite different from those of the preschooler or the adolescent. At birth, the head comprises one-fourth of the body length because of the rapid growth of the central nervous system during fetal life. During the toddler and early preschool years, the rapid increase in trunk length gives the child a top-heavy appearance. During the late preschool years, the extremities begin to grow rapidly, and the child appears to "thin out." By 6 years of age, the child is able to put an arm over the head and touch the opposite ear. By 7 years of age, parents often describe the child as being gangly and awkward and begin to complain about the expense of keeping the child in shoes and clothes that fit. The extremities

FIGURE 20–1.
(A) *These girls (8, 11, and 18 years of age) are all the same height.* (B) *The influence of genetics is readily apparent 6 years later when they are again seen standing with their fathers.* (C) *As young adults (20, 22, and 30 years of age), these women exhibit the influence of their fathers on their final height.*

continue to grow rapidly during the school-age years, with particular rapidity during the early pubertal period. During the later pubertal years, trunk growth begins to accelerate again (Fig. 20-2).

For many individuals, the school years represent one of the healthiest periods of life. Children of this age are able to fight off infections easily and tend to recover quickly when ill.

The increase in organ maturity and in general body size enables the child to respond physiologically to illness in a more adult manner. In the school-age child, for example, the danger of occlusion of the airway during an infection of the respiratory tract, the incidence of seizures that accompany high temperatures, and the chance of dehydration during an illness that involves vomiting or diarrhea are all greatly re-

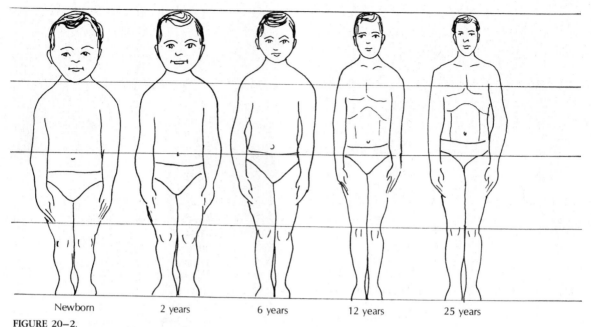

FIGURE 20–2.
Body proportions and form change as individuals progress through the early years of the life span.

duced. As the body size increases, body surface is less in proportion to the body mass; this fact combined with maturation of the skin decreases insensible water loss.

SOMATIC DEVELOPMENT

Skeletal System

The most rapid hyperplastic growth of the school-age years is experienced by the skeletal system. This growth is particularly obvious in the long bones of the extremities and in the development of the facial bones. The rapid growth of the preschool years now slows to a height gain of 2 to 2½ inches per year if nutrition is optimal and no disease processes interfere.[4, 21] Growth is most rapid in the spring and the fall. Girls begin to surpass boys in height and weight around 11 years of age and remain taller until male peers enter the adolescent growth spurt that heralds their pubertal period (Fig. 20-3).[21]

Because the long bones are growing faster than the adjacent muscles, many children experience "growing pains," or muscle and ligament aches, caused by stretching of these softer tissues.[42] Children are most likely to complain of pain when lying down at night. Although such pain is thought to be a normal phenomenon by some people, persistent complaints of pain should be checked by a physician because bone cancer, childhood arthritis, rheumatic fever, and other disease processes may exhibit similar symptoms in their early stages.[42] Taut, stretched muscles also have a tendency to respond with quick, jerky movements,[43] a fact which explains some of the continued uncoordination during these years.

Posture

The curvature of the spine reflects the body's health state and balance. It changes throughout childhood as the center of gravity moves down the body and as muscle strength increases. Until strength of adjacent muscles and ligaments is adequate, a child may appear to be loose-jointed, gangly, and swaybacked.[42] During the early school-age years, the child gradually loses the potbellied, swaybacked appearance (lordosis) of the early childhood years. The child's posture becomes straighter as the pelvis tips backward and the abdominal muscles become stronger.[4] A convex curvature begins to appear in the thoracic spine area.[16] The shoulders continue to have a rounded appearance.[21] Although the neck appears to

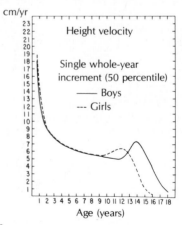

FIGURE 20–3.
Average height gained each year from birth through 18 years of age. (From Lowrey, G. H. [1978]. Growth and development of children [7th ed.]. Chicago: Year Book. With permission.)

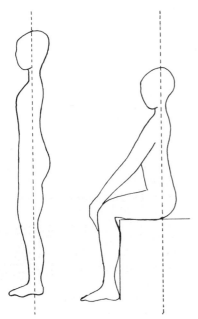

FIGURE 20–4.
Correct standing and sitting positions for adolescents and adults. Good body alignment, whether standing or sitting, should allow a straight line to be drawn through ear, shoulder, and hip.

The toddler normally assumes a wide base or stance when standing. The toes point outward because of an outward rotation of the legs at the hip. As the lower extremities gradually rotate inward, flexibility for voluntary rotation increases. By the school years, the child is usually able to rotate the foot 30° inward and 60° outward,[16] valuable assets for ballet. If the leg rotates too far, the child may exhibit **pigeon-toed** walking (toes pointing inward). Although this phenomenon is occasionally related to a pathological problem, most cases are developmental and disappear spontaneously without treatment, especially if they are related to the "grip phenomenon," which uses the big toe for balance and for pushing off during walking. Both corrective shoes and poorly fitted regular shoes may increase stress points on the growing skeleton; thus, the former alter skeletal development therapeutically and the latter negatively. Rapid growth of the foot in the late school years is one of the first indications of the onset of the adolescent growth spurt. The feet reach their final growth 1 to 2 years before the long bones of the legs.[34]

Ossification

Ossification, the formation of bone, continues at a rather steady pace throughout the school years. Fractures usually heal quickly because the body is already metabolizing the necessary constituents of bone tissue.[7]

All the primary ossification centers of the long, tubular bones appeared during fetal life.[6] The body laid down a transverse disc along the cartilaginous tissues that are precursors to bone development. These discs serve as foundation structures for calcification, or bone formation, during the next two decades of life. The discs gradually increase in length. The constant addition of cartilage at the ends of the ossification points allows continued extension of bone length. Secondary ossification points appear after birth at the ends of bones. These oval discs grow medially and distally very slowly toward the **epiphysis**, the final point of ossification of the long bones.[6] The shaft of the long bone and the cap fuse at, or near, the onset of true puberty. In fact, the maturation of the skeletal system and that of the reproductive system are synchronized. This fact is most easily observed in girls. Menarche (the first menstrual period) usually occurs slightly before final epiphyseal fusion. The maximum increment in growth of the long bones occurs in the year before the onset of menarche. Linear growth of the long bones generally ceases within 2 years after menarche. Those individuals who mature early usually experience an earlier growth spurt but usually end up shorter than their peers in adult life.[21]

Successive x-ray films of the hand reveal a definite schedule in the appearance and the union of the wrist bones (Fig. 20-5). These x-rays can be used to assess biological age. However, by 10 years of age, it is common to have as much as a 2-year discrepancy between bone age (skeletal maturity) and chronological age.[21] The determination of bone age can be valuable in estimating biological age for predicting the onset of puberty. Children who experience either delayed or premature maturation can be identified by comparing the maturity of the bone development with their chronological age.

elongate and the chest becomes broader and flatter, a "military posture" (head erect, shoulders back, stomach in, chest out) does not appear naturally until further growth of the trunk and its muscles during the adolescent years (Fig. 20-4).[16]

Adequate exercise is needed to develop strength and flexibility and to encourage muscular development during the school-age years. However, exercise has minimal influence on posture because the vertebral curves are not fully under voluntary control. "Posture, to a degree, reflects strength and health, and these factors are the more basic conditions which should receive our consideration. The old idea of admonishing school children to 'stand straight' or 'sit straight' in the interest of better posture often confuses cause and effect. A child typically adopts the posture which keeps the parts of his body in proper balance. Frequent action and change of activity in school are excellent preventives of faulty posture."[21] Erect posture may be considered satisfactory if one is able to draw a straight line from the ear through the shoulders and then through the greater trochanter (hip) to the anterior part of the long arch of the foot.[21] Although parents and teachers may encourage this positioning, it should not be forced on the child. One should keep in mind that the posture assumed is usually reflective of body growth.

Poor posture can reflect fatigue as well as a major or minor skeletal defect. School-age children, especially females during the late school years and early adolescence, should have periodic checks for **scoliosis** (abnormal curvature of the spine). This simple procedure consists of checking for evenness of hips (pelvic tilt) and shoulders and for abnormal curvatures of the spine in standing and bending positions.

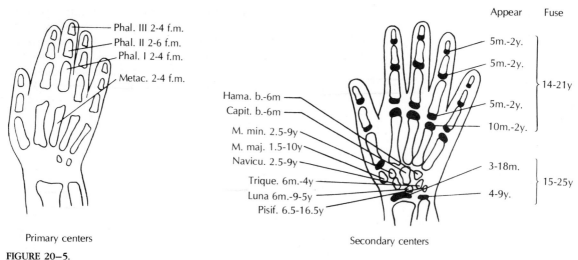

Appear   Fuse

Phal. III 2-4 f.m.
Phal. II 2-6 f.m.
Phal. I 2-4 f.m.
Metac. 2-4 f.m.

5m.-2y.
5m.-2y.
5m.-2y.
10m.-2y.

14-21y

Hama. b.-6m
Capit. b.-6m
M. min. 2.5-9y
M. maj. 1.5-10y
Navicu. 2.5-9y
Trique. 6m.-4y
Luna 6m.-9-5y
Pisif. 6.5-16.5y

3-18m.
4-9y.

15-25y

Primary centers

Secondary centers

FIGURE 20–5.
Time schedule for the appearance of primary and secondary ossification centers and the fusion of secondary centers with the shafts in the hands. Key: f.m. = fetal month; b = birth. (From Caffey J. et al., [1978]. Pediatric x-ray diagnosis *[7th ed.]. Chicago: Year Book. [Modified from Scammon in Morris;* Human anatomy.*] With permission.)*

Both gender and race affect bone maturation. Girls generally mature 2 years earlier than boys, and black children mature more rapidly than white children.[21] Bone age can also be altered (usually delayed) by disease, nutrition, or metabolic factors (Figs. 20-6 and 20-7).

Facial Development

Since the head attains 91% of its adult size by 6 years of age, and 94% by 10 years, only a minimal increase (about ½ inch) in the circumference of the skull occurs during the school-age years.[21] However, between 6 and 11 years of age, the head *appears* to enlarge greatly, and facial features exhibit marked changes because of the growth of the facial bones, in particular, the sinuses, the maxilla (upper jaw), and the mandible (lower jaw). The face literally grows away or out from the skull (Fig. 20-8).

Between 5 and 7 years of age, the frontal sinuses become well developed. Sinal growth continues rapidly over the next 5 to 6 years; by 12 years of age, adult size is nearly attained.[6] Although the sinuses strengthen the architectural structure of the face, reduce the weight of the head, and assist in providing resonance to the voice, they also offer potential foci for infection, since they provide a warm, dark, moist area that is conducive to bacterial growth. Some children experience an increase in upper respiratory infections during the early school years as a result of the increase in exposure to communicable diseases after entering school as well as the development of the sinal cavities.

The mandible grows downward, forward, and away from the cranial vault. Concomitant growth of the maxilla and the nasal passageways allows for greater exchange of air to meet the needs of the growing, active body. Room is also made for the permanent molars and other secondary teeth. Temporary disproportions in the shape of the face frequently lead school-

agers to consider themselves "ugly ducklings." About 90% of facial growth is attained by age 12.[21]

Muscular System

Muscle mass and strength gradually increase, and the body takes on a leaner appearance as "baby fat" decreases. During the middle childhood years, the child gains about to 3 to 3½ kg (5–7 lb) per year. A formula sometimes used for predicting weight (in pounds) for children 8 to 12 years of age is to multiply the age by 7 and then add 5 ([age × 7] + 5).[21] Thus, a 9-year-old child can be expected to weigh roughly 68 lb. This weight increase is caused mainly by increase in the size of the skeletal and muscular systems as well as increases in the size of some body organs. The loose movements, "knock knees," and lordosis of early childhood disappear as muscle tone increases. At all ages, males have a greater number of muscle cells than females, apparently as a result of the higher levels of androgens (male hormone).[34] Because of their greater number of muscle cells, males at all ages are usually stronger than females.[4] Although females generally have more adipose (fat) tissue, the balance between muscular and adipose tissue in the child seems to be more closely related to the amount of exercise and activity than to gender.[7] Children double their strength and physical capabilities during these years.[43] The increase in muscular strength results from both genetic factors, which cause hyperplastic growth, and exercise, which facilitates hypertrophic growth.

Athletic prowess in a child is more closely related to biological age and gender than to chronological age;[9] this factor should be considered before children are allowed to participate in competitive, strength, and endurance sports. Muscles are still immature and are easily injured. In other words, athletic activities should be chosen according to the

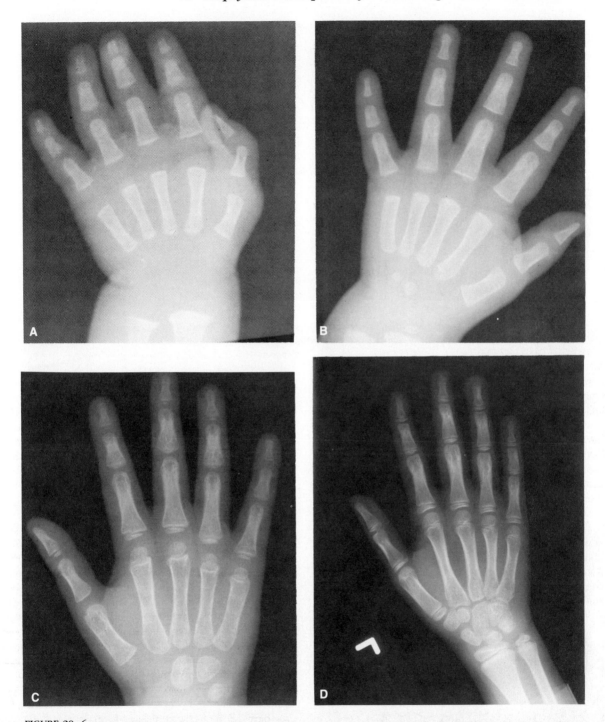

FIGURE 20–6.
X-rays of the hand, showing ossification of the wrist bones. (A) *5 weeks;* (B) *1 year;* (C) *4 years;* (D) *8 years. (Courtesy Department of Radiology, The Children's Hospital, Columbus, Ohio.)*

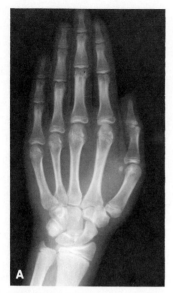
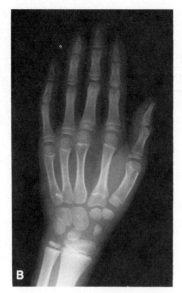
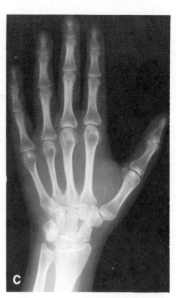

FIGURE 20–7.
X-rays of the hand, showing ossification of the wrist bones. (A) *10-year-old female;* (B) *10-year-old-male;* (C) *20 year old. (Courtesy Department of Radiology, The Children's Hospital, Columbus, Ohio.)*

physical abilities of the child, not by peer, parental, or community pressures. This factor also needs to be assessed when a child is considering participation in coeducational sports. Boys tend to excel in activities that require strength, endurance, and gross movements (e.g., running, jumping, throwing). Girls tend to excel in activities that require coordination, balance, and fine-motor movements (e.g., balance beam, skipping, and crafts).[9] These differences are due to musculoskeletal development, opportunity for motor activity practice, and nervous system maturity.

With the current interest in physical health, many adults engage in regular exercise programs or jogging. Parents frequently encourage their school-agers to join them. School-agers can develop stress fractures or suffer heat injuries if engaged in distance running or trying to keep pace with the adults.[35] Fortunately, most preadolescent children "will stop,

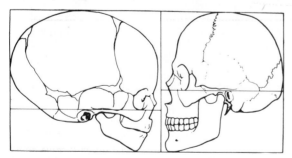

FIGURE 20–8.
Facial growth. The skull of a neonate (left) and that of an adult (right). The horizontal lines cross the same bony landmarks in each illustration. (From Lowrey, G. H. [1978]. Growth and development of children [7th ed.] Chicago: Year Book. With permission.)

sit down, or pass out before creating significant physical injury."[35] Adults are cautioned to slow the pace and shorten the distance if children younger than 14 are included in running or jogging activities. Strenuous activity should be avoided during periods of high temperature or humidity because of the child's still limited ability to cool the body by evaporation cooling (sweating).[35]

Nervous System

The continuing maturation of the central nervous system allows for the performance of increasingly complex gross- and fine-motor skills. Although the brain has reached 90% of its adult size by 7 years of age,[21] the sulci (fissures or grooves) of the cortex of the brain continue to develop as intellectual functions expand.[7] The growth rate of the brain is greatly slowed, with 95% of brain growth achieved by age 9, and full growth achieved during adolescence.[8] Improvement in diet cannot make up for nutritional deficits that have affected hyperplastic growth of the brain during the late fetal or early infancy periods of life (see Chap. 3). Since head circumference correlates well with the deoxyribonucleic acid (DNA) content of the brain, heads that measure more than two standard deviations below the expected norm are indicative of potential cellular deficiency. In general, the smaller the size of the head, the lower the intelligence.[21,34] Children with superior intelligence quotients (IQ) often have larger than average head circumferences.[21]

Myelinization

The transformation of the clumsy 6 year old into the coordinated 12 year old is due in part to the maturation of the central nervous system and the improved transmission of nerve impulses to the muscles involved. **Myelinization,** the development of the myelin sheath around the axons (arms) of nerve cells, continues during the school years. It is about 90% completed by 7 years of age. The percentage of attainment of final development appears to be synchronized with growth of the brain. As the thickness of this insulating sheath increases, the conduction of nerve impulses improves. Experience in using the motor pathways affects ease and skill of coordination.

Gross-Motor Activity

The gross-motor (large-muscle) skills of the 6 to 7 year old far outstrip fine-motor (small-muscle) coordination. The child of this age is full of energy, enjoys gross-motor activity, and is enthralled with the world; the sky is the limit. Since control of impulses and fear of dangers may still be limited, anything and everything must be tried—hopping, roller skating, bike riding, running, climbing, wrestling, and so on (Fig. 20-9). Even when the 6 year old is sitting in a chair or lying on the beach (or in bed), the child seems to be in perpetual motion.

The child is more aware of the physical self and its control than the emotional, social, or cognitive self. The 6 year

old becomes so engrossed in activities that he or she often does not recognize tiredness when it occurs. Fatigue may be exhibited later in quarrelsomeness, crying, or a lack of interest in eating. The emotional roller coaster of the 6 year old may be due in part to this sustained activity followed by the physical exhaustion of overactivity. Adults still need to set firm guidelines to protect the child both physically and emotionally and use the scenarios to help the child become more aware of the relationship between the physical and emotional domains.

Seven- and 8-year-old children exhibit less restlessness. Although the energy level of these older children is just as high, their activities are more subdued and directed. Increased attention span and awareness of cognitive skills enhance their enjoyment of sit-down games. Bicycles begin to be used for errands and transportation, not just for something to do. Increased myelinization improves reaction time, which makes participation in group sports easier. The 6 year old can throw and catch a ball with a fair amount of control; the 7 year old begins to make connections between the bat and the ball. Running is directed toward races or to getting somewhere in a hurry, not just running for the sake of running. Swimming movements become more coordinated. In general, the 7 year old uses a more cautious (and a more serious) approach to activities. Gross-motor activities seem to come under the control of both conscious will and cognitive skills (Fig. 20-10).

Children between 8 and 10 years of age gradually exhibit greater rhythm, smoothness, and gracefulness of muscular movements. They consciously work to coordinate and perfect physical skills. Strength and endurance increase. These children engage in physical activities that require longer and more concentrated attention and effort, such as baseball and hiking. Hours are spent practicing new gymnastic stunts, ballet positions, batting and pitching skills, break dancing, or judo and wrestling maneuvers (see Fig. 20-10). They compete individually in races, on foot, or on a bicycle to test their strength; they try to outdo one another in complexity or bravery on the skate board or in climbing trees. Children begin to appreciate their individuality and seek opportunities to show off a newly acquired skill, whether a "Tarzan swing" or riding the bicycle "without hands." Group games in school or in the community provide opportunities to develop and to test skills, as well as an arena for social recognition and approval. Admiration of the skill by an adult or peers enhances the child's self-esteem and spurs more effort into perfecting the skill. Greater individuality is also exhibited during these years. As restlessness decreases, many children begin to prefer quieter activities, such as reading.

Between 10 and 12 years of age (the pubescent years for girls), energy levels remain high but are better directed and controlled. The pubescent possesses physical skills almost equal to those of the adult, all that is required at this stage is practice. The body does what the brain tells it to do. Further growth and development of the muscular and skeletal systems during adolescence increases strength and endurance. Greater self-mastery is reflected in repetitious practice, increased self-confidence, and interest in self-development

FIGURE 20–9.
The young school-ager may not exhibit extraordinary skill but loves to show off. Such early efforts need to be reinforced as a foundation for attempting more complex feats later.

FIGURE 20–10. (A)
Six- and seven-year-old children possess an excessive amount of energy, which is frequently directed into gross-motor activities that may allow competition and cooperation with peers. During the late school years, children participate in controlled gross-motor activities (in this case, break-dancing) that allow them to refine movements and increase strength. (Photo on right by Ed Slaman.)

through physical activities. Although the pubescent child can sit still for prolonged periods of time, discharge of excess energy frequently occurs through foot tapping, finger drumming, and leg swinging—much to the distraction of parents and teachers.

Since the metabolic rate of children is higher per mass unit than that of adults, and their sweating capacity is still limited, they have more difficulty adjusting to extremes of temperature when exercising.[2] Dehydration and overheating create genuine threats to the child's health and life. Full hydration, frequent rests, and light clothing are essential during periods of physical exercise.

Fine-Motor Activity

Increased myelinization of the central nervous system is reflected in the marked improvement of fine-motor or manipulative skills. Balance and eye–hand coordination improve linearly with myelinization and practice. The hands are used more adroitly as tools. The 6 year old is able to hammer, to

paste, to tie shoes, and to fasten clothes. However, the neurologically immature child may continue to have difficulty with tying anything for several years (Fig. 20-11). The school-ager needs to be able to use the hands and fingers without having to concentrate on the muscle movements essential to make the pencil move in a specific direction or with a specific *degree* of intensity. Consequently, handedness should be firmly established by age 4, allowing the child to concentrate on control of muscle movements during the preschool years and on the finished **product** rather than the **process** of writing, drawing, or material manipulation during the school-age years.

By 7 years of age, the child's hands become steadier. The child of this age prefers a pencil to a crayon for printing, and reversal of letters during writing is less common. Printing becomes smaller. Many children exhibit sufficient finger coordination to begin music lessons on a piano, woodwind, brass, or stringed instrument. The 7 year old is usually completely self-sufficient in dressing.

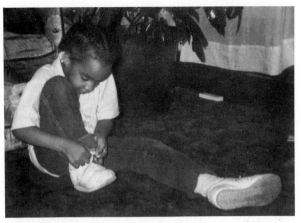

FIGURE 20–11.
Some late preschoolers are able to tie their shoes; however, most children do not master this feat until the early school years because of the complex cognitive skills as well as the fine-motor skills involved.

Between 8 and 10 years of age, the hands can be used independently with more ease and precision. Sufficient coordination develops to enable the child to write rather than print words. Letter size continues to become smaller and more even (Fig. 20-12). Special abilities become more obvious and differentiated; that is, children begin to use fine-motor skills to express cognitive and cultural interests through activities such as sewing, model building, weaving, or other crafts. Parents are grateful to see improved eating skills at the table. Children should become completely self-sufficient in self-care during these years, including complete bathing and hair washing.

The child between 10 and 12 years of age begins to exhibit manipulative skills comparable to the precision exhibited by adults. The complex, intricate, and rapid movements essential for producing fine-quality handcrafts or executing a difficult number on a musical instrument may be mastered. Talent and practice become the keys to proficiency. Recitals or exhibitions of their work help to foster positive self-regard in

FIGURE 20–12.
Improvement of fine-motor control is evidenced by changes in handwriting. These children were asked to write their names on a blank piece of paper. With increasing age, the size of their writing becomes smaller, and the evenness and the uniformity of letter configurations improve. Females generally exhibit more highly developed fine-motor skills during these years because of advanced neurological development. Note the immaturity in discrimination as well as coordination of the 4 year olds; the reversal of letters of a 6 year old (Bridget); the mixture of upper- and lower-case letters of the 6 year olds; and the letter dropping of the 8 year old. All are common phenomena for the ages of the children.

children with such accomplishments. Physical maturation and the social environment work together to help the child achieve Erikson's task of industry. As children concentrate on a product or skill, they learn how to work; they learn not only what they can do, but also what they are interested in doing, and what activities have intrinsic and extrinsic value. A foundation is being laid for the emerging sense of identity, the central task of the adolescent years.

Perceptual Skills

Intact perceptual skills are critical to learning and performing in school. Five modalities are recognized that may be used in learning: visual (discussed in the next section), auditory, haptic (touch), olfactory (smell), and gustatory (taste). The sense of taste and smell are fully developed before the school-age years. These senses are more commonly used as modes of learning in the preschool years, but they continue to offer valuable sources of information about objects throughout life. The young school-ager should be able to feel, identify, and locate points of cold, heat, skin touch, and pinprick on every body surface. The young school-ager should also be able to identify common unseen objects by touch (**stereognosis**). This skill provides the basis for many "feely box" games in kindergarten through second grade.

Auditory perception is normally acute during both the preschool and the school-age years. The child should be able to discriminate fine differences in articulated sounds and voice pitch. Because of the ability to hear and duplicate phonetic utterances and to comprehend translations, the school years are an optimal time to learn a foreign language. Children who are introduced to a second language during the preschool or school-age years frequently learn to speak the language as fluently and easily as a native. The ability to duplicate foreign sounds exactly may be lost after puberty (about age 12). Children who move to a foreign country or who learn a second language during adolescence frequently retain an accent, especially when under stress, even if the new language becomes their primary form of verbal communication.[25] Evidence strongly suggests that foreign languages should be introduced during the primary school years.

Discrimination ability improves with practice. Left–right discrimination is more difficult than up–down discrimination and can lead to reading problems such as dyslexia.[31] Reversal problems in both reading and writing decrease gradually through 10 and 11 years of age.[31]

Development of the Eye

During infancy and the toddler years, the eye is normally **hyperopic.** Because of the shortness of the eye from front to back, the image of an object focuses behind the retina, a situation that leads to farsightedness. However, the extreme malleability of the lens during early childhood allows the eye to refocus the image rapidly on the retina. In fact, during infancy, the flexibility of the lens allows the baby to accommodate for objects held only a few inches from the nose or at a great distance.[16] During the preschool years, the normally developing eye becomes **emmetropic;** the image of an ob-

ject focuses on the retina without any accommodative effort from the lens. If the eye grows too much, the image focuses in front of the retina, producing **myopia** (nearsightedness) (Fig. 20-13). Any time the image is not focused directly on the retina, vision is blurred. The length of the eyeball appears to be genetically controlled; therefore, nearsightedness (myopia) and farsightedness (hyperopia) frequently appear in several generations of a family. The eye may have a slight growth spurt during early adolescence, which may be responsible for an increased frequency of myopia during the pubertal period.[37] Many young adults experience changes again during late adolescence or the early 20s.

Most children with normal vision achieve 20/20 visual acuity by age 5; this means that the child (and those with normal vision) is able to see a particular object clearly at 20 ft. Visual acuity of 20/40 means that an individual can see an object clearly only at 20 ft that other people can see clearly at 40 ft (this measurement is the estimated visual acuity of the 2

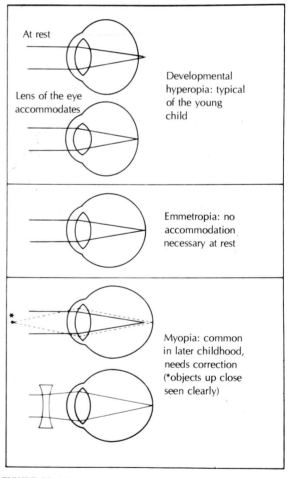

FIGURE 20–13.

Changes in the eye during childhood. (From Smith, D. W., Bierman, E. L., & Robinson, N. M. [1978]. The biologic ages of man: From conception through old age. Philadelphia: W. B. Saunders. With permission.)

year old). Visual acuity of 20/200 indicates that an individual can identify an object from a distance of only 20 ft that other people can identify at 200 ft (this measurement is the estimated acuity of the 3-month-old child,[27] and is also the definition of legal blindness). Improvements in vision during the toddler and preschool years appear to be due more to increased discrimination skills and learning than to changes in the eye per se.[16]

Depth perception (**stereopsis**) requires the coordinated use of both eyes (binocular vision). The optic center of the brain must fuse the two images. This ability is not present at birth; consequently, **strabismus** (crossed eyes) is common during early infancy. As visual acuity and control of eye movements by the ocular muscles improve, the brain learns to fuse the images. Binocular vision begins to emerge around 4 to 5 months of age,[27,45] becomes functional around 10 months, and stabilizes between 4 and 6 years.[21] Strabismus that continues through the toddler and preschool years can be due to weak eye muscles, an inability of the brain to fuse the images, or to a decreased acuity in the deviating eye.[21] Strabismus causes a double image to appear. This result in turn affects depth–distance assessment, object location, and understanding of spatial relationships. Children should be asked to indicate if they see a single image when looking at objects. A double image can interfere with acquiring reading skills, eye–hand coordination, and participation in sports. Any strabismus beyond 3 months (even if it only appears when the child is tired) should be checked by a pediatric ophthalmologist.[27]

Visual maturity is usually reached between 6 and 7 years of age. Peripheral vision is fully developed, and the child is able to discriminate fine differences in color.[7] Large-print books are not essential to aid in visualization. However, since differences in shapes and positions of letters are more obvious, large print helps the child who is just learning to read to discriminate letters and words more easily. Although visual screening tests (by professional or paraprofessional people) are recommended during the preschool years, only one third of the children who need visual correction are identified during these years.[18] Consequently, on entering school, all children should have a visual examination by an ophthalmologist. The child with a vision problem usually does not complain of poor vision because he or she has known nothing else. Although adults see details like leaves on trees, letters on signs, and features on faces, the child seems to assume that such powers of discrimination are yet to come. When peers exhibit discrimination competencies, the child with acuity problems may accept such skills as another sign of individual differences. Most visual problems can be easily corrected with eyeglasses.

Cardiovascular System

By 5 years of age, the heart has quadrupled its birth size. At 9 years, it is 6 times the birth weight, and by puberty it is almost 10 times the birth weight.[21] Obviously, much cardiac growth takes place during the school years. However, the size of the heart is smaller, proportionately, to body size than at any other period of life. This fact accounts in part for the easy tiring.[43] Increased cardiac function is essential to meet the oxygen and circulatory needs of the growing, active body. As the heart grows, it assumes a more vertical position within the thoracic cavity. The diaphragm descends, allowing more room for both cardiac action and respiratory expansion.

Pulse and respiratory rates are affected by size, gender, and activity of the child (see Appendix E). As the rhythm of the heartbeat gradually comes under the influence of the vagus nerve, the cardiac rate slows.[21] "Functional" or "innocent" heart murmurs are present in as many as 50% of children during the school years. These soft, "blowing" heart sounds are caused by the blood passing through normal heart valves.[16] These sounds, which have no particular significance, occasionally persist into the adolescent or adult years. Blood pressure increases as the left ventricle of the heart develops.

Minimal changes are experienced in the constituents of the blood from infancy through 12 years of age. The hemoglobin and hematocrit are increased slightly, and the white blood cell count is reduced slightly from preschool levels.

Respiratory System

At birth, the lungs have about 20 million alveoli. This number gradually decreases. The adult complement of 200 to 600 alveoli is reached by 8 years of age.[17] However, lung capacity is proportional to body size. The 200 mL capacity of the newborn has expanded to 2.2 L at 8 years, but increased size of each alveoli allows the lungs to hold close to 5.5 L at 25 years.[17] The respiratory rate slows as the lungs' **tidal volume** (the amount of air exchange with each breath) doubles between ages 5 and 10, thus increasing tolerance and resilience for gross-motor activities.[21]

Gastrointestinal System

The gastrointestinal system achieves adult functional maturity during the school years.[16] Upset stomachs occur less frequently. The toddler's "cow's-horn" shaped stomach assumes a "fish-hook" shape between 7 and 9 years of age. The adult "bagpipe" shape appears during pubescence (10–12 years). The stomach is able to tolerate all foods, but dietary intake needs to be geared to the growth and metabolic needs of the child (see the following section on maintaining health). The increased capacity allows children to go longer between meals. Abdominal pain is a common childhood complaint. Since this pain can be a symptom of either psychogenic or physical pathology, medical consultation should be sought for recurring complaints.

Genitourinary System

The urinary system is functionally mature during the school years. The kidneys double in size between the 5th and 10th years to keep up with the increased metabolic wastes of the body. The renal system is able to conserve water adequately to maintain stable fluid and electrolyte balances.[7] The constituents and specific gravity of the urine are similar to those of the adult. Five percent to 20% of school-age children have small amounts of **albuminuria** (protein in the urine); it is found most commonly in children with marked lordosis. The reason is unknown, but it appears to be related to the impaired venous blood circulation experienced by the kidney when the child is standing. This phenomenon normally disappears by puberty.[21]

Fifteen percent of 5 year olds, 5% to 6% of 10 year olds, 2% to 3% of 12 to 14 year olds, and 1% to 2% of 15 to 18 year olds have **nocturnal enuresis** (involuntarily wetting the bed during sleep).[5] Boys are 30% more likely to have enuresis than girls.[38] Although a genetic factor appears to be at play in some situations (more common in monozygous twins than dizygous twins and more common if both parents were bed-wetters than if only one or neither had nocturnal enuresis), most cases show no organic cause, and the etiology is unknown.[5] Some children have not been taught that cleanliness is prized and wetting is inappropriate! Evidence indicates that some children may have delayed neurological development, a chronic bladder infection, or a small bladder capacity.[30] Some children sleep so soundly that they are unaware of physical stimuli. Other children may experience fear of the dark or other emotional reactions that prevent them from assuming control of the situation; they find less fear and trauma in the wet bed than in the known or unknown consequences.

A higher incidence of bed-wetting is found in distressed homes or families that are facing other stressors, such as divorce, a move, hospitalization, or a new sibling.[5] The behavior in turn increases or creates intrafamily tensions that can lead to social and emotional problems for the child. The child may not be able to participate in school trips or any overnight visits because of the social problems associated with enuresis.

Most cases are self-limited, and the child experiences a spontaneous "cure" before puberty. Several treatments are available. The bed-alarm conditioning device appears to show the most promise.[30] (A bell or buzzer sounds as soon as the device begins to get wet.) Meanwhile, the school-age child is old enough to assume responsibility for the behavior and can be expected to change the bed and wash the linens (with help if under age 8). The family needs to offer warm support of the child's efforts and understanding of the fears and embarrassment.

Immunological System

The immunological system becomes functionally mature during the early school years. Lymphoid tissues, the producer of antibodies, reach a peak in size between 6 and 7 years of age. Enlargement of the adenoid and tonsillar lymphoid tissues makes these tissues appear to be hypertrophied, but enlargement is normal for the child 5 to 7 years of age. Maximal development of these tissues coincides with the time when acute infections of the respiratory and alimentary tract are most common. Tonsillectomies and adenoidectomies are fre-

quently incorrectly recommended because of the use of adult standards for evaluating "normal" size.[3] These tissues do not need to be removed unless they are precipitating serious middle-ear infections, are obstructing swallowing or breathing, or are the foci for frequent, persistent infections. Growth of these tissues ceases after 7 years of age. Normal involution makes them appear small by puberty.

Once an individual has produced an antibody against a particular antigen (foreign material), the template is retained. The body can resynthesize antibodies against that antigen at a later date rapidly and in large quantities. Consequently, the number of major infections usually decreases with age, because the body can fight the antigen at an earlier stage. The body is able to localize infections well, but the school-ager still experiences 3½ significant infections per year. Colds, gastrointestinal system infections, allergic disorders, communicable diseases, and pneumonia account for more than 70% of school absenteeism.[16]

MAINTAINING HEALTH

One third of our lives is spent in preparation for the other two thirds. During the school years, the child is rapidly learning how to use the strengths and to compensate for the limitations of his or her own body. Maximal development of the cognitive, social, and emotional domains depends highly on adequate functioning of the biophysical domain. The child who is ill, who has a low energy level, or who is physically incapable of learning a particular skill is limited in the ability to take full advantage of educational and social opportunities (see Chap. 17). An understanding of basic health needs can help to prevent many health problems. Regular health checkups can identify minor problems early, before they become more serious.

Metabolic Needs

Physical development is more significant than chronological age in determining the basal (resting) metabolic rate (BMR). The basal metabolic rate is highest during periods of most rapid growth. Since males have more muscle mass than females, they generally have a higher basal metabolic rate. Total metabolic needs (resting and energy) are affected by the energy expenditure of the individual child. The quiet, sedentary child who prefers fine-motor activity requires fewer calories than the athletically oriented child who uses every opportunity to express or exhibit gross-motor prowess (Fig. 20-14).

Nutritional Needs

As children grow, they gradually require less food per unit of body weight; however, the total amount of food consumed increases until after the pubertal period (see Appendix E). Adequate nutrition is needed for six reasons during this period of life:

FIGURE 20-14.
Good eating habits established during the preschool years need to be continued during the school-age years. Children who are allowed to be "picky" eaters may have poor nutritional habits for the rest of their lives, a factor that will affect energy levels, health status, and longevity.

1. To meet the basal metabolic needs of the body. A certain amount of energy is needed just to keep the body functioning.
2. To meet the body's energy needs. Great variation is seen among children in this area.
3. To meet cellular growth needs. Some hyperplastic growth is continuing, but much hypertrophic growth occurs during the school years.
4. To prepare for the physiological changes of the pubertal period.[20]
5. To meet cellular replacement needs. Some cells are already beginning to exhibit signs of aging and must be replaced, if possible, to maintain optimal functioning of the system.
6. To meet cellular repair needs. Injuries—minor and major—are common during the school years. Even a hangnail requires extra calories for repair.

A formula sometimes used to predict caloric needs of children of this age is 1000 plus 100 times the child's age (1000 + [100 × age]).[42] Thus, a 9-year-old child would require roughly 1900 calories. The protein, calcium, vitamin, and mineral requirements are particularly high during these years to ensure adequate materials for growth of the muscular and skeletal systems. Although vitamins may not be essential if the child eats a well-balanced diet, many health care practitioners recommend daily vitamins to ensure adequate vitamin and mineral intake. Table 20-1 gives the recommended daily minimal intake of different types of food for the school-age child. If the child is involved in sports and exercise programs, then special consideration should be given to an adequate intake of not only calories and fluids but also to the right proportion of fat, carbohydrates, and protein.[23]

Since obesity in childhood is closely correlated with obesity during the adult years, parents are advised to maintain their child's weight within normal limits. Children whose diets are high in fat increase their risk of obesity, high blood cholesterol, and cardiac disease unless active steps are taken to lower intake levels. Three percent to 25% of school-age children have elevated blood cholesterol or lipid levels, which increase the risk of cardiovascular disease.[15] The National Institute of Health recommends that saturated fats make up no more than one third of the child's daily fat intake.[40] Limiting cholesterol intake to 300 mg/day is recommended by the American Heart Association to lower the risk of heart disease.[44]

Eating habits are a critical factor in life-span health maintenance. Food preferences and dislikes become strongly established during the school years; dietary habits are the result of cultural influences, family attitudes toward food, parental example, and individual tastes. Education and guidance offered to the child by the parents regarding nutritional intake strongly influences intake at this time and later in their lives. Some children eat foods mainly composed of high amounts of sugar and starches and avoid vegetable and protein foods

TABLE 20-1. RECOMMENDED MINIMUM DAILY INTAKE FOR SCHOOL-AGERS*

Type of Food	*Amount*
Milk	2–3 cups
Meat	2–3 servings
Fruit and vegetables	4–5 servings
Bread and cereal	4–5 servings

* Extra foods need to be added in each group to ensure adequate caloric intake.

because of inadequate guidance. Other children may begin to use food as an emotional weapon against the parents. As in every other aspect of the parent–child relationship, the parents must know themselves well, be secure in their own goals, and offer a good model to prevent and to remedy mealtime problems.

School-agers frequently become so involved in their activities that they neglect or forget to eat. Parents must establish a fairly regular schedule to ensure that the child obtains adequate intake to prevent undue fatigue and illness. Breakfast is critical for providing adequate calories to start the day. The child who attends school without breakfast exhibits fatigue and poor attention; learning obviously is affected. Many schools have established breakfast or lunch programs, or both, to assist with this problem when a large number of their children come from homes where breakfast is not offered or encouraged. Children also need after-school and between-meal snacks. Energy expenditure and growth needs are so high during childhood and adolescence that the fasting period between meals may be too long. If a child eats lunch at 11:30 AM at school and does not have supper until 6 or 6:30 PM, a substantial after-school snack is essential. Small, frequent feedings of nutrient- and energy-dense foods are crucial for the active child.[20] Low-energy levels can precipitate irritability, headache, and lassitude, factors that can lead to poor academic achievement and family dissension. Illness, fatigue, excitement, and temporary emotional disturbances can all cause temporary decreases in food intake or changes in food habits. Good nutritional habits established at this age help set a pattern for a lifetime of healthy food intake.[20]

Table manners show interesting changes with age. The 6 year old who is going through a brief growth spurt, who has a high energy level, and who is experiencing an expanding world generally has a good appetite. However, since so many things are more interesting than eating, the 6 year old's table manners may consist of grabbing the food, stuffing it in the mouth, and then talking with the mouth full of food (Fig. 20-15). Jerky motor coordination also means that spills are frequent. Life seems too exciting to waste much time eating.

The 7 year old, as in other areas of life, becomes less expansive. Talking at mealtime decreases, but food continues to be eaten quickly to rejoin the gang outside. The 8- to 9-year-old child begins to slow down. Manners generally improve (in those homes where they are encouraged), and the meal can become a time of brief socialization. The pubescent child may once again begin to eat rapidly to join (or rejoin) friends, but improved coordination improves manners and prevents spills of earlier years. A better perspective of time coupled with parental guidance can help make the dinner hour a pleasant social activity.

Mealtimes are more than periods of physical refueling. Mealtimes become significant memories of childhood. Effective communication, turntaking, listening, and sharing are critical elements for solidifying the parent–child bond. Thus, mealtimes are also a time for emotional and social refueling.

Serious illness or dietary deficiencies can cause temporary setbacks in growth during the early years. However, since the majority of growth after age 6 is hypertrophic in nature, catch-up growth can occur once an adequate diet is provided. Unless significant damage has occurred because of malnutrition, replacement of the missing factor (nutritional or hormonal) usually results in dramatic acceleration of growth.[34]

FIGURE 20–15.
The young school-ager is too busy attending to social and play events to concentrate on etiquette or refine fine-motor skills. Mealtimes may be viewed as a "necessary evil" imposed by adults and the body that interrupts what they really *want to do.*

Adequate growth after an illness or a deficiency depends on the age of the child, the severity and duration of the problem, and the actual tissue (or tissues) involved. The humoral negative feedback system (in which the cells secrete a particular protein that has an antimitotic effect when a certain level is reached) allows the cells to grow until the expected levels for the child's development are reached, and then growth continues at a more normal pace.[21,34] As mentioned in Chapter 3, not all tissues develop at the same time; each has its own critical growth period. Deficiencies that occur during periods of critical hyperplastic growth usually cannot be compensated (e.g., brain growth during early infancy).

Sleep Needs

Inadequate sleep can lead to daytime irritability, fatigue, lack of endurance, inattention, and poor learning. The 6 year old needs about 12 hours of sleep per night; some children also continue to need an afternoon quiet time or nap to allow them to restore their energy levels. The 12 year old needs about 10 hours of sleep at night.[22] Evening television programs often compete for sleep time.

Children of this age may continue to have nightmares. Many different theories are given for the occurrence of nightmares: some postulate that they occur because of the maturation of the child's concept of death; some feel that they are related to indiscriminate watching of violence on television; others feel that they are related to energy expenditure and the continued search for one's own strengths and skills; still others feel that nightmares are a warning or indicator of excessive stressors in the child's life. Parents are urged to evaluate the child's environment in terms of his or her coping level. Bedtime is an excellent time to foster parent–child confidences. The activities of the day can be shared, and conflicts can be discussed and resolved. Ways to help the child relax before sleep include story time, religious readings and prayers, physical ministrations (e.g., bathing, back rubs), and exchange of loving affirmations. Quiet music is relaxing, and a night light helps to reduce fears.

Health Care

Continued health care surveillance by parents is essential to maintain a high level of physical health. Younger school-agers are too busy with the world to take time out for bathing or for washing faces, hands, or ears; many would wear the same clothes all week if the parents did not intervene. Fortunately, school-agers eventually begin to assume more interest in self-care. They also become more sensitive to exposure of the body and express interest in their own physical changes. By about 11 years of age, they begin to become concerned about personal hygiene and dress for social reasons.

Irritations and minor infections of the genitalia are relatively common, especially in females. Even though the child may experience vaginal itchiness or odor and even some discharge, she may not tell an adult.[7] Education in hygiene, health, and sexual functioning are essential, both by the family and the school, especially as puberty approaches. Of particular importance is teaching the young female to wipe from front to back (toward the rectum) after urination and defecation, to decrease the possibility of introducing bacteria into the vagina or urethra. Bubble baths are discouraged since the bubbles tend to increase the chance of introduction of bacteria to vaginal and urethral areas.

Other health maintenance measures include the provision of adequate nonglare lighting for reading and the avoidance of sudden loud noises or blaring music, which can damage the inner ear and cause hearing loss.

Health Supervision

School-age children should have one complete physical examination per year to assess growth patterns and to detect early signs of illness (see Table 6-4). Most children visit their physicians several additional times each year for minor illnesses, infections, or injuries.

Accidents

Accidents are the leading cause of death in this age group. Curiosity, incomplete control over motor activities, delayed responses, impulsiveness, inadequate knowledge, and poor planning or problem-solving skills are all interrelated. Education, example, and discipline are all needed to help avoid accidents. Although the child may vehemently resist parental guidance, parents are wise to establish guidelines that govern the activities and whereabouts of the school-ager. Public concern has encouraged laws that require fireproof nightclothes, fences around swimming pools, seat belts, and helmets for motorbike riding to help protect younger children. As the child begins to consciously separate the cognitive and social domains from the affective domain, impulsiveness decreases and self-discipline finally becomes stronger than curiosity. As the child gradually internalizes parental rules, increased freedom can be safely allowed.

The "accident-prone" child (the child who is involved in many minor accidents) needs to be evaluated. Neurological deficits may be a causative factor. Psychological and social factors also may be major precipitants of physically traumatizing events. (Is the child a daredevil? Why? Does the child lack self-discipline? Why?) An accident-prone child may consciously or unconsciously be seeking more adult attention. Depression may prevent some children from foreseeing the results of an activity. Other children may be exhibiting an inability to correlate the cause and effect relationships of their behaviors, a mild form of the helplessness syndrome.

Dentition

The child's face and permanent teeth develop so rapidly during the school years that dental checkups are recommended every 6 months.[33] The loss of the first tooth can be frightening to the child who is unprepared for the event. To the child who is prepared, it is one of the first tangible signs of

DENNIS the MENACE

"NAW...THE TOOTH FAIRY WON'T CARE IF IT GOT KNOCKED OUT IN A FIGHT. IT ALL PAYS THE SAME."

FIGURE 20–16.
(Reprinted courtesy of Dennis the Menace. *Copyright Field Newspaper Syndicate, T.M.®)*

Tetracycline binds to the dentin during the process of active calcification, causing a brown staining. Consequently, it should be avoided until after the seventh birthday to prevent negative cosmetic effects.[26]

Young children and adolescents frequently experience tooth pain or sensitivity, even though no disease is present. A response to highly concentrated sugars or to temperature differences occurs because the large nerve of the young tooth is closer to the surface of the tooth. As the tooth ages, the nerve not only becomes less excitable, but the nerve also begins to shrink, putting more distance between it and the tooth surface, thus rendering it less sensitive to environmental influences.

Malocclusion

More than 75% of children have some form or degree of occlusive disharmony; at least 15% of them need treatment.[36] Normally the cusps (prominent structures) interdigitate with the fossae (depressions in teeth) to create a comfortable, tight, chewing surface. When cusps meet and prevent the close interdigitation essential for chewing or interfere with the relaxation of facial muscles or an attractive appearance, treatment is indicated. Malocclusions may be either skeletal or dental in origin. Disharmonies of bone growth frequently result from a mixed racial background.[21] The malposition of teeth may be due to: prolonged sucking, which can cause open bite or tongue thrust; the early loss of primary teeth because of improper care, which allows permanent teeth to drift into abnormal positions; or a disproportionate relationship between jaw length and tooth size, which causes either wide spacing or overcrowding.[19] Primary teeth should not be pulled unless absolutely necessary, because they affect the alignment of the other teeth; this effect in turn can cause alignment problems when the permanent teeth emerge. Misaligned teeth need to be straightened, since recurrent impact that is not on the long axis of the tooth can lead to dental problems, including bone degeneration, during the adult years.

"growing up," and the event is greeted with much enthusiasm (Fig. 20-16). Children soon learn how squeamish many adults are about loose teeth and blood and take great delight in wiggling the loose tooth for parents or relatives. When the first permanent central incisors emerge, they appear much too large for the mouth and face, another factor that contributes to the "ugly duckling syndrome." Generally, the teeth of boys are larger than those of girls (Figs. 20-17 and 20-18).[21]

FIGURE 20–17.
Eruption of the permanent teeth. (From Marlow, D. R. [1977]. Textbook of pediatric nursing *[5th ed.]. Philadelphia: W. B. Saunders. With permission.)*

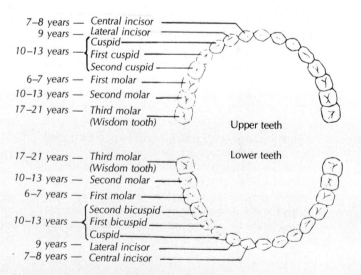

7–8 years —	Central incisor
9 years —	Lateral incisor
10–13 years —	Cuspid / First cuspid / Second cuspid
6–7 years —	First molar
10–13 years —	Second molar
17–21 years —	Third molar (Wisdom tooth)

Upper teeth

Lower teeth

17–21 years —	Third molar (Wisdom tooth)
10–13 years —	Second molar
6–7 years —	First molar
10–13 years —	Second bicuspid / First bicuspid / Cuspid
9 years —	Lateral incisor
7–8 years —	Central incisor

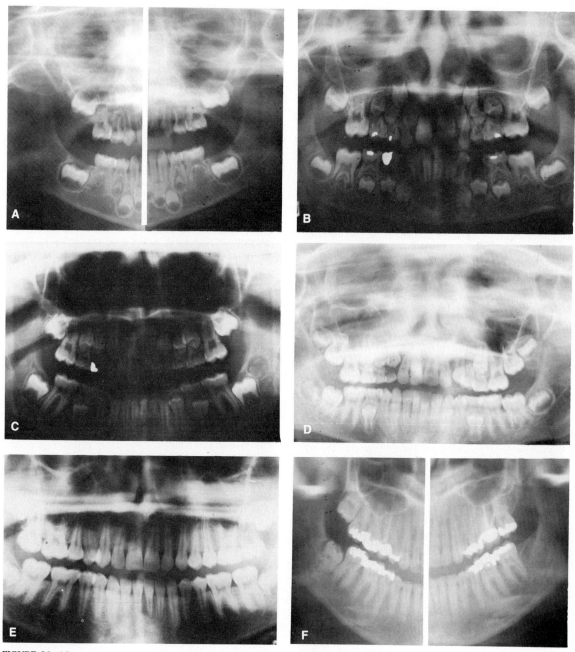

FIGURE 20–18.
X-rays of the deciduous and permanent teeth. (A) *3 years;* (B) *6 years;* (C) *8 years;* (D) *10 years;* (E) *14 years;* (F) *23 years.*

Bruxism

Some children grind their teeth while they sleep. This action sometimes creates enough noise to be heard in the next room. Over a period of time, the child can grind away some of the enamel and dentin. Some people think that bruxism is a sign of severe tension in the child's life. However, this behavior may be precipitated by the need to reposition malaligned teeth and can help facilitate a good occlusion of permanent teeth. When teeth are malpositioned, bruxism is an attempt at self-righting. A dental evaluation should be obtained.

Caries

Although the reduction in tooth decay has been 40% to 60% since the addition of fluoride to drinking water in the 1960s, tooth decay is still the leading "disease" in the United States.[10] Caries (tooth decay) are the end result of demineralization of the enamel and dentin of the tooth.[33] The teeth and mouth are constantly bathed in saliva and covered with bacteria, which aid in the initial digestion of food. Colonies of bacteria coalesce to form a soft, nonmineralized mass, known as dental plaque.[33] These bacteria produce organic acids when they are in contact with food residues, especially fermentable carbohydrates. If these carbohydrates remain in contact with the teeth (food particles get caught in cavities and crevices of teeth) for more than 15 minutes, the organic acids begin to diffuse into the tooth surfaces at the point of contact, creating an "acid challenge" to the subsurface mineral crystals and a gradual breakdown of tooth structure. Once the process is initiated, it continues until the crown is destroyed and the pulp is infected.[33] Only replacement of the diseased area by a dentist can halt the process once it has started.

Since the introduction of fluoride toothpaste and the greater emphasis on oral hygiene in the 1970s, another 40% to 60% reduction in caries has been found.[10] Fluoride augments the tooth's resistance to acids and helps with the remineralization of enamel and dentin. Some evidence suggests that adequate fluoride intake may also strengthen the bone structure and reduce fractures in the elderly. Thirty percent of teens are now free of caries, and another 30% have only a few caries.[10] Caries should receive prompt attention. They can become the foci of infection, sending toxins (poisons) throughout the body system if untreated.

The two best ways to prevent caries are the avoidance of high-sugar foods and the brushing of teeth, especially immediately after eating or snacking and before bedtime. The use of dental floss helps to remove food particles and to reduce plaque in areas the toothbrush cannot reach. However, even thorough and vigorous mouth care cannot remove all plaque, so regular dental visits for tooth cleaning and plaque removal are essential. The average 7 year old is capable of assuming full responsibility for dental hygiene, including the use of dental floss. Baking soda or salt may be substituted for toothpaste.

Some foods, such as cheeses, have a neutralizing or buffering action on plaque acids and consequently make a good snack food when one cannot brush.[10] Eating crispy foods such as apples, celery, and carrots also help to remove food particles after snacking. Sugarless gum after snacks helps to reduce caries formation by changing the pH of the plaque, increasing the flow of saliva, and dislodging food residue.[33] Rinsing with water can dislodge some particles and thus reduces the chance of cavity formation. When children learn these precautions, they tend to carry them on into the adult years as part of their oral hygiene and thus can reduce cavity formation during adult years. Bacteria and plaque are normal to the oral cavity. Since they cannot be eliminated, good oral hygiene is essential to reduce cavity formation. Avoidance of kissing babies on the mouth can delay the introduction of the more potent cariogenic bacteria.

Health Screening

Many schools require or provide health and dental screening before entrance to school and periodically during the school years. Poor health status or deficient functioning of the senses can reduce the child's ability to learn at school. School systems require adequate immunization as a prerequisite for admission to, or staying in, school. If a child has completed all immunizations before school, none may be needed during the school years except on special occasions, such as influenza shots recommended to prevent epidemics (see Table 6-3). Adequate surveillance of health status during childhood can help to maintain high-level wellness and can also help to prevent some chronic residual problems of the adult years.

Vision

Five percent of children develop eye problems during the first two years of life (usually strabismus),[27] and 25% of children need eyeglasses at some point during their school years to correct for accommodation problems, strabismus, or an astigmatism.[16] An **astigmatism** (uneven refraction of an object on the retina) can cause distortion and blurring of letters and numbers. All visual problems should be corrected as soon as possible because of their negative effect on learning. Visual screening should be continued throughout one's lifetime.

Hearing

Significant hearing loss is the most commonly overlooked serious handicap in young children.[16] The child may exhibit a mild to marked speech defect secondary to the hearing loss. The parents often feel that the child "is just not paying attention," "doesn't understand," or "forgets easily." Recurrent or chronic ear infections, fluid in the middle ear, frequent exposure to sudden loud noise, and illnesses, such as measles or mumps, can lead to decreases in auditory acuity. Five percent of children do not pass auditory screening tests.[16] Many hearing losses are temporary, due to mild infections or allergies. Loss of hearing in one ear may create difficulty in picking up sounds and in determining direction or location of the source of a sound.

Urinalysis

Urine tests can detect diabetes and silent or chronic urinary tract infection. One percent of females may have infections without symptoms.[16] Many adult urinary tract problems have their beginnings in untreated childhood infections.

Hematology

Blood tests may reveal an iron-deficiency anemia, a problem usually associated with inadequate nutrition. Increased susceptibility to infections, irritability, easy fatigability, and inadequate attention span are frequently associated with anemia. Once identified, anemia can be easily treated with an iron supplement and the addition of iron-rich foods to the diet (e.g., raisins, spinach, liver, egg yolk).

Blood Pressure

Blood pressure screening of children has received more attention in the last few years. High blood pressure may be found in children as young as 6 years of age. Untreated, it may escalate and contribute to adult hypertensive health problems. African American children tend to have higher blood pressure readings than white children. Most cases can be treated by diet.[24]

ALLERGIES IN CHILDREN
This section by James Abel

Allergy is the most common chronic health problem that occurs in children from newborns through age 17.[32] The incidence of major allergies in children is reported to range as high as 28.5% to 35% of children younger than 17 years of age.[14,32] Allergic symptoms are frequently associated with other illnesses (such as colds) in children and adolescents. The total time lost from school because of recurring health conditions amounts to at least 33 million days, with asthma being responsible for more than 7.5 million days, and hay fever or other allergic illness accounting for 1.5 million days.[32] Thus, more than one fourth of the days lost from school because of recurring health problems are associated with allergic disorders.

The frequency with which hay fever or asthma occurs in children whose parent (or parents) also had hay fever or asthma is about 30% to 60%. In contrast, the incidence in a matched group of individuals whose parents did not have hay fever or asthma only averages 6.4%.[39] These data strongly suggest that allergic conditions are transmitted by hereditary factors. It is the general opinion that the predisposition to allergy is what is inherited, rather than a specific allergic disease. Evidence seems to indicate that the factor is transmitted through incomplete dominance by two genes: H, an incomplete dominant gene for nonallergic individuals, and h, a recessive gene (see Chap. 3). People who have HH genetic compositions are not allergic; those with hh genetic material are allergic. An individual with Hh may or may not be allergic, but even if the person is nonallergic the h factor could be passed to an offspring and, thereby, account for the appearance of an allergic individual in a family with no history for allergy. In fact, large numbers of allergic individuals are found in nonallergic families. On the other hand, some people believe that it is difficult to dissociate acquired factors from genetic ones, and they postulate that allergy may also be acquired.

Two general types of allergic responses have been described. One is the **immediate reaction** (type I), which occurs quite suddenly after exposure to an **antigen** (foreign body) for which the person is sensitized. Common examples of the immediate type of reaction include urticaria ("hives"), allergic rhinitis ("runny nose"), eczema (skin rash), and asthma (the major allergic disease in children).

The other type of response is the **delayed reaction** (type II); in this case, the observed reaction is postponed a number of hours or days, and there are no demonstrable circulating antibodies. Included among the delayed forms are fungus allergy, allergic contact dermatitis, and the tuberculin type of bacterial allergy.

The usual type I allergic reaction features the unification of an antigen (the offending agent) with an antibody (the protein produced by the body's immune response to the offending agent). This combination results in the formation of a soluble complex. The presence of antigen–antibody complex with blood components (known as complement) causes the sensitized cells in the shock organ and tissue to undergo a proteolytic reaction (disintegration of proteins) that results in the release of chemical mediators found within these cells. These mediators are then responsible for the ensuing allergic reaction either entirely or in part, depending on the site of the reaction. Chemical mediators produce symptoms of allergy primarily by their influence on smooth muscles, capillary blood vessels, collagen, and mucous glands. The usual results are constriction of smooth muscles, dilation of blood vessels, and associated increase in capillary permeability, inflammatory reactions in collagen tissues, and increased mucus secretion.

The responses produced in type II reactions are mediated by an interaction of locally deposited antigen with antibody that was produced by, and bound to, a sensitized lymphocyte. This reaction is induced by special routes of antigen administration (subcutaneous or intracutaneous), after contact of the antigen with the skin (e.g., poison ivy dermatitis), with antigens that are living agents (e.g., the tubercle bacillus), or through certain chemical agents called adjuvants that enhance the development and production of hypersensitivity. Serum antibodies are not demonstrable in delayed hypersensitivity reactions, and special shock tissues or organs are not identified. However, many body tissue cells are susceptible to injury from these delayed reactions.

The preceding information makes it easier to understand allergic reactions. If one knows (1) the nature of the antigen, (2) the location of the antibody-containing cells, shock tissues, or organs, and (3) the character, concentration, and route of entry of the specific antigen, then one can anticipate the type of allergic response. Various kinds of predictable reactions are outlined in Table 20-2. In addition, a comparison of the actions of the different chemical mediators can serve to explain the various clinical manifestations of allergic reactions that occur, depending on the mediator involved. Table 20-3 gives an analogy of two chemical mediators and the clinical symptomatology evoked by them.

These two tables make it more apparent that different allergic reactions are similar in many respects except for the location of the shock (target) organ, tissue, or sensitized cells. It also discloses how the diagnosis, essential characteristics, and treatment of many of the different allergic ailments can be similar (e.g., avoidance of the antigen). In addition, it is evident that more than one shock organ or tissue may be pro-

TABLE 20-2. VARIABLE ALLERGIC RESPONSES TO DIFFERENT ANTIGENS

Nature of Antigen	Specific Antigen	affecting ⟶	Shock (Target) Organ or Tissue	to produce ⟶	Clinical Manifestation
Inhalants	Pollens (trees, grasses, flowers)		Eye		Lacrimation, visual disturbances, conjunctivitis, iritis, uveitis, blepharitis
	House dust Mold		Nose		Seasonal and/or perennial rhinitis, nasal polyposis
	Spores		Ear		Partial or complete hearing loss, serous otitis media
	Any animal dander (e.g., cat, dog, horse, gerbil, guinea pig)		Throat		Itching of mouth or tongue, sore throat, croup, edema of glottis and epiglottis, enlarged tonsils and adenoids, cough, salivation, swollen lips, mouth, or tongue
			Bronchi and lungs		Asthma, bronchitis, asthmatic bronchitis, Löffler's syndrome, pneumonitis, pleural effusion, pleurisy
Ingestants	Any food Any drug Any swallowed inhalant Any food additive (intentional or unintentional)		Gastrointestinal system		Aphthous stomatitis or canker sores, cheilitis, geographic tongue, gastritis, duodenitis, jejunitis, ileitis, colitis, infammatory bowel disease, diarrhea, constipation, vomiting, colic, abdominal pain, bloating, melena, proctalgia, pruritus ani, cyclic vomiting
			Musculoskeletal system		Arthritis, arthralgia, palindromic rheumatism, intermittent hydroarthrosis, myalgia, "leg pains"
			Skin		Angioedema, eczema, urticaria, purpura, erythema multiforme, drug rashes, contact dermatitis, Arthus reactions
			Blood		Thrombocytopenic purpura, hemolytic anemia, leukopenia, agranulocytosis, eosinophilia
			Genitourinary system		Dysuria, frequency of urine, enuresis, vulvovaginitis, urethritis, pruritus vulvae, orthostatic and idiopathic albuminuria, idiopathic renal bleeding
			Nervous system		Headache (including migraine), convulsions, tremors, tension, fatigue, hyperactivity, lethargy, mental apathy and dullness, confusion, poor attention span, vertigo, mood changes, narcolepsy, insomnia, Meniere's disease, neuralgia
			Miscellaneous		Anaphylactic shock, Henoch-Schönlein purpura, fever, enlarged lymph nodes, flushing, pallor
Contactants	Plant oils (poison ivy) Cosmetics Clothing		Skin		Contact dermatitis
Injectants	Drugs Foreign serum		All tissues		Serum sickness or drug allergy
Infectants	Viruses Bacteria Bacterialike organisms		All tissues		"Bacterial" allergy

voked by a single antigen to produce a combination of symptoms, or several different antigens may induce the same reaction in a given target organ or tissue. Finally, clinical examples of immediate and delayed forms of hypersensitivity may exist either together or at different times, and these reactions may occur as a result of exposure to the same antigen. Thus, there are no restrictions as to the types of agents that can act as antigens to produce or enhance the manifestations of allergy, and any organ, tissue, or system may be affected. The combination of manifestations that may result is unlimited.

Lucretius stated in *De Rerum Natura*, in 65 BC, "What is food to one man may be fierce poison to others." What has been said of antigenic inhalants, drugs, contactants, injectants, and infectants applies equally to foods and agents intentionally or unintentionally added to foods. One of the more troublesome problems of infant and child care is that of food allergy. Unfortunately, knowledge about this condition is far

TABLE 20-3. COMPARISON OF SOME OF THE ACTIONS OF HISTAMINE AND ACETYLCHOLINE TO PRODUCE CLINICAL ALLERGY MANIFESTATIONS

Target Organ or Tissue	Histamine	Acetylcholine	Clinical Allergy Manifestation
Nervous system	Headache	Headache Excitement Depression	Headache Tension Fatigue
Respiratory system	Bronchospasm Increased mucus secretion	Brochospasm Cough Increased mucus secretion	Asthma Bronchitis Asthmatic bronchitis

Gastrointestinal system	Stimulates acid production
	Stimulaes other
	    gastrointestinal glands
		Stimulation of gastrointestinal
		    glands
			Gastritis
			Pylorospasm
			Esophagitis
			Duodenitis
			Ileitis
			Colitis

Genitourinary system		Increased bladder tone	Frequency Enuresis
Cardiovascular system	Vasodilation Hypotension Whealing	Vasodilation Hypotension	Flushing Shocklike lowering of blood pressure Hives
Salivary glands	Salivation	Salivation	Salivation Drooling
Sweat glands		Increased stimulation	Increased sweating
Lacrimal glands		Increased lacrimation	Tearing
Skeletal muscle		Asynchronous fasciculation	Tremors

from complete, and many differences of opinion exist about food allergy disorders.

Two principal kinds of food allergies exist: an immediate reaction that manifests itself within a few seconds or minutes after exposure to the offending agent, or a delayed reaction that appears several hours or days later. With the immediate type of reaction, it is more likely that the antigen is a whole food or food additive; whereas in the delayed reaction, the antagonizing agent may be some breakdown product produced during the process of digestion. In either case, the insulting factor serves as an antigen. It must be realized that the development of so many varieties of processed foods and chemical additives* has produced a vast number of substances that can be antigenic in themselves or can act as antigens to cause a variety of allergic reactions.[28] In each case of food intolerance, an attempt must be made to determine whether or not the reaction is a true allergy. This task can be

arduous, but differences are found between intolerance for food secondary to a number of specific or nonspecific causes and a true food allergy generated by an antigen–antibody mechanism. In the former instance, symptoms induced by the ingestion of the food are usually caused by a deficiency in the digestive mechanism or a disturbance in digestive physiology.

Allergy can be responsible for many clinical manifestations (see Table 20-2). Of interest are the neurologic, neurotic, and psychoneurotic manifestations described in the allergy-mediated disorder of "allergic toxemia" (or tension-fatigue syndrome). This disorder is characterized by such symptoms as lethargy, fatigue, irritability, restlessness, mental confusion, headache, gastrointestinal symptoms, and body aches or pains.[11, 12, 13, 28, 29, 41]

Children who have the more diffuse constitutional allergic traits (e.g., tension, fatigue, hyperactivity, excessive sweating, salivation, pallor, lacrimation, enuresis, or vague aches and pains) are sometimes considered to be neurotic, hypochondriacal, or structurally inferior. When other reasons for such symptoms cannot be ascertained, the possibility of a syndrome caused by allergy should be investigated. If symptoms such as nervousness, irritability, hyperactivity, mental or physical fatigue, and sluggishness appear in children, the possibility that these symptoms are related to an allergic disorder may be substantiated if the symptoms improve or disappear after elimination of the suspected allergen, and reappears with its reintroduction. A child's symptoms deserve

---

(*) An inventory of food additives compiled by the Food Protection Committee of the National Research Council lists more than 2700 substances that are being added to American foods. These additives include preservatives, nutritive supplements, non-nutritive sweeteners, antioxidants, surface acting agents, emulsifiers, stabilizers, bleaches, food coloring and dyeing agents, buffers, texturizers, firming agents, anticaking agents, binders, enzymes, and natural or artificial flavorings.

to be approached with an open mind and a willingness to consider the possibility that they may be of allergic origin.

Allergy is one of the great medical masqueraders for illness and behavioral disorders in childhood. A typical sequence of ailments in an allergic child might be as follows: First, the infant may experience feeding problems because of a reaction to cow's milk with symptoms of colic, vomiting, diarrhea, constipation, or failure-to-thrive. Later, eczema may appear, and the child may begin to develop frequent "colds" characterized by rhinitis, cough, and congestion. Perhaps numerous bouts of ear infections begin, and recurring or persistent fluid in the middle-ear space becomes a problem. Intermittent episodes of bronchiolitis, croup, bronchitis, or pneumonia may appear. Concurrently or subsequently, the child may develop hay fever or asthma with all of their complications. It is possible that sinusitis, migraine headaches, abdominal pain, or inflammatory bowel disorders also become issues. Interspersed with this succession of events may be problems such as bed-wetting, leg pains, hyperactivity, urethritis or vaginitis, fatigue, learning disabilities, a seizure disorder, bouts of unexplained fevers, and behavioral disorders at home or school. The child may also suffer from canker sores, menstrual irregularity, dysuria, nasal polyps, arthritis, vertigo, sleep disorders, or hives. All the aforementioned ailments, and many more, could be caused by one or more allergies. The potential combination of disorders, diseases, or disabilities is uncountable.

Allergy can precipitate a plethora of diverse ailments. When faced with a child who manifests an unusual disparity or strange profusion of symptoms, the practitioner should consider the possibility of an underlying allergic provocation and should consider evaluating the child for an allergy disorder.

CONCLUSION

Growth is slower and more uniform during the early school years than during the preschool and adolescent years. Norms are valuable to indicate growth trends, but individual variance as affected by hereditary factors, gender, and environmental conditions must be kept in mind when growth tables are used. Measurements taken only one time may give undue cause for alarm or a false sense of security; measurements need to be taken several times to identify the child's pattern of growth. Individual differences increase with age in all domains, including the biophysical. No child fits the norms in all aspects.

The care, modeling, and support provided by the parents has a marked influence on the child's ability to maximize potentials during these years. A poor state of health can affect the learning processes. Good nutrition, careful hygiene, and regular physical and dental checkups are essential to maintain high-level wellness. There is increasing concern about the physical welfare of children and the implications for their health as adults. In the past 20 years, children 6 to 9 years of age have experienced a 54% increase in the prevalence of obesity and a 98% increase in the prevalence of super-obesity.[46] A decrease in formal physical education at school

has not been compensated by parental or community activities. Children spend more time watching TV and less time in active physical involvement. Less than 30% of their parents engage in moderate to vigorous exercise at least three times a week, and 50% do not exercise even once a week.[46] Consequently, children have neither the model nor the partnership with parents to encourage habits of physical activity. Since lack of adequate exercise is associated with coronary artery diseases, obesity, elevated blood pressure, diabetes, and osteoporosis, there is increasing concern about the potential latent effects on national health status when people grow up without adequate exercise to provide for "optimal functioning of all physiological systems of the body."[1] "Childhood represents a period of time when habits are formed. A program of physical activity that is enjoyable in childhood will probably be continued throughout the adult years for lifelong preventive health."[20]

Although physical growth appears to take a moratorium during the school-age years, it is a period of stabilizing, refining, and strengthening of functioning in preparation for the adolescent growth spurt and final maturation. The organs are increasing in size and ability to meet the needs of a mature body.

The child, because of increased cognitive skills and a widening social world, moves away from preoccupation with self and concentrates more on the use of the body as a tool for satisfying curiosity, performing new skills, and achieving higher goals. Gross-motor and fine-motor skills and coordination increase greatly during these years, allowing the child to pursue almost any activity with the potential of high-level performance if adequate practice and experience are pursued.

REFERENCES

1. American Academy of Pediatrics. (1987). Physical fitness and schools. *Pediatrics, 80,* 449–450.
2. American Academy of Pediatrics, Committee on Sports Medicine. (1982). Climatic heat stress and the exercising child. *Pediatrics, 69,* 808.
3. Behrman, R. E., Vaughan, V. C., & Nelson, W. E. (Eds.). (1987). *Nelson textbook of pediatrics* (13th ed.). Philadelphia: W. B. Saunders.
4. Brower, E. W., & Nash, C. L., Jr. (1979). Evaluating growth and posture in school-age children. *Nursing 79, 9*(4), 58.
5. Butler, R. J. (1987). *Nocturnal enuresis: Psychological perspectives.* Bristol, UK: Wright.
6. Caffey, J. P. (1985). *Pediatric x-ray diagnosis* (8th ed., F. N. Silvelrman, Ed.). Chicago: Year Book.
7. Chinn, P. L. (1979). *Child health maintenance: Concepts in family-centered care* (2nd ed.). St. Louis: C. V. Mosby.
8. Cooke, R. E. (Ed.). (1968). *The biological basis of pediatric practice.* New York: McGraw-Hill.
9. Eckert, H. M. (1987). *Motor development* (3rd ed.). Indianapolis, IN: Benchmark Press.
10. Featherstone, J. D. B. (1987). The mechanisms of dental decay. *Nutrition Today, 22*(3), 10–16.

11. Feingold, B. F. (1973). *Introduction to clinical allergy.* Springfield, IL: Thomas.

12. Feingold, B. F. (1985). *Why your child is hyperactive.* New York: Random House.

13. Frazier, C. A. (1985). *Coping with food allergy* (rev. ed.). New York: Times Books.

14. Freeman, G. L., & Johnson, S. (1969). Allergic diseases in adolescents. *American Journal of Diseases of Children, 107,* 549.

15. Glueck, C. J., et al. (1980). Risk factors for coronary artery disease in children: Recognition, evaluation and therapy. *Pediatric Review, 2,* 131–138.

16. Holm, V. A., & Wiltz, N. A. (1973). Childhood. In D. W. Smith & E. L. Bierman (Eds.), *The biologic ages of man from conception through old age.* Philadelphia: W. B. Saunders.

17. Hubbell, K. M., & Webster, H. F. (1986). Respiratory management of the neonate. In N. S. Streeter (Ed.), *High-risk neonatal care* (pp. 107–141). Rockville, MD: Aspen.

18. Ismail, H., & Lall, P. (1981). Visual acuity of school entrants. *Child: Care, Health and Development, 7,* 127.

19. Kilman, C., & Helpin, M. L. (1983). Recognizing dental malocclusion in children. *Pediatric Nursing, 9,* 204.

20. Kris-Etherton, P. M. (1986). Nutrition and the exercising female. *Nutrition Today, 21*(2), 6–16.

21. Lowrey, G. H. (1986). *Growth and development of children* (8th ed.). Chicago: Year Book.

22. Marlow, D. R., & Redding, B. A. (1988). *Textbook of pediatric nursing* (6th ed.). Philadelphia: W. B. Saunders.

23. Narins, D. M., Belkengren, R. P., & Sapala, S. (1983). Nutrition and the growing child. *Pediatric Nursing, 9,* 163.

24. National Heart, Lung, and Blood Institute's Task Force on Blood Pressure Control in Children. (1977). Report to the Task Force on Blood Pressure Control in Children. *Pediatrics, 59*(Suppl. 5).

25. Oyama, S. (1976). A sensitive period for the acquisition of a non-native phonological system. *Journal of Psycholinguistic Research, 5*(3), 261.

26. Physician's Desk Reference. (1990). *Physician's desk reference.* Oradell, NJ: Medical Economics.

27. Pushkar, R. G. (1988). What baby sees. *Parents Magazine, 63*(3), 90–94.

28. Randolph, T. G. (1978). *Human ecology and susceptibility to the chemical environment.* Springfield, IL: Thomas.

29. Rowe, A. H. (1972). *Food allergy: Its manifestations and control and the elimination diets.* Springfield, IL: Thomas.

30. Ruble, J. A. (1981). Childhood nocturnal enuresis. *MCN: The American Journal of Maternal/Child Nursing, 6,* 26.

31. Rudel, R. G., & Teuber, H. C. (1963). Discrimination of direction of line in children. *Journal of Comparative and Physiological Psychology, 56,* 892–898.

32. Schiffer, C. G., & Hunt, E. P. (1963). *Illness among children* (U.S. Children's Bureau Publication No. 405). Washington, DC: U.S. Government Printing Office.

33. Shaw, J. H. (1987). Causes and control of dental caries. *New England Journal of Medicine, 317,* 996–1004.

34. Smith, D. W., Bierman, E. L., & Robinson, N. M. (Eds.). (1978). *The biologic ages of man: From conception through old age* (2nd ed.). Philadelphia: W. B. Saunders.

35. Smith, N. (1986). Should children run in distance events? *Journal of the American Medical Association, 255,* 820.

36. Stewart, R. E., et al. (Eds.). (1982). *Pediatric dentistry: Scientific and clinical practice.* St. Louis: C. V. Mosby.

37. Tanner, J. M. (1989). *Foetus into man: Physical growth from conception to maturity* (rev. ed.). Cambridge, MA: Harvard University Press.

38. Tissier, G. (1983). Bedwetting at 5 years of age. *Health Visitor, 56,* 333–335.

39. Tuft, L., & Mueller, H. L. (1970). *Allergy in children.* Philadelphia: W. B. Saunders.

40. U.S. National Institutes of Health, Office of Medical Applications of Research. (1985). Lowering blood cholesterol to prevent heart disease. *Journal of the American Medical Association, 253,* 2080–2086.

41. Von Hilsheimer, G. (1974). *Allergy, toxins, and the learning-disabled child.* San Rafael, CA: Academic Therapy Publications.

42. Waechter, E. H., Phillips, J., & Holaday, B. (1985). *Nursing care of children* (10th ed.). Philadelphia: J. B. Lippincott.

43. Whaley, L. F., & Wong, D. L. (1989). *Essentials of pediatric nursing* (3rd ed.). St. Louis: C. V. Mosby.

44. Wiedman, W., et al. (1983). Diet in the healthy child. *Circulation, 67,* 1411–1414.

45. Yonas, A., & Granrud, C. E. (1985). Reading as a measure of infant spatial perception. In G. Gottlieb & N. A. Krasnegor (Eds.), *Measurement of audition and vision in the first year of postnatal life* (pp. 301–322). Norwood, NJ: Ablex.

46. Zylke, J. W. (1988). Does physical fitness of today's children foretell the shape of tomorrow's adult American? *Journal of the American Medical Association, 259,* 2344–2349.

Cognitive Development During the School-Age Years

Keith Holly and Clara S. Schuster

Just as the goals of education go beyond memorizing the alphabet, the rules of grammar, the multiplication tables, and the correct pronunciation of words, our interest in children's development goes beyond the labeling and classification of children into various developmental stages, or pigeonholing them into categories based on intelligence test results. Our concern is to find ways to understand and encourage a child's uniqueness and to stimulate creativity. Study of cognitive development of school-age children must include the effect of sociocultural factors on cognition (and vice versa) as well as the strategies and styles employed in processing information. Clues to the school-ager's thinking process are extracted from the questions they ask and the analogies, metaphors, and reasoning they use in interacting with others.

Today's children enter school with more diverse experiences than their predecessors. Television, movies, computers, mechanical toys, and travel provide contemporary children with experiences beyond the thoughts or dreams of their parents and teachers at the same age. These encounters with the world affect the child's perceptions, the information processed, and the alternatives considered for solving problems or for facing the activities of daily living.

During the school years, children gain new knowledge, new insights, greater mental flexibility, and increased potential for creative productions. Although the rate of intellectual development may differ somewhat according to family and culture, the patterns are similar. This chapter examines some of the theories and models of intelligence and the factors that affect learning.

CONCEPTS OF COGNITIVE DEVELOPMENT

Bruner's Theory

Jerome Bruner observes that children gradually learn strategies for hypothesis testing during the school years.[7] Consequently, problem solving becomes more efficient, consistent, and reliable than the random guessing of the preschooler. The young school-ager still has difficulty forming hypotheses or tentative concepts necessary for solving problems, however. For example, when children play the game "animal, vegetable, or mineral?" they try to guess the word or concept the other has in mind by initially asking whether the object is an animal, vegetable, or mineral. The goal is to guess the correct answer with the fewest questions. The strategy of going from general categories to subcategories, and then to specific questions that lead to identification is much easier for a 10 to 12 year old than for a 7 year old, who has less ability to form concept categories and thus must rely on random guessing.

Piaget's Concrete Operational Thought

A child's thoughts take on wings when they make the transition from the intuitive thought processes of the preschooler to the logical operations of the school-ager. No longer are one's thoughts and understandings restricted by cognitive egocentrism, centration, or the perceptual qualities of a stimulus. Faced with differing interpretations of reality by peers and adults, the school-ager begins to recognize differing points of view and to distinguish his own from that of others.[47] Thought moves from preoperational affective reasoning and imitation to operational reflection. Thus, the child begins to develop "logical socialized thought." Piaget states that a permanent, progressive equilibration is finally established as the processes of assimilation and accommodation are integrated.[47]

Interpretations of reality lose their mysticism as the child realizes that a physical cause or explanation is behind every event (hence the growing skepticism about Santa Claus and the Tooth Fairy). "Why?" and "How?" become the predominant themes of these years as the child searches for the rules of logic. The school-ager, in looking for the functional links between objects and events, may make inferences, but *systematic search* for "the truth" is still limited.[52] With the wedding of naïve logic and classification skills, the child gradually develops a consistency of reasoning. Reasoning is limited to concrete objects and actions (what is), however, since verbal propositions and abstract issues (what might be) are not yet comprehended. The child cannot yet analyze his or her own thoughts or anticipate problems of the future.

New Skills

Concrete operational processes do not appear all at once. The child may use operational thought in some areas but preoperational in others. Skills continue to emerge over the entire period and beyond.

Concept Formation

Because of extreme cognitive egocentrism, *preoperational* concepts and thought were limited to the perceptual qualities of objects and actions of the moment. Most of the problem-solving approaches were limited to one-to-one correspondence of perceptual qualities (see Fig. 10-3). With *concrete* operations, the child becomes more organized and can attend to multiple environmental stimuli. Consequently, the child is able to group several observations and operations into one concept, eclipsing the need to physically manipulate the transformation from one state to another. The child begins to examine and attend to what is important and ignore the irrelevant, thus discriminating the distinguishing features essential for logical groupings. The child realizes the need to mentally reverse himself or herself to place the right shoe on the right foot of the other person. The loss of egocentricity and centration result in marked increase in flexibility of thinking, conceptualizing, and, thus, learning about the environment.

Decentration

One of the cardinal skills of the concrete operational period is the ability to decentrate. No longer is the child tied to just one feature or one dimension of an object or event for thinking purposes. Several features or relationships can be kept in mind simultaneously, compared, or grouped as necessary for identifying relationships. Patterns of relationships can be visualized in the groupings of smaller objects. Decentration is essential for solving conservation tasks. The school-ager understands that a nickel is worth less than a dime since he or she no longer centrates on the size but on the concept of exchange value that has emerged with the development of a concept of stability of number. Suddenly, an adult male can be a brother, father, husband, and uncle all at the same time (but to different people) even though he is the child's grandfather.

Transitivity

Transitivity or "transformational reasoning" is the ability "to follow successive changes with all their possible detours and reversals."[52] One can start at point A and understand all the steps to arrive at point B. At this stage, the child is able to show the position of a pencil halfway through the process of falling from a perpendicular to a horizontal position, and he or she can put a series of 4 to 5 pictures in sequential order (e.g., an apple from whole to core state).

"Transitivity of equality" emerges in the late school years. The child reasons, "if A = B, and B = C, then A = C." B is used to facilitate grouping of the two equations. Thus, the skill of transitivity is essential for the emergence of logical operations.

Reversibility

Once the child is able to trace the steps of a transformation from point or condition A to point or condition B, then these steps can be retraced, and the whole process can be reversed. Piaget identifies this skill as the "manifestation of a permanent equilibration between the assimilation of things to the mind and the accommodation of the mind to things."[49] The child can fold a paper up into an airplane or a bird and reverse the process to see the fold lines, use a musical scale to go up or down, melt Jello, take a toy apart and put it back together, and walk to school and back without getting lost. This skill is essential for understanding addition and subtraction (e.g., $3 + 5 = 8, 8 - 5 = 3$).

Seriation

Seriation is the ability to organize objects into a continuum based on quantitative changes in one dimension, such as length, weight, color shades, or height. The older preschooler might be able to make some orderly arrangements through creating general groupings (larger versus smaller sticks) or through trial and error, but the school-ager understands the task before actively solving it and creates a plan of attack before beginning (find the heaviest or darkest object in the group yet to be sorted).

Equivalency

When the seriation skill is combined with the skill of transitivity of equality, the child is able to combine two seriated groups with a one-to-one correspondence on the same dimension (e.g., matching differing sizes of balls to go with descending sizes of bats; fitting different sizes of toys into ascending sizes of boxes; or matching intensity of color changes in two or more colors). The notion of **equivalency** builds quickly from this new combinatorial ability and enables the child to find all the numbers, which when added together, add up to X. Concepts of money denominations (ten pennies = 2 nickels = 1 dime), counting by 2's or 5's, and the foundations for algebra skills all lie in the burgeoning skill of equivalency. Even the simple skills of weighing or balancing a scale depend on the notion of equivalency (Fig. 21-1).

Classification

Greater attention to the fine differences between objects enables the child to group and organize them into classes according to some stable criterion. As objects develop a stable identity, they can be divided into groupings using "scientific" criteria. Increased sophistication in cognitive processes enable the child to arrange them into hierarchical relationships as the child begins to attend to similarities as well as differences. Subclasses and multiple classifications are recognized. This skill has marked implications for the learning of botany and biology, even of family genealogies (e.g., try to convince a preschooler that a poodle and a wolf belong to the same family of animals). The child begins to be able to count by 5's and 10's around 7 years, and by 2's around 8 years.

Conservation

As the child begins to understand the permanence of the identity of objects, perceptual (especially visual) thinking is replaced by cognitive reasoning. The child realizes that some salient quantitative property of the object continues to exist even though other dimensions of the object change. Irrelevant changes can be ignored while attention is focused toward the significant factor. The skills of conservation do not appear all at once. The simpler, more concrete conservations appear first, and the more complex and abstract appear later. Seriation skills on various dimensions appear to emerge at about the same time as the corresponding conservation skill.

Number. Children's concept of number "goes hand in hand with the development of logic."[48] This skill is essentially the first concrete operational one to emerge. The classic experiment is to put two sets of six pebbles, checkers, pennies, or whatever in front of the child in equal length lines. The one-to-one correspondence can be pointed out. If the examiner asks, "Which line has more?" the preschool child looks amazed and laughs, saying that they are the same. Now the examiner lengthens one line by spreading out the objects and repeats the question. The centrating preschooler says that the longer line contains more objects. The child who is able to conserve number looks at the examiner with incredulity, wondering about his or her intelligence level! One study

FIGURE 21–1.
New cognitive skills enable school-agers to expand their understanding of the world and significant concepts. It is easier to remain focused on a task if parents are involved, interested, and supportive.

indicates that "84% of 5-year olds, 94% of 6-year-olds, and 98% of 7-year-olds are able to conserve number."[45] As the child's concept of number becomes stabilized, he or she is able to do simple additions and subtractions. Manipulation of blocks, pictures, game pieces, and other concrete objects facilitates early counting and mathematical skill mastery.[33]

Mass. The second conservation skill to emerge (shortly after the first) is that of mass. The child now understands that changing a ball of clay into a sausage or a pancake does not change the quantity of mass. Combined with the skill of reversibility, the child now realizes that it can be changed back into the ball and will be the same size as the original ball.

Weight. Around 9 to 10 years of age, the child realizes that weight is a constant factor regardless of the type of object weighed, the shape, or the number of pieces the original object may be broken into.[49] The child now knows that two balls of clay remain the same weight even if one is cut into multiple pieces or flattened into a pancake. The classic question used to tease children is, "Which weighs more, a pound of feathers or a pound of rocks?" The nonconserving child takes the question seriously, the conserver may get angry at the stupidity of the question.

Volume. The skill of conservation of volume is more abstract and consequently does not emerge until the end of the concrete operational period (11–12 years of age).[49] The classic experiment is to present the child with two test tubes filled with equal amounts of colored fluid. One test tube is then poured into a petri dish and the child is asked which container has the most fluid. The nonconserver focuses on one perceptual dimension and makes a choice between the two, "because it is taller, or fatter."

Another way conservation of volume is assessed is to provide the child with equal-size containers of water and then provide the child with two obviously different-size objects (e.g., a small, heavy rock and a large piece of wood) to place in the water and ask, "Which object will make the water rise higher?" The nonconserver tends to concentrate on the weight of the object.[50] The 7 to 8 year old says that the heavy object will cause the water to rise, regardless of the size of the second object. The 7 to 9 year old still concentrates on the weight, saying that the rock is heavy on the bottom, the wood is heavy on the top of the water (still assimilating to their own concept of volume). The conserver (about 10–11 years) can correctly explain that volume, not weight, causes the water to rise.[50] However, it is not until 11 to 12 years that the child has a stable sense of conservation of volume. At this point, the child is able to take two balls of clay, flatten one into a pancake, and correctly predict that they will both displace the same amount of water in the container.[50]

Perceptual and Spatial Organization

Cognitive Maps. Cognitive maps are mental images about spatial relationships. They are built from the retained perceptual skills of the preschooler combined with the transitivity skill of concrete operations. Cognitive maps help col-lect, organize, store, recall, and manipulate information about the spatial environment.[14] Cognitive maps are used to get around in houses, locate objects in the yard, and to go from one location to another in towns and cities. When someone asks the way to a particular store, one must first get a mental image of the streets and significant structures or landmarks that will help to guide the person step by step to his destination. The 10- to 12-year-old child is more efficient at identifying significant landmarks, estimating distance, discovering and correcting navigation errors, and using sophisticated spatial reasoning abilities than younger school-age children.[11,67]

Cognitive mapping has been used as a memory tool by students to recreate pictures, diagrams, or flow charts for recall on tests. Cognitive mapping is a prerequisite to the higher skill used in solving geometry problems. "Graphic representations" are visual maps of concept and relationships, such as the life cycle of a butterfly, flow chart of an automobile plant, pie charts of data, or a pictorial family tree. Cognitive maps are fundamental to skilled thinking because they provide information and opportunities for analysis that reading alone or linear outlining cannot provide. Many learning disabled and dyslexic children experience difficulty with this skill.

Figure-Ground Activities. Children's perceptions of the world are initially global in scope because they see whole objects such as trees, houses, or cars rather than their component parts. With development, perception becomes more selective, analytical, and finally integrative in gaining new perceptions. The ability to isolate a specific stimulus from its background is called "figure-ground segregation." Decentration enables the school-ager to identify increasingly obscure objects in complex pictures or to identify that the same lines can simultaneously represent the boundaries or parts of two objects. School-agers like to practice this skill through "find the hidden picture" or "find the camouflaged object" games by separating imbedded figures from their backgrounds. Auditory figure-ground activities (more commonly referred to as auditory discrimination) include identifying the instruments that are being played in a band or orchestra.

Time, Distance, and Speed. **Time** cannot be perceived through the five senses; a logical concept of time must be developed by coordination of perceptually based cues such as succession of activities. Initially, time is understood only in terms of the relation of one activity to another routine activity in the child's life (e.g., before or after lunch, nap). Gradually this understanding is extended to weekly activities (e.g., before or after church) and then to seasonal relationships. The seasons of the year are identified by temperature, color of leaves, the variety of plants living, and other discrete perceptions about nature. Their sequential order provides a sense of the passage of time. During the school years, "temporal relations are merged in the single notion of time."[52] Now the child can begin to understand and use clock time. However, although dates are memorized, concepts of historical time (continuity of eras outside one's life span) are still elusive.

Piaget contends that length and **distance** are psychologically distinct although they are interdependent. An understanding of distance is central to understanding space. A child of 9 to 10 years of age is beginning to make comparisons of distance with the amount of time it takes to get from one location to another. Children's judgment of distance seems to be influenced by many variables in addition to the time it takes to get from point A to point B. (If I walk slow, it is a long distance. If I walk fast, it is a short distance.) Barriers in the pathway, different starting and stopping points, the attractiveness (or unattractiveness) of the pathway, and the motivation of the child still influence the judgment of distance.

Piaget used toy trains to experiment with children's concept of **speed**. He asked children to watch two toy trains starting at different points on the track to determine which train went faster. Four and five year olds concentrated on stopping points of the two trains and seemed to ignore starting points. Only when a train came from behind and passed the other train did the child declare it was faster. Older children are able to consider both starting and stopping points to determine train velocity when time is held constant. At about 8 years of age, the child begins to understand that speed is the relationship between time and distance traveled.[49] It is not until formal operations are mastered (during adolescence) that a person is able to coordinate time, speed, and distance to solve the unknown factor.

Application

The new cognitive skills of the school-ager serve as intrinsic motivators for learning how to work. The child's curiosity and perseverance spur increased mastery over the environment. A supportive environment provides adequate experiences and materials, teaches approaches to problem solving, encourages reflection, allows for trial-and-error learning, and provides corrective feedback, success, and encouragement.

Money Management

Teaching children how to manage money is a direct application of mathematical skills. Allowances help children understand the relative value of money. Grade-school children become increasingly more capable of planning and making financial choices. Taking children on shopping trips to discuss sales, prices, quality, and quantity of goods helps them learn about the responsibilities of money. Having them plan ahead for purchases, keep a ledger, and make purchases helps them learn to handle money judiciously. By the age of 8 or 9, children can manage a savings account and begin to understand the control of withdrawals and deposits and the way accounts earn interest. By 10 to 12 years, many children start working for neighbors by doing odd jobs such as lawn work, washing cars, and walking dogs. Being paid for work and handling money gives children a new appreciation of and responsibility for money management.

Memory Tasks

As children get older they are expected to recognize and recall more information. Children delight in games of memory such as Memory, Concentration, or Follow-the-Leader Sentence (i.e., I went to London and saw a *pig*; the next child adds onto the sentence saying, "I went to London and saw a pig and a *horse*," and so on, until the sentence becomes quite lengthy and difficult to recall). A young child given the numbers 1, 5, 9, 13, 17, and 21 tries to parrot the numbers but without seeing relationships. If the child can count, he or she may perceive a serial order according to numerical size. In a later developmental stage, he or she may remember the numbers as all odd numbers. Memory is most effective when the set of numbers is recognized as a pattern that adds 4 to each previous number. When a child learns to use memory cues and clues to store and retrieve information instead of using "rote memory," learning is markedly increased. School-agers also are fascinated with learning special communication codes such as the Morse code, American Sign Language, a foreign language, or Braille (Fig. 21-2).

Games and Hobbies

To Piaget, play and cognition are inseparable and interdependent; each supports the growth of the other.[47] Any time a new skill is acquired and the individual practices the skill purely for the sake of pleasure at mastery, play is the result. Play is pure assimilation, the repetition of a behavior or exercise of a schema solely for the pleasure of feeling virtuosity or power over the skill.[47]

Piaget identified three major types of play. **Practice play,** found predominantly at the sensorimotor and preoperational

FIGURE 21–2.
This girl is using sensorimotor memory skills to assist her with the memorization of highly abstract representational symbols (musical notes in this case).

stage, includes physical skills such as running, jumping, lifting objects, and throwing objects. It also includes mental skills such as asking "why?" questions, playing alliteration or synonym games, or making up stories. (This type of play may include making up stories about the cause of situations to see if an adult will believe them. The adult calls this "lying," but the child sees it as practicing the art of getting someone to believe what is not true by controlling behavior and vocal intonations.)[18] In **symbolic games,** objects are used as make-believe representations of the real world. The child may play "cowboy" by using a stick for a horse, string for the horse's bridle, and a rock or carrot for a gun. **Games with rules** begin to emerge during the concrete operational stage. Initially, children try to impose their rules on others, even changing rules as the game progresses to ensure winning. Gradually, they understand that games use regulated stable rules of agreement between the players or a code of rules handed down from earlier generations (e.g., hide-and-go-seek, baseball, checkers, "Sorry").[47] Games enable the child to deal with competition, loss, success, and strategy development within a confined context—great preparation for life's realities. School-aged children also begin to take on and play out predesigned roles and are competitive with their peers to see who can throw farthest, run fastest, or jump highest.

A fourth category, **constructional games** or **model-building games,** is identified by Piaget, although he specifies that it includes the element of accommodation or work and therefore is not pure play as are the other three categories. Mastery of skills during this period may lay the foundation for a hobby that can last a lifetime (e.g., building model airplanes or cars, needlework, pet breeding, woodcarving, poetry writing, art, plant growing). Some older children and adults progress from models to building the real objects, such as rebuilding antique cars and old houses. For some, a hobby may turn into a career. Playing games and getting involved in hobbies help children develop their muscle and motor skills, as well as concepts of size, color, shape, texture, weight, mass, and time. They become more proficient in classifying and sequencing of objects. They learn how to work and how to concentrate and persevere at a task. They also can learn social skills and why to obey codes of conduct and rules of behavior (Fig. 21-3).

Humor

A relationship appears to exist between a child's level of cognitive development and the type of humor appreciated. Humor depends on the elements of surprise, incongruity, and discrepancy from the expected. The ability of children to resolve incongruities to enjoy a joke usually emerges between the ages of 6 and 8 years. At the preoperational level, children may laugh at jokes because everyone else does, but they cannot explain why the joke is funny. The concrete operational child can give more logical explanations of jokes. Humor is based on language that can have multiple meanings, such as that used in ambiguities, analogies, and puns (e.g., "I

FIGURE 21–3.
It is critical that children receive adequate instruction and develop a healthy sense of safety precautions before they use new equipment.

saw a man-eating gray shark at the beach. That's nothing, I saw a man eating pink salmon at the picnic table!"). Jokes that take time to figure out and are moderately hard for young children to understand are often funniest to older children because it gives them the opportunity to demonstrate their superior cognitive development. The mastery of symbolic functioning as well as the beginning of logic enables children to appreciate a play on words.

Safety

During early childhood, children are learning to obey the rules for safety enforced by parents. Gradually, as concrete operations emerge, the child is able to consolidate the rules into schemata for "safe" or "unsafe" behaviors, objects, places, and situations. The ability to exert self-discipline can now override curiosity, thus decreasing impulsiveness. Increased understanding of cause–effect relationships and the ability to judge spatial relationships help the child accommodate to the realities of environmental dangers and the safe use of tools such as knives and lawn mowers. However, new situations may require new solutions, and the child's processing of the situation may be too slow to avoid the danger. In moments of stress or excitement, the child may revert to the impulsive, intuitive thinking of preschool years (Fig. 21-4). Consequently, safety rules and supervision are still essential for this age group. The school-age years are a critical time to teach and reinforce pedestrian, vehicular, and fire safety, drug avoidance, familial values on sex, and phone and stranger safety. Every child should know how to obtain help (e.g., 911 emergency phone number) and to give basic first aid (e.g., how to stop bleeding and give artificial respiration).

FIGURE 21–4.
School-agers are easily distracted and frequently forget to look where they are going, a fact that precipitates many mishaps.

Beliefs

As school-agers begin to realize that specific, explainable causes are behind every event, they gradually lose their belief in the power of magical thought, myths, and magic. "How did the tooth fairy know that I lost a tooth today?" "How does Santa get in the house when we don't have a fireplace?" "How can he deliver presents to ALL the children in ALL the world in one night?" They begin to understand the role of parents and other adults in the continuation of cultural myths.

Assumptive Realities. As the school-ager develops new cognitive skills, unique insights into "the secrets of the adult world" emerge. However, even though the child is not yet able to differentiate between assumption and fact, these new revelations may be treated as eternal verities.[19] When the child's unvalidated hypothesis is confused with reality, it results in exaggerated beliefs, **assumptive realities.**[19] The discovery of *the truth* makes a profound impression on the global, diffuse ideation typical of preoperational thought, creating a ripple effect on other schemata as the ideas that surround a

focus undergo "abrupt transformation on the basis of changes in an isolated idea."[10] A new form of egocentrism—pride and assurance in one's own cognitive skills—emerges. This form of egocentrism, which is characteristic of concrete operations, forces the child to refuse to alter a hypothesis or belief even in the face of contradictory evidence. If evidence contradicts the hypothesis, it is rejected, argued away, or assimilated into the hypothesis. The child's assumption *cannot* be wrong![19] The child often "takes rules as a challenge to his own cleverness and attempts to break them without getting caught"[19] as a means of proving his or her cleverness.

Cognitive Conceit Versus Cognitive Ineptitude. One manifestation of assumptive realities, according to David Elkind, is **cognitive conceit.**[19] As the child's newly acquired "concrete operational vision penetrates the aura of omniscience and omnipotence surrounding adults,"[10] the child begins to realize that adults do not know everything and they are not able to do everything as the child had believed during the preschool years. This awakening can lead to an exaggerated confidence in one's own cognitive powers, with a frequent pitting of wits against those of adults. The child may try to "catch" adults in verbal games (e.g., "I *did* wash my hands. You *didn't* tell me to use soap!") to prove their hypothesis or to increase their own sense of skill.

Awareness of the adult's "humanness" may reawaken the vulnerability experienced during the separation–individuation crisis, spurring the need to develop strategies for facing the world: "If my parents cannot perpetually protect me, then I must find ways to protect myself."

Children who persist in the preoperational belief that others know everything and that they know nothing develop what Elkind refers to as **cognitive ineptitude.**[19] This description fits well with Erikson's concept of **inferiority** (see Chap. 22). Many school-agers identify with or become engrossed by games or stories that exploit the talents and virtues of school-agers and pubescents (e.g., *The Babysitter's Club* and *The Hardy Boys* mysteries, Nintendo, Teenage Mutant Ninja Turtles, Superboy). Such sagas enable young people to identify with the characters, imagine themselves as strong or adroit, work out problems or fears at their own pace in a play forum, or provide a temporary escape from their own perceived weaknesses. Cognitive conceit may also lead the child to find external reasons why he or she lost a game and to brag excessively when he or she wins, especially in a game against adults.[19]

The Foundling Fantasy. The **foundling fantasy,** an apparent by-product of cognitive conceit, leads some children to imagine themselves to be the child of a wealthy, famous, or aristocratic person. They believe themselves to be adopted, or they believe that their identity was confused in the hospital or shortly thereafter. They only need someone who knows the truth to reveal the facts to release them from the "tyranny and unbearable suffering" (even the best of parents suffer through this normal delusion) of their present home and elevate them to their proper status as heirs to power and wealth.

INTELLIGENCE AND LEARNING

Models of Intelligence

Binet's "Global" Model

In 1905, Alfred Binet and Theodore Simon were commissioned by the Minister of Education in Paris to find a way to identify mentally retarded children to offer them special education programs.[4] They developed the first known intelligence tests and model of intelligence to facilitate the process. In 1916, these intelligence tests were revised and expanded by Terman and Merrill from Stanford University and became known as the Stanford-Binet Intelligence Scale, which still is one of the most popular intelligence tests used by psychologists today. It represents the *"global" model of intelligence* because it summarizes the various abilities and skills into a single score, known as the Intelligence Quotient (IQ) or, in more recent years, as a Standard Age Score (SAS).[70]

"Two-Factor" Theory

While Binet was developing his tests, a prominent English psychologist, C. E. Spearman, developed a *"two-factor" theory of intelligence,* consisting of "general capacity" (g) and "specific capacity" (s) (Fig. 21-5).[61]

Guilford's "Structure-of-Intellect"

In 1967, J. P. Guilford and his colleagues at the University of Southern California proposed a three-dimensional "structure-of-intellect" (SI) model of intelligence composed of operations, contents, and products, each of which was comprised of multiple sub-components (Fig. 21-6).[28].

The five operations times the four contents times the six products equaled 120 total factors. Guilford attempted to

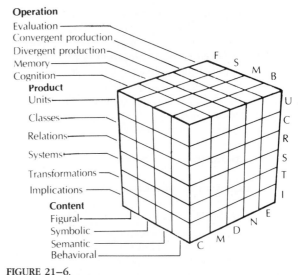

FIGURE 21–6.
The structure-of-intellect model and definitions of its categories.

describe, isolate, and assess each of the 120 units separately. For example, one of the 120 factors called "MSU" (Memory [M], Symbolic [S], Units [U]) might be measured by recall of a set of numbers. Solving an arithmetic problem might assess the "NSC" factor (Convergent [N], Symbolic [S], Classes [C]). The strength of the SI model is the diversity of intelligences that can be imagined, described, and possibly strengthened through individualized learning experiences.

"Multiple Intelligence" Model

In 1983, Gardner proposed a "multiple intelligence" model that consists of seven distinct intelligences: linguistic, logical-mathematical, spatial, musical, bodily-kinesthetic, interpersonal, and intrapersonal.[25] This view claims that these seven intelligences form the core capacities involved in all cultural roles, ranging from parenting to a variety of adaptational and occupational skills. Achievements in each area depend on basic genetic potentials interacting with environmental opportunities and experiences.

Sternberg's Triarchic Theory

Robert Sternberg, one of the newest theorists on intellectual functioning, sees intelligence as a multi-factored, as yet poorly understood, entity.[63] He feels that measures of the intelligence quotient offer a limited picture of one's cognitive functioning.[71] Sternberg notes the difference between academic or "schoolhouse" intelligence, based on memorization, critical thinking, and use of processing skills in the academic setting, and practical or "street-smart" intelligence, which emphasizes application of knowledge to the realities of one's environment and lifestyle.[65] In his search for differences between the two, Sternberg developed the Triarchic Theory of Human Intelligence, which consists of three functions or subtheories.[63]

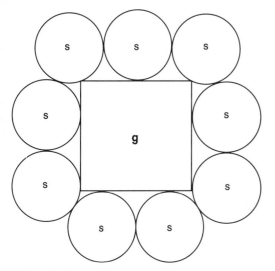

FIGURE 21–5.
Spearman's two-factor theory of intelligence.

The **componential subtheory** "specifies the structures and mechanics that underlie intelligent behavior."[63] This subtheory is broken down into three components: (1) **knowledge acquisition components**, which (a) *selectively encode* information (separate relevant from irrelevant information), (b) *selectively compare* the new information with what one already knows, and (c) *selectively combine* or integrate relevant knowledge to make new cognitive structures; (2) the **meta-components**, which control information processing, construct plans, and monitor one's functioning; and (3) the **performance components**, which execute the plan.[65]

The **experiential subtheory** looks at the role of past experience in knowledge use. This form of intelligence is expressed by (a) the ability to *deal with novelty* and (b) the ability to *automatize performance* on a given task or situation in order to expend one's cognitive energies on dealing with the novel factors involved. As greater expertise develops, more knowledge and processing issues are packed into a processing system to reduce energy expenditure. This process corresponds with Piaget's schemata. Insight is a critical factor in adaptation to novelty. The degree to which one is insightful allows one to select facts and information or a combination of facts and information from a wide variety of choices that are pertinent to the situation. Insight enables one to see relationships and to construct a working subtheory or processing system. Insight is actually the effective use of selective encoding, selective comparison, and selective combination.[71] Gifted children are noted to have exceptional ability to deal with novelty because of their insight skills,[64] whereas retarded people are noted to have inadequate automatization skills.[63]

The third subtheory of Sternberg's model, **contextual intelligence**, emphasizes the interface with the external world through (a) *adaptation* (changing one's self to meet the demands of the situation), (b) *selection* of a more appropriate environment or situation, or (c) *shaping* the situation to meet one's own needs and goals when a change cannot be made. An example of the latter would be finding a way to convince parents to allow a pet when they do not want one.

Sternberg recognizes that people may have strengths in one function and weaknesses in the others. Children whose strengths are "componential" may receive high scores on multiple choice tests and activities that emphasize analytic thinking. "Experientially" strong children may show insight and creativity in situations that appear to be routine to other children. Creativity and IQ are not synonymous, according to Sternberg.[63] A child strong in "contextual" intelligence learns to "play the game," attending to environmental feedback and the success of others to adapt successfully to the demands of the situation. This child would be described as having "street smarts." Sternberg emphasizes that truly intelligent behavior involves all three subcomponents and therefore can only be understood in context; it is how one exploits available resources to meet one's goals.[63] The "gifted" child is "more effective in all three processes of knowledge acquisition."[65]

Sternberg shares that his theory does not negate the concept of qualitatively different cognitive stages.[63] He gives acknowledgment frequently to the necessity of mastering Piaget's formal operational stage for the processing of higher-level analogies and abstract problems. Personality, rather than intelligence per se, is seen as the critical factor in balancing the three functions.[65]

Intelligence and Cognition Testing

The Intelligence Quotient

Intelligence is usually interpreted as the ability to solve problems related to one's cultural and environmental demands. More advanced societies have developed assessment tools to determine the match between the two. Dozens of individual and group tests are available to assess various age groups under different conditions. Schools are the largest users of intelligence tests. Although IQ tests were originally designed to be used for academic placement of students, their popularity has spread to industry and community agencies.

Computation and Interpretation of IQ Scores

A child's mental age (MA) is determined by questions answered on a standardized test. The mental age represents the "norm" or average score for a representative sample of children. A "ratio IQ" is derived by dividing the mental age (MA) by the chronological age (CA) times 100, using the following formula: $MA/CA \times 100 = IQ$.

Most intelligence tests employ a "deviation IQ" to interpret the meaning of the ratio score. This deviation assumes that the mathematical (mean) is an IQ of 100 with a standard deviation of 15 (or 16) IQ points. Average IQs range from 84 (or 85) to 115 (or 116) (Fig. 21-7).

The mentally gifted are usually considered to be two standard deviations above the mean for the IQ test (the upper 2%–3% of the population) or an IQ score above 130 to 132. The mentally retarded are usually considered to be two standard deviations below the mean (the lower 2%–3% of the population), which translates into an IQ score below 68 to 70.

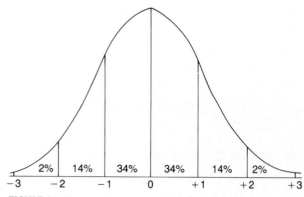

FIGURE 21–7.
IQ distribution.

Since scores on intelligence tests depend on many factors, any one IQ score reflects a person's performance on that particular test at that particular time. Standardized individual intelligence tests, such as the Stanford-Binet or the Wechsler (given in a one-to-one situation), are usually more valid than group tests because they are more sensitive to the needs of the individual child and are broader in scope.

Intelligence tests are often described as biased against minorities, non-English speaking children or adults, and lower socioeconomic groups. The original norms on intelligence tests in America were made on predominantly middle and upper class white children. Attempts have been made to eliminate cultural biases and to construct "culture free tests." However, these attempts have become an impossible dream. "Culture-fair tests" by Cattell, the Ravens Progressive Matrices, Goodenough-Harris Drawing Test, and the Leiter International Performance Scale are used to reduce the language and verbal aspects that increase cultural biases because of language or culture.[9] In an effort to provide fair assessments for disadvantaged blacks, the "Counterbalance General Intelligence Tests"[13] and the "Black Intelligence Test of Cultural Homogeneity"[77] for lower class blacks were developed. These tests attempt to use words and life experiences common to the African American culture. However, African Americans do not represent a unified cultural experience.

Nature–Nurture of Intelligence

Is intelligence inherited? Evidence that indicates a genetic factor includes correlations between IQ scores for people with varying degrees of genetic similarity. Studies of identical twins find correlations from .7 to .9, and of fraternal twins from .5 to .7.[5] Median correlations of identical twins reared together is .87, identical twins reared apart, .75; fraternal twins reared together, .58; parents and their children, .40; siblings reared together, .36; unrelated children reared together, .30; and unrelated children reared apart, essentially .00.[35]

Does the environment determine intellectual potentials? Research consistently shows positive correlations between IQ and socioeconomic status (e.g., income, education, occupation). Higher IQs generally are found in children of higher social classes. Since socioeconomic status and educational levels are closely related, it is difficult to determine if the IQs are due to educational difference or other socioeconomic factors. Children raised in poverty tend to have lower IQs.[69] Poor people tend to have larger families and thus less time for individualized attention. Lower income also decreases the likelihood of providing opportunities for stimulating experiences. Affluent and educated people tend to buy more books, newspapers, and magazines and to provide their children with more educational opportunities than poor people. In one study, 25 children, all considered mentally retarded and unadoptable, were moved from an orphanage to an institution where they received more personalized attention.[59] Later, when these supposedly retarded children were adopted by parents who provided a loving and socially stimu-lating environment, they showed an average *gain* of 29 IQ points! The children who remained in the orphanage *lost* an average of 26 IQ points.

It has been known for some years that on IQ tests Oriental immigrants score as high as or higher than Caucasian children in the United States. Nationality and ethnic studies have indicated about 11 IQ points of superiority of native Japanese children over native American children.[40] Asian students out-perform their American counterparts in mathematics and sciences.[66] Comparison of Asian social and scholastic environments reveals that (1) there is much parental and social pressure toward a career trajectory, (2) the curriculum stresses math and science comprehension, and (3) school-agers spend more time each day, more hours each week, and more weeks per year on in-class and out-of-class math and science activities.[66] It would appear that the child-rearing practices, good health and nutrition, high goal expectations, and the opportunity to practice and apply concepts can help to account for superior results on intelligence and academic tests.

Uses and Values of IQ Scores

In addition to identifying mentally retarded people who need additional educational assistance, intelligence tests are used to identify gifted children and children with learning problems; they are used for assisting with the diagnosis of neurological problems, mental disorders, and anxiety and emotional states and for a variety of clinical purposes. In actuality, IQ tests measure how much a person has learned, the person's ability to retrieve that information appropriately, and his or her ability to take a test. Although intelligence test scores tend to be correlated with academic progress (e.g., reading, spelling, arithmetic), to base a person's worth or career future on IQ scores alone is naïve and unfair. Self-confidence, creativity, and social skills are equally important in the expression of cognitive adaptive processes.

Exceptional Learners

Exceptional learners are those who deviate from the average to such an extent that they require modification of educational practices.

Gifted

Children who are gifted possess superior intellectual potential. These children have a greater capacity for memory, a more developed ability to scan quickly, have more efficient encoding and superior automatization of thought processes, and faster retrieval of information from memory.[58] Most general intelligence tests emphasize verbal and abstract reasoning; consequently, they may not predict a child's unusual talent in other meaningful areas such as chemistry, music, creative writing, or mathematics.[73]

Many parents and teachers equate high achievement with "giftedness." However, "high achievers" may be less creative but more persevering and conforming to standards than those of high intelligence. Some gifted children do poorly in school because they "march to a different beat of the drum." They are bored and lack motivation to complete what they perceive to be pedantic, unchallenging, unrewarding assignments. Giftedness involves social and motivational properties as well as cognitive qualities (Fig. 21-8).[58]

Most students, regardless of age, desire teachers who promote and allow for divergence in learning experiences by offering opportunities for creative writing and experimenting in the visual and performing arts, the sciences, history, philosophy, and many other areas that are often overlooked in regular classes. Using Guilford's structure-of-intellect as a model, teachers may set up learning centers and use educational experiences that encourage creative thinking, such as fluency (production of ideas), originality (uniqueness of ideas), transformation (variation of ideas), flexibility (modification of ideas), and elaboration (extension of ideas). "Creativity" as expressed by Guilford's model is the "divergent" mental operation and is not necessarily valued in American schools because it is difficult to empirically measure. The traditional classroom teacher stresses memory and convergent thinking because they are easier to measure and use as a basis for evaluating academic performance and grades.

Many states have implemented nontest methods as criteria for giftedness to increase the number of students identified from minority and low-level socioeconomic groups. In addition to superior cognitive skills as identified by IQ tests, schools may include evaluations of academic performance, creative thinking, visual and performing arts, psychomotor skills, and leadership. Affective assessments have been used to determine students' self-concepts, locus of control, need for achievement (motivation), and attitudes toward school. School systems are assuming increasing responsibility for the development of special talents and cognitive skills.

Cognitive maturity is not to be equated with social maturity. They are separate domains and require different experiences to develop. Although some gifted children may be social misfits, as a whole, cognitively precocious children are psychologically and socially mature for their age.[34, 68] Advanced cognitive processes enable them to extract essential social rules. Vice versa, the ability to harness and focus social energies, factors that provide an appearance of maturity, have also enabled the child to attend to and learn from opportunities available in the environment. Studies have shown that gifted children are sensitive to peer behavior and offer more ideas about ways to solve social conflicts and to interact cooperatively.[23, 44] This same sensitivity, and sense of uniqueness, can precipitate depression, suicide, school dropout and criminal activity.[42, 75] Gifted children tend to prefer strategy and computer games, chess, puzzles, and reading.

Kohlberg's work on moral judgments within a social-cognitive framework indicates that children with higher IQs tend to make higher moral decisions than other children of the same age.[37] However, one must recall that Kohlberg's theory was based on Piaget's model of cognitive development, so it has a built-in assumption that higher levels of mental functioning are related to higher levels of moral judgment. However, cognitive developmental levels are frequently higher than moral levels because of the influence of peer pressure and need for social acceptance. Intellectually gifted preadolescent children tend to show average or superior adjustment in self-direction, independence, social skills, freedom from psychopathic trends, sociability, social values, social preferences, and attitudes. Gifted children usually have fewer aggressive and withdrawal tendencies and are less involved in social delinquency (performing minor crimes as a way to achieve or maintain peer relationships) than nongifted children.[39] Intellectually gifted children in elementary school tend to have higher concepts of self-worth, self-esteem, and individualism than nongifted children. Most assessments of general psychosocial competency and adjustment show that

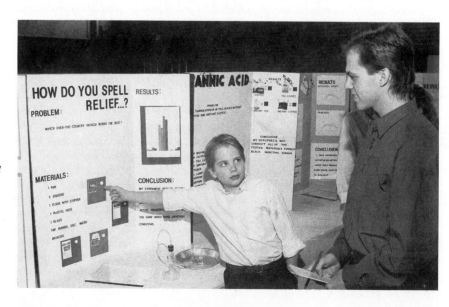

FIGURE 21–8.
School, boys and girls clubs, and other organized programs enable young people to exploit their special interests, talents, and gifts.

intellectually gifted children are at least comparable or superior to those not so designated.[34]

Learning Disabled

Many children have mild to severe learning problems, but they are not mentally retarded. **Learning disability** is a description of a broad category of problems that affects a child's ability to learn, or, as Piaget would see it, the child has difficulty accommodating new material (assimilation still has primacy over accommodation). "Academic skills disorders" may be limited to a specific area, such as arithmetic, expressive writing, or reading. An "attention-deficit disorder" (with or without hyperactivity) may create pervasive learning problems through inattention and impulsiveness. The learning problems may be caused by neurological dysfunctions (caused by chemical imbalance, minimal brain damage, allergy, seizure disorder, or birth defect), an innate processing deficiency, environmental deprivations, helplessness syndrome, failure to "learn how to learn," or critical emotional problems. Most of the time, the etiology is unknown.

Learning disabilities are often identified through a battery of assessments that include personality, IQ, and achievement tests. The child often scores at the normal or above normal range on individual IQ tests, but in achievement tests (e.g., math, reading, spelling) he or she scores two or more grade levels below the expected in academic skills. For example, Larry, a 10-year-old fourth-grader, has a verbal IQ of 120 and a performance IQ of 117 (or a composite IQ of 118). However, his reading vocabulary and reading comprehension scores are at the first-grade level, and his arithmetic scores are at the second-grade level. He also displays mirror writing (writing from right to left and backwards). He is hyperactive and has difficulty following directions. Several neurologists offered a tentative diagnosis of "minimal brain damage" because he sustained a high fever at 11 months of age. After evaluations by the school psychologist, a neurologist, and his family doctor and observational reports from his teacher and parents, he is enrolled in the Educationally Handicapped Class where he can receive special tutorial help from a reading and math specialist to help build sufficient self-confidence and self-esteem to enable him to experience success in school.

The learning disabled may experience multiple learning handicaps. They often are poor listeners, cannot separate significant from irrelevant factors, don't know how to take notes, are unable to work independently or follow through with directions, and are easily distracted. The lack of success in the academic setting precipitates feelings of hopelessness, reduced effort, boredom, detachment from school, and low self-esteem.

Mentally Retarded

The American Association on Mental Deficiency (AAMD) defines "mental retardation" as: "(1) significant subaverage general intellectual functioning; (2) concurrent deficits or impairments in adaptive functioning; (3) onset before the age of 18."[3]

The classification levels of retardation based on the degree of severity are the following:

Mild: 50–55 to 70 level of IQ
Moderate: 35–40 to 50–55 level of IQ
Severe: 20–25 to 35–40 level of IQ
Profound: lower than 20–25 level of IQ

Public schools often have two separate programs for special education of mentally retarded children. Educable Mentally Retarded (EMR) classes are for people with IQs ranging from about 50 to 75. These people often have poor social adaptive behavior skills but usually are capable of reading, writing, and arithmetic skills as high as the sixth grade level when they graduate from school. Trainable Mentally Retarded (TMR) classes are available for people with IQs below 50. Many are able to read simple signs and benefit from special training in caring for self and performing simple job skills.

Some schools offer a separate full or part-time class for "slow learners" (IQ 75–90), whereas others prefer to mainstream (integrate) the children with the regular classes and provide academic assistance from peers as well as the teacher.

For many children, the school is seen as an extension of the family for continued enculturation and socialization. However, there may be a marked discontinuity between the home and the school, especially if the teacher or administration does not appreciate the child's culture or language. As a result, children may fail to do well in school because they have had different life experiences, they do not understand the demands of the school, or they have a different value system. A child may enter school with a different complex of general knowledge and repertoire of competencies. Although potential for success may be high, many of these children have been labeled "slow learners" or "retarded" purely because they do not possess the desired competencies, and subsequently they may be given inferior educational opportunities.

Like giftedness, the diagnosis, identification, and classification of mental retardation can no longer be made solely on the basis of IQ test scores. Other data such as socialization skills, personal adjustment, and self-help skills must be considered. Many public schools use the *Adaptive Behavior Scale,* which assesses factors such as independent functioning, sense of responsibility, physical development, practical intelligence, language development, vocational abilities, and self-direction as part of a test battery to determine eligibility or need for special education.[38] A more recent instrument, *Vineland Adaptive Behavior Scale,* is available in three versions.[60] This scale evaluates communications, daily living skills, socialization, motor skills, and maladaptive behavior.

FACTORS THAT AFFECT LEARNING

Cognitive *processing* consists of using the five senses to take in, decode, mediate, store, and then retrieve information to solve problems. *Learning* is defined as a relatively permanent behavior change resulting from interaction with the environment.

Cognitive Processing

Neurons are tied together in complex networks that allow them to recall past memory patterns of touch, taste, sound, smell, and visual images. These sensory signals are the keys to recognition, categorization, and storage of information. The brain's ability to recognize patterns that are slightly different or incomplete as nonetheless belonging to the same overall group makes problem-solving alternatives almost unlimited. For example, the sight of a part of a chair, or a type of chair never seen before, still can trigger the brain to remember the concept of "chair." The cognitive processing of information includes (1) attending to sensory (e.g., visual, auditory or haptic) stimuli, (2) encoding, (3) storing, and (4) retrieving of information. It also includes (5) planning, (6) making decisions in problem-solving situations, and (7) communicating ideas to others. Cognitive processing may also include (8) using dreams and fantasies creatively to give variety to life experiences (Fig. 21-9).

Metaknowledge

Metacognition refers to awareness of, sensitivity to, and control of one's thinking. Although true metacognition or "thinking about thinking" (making one's own reasoning process the object of introspection) does not appear until the achievement of formal operational thought,[51] several components or precursor (**metaknowledge**) skills begin to emerge during the school-age years, as one becomes aware of the ability to control what is learned and develops ways to enhance memory. School-agers tend not to use metacognitive

FIGURE 21–9.
The young school-ager, who still possesses many learning characteristics of the preoperational child, needs many "hands on" experiences to maintain interest in and to understand topics of study.

processes or "feeling of knowing" judgments unless asked to do so.[8] However, when taught or encouraged to use specific strategies to actively monitor, regulate, and direct learning, the effects are more likely to be efficient and long-lasting.

Metaknowledge operations help the learner to: (1) *predict* the consequences of an action or event; (2) *check* the results of one's actions (to determine whether or not they worked and had the desired effect); (3) *monitor* one's ongoing activities (to assess mastery toward goals); (4) *reality test* to determine whether the activity makes sense to self and others; and (5) *coordinate and control* deliberate attempts to learn and solve problems.[22]

Metaknowledge consists of at least three subdivisions that are closely related to each other: meta-attention, meta-perception, and meta-memory.

Meta-attention

Meta-attention, the awareness and regulation of one's attention level, builds off of the preschooler's task of learning how to harness and focus energies. Past experiences affect one's attention to task. A siren on an ambulance or police car captures our attention, whereas those living in heavily traveled areas may habituate to the sound of cars on a busy street, the sound of a train, or of a plane. Older children learn to focus or refocus on the *important task,* realizing that daydreaming penalizes their problem-solving abilities. The ultimate goal of meta-attention is to discern the relevant from the irrelevant, so that one's energy can be focused on the appropriate task at the appropriate time. The young and inexperienced learner doesn't realize that different tasks require different attention levels. For example, when one reads for pleasure, there is no need to focus on details as one would for material that one will be tested on later. When the stakes are high, the ultimate attention experience is sought. Because attention and memory capacities are limited, it is impossible to remember everything; therefore, it is imperative that one learns to scan, select, and focus on the pertinent factors. To learn this flexibility, school-age children need the opportunity to practice monitoring, controlling, and using different attention levels. This skill is one of the major issues in learning how to work, a critical task for the school-age years. Children's self-regulation relative to meta-attention is to select and control their commitment and attitudes concerning learning tasks.

Teachers, parents, and other significant adults can assist children by helping them to use strategies that increase attention span, avoid distractions, and focus attention on significant stimuli.[22] Enhancing children's visual, auditory, and haptic (touch) search strategies also helps increase attention capacity.

Meta-perception

Meta-perception focuses on the child's awareness and knowledge of his or her perceptions. In early childhood, a child gives an automatic response or reaction with little thought to the reasons why he or she responded to the sensory stimuli in that manner. As the child becomes older, he or she begins to realize that many other interpretations and potential responses are possible. This awareness of alternate views is the beginning of meta-perception, the ability to de-center, to include the perceptions of others, and to consider multiple perceptions simultaneously. As children start asking questions to clarify their perceptions, adults need to be patient, to reinforce them for asking questions (rather than making them feel dumb, incompetent, or stupid for their lack of understanding). Repeated devaluation and negative labeling have a damaging effect on the child's self-esteem and negatively affect intellectual growth and academic achievement.

Teachers and parents can facilitate the meta-perception process by encouraging children to explore their "perceptions" and by being generous in the interpretation of the child's perceptions as he or she goes beyond synesthesia to integrate multiple perceptions from the same or differing modalities.

Meta-memory

Meta-memory is the awareness of one's ability to retain or store information. Young children approach a task that requires memory with enthusiasm, optimistic that they will always remember the information. They seem unaware of a need to use memory pegs or retrieval cues to assist them in the recall process. As children get older and experience the frustration of the inability to retrieve important information, phone numbers, recital pieces, and names, the "need for memory" becomes evident to them. From fourth grade on, children can generally estimate their recall ability about as well as adults.[36] Older children become sensitive to cues and clues that will help them memorize critical information. The ability to associate "new learning" with "old learning" may facilitate the memory process if the child's emotional and attitudinal experiences are positively associated with the old learning. The complexity of memory and meta-memory skills varies with cognitive sophistication, past experiences, and motivations.

Parents, teachers, and others can assist with memory building in the school-age child by sharing techniques such as the use of mnemonic devices (e.g., using Roy G. Biv to remember the colors of the light spectrum in order: red, orange, yellow, green, blue, indigo, and violet; HOMES to remember the names of the Great Lakes: Huron, Ontario, Michigan, Erie, and Superior; or running through the alphabet to remember the first letter of a person's name). Practice in memorizing poetry, Scripture, multiplication tables, and a second language also builds up a child's memory skills.

Cognitive Styles

Individual differences in modes of perceiving, remembering, and thinking are known as "cognitive styles." The term implies that children develop distinctive ways of obtaining, storing, transforming, and using information. Children's styles for processing information are influenced by levels of anxiety,

courage, energy, risk-taking, and motivations. These styles become habits, or automatic thought patterns, through persistent use.

Children tend to be either impulsive or reflective in their approach to learning and problem solving. The interplay between cognitive, social, and emotional factors is heavy. Impulsive children tend to be hurried and unconcerned about error. Much of their thinking still remains in the pre-operational stage. The reflective child makes fewer errors because of taking time to ponder the facts before responding or acting. This child seems to be more concerned about errors. Most of these children exhibit concrete operational thought patterns, especially in the area of the conservations.[16]

Knowledge of cognitive styles may help parents and teachers broaden educational goals and outcomes, expand opportunities for decision-making choices, and provide a variety of instructional methods individualized to the child's needs.

Right–Left Brain Processing

Recent findings in brain science (aided by new computer programs that can stimulate brain cells into action) are revealing that "the brain is far more intricate than any mechanistic device imaginable."[2] Split-brain research shows that, when the connection between the right and left hemispheres is severed by cutting of the corpus callosum, the two hemispheres operate independently of each other.[17] Each hemisphere has a separate consciousness, "its own separate and private sensations; its own perceptions; its own concepts; and its own impulses to act."[62] After the severing of the corpus callosum, each hemisphere has its own schemata that are inaccessible to the other side. In 95% of the population, the two hemispheres show the functional specialties noted in Table 21-1. The right hemisphere interprets and coordinates emotional and creative components (intuition, inspiration, and imagination), and the left hemisphere deals with rational, analytical factors (reading, writing, and arithmetic).[17] Lateralization is more marked in men than in women.[17]

Studies seem to indicate that creative professional people (e.g., artists, lawyers, sculptors, authors) are neither right- nor left-brain dominant, but they tap the skills of both hemispheres.[53] For all of us, the two hemispheres function in tandem to accomplish daily tasks.

Approaches to Problems

Problem Solving

Problem solving is a generic term that covers a wide scope of complex behaviors. Problem-solving skills are tapped when the solution to a problem or goal isn't readily apparent. Problem solving may involve the application of new responses to an old problem or old responses to a new problem.

Numerous problem solving models can be applied to learning processes. Problem solving, using Guilford's structure-of-intellect model (see Fig. 21-6), focuses on specific

TABLE 21-1. HEMISPHERIC FUNCTIONS

Left Side of Brain	*Right Side of Brain*
Motor control and sensory interpretation of right side of body	Motor control and sensory interpretation of left side of body
Abstract, analytical	Concrete, holistic
Reality oriented	Intuitive
Expressive language skills	Nonverbal (prosody) expression
Comprehension of language	Comprehension of emotions
Writing skills	Artistic
Mathematical skills	Perceptual skills
Reading abilities	Musical abilities; recognizes melodies
Time orientation	Spatial orientation; recognizes visual patterns and faces; picture drawing; matching patterns and puzzle pieces
	Metaphorical expressions and puns

applications of the three major dimensions: *operations, contents,* and *products.*

Other problem-solving approaches focus on steps or stages. They begin by (1) defining the problem, followed by (2) identifying strategies, (3) selecting the best idea, and then (4) trying it out. The final and equally critical steps are to (5) evaluate and (6) monitor one's own progress.[76]

Piaget proposes that all problem solving is a creative experience for the child who must *invent* a solution to each problem faced. Even if the solution turns out to be incorrect, the process is a learning experience. From a Piagetian view, problem solving is an accommodative process that uses differentiating, classifying, and discovering concepts.

Single-Dimensional Problem Solving
Younger school-agers make many premature closures.[1] They do not yet have sufficient experience or mental flexibility to generate multiple alternatives in problem solving. They tend to imitate what they have seen done by others, regardless of its appropriateness, or to follow a rule carefully without thinking about the side effects of the behavior. Many of their solutions to practical problems seem logical to them; however, since they do not assess all the pros and cons of the alternatives before implementing the action, disastrous or negative side effects may outweigh the positive goal. One child may write his name in indelible ink on the inside of a brand-new jacket to prevent a repeat episode of a lost jacket and mother's anger and to prevent having to rewrite the name after it is laundered. The child has no awareness that the ink bleeds through to the outside or that the printing can also be seen when the collar is open. Another child may try to "even up" the ragged edge of a torn window curtain, unaware that he or she is only making the hole larger in the process. In each case, the child is taking initiative for positive reasons. However, the child was able to concentrate on only one dimension of the problem at a time. Self-esteem is threatened when the adult is unable to acknowledge the intent and only punishes the behavior and belittles the child.

As children get older and become exposed to a greater variety of experiences, their problem-solving skills generally improve. They are better able to generate multiple solutions and to anticipate consequences.[1] Supportive, corrective feedback substantially improves the frequency with which first-through fifth-graders detect multiple solutions. However, the possibility of more than one correct solution does not appear until about sixth grade, when formal operational thought emerges.[1]

Logic and Reasoning
The ability to use formal reasoning and abstract logic does not appear until the emergence of Piaget's formal operational level (about 11–12 years of age). During the school-age years, deductive (from general to specific) and especially inductive (from specific to general) reasoning are weak. Children love practicing the use of syllogisms (two premises and a conclusion). The classic example states: All horses have four legs, that animal has four legs, therefore it is a horse. Since categorization and reversibility skills are still not stabilized, their "logical conclusions" are frequently erroneous (all horses may be animals, but all animals are not horses). School-agers know that the conclusion is wrong but love "proving" the absurd. Even by 11 years of age, few children can use deductive reasoning to explicitly describe the illogicality.[43]

The rules children use to solve problems become increasingly complex throughout the middle childhood years. Children were asked which side would go down when weights were placed at various distances from the fulcrum of a balance scale. Four rules emerged:[57]

Rule 1: The side with the greater weight will go down.
Rule 2: If the weights are equal, the side with the weight farthest from the fulcrum will go down.
Rule 3: If one side has more weight, but the other side has a weight farther away from the fulcrum, guess.
Rule 4: Multiply weight times distance from the fulcrum to determine which side goes down.

"Five-year-olds most often used Rule 1 and failed to solve the more difficult ones. Nine-year-olds used Rule II or III, while 13 to 17 year olds most often used Rule III. Most did not use Rule IV. Therefore, problem solving using logic and reasoning develop increasingly complex rules to integrate information in problem solving situations," requiring a logical approach.[57]

Creativity

Creativity is often confused with intelligence, but researchers have shown that highly creative children don't always score high on IQ tests, and that those with high IQs don't always score high on creativity tests.[26] "Creativity" appears to be a broad and general concept with multiple meanings. Except for Guilford's structure-of-intellect model, most theories and models of intelligence do not tap the creativity dimension. In the Guilford model, *operations* that appear to tap creativity include "divergent productions" and "evaluations," while the *content* dimensions vary according to the situation. Under *products,* creativity can be tapped under "transformations" and "implications." Some examples of creative test items from Guilford's SI Model are the following:

> Example A:
> Divergent (D) Semantic (M), Transformations (T) or DMT: (1) Write clever titles to a short story. (2) Give clever solutions to 'X' riddle.
> Example B:
> Divergent (D) Semantic (M) Implications (I) or DMI: (1) Suggest ten different occupations for people interested in animals. (2) What symbols or emblems might best represent aggression and hostility?

Other traits of creative individuals are given in Table 21-2.

Children are often more creative than adults because of their open attitude for seeking new discoveries and resiliency to failure. Obstacles that may block children's creativity are fear of criticism from others, limited time availability, limited information on the problem, and entrenchment in habit patterns that eclipse one's ability to create novel approaches.

Creative children seem to be more assertive and have greater self-confidence than noncreative children. They show an openness, independence of judgment, initiative, and often display leadership in a group. They ask questions and offer suggestions, often using humor to convey their messages. Creative children often produce solutions that go beyond the usual constraints of time, place, common materials, and uses of objects.

When creativity deals with dimensions of divergent ability, originality, uniqueness, and spontaneous flexibility, females have a slight edge over males, but the differences are insignificant. If the creative tasks involve mathematics or scientific content, males seem to have the edge; whereas females seem to have the edge in content of literature and creative writing. Overall, there appears to be little difference in creative ability between males and females.[12, 28, 41]

TABLE 21-2. TRAITS OF CREATIVE PEOPLE

Sensitivity to problems
Insightful
Expansive imagination
Observant of details, discrepancies
Curiosity
Interest in new experiences
Rich sense of humor
Inquisitive about people
Generation of novel or original ideas, approaches
Fluency—flow of ideas
Flexibility—readiness to change directions or to modify information
Ability to synthesize
Openmindedness
Ability to reorganize or redefine
Ability to elaborate or give a variety of implications
Initiative
High-risk takers
Hesitancy to conform
Search for and joy in the unusual
Avoidance of functional-fixedness situations

It would appear that creative people have a certain freedom of spirit or willingness to take risks that goes beyond the conventional ideas accepted by society. Some may appear to be creating a "dreamworld" by using divergent thinking to go off on tangents. All show flexibility and diversity and provide multiple hypotheses in problem-solving situations. They seem to use metaphors, analogies, puns, and similes more often than noncreative children (Fig. 21-10).[28]

Parents, teachers, and others involved in the education of children can improve the creative potential of young people in the following ways:

1. Creating an environment and an atmosphere of freedom that encourages questions, hypotheses, and multiple solutions to problems.

2. Avoiding strong criticism while encouraging children to take risks, to dream, to imagine, and to carry out new ideas.

3. Providing opportunities for (a) brainstorming (creating a large number of ideas or solutions), (b) translation training (how to transform ideas, words, sentences, and so on into alternative representations or metaphors), (c) strategy training (how to devise and monitor potential solutions), and (d) logic training (how to use deductive and inductive reasoning to solve problems).

4. Encouraging the creation of new classifications and new systematizations of knowledge that differ from conventional ones (e.g., new classification of animals).

5. Modeling creative problem solving for children when confronting everyday situations (i.e., practice what is preached). Verbalize the thoughts and steps undertaken to resolve a problem. Encourage the child to provide input.

6. Reinforcing and rewarding multiple responses, unusual

FIGURE 21–10.
Creativity comes in many forms. Art projects supposedly tap right-brain functioning and offer the opportunity to develop all domains.

responses, flexibility in thinking, open-mindedness, a wide range of interests, use of logic, and other characteristics associated with creativity (Fig. 21-11).

When 6- to 10-year-old children were asked to "imagine you're clever," they improved their reflective responses significantly in problem-solving situations. This finding suggests that we may set limits on children's creativity by communicating low levels of expectations for creative productions.[30]

Special Talent

"Average" children, as well as those of superior intelligence, may be talented in a specific field such as music, art, writing, drama, or mechanics. Talents often represent clusters of abilities, such as artistic talent (painting, sculpturing, sketching, music, dance, and drama). Children may have scientific, social, physical, linguistic, or academic talents. The origin of special talent is unclear. Some theorists assume a genetic factor, others stress environmental issues. However, it is obvious that no child develops a talent without instruction and practice. Some children have more ability or talent to use the opportunities available to them; some never develop a particular skill no matter how hard they try! Therefore, some underlying exceptional aptitude or neurological substrate is involved in all exceptional performance.[20, 21] Many talents appear to have a critical period for development. "Puberty appears to be a crucial point with respect to the development of talent...the hormonal influences, presumably on the brain, can facilitate development of the talent for a few, but inhibit it for all others" (Fig. 21-12).[21]

Music

Gardner's model of intelligence; includes musical intelligence as one of the seven distinct types of intelligence.[25]

FIGURE 21–11.
Group projects offer opportunities to develop creativity, memory, and talents in many areas while promoting the social skills of negotiation and cooperation.

FIGURE 21–12.
Each child has some special talent. It is a challenge to parents and educators to help the child discover and develop his or her special "gift."

Guilford's model provides for several factors that account for proficiency in music.[28] There are strong parallels between developmental stages of music and Piaget's stages of cognitive development.[29] During the first year of life, children react to musical sounds. A 6-month-old child can vocally match pitch and remember melodies.[55] By 2 and 3 years, most can spontaneously reproduce phrases of songs heard. By 3 and 4 years, they can usually follow the general plan of the melody, and at 4 and 5 years, they can discriminate register of pitches and tap back simple rhythms. At 5 and 6, they can normally discriminate tonal and rhythm patterns. At 7 and 8, they appreciate consonance versus dissonance concepts and have developed harmonic skills by the age of 10 and 11.[55, 56] Musical conservation skills are similar to other cognitive conservations. Most children younger than 7 or 8 are unable to conserve a melody if the tempo or rhythm is changed. By 10 or 12, they are able to conserve melody, meter, and rhythm.[55]

Some feel that musical ability is learned rather than innate.[55] Children identified as gifted musicians have unusual capacity for representing musical relations in their everyday life and extraordinary abilities for all-at-once imitation.[24, 29] Child prodigies in music seem to rely exclusively on figural representations. Many were writing and composing during their childhood. They seem to possess superior understanding of musical events in relationship to one another.[24, 29] Most

outstanding musicians are discovered at an early age, usually before 6 and often as early as 2 or 3 years of age. "A Hungarian musical prodigy, Enuis Nyireguhazi, when not yet 1, exhibited a tendency to imitate singing; in the second year of life, he could imitate melodies, even though his capacity for verbal expression was poor. He had absolute pitch, at 4 took lessons, and at 7 he was able to transpose, to sight read difficult pieces, and to remember complex ones. He began to compose at 6, and at 12 emerged with his own composition."[24] One unusual young girl was noted to hum a song in its entirety at 7 months. By 12 months, she could replicate any tune on pitch.

Musical ability, mathematical skills, and language competence are frequently associated, as if related to some underlying construct.

Idiot Savant

Special abilities in one isolated area, such as music, art, rote memory, pictorial memory, and other specific proficiency skills, have been noted in some severely mentally retarded people ("idiot savant"). For example, one 3½-year-old autistic child made animal drawings comparable in skill to an adult artist. Others have been known to reproduce intricate piano music or lifelike clay sculptures.[54]

Sociocultural Factors

Competition and comparisons of self to others affects *what* we learn and *how* we learn it. One's family's attitude toward education and learning, their support, peer attitudes, and environmental opportunities for learning directly and indirectly affect one's progress in school and one's ability to maximize potentials.

Environmental Stress

Anxiety and stress may provide motivation for change by providing the driving power for problem solving. However, too much stress can drain the affective energy sources needed for accommodation of new material. Children who face the divorce of parents, death of a close friend, a move to a new community, or even ridicule and teasing by peers may experience anxiety, depression, or attention-deficit disorders, all of which tend to heighten frustration, lower self-esteem, and lower academic achievements.

Family

The relationship of children to their parents and siblings can positively or negatively affect the child's cognitive development. High academic achievement tends to be positively correlated with a stable marriage relationship of the parents, a democratic parenting style, positive mental and physical health of family members, and positive coping strategies for facing crises experiences.[6, 31, 74] Small family size, family values on education, and nonghetto residential locations also tend to be positively correlated with higher IQ scores and academic performance.[15, 32, 72] High-achieving students tend to have strong, dominating mothers. Families who value education and become involved in the child's interests, concerns, and progress, facilitate maximization of the child's cognitive potentials and positive attitudes toward learning.

Schools

The student–teacher relationship is one of the key factors related to cognitive development and success in school. Teachers who are warm and understanding, show interest, and have the ability to communicate at the child's pace and level of comprehension challenge and inspire students to want to please the teacher, to receive recognition and warm praise. A superior learning situation results from a meshing of student and teacher role expectations. "Personality clashes" or autocratic discipline approaches tend to decrease the child's motivation to invest in the difficult task of learning new material (Fig. 21-13).

Peers

The influence of peer groups (age mates, classmates, neighborhood friends) becomes stronger as a child progresses through school. Peer values and competition add strong motivating components to learning. However, peer influence can have detrimental effects when conformity to "peer norms" causes children to become victims of "group think," thus reducing motivation for divergent thinking or creative problem solving. Other children resist doing well in school for fear of social rejection from peers for being "teacher's pet" or for making others look "dumb." The wise teacher creates opportunities for cooperative activities in which everyone's talents and interests can be tapped and challenged. When peers work together at complex tasks, a positive effect on retention is found.[46]

Mass Media

Of all the forms of mass media, television is probably the most popular. The presence of VCRs in the home and the ready

FIGURE 21–13.
The focused, synchronized attention of a caring adult can facilitate learning. The enthusiastic response of an adult can give wings to a child's efforts.

availability of videotapes will probably increase television watching by children. Although many tapes offer pure entertainment, a large variety of educational programs are available that can stimulate intellectual development (e.g., National Geographic, studies of animal behavior, and a wide range of programs on mathematics, literature, creative writing, art, music, travel, pet care, and hobbies). Instructional television and educational films for home or classroom use have increased exponentially in the past 10 years. Many of these programs are available for free loan from local public libraries. These forms of mass media have given children from disadvantaged environments the opportunity for many vicarious learning experiences. Many children with learning disabilities also find that these more graphic approaches to information facilitate learning new material.

Motivation

Traditionally, the psychology of motivation was tied to basic physiological drives and biological needs, such as food, water, physical comfort, and sex. The concept of motivation, as Piaget uses it, is essentially synonymous with "curiosity" or an innate drive to find solutions. When the child is in a state of disequilibrium, he or she is energized to satisfy his or her uneasiness by searching for a solution (more information or new approach). When the new solution is found, the child is satisfied and returns to a state of equilibrium, thus reducing motivation to learn new material. Intrinsic motivation to learn a new skill or information enhances the learning process.[27] The child is motivated to learn for the reward of skill mastery and self-competence, not by an extrinsic reward from a teacher or parent (although adult praise and recognition remain important).

Computer Use

Computers are providing new avenues for adapting instruction to individual differences in intelligence, cognitive styles, and motivation. Well-constructed computer programs offer a variety of processing modes, such as exploratory programs that use branching systems or structured programs designed to give precise answers. A variety of content modes (affective, symbolic, graphic, and semantic) are available to match individual student learning modes. Some of the distinct advantages of computers are that they provide instantaneous feedback and never lose patience, thus allowing multiple repetitions of a task until the child thoroughly understands it. Computers can provide the kind of instruction one might receive from tutors and thus appear to be a valuable supplementary tool for learning. Children seem to love working with computers, and the social stigma associated with wrong answers offered in a group setting is eliminated. Thus, energies are freed for learning, energies that might otherwise be used to maintain self-esteem and peer respect (Fig. 21-14).

The fear that computers might replace the "human element" has not been substantiated in schools or homes. The

FIGURE 21–14.
Computers are taking their place beside the basic "three R's" in classrooms.

fear that children would become "mechanical and robotlike" is equally unjustified since children often invite their friends to share in the computer games and programs, thus promoting social interaction rather than discouraging it. The concern that economically deprived families and schools in poorer areas will fall further behind because they are not able to afford computers also appears to be unjustified. Computers are becoming a standard part of school and library equipment as the purchase prices decrease. However, as with television, children may neglect their social and academic responsibilities if they spend too much time with computers.

IMPLICATIONS

Family

Parental modeling and support are crucial to the child's progress in school. Parents are in a key position to encourage the child to learn the skills of conservation, classification, and figure-ground discrimination through special activities and, more significantly, through the challenges offered in the activities of daily living. Parents can encourage involvement in sports, hobbies, and clubs that promote the recognition and development of a child's special interests and skills. By taking pride in the child's pursuits and sharing hobbies and activities as a family, the potential negative effects of peers can be thwarted and their positive effects enhanced. By gradually encouraging the child to become a partner in family decision-making processes, the child learns both social and cognitive skills essential for successful coping during these years as well as during adolescent and adult years. Reading or watching TV together enables the child to increase his or her knowledge as well as to begin to apply information learned to his or her own life experiences. Table games, especially strategy games, are fun, but they also teach cognitive dexterity and self-discipline skills. Family field trips or vacations, home computers, educational videotapes, books, magazines, and newspapers can supplement and enrich the experience of children, providing the parents help to put the experiences into a meaningful context. Exposure alone is not sufficient.

Schools

The models of intelligence by Guilford, Gardner, and Sternberg include abilities in the arts (e.g., music, art, drama), intrapersonal and interpersonal relationships (e.g., social, attitudinal, emotional, behavioral), critical thinking ability, meta-components of problem solving, insight, creative thinking, and many other abilities. Thus, schools that concentrate only on academics fail to tap the full range of the school-ager's potentials. New understandings of the range of school-agers' intellectual and cognitive abilities should be evident in curriculums, methods of teaching, and learning environments.

Readiness for various learning tasks is critical. A cognitively delayed child should not be stressed by tasks beyond his or her capacity any more than a gifted child should be held back from realizing his or her full potential. Teachers who are flexible and patient with individual learning differences and who respect each child as a learner and thinker provide flexible opportunities for experiencing success in school. The role of the teacher is to facilitate thinking not just to reinforce rote memorization or correct the wrong responses. The teacher needs to raise open-ended questions to stimulate children's independent investigations, to make a diagnosis of each child's progress through the cognitive stages (observing levels of operation, styles of learning, information processing and problem-solving abilities), and to determine the instructional strategies appropriate for each child. Teaching objectives can be personalized based on the teacher's expert

knowledge of each child's ability, developmental level, and learning style. Parents and teachers need to work together to maximize the learning potentials of children.

Community

Children are the citizens of tomorrow. A community concerned about its future invests in schools, recreational programs, museums, and libraries. However, the availability of programs alone is insufficient if they are not geared to the child's unique interests and cognitive needs. Community support for educational programs, musical and dramatic productions, teachers, books, and so on, may require more tax dollars, but the investment can have both short-term effects (e.g., reduced delinquency rates) as well as long-term effects (e.g., a future with a more educated, involved, prepared citizenry) (Fig. 21-15).

In addition to the financial investment are the investments of time and love from caring, understanding community people who are willing to serve as models and mentors for these "people-in-process." Opportunities for multi-

FIGURE 21–15.
The school years are an excellent time to teach safety and to interact positively with community helpers. Attitudes and habits established during these years tend to persist throughout life.

cultural, multiracial, and multi-age groupings and support of equal opportunity for all children regardless of race, color, creed, disability, or socioeconomic status help to ensure both the experiences and the social and emotional support that allow a child to maximize cognitive potentials. A supportive community helps each child to find another person "marching to the same drum" that will enable each child to reach his or her highest potential.

REFERENCES

1. Acredolo, C., & Horobin, K. (1987). Development relational reasoning and avoidance of premature closure. *Developmental Psychology, 23,* 13–21.
2. Allman, W. F. (1988). How the brain really works its wonders. *U.S. News and World Report, 104*(25), 48–54.
3. American Association of Mental Deficiency. (1977). *Manual on terminology and classification in mental retardation* (1977 rev.). Washington, DC: American Association of Mental Deficiency.
4. Anastasi, A. (1988). *Psychological testing* (6th ed.). New York: Macmillan.
5. Bouchard, T. J., & McGue, M. (1981). Familial studies of intelligence. *Science, 212,* 1055–1059.
6. Boyd, D. A., & Parish, T. S. (1985). An examination of academic achievement in light of familial configuration. *Education, 106*(2), 228–230.
7. Bruner, J. S., Goodnow, J. J., & Austin, G. A. (1986). *A study of thinking.* New Brunswick, NJ: Transaction Books.
8. Butterfield, E. C., Nelson, T. O., & Peck, V. (1988). Developmental aspects of the feeling of knowing. *Developmental Psychology, 24,* 654–663.
9. Cattell, R. B. (1959). *Handbook for culture fair intelligence test: A measure of "g".* Champaign, IL: Institute of Personality & Ability Testing.
10. Clifford, T. (1986). Cognitive development of the school-ager. In C. S. Schuster & S. A. Ashburn (Eds.), *The process of human development: A holistic life-span approach* (2nd ed., pp. 465–486). Boston: Little, Brown.
11. Cornell, E. H., Heth, C. D., & Broda, L. S. (1989). Children's wayfinding: Response to instructions to use environmental landmarks. *Developmental Psychology, 25,* 755–764.
12. Dhillon, P. K., & Mehra, D. (1987). The influence of social class and sex on primary school children's creative thinking. *Asian Journal of Psychology and Education, 19*(2–3), 1–10.
13. Dove, A. (1986). Taking the chitlings test. *Newsweek, 72*(3), 51–52.
14. Downs, R. M., & Stea, D. (1977). *Maps in minds: Reflections on cognitive mapping.* New York: Harper and Row.
15. Drews, E., & Teahan, J. E. (1957). Parental attitudes and academic achievement. *Journal of Clinical Psychology, 13,* 328–332.
16. Duryea, E. J., & Glover, J. A. (1982). A review of the research on reflection and impulsivity in children. *General Psychology Monograph, 106*(2), 217–237.
17. Ehrenwald, J. (1986). *Anatomy of genius: Split brains and global minds.* New York: Human Sciences Press.
18. Ekman, P. (1989). *Why kids lie: How parents can encourage truthfulness.* New York: Charles Scribner's Sons.
19. Elkind, D. (1981). *Children and adolescents: Interpretative essays of Jean Piaget* (3rd ed.). New York: Oxford University Press.
20. Ericsson, K. A., & Faivre, I. A. (1988). What's exceptional about exceptional abilities? In L. K. Obler & D. Fein (Eds.), *The exceptional brain: Neuropsychology of talent and special abilities* (pp. 436–473). New York: Guilford Press.
21. Fein, D., & Obler, L. K. (1988). Neuropsychological study of talent: A developing field. In L. K. Obler & D. Fein (Eds.), *The exceptional brain: Neuropsychology of talent and special abilities* (pp. 3–15). New York: Guilford Press.
22. Fry, P. S., & Lupart, J. L. (1987). *Cognitive processes in children learning.* Springfield, IL: Charles C. Thomas.
23. Gallagher, J. J. (1958). Social status of children related to intelligence, propinquity, and social perceptions. *Elementary School Journal, 58,* 225–231.
24. Gardner, H. (1973). *The arts and human development.* New York: Wiley.
25. Gardner, H. (1983). *Frames of mind: The theory of multiple intelligences.* New York: Basic Books.
26. Getzels, J. W., & Jackson, P. W. (1968). *Creativity and intelligence: Explorations with gifted students.* New York: Wiley.
27. Gottfried, A. E. (1983). Intrinsic motivation in young children. *Young Children, 39*(1), 64–73.
28. Guilford, J. P. (1967). *The nature of human intelligence.* New York: McGraw-Hill.
29. Hargreaves, D. (1987). *The developmental psychology of music.* New York: Cambridge University Press.
30. Hartley, R. (1986). Imagine you're clever. *Journal of Child Psychology and Psychiatry and Allied Disciplines, 27*(3), 383–398.
31. Hess, R. D., & Holloway, S. D. (1984). Family and school educational institutions. In R. D. Park (Ed.), *Review of child development research* (pp. 179–222). Chicago: University of Chicago Press.
32. Higgins, J. V., Reed, E. W., & Reed, S. C. (1982). Intelligence and family size: A paradox resolved. *Social Biology, 29,* 193–199.
33. Hughes, M. (1986). *Children and number: Difficulties in learning mathematics.* New York: Basil Blackwell.
34. Janos, P. M., & Robinson, N. M. (1985). Psychosocial development in intellectually gifted children. In F. D. Horowitz & M. O'Brien (Eds.), *The gifted and talented: Developmental perspectives.* Washington, DC: American Psychological Association.
35. Jarvik, L. F., & Erlenmeyer, K. L. (1967). Survey of familial correlations in measured intellectual functions. In J. Zubin & G. A. Jervis (Eds.), *Psychopathology of mental development.* New York: Grune and Stratton.
36. Kail, R. (1990). *The development of memory in children* (3rd ed.). New York: W. H. Freeman.
37. Kohlberg, L. A. (1980). *The meaning and measurement of moral development.* Worchester, MA: Clark University Press.
38. Lambert, N. M. (1978). The adaptive behavior scale—public school version: An overview. In W. A. Coulter & H. W. Morrow (Eds.), *Adaptive behavior: Concepts and measurement* (pp. 157–183). Orlando, FL: Grune and Stratton.
39. Liddle, G. (1958). Overlap among desirable and undesirable characteristics in gifted children. *Journal of Educational Psychology, 49,* 219–223.
40. Lynn, R. (1982). IQ in Japan and The United States shows a growing disparity. *Nature, 197,* 222–223.
41. Maccoby, E. E., & Jacklin, C. N. (1978). *The psychology of sex differences.* Palo Alto, CA: Stanford University Press.
42. Mallis, J. (1983). *Diamonds in the rough.* Austin, TX: Multimedia Arts.
43. Markovits, H., Schleifer, M., & Fortier, L. (1989). Development of elementary deductive reasoning in young children. *Developmental Psychology, 25,* 787–793.

44. Miller, R. (1956). Social status and socioeconomic differences among mentally superior, mentally typical, and mentally retarded children. *Exceptional Children, 23,* 114–119.

45. Nelson, L. N. (1974). The development of cognitive operations in young children. *The Journal of Educational Research, 68*(1), 116–123.

46. Perlmutter, M., Behrend, S. D., Kuo, F., & Muller, A. (1989). Social influences on children's problem solving. *Developmental Psychology, 25,* 744–754.

47. Piaget, J. (1962). *Play, dreams and imitation in childhood* (C. Gattegno & F. M. Hodgson, Trans.). New York: W. W. Norton.

48. Piaget, J. (1965). *The child's concept of number.* New York: W. W. Norton.

49. Piaget, J. (1967). *Six psychological studies* (A. Tenzer, Trans., & D. Elkind, Ed.). New York: Vintage Books. (Original work published 1964)

50. Piaget, J. (1969). *The child's conception of physical causality.* (M. Gabain, Trans.). Totowa, NJ: Littlefield, Adams.

51. Piaget, J. (1969). *Judgment and reasoning in the child* (M. Warden, Trans.). Totowa, NJ: Littlefield, Adams.

52. Piaget, J. (1976). *The psychology of intelligence* (M. Piercy & D. E. Berlyne, Trans.). Totowa, NJ: Littlefield, Adams. (Original work published 1947)

53. Quen, J. M. (Ed.). (1986). *Split minds/split brains: Historical and current perspectives.* New York: New York University Press.

54. Rimland, B., & Fein, D. (1988). Special talents of autistic savants. In L. K. Obler & D. Fein (Eds.), *The exceptional brain: Neuropsychology of talent and special abilities* (pp. 474–492). New York: Guilford Press.

55. Serafine, M. L. (1986). Music. In R. F. Dillon & R. J. Sternberg (Eds.), *Cognition and instruction* (pp. 299–342). San Diego: Academic Press.

56. Shuter-Dyson, R., & Gabriel, C. (1981). *The psychology of musical ability* (2nd ed.). London, UK Methuen.

57. Siegler, R. S. (1983). Information-processing approaches to development. In W. Kessen (Ed.), *Handbook of child psychology, 1* (pp. 129–211). New York: Wiley.

58. Siegler, R. S., & Kotovsky, K. (1986). Two levels of giftedness: Shall ever the twain meet? In R. J. Steinberg & J. E. Davidson (Eds.), *Conceptions of giftedness* (pp. 417–435). New York: Cambridge University.

59. Skeels, H. M. (1966). Adult status of children with contrasting early life experiences. *Monographs of the Society for Research in Child Development, 31*(Serial No. 3).

60. Sparrow, S. S., Balla, D. A., & Cicchetti, D. V. (1985). *Vineland adaptive behavior scales.* Circle Pines, MN: American Guidance Service.

61. Spearman, C. (1927). *The abilities of man.* New York: McMillan.

62. Sperry, R. W. (1969). A modified concept of consciousness. *Psychological Review, 76,* 532–536.

63. Sternberg, R. J. (1985). *Beyond IQ: A triarchic theory of human intelligence.* New York: Cambridge University Press.

64. Sternberg, R. J. (1986). A triarchic theory of intellectual giftedness. In R. J. Sternberg & J. E. Davidson (Eds.), *Conceptions of giftedness* (pp. 223–243). New York: Cambridge University Press.

65. Sternberg, R. J., & Wagner, R. K. (1989). Individual differences in practical knowledge and its application. In P. L. Ackerman, R. J. Sternberg, & R. Glaser (Eds.), *Learning and individual differences: Advances in theory and research* (pp. 255–278). New York: W. H. Freeman.

66. Stigler, J. W., Lee, S., & Stevenson, H. W. (1987). Mathematics classrooms in Japan, Taiwan, and The United States. *Child Development, 58,* 1272–1285.

67. Stiles-Davis, J., Kritchevsky, M., & Bellugi, U. (Eds.). (1988). *Spatial cognition: Brain bases and development.* Hillsdale, NJ: Erlbaum.

68. Terman, L. M. (1925). Mental and physical traits of a thousand gifted children. In L. M. Terman (Ed.), *Genetic studies of genius.* Stanford, CA: Stanford University Press.

69. Thomas, G. E., Alexander, K. L., & Eckland, B. K. (1979). Access to higher education: The importance of race, sex, social class, and academic credentials. *School Review, 87,* 133–156.

70. Thorndike, R. L., Hagen, E. P., & Sattler, J. M. (1986). *Stanford-Binet Intelligence Scale: Guide for administering and scoring the fourth edition.* Chicago: Riverside.

71. Trotter, R. J. (1986). Three heads are better than one. *Psychology Today, 20*(8), 56–62.

72. Wagner, M. E., Schubert, H. J., & Schubert, D. S. (1985). Family size effects: A review. *Journal of Genetic Psychology, 146*(1), 65–78.

73. Wallach, L. (1985). Creativity testing and giftedness. In F. D. Horowitz & M. O'Brien (Eds.), *The gifted and talented: Developmental perspectives.* Washington, DC: American Psychological Association.

74. Watson, T., Brown, M., & Swick, K. J. (1983). The relationship of parents' support to children's school achievement. *Child Welfare, 62*(2), 175–180.

75. Webb, J. T., Meckstroth, B. A., & Tolan, S. S. (1982). *Guiding the gifted child.* Columbus, OH: Ohio Psychology Publishing.

76. Wessells, M. G. (1982). *Cognitive psychology.* New York: Harper and Row.

77. Williams, R. L. (1975). The BITCH-100: A culture-specific test. *Journal of Afro-American Issues, 3,* 103–116.

22

Far from wanting to shine, I laughed in chorus with the others, I repeated their catchwords and phrases, I kept quiet, I obeyed, I imitated my neighbors' gestures, I had only one desire, to be integrated.

—JEAN-PAUL SARTRE,
THE WORDS

Psychosocial Development During School-Age Years

Helen Bray-Garretson and Kaye V. Cook

Entrance into school dramatically challenges the child to develop new social and cognitive skills. There is increasing awareness of who one is and of the rules and conventions governing behavior as one enters more complex relationships. Special peer friendships bring a new understanding of trust and reciprocity within relationships. Changes in the relationships to self and parents accompany the child's increasingly competent participation in the wider world of peers and school experiences. With increasing age and maturity, the child becomes more independent, seeking peer contacts by telephone, making decisions on money and time management, participating in overnight visits, or attending summer camps. By the end of the school years, children are actively practicing the skills of compromise and competition through clubs and social groups, in preparation for the increased social pressures of adolescence and adulthood.

The child quickly realizes that school rules are different from those at home, requiring adaptations in behavior. Gradually, the rules are more clearly understood and internalized as academic and social expectations become more complex. The child's self-knowledge parallels the changing awareness of social rules, friendships, and gender roles.

When a child is offered a healthy, supportive environment, the middle childhood years provide opportunities to begin to know one's self, abilities, and interests. The development of positive self-esteem and self-image occurs through three major avenues. First, children test out personal competencies by actively meeting the objective challenges set by school, home, and the self. In short, children learn how to work, sacrificing immediate pleasures in the service of specific goals. As children work, they develop competencies in selected areas, taking pride in their mastery. Second, children derive a sense of belonging to a society larger than that represented by the family of origin. Contacts with peers, teachers, and other representatives of the culture help children to begin to understand themselves in the context of their society, culture, and world (Fig. 22-1). They begin to participate in and identify with cultural traditions, developing a sense of security in the richness of the flow of life from generation to generation. Third, the child elaborates horizontal relationships, practicing social skills of cooperation and competition with peers, allowing for the emergence of self-monitoring, moral conscience and self-disciplining for the benefit of others besides one's self.

Successful mastery of these tasks enables the child to enter the adolescent years with a sense of purpose and self-confidence. These years involve more than treading water. They are a springboard for all that comes later in the life span. The child is discovering, learning, strengthening, and stabilizing many concepts of the self and of interpersonal relationships.

FIGURE 22–1.
During the school-age years, children begin to learn the traditions, sagas, and values of their culture (encultura-tion).

THEORETICAL PERSPECTIVES ON MIDDLE CHILDHOOD

By age 6, the healthy child has developed a strong sense of the self as separate from significant people in the family. The challenge of the school-age period is to elaborate the dimensions of that self. This occurs through association with people like oneself, emphasizing the process of belonging and fostering self-acceptance by determining that "I am like others" through clubs, gender-groupings, and friends with similar interests. Various theories, however, put different emphases on the way self-concept develops.

Psychodynamic Theorists

Freud

Sigmund Freud described the middle childhood years as a time of relative calm between the major developmental hurdles of the Oedipal conflict and the onset of puberty and sexual awareness. He used the term **latency** to denote that the struggle to deal with the "libido" or sexualized energy is apparently dormant during this period. With the resolution of the Oedipal complex, usually by age 6, the child identifies with the same-sex parent and develops a superego strong enough to thoroughly and adaptively repress sexual and aggressive impulses. This allows the child to redirect emotional energy and provides social space to explore other avenues of self-definition, through developing same-gender friends, learning academic skills, practicing individual talents, and pursuing personal preferences in activities (Fig. 22-2).

Later psychodynamic theorists indicate that endogenous emotional factors other than repressed sexual energies stimu-late the healthy development of self. Adler focuses on the school-ager's innate need to strive for mastery or competence.[3] Others claim this phase is marked by a search for emotional and cognitive coherence. This view contends that the child is assimilating new information, new emotions, and new perceptions of relationships that are paired with existing emotional schemata until a conflict forces a change in the self-structure of the child.[37] Regardless of the explanation, it is obvious that ego resources and ego strengths are built up as cognitive, emotional, and social growth occurs in the child, especially in the context of stable, nurturing relationships.

Erikson

Erik Erikson identifies the focal task of the school-age years as **industry**.[30] During this period, children learn to "work" at chores, school, crafts, talents, hobbies, and athletics, receiving intrinsic satisfaction in their activities and in the results of their work. During the school years, then, the child redirects the drive and energy of play into concrete pursuits and approved goals.[31]

During the earlier years, play was a child's "work," facilitating the learning of specific motor and social skills. Pre-school-age children learned to take initiative and set some goals for themselves. Some of the goals were unrealistic; most were goals that dealt with meeting immediate needs and pleasures, or tasks that could be accomplished within a short period of time. The school-ager now sets challenges that negate immediate pleasures and may take several sessions or even several years to master. Motor, cognitive, and social skills are refined as the child systematically and repeatedly attempts to master the abilities to read, ride a bike, thread a needle, bake a cake, balance on a skateboard, play an instrument,

FIGURE 22–2.
Participation in community events is part of the process of bonding to one's culture.

draw a horse, bat a ball, or play chess. Each child, each family, and each culture has its own valued goals. As the child systematically directs efforts toward mastering the desired goal, a sense of competence and self-confidence emerges. The child begins to discover his or her unique qualities and gains a sense of belonging to and acceptance by the community. The child is able to see the self as "a person in process." The school-age years are a time for making, doing, performing, and finishing so that the child can positively reflect, "well done!"

In most cultures, the child's eagerness for knowledge is met by the provision of formal educational programs. Parents and society work with the children to help prepare them for successful adulthood. The child who develops a positive sense of competency during these years of increasing industry lays the foundation for the more abstract and stable identities of the adolescent years. Mastery of Erikson's task of indus-

try is pivotal to positive self-esteem and self-confidence in the years ahead.

But not every child is ready or able to master Erikson's industry. Children reared with environmental deprivation, shaky attachments to parents, or with abusive, restrictive, or nonresponsive parents, may not have developed the ability to take initiative, or to harness and focus their energies toward mastery of short-term tasks. They enter the school years at a disadvantage. They are unable to organize themselves to harness energies in response to assigned tasks. If the child is not ready to begin productivity, or if persons in the environment demand competencies (e.g., an overly demanding teacher) for which the child is not ready, the child may be left with an impression that he or she is "never quite good enough."

Sometimes the environment inadequately supports a child's attempts at talent development or pursuit of an interest (e.g., poverty precludes music or gymnastic lessons) or thwarts the gaining of new skills (e.g., the parents may feel an activity like ballet is inappropriate for a boy), thus setting the stage for the development of feelings of **inferiority,** the counterpoint of Erikson's industry. The child does not learn what he or she can do, may feel stigmatized, or does not feel valued, unique, or competent within the culture. These deficits may seriously affect entry into adolescence with its own inherent anxieties and tensions.

When one masters Erikson's task of industry, the resulting sense of competence allows one to face others and life's exigencies with confidence. Thus, positive social relationships, according to Erikson, are an outgrowth of one's self-esteem and depend on a sense of increasing autonomy, control, and competence. Middle childhood is a crucial stage for the acceptance of responsibility for personal effort and forms the basis for cooperative and productive adolescent and adult relationships. There is a new freedom that emerges in the awareness of "a world shared with others" (versus duty-dependence) and a "sense of self that can be safely extended into this broader social world" (versus excessive self-restraint) (Fig. 22-3).[34]

Constructivism Theory

The constructivist perspective of development recognizes that children are active participants in their own development, not just passive recipients molded by their biological predispositions or environmental experience.[22] Initially rules are established by family members, but become modified and altered by experiences in the larger community. Children's increasing abilities to participate in their social world depend on expanded knowledge of the rules and regularities of their social world and on active efforts to achieve competence in logical thinking.[84] The school-age child actively *constructs* a personal view of the world and selects a response to it, based on a sense of self and of the rules and conventions that govern the world.[23]

Social cognitivists assume that cognitive development is

FIGURE 22–3.
School-agers become aware of cultural differences as adults introduce them to new foods, costumes, customs, and languages. Their attitude toward differences is colored by the attitudes of the adults.

central to social development, and that changing cognitive abilities bring parallel changes in social behaviors. Social cognitivists study children's behaviors using the methodology and paradigms developed by Piaget and modified by many others. Self-concept or social competence is rooted in a sense of oneself, *both* as an individual and as a participant in a social world.

To the constructivist, both internal and external factors are important in developing self-esteem. Social competence consists of four defining issues, each of which has a self-assertive and an integrative goal: **identity, control, social comparison,** and **resource allocation** (Table 22-1).[79]

The self-assertive goal of **identity** refers to the ability to develop and express one's *individuality*; its integrative aspect is *belongingness,* or the ability to create, maintain, or enhance social units of which one is a part. For example, a child may know she has artistic talent and derive satisfaction in expressing this skill by participating in the group mural project. In **control,** *self-determination* is the self-assertive goal (i.e., beginning to establish and maintain personal control over life circumstances and regain control when it is lost). The integrative aspect is *social responsibility,* which occurs in situations when one has particular duties, commitments, or roles; for example, when one chooses to do homework immediately after school so that one can participate in the Little League

baseball game that evening. **Social comparison** is defined by *superiority* in the self-assertive goal and *equity* in the integrative goal. Superiority occurs most often in competitive situations with peers; equity occurs where powerful norms are important in maintaining positive relationships. For example, a fifth grader may know that he is the best writer for the school newspaper, but recognizes that the newspaper only gets out when everyone works on the nitty-gritty tasks in an equitable way. Finally, **resource allocation** shares a self-assertive goal of *resource acquisition* and an integrative goal of *resource provision*. For example, friendships are maintained when a child both receives and gives something in the relationship, whether it be tangible (sharing treats) or abstract (giving assistance). The social constructivism theory may feel cumbersome because it attempts to address the complexity of a child's experience by including cognitive components and social experience along with internal perceptions.

Learning Theories

Learning theory assumes that one's behavior is under the control of environmental contingencies. Classical and operant conditioning situations set the stage for the development of behaviors that become patterns expressed throughout life.

TABLE 22–1. INTERNAL FACTORS INFLUENCING SOCIAL COMPETENCE

Factor	*Self-Assertive Goal*	*Integrative Goal*
Identity	Individuality	Belongingness
Control	Self-determination	Social responsibility
Social comparison	Superiority	Equity
Resource allocation	Resource acquisition	Resource provision

(Ford, M. E., & Ford, D. H. (eds.). (1987). Humans as Self-Constructing Living Systems. Hillsdale, NJ: Erlbaum.)

Children of school-age will produce behavior that earns reinforcement. Associations once learned are difficult to change without specific manipulation of reinforcement patterns. For instance, if a child learns that whining in the grocery line earns him a choice from the candy rack to keep quiet and stem a tantrum, whining is reinforced in that situation and may generalize to other situations. Many maladaptive behaviors, such as throwing tantrums, lying, cheating, or bossiness, are learned in this way, as are many adaptive behaviors such as doing homework, expressing feelings, playing cooperatively, or being polite. Parental discipline plays a crucial role in behavior and attitude development (see Chap. 16).

Social Learning Theory

Some behavioral patterns are learned indirectly by observing other people. Children will imitate what they see adults or more powerful peers do, even though they may believe it to be a negative action. For example, if they observe another child striking a Bobo doll viciously, they are likely to do the same when they are in the presence of a Bobo doll.[5]

Bandura's model of **reciprocal determinism** indicates that three components enter into the development of the self-system: individual qualities, the environment, and overt behavior.[6] These interact in a dynamic, synergistic way in the social environment. Thus, a child's choice of environment or activity influences the learning opportunities available. For example, girls spend more time in highly structured, adult-oriented behaviors than boys, providing them with more opportunities for learning communication, negotiation, and cooperation skills required in social situations.[48] Bandura also suggests that cognitive factors predict social learning and emphasizes the role of perceived **self-efficacy** (the belief that one can master a situation and produce a positive outcome).[5] A child who expects to do well, and tells herself, "I **can** do this," will generally do better than if she lacks confidence. As she takes risks and tries something new, she meets with some new successes, enhancing her sense of self-efficacy.

The concept of self-efficacy is similar to the concept of **internal locus of control,** which is the sense that events, situations, outcome or attitudes are based on resources from within oneself. An understanding of locus of control increases with age. Preschoolers often attribute physical and cognitive accomplishments to magical processes, or events outside one's own control (external locus of control). During the school years, children begin to understand more complicated and abstract cognitive and social cause–effect relationships. Children with a sense of internal locus of control tend to do well on tasks of self-control, such as waiting patiently or working more carefully to achieve a better product or result.

Every child needs to experience success. Children need to feel they are responsible for doing an excellent job in some aspects of their lives. Children may feel inferior because they compare themselves too harshly with peers, caregivers, teachers, and parents. Adults can facilitate the development of self-efficacy and internal locus of control by (1) providing opportunities to participate in decisions that directly affect a child's life, (2) by pointing out the child's responsibility for his or her own behaviors, and (3) by recognizing and appreciating a good performance, even though it may not be perfect. **One can be proud of "doing one's best," even if it is not "the best" when compared to others.**

Ecological Approach

The ecological approach reminds us that learning occurs in interaction with an ever-widening suprasystem.[49] As illustrated in Figure 22-4, there are multiple layers of influence that affect children's behaviors. For instance, children will drink milk because their bodies are internally calling out for it, their parents serve it at every meal, they watch classmates drink it for lunch at school, they see "pep talk" commercials for milk on television, and they know that our culture highly values personal health actions.

According to Urie Bronfenbrenner's model, the **microsystem** incorporates the settings in which the child lives, including family, school, peers, and neighborhood.[12] The child continues to expand, elaborate, and integrate the social and affective support available within the microsystem during the middle childhood period.

The **mesosystem** consists of the relations between the various microsystems of the child's life. For example, parents of a child who does poorly in school can help the child improve academic performance by keeping in close contact with teachers, assisting the child with homework, and participating in supportive projects such as reading or playing with math facts.

The **exosystem** describes settings in which the child does not have an active role but which influence the child's immediate experience. For example, the federal government may fund an after-school program for latchkey children, remedial academics, or cultural enrichment. The **macrosystem** is the most abstract level of influence—the attitudes and ideologies of the culture that have an impact on the microsystems. For example, recent comparisons of American and Asian education suggest that the less structured American educational system encourages creative thinking, but does not facilitate formal or informal learning of math concepts and abilities as well as the Asian culture.[72] American children spend less time in school, in math class, and in formal math instruction, than other technologically advanced societies.[75]

Descriptions of Self

Children's concept of self is not well-integrated with cultural values until approximately 8 years of age.[41] Thus, a young obese child may recognize that he or she is overweight and may report that obese children are less well-liked, but self-esteem may not suffer as a result of this knowledge until after the eighth birthday. Only then do children begin to tie all the facts together (personal discomfort, social ostracism, body image, and critical feedback) to see themselves as inferior because they are obese (or disabled, or a member of any

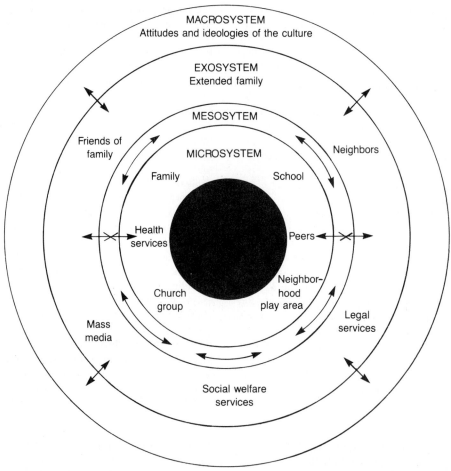

FIGURE 22–4.
Ecological influences on children's behavior. Bronfenbrenner's ecological model. (From Gar-barino, J., [1980] in C. Kopp and J. Krakow [Eds.] Child development in social context, Read-ing, MA: Addison-Wesley, with permission.)

minority group). Assessing personal values by negative facts (unfortunately) produces low self-esteem (see Chap. 17). By age 10, children reflect on their emotional selves and are able to comment on feelings and mood.[73] These self-conceptions change and stabilize during adolescence when they become capable of integrating abstract information into an individu-alized, conceptual sense of who they are.[40]

In the preschool years, children describe themselves by external appearances; they are concrete thinkers; they are what they can see (e.g., boy with brown hair). By the early school years, children begin to include skills, status (age and school grade), and preferences more often as part of their self-description ("I can throw a ball across the yard," or "I like to eat sushi"). As they mature, their descriptions of themselves begin to include talents (e.g., play the piano, good in math). Eventually (during adolescence), self-description includes abstract issues ("I am shy," or "I am empathetic.") Generally it

is not until late adolescence that one is able to share values and beliefs that may be contrary to the values of others (e.g., "I believe in a personal God") or that cause much pain (e.g., "I feel inferior to other people").

As children move from an undifferentiated to a more individualized and complex sense of self, they make value judgments about themselves.[51] Coopersmith interviewed school-age children and their parents to pinpoint the ante-cedents of self-esteem, and he suggested that children mea-sure themselves on four dimensions: being loved by others, feeling competent at work, being in tune with the values of the culture, and feeling powerful, able to control one's self and others.[18] Once established, self-esteem is resistant to change. High self-esteem tends to be stable over time and predicts many positive aspects of a person's life. Children with good self-esteem generally approach the world positively, and ex-perience success in other areas, for example, reading ability.[52]

High self-esteem provides a reservoir of emotional energy which enables persistence to task and resiliency when "the going gets tough."

Balancing Dependence and Independence

Skills are developing very rapidly in all areas, and there is a desire, if not need, to prove one's competence and ability to face life independently. However, the school-ager, for all the daring and bravado, is still very aware of his or her vulnerability. The insecurity and transitions of childhood can be seen in their contradictory behaviors. Children's bravado shows up in their saying, "I dare you," when they have only begun to learn the skill themselves. Bravado during the day may be counterbalanced by nightmares, or by fears of the parents' deaths or divorce. To make themselves feel safer, they may identify with a super hero (e.g., GI Joe or Ninja turtles) (see "Cognitive Conceit," Chap. 21) or take on adult-type behaviors (e.g., wearing makeup and high heels) (Fig. 22-5). Shows of cockiness, false assurance, or even rudeness may be weak attempts to cover up the fear of failure, insecurity, and a continued need for protection and guidance. Alert adults can help the child negotiate this emotional ambivalence by responding with flexibility and by encouraging the child to take on new challenges with clear assurances of safety and support.

GAINING SOCIAL SKILLS THROUGH WIDENING SOCIAL RELATIONSHIPS

Intrafamilial Dynamics

During the school-age years the child's major context for emotional nurturance continues to be the family. A new balance between family, peers, society and self is negotiated. For the well-developing child, the balance between dependence and independence gradually leads to increased autonomy and self-confidence.

Relationship to Parents

The balance between dependence on and independence from the parents must be renegotiated repeatedly. Every perceived failure may be seen as a validation of one's vulnerability or dependence on the parents. However, both failures and achievements are opportunities for increased awareness of one's separateness, responsibility for personal efforts, and social–emotional growth.

For instance, when a first grader makes a new friend, there is a validation of one's personhood and acceptance by others. Self-esteem and independence are enhanced. But when she gets arithmetic problems wrong, the child faces the challenge of learning to accept objective criticism without turning to one's mother for protection. The child may need to discuss feelings and disappointment later with the parents,

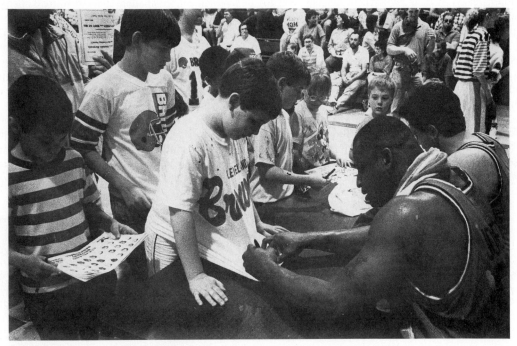

FIGURE 22–5.
Athletes and other "heroes" provide role models as well as vicarious experiences of strength and expertise.

but most first graders can accept the feedback from other caregivers independently. The challenge for parents is to provide the support necessary to sustain the child without stepping in to take over. Dealing with experiences of failure and success in the outer world with the assurance of continued secure acceptance from one's parents, helps the child to build a clearer sense of personal skills and weaknesses. This approach ultimately contributes to a realistic evaluation of one's abilities without infringing on one's value as a person.

VARIATIONS OF PARENTING PATTERNS. In our culture, children widen their social relationships beyond the family at an earlier age and at a more intense level because more people are involved in the caregiving process. Of children born in 1988, only 12% will grow up in traditional nuclear families where fathers go to work every day and mothers stay home.[44] The majority of today's children grow up with a variety of caregivers due to maternal employment, divorce, single parenting, paternal job loss, foster or adoptive placement, and so forth.[53]

Maternal Employment. Most Western families today are dual-income families. Over half of the mothers of school-age children in the United States work outside the home.[46] Working may produce an emotional drain on mothers who feel pressured to be both excellent employees at work and excellent mothers at home. However, if the mother is comfortable with her role at work and the father stays actively involved in the life of his children, the children, especially girls, tend to become more secure, mature, and independent.[45,46]

Children raised in dual-employment families tend to have fewer gender-stereotyped views.[46] The quality of the marital relationship, the arrangements provided for the care of these children (e.g., after-school programs), the child's characteristics, the availability of the father, and the father's working conditions are all factors that impact on the child's development.[20] When both parents are employed outside the home, they must work together to provide a supportive nexus for their children's social and emotional development. The term **latchkey children** refers to children whose time after school, before parents return from work, is essentially self-supervised. While many parents may use neighbors or friends for backup if the children feel they need help, they do not

provide on-site caregivers. Seven percent of preschool-age children and 40% of 8- to 10-year-old children must fend for themselves for part or all of the day.[67] For the older child, the chance to stay alone for two or three hours may represent an opportunity to demonstrate responsibility and autonomy, but younger children need clearer solutions to loneliness or minor problems that might arise within the house. Many children experience fear and have difficulty with self-discipline when adults are not readily available (Fig. 22-6). Older children without adult supervision are more susceptible to peer pressure to participate in antisocial behaviors.[74] In response to this pressing need for dependable, supportive supervision, many communities have begun to offer after-school activities for a reasonable cost.

Children of Marital Transitions: Divorce and Remarriage. The frequency of divorce today suggests that almost 50% of children will have at least some experience with single parenting as a result of parental divorce and marital transitions.[44] These relationship discontinuities are inevitably stressful on children. For some children, schoolwork may suffer when parents are feuding, either in the year before divorce, or if conflict continues during and after the divorce. Children facing divorce have less energy available to use in other ways and may have unexpected difficulty with developmental transitions, such as entering school, facing new classes or peers, or coping with the physical changes of early adolescence. Although many children appear to cope well with these stresses, recent research documents more long-term effects than previously recognized, including lower school achievement, continuing affective distress, behavior problems, and relationship problems during adolescent and adult years.[82] It takes children 2 to 3 years to "recover" from the stress of parental divorce. Even 5 years after parental divorce, one study discovered that only 34% reported that they were "happy," thriving, and doing well. Thirty-seven percent reported that they were "intensely unhappy," lonely, depressed, and angry.[83]

Most divorced parents remarry within 5 years, creating another crisis, despite the potential benefits. It may take longer for children to adjust to parental remarriage than to the original divorce.[44] Blended families with stepchildren from both sides add new sources of sibling tension, but also

FIGURE 22–6.
When children are left without adult supervision, temptation sometimes overpowers judgment, leading children into potentially dangerous situations.

offer new opportunities for sibling bonding. Repeating the cycle of divorce and remarriage for a second or third time is not uncommon, and it magnifies the stress with which children must cope and discourages commitment or emotional investment in relationships as adults. Parental divorce shakes the child's sense of identity, including who the child will become, and what is right and wrong.[17]

In middle childhood, children begin to comprehend the complexity of relationships and feel more complex emotions. Consequently, they may be more susceptible to stress. They are more sensitive to parental emotions and may become more aligned with one parent than the other. The younger child may cognitively interpret the implications of the divorce more concretely and literally (asking, for example, "If Mom and Dad get divorced, will he still be my Dad?"). In later middle childhood years, they usually are able to understand the relationships and can make better use of extended support systems, including other adults, grandparents, and friends. School may become an escape system.

Several crucial psychological tasks confront children following their parents' divorce:[82]

1. To understand the divorce.
2. To go on with their lives as children.
3. To grieve and cope with the loss of the intact family and often the loss of one parent.
4. To deal with anger and a sense of unfairness.
5. To absolve oneself of any responsibility for the divorce and work through a sense of guilt.
6. To accept the permanence of the divorce.
7. To understand the nature of love and caring in order to invest oneself in new relationships.

Healthy post-divorce adjustment is facilitated if parents minimize overt conflict, if the children maintain a close relationship with **both** parents, if children are provided with a secure and predictable environment, if parents exercise flexibility in redefining their roles in relationship to the children, and if the children have extensive social support networks.[15]

Single Parenting. Children in single-parent, mother-headed households face special challenges and unique opportunities in their development. The situation of single parenting, for any length of time, is often very stressful for both parent and child. Typically the mother experiences a loss of both economic and emotional support at just the time when she needs increased levels of support to deal with the challenges of rearing her children. Dealing with children who face the internal turmoil caused by the disruption in family relationships may increase her sense of guilt and her sense of loneliness. She may overly develop her relationship with the children as a "social pacifier" that substitutes for adequate meaningful adult contacts. In this situation it is difficult for a child to assess the rightful role as "child" in the family and to extend efforts toward his or her own development.

In an effort to identify the new rules or to express their own anger about parental separation, the children may test the mother's ability to set limits and provide discipline by acting in noncompliant or demanding ways. Of crucial importance is the quality of the parent's adjustment to singleness and the warmth of the parent–child relationship. Consistently nurturant interactions and parental willingness to discuss, nonjudgmentally, the child's feelings will strongly affect the emotional outcome for the children in a positive, adaptive way.

FACILITATING POSITIVE (HEALTHY) RELATIONSHIPS. Regardless of the family structure, some factors are crucial to healthy development of the children (many of these factors are discussed in Chap. 32). Adults in nontraditional families need to recognize that the children are still children, thus requiring:

1. Reassurances of continuation of the love-bond with both parents and all grandparents.
2. Maintenance of contact with a noncustodial parent.
3. Clear, growth-inducing rules.
4. Adults who listen.
5. Opportunities to continue with their own social life and opportunities to develop talents and interests.
6. Continued protection from situations, responsibilities beyond the child's adaptational skills.
7. Recognition of individuality, vulnerabilities, and strengths.
8. Freedom from concerns about meeting basic necessities of life.

Sibling Influence

Siblings usually provide the first and the most intense peer relationship.[60] During middle childhood, siblings exert a power second only to that of parents. Siblings provide a continuing relationship through crucial stages of development and family experiences. They also provide a forum for learning social skills, personality development, expression of feelings, and collaboration.[60] The sibling relationship may last 60 to 80 years, consequently, it behooves parents to foster a healthy, cooperative companionship in the children.

Sibling relationships are both horizontal and vertical, reciprocal and complementary.[26] Siblings engage in "give and take" interactions, shifting the responsibility for initiating the type (playful or task-oriented) and tone (positive or antagonistic) of the time together. At times, the older sibling takes on a parentlike role, giving instructions and demanding compliance from younger siblings.[8] Older siblings are more often the initiators of the relationships with young siblings, particularly of aggressive behaviors, while younger siblings imitate more.[2] Sibling rivalry is likely to occur if the siblings are jealous of perceived privileges and more lenient discipline the other child receives from the parents. When the interaction between parents and children is positive and characterized by individualized attention and respect, sibling quarrels decrease.

Longitudinal studies of siblings suggest that the sibling

bond is generally positive, even in mixed-gender dyads.[2] Children may have antagonistic moments, but those times do not jeopardize the intensity of the relationship. Children within a family stick together and often describe each other as best friends. The sibling bond tends to become stronger under chaotic situations such as marital transitions, alcoholism, or economic distress.[7] With siblings, children have the opportunity to practice social skills and coping strategies that facilitate interactions with peers. Older siblings are more likely to step into dominant positions in peer relationships, and younger siblings often have more extensive friendship circles because they have learned to adjust and compromise in response to their older siblings.[2] The influence of siblings seems to be stronger during middle childhood than at later developmental stages.

Effect of Ordinal Position

For generations, parents have been aware that, despite their best efforts, each child in the family develops a unique interactional pattern, even if two are identical twins. In a moment of either awe or frustration, the parents may ask, "How can two children be so different when they are raised in the same family?" Parents often try very hard to be fair and to treat each child equally. At Christmas or on the other special occasions, each child may receive *exactly* the same gift (except for a different color), but one child will still feel that the occasion is somehow unfair—and it probably is. One child may not have really wanted that particular gift, or the older child may resent the fact that the younger child is receiving a privilege at an earlier chronological age.

The truth is that **no two children are ever born into the same family,** even though they share the same parents and the same experiences. The simple fact that one child is born first may allow him or her the privileges of uncontested parental attention in the early years. A child may be the oldest of five, the second of two, the last of six, or the fifth of nine; each child experiences an entirely different family milieu.

Oldest Children. What is it like being the oldest kid in the family? According to Julia, age 7, "Nice, because I get to do more stuff than my sister." But Kevin, age 11, sees it differently: "Rotten. I have to take care of my baby brother if he cries too much . . . and he always cries when Mom is cooking dinner."

Oldest children in any family are more adult-oriented and are given more privileges (as their younger siblings point out) and more responsibility (as they are quick to point out). They identify more strongly with adult values and therefore develop strong personality patterns such as competitiveness, self-confidence, conformity, and conscientiousness. Firstborns have a few years in which they are the undisputed center of the household. When siblings arrive, they may feel ousted or relegated to an inferior position. By the time they are in school, oldest children, especially girls, may be taking on increased responsibilities for child care, for example, watching young children to be sure they "don't get into mischief" (e.g., playing in the bathroom or eating crayons). Oldest

children often help out more around the house. Parenting styles may alternate between supportive pampering to setting high expectations and strict rules for the first child. This combination of factors generally produces higher childhood and adulthood achievement patterns in firstborns.

Middle Children. In contrast, middle siblings have to struggle to get individualized, uninterrupted attention from the parents. Middle children may feel "lost in the shuffle" and a step behind the older siblings. "We try harder" seems to be their theme. Middle children spend more time with other children, especially older children. Consequently, middle children are more sensitive than firstborns to the values and preferences of peers, and are more oriented toward peers than adults. They may choose older siblings as role models, particularly in academic contexts. For instance, it is common for a first grader to pretend to read aloud by looking at the pictures in imitation of the fourth grader who is reading for the requirements of homework. Because middle children function as part of a group of children within the family (made up of those who are more competent and others who are less competent), they have many opportunities to learn how to be flexible and adaptable, and to negotiate and compromise. In school, middle children seem to exhibit the fewest behavior problems and show a relatively good adjustment to general life stress.[78]

Youngest Children. People who are the youngest in their families, the "babies," no matter how old they are, may never receive the parent's undivided attention until all the other children have left home. However, they are often the focus for the whole family's attention. Because there are more caregivers, it is generally easier for them to find someone ready to engage in play or in meeting specific needs. For some children, being pampered might encourage them to retain babyish mannerisms or to lag behind in self-sufficiency to guarantee the closeness of caregivers. They are less likely than middle children to be caught up in the rivalry or competition with older siblings and seem freer to forge their own individualistic way in the world. They may be more likely to act out because they have not been disciplined consistently and because they know someone in the family will be supportive of them, even if they are in trouble.[78]

Only Children. "Only" children find themselves in a unique position because they pick up the most salient characteristics of all three categories of birth order. "Only" children, like firstborns, are the depository of the parent's highest hopes and enduring expectations. Like middle children, they may develop mediation skills as they are the focus of the family triangle. And like the youngest in a family, they find themselves the focus of sustained nurturance. By school-age, only children tend to display a positive self-regard reflective of this high support, and consequently, experience a high degree of achievement and emotional stability in later years.

FACTORS MEDIATING BIRTH ORDER. Family size and socioeconomic status mediate the effects of birth order. In smaller families there may only be a firstborn and a youngest child.

Parenting experience and financial status of the parents at the time of the children's birth, and again during the teen years, can provide a "different family" for both of them. In larger families, financial resources and parental attention are often stretched between children, diluting attention and providing less focused expectations. Other factors such as school experiences, gender, ethnic background, urban or rural location, spacing of children, and religious training further mediate birth order effects.

MODERATING BIRTH ORDER EFFECTS. Positive relationships within the sibling subsystem can be facilitated by offering a variety of interactional opportunities within the family. Children should not be frozen into a unidimensional role with one of their siblings (e.g., the oldest girl *always* feeds the baby). Rotating or sharing family responsibilities teaches the skills of negotiation and compromise. Although family activities, especially those centered on having fun in active, participatory ways, build up trust between family members, each sibling also needs time alone to develop personal skills and preferences. Parents who can relate warmly to each child as an individual and also provide attention to the siblings as a group, will foster positive family relationships.

Extended Family Members

Inclusion of extended family members usually enriches family interactions. Grandparents are storehouses of information and ideas that represent significant personal and family history. The values and traditions they bring to the family circle provide rich resources to the developing child who is in the process of formulating personal values and goals. Visits with

aunts, uncles, and cousins remind children of the circle of family safety that backs up their nuclear family. Families whose extended relatives are at a distance may choose to widen their social family to include neighbors, fellow church or club members, foster children, exchange students, or people in need of emotional support networks (Fig. 22-7). For children, the richness of these extended family connections facilitate psychosocial development in modeling a variety of attitudes, choices, and styles of relating that can be integrated into the child's self-image.

Understanding One's Culture Beyond the Home

The School Environment

The school presents a new environment for the child, much larger and more complex than previously experienced. For many of us, memories of the first day of school still may evoke a sense of anticipation or fear, unrivalled in the rest of our development. It is one's formal initiation into a world beyond the home, a world in which we may not be treated as gently or regarded as positively as in the home environment. Although educational philosophy specifies that school is to be a safe, nurturant place where children are lead into an understanding of the basic tools of our culture, school is often experienced as a place where demands and expectations are unrealistic and where children are evaluated according to a rigid set of expectations.

During the elementary school years, the influence of the teacher on the child's values and self-esteem increases. In the

FIGURE 22–7.
Having an exchange student join the family is an excellent way to share and understand both cultural diversity and human likenesses.

current typical model of education in the United States, the elementary teacher is female and takes on a variety of roles, perceived by the children as limit-setter and judge on one hand and as guide and role model on the other. The teacher exerts influence in both direct and indirect ways. Most obvious are her choices about classroom structure, varying from the rectangular lineup of desks with students in alphabetical order, to the open classroom where learning stations allow free choice and mobility. Open classrooms tend to encourage prosocial behavior. Children in these classrooms have more varied relationships, participate in more school activities, cause fewer disciplinary confrontations, and produce more imaginative play.[54] However, for the anxious child who benefits from clarity and predictability, the structured classroom may be more conducive to learning. Thus, neither classroom arrangement guarantees more effective learning or academic achievements. A classroom that offers some flexibility within a clear structure is most likely to enhance the psychosocial development of most children.

Teachers sometimes develop and maintain expectancies of their students. Dubbed the "self-fulfilling prophecy," these expectations may be formed on the basis of first impressions and are subject to personal bias. In a now classic study, Rosenthal and Jacobson told teachers that specific students were "late bloomers" who should show tremendous academic gains during the year.[63] Although the children had been chosen randomly without any information on their intellectual potential, these children showed a significantly increased IQ score at the end of the year in comparison to their initial testing! Grades on report cards and comments on behavior followed suit: These children were evaluated more positively and maintained their advantage for several years. When teachers believe in the success of students, students may be more likely to become successful. Unfortunately the flip side of this position may also be true, although, for ethical reasons, it cannot be tested: Students considered to be "without promise" are more likely to underachieve relative to their abilities. The strength of the influence of teacher expectations has been hotly debated, and many argue that parental and self-expectations maintain a far greater impact. Nevertheless, teachers who support their students and believe in their abilities are more likely to maximize their potential.

Children from low socioeconomic homes or racial minorities are more likely to feel unsupported in traditional classrooms. It is unclear if this is related to children's misinterpretations of their experience or to actual differences in classroom dynamics. Representatives from all areas of the school system should make conscious efforts to provide developmentally appropriate curriculum materials and stimulate thoughtful discussions. They should integrate cultural arts and language, as well as specific interests of minority students, in an effort to enhance the children's motivation to learn.

Some students from lower socioeconomic backgrounds may enter the school scene without adequate preparation because the parents do not know what or how to teach the young child, do not have money to provide cultural exposure, or believe that the school will teach the child everything. Children from chaotic, poorly supervised homes may not understand the unspoken cultural expectations for social behavior and may not be motivated to learn them. In the structured school environment, these children may start off with an overload of negative, disciplinary comments.[25]

Even the well-behaved child may perceive the school setting as a forum for being judged. Elementary school children are very sensitive to being evaluated as inadequate. Every quiz, every test, any piece of homework, can be a minitrauma, especially for an anxious child. Anxiety about test taking is heightened when work is under a time pressure, when the examination is unexpected, or when teachers emphasize the critical nature of the exam.[56] Report cards with letter grades can make children dissatisfied with themselves and may, at least in the early grades, contribute to decreased motivation for learning.

It is critically important for teachers, administrators, and parents to work together, especially in the lower grades, to support children's learning and to maximize their willingness to assume more responsibility for their own learning process (Fig. 22-8). Parents need to be involved in school meetings, monitoring homework, and talking with teachers to prevent and help solve behavior and school adjustment problems.[68]

The Influence of Television

Television exerts a major socializing influence on school-age children simply because they spend a lot of time watching it. The average television in the United States runs for 6 hours a day.[74] Children between the ages of 2 and 5 average $23\frac{1}{2}$ hours of viewing time per week, and children 6 to 11 average $27\frac{1}{2}$ hours per week in front of the television.[17] It is estimated that by adolescence, children will have spent more time watching television (22,000 hours) than they have spent in school or in any other activity except for sleeping.[50, 71] Television watching often substitutes for family-oriented activities such as playing games and talking, and for outdoor activities and sports, reading, helping out with household chores, or development of talents and creative hobbies.

Only 11% of the viewing time of 2- to 11-year-olds is spent watching programs produced for children.[1] Since reality is still poorly defined through third grade, many children still accept much of what is viewed as real.[61] Heavy viewers (over 4 hours per day) tend to view the world as a more violent place than light viewers. They also exhibit more stereotyped gender roles as early as age 3.[17] Most parents do not consciously help children compare the values presented on television to those of the family. Stereotyping on the basis of racial categories and gender is a persistent problem and can carry over into real life attitudes.[50] Television offers images of sexuality and sexual activity that are impossible for the school-age child to understand and dangerous for the adolescent to emulate. Sexual portrayals often provide the raw material that goes into middle childhood's crude and rude jokes, gestures, and terms that the child really does not comprehend. The

FIGURE 22–8.
This young lady will have many experiences in the next 12 years that will affect her ability to meet the cultural expectations of adulthood. The ability of parents, community, and school to work cooperatively can determine the success of her efforts.

mimic super heroes, integrating this material into free play routines. Some children are sensitive to visual images intended to evoke fear and may question parents about whether or not the images, especially dragons, dinosaurs, trolls, evil spirits, and witches, are real or pretend. These images often carry over into nightmares, especially for the anxious child. Children who are less competent in school tend to watch more television (or vice versa), and are more likely to believe that the content is real.[17,32]

Television capitalizes on acts of physical or verbal aggression. Children between 8 and 12 years of age appear to be particularly sensitive to television violence.[33] Weekend daytime programs designed for children have a high aggressive content: 93% with violence at a rate of 17.6 incidents per hour.[86] Many cartoons are virtually non-stop acts of aggression by magical creatures in a fantasy setting. Music videos tend to capitalize on violence, sex, gender stereotypes, and anti-establishment themes. Fifty percent show antisocial behavior, 20% involve social protest, and 57% portray marriage negatively.[14]

Exposure to violence on television increases the chances that children will endorse aggressive attitudes on a self-report questionnaire, or act violently immediately afterwards in a laboratory setting, or in generalized aggressive behavior at school.[32] Children learn from television that violence is effective: it works for both the good guys and the bad guys. This makes it more likely that children in stressful situations will identify with the violent cues, (e.g., angry tone, verbalizations of hate or revenge), and act out in an aggressive way. Children who identify with a hero who uses force to win are more likely to be aggressive and eventually get caught in a vicious cycle: aggressive children prefer aggressive programs on television.[32]

Watching violence on television may cause indifference to violence in real life and desensitize its watchers to anxiety about dreadful acts. The viewer may feel aroused by the violent action, but while sitting in a relaxed setting, the discomfort eases relatively quickly. As children become less sensitized to violence and pain when they see it on television, they may become less concerned about real life violence and pain.

The lifestyle, clothing, and wealth displayed by many television characters provide an unrealistic touchstone for "successful" living. Older children may devalue their own parents or culture because of the discrepancies or may begin to resort to illegitimate means (e.g., stealing, drug-selling) to obtain an income that can surround them with assurances of value. In the absence of healthy family relationships and support, these televised standards may continue to serve as the person's idealized image of successful living as an adult, thereby leading the viewer to a low self-esteem or a life of manipulation and crime.

Although caregivers cannot totally shield a child from television without risking the child's alienation from peer culture, they can help a child understand the scenarios. Parents can limit viewing time, monitor program selection, dis-

visual images, often of an explicit nature, may even encourage precocious sexual exploration and undermine the natural development of respectful sexual intimacy within the value of a committed relationship. Children believe that what they see is a real and acceptable way of life.[17]

Advertisements portray a spirit of material acquisitiveness that is accepted as normative. Children demand the latest sneaker or clothing fashions, or the most gruesome set of outer space invaders as soon as they see them on television, regardless of the stash of clothing or ignored toys in the closet. Children in the early grades cannot apply logical analyses to the commercial glamour. They do not realize that advertisements often endorse products that are easily broken, hazardous, or non-nutritional. They may engage parents in emotional struggles for the advertised product, accusing parents as "uncaring" when they refuse to purchase the desired goods.

Children in the lower grades often identify with and

cuss the values and information presented on television within their own value system, decrease confusions by clarifying truth and reality versus fantasy, teach critical viewing skills, and discuss how what is viewed affects personal and community life.[17]

Peer Relations and Social Behavior

A child's sense of self takes shape in the context of relationships with others. Relationships with peers provide distinctive experiences, unlike those with parents or siblings. Friends provide opportunities for experimenting with new styles of relating, experiencing new qualities of trust in others, and learning new sensitivities within oneself. Peers serve as a mirror for testing one's acceptability and as competitors that help sharpen one's skills (Fig. 22-9).[42]

Social Cognitive Theory

During the school years, the child undergoes a decentering process, learning to differentiate between the perspectives of the self and others. This awareness develops in several stages.[69] By age 6, children become more adept at *predicting* the needs or preferences of another person and thus may describe mother's desires in terms of something he or she heard mother say. The 6-year-old who watches his father wrapping a handbag may say, "Mother won't like that; it doesn't have pockets," because he heard her complain one day as she scrounged through her pocketbook for a pen.

Around age 8, *reciprocal skills* develop. Children begin to recognize that conflict erupts with a friend when they view a situation differently, and thus, impetus is given to try to predict the other's perspective. They begin to consciously look for responses in the facial expressions of others.[39] Some may change their behavior based on their predictions of another's response. Around age 10, *mutuality* develops, and a child can perceive how a third person may interpret or feel about some action of the two close friends (e.g., how a teacher may feel about them whispering in class). By adolescence, children can produce *in-depth perspectives* showing awareness of complicated interactions of groups of people within complicated systems. As children attain higher levels of perspective taking, they become capable of more complicated and rich relationships.

Sullivan's Theory

Sullivan observes that children have a growing need for friends, or "compeers."[76] Children in the "juvenile era" participate in a gradually expanding world, which provides self-knowledge and confrontation between the self and the rules of the world. Very early, children become aware of competition and realize that their status in the group hinges on their performance. They recognize the social implications of titles such as "high achiever," "campus clown," "good dresser," or "delinquent," and become vulnerable to teasing.

Some time between 8½ and 12 years of age, the juvenile moves into the preadolescence era, which is characterized by **isophilic intimacy.** Sullivan contrasts isophilic intimacy, loving a member of the same gender, with **autophilic** (self love) and **heterophilic** (loving a member of the other gender) intimacy. This is the first love relationship outside the family, and confirms one's "lovability." By isophilic intimacy, Sullivan does not mean *homosexual* physical intimacy, but deep *homosocial* friendship. The same-sex person who meets these emotional/social intimacy needs is described as a "chum or best friend." Isophilic intimacy furthers self-identity and helps to lay a foundation for heterophilic intimacy. According to Sullivan, preadolescence ends not with the establishment of the homosocial relationship, but with puberty and lust—the awareness of a desire for satisfaction of sexual drives.

Developing Friendships

Many skills are involved in learning to be a good friend and a participant in social interactions. Children are drawn together on the basis of shared interests and become friends by participating in trust-building experiences.[35] Popular children are friendly and skilled in initiating and maintaining relationships. They learn how to greet newcomers, begin conversations, and invite children to join their activities. Social competence and self-esteem emerge as the child learns the skills of

FIGURE 22–9.
School-agers typically strive for homogeneity to support their own developing ego (e.g., same-gender grouping, all have bangs, long straight hair, short-sleeved tops).

when to cooperate and when to compete.[28] Popular children learn to maintain friendships by communicating clearly, telling another when their message is incomplete, and negotiating conflict.

As children grow older, their understanding of friendship changes. To 6- and 7-year-olds, friendship consists of playing with the same toys or doing things together. Children 9 or 10 years of age describe friendship as the sharing of thoughts and feelings. Friendship, they realize, is not simply being together. Friends recognize warm feelings and commitments toward one another and make decisions with the other in mind. A 10-year-old may therefore decide to visit her sick friend rather than go to a party, explaining that "I had to; she's my friend." At 11 or 12 years, friendships are characterized by sharing problems, emotional support, trust, and loyalty. By this age, friends know the likes, dislikes, and concerns of one another. When a friend gets a good grade, they rejoice, knowing how much the friend studied. When giving gifts, they work hard to choose something the other will like.

Friends are crucial to healthy psychosocial development, and most school-agers have at least one good friend. Friendship attachments often remain stable during the primary grades.[9] These friends become increasingly important during the middle school years, and parents become less important. Friends elicit stronger emotional responses than others, and engage more deeply in play. They share, talk, practice fighting, negotiation, and making up, and strong bonds are formed. They experience vicarious delight and sadness. Friends teach children the "scripts" they will use in future relationships.

Acceptance into a peer group may be influenced by many factors, such as attractiveness, age, gender, talent, communication skills, or ability to arbitrate decisions for a group.[64] While every child may at times be the brunt of peer cruelty, children with solid self-esteem and flexibility are able to endure until it passes on to another child. Many children who do not fit into the most popular clique at school still develop satisfying friendship groups both at school and in their neighborhoods.

Although aggression should not be the predominant mode of interaction, conflict may actually play a positive role in children's early peer relationships.[70] Indeed, children may have *more* angry arguments with their closest friends. "Rough and tumble" friendships provide conflict that strengthen affiliation, as children resolve differences of opinion.[47]

Facilitating Development of Social Skills

Children with poor social skills may need assistance in bolstering their understanding of social interactions. The simplest intervention for developing social skills is to provide a friend. Children who interact regularly with at least one other child generally learn the skills necessary to maintain a relationship. Children also benefit from advice and the direct teaching of social skills.[16] Dodge has described children's response to social information in five steps: decoding of social cues, interpretation, response search, selecting an optimal response, and enactment.[24] For children with poor social skills, isolating the inappropriate behavior and suggesting an alternative adaptive response may be enough to change the behavior. For example, aggressive boys are more likely to perceive another child's advance as hostile. When more positive reasons for behaviors are explained, aggressive boys often develop more empathy and thus exhibit more positive responses to overtures. If children are taught how to greet peers, how to negotiate conflict, or give positive feedback, they are more likely to get and keep friends. This in turn raises self-esteem, and a positive social cycle can be initiated.

Identifying One's Self Through One's Peers

During the school-age years, children may become painfully aware of their inadequacies and search for ways to bolster their esteem in the eyes of others (see "Cognitive Ineptitude," Chap. 21). Thus, children of middle childhood may boast of their abilities, claiming outrageous strength or precision ("I can beat up your big brother!" or "I'm smarter than you are," when, in fact, grades are poor). Such boasts are an attempt to defend themselves when they feel threatened. Children may need ego protection and reassurances of continued acceptance while they experiment with alternative behaviors.

Although facing reality is essential, emphasizing or encouraging acknowledgment of real strengths, combined with humor and tolerance, can help a child feel supported and prevent feelings of devastation over the failure to live up to impossible standards. Because middle school children spend so much of their time practicing new skills, this becomes a good time to talk with children about "sharing" and "including" those who are different, and opening their world to people, activities, food, cultures, and ideas that are "different" from their own experience.

A significant area of stereotyping is in gender roles. When children identify that they are male or female, they begin to choose behaviors deemed culturally appropriate for their gender. They identify with the same-gender parent, quickly label the gender of others, and respond differentially to another's gender. At the same time, boys, more quickly than girls, develop increasingly stereotyped gender behaviors (Fig. 22-10).[38] Girls who prefer the activities of boys are not treated as harshly by peers. They may be ignored or accepted rather than criticized. As children encounter a greater variety of people, roles, and preferences, and as they mature, they demonstrate greater awareness that gender roles are flexible.

Because of the need to associate with people with whom the child can identify, the play and social groups of school-age children tend to become increasingly gender segregated until puberty. Girls tend to stay with dyads or triads of girls; boys tend to play in larger groups of boys. Boys devote more energy to setting and administering rules and regulations; girls focus more on the patterns of social interaction that may include or exclude others. Thus, girls in their play focus on social relatedness, whereas boys play at competency and competition. Both social relatedness and a sense of personal competency are necessary as the child fits into the wider cultural context.

FIGURE 22–10.
Young boys tend to shun girls to pursue more "masculine" activities and environments. Running around with "the boys" helps with the continued weaning from parental supervision.

Children gradually learn to balance the internal drive for expression and the external demand for conformity in social behavior. Children growing up in families with strong family traditions or associations with cultural traditions, such as their own ethnic heritage or church involvement, often learn to perceive themselves and express themselves in a more differentiated way. They know they are both part of a valuable group of people and yet are separate individuals within that group. A child who understands and accepts the traditions and skills of his or her culture or subculture has a better chance at negotiating a personally satisfying niche in that social structure.

Third-Culture Kids

One of the major tasks of the school-age years is to "participate in and identify with cultural traditions" (Fig. 22-11). School-agers thrive on learning the music, lingo, traditions, holidays, sagas, games, values, gender roles, and social nuances of the culture. They derive a sense of belonging from this close association and identification with others. They learn the basic skills valued by the culture. Friendships are made, niches found, secrets and special experiences are shared, all laying the foundations for special memories and long-term relationships. Continuity of culture, people, and relationships offers stability and an arena for practicing social skills, exploring one's special talents, uniquenesses, and separate identity.

However, in today's world, a child may spend part or all of the developmental years in "a culture other than his own and has a sense of identity to both or all cultures. He takes pieces of those cultures and has a sense of identity with each of them, but doesn't have a sense of ownership in any of them."[58] From these two (or more) cultural exposures, the child forms his own unique blending—a third culture.[80] Children of diplo-

matic personnel, missionaries, international businessmen, and military personnel may have a difficult time answering the question, "Where do you come from?" They may feel that they have two or more "homes," yet feel like an alien in both. Each time the child returns "Stateside," this "global nomad" may experience unresolved grief because of the multiple simultaneous losses that no one understands or supports.[57]

There are many advantages to being a Third-Culture Kid (TCK). Ninety percent speak more than one language.[57] As they mature, they have increased powers of observation, greater flexibility, the ability to withhold judgment, and greater empathy because of their experiences. However, TCKs also may experience rootlessness, insecurity, ongoing sadness due to unresolved grief, and a feeling of being out of step with others.[59] They have a different knowledge base, may not know expected etiquette or clothing styles, and function from a different social value system and interest base. They have learned to make friends easily, but the repeated fractured relations prevent the time and energy investment necessary for depth of relationships or for developing the skills essential for conflict resolution. At the same time, a TCK may find monocultural friends shallow or boring. The truth is that the TCK may not really know who he or she is.[10, 27] Study of TCKs reveals the importance of identifying one's self within the context of a stable group in order to individuate with maturity. The stability of the parents' relationship becomes a critical factor in the child's security when all else seems unstable. Many TCKs continue to experience a feeling of rootlessness and alienation into their adult years, seeking other TCKs for meaningful, synchronous relationships. Additional information can be obtained from the Institute for International Studies in Education, Erickson Hall, Michigan State University, East Lansing, MI 48824.

STRESSORS OF SCHOOL-AGE YEARS

Stress is endemic to humanness: children are not protected from stress by virtue of their age. For the school-age child, stress occurs with divorce, uniqueness, homelessness, abuse, pressure to perform well in school, moving, growth spurts, new challenges, and many other factors. Growing up is stressful, even for well-adjusted children. Children experience stress as an integral part of school, family, or peer experiences, as well as from normal physical, cognitive and emotional changes. In Western societies, 40% to 48% of 6- to 11-year-olds exhibit moderate to high amounts of stress; 35% of children experience stress-related health problems.[13] These challenges can positively impact a child's development if parents and teachers are sensitive to the child's needs as they occur.

School Factors

Achievement Pressure

School is a common source of pressure. Achievement is heavily emphasized in American society. Yet achievement depends upon a complex interaction of factors, and children

FIGURE 22–11.
During the school years, children invest themselves in learning the traditions of their culture. When these traditions can be shared with others, self-esteem and early generativity are fostered. (Photograph courtesy of African Children's Choir, sponsored by Friends in the West, Arlington, WA.)

within the same family may differ widely in achievement levels. Everyone knows children who, though lacking academic skills, compensate by working hard; and conversely, of children who are capable but do poorly in school. The difference between these two children is their motivation to do well, their need for achievement. High achievers may excel under pressure, developing new talents and maintaining good grades. Poor achievers may find that pressure interferes with performance. These children often have a lower need for achievement, a more external locus of control, difficulty setting goals, and an impulsive cognitive style.

Middle-class parents tend to encourage high academic achievement as a value more than lower-class parents. Parents who are better educated often believe that education is necessary for getting ahead in the world. When they provide an enriched learning environment, their children are better prepared for starting school.

The first year of schooling can be a "period of considerable consequences for shaping subsequent achievement trajectories."[4] When parents are involved and support the child's learning process right from the beginning, the child has a better chance at maximizing intellectual and social potentials. Teachers can affect their students' performance (the Rosenthal effect), although the magnitude of this effect is not

clear. If teachers expect more of whites than blacks, of boys than girls, and of middle-class than lower-class students, then students tend to align their behaviors with teacher expectations. Children tend to shape their self-expectations to teacher expectations during the early school years. First graders in one study were aware that teachers treated high and low achievers differently, and matched their self-expectations to teacher expectations.[85] In this study, fifth graders were even more likely to mirror teacher expectations in their self-descriptions.

Underachievement is a complex problem resulting in a cyclic process of failure, censure, and decreased efforts. The experience of negative feedback from parents, teachers, and peers is unlikely to inspire any student to improve and may cement an oppositional response style to parental or teacher authority. Parents of underachievers must coordinate efforts with the school and with the child to address a realistic plan for helping the child to experience success, manage homework, or study for tests. Helping the child to be in control, experience success, see improvement, and receive legitimate praise are the crucial keys to reversing a pattern of underachievement.

Underachievement may also be precipitated by the American tendency to speed children's development (the "hurried child").[29] We provide children with enriching experiences from the cradle, exult over every milestone passed and every skill mastered, searching for markers that our child is more "brilliant" or more "athletic" than the next, visiting on the child our own inadequacies. We pressure the child into dance, music, sports, and art lessons, usurping time needed for developing peer relationships or stabilizing present skills.

The pressure for early maturation is intensified by increasingly early evaluations. Many school systems now give children readiness assessments to measure their knowledge of kindergarten or first-grade skills. Although early evaluation can provide useful information when special services are needed, early abilities do not necessarily predict later achievement. The anxiety that inaccurate interpretation of early tests can cause parents may outweigh the potential beneficial effects for some children. High achieving or gifted parents do not necessarily have gifted children, and it is wise to remember that pressuring children in academic pursuits can interfere with emotional and social development. Waiting a year to start school frequently allows for a better match between the child's readiness and learning experiences. *Early success, not early starting, facilitates higher achievement in later grades.*

Pressures for early maturation and extraordinary excellence are not limited to the academic arena. In middle childhood, and even earlier, children are teased about having "boyfriends" and "girlfriends," or parental approval is voiced over "little adult" hair and clothing fashions (Fig. 22-12). These pressures rob children of the joys inherent in childhood and force them to assume premature sexual roles and social sophistication; thus depriving children of the time, opportunities, and experiences essential to self-knowledge

by encouraging attention to superficial, artificial criteria, which may become the touchstones for identity and adulthood. "Good parents" provide opportunities for children to enjoy structured and unstructured social relationships with people of all ages. They encourage children to develop their unique talents and interests without involving them in so many scheduled activities (e.g., Little League, music lessons, Scouts) that family meals, social times, and self-esteem suffer.[21]

Family Factors

Parent–Parent Relationship

The relationship between the parents is a crucial factor in a child's social–emotional development. Frequent bickering or outright conflict erodes a child's sense of security, elevates concerns about family dissolution, denies continued "refueling" opportunities, and saps energies needed to face other stressors of life. Some parents, although physically present, may be emotionally unavailable to their children because they are consumed by their own stresses. This is especially true when marital conflict precipitates maternal depression.[19] Distressed fathers tend to become more intrusive on a child's activities, thus decreasing learning.[11]

Conflicting rules and values from the parents lead to confusion for the child trying to discover the more complex cause–effect relationships of life. If parents argue repeatedly, children may express their tension and insecurity by poor school performance or emotional concerns. Behaviors observed between feuding parents may be reenacted with siblings or peers, or later in one's own marital relationship.

FIGURE 22–12.
Older school-agers begin to learn skills that facilitate heterosocial relationships.

When parents seriously work to limit conflict, avoid verbal aggression, and develop negotiation approaches that facilitate resolution of conflict, confrontation can have a positive impact on developing children. Harmony and cooperation between parents facilitates positive emotional and social development of the children (see Chaps. 29 and 32).

Child Neglect and Abuse

Mistreatment of school-age children, often by someone in their family, has increased in frequency and intensity in the United States during the past 50 years. **Neglect** (failure to provide adequate care for children) and **abuse** (discipline or treatment that is so forceful it hurts the child) may occur when parents feel overwhelmed, frustrated, or angry, or when they overreact to noncompliance, normal developmental curiosity, immaturity, or a negative behavior on the part of the child. Unfortunately, abuse and neglect have long-term developmental implications, and children who learn from parents that violence is a powerful way to get what they want are more likely to replicate hostile, aggressive patterns in their social relationships as adults and in their own efforts at rearing children.

Child sexual abuse during the school-age years is currently reported by at least 20% of American adults. Girls are 4 times more likely than boys to be victims of sexual abuse. Abuse is perpetrated primarily by men, and often by men who are social caregivers of the child.[81] For the child, the effects of sexual abuse may show up immediately in the form of withdrawal, guilt, depression, regressive behaviors, inappropriate sexual acting out, aggression, inability to concentrate, poor peer relations, and self-destructive or counterproductive behaviors. Sexual abuse has serious long-term emotional and behavioral effects. The child's sense of betrayal will affect future trust relations and the development of a secure sexual identity. The child often develops low self-esteem from the stigmatization and guilt of the experience. A sense of disempowerment may develop as the child experiences a loss of personal effectiveness and choice-making as a result of the personal effectiveness and choice-making as a result of the victimization experience.

Child Factors

Hyperactivity

Some children always seem to be getting into mischief. They run when they should walk, they talk when they should listen, and they do homework, but not the right page. Overactivity and inattentiveness are the hallmarks of children with an *attention deficit disorder* (also known as hyperkinesis, minimal brain dysfunction, and hyperactivity). Children who have difficulty prioritizing parental or teacher requests, or who cannot develop self-control of impulses, are at risk for developing conduct problems in junior high school.[43] Teaching the child how to slow down and focus in very concrete ways can improve performance at school. Teaching self-control strategies such as talking oneself through an activity or respon-

sibility, closing one's eyes when listening to instructions, or using a calming routine can help the child learn to control impulsive actions. Some children also "slow down" when they discover that the parent or teacher is willing to listen with full attention and provide responsive, active feedback for as long as it takes to communicate a message.

Depression and Anxiety in Children

Every school-age child experiences moments of sadness. These sad moods occur after the child sustains a loss, which may be large, such as the death of a family member, or small, as in the misplacement of a favorite pencil. Although children may feel distressed enough to cry, in early middle childhood, they may not be able to label their feelings accurately nor verbalize the causes of their pain. They live in the "here and now" and cannot project themselves into the future and perceive feeling any different. As they approach adolescence, cognitive processes enable them to see themselves in a more objective, coherent way and thus to report feelings and depressive moods. One out of 14 children, and one out of every seven adolescents, is seriously depressed.[62] Any child who is chronically upset, lonely, sad, or low in energy during middle childhood may develop clinical depression requiring therapy during adolescence.[65, 88] Accident-proneness and nebulous health problems are also clues to depression.[17]

Caregivers can help children sort out their emotions at a level that meets the child's ability to verbalize experience. When children report that they have no friends, that nobody loves them, that they never get to do what they want, the parent should not ignore these comments as "silly talk," especially if these themes are repeated frequently. Provision of warm responsive support and redirection of energies into an enjoyable activity can help to dissipate the negative energies of the moment. Sitting down later when the child is calm and talking about these emotional impressions with an attitude of warmth and caring can help the child to find alternative ways to face life, understand self, and resist viewing the self as helpless or hopeless. A disturbed parent–child relationship is the most common cause of severe stress and depression. Therefore, improving the relationship is critical to both therapy and prevention (Fig. 22-13).[17]

Children under 6 years tend to view emotions as an innate part of a situation. By 10 years of age they begin to realize that emotions are individualized reactions to events as mediated by perceptual and mental processes.[39] This awareness enables them to use cognitive approaches to "cheer up" by thinking positively or forgetting about the bad.

Crises and Transitions

School-age children need stable, predictable environments. At times, illness or fractionalization of the family may interfere with their stability. Foster parenting is provided when parents abuse or are unable to provide for children. Unfortunately, children often are placed in unfamiliar homes, and none of their siblings may be present. Some children experience

FIGURE 22–13.
The best immunization against depression and vulnerability is a healthy, loving home, where parents and children have some common goals that encourage them to spend time working together.

multiple foster placements during their lifetime, and thus miss the continuity so essential to stabilization of their own immature identity. The sense of abandonment can increase their sense of vulnerability, lower self-esteem, and increase aggressive defensiveness.

Homelessness is becoming an increasing problem. The National Coalition for the Homeless estimates that 500 to 800 thousand homeless persons are children.[55] As in foster parenting, children experience serious disruption in their lives. Homelessness is accompanied by a myriad of other problems, including lack of continuity in academic learning, lack of "belonging" to a peer group, inability to develop a talent or interest, family disruption, inadequate health care or nutrition, and perpetual financial crisis.

Children with extended or frequent hospitalizations may be "at-risk" in the areas of identity development, attachment, and maturity. Threats to identity development may be minimized by providing children as much stability and continuity as possible, inside and out of the hospital. Children may fear losing their parents, as well as functioning, body parts, or life itself. Thus parents should be readily available to hospitalized children and should explain hospital procedures as completely as possible. Academic learning should also be maintained as much as possible in the hospital and during recuperative periods to prevent the stress that emerges from academic failure or inability to keep up with peers.

The school-age child, whose developing self-concept is based on concrete experiences, should be provided with as much continuity as possible in the face of these and other disruptions. If possible, children should be kept in the same school system or provided individual support to help them through the transition. They should be allowed to carry with them objects that symbolize home and family.

The Resilient Child

The term *stress* inherently connotes negative effects and elicits immediate concern for children's development and health status. Yet some children respond well to stressors. These children, described as *resilient* or *invulnerable* children, can maintain equilibrium in the face of stress that creates significant problems for other children.[36]

A child's resilience is a complex function of his or her temperament and response style, as well as family characteristics and external stressors. Temperament is generally assumed to be a biologically built-in, relatively stable characteristic of children. Thomas and Chess, in their classic New York Longitudinal Study, differentiated between temperamentally "difficult," "easy," and "slow to warm up" children.[77] "Difficult" children show sleep, feeding, and elimination irregularities, inflexibility, slow adaptability, and negative moods. In contrast, "easy" babies are friendly, happy, and adaptable. "Slow to warm up" children seem anxious until they settle in and the situation and environment seem familiar. Children in the same family often show different temperaments.

Temperamentally difficult children are less adaptable, more vulnerable to adversity, and more likely to produce and elicit adverse responses. Temperamentally easy or adaptable children are less likely to be the recipient of hostility, anger, or adult anxiety, and are better able to cope with negative situations, partly because they generally develop more extensive positive support systems.

Although difficult children may be at greater risk for later social and emotional problems, the development of these problems depends on a variety of other factors, including parenting style. In some cases, a child's temperament matches parenting style, a parallel that Thomas and Chess described as "goodness of fit." When there is a match, the child's development is optimized. Parents who provide patient, firm, consistent, and tolerant parenting best protect difficult children from developing maladaptive behaviors.

As indicated in the *Stress Scale for Children,*[66] children, like adults, are sensitive to changes that impact on daily life experiences, especially if these changes occur in relationships (see Social Readjustment Rating Scale, Chap. 39). Loss of a parent, whether through death, desertion, or marital transition, is considered to be the most stressful experience for a child.[66] Emotional upsets, negative behaviors, persistent fears, and regression to immature behaviors often signal a child's inability to cope with their experiences. Children may withdraw socially, develop unexplained aches and pains, or act out in covert ways.

Adult perception of stress does not necessarily match a child's perception. When fourth to sixth graders were asked to rank life events according to their degree of stress, they paralleled many of the adult rankings of stress, but included other sources of stress, most notably, events which engendered public embarrassment.[87]

Temperament and response style may predispose a child towards vulnerability or invulnerability, but effective parenting can moderate the effects of stressors. Parents who provide constructive environments better prepare their children for the inevitable stresses that all people face. As children develop competencies in self-control and awareness of their social world, they often become better able to resolve stress appropriately. Resiliency can be developed by providing a stable family environment, facilitating the emergence of positive self-esteem, supporting the child's problem-solving abilities, and by teaching self-soothing, relaxation, and coping strategies.

IMPLICATIONS

The school-ager confronts a series of developmental tasks that, in the presence of supportive parents, are easily resolved. Resolution of social–emotional tasks depends on the child's increasing cognitive abilities, which in turn form the basis for an increasing awareness of the larger world and of the rules and relationships within it. Although the child has not yet developed a stable sense of self-identity, the experiences of the middle childhood years lay a foundation for identifying one's interests and special abilities—prerequisites for organized self-awareness. Participating in activities, developing hobbies, and accomplishing school objectives gives the child a sense of work well done. The healthy child becomes an increasingly industrious participant in life and a flexible and positive contributor to the lives of others.

As school-agers continually widen and broaden their awareness of persons and institutions, their world changes markedly. Over time, they master the rules of school and the changing content of their school's curriculum. They learn to participate in both one-on-one and group peer relationships

and to understand others' perspectives, even those with whom they have little contact. They participate in organizations, begin to pledge their allegiance, and actively seek to understand attitudes and values. Parents continue to contribute to the child's personality, self-esteem, and values by the way they offer discipline, moral teaching, social relationships, protection, love, and opportunities to maximize potentials. Schools and friends provide situations that further challenge and nurture cognitive, social, and spiritual development in an individualistic, self-differentiated way.

Today's school-age children are under more stress than in previous eras owing to: (1) a broader exposure to the problems of today's society as addressed in mass media, (2) the influence of rapid changes in technology, (3) the need for increased information and higher performance output to succeed in today's culture, (4) the increased mobility and instability of the family, and (5) the threats of nuclear war, environmental pollution, and crime. Children seem to be required to live in and through a whirlwind of changes, some of which may seem hostile to their developing concept of self. Every school-age child has the capacity to be resilient, to meet challenges by developing coping skills that eventually contribute to adaptive skills for adolescence and adulthood. But it is up to the significant adults to help children develop that resiliency by assisting them in their efforts to "learn how to work." Children are eager to move forward into an increasingly larger, more exciting, and more responsive world. We as a society, as parents, and as caregivers, need to provide them with as broad a base of experience as possible. We need to nurture our children's self-esteem appropriately as they move forward into the larger world as a person-in-process, sorting out who they are and who they choose to become.

REFERENCES

1. Abelman, R. (1987). TV literacy II: Amplifying the affective level effect of television's prosocial face value through curriculum intervention. *Journal of Research and Development in Education, 20,* 40–49.
2. Abramovitch, R., Corter, C., Pepler, D. J., & Stanhope, L. (1986). Sibling and peer interaction: A final follow-up and a comparison. *Child Development, 57*(1), 217–229.
3. Adler, A. (1956). *The individual psychology of Alfred Adler.* Edited and annotated by H. L. Ansbacher and R. R. Ansbacher. New York: Harper and Row.
4. Alexander, K. L., & Entwisle, D. R. (Eds.). (1988). Achievement in the first two years of school: Patterns and processes. *Monograph of the Society for Research in Child Development, 53,*(2).
5. Bandura, A. (1977). *Social learning theory.* Englewood Cliffs, NJ: Prentice-Hall.
6. Bandura, A. (1978). The self system in reciprocal determinism. *American Psychologist, 33,* 344–358.
7. Bank, S., & Khan, M. (1982). *The sibling bond.* New York: Basic Books.
8. Berndt, T., & Bulleit, T. (1985). Effects of sibling relationships on preschoolers' behavior at home and at school. *Development Psychology, 21,* 761–767.

9. Berndt, T., Hawkins, J., & Hoyle, S. (1986). Changes in friendship during a school year; Effects on children's and adolescents' impressions of friendship and sharing with friends. *Child Development, 57,* 1284–1297.

10. Brislin, R. W., & Van Buren, H, (1987). Can they go home again? In G. R. Weaver (Ed.), *Readings in Cross-Cultural Communication* (2nd ed.) (pp. 269–278). Lexington, MA: Ginn Press.

11. Brody, G. H., Pillegrini, A. D., & Sigel, I. E. (1986). Marital qualities and mother-child and father-child interactions with school-aged children. *Developmental Psychology, 22*(3), 291–296.

12. Bronfenbrenner, U. (1979). *The ecology of human development: Experiments by nature and design.* Cambridge, MA: Harvard University Press.

13. Brown, B., & Rosenbaum, L. (1984). Stress and competence. In J. H. Humphrey (Ed.), *Stress in childhood.* New York: A.M.S. Press.

14. Brown, J. D., & Campbell, K. (1986). Race and gender in music videos: The same beat but a different drummer. *Journal of Communication, 36,* 94–106.

15. Camara, K., & Resnick, G. (1988). Interpersonal conflict and cooperation: Factors moderating children's post-divorce adjustment. In E. Hetherington & J. Arasteh (Eds.), *Impact of divorce, single parenting, and step parenting on children.* Hillsdale, NJ: Erlbaum.

16. Cartledge, G., & Milburn, J. (1986). *Teaching social skills to children: Innovative approaches* (2nd ed.). New York: Pergamon.

17. Clapp, G. (1988). *Child study research: Current perspectives and applications.* Lexington, MA: Lexington Books.

18. Coopersmith, S. (1967). *The antecedents of self-esteem.* San Francisco: Freeman.

19. Cox, A. D. (1988). Maternal depression and impact on children's development. *Archives of Disease in Childhood, 63,* 90–95.

20. Crouter, A. C., & Perry-Jenkins, M. (1986). Working it out: Effects of work on parents and children. In M. W. Yogman & T. B. Brazelton (Eds.), *In support of families.* Cambridge, MA: Harvard University Press.

21. Curran, D. D. (1983). *Traits of a healthy family: Fifteen traits commonly found in healthy families by those who work with them.* Minneapolis, MN: Winston Press.

22. Damon, W. (1977). *The social world of the child.* San Francisco: Jossey-Bass.

23. Damon, W., & Hart, D. (1982). The development of self-understanding from infancy through adolescence. *Child Development, 53,* 841–864.

24. Dodge, K. A. (1983). Behavioral antecedents of peer social status. *Child Development, 54,* 1386–1399.

25. Dumas, J. (1989). Treating antisocial behaviors in children: Child in family approaches. *Clinical Psychology Review, 9,* 197–222.

26. Dunn, J. (1983). Sibling relationships in early childhood. *Child Development, 54,* 787–811.

27. Eakin, D. B. (1979). The real culture shock: Adolescent reentry to the U. S. *Foreign Service Journal, August,* 20–22.

28. Eisenberg, N., Shell, R., Pasternack, J., Lennon, R., Beller, R., & Mathy, R. (1987). Prosocial development in middle childhood: A longitudinal study. *Developmental Psychology, 23,* 712–718.

29. Elkind, D. (1988). *The hurried child* (rev. ed.). Reading, MA: Addison-Wesley.

30. Erikson, E. (1963). *Childhood and society* (2nd ed.). New York: W.W. Norton.

31. Erikson, E. (1968). *Identity: Youth and Crisis.* New York: W.W. Norton.

32. Eron, L.D. (1982). Parent-child interaction, television violence, and aggression of children. *American Psychologist, 37*(2), 197–211.

33. Eron, L.D., & Huesmann, L.R. (1986). The role of television in the development of prosocial and antisocial behavior. In D. Olweus, J. Block, & M. Radke-Yarrow (Eds.), *The development of antisocial and prosocial behavior: Research, theories, and issues.* New York: Academic Press.

34. Franz, C., & White, K. (1985). Individuation and attachment in personality development: Extending Erikson's theory. *Journal of Personality, 53,* 224–256.

35. Furman, W. (1987). Acquaintanceship in middle childhood. *Developmental Psychology, 23*(4), 563–570.

36. Gamezy, N. (1983). Stressors of childhood. In N. Gamezy & M. Rutter (Eds.), *Stress, coping and development in children.* New York: McGraw-Hill.

37. Guidano, V., & Liotti, G. (1983). *Cognitive processes and emotional disorders.* New York: Guilford.

38. Guttentag, M., & Bray, H. (1976). *Undoing sex stereotypes: Research and resources for educators.* New York: McGraw-Hill.

39. Harris, P.L. (1989). *Children and emotion: The development of psychological understanding.* New York: Basil Blackwell.

40. Hart, D., Maloney, J., & Damon, W. (1987). The meaning and development of identity. In T. Honess & K. Yardley (Eds.), *Self and identity: Perspectives across the lifespan.* London: Routledge and Kegan Paul.

41. Harter, S. (1983). Developmental perspectives on the self system. In P. H. Mussen (Ed.), *Handbook of child psychology* (4th ed., Vol. 4). New York: Wiley.

42. Hartup, W. (1989). Social relationships and their developmental significance. *American Psychologists, 44,* 120–126.

43. Henker, B., & Whalen, C. (1989). Hyperactivity and attention deficits. *American Psychologist, 44,* 216–223.

44. Hetherington, E. M., Stanley-Hagan, M., & Anderson, E. (1989). Marital transitions: A child's perspective. *American Psychologist, 44,* 303–312.

45. Hoffman, L. W. (1984). Work, family and the socialization of the child. In R. D. Parke (Ed.), *Review of child development research* (Vol. VII, The family). Chicago: University of Chicago Press.

46. Hoffman, L. W. (1989). Effects of maternal employment in the two-parent family. *American Psychologist., 44,* 283–292.

47. Humphreys, A. P., & Smith, P. K. (1987). Rough and tumble friendship, and dominance in schoolchildren: Evidence for continuity and change with age. *Child Development, 58*(1), 201–212.

48. Huston, A. C., Carpenter, C. J., Atwater, J. B., & Johnson, L. M. (1986). Gender, adult structuring of activities, and social behavior in middle childhood. *Child Development, 57*(5), 1200–1209.

49. Kopp, C., & Krakow, J. (Eds.). (1980). *Child development in social context.* Reading, MA: Addison-Wesley.

50. Leibert, R. M., & Sprafkin, J. (1988). *The early window effects of television on children and youth* (3rd ed.). New York: Pergamon Press.

51. Mack, J., & Ablon, S. (1983). *The development and sustenance of self-esteem in childhood.* New York: International Universities Press.

52. Markus, H., & Nurius, P. (1984). Self-understanding and self-regulation in middle childhood. In W. A. Collins (Ed.), *Development in middle childhood.* Washington, DC: National Academy Press.

53. McLoyd, V. (1989). The effects of paternal job and income loss on children. *American Psychologist, 44,* 293–302.

54. Minuchin, P., & Shapiro, E. (1983). The school as a context for social development. In P. H. Mussen (Ed.), *Handbook of child psychology* (Vol. 4). New York: Wiley.

55. National Coalition for the Homeless. (1989).

56. Plass, J., & Hill, K. (1986). Children's achievement strategies and test performance: the role of time pressure, evaluation anxiety, and sex. *Developmental Psychology, 22*(1), 31–36.

57. Pollock, D. C. (1986, March). *The care and feeding of TCKs.* Unpublished paper presented to the Christian and Missionary Alliance Council.

58. Pollock, D. C. (1987). Third-culture kid. *Trans World Radio, 8*(5), 15–19.

59. Pollock, D. C. (1989). *Third-culture kids.* Lecture. Washington, D. C.: American University.

60. Powell, T. H., & Ogle, P. A. (1985). *Brothers and sisters—a special part of exceptional families.* Baltimore, MD: Paul H. Brooks.

61. Quarforth, J. M. (1979). Children's understanding of the nature of television characters. *Journal of Communication, 29,* 210–218.

62. Reynolds, W. M. (1985). Depression in childhood and adolescence: Diagnosis, assessment, intervention strategies and research. In T. R. Kratochwill (Ed.), *Advances in school psychology* (Vol. 4). Hillsdale, NJ: Laurence Erlbaum.

63. Rosenthal, R., & Jacobson, L. (1988). *Pygmalian in the classroom* (enl. ed.). New York: Irvington.

64. Rubin, Z. (1980). *Children's friendships.* Glasgow, G.B.: Fontana.

65. Rutter, M. (1988). Depressive disorders. In M. Rutter, A. H. Tuma, & I. Lann (Eds.), *Assessment and diagnosis in child psychopathology.* New York: Guilford.

66. Saunders, A., & Remsburg, B. (1984). *The stress-proof child: A loving parent's guide.* New York: Holt, Rinehart & Winston.

67. Scarr, S., & Weinberg, R. A. (1986). The early childhood enterprise: Care and education of the young. *American Psychologist, 41,* 1140–1146.

68. Schimmels, C. (1989). Understanding (and working with) your child's teacher. *Christian Parenting, 2*(1), 49, 50, 53, 54, 73.

69. Selman, R. (1980). *The growth of interpersonal understanding: Developmental and clinical analysis.* New York: Academic Press.

70. Shantz, C. V. (1987). Conflicts between children. *Child Development, 58*(2), 283–305.

71. Sheppard, S. (1989). Television: The prime time invader. *Christian Parenting, 2*(1), 37+.

72. Song, M. J., & Ginsburg, H. P. (1987). The development of informal and formal mathematical thinking in Korean and U. S. children. *Child Development, 58,* 1286–1296.

73. Sroufe, L. A., Cooper, R. G., & Marshall, M. E. (1988). *Child development: Its nature and course.* New York: Knopf.

74. Steinberg, L. (1986). Latchkey children and susceptibility to peer pressure: an ecological analysis. *Developmental Psychology, 22*(4), 433–439.

75. Stigler, J. W., Lee, S. Y., & Stevenson, H. W. (1987). Mathematics classrooms in Japan, Taiwan, and The United States. *Child Development, 58,* 1272–1285.

76. Sullivan, H. S. (1953). *The interpersonal theory of psychiatry* (Ed. by H. S. Perry and M. L. Gawel). New York: Norton.

77. Thomas, A., & Chess, S. (1977). *Temperament and development.* New York: Brunner/Mazel.

78. Touliatos, J., & Lindholm, B. W. (1980). Birth order, family size, and children's mental health. *Psychological Reports, 46,* 1097.

79. Urban, H. B. (1987). Dysfunctional systems: Understanding pathology. In M. E. Ford & D. H. Ford (Eds.), *Humans as self-constructing living systems* (pp. 313–341). Hillsdale, NJ: Erlbaum.

80. Useem, R., & Downie, R. (1976). Third-culture kids. *Today's Education,* (September-October), 103.

81. Walker, C., Bonner, B., & Kaufman, K. (1988). *The physically and sexually abused child: evolution and treatment.* New York: Pergamon Press.

82. Wallerstein, J. S., & Blakeslee, S. (1989). *Second chances: Men, women, and children a decade after divorce.* New York: Ticknor and Fields.

83. Wallerstein, J. S., & Kelly, J. B. (1980). *Surviving the breakup.* New York: Basic Books.

84. Waters, E., & Sroufe, L. A. (1983). Social competence as a developmental construct. *Developmental Review, 3,* 79–97.

85. Weinstein, R. S., Marshall, H. M., Sharp, L., & Batkin, M. (1987). Pygmalian and the student: Age and class differences in children's awareness of teacher expectations. *Child Development, 54*(4), 1079–1093.

86. Williams, T., Zabrack, M., & Joy, L. (1982). The portrayal of aggression on North American television. *Journal of Applied Social Psychology, 12,* 360–380.

87. Yamamoto, K. (1979). Children's ratings of the stressfulness of experiences. *Developmental Psychology, 15,* 459–472.

88. Zeitlin, H. (1986). *The natural history of psychiatric disorder in children* (Maudsley Monograph 29). Oxford: Oxford University Press.

VII

ADOLESCENCE

One of the most dramatic milestones in the development of the individual is the transition from childhood to adulthood. All five domains assume new possibilities and perspectives during this period. Many cultures have dramatic rites to celebrate the young person's abrupt initiation into the adult world. Western societies do not have such clearly defined launching points into the rights and responsibilities of adulthood; nevertheless, each individual is expected to gradually assume more adult roles. Even with the best foundation, however, this transition is not always smooth.

Adolescence is one of the most difficult and, at the same time, most exciting periods of life. The young person gains the physical body of an adult whether or not he or she is ready to assume the social mantle of adult responsibilities. The internal emotional conflicts precipitated by this discrepancy can be quite painful as the young person struggles to bring body, mind, and emotions under conscious, controlled (or at least predictable) subjection.

The vulnerabilities awakened by the realization of physical and psychological separateness from parents, which were inherent in the separation-individuation processes of early childhood, are again aroused as the young person begins to realize more intensely his or her physiological and psychological differences from peers and the eminent need to separate from dependence on the family. The "dart and catch" games with parents which were so typical of the toddler period are reenacted during adolescence as the young person eagerly reaches out to encompass the perceived privileges and pursuits of the adult years, only to retreat to the safety of the family when facing unexpected challenges. Confrontations with differences in skills, interests, and concerns force the young person to evaluate the foundations of his or her values and priorities, and to develop independence in thinking as well as in the activities of daily living.

The possibilities of adolescence are limitless if the young person is willing to invest adequate time, energy, and resources. With commitment and a creative approach, adolescents in Western cultures can pursue almost any career trajectory to optimize their talents and goals. With all their energy and enthusiasm, however, adolescents still need supportive families and communities to help them to actualize dreams and master developmental tasks. The success of mastering the tasks of adolescence depends highly on the extent to which preceding tasks were mastered. The success of the adult years is likewise dependent on the ability to invest oneself in the mastery of these adolescent tasks.

Developmental Tasks of Adolescence

*1. Appreciate own uniqueness:
> identify interests, skills, and talents
> identify differences from peers
> accept strengths and limitations
> challenge own skill levels

*2. Develop independent, internal identity:
> value self as a person
> separate physical self from psychological self
> differentiate personal worth from cultural stereotypes
> separate internal value from societal feedback

*3. Determine own value system:
> identify options
> establish priorities
> commit self to decisions made
> translate values into behaviors
> resist peer and cultural pressure to conform to their value system
> find comfortable balance between own and peer/cultural standards, behaviors, and needs

*4. Develop self-evaluation skills:
> develop basis for self-evaluation and monitoring
> evaluate quality of products
> assess approach to tasks and responsibilities
> develop sensitivity to intrapersonal relationships
> evaluate dynamics of interpersonal relationships

*5. Assume increasing responsibility for own behavior:
> quality of work/chores
> emotional tone
> money management
> time management
> decision making
> personal habits
> social behaviors

6. Find meaning in life:
> accept and integrate meaning of death
> develop philosophy of life
> begin to identify life or career goals

7. Acquire skills essential for adult living:
> acquire skills essential to independent living
> develop social/emotional abilities and temperament
> refine sociocultural amenities
> identify and experiment with alternatives for facing life
> acquire employment skills
> seek growth-inducing activities

8. Seek affiliations outside of family of origin:
> seek companionship with compatible peers
> affiliate with organizations that support uniqueness
> actively seek models or mentors
> identify potential emotional support systems
> differentiate between acquaintances and friends
> identify ways to express one's sexuality

9. Adapt to adult body functioning:
> adapt to somatic changes
> refine balance and coordination
> develop physical strength
> consider sexuality and reproduction issues

---

*Tasks deemed most crucial to continued maturation are marked with an asterisk.

Biophysical Development of the Adolescent

Clara S. Schuster

Adolescence is the term used to identify the period of transition from childhood to adulthood and includes the marked changes occurring in all five domains. Adolescence is recognized as the period of life during which the individual is forging a sense of personal identity and gaining emancipation from the family unit. As such, it is primarily a cognitive, sociological, affective, and spiritual process, rather than a physical phenomenon. In Western cultures, adolescence has no clear-cut beginning or end. However, to establish more definitive parameters—at least for the discussion of the development of the biophysical domain—the authors have arbitrarily chosen the years from 11 through 19 to represent the period of adolescence, with the specific understanding that the boundaries can be extended or collapsed at either end to encompass the variations in development found in individuals. Some persons may continue to function as adolescents for many years beyond the twentieth birthday.

The term **puberty,** on the other hand, is restricted to physiological development, particularly those phenomena associated with final maturation of the reproductive system. The **pubertal period** refers to the 3 to 5 years of most rapid development surrounding **true puberty**—the point at which reproduction is first possible. Unfortunately, it is difficult to identify that point precisely because both ovulation and spermatogenesis are internal phenomena. Consequently, most persons use external phenomena to identify the point of puberty rather than attempt to identify the point of true puberty. **Menarche** (the first menstrual period) is the identification point used to divide the prepubertal from the postpubertal female; the onset of **nocturnal emissions** ("wet dreams" or involuntary orgasm with release of semen during sleep) is frequently used as an arbitrary division between prepubertal and postpubertal males. Some authorities use coarsening and curling of pubic hair, appearance of facial hair, or the deepening of the voice as the point of puberty in males, since these phenomena frequently coincide with spermatogenesis. However, none of these external phenomena indicates that the individual is biologically capable of reproduction, since gametogenesis is usually delayed 1 or 2 years after the external phenomena are exhibited. Adolescence and puberty, then, are separate but interdependent developmental processes.

The early years of adolescence are characterized by very rapid growth. The individual is usually very interested in bodily development, is frequently confused by it, and is curious about the final outcome. The physiological changes mandate a change in one's body image and concept of self. Chronological age is an inadequate parameter for biophysical development; in a group of 13-year-olds, a 4-year spread in sexual and somatic development is not uncommon. These variations in growth may cause concern over the normalcy of one's body, sexuality, the ability to compete in athletics, and social and peer relationships. At a time when blending with one's peers is still so important psychosocially, variations in biophysical maturity can create major social hurdles. In short, the physical changes of adolescence constitute a major developmental crisis for the individual.

Imbalances in biophysical growth as well as among the domains are common. The adolescent may be awkward in gross-motor activity—it takes time to get used to one's new body. Many adolescents experience temporary discoordination in adapting to the changes. A marked increase in modesty frequently accompanies sexual changes (even though contemporary television and music videos may encourage girls to dress very suggestively without understanding what it means). Many teens become sharply critical of their own features. One's hands, feet, or nose—all of which increase in size before the arms, legs, or the rest of the face "catch up"— are common sources of embarrassment to the adolescent. Some adolescents are embarrassed and fear ridicule because of excessive height or shortness, breast development, or a squeaky voice.

These changes, along with fluctuations in hormonal balance, frequently lead to heightened emotionality in the adolescent. The inability to control the changes may reactivate symptoms of the helplessness syndrome or cause strict adherence to reduction diets to gain control. Peers and other social contacts frequently interact differently with an individual who appears to be physically mature. The new role expectations, combined with the essential psychological readjustments, can lead to symptoms of stress.

Adolescents need much supportive reassurance during the pubertal period, and they need to understand how and why changes occur. An understanding of the concept of variability of normal development is essential to facilitate adjustment. Comparisons can be devastating. **At no point in a person's development should the concept of individuality be stressed as much as during early adolescence.**

THE PUBERTAL PERIOD

The *pubertal period*—the period of maturation of the reproductive system—includes all the primary and secondary sexual developments precipitated by the endocrine changes in the individual. Sexual maturation has been held in abeyance since fetal life when the hypothalamus was "imprinted" to respond to male or female hormones.[45] Before the second birthday, the hypothalamus reaches a very sensitive "set point," which establishes a negative feedback system to inhibit production of sex steroids.[19] The pubertal period is initiated when the hypothalamus matures sufficiently to reset or override the inhibitory effects of the gonadostat which has suppressed the release of *gonadotropin-releasing hormone* (GnRH).[45] Readjustment of the set point allows for higher concentrations of sex hormones and the establishment of a positive feedback control mechanism.[19] This in turn leads to maturation of the reproductive system and changes in other body cells.[24] The pubertal period may last 8 to 10 years, although 3 to 5 years is more common.[61] **Primary sexual development** includes the maturational changes occurring in all those organs directly related to reproduction (e.g.,

penis, testes, ovaries, breasts, uterus). **Secondary sexual development** includes the physiological changes that occur in other parts of the body as a direct result of changes in hormonal balance (e.g., development of facial and pubic hair, voice changes, fat deposits).

Hormonal Control

During early childhood, males and females have small amounts of both estrogen (female hormone) and androgen (male hormone).[39] At about age 7 to 8 years, both of these hormones begin to increase gradually until **pubescence** (the first half of the pubertal period, which precedes the onset of external puberty). During pubescence, females experience a rapid increase in the production of estrogen, whereas males have a rapid increase in the production of androgens.

The mechanics that initiate the pubertal process are as yet poorly understood. It appears that the maturation of the hypothalamus initiates the process through secretion of neurohumoral releasing factors (chemicals released into the hypophysial portal vessels and neurons connecting the hypothalamus and pituitary).[24] This causes the anterior pituitary gland to release GnRH and *follicle-stimulating hormone* (FSH), which in turn stimulates the gonads to release *leutenizing hormone* (LH) (see Chap. 3). Gradually, an effective positive feedback system is established, and increasing amounts of FSH are released.[45]

Two other hormones secreted by the anterior pituitary are *pituitary growth hormone* (GH) and *thyroid-stimulating hormone* (TSH). Growth hormone levels remain relatively constant throughout life.[30] The main function of GH appears to be the stimulation of deoxyribonucleic acid (DNA) synthesis and hyperplastic cell growth, particularly of the bones and cartilage. Since the increased androgen levels that accompany puberty in both males and females are antagonistic to GH, increased androgen levels are partially responsible for the decrease in the rate of body growth.

Adequate thyroxin levels are essential throughout life for (1) hypertrophic and hyperplastic cell growth of all body systems, especially the brain and skeletal systems, and (2) primary and secondary sexual development. During the pubertal period, there is an increase in thyroxin secretion by the thyroid under the influence of TSH.[30] Thyroxin levels directly increase body metabolism. The increased metabolic rate leads to a higher body temperature, which frequently causes teenagers to complain of feeling too warm (thus explaining their rejection of an extra sweater offered by a concerned parent).

It is important to realize that the secretion of each of these hormones is interdependent with the levels of other hormones through a delicate feedback mechanism (Fig. 23-1). During the pubertal process, imbalances in hormonal levels are common. Because of their intimate relationship to the hypothalamus, emotional states in an individual, such as fear or anxiety, can directly affect the efficiency of the total process. Normal maturation depends on a complicated and

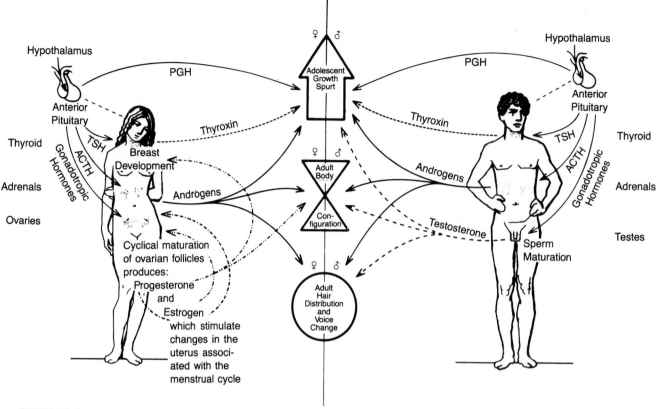

FIGURE 23–1.

The endocrine system at puberty. (From I. Valadian and D. Porter, Physical Growth and Development From Conception to Maturity.
Boston: Little, Brown, 1977. With permission.)

sensitive balance among the endocrine glands—an excellent example of General Systems Theory (see Chap. 2).

Somatic Changes

Although the point of onset and rate of development of the pubertal process varies greatly from one individual to another, the sequence of events, once started, is fairly predictable. The maturational pattern of males parallels that of females. In discussing the sequence of these events, it is important to keep in mind that one phenomenon is not complete before another begins. Each characteristic may take 1 or 2 years to reach its adult maturity level.

Factors Affecting Onset of Puberty

The most crucial factor controlling onset of the pubertal process is the gender of the individual; females mature an average of 2 years earlier than males. It is postulated that this difference is caused by the more rapid maturation of the central nervous system in females. Many factors appear to affect the onset of puberty. Hereditary factors and climate show significant correlation with the onset of menarche, which occurs later in colder climates.[45] Chronic disease, such as diabetes, is known to delay the onset of puberty. Black

females tend to initiate the menstrual cycle a few months earlier than white females. However, when females from various racial backgrounds are exposed to similar environment and living conditions, differences in the onset of menarche disappear. Some research indicates that females have an earlier menarche if they have fewer siblings, are blind, 20% to 30% overweight, or live at lower altitudes or in urban settings.[45]

An improvement in the nutritional and health status of children in Western cultures is reflected in the gradual decrease of the age of menarche from 17 years in Europe in 1850 to 14.5 years in the United States in 1900.[30] The current average age of 12.5 to 12.8 years for menarche has remained stable for the past 30 years, suggesting that, overall, adolescents are approximating optimal nutritional and health levels.

Nutrition and health status have a marked influence on the maturational process. Evidence indicates that a minimal weight for height is essential for the initiation and maintenance of the menstrual cycle.[16] Although two females may vary widely in height, the percentage of body weight to fat is essentially identical at menarche. This is one of the explanations for delayed menarche in young female dancers and athletes—they have a very low body–fat ratio.[46] Female ballet dancers, swimmers, and runners generally do not experience menarche until they are 15 years of age.[45] This *critical-fat theory* explains why females in poverty situations tend to have delayed menarche as well as delayed resumption of the menses following childbirth and lactation. The critical-fat theory also explains why there has been a decrease in the age of menarche in advanced industrial nations.

Menarche that occurs any time between 9.5 and 15.5 years is considered to be within normal limits, although menarche before 11 years of age is considered early. Many males experience nocturnal emissions at about 14.5 years; 11.5 to 17.5 years is considered the normal range for regular onset of this phenomenon (see Table 23-1). Although the neural pathways underlying orgasm are present much earlier, true ejaculations do not occur prior to external puberty.[54]

Sequence of Changes

The earliest hormonal changes are so minute and gradual that external physical and emotional correlates usually are not recognizable. However, young females may have minor fluctuations in hormonal levels with corresponding physical and emotional manifestations discernible to the astute observer. When the author's daughter was about 8 years old, her mother began to notice temporary withdrawal behaviors and a single pimple on the side of her nose, occurring at about 6-week intervals. One day the daughter came to her mother, greatly disturbed because "I am so depressed and I don't know why." They mutually explored many potential sources of her depression, all of which proved to be unfounded. After exhausting the various avenues, her mother said, "Have you noticed that you have a pimple on the side of your nose?" The daughter reached up to feel, wondering how a pimple could relate to her depression. Her mother then went on to explain briefly the cyclic effect of hormones in a woman's body, ending with the comment, "I don't think anything is wrong with you. I think your depression is just the result of your hormonal balance." Relief and a huge smile flooded her face. She hugged her mother and responded, "I'm so glad I talked to you about it. Now I am happy and excited about feeling depressed. I'm growing up!" So goes the paradox of maturation—one is happy about being depressed!

The first overt sign that the pubertal process is under way is usually the maturation of the eccrine and apocrine glands. The young person who typically hates to take time out to bathe now **must** wash and use deodorant regularly to protect both clothes and friendships.

The second physiological phenomenon experienced by males and females is pelvic enlargement. Males have a thickening and strengthening of the bone structure; in the female

there is an increase in the diameter of the internal pelvis, preparatory for the birth process. These anatomical differences are clearly distinguishable by 10 years of age.[30]

The third step in the somatic maturation of females is enlargement of the ovaries and uterus. The male experiences a corresponding increase in testicular and scrotal size. The testes become very sensitive to touch at this time. Most young men find an athletic support comfortable as well as protective for sports activities. Androgens may also cause the scrotum to begin to darken at this time. Many health care personnel advocate that regular testicular self-examination (TSE) is as critical to males for early detection of tumor growth as breast self-examination (BSE) is to females.[60] Most testicular cancer occurs between age 20 and 30. The American Cancer Society provides (free of charge) excellent pamphlets on both procedures.

The fourth developmental characteristic to appear is hyperplastic and hypertrophic growth of the fatty and connective tissues between and within the 15 to 20 lobes that make up each breast.[34] About 33% of males have some degree of unilateral or bilateral breast tissue enlargement,[39] which may be a source of much embarrassment. It usually disappears after several months. However, it should be checked by a physician if it persists.

Female breast development occurs in five stages, starting about 2 years before menarche:[32, 45] (1) preadolescent breast bud; (2) increase in areolar diameter, slight breast mound; (3) breast and areola enlargement; (4) continued enlargement with secondary mound for areola; and (5) mature breast with projecting nipple. Although there may be some growth of the lobes, growth of the alveoli does not occur until a pregnancy.[34] The breast continues to experience growth and contour changes for 3 to 5 years after the breast buds appear. The breasts are frequently tender during the early phases of growth (Fig. 23-2). Slight difference in the size of the breasts is normal, since one breast may respond more rapidly to circulating hormones than the other. Females should be encouraged to begin breast self-examination each month *after* the menstrual period.

The fifth characteristic is the growth of pubic hair. This also occurs over a period of 2 to 5 years in 5 stages from (1) no hair to (2) light labial hair, (3) hair on mons pubis (4) lateral spread with thickening, curling, and coarsening, and (5) spread to the thigh areas.[32]

The sixth area to exhibit changes is the external genitalia. The penis now "catches up" to the growth experienced earlier is scrotal size. Young males need reassurance that the size of the nonerect penis has no relationship to the size of the erect penis or to the sexual satisfaction of either partner during sexual intercourse. Females experience growth in the labia and the size of the vagina. Many begin to secrete a thin, milky-colored fluid as early as 12 months before menarche. The amount secreted is often cyclic in pattern, reflecting changes in the hormonal levels. This secretion may cause a yellow staining of the underpants, leading some mothers to question their daughters about "wetting their pants" or having poor hygiene habits.

TABLE 23–1. EXTERNAL PHENOMENA MARKING THE POINT OF PUBERTY

Phenomenon	Normal Age Range (yr)
Menarche (female)	12.5 ± 3
Nocturnal emissions (male)	14.5 ± 3

FIGURE 23–2.
Young girls and women generally find the wearing of a bras-
siere provides comfort and support, especially when partici-
pating in sports.

Midway through the pubertal period, about the time the pubic hair begins to curl, females experience their first menses and males may begin to experience regular nocturnal emissions. However, the onset of menarche does not indicate sexual maturity. The early menses are often irregular, both in frequency of onset and in the duration and characteristics of flow. This irregularity is probably caused by a lack of the modifying influence of progesterone, since progesterone is not produced until ovulation occurs. Early menstruation is caused by cyclic fluctuation of estrogen levels or estradiol rhythms because progesterone is not yet formed in the ovaries.[45] Nocturnal emission is also a poor indicator of the onset of true puberty in the male. Some males may experience nocturnal emissions fairly regularly during the late school-age years. The emissions, usually occurring every 1 or 2 weeks, are independent of sexual stimulation. Nocturnal emissions, like menarche, can create a developmental crisis if the young person is not prepared for the event. Young males may experience either deep shame and guilt or pride about the phenomenon, depending on family and peer attitudes and pressures. Others may fear or even receive punishment from their parents for "wetting the bed." Spontaneous erections and ejaculations can be puzzling, troublesome, and embarrassing to the adolescent male, especially if they occur in a mixed social setting. However, nocturnal and spontaneous erections are as normal for males as menstruation is for females. Both should be accepted as signs of healthy development of the reproductive system. Some persons suggest that occasional masturbation activities can relieve genital tensions in both males and females, and provide the adolescent with information on how the body works.

The eighth pubertal characteristic to appear is axillary hair. Hair holds odor, which makes good hygiene mandatory. In North America, many girls prefer to shave the axillary hair for reasons of both hygiene and appearance. For some, axillary hair may occur earlier in the sequence of events, even before the appearance of pubic hair. General body hair increases throughout puberty on both boys and girls. Because of the higher level of androgens, however, boys of most races develop much more hair, including facial hair.

Gametogenesis generally occurs 12 to 24 months after the external indicators of puberty appear. Occasionally, ovulation may precede menarche. Male gametogenesis can be confirmed by finding mature sperm in the urine or seminal fluid.

The last major physiological change is broadening of the body frame. Females have broadening of the hips and males experience broadening of the shoulders, giving each the mature body contours of the adult. Although the internal diameter of the pelvis continues to broaden for at least 3 years after menarche, the final growth is usually not complete until after the eighteenth birthday.[35] This is a major reason why adolescents have a higher incidence of difficult childbirth.

Both males and females experience vocal-pitch changes with laryngeal growth and thickening of the vocal chords. In just 12 months, the laryngeal membranes grow from 8 mm to 16 mm.[59] Males characteristically experience dramatic changes, with "cracking" of the voice. Females may also experience vocal cracking but to a lesser degree. These changes occur throughout the pubertal process. Like facial hair in the male, vocal changes in males and females usually begin to occur at the point of true puberty, although they may not occur until the end of the pubertal period.

Hormonal changes and rapid growth cause about one third of all adolescents to develop striae (stretch marks) on gluteal areas, thighs, and lower abdomen. They are a deep reddish purple when they first appear but gradually fade to near invisibility.[30] The changes of the pubertal period in males and females are summarized in Table 23-2.

The Menstrual Cycle

The anticipation of and the onset of menarche raise many questions in a young female's mind. Foremost is the question, "Am I normal?" Inherent in this question are concerns about sexuality, health status, and childbearing ability, as well as curiosity about the unknown. A knowledge about normal physiology and characteristics of the menstrual cycle with its variations can greatly reassure the young woman who is learning to deal with her new body functions.

Normal Characteristics

During the first year following menarche, the length of the **menstrual cycle** (onset of one menses until the onset of the next menses) is frequently irregular. After the establishment of a regular pattern, a cycle may range from 21 to 35 days and still be within normal limits. Variations from month to month are also common: 60% of females experience cycles which vary as much as 5 days from the expected date of onset.[42]

There are three distinct phases of the menstrual flow: premenstrual discharge, major discharge, and postmenstrual discharge. Premenstrual discharge may be pink-mucoid to dark brown in color, lasting up to 1½ days. The major discharge, which is bright to deep red in color, lasts an average of 3 to 5 days. Many women experience a postmenstrual discharge, lasting up to 2 days. This last type takes several forms: pink-mucoid secretion, yellow-brown serous fluid, red watery fluid, or thick brown secretions. Some women may experience very little or no premenstrual or postmenstrual discharge. Women report that the total menstrual flow period lasts 4 to 8 days when the premenstrual and postmenstrual flows are included; the average is 5 to 6 days.[47]

The major flow is a bloody, nonclotting, viscous fluid with occasional tissue particles and mucus. The average blood loss is about 44 mL (1½ oz); young adolescents average about 34 mL (1 oz).[21] Small clots and pieces of the endometrial lining are not unusual during the first 24 hours. However, large clots or pus are indicators that medical attention is needed. The odor of the menstrual flow is bloody, musty, and "earthy." Fever, severe abdominal pain, or a fishy or foul odor are signs of infection and must be evaluated by a health practitioner immediately. Untreated infections are a common cause of infertility. An unpleasant odor develops when the flow comes in contact with air. Good hygiene is essential to prevent both odor and infections. Menstrual pads or tampons can be a reservoir of bacteria and potential infection if not changed frequently (at least 3 to 4 times daily, or every 3 to 4 hours during heavy flow).

Premenstrual Syndrome

The drop in estrogen and progesterone levels prior to the onset of the menses is often accompanied by both physical and emotional symptoms. Approximately 80% of women experience some degree of distress prior to their menses; 20% to 40% have severe, debilitating symptoms.[56] The most common symptoms are anxiety, emotional lability, and irritability.[56] The woman may feel as if she has a dual personality because of the dramatic difference in her ability to deal with stress. Over one third of women have symptoms of depression and withdrawal.[56] The tension and feelings of imbalance may lead some women to express suicide ideation. Suicide attempts, and absenteeism from school and work, are higher at this time of the month.[56] There is an increase in accidents and lower grades on tests.[56]

The symptoms of premenstrual syndrome (PMS) are

TABLE 23–2. SOMATIC CHANGES OF THE PUBERTAL PERIOD

Step	Females	Both Genders	Males
1		Apocrine gland development	
2	Increased diameter of internal pelvis	Pelvic changes	Thickening and strengthening of bone structure
3	Growth of ovaries and uterus	Growth in gonad size	Growth of testes and scrotum
4		Breast enlargement	
5		Appearance of pubic hair	
6	Growth of labia and vagina	Growth of external genitalia	Growth of penis
7	Menarche	External puberty	Nocturnal emissions
8		Axillary hair	
9	Oogenesis, ovulation	True puberty	Spermatogenesis, sperm in urine and semen
10	Broadening of hips	Broadening of body frame	Broadening of shoulders
11		Vocal changes throughout	

related to decreased hormonal levels that cause fluid retention. This factor is responsible for temporary weight gain (often as much as 5 pounds), sensitivity of the breasts, abdominal enlargement, and headache. Some women, especially those who sing, may note minor changes in vocal quality before or during the menses due to edema of the vocal chords. Women who use their eyes for fine details such as needlework or for extensive reading, may become aware of visual acuity changes before and during the menses. The extra fluid is lost through increased urine production during the first 2 days after onset of the menses.

Decreased blood flow to the uterus and uterine contractions appear to be responsible for pelvic discomfort, cramping, and backache. Forty percent to 50% of women experience mild hypoglycemia (low blood sugar) as part of the premenstrual syndrome, which may be partially responsible for fatigue and dizziness as well as nausea, paleness, sweating, weakness, and a craving for sweets.[56]

The decrease in ovarian hormones appears to affect the smooth muscle of the gastrointestinal system as well as the uterine muscles. One out of three women experiences constipation, and almost 50% report diarrhea symptoms (increased looseness or increased frequency) with the onset of the menses.[50] Nausea, vomiting, and decreased appetite are also frequent.[22, 50] The incidence of PMS increases with age, peaking around 33 years of age.[56] Nonmedical treatment may include extra sleep and rest, stress reduction activities, small, frequent high-protein meals (to prevent hypoglycemia), decreased fluid, sugar, and salt intake, increased physical exercise, and decreased caffeine and nicotine intake. Medical treatment may include biofeedback, hormonal therapy, and medication.

Dysmenorrhea

Dysmenorrhea (painful menstruation) is experienced by about 33% of adolescent females once ovulation occurs.[9] Anovulatory cycles do not cause hypertrophy of the secretory endometrial lining and consequently are relatively painless.[58] **Primary dysmenorrhea** is experienced as spasmodic uterine or lower abdominal and back pain during the first 12 to 24 hours of the major menstrual flow.[40] The etiology and mechanisms of primary dysmenorrhea are unknown, but there appear to be several contributing factors. Recent research indicates that the secretory endometrium produces prostaglandin, which causes contraction of the smooth muscles (uterus and blood vessels).[1] The pain may also be due to ischemia (lack of oxygen) of the uterine muscles. Because of the anatomical position of the blood vessels, the blood supply is decreased when the uterine muscles contract. This phenomenon is an essential asset during and following childbirth but is somewhat of a nuisance at other times. Contractions of the round ligaments that support the uterine body by attaching to the spinal column are responsible for the backache. Primary dysmenorrhea often disappears spontaneously at about 24 years of age when uterine maturation is complete or after the birth of a baby as the result of dilation of the cervix.[58] The small cervix of the nulliparous woman causes the uterus to work harder to rid itself of the menstrual contents.

Primary dysmenorrhea should be evaluated by a physician to rule out any organic problems and to offer emotional support to the young woman. The fact that only ovulating women experience primary dysmenorrhea can be reassuring to the young female.

The treatment of dysmenorrhea may include warmth (e.g., application of a heating pad) to increase the blood supply to the uterus, or a mild analgesic, such as aspirin or ibuprofen. Exercise throughout the month maintains good muscle tone and flexibility; exercise during the menses is helpful in alleviating backache (Fig. 23-3). Occasionally, physicians will recommend a diuretic to reduce symptoms due to fluid retention, an oral contraceptive to be taken for 3 to 6

FIGURE 23–3.
Regular exercise helps prevent or reduce the discomfort of menstruation. Balance reflexes are refined through the challenge of new positions and exploits.

months to produce anovulatory cycles, or an antiprostaglandin medication to relax the uterine musculature. If dysmenorrhea is associated with the first menstrual period, the young female should be seen immediately by a physician.[1] There may be an infection or anatomical abnormality.

Secondary dysmenorrhea is characterized by severe, constant, or radiating pain (pain that appears to "shoot" down the leg), which may begin 2 to 3 days before the onset of the menses or may extend beyond the first 24 hours. These are symptoms that should be evaluated by a physician, again to rule out a physiological abnormality, endometriosis, or infection.

Amenorrhea

Five percent of adolescent girls experience amenorrhea.[27] If a girl has not menstruated by age 16½ **(primary amenorrhea),** she should see a physician.[10] In fact, every girl should have a perineal inspection by 12 years of age to rule out the possibility of an imperforate hymen (the hymen has no opening to allow menstrual flow to escape). Skipping a menstrual period is frequent during the first year after the onset of menarche. However, **secondary amenorrhea** (absence of menses for 6 months or more) is not normal. It can be caused by emotional factors, such as unresolved stressors that lead to anxiety.[11] Fear and fatigue also can cause amenorrhea. Once the menstrual cycle is clearly established, the most common cause of amenorrhea is pregnancy. **Oligomenorrhea** (cycles of 35 to 90 days) and amenorrhea are more prevalent in college students than in the general population.[4] Numerous female college students have told the author that they never have a menstrual period during the academic quarter or semester; however, when their examinations are over and they return home for a well-deserved vacation, the menstrual period returns. Female inmates of penal institutions report similar menstrual behaviors. Twenty percent of regularly exercising women and 50% of competitive female athletes experience amenorrhea or oligomenorrhea.[27] Particular attention needs to be paid to calcium intake. Female athletes may need as much as 1500 mg of calcium daily to achieve a positive calcium balance to support bone mass and offset amenorrhea problems.[27] Cases of amenorrhea should be checked by a physician or nurse practitioner, however, since amenorrhea can be a symptom of a pathological disease process (such as diabetes mellitus or thyroid disorder) or pregnancy.[11]

SOMATIC DEVELOPMENT

About 2 to 4 years before the onset of external puberty, the child enters the pubescent period, which is characterized by a rapid acceleration in the rate of body growth. At the beginning of this period, most children have already attained 75% to 80% of their height, and 50% of adult weight.[9] Body configuration changes because of the accretion of skeletal, muscle and adipose tissue. Girls have 40% to 50% more body fat than boys.[27] Although all body systems undergo rapid maturational changes, growth is most easily observed in body height.

The prepubertal growth spurt is arbitrarily divided into two stages. The first stage, *the adolescent growth spurt,* is identified by an increase in the growth rate of the arms and legs. This growth spurt is basically the product of increased hormonal activity. The second stage of prepubertal growth, *the maximal growth spurt,* begins about a year before the onset of true puberty. The individual experiences a marked acceleration in the rate of height increase. The peak height velocity for most European and North American boys is about 14 years of age, when they gain about 8 to 10 cm per year.[7] Growth continues at a rapid pace until it reaches a peak that generally coincides with the onset of external puberty, followed by a rapid decrease in the growth rate (Fig. 23-4).

Early maturation of girls can lead to social stresses for which they are usually psychologically unprepared. Boys interested in sports activities may find early maturation an asset in self-evaluation and social status.[7] Another interesting change that occurs during the pubescent period is the change in hairline. During childhood, the hairline of both males and females circles evenly around the face at the temples. During pubescence and the early adolescent years, the hairline on males begins to recede at the temples, giving the face a more rectangular appearance.

During adolescence, the organs function at widely varying levels of maturity, even within the same system (Table 23-3). These variances can and do lead to temporary metabolic, hormonal, and functional imbalances.

Skeletal System

The correlation between the maturation of the skeletal system and that of the reproductive system is very high, probably because they are both under the influence of the hypothalamus.[9,30] Activation of the hypothalamus appears to initiate sequential growth changes in the young adolescent. The feet and hands are the first to experience rapid growth, followed by the long bones of the arms and legs. Before puberty, both males and females experience lengthening and broadening of the body frame. After onset of the external signs of

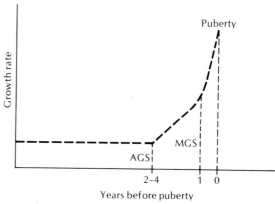

FIGURE 23–4.
The prepubertal growth spurt. AGS = adolescent growth spurt; MGS = maximal growth spurt.

TABLE 23–3. AVERAGE WEIGHTS OF ORGANS AT DIFFERENT AGES (g)

	Newborn	*1 Year*	*6 Years*	*Puberty*	*Adult*
Brain	350	910	1200	1300	1350
Heart	24	45	95	220	300
Thymus	12	20	24	30	0–15
Kidneys (both)	25	70	120	170	300
Liver	150	300	550	1500	1600
Lungs (both)	60	130	260	410	1200
Pancreas	3	9	20	40	90
Spleen	10	30	55	95	155
Stomach	8	30	60	80	135

(Lowrey, G. H. [1978]. Growth and development of children [7th ed.]. Chicago: Year Book)

puberty, ossification slows, and the epiphyseal areas of the long bones mature under the influence of the sex hormones. Consequently, long-bone growth stops. The African youth has longer legs and arms in proportion to sitting height, more muscle, and heavier bones per unit size than white youths, giving many blacks a marked advantage in racing and other sports.[30, 54]

Although the adolescent may grow 2 to 3 more inches following the onset of menarche or nocturnal emissions, much of this growth is caused by continued increase in length of the trunk rather than the long bones.[7, 45] The longer pre-pubertal growth stage experienced by males allows for greater limb growth and final height.[52]

One third of the females and one half of the males of high-school age participate in some competitive sports.[37] Since androgen influences the density of skeletal structure, the bones of males are more dense than those of females. For example, the humerus of the male is one-third more dense than that of the female.[9] The implications for contact sports or activities requiring leverage are obvious. "Sports physicals" may be discouraging for the physically immature boy, but this screening is essential to ensure that participants are physic-ally mature enough to endure the hardships of pummeling and impact.[26] A lifetime of good health is at stake. Physically immature adolescents can be directed into alternative, more physically appropriate sports activities, such as tennis, swim-ming or horsemanship. Weight-lifting is especially dangerous if the body is not physiologically ready for the stress.

Fractures of the long bones—especially in the epiphyseal area—during the prepubertal growth spurt can create a growth imbalance by arresting growth of the affected bone and can predispose the person to osetoarthritis later in life.[49] Female ballet dancers who experience delayed menarche also experi-ence a marked increase in bone fractures and scoliosis because of the hypoestrogenemia associated with reduced weight gains and the bone stress associated with dancing.[57] Adequate nutri-tion and calcium intake are essential.

Not all fractures are easily recognized. Many adolescent athletes develop stress fractures from impact stress on young

bones. Radiographic examination may show no bone changes, but the child can continue to complain of generalized pain in the leg or adjacent joints. Some may have focal tenderness, swelling, or decreased range of motion. Resting the bone is critical to healing and to prevention of a complete fracture. A switch to swimming will result in minimal disruption of training and prevent loss of muscle tone.[44]

Since growth in both height and weight is closely related to maturation of the reproductive system, the onset of which is genetically as well as environmentally determined, the estab-lishment of norms for this age group is very difficult. One child might grow 6 to 7 inches in one year, while a peer may grow only 1 inch (Fig. 23-5). Growth assessment must be highly individualized, taking into account parental height, previous growth pattern, sexual maturity, and environmental conditions (see the grids in Appendixes D and E for growth

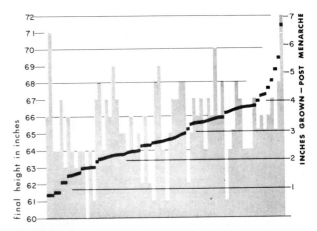

FIGURE 23–5.

Growth following menarche in 68 normal American girls. The dark line indicates the final height; the shaded areas indicate the inches grown after menarche. There does not appear to be any correlation with final height. (Lowrey, G. H. Growth and Development of Children [7th ed.]. Chicago: Year Book, 1978. With permission.)

trends). Males may continue to increase in height through their early twenties.

Muscular System

Before the pubertal period, males and females experience only minor differences in muscle mass.[9] The maximal growth of muscle mass correlates with the maximal growth of the skeletal system.[30] The peak period of growth in females occurs 1 year before menarche, and, in males, about 6 months before puberty.[9] Muscular strength of girls improves linearly through about age 15 (when they reach a plateau). Boys experience a marked increase in strength from age 14 to 19. By 17 years of age, muscle mass is about two times greater in males than in females, causing the average male to be two to four times stronger than the average female.[9] This is particularly true of the upper extremities and trunk.[7] The implications for coeducational sports are obvious. Physical condition and strength should be evaluated carefully before any person participates in competitive contact activities.

Increase in muscle mass appears to be directly related to the presence of androgens. Exercise facilitates development of muscle size, strength, and endurance. Therefore, regular and appropriate exercise is essential. The press has given much attention lately to the abuses of androgenic anabolic corticosteroids and human growth hormone by young athletes to improve their physical appearance, to facilitate the growth of musculature, and to enhance aerobic performance and strength. It is reported that 6.6% to 11% of high school males use anabolic steroids.[15] These drugs have a marked negative impact on natural hormone production and on the delicate hormonal feedback system. Elevated levels of the steroids may cause premature fusion of the long bones, and thus, shortened adult height.[15] Fertility and liver function may be impaired. Mood swings, severe acne, high blood pressure, cardiovascular disease, and possible cancer of the liver and testicles have also been associated with the abuse of steroids. Those sharing needles and drug equipment also run the risk of contracting AIDS.[2]

Central Nervous System

The growth of the cerebrum, cerebellum, and brain stem is essentially complete by the end of the tenth year of life.[30] Consequently, in contrast to the other systems of the body, the central nervous system does not experience a sudden growth spurt during the pubertal period. However, the myelinization of the greater cerebral commissurae and reticular formation of the central nervous system continue until the middle adult years.[8] Brain tissue appears to reach quantitative and qualitative maturity with puberty. The gradual increases in fine-motor control and intellectual capacity discernible during the adolescent years appear to be due to education and practice (Fig. 23-6).

Adolescents are capable of any skill an adult can perform. The social and familial context become very significant in

FIGURE 23–6.
Completion of the myelinization process allows for the precise neuromuscular control that enables adolescents to engage in intricate fine-motor skills. Training and practice are the keys to competency.

determining what skills are valued and reinforced. Although neurologically the person may be capable of the intricate movements necessary for a particular skill, maximal performance may not appear until the young adult years, when muscular strength and physiological endurance reach their peak. Many Olympic champions in sports requiring agility and precise coordination are still adolescents.

Cardiovascular System

The heart experiences a growth spurt during the prepubertal growth period. This growth enables the heart to pump the blood with increased strength, thereby elevating the blood pressure. Although the pulse rate may exhibit a transient increase during the peak periods of growth, the increased size allows the pulse rate to stabilize at a lower rate. Females generally maintain a pulse rate about 10% higher than males.[8] Blood volume, which is directly related to weight, increases more rapidly in the male. In late adolescence, males average

5500 mL and females 4200 mL of blood.[30] There is an increase in the length and the thickness of the blood vessel walls and in the size of the heart. The heart growth is relatively greater, however, than the growth in the diameter of the veins and the arteries. This delay in increase in the size of blood vessels, combined with the increased heart size, stroke strength, and blood volume, may cause the young adolescent to experience transient chest discomfort or fullness combined with "thumping," especially after periods of activity. Hormonal changes also create some differentiation of blood values (see Appendix E).

There is increasing concern that children and adolescents be educated and encouraged to adopt health habits and behaviors that will lower the risk or prevent adult cardiovascular disease. These include avoiding tobacco, alcohol, obesity, physical inactivity, high cholesterol foods, and adopting dietary measures to prevent high blood pressure.[43]

Respiratory System

The increase in *vital capacity* (the greatest volume of air that can be expressed from the lungs following a maximal intake of air) correlates with the structural frame: the greater the height of an individual, the larger the vital capacity and the slower the respiratory rate, regardless of gender.[8] On the average, however, males breathe more slowly than females.

Gastrointestinal System

The adolescent growth spurt requires a corresponding increase in the size of the stomach to accommodate the increased need for food required to support body growth and development. The stomach becomes both longer and wider and also experiences an increase in gastric acidity to facilitate digestion of the increased intake.[52] This increased acidity frequently causes abdominal pain and may occasionally lead to symptoms of gastric ulcers in adolescents. The stress of coping with the myriad of physiological changes may also increase gastric secretions and thus bring about ulcer symptoms. Frequent small meals, or the occasional use of an antacid tablet can help to relieve gastric discomfort.

Basal Metabolic Rate

The *basal metabolic rate* (BMR) is the rate at which the body uses calories to maintain body function when at rest. The BMR correlates closely with the rate of body growth. It increases with periods of growth spurt, reaching a peak at external puberty, and declining gradually as the growth rate decelerates. At the end of adolescence, the BMR of males is about 10% higher than that of females.[30] One theory for the gender difference is the greater muscle mass in males; another is that increased BMR is a direct result of higher androgen levels.[8]

Because of very rapid growth, the pubescent child may not have sufficient energy left for strenuous activities. He or she tires easily and may frequently complain of needing to sit down. Gradually the child is able to increase both speed and stamina during exercise. An increase in muscular and skeletal strength, as well as the increased ability of the lungs and heart to provide adequate oxygen to the tissues, facilitate the maintenance of homeostasis and the rate of recovery after exercise. The body reaches its peak of physiological resilience during late adolescence and early adulthood.[8] Evidence of this peak is reflected in the age of many Olympic competitors. Both strength and the tolerance for strenuous activity can be increased by regular physical training and an individualized conditioning program.

Nutritional Needs

An increase in caloric needs parallels the rate of body growth and the increased metabolic rate. Teenagers frequently feel as if they can never get enough to eat. Meals are frequent and voluminous. Parents are awed and sometimes angered at the amount of food their adolescents consume. At peak growth periods, females may consume as much as 2600 calories per day, and males may take in 3600 calories or more (Fig. 23-7) (see Appendix E for further details).[9] Work schedules, odd class scheduling, concern about weight gain, peer activities, and inadequate knowledge of nutritional needs leads over 50% of adolescents to skip at least one meal a day, usually breakfast.[31] Intake is influenced by peers, family, culture, individual preferences, and fads. They may rely on quick-energy foods, such as carbonated beverages and snack chips. It is estimated that one-fourth to one-third of an adolescent's

FIGURE 23–7.
A large volume of food does not ensure nutritional adequacy. Adolescents need to be sure to include complete proteins and all four food groups in their diets.

calories come from snack foods.[31] Inadequate nutritional intake is common even though calories may be adequate. Consequently, careful attention should be given to fluid, protein, iron, and calcium needs. A daily vitamin supplement can help ensure the adequate intake of essential vitamins.

Protein needs are closely related to the growth rate. During adolescence, proteins should comprise 12% to 16% of the total daily energy intake, with higher proportions during the earlier years, when growth is most rapid.[41] Protein needs may not be met if the adolescent is on a severe reducing diet, is from a lower socioeconomic environment, or is on a diet that eliminates animal proteins. Strict vegetarian diets can also lead to deficiencies in vitamins and minerals.

Adequate calcium intake is essential for continued bone growth and formation of teeth. Males need 400 mg and females need 250 mg of calcium daily during adolescence.[27] Inadequate dietary calcium places the young person at risk for bone density loss—especially young amenorrheic female athletes. Adolescents, especially males, are at risk for suboptimal calcium intake during periods of rapid skeletal growth. The weight-conscious female may also unknowingly reduce her calcium intake, placing herself at risk for problems associated with low calcium. Milk and cheese are the richest sources of calcium.

The female's iron needs vary according to the blood loss during her menses; a daily intake of 1.2 g of iron is recommended for replacement and maintenance needs.[38] Adolescent boys need approximately 1.1 mg of daily iron.[27] Periodic blood checks will indicate if additional intake is needed. Many physicians recommend a regular iron supplement even when dietary intake appears to be adequate. Inadequate vitamin C is another frequent nutritional problem, since fruit juices, fresh fruit, and vegetables may be overlooked. High consumption of soft drinks can interfere with drinking enough milk to meet calcium needs. Recent studies at Washington State University also show that the caffeine and sugar in a soda can cause a 30 mg calcium loss over the following 3 hours.[31]

Caloric needs are further increased if the adolescent is involved in sports. The amount and the frequency of food intake can affect the athlete's strength and endurance. Female athletes may consume as much as 4000 calories, and males as high as 6000 calories, in one day.[27] The recommended pattern of food intake for athletes is 15% protein, 30% fat, and 55% carbohydrate.[37] Fat and carbohydrate, but not protein, are converted to immediate energy. Paying attention to adequate hydration and salt intake is also important for athletes (Fig. 23-8). If energy expenditure exceeds energy intake, the young athlete may lose significant lean tissue rather than fat, may compromise physical growth and development, impair performance, and endanger health.[27] High-energy foods are recommended to ensure adequate caloric intake. Adolescent athletes should concentrate on nutrition, not weight control.

The recommended minimal daily intake for adolescents in the four basic food groups is given in Table 23-4. If a young person is involved in athletics or if a young woman is pregnant, caloric intake will need to be increased.

Fatigue

Easy fatigability was mentioned earlier as a side effect of the usurping of calories by the body for growth; fatigue may also be precipitated by overactivity. There is so much for the young adolescent to do and to become involved in that he or she may not set appropriate limits on activity or involvement. The adolescent needs to plan some quiet time every day to allow for both physiological and psychological rest. Many adolescents hate to go to bed—and hate to get up in the morning. All the interesting things happen at night (or so it seems). The lack of adequate sleep can also lead to a feeling of chronic fatigue. Adolescents need 8 to 9 hours of sleep at night.

Faulty nutrition is another major cause of fatigue. Poor eating habits established during the school-age years, combined with the typical quick-service, quick-energy food consumption patterns of adolescents, frequently lead to anemia. Females must be especially careful to obtain adequate iron intake because of the loss during each menses. Testosterone levels in males help to retain higher hemoglobin levels.[52]

COMMON PROBLEMS ASSOCIATED WITH ADOLESCENT GROWTH

A number of common problems during adolescence present additional hurdles to the establishment of a positive self-concept and body image. Although these conditions are not unique to adolescence, they seem to occur more frequently during these years, creating more stress in a period that is already full of stressors and crises.

Juvenile Obesity

Approximately 20% of adolescents are overweight.[27] Obesity can be a serious health problem because it increases the incidence of some diseases, elevates blood pressure, heightens surgical risks, and augments death rates.[13] It is difficult to normalize weight during adulthood if obesity has been the pattern during adolescence.[27] Obesity also can be a serious social problem because it increases the incidence of teasing and name calling, heightens a sense of stigma and discrimination, and creates difficulties finding clothing or dates. Obesity is defined as a body weight 20% or more above the recommended desirable weight for one's height.[14] Many pubescents deposit extra fat in preparation for the adolescent growth spurt. Those who consistently overeat and select nutritionally unbalanced foods may accumulate too much body fat. Once these additional cells are formed, they may predispose the individual to lifelong obesity. Ten percent to 16% of adolescent females are more than 20% overweight for their height;[52] 80% of these females will remain overweight as adults. Obesity may occasionally be caused by a malfunction in metabolism; calories may be converted into fat instead of heat or energy. Although obesity is associated with inadequate exercise, the major cause of obesity is hyperphagia (overeating).[27]

Food consumption patterns may facilitate storage rather

FIGURE 23–8.
Adequate exercise continues to be critical for maximal development and functioning of all body systems.

than use of energy. Some teenagers have the *night eating syndrome*; in the mornings they do not feel like eating, so breakfast is skipped, and when they are unable to sleep at night, they eat. Eating before sleeping leads to storage of the calories, since they are not needed for energy. Many teenagers and up to 64% of college males and 90% of college females

TABLE 23–4. RECOMMENDED DAILY INTAKE FOR ADOLESCENTS*

Food Group	Amount	
Milk	3–4	cups
Meat	3–4	servings
Fruit and vegetables	5–6	servings
Bread and cereals	4–5	servings

Extra foods may be added in each group to ensure adequate caloric intake.

face stress with the *eating binge syndrome.*[25] They consume great quantities of food in short periods of time and subsequently suffer severe discomfort and self-criticism. Their attempts at reduction diets are short-lived, since intermittent stress precipitates the eating binge again. The adolescent may develop negative feelings about the self because of being fat, or disgust because of the lack of self-discipline, yet he or she attempts to comfort the self with food. Thus a vicious cycle can be established. The teenager with the *eating without satiation syndrome* finds it very difficult to stop once eating is started—the food just "feels so good going down." This type of hyperphagia usually has no correlation with stress, and the individual expresses little or no self-criticism after the spree.

There is a direct correlation between the amount of television viewing and the prevalence of both childhood and adolescent obesity. However, other sedentary activities, such as reading and radio listening are not related.[13] Television viewing may be an indicator of lack of active involvement in other activities, and also provides opportunity to eat.

Weight Loss

The treatment of juvenile obesity is very difficult during periods of rapid growth. Good nutrition—a diet that includes the basic four food groups—is essential. Many health professionals try to assist the adolescent to maintain rather than lose weight until the growth spurt is completed. This policy often results in an appearance of weight loss, since the adolescent gains in height what is lost in width. Athletes who try to lose weight to fit into another weight category also lose muscle strength. They should limit weight loss to no more than 2 pounds per week.[37] Caloric intake is usually reduced in the form of foods high in carbohydrates (sugars and starches). Adolescents can lose 1.5 pounds weekly by reducing daily caloric intake by 500 kcal (soft drink and slice of cake, or pie; bag of chips and candy bar) and increasing daily energy expenditure by 300 kcal (walk about 3 miles) per day.[27]

Over 50% of college students indicate they are or have been on a diet.[31] Some will use diet pills, laxatives, or even diuretics to speed up the process. Persons who go on fad diets or use these methods endanger themselves and may cause irreparable damage.[31] Consequently, before going on a weight control program, it is wise to consult with a physician, nurse practitioner, or dietitian.

Some young people may benefit from attending camps or "rap-session" groups for overweight children and adolescents. They are encouraged to lose weight by learning how to establish good eating and exercise habits. Dieting and exercise are very difficult for the adolescent who developmentally wants instant results. These programs include group discussion periods for the sharing of common problems and concerns. The "fat" adolescent rarely uses normal peer groups for support and physical activity.[28] Their embarrassment over their physical condition often sentences them to a life of loneliness, thus affecting social–emotional development. Obese adolescents need adult assistance in recognizing what they can eat when out with the gang. Group activities need to be provided that focus on constructive experiences that will assist the participants to recognize and to mobilize their potentials or assets.

Anorexia Nervosa

One to 3% of adolescents become sufficiently obsessed with the idea of losing weight that they restrict their intake and increase their activity level so severely that their very lives are threatened by the weight loss. A distorted perception of personal appearance convinces the victims they are obese, although in reality, emaciation (25% or more weight loss) may threaten survival.[51] Ninety percent of the anorexia nervosa population is female.[3] The etiology is unknown, but it is hypothesized that anorexia nervosa is a reactivation of the separation-individuation issue precipitated by events of puberty or independent living, since the peak periods of incidence are between age 12 and 13 and between age 19 and 20. These adolescents are usually "ideal" children prior to onset of symptoms. They have been rigidly obedient to parental and

societal (external) expectations. The anorexia appears to be an attempt to extricate themselves from parental control and to maintain rigid control of what happens to their emerging adult bodies.[25] They also attempt to achieve the cultural ideal of the slender body and avoid the cultural stigma associated with "fat."[6,51] This control offers a sense of effectiveness in the face of developmental and maturational crises beyond their control. Anorexics may avoid school as a way to prevent control by teachers.

Anorexia nervosa is not an attempt at suicide but at psychological self-preservation.[25] The irony is that the physical self is dying while the psychological self is trying to emerge. *The anorexia takes on a life of its own* once it gets started. Physical changes include decreased weight, blood pressure, pulse rate, and temperature. The individual has dry flaky skin and may develop lanugo (fine downy body hair). Females experience amenorrhea as their weight falls below the critical-fat level. They also experience constipation, abdominal pain, and cold temperature intolerance. There is a denial of hunger along with sensations of fatigue and depression. Yet the person may exhibit much energy in scholastic work and even in exercise regimens.[51] Attempts to reason with anorexic individuals and to present facts and norms are useless. Dichotomous reasoning (black-white thinking) is common in all aspects of their life—evaluation of self, circumstances, and others.[51] Many are obsessive-compulsive in their behaviors, demanding physical and environmental order and cleanliness, or engaging in compulsive studying and ritualistic activities.[51] They are proud of their strict, stoic, Spartan existence. As many as 15% to 21% of anorexics may die from the disorder.[36]

Many disciplines need to work together to help the anorexic adolescent to return to a safe weight and to gain a balanced sense of self-control, pride, and independence. All of the members of the family must be involved in the therapy, since a careful assessment of family dynamics frequently reveals inadequate individuation and gross overprotectiveness. Anorexics who are "cured" tend to stabilize at 85% to 90% of ideal weight for their height.[51]

Bulimia

Some adolescents maintain or lose weight through self-induced vomiting, which may be used regularly or only after an eating binge. This disorder tends to emerge in late adolescence and early adult years.[51] Some studies report that up to 20% of college-age females and 6% of college-age males use this method of weight control. The behavior may continue into the adult years, but at a lower incidence and usually at a more sporadic pattern.[25] Like anorexia, the origin of bulimia is hypothesized to be in the early mother–child interaction. Whereas anorexia is seen as an attempt to shut out overinvolvement, bulimia reflects an adaptive response to maternal under-involvement.[25] Both disorders are interpreted by the psychoanalytic view as the unsuccessful resolution of Mahler's separation-individuation process.[48,51] There is also evidence to indicate that bulimics experience difficulty accepting a positive feminine sexual identity and experience.[48] Bulimics may be obese, average, or underweight. The physical, endocrine, social, and emotional symptoms seen in the starved or semi-starved state of anorexics is also observed in many bulimics. Some bulimics may experience throat irritation or an erosion of tooth enamel because of the frequent vomiting (stomach acids eat the enamel away). Cardiac and menstrual irregularities are common, due to endocrine and electrolyte imbalances. Death may also occur.[51] Many bulimics have associated behavior problems, such as alcoholism, drug abuse, promiscuity, and stealing (all abnormal "taking in" activities).[3,51] Most bulimics realize their behavior is abnormal and attempt to prevent discovery of their actions.

Since 23% of bulimics may attempt suicide, referral to counseling is strongly suggested when bulimia is discovered.[18] Both anorexics and bulimics should be referred for medical evaluation because of the threat to life. Both also need intensive counseling to help them to renegotiate the parent–child relationship, reevaluate their body image, and to rework their identity. Additional information can be obtained through the National Association of Anorexia Nervosa and Associated Disorders, Box 271, Highland Park, IL 60035.

Acne

More than 80% of adolescents experience some degree of *acne vulgaris* (or "zits") between 9 and 20 years of age.[53] The increased androgen levels at puberty stimulate the production of sebum by the sebaceous glands of the face, neck, shoulders, and upper chest. The small, immature ducts leading from the glands to the surface of the skin may be inadequate to transport the large amounts of material produced, forcing the sebum to occlude the ducts and to dilate the glands. The normal bacteria of the skin colonize the sebaceous follicle, releasing free fatty acid as a substance that irritates surrounding tissue. The closed comedo (whitehead) has two fates. It can continue to dilate until it becomes an open comedo (blackhead), or it can rupture below the skin surface, spreading its contents into surrounding tissue. The skin sets up a localized foreign-body response to the comedonal core and the acids from the ruptured comedos. Occasionally, two or three comedos may merge, creating nodules or cysts. When bacteria are involved, abscesses may form.

Most cases of acne disappear spontaneously sometime after the twentieth birthday. Although there appears to be a genetic predisposition toward acne vulgaris, it can be precipitated or aggravated by poor hygiene, working in a greasy environment, or the use of ordinary cosmetics. Forehead acne has been reported from the use of pomade or oils on the hair, and perioral acne from the use of fluoridated toothpastes.

The general management of acne includes a well-balanced diet, good hygiene to remove surface pore blocks and to reduce bacteria count, the avoidance of known irritants, and the reduction of emotional tension and anxiety. Research does not document the need for dietary restrictions.[53] How-

ever, individuals may find that particular foods appear to be associated with increased comedo formation, and that adequate sleep and exposure to sunlight appear to help.[38] Pinching and squeezing may spread the contents into the adjacent tissues, thus increasing the chances of infection and scarring. Superficial pustules may resolve more quickly, however, if the contents are squeezed out to the surface, using gentle pressure and clean hands.[53]

Several breakthroughs have been made in controlling the formation and the treatment of acne. For severe cases, antibiotics may be used. Both oral and topical medications are available to help reduce the severity of acne. Accutane, once highly recommended, is now discouraged because of its teratogenic effect on developing fetuses and multiple side effects on the users (e.g., intercranial tension, headaches, nausea, seizures, emotional instability, drowsiness, depression, and blood and skin changes).[55] Adolescents are encouraged to obtain medical consultation for advice or assistance in controlling the condition of the skin during this period of life, since acne may create social discomfort as well as permanent facial scarring.

Poor Posture

Poor posture is a common phenomenon of both male and female adolescents. One causative factor is the rapid skeletal growth. Since the long bones grow faster than the adjacent muscles, keeping the joints bent relieves tension on stretched muscles. Many young adolescents complain of muscle cramps or leg aches for the same reason. Some adolescents are uncomfortable with, or ashamed of, their height and will slump to appear shorter. Some females who are embarrassed by an increase in breast size may round their shoulders and lean forward slightly to deemphasize their maturing figure. There is also speculation that some poor posture is due to inadequate exercise and too much sitting to watch television. Poor posture may also be caused by unequal leg length. A difference of one-half inch at maturity is normal, but may precipitate muscle imbalance.[17] Frequently a shoe lift is all that is necessary to achieve balance.

Medical evaluation may be appropriate to rule out the presence of a skeletal anomaly. *Scoliosis,* a lateral deviation of the spine, is often first diagnosed in early adolescence. Since it is progressive and can lead to complications, early intervention is warranted. Although evidence now suggests some genetic basis for scoliosis, the exact mechanisms and underlying causes are unknown.[17] Many physicians recommend routine screening for scoliosis during the junior high school years.

Dentition

Permanent dentition is usually completed during the late adolescent years. The third molar (wisdom tooth) usually erupts earlier in females. Many young adults need to have one or more wisdom teeth removed because there may be inadequate room in the dental arch to support the extra tooth. Removal prevents overcrowding of teeth and resultant malocclusion. Also, since the third molar is the last tooth to develop, calcification may cease before the enamel is complete. Eruption of the poorly calcified tooth leads to rapid decay, necessitating removal.

Adolescents are frequently in need of dental attention to prevent or to cure *malocclusion,* a significant deviation of the normal alignment of teeth that causes poor bite. Some young people develop *bruxism,* or grinding of teeth, especially at night, as a mechanism for realigning maloccluded teeth. However, bruxism also results from tension. Bruxism among college students is 20.5% (an increase of 400% since 1966), presumably due to increased stress associated with changes in cultural attitudes and lifestyles.[23]

Straightening of the teeth is usually done during adolescence when the supportive structures are still soft enough to allow gradual repositioning of the teeth. Straightening of the teeth can help correct some speech defects caused by poor tooth alignment; it can also decrease the occurrence of emotional trauma due to unattractive appearance.

Headache

Forty percent of children experience headache by 7 years of age.[20] Ninety-one percent of men and 95% of women have headaches at least once a year during their adolescent and young adult years, 90% of which are benign.[5] Twenty-nine percent of boys and 32% of girls have at least one headache per month during adolescence. Four percent of boys and 7% of girls suffer migraine headaches during adolescence.[29]

Headaches can be divided into three categories: symptomatic, psychogenic, and vascular (migraine). **Symptomatic headaches** are secondary to problems such as infection, trauma, sinusitis, metabolic imbalances, eye strain, head injury, fever, allergies, brain tumor, bruxism, hunger, or encephalitis. **Psychogenic headaches,** or tension headaches, are the most frequent recurrent form of headache. Tension headaches are rare before adolescence.[33] The individual tenses the muscles, especially those of the neck and the scalp, in response to stress. A headache ensues, which may last from several hours to several days. The average is about 5½ hours for adolescents.[29] It is frequently a dull, persistent, band-like pain felt on both sides of the head (Fig. 23-9).

Seventy percent of those experiencing vascular or **migraine headaches** have a family history of similar headaches.[5] These headaches may begin during the toddler years; by 15 years of age, the incidence is about 5%.[12,33] Vascular headaches typically have three phases. In the preheadache phase, the individual may experience an *aura* that consists of transient neurological signs, distorted perceptual processes (strange sounds or lights), and difficulty thinking. During the second phase, the scalp vessels become dilated and pulsatile, producing a unilateral, pounding headache, which may spread to the entire head. In the third phase, edema of the vessel walls and tightening of the muscles leads to a steady, intractable, tension-type headache. The causes of vascular headaches are unknown, but stress, fatigue, loss of sleep, hormonal imbal-

FIGURE 23–9.
Adolescents tend to become involved in so many different activities that parents may need to help them set some limits. Adequate rest can prevent fatigue and the depression or the discouragement that will sometimes accompany it.

ance, bright lights, eye strain, alcohol, and foods with tyramine (milk products, chocolate, coffee, cola beverages) are known to trigger these headaches.[33]

Recurring headaches in children and adolescents should be evaluated by a physician, since any headache can signify a serious health problem, and most can be treated prophylactically or symptomatically. The person's total lifestyle and lifespace needs to be considered in the assessment, including school grades, peer relations, potential environmental toxins, and the parents' marital adjustment.

CONCLUSION

Adolescence can be a time of great happiness as the young person anticipates adult characteristics and responsibilities. But the pubertal period can also be one of intense anxiety and apprehension as the young person observes the unfolding of adult body configuration and functions. Although the total changes occur over a space of 8 to 10 years, the young person may be consciously aware only of those events that represent the most dramatic changes over a 2- to 3-year span of time. Menarche is the most clearly defined overt sign of female puberty, but true puberty usually does not occur until 1 to 2 years later, when the ovaries begin to produce viable ova. Males have no clear demarcation for identifying the onset of true puberty, unless the urine is tested regularly for the presence of viable sperm.

The fact that most girls experience puberty during the junior high school years has implications for both parents and the educational system. Confrontation with menarche without warning can be a terrifying experience. The young girl may fear that she has injured herself, or even that she has a terminal disease. The plethora of emotions and feelings accompanying male and female puberty complicate self-understanding and social relationships. Clear, complete, positive prophylactic health education from parents and educational systems (during late school-age years as well as continuing during adolescence) is essential to prevent confusion and to enable healthy handling of the emerging adult body and emotions. It is crucial that young people understand these changes within a healthy value system and social context, so they can respond positively to this new dimension of their expanding life.

Nutrition requirements during adolescence are directly related to the rate and the stage of growth, with the highest requirements at the peak rate of growth. Adolescents may need guidance in how to care for and use their bodies appropriately to maximize their potentials. All females should be encouraged to have a pelvic examination and Pap smear annually after 18 years of age, or sooner if they are sexually active. Dental visits should continue at 6-month intervals, and a complete physical examination should be obtained at least once a year (see Table 6-4). Measles and diptheria-tetanus "booster" immunizations are recommended during adolescence (see Table 6-3). Health education classes can provide adolescents with information that will help them understand body functioning and become more independent in health maintenance.

At no time is individuality more critical than during adolescence. The young person needs to be assured of his or her normalcy and appreciated for the individual variations contributing to uniqueness. Adolescents should continue to be assessed in terms of individual health status and abilities. Because of the rapid changes, continued regular health care is essential to identify potential problems and to provide preventive intervention and reassurances of normalcy.

A carefully planned, individualized athletic program should be provided for each adolescent, including proper conditioning, competent coaching instruction, rigid regulations to protect the athlete's safety, and promotion of the enjoyment of the activity. Each individual needs to learn to appreciate, to use, and to care for the body properly during adolescence so that it can be used as a tool for positive self-expression in the years ahead.

REFERENCES

1. Adolescent Gynecology. (1977). *Report of the 7th Ross Roundtable.* Columbus, OH: Ross Laboratories.
2. Amsel, Z., Genser, S. G., & Haverkos, H. W. (1989). Anabolic steroid use among male high school students. *Journal of the American Medical Association, 261,* 2639.
3. Andersen, A. (1983). Anorexia and bulimia. *Journal of Adolescent Health Care, 4*(1), 15.
4. Bachmann, G. A., & Kemmann, E. (1982). Prevalence of oligomenorrhea and amenorrhea in a college population. *American Journal of Obstetrics and Gynecology, 143,* 98.
5. Barrett-Griesemer, P., Meisel, S., & Rute, R. (1981). A guide to headaches-and how to relieve their pain. *American Journal of Nursing, 81,* 50.
6. Beumont, P. J. V., & Touyz, S. W. (1987). Anorexia and bulimia nervosa: A personal perspective. In P. J. V. Beumont, G. D. Burrows, & R. C. Casper (Eds.), *Handbook of eating disorders: Part I: Anorexia and bulimia nervosa* (pp. 1–11). New York: Elsevier.
7. Beunen, G. P., Malina, R. M., Van't Hof, M. A., Simon, J., Ostyn, M., Renson, R., & VanGerven, D. (1988). *Adolescent growth and motor performance: A longitudinal study of Belgian boys.* Champaign, IL: Human Kinetics Books.
8. Chinn, P. L. (1979). *Child health maintenance: Concepts in family-centered care* (2nd ed.). St. Louis: Mosby.
9. Cooke, R. E. (Ed.). (1968). *The biologic basis of pediatric practice.* New York: McGraw-Hill.
10. Davajan, V., & Kletzky, O. A. (1986). Primary amenorrhea. In D. R. Mishell, Jr. & R. P. Marrs (Eds.), *Infertility, contraception and reproductive endocrinology* (2nd ed., pp. 237–252). Oradell, NJ: Medical Economics Books.
11. Davajan, V., & Kletzky, O. A. (1986). Secondary amenorrhea. In D. R. Mishell, Jr. & V. Davajan (Eds.), *Infertility, contraception and reproductive endocrinology* (2nd ed., pp. 253–274). Oradell, NJ: Medical Economics Books.
12. Debrun, S. R. (1981). Headaches in adolescents. *MCN: American Journal of Maternal Child Nursing, 6,* 407.
13. Dietz, W. H. (1988). Childhood and adolescent obesity. In R. T.

Frankle & M. U. Yang (Eds.), *Obesity and weight control: The health professional's guide to understanding and treatment* (pp. 345–359). Rockville, MD: Aspen.

14. Domangue, B. B. (1987). Biological considerations in the treatment of adult obesity. In H. L. Field & B. B. Domangue (Eds.), *Eating disorders throughout the life span* (pp. 71–89). New York: Praeger.

15. Engel, N. S. (1989). Anabolic steroid use among high school athletes. *MCN: The American Journal of Maternal Child Nursing, 14,* 417.

16. Frisch, R. E., & McArthur, J. W. (1981). Menstrual cycles: Fatness as a determinant of minimum weight for height necessary for their maintenance or onset. *Science, 185,* 949.

17. Gallagher, J. R., Heald, F. P., & Garell, D. C. (1976). *Medical care of the adolescent* (3rd ed.). New York: Appleton.

18. Garfinkel, P. E., et al. (1980). The heterogeneity of anorexia nervosa: Bulimia as a distinct subgroup. *Archives of General Psychiatry, 37,* 1036.

19. Goebelsmann, U. (1986). The menstrual cycle. In D. R. Mishell, Jr. & V. Davajan (Eds.), *Infertility, contraception and reproductive endocrinology* (2nd ed., pp. 69–89). Oradell, NJ: Medical Economics Books.

20. Golden, G. S. (1982). The child with headaches. *Developmental and Behavioral Pediatrics, 3*(2), 114.

21. Hallberg, L., et al. (1966). Menstrual blood loss: A population study. *Acta Obstetricia et Gynecologica Scandinavica, 45,* 320.

22. Heitkemper, M. M., Shaver, J. F., & Mitchell, E. S. (1988). Gastrointestinal symptoms and bowel patterns across the menstrual cycle in dysmenorrhea. *Nursing Research, 37*(2), 108–113.

23. Hicks, R. A., & Conti, P. A. (1989). Changes in the incidence of nocturnal bruxism in college students: 1966–1989. *Perceptual and Motor Skills, 69,* 481–482.

24. Hockfelt, T., Tsuruo, Y., Meister, B., Melander, T., Schalling, M., & Everitt, B. (1987). Localization of neuroactive substances in the hypothalamus with special reference to coexistence of messenger molecules. In V. B. Mahesh, D. S. Dhindsa, E. Anderson, & S. P. Kalra (Eds.), *Regulation of ovarian and testicular function* (pp. 21–45). New York: Plenum Press.

25. Johnson, C., & Connors, M. E. (1987). *The etiology and treatment of bulemia nervosa: a biological perspective.* New York: Basic Books.

26. Kreipe, R. E., & Gewanter, H. L. (1985). Physical maturity screening for participation in sports. *Pediatrics, 75,* 1076–1080.

27. Kris-Etherton, P. M. (1986). Nutrition and the exercising female. *Nutrition today, 21*(2), 6–16.

28. Langford, R. W. (1981). Teenagers and obesity. *American Journal of Nursing, 81,* 556.

29. Linet, M. S., Stewart, W. F., Celentano, D. D., Ziegler, D., & Sprecher, M. (1989). An epidemiological study of headaches among adolescents and young adults. *Journal of the American Medical Association, 261,* 2211–2216.

30. Lowrey, G. H. (1986). *Growth and development of children* (8th ed.). Chicago: Year Book.

31. Marrale, J. C., Shipman, J. H., & Rhodes, M. L. (1986). What some college students eat. *Nutrition Today, 21*(1), 16–21.

32. Marshall, W. A., & Tanner, J. M. (1969). Variations in patterns of pubertal changes in girls. *Archives of Disease in Childhood, 44,* 291.

33. McCarthy, A. M. (1982). Chronic headaches in children. *Pediatric Nursing, 8*(2), 88.

34. Mishell, D. R., Jr., & Marrs, R. P. (1986). Endocrinology of lactation on the puerperium. In D. R. Mishell, Jr. & V. Davajan (Eds.), *Infertility, contraception and reproductive endocrinology* (2nd ed., pp. 143–162). Oradell, NJ: Medical Economics Books.

35. Moerman, M. L. (1982). Growth of the birth canal in adolescent girls. *American Journal of Obstetrics and Gynecology, 142,* 528.

36. Moore, J. A., & Coulman, M. U. (1981). Anorexia nervosa: The patient, her family, and key family therapy interventions. *Journal of Psychiatric Nursing, 19*(5), 9.

37. Nairns, D. M., Belkengren, R. P., & Sapala, S. (1983). Nutrition and the growing athlete. *Pediatric Nursing, 9,* 163.

38. National Research Council. (U.S.) Subcommittee on the Tenth Edition of the RDAs. (1989). *Recommended dietary allowances* (10th rev. ed.). Washington, DC: National Academy Press.

39. Nelson, W. E., Behrman, R. E., & Vaughan, V. C. (Eds.). (1987). *Nelson Textbook of Pediatrics* (13th ed.). Philadelphia: W. B. Saunders.

40. Oriatti, M. D. (1975). Dysmenorrhea. *Pediatric Annals, 4*(1), 60.

41. Pipes, P. L. (Ed.). (1989). *Nutrition in infancy and childhood* (4th ed.). St. Louis: Times Mirror/Mosby.

42. Reeder, S. J., & Martin, L. L. (1987). *Maternity nursing: Family, newborn, and women's health care* (16th ed.). Philadelphia: J. B. Lippincott.

43. Remington, P., Anda, R., & Marks, J. (1988). Cardiovascular risk factors and the adolescent. *Journal of the American Medical Association, 259,* 44–45.

44. Rosen, P. R., Micheli, L. J., & Treves, S. (1982). Early scintigraphic diagnosis of bone stress and fractures in athletic adolescents. *Pediatrics, 70*(1), 11.

45. Roy, S., & Benner, P. F. (1986). Puberty. In D. R. Mishell, Jr. & V. Davajan (Eds.), *Infertility, contraception and reproductive endocrinology* (2nd ed., pp. 163–178). Oradell, NJ: Medical Economics Books.

46. Sanborn, C. F., Martin, B. J., & Wagner, W. W. (1982). Is athletic amenorrhea specific to runners? *American Journal of Obstetrics and Gynecology, 142,* 859.

47. Schuster, C. S. (1974). *Characteristics of the menstrual period.* Unpublished research.

48. Schwartz, H. J. (1987). Bulimia: Dynamic considerations. In H. L. Field & B. B. Domangue (Eds.), *Eating disorders through the life span* (pp. 59–68). New York: Praeger.

49. Shapiro, F. (1987). Epiphyseal disorders. *New England Journal of Medicine, 317,* 1702–1710.

50. Shaver, J. F., Woods, N. F., Wolf-Wilets, V., & Heitkemper, M. M. (1987). Menstrual experiences in dysmenorrheic and nondysmenorrheic women. *Western Journal of Nursing Research, 9,* 423–439.

51. Sholevar, G. P. (1987). Anorexia nervosa and bulimia. In H. L. Field & B. B. Domangue (Eds.), *Eating disorders throughout the life span* (pp. 31–47). New York: Praeger.

52. Smith, D. W., Bierman, E. L., & Robinson, N. M. (Eds.). (1978). *The biologic ages of man: From conception through old age* (2nd ed.). Philadelphia: W. B. Saunders.

53. Stone, A. C. (1982). Facing up to acne. *Pediatric Nursing, 8,* 229.

54. Tanner, J. M. (1989). *Foetus into man: Physical growth from conception to maturity* (rev. & enl.). Cambridge, MA: Harvard University Press.

55. Thompson, E. J., & Cordero, J. F. (1989). The new teratogens: Accutane and other vitamin-A analogs. *MCN: American Journal of Maternal Child Nursing, 14,* 244–248.

56. Vargyas, J. M. (1986). Premenstrual syndrome: The neuroendocrine control of mood and behavior. In D. R. Mishell, Jr. & V. Davajan (Eds.), *Infertility, contraception and reproductive endocrinology* (2nd ed., pp. 353–364). Oradell, NJ: Medical Economics Books.

57. Warren, M. P., Brooks-Gunn, J., Hamilton, L. H., Warren, L. F., & Hamilton, W. G. (1986). Scoliosis and fractures in young ballet dancers: Relation to delayed menarche and secondary amenorrhea. *New England Journal of Medicine, 314,* 1348–1353.

58. Watson, J. E., & Royle, J. R. (1987). *Medical-surgical nursing and related physiology* (3rd ed.). Philadelphia: Brailliere Tindall.

59. Wieczorek, R. R., & Natapoff, J. N. (1981). *A conceptual approach to the nursing of children: Health care from birth through adolescence.* Philadelphia: J. B. Lippincott.

60. Williams, H. A. (1981). Screening for testicular cancer. *Pediatric Nursing, 7*(5), 38.

61. Wyngaarden, J. B., & Smith, L. H. (Eds.). (1988). *Textbook of medicine* (18th ed.). Philadelphia: W. B. Saunders.

Cognitive Development During Adolescence

Randy L. Cronk

The abilities to reason, solve problems, and imagine the future begin to blossom during adolescence. The development in each of the domains is mutually influential and complex. Affective responses influence the way the adolescent responds socially and cognitively, and, in turn, thought processes influence affective responses. This chapter will examine the emerging cognitive skills and structural changes that accompany the transition into adolescence and the adultlike thinking of which the adolescent becomes capable.

The first systematic approach to studying adolescent cognitive development focused on intellectual performance and cognitive content.[4] This *psychometric* approach assessed adolescents' intelligence through standardized tests (e.g., the Stanford-Binet Intelligence Scale). Psychometrics is concerned with identifying quantitative changes in knowledge; that is, changes in the *amount* of a particular intellectual skill or ability.

Early psychometric research indicated that general intelligence scores tended to stabilize by the time the individual reached adolescence.[52] However, changes in the adolescent's life circumstances can dramatically affect functioning. For example, a prolonged illness lowers the energy level necessary to tap intellectual potentials, and an adolescent who associates with a peer group that does not value education may show a relative decline in performance. The onset of a physical growth spurt does not imply an intellectual growth spurt. The onset of pubescence is not correlated with intelligence.[50]

During adolescence, special skills and abilities in areas such as science, math, literature, and the arts become increasingly noticeable. Some of the differentiation and specialization of cognitive abilities is heavily influenced by sociocultural factors. Despite recent cultural emphasis on equality of education and opportunity, females exhibit relative superiority in verbal skills and males in math and the sciences.[6] Although differential neurological development may influence these noted sex differences, one must recognize the cultural expectations and pressures in the form of sex-role stereotypes that influence the development of associated skills. It has been suggested that girls' IQ scores tend to decline more than boys' during adolescence because of the lack of support and encouragement many girls receive for independence, initiative, and intellectual growth.[7]

The psychometric approach is informative and valuable; however, it is rather static because it does not explain the emerging and changing individual. To address issues related to life-span development and the processes of cognitive development, our discussion turns to *qualitative* changes in thinking as hypothesized by Piaget.

FORMAL OPERATIONAL THOUGHT

According to Piaget, the individual's cognitive structures reach maturity during adolescence.[19, 26, 41, 42] With acquisition of formal operational thought, Piaget proposes that the individual's potential, in terms of quality of thought, is at its maximum. There are no further structural improvements in cognitive organization. The adolescent acquires the cognitive structural equipment to think as an adult thinks. This does not mean that the adolescent thinks as well as an adult thinks in any given instance. It does mean, however, that the adolescent now possesses the ability to use the same approaches to problem solving. After the acquisition of formal operations, any changes in thinking abilities are quantitative rather than qualitative with respect to logical operations. Although according to Piaget, cognitive structures make no further improvements, the content and function of thought continue to change and improve beyond adolescence with increased experience.

Both formal operational thought and concrete operational thought use logical operations (see Chap. 21). A primary difference between them is that concrete thought is bound to the situational present and the concrete qualities of the environment. The individual capable of formal thought can deal with abstract and complex verbal problems, hypothetical problems, and problems of the present, past, and future. Formal operations liberate one from the specific content of problems. Adolescents recognize that logically derived conclusions have a validity independent of empirical observations. The power of formal operational thought is in its freedom from the physical. Although formal operational thought may begin as early as eleven or twelve years of age, most adolescents are not fully into this stage until they are approximately 15 years old.[26] Although the timing and pervasiveness of formal operational thought may vary, the nature of formal reasoning is invariant. It is also important to bear in mind that not all adolescents (or adults) will consistently use formal operational thinking.[2, 5, 53] Stimulus situations that are novel, as well as other factors such as stress, are likely to inhibit the use of formal operations.

Characteristics of Formal Operational Thought

Formal operational thought is a "higher-order" process in that it involves (1) easily moving from the reality of the present to the heights of possibility, (2) abstract reasoning, (3) systematic problem solving, (4) multidimensional reasoning, (5) hypothetical-deductive thinking, and (6) thinking about one's own thoughts.

Reality and Possibility

According to Inhelder and Piaget, the most distinctive qualitative dimension of formal operational thought is the new found ability to deal with the *possible* as well as the *real*.[26] Instead of thinking about things as they *are,* the adolescent can now think about how things *might be, could be,* or *should be*. With concrete thinking, possibility is synonymous with reality; with formal thinking, reality is but one of numerous possibilities and is subordinate to the possible. The formal thinker is not content to deal with the immediate experience, but is continually thinking about alternatives. Put differently, the concrete reasoner observes his or her environment and asks the question "what?" or "why?" The formal reasoner imagines the environment as it could be and asks the questions "What if?" or "Why not?"

Adolescents become eager to apply this new cognitive ability of envisioning possibilities to many areas of life, including politics, religion, education, career, sports, social relationships, and development of their own identity. Liberated from reality, the adolescent begins to think about ideas, ideals, ideologies, and ideal states. Possibilities, however, have not yet been tempered in the refining furnace of reality. This *adolescent idealism* often leads adults to criticize the adolescent for "living in a dream world or utopia," being "unrealistic," "impractical," or "out-of-touch with reality." Yet those very ideals are what spur inventions and social change. The most frustrating response to the creative, perhaps idealistic thinker is, "This is the way we have always done it." Rigidity of "the system" can stifle ideas or lead to rebellious behaviors.

Possibility thinking enables adolescents to create and entertain alternative options or solutions to problems. They begin to realize that there is more than one way to solve a problem. This new *flexibility* in thinking allows them to deal with concrete and abstract ideas from many perspectives. They can now think about the impossible, the opposite position, or in a manner contrary to reality issues. They are able to anticipate the viewpoint or position of a person with whom they disagree and to formulate a counter argument. This new skill is admired on the school's debate team, but deplored by parents who are challenged to provide better rationale for their directives. Thinking about possibilities is evidenced in the adolescent's emerging concern with his or her future. Older adolescents assume a new appreciation of how present choices and decisions may shape the future. They become concerned with forming goals and organizing their activities to achieve these goals. They begin to recognize that the consequences of their behaviors are not limited to the present, and that most options simultaneously have both positive and negative effects.

Another result of thinking about ideals is the often disturbingly uncomfortable comparisons made between "what is" and "what should/could be." Such comparisons often produce intense political, social, and religious activism. Adolescents, equipped with their "dreams of a better tomorrow," are able to become zealots to a broad spectrum of issues and causes. They may become intensely concerned about environmental issues, human rights, or religious principles, as well as other moral and ethical issues. The cognitive detachment from the present circumstances accompanying this new concern for the ideal allows many adolescents to undergo intense and meaningful religious experiences. They can now become committed to a specific value system or an ideal future, and structure their goals and behaviors accordingly. This ability to envision the possible makes clear why advanced moral reasoning is based upon formal thinking abilities (see Chap. 16).[33]

Adolescent idealism can be a significant source of conflict. The adolescent's ideals are often the basis for major or minor conflicts with parents, teachers, and individuals in authoritative and leadership roles. Adults need to recognize and appreciate the adolescent's view. Helping the adolescent recognize and understand the gap between the ideal and real and find alternative goals or strategies can alleviate some of the dissonance and strife he or she experiences.

Abstract Reasoning

In concrete operational thought, children think with symbols that enable them to readily master the mathematical operations of addition, subtraction, multiplication, and division of whole numbers. Children use the symbols for concrete referents. Consequently, their reasoning is referred to as "first-order" operational thinking. Formal operational thinkers, however, possess the ability to think about "symbols that represent other symbols" (e.g., the variables X and Y that represent the first-order numerical symbols 1, 2, 3, etc.). The formal operational thinker no longer needs concrete examples or symbols to reason. In essence, he or she can now deal with the abstract or nonconcrete. Abstract reasoning involves the logical manipulation of propositions or symbols that are derived from or based on concrete reality, "second-order" operational thinking.[26]

The abstract reasoning abilities of the adolescent are demonstrated in the ability to deal with verbal representations of the concrete. For example, if an adolescent is presented with the statement, "Joe is taller than Lisa and Bob is shorter than Lisa," the ability to reason with the verbally abstract will allow them to evaluate the relationship between Joe and Bob. The concrete operational child will have difficulty arriving at the logical conclusion. Since thinking is no longer limited to concrete symbols, adolescents are free to reason about the abstract. They can now understand abstract concepts or philosophies such as democracy, faith, and integrity. The adolescent is also capable of having feelings about ideals and concepts instead of only toward objects and people.

Combinatorial Thinking

Another important qualitative characteristic of formal thinking is its potential for *combinatorial reasoning.* Inhelder and Piaget demonstrated this attribute of formal thought in a chemical-combinations problem.[26] The individual is presented with five jars containing colorless liquids. One combination of three of the liquids produces a yellow color. Of the two remaining jars, one contains a bleaching agent that will not permit the color to appear and the other contains water (which has no effect on the other liquids). The individual is shown the colored liquid that can be produced but does not

see how it is obtained. If a child, functioning at the concrete operational stage, is asked to produce the yellow liquid, he or she usually proceeds by combining only two liquids at a time. After combining a few of the possible pairs, the systematic nature of their search for the solution stops. Any subsequent combinations are haphazardly produced, some are duplicated, and many combinations (3 to 5 at a time) are never attempted. The formal-operational adolescent, however, is able to envision and systematically test all possible combinations (2, 3, 4, and 5) of the liquids; nor does the adolescent always stop when the correct three chemicals are mixed. Formal operation thought allows the adolescent to reflect upon the necessity and sufficiency of causal events. That is, the adolescent can recognize that the three-chemical mixture that first produces a yellow liquid is sufficient to produce the color, but may not be necessary. The adolescent may continue testing to see if other combinations produce the yellow liquid (Fig. 24-1).

The formal thinker reasons similarly in a multitude of situations. For example, an adolescent recognizes that a nail is sufficient to produce a flat tire, but it is not necessary; a piece of glass, metal object, or sharp stone may simultaneously contribute to the flat tire. He or she knows that there are multiple causes to events and that causal agents can interact in

FIGURE 24-1.
The adolescent is able to engage in systematic combinatorial thinking, a skill that opens the door to scientific research and experimentation.

unique ways. Adolescents can understand that the combined effects of alcohol and barbiturates are much more serious than their individual effects.

The ability to form combinations may at first appear to be a rather unimportant cognitive skill, unless one is faced with a problem that requires the systematic pairing of events (like arranging a round-robin play-off schedule in a sporting event or attempting to reconnect a few accidentally confused spark-plug wires). However, combinatorial reasoning is significant in a broader way, in that it represents the adolescent's increased flexibility and capacity for generating and evaluating multiple viewpoints or solutions to problems.

Multidimensional Reasoning

Multidimensional reasoning builds off of the previous three skills, especially possibility generation and combinatorial thinking. When faced with a problem, the adolescent is able to generate multiple potential solutions. Multidimensional thinking enables the person to project the potential positive and negative side effects of each solution *simultaneously* and to weigh the potential results against each other. This enables the person to prioritize and choose the most appropriate alternative to meet a specific goal with the least adverse effects. Such skill is essential for long-range planning.

Most adolescents do not have enough knowledge and experience to enable them to anticipate all the consequences of an action. It is in this area that a mentor is most valuable—to help the adolescent to identify other options and to anticipate all the side effects: "Have you thought about . . . ?" or "What will you do if . . . ?" Such questions expand the adolescent's ability to use this higher-level cognitive skill. This ability continues to develop during the adult years.

Hypothetical-Deductive Thinking

The characteristics of formal thinking are not independent of one another. The interdependence of the structural dimensions of formal thought becomes more obvious as we see how the ability to think abstractly, imagine possibilities, and form combinations allow for hypothetical-deductive reasoning.

Hypothetical-deductive thinking requires the adolescent to reason from the empirically real to the possible and back to the empirically real (Fig.24-2). This form of thinking is the basis of most scientific work and can generally be described in terms of hypotheses that are in the form of "if-then" statements. The "if" part of the statement constructs some abstract theoretical idea (a possibility). The "then" part of the statement is what the person expects to find if the theoretical idea is true. Hypothetical thinking also involves the ability to extract some core thread or characteristic of a group of seemingly unrelated objects or events to form a new, "umbrella" category or theory. "If" the categorization or theory is valid, "then" (by deductive thinking) it should be able to predict other objects belonging to the category, events, or behaviors. For example, *if* I hypothesize that reinforcement increases the frequency of a behavior, *then* some behavior that I observe to be reinforced ought to increase in frequency. The formal operational thinker evaluates his or her theoretical idea in

FIGURE 24–2.
Working on complex problems, such as motor repair, requires hypothetical-deductive *problem solving approaches.*

light of their real-world observations. Hypothetical thinking enables the establishment of philosophies, values, and goals.

Metacognition

Metacognition is the ability to turn thoughts inward and think introspectively about one's own thought processes. The adolescent becomes aware of cognitive activity and how it could be used in another way. A person can follow a train of thought and identify the sequential steps of reasoning. "How did I come to that thought or conclusion?" This dimension is conceptually related to the others, particularly to the ability to think abstractly. The adolescent becomes increasingly capable of thinking about psychological processes such as language, memory, communication patterns, feelings, relationships, attention factors, and perception. Many adolescents become intensely introspective. They are awed by their new insights. When they so choose, they are able to articulate their thoughts and feelings on a wide range of subjects. Their ability to think introspectively enables them to separate their thinking from their emotions, to benefit from counseling, and to deal with damaged emotions from earlier years (Fig. 24-3).

Manifestations of Formal Operational Thought

The characteristics of formal operational thought result in new and unique cognitive, emotional, and psychosocial outcomes.

Idealism

Possibility thinking moves the adolescent into the realm of envisioning an idealistic world. As mentioned above, this "wish for a better world" motivates many adolescents to become promoters of political, religious, social, and family reform.

FIGURE 24–3.
The imaginary friends of pre-schoolers give way to the fantasies of schoolagers. During preadolescence, time is spent in day dreaming, and during adolescence, in dream building.

Adolescents frequently have a great deal of emotional energy bound to their idealistic concepts. Subsequently, a great deal of urgency accompanies their expression of ideals. They are exceedingly anxious for the changes prescribed by their idealism to occur. In earnest, they demand that changes that would foster a better education, a more harmonious family life, and so forth, be made immediately. Limited experience tends to give them "tunnel vision," when the issue is not seen in context. Their solutions seem so obvious and simple to them that implementation should be no problem—if only others would cooperate and "do the *right* thing." Delays in action spur anger, cynicism, disillusionment, or despair. Their patience with the developmental pace of institutions, government, church, and the family often grows short. Subsequently, many a well-intended and socially desirable dream of the adolescent becomes abandoned. Hopefully, their discouragement will not become so pervasive that a sense of helplessness overcomes them and they abandon any future attempts to fulfill their goals and dreams, or even worse, that they lack the motivation to even develop and possess ideals. The prescription for parents and society seems obvious: be aware of adolescent urgency, help them realize their goals by sharing helpful information, resources and opportunities, and attempt to foster patience with praise and encouragement (Fig. 24-4).

Egocentrism

A second important manifestation of formal thought specific to adolescence is **affective egocentrism.** *Physical egocentrism* is seen during infancy because infant thought is bound to sensual and motor experiences. In early childhood, *cognitive*

FIGURE 24–4.
During adolescence, the parent begins to assume a mentor role, encouraging the adolescent to consider alternatives and outcomes when facing issues of life.

egocentric thought is exhibited in the child's inability to imagine how another person might experience or interpret the environment. They cannot readily take on a perspective or role different from their own. For adolescents, egocentrism arises from a preoccupation with their own power of thought.[26] By giving undue attention to their own cognitive capabilities, the adolescent magnifies and intensifies the importance of his or her own ideas. Ideas are created and "owned" and therefore emotionally invested. Thus, the adolescent displays a type of cognitive arrogance, conceit, or aggrandizement. Their ideas have been thought through so well that there could be no other logical conclusion. To entertain the conclusions of another is a form of self-betrayal. Consequently, the affective domain, in service to the cognitive domain, refuses to listen to, understand, or accept another's view and will go to extremes to prove the other (especially a parent) wrong. When someone rejects an idea (e.g., in a brainstorming session), the adolescent may feel a personal rejection—a potential source of many hurt feelings.

IMAGINARY AUDIENCE. Elkind has expanded on the concept of adolescent egocentrism and its ramifications.[13, 14, 16] Elkind observed that adolescents assume that everyone else is as preoccupied with the adolescents' thoughts and actions as they are themselves. Since the adolescent is concerned about him- or herself, everyone else must be equally concerned about them. The adolescent is thus overwhelmed with self-consciousness and feels as though he or she is on stage for everyone's viewing. Adolescents obsessed by this extreme self-consciousness are said to have constructed an *imaginary audience*. The effects of this imaginary audience are evidenced in the adolescent's increased concern with physical characteristics and appearance. Exorbitant attention is often placed upon complexion, hair style, or clothing, in order to "blend in" with others and decrease the focused attention.

Some adolescents are constantly sharing their thoughts, observations, criticisms, and dreams. They are enamored with their new cognitive powers and are positive everyone else is as interested in their new observations and insights as they are. Feeling continuously watched, and fearing the judgment and ridicule of the imaginary audience, other adolescents become reluctant to express their thoughts and prefer being alone to interacting with others. Their self-confidence can go up or down rapidly as the result of imagined social approval or criticism. A most common way of dealing with the sense of being the subject of everyone's viewing is for the adolescent to become indistinguishable and conform to their peers. Since "everyone is doing it," the young (or immature) adolescent reasons that social persecution will follow if he or she does not conform to the relevant and important norms. For the adolescent, conformity is the means to receive important positive attention and avoid the dreaded disdain of others. The reassurance and counter arguments of parents are generally of no avail to an adolescent holding tight to the perception of an imaginary audience.

PERSONAL FABLE. Another important aspect of adolescent egocentrism is called the *personal fable*. Adolescents become so consumed with thinking about themselves that they begin to believe that their thoughts and feelings are special. Thus, they claim "You can't possibly know how I feel" or "I've invented (or discovered) something really great (or unique)." Another dimension of the personal fable is the conviction that no harm or misfortune can befall oneself (impunity). The detrimental outcomes of such beliefs are not to be ignored nor trivialized. For example, adhering to the personal fable can contribute to lax attitudes toward sexual behaviors, careless attitudes about automobile safety, daring alcohol and drug usage, and so forth. The adolescent exemplifies the personal fable with comments such as "I won't get pregnant"; "Other people get sexually transmitted diseases"; and "Don't worry, I can handle my alcohol." They find it difficult to appreciate the experience, warnings, creations, and ideas of others (Fig. 24-5).

Adolescent egocentrism is pervasive and results in a variety of commonly observed behaviors: self-criticism, modesty, need for privacy, conformity, concern for hygiene and appearance, and frequent embarrassment, shame, and arrogance. Adolescent egocentrism eventually is outgrown with maturation and experience in social perspective taking.[8, 14, 17] Social perspective-taking activities such as role playing or arguing from someone else's point of view gradually allow adolescents to differentiate between their thoughts and feelings and those of others. Older adolescents display significantly fewer egocentric behaviors then younger adolescents.

Pseudostupidity

Sometimes adolescents will examine a particular problem so thoroughly that they become unable to make a decision at all, or will attribute overly complicated motives to someone else's behavior when a simple explanation seems so obvious. Elkind has referred to these aspects of the adolescent personality as examples of *pseudostupidity*.[14, 15] Because formal operational thinking allows the adolescent to evaluate many possibilities simultaneously, they may reason in overly complex ways about relatively simple issues. Adolescents sometimes handicap themselves and become unable to make decisions because they literally are thinking too much. Similarly, adolescents think too much about the behavior of others and overcomplicate other's motives. For example, an adolescent might distort a simple request made by a parent as a sign of the parents' intent to undermine the adolescent's independence and competence.

Elkind points out that although these behaviors appear "stupid," they do not reflect any sort of intellectual deficiency. Pseudostupid behavior is the natural consequence of the adolescent's new cognitive capabilities coupled with a lack of experience—neither of which are controllable by the adolescent. The prescriptions for responding to "pseudostupid" adolescent behaviors become clear: Adults should not view the adolescent's behavior as senseless or intentionally irrational and annoying. Instead, the adult should recognize that the cognitive capabilities of the adolescent have tempor-

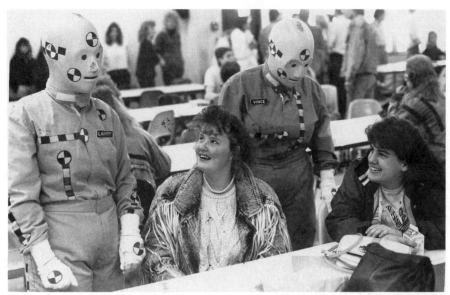

FIGURE 24–5.
Community safety education programs attempt to break through the adolescent's aura of impunity by means of humor, sense of camaraderie, concreteness, and appeals to reason.

arily developed beyond what they have learned through experience.

Social Cognition

The final manifestations of formal operational thought deal with cognitions as they relate to social phenomena. In general, social cognition is the study of how we interpret, analyze, remember, and use information about individuals, groups, and social events.

The adolescent's cognitions about social phenomena go beyond the concrete, immediately observable attributes of themselves, others, and social interactions.[20] The adolescent begins to use overt behavior as well as other evidence to make inferences about covert sociopsychological processes and causes that underlie observed behaviors. Also, the adolescent gains the ability to attend to and consider the importance of numerous pieces of social information, whereas the child's cognitions dealt with only the most obvious and highly salient features of the person or event. For example, a child can perceive obvious signs of happiness in someone else. However, the adolescent can detect the subtle, nonverbal clues that indicate that this person's happiness is a forced facade.

Finally, a conservation of social information develops as well. Developing individuals gradually come to think of themselves and others as "stable human beings who conserve, over time and circumstances, their personhoods, personalities, social and sexual roles and identities, and many other attributes."[20] The discussion of social cognition topics that follows applies jointly to adolescent and adult social cognition processes and effects. Research supporting the conclusions has primarily used college-age subjects.

COGNITIVE MISERS: SHORT-CUTS IN THINKING. A basic premise of cognition theory is that individuals experience information overload. Even during routine interactions we are confronted with more bits of social information than we are capable of processing. How do we cope with this? We cognitively streamline and gain efficiency by using numerous short-cuts. The use of short-cuts is so pervasive and necessary that some psychologists portray the individual as a *cognitive miser*.[18] This means that people will frequently think as little as possible, and that once a conclusion is drawn or an opinion is formed, they are reluctant to change their mind. (Notice the consistency between this conclusion and Piaget's own suggestion that accommodation is attempted secondary to assimilation.) Hand-in-hand with the conclusion that we are cognitive economists is the fact that people are often unaware of the mental processes they are using.[38] That is, people are often unable to report how they reasoned or why they behaved as they did.

To be useful, the cognitive miser strategy must not only provide a simple way of dealing with information, but it must also be reasonably accurate most of the time. However, recalling some of the short-cuts you have attempted in your own life, you will realize there is often a trade-off between accuracy and simplicity. A common way of detecting if a short-cut has been used is to identify biases, errors, or distortions that surface when people think about social information.

The Representative Heuristic. Several strategies or decision-making principles are used to quickly make inferences or easily draw conclusions.[55] These cognitive strategies are called heuristics. The *representative heuristic* means that one makes a judgment or inference about a social object based on that object's resemblance to typical cases. For example, imagine you meet a male stranger who has a rich vocabulary, is short in stature, dresses neatly, enjoys reading, and speaks quietly. Is he a nurse, a truck driver, a librarian, or a fisherman? If you proceed in identifying the man's trade by comparing his traits with the "typical" traits of each of the occupations, you are using the representative heuristic. The heuristic allows you to make a quick "best guess" based on the resemblance between the object and the characteristics of a pre-constructed category. However, errors can occur. The man you meet might be a truck driver. In this example, the representative heuristic functions much like a "stereotype." We are also well aware of the fallibility of stereotypes and the errors that result from judging all members of a category similarly.

The Availability Heuristic. A second cognitive decision-making strategy is the *availability heuristic.*[55] Here, the individual economizes by making judgments based on how easily an instance comes to mind. Thus, a teacher's evaluation of a student may be overly influenced by the memory of a recently missed deadline.

Other factors, such as the vividness, importance, or distinctiveness of memory information can make the information more cognitively "available," and subsequently affect the decision. For example, if a series of tragic airline crashes is highly publicized, airlines are likely to experience a reduction in passengers. This is likely to occur even though statistics indicate that flying is one of the safest modes of transportation. The risks involved in flying become increasingly available to us because of the distinctiveness and importance of the publicized crashes, and, subsequently, our decisions are influenced.

Priming. Priming, one way of manipulating availability, is done when you expose people to ideas or categories that affect memory information, and subsequently affect judgments. A simple illustration might be that if an individual had recently been viewing drawings of people and was then asked to examine an abstract drawing, he or she would be more likely to see human features in the abstract drawing than if he or she had previously been viewing landscapes or still-life drawings. Here, the individual economizes by using the most accessible category to process the information, rather than searching for a more appropriate category.

The ramifications of the *priming effect* are of notable social consequence if we recognize that behavior often appears quite ambiguous.[25] For example, a man who has recently consumed pornography might interpret a woman's fleeting glance and smile (or other behavioral cues) differently than a man who has just watched a rerun of "I Love Lucy."

Theory Perseverance. Theory perseverance means that people will cling to their idea or belief even after the evidence that once supported their idea is discredited or no longer exists.[45] Although theory perseverance is not the active implementation of a strategy, it still depicts the individual as a cognitive miser. Here, the short-cut is achieved by refusing to engage in further cognitive activity. Once the mind has a particular idea, it refuses to give it up.

Theory perseverance was demonstrated clearly in a study where college students were lead to believe that good firefighters either readily took risks or were very cautious.[1] Consistent with the "good firefighter theory" that they heard, subjects then generated reasons for why effective firefighters should have the "risky" or "cautious" trait. After generating their rationale, subjects were told that there was really no truth to the initial claim that the exceptional firefighter took risks or was extremely cautious. In spite of the now denounced and discredited notions, subjects persisted to hold tight to their initial idea of a good firefighter—the theory persisted.

In summary, we recognize that individuals do not always make use of the reasoning powers available to them. They tend to rely on short-cuts to process the abundance of social information encountered. Additional cognitive biases and errors will be discussed later in the chapter.

ATTRIBUTION: EXPLAINING BEHAVIOR. Freed from the concrete, observable present, the adolescent and adult reason about the hypothetical causes of behavior. The person observes his or her own behavior or the behavior of others and attempts to answer the question "why?" This tendency to explain behaviors—to make attributions—is so pervasive that some would label all of us "naïve psychologists."[24]

When explaining the behaviors of oneself and others, one may attribute the cause of the behavior to the person, to the environment, or to a combination of the two. Attributing the cause of the behavior to the person is an *internal* or *dispositional attribution,* and attributing the cause to something in the environment is an *external* or *situational attribution.* For example, a student may attribute a failing grade on an exam to poor management of study time or lack of interest in the material—internal attributions. Conversely, the student may believe the exam questions were ambiguously written and the professor did not adequately discuss the material—external attributions. Alternatively, the student may attribute the failure to some combination of the two kinds of attributions.

People use information about "consistency," "distinctiveness," and "consensus" in assigning internal or external attributions.[32] For example, when explaining someone's behavior (e.g., why did Ted trip over the feet of his dancing partner, Carol?), most people look at consistency (does Ted frequently trip over Carol's feet?), distinctiveness (does Ted trip over the feet of other people he dances with?), and consensus information (do other men trip over Carol's feet?). If Ted consistently trips over Carol's feet as well as the feet of all his dance partners, whereas few others experience such difficulty, we attribute the ungraceful event to Ted. However, we would not attribute clumsiness to Ted if he experienced no such difficulty with other partners and if other men were similarly embarrassed when dancing with Carol.

The theory of *correspondent inference* focuses on three types of behavioral information that allow us to make an inference about people's traits or internal attributions.[29] First, only behaviors that seem to be freely chosen are considered. Thus, we do not attribute "neatness" or "untidiness" to someone who was bribed or forced into cleaning up a room. Second, we pay close attention to behaviors that produce unique outcomes.

Does a person consistently choose to be around other people, or does he or she prefer to enjoy private activities? Does the person frequently attend musical cultural events or sports activities? If a person who lives in a rural area with limited transportation is requested by the parents to chauffeur a sibling to events, then the element of choice is eliminated, negating the behavior's ability to reflect internal attributes.

Finally, we make judgments based on actions that are out of the ordinary and discouraged by society. For example, if you see someone jogging on a lovely sunny day, you may hesitate to draw any conclusions about the runner's stable traits. However, you may draw inferences concerning the runner's dedication and commitment if you encounter him or her weathering a cold, snowy, blustery day. There is correspondence between the individual's behavior and their inferred trait of "dedicated" (or as some would have it—"compulsive") behavior. Behaviors that are informative about a person's traits are freely chosen, yield unique outcomes, and are low in social desirability.

COGNITIVE BIASES AND ERRORS. Thus far, our discussion of attributional processes has implied that individuals are highly rational in identifying the causes of behavior. A significant finding of research, however, is that individuals are influenced by cognitive biases that can lead to error in judging the causes of behavior.

The Fundamental Attribution Error. Suppose that while picnicking at the park you hear a scream from a nearby table and turn just in time to see a lady pouring a jug of ice-tea over someone's head. How would you explain this behavior? Research suggests that you would tend to attribute the woman's actions to her temper, playfulness, or some other dispositional factor. You would tend not to use situational explanations, such as strong provocation by the soaked recipient. This tendency for observers to underestimate situational influences and overestimate dispositional influences is called the *fundamental attribution error.*[44] The effect is so pervasive that even when individuals are made aware of situational constraints that shape the behavior, they continue to overattribute the cause of the behavior to the individual.[22,30] If someone reads an essay written by a stranger, they tend to assume that the essay reflects the person's opinions and attitudes, even if they had been instructed that the writer was assigned the essay topic.[57] The attribution error is fundamental because it affects one's attitudes and behaviors.

The implications of the fundamental attribution error are important. It suggests that even if we are aware of the situational variables that adversely affect disadvantaged groups (e.g., minorities, the homeless, the physically ill and handicapped, the victims of abuse and violence, and economically and educationally deprived people, to name a few), we may still perceive these individuals to be responsible for their plight. The social consequences of this error are serious and should not be trivialized.

The Actor-Observer Effect. A second attributional error concerns the person who is being evaluated. If an adolescent boy observes a peer trip on the stairs, how would he explain the behavior? As an "observer," he would probably attribute the behavior to dispositional factors, such as clumsiness or a lack of attentiveness. If, however, the boy were the one who had tripped, he would probably invoke a situational explanation. As the "actor," he would blame the incident on tattered carpet, poor lighting, slippery shoes, or some other external factor.

This tendency to attribute one's own behavior to situational factors and the behavior of others to internal causes is generally called the *actor-observer effect.*[31] The effect seems in part to result from the actor's perceptual awareness of situational factors. The actor is most aware of the environmental forces acting on him or her. The observer's attention, however, is focused upon the individual, and there is limited awareness of situational constraints. Enhancing awareness that others do behave in an environment that "pushes and pulls" reduces this biased effect.

Self-Serving Attributional Biases. A third attributional effect, known as the *self-serving bias,* recognizes that people tend to perceive themselves favorably.[34] Repeatedly, psychologists have found that individuals readily take the credit for their success, attributing their fortune to their ability and effort, yet explain their failures away by citing external factors such as bad luck and the inherent difficulty of the problem. The prevalence and potency of this effect is emphasized by the conclusion that "the need to view oneself in a favorable way following a success or failure . . . may be one of the best established, most often replicated, findings in social psychology."[46]

Because of the obvious win–lose outcome of sporting events, examples of the self-serving bias abound in athletics. (This is not to suggest that work, family, school, and so on, are not abundant with positive and negative performance feedback). How does the athlete explain his or her winning performance? "Of course" their superior performance is the result of personal factors like determination, hard work and effort, extensive practice, and devotion. On the other hand, the less fortunate athlete avoids self-deprecating internal attributions and blames his or her recent failure on situational factors like bad luck, a tough schedule, poor training conditions, or biased officiating. Whether one has succeeded or failed, people appear to be motivated in both outcomes to protect and enhance their self-esteem and to improve their public image.

The self-serving attributional error, however, is just one of many tactics of *self-presentation* or *impression management* that people employ.[47] People will also use flattery, pretend to be interested, agree with what others are saying, carefully control nonverbal behaviors, and much more, to present the desired picture of themselves to others. Thus, cognitive issues mediate social behaviors.

Other Self-Serving Tendencies. Sociopsychological research has revealed that individuals attempt to enhance their self-esteem or self-concept in numerous ways.[37] In addition to self-serving attributions, individuals are biased in the comparisons they make between themselves and others. Self-complimenting comparisons made by adolescents include judging themselves as fairer in social exchanges, as having greater athletic talent, or believing they are more intelligent than the average peer. "Average" people see themselves as "above average" on most socially desirable and subjective dimensions.[37]

Other self-edifying tendencies include a ready acceptance of flattering information, a disbelief in critical evaluations, a tendency to overestimate the social desirability of one's own behavior, and "cognitive conceit" demonstrated by overestimating the accuracy of personal decisions and beliefs. People also tend to reconstruct memories in self-enhancing ways, and if they cannot "misremember" their past they will attempt to justify it.

Furthermore, the more people approve of themselves on some dimension (e.g., athletic skill, intelligence, or sense of humor), the more likely they are to judge others along that dimension. Similarly, if they receive a positive evaluation from some source, they are likely to view that source as reliable and credible. Although some actions may not be desirable, they tend to see their underlying motives as good, while being less generous with their judgments of other people's motives. Also, not only do they attribute positive personality traits to attractive people, they believe attractive people have traits more like their own than do unattractive people.

Self-serving tendencies may also grow out of the egocentrism of adolescents. The previously discussed concept, "personal fable," relates to the finding that college students are very optimistic about their future. They believe they are more likely than their peers to get the best jobs and the highest salaries, and less likely to experience divorce, illness, unemployment, or some other negative outcome.[39] Such idealistic optimism can decrease efforts essential for success. Success requires enough optimism to envision a goal, tempered with enough fear of failure to motivate the individual.

A final, self-serving tendency is to either overestimate or underestimate how much others think and act as we do. On matters of opinion (e.g., what is the best football team, or who should be homecoming queen) or when we blunder or fail, we console ourselves by thinking that such beliefs or behaviors are the norm. This overestimation of the commonality of one's opinions and undesirable behaviors is called the *false consensus effect*. Alternatively, a *false uniqueness effect* occurs when we underestimate the commonality of our virtues and

skills. Our talents and admirable actions are seen as relatively rare.

It is important to recognize exceptions to the egocentric and self-bolstering behaviors discussed. After all, are there not people who behave modestly or even become self-deprecating? Many people have exclaimed at some time, "I'm really not that good," or "I haven't had much time to practice." Sometimes, however, *self-handicapping* behaviors such as these are used to protect one's self-images.[28] A fear of failure can be so intense in people that they intentionally handicap themselves so as to have a ready excuse in case failure occurs. Thus, not feeling well on a first date or looking for distractor tasks prior to a major exam provides the justification for failure. Self-handicapping protects one's self-esteem by providing an excuse for poor performance.

There are three suggestions why self-serving behaviors occur. First, people present themselves in ways designed to create a good impression and wish others to think well of them. Second, self-serving tendencies are the by-product of how people process and remember information. Information is gathered from only one perspective—personal experiences guided by personal values, attitudes, and expectations. Third, we are motivated to both protect and enhance our self-esteem and self-concept.

Not everyone displays self-serving tendencies to the same degree. Some people have inordinately poor self-concepts and must use them to remain functional. Self-serving biases are not lies, but self-deceptions—deceptions that distort reality to provide self-confidence and bolster self-esteem.

INFORMATION PROCESSING

The psychometric approach focuses on *content*; the Piagetian approach on *structure*. The information-processing approach focuses on the means by which people, regardless of age, *process* information (Fig. 24-6). Heavily influenced by recent developments in communication engineering and computer science, psychologists have found a useful analogy between the information-processing functions of computers and humans.[21] As one of the most significant developments in contemporary psychology, the information-processing approach is receiving much attention in cognitive science today.

The analogy between a computer and a person begins with the flow of information. First, information must be *encoded* or translated into a form either the computer or person can recognize. Just as keystrokes are transformed into the computer's electronic language, sensory information (i.e., hearing, vision) is converted into the brain's neural language. Second, information must be *stored* in the system's memory. Third, the system must be able to *retrieve* information when needed. The analogy continues as we compare the computer's hardware to the person's own central processing unit (CPU), the brain. Software, or computer programs, are analogous to our cognitive operations, plans, and strategies. It is important to note that the analogy does not equate computers and humans. It does, however, point to the centrality that

FIGURE 24–6.
Adolescents work very hard at both understanding content and processing information.

memory and the processes of encoding, storage, and retrieval play in cognition. The model allows us to organize and simplify a great number of observations about how people process information.

The Memory System

The central focus of information-processing theories is memory. The most widely accepted model of human memory assumes we have three distinct memory systems: sensory memory, short-term memory (STM), and long-term memory (LTM) (Table 24-1).[3] Information is passed from one storage structure to another by means of control operations such as attention, rehearsal, organization, and elaboration. The theory addresses how information is represented, how long it is retained, how much information can be held, and why information is forgotten in each of these memory systems. Figure 24-7 illustrates the flow of information through various systems and indicates several significant processes that occur in memory.

TABLE 24–1. MEMORY PATTERNS

	Sensory	*STM*	*LTM*
Duration	Visual: $1/3$ sec Auditory: 2–3 sec	15–20 sec	Unlimited
Form of Information	Sensory	Verbal	Visual semantic
Capacity	Relatively large	Small 7 ± 2 items	Unlimited

Sensory Memory

The sensory memory, or *sensory register* as it is often called, allows the effects of a stimulus to be held briefly after the stimulus itself has disappeared. Two sensory memory systems have received the greatest amount of attention: iconic memory and echoic memory. *Iconic memory* holds visual information, whereas *echoic memory* contains auditory information. Both of these systems hold information in a form similar to the stimulus itself. Thus, it is as though there is a photographic image in iconic memory, and a tape recording or echo in echoic memory.

ICONIC MEMORY. Over three decades ago, Sperling gathered impressive evidence for the existence of iconic memory.[48] In what is now considered one of the classic studies in cognitive psychology, Sperling demonstrated that people briefly have more visual information available in iconic memory than they are able to report. To demonstrate this, he used what is called the *partial report technique,* in which subjects were shown three rows of four symbols (numbers and letters) for a very brief amount of time (less than one-tenth of a second). Sperling then asked subjects to either recall the entire matrix (*whole part*) or he signalled them to recall one of the rows (*cued partial report*). Sperling demonstrated that as the time between the termination of the matrix and the presentation of the recall cue increased, recall performance decreased (Fig. 24-8). Since subjects did not know which row was to be cued, Sperling concluded that the proportion of symbols recalled in a randomly selected row was proportional to the total amount of information available in iconic memory.

Sperling's research demonstrates two important characteristics of iconic memory. First, iconic memory can hold

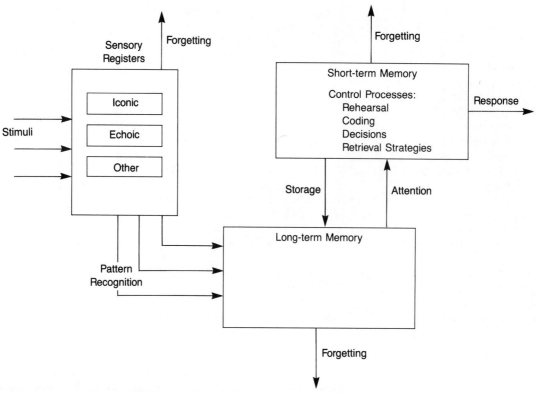

FIGURE 24–7.
The memory system. (Atkinson, R. C., & Shiffrin, R. M. [1968]. Human memory: A proposed system and its control processes. In K. W. Spence & J. T. Spence, [Eds.], The psychology of learning and motivation *[Vol. 2]. Orlando, FL: Academic Press.)*

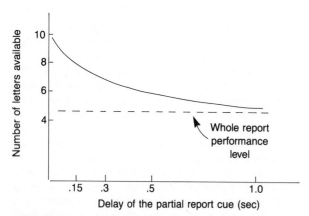

FIGURE 24–8.
In Sperling's partial report experiment, the number of letters recalled declines as the signal to report is delayed. (Adapted from Sperling, G. [1960]. The information available in brief visual presentations. *Psychological Monographs, 74, 1–29.)*

more information than we are capable of reporting. Second, visual information decays rapidly in iconic memory. It is generally accepted that iconic memory has a duration of one-third to one-half second. Thus, if one is going to use or remember iconic information they need to process it immediately. For example, if you want to remember a license plate number you briefly saw, you need to verbally rehearse the number to yourself until you can write it down. In addition, you cannot look at any other license plates until you are verbally rehearsing the first one. Since iconic memory works *automatically,* looking at a second stimulus covers up or *masks* the first image.

ECHOIC MEMORY. Research analogous to Sperling's has examined the characteristics of echoic memory.[11] Results indicate that echoic memory holds auditory information about 2 or 3 seconds and that it holds slightly more information than we are able to report. Similar to iconic memory, echoic memory functions automatically, and whenever new information is encountered it covers and serves to mask the first message. This process perpetually repeats itself. Thus, echoic memory functions like a delayed playback tape recorder where auditory information is repeatedly placed on a very short tape. So short is the tape that we end up recording on top of old information after only a few seconds. A person can immediately repeat the last few words uttered by someone, even if not initially attending to the communication. However, the person would be unable to repeat what had been said three or four sentences previously.

Echoic memory can be demonstrated easily with a technique called the *stimulus suffix effect*.[10] First, obtain the consent of several of your friends to help you. Prepare eight lists of nine digits, each list containing the digits one to nine in a different random arrangement. Inform your friends that you are going to read a list of nine numbers to them at a pace of about 2 numbers per second. After each list they will be cued to recall the nine digits in order. At the end of four of the lists you will clap your hands, while at the end of the other four lists you will say the word "zero." The clap or the word "zero" each serve as cues for your friends to write down, in order from left-to-right, the nine digits they just heard. After you have completed the eight trials, compare how many of the digits were recalled in each of the nine positions for the "clap" and the "zero" conditions. You are especially interested in the ninth position. It is expected that more digits in the last position will be recalled when a clap was the recall cue than when "zero" was the cue. Why? The word "zero" enters the echoic memory as one of the items in the list and in a sense covers up (masks) the true end item, the ninth digit. The presence and nature of echoic memory are demonstrated.

In summary, we see that the duration of information in the sensory memories is very brief. Information is lost or forgotten primarily because of decay (its short duration), but also because of interference (new information masking old information). The information is held in a form that is the same as the stimulus itself, and the capacity of the sensory memories is relatively small.

Short-Term Memory

Short-term memory (STM) is often called *working memory* because it is the place where we consciously and actively process information. For example, you are using and occupying STM space when you read this sentence, rehearse a telephone number prior to dialing it, attempt to work a math problem in your head, or reflect on a day at the beach last summer.

One important characteristic of STM is its extremely limited capacity. It is clear that no matter what kind of information is held in STM (e.g., words, colors, numbers, or geometric shapes), the memory span is limited to seven items plus or minus two.[35] For example, memory span is being taxed if one hears a new nine-digit zip code. Subsequently, errors are likely in transcribing it onto an envelope.

Demonstrating STM capacity is relatively simple. Generate several lists of randomly arranged consonants varying in length from five to ten letters. Read each list to a friend and request that he or she immediately write down each list in

order. You will find that accuracy decreases dramatically as list length increases.

The capacity limitations of STM can be overcome to a degree. By *chunking* related pieces of information together, the functional capacity of STM is increased. Chunking benefits from previously encountered patterns of information that have been stored in long-term or permanent memory. To illustrate, read to a friend the following 12 letters grouped in this way: YM-CAF-BIU-FOC-BS. Next read to another person the same 12 letters grouped in a different way: YMCA-FBI-UFO-CBS. Ask each friend to recall the letters in order. The second individual can make use of information already stored in LTM and chunk the 12 letters into four meaningful units. Subsequently, recall accuracy is greater. Thus, STM capacity is measured in chunks rather than in individual items.

The implications are that one can increase working memory space for information by clustering meaningful and related pieces of information together (Fig. 24-9). Extensive experience with related information results in permanent storage of these chunks. Thus, we find that musicians, master chess players, electrical engineers, and others, have functionally greater capacity to remember information related to their field of expertise. An individual's capacity to recall and think about information increases with experience in chunking.

Some have suggested that the total processing space in STM is the same for adolescents and children. The space in STM is used not only to hold bits or chunks of information, but also to hold operations necessary to process the information. Thus, total STM space is divided between operating space and storage space. The reason adolescents appear to have greater STM capacity than school-agers is because they have greater operational efficiency. This idea of developing STM operational efficiency is hypothesized as an explanation of Piagetian stage development. The operational efficiency of STM, like stage development, is the result of practice, maturation, and general experience.

The label *short-term memory* indicates that information in STM is rapidly forgotten unless it is reviewed or placed in long-term memory (LTM). The brief duration of STM was first demonstrated by having subjects hear three letters and then perform a brief distractor task (count backwards from a three-digit number) before being cued to recall the three letters.[40] Results showed that after only 15 to 20 seconds, few three-letter combinations could be recalled.

This rapid rate of forgetting can be very frustrating, but also has its advantages. Forgetting the name of a new acquaintance just seconds after introductions can be embarrassing. On the other hand, retrieval might be cumbersome if every telephone number ever dialed were stored in LTM.

Research suggests that interference is the primary reason why STM information is forgotten so quickly.[56] Essentially, STM information is forgotten because new information continually produces STM capacity overload. With limited STM capacity, new information quickly displaces old information.

FIGURE 24–9.
"Chunking" information enables a musician to play music smoothly while looking ahead to the next measure or musical phrase.

Thus, to minimize loss of STM information, eliminate interference. To be sure that thoughts and ideas are not lost while concentrating on an activity like writing a paper, the adolescent should move to a nondistracting environment.

Finally, it is important to note that STM information is generally represented verbally. When consciously solving a problem or rehearsing information, the information is in verbal form. Although a telephone number is seen in the directory, people verbalize the number to retain it in STM long enough to place the call.

Long-Term Memory

Long-term memory is distinguished from sensory and short-term memory in several ways. First, its capacity is functionally unlimited. To date, no one has been identified as having an overloaded LTM. Second, information in LTM has been extensively processed and is interassociated. Information in LTM is largely *semantic,* meaning that representations or meanings abstracted from experience are what is stored. A consequence of the interconnectedness and semantic nature of LTM information is the potential for biases and distortions. Thus, LTM memories often fail to correspond with the facts. Third, LTM information is highly resistant to forgetting. The impressive durability and accuracy of LTM for visual information was demonstrated in one study where subjects viewed 2,560 pictures for a few seconds each. One year later they recognized them with 63% accuracy.[49]

Some interesting clinical and neuropsychological evidence supports the distinction between the STM and LTM systems. First, older people often report difficulty storing new permanent memories. A senile person is able to recall his or her past, yet seems unable to restore new information. Second, a type of memory loss known as *retrograde amnesia* supports the idea of two separate memory systems. Retrograde amnesia occurs when people are unable to recall events prior to neural-electrical shock produced by intense physical, electrical, or chemical stimuli. Events processed after the trauma are retained normally. Often, the individual recovers memories closer and closer to the accident as time passes.

Third, some types of brain damage seem to render individuals unable to place new information in LTM. In one case, a young man lost part of his temporal lobes and hippocampus in a brain operation undergone to relieve epilepsy.[36] The operation had no effect on his above average intelligence. However, after the operation, he suffered from *anterograde amnesia;* he was unable to store new information in LTM although he could easily remember information stored before the operation. Following the operation, he would work the same jigsaw puzzle day after day without showing benefit of practice and read the same magazines over and over again as though each reading were the first. For him, life was like "walking through a dream" because "yesterday" never really came.

Thousands of other people experience anterograde amnesia as victims of *Korsakoff's syndrome*. These people have inflicted brain damage on themselves through severe alcoholism. This brain pathology results from the thiamine (vitamin B_1) deficiency that accompanies the poor dietary habits of alcoholics. Work with anterograde amnesic individuals suggests that they may be able to learn but are unable to report the new information or bring it to consciousness.[23]

MEASURING LTM. There are three differentially sensitive measures used to determine if something has been retained in LTM. First, retention can be measured by simply requesting an individual to *recall* information. However, experience tells us that people often know more than they can report. We all have experienced the *tip-of-the-tongue phenomena* where we know information but just cannot bring it to consciousness at the moment (expressive memory). A second and more sensitive measure of retention is *recognition*. Here the individual must select the remembered information from an array of provided information (receptive memory). Examples include finding one's bicycle in a crowded bicycle rack or selecting the correct answer on a multiple-choice exam. The most sensitive yet seldom used measure of retention is *relearning*. It is hypothesized that if the time it takes to relearn a given amount of material is less than the time it took to learn the material the first time, some retention has occurred. For example, if retention has occurred, review of material for a biology exam or relearning the same role in a play performed several years prior ought to take less time.

LTM FORGETTING. Forgetting is the inability to recall a piece of information accurately. The first systematic studies in memory and forgetting were conducted by Herman Ebbinghaus over 100 years ago.[12] Serving as his own subject, Ebbinghaus studied lists of nonsense syllables—three-letter syllables consisting of a vowel between two consonants. Ebbinghaus used nonsense syllables to minimize the effects that prior knowledge has on retention. He would master lists of these nonsense syllables and then wait for varying amounts of time and test his ability to recall the lists. As Figure 24-10 illustrates, Ebbinghaus discovered that most forgetting occurs soon after the material is initially learned and rehearsal has terminated.

Since the pioneering work of Ebbinghaus, psychologists have proposed three major theories of forgetting.

First, *decay theory* proposes that memory information spontaneously fades or decays with the passing of time. Repeated use of memory information is the only way to keep the memory. You either use it or lose it. However, evidence suggests that reasons other than decay are primarily responsible for forgetting.

Second, *interference theory* claims that the reason people cannot remember information is because other information, especially similar information, interferes with recall. A simple experiment provided initial support for this theory.[27] In one condition, subjects learned a list of nonsense syllables before going to sleep, a condition felt to minimize the number of interfering events. In the second condition, subjects continued with their normal waking activities following their mastery of the list. At various retention intervals, each subject's memory of the material was tested. Subjects who went to sleep could recall more information (Fig. 24-11).

When old memory information interferes with retention of new information, it is called *proactive interference*. Individuals who have encountered a new keyboard configuration on a computer or typewriter are familiar with the frustration of proactive interference. Even with extensive practice, they occasionally find themselves placing their fingers according to the old keyboard arrangement. Alternatively, when new information inhibits one's ability to recall old information, *retroactive interference* has occurred. For example, learning several

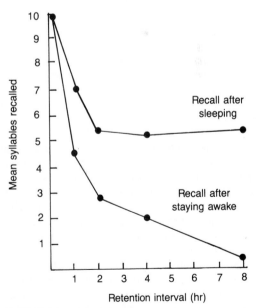

FIGURE 24–11.
Mean number of nonsense syllables recalled by subjects as a function of number of hours awake or asleep after learning. (Jenkins, J. G., & Dallenbach, K. M. [1924]. Oblivescence during sleep and waking. American Journal of Psychology, 35, *605–612.)*

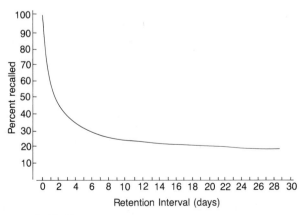

FIGURE 24–10.
The Ebbinghaus' forgetting curve. (Adapted from Ebbinghaus, H. [1964]. Memory: A contribution to experimental psychology. New York: Dover [originally published in 1885].)

new telephone numbers may make it more difficult to accurately remember some older phone numbers.

Third, *retrieval failure theory* suggests that when memories cannot be recalled it is because the proper retrieval cues are not available. This cue-dependent theory recognizes that the cues present during recall are often different than the cues that were present during the initial learning. To the extent that we can reinstate the original cues, we can facilitate recall. One version of this notion is referred to as the *encoding specificity principle* and is stated as follows: "Specific encoding operations performed on what is perceived determines what is stored, and what is stored determines what retrieval cues are effective in providing access to what is stored."[54]

REPRESENTATION OF LTM INFORMATION. Psychologists believe there are two basic types of memory information: declarative and procedural. The difference between declarative and procedural knowledge is the difference between "knowing what" and "knowing how."

Declarative memory contains facts and specific information. It is divided into episodic and semantic memory. *Episodic memory* is autobiographical in nature and stores information about events in one's life. It holds information about the time and place of happenings. In contrast, *semantic memory* holds factual information that is independent of time and space. Whereas episodic memory allows one to recall information about high school graduation, semantic memory allows one to recall the meaning of a word or the capital of the state, or the scientific name of a dinosaur.

Procedural memory is knowing how to do things. In contrast to declarative knowledge, procedural knowledge is acquired slowly, may be partially possessed, and can be demonstrated. For example, the skills of an athlete, mathematician, or musician are acquired slowly and gradually. Often, they must be demonstrated rather than explained, as it is very difficult to provide a verbal account of complex actions (Fig. 24-12).

FIGURE 24–12.
The ability to play a musical instrument requires procedural memory—learning how to make desired notes, learning to read and then play written music, and playing in concert with others.

STORING INFORMATION IN LTM. Rehearsal is a primary control process in the information processing model. *Maintenance rehearsal* is the rote repetition of information and is useful in keeping information salient in STM. However, more extensive processing is generally necessary to move information into LTM. Such *elaborative rehearsal* requires effort and involves relating new information to information already held in LTM. Consider the mental tasks that could be done with a list of words. Shallow processing tasks would include simply pronouncing each word, counting the number of vowels in each word, or finding words that rhyme. Deeper processing tasks like using the word in a sentence or defining the word would be more facilitative in transferring the words into LTM.[9]

Not all information enters LTM as the result of deep and elaborative processing. Some processing is done *automatically*—without intention, without our awareness, and without interfering with other mental activities.[43] Some tasks initially require a lot of mental effort but later become fairly automatic, like riding a bike, writing one's name, or reading. In fact, the automaticity is difficult to stop. For example, consider the task where words are printed in red, yellow, or blue ink and the objective is to name the color of the ink. Not too difficult, unless the words are names of other colors (such as "red" printed in green ink). Looking at the word automatically accesses the meaning of the word which then competes with the response of naming the color of the ink. The competing responses slow down performance on what is commonly referred to as the *Stroop task*.[51]

Improving Memory

Along with research in other areas of psychology, the information processing perspective provides some useful techniques and prescriptions for improving memory. These are especially applicable to adolescents and college students who are in educational environments placing great emphasis on learning and acquiring new information.

REDUCE INTERFERENCE. Eliminate internal distractions such as anxiety. Dispense with external distractions like music, television, distracting conversations, food, and so forth.

ATTACH MEANINGFULNESS. When encountering new information, attempt to relate it to something already known. For example, an adolescent might better remember a new schoolmate's name, Jim Strong, if he or she thought about what a "strong" athlete Jim was and how they met in front of the gym.

DISTRIBUTE PRACTICE. Distributing practice over several sessions allows the individual to identify what material was forgotten since the last practice. Subsequently, he or she can focus efforts on the unmastered material. It also reduces proactive interference that builds during single study sessions.

MASTER PARTS. Break large tasks into manageable tasks, much like an actor or actress would focus on remembering parts of a play rather than the entire play at once.

PARAPHRASE. To be able to explain something in one's own words requires a deeper knowledge of the material than a rote repetition of information. Paraphrasing attaches personal meaning to the events and issues. Later on, it will be one's own meaning that will be recalled.

IDENTIFY LOGICAL CONTENT OR ORGANIZATION. If structure or organization can be found in the material, recall will be facilitated (chunking). Discovering structure leads to a simplification. For example, a 12-item grocery list may be difficult to recall. But if one recognized that four items were from each of three categories (e.g., dairy, fruit and vegetables, and bakery), the task will be less difficult.

REINSTATE ORIGINAL LEARNING CUES. The encoding specificity principle suggests that cues associated with the information when encoded will be the cues helpful during recall. Thus, the student who will take an afternoon exam in class ought to study in the presence of the stimulus cues that will be present during testing. Theater directors recognize the importance of cues, and subsequently require dress rehearsal.

MNEMONIC DEVICES. Mnemonic devices work well because they create meaningful and often vivid or distinctive memories. They also often result in a dual code; that is, a visual and verbal memory code of the information.

One of the most common mnemonic tools is the use of *acronyms*. Many an adolescent learned to multiply algebraic equations by remembering "FOIL" (multiplying the first, outer, inner, and last numbers), or recalled the colors of the visual spectrum with the help of a name "ROY G. BIV" (red, orange, yellow, green, blue, indigo, violet).

The *method of loci* requires the pairing of to-be-remembered items with locations already stored in memory. For example, suppose that when a teen-ager comes home from school he or she always checks the mailbox, inserts the key in the doorknob, goes to the closet, and then marches straight to the refrigerator. The parent asks the adolescent to stop at the grocery store after school and pick up eggs, milk, ravioli, and spinach. How can these items be remembered? First, one can create vivid images such as milk running out of the mailbox when opened, egg yolks on the door knob, an Italian feast inside the closet and an avalanche of spinach falling out of the opened refrigerator. Then, the adolescent only needs to mentally follow the movement from location to location at home when selecting items. The person may choose to create an acronym (e.g., REMS) to remember the items.

Another useful mnemonic is the *memory-peg technique*. Here a prememorized set of words serves as mental "pegs" on which the new material is "hung." First of all, one memorizes a list of peg words like "one is a bun, two is a shoe, three is a tree, four is a door," and so on. Next, they vividly and interactively image each new word with one of the peg words. Later on, recalling the peg words will serve as cues for the key memory words.

Additional mnemonic techniques include learning songs (e.g., the ABC song) or creating rhymes (e.g., "Thirty days hath September" or "Columbus sailed the ocean blue in 1492").

The *key word* method is useful in learning a foreign language or the definitions of words. This is a word association technique in which an already known word (keyword) sounds like the word to be learned. An example would be attempting to learn the Spanish word "plato" which translates as "duck". The keyword here might be "plate." The student creates an image of a roasted duck sitting on a plate. When a translation of "duck" to "plato" is required, the key word, "plate," will take them to the answer.

IMPLICATIONS

The potential to use formal reasoning does not imply that the adolescent is an intellectually mature individual. Despite the vast amount of knowledge they have accumulated, adolescents lack the breadth of experience necessary to form the firm foundations of wisdom. Solving complex and multifaceted problems at home, school, work, community, and the church prepares the adolescent for the cognitive challenges of adulthood. The adolescent's ability to learn, make decisions, and solve problems is still very much influenced by other domains. Social pressures by peers, personal and family expectations, institutional pressures and expectations, emotions, and motivational drives all have significant impact upon the adolescent's ability to tap cognitive potentials (Fig. 24-13).

Adolescents have limited patience with the progress of society and their own lives. They are anxious for major changes to occur, and yet dependent on the stability of parents. Often, the pressure to realize immediate goals and to

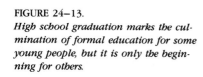

FIGURE 24–13.
*High school graduation marks the cul-
mination of formal education for some
young people, but it is only the beginning for others.*

gratify desires outweighs any consideration of long-term consequences.

How can the adult facilitate the adolescent's use of formal operational thought and appreciate the consequences of behaviors? It is recognized that there are no absolute answers to these questions, only general guidelines. How the parent structures the adolescent's environment is important. A major role of parents is to help the adolescent identify alternative goal strategies and to look at the crucial consequences of each option. Adolescents need opportunities to choose, to make decisions, and to experience the consequences of their decisions. Limits on independence should be provided to protect the adolescent from severe trauma, but a gradual lifting of rules helps prepare the adolescent for a smooth transition into adulthood and responsible independence.

By participating as a mentor and role model, parents can be very effective in providing guidance to the adolescent. As an individual with formal operational abilities, the adolescent is less in need of an autocratic parent who thinks for them and more in need of a challenger, counselor, and encourager. The adolescent is capable, but still weak and inexperienced. Adolescents are not yet aware of the complexity of decisions. A supportive and encouraging environment will facilitate their development into a self-confident, responsible, thinking adult.

REFERENCES

1. Anderson, C. A., Lepper, M. R., & Ross, L. (1980). Perseverance of social theories: The role of explanation in the persistence of discredited information. *Journal of Personality and Social Psychology, 39,* 1037–1049.
2. Arlin, P. K. (1975). Cognitive development in adulthood: A fifth stage? *Developmental Psychology, 11,* 602–606.
3. Atkinson, R. C., & Shiffrin, R. M. (1968). Human memory: A proposed system and its control processes. In K. W. Spence & J. T. Spence (Eds.), *The psychology of learning and motivation* (Vol. 2). Orlando, FL: Academic Press.
4. Ausubel, D. P. (1954). *Theory and problems of adolescent development.* Princeton, NJ: Van Nostrand.
5. Blasi, A., & Hoeffel, E. C. (1974). Adolescence and formal operations. *Human Development, 17,* 344–363.
6. Bradway, K. P., & Thompson, C. W. (1962). Intelligence at adulthood: A twenty-five year follow-up: *Journal of Educational Psychology, 53,* 1–14.
7. Campbell, P. (1976). Adolescent intellectual decline. *Adolescence, 11,* 629–635.
8. Chandler, M. J. (1975). Egocentrism and anti-social behavior: The assessment and training of social perspective-taking skills. *Developmental Psychology, 9,* 326–332.
9. Craik, F. I. M., & Tulving, E. (1975). Depth of processing and the retention of words in episodic memory. *Journal of Experimental Psychology: General, 104,* 268–294.
10. Crowder, R. G., & Morton, J. (1969) Precategorical acoustic storage (PAS). *Perception & Psychophysics, 5,* 365–373.
11. Darwin, C. J., Turvey, M. T., and Crowder, R. G. (1972). An auditory analogue of the Sperling partial report procedure: Evidence for brief auditory storage. *Cognitive Psychology, 3,* 255–267.
12. Ebbinghaus, H. (1964). Memory: A contribution to experimental psychology. New York: Dover (originally published in 1885.)
13. Elkind, D. (1967). Egocentrism in adolescence. *Child Development, 38,* 1025–1034.
14. Elkind, D. (1974). *Children and adolescents: Interpretive essays on Jean Piaget* (2nd ed.). New York: Oxford.
15. Elkind, D. (1978). *The child's reality: Three developmental themes.* Hillsdale, NJ: Erlbaum.
16. Elkind, D. (1984). *All grown up and no place to go: Teenagers in crisis.* Reading, MA: Addision-Wesley.
17. Enright, R. D., Lapsley, D. K., & Shukla, D. G. (1979). Adolescent egocentrism in early and late adolescence. *Adolescence, 14,* 687–695.
18. Fiske, S. T., & Taylor, S. E. (1984). *Social cognition.* Reading, MA: Addision-Wesley.
19. Flavell, J. (1963). *The development psychology of Jean Piaget,* Princeton, NJ: Van Nostrand.
20. Flavell, J. (1977). *Cognitive development.* Englewood Cliffs, NJ: Prentice-Hall.
21. Gardner, H. (1985). *The minds new science: A history of the cognitive revolution.* New York: Basic Books.
22. Gilbert, D. T., & Jones, E. E. (1986). Perceived-induced constraint: Interpretations of self-generated reality. *Journal of Personality and Social Psychology, 50,* 269–280.

23. Graf, P., Squire, L. R., & Mandler, G. (1984). The information that amnesic patients do not forget. *Journal of Experimental Psychology: Learning, Memory, and Cognition, 10,* 164–178.

24. Heider, F. (1958). *The psychology of interpersonal relations.* New York: Wiley.

25. Higgins, E. T., Rholes, W. S., & Jones, C. R. (1977). Category accessibility and impression formation. *Journal of Experimental Social Psychology, 13,* 141–154.

26. Inhelder, B. and Piaget, J. (1958). *The growth of logical thinking.* New York: Basic Books.

27. Jenkins, J. G., & Dallenbach, K. M. (1924). Obliviscence during sleep and waking. *American Journal of Psychology, 35,* 605–612.

28. Jones, E. E., & Berglas, S. (1978). Control of attribution about the self through self-handicapping strategies: The appeal of alcohol and the role of underachievement. *Personality and Social Psychology, 4,* 200–206.

29. Jones, E. E., & Davis, K. E. (1965). From acts of dispositions: The attribution process in person perception. In L. Berkowitz (Ed.), *Advances in experimental social psychology* (Vol. 2). New York: Academic Press.

30. Jones, E. E., & Harris, V. A. (1967). The attribution of attitudes. *Journal of Experimental Social Psychology, 3,* 2–24.

31. Jones, E. E., & Nisbett, R. E. (1971). *The actor and the observer: Divergent perceptions of the causes of behavior.* Morristown, NJ: General Learning Press.

32. Kelley, H. H. (1972). Attribution in social interaction. In E. E. Jones, D. E. Kanouse, H. H. Kelley, R. E. Nisbett, S. Valins, & B. Weiner (Eds.), *Attribution: Perceiving the causes of behavior.* Morristown, NJ: General Learning Press.

33. Kohlberg, L. (1973). Continuities in childhood and adult moral development revisited. In P. B. Baltes and K. W. Schaie (Eds.), *Life-span development psychology: Personality and socialization* (pp. 179–204). New York: Academic Press.

34. Miller, D. T., & Ross, M. (1975). Self-serving biases in the attribution of causality: Fact or fiction? *Psychological Bulletin, 82,* 213–225.

35. Miller, G. A. (1956). The magical number seven, plus or minus two: Some limits on our capacity for processing information. *Psychological Review, 63,* 81–97.

36. Milner, B. (1966). Amnesia following operation on the temporal lobes. In C. W. M. Whitty & O. L. Zangwill (Eds.), *Amnesia.* London: Butterworths.

37. Myers, D. G. (1987). *Social psychology* (2nd ed.). New York: McGraw-Hill.

38. Nisbett, R. E., & Wilson, T. D. (1977). Telling more than we know: Verbal reports on mental processes. *Psychological Review, 84,* 231–259.

39. Perloff, L. S. (1988) Social comparison and illusions of invulnerability. In C. R. Snyder & C. Ford (Eds.), *Clinical and social psychological perspectives on negative life events.* Orlando, FL: Academic Press.

40. Peterson, L. R., & Peterson, M. J. (1959). Short-term retention of individual verbal items. *Journal of Experimental Psychology, 58,* 193–198.

41. Piaget, J. (1969). The intellectual development of the adolescent. In G. Caplain and S. Lebovici (Eds.), *Adolescence: Psychological perspectives* (pp. 22–26). New York: Basic Books.

42. Piaget, J. (1981). *The psychology of intelligence.* Totowa, NJ: Littlefield, Adams.

43. Posner, M. I., & Snyder, C. R. R. (1975). Attention and cognitive control. In R. L. Solso (Ed.), *Information processing and cognition: The Loyola Symposium.* Hillsdale, NJ: Erlbaum.

44. Ross, L. (1977). The intuitive psychologist and his shortcomings: Distortions in the attribution process. In L. Berkowitz (Ed.), *Advances in experimental social psychology* (Vol. 10). New York: Academic Press.

45. Ross, L., Lepper, M. R., & Hubbard, M. (1975). Perseverance in self-perception and social perception: Biased attributional process in the debriefing paradigm. *Journal of Personality and Social Psychology, 32,* 880–892.

46. Ross, M., & Fletcher, G. J. O. (1985). Attribution and social perception. In G. Lindzey & E. Aronson (Eds.), *The handbook of social psychology* (3rd ed.). New York: Random House.

47. Schlenker, B. R. (1980). *Impression management: The self-concept, social identity, and interpersonal relations.* Belmont, CA: Brooks/Cole.

48. Sperling, G. (1960). The information available in brief visual presentations. *Psychological Monographs, 74,* 1–29.

49. Standing, L., Canezio, J., & Haber, R. N. (1970). Perception and memory for pictures: Single-trial learning of 2,560 visual stimuli. *Psychonomic Science, 19,* 73–74.

50. Stone, C. P. and Barker, R. G. (1937). Aspects of personality and intelligence in postmenarcheal and premenarcheal girls of the same chronological age. *Journal of Comparative and Physiological Psychology, 23,* 439–445.

51. Stroop, J. R. (1935). Studies in interferences in serial verbal learning. *Journal of Experimental Psychology, 18,* 643–662.

52. Thorndike, E. L. (1926). On the improvement of intelligence scores from thirteen to nineteen. *Journal of Educational Psychology, 17,* 73–76.

53. Tomlinson-Keasey, C. (1972). Formal operations in females ages 11 to 54 years of age. *Developmental Psychology, 60,* 364.

54. Tulving, E., & Thomson, D. M. (1973). Encoding specificity and retrieval processes in episodic memory. *Psychological Review, 80,* 352–373.

55. Tversky, A., & Kahneman, D. (1974). Judgment under uncertainty: Heuristics and biases. *Science, 185,* 1123–1131.

56. Waugh, N. C., & Norman, D. A. (1965). Primary memory. *Psychological Review, 72,* 89–104.

57. Yandrell, B., & Insko, C. A. (1977). Attributions of attitudes to speakers and listeners under assigned-behavior conditions: Does behavior engulf the field? *Journal of Experimental Social Psychology, 13,* 269–278.

There is no ache more deadly than the striving to be oneself.
—YEVGENIY VINOKUROV

Psychosocial Development During Adolescence

Clara S. Schuster, Randy Cronk, and F. Wayne Reno

Adolescence marks the end of childhood. During adolescence, the roles, interests, and identities developed during childhood must be reworked into the roles, responsibilities, and identities of adulthood.[7] Every adolescent confronts a broad range of new experiences, each seeming to call for immediate solution. A new body and sensual self demand attention and respect; burgeoning cognitive skills cry for opportunities for creativity and control; growing awareness of one's inner self demands final individuation from parents and other authority figures; and increased knowledge and broader social awareness leads one to question childhood values and traditions, frequently setting the stage for generational conflict and feelings of alienation. Underlying these confrontations is the adolescent's need and attempt to identify his or her own uniqueness, value, and values. The search for one's inner identity and "niche" in the social world can be a long, even painful, struggle, especially for the young person who seriously assumes full responsibility for the custodianship of his or her own life—its decisions, directions, and destiny.

Period of Transition

Technological societies allow for a prolonged period of transition from childhood to adult identities.[19] This period of time between the onset of puberty and the cultural expectation for the assumption of adult responsibilities, such as career, marriage, and child-rearing, allows young people to explore their unique talents, interests, ideologies, and identifications. The person emerging from high school or college is a very different individual from the young person entering adolescence at the age of 11 or 12.

As young people enter the junior high school years, they find themselves in a new world. They are not "big children," for their interests and needs have changed. Nor are they "little adults," for they are not yet ready to face the complexities of the adult world. Consequently, many feel compelled to create their own culture in the arena of a peer group, where they can experiment with new roles and search for their unique identity.

Adolescence is frequently described as a period of "storm and stress."[7] Although every adolescent faces some predictable stressors, the majority of persons do not find adolescence to be any more difficult than any other period of life.[29,45] Depending on temperament, parent–adolescent relationship, and experiences or opportunities offered by the social environment, some adolescents may be relatively untouched by the stereotypic storm and stress syndrome, whereas others may find this the most difficult period of their lives. Those young people who have developed a strong, supportive relationship with their parents during the preschool and school-age years are in the best position to weather the stresses of the adolescent period.

Parental modeling and the family atmosphere influence adolescent values, beliefs, and behaviors. Most adolescents continue to seek the positive, strong support of their parents. Healthy families with adolescents exchange warm affection and enjoy spending time together.[4] Clearly identified roles and expectations can facilitate the transition to adulthood. However, guidelines rather than prescriptions are in order. The adolescent must be allowed to take an active role in the development of his or her own relationships and values to emerge as a strong, stable, secure adult.[30]

Substages of Adolescence

Hormonal factors and physical development associated with puberty appear to have a marked impact on emotionality, aggressiveness, interest in the opposite gender, anxiety, impulse control, anger, and depression.[1, 21, 47] Thus, differences in the timing of puberty, rather than chronological age, account for differences in adolescent social and emotional behaviors. Adolescence may be divided roughly into three substages, each moderately definable and yet overlapping. By the end of the teen years, the differences between early and late maturers tend to smooth out (Fig. 25-1).

The **young adolescent** is making a transition to adolescence as well as to future adulthood.[4] Boys, as a whole, enter this stage 1 to 2 years later than girls. The pubescent, undergo-

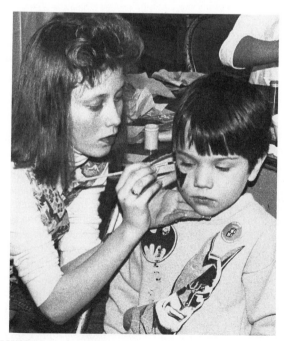

FIGURE 25–1.
Teens who have developed talents during school-age years find that these skills can facilitate transition through adolescent years. They are able to concentrate on how to use the skills rather than their own acceptability to others (abundance versus deficiency orientation).

ing dramatic physical and hormonal changes, is concerned about the normalcy and acceptability of the emerging adult body, emotions, and skills. Consequently, the healthy young adolescent tends to concentrate on *homosocial* relationships, (i.e., social relationships with the same gender). The adolescent reasons, "By associating with persons as much like myself as possible, I am able to compare myself to them and compete on an equal basis with them. I assure myself of my normalcy and acceptability." Some studies indicate a lowering of self-esteem during these years as the adult body is unfolding.[45] Girls, because of the dramatic changes in body configuration and functioning, especially need to construct a new self-image with puberty and thus find homosocial relationships crucial to self-evaluation and support.

Middle adolescence generally begins around age 14 or 15. Cutting of the psychological umbilical cord with parents embodies a grieving for the loss of childhood,[22] as well as a shift toward experimentation with alternative roles—roles that enhance the adolescent's sense of independence, encourage *heterosocial* relationships (i.e., social affiliation with the opposite gender), and initiate the search for self-knowledge. The breaking up of old relationships and the search for a new identity is psychologically stressful, frequently leading to moodiness, irritability, and depression. New moral dilemmas (e.g., dealing with drugs and sex), differing value systems, and peer pressures for conformity, challenge one's ability to "fit in" academically and socially. The young person who begins to conceive of the self as "personal property,"[14] resists forces that would fit him or her into a stereotyped mold or keep him or her as an extension of another's identity or value system. Self-esteem increases as the young person adapts to the adult body configuration and gains higher level physical, academic, and social skills.[45] The driver's license serves as a "rite of passage" for many young people in contemporary culture.

Around age 17 or 18, the adolescent confronts the reality of imminent adulthood. The **older adolescent** begins to assume increased responsibility for personal behavior and its consequences, and consciously works on acquiring the academic, occupational, personal, and social skills deemed essential to adult living. During this period one begins to identify those factors most crucial to one's identity, such as an intrinsic value system, sexual orientation, occupational identity, and the meaning of life.

Although "adolescence" culturally or legally may end at 18 or 21, some may extend adolescence into a fourth stage, **youth,** because of continued financial or social dependence on the family and a delay in assuming responsibilities of career and social relationships while pursuing one's education.[6] However, this extended moratorium on assumption of culturally desired responsibilities does not negate the assumption of internalized responsibility for one's value position, interpersonal relationships, and direction in life. On the other hand, even though a person may marry and hold down a secure job, the task of consolidating a coherent, independent, internal identity that gives proactive direction and meaning to life may not occur until the mid-twenties or later,[7, 15, 18] when the person faces a life crisis, requiring a restructuring of value system and priorities. Psychosocially, adolescence ends when the person finds a comfortable fit between the "I" and a "belief system that clarifies the individual's place in an infinite and timeless universe."[8] The person then is able to articulate what he or she believes in or has stood for, and to rise above self-consciousness to a commitment to persons, ideologies, or concerns beyond one's self.[7] Some persons never adequately resolve the issue of identity, a factor that affects the quality of adult life.[7]

THE QUEST FOR IDENTITY

Identity versus Role Confusion

The central crisis of one's life, the fifth rung of Erikson's ladder of social–emotional development, is the issue of **identity.**[7,8,23] It is not until adolescence that the individual develops "the prerequisites in physiological growth, mental maturation, and social responsibility to experience and pass through the crisis of identity."[7] All the previous crises lead toward the development of a unique identity. As in the resolution of previous crises, the healthy personality assumes an active role in mastering the conflicts between self and the environment. Those who have incompletely or negatively resolved the previous crises may take a maladaptive stance of fanaticism or rejection of cultural standards, or may find safety in a passive stance resulting in bewilderment or **role confusion.**[7,8,22] Regardless of the polarity one assumes, there is a major reorganization of personality as one leans on the securities and resolutions of childhood while reaching toward the anticipated freedoms and responsibilities of adulthood (Fig. 25-2).

Building on the Past

In Erikson's theory, identity development is a lifelong process. Each previous stage contributes to one's sense of selfhood. During the school-age years, the well-developing person explored and mastered multiple skills and roles, each of which contributed to an identity based largely on concrete descriptors of one's physical characteristics and competencies. The new cognitive skills of abstraction and hierarchical organization enable one to consolidate these multiple concrete identities into a more abstract, conceptual and internalized sense of self. Thus, a child who plays baseball, runs fast, and likes to swim, begins to identify the self as athletic. One who collects butterflies, knows all the bones and organs of the body, and likes to experiment with chemicals, begins to identify the self as a scientist. This awareness of conceptual identities (e.g., leader, dramatist, artist, problem solver, poet, mathematician, comedian) and characteristics (dependable, optimistic, creative, and so forth) enables the adolescent to begin to systematically and realistically identify career options, focus energies, expand skills, and modify personal characteristics to actuate a chosen, desired self.

FIGURE 25–2.
Participation in events valued by one's culture helps the young person prepare for the responsibilities, social relationships, and knowledge base expected in their circle of acquaintances.

During adolescence, Erikson's four earlier stages assume new forms and are reworked as an integral part of the identity crisis.[7]

STAGE I (TRUST): *Temporal perspective versus time confusion.* Adolescents find it difficult to trust time. Nothing comes fast enough, and there is a great temptation to take shortcuts or make premature commitments to marriage, career, or parenthood. Ironically, these premature commitments tend to delay self-discovery and identity resolution. A second aspect of the reworked trust crisis is that the trust learned in infancy is now refocused in the trusts of adulthood—the search for a self-chosen love, the capacity for faith, or an in-depth religious experience.

STAGE II (AUTONOMY): *Self-certainty versus self-consciousness.* The adolescent strives for renewed emancipation from the parents, needing to establish his or her own rules and regulations. In this search for autonomy in problem solving, identity, and value formation, the adolescent often rejects the guidance of authority figures such as parents, teachers, and society, substituting the peer group as the authority. Even though the peer group may appear to foster values counter to parents' needs, wishes, and values, it may provide a protective setting where there is room to experiment with other social roles and variations on cultural values. Self-discipline is exerted to achieve one's goals and to squelch impulsivity. This may result in transient periods of compulsivity.

Self-consciousness is exhibited in the phenomenon of "imaginary audience" (see Chap. 24) and the efforts to blend with peers. There is a marked increase in personal agony, which can be covered up by arrogance to hide one's sense of insecurity. The adolescent "is mortally afraid of being forced into activities in which he would feel exposed to ridicule or self-doubt . . . He would rather act shamelessly in the eyes of his elders, out of free choice, than be forced into activities which would be shameful in his own eyes or in those of his peers."[7]

STAGE III (INITIATIVE): *Role experimentation versus role fixation.* The grandiose ideas and plans of adolescence are frequently unmatched by their skills or perseverance. The adolescent may play the role of an aristocrat one day, and a recluse the next. Behaviors or attitudes portrayed in mass media or reading may be "tried on" in social relationships or used for problem solving.

Freud observed that adolescents express a range of relationships, from excessive egocentrism to idealistic altruism; from regarding themselves as the center of the universe to being extremely self-sacrificing and devoted; from forming passionate love relationships one day to breaking them the next; from an overpowering longing for solitude to throwing themselves enthusiastically into the life of the community; and from being a whiny kid one day to a sophisticated, mature person the next.[10] Such contrasts are as confusing to adolescents as to the adults living and working with them. However, there is a tendency to choose "safe" roles set by others to avoid embarrassment, disorder and guilt.

STAGE IV (INDUSTRY): *Apprenticeship versus work paralysis.* The adolescent begins to focus on the more sophisticated social and career skills needed for successful adulthood. Mentors and continued parental support are essential during these years. The industry of adolescence demands a lot of enthusiasm, hard work, and self-discipline. School and community support of burgeoning skills are crucial to the development of talents and potentials. Adolescents need opportunities for gainful employment in the community as they explore interests and abilities, develop work habits and social relationships, and increase independence from their families (Fig. 25-3).

Looking Toward the Future

While the adolescent is continuing to struggle with and reexamine past struggles, he or she is also laying the foundation for and exhibiting precursor skills for resolution of Erikson's next three stages.[8, 15]

FIGURE 25–3.
Paid work experiences provide increasing financial independence and are an important facet in the preparation for adulthood.

STAGE VI (INTIMACY): *Sexual polarization versus bisexual confusion.* Erikson's concept of psychosocial intimacy is not synonymous with the popular use of the word to represent physical or sexual contact. Nevertheless, the adolescent is facing and resolving issues of gender-identity, gender-orientation, and gender-expression (see Chap. 14). Sexual activity undertaken during adolescence is seen by Erikson as "the self-seeking, identity-hungry kind; each partner is trying only to reach himself."[7] Physical intimacy without psychosocial intimacy may cause foreclosure of identity development and confusion of values because the pursuit of physical affirmation and excitement eclipses the emotional intimacy so essential to knowing and being known, to sorting values, establishing priorities, strengthening self-discipline, and developing social and negotiation skills—all requisite components in the task of identity homework. If one's identity is not clear, one can become a "chameleon" in social relationships, losing one's identity to that of the other.

The adolescent must begin to share viewpoints, concerns, and feelings to get sufficient feedback to see the self more clearly. The young person strives to find a mirror for and understanding of the self through talking (thus, the constant

FIGURE 25–4.
Some parents are convinced that the telephone is a permanent appendage on the adolescent's ear.

use of the telephone!) (Fig. 25-4). The self-centered intimacies of adolescence help shape and sharpen one's identity through the exchange of ideas, the negotiation of behaviors, and the exploration of ideological stances.

STAGE VII (GENERATIVITY): *Leadership and followership versus authority confusion.* The adolescent is already beginning to reveal allocentric orientation through involvement in projects that benefit others without concern for self-enhancement. Male and female adolescents are equally altruistic.[41] Those with low altruistic orientation may become involved in group projects, but will direct energies toward the adult in charge to achieve a "good boy" image.[41] The healthy adolescent is not a "blind follower" but a conscientious volunteer or cooperative follower. There is an awareness of self-expression in the opportunities to work with others.

STAGE VIII (INTEGRITY): *Ideological commitment versus confusion of values.* Most people identify what they are *against* before they are able to clarify what they are *for* and why.[15] The adolescent "must repudiate some 'foreign' values in order to focus his or her beliefs on some chosen identity."[7] The healthy adolescent begins to stand up for or against something based on a chosen identity and values. Ideologies at this point tend to be simplistic views that will be modified or fleshed out through the rest of life. But they provide a compelling power and source of commitment that contribute to vital involvement in life. Without commitment, people become pawns of the environment, and values lack integrity.

Identifying One's Uniqueness

Identity Homework

The forging of one's unique identity from the raw materials and experiences of childhood is known as **identity homework.** It involves the identification of one's potentials, the evaluation of strengths and weaknesses, the search for values to live by, and the choice of a source of identity. "I am the blacksmith of my own identity."[15] Each problem we confront asks us for our identity. The values we use to face the conflicts of life gradually reveal our priorities and shape our behavior. Identity homework requires the person to consciously evaluate relationships, conflicting values, reactions, and so forth, to compare one's real self or behavior to the desired or ideal self. It involves establishing priorities and admitting one's weaknesses and errors, as well as formulating active steps to focus energies in the desired direction. Facing and admitting one's inadequacies is difficult, threatening, and painful. Consequently, many people avoid the process, preferring instead to accept the values and behaviors proffered by peers or the culture (school-age mentality). The process is frequently most painful right before resolution of one's inner identity,[7] partly because feelings of loss and mourning accompany the dissolution of old relationships, values, and security props.[22] Identity homework answers three questions: (1) Who am I? (2) What do I have to offer? (3) What am I going to do with it?[7] Eventually, all the intangible aspects of self—values, priorities, and ideologies—are identified and integrated into a working philosophy and identity. From this base, one is able to tap into the "authentic self" or "existential" aspects of self and is ready to move toward positive resolution of Erikson's next crisis—intimacy.[8, 23] Although the foundations of identity are established in healthy individuals during adolescence and young adulthood, **identity homework continues throughout life as chosen values are reevaluated or prioritized in light of current problems and situations.**

Coping with Varieties of Differences

Because the ego is still weak, young adolescents tend to try to be like their peers, wearing similar clothing and hair styles, and pursuing similar activities and interests. As they get older, they begin to identify, appreciate, and value their uniqueness.

The process of a separate identity formation usually begins by developing one's unique talents and interests. However, talents and special abilities may be overlooked or neglected because of the amount of time or energy necessary to develop them. Many adolescents are gifted in science, math, music, art, social leadership, or neuromuscular coordination. However, inadequate resolution of Erikson's task of industry undermines the strength, drive, determination, and perseverance necessary to develop them.

Regardless of the category of defining characteristics—our differences are important. Eventually, differences caused by exceptionality (see Chap. 17), economic or social status, opportunities, education, social or travel experiences, intellectual potentials, physique, temperament, gender, religious training, ordinal position, and so forth, must all be faced and forged into a positive, working concept of self. It is important to "dare to be different" to maximize our potentials for either our own or society's benefit.

Establishing the Source of One's Identity

Sources of Identity

For many people, establishing one's identity is very difficult because it requires development of self-evaluation and self-discipline skills. Not only must one's strengths be faced, but one must admit weaknesses and internal value conflicts. One must also choose values to live by. The well-developing person will then translate these values into behaviors consistent with one's goals.

One can choose to master stereotypic skills, behaviors, and attitudes associated with a particular career or social role (restrictive approach), or one can choose a particular career or social role based on one's identified values, interests, and talents (expressive approach). The restrictive approach can lead to feelings of security and competence. However, when one uses the role behaviors as a crutch for identity, the deeper issues of self-evaluation are usually neglected, leaving the person vulnerable to environmental pressures later in life. The person using an expressive approach identifies many ways to express the unique self and finds more resiliency when the exigencies of life close doors. In the former ap-

proach, "life is happening to the individual," but in the latter, life is "being lived by his initiative."[7]

The search for identity and meaning in one's life often gets sidetracked by the issues of daily living. Adolescents are caught up in issues of social acceptance and peer pressure, career concerns and parental pressure, fear of failure and sexual pressure, financial insecurities and media pressure. Consequently, by choice or by default, many adolescents (and many adults) substitute their public identity for their private identity. Although societal roles may offer guidelines or a frame for making a transition to a deeper exploration and evaluation of one's selfhood, there is a real danger of getting stuck in the behavior patterns accompanying the external source of identity. Social security and emotional comfort become the guiding values for life, rather than internal integrity. Decisions, relationships, and behaviors are focused toward maintaining the external identity source.

Schuster offers 16 potential sources of identity. Individuals typically exhibit characteristics of these sources as they transit the adolescent years:

1. PLEASURE. "I am what pleases me." This is one of the most primitive forms of identity. The only times this person feels "fully alive" is when the adrenalin levels are high or the senses are maximally stimulated. Consequently, the person tries to stay in touch with the self by seeking sensual and exciting experiences (sports, roller coasters, sex, drugs, daring feats) (Fig. 25-5). Between activities the person may feel depressed or bored. Sedentary, routine, or cognitive activities may be shunned in the search for physical stimulation. The person may allow or dwell on vague anxieties, hypothetical worries, or presumed injustices or social insults because of the increased contact with the physical self accompanying the increased tension. As an adult, this person may pursue a career focused on a "playtime" lifestyle (e.g., surfboard instructor, race car driver).

2. PARENTS. "I am a replica of my parents." Failure to resolve the separation/individuation process causes the young person to continue to consciously or unconsciously live out the parents' value system.[32] This person may be "too good to be true" as an adolescent and may become depressed during adulthood—especially if the spouse is seen as an inadequate substitute for parental values and behaviors.[22] Most adolescents appreciate (even though they may loudly protest) the parent who sets firm guidelines for social behaviors, curfews, and activities, since these parental values can be used as an excuse to avoid participation in activities without stigmatizing the adolescent who is not yet strong enough to resist peer pressure independently.[6] However, there comes a point when a young person must take a stand based on personal values and needs. Some young adults in an attempt to individuate may merely exchange their parental attachment to a mentor or spiritual leader for discipleship, thus becoming an extension of the new person's world views, values, and behaviors. Find-

FIGURE 25–5.
Adolescent: "I am what pleases me."

ing a value system different from that of one's parents, even if found in a solid religious philosophy, does not equate with identity homework unless it has been uniquely worked out for oneself. The conscious, free choice of a value system similar to that of the parents is not synonymous with being an extension of them.

3. PERSONS. "I am who I affiliate with." Identity is found in associating with persons of greater strength, higher visibility, or more significant achievement. This source of identity facilitates separation from parental identity. Dating a prestigious person (e.g., cheerleader or sports star) increases one's social value. Some teens carry and share a wallet full of pictures which help to validate their acceptability. The adolescent may "fall head over heels in love so as to 'lose' the self in another person."[22] But dependence on love, romance, or sexual excitement does little to insulate against depression, loneliness, or loss because of the lack of development of inner strength or coping mechanisms.[22] Marriages based on this source are potentially disastrous (see Chap. 29).

4. PHYSIQUE. "I am my body." Intraindividual separation of domains is weak or nonexistent. One may be very proud of or very embarrassed by facial or body appearance. The person may work hard at developing the physical self through diet

management or exercise, and may even resort to drugs or surgery to ensure acceptability. The onset of puberty is a critical factor. Late developing males and early maturing females are most likely to receive negative peer and adult evaluation and feedback.[48] Physically attractive adolescents are seen more positively than "normal" or unattractive peers.[26] It is typical for the immature adolescent to use a unique characteristic to define one's total identity—a disability, striking hair color, distinctive voice, height, or attractive physical attribute. All other aspects of life are assimilated into the valued or detested characteristic. Younger teens, still adapting to their developing bodies, are especially vulnerable to adopting this source of identity. There is agony over "zits," body parts that are "too large," and others that are "too small." There is a strong sense of stigmatization by disabilities or deformities (see Chap. 17). There may be an unearned sense of superiority in the fortuitous granting of a "body beautiful." This is a "superficial/exterior response that tends to short circuit genuine strength."[22] Many young people today are having plastic surgery to "correct" those parts of their bodies deemed undesirable, leading to the concept of "designer bodies." The person with anorexia nervosa may be stuck on this source of identity.

5. PACKAGING. "I am what I look like"—whether wild hairdo, behaviors and clothes, or very reserved appearance and behaviors. One packages and presents the self to others in conformity with current fads or stereotyped cultural appearances. By attending to details of appearance, the young person thinks maybe "I can camouflage a detested characteristic or maybe others will graciously overlook the embarrassing factor." Adolescents spend much time on makeup, grooming, and hygiene to ensure social acceptability. No hair must be out of place; colors must exactly coordinate. "If I dare to be different, it must be in a way envied by my friends."

6. PRODIGY. "I am what I can do." The individual finds identity through the acceptance and praise offered for the possession and development of a special talent. The early developing male is in an enviable position because of his ability to participate in competitive sports events. Others are admired because of musical or artistic skill, academic prowess, or other socially valued ability (Fig. 25-6). This young person may become overly dependent on the recognition and admiration of others and fail to develop other skills essential to healthy social relationships and intrapsychic development. There may be bouts of confusion and depression during young adult years, when the skills of peers catch up and the special recognition is no longer offered.

7. POSSESSIONS. "I am what I own." Social desirability and value are ensured by surrounding oneself with things money can buy: clothes, electronic equipment, cars, and so forth. One relates to others through these material objects. Older persons may use a home, heirlooms, or other special objects as part of their "credentialling" process.[8] Suicides associated

FIGURE 25–6.
Special talents continue to be developed during adolescence, leading to another avenue for discovering uniqueness.

with financial failure (e.g., Wall Street crashes) can be attributed to loss of this source of identity.

8. POWER. "I am what I control." One finds safety or security in the ability to control events or people. Identity is based on creating a sense of invulnerability. Once in a position of power or leadership, the person may use the opportunity for self-aggrandizement rather than service. Other people may be seen as less human, or as pawns for one's own needs, plans, or desires. History is replete with examples of this source of identity (e.g., Adolph Hitler, Joseph Stalin, Jim Jones, Ho Chi Minh, Nicolae Ceausescu of Romania, and Saddam Hussein of Iraq).

9. PRIVILEGE. "I am what I have inherited." Family origin, social class, gender, and ordinal position can grant social recognition and provide access to privileges not available to others. One sees status as ensuring social acceptability and establishing life roles. Privilege brings responsibility which can either serve as a prescriptive frame (restrictive approach) or offer opportunities to place one's unique stamp on the role (expressive approach).

10. PROTOCOL. "I am what I do." This person conforms to the social expectations of the culture. They study and learn the social nuances—how to position one's body, the special tenor and inflections of the voice, the "proper" way to express oneself in writing or in face-to-face interactions. This person appears to have memorized Amy Vanderbilt's etiquette book, knows how to make other people feel relaxed, and is an expert in soothing conflict or hurt feelings. Yet with all the "smoothness," authenticity and empathy often appear to be missing.

11. PRESTIGE. "I am what I belong to." One joins the "right" club, attends the "right" school, is elected to the "right" office, or is published in the "right" journals. An adolescent may seek to become a cheerleader, join the marching band, or strive to be on the school's academic trivia competition team. Identity is based on achieving the most desired status—or even in serving others through recognized social agencies, such as the American Red Cross or one's religious affiliation.

12. PROFESSION. "I am what my career demands." Imagining oneself in a particular role can be an invitation to foster growth.[23] The young person begins to assume the attitudes, interests, and behaviors relevant to a career, whether the career is medical doctor, automobile mechanic, parent, or teacher. Other people frequently reinforce the behavior or career goal through differential treatment. Eventually, as technical skills are mastered, technique and knowledge are taken for granted, and roles fall away in an unselfconscious way to allow the person to make the career but one aspect of self expression.[23] Occupational roles frequently continue to be a strong source of identity, especially for men, thus creating major questions about one's value or roles during a time of unemployment or retirement.

13. PRODUCTS. "I am what I create." Providing an object or a service that is appreciated, admired, or of value to others, is accompanied by a feeling of affirmation and acceptance. The person may begin to base personal value and acceptability on the ability to produce the unique or valued product, striving always to make it better or "the best." When an idea, poem, art piece, or bid to assist is "second best," critiqued, or bypassed, the sense of personal rejection may precipitate social withdrawal or depression. This person cannot separate one's personage from one's products because he or she concentrates on "being the best," rather than "doing one's best." Adolescents are particularly vulnerable as they begin to take initiative to provide or produce something unique that expresses their inner values, insights, pain or aesthetic talent.

14. PROGENY. "I am my children." One's offspring, their antics and achievements, become the central focus of identity and become the source of justification for existence. Self-pride or reproach is bound to the successes and failures of the children. This source of identity is generally reserved until the young adult years, but may be a source of identity for adolescent girls who see no other future. They may purposefully become pregnant to actualize their identity and secure their future value.[35]

15. PHILOSOPHY. "I am what I believe in." One attaches to a cause such as animal rights, an abortion position, the AIDS crisis, environmental pollution, or an ideology as expressed by a religious belief or charismatic leader. All of one's energies become focused toward that end, and all events are interpreted from the targeted perspective. The young person can develop either a fanatical or very positive lifestyle, depending on the ideology chosen.

16. PSYCHE. "I am who I am!" Of all the potential sources for self-evaluation and direction, this is the only one which deals with the true, internal identity of the person. This is the ultimate goal of all identity homework. It involves the deepest intimacy with the self in the search for integrating beliefs, values, priorities, and goals. From this search emerges authenticity, commitment, and the ability to be intimate with others.

As the young person travels through the adolescent years, he or she may simultaneously or sequentially find identity in any of these sources. They can provide a temporary "crutch" as one is involved in identity homework. However, a person can get caught up in the comfort of a particular identity and settle on it for a lifetime, rather than expend energies on and face the pain and insecurities of identity homework. The question of identity "is never completely answered, and can't be, even partially, until the person makes a commitment and lives it out for a number of years . . . when the person's energy is devoted more to the commitment than to the identity issues of the previous stages, one could be said to be past the identity crisis."[23]

Search for Meaningful Values

Values are tied not only to our identity system, but also to our moral system and what we are willing to do to maintain our source of strength or confidence to face life. The search for values is closely tied to faith development (see Chap. 2). The search for meaningful values does not happen easily or all at once. It takes a lifetime of continual searching, modifying, and maturing. But the basic value system and evaluation process structures are resolved during the identity crisis. Those who are particularly sensitive to the needs of those around them, or have a high I.Q., frequently find that this time of identity search and value clarification is prolonged because they are more aware of other issues that need to be simultaneously evaluated for a comprehensive view.[7]

Long-Range Effects of Source of Identity

The immature sources of identity (e.g., persons, pleasure, physique) should begin to be replaced by philosophical and psyche sources as the person gets a clearer picture of potentials and inner value system. When one's identity and sense of self-approval come from within, then identity remains stable through the exigencies of adult life (e.g., unemployment, illness, family death, disaster, birth of disabled child). There is an inner resiliency that does not collapse when the world does. Those who have not resolved the identity issue continue to have major identity crises when facing life's problems (e.g., severe depression on loss of spouse or "empty nest," or divorce following birth of a disabled child). Midlife changes are less likely to become a crisis when the person has already released physique or progeny as sources of identity.

Negative Identities

Approximately three fourths of adolescents negotiate this life phase fairly successfully. The remaining quarter experience problems of delinquency, drug or alcohol dependency, school failures, sexual involvements, conflict with parents, and generalized expressions of depression or aggression.[22] When a person believes that expectations of the self, peer, or parents cannot be met, a negative identity may develop.[7] Adolescents may feel that they are not good enough, expect failure, and therefore give up trying to achieve the culturally desirable roles. Some may assume a rebellious stance, acting out, or exhibiting behaviors in direct defiance of authority figures as a way to maintain self-esteem and control. The culturally undesirable or dangerous roles may appear to be the most realistic. Thus, a child with devoutly religious parents may engage in stealing, taking drugs, or other anti-establishment behaviors. The young person may focus energies on "being the best at being bad," to achieve self-satisfaction, control, or attention.

FACTORS INHIBITING HEALTHY IDENTITY FORMATION. There are many factors that may seriously inhibit identity formation. Poverty and abuse both tend to have adverse effects on development. If the young person perceives that the parents do not like or support him or her, then who will? The person may continue to feel "not quite good enough" throughout adult life.[44] When one loses a sense of the basic goodness of life and of hope in the future and society, there is no energy left for identity homework and value resolution. Energies are used for self-protection and assurances of acceptability.

One copes with the fear of failure ("I am vulnerable without adult support") by using tactics that avoid the heavy responsibility and pain of identity homework. Keeping oneself busy with social activities, sports, school work, listening to music, concentrating on enhancing physical attractiveness, involvement in drugs, alcohol, and sex, all tend to divert energies away from thinking about deeper issues of value conflicts, future goals, and adult responsibilities. The end result is that the individual is unprepared to assume the mantle of responsible, successful adulthood. Adolescents need appropriate psychosocial challenges and private time, away from television and people, to think about critical life issues and direction.

ROLE CONFUSION (IDENTITY DIFFUSION). The person who does not clarify and commit oneself to an inner value system becomes prey to multiple external pressures to their behavior or value codes. The resulting **role confusion** represents the negative counterpart of Erikson's task of identity.[7] It is characterized by having few commitments, goals, or values. The trademark of this individual is apathy. The person may not be able to muster the energy or will to "get going" or may experience immobilizing panic in the face of life's problems. Role confusion evidences itself in difficulty with finishing assignments, making friends, or thinking about the future. The person also is at the whim of peer pressure—going along with the crowd, regardless of potential consequences to the self or others. "Wilding," the unprovoked attack on innocent persons by a group of adolescents seeking the "thrill" of beating up someone, is an extreme example of this phenomenon.

DESTRUCTIVE SEARCHES. Young people face many moral issues in their search for identity. It is easier to go along with another's decisions to ease the loneliness of adolescent individuation and to block out the awareness of vulnerability. In contemporary society, sexual behavior and the use of illegal drugs comprise two major moral dilemmas for adolescents. Visions of grandeur and the attitudes of impunity and immunity to the laws of mortality and probability (sometimes referred to as the *invincibility fable*) result in risk-taking of all kinds. A false security develops when the adolescent believes that bad consequences happen only to other people, but never to him or her. Reality is denied when it interferes with one's own hopes and fantasies.

Kohlberg's postconventional level of morality is usually reached later in life, long after the adolescent period (see Chap. 16). Therefore, the emotional, cognitive, and moral underpinnings to maintain a stance of abstinence are weak. Moral choices based merely on the avoidance of negative consequences may be a valid, but insufficient, reason for making the decision to "just say no" to peers or to avoid promiscuous, recreational, or casual sex. Parents and others need to teach their basic moral values early in the child's life, facilitate the development of self-discipline, provide alternative activities, support the young person's ability to take a stand, and provide a warm atmosphere for communication and enlightenment.

Sexual Behavior. Sexual behavior is a major concern during adolescence. The cognitive ability to think about "possibilities" is, in a large number of adolescents, underdeveloped. This, combined with the invincibility fable, results in illogical thinking, causing them to fail to consider "what if" questions, such as "What if your partner has a sexually transmitted disease (STD)?" or "What if you or your partner become pregnant?" Now that they possess adult bodies, adolescents want to experience adult "rights." For many, the concept of abstinence or waiting is difficult when time drags. Self-discipline is poorly developed, and personal, guiding values are not yet internalized.

Because of the invincibility fable, sexually active adolescents often fail to use contraception. Boys typically regard pregnancy as the girl's problem, and girls typically consider the problem nonexistent. Only about one third of teenagers use contraception, and one half of them use faulty methods (e.g., withdrawal).[49] Therefore, over 80% of sexually active teenagers are at high risk for pregnancy. Of sexually active teens, 35% to 40% become pregnant, the highest percentage being among the younger ages (15 and under).[24] Each year in the United States, one out of every 10 girls between 15 and 19 become pregnant, 92% premaritally.[49] Annually, over 1 million teenagers become pregnant, and approximately half a million become mothers.[37]

When pregnancy does occur, the young girl may be emotionally immobilized, avoiding medical care or professional consultation. Even the outwardly rebellious girl may be too ashamed to tell her parents—thus placing both herself and the baby at biological risk.[9] Social risk is also obvious when one realizes that 34% of girls 15 to 19 years of age who marry before childbirth are separated or divorced by the time their infant is 6 months old.[37] There also is a marked discrepancy in educational achievement of these women 11 years later.[37] Adolescent fathers also exhibit impoverished educational and employment records.[16] The wasted human potential of premature sexuality has become a national as well as a family and personal concern.[16]

Substance Abuse. Alcohol remains the number one "drug of choice" among high school students. Cigarettes rank second, followed by marijuana. Alcohol and cocaine use are increasing. Adolescents are substituting the less expensive and extremely addictive form of "crack" for cocaine.[5] Many adolescents use drugs and alcohol as a way to avoid facing the realities or problems of life. For the time they feel better, escape the pain, or forget about the trauma. Consequently, not only does the drug become a physical habit, but an emotional one as well. **The very problems that challenge them to face themselves and their identity—that help prepare them to face the realities of adult life—are avoided, truncating social and emotional development.** Later, when they attempt to break the dependencies, they find themselves emotionally immature, compounding the issues faced in trying to break the habit and face life successfully. Drug use and irresponsible sexuality tend to go hand in hand. Responsibility in one area carries over to responsibility in the other. Self-discipline and a sense of responsibility for the custodianship of one's life appear to be key factors in a commitment to abstinence.

Group Identity. Identity homework is a lonely, difficult, and disconcerting task. Consequently, many adolescents continue to use their affiliations with peers as a source of social and emotional protection (Fig. 25-7). The middle teen typically becomes a part of a clique or gang that develops its own code of conduct, rites of passage, and value system, distinguishing it as unique from the broader teen scene. Within this new system, the adolescent finds a temporary haven from the onslaught of environmental pressures.

Group identity can have a positive valence in that it serves as a bridge between the family and the larger society. Peers facilitate the final individuation process—that is, if it is ever truly final. Many of us continue to find our parents a significant refueling source, even in middle adulthood! Separation from the parents becomes easier as the young person goes on to college, a job, marriage, or the military. Peers also provide an arena for practicing and refining emerging adult social skills in an accepting, yet reflecting environment.

As the teenager passes into the late adolescent phases, becoming more concerned about abstract philosophical issues, there is a breaking away from group dependency (sometimes forced by graduation from high school). The teenager begins a conscious search for a mentor or role model to facilitate attaining the knowledge and skills needed to face adulthood. A mentor helps establish meaningful values and goals to direct one's life. This is an extremely positive step toward maturity, as long as the young person maintains responsibility for evaluating and actively choosing the values and behaviors affecting his or her life. There is danger in releasing responsibility for decisions to the other person (e.g., spiritual leader or spouse), because of the temptation to avoid further identity homework. One can become an extension of the other's will, rather than continuing to pursue successfully his or her own identity.

Issues of Negative Identities. The transition from a child-

FIGURE 25–7.
Adolescents continue to seek homosocial relationships for cooperative and competitive activities in a friendly, supportive group.

hood identity to an adult identity is obviously laden with some difficult hurdles and pitfalls. The breaking up of old securities leaves the young person vulnerable to the predators of cultural pressures and of their own minds. Young people may defy the adult culture and remain in control of events by engaging in delinquent acts, or they may avoid adult culture and the pain of identity homework through suicide.

Delinquency Acts. About 80% of all adolescents in North America and Great Britain engage in minor misdemeanors.[40] The taunting, fighting, and open confrontations of childhood have shifted to more covert antisocial behaviors during the adolescent years (e.g., using someone else's I.D. card, vandalism, drug use, truancy, stealing, running away, and sexual acting out). However, many adolescent crimes are not minor. Forty-seven percent of the arrests for murder, assault, and robbery involve youths under age 21.[51] Though not causative, two factors correlate highly with the incidence of delinquency: poor school achievement and low socioeconomic status. The rate of delinquent crimes by adolescent males climbs steadily, outnumbering delinquent acts by females.[42] Delinquents roughly fall into three categories:[42]

1. Teens who are "normal" but have been socialized in communities where antisocial behaviors are tolerated, accepted, or even expected. In some subcultures, boys may even be encouraged to engage in illegal acts as a way to establish independence and to assert masculinity.

2. "Maladaptive" adolescents appear to be incapable of delaying gratification. They have character disorders which allow them to inflict pain on others without remorse. These are persons considered to be "amoral"— or without the culturally desired moral code.

3. "Rebellious" adolescents generally have middle class advantages, but often have been victims of exploitation by their parents. They choose to flout the rules they have been taught, and are thus considered to be "immoral."

Theories of the cause of juvenile crimes (both individual and group crimes) are numerous. Four of the most accepted views follow.[20]

1. The Nonintegration Theory. This view observes that these adolescents have no allegiance to a social and economic system (amoral view).

2. The Limited Opportunities or Poverty Theory. This view holds that delinquency emerges from racial prejudice, lack of equality in education and employment, and family disorganization. Adolescents therefore are forced to resort to illegitimate means to support themselves and their causes (survival view).

3. The Reputation ("rep") Theory. These individuals are not as interested in economic gain as they are in establishing a reputation. Delinquent acts stem from a need for power and prestige. In delinquent subcultures, the more daring and brave achieve greater status and leadership positions (status view).

4. The Labeling Theory. Societal labeling of a person as "delinquent" may create a self-fulfilling prophecy. Negative labels are tantamount to sealing the adolescent's future. If parents, judges, teachers, and the police repeatedly tell a young person that he or she is delinquent, their opinion is believed and acted on (fulfillment view).

Delinquents often develop an elaborate code of rationalizations for their activities:[20]

1. Denial of Responsibility: They cite being unable to read, living in a fatherless home, or growing up in an abusive environment.

2. Denial of Injury: "Stealing goods from a store does not really hurt anyone."

3. Denial of Victim: The teacher or storekeeper who is assaulted "deserves it" for resisting the delinquents or for treating them poorly.

4. Condemning the Condemner: They cite the hypocrisy of those in power, such as "cops on the take," or unfairness in the system.

Suicide. Suicide is the third leading cause of death in adolescents.[54] The cognitive ability to be introspective increases the adolescent's awareness of shortcomings. Difficulty in separating one's own feelings from those of others (inadequate individuation) and the difficulty involved in creating a new self-image (inadequate identity homework) increase the adolescent's inner turmoil.[43] Consequently, thoughts of death, dying, and killing oneself and judging the family to be better off without them are common phenomena of adolescence.[52] Even though the majority of adolescents think about suicide as a potential solution to life's stresses,[43] successful suicide occurs at the rate of only 1 in 10,000 every year.[50] Three times as many girls as boys attempt suicide, but three times as many males as females are successful at the attempt (due to the choice of more violent methods).[43]

One half to two thirds of suicidal adolescents are from divorced families, and drugs are a factor in about 50% of suicide cases.[43] Researchers have found that most adolescent suicides are preceded by a sequence of negative events including family abuse,[18] breakdowns in communication among family members, and a sense of "being in the way."[43] One third of adolescents have suicidal thoughts following the death of a sibling.[2] Suicide is not limited to adolescence, however. Children as young as 5 years of age have been known to attempt or commit suicide.[54]

Eighty percent of suicide attempters give clear signs of their intention.[43] Suicide prevention requires heeding the preliminary warning signs, including the following:

1. A sudden decline in school attendance and achievement, especially in students of better than average ability.

2. A break in a love relationship (a precipitating event for many adolescent suicides).

3. Depression, expressions of hopelessness, unsolvable problems, multiple losses, and rejection. The young person may be "repulsed by life."

4. Withdrawal from social relationships, especially if the adolescent seems no longer to care about social interaction and appearance.

5. An attempted suicide (often a bid for increased attention or an attempt to see if people really care or are listening).

6. A keen interest in the suicides of other adolescents. Cluster suicides sometimes influence the adolescent's natural egocentrism. Identification with the deceased and the attendant grief and eulogizing of survivors may precipitate suicide attempts in survivors.

7. Verbal warnings.

Some suicides are secondary to other adolescent issues such as attitudes of impunity and characteristics of impulsivity. The young person may drive dangerously as a way of proving competency or bravado. Fantasies of rebirth, return, or reunion into a new, happier family may eclipse an understanding of the permanency of death.[18] Others see suicide as a last desperate attempt to gain parental attention or to gain control over their own lives.[18] Professional help for suicidal adolescents and their families can often open up channels of communication that have been blocked by a combination of parental insensitivity and adolescent self-absorption. Therapy also enables the would-be suicide to find ways to express anguish, "untie knots that bind them to past unhappiness, seek satisfaction in new possibilities, and in so doing accept the promise of a future."[18] In short, counseling provides assistance with the process of identity homework.

NEGATIVE IDENTITIES RESOLVED. The resolution of a negative identity takes time. The person generally finds himself or herself unprepared for the responsibilities of adulthood. Fortunately this is not an insurmountable problem. Erikson's belief in *invariant sequence* is not as rigid as that of Freud and Piaget. That is, if the resolution of one stage of development does not occur on time or is not resolved in a healthy manner, it may, with encouragement, challenge, motivation, and opportunity be resolved later in life—a very optimistic viewpoint! Lack of resolution does not necessarily negate the assumption of or even enjoyment of adult responsibilities, but does restrict the person's ability to find intra- and interpersonal freedom.

Identity Consolidation

The healthy adolescent is able to weather the stressors of these transition years. Through facing challenges, trying on differing roles, and searching for meaning to one's life, one's uniqueness becomes appreciated and one's identity begins to consolidate and stabilize.

James Marcia describes four major levels of identity.[33] He uses two criteria to establish whether the person has attained a mature identity: crisis and commitment. **Crisis** is defined as engagement in choosing among many meaningful alternatives. **Commitment** is defined as the degree of personal investment the individual exhibits.[38] Maturity is achieved through experiencing a crisis, making a choice, and then becoming committed to a person, occupation, or ideology.

Many adolescents avoid facing crises by premature commitment to roles, rather than to goals or values. The result is **foreclosure**[7]—they adopt an externally-based identity. The adolescent accepts earlier roles and parental values wholesale, failing to explore alternatives and failing to forge a unique personal identity. For example, an adolescent realizes that his father is a medical doctor, as are his grandfathers on both sides. Two of his older brothers have chosen medicine, and his sister is in medical school. Such a person may follow a medical career for which he may not be temperamentally suited and for which he really has very little interest. The same scenario repeats itself with many adolescent girls reared by welfare dependent mothers.[39]

The **identity-diffuse** adolescent (role-confusion) may be aware of the crisis, and even some of the options; however, he or she is unable to establish priorities and make a commit-

ment. This person is directionless and aimless, taking the easiest path of the moment—the one that appears to offer the most comfort and the least stress. This individual is easily influenced by pressure from parents, peers, advertising, and charismatic personalities. This person may seek a lifestyle of pleasure or play to avoid commitment to long-range goals.

Both Marcia and Erikson refer to a state of **moratorium**.[7,33] This is a form of "time-out" to explore the potential options before making a commitment to adult responsibilities or even a definitive value system: time out to go to college, time out in the military, time out to travel and explore the world, or time out to "taste" and test options in the world of work. The moratorium is relatively common and can have very positive results. Erikson reports that the adolescent may become absorbed in a previously unknown or unconsidered, but interesting, life-long pursuit as a result of this time out to experiment. On the other hand, some people turn the young adult years into a permanent moratorium, choosing a pleasure or play-oriented lifestyle and continued avoidance of commitment to adult responsibilities and identity.

Identity achievement is Marcia's fourth and most advanced level of identity consolidation. Through identity homework, each crisis is squarely faced and resolved through conscious construction of alternatives, weighing of options, consideration of consequences, and commitment to a goal or value. This affective task is made possible by the cognitive skill of combinatorial reasoning (see Chap. 24).

Identity formation is not mastered once and forever. It is a life-long process in which crises are continually faced and new commitments are made or old ones are solidified. Future development consists of increasing differentiation and refinement.

Societies do two things for the developing person. First, they provide values that have stood the test of time, and, second, they provide social structures and customs that ease the transition from childhood to adulthood. Those who choose the **foreclosure** or **moratorium** paths may find themselves refacing identity issues later in life, after environmental supports for identity homework fall away.

FACTORS AFFECTING THE SEARCH FOR IDENTITY

Parents

The major support of identity homework is the family.[6,55] Belief in the myth that adolescents and their parents are alienated from one another by a "generation gap" has many parents overwhelmed with anxiety as their youngsters approach puberty. However, research provides no real evidence of a generation gap.[57,58] Although adolescent–parent relationships may involve conflict, teenagers still have more common values, attitudes, and beliefs with parents than with their friends.[31] Adolescents agree with their parents on most basic values and seek their parents' advice on important issues. Consulting with friends is generally reserved for superficial "peer culture" issues, such as how to dress, what music to listen to, and so forth. When parents understand the teen's mania for conformity, they are able to accept temporary fads, thus reducing the stress on both sides (Fig. 25-8).[6]

Many parents decide to "let go" when the adolescent begins to push the limits of parental guidelines. Yet "a strong, positive family connection is still vital to the teenager's sense of security and well-being, and giving first priority to spending time with friends doesn't mean he doesn't value his family."[6] The family provides several basic functions throughout adolescence that are never fully replaced by peer groups or any other social structure.[36, 57] First, the family provides a sense of *closeness.* Conditions of intimacy, trust, and support create an emotional bonding that allows the adolescent to safely identify with a basic primary group. Independence and identity are established in concert with parental support, trust, and understanding. The importance of closeness is indicated by adolescents when they cite "just talking" as the activity they most enjoy with parents.[58] **The parent needs to remain available when the adolescent feels the need, and not just when it is convenient for the parent.** To the extent that parents and adolescents communicate, adolescents move closer to an adult view of the world. The parent needs to maintain the synchrony of turntaking and the ability to serve as a refueler developed during the child's infancy and toddler years. However, a balance must be found. Too much closeness is likely to enmesh the adolescent in his or her family, whereas insufficient closeness creates a feeling of separation or lack of caring by parents.

Family and community poverty are often associated with increased problems during the adolescent period (drugs, delinquency, pregnancy, running away, truancy). However, poverty per se is not the problem. True, the poor adolescent has fewer resources available for positive mentors and development of interests and potentials. But many of those who grow up with inner-city poverty become model citizens. The key is the parent–child relationship. "Many young people who do well despite their disadvantages have been more or less sheltered from prolonged competition on the streets . . . The influence of family values even in the absence of material support, the relative security of religious belief and practice, fortunate experiences with teachers and schools— all of these factors are important in shaping the life chances of young achievers . . . It is the adult role models, together with positive values assimilated in childhood, that makes the difference."[55]

A second function served by the family is as a *model of adaptability.* Parents provide adolescents with norms and rationales, information that adolescents will find helpful as they extend their parameters of interaction. The family illustrates how a power structure can change, how roles develop, and how relationship norms are formed. Again, a balance must be struck. Rigid (low-adaptability) families are likely to produce adolescents who internalize a rigid interaction style. Alternately, too much adaptability may produce adolescents who lack focus and purpose and have a chaotic interaction style.

Finally, the family provides essential *communication* functions—a prerequisite for mutual understanding. The adolescent learns valuable skills in the areas of speaking, listening, and negotiation. Parents as well as adolescents can mature as they discuss school issues, career options, world events, family issues, ethical conflicts, financial management, peer conflicts, and personal problems. Such intimate sharing— especially with fathers—is highly correlated with high self-esteem and positive psychosocial development.[28]

Modeling

Parents are a key source of guidance and encouragement. By design or default, parents are continual models of the adult world and adaptation to life. The adolescent, looking for life's verities, and "turned off" by hypocrisy, becomes keenly aware of any discrepancies between what parents "practice" and

FIGURE 25–8.
Adolescents who feel in control of their lives, who are actively contributing to their future, and who have supportive, loving parents are least likely to attempt to escape the trials and responsibilities of life through suicide or drugs.

what they "preach." Parents sensitive to the importance of modeling monitor their own behaviors to reflect values, beliefs, and attitudes they wish their adolescent to adopt.

The role that social learning or modeling plays in the acquisition and elicitation of behaviors is significant and well-documented.[3] The adolescent, vigorously constructing a viable identity, is searching for social information that will facilitate the establishment of that identity. As models, parents are key sources of social information. Thus, identity information that parents model has the potential of being relatively easily integrated into the adolescent's identity. Alternatively, recognizing their limits as models, it is important that parents uphold alternative models and encourage the adolescent to develop relationships with other adults who can model or teach desirable skills.

Mentoring

The relationship of parents toward their adolescents may be characterized as either mentoring or meddling. Careful, understanding, sensitive, and respectful interaction is identified as **mentoring.** Actually, any adult may serve as a mentor. This person provides key assistance and encouragement that enables the adolescent to become increasingly independent in such areas as decision making, time and money management, information gathering, skill development, and independent living skills. Mentoring parents are neither short-sighted in their response to the adolescent's problems, nor do they possess an overly simple, shallow, or narrow view of the adolescent's problems and concerns. The mentor helps the adolescent to identify options and key questions to ask when facing decisions.

The overzealous, protective, or demanding parent can become a meddler and thus interfere with the adolescent's ability to establish a healthy identity. The parent who is dissat-isfied with his or her own self is likely to try to make the child into a surrogate self. Meddling or enmeshed parents push their child to live out their dreams in the classroom, on the athletic field, and so forth. They make decisions for the child, thus denying the adolescent opportunities to weigh options and make choices. Unwittingly, they foster dependency and hostility on the part of their offspring, thus increasing parent–child stress. Children are forced to become socially aggressive to break the parental umbilical cord. Making life too easy by removing the challenges of earning money, living with the consequences of decisions, and absorbing self-care responsibilities merely serves to delay the adolescent's motivation to assume adult responsibilities (Fig. 25-9).

Healthy parents gradually release responsibilities and privileges to the teen to build up the child's ability to manage stress, organize time, and exert self-discipline. They nurture the adolescent's sense of responsibility by setting limits and rules, by expecting increased participation in household management, and by allowing the adolescent to live with the consequences of behavior and decisions. However, recognizing the adolescent's immaturity, impunity, and impulsivity, most parents will judiciously step in to prevent disastrous results.[6]

Dolores Curran notes that healthy parents:[6]

1. relinquish rule-setting and guidelines gradually as the adolescent matures and exhibits the ability to handle increased responsibility for his or her life;

2. provide specific, clear guidelines on sexuality;

3. encourage and respect opinions that differ from their own;

4. reserve criticism for issues of basic values, not superficial differences;

FIGURE 25–9.
Precursors of generativity are fostered by helping adolescents to become involved in group projects that benefit their school or a community group.

5. monitor their children's friends, activities, and influences—offering guidance as necessary;

6. spend individualized time with each child; and

7. help the adolescent to leave home both physically and emotionally.

In this environment, stress is reduced, mentoring is maximized, meddling is minimized, and the adolescent is best prepared to face his or her own adulthood successfully.

Divorce

Although the long-term effects of divorce are not easy to predict, divorce presents the adolescent with stresses that can affect their quest for identity.[57] Contact with both parents is altered. The custodial parent, in the absence of an adult partner, may become exceptionally close to the children, thus interfering with the individuation process. The ever-increasing frequency of blended families presents new challenges to loyalties and belonging. The necessity of maternal employment also changes the family dynamics.

Although divorce cannot be implicated as the single culprit in adolescent maladaptive development, it has been linked to increased risk for delinquency, hostility and acting out behaviors, lower self-esteem, early home-leaving, and poor self-restraint and social adjustment.[11] It is important that society guard against projecting its anxieties about divorce onto the children of divorce. It is the adolescent's own perceptions that are crucial. Research has consistently found that 3 out of 4 adolescents view their parents' divorce as the correct action.[34] Although divorce is almost always traumatic, the effects of a conflict-ridden home can be even more damaging. For the adolescent, the quality or process of family life appears to be more important than the structure of family life.

Although adolescents are less likely than younger children to internalize and feel guilty for the divorce, their healthy adjustment depends on quality support both in and out of the home. Parents are cautioned about disclosing too much intimate information to their adolescent. Although the adolescent appears to be mature in many ways, emotional structures are still too weak to serve as a confidant to the parents. The adolescent is still working too hard on his or her own identity to help the parents clarify or rework their own. Parents, despite their own pain and conflict, need to continue to offer supportive acceptance of the adolescent to help the adolescent emerge from the stresses of divorce with a healthy identity.

Peers

With increasing age, adolescents spend more time with peers and less time with parents. They find peer interactions relaxing and a source of entertainment, as well as a challenge. Because peers usually come from the same social environment—the same neighborhood, similar ethnic and cultural heritage, and the same socioeconomic status—peer groups tend to reflect the values of the parent culture. This tendency to affiliate with friends who share values thus reinforces many values instilled by parents. Although the desire to affiliate with same-gender friends is strong throughout adolescence, the desire to affiliate with opposite-gender friends grows with increasing age (Fig. 25-10).

Value of Peers

The importance of peers can vary significantly from adolescent to adolescent. As mentioned previously, peers influence matters of taste, dress, speech, and leisure activity. When there is a stressful, unsupportive, or chaotic environment at home, the adolescent's peer group may gain prominence over the parents in identity nurturing. The peer group is perhaps best viewed as an auxiliary to the family, a bridge between the dependence of childhood and the independence of adulthood.

One major function of peer groups is to provide a context in which adolescents can learn and test their developing interpersonal and social skills. In the peer setting, adolescents learn what to expect from friends; shape their identities by comparing themselves with peers; experiment with roles and behaviors; practice leadership and conformity skills; gain and give social support to others; learn how to cope with social rejection and failure; resolve interpersonal problems; and learn how to hold themselves and others in esteem. In essence, peer groups serve a major socialization function in the life of the adolescent.

FIGURE 25–10.
Heterosocial relationships enable adolescents to practice the social skills that contribute to comfortable and healthy adult relationships.

Peer Pressure

Throughout life we are assaulted by peer pressures to conform. Conforming behavior may be exhibited to obtain the social praise and recognition of peers. Alternatively, much conforming behavior can be viewed as avoidance behavior. The primary motive directing many an adolescent's behavior is to avoid the rejection and disapproval of their peers. Additionally, some conforming behavior may be viewed as an information-seeking response. When in doubt about what to do in a novel or unfamiliar social situation, look to others and do as they do. Conformity can be a very adaptive response.

Conformity is an essential social phenomena. The issue becomes "whose norms" or "what norms?" When adolescents conform to the expectations of parents and teachers, the cultural status quo is maintained and cultural stability is assured. It is only when peer expectations conflict with those of adults that cries of peer pressure are heard. In areas where social values are changing rapidly and immediate consequences are anticipated, adolescents tend to side with their peers. One important example is the attitude toward sexual activity, which involves the interface of hormonal, peer, media, and cultural pressures. The age of first coitus is gradually decreasing, and the number of sexually active teens is increasing,[46] creating physical, social, medical, emotional, and financial problems unanticipated by the teen immersed in impunity reasoning.

It is important to note that there are different types of conformity. While some conforming behaviors are rather benign in their outcome, others can be labeled as either prosocial or antisocial. The majority of conforming behavior (e.g., clothing and hair styles) does not deserve the label of antisocial.

Society

Schools

Following the family, schools are probably the most influential social institution in the adolescent's life. Schools serve to socialize as well as educate youth. The heterogeneous nature of the school environment provides youth with formal and informal information to evaluate and prioritize.

The high school dropout rate of 20% that society faces today is a problem of crisis proportions. The rate is doubled for some minority and ethnic groups. With our changing technological and information-oriented society, the lack of education puts millions of American youths at a tremendous economic disadvantage. In 1989, Elizabeth Dole, U.S. Labor Secretary, estimated that over half of the jobs available in the year 2000 will require education beyond high school. Currently, few programs have been able to reverse the problem. One step taken by some states is to void the driver's license of anyone under 18 who drops out of school. This law cut the dropout rate by 30% in West Virginia, but it has a limited effect on urban youths who have little opportunity for owning and operating an automobile. Educators are becoming increasingly aware of the importance of involving parents in the educational process (Fig. 25-11). The effects are significant. As parents become involved in their child's education, the child's academic achievement increases.

There seems to be little doubt that one of the key variables on which the education of our youth hinges is the effectiveness of teachers. Good teachers of adolescents recognize and appreciate individuality. Effective teachers engender respect and are positive role models with whom the students can identify. Effective teachers also recognize that adolescents benefit from a variety of learning styles—thinking, watching, doing, or feeling—and engage students in a variety of tasks that let each of them exploit their own learning style strengths.[25, 27] Most communities now offer special programs for adolescent girls who become mothers prematurely. The programs offer classes on child development and care, as well as academic subjects. Both the mother and her child benefit by providing her with more information to face life and improve her employment marketability (Fig. 25-12).

The Urban Superintendents Network has suggested that schools need to foster teamwork with the community. They observe that the absence of legitimate employment serves as the biggest barrier to successful transition of poverty-raised adolescents into adulthood.[55] In many urban communities, private industry is assuming more responsibility for encouraging students to stay in high school by offering mentoring, part-time jobs, and promising employment opportunities on graduation. Other companies offer college tuition benefits for long-term high school employees. Both the adolescent and industry benefit from the arrangement.[12] Because the adolescent is able to get a clearer picture of what he or she *could be,* the student is more likely to strive for better grades and to complete a basic education, laying a firmer foundation for adult life.[56] The companies enjoy a better employee pool. When students believe their efforts will be rewarded, they are willing to exert the effort for a better future.

FIGURE 25–11.
Although adolescents need to assume responsibility for remembering and completing homework, a supportive parent who is available to assist "when the going gets tough" can provide that extra boost while strengthening the parent–teen bond.

FIGURE 25–12.
Pregnancy presents a major crisis to a young woman's life. It is important to attempt to look at all aspects of the situation when making a decision that will permanently affect the lives of all persons involved (the girl, the father, the baby, and the baby's biological grandparents).

The Media

The media, given its central position in our culture, has the potential to significantly impact the development of the adolescent's identity. By the time the average American adolescent graduates from high school, he or she will have spent more time watching television than in the classroom.

On the positive side, television has the potential for enlarging the adolescent's understanding of the world, stimulating creative ideas and new interests, and providing information as well as entertainment. Such positive outcomes have not concerned researchers nearly as much as the potential damaging effects of television. Violence and aggression on television are consistently linked with increases in child and adolescent episodes of violence.[53] Yet 8 of 10 programs contain violence, and prime-time programs average 5 violent acts per hour.[13] Violence becomes an acceptable means of treating people and solving problems. The effects of violence are often trivialized or even ignored. The "good guys" are just as likely to be rewarded for their aggressive acts as the "bad guys" are to be punished. Viewing antisocial scenarios in the media has been shown to be highly associated with antisocial behavior.[17]

Television stars model daring and dangerous lifestyles in action-packed drama. The dangerous and reckless operation

of automobiles is lauded. Quick acceleration, fast braking, squealing tires, and speeding that endangers the lives of the perpetrator as well as the innocent are seldom followed by injury or legal penalty. Rarely is the use of seatbelts depicted, and the stereotypical roles of female as passenger and male as driver are perpetuated.

Relationships are often trivialized and presented as disposable—like too many products marketed in the media. Wealth and glamour are overrepresented. Women typically portray stereotypical roles where they are thin, young, attractive, and primarily concerned with attracting men. Men, however, are often depicted as strong, aggressive, competent, achievement-oriented, and only secondarily concerned about women. An overly simplistic view of relationships is presented, as problems are happily resolved in 60 minutes or less.

The media, through programming and advertising, suggests that the "good life" of beauty, romance, wealth, and alcohol are the standard for evaluating success. Immediate gratification is the order of the day—rather than self-restraint and discipline. It is no wonder that the gap between the adolescent's media-instilled "ideal" world and their "real" world leaves many adolescents dissatisfied and depressed,[55] setting fertile ground for the teenager to contemplate and act on contemporary rock stars' lyrics of suicide.

Not only does the media impact identity formation in an overt way with its unrealistic messages about violence, danger, power, wealth, and immediate self-gratification; but the indirect effects on identity formation are underestimated. For each hour the adolescent passively consumes the media (or the media consumes the adolescent), the adolescent relinquishes one hour he or she could have engaged in an activity stimulating physical, cognitive, or social growth. The concerned parent needs to continue to be informed, to consider the information and issues carefully, and to attempt to provide an environment that will facilitate the positive growth of children.

CONCLUSION

Adolescence is a period of marked intrapersonal and interpersonal changes. One's changing body size and configuration evoke a new set of reactions and expectations from parents, peers, and society. Hormonal fluctuations precipitate new feelings and emotional responses, and may take the adolescent by surprise, giving rise to doubts about normalcy, self-discipline, or social acceptability.

Societal and intrapersonal pressures to individuate from parents is counterbalanced by a recognition of vulnerability. The rights of adulthood are enticing, but the responsibilities may seem oppressive. There is a need to be recognized as a unique individual, yet a fear of being "different." Investing two, four, or more years in one's future conflicts with the desire to "get on with the business of living." Forcing oneself to sit down and study is difficult when there are so many new urges, interests, options, and potentials to explore. Adolescents want to taste and test the world, often coming into conflict with parents, teachers, or societal rules that attempt to curb their impulsivity or remind them of consequences.

Yet, through all this, the adolescent is asking the age-old questions of "Who am I?" and "Where do I fit in this world?" Young people who have learned how to harness and focus energies, who have learned how to exert self-discipline, who have learned how to work and develop talents, and who have experienced a warm, synchronized, respectful relationship with their parents appear to be in the best position to face the pressures of the adolescent years.

Healthy parents gradually provide the adolescent with more responsibility for decision-making, yet continue to set behavioral guidelines that provide direction and social security for the immature adult-in-the-making. Parents assume a role of mentorship, presenting the burgeoning adult with significant questions to answer, viable options to consider, and information to incorporate when making decisions. In this environment, the adolescent begins to identify his or her own values, goals, and priorities, begins to evaluate personal strengths and weaknesses, and begins to acquire the intrapersonal skills essential to individuation from parents and peers. In this climate, the adolescent most easily begins to answer the question, "Who am I?" in a positive, constructive manner.

Obviously, many young people are not offered such support, even in intact families. Thus it becomes difficult to sort out the crucial options and anticipate long-range or unexpected results. Consequently, the young person may settle for a more external, concrete, but immature or negative identity, or may prolong the process of identity homework well beyond the teen or even young adult years.

Entrance into the twenties or even the thirties does not confer an adult socioaffective state. Many persons continue throughout life never having adequately resolved the identity crisis. If one adds alcohol or drugs to the equation, then the young person may feel as if he or she is in the middle of a psycho-social tornado. Life may be eclipsed before it begins.

Self-intimacy, though frequently painful and difficult, is essential to successful negotiation of the identity issue. Each time one faces a problem, conflict, or crisis, a decision must be made—by conscious choice or by default. Those who travel the road of **expediency** choose to respond by default—they do what is easiest under the circumstances or follow along with what others are doing. This person is vulnerable to peer pressure and, often, feelings of recrimination or remorse later. Those who make a conscious choice, think for themselves, look at the options and consequences, consider the long-range effects or the implications on others—look at the values involved and carefully choose the priority value before acting. The decision may alienate peers, but the young person has faced the decision successfully and knows that he or she can live with the consequences. The person maintains control of his or her own emotional and social destiny. Each of these decisions begins to build into personal habits and social reputation. One is comfortable with the self because **integrity** is maintained, identity is solidified, and consequences are manageable. Adolescence is both a practice ground and an exciting launching point for adult life; the possibilities are unlimited.

REFERENCES

1. Aro, H., & Taipale, V. (1987). The impact of timing of puberty on psychosomatic symptoms among fourteen-to sixteen-year-old Finnish girls. *Child Development, 58,* 261–268.
2. Balk, D. (1983). How teenagers cope with sibling death: Some implications for school counselors. *The School Counselor, 31,* 150–158.
3. Bandura, A., & Walters, R. H. (1963). *Social learning and personality development.* New York: Holt, Rinehart and Winston.
4. Benson, P. L., Williams, D. L., & Johnson, A. L. (1987). *The quicksilver years: The hopes and fears of early adolescence.* New York: Harper and Row.
5. Berger, K. S. (1988). *The developing person through the life span* (2nd ed.). New York: Worth Publishers.
6. Curran, D. D. (1985). *Stress and the healthy family.* Minneapolis, MN: Winston Press.
7. Erikson, E. H. (1968). *Identity, youth, and crisis.* New York: Norton.
8. Erikson, E. H., Erikson, J. M., & Kivnick, H. Q. (1986). *Vital involvement in old age.* New York: W. W. Norton.
9. Foster, S. (1988). *The one girl in ten: A self portrait of the teen-age mother.* Washington, DC: Child Welfare League of America.
10. Freud, A. (1968). Adolescence. In A. E. Winder & D. I. Angus (Eds.), *Adolescence: Contemporary studies.* New York: American Books.
11. Fuhrman, B. S. (1986). *Adolescence, adolescents.* Boston: Little, Brown.
12. Galiano, D. A., & Nearine, R. J. (1988). Blight flight: Inner-city students aim for college. *Educational Record, 68(4)/69(1),* 36–41.
13. Gerbner, G., Gross, L., Morgan. M., & Signorielli, N. (1986). Living with television: The dynamics of the cultivation process. In J. Bryant & D. Zillman (Eds.), *Perspectives on media effects.* Hillsdale, NJ: Erlbaum.
14. Goldston, R. (1987). The child's concept of death. In J. E. Schowalter, P. Buschman, P. R. Patterson, A. H. Kutscher, M. Tallmer, & R. G. Stevenson (Eds.), *Children and death: Perspectives from birth through adolescence* (pp. 41–43). New York: Praeger.
15. Gross, F. L., Jr. (1987). *Introducing Erik Erikson: An introduction to his thinking.* Lanham, MD: University Press of America.
16. Hardy, J. B., & Duggan, A. K. (1988). Teenage fathers and the fathers of infants of urban, teenage mothers. *American Journal of Public Health, 78(8),* 919–922.
17. Hearold, S. (1986). A synthesis of 1043 effects of television on social behavior. In G. Comstock (Ed.), *Public communication and behavior* (Vol. 1). Orlando, FL: Academic Press.
18. Hendin, H. (1987). Youth suicide: A psychosocial perspective. *Suicide and Life-Threatening Behavior, 17(2),* 151–165.
19. Hurrelmann, K., & Engel, U. (Eds.). (1989). *The social world of adolescents: International perspectives.* New York: Walter de Gruyter.
20. Ingersoll, G. M. (1989). *Adolescents* (2nd ed.). Englewood Cliffs, NJ: Prentice-Hall.
21. Inoff-Germain, G., Arnold, G. S., Nottelmann, E. D., Susman, E. J., Cutler, G. B., Jr., & Chrousos, G. P. (1988). Relations between hormone levels and observational measures of aggressive be-

havior of young adolescents in family interactions. *Developmental Psychology, 24,* 129–139.

22. Klimek, D., & Anderson, M. (1988). *Inner world, outer world: Understanding the struggles of adolescence.* Washington, DC: Office of Educational Research and Improvement. (ED 290 118)

23. Knowles, R. (1986). *Human development and human possibility: Erikson in the light of Heidegger.* New York: University Press of America.

24. Koenig, M.A., & Zelnik, M. (1982). The risk of premarital first pregnancy among metropolitan-area teenagers: 1976 and 1979. *Family Planning Prospectives, 14,* 239–247.

25. Kolb, D.A. (1984). *Experimental learning: Experiences as the source of learning and development.* Englewood Cliffs, NJ: Prentice-Hall.

26. Langolis, J.H., & Stephan, C.W. (1981). Beauty and the beast: The role of physical attraction in peer relationships and social behavior. In S. S. Brehm, S. M. Kassin, & S. X. Gibbons (Eds.), *Developmental social psychology: Theory and research.* New York: Oxford University Press.

27. Lawrence, G. (1982). *People types and tiger stripes: A practical guide to learning styles* (2nd ed.). Gainesville, FL: Center for Applications of Psychological Types.

28. LeCroy, C. W. (1988). Parent-adolescent intimacy: Impact on adolescent functioning. *Adolescence, 23,* 137–147

29. Lefstein, L. (1986). *A portrait of young adolescents in the 1980's* (ED 294 649). Chapel Hill, NC: Center for Early Adolescence. (Paper presented at the Lilly Endowment Leadership Education Conference, "Building Leadership for Youth: A Shared Vision," Indianapolis, IN: September 30, 1986)

30. Lerner, R. M. (1987). A life-span perspective for early adolescence. In R. M. Lerner & T. T. Foch (Eds.), *Biological-psychosocial interactions in early adolescence: an overview of the issues* (pp. 9–34). Hillsdale, NJ: Erlbaum.

31. Lerner, R. M., Karson, M., Meisels, M., & Knapp, J. R. (1975). Actual and perceived attitudes of late adolescence: The phenomenon of the generation gaps. *Journal of Genetic Psychology, 126,* 197–204.

32. Mahler, M. S., Pine, F., & Bergman, A. (1975). *The psychological birth of the human infant: Symbiosis and individuation.* New York: Basic Books.

33. Marcia, J. (1966). Development and validation of ego identity status. *Journal of Personality and Social Psychology, 3,* 551–558.

34. McLaughlin, D., & Whitfield, R. (1985). Adolescents and their experience of parental divorce. *Journal of Adolescence, 1,* 155–170.

35. Michaels, G. Y. (1988). Motivational factors in pregnancy. In G. Y. Michaels & W. A. Goldberg (Eds.), *The transition to parenthood: Current theory and research.* New York: Cambridge University Press.

36. Olsen, D. H., Russell, C. S., & Sprenkle, D. H. (1980). Marital and family therapy: A decade review. *Journal of Marriage and the Family, 42,* 973–994.

37. Osofsky, J. D., Osofsky, H. J., & Diamond, M. O. (1988). The transition to parenthood: Special tasks and risk factors for adolescent parents. In G. Y. Michaels & W. A. Goldberg (Eds.), *The transition to parenthood; Current theory and research* (pp. 209–232). New York: Cambridge University Press.

38. Rice, F. P. (1990). *The adolescent: Development, relationships, and culture* (6th ed.). Baton Rouge, LA: Allyn and Bacon.

39. Roesel, R. (1987). Poor and at risk for pregnancy. *Educational Horizons, 65,* 118–120.

40. Rutter, M., & Giller, H. (1984). *Juvenile delinquency: Trends and perspectives.* New York: Guilford Press.

41. Savin-Williams, R. C. (1987). *Adolescence: An ethological perspective.* New York: Springer-Verlag.

42. Schiamberg, L. B. (1988). *Child and adolescent development.* New York: Macmillan.

43. Schowalter, J. E. (1987). Adolescents' concepts of death and how these can kill them. In J. E. Schowalter, P. Buschman, P. R. Patterson, A. H. Kutscher, M. Tallmer, & R. G. Stevenson (Eds.), *Children and death: Perspectives from birth through adolescence* (pp. 3–9). New York: Praeger.

44. Silvious, J. (1990). Never quite good enough. *Today's Christian Woman, 12*(5), 53–54.

45. Simmons, R. G., & Blyth, D. A. (1987). *Moving into adolescence: The impact of pubertal change and school context.* New York: Aldine De Gruyter.

46. Smith, E. A. (1989). A biosocial mode of adolescent sexual behavior. In G. R. Adams, R. Montemayor, & T. P. Gullotta (Eds.). *Biology of adolescent behavior and development* (pp. 143–167). Newbury Park, CA: Sage Publications.

47. Susman, E. J., Inoff-Germain, G., Nottelmann, E. D., Loriaux, D. L., Cutler, G. B., & Chrousos, G. P. (1987). Hormones, emotional dispositions and aggressive attributes in young adolescents. *Child Development, 58,* 1114–1134.

48. Tobin-Richards, M. H., Boxer, A. M., & Peterson, A. C. (1983). The psychological significance of pubertal change: Sex differences in perceptions of self during early adolescence. In J. Brooks-Gunn & A. C. Peterson (Eds.), *Girls at puberty* (pp. 123–154). New York: Plenum Press.

49. Trussell, J. (1988). Teenage pregnancy in the United States. *Family Planning Perspectives, 20*(6), 262–272.

50. U. S. Department of Education. (1988). *Youth Indicators 1988: Trends in the well-being of American Youth.* Washington, D.C.: U. S. Government Printing Office.

51. U.S. Department of Justice. (1984). *Crime in the United States.* Washington, DC: Federal Bureau of Investigation.

52. Velez, C. N., & Cohen, P. (1988). Suicidal behavior and ideation in a community sample of children: Maternal and youth reports. *Journal of the Academy of Child and Adolescent Psychiatry, 27,* 349–356.

53. Viemero, V. (1986). *Violence viewing and adolescent aggression: A longitudinal study.* (Paper presented at the International Television Studies Conference, London, April 10–12, 1989. [ED 294 555].)

54. Wass, H., & Stillion, J. M. (1987). Death in the lives of children and adolescents. In H. Wass, F. M. Berardo, & R. A. Neimeyer (Eds.), *Dying: Facing the facts* (2nd ed., pp 201–228). Washington, DC: Hemisphere.

55. Williams, T. M., & Kornblum, W. (1985). *Growing up poor.* Lexington, MA: Lexington Books.

56. Wilson, A. B. (1989). Theory into practice: An effective program for urban youth. *Educational Horizons, 67,* 136–144.

57. Youniss, J. (1988). *Mutuality in parent-adolescent relationships.* Washington, DC: William T. Grant Foundation; Commission on Work, Family, and Citizenship.

58. Youniss, J., & Smollar, J. (1985). *Adolescent relations with mothers, fathers, and friends.* Chicago: University of Chicago Press.

VIII THE EARLY ADULT YEARS

Finally, the young adult years have arrived—the years glorified by the media, the years that have been dreamed of for so long, and have seemed so elusive. Entrance into these years may be gradual or abrupt, partial or complete, for chronological age alone is an insufficient criterion for the definition of adulthood.

There is an element of excitement as the young person prepares to "leave the nest" and launch out to establish a home and life independent of the family of origin. At the same time, inadequate skill and task mastery give rise to insecurities and renewed awareness of one's vulnerability to the exigencies of life. Continued warm emotional support and mentoring from parents and other adults facilitates adjustment and engenders feelings of trust in the environment and one's own abilities to face life as an adult successfully.

The cumulative effect of previous experiences play themselves out as the young person assumes full custodianship for his or her life. The individual begins to consciously control and integrate the five domains in the search for an optimal lifestyle and expression of one's uniqueness. Crucial decisions are made during these years—marriage, career, children, religion, financial investments, and social affiliations—that will impact the quality of life for the rest of the adult years. The challenges of the developmental years have helped to prepare one to face the responsibilities of full adulthood. However, premature assumption of adult responsibilities can thwart reaching one's goals. On the other hand, perpetual postponement of assuming full responsibilities can prevent optimization of one's potentials.

As the person assumes the mantle of adulthood, he or she begins to realize that the presumed rights and privileges which were associated with these years include responsibility and self-discipline. An idealized concept of adulthood is gradually replaced by the responsibilities inherent in the more complex relationships of one's chosen family and community bonds. The challenges of life foster continued identity homework and refinement of one's goals and value system. The person begins to find satisfaction and happiness in reaching out to and meeting the needs of others rather than focusing purely on one's own pleasure of the moment.

The young adult years are indeed rich, meaningful, and rewarding, but in ways unseen or undreamed of by the adolescent.

Developmental Tasks of Early Adulthood

*1. Achieve independence from, or establish contributory interdependence with family of origin:
>   finances
>   residence
>   health maintance of all five domains

*2. Identify the basis of own personal worth:
>   solidify personal identity
>   separate identity from career, affiliations, or financial status
>   resolve integrity versus expediency issues

*3. Develop ability to share inner self with others to increase understanding and cooperation (emotional intimacy):
>   values/philosophies
>   goals/needs
>   concerns/fears
>   refine negotiation skills

*4. Find something higher than self to live for:
>   solidify value system and concept of God
>   identify a life goal or dream
>   integrate own concept of death and eternity into a philosophy of life
>   sacrifice immediate goals in light of life goals
>   assist other people as able and as opportunities arise
>   affiliate with organizations or groups holding similar value systems
>   commit one's self to the welfare of one or more persons (usually toward family of creation)

5. Develop satisfying social relationships
>   develop an awareness of the solitariness of life
>   seek affiliation with all age groups
>   differentiate between love and friendship
>   differentiate between affective and erotic intimacy
>   develop a close friendship with 1 or 2 other people
>   decide on issues of marriage and child-bearing
>   forge new relationship to families of origin and creation

6. Balance expression of personal needs and interests with the expectations and opportunities of the culture
>   find productive and refreshing leisure time activities
>   identify career options that allow expression of uniqueness and inner self
>   weigh personal rights against communal responsibilities
>   create opportunities for expression of uniqueness

7. Assume responsibility for independent decision making
>   realistically evaluate and accept own limitations
>   seek assistance as necessary
>   identify and explore multiple options and potential outcomes
>   maintain openness to opinions and values of others
>   modify personal convictions as new insights occur
>   make decisions based on personal convictions and not on peer opinion or social pressures
>   put decisions into long-range context
>   assume responsibility for outcome of decisions

8. Develop expertise in career (includes parenting)
>   seek appropriate education
>   entertain alternative approaches
>   take pride in process as well as product
>   seek career mentor
>   evaluate and redirect career progress as necessary

---

*Tasks deemed most crucial to continued maturation are marked with an asterisk.

26

The secret is not to live less intensely, but more intelligently.

—HANS SELYE
THE STRESS OF LIFE

Biophysical Development During Early Adulthood

Shirley S. Ashburn

Each system of the body matures at a different rate; the systems do not all "peak" during childhood. Nonetheless, by young adulthood, the organs have all achieved maturity, and, consequently, these years are considered to be a period of optimal biophysical functioning. Most Olympic or professional athletes who compete in sports events demanding extreme strength, speed, or agility are in this age group. Gradual biophysical changes continue to occur during the twenties and thirties. Since the capacity of human organs is much greater than needed for routine daily activities, it takes time to notice these changes. However, 20 years later, as people exit this stage, they begin to become aware of changes in biophysical functioning.

Both attaining and maintaining high-level functioning during this period of life depend on understanding the body's unique needs and on consistently providing appropriate care to meet those needs. Paradoxically, it is during these early adult years that psychosocial pressures and cognitive challenges tempt one to misuse and abuse the body. Adult students may spend night after night studying or socializing, thereby denying themselves the sleep they need to function "at their best." Young mothers or fathers who are also students may skip meals and appropriate exercise to finish housework or schoolwork while their children nap. Young adults, whether struggling to "just survive and make ends meet," or pushing toward "success," often declare, "I'm too young to worry about overdoing it," as an attempt to justify their actions. Yet, the lifestyle the young adult chooses to live now will affect the quality of life during both middlescence and late adulthood.

SOMATIC DEVELOPMENT

Physical appearance is influenced by genetic endowment, interaction with the environment, and one's health maintenance practices.

Skeletal System

Women usually attain their full height before they enter their twenties. Men continue in grow in height for a longer period, a fact which accounts for much of the height differences between genders. They attain full adult height in the early twenties. The vertebral column may continue to grow in some individuals until the thirties, adding another 3 to 5 mm to their height.[28,63] The legs are approximately one half of the adult's height.[34] Breadth proportions (e.g., hips and shoulders) may continue to mature into the mid-twenties. Another few millimeters may be added to the width of the head, facial diameter, hands, and legs by surface deposition of bone.[28] Peak bone mass is reached in both genders at approximately 35 years; the rate of bone mass loss after that is statistically greater and faster in women than in men (see the discussion of osteoporosis in Chap. 35).[59] Although skeletal growth ceases, bone retains the ability to replace itself, an ability that is essential to the healing of fractures.[66] Sudden, hard impact, repetitive neuro-muscular activities, or the incorrect performance of an unfamiliar task can precipitate musculoskeletal injury. Professional athletes are prone to injuries due to excessive use.[55]

Muscular System

Muscle mass is influenced by genetic factors, insulin level, nutrition, growth hormones, testosterone, and exercise.[23, 50] Testosterone, present in both males and females, not only increases muscle mass, but also bone density (mass). Consequently, since males have more testosterone than females, gender differences in muscle mass are significant.

Muscles increase in length as long as the skeleton elongates. However, the muscle fibers increase in size, not number. A muscle will increase in diameter and mass, depending on the intensity of activity to which it is subjected. This is why the person who begins to exercise regularly may initially gain weight. If the person is trying to lose weight, the weight loss will eventually occur as the fat is metabolized.

The peak of muscular strength occurs around 25 to 30 years, and then gradually declines approximately 10% between ages 30 and 60.[18] Most of this decrease occurs in the muscles of the back and legs, with less occurring in the arms. Some professional athletes continue their careers into their thirties, but athletes whose performance involves speed and agility begin to realize that they are "past their prime." However, since the potential for endurance peaks during the thirties, athletes over 30 excel in such events as long-distance running, walking, and weight-lifting (Fig. 26-1).[58] Manual dexterity peaks in the twenties and starts to decline in the middle thirties.[28]

During the early adult years, most injured muscles will repair themselves if they receive appropriate rest and immobilization. Healed muscles need progressive exercise to resume their pre-injury functional state.[7]

Low Back Pain During Early Adulthood
Back problems rank second only to the common cold as the most prevalent cause of sick leave in the United States.[64] The majority of backaches during young adulthood and early middlescence stem from preventable muscular and ligament problems. The pain usually originates in the lumbar region, because that area contains the largest skeletal curve and supports the most weight compared to other parts of the spine. This low back pain is usually alleviated with improvements in posture, exercise, weight control, and attention to body mechanics (Fig. 26-2).

Body Composition
Body mass consists of two types of tissue: lean (muscle, bone, and organs) and fat (adipose tissue). Relative percentages of lean and adipose tissue that comprise body mass give a measure of body composition. During early adulthood, the **per-**

FIGURE 26–1.
Musculoskeletal strength and endurance are at their peak during the early adult years. Optimal functioning is dependent on conditioning and exercise.

centage of body weight that is muscle decreases in the average individual, reflecting not a loss of muscle, but rather an increase in fat weight.[28] Most authorities recommend a maximum body fat of 15% to 18% of total weight for men, and 20% to 25% for women.[3, 55] Women tend to have fat deposits over the shoulders, breasts, buttocks, and thighs; men tend to have fat more evenly distributed throughout the body.[36] Body composition is directly related to physical fitness and high-level wellness. Overweight people experience more difficulty with physical work and take longer to recover from illness.[28] Excess weight adds to a person's workload and limits range of motion. Obesity places an individual at risk of suffering coronary heart and artery disease, cerebrovascular accident

FIGURE 26–2.
Proper equipment and body mechanics are essential for prevention of back pain and injury.

(stroke), and hypertension (high blood pressure.) Even mild to moderate obesity leads to increased risk of coronary disease.[37] Excessive adipose tissue around the waist or abdomen places the individual at higher risk than fat on the thighs, buttocks, and limbs.[55]

Since physical appearance and activity are valued in the United States, body composition influences feelings about oneself. When one cannot participate in group activities, or if appearance violates cultural biases, excessive adipose tissue can affect negatively one's body image and self-concept, as well as social relationships.

Body Measurements

Obesity is generally judged by comparing one's actual weight to a desirable weight on a chart prepared by the Metropolitan Life Insurance Company (see Appendix F). "Desirable weight" is based on the weights with the lowest mortality for a given height. To use this chart effectively, one must determine frame size. A relatively reliable guide to frame size is evaluation of elbow breadth. The National Institute of Health views the body mass index (BMI) as the most valid way to determine ideal weight because it compares weight with body fat.[60] The BMI does not tell a person how much he or she should weigh; it allows the individual to choose the weight at which he or she feels best.

Neurological System

Cell Development

Although the brain reaches physical maturity before 20 years of age, final myelinization and differentiation of the central nervous system occurs at about 25 years of age.[66] The weight of the brain declines about 1 g per year beginning at 30 years, but the size or weight of the brain is no indication of intelligence or wisdom.[61] Neurologists believe that humans use a very small amount of their available brain cells. The relative weight of the adult's central nervous system is one fiftieth of total body weight.[34]

The brain has the highest energy metabolism of all body organs, a fact reflected in its blood supply and oxygen use. The adult brain requires 20% of the oxygen and receives 30% of the heart's output of blood when the body is at rest.[34] The brain depends on glucose as its primary source of energy, but in fasting conditions it can metabolize ketones. Although brain cells do not replace themselves if they die, there is a constant turnover of the amino acids of the brain, resulting in replacement of half of the brain's total protein every 6 weeks.[19] The brain's metabolic rate is relatively constant over each 24-hour period.

Although some researchers have attempted to find gender differences, there is little justification for use of the terms "male brain" or "female brain" in humans, beyond the fact that the brain is physically housed in either a male or a female body.[59]

During early adulthood, as in any other stage of the life span, there is little or no regenerative potential for the cells of the central nervous system.[52] A damaged brain cannot be completely restored. When the peripheral nervous system has been damaged, regardless of age, potential for nerve cell repair exists only as long as the nerve cells are still viable.[52] However, rehabilitive therapy programs can often develop alternate pathways to accomplish the same goal.

Sensory Organ Development

Because the lens of the eye continues to grow without shedding older cells, it gradually becomes thicker, less elastic, and more opaque.[68] This aging affects lens accommodation sufficiently that by 40 years of age the person may notice some difficulty reading small print. Many say that the words are blurred until they blink their eyes several times in an attempt to focus.

Hearing acuity usually peaks around age 20, and thereafter gradually declines. The high tones are often lost first, followed by the lower ones.[68] In most cases, the inaudible sounds have little significance to the activities of daily living. Many factors, such as nutrition, environment, and heredity, affect how much and how fast hearing is lost. Excessive noise levels (such as loud music, noisy work places) can accelerate progression of hearing loss (Fig. 26-3).

The senses of taste, smell, touch, and awareness of temperature and pain remain keen until middlescence.

FIGURE 26–3.
Protection of hearing is essential in high-sound occupations or environments (note ear protectors).

Pain

Pain is the most common and compelling reason for seeking health care.[7] Its presence impacts upon all domains of human experience (see Chap. 5 for discussion of pain perception). Since pain is an individualized, subjective experience, an operational definition must be used. *Pain* is whatever an individual perceives as physical discomfort in response to a stimulus. Perception is influenced by past experiences, attitudes, and culture, as well as by the nature of the stimulus.[7, 40] Pain can be described by its duration (continuous or intermittent), its intensity (severe or mild), the nature of its feeling (dull or sharp), and its location (specific to one body area or generalized). The phenomenon of pain has four components: (1) reception of the pain stimulus by pain receptors, (2) conduction of the pain stimulus to the brain by the nerves, (3) perception of the pain in the higher centers of the brain, and (4) interpretation and reaction to the pain (physical and psychosocial processes).

All pain is real, regardless of its cause—even if the cause is unknown. "Pure" psychogenic pain (caused by emotional events) is probably rare; "pure" organic pain (caused by physical stimuli) is, in all likelihood, also rare. Most pain perception is a combination of both. An individual's attitude toward the self as well as the origin of the pain-producing stimulus affects the intensity of discomfort. For example, a woman who sees the birth process as a healthy, normal experience, prepares for it, and looks forward to it, generally perceives less discomfort than a woman whose culture steeps childbearing in taboos and secretive fears.

The physical reaction to pain can be divided into autonomic or skeletal muscle reactions. Autonomic reactions include increased blood pressure and heart rate, which serve to increase blood flow to the brain and muscles; rapid, irregular respirations, which increase the oxygen supply to the brain and muscles; dilation of the pupils, which allows for an increased amount of light entering the eye; and increased perspiration, which carries away body heat produced by the increased metabolism.[56] Skeletal muscle response involves an increase in muscle tension, which prepares the body for neuromuscular and skeletal movement. These physiological responses prepare the body to "fight or flee" the painful stimulus (see discussion of stress in Chaps. 35 and 36).

Pain specialists categorize pain as either acute or chronic. The difference between the two has implications for both assessment and intervention. *Acute pain,* often a common, daily occurrence, is defined as an episode that lasts from a split second to about 6 months.[41, 49] It warns the person that the body has experienced or is in danger of experiencing damage to body cells. Anxiety is often associated with acute pain.[26] *Chronic pain* is defined as pain that lasts for 6 months or longer, although this time frame is arbitrary.[41, 49] Chronic pain may be associated with some diseases such as arthritis, but often has no known cause. When it persists, pain becomes a major disorder in and of itself. Depression often accompanies chronic pain.[35]

The discovery of endorphins has done much to add to the understanding of how the mind and body work together to produce natural analgesia.[21, 73] The term *endorphin* is a combination of two words: *endogenous* and *morphine*. Endorphins are compounds with opiate-like properties that include the potential to alter pain perception and mood.[77] Located in the synapses (places where nerve impulses are transmitted from one nerve cell to another), endorphins are thought to inhibit pain perception by blocking transmission of pain impulses in the brain and spinal cord.[7]

Some people have higher endorphin levels than others. The release of endorphins can be encouraged by exercise, physical stimuli (such as electrical nerve stimulation, pressure at acupuncture points, or massage), and by specific relaxation techniques.[77] Psychological mechanisms, such as giving the individual anxiety-reducing information ("this ice pack should make the swelling go down") and distraction (using guided imagery to focus on pleasant thoughts), also are believed to induce the flow of endorphins.

Cardiovascular System

By the time a person enters early adulthood, the cardiovascular system has established adult size and rhythm. The optimal efficiency of cardiac output (the amount of blood the heart pumps per minute) should continue throughout young adulthood.[18] Blood pressure is stabilized by the early adult years (see Appendix E).

By the third decade of life, selected areas of arteries have begun to thicken. Fat accumulates on these thickened areas, and forms soft fatty streaks.[55] These streaks (plaques) are thought to be precursors of *atherosclerosis,* an abnormal accumulation of lipids (fats), minerals, and fibrous tissues in blood vessel walls that narrows their lumen (internal diameter) and thus reduces blood flow.[7] Coronary atherosclerosis involves the blood flow that nourishes the heart and is the most common cause of heart disorders in the United States. Atherosclerosis is a form of *arteriosclerosis,* which means "hardening of the arteries."

This early plaque formation is largely preventable and reversible through lifestyle changes.[55] Major controllable factors that place the person at risk for atherosclerosis and cardiovascular disease include high cholesterol level, high salt intake, alcohol consumption, high blood pressure, high level of stress, inadequate exercise, smoking (effects of nicotine and tar), and obesity.

Respiratory System

A man's lung function reaches its peak at about 25 years; a woman's peak is at about 20 years.[32] Although many organs of the body thrive on work and increase their functioning mass (hypertrophy) when challenged by a long-term work load, the lungs' capacity to do so is limited. The body's ability to use oxygen optimally is more dependent on the efficiency of the cardiovascular system and the functioning of the oxygen uptake of the skeletal muscles (especially those of the chest, back, and neck) than on the size of the lungs.[7, 35, 46] With proper conditioning, the oxygen uptake is sufficient to meet young adult body needs, even during a rigorous game of racquetball (Fig. 26-4).

A gradual loss of alveoli elasticity begins during the thirties. This loss eventually contributes to a decrease in vital capacity (volume of air that can be expelled following a full inspiration).[70] Aerobic exercise augments vital capacity.[12] Vital capacity will diminish at a faster rate if the person is a cigarette smoker. Young adults tend to get fewer respiratory infections than they did during childhood, and nonsmokers tend to experience fewer respiratory infections than smokers.

Since oxygen concentration in the air is lower in high-altitude environments, mobile, active young adults who are attracted to skiing, hang-gliding, piloting, or mountain climbing may initially feel short-of-breath or fatigued when attempting strenuous physical activity. The natives of high-altitude climates possess slightly larger lungs than do those who reside closer to

FIGURE 26–4.
Improved health status and social climate enable many women today to pursue activities and careers once exclusively reserved for men.

sea level. The lungs of these natives also have an increased oxygen-diffusing capacity compared with those of their sea-level visitors.[12]

Integumentary System

After adolescence, the skin begins to lose moisture, gradually becoming more dry and wrinkled with age. Women begin to notice "smile lines" in their late twenties; they gain lines at the outer corners of their eyes ("crow's feet") in their thirties. Because men have more body oil (in the sebaceous glands) than women, their skin is slower to dry and wrinkle. Shaving seems to have a rejuvenating effect on the thicker skin of the male by removing dead skin cells.[50] Consequently, a man may not notice wrinkles until his thirties, usually starting on the forehead. "Smile lines" in men also occur during their thirties.

Many factors—heredity, climate, cigarette smoking, sun exposure, hormonal balance, and general health—affect how quickly skin ages.[2, 59] Women whose mothers had soft skin with limited wrinkling can anticipate the same. A dry climate and increased sun exposure can make skin leathery and wrinkled, causing a person to look older than the chronological age. Women who smoke often have very pronounced wrinkling at an early age; the reason for this is unknown, but it is believed to be related to the fact that smoking lowers estrogen levels.[31] All of the moisturizers and creams, even those containing estrogen, cannot reverse the aging process. Oils, moisturizers, liposomes, and emollients may soften and smooth, but they do not actually feed the skin. All of the skin's nourishment comes from the tiny blood vessels in the dermis (the "true" skin underlying the external layer of skin that is visible). Diet plays an important role in maintaining healthy skin. Deficiencies in water and vitamins A, B, and C result in dry, rough skin.

Acne

While severe acne cases can occur during adolescence and then "clear up" in the early twenties, many men and women are plagued by this skin disorder during early adulthood. Some of these people may never have had a pimple as a teenager. Others are troubled with acne most of their lives. Many women combat eruptions of premenstrual acne. The use of cosmetics containing fatty acids (e.g., isopropyl myristate, isopropyl isostearate, sodium lauryl sulfate, butyl stearate) may aggravate the condition for women who have had acne since adolescence or who have bouts of premenstrual acne.[24, 59] Some women develop *acne cosmetica* from contaminated or old cosmetics.

Another type of skin disorder, *acne rosacea,* ("brandy face" or "brandy nose") is a chronic dermatosis characterized by dilation of cutaneous blood vessels, especially of the nose. This condition most commonly begins in oily-skinned, fair-complexioned persons during their thirties.[33] Although women are affected 3 times more frequently than men, males may develop a more severe form of this acne.[2] Alcohol consumption exacerbates the problem by increasing vasodilation.

Skin and Sun

The sun affects the appearance of the skin, including freckles. Freckles are an inherited, normal alteration in pigmentation that is accentuated by sun exposure. There are advantages and disadvantages to sun exposure.

THE SUN: A HARMFUL FORCE. Sunlight is potentially dangerous. Premature aging of the skin, sunburn, and skin cancer are directly related to the length of time in the sun, intensity of the sunlight, the natural protection of the individual, and the adequacy of sun-protection factors.[62] The sun releases ultraviolet rays (UVR), which are believed to stimulate release of free radicals (highly reactive atoms) in the skin. These free radicals damage DNA. If the body is unable to repair DNA, mutations develop and cancer may result. Any substance that produces free radicals in the body is considered to be potentially carcinogenic.[62] Presently, persons in their twenties are among the groups with the fastest growing number of new skin cancer cases.[60]

Tanning beds and booths make use of ultraviolet rays. These UVRs tan the skin at a very slow pace, but this does not make them safer. On the contrary, a person must spend a longer period of time in these booths to tan, which can lead to excessive wrinkling and cancer. Many prescription drugs (e.g., tetracycline, bactrim) interact with UVR to further increase their negative effects. A pregnant woman should not use these booths—she may be potentially harming herself as well as the baby she is carrying.

When skin is exposed to the sun, its top layer produces a protective pigment called melanin (which darkens the natural skin color, "tan") (Fig. 26-5). Those individuals who are "fair" in complexion or those who stay out too long in the sun cannot produce melanin fast enough. Dilated blood vessels in the dermis cause increased blood flow to the area resulting in redness and swelling. Individuals often forget to protect their eyes, lips, and hair from sunlight. Lips lack the protective melanin layer of other skin surfaces, so they burn easily and are especially prone to skin cancer. The skin around the eyes is especially sensitive to sunlight and prone to excessive wrinkling.

THE SUN: A HEALING POWER. In moderation, sunlight has some beneficial effects. Sun exposure assists many mild cases of acne because when the surface layer peels off, it carries away blackheads and potential comedones. Severe cases of acne, however, are aggravated by sun exposure.[2] Natural sunlight absorbed through the skin helps the body use vitamin D to keep bones strong and healthy.[62] Sunlight appears to influence the excretion of a hormone in the brain, melatonin, that elevates one's moods and improves emotional stability.[60]

Hair

Many people are concerned about the hair on the head—too much for some people, not enough for others. Color, texture, thickness, and curliness are topics of discussion and targets for change. Hair, like nails, is composed of dead cells. Each hair is produced by a hair bulb encapsulated in a hair follicle located under the skin. The hair bulb produces hair cells, pushing them toward the surface to form a single strand of hair. Each

FIGURE 26–5.
Dark-skinned persons are just as vulnerable to the effects of ultraviolet rays as are light-skinned persons.

bulb remains active for about 4 to 6 years, producing scalp hairs of about 3 feet in length, although hair length up to 10 feet has been documented.[54] When the hair bulb dies or goes into a resting phase, a new one is formed underneath and replicates the process, starting a new strand of hair.[54] Although hair is inert, each follicle depends on an adequate blood and oxygen supply for nourishment and production of healthy hair. Heredity, more than any other factor, affects thickness, length, curliness, and abundance of hair. Nutrition, health status, and care will affect the health and beauty of the hair.

Each strand of hair has three layers: the cuticle (outside), the medulla (center), and the cortex (between the cuticle and medulla).[54] The cuticle cells, layered like shingles on a roof, protect and, if intact, preserve moisture. They are composed of keratin, a strong protein. When the layers lie flat, they reflect light and give the hair a shiny appearance; if the layers are damaged, the hair will look dry and dull. Since hair is 65% to 95% protein, it is very sensitive to dietary inadequacies.[54] Hair begins to deteriorate as early as the second or third day of a strict reducing diet.[60] Too much sun, too much heat, or overprocessing with chemicals will also damage hair.

Hair gets its color from melanocytes—cells that deposit their pigment in the hair cortex. The actual color depends on the size, number, and kind of melanocytes and on the presence or absence of air bubbles in the hair cortex.[59] White hair is caused by the progressive reduction in pigment production. When white hairs mix with partially pigmented and fully colored hairs, that particular section of hair appears gray. Actual gray hairs are rare, but exist when bubbles occur in partially pigmented hair that originally contained black-brown pigment.[31, 59] The onset of loss of hair pigment is determined genetically and may begin to occur before early adulthood. Graying of hair, as a process, is irreversible; no diet or medication can change what has already occurred. Malnutrition can cause changes in the hair, including temporary loss of pigmentation. Stress, as an entity in itself, has not been proven as a factor that accelerates graying.[31, 59]

Some thinning of the hair of the head in both genders is normal during early adulthood because there is a progressive increase in the number of follicles that are in a resting phase as one grows older. Fifty to 100 strands of scalp hair are normally lost each day.[31, 50, 59] However, excessive hair loss does not usually occur during early adulthood. Although hair grows faster in length between the ages of 16 and 46, there is a gradual decrease in hair density, especially at the temples.[59] Baldness is approximately 6 times more prevalent in men than in women. Excessive hair loss is rarely caused by disease; usually it is caused by an X-linked genetic factor. Male-pattern baldness, the most prevalent form of baldness, may start on the back of the head or as a receding hairline. As hair loss continues, the separate balding areas may meet.[50, 59] Baldness can begin in males anytime after puberty. It is ironic and still remains a mystery that androgen, responsible for hair growth, is also responsible for hair loss when the genetic

predisposition is present.[50, 76] Minoxidil, a topical solution has stimulated hair growth in some men, but is not a cure for baldness.[50]

Healing

Most tissues of the body can repair themselves through regeneration of body cells. Different types of cells possess varying abilities for regeneration. Those cells that multiply and continually replace themselves usually regenerate without difficulty following injury. Such cells, called *labile cells,* include those found in the respiratory and gastrointestinal tracts as well as those in bone marrow and parts of the reproductive system. Cells that regenerate only after injury—*stable cells*—are found in the liver, kidneys, pancreas, and endocrine glands.

Some cells do not regenerate at all; they are called *permanent cells.* Neurons in the central nervous system and myocardial cells of the heart are examples. Once these tissues are damaged, only scar tissue develops. The original cells are dead; the scar tissue is nonfunctional; thus the organ of which these dead cells were a part operates less efficiently.[35]

Fortunately, many of the physical injuries resulting from accidents leave little or no residual impairment in the activities of daily living. The healing of a simple skin wound can be divided into three phases, although the complexity of the healing process depends, of course, on the severity of the wound.[35]

The first phase of the process, **traumatic inflammation,** is characterized by the sealing together of the wound edges (or traumatized area) by a fibrous clot. This seal is formed by the interaction of fibrinogen, a component of the hemorrhaging blood, with other body proteins; these two elements dry to form a seal that prevents fluid loss and bacterial invasion. The capillaries (small blood vessels) along the edge of the wound dilate, causing redness and swelling. At the same time that this process is occurring, the second phase of healing is under way.

During this **destructive phase,** white blood cells (leukocytes and macrophages) come to the scene and ingest dead and dying tissue. These first two phases together take 4 to 6 days. The third phase is concerned with replacing and restoring the injured tissue; it is aptly called the **proliferation phase.** The existing capillaries sprout new offshoots, and collagen is laid down by fibroblasts to reinforce and to strengthen the bond between the wound edges. This whole process takes about 14 days.

Healing can be further categorized by first, second, or third intention. **First intention healing** refers to the simple closure of an uncomplicated wound (or one in which little tissue destruction has occurred). Healing by **second intention** takes longer and is necessary when the wound is complicated by infection or size. (Infection interrupts the simpler healing mechanisms.) Large or deep wounds require the body to produce granulation (scar) tissue to close the gap; healing is complete when new skin grows over the granulations. Often, if a wound is large, sutures (stitches) or skin grafting will be used to aid the healing process (healing by **third intention**). In addition to infection, conditions such as inadequate nutrition, body overactivity, poor circulation, and systemic diseases, such as diabetes, can delay or inhibit the healing process.[7]

Hematological System

Blood consists of erythrocytes (red cells), leukocytes (white cells), thrombocytes (platelets), clotting factors, water, oxygen, carbon dioxide, electrolytes, vitamins, minerals, sugar, proteins, fats, cholesterol, hormones, antibodies, and other chemical substances, as well as waste products. The quality and quantity of blood contribute directly to the person's level of wellness.

Acid–Base Balance

Imbalance of blood pH results in disruption of healthy cellular function throughout the body. There are three regulators that work interdependently to maintain acid-base balance: a chemical buffering mechanism, the lungs, and the kidneys. The buffer mechanism neutralizes strong acids and bases in body fluids; the lungs regulate acid excretion or retention by hyper- or hypoventilation; and the kidneys excrete acid or alkaline urine as needed to restore equilibrium.[38]

Blood Volume

The total blood volume in a young adult is 70 to 85 mL per kg of body weight.[34] After age 30, the blood volume comprises 7.5% and 6.5% of body weight, respectively, for men and women.[23] Adipose tissue has a poorer blood supply than muscle or body organs, so relative blood volume will vary inversely with the amount of body fat.

Bone Marrow

Hematopoiesis (the formation of blood cells) is the primary function of bone marrow. Bone marrow is contained inside all bones of the body. Although there are two kinds of bone marrow in adults (red and yellow), only red marrow makes blood cells. By 25 years of age, adult red bone marrow distribution is attained in the pelvic bones, sternum (breast-bone), ribs, cranium (skull), ends of long bones, and vertebrae (back-bone).[33] Yellow bone marrow is red marrow that has changed to fat.

Immunological System

Early adulthood is potentially the healthiest portion of the life span. Many young adults have become desensitized to childhood allergies, with the exceptions of asthma and "hay fever." By age 20, people have developed immunity to many of the infectious agents causing illness in children. When a person's immunizations are up-to-date, and stress is within workable boundaries, the young adult's body mechanisms for defense and restoration are impressive.

Lymphatic System

The lymphatic system plays a key role in the body's defense against microorganisms. Tiny lymphatic capillaries collect microorganisms found in body tissues and carry them by way of lymphatic fluid to the lymph nodes, where lymphocytes and macrophages remove bacteria and other foreign substances. Filtered lymph fluid is then emptied into the venous system for disposal or recirculation.[8]

The Spleen

The largest lymphatic organ is the spleen. Located in the left upper abdomen, it filters and stores blood, traps foreign particles, and destroys bacteria and viruses. The spleen operates optimally during early adulthood. If the individual's spleen is injured (e.g., from trauma) to the point that it must be removed surgically, the person is at increased risk of having pneumococcal infections. To counteract this organism, the person should receive pneumococcal vaccine.[7]

Gastrointestinal System

Although the production of some digestive juices decreases after 30 years of age, healthy young adults do not experience significant changes in their pattern of digestion or elimination.[7,55] The rate at which food travels through the gastrointestinal tract is still influenced by factors such as the nature of the food (e.g., high fiber content travels faster than saturated fat) and the state of physical health. The previously established habits of elimination should persist (i.e., frequency, consistency, and color of bowel movements). Most stools are brown owing to bile pigmentation. Various foods and medications affect stool color. Stools that are externally coated with bright red blood might be a symptom of hemorrhoids, especially in pregnant females, and should be checked by a physician. Emotional stress can lead to ulcers or colitis.

Dentition: The Third Decade

The appearance of "wisdom teeth," or third molars, is another change in the alimentary canal. These molars normally erupt between 19 and 21 years. Their roots mature anywhere between 18 and 25 years.[34] There are normally 4 third molars, although some individuals may not fully develop all four. These teeth frequently create problems. It is not unusual for wisdom teeth to come in sideways, or facing any direction. They also can force the other teeth out of alignment, making chewing difficult and painful. Dental assistance may be necessary to facilitate eruption. Often, the third molars must be removed because of gum swelling, local infection, and pain, or to provide proper occlusion of the jaws.

Dentition: The Fourth Decade

Toward the end of early adulthood, many persons notice a slight change in the color of their natural teeth. This is due to thinning of tooth enamel, inefficient dental hygiene, and the person's choice of food and drink (coffee and tea drinkers as well as smokers will have darker-colored teeth).[60] As teeth or old fillings start to crack or break off, the person may choose to have a new filling or a porcelain cap (crown) inserted. Others prefer a bridge or partial dental plate to replace the tooth or teeth.

Flossing is essential to prevent caries from occurring on the adjacent surfaces of teeth. The soft tissues of the mouth (especially the gums) become inflamed, swollen, and tend to bleed in the presence of high concentrations of bacterial plaque. This infection is called *gingivitis*. Effective flossing and brushing help to remove the plaque (which can harden into tartar, which encourages more plaque formation) and reduces places for residual bacteria to multiply (thus helping to prevent gum tissue infections).[11] Regular cleaning of teeth by a dentist or dental hygienist is essential to remove the built-up tartar which regular brushing cannot remove and to prevent premature yellowing of the teeth. Pregnant women may experience swollen gums that bleed easily ("pregnancy gingivitis") because of hormone changes. This condition may be improved by taking vitamin C (amount prescribed by a doctor) and should disappear spontaneously after delivery.[59] Gingivitis, untreated, can lead to *peridontitis,* an infection of the gums, bone, and supporting tissues of the teeth.

Urinary System

Renal Functioning
The kidneys play a dominant role in maintaining physiological homeostasis. They aid in excreting metabolic waste products and in regulating the water content, salts, and acid–base balance of the body.

Fluid and Electrolyte Regulation
The regulation of fluids and electrolytes is a good example of how the body strives to maintain equilibrium or homeostasis. The ability to maintain stability of body fluids is greatest during early adulthood, and is least stable at both ends of the human life span.[38] Water is essential for nutrient digestion and distribution, waste disposal, body cooling, joint and membrane lubrication, and fighting disease. Blood is made primarily of water, as are cells, muscles, and most body parts. The total amount of body water in healthy, young adults is 60% of body weight (i.e., approximately 40 liters in a 70-kg person). The young adult brain is 74% water.[60] Water is distributed in a ratio of one-third extracellular to two-thirds intracellular.[70] Regulatory mechanisms for water balance include thirst, antidiuretic hormone, and selective cell and capillary membrane permeability.

Daily intake of water during early adulthood should be approximately 2100 to 2800 mL.[75] This does not, however, mean that 2800 mL (over 11 full 8-oz glasses!) of actual water needs to be consumed. Rather, sources of water should include drinking approximately 1500 mL (six 8-oz glasses) of fluids and eating foods containing water (e.g., fruits and vegetables, meats). Water is also synthesized by the body as a result of carbohydrate, protein, and fat catabolism (approximately 300 mL/day).[75]

Output of water should equal intake. Body water losses consist of two types: obligatory and facultative. *Obligatory* (necessary) water losses are those essential to the excretion of body wastes. These include urinary output (approximately 1200 mL/day) and fecal output (about 100 mL/day). Other obligatory losses include water loss through the lungs and skin (also known as **insensible water loss**). Insensible water loss (IWL) equals approximately 800 mL/day in early adulthood and increases when body temperature increases; thus, IWL is important in the regulation of body temperature. *Facultative* water losses represent the water reserve available to the kidneys and lungs for maintenance of the extracellular fluid and normothermia. The kidney reserve volume is 500 mL/day, and insensible reserve volumes are equal to 200 mL/day.[75] Fluid losses need to be continuously replaced. The best replacement fluid is water (Fig. 26-6). Sweet drinks (sodas, juices, alcohol) should be avoided when a person is thirsty or underhydrated; sugar reduces the amount of water in one's bloodstream and body tissues by drawing fluid into the digestive tract. Caffeine and alcohol are diuretics and actually increase water loss.[60]

FIGURE 26–6.
Because of obligatory water losses, people working in hot environments or engaging in strenuous exercise need to pay special attention to fluid and salt intake.

Endocrine System

The endocrine system is a conglomerate of glands that are not anatomically contiguous, but are chemically interrelated so that they function as a single-organ system. The endocrine system links all the body systems and affects nearly all biophysical functioning throughout the life span.[33] The tasks of the endocrine system are fourfold: (1) maintenance of the body's internal environment; (2) mobilization of responses to internal and external challenges (stress infection, trauma); (3) regulation of growth and development; and (4) sexual reproduction.[76]

The primary functional units of the system are the endocrine glands: the pituitary, thyroid, parathyroid, adrenal, and pineal glands; the cells of the islets of Langerhans in the pancreas; the gonads, ovaries, and testes; and the thymus. Some of these subsystems are totally endocrine in function, whereas others form parts of larger organs that perform more than just endocrine functions. The thymus, for example, produces hormones but is also a part of the immune system.

Prostaglandin is an example of an endocrine hormone produced throughout the body: if secreted by the uterus, it stimulates uterine muscle contractions (causing either menstrual cramps or helping to initiate labor); if produced by the kidneys, it helps maintain body fluid balance and blood pressure. Many scientists believe that almost every bodily process that involves hormones is affected by prostaglandins.[31]

Both the basal metabolic rate (BMR) (the body's consumption of oxygen at rest) and secretions of thyroid hormones slowly decrease as a person approaches mid-adulthood. This decrease in the BMR is related to the decrease in muscle mass (which is a large oxygen-consuming tissue). The decrease in thyroid hormones (which assist in regulating the BMR) is the result of the slower rate at which they are broken down and removed from the blood.[30] Therefore, the young adult's body is burning up fewer calories per unit of body weight in a resting state than it was during adolescence, a situation that can cause weight gain unless caloric intake is decreased or exercise is increased.

Reproductive System

Biophysically, the ideal age for a woman to become pregnant for the first time is in her twenties.[51,66] Her reproductive as well as the other systems in her body are mature and more coordinated during early adulthood than at any other time of her life span. Young adult women are more likely to produce fertilizable eggs. Her hormone cycle is more dependable and her uterus and pelvis are more receptive to sustaining a pregnancy and facilitating the safe delivery of a healthy baby.

In men, testosterone production reaches its maximum daily output during the twenties.[20,50] Since spermatogenesis continues throughout adulthood, the young man's biophysical ability to father a child should not be affected by any developmental somatic changes.

The Healthy Female Reproductive System

The female reproductive system is regulated by both the neurological and endocrine systems. The hormones involved in this feedback system affect several other parts of the body (see Chaps. 3 and 23).

The *hymen* (or hymenal ring) is an irregularly-shaped membrane that surrounds and partially occludes the vaginal opening. The size and strength of the hymen varies among individuals. Surgery may be necessary to perforate a thick hymen to allow intercourse or pelvic examination. Surgery will also be necessary if the hymen prevents excretion of menstrual flow. This membrane generally is perforated at the time of a woman's first coital experience. The hymen may sometimes be broken through strenuous physical activity, masturbation, or the misuse of tampons.

The perineum includes the skin and muscles between the vaginal opening and the anal orifice. Since the contractions of these muscles serve as the major organs of response during orgasm, a woman who has had her uterus and ovaries removed can still experience orgasms.[33]

The vagina is acidic from menarche to menopause; its surface is moist from fluid secreted by the vaginal epithelium.[59] Most practitioners today do not recommend routine douching (vaginal irrigation). Douching can destroy the natural protection and actually push bacteria further into the reproductive tract, thus leading to infection. A woman should follow her physician's recommendation for frequency and type of solution to use. Vaginal sprays are also unnecessary and can cause infection, itching, burning, irritation, vaginal discharge, and rashes.[48] Keeping genitalia clean with plain soap and water is the most effective way of "keeping fresh."

FEMALE BREASTS. Female breasts reach maturity in the twenties (see Chap. 31). The erectile tissue of the nipple responds to sexual excitement, cold, friction, pregnancy, and menses by becoming more rigid and prominent.[33]

BREAST SELF-EXAMINATION (BSE). Worldwide, breast cancer is diagnosed in approximately 1 million women annually.[7] In the United States, 44,300 new cases are detected annually—300 of them in men. More than 1 in every 10 women develop breast cancer during their lifetime, and approximately 20% of these women will die from the cancer because it advances too far before it is detected.[15] Some women develop breast cancer in their late teens or early twenties. Early detection of breast cancer may be the difference between life and death. The woman should perform BSE at the same time each month, since the size and texture of the breasts vary during the menstrual cycle. The best time is immediately after the monthly menstrual flow has ceased—when the breasts are not swollen. A health professional can teach a woman the correct BSE procedure; brochures are also available from the American Cancer Society. Mammography can detect cancer nodules several years before it can be picked up by BSE (see Chap. 35).

The Healthy Male Reproductive System

Most men have less knowledge about the male reproductive system than women have about the female reproductive system (see Chap. 3 for a review of the male reproductive system).[60] Males who have not been circumcised should gently retract the foreskin and wash with soap and water to maintain cleanliness. The male urethra is a passageway for both urine and semen, but not at the same time. During ejaculation, a small valve closes internally to allow only the sperm and semen to be discharged. A man may awaken from sleep with an erection stimulated by the need to urinate. This erection will resolve after urinating (see Chap. 23).

The Leydig cells (one of the sources of testosterone) begin to decline slowly in number after the man is approximately 25 years old.[20] Although testosterone reduction may affect sexual response, the changes are not readily apparent in the healthy young adult male. All domains—not just the biophysical realm—affect sexual response and expression. The decline in testosterone does result in a gradual decrease in muscle mass, bone density, hair growth, skin thickness, metabolic rate, and vocal timbre; the extent of these changes varies among individuals.[33]

The prostate gland encircles a part of the urethra. This gland is under both neural and endocrine control. It is subject to hyperplasia which can occur in males of all ages, although it is more prevalent in older men. It can be easily felt during a physical exam.

The left testicle usually hangs a little lower than the right because of a heavier blood supply.[53, 60] If a man had an undescended testicle as a child that either descended spontaneously or was corrected surgically, a weak spot may be left in the muscle layer in the lower abdomen (original site of the testicle). This spot is a potential place for a hernia (bulging intestine through the muscle) to develop.

TESTICULAR SELF-EXAMINATION. Men are encouraged to perform a monthly testicular self-examination (TSE) to identify pathological conditions such as cancer. Testicular cancer is common between 15 and 35 years of age; it ranks first in cancer deaths among young adult males.[7] If detected early, testicular cancer is second only to skin cancer in terms of successful cure rate.[60] Testicular cancer is almost always painless, so a young man should not wait until he feels pain (or until a lump grows larger) before he consults a doctor. Health professionals can teach young men how to perform TSE. Just as adolescent girls should be taught BSE, teen-age boys should be taught how to perform TSE.

MALE BREASTS. Male breasts obviously do not serve a nutritive or functional reproductive purpose. In some men, they are a source of sexual arousal and pleasure. Many men, especially those who are overweight, may experience slightly enlarged breasts. Because of the possibility of breast cancer in men, they are encouraged to check periodically for abnormal lumps and, if discovered, to have these evaluated by a physician.

Physiology of Sexual Response

Masters and Johnson (who extensively studied the human sexual response patterns) discovered that the sexual response cycle in both men and women can be divided into four stages: excitation, plateau, orgasm, and resolution.[39] Phase 1, **excitation** (sometimes lasting hours), can be elicited by any source of somatogenic or psychogenic stimulation and usually takes place more rapidly in men than in women. Phases 1 and 2 can occur during REM sleep (see later discussion) even if dreams are nonsexual in nature.[10, 72]

FEMALE SEXUAL RESPONSE. The first sign of sexual response in women is vaginal lubrication, as the Bartholin glands on each side of the vagina contract to release fluid. An increased blood supply occurs in the labia minora and majora. The head (glans) of the clitoris enlarges and its shaft elongates. There is upward and backward movement of the cervix and uterus, erection of the breast nipples, and an increase in the size of the breast alveoli (glandular tissue). The breasts and the labia minora may also become flushed.[39, 48]

If the woman is not distracted and she continues to be adequately stimulated, the intensified **plateau** phase follows. The outer third of the vagina becomes engorged, decreasing its opening in preparation for orgasm. The labia minora's color deepens to a bright red; the clitoris retracts; heart rate and blood pressure increase.

Orgasm, the third phase, is characterized by rhythmic contractions of the clitoris, vagina, uterus, perineum, and sometimes the rectal sphincter. Rhythmic contractions sometimes occur in the arms, legs, abdomen, and buttocks. The woman's respiratory rate can increase to as high as 40 breaths per minute and the heart rate to 180 beats per minute. Systolic blood pressure (the numerator in the blood pressure fraction) can increase by 30 to 45 mmHg.[55] Women's descriptions of orgasm vary from a slightly pleasurable movement sensation to passionate throbbing. A woman's orgasmic experience is influenced by her sociocultural upbringing, affective state, physical health, sexual motivation, past sexual experiences, sexual education, and environmental distractions; it is normal for a woman to have variation in her sexual interest, activity, and response. A woman may not experience orgasm during one particular coital act, but she may experience one or multiple orgasms of varying intensity (without dropping below the plateau phase) the next time.

The fourth phase, **resolution,** is manifested by a return to the preexcitement phase. Within 10 to 15 seconds, the clitoris loses its swelling, and normal color returns to the labia minora. Ten to fifteen minutes are required for the vagina to resolve to "normal"; 30 minutes are required for the cervical opening to decrease to its preexcitement state.[8] If orgasm did not occur, the lingering engorgement may cause feelings of pelvic fullness and pressure that take longer to resolve.[48]

MALE SEXUAL RESPONSE. The male sexual response includes two distinct components: a genital vasocongestive reaction (which produces penile erection) and reflex muscular contractions (which result in orgasm). This distinction can be important in diagnosing and treating sexual dysfunction because they involve different systems of the body and are enervated by different parts of the nervous system.

The erectile component of the sexual response is initiated in the **excitement** phase by physical stimulation of the genitals, psychic stimulation, or a combination of both. Once attained, the healthy male can maintain erection for long periods of time during the **plateau.** The young adult male may achieve and lose an erection several times during lovemaking as a normal pattern.

The male **orgasm** is divided into 2 phases—emission (of seminal fluid into the man's urethra) and ejaculation (contractions that cause semen to spurt from the penis). Once emission occurs, it is difficult for the man to voluntarily postpone ejaculation. Although ejaculation usually follows erection, ejaculation can occur in the absence of an erection.[33] Following ejaculation, almost all men experience a refractory period as part of the **resolution** phase.[48] This period, lasting a few minutes in young men to several hours for an older man, is a time when the man is biophysically unable to achieve another erection.[8, 55] Some young men, however, can achieve two or more ejaculations with such a short refractory time between them that it appears to be a multiple orgasm. Men, like women, experience an increase in respiratory rate, heart rate, and blood pressure during sexual intercourse.

Prolonged sexual plateau without orgasm can sometimes cause painful cramping in the man's testicles or urinary tract. Contrary to popular belief, a man will not be "hurt" or "ruined for life" if, after having engaged in active foreplay, he does not proceed to have sexual intercourse.

FACTORS INFLUENCING HIGH-LEVEL WELLNESS

At the threshold of the 21st century, much is known about how to maintain a healthy body. The young adult who makes intelligent choices for maintenance of high-level wellness must integrate this information into a healthy lifestyle.

Nutrition

Because of increased appreciation for ethnic preferences, and improved agricultural techniques, food storage, and transportation, the public is provided with many food selections unknown just 5 years ago. However, in the presence of abundance, a person may still experience a subnutritional status if wise choices are not made, or if economic status limits choices.

Calories

During early adulthood, when an individual has, for all practical purposes, completed biophysical growth, the large number of calories required during adolescence are no longer necessary. The young adult needs only enough calories for cell repair and replacement, energy, protection from

illness, and maintenance of body functioning. Caloric needs vary according to age, gender, body size, amount of physical activity expended in one's occupation or exercise, affective state, metabolism (which can be affected by medications), stress, and climate.

Protein

Ten percent to fifteen percent of the daily caloric intake of the young adult should be protein.[75] The body needs 20 amino acids (the "building blocks" of proteins), 11 of which are synthesized naturally by the body. The other nine must be consumed in one's food.[27] If a food contains all nine of these essential amino acids, it is called a *complete protein* (e.g., meats and dairy products). A food that contains eight or fewer amino acids is called an *incomplete protein* (e.g., grains and vegetables). People, especially those who are vegetarians, need to combine incomplete proteins to ensure that all nine of these essential amino acids are available in the same meal (e.g., rice and beans, peanut butter and bread). If not, the food cannot be metabolized by the body and some nutritional value is lost.

Protein, which is necessary for growth and repair of body tissues as well as the production of hormones and enzymes, becomes an energy source if a person does not consume enough carbohydrates and fats. Too much protein (a common problem in Western nations) can, over time, damage kidneys, or will be converted to excessive free calories which are then stored as body fat.[4, 23, 69, 74]

Fat

Fats (lipids) are necessary and beneficial in appropriate quantities, supplying energy, thermal insulation, vital organ protection, nerve impulse transmission, tissue and membrane structure, and cell and enzyme metabolism.[75] Fats are divided into several subgroups, with dietary *triglycerides* composing the largest subgroup.

Type and amount of dietary fat ingested can affect level of wellness. Relatively large amounts of fats (especially saturated fat) are risk factors for cardiovascular disease, diabetes mellitus, cancer, and other general health problems.[44, 47, 75]

Cholesterol, a chemical found in fats, provides no calories,[25] but is essential in the production of sex hormones, cell membranes, vitamin D, and bile acids.[75] It serves as a structural component of every cell of the body, and is especially important for the proper functioning of brain and nerve tissues and liver cells.[75] Cholesterol occurs naturally in all animal-based foods, but is not present in plants. Saturated fats tend to be high in cholesterol content and thus elevate a person's blood cholesterol level. However the healthy human body synthesizes cholesterol in the liver, even if a person consumes no cholesterol (Fig. 26-7).

The cells of the intestine and the liver manufacture microscopic carriers (lipoproteins) composed of fat, cholesterol, and protein to transport cholesterol. Although *low-density lipoproteins* (LDL), the "bad cholesterol," return essential fats and cholesterol to the cells of the body for the

FIGURE 26–7.
Nutritional habits established during the early adult years can have a significant effect on the quality of one's life.

synthesis of hormones and cell membranes, they also deposit cholesterol on the arterial walls as plaque, leading to atherosclerosis.[25] Atherosclerosis is not just a disease of middlescence or late adulthood. Plaque accumulates at the rate of 1% to 2% per year throughout life.[25] Fortunately, *high-density lipoprotein* (HDL), the "good cholesterol," cleans this plaque from the blood vessel walls and returns it to the liver where it can be processed and excreted from the body.[25] Thus, depressing LDL levels and increasing HDL levels can reduce atherosclerosis. Other actions that may decrease the buildup of plaque are increasing vitamin C, reducing saturated fats, increasing fiber intake, and exercising.[75]

Most dietitians recommend eating fewer cholesterol-laden foods, especially if an individual has a family history of cardiovascular disease. The American Heart Association recommends a preventive diet (formerly called the "prudent diet") with a daily *maximum* fat intake of only 30% of the total calories (with approximately 10% coming from each type of fat: saturated, monounsaturated, and polyunsaturated), and to reduce cholesterol intake below 300 mg per day.[1, 9, 16] Unfortunately, most Americans (especially young adults eating "fast foods") consume between 35% and 45% of their daily calories as saturated fat.[75] Most fat in American meals and snacks comes from animal fats, dairy products (including ice cream, cheese, milk), and nuts (especially peanut butter).[74, 75] Healthy adults should maintain a serum cholesterol level below 200 mg/dL, with the HDL level higher than the LDL.[33]

Carbohydrates

Carbohydrates should be a person's major source of energy so that proteins can be used to perform their unique functions. The young adult should choose from 50% to 60% of the daily calories from carbohydrates.[75] All carbohydrates are composed of simple sugars that are divided into three different categories according to their size. The two small carbohydrates groups, both known as **simple carbohydrates,** include glucose, and are found in molasses, corn syrup, honey, white sugar, and the sugar in fruits and milk. The largest group, **complex carbohydrates,** are composed mainly of starches, which consist of strings of glucose. These elements are found in pasta, potatoes, rice, grains, and beans. Foods that contain complex carbohydrates also contain protein, vitamins, and minerals, and are often found in high-fiber content foods.

As the body metabolizes carbohydrates, it forms glucose (measured as blood sugar) and then converts some glucose into glycogen (stored by the liver for use later). Every cell in the body needs glucose; the brain and central nervous system depend solely on glucose for energy. Glucose is essential to maintaining affective well-being, biophysical energy, and cognitive alertness. Infection, healing, growth, and stress increase a person's need for glucose. During adolescence and early adulthood, the normal blood sugar is 60 to 110 mg/dL (1 dL = 100 mL) if the person has not eaten for about 8 hours; for late adulthood, 60 to 125 mg/dL; for children other than neonates, 60 to 100 mg/dL.[67] Because complex carbohydrates take longer to digest, they do not cause the rapid rise in blood sugar levels that simple carbohydrates cause.

Fiber

Dietary fiber, an indigestible form of the complex carbohydrates, is found in plant foods (e.g., cellulose, pectins, gums). Since some fibers contain absorbable products, they are not totally without calories, but their energy contribution, in general, is negligible. There are many beneficial aspects of including fiber in one's daily food. Its water-holding capacity causes feelings of fullness, which promote satiety, thus reducing intake of calorie-laden fats and sweets. Fiber exercises the muscles of the gastrointestinal tract, thus improving their tone; it speeds the transit of food laden with potential cancer-causing agents; it binds fats and cholesterol and disposes of them with the feces; and it can even slow the absorption of sugars, thus facilitating a more even rise in blood sugar.[75] Some fibers relieve constipation (and hemorrhoids) by attracting water into the digestive tract, thus softening stools; other fibers help to solidify watery stools and decrease diarrhea.

There are disadvantages in eating too much daily fiber, although the effects can be highly individualized (e.g., a vegetarian may become "full" quickly of fiber and consequently may not eat enough protein; another person may experience several loose bowel movements).

Vitamins and Minerals

Vitamins and minerals are substances that have no caloric value but are essential for growth, maintenance, and the functioning of body processes. Too much or too little of either causes chemical disequilibrium and illness.

Because of a larger body, the young adult male needs more protein, vitamins B_2 (riboflavin), and B_6 than the adolescent male.[27] Smokers, people who consume excessive sweets, and women taking birth control pills need to increase their B and C vitamins because their bodies metabolize these vitamins differently.[75] Those who drink more than the equivalent of two 6-oz cups of brewed coffee (about 166 mg caffeine) need additional B vitamins, vitamin C, calcium, zinc, magnesium, potassium, and iron.[62] Caffeine is a diuretic that promotes excretion of these water-soluble nutrients. Runners, athletes, and aerobic exercisers must ensure adequate calcium intake for maximal bone density.

Sodium

Sodium is essential for metabolism of water and minerals. The average American (regardless of age) consumes enough sodium (actually, an excess amount) without adding table salt (sodium chloride) to daily meals or snacks. Sodium also is found in soy sauce, monosodium glutamate (MSG), baking powder, baking soda, and some preservatives. Excessive sodium can raise blood pressure, which in turn can precipitate strokes and heart attacks. Too much sodium can also cause or increase the severity of fluid retention, headaches, mental confusion, premenstrual syndrome (PMS), and kidney problems.[38, 62, 75] Herbs may serve as a tasty substitute for salt in the preparation of food. After heavy perspiration (e.g., intensive exercise), an individual needs to ingest more fluids, sodium, and potassium from a natural source (e.g., oranges) rather than salt alone.[38, 60]

Dietary Planning

One of the most familiar ways of grouping foods in the United States has been to categorize foods into four major groups: meat (2 servings), milk and milk products (2 servings), fruit and vegetables (4 servings), and grains (4 servings). This guideline provides the basic foundation for evaluating intake.

Since it provides only about 1200 kcal, additional foods must be added to ensure adequate nutritional value and to individualize for caloric need. A person can follow all the rules, but ingest too much animal protein and still fail to meet daily needs for many nutrients, including vitamin B_6, iron, magnesium, and zinc.[75] It is therefore crucial for a person to carefully select food to ensure adequate nutrition.

Sleep and Rest

Although we spend approximately one third of our lives sleeping, the exact biophysical mechanisms involved in sleep and even the reasons why people need to sleep are not known.[17] It is known that sleep deprivation results in inefficient use of biophysical, cognitive, and affective potentials; it can even lead to illness. Sleep is not the lack of activity; rather, it is an altered state of consciousness composed of complex biophysical, psychosocial, and cognitive (some would add spiritual) activities essential to an individual's high-level wellness. Understanding a person's sleep-wakefulness cycle can facilitate high-level wellness.

Many factors influence the need for rest and sleep: physical health, affective mood, cognitive energy expenditure, type of occupation, nutritional status, impact of stress, and amount of daily exercise. No gender differences are found in sleep patterns.[10] Most young adults do not take time to rest during their waking hours—perhaps a continuation of the "not knowing when to stop" syndrome of adolescence. However, people can actually increase productivity if they plan for adequate rest periods during the day and sleep at night. Resting before a person is tired will prevent fatigue. This is especially significant for the adult who is the primary caregiver of an infant or young children—this adult needs to rest or "grab forty winks" when the baby sleeps. It is imperative for a pregnant woman to obtain adequate sleep and rest for the benefit of herself and her unborn child.

Electroencephalograms (EEGs) have been used to compare brain-wave activity during waking and sleeping states. Electroencephalograms display rapid, irregular waves while we are awake and alert. As we begin to rest, these waves change to **alpha rhythm,** a regular pattern of low voltage with frequencies of 8 to 12 cycles/sec. In deep sleep, a **delta** rhythm occurs, which is a slow pattern of high voltage and 1 to 2 cycles/sec. During certain stages of slumber, sleep spindles, or sudden, short bursts of sharply pointed alpha waves, occur with frequencies of 14 to 16 cycles/sec.[6, 17, 71] Electroencephalogram tracings demonstrate that young children experience the same stages of sleep as do adults. The difference between children and adults lies in the amount of time spent in each stage.

There are two basic types of sleep: REM and non-REM sleep, which respectively evolve from the "active" (state 2) and "quiet" (state 1) sleep states of the infant (see Chap. 4).[78] Rapid eye movement (REM) sleep, a term coined in the 1950s, refers to the eye movements beneath closed eyelids. It is also known as "active sleep" because it is accompanied by increased heart beat and blood pressure, involuntary muscle twitching, and erratic breathing. Most but not all dreams occur during REM sleep. A newborn baby spends about 50% of sleep time in REM sleep. The amount of time spent in REM sleep decreases gradually during the life span.[19] Higher amounts of REM sleep correspond to the time during which brain cells are growing or developing and repairing themselves most rapidly (e.g., childhood, after injury, or during drug withdrawal).[19] Brain protein synthesis occurs during sleep. The relationship of REM sleep to cognitive growth is still under study. The amount of REM sleep appears to be correlated with intellectual functioning in adults.[10] Inadequate REM sleep interferes with memory.[19]

Under normal circumstances, 20% of the total sleep time of young adults consists of REM sleep,[71] which usually occurs 4 to 6 times during the night, at intervals of 90 to 120 minutes.[10] The first episode of REM sleep lasts about 1 to 5 minutes, but by the end of the sleep session, REM sleep segments may last up to 1 hour.[10] The exact physiological reason is unknown, but the amount of REM sleep determines the amount of actual rest. When REM sleep is not achieved, or is interrupted consistently, extreme tiredness and serious neurotic tendencies can develop.[17, 71]

When a sleeper is not experiencing REMs, is breathing slowly and regularly, and has little or no muscle movement, he or she is experiencing "quiet sleep" or non-rapid eye movement (NREM) sleep. This kind of sleep comprises 75% to 80% of sleep time and is divided into four progressively deeper stages, with REM sleep recycling intermittently between the NREM sleep periods.[10] Each person has a particular sleep pattern; this pattern changes throughout the life cycle. However, the percentage of REM sleep in relation to NREM sleep does not change during the the adult years.[10] During stage 1 NREM sleep (2%–5% of sleep), the heart rate, arterial blood pressure, and basal metabolic rate all decrease, whereas during REM sleep, there is excitation of the brain and the autonomic nervous system. Most people spend less than 7 minutes in stage one NREM sleep, the transitional state.[10] We may feel we are awake, but our reactions to external stimuli decrease and our thoughts drift.

Stage 2 (45%–55% of sleep), or medium-depth sleep, constitutes the majority of an adult's sleep time. Stages 3 (3%–8% of sleep) and 4 (10%–15% of sleep), the deepest stages, are often grouped together as delta sleep. Delta sleep is prevalent during the first half of the sleep session; many young adults enter this stage 30 to 45 minutes after sleep onset and become difficult to waken.[71] This deep sleep begins to be replaced with longer periods of lighter sleep after 30 years of age.[6, 71]

Sleep patterns, as well as types of dreams, often change during pregnancy. The drowsiness of early pregnancy may be caused by increased estrogen levels, which augment sensitivity to serotonin, the brain's tranquilizer.[62, 71] By the third trimester, some women may have become desensitized to serotonin, leading to a withdrawal that includes insomnia.[59, 62]

Some young adults function best (i.e., optimal alertness) with 7 to 9 hours of sleep; others appear to do well with less.

How well one functions the next day, not the number of hours slept, is the touchstone of adequacy.

Although a sleeping person does not normally interact with the environment, the sleeper does continue to monitor the environment.[10] Thus, a person will hear and often become alert on hearing his or her name whispered, and a mother will hear and respond to her crying infant. An attractive concept to business persons and college students is the notion of "sleep learning"—the idea that one can learn material from audiotapes played while one is sleeping. Research evidence does *not* support this "painless" approach to learning.[19]

At one time or another, most individuals suffer from mild sleep disturbances. Research has identified several principles that increase a person's ability to benefit from sleeping time (Table 26-1).[60]

Chronic insomnia as well as habitual nightmares, night

TABLE 26–1. WAYS TO FACILITATE SLEEP

1. Maintain a regular sleep schedule.
2. Incorporate pre-sleep rituals (whether it's brushing teeth, setting the clock, listening to music, doing some light reading). Do something that orients mind and body toward the relaxation of sleep.
3. Sleep in a dark, quiet place.
4. Sleep only at night. Don't plan to habitually "catch up" with long naps during the day—this will interrupt internal rhythms.
5. Use the body, and not someone else's behavior, as a guide for sleep needs.
6. Avoid caffeine and other stimulants near bedtime. The nicotine in cigarettes is as much a stimulant as is caffeine.
7. Avoid alcohol. A drink may make a person sleepy, but alcohol actually disrupts sleep. It exacerbates existing breathing problems and can cause withdrawal headaches, thirst, or a need to urinate during the night.
8. Avoid excessive liquid intake during the evening (a full bladder frequently awakens one).
9. Avoid sleeping pills, even over-the-counter (OTC) drugs. OTC drugs only make a person groggy; they don't induce sleep. They can become addictive with subsequent withdrawal symptoms that last for weeks. Prescription hypnotics decrease REM sleep and can be addicting. One may even experience a "hangover" effect from a sedative. When the medication is stopped, "boomerang" or "rebound" insomnia can occur. Neither OTC nor prescription drugs mix safely with other medications or alcohol, and much too easily lead to overdosing and death. L-tryptophan supplements (amino acids dubbed "Mother Nature's sleeping pill"), have lead to eosinophilia, a blood condition that can cause death.[29, 42, 57] The exact reason is not yet known, but appears to be a manufacturing issue.[5] A health care practitioner should be consulted before taking this or any medication.
10. Avoid heavy meals near bedtime. Fats are difficult to digest; carbohydrates will boost energy and keep one awake. If one is hungry in the evening, a light protein (warm nonfat or low-fat milk which contains natural L-tryptophan) may help, as long as several ounces don't fill the bladder too quickly.
11. Refrain from vigorous physical exercise just before bedtime. Exercise increases oxygen supply to the brain and body, raises metabolism and body temperature, and, in general, awakens the body. Exercise earlier in the day, however, can positively influence sleep quality.

terrors (awakening with extreme anxiety), and sleepwalking can be the result of biophysical disequilibrium as well as long-term psychological disturbances. The person experiencing any of them, regardless of age, should consult a health professional who specializes in treating sleep disturbances.[6, 43]

Exercise

After nutrition, the most significant lifestyle factor affecting high-level wellness is the type, amount, and frequency of exercise. Increasing numbers of adults state that they are exercising routinely, reflecting a change in priorities toward a healthy body. Once a person is "hooked" on exercise, he or she tends to continue exercise throughout life. Many young adults first become interested in exercise as a means of improving physical attractiveness; some are physical fitness "buffs," others recognize exercise as a way to increase energy and decrease one's risk of degenerative diseases.

Benefits

Exercise can positively impact every system of the body and aid in maximizing potentials of all five domains. Benefits of exercise include the following: increased lung capacity, enhanced efficiency in handling oxygen, lower breathing rate, increased blood volume per heartbeat, lower blood pressure, lower LDL cholesterol levels, higher HDL cholesterol levels, lower triglyceride levels, lower uric acid levels (decreasing incidence/severity of gout and kidney stones), decreased platelet stickiness (lessening risk of heart attack, stroke, gangrene, and prompting better flow of blood), increased hormone-related capacity of pituitary and adrenal glands (enabling a person to react more efficiently to stress), increased muscle strength, increased physical skills, increased sense of physical well-being, increased amount of delta sleep, increased cognitive alertness and accuracy, and reduced depression and anxiety.[3, 12, 18, 23, 28, 55, 60] This is only a partial listing of the benefits of exercise. Exercise can help prevent many diseases (e.g., heart attacks, high blood pressure, osteoporosis) and it can also aid weight loss. It can even help those who wish to control alcoholism and other forms of substance abuse.

Types

Physical exercise can be divided into aerobic and anaerobic exercise, depending on how the body supplies energy to the muscles. Both forms use large amounts of glucose and oxygen. In **aerobic** exercise, the body is able (through the lungs, metabolism, heart, and blood stream) to keep pace with the consumption of energy by the muscles. Endurance activities (e.g., running, walking, jumping jacks, swimming, cycling) are typical forms of aerobic exercise. Aerobic exercises strengthen the cardiovascular system, build up endurance, and tone or strengthen body muscles depending on the type and amount of exercise involved.

Anaerobic exercise (meaning "without oxygen") involves using the oxygen and glucose stored in the muscles; this energy can be generated quickly when the type of exer-

cise consumes oxygen and glucose more quickly than the heart and lungs can respond. This form of exercise can be sustained for only short periods of time (e.g., 50-yard dash, weight-lifting), usually for less than 2 minutes. Anaerobic exercises are used to strengthen muscles (Fig. 26-8). Since they involve stress to the muscles, tolerance and strength need to be built gradually over time.

Safe Exercise

Recent research has helped us to understand what constitutes the proper type and frequency of exercise for selected groups of people, along with criteria for when to cease and when to advance to a more difficult level. Exercise techniques, routines (e.g., warming up, cooling down), equipment, even clothing, should be individualized for each person and orchestrated by a knowledgeable CPR-certified instructor/trainer. A thorough physical exam by a qualified health professional is a must before any person, regardless of age, undertakes any form of physical activity or exercise program. A treadmill test to assess cardiovascular status is mandatory for any individual over 30.[55] Other significant areas to assess before undertaking a personal exercise program (and to reevaluate whenever necessary) are nutrition, bodily response, lifestyle, and time commitment/management. Exercise during pregnancy is covered in Chapter 30.

Ongoing Health Care

As with the care of any fine machine, preventive maintenance for the body can play a major role in ensuring high-level wellness during early adulthood. Health maintenance is often neglected, if the young adult feels immune to illness. Annual physical assessments are recommended, including physical examinations, weight, blood pressure, rectal exam, diet eval-

FIGURE 26–8.
Anaerobic exercise is used to strengthen specific muscles, but it has a limited effect on the functioning of the heart and lungs.

uation, sleep pattern assessment, and assessment of any other concerns. Males should have a testicular exam performed yearly by a health professional. Women are encouraged to have annual Pap tests (checks for cancer of the uterine cervix). This procedure, which also includes a pelvic exam, can facilitate the detection of many other gynecological problems. Females should have a breast examination performed yearly by the health professional. Every woman should have a mammogram (breast x-ray) to determine a baseline reading some time between 35 and 40 years of age (earlier than this if there is a family history of breast cancer).

Persons who completed the primary series of immunizations should have a booster immunization against diphtheria and tetanus every 10 years. If the individual has no record of immunization, no documented history of the disease, or no laboratory evidence of immunity to measles, mumps, and rubella (MMR), he or she should also have the MMR vaccination. There are many young adults who either were vaccinated for the MMR before 15 months of age, or they received the MMR vaccination from an ineffective lot (thus, giving inadequate protection against the disease).[65] See Chapter 6 for immunization maintenance recommendations throughout the life span.

Those young adults who live in close proximity to each other, as well as those individuals who are exposed to large populations of people (e.g., health professionals, police, school teachers, etc.) are at high risk for influenza exposure and should receive influenza vaccine annually. The hepatitis B vaccination (series of three shots) is advised for any individual who has frequent exposure to blood, multiple sexual partners, special high-risk populations, or shared needles. Overseas travel also may require an update on immunizations. Since specific requirements vary from country to country, current recommendations may be obtained from the local health department.

Dental examinations should be performed on a 6-month basis for cleaning, prophylactic care, and early detection of tooth or gum disease. Routine eye examinations every 2 years are encouraged.

For young adults who are on limited incomes, many clinics are available across the country that provide low-cost medical attention. Planned Parenthood, family health centers, and hospital satellite clinics are only a few examples of these facilities.

Accidents

Accidents are the leading cause of disability and death in this age group.[7, 18] Disabling injuries have many sources, including work-related incidents, thrill-seeking pleasures (which may include substance abuse), interpersonal violence, vehicle-related incidents, and sports injuries (Fig. 26-9). Since an accident is most likely to occur when a person is experiencing stress, and since many young adults are under duress either voluntarily or involuntarily, it is easy to understand the incidence of accidents in this age group.

Because of their age, physical stamina, and quick reflexes, young adults are the most likely candidates to be hired for positions requiring physical ability. Many young adults also desire exciting challenges so they frequently accept potentially hazardous employment (e.g., working on high bridges, offshore drilling rigs, in coal mines, and construction). No one should be allowed to work in occupational settings without being informed of work-site hazards and being provided with educational training to reduce those hazards. Pregnant women may unknowingly expose the fetus to industrial substances that are harmful. Proper evaluation and temporary reassignment may be necessary.

Many accidents occur at home. Taking the time to read instructions about proper handling of appliances can prevent

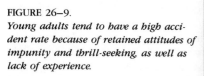

FIGURE 26–9.
Young adults tend to have a high accident rate because of retained attitudes of impunity and thrill-seeking, as well as lack of experience.

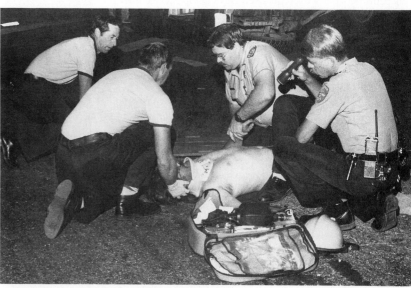

many injuries. Attempting to use the equipment when tired or while drinking is another cause of many accidents, whether at home, work, or play. The enthusiasm and spontaneity of youth are not always tempered by experience or wisdom. Helmets while riding "bikes" or seat belts in motor vehicles do not prevent accidents, but they can prevent disabling injury or even death.

Substance Abuse

Throughout history, societies have been plagued by those who use pharmacologically active substances for nontherapeutic or "recreational" purposes. This abuse is a complex problem whose symptoms can range from minor physical or psychological difficulties to complete dependency and severe biophysical, psychosocial, cognitive, and spiritual dissonances. Substance abusers, broadly defined, are persons who use psychoactive products without medical sanction. Motivating factors include curiosity, peer pressure, pain relief, anxiety, fatigue, a search for ecstasy, or an attempt to escape from stress or boredom. Many persons tend to abuse more than one substance at a time, creating a dangerous situation for the abuser, the people around the abuser, and potential offspring (whether they are already conceived or not).

Abuse easily leads to addiction, a behavioral state characterized by loss of ability to control a drive or craving for the substance. There are two types of dependency—psychological and physical. The first is a compulsion to use a substance on a continuous or sporadic basis to achieve a psychological effect (e.g., to avoid anxiety or to feel the exhilaration). Use of the psychoactive agent creates an altered biophysical state leading to physical dependence. Consequently, if the blood chemical levels are not maintained, drug-specific withdrawal reactions will result. (It is important to note that when people develop tolerance to a drug given for medical purposes, thereby needing to increase the amount of medicine taken to achieve the same effects experienced from a previously smaller dose, they are not necessarily physically dependent on the drug).[62] Substance abuse can negatively affect every cell, organ, and system in the human body.

Nicotine
Twenty-nine percent of adults in the United States smoke cigarettes.[22] Nicotine, the active ingredient in tobacco, is considered the most widespread, costly, and physically addictive substance of abuse in the United States.[18, 55, 62] Nicotine is a carcinogen (cancer-producing agent) linked to many cancers occurring in several systems of the body, including the cardiovascular, respiratory, gastrointestinal (including gums and jaws), neural, and genitourinary systems.[62] Smoking increases the risk of emphysema and respiratory problems. Cancer and other diseases caused by nicotine can occur whether it is smoked (cigarette, cigar, pipe), chewed (tobacco, nicotine-containing gum), or held on the inside of the mouth (snuff). Other family members, especially children, have increased allergies, respi-

ratory problems, and asthma when exposed to second-hand smoke. (See Chap. 35 for further discussion of smoking.)

The pharmacological effects of nicotine are complex, sometimes causing stimulation and at other times, depression of various biophysical systems. The nicotine-stimulated release of epinephrine from the adrenal glands accelerates heart rate and elevates blood pressure. Small amounts of nicotine stimulate nerve cells of the peripheral nervous system, outside of the brain and spinal cord; larger doses first stimulate then block transmissions of impulses.

The central nervous system (CNS) is greatly stimulated by nicotine and can cause hyperventilation and vomiting.[62] The cardiovascular system reacts to nicotine by constricting blood vessels that carry oxygen and nutrients to the rest of the body, thus raising the heart rate in compensation, and increasing cardiac workload. Stimulation of the gastrointestinal tract may result in diarrhea.

Approximately 1.3 million people successfully stop smoking each year.[22] Some experience irritability, hostility, emotional depression, and difficulty in concentration when they try to quit smoking.[62] Although these symptoms can last for several days after the person stops intake of nicotine, they usually resolve without drug therapy.

Alcohol
Ethyl alcohol (ethanol, grain alcohol, ETOH) is the active ingredient in alcoholic beverages such as wines and beers; ETOH is a potent CNS depressant with tranquilizing, hypnotic (causing partial or complete unconsciousness), and anesthetic properties. In general, ETOH is toxic to most cells in the human body and can produce both acute and chronic medical problems. In addition to creating strained interpersonal relations, the most common complications of imbibing ETOH are dehydration, headache ("hangover"), and impaired cognitive judgment. Acute toxicity can cause death due to cardiovascular collapse and severe CNS depression. Chronic alcoholism predisposes to degeneration of all systems of the body, especially the nervous system, liver, pancreas, and heart. High blood pressure and gastrointestinal ulcers are also prevalent. Alcoholism also increases the risk for certain forms of cancer.[62] Chronic alcoholics may develop both obesity from excess caloric consumption and malnutrition due to nutritional deficiencies. Alcohol used during pregnancy can cause physical malformations of the fetus as well as mental and growth retardation (fetal alcohol syndrome, see Chap. 3). The amount of ETOH in one can of beer is equivalent to one 8-oz glass of wine or 2 oz of hard liquor in a typical mixed drink.[60] The average person can metabolize approximately 2 oz of ETOH within 1 hour;[75] this metabolism is, however, affected by factors such as gender, body weight, amount and type of food in the stomach, and presence of medication in the bloodstream.

Caffeine
Caffeine is the third most abused substance in the United States.[55] It is present in coffee, tea, cola (a drink does not have

to be dark in color to contain caffeine), chocolate, over-the-counter drugs, and prescription drugs. Even "decaffeinated coffee" contains small amounts. Caffeine affects different people in different ways. Caffeine can be used for medicinal purposes. For example, its vasoconstrictive properties can stop a headache associated with dilated blood vessels; its dilating properties of bronchi can bring relief to some people who have a chronic obstructive airway disease.[62]

In addition to being a diuretic, caffeine is a CNS stimulant; it can make a person hyperactive or jittery. It can exacerbate the symptoms of psychotic states and panic disorders. Caffeine can increase the frequency of seizures in a person who has a seizure disorder.[62] It increases the heart rate, irritates the gastrointestinal tract, and interrupts the natural biorhythms of sleep. It also is associated with increased risk of fibrocystic breasts (see Chap. 35). Caffeine is also known to be addictive to some people, resulting in severe headaches and other symptoms if the person tries to stop using caffeine products.

Marijuana

It is speculated that cannabis (marijuana, hashish, hashish oil) is the fourth most abused drug in our society.[18, 55] Granted, there are some legitimate, medicinal uses for marijuana (e.g., to counteract nausea and vomiting in patients with cancer; to decrease pressure inside the eye of a patient with glaucoma). People show various responses to marijuana. The major pharmacological actions of marijuana include stimulation of the cardiovascular system (increased heart rate, blood pressure), cold extremities, dry mucous membranes (especially of the mouth and eyes, which are then vulnerable to infection), and alterations of CNS functioning (initial body relaxation, loss of motor coordination, rapid emotional changes, impaired memory, short or dulled attention span, and hallucinations).[62] Lung tissues of long-term marijuana smokers show elevated levels of precancerous cellular change.[8, 62] Many users suffer from bronchitis and inflammation of the respiratory tract. Research is currently being conducted to determine the effects of marijuana on the immune and reproductive systems. Since marijuana is fat-soluble, it remains in the body for several weeks (unlike water-soluble drugs that are more quickly flushed out of the body), potentially causing delayed effects or "flashbacks" when least expected.

Disability

Nearly 5.5 million adults living in the community need assistance with everyday activities such as bathing, feeding, and shopping.[13] Spinal cord injury can be a serious problem, depending on the location of the injury. Some temporary or permanent disabilities are severe enough to require special equipment or assistance with activities of daily living such as getting in and out of bed or using the toilet. Preparing meals, completing household chores, or driving a car may be impossible for some individuals unless extraordinary assistive devices are employed. Aside from the psychosocial assault,

which plays a crucial part in adjustment (see Chap. 17), the disabled young adult has serious physical threats with which to contend.

Humans are intended to be ambulatory creatures. When mobility is reduced, every body system is affected. There is a threat to life when a person is confined to a bed or wheelchair. The efficiency of the neuromuscular and skeletal systems decreases if immobility is prolonged. It takes the average healthy adult 6 weeks of mobility to reverse the cardiovascular changes that are acquired when immobilized for only 3 weeks. Three physiological effects on the respiratory system may occur as a result of immobility: decreased respiratory movement, decreased movement of secretions, and disturbed oxygen-carbon dioxide balance. For many individuals, immobility leads to problems with ingestion, digestion, and elimination. Metabolic homeostasis is threatened when a person cannot move about in an accustomed manner. The immobilized person is vulnerable to urinary tract infections and kidney stones if sufficient fluid is not consumed and if the daily diet contains an excess of minerals and amino acids, such as calcium phosphate and cystine. The skin is subject to breakdown if an immobile person does not remove pressure from the area of contact at least once every 2 to 3 hours.

Many physical barriers can be overcome, but the process is not easy (Fig. 26-10). Various self-help items (e.g., modified eating utensils, books recorded on cassettes, modified automobile controls) are available for those who need them. Cosmetic and functional prostheses for amputees can be purchased. Financial assistance and vocational training also are made possible through supportive systems at the local, state, and federal levels.

A crucial facet of rehabilitation for the young adult is the resumption (or initiation) of a healthy sexual relationship. Physical disability is *not* synonymous with sexual impotence.[13] Sexual partners should be included in counseling sessions, so that emotions and alternative means of gratification can be explored and worked through. Variation in positions or techniques for coitus and sexual satisfaction can solve most difficulties. The major hurdle in sexual activity is the acceptance by both partners of the missing limbs (stumps), paralysis, or disfigurement, since body image is an important part of a satisfying relationship. It is essential for the partners to keep an open mind and a sense of humor, and to remember that sexual intimacy can be reached in many ways.

Common Health Concerns

For the most part, early adulthood is the healthiest portion of the life cycle. Nevertheless, there are some common problems.

Headaches

The most common headaches—muscle-tension and migraine—are predominantly afflictions of early adulthood (many begin during childhood). The frequency and severity of these headaches peak during early adulthood; they continue throughout life for some individuals.[45]

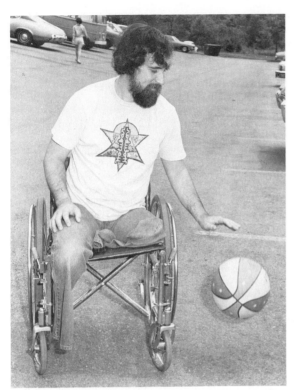

FIGURE 26–10.
Disabled young adults face multiple barriers to full participation in life. However, with creativity and perseverance, most can pursue their interests satisfactorily.

Muscle-tension headaches usually begin gradually with a dull pain that builds to a persistent ache. They are felt in the shoulders, neck, and scalp. These muscle spasm headaches are associated with distress, anxiety, and depression—many times the result of living life "too fast," setting personal goals too high, experiencing the threat of failure, or being bombarded by too many stressors at the same time.

Migraine headache is a very painful condition caused by alternating constriction and dilation of scalp, retinal, and cerebral arteries that supply blood to the brain.[7,8] The extreme constriction and dilation precipitate other symptoms. At the onset of a migraine headache, some sufferers experience disturbances of vision, hearing, touch, smell, or speech (aura). Some feel light-headed, dizzy, or euphoric. During the early phase of a migraine attack, a person may suffer numbness, weakness, or even temporary paralysis in one or more parts of the body. Then the excruciating, constant, piercing, throbbing pain begins, usually on one side of the forehead, then maybe becoming generalized—but lasting for hours or days.[45] Unlike muscle-tension headaches which usually occur late in the day, migraine attacks may disrupt sleep, appear within minutes after awakening, or occur at any point during the day. Some individuals who suffer from migraines also get muscle-tension headaches.

Migraines are usually accompanied by other symptoms: nausea, vomiting, loss of appetite, diarrhea, tremor, and alternating spells of perspiration and chills. Fingertips may turn cyanotic (blue) and hands may feel icy. Tears flow from the eye closer to the pain area or from both eyes; the sufferer's face may become pale. One or both of the arteries in the temples may become so distended that their pulsations are visible to an observer several feet away. Blood pressure is elevated. Heart rate increases. Some people may even experience bleeding from the nose or ears.[45] Others may retain excessive sodium and water; hands and feet can become visibly swollen; temporary weight gains may occur.[45] This "almost unconscious with pain" headache affects other domains, and many victims experience impaired judgment, irritability, hostility, or psychological prostration. Migraines usually do not occur simultaneously with intense stress, but afterwards. Predictable environmental factors can trigger migraines in sensitive persons: lack of sleep, excessive sleep, emotional tension, a long session of critical thinking, physical exertion and fatigue, intense light and glare, head injury, ovulation, menstruation and menopause, oral contraceptives, hunger, ETOH, certain foods, cold foods, high altitude, pungent odors, weather changes, and many other factors.[45]

Regardless of what triggered either the muscle tension or migraine headache, stress reduction practices can offer varying degrees of relief to those who suffer from them. Medical treatment of migraines takes two forms: abortive, attempting to stop the pain once it begins; and prophylactic, attempting to prevent future pains.

Infections

Throughout life, our bodies wage war against infectious forces that threaten our defenses. The early adult years are no exception. Like headaches, infections are often the result of an external stress which consumes enough energy to weaken our internal defenses. The most common infections that occur during these years affect the respiratory, gastrointestinal, and genitourinary systems.

Sexually transmitted diseases (STDs) have an increased incidence (and often begin) during early adulthood. Some can be contracted in ways other than sexual contact; some can be cured, others cannot. The most prevalent STDs in the United States are chlamydia, gonorrhea, syphilis, herpes, venereal warts, hepatitis type B, and pubic lice ("crabs").[60] Human immunodeficiency virus (HIV), the newest STD, has attracted wide attention and concern because it is increasing in incidence and is fatal.

With all of the infections mentioned, prevention is a priority. Many of the stressors mentioned in this chapter lower a person's resistance to infection or place a person in a situation which is high-risk for injury or infection (e.g., overeating or undernutrition; fatigue or sleep deprivation; lack of exercise or unsafe exercise practices; failure to be properly immunized; failure to see a health professional for checkups on a regular basis or when needed; multiple sexual partners; attitudes of impunity or invulnerability; and substance abuse).

CONCLUSION

Early adulthood is the stage of life when a person should be able to experience peak physical fitness, intellectual performance, and interpersonal relationships. High-level biophysical functioning can be maintained for many years with judicious health care. Assuming full responsibility for the care of one's body includes accepting the challenges of maintaining sensitivity to changes in functioning, seeking medical care and new information as needed to maintain high-level functioning, treating one's body with respect, and becoming aware of stressors and how to control them. It also means realizing that a person's biophysical health is directly affected by how one lives, loves, works, relates, and believes. One's physical health must not be taken for granted. It must be protected and nurtured to function at optimal levels. Clinical evidence suggests that humor and laughter can aid in controlling pain, speeding recovery, and decreasing the effects of negative stressors.[1] Stress can be diminished by distracting attention, reducing muscle tension, encouraging a more positive outlook on life, and increasing production of endorphins. A sense of humor can aid a person in attaining, maintaining, or regaining high-level wellness. How a person lives one's life during early adulthood is critical not only to longevity, but is also pivotal to the quality of life that same person will experience during the middlescent and late adult years.

REFERENCES

1. American Heart Association Nutrition Committee. (1982). Rationale of the diet-heart statement of the American Heart Association. *Arteriosclerosis, 4,* 177.
2. Arndt, K. A. (1988). *Manual of dermatologic therapeutics with essentials of diagnosis* (4th ed.). Boston: Little, Brown.
3. Bailey, C. (1984). *The fit-or-fat target diet.* Boston: Houghton Mifflin.
4. Beck, M., Hager, M., Miller, M., Hutchinson, S., Hackett, G., and Joseph, N. (1989). Warning! Your food, nutritious and delicious, may be hazardous to your health. *Newsweek, 113*(13), 16–19.
5. Belongia, E. A., Hedberg, C. W., Gleich, G. J., White, K. E., Mayeno, A. N., & Loengering, D. A., et al. (1990). An investigation of the cause of the eosinophilia-myalgia syndrome associated with tryptophan use. *New England Journal of Medicine, 323,* 357–365.
6. Boxer, S. (1989). Inside our sleeping minds. *Modern Maturity, 32*(5), 48–54.
7. Brunner, L. S., & Suddarth, D. S. (1988). *Textbook of medical-surgical nursing* (6th ed.). Philadelphia: Lippincott.
8. Bullock, B. L., & Rosendahl, P. P. (1988). *Pathophysiology: Adaptations and alterations in function* (2nd ed.). Glenview, IL: Scott, Foresman, Little, Brown.
9. Byrne, G. (1988). Surgeon General takes aim at saturated fats. *Science, 241,* 651.
10. Carskadon, M. A., & Dement, W. C. (1989). Normal human sleep: An overview. In M. H. Kryger, T. Roth, & W. C. Dement (Eds.), *Principles and practice of sleep medicine* (pp. 3–13). Philadelphia: W. B. Saunders.
11. Clark, J. W. (1986). *Clinical dentistry* (Vol. II). Philadelphia: Harper and Row.
12. Cooper, K. H. (1983). *The aerobics program for total well-being.* New York: Bantam Books.
13. Cornelius, D. A. (1982). *Who cares? A handbook on sex education and counseling services for disabled people* (2nd ed.). Baltimore: University Park.
14. Cousins, N. (1981). *Human options: An autobiographical notebook.* New York: Norton.
15. Devita, V. T., Hellman, S., & Rosenberg, S. A. (1989). *Cancer: Principles and practice of oncology* (Vol. I, 3rd ed.). Philadelphia: J. B. Lippincott.
16. Dietary Guidelines. (1985). Dietary Guidelines Advisory Committee reports. *Nutrition Today, 20*(3), 8.
17. Dinner, D. S. (1982). Physiology of sleep. *American Journal of EEG Technology, 22*(2), 85.
18. Edelman, C. L., & Mandle, C. L. (Eds.). (1986). *Health promotion throughout the lifespan* (2nd ed.). St. Louis: C. V. Mosby.
19. Empson, J. (1986). *Human Brainwaves: The psychological significance of electroencephalogram.* New York: Stockton Press.
20. Ewing, L. (1983). Leydig cells. In L. Lipschultz & S. S. Howard (Eds.), *Infertility in the male.* New York: Churchill-Livingstone.
21. Fields, H. L., et al. (1985). *Proceedings of the Fourth World Congress on Pain: Advances in pain research and therapy* (Vol. 9). New York: Raven Press.
22. Fiore, M. C., Novotny, T. E., Pierce, J. P., Giovino, G. A., Hatziandreu, E. J., & Newcomb, P. A., et al. (1990). Methods used to quit smoking in the United States. *Journal of the American Medical Association, 263,* 2760–2765.
23. Forbes, G. B. (1987). *Human body composition: Growth, aging, nutrition, and activity.* New York: Springer-Verlag.
24. Fulton, J. D., & Black, E. (1983). *Dr. Fulton's step-by-step program for clearing acne.* New York: Harper and Row.
25. Garrison, R. H., & Somer, E. (1990). *The nutrition desk reference* (rev. ed.). New Canaan, CT: Keats.
26. Goldberg, I. K., Kutscher, A. H., & Malitz, S. (1986). *Pain, anxiety, and grief.* New York: Columbia University Press.
27. Guthrie, H. A. (1989). *Introductory nutrition* (7th ed.). St. Louis: C. V. Mosby.
28. Haywood, K. M. (1986). *Life span motor development.* Champaign, IL: Human Kinetics.
29. Hertzman, P.A., Blevins, W. L., Mayer, J., Greenfield, B., Ting, M., & Gleich, G. J. (1990). Association of the eosinophilia-myalgia syndrome with the ingestion of tryptophan. *New England Journal of Medicine, 322,* 869–873.
30. Ingbar, S. H., & Woeber, K. A. (1985). The thyroid gland. In J. D. Wilson & D. W. Foster (Eds.), *Williams textbook of endocrinology* (7th ed.). Philadelphia: W. B. Saunders.
31. Jovanovic, L., & Subak-Sharpe, G. J. (1987). *Hormones: The woman's answerbook.* New York: Fawcett Columbine.
32. Kiernan, J. (Ed.). (1981, Dec.). No end to love. *The American Lung Association Bulletin.*
33. Kneisl, C. R., & Ames, S. W. (1986). *Adult health nursing: A biopsychosocial approach.* Reading, MA: Addison-Wesley.
34. Lowrey, G. H. (1986). *Growth and development of children* (8th ed.). Chicago: Year Book.
35. Luckmann, J., & Sorenson, K. C. (1987). *Medical surgical nursing: A psychological approach* (3rd ed.). Philadelphia: W. B. Saunders.
36. Malasanos, L., et al. (1986). *Health assessment.* St. Louis: C. V. Mosby.
37. Manson, J. E., Colditz, G. A., Stampfer, M. J., Willett, W. C., Rosner, B., Monson, R. R., Speizer, F. E., & Hennekens, C. H. (1990). A

prospective study of obesity and risk of coronary heart disease in women. *New England Journal of Medicine, 322*(13), 882–889.

38. Masiak, M. J., Naylor, M. D., & Hayman, L. L. (1985). *Fluids and electrolytes through the life cycle.* Norwalk, CT: Appleton-Century-Crofts.

39. Masters, W. H., & Johnson, V. E. (1966). *Human sexual response.* Boston: Little, Brown.

40. McCaffery, M. (1980). Understanding our patients' pain. *Nursing '80, 10*(9), 26.

41. McGuire, D. B. (1984). The measurement of clinical pain. *Nursing Research, 33*(3), 152–156.

42. Medsger, T. A. (1990). Tryptophan-induced eosinophilia-myalgia syndrome. *New England Journal of Medicine, 322,* 926–928.

43. Melnechuk, T. (1983). The dream machine. *Psychology Today, 17*(11), 22–34.

44. Miller, S. A., & Stephenson, M. G. (1987). The 1990 national nutrition objectives: Lessons for the future. *Journal of the American Dietetic Association, 87*(12), 1665.

45. Murphy, W. B. (1982). *Dealing with headaches.* Alexandria, VA: Time-Life Books.

46. Murray, J. F. (1986). *The normal lung: The basis for diagnosis and treatment of pulmonary disease* (2nd ed.). Philadelphia: Saunders.

47. Newell, G. R. (1985). Cancer prevention: Update for physicians, four years later. *Cancer Bulletin, 37,* 103.

48. Olds, S. B., London, M. L., & Ladewig, P. A. (1988). *Maternal-newborn nursing: a family-centered approach.* Menlo Park, CA: Addison-Wesley.

49. Payne, R., & Foley, K. M., (Eds.). (1987). Cancer pain (symposium). *Medical Clinics of North America, 71*(2), 153–348.

50. Pesmen, C. (1984). *How a man ages.* New York: Ballantine Books.

51. Pillitteri, A. (1985). *Maternal-newborn nursing: Care of the growing family* (3rd ed.). Boston: Little, Brown.

52. Price, S. A., & Wilson, L. M. (1986). *Pathophysiology: Clinical concepts of disease processes* (3rd ed.). New York: McGraw-Hill.

53. Ramsey, F. B. (1986). Testicular self-examination. *Postgraduate Medicine, 80*(4), 172.

54. Robbins, C. R. (1988). *Chemical and physical behavior of human hair* (2nd ed.). New York: Springer-Verlag.

55. Samuels, M., & Samuels, N. (1988). *The well adult.* New York: Summit Books.

56. Schafer, W. (1987). *Stress management for wellness.* New York: Holt, Rinehart, & Winston.

57. Silver, R. M., Heyes, M. P., Maize, J. C., Quearry, B., Vionnet-Fuasset, M., & Sternberg, E. M. (1990). Scleroderma, fasciitis, and eosinophilia associated with the ingestion of tryptophan. *New England Journal of Medicine, 322,* 874–881.

58. Skolnick, A. (1986). *The psychology of human development.* San Diego: Harcourt, Brace, Jovanovich.

59. Sloane, E. (1985). *Biology of women* (2nd ed.). New York: Wiley.

60. Smith, S., & Smith, C. (1988). *The college student's health guide.* Los Altos, CA: Westchester Publishing.

61. Spence, A. P. (1989). *Biology of human aging.* Englewood Cliffs, NJ: Prentice-Hall.

62. Spencer, R. T., Nichols, L. W., Lipkin, G. B., Sabo, H. M., & West, F. M. (Eds.). (1989). *Clinical pharmacology and nursing management* (3rd ed.). Philadelphia: J. B. Lippincott.

63. Tanner, J. M. (1989). *Foetus into man: Physical growth from conception to maturity* (rev. and enl.). Cambridge, MA: Harvard University Press.

64. The Fit Back. (1988). *The fit back: prevention and repair.* Alexandria, VA: Time-Life.

65. The Medical Letter, Inc. (1989). Measles revaccination. *Medical Letter on Drugs and Therapeutics, 31*(797), 69–70.

66. Timiras, P. S. (1972). *Developmental physiology and aging.* New York: Macmillan.

67. Treseler, K. M. (1982). *Clinical laboratory tests: Significance and implications for nursing.* Englewood Cliffs, NJ: Prentice-Hall.

68. Troll, L. E. (1985). *Early and middle adulthood: The best is yet to be—maybe* (2nd ed.). Monterey, CA: Brooks/Cole.

69. United States. Department of Health and Human Services. (1988). *The Surgeon General's report on nutrition and health.* Washington, DC: U.S. Department of Health and Human Services, Public Health Service.

70. Van De Graaf, K. M., & Fox, S. I. (1989). *Concepts of human anatomy and physiology* (2nd ed.). Dubuque, IA: Wm. C. Brown.

71. Walsleben, J. (1982). Sleep disorders. *American Journal of Nursing, 82*(6), 936–940.

72. Ware, J. C. (1981). Monitoring exertions during sleep. In M. H. Kryger, T. Roth, & W. C. Dement (Eds.), *Principles and practice of sleep medicine* (pp. 689–695). Philadelphia: W. B. Saunders.

73. West, B. A. (1981). Understanding endorphins: Our natural pain relief system. *Nursing '81, 11*(2), 50.

74. Whitney, E. N., et al. (1987). *Understanding normal and clinical nutrition* (2nd ed.). St. Paul: West.

75. Williams, S. R. (1990). *Essentials of nutrition and diet therapy* (5th ed.). St. Louis: Times Mirror/Mosby College Publishing.

76. Wilson, J. D., & Foster, D. W. (Eds.). (1985). *Williams textbook of endocrinology* (7th ed.). Philadelphia: W. B. Saunders.

77. Wilson, R. W., & Elmassian, B. J. (1981). Endorphins. *American Journal of Nursing, 81,* 722.

78. Zepelin, H. (1983). A life span perspective on sleep. In A. Mayes (Ed.), *Sleep mechanisms and functions in humans and animals: An evolutionary perspective.* Wokingham, Eng: Van Nostrand Reinhold.

27

Men occasionally stumble over the truth, but most of them pick themselves up and hurry off as if nothing had happened.

—WINSTON CHURCHILL

Cognitive Development During the Adult Years

Robert Bornstein and Clara S. Schuster

The culture is laden with myths regarding cognitive development during adulthood. One is that intellectual development ends with completion of one's formal education. A second is that the early adult years represent the period of highest intellectual functioning (Fig. 27-1); a third claims that middlescents tend to bask in the glory of earlier accomplishments and, therefore, avoid involvement in activities that require strenuous intellectual activity. A fourth myth views adults as less open to new ideas and more "set in their ways" as they get older. A fifth myth holds that senior adults experience decreased intellectual functioning and eventually need assistance in decision making and problem solving. Current research indicates that although one or more of these statements may be true for a specific individual, they do not represent the "norm," nor do they represent functioning patterns of "healthy" individuals.

Although most of us tend to think of "intellectual" and "cognitive" abilities as synonymous, the two terms actually reflect somewhat different aspects of mental activity. **Intelligence** is basically an estimate of "what and how much people know," as identified through the discipline of *psychometrics* (the measurement of intelligence). "Intelligence" usually means "the capacity or combination of psychological capacities which equip the individual to master school-like subject matter if given proper instruction and motivation."[14] Psychometricians make four assumptions: (1) there is a consensually agreed on body of knowledge (things people can know); (2) this body of knowledge can be sampled through the construction of a test; (3) everyone who takes the test has had equal opportunity to acquire the identified knowledge; (4) consequently, the differences in the scores people receive on the test are a reflection of differences in ability to acquire knowledge. A higher IQ score is assumed to reflect "a greater ability to acquire knowledge." The question becomes, "do intellectual abilities change over the 40- to 70-year span of adult life?"

A second question in psychometric studies deals with whether intellectual ability is singular and global or if it is comprised of numerous capacities, each attuned to different aspects of knowledge (see Chap. 21). We are interested in whether the number and nature of intellectual abilities change over time, and, if so, do different abilities reveal different patterns of change?

While measurements of *intelligence* tend to concentrate on content, measurements of *cognition* concentrate on problem solving and information processing. **Cognition** focuses on *how* and *why* people know, rather than *what* and *how much* they know. Thus, cognition is evaluated or assessed indirectly by drawing inferences from performances on tasks and problems that involve the processing of information (e.g., gathering, encoding, storage, manipulation, and retrieval of information). We are interested in whether or not these processes change over time and, if so, how and why.

The questions seem quite simple and straightforward. However, the conduct of formal research raises numerous problems and issues that, singularly or in interaction, produce results that are frequently ambiguous and open to multiple interpretations. A brief simplified sampling of these problems facilitates reader understanding of intellectual and cognitive development during the adult years.

PROBLEMS IN ASSESSMENT

Ecological Validity of Assessment Devices

The validity of intelligence tests has been and continues to be questioned based on the first three assumptions of psychometricians. The validity of their use with older adults is also questioned, since the standardized tests most frequently used in assessing intelligence were originally designed to tap the educational aptitude of relatively young individuals. Do the tests yield equally valid measures of the intelligence of older adults, who have experienced different histories, live in quite different situational contexts, and have different life goals or interests? The use of short-term memory and retention tasks to assess cognitive functioning might automatically favor younger, college-age adults, since it is they who have had relatively recent experience with the short-term memorization of previously unfamiliar materials (e.g., preparing to pass an exam). As people move into the adult years, their life goals and developmental tasks may be less oriented toward intellectual development as a goal in itself (as it is for children and adolescents).[8] Most adults are more concerned about the pragmatic aspects of adaptation to the exigencies of life. As with the other skills of life, once a cognitive skill is mastered and practiced, it slips into the background of habit, and the task at hand becomes the critical focus. Thus, middlescent and older adults are less likely to expend time and energy developing short-term memory skills and are more likely to use memory aides, such as written lists. (Written lists are fail safe, and their use is not a form of "cheating" in the real day-to-day world.)

Population Sampling

The Issue of Normal Aging Versus Disease Processes

Chronological aging is intrinsically associated with an increased incidence or frequency of illness. Thus, researchers are forced to make a very fine and difficult distinction. They would like to be able to study "normal" intellectual and cognitive development without introducing the biasing effects of "abnormal" disease processes; yet, the practice of eliminating subjects with known illnesses may actually serve to create another bias (i.e, an overly positive picture).[61]

Selective Survival

Not everyone born on the same date has an equal likelihood or probability of living into middle or old age. In this society, whites, females, and members of the middle and

FIGURE 27–1.
Increases in technology require that many people obtain advanced education to pursue the career of their choice.

upper socioeconomic classes have greater life expectancies at birth than do blacks, males, and members of the lower classes. For whatever reasons, people with more formal education and greater intelligence also appear to out-survive those who are intellectually duller and receive less education.[46] Thus, samples of subjects studied at progressively older ages are increasingly biased because more people with the aforementioned characteristics have survived to those ages.

Developmental Research Strategies and Problems of Interpretation

The ultimate goal of developmental research is to describe and explain *ontogenetic age changes* (e.g., changes in individuals that accompany or are associated with growing older). The primary methodological problem lies in the fact that the measurement of changes requires the study of individuals of different chronological ages that are confounded with differences in both historical and current circumstances. The task for the developmental researcher, then, is to sort out this complex web of determinants.

The Cross-Sectional Research Strategy

The vast majority of developmental research studies employ the cross-sectional strategy, which entails the simultaneous study of several different age groups of individuals. With this strategy, any differences are usually considered to be reflective of *age differences* rather than age changes. Noting, for example, that 60-year-olds score higher on a specific factor than 20-year-olds does not automatically mean that a real age change has occurred. It is possible that the score earned by the current 60-year-olds might be identical to the score they would have earned had they been evaluated when they were 20. Since each age group is only evaluated once, researchers can only state that an age difference exists.

Differences may arise from cohort–generational effects. Consider a hypothetical 1990 study: the 20-year-olds were born in 1970, the 40-year-olds in 1950, the 60-year-olds in 1930, and the 80-year-olds in 1910. Individuals born in 1970 might have some dim childhood recollections of the Vietnam War, and they most certainly have heard or read about it, but their experience of that conflict and the impact it had on American society is probably quite different from that of individuals who were born earlier and were therefore older at the time of its occurrence. Indeed, it is only the 40-year-olds who are likely to have experienced the horrors of that war on a firsthand, combatant basis. In a similar vein, the 60 and 80 year olds lived through World War II and had firsthand experience with the Great Depression of the 1930s and the New Deal politics that followed; the others did not.

Other historical differences are more subtle in nature but may be even more influential. Successive generations of Americans have acquired more formal education (shifts have been made in educational programs as well); this factor has been causally linked to differences in measured intelligence, attitudes, values, and socioeconomic class status (see Fig. 27-1). Specific child-rearing practices as well as parental attitudes also have shifted over time. Improvements in medical care and nutrition have produced successive generations that are bigger and healthier. Mass media and technology have had their impact. This list of differences in historical circumstances could be greatly expanded, but the crucial point is probably already obvious. Different age groups have different life histories. Thus, the data from cross-sectional studies are always open to interpretation because differences may result from different life histories (cohort–generational differences) rather than the effects of aging per se.

The Longitudinal Research Strategy

Few developmental studies are longitudinal in design. This research strategy entails the use of a single group of subjects who are periodically assessed at different points in time. A hypothetical example would be a study begun in 1930 when the research subjects were 20 years old and completed in 1990 when they were 80. Assessments could have been made in 1930, 1950, 1970, and 1990 at subject ages 20, 40, 60, and 80.

The obvious advantage of the longitudinal approach is that differences can be logically interpreted as *age changes,* since the scores earned at one chronological age can be directly compared to those earned by the same subjects at both earlier and later ages. Cohort–generational effects are negated by the fact that all subjects belong to the same generation and presumably share a common history regardless of the age at which the assessment is made. However, differences can be magnified by selective attrition, which, like survival, tends to be higher among the "less advantaged" members of any given cohort. Therefore, successive assessment periods use fewer and fewer of the original subjects, and those who continue tend to increasingly represent "the cream of the crop."

"Time of testing" effects present two additional problems: changes in performances over successive assessments may represent the effects of repeated practice and whatever learning may be derived from it, or they may come from shifts in cultural factors that influence one's perspective or at least one's response to test questions. Societies do not remain static. People's values, attitudes, and the social institutions that reflect them undergo changes over time. Thus, at any given point in history, a society might be more or less religiously oriented, more or less concerned about peace and the threat of nuclear war, more or less satisfied with the functioning of its government, or more conservative or liberal with regard to issues such as individual rights.

It also is obvious that practical considerations limit the number and variety of people who can be studied at any one time. Researchers therefore select research subjects with the hope and intent of being able to generalize research findings to as large and diverse a population as possible (external validity). In the case of longitudinal studies, all the subjects come from the same cohort or generation, thus making generalizations to people born to other cohorts or generations impossible—unless, of course, the researcher can demonstrate that cohort–generational effects are inconsequential for the factor assessed.

The other major drawback to conducting developmental research via the longitudinal strategy is purely practical in nature. Final results of a longitudinal study are not known until years after its inception, 60 years to be exact in our hypothetical example. Time, financial, and personnel commitment and costs are high.

The Distinction Between Performance and Competence

Even with the best research design, one can only measure what is directly observable—in this case, performances on tests of intelligence or cognition and problem solving. Some researchers argue that the *intellectual performance* of older subjects is often an inaccurate reflection of *intellectual competence* or capacity (internal ability). From their point of view, one's intellectual competence cannot be directly inferred from intellectual performance until all of the factors that intervene between the two are clearly identified and fully functioning. When any one or more of these intervening factors are at less than optimal level, intellectual performance is reduced regardless of how intellectually competent the individual may actually be.

The extensive literature that describes the comparison of younger and older adults to each other on a wide variety of cognitive tasks leaves little doubt that younger adults are generally and consistently superior to older ones in cognitive performances. Nevertheless, gerontologists often find themselves in disagreement about the meaning of these differences. Both age differences and age changes in motivational and arousal states are found. It can be argued, therefore, that any reduced intellectual performance in older adults reflects a difference or change in motivational or arousal state and not a real decline in intellectual capacities.

Age-related declines or decrements in intellectual performance may originate from a host of so-called "situational determinants," such as sensory-perceptual or motor skill changes. The important point is that, since countless such uncontrollable variables exist, it is often possible to claim that reduced intellectual performances of older subjects are reflective of the negative influence of these variables while still claiming that intellectual competence remains undiminished over time.

On the other hand, some consider performance to be an accurate reflection of competence. These researchers often point out that, when intervening variables are adequately controlled age differences and age changes that tend to favor younger people still exist. Furthermore, they argue that the assessments reflect what one is capable of doing under real life circumstances. Since no one functions under totally optimal conditions all the time, it is nonsensical to try to assess intellectual competence or capacity as though it were independent of the influence of such intervening variables.

CHANGES IN ADULT INTELLIGENCE AND COGNITION

Identifying Specific Intellectual Changes

Answers to questions about how much (and in what direction) intelligence changes during adulthood depend on the factors measured. The earliest life-span studies measured intelligence cross-sectionally and used a single measure of general intelligence as computed from so-called "omnibus" tests. These data suggested that intelligence peaked during the late teens and then progressively declined throughout adulthood.[9] Somewhat later, longitudinal studies, again using the single intelligence score, suggested that intelligence peaked during the early twenties, held relatively stable through the late thirties, and then began to progressively decline.[9] Thus, developmentalists believed that intelligence declined throughout much of adulthood, starting in either early adulthood (cross-sectional studies) or in middle-age (longitudinal studies).

Performance and Verbal IQ

When researchers began to subdivide the single intelligence measure into two broad classes of ability, the *performance IQ* and the *verbal IQ*, a different pattern of development emerged for each. The performance IQ began to decline quite dramatically in early adulthood, while the verbal IQ sometimes began to decline during middlescence, sometimes remained stable, and sometimes actually increased throughout adulthood!

Crystallized and Fluid Intelligence

According to a construct proposed by Cattell and Horn, fluid intelligence (Gf) consists of those abilities that reflect the cumulative effects of casual (informal) learning experiences.[20, 51] This broad form of intelligence includes the abilities to see relationships and to comprehend implications. Fluid intelligence thus includes features such as perceiving spatial relationships (e.g., geometric figures, hidden figures, matrices), short-term nonsensical memory, memory span, general reasoning, associative power, abstraction, and problem solving. These features are developed independently from the systematic influences of education and culture.

In contrast, **crystallized intelligence** (Gc) consists of those abilities that are the product of formal education, systematic socialization experiences, and enculturation. Crystallized intelligence reflects the accumulation of specific knowledge. Many of these educational and enculturation influences, such as home, school, and work environments, function to produce interindividual differences in personal adjustment, motivation, and culturally based knowledge and sophistication. This broad form of intelligence includes the abilities of formal reasoning and communication. Crystallized intelligence thus includes features such as verbal comprehension, general understanding, information base, number facility, concept formation, systematic logic, inductive reasoning, flexibility, and integration.

Fluid and crystallized intelligence tend to become increasingly distinguishable with age. Fluid intelligence, which is reflected in the Wechsler Adult Intelligence Scale (WAIS) performance scores, tends to peak in early adulthood and then gradually decline. Crystallized intelligence, on the other hand, tends to remain stable or even to increase with age in the face of continued education, a stimulating, varied environment, or with the challenge of complex responsibilities or career.[68, 82, 87] Crystallized intelligence also is reflected in the WAIS verbal score. Both Gf and Gc are affected by health status and lifestyles. Those with higher educational levels and responsible careers tend to retain high functioning for a longer period of time.[68, 69] It is also observed that people who are forceful, intense, and relatively strong in interpersonal relations tend to have IQs that increase with age.[57] However, this observation is not to be interpreted that education or a healthy lifestyle automatically translate into a longer period of optimal intellectual functioning. But people with high intelligence, high verve, greater self-discipline, and high motivation and commitment are more likely to seek a college education, a challenging career, stimulating experiences, continued individualized education, and a disciplined lifestyle, all of which promote continued high-level intellectual functioning (Fig. 27-2).

The Great Debate

Although some great minds continue to struggle with the issue of whether or not intellectual declines accompany adult aging, some points are apparent.[8, 9, 10, 52, 53] There is a decline in many psychometrically assessed intellectual abilities for most aging individuals. It also is evident that these declines start later in life and are smaller in magnitude than was previously thought. It is clear that significant declines do not normally begin within the period of young adulthood or perhaps even by the onset of middle age as previously thought. Furthermore, different types or clusters of intellectual abilities appear to age differently; most may decline, but some remain relatively stable or are even enhanced throughout most of adulthood. Lastly, it is noted that differences between individuals are important; some individuals continue to improve in some intellectual abilities into their eighties (see Fig. 27-3).[84] What must be kept in mind is the fact that this combined variability is so great that no single generalized statement about the course of intellectual development will provide an accurate prediction for all adults.

FIGURE 27–3.
The "vitally involved" person will continue intellectual pursuits into the late adult years. Life's experiences and knowledge sometimes take on new meanings with the perspective of age.

Theories of Cognitive/Intellectual Development

Piaget

The most complete theoretical account of cognitive development is that proposed by Jean Piaget. Piaget is not concerned with the content of thought or "body of knowledge" per se but the operational structure used for processing information. He proposes an invariant sequence of four qualitatively different stages, the last of which, "formal operational thought," emerges during adolescence (see Chap. 24). Piaget saw the late adolescent and young adult years as a time for refining the formal

FIGURE 27–2.
Continuing education is essential in most jobs to maintain efficiency, decrease accident rates, and keep abreast with technology and legislation. Many adults find that continuing education also provides an intellectual stimulus in their lives.

operational approach to problem solving.[40] He asserted that any cognitive advancement beyond the acquisition of formal operations represented quantitative rather than qualitative change; that is, the same cognitive operations are applied throughout adulthood to an ever expanding and more complex array of experiences and problems.[74]

The adult becomes increasingly adroit at combinatorial reasoning and in integrating the mental steps involved in problem solving. The alternative solutions to a situation are evaluated, prioritized, and synchronized with one's past experiences, value system, and goals. The end result is a unique product for each person, even though the processes used are the same. The adult, because of reduced egocentrism, is able to approach issues more objectively, enabling him or her to draw more effectively on education and experience as well as on all the cognitive operations available. The adult who is able to generate and entertain more options and realistically hypothesize the potential effects of each option (multidimensional thinking) is better able to choose a "best fit" solution that considers all known current and long-range factors.

Because of inadequate environmental stimulation or intellectual limitations, some people fail to master formal operational thought. Others may not master the skills until the adult years when faced with more complex and frequent issues that require hypothetical–deductive thinking. Once acquired, the use of formal operational thought may be limited or even abandoned, depending on a person's response to environmental challenges.

Cognitive processing is affected by the health of the other domains. In a social climate where "difference" or individuality is frowned on, a person may repress use of creative or formal operational thought. Social convention forces the person to use ready-made solutions to problems. However, use or apparent nonuse of formal operational thought is not to be equated with knowledge or solutions. None of us, even the most gifted, uses formal operational thought all the time. Even Piaget noted: " . . . I am, for example, at an operatory level for only a small part of the day . . . the rest of the time I am dealing with empirical trial and error."[73] Most of the activities of daily living involve the use of habit patterns or concrete operational thought developed during the school years. Most of us resort to sensorimotor thought when trying to give directions or in describing or thinking about a favorite meal.

Cognitive processing is also influenced by one's physical and emotional status. Formal operational thought takes much energy. Reduced physical or emotional health reduces energies available to process more complex issues and problems, a factor that may be significant in precipitating accidents or other "stupid" decisions and behaviors.

Piaget notes marked differences in the levels of development attained by people. During adolescence, individual differences in education, experience, aptitude, motivation, talents, and interests begin to become significant in shaping the direction of formal operational thought. Piaget feels that these differences influence a person's career choice. Thereafter, he feels that the working environment contributes to one's knowledge base and to the use or nonuse of formal operations.[74] Law students build their career on their ability to apply precise logic to abstract concepts. Auto mechanics and physicians alike build their careers on the ability to hypothesize the source of a problem and then to systematically intervene to "cure" the ill (Fig. 27-4). It is important to note that although career *choice* may be based on one's interests, motivations, special talents, education, and competence, job *success* is largely determined by attitude, emotional maturity, and interpersonal relationship skills.

Although Piaget's framework for describing the processing of information appears to have universal applicability, the individual's data base is heavily influenced by culture and life experiences. A person who may be considered "intelligent" in one society may be thought to be quite naïve in a cultural context that requires a different knowledge base and adaptational skills.

Beyond Piaget

Riegel and Arlin

Several writers disagree with Piaget's concept that qualitative changes culminate with formal operational thought. K. F. Riegel, for example, has noted that the motivational force that underlies

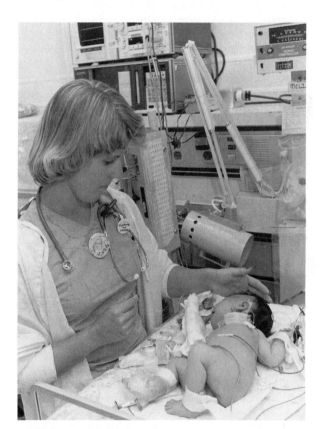

FIGURE 27–4.
Hypothetical–deductive and combinatorial thinking skills are essential prerequisites for the detective work inherent in many careers.

Piaget's frame for cognitive development is the need to resolve disequilibria (i.e., the desire to bridge discrepancies or contradictions between what the individual knows or understands and what is being communicated by some aspect of the individual's environment).[81] Riegel's position is that the hallmark of adult cognition is the seeking out of contradictions. He therefore proposes that adulthood is characterized by a shift in motivations that produces a fifth or "dialectic" stage of cognitive development. In a similar vein, Arlin refers to postformal operational thought as a "problem finding stage" in which the individual is concerned with discovering new questions rather than seeking well-defined answers to old questions.[3, 4] However, since neither Riegel nor Arlin addresses a change in the hierarchical structure of Piaget's theory, serious questions are raised as to whether either of these theories proposes a true postformal operation stage of cognitive development. In fact, they may represent a parallel form of cognition, since both of their emphasized characteristics can be found during Piaget's earlier stages and are not dependent on mastery of formal operational thought.[22, 81]

Commons

Michael Commons proposes two postformal operational stages that are hierarchically related to Piaget's four stages.[22] Each of Piaget's stages performs higher-level operations on the organization, rules, and relationships of the previous stage (Table 27-1). Commons' two *structural analytic stages* are found only in cognitively mature people. Like Piaget's theory, these stages involve cognitive operations on the structures or operations of lower stages. **Systematic operations** "consist of exhaustive operations on classes or relations of classes or relations," or the creation of systems.[22] Thus, the person creates holistic abstract representational systems by building operations on top of operations. Theory development falls into this category. **Metasystematic operations** consists of cognitions about the systems created. Such reasoning is essential for comparing and contrasting one system with another. Recognition of isomorphic properties of seemingly dissimilar philosophies, theories, and ideas involves metasystematic thinking because such thought is distinct and a step higher than understanding of the individual systems involved. **Metatheory** development is the end product. One is able to construct a supersystem and systematically analyze the subsystems or theories contained therein.[22] Einstein's general theory of relativity falls into this category (coordinates theories of inertial mass and gravitation). Von Bertalanffy's General Systems Theory also falls into this category (see Chap. 2).

Although Commons presents some substantial research data to support his theory, it is not yet clear whether these proposed stages require qualitatively different operations from Piaget's formal operations or if they are merely an application of the characteristics of formal operational thought (e.g., possibility thinking and combinatorial reasoning) to broader and more abstract issues. After all, Piaget's concept of conservation continues to emerge over a 6 year period and still may not be completed in all areas, even in young adulthood (e.g., 92% of college students conserve mass and weight, but only 58% conserve volume!).[39] Perhaps systematic operations is a sophisticated manifestation of hypothetical–deductive thinking (the ability to inductively create a new system) and metasystematic operations represents intricate multidimensional thinking (the ability to apply combinatorial reasoning to the new systems created). Perhaps it is our own cognitive limitations that hinder us from understanding or appreciating what Commons has to present! Commons states that, "exposure to and experience with problems that require abstract representational modes of analysis are undoubtedly necessary factors [for the development of his two stages], but just how native ability, education, and experience interact in this regard is a difficult issue to address."[22] Because of the intensity of these levels, "systematic and metasystematic reasoning is limited to the domain of formal, abstract, as opposed to everyday thought, in contrast to Piaget's formal operations, which are discernible in everyday thinking."[22]

Baltes

Baltes postulates that dual processes account for intelligence development across the life span.[7] The "mechanics" of intelligence involve the basic skills that closely parallel those previously referred to as fluid intelligence. "Pragmatics," on the other hand, reflect organized systems of knowledge, like social intelligence and wisdom, that are more concerned with specific situations and contexts and are, therefore, applied and adaptive in nature (crystallized intelligence). According to Baltes, intellectual development during infancy, childhood, and adolescence is characterized by the acquisition and development of mechanics, while that of adulthood is focused on both adjusting to age-related losses in mechanics and developing one's pragmatics to fit changing personal goals and situational contexts. The latter is considered the bellwether of adult intelligence.

According to this theory, adult intelligence is rather idiographic, that is, past life history, current life circumstances, and personal interests, values, needs, and desires all influence how each individual copes with life. Adult intelligence, con-

TABLE 27–1. COMMONS' CONSTRUCT OF HIERARCHICAL INTEGRATION OF COGNITIVE PROCESSES*

Stage	Operation
Sensorimotor	Action on material objects
Preoperational	Action with symbolic representations of material objects
Concrete operations	Organization of symbolic representations into classes and relations
Formal operations	Abstraction and further organization of classes and relations
Systematic operations	Creation of systems and theories from classes and relations
Metasystematic operations	Operations on systems and development of metatheories

*The first four stages were identified by Piaget.

ceptualized this way, can be assumed to be ecologically valid since it is measured in terms of an individual's adaptation within his or her "real world." Intelligence as psychometrically measured by standardized tests presumably measures something far different.

Schaie

K.W. Schaie also offers a life-span view of intellectual development, which he presents as a stage theory.[83, 84] However, the stages are defined in terms of external context rather than in terms of internal organizational structuring as found in Piaget's theory. According to Schaie, the intelligence of childhood and adolescence is one of acquiring and forming basic skills and abilities. In young adulthood, these skills and abilities begin to be "applied" to the solution of real life problems. Intellectual development continues as long as this application holds true. The "responsible" stage of middle age involves the application of skills and abilities to the management of "increasingly complex environmental demands." This phase meshes well with Daniel Levinson's description of individual life structure (see Chap. 38). In midlife, the adult is busy with an ever expanding set of responsibilities, each of which contains its own elements of change over time. The adult spends time reviewing previous decisions, undergoing personal change in the form of the disillusionment process, and beginning to plan for a future life that will be commensurate with his or her values. Worded differently, the middle-age adult balances and juggles past, present, and future considerations of the multiple roles of worker, parent, spouse, child to one's own aging parents, friend, mentor, and concerned citizen.

At the same time, some individuals, particularly those in the higher social strata as defined by education and vocation, may also be in the "executive" stage, in which their skills are directed toward decisions that extend beyond self and family to affect others. The final stage, the "reintegrative," is one in which intellect is applied to the solution of highly personal and pragmatic tasks. Intelligence during this stage is characterized by restricting one's attention to those aspects of the environment that remain salient and adaptive while ignoring those that are no longer of interest or relevance. It is further characterized by "intellectual integrity," which is a melding of everything that has been experienced in life up to that point, a concept similar to Erikson's "ego integrity."

COGNITION AND PROBLEM SOLVING

"People motivate and guide their actions anticipatorily through the exercise of forethought. They anticipate likely outcomes of prospective actions, set goals for themselves, and plan courses of action designed to realize valued futures . . . By cognitive representation in the present, conceived future events are converted into current motivators and regulators of behavior . . . The stronger the perceived self-efficacy, the higher the goals that people set for themselves and the firmer their commitment to those goals."[11]

The Young Adult Years

Freud suggested that the mature adult must balance two critical themes to find success and happiness: love and work.[43]

Although the five domains should be well differentiated by this point, they have developed networks that allow higher level integration and thus mutual support of continued development. The cognitive domain, as the executive domain of the person's system, is a critical factor in choices that affect career (work) and leisure (love). Choices made during the late adolescent and young adult years can, and usually do, affect the course of one's adulthood.

Career Choices

The young adult years are both exciting and frightening for many people as they make career choices. One's intellect is not the only factor in career choices. Although one's aptitude, knowledge base, and interests are critical factors, so are self-discipline, previous experiences, social and emotional maturity, and opportunities available in the community or the person's social and financial world. Little research is available on how most young adults choose a career. Obviously, propinquity plays a major role. A person who grows up in a mid-American community is more likely to become a farmer, mechanic, or teacher than a marine biologist, international lawyer, or scuba diver instructor. School guidance counselors help young people identify careers compatible with interest and aptitude strengths, often introducing careers a person never knew existed. For some, a career choice may be seen as an expression of one's personality, thus, a person who derives satisfaction out of helping other people may go into nursing, religious work, social services, or teaching.

Intelligence becomes a critical factor in career choice in that each line of work embraces its own body of knowledge, which must be mastered to perform adequately. Consequently, entrance into the job market may require certification of completion of an educational program or a competency exam. Even a fast-food service may require passing a simple reading or math test. Other careers may require evidence of the ability to do research, to resolve complicated problems, or to make "wise" decisions.

College

Approximately 35% of young adults attend college or technical schools,[96] some to prepare themselves for a specific career, others to explore interest options with the hope that a career choice will eventually emerge, some to provide a moratorium on assuming adult responsibilities, and a few, admittedly, to "find a mate." Whatever the reason, college courses should expand young people's awareness of their own cognitive abilities and interests as well as their awareness of the ideas, theories, and works of other great minds. Students and faculty alike sharpen their understandings and clarify their own positions by discussing and sharing conflicting views or philosophies.

There are a few secrets to obtaining and maintaining a

high grade point average. The most obvious is organizing one's time adequately to complete all the readings and assignments in a timely fashion. A rule of thumb is a minimum of 2 hours of outside study time for every 1 hour of class time. Those who experience poor grades because of high test anxiety are reassured to learn that participation in relaxation exercises three times a week can decrease test anxiety. However, participation in aerobic exercises three times a week can result in both decreased test anxiety *and* increased physical fitness.[92] Physical exercise also can increase a person's speed. However, it will not increase accuracy unless accompanied by appropriate study techniques.[12]

A person's receptivity to new ideas partially depends on affective development, the individual's outlook on the world, and self-esteem. The more affectively mature and secure person often seeks differing opinions or viewpoints that challenge previously held concepts and expand knowledge. The emotionally secure person does not feel a need to defend his or her own view or ideas and thus can concentrate more effectively on intellectual activities that modify or expand previous ideas to achieve a more holistic picture.

Often, the initial insight into or discovery of a concept occurs during the early adult years. Many people then spend a lifetime implementing the salient principles, elaborating on the concept, or further exploring possibilities. Albert Einstein is supposed to have shared that he only had two worthy ideas during his lifetime, both during early adulthood. He spent the remainder of his life exploring the significance of those ideas.

Although some financial remuneration is essential, it is not the only criterion for career choice. Many adults find that a career choice and subsequent educational pursuits are based more on the perceived challenge, meaningfulness, and ability to exploit one's cognitive, affective, and social skills than on salary potentials alone. Many young adults are willing to sacrifice or delay personal pleasures, material possessions, and social relationships in the pursuit of an education that will enable them to secure a more challenging and rewarding career. For some, cognitive challenge takes on a life of its own, often turning into a career of research or a lifelong pursuit of knowledge as found in college teaching or research.

Noncollege Adults

Many persons choose not to go to college but to pursue other forms of job security. Some end up in blue collar, semiskilled, or unskilled jobs by default rather than by choice. Premature assumption of marital or family responsibilities often precludes pursuit of higher education (Fig. 27-5). Failure to finish high school or the inability to read also prevents some people from developing cognitive and interest potentials for a specific career. Some may find a position as custodian, waitress, receptionist, or construction worker to be satisfying and adequately challenging. Others desire more cognitive challenge, self-fulfillment, or opportunity for self-expression than such careers offer. Inadequate preparation or opportunities set the stage for conflict, job hopping, or even unemployment. Although it may mean much personal sacrifice, and even hard-

FIGURE 27–5.
Many choices and responsibilities undertaken during the early adult years make pursuit of education difficult, but not impossible.

ship, young people who are dissatisfied with their current career options are encouraged to go back to school to pursue a specific interest to open up career, cognitive, and financial opportunities.

Determining Success

One of the myths of western cultures is that hard work will bring success. While this statement may be true in some situations, many of the hardest working people are never recognized or adequately compensated. "Trying" is not always enough. Promotions or opportunities many times are based more on networking or on who one knows, "the right connections," than on one's personal ability or even contribution. Although this fact is hard to face, it is one of the realities of adult life. Many young adults also begin to realize that usually there is more than one way to do things—not just a right and wrong way, but good and better ways. Finding the "better way" provides a cognitive challenge and job satisfaction not contingent on financial award. Employers who allow employees the freedom to contribute to the improvement of their work environment, product, service, or management, usually find greater loyalty, productivity and longevity; witness the changes in Eastern Europe. One's satisfaction and morale are generally highest when cognitive interests and skills match the employer's and society's needs. Those who do not find intrinsic satisfaction in their jobs often find that other factors (e.g., salary, vacation policies, insurance) provide adequate compensation to allow them to pursue their avocational interests, which contribute to their own, their family's, or the community's welfare through exploitation of their cognitive skills in different settings.

Leisure

Researchers have struggled to come up with a workable definition of leisure. Among those tried (and found to be lacking in one or another aspect) are: (1) distinguishing between *instrumental (extrinsic)* activities, in which future gratification is sought or the sources of reward are external to the activity itself, versus *expressive (intrinsic)* activities, in which the pleasure, satisfaction, and reward are immediate and derived from the process of doing; (2) defining leisure as relaxation from the stresses and strains that accompany one's daily regimes; or (3) looking at how people spend their discretionary time, that is, time not spent at compensated work.

Leisure time can obviously be used to pursue one's intellectual interests, whether they are career related or not. One can also engage in activities that foster cognitive skills and talents that serve to keep the individual up to date during a time of rapid societal change in both technology and knowledge bases. Staying current can, in turn, either bolster one's ongoing career or lay the foundation for a possible shift in careers. Leisure time may also be used as an outlet for creative talents and urges that are either ignored or stifled in the work place.

Whatever the intellectual, cognitive, or creative benefit, leisure ought to serve to enhance the affective domain. Leisure activities that are subjectively perceived as personally meaningful and emotionally satisfying are known to facilitate psychological well-being.[70] Also, recall Freud's suggestion that mature adults must balance love and work to find success and happiness. Part of loving may involve taking care of one's own affective domain by finding time to play as a balance against overworking.

Over time, leisure preferences shift away from the more physically active interests of younger adults toward pursuits that are increasingly sedentary and passive. This trend is unfortunate. It has long been considered a factor that contributes to age-related declines in biological functioning and general health status; it is becoming increasingly clear that sedentary activities are also detrimental to intellectual and cognitive functioning. Aerobic exercise programs contribute to relieving psychological stress symptoms and improvements in reaction times, attention, several memory indices, and some measures of mental flexibility in older adults.[67]

The good news is that old and young alike, even those who are totally "out of shape," can benefit dramatically from such programs. The bad news is that it is extremely difficult to initiate and then maintain the motivation to do so in older adults who are not exercise oriented. Generally speaking, older people have difficulty establishing satisfying leisure time activities once the time becomes available (as in retirement) if they have not developed a leisure time regimen earlier in life. The key, then, is to institute such programs early in life; the formation of habit together with the realization of benefits derived and losses experienced on nonparticipation serve to strengthen and maintain the motivation.

The Middle Adult Years

Current studies indicate that general intelligence is maintained or even increases slightly up to about 55 to 60 years of age.[26, 68, 85] Intelligence continues to develop, resulting in functioning that is stable or superior to that exhibited by younger adults throughout the period of middlescence and into the beginnings of old age.[8, 86] The differences in assessment scores may actually reflect the life history advantage of middlescent over younger people. Recent generations have been exposed to a society that places a greater demand on individuals for heightened intellectual performance. It is also assumed that the continued use of intellectual functions results in greater stability or at least less decline in these abilities throughout the middle and later years. Middlescent adults also show the effects of individual specialization and the interindividual differentiation of life trajectories.[8] Research findings indicate that little or no long-term memory deficit occurs during the period of adulthood,[42] and that significant short-term memory losses occur only at quite old ages.[50]

Learning, Problem Solving, and Productivity

Middle-age adults who are still relatively attuned to the procedures of formal education and who are still oriented toward general achievement motives are more likely to be highly motivated to perform well on the problem-solving and learning tasks presented to them during formal assessments. Middlescents who find the tasks totally irrelevant to their personal motivations and concerns may do poorly on laboratory tasks, thus appearing to have a reduced intellectual functioning.

Because it is so difficult to untangle the effects produced by generational differences, task characteristics, and motivational status from those produced by true age-related changes in learning ability and problem-solving capacity, it seems logical to move away from laboratory-based research findings to gain additional perspective. Middle-age adults, because of life history, exhibit a greater fund of knowledge during the midlife period than they did at younger ages. There is also a clear consensus that measures of general productivity, achievement, and community and work involvement reach a peak during middlescence. Such real-life measures of performance, when contrasted with the performance given in laboratory settings, clearly imply that middle-age adults are at the height of their competency with regard to the type of learning and problem solving that applies to their everyday lives. The competence exhibited in real-life situations by middle-age adults is the interface of functioning of all five domains.

Increased differentiation of the domains and greater emotional maturity generally enable the middlescent adult to develop the skill of wisdom (discussed later).

Continued Education

Many companies require and provide continued education for their employees to ensure competent performance in their positions and to offer opportunity for advancement (Fig. 27-6). Changes in technology render some jobs or job skills obsolete, precipitating the need for further education or facing of the unemployment lines. Many women find themselves lacking adequate employment skills when widowed or divorced and return to school as a way to ensure future financial security. Dissatisfaction with one's original career choice or a desire to enlarge one's professional horizons sends many middlescent adults back to school. Other middlescents find that, once their children are older, they are free to pursue earlier career goals and subsequently return to college.

Many middlescents are quite apprehensive about returning to the academic world. They remember the struggles they had with courses during adolescence and often believe the myth that middlescents experience a decrease in intelligence. The fear of failure also plagues them with concern of personal embarrassment before friends and family. Once enrolled, most middlescent students discover that their increased personal maturity and experience tend to make concepts easier to understand and, thus, material easier to remember (Fig. 27-7). Many of these students excel as they rediscover the joy of concentrating on development of the cognitive domain.

The Older Adult

Of paramount concern in regard to cognitive functioning of older adults is the distinction between performance and competence. Many gerontologists argue that the inferior performance of older adults is due to motivational problems or troublesome situational determinants rather than to deficits in cognitive competence per se. What follows is a discussion of these types of variables together with an exploration of possible differences in competency factors.

Situational Determinants

Pacing Effects

Laboratory assessments of cognitive functioning and problem solving are almost always time rather than power based (how much or how well can you do with unlimited time). It is a well-established fact that when tasks are rapidly paced, the performance of younger subjects is clearly superior to that of older subjects, while slower pacing results in a more even (but still not equal) performance.

Under typical laboratory conditions, two types of errors are possible: so-called "errors of commission" occur when responses are inaccurate or wrong; and "errors of omission," when the subject simply fails to respond at all. Under rapid pacing conditions, the rate of commission errors is about equal for the two age groups, whereas the omission error rate is much greater for the elderly subjects.[16] While both age

FIGURE 27-6.
Although new technology and skills may seem threatening to learn at first, most adults find the new skills fun as well as supportive of the expanded responsibilities of their careers.

FIGURE 27-7.
Non-traditional students bring maturity and experience to the classroom—factors which help them place new information into a broader context and provide it with meaning beyond campus life.

groups appear to benefit about equally from slower pacing in terms of commission errors, it is the older people who benefit the most in terms of improving their omission error rates.[1,36] One can therefore infer that older people are as competent as younger adults in mastering tasks, but they just require more time to do so. Taken collectively, studies suggest that the performance deficit that remains after the pace of a task has been manipulated is due to the relatively greater difficulty that older subjects have in retrieving previously acquired information, a cognitive capacity and competence factor.[2,18,55,58,66] This inference seems to be compatible with the established findings of a slowdown in biological function and an increase in reaction time with advancing age. Other data, however, suggest that this inference may be overly simplified.

Task Relevance and Meaningfulness

An increasing number of criticisms about lack of ecological validity and the use of "arbitrary laboratory trivia" have been leveled at researchers.[5] It has been pointed out that standardized cognitive and learning-memory tasks, amenable to the demands for formal education, are positively biased in favor of younger subjects. It is claimed that older subjects find such tasks, especially those using unfamiliar, novel, or "nonsense" materials, to be irrelevant to the conduct of their lives. This lack of relevancy or meaningfulness, in turn, introduces motivational differences that once again tend to favor younger adults.[6,23] Attempts to enhance the relevancy or meaningfulness of task materials often produce a marked improvement in older subjects' performances. On the other hand, these studies also reveal that the performance of these older subjects rarely reaches a level comparable to that of the younger subjects; still other studies suggest that dramatically increased meaningfulness actually exaggerates the deficits of the elderly.[13,17,30,44,77] Thus, the use of novel, unfamiliar, or meaningless materials does not appear to be the sole determinant of the performance deficit of older persons.

Motivation

It has already been suggested that the reduced performances of older adults may be an artifact of age differences or age changes in motivation rather than time-related declines or deficits in cognitive capacity or competence.[16,38] Older people may be more cautious, less involved, or overaroused and threatened by laboratory tasks.[38]

Increased Cautiousness. Part of the attractiveness of this hypothesis is its congruence with two motivational shifts discussed in Chapter 38: the shift from an expansive to a constrictive orientation and the shift from active to passive mastery. Both clearly suggest that older adults manifest greater caution in a wide variety of situations than young adults. One manifestation of the age-related increase in cautiousness is an increased concern among older subjects about the accuracy or correctness of their responses. When assessments are timed, people sometimes feel forced to choose between being accurate or being fast. Because older adults are more concerned with accuracy, they often fail to respond

to all the items within the time limits imposed on them. By virtue of being less cautious, younger adults are willing to accept reduced accuracy to comply with the pacing demands of the task.

Other researchers have attempted to test the hypothesis of increased cautiousness by more direct means: the application of a methodology derived from **signal detection theory.** This methodology enables a researcher to estimate the degree of confidence that subjects must have about the correctness of their response before they are willing to actually venture an answer. Cautious subjects should adopt more stringent (higher) confidence levels than noncautious subjects. Some studies report significant age difference in cautiousness,[56,93] while others report no differences;[47,48,94] still others suggest the existence of a complex relationship between cautiousness, age, and ability levels.[27]

Underarousal. Some researchers noted that many of their oldest subjects appeared to be resentful and lacked interest in the assessment items and, therefore, were less inclined to make full use of their cognitive skills in the performance of the tasks presented to them.[54] When given a choice, a large percentage of older adults simply refused to make the effort to memorize word-to-letter pairs of stimuli. When researchers changed the stimulus materials to occupation name pairs, the elderly subjects participated more willingly in the study.[54] While the shift of stimuli can be viewed as a manipulation of task meaningfulness, it also points to the fact that older subjects become more involved in or more motivated to perform tasks when they are perceived to be relevant, meaningful, and ecologically valid.

Several research studies have attempted to increase task involvement (or decrease task cautiousness) via the use of monetary incentives.[28,41,49] The results of these studies are mixed, leading researchers to conclude that it is difficult to facilitate the cognitive performances of elderly adults via the noncognitive manipulation of motivation.[29]

Some studies have used "bioelectric" measures (the galvanic skin response, heart rate, vasoconstriction) of autonomic nervous system function to assess the level of physiological arousal in older subjects during testing. Evidence has supported the underarousal hypothesis.[65]

Overarousal. Some gerontologists believe that stress or anxiety is responsible for poor test performance. Thus, response inhibition is due to heightened anxiety or overarousal, the same reason given by many students for "blocking" or "going blank" on a critical exam when the material is clearly understood. Some of the most convincing evidence in support of the "overarousal" or the "heightened anxiety" hypothesis comes from studies that find the overall performance of elderly subjects to improve and the number of omission errors to dramatically decrease when the pacing of task trials is slowed down.[35] The interpretation is that the slower pacing reduces overall test anxiety.

The poorer performance of elderly subjects under rapid pacing conditions also was discovered to be accompanied by, or associated with, an increased level of physiological arousal as evidenced by an assessment of blood plasma levels of free fatty acids.[78] To demonstrate that anxiety was inhibiting performance, the researchers attempted to experimentally lower the arousal by administering Propanol, a drug that blocks autonomic nervous system (ANS) arousal.[37] As hypothesized, a significant reduction was seen in both fatty acid levels and in the total number of errors committed.

In summary, hypotheses of underarousal or overarousal appear to merit about the same status as the hypothesis of increased cautiousness. It appears unlikely that any one or combination of the three theories fully explains the deficits that characterize the problem-solving performances of the elderly. For this reason, we now turn to a discussion of possible age-related differences in competency factors.

Cognitive Competency Factors

Central Nervous System Slowdown
Several of the factors already discussed (pacing effects, commission versus omission errors, and overarousal) can be reinterpreted as reflections of an age-related decline in the speed of central nervous system processing. First, studies that seek to establish the source of the age-related increase in reaction time suggest that central rather than peripheral processes are involved; that is, the increase in reaction time lies in the processing of the information and not the time required to either stimulate the senses or execute motor responses (Fig. 27-8).[95] The gap between the reaction times of older and younger adults widens as the task becomes increasingly complex, that is, when more information needs to be processed. Secondly, developmental studies of the brain's overall electrical activity also suggest that aging is accompanied by a change in brain wave patterns that are indicative of "slowed activity."[16]

Memory
One current view of the memory system is that it consists of (1) sensory register, (2) primary memory, (3) secondary memory, and (4) tertiary memory "stores," as well as the processes for registration, encoding, and retrieval of information from the four "stores."[76] The last "store" is synonymous with long-term memory, while the middle two seem to collectively represent what has been referred to as short-term memory.

Some researchers, however, prefer to think about memory purely in terms of "processes" rather than "stores."[24] According to this theory of memory, information is retained in memory as long as it is actively attended to (the primary memory process). Once attention is diverted, however, the information is lost from memory at a rate commensurate with the depth at which the information was processed (the secondary memory process) while it was attended to. Note the possibility for confusion between primary memory as one of the four hypothesized "stores" and the view of primary memory as a temporary holding and organizing process.

Little evidence suggests that age differences or age changes occur in the sensory store (perceptual memory),

FIGURE 27–8.
Healthy older adults tend to maintain excellent cognitive and motor functions, which enable them to pursue avocational interests well into the retirement years.

where information is processed in terms of its physical qualities (e.g., loudness, location, or form) and held for relatively short durations, and where capacity is limited to two to four discrete bits of information. Nor is there clear-cut evidence that age differences or age changes occur in the tertiary memory store which is believed to have a large or unlimited capacity, and where information is assumed to be permanently stored. When age differences in tertiary memory are found, they are more likely to favor older adults who may remember distant events in detail, even though they may concurrently experience difficulty following the story line of a television program.[72]

Age differences and age changes that clearly and consistently favor younger adults can be demonstrated only for the secondary memory store, which is used when the capacity for the primary store is exceeded. Its capacity is estimated to be five to nine discrete bits of information, which are stored for relatively short durations (minutes). The age differences and changes in secondary memory tend to be rather small when measured via recognition tasks (receptive memory) and rather substantial when recall tasks (expressive memory) are used. Older adults encounter the least difficulty in memory when asked to recall events or day-to-day events that involve action, since sensorimotor involvement seems to facilitate memory.[59, 80]

Recognition tasks (like true–false or multiple choice

tests) provide the individual with definitive cues that can be used to direct retrieval (receptive memory). *Recall tasks* (like "tell me all that you can remember about X") provide fewer and less definitive retrieval cues (expressive memory). The greater deficit for older adults under recall relative to recognition conditions suggests that retrieval is the primary culprit. However, since retrieval and the use of retrieval cues are likely to depend on the way the information was originally put into the "store," the encoding process of older adults (how meaning is given to incoming information) is held suspect as well.

Attention

Part of the problem that older adults have with short-term memory may result from deficits in attention. Few if any age differences or changes in short-term memory are found in tasks that involve information that humans appear to process automatically and effortlessly (e.g., spatial, temporal, and frequency issues). Age differences or changes are much greater (and in favor of younger adults) when the tasks require effortful attention, especially when that attention also must be selective, such as when paying attention to multiple stimuli or discriminating between relevant and irrelevant information.[25,71,75] Simply stated, it can be argued that short-term memory tasks that involve effortful processing are more of a drain on the capacity of elderly adults, thus limiting their ability to simultaneously engage in other important cognitive activities. This idea fits with the hypothesis that information begins to be lost from memory as soon as it is no longer used (the "use it or lose it" hypothesis).

Rehearsal, Mediation, Depth of Processing, and Organizational Structures

A number of studies suggest that the memory system of older adults may be deficient in other ways. For one, older people appear to rehearse new material less frequently, sometimes with just a single repetition of the information.

When memorizing a list composed of the words plate, bicycle, fork, napkin, car, and ferry, one can separately process each of the six words or create a verbal or visual association between them that would help to categorize or organize them in such a way that one word provides storage and retrieval cues for the others. Verbal or visual associations that are used this way are called "mediators," and their use dramatically facilitates learning and performance. In the above example, one might think about "items of transportation" and "eating implements," or one might picture a ferryboat on which sits a car with bicycle atop and driver sitting inside with napkin and plate on her lap and fork in hand. Younger adults tend to spontaneously generate such mediators. Older adults generate and use mediators less frequently during encoding. However, they are capable of doing so on request or when taught how to do so.[16] When and if older people do process information deeply, they appear to be as efficient as younger adults in putting information into long-term memory and keeping it there. This ability helps to account for the lack of age differences or changes in tertiary memory.

Some studies suggest that older adults appear to generate and process information at shallower levels, and they use different organizational strategies or structures than do younger people. When the knowledge structures of younger adults is accepted as the standard for assessment, then older adults can be considered deficient or less effective. However, when it is acknowledged that older adults have created knowledge structures that are appropriate to their needs, interests, lifestyles, and circumstances, then the knowledge structures of older people may be seen as being about as efficient to their lives as are those of younger adults. Again, the notion of an aging deficit is, to a degree, contextually bound. Whether the knowledge structures of the elderly are really deficient or contextually efficient depends on the degree to which such laboratory materials and tasks are ecologically valid indicators of real life for a developmentally older age.

Factors Associated With the Notion of Mental Rigidity

Scattered throughout the literature, references can be found to an age-related increase in mental rigidity, an assumption for which empirical support is mixed and no consensual agreement can be reached.[16] However, some factors may play a role in any apparent decline in intellectual functioning, since the individual resists creative flexibility in problem solving. **Resistance to extinction** refers to the strength of a "conditioned" response or behavior. When a behavior has been rewarded or successful most of the time (close to 100%), it is established rapidly but is also weakened or lost more rapidly once reinforcement is stopped. When reinforcement is less frequent (the usual course of life events), responses are acquired more slowly but are also more resistant to extinction. The person attempts to replicate earlier successes through continued use of the behavior. Older people are more likely than younger people to persist in the production of behaviors that no longer earn rewards and to use old responses to solve novel problems, perhaps because they have found it so effective in the past and perhaps because systematic evaluation of a novel situation and the creation of an effective novel response may take more energy than the person is willing to expend.

Sets and expectancies refer to the tendency to "assimilate" a problem into current expectancies and to call on old habits to solve the problem. Performance, therefore, should be facilitated when the individual's predetermined responses (habits) coincide with the proper solution to the current problem (positive transfer); performance is hindered when the individual's predetermined responses or mind set provide an unrealistic or maladaptive solution to a current problem (negative transfer). It may be more difficult to identify laboratory tasks appropriate for the sets and expectancies of older adults;[15,64] therefore, differential positive and negative transfer effects may be found for younger and older adults.[45]

Functional fixedness refers to a specific form of learning set or expectancy, one in which the individual is unable to use a particular object for anything other than its traditional use or function. Such fixedness should increase with age, since more time has been spent using a particular object in its customary or usual fashion. Therefore, when problems call for the creative use of objects in terms of their abstract rather than their functional properties, elderly adults may be affected more negatively than younger ones.

In truth, most older adults (60–80 year olds) exhibit much plasticity in functioning and even in learning. Cognitive training studies show a gain in performance levels.[8] Research in brain anatomy (mostly through animal research) provides evidence that, at any stage of life, an enriched, more challenging environment stimulates a thicker cortex and larger neurons, factors that facilitate more accurate problem solving.[33]

Everyday Functioning of Older Adults

It is important to note that the entire discussion of competency and production deficits is based on measures derived from formalized laboratory-type tasks and procedures. What about cognitive processes and change in relation to the activities of daily living? Some early findings derived from "naturalistic" studies suggest that the elderly define their problems differently than do the young: they are more likely to recognize the necessity for taking advice, conserving time and resources, and distinguishing between critical and extraneous tasks and demands.[61] Their functioning is influenced by a different set of life experiences and, consequently, a different set of values and priorities. Most still believe that they are able to learn and improve their performance with effort but may relinquish some tasks to others whom they see as more competent.[61]

In considering the real life performance of older people, it is naïve to regard them as passive victims of cognitive degeneration. On the contrary, older people are observed to conserve and exploit their intellectual resources more fully than do the young and to have a more subtle perception of the points at which the complexity of decisions exceeds their capacities, and thereby they avoid unnecessary blunders. It is fitting to conclude with this reminder: The study of performance is not merely the study of "'decrements in performance.' Unless we recognize that it is also the study of 'adaptation' to decrements of performance, we shall entirely miss the point."[79]

Summary Statement on Cognition and Problem Solving of Older Persons

There is little doubt that younger adults out-perform their older counterparts on almost all traditionally used measures of cognition and problem solving. It is also obvious that a number of performance-related factors can be manipulated either to widen or close this gap. Even under optimal performance conditions, however, some degree of gap still remains, thus leading to the conclusion that genuine, though usually small, age differences and changes in cognitive competency exist. Nevertheless, "there is no general (across abilities) and normative (applicable to most persons) change in the capacity of adult individuals until they reach age 60–70,"[8] and even

then, the declines are usually insignificant.[61] Most people function within the "normal" range of cognitive processing until late old age or death.

It is one thing to say that an older learner or problem solver is not as efficient as a younger one; it is an entirely different matter to say that the older adult is incapable of either learning or problem solving. The fact that older adults are less likely to spontaneously use mediators or to process information at deeper levels, but can do so when either instructed or taught how to do so, suggests that many of these deficits are in production rather than competency per se. This distinction is not trivial! Although learning and problem solving may not be as efficient in old age as in youth or middle age, both processes are active to a greater extent than is usually portrayed in stereotypes about the cognitive functioning of older adults. Furthermore, to the degree that we believe that optimization of one's functioning is the right of individuals of all ages, it behooves us to consider the various manipulations necessary for the creation of an optimal learning and problem-solving environment for the older adult.

Wisdom

From the perspective of day-to-day living, intellectual and cognitive functioning represents more than the accretion of formal knowledge and/or problem-solving techniques. It also includes the acquisition and use of what we commonly refer to as **wisdom.** Wisdom is not automatic with age. It requires the loss of adolescent egocentrism and the growth of the ability to separate the emotional, social, and cognitive domains for effective decision making (Fig. 27-9). Wisdom may be seen as the "fine tuning" of reasoning or the judicious application of knowledge for the resolution of the problems of daily living.

The person of wisdom has begun to extract meaning from experiences and can creatively explore multiple options. The person of wisdom broadens the horizons of time and meaning beyond the immediate situation or Freud's "pleasure principle" when making a decision. He or she is able to see the problem in the context of long-range implications as well as to appreciate the perspective or needs of other persons. The "wise" person can anticipate the unexpected, taking those factors into account when making a decision.

In short, wisdom is not based on intelligence (although a basic body of knowledge is essential for effective decisions) as much as the ability to free oneself from the emotional overtones of the situation to make a "best-fit" decision in light of one's needs, values, and goals, the needs of other people, the long-range implications, and the specifics of the situation. The key is one's ability to logically and humanely prioritize all the factors involved and, through combinatorial and multidimensional thought, to arrive at a solution that achieves the goal while offering the fewest negative side effects. As such, wisdom is predicated on affective maturity, not just cognitive maturity.

FIGURE 27–9.
Communities and employers appreciate those who show wisdom and allocentrism in the performance of "routine" responsibilities. Because of them, our communities are better places to live.

THE EXCEPTIONAL ADULT

The Intellectually Gifted Adult

In 1921, Lewis B. Terman began a longitudinal study of 1528 children ages 3 to 19, all of whom had IQs above 135 (average IQ 150).[91] Follow-ups were conducted every 5 to 12 years and again in 1982, when many of the subjects were in their seventies. These data provide a rare opportunity to look at the course of adult development in a group of intellectually gifted individuals.

"The number [of men] who became research scientists, engineers, physicians, lawyers, or college teachers, or who were highly successful in business and other fields, is in each case many times the number a random group would have provided."[91] The women appeared to be "ahead of their time" in that they joined the work force in larger numbers than was expected of women in that era. More of them also remained single, delayed marriage and parenthood, or chose to remain childless. A higher than usual proportion of them moved into professional and managerial positions, and they appeared to be much happier in their work than reported by other working women.[46]

Starting with the 1960 follow-up, an attempt was made to compare the most and least successful male members of the original population. The terms "most" and "least" successful are clearly relative, since almost all subjects equalled or exceeded the general population in terms of occupational status and income. Nevertheless, some significant and provocative differences between the two subgroups were discovered. While both subgroups scored about the same on the original intelligence tests in 1921, as children, the members of the most successful subgroup skipped more grades, graduated earlier from high school, and received more graduate or professional training. As adults, their occupational status and income level was significantly higher, they belonged to a greater number of professional and civic organizations, they were more physically active, preferring participation sports to

spectator sports, they experienced lower mortality rates, they possessed a broader range of interests, *and they grew progressively smarter as they grew older.*[46] In midlife, they also had better personal and marital adjustment and were happier and more satisfied with family life, self, and work (listed in order of reported importance to these men).

The key background difference between the two subgroups appears to have been the *greater willpower, perseverance, and desire to excel demonstrated by the members of the most successful subgroup,* a set of traits clearly present in childhood and apparently fostered by parents who encouraged ambition, initiative, and independence, and who applied more pressure to excel. **Success was related to emotional and social factors, not to intellect alone** (Fig. 27-10). These people possessed a verve for life, had discovered the joy of living, were active, not passive, participants in life. Now well into old age, this population of intellectually gifted individuals continues to be smarter, happier, healthier, more active, and richer and to have lower incidence of suicide, mortality, alcoholism, or divorce than the general population. Fewer of them are fully retired, and they continue to outstrip the general population on all measures of productivity.[46]

The Intellectually Impaired Adult

One is tempted to speculate that a group of school-age children selected on the basis of below average intelligence would, during adulthood, possess the opposite characteristics of Terman's sample on measures of occupational status, income, physical and mental health status, personal sense of happiness, and mortality rates. In spite of this negative assumption, many such individuals successfully attain and maintain significant positions in the social, civic, and work arenas that are essential to the well-being of themselves and society as a whole. High self-ratings on success and happiness are not automatically tied to intellectual giftedness, as witnessed by the differences between Terman's least and most successful subgroups. Improved social, educational, and habilitative ser-

FIGURE 27–10.
Success in college pursuits or life itself depends on the person's commitment and perseverance, not intellect alone. The brightest student can fail if he or she has insufficient self-discipline to complete assignments.

vices and programs for people with suboptimal intelligence are increasing both productivity and life satisfaction. The key to perceived success is whether or not one finds a comfortable match between potentials/ambitions and opportunities/rewards. It clearly behooves us, then, to strive to maximize and appreciate the potential of each of society's members for productivity, success, and personal happiness.

Creativity Across Adulthood

The first systematic attempt to study creativity in nonacademic as well as scholarly areas across adulthood is represented by the work of Lehman.[62,63] According to his data, maximum creativity was achieved in early adulthood but declined rapidly from age 30 onward. Furthermore, he documented this pattern across quite diverse disciplines. He contended that the creative output of chemists and orchestral composers at age 60 was only about one fifth of the peak rates established before age 30. This rather negative picture of creativity across adulthood was immediately challenged on the basis of his failure to control for individual differences in longevity. Since the works of relatively short-lived individuals were combined with those of relatively long-lived persons, there was a built-in statistical bias for greater productivity in the earlier decades of adulthood.

When the creative productivity of individuals who lived to age 79 and beyond is considered, the findings turn out to be quite different.[31,32] Midlife, defined as the decades of the forties and fifties, is the most productive period for most professions, while historians and philosophers (scholars) are most productive in their sixties! Research on creative productivity in the arts suggests that poets and composers of classical music tend to produce their best works in their late thirties, while the writing of imaginative and informative prose peaks in the early to mid-40s and age 50 respectively.[89,90] Data also reveals that creativity declines quite gradually; that is, the consistency in both productivity levels and the production of highly creative works continues throughout adulthood.[89,90] Research findings on creative productivity in scientists and mathematicians indicates that the age of peak productivity is achieved in the 40s and begins to decline gradually around age 50.[21] Furthermore, a significant amount of stability is found among individual mathematicians in both productivity levels and in the production of high-quality works.

Taken as a whole, these findings are quite impressive, since they reflect more than intelligence or creative capacity per se. The maintenance of high activity and energy levels and proper motivation are also crucial, especially at a time of life when circumstances are often said to conspire to favor "youth."

Interestingly, it does not appear that a single individual in Terman's group could be deemed a creative genius of the magnitude of an Einstein, Mendel, Pasteur, Beethoven, or Picasso. One or more such individuals may yet be identified, since it often takes years to fully recognize, understand, and appreciate such contributions. However, it is also possible that none exist in this group. Fewer than 1% of adults have achievements labeled as "creative-productive," and then it may be in such a narrow field as to go unrecognized by most of the world.[88] While creativity and intelligence are clearly related, IQ scores are inadequate for assessment of creativity. Social and emotional factors, such as committedness, are also significant.[88] Since Terman's group was selected solely on the basis of very high IQ, it is possible that exceptionally creative individuals with somewhat lower IQs who did develop special creativity were screened out. Then again, some potentially creative people never find the right opportunity or are never recognized beyond their own families or communities (Fig. 27-11).

FIGURE 27–11.
Some careers require a unique combination of talent and creativity, as well as opportunity and the willingness to work long hours.

The Talented Adult

Children of exceptional talent do not necessarily maintain exceptionality in that area as an adult, since many other adults, with education and practice, tend to "catch up" in skill levels. The child prodigy may lose motivation to excel or further develop a talent when special acclaim begins to fall away and personal effort based on self-discipline becomes more critical. However, many of the "talents" do become avocations that break the intensity of career pursuits and allow for expressions of creativity and individuality as mentioned in the section on adult leisure.

The Illiterate Adult

Twenty percent of adults in our society are functionally illiterate. They do not possess the reading and writing skills necessary to be self-confident and self-sufficient participants in their homes, communities, and society. It is estimated that 35 million or more American adults do not possess the minimal reading skills needed to survive independently.[60] Illiteracy is a disaster of national proportions in a technological society. Illiteracy and poverty are highly correlated.

Functional Illiteracy

Many nonreaders have grown up in socioeconomically disadvantaged areas with parents and peers who have not encouraged academic skills or who have not helped them to develop their cognitive talents. Many disabled persons were formerly denied educational services as a child ("weak body, weak mind") or were sheltered from the community because the family was embarrassed or lacked confidence in the child's ability to learn (thus creating a doubly handicapped adult).

An alarming number of functionally illiterate individuals attended elementary school, and many of them have been awarded high-school diplomas. However, they never learned to read or write sufficiently to be able to satisfactorily compose letters, fill out employment applications, write a check, find a number in the telephone directory, or read directions on a package, a note from their child's teacher, or the front page of a newspaper, let alone any leisure reading. Grocery shopping and food preparation may be difficult. In addition, many of these functionally illiterate individuals cannot perform simple arithmetic, creating problems in financial management. Low literacy skills make many young people unfit for military service. School was merely a holding pen for ± 12 years. No one ever took the time to care enough to adequately assess or to individualize teaching to the developing citizen's needs. The parents, for whatever reason, did not adequately monitor the child's school progress. The result is an adult inadequately prepared to assume the full mantle of adulthood in the Western culture. Television becomes a major source of information.

The functionally illiterate adult usually possesses a low self-esteem and, feeling ignorant, is afraid that others will discover the problem and make fun of or take advantage of him or her. Although their children come home from school learning to read and to do simple math, many illiterate parents make no attempt to learn from their children. Other illiterate parents try to hide their deficit from their children. Moreover, some parents may make fun of learning and instill a disrespect for education in their children, perpetuating the mentality of illiteracy to another generation. In the "land of equal opportunity," illiteracy shuts them off from the mainstream of American life.

Non–English-Speaking Adults in American Society

Immigrants and other persons to whom English is a second language face many of the same problems as the functionally illiterate adult. Even blind persons, though competent in Braille, experience difficulty in tasks that require skill in the printed language. Non-English speakers, even highly educated professionals, face discrimination in employment and are often relegated to low-paying positions that perpetuate their poverty status. Inability to understand street signs, the newspaper, advertisements, and other pieces of information limits their ability to take advantage of special sales, sets them up for getting lost in a strange environment, or increases their vulnerability to accidents. They may be unable to seek essential financial assistance from social agencies or to fill out the required forms. Food purchasing depends on pictures, and even television and magazines cannot be enjoyed if one does not understand the language.

Most debilitating is the inability to communicate with other people in the community or work world. Feelings, fears, pleasures, observations must all be kept to oneself, creating a lonely, depressing existence. The more intelligent the person, the more difficult is the lack of meaningful communication for the individual. Many express feeling like "big children" in the adult world.

Opportunities for Learning

Most illiterate adults can learn to read and write by enrolling in special classes or tutoring programs offered by departments of adult education in community school districts. Most communities also have courses designed to help the 28.5% of Americans who dropped out of high school to prepare for the high-school equivalency exam.[96] Some community colleges accept adults who have not finished high school and provide essential classes to enable them to graduate from college with either certification in a special area of training or an associate degree in an occupation. Many communities offer classes in English as a Second Language (ESL). These classes may be offered through churches, social agencies, and The American Red Cross, as well as community colleges and local adult education programs. The basic language acquisition takes about 500 hours of instruction; after that, it is a matter of vocabulary expansion.[19] A second language is best learned in context or with daily usage.

Persons with special vocational interests and aptitudes can take advantage of training made available through the continued education workshops offered by employers or adult education programs or specialized schools. The military services provide other sources of work and educational opportunities.

IMPLICATIONS

Embedded within the literature covered in this chapter are several threads that can be combined to provide a general prescription for increasing the likelihood of maintaining relatively high levels of intellectual, cognitive, and creative functioning well into the later years of adulthood. Simply stated, the prescription is that "practice helps to make perfect." Individuals who function well during the late adult years tend to have been relatively bright as youngsters and to have gained a greater than average number of years of formal education. In addition, they also tend to acquire and nurture an adult lifestyle that can best be described as intellectually, cognitively, and creatively challenging and stimulating; that is, they virtually guarantee themselves the opportunity to continue practicing and developing their abilities and talents.

Establishing such a lifestyle depends on more than just being bright and well-educated. It often requires some measure of luck, and it clearly depends on the careful nurturing of all the domains to establish a basic zest or verve for the fullness of life. Recall, for example, the importance of the affective domain and the need to balance love and work. Also note the benefits derived from incorporating programs of aerobic exercise as a regular feature of one's leisure-time activities: enhanced feelings of well-being, better biological functioning and general health status, and improved intellectual–cognitive performance.

Career success appears to be related to three interdependent factors, each of which can be systematically evaluated and strengthened:[34]

Declarative Knowledge: The "grammar," "rules," and "principles," or specific information one needs to know to function effectively.

Procedural Knowledge: The "processes," "reasoning," and "comprehension" or specific decision-making skills one needs to function effectively.

Metaself Knowledge: The "executive processes" of meta-cognition and meta-memory that one uses to tap into strengths, knowledge, and skills to function effectively. This factor also includes awareness of one's weaknesses, responses to stress, and perseverance, factors that alter performance.

Young adults can learn about successful life through observation and by seeking out older persons who can serve as role models and mentors. In so doing, the young person offers the other person an opportunity to express **generativity.**

REFERENCES

1. Arenberg, D. (1965). Anticipation interval and age differences in verbal learning. *Journal of Abnormal Psychology, 70,* 419–425.
2. Arenberg, D. (1967). Age differences in retroaction. *Journal of Gerontology, 22,* 88–93.

3. Arlin, P. K. (1975). Cognitive development in adulthood: A fifth stage. *Developmental Psychology, 11,* 602–606.

4. Arlin P. K. (1984). Adolescent and adult thought: A structural interpretation. In M. L. Commons, F. A. Richards, & C. Armon (Eds.), *Beyond formal operations: Late adolescent and adult cognitive development.* New York: Praeger.

5. Bächman, L., & Molander, B. (1989). The relationship between level of arousal and cognitive operations during motor behavior in young and older adults. In A. C. Ostrow (Ed.), *Aging and motor behavior* (pp. 3–33). Indianapolis, IN: Benchmark Press.

6. Bächman, L., & Nilsson, L. G. (1984). Aging effects in free recall: An exception to the rule. *Human Learning, 3,* 53–69.

7. Baltes, P. B., Dittmann-Kohli, F., & Dixon, R. A. (1984). New perspectives on the development of intelligence in adulthood: Toward a dual process conception and a model of selective optimization with compensation. In P. Baltes & O. Brim (Eds.), *Life-span development and behavior* (Vol. 6). New York: Academic Press.

8. Baltes, P. B., Dittmann-Kohli, F., & Dixon, R. A. (1986). Multidisciplinary propositions on the development of intelligence during adulthood and old age. In A. B. Srenson, F. E. Weinert, & L. R. Sherrod (Eds.), *Human development and the life course: Multidisciplinary perspectives* (pp. 467–507). Hillside, NJ: Lawrence Erlbaum.

9. Baltes, P. B., & Schaie, K. W. (1974). Aging and IQ: Twilight years. *Psychology Today, 40,* 35–39.

10. Baltes, P. B., & Schaie, K. W. (1976). On the plasticity of intelligence in adulthood and old age: When Horn and Donaldson fail. *American Psychologist, 31,* 720–725.

11. Bandura, A. (1989). Regulation of cognitive processes through perceived self-efficacy. *Development Psychology, 25,* 729–735.

12. Beh, H. C. (1989). Mental performance following exercise. *Perceptual and Motor Skills, 69,* 42.

13. Belmore, S. M. (1981). Age-related changes in processing explicit and implicit language. *Journal of Gerontology, 36,* 316–322.

14. Birren, J. E. (1964). *The psychology of aging.* Englewood Cliffs, NJ: Prentice-Hall.

15. Botwinick, J. (1959). Drives, expectancies, and emotions. In J. E. Birren (Ed.), *Handbook of aging and the individual.* Chicago: University of Chicago Press.

16. Botwinick, J. (1984). *Aging and behavior* (3rd ed.). New York: Springer.

17. Botwinick, J., & Storandt, M. (1980). Recall and recognition of old information in relation to age and sex. *Journal of Gerontology, 35,* 70–76.

18. Canestrari, R. E. (1963). Paced and self-paced learning in young and elderly adults. *Journal of Gerontology, 18,* 165–168.

19. Carroll, J. B. (1986). Second language. In R. F. Dillon & R. J. Sternberg (Eds.), *Cognition and instruction* (pp. 83–126). San Diego: Academic Press.

20. Cattell, R. B. (1971). *Abilities: Their structure, growth and action.* Boston: Houghton-Mifflin.

21. Cole, S. (1979). Age and scientific performance. *American Journal of Sociology, 84,* 958–977.

22. Commons, M. L., Richards, F. A., & Kuhn, D. (1982). Systematic and metasystematic reasoning: A case for levels of reasoning beyond Piaget's stage of formal operations. *Child Development, 53,* 1058–1069.

23. Cornelius, S. W. (1984). Classic pattern of intellectual aging: Test familiarity, difficulty, and performance. *Journal of Gerontology, 39,* 201–216.

24. Craik, F. I. M., & Lockhart, R. S. (1972). Levels of processing: A framework for memory research. *Journal of Verbal Learning and Verbal Behavior, 11,* 671–684.

25. Craik, F. I. M., & Simon, E. (1980). Age differences in memory: The roles of attention and depth of processing. In L. Poon, J. Fozard, L. Germak, D. Arenberg, & L. Thompson (Eds.), *New directions in memory and aging.* Hillsdale, NJ: Lawrence Erlbaum.

26. Cunningham, W. R., & Owens, W. A. (1981). The Iowa State study of intellectual abilities. In K. W. Schaie (Ed.), *Longitudinal studies of adult psychological development.* New York: Guilford Press.

27. Danziger, W. L., & Botwinick, J. (1980). Age and sex differences in sensitivity and response bias in a weight discrimination task. *Journal of Gerontology, 35,* 388–394.

28. Denney, N. W. (1980). The effect of the manipulation of peripheral, noncognitive variables on problem-solving performance among the elderly. *Human Development, 23,* 268–277.

29. Denney, N. W. (1982). Aging and cognitive changes. In B. B. Wolman (Ed.), *Handbook of developmental psychology.* Englewood Cliffs, NJ: Prentice-Hall.

30. Denney, N. W., & Palmer, A. M. (1981). Adult age differences on traditional and practical problem-solving measures. *Journal of Gerontology, 36,* 323–328.

31. Dennis, W. (1958). The age decrement in outstanding scientific contributions: Fact or artifact. *American Psychologist, 13,* 457–460.

32. Dennis, W. (1966). Creativity productivity between the ages of 20 and 80 years. *Journal of Gerontology, 21,* 1–8.

33. Diamond, M. C. (1988). *Enriching heredity: The impact of the environment on the anatomy of the brain.* New York: Free Press.

34. Dillon, R. F. (1986). Issues in cognitive psychology and instruction. In R. F. Dillon & R. J. Sternberg (Eds.), *Cognition and instruction* (pp. 1–12). San Diego: Academic Press.

35. Eisdorfer, C. (1968). Arousal and performance: Experiments in verbal learning and a tentative theory. In G. Talland (Ed.), *Human behavior and aging: Recent advances in research and theory.* New York: Academic Press.

36. Eisdorfer, C., Axelrod, S., & Wilkie, F. L. (1963). Stimulus exposure times as a factor in serial learning in an aged sample. *Journal of Abnormal and Social Psychology, 67,* 597–600.

37. Eisdorfer, C., Newlin, J. B., & Wilkie, F. (1970). Improvement of learning in the aged by modification of autonomic nervous system activity. *Science, 170,* 1327–1329.

38. Elias, M. F., Elias, P. K., & Elias, J. W. (1977). *Basic processes in adult developmental psychology.* St. Louis: C. V. Mosby.

39. Elkind, D. (1962). Quantity concepts in college students. *Journal of Social Psychology, 57,* 459.

40. Elkind, D. (1981). *Children and adolescents: Interpretive essays on Jean Piaget* (3rd ed.). New York: Oxford University Press.

41. Erber, J., Feely, C., & Botwinick, J. (1980). Reward conditions and socioeconomic status in the learning of older adults. *Journal of Gerontology, 35,* 565–570.

42. Feldman, H. (1964). *Development of the husband-wife relationship: A research report.* Ithaca, NY: Cornell University Press.

43. Fenichel, O. (1946). *The psychoanalytic theory of neurosis.* New York: Norton.

44. Gardner, E. F., & Monge, R. H. (1977). Adult age differences in

cognitive abilities and educational background. *Experimental Aging Research, 3,* 337–383.

45. Gladis, M., & Braun, H. W. (1958). Age differences in transfer and retroaction as a function of intertask response similarity. *Journal of Experimental Psychology, 55,* 25–32.

46. Goleman, D. (1980). 1,528 little geniuses and how they grew. *Psychology Today, 13*(9), 28–53.

47. Gordon, S. K., & Clark, W. C. (1974). Application of signal detection theory to prose recall and recognition in elderly and young adults. *Journal of Gerontology, 29,* 64–72.

48. Harkins, S. W., Chapman, C. R., & Eisdorfer, C. (1979). Memory loss and response bias in senescence. *Journal of Gerontology, 34,* 66–72

49. Hartley, J. T., & Walsh, D. A. (1980). The effect of monetary incentive on amount and rate of free recall in older and younger adults. *Journal of Gerontology, 35,* 899–905.

50. Horn, J. L. (1970). Organization of data on life-span development of human abilities. In L. R. Gowet & P. B. Baltes (Eds.), *Life-span developmental psychology.* New York: Academic Press.

51. Horn, J. L. (1980). Concepts of intellect in relation to learning and adult development. *Intelligence, 4,* 285–317.

52. Horn, J. L., & Donaldson, G. V. (1976). On the myth of intellectual decline in adulthood. *American Psychologist, 31,* 701–719.

53. Horn, J. L., & Donaldson, G. V. (1977). Faith is not enough: A response to the Baltes-Schaie claim that intelligence does not wane. *American Psychologist, 32,* 369–373.

54. Hulicka, I. M. (1967). Age changes and age differences in memory functioning. *The Gerontologist, 7,* 46–54.

55. Hulicka, I. M., Sterne, H., & Grossman, J. (1967). Age-group comparisons of paired-associate learning as a function of paced and self-paced association and response time. *Journal of Gerontology, 22,* 274–280.

56. Hutman, L. P., & Sekuler, R. (1980). Spatial vision and aging: II. Criterion effects. *Journal of Gerontology, 35,* 700–706.

57. Jarvik, L. F., Eisdorfer, C., & Blum, J. E. (1973). *Intellectual functioning in adults: Psychological and biological influences.* New York: Springer.

58. Kinsbourne, M., & Berrhill, J. (1972). The nature of the interaction between pacing and the age decrement in learning. *Journal of Gerontology, 27,* 471–477.

59. Knopf, M., & Neidhardt, E. (1989). Aging and memory for action events: The role of familiarity. *Developmental Psychology, 25,* 780–786.

60. Kozol, J. (1985). *Illiterate America.* Garden City, NY: Anchor Press.

61. Lachman, M. E., & Leff, R. (1989). Perceived control and intellectual functioning in the elderly: A 5-year longitudinal study. *Developmental Psychology, 25,* 722–728.

62. Lehman, H. C. (1953). *Age and achievement.* Philadelphia: American Philosophical Society.

63. Lehman, H. C. (1960). The age decrement in outstanding scientific creativity. *American Psychologist, 15,* 128–138.

64. Levinson, B., & Reese, H. W. (Eds.). (1967). Patterns of discrimination learning set in preschool children, fifth graders, college freshmen, and the aged. *Monographs of the Society for Research in Child Development, 32*(7).

65. Marsh, G. R., & Thompson, L. W. (1977). Psychophysiology of aging. In J. E. Birren & K. W. Schaie (Eds.), *Handbook of the psychology of aging.* New York: Van Nostrand Reinhold.

66. Monge, R. H., & Hultsch, D. F. (1971). Paired associate learning as a function of adult age and the length of the anticipation and inspection intervals. *Journal of Gerontology, 26,* 157–162.

67. Ostrow, A. C. (1989). *Aging and motor behavior.* Indianapolis, IN: Benchmark Press.

68. Owens, W. A. (1966). Age and mental abilities: A second adult follow up. *Journal of Educational Psychology, 57,* 311.

69. Palmore, E. B. (Ed.). (1974). *Normal aging: II. Reports from the Duke longitudinal studies, 1970–1973.* Durham, NC: Duke University Press.

70. Peacock, E. W., & Talley, W. M. (1985). Developing leisure competence: A goal for late adulthood. *Educational Gerontology, 11,* 261–276.

71. Perlmutter, M. (1983). Learning and memory through adulthood. In M. W. Riley, B. B. Hess, & K. Bonds (Eds.), *Aging in society.* Hillsdale, NJ: Lawrence Erlbaum.

72. Perlmutter, M., & Mitchell, D. (1982). The appearance and disappearance of age differences in adult memory. In I. M. Craik & S. Trehub (Eds.), *Aging and cognitive processes.* New York: Plenum.

73. Piaget, J. (1960). The definition of stages of development. In J. Tanner & B. Inhelder (Eds.), *Discussions on child development* (Vol. 4). New York: International University Press.

74. Piaget, J. (1972). Intellectual evolution from adolescence to adulthood. *Human Development, 15*(1), 1.

75. Plude, D. J., & Hoyer, W. L. (1981). Adult age differences in visual search as a function of stimulus mapping and processing level. *Journal of Gerontology, 36,* 589–604.

76. Poon, L. W. (1985). Differences in human memory with aging. In J. E. Birren & K. W. Schaie (Eds.), *Handbook of the psychology of aging.* New York: Van Nostrand Reinhold.

77. Poon, L. W., & Fozard, J. L. (1978). Speed of retrieval from long-term memory in relation to age, familiarity, and datedness of information. *Journal of Gerontology, 33,* 711–717.

78. Powell, A. H., Eisdorfer, C., & Bogdonoff, M. D. (1964). Physiologic response patterns observed in a learning task. *Archives of General Psychiatry, 10,* 192–195.

79. Rabbitt, P. (1977). Changes in problem-solving ability in old age. In J. E. Birren & K. W. Schaie (Eds.), *Handbook of the psychology of aging.* New York: Van Nostrand Reinhold.

80. Ratner, H. H., Padgett, R. J., & Bushey, N. (1988). Old and young adults' recall of events. *Developmental Psychology, 24,* 664–671.

81. Riegel, K. F. (1973). Developmental psychology and society: Some historical and ethical considerations. In J. R. Nesselroade & P. B. Baltes (Eds.), *Life-span developmental psychology: Methodological issues.* New York: Academic Press.

82. Schaie, K. W. (1975). Age changes in adult intelligence. In D. S. Woodruff & J. E. Birren (Eds.), *Aging: Scientific perspectives and social issues.* New York: Van Nostrand Reinhold.

83. Schaie, K. W. (1978). Toward a stage theory of adult cognitive development. *Aging and Human Development, 8,* 129–138.

84. Schaie, K. W. (1979). The primary mental abilities in adulthood: An exploration in the development of psychometric intelligence. In P. Bactes & O. Brim (Eds.), *Life-span development and behavior* (Vol. 2). New York: Academic Press.

85. Schaie, K. W. (1983). *Longitudinal studies of adult psychological development.* New York: Guilford Press.

86. Schaie, K. W. (1983). The Seattle longitudinal study: A twenty-one year exploration of psychometric intelligence in adulthood. In K. W. Schaie (Ed.), *Longitudinal studies of adult psychological development.* New York: Guilford Press.

87. Schaie, K. W., & Willis, S. L. (1986). *Adult development and aging* (2nd ed.). Boston: Little, Brown.

88. Siegler, R. S., & Kotovsky, K. (1986). Two levels of giftedness: Shall ever the twain meet? In R. J. Sternberg & J. E. Davidson (Eds.), *Conceptions of giftedness* (pp. 417–435). New York: Cambridge University Press.

89. Simonton, D. K. (1975). Age and literacy creativity: A cross-cultural and trans-historical survey. *Journal of Cross-Cultural Psychology, 6,* 259–277.

90. Simonton, D. K. (1977). Creative productivity, age and stress: A biographical time series analysis of 10 classical composers. *Journal of Personality and Social Psychology, 35,* 791–804.

91. Terman, L. M. (1954). Scientists and non-scientists in a group of 800 gifted men. *Psychology Monographs, 68,* 1–44.

92. Topp, R. (1989). Effect of relaxation or exercise on undergraduates' test anxiety. *Perceptual and Motor Skills, 69,* 35–41.

93. Wallach, H. F., Riege, W. H., & Chohen, M. J. (1980). Recognition memory for emotional words: A comparative study of young, middle-aged and older persons. *Journal of Gerontology, 35,* 371–375.

94. Watson, C. W., Turpenoff, C. M., Kelly, W. J., & Botwinick, J. (1979). Age differences in resolving power and decision strategies in a weight discrimination task. *Journal of Gerontology, 34,* 547–552.

95. Welford, A. T. (1977). Motor performance. In J. E. Birren & K. W. Schaie (Eds.), *Handbook of the psychology of aging.* New York: Van Nostrand Reinhold.

96. World Almanac. (1989). *World almanac and book of facts, 1989.* New York: World Almanac.

To feel that one counts for something with other people is one of the joys of life. What matters is not how many friends we have, but how deeply we are attached to them. Above all, personal relationships count for more than anything else.

—DIETRICH BONHOEFFER

Psychosocial Development During Early Adult Years

Cecil R. Paul

The hills have been climbed and the valleys traversed, and what one had assumed to be a peak is but another hill in the ongoing struggle to be and to become. Like those experiences one has in hiking, of climbing up and down the approach hills to a slope, the adolescent period is a struggling experience, with high points of perspective and hope followed by low points of task diffusion and relational frustration. As the young adult years emerge, many of these small hills have been conquered and one feels that they have been a good preparation for the steady upward climb toward the pinnacle of what has begun to be perceived as the measure of success and fulfillment: adulthood.

However, as young adults enter these years, they may experience an initial sense of letdown. Adulthood is not what they anticipated, or, by "skirting around the foothills," they find themselves unprepared for the serious climb. They did not get all the experience or equipment they needed along the way (education, personal skills), or they have picked up extra, burdensome baggage (substance abuse, children) that slows down the climb and may prevent reaching their ultimate goal. During their struggle they have left behind some familiar road marks and faces. The journey ahead looms frightening and lonely.

Robert Havighurst observes that the young adult years constitute one of the most difficult periods in an individual's life.[16] Before this time, many activities, responsibilities, and roles were determined by chronological age or grade in school. New privileges and responsibilities were regularly attained, earned, and bestowed when predetermined milestones had been reached (Fig. 28-1). The pinnacle—perhaps the 18th birthday or graduation from high school—was seen as the ultimate goal or achievement, the signal of transition out of childhood into adulthood. However, many young people discover when they have reached the end of this path that they are stepping off into a nebulous world without preestablished goals, which if achieved would bring recognition. Prestige and power are no longer conferred automatically with the passage of time or the move to a new class. Some young adults discover that privileges and opportunities are based on family connections rather than on innate potentials, skills, or hard work.

For 18 years (or more), the individual has been waiting to "grow up," to reach that point where he or she would "know," "understand," and "be in control." (Parents often tell the child, "When you grow up, you'll understand . . . ") That time has arrived, yet the young person realizes that little has changed on the inside, and he or she faces many questions in making major decisions, such as investing in an education, selecting a mate, launching a career, bearing children, and managing a home. Many frustrated young adults criticize their educational and family experiences for failing to prepare them adequately with the life skills they need during these years of transition.

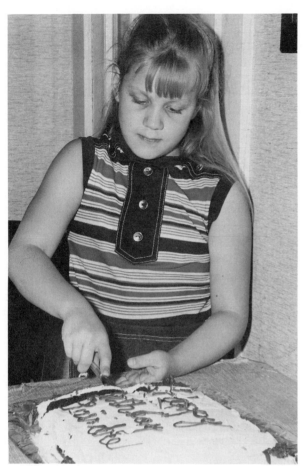

FIGURE 28–1.
During the adult years, "success" is no longer ensured by another birthday or grade in school. Personal achievements secured by goal setting, self-discipline, and hard work become the criteria.

During the transition, young adults face the initial demands of assuming the responsibility to "plug in" and "settle down." It is a time for the experiences of the long journey to be integrated into new adult objectives that connect one with society. The individual begins to realize that the struggles continue with new hills and valleys that hold new risks and pressures. The hazy hills of adulthood are not as clearly visible as anticipated; new tasks and crises await the weary traveler. Circumstances demand that the young adult depend on past experience while developing a new sensitivity and sense of responsibility toward the surrounding community and environment. The new tasks involve the integration of previous experiences of dependence and independence into more complex levels of interdependence.

The deep need for independence leads many young people to break away from their family and community support systems. While the strengths and resources of each family differ, this separation leaves many young people with little support or guidance. Frequently, this vacuum draws them into affiliations based on shared deficiencies, frustrations, and anger. At a time when they are motivated to use help (from other than family), many discover that minimal resources are available to help them gain essential skills and establish appropriate goals.

As a result, many young adults go through a period some call a **moratorium,** a delay in a commitment to or the pursuit of the tasks and goals of mature adulthood.[8, 19] Although it may take many behavioral forms, internally, the young adult is caught in the cross currents of the security of structured goals and family identity versus individualized goals and personal identity. A moratorium period provides time and a forum for the process of focusing objectives and experimenting with choices. This interim period—"youth"—can be one of intense searching for one's unique identity, goals, and affiliations (see Chap. 25). New understandings of life during these years forces one to redefine the meaning of adulthood and maturity. The individual begins to solidify a personal identity and to define an adult role.

When is one an adult? Legally, it may be at 16, 18, or 21 years of age; but is it only a matter of age, as is so commonly expressed? Those cultures that set a chronological age to herald the entrance into adulthood generally mark the event with specific rituals, celebrations, or pubertal rites and establish specific expectations or roles and functions to be assumed when the age is reached.

However, in Western cultures, designations between youth and adulthood are not as clear. Different contingencies operate in the lives of a financially independent, fully employed, married 19-year-old person as compared to the 23-year-old college student who is financially dependent on his or her parents. How does one define adulthood for a 25-year-old mentally retarded person? Is a 16-year-old female an adult because she is the mother of twins? These questions help us realize that the old definitions and norms based on simple groupings of criteria are inadequate. The transition into adulthood is both complex and gradual and reflects individual and cultural differences. Physical development, chronological age, individual achievements, and societal expectations mesh to play a significant role in whether or not an individual is accepted as a mature adult.

Definitions of maturity emphasize tasks, crises, and adjustments. The adjustments that an individual is expected to make in becoming mature involve three general dimensions of life. First, the **intrapersonal** demands of the emerging self are examined in terms of the pressures to differentiate and integrate the unique aspects of one's self-system. The second dimension is **interpersonal,** in which one is learning how to deal with the reciprocal relationship between personal needs and the needs and expectations of others. The third area of adjustment is **environmental,** which addresses the ability to manage the economic and physical needs of life. Thus, maturity involves processes of differentiating, integrating, relating, and coping.

THE QUEST FOR INTIMACY

Erikson's Theory

Erik Erikson's theory assumes a central position in the exploration of the psychosocial dimensions of early adult life.[6] Erikson's first five stages have focused inward as the individual gradually learns more about himself or herself, and how others view himself or herself, and begins to mesh the two into a healthy identity. At this stage, as Erikson's earlier tasks are resolved, the person begins to focus outward, to know and to be known by others. The core task of the early adult years as identified by Erikson is **intimacy.** If the ego has not adequately mastered the skills of the prior psychosocial stages, the person becomes caught in a conflict between the lack of readiness and the demands of this new stage.

It is critically important that the task of identity be adequately addressed in preparation for the pressures toward intimacy. The ability to be intimate with others is predicated on knowing one's self intimately. Intimacy involves the sharing of one's *inner* self, who one *really* is. If one's identity is based on the superficial criteria of power, prestige, possessions, persons, and so forth (see Chap. 25), then external social pressures and internal drives to maintain continuity and security eclipse true knowledge of one's self. The capacity to build meaningful, deep intimacies that involve fidelity or commitment is seriously weakened when the question of identity has not been actively and positively addressed.

Intimacy Versus Isolation

As a young person begins to feel more secure in his or her unique identity, he or she is able to establish both internal and external intimacy. **Internal intimacy** is the ability to recognize and accept one's own unique feelings and reactions to life events, regardless of how unusual, unexpected, painful, or ugly they may be. **External intimacy** is the ability and willingness to share one's feelings, dreams, needs, disappointments, desires, values, reactions, evaluations, opinions, goals, aspirations, fears, and frustrations in an open, honest dialogue. This definition does not mean "verbal or emotional diarrhea," in which the person indiscriminately blurts out all inner feelings to whomever is available, but indicates *selective* sharing of feelings and reactions to facilitate understanding, communication, knowledge, or appreciation between two people.

Intimacy, as discussed by Erikson, focuses on the affective and social domains, not the biophysical. Sexual intimacy is not the issue. True **intimacy** is the ability to let others see one's inner self without fear of disintegration, role confusion, or emotional destruction if the other person disagrees with or criticizes what is shared. The risks inherent in intimacy lead many individuals to shrink away in fear as the relationship demands greater revelation of the true self. The closer one becomes to another person, the greater is the danger of taking advantage and being taken advantage of.[21] "Any close relationship involves the exchange of demands and expectations, some of which are difficult and unpleasant. More impor-

tantly, getting to know someone intimately always involves hurt when illusions are dashed or expectations unfulfilled; and it always involves unpleasant insight into one's own weaknesses."[20] If the threat to one's ego identity is too strong, the person may retreat to the safety of traditional roles, discussion of culturally acceptable views, physical intimacies, or high intensity leisure-time activities.

When one fears to share private inner issues, then a sense of **isolation** develops from the inability to have genuine exchanges with others who could offer empathy, understanding, encouragement, insight, or support. Cooperation or intimate sharing of the self with another may make the person feel that he or she is losing a part of the self or that the other will engulf his or her personhood. Therefore, "the counterpart of intimacy is distantation: the readiness to repudiate, isolate, and if necessary, destroy those forces and people whose essence seems dangerous to one's own."[7] A relationship that may have begun with some anticipation of success disintegrates as communication breaks down. Emotional isolation perpetuates the shallow, lonely, stereotyped existence based on the pseudoidentities of the last crisis. Many people live all their lives caught in the web of unresolved earlier crises.

Reintegration of Previous Tasks

The complex and continuing relationship between the earlier stages of development and intimacy is vital to understanding the young adult years. Erikson draws an analogy to the physiological development of the fetal period of development.[6] If the prenatal environment is not conducive to the division and maturation of cells in one or more of the organ systems, a developmental arrest occurs and frequently cannot be remedied or compensated for at a later stage; thus, it has a continuing debilitating effect on the individual's biophysical functioning (see Chap. 3). Erikson observes a pattern of emotional development that appears to follow inner laws of emergence but is equally influenced by the social–emotional environment. This development creates a succession of potentialities for significant interaction with others and a gradual blossoming of self-awareness. The expectations and challenges of the surrounding culture create pressures for adjustment to which the developing ego must respond and adapt (Fig. 28-2).

The problem of timing is as critical for the developing personality as it is for the developing embryo. When the environment is conducive to growth, and the ego makes the necessary adaptations, the sequence of psychosocial development continues on in health toward the next crisis. However, if the crisis is not met and the ego has not adapted, the tensions and scars of that stage continue to influence successive stages of psychosocial development. It is difficult to repair them later in life. The degree of success in resolution of each of the earlier stages has a profound impact on the characteristics and directions of intimacy. When successfully mastered, the forces of trust, autonomy, initiative, industry, and identity become power sources, enhancing the experience and expression of

FIGURE 28–2.
The separation–individuation process surfaces once again as the young adult leaves home for college, career, or military service. Security items from home help quell the sense of vulnerability in the new environment.

intimacy. The issue of trust, for example, is essential to the sharing of one's "secrets" with another person, as well as to loving the other fully and allowing one's self to accept another's love without suspicion. If one has fears (real or imagined) that the other will break confidentiality or use the information or relationship as a weapon to destroy social, career, or marital relationships, or even to destroy one's self-trust, the intimacy will be withheld in self-protection.

In many ways, the forces of isolation seem to be a repetition of the autonomy issue of the toddler phase, "me do" and "don't engulf me." Somehow, being known is equated with control by others and represents a loss of freedom or a return to dependency on them and their opinion. "If they don't know what I think, then I am master of myself and my destiny." When one's identity is not yet solidified, when one is not yet able to explain the rationale behind an opinion or reaction, then elements of shame, doubt, or even guilt may be experienced. These same three feelings may be experienced if one is unable to differentiate between the problem and the person, equating the problem with the person's value. Incomplete resolution of Mahler's individuation issues may also play a role.[24] If a person is unable to clearly differentiate between the sharing of a problem and the responsibility for its resolution, then the person may share all (verbal diarrhea) with nescient hope that the other will assume the responsibility for resolving the problem. Others, unable to differentiate between empathic listening and responsibility assumption,

avoid intimacy for fear that others will "dump their problems on me" and expose their weaknesses. Shame, doubt, or guilt about one's inner feelings raise fears of devaluation in the eyes of the other and prevent sharing. Thus, when the negative counterparts of Erikson's crises prevail, the person is more likely to lean toward isolation.

Interdependence of Identity and Intimacy

One's identity is a dynamic entity, undergoing evaluation and refinement over one's lifetime as new experiences and challenges are faced. However, one's basic identity and the skills necessary for self-evaluation and inner conflict resolution should be established during the late adolescent and early adult years. Many adolescents and young adults avoid their "identity homework" by accepting without question the values of their parents, church, or culture or by remaining undecided and noncommittal, to "hang loose." The truth is, such stances represent a failure (through fear, naïveté, laziness, or inadequate environmental support) to be intimate with the self, to explore one's inner beliefs and relationships. Eventually, everyone must face themselves. We are not alone in our questions and fears. During stage 5, as we use others as a sounding board or mirror of our own feelings, questions, values, goals, and evaluations, we *begin to know ourselves,* to strengthen our inner identity, and to clarify what we really value and believe. Gradually, the focus changes (we enter stage 6), and we begin to engage in true intimacy with others, *to allow others to know us and to get to know other people.* We have developed a sense of separateness, uniqueness, and value that is not lost or stolen in the sharing of that self with others. They do not engulf us with their will, feelings, reactions, or criticisms. The paradox is that we grow closer as we reveal our uniqueness to the other. A new freedom emerges and enables us to move toward self-actualization. Failure to be intimate truncates growth and undermines the sense of a stable identity.[21]

Mature intimacy is founded on an identity strength that enables the individual to free others to be wholly themselves, not a dependent appendage. Identity strength allows one to appreciate the differences of others without a need to change them or their values into a common system. The differences of experience, education, values, viewpoints, or goals enrich rather than destroy a relationship. In stage 7 (generativity), one shares for the benefit of the other, for the growth and enhancement of the other's life. The potential polarizations in any intimate relationship are overcome by identity strength. When it is missing, polarizations dominate the relationship and often lead to separation, divorce, and loneliness.

Unresolved Identity Issues

Unresolved identity questions lead to major problems with young adult tasks, such as selecting a mate, developing satisfying social relationships, or resolving conflicts. Some individuals cannot deal with the question of intimacy; consequently, progress toward self-actualization, generativity, and maturity becomes truncated. Problems are evidenced through two patterns of isolation.

The individual may function in **expressive isolation,** which protects the image one shows to other people. "Even when living with someone, they are often really living alone. They don't share their thoughts and intimate feelings for fear that their partner might use what they expose against them. They keep themselves busy at work or become so involved in other activities—golf, tennis, exercising—that there isn't much time or energy left for intimacy."[12] This person can function within socially acceptable, defined roles, always *doing the right thing.* He or she may be socially charming but, in close relationships, is shallow or subservient to the ideas and the values of the other person, unable to express true feelings, values, or opinions for fear of criticism. The ego strength and mood of the moment depend on the approval of others, regardless of cost (Fig. 28-3). The person, caught in his or her own web, doesn't understand the difference between *doing* and *being* and is baffled by the partner's complaints of inadequate communication or lack of substance to the relationship.

The characteristics of expressive isolation makes it unlikely that the interpersonal tasks that confront the young adult will be managed successfully. This individual may aggressively function as though in charge or in control of his or her life, only to fall apart or to become rigid and testy at the unexpected or during crisis events. Some may gain popularity by working for others, expressing the other's views, and taking their cues from environmental circumstances, only to withdraw when there is no model to follow.

Attempts to compensate for feelings of emotional inadequacy may lead the individual into pseudointimacy, which becomes manifest in forms of heterosexual conquest and control. Reciprocal sharing of identity and care is avoided. The "swinging single" pursues pseudointimacies that protect the person from disclosure and responsibility. Rather than alleviating loneliness, this form of "togetherness" merely accentuates one's sense of isolation.[21] The use of others in the name of "making love" is a common theme of this person in the courtship rituals of contemporary society. The substitution of physical for psychosocial intimacy reveals its inadequacy too late, after marriage has already taken place, as is evidenced in a higher divorce rate for people who have engaged in premarital sex.[18] The couple struggles with deficient communication and problem-solving patterns. When a person has children, the challenge is to expand care and commitment beyond the preoccupation with self-protective patterns of socialization to systematic guidance of the children toward values and behaviors the person finds to be a working part of one's own psychosocial development. However, if one has not solidified his or her own value system, how can he or she effectively guide the next generation? Parenting is confusing and ineffectual.

Although it is not considered pathological in nature, expressive isolation involves anxiety that inhibits and undermines the adjustments appropriate to adult life. It certainly blocks the possibilities for the individual to become a fully functioning personality; energies are invested in defensive rather than actualization processes.

A more severe and pathological form of isolation is **receptive isolation.** In this pattern of behavior, the defensiveness is expressed in the distortion of social and environmental stimuli. Environmental events are translated to fit into the individual's expectations (Piaget's assimilation), regardless of how contradictory the original stimulus may have been. Reactions are based on the perceived rather than the actual stimulus. This person is deeply and emotionally invested in each experience and thus is unable to take the self-objective approach that would help clarify interaction patterns.

Communication problems are frequent as the person reinterprets what the other says to fit his or her own needs, interests, or biases. Negotiation and resolution of conflict of interest problems may be impossible. Hurt feelings and exposed vulnerabilities lead to further isolation. This individual, locked away in the isolation of self, misses the joy and stimulus of growth-producing intimacies. The individual carries this isolation into midlife, during which it continues to be expressed in dysfunctional ways. An anxious self-absorption undermines healthy self-awareness and emotional development. The individual stagnates, failing to become creatively involved in the social order.

The process of differentiating and integrating a sense of identity prepares one for the task of integrating a sense of intimacy. The individual's struggle with the intimacy–isolation crisis is further complicated by the ongoing tasks of relating the self to the surrounding culture. Where does one fit in, and how will one's values and purpose for living be expressed?

FIGURE 28–3.
People who are secure in their identity are not concerned about the reactions of others when they assume unconventional responsibilities. Interest and need serve as guidelines for behavior, not stereotyped gender roles.

Resolving the Issues of Intimacy

Avenues of Search

Family and friendship experiences in early childhood and adolescence are vital to the expression of intimacy. Again, we see the critical importance of how the tasks and crises of each psychosocial stage of development are experienced. The positive psychic elements of trust, autonomy, initiative, industry, and identity enrich the meaning of intimacy and transcend a strict psychosexual interpretation. The quality of friendships and partnerships in the life of the mature adult are enriched by this history. The psychic sharing of self is at the heart of healthy intimacies.

There is a "distinction between desire for interpersonal contact and the social skills needed to act on the desire."[17] The internal drive appears to be innate. However, its expression is heavily influenced by both family experience and the culture. This distinction is critically important to how we interpret the problem of limited social contact for the fulfillment of affiliation motivation. Behaviors that seem to signal a movement toward isolation may reflect decreased opportunities, cultural training, or anxiety over how to pursue a deep sense of affiliation motivation, rather than a lack of awareness or willingness to share the deeper self. Shyness or discomfort in sharing with a group of people is not synonymous with isolation. On a one-to-one basis, in the right circumstances, the same person may be highly intimate and show in-depth self–other awareness.

The process of maturing moves one into a readiness for deeper, enriched, and more complex intimacies. When one shares the inner self with other selected persons on a deep personal level, revealing one's true identity, the gender or age of the person becomes irrelevant. It is one person reaching out to another with mutual openness. Intimacy can occur on all levels: one-to-one friendships, small groups, or even community involvement. Thus, one can have many intimate heterosocial and homosocial relationships without physical intimacy. Physical intimacy is but one facet of self-sharing, not the focus of it. At its best, physical intimacy is predicated on a mature, reciprocal social–emotional intimacy that has forged a growing and enduring commitment to the other. Sexual intimacy is conspicuously absent in most of the deepest relationships of life (grandparent–grandchild, parent–child, teacher–student, best friends).

Discussions of identity and intimacy have not given adequate attention to differences in how males and females approach these tasks and questions in their lives.[10, 13] Carol Gilligan argues, "While for men, identity precedes intimacy and generativity in the optimal cycle of human separation and attachment, for women these tasks seem instead to be focused. Intimacy goes along with identity, as the female comes to know herself as she is known, through her relationship with others."[13] It is her observation that "women bring to the life cycle a different point of view and order human experiences in terms of different priorities."[13]

She emphasizes that women base their journey into and through identity and intimacy on the centrality of **affiliations** and **attachments.** Thus, the loss of intimacies through separation and divorce are experienced as the loss of self. One needs to recognize that men can experience these dynamics as well. However, Erikson's concept of intimacy is not necessarily synonymous with affiliation and attachment. Intimacy is idea centered, whereas affiliation and attachment are person centered. However, female self-esteem frequently depends on success in relationships.[5] Because of this need, she may be more likely to communicate negative as well as positive feelings in hopes of "fixing what is wrong." The more defensive, less expressive male may thwart her efforts, increasing the strain on a relationship.[12] Increased sensitivity to the other's feelings helps to reward efforts at emotional expressions and facilitates a happier relationship.[5] Gilligan notes that men's concern with justice and women's concern with care and relationships need to and do converge. She notes, "This dialogue between fairness and care not only provides a better understanding of relations between the sexes, but also gives rise to a more comprehensive portrayal of adult work and family relationships."[13]

In the discussion of approaches to intimacy, the role of birth order and sibling relationships may be more important than we have previously understood. Older females of sibling dyads tend to engage in more positive physical contact than do older brothers. Cultural norms appear to sanction positive physical contact for females and discourage it for males. It is also noted that affective and gender-stereotyped behaviors of younger and older siblings is strongly correlated. Thus, as the older sibling within a pair demonstrates positive or negative affect, male or female interests, the younger sibling tends to follow suit.[32]

Marriage

Many young people, unnerved by the hills still ahead, unsettled by the obscurity of the path or feeling the loneliness of the journey, rush into marriage as the solution to their personal crises. With marriage, they have someone to help them set goals, to "read the map," to talk to along the journey. Unconsciously, they may reason that this external relationship will quell the rising insecurities of facing adulthood or substitute for forging an individualized, mature identity. Consciously, they may believe that marriage provides the forum for personal happiness and fulfillment or that it provides them with a reason to live. In reality, they may try to resolve the intimacy issue through close living, a shared bed, and even children.

The rising divorce rate poignantly reveals that a ceremony and a common name do not automatically confer intimacy, commitment, and unity. As the couple gets beyond the thrill of the physical relationship and faces the realities of family goal setting, financial management, and child rearing, the strength of their individual identities and skill at intimate communication become apparent. Those who have founded their relationship on genuine psychosocial intimacy find a deepening appreciation of self and partner as the hills and journey are faced. Because each has a strong separate identity, they can tap into each other's strengths to face the journey. Map reading is indeed easier. They share skills, knowledge, and equipment, and the path is less lonely. However, if identities are weak and intimacy superficial, vulnerabilities rather than strengths are revealed as they turn to each other. Even within marriage, each experiences emotional isolation. The couple begins to hide behind roles, retaining their loneliness. Many opt to leave the relationship, often never really understanding why communication and negotiation were so difficult (see Chap. 29). The best insurance policy for successful marriage is a deep friendship and commitment before the exchanging of "I do." It needs to be restated at this point that intimacy is not an issue of marriage or sexuality, but of mutuality and love. Marriage is enriched when intimacy is established. However, intimacy can also exist outside the context of marriage, enriching the lives of those who have found a close friend.

One's search for intimacy goes beyond the commitment to the marital partner or other close friendships. "We maintain covenantal commitment to the community as well. Our sense of fidelity must transcend the one-on-one relationship to include the larger community that is impacted by our lives. We do not make our choices in isolation, nor are the effects of our choices limited to one relationship."[28]

Friendship and Community

One of the most important questions young adults face is, "Who will be my people?" Repeatedly they deal with finding their sense of community by developing friendships and fellowship bonds. Erikson's approach to intimacy is expressed through affiliation and partnership.[8] The term affiliation is used to indicate the meaning of intimacy as inclusive of friendships and partnerships. These friendships and partnerships are based on choice rather than the "blood bonds" of family. The capacity to affiliate and negotiate reciprocal partnerships in the various facets of family, friendship, work, and community relationships is essential to high-level personal and professional maturity. This ability to establish bonds with a congenial social group leads to further discovery of self and others. The small support-group experience plays an important place in revealing breadth and depth in addressing the task of intimacy. We find a new sense of personhood as we share or lose ourselves in serving others.

Erikson states, "From here on ego-strength depends on an affiliation with others who are equally ready and able to share in the task of caring for offspring, products, and ideas" (generativity).[7] Thus, as identity is the prerequisite for intimacy, intimacy is the prerequisite for generativity (see Fig. 28-4).

Pseudointimate Relationships

When one's identity is not well established, it becomes easier to base close relationships on the external issues that define the self. Thus, two people can become involved in sharing mutual interests, career goals, ways to get the most for one's money, rearing children, or ways to climb the social career ladder. Discussions center around stereotyped, socially acceptable topics and behaviors, mutual dislikes, or common concerns. Opinions are expressed only if one has heard another share the same view. Thus, one can align with that

FIGURE 28–4.
Value identification is a crucial factor in identity homework. When a person "knows where he or she is coming from," then that value can be translated into social behavior without apologies. When polarities are recognized, it takes courage to share publicly one's intimate values and philosophies.

person if a confrontation arises with a third person. One reserves expression of opinions to those known to be acceptable to the other party. The pseudointimate person hides behind the accepted roles and behaviors of the culture. Stereotyped responses are used to ensure (but in actuality replace) security in relationships.

The two almost always agree because of acquiescence or subservience on the part of one or both to the ideas, needs, opinions, reactions, or goals of the other. However, as a friend once shared, "If two people always agree, one of them is unnecessary."[2] The identity of one or both is subsumed by the other, preventing the development of true intimacy, the open exchange of two mature identities.

Some people never differentiate between acquaintances and friendships. As a result, everyone is a "friend." They dissipate their intimacy energies, ending up with many pseudointimacies or "emotional diarrhea" because of the inability to discriminate in the intimacy process. They have not discovered the goal of an intimate relationship: continued growth of both individuals. One may have many acquaintances but few in-depth friends over a lifetime. In pseudointimate relationships, the individual uses physical and sexual intimacy as a way of avoiding the depths of emotional intimacy. Emotional intimacy is hard work, it is risky. Therefore, one exchanges the satisfying depth of relationships for superficial breadth of relationships. The thrill of physical response replaces the thrill of emotional response. Sensuality is used to ensure but actually replaces security in the relationship.

Mentors

Studies of the young adult highlight another major task of these years, that of finding a "mentor."[22] The transition from the dependency of childhood to the independence of a mature adult often includes adjustment demands for which the earlier years did not prepare the young person. Unanticipated challenges arise. The change in the nature of the relationship with the family of origin or the loss of the community networks that were a part of development leave the young adult with a vacuum of models and close consultants. Yet, the need still exists for someone to help us be objective about ourselves and to help us put life's problems into perspective. There is a deep need to consult with a person who blends personal and professional life experience with the capacity to communicate with empathy and objectivity. The mentor assists with the transition through intimate communication of his or her observations of the young adult as well as intimate sharing of "life's secrets," the keys of successful adult or professional living. Not everyone can be a mentor, only those who have traveled through the hills successfully (Fig. 28-5). Wise choice of a mentor can facilitate resolution of the task of intimacy as well as progress toward personal and professional goals.

Dimensions of Intimacy

Howard and Charlotte Clinebell expanded Erikson's task of intimacy into 12 dimensions or facets.[3] The facet of **physical intimacy** is far more complex and important than sexual intimacy. The touch of the hand and the warmth of a hug are

FIGURE 28–5.
Mentor relationships facilitate the maturation process of both the mentor and the one being guided.

vital to meaningful intimacy and are not limited to sexual expression. **Emotional intimacy** refers to the capacity to perceive, nondefensively, the meaning and focus of the emotion that the other person is expressing. **Intellectual intimacy** is the sharing of ideas without polarization of the relationship and is characterized by a genuine desire to understand the other's point of view, with a willingness to negotiate if necessary to resolve mutual problems.

Even times of crisis and conflict are important in building depth and character strength into relationships. When crises come into the life experience of the other person in the form of loss or tragedy, the way we respond to one another signals what levels of **crisis intimacy** exists in that relationship. When differences of perspective, interest, values, and choices become apparent, they become the occasion for **conflict intimacy.** These are important tests of a mature intimate relationship and generally reveal strength in the other facets of intimacy.

The capacity to share aesthetic facets of life and to act together in creative ways are two complementary dimensions of intimacy that enrich friendship, family, and marital relationships. These two facets are expressed as **aesthetic intimacy** and **creative intimacy.** Erikson, like Freud, stresses the importance of love and work in the healthy, mature adult.[8] Clinebell brings these together in the capacity of a couple to be close in sharing common tasks through **work intimacy.** These are complemented by the capacity to add the times of fun and play through **recreational intimacy.** The combined strengths of **shared commitment** and **ultimate concern** facilitate growth in the relationship and within each individual. The facet on which all the others depend is the quality of **communication intimacy.**

These dimensions of intimacy are most meaningfully expressed within the extended family, friendship circles, and general community. Intellectual intimacy provides us with a facet for ongoing growth in all of our relationships. This sharing of ideas challenges personal growth throughout our development and thereby positively affects the health of the surrounding community. The expression of one's creativity often demands friendships and circles of relationships that nurture the aesthetic sensitivity. Play is a vital part of our lives, providing us with means of stress reduction and health. The family that plays together stays together, and the community that expresses itself in celebrative play provides a healthy climate for the next generation. The intimacy of work through sharing tasks and goals is an important way for a community to express itself and to create a greater sense of unity and purpose.

Questions of Self and Culture

The relationship between our sense of self and the culture holds significant implications for the way we handle commitments to marriage, family, work, and recreation. The intensity of the struggle for identity is often carried into the young adult years, during which time the task of adapting to the culture becomes a central issue. Kenneth Keniston has conceptualized a separate phase of development for many individuals in their 20s.[19] He proposed that "youth" are caught in a conflict between their personality, their values, and the institutions of culture. The person in this phase of development has great difficulty in accepting society's demands and expectations. Keniston feels that "the awareness of the actual or potential conflict, disparity, lack of congruence between what one is (one's identity, values, integrity) and the resources and demands of the existing society increases. The adolescent is struggling to define who he is; the youth begins to sense who he is and thus to recognize the possibility of conflict and disparity between his emerging selfhood and this social order."[15]

According to Keniston, the young adult is involved in three major tasks. The first is *the continuing quest to operationalize a sense of identity;* this task is often reflected in how the individual focuses vocational objectives. Many approach this task in economic terms. It becomes the means for meeting primary needs and also the secondary needs of socialization and recreation. Many allow their work or career to define who they are, conforming to the stereotyped representation of the job, its financial status, and prestige value. Those with a well-defined identity approach work as an expression of who they are and what they value. The second is the *quest for authentic or fulfilling intimacy,* which has occupied most of the chapter discussion so far.

Keniston's third task is that of *relating self to culture.* His research suggests that during the 20s many young adults struggle with this central question. They generally seek solutions in one of three directions. One option is **radical activism,** or the revolution solution in which the individual seeks to change the culture in some dramatic and critical way. Keniston's studies of radical activist groups reveals combinations of idealism, frustration, and an often unrecognized dogmatism operating in their response to the culture (identity based on philosophy). The institutions of the social order

become the focus of confrontation; basic to this confrontation is a conflict in values. Young adults who have attained high levels of academic success may become polarized with the values of society. For example, during the 1960s, the focus of such polarization was the war in Vietnam together with the issue of civil rights. Many young adults invested great time and energy attacking perceived injustices. The traditional young adult tasks shrink in relative significance and may be postponed while these individuals seek to change the social order.

Expectations of the established order also are flagrantly opposed through a radical style change (e.g., clothing, hair style, language, use of drugs, music). If the tasks of marriage and family are pursued, the radical style may evidence itself in variation on family lifestyle and in the ways needs and crises of other members of the family are met. Without the support of the larger culture and social groups to provide stability and affirmation, the alternative lifestyle and "forging one's own way" can become the source of great stress and adjustment difficulty.

A second approach to negotiating the relationship between self and culture is the **separation solution.** Some young adults may be so ambivalent toward society that they make a choice to separate themselves and their lifestyles from the mainstream. They may have tried the radical activist approach and have become disillusioned as to its efficacy. Inasmuch as their basic sense of identity has been focused on self perceptions, rationalizations, and values (disregarding family and cultural pressures), they often seek to establish their own community with other individuals who share this polarization from the institutions of society. The in-grouping may be so strong that a separate communal lifestyle is established. Communes sprang up throughout our country in the 1960s and into the late 1970s. The timetable for dealing with tasks of intimacy, including marriage, family, and community life, was important. However, the style or approach to these tasks departed from traditional ways. Commune participation provided a moratorium period for many. Communes generally have retention problems. Having served their purpose, communes are abandoned as a structure for ongoing task fulfillment. The rapid turnover in membership evidenced their failure to facilitate task fulfillment during the young adult years. With time, the young person reevaluated identity issues, finding more commonness and intimacy with the broader culture than the person formerly recognized.

Perhaps what is observed in the second approach is a cognitive conflict rather than a psychosocial problem. As young people are exposed to new information, ideas, and values, these must be integrated into their current value structures. The cognitive conflicts can be emotionally wrenching as individuals try to acknowledge differing viewpoints without violating their current value systems or feeling forced to replicate family, peers, or even society stereotypes. Participation in activist groups and communes minimizes the dissonance while individuals readjust value orientations. King Solomon warned us that with knowledge one must also seek understanding. Perhaps as young people are able to embody their values within a larger structure, to establish firm identities, and to set priorities, the importance and power of the commune or reactionary organization becomes unnecessary.

The third approach to negotiating the relationship between self and culture is to compromise or adapt, the **adaptations solution.** This approach may follow the exploration of the first and second attempts at solutions and negotiations. One young man spent 2 years as a member of a radical revolutionary organization after an initial involvement in the peace movement. Disillusioned with this group, and beginning to confront the tasks and demands of marriage and parenthood, he took his family into a communal setting. It was less than 1 year before his own values and interests led him away from the commune. As he approached age 30, he and his wife rejoined the mainstream of society, entering a human service occupation.

Another option for negotiating a relationship between self and culture demands a level of maturity and social concern that enables the individual to move beyond the tendency toward narcissism. This fourth negotiation is well identified as the **servant solution.** Individual identity is expressed through compassionate investment of time, energy, and talent in improving the lot of humanity and responding to the needs, tasks, and crises of others (Fig. 28-6).

The negotiation process involves some ongoing problems with time perspective. The individual's past experience and the present society demand renegotiations as to where his or her identity connects. The individual seeks to preserve the integrity of personal values and goals while finding an avenue of creative expression within society. The investment of this young adult in a reexamination of the cultural inheritance is vital to society. If the renegotiation is achieved, the young adult contributes to society the strengths of intelligence, ethical sensitivity, and energy.

This process of renegotiation and reinvestment is an outgrowth of the fulfillment of the tasks of identity and intimacy. Keniston's concept of the tasks of negotiating a relationship between self and culture is consistent with Erikson's emphasis on the tension between intimacy and isolation in the young adult years. Whether or not to become an integral part of the community, and how to do so, are central questions of the young adult years. When positively accepted, this bonding leads to "generativity" in the middle years, which is an investment in the next generation.

ADAPTATION TO ADULTHOOD

Vocational Tasks

Job or Career Choice

The early psychosocial experiences with trust, autonomy, initiative, industry, and identity are critically important to the processes of identifying one's interests and talents, harnessing one's energies, and focusing them into a channel for work and its related responsibilities. With the dramatic changes in technology, the development of employment competency is far more complex than it was in the agrarian or industrial family traditions, in which learning a set of specific skills would provide employment options for life. More important than specific skills are the experiences with models, mentors, and other support systems that enable the individual to clarify an identity that begs to be expressed in the work experience. In other words, *work should be an outgrowth of one's identity*, not what forms one's identity (Fig. 28-7).

Work provides the young adult with an opportunity to become an economically independent and responsible individual, thus facilitating continuing psychosocial maturation. The choices an individual makes in this area are not made in

FIGURE 28–6.
Many young adults seek outlets for service to others without any expectation of compensation except the joy of knowing they have made life a little easier for someone else.

FIGURE 28–7.
The most successful careers are expressions of the person's interests, personality, talents, and goals.

isolation from past psychosocial experience or the socio-economic realities of society, which sometimes place limits on the options available. The choice continues to effect changes in psychosocial identity and lifestyle in the years ahead.

Vision or Higher Cause

A central task for the young adult is to find something higher than the self to live for. The vision takes on different meanings for each individual. For some, it is a commitment to another person, a child, friend, or spouse. For others, it takes the form of commitment to an ideal or a cause.[21] Energies are focused toward meeting the needs of the person or cause as a part of the self. Healthy commitment involves the balanced expression of personal needs and interests with the expectations and opportunities of the institutions of the culture.

Young adults are challenged to identify career options that allow for the expression of their unique skills and motivation for the good of the social units of the culture. However, for many, the level at which this task is addressed is the need for money or "making it" socially in the market place. But "working well" involves more than a job. The complex relationship between viewing work as a job and the need for a vision or dream to live by is a potential crisis for the young adult.

The task of finding a career that meets the socioeconomic demands as well as the visionary needs of the individual requires appropriate training and education. The young adult years generally involve both the pursuit of such experiences and an evaluation of the "fit" between one's competencies and interests and the demands and satisfactions of the job. Many young adults have periods of second-guessing their educational experiences and choices. The jobs they planned for are not available or do not provide the expected fulfillment. The need to role play and explore options continues to be a part of development, although with less freedom for expression than in childhood and adolescence.

The reality is that people seek to validate their existence and worth through activation of their value systems.[29] For some, it takes the form of being productive and enjoying the securities and comforts that money will buy. Others find their vision in service to others and struggle with the tension created by inadequate remuneration, seeking a career that combines them in a meaningful and effective way.

Family and Cultural Influences

The ongoing expression and development of one's value system is essential to the young adult growth experience. The pursuit of education and career choices involves balancing personal rights and the rights and needs of others within community.

While adulthood is often discussed in terms of independence, adaptation to adulthood continues to involve one's relationships with parents and siblings. The process of maturity involves forging new relationships with both the families of origin as well as one's newly created family and friendship networks.

It has long been assumed that independence means movement out of the home of the parents. While this move continues to be the case for the majority in Western cultures, many young adults continue to reside in the parental home or return to the family of origin after completing educational pursuits or the breakup of their family of creation. In 1984, 37% of people 18 to 29 years of age resided with their parents (18 million of the 50 million people in that age group!).[14] The reasons are myriad. Since the early 1970s, the growth of the American economy has slowed down, and more young people are postponing marriages. The cost of housing has increased, and the divorce rate has gone up rapidly. Young adults born during the 1960s "baby boom" are faced with high unemployment rates because of limited availability of entry level positions. While a lower proportion of black than white young adults were living with their parents in 1940, this proportion has reversed, reflecting continuing socio-economic disadvantages for the adolescent and young adult black members of society.

The separated young adult is more likely to move in with parents than the divorced. It is more common for separated or divorced men to live with their parents than separated or divorced women. This fact may reflect the reality that most women carry responsibility for the children and that men have greater freedom to move in with parents.

The greatest percentage of young adults (77%) between the ages of 20 and 34 do not live with their parents. However, if the realities of unemployment and divorce increase, one might expect continuing changes in these patterns of living.[14]

Polarities of the Thirties

Many young adults make the transition into their thirties without major crises, while others experience anxiety because of unfulfilled tasks and losses. Throughout the life span, the degree to which one has effectively dealt with the tasks and crises of previous psychosocial stages is a major determining influence on the nature of this passage.

Establishing and Maintaining Roots

While intimacy is the major focus of the twenties, it takes on new significance in the thirties. There is a deep need to develop and maintain a close, growth-inducing, goal-achieving relationship with at least one other person. When this is achieved, then the security of that relationship becomes the root or the springboard for community with a group or a larger number of people outside the significant immediate family or relationship. The question, "who will be my people?" usually has changed to "who will be *our people*?" Where will we establish our sense of community, bonding, and territory?

The individual may experience blocks and frustration in resolving the task of discovering networks and a larger sense of belonging as the nuclear unit collapses. Those caught in the throes of separation or divorce may experience a sense of mistrust, shame, doubt, and guilt, factors that can interfere with both identity and intimacy. The increase in "blended family" experiences has created new intimacy and commitment pressures on all age groups of the extended families involved. Such separations and losses involve friendships and community experiences as well. For many, the sense of failure, disappointment, anger, and guilt make the task of establishing roots in the thirties complicated. Trust and self-confidence are tested and individuals revisit the old question of identity.

Though usually not identified as such, *parenting is a career*. No woman need be ashamed or feel worthless because her energies are invested full time in "creating a person" and providing an environment conductive to the maximization of the potentials of each member of the family, including herself. Sheehy notes, "One common reaction into the thirties is tearing up the life one spent most of the twenties putting together."[32] As the children enter school, many women begin to explore educational and career options. Individuals bored by their employment may reevaluate career and family options. As the individual experiences separations, tragedies, losses, and the realities of survival, he or she becomes more introspective, evaluating again one's values and goals, friendships, and lifestyle. New revelations about self and life frequently lead to a new identity and priorities and resultant changes in career or lifestyle directions.

Advancement Demands

While the pursuit of roots is critically important, whether man or woman, the continuing task of finding and succeeding in a career becomes the focus of both internal and external evaluation. The *ins* of establishing roots and the *ups* of career success and validation frequently come into conflict. Clinical counseling with individuals and couples in their thirties focuses on a range of case illustrations:

Married men and women may become more invested in the pursuit of success than in maintaining marital bonds and strong family roots.

The woman who set aside her own vision for a vocation may find her husband devaluing the marriage that she has given her all to nurture. She may have sacrificed for years to enable him to pursue the dream of his career. With divorce, she confronts the task of identity and intimacy again, but complicated by enlarged responsibilities, family needs, and uncertain resources.

The single young adult parent may struggle with complicated new intimacy needs without a sense of community or support group.

The man who sacrificed marriage and family life for career and upward mobility may discover it doesn't mean anything to anyone anymore, including himself. He has missed the more important things of life—intimacy with a loving family.

The woman may have retaliated in response to her husband's unfaithfulness and made reckless intimacy choices only to find the experiences have left her depressed and unfulfilled.

Many singles in their thirties begin to feel the pressure of time and age as they contemplate whether they want to find a marriage partner and establish a family.

The sharing and balance of these tasks and commitments of the thirties are complex. Within relationships, it is complicated by the reality that a man and the woman may be at different stages of maturity and may be facing different crises at the same time. While communication is essential, it is threatening since exploring critical issues exposes the pain of one's vulnerabilities.

Anticipation of Midlife

When does the young adult stage end and middle age begin? The thirties represent a period between the early young adult and the middle adult years. A sense of transition is felt between youth and the aging process. During the 1960s and 70s, early young adults were critical of those "over 30," saying they were out of touch with life's central issues.

Sex differences and age variables need far more careful research before we can fully understand how the tensions of the thirties are experienced and processed. What impact does a delay in responding to the tasks of the twenties have on the tasks of establishing roots and achieving success and social advancement? What impact does an age difference of several years between the male and female have on the manner in which they individually and jointly resolve these tasks? Does the male anticipate the midlife experience with a different combination of concerns than the female? What influence do the cultural and institutional contexts and support systems have?

These questions are the beginnings of what is experienced as midlife tasks and crises. Three major processes that begin to take place in the thirties become far more central as critical tasks in midlife:

Refocusing of the identity question
Reevaluation of the vision or dream
Renegotiation of the intimacies of one's life

It is important to underline the positive aspects inherent in the years of the thirties. For those who have addressed the key questions of the twenties and prepared solid foundations in areas of intimacies and career or service, these years are often the most productive ones of life. These are the years when life seems most vibrant, promises are realized, and experiences are the richest. One has enough breadth of experience and practical wisdom to put events, chosen or unexpected, into context. Those who have explored and experienced the process of maturation are able to manage the unpredictable changes and crises that visit us all and "come out on top." Exciting fulfillments come through balanced, holistic living during the "thirty-something" phase (Fig. 28-8).

FIGURE 28–8.
People in their thirties tend to become involved in critical community issues, such as the educational programs offered to their children.

DEVELOPING MATURITY

Theories of Psychosocial Maturity

Perspectives on Maturity

Many models for understanding personality can be used to explore the nature and process of maturity. Inherent to most personality theories is the goal of maturing or becoming. Salvatore Maddi has grouped the major theories into three viewpoints: the **conflict, consistency,** and **fulfillment** theories.[23] (These correspond with the psychodynamic, behaviorist, and humanistic views presented in Chapter 1.)

Conflict

The conflict view proposes that the person is caught between two powerful opposing forces that are never fully resolved. Basically, the hypothesis states that conflicting forces impinge on the developing personality, either pushing the individual forward toward maturity or blocking that process and leading to pathology. Consequently, life is a process of attempting to balance these forces in such a way that the individual is able to function with some degree of satisfaction without becoming the victim of paralyzing anxiety and guilt. The most significant example of this approach is Sigmund Freud's psychoanalytical model.

Freud did not give much attention to the adult years as a stage of continuing evolvement, nor did he present tasks beyond the genital psychosexual dynamics that began at pubescence.[11] The concept of **defensiveness** is essential to his view of personality and thus of adjustment and maturity. According to Freud, maturity is the process of adjusting to the demands and pressures of both the instincts and society. At best, maturity is the maintenance of some workable balance between the two, but it is not without its price. The defensive posture protects the individual from an awareness of instincts and blocks out feelings of guilt and anxiety precipitated by nonconformity to society's expectations. The concept of de-

gree is important in distinguishing between adjustment and pathology. The greater the defensiveness, the greater the pathology. If the degree of defensiveness weakens one's awareness of reality, it undermines the individual's ability to become both a productive member of society and a fulfilled person.

Freud also offers a more positive conflict for understanding adult functioning. He proposed that the balance of maturity is between love and work.[8] The maturity of love is expressed in sexual intimacy, friendships, and nurturing; the maturity of work is expressed in productive social and cultural involvement.

Consistency

Salvatore Maddi contrasts his own theory of consistency with the conflict theory, noting that "in the consistency model, there is little emphasis upon great forces be they single or dual, in conflict or not. Rather there is an emphasis upon the formative influence of feedback from the external world."[23] As in the general field of learning theories and behavioral models, Maddi's stress is on the stimulus–response relationship. Conflict is not viewed as inevitable, nor do predetermined possibilities or ideals serve as the indicators of meaningful living. The theory is basically a homeostatic view of the individual. Maddi's central emphasis is on the activation level of the personality. The personality is shaped in early childhood to expect a particular level of activation (stimuli or involvement); thereafter, the person seeks to maintain the level of activation to which he or she is accustomed. Behavior may serve the purpose of either increasing or decreasing the level of activity, depending on what is most familiar.

Maddi identifies two basic types of personality: high-activation people and low-activation people. According to Maddi, "High-activation people will spend the major part of their time and effort pursuing stimulus impact in order to keep their actual activation levels from falling too low, whereas low-activation people will spend the major part of their time and effort avoiding impact so as to keep their actual activation level from getting too high."[23] The high-activation type has a need for intensity, variety, and meaningfulness in life. If a person is more external in his or her orientation, this need is expressed through the external environment, via both physical and social behaviors. If a person is more internal in orientation, these high needs are expressed in cognitive and emotional pursuits. The low-activation type avoids intensity, variety, and meaningfulness. If characterized by external orientation, the individual seeks the uncomplicated life, in which excess and indulgence are avoided. If characterized by an internal orientation, the person seeks to minimize anxiety precipitated by ideology evaluations or self-exploration. This type of person can become the classic "couch potato."

Little evidence of a developmental theory is seen in the consistency model. Once the formative years are behind, the developing person uses both differentiation and integration to manage the impact of the external world. If maturity is defined in terms of adjustment, there are problems in defining the characteristics of the mature person according to this model. The definition of maturity would depend on an individual's activation type and whether he or she is an external or internal type of personality. The consistency model does not provide us with a statement on the nature and the process of maturity, nor does it offer a significant stage theory with specific tasks and adjustment demands for the adult years. Perhaps it could be said that, in general, the mature person is coping most effectively with maintaining a customary level of adjustment within the context of social forces.

Fulfillment

Some theories interpret personality as the natural unfolding of the potentials of the individual. These potentials might be in the form of a genetic blueprint that blossoms almost automatically, given a supportive environment. Other slightly different theories emphasize idealistic (philosophical or aesthetic) goals toward which an individual strives. These theories focus on the processes of individualized potentials and their actualizations, which are neglected by both conflict and consistency theories. Gordon Allport,[1] Carl Rogers,[31] Arthur Combs,[4] and Abraham Maslow[25] are four of the most influential theorists of maturity as an actualization or "becoming" process. These theorists go beyond the repressive determinism views of the conflict and consistency theories, which blame adult behavior on early childhood and adolescent experiences. Fulfillment theorists observe that, in healthy individuals, the dynamic process of development continues throughout life, even until the moment of death. The person continually presses onward, attempting to become "all that you can be." These writers have much to say to us in our endeavor to understand maturity and the nature of the individual's being and becoming.

Conflict theorists identify maturity in terms of compromise and adjustment in the struggle between personal drives and the expectations of society. **Consistency theorists** emphasize the process of maintaining customary levels of

activation in sorting out the feedback of the environment. For the **fulfillment theorists,** maturity is expressed as a natural unfolding of potentials and the actualization of human ideals. Inasmuch as this view is highly optimistic, it has strong appeal to the young adult who is looking for goals and a sense of hope in confronting the tasks and crises of this phase of development. At no other point in life are individuals more keenly aware of their potentials and of the possibilities and pressures that confront them.

The Process of Self-actualization

Carl Rogers[31] and Abraham Maslow[25] developed their theories of personality around the concept of self-actualization. In describing his view of human development, Rogers writes: "The organism has one basic tendency and striving—to actualize, maintain, and enhance the experiencing organism."[30] Rogers' view is highly optimistic: he sees the individual as being capable of growth toward self-reliance, autonomy, and self-government. This tendency toward self-actualization is present throughout development from the time of conception to maturity. Development is an ongoing process throughout adult life, wherein the person is seen as a "fluid process, not a fixed and static entity; a flowing river of change, not a block of solid material; a continually changing constellation of potentialities, not a fixed quantity of traits."[31] Rogers perceives maturity as an ongoing process that is both exciting and threatening; it is an ever-growing process of self-discovery.

The term **becoming** is highly expressive of how both Allport and Rogers view human development; less emphasis is placed on general norms for development and more emphasis on the uniqueness of each individual's process of becoming.[1] Fulfillment theorists place limited emphasis on a developmental stage theory and concentrate more on the themes of actualization and maturity. Idealism permeates their work: conflict is discussed only minimally as a barrier, and challenges afford opportunities to the process of actualization. Although the importance of nurturing relationships is recognized by these "personologists," the thrust of their approach is on the resources within the individual for actualization.

Maslow's concept of the **hierarchy of needs** provides us with a model for identifying five different levels of need that motivate behavior. Consequently, a wide range of lifestyles and values is seen in adult life. While Maslow maintains his idealism throughout, the potency of lower-level needs brings the realities of the individual's circumstances into focus. Maslow establishes the primacy of **physiological needs** in his motivational theory. This concept has a homeostatic basis, since the human organism demonstrates "automatic efforts to maintain a constant, normal state of the blood stream."[26] Most of Maslow's emphasis within the first level in the hierarchy deals with *life-sustaining* behaviors, such as those that seek sleep, oxygen, water, and food. He also notes the existence of *life-enhancing* physiological needs, such as coition and comfort.[26]

An individual's perspective on life is significantly influenced by the level of need that dominates. If the adult is dominated by physiological needs, then these needs become reflected in the lifestyle and the focus of activities. As observed in news broadcasts and stories from Ethiopia, Bangladesh, and other areas of famine, the individual with significant food deprivation evidences little concern over the higher level needs; he or she is preoccupied in both thought and behavior with physiological need gratification, basic survival.

The unemployed young adult male who is without family support may find himself preoccupied with meeting his basic physical needs. The situation makes it difficult for him to deal with the tasks of building a meaningful intimacy and establishing a family. If he is married and has a family, his unemployment demands a concentration of thoughts on this lowest level of needs for both his own and his family's survival. The consequences of this stressor can be seen in both urban and rural areas of socioeconomic decline that have high unemployment rates.

What are the possibilities for higher-level functioning for a pregnant young woman recently rejected by her boyfriend and family or for an abandoned mother of four? These people are preoccupied with securing food and shelter for themselves and their children. The chronically ill individual is likely to be depressed by the dominance of illness over the capacity to rise to new levels of need fulfillment. When personal and family health problems are critical, the idealism of youth is easily lost. It is when these physiological needs are relatively ensured that the individual can move to higher levels of need experience and pursuit. The new unsatisfied needs then dominate the individual's behavior, and when these needs have been satisfied, the next level of yet-to-be-satisfied needs emerges.

The tremendous rise in the use and abuse of drugs further complicates the process of movement within this hierarchy of needs. It is evident that the use of drugs to escape the pressures and demands of confronting these various levels of needs serves to sabotage the process of being and becoming both for the individual and for other members of the family. This result is not only true of the physiological level of needs, but even at higher levels of need and goal pursuit as well.

Assuming that the first level of physiological needs are at least minimally met, an awareness of **safety** emerges as evidenced in those patterns of behavior that are self-protective and cautious. A fear of helplessness and environmental crisis exists. These safety needs are most clearly revealed in the helpless child who has a high refueling need. Looking at the adult in our society, Maslow writes, "The healthy, normal, fortunate adult in our culture is largely satisfied in his safety needs. The peaceful, smoothly running, good society ordinarily makes its members feel safe enough from wild animals, extremes of temperature, criminal assault, murder, tyranny, etc . . . Therefore, in a very real sense he no longer has any safety needs, as active motivation."[26] This statement is helpful in understanding the impact of one's general cultural milieu and environment. When a community or country is torn by

civil strife, social instability, political repression, or environmental extremes, the necessity of concentrating on this level of need stifles further development.

One might take some exception to Maslow by stating that for many safety needs no longer operate as sources of active motivation. Again, let's return to the use and abuse of drugs, which leads to assault, theft, rape, and other forms of violence. As increasing numbers of people move to the cities, there is a rise in the threat to safety for an increasing percentage of people. Unless socioeconomic development and employment possibilities are made available to everyone, the threat to both physiological and safety need satisfaction increases.

When physiological and safety needs are relatively satisfied, the need **for belongingness and love** becomes the focus. This need for affection may become the dominant theme of the individual's thought and behavior. At this stage, it is easier to share intimately with others. The need for love is assumed by many theologians, philosophers, and psychologists to be the most central need of mankind and the highest expression of human values. The different levels of love must be differentiated: infantile (self-serving, grasping, dependent) love is quite different from mature (life-giving, nurturing, responsible) love, a fact that reveals important differences in self-awareness and insight. Mature and well-adjusted members of society have a sense of belonging and evidence reciprocity in the loving and caring dimensions of social life.

Beyond the belonging needs, the developing personality reaches the level of **esteem** needs. Maslow sees the need to be valued and appreciated as a mixture of the need for achievement, competence, and recognition. The contrasting situation is that of being locked into a syndrome of low self-esteem, inferiority feelings, and blocked motivation due to feelings of inadequacy. An individual reaches relative satisfaction when he or she is moving away from these crippling feelings.

The satisfaction of the other levels of need in the hierarchy does not lead to a state of quiet reflection and satisfaction as though the final stage has been attained. Instead, individuals are pushed forward by the need to be all they are capable of being, the **self-actualization needs.** They begin to establish goals for the actualization of their potentials. The concept of "metaneeds" was developed by Maslow to identify the "being values" of the individual; it is the process of working at fulfilling one's destiny or calling in life. The goal of growth-motivated individuals is to fulfill their vocation for purposes of ultimate satisfaction.[27] This concept raises questions as to the basic characteristics of what Maslow refers to as the "self-actualizing" person or what Rogers refers to as the "fully functioning" person. Allport's concept of a "mature sentiment"[1] and Combs' concept of the adequate personality[4] add depth and breadth to the meaning and nature of maturity.

Characteristics of the Mature Personality

Allport, Rogers, Combs, and Maslow (fulfillment theorists) have given considerable attention to defining the specific characteristics of maturity. Their approaches are of particular value, since they fundamentally agree about the basic characteristics of maturity. The achievement of *independence from* or the establishment of contributory financial, social, and emotional *interindependence with the family of origin* is a given. The person no longer sees himself or herself as a dependent member of the childhood family.

All the fulfillment theorists give primary attention to the importance of being *open to experience*. Rogers sees the fully functioning person as nondefensive, open to change, flexible, and able to tolerate ambiguity. The mature person is open to what is going on in his or her current life process. Allport characterizes the immature personality as one who is dominated by biological drives and immediate gratification; the mature personality would be one who has mastered impulse control and whose behavior reflects this.

All these theorists see the *absence of defensiveness* as being characteristic of the self-actualizing or fully functioning mature adult; this concept implies being more open to reality and to others. The tasks on which Havighurst or Schuster focus are obviously more likely to be fulfilled by this type of person. To share the inner self with others, to make a marriage work, to develop satisfying social relationships, and to balance the expressions of personal needs and interests with the expectations and opportunities of the culture all require the energy and investment of a relatively nondefensive personality. The capacity to view life with a combination of insight and humor is another way of expressing nondefensive living.

Another area of agreement among these theorists is their emphasis on the quality of **self-acceptance** or **self-objectivity.** The mature person is "better able to permit his total organism, his conscious thought participating, to consider, weigh and balance each stimulus, need and demand, and its relative weight and intensity."[31] Self-acceptance is the process of listening to oneself to let the inner self emerge. It might be added that a media-oriented culture tends to interfere with this process. Can individuals become psychologically mature if they seldom meditate or listen to their inner needs and potential to become? Beyond self-acceptance is the capacity to be self-objective, which is the ability to look at one's self from another perspective, to emotionally separate one's self from an interaction, and to view the self as a third person. One has the advantage of seeing external behavior as well as internal thoughts and motives. The individual who is able to be self-objective is less likely to become emotionally enmeshed in a scenario and is able to remain more objective and thus more sensitive to the needs of all involved, including the self. The mature personality has "the ability to objectify oneself, to be reflective and insightful about one's own life. The individual with insight sees himself as others see him, and at certain points (seems) to glimpse himself in a kind of cosmic perspective."[1] This person is thus able to identify the basis of his or her own personal worth.

The apex of this process of self-objectification is what Maslow identifies as a "peak experience," which is most likely to occur when a person is facing a crisis with a full awareness of all the dimensions involved and a full use of capacities. It is the obverse of the acute helplessness syndrome. Because the individual is able to think clearly, he or she is able to respond in synchrony to the needs of the immediate situation while keeping in mind the long-range effects. This reaction is in contrast to the person who reacts when a person or an event touches a "trigger button."

A related characteristic of the mature personality is that of *assuming responsibility* for one's own life in an honest manner. This characteristic also means that one expects and allows other people to take responsibility for their own lives, actions, and values. The open and self-objective person confronts reality and the tasks of life in a responsible manner. In discussing the fully functioning person, Rogers identifies this quality as possessing an "internal locus of evaluation."[31] Individuals are no longer driven by the dictates of a severe conscience, the traditions of the culture, or the pressures from peers; rather, they have sorted out and integrated those values that are most important to their own becoming. They assume responsibility for their own lives and decisions. Maslow suggests that such individuals may have to be nonconformists and swim upstream against the currents of conformity. To put this concept in the language of a contemporary moral theorist, Lawrence Kohlberg, the individual has moved beyond the law-and-order approach of morality to the level of principled living. This self-aware internalization is reflected in an individual's sensitivity to justice and *reciprocity in relationships* with others (see Chap. 16). Obviously, such a person is most capable of fulfilling the tasks of assuming civic responsibility and establishing reciprocal social care. The mature individual *commits oneself to intimacies and responsibilities* more completely and effectively. Events, such as selecting a mate, building a marriage, and creating a family life experience that is mutually enjoyable and fulfilling, are far more likely to occur in the life of such a person. Assuming responsibility for independent decision making, developing expertise in a career, and participating in the general family and community life are expressions of affective maturity.

The mature person views life as involving *ongoing change* and is willing to be a significant part of that process. Changes in culture and the institutions of society do not overwhelm the person. He or she is able to maintain integrity while expanding a sense of identity. This capacity is particularly important in the life of significant changes in gender-role and marital-role expectancy in our society. Rather than becoming defensive or isolated, the mature person participates in the process of differentiating and integrating roles that are mutually beneficial. Thus, the mature man whose wife is seeking the fulfillment of her deferred educational and vocational objectives is capable of entering into that process in a supportive, contributory, and mutually rewarding manner. This maturity may be reflected in a cooperative endeavor to fulfill the ongoing tasks of rearing children and managing the home.

These theorists agree about the critical importance of a **philosophy of life** that is both unifying and directing. Allport sees the attributes of humor and religion as complementary and balancing functions in the mature personality. This "mature religious sentiment" or philosophy of life is rich in its diversification because of a combination of discriminations and reorganizations. While it is shaped by formative childhood experiences, it is dynamic and fundamentally autonomous of its origins. This philosophy of life is unifying because it is "productive of consistent morality." The mature outlook is one that endeavors to take into consideration all other perspectives and data. *The mature person has a quality of tolerance that saves the individual from a narrow dogmatism that would reject the views and opinions of others.*[1] (The immature person becomes defensive as a way to protect the insecure self.) This philosophy is comprehensive inasmuch as it makes sense out of life for each person, including coming to grips with the major dilemmas of human suffering and death. The individual is able to function wholeheartedly even without absolute certainty.

In the face of life's complexities and humanity's sufferings, the mature person demonstrates the *capacity to take risks* for the good of his fellow man (Fig. 28-9). "To the genuinely mature personality a full-faced view of reality in its grimmest aspects is not incompatible with an heuristic commitment that has the power to turn desperation into active purpose."[1] People involved in the helping and healing professions are constantly confronted with these dilemmas. Providing both medical care and strength of character in the face of an individual's suffering and pain is a challenge that confronts the medical and psychiatric practitioner. This challenge may also confront a young couple who face the grim reality of a chronic disease process in their child, or a young man whose

wife has just died, leaving him with the care of two young children. *A comprehensive philosophy of life, and finding something higher than the self to live for* provide a sense of hope and purpose that enables the individual to continue to function even in the presence of tragedy, disaster, sickness, and death.

The experience of becoming fully functioning or self-actualizing is ongoing. However, it is attained to a relative extent in the development of the characteristics discussed. The fully functioning individual is **actualizing potentials.** Such self-actualization is possible only if Maslow's lower-level needs are met; if they are not met, the individual has a pattern of **deficiency motivation.** All relationships and behaviors become based on the question: "How does this contribute to my welfare?" The quality of the individual's life and that of others becomes negatively influenced. The **growth motivation** required to effectively establish intimate and mutually responsible relationships in marriage and family is missing, as is the growth motivation essential to building community. The growth-motivated person, on the other hand, is expressing self rather than simply adapting; relationships with others are spontaneous and natural rather than forced or defensive. Relationships and behavior flow out of the abundance of one's joy and satisfaction with life and answer the question: "How can I contribute to the welfare of the other?" Family and community life are greatly enriched by the presence of these people who put the needs of others before their own and exude the joy of life and living.

Maslow has an appreciation for the ongoing need for the renewal of the human spirit in its struggle to become self-actualized. This renewal is expressed in spiritual rather than in traditional religious ways. Maslow sees the need for individuals periodically to achieve a peak experience (or self-transcending) that is mystical in nature. Although such an experience is transient, it has a powerful influence on the ongoing process of actualization.

Gaps: Expectations and Realities

Differences are seen in the nature of developmental tasks and the timing of the psychosocial crises for each stage of development. These differences create gaps in time perspective and energy investment and may lead in turn to major differences in values and priorities in life style. A "generation gap" may occur when two people do not understand or appreciate their differences in values and priorities. However, the generation gap is not primarily chronological, any more than a chronological definition of either adolescence or maturity is adequate. A gap may occur between two people of the same chronological age who have markedly differing developmental levels or primary value systems. These gaps are often manifest in the major areas of differentiation and integration of identity and the establishment of psychosocial reciprocity.

One of the major gaps exists in the area of role definitions

FIGURE 28–9.
Artistry and creativity open one up to potential criticisms, but provide an important outlet for expression of one's inner self.

and expectations. Young adults in their thirties who have adolescent children often find themselves polarized around style, values, and choices. The young adult is becoming much more goal-oriented than the adolescent. The adolescent is still investing time and energy in sorting out roles, strengths, and capacities. This process of differentiation and integration often involves role playing and role experimentation, which are evidenced in everything from clothing styles to fluctuating interests in various activities. The adolescent is faced with the dilemma of finding a role in relation to a changing culture and social expectations. It is somewhat like boarding a moving vehicle when you have not had enough time to decide whether or not you want to go in the direction it is heading. For the adolescent, dealing with goals and values is secondary to finding a role. However, roles are constantly shifting as the culture, its institutions, and even personal relationships are shaped by technology and the media. The adult may have great difficulty understanding or relating to the adolescent who does not yet demonstrate stability and direction in goals. This relationship is complicated by the recent parallel tasks and crises with which this young adult has been struggling and may not yet be comfortable.

The polarizations that characterize the psychosocial experience of the adolescent are relatively resolved in the young adult, enabling the person to move ahead with the intimacies of marriage, friendship, and community. The mature young adult has already dealt with the differentiation of personal drives, individual abilities, and the place of family and peer group in his or her value system. Experimentation with the capacity to fulfill certain roles is generally behind the young adult, enabling a move toward consideration of direction or goal orientation for the continuing expression of a clearer sense of identity and personhood.

Gaps exist on intrapersonal as well as interpersonal levels. There are problems with time diffusion in the experience of the adolescent; the pressures are so great that time may go out of focus. Integrating the past into the present as well as responding to the demands of others to make future choices becomes an overwhelming task. The mature young adult maintains a focus on tasks that involve both present commitments and future goals. The young adult is able to invest time and energy with less diffusion in accomplishing the tasks that society expects this individual to fulfill. Undertaking marital and family responsibilities during adolescence poses a much higher risk than it does in the young adult years.

Gaps also exist within the experience of the young adult. Those who have not mastered prior tasks and psychosocial crises experience gaps between current expectations and their resources to respond. These early psychosocial experiences have been discussed as key factors that impact the transition into maturity. Other gaps exist that are due to combinations of environmental and decision-making problems; perhaps the attainments of an individual do not measure up to self-expectations. There may be a recurrence of old task demands because of failures or breakdowns in those

tasks that were once thought to be completed. A crisis such as job loss, marital discord, or child-rearing complications might trigger the recurrence of these old themes and a reworking of identity.

One of the most common experiences is failure to make a marriage work. Separation and divorce are on the increase in our society and leave individuals with ego problems as well as problems with role and goal conflicts. The 30-year-old man who is now back in the single group, separated from his wife and family, has trouble sorting out roles and goals. He experiences a type of regressive episode in his psychosocial development; he is back climbing old hills and struggling through valleys of identity diffusion he thought he had conquered. At the same time, he feels the demands from self, children, and society to function as a good father. How is he to put it all together? Feelings of failure, loss, hurt, and bitterness over a lost marriage may block the fulfillment of the task of finding another partner and making a second marriage work. The response of the surrounding community may compound the problem. The divorced woman who joins community organizations for the sake of her children may find herself forced into isolation; she may be viewed as a threat to the stability of other marriages and rejected by couples. One of the major problems in such situations is to find a congenial social group that will help the divorced young adult cope with the ongoing demands of social and family responsibilities.

The failure to make a marriage work generally includes the sense of failure in rearing children, particularly as custody and related issues are addressed. Gaps are found between what one had anticipated in parenting and the realities of separation. The breakdown in the time and space dimensions of the relationship involves a separation of shared growth experience. Failure in parenting adds to the feelings of defeat and loss that began with the disruption of the marriage. In addition, the task of vocational fulfillment may break down into the frustrations of job inadequacy to meet the economic pressures of marital and family separation. Thus, the loss of a role often throws the sense of goals into a new state of diffusion.

In each case, the young adult is faced once again with the issues of identity: Who am I? What do I value? What are my goals? What are my priorities? On what do I base my worth? As these issues are clarified, then the issues of intimacy once more become the focus of affective energies: To whom, to what do I commit myself? Who will be my people? Who will be my confidant? How much do I share? What career options allow me to best express my interests, potentials, and goals? How do I activate my value system?

As one faces bravely and openly the recurring issues of identity (whether because of marital breakdown, job loss, severe personal illness, a challenging adolescent, or family death), opportunity is found for personal growth that transcends the pain and renewed personal satisfactions that come only from confidence in one's ability to face the realities of life—no matter how difficult (Fig. 28-10).

FIGURE 28–10.
A talent or interest (e.g., musical ability) can be expressed in multiple ways. The challenge is to find a compatible peer group for development of the skill and a cultural setting that appreciates the specific form of expression.

CONCLUSION

Knowledge and acceptance of one's self free us to know and be known by others. From the experience of affective intimacy, we not only strengthen our self-knowledge, but continue to reveal new aspects of our inner self, interests, and values as we exchange viewpoints, reactions, and opinions. We sharpen our identity as we answer the challenges presented by others willing to confront our will, behaviors, or values. Respect and mutuality emerge as reciprocal exchanges occur and ideas spur reflection, insight, and personal growth. Erikson hypothesizes that commitment and love emerge as vital strengths.[9]

One cannot force one's self to love, it is beyond mere willing; it is a spontaneous, existential experience, the outgrowth of the integration and harmonizing of intimacy.[21] Mutuality provides freedom and wings to accept the other as one accepts the self. The sense of separateness realized during infancy is finally transcended, yet individual distinctiveness is confirmed.[9] Two can be one again without loss of the self. This love sets the foundation to want to serve the other, to protect and care for the concerns of someone other than self. For many, this intimacy and sense of generativity goes beyond the immediate family to include serving the community through its institutions (e.g., schools, American Red Cross, church).

Not everyone masters the crisis of intimacy during the early adult years. Many, because of insufficient identity resolution, may not focus on true intimacy until the middle years or later. However, when identity is adequately resolved, defensiveness recedes, and the person experiences a new freedom, a new birth of the self that transforms all relationships and allows, for the first time, the actualization of one's full potentials as a mature human.

REFERENCES

1. Allport, G. W. (1937). *Personality: A psychological interpretation.* New York: Holt.
2. Archer, J. (1980). Personal communication.
3. Clinebell, J. H., & Clinebell, C. H. (1970). *The intimate marriage.* New York: Harper and Row.
4. Combs, A. W., Richards, A. C., & Richards, F. (1976). *Perceptual psychology: A humanistic approach to the study of persons.* New York: Harper and Row.
5. Diedrick, P. (1984). *Gender differences in communication.* (ERIC Document Reproduction Service No. ED 289 126)
6. Erikson, E. H. (1963). *Childhood and society* (2nd ed.). New York: Norton.
7. Erikson, E. H. (1966). *Insight and responsibility.* London: Faber.
8. Erikson, E. H. (1968). *Identity, youth and crisis.* New York: Norton.
9. Erikson, E. H., Erikson, J. M., & Kivnick, H. Q. (1986). *Vital involvement in old age.* New York: W. W. Norton.
10. Franz, C. E., & White, K. E. (1985). Individuation and attachment in personality development: Extending Erikson's theory. *Journal of Personality, 53,* 224–256.
11. Freud, S. (1935). *A general introduction to psycho-analysis* (Authorized English translation of the revised edition by J. Rivière). New York: Liveright.
12. Freudenberger, H. J. (1987). Today's troubled man. *Psychology Today, 21*(12), 46–47.
13. Gilligan, C. (1984). *In a different voice.* Cambridge, MA: Harvard University Press.
14. Glick, P. C., & Linn, S. L. (1986). More young adults are living with their parents: Who are they? *Journal of Marriage and the Family, 48*(1), 107–112.
15. Gould, R. L. (1978). *Transformations.* New York: Simon and Schuster.
16. Havighurst, R. J. (1972). *Developmental tasks and education* (3rd ed.). New York: McKay.
17. Hill, C. (1987). Affiliation motivation: People who need people . . . but in different ways. *Journal of Personality and Social Psychology, 52,* 1008–1018.
18. Kelly, E. L., & Conley, J. J. (1987). Personality and compatibility: A prospective analysis of marital stability and marital satisfaction. *Journal of Personality and Social Psychology, 52,* 27–40.
19. Keniston, K. (1971). *Youth and dissent: The rise of a new opposition.* New York: Harcourt, Brace and Jovanovich.
20. Kiefer, C. W. (1988). *The mantle of maturity: A history of ideas about character development.* Albany, NY: State University of New York Press.
21. Knowles, R. T. (1986). *Human development and human possibility: Erikson in the light of Heiddeger.* Lanham, MD: University Press of America.
22. Levinson, D. J., et al. (1978). *The seasons of a man's life.* New York: Knopf.
23. Maddi, S. R. (1989). *Personality theories: A comparative analysis* (5th ed.). Chicago: Dorsey Press.
24. Mahler, M. S., Pine, F., & Bergman, A. (1975). *The psychological birth of the human infant: Symbiosis and individuation.* New York: Basic Books.
25. Maslow, A. H. (1968). *Toward a psychology of being* (2nd ed.). New York: Van Nostrand.
26. Maslow, A. H. (1971). *The farther reaches of human nature.* New York: Viking.
27. Maslow, A. H. (1987). *Motivation and personality* (3rd ed.). New York: Harper and Row.
28. Paul, C. R., & Lanham, J. (1982). *Choices: In pursuit of wholeness.* Kansas City, MO: Beacon Hill Press of Kansas City.
29. Pruyser, P. (1976). *The minister as diagnostician.* Philadelphia: Westminster Press.
30. Rogers, C. R. (1951). *Client-centered therapy.* Boston: Houghton Mifflin.
31. Rogers, C. R. (1961). *On becoming a person: A therapist's view of psychotherapy.* Boston: Houghton Mifflin.
32. Sheehy, G. (1976). *Passages: Predictable crises of adult life.* New York: Dutton.

IX THE FAMILY

The family is the bedrock of society. It produces, nurtures, trains, and teaches the citizens of tomorrow. It is the family that "civilizes" children, teaches them how to love, to share, to empathize, to help others, and to negotiate conflicts. It is the family that teaches children its own traditions and those of the culture. It is the family that prepares children to face their own adult years: it prepares them to assume emotional and financial independence, to set goals and to discipline oneself to achieve them, to work, to initiate and maintain their own family, and to face the exigencies of life.

The problems of societies are, to a large extent, reflections of the failure of families to raise mature, allocentric, cooperative, generative offspring. Crime, lack of integrity in government and business, family abuse, disintegration of families, substance abuse, and even environmental pollution are major indicators of the immaturity of persons–identity is found in self-gratification and self-aggrandizement rather than in the ability to find something higher than oneself to live for and concern for other's welfare.

Most of us receive more specific preparation for professional development than for family development. Yet, it is within the context of social relationships, especially those of the family, that we receive our major satisfactions in life. Careers may flourish, but if personal relationships falter, most of us become very disillusioned with the meaning of life. Thus, for both personal and societal reasons, it behooves us to understand, support, and maintain healthy family relationships and functioning.

It is paradoxical that in healthy families, the members "belong" to each other, a factor which provides special privileges of communication and responsibility, yet the members defend the right of individuality in the expression of opinions and potentials. Since most of us have intimate contact with only 2 or 3 families during our developmental years, we may not know what a "healthy" family can be. As a result, we replicate in our family of creation what was modeled in our family of origin. Although all problems cannot be avoided, persons who approach family initiation and development with as much objectivity as career choice and development, find that the family can become an outlet for creativity as well as a refreshing oasis as one travels through life. The healthy family positively and patiently prods, protects, and provides for its members who are bonded in love, committed to the welfare of each other.

Developmental Tasks of Families

*1. Identify clearly who does and who does not belong to the family system:
> selectively admit persons into the primary family unit
> differentiate between advice-giving and decision-making powers of extended family members
> develop interdependent relationships with extended family members
> prevent intrusion on the family resources by non-family members

*2. Develop deep commitment to the welfare of the family unit as well as to each of its members:
> postpone or delay own gratification for the welfare of the family
> balance own rights as a person against those of other family members and against one's responsibilities as a family member
> develop a willingness to sacrifice own gratifications for the development of another family member

*3. Maintain open communication for expression of needs, values, frustrations, disappointments, excitements, ideas, interests, etc.:
> respect expressions of feelings and needs
> provide and protect individualized time for each family dyad
> provide for family sharing/conference times

*4. Appreciate and support the uniqueness of each family member:
> assist with the identification and support of each member's unique interests, needs, talents, relationships, and goals
> provide for protection and respect of each person's ideas, property, privacy, values, territory, and time

*5. Establish common philosophies, values, and goals:
> protect the right and responsibility of the family to develop its own rules, traditions, values, talents, interests, etc.
> provide opportunities for family work, leisure, and cultural pursuits
> provide for joint decision-making opportunities to resolve issues of conflict, activities of family living, problems, careers, education, spiritual development, etc.
> discuss community, national, world issues and problems
> guide ethical and moral development of members
> provide for esthetic and value development

*6. Establish rules regulating conduct and relationships consistent with family philosophies, values, and goals:
> relationships within the family
> approaches to conflict negotiation
> role modeling and training
> relationships with persons outside the family
> philosophy and approaches for enforcement of rules

*7. Divide responsibilities for maintenance of the family as an effective functioning unit:
> provision for each member, regardless of age, to contribute to the family welfare according to the individual's interests as well as abilities
> provide increasingly more complex challenges as individual members mature
> balance the division of family resources according to individual needs

---

*Tasks deemed most crucial to continued maturation are marked with an asterisk.

623

Initiating a Family Unit

Clara S. Schuster

Many couples who contemplate initiation of a new family unit are dedicated to the concept of the "ideal" relationship. They are "in love." In spite of the problems they may have observed within their parents' marriages or even in those of their peers, they are convinced that their relationship is unique and therefore immune to the boredom and destructive conflicts that destroy so many marriages. Many married couples *are* able to achieve a special relationship—not because they are free from cultural stressors, or the exigencies of life, but because they recognize and work with their strengths and weaknesses. After 3, 12, 26, or 54 years of marriage, these couples say that they are more in love than when they left for their honeymoon.

A successful union does not happen just because the individuals wish for it. A successfully functioning family unit requires realistic appraisal, sacrifice, forgiveness, commitment, and planning. In short, a good relationship is earned—it is worked for—and does not automatically happen because two people love each other (Fig. 29-1).

A good union begins long before a couple pledges their marriage vows. It starts with two people who have done their "identity homework" (see Chap. 25). They have learned to know themselves, their goals, and their value systems. These factors become guidelines during courtship as they look for someone with compatible goals, values, and approaches to share the journey through life. Gradually, through an honest and open communion, two people develop a mutual respect that cherishes the uniqueness of each one and yet binds them together in their understanding of life and hopes for the future.

THE FAMILY AS A SYSTEM

The family is a social system composed of two or more interdependent persons that remains united over time and serves as a mediator between the needs of its members and the forces, demands, and obligations of society.[22] As a system, all the characteristics of open systems discussed in Chapter 2 are pertinent to describing, explaining, and assessing the levels of family functioning.

Role of Family in Society

As a system, the family experiences dynamic interaction with other families and social systems of the culture. Each family affects and is affected by this contact with the suprasystem. Each society identifies specific responsibilities for its families that, when fulfilled, enhance the total functioning of the society. Each family, however, functions independently and puts its own stamp on the task.

PEANUTS

FIGURE 29–1.
Reprinted courtesy of Peanuts. *Copyright 1989, United Feature Syndicate, Inc.*

Functions of the Family System

Companionship

The primary function of the family in society is to provide companionship. Humans are gregarious and need affiliation with other humans to fully realize their own potentials. We each need to know and be known as an individual to appreciate and to value our own uniqueness. The world is too large for us to know and be known in detail by each person with whom we have contact. Consequently, we play a role or present a pseudoself to the world at large. It is only with a small, intimate group of people that we have the time or inclination to reveal our true selves. Within the family, a multiplicity of experiences occur over an extended period of time that facilitate the required peeling away of roles and pseudoselves to extract full value from relationships and promote optimal personal growth.

The consistency with which other people respond enables us to develop a sense of trust, which lays the foundation for attachment, loyalty, and love—the bedrock of feelings of kinship and the springboard for personal development. Self-esteem is enhanced as family members affirm the presence and value of one another. No matter how badly we fail, in a *well-functioning family* the other members value our efforts, sympathize with our pain, and continue to accept us.

Many observe that companionship is even more critical than sexual compatibility in marital satisfaction.[3, 18] Genuine companionship fosters an emotional intimacy that stimulates the growth of the individuals while binding them still closer together. When two people are true friends, they are able to share themselves on a personal level. They can share their dreams, disappointments, fears, values, reactions, triumphs, and failures openly without fear of reprisal, ridicule, or loss of face. Unconditional acceptance characterizes the relationship.

True companionship is predicated on an equality in the relationship between two people. It requires an intimate knowledge of both one's self and the other person, so that a sensitive reciprocity is established. It means responding to the total person and not simply to the role or the concern of the moment. Such intimacy and companionship takes time—even years—to develop. It begins with courtship and can, if worked on, continue through the childbearing years and into the post–child-rearing period. However, many individuals become so involved in their bread-winning, homemaking, or child-rearing roles that the companionship roles are underdeveloped, leading to antagonism because of a lack of understanding or appreciation for the other. Cultural and personal factors that advocate rigid gender-role stereotypes tend to keep husband and wife in their own worlds, spending time with same-gender friends for companionship and advice, thus usurping spousal companionship.[18] As our society becomes more impersonal, the companionship role within the family takes on more importance.

Sexual Relations

Human sexuality serves three functions, each of which can deepen the tie between the couple: reproduction, pleasure, and communication.[34] Every culture has developed its own set of rules to guide sexual expression. Infant betrothals, child marriages, and chaperones are all efforts to restrict premarital experimentation. Incest taboos and laws that prohibit intrafamily and clan sexual relations are also attempts to control potentially disastrous outcomes.

In most cultures, marriage legitimizes sexual relations and expression. The spouses have free access to a sexual partner, except when medical conditions or religious beliefs prescribe brief periods of abstinence. In most cultures, fidelity is expected. That is, the spouses are expected to be faithful to each other. However, in some cultures, a double standard may allow the husband (but not the wife) to seek other sources of sexual outlet to "relieve the wife of her burden."

Economic Cooperation and Protection

Two hundred years ago, household responsibilities were, of necessity, gender-related. The greater physical strength of the male was essential to provide for the safety of the home and meat for the table. The female, staying close to the home because of the need to care for young children, provided clothing, food preservation and preparation, and meals. Today, so many tasks have been automated (e.g., washing clothes, transportation) or can be purchased (e.g., fresh meat, ready-made clothing) that one can live easily and successfully without an adult partner to provide the essentials of survival. However, in spite of this potentiality for independent living, most people still find they can live more cheaply or comfortably when a second person shares expenses, home maintenance, and child-care responsibilities. Most adults also find intimacy, shared goals, and emotional support a critical factor in deciding to choose a life partner or companion.

Legitimate Procreation

A universal and historical function of family life is the reproduction of the human race, the provision of future workers for the maintenance of society. "Society's concern with legitimacy is not an effort to brand or embarrass children born out of wedlock, but a well-intentioned attempt to ensure the welfare of the children in each new generation."[18] Legitimacy provides for the orderly transfer of property, wealth, titles, or position. Blood kinship also assigns primary responsibility for the care of children, the ill, the disabled, and the elderly.

Socialization of Offspring

The family is the child's training ground for adult responsibilities. It is within the family that one develops self-discipline and a respect for other people. The child gradually learns and internalizes rules, roles, and responsibilities through the privileges and responsibilities of ordinal position and the models and guidance offered by the parents.

Enculturation of Citizens

The family teaches its members the traditions, taboos, and values of the culture. Each subculture or family has its own unique status and traditions within the community. Socioeconomic status and ethnic or religious background give the family its unique orientation to the culture at large. The values and identities learned during childhood shape our expectations of the adult years.

Social Control

Whenever two or more people interact, some common rules must be accepted by all parties for continued cooperative effort and maintenance of individual rights. Families are expected to help their members learn and abide by the rules of society. Successful adaptation to rules within the family is a prelude to successful adaptation to societal rules. When the family cannot, or will not, control the behavior of its members, then society is forced to impose sanctions.

Family Structure

The family is universal because the needs to which it responds are universal. Its structure varies to meet the needs of particular people as well as the society and culture. Agricultural societies and many ethnic or inner city families tend to have **extended families.** A bride or groom may join the new spouse's household as another member, both physically and psychologically, or the couple may set up a separate home contiguous to the family of one spouse. The extended family may function as an economically cooperative unit. Boundaries between the new couple as a separate unit and the parents can become blurred unless carefully guarded. Close kinship ties are fostered, a factor that can have both positive and negative aspects, depending on the people involved.

In industrial societies, small mobile family units are essential for economic survival. The new couple (family of creation) separates physically from their families of origin. The **nuclear family** (the couple and their children) comprises an economically and psychologically independent unit. This unit has been the typical family structure in the United States for the past century. Unfortunately, this arrangement tends to separate family members from significant role models, emotional support, financial assistance, and affirmation during times of crisis.

With the emergence of a technological society, family structure may change again. Although the independent nuclear family still appears to be the cultural ideal, awareness of the value of the extended family has increased. Advances in computer technology may allow many people to work at home at a terminal instead of moving from city to city when they change jobs.[43] This option can allow today's family to combine the best of both basic family structures: they maintain the economic and psychological integrity of the nuclear family while preserving accessibility to the extended family for continued affirmation and support.

Significance of Marital Choice

In primitive, agricultural, and early industrial societies, families were and are often held together by necessity.[43] Men and women need each other for survival. They are a working partnership. However, gender roles can be so rigidly maintained that one cannot survive without access to the services of the other. Today, in Western societies marriages are more likely to be held together by mutual affection, rather than by formal stereotyped gender roles. Although marriages may remain intact for financial, social, or convenience reasons, for a marriage to survive successfully, the individuals involved must be able to relate to each other as people, not just as roles. Consequently, they need to establish not only a working partnership but a deep friendship as well.

Although it appears to be comparatively easy to obtain the dissolution of a marriage from a legal standpoint, an unhappy marriage or divorce is a severe, emotionally traumatic event. Therefore, it is wise to be fully aware of the implications of one's marital decision and to know both one's self and the other person as well as possible before the final step is taken.

CHOOSING A PARTNER

Social Factors That Affect Courtship

To persons raised with individual freedoms, the personal choice of a marital partner appears to be an inalienable right. However, for parts of the world, and for most of recorded history, people have had little personal input in this decision. Even if free choice appears to be a right, however, many factors narrow the field of choice.

Cultural Mores

The mode of choosing a marital partner is frequently dictated by the culture. In some, it is strictly by parental choice, arranged to meet societal needs or religious goals, to prevent war, to distribute or retain wealth, to honor ancestors, or to ensure purity of blood lines. Therefore, happiness is not a factor in determining the success of a marriage, and divorce is not allowed. Gender roles are critical and strictly enforced. Some spouses may never meet before the wedding. In India, some females may be betrothed during infancy. To ensure compatibility (at least in skill performance), she may assume residence with her parents-in-law by 10 or 11 years of age and become married with the onset of menarche.

In other cultures, marital choice is a **joint venture.** The parents exercise considerable influence, but the child also has a voice in the final choice. The final decision may be made by either party. Meanwhile, considerable effort is taken to prevent promiscuity. Males and females are segregated for all casual and formal social events, and chaperones may be employed when dating begins.

Many cultures allow unlimited social and sexual access. The choice is left to the individual, but cultural overtones may still be strong or parental approval may be required. In some cultures, the male or the female must prove their eligibility for marriage by achieving pregnancy. In other cultures, premarital pregnancy is linked with religious or social depravity. It is common for individuals in Western cultures to seek parental input, or at least approval, but they usually make their own choice of marital partners.

Socioeconomic Factors

The choice of a partner may be a personal affair, but it is strongly influenced by the values and orientation of one's culture, family, and social class. Each class, ethnic group, neighborhood, or social circle has its own values and expectations:[26]

Upper Class: Graceful living
Upper Middle Class: Career, education
Lower Middle Class: Respectability and stability of job
Working Class: Financial survival, available job
Lower Class: Physical survival

Upper-class families tend to maintain supervision and control over their offspring's mate selection.[14,34] The children often attend private school (a form of social isolation), and, when they leave home for college, the exclusivity patterns tend to persist. Most upper-class young adults marry in their mid- to late-twenties, after completion of college and the initial establishment of a career.

Middle- and working-class families also may provide supervision by encouraging group activities at church, school, or with the family. "Commercial" dating (e.g., skating, dancing, sports) is common. Formal engagement and wedding activities are important social events. Most middle-class young adults marry in their early- to mid-20s, often during or immediately following college or career training.

Lower-class families tend to provide less supervision of dating.[34] Engagements are generally informal, and marriage often occurs with pregnancy. Most of these individuals marry in their teens or early twenties before completing their education. The reader is reminded that such broad categorizations are used to observe trends and should not be used to stereotype specific individuals.

Choice to Remain Single

Some people make a conscious choice to remain single. They acknowledge a determined focus in their approach to life and find that their careers take precedence over any desire to marry. Others recognize a strong desire for independence and self-direction, which would be jeopardized by the unity of the marriage bond. Still others, recognizing their own unique personalities, goals, and values, decide that finding a suitable spouse to meet their unique needs is unlikely and consequently decide not to look. Some people enjoy the freedom of multiple relationships and find the focus on one relationship a stifling experience. Others would like to marry but are unwilling to take "just anyone." For these individuals, remaining single is preferable to marriage to the wrong person.

In a marriage-oriented society, it is difficult for the individual to admit to the self or to others that he or she does not want to marry, is afraid of marriage, cannot find a suitable partner, or would not make a suitable marriage partner. If the unmarried person interprets singlehood as undesirable, he or she may suffer episodes of low self-esteem.

Some people choose a temporary or permanent single lifestyle for positive reasons; others avoid marriage for negative reasons. Emotional intimacy frightens many people. These people may have fears of: losing personal boundaries or identity; being known too well (the possibility of being revealed as weak, inadequate, or undesirable); being attacked for personal values; being abandoned by one entrusted with intimate thoughts and feelings; or injuring another emotionally or being injured. Those people who have been victims of incest or exploitation may have developed such a deep fear or hatred of the opposite gender that the idea of a gentle, considerate, loving relationship is incompatible with any previous experience. Individuals who have previously experienced an intense, emotionally intimate relationship may feel so betrayed by the former partner that to place trust in a second person, or to become vulnerable a second time and chance the agony of another rejection, may be impossible for them. These people may be greatly helped by good counseling. Unresolved conflicts of this nature continue to affect all one's relationships, even the relationship with oneself.

The single person faces some unique social problems. Food packaging and housing options favor married people and families. Many singles want to enjoy a relationship with peers but may not enjoy the singles' bar, the holiday ski resort, or beach atmospheres. If the single person engages in an honest, intimate exchange with a married person of the opposite gender, he or she may be suspected of spouse snatching; if the exchange is with someone of the same gender, the individual may be suspected of homosexuality. Consequently, many single people are prevented from having intimate, growth-producing relationships and feel isolated from society. Parents frequently continue to relate to their unmarried son or daughter as if he or she were not yet fully adult. Single-parent adoptions can help to offset some of this isolation, but they cannot make up for the lack of peer intimacy. However, many singles find greater acceptance by both family and married peers after an adoption.

Traditional Steps That Lead to Marriage

The method of choosing a marital partner has changed radically in Western cultures during the past two generations. Today, marriage is preceded by a period of increasingly intense social pairing, which offers the opportunity to gradually narrow the potential options for choice of a permanent partner.

Dating

Most individuals date several people before marriage with no commitment beyond the actual agreement for the date itself. Many people date purely for the fun of it. In some cultures (many of which are minority groups within Western cultures), it is considered unusual and immoral to date without a marriage commitment or without at least an interest in exploring that option.[10]

The nature and character of a date is highly influenced by the age as well as the social and financial position of the participants. Most people begin dating in junior or senior high school and continue until they marry. Younger daters frequently are involved in group activities, such as roller skating, school dances, or a spontaneous get-together at the local McDonald's. Older daters tend to prefer more solitary activities that allow them to explore a common interest (e.g., a concert, boating activities) or that facilitate communication to enhance their knowledge of each other and themselves.

Functions of Dating

Dating serves several important functions:

1. Dating provides activity for leisure time. Dating offers opportunities for entertainment, recreation, even educa-

tion, as the couple pursues a common hobby or interest together.

2. Dating can offer status to the individuals involved. A date with the star football player or a cheerleader may offer as much status to the adolescent as a date with the community's leading attorney or TV newsperson may provide to an adult.

3. Dating offers the opportunity to learn interpersonal skills. Individuals get to know how others think and react to events. They learn that there are differences in emotional responses and expressions. They teach each other how to adjust their behavior to meet the other's needs and how to behave in a new situation. They learn negotiation, the give and take so essential in a working relationship.

4. Some people date to pursue a friendship. They thoroughly enjoy the companionship of a particular person, who they date with no thought of a permanent relationship. Both individuals can mature as they share their lives, values, and goals.

5. Still others may date to engage in sexual intimacy. It may be an immature but honest search for love and security, or it may be purely for exploitative reasons with no intention of follow-through and responsibility nor any idea of the long-range effects on the other person or the self.

6. Most importantly, dating helps the individual to learn about himself or herself. Confrontations with the values, concerns, interests, and questions of another help one to clarify one's own value system.

7. Dating lays a groundwork for courtship by helping one to identify what type of person is most compatible with one's personality, goals, and values. Dating sharpens one's ability to see people as individuals. All men and all women are *not* alike. The ability to make fine discriminations between them enables one to make a marital choice that is based on identification of the most compatible factors.

8. Dating also constitutes a form of courtship, especially as one matures. Each date holds the potential for meeting one's future partner. Dating permits the individual to select his or her partner on the basis of personal preference and paves the way for the eventual decision to marry a specific person or to remain single.

Process of Dating

Initiating a date increases vulnerability; thus, it is difficult for a shy or insecure person. Even a legitimate rejection may be interpreted as personal devaluation. The first date with an idealized "special" person may be fraught with so much anxiety that communication is inhibited. Dates structured around group activities tend to reduce the strain on a couple by spreading the responsibility for conversation and activity and reducing the focus on the individuals involved.

On their first few dates with each other, individuals tend to use formal or stereotyped behaviors. Gradually, as each begins to know the other better, they move toward more relaxed, individualized, and personalized behavior. The relationship becomes more meaningful as they dare to be honest with each other about feelings and values. The more affirming and committed they become to the relationship, the more they dare to be themselves.

Each relationship is a learning experience for future relationships as one gets to know one's self and how to negotiate conflicts of interest. This is a time to become aware of potential abuse problems. Abusive patterns experienced in one's family of origin tend to be repeated in new relationships. Verbal and emotional abuse tend to escalate over time. Unless therapy is received (and it is not always successful), exposure to abuse as a child sets one up to be either a recipient or giver of abuse as an adult.[30]

The benefits of dating include learning how to deal with frustrations and difficult partners, learning how to communicate thoughts effectively, learning how to empathize with another's feelings, learning how to resolve a problem and come to a common decision, and learning how to commit one's self to another. In addition, dating provides an avenue for emotional weaning from parents.

Courtship

Courtship begins when at least one member of the dyad has marriage in mind, even though this intention may not yet be verbalized. Often there is no sharp line between dating and courtship.

The Filtering Process

The choice of a mate naturally begins with who is available. The individual's contact group tends to bring together people of similar class, interests, educations, and goals. From this pool of eligibles, one tends to select or to eliminate potential partners on the basis of physical appearance, height, age, race, energy level, or social habits. Because people are socialized to value certain traits, they tend to marry someone who exhibits similar characteristics and values (homogamy). When a couple shares a similar background, they have "organized their stock of experience in a similar fashion,"[40] a factor that facilitates communication and reduces conflict of values. Physical attractiveness and personality are primary components in the initial choice. As the relationship becomes more complex, lifestyle, aesthetic interests, hobbies, communication sensitivity, and leisure-time activities tend to maintain or decrease interest in the relationship. As companionship is intensified, values, religious beliefs, goals, family relationships, and ethics are explored for compatibility (Fig. 29-2).

Essence of Love

Eventually a couple decides that they are "in love." Love is the most acceptable reason for marriage in Western culture. Religious institutions teach that love nurtures marital happiness and family solidarity and therefore emphasize that love must prevail in family relationships.[9] Immature people may view the experience from the standpoint of "being loved," rather than "sharing love," or "giving love." They may assume that it is easy to love but difficult to find the right person to love.

FIGURE 29–2.
True love, mutual respect, and open, intimate communication foster a genuine companionship, a foundation for marital satisfaction, and a springboard for personal growth through the years.

Consequently, these individuals may fail to learn "how" to love.[16] Once they fall in love, they may assume it is permanent and fail to extend the effort required to stay in love.

Although it is recognized that love makes a positive contribution to our lives, love is an elusive concept because of its highly personal quality. Infatuation, puppy love, sexual attention, and crushes can elicit many of the same physical responses that are interpreted by the individual as true love. **True love** is variously defined as a deep and tender feeling of affection or devotion, an intense emotional attachment, or a *commitment to the welfare of another*. A **crush** is a *one-sided love* that is usually based on the *idealized image of another*. **Puppy love** may be quite *genuine but immature* as yet because of the developmental level and experiential background of the two people involved. **Infatuation** is a *self-centered* form of love that grows out of a *need to belong to someone*. "The other person is a hook on which these self-generated emotions are hung."[5] Identification with the idealized qualities of the other enhances one's own self-esteem.

Infatuation Versus Love

The idea of love at first sight is a myth. Mature love emerges gradually as the uniqueness of the individual is recognized. Infatuation tends to ignore reality and to idealize the loved one while focusing on physical characteristics or special skills. There is minimal or no emotional intimacy, which is so essential to develop reciprocity or to validate assumptions. The individual often has a blind sense of security or jealousy or refuses to look at the relationship or the other person more deeply for fear of losing the idealized image. The person is actually "in love with love" and is more concerned about self-enhancement and pleasure than about the welfare of the other or the long-range implications of the relationship.

Infatuation plays an important role in the courtship process in that people generally "fall in love with love" several times before they marry. Love may begin with infatuation, but real love arises from an appraisal of the total person. The deeper one knows the other, the more intense and committed the love and the relationship become. Real love also idealizes the loved one, but this image can be checked against reality without a sense of loss because mature love can allow the partner to be wholly himself or herself (complete with flaws) without feeling a need to make the person fit into one's own image or value system. Eric Fromm observes that the paradox of mature love is that two people become one while remaining separate (Fig. 29-3).[16]

Physical attraction is important, especially in the beginning, but it plays a relatively minor role in an evolving relationship, in which personality attraction assumes the significant role. Feelings of trust and a sense of security are fostered in a mutually affirming relationship, in which each looks for ways to enhance the functioning of the other and to strengthen the relationship.

Definitions of Love

Eric Fromm postulates that true love is an art that must be learned.[16] We *learn* to love a specific person as we get to know his or her strengths and weaknesses.[21] We accept and love the *total* person. Just as individuals must perform "grief work" (see Chap. 19) when they experience the loss of someone to whom they are attached, persons who are creating a new attachment have to engage in "love work." "Love is a constructed experience built with feelings, ideas, and cultural symbols."[36] We allow ourselves to "fall in love" with people who meet our cultural, social, and personal criteria for a potential partner, but it takes effort to establish mutuality and maintain that love as we get to know that person as a unique, respected individual.

Mature love expands the sensitivity and expression of all five domains. The physical domain is energized for activity. Love adds "wings to our feet" and craves satisfaction. The affective domain achieves heights never before experienced by enlarging one's emotional capacity. A partner allows one to give of the self, providing opportunity for the centering of altruistic, allocentric behaviors. This love overflows in relationships with other people. Fromm states, "Giving is the highest expression of potency. In the very act of giving, I experience my strength, my wealth, my power. This experience of heightened vitality and potency fills me with joy. I experience myself as overflowing, spending, alive, hence as joyous. Giving is more joyous than receiving, not because it is a deprivation, but because in the act of giving, lies the expression of my aliveness."[16] The social domain finds expansion through a friendship and companionship that relaxes the mood and thus the body through a sense of security; one's horizons are also expanded through new acquaintances and experiences.

The cognitive domain is involved through confirmation of the other's right to express feelings, goals, and values wholly and the reciprocal affirmation by the other of one's own self, feelings, goals, and values. This role of love indicates that it must be a bidirectional relationship or else it will disintegrate. Each person must maintain control over his or her own life, actions, values, direction, and energy. With this foundation, problems can be identified, and issues negotiated as necessary. Mature love includes responsibility, commitment, unselfish acceptance of the other person's strengths and weaknesses, and mutual respect. The spiritual domain is also sensitized by an increased awareness of aesthetic experiences and the miracle of finding "someone who loves me" and someone who is "worth the investment" of time, energy,

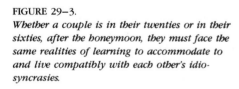

FIGURE 29–3.
Whether a couple is in their twenties or in their sixties, after the honeymoon, they must face the same realities of learning to accommodate to and live compatibly with each other's idiosyncrasies.

and intimacies. Erikson sees love as the spontaneous virtue springing from the resolution of the task of intimacy; it cannot be forced or willed into existence.[13] It transcends the mundane aspects of life and is thus the essence of the spiritual domain.

Model of Love

Robert Sternberg proposes a three-sided model of love, which represents the cognitive, affective, and motivational components of love, consisting of commitment, intimacy, and passion.[41, 44] The size and shape of the three sides of the triangle change as the components increase or decrease. Each love relationship of our life taps and emphasizes the three components to different degrees. Most of our relationships do not involve love, so none of these components is present. Consummate, or complete, love exists and continues to grow when all three factors are present. If one or more sides is missing, the relationship assumes a different character. Thus, a deep friendship may include commitment and intimacy, but not passion. Passion by itself would result in infatuation; combined with intimacy would be romantic love. Many marriages that begin as consummate love may lose the passion components over the years to become companion love. If intimacy is also lost, the love is empty and the couple remain together because of habit or roles. In healthy relationships, commitment and intimacy tend to increase gradually over the years, whereas passion tends to decrease (not disappear!). It is important to continue to express love in one's behavior or even the greatest of loves can die.[44]

Types of Love

As we travel through life, we experience several types of love that are affected by the power or caregiving relationship as well as mutuality. Feelings of love may transfer or generalize from one person to another, but the uniqueness of each relationship modifies the character and the expression of those feelings.

Filial Love. The love for one's parents is based on dependency, trust, gratitude, vulnerability, and appreciation for the care and sacrifices they have made for us. Adult love relationships appear to follow the same attachment patterns and prevalence that Bowlby and Ainsworth define for infancy.[20] Memories of one's relationship with parents (responsive and caring, cold and rejecting, positive or negative) tend to correlate with the three adult attachment patterns and support claims that one's experience of love with parents provides the foundation and framework for love as an adult.[20] About 55% of adults have a *secure* attachment based on trust, responsiveness, and caring. Twenty-five percent experience an *avoidant* attachment pattern, which lacks trust, closeness, and belief in permanence. About 20% of adult romantic relationships are characterized as *anxious/ambivalent*. These people experience a "preoccupying, almost painfully exciting struggle to merge with another person."[20] They fall in love frequently and easily but find it difficult to find true love. They are vulnerable to loneliness.

Sibling Love. The love for one's brothers and sisters is based on companionship, shared experiences, rivalry, and competition. The quality varies with the culture, gender, ordinal position, and the family; however, there is a tendency to feel a genuine kinship and desire to support one another as necessary throughout life regardless of previous altercations.

Parental Love. This is the love felt for a dependent person, particularly one's own children. Feelings range from a sense of power or control (the other is unconsciously viewed as an extension of self) to servanthood (one exists to be an extension of the other).

Spousal Love. This love, the chosen relationship with a peer, takes many forms that may be a transient or a permanent approach to the relationship:

Erotic love (Sternberg's passion) focuses on the physical component and is generally short-lived, or it dies quickly once the physical attraction has disappeared.

Romantic love is a commitment to an idealized image of the spouse or love relationship. It spawns selfless devotion and continued courtship behaviors.

Manic love is a combination of erotic and romantic love. It is often characterized by obsessive feelings of jealousy. This person's personal immaturity is obvious. The lover is needed to complete his or her sense of identity and security. The individual often feels that life without the partner would be meaningless and goes to extremes to maintain the relationship.

Pragmatic love is practical and realistic. The goal is mutual contentment with a focusing of energies toward compatibility and mutual problem solving. Many arranged marriages and long-term marriages evolve to this relationship when passion is absent.

Ludic (playful) **love** avoids a deep emotional commitment. Fun, not rapport, is the goal. It is soon outgrown as interests change.

Philos love focuses on commitment, closeness, shared experiences, and friendship. A deep, enduring companionship is expressed as mutual caring, affection, and support—precious commodities of a solid relationship.

Stogic love lacks the intimacy of philos love. Although a solid relationship exists, it is basically unexciting and uneventful.

Altruistic love parallels parental love in that the need to provide nurturing to the other takes precedence over one's own welfare. Feelings of humility may be evolved by the honor of caring for the other.

Agape love is an intellectual or spiritual love. It seeks not to possess, but to give. It is a self-spending love that places relationships in the context of eternal issues. It is more frequently found in a commitment to principles of a Being higher than self than in the spousal relationship.

Identifying Potential Partners

Many people are frustrated by the inability to find suitable potential partners. Previous life experiences may have left the person "gun shy," or current social contacts may be too limited. One should seek opportunities to meet people with similar interests and values while continuing to be friendly, outgoing, warm, and enthusiastic. Too often in the search for a potential partner, a person concentrates on "what I want." This self-centeredness shows in the individual's relationships. One needs to continue to develop the self, working on interests, education, career, and identity. One must treat others with respect and concentrate on "what I have to offer." This allocentric approach is both more appealing and more mature. If one never marries, the identity homework will provide a foundation for a richer, fuller life.

Premarital Sex

Sexual attraction is a normal part of any relationship. At some point, each couple must face the question of how fast and how far their physical intimacies should progress. They must decide on the meaning of sexual intimacy and how and when this is most appropriately achieved for them. This approach implies choice. "Unless freedom of choice is based on an understanding of the alternatives from which the choice is to be made, it cannot be truly free."[5] If our freedom of choice injures or deprives another of freedom of choice, then ultimately freedom of choice ceases to exist. Both parties must carefully think through the available facts and personal values and accept full responsibility for their own behavior.[5] This responsibility is predicated on a mature understanding of one's value system, motivations, and potential emotional, social, and physical consequences.

About 95% of men and 80% of women participate in intercourse before marriage.[29] However, sexual intercourse may have a different meaning for each person. Males tend to focus on eroticism, whereas females may be more concerned with romanticism. Men play with love to get sex, women play with sex to get love. Consequently, the motivation may differ greatly, creating fertile ground for misunderstandings of intention and hurt feelings. When the female interprets a bid for sex in light of her own romantic notions of love, she may impart a more serious note to the relationship than is felt by the male.

For some individuals, intercourse may be seen as a way to prove masculinity or femininity. Thus, it is a means to an end. Being a "real man" or a "real woman" involves more than the ability to copulate. The anticipation of sexual demands by one individual may put the other on guard and thus serve as a barrier to the development of a viable relationship.

The age of the participants is another factor that affects the character of a physically intimate relationship. The 15-year-old who seeks security, status, or identity places quite a different meaning on sexual intimacy than the 35-year-old divorcée who seeks companionship, recreation, or personal expression.

The individual's decision to participate in sexual inter-course appears to be consistent with a total outlook on life. "In conservative circles, those who think highly of themselves tend to refrain from intimacies that violate their convictions; conservative women who engage in sexual relations tend to be those whose self-esteem is so low that they are desperate for anything remotely resembling affection and acceptance from men."[2] In liberal circles, those with low self-esteem are the least likely to have sex.[2]

Religious affiliation does not appear to make a significant difference in premarital sexual behavior; however, the individual's degree of devotedness to a concept of God and participation in religious activities is highly correlated. The more "religious" a person is, the more internalized are the values of his or her religion, the more likely the individual is to avoid coitus before marriage.[38]

It is difficult to make an unbiased decision about premarital sex. Parental culture and religious affiliation give one standard; peer culture and mass media offer one at the opposing end of the continuum. Sex is a marketable commodity. "The mass media often function like a lens, dissecting out and magnifying small groups and making them appear to be entire populations."[5] "Sexploitation," especially of women, can affect women's views of themselves as well as men's views of women. Adolescents frequently are led to believe that "everybody is doing it," and that sex is an essential part of adult life. What one believes about sexual needs affects behavior. If one believes it is a form of self-preservation and that dire consequences will result from the denial of basic urges, then one may feel it is acceptable to pressure another person into intercourse. The underlying questions are: "What controls whom?" and "Who controls what?" Does the individual control sex or vice versa? Young people who have learned how to deal effectively with frustrations, to separate feelings and behaviors, to discipline one's self, and to live with the consequences of their decisions and behavior find it easier to resist the temptations of illicit sex.

Sexual behavior tends to occur in a step-wise fashion. One begins with hand-holding and moves to kissing, various forms of light and heavy petting, and finally to intercourse. Once a barrier is broken, it is easier to engage in the same activity again. Fears and inhibitions are overruled, and sensual pleasure presides. The longer a person is at one level, the less interesting the activity becomes, and normal physical responses impel the person to engage in a more erotic activity. This is a major reason why parents are encouraged to delay dating behavior for their children until the middle or later teen years.

At some point, the couple must make a decision on the limits of their behavior. Decisions work best when they are made *before* one is in a situation in which the decision must be enforced. Couples need to engage in a full and free discussion of their feelings, values, and the implications of each step. It is better to move too slowly than too fast because one of the partners (especially the woman) may become angry, disgusted, depressed, or disillusioned if pushed too fast.[2] Ambiguous standards tend to invite infractions by an eager partner, a reason why one must think through his or her personal values and standards and not leave the decision to the whims of another. Thus, a healthy relationship is predicated on mastery of "identity homework" before mutual exchange of viewpoints can occur. The negotiation and teamwork involved in making and implementing a decision may be more significant than the nature of the decision per se.

The only way to preserve self-respect and personal integrity is to stick to one's beliefs. If the experience evokes feelings of guilt, it will retard rather than enhance the relationship.[26] "A person who feels something must be done because others are doing it has sacrificed freedom of choice just as much as the individual who refrains from doing something because others have prohibited it."[5] "A person who seeks mature, integrated behavior patterns seeks to be consistent in his value judgments, his personal and social relationships, and his sexual behavior."[26] Therefore, one's relationships, decisions, and behaviors must be consistent with a core value system. The individual cannot override basic values and be at ease with the self. "To remove sexual behavior from the ethical context is to oversimplify and dehumanize the individual."[26]

Some people feel that they prefer to prove their love and respect for the partner by refraining from sex. This behavior avoids any hint of exploitation and enhances the affective and cognitive aspects of intimacy. In one major study, only 4.5% of the males reported that sex strengthened interpersonal relationships with their partner.[28] Longitudinal studies indicate that premarital abstinence is associated with a lower divorce rate.[25]

Engagement

With the announcement of a couple's plan to marry, they enter a new world. The couple has confirmed for themselves and for others their commitment and intention. Their courtship has become public (Fig. 29-4). Their relationship as-

FIGURE 29–4.
She said, "Yes!"

sumes greater seriousness and responsibility. They begin to be viewed and to be responded to by others as a single unit. This new label influences their concept of self and their relationship. While engagement offers greater security to the couple, it also affords numerous opportunities for increased tension and conflict as they begin to work together in earnest toward common goals.

The engagement period is ostensibly to prepare for the wedding: arranging for the official to perform the ceremony, developing a guest list, obtaining a marriage license, submitting to a blood test, and so on. However, the engagement is in reality the beginning of the couple's formal unity, while at the same time it offers them the opportunity to assess their compatibility and to take appropriate action if necessary before the final step is taken.

Functions of the Engagement Period

The engagement period fulfills four major requirements.

Strengthening of the Relationship. The increased commitment encourages heightened openness and intimacy. How well do they really know each other? The sharing of feelings, opinions, and values provides the opportunity for increased closeness, but it also risks the possibility of rejection by the other. For this reason, it is critical that each person know himself or herself well before making a marriage commitment (see Chaps. 25 and 28).

When one's identity is secure, then he or she brings a healthy, positive outlook to the relationship. One's values and goals are not tied to the whims, needs, or strengths of the other. The individual is able to be fully herself or himself, offering enough flexibility to be compatible and cooperative, yet with an individuality that brings stimulation and stability to the relationship. A secure identity means that one has the ability to be honest with oneself about one's own deep feelings and therefore can be honest with others. Only through honesty in self-identity is one able to evaluate self and to hear the other person's view fully. Then love can spring from "being-love" (giving) rather than "deficiency-love" (taking) to create a healthy, growth-producing relationship.[31] Deficiency-love is a selfish love characteristic of people with poor self-concept. These individuals must "borrow" from the other person to feel complete. Being-love gives from its abundance, the overflow of its joy with life and living. Being-love shares a peer relationship; each partner can give reciprocally for the benefit of the other. Thus, both are enhanced.

Pseudomutuality may develop when one person is unable to tolerate the unique interests, values, and goals of the other. When differences are recognized and appreciated, they can enrich the relationship. When one person feels threatened by the differences, then the couple may extend their energies toward meeting role expectations rather than exploring, developing, and integrating their unique identities.[42] The relationship becomes static because change is seen as a threat. Although the couple may feel unhappy, frustrated, or unfulfilled, they may refuse or may be unable to seek a real solution to their problems (which increase with marriage). If

a husband and wife relate to one another only on the basis of roles, the marriage tends to erode.

During the engagement, the couple begins to develop their own traditions—the special song, place, activity, poem, phrases, pet words, and so on. These become a bond of uniqueness that helps to bind them together. They usually begin to think about finances more seriously.

Sometimes an individual feels the need to reveal his or her past in its entirety. If the partner is likely to learn of significant information through a third party, then it is best to share it honestly from the beginning.[5] However, indiscriminate sharing to obtain emotional release is both unwise and immature. Information should be shared because it can help the couple to develop a deeper understanding and appreciation of each other that will ultimately enhance their relationship as they work through issues together. During courtship, the couple should evaluate the emotional maturity and health of one another. The couple may need to seek counseling if they are concerned over these issues. A lack of emotional maturity or stability is highly associated with marital discord.[25, 26]

Marriage to an overly sensitive or neurotic person can be difficult. This trait will not change after marriage; therefore, discord during courtship can serve as a warning.

Redefinition of One's Social World. Psychologically and socially, the engaged couple become a unit. The individual's orientation changes from the family of origin or a first marriage to the new relationship. If the emotional commitment and focus of energies do not change, the new relationship is at risk. Marriage is not just a union between two isolated people. It is a union between two families.[42] One must meet and become integrated (as much as possible) with the in-laws. The better the relationship with the future in-laws, the more support and encouragement the couple will receive in the years ahead (Fig. 29-5). Parents can ease the normal anxiety and stress of the engagement period, as well as offer a hand (or a shoulder) when problems arise later. Parents generally begin to treat their child in a more adult manner and the espoused as a member of the family.

During this period, one also has a chance to see how the intended mate relates to his or her own parents and siblings. How a man treats his mother is a good indicator of how he may treat his wife. A person's relationship to animals, young children, and disabled people also gives clues to the potential partner's sensitivity, allocentrism, and generativity leanings. The parents' relationship can give clues to one's own marital relationship, since the modeled patterns tend to be replicated. The individual's relationship with the in-laws also gives a foretaste of the years to come. When in-laws disapprove of a potential mate, it is a sign of trouble ahead. Secret marriages to avoid parental criticism tend to aggravate rather than alleviate the problem. The parents are hurt by the lack of trust and confidence expressed by the couple, and the individual then has two hurdles to overcome to reestablish a working relationship with the in-laws.

During this time, the couple also becomes more inti-

FIGURE 29–5.
Maintaining contact with in-laws can provide support and encouragement during times of stress and excitement.

mately acquainted with the other's friends and social world. Adjustments begin to occur as each drops some old acquaintances and makes new friends with more compatible interests. Social habits begin to change as they assume a more serious stance. Each begins to see the other in more diverse situations and to project what marriage to the other person will be like.

Preparation for Married Life. The couple begins to consider the types of responsibilities associated with their decision and to learn the skills deemed essential to their new roles (e.g., cooking, home repairs, gardening, housekeeping, shopping). Some of the ideas a couple should explore include money management, career goals, religious involvement, household work division, number and spacing of children, feelings about infertility and adoption, values and moral standards, role expectations, discipline of children, leisure-time activities, educational plans, and where to live.

Differing values and maturity levels strain a relationship over the years. Obviously, most couples are not going to agree on every issue, but these discussions are part of the preparation for marriage: to learn how to negotiate an issue so that neither one feels subjected to the other's view. Issues of power and control emerge as the couple shares information and

learns to work together at short-range goals and chores. For understanding and compatibility, individuals need sufficient time with each other to explore these issues. If one partner in the relationship is in military service or away at college, then communication may be carried out by letter and telephone. However, couples should be aware that it is relatively easy for a completely incompatible couple to have a smooth relationship when they are far apart most of the time.[15]

One of the biggest dangers to a relationship is the overly agreeable couple. Often this condition occurs because one is always holding back until he or she knows what the other expects or wants. One person may be overly concerned about presenting a positive image of the self to the loved one. As a result, one (the weaker personality), in essence, becomes an extension of the other (the stronger personality). They become two strangers in love because of the lack of honesty, naturalness, and genuine mutuality. It is a superficial intimacy that is more concerned with the self being conveyed than the self one truly is! A wise friend once remarked, "If two people always agree, one of them is unnecessary." Each relationship needs the stimulating, balancing input of both people. Interaction patterns become apparent only with time and exposure. The best marital success is enjoyed by those who have known each other at least 2 years and who have been engaged 6 to 12 months.[15,35]

In-depth Assessment of Compatibility. The "halo effect" may mask behaviors that will be interpreted differently after a few months or a few years of marriage. "Problems that present themselves during the planning stages will appear unmasked and more severe after the couple has been formally united."[15]

A similarity of affiliation needs and emotional stability facilitates marital compatibility. The couple also must assess their authority and submission needs. Conflicts may arise over who is "boss." Male or female leadership of the relationship is irrelevant, but comfort with the decision-making process is critical. The degree of participation in decision making during dating can give a person a feel for the partner's creativity and flexibility. One can be dominant without being domineering. Many circumstances require mutual decision making, such as washing the car and deciding which set of parents to visit for the holiday, where to spend the honeymoon, or who should change residence or jobs after the marriage.

Intelligence and educational level are critical factors in a long-term relationship because they affect the uniqueness of input, problem-solving skills, and the ability to work together as partners.[2,46] A quick wit can sharpen the other's wit and increase life's enjoyment when it is equally matched, but it can be a sword that severs the relationship in a mismatched pair. The less educated or less intelligent partner may feel threatened or incompetent; the more gifted may feel the need to inhibit the expression of ideas that are misinterpreted or not comprehended. The gifted can stagnate without adequate challenge. This stagnation is especially true for the woman, who is more likely to remain at home during the child-rearing years with a subsequent decrease in adult peer contact. Playing table games is one way to assess intellectual and emotional compatibility. The **Ungame*** and **Reunion*** offer excellent mediums for getting to know another person. Another resource for exploring compatibility and life is "Engaged Encounter." For information, contact Dave and Sue Edwards, 1509 South Forest Street, Denver, CO 80222.

Sexual expression and compatibility are other areas of concern to many couples. Many who abstained during earlier courtship may now participate in physical intimacies as an outgrowth of their new devotion and commitment. Since most couples are able to make a sexual adjustment, one's spouse should be chosen for other reasons.[26, 46] "If sexual compatibility were a question of physique, this evidence would be crucial. However, this is not the case. Human beings of almost any shape and size can relate sexually. For this reason, it is not necessary to 'try each other out for size.' "[2] Since about 50% of engagements are eventually broken, some individuals may find that "physical intimacy before marriage can make an advisable separation difficult and painful to carry out, and leave the participants guilt-ridden."[35] Other individuals, of course, may feel otherwise, depending on their value systems.

Another area frequently overlooked by a couple is the energy level or life tempo of the other. One's energy level can either intensify or dull the most routine activity. An individual's zest for life and living can exhilarate, exhaust, or bore the partner as the years roll by. One needs a high degree of flexibility to keep up with a partner who has a high verve for life.

Many couples live together without marriage (cohabitation) as a way to assess their compatibility. This arrangement is usually an extension of the courtship process rather than an alternative to marriage. Marriage changes the relationship so much that even living together cannot reveal some of the later relationship problems.[46]

Prerequisites of a Successful Marriage

Most people experience homogamous marriages (marriage within their same social group). Homogamy facilitates the compatible blending of interests, values, traditions, and experiences. Common social, religious, and leisure-time contacts tend to lend support to the stability of the relationship. Despite cultural pressures, many individuals choose a mate with a radically different background, an act that provides stimulation and novelty for years (Fig. 29-5). These people have defined their own set of values and can create a rich, meaningful relationship.

Mixed marriages include not only interracial marriages, but intergeneration, interfaith, international, and interclass marriages. In truth, however, **every marriage is a mixed marriage,** for it brings together two people of different family origins, traditions, experiences, kin, relationships, and value systems. For any marriage to be successful, certain prerequisites are essential.[2, 15, 32]

FIGURE 29–6.
Intercultural marriages can provide a wide variety of family traditions for individuals to draw on while developing their own. Childhood stories can entertain the couple and their children for years to come.

Emotional Maturity. One needs self-objective knowledge of one's own skills, weaknesses, values, goals, and feelings. Maturity includes the characteristics of self-discipline, self-objectivity, and self-responsibility. Persons with emotional instability, high physiological arousal during conflict, poor impulse control, and neurotic tendencies before marriage have low marital adjustment scores and high divorce rates.[25] Identity homework is a given for gaining adequate emotional maturity to enter and maintain a successful marriage.

Love. Genuine, altruistic, being-love based on realistic appraisal of the total person is necessary. "An emotionally healthy person would rather risk the death of love than allow love to develop on an unreal foundation."[2] Erotic love may be a part of the relationship, but success comes from philos, altruistic, and agape love.

Compatibility. Similarity of interests, values, goals, energy, intellectual skills, and lifestyles is discovered only through affective intimacy.

Skill. Communication, negotiation, and problem-solving

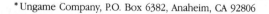

*Ungame Company, P.O. Box 6382, Anaheim, CA 92806

abilities, empathy, and compassion are learned through the context of one's family of origin and refined during the dating and courtship period.

Effort. Willingness to sacrifice and focus all energies toward resolution of problems is essential.

Commitment. The determination to make it work, to "hang in there" during the tough times (all marriages have them) is essential. "The degree of their commitment to the marriage will be the measure of its stability while they are learning to cope with the problems plaguing them."[15]

Support. The affirmation offered by family, friends, and community is important. Most couples have a hard time "making it on their own."

Flexibility. The ability to adapt to changes in the other person or circumstances and to meet life's problems is necessary. The couple may work together to create change through dialogue, reading, or counseling. Each should accept the differences of the other as stimulating, exciting, and helping to expand one's world.

Caring. The ability to be concerned about the welfare of the other, to want to care for and to make life better for the other person is crucial. Marriage is not a 50:50 proposition, but an 80:80 relationship, each giving more than he or she expects to receive in return.

ESTABLISHING A SUCCESSFUL ADULT–ADULT RELATIONSHIP

The wedding signifies the legal beginning of "oneness." A public ceremony allows family and friends to celebrate the event with the couple. In the United States, the average male is 24.8 years of age and the female 23 years of age at the time of their first marriage.[39] Eighty-four percent of couples opt for a religious ceremony.[37]

Honeymoon

The wedding is frequently followed by a vacation trip, which allows the couple time to concentrate on and invest in each other. The honeymoon needs to provide leisure, privacy, and novelty. Even if it is short, it will be a special memory later. The honeymoon serves two basic functions: it facilitates the establishment of marital sexual expression and encourages the couple to make the transition from dual independence to mutual interdependence.

Marital Sexuality

Both partners must develop sensitivity and competence as an intimate sexual partner if the couple is going to enjoy a satisfying sexual relationship. Neither partner should expect instantaneous success, even if they have had prior sexual experience. It may take 2 weeks to more than 9 years before a particular couple achieves a mutually satisfying sexual adjustment.[19] Prior knowledge about anatomy and techniques facilitates adjustment. The new husband may find that the stress of the moment overrides his eagerness, preventing the attainment of a full or prolonged erection. The new wife may find

that old taboos interfere with her ability to relax and appreciate the new freedom of marriage. The honeymoon is a time to become comfortable sharing each other's bodies. Light and heavy petting need to continue as preludes to copulation. When bypassed, sexual dysfunctions may occur.[2]

The ability to communicate openly about likes and dislikes and the willingness to be creative also can enhance sexual enjoyment. The couple should remember that sexual freedom does not license exploitation or abuse. Continued mutual respect; flirting, dressing, and grooming to please the other; and spontaneous smiles, compliments, hugs, kisses, and caresses throughout the day all make the time in bed more desirable to both.

Young couples tend to have intercourse frequently. They may try several times daily during the honeymoon and gradually taper off to three to four times per week. Frequency varies with the couple and their age, but the average appears to be twice a week after several years of marriage.[45] Fifty percent of women experience orgasm within the first month of marriage, and 75% within the first year. Orgasm may not be associated with the sexual act but may occur spontaneously the next day.[27] Only 53% of women report orgasm almost every time they have intercourse.[23] Satisfaction, however, is more than orgasm: "The couple will not be able to find sexual satisfaction if they do not find happiness in other ways; but their companionship will find richer meaning and interpretation through their sexual union."[26]

Mutual Interdependence

Marriage is fraught with big and little decisions. The couple must merge their independent habits into a mutually compatible routine. Who fixes breakfast? Who uses the bathroom first, and what shelf holds whose paraphernalia? What time do we go to bed or get up? How often and when do we have sex, go to church, eat?

During the honeymoon, the couple begins to realign priorities so that the needs of both may be met, and they begin to turn first to each other rather than to parents or peers for support, stability, and encouragement. During this time, the friendship experienced before marriage can become even stronger. In a healthy marriage, the two become the best of friends, mutually dependent on each other for advice and confidence. Gradually, a new oneness emerges, and the marriage relationship becomes more important than the individuals within it.[5] This oneness does not mean an annihilation of the individuality of either, but rather a respect for the needs of both for the good of the whole. They establish a duet in which each blends in a balanced way with the skills and needs of the other. As they practice and get to know each other better, the harmony becomes even more evident to both themselves and others.

Establishing the New Family Unit

Once the bride and groom return from the honeymoon, they must get down to the serious business of establishing a home. The establishment of a home includes mundane tasks, such as cleaning out an apartment and setting up housekeeping; it also means the more complicated tasks of establishing their new roles as husband and wife. Some of these tasks or adjustments include the following:[26]

1. Establishing routines for daily living
2. Learning how to make purposeful decisions together
3. Building new friendships as a couple
4. Developing relationships with in-laws
5. Establishing a working family budget
6. Developing a "double-person" spending and shopping mentality
7. Establishing religious habits
8. Deciding on children and contraceptive methods
9. Learning how to negotiate conflicts
10. Learning the give and take of living together
11. Allocating responsibilities
12. Developing effective communication patterns
13. Establishing a shared core-value system
14. Identifying family "rules"
15. Creating common goals
16. Deciding on leisure-time activities and community involvement
17. Establishing financial credit
18. Developing a satisfying sex life
19. Establishing a balance between togetherness and respect for individuality
20. Establishing traditions as a family

The key to satisfactory and successful negotiation of these and other tasks is the couple's ability to communicate openly and honestly with each other.

Communication Between Partners

Several characteristics are found in all successful adult–adult relationships: mutual respect, allocentrism, common interests, self-disclosure, and spontaneity. Self-disclosure is most critical to effective communication. Most of our relationships involve fulfilling a role (e.g., student, employee, neighbor, consumer, attender, teacher). If we continue to relate to all people in a role capacity, then we relegate ourselves to the position of actor rather than person. As we hide our true feelings and responses from others, we also hide them from ourselves and as a result may lose the ability (or never gain the ability) to know our true feelings, values, and goals (see Chap. 28).[24]

It is in the process of revealing ourselves to others that we discover who we really are.[42] "Alienation from one's real self not only arrests personal growth, it tends to make a farce out of one's relationship with people."[24] When we fail to share ourselves, we become difficult to know or to predict and therefore difficult to love. Self-disclosure by one partner encourages reciprocal disclosure by the other. Thus, we "touch

base" and enhance our appreciation for the uniqueness of ourself and the other. Self-boundaries become clearer and mutual respect is enhanced. When each partner remains emotionally isolated, untouched by the other, the couple retains a role relationship. They may be married, but they can experience an overwhelming sense of loneliness because contact is not genuine. "The loneliest loneliness is to be alone with someone with whom one wants to feel close."[42]

Marriage survival depends partly on the development of clear and healthy identities.[19] Each partner must have achieved Erikson's earlier developmental tasks successfully and have his or her self-identity firmly in hand (see Chap. 25).[12] One must know who one is before fully appreciating the self or sharing that self with another. One must be honest with the self about deep feelings before one can be open and honest with others.[33] The individual must know who "I" is before he or she can say with genuine honesty, "I love you."[42] Getting to know one's self and personal values, goals, preferences, strengths, and weaknesses is a task many people avoid or only partially fulfill. Yet, self-knowledge is the bare foundation of all other relationships. If the individual knows and accepts the self, then he or she can accept the other, and both lives are enriched through the relationship.

If a person has not completed "identity homework," the concept of self may be cloudy or weak. Erikson identifies this person as one who tends to retreat or withdraw from honest communication with others.[12] The low self-esteem that began in childhood continues to color the adult life. "To be married to a person with a poor self-image is horrendous. Marriage does not produce this low self-esteem, but it can reinforce it."[19] If one partner is constantly subjected to abuse, put downs, and lack of respect by the other, then self-esteem can be eroded after marriage. If one partner has severe neurotic problems and is constantly rationalizing personal difficulties or projecting them onto others, then this problem also severely strains the relationship.[26]

In both of these situations, the immature or disturbed partner may avoid discussing any problems as a way to avoid emotional discomfort. Facts may become heavily tinged with personal values and feelings. Consequently, mutually satisfying resolution of conflict may become impossible. If both persons are immature or neurotic, then their common inadequacies tend to compound their problems.[25, 26]

The partner's self-esteem can be enhanced through continual affirmation of his or her value and presence, reassurance, recognition of strengths and talents, minimization of weaknesses, and by signs of appreciation and encouragement. If one person is building up the other partner, the partner doing the building should not be self-deprecating in the process. Each can continue personal growth through reading, acceptance of responsibility, reaching out to other people, continued openness, and involvement in activities that bring pleasure or satisfaction in achievement. Outside friends can reduce the burden of friendship on a marriage, but one must be careful not to allow friends to dilute the strength of the marital bond.[19]

Balancing Unity and Separateness

Families struggle with two opposing psychological forces: **togetherness,** the need for love, approval, agreement, and sharing; and **individuality,** the need for autonomy, separateness, and recognition of uniqueness.[4] These two forces actually compose a single continuum, representing the ability of the family to see and to appreciate the boundaries between the subsystems of the family.[17] Families with low cohesion and inappropriately rigid boundaries make up the "disengaged" end of the continuum. At the opposite "enmeshed" end, high cohesion and diffuse boundaries are found. In the middle "normal" range, boundaries are clear, differences are respected, yet appreciation is strong. The key to the continuum is the degree of personal identity mastered by each member and the ability to communicate this identity to others.

Disengaged Relationships

These family members adamantly assert their independence. They are so concerned about self-recognition and self-enhancement that bonding, or empathy, for others may be minimal. They may demand their "rights" but do not acknowledge responsibilities to other members. They seldom share their true feelings or values in such a way that understanding is enhanced. Each member is an independent psychological subsystem. Communication is task-oriented, consequently each family member lives a role relationship. They do not really know one another because genuine intimacy is not fostered. Family responsibilities tend to be rigidly divided into "your" jobs and "my" jobs, with little sense of caring for the needs or interests of each other.

Enmeshed Relationships

Intimacy can become confused with an unhealthy togetherness or an extreme cohesion that results in a loss of personal boundaries and identity.[17] High self-disclosure and inappropriate disclosure (e.g., sharing with the wrong subsystem) can tie the members so closely that boundaries become blurred. Each member is expected to be like the other, to have the same feelings, concerns, and values. One person's problems become everyone's business. Reality and individual differences are submerged in the demand for self-confirmation, or reflection, in the lives of others. Such intimacy becomes smothering.[17] Enmeshed relationships often include extended family members (or clan) because the couple has not clearly identified who does and does not belong to their family system. They allow in-laws inappropriate access to family information and allow them to interfere with problems and decision making.

This kind of relationship occurs when none of the individuals has developed a strong or healthy sense of personal identity. Instead, each develops a pseudoself, an identity based on external pressures or roles instead of internalized assessment, values, and goals. The couple merges their pseudoselves in marriage. They become involved in playing their roles and being what they think the other person or "society" wants them to be. At the same time, each unwittingly demands that the other enhance the functioning of his or her self. However, since neither individual knows the self well enough to identify personal needs or to communicate adequately to the other who he or she is and what may be needed, neither individual truly develops identity even within marriage or takes full responsibility for personal development. The couple, and eventually their children, develop a **mass ego identity** in which all family members are expected to have the same feelings, reactions, opinions, values, and enemies as the other members.

Poorly defined individuals feel that they cannot live without the other person because each needs the other for strength or direction. They have difficulty with independent problem solving and decision making. If one experiences injustice or anger, the partner is expected to feel the pain just as acutely as the aggrieved and thus help to dissipate some of the intensity of emotion. This "no-self" individual laughs when others laugh but without understanding. The person has no separate joys, goals, or independent value system and is unable to offer an objective or unique perspective to discussions. Such a person is *very* apt at getting along with others and is well liked, even sought out, because of the tendency to affirm and to support the views of others. Consequently, the no-self person may be well liked at work or in social life, where he or she can play a role. In the deeper intimacy of marriage, however, in which each must carry part of the responsibility for decision making and value clarification, this individual may be a complete failure. The poor differentiation of self makes him or her merely an extension of the other person. He or she lives vicariously.

The no-self person can be a strong, demanding, flamboyant individual who draws strength and courage from the partner to face the world with confidence, a quiet, hard-working "back-seater," or a friendly, joke-filled alcoholic. They all have one thing in common: the strength to face each day and its problems is external to themselves. These individuals do not face stress well, tend to blame other people for their failures, and may retaliate quickly if they perceive support is decaying.

The person who provides the emotional strength, who "gives in," finds it draining to be the thinker, organizer, decision-maker, and guide for two people. Many of these persons experience high stress or dysfunction because of the erosion of their emotional strength.[4] Other people may thrive on the sense of importance and power the relationship gives them (Fig. 29-7).

An enmeshed relationship can change only when a person begins to clearly define and openly state inner conviction, values, principles, and goals that differ from those of the spouse or family and begins to take responsible action based on these convictions, regardless of the behaviors or feelings of others. He or she must be able to maintain a separate sense of self in the face of emotional pressure from the others and to assume responsibility for his or her own emotional reactions. The individual must be able to emotionally step back from an interaction and observe the interplay, much as a third person

FIGURE 29–7.
The most successful relationships are between two people with clearly defined identities who have learned the skill of commitment, self-discipline, negotiation, compromise, and cooperation during their developmental years.

might do, and concentrate on the process, not just the product, of the interaction. He or she must get beyond feelings and emotions to look at the situation realistically and differentiate between facts, beliefs, opinions, and convictions. In this way, the dynamics of the situation can be analyzed.

An individual can extricate herself or himself from an unhealthy relationship by trying to develop a person-to-person relationship, in which discussions are about one's own values, ideas, and opinions, rather than people, events, and things. As one becomes aware of personal feelings and reactions, they can be brought under control. One broadens perspectives by listening to all sides, refusing to align oneself with another's position, or defending one's own. Counterattack is counterproductive. An emotional distance is essential to think about the events of a relationship. Emotional issues are best discussed at a nonemotional time, when the facts and the communication process can be more clearly evaluated.

Normal Range

Marital adjustment and balance are closely related to the couple's ability to communicate. The more open they can be and the more areas they are free to discuss, the closer their relationship will be. Two factors facilitate intimacy. The sharing of information, which is difficult to obtain from other sources, tends to escalate and become deeper with time. *Self-disclosure* is the foundation of appreciating individuality. *Affirmation,* the second factor that facilitates intimacy, is the foundation for togetherness. It is expressed through the many ways one recognizes the existence of the other: responding relevantly to communications, accepting the other's self-experiences, involving oneself in the other's interests, and personalizing one's interactions.

The fear of rejection and other barriers to emotional intimacy can be overcome by the affirming support offered by a warm, sensitive partner. Each person has a right and a responsibility to personal feelings and to differentiate the self from others. We cannot find ourself in other people, we cannot live life for them, nor use them for our own selfish purposes of self-affirmation.[6] We must show appreciation for the right of other people to determine their own direction.

Conflict Management

No two people see eye to eye on every issue. It is ironic that the relationship that produces the greatest satisfaction in life also produces the greatest conflict. In fact, the more intimate a relationship, the more prone a couple is to conflict.[36] As they relate to more issues and involve deeper layers of their personalities, conflict is inevitable. As they reveal more of the self to the other, each becomes more vulnerable to hurt and affirmation. It is only as each one discloses personal feelings, preferences, construction of reality, mistakes, and limits, however, that personal space is defined and mutual respect fostered.

Cultural tradition encourages the suppression and repression of conflict. This tradition can put a secondary strain on a couple who feels that the marriage is deteriorating when differences emerge. The avoidance of conflict through suppression of self-disclosure leads to the isolation of the individuals, misunderstanding, resentment, anger, hostility, bitterness, hatred, and scapegoating.[7] The couple may develop "pseudomutuality" to decrease the occasions of conflict. They retreat to roles and decrease their intimate exchanges, acts that merely blur the problems and move the couple toward one end or the other of the togetherness–separateness continuum. On the surface, they have a good relationship, but, in reality, they miss a healthy relationship (see Chap. 32). Other couples may develop a "pseudohostility." They bicker over trivia and discharge the negative energy that comes from the tension of covering up the real conflicts. Intimacy is again thwarted.

If two people live together and are honest with each other, the uniqueness of their individual needs will clash. Conflict in and of itself is not destructive. In fact, conflict is essential to growth, for it "necessitates the continual negotiation and renegotiation of values, beliefs, and goals."[11] It is the handling of the conflict that is constructive or destructive. When conflict is successfully negotiated, the individuals have a decrease in anxiety that can lead to growth and personal optimism. Conflict does not dull love. *It is indifference to the partner's frustration, needs, and values that kills love.* The honest, even heated, sharing of conflicting needs is growth producing. The avoidance of conflict only compounds the issue by storing up tensions from unresolved conflicts ("gunny sacking"). These stored-up tensions typically emerge as a single large explosion at some later point, over some "straw that breaks the camel's back."

Many arguments are worthwhile because they enable a person to get in touch with the real self before arriving at a solution, expose the underlying problem, clear the air, enable one to reevaluate the self or one's partner, foster the mutual facing of a problem, and encourage the creation of joint solutions that can draw the couple closer together.[26] If an argument is to be constructive, however, it must be part of the problem-solving sequence. "Hit and run" tactics are destructive, and no growth is possible. Conflict, if resolved, helps to assure that neither individual is "swallowed up" by the other.[42] A good argument can sharpen one's wit and provide a source of healthy stimulation. When two people have healthy self-identities, they can share without fear of losing face or power in the relationship. They meet as equals, each trying to understand and enhance the other.

Successful family conflict moves through five stages.[17]

Prior Condition Stage

In addition to differences of personality and experiences, prior conditions, such as ambiguous roles and responsibilities, scarcity of essential resources, unhealthy dependency and independence, poorly defined rules, and inadequate information all set the stage for tension. Consequently, self-disclosure and communication are critical factors in reducing surprises and thus the occasion for conflict. Curran, in her book *Stress and the Healthy Family,* presents excellent examples of conflict avoidance through anticipatory action.[8]

Frustration Awareness Stage

Individual perceptions affect sensitivity to tension or conflicts. Inaccurate perceptions can create conflict where none exists. It is critical at this stage to share and to validate perceptions. Couples miscommunicate about 20% of the time.[42] Clarification can avoid unnecessary conflicts. Conflict also can be avoided if one decides the negative consequences of confrontation outweigh the positive outcomes. "Backing off" does not resolve the issue but may be the better part of valor under certain circumstances. Getting caught up in the minor issues of life can block one's view of and appreciation for the whole picture. Humor can often defuse impending conflict by plac-

ing the "facts" into a new context, thus changing sensitivity thresholds or the perspective on and therefore meaning of events.

Active Conflict Stage

Nothing can be resolved if a couple refuses or is unable to communicate with each other effectively. To remain constructive, the couple *must* communicate, which includes active listening and empathizing as well as honest self-disclosure. The ground rules for fair fighting are: (1) make allowances for circumstances; (2) do not confront the other when ill or tired; (3) get the consent to confrontation of both people; (4) meet face-to-face; (5) keep the subject current; (6) keeping it private; (7) separate fighting and lovemaking; (8) using "I" statements; (9) listen without interrupting; (10) deal with negative feelings; (11) be honest—why are you really angry?; (12) do not blame; (13) do not generalize (i.e., "always," "never"); (14) be creative; (15) stick to resolvable issues; and (16) do not leave scars by accusations or verbal or physical abuse.

When the differences are not negotiated satisfactorily, one of the persons may resort to coercive efforts to obtain compliance. Cultural traditions and Judeo-Christian teaching support male leadership in the family. Many people quote Saint Paul's admonition to wives to "submit yourselves unto your own husbands" (Ephesians 5:22). They use this verse as a foundation for unmitigated authority, which demands compliance and obedience. In essence, the wife becomes an extension of the husband's needs, desires, values, and goals.

By taking this statement out of context, people forget that Saint Paul goes on to say that husbands are to "love their wives as their own bodies" (Ephesians 5:28). This statement advises a mutual respect for her needs and values as if they were his own. The teaching does not leave room for coercion or dictatorship but emphasizes a genuine partnership in which both respect the needs, values, and goals of the other. Each is nourished, cherished, and enhanced in such a relationship. The will of the other is sought as a valued contribution to the partnership. The more egalitarian the relationship, the better the communication and the better the conflict resolution. If a couple suppresses negative feelings and avoids the conflict and satisfactory resolution, then resentments compound to poison the relationship. Loss of self occurs as the relationship erodes.

Solution Stage

Rationality must replace subjective, paranoid, or authoritative feelings if a mutually satisfactory solution is to be found. Both must participate in the brainstorming of alternative solutions and potential consequences. Peacemaking is too heavy a burden for one person to carry alone. When both participate, neither one loses; both win, and self-esteem is enhanced. The steps to effective resolution include: (1) defining the problem (each may see it differently), (2) trying to understand underlying causes, (3) identifying priorities or critical factors for each individual, (4) brainstorming possible solutions, (5) agreeing on the best approach, and (6) demonstrating a willingness to

FIGURE 29–8.
*Common goals, hard work, and humor charac-
terize healthy relationships.*

implement the solution. The couple does not need to agree on everything or every issue, but they do need to be able to work out a mutually satisfactory compromise. If personal desires, selfish whims, and hurt feelings take precedence over the success of the partnership, then perspective is lost, compromise is impossible, and the relationship is jeopardized. The parts have become more important than the whole. Poor conflict resolution leads to warfare or withdrawal, both of which are self-defeating.

Each person must have sufficient commitment to the relationship to carry him or her over the difficult times. The involvement of either individual in extramarital affairs tends to undermine trust in the relationship and to divert energy away from a resolution of the couple's conflicts.[32] Consequently, it erodes the unity of a couple toward a common goal and mutual satisfaction.

Follow-up Stage

For conflict resolution to be successful, both partners must follow through with their end of agreed-on behavior changes or responsibilities. The patterns of conflict negotiation used in earlier confrontations tend to be repeated. Consequently, the early months of marriage are critical to establishing healthy approaches to communication and conflict management. If a couple finds that their confrontations are destructive rather than growth producing, then marital counseling should be sought early, before permanent scars are left by sharp tongues and immature behaviors.

Maintaining Vitality

Psychologists and marriage counselors offer multiple suggestions for maintaining and nurturing love in a relationship. Communication cannot be effective unless the couple has

sufficient time with each other. Busy schedules, careers, and children or family responsibilities can eclipse quality time with each other. Gradually, the relationship disintegrates as the two become emotional strangers. Most couples need to plan time with each other—to continue to "court" and "date" each other even though married—to provide times of romance and intimate communication. These "escapades" need not be expensive: a candlelight supper at home, a daily walk together, written notes tucked into a briefcase or lunch bag or taped on the bathroom mirror evoke positive feelings. Reading, puzzle construction, pursuing a hobby together, or redecorating the home can provide time together but must not usurp time for quiet sharing of events, problems, and concerns (Fig. 29-8). Most couples need at least one time a week to sit and talk without interruption about vital issues.

An annual weekend "honeymoon" or "retreat" is seen as essential for some couples. During this time, they reassess the direction of their relationship and their trajectory as a family. Concrete long-range goals are established (e.g., family planning, home repairs, career moves, financial investments) and annual plans are made to achieve the goals. Time is set aside on a monthly basis to review and retrench the relationship and plans. These couples approach the marriage as a serious business partnership within the context of a close personal relationship, attempting to maximize the benefits of both.

CONCLUSION

There is no rational reason why anyone needs to marry in the United States today. Roles, responsibilities, and job opportunities are no longer dependent on gender. With technological advances, all needs can be purchased or performed by oneself with simplified devices. However, "the very technological advances that have made it possible to live as an unattached individual have created a cold, impersonal world that makes us crave intimate relationships. At the same time, these conditions make it hard to find and sustain them."[36] Consequently, love, companionship, and good communication are essential ingredients in initiating and maintaining a meaningful, long-term working relationship. If a marriage is to last, it must be approached carefully, for such a relationship is all-embracing.

Marriage is a new reality. It is a constantly emerging, developing relationship that is constructed by the unique interaction of the partners. "Two strangers come together and redefine themselves."[1] A healthy marriage begins with two people with strong personal identities. This comfort with one's self is discreetly shared with family and close associates. One does not need to continue to play a role in intimate interactions. As one shares inner values, opinions, hurts, and ecstasies, mutual respect and appreciation are developed. Love springs from a desire to share the self and to enhance the other (being-love), rather than from a need to fulfill one's self in another (deficiency-love).[31]

The "responsible I" assumes responsibility for one's own happiness and comfort and does not blame others for failure or unhappiness. It is in the context of two people with healthy identities that true intimacy evolves into a rich, lasting marriage that fosters the continued growth of each member. Conflict actually helps the couple to grow closer together while it more clearly defines the individual boundaries. Marriage is not an easy relationship. At its best, it is an intense relationship between two separate people. It takes hard work and compromise to develop a mutually respectful and enhancing relationship. It inevitably involves the total personality of both partners in face-to-face contact.[46] It is only in this context that Schuster's seven family tasks will be mastered.

REFERENCES

1. Berger, P., & Kellner, H. (1977). Marriage and the construction of reality: An exercise in the microsociology of knowledge. In P. J. Stein, J. Richman, & N. Hannon (Eds.), *The family: Functions, conflicts and symbols.* Reading, MA: Addison-Wesley.

2. Blood, B., & Blood, M. (1978). *Marriage* (3rd ed.). New York: Free Press.

3. Blood, R. O., & Wolfe, D. M. (1978). *Husbands and wives: The dynamics of married living.* Westport, CT: Greenwood Press.

4. Bowen, M. (1985). *Family therapy in clinical practice.* New York: Jason Aronson.

5. Bowman, H. A., & Spanier, G. B. (1978). *Modern marriage* (8th ed.). New York: McGraw-Hill.

6. Buscaglia, L. (1982). *Personhood: The art of being fully human.* New York: Fawcett Columbine.

7. Crosby, J. F. (1976). Conflict resolution: An entrée into self. In E. A. Powers, and Lees, M. W. (Eds.), *Process in relationship: Marriage and family* (2nd ed.). St. Paul, MN: West.

8. Curran, D. D. (1985). *Stress and the healthy family.* Minneapolis: Winston Press.

9. D'Antonio, W. V. (1980). The family and religion: Exploring a changing relationship. *Journal for the Scientific Study of Religion, 19,* 89.

10. Duvall, E. R. M. (1985). *Marriage and family development* (6th ed.). New York: Harper and Row.

11. Eisenman, E. P. (1977). The origins and practice of family therapy. In P. J. Stein, J. Richman, & N. Hannon (Eds.), *The family: Functions, conflicts and symbols.* Reading, MA: Addison-Wesley.

12. Erikson, E. H. (1963). *Childhood and society* (2nd ed.). New York: Norton.

13. Erikson, E. H., Erikson, J. M., & Kivnick, H. Q. (1986). *Vital involvement in old age.* New York: W.W. Norton.

14. Eshleman, J. R. (1988). *The family: An introduction* (5th ed.). Boston: Allyn & Bacon.

15. Folkman, J. D., & Clatworthy, N. M. (1970). *Marriage has many faces.* Columbus, OH: Merrill.

16. Fromm, E. (1956). *The art of loving.* New York: Harper.

17. Galvin, K. M., & Brommel, B. J. (1986). *Family communication: Cohesion and change* (2nd ed.). Glenview, IL: Scott, Foresman.

18. Garrett, W. R. (1982). *Seasons of marriage and family life.* New York: Holt, Rinehart and Winston.

19. Garrett, Y. (1981). *The newlywed handbook: A refreshing, practical guide for living together.* Waco, TX: Word Books.

20. Hazan, C., & Shaver, P. (1987). Romantic love conceptualized as an attachment process. *Journal of Personality and Social Psychology, 52,* 511–524.

21. Hendrick, C., & Hendrick, S. (1983). *Liking, loving and relating.* Monterey, CA: Brooks/Cole.

22. Horton, T. E. (1977). Conceptual basis for nursing intervention with human systems: Families. In J. E. Hall & B. R. Weaver (Eds.), *Distributive nursing practice: A systems approach to community health.* Philadelphia: J. B. Lippincott.

23. Hunt, M. (1975). *Sexual behavior in the 1970s.* New York: Dell.

24. Jourard, S. M. (1971). *The transparent self* (rev. ed.). New York: Van Nostrand Reinhold.

25. Kelly, E. L., & Conley, J. J. (1987). Personality and compatibility: A prospective analysis of marital stability and marital satisfaction. *Journal of Personality and Social Psychology, 52,* 27–40.

26. Kelly, R. K. (1979). *Courtship, marriage and the family* (3rd ed.). New York: Harcourt Brace Jovanovich.

27. Kinsey, A. C., et al. (1953). *Sexual behavior in the human female.* Philadelphia: W. B. Saunders.

28. Kirkendall, L. A. (1984). *Premarital intercourse and interpersonal relationships.* Westport, CT: Greenwood Press.

29. Levitan, S. A., Belous, R. S., & Gallo, F. (1988). *What's happening to the American family? Tensions, hopes, realities* (rev. ed.). Baltimore: Johns Hopkins University Press.

30. Marshall, L. L., & Rose, P. (1988). Family of origin violence and courtship abuse. *Journal of Counseling and Development, 66,* 414–418.

31. Maslow, A. (1982). *Toward a psychology of being* (2nd ed.). New York: Van Nostrand Reinhold.

32. Masters, W. H., & Johnson, V. E. (1975). *The pleasure bond: A new look at sexuality and commitment.* Boston: Little, Brown.

33. Rogers, C. R. (1961). *On becoming a person.* Boston: Houghton Mifflin.

34. Saxton, L. (1990). *The individual, marriage and the family* (7th ed.). Belmont, CA: Wadsworth.

35. Sell, C. M. (1981). *Family ministry: The enrichment of family life through the church.* Grand Rapids, MI: Zondervan.

36. Skolnick, A. S. (1987). *The intimate environment: Exploring marriage and the family* (4th ed.). Boston: Little, Brown.

37. Smith, H. I. (1983). *More than "I do": A pastor's resource book for premarital counseling*. Kansas City, MO: Beacon Hill Press of Kansas City.

38. Spanier, G. B. (1973). *Sexual socialization and premarital sexual behavior: An empirical investigation of the impact of formal and informal sex education* (Doctoral dissertation, Northwestern University). Evanston, IL: Northwestern University.

39. Statistical Abstract of the U.S. (1989). *Statistical abstract of the United States, 1989* (109th ed.). Washington, DC: U.S. Government Printing Office.

40. Stein, P. J., Richman, J., & Hanson, N. (1977). *The family: Functions, conflicts and symbols*. Reading, MA: Addison-Wesley.

41. Sternberg, R. J., & Barnes, M. L. (1989). *The psychology of love*. New Haven, CT: Yale University Press.

42. Strong, B., & DeVault, C. (1989). *The marriage and family experience* (4th ed.). St. Paul, MN: West.

43. Toffler, A. (1980). *The third wave*. New York: Morrow.

44. Trotter, R. J. (1986). The three faces of love. *Psychology Today, 20*(9), 46–50, 54.

45. Trussell, J., & Westhoff, C. F. (1980). Contraceptive practice and trends in coital frequency. *Family Planning Perspectives, 12*, 246–249.

46. Whipple, C. M., & Whittle, D. (1976). *The compatibility test: How to choose the right person and make your marriage a success*. Englewood Cliffs, NJ: Prentice-Hall.

The Decision To Be or Not To Be Parents

Clara S. Schuster

Although parenthood is a statistically normative phenomenon in the lives of young adults, it is a singularly momentous event to the individuals involved. The decision (or lack of it) of whether or not to have a child is probably one of the most significant decisions in an individual's life, since the ripple effect will profoundly influence the lives of many other people, including the life of the child produced.

Although most couples want or plan to have children "someday," many feel a need to complete other tasks and goals (e.g., education, career, financial obligations, personal development) before assuming the responsibilities of parenthood. Subtle—and not so subtle—pressures are placed on the couple if they wait too long. The in-laws want to see their grandchildren before they die. The husband's friends may tease him about his virility, or the dedication of the wife to her "feminine role." Some couples may even receive subtle questions about consummation of the marriage. Friends and family members may pressure the couple to become a "complete" family—inferring that the couple is not a family by itself. The couple may feel stigmatized as abnormal, materialistic, selfish, neurotic, inadequate, incomplete, immoral, or immature.[20, 120]

On the other hand, concern about zero population growth has created pressure for the couple who have or want to have three or more children. "Don't you know when to stop?" "Did you ever hear of birth control?" "What else do you and your husband (or wife) do in the evening?" are all common questions to which the couple may be subjected (Fig. 30-1). Some parents indicate that they are treated as if they have committed a crime by producing a large family, even though they may be socially, emotionally, and financially able to provide for their own and the children's needs.

Some individuals choose to become parents because it will offer another outlet for their own creativity and psychosocial-sexual development; they see parenthood as another opportunity to share themselves intimately with others. They may view parenthood as an art—the chance to become actively involved in the creation of another person, not just physically, but socially, cognitively, emotionally, and spiritually. Parenthood offers the potential of another exciting adventure in life—another avenue for self-actualization and psychological fulfillment. They may receive emotional satisfaction in doing things for others or may feel that they are obtaining a second chance to accomplish (through the child) what they wanted to do or felt they missed the first time through. Some women have children to dissipate loneliness or to provide a face-saving escape from unsatisfying employment (Fig. 30-2).

An individual couple may want children because they feel that the child gives them a common goal—a shared interest—that will help to solidify and to maintain the union. Conversely, a couple may decide against becoming parents because they feel a child would add too much stress or interfere with their current relationship.

FIGURE 30–1.
Reprinted courtesy of Hi and Lois. Copyright King Features Syndicate, Inc.

Some couples become parents because they feel that children help to bond the generations: Through pregnancy and parenthood, the couple shares a common experience with their own parents, and grandparents may become more willing to accept the young couple as adults. Unfortunately, some individuals find that the grandparents do not adequately respect the new family system and continue to interfere with functioning and decision-making by the couple. For other couples, memories of their own negative childhood experiences continue to impede their relationship with the new child.

Some couples and cultural groups feel that children offer security for the later years of life, while others may see children as their hold on immortality—someone to carry on the family name, traditions, or business or to receive the inheritance. Children may be seen to offer a person status: Parenthood provides proof of one's adulthood, or the child may offer a means of displaying the parents' financial success through the quantity or quality of the child's clothing, toys, or education.

Deciding to have a child is a family affair that should be thoughtfully considered, both individually and collectively. If a child prevents the other members of the family from reaching their personal goals, resentment may develop and interfere with the total family dynamics. If the child allows the individual family members to expand the alternatives for goal achievement, then the enriched family system can enhance its cohesiveness, joy, and maturity level.

The quality of the parent-child relationship and the emotional satisfaction received by the parents will depend heavily on the individual parent's level of development, motivation for parenthood, ability to empathize, and willingness to make personal sacrifices for the benefit of another. The child demands and needs much personal attention during the early months of life; the interdependent relationship is heavily skewed toward dependence on the part of the infant. Parents who are expecting more positive feedback may find parenting a disappointing or draining experience. Other priorities, goals, and concerns may cause the parent to begin resenting the amount of time and energy demanded by the child.

DECISION AGAINST INCREASING THE FAMILY

The decision for voluntary childlessness has become an increasingly popular option among couples in first-world cultures. Concern over population increases and personal development of the individuals involved are major factors in the decision.

Voluntary Childlessness

According to the U.S. Census Bureau's annual report on fertility rates, in 1987, 10% of American women ages 18 to 34 expected never to bear children.[118] These couples generally

FIGURE 30–2.
Pregnancy may offer some women a welcome relief from a hectic or boring office routine. However, many of them find that they have merely "jumped from the frying pan into the fire."

have an above-average education and intelligence, marry at a later age, enjoy more financial stability, share a more egalitarian relationship, and have high marital satisfaction and good communication skills.[20, 35, 120]

One third of childless couples decide prior to marriage to remain child free.[120] In fact, many of them make the decision during their teenage years.[20] It is not until they are older that they realize the rejection of parenthood is not synonymous with the rejection of marriage. The other two thirds slip into a childless marriage because of prolonged postponement.[120] Children are postponed for a definite period while the couple accomplishes a goal, such as travel, home purchase, or career establishment. In the second stage, they still plan to have children "someday," but postpone the event for an indefinite period until they can "afford it," or "feel more ready." During the third stage, the couple begins to deliberate on the pros and cons of parenthood. They realize that it is an irrevocable decision. There are no periods of trial parenthood. There is no choice of the type of child. They decide to make the decision later when their lives will suffer less disruption. In the final stage, they accept the state of permanent childlessness. They may suddenly realize that they have waited too long when they face infertility issues or menopause.[20] Others have weighed the pros and cons and have decided parenthood is not the right decision for them. Some wish to avoid the penalties of parenthood, others prefer to protect the rewards of childlessness.[20] As a couple, they may feel that their contribution to society is more constructive by pursuing a career than by raising children. This is not necessarily a selfish decision or a reaction to parenthood per se. It may be a very realistic evaluation of the couple's strengths, weaknesses, values, and goals.

Factors Affecting the Decision

Parenthood demands a long-term commitment of energy, time, and material resources. The financial obligations involved in child-rearing are increasing. Estimates indicate that it costs from $70,000 to $200,000 to raise one child from birth to 18 years of age, depending on family income, goals, and lifestyle,[60, ;67] averaging $86,000–$92,000 in 1986.[119] These figures do not include college expenses or the indirect cost of the parent's lost income if a decision is made to stay at home (which may be $200,000 or more). If the parent returns to work, there is the added expense of child care. Second and third children cost proportionately less than the first child because of shared resources, but the additional expense, especially in loss of maternal employment, still discourages large families in today's society. In 1987, 61.4 percent of first-time mothers returned to work within the year; however, only 44.2 percent of mothers of 2 or more children returned to work within the year after birth of the youngest child.[118]

Worldwide population was 5,000 million in 1987, increasing at a rate of 1 million persons every 5 days.[93] At this rate, it will top 6,000 million by the year 2000 and triple or quadruple in the 21st century.[93] Even though China has re-

duced its birth rate by almost 50% in the past 15 years, with the one child per family policy, improved medical care and increased life spans will create a 200 million population increase in the next 20 years.[93] The current world growth rate of 1.8 percent per year means a doubling of world population every 39 years.[36]

For those concerned with population trends, an average of 2.1 children per female is considered to be the replacement rate.[67] The current U.S. rate of 1.8 children per female places us below zero population growth. Although the United States can support a much larger population than its current 248,000,000 people, there is a concern that the potential problems (e.g., environmental pollution, population density) may dilute the quality of life to an unacceptable level.

A shaky marital relationship also discourages some couples.[49] They may feel the need to concentrate their energies on each other or are concerned about the negative effects of a potential divorce on a child. Many couples begin to recognize that the parenthood mystique is "not all it is cracked up to be." They see the sacrifices made by their parents and peers and realize that their own lives are happier as they are,[20] which does not mean they dislike children. Many of these individuals are successful nurses or school teachers. They are merely aficionados of their adult-centered lifestyle.[120]

Ann Landers asked her readers a simple question: "If you had it to do over again, would you have children?" She received an unprecedented 10,000 letters, 70 percent of which responded "No!"[65] The myth of parenthood was shattered; it became clear that the fairy tale "and they lived happily ever after" ended with the birth of a baby. The "no" mail fell into four categories:

1. Some parents were concerned about world tensions and the effects of overpopulation on quality of life.

2. Other parents felt that the children had ruined their relationship with each other. Many felt that personal time and energy were so heavily drained that they were no longer free to experience life as an individual in their own right. Mothers expressed more concern over this aspect than did fathers. Fathers may resent the financial cost; mothers are concerned with the personal cost. Surveys of stress and life satisfaction indicated that the parents of young children feel significantly more stress than individuals in other phases of life. Research also indicates that satisfaction with life (especially for women) drops with the birth of the first child. Stressors decrease and general life satisfaction increases as the children become older, and many parents express marked increase in life satisfaction when the children leave home.[19]

3. The saddest letters came from parents whose children had essentially broken their emotional ties when they left home. The parents felt that the children had forgotten them. Some older persons want their children to express gratitude to them for having devoted years of labor to their upbringing; other older persons seek and need the companionship of their children; still others

feel they have lost a friend. This last attitude is perhaps the most painful. Whether real or perceived, lack of attention is interpreted as rejection.

4.   Bitter letters were received from disenchanted parents whose children did not match their dreams; they felt that the children had failed them. Their children did not possess a prized skill or physical attractiveness, or they were delinquent, colicky, or had crooked teeth requiring expensive dental work. These parents found it impossible to relive their own lives through the children's social activities. They felt they had done "all the right things," had even "lived by the book," but they were disappointed by the results.

Although one must acknowledge that such a survey is biased by the intensity of the feelings of those who responded, their reactions to parenthood are, nevertheless, significant and should be considered by couples who are assessing their assets, liabilities, and motivations for parenthood. Parenthood is not all fun and games or even a job that can be laid aside at the end of the day. There is no "magic formula," and results are not guaranteed. It may be that Landers' letters reflect the immaturity of the parents who responded, and highlight the need for education/counseling about the realities of parenting. Yet, a controlled study in England and the United States revealed similar results. Only 38% of mothers of preschoolers felt fulfilled by the role, 10% were satisfied, 20% in conflict, and 32% felt alienated from the role.[15] Successful parenting requires dedication of oneself to another, a task that demands considerable maturity. Joys are frequent when expectations are realistic and motivations are not self-serving. The pleasure comes from a job well done, but concrete evidence of the success of one's efforts may not be clear until the child's adult years.

Contraception

Although couples have attempted to control conception for centuries through techniques such as the ingestion of special herbs, insertion of foreign objects in the uterus, or timing coitus with the phases of the moon, effective methods of contraception have been available only since 1930. Reliable, efficient methods emerged in 1960 when "the pill" was released.[84]

Many doctors and psychologists feel that an interval of 2 to 3 years between children is beneficial to both the mother and the child. Effective family-planning techniques are essential in order to space children and to avoid having unwanted children who may cause additional stress on the family unit. The mother of an unwanted child may avoid getting adequate prenatal care and may give minimal attention to the child after its birth. Unwanted children are more likely to be battered, they experience a higher mortality rate, and have a higher juvenile delinquency rate.

Choice of Method

Although most men tend to leave the decision for birth control to the woman, in an egalitarian relationship it is a dual responsibility that needs a specific discussion.[113] There is no single ideal method of contraception; every method has its drawbacks.[84] Each couple must weigh the advantages, disadvantages, and side effects of each method, taking into account religious and moral values and personal and aesthetic factors when making the decision. The safest and most effective method of birth control obviously is abstinence. However, most people do not find this method personally appealing!

The sexually active couple needs to have a clear understanding of the reproductive system and the ovarian cycle (see Chap. 3), both to enhance their satisfaction and to increase their success in the use of the method they choose. **The single most critical factor in the success of a method is conscientious acceptance of responsibility for implementation.**[47,89] The method chosen may be very effective, but it cannot be expected to be efficient if it is used haphazardly.

When choosing a method of contraception, the couple needs to consider (1) the mechanism of action (i.e., how and when the method works), (2) undesirable side effects of the method (and what to do about them), (3) the effectiveness rate of the method, and (4) whether or not they eventually want to conceive a child. Effectiveness of a contraceptive method is indicated by the number of pregnancies per 100 women years of use; this number can be translated into a percentage. The natural fertility rate (if no method of contraception is used) for women 20–24 years of age is 86 (i.e., a woman has an 86% chance of becoming pregnant in 12 months of unprotected intercourse.)[28] Natural fertility decreases with age, especially after age 35.[28]

There is frequently a difference between the theoretical and the actual effectiveness of a contraceptive method. For instance, the pregnancy rate for women who use an oral contraceptive is theoretically close to zero. However, in actuality, effectiveness is reduced because many women forget to take the pill. The most frequently used contraceptive methods are compared in Table 30-1.

Preconceptual Methods

Prevention of Ovulation

Ovulation can be prevented through hormonal control of the menstrual cycle (see Chap. 3 for a review of this subject). About 29 percent of women in the United States rely on the **oral contraceptive pill** for birth control.[47] Hormonal contraceptives are composed of a combination of estrogen and progesterone. The artificial maintenance of estrogen and progesterone levels suppresses the maturation of primary follicles, interferes with the release of luteinizing hormone (LH) by the pituitary, effects changes in endometrium development, and effects cervical mucosa changes. Ovulation may still occur when estrogen dosage is too low. The sudden drop in

TABLE 30–1. COMPARISON OF BIRTH CONTROL METHODS

Method	Chance of Pregnancy*	Advantages	Disadvantages	Contraindications
Chance (natural fertility)	52–86			
Oral contraceptives Combined pill	0.2–10	May eliminate cramps, acne; no action required at coitus; regularity of menstrual cycle	Must be taken every day; requires prescription; increased risk of blood clotting	Smoking Sickle cell anemia Hepatitis Breast feeding Older than age 40 Diabetes Hypertension
Withdrawal	6.7–25	No cost	Sperm in preejaculatory fluid; interruption of sexual activity	
Rhythm (calendar)	10–27	Nothing to be purchased	Long periods of abstinence	Irregular periods
Condom with spermicide	0.4–20	May be purchased at any drugstore; protects against venereal disease	Must be removed carefully to prevent spilling; dulls penile sensation	
Diaphragm with jelly or cream	1.9–18	Nothing ingested; may be inserted several hours before coitus; used for coitus during menses	Cream must be reapplied within 1 hour before coitus; must be left in 6–8 hours after coitus; requires professional fitting and prescription	Severely displaced uterus Cystocele
Cervical cap	9	Can be left in place	Cervical ulcers, infection	
Sponge	9–17	Can be inserted up to 24 hours before intercourse	May lead to infections, toxic shock syndrome	
Foams, jellies, creams	5–22	May be purchased at any drugstore	Must be used within 1 hour before coitus; messy; must be deposited at entrance to cervix	Allergy to solution
Sterilization Male Female	 0.02 0.13	Most effective method; permanent	Surgery required; expensive; effects not immediate for male	Desire for children later
Intrauterine device (IUD)	1.2–5	No need for daily concern; separated from coitus	May cause cramps or longer menses; may need to check for "tail" of device before coitus	Women who have long, crampy periods Cervicitis Venereal disease Endometriosis Anticoagulant therapy
Morning after pill	1–5	Effective for unprotected coitus	Nausea and vomiting; ectopic pregnancy	

*Pregnancies per 100 woman years. The wide range represents theoretical versus actual effectiveness based on carelessness in use.

progesterone level that occurs when the pill is stopped simulates the normal hormonal drop preceding the menses and usually precipitates degeneration of the endometrial lining.

Every pill has a different ratio of the two hormones. The side effects or undesirable effects from the contraceptive pill are determined by the balance of hormones in any given woman. If a woman has a naturally high level of estrogen and is taking an estrogen-dominant pill, she may develop symptoms of estrogen excess, progesterone deficiency, or both. The reverse may also be true. If symptoms develop, the solution is to switch to a pill with a different balance rather than to discontinue the pill. "The pill" is a set of choices, not one choice.

The contraceptive pill is generally contraindicated (not recommended) if a woman is breast-feeding, since some women find that it interferes with milk production. Some women find that the menstrual period is greatly shortened and the flow lightened when they are taking the pill. Occasionally, the menses will disappear altogether, and the woman may be temporarily infertile following use of the pill.[121] Diabetes and sickle cell anemia may also be aggravated by the pill. Since oral contraceptives may increase the blood-clotting factors in some women, their use is not advisable for women with a history of phlebitis or other clotting problems.[33] Smoking is strongly discouraged for women using oral contraceptives.[33, 47, 89] There is evidence of a decreased risk for developing ovarian and endometrial cancer in women who have used oral contraceptives.[47, 54, 121] There is evidence of decreased pelvic inflammatory disease and rheumatoid arthritis.[33] There is no evidence of increased risk of breast cancer in women who used oral contraceptives before the birth of the first child,[104] but there is a slight increase in current users.[54, 68]

Hormonal suppression of ovulation can also be achieved by **subcutaneous implant** of time-release hormone rods.[85] The minute, sustained release of estrogen allows for lower doses and fewer side effects. It is effective and efficient, since it removes the human error of forgetting. Some women experience menstrual irregularity. Pregnancy rates are under 0.5.[85]

Hormone-impregnated vaginal rings also are available at some clinics and negate the need for daily remembering. They are left in place for 3 weeks and then removed during menstruation. Pregnancy rates have been low (1–2%), and user acceptance high.[85]

Steroid injections (e.g., DMPA and depo-Provera) can suppress ovulation for up to 12 months, depending on the form of administration and dosage.[38] Forty percent of women experience amenorrhea for 3 or more months, and many have menstrual irregularities.[85] The steroid administration may be accompanied by dizziness, weight gain, headaches and nervousness. Delay of return of fertility causes concern as does the virilizing effect on female babies should the woman become pregnant.[38]

Prevention of Spermatogenesis

Male contraceptives are still in experimental stages of development. Current hormone-therapy regimens achieve significant oligospermia but may not achieve azoospermia. Since sperm take up to 3 months to develop, an implant or injection may take 12 weeks before fertility is adequately affected.[55] The same delay is observed when therapy is discontinued. Because current hormone therapy affects libido (sexual desire) and potency, it is considered undesirable.[50, 55]

Gossypol, a compound extracted from cottonseed, has been used in China and demonstrates potential for reducing the sperm count without reducing libido.[50] It has a 99% effectiveness rate in causing azoospermia or oligospermia.[55] However, its effects on the cardiac and respiratory systems may prove it undesirable. There is a thin line between inadequate,[16] therapeutic, and toxic doses. Ten to twenty percent of men become permanently sterile.[55]

Prevention of Union of the Sperm and Egg

If the couple prefers not to tamper with the hormonal balance, they may elect a method that prevents the sperm from reaching the egg. As mentioned earlier, **abstinence** is an extremely effective method. However, if the couple engages in other noncoital sexual activities, sperm, can be accidentally

transferred from the male to the vaginal area, and pregnancy, although unlikely, could still occur. Some couples rely on **coitus interruptus.** In this method, the penis is withdrawn just prior to ejaculation. The couple should be aware that ejaculation may be hard to control or to predict, and that sperm may be present in the preejaculatory secretions. Couples also find this method to be psychologically frustrating. Those who plan to use this method should become familiar with the squeeze technique popularized by Masters and Johnson to prevent imminent ejaculation.

Natural Family Planning Methods. The **"rhythm"** or **"natural"** family planning method combines knowledge of the ovarian cycle with abstinence. The aim is to avoid intercourse on the days surrounding ovulation. Predicting ovulation by the calendar alone (see Chap. 3) has a pregnancy rate of 10 to 30 percent; the rate decreases when using the basal temperature records and assessment of cervical mucus.[37, 47]

In the **calendar method,** the woman keeps a record of the menses for at least 6 months and then performs the following calculations: She subtracts 20 from the number of days of the shortest cycle (this represents the first unsafe day) and then subtracts 11 days from the number of days in the longest cycle (this represents the last unsafe day). Unprotected intercourse should be avoided during the interval between those two days of the cycle.[37] Ovulation can be more precisely identified if the woman takes her **basal body temperature (BBT)** before rising in the morning (Fig. 30-3). The basal temperature usually remains below 36.6°C (98°F) during the follicular phase of the cycle and rises 0.2–0.6°C (0.5 to 1.2°F) with ovulation.[37] Unprotected intercourse should be avoided for 3 days before ovulation is expected and can be resumed 3 days after the temperature rises. Many women subtract six from the earliest recorded day of temperature elevation just to be sure (if the first day of temperature elevation is day 17, then the first 11 days are considered to be safe).

Assessment of the **cervical mucus** (the Billings method) can add further accuracy to pinpointing the day of ovulation.[12, 47] Advocates of this method indicate that it can be used effectively with irregular cycles and that it allows more "safe" days than the other two methods. As ovulation approaches, the mucus becomes thinner, clearer, stretchier and more slippery,[37] like raw egg white. **Spinnbarkeit** is the term used to describe the stretchability of the mucus. Ovulation occurs 1 to 3 days after maximum spinnbarkeit.[37] By removing some of the mucus with an applicator or her finger, a woman can learn to assess her degree of spinnbarkeit. Intercourse is avoided when the mucus becomes moist and slippery.

There are three other methods a woman can use to pinpoint the day of ovulation: (1) judge the consistency of the cervical os by touch (it is soft, like the lips, at ovulation and firm, like the nose, soon afterwards);[37] (2) touch diabetic test tape to the cervix (it turns from yellow to dark blue at the time of ovulation); and (3) look at the cervical mucus under a microscope (at ovulation the pattern will resemble a fern, but this pattern disappears in 2 or 3 days). Natural methods are

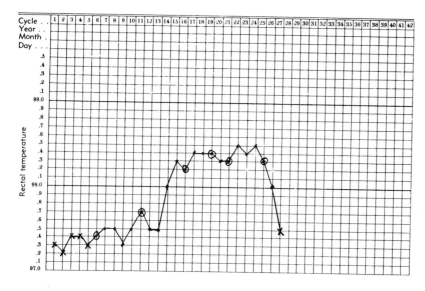

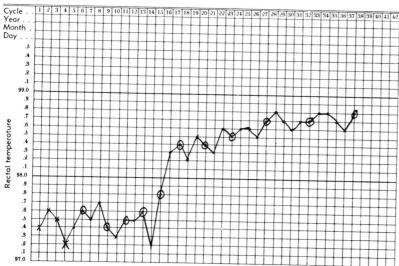

FIGURE 30–3.
Basal temperature chart. Cross marks indicate menses; circles indicate intercourse. Upper chart: ovulation occurred on day 14, no pregnancy occurred. Lower chart: Ovulation occurred on day 15. Continued elevation of temperature beyond 16 days after ovulation indicates a possible conception.

still crude and inaccurate and require much motivation and self-discipline to be effective since abstinence may be necessary one third to one half of the cycle.[47]

Barrier Methods. Mechanical barriers to contraception are the condom for males and the diaphragm, cervical cap, and vaginal sponge for females. These methods are more effective if they are used in combination with chemical contraceptives. The **condom** is the only reliable temporary male contraceptive. Rubber/latex condoms serve as a barrier to both sperm and venereal disease.[47] Female partners also have a reduced risk for cervical cancer.[47] The man should put the condom on during foreplay and after erection, but before inserting the penis into the vagina. There should be a space between the end of the condom and the penis for receiving sperm. A condom should be used only once. Extreme caution must be taken not to spill the contents.

Diaphragms require a vaginal examination for fitting and a prescription. The woman must be taught how to insert and remove the diaphragm properly. If it is inserted improperly, the cervix may actually be pushed into a position that will facilitate entrance of the sperm into the uterus. The woman is usually advised to insert the diaphragm regularly each evening as a part of bedtime routine or within an hour before coitus. It must be left in place for at least 6 to 8 hours after coitus. Many women do not like to manipulate the genitalia for insertion, but users indicate that the diaphragm does not interfere with enjoyment of intercourse. A woman needs to be refitted after each pregnancy or after any pelvic surgery or weight change of 10 pounds or more. The diaphragm can be used during menstruation.

The **cervical cap,** used with spermicide, fits directly over the cervix, blocking the opening by suction adherence.[97]

It is difficult to insert, but can be left in place for prolonged periods of time. It needs to be removed and cleaned at least every 72 hours to prevent ulcerations, odor, and infections.[84]

The **vaginal sponge** provides both a mechanical barrier and a spermicide. There is some concern about pelvic infections and toxic shock syndrome if it is used improperly or left in place beyond the recommended length of time.[34,95] It can be used for multiple copulations, but has a high failure rate.[47]

The **female condom** is a plastic pouch which lines the whole vaginal surface. There is some reduction in sexually transmitted disease, but effectiveness studies are not available.[16]

Spermicides prevent union of the sperm and ovum by immobilizing or killing the sperm. Creams, jellies, foams, or suppositories can be used alone or with a mechanical barrier. To be effective, they must be applied near the cervix and within 1 hour before coitus. Some people feel that spermicides are messy; others may experience burning, irritation, or even allergic reactions. Spermicides also provide some protective action against venereal diseases.[47]

Other methods. **Douching** is generally considered to be an ineffective method because sperm can enter the cervix after intercourse much more rapidly than the woman can administer the douche solution.

The development of a **birth control vaccine** has been plagued with many problems. Such a vaccine, when available, would work on the antibody–antigen principle discussed in Chapter 20. It is difficult to develop antibodies specific to the reproductive system that are also safe, effective, and reversible. Vaccines specific to chorionic gonadotrophin would function as a post-conception method. Other vaccines stimulate the production of sperm antibodies. "It is likely that it will be the women who will probably have to take the male pill!"[55]

Sterilization

One third of couples choose surgical contraception, or sterilization, to provide permanent birth control.[47,84] So far, the attempts to reverse these procedures have had only about a 50% rate of success in men, and a lower rate in women.[51,89,98] Premature sterilization may be a source of regret.[92] In spite of the safety, effectiveness, and low cost of sterilization available to men, women are twice as likely to have their "tubes tied" than men are to have a vasectomy.[47]

Vasectomy involves the severing of the vas deferens, the two tubes that carry sperm from each testicle. Men report some pain the day of the procedure and the day after. At least three successive ejaculations must be free of healthy, mature sperm before other methods of contraception can be discontinued (a process that may take 10 to 16 weeks).[51] Contrary to the beliefs of some men, vasectomy does not interfere with ejaculation, orgasm, or sex drive. In fact, many men indicate an increase in sexual arousal because of the perceived freedom from impregnation of the partner. One percent of the tubes can "recanulize," spontaneously reversing the process.[1,51,106]

A variety of sterilization methods are available to women.

Most of these methods involve abdominal **tubal ligation** and cauterization by laparoscopy or minilaparotomy. These methods generally require hospitalization; however, they are increasingly performed on an outpatient basis. Abdominal tubal ligation, which is often performed immediately postpartum, involves the tying and cutting of the fallopian tubes. It is a relatively simple surgery. Because the incisions are so small, they can be covered by Band-Aids.

Postconception Methods

In spite of the advances in contraceptive techniques and the ready availability of information and equipment, many couples engage in unprotected intercourse or conceive an unplanned or unwanted child. Many young women, caught up in the interests and concerns of the immediate environment, do not connect coitus with pregnancy until after conception. They may believe that they are too young to become pregnant, that, "it can't happen to **me,**" or that one has to engage in intercourse many times before a pregnancy will occur. Many young people receive little or no family planning information because the discussion of sex is still a taboo topic in many families and cultural groups. Some may see the use of contraceptive measures, especially by unmarried couples, as a "sin" since it means that one "planned" to engage in illicit sex. Others use alternative "old wives' tale" methods based on inadequate understanding of anatomy and the process of conception (e.g., sitting on the toilet will "drain it all out"). Some women (and men) may secretly or unconsciously desire a pregnancy, leading them to use contraceptive methods erratically. It is not uncommon for a woman to continue to use the same ineffective method of birth control that she practiced before an unwanted conception (ignorance or helplessness syndrome).

Mechanical Interference with Implantation

The **intrauterine device (IUD)** is a small object that is placed inside the uterus by a physician or health practitioner. Today most IUDs are impregnated with progesterone or copper to increase their effectiveness. The IUD functions by two actions: It (1) establishes a local sterile inflammatory response which is spermicidal, and (2) prevents implantation of the blastocyst if conception should occur.[83] Cramps may occur with insertion of the IUD and even afterward. An over-the-counter aspirin substitute may be recommended for easing discomfort. The first menses may be heavier than usual, and subsequent menstrual periods may also be longer and heavier than those prior to the IUD insertion. Special attention should be paid to vitamin C and iron in the diet, a lack of which is associated with increased menstrual flow.

Women usually are taught to feel for the IUD "tail" in the vagina to make sure it is in place, since the expulsion rate is about 10%.[83] However, the tails may be coated with vaginal discharge, so the fact that they are not felt does not always mean that the IUD is not in place. The placement should be checked by a health practitioner as soon as possible if the woman suspects that the device has been expelled. The woman needs to return for a checkup every year. Some IUDs must be changed every 1 or 2 years, while others may be left in place longer. In order to be sure that she is aware of any spontaneous expulsion of the IUD, the woman should check all tampons or sanitary pads before disposal. Expulsion of the device is most likely to occur in the first 3 months of use and during menstruation.

Because of its ability to interfere with implantation, an IUD may be effectively inserted within 5 days after unprotected intercourse if the woman would like continued protection.[47,125]

Chemical Interference with Implantation

Prostaglandins, a group of naturally occurring fatty acids, can interfere with implantation of the blastocyst by increasing uterine activity. This will decrease the blood supply to the uterus and consequently decrease the oxygen available to the young embryo. Prostaglandin therapy is especially effective the first 2 weeks, prior to the onset of the menses.[50]

Postcoital contraception also includes the **"morning-after" pill.** Several regimes are used. The medication must be started within 36 to 48 hours of intercourse, and continued for 5 days.[85,122,125] There is a high number of ectopic pregnancies among the 1% to 5% failure rate.[125]

Abortion

Birth control may be extended beyond implantation through the use of abortion. Advocates for or against abortion base their stand on philosophical, religious, ethical, eugenic, social, political, psychological, or medical issues. Opinions regarding abortion can be divided into four major viewpoints,[53] as discussed in the following sections.

No Grounds for Abortion. Some people feel that there are no grounds for termination of a pregnancy; each life is considered sacred and every human has a right to live. Advocates of this view indicate they do not know when an individual becomes uniquely human in the spiritual or emotional domain versus being purely animal in the physical, cognitive, or social sense.

There are many opposing views on the beginning of a valued human life, which these individuals have considered and questioned. Is it (1) during the preschool years, when the child begins to develop a concept of right from wrong; (2) during the toddler years, when the child begins to use language or to develop autonomy from the mother; or (3) at the moment of birth? If birth, then physical separation from the mother would apply to a fetus of any age. However, birth is generally thought of in terms of a full-term infant; thus premature infants may be viewed differently in terms of humanness! (4) Others feel that "life" begins at the point when the fetus is mature enough to sustain extrauterine life. In the medical field, this is usually considered to occur between 24 and 28 weeks of gestation. However, with advances in medical science, younger fetuses are now beginning to survive. (5) Some mothers acknowledge individuality of the fetus when they experience "quickening"—fetal movement at about 20 to 24

weeks. However, fetal movement has been occurring freely since the third month of gestation. (6) Others advocate that since the criteria for death is now based on "brain death," the criteria for life should be based on "brain life." Brain function appears to be present by 8 weeks of gestation based on electroencephalographic readings.[42] They feel the fetus, which is dependent on the placenta at this point, is as much a human as an 80-year-old on a ventilator. (7) Another view is that human life begins when the heart begins to beat (22 days after conception), which is less than 1 week after the first missed menstrual period. It is the ambiguity of these commonly held views on the beginning of human life that leads advocates of this viewpoint to believe that (8) the child is a human entity from the moment of conception.

Medical Grounds for Abortion. When the life of the mother is threatened, those who hold the first view may be forced to reassess priority of right to life. Continuation of a pregnancy may cause the death of both mother and child. Others feel that when there is evidence that the child will be born with a severe physical or mental abnormality, termination is desirable. They feel that the quality of life of the individual and the family is as significant as the principle of life itself, and that support of life at any cost is not a valid goal in and of itself.

Social Grounds for Abortion. Circumstances (e.g., out-of-wedlock pregnancy, rape, incest, maternal age) or other priorities (e.g., financial needs, education, career) may make child-rearing unacceptable. The quality of family life is considered to be significant in this view.

Advocates of the earlier views may feel that social grounds or abortion for "convenience" are unacceptable criteria for abortion and would encourage the woman to respect the human life through childbirth and then to release the child for adoption. However, even going through the pregnancy may cause serious social difficulties that are deemed detrimental to the woman's emotional health.

General Availability of Abortion. Many people feel that abortion should be freely available at the request of the woman for any reason. Persons who believe that all babies should be wanted support the view of "abortion on request" when other methods of birth control have failed. The woman feels that she should have the right to terminate the pregnancy before she has developed a personalized image of the fetus. Pro-life advocates are especially incensed when babies are aborted purely for the convenience of the mother, or because the infant is the "wrong" gender.

Long-term Effects of Abortion. Counseling prior to and after an abortion is essential to help a woman and her partner to explore the issue honestly and holistically, to identify the true reasons for desiring the abortion, and to discuss alternatives.[27,103] Unfortunately, many women are so overwhelmed by the circumstances that they refuse or are unable to fully benefit from counseling.[36] They may indicate an immediate sense of relief to be freed of the pregnancy, but many experience recurring bouts of guilt when they begin to think about events.[36] Feelings of grief and depression are normal and common following abortion. Many women suffer from "post-traumatic stress disorder" following an abortion.[102] This is characterized by sleep disorders, reenactments of the traumatic event, impaired memory and concentration—especially on the anniversary of the abortion. Some women indicate having nightmares and guilt feelings many years after an abortion when the issues have not been adequately resolved. Adolescent women are particularly prone to long-range negative sequela, such as personality disorders, drug abuse, and nightmares.[21] The abortion may become a ghost of the past she must deal with in a subsequent pregnancy, labor, and delivery.[48, 115]

Studies indicate that the incidence of serious post-abortion emotional disturbance is highest when the woman (1) is ambivalent about the decision, (2) is coerced into the decision, (3) is forced to have the abortion because of medical problems, or (4) already has symptoms of severe personality disorganization.[32]

Research indicates that some women who have had elective vaginal abortions with cervical dilation have twice as high a risk of losing subsequent pregnancies as a result of cervical incompetence. There is also a higher rate of complications during pregnancy (e.g., ectopic pregnancy, spontaneous abortion) and higher prematurity and perinatal death rates in subsequent pregnancies.[27, 36, 70]

"Abortion is a far greater dilemma for men than researchers, counselors, and women have even begun to realize."[103] Seventy-five percent express they had a difficult time with the experience, and many report "persistent day and night dreams about the child that never was, and considerable guilt, remorse, and sadness."[103] A man may actually need as much support as the woman to resolve the feelings of loss and emptiness, but is generally forgotten for his role as a father of a lost child. Difficulty with trust, communication, joint problem solving, honesty, true intimacy, and mutual support leaves the issue unresolved for both the woman and the man, leading to failure of 70% of relationships within 1 month of the abortion.[103]

DECISION TO INCREASE THE FAMILY

Biological procreation is not synonymous with true parenthood. Children whose parents choose to have them as an outgrowth of their own abundance, life satisfaction, and creativity are fortunate indeed. Unfortunately, many parents ignore or are grossly ignorant of their influence on their child's development.[3] A parent who is still involved in his or her own identity crisis may not be sufficiently flexible to meet the child's changing needs. Parents who have not yet resolved their own identities may experience much more difficulty in allowing their child to have a separate identity. Developmental level rather than chronological age, then, becomes a critical factor in parenting success.

As indicated earlier, a couple's decision to have children may be strongly influenced by cultural standards—they feel that it is the thing to do after marriage. Such a decision is based on roles rather than goals for the couple. A new family member will change the direction and reciprocity of communication, which can lead either to firmer commitments or to rivalries. Insecurity or weak identity in one parent can be compensated for by the strength of the other, but if the interdependence of the couple is so lopsided that it approaches dependence on the part of one member, it may threaten the success of both the marriage and the potential for parenthood.[56] "The optimal condition for parenthood is marriage based on a compatible partnership, which can reduce the frustration, anxiety, and anger of everyday life to a tolerable minimum and which at the same time can provide a creative reciprocity and spontaneous solidarity."[56]

It is obvious that a couple should assess their financial resources. Will they be able to live on only one income? If both parents want or need to continue working, who will care for the child, and how much will it cost? Will the individual parents be able to complete their own education or career goals? Parenting is easier when these questions have been successfully resolved. A planned pregnancy that has been achieved after careful weighing of both family and personal resources can offer a period of great joy, excitement, anticipation, and strength for the couple.

Though rarely done, a couple should receive counseling before pregnancy in order to ensure the health status of the mother and improve the outcome for the infant.[24] The mother, in particular, needs to be aware of potential risks to herself or the child engendered by health history, life styles, age, nutrition, etc.[24] When prenatal care includes the 3 months before pregnancy as well as the 9 months of pregnancy, the parents are more likely to avoid alcohol, x-rays, drugs, communicable disease, and other factors that may affect the fetus.[14]

Twenty-one percent of births to women over age 30 are a first child.[41] With greater emphasis on career preparation and building, many women are waiting until their late 30s to have the first child. Financial concerns in today's world and the desire to have a child within the context of a late marriage or with a second spouse is also increasing the number of mature women having babies. During the 1980s, births to women over 35 have increased 68%.[124] Although the risk of chromosomal anomalies is increased, when health status, nutrition, and medical support are adequate, they can compensate for the negative effects of issues such as advanced maternal age and short interpregnancy interval.[61, 62]

Pregnancy

Pregnancy is a biologically normal but exceptional period in life. The first sign that a woman has become pregnant is usually a missed menstrual period. Both her physical and psychological responses to this event may be colored by whether it was planned or "accidental," whether she is married or single. For both the man and woman, pregnancy may declare adulthood and independence, verify masculine or feminine role, confirm love, extend dreams, confer status, engender fear, or present major physical, social, or psychological problems (Fig. 30-4).

Signs of Pregnancy

The **presumptive signs** of pregnancy, which appear during the first trimester, are mainly the result of changes in the hormone balance.[58] Other factors, including birth control pills, can cause one or several of the same signs. Consequently, these signs are not definitive indicators of pregnancy: amenorrhea, fatigue, frequency of urination, morning sickness, enlargement and tingling of breasts, weight gain (although some women may lose weight during the first trimester because of nausea and vomiting), increase in basal body temperature.

The **probable signs** of pregnancy usually appear in the second trimester: quickening—movement of the fetus felt by the mother, uterine and abdominal enlargement, Hegar's sign (softening of cervix), positive pregnancy test. Since these symptoms may occasionally appear without a pregnancy, they also are not considered confirmatory. Pseudocyesis (false pregnancy) can replicate the presumptive and probable signs of pregnancy so closely that one third of these individuals may be erroneously diagnosed as pregnant by competent physicians.[5] The symptoms of pseudocyesis are psychogenic in origin; some studies indicate that psychological factors acting on the anterior pituitary can initiate maintenance of the corpus luteum even though conception has not occurred.[5]

The **positive signs** of pregnancy are dependent on confirmation by a qualified health professional. These signs are usually not discernible until the second trimester: auscultation of fetal heart, palpation of fetal parts and movement, visualization of the fetus by ultrasound or x-ray.

Physiological Changes

Pregnancy affects almost every system of the woman's body. The average weight gain is 10 to 12.5 kg. (22–27.5 lbs.), much of which is fluid.[45]

Endocrine System

Increased levels of progesterone and enlargement of the thyroid increase the basal metabolic rate of the body to 20 percent above the non-pregnant state. Progressive hyperinsulinemia (elevated insulin levels) may cause hypoglycemia (low blood sugar), which can lead to fainting and nausea.[26] Many women experience symptoms of diabetes during pregnancy. Having frequent, small, high-protein meals and eating crackers before arising to activity in the morning or after a nap can reduce the symptoms. Nutritional intake needs to be increased to meet the needs of both the mother and the fetus.

Integumentary System

Adrenal, placental and pituitary hormones cause darkening of areas of the skin.[126] The nipple and areola are universal targets for darkening. Many women also develop a line between the umbilicus and the symphysis pubis, known as the *linea nigra*. Pigmentation of the cheeks and forehead is known as *chloasma* or the "mask of pregnancy." Some women merely become more freckled.

The sebaceous and sweat glands become more active, increasing hygienic needs and reactivating acne problems in some women. The increase in total body hair growth may make some women self-conscious. An increased rate of hair loss after the birth of the baby is caused by a sudden decrease in the number of active growing hair follicles in the scalp.

Increased activity of the adrenal cortex may lead to the development of *striae* (stretch marks). Unfortunately, creams do not appear to prevent or to remove these marks, which appear as reddish-purple, wavy, shiny, depressed streaks on the abdomen, buttocks, thighs, and breasts. Many of the stretch marks will disappear after pregnancy, but some will remain as smaller, pale, shiny stripes.

Cardiovascular System

Blood volume increases 45% to 55% to meet the needs of the enlarging breasts and uterus.[4, 26] The non-pregnant woman has approximately 2500 cc of blood, the pregnant woman 3900 cc.[4] This change increases the work load of the heart. The pulse rate may increase about 15 beats per minute[4], but the blood pressure should not change. This blood volume change may be responsible for lightheadedness on arising.

FIGURE 30–4.
Both the father and the mother experience dreams, aspirations, and fears of the future with a new baby. Pregnancy can help to draw the couple closer together. Increasing numbers of mature couples are entering parenthood as a planned experience.

Increased blood volume can also precipitate headaches. Persistent headaches—especially toward the end of pregnancy—should be reported to the physician. Redness of the palms and soles as well as nosebleeds also are attributed to the increased blood flow. Increased blood flow to the vocal cords may cause deepening of the voice and hoarseness.

The increased blood volume, combined with increased uterine size and pressure, can reduce the return flow of blood from the legs and lower areas of the body, which in turn can lead to edema and varicose veins. Elevation of the legs and the use of support hose can alleviate discomfort and prevent problems. Persistent edema, especially toward the end of pregnancy, should be reported to the physician.

Hematocrit and hemoglobin levels may drop quite low during pregnancy because of the dilution of the red blood cells,[26] in spite of a 25% increase in total number of red blood cells.[4] Iron intake should be at least 60 mg daily to ensure that the needs of both mother and fetus are met.[45]

Respiratory System

The total air volume of the lungs increases 40% during pregnancy, facilitating the exchange of oxygen and carbon dioxide with only minimal increase in the respiratory rate.[26] During the third trimester, pressure of the uterus against the diaphragm and rib cage may make the woman feel uncomfortable and short of breath. "Lightening" (tilting and lowering of the uterus during the last weeks of pregnancy) greatly alleviates the discomfort.

Gastrointestinal System

Progesterone appears to relax the walls of the gastrointestinal tract as well as the uterus. Consequently, motility is slowed, and the sphincters are relaxed. As a result, stomach emptying occurs more slowly. Escape of stomach contents into the esophagus may cause heartburn.[126] Increasing uterine size may prevent large meals and interfere with evacuation of the bowel during the last trimester. Increased fluids and dietary bulk can help to alleviate the difficulty. The gums may swell, bleed easily, and develop gingivitis.[126] Good oral hygiene and dental visits are imperative.

Genitourinary System

Pressure of the uterus on the bladder during early pregnancy and again during late pregnancy after lightening may necessitate frequent urination and thus disrupt sleep. The kidney pelves and ureters dilate, leading to stagnation of urine.[126] The relaxing effect of progesterone on the urinary tract sphincters may allow passage of bacteria into the bladder, leading to bladder and kidney infections.

Bed rest allows the fluid accumulated as leg edema to return to the circulatory system, where it can be excreted by the kidneys. The woman's salt intake may be limited by some physicians with the intent of reducing the work load of both the heart and the kidneys. Side-lying positions reduce the pressure of the uterus against the ureters (such pressure can trap the urine in the kidney and cause pain) and against the inferior vena cava (this pressure can slow the return of blood to the heart and cause faintness).

Musculoskeletal System

Progesterone causes softening of the cartilages, especially of the hips and symphysis pubis. Toward the end of pregnancy the mother may appear to "waddle" as a result of loose joints.[126] This loosening allows for expansion of the birth passage during the birth of the baby. The increasing size of the uterus creates strain on the support ligaments, and changes the mother's posture as the center of gravity changes. The resultant backache can be alleviated by mild exercises, low-heeled shoes, and good posture. Muscle cramps of the legs can be stopped by straightening the leg and pressing the toe upward, toward the knee.

Exercise During Pregnancy

Most physicians recommend continued exercises in moderation.[58] Exercise tones and strengthens muscles, increases circulation, decreases varicose veins, and promotes better relaxation and sleep. There is some concern about adequate blood flow to the fetus.[4] Strenuous, weight-bearing exercises can decrease uterine blood flow by as much as 70%[59] and slowed fetal heart rates have been recorded after strenuous or prolonged exercise.[22] Consequently, it is generally recommended that aerobic exercises be limited to those which do not elevate the mother's heart rate above 140 or her temperature more than 1.5 to 2.0°F.[4,30] Liquids should be taken frequently and activity limited to 15 minute segments.

It is recommended that the mother limit walking to 2 miles per day during the first trimester, and 1.5 to 2.5 miles per day thereafter.[4] Jogging is contraindicated if the temperature or humidity is high. Mothers should warm up and cool down slowly to prevent stress to the fetus. Stationary bicycles are considered safe and swimming is promoted as the "perfect exercise."[4] However, jacuzzi baths in temperatures above 38.5°C are potentially dangerous to the fetus.[4]

The mother should be cautioned against jerky, bouncing movements or any activity that may allow air to enter the vagina (e.g., shoulder standing, bicycle pump, knee-chest and abductor stretching), since this may precipitate an air embolism and death.[30] Double leg raises and sit-ups can split the weakened abdominal muscles.[30] The physician should be consulted immediately for any unusual effects following exercise (e.g., dizziness, uterine contractions, spotting, tachycardia, headache, decreased fetal activity).

Women are encouraged to wear lap-shoulder seat belts with the strap across the hips—not across the uterus when riding in cars.[58]

Psychosocial Changes in the Expectant Couple

Pregnancy is a critical phase in the life span of the couple, requiring psychological adaptations leading to new levels of integration that normally represent development. Pregnancy is a normal developmental event; however, one "becomes a parent" only once in a lifetime.[99] With subsequent pregnancies, one is already a parent. As with any new experience, the couple usually finds the adaptive and integrative tasks to be more difficult with the first child. This situation may be compounded by a lack of exposure to child care during their developmental years. Parenthood offers an opportunity for personal and social growth. However, it can also be traumatic to those who have not accomplished successfully the earlier developmental tasks.

If the pregnancy was planned, and if the child is wanted by both parents (not all planned pregnancies are really wanted), "the oneness of the pregnant woman with her mate encompasses their yet unborn child, creating the psychodynamic foundation of the triad: father-mother-child."[8] This confirmation of the couple's love can deepen the bond between them. Both of them will begin to fantasize and to identify with a dream of their child to be. On the other hand, insecurity about the foundations of one's identity and ambivalence toward the pregnancy may undermine the meaning of the marriage and affect the emotional climate awaiting the unborn child. Second-time mothers find themselves so involved in the daily activities of the first child that they spend less time thinking about and preparing for the second child.[81]

Since parenthood implies a lifelong commitment, the parents may feel trapped, unable to return to their own childhood and interests. Other expectant parents may "revive their memories of childhood and discover a new order of reconciliation with their parents within their own experience of becoming parents."[56] Interests and social relationships change as the couple assumes a new family identity.

Psychosocial Changes in the Pregnant Woman

The pregnant woman is frequently described as being moody and emotionally labile.[66] The constant redefining and integrative tasks absorb much of her emotional energy. The task is easier if the pregnancy was planned and she has a supportive, encouraging family.[18] Women need much support and emotional input during their pregnancy; it is as if they are storing up emotional energy to share later with the neonate. Stressors and anxieties can interfere with this process. Fortunately for the pregnant woman, many other people who accept her pregnancy positively also become protective of her. They are concerned about fatiguing work, her diet, and her comfort. They may even treat her as if she were marginally ill, encouraging her to rest and to avoid bad news and generally pampering her. People she has never met may strike up a conversation centering on her pregnancy. Some women resent this personal intrusion; others welcome the attention.

The classic studies of Grete Bibring[9] on psychological processes during pregnancy indicate that pregnancy is a crisis precipitating profound psychological as well as somatic changes. Bibring observed that many women exhibit symptoms of "borderline psychosis" during pregnancy even if they appear to have had good mental health prior to pregnancy and want the baby very much. A first pregnancy is a very

cosmic experience. Most women are in awe of the conception. "They are the pregnancy, and the pregnancy is them."[48] Pregnancy heralds a point of no return;[10] the woman can no longer return to her nonpregnant, never-pregnant self. Acute disequilibrium may accompany her attempts to reorganize her self-concept. This phenomenon should be viewed as a normal developmental process that is essential to assuming a new identity and a new role. This disequilibrium is especially poignant in the change from "Mary" to "mother," or with the first pregnancy.

The pregnant woman emerges from this phase with a new relationship with herself. Pregnancy can reactivate previously unresolved or partially resolved developmental conflicts. The reintegration of the past, present, and future can lead to maturation. The pregnant woman needs extra support and encouragement during this time in order to recognize, to resolve, and to enjoy the developmental phenomena peculiar to pregnancy. The course of the postpartum period is based on the ego strength of the woman, her relationship to her mother, and the quality of the marital support she receives.[48] The person who has not worked through these crises may find the parent-infant relationship unsatisfying. An unhappy marriage increases the probability of postpartum depression.[48] The more egalitarian marital styles increase the flexibility of roles and therefore ego strength and comfort.

Psychoanalytical studies indicate that increases in the progesterone levels during pregnancy cause the woman to have an increased sense of relaxation and well-being. This phenomenon is also associated with a decrease in anxieties and a retentive tendency, leading to increases in self-centeredness, primary narcissism, and fantasies.[8] A spontaneous interest in her own past, other children and babies, and looking at baby books helps the woman to develop a more concrete image of her fantasized child. This fosters an attachment to the unborn child and facilitates bonding after birth. She will rub her abdomen to touch fetal parts or to soothe the fetus,[88] she may sing, read, or play music for it. Many parents give the baby a nickname to help personalize the relationship.[66] There is much professional interest in stimulating mother-infant attachment before birth as a way to prevent child abuse.[39]

Women over age 35 appear to view pregnancy in a much more deliberate and thoughtful way than the younger mother, often approaching it as a "project."[124] They have planned and been in control of other aspects of their lives, and they continue to use the same approach to pregnancy. They plan for "the right time," obtain maximal relevant information, assume responsibility for optimal prenatal care, savor the experience and work at integrating their concept of motherhood into their expanded self-image.[124]

Reva Rubin has identified two mutually independent but highly correlated questions that modify perception of stimuli and behavior throughout pregnancy.[101] The first deals with the woman's perception of time within the life space, presupposing that the woman wants a child "someday." The second question is concerned with the woman's personal sense of identity—her femininity or womanhood, which is established by the biological fulfillment of pregnancy. These two questions can be followed through five separate stages of the childbearing process, as discussed in the following sections (Table 30-2).

Prepregnancy

"Someday" is seen in the abstract future. A woman who has never achieved a pregnancy may question her sexual and procreative ability. Even a woman who has achieved one pregnancy may feel that it was accidental and may want a second pregnancy to prove her functional ability.

First Trimester

The first missed menses and the awareness of potential pregnancy come as a shock. "Who, me? Now?" Even the woman desirous of the pregnancy may become aware of other priorities that need to be attended to before the addition of a family member. Financial resources, educational and career goals, and other plans suddenly assume major importance. The ramifications of childbirth and parenting may suddenly seem overwhelming, and the woman may question her motives, wondering if it is too late to back out. The pregnancy offers proof of her sexuality and reassurance against the fear of infertility. However, the wish to be pregnant may not be synonymous with the desire to have a child or to become a mother. The lack of positive signs at this stage makes the woman look inward for evidence of proof of the pregnancy. The lack of concrete evidence may prevent her from telling others for fear that just the telling will prevent its occurrence, or she may proudly announce that she is pregnant, yet secretly fear (or hope) that she is not. She may be ecstatic, afraid, disbelieving, or resigned. Each woman is unique in her reaction and her level of acceptance.

Second Trimester

When the baby begins to move, it becomes a physical reality to the woman. The movement signifies a form of communication between them, and mothers-to-be begin the process of attachment to the fetus.[23] The abdomen enlarges to the extent that maternity clothing becomes necessary. Others become aware of her pregnancy, whether she has told them or not. "Yes, it has happened to me! Now!" The woman who is unable to accept her pregnant state may refuse to wear maternity clothes until the third trimester.

This stage offers several tasks that are unique to pregnancy:[56]

1. The woman becomes acutely aware of herself as a link between the past and the future. The life-cycle assumes a new perspective.
2. She needs to redefine femininity and body image.
3. Reassessment of life-span role and maturity level leads to a new self-identity.
4. Personal and family goals will need to be reassessed in light of resources and new responsibilities.
5. Marital and parental relationships are reassessed. Some wives (and husbands) become acutely aware that they will never again be alone with their spouse.

Third Trimester

The fantasy image of the unborn child becomes very real during the third trimester. The woman may fear the baby's loss and may become very protective of herself both physically and psychologically. "Me" changes to "us." She wants the "someday" to be "now!" Time seems to pass slowly. The woman keeps herself busy to keep from thinking about the baby, but her thoughts are constantly there. Mothers are noted to touch and rub their abdomens during the third trimester. Those who make this gentle massaging and stroking a daily occurrence show greater comfort with, touching of, and talking to their babies after birth.[23] Such activity appears to strengthen the bonding process by facilitating recognition of the reality of the child's growth[116] and individuality. Many mothers prepare themselves for childbirth and motherhood by attending classes; others are unable to project themselves beyond the delivery. Lack of preparation for the baby may signify a disbelief on the part of the woman in her ability to produce a child, or an unconscious rejection of the child.[56] Women in some cultural groups do not obtain baby supplies until after the birth, feeling that it would bring bad luck.

About 30% of pregnant women suffer mild depression, and almost 20% have moderate to severe depression during pregnancy.[31] This may be a reaction to a sense of inadequacy

TABLE 30–2. PSYCHOSOCIAL CHANGES OF PREGNANCY

Stages of the Childbearing Process	"Life-Space" (Timing)	Personal Sense of Identity
Prepregnancy	Someday (abstract future)	Can I?
First trimester	Not now! (someday)	Who—me?
Second trimester	Now!	Yes, me!
Third trimester	Make someday now!	Me—us
Labor	Now?	Who—me?
Delivery	Questions resolved	

as a mother, or a continuation of preexisting emotional problems. Many women express anxiety that they are unprepared and will not be as good a parent as their own mother.[40] The woman may fear the birth of a defective child or may fear her own death during childbirth. As delivery draws closer, these thoughts may increase or may become submerged under thoughts of the immediacy of her child-to-be. Toward the end of pregnancy, some mothers may feel that the fetus is an enemy. They find the kicking painful, and breathing difficult. The antagonism may be aggravated by lack of sleep caused by the movement of the fetus when the mother lies down to rest. Prenatal depression, regardless of cause, has a close correlation with postpartal depression.[31] A poor marital relationship appears to predispose the mother to depression, and a good relationship appears to insulate her from depression.[31]

During the last month, most mothers become impatient and anxious for the physical separation. They want to see their baby, to hold it in their arms, to assume a new form of love and communication. Many express the idea that they feel like a child waiting for a Christmas gift. Many mothers have a burst of energy toward the end of pregnancy and often spend considerable time cleaning and preparing the home as if a significant guest is about to arrive.

Labor and Delivery

The woman frequently returns to the same three questions during labor and delivery. During the early stages she again asks, "Who, me? Not now—someday." After waiting so long, it is hard for her to believe the time has finally arrived. When labor is active she becomes very assured that "It is **me** and it is **now!**" Toward the end of labor, the mother is saying, "Make it now! Let there be a separation of us!" The questions are resolved with the reality of the delivery.

Psychosocial Changes in the Expectant Father

Fatherhood is not synonymous with motherhood. Fatherhood is socially and emotionally significant in its own right. The culture and childhood experiences do not prepare men for parenthood in the same way it prepares women. Men are much less likely than women to see parenting as an integral part of their gender role.[82] The provider and protector roles are emphasized more than the creative and nurturing roles. As a result, pregnancy may become an emotional experience fraught with ambivalence for the father as well as the mother.[88]

Fathers indicate that their mate's pregnancy touches virtually every facet of living, including their self-image, their role as a husband, their social contacts, and even their work relationships. Like mothers, fathers are concerned about loss of free time, their ability to meet the child's needs, career conflicts, and their ability to adjust to marital and life-style changes with a baby.[52,114] Their concerns over possible defects are as great as women's during the pregnancy.[96,105] Even though it may engender fears regarding the financial security of the home, the woman's pregnancy is almost always a source of pride to the man; he sees it as evidence of his power to share in the creation of life and of his masculinity. Many men

become more health conscious (e.g., a decrease in smoking). They feel the need to take care of themselves so they will be ready for the new responsibility.[96] Some fathers may feel a sense of envy or jealousy over the wife's ability to carry their child, sometimes precipitating dreams about changes in his own body, even imagining the pregnancy experience.[88] Most men feel that they will be as good, or a better parent, than their own father.[40]

Changes in gender-related, culturally imposed roles and physical removal from the extended family both allow and require the man to become more involved in his partner's pregnancy. The degree of involvement is dependent on developmental level, personal style, and the marital relationship. Three detachment/involvement styles adopted during pregnancy have been identified:[76]

1. THE OBSERVER STYLE: This is the wife's pregnancy. He may be supportive, but does not interfere in what he considers to be her domain of decision making. There is minimal emotional investment in the pregnancy even though he may be proud to be expecting a family increase.

2. THE INSTRUMENTAL STYLE: It is his responsibility to organize, coordinate, manage events. Clinic appointments and childbirth classes are attended as a part of his "responsibilities," not for the "experience" of sharing with his partner.

3. THE EXPRESSIVE STYLE: "We are pregnant." There is a sense of mutuality and full involvement in events. This father tries to share, experience, and sensitively support the mother in every way possible.

The tough, domineering, unemotional "real man" portrayed by the mass media may put the father in conflict with how he really wants to act and to react. He may question his own gender identity, feeling that he will be seen as effeminate if he is "soft."[19] This reaction may prevent him from giving his wife the tenderness and sensitive support she needs during this time.

There are three basic orientations that can strongly influence the man's response to and involvement in pregnancy:[11,56]

1. The man with an immature **romantic orientation** to his mate may experience a sharp maturational crisis with the advent of pregnancy. The need to assume more and new responsibilities may leave him with a sense of awe. He is frightened by the threatened loss of freedom. His casualness may precipitate marital and in-law crises. Juvenile notions of masculinity may be reassessed. The need for renewed identity homework may be extremely difficult. He may find his wife's changing figure less attractive, even repulsive. Fortunately, only about 5% of men feel negatively about the changes.[40]

2. The **career-oriented** man may resent the intrusion of the pregnancy, feeling that "it" is a burden that will interfere with his life goals. This is especially true if he is

still engaged in educational preparations. His more ritualistic approach to life makes him want to retain the locus of control. He may see his old self to be quite adequate and will resist changes in his self-identity, especially when imposed by his wife, in-laws, and friends. He tends to continue old habits including motorcycling and camping with his wife. A detached attitude is common. The pregnancy is his wife's career, not his. Men who experience little interest in having children usually have very negative memories of their own parents.[40]

3. The **family-oriented** man accepts pregnancy as a gift. Fatherhood is an avenue to fulfillment of life. He assumes anticipatory fatherhood behaviors during the pregnancy. He thrills at the changes in his wife. Together they watch and feel the baby move, look at and read books, and attend parenting classes. Like the mother, he begins to watch other children more, to seek out couples with children, to talk to other people's babies, and to ask questions of his own parents. Development of an expanded self-identity is easier by his participation in the pregnancy and his anticipation of new responsibilities. The relationship with his wife evolves into a new and richer partnership (Fig. 30-5).

Regardless of their orientation, some men feel that they lose their own identity as the woman's pregnancy becomes the focus of their lifestyle, attention and conversation by friends and relatives. He may feel left out and insignificant unless health care agencies, family, and friends consciously include him in the preparation and interests. He may feel that

FIGURE 30–5.
The father can be an active member of the pregnancy. Both the father and the mother begin to know their baby before it is born by noting its activity level and response to stimuli. Such shared experiences help to prepare them for the emotional investment that is essential to the infant's (and their own) socio-affective development in the months ahead.

the obstetrician has replaced him in importance to his wife and may come to resent the pregnancy and the child. Some men will cover up or deny their reactions by becoming over involved in work or initiating their own creative project (write book, raise dogs, plant garden, etc.) as a way to compensate for rivalrous feelings.[90] Participation in prenatal classes or father's groups that explore men's feelings and the couple's relationship can help men to work through feelings precipitated by the pregnancy, improve marital quality, and enhance bonding to the baby.[114]

The Couvade Syndrome

Twenty percent to twenty-five percent of men may identify so closely with the woman's pregnancy that they develop symptoms mimicking pregnancy or develop other physical problems.[59, 117] Some researchers report that the incidence may be as high as 65% of men.[78] Loss of appetite, toothache, nausea, vomiting, food cravings, and weight gain are common—even abdominal pain and distention. Some professionals feel that the symptoms are an unconscious bid for continued time and attention spawned by a reevaluation of his own needs for support, nurturance, and dependency,[90] or a result of envy of the woman's ability to conceive.[78, 90] Other professionals feel that the majority of symptoms appear to be caused by anxiety (usually unperceived) felt by the man for the woman.[117] Because men tend to keep concerns and feelings to themselves, they may feel isolated or alienated.[78, 90] Still others see the couvade syndrome as a positive identification on the part of the man with what the woman is experiencing.[78] A fourth view "reflects the male's identification with the nurturant side of himself in response to pregnancy," but he may not know how to activate his feelings.[77, 78] Occasionally, other relatives, including siblings of the baby-to-be may experience an increase of physical problems. The man may be very sensitive to any teasing about his symptoms and needs a warm and accepting approach from anyone trying to help him to handle his symptoms. Medical personnel need to take the couple's pregnancy into account when planning any medical care for the father.[78] Almost 30% of men experience depression during their wife's pregnancy, and almost 50% report a reduction in self-esteem![90] Like the wife, he is reworking his identity and spousal relationship.

Sex During Pregnancy

Most couples experience changes in their sexual relationship after the advent of pregnancy. Changes in hormonal balance cause some women to lose sexual interest during the first trimester.[108] The husband may be puzzled or feel rejected by her passivity. During the second trimester, many women desire more sexual activity.[74, 88, 108] By now, the man may feel it is immoral, improper, or unclean to have sex during pregnancy, and experience guilt for desiring her.[108] Superstitions and fears of fetal loss or damage discourage some couples.[90] For some men, abstinence may be seen as an excuse to seek extramarital affairs. For others, it may be the "ultimate sacrifice" to ensure a successful birth.[96] Intercourse becomes increasingly awkward as the pregnancy advances. A broad repertoire of techniques and alternatives as well as a sense of humor can help the couple through the later months.

The woman's changing body shape requires a redefinition of body image and sexuality for both the pregnant woman and her mate. Some men find the pregnant woman to be attractive and desirable; others find her grossly repulsive. The latter attitude can create great strain on the union. The woman likewise may feel herself to be very attractive, or she may feel "like an elephant." Her self-concept will affect the relationship with her partner.

Most physicians place no sexual restrictions on their couples as long as they are comfortable and there are no cervical changes. This approach is appreciated by the couple who experience heightened sexual drive with the onset of early labor. Most women (over 80%) report no pain during intercourse.[110] Other pregnant women may experience a sense of fullness or even pain for as long as 30 minutes after sexual arousal.[43] Orgasm in the female is associated with uterine contractions.[13] Consequently, women who are prone to spontaneous abortion in early pregnancy may be advised to avoid orgasms. Research indicates that orgasm in late pregnancy may increase Braxton-Hicks contractions or even lead to premature labor.[43] In fact, some cultures use the stimulation of orgasm as a method to induce labor.

Abstinence may be recommended by some physicians for the last 2 to 6 weeks of pregnancy because of the possibility of infection, premature rupture of the membranes, or bleeding.[27] Although rare, there is some evidence that air may be introduced into the vagina during sexual foreplay or douching, which can lead to death of the mother as a result of air embolism.[27,43] These dangers may require reassessment of priorities and sexuality for the couple.

INFERTILITY

Infertility, the inability to achieve a pregnancy after one year of sexual relations without contraception, is a problem for 20% to 25% of couples today.[7,27] About 40% of infertility problems are of male origin, and 40% of female origin. The other 20% are of combined problems or of unknown origin.[28] Couples who have never produced a child are said to have **primary infertility.** Couples who have conceived at least once are classified under **secondary infertility.** The term **sterility** is reserved for those conditions producing irreversible infertility.

Females usually achieve maximum fertility at about age 24 and males at age 25.[28] Fertility rates begin to diminish rapidly in females after age 30 and in males after age 45, although men in their eighties have been known to father children.

Response of the Couple to Infertility

Approximately 95% of newly married couples expect to have their own children someday.[75] The fact of infertility comes as a shock and constitutes a critical and complex life crisis. How does one master Erikson's task of generativity without someone to guide, love, and protect?[80,109] The individuals involved feel as if the future is out of their control. This forced helplessness is a grave threat to ego-identity and integrity. Infertility may also pose a threat to the individual's sexual integrity, necessitating a redefining of sexuality as well as of roles, goals, and worthiness.[69,75,107] These internal stressors, combined with the external social, cultural, and family pressures to have children, may precipitate a psychological crisis that can be severe enough to interfere with functioning in all five domains. The woman may feel that she has been "cheated" out of her career. The man may feel guilty for "theft" of the woman's rights.[79]

Involuntary infertility is the loss of a dream, hopes, and plans for the future.[107] Each month the hope builds against increasing odds, only to crumble along with the disintegrating endometrium. Each may feel intense pain or grief, yet there is no socially recognized way to express the loss or to vent the anger and frustration.[80,107] Discussing one's feelings with friends and family who may not understand the fears, agony, or confusion in facing the unknown, leaves the infertile person open to unwanted pity, patronization, or trivialization of the crisis. Consequently, most carry their burdens alone, talking only with each other and medical personnel. Suddenly the most intimate details of their life must be recorded and discussed. Spontaneity and romance give way to a perfunctory, clinical approach in the bedroom, increasing the stress on the couple.[94] Infertility regimes can be time consuming and exhausting, invading thoughts and disrupting the routine activities of daily living. They become vulnerable to every "cure" no matter how silly or ridiculous.[94]

When infertility persists, despite rigorous and expensive efforts to identify and correct the problem, "nascent hope (is) followed by depressing frustration and despair."[17] The woman, because social forces inculcate motherhood since birth, generally has more emotional struggle/upheaval than the man.[111] Anger and grief can be overwhelming as the couple let go of the child they will never have, rework their internal identity, readjust role commitments, and decide upon what course of action is best for them. The need to redefine themselves, the meaning and purpose of their marriage, and the realities of life bring half of the couples closer together.[46] The couples are challenged to separate their self-esteem and sexuality from child bearing,[107] a factor which can lead to higher levels of self-knowledge and more mature identity. A self-help organization, RESOLVE (5 Water St., Dept. A., Arlington, MA 02174), offers infertile couples throughout North America information, referrals, and support.

Causes of Infertility

Infertility has increased from one out of nine to one out of four to five couples in the last generation. Increased sexual freedom has lead to a corresponding rise in venereal diseases, many of which go undetected until damage is done to the reproductive system. Career stress, legalized abortion, and planned delays in childbearing also contribute to the increase.[7] In 1965, 76% of women had borne their first child by their 25th birthday. In 1985, only 39% had done so.[63]

Eighty percent or more of infertile couples can be "cured" with today's technology. The solution may be as simple as gaining a better understanding of anatomy and the process of conception. Others may require medical or surgical assistance or even psychotherapy. Success rates depend on many factors: age of mother, length of infertility, causes, options available, etc. During the first visit for infertility assistance, the husband and wife are usually counseled about male and female anatomy (see Chap. 3) and coital techniques. Occasionally couples are identified who have not achieved full male penetration, even after several years of marriage. Some women routinely douche immediately before coitus: the resulting change in pH may prevent conception by killing the sperm.

The couple is also counseled on the ovarian cycle (see Chap. 3) and the viability of the ovum. Some couples have thought that the fertile period occurred at the end of the menses, like the estrus cycle of a cat or a dog. A clear understanding of the timing of coitus in relation to ovulation may be sufficient to achieve a pregnancy. The woman is usually given a chart to keep a record of her early morning temperature in order to identify an ovulatory pattern (see Fig. 30-3). A computerized thermometer (Rabbit ©, 1-800-999-1220, extension L) can help a couple to identify the fertile period without elaborate chart keeping. A newly marketed urine test (First Response {TM} by Tampax) purports to identify ovulation 12 to 24 hours *before* it occurs. Evaluation of spinnbarkeit is also an excellent way for a couple to identify the fertile period.

The husband and wife are asked to implement any new information they may have obtained at the interview. The couple should also obtain a complete medical checkup and examination of the reproductive system to rule out any obvious organic causes of infertility. Subsequent visits are under the direct supervision of a medical doctor.

Male Factors

The doctor will usually request a semen analysis to check male fertility. This specimen is easily obtained from the man by wearing a condom during intercourse or through self-stimulation and ejaculation into a clean receptacle. The average volume is 3 ml per ejaculate (less than 1 teaspoon), with about 100,000 sperm per cubic centimeter. All the sperm are not completely or well formed (morphology), but at least 60% must be normal in order to achieve a pregnancy (Table 30-3). If the results from the semen analysis are poor, some changes in environmental factors may lead to improvement. Attention to adequate diet and vitamins may improve morphology. Thyroid extract can improve the concentration. Alcohol consumption, smoking, and street drugs are suspected of causing some types of infertility.

Motility of the sperm can be affected by heat. The testes develop in the fetal abdominal cavity and descend into the scrotal sac before or shortly after birth. The scrotum is a physiologically active muscle covering the testes and spermatic cords that maintains the testicular temperature approximately 2.2°C lower than the abdominal temperature. As body temperature increases because of exercise or environmental temperature, the scrotum relaxes and allows the testes to be lowered and cooled. In cooler conditions, the scrotum draws the testes close to the body to maintain their temperature. Exposure to heat can damage developing sperm; recovery may require 2 to 3 months. Repeated exposure to high temperatures can cause permanent damage. Counseling can frequently identify heat-related causes of decreased motility; for example, the man may have been taking frequent very hot baths, wearing jockey shorts or an athletic support. A Testicular Hypothermia Device has been approved by the FDA for helping men to reduce testicular temperature.[71] Other common preventable causes of male infertility include exposure to heavy metals (lead, iron, zinc, copper) or gas fumes, and obesity.[7]

Common preventable causes of male sterility includes postpubertal mumps, exposure to x-rays, undescended testicles, and venereal disease.

Female Factors

One of the first goals of the physician is to discover whether the woman is ovulating. Evaluation of the temperature chart can give some clues: The first and last half of an anovulatory cycle may show minimal change in average temperature. Most

TABLE 30–3. NORMAL SEMEN ANALYSIS

Factor	Normal Values	Lowest Value Needed to Achieve Conception
Volume	2–5 mL	1 mL
Motility		
Percentage	More than 60%	50%
Rate (evaluated on a scale of 1–10)	8–10	5
Concentration	40–250 million/mL	20 million/mL
Total sperm count	Variable	50,000,000/ejaculate
Morphology	More than 70% normal and mature sperm	60% normal and mature sperm

women experience one or two anovulatory cycles per year. Two medications are available to stimulate the ovulatory function of the ovary. Injections of menotropins (Pergonal) followed by HCG stimulate growth and maturation of the graafian follicle. Chlomiphene citrate (Clomid), taken orally, stimulates the pituitary to release FSH. Both treatments, especially Pergonal, are associated with a 10 times higher than average multiple birth rate because of multiple ovulation.[86]

A second major cause of female infertility, blockage of the fallopian tubes owing to a previous infection (especially gonorrhea), pelvic inflammatory disease, or endometriosis, can be identified through relatively simple procedures. The success rate of surgical repair is variable, depending heavily on the extent of the damage.

Women who are able to conceive but have difficulty maintaining the pregnancy may be assisted by hormonal therapy (progesterone) during the first trimester. Spontaneous abortion caused by an incompetent cervix may be prevented by suturing of the cervix until term.

Common preventable causes of female infertility or sterility include jogging over 30 miles per week, being under weight, obesity, using street drugs, and venereal diseases.

Male-Female Problems

Some infertility problems result from the unique combination of two otherwise normal individuals. A high percentage of joint infertility is caused by antigen-antibody reaction: The woman's body may form antibodies against the husband's semen, thus killing the sperm.[29] Diagnosis is made by microscopic evaluation of semen removed from the vagina approximately 1 hour after intercourse. The antibody level can be reduced by preventing contact for 3 to 12 months (most couples prefer to use a condom rather than abstinence). The cervical mucous can be bypassed by artificial insemination with the husband's sperm (AIH).

Faulty understanding of spermatogenesis may also decrease the chances of pregnancy. A couple may attempt to "save up" sperm by avoiding intercourse until the time of ovulation. Since sperm have a high mortality rate after 3 weeks of storage, the couple may actually be implanting only dead sperm. On the other hand, the couple may have intercourse daily or several times daily around the time of ovulation. Because of inadequate opportunity to build up a reserve supply, the total sperm count may be too low to achieve a pregnancy. Couples are usually encouraged to maintain a normal pattern of sexual activity throughout the month and then to have intercourse every other day around the time of ovulation as indicated by the temperature chart.[28] The woman is also encouraged to remain on her back for at least 30 minutes after intercourse to facilitate bathing of the cervix with the semen.

Psychogenic Infertility

Occasionally, infertility can be the result of an unconscious desire to avoid parenthood, even though on the conscious level the individual may express an intense desire for pregnancy. Emotional factors can produce physiological changes (e.g., tubal spasm, anovulation, reduced sperm count), which can prevent conception.[100] Some individuals may subtly avoid coitus during potentially fertile times. Counseling can be very helpful in identifying their true feelings. Women may fear dying in childbirth or having an abnormal child; they may also be afraid of losing their mate during pregnancy because of decreased attractiveness or after the birth because of competition. Both male and female infertility may stem from hostility or marked ambivalence toward one's own mother[100] as well as week self-identity. Psychotherapy and reeducation in interpersonal relationships may help such persons to resolve old conflicts and resulting guilt, thus enabling the individual to achieve pregnancy and meet parenthood responsibilities more successfully.

Alternatives

Artificial Insemination

Artificial insemination with the husband's sperm (AIH) can be used when the man's sperm count or concentration is low. The husband's semen is centrifuged to increase the concentration and then frozen in nitrogen vapor until needed. Pregnancy may be achieved if sperm from three or four ejaculates are concentrated and combined. Frozen sperm may maintain motility indefinitely; a woman in England conceived a child through AIH 8 months after her husband's death.[2]

If the husband's semen analysis is very poor, the couple may choose artificial insemination with donor sperm (AID). Because of the religious, ethical, and legal issues involved, intensive counseling should accompany this form of semiadoption. The physician usually chooses a donor who is physically similar to the husband. Mixing of the husband's semen with that of the anonymous donor frequently helps to offset adverse psychological reactions. Because so many diseases (e.g., AIDS, syphilis, hepatitis) can be passed through the semen, most physicians prefer to use frozen and tested rather than fresh semen.[73]

Sperm banks have been established as repositories for donor sperm. One of these banks specializes in storing sperm of Nobel Prize winners and other eminent, intelligent men.[2]

In Vitro Fertilization (IVF)

The advances in medical science now allow a physician to remove a ripe ovum from the ovary, mix it with sperm, allow it to grow briefly (2 to 8 cell stage), and then place it in a woman's uterus (test tube babies).[72] There is a 20% to 25% success rate with this method,[57, 112] a rate which can be increased when 2 or more embryos are implanted at the same time.[72]

Gamete Intrafallopian Transfer (GIFT)

GIFT is similar to IVF in the retrieval of ova and joining of sperm, but the conceptus is placed in the fallopian tube where it can continue the normal transport and implantation process. Success rates are higher with GIFT than with IVF (Fig. 30-6).

FIGURE 30–6.
Reprinted courtesy of Jim Borgman. Copyright King Features Syndicate, Inc.

Surrogate Motherhood

Surrogate motherhood, the bearing of a child for a couple because of the wife's infertility, is as old as history itself.[44] Although a pregnancy can be established and maintained until term through hormone replacement when a woman has no ovaries[87], if she has no uterus, then the couple may opt to "rent" a womb for IVF, or a woman may agree to artificial insemination with a man's sperm with the purpose of releasing the baby to the man and his wife after birth. Some women agree to this because they truly enjoy pregnancy, or out of an unselfish desire to help others; others because they see it as a way to earn money.[91] There are many legal as well as moral and religious issues raised. The surrogate mother often needs counseling to help her to resolve the loss.

Lavage and Implantation

Some couples are opting for another form of semi-adoption or surrogacy. If the wife has blocked fallopian tubes or a problem with ovum production, then the husband's sperm may be used to fertilize another woman's ovum. Before the conceptus is able to implant in the donor endometrium, it is "washed" from her uterus and placed in the uterus of the sperm donor's wife.[60]

Other

The future may see other alternatives emerge. One offers a viable option for women who wish to postpone childbearing until their career is well established. Through IVF or lavage, a conceptus is obtained and frozen until the woman is ready to host the fetus. In this way she can avoid some of the problems associated with the aging ovum.

Some persons have talked about the possibility of cloning—a procedure which is still in the science fiction stage.[60] A current possibility, though fraught with risk, is the implantation of the young embryo onto the intestine of a woman or man. The placenta would attach to the bowel, and birth would occur by Cesarean section.[60]

Adoption

Each year in the United States, about three million couples decide to increase their family through adoption.[94] Again, intensive counseling is advised in this situation. By the time the infertile couple is willing to admit their situation and consider adoption, they often face feelings of desperation, helplessness, and low self-esteem. They may be financially and emotionally exhausted when they apply for adoption. They frequently feel lonely and isolated. Individuals who have children (or who do not want children) do not understand the emotional pain the couple is experiencing and may offer platitudes rather than real support. Couples are often embarrassed to discuss their infertility even with each other, let alone with parents or friends. Misinformation may prolong the delay in seeking professional help. Friends and family may suggest that the infertility is "all in the head" or that the couple just needs a change of pace or a second honeymoon. The woman may feel shame and guilt that she is "not fulfilled" and the man because he is "not virile." These reactions need to be resolved.

Couples (and some single persons) can legally adopt children through agencies or private sources. The decline in the number of children available for adoption, however, may constitute still another threat to the psychological health of the infertile couple, because this situation once more places them out of control of their own destiny. Anxiety is increased even more when they realize that agencies concentrate on finding the right family for the child rather than vice versa.[6] They wonder if they can "measure up," and may begin to strive for perfection, to play roles, thus increasing stress and potentially reducing intimacy.

All states designate a division of the welfare department or children's services to handle adoptions. Private agencies also offer adoption services. Although each agency sets its own policies, procedures, and price, each is subject to state law. Private adoptions are legal in some states and may be arranged through a lawyer or a physician. The cost of private adoptions is generally higher. "Open adoptions" are increasingly popular. The birth mother and adoptive parents meet, often before birth. The adoptive parents may attend the labor and delivery of the baby.[25] The birth mother may request contact with the parents and baby in the years ahead. State agencies usually offer the couple greater security; occasionally private adoptions may be challenged because of legal loopholes or inadequate release procedures.

Most states require an adjustment period of 6 months to 1 year before the adoption can be finalized. The couple may see this as another anxiety-producing situation, fearing that the child with whom they are falling in love may be removed from their home (which is, however, very rare).

Couples who are unwilling to wait 3 to 5 years for an infant may choose to adopt an older child, a biracial child, or a "handicapped" child. More than half of adopted children are over 2 years of age.[6] Some states have subsidized adoption plans that will assist the couple with the medical expenses of a physically disabled child. About 10% of couples choose an international adoption—around 9000 per year.[6]

Adoption presents an emotional barrier to some couples who feel strongly about blood lines or whose concept of sexuality is tied to their ability to procreate. Such a couple may need to redefine their concept of sexuality as well as their values, priorities, and goals. Unsound motives for adoption and unresolved conflicts about infertility may affect the quality of the parent-child relationship. The chances of success in adoption are as great as those with natural-born children when the parents have accepted their infertility realistically, without guilt or other anxiety, and when the child is accepted unreservedly as an individual to be loved, nurtured, guided, and enjoyed.

IMPLICATIONS

There is a major gap between the medical technologies of the 1990s and cultural values.[123] The process of marital unity, procreation, childbearing, and child rearing no longer need

to be seen as one. The links can be substituted at any point. This raises ethical, religious, medical, and legal issues for each couple and even for society. We do not yet have legal or cultural guidelines or principles to help with the decisions involved. Even religious organizations are just beginning to face the reality of these options in light of their philosophical stance. A husband's sperm may fertilize a donor's ovum and be implanted in the wife.[87] A husband's sperm and a wife's ovum may even be implanted in a surrogate mother after conception to bypass the problem of habitual abortion. The medical possibilities for infertile couples are endless. Many medical centers are now freezing young embryos for implantation at a later date when the uterus is more prepared to receive it, or as a backup in case of failure of the first implant.[72] What is the legal status of a frozen embryo if the parents die before implantation? The Australian state legislature ruled they were to go anonymously to prospective parents.[64] Tennessee Judge W. Dale Young ruled in September of 1989 that life began at conception, and subsequently gave custody of seven frozen embryos to the wife in a divorce case.

Procreation is not synonymous with parenthood. Successful parenthood requires sufficient personal maturity to become unselfishly involved in facilitating the growth and development of another person. But parenthood is only one avenue for achieving Erikson's task of generativity. Many couples achieve generativity through their careers, community service, and hobbies. "It is in everyone's best interest to make having children the result of a deliberate choice, rather than of sexual happenstance."[117] The childless marriage is equally viable and satisfying to a couple if it is a **chosen** lifestyle.[35] It can be devastating if it results from involuntary infertility. The decision to have a child should be jointly resolved by the couple through a weighing of personal and family assets, values, goals, and priorities: "Every pregnancy, no matter how enthusiastically welcomed and experienced, requires the prospective parents to perform a significant amount of psychological 'work' in order to prepare themselves physically and emotionally for the arrival of their new child. This work consists of personal change and growth and necessarily causes some amount of anxiety."[48] Different maturity levels, degrees of involvement, and social pressures may influence the reactions of the couple individually and jointly.

One's level of personal identity and maturity come into focus in the question of whether to be parents. Inadequate communication is the most critical barrier to effective family planning. Some couples fail to communicate their intentions and end up with a pregnancy by default. Infertility problems force communication, but the tensions and guilt involved may actually decrease emotional intimacy. During either infertility or pregnancy, each person may become so involved in his or her own sphere of concerns that intimacy can be eclipsed. "Fears about intimacy or loss of one's individuality or becoming engulfed in the relationship can limit each partner's incentive to provide support. Individuals may lack the social skills to relate effectively, and emotions such as unresolved anger or resentment can impede improving marital quality and support."[18] A person who has mastered the skill of identity homework is able to communicate his or her needs, desires, and concerns to the partner. This person is also able to be sensitive and supportive of the other without fearing loss of identity in facing the crisis of infertility or of adding a new member to the family unit.

Pregnancy and childbirth provide one more avenue of emotional involvement between the husband and wife. The experience tends to bring out the "hidden side" of masculinity. Expressions of caring, concern, and tenderness emerge, and feelings of empathy, fear, weakness, and sympathy are expressed.[96]

Both the mother and the father find pregnancy a sobering and maturing yet exciting and fulfilling experience when a child is wanted and planned for. Childbearing provides another avenue of personal growth and maturity for adults.

REFERENCES

1. Alderman, P. M. (1988). The lurking sperm. *Journal of the American Medical Association, 259,* 3142–3144.
2. Anderson, J. K. (1982). *Genetic engineering.* Grand Rapids, MI: Zondervan.
3. Anthony, E. J., & Benedek, T. (1970). *Parenthood: Its psychology and psychopathology.* Boston: Little, Brown.
4. Artal, R. M., & Wiswell, R. A. (Eds.). (1986). *Exercise in pregnancy.* Baltimore, MD: Williams & Wilkins.
5. Barglow, P., & Brown, E. (1972). Pseudocyesis. In J. G. Howells (Ed.), *Modern perspectives in psycho-obstetrics.* New York: Brunner/Mazel.
6. Barth, R. P., & Berry, M. (1988). *Adoption and disruption: Rates, risks, and responses.* New York: Aldine de Gruyter.
7. Behrman, S. J., & Patton, G. W. (1988). Evaluation of infertility in the 1980s. In S. J. Behrman & R. W. Kistner (Eds.), *Progress in infertility* (3rd ed., pp. 1–22). Boston: Little, Brown.
8. Benedek, T. (1970). The psychobiology of pregnancy. In E. J. Anthony & T. Benedek (Eds.), *Parenthood: Its psychology and psychopathology* (pp. 137–151). Boston: Little, Brown.
9. Bibring, G. L. (1959). Some considerations of the psychological processes in pregnancy. In *Psychoanalytic study of the child* (Vol. 14, pp. 113–121). New York: International Universities Press.
10. Bibring, G. L., Dwyer, T. F., Huntington, D. S., and Valenstein, A. F. (1961). A study of the psychological process in pregnancy and of the earliest mother-child relationship. In *Psychoanalytic study of the child* (Vol. 16, pp. 9–24). New York: International Universities Press.
11. Biller, H. M., & Meredith, D. (1975). *Father power.* New York: David McKay.
12. Billings, J. J. (1983). *The ovulation method: the achievement or avoidance of pregnancy by a technique which is safe, reliable and universally acceptable* (7th ed.). Melbourne: Advocate Press Pty.
13. Birns, B., & Hay, D. F. (Eds.). (1988). *The different faces of motherhood.* New York: Plenum Press.
14. Bobrowsky, S. (1987, April). Nine months plus three. *Military Lifestyle,* pp. 34–35, 38, 40, 57.
15. Boulton, M. G. (1983). *On being a mother: A study of women with preschool children.* New York: Tavistock.
16. Bounds, W. (1989). Male and female barrier contraceptive methods. In M. Filshie & J. Guillebaud (Eds.), *Contraception: Science and practice* (pp. 172–202). Boston: Butterworths.
17. Bradney, N. (1986). But not alone. *Journal of the American Medical Association, 255*(1), 41.
18. Brown, M. A. (1987). How fathers and mothers perceive prenatal support. *MCN: American Journal of Maternal/Child Nursing, 12,* 414–418.
19. Campbell, A. (1975). The American way of mating: Marriage si, children only maybe. *Psychology Today, 8*(12), 37.
20. Campbell, E. (1985). *The childless marriage: An exploratory study of couples who do not want children.* New York: Tavistock.
21. Campbell, N. B., Franco, K., & Jurs, S. (1988). Abortion in adolescence. *Adolescence, 23*(92), 813–23.
22. Carpenter, M. W., Sady, S. P., Hoegsberg, B., Sady, M. A., Haydon, B., Cullinane, E. M., Coustan, D. R., & Thompson, P. D., (1988). Fetal heart rate response to maternal exertion. *Journal of the American Medical Association, 259,* 3006–3009.
23. Carter-Jessop, L. (1981). Promoting maternal attachment through parental intervention. *MCN: American Journal of Maternal/Child Nursing, 6,* 107.
24. Cefalo, R. C., & Moos, M. K. (1988). *Preconceptual health promotion: A practical guide.* Rockville, MD: Aspen Publishers.
25. Colt, G. H., & Grant, M. (1987). At last—It's a boy! A new kind of adoption leads this couple into the delivery room. *Life, 10*(6), 28–34.
26. Creasy, R. K., & Resnik, R. (1989). *Maternal-fetal medicine: Principles and practice* (2nd ed.). Philadelphia: W. B. Saunders.
27. Cunningham, F. G., MacDonald, P. C., & Grant, N. F. (1989). *Williams obstetrics* (18th ed.). Norwalk, CT: Appleton and Lange.
28. Davajan, V., & Mishell, D. R., Jr. (1986). Evaluation of the infertile couple. In D. R. Mishell, Jr & V. Davajan (Eds.), *Infertility, contraception and reproductive endocrinology.* (2nd ed., pp. 381–387). Oradell, NJ: Medical Economics Books.
29. Davajan, V., Nakamura, R. M., & Bernstein, G. S. (1986). Role of immunology in infertility. In D. R. Mishell, Jr. & V. Davajan (Eds.), *Infertility, contraception and reproductive endocrinology* (2nd ed., pp. 521–530). Oradell, NJ: Medical Economics Books.
30. DeGrez, S. A. (1988). Bend and stretch. *MCN: American Journal of Maternal/Child Nursing, 13,* 357–359.
31. Dimitrovsky, L., Perez-Hirshberg, M., & Itskowitz, R. (1987). Depression during and following pregnancy: Quality of family relationships. *Journal of Psychology, 12*(3), 213–218.
32. Donovan, C. M., Greenspan, R., & Mittleman, F. (1974). The decision-making process, and the outcome of therapeutic abortion. *American Journal of Psychiatry, 131,* 1332.
33. Drife, J. (1989). Complications of combined oral contraception. In M. Filshie & J. Guillebaud (Eds.), *Contraception: Science and practice* (pp. 39–51). Boston: Butterworths.
34. Faich, G., Pearson, K., Fleming, D., Sobel, S., & Anello, C (1986). Toxic shock syndrome and the vaginal contraceptive sponge. *Journal of the American Medical Association, 255*(2), 216.
35. Feldman, H. (1981). A comparison of intentional parents and intentionally childless couples. *Journal of Marriage and the Family, 43,* 593.
36. Filshie, G. M. (1989). Abortion. In M. Filshie & J. Guillebaud (Eds.), *Contraception: Science and practice* (pp. 250–274). Boston: Butterworths.
37. Flynn, A. M., & Bonnar, J. (1989). Natural family planning. In M. Filshie & J. Guillebaud (Eds.), *Contraception: Science and practice* (pp. 203–223). Boston: Butterworths.
38. Fraser, I. S. (1989). Systemic hormonal contraception by non-

oral routes. In M. Filshie & J. Guillebaud (Eds.), *Contraception: Science and practice* (pp. 109–125). Boston: Butterworths.

39. Gaffney, K. F. (1988). Prenatal maternal attachment. *IMAGE: Journal of Nursing Scholarship, 20*(2), 106–109.

40. Gerson, M. J. (1989). Tomorrow's fathers: The anticipation of fatherhood. In S. H. Cath, A. Gurwitt, & L. Gunsberg (Eds.), *Fathers and their families* (pp. 127–144). Hillsdale, NJ: Analytic Press.

41. Goldberg, W. A. (1988). Introduction: Perspectives on the transition to parenthood. In G. Y. Michaels & W. A. Goldberg (Eds.), *The transition to parenthood: Current theory and research* (pp. 1–20). New York: Cambridge University Press.

42. Goldenring, J. M. (1982). Letter to the editor. *New England Journal of Medicine, 307*(9), 564C.

43. Goodlin, R. C. (1976). Can sex in pregnancy harm the fetus? *Contemporary Obstetrics/Gynecology, 8*(5), 21.

44. Götz, I. L. (1988). Surrogate motherhood. *Theology Today, 45*(2), 189–195.

45. Grannum, P., & Copel, J. A. (1989). Antepartum care. In R. E. Rankel (Ed.), *Conn's current therapy* (pp. 883–890). Philadelphia: W. B. Saunders.

46. Greil, A. (et al.). (1987). *Sex and intimacy among infertile couples.* Paper presented at the 37th Annual Meeting of the Society for the Study of Social Problems. Chicago: August 14–16, 1987. (ED 294 820)

47. Grimes, D. A. (1986). Reversible contraception for the 1980s. *Journal of the American Medical Association, 255*(1), 69–75.

48. Grossman, F. K., Eichler, L. S., & Winickoff, S. A. (1980). *Pregnancy, birth, and parenthood.* San Francisco: Joseey-Bass.

49. Gurwitt, A. (1989). Flight from fatherhood. In S. H. Cath, A. Gurwitt, & L. Gunsberg (Eds.), *Fathers and their families* (pp. 167–188). Hillsdale, NJ: Analytic Press.

50. Harper, M. J. K. (1983). *Birth control technologies: Prospects by the year 2000.* Austin, TX: University of Texas Press.

51. Hendry, W. F. (1989). Vasectomy and vasectomy reversal. In M. Filshie & J. Guillebaud (Eds.), *Contraception: Science and practice* (pp. 292–304). Boston: Butterworths.

52. Hoffman, L. W. (1975). The value of children to parents and the decrease in family size. *Proceedings of the American Philosophical Society, 119,* 430–438.

53. Howells, J. G. (1972). Termination of pregnancy. In J. G. Howells (Ed.), *Modern perspectives in psycho-obstetrics* (pp. 205–232). New York: Brunner/Mazel.

54. International Committee for Research in Reproduction. (1989). Oral contraceptives and breast cancer. *Journal of the American Medical Association, 2,* 206–207.

55. Jeffcoate, S. L. (1989). Progress towards a systemic male contraceptive. In M. Filshie & J. Guillebaud (Eds.), *Contraception: Science and practice* (pp. 305–309). Boston: Butterworths.

56. Jessner, L., Weigert, E., & Foy, J. L. (1970). The development of parental attitudes during pregnancy. In E. J. Anthony & T. Benedek (Eds.), *Parenthood: Its psychology and psychopathology* (pp. 209–244). Boston: Little, Brown.

57. Jones, H. W. (1986). In vitro fertilization. *Journal of the American Medical Association, 255,* 106.

58. Kanwit, E., & Brunel, L. E. (1987). Prenatal care. In K. R. Niswander (Ed.), *Manual of obstetrics: Diagnosis and therapy* (3rd ed., pp. 28–37). Boston: Little, Brown.

59. Ketter, D. E., & Shelton, B. J. (1984). Pregnant and physically fit, too. *MCN: American Journal of Maternal/Child Nursing, 9,* 120.

60. Kimball, G. (1988). *50-50 parenting: Sharing family rewards and responsibilities.* Lexington, MA: Lexington Books.

61. Kirz, D. S., Dorchester, W., & Freeman, R. K. (1985). Advanced maternal age: The mature gravida. *American Journal of Obstetrics and Gynecology, 152*(1), 7–12.

62. Klebanoff, M. A. (1988). Short interpregnancy interval and the risk of low birthweight. *American Journal of Public Health, 78,* 667–670.

63. Kuchner, J. F., & Porcino, J. (1988). Delayed motherhood. In B. Birns & D. F. Hay (Eds.), *The different faces of motherhood* (pp. 259–280). New York: Plenum Press.

64. Kutscher, A. H., Carr, A. C., & Kutscher, L. G. (1987). *Principles of thanatology.* New York: Columbia University Press.

65. Landers, A. (1976). If you had it to do over again, would you have children? *Good Housekeeping, 182*(6), 100.

66. Lederman, R. P. (1984). *Psychosocial adaptation in pregnancy.* Englewood Cliffs, NJ: Prentice-Hall.

67. Levitan, S. H., Belous, R. S., & Gallo, F. (1988). *What's happening to the American family? Tensions, hopes, realities* (rev. ed.). Baltimore, MD: Johns Hopkins University Press.

68. Lipnick, R. J., Buring, J. E., Hennekens, C. H., Rosner, B., Willett, W., Bain, C., Stampfer, M. J., Colditz, G. A., Peto, R., & Speizer, F. E. (1986) Oral contraceptives and breast cancer. *Journal of the American Medical Association, 255,* 58–61.

69. Love, V. (1984). *Childless is not less.* Minneapolis, MN: Bethany House.

70. Madore, C., et al. (1981). A study on the effects of induced abortion on subsequent pregnancy outcome. *American Journal of Obstetrics and Gynecology, 139,* 516.

71. Mann, P. (1986, Jan.). New help for the childless. *Reader's Digest,* pp. 135–140.

72. Marrs, R. P., & Vargyas, J. M. (1986). Human in vitro fertilization: State of the art. In D. R. Mishell, Jr. & V. Davajan (Eds.), *Infertility, contraception and reproductive endocrinology* (2nd ed., pp. 565–580). Oradell, NJ: Medical Economics Books.

73. Mascola, L., & Guinan, M. E. (1986). Screening to reduce transmission of sexually transmitted diseases in semen used for artificial insemination. *New England Journal of Medicine, 314,* 1354–1359.

74. Masters, W., & Johnson, V. (1966). *Human sexual response.* Boston: Little, Brown.

75. Matthews, R., & Matthews, A. M. (1986). Infertility and involuntary childlessness: The transition to nonparenthood. *Journal of Marriage and the Family, 48,* 641–649.

76. May, K. A. (1980). A typology of detachment/involvement styles adopted by first-time expectant fathers. *Western Journal of Nursing Research, 2*(2), 445–453.

77. May, K. A. (1987). Men's sexuality during the childbearing year: Implications of recent research findings. *Holistic Nursing Practitioner, 1*(4), 60–66.

78. May, K. A., & Perrin, S. P. (1985). Prelude: Pregnancy and birth. In S. M. H. Hanson & F. W. Bozett (Eds.), *Dimensions of fatherhood* (pp. 64–91). Beverly Hills, CA: Sage.

79. McKee, L., & O'Brien, M. (1982). The father figure: Some current orientations and historical perspectives. In L. McKee & M. O'Brien (Eds.), *The father figure.* New York: Tavistock.

80. Menning, B. E. (1988). *Infertility: A guide for the childless couple* (2nd ed.). New York: Prentice-Hall.

81. Merilo, K. F. (1988). Is it better the second time around? *MCN: American Journal of Maternal/Child Nursing, 13,* 200–204.

82. Michaels, G. Y., & Goldberg, W. A. (Eds.). (1988). *The transition to parenthood: current theory and research.* New York: Cambridge University Press.

83. Mishell, D. R., Jr. (1986). Intrauterine devices. In D. R. Mishell, Jr. (Ed.), *Infertility, contraceptives and reproductive endo-*

crinology (2nd ed., pp. 639–657). Oradell, NJ: Medical Economics Books.

84. Mishell, D. R., Jr. (1986). Contraceptive use and effectiveness. In D. R. Mishell, Jr. & V. Davajan (Eds.), *Infertility, contraception and reproductive endocrinology* (2nd ed., pp. 583–591). Oradell, NJ: Medical Economics Books.

85. Mishell, D. R., Jr. (1986). Long-acting contraceptive steroids and interception. In D. R. Mishell, Jr. & V. Davajan (Eds.), *Contraception and reproductive endocrinology* (2nd ed., pp. 623–638). Oradell, NJ: Medical Economics Books.

86. Moore, K. L. (1988). *The developing human: Clinically oriented embryology* (4th ed.). Philadelphia: W. B. Saunders.

87. Navot, D., Laufer, N., Kopolovic, J., Rabinowitz, R., Birkenfeld, A., Lewin, A., Granat, M., Margalioth, E. J., & Schenker, J. G. (1986). Artificially induced endometrial cycles and establishment of pregnancies in the absence of ovaries. *New England Journal of Medicine, 314,* 806–810.

88. Nichols, F. H., & Humenick, S. S. (1988). *Childbirth education: Practice, research, and theory.* Philadelphia: W. B. Saunders.

89. Niswander, K. R. (1987). Contraception, abortion, and sterilization. In K. R. Niswander (Ed.), *Manual of obstetrics: Diagnosis and therapy* (3rd. ed., pp. 3–27). Boston: Little, Brown.

90. Osofsky, H. J., & Culp, R. E. (1989). Risk factors in the transition to fatherhood. In S. H. Cath, A. Gurwitt,, & L. Gunsberg (Eds.), *Fathers and their families* (pp. 145–165). Hillsdale, NJ: Analytic Press.

91. Overvold, A. Z. (1988). *Surrogate parenting.* New York: Pharos Books.

92. Potts, M. (1988). Birth control methods in the United States. *Family Planning Perspectives, 20*(6), 288–297.

93. Potts, M., & Bhiwandiwala, P. (1989). Birth control: A world view. In M. Filshie & J. Guillebaud (Eds.). *Contraception: Science and practice* (pp. 1–10). Boston: Butterworths.

94. Quindlen, A. (1987). Baby craving: Facing widespread infertility, a generation passes the limits of medicine and morality. *Life, 10*(6), 23–26.

95. Reingold, A. L. (1986). Toxic shock syndrome and the contraceptive sponge. *Journal of the American Medical Association, 255*(2), 242.

96. Richman, J. (1982). Men's experience of pregnancy and childbirth. In L. McKee & M. O'Brien (Eds.), *The father figure.* New York: Tavistock.

97. Richwald, G. A., Greenland, S., Gerker, M. M., Potik, R., Kersey, L., & Comas, M. A. (1989). Effectiveness of the cavity-rim cervical cap: Results of a large clinical study. *Obstetrics and Gynecology, 74*(2), 143–148.

98. Rioux, J. E. (1989). Female sterilization and its reversal. In M. Filshie & J. Guillebaud (Eds.), *Contraception: Science and practice* (pp. 275–291). Boston: Butterworths.

99. Roopnarine, J. L., & Miller, B. C. (1985). Transition to fatherhood. In S. M. H. Hanson & F. W. Bozett (Eds.), *Dimensions of fatherhood* (pp. 49–63). Beverly Hills, CA: Sage.

100. Rothman, D., & Kaplan, A. H. (1972). Psychosomatic infertility in the male and female. In J. G. Howells (Ed.), *Modern perspectives in psycho-obstetrics* (pp. 31–52). New York: Bruner/Mazel.

101. Rubin, R. (1970). Cognitive style in pregnancy. *American Journal of Nursing, 70,* 502.

102. Rue, V. (1985). *Mourning responses, reconciliation and abortion.* Washington, DC: Family Research Council.

103. Rue, V. (1986). *Forgotten fathers: Men and abortion.* Lewiston, NY: Life Cycle Books.

104. Schlesselman, J. J., Stadel, B. V., Murray, P., & Lai, S. (1988). Breast cancer in relation to early use of oral contraceptives. *Journal of the American Medical Association, 259,* 1828–1833.

105. Schuster, C. S. (1980). Unpublished research.

106. Sharlip, I. D. (1986). Late spontaneous reversal of vasectomy. *Journal of the American Medical Association, 255*(6), 820.

107. Sherrod, R. A. (1988). Coping with infertility: A personal perspective turned professional. *MCN: American Journal of Maternal/Child Nursing, 13,* 191–194.

108. Sherwen, L. N. (1987). *Psychosocial dimensions of the pregnant family.* New York: Springer.

109. Snarey, J., Son, L., Kuehne, V. S., Hauser, S., & Vaillant, G. (1987). The role of parenting in men's psychosocial development: A longitudinal study of early adulthood infertility and midlife generativity. *Developmental Psychology, 23,* 593–603.

110. Steege, J. F., & Jelousek, F. R. (1982). Sexual behavior during pregnancy. *Obstetrics and Gynecology, 60,* 168–182.

111. Still, B. F. (1989). Married, no children, infertility: A special kind of loss. *Focus on the Family,* April, 2–4.

112. Stone, B. A., Tan, T. T., Koopersmith, T. B., Quinn, K., & Marrs, R. P. (1988). Luteotropic activity in serum of women following embryo or gamete transfer in a program of assisted conception. *Journal of In Vitro Fertilization and Embryo Transfer., 5*(5), 275–281.

113. Swanson, J. M. (1985). Men and family planning. In S. M. H. Hanson & F. W. Bozett (Eds.), *Dimensions of fatherhood* (pp. 21–48). Beverly Hills, CA: Sage.

114. Taubenheim, A. M., & Silbernagel, T. (1988). Meeting the needs of expectant fathers. *MCN: American Journal of Maternal/Child Nursing, 13,* 110–113.

115. Tipping, V. G. (1981). The vulnerability of a primipara during the antenatal period. *MCN: American Journal of Maternal/Child Nursing, 10,* 61.

116. Trabert, C. (1981). Prenatal tactile intervention can be encouraged. *MCN: American Journal of Maternal/Child Nursing, 6,* 108.

117. Trethowan, W. H. (1972). The Couvade syndrome. In J. C. Howells (Ed.), *Modern perspectives in psycho-obstetrics.* New York: Brunner/Mazel.

118. U.S. Bureau of the Census. (1987). *Annual report on fertility rates.* Washington, DC: United States Government Printing Office.

119. U.S. Department of Education. (1988). *Youth indicators, 1988: Trends in the well-being of American youth.* Washington, DC: Superintendent of Documents.

120. Veevers, J. E. (1980). *Childless by choice.* Toronto: Butterworth.

121. Vessey, M. P. (1989). Oral contraception and cancer. In M. Filshie & J. Guillebaud (Eds.), *Contraception: Science and practice* (pp 52–68). Boston: Butterworths.

122. Walden, W. D. (1989). Abortion. In R. E Rankel (Ed.), *Conn's current therapy* (pp. 890–896). Philadelphia: W. B. Saunders.

123. Whiteford, L. M., & Poland, M. L. (1989). *New approaches to human reproduction: Social and ethical dimensions.* Boulder, CO: Westview Press.

124. Winslow, W. (1987). First pregnancy after 35: What is the experience? *MCN: American Journal of Maternal/Child Nursing, 12,* 92–96.

125. Yuzpe, A., & Kubba, A. (1989). Postcoital contraception. In M. Filshie & J. Guillebaud (Eds.), *Contraception: Science and practice* (pp. 126–143). Boston: Butterworths.

126. Ziegel, E. E., & Cranley, M. S. (1984). *Obstetric nursing* (8th ed.). New York: Macmillan.

The Expanding Family

Clara S. Schuster

Preparation for parenthood begins long before the birth of a new baby, in fact, even before conception. It begins with one's own infancy and the relationship with one's parents throughout childhood and adolescence. Pregnancy and childbirth merely intensify the process. The experience of parenting varies with age, marital status and quality of the relationship, finances, ethnicity, health, education, career goals, commitment to role, value system, earlier socialization experiences, support from family of origin, uniqueness of the child, resources, and so on.[9, 98] All these issues play a role in the meaning of the child to the parents and the decisions the couple will make regarding child care and the new family relationships.

A number of significant decisions need to be made when a couple is expecting a child. One decision concerns employment: How long will the woman continue to work, and when will she return to the job market, if at all? Should she return to work while the husband remains at home for child care? If both parents return to work, what arrangements are available for child care; should they use grandparents, a babysitter, or a day care nursery?[69] Is the cost of child care adequately offset by the woman's salary to make her return to work worthwhile? (A woman must earn twice what she pays for hired help *after* taxes to break even!)[67] Can part-time work, home-based work, or alternating hours for husband and wife be arranged? Though innocuous on the surface, these decisions may be critical to the optimal development of the child, and they can be a source of crisis and conflict for couples who feel that the woman's place is in the home, while financial conditions still require her assistance in supplementing the family income.

Another major decision involves the method of infant feeding. For some women, the commitment to breast-feeding or bottle-feeding is established long before pregnancy is confirmed by previous experiences, psychosexual development, and the meaning of the breast to the woman. However, even though the decision is hers finally, it is not hers alone. The support of her mother, the attitude of the husband, and even the opinion of friends become significant in both the woman's decision and her success at breast-feeding.[7] Some women are greatly repulsed by the idea of breast-feeding, feeling that it is "animalistic." Some husbands are possessive of the wife's breasts and do not want them shared by the baby, especially sons. Older children in the family may feel that breast-feeding is embarrassing, "weird," or "sick." The negative attitudes of others are conveyed overtly and covertly to the breast-feeding mother, potentially undermining her commitment. Because of all the adjustments she is making to new responsibilities and relationships, the new mother is vulnerable to the opinions of others.

A third major decision centers around health care for the childbirth experience. For most couples, pregnancy and childbirth should be approached as a normal process and as a social event rather than as an illness or disease state that requires extensive medical direction and intervention to maintain or to regain high-level wellness. How much do the woman and her partner want to participate in the birth experience? Do they want to have the baby at home, at a childbirth center, or in a hospital? Couples are encouraged to choose a physician who supports their views on the childbearing process. It is essential at this time that the woman (and her partner) have absolute confidence in the skill and integrity of the physician. Because of their commitment to the family-centered approach while offering high-quality care to the healthy expectant couple, midwives are gaining more acceptance in the U.S.

PREPARATION FOR CHILDBIRTH AND PARENTING

Almost all couples engage in some preparation for childbirth and child care. For many, it involves only the purchasing of essential clothing and supplies; other may discuss the upcoming childbirth experience with their friends and family members. Unfortunately, these sources frequently have a variety of "horror stories" to tell, which increase the pregnant woman's fears rather than help her prepare realistically and constructively for childbirth. Many pregnant couples read pamphlets from the physician's office, but what is shared by friends has more reality than the contents of an impersonal booklet. Some women systematically write down questions to ask the obstetrician. Others find the public library to be a rich source of information on fetal development, childbirth, and child care.

Instruction in Child Care and Parenting

A growing number of parents take advantage of formal classes offered in the community. Many public school systems include parenting courses as a part of their health education

curriculum, a trend the author highly supports. Adult education programs, hospitals, and some doctors sponsor classes on parenting. The American Red Cross offers, free of charge, an excellent preparation-for-parenthood class for mothers and their partners (Fig. 31-1). A number of hospitals have successfully inaugurated innovative prenatal education classes for children that help prepare them for the arrival of a new sibling.[144] The process of pregnancy, childbirth, and sibling rivalry are all covered in detail. Some hospitals make provision to allow siblings to attend the birth.[112] Classes for grandparents are offered to help acquaint them with changes in medical practice and child care philosophies and to facilitate their ability to support their son or daughter.[96]

Many parents-to-be are unable to project themselves beyond the birth experience and consequently obtain little knowledge about the techniques of child care. These individuals depend on the hospital staff, their mothers, or friends to tell them what to do and how to care for the baby. With shortened hospital stays after childbirth (many return home within 36 hours of birth), parents need referral to other community resources, such as public health nurses, Child Conservation League (CCL), extension courses from colleges and universities, and adult education courses sponsored by the local school systems and the American Red Cross. The American Red Cross First Aid Course is also recommended to parents because it can help prepare them to handle some of the crises and minor injuries all children receive in the process of growing up.

Preparation for Childbirth

Most communities have at least one organized program to help parents acquire the knowledge and skills for both the woman and her partner to participate actively in her labor and the delivery of their baby. These classes usually include infor-

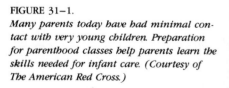

FIGURE 31–1.
Many parents today have had minimal contact with very young children. Preparation for parenthood classes help parents learn the skills needed for infant care. (Courtesy of The American Red Cross.)

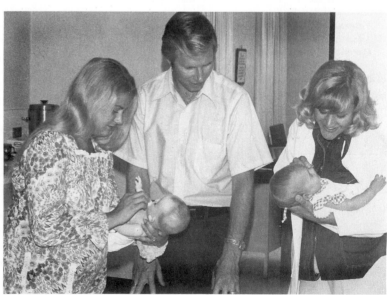

mation on anatomy and the birth process as well as special techniques of relaxation and breathing. The **psychophysical** (Dick-Reed) method encourages mental dissociation from the body with relaxation and breathing activities. Education and exercises are used effectively to break the fear-tension-pain cycle. The **psychoprophylactic** (Lamaze) method applies classic Pavlovian conditioning to childbirth. Through conditioning, discipline, and concentration, new responses are taught to block out the perception of pain. In both these methods, and in the **Bradley** method, the couple learn a new appreciation for the functioning of the body during labor. All these methods teach the couple how to work with, rather than against, the body to facilitate the labor process (Fig. 31-2). Participants indicate they have reduced anxiety, heightened concentration, and decreased pain during the childbirth process.

The provision of a physically and socially supportive environment by the husband or other meaningful person reduces the woman's stressors and facilitates her ability to work cooperatively with her labor process. Fatigue is minimized, and the sense of being in control is maximized. She draws emotional energy from the other to face the labor process. Husband and wife may feel a new bond of sharing and commitment.

Although the purist would advocate that these "natural childbirth" methods be substituted for medication during labor and delivery, most instructors of the methods, doctors, and mothers themselves see the use of these methods as a way to reduce, not to eliminate, medication, a way to remain in control of the labor, rather than to be controlled by it. Research indicates that prepared women have shorter labors, need less medication, and enjoy the birth experience more.[81, 109]

Classes in parenting and preparation for childbirth also give the parents an opportunity to meet with other young couples and thus to share ideas and fears under the guidance of a knowledgeable person. Contact with other expectant couples can help them to assess their own changing roles and goals. The peer group can offer a support system that substitutes for the guidance and socialization formerly offered by the extended family.

Not all parents attend classes, although they may be available in the community. Factors, such as a lack of time, previous knowledge and experience, lack of interest, or cultural conditioning, may prevent attendance. Some mothers feel that they do not need preparation (childbirth is a "natural event"); some are afraid that classes will increase their fear (they want to avoid the experience); others do not believe that anything can really help (the helplessness syndrome). It should be strongly emphasized that classes can and do help even the most fearful, the most naïve, and the most unbelieving to experience easier, more satisfying childbirth and child care experiences. Even multiparous parents state that preparation-for-childbirth classes offer them the opportunity to be more intelligent health care consumers.

THE BIRTH PROCESS

Several events may occur toward the end of gestation that give the mother and her physician clues that labor is imminent:

1. Descent of the baby's head into the pelvic cavity causes a slight forward tilt of the uterus (**lightening** or "dropping"). This movement greatly relieves pressure on the rib cage and diaphragm, so that breathing is easier; however, it increases the pressure on the bladder.
2. "Ripening," or softening, of the cervix occurs in response to both the pressure of the fetus and hormonal influences. Most women have **effacement** (thinning of the cervical walls) and some **dilatation** (opening of the cervix) before the onset of labor.
3. Changes in hormonal levels may make the woman alternately very tired or full of energy. The instability of her

FIGURE 31–2.
Parents who participate in childbirth classes find themselves better prepared for the experience. Childbirth can be as encompassing for the father as it is for the mother when the couple works together in the birth of their child. (Courtesy of Beth Israel Hospital, Boston. Photograph by Michael Lutch.)

energy level may be confusing to both the woman and those around her.

4. The frequency and strength of **Braxton-Hicks contractions** (the irregular uterine contractions experienced throughout pregnancy) increase. Occasionally, these contractions may be regular enough and strong enough to cause the mother to believe she is in early labor. She may be hospitalized for several hours before the phenomenon known as **false labor** is identified. Although painful, these contractions are not strong enough to cause the essential effacement and dilation. The disappointed mother is sent home to await the onset of true labor.

Initiation of Labor

The initiation of labor depends on a constellation of interrelated maternal and fetal events not yet fully understood. No one factor is responsible for the total process of initiating labor. It is the synchronization of several factors that appears to trigger labor. The contraction of one uterine muscle cell triggers contractions of adjacent cells as hormonal balances change.[36] Sensitivity to contractions is influenced by chemical, mechanical, and neurologic factors. The major components appear to be the following:[24, 36, 51, 64, 138]

1. The fetus may signal the mother's body to initiate labor by the secretion of adrenocorticotropic hormone (ACTH) from the fetal pituitary after key maturational events have occurred. ACTH stimulates the fetal adrenals to increase cortisol production, which in turn increases maternal production of estrogen.

2. A rise in maternal estrogen levels increases the vascularity of the uterus and also appears to stimulate prostaglandin production. Prostaglandin can evoke contractions of the uterus at any stage of pregnancy.

3. The placental aging process results in the production of less progesterone (which decreased uterine contractibility during the pregnancy). Decreased progesterone levels allow the lysosomes to release arachidonic acid, which is a precursor of prostaglandin synthesis, and also increase the sensitivity of the uterus to oxytocin.

4. The decidua (endometrial lining) begins production of **prostaglandin,** which in turn sustains estrogen levels. Semen also has a high **prostaglandin** level and may play a role in initiating labor after intercourse in late pregnancy.[26]

5. As contractions resume, the fetus is pushed toward the cervical opening. Pressure from the baby's head irritates the cervix, leading to reflexive contractions by the uterus, which in turn exert further pressure on the cervix and cervical dilation. Neurohormonal action from the dilated cervix to the hypothalamus (Ferguson's reflex) causes release of oxytocin and further contractions.

6. Oxytocin appears to be the main hormone that produces effective uterine contractions. It is excreted by the hypothalamus of both the mother and the fetus but stored and released by the posterior pituitary. Change in oxytocin levels is minimal before or with the onset of labor. However, with decreased progesterone levels, the uterus becomes more sensitive and reactive to the oxytocin. Increased oxytocin levels are observed in response to Ferguson's reflex and also to nipple stimulation. Nipple stimulation can be used to "soften" the cervix or to initiate labor.[51]

There are three classic signs of the initiation of labor. An individual woman may experience one, two, or all three of them. The three signs are as follows:

1. The appearance of **bloody discharge** ("show") caused by the loosening of the mucoid plug that has sealed the cervix during pregnancy.

2. The occurrence of **uterine contractions,** gradually increasing in frequency and intensity. Tightening may be felt in the back and lower abdomen, similar to that felt with menstrual cramps.

3. The **rupture of the "bag of waters"** that envelopes the fetus, allowing passage of fluid through the vagina. This fluid may seep slowly, or a large amount may be emitted at once. The woman may confuse this event with urinary incontinence. There is no warning or pain. Women are encouraged to cover their mattresses with a plastic protector during the last month of pregnancy and to wear a sanitary pad when they are out in public.

Labor and Delivery

Each woman's labor is uniquely her own. To compare experiences is unfair, but certain common elements do emerge. Many factors can influence both the duration of each stage and the mother's psychological response to that stage. During the first stage, the cervix is dilating to allow extrusion of the fetus; during the second stage, the fetus passes through the birth canal (vagina); during the third stage, the placenta is delivered. Some nurses call the first hours after delivery the "fourth stage," when the mother is still evacuating large amounts of blood and fluids from her body.

The first stage of labor is subdivided into three phases. The mother usually enters the health care system or calls for her childbirth assistant during the first or second phase. The contractions in this phase are not painful or prolonged (20 to 45 seconds). The rest periods between contractions gradually shorten from 20 minutes to about 5 minutes. The woman is usually comfortable and can walk around or even keep herself busy with household activities, reading, or sewing. She is generally excited and talkative. ("Who me? Now? Maybe it is only false labor.") There is an element of disbelief and ambivalence. ("Am I ready?") If possible, the mother should be encouraged to rest between contractions to conserve energy for the work to come. During this phase, the cervix becomes effaced and dilates to about 4 cm.

In the second phase, the woman loses her mood of

excitement and entertainment; she becomes serious and introverted, concentrating on herself and her contractions. As the contractions become stronger, longer, and more frequent; doubt no longer exists ("Ready or not, it is *me* and it is *now!*") There is not much time for rest when the contractions occur every 3 to 5 minutes. However, the prepared mother is able to focus her energies to work with the contractions and to relax and refresh herself between them. A strong, quiet, supportive environment greatly improves her confidence and her ability to concentrate. If the mother has chosen a hospital setting, fetal monitors (see Chap. 4) are frequently attached to assess the fetal response to the stressors of labor. Each contraction of the uterine muscles causes a temporary decrease or cessation of blood flow to the placental site. Consequently, monitoring of the duration of contractions and the fetal heart rate is recommended to assess the oxygen status of the fetus (see Fig. 4-4).

Contraction patterns have four distinct phases. The onset of the contraction is characterized by a gradual increase in intensity. The uterus can be felt to harden as the muscles contract. During the acme, or peak, of the contractions, the uterus appears to raise itself upward, away from the vertebrae. If the woman is fearful, she tightens her body, including her abdominal muscles, thus counteracting the effectiveness of the uterine activity and increasing the pain. The intensity of the contraction is released during the decrement phase. Associated pain disappears, and blood flow returns to the placental site. The rest phase between active contractions is essential for both fetal and maternal recuperation.

The contractions of the second phase of the first stage of labor bring about complete effacement and dilate the cervix to 7 cm. These first two phases last about 10 to 12 hours for the primiparous woman (first baby) and are considerably shorter for the multiparous woman. Fortunately, the transition or third phase of the first stage of labor is brief (30 minutes to 1 hour). The 60- to 80-second contractions are intense and frequent (every 2 to 3 minutes), and the final dilation (8 to 10 cm) is hard work. A prepared partner (usually the spouse) can greatly facilitate the mother's ability to work with her body and to remain in control of the birth process. The close support of the father can be meaningful to both of them at this time. The most effective focal point for the mother is her partner's eyes. The mature, well-prepared couple function as a synchronized team, a factor that helps to strengthen their commitment to each other and to the new baby.

Pain medication, if administered, is usually given just before the transition phase. Intense concentration on breathing techniques can increase oxygen to the fetus and decrease pain perception by the mother. The unprepared, uncooperative mother frequently recalls this phase with fear and embarrassment and as a point of disintegration. The prepared mother recalls it as having been difficult but feels proud that she was able to maintain control. These two alternative responses can leave their mark on the woman's concept of her self-identity and sexuality. They may even affect her relationship with the baby or the father.

The mother's perception of her performance during childbirth can be a sign to her of her later capabilities as a mother.[98] Consequently, the mother who has a cesarean section may experience depression from a sense of failure. Some may even feel a sense of rejection toward the child for "doing this to me" or highlighting her vulnerabilities, factors that can interfere with the parent–infant relationship.[98]

Once the cervix is completely dilated, the baby begins to pass through the pelvic canal (see Fig. 4-3). Contractions during the second stage remain long (60–90 seconds) but are further apart (3–4 minutes). Up to this point, the mother's main task was to concentrate on breathing patterns that would facilitate relaxation and increase the oxygen available to the fetus. At this point, as she feels the descending baby press against the lower colon, she takes a deep breath and pushes downward with all her strength to help push the baby along. The pain of the last phase of stage 1 is gone and is replaced by physically hard work. During the first stage, the mother could not do anything to stop the contractions or speed the delivery; at this stage, she can actively work with the contractions to assist the process. The woman is generally advised against pushing as the baby "crowns" (passes through the perineal opening) (see Fig. 4-5). Gradual stretching of the tissues and an episiotomy (a short cut made to enlarge the opening) can reduce pain and prevent tearing or problems after delivery. This second stage generally lasts 30 to 60 minutes for the primipara but may take only 10 minutes for the multiparous woman. Although concentrating heavily on the task in which she is involved, the woman in this stage frequently engages in conversation between contractions. Her birth time is close. Her excitement is contained.

When medications have been minimal and involvement high, the signs of stress are eased with the birth of the baby. Joy floods the mother's face; her eyes sparkle; her excitement is no longer contained. The prepared mother seems infused with a new pride and heightened self-esteem ("I did it!"). She exchanges conversation with her partner and the doctor. The focus is no longer herself, but the baby. The unprepared mother may express relief ("It's over—I survived!").

While the mother is talking and watching or holding her baby, the uterus resumes contractions. Within 5 to 20 minutes, the placenta is expelled, a rather anticlimactic event that many mothers say hurts more than the birth itself, since attention is no longer focused on working with their bodies (see Fig. 3-18).

The mother and father who have participated actively in the childbirth process experience an indefatigable elation. They talk to anyone and everyone, reliving the experience with enthusiasm and joy. Days, weeks, even years later, the woman and her husband revel in the richness of the experience they shared. A new dimension has been added to their relationship. Even the child will be told of the details of his or her own birth.

Because of the pioneer work performed by the physicians John Kennell and Marshall Klaus,[83] many hospitals and most birthing centers encourage close contact between mother and infant during the hour after birth (Fig. 31-3). When the father also is involved during this period, enriched family relationships can develop that appear to have substantial positive long-range effects on family relationships and the child's development. Allowing the father to be present during cesarean childbirth or to have close contact with the baby immediately after delivery also fosters greater bonding and involvement of the father.[105, 123]

THE PUERPERIUM

The puerperium, sometimes known as the "fourth trimester," is the 6-week period after delivery of the baby. During this time, the uterus gradually returns to its prepregnant state. Uterine involution (a process thought to take about 6 weeks) is most rapid during the first 2 weeks after delivery. During this time the **lochia** (bloody discharge) gradually changes in color from bright red to creamy white. Some discharge may continue for 2 to 4 weeks after delivery. Couples are usually advised against intercourse for 2 to 6 weeks after the birth (depending on both the physician and the mother) to avoid infections or an unplanned pregnancy. Ovulation may resume in 28 days or may be delayed several months. Complete breast-feeding suppresses ovulation for at least 10 weeks.[102] Most women reinitiate menses 6 to 10 weeks after delivery unless they are breast-feeding, in which case the menses may be delayed until weaning.[102] However, anovulation is not assured, and breast-feeding women are advised to consult their physician about appropriate methods of birth control.

Many women are concerned about a "flabby belly." The stretched abdominal muscles take time to resume good tone, although the process can be facilitated through specific postpartum exercises and tightening of the abdominal muscles. The existence of weak abdominal muscles 6 months later is caused by lack of exercise; it is not a natural consequence of pregnancy.

Postpartum Depression

Depression During the First Week ("Postpartum Blues")

Fifty percent to eighty-four percent of mothers experience a letdown or episodes of sadness during the first week.[12, 27, 42] They may experience irritability, headache, anxiety, insomnia, confusion, and even negative feelings toward the baby.[27] Several theories are offered to explain this depression; one factor appears to be the rapid decrease in estrogen and progesterone levels following delivery. **Temporary imbalance of the hormonal system** appears to reduce energy levels and foster emotional lability. A second theory indicates that the mother may be experiencing **sleep deprivation syndrome.**[151] The expectant mother needs more sleep toward the end of pregnancy, but she frequently finds it difficult to assume a comfortable resting position; she may be kept awake by the movement of the baby (some mothers find that fetal movements are decreased if they lie on their side and leave a lighted flashlight under the covers!) or the excitement of her own thoughts. The mother may go into labor after a full day awake; she may then be awake and working hard for 12 or more hours of labor. After the baby is born, her euphoria and need to relive the experience verbally may prevent sleep. Other factors, such as hospital routines, physical discomfort, or concern over the baby or herself, may also prevent the mother from obtaining adequate sleep. It is not unusual for a new mother to have gone 36 to 48 hours without sleep in the period of time that surrounds her labor and delivery. When she returns home to resume responsibility for household tasks, care of the new baby (who may want to be fed every 3 hours), and her own physical recuperation, she may be in a serious state of sleep deprivation; thus, it is not surprising if she becomes irritable, headachy, restless, emotionally labile, or depressed. Health care facilities and family members can be helpful by assuring uninterrupted periods of sleep and assuming routine responsibilities for the woman so that she

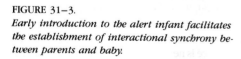

FIGURE 31–3.
Early introduction to the alert infant facilitates the establishment of interactional synchrony between parents and baby.

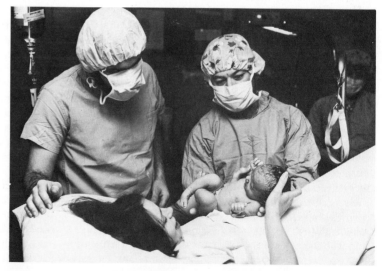

can devote her energies to her own restoration and the process of bonding with her new baby.

A third theory on postpartum depression is offered by Klaus and Kennell, advocates of early mother–infant contact.[78, 80, 81, 83] They feel that the phenomenon may be due to **inadequate contact with the infant** during the hospital stay. The mother is given inadequate opportunity to channel her emotional energies toward forming affectional ties to her new baby. Hospital routines and other people caring for the infant can deprive the mother of opportunities to get to know her baby and to develop competence in child care techniques.

This theory is also supported by James and Joyce Robertson.[119] They theorize that heightened anxiety is a normal phenomenon that accompanies the hormonal changes after birth. The intensity of maternal anxiety would be identified as psychotic at any other time but serves to direct the mother's attention toward the baby immediately after birth. This heightened anxiety assures close proximity of the mother and attention to the infant's interactional cues, essential ingredients for the infant's survival and normal development. The Robertsons observe that it is abnormal if a mother does *not* experience heightened anxiety. They also feel that mother-neonate separation interferes with the effective focusing of the heightened anxiety, leading to depression and possibly becoming a barrier to sensitive bonding with the infant, since it is the mother's frequent contact with the infant and her repeated experience with success in care and comforting that increase self-confidence and facilitate bonding.[119] By the fourth month after birth, the heightened anxiety has decreased; however, because confidence in her own skills is increased, sensitive interaction is maintained by the empathy developed by the mother during the early months.

T. Berry Brazelton offers a fourth theory about postpartum depression, which indicates that the mother is experiencing a conflict between the idealized image of motherhood and the reality of her own competencies.[81, 82] The mother may feel that the child's total welfare and outcome depends on her competency. She may experience **unrealistic expectations of herself as a mother,** and the conscious or subconscious recognition of this credibility gap can elicit feelings of helplessness or self-criticism, which lead to depression.

The author has heard many new mothers express that they were upset or depressed because their husband was not able to share this special time with them. His working hours or hospital policies prevented adequate contact time. For some mothers, delivery was their first experience with hospitalization, and, for a few, the first time ever to be separated from the family overnight (they had never gone to a summer camp or spent the night at a friend's home). Therefore, the depression may actually represent a form of **separation anxiety.**

Delayed Depression (Nonpsychotic Postpartum Depression)

One fourth to one half of mothers experience a sense of depression (anxiety, sense of guilt over lack of love for the child, or inadequacy in mothering role) several weeks or months after delivery.[12, 38, 42] The mother may exhibit panic attacks, anorexia, extreme irritability, fear of the baby's death, crying, and inability to manage the activities of daily living.[27] Fatigue may play a role since the mother seldom obtains more than 5 consecutive hours of sleep, and she may find it difficult or impossible to nap during the day. Some mothers have experienced inadequate coping patterns before pregnancy and motherhood. There may be long standing emotional or personality disorders, drug or alcohol abuse, or other signs of disorganization or inadequate coping with life's stressors.[139] The responsibility for another person who demands and needs her constant attention may prove to be overwhelming.

Ramona Mercer observes that a mother may go through a period of grief as she relinquishes the fantasies and expectations of pregnancy and adapts to the realities of the baby, the associated workload, and her physical appearance (her figure may not return instantly with fashion-model curves).[97] In some cases, the mother may not be able to adjust her prenatally formed mental image of the infant (e.g., coloration or gender) with the real baby.[23, 78] Her dream may have consisted of a fat, happy, cuddly baby who slept all night, was fed four times daily, and enjoyed a bath every day. Instead, the baby may appear thin, cry frequently, stiffen when held, wake twice during the night, demand to be fed every 3 to 4 hours, and cry all through the bath!

The redefinition of herself as a mother and changes in the relationship with her husband require energy investment. The identity homework (see Chap. 25) of this period is not accomplished easily nor automatically. Many women express that it may take more than a year before they have adequately integrated past, present, and anticipated future experiences to sufficiently identify themselves as "mother." Lack of adequate social support and structured roles and rituals may increase role ambivalence and thus increase a woman's sense of depression.[31, 38] A poor relationship with one's spouse or mother increases the risk of postpartal depression in Western cultures.[30, 38]

The learning of new skills is draining. The small nuclear family may have failed to provide her with adequate experience in the care of young children. The mother may not have enough knowledge to know what behaviors are normal or enough experience to be comfortable in handling the baby. Extended family or supportive friends are essential to help answer questions or to relieve some of her anxieties and responsibilities. Physical recovery is slowed when adequate rest is not obtained. The maintenance of ongoing responsibilities while assuming new ones may seem overwhelming. Most new mothers are unprepared for how tired they feel and how much assistance is needed in the first weeks as they make the transition to motherhood.[97] The initial 4 to 6 weeks appear to be the period of peak adjustment. After that (when the baby begins to sleep longer at night), parents begin to focus beyond immediate needs to the growth and developmental needs of the infant.[141]

A pause at this point is appropriate, lest the reader think that transition to parenthood is an overwhelming task successfully transcended only by the brave and mighty or the idealistic or naïve. Two themes flow through the response to the new role: the response to the *day-to-day child care* and relationship with a young child; and the response to the *long-term relationship*.[12] The themes involve the meaning and purpose a child gives to one's life and the sense of commitment to the needs of another, and the pride one takes in the children's accomplishments or the sense of pleasure one receives in service to another. Most mothers see motherhood positively. Although they may not like the chores involved and may find the role socially stifling, they find the new relationship, the opportunity to give and receive love, rewarding.[12]

Building on Brazelton's idea, some mothers experience an abrupt confrontation with reality after bringing the baby home. The baby's temperamental difficulties (e.g., easily stressed, colicky, difficult to comfort, poor state control) may strongly contribute to the mother's anxiety and depression.[35] Her anxieties may be translated into body language and transmitted to the infant, increasing the infant's anxiety (see Sullivan's theory in Chap. 8). The harder she tries, the more upset the baby seems to be. She begins to doubt her own ability to be a mother. This baby does not match her dreams. Adequate social support is essential.[35]

Motherhood itself may also fail to match the woman's dreams. When the novelty wears off, she may find herself feeling tired, bored, and unchallenged. Attempts to breast-feed may be aborted; the baby may be colicky. The lay literature abounds with articles and books about the bounties of motherhood. A woman may expect to have instant, overpowering love for the infant; she is surprised to discover that the birth experience did not suddenly turn her into a knowledgeable and loving mother. She may begin to question her sexuality, her motives, her ability to love. A mother or father frequently does not begin to feel love or a feeling of emotional reciprocity until the baby begins to socialize overtly with others.[122] A deep relationship takes time to develop; it evolves slowly, and many factors can block or facilitate that process (early contact after birth appears to facilitate the process). The bonding process is discussed later in this chapter.

Perhaps for the first time in her life, the new mother is responsible for someone else, not just for a few hours or a few days, but 24 hours a day, for a year, 5 years, 15 years, or more. This fact may have overwhelming ramifications for the woman if she feels that the child will continue to require as much care as has been necessary during the first few weeks or months of life. She may feel a loss of her own identity in the press of all the responsibility. During her pregnancy (and perhaps all her life), she has been cared for. Others concerned themselves about *her* safety, *her* emotions, and *her* diet, catering to *her* whims and needs. This time she is the caregiver. She is no longer the recipient but the giver of nurturance.

During pregnancy she was the center of attention. (How did she feel? Was she comfortable? Could anything be done to help her? How much longer did she have to go?) Now the baby is the focus. (How is his or her health? How much does he or she eat? Is the baby warm enough? How much does the baby weigh now?) The mother takes a back seat. The attention she does get is tangential to the infant's health and development.

One of the major precipitating factors of postpartum depression, especially for the primiparous woman, is the dramatic change in lifestyle. If the mother was working before the baby was born, she enjoyed a fixed schedule or routine. She could plan her day or her week. Now her schedule is unpredictable and out of her control. When she wants to sleep, the baby wants to eat; when she wants to watch television or spend time with her spouse, the baby demands attention. During the first months, she may feel that she is controlled by her offspring, a feeling that is especially true for parents of twins.[46] Fortunately, most infants begin to establish a predictable wake–sleep pattern by 3 months of age.

Another dramatic change in lifestyle that may be precipitated by the birth is the loss of adult contact, especially for the woman who had previously worked outside of the home. Her world now centers around the home and the baby. As the novelty wears off, the mother may experience sensory deprivation. She may feel isolated and depressed by the lack of adult contact. She needs stimulating conversation to keep her mind active and satiated; she needs to voice her own opinions to maintain a sense of self-identity and to test reality.

Another major precipitating factor of postpartum disturbance may be the mother's perception of her own time within the life space. To many women, childbirth signifies the point of transition from youth to adulthood. The new mother may suddenly realize that she is no longer looking ahead to what her life will be; she is there. She suddenly realizes how rapidly the preceding years have passed and may telescope the future. She is at a crisis point in life. Time seems to be passing too quickly (or, in some cases, too slowly). Thoughts of her own mortality are common, even though she realizes with gratitude that she survived the childbirth experience. She must face her own mortality and integrate this concept into her approach to life; she must complete the crisis of reintegration of her past, present, and future that was initiated by the pregnancy.

Many potential emotional hazards exist for the new mother. The older mother (in her thirties or forties) may find the change especially difficult. Her self-identity is undergoing dramatic modifications as her role, responsibilities, and relationships change. After years of competence in a career, she may be upset with her own lack of competence and expertise in infant care, or she may not feel comfortable playing with a baby.[86] Even the well-prepared mother of a much-wanted child faces these critical adjustment tasks. The transformation in self-identity to the role of a competent mother does not occur overnight. Most mothers begin to feel comfortable with their new role within 3 to 4 months.[122]

Cultural emphasis on production rather than reproduction also tends to make some mothers devalue their role as the caregiver and creator of a new generation, increasing feelings of depression. Many mature mothers, however, feel more prepared for parenting than young mothers and have a stronger sense of self-identity and autonomy, increased financial security and sense of control.[48] Their marriages are stronger, and the woman does not feel a need to consult the husband on everything.[86] These qualities help to minimize stressors and shorten the adjustment period.

Mercer identifies four stages in the adaptation to the maternal role:[98]

0 to 2 months: *Physical recovery.* The mother is attempting to meet the infant's basic needs while her own body is recovering.

2 to 4 months: *Achievement.* The mother begins to develop a sense of competence in infant care skills.

5 to 8 months: *Disruption.* As the infant's needs change, the mother must increase her flexibility in meeting the needs.

9 to 12 months: *Reorganization.* The mother sees herself, the child, and the world in a new way, restructuring her time and energies to meet her own and the child's needs.

Mothers who experience depression or difficulty with transition may call the Depression After Delivery and Postpartum Support International hot line for counseling, referral to support groups, or literature (215-295-3994).

Early, even severe, short-term depression does not appear to have long-term psychiatric effects on the child, although cognitive and language development may be delayed if parental responsiveness is inadequate in the early months.[30]

Psychotic Depression

True **puerperal psychosis** is rare.[27, 42] These mothers experience marked depression or severe adjustment difficulties to the new relationships and responsibilities.[30] Marked mood swings, severe irritability, bizarre behavior, paranoia, cognitive disorganization, and even hallucinations may be found.[27] Careful evaluation is essential to provide appropriate intervention to protect the infant and facilitate the mother's coping.[139] Counseling is essential and hospitalization is common. Untreated or unresolved severe maternal depression results in psychiatric disturbance in 30% to 50% of the children.[30]

Lactation

The American Academy of Pediatrics and several other leading medical societies strongly recommend the promotion of breast-feeding in the United States and throughout the world[66] because of the physiological advantages of breast-feeding for both the mother (e.g., decreased uterine involution time and delayed ovulation)[102] and the infant (e.g., species-specific nutritional composition of human breast milk, the nonallergenic and allergic protective properties of breast milk, and reception of antibodies in early breast milk).[106, 132, 143] In the long run, however, except for situations in which the infant is allergic to formula or it is difficult to maintain a sterile fresh supply of milk, the attitude of the mother toward herself, her infant, and her choice of feeding technique is more

significant than the actual method she uses to provide physical nourishment to the infant (Fig. 31-4).

Today, 62% percent of mothers in the United States choose to breast-feed.[132] The reasons against breast-feeding were cited in this chapter's introduction. The educated woman from a middle- or upper-income level is most likely to choose breast-feeding.[68] She may see breast-feeding as a natural part of her role as a mother and a normal extension of pregnancy and her psychosexual development. Her extended family may offer supportive encouragement, and her husband may express pride in her desire and ability to nurture the infant in this way. Some mothers choose to breast-feed because of peer pressure or as a status symbol. Others may breast-feed because their mothers, best friends, or husbands expect them to do so. The mother herself may feel that breast-feeding is the only way to be a "real" mother. However, if she harbors unconscious reservations about the exposure and touching of her breasts, her attitude will be transmitted to the baby, and the experience will prove to be unsatisfactory for both.

Some mothers may choose to breast-feed because it is easier, more convenient, and cheaper than bottle-feeding. However, dietary intake is important to the mother's health; she needs to add 130 calories to her intake for every 100 mL of milk she produces. Average daily milk production the first 4 months is 750 to 800 mL.[52] At full lactation, she produces 850 to 1200 mL of breast milk per day.[143] An additional 500 to 800 calories, 20 g of protein, adequate fluids, calcium, and vitamins must be provided.[143]

FIGURE 31-4.
Breast-feeding provides an excellent opportunity to provide sex education to young children. Preschool-age children often want to try to suckle.

About 40% to 50% of breast-feeding mothers continue to nurse their babies through the fourth month.[132] To be successful, the mother must first of all really want to breast-feed. Second, she must believe in her own ability to produce milk. All new mothers have some doubt about this phenomenon (and the breast does not have ounce markers to help her evaluate how much milk the baby is actually receiving). Her best assurance that the baby is adequately fed is the baby's response. Is the baby satisfied after feedings? Is the baby sleeping between feedings? Is the baby wetting diapers and gaining weight? If so, then the baby is getting enough to eat. Weighing after each nursing is unnecessary.

Many mothers say that they stopped nursing because their milk was "not rich enough," their breasts were not large enough, or they did not have enough milk.[132] In reality, the size of the breasts has no correlation with the amount of functional breast tissue. Most of what provides the breast contour is fat and connective tissue, not functional tissue. Breast milk is normally a translucent bluish white, watery fluid. Adequate production depends on adequate fluid intake and adequate suckling.[87] However, in our culture it is more acceptable to blame a physical malfunction than to admit self-doubt, embarrassment, or sexual anxiety as the real reason for failure.

Successful breast-feeding is ensured when the woman has enough knowledge about the process of lactation to be able to understand and work with her body. The breast undergoes preparation for lactation during pregnancy. There is growth of the secretory alveoli or acini of the breast and frequently some secretion of **colostrum,** the precursor of breast milk.[52] This yellowish fluid is high in protein, fat, sugar, salts, and antibodies. After delivery, psychic factors and the suckling of the breast stimulate a neurohormonal reflex of the nipple, which in turn causes the posterior pituitary to continue production of oxytocin.[102] Oxytocin appears to stimulate production of prolactin by the anterior pituitary. Prolactin, in turn, stimulates the secretion of milk by the cells that line the mammary alveoli.[52, 102] Oxytocin, the hormone that caused the contraction of uterine muscles during labor, continues to help the uterus to return to prepregnant size. During the first week after delivery, many breast-feeding mothers experience uterine cramps while nursing the infant. Oxytocin also causes contraction of the muscles that surround the milk glands and ducts, which accounts for the "milk letdown reflex" experienced by mothers and facilitates the flow of milk from the nipple.[52, 102]

The marvelous reflexive process of milk production allows the mothers to breast-feed under unusual circumstances. Occasionally, because of maternal illness, neonate illness, or a late decision to breast-feed, the mother may not nurse for 2 weeks or more after delivery. However, even in the absence of any previous stimulation, lactation can be established successfully at this late date. In fact, even the mother who has not delivered a baby but is increasing her family through adoption can initiate the same neurohormonal reflex and cause her breasts to begin lactation. Although it may take

her several weeks of persistent nursing effort, she can stimulate production of enough milk to meet much of the baby's nutritional needs.[18, 87, 90, 155]

Continued production of milk depends on emptying at least one breast at each feeding.[143] Milk is produced continually in the alveoli during lactation. The milk is transported through tiny ducts to 15 to 20 large sinuses behind the nipple, which function as reservoirs for the milk until suckling occurs. Emptying of the reservoirs depends on both suction and compression during nursing. The infant empties the sinuses of milk in 5 to 10 minutes of vigorous suckling, but mothers usually suckle the baby longer after the nipples "toughen" to satisfy the baby's need to suck as well as to provide nourishment. This suckling period also offers a special time for the mother and infant to communicate with each other.

Complete emptying of the breast appears to stimulate continued production of milk. Frequent emptying increases the speed of production, whereas infrequent nursing slows down production. During the first 2 to 3 weeks, the neonate may nurse 10 to 12 times a day.[68] Most infants nurse about every 3 hours. Mothers can successfully breast-feed twins or even triplets by this mechanism.[87] The other children or even her husband may want to suckle. These are normal events, and they do not reduce the amount of milk available to the infant. Women can continue to lactate for years if they are adequately stimulated,[90] although most mothers prefer to transfer the baby to a cup by the time the child is 10 to 12 months of age.

Weaning should be a gradual rather than an abrupt process for both the mother and the infant. Abrupt cessation of nursing causes an excessive and painful accumulation of milk in the lactiferous sinuses and can lead to mastitis. It may also precipitate maternal depression.[106] Even when ill, most mothers can and are encouraged to continue breast-feeding.[68] A woman may continue to excrete small amounts of milk for 4 to 5 years after cessation of breast-feeding.

Some medications taken by a breast-feeding mother pass through the milk and are potentially harmful to the infant. Consequently, any recommended medications should be checked for potential effects on the infant before administration. If it is potentially harmful to the infant, breast-feeding can be temporarily discontinued, but lactation maintained through pumping until the medication is discontinued.[19, 106]

The mother and baby are most ready to nurse immediately after delivery (Fig. 31-5).[132, 143] The infant in state 4 is able to respond eagerly and to coordinate sucking and swallowing reflexes. The licking and suckling stimulation of the nipple encourages early production of milk (within 2 to 3 days). When the mother is forced to wait 12 to 24 hours before nursing, the infant is frequently too sleepy or too agitated to take the nipple easily, sucking and swallowing reflexes may be poorly coordinated, and the nipple inadequately stimulated. Milk production, therefore, may be delayed until the fourth or fifth day after delivery.

Many breast-feeding mothers experience nipple tenderness. One of the most critical factors is the "latching on" process. The infant must have sufficient nipple in the mouth to

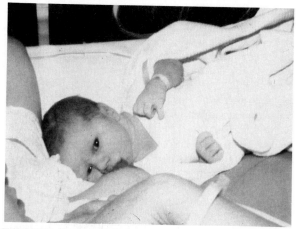

FIGURE 31–5.
When offered the breast within the first hour after birth, the baby is usually alert and able to coordinate the sucking and swallowing reflexes. Immediate breast-feeding not only fosters earlier production of milk but also facilitates the mother–infant bonding process.

be able to compress the milk sinuses and to extract the milk (Fig. 31-6). It is necessary that a large part of the areola be included in the "bite." If only the nipple is inserted, vigorous sucking action is required to obtain milk, resulting in excessive friction on the nipple as well as incomplete emptying of the sinuses.

Mothers are usually encouraged to alternate breasts at each feeding to assure adequate emptying and to prevent soreness to the nipples. Changing the position of the baby during nursing (e.g., lying down versus sitting up) can also help to prevent or alleviate nipple tenderness.[68, 87, 114, 132] Rubbing the nipples gently with a towel during pregnancy and limiting nursing time to 10 minutes during the early feedings

may help to avoid soreness. Even with these precautions, however, many mothers experience some soreness or even nipple bleeding between the sixth and tenth day after delivery. These symptoms disappear as the nipples "toughen." Release of the suction by inserting a finger into the corner of the baby's mouth before removal from the breast can help to avoid nipple irritation throughout the nursing period.[147]

Both lactating and nonlactating mothers experience **primary engorgement** 2 to 3 days after delivery, which is caused by increased blood flow to the breasts in preparation for milk production. Women may complain of tenderness in the breasts and the armpits. Although postdelivery medication can help to reduce the intensity of primary engorgement, little can be done to offer relief for the discomfort except to take pain medication. Primary engorgement subsides gradually after 2 to 3 days. The breasts of nonlactating mothers return to normal size about 3 weeks after delivery.

Secondary engorgement occurs after the breasts begin to produce milk. Before this time, the baby receives colostrum during nursing. When the milk "comes in," the mammary ducts and lactiferous sinuses may fill rapidly. Discomfort due to secondary engorgement can be relieved through frequent, brief nursing to prevent over distention of the sinuses. Once the sinuses have been stretched, the filling preceding each nursing is no longer painful, even though the breast may feel firm to the touch.

Lactating mothers also experience a decrease in breast size in 2 to 3 weeks. This phenomenon, combined with the baby's "appetite spurt" and need for more milk, may cause the mother to believe that her milk has "dried up." Adequate rest, fluids, diet, and frequent nursing ensure continued production. Supplemental bottles are usually discouraged during the first month, since they may interfere with the establishment of the balance between supply and demand. "Mature milk" is not produced until about 2 weeks, and compositional alterations may continue until about 12 weeks.[52] Supplemental

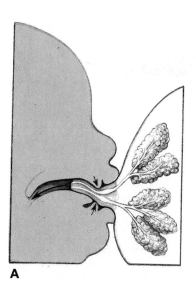

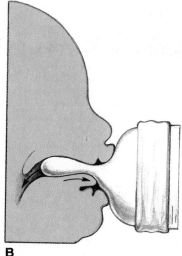

FIGURE 31–6.
Correct position of the baby's mouth on the nipple.

A   **B**

bottles are also discouraged because a different type of sucking action is required to extract the milk. Some believe the binipple experience can be confusing to the young baby.[68, 143]

Milk production is sensitive to psychic influences. Suckling, sleep, and sexual intercourse increase prolactin production.[90] Fatigue, fear, pain, anxiety, or emotional stress can inhibit the "letdown reflex" and decrease milk production. Thinking about nursing or hearing the baby cry can elicit the letdown reflex, causing a tingling sensation and release of milk. The oxytocin-induced letdown reflex can actually cause the milk to squirt 3 to 4 feet from the uncovered breast. Gentle pressure against the nipple effectively stops the leakage. (If the mother is out for a formal evening, crossing of the arms over the breasts can effectively and discreetly apply pressure against the nipples.)

Breast-feeding is an exciting and positive experience for the woman who is secure in her own psychosexual development and who views nursing as a natural sequela to pregnancy. Such a woman finds breast-feeding emotionally satisfying and an aid to communication with and attachment to her new baby. Relaxin, a hormone released during the suckling, can also help the mother feel more relaxed and secure in her role as primary caregiver, nurturer, and mother of the neonate.

La Leche League International (9616 Minneapolis Avenue, Franklin Park, IL 60131, 312-455-7730) is an organization established by mothers to evaluate and disseminate information on breast-feeding to mothers and professional people. This organization has branches throughout the United States and even overseas where mothers meet together to offer mutual support and understanding.

THE NEW FAMILY

Most parents experience a feeling of awe and reverence at the birth of their child. They are overwhelmed by the miracle of birth and gaze in amazement at the tiny creature they were instrumental in creating. Prepared parents who participated actively in the birth experience talk to anyone and everyone who will listen for days and weeks after the birth as if trying to validate and absorb the reality of the event. They experience a "high" that extends beyond the birth and helps in the establishment of a positive relationship with the baby. The maturing individual who is successfully integrating past, present, and future is able to transfer the love for the fantasy child to the real child. The new infant is seen as a part of self, a part of the mate, and yet as an individual entity.[8]

Bonding

The early verbal and nonverbal experiences between infant and parents create a pattern of mutuality that subconsciously establishes the tone for interpersonal relationships and their intrapsychic coloring throughout life. Attachment of the infant to the parent has been discussed in Chapter 8. Specific characteristics of the infant, such as head shape, body movement,

and vocalization appear to serve as "biological releasers" of adult caregiving behaviors.[137] Because dependence during infancy is almost absolute, it is essential that strong affectional ties are established by the parents toward the infant to ensure adequate physical and affectional nurturing during the early months of life. Parents exhibit their affectional ties to the infant through nonverbal behaviors such as vocalizing, rocking, preening and fondling, kissing, attending promptly, providing body and breath warmth, cuddling, and prolonged gazing. These parental behaviors appear to be essential to the early security and thus to the development of the infant (Fig. 31-7).[81, 152]

Brazelton,[17] Bowlby,[13] and Mahler[95] have written quite profusely and elegantly on the mother–infant dyad or bonding process—the intimate attachment of each to the other—that is characterized during the early months by a mutual focusing on the infant's needs. This process is followed by a gradual decentering, with mutually reciprocal interaction. The individuation of the two members of the system is usually completed by 3 years, but they continue to maintain a heavy emotional investment in each other throughout life.[95] This ability of the parent to become and to remain socially attached to the infant ensures the survival of the young. "The caregiver's responsiveness to the infant's signals predicts the quality of attachment."[142] Research is beginning to indicate that infantile autism, nonorganic failure-to-thrive, learning disabilities, and the battered child syndrome may be related to inadequate responsiveness of the mother to her infant.*[22, 47, 119]

Early interaction appears to be facilitated through the possession of specific characteristics, or "tools," on the part of both the parent and the infant. When functioning optimally, the reciprocal use of these tools can lead to an intense, mutually satisfying relationship. Infant tools have already been described in Chapter 7. The infant's use of these tools helps to affirm parenting efforts and empathy, endear the child to the parent, and encourage continued investment of time and energies to meet the infant's physical and social needs.[17, 107] However, parenting behaviors are influenced more by the parents' temperament personality profile (self-concept, empathy, flexibility, allocentrism) than the infant's temperament.[98] Sensitivity, empathy, and responsivity appear to be the critical personality traits.[135] The most effective parents balance empathy (child's experience) with objectivity (parents' experience).[131] Even the best mothers only respond to about 55% of the infant's crying.[135] Parents become "flexibly

---

* This inadequate response does not mean that the mother does not love her child, nor does it rule out organic or attachment-tool deficits on the part of the infant that may set up barriers to parental bonding. It takes **two persons** to establish the synchrony of interaction. Many of these infant–parent dyads fail to establish this critical synchrony during the early weeks after birth, when maternal heightened axiety is at its peak. Negative experiences or faulty expectancies on the part of either parent or infant can lead to maladaptive behaviors and inappropriate cueing and responding on the part of either or both.

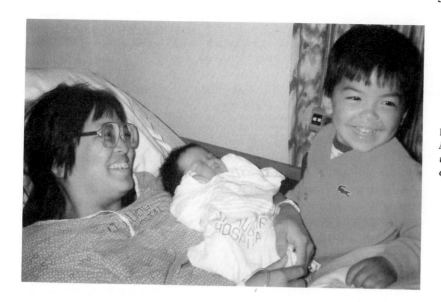

FIGURE 31-7.
Many hospitals encourage siblings to visit to facilitate bonding and to decrease rivalry.

available" to provide security and challenge for learning and for autonomy.[6]

Parental Tools

Contact with an appealing baby appears to elicit specific responses from adults, even when previous contact with babies has been minimal or absent. Whether these responses are imitated by watching others (learned), remembered from mothering received as a child (memory traces), or instinctual in nature (innate), no one knows. The stability of these characteristics across cultures and centuries leads one to believe that they are innate. However, humans are so strongly influenced by culture, experience, and preconceived views of others that innate behaviors are easily submerged or extinguished by stress, traditions, or perceived roles. Some behaviors appear to help make the infant more alert and to foster increased quantity and quality of interaction.

The use of a **high-pitched voice** is the most fascinating of all phenomena to observe. When an adult (and even many children) is facing and talking to an infant, the voice immediately softens and elevates. In the middle of a sentence, the person may turn to an adult or child in the room and, without taking a breath, drop to normal-pitched speech. The episode is reversed just as rapidly. Data clearly indicate that infants have a strong preference for the high-pitched female voice.[49] Many mothers have an insatiable desire to talk to the baby, especially to repeat the name frequently as if to connect the two, to reassure themselves of the reality of this new life in their care, to confirm the miracle. With the neonate's ability to turn to sound and to synchronize movements with speech rhythms, the mother is reinforced to repeat the behavior.[28]

Rocking behavior is usually observed when a baby is held even if the child is asleep. Those with strong parental instincts are even noted to rock and "jiggle" a baby doll in child care classes when learning infant care. This rocking behavior, in addition to soothing the child and significantly increasing visual scanning behavior up to 71% when accompanied by elevation to the shoulder, is thought to excite vestibular stimulation, thus facilitating coordination and voluntary control of movements.[85] Harlow has shown that monkeys raised in isolation with a stationary, nonmovable "mother" develop severe autostimulatory behaviors, including self-cuddling, self-rocking, biting, scratching, and hair pulling.[4] When approached by another monkey or a human, they withdraw in marked fear. If physical contact is made, they react with immediate, uncontrolled, aggressive, hostile behaviors. Monkeys with movable "mothers" did not exhibit these behaviors. Rocking activity, then, appears to be essential to the coordination and development of the physical, affective, social, and cognitive domains. Evidence derived from growth patterns of premature infants indicates that weight gains are accelerated when the infant is stimulated by regular rocking or movement in moderate amounts (e.g., use of water beds).

Attending is another characteristic observed in parents who are bonding to their infant. They may spend up to 90% of interaction time just looking at the infant.[135] It is as if they are visually engulfing the child, making him or her a part of themselves. Since infants prefer a facial pattern, they are stimulated to return the attending behavior. Assumption of the **en face position** (the full-face eye-to-eye position) is also characteristic of parents who are developing an attachment to their infant (Fig. 31-8). Eye-to-eye contact holds the infant's attention for longer periods of time and helps the parent to feel accepted by and closer to the infant.[12, 120, 134] When the adult's and infant's faces are at cross planes rather than parallel to each other, the infant does not attend as easily or as long.

Smiling and **highly exaggerated mouth and eye movements** also elicit longer fixation responses from the infant, especially after the neonatal period.[120, 140] This activity again is mutually reinforcing, especially when combined with adult vocalization.

Enfolding is a more complex behavior, incorporating

FIGURE 31–8.
En face position; the mother's and baby's eyes are parallel.

several other patterns that are more difficult to identify, such as touch, muscle tone, and body blending. Infants become quiet with a gentle, relaxed touch. They also are quieted by the low, rhythmic beating of the heart heard when they are held close to the caregiver's chest. This close contact allows for stimulation of the olfactory sense and provision of warmth. Ashley Montagu speaks of the importance of touch in communication.[103] Tactile-kinesthetic stimulation, appropriately given, facilitates relaxation in the neonate. This relaxation of infant muscle tone is a tactile as well as an affective reinforcer to the caregiver.

Moderation of stimuli is observed in sensitive parents. By **pacing** the intensity and frequency of the stimuli they offer the baby, based on the infant's cues, they are able to help the infant to maintain an optimally alert state to interact with the environment.[135] If the tempo is too fast, it exceeds the infant's ability to process information, leading to overload, irritability, and delayed affective and cognitive development. Sensitivity to the current developmental level, signals, and needs of the child enables the parent to facilitate developmental maturation.[135]

The parent, like the infant (as described in Chap. 7), is in possession of critical tools that facilitate parent-infant interaction and bonding. As the baby uses a tool, the caregiver reciprocates with a reinforcing tool that encourages the infant to repeat the behavior or to continue the interaction; thus, a ballet of interaction can be observed and objectively recorded. The foundation is established for a mutually rewarding relationship that supports the development of the infant. The development of parental bonding can be facilitated by helping parents to become aware of and sensitive to the interaction cues emitted by the infant and to use reciprocal behaviors appropriately to elicit infant responses.[15,99] Too much or too little use of parental tools can tire or understimulate the baby (see Chap. 13). Paternal bonding and maternal bonding appear to

be parallel processes.[93,137] However, biophysical and social/cultural issues can create different paths or ways to express and develop their bonds.

Maternal Bonding

Because of biological, socialization, and cultural issues, parenthood tends to have a greater impact on women than on men.[12,137,150] After the birth of the baby, the mother must accomplish the critical task of establishing a mutually satisfactory, symbiotic affectional relationship with the baby. Contrary to popular thought, this task often is not accomplished instantaneously nor easily. The attachment process begins during pregnancy. When fetal movements begin to be felt, a form of communication is sensed by the mother, and even the unwanted baby usually begins to be accepted.[80] Immediately after delivery, the mother's body undergoes dramatic changes in hormonal balance, fluid shifts, and repositioning of body organs; dramatic changes in intrapersonal and interpersonal relationships occur as well. All these factors appear to predispose her to a state of "heightened maternal anxiety," in which cognitive and affective energies are focused toward the infant's welfare.[12] This anxiety tends to keep the mother near her infant and highly responsive to the infant's cues. Prolonged and multiple contacts with the infant during this time appear to facilitate maternal bonding.[14]

The affectional attachment process is fragile and tenuous. Not all mothers feel instantaneous connectedness.[121] Some may feel trapped by the infant's dependency and fear losing their own autonomy.[6] Others feel an immediate comfortable reciprocity with the infant. Still others find it difficult to believe that this child *really* belongs to them, never to be given back to another.

Mothers from disrupted families of origin (e.g., divorce, death before age 16) are less contingent in their responses to their infant and talk, smile, touch, or present objects to the infant less frequently even though the baby may be responsive. At 5 months, these mothers are less likely to see the child as a person.[111] Perhaps they are afraid to lose their heart to another for fear of repeated loss. Although cultural and social class differences in the degree of maternal-infant bonding or sensitivity of interaction with neonates and infants are documented, they are based on education and social-emotional developmental level and not on economic issues per se.[45]

"While bonds of affection are still forming, they can be easily retarded, altered or permanently damaged."[80] Minor problems during pregnancy, a difficult labor and delivery, premature birth, or minor problems after birth can interfere with the bonding process of the mother. She may resent the child who has caused her so much pain and anxiety or may resist attachment for fear she will lose the child. This feeling is a normal defense against the pain of loss.

At the turn of the century, Budin noted that premature infants were frequently abandoned by their mothers when they were not allowed to see the baby or to participate in their care.[15] Cooney made the same observations in the 1930s. Klaus and Kennell observed that an inordinately high proportion of healthy premature infants from their hospital became victims of parental abuse and neglect.[79] A search of the literature revealed that 13% to 36% of children who are severely neglected or abused were premature or experienced prolonged separation from the mothers. They postulated the existence of a biologically determined "sensitive period" for attachment and bonding by the mother.

Klaus and his associates set up an experiment that involved 14 mothers of normal newborn infants.[83] The mothers were given 1 hour of private contact time with their nude infant during the first 2 hours after birth; they were also given the nude baby for 5 extra hours per day on each of the next 3 days of life for a total of 14 extra hours of contact time during the hospital stay. The interaction of these mothers with their infants was then compared to the interaction of control mothers who did not experience this extra time. Mothers who had early and frequent contact with the infant showed more attachment behaviors (looking at the infant; smiling at the infant; holding the infant closely; rocking, talking to, and caressing the infant) at 1 month after discharge than mothers who experienced minimal contact or prolonged separation.[83] These mothers were also much more reluctant to leave the infant with another caregiver to go out for an afternoon or an evening. Not all replications of this study have supported the "sensitive-period" theory.[81] For high-risk babies or mothers, however, the early contact appears to make a profound difference in the quality of mother–infant interaction.

Early maternal contact also appears to be highly correlated with the later exploratory behavior of the infant.[83] When the children from Klaus' study were 2 years old, the mothers offered fewer verbal commands but asked more questions of their children.[118] When these same children were 5 years old, they had significantly higher IQs and advanced scores on two language tests.[117] Thus, the child's cognitive, affective, social, and even physical development may be indirectly facilitated by early and extended mother–infant contact.

The rooming-in experience in the hospital allows both the mother and father frequent and prolonged contact with their baby. Lactation induces an emotional state that intensifies the receptive and retentive tendencies that are experienced during pregnancy and heightened with a positive childbirth experience, thereby facilitating affectional symbiosis. "Frequent and intimate contact with a thriving infant has a stimulating and integrating effect on motherliness."[5] It is evident that early contact with an alert baby promotes positive feelings. In addition, knowledge of infant care and characteristics offsets maternal insecurity.

Mothers are noted to progress through an orderly sequence of behaviors on introduction to their new baby after delivery. Klaus and Kennell describe the first step as "looking." The mother seeks eye-to-eye contact with the infant; she assumes the en face position and appears to "engulf" the baby visually. This behavior is noted to be present in some mothers for months. It is as if they are visually reassuring themselves of the reality of the infant's presence. Mothers who are attaching express the feeling that they cannot seem to satiate their need to look at the child; every movement and every breath are noted. The bonding process is facilitated when this introduction occurs immediately after birth, since both the mother and infant are in heightened states of alertness and receptivity. The infant's open, alert eyes associated with state 4 enhance the mother's feelings that the infant is looking at, accepting, and getting to know her.

When the naked baby is placed in close proximity to the mother, she begins to touch the infant's extremities with her fingertips for about 4 to 8 minutes.[83] The fully clothed and wrapped baby may be "finger-tipped" for a longer period of time. She gradually progresses to the "palming" stage, in which the mother begins to touch the baby with her whole hand, starting first with the arms and legs and then moving to the trunk with caressing and massaging movements. Reva Rubin identifies these behaviors as being associated with the "taking in" phase of attachment.[128]

During the "taking-hold" phase (which lasts about 10 days), the mother begins to enfold the baby and to mold more easily to the infant's contours. She is beginning to recognize the little signs that indicate discomfort, hunger, or the desire to be held. During this phase, the mother is full of questions and is receptive to teaching: she needs encouragement and support in feeling competent to care for this new life. All her attention and energies are focused on the needs of the infant. The mother may focus so much attention on the infant that she ignores her own needs for rest. She is usually discharged from the health care facility during this time. Family members need to provide adequate care and support to prevent overtiring, especially if other children are in the home.

Although still in Mahler's autistic period, the mother gradually begins to "let go" about 2 weeks after delivery.[128] She begins to regard the infant as a separate individual and to attend to some of her own unique needs (e.g., she may have her hair done at the beauty parlor or fix a special dinner for her husband). Some mothers take longer to reach this third phase. Mothers who continue with high intensity responsiveness begin to show signs of "burn out." It is important to the development of both the baby and the mother that she take the initial steps toward separation.[6, 16, 95, 131]

Because amniocentesis and ultrasonography are available, parents frequently know their infant's gender before birth. Evidence indicates that feelings of well-being and attachment to the fetus increase after viewing the infant by sonography and the assurance that the baby appears to be healthy.[84, 100] However, a study of the effect of this knowledge on the mother's behavior 2 to 5 days after delivery indicates no significant difference in the bonding behaviors exhibited by the mothers.[57]

The confident, secure mother is able to "lose" herself, "regress" to the service of the infant, yet retain her own individuality while achieving essential empathy and intimacy with her infant.[6] Motherliness is a dynamic reciprocal state that requires changes in the quantity and quality of the relationship with age, situation, and maturation of both the child and the mother.

Paternal Bonding

No matter how egalitarian a relationship, birth of the first child tends to divide the responsibilities into more traditional roles.[104, 108, 124] The couple changes its focus from romantic involvement to a partnership in the "business" of raising a child. Although the basic emotional reactions to parenthood are similar in many ways, and both parents derive positive feelings from the assumption of parenting responsibilities, some critical differences in how these feelings may be expressed or acted on are noted.[75, 124] **Fatherliness is not synonymous with motherliness.**

Women repeatedly report that they have the final responsibility for the care of the children regardless of whether or not they are employed outside the home.[12, 88, 89] The father is seen and sees himself as a helper or facilitator. The mother who has respite assistance or another adult in the home is less irritable, warmer, and more emotionally stable in dealing with the infant and expresses increased life-satisfaction.[12]

Most women are socialized all their life for motherhood.[12] However, men don't have as much support throughout life to develop a paternal role, image, and identity because the culture tends to shut the man out of the "woman's domain."[54] Traditionally, men have been seen as the bread winners, protectors, sex-role models, leaders, and the bridges to the outside world.[25] The image of "manliness" portrayed by the mass media rarely includes the warm, tender, affectionate, involved, responsible father. When these characteristics are portrayed, it is often with humor, a hint of weakness, or as character flaws that rob the man of his ability to think objectively or retain power or respect.

It is only during the last generation that men in Western societies have been encouraged to assume an active, nurturing, responsible caregiving role.[88] The more autonomous and mature men are breaking with tradition to assume new responsibilities and to establish sensitive relationships with their children.[61, 88, 91, 110] Feelings of warmth, devotion, protectiveness, and pleasure at physical contact are expected of mothers. However, these qualities have not been culturally fostered in men. However, *the capacities to empathize and respond emotionally to others and the ability to value a love object more than the self are human characteristics* essential to healthy interpersonal relationships (Fig. 31-9).[74]

"Though young men today may be liberated to act more nurturant to newborns, internal psychological resources accompanying that mode of relating may not be readily available to them."[54] A father, insecure in his new role or identity, may feel confused as he tries to sort out these new feelings, his masculinity, and his new responsibilities. One third of new fathers suffer depression, due to financial concerns, anxiety over the wife's or infant's welfare, feelings of incompetence, conflicting pulls of employment and home, or the sexual readjustment.[71, 108, 154]

Those with high marital satisfaction are most likely to become actively involved in the parenting roles.[44, 91] Increased emotional involvement with their mates allows the man to get in touch with the "hidden side" of masculinity by

FIGURE 31–9.
Feelings of tenderness and gentleness are human characteristics, not the prerogatives of women.

tapping feelings of empathy, fear, and sympathy and by encouraging expressions of caring, concern, and tenderness.[116] Pregnancy and childbirth provide men as well as women with a new meaning and direction to life and another avenue for maturation (Fig. 31-10).[108]

New mothers and fathers feel equally incompetent and anxious at first; however, when the man has decreased opportunity to master child care and interactive skills (e.g., because he must got to work to ensure financial stability of the family, arrives home late, or mother "shuts him out"), he often decreases his attempts at child care, gradually feeling less competent while the mother increases her comfort in parenting.[63, 88, 93] Although men and women show equal concern by responding to infant crying with increased heart rate and blood pressure, many men are uncomfortable with the care of a small, weak baby.[11] Despite all the hype about father involvement, 40% of fathers have never even changed a diaper.[92] Mothers serve as the "gatekeeper" of paternal involvement.[63, 110] Forty percent of fathers express that they would like to be more involved in infant care; however, 60% to 80% of mothers are unwilling to allow them more involvement.[72, 115] Many mothers see child care as their role. A request for father assistance may be viewed as an admission of their own incompetence or a demasculinization of her partner, a view still held by some men.[12, 88] The process of decision making and negotiation is more important than who does what.[108]

Many men feel cheated out of one of life's most precious experiences. However, even though fathers may have limited involvement in the *physical* care of their offspring, most mothers and 80% of fathers say that he is *emotionally* involved in the child's welfare and guidance, especially with sons.[12, 88]

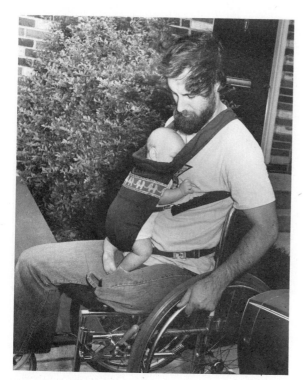

FIGURE 31–10.
Fathers can and do provide sensitive care to young children. Children tend to have higher cognitive functioning when fathers are actively involved in caregiving and parenting.

Fathers tend to become more involved as the child begins to walk, talk, and engage in social games.[93, 124] Although fathers today spend only about 20% to 30% as much time with their children as mothers in one-to-one interaction,[89] two thirds of women say that the fathers enjoy the children as much or more than they do.[12] Because fathers are not swamped by the moment-by-moment demands of parenting, they engage in more play activities and have time to be more reflective about the problems faced, placing issues into broader context.[12]

When fathers are actively involved during the pregnancy, delivery, and postpartum periods, their attachment to the neonate appears to be as strong as the mother's.[58, 59] The period immediately after delivery is especially conducive to the development of affectional ties. When fathers are present at the delivery, they go through a period of **engrossment**— intense preoccupation with thoughts of the infant—similar to that experienced by the mother.[59] Strong paternal affectional bonds are enhanced by early contact with the open-eyed, alert infant. Like the mother, fathers who are separated from their offspring during the early days, weeks, or months of life have more difficulty developing strong emotional ties and showing affection to their offspring.[59]

Sensitivity appears to be a consequence of contact with the baby rather than a precursor to involvement.[50] "Love develops through simple everyday actions—such as feeding, comforting, bathing, or playing with the child."[70] Studies of fathers as primary caregivers have revealed them to be just as sensitive and responsive as mothers to infant cues and equally competent in providing affection, stimulation, and physical care.[113, 133] Their behaviors are not replicas of mothering behavior but are complimentary, unique to their own experience and personality. Fathers who are primary caregivers find parenting to be a positive, growth-producing experience.[113] They experience an increase in empathy and flexibility and increased confidence in themselves as capable, generous persons.[58, 113]

Father behaviors tend to be more exciting and stimulating, motivating the child toward active involvement in the environment.[58, 75, 153] Mothers tend to have gentler, more soothing behaviors that console or succor the child. The infant is aware of these differences in interaction, seeking the father for play and the mother when frightened.[93] This difference in parental focus continues through middle childhood.[130] Children with highly involved fathers (40% or more of child care) tend to exhibit higher cognitive competence, advanced developmental functioning, increased empathy, decreased sex-stereotyped beliefs, better peer relations, higher self-esteem, increased confidence, higher leadership skills, and increased internal locus of control.[58, 88, 89, 113]

The bonded, committed father plays multiple roles, influencing directly (or indirectly through support of the mother) the development of the child in the following ways:[25]

1. Provides physical caregiving
2. Serves as an alternative attachment figure
3. Provides for basic needs: food, shelter, clothing
4. Modulates the child's affect
5. Facilitates gender identity
6. Models communication and negotiation patterns
7. Assists with group relatedness
8. Facilitates the separation–individuation process
9. Sets standards and guidelines for behavior
10. Enforces discipline
11. Supports and relieves mother's role
12. Influences the social and emotional climate
13. Guides toward growth-producing experiences
14. Mediates conflicts with others (mother, school)

In the small nuclear family, the father's involvement in child nurturing is essential for maximal development of all family members. When given the chance, the father's bond and responsiveness to the cues of the young infant are as sensitive as the mother's.[60] Skill, not gender, becomes the criterion for effective parenting. As a man becomes more involved in child care, both he and the child experience increased options for the expression of their own uniqueness. Both begin to see themselves as competent, a factor that has a cumulatively positive effect.[60] "Many [men] are beginning to recognize the value of male parenthood not only for their children and families as a unit, but for their own personal growth and fulfillment. Indeed, men are discovering that parenting is self-actualizing."[65]

Adoptive Parenting

The question has been raised about whether or not it is the delay in the introduction of a child to adoptive parents that may account for some of the difficulties adoptive parents express in completing the bonding process successfully.[59,81] Adoption does present some unique barriers, but most components parallel those of bonding in biological parents. The key is the adoptive parents' commitment to the new child.[148]

1. A healthy parental attachment depends on a sense of **entitlement** to be a parent to the child. Those who see kinship limited to blood ties experience more difficulty admitting the child to the emotional bond of the family. Fear that the child may be removed from the home may "keep love at arm's length."[136] Once a child is legally and morally free for adoption, the parents can invest themselves without fear of loss. Most biological parents never face the entitlement crisis. However, some women face this in out-of-wedlock pregnancies.

2. Couples need a **validation** of parenthood. The pregnant couple with a wanted child find that friends and family offer support. After the baby is born, announcements are circulated and the child is greeted by the community. Adoptive parents need this same reassurance of acceptance by significant other people.

3. Adoptive parents need assistance with **preparation** for parenthood as much as biological couples.[94] They also need opportunities to talk about the feelings and the role changes that emerge with an expanded family.[146]

4. When a new baby is born, the relatives engage in **claiming behaviors** that help to identify the child as a family member; name choosing, pointing out family resemblances, and religious ceremonies all facilitate bonding. Some of these same events occur with adoption. Pictures are placed on walls and stories are shared to help claim the adopted child into the nuclear family.[148] Some parents consciously or unconsciously refuse to acknowledge the child's biological or hereditary differences. It is a painful reminder of their own infertility or raises fears of losing the child's love.[136] "Hereditary ghosts" can interfere with the process of entitlement as well as the child's sense of generational continuity. Adoptive parents need to acknowledge and openly communicate the child's adoptive status. The need to discuss the child's biological and ethnic background often increases with age as cognitive processes mature and identity issues are actively faced.[136]

5. **Love** develops gradually over time as synchrony of interaction is established (Fig. 31-11). **Commitment** to the child's day-to-day care, mutual enjoyment of leisure time, and joint mastery of goals endear the parent and child to each other as they get to know each other as unique

FIGURE 31–11.
Whether adopted or biological, it is important for parents to spend enough time with the child, interacting at his or her level of interest and development, so that each can understand and "love" the other.

people. When the other criteria are satisfied, 75% to 87% of adoptive parents feel that the child (even an older child) is their own within 1 month after placement.[43]

Parental Attachment Patterns

So far, we have written as if bonding always occurs immediately and in the hospital setting. Lest we be accused of perpetuating the "motherhood or parenthood myth," a few more observations need to be made. **Bonding,** or the affectional sacrificial commitment of one person to the welfare and needs of another, is a *gradual process.* What we have discussed so far are the precursors to that process and the environmental conditions that appear to influence the strength of the bond.

Components of parental attachment or bonding include feelings of warmth; a sense of possession; feelings of devotion, protectiveness, and concern; acceptance of inconveniences; a positive anticipation of prolonged contact; pleasure in the interaction; and a sense of loss over real or imagined absence.[122] These feelings are not automatically present with the birth or adoption of the baby or child; they develop over time in a fairly regular pattern.

Research by Robson and Moss indicates that, at first contact, 34% of mothers reported having no special attachment feelings at all.[122] (This finding is not necessarily contradictory to the observation that new mothers frequently experience a great sense of awe on first contact with their offspring; one can feel awe without having a feeling of belonging.) Seven percent of the mothers reported negative feelings, and 55% reported positive feelings. Only 4% indicated experiencing a real "love" at first sight. During the first few days, as many as 75% of mothers and 50% of fathers report experiencing a feeling of estrangement.[93] The neonate may be seen as inanimate or subhuman. Mothers attempt to make meaningful contact and often personalize the infant's behaviors. Flailing of the arms may be interpreted as "waving at me," eye-to-eye contact interpreted as "waking up for me."[122]

During the first month, the mothers are tired and often feel insecure and unable to control the crying, eating, sleeping, and stooling patterns. An irritable, crying infant tends to increase the father's anxiety about competency and lifestyle changes even more than it does for mothers, issues that increase marital tension.[150] When parents are unable to communicate with their infants, they look for the little signs of fleeting smiles, eye-to-eye contact, and vocalization efforts as reinforcers for being a "good parent." Many mothers question their decision to have a baby during that first month.[122] As the infant's tools strengthen, positive feelings begin to emerge. Between the fourth and sixth weeks, the infant becomes a *person* to parents. They begin to feel that their efforts are rewarded with reciprocal attention, a factor that increases feelings of rapport.[122]

Mothers begin to feel important and needed when they observe differential responses of the infant to them versus other people. By the end of 3 months, most feel strongly attached to the infant.[122] Even mothers who experience very negative feelings toward the infant during the first 6 weeks can begin to feel just as strongly in a positive way once the infant begins to respond more definitively.

The attachment process appears to be affected by the mother's personality and level of emotional development, the mother's life experiences and preparation for the birth, and the infant's behavioral characteristics or use of tools.[122] For mothers who experience early attachment (during the first 2 days of life), the infant's social behaviors are insignificant; the critical factor is the intensity of the mother's desire for the baby.[122] These mothers are calm, secure, and competent and experienced in child care, and they see the infant as a part of themselves and yet as a unique entity. The infant's social skills become critical to maintaining the attachment. Late attachers typically have ambivalent feelings about having a baby or becoming a mother and exhibit more anxiety. Their babies may be difficult to care for, or they give little cause for love or inadequate response to the mothers' caregiving efforts. Some mothers simply do not want the baby. The attachment bond becomes stronger as the infant responds to care. The infant's ability to smile and give eye-to-eye contact appears to have central importance in the mother's development of attachment.[122]

Rivalry in the Family

When a relationship is particularly close and meaningful or is perceived as essential to one's own well-being, competition for attention may lead to jealousy (fear of losing to the competitor) or rivalry (hatred or dislike of those with a perceived

advantage).[76] This antagonism, usually one-sided, results from fear of replacement or a loss of status in the previous relationship. The aggrieved family member may begin to make unreasonable demands for time and attention to regain or ensure status. Although we usually think of rivalry as occurring between siblings, it can occur with any relationship at any age when friendships expand and change. Even animals may express increased needs for attention when a new baby arrives.[2] Rivalry exemplifies a desire to maintain the security of the status quo.

Rivalry is commonly felt by the husband or wife when a new baby arrives. Each needs to remain sensitive to the continued emotional needs of the spouse as a separate individual, not just as a parent. Sometimes parents become so involved in the novelty and thrill of parenthood that all their attention and emotional energies become focused on the new baby. Even parents who desperately wanted and planned for the baby may begin to feel some resentment at the need to consider the new baby when making a decision to go out for the evening or just to spend some time alone together. As a result, marital happiness may decline. It takes time for the parents to adjust to the idea of being a larger family, not just a couple (Fig. 31-12). They need to be reminded to continue to spend time alone with each other, even if only for a 20-minute walk.

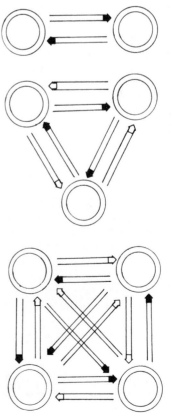

FIGURE 31–12.
The communication system within a family becomes infinitely more complex each time a new member is added.

Children between the ages of 18 months and 3½ years are most likely to feel and express rivalry with the new baby, especially if the parents have been oversolicitous or inconsistent in discipline. Children of this age are beginning to realize that the mother is not a part or an extension of themselves, but she is still essential to their security and independence. It is difficult for them to comprehend the need to wait until later for attention. Sibling rivalry may be expressed by avoiding any form of contact with the new baby, by verbal rejection, or even by physical abuse of either the baby or the mother. Some children become destructive of property or abusive to pets, actions that are a form of scapegoating (Fig. 31-13).

Rivalry can be prevented by including the current family members in the birth preparations as much as possible.[1, 21, 101, 125]

When and how a child is told about the new arrival is predicated on the age and comprehension level of the child. Storybooks can facilitate this process.[53] The new baby should be thought of and spoken of as "ours" rather than as only the mother's, with comments such as "we are pregnant"; this inclusion prevents a feeling of being "shut out" from the event, a precipitator of jealousy for both husband and children.[125] Switching of rooms, beds, or moving to a new residence should be accomplished as long as possible *before* the new baby arrives so that younger children do not feel physically displaced by the baby. Many families and hospitals are including children in the birth experience.[112] However, actual presence at a sibling's birth does not appear to impact adjustment issues for the child.[37] Families are encouraged to include siblings in postpartum visits to the hospital.[145] Children, when allowed, tend to go through the same sequences of awe and gentle fingertip, extremity touching that adults experience.[1] There is a marked reduction in noncompliant, restless, and clinging behaviors, and a marked increase in filial attachment are seen when children are included and spared separation experiences from the mother.[1] The father's active involvement with the older child (or children) also helps the child to adjust more easily.[10]

When the mother returns from the hospital, her first concern should be to let the older child know how much he or she was missed and to renew the bond between them.[1] After the older child is ready, the new baby can be introduced (Fig. 31-14). After the baby arrives home, unity is fostered by involvement of the other family members. Children who share in the infant care and household chores (according to age) are elevated to the status of "competent helpers." Both the father and siblings should have the opportunity to assist in showing off the new baby and should be allowed to participate in the conversations with guests. Younger children often enjoy imitating child care activities with a special doll. Role playing helps them understand and integrate the new experience into their own lives. Dramatic play with bathing, bottle-feeding, and even attempts to breast-feed are common and therapeutic.

A new baby does require a lot of time and attention. Laughing about the inconvenience and messiness of diapering helps older children to take these in stride. Emphasizing that the mother performed the same tasks for the older children when they were infants takes the sting off the perceived extra attention given to the baby and offers a foundation for emphasizing how much the older ones have grown up in skills, interests, and communication abilities. The birth of the sibling thus heightens the distinction between self–nonself, but the feelings evoked by this distinction can be channeled into a warm, affectionate tie between the siblings by the understanding and continued affirmation shown by the parents.[39] It is essential to find time to maintain the closeness of the previous one-to-one relationship, especially with young children. This time can be spent, for example, reading to the older child while feeding the baby or walking to the park with the baby in a carriage. Planned "private time" with a parent is

FIGURE 31–13.
Sibling rivalry that is inadequately handled during the early years can continue to create interactional problems in the years ahead.

FIGURE 31–14.
The first meeting. Sibling rivalry can be reduced by the introduction of the older child to the new family member at a pace and in a way suited to the child's interactional style.

critical to maintaining communication and assuring desirability.[34, 62, 127]

The parents need to consider the young child's concept of a baby. All that an older sibling often sees is a head and a blanket. What is underneath? Children may pinch, pull, and pick at a baby during the first week, not because of jealousy but from **curiosity.** A parent should show the child the new baby naked and state that "you looked just like that when you were a baby." A new baby in the family offers many natural opportunities for sex education and preparation for their own parenting. Children are usually fascinated to learn that they were once attached to the mother by the umbilical cord.[144]

A child may become jealous of the mother's role and develop a "little mother" complex characterized by possessiveness and a desire to give all the child care (Fig. 31-15). Possessiveness in early childhood is natural. The school-age child may see the baby as a real live "baby doll," a dream come true. The adolescent may wish to assume an adult role early. Parental handling of such situations depends on the age of the child. All should be allowed to participate in the care of the baby, but relationships must be kept clear, and the child should be encouraged to develop skills and interests that are age-appropriate. Usually, the novelty wears off and family

FIGURE 31–15.
Adolescent female sibling of a new infant may develop a "little mother" complex. While the desire to be actively involved in the care of the new baby is typical for children of all ages, it must not prevent the pursuit of activities that are more normal and growth producing for their ages.

relations begin to assume normalcy. Parents need to assist children with positive interactions, sharing, and negotiations. They may also need to establish rules, such as "We do not hurt anyone in the family," when a more competitive relationship exists.[21] It is OK to be jealous (normal feeling). It is not OK to hit (socialization of feelings).[127]

Some mothers allow a teen-age sibling to assume a mother's role, since it reduces their work load and they have a built-in babysitter. The baby may become more attached to the older sibling than to the mother. However, when the sibling leaves for college, marriage, or a job, the separation can be traumatic for all three: the teen-ager leaves a part of the self, the young child may feel abandoned and forced to develop new emotional attachments, and the real mother has to assume a new role that she may resent.

The family is a forum for learning problem-solving and negotiation skills, empathy, and sensitivity to others. When parents experience marital discord, the children tend to have higher levels of antagonistic behavior, since children use the parental behaviors as a guide to their own.[20]

Younger children are especially vulnerable. Parents are in a unique position to effect the sibling relationship for a lifetime. Although some competition is healthy and normal, if love and acceptance are contingent on the child's ability to meet a parent's need, or if self-worth becomes relative by frequent comparing of children to one another, then validation of individuality and worth are arbitrary, creating fertile ground for severe sibling rivalry.[34, 41, 126, 149] "If I can't be best at being best, I'll be best at being worst."[41] Severe sibling rivalry can continue into adulthood, affecting the quality of the sibling relationship for the next 60 to 80 years![3, 149] The need for continuous warm, supportive parental acceptance and love is paramount to healthy emotional development.[77]

When parents are psychologically unavailable to the children, the children can form such a tight, loyal, mutual support group that the development of a healthy individual identity may be impeded by the closeness.[3] Other people, even spouses, may be shut out later in life. Parents are in a key position to help children learn how to negotiate differences, to cooperate, to appreciate one another's strengths and weaknesses, and to affirm the value of others.[33, 73] Recognition of individuality is the key factor.[34, 127] Attempts to "be fair" by provision of matching gifts or experiences tends to blur personalities.[21] Favoring can be equally damaging. When individuality is appreciated, love freely offered, and feelings recognized, siblings can become supportive friends for a lifetime.[41, 73]

IMPLICATIONS

Parenting is one of the most difficult yet potentially the most gratifying role in a person's life.[25, 98] It is not a permanent babysitting job that focuses on physical care but, rather, is *an opportunity to create a person,* socially, emotionally, and spiritually. No career is more important. Consequently, parenthood should not be entered lightly or by accident. It should be a planned event if each family member is to thrive and mature optimally. Mothers, because of biological and sociological factors, are faced with the greatest adjustments during this period. Intimate support from her husband or partner is the most significant factor in her adjustment.[32] He is able to serve as a buffer to other responsibilities and demands on her time, thus allowing her to concentrate on the new relationship and responsibilities. When husbands are fully supportive, women experience more comfort with mothering, less depression, and much less parental stress.[29, 42, 55] When the woman does more of the housework and child care than she had expected, negative feelings emerge and interfere with the marital relationship, as well as with positive parenting.[129]

Parenthood asks us for our identity and challenges our value system. As such, initiation into parenthood can foster personal growth or precipitate disintegrated functioning. Unresolved dependency needs are exacerbated by the dependency needs of a baby.[56] Psychoanalytic theory postulates that children contribute to adult development because parental love, at its roots, is narcissistic.[107] The child is viewed as an extension of the self and, therefore, a form of self-care. As such, an attractive, responsive infant contributes to the parents' sense of competence and self-esteem and fosters feelings of bonding to the child (another expression of the self).[137]

Humanists see the infant as a separate individual, even during gestation. The parents actualize their own potentials as they creatively respond to the infant and provide an environment conducive to maximizing the child's potentials. *The first and most critical task of the parent is to establish interactional synchrony with the new child,* regardless of his or her age. From this sensitive mutual responsivity emerges the infant's attachment and the foundation for the healthy development of the child of any age. Most parents, regardless of educational or financial differences, want a better life and better world for their children.[98] They attempt to foster independence, creativity, and integrity as well as cognitive and motor skill development.[98] To be successful, to help each member thrive and mature optimally, the parents need to have strong self-identities and adequate community resources to draw on as necessary.

The adaptation to parenting twins or triplets is especially difficult because of the amount of physical care involved, as well as the difficulty in identifying and responding to the uniqueness of each child, a factor that can impede bonding.[55, 71] Intimate support of the spouse becomes even more critical to successful transition to parenthood of multiple births.[55] Parenthood support groups include the following:

National Organization of Mothers of Twins Club
12404 Princess Jeanne N.E.
Albuquerque, NM 87112-4640
505-275-0955

Twinline/Warmline
415-644-0863

The Triplet Connection
P.O.Box 99571
Stockton, CA 95209
209-474-3073 or 209-474-0885

The addition of a new member to the family places stress on the family system as new relationships and lines of communication are established. Many new parents are completely unaware and unprepared for the dramatic change of lifestyle.[98] The addition of a second child is generally easier.[56] Family members must retain their individuality while taking into account the needs of others. Parents and older siblings begin to realize their own strengths as they meet the needs of another. Erikson observes that generativity "is concerned with new beings as well as new products and new ideas and which, as a link between the generations, is as indispensable for the renewal of the adult generation's own life as it is for that of the next generation."[40]

REFERENCES

1. Anderberg, G. J. (1988). Initial acquaintance and attachment behavior of siblings with the newborn. *Journal of Obstetric, Gynecologic, and Neonatal Nursing, 17*(1), 49–54.
2. Bahr, J. E. (1981). Canine and feline rivalry: Another form of sibling rivalry. *Pediatric Nursing, 7*(4), 18.
3. Bank, S. P., & Kahn, M. D. (1982). *The sibling bond.* New York: Basic Books.
4. BBC-TV. (1975). *Rock-a-bye-baby* [Film]. BBC-TV: Time-Life.
5. Benedek, T. (1970). Motherhood and nurturing. In E. J. Anthony & T. Benedek (Eds.), *Parenthood: Its psychology and psychopathology* (pp. 153–165). Boston: Little, Brown.
6. Bergman, A. (1985). The mother's experience during the earliest phases of infant development. In E. J. Anthony & G. H. Pollock (Eds.), *Parental influences: In health, in disease* (pp. 165–181). Boston: Little, Brown.
7. Beske, E. J., & Garvis, M. S. (1982). Important factors in breastfeeding success. *MCN: American Journal of Maternal/Child Nursing, 7,* 174.
8. Bibring, G. L. (1959). Some considerations of the psychological process in pregnancy. In *Psychoanalytic study of the child* (Vol. 14, pp. 113–121). New York: International Universities Press.
9. Birns, B., & Hay, D. F. (Eds.). (1988). *The different faces of motherhood.* New York: Plenum Press.
10. Bittman, S. J., & Zalk, S. R. (1978). *Expectant fathers.* New York: Hawthorne Books.
11. Boukydis, C. F. Z., & Burgess, R. L. (1982). Adult physiological responsiveness to infant cries: Effects of temperament of infant, parental status and gender. *Child Development, 53,* 1291–1298.
12. Boulton, M. G. (1983). *On being a mother: A study of women with pre-school children.* New York: Tavistock Publications.
13. Bowlby, J. (1969). *Attachment and loss: I. Attachment.* London: Hogarth Press.
14. Bowlby, J. (1977). The making and breaking of affectional bonds: Aetiology and psychopathology in the light of attachment theory. *British Journal of Psychiatry, 130,* 201–210.
15. Brazelton, T. B. (1978). The remarkable talents of the newborn. *Birth and Family Journal, 5,* 187.
16. Brazelton, T. B. (1983). Precursors for the development of

emotions in early infancy. In R. Plutchik & H. Kellerman (Eds.), *Emotions: Theory, research and experience* (Vol. 2). New York: Academic Press.

17. Brazelton, T. B. (1986). *On becoming a family: The growth of attachment.* New York: Dell.

18. Brewster, D. P. (1979). *You can breastfeed your baby . . . even in special circumstances.* Emmaus, PA: Rodale Press.

19. Briggs, G. G., Freeman, R. K., & Yaffee, S. J. (1986). *Drugs in pregnancy and lactation: A reference guide to fetal and neonatal risk* (2nd ed.). Baltimore: Williams and Wilkins.

20. Brody, G. H., Stoneman, Z., & Burke, M. (1987). Family system and individual child correlates of sibling behavior. *American Journal of Orthopsychiatry, 57,* 561–569.

21. Calladine, C., & Calladine, A. (1979). *Raising siblings: A sane and sensible approach to raising brothers and sisters without raising the roof.* New York: Delacorte Press.

22. Campbell, B. K. (1979, April). *The psychotic child: Early identification of psychosis in the first years of life.* Address presented at the conference "An Interdisciplinary Approach to the Optimal Development of Infants: The Special Child," Ann Arbor, MI.

23. Carek, D. J., & Capelli, A. J. (1981). Mother's reactions to their newborn infants. *Journal of the American Academy of Child Psychiatry, 20,* 16.

24. Casey, M. L., & MacDonald, P. C. (1986). Initiation of labor in women. In G. Huszar (Ed.), *The physiology and biochemistry of the uterus in pregnancy and labor* (pp. 155–161). Boca Raton, FL: C. R. C. Press.

25. Cath, S. H., Gurwitt, A., & Gunsberg, L. (Eds.). (1989). *Fathers and their families.* Hillsdale, NJ: Analytic Press.

26. Chez, R. A. (1975). Sex in pregnancy. *Contemporary Obstetrics & Gynecology, 6*(2), 99.

27. Cohen, R. L. (1988). Emotional disorders and mental illness associated with pregnancy and postpartum period. In R. L. Cohen (Ed.), *Psychiatric consultation in childbirth settings: Parent- and child-oriented approaches* (pp. 71–84). New York: Plenum.

28. Condon, W. S., & Sander, L. W. (1974). Neonatal movement is synchronized with adult speech: Interactional participation and language acquisition. *Science, 183,* 99.

29. Cowan, C. P., & Cowan, P. A. (1987). A preventive intervention for couples becoming parents. In C. F. Z. Boukydis (Ed.), *Research on support for parents and infants in the postnatal period* (pp. 225–251). Norwood, NJ: Ablex.

30. Cox, A. D. (1988). Maternal depression and impact on children's development. *Archives of Disease in Childhood, 63,* 90–95.

31. Cox, J. L. (1988). Childbirth as a life event: Sociocultural aspects of postnatal depression. *Acta Psychiatrica Scandinavica, 344*(Suppl.), 75–83.

32. Crnic, K., & Greenberg, M. (1987). Maternal stress, social support, and coping: Influences on the early mother–infant relationship. In C. F. Z. Boukydis (Ed.), *Research on support for parents and infants in the postnatal period* (pp. 25–40). Norwood, NJ: Ablex.

33. Curran, D. (1983). *Traits of a healthy family: Fifteen traits commonly found in healthy families by those who work with them.* San Francisco: Harper and Row.

34. Curran, D. (1985). *Stress and the healthy family.* Minneapolis, MN: Winston Press.

35. Cutrona, C. E., & Troutman, B. R. (1986). Social support,

infant temperament, and parenting self-efficacy: A mediational model of postpartum depression. *Child Development, 57,* 1507–1518.

36. Danforth, D. N., & Ueland, K. (1986). Physiology of uterine action. In D. N. Danforth & J. R. Scott (Eds.), *Obstetrics and gynecology* (5th ed., pp. 582–628). Philadelphia: J. B. Lippincott.

37. DelGuidice, G. (1986). The relationship between sibling jealousy and presence at a sibling's birth. *Birth: Issues in Perinatal Care and Education, 13*(4), 250–254.

38. Dimitrovsky, L., Perez-Hirshberg, M., & Itskowitz, R. (1987). Depression during and following pregnancy: Quality of family relationships. *Journal of Psychology, 121*(3), 213–218.

39. Dunn, J., & Kendrick, C. (1982). *Siblings: Love, envy and understanding.* Cambridge, MA: Harvard University Press.

40. Erikson, E. (1980). On the generational cycle: An address. *International Journal of Psychoanalysis, 61,* 213.

41. Faber, A., & Mazlish, E. (1987). The perils of comparisons. *Parents Magazine, 62*(5), 82–86.

42. Fedele, N. M., Golding, E. R., Grossman, F. K., & Pollack, W. S. (1988). Psychological issues in adjustment to first parenthood. In G. Y. Michaels & W. A. Goldberg (Eds.), *The transition to parenthood: Current theory and research* (pp. 85–113). New York: Cambridge University Press.

43. Feigelman, W., & Silverman, A. R. (1979). Preferential adoption: A new family formation. *Social Casework, 60,* 302.

44. Feldman, S. S., Nash, S. C., & Aschenbrenner, B. G. (1983). Antecedents of fathering. *Child Development, 54,* 1628–1636.

45. Field, T. M., & Pawlby, S. (1980). Early face to face interactions of British and American working and middle-class mother–infant dyads. *Child Development, 51*(1), 250–253.

46. Foley, K. L. (1979). Caring for the parents of newborn twins. *MCN: American Journal of Maternal/Child Nursing, 4,* 221.

47. Fraiberg, S. (1979, April). *Clinical issues in infant assessment.* Address presented at the conference "An Interdisciplinary Approach to the Optimal Development of Infants: The Special Child," Ann Arbor, MI.

48. Frank, S., Hole, C. B., Jacobson, S., Justkowski, R., & Huyck, M. (1986). Psychological predictors of parents' sense of confidence and control and self-versus child-focused gratifications. *Developmental Psychology, 22*(3), 348–355.

49. Freedman, D. G. (1974). *Human infancy: An evaluationary perspective.* New York: Halsted Press.

50. Frodi, A. M. (1980). Paternal-baby responsiveness and involvement. *Infant Mental Health Journal, 1,* 150.

51. Fuchs, A. R. (1986). The role of oxytocin in parturition. In G. Huszar (Ed.), *The physiology and biochemistry of the uterus in pregnancy and labor* (pp. 163–183). Boca Raton, FL: C.R.C. Press.

52. Garza, C. G., & Hopkinson, J. (1988). Physiology of lactation. In R. C. Tsong & B. L. Nichols (Eds.), *Nutrition during infancy* (pp. 20–32). Philadelphia: Hanley and Belfus.

53. Gates, S. (1980). Children's literature: It can help children cope with sibling rivalry. *MCN: American Journal of Maternal/Child Nursing, 5,* 351.

54. Gerson, M. J. (1989). Tomorrow's fathers: The anticipation of fatherhood. In S. H. Cath, A. Gurwitt, & L. Gunsberg (Eds.), *Fathers and their families* (pp. 127–144). Hillsdale, NJ: The Analytic Press.

55. Glaser, K. (1987). A comparative study of social support for new mothers of twins. In C. F. Z. Boukydis (Ed.), *Research on*

support for parents and infants in the postnatal period (pp. 41–60). Norwood, NJ: Ablex.

56. Goldberg, W. A., & Michaels, G. Y. (1988). Conclusion: The transition to parenthood: Synthesis and future directions. In G. Y. Michaels & W. A. Goldberg (Eds.), *The transition to parenthood: Current theory and research* (pp. 342–360). New York: Cambridge University Press.

57. Grace, J. T. (1984). Does a mother's knowledge of fetal gender affect attachment? *MCN: American Journal of Maternal/Child Nursing, 9,* 42.

58. Greenberg, M. H. (1986). *Birth of a father.* New York: Avon Books.

59. Greenberg, M. H., & Morris, N. (1974). Engrossment: The newborn's impact upon the father. *American Journal of Orthopsychiatry, 44,* 520.

60. Greif, G. L. (1985). *Single fathers.* Lexington, MA: Lexington Books.

61. Grossman, F. K., Pollack, W. S., & Golding, E. (1988). Fathers and children: Predicting the quality and quantity of fathering. *Developmental Psychology, 24*(1), 82–91.

62. Guidry, J. (1987). Our breakfast club: A new baby, a jealous sibling: What's an overworked mother to do? *Parents Magazine, 62*(12), 84.

63. Gurwitt, A. (1989). Prelude. In S. H. Cath, A. Gurwitt, & L. Gunsberg (Eds.), *Fathers and their families* (pp. 3–10). Hillsdale, NJ: The Analytic Press.

64. Guyton, A. C. (1987). *Human physiology and mechanisms of disease* (4th ed.). Philadelphia: W. B. Saunders.

65. Hanson, S. M. H., & Bozett, F. W. (1985). Preface. In S. M. H. Hanson & F. W. Bozett (Eds.), *Dimensions of fatherhood* (pp. 14–16). Beverly Hills, CA: Sage Publications.

66. Hendershot, G. E. (1984). Domestic Review: Trends in breastfeeding: Report of the Task Force on the Assessment of the Scientific Evidence Relating to Infant-Feeding Practices and Infant Health. *Pediatrics, 4*(74), 591–602.

67. Hertz, R. (1986). *More equal than others: Women and men in dual-career marriages.* Berkeley, CA: University of California Press.

68. Hopkinson, J. M., & Garza, C. (1988). Management of breastfeeding. In R. C. Tsang & B. L. Nichols (Eds.), *Nutrition during infancy* (pp. 298–313). Philadelphia: Hanley and Belfus.

69. Howes, C. (1989, September). Infant child care. *Young Children,* pp. 24–28.

70. Hwang, C. P. (1987). The changing role of Swedish fathers. In M. E. Lamb (Ed.), *The father's role: Cross-cultural perspectives* (pp. 115–138). Hillsdale, NJ: Lawrence Erlbaum Associates.

71. Hynan, M. T. (1987). *The pain of premature parents: A psychological guide for coping.* New York: University Press of America.

72. Jackson, S. (1987). Great Britain. In M. E. Lamb (Ed.), *The father's role: Cross-cultural perspectives* (pp. 29–57). Hillsdale, NJ: Lawrence Erlbaum Associates.

73. Jacobbi, M. (1987). Ten ways to help your kids become friends. *McCalls, 145*(6), 57.

74. Jessner, L., Weigert, E., & Foy, J. L. (1970). The development of parental attitudes during pregnancy. In E. J. Anthony & T. Benedek (Eds.), *Parenthood: Its psychology and psychopathology* (pp. 209–244). Boston: Little, Brown.

75. Jones, L. C. (1985). Father–infant relationships in the first year of life. In S. M. H. Hanson & F. W. Bozett (Eds.), *Dimensions of fatherhood* (pp. 92–114). Beverly Hills, CA: Sage Publications.

76. Katz, L. G. (1981). Brotherhood/sisterhood begins at home: Notes on sibling rivalry. *Journal of the Canadian Association for Young Children, 7,* 20.

77. Keiffer, E. (1986). Making friends in the family. *Reader's Digest, 130*(1), 77.

78. Klaus, M. H. (1978). The biology of parent-to-infant attachment. *Birth and Family Journal, 5,* 200.

79. Klaus, M. H., & Kennell, J. H. (1970). Mothers separated from their newborn infants. *Pediatric Clinics of North America, 17,* 1015.

80. Klaus, M. H., & Kennell, J. H. (1977). Mothers separated from their newborn infants. In J. L. Schwartz & L. H. Schwartz (Eds.), *Vulnerable infants: A psychosocial dilemma.* New York: McGraw-Hill.

81. Klaus, M. H., & Kennell, J. H. (1982). Labor, birth, and bonding. In M. H. Klaus & J. H. Kennell (Eds.), *Parent–infant bonding.* St. Louis, MO: C. V. Mosby.

82. Klaus, M. H., Leger, T., & Trause, M. A. (Eds.). (1975). *Maternal attachment and mothering disorders: A round table.* Sausalito, CA: Johnson & Johnson.

83. Klaus, M. H., Jerauld, R., Kreger, N., McAlpine, W., Steffa, M., and Kennell, J. H. (1972). Maternal attachment: Importance of the first post-partum days. *New England Journal of Medicine, 286,* 460–463.

84. Kohn, C. L., et al. (1980). Gravidas responses to realtime ultrasound fetal image. *Journal of Obstetric Gynecological Nursing, 9,* 77.

85. Korner, A. F., & Thoman, E. B. (1973). Visual alertness in neonates as evoked by maternal care. In L. J. Stone, H. T. Smith, & L. B. Murphy (Eds.), *The competent infant: Research and commentary* (pp. 1057–1070). New York: Basic Books.

86. Kuchner, J. F., & Porcino, J. (1988). Delayed motherhood. In B. Birns & D. F. Hay (Eds.), *The different faces of motherhood* (pp. 259–280). New York: Plenum Press.

87. La Leche League International. (1987). *The womanly art of breastfeeding* (4th rev. ed.). Franklin Park, IL: La Leche League International.

88. Lamb, M. E. (1987). Introduction: The emergent American father. In M. E. Lamb (Ed.), *The father's role: Cross-cultural perspectives* (pp. 3–25). Hillsdale, NJ: Lawrence Erlbaum Associates.

89. Lamb, M. E., & Oppenheim, D. (1989). Fatherhood and father–child relationships: Five years of research. In S. H. Cath, A. Gurwitt, & L. Gunsberg (Eds.), *Fathers and their families* (pp. 11–26). Hillsdale, NJ: The Analytic Press.

90. Lawrence, R. A. (1989). *Breastfeeding: A guide for the medical profession* (3rd ed.). St. Louis: C. V. Mosby.

91. Levy-Shiff, R., & Israelashvili, R. (1988). Antecedents of fathering: Some further exploration. *Developmental Psychology, 24*(3), 434–440.

92. Lewis, C. (1984, September). *Men's involvement in fatherhood: Historical and gender issues.* Paper presented to Developmental Section of the conference of the British Psychological Society, Lancaster, England.

93. Lewis, C. (1986). The role of the father in the human family. In W. Sluckin & M. Herbert (Eds.), *Parental behavior* (pp. 228–258). New York: Basil Blackwell.

94. Lockhart, B. (1982). When couples adopt, they too need parenting classes. *MCN: American Journal of Maternal/Child Nursing, 7,* 116.

95. Mahler, M. S., Pine, F., & Bergman, A. (1975). *The psychological birth of the human infant.* New York: Basic Books.

96. Maloni, J. A., McIndoe, J. E., & Rubenstien, G. (1987). Expectant

grandparents class. *Journal of Obstetric, Gynecologic, and Neonatal Nursing, 16,* 26–29.

97. Mercer, R. T. (1981). The nurse and maternal tasks of early postpartum. *MCN: American Journal of Maternal/Child Nursing, 6,* 341.

98. Mercer, R. T. (1986). *First-time motherhood: Experiences from teens to forties.* New York: Springer.

99. Meyers, B. (1982). Early intervention using Brazelton training with middle-class mothers and fathers of newborns. *Child Development, 53,* 462.

100. Milne, L. S., & Rich, O. J. (1981). Cognitive and affective aspects of the responses of pregnant women to sonography. *MCN:American Journal of Maternal/Child Nursing, 10,* 15.

101. Mintzer, M. (1987). Social Security. *Health, 19*(10), 22.

102. Mishell, D. R., Jr., & Marrs, R. P. (1986). Endocrinology of lactation and the puerperium. In D. R. Mishell, Jr. & V. Davajan (Eds.), *Infertility, contraception and reproductive endocrinology* (2nd ed., pp. 143–162). Oradell, NJ: Medical Economics Books.

103. Montagu, A. (1986). *Touching: The human significance of the skin* (3rd ed.). New York: Perennial Library.

104. Muri, R. (1989). Fatherhood from the perspective of object relations theory and relational systems theory. In S. H. Cath, A. Gurwitt, & L. Gunsberg (Eds.), *Fathers and their families* (pp. 47–61). Hillsdale, NJ: Analytic Press.

105. National Institutes of Health. (1980). *Caesarean childbirth: Consensus Development Conference summary.* Bethesda, MD.

106. Nice, F. J. (1989). Can a breast-feeding mother take medication without harming her infant? *MCN: American Journal of Maternal/Child Nursing, 14*(1), 27–31.

107. Ornstein, A., & Ornstein, P. H. (1985). Parenting as a function of the adult self: A psychoanalytic developmental perspective. In E. J. Anthony & G. H. Pollock (Eds.), *Parental influences: In health, in disease* (pp. 183–232). Boston: Little, Brown.

108. Osofsky, H. J., & Culp, R. E. (1989). Risk factors in the transition to fatherhood. In S. H. Cath, A. Gurwitt, & L. Gunsberg (Eds.), *Fathers and their families* (pp. 145–165). Hillsdale, NJ: The Analytic Press.

109. Parke, R. D. (1981). *Fathers.* Cambridge, MA: Harvard University Press.

110. Parke, R. D., & Tinsley, B. J. (1987). Fathers as agents and recipients of support in the postnatal period. In C. F. Z. Boukydis (Ed.), *Research on support for parents and infants in the postnatal period* (pp. 84–113). Norwood, NJ: Ablex Publishing Corporation.

111. Pawlby, S. J., & Hall, F. (1980). Early interactions and later language development of children whose mothers came from disrupted families of origin. In T. M. Field (Ed.), *High-risk infants and children: Adult and peer interactions* (pp. 61–75). New York: Academic Press.

112. Perez, P. (1979). Nurturing children who attend to birth of a sibling. *MCN: American Journal of Maternal/Child Nursing, 4,* 215.

113. Pruett, K. D. (1989). The nurturing male: A longitudinal study of primary nurturing fathers. In S. H. Cath, A. Gurwitt, & L. Gunsberg (Eds.), *Fathers and their families* (pp. 389–405). Hillsdale, NJ: The Analytic Press.

114. Pryor, K. W. (1980). *Nursing your baby.* New York: Pocket Books.

115. Quinn, R. P., & Staines, G. L. (1979). *The 1977 quality of employment survey.* Ann Arbor, MI: Survey Research Center.

116. Richman, J. (1982). Men's experience of pregnancy and childbirth. In L. McKee & M. O'Brien (Eds.), *The father figure.* New York: Tavistock.

117. Ringler, N. M., Trause, M. A., & Klaus, M. H. (1976). Mother's speech to her two-year-old, its effect on speech and language comprehension at 5 years. *Pediatrics Research, 10,* 307.

118. Ringler, N. M., Kennell, J. H., Jarvella, R., Navojosky, B. J., and Klaus, M. H. (1975). Mother-to-child speech at 2 years—effects of early postnatal contact. *Journal of Pediatrics, 86,* 141–144.

119. Robertson, J., & Robertson, J. (1979, April). *From birth to three: The vulnerable years.* Address at the conference "An Interdisciplinary Approach to the Optimal Development of Infants: The Special Child," Ann Arbor, MI.

120. Robson, K. S. (1967). The role of eye-to-eye contact in maternal–infant attachment. *Journal of Child Psychology and Psychiatry, 8,* 13.

121. Robson, K. S., & Kumar, H. A. (1980). Delayed onset of maternal affection after childbirth. *British Journal of Psychiatry, 136,* 347–353.

122. Robson, K. S., & Moss, H. A. (1970). Patterns and determinants of maternal attachment. *Journal of Pediatrics, 77,* 976.

123. Rodholm, M. (1981). Effects of father–infant postpartum contact on their interaction 3 months after birth. *Early Human Development, 5,* 79.

124. Roopnarine, J. L., & Miller, B. C. (1985). Transitions to fatherhood. In S. M. H. Hanson & F. W. Bozett (Eds.), *Dimensions of fatherhood* (pp. 49–63). Beverly Hills, CA: Sage Publications.

125. Rosemond, J. K. (1987). And baby makes four: Preparing your first child for the second. *Better Homes and Gardens, 65*(1), 38.

126. Rubin, N. (1986). Mom and dad always liked you better. *Parents Magazine, 61*(6), 86–92.

127. Rubin, N. (1988). Kids' fights. *Parents Magazine, 63*(3), 96–99.

128. Rubin, R. (1963). Maternal touch. *Nursing Outlook, 11,* 828.

129. Ruble, D. N., Fleming, A. S., Hackel, L. S., & Strangor, C. (1988). Changes in the marital relationship during transition to first time motherhood: Effects of violated expectations concerning division of household labor. *Journal of Personality and Social Psychiatry, 55*(1), 78–87.

130. Russell, G., & Russell, A. (1987). Mother–child and father–child relationships in middle childhood. *Child Development, 58,* 1573, 1585

131. Sander, L. W. (1976). Issues in early mother–child interaction. In E. N. Rexford, L. W. Sander, & T. Shapiro (Eds.), *Infant psychiatry.* New Haven, CT: Yale University Press.

132. Saunders, S. E., Carroll, J. M., & Johnson, C. E. (1988). *Breast-feeding: A problem-solving manual.* Amityville, NY: Essential Medical Information Systems.

133. Sawin, D. B., & Parke, R. D. (1979). Father's affectionate stimulation and caregiving behaviors with newborn infants. *Family Coordinator, 28,* 509.

134. Schaffer, H. R. (1984). *The child's entry into the social world.* London: Academic Press.

135. Schaffer, H. R., & Collis, G. M. (1986). Parental responsiveness and child behavior. In W. Sluckin & M. Herbert (Eds.), *Parental behavior* (pp. 283–315). New York: Basil Blackwell.

136. Shaw, M. (1986). Substitute parenting. In W. Sluckin & M. Herbert (Eds.), *Parental behavior* (pp. 259–283). New York: Basil Blackwell.

137. Sluckin, W. (1986). Human mother-to-infant bonds. In W. Sluckin & M. Herbert (Eds.), *A comparative view of parental behavior* (pp. 208–227). New York: Basil Blackwell.

138. Speroff, L. (1976). What initiates labor? *Contemporary Obstetrics & Gynecology, 7*(5), 113.

139. Spietz, A. (1988). Working with depressed moms. *NCAST National News, 4*(1), 1–5.

140. Stern, D. N. (1977). *The first relationship.* Cambridge, MA: Harvard University Press.

141. Stranik, M. K., & Hogberg, B. L. (1979). Transition into parenthood. *American Journal of Nursing, 79,* 90.

142. Stroufe, L. A., & Waters, E. (1982). Issues of temperament and attachment. *American Journal of Orthopsychiatry, 52,* 743–746.

143. Sutphen, J. L., & Siden, A. A. (1989). Normal infant feeding. In R. E. Rankel (Ed.), *Conn's current therapy* (pp. 933–936). Philadelphia: W. B. Saunders.

144. Sweet, P. T. (1979). Prenatal classes especially for children. *MCN: American Journal of Maternal/Child Nursing, 4,* 82.

145. Trause, M. A., et al. (1981). Separation for childbirth: The effect on the sibling. *Child Psychiatry and Human Development, 12,* 32.

146. Walker, L. O. (1981). Identifying parents in need: An approach to adoptive parenting. *MCN: American Journal of Maternal/Child Nursing, 6,* 118.

147. Walker, M., & Driscoll, J. W. (1989). Sore nipples: The new mother's nemesis. *MCN: American Journal of Maternal/Child Nursing, 14,* 260–265.

148. Ward, M. (1981). Parental bonding in older-child adoptions. *Child Welfare, 60,* 24.

149. Wiley, K. W. (1988). My sister myself. *Health, 20*(4), 46.

150. Wilkie, C. F., & Ames, E. W. (1986). The relationship of infant crying to parental stress in the transition to parenthood. *Journal of Marriage and the Family, 48,* 545–550.

151. Williams, B. (1967). Sleep needs during the maternity cycle. *Nursing Outlook, 15*(2), 53.

152. Winnicott, D. W. (1970). The mother–infant experience of maternity. In E. J. Anthony & T. Benedek (Eds.), *Parenthood: Its psychology and psychopathology.* Boston: Little, Brown.

153. Yogman, M. V. (1982). Observations on the father–infant relationship. In S. H. Cath, A. Gurwitt, & J. M. Ross (Eds.), *Father and child* (pp. 101–122). Boston: Little, Brown.

154. Zaslow, M., Pederson, P., Kramer, E., Suwalsky, J., & Fivel, M. (1981, April). *Depressed mood in new fathers: Interview and behavior correlates.* Paper presented to the Society for Research in Child Development, Boston, MA.

155. Zimmerman, M. A. (1981). Breast-feeding the adopted newborn. *Pediatric Nursing, 7*(1), 9.

There are two lasting bequests we should leave our children . . . One is roots and the other is wings.

—HODDING CARTER, JR.

Maintaining Family Unity

Clara S. Schuster

The headline reads: "Man kills parents, two brothers, and himself." The media commentator reflects the whispers of the shocked suburban neighbors: "The neighborhood is paralyzed tonight by this grisly event. Former teachers described the alleged murderer as a quiet, well-behaved honor student coming from a **good** family. The parents, both professional people, were actively involved in community as well as church activities. Just last week the father was honored . . . " We all know this scenario, yet we are stunned anew with each recurrence.

A less visible, yet more common, vignette centers on lonely, aging parents, people who have raised one or more children to adulthood only to see them swallowed up by peer groups, cultural enticements, and the exigencies of daily life. With sad, bitter hearts, they protest to sympathetic ears, "I did *everything* for them when they were little. Why can't they remember me now? We had such a **good** family."

How often we hear the words, "It was such a **good** family!" Yet **good** families have children who become heavily involved in drugs or other delinquent or criminal activities. **Good** families have children who run away from them. **Good** families suffer the pains of separation and divorce. Each time a **good** family experiences one of these tragedies, we wince, realizing our own vulnerability and not knowing quite how to predict or to prevent these devastating plights.

We are also aware of individuals of historical renown or even within our own communities who, in spite of growing up in adverse circumstances, such as with single parentage, poverty, social disadvantage, or inadequate cultural modeling, turn out to be "giants" in society through their allocentric (other-centered), mature, self-sufficient, and warm human approach to life.

The family, as a system, is a prototype of society. Through its hierarchical relationships, rules, values, and communication patterns, children learn and test skills that they will use when relating to the larger society. The family is the bedrock of society. It is the garden in which personalities germinate, grow, and mature. The family supplies the nation with citizens: workers, consumers, taxpayers, and leaders. The health of the nation depends on the health of its citizens.[14] The health of the citizens depends on the health of the family.[1,2,7]

If these suppositions are valid, then we must safeguard the health of the family as a whole with as much vigor as we support the development of the individuals within it. We must identify ways to foster the unity of the family without neglecting the individuals within it. We must reevaluate our criteria of **good** families to differentiate the characteristics of **healthy** families. Only then can the potentials of family life be maximized and provide high-quality life for the individuals who comprise the family system.

MAINTAINING THE ADULT–ADULT RELATIONSHIP

When a couple marries, they promise to love, cherish, and honor each other "till death us do part." They are caught up, as they should be, in the joys of physical and social intimacies. They are enveloped in the task of "becoming one." Unity, however, does not refer to the fusion of selves that may occur between poorly differentiated spouses. Nor does it refer to the development of a pseudoself in which one (or both) depends on an attachment to the other person for self-identity.[1] Both situations are potentially disastrous. In the first, both parties become involved in being what they think the other expects them to be, yet each demands changes in the other to enhance his or her own functioning. Each enters the relationship with the naïve assumption that they will hold the same views, opinions, and goals: they will think as one. Communication of vital values, priorities, and expectations is limited since the other is supposed to automatically "know" what is important. Neither person assumes full responsibility for self or communication.[1] Confusion, disappointment, and anger erupt as differences emerge or expectations are not matched. In the second situation, one person becomes an extension of the other. No sense of goals or power or even strength for daily living exists except as ego strength is borrowed from the other (fused ego boundaries). One's reason to be, one's sense of self, depends on the achievements of the other or the affirmation and stability offered by the spouse. In both of these situations, the individuals have failed to do sufficient "identity homework" to know their own values, goals, and feelings (see Chap. 25). The relationship is based on a state of personal *deficiency* or ego needs, rather than from the *abundance* of what each can contribute to a new family system.

Genuine unity recognizes, cherishes, and safeguards the individuality of each member. Because ego boundaries are clear, the partners are able to share a comfortable, non-threatening emotional closeness without fear of loss of self or submersion into the ego deficiencies of the other. The couple that negotiates this task of intimacy early in their relationship is well on the way to a lifetime of family unity (see Chap. 28).

The good feelings and lofty intentions of honeymooners do not ensure a healthy family unit. Reality soon sets in, and egocentric, idealistic thinking is confronted with new tasks, relationships, and challenges. When families are no longer held together by necessity (i.e., when a man and a woman need each other to perform the tasks of life that could not be accomplished alone), the establishment of companionship is imperative for the health of the union and for vibrant survival in the years ahead. The longevity of a marriage, as well as the joy and the strength derived from it, is enhanced when the couple are the best of friends and not just role partners.

Adjusting to the Expanding Family

The early years of marriage offer the couple the opportunity to get to know each other more deeply and to learn how to meet and resolve problems when they arise (see Chap. 29). The couple can direct their energies toward accepting, defining, and refining their roles as husband, wife, and companions. Because these years usually are fairly free of responsibility, the couple can share many hours of uninterrupted companionship and spontaneous leisure activities; it is a time to bond, to solidly commit themselves to the union and welfare of the other.

The arrival of the first child creates marked changes in lifestyle, time availability, and priorities for the couple. For many individuals, this is the first time they have had anyone dependent on them for 24 hours a day, 7 days a week. Studies consistently indicate that marital happiness and adjustment decrease with the birth of the first child.[34,35] Some of the factors that decrease marital happiness are obvious, such as reduced leisure time as a couple or as individuals, fatigue, concerns over the financial integrity of the family, and even rivalry between partners as discussed in Chapter 31.

Other factors are more subtle, such as increased time with in-laws (who may offer much unsolicited advice), decreased time for conversation and social intimacy, delayed plans, decreased spontaneous lovemaking because of tiredness or fear of interruptions, and fewer contacts with the "outside world" because of all the paraphernalia that must accompany travel with the baby. Many couples find they have outgrown their friends who do not yet have children or who live more spontaneous lifestyles. The couple that is not yet ready to "settle down" or individuals who are more concerned with their own lifestyles and development than with that of others find the adjustment most difficult.

However, *marital satisfaction and family satisfaction are not synonymous,* and the decrease in marital satisfaction after becoming parents is not sufficient to destroy most marriages.[33] When both parents are secure in the love of the other and have a good sense of personal identity, parental satisfaction offsets marital disappointment. In fact, many marriages become even more satisfying after children are born because of a sense of fulfillment, a new way to share love. Children give parents the opportunity to "reaffirm and rejuvenate their basic commitments to love, life, work, and play."[13] The couple has a common goal toward which to strive, that of raising their children to successful adulthood.

Mature individuals who have achieved a sense of unity are able to expand their concept of the family system to include the new members as unique individuals. The readjustment of priorities can be seen either as a temporary inconvenience or as a growth-producing challenge that accompanies the transition from being a couple to being a family. The latter leads toward higher levels of both personal and family functioning.

Maintaining Vitality

Some couples can become so engrossed in the joys or responsibilities of parenthood that they forget the original purpose of their union—permanent, in-depth companionship. After children arrive, they may find that the husband gets caught up in earning sufficient money to provide for the needs of the family; the wife becomes involved in child care, home-making, and/or her own career. As the years progress, they become strangers sharing the same bedroom. Each is involved in his or her separate responsibilities. If both spouses work outside the home, they may begin to relate to each other as roles rather than as people because of insufficient private couple time. There are so many interruptions when they are together that sharing behaviors are gradually extinguished. They begin to approach the family in a stereotyped manner, as a single unit rather than recognizing the unique needs and contributions of each member as a separate individual. Suddenly, parents may feel a loss of their own identity within the family system: they play a role, but they do not feel that they are recognized or appreciated for their unique personal qualities or the contributions they make. Communication and commitment disintegrate under the stress of maintaining one's sense of identity and esteem.

The nuclear family, as a system, is self-limited. It has a beginning, a period of growing, and then a shrinking as it begins to release members to society. Eventually, the two senior members die and that family ceases to exist. If the couple does not maintain the vital companionship of earlier years, the family will self-destruct when the children leave home (or even earlier). The couple lives separate lives and live in different worlds. They may be lonely and sexually frustrated.[5] The parents may literally find themselves strangers to each other with no common goals or meanings to life. Because wives are usually more personally involved in the management of the home and children, they are more vulnerable to family problems.[26]

In the midst of child rearing, the parents need to separate the spousal subsystem from the parent–child subsystems.[33] The elusive yet all-vital quality of marital love must be maintained. This love does not survive merely because it existed when vows were exchanged. It survives and grows because the couple works at nurturing each other. The couple must actively engage in "love homework," continuing the process of knowing each other on increasingly deeper levels, keeping abreast with the circumstantial and developmental changes each is experiencing in facing crises and the activities of daily living. What new insights, priorities, or concerns does each face?

Successful marriages have husbands and wives who are not tied to traditional roles.[13] Each respects the individual needs, talents, and interests of the other and works these into the division of responsibilities. The lover–companion relationship is enhanced when each is able to provide stimulation, challenge, encouragement, solace, and spiritual nourishment for the other.

In a vital marriage, the partners look for opportunities to spend time alone as a couple. Even though both of them may work and feel swamped with responsibility, they **make** time for each other.[8] They may share family chores, such as shopping, doing dishes, or wrapping Christmas gifts, or they may merely sit and talk, watch television, or jog together. The sharing of a joke or incidents from the day and brief ex-

FIGURE 32–1.
Each couple needs to find time away from the children to refresh and strengthen their relationship.

changes of affection indicate a recognition of and appreciation for the presence of the other person. But the couple also needs special time alone to enjoy their relationship without interruption, to renew their commitment, to rejuvenate their relationship. Depending on the couple's financial resources, this time can take many forms. Attending a concert, a sports event, or an auction can help to relieve the stresses of everyday life (Fig. 32-1). Most women appreciate the opportunity to eat at a restaurant. An evening at a motel or a weekend away from home can provide the time to revitalize a relationship. Some counselors recommend that married couples continue to "date" once a week. It may only be a picnic or long walk to the park topped off by an ice cream cone, but it is time alone together. A minimum commitment of one evening each month should be reserved to spend exclusively with each other in a mutually pleasurable activity. Some counselors recommend one weekend per year in "executive retreat" to assess family problems, finances, assets, strengths, to set priorities, and to plan strategies for meeting goals over the next year. When planned ahead, both partners can look forward to the break from everyday routines and responsibilities. Children grow to appreciate and respect their parents' time alone.

A satisfying marriage takes years to develop.[5] It is so easy to give up during the early years when financial and child-rearing issues are confronted and one is still fairly heavily invested in his or her own identity homework and its challenges. No marriage is a honeymoon forever. But the advantages of the struggle far outweigh the disadvantages of a fractured relationship.

Adjusting to the Decreasing Family

The couple that has maintained a vital, caring, open, sensitive relationship during the childbearing and child-caring years finds that they not only cope more effectively with the normal psychological tensions of family living, but they are still friends after the children leave home. Since they probably have another 20 years of living together as a couple after the children leave home, the time spent in getting to know each other becomes an investment in life itself. The love shared in the early years takes on a new and deeper meaning with the sharing of experiences, crises, and memories. If mutual respect has developed, then each can rise to new heights of personal fulfillment. This time of life is one of new beginnings, not of the "empty nest"! Each partner has more energy to pursue his or her career. For women who saw motherhood as their career, the change can be frightening, but the loving support of a lifelong companion can make her transition easier and more exciting.

The postparental period allows a couple to focus on their relationship to each other, to do all those things they didn't have time or money to do while they were still actively involved in child rearing. Some may even experience a "honeymoon" period with an enriched relationship and deeper tolerances.[20] Because they no longer feel the need to be models for the children or to be alert to their children's needs for guidance, the parents tend to relax in their roles and expectancies of each other, a phenomenon known as "mellowing." When differences arise, they can resolve them more directly and quickly without fear of being overheard by "the children."

PARENTAL RELATIONSHIPS WITH CHILDREN

Each of us wants to have a healthy, satisfying family life. Yet we have few models on which to base our created relationships. Most of us have had an intimate acquaintance with only one or two families before initiating our own: our family of origin and perhaps that of a good friend. Most families are seen only as they present themselves to the outside world. We may judge our own family as "good" or "bad" based on our subjective experience within it, yet a sibling may have an opposing opinion. It is here that we get to the heart of the question, "What is a **good** family?" We can look around to identify those families who are financially secure in the community, yet affluence is not enough if the relationship is devoid of social meaning to the individuals within that family.

Because our culture places so much emphasis on material goods and social position, we are tempted to use these artificial standards to identify a **good** family. As we examine these criteria more critically, however, we begin to realize their superficiality. Family satisfaction was actually increased during the Depression years because the members of families had more time to spend with one another.[5] Many people from the poorest states (Southeast) report the most positive affects.[4] Although abject poverty may increase stressors, wealth beyond necessity does not ensure conjugal peace.

The fundamental determinant of the quality of subjective human life is the presence or absence of meaningful interpersonal exchanges that provide psychological support.[4] Many families experience pseudomutuality. They look good to others because of their social sophistication. They participate in community, educational, civic, and religious organizations and are friendly to neighbors, but little, if any, honest interaction occurs among the family members.[7] These families may avoid conflict by suppressing negative reactions and behaviors. The members do not share personal feelings or values with one another because of fear of censure or the anxiety such sharing causes other family members. Their lives may become painful because of a lack of mutual respect, which, if severe enough, can rob them of the energy to face even the simplest of daily tasks. When people experience true companionship (see Chaps. 28 and 29), they are freed to create even more satisfying existences.

Approaches to Assessing Family Functioning

The quality of family functioning can be assessed by five major approaches. The **developmental family task approach** is used by Evelyn Duvall.[9] This approach assesses the ability of a family to master specific tasks and responsibilities associated with the age of its children (see Appendix C).

The developmental family task approach concentrates on output, or the interface with the supersystem (see Chap. 2). Throughput is secondary to the output. Goals appear to be heavily influenced by external sources.

The **interactional approach** is discussed by Dolores Curran.[7] This approach can be used to assess the quality of interaction between members of the family system.

The interactional approach focuses not on the total unit but on the intrafamily dynamics among the subsystems (adult–adult, adult–child, child–child). The health of these interactions is assumed to reflect the degree of differentiation and articulation achieved by the family as a system. The healthier the interaction, the more success the family as a whole experiences in meeting family tasks. This approach concentrates on throughput and is concerned with the affective, social, and spiritual domains. Goals are determined by internal sources.

As sociologists, both Duvall and Curran had extensive experience with families and were involved in major research projects before presenting their ideas. Each set of characteristics was influenced by the philosophical views of the culture of their era. Although Duvall's tasks may be seen as too traditional by some, it is hard to deny the necessity for successful resolution of the tasks she identifies. Curran's frame was developed when society was moving from an emphasis on roles to an emphasis on goals. Consequently, the criteria are more difficult to objectively assess, yet more crucial to maximization of both individual and family potentials.

The **system maturity approach** uses Werner's dimensions presented in Chapter 2. This approach enables one to look objectively at family membership and clarity of roles. It emphasizes the degree of differentiation attained by a system, the differentiation from the supersystem as well as the differentiation of its component parts. Werner's continuums allow for an objective assessment of the degree of differentiation attained (see Table 33-1). This approach also concentrates on the family's interface with the supersystem.

Tapia's frame presented in Chapter 33 (see Table 33-4) enables one to look at the family's **developmental level.** Whereas the developmental family task and system maturity approaches deal with all five domains (physical, intellectual, social, emotional, and spiritual), the developmental level approach focuses mainly on the affective and social domains.

The **holistic family task approach** suggested by Schuster in the unit introduction deals with all five domains, intrafamilial and extrafamilial relationships, individuals, and the family as a whole.

It quickly becomes apparent that the *structure* of a family (as discussed in Chap. 33) is an insufficient criterion for evaluating family health or *functioning.* Such structural definitions of family health are heavily biased culturally and are not flexible enough to be used in a situation in which roles are being questioned or are changing rapidly. As in most situations, the practitioner must be committed to pluralism when working with individuals and families. Each approach makes a contribution to our understanding of family functioning.

Characteristics of Good Families

The family is a dynamic system. The members within it are in perpetual change as they progress through physical, cognitive, emotional, social, and spiritual development. Changes in one member of the family necessitate changes in other members and, consequently, in the total family system. Duvall identified eight discrete family stages. The needs and experiences of each stage are distinctly different from those that precede or follow it. The stage is usually based on the age of the oldest child in the family. Parents may find themselves in two or more stages simultaneously if they have more than one child:[9]

1. Beginning family
2. Childbearing family
3. Family with preschool child
4. Family with school-ager
5. Family with adolescent
6. Family as a launching center
7. Family in middle years
8. Aging family

Successful parents exhibit flexibility and resiliency as

they meet the needs of their rapidly developing children. Parents change too, however, as they meet new challenges. As families progress through these developmental stages, Duvall proposes that the basic responsibilities remain constant, but that the focus differs for each stage. Although these tasks were developed for Western cultures, in some manner, every culture must provide a means for mastering them. In the nuclear family, the responsibility for orchestrating the mastery of tasks falls on the shoulders of the adult members or the administrative head of the family system. If they fail to meet the tasks, then the tasks may be assumed by the extended family, the commune, or the community (e.g., children's services).

Family Tasks According to Duvall

PHYSICAL MAINTENANCE. The family must provide for the basic life support needs of its members. These include provision of food, shelter, clothing, health care, and so forth. The quality of these services depends on the cultural context as well as the financial status of the family. When the nuclear family is unable to provide these services, the local welfare department may become involved to assist the family in ensuring that survival needs are met.

ALLOCATION OF RESOURCES. The family apportions possessions, space, time, and affection to its individual members based on the perception of the individual members' needs and the value assigned to each member. Some parents do not realize their children's need for toys or even for their own beds. The parents themselves may have grown up in deprived environments and therefore give their children only the essentials or what is left over after meeting their own needs. Other parents provide the children with "what I never had." The children, unaware of the sacrifices involved, become demanding of more.

Mature parents share resources with the children, helping them to become aware of financial and time limitations and expecting reciprocal sacrifices on the part of the children.[8] The children may not have the same toys or jackets as the children down the street, but they realize that the parents share freely and fairly of what they have. Because the parents share affection with their children and respect their children's personhoods as well as their belongings, self-esteem is enhanced and unity is fostered.

DIVISION OF LABOR. This task is frequently a source of friction in families. Each of the parents, coming from differing families of origin, may have different concepts about the husband's or the wife's role within the family. The traditional roles of the culture may be in conflict with the individual parent's personality or the needs of the family. Together the couple must decide on the responsibilities of procuring an income for the family, managing household chores, and caring for the children. Under these headings would come mundane tasks, such as washing out the bathtub after use, changing the baby's diapers, polishing shoes, washing clothes, paying the bills, or fixing breakfast.

When the parents can discuss these issues openly, match needs with skills or interests, and show flexibility and fairness in the division of tasks, unity is enhanced. As children mature, they are given responsibilities commensurate with their understanding and level of skill. They participate as partners in the business of making the family run smoothly. Unity is not enhanced if children feel that the parents are shirking their fair share. When all members participate fairly in the division of work, then more time is available to share leisure-time activities (Fig. 32-2).

SOCIALIZATION OF FAMILY MEMBERS. Parents gradually guide children into increasingly mature patterns of behavior that become internalized and self-monitored. Aggression, sleep habits, chores, elimination, schoolwork, and sexual drive are gradually brought under voluntary control. The norms and expectations of the community as well as those of the family set a standard for behaviors. Complex behaviors that involve attitudes, social orientation, biases, and involvement are learned through observation. Parents cannot expect behaviors from their children if they are not exhibiting the desired characteristics themselves. It is difficult for a child to value hard work or prudent use of time if the parents watch television all evening while the child studies. It is also difficult for a child to say "no" to drugs, cigarettes, or alcohol if they observe their own parents smoking or taking a drink after work to "wind down."

REPRODUCTION, RECRUITMENT, AND RELEASE OF FAMILY MEMBERS. Parents increase the family size through birth and adoption. The goal of the childbearing family is to release self-sufficient, productive individuals into society at maturity. Temporary increases may occur through caring for foster children or accepting an exchange student.

Circumstances may necessitate the inclusion of in-laws or friends. Rules have to be established to protect the boundaries of the nuclear family system and the relationship among members. If boundaries are not clearly contained, unity is jeopardized. Unity thrives on continuous relationships with a stable group of people, in which identity and relationships are clearly differentiated, articulated, and respected. When new members are accepted (e.g., daughter- or son-in-law) and valued for their unique contribution to the family system, unity is enhanced. At the same time, a new couple needs to accept both of the in-law families as their own, but also as part of the suprasystem to protect their newly established family system. When in-laws are allowed to make decisions for the couple, the new system's integrity is compromised.

MAINTENANCE OF ORDER. Every family has a hierarchical system usually based on age, sex, and skills. A decision-maker (usually one of the parents) is responsible for coordinating the activities of daily life. Rules for conduct and relationships are present even if unspoken. Smooth functioning is facilitated when communication is open and clear. Each member is respected for his or her unique needs, opinions, and goals. When a conflict over needs occurs, the individuals involved are able to share their points of view freely. Negotiation and mutual compromise are encouraged. When alternative solutions cannot be identified, then the decision-maker considers what is best for the total family. Because of mutual respect, the members of the family accept the decision, even though it is not the most desirable one for some of the members. Mutual respect enhances unity.

FIGURE 32–2.
Each family defines its own concept of relaxation and leisure-time activity.

Evaluation of Functioning

The success of a family, according to Duvall, is based on how well the family meets its short-term aspirations, attains the goals society sets for it, and masters the developmental tasks at each stage.

Although Duvall's tasks concentrate on specific, identifiable behaviors of the family system as orchestrated by the administrative subsystem, one must acknowledge that successful meeting of these tasks can facilitate the intangible bonding, or unity, that occurs among its members. Unity is enhanced not only across generational lines but also between members of sibling subsystems as well.

Many families, however, appear to meet all these tasks with success and still do not achieve genuine unity among their members. These are the **good** families portrayed in the introduction. Something is still missing.

Characteristics of Healthy Families

Psychologists and family development specialists are realizing that the evaluation of families according to their ability to meet the expectations of culturally determined roles is an anachronism. Families no longer are held together by necessity. Women are able to earn a living through gainful employment, and men are able to cook and to launder clothes. "Today the major function of family is relational. Our needs are emotional, not physical."[7] Fractionization of a family was formerly caused by the failure of its members to fulfill roles. Today, it is more commonly caused by a failure to achieve goals or to meet the social and emotional expectations and needs of the spouses.

A Harris survey in January 1980 found that family success was more important than financial success to 96% of the American population surveyed.[7] Most of our daily contacts involve using a formal, impersonal "role" self. Consequently, each person needs a small, intimate, private group that accepts idiosyncrasies and allows relaxation and the "peeling away" of these multiple impersonal roles. If Maslow's lower-level needs of survival, safety, and security are met, individuals begin to search to meet their needs for belonging and affection, esteem and self-respect, and self-actualization through the structure of family relationships.[28]

Several practitioners have attempted to identify the characteristics of **healthy** families.[7,26,36] The most complete listing was developed by Dolores Curran from a survey of professional people (e.g., doctors, scout leaders, school personnel, psychologists, ministers) who had daily, intimate contact with families. From their observations, Curran identified 15 traits of psychologically and socially healthy families, families that release healthy, productive citizens into society. She consolidated these characteristics into 12 major areas that represent the interactions among members of families.[7] No family is perfect, but these traits provide information and guidelines for distinguishing between "healthy" and "good" families.

FIGURE 32–3.
Participation of the family members in community activities enhances their sense of belonging to the broader culture.

PLACEMENT OF MEMBERS IN THE LARGER SOCIETY. Parents provide a "minisociety" that prepares children to interface with the broader culture. The family teaches children how to interact with both vertical and horizontal relationships. The parents introduce the child to the community's parks, stores, entertainment facilities, and transportation system. They prepare the child for school and influence his or her adjustment to it by their own attitude and the amount of support they extend to both the child and the school system. The parents' attitude toward and involvement in church, community organizations, and political systems influence the child's attitude toward the institutions and the values of the broader culture. Parents who are interested in news events, value systems, and their cultural heritage and who discuss these with their children help them to become more aware of their own identities and value system within the culture. Sharing and preparation enhance unity and offer security to children by minimizing surprises when they are confronted with the realities of "life in the big world" (Fig. 32-3).

MAINTENANCE OF MOTIVATION AND MORALE. All persons need to be recognized for their uniqueness. When family members affirm one another's efforts, confidence is enhanced, and creativity is encouraged. When support and affection are given routinely, unity is maintained during crises. Family rituals, gatherings, and festivals help the members appreciate their heritage and anticipate their future. A sense of kinship and loyalty is fostered. These periods of sharing help family members refine their philosophies of life and identify what they have in common. The good feelings engendered by mutually enjoyed work and leisure activities help to carry the family through the difficult times that are common to all families.

ENCOURAGEMENT OF OPEN COMMUNICATION. Every commentator on healthy family dynamics identifies communication as the key to family health. Through honest, open communication, the members are able to solidify their own individuality and that of others. Healthy individuals not only express their values and feelings but listen sensitively to those of other family members. They encourage independent thinking and feelings. When confrontations arise, they use approaches that not only resolve the conflict but restore the mutuality of the relationship. These family members value the time spent conversing with one another and use every opportunity to share events, aspirations, disappointments, and feelings. The television is not allowed to usurp their relationship time. Nonverbal messages are decoded, and members are careful not to use turnoff words or putdown phrases that would stifle free and creative expression of the authentic self.

Through careful listening, the parent gives the child permission to express what he or she is feeling and helps to clarify problem situations. Since the feeling system links the affective and cognitive domains,[1] this technique facilitates greater self-understanding and autonomous problem solving. By using **active listening** techniques, parents listen for the feelings and meaning of a communication from the child without inserting judgmental overtones.[16] This approach fosters self-disclosure, focuses on identification of the specific underlying problem, and maintains self-respect when conflict surfaces.

It is critical to identify the "ownership" of a problem to maintain objectivity and protect individuality.[16] This identification is facilitated through the use of "I messages," which are statements that explain how a behavior or situation makes the speaker feel or affects the speaker's life (e.g., "I am feeling very angry right now because . . . ," or "If you get a cold because you don't wear a rain coat today, I will have to stay home to take care of you. That means that I will not get paid for that day of work and we will not be able to . . . "). This honest, open approach allows two persons to develop an authentic relationship, which fosters negotiations for a mutually acceptable solution. Conflict-of-needs is no longer a power struggle in which one person "wins" while the other capitulates. It is a "no-loser" approach that enables both parties to know and to respect each other better.[16] Their mutual respect thus leads to an increased differentiation as well as an increased integration of the parent–child subsystem, which fosters unity.

PROVISION OF AFFIRMATION AND SUPPORT. The members of a healthy family make opportunities both to affirm and to support the value and uniqueness of each member. They like one another and say so. They extend appreciation for the *efforts* of the other person even if the final product is not commendable. They support the other members' goals even when it may require some sacrifice on their part (e.g., listening to a third-grader learning to play a violin or shifting schedules and responsibilities to accommodate a parent returning to school). The basic mood of this family is positive. They know that, even if they fail to achieve a personal goal, the other members will extend empathy and understanding rather than criticism or ridicule. The whole family suffers if members cannot affirm one another because self-esteem is lowered.[13] The healthy family extends support to community institutions, but not automatically, for they expect the same open communication, affirmation, and respect from the institution as is found in their own family (Fig. 32-4).

FIGURE 32-4.
Working with real materials and sharing in genuine family or community projects helps to socialize children, refines their sensorimotor skills, prepares them to assume adult responsibilities, and increases their sense of self-worth.

ENCOURAGEMENT OF MUTUAL RESPECT. The healthy family values and respects each member regardless of age, disability, or eccentricity. Because of the respect shown and the affirmation offered, each person grows in self-respect, a self-respect that fosters the cherished care of one's own physical and psychic selves. This respect generalizes and transfers to institutions and people outside the family, and not only to those with whom they agree or find things in common. Sex, creed, color, career, disability, or social orientation do not interfere with the respect that is afforded each person with whom they have contact. These individuals show respect but are not obsequious. They respect people, not positions. Each member has learned within the context of the family to approach every person with the same gentleness, tenderness, and respect that they themselves cherish and thrive on. This respect extends to the personal property and mail of other people as well as each person's right to solve his or her own problems, to make mistakes, to identify friends, or to experience periods of solitude. These individuals do not invade the "personal space" of another person. In short, the subsystems are clearly delineated and members do not try to make others an extension of their own egos. They demand respect for their own selves by their deportment and their authenticity of interaction. Mutual respect is one of the strongest aspects of family unity.[20]

GENERATION OF TRUST. Trust is recognized as a precious possession. It is the foundation of intimate relationships. The husband and wife trust the commitment of the other to the marriage. The children trust the parents' intentions and guidance to keep them safe (socially, emotionally, and spiritually, as well as physically), even though it may mean the frustration of a particular goal. The parents trust the ability of the child to gradually assume more self-direction. Members also recognize the essence of confidentiality. Confidences are cherished and maintained.

SHARING OF TIME. Lack of time is probably the most pervasive enemy of the healthy family.[7] The activities of daily living, work, and community commitments may encroach on this precious, limited commodity. A strong sense of family rests on the time spent together; the experiences and responsibilities shared; and the goals, values, and priorities developed in tandem. If members do not make time for one another and for family activities, they become "ships passing in the night." Consequently, allegiance, socialization, and the establishment of values are turned over to other systems, such as the school, clubs, church, scouts, neighbors, or peers.

The high fractionization rate of families may actually be an artifact of society more than it is a conflict of personalities. The family that values its unity must take an assertive stance against intruding pressures.[8] Each member must find a balance among extrafamilial, intrafamilial, and personal commitment times. They must not allow business or civic responsibilities to infringe regularly on family life. At some point, an individual must reassess priorities. If maintaining family integrity and unity is important, then the courage must be summoned to use that small but emphatic word "no." The decision must be made as to which is more important, a public image or family relationships. If external forces are allowed to direct the individual's time, he or she in essence is saying "no" to the family and offering its members "leftover" time. Sandra and Harry Chapin's song "Cat's in the Cradle" poignantly catches the rhythm of this lifestyle (Fig. 32-5). Sometimes a career, or at least an employer, needs to be changed so that the individual is able to work to live and not live to work.

Men and women can "burn out" as they juggle home, work, and family responsibilities and activities. It is only as they develop a clear sense of their own boundaries and priorities that they can balance their stressors and assets and proceed on a relatively smooth course. Adults also have to be careful not to overload children in the push to maximize potentials. A child should be involved in only one activity at a time that requires practice (e.g., piano, ballet, football, or band).[7] That activity should have intrinsic value to the child, so that parental time is not "zapped" by forced spectator roles or supervision.

Healthy families structure time for each interactional subsystem to develop appreciation for the other. They prize time alone with individual members. Charles and John Wesley, outstanding humanists and theologians of the 1700s, came from an impoverished family of 19 children. When Suzanna, their mother, was asked how she accounted for her sons' self-confidence, personality, and spiritual success, she replied that she scheduled 1 hour each week to be spent alone with each child and engaged in activities that he or she wanted or needed to do. This individual time was respected and jealously guarded by each member of the family. No intrusions were allowed except for emergencies.[38] Time must be made for the parent and the child to get to know and like each other. **Special time with each child is not a luxury but a necessity.**[7] Parents must keep time in balance for each child even if one is gifted or disabled. Time cannot evolve disproportionately around any one member of the family.

The family needs to plan group time together. Sharing of responsibilities can heighten the sense of intimacy.[1] Work activities can be turned into play (e.g., yard work, car wash, redecorating, food preparation). A sprinkling of humor throughout the activities of daily living relieves drudgery, depression, and conflicts. Pure play activities should be planned regularly into the schedule, such as trips to museums, a picnic (even in the snow), a trip to the beach, volleyball games, bike trips, bowling, or fishing. These excursions need not be expensive; they are only the media that provide the time together to share ideas. Window-shopping after the stores have closed for the day can be more fun than the actual purchasing of goods. Brief activities can be worked into the daily schedule. Memories are made from the sharing of simple, fun events. (Parents who need ideas might start with *Let's Make a Memory* by Gloria Gaither and Shirley Dobson.[11]) A weekly ethnic meal can provide variety and

Cat's in the Cradle

By Sandy and Harry Chapin

My child arrived just the other day
  he came to the world in the usual way—
  But there were planes to catch and bills to pay
  he learned to walk while I was away
    and he was talkin fore I knew it and as he grew
          he'd say

    I'm gonna be like you, Dad
    you know I'm gonna be like you.

and the cat's in the cradle and the silver spoon
Little boy blue and the man in the moon
when you comin' home, Dad
    I don't know when
      but we'll get together then—
  you know we'll have a good time then

My son turned 10 just the other day
  he said, Thanks for the ball, Dad, com'on let's play
  Can you teach me to throw?
  I said not today, I got a lot to do
  He said, That's okay
    and he walked away
      but his smile never dimmed
  it said I'm gonna be like him, yeah
    you know I'm gonna be like him

and the cat's in the cradle and the silver spoon
Little boy blue and the man in the moon
when you comin' home, Dad
    I don't know when
      but we'll get together then—
  you know we'll have a good time then

Well he came home from college just the other day
  so much like a man I just had to say
  Son, I'm proud of you, can you sit for awhile
  He shook his head and said with a smile—
  what I'd really like, Dad, is to borrow the car keys
  see you later, can I have them please?

When you comin home, Son?
    I don't know when
    but we'll get together then
  you know we'll have a good time then

I've long since retired, my son's moved away
  I called him up just the other day
  I said I'd like to see you if you don't mind
  He said, I'd love to, Dad—if I can find the time

You see my new job's a hassle
  and the kids have the flu
  but it's sure nice talkin to you, Dad
  It's been nice talking to you

And as I hung up the phone, it occurred to me—
  he'd grown up just like me; my boy was just like me

and the cat's in the cradle and the silver spoon
Little boy blue and the man in the moon
when you comin home, Son?
    I don't know when
    but we'll get together then, Dad,
  we're gonna have a good time then

FIGURE 32–5.

Cat's in the Cradle. (Words and music by Sandy and Harry Chapin. Copyright © 1974 Story Songs, Ltd. All rights reserved. With permission.)

much discussion around the table. Reading a book or watching a special television program together also provides fuel for animated, authentic conversations that center on feelings and value systems. It can be enlightening and entertaining to speculate how one would allocate monies received from a hypothetical sweepstakes or inheritance.

FOSTERING OF RESPONSIBILITY. Children need challenges to grow. Because the parents understand the relationship between responsibility and self-esteem, they gear responsibilities to the child's capabilities and then support the child's efforts. They do not remove the obstacles in their children's lives that can foster growth. They do not cover up for the

child's neglected or forgotten responsibilities but allow the child to live with the natural consequences of irresponsibility. They help the child recognize the self as a partner in the tasks and responsibilities of the family system. In this way, children learn not only the psychomotor skills essential to successful independent adult living but also the problem-solving and self-discipline skills essential to successful goal-setting and achievement. Genuine happiness and contentment result from the confidence of knowing that one has mastered difficult skills and situations and can continue to do so.

TEACHING OF MORALS. Curran observes that too many people emphasize "doing your own thing" over an evaluation of the ripple effect of the behavior on one's long-range lifestyle and goals or the effect of the behavior on the lives of others. This emphasis tends to create a self-centered, hedonistic culture.[15] The source of authority becomes the person alone. Parents need to teach specific guidelines about right and wrong and to share with their children values and principles to believe in and to guide behavior. At the same time, parents need to realize that intent is crucial in judging behavior and must take time to understand the child's frame of reference, using infractions as opportunities for teaching rather than punishment, as the child learns to balance self-will with the needs and feelings of others. Both autonomy and unity are fostered when parents have clearly defined values and standards that are comfortably integrated into their own behavior and openly shared with their children. The children are able to see the benefits, not just the restrictions, of self-discipline.

SHARING OF RELIGIOUS BELIEFS. Religious participation correlates positively with increased marital satisfaction, happiness, and adjustment.[22] Sharing religious beliefs is more than teaching the nuances of church doctrines or institutionalized faith as practiced through rituals, memorized prayers, and participation in corporate worship. Healthy families share their religious beliefs because of the difference it makes in everyday family life. A vital religious core provides common values and a sense of meaning and purpose, or direction, to life. Families, like individuals, need the hope and strength that come from a belief in something higher than self. The family that pursues only material objects or goals may be a candidate for self-destruction either from the eventual boredom of material pursuits or the inability to meet a crisis when it arises.[7]

The healthy family does not have a rigid set of rules and prohibitions.[13] Rather, the internalized principles are woven comfortably into the fabric of daily living. The members recognize the difference between breaking conventions and breaking convictions. The peace of mind enjoyed by those who have made a commitment to something higher than themselves and who have internalized a positive value system enables them to extend more energy toward other people, affirming and supporting their growth.

A 1981 Gallup survey of youth found that parents who placed a high value on religion were more likely to help children with their homework, share physical affection with their children, tell them they were loved, praise them, and talk with them about their daily activities.[12] Children are more likely to embrace the parents' value system if they see that it sustains their parents through crises. Curran observes that "we must ask ourselves if those drawn to the cults are not really seeking a sense of family, complete with its traditions and value systems, which may have been missing in their own childhood families."[7]

The way we translate our values and religious beliefs into everyday living is the way we pass on our faith, or lack of it. Many religious doctrines teach that love must prevail in family relationships, thereby nurturing marital happiness and family solidarity. However, some doctrines also prescribe gender-role behaviors that may actually undermine family relationships by failing to recognize the individuality of members.

ENJOYMENT OF TRADITIONS. The healthy family views itself as a link between the past and the future. It shares stories both funny and sad about the history of the family. Grandparents are seen as valuable sources of family history, folklore, and cultural preserves. The family leans heavily on its religious and ethnic traditions for a sense of identity as well as its relationship to the broader culture. It also develops its own unique traditions based on rituals learned in the family of origin, spontaneous events, or personal desires. Young couples frequently experience conflict over rituals surrounding significant events, such as Christmas (e.g., whether to open presents on Christmas Eve or on Christmas morning). As the family develops its own traditions, the members eagerly anticipate the next occurrence of the event, jealously guarding against any changes in the rituals or intrusions on the family time. The anticipation of holidays and other periodically recurring special events relieves the boredom and drudgery of routine events and responsibilities. The sharing of ethnic customs, rituals, food, or even language provides a sense of kinship that sustains during periods of crisis. Such close, shared experiences provide a life-long base of love and support.

RESPECT FOR PRIVACY. In the midst of sharing time with one another, family members must respect the need of each to share time with the self. Private time is essential for unwinding and processing events. The individual must have the opportunity to get to know and like the self. The healthy family protects and encourages the right of each member to be their own person and to be alone. Each member can choose their own friends, follow their own fads, keep or dispose of their own material possessions as long as it does not violate the rights of others or create a safety issue. Permissiveness does not mean indulgence but freedom to be one's self. Mutuality is still expected and fostered.

VALUE SERVICE. Healthy families stress cooperativeness, not competition, in relationships. Because members are at peace with themselves, they enjoy sharing their abundance of ego with others. They are alert to the needs and stressors of others and take active measures to assist by opening doors for a package-laden parent, running telephone interference for a distressed sibling, singing for a lonely grandparent, or retrieving a toy for a young child. The empathic and altruistic orientation developed within the family impels them to serve others in concrete ways. Neighborhood children, foster children, exchange students, lonely college students, all are made to feel welcome in their home. There is always enough love, affirmation, and good will to include another. (Conversely, new members or visitors may serve as distracters or substitute gratifiers in a dysfunctional or unhappy family system.) Members of healthy families donate blood, time, or expertise to improve the quality of life in the community. However, even volunteer time is kept in balance with family responsibilities and relationships. Through giving of the self in service to others, the individual actually receives more ego strength.

SEEKING OF HELP. The healthy family is aware of its own limits and seeks help when necessary. It recognizes that no family is perfect and does not strive for an impossible, self-imposed standard (a self-defeating mentality). Family members expect problems and consider them a normal part of intimate, honest relationships. They develop techniques for preventing problems and for dealing with specific problems as they arise.[8] They seek help in the early stages of a problem before it reaches unresolvable dimensions. Unity is enhanced because each member feels a responsibility to contribute to the resolution of problems and conflict-of-need situations.

When Children Become Adults

In spite of the aesthetic appeal of Curran's major areas of family interaction, no magic formula can assure a positive outcome to the efforts of child rearing. A child may grow up and appear to be successful but still be stunted inside.[25] The unique personality structure and ego intensity of each individual dynamically create a different relationship with each member of the family. Biological factors, health status, educational and cultural opportunities, cultural standards, peers, adult role models, kinship contacts, and financial security are all factors that make a contribution to the final outcome. However, despite these potential influences, the family (by its value system and interactional patterns) is the most significant influence in a person's life, since it lays the foundation for adaptation to life.[25] It is within the family that the individual learns to face stressors, to negotiate conflicts, and to accept one's self as a person. Even the early parent–child relationship continues to affect the quality of one's life because of the effects on the person's personality development,[21] the creation of memories, and because the quality of the interaction of grown children with their parents tends to endure over time. Because one's personality effects future relationships and parenting style, the quality of the original parent–child relationship indirectly effects the personality of the next generation.[21] People bring templates of past experiences to current situations that are based on selective reconstruction of events.[29] These memories become a part of each interactional equation, affecting interpretation and behaviors in situations with their own family members. Attention to Curran's characteristics increases the chances of survival of the nuclear family and of a positive outcome for the children.

One of the most difficult tasks of parenthood is the pacing of efforts to foster independence. When parents release the authority and the responsibility for guidance too early in a child's life, it makes it more difficult for the maturing offspring to accept the rules and regulations of other people and institutions.[24] It also decreases the sense of caring between parents and child and thus the bonding with one another. On the other hand, independence and self-esteem

are decreased and conflict is increased when parents continue to rule adolescent and adult children.

Bowen, a renowned psychiatrist, observes that families are constantly balancing two opposing forces: togetherness (the need for love, approval, acceptance, and agreement) and individuality (the need for autonomy, productivity, and creativity).[1] If *togetherness* predominates, a fusion of selves (undifferentiated family ego mass) prevents independence and the maximization of the potentials of individual members. This kind of family expects everyone to hold the same opinion or to feel equally disturbed when one person perceives an insult from an outside source. Alternate viewpoints or even a clarification of the facts are not easily tolerated; subjective, self-effacing overtones color both intrafamilial and extrafamilial relationships. A severe pathology of the family as well as its individual members can develop. If *individuality* prevails, then perspective is lost: the parts become more important than the whole, and the bond is weakened. The members of this family have no sense of belonging to or caring for one another. Mutuality is lost. Limited commitment to family goals and welfare limits the willingness or ability of its members to sacrifice or delay personal goals for the benefit of others (see Chap. 29).

The healthy family supports autonomy and gradual assumption of responsibility. Its goal is to prepare the children for a successful, independent adulthood (Fig. 32-6). Both the

FIGURE 32–6.
Young people from healthy families enter the adult world with enthusiasm and confidence.

children and the parents take pride in the burgeoning abilities to assume responsibility for problem solving, interpersonal relationships, time and money management, as well as personal care and household responsibilities.

Grown children tend to reproduce the parents' culture if they have had a close relationship with good identification.[14] They continue to use the parents as a resource for decision making. Superordinate–subordinate roles are released. The relationship becomes one of a friendship or a mentor relationship over time because mutual respect has been established and each individual's uniqueness has been recognized and fostered. When contact between the generations is rewarding, it continues over time.[20]

STRESS AND FAMILY UNITY

Every family is barraged by stressors, big and little, life-changing and inconsequential, unanticipated, and predictable. Birth of a child, father absence, conflict of needs, illness of the spouse, financial concerns, employment demands, sibling squabbles, death of a relative, toddler and adolescent strivings for autonomy, business failure or unemployment, home maintenance tasks, social obligations, and the developmental needs of children all create stress for parents and their children. "Tensions stem from the need to provide a stable family for the rearing of children and for preserving the vitality of American society without infringing upon personal freedoms."[25] Parents who have worked through their own identities and see life realistically, expect life to have its ups and downs. In spite of life's difficulties, they face situations with a confidence that they have the resources to meet and rise above the stressors.[8] *Healthy or stress-effective families view stress as temporary and normal, not as a sign of weakness or failure.* They work together to seek positive solutions to the problems faced. As a result, the family emerges stronger and better prepared to meet the next stressor as its repertoire of stress skills builds. Dysfunctional or distressed families wallow in self-pity or anger as they try to affix blame. They have a sense of guilt or lowered self-esteem for "permitting the stress to exist." They often focus on the family's weaknesses rather than its strengths and, thus, in discouragement give up efforts to resolve the issue. The buildup of unresolved stress thus frequently creates an aversion to family life.[8]

Common Family Stressors

Curran surveyed married men, married women, and single mothers to identify what parents see as the most stressful elements in their lives.[8] Although, as one would expect, differences were found in both the factors identified and their stress value, the three groups also had much in common. Interestingly, rather than naming factors beyond their control, such as a disabled child, unemployment, or natural disaster, these families identified factors inherent in living together as a family, such as the coordination of time, money, and rela-

tionships. The top ten stressors, in order of priority, are identified in the following sections.[8]

ECONOMICS, FINANCES, BUDGETING. All families struggle with insufficient money to meet the family's desired lifestyle. However, stress is related to issues of planning, self-discipline, and budgeting rather than the amount available. Healthy families do not equate self-esteem or power with either individual or family income. Each person is respected for his or her contribution to the family and community. "Wealth" is shared according to need. The family discusses their needs and desires and works these into a budget. Children are taught how to manage money effectively, and *credit card use is discouraged.*

CHILDREN'S BEHAVIOR, DISCIPLINE, SIBLING FIGHTING. In her interviews with healthy families, Curran was impressed with the fact that stress-effective parents truly enjoy their children. In spite of the additional work, discipline problems, and inconveniences inherent in the parenting role, they considered parenting to be a major source of pleasure and satisfaction. Because these parents have resolved their own identity issues, *they are confident in their right to establish clear rules and guidelines,* to make the final decision, and to be the leader in the home. Comfort with their roles enables them to listen to the child's viewpoint, admit mistakes, and be flexible in rule enforcement without loss of respect. This comfort with parenting sets a model for social relationships that fosters respect, self-discipline, and mature behavior in their children. The parents in healthy families use an authoritative approach; they are not afraid to establish firm limits.[8, 19, 23] They also encourage their children to assume responsibility for the consequences of their behaviors, and they "let go" of responsibility for decision making as the children exhibit readiness to assume the responsibility. In healthy families, the parents form a "parenting unit," each supporting the other, providing care, offering direction, and ensuring consequences as necessary.[30] Even though they may have differing discipline styles, they present a united front to the children, facilitating rule learning and self-discipline. Step-parent families experience considerable difficulty in the area of child guidance and discipline. "In general, the best strategy of a step-father to gain acceptance by step-children seems to be one where there is no initial active attempt to take over and/or actively to control the child's behavior, either through authoritarian or the more desirable authoritative techniques. Instead, the new father should first work at establishing a relationship with the child and support the mother in her parenting. This period can be effectively followed later by more active authoritative parenting, which leads to constructive outcomes, at least for boys."[19]

INSUFFICIENT COUPLE TIME. When parents do not find enough time to spend with each other, the entire family suffers. Work schedules and child care responsibilities usurp emotional and physical energies. "Time for each other is secondary to time for work or for unwinding from work. Friendship between them begins to diminish. They no longer share deep feelings because doing so would require time and commitment. They eventually become roommates or strangers who simply live together rather than intimates who are willing to become vulnerable by sharing their deepest feelings."[8] Thus, distressed families have a weaker spousal bond. This weakness may not be blatantly apparent during the normal activities of daily living, but an increasing number of minor conflicts and the lack of bonding become obvious during times of stress.[6] Issues of child guidance and discipline are aggravated. "Marital discord prevents the spouses from establishing the unified alliance necessary for parental leadership. The functioning of the executive system of the home is weakened by internal division: the two most experienced and capable members may be unable to work together to solve the problems of family life. Specifically, the parents may be unable to join together to provide consistent direction, guidance, and discipline for the children."[6] The children, consequently, may assume too much power, undermining parental authority and further interfering with the marital relationship.

Healthy families value and protect couple time. They realize that love and cooperation die if they are not nurtured. Consequently, they schedule time for each other—time to discuss problems, time for physical intimacy, time for fun, time to share interests, feelings, and personal growth. The refreshment of these moments provides resiliency for facing the other stressors of life. Couples that wish to revitalize their relationship are encouraged to attend a Marriage Encounter retreat or workshop (c/o Luther and Kay Wallace, 7050 S. Steele St., Littleton, CO 80122).

LACK OF SHARED RESPONSIBILITY IN THE FAMILY. Stress-effective families reduce stress by sharing responsibility. "Many hands make hard work easy." When one person assumes the major responsibility for the organization and management of family responsibilities and chores, resentment and tension build to create additional stress. Fatigue and decreased esteem undermine productivity and relationship satisfaction. When parents (especially mothers) feel that the child's success or failure rests entirely on the parent, then he or she may do so much for the child that (1) the child will not learn how to do for himself or herself (spoiled) and (2) the parent will "burn out."[32] In truth, these parents are more concerned with how the child reflects on them and their skills at providing and caregiving than they are about the maturing needs of the child. When everyone shares, then more time is available for family leisure. No one "uses" mother or any other family member. Each person assumes responsibility as age, interests, and time permit. Stress is reduced, mutuality and intimacy are enhanced.[23]

Curran notes that "the most striking difference between healthy parents and others is that the father plays an active role in parenting his children."[8] This participation relieves the burden on the mother but also provides children with a unified front and alternative approaches to dealing with life and its relationships, stressors, and responsibilities. Although egalitarian couples may try hard to participate equally in child care, previous cultural training, work schedules, and interests of the persons involved tend to draw them toward traditional roles.[23] Although the father may be available for answering questions, providing supervision, or rendering emotional support, the average father with a working wife spends only 15 to 25 minutes per day in direct child care.[31] Sharing of parenting responsibilities not only has multiple beneficial effects on the children's short-range and long-range development but also enhances the marital relationship.[17,23] Sharing of responsibility for parenting is especially critical after a divorce. The marital relationship must be separated from the parental relationship for the benefit of the children.[18] Urie Bronfenbrenner notes that the major difference between successful and unsuccessful children of divorced parents is the continued active involvement of the father and his support of their mother.[3]

COMMUNICATING WITH CHILDREN. Stress-effective parents "accept their children as they are and let them know this in a thousand little ways."[8] Distressed parents are absorbed within themselves. "So much time is spent coping with the daily stress of living that there is little strength or enthusiasm left over for parenting."[10] In healthy families, both parents spend time with the children because they enjoy them and want to develop a close relationship. The father is comfortable "turntaking" with the infant, playing "trucks" with a toddler, "racing" with the preschooler, losing a game of checkers to the school-ager, or riding bikes with a teen (Fig. 32-7). Involved, caring fathers can kiss a "boo-boo," bandage a doll, or cradle a crying adolescent. Parents, especially fathers, who are actively involved with their children set the foundation for a warm, open relationship that reaps positive results during adolescence and later in life.[8] Some parents try to assure *quality* time by scheduling in a *quantity* of time each day or week. Children *do* need to have uninterrupted private time with each parent on a regular basis. However, "This assumes that a child's needs can be scheduled to fit into our time availability. Healthy parents know this isn't always possible. Children need us when they **need** us, not only when we're available."[8]

The younger the child, the more difficult it is to wait for attention. Children need to know that parents are available when *they* need the parent. Mahler's concept of emotional refueling[27] extends through the adolescent years. When parents are at work or are separated or divorced, stress is reduced and emotional security enhanced when the child is able to reach a parent by phone.

Communication, to be effective, must be reciprocal. Healthy families listen to each other, and they acknowledge the feelings, disappointments, and needs of the others. Stress-effective families admit mistakes and problems, they affirm each other, they attend to nonverbal cues, and they maintain confidentialities. In short, stress-effective families concentrate on developing and maintaining satisfying, supportive, and meaningful relationships with each other. By establishing rules before problems occur and by facing conflicts openly, they are able to avoid many of the problems that plague

FIGURE 32–7.
The quality of the relationship between a parent and child is more crucial than the quantity. The quality is determined by the parent's ability to participate in activities at the child's level of development. The synchrony established during these early years is the foundation of solid family relationships that emerge into close friendships during later years. (Photo by Ed Slaman.)

distressed families. The respect developed during the early years reduces conflicts during the adolescent years as the parents and teens renegotiate rules, roles, and relationships.

INSUFFICIENT "ME" TIME. Once children enter the home, many parents feel that they lose their own identities. They give up pursuit of their own hobbies, interests, and leisure-time activities to meet the needs and demands of the children. Healthy families encourage their members to maintain or develop their own activities and friendships and protect the individual's right to personal time, space, and property, even in the early years. The stress-effective family encourages its members to "get away" for an evening, overnight, or a weekend or to a camp to pursue activities that refresh and relax.[8]

GUILT FOR NOT ACCOMPLISHING MORE. Somehow in the process of growing up, many of us extract the opinion that adults "know it all" and "can do it all." Cultural ideals created and transmitted by mass media or uniquely processed within our own minds lead us to believe that the man earns top salary, yet, because of flexible working demands, he is able to spend hours in community volunteer activities and hours nurturing and playing with his children each week. The mythical "super mom" works full time, maintains an immaculate home, attends every parent–teacher meeting, is available for her children, and manages to continue to look appealing for her husband. When parents don't match the ideal, something has to give. As standards relax, the "guilties" set in. Healthy families reevaluate standards and roles. They focus their energies on finding workable solutions. Priorities are reestablished with goals and relationships taking priority over traditional roles, impossible standards, and peer pressure. "Dishes wait, children don't." Changes may include a change of job, a

reduction in expenditures, or a reassignment of responsibilities within the family. Healthy families recognize their humanness and learn to live productively within their limits.

SPOUSAL RELATIONSHIPS (COMMUNICATION, FRIENDSHIP, SEX). Healthy couples "communicate on a *feeling* level as well as on a *verbal* level."[8] Their identity is secure enough to risk intimate discussion of feelings, reactions, concerns, problems. Rather than destroying the relationship, the discussions draw the couple closer as they understand and respect each other's position. They continue to do their "love homework" by finding time to share, through telephone calls, notes, special looks, and words that say "you are the most important person in the world to me." They spend a weekend away from the children to enjoy their love and friendship. Loneliness does not exist in this relationship. Children are offered a model of a healthy relationship and grow secure within their parents' love. The couple finds energy to face the other issues of life from their support and love of each other.

INSUFFICIENT FAMILY PLAYTIME. When the bad times come— and they do for all families—the family that plays together, stays together; they have warm, rich memories to draw on; they know they are friends in spite of the current problem they are facing. The "playing" family does not have unlimited leisure time. They have learned to schedule work and home commitments to allow free time for family outings or an evening of games. *They turn work into play* (e.g., washing the car together, gardening, community cleanup project, helping a child with a school assignment). "In short, this family makes fun and creates bondedness out of what other families might perceive as work."[8] Play need not be expensive. They may read a book and talk about its contents, attend a school concert or ball game, put a puzzle together, or pitch tents in the backyard (Fig. 32-8). The point is that they do it together, each enjoying the experience in his or her own way. Humor is also critical. Finding the funny side of a difficult situation can make it much easier to live with. Curran discovered that, during adolescent years, young people with stress-effective parents and healthy home environments continued to enjoy their families and frequently brought other young people home to enjoy life with them. Why should adolescents want to stick around a boring, stress-filled family?

OVERSCHEDULED FAMILY CALENDAR. Even healthy families can become overscheduled. Healthy families are filled with individuals excited about life and living, persons, pursuing individual talents and interests, investing themselves in the lives of others. This very enthusiasm, however, can be the family's downfall. After awhile, so much time can be spent out of the home giving to the needs of others that intrafamily relationships suffer. Family members begin to burn out, they become irritable, they become strangers living in the same household. The distressed family begins to feel hurried, haggard, and harassed. Escape is the only solution to what "they" are doing to "me." Stress-effective families acknowledge and deal with the issues before they disable the family. They recognize that they have scheduled themselves "into this mess." It was a *choice*! Consequently, they sit down and discuss the needs and interests of family members, finding a balance between the needs of each person, the needs of the family, and the needs of the community. The stress-effective family looks at long-range as well as weekly calendars to ensure sufficient family time for work, communication, play, and respite. They "unschedule"

FIGURE 32–8.
Dual-career families frequently need to schedule family time to ensure time together as a family, an essential ingredient of family unity.

themselves as they reestablish priorities and coordinate schedules to provide time to be a family.

The "Successful" Family

The stability of society is threatened by the increasing number of people raised in unstable homes. Children carry the scars left by distressed families for the rest of their lives.[25] It is critical to understand factors that differentiate between successful and unsuccessful families to be able to offer intervention ideas.

People are beginning to realize that success cannot be measured in terms of how much money one earns, how many honors one is awarded by the community, how well a person or family meets the artificial standards or roles established by peers or the culture, the number of children sired, or any other quantitative measure that signals cultural ideals. Single parents, dual-career families, older parents, blended families, and families in poverty or with disabled members do not automatically qualify for the status of "unsuccessful family" by nature of the family complex. The success or health of a family is not measured by its structure or the number of problems or stressors it faces. Rather, the success of a family is more closely related to its ability to deal with stress and to develop meaningful, supportive relationships between its members.[8] Successful, or healthy, families find ways to meet and reduce stressors to maximize family relationship potentials. These solutions are not based on ethnic origin, number of persons in the family, or the uniqueness of the stressors faced but are based only on the openness and willingness of the people to face the stressors. Such intimacy is predicated on the emotional health and maturity of its leaders, the parents. The parents must do their own "identity homework" before they can fully involve themselves in their "love homework" or their "family homework." Life as an individual or as a member of a family is a continuous struggle, but the pathway is easier when parents have enabled us to develop the emotional, social, personal, career, and spiritual skills necessary to invest ourselves in our spouses and children without loss of our own identities.

CONCLUSION

The *good* family is not synonymous with the **healthy** family. A definition of the former typically employs culturally imposed external status symbols, such as wealth, education, or position. A definition of healthy families, on the other hand, is based on the intrapersonal dynamics of the family, an internal factor observed only by people with intimate contact with the family.

Since children have a tendency to emulate parental behaviors, interaction patterns are transmitted from generation to generation. Thus, the micro-culture of the family system provides a medium for "inheriting" mental health or illness.[1,2] Family unity is not a given because two people fall in love and marry: they have to work daily at maintaining respect and communication. It involves the reciprocal activities of open sharing and active listening. A healthy family shares a mutual respect and an open communication that lead to deeper understanding and appreciation of each individual's feelings and value system. Respect and communication lead to greater unity, or bonding, among the members, enabling them to transfer this same respect and allocentrism to persons outside the family system. The success of parenting often depends on the quality of the social environment and the community support.[13] The involvement in too many community activities or extracurricular activities connected with one's employment can overburden the family system, while the availability of support resources can help to relieve family conflict.

Divorce is frequently the result of a couple's inability to establish open communication with each other. Divorce usually does not completely sever the relationship between spouses, however, especially if children are involved. The postmarital relationship can be enduring and amazingly resilient, much like a kinship relationship.[37] The parents must continue to cooperate for the sake of the children. When a child has free access to both parents, the long-term negative effects of a fractionized family are minimized.

The paradox of family unity is that it is strongest when family members recognize and appreciate the uniqueness of one another.

REFERENCES

1. Bowen, M. (1985). *Family therapy in clinical practice.* New York: Jason Aronson.
2. Bowlby, J. (1973). *Attachment and loss* (Vol. 2). New York: Basic Books.
3. Bronfenbrenner, U. (1979). *An ecological perspective, the American family: Current perspectives.* Cambridge, MA: Harvard University Press. (Harvard Seminar Series)
4. Campbell, A. (1976). Subjective measures of well-being. *American Psychologist, 31,* 117.
5. Caplow, T., & Bahr, H. M. (1982). *Middletown families: Fifty years of change and continuity.* Minneapolis: University of Minnesota Press.
6. Christensen, A., & Margolin. (1985). Conflict and alliance in distressed and non-distressed families. In R. A. Hinde & J. Stevenson-Hinde (Eds.), *Relationships within families: Mutual influences* (pp. 263–282). New York: Oxford University Press.
7. Curran, D. D. (1983). *Traits of a healthy family: Fifteen traits commonly found in healthy families by those who work with them.* Minneapolis, MN: Winston Press.
8. Curran, D. D. (1985). *Stress and the healthy family.* Minneapolis: Winston Press.
9. Duvall, E. R. M. (1971). *Family development* (4th ed.). Philadelphia: J. B. Lippincott.
10. Elkind, D. (1983). The loss of innocence. Cited in D. Curran (Ed.), *Stress and the healthy family* (p. 111). Minneapolis, MN: Winston Press.
11. Gaither, G., & Dobson, S. (1983). *Let's make a memory: Great ideas for building family traditions and togetherness.* Waco, TX: Word Books.
12. Gallup, G., Jr. (1981). *Gallup youth survey.* New York: Associated Press.
13. Garbarino, J. (1982). *Children and families in the social environment.* New York: Aldine.
14. Garrett, W. R. (1982). *Seasons of marriage and family life.* New York: Holt, Rinehart and Winston.
15. Glasser, L. N., & Glasser, P. H. (1977). Hedonism and the family: Conflict in values. *Journal of Marriage and Family Counseling, 4,* 11.
16. Gordon, T. (1970). *P.E.T., Parent effectiveness training: The tested new way to raise responsible children.* New York: Wyden.
17. Gray-Little, B., & Burks, N. (1983). Power and satisfaction in marriage: A review and critique. *Psychological Bulletin, 93,* 513–538.
18. Greif, G. L. (1985). *Single fathers.* Lexington, MA: Lexington Books.
19. Heatherington, E. M. (1985). Parents, children and siblings: Six years after divorce. In R. A. Hinde & J. Stevenson-Hinde (Eds.), *Relationships within families: Mutual influences* (pp. 311–331). New York: Oxford University Press.
20. Hess, B. B., & Waring, J. M. (1978). Changing patterns of aging and family bonds in later life. *Family Coordinator, 27,* 304.
21. Hinde, R. A. (1985). Introduction. In R. A. Hinde & J. Stevenson-Hinde (Eds.), *Relationships within families: Mutual influences* (pp. 1–6). New York: Oxford University Press.
22. Hunt, R. A., & King, M. B. (1978). Religiosity and marriage. *Journal for the Scientific Study of Religion, 17,* 397.
23. Kimball, G. (1988). *50-50 parenting: Sharing family rewards and responsibilities* (rev. ed.). Baltimore: Johns Hopkins University Press.
24. Lasch, C. (1979). *Haven in a heartless world: The family besieged.* New York: Basic Books.
25. Levitan, S. A., Belous, R. S., & Gallo, F. (1988). *What's happening to the American family? Tensions, hopes, realities* (rev. ed.). Baltimore: Johns Hopkins University Press.
26. Lewis, J. M., et al. (1976). *No single thread: Psychological health in family systems.* New York: Brunner/Mazel.
27. Mahler, M. S., Pine, F., & Bergman, A. (1975). *Psychological birth of the human infant.* New York: Basic Books.
28. Maslow, A. H. (1968). *Toward a psychology of being* (2nd ed.). Princeton, NJ: Van Nostrand.
29. Minuchin, P. (1985). Relations within the family: A systems perspective on development. In R. A. Hinde & J. Stevenson-Hinde (Eds.), *Relationships within families* (pp. 7–26). New York: Oxford University Press.
30. Ornstein, A., & Ornstein, P. H. (1985). Parenting as a function of the adult self: A psychoanalytic developmental perspective. In E. J. Anthony & G. H. Pollack (Eds.), *Parental influences: In health and disease* (pp. 183–232). Boston: Little, Brown.
31. Pleck, J. (1985). *Working wives/working husbands.* Beverly Hills, CA: Saga.
32. Procaccini, J. (1983, October). The new energy crisis: Parent burnout. *Marriage and Family Living,* 45.
33. Reiss, I. L. (1988). *Family systems in America* (4th ed.). New York: Holt, Rinehart and Winston.
34. Rollins, B. C., & Feldman, H. (1970). Marital satisfaction over the family life cycle. *Journal of Marriage and the Family, 32,* 20.
35. Spanier, G. B., Lewis, R. A., & Cole, C. L. (1975). Marital adjustment over the family life cycle: The issue of curvilinearity. *Journal of Marriage and the Family, 37,* 263.
36. Stinnett, N., Chesser, B., & DeFrain, J. (1979). *Building family strengths: Blueprint for action.* Lincoln, NE: University of Nebraska Press.
37. Strong, B., & DeVault, C. (1989). *The marriage and family experience* (4th ed.). St. Paul, MN: West.
38. Wesley, J. (1958). *The works of John Wesley* (Vol. 9). Kansas City, MO: Nazarene Publishing House.

33

Most of the problems individuals have either begin or end up in the family. As a result, families today are encountering endless challenges and frustrations that both threaten their current structures and strain their available resources. To complicate their problems, society gives only lip service to the importance of families and comes to their rescue only when they are under intense stress and unable to cope effectively.

—DAVID OLSON

Variations in the Family Experience

Perle Slavik Cowen

The ancient Chinese curse "May you live in changing times" seems to have been actualized in the American culture of the last 20 years. Although the composition and relationships of families have been in a state of transition and evolution for more than 300 years, the past two decades have witnessed an accelerated rate of change. Even the word "family" may no longer conjure up the image of the "traditional" American family with a single breadwinner, two parents, and one or more children under the age of 18. Today's family may have its structure described in such terms as traditional, reconstituted, blended, single parent, or shared custody.

The Bureau of the Census defines the family as "two or more people, related by birth, marriage, or adoption residing together in a household."[74] Although this statement does not describe the many variations the family may experience in both structure and function, it does provide a definition that allows statistics on family to be collected and examined. Recent trends indicate that the percentage of "traditional families" has decreased in America because of increased rates of divorce, later first marriages, fewer children per family, and postponed childbirth.[14] Of the 250 million people in the United States in 1989, about 208 million (83%) lived in families. The total number of families was 66 million, resulting in a median family size of 3.16.[74] About 50% of families include children younger than age 18. The stereotypical household of a married couple with children made up 77% of the total families with children in 1988.[74]

Single-female headed homes have increased from 10% of all families in 1960 to about 16% in 1990.[74] Sixty percent of these families have children younger than age 18 in the household, and the remaining 40% are single females with other relatives, such as an aged parent, in their home.[74] The pie chart in Figure 33-1 shows that more married couples live without children than with children. This figure obviously includes newly married as well as "empty nest" families. Couples today are likely to live in an "empty nest" family as long or longer than they lived with children in the home.

What do these figures tell us about today's family? Is it changing and adapting to the new pressures of today's environment or is it in "decline and crisis," as proph-

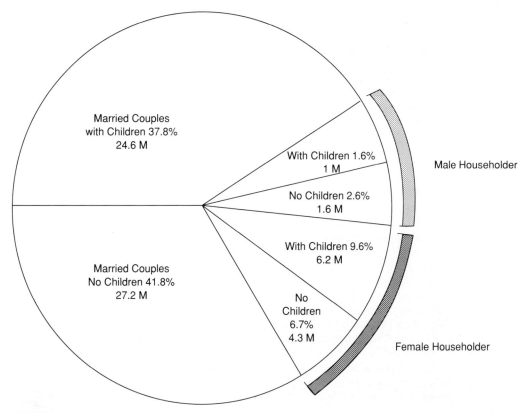

Married Couples
with Children 37.8%
24.6 M

Married Couples
No Children 41.8%
27.2 M

With Children 1.6%
1 M

No Children 2.6%
1.6 M

With Children 9.6%
6.2 M

No
Children
6.7%
4.3 M

Male Householder

Female Householder

FIGURE 33–1.
Typography of 65 million families in the U.S. (1990 Bureau of Census).

esied in the popular press? Do today's changes reflect a long-term trend toward a variety of families that are socially, legally, and economically viable?[14] Or do they represent failure of individuals or society? The stereotypical American family that forms the basis for "ideal family life" may be the result of media presentation of families from the 1940s and 1950s. The stability of the families of that era may have been an artifact of the larger historical picture. The parents were raised during the austerity of the post–World War II depression when family relations were facilitated by the need to find comfort and companionship in each other. They entered adulthood at a time of sustained prosperity. The sudden turnabout in their fortunes allowed them to marry earlier and to have more children than any generation before or since.[15] The stability and hardships of their youth provided resiliency and commitment to their family of creation. Financial prosperity fostered an attitude that hard work was sufficient to create the idyllic life portrayed by storybook tales. The "American dream" seemed to have become a reality.

Just as social changes had a marked effect on families of that era, accelerated changes in our current economic and sociocultural environments have had a profound effect on today's family and its ability to maintain its equilibrium. The family unit has had to face financial, technological, and social

changes over time that have created new stressors and opportunities. In 1947, only 32% of all adult females were in the labor force. By 1980, this percentage increased to 52%, resulting in the majority of America's 22 million children growing up in homes in which both parents, or the sole parent, were employed outside of the home.[18]

As families have attempted to adapt to the rapid changes in contemporary society, inadequate resources and the stress that accompanies one's attempts to meet the responsibilities of individual and community roles (role stress) have become issues. Community problems include the lack of adequate child or dependent adult day care and the need for more adolescent parenting programs. Signs of dysfunction, such as drug and alcohol abuse, homelessness, family violence (child, spouse, and elder abuse), and high infant mortality rates, have reached crisis proportions while intervention programs are increasingly competing for an ever shrinking pool of funding sources.

The family occupies a position between the individual and society and thus its basic functions are twofold: to meet the needs of the individuals in it and to meet the needs of the society of which it is a part.[26] While many families may be able to cope with rapid changes and increased pressures, a rising number require help to maintain or achieve healthy family functioning. "Healthy" family functioning is not described by a legal, structure-based definition or in the mastery of a specific set of objective tasks. The intrafamilial dynamics are the critical factors in determining the family's health, needs, and successes (see Chap. 32).[20] In our pluralistic society, with its multiplicity of needs, attitudes, values, behaviors, and life-styles, a variety of family structures and methods exists for fulfilling the individual's and family's needs. From this diversity many variations in family life have emerged.

STUDY OF THE FAMILY

Many reasons can be given for the importance of examining and using family theories in any discussion of the family: (1) theories provide a framework for the collection, organization, and clarification of information concerning a family's structure and functioning; (2) theories provide a structure for the categorization and analysis of data that has been collected; (3) theories provide perspective and meaning to information and provide direction for further investigation; and (4) theory directs practice in a systematic, cohesive, and consistent manner and thereby serves as a guide in the formulation of intervention plans for families that need help. Anytime a practitioner works with a client, it must be remembered that the client functions in the context of a family and the relationship with these other family members has a significant input on the client's functional level.

Theoretical Approaches

The direction and perspective that theories provide are usually reflective of the area of study from which they originated. Many perspectives have been used to study the family, including anthropological, structural, functional, situational, psychoanalytic, economic, social-psychological, institutional, interactional, developmental, and legal.[56] All of these approaches have contributed significantly to what we know about families. However, three major approaches are particularly useful in developing an understanding of the family.

Family Task Approach
Duvall's developmental family task approach focuses on an analysis of the responsibilities of the family as a small group, progressing and changing through life span stages, from its inception through old age and dissolution. Duvall identified eight successive developmental stages of the family (see Appendix C). Although the tasks remain the same at each level, transition from one stage to another presents challenges and stresses as families assume new roles and strive to develop new methods of relating to each other and to their environment (see Chap. 32). The challenge for the family is to meet each member's needs, as well as those of the family as a unit, while balancing them against the pressures or expectations of the extended family and society. This meshing is often difficult and may become a source of great conflict. For instance, a middle-aged new parent may face tasks relating to care re-

sponsibilities for frail, elderly parents that conflict with the task of parenting a newborn infant (and other children in the family) while simultaneously maintaining a satisfying marital relationship and, perhaps, even working outside of the home to ensure adequate income.

As discussed in Chapter 32, Duvall views each stage of family development as having major tasks to master in order to meet its biological requirements, its cultural imperatives, and its own aspirations and values. Family tasks can be mastered when the family strives as a unit to meet the demands and needs of family survival, stability, and successes while its members in turn are striving to meet their individual developmental requisites. Family tasks are also created by community pressures for the family and its members to conform to the expectations of the family's reference group and the wider society. If the family does not successfully accomplish the tasks associated with each stage, it can experience difficulty in negotiating the tasks of the next stage. Nontraditional families must negotiate additional tasks at various stages of their development.[13, 38, 49]

Duvall's *developmental family task approach* helps us assess the family's performance of the responsibilities appropriate to its particular stage while providing guidelines for determining support needs. However, it is based on the general features of a nuclear family with children and can be criticized for its assumption of traditional structure, its middle-class bias, and its lack of adequate attention to intrafamilial dynamics. It is obvious that not everyone "fits" into normative family life stages. The increasing variation in family structures (including childless marriages, single parenthood, and remarriage) results in altered life span family stages and more complex issues for the family to face.

Murdock identifies four *universal family tasks:* sexual, economic, reproductive, and educational.[51] Most theorists have expanded on these basic requisites. However, if the family has no children, the third and fourth tasks may not apply. Schuster's *holistic family tasks* are presented in the unit introduction and again in Appendix A. These tasks address the complexity of issues that all families (with or without children) face in the process of striving toward high-level wellness.

To accomplish its major tasks, the family must meet the needs of both individual family members and the wider society. In modern societies, many of the basic functions are assumed by social agencies when the family is unable to meet the essential needs of its members. However, some tasks that form the very heart of family relationships cannot be assumed by others (e.g., commitment and communication).

Interactional Approach
The interactional conceptual framework is a social-psychological approach that strives to interpret family phenomena in terms of internal dynamics.[20, 70] These dynamics or processes consist of communication patterns, decision making, coping patterns, and socialization, with the assessment of roles and communication processes forming the core of the frame-

work. Although individual personality and culture are also viewed as concerns of this framework, the family is not examined within its external environment or its interfaces with the external social system.[66] Thus, the attention is focused on how the family members interact between and among each other. This approach is useful in providing a way to assess sources of difficulty in family communication patterns. However, the family does not operate in a vacuum but maintains a dynamic relationship with the environment that must be considered if comprehensive assessment and treatment are to be provided. It is assumed that if internal communication patterns and roles are healthy, it is reflected in relationships with the broader culture.[20]

Structural–Functional Approaches

Structural–functional approaches primarily analyze the family's structural characteristics (organizational dimensions) and the functions it performs for both society and its subsystems. The general assumptions are that: (1) a family is a social system with functional requirements; (2) a family is a small group that possesses generic features common to all small groups; (3) the family as a social system serves both the individual and the society in which it is embedded.[24]

The *structure* of the family refers to who is considered a member of the family, their roles, lines of communication, and how its members use power and affiliation to relate to each other. A structural analysis often applies general systems theory (see Chap. 2) to the family. It focuses on the family as a unit, seeing its relationship to other systems and acknowledging its dynamic, changing state.[71] In this analysis, the family is seen as a dynamic social system that is constantly evolving in structure. It has subsystems (e.g., mother–child, husband–wife) and a suprasystem (community) that can be objectively identified and analyzed. Analysis of subsystems (see p. 43) may target role structure, value systems, communication patterns, and power structure, as well as the specific individuals who make up the system.[26]

Family *functioning* is assessed by examining the specific sources of difficulty or strength in individual role expectations, role taking, and responsibilities that members are expected to meet, both within and outside the family. These functions may be grouped into three major categories: affective, socialization, and health care. The affective function refers to the responsibility of the family to meet the psychosocial needs of its members; the socialization function is concerned with teaching children the responsibilities of being productive members of society; and the health care function encompasses the provision of food, clothing, shelter, and health care services.[25] Family functioning, even with the many variations in structural form, is ultimately evaluated by how well the family is able to fulfill its responsibilities. Family functions change as input from the suprasystem requires the family to modify goals or behaviors. The healthy family is continuously evolving toward greater acceptance of the uniqueness of its members and greater integration of the members for cooperative goals and functioning.

Relationships Between Family Structure and Function

Family structure (organization) relates to the composition and organization of the family. Although each family can be approached as a system, in today's society family structure, with the many possible variations in form, is ultimately evaluated by how well the family is able to fulfill its family functions.

Variations in Family Structure

Although still the most prevalent family form in the United States, the percentage of traditional families has declined. Recently, William Bennett, U.S. Secretary of Education, stated that, of 100 randomly selected children born in 1986, "12 have been born to unmarried parents; 40 have been born to parents who will divorce before the child is 18 years old; 5 have parents who will separate; and 2 have been born to parents one of whom will die during the child's first 18 years"; thus, only 41 of these 100 children will reach their 18th birthdays living with both biological parents.[76] Multiple family structures have emerged, such as blended, serial, communal, homosexual, single-parent, extended, joint custody, and househusband, to name a few.[45]

Divorce is the major disrupter of the traditional family unit. With the divorce rate of first marriages at 40%,[45] and of later marriages at 61%,[32] it is obvious that the family members face multiple shifts in membership, roles, and environments that require a major reorganization of the family system. Although about 45% of divorces occur between childless couples, the majority involve children.[53] Initially, emotional distress is high. The children tend to exhibit behavior problems and disruptions in functioning. Most adjust reasonably well within 24 months, but there is still a higher risk of antisocial behavior, acting out, noncompliance, and underachievement problems at school, especially for sons in the custody of their mothers.[35] Mothers tend to have an ambivalent relationship with the sons, which results in inconsistent discipline, decreased monitoring, and increased distancing 6 years later.[35]

About 23% of all United States families with children younger than age 18 are now **single-parent families.**[74] This percentage may be due to the birth of a child to an unmarried woman; death, divorce, or separation from a spouse; or adoption by an unmarried person. The largest subgroups are headed by divorced mothers (37%), never-married mothers (25%), and separated mothers (17%). Eighty-eight percent of single-parent families are headed by women, and 12% are headed by men.[57] The demographic trends of increasing numbers of never-married mothers is raising concerns. In the general population, children born to unmarried mothers rose from 5% in 1960 to 11% in 1970, 18% in 1980, and 24.5% in 1987. More than 62% of the black infants born in 1987 were born to unmarried mothers, while the figure for whites was 16.7%. Thirty-two percent of unmarried-mother births are to women younger than 20 years of age.[74] Combining the incidence of divorce, widowhood, and single parenthood, 59% of the children born in America today will be raised by a single parent for part of their lives.[76]

The many variations of single-parent families make it impossible to generalize about this group as a whole. Each of these subgroups has different issues and concerns with respect to both resources and abilities. The economic, emotional, and social support available to single-parent families is of primary importance in determining the quality of life these families will experience. For families in which the noncustodial parent, usually the father, is actively supportive in both the emotional and financial areas, the quality of life for the children is higher.[34] However, for many families this structural variation has been associated with harsh economic realities. About 21% of the children in female-headed households receive child support, and 34% receive Aid to Families with Dependent Children (Fig. 33-2).[55] With women and children making up the majority of the 13% of Americans who live below the poverty level, this group represents the "new poor" in the United States.[76]

Because 80% of divorced people remarry, the **reconstituted** or **blended family** is emerging as a major family structure in contemporary society.[45] These single-parent families are formed when a step-parent joins a family or, in the more complex situations, when two single-parent families join to create a new family unit. Eighty-three percent of divorced men and 75% of divorced women remarry, and 60% of these have children.[45] It is estimated that one child in five younger than the age of 18 is a step-child and that by the year 2000 this family structure will outnumber all other kinds of American families.[32, 33] These families face unique challenges and tasks, including reassignment of responsibilities, maintaining permeable boundaries to permit the shifting of household memberships, reworking ordinal position relationships, working for open lines of communication between all sets of families and extended families, and establishing new traditions, roles, rules, and relationships.

Variations in Family Functioning

In many families, the freedom to choose an alternative family structure actually strengthens family functioning. Other families become dysfunctional or enter into cycles of poverty. The challenge to the practitioner is to optimize family functioning, regardless of structure, based on the resources and strengths of the individual family.

> It is imperative that therapists at least recognize the extent of change and variations in the norm that are now widespread and that they help families to stop comparing their structure and life cycle course with that of the family of the 1950s. While relationship patterns and family themes may continue to sound familiar, the structure, ages, stages and form of the American family has changed radically.[13]

The ability of the family to provide for the welfare of its members is a primary indicator of how well the family is

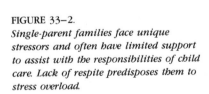

FIGURE 33–2.
Single-parent families face unique stressors and often have limited support to assist with the responsibilities of child care. Lack of respite predisposes them to stress overload.

functioning. The functional abilities of families vary greatly, both between families and within each family's experiences.

Tapia's Model of Family Functioning

Tapia identifies five developmental levels that can be used to assess the family's ability to function adaptively with society to meet its needs.[71] These levels are similar to the stages of development identified by Erikson and are described in the following sections.

Level 1: Infancy or the Chaotic Family. This stage represents the least mature level of family functioning, and it is characterized by disorganization in family life, undifferentiated roles and inability to assume roles, limited adaptive skills, inability to use community services, and lack of goals or a bonding orientation. The parents barely meet the family needs for security and physical survival and demonstrate a general inability to provide adequate financial resources, shelter, nutrition, and hygiene. They may engage in socially deviant behavior, including child abuse and neglect, and substance abuse. The children are deprived of functional role models and may experience role reversal, in which they take over many of the adult tasks and roles because of parental incompetency. The family basically distrusts outsiders, and the members may use ritualism, defensiveness, and distortion as devices to discourage social agencies from attempting to assist them. They are unable to provide for support and growth of the individual members because of the psychosocial immaturity of the adult members.

Level 2: Childhood or the Intermediate Family. This level of family functioning is slightly less disorganized and is characterized by financial stress (even though finances are adequate to meet needs if managed properly), rigid role differentiation that is used to preserve individual identity rather than to promote family integrity, limited adaptive skills, lack of initiative, and possible engagement in socially deviant behavior. They exhibit more skill in meeting the needs for security and survival. These parents are more willing to work together for the benefit of the family; however, because they lack examples, information, or experience, they require much assistance before they are able to acknowledge their problems realistically or develop viable approaches for their resolution. The family does not actively seek help and may appear defensive and fearful to outside agencies, although they do have more ability to trust than level 1 families. This type of family is unable to support and promote the growth of its members. They tend to exhibit enmeshed relationships (see Chaps. 29 and 32).[7] Harsh discipline may be directed toward family members who interfere with one's goals or comfort. It is significant to note that family functioning level is not contingent on financial status. The Ewing family on "Dallas," a popular television serial, functions at level 2. Their ability to purchase services of household help and fancy cars tends to cover for dysfunctional family relationships.

Level 3: Adolescence or the Family With Problems. This family is essentially normal but has a substantial number of conflicts and problems. It is characterized by an ability to provide for the survival and security needs of its members, greater trust in people, ability to use community resources, and less open hostility to outsiders. However, the parents seem unable to predict and thus take action to avoid many developmental or role conflict issues. Typically, one parent is more mature than the other, but both parents may be unsure of their own identities. Therefore, they have difficulty in helping the children find their identities. Punishment or permissiveness is more common than guidance of children. Although many of the members are industrious, the identities and roles of the members and the goals of the family may still not be clearly defined. They exist in the vacuum of present time, seemingly unaware of their history or the creative potential of their future.

Level 4: Adulthood or the Family With Solutions. Families at this level may be described as stable, healthy, and happy with fewer problems and conflicts because of their ability to predict, avoid, or handle problems as they arise. These parents have done much of their identity homework (see Chap. 25) and thus have a sense of direction. They are not afraid to pass their values and rules on to their children. This family is characterized by an ability to provide for survival and security needs, emotional and social expression, and mature role models. They are capable of identifying, setting, and striving toward family goals. The main concerns of this family center around the stages of growth and development of the children. In discipline, guidance takes precedence over punishment. These parents refer themselves to outside help if problems or crises occur. The needs of the individual members and the family needs and goals are usually balanced by this family.

Level 5: Maturity or the Ideal Family. This family is described as emotionally healthy and is characterized as meeting all family tasks; providing a healthy balance of individual and group goals, activities, participation, and concerns; promoting adaptive flexibility; and agreeing on role structure and stability of goals. In times of crisis, this family can ask for and use help from appropriate sources. Members describe satisfaction with the family because it meets the physical and emotional needs of its members and moves toward collectively perceived and shared goals. Curran observes that these families produce well-adjusted, productive, mature adolescents.[20] Again, financial status is *not* the determining factor; rather, the intrafamilial communication, commitment, love, and support are. Table 33-1 compares the ability of families at each of Tapia's five levels to meet basic family tasks.

Werner's System Maturity

Family functioning can also be assessed by evaluating the family's maturity level. Werner's continuums (see Chap. 2) may be adapted to reflect the specific developmental levels of a family:[80]

1. Individualization and role independence of the subsystems in the family.

2. Efficiency of the family in allocating resources and making decisions.

TABLE 33–1. ABILITY OF FAMILIES TO MEET BASIC FAMILY NEEDS

Basic Needs	Family Level				
	I	II	III	IV	V
1 Survival	Bare	Minimal	Adequate	Good	Excellent
Security	—	Some	Adequate	Good	Reasonable
2 Social	Unclear	Rigid	Clear	Good	Excellent
Emotional	—	—	Limited	Good	Excellent
3 Sexuality	—	Barely	Rigid	Adequate	Excellent
Training	—	—	Limited	Good	Excellent
4 Support	—	—	Rarely	Adequate	Excellent
Growth	—	—	—	Adequate	Excellent

3. Intrafamily organizational patterns for communication and cooperation.

4. Interpretation and processing of events, and the resultant interface of the family with the environment and culture.

5. Generation and use of alternative means for goal achievement.

6. Independence of the family from other persons or agencies in goal setting and the ability to focus energies toward goal achievement.

When one evaluates families for their ability to function as a mature system, one finds them at all levels along these continua, from those unable to meet their responsibilities as an independent system to those who are able to meet them in healthful, ideal ways. Families develop their own special patterns in performing these functions, and these patterns become a major focus for determining successful task outcome. Although the family's structure may take many forms, its stage of development or maturity as a system is most significant in influencing family functioning. Table 33-2 indicates the characteristics of each family level along Werner's system maturity continua.

STRESSORS TO THE FAMILY BOND

In contemporary society, many economic and technological pressures predispose people toward role stress and strain. These pressures operate in addition to the many changes, adaptations, and pressures that families face as part of the normal developmental processes of family life. While many families may be able to cope with rapid changes and increased pressures, a rising number require help to achieve or maintain healthy family functioning. This section examines acute and chronic stressors that present problems to families.

Acute Stressors

A **stressor** is a temporary or prolonged situation that requires people to use alternative adaptational responses to meet the immediate and ongoing needs of life. Family members may interpret stressors to be positive, negative, or neutral depending on their perceptions and adaptational skills. A crisis occurs when a stressor is so severe that the individual or family reaches a state of disorganization in which the ability to function deteriorates.[42] Family functioning may be described as disorganized and dysfunctional during a crisis episode. It takes time to fully assess the situation, one's values, and potential approaches for resolution or amelioration of the situation. Many individuals, especially those who are undergoing a severe crisis, need outside assistance to sort out relevant issues and develop positive adaptive approaches (see Fig. 36-10). Crisis is most often seen as a negative factor in one's life because of the strain on one's coping abilities and the pain of facing one's inadequacy to control events. However, crisis can have a *very* positive outcome. As challenges are realistically faced, one is forced to reevaluate goals and priorities. This reevaluation can produce much growth and a new centering of strength within the family members individually and collectively. As a result, the family can emerge from the crisis more mature, resilient, and cohesive. If the crisis is not faced openly and honestly, then degeneration of the family or person within it may be the sequela.

In general, crisis can be classified as developmental or situational.

Developmental Crises

Developmental crises are defined as expected events that occur normally to most individuals in the course of living.[10] These events have been dealt with by a number of theorists: Erikson described eight critical tasks of the life span that must

TABLE 33–2. RELATIONSHIP OF WERNER'S SYSTEMS DEVELOPMENT THEORY TO TAPIA'S LEVELS OF FAMILY FUNCTIONING

Werner's Continuum Factors (see p. 41)	*Tapia's Family Levels*				
	I	II	III	IV	V
1	Mass ego identity	Confused relationships	Some individuation	Clear identities	Differences respected
2	No real leadership	Autocratic leadership	Authoritative leadership	Flexible leadership	Cooperative leadership
3	Poor communication	Rudimentary efforts	Weak patterns	Cooperative milieu	Integrated interdependent
4	Everything personal attack	Weak differentiation	Family-other clear	Focused on stimulus	Discrete responses
5	Limited, rigid skills	Rigid approaches	Limited flexibility	Adaptive approaches	Flexible, creative approaches
6	Highly suggestible	Labile goals	Weak self-direction	Independent	Stable goals

be resolved by individuals if emotional-social maturity is to be achieved; Duvall conceptualized eight developmental stages that characterize the life span of families; Schuster describes age-specific tasks throughout this text; and this chapter has discussed family tasks that are relevant to all cultures. Each of these developmental tasks has a potential for crisis associated with it, as do the transitions between the various developmental stages.

Situational Crises

Situational crises are considered extratemporal in that they occur randomly and are independent of any developmental stage.[65] They are more individualistic, less predictable, less universal, and, because they are seldom anticipated, they take people by surprise. Three precipitants of external crisis are: (1) loss of a source for satisfying basic needs (e.g., unexpected death, departure of a significant other, a serious illness or injury, unemployment); (2) the possibility of such a loss; and (3) a challenge that overtaxes one's capacities, such as birth of a disabled child, disaster, or a required move to a new community.[12]

Mobility

Americans are among the most mobile people on earth. One out of five American families changes residence each year. Families may move for a variety of reasons, including promotions in the work place, corporate policies that dictate rotation of employees, desire for a better home, migratory jobs, and employment opportunities in areas reputed to be "job rich." These relocations are stressful events for a number of reasons. Additional family tasks include establishing a new household, developing new community ties (e.g., doctor, church, schools, bank), establishing social peer group rela-

tions, and assisting children to establish themselves in new schools and develop new peer relations. Significant problems are related to moves that distance the family from its kin network. Teen-agers are more likely to run away from home when they can no longer seek refuge with nearby kin, and resources for practical knowledge of child care declines with increasing isolation from the extended family group.

Unemployment

The loss of a job or a temporary layoff is a humiliating and frightening experience both for the individual and the family, for it is a painful reminder that the individual is expendable. According to a Johns Hopkins University study, a New York community that experiences a 1% rise in unemployment can expect 5% more suicides, 3% to 4% more hospitalizations for mental illness, 4% to 6% more homicides, 6% to 7% more prison incarcerations, and a 2% increase in the overall death rate.[42] The scope of economic decline (e.g., national, regional, or local) greatly affects the resources and opportunities that families can use. Jobs that are lost because of technological changes or reduced demand for products may be permanent in nature and require the individual either to retrain or relocate to become employable.

Whenever economic adversity is widespread, mental health facilities report an increase in the number of people who seek help.[42] Family conflict, loss of morale and self-esteem, feelings of deprivation, and loss of roles are some of the problems these families face. The economic deprivation may effect many aspects of each family member's life in ways that stretch the family's coping ability. For example, when a registration fee prevents children from participating in activities such as baseball or bars them from activities such as science projects or school outings, self-esteem and socialization opportunities are lost, as is the opportunity to develop one's skills or interests. The children may feel considerable anger toward or disrespect for parents whom they deem as incompetent providers or toward a society that they feel has dealt with them unfairly.

Death of a Significant Other

Death of a significant other may occur at any time. When it occurs, a series of events are initiated. First, death is an acute crisis that affects each family member as well as the family structure itself. The overall effect depends on such variables as anticipated versus unexpected death; the status of the family at the time of death (functional versus dysfunctional); the financial and social stability of the family; the closeness of the family members; the impact on the role functions of the members; the coping abilities of each family member; the potential for changes in normal role and interaction patterns within the family; and the family's prior pattern of crisis resolution.

Secondly, loss and death disrupt family equilibrium and result in the need for reorganization or roles, power, and communication lines. It is important to remember that, although the death affects each family member differently, it equally influences all family relations. Unresolved feelings can affect a family for generations to come. Even more crucial is the fact that, if resolution does not occur, a "ghost" becomes an integral part of the family system.[29] Fears of intimate relationships and divorce may be long-range effects.

Divorce

The ripple effect of divorce produces a disequilibrium of all family members in both the nuclear and extended family systems. This disruption is associated with myriad shifts in membership roles and boundaries that require a major reorganization in the family system. Divorce permanently alters the structure of the family and requires family members to develop new methods of functioning to accomplish family tasks. Research indicates that the family system requires 2 to 3 years to complete this complex process and restabilize in its new roles and relationships.[17,59] However, this restabilization does not mean that fears have disappeared or that the individuals involved are thriving and "happy." Five years later, only 34% of the children are categorized as "happy" and coping well.[79] Long-range effects include an increased incidence of aggression, anxiety, sexual promiscuity, fear of betrayal, and divorce in the children's marriages.[17] Children may have much trouble working through feelings. "Ghosts" may arise in late adolescence or the young adult years and interfere with a sense of trust and choice of a partner, even 20 to 30 years later.[78]

The process of terminating the marital relationship while maintaining cooperative, interdependent roles as parents is difficult. The results of many different studies indicate that the postdivorce relationship between the parents is the most critical factor in the healthy adaptation of the children.[59] In fact, the level of parental conflict may be more important to

the children's adjustment than absence of the noncustodial parent or the divorce itself.[23] A 5-year study that examined the nature of postdivorce relationships around parenting issues found that 12% were "perfect pals," 38% "cooperative colleagues," 25% "angry associates," and 25% "fiery foes."[1] The most important characteristic of a successful coparenting relationship is mutual respect, which seems to insure the needed flexibility for the negotiation of child-related issues.[59]

Chronic Stressors

A chronic stressor may be an acute stressor that was not resolved and thus continues to create disruption; a stressor that was resolved in a dysfunctional manner and thus has created other long-term problems; a stressor for which personal or community resources are inadequate to resolve effectively; or a stressor that continues to present additional problems for the family, such as living with a disabled member, maternal employment, or single parenthood.

Maternal Employment

Modern society has created both the opportunity and the need for expanding the roles of family members. The changes, stresses, and rewards of each family member's role expansion affect not only the role functioning of other members but of the family unit as well. Contemporary economic realities have necessitated the entry or reentry of many mothers into the labor market. In the past 35 years, unparalleled numbers of married and single mothers of young children have entered the paid labor force outside of the home. In 1947, only 32% of all adult females were in the labor force; by 1988, this percentage had increased to 57%. Sixty-five percent of women with children younger than 18, 55% of those with children younger than 3, and 52% of women with children younger than 12 months are employed outside of the home.[74] Not all of these mothers work full time, however. Although women join the work force for a variety of reasons, including development of a career, personal fulfillment, and the desire for supplemental income, the majority of working mothers work to maintain their family's standard of living. Less than 18% of all employed Americans earn $30,000 or more per year.[75] The average annual salary for women in 1990 was $16,380.[74]

The current economic climate appears to require the earnings of both husband and wife to match inflation and maintain the economic status of the family. In two-parent households, more than 65% of both parents are working, 78% of women separated from their husbands are working, and 85% of all divorced women are working.[67] Most single-wage families are at a distinct economic disadvantage. However, families in which the woman is the single wage earner have considerably lower median annual incomes than those with men as the sole wage earner. This fact, in a great part, is caused by a lower level of education and less work experience than men of the same age. Demographic data indicate that these numbers will continue to rise. The fastest growing group of women in the labor market is mothers with infants.[47] It is projected that, by the year 2000, 75% of all mothers will reenter the paid labor force before the baby's first birthday.[6]

The majority of America's 22 million children are growing up in homes in which both parents, or the sole parent, are employed outside of the home. The most alarming statistics pertain to children who are not provided with supervised care while their parents are at work. It is estimated that 7% of preschoolers (or as many as 50,000) and 40% of school-age children (or up to 4 million) are left in self-care while their parents are at work (latch-key kids).[18,64]

Many are concerned about the long-range well being of infants and children who are cared for by persons other than their parents. Research results are still equivocal depending on the age of the child (infants are more likely to have negative effects, see Chap. 8), quality of care, number of hours per week that the child is away from the parents, warmth, support, and reciprocity of the parents and caregivers, and the biases of the researchers or the factors studied. Differing concepts of "healthy development" (and significant indicators of such) influence the outcome variables studied. Certain factors may have a prolonged "sleeper" effect on the developing and emerging personality, and interim variables can ameliorate or aggravate potential negative effects. When children receive adequate day care, most studies are unable to identify marked adverse effects.[17]

No significant negative effects have been observed in children in terms of parent–child bonding, adjustment, school achievement and intelligence, career aspirations, and sex-role concepts. The attitudes of children toward their parents appear to be no different for children of employed mothers and children of homemakers. All of these findings are moderated, however, by the variable of child care. Available evidence indicates that when quality day care is available from friends, relatives or an institutional source, no negative effects are observed. In fact, in children from less advantaged homes, high quality day care may lead to increases in IQ . . . and daughters of working mothers, in general consistently indicate higher educational and career aspirations.[19]

Although no serious negative effects are identified for children, many problems do exist because of increased role expectations for the parents. These include psychological and physical weariness from the performance of multiple roles, time pressures, inter-role and inner conflict, and guilt.[19] These problems become magnified when adequate and affordable child care is lacking or when a single parent has limited social support (Fig. 33–3).

Dual Career

There has been a marked increase in the number of "dual-career" families in which "both heads of household pursue careers and at the same time maintain a family life together."[63] This family is distinguishable from most families in which both spouses are employed because the wife's career is an integral part of her identity, demands professional commitment, and is not simply a way to earn supplemental income

FIGURE 33–3.
Fathers must assume more responsibility for child care when the mother is employed. This responsibility can lead to closer father–child relationships. Children of dual-career families generally experience more contact with the wider culture because of the parents' broader interests and contacts.

for the family.[36] This family is in contrast with the "dual-work" or "two-paycheck" family, in which the wife's work is classified as a job rather than as a career.[37] In a true dual-career family, both parents share the housework and child care.[31]

Dual-career families face both internal and external strain.[36,68] Internal strain arises from within the family itself and includes issues of work overload, role identity confusion, conflicting schedules and needs of career and family, and nuclear family limitations. Thus, these families may have difficulty balancing career and home life, feeling comfortable about stepping outside of the traditional husband and wife roles, meshing individual career trajectories with family development needs, and finding satisfactory child care arrangements.[36,37] Conflicts may necessitate value prioritization: Which career is more important, that of parenting or the one that provides a salary and job satisfaction? Children need attention and care from their parents. "The world is full of fathers who rarely see their children [because of their careers]; for mothers [with careers] to do the same is not the answer."[61] It may be a difficult balance for some families.

External strains are those that result from conflict between the dual-career family and other societal structures such as disparity between dual-career lifestyles and traditional family norms, the demands for geographic mobility when career advancement is continuous, and the dilemma of finding time for interaction with friends and relatives in addition to career and family.[37] Some dual-career families are forced to maintain two homes because of careers located in different geographic locations. Some have only weekends together.[36]

Eighty-five percent of dual-career families want to have or do have children, although many postpone children until their thirties.[36] They do not feel that they should have to make a choice between career and parenthood. Few men say that children influence their career development; however, many career women indicate that the choice to have children does affect their career, and they tend to develop their careers more slowly after children arrive.[31]

Both research and popular literature continue to emphasize the chronic stress associated with women who combine careers and families. The role conflicts that arise from the numerous tasks associated with both roles have been cited as the root of this chronic stress. One study found that women in two-job families experienced significantly more work and family role strain than did the men in these families and that women were significantly more depressed than men.[44] Although it is unclear whether women in two-job families experience more or less stress than those in dual-career families, it has been discovered that women who derive high satisfaction from their professional and maternal roles found the combination to be rewarding.[31] Thus, it may be that the cost for dual-career and dual-job women is the same, but the payoff is greater for career women, and they therefore experience less depression.[37] Higher salaries enable career women to hire assistance with home and child care, thus reducing the workload and resultant strain. The housekeeper or child caregiver may become a quasi-family member,[36] thus creating one more variation on family structure.

Older-Parent Families

Births to women older than age 30 have increased by 35% in recent years.[50] Many are born to dual-career families or single mothers who postponed childbearing until educations were completed and careers well established. Consequently, many of these children enter families with the increased advantages of ambitious parents with adequate finances. Others are born to couples in second marriages. Some are "caboose" children, both planned and unexpected. Parents generally feel that the children of their "mature years" should benefit from their better education, greater affluence, and increased maturity, judgment, and emotional stability.[50] However, one research study indicates that 50% of the children felt that the parents' increased age had a negative impact on their lives. The other 50% expressed positive or neutral feelings (Fig. 33-4).[50]

Older mothers tend to be more sensitive and receptive to the children's needs but, at the same time, more "uptight" and conservative. Greater parental attention and stimulation facilitated higher achievement, but some children felt parental pressure to succeed.[50] The parents were much less likely to divorce, thus providing stability, but many children were embarrassed by the parents' "oldness" during school and adolescent years, when conformity is so important to them. They felt stigmatized by the family's uniqueness, especially

FIGURE 33–4.
Older parents generally bring greater maturity to the career of parenting, a factor that usually benefits the development of the child.

when their parents were thought to be their grandparents.[50] Some were proud of their parents because of the respect offered by the community. They often behaved like "little adults" because of their open communication with parents. Others felt cheated because the parents were unable or unwilling to engage in camping, sports, and so on.[50]

The sense of deprivation was intensified when parents substituted material goods for parental time. Those who were most content and secure during childhood were those whose parents gave of themselves and their time.[50] Only children and children of single parents felt especially disadvantaged because they had no other children to grow up with or they were concerned about parental death. Morris offers 10 tips for older parents:[50]

1. Develop extra rapport with the child.
2. Schedule fun time together.
3. Maintain a personal fitness program.
4. Spend time together.
5. Provide comforts and pleasures, but don't spoil.
6. Discuss concerns about mortality.
7. Broaden contacts with other people of all ages.

8. Talk to the child.

9. Participate in the child's interests.

10. Spend time together throughout life, not just during infancy.

Single-Parent Families

There are many variations in the routes to single parenthood. These include two-parent families who as a result of separation, divorce, desertion, or death become single parents, and single-parent families in which a single person chooses to adopt a child or in which a woman delivers and keeps her own child. Despite the differences in these routes, single-parent families are frequently viewed as alike because of common experiences, such as reduced family income, a sense of isolation and loneliness, role overload, and unequal access to the material and social resources more easily available to two-parent families.

However, these families are not homogeneous and many variables must be assessed to understand their needs. They may differ in the sex of the custodial parent, the paths along which the family evolved, the extent of support from the noncustodial parent, the manner and level of functioning, patterns of interaction, acceptance and support of extended family members, socioeconomic status, community resources, educational level, racial and ethnic background, and age of parent.[73] Thus, these families have a variety of individual characteristics and functional abilities.

Studies that examine family functioning have provided some insight into what life is like inside single-parent families. When one parent leaves the family, two dramatic changes follow. First, as the social distance between the custodial parent and the children decreases, the "echelon structure" collapses, and the children are essentially promoted to junior partners. They assume an expanded role characterized by increased responsibility within the family. Second, the decomposition of the authority structure fosters a parent–child relationship characterized by greater equity, more frequent interaction, and greater intimacy and companionship.[73]

Conclusive data document the low economic status of single-parent families. They are at greater risk for low incomes, high rates of poverty, and fewer employment opportunities than two-parent families. Factors associated with reduced risk and more successful single-parent families include increased age of the parent and children, higher educational levels of the parent, adequate family income, residential stability, development of an adaptive informal support system, separation of marital and parenting roles, ability to manage conflict, supportive interaction from the noncustodial parent, the ability to establish new family rules, and accessibility to child care alternatives.

Adolescent Families

The incidence of adolescent pregnancy has risen to epidemic proportions. About 16% of the total number of births and 28% of first births are to adolescent parents. About 87% of unwed mothers kept their infants in 1971, and more than 96% did in 1987.[16] About 9600 babies were born to girls younger than 15 years of age in 1987![74] These parents face multiple stressors, including the normal developmental crises of adolescence, the situational crisis of unplanned parenthood, and the chronic stressors associated with meeting the developmental needs of the infant while meeting their own needs. Most adolescents, especially the younger ones, lack the physical, emotional, economic, and educational resources necessary for parenting (Fig. 33-5). How the adolescent responds to the demands of this new role is determined to a large extent by the quality of social support available.[3] Many adolescent mothers drop out of school, a major factor that precipitates poverty for her and her child.

Some pregnant adolescents use drugs, alcohol, or tobacco; many do not seek prenatal care until late in the pregnancy, thereby increasing the risk of toxemia, birth defects, and nutritional and illness-related complications for both the mother and infant. Avoidance of adequate health care may be related to a variety of problems, including denial of the pregnancy, fear, naïveté, mistrust of authority figures, ignorance, uncertainty of how to tap into the health care system, and inadequate finances. The adolescent father exhibits many of the same emotional problems. In addition, he may have feelings of guilt and anxiety as a result of his denial of involvement with the mother. If the adolescent father does make an emotional and financial commitment, it may necessitate his

FIGURE 33–5.
Adolescent parents must continue to meet their own developmental and educational needs while simultaneously fostering the child's development.

dropping out of school and settling for jobs that pay poorly. Whether the couple marries or not, the custodial parents face many hard realities in attempting to assume a role for which they are not yet developmentally ready.

Between 76% and 95% of single adolescent parents continue to live with and receive support from their families.[69] Three distinct patterns of interaction may result from this arrangement: **role sharing,** in which the family shares the duties and responsibilities for the infant's care; **role binding,** in which the child-caring tasks, decisions, and responsibilities are delegated to the young parent alone; and **role blocking,** in which the family may usurp the role of primary caregiver or the adolescent may willingly relinquish responsibility for the infant and assume a sibling role to the infant.[69] Care arrangements are further complicated when the adolescent gives birth to a high-risk infant. Adolescents have a higher incidence of premature and small-for-gestational-age babies and may be separated from the baby during long-term intensive care. These infants may have additional needs such as frequent feedings, difficulty establishing a sleep–rest cycle, and long-term health problems, and they may be less responsive to the parents' interactions than the average infant.

Observations of parent–infant interactions note a wide range of connectedness between the adolescent parent and the infant. Adolescent mothers who subsequently do well as parents are actively involved with their infant, even in the first days of life. They look at, touch, smile at, and talk to the baby frequently. Play and teaching are paced to the baby's interests and energy level.[3] More commonly, however, the adolescent mother (still heavily involved in her own egocentric adolescent needs) is unable to focus on the child as a separate individual with his or her own developmental needs. This mother tends to be quiet and rarely smiles at or plays with the baby. The lack of talking is evident in diminished teaching and praise of the young child.[3] Regardless of how the mother–infant synchrony may be assessed, there is "substantial stability in maternal behavior from the newborn period through five years following birth."[3]

During the preschool and school years, children of nonsensitive mothers are found to have a higher incidence of cognitive and social delays, accidents, and child abuse and neglect.[8,11,52,72] Issues that arise from adolescent parenting are altered role performance, ineffective coping, knowledge deficits, inadequate provision of basic care needs for both the adolescent and the infant, social isolation, and altered psychosocial growth and development for both the adolescent and her child. These are best addressed through extensive social service programs that include financial support, job training opportunities, high school completion programs, and parenting programs. Adolescents need parenting information focused on communication, that is, positive attention toward the child and teaching techniques. Reciprocity potentials of the dyad must be recognized and established before negative interaction patterns are fixed. Parenting programs that provide the most positive gains are those that have weekly contact with the adolescent over a 1- to 3-year period, capitalize on the adolescent mother's natural enthusiasm, energy, and feelings of love, and include routine health screening and developmental testing for the child, instruction in or modeling of basic child care techniques, enhancement of the mother's system of formal supports, and regular home visits.[22]

Blended Families

In addition to the usual family tasks, the blended family has some unique tasks to face. Blended families must deal with issues of loss and separation from the noncustodial parent, violation of trust, conflicts of loyalty and authority, role adjustments, and the challenge of developing a new family identity that may include her children, his children, and their children. The first 2 years frequently are marked by increased conflict with one's children, especially for daughters and mothers. The new stepfather may feel like an intruder.[35] "In general, the best strategy of a stepfather to gain acceptance by stepchildren seems to be one where there is no initial active attempt to take over and/or actively to control the child's behavior, either through authoritarian or the more desirable authoritative techniques. Instead, the new father should first work at establishing a relationship with the child and support the mother in her parenting. This period can be effectively followed later by more active authoritative parenting, which leads to constructive outcomes, at least for boys."[35]

Many adults underestimate the problems associated with these issues and enter their succeeding marriages with the naïve, unrealistic expectation that a cohesive new family unit ("Brady Bunch") will spring effortlessly into existence. Adjusting to new personalities, roles, responsibilities, communication styles, and relationships is not easy. While first divorces are typically related to spousal conflicts, second divorces more often are related to parental conflicts exacerbated by the ambiguities of role relationships in the new family, undermining of the spousal relationship by the children, and the baggage of unresolved issues from the previous family.[45,48] Children in blended families tend to have more rivalry and relationship problems than children in "natural" families. Girls exhibit more avoidance behaviors and boys, more aggressive behaviors. Only 10% exhibit protective, empathetic, nurturing relationships; 33% have open communication and a caring companionship; 35% have high involvement and concern mixed with moderate levels of aggression, but intense loyalty against outside forces; 22% are critical and openly hostile (Fig. 33-6).[35]

Adaptational difficulties between the new husband and wife, anxiety over the new relationship and responsibilities as a step-parent, reworked relationships with former spouses, and manipulative behavior by the children may all create additional stressors.[77] Both the quality and the rate of adjustment by the blended family are influenced by support from the social environment and the maturity of the persons involved. Counseling can be a valuable resource for reworking old relationships and establishing new ones (Table 33-3). The younger the children, the easier their adaptation to the new family.[45] The parents need to be strong in themselves and

FIGURE 33–6.
It take time for step-siblings to develop a positive, cooperative sibling bond. Parents can facilitate the process by orchestrating experiences that both children enjoy.

need to work at nourishing the couple bond to maintain a strong relationship.[45] Support, information, and literature are available from Stepfamily Foundation, 333 West End Ave., New York, NY 10023.

Poverty

The economic hardship of poverty is a particularly threatening force that is straining families today. Twenty percent of children and 10.7% of all families had incomes that fell below the federal poverty level in 1987.[74] (The official poverty line for the United States in 1990 was: family of 2, $8,420; family of 3, $10,560; family of 4, $12,700; family of 5, $14,840.) The structure of low-income families is often different from that of the professional classes. Although legally it may be a single-parent family, in actuality, it is often an extended three- or four-generational network of kin.[27] These family structures may appear to be disorganized when they are compared to traditional, nuclear families. However, recent studies describe these "extended families" as highly functional. For example, low-income black families tend to consist of large networks of kin who exchange material and service resources through "swapping" of goods and "child keeping." The activities of these kinship organizations are adaptive strategies to the conditions of poverty.[27]

The adaptation of multi-problem, poor families to the stark political, social, and economic suprasystem has produced a family development pattern that varies significantly from the middle-class paradigm (Fig. 33-7).[13]

Hines breaks the family life span of the poor into three phases:[39]

1. Adolescence or Unattached Young Adult (may begin when the person is only 11 or 12 years old): This school-age child is virtually on his or her own, unaccountable to adults. He or she may or may not live in the home of the parents.

2. The Family With Young Children: A phase that occupies most of the life span and commonly includes three- and four-generation households.

3. The Family in Later Life: The grandmother is still involved in the central child-rearing role and still actively in charge of the younger generations.

This variation in family life development tends to blur lines of responsibility for normative family tasks and creates the reality of the multi-problem family.[39] The heightened, multiple variations in both developmental and situational

---

TABLE 33–3. STEPFAMILY CHARACTERISTICS, STEPFAMILY TASKS

Stepfamily Characteristics	*Stepfamily Tasks*
1. Begins after many losses and changes	1. Dealing with losses and changes
2. Incongruent individual, marital, family life cycles	2. Negotiating different developmental needs
3. Children and adults all come with expectations from previous families	3. Establishing new traditions
4. Parent–child relationships predate the new couple	4. Developing a solid couple bond and forming new relationships
5. Biological parent elsewhere	5. Creating a "parenting coalition"
6. Children often members of two households	6. Accepting continual shifts in household composition
7. Legal relationship between step-parent and children is ambiguous or nonexistent	7. Risking involvement despite little societal support

Visher, E. B., & Visher, J. S. (1988). Old loyalties, new ties (p. 10). New York: Brunner/Mazel.

FIGURE 33–7.
Even in the midst of poverty, families can have amazing resiliency.

stressors of these families create barriers to healthy development and produce an environment of conflict and loss.

Homelessness

According to the National Governors' Association, a homeless person is "an undomiciled person who is unable to secure permanent and stable housing without special assistance."[21] It is both horrifying and alarming that families are the fastest growing segment of the homeless population. National estimates claim that 30% of homeless people are part of a family group. Eighty-five percent of these families are made up of single mothers with children.[4] These mothers often have had chaotic childhoods themselves. Of those studied, one-third have suffered physical abuse and one in nine, sexual abuse.[4] The average age of these mothers is 27, they have an average of two to three children, and they many receive Aid to Families with Dependent Children.[62] Others are unable to receive assistance because local guidelines may require a permanent address to receive funds.

It is not known how many of these families became single-parent as a result of the strain of poverty and homelessness or vice versa. Even two-parent homeless families face tremendous chronic stress every day, increasing the risk for conflict and dissolution. Experts in the field identify deficits in social support as a hallmark of homelessness. One psychiatrist notes that "the lack of a home is symptomatic of profound disconnection from supportive people and institutions."[4]

Factors that precipitate homelessness of families are many and varied, including family instability, drug and alcohol addiction, declining national and local economies, unemploy-

ment, reduced government aid to families, culture of poverty, teen pregnancies, chronic mental illness, poor money management, and severe shortages of low-income housing. The physical and mental health of most homeless families is precarious. Facing the daily hardships with inadequate resources to meet even the most basic needs of food, shelter, and health care extracts a high price in all areas of individual and family functioning.

The National Coalition for the Homeless estimates that 750,000 school-age children are homeless and that up to 60% do not attend school. Many are developmentally delayed, never receive immunizations or basic health care, suffer from malnutrition, respiratory problems, and other preventable illnesses, contract sexually transmitted diseases, are victims of assault and trauma, and die as a result of their hazardous surroundings.[5, 62] Many are depressed, suicidal, and exhibit extreme emotional stress.[5] Infants born to homeless women are at particular risk because of inadequate prenatal care and nutrition. Even those adults and children who enter the homeless environment in good health face ominous obstacles in maintaining even marginal health because of the poor living conditions in the "homeless hotels." These care areas are often overcrowded, and many are poorly ventilated, unhygienic, dimly lit areas that provide an ideal environment for the spread of infectious diseases.[5, 62]

The reduction of federal social programs in the 1980s eliminated resources for many marginally functioning families and also cut into the staffing budgets of those agencies left to deal with poverty issues. As a result, there has been widespread criticism of both the inadequate resources and excessive "red tape" involved in supplying aid to these high-risk families. The "bottomless bureaucratic trap" that often surrounds these families is described by some authors as contributing to the physical and mental decline that many suffer while receiving "help." Note the following scenario:

> Homeless families in the Martinique Hotel are told they must not cook within their rooms. They are then assigned a "restaurant allowance" which, however, they are told, it would be unwise to use in restaurants. In time, they realize that the restaurant allowance is intended to buy groceries they cannot cook in kitchens they don't have and must therefore try somehow to cook on hot plates they are not officially permitted to possess. If they use the restaurant allowance in a restaurant, their children will soon starve. If they cook within their rooms, they break a rule to which they have agreed. If they are discovered in infraction of a rule, they are at the mercy of the guard who has discovered their offense.[46]

Effects of Stress on the Family

Stress is an unavoidable fact of life. Disabling stress and maladaptive coping may create family conflicts that are destructive and dysfunctional for all members of the family. These conflicts too often culminate in violence. Every year 6 million women, children, and men are victims of severe physical abuse at the hands of their parents, spouses, siblings, or children.[30] More than 50% of women are battered at some point in their lives, 16% per year. Two thousand to four thousand women are beaten to death annually. Sixty percent of men batter at some point in their lives.[9, 58] Several factors are related to family violence, including the intergenerational transmission of violence, financial strain, social and structural stress, social isolation and low community embeddedness, low self-concept, personality problems, and psychopathology.[30] Violence, though more common in lower socioeconomic status families, is also found in high income and professional families. The presence of risk factors, especially multiple risk factors, indicates that the family is vulnerable to ineffective or maladaptive coping behaviors and methods of providing for the family's welfare.

The ecological model of child maltreatment proposes that maltreatment arises out of a mismatch of parent, child, and family to the neighborhood and community in which they are embedded.[28] The model rests on three levels of analysis: the relationship between the family and the environment, the interacting and overlapping systems in which human development occurs, and the quality of the environment.[28] This model has been further refined to account for the temporal effect of life events, stress, and social support (Fig. 33-8).[40] When stress factors become greater or when they are not matched by adaptive behaviors, the risk for abuse is high. Intervention by social support systems or social networks is critical in mediating abuse.

About 1.7 million child abuse cases are reported per year, with a mortality between 2000 and 5000.[54] About half of these children die as a result of the cumulative effects of repeated beatings or from a single violent episode. The other half of the victims die as a result of child neglect, because the parents have failed to provide for the child's basic needs (e.g., failure to secure needed medical care or inadequate supervision). Children reported as child abuse fatalities are much younger, on the average, than those children reported for maltreatment: 2.6 years versus 7.2 years of age.[2] Comparisons of reported child abuse fatalities to those children reported

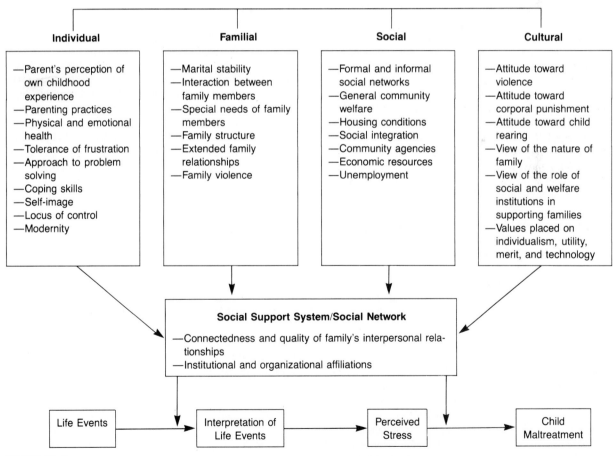

FIGURE 33–8.
The ecological model of child maltreatment. (Howze, D. C., & Kotch, J. B. (1984). Disentangling life events, stress and social support: Implications for the primary prevention of child abuse and neglect. Child Abuse & Neglect, 8(4), 401–409.)

for maltreatment suggest that children who die as a result of abuse or neglect are more likely to come from families in which two caregivers are present (69% compared to 56%) and in which the caregivers are 16 to 20 years of age (21% compared to 9% for adults older than 20 years of age). Evidence also shows that minority children who live in low-income households are over-represented in the fatality statistics, as are children who live with chronic drug abusers.[54]

Four types of cognitive disturbances in parents are related to child abuse: unrealistic expectations of the child's performance abilities, poor problem solving and processing of events, immature methods for handling frustration (e.g., Spitz's physical aggression stages, see Chap. 11), and negative attribution for the child's motivation (e.g., "my baby cries because she hates me").

Many of these same issues are associated with spouse abuse. The majority of the victims of spouse abuse are women. About 5% of all American women (3–4 million in the United States and 500,000 in Canada) seek medical attention or police assistance for physical abuse annually.[41] The number who are abused is probably much higher since the majority of abuse scenarios go unreported. No socioeconomic level is exempt from abuse. The modeling of violence in families of origin predisposes a woman to the victim role or a man to the aggressor role. Chronic stressors such as unemployment, drug and alcohol abuse, poverty, role stress, and dysfunctional family relations also contribute to this recurring cycle. The primary reason why women remain in abusive relationships is economic; they are fearful that they will be unable to provide for their own or their children's basic care needs. The self-esteem of many abused women is so low that they lack the confidence that they would be able to survive independently of the abusing spouse.

Family abuse may be directed toward any person who is seen as dependent or as a source of frustration. It is estimated that between 500,000 to 2 million elderly people are abused each year. The majority of the offenders are family members: 42% are sons or daughters, 15% are spouses, 19% are grandchildren, 4% are other relatives, and 20% are nonrelatives.[60] The typical offender is a middle-age, middle class, white female who lives with the victim, is an alcohol or drug addict, has long-term financial problems, and has high stress levels and low frustration tolerance.[60] These adult abusers frequently have a history of being abused by the parent who at this point depends on them.

It is apparent that dysfunctional family behavior is grounded in inadequate and dysfunctional role performance of individuals, maladaptive coping responses to stress, inadequate communication and concern for the well-being of others, economic stressors, and inadequate social support. The keys to preventing violence in the family lie in the prevention of child abuse and neglect and the development of an individual's coping skills. Increased funding for education and support services offers the best hope for facilitating healthy family functioning in future generations.

THERAPEUTIC APPROACHES TO WORKING WITH FAMILIES

The professional person comes in contact with many different family structures in the course of work. Whether the focus of interaction with a family is from an educational, medical, social, legal, or counseling viewpoint, the professional needs to identify what the individual and family functional levels and needs may be. Family assessment approaches depend on the reason for interaction, the goals of the intervention, and the background of the practitioner. Usually, each profession develops its own tools for assessment. An interdisciplinary approach to family assessment may involve the evaluation of the family's ability to meet Murdock's four basic tasks, Duvall's eight tasks, Schuster's seven tasks, Tapia's five levels of family functioning, or Curran's 12 traits of a healthy family (see Chap. 32). Evaluation according to task management allows the practitioner to determine objectively the basic strengths and weaknesses of the family as a system. Assessment of the level of family functioning according to Tapia's paradigm allows the tailoring of appropriately paced intervention approaches.

Practitioner Roles

The family's level of functioning is indicative of its overall state of psychosocial health. Improvements in the level of functioning allow the practitioner to determine the effectiveness of interventions and support services. Regardless of a family's structure, abilities, or functional level, the practitioner can help the members mobilize their resources by developing strategies based on specific theories or tasks. Practitioners can help a family increase its functional level and provide a healthy environment for the individuals within the family.

Tapia has identified that the various levels of family functioning require different skills and relationships from the practitioner.[71] Every family cannot be approached with the assumption that they will joyfully receive and independently act on all information offered. Even with the threat of removal of the children, the parents may be too stressed to clean the home, attend parenting classes, or even secure a new dwelling. Table 33-4 meshes the family level with the practitioner's approach.

Level 1: Infancy or the Chaotic Family
The focus of intervention with this family is the establishment of a trusting relationship. Families at this level have a difficult time accepting help because of their fear and distrust of outside people and agencies. The practitioner who cannot establish a trusting relationship with these families will not be effective in setting goals or implementing interventions. The practitioner needs to become a "good parent" to the family, attempting to engender trust. This process requires patience, warm support, consistency of attention, approach, and responses, clarification of roles, and noncontingent acceptance of the family and the idiosyncrasies of individual members.

TABLE 33–4. MODEL FOR ASSESSMENT OF AND APPROACH TO FAMILIES

Helping Activities	Trust	Counseling	Complex of Skills	Prevention	None
Continuum of Skills				Anticipated problem areas studied, teaching of available resources, assistance in family-group understanding, maturity, and foresight	
Practitioner and Family—Partners					
Partnership	Acceptance and trust, maturity and patience, clarification of role, limit setting, constant evaluation of relationship and progress				
Partnership Stressing Family's Ability		Based on trust relationship, uses counseling, and interpersonal skills to help family begin to understand itself and define its problems. Practitioner uses honesty, genuineness, and self-evaluation			
Practitioner—Expert and Partner			Information, coordination, teamwork, teaching; uses special skills, helps family in making decisions and finding solutions		*Family Independent* *Help Not Needed*
Practitioner—Expert and Partner with Family					
Practitioner—Adult Helper to Family					Ideal family, homeostatic, balance between individual and group goals and activities. Family meets its tasks and roles well, they are able to seek appropriate help when needed
Practitioner and Family—Siblings				Family has solutions, are stable and healthy with fewer conflicts or problems, very capable providers of physical and emotional supports. Parents mature and confident, fewer difficulties in training of children, able to seek help, future-oriented, enjoy present	
Practitioner—Good Parent to Family			Normal family but with many conflicts and problems, variation in economic levels, greater trust and ability to seek and use help. Parents more mature, but still have emotional conflicts. Do have successes and achievements, and are more willing to seek solutions to problems, future-oriented		
Continuum of Family Functioning	Chaotic family, barely surviving, inadequate provision of physical and emotional supports. Alienation from community, deviant behavior, distortion and confusion of roles, immaturity, child neglect, depression-failure	Intermediate family, slightly above survival level, variation in economic provisions, alienation but with more ability to trust. Child neglect not as great, defensive but slightly more willing to accept help			
Family Levels	**I Infancy**	**II Childhood**	**III Adolescence**	**IV Adulthood**	**V Maturity**

Tapia, J. A. (1972). The nursing process in family health. Nursing Outlook, 20, *267. With permission.*

The practitioner, like a parent, may have to do much for the family to ensure meeting of basic needs and to enable them to learn essential skills through the consistent modeling of the essential skills. Acute helplessness syndrome (see Chap. 13) may prevent them from taking definitive action on their own behalf.

Level 2: Childhood or the Intermediate Family

The trust established in the previous level is the basis for the practitioner to begin to foster autonomy by mobilizing the family to review their problems and to begin to understand themselves more clearly. This family is still quite dependent but can contact resources identified by the practitioner. Problems that are identified by the practitioner may not be accepted by the family, and thus interventions must focus on what the family identifies as its own needs and priorities, with the practitioner functioning as an older sibling to the family. This process strengthens the therapeutic relationship and eventually leads to more realistic priorities for family functioning. This stage requires accurate diagnosis of family problems. The goal is to help the family grow to the level at which they can establish goals, help to identify options, and then work independently for solutions to some of their problems. Progress is identified when the family begins to feel more like a family rather than a group of isolated individuals. This family experiences the practitioner in a sibling role, allowing for fluctuation between dependence and independence by the family.

Level 3: Adolescence or the Family With Problems

Most families function at this level. Although many of them never seek assistance, most are receptive to assistance or recommendation for referral to another resource or agency when it is supportively offered by a teacher, health practitioner, or friend. A number of intervention strategies are useful in assisting this family to solve its recognized problems. Assistance may be provided through teaching, information, coordination of referrals, teamwork, or special technical skills that enable the family to establish realistic goals and seek help independently to reach those goals. The family should be encouraged to start with the easiest problems first to generate some increased self-esteem through goal achievement. The practitioner's role in these interaction activities demands a wealth of technical and interpersonal skills as well as knowledge of community resources and the ability to coordinate and cooperate with a multidisciplinary team. The practitioner is viewed by the family as an adult helper who assists them in trying out their decisions and evaluating their outcomes. Control is important to this family. Consequently, a patronizing approach or the giving of ultimatums is resented and resisted. Anticipatory guidance and assistance with the evaluation of the alternatives are supportive.

Level 4: Adulthood or the Family With Solutions

The practitioner's primary role with these families is one of preventive teaching directed at enabling the family to maintain its health. Interventions are directed at helping family members anticipate and avoid problem areas, independently generate possible alternatives, and realistically examine the effects of these alternatives. These families usually are able to identify crisis or impending crisis and seek assistance appropriately as needed. The practitioner's role requires broad knowledge of potential problems and potential community resources for both health maintenance and crisis intervention. The family views the practitioner as an expert teacher and partner.

Level 5: Maturity or the Ideal Family

This family anticipates developmental challenges and takes appropriate preventive actions or seeks assistance to decrease the stress. Intervention is not necessary for this family unless a major crisis occurs, such as the birth of a disabled child, fire, or death of a family member. At such times, the family recognizes its need for assistance and independently seeks appropriate community resources. If services are required, the role of the practitioner would be to help families identify relevant factors and potential solutions and resources for facing the crisis and regaining their equilibrium.

Therapeutic Strategies

Family counseling can help an individual or family cope more effectively with their life situation. Counseling can help many families resolve communication problems and reach a higher level of maturity, greater self-esteem, and closer relationships. The ultimate aim of counseling is to help the individual and family attain healthy family functioning in meeting life-span tasks.

Counseling strategies fall into four basic categories: relationship strategies, communication strategies, problem-solving strategies, and personal strategies.[43] Each of these requires different counseling techniques:

1. Relationship Strategies: Help the family establish a trusting relationship by using a family-centered approach for clarifying expectations and performing as a good role model. The family members may bond to the practitioner as a transition to bonding with each other. This bond requires the establishment of a trusting practitioner–family relationship but also the development of a plan for transfer of feelings back to each other and termination of the professional relationship.

2. Communication Strategies: Help the family develop better communication skills, learn how to be good listeners, provide new information, and learn how to use positive reinforcement. The practitioner must model these skills as well as facilitate their development.

3. Problem-Solving Strategies: Help the family become problem solvers, define the problem, use confrontation and feedback when appropriate, develop negotiation skills, build on family strengths, and manipulate the environment when necessary. The practitioner makes appropriate referrals and develops parent support groups as necessary to augment the counseling program.

4. Personal Strategies: Facilitates the ability of people to look at themselves, get assistance as needed, and be responsible for their own decisions and behaviors. The practitioner must be careful to avoid an attitude of omnipotence and must become aware of personal "burn out" in counseling programs that require high personal involvement. The practitioner must know how to cope with personal stress to assist clients effectively.[43]

A therapeutic interview is typically the first step in determining needs and strategies. Areas of family assessment that should be considered include the family's history, structure, economic resources, roles, boundaries, communication patterns, conflict resolution patterns, power distribution, values, emotional climate, division of labor, support systems, stressors, socialization of children, intrafamily relationships, and health status of the individual members. This data, which is obtained in a nonthreatening, supportive manner or through direct observation of family interactions, allows the practitioner to determine the basic functional level of the family and to determine the needs of both the individual and the family as a group. The practitioner may then assume the most appropriate role relationship with the family and begin implementing intervention counseling strategies that will move the family to a higher functional level for all members.

CONCLUSION

This chapter has covered briefly some of the theories about the family and how the family may experience differences in both structure and function. It has discussed ways one can identify and assess those differences, has given guidelines for assessing malfunctioning and dysfunctioning families, and has suggested tools to use in working with them based on their developmental or functional level. This chapter also discussed some of the stressors associated with variations in family experience with life in contemporary society.

The wide variety of family structures present in America today are challenging current family life-span theories to adopt a more realistic view of essential family tasks. Strategies aimed at helping to achieve traditional nuclear family lifestyles are not appropriate for nontraditional families and are insensitive to their unique stressors and needs.

The factor that offers the most hope for helping dysfunctional families is in the area of child abuse prevention. Family nurturing programs and information on family growth and development that teach and model basic supportive parent–child relationships need to be offered in high schools, colleges, and communities. These provide the best hope for future generations of all people. The cycle of violence, poverty, helplessness, and dysfunction can best be broken through attention to the environment and home life provided to our youngest citizens.[17]

REFERENCES

1. Ahrons, C. R. (1981). The continuing co-parental relationship between divorced spouses. *American Journal of Orthopsychiatry, 59,* 415–427.
2. American Humane Association, Child Protection Division. (1984). *Highlights of official child neglect and abuse reporting, 1982.* Denver, CO: American Humane Association, Child Protection Division.
3. Aten, M. J. (1988). Teenage mother–infant interactions: A challenge for early intervention. *NCAST National News, 4*(2), 1–5.
4. Bassuk, I. E., et al. (1986). Characteristics of sheltered homeless families. *American Journal of Public Health, 76,* 1097–1101.
5. Berne, A. S., Dato, C., Mason, D. J., & Rafferty, M. (1990). A nursing model for addressing the health needs of homeless families. *Image: Journal of Nursing Scholarship, 22*(1), 8–13.
6. Blank, H. (1986). Child care in the year 2000. In C. H. Thomas (Ed.), *Current issues in day care: Readings and resources.* Phoenix, AZ: Oryx Press.
7. Bowen, M. (1985). *Family therapy in clinical practice.* New York: Jason Aronson.
8. Brooks-Gunn, J., & Furstenberg, F. F. (1986). The children of adolescent mothers: Physical, academic, and psychological outcomes. *Developmental Review, 6,* 224–251.
9. Browne, A. (1987). *When battered women kill.* New York: Free Press.
10. Burgess, A. W., & Lazare, A. (1976). *Community mental health: Target populations.* Englewood Cliffs, NJ: Prentice-Hall.
11. Camp, B. W., et al. (1984). Infants of adolescent mothers: Maternal characteristic and developmental status at one year of age. *American Journal of Diseases of Children, 138,* 243–246.
12. Caplan, G. (1974). *Support systems and community mental health: Lectures on concept development.* New York: Behavioral Publications.
13. Carter, B., & McGoldrick, M. (Eds.). (1988). *The changing family life cycle: A framework for family therapy.* New York: Gardner Press.
14. Chamberlin, R. M. (1987). Our nation's families: A sociological perspective. *Human Values, 2*(2), 13–18.
15. Cherlin, A. (1981). *Marriage, divorce, remarriage.* Cambridge, MA: Harvard University Press.
16. Children's Defense Fund, 1987. (1987). *A high price to pay: Teenage pregnancy in Ohio.* Columbus, OH: Ohio Printing.
17. Clapp, G. (1988). *Child study research: Current perspectives and applications.* Lexington, MA: Lexington Books.
18. Coolsen, P. (1983). *Strengthening families through the workplace.* Chicago: National Committee for the Prevention of Child Abuse.
19. Cramer, S. H., Keitel, M. A., & Rossberg, R. H. (1986). The family and employed mothers. *International Journal of Family Psychiatry, 7*(1), 17–34.
20. Curran, D. (1985). *Stress and the healthy family.* Minneapolis, MN: Winston Press.

21. Damrosch, S. P., Sullivan, P. A., Scholler, A., & Gaines, J. (1988). On behalf of homeless families. *Maternal Child Nursing, 13,* 259–263.

22. Daro, D. (1988). *Confronting child abuse: Research for effective program design.* New York: Free Press, Macmillan.

23. Emery, R. (1982). Interparental conflict and the children of discord and divorce. *Psychological Bulletin, 91,* 12–20.

24. Eshelman, J. R. (1974). *The family: An introduction.* Boston: Allyn and Bacon.

25. Friedman, M. (1986). *Family assessment: Theory and assessment* (2nd ed.). New York: Appleton-Century-Crofts.

26. Friedman, M. (1986). *Family nursing: Theory and assessment* (2nd ed.). New York: Appleton-Century-Crofts.

27. Fulmer, R. H. (1988). Lower-income and professional families: A comparison of structure and life cycle process. In B. Carter & M. McGoldrick (Eds.), *The changing family life cycle* (pp. 545–578). New York: Gardner Press.

28. Garbarino, J. (1976). The human ecology of child maltreatment. *Journal of Marriage and the Family, 39,* 721–735.

29. Gelcer, F. (1983). Mourning is a family affair. *Family Process, 22,* 501.

30. Gelles, R. J. (1987). *Family violence.* Newbury Park, CA: Sage Publications.

31. Gilbert, L. A. (1985). *Men in dual-career families: Current realities and future prospects.* Hillsdale, NJ: Lawrence Erlbaum.

32. Glick, P. C. (1984). Marriage, divorce, and living arrangements: Prospective changes. *Journal of Family Issues, 5,* 7–26.

33. Glick, P. C., & Lin, S. L. (1986). Recent changes in divorce and remarriage. *Journal of Marriage and the Family, 48,* 737–747.

34. Hanson, S. M. H., & Sporakowski, M. J. (1986). Single parent families. *Family Relations, 35,* 3–8.

35. Heatherington, E. M. (1988). Parents, children, and siblings: Six years after divorce. In R. A. Hinde & J. Stevenson-Hinde (Eds.), *Relationships within families: Mutual influences* (pp. 311–331). New York: Oxford University Press.

36. Hertz, R. (1986). *More equal than others: Women and men in dual-career marriages.* Berkeley, CA: University of California Press.

37. Hicks, M. W., Hansen, S. L., & Cristie, L. A. (1983). Dual career/dual work families: A systems approach. In F. D. Macklin & R. N. Rubin (Eds.), *Contemporary families and alternative lifestyles* (pp. 164–179). Beverly Hills, CA: Sage Publications.

38. Hill, R. (1986). Life cycle stages for types of single parent families: Of family development theory. *Family Relations, 35,* 19–29.

39. Hines, P. (1988). The family life cycle of poor black families. In B. Carter & M. McGoldrick (Eds.), *The changing family life cycle* (pp. 513–544). New York: Gardner Press.

40. Howze, D. C., & Kotch, J. B. (1984). Disentangling life events, stress and social support: Implications for the primary prevention of child abuse and neglect. *Child Abuse and Neglect, 8,* 401–409.

41. Jaffe, P. J., Wolfe, D. A., & Wilson, S. K. (1990). *Children of battered women.* Newbury Park, CA: Sage Publications.

42. Janosik, E. H. (1986). *Crisis counseling: A contemporary approach.* Boston: Jones and Bartlett.

43. Johnson, S. H. (1986). *Nursing assessment and strategies for the family at risk: High-risk parenting* (2nd ed.). Philadelphia: J. B. Lippincott.

44. Keith, P., & Schafer, R. B. (1980). Role strain and depression in two-job families. *Family Relations, 29,* 483–488.

45. Kimball, G. (1988). *50-50 parenting: Sharing family rewards and responsibilities.* Lexington, MA: Lexington Books.

46. Kozol, J. (1988). *Rachel and her children: Homeless families in America.* New York: Crown.

47. Maynard, F. (1985). *The child care crisis.* Markham, ONT: Viking.

48. Messinger, L. (1984). *Remarriage.* New York: Plenum Press.

49. Mills, D. M. (1984). A model for stepfamily development. *Family Relations, 33,* 365–372.

50. Morris, M. (1988). *Last chance children: Growing up with older parents.* New York: Columbia University Press.

51. Murdock, G. P. (1968). The universality of the nuclear family. In N. W. Bell & E. F. Vogel (Eds.), *A modern introduction to the family* (rev. ed.). New York: Free Press.

52. Musick, J. S., et al. (1987, December). A chain of enablements: Using community based programs to strengthen relationships between teen parents and their infants. *Zero to Three,* pp. 1–5.

53. National Center for Health Statistics. (1984). Births, marriages, divorces and deaths, U.S. 1983. *Monthly Vital Statistics Report, 32,* 84–112. (DHHS Publication Number PHS 84-112).

54. National Committee for Prevention of Child Abuse. (1987, July). *NCPCA Fact Sheet, 9.*

55. Norton, A. J., & Glick, P. C. (1986). One parent families: A social and economic profile. *Family Relations, 35,* 9–17.

56. Nye, I., & Bernardo, F. (1966). *Conceptual frameworks for the study of the family.* New York: Macmillan.

57. Parents Without Partners. (1986). *Facts about single parent families.* Single Parent Clearinghouse.

58. Peachey, R. (1988). *Statistics.* Philadelphia: National Clearinghouse for the Defense of Battered Women.

59. Peck, J. S. (1989). The impact of divorce on children at various stages of the family life cycle. *Journal of Divorce, 12*(2–3), 81–106.

60. Pollick, M. F. (1987). Abuse of the elderly: A review. *Holistic Nursing Practice, 2,* 43–53.

61. Poloma, M. M., Pendleton, B. F., & Garland, T. N. (1982). Reconsidering the dual-career marriage: A longitudinal approach. In J. Aldous (Ed.), *Two paychecks: Life in dual-earner families* (pp. 173–192). Beverly Hills, CA: Sage Publications.

62. Raferty, M. (1989). Standing up for America's homeless. *American Journal of Nursing, 12,* 1614–1617.

63. Rapoport, R., & Rapoport, R. N. (1969). Dual career family. *Human Relations, 22,* 3–30.

64. Scarr, S., & Weinberg, R. A. (1986). The early childhood enterprise: Care and education of the young. *American Psychologist, 41,* 1140–1146.

65. Schneidman, F. (1973). Crisis intervention: Some thoughts and perspectives. In G. Spector & W. Claiborn (Eds.), *Crisis intervention.* New York: Behavior Publications.

66. Schvaneveldt, J. D. (1966). The interactional framework in the study of the family. In F. I. Nye & F. M. Bernardo (Eds.), *Emerging conceptual frameworks in the family analysis.* New York: Macmillan.

67. Sells, C. J., & Paeth, S. (1987). Health and safety in daycare. *Topics in Early Childhood Special Education, 7*(1), 61–72.

68. Skinner, D. A. (1980). Dual-career family stress and coping: A literature review. *Family Relations, 29*(4), 473–481.

69. Smith, J. B. (1983). Care of the hospitalized abused child and family. *Nursing Clinics of North America, 16,* 127–137.

70. Stryker, S. (1964). The interactional and situational approaches. In H. T. Christensen (Ed.), *Handbook of marriage and the family.* Chicago: Rand McNally.

71. Tapia, J. A. (1986). Fractionalization of the family unit. In C. S. Schuster & S. S. Ashburn (Eds.), *The process of human development* (2nd ed., pp. 697–718). Boston: Little, Brown.

72. Taylor, B., et al. (1983). Teenage mothering, admission to hospital and accidents during the first five years. *Archives of Disease in Childhood, 58,* 6–11.

73. Thompson, F. H., & Gongla, P. A. (1983). Single-parent families: In the mainstream of American society. In E. D. Macklin & R. H. Rubin (Eds.), *Contemporary families and alternative lifestyles* (pp. 97–124). Beverly Hills, CA: Sage Publications.

74. U.S. Bureau of the Census. (1990). *Statistical Abstract of the United States: 1990* (110th ed.). Washington, DC: Superintendent of Documents.

75. Uchitelle, L. (1987, October 11). Making a living is now a family enterprise. *New York Times,* Sect. 12, pp. 1–8.

76. Vincent, L. J. (1988). Changing economic and social influences on family involvement. *Topics in Early Childhood Special Education, 8*(1), 48–59.

77. Visher, E. B., & Visher, J. S. (1988). *Old loyalties, new ties.* New York: Brunner/Mazel.

78. Wallerstein, J. S., & Blakeslee, S. (1989). *Second chances: Men, women and children a decade after divorce.* New York: Ticknor and Fields.

79. Wallerstein, J. S., & Kelly, J. B. (1980). *Surviving the breakup.* New York: Basic Books.

80. Werner, H., & Kaplan, B. (1963). *Symbol formation.* New York: John Wiley.

The Family With a Disabled Member

Clara S. Schuster

Approximately 25% of the population is directly or indirectly (family member) affected by disability or chronic illness.[82] The presence of a disabled person within the family increases the stress load of the family but does not necessarily create a deviant or "handicapped family."[48,61] However, "courtesy stigma" may be extended to the family members of a disabled person, affecting their social image and acceptability in the community.[53,80] Family members may become victims of stress as they attempt to cope with the consequences of the disability as well as the social isolation and rejection.[60] Families may experience some difficulty in coping with a catastrophic event,[27,30] but they are not "doomed to dysfunction."[67]

Their response is the result of ongoing adjustment to chronic stress and consequently includes past experiences, attitudes, biases, and values; future goals and expectations; as well as current realities, problems, and concerns. Most families cope or adapt amazingly well or may even thrive with the challenges.[17,67] However, the presence of a disabled family member presents one more occasion for "identity homework" (see Chap. 25). Juxtaposition of values is not an easy task and requires much sensitivity from practitioners while people are reassessing their values.

By understanding the unique stressors and adjustment patterns used to cope with disability, practitioners can be more supportive to family members. In their lack of understanding, practitioners can convey to family members a feeling that their behavior is "inappropriate" or "pathological." Many family members have been erroneously labeled "hysterical," "overprotective," or "nonaccepting" by insensitive professionals.[61] Such negative labeling of intense, but normal, responses can increase family stress and reduce effective coping during the crisis as well as in the ensuring years.

RESPONSES TO DISABILITY

Birth of an Impaired Child

Throughout pregnancy most parents, especially the mother, invest extensive amounts of energy in physical and psychological preparation for the new baby.[14] "Nest building" activities, such as preparation of the infant's room, collecting a layette, and making articles by hand for the baby, all imply a joyful anticipation of the event. Grandparents, siblings, and friends frequently contribute to the preparation, indicating the high social value of the addition to the family.

Parents, especially the mother, begin to fantasize about the new baby, formulating consciously or unconsciously, a concept of the baby's appearance, behavior characteristics, gender, special talents, intellectual potential, and even future contributions to the family or society. These daydreams create an "ideal child." The parents dream of giving the child what they did not have during their own childhood, replicating favorite activities, or experiencing new companionships.

The ability of the parents to produce an unimpaired child is psychologically and culturally critical to their sense of personal adequacy. Thus, narcissistic investment in the fetus predisposes the parents to dream of a "perfect child" because the baby becomes so closely tied to feelings of achievement and self-worth.[14] However, whether the pregnancy is desired or rejected, fear that the child may have abnormalities appears to be a universal concern.[68] Many parents are reluctant to mention these anxieties lest the very expression of the fear precipitate the event. Most parents are able to minimize these fears and to anticipate a happy outcome.

When the child is born "healthy," the two initial tasks of parenthood are made infinitely easier: (1) to become attached to the child (it is difficult to reject what is perceived as a part of or an extension of the self); and (2) to develop a new self-image as an adult responsible for another life, that is, a parent. The mother may see the infant as something she has made, a gift that she presents to her family, husband, or society.[62]

The birth of an infant, especially the first one, is a crisis event for any family. When the new infant does not match the ideal infant, the parent is challenged to blend, or to bend, the ideal to meet the reality. Sometimes, the gap involves a superficial factor; for example, the author and her husband expected a brown-haired baby but had a blonde one instead. We were not even aware of our preconceived expectation until after her birth, when we recognized our shock reaction. It was a small, superficial difference, but one that nevertheless required an adjustment of our concepts about "our baby." At other times, the gap between the ideal and the real is so great that every coping skill a parent possesses is called on, and even then these skills may not be sufficient to bridge the gap readily or comfortably. The gender of the child sometimes falls into this category. When the infant turns out to be the "wrong" gender, it may take days, weeks, or even years for the parents to *forgive* the child for *defying* their dreams.

When an infant is born with a defect that is obvious at birth or shortly thereafter, the crisis of the birth and the necessity of bridging the gap between the real infant and the ideal one may present seemingly insurmountable obstacles to the parents. Since the "cuteness" of a baby is a factor known to aid in the parents' positive feelings toward an infant, atypical physical appearance or behavior can present a barrier to bonding, a factor that ultimately affects the development of

both the child and the parents.[31, 40, 53] At a time when parents should be getting to know their new child as a separate individual, their emotional energy may be usurped to cope with the psychological "pain gap," grief, and value reassessment.

To be successful both as individuals and as parents, the two initial tasks of parenthood must be mastered in spite of the gap. Unless the parents are able to cope with the assault to their parental ego, a healthy attachment to the infant will be difficult, if not impossible.[40] Parents find it difficult to meet even the most basic nutritive needs of the infant, let alone the socialization and specialized needs of the child if their energies are completely invested in identifying and supporting their own identity and self-esteem. Parental grief over the disability may inhibit the warm, consistent, nurturing attention and synchronized responses the infant needs during these critical early months and, thus, effectively prevents the child's ability to predict events, master effective signaling systems, imitate, and learn how to learn.[48] Many, if not most, parents need counseling to help them put roles, relationships, and identities back into a healthy perspective. Unfortunately, many parents do not take advantage of counseling services even when they are available. See Appendix G for potential resources (Fig. 34-1).

FIGURE 34–1.
Parents are challenged to redefine priorities and to identify and pursue common interests when a child has physical or cognitive limitations. However, the broadening of horizons can contribute to both their lives.

Impact on the Parents

When the parents learn that their baby is impaired in some way, their dream of living "happily ever after" is shattered. The normal period of disequilibrium following birth and adjustment to new roles is intensified. New goals may need to be established for the child, themselves, and for the total family. The couple, individually and collectively, assumes a new self-image. The parents find that their relationships with spouse, family, friends, and professionals change. They often feel an intense isolation from the infant, from each other, from the extended family, and from people in general. The spontaneous joy and atmosphere of celebration after the birth of a healthy child may be sharply muted by the parents and others. For some families, it may feel more like a funeral, requiring time to grieve before moving forward with life.[35] Anxiety and vulnerability build as parents attempt to establish a semblance of equilibrium.

The mother, because of her greater narcissistic investment, may react more strongly than the father, at least outwardly. The fact that the father usually has a job to which he can "escape" helps him retain some stability of schedule and emotional distance from the event. The culture socializes men to handle stress in a different manner. Many men are less willing to talk about the disability, but indications are that they feel the pain as greatly as the mothers.[3] When they are not involved in their child's care or are not included in therapy or counseling sessions, they may lack an understanding of their child's needs.[13, 48, 49] In an attempt to protect their own ego from the narcissistic hurt, they may pretend that the situation is less severe than it really is. This pretense is a potential source of contention between the parents, since the mother may interpret the father's more stoic approach as a lack of concern. However, when the truth finally hits, "it hurts all the more for the length of the deception."[75] Many men express that they feel "richer" once they are able to recognize and express their feelings. "It's like before I was half a person and now I'm whole."[75] This response is but one of the benefits of parenting a disabled child.

The ego-identity of both parents may be severely threatened. The concept of their own or their spouse's sexuality may be in question. They may interpret the loss of the perfect child as a defect in their own humanness or integrity or in their ability to produce a "whole child."[40] Some feel personally responsible for "inflicting" the child on society.[80] The defective child may be seen as an ineradicable stigma and a reflection on their own adequacy, identity, procreative ability, or ancestral background. They cannot "make right" what has happened. The father may feel overwhelmed with the financial responsibilities involved in caring for the child and may wonder if he can continue to provide for the needs of his family. He may resist asking for financial aid because to ask is a further acknowledgement of his inadequacy.

The mother may also feel overwhelmingly inadequate, especially if she saw her career as that of being a mother. At the onset of her career, she has created a "bad child." She has lost status in her own eyes at a time when she was expecting a "promotion." She may have felt somewhat unprepared but challenged by the idea of learning how to care for a normal infant; she is overwhelmed and devastated at the idea of caring for a disabled infant. She has failed before she started. How can she turn out an exemplary product to society at the end of 18 to 20 years when she begins with defective material? The future may loom ominously to both parents.

The birth of an impaired child appears to be less devastating if the family already has one normal child. The couple has already proved their soundness of body, adulthood, and sexuality, and they have also been inducted successfully into the status of parenthood. At that point, they are merely expanding their responsibilities, not changing them. Realization that a pregnancy may result in the birth of another disabled child can have a negative effect on the parents' sex life. Many parents may not have the courage to risk another pregnancy,[4, 35] thus the issues of soundness and sexuality for first-time parents may never be completely or adequately resolved.

Disability After the Neonatal Period

Late-Appearing Congenital Anomalies

Many hereditary traits and congenital disabilities, such as deafness and cerebral palsy, do not become apparent until several months after the child's birth. Others, such as diabetes or mental retardation, may take several years before the parents recognize a problem and professionals document it. In these cases, the parents have had an opportunity to bond to the infant. They have been able to integrate some of their ideal infant into the real child. An awareness that something is wrong unfolds gradually as the parents observe that the child is not achieving the expected milestones, fails to respond in an expected manner, or begins to develop an unexpected behavior.

Unfortunately, the parents' initial observations and concerns frequently are ignored or treated lightly by the professionals as the projections of overanxious, neurotic parents.[81] Many parents report that they are told, "Don't worry, everything is fine," or, "He'll outgrow it." Professional denial only increases parental stress.[53] Many feel forced into an aggressive advocacy role for their child, a stance that precipitates personality changes as they "fight the system," trying to secure diagnosis, treatment, or information.[48, 81] The search for assistance for their child may consume much energy and time, cutting into a healthy relationship with the child or between the spouses. They are forced to tell their story repeatedly as they seek assistance. Once the diagnosis has been made, rather than devastating the parents, most express a tremendous sense of relief.[81] The truth sets them free to focus their energies on appropriate intervention strategies. The parents have a sense of accomplishment. They have fought a battle for their child and won. No longer do they fear being stigmatized as neurotic parents; their efforts and behaviors have been vindicated.

Traumatic Injury or Illness

The immediate effects of a serious injury or illness of a child cannot be disputed by either parents or professionals. The parents deeply fear the loss of the child they know and love. They also face intense fears about the future. When disastrous sequelae appear (e.g., permanent disability, emotional problems, or cognitive deficits), the parents feel the loss of their normal child just as acutely as if the child had died.

When an older child, adolescent, or young adult is injured, the parents may face having a dependent child once again at a time in their lives when they were beginning to enjoy more freedom from active parenting responsibilities. The dependent person may seriously interrupt the parents' goals and lifestyle, a factor that can lead to marked resentment.

When a family member is temporarily or permanently disabled or ill, role changes occur in all other family members. Not only is the family workload increased by the care for the invalid, but the normal responsibilities of the disabled member must be assumed by the other members of the system. When an adult is disabled, the family may need to seek alternative sources of income to maintain living expenses. The additional responsibilities may lead to fatigue, anger, or depression as the caregiver experiences responsibility overload. Disability in a spouse at any age disrupts plans and dreams. Side effects may include role reversals, financial hardships, decrease in companionship, loss of a sexual partner, and identity changes.

The question that haunts family members is, "Why?" When the disability is caused by an accident or illness, a family member may assume or assign the guilt, identifying ways the trauma could have been prevented: "If only I had . . ." Guilt, whether directed at one's self, the spouse, sibling, or another, can devastate the family unit. Crisis counseling is essential.

Factors That Affect the Response of Family Members

The response of family members to a disability depends on many variables. Most of the responses are attempts to maintain psychological equilibrium and ego-identity. The previous relationship with the disabled person is a critical factor. In general, the older the child when the disability becomes known, the stronger the attachment bond and, therefore, the greater the resistance to fractionization. Loving attention continues to be showered on the child in spite of the child's limited responsiveness or ability to reinforce parental efforts. The strength of one's premorbidity marital bond likewise impacts the quality of the commitment of spouses.

Relationship With Practitioners

How family members are told about a disability and the type of affective support given them at the time are crucial to the family members' future relationships with one another, the disabled person, and professional people.[44, 81, 83] In many cases, individuals may not remember exactly *what* was said to them but vividly recall years later *how* they were told (or not told) about the disability of a family member. Family members appreciate staff members who make themselves available to answer questions, to listen, and to talk about the disabled person's positive aspects. People desire the truth, sensitively presented; optimism and hope must be maintained, however, and new roles simply and gently described.[18, 44] The brisk, hurried, impersonal practitioner can leave an individual feeling isolated and angry.[79] Furtive looks, avoidance behavior, whispers, or tightly drawn faces of embarrassed, grieving, curious, or insecure staff members can increase the family members' sense of stress, stigma, and isolation, factors that may be more incapacitating to the family members than the disability itself. People indicate that anxieties are frequently reduced after seeing a deformed neonate or an injured family member because the infant, child, or adult does not look as bad as their imaginations conjectured.

Type of Disability

The type of disability affects family responses. What is the trajectory of the condition in terms of quality or length of life?[11, 43] Is it correctable or life threatening? Parents may experience marked difficulty bonding to a child they expect to die. Investing heavily now will hurt intensely later. Anticipatory grief (see Chap. 19) may prevent continued intense emotional investment in or commitment to a person with Alzheimer's disease, a stroke, or any terminal illness.

Do any other family members have the same or other problems? Has previous contact with this or other disabilities been positive or negative? No clear correlation is found between the degree of deformity or disability and the intensity of family members' responses. It is the meaning of the disability rather than the degree of involvement that is significant. One parent may be more disturbed by a facial birthmark than by a metabolic imbalance or a club foot. A wife may be more upset by her husband's diabetes or high cholesterol because of the dietary changes than surgery for prostatic cancer. A mentally retarded child often creates more psychological stress and stigma than a physically impaired child.[44] Consequently, when parents have a child with both physical and cognitive defects, they tend to use the physical disability as an excuse for the developmental delay. Orthopedic anomalies and blindness create the greatest barriers to maternal bonding because of the obvious discrepancy from the normal child, anticipated inability to perform self-help skills, or the inability of the infant to establish eye-to-eye contact (a significant reinforcer for maternal caregiving).[21] Parents may experience grief and anger that they will never be free of the intense caregiving responsibilities to pursue their own interests.[24] The spouse of a disabled person may feel anger at being "cheated" out of life dreams or planned retirement and leisure activities.

The value system of the family also affects their responses to chronic illness or impairment, in part because the couple's reasons for marrying or having a baby are incorporated into this system. Those who place high value on physical perfection and beauty may find a mastectomy, cleft lip, or facial burns especially difficult to accept. Mental retardation and mental illness may be difficult for highly educated, ambitious families. Cerebral palsy, amputation, or paralysis may be difficult for the physically or sports oriented family. Impairment, disability, or chronic illness force an abrupt confrontation with and reworking of one's value system.[35]

Degree of Maturity

An individual's degree of maturity at the time of the entrance of the disabled person into the family heavily affects acceptance and coping skills. Children tend to reflect the **true** attitude of the adults around them, especially the mother's.[13, 64] Younger children tend to accept the disability, although they may be disappointed or confused by the loss of a playmate or companion. The preschooler, with incomplete concepts of causality, may attribute the anomaly or injury to his or her own negative feelings that stem from sibling or parental rivalry. Young elementary children at home or in the community may be afraid to associate with the disabled child or adult for fear of "catching" whatever the disabled person has. Older school-agers and adolescents may experience embarrassment from the perceived stigma associated with a disabled person. They may refuse to have friends or a date visit the home, or they may refuse to accompany the family to social events when the disabled person is included.[65] Adolescents may also resent the increased workload associated with the reallocation of responsibilities, feeling forced to grow up too soon.[64] Many people, regardless of age, become more serious and mature as they develop sensitivity to the needs of someone besides themselves.

The emotional maturity of the parents is critical in their response to a child's disability. Those who have not yet successfully resolved Erikson's task of identity may be especially vulnerable and need much assistance in separating their personal integrity from the event. Other young or immature parents may still be too involved in their own development to recognize the *significance* of their child's impairment. Fear of the truth, role confusion, feelings of worthlessness, or naïveté may prevent parents from seeking help for themselves or the child. Sensitive, client-paced, synchronized assistance from practitioners can help reduce feelings of vulnerability and help family members develop insights, clarify values, and develop new depths of self-understanding.

The ability of a couple to give mutual support is crucial in their ability to mobilize effective coping strategies. The communication patterns established before the event may facilitate or hinder their ability to express their grief and to mitigate a sense of personal isolation. When people are able to share how they feel without criticism from the partner, commitment is strengthened and personal growth facilitated. Families that are able to support the integrity of each member can emerge from the situation as a more cohesive unit. The couple often feels that no one else can really understand or

share the burden; they are alone, but at least they have each other. However, if each person retreats into his or her own private world, the burden is compounded and the chance of fractionization of the family is increased. Many people may want and need to be left alone for short periods of time while they attempt to absorb the reality of what has happened and try to gain some new internal perspectives. However, to "crawl into a shell" is unhealthy and is an indication of the need for intensive professional counseling.

Families frequently find that they are not united in their efforts to solve the disabled member's problems.[49] Their ability to communicate their thoughts and feelings becomes a valuable tool for identifying stressors and resolving the pain. This skill may need to be encouraged and fostered in individuals who are not yet comfortable with Erikson's task of intimacy. The practitioner may need to assure family members of the acceptability and the normalcy of their socially taboo thoughts and feelings before they can feel free to disclose negative reactions toward the disabled family member and life in general. The counselor may even need to identify typical reactions for people before they are able to identify or to admit, even to themselves, their true feelings.

Feelings of alienation may temporarily impair communication between husband and wife.[47] Although they may share food and space, they may become virtual strangers because of the inability to share their thoughts and feelings. The severe injury or chronic illness of a spouse may precipitate an annulment or divorce when a partner feels cheated out of companionship, sexual relations, or a shared workload. Couples that are able to reestablish the bridges of communication find that they can develop "emotional bonds of great depth and enduring strength."[47]

Religious Orientation

A serious illness, injury, or birth of a defective child almost always awakens questions that involve the spiritual domain.[17] The religious orientation or values of the individual may either hinder or facilitate coping skills. People universally ask, "Why me?" If their concept of God is that of an overseer, judge, and punisher, they may search their own background for a serious "sin" that they committed. This concept of God can evoke a high level of guilt that is difficult for the individual to resolve. Premarital sex frequently becomes the presumed behavior for which one is being punished. When the person feels that the "sin" cannot be shared or discussed with anyone, not even the spouse, feelings of isolation are increased. Sensitive counseling may be required to help such an individual put events into realistic perspective and to alleviate the guilt. Counseling by a clergy person may be helpful.

People may experience much conflict over how God fits into the picture. Friends may comment on how lucky a child is that God provided a specific, capable set of parents. Although on the surface, the friend's comment is offered as a compliment, and it may be helpful to some parents, it raises several critical philosophical questions: (1) Does God deliberately create a defective child and then look for suitable parents? (2)

Does God have a certain number of "flawed models" that are bestowed on the most worthy (or most sinful)? (3) Does God deliberately test our strength and tolerance levels through pain, illness, and deformity?

Other well-meaning friends, attempting to offer a glimmer of hope, share the idea that, "If you live close enough to God and *really* have faith, then the person will be cured." This possibility is exciting to family members who may spend much time in religious pursuits (e.g., prayer and church attendance) or seek the assistance of faith healers. Although the author is aware of miraculous cures and would not negate the power of a living, loving God, one must face the questions raised if the person is not cured. Is it a result of a person's lack of closeness to God? If so, then one's own spiritual health is in jeopardy, or the family member's inadequate spiritual growth is keeping the disabled or chronically ill person from being cured. This belief can lead to too much guilt for any person to live with. Individuals of this persuasion might be cautioned to pray, "Thy will be done," and leave the matter in God's hands.

At the other end of the continuum are those who feel that God is a companion, a helper, or a guide in times of stress. They feel that God does not purposefully create a defective child or deliberately cause a serious accident or debilitating illness; this idea, to them, would imply a cruel God. They believe that, through the laws of physical nature, people are subject to natural disasters, developmental problems, and genetic mutations. Being human offers no immunities or special privileges over any other species, except that it provides the ability to think creatively and to communicate with God. Some may feel that God could and would cure if He wanted to, but why would God cure one person and not another? The issue is resolved by accepting the fact of the disability and the philosophy that God gives inner strength each day to face the responsibilities and sorrows, not just somehow, but triumphantly and confidently.

Decision to Institutionalize

Most families experience extreme conflict about the decision to tap into community resources. Their sense of family responsibility may be so great that caregivers are reluctant to use help from either friends or agencies.[11] The grandparents of a disabled child or the adult children of an ailing middlescent may not be aware of the depth of the problem. The stress of caregiving may be so insidious or so slowly cumulative that one is not aware of the degree of stress until it is too late.[11] It is easy to begin to center life around the disabled family member.[4] However, everyone (spouse, siblings, parents, caregiver, and the disabled person) suffers when one person is allowed to usurp a disproportional wedge of time, resources, and energies.[65]

Caregivers may be confused by feelings of pity or love, a sense of obligation, concern for the welfare of the individual, and reactions of other family members (immediate and extended) and the community. Each situation must be handled individually. Placing a disabled child or grandparent out of the home may raise feelings of guilt on the part of siblings (young and old) and may even increase their fears of a similar fate.[13] Some people do require specialized care, but a premature or inappropriately timed placement may result in adverse long-term psychological effects to all concerned. Most developmentalists recommend caring for a child at home as long as possible because parents are generally more sensitive and synchronized to the child's needs, factors that help develop a sense of selfhood and security in the child. This foundation is essential for learning about one's own potentials and the environment. When a disabled spouse is placed in a community care facility, family members frequently find that they have more quality time to spend with the person. Some elderly couples may move to a care facility together so that they have the additional care that they need yet can remain together even though one is still quite capable of self-care.

Response Patterns of Family Members

Even though parents have not seen their baby, attachment has been made during the prenatal period to an idealized infant.[37] With the birth of an impaired infant or the injury of a child, the parents' worst fears are realized. The parents are consequently presented with two major tasks: to relinquish the idealized child and to accept the reality of their new child. The highly charged longings for the normal child are recalled and intensely felt while they are gradually released and reinvested in the real child.[77] The strenuous "grief work" associated with release of the ideal child is a process that some parents may never complete because of the pain involved.

When an adult is injured, the family assumes he or she will either die or fully recover. Awareness of permanent disability is a shock. Adjustment to having a disabled family member is a slow and painful process.[28, 40] It is difficult to release the previous relationship or concept of the "ideal" child and reinvest in the new realities at the same time.[19] Each contact with the disabled person may serve as a reminder of what one has lost and may consequently interfere with resolution of the loss.[79]

Stages of Adaptation

Although variation in the magnitude of expressed behaviors and their duration is wide, family grief processes progress rather predictably through six stages. Some families or individuals may seem to skip through the early stages, whereas others may show all the classic behaviors. Some family members may not be able to complete each stage successfully and may continue to exhibit behaviors typical of an early stage for many years.[79] A person may exhibit behaviors of more than one stage or may return to an earlier stage while attempting to complete grief work or when new developmental challenges arise.[76] Asynchronous movement of family members through the stages may cause tension by creating communication barriers. Eventually, most families reach a compromise between the disabled person's needs and the desire to grow as individuals and as a family.[79] Many express that facing chronic illness or disability becomes a positive, strengthening experience.[13]

STAGE 1. When family members learn of the disability, they characteristically exhibit symptoms of shock and denial. "It can't be true." "Are you sure it's the right baby?" Numbness and disbelief set in; the whole world seems unreal; feelings of detachment and unreality predominate. They hear, but don't really listen to what is said; it is too much to take in all at once. Family members may put the existence of the loved one's disability out of their minds, repressing it as a defense against emotional pain. "The physician might be wrong." "There might be a miracle." They may need to have the situation explained a third, fourth, or fifth time, simply and honestly, because shock and grief can prevent a clear understanding the first time a person is informed.

This stage includes feelings of sorrow, emptiness, and helplessness. Uncontrollable spontaneous weeping or complete apathy may be observed. The family may deny the existence of the disability while mourning the death of the ideal child or the loss of their dreams and former relationships. Their thoughts focus on their own personal loss. Denial is healthy in that it allows the family members to absorb the reality slowly, at their own pace. Obtaining a second opinion during this period helps to confirm the reality of the situation and also helps to engender confidence and trust in the physician. The phase of shock and denial may last several days to several months. A family that continues in the denial phase for years may exhaust themselves physically, emotionally, and financially while searching for a doctor who will deny the diagnosis or promise a "miracle cure." Stage 1 is characterized by both *cognitive and affective denial.*

STAGE 2. Stage 2 is characterized by *cognitive awareness* of the deviation from the dream child but continued *affective denial.* This awareness results in intense anger, hostility, and the need to fight anything or anyone who is connected with the disability or who imposes confrontation with reality.[13] As family members continue to search for an answer to "Why me?" and to affix blame to an event or person, they may become angry with each other, other (normal) children, professionals, society in general, or themselves. Seventy percent to 80% of parents admit to having some feelings of revulsion during the first months of a disabled child's life. Some even admit that they wished the child would die.[13] These feelings, though normal, can lead to guilt, anger, depression, or overcompensation through solicitousness. Anger toward God may be expressed through refusal to attend church or to pray. Since anger toward the disabled person or God may be felt, but is difficult to express, other adults and especially professionals may be used as "safe" emotional scapegoats for the displaced anger.[46] Professionals who are able to recognize that the anger is not a personal attack (even though it may be so verbalized) find it much easier to deal constructively with grief-induced anger. Counterattack or "knee-jerk" responses only increase feelings of guilt and

intensify or prolong family grief. Patient acceptance from professionals is vital.

Anger may also result from a perceived incompetence to produce a whole child or to prevent an accident as well as feelings of incompetence to care for a family member with special needs. The parent may feel hatred toward the child as a source of the threat to self-esteem. Hatred in turn may precipitate feelings of anger and guilt. Encouragement of physical activities that simulate a normal routine and help family members learn any special procedures essential to the care of their loved one may increase feelings of competence and help offset some of the excessive energy generated by feelings of helplessness and anger.

STAGE 3. Stage 3 is characterized by appeals for help. Negative energies generated by *affective awareness* of the reality of the situation are channeled into *cognitive rebellion* and the search for ways to ameliorate the impact of the disability on the person's life. The family may begin to reach out to the physician (provided the relationship is still intact) to explore other diagnostic possibilities or to find a new treatment. Others may spare no expense in their search for an "educational or therapeutic cure." The mother may feel that if she gives the child enough love and attention, the problem will resolve itself, an attitude reminiscent of the magical thought powers of the preschooler.

Families may also begin to bargain with God through increased prayer and church attendance. Pleas are made to God to cure the person in exchange for promises of obedience, service, or financial support. Disenchantment may ensue when no cure is forthcoming.

The positive aspect of stage 3 is that energies are focused toward the reality of the situation rather than toward the loss or a person's own narcissistic hurt.

STAGE 4. Stages 3 and 4 are frequently interchanged and revisited. When all active coping strategies have failed to remove the problem, the family members may lapse into a deep depression, withdrawal, despair, and disorganization. This stage represents the family's complete exhaustion. They have not yet completely accepted reality, but the facts have imposed themselves to the point at which they can no longer be resisted.[13] Defensive retreat—a dulling of reality—appears to be an essential prelude to reorganization and mobilization of constructive coping strategies. There is a final letting go of the ideal in this stage, a very painful process. Olshansky indicates that many parents are never completely able to release the idealized child and continue through life in a state of chronic sorrow.[58] *Cognitively,* the family member has *adapted* to the reality of the situation, but *affective rebellion* leads to sensitivity and vulnerability. The unfairness of life is faced as the person tries to answer, "Why me?" and reassess life values and goals.[69] Bitterness is past, but maintaining optimism and realism is a "full time balancing act."[57]

Rearing a disabled child is a dynamic process in which the parents may need to renegotiate their acceptance of the child and the disability at each major new challenge.[55] Most parents experience residual elements of stage 4 when the child enters a new developmental stage or is faced with new tasks. Periodic grief reactions are normal in the "best adjusted" parents.[38, 85] It is not a denial of facts, but a facing of reality to feel sorrow for the child who experiences difficulty with new tasks (e.g., the tying of shoes by the blind child); is unable to join in an activity enjoyed by the parents (e.g., inability of a deaf child to enjoy a rendition of Handel's *Messiah*; or faces a developmental milestone, e.g., menarche in a Down's syndrome daughter).

Around the child's 18th or 21st birthday, parents may reexperience stress as great as that experienced at the time of the initial diagnosis.[33, 67, 84] When other young adults are leaving home, the parent may feel stress from the lack of independence, yet they may feel that allowing the young person to live in a group home is a form of rejection.[7] Parents may also feel increased stigma from society. There is a big difference between pushing a cute 4 year old versus a gangly 24 year old in a stroller through a shopping mall (Fig. 34-2).[7]

The critical times for parents are (1) when they first suspect or discover a disability; (2) when the child enters public school (5–6 years of age); (3) when the child reaches puberty;[76] (4) when the child leaves school and seeks employment or independent living (18–21 years of age); and (5) when the parents are unable to continue caring for a child because of age or illness. Even parents of normal children feel a sense of loss and stress at these times. Parents of disabled children are forced to face the widening gap between the ideal and the real child once more and make appropriate adjustments without role models and usually with inadequate professional assistance.

Complete resolution of stage 4 may take many months, or even years. How can one realistically accept an uncertain,

FIGURE 34–2.
Parents of severely disabled children are challenged to find appropriate adaptive equipment to enable their disabled child to participate in age-appropriate activities.

unpredictable future? Some family members may never fully resolve this stage.

STAGE 5. Even though family members may retain some residual feelings or behaviors from previous stages, they *cognitively* are able to *accept* the impairment. Even though they may be unhappy about the situation, *affectively,* they are able to *adapt* constructively to the realities of life as they find it. Cognitive acceptance does not mean resignation to the disability but a capacity to appreciate the person's abilities and to develop these, while making realistic modifications in approaches and goals for the person's limitations. The focus becomes maximization of potentials as family members assume roles as active members of the habilitation or rehabilitation team.

STAGE 6. People who reach stage 6 maintain all the positive qualities of stage 5. They are able to mobilize and reorganize priorities, values, and coping strategies sufficiently to be able to *cognitively and affectively accept* the disability. "Acceptance is not a process of denying . . . feelings, but rather of weaving the fact of special needs into your overall lifestyle and getting on with the business of living."[27] Individuals who master stage six transcend the hard realities of life by finding joy in the relationship and pride in the person's accomplishments, however small. No matter how severe the disability, they learn to see beyond the impairment, appreciate the person for what he or she can do, and love the person purely for being who he or she is.[8, 15] These family members actually attain an **attitude of gratitude,** realizing the benefits the challenge has contributed to their own lives and to that of the family. They find themselves richer, deeper, more perceptive and sensitive persons for the challenges faced and the love shared.[3, 10, 15]

Long-Range Adaptations of Parents
Successful completion of the parental grief process requires not only the release of the idealized child but also acceptance of both the **personhood** and **limitations** of the real child. Various combinations of acceptance and denial lead to different long-term parent–child relationships (Table 34-1).

1. When the idealized child is not released, the parents (or parent) may not be able to accept the real child or the disability. For example, 10% of parents place their Down syndrome baby into long-term foster care or adoption. Another 10% to 20% never fully accept the child.[13] Parents are unable to establish synchrony of communication with the *rejected* child and professional assistance may be resisted. Children of these parents are high-risk candidates for failure-to-thrive syndrome. The child may receive adequate physical care but inadequate emotional and social stimulation. The child may be related to more as a bothersome pet than as a respected, cherished person. Some may be physically neglected or their care

TABLE 34–1. LONG-RANGE PARENTAL REACTIONS TO A CHILD WITH A DISABILITY

Type of Reaction	Attitude Toward Child	Attitude Toward Disability	Manifestation of Reaction
Rejection	Rejected	Denied	Neglect of child
Idealization	Accepted	Denied	"Pushing" the child
Pity	Rejected	Accepted	"Smothering" the child
Realistic acceptance	Accepted	Accepted	Constructive guidance

may be relegated to the care of an older sibling, relative, or friend.[52]

2. Some parents retain the *idealized* image of the child and transfer these dreams to the real child. The disability is denied or ignored as the expectations remain unchanged even though the disabled child is unable to fulfill them. The parents may feel that the social stigma of having a disabled child is unbearable and may focus their energies toward retaining their own self-esteem rather than maximizing the child's actual potentials. They may be hostile toward the child and use abusive methods of discipline in trying to make the child meet their goals, partially explaining the increased incidence of child abuse in the disabled population.[87] These parents may continue to seek a miracle cure and to refuse special medical, habilitative, or educational assistance. Some children, picking up on parental discomfort with the disability, avoid sharing concerns about their disability to reduce parental worry or hostility, thus increasing their own stress.[45]

3. A third group of parents completely lose contact with their idealized child. The disability assumes primacy over the personhood of the child.[48] "We have a **disabled** child." The child's "normal" characteristics, uniquenesses, and individuality are eclipsed by the parents' sorrow over the child's defect and in the stereotyped behaviors, limitations or responses they attach to the defect. Their own feelings of guilt may also cause them to concentrate on the disability, or they may attempt to cover up for conscious or subconscious feelings of disgust or rejection toward the child. The end result is intense *pity* for the child who has to live with this burden. Overprotective and smothering behaviors hide or atone for their own negative feelings. The parents attempt to remove all further problems and frustrations from the child. They may become so devoted in their attention that they do not allow the child challenging opportunities for growth; they make the child dependent on them, thus they *create* a handicapped individual. The parents may lose their own identity as they become slaves to the disabling condition or an extension of the child's will. Some parents feel that the disability with its attendant special care needs gives them special status and, thus, may invest their identity and self-worth wholly in the

child,[27] even resisting the child's attempts to become more independent.

4. The parent who is able to release the idealized child and "come to terms" with both the child and the disability is in the best position to deal with the circumstances *realistically* and constructively.[13] This attitude does not imply that all grief over the loss is eradicated, but it does mean that the parent is able to identify both the strengths and needs of the child and extricate the self from narcissistic delusions and personal guilt. This parent may still become irritable from fatigue, depressed by financial concerns, or discouraged by slow progress. However, the child and parent work together to identify and employ compensatory mechanisms to achieve tasks with the parent giving help and guidance only as necessary.[53]

The issues of neglect, unrealistic expectations, lack of synchrony, removal of challenges, denial of individuality, failure to see one's talents and interests, and abuse that are found as expressions of the first three parental attitudes have profound negative effects on the child's development irrespective of disability.[48] These parental behaviors may prove to be more disabling in the long run than the impairment per se.

LIVING WITH A DISABLED FAMILY MEMBER

Entrance of a disabled person into the family alters almost every aspect of family life. Whether the disabled or chronically ill person is a child or an adult, some common problems arise in families.[40, 59] One of the greatest issues concerns finances. At a time when financial needs are increased, the ability of family members to secure employment may be curtailed by the caregiving activities. Many of the expenses, such as transportation to therapy programs or special equipment, are not covered by insurance. Other expenses are hidden, such as long-distance telephone calls for making medical appointments or calls home to the grandparents, siblings, or clergy when a person is hospitalized. Meals away from home during hospitalizations or babysitters for the other children while attending therapy sessions also increase financial output. Extra laundry, damaged clothing and furniture, extra heating, the need for additional domestic help or respite care, as well as essential medical care or therapy not covered by insurance all increase the financial burden of the family (Fig. 34-3).[61] The caregiver may be overwhelmed by the burden of work, and some become housebound because of the disabled person's needs.

The daily grind of care without hope of a letup may lead to "burn out,"[25, 61, 81] especially for single parents.[67] Fifty-two percent of families with mentally handicapped children indicate that they are unable to obtain a babysitter.[61] Families, especially those with young, severely handicapped children or those with aging parents, need referral to respite care centers that offer temporary relief.[5, 22, 34] Unfortunately, not enough care centers are available. Extended care facilities and nursing homes can offer some relief while family members take a well-earned vacation or parents recuperate from their own illnesses.

Disabled Child

Effect on Parents

Approximately one out of every seven families has a handicapped child. The parents face much more than the process of mourning the loss of the dream child and accepting the disabled child; parents wish it were that simple. The mother may feel compelled to stay at home with the child, although

FIGURE 34–3.
One "hidden cost" of disability is the remodeling that may be necessary to accommodate to the special needs of the disabled person.

she had planned to return to work or develop a career. Consequently, the financial base is eroded as well as the potential for career fulfillment. The father may feel a need to find a second job to meet the additional expenses, yet, in actuality, fewer fathers of severely disabled children hold full-time or second jobs in order to be more available at home.[45, 48] Some parents may decide to change jobs to obtain a higher income even though the employment may not meet their own actualization needs. Other families may feel the need to move or to remain in an area where more appropriate medical or educational resources are available, even though it does not offer the opportunities for career advancement or adequate contact with the extended family.

Travel time to and from doctors' offices, clinics, and special education programs can be physically exhausting. Hoping against the odds and facing the uncertainty of the future can be emotionally exhausting. Caring for a child who requires special care or exercises or who is frequently in pain exacts its toll even from an exceptionally stable and mature parent. It is usually the mother who must absorb the pressures of day-to-day care of the severely disabled child, and it is she who "pays the price in terms of stress, social isolation, and sheer hard work."[61] The father usually maintains a fairly routine schedule of employment outside the home, but the mother's responsibilities gradually increase as she must drive the child to clinics, ongoing therapy programs, and preschool programs. It is usually the mother who remains at the hospital with the child if surgery is scheduled or if serious complications require specialized care.[38, 49] It is also usually the mother who searches the stores for special food products or equipment to meet the child's needs, implements a therapy program at home, cooks the special diet, or performs the dressing, toilet care, and general activities of daily living that the child is unable to perform. All of these activities are added to the mother's other responsibilities of managing the home and caring for other children. No wonder she feels as if she needs a private secretary to keep it all straight and to help orchestrate events. Unless the father is able to give her intimate emotional support and some relief from these responsibilities, she may have little or no time for the development of her own interests or for meeting her own needs as an individual.[48, 51, 67] His emotional warmth is crucial to her mental health. About 50% of fathers, because of family structure, parenting concepts, or work hours, may be excluded from the parenting role but may still play a significant role in supporting the spousal relationship.[36, 48] Adolescent siblings offer the most help within the home, but when they leave home for college or career, the parental burden is once more increased.[61]

The delay in the infant's use of interactional tools may discourage the parents who need reinforcement that they are "being good parents."[48] Family interaction time, leisure-time activities, pursuit of personal interests, and private time are reduced or thwarted. When outings are planned, the parents with a severely disabled child may have to pack a wheel chair, special eating utensils, extra clothes, medications, special toys, and other accoutrements essential to the functioning, care, or independence of the child. Physical and emotional exhaustion, fear of another pregnancy, and limited amounts of time available for intimate privacy may interfere with the parent's sexual life, again increasing their sense of personal isolation.[47] Parents who find personal "release time" through family, friends, or temporary respite care services are able to engage in activities that allow them to communicate more effectively and enjoy each other's companionship. Some parents are so entrenched in care that they don't know what to do with the time when respite is offered. At times, respite can increase marital discord because the couple have used the busy schedule to mask or avoid facing problems.[67] Parents need to take time to pursue their couple relationship separate from their role as parents.[75] Many counselors recommend that parents continue to "date" each other at least once a month to maintain their love relationship. Those who experience more control over their lives are able to have warmer, more satisfying relationships with their child.[32] In spite of the increased stress, however, an increased incidence of divorce is not documented in recent literature.[13, 45, 48, 66, 73, 79] When it does occur, it is generally due to preexisting problems aggravated by the new stressor or inadequate communication time.[53, 75] Most parents of disabled children report a strengthening of their relationship and feel that they have become "better people" for the experience.[79]

Parents who have only one (disabled) child need to consider the kind of life they will have in 20 years. Some parents involve themselves in the needs of their disabled child so much that other aspects of their lives are neglected. Personal pursuits may be eclipsed by the needs of the child. If the child dies or is institutionalized later, the parents may suddenly feel abandoned; they have fought against the odds through the years and are left with nothing. They may feel that their lives have been wasted on an individual who could never adequately repay their efforts by becoming more independent. They may feel that they are left without an identity or a future. The parents may find they are strangers to each other and may feel alienated again, or still. A second child may help to give them a sense of personal worth and accomplishment, help to maintain a sense of normalcy in family life, and offer relief from the intensity of care and entertainment the disabled child may need. A physically and mentally normal child can draw out, nurture, and challenge the disabled child in ways the parents never dreamed.[63] Everyone can have healthier lives with a second or a third child. Siblings can have a normalizing effect on the whole family.[74] On the other hand, if the parents have a second child to "compensate" for the loss of the ideal child, then everyone can be negatively affected.[53] If the risk of another disabled child is too great, children can be added by adoption. The family with a disabled child may find life difficult, but life can also be enormously enriched by the child's presence.

Effect on Siblings

Children are effected negatively or positively by the presence of a disabled family member depending on parental handling.[23, 63, 70, 79] If the parents attempt to hide the fact of the

disability, the truth may be distorted by youthful imaginations working overtime.[50] They may begin to wonder if the disability is their fault or if it might happen to them also.[65] As children get older, other issues arise, such as concerns about their own offspring and future responsibilities to the disabled sibling.[40] When the impairment is the result of a genetic factor, the siblings and extended family members should have genetic counseling to help them with family planning. Adult siblings are frequently concerned about the long-term and postparental care of the disabled sibling.[63]

Some siblings are able to take life with a disabled family member in stride and include the disabled individual as much as possible in the normal activities of family life and daily living. Others have unique problems to face when the impaired child bites, breaks toys, masturbates in public, or screeches unexpectedly.[62] They have to face peer teasing, or they may even be justifiably afraid of the handicapped sibling.[50] They may feel caught between the need for peer group identity and the need to protect the atypical sibling.[12] Siblings may experience loneliness and the same array of feelings that parents experience.[23, 50, 63] Some even feel guilty about their own good health.[64, 67] Some try to protect their parents from additional burdens by keeping feelings and problems to themselves.[23] They may also feel anger toward the disabled child for causing the parents' pain.[13] Children adapt and accept the situation as the parents adjust (Fig. 34-4).

Sibling rivalry can be intense if the child has to compete for parental resources and attention.[23, 51, 53, 63] Some "normal" children may resent the abnormal home life and the intrusion

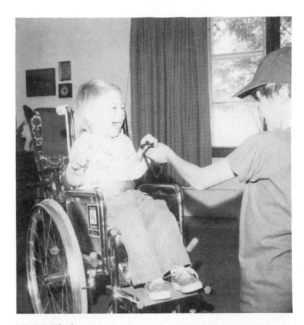

FIGURE 34–4.
The presence of a disabled person within the home can help children become more empathetic and sensitive to the needs of others. The experience can help hasten the transition from an egocentric to an allocentric orientation.

on their own developmental experiences or the extra time the handicapped child extracts from the parents.[63] When each child is given individual time with the parents, stress can be reduced.[23,64,65] Siblings need to be encouraged to pursue their own interests, activities, and friends separate from the disabled child.[23,48,51,64] Siblings need respite too!

Mutual sharing of feelings, mutual planning for the future, and mutual involvement in the habilitation program can help siblings develop mature responsibility and respect for human rights and dignity.[50] It should be emphasized again that the total family can be drawn closer together by the event when communication lines remain open and individuality is respected.

A potential source of problems is the sibling who becomes overinvolved in the care or responsibility for the disabled child. They may in reality function as a surrogate parent.[13,53,63] Some young adults may change their life plans to continue to care for a disabled family member. Other siblings may feel an obligation to compensate for all the parental frustrations and disappointments.[53,63,65] Parents should encourage each child to seek and develop individual talents and interests.[4]

Some siblings try to make life easier for the disabled member by "taking over" for the person. They may speak for them, do their chores, or absorb mistakes and misdemeanors, thus unwittingly hindering efforts toward independence. They need to learn to share in the joy of *helping* the disabled person become more independent through facing the challenges of life on their own, complete with mistakes. By including the disabled sibling in games of pretending and in the normal bantering or teasing that occurs in families and by allowing the disabled sibling opportunities for both winning and losing at games, the other siblings can help prepare the disabled child to face the reactions of acquaintances or strangers and the adult world with greater flexibility and resiliency.[50] A sense of humor is invaluable in facing the stressors of life.

Seventy-five percent of parents feel that the siblings are better for the experience of living with a disabled child.[61] Siblings of disabled children tend to show increased acceptance of human differences, greater maturity, and less casual acceptance of good health.[23,48,50,53,63] Many seek careers in which they can advocate and protect the rights of disabled people. Their "on the job training" makes them excellent respite caregivers for other families even during their adolescent years.[63]

Thus far, the chapter's discussion has been limited to the primary family. However, the family does not live in a vacuum. Relationships with the extended family or the community can also facilitate or hinder the parents' long-range adjustment.

Effect on Grandparents

At a time when the parents need someone strong and wise to confide in, 40% find that their own parents may increase rather than share the burden.[13] The grandparents may continue to deny the problem, or they may offer suggestions for care and guidance that may be contrary to professional advice,

thus interfering with the parents' ability to cope realistically with the child's limitations. Occasionally, grandparents may become so distraught that role reversals occur, and the parents end up comforting the grandparents.

Some grandparents may feel embarrassed by the situation and may seek to prevent the news from leaking out to friends and neighbors, especially if the child has a hereditary disorder. One family kept their secret from both sets of in-laws and all friends for more than 10 years by institutionalizing the impaired child at birth. Grandparents may react in anger and attempt to fix the blame to the "poor family stock" of the spouse.[53] "I told you not to marry —." "You might have expected your child to be blind because your wife wears glasses!" (Even though both the father and grandmother wear glasses.) Some grandparents may ignore the existence of the disabled child, relating only to the "normal" grandchildren. These grandparents appear to suffer from even more narcissistic hurt than the parents.

Fortunately, there are also those grandparents who care more deeply about the child than about their hereditary pride and thus attempt to support the parents. The grandparents' pain can be reduced and their support capabilities strengthened if the parents are able to include them in all the information shared by the physician and in the working through of plans. If they live close enough, they can attend medical, therapy, or educational sessions with the parents and provide significant help to the parents by assuming some of the home care activities and by providing transportation and babysitting relief. Paternal grandparent involvement seems to increase the father's involvement with his child.[48] Parents who are isolated from extended family members may find that the emotional and physical burdens of raising a severely disabled child without ready assistance can be taxing on their physical and emotional health.

Effect on Friends

Close friends may experience a grief process similar to that experienced by the parents, grandparents, and siblings. Because of greater distance, however, the reaction is usually not as intense. Some friends are able to empathize with and offer support to the parents. Many others, however, may be so consumed by their own grief, or so concerned that they will increase the parents' stress if they say the wrong thing, that they may avoid the couple to avoid an awkward situation. When they meet on the street, eyes are averted and faces become rigid. The couple suddenly feels as if they have done something terribly wrong, that they are contagious or grossly inferior. Their friends are avoiding them, and they are too stunned or too busy to reach out for help. Their sense of alienation is too intense for words. Families are fortunate indeed who have friends that are still able to see them simply as John and Mary, not as the couple with the **defective** baby, or as if they had ceased to exist. All the parents may need is a shoulder to cry on or someone to listen or to confide in.[26,33,61] Just a friend who listens, no fancy counseling or expert advice, may be all that is needed.

Acquaintances and community members are frequently

curious; this phenomenon is normal but also distressing to the parents, who suddenly feel that they are on public display. Parents may avoid leaving home except for essentials, such as grocery shopping, thus feeling imprisoned in their own homes, another factor that increases feelings of alienation and depression.

Although friends and community members are curious at first, the parents' attitude becomes crucial to the child's acceptance by the community. "The child must depend on his parents to take a stand, to assert his identity as a worthwhile individual."[47] The parents function as role models for the rest of the community in relating to the child. This process is difficult for parents who have no guidelines for themselves. The parents' personal identity must be strong and their acceptance of the child's disability must be high to help change the attitude of the public from one of curiosity and stigma to one of respect, understanding, and acceptance. This change becomes a lifetime process. Contact with other parents of special needs children can facilitate adaptation.[2,72]

Disabled Adult

As people age, the percentage of those with disability increases. Not only do disabled children become disabled adults, but, over time, more people become disabled or chronically ill. Twenty-four percent of people 45 to 64 years of age, and more than half of those older than age 65 are limited by one or more disabling conditions.[43] Although medical advances may increase life spans and the quality of life, in many conditions the state of the art is still inadequate to restore the person to previous functioning levels.

Disabled Parent

When a person with children in the home is disabled, the responsibilities for maintaining the family system frequently need to be reassigned.[56] The nondisabled parent may "burn out" from the increased load (Fig. 34-5). Children may have to assume responsibilities beyond their years. Children may feel obligated to abbreviate their educational pursuits because of limited financial resources or the need for home care assistance while the nondisabled parent works. Depending on the degree of disability and dependency, the nondisabled parent may feel that the responsibilities are too great to maintain the family as a separate system, forcing the disabled member back to the family of origin or into a nursing home.

The extent of the disability, financial security, age of the children, and availability of extended family or close friends to assist with the reassignment of family tasks (as well as the new responsibilities) are critical components in the ability of the family to adapt to the new circumstances. Children may become resentful of the usurpation of their time or may rally to the task, achieving new levels of self-understanding and maturity. Their reactions depend on the previous child–parent relationship as well as parental handling at the time. The nondisabled parent may try to manage the grief, fear, or questions of the children without having resolved them personally. Some children, especially those with mentally ill mothers, may be scarred for life.[20,29,56] Professional counseling is valuable as the children grieve the loss of the old (the known parent and lifestyle) while adjusting to the new (disabled parent and assumption of responsibilities).

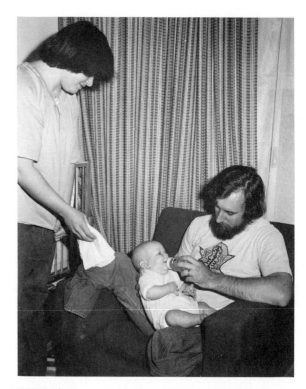

FIGURE 34–5.
Most disabilities do not prevent active participation in family or parenting responsibilities, although modifications of approach may be necessary (see Chap. 17).

Disabled Spouse

The spouse also needs counseling and time to work through the grief of losing the known partner and adjusting to the new. Sex life may become nonexistent; financial stability may be eroded; the individual may feel inadequately prepared to assume the necessary responsibilities; social contacts may be curtailed while interaction with professionals is increased. In short, the person mourns what the person started out to be in addition to the companionship and goals lost to the disability.[1,39] Family dynamics, locus of power, communication patterns, financial status, and personal identity may all be affected.[1] A sharp decrease in the quality of life as well as life satisfaction may occur as goals and leisure-time activities are released. Medical personnel find that they must deal with *two* patients: "Patient at home, partner now at risk."[9] Six new tasks arise for the nondisabled spouse:[56]

1.   Deal with the ill partner's pain, disfigurement, disability.
2.   Deal with the partner's emotional response to the illness.

3. Deal with medical personnel and procedures.
4. Preserve a positive image of and relationship with the partner.
5. Meet own social needs.
6. Maintain balanced perspective on life

In spite of all these barriers, most families with disabled adults find highly adaptive lifestyles. Some may even emerge enriched by the experience as they undergo major adjustments in their value systems and priorities, which in turn enable them to appreciate in a new way the value of health, family, and friends as well as a deeper purpose in life.

Older Adults

Both the older person and the family member enter into the new relationship with a history of interactions that may facilitate or impede the new relationship.[71] Typically, caring for dependent older adults is associated with high levels of interpersonal and intrapersonal tension and increased physical complaints.[6] Role reversals, increased responsibilities, conflict over money or inheritance, and resentment toward uninvolved family members all elevate stress levels.[78]

Alzheimer's disease or senile dementia creates special problems for the family because of the loss of memory, disorientation, personality changes, and loosening of inhibitions.[25, 54] Family members frequently experience increased frustration or embarrassment when the person's public behaviors break social conventions. Loss of a communication partner and decreased social contacts lead to loneliness for the spouse. Forgetfulness, night wanderings, poor judgment, and demands for attention may require constant vigilance. Incontinence, poor eating habits, and inability to care for or entertain one's self increase the partner's workload. Stress may be compounded when it is difficult to determine if negative behaviors are part of the medical problem or deliberate provocations.[25, 78] Caregiver stress is greatly decreased when affection, appreciation, and support can be offered by the disabled partner or other people.[54, 71]

MAXIMIZING FAMILY POTENTIALS

Broad-based support of the total family system, with its own cultural and ethnic influences and goals, has more positive results than the traditional therapy-centered approach.[16, 42, 83] Concentration on facilitating activities of daily living seems to be more effective than a pure therapy–exercise regime.[33] "Intervention may be seen as 'part of the burden of care' rather than part of the solution"[48] unless a holistic approach is employed. Including family members as integral, respected members of the team is crucial since they have continuity with the client and often are the determining factor in the success of a program. Family members need information about issues beyond therapy: concerns about normal child development, discipline, realistic expectations, communication techniques, sexuality, finances, educational options, respite care, and personal depression may outweigh concerns about the client's

muscle tone or dietary restrictions. Timely, effective counseling can help to maintain family integrity and personal growth of the individual members.

Immediate Assistance to Families

Whether the practitioner is a physician, nurse, psychologist, minister, social worker, therapist, or teacher, three fundamental concepts of successful counseling are offered:

1. **Acceptance** of feelings, perceptions, and cultural values of the client. This concept does not mean that the practitioner agrees with these feelings but that one must acknowledge the feelings as real and painful (and usually normal) to the client and accept them on that basis.
2. **Assistance** for the client to see the reality of the situation in a healthy, constructive way. This concept may require reassessment of values and priorities, which is a difficult task that involves disequilibrium before reintegration of the self-system.
3. **Empowerment** of family members to maintain control over important aspects of family functioning and therapy.

The counselor cannot force a client to agree with new views; neither can the practitioner help the client see reality if the practitioner does not openly accept and deal with the client's viewpoint and feelings. The client must feel respected, accepted, and understood before sufficient energy is available to accept, understand, and implement ideas that the practitioner has to offer.

Since no one can predict with complete accuracy, negative predictions that tend to increase anxiety unnecessarily should be avoided. However, family members should be informed of realistic alternatives and the critical factors, such as education, interpersonal relationships, and therapy, that can influence quality of life and the disabled person's future. Discuss the disabled person's condition in terms of the present and the near future, emphasizing the family's role in maximizing the person's current potentials.

The practitioner can offer the family members support in their expressions of grief. Reassuring them that such feelings are normal can be therapeutic; stoicism may be a pathological behavior, not a healthy one (see Chap. 19). Physical symptoms, such as fatigue, weakness, aching, emptiness, headache, frequent sighing, or shortness and tightness of breath, can all be closely related to grief and need to be treated accordingly.[41]

Two helpful hints can be shared with family members. The first is to **take one day at a time.** When people try to see the whole future at once, they are overwhelmed. Many anticipated problems never materialize when the needs of each day are met successfully. Second, in the case of a disabled child, the parents should **see the child as a person first and interact on that basis,** at times pretending a bit if they must (e.g., it may make parents feel better to hang a mobile over the crib of a blind infant). The parents should be encouraged to play with and talk to the child (even the deaf child) and to *vary their care and attention only as absolutely dictated by the disability.* In short, the family should **enjoy the child as a person.**

Parents may need much support in recognizing the emotional needs of the infant or child. Although disabled, **the infant still exhibits more normalcy than deviancy.** Families are frequently told to "treat him or her as you would any other baby." Although this advice is good for most situations, it may be difficult for parents to understand or accept (Fig. 37-6). The infant still needs food, shelter, clothing, and protection. Most of all, the child needs the same discipline, challenges, reciprocity, playtime, warmth, and love that is offered to every other child. **The individual will continue to grow up with or without the parents' help, and the impairment will still be there when the individual reaches adulthood. However, a child will grow up more successfully and better able to face life independently if he or she has had the parents' love, accep-**

FIGURE 34–6.
When disabled family members are fully integrated into family and community life, their sense of life satisfaction is increased and the negative effects of stigmatization are decreased. They help the community become aware of their "humanness" and "abilities," rather than the disabilities.

tance, and realistic guidance as an infant and young child. Inadequate parental acceptance and support can prevent realization of the child's full potentials.

Long-Range Assistance for Family Members

Developmental tasks remain the same for individuals and families in spite of disability.[27] Finding alternative strategies for achieving physical and developmental tasks can offer a challenge to the creativity of practitioners and family members, increasing self-esteem when they are successful. Diary keeping can help make progress evident when day-to-day changes are minimal.

Families need to be in touch with agencies that can give them specific ideas or support in meeting the disabled person's special needs. The person gives the family members a diagnosis also a moral responsibility to offer them referral to potential sources of assistance. Too many families are left to find these limited sources on their own. Newly diagnosed individuals and their families can receive very real support from someone else who has been through the same experience, and their sense of isolation can be greatly reduced. Early contact with the local school system can facilitate the early planning for appropriate services, placement, and equipment. All states have Early Intervention Programs (EIP) for disabled children that start at birth. The state Bureau of Vocational Rehabilitation offers training and educational services for disabled adults.

CONCLUSION

The entrance of a disabled member into the family is one of the most pervasive and stressful experiences that a family can face. It is a multidimensional event that will ultimately influence almost every aspect of family life.[86] The disabled person needs to be challenged and supported in efforts to become or remain an active member of the family system (see Appendix G for resources). Complete dependency is demoralizing and stifling to all involved.

The attitude of the parents profoundly affects the degree of independence, physically and emotionally, that a child will achieve by the young adult years. The parents need to accept the disability before the child can accept it; the child needs to accept the disability before he or she can accept the self; he or she needs to accept the self before he or she can enjoy the environment; and he or she needs to enjoy the environment before he or she can learn effectively from it.

One of the practitioner's roles is to support the family's expressions of grief while helping members identify strengths in both themselves and in the disabled family member. Many families find it helpful to have contact with an older child or adult with the same disability who is adapting successfully to the activities of daily living. It helps both the family members and the disabled person to realistically identify ways to minimize (not eliminate) disabilities by maximizing abilities. Effective counseling can help families establish effective coping patterns and find new directions and meanings to life that are crucial to the successful long-range adaptation of each family member. *Each member can bring unique pleasure and rewards to the family, but only if given the chance.*

"Sorrow fully accepted brings its own gifts."
—Pearl Buck

REFERENCES

1. Anderson, R., & Bury, M. (Eds.). (1988). *Living with chronic illness: The experience of patients and their families.* London, UK: Unwin Hyman.

2. Association for the Care of Children's Health. (1987). *Parent resource directory for parents and professionals caring for children with chronic illness or disabilities.* Rockville, MD: Office for Maternal and Child Health Services. (ERIC Document Reproduction Service No. ED 289 269)

3. Avini, M. (1988). Ears that listen and understand perfectly. *Education of the Visually Handicapped, 20*(2), 72–73.

4. Baird, D. I. (1987). *Dorothee, the silent teacher: A family forgives disaster.* Kansas City, MO: Beacon Hill Press of Kansas City.

5. Biklen, D., & Knoll, J. (1987). The disabled minority. In S. J. Taylor, D. Biklen, & J. Knoll (Eds.), *Community integration for people with severe disabilities* (pp. 3–24). New York: Teacher's College Press.

6. Brody, E. (1985). Patient care as a normative family stress. *The Gerontologist, 25,* 19–29.

7. Brotherson, M. J., Backus, L. H., Summers, J. A., & Turnbull, A. P. (1986). Transition to adulthood. In J. A. Summers (Ed.), *The right to grow up: An introduction to adults with developmental disabilities* (pp. 17–44). Baltimore: Paul H. Brookes.

8. Buck, P. S. (1973). *The child who never grew.* Bath, England: Chivers.

9. Bury, M. (1988). Meanings at risk: The experience of arthritis. In R. Anderson & M. Bury (Eds.), *Living with chronic illness: The experience of patients and their families* (pp. 89–116). London: Unwin Hyman.

10. Buscaglia, L. (Ed.). (1983). *The disabled and their parents: A counseling challenge.* Thorofare, NJ: Slack.

11. Corbin, J. M., & Strauss, A. (1988). *Unending work and care: Managing chronic illness at home.* San Francisco: Josey-Bass.

12. Crouthamel, C. S. (1988). Siblings of handicapped children. *Early Childhood Development and Care, 37,* 119–131.

13. Cunningham, C. (1987). *Down's syndrome: An introduction for parents* (rev. ed.). Cambridge, MA: Brookline Books.

14. Deutsch, H. (1945). *The psychology of women* (Vol. II). New York: Grune and Stratton.

15. DeVinick, C. (1988). *The power of the powerless.* New York: Doubleday.

16. Dunst, C. J., Trivette, C. M., & Deal, A. G. (1988). *Enabling and empowering families: Principles and guidelines for practice.* Cambridge, MA: Brookline Books.

17. Dyson, L. (1987, November). *Parent stress, family functioning and social support in families of young handicapped children.* Paper presented at the National Early Childhood Conference on Children With Special Needs, Denver, CO. (ERIC Document Reproduction Service No. ED 294 335)

18. Dyson, L., & Fewell, R. R. (1986). Stress and adaptation in parents of young handicapped and nonhandicapped children: A comparative study. *Journal of the Division for Early Childhood, 10*(1), 25–34.

19. Engel, G. L. (1961). Grief and grieving. *American Journal of Nursing, 64*(9), 93.

20. Feldman, R. A., Stiffman, A. R., & Jung, K. G. (1987). *Children at risk: In the web of parental mental illness.* New Brunswick, NJ: Rutgers University Press.

21. Fraiberg, S. (1974). Blind infants and their mothers. In M. Lewis & L. A. Rosenblum (Eds.), *The effect of the infant on its caregiver.* New York: Wiley.

22. Gafford, L. S. (1987). Respite care. In H. M. Wallace, R. F. Biehl, L. Taft, & A. C. Oglesby (Eds.), *Handicapped children and youth: A comprehensive community and clinical approach* (pp. 239–250). New York: Human Services Press.

23. Gallo, A. M. (1988). The special sibling relationship in chronic illness and disability: Parental communication with well siblings. *Holistic Nursing Practice, 2*(2), 28–37.

24. Gerring, J. P. (1988). Behavioral and emotional conditions of handicapped adolescents. In J. P. Gerring & L. P. McCarthy (Eds.), *The psychiatry of handicapped children and adolescents* (pp. 73–99). Boston: Little, Brown.

25. Gilhooly, M. L. M. (1987). Senile dementia and the family. In J. Orford (Ed.), *Treating the disorder, treating the family* (pp. 138–168). Baltimore: The John Hopkins University Press.

26. Goar, A. (1988). Information has been the most valuable thing. *Education of the Visually Handicapped, 20*(2), 73–74.

27. Goldfarb, L. A., Brotherson, M. J., Summers, J. A., & Turnbull, A. P. (1986). *Meeting the challenge of disability or chronic illness: A family guide.* Baltimore: Paul H. Brookes.

28. Goldiamond, B. (1982). Families of the disabled: Sometimes insiders in rehabilitation, always outsiders in policy planning. In M. G. Eisenberg, C. Griggins, & R. J. Duval (Eds.), *Disabled people as second class citizens* (pp. 152–170). New York: Springer.

29. Goodman, S. H. (1987, April). *The developmental course of young children with emotionally disturbed mothers.* Paper presented at the biennial meeting of the Society for Research in Child Development, Baltimore, MD. (ERIC Document Reproduction Service No. ED 294 401)

30. Hatfield, A. B., & Lefley, H. P. (Eds.). (1987). *Families of the mentally ill: Coping and adaptation.* New York: The Guilford Press.

31. Hildebrandt, K. A., & Fitzgerald, H. E. (1983). The infant's physical attractiveness: Its effect on bonding and attachment. *Infant Mental Health Journal, 4,* 3.

32. Huntington, G. S. (1987, April). *Maternal and handicapped child characteristics associated with maternal involvement behavior.* Paper presented at the biennial meeting of the Society for Research in Child Development. Baltimore, MD. (ERIC Document Reproduction Service No. ED 290 274)

33. Hutinger, P. (1988). Stress: Is it an inevitable condition for families of children at risk? *Teaching Exceptional Children. Summer,* 36–39.

34. Janicki, M. P., Krauss, M. W., Cotten, P. D., & Seltzer, M. M. (1986). Respite services and older adults with developmental disabilities. In C. L. Salisbury & J. Intagliata (Eds.), *Respite care: Support for persons with developmental disabilities and their families* (pp. 51–67). Baltimore: Paul H. Brookes.

35. Kanat, J. (1987). *Bittersweet baby.* Minneapolis, MN: CompCare Publishers.

36. Kazak, A. E., & Marvin, R. S. (1984). Differences, difficulties and

adaptation: Stress and social networks in families with a handicapped child. *Family Relations, 33*(1), 67–78.

37. Kennell, J., Slyter, H., & Klaus, M. (1970). The mourning response of parents to the death of a newborn infant. *New England Journal of Medicine, 283,* 344.

38. Knafl, K. A., Deatrick, J. A., & Kodadek, S. (1982). How parents manage jobs and a child's hospitalization. *Maternal Child Nursing, 7,* 125

39. Lefley, H. P. (1987). The family's response to mental illness in a relative. In A. B. Hatfield (Ed.), *Families of the mentally ill: Meeting the challenges* (pp. 3–21). San Francisco: Josey-Bass.

40. Levy, J. M. (1988). Family response and adaptation to a handicap. In J. P. Gerring & L. P. McCarthy (Eds.), *The psychiatry of handicapped children and adolescents* (pp. 215–246). Boston: Little, Brown.

41. Lindemann, E. (1965). Acute grief: Symptoms and management. *Child and Family, 4,* 73.

42. Lipsky, D. K. (Ed.). (1987). *Family supports for families with a disabled member* (Monograph No. 39). New York: International Exchange of Experts and Information in Rehabilitation, World Rehabilitation Fund. (ERIC Document Reproduction Service No. ED 287 264)

43. Lubkin, I. M. (1986). *Chronic illness: Impact and interventions.* Boston: Jones and Bartlett.

44. Lynch, E. C., & Staloch, N. H. (1988). Parental perceptions of physicians communication in the informing process. *Mental Retardation, 26*(2), 77–81.

45. Madge, N., & Fassam, M. (1982). *Ask the children: Experiences of physical disability in the school years.* London, UK: Batsford Academic and Educational Limited.

46. Margolis, H., Shapiro, A., & Brown, G. (1987). Resolving conflicts with parents of handicapped children. *The Urban Review, 19,* 209–221.

47. McCollum, A. T. (1975). *Coping with prolonged health impairment in your child.* Boston: Little, Brown.

48. McConachie, H. (1986). *Parents and young mentally handicapped children: A review of research issues.* Cambridge, MA: Brookline Books.

49. McKeever, P. T. (1981). Fathering the chronically ill child. *Maternal Child Nursing, 6,* 124.

50. Meyer, D. J., Vadasy, P. F., & Fewell, R. R. (1985). *Living with a brother or sister with special needs: A book for sibs.* Seattle: University of Washington Press.

51. Millard, D. M. (1984). *Daily living with a handicapped child.* London, UK: Croom Helm.

52. Monsen, R. (1986). Phases in the caring relationship: From adversary to ally to coordinator. *Maternal Child Nursing, 11,* 316–318.

53. Murphy, A., & Crocker, A. C. (1987). Impact of handicapping conditions on the child and family. In H. M. Wallace, R. F. Biehl, L. Taft, & A. C. Oglesby (Eds.), *Handicapped children and youth: A comprehensive community and clinical approach* (pp. 26–41). New York: Human Services Press.

54. Murphy, C. (1988). *Day to day: Spiritual help when someone you love has Alzheimer's.* Philadelphia: The Westminster Press.

55. Murphy, M. A. (1982). The family with a handicapped child: A review of the literature. *Developmental and Behavioral Pediatrics, 3*(2), 73.

56. Nichols, K. A. (1987). Chronic physical disorder in adults. In J. Orford (Ed.), *Treating the disorder, treating the family* (pp. 62–85). Baltimore: The Johns Hopkins University Press.

57. Norgel, M. J. (1988). My goal: Keeping things in perspective. *Education of the Visually Handicapped, 20*(2), 76–77.

58. Olshansky, S. (1962). Chronic sorrow: A response to having a mentally defective child. *Social Casework, 43,* 190.

59. Orford, J. (1987). Integration: A general account of families coping with disorders. In J. Orford (Ed.), *Treating the disorder, treating the family* (pp. 266–293). Baltimore: The Johns Hopkins University Press.

60. Orford, J. (1987). Introduction. In J. Orford (Ed.), *Treating the disorder, treating the family* (pp. 1–6). Baltimore: The Johns Hopkins University Press.

61. Pahl, J., & Quine, L. (1987). Families with mentally handicapped children. In J. Orford (Ed.), *Treating the disorder, treating the family* (pp. 39–61). Baltimore: The John Hopkins University Press.

62. Powell, T. H., & Hecimovic, A. (1981). *Respite care for the handicapped: Helping individuals and their families.* Springfield, IL: Thomas.

63. Powell, T. H., & Ogle, P. A. (1985). *Brothers and sisters: A special part of exceptional families.* Baltimore: Paul H. Brookes.

64. Powell, T. H., & Ogle, P. A. (1986). Brothers and sisters: Addressing unique needs through respite care services. In C. L. Salisbury & J. Intagliata (Eds.), *Respite care: Support for persons with developmental disabilities and their families* (pp. 29–49). Baltimore: Paul H. Brookes.

65. Russell, P. (1985). *The wheelchair child: How handicapped children can enjoy life to its fullest.* Englewood Cliffs, NJ: Prentice-Hall.

66. Sabbeth, B. F., & Leventhal, J. M. (1984). Marital adjustment to chronic childhood illness: A critique of the literature. *Pediatrics, 73,* 762–768.

67. Salisbury, C. L. (1986). Parenthood and the need for respite. In C. L. Salisbury & J. Intagliata (Eds.), *Respite care: Support for persons with developmental disabilities and their families* (pp. 3–28). Baltimore: Paul H. Brookes.

68. Schuster, C. S. (1981). Unpublished research.

69. Schuster, C. S. (1989). Why me, God? *Christian Parenting, 1*(3), 19–20.

70. Senapati, R., & Hayes, A. (1988). Sibling relationships of handicapped children: A review of conceptual and methodological issues. *International Journal of Behavioral Development, 11*(1), 89–115.

71. Sheehan, N. W., & Nuttall, P. (1988). Conflict, emotion, and personal strain among family caregivers. *Family Relations, 37,* 92–98.

72. Shelton, T. L. (1987). *Family-centered care for children with special health care needs.* Rockville, MD: Office for Maternal and Child Health Services. (ERIC Document Reproduction Service No. ED 288 321)

73. Silbert, A. R., Newberger, J. W., & Flyer, D. C. (1982). Marital stability and congenital heart disease. *Pediatrics, 69,* 747–750.

74. Simeonsson, R. J., & McHale, S. M. (1981). Review: Research on handicapped children: Sibling relationships. *Child: Care, Health and Development, 7,* 153.

75. Simons, R. (1987). *After the tears.* San Diego: Harcourt Brace Jovanovich.

76. Smith, S. (1983). The link between sexual maturation and "adolescent grieving" in parents of the dependent disabled. *Sexuality and Disability, 6*(3/4), 150–154.

77. Solnit, A. J., & Stark, M. H. (1961). Mourning and the birth of a defective child. *Psychoanalytical Study of the Child, 16,* 523.

78. Springer, D., & Brubaker, T. (Eds.). (1984). *Family care and dependent elderly: Minimizing stress and maximizing independence.* Beverly Hills, CA: Sage.

79. Thomas, R. B. (1987). Family adaptation to a child with a chronic illness. In M. H. Rose & R. B. Thomas (Eds.), *Children with chronic conditions: Nursing in a family and community context* (pp. 29–54). Orlando, FL: Grune and Stratton.

80. Thomas, R. B. (1987). Introduction and conceptual frame. In M. H. Rose & R. B. Thomas (Eds.), *Children with chronic conditions: Nursing in a family and community context* (pp. 3–12). Orlando, FL: Grune and Stratton.

81. Turnbull, A. P., & Turnbull, H. R. (1978). *Parents speak out: Views from the other side of the two-way mirror.* Columbus, OH: Charles C. Merrill.

82. United Nations. (1986). *Disability: Solution, strategies and policies: United Nations decade of disabled persons, 1983–1992.* New York: United Nations Department of International Economic and Social Affairs.

83. Werth, L. H., & Oseroff, A. B. (1987). Continual counselling intervention: Lifetime support for the family with a handicapped member. *The American Journal of Family Therapy, 15,* 333–342.

84. Wikler, L. (1981). Chronic stress of families of mentally retarded children. *Family relations, 30,* 281–288.

85. Winkler, L., Waslow, M., & Hatfield, E. (1981). Chronic sorrow revisited: Parent vs. professional depiction of the adjustment of parents of mentally retarded children. *American Journal of Orthopsychiatry, 51,* 63.

86. Woods, N. F., Yates, B. C., & Primomo, J. (1989). Supporting families during chronic illness. *Image: Journal of Nursing Scholarship, 21*(1), 46–50.

87. Zantal-Wiener, K. (1987). *Child abuse and the handicapped child* (Digest #446). Reston, VA: Clearinghouse on Handicapped and Gifted Children. (ERIC Document Reproduction Service No. ED 287 262)

X
THE MIDDLE ADULT YEARS

Contrary to stereotyped cultural beliefs and the influence of mass media, which tout the merits and glories of the young adult years, middlescence can and does encompass the best years of one's life. Many of the pseudoidentities of earlier years have been superseded by an appreciation for the deeper realities of life. Decisions of career, life partner, family, geographic location, and so on have been made. Energies that were focused toward learning the skills, intricacies, and nuances of one's career position or in meeting the dependent, constantly changing needs of children can now be redirected toward continued personal development (hobbies, interests, talents) or toward the broader community (volunteer projects, community development and welfare). As a result, the middlescent years open new doors for personal development, creativity, mentoring, career achievements, and social relationships.

Experience, the perspective of time, and increased knowledge enable middlescents to face life with greater wisdom and equanimity. Even serious issues do not assume the same urgency or consume as much energy as during earlier years. As a result, healthy middlescents tend to take a broader view of their "world," to appreciate life more fully, and to tap into their assets more completely than younger adults. The physical energy, stamina, and abilities of most middlescents remain high with regular exercise, attention to nutrition, and routine health care. In short, middlescents reach peak productivity and satisfaction because of their ability to maximize potentials with minimal use of energy; maturity is finally achieved.

Developmental Tasks of Middlescence

*1. Find self-confidence in inner identity, values
- Reevaluate and solidify or modify personal convictions
- Differentiate between self-worth and external problems
- Separate personal value from career success or financial status

*2. Balance or come to grips with discrepancies among dreams, goals, and realities
- Readjust goals as necessary
- Put experiences into context of continuities of life
- Make proactive midcourse adjustments

*3. Develop a philosophy for dealing with own mortality
- Expand avenues for spiritual development
- Resolve meaning of death

*4. Identify and share factors that give life meaning and continuity
- Identify and develop active and latent talents and interests
- Evaluate keys to personal success
- Share traditions, culture, folklore, and skills with younger generations
- Provide formal and informal mentor relationships
- Assume leadership roles

*5. Extend sense of caring and responsibility beyond the immediate
- Families of origin or creation
- Neighborhood
- Church and organizations
- Immediate community
- Extended community (state, national, international)

6. Develop wisdom
- Separate affective from cognitive domain for decision making
- Appreciate needs and views of others
- Evaluate issues in the context of time

7. Establish new relationships with other people
- Revise bonding and commitment to family of creation
- Encourage independence in offspring
- Integrate new persons into family system
- Rebalance power and responsibility as family membership and needs change
- Adjust to aging and death of parents
- Enjoy an active social life with persons of all ages
- Maintain a confidant(e) relationship

8. Find satisfaction in career or job
- Share expertise with younger workers
- Discover ways to improve knowledge and competence
- Plan for retirement

9. Adapt to changes in physical domain
- Climacterium
- Decreased strength and stamina
- Physical appearance
- Biological changes

10. Assume active responsibility for maintaining high-level wellness in all five domains
- Develop self-renewing ability
- Seek new information to maintain currency and promote continued development
- Assume prophylactic health maintenance habits
- Seek consultation as necessary
- Balance work and leisure time
- Balance family and self time
- Develop meaningful leisure-time activities

---

*Tasks marked with an asterisk are deemed most crucial to continued maturation.

Biophysical Development During Middlescence

Shirley S. Ashburn

The physical vigor of youth may have passed, but most middlescents nevertheless continue to experience and enjoy a healthy body throughout midlife. "Middlescence," a term synonymous with both middle-age and midlife, means being in the middle of the age continuum, arbitrarily that period of life between 40 and 60 years of age.

Even though middlescence is characterized by changes in the way the body looks and works, these biophysical changes vary in how and when they appear, being more obvious in some individuals than others. Primary (normal) aging refers to universal changes inherent to the process of aging. Secondary (pathologic) aging results from illness, disease, and other environmental factors that may hasten the aging process.

The quality and quantity of health maintenance behaviors through childhood and early adulthood (e.g., nutrition, treatment of disease, and exercise) directly affect the level of wellness that the middlescent experiences. Those who have cared for their bodies during the early adult years are more likely to enjoy continued good health during middlescence. Likewise, the middlescent who takes proper care of the body during midlife generally is healthier during late adulthood. Yet, despite the best of care, our bodies still age and eventually die. Why?

THEORIES OF HUMAN AGING

No single factor has been isolated to satisfactorily explain all possible causes of aging.[18, 53, 76] Because the domains are interdependent, aging is not solely a function of biophysiology. Although many theories describe how and why aging occurs, no *one* theory is universally accepted by researchers. The aging process is better explained if several of these theories are integrated. This chapter reviews biophysical theories that postulate how aging occurs at either the cellular or organ level.

All individuals go through similar aging processes, but it is not known why some individuals show marked age-related changes at much earlier ages than others, nor why there may be such wide variations in aging among persons in the same family and in similar environments and societies. Starting in infancy, the body is already beginning to age. The body not only ages overtly, but a variety of covert aging changes are constantly occurring (e.g., blood cells go through about 120-day life cycles; the epithelial cells that line the intestines and the skin go through their own specific cycles).[9] It may be difficult to ascertain which are intrinsic and inevitable changes and which are changes imposed on the tissues by common or uncommon external factors (e.g., drugs, stress, illness, accidents, solar exposure, environmental pollutants).

Biological Programming Theory of Aging

The premise of this theory is that each human body contains an **aging chronometer** ("biological clock") that controls the speed of metabolic processes and, ultimately, aging. Some researchers believe this control site is located in the hypothalamus, sending information throughout the body via hormones and neurons. As the organism grows older, the ability of either of these means to transmit information may decline.[76] Other researchers think that an aging control center is located in each body cell, determining the exact number of cell divisions that an individual cell can undergo before dying.[29, 76]

Gene Theory

The gene theory proposes that one or more genes within a person are programmed to initiate or stop functioning of specific processes throughout a person's life span.[27] Since genetic material is passed from generation to generation, this theory is used to explain how aging characteristics and longevity are transmitted from parents to offspring. A person can estimate longevity with a fair degree of accuracy by averaging the natural death age of the four grandparents and two parents.[26]

Gene Mutation Theory

Gene mutations occur spontaneously during cell reproduction or as the result of natural environmental irradiation. Since gene mutations are reproduced in successive body cells, they can result in defective cells or functioning. As successive generations of these transformed cells accumulate, the altered cells modify the functional ability of the tissue or organ of which they are a part and eventually the functional capacity of the person.

Cross-Linkage Theory

The cross-linkage theory proposes that with age the molecular strands of selected cellular proteins (i.e., DNA, collagen, enzymes) connect crosswise (often in the form of chemical bonds between hydrogen atoms).[66] Over time, with the formation of new cross-links, some of these proteins are irreversibly altered structurally and functionally. This alteration, in turn, ultimately causes failure in the cells, tissues, and organs of which the proteins are a part. If DNA becomes cross-linked, it results in damaged chromosomes, and the ability to direct protein synthesis may be adversely affected, including disruption of normal immunological responses by the body. Thus, the person may be unable to adequately fight antigens. Cross-bonding of DNA may also lead to cellular death if it cannot be repaired.[66]

Free Radical Theory

Free radicals, formed as by-products of normal cellular processes, are chemicals that not only alter the molecules of cell membranes but also cause chromosomal mutations. Either way, their cumulative effect may be a gradual contribution to changes commonly associated with aging by reducing cellular function and regenerative mechanisms.[28, 66]

Cellular Garbage Theory

Another theory that involves cellular metabolic by-products is the cellular garbage theory. The accumulation of these wastes eventually "poisons" the cells and decreases their functional ability. These substances, unlike reactive free radicals, are chemically inert.[15] However, they begin to interfere with normal functioning and regenerative cycling of the cell and thus contribute to aging characteristics. One such by-product, lipofuscin, a yellow-brown pigment, is found so commonly in aging cells that it is often referred to as "age pigment."[76] The accumulation of harmful, metabolic by-products and the effects of faulty enzymes due to random errors also contribute to aging changes.

Wear-and-Tear Theories

Wear-and-tear theories support the idea that aging is a programmed process. They propose that each individual, and perhaps each cell, has a specific amount of metabolic energy available, and the rate at which this energy is used determines the person's length of life.[42] When the energy is depleted, cell function stops. Continued functioning depends on the ability of the body to replace the worn-out cells. When enough cells cease to function, and replacement cannot maintain pace with body needs, the organism dies.

Autoimmune Theories

Autoimmune theories state that, as age advances, the immune system is no longer able to correctly distinguish harmful substances (antigens) from normal body proteins. Therefore, the body may begin to form antibodies against its own proteins. This formation results in the body's immune system attacking and destroying its own body cells.[76, 81]

SOMATIC CHANGES

Midlife is not characterized by a sharp turning point when the individual's body suddenly experiences rapid decline and deterioration. Rather, it covers a span of about 20 years when the biophysical balance begins to shift, gradually and inevitably, from peak physical performance to changes that may present new challenges. How well the middlescent body functions is directly correlated with genetic constitution, nutrition, exercise, rest, cognitive awareness, emotional outlook, stress, and concomitant disease or disabilities.

Skeletal System

Bone mass begins to decrease once skeletal growth ceases in early adulthood. Women lose calcium from bone tissues after menopause, resulting in a reduction of 1% to 1.5% decrease in bone density and mass (osteoporosis) each year.[56]

Effects of this bone "softening" leads to an increased risk of osteoporotic fractures.[46] By age 60, 25% of white and Oriental women develop spinal compression fractures; femoral neck fractures begin about 70 to 75 years of age; and by 90, 20% of all white women have experienced a hip fracture. Complications cause one sixth of these women to die within 3 months.[56] The osteoporotic process is reduced when women ingest adequate calcium, engage in weight-bearing exercise, and, after menopause, take estrogen until 75 or 80 years of age.[46, 56]

Males also lose calcium from their bones, but male bone loss may not start until the seventies or eighties and occurs at a slower rate.[76] Since men are not subject to the menopausal hormonal changes, and because their skeletons contain more calcium and are heavier than that of women of the same size, middlescent males possess more bone strength than middlescent females.

As people age, the pressure of gravity gradually compresses the spinal vertebrae. The cartilage between all the vertebrae and both hip joints becomes more limited in regenerating itself; it loses water; it becomes less elastic because of hardening of its collagen fibers.[76] Also, a change in the normal 130° to 135° angle of the hip joints results in a more acute angle (Fig. 35-1).[74] All of these changes result in a slight height decrease. Women who take estrogen before menopause do not experience the height decrease experienced by women who do not take estrogen.[56]

Under the burden of the body's weight and activity, the forefoot (metatarsus) tends to spread. A "bunion" (hallux valgus) develops when the great toe deviates laterally, the metatarsal toe joint hypertrophies, and inflammation of joint tissues ensues. Etiological factors include heredity, lifestyle, and presence of arthritis. Treatment depends on the degree and severity of the deformity. Because many shoes are designed to be narrower in the forefoot than the foot itself, the middlescent can avoid much pain by wearing a properly fitting shoe that provides balance.

Middlescents are prone to "stiff joints," caused by the normal loss of fluid and thinning cartilage in the joints. The key to keeping joint stiffness to a minimum during the middle years is to keep them active. When a joint moves, the bones on either side of it squeeze the cartilage, force metabolic wastes out of the joint, release rich nutrients from the ends of the bones, and redistribute the joint fluid.[53] All of these actions contribute to smoother, more comfortable motion.

Muscular System

Muscle Mass

After early adulthood, skeletal muscle mass begins to reduce, resulting in a decrease in both the number of muscle fibers and in the diameter of the remaining fibers.[76] The number of muscle cells an individual actually loses (and the amount of fat tissue he or she may gain) depends on several factors, including the person's heredity, exercise, and nutrition.

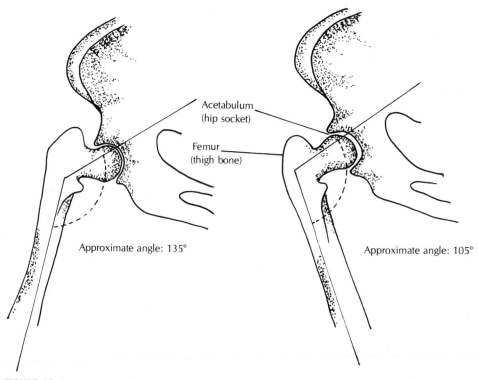

Acetabulum (hip socket)

Femur (thigh bone)

Approximate angle: 135°

Approximate angle: 105°

FIGURE 35–1.
Changes in the hip joint associated with age.

Lower back pain among middlescents may be related to impaired flexibility of the hip and back joints and reduced elasticity of the hamstring muscles.[67, 74] The middlescent who wishes to reduce muscle loss must exercise to maintain or increase muscle tone.

Muscle Strength

With the loss of muscle mass goes an age-related reduction in skeletal muscle strength. The amount of strength that is lost in most people, however, is only about 10% to 20% by the time they reach their 70s.[76] The amount of strength lost differs between individuals; it depends on the level of activity that the person has maintained throughout his or her lifetime. Again, efficient exercise tends to retard atrophy and may actually facilitate gain in muscle strength.[76]

Body Shape and Composition

Many people assume that middlescents experience "middle-age spread," referring to thickened waistlines, protuberant abdomens, and widened derrières. Although it is easy for middlescents to acquire such contour changes, these changes can be avoided through proper diet and adequate exercise.

When an individual loses muscle, whether from aging, a decrease in physical activity, or both, fewer calories are burned. In addition to the normal loss of lean muscle tissue associated with the aging process, unused muscles atrophy and lose many of the enzymes necessary to burn calories.[14, 86] If that person continues to consume the same number of calories, then the unused calories are stored as fat. Initially, the atrophied muscle cells are replaced by fat. This replacement alters the firm contour of the muscle. As additional calories are turned to fat, it is deposited outside the muscle and under the skin (subcutaneous fat). People deposit this excess fat in different places on their bodies.[14] Middlescents in general tend to deposit fat in the thighs, abdomen, waist, back, and upper arms. Females, in general, acquire more body fat than males.[21] Estrogen in women (and androgen that has converted to estrogen in obese males) increases deposition of fat in all subcutaneous tissues, particularly in the buttocks, thighs, and breasts.[21, 74] Most middlescents can prevent this additional fat distribution by appropriate type and amount of exercise and by consuming fewer calories.

Weight

It is obvious from the previous discussion that weight tends to change during midlife. When fat first begins to replace muscle cells, the person may lose weight because fat weighs less than muscle.[76] In terms of body fat content, this individual may be *overfat,* but not necessarily *overweight.* It is when additional fat begins to deposit outside the muscle that the person gains weight.

Neurological System

The functioning of the central nervous system through the early middlescent years is normally maintained at the same high level achieved in young adulthood. Although neurons are lost with aging within the total nervous system, some neurons appear to grow new axons and establish new synapses to compensate for degenerated neurons.[71, 76] The individual may be slower in responding to sudden changes in the environment (this slowness may be due, in part, to the individual's attempt to select the best response), but deep reflexes (e.g., jerk reflexes) remain relatively intact up to age 60.[76]

Visual Changes

Visual changes become noticeable during early middlescence primarily because of **presbyopia,** a gradual decline in the ability to focus on close objects.[37] Other symptoms of decreasing accommodation are eyestrain and fatigue after close work. People who are nearsighted and already wear glasses may begin to find themselves taking their glasses off to read more comfortably. Others find themselves holding reading materials further away. Most middlescents also notice that objects in the distance are initially blurred when they look up from close work. The lens changes shape more slowly in response to ciliary muscle relaxation.[46]

Eyeglasses or contact lenses usually correct these situations. Both nearsighted and farsighted people eventually need either two pairs of glasses (one for reading, one for distance) or bifocals. Some people prefer to substitute contact lenses for glasses. Trifocal glasses allow for clear close, distant, and "arm's length" sight.

Although magnifying lenses and reading glasses are sold over the counter (without prescription), it is best for individuals to have eye examinations by a professional. The visual acuity of the two eyes can vary, and this variation can be diagnosed and treated only by an optometrist or ophthalmologist.

The cells that cover the eyeball and those in the upper and lower eyelid lose moisture during middlescence.[76] Those individuals who perform close work may find the use of lubricating eye drops ("artificial tears") soothing.

The size of the pupil becomes smaller around age 50, resulting in less light entering the eyes.[40] As the eyes' blood supply diminishes in the 50s, a person's visual field is reduced and the retina may become less sensitive to low levels of illumination.[13] This process may lead to "night blindness," or difficulty driving after sundown. Most people discover that increased levels of illumination increase their visual performance. Problems with depth perception, recovery from glare, and adaptation to darkness may also occur (Fig. 35-2).[80]

The normally clear lens of the eye may gradually become more opaque, creating a **cataract.** Cataracts vary in density and size and, if present, are almost always bilateral. Cataracts can accompany diseases such as diabetes but usually are the result of aging and most commonly occur after the age of 50.[87] Eventually, most cataracts are removed because of severely decreased visual acuity.

Auditory Changes

One auditory change of late middlescence is **presbycusis,** a progressive loss of hearing primarily caused by thickening of the capillaries that supply nutrients to the inner-ear struc-

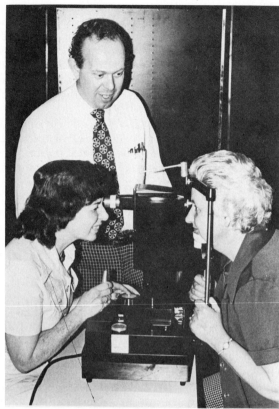

FIGURE 35–2.
Regular visual checkups are critical during middlescence to catch early signs of glaucoma and to make corrective changes in eye glasses or contact lenses to ensure maximal visual acuity.

tures.[76] Presbycusis, sometimes beginning around age 40, occurs more frequently in men than in women. Middlescents with mild presbycusis merely need to place themselves closer to or turn up the source of sound. Presbycusis tends to progress with age, eventually resulting in the need for a hearing aid, but not until the late adult years. People who have abused their auditory system during earlier years through loud music or noisy occupational environments may begin to notice hearing losses.

Other Sensory Changes

Beginning in the middle years, the senses of taste and smell begin to diminish gradually. To date, it is unclear whether these reductions are due to a decrease in taste buds and receptor cells or to other factors.[76]

Cardiovascular System

Heart size does not increase beyond the normal "fist" size in the average middlescent person. However, as middlescence progresses, changes in heart size may be noted in some individuals, with hypertrophy (enlargement) occurring primarily in the left ventricle. Left ventricular hypertrophy may occur independently or may be secondary to arterial hardening. (The left side of the heart must increase its size and muscle mass to force the blood through the narrowed [atherosclerotic] or less resilient [arteriosclerotic] arteries.) The heart chambers gradually become stiffer and more collagen-filled during midlife.[76] These changes may cause both the systolic and diastolic blood pressures to rise during middlescence. It is desirable to keep the blood pressure below 140/90.[16] (Refer to Appendix E for other biophysical parameters.)

These changes gradually slow the amount of blood that passes through the heart each minute. The heart rate at rest and the maximum heart rate during strenuous exercise also decrease. As a result, cardiac output normally decreases about 1% per year.[36] This reduction in cardiac output results in less blood flowing through the arteries and, therefore, reduced oxygen available to the cells in the body.

All of these age-related changes accentuate the importance of following a continuous exercise program to maintain contractibility of the left ventricle, increase cardiac output, improve peripheral circulation, and, therefore, increase oxygen flow to the body.

Some middlescents experience varicose veins. Veins have one-way valves that prevent a backward flow of blood. When these valves become incompetent, some of the blood backflows and causes ballooning of the vein. **Varicose veins** are dilated, tortuous, superficial veins found most commonly on the calves and thighs. Primary varicose veins may develop from hereditary predisposition, pregnancy, standing for long periods of time, or obesity.[7] Signs and symptoms of varicose veins range from cosmetic discoloration to pain, a feeling of heaviness, fatigue, and swelling. If varicose veins are not treated, they can lead to inflamed veins (phlebitis) or a blood clot (thrombophlebitis). Support stockings help some individuals bring these symptoms under control; other people require surgery.

Hematological System

During middlescence, no major changes occur in the blood values, cells, or platelets of the healthy person. Chemical composition of the plasma remains essentially the same as in younger people.[76] The levels of cholesterol, lipids, and low-density lipoproteins (see Chap. 26) tend to increase with age, but regular exercise can help to lower their accumulation on the blood vessel walls.[76]

Respiratory System

The respiratory tissues maintain full vital respiratory capacity (maximum breathing capacity) throughout early middlescence, barring repeated contact with respiratory illnesses, such as pneumonia, asthma, bronchitis, and the common cold. Of these diseases, the first three may cause some residual loss of functioning lung tissue. The functioning of respiratory tissues may be predicated on whether or not the person is a smoker and, if so, the extent and duration of smoking activities. Smoking increases the risk of respiratory diseases and decreases respiratory efficiency.

As the years advance, lung tissue becomes less elastic, resulting in gradually decreased breathing capacity. Respiratory rates increase in response to decreasing pulmonary function (and perhaps decreasing cardiovascular functioning) to maintain adequate cellular and tissue perfusion of oxygen. It is important that the middlescent be "in tune" with the signals his or her body sends at this time and that he or she learns to "pace" the self so as not to become overtired.

Integumentary System

One of the first observations noted about people is the appearance of their skin. Several age-related changes are characteristic of middlescence, although any one individual may display only a few of them.

Elastic fibers in the dermis become less resilient, and skin no longer stretches as tightly across muscles and bones, causing some sagging and wrinkling. During the early adult years, the skin is relatively elastic and follows the receding tissues from which excess fat tissue disappears with weight reduction. Around the age of 40 years, however, an individual who has just completed a significant (and often too-rapid) weight reduction may feel (and act) younger, but actually appears older. This phenomenon is caused by the loose skin folds that cannot recede as readily to accommodate the loss of fat. Flabby skin connotes the presence of an aging integumentary system.[74]

"Bags" under the eyes often accompany middlescence. They are caused by weakening of the underlying muscle and fibrous tissue. Consequently, the subcutaneous fat herniates the weakened tissues, and the skin balloons. The loss of subcutaneous fat as well as diminished skin elasticity can result in the formation of jowls, "double chins," and neck folds. A triangular arch of skin folds also forms below and above the corners of the mouth, travelling upward to the sides of the nose.

Both the dermis and epidermis begin to lose cells at a pace that cannot be replaced. Consequently, the skin begins to thin and may allow substances to permeate the surface cells more easily. Pores enlarge. A middle-age woman may notice that her makeup "goes on" differently. Many women, during late middlescence, outline their lips with a cosmetic lip pencil to prevent lipstick from seeping into the facial tissues that surround the lips. A person may notice that he or she becomes sunburned more easily. It is no surprise that the regular use of the vitamin A derivative, tretinoin ("Retin-A"), which speeds up regeneration of surface skin cells, has become so popular. After the forties, women begin to have thinner skin and less skin collagen than men.[60]

It is ironic that, although subcutaneous fat tends to deposit in some parts of the body, it is lost in other parts. By the time the fourth decade has passed, some subcutaneous tissues just beneath the skin have begun to lose fat. This loss occurs in both males and females and even in obese people. Loss is usually noticed first over the tibia (shin). Loss of subcutaneous fat causes the skin to wrinkle and sag.

As integumentary tissue loses moisture during midlife, it becomes thinner, drier, and more easily bruised or cracked.[74] Increased exposure to the sun over prolonged periods of time accelerates the appearance of dry skin and wrinkles. Wrinkling tends to be less marked and tends to occur later in life in dark-skinned people.[53] Those individuals who have had much exposure to the sun are at high risk to develop skin cancer (see Chap. 26).[76]

As a person grows older, the melanocytes in the epidermis gradually decrease in number, resulting in two age-related skin variations.[76] First, pale patches of skin, called **vitiligo,** may appear where there is not enough melanin to give the usual skin color. Vitiligo may affect any part of the body. It is particularly conspicuous when it occurs among dark-skinned people or when light-skinned people become tanned (except where the melanocytes have been lost). Vitiligo does not disappear, but cosmetic products can easily diminish the contrast between affected areas and the rest of the skin. Those melanocytes still present tend to be larger and group together, forming dark pigmented plaques known as **age spots.**

A **callous,** a thickening of the outer layer of the skin, may be formed where excessive pressure and friction are found. On the feet, a callous may be related to long hours of standing or walking, improper footwear, metatarsal spread, obesity, imbalance of the foot, or arthritis.[7] The uncomfortable sensation of burning underneath a callous is due to pressure on adjacent nerve endings.

Corns are a form of callous that appear on or between the toes. Self-care includes warm soaks and alleviating the cause of pressure and friction. Anyone who suffers from a circulatory disease or diabetes should consult a health professional before attempting treatment.

Hair

Hair color usually darkens with age, but the process is reversed with the onset of graying. Half of the population older than age 50 has at least 50% gray scalp hair, regardless of gender or original hair color.[53] Graying usually begins at the temples of the head.

Hair growth and distribution also change during midlife. A decrease in the number and activity of hair follicles causes a generalized loss or slower growth of most body hair, especially on the scalp.[60, 74] Therefore, scalp hair becomes thinner. The amount and distribution of hair are determined by racial, genetic, and sex-linked factors; almost everyone eventually experiences a diminution of body hair except on the face.

As estrogen production decreases in the female, unopposed adrenal androgens cause coarse facial hair to grow, especially on the chin and around the lips. Some women occasionally grow coarse hairs on their breasts.[34] In males, the hairs of the eyebrows, ears, and nostrils grow faster and become more coarse. Electrolysis can remove hair permanently because it destroys the follicle; shaving, depilatories, or waxing are temporary measures.

Nails

A person's nail growth may slow during middlescence. Nails can become dry and brittle if exposed to chemicals or drying agents, including excessive use of nail polish removers and adhesives.[34]

Cosmetic Surgery

Many men and women choose to alter their bodies through cosmetic surgery. The more popular procedures include rhytidoplasty ("face lift"), rhinoplasty (nose alteration), breast enlargement, breast reduction, and liposuction. Any such procedures should be performed by a physician who is certified by the American Board of Plastic Surgery. Although liposuction permanently alters the body's contours by removing fat cells, it cannot change the dimpled appearance of skin commonly known as cellulite or the deposit of new fat cells. Since aging processes continue, a "face lift" only lasts for 5 to 10 years.[38]

Altered body shape may have both physiological and psychosocial implications. Many people are pleased with the results of their cosmetic surgery. Most of them do not anticipate that the surgery will change their lives; they merely want to improve parts of their bodies that did not match their body concept or that created health problems for them.

Immunological System

Most lymphoid tissue undergoes structural change as a person grows older. Although red bone marrow is slowly replaced by yellow bone marrow as a person ages, the lymphocytes manufactured in the marrow don't appear to decline significantly in number or function during middlescence.[76]

The pharyngeal tonsils are almost completely atrophied in an adult.[76] Many middlescents in the United States do not have their palatine tonsils because they were removed surgically during childhood. It is debatable as to how effective they are in fighting infection during adulthood.

Injured parts of the middlescent's body may take longer to heal than they did in early adulthood. Cellular repair and regeneration appear to have slowed. The middle-age person's body may be more vulnerable to certain diseases than in earlier years.[67,76] However, the average middlescent's ability to resist illness does not depend solely on the biophysical status of the immune system. Those who exercise regularly and receive social support are better able to buffer stress and reduce illness.[39] Middle-age individuals who possess a sense of commitment (as opposed to alienation) and control (rather than powerlessness) and who perceive problems as challenges (instead of threats) are less likely to become ill while experiencing the stress of situational crisis.[47] **Psychoneuro-immunology** explores the connection between psychoso-

cial factors, such as attitudes and emotions, the neurological system, and the immune system. (Refer to discussion of the Holmes and Rahe Social Adjustment Rating Scale in Chap. 39.)

Gastrointestinal System

Dentition

Middlescents begin to develop new dental concerns. For example, new oral bacteria (that are not usually present during early adulthood) may attack teeth near the gum line, causing periodontal diseases.[11,65] Adults who did not have the advantage of fluoride and modern preventive dental care during their earlier years often have secondary decay around old fillings and tooth roots. Tartar on the tooth surface at and below the gum line can lead to gingivitis and periodontal disease. If allowed to continue, the affected teeth start to loosen as the gum tissue recedes. Treatment is largely preventive via rigorous plaque control, which includes use of fluoride products, regular flossing and cleaning, and mechanical scaling (scraping tartar by a dentist or dental hygienist).[57] Root planing (smoothing root surfaces so gum tissue can reattach) is a specific treatment to bring the disease under control.

Adults may still elect to have their teeth repositioned with orthodontics (e.g., braces, retainers). However, the process takes much longer than it does for adolescents. With age, teeth may discolor; some individuals seek special procedures from their dentists to help whiten their teeth.

Stomach

Since early adulthood, the production of hydrochloric acid and pepsin has gradually declined. This decline may reduce the speed of protein digestion. Diminished secretion of acid and pepsin may reduce the absorption of iron, calcium, and vitamin B_{12}.[83,86] Because the motility of the gastrointestinal tract decreases with age, such food appears to "just sit" in the stomach. As a result, some middlescents may begin to experience "acid indigestion" and omit certain foods from the daily diet that "disagree" with them. Some experience discomfort when gas-producing foods pass through the stomach and intestines more slowly.

Intestines

If the middlescent leads a sedentary lifestyle and eats many refined foods (low in fiber), then the already slowing gastrointestinal tract predisposes the person to bouts of constipation. In addition, many adults don't drink enough water to ensure healthy elimination.[83,86]

Constipation may precipitate hemorrhoids (varicose veins in the anal canal). Middlescents who are obese, who have had several pregnancies, who sit or stand for long periods of time, who have varicose veins in their legs, or who are experiencing severe personal stress are vulnerable to developing hemorrhoids. Hemorrhoids cause anal itching, bleeding during bowel movements, and pain. Treatment may be medical or surgical depending on severity.

Some middlescents develop lactose intolerance, an inability to digest lactose, which is a sugar found in milk and milk products.[86] The ingested lactose remains unabsorbed in the intestine, where it absorbs water and causes abdominal distention, cramping, flatulence (gas), and diarrhea. The severity of symptoms depends on the degree of enzyme deficiency. Treatment primarily focuses on eliminating lactose from the diet. Some adults are able to benefit from taking the lactase enzyme in tablet form when eating lactose-laden foods.

Urinary System

Kidney

Structural changes in the kidney begin in early adulthood and slowly continue through midlife and into late adulthood.[76] As blood vessels to the kidney thicken, blood supply is reduced. Nephrons, the functional units of the kidneys that include the tubules through which the blood passes, decrease in number and thicken in part because of fat deposition. Thus, the glomerular filtration rate (the rate at which the kidneys filter wastes from the blood) begins to decline gradually after 40 years.[76] However, middle-age people normally experience no kidney dysfunction because the kidneys have extensive reserve capacity.

Bladder

The muscles in the walls of the bladder and urethra gradually tend to weaken and lose elasticity. This slow decrease in tone limits bladder capacity. Consequently, the middlescent feels the need to urinate more frequently. By the time a person reaches his or her seventies, the bladder capacity is less than half of what it was during early adulthood.[60, 76]

As women age, increasing weakness of the muscles that form the pelvic floor may reduce the effectiveness of the external urethral sphincter. Since these muscles close the outlet of the bladder, their weakness contributes to leakage of urine. This leakage may occur when the woman sneezes, coughs, or is suddenly startled (**stress incontinence**). It may occur earlier than middlescence in multiparous women.[74] In addition to increasing the risk of bladder and skin infection, stress incontinence is both an inconvenience and an embarrassment. It can be either alleviated or its frequency reduced by the regular performance of pelvic floor tightening exercises ("Kegel exercises"). Surgical correction may be required for some women.

As men age, the prostate gland normally begins to enlarge and develop nodules within it (benign prostate hyperplasia). In 10% of all men older than age 50, the prostate enlarges enough to interfere with smooth flow of urine during urination.[60, 76] Surgery may be necessary.

Body Water

As one ages, a decrease in the number of body cells and an increase in adipose tissue, which contains less water, result in a decrease of total body water. The greatest amount of water is still located within the cells. Total body water of middlescent males is about 54.7% of body weight; of females, 47%.[50] Middlescents need to continue to drink about 1500 mL of water daily to ensure healthy kidney functioning and general homeostasis.[50]

Electrolytes

Healthy renal function helps to maintain all fluid and electrolyte balance with the exception of calcium and magnesium.[48] To maintain a positive calcium balance and decrease bone loss, both young and middle-age adults need a daily calcium intake of 1500 mg.[49, 63] A dietary deficiency of magnesium is rare in a healthy individual, but a magnesium deficiency can occur as a result of vomiting, diarrhea, alcohol abuse, or the use of diuretics.[83] Large amounts of magnesium are found in green and yellow vegetables.

Endocrine System

Except for changes in the woman's ability to produce progesterone and estrogen, the ability of the endocrine glands to produce hormones during middlescence remains high in the healthy person. Cortisol (hydrocortisone) secretion by the adrenal glands decreases with age.[76] Plasma cortisol levels remain virtually unchanged, however, because it is broken down and removed more slowly by the liver, allowing people to continue to respond quickly to stress, even as they grow older.[77]

Since metabolic needs are lower in midlife, less thyroxine (the chief thyroid hormone that governs metabolic rate) is secreted by the body. Many middlescents begin to feel the difference of a lower basal metabolic rate (may fatigue more quickly than in early adult years), or they may see the difference (may gain weight if they continue to eat the same amount they did during early adulthood without increasing physical activity).

Human Energy Output

The two major contributors to human energy output are metabolic processes and motor activities. To estimate the total energy a person spends requires evaluating these components individually, then adding them together.

Metabolic processes normally account for at least two-thirds of the energy spent in 24 hours and consist of the energy spent to keep the heart beating, the lungs inhaling and exhaling, the cells conducting their metabolic activities, the nerves generating their electrical impulses, and, essentially, all the processes that support life.[83] The **basal metabolic rate** (BMR) is the rate at which energy is spent for these maintenance activities (usually expressed as Kcal per hour) when the individual is at rest (see Chap. 6). The BMR varies among individuals and may vary for one individual with a change in level of wellness.

The BMR is highest in the young and decreases by about 2% per decade after physical growth has stopped in early adulthood. It decreases more rapidly in late adulthood.[76] The

BMR is higher in people with larger body surface areas. For example, if two people weigh the same, the taller, thinner person has a faster metabolic rate because of a larger skin surface through which heat is lost by radiation. The BMR is usually slower in females, even though controlled for height and weight with men, because women have a higher percentage of body fat.[86] The lean body tissue (fat-free, which includes muscle) of men is more active metabolically than the fat of women (even when the body is at rest).

The second component of energy output is physical activity. The amount of energy needed for an activity like swimming or studying for an exam depends on how many muscles are involved and on how intensely and how long they have to work (Fig. 35-3). An obese person usually uses more energy to perform a task than does a nonobese person because it takes extra effort for the heavier person to move the additional body weight. A person who is skilled in performing a task expends less energy than a person who is learning to perform the task. The decrease in voluntary activity that has traditionally characterized middle-age accounts for another 5% reduction per decade in the amount of energy used.[76, 83]

FIGURE 35–3.
With regular exercise, strenuous work can be continued into the middlescent years. Adequate calories need to be consumed to prevent weight loss.

Pancreas

Normally, the level of glucose in the blood regulates the amount of insulin that is released by the pancreas. As many people age, their ability to move this glucose to the cells of the body for energy is decreased because a high blood glucose level no longer triggers release of adequate insulin (diabetes mellitus).[54, 62] Diabetes mellitus increases in frequency with every decade of life.

Two types of diabetes mellitus exist. **Juvenile-onset** (type I or insulin-dependent) diabetes, more common in young people, is caused by pathological changes in the pancreas that reduce insulin production. **Maturity-onset** (type II or non–insulin-dependent) diabetes is the most prevalent endocrine disorder in older people. With maturity-onset diabetes, a reduced amount of glucose enters body cells, thought to occur because the body cells lose sensitivity to insulin.[76] Therefore, with maturity-onset diabetes, the pancreas must generally produce extra insulin, attempting to compensate for the cellular insensitivity.

In untreated diabetes mellitus, the glucose remains in the blood stream because body cells are unable to absorb enough glucose for metabolism. Although hyperglycemia (excessive glucose in blood), or "high blood sugar," can cause life-threatening physical complications, a person may be unaware of maturity-onset diabetes until it is discovered during a physical exam or routine diabetes screening. Although several factors can contribute to the onset of diabetes (e.g., increasing age, obesity, high carbohydrate diet, physical inactivity, stress, hormonal imbalance, drugs, infection), only a person who is predisposed genetically will actually develop the disease.[7]

Drug treatment of maturity-onset diabetes includes agents that promote the release of insulin from the pancreas, diet modification, and weight loss. Exercise decreases blood glucose and facilitates its entry into body cells.[76]

Reproductive System

As individuals progress through middlescence, reduced sex hormone production (testosterone, estrogen, progesterone) results in marked biophysical change. **Climacteric** is the term used to describe this transitional period or process. It begins when sex hormone production significantly declines and terminates when the individual's ability to reproduce offspring ceases.

Female

Climacteric

The female climacteric (or menopausal period) does not occur overnight; it is a gradual process that takes from 5 to 20 years, during which the function of the ovaries begins to diminish and then finally ceases.[34, 74] During this time the uterus gradually abandons the monthly process of shedding and regenerating its lining. Menopause per se is the permanent cessation of menses due to decreased ovarian functioning.

Throughout life, the number of ovarian follicles, or egg-forming cells with which a woman was born, progressively decreases by either ovulation or retrogression. Because of age-related degeneration of the theca cells, the follicles are no longer able to react to the gonadotropin, follicle-stimulating hormone (FSH). As a result, estrogen production gradually decreases. The pituitary gland increases production of FSH in an effort to stimulate the ovary to produce more estrogen. Even though more FSH and luteinizing hormone (LH) are produced, ovulation does not always occur.[41] If ovulation does not occur, then no progesterone, which is secreted after the rupture of the egg from its follicle, is produced. Decreased levels of estrogen and progesterone are responsible for multiple symptoms and changes in the climacteric woman.

Natural (as opposed to surgical or "artificial") menopause (or more correctly, the menopausal period) is not a single event or an illness; it is a gradual process that is divided into three stages. During the first stage, **premenopause,** the ovaries gradually decrease their hormone production. This decrease often begins around 40 years of age and lasts until menstrual periods cease.[61, 76] At first, the woman may not notice any change in either her cycle length or flow, or she may become aware that the cycles are gradually lengthened (e.g., every 5 to 6 weeks instead of the usual 4-week pattern). Other women find that their periods come more frequently for an extended period of time (e.g., every 3 weeks). Still others become irregular (e.g., they may have two periods of 2 or 3 weeks apart, then go 6 or 8 weeks without one).[34] Some women may experience all three patterns before finally completing their menstrual cycles permanently. Others experience no changes. They merely stop menstruating one month and never start again!

The menstrual flow also changes. Many women notice that their periods become lighter with fewer pieces of tissue. This change is caused by decreased progesterone. Other women find they have an extremely heavy flow for 1 or 2 days, then several days of thin spotting. Some women have numerous days of spotting before menstruation. Still others occasionally have heavy bleeding for several days because of an aberrantly high level of estrogen, as if the body is giving one final surge to regain the previous hormonal balance.

Because of the inconsistent flow of estrogen and the body's irregular attempts to adjust to it, "premenstrual syndrome" (PMS) symptoms, such as breast tenderness and fluid retention, may be heightened. Excess fluid often leads to a bloated feeling in the abdomen. Women tend to gain weight during menopause (and they tend to gain fat during postmenopause). Some of the fat converts androgens in their bodies to estrogen, which, in turn, promotes fluid retention.[14, 21, 72, 76] Restricting salt intake and getting regular exercise helps many women overcome fluid retention.

If her menstrual period is late, the woman may wonder if she is pregnant. At-home urine tests are more likely to give a false positive reading in premenopausal women, therefore, further testing is needed before making the assumption that pregnancy is the reason for the lack of menstruation.[34] After determining that the woman is not pregnant, some doctors prescribe a diuretic (water pill) to reduce swelling. In some cases, doctors may prescribe a dose of progesterone to interrupt the flow of estrogen, produce menses, and start a new cycle.

As menstrual periods cease and hormonal levels stabilize during postmenopause, PMS symptoms subside. It is helpful if the woman keeps a record of when her menstrual periods occur, how long they last, the type of flow, and any other symptoms or changes she may notice.

The second stage is **menopause** itself. Ovaries cease production of ova, hormonal production diminishes further, and menstrual periods cease. The woman obviously becomes sterile at this point. However, she may still ovulate sporadically in the absence of a menses. Menopause is generally considered complete (pregnancy no longer possible) after one year of amenorrhea.[8, 74] The average age for menopause in the United States is 51.4 years.[8] Ninety-five percent of women are between 45 and 55 at the time of menopause.[56]

The actual time at which menopause occurs in a woman cannot be predicted, although daughters tend to follow age trends similar to those of their mothers.[8] The age of onset appears to be genetically predetermined, but it is also influenced by health status. It is not related to the number of previous pregnancies, lactation, race, education, socioeconomic status, age of menarche, or height and weight.[56] However, those who are malnourished or who smoke tend to have an earlier menopause.[56] In industrialized countries, the mean age of menopause has shifted from 40 to 50 years of age in the last 100 years.[56] Women in first world nations spend about one third of their lives in the **postmenopausal stage.**

Health Alterations Associated With Natural Menopause. About 80% of women experience one or more symptoms attributable to the hormonal changes of menopause.[46] Since some of the symptoms can be caused by factors other than the hormonal changes, they should be evaluated by a health professional.

A woman is not completely without estrogens even during postmenopause. Some estrogen still is produced by the adrenals.[74] Women who are overweight sometimes lack many of the symptoms of estrogen deficiency because their body fat produces estrogen after the ovaries stop functioning.[14, 21, 56, 74]

Seventy-five percent of perimenopausal women experience **hot flashes** and **flushes.**[56] Decreased estrogen appears to cause vasomotor instability, resulting in transient vasodilation of capillaries. Blood rushes to the skin surface as the vessels dilate (usually starting on the chest and spreading to the neck, face, and arms), causing a wave of heat (hot flash) or pinking of the skin (hot flush). Afterward, as the perspiration evaporates and vessels constrict, the woman may experience a "chill." Hot flashes may occur once a month or more than 20 times a day; about 50% of women experience hot flashes once a day, and 20% more than once daily.[56] They may last for a few seconds or, more commonly, up to about 4 minutes. If they occur during the night (the most frequent time), they are called "night sweats." Dressing "in layers," avoiding high necklines, and using cotton clothing and bed linens allow heat to escape from the woman during hot flashes. Hot flashes and flushes usually disappear after 2 to 3 years and rarely last more than 5 years.[56]

Many women state that they experience periods of rapid heartbeat, or **palpitations,** during the climacteric, especially when tense or tired or in conjunction with a hot flash.[8] Heart disease should be ruled out by a doctor.

With decreased estrogen, the woman may notice a loss of muscle strength. Regular exercise can help counteract this loss (Fig. 35-4). Reduced estrogen levels also decrease elasticity in the skin's connective tissue, ultimately resulting in different degrees of wrinkling and sagging of tissue.[4] Some women find these changes in physical appearance distressing. Limiting exposure to the sun and maintaining regular exercise help reduce some of these effects.

Androgens, androsterone, and testosterone continue to be produced by the woman because of increased LH levels. These hormones, together with increased levels of cortisone

FIGURE 35–4.
Middlescent women can help maintain their figure, energy, and sense of well-being by engaging in a regular exercise program.

and corticotropin (ACTH) lead to **increased facial hair** in many women during the postmenopausal phase.[56] Body fat is redistributed. As estrogen levels decrease, the woman has an increased risk for atherosclerosis, which leads to an increased incidence of thrombosis and myocardial infarction in the postmenopausal phase.[46, 56]

With the decrease in estrogen, other physical changes may occur. **Atrophy of the vagina** occurs gradually and may be accompanied by **decreased lubrication** by the Bartholin glands. These changes can lead to vaginal dryness, itching, burning, vaginitis, dyspareunia (painful intercourse), and vaginal bleeding.[56] **Atrophy of the trigone of the bladder** can result in dysuria, urinary frequency, and urgency incontinence. **Loss of tone of the perineal elastic tissue** frequently eventually results in urinary stress incontinence.[56] Some women experience an increase in **arthralgia** and **arthritis** (joint pain and inflammation).[46, 56] However, most of these symptoms do not appear until late adulthood.

Some women experience a variety of **affective symptoms.** They may feel nervous, dizzy, short-tempered, depressed, or may experience headaches. Some women may experience transient episodes of intense anxiety or even feelings of panic or a sense of impending doom owing to the effects of unstable hormonal balances. Such feelings may be correlated to changes in hormone levels or to the physical symptoms these changes produce. Mood swings also may be aggravated by changes in lifestyle at this time.[19] Periods of intense alertness and loss of sleep may later precipitate periods of intense fatigue or irritability. Decreased estrogen makes some women more vulnerable to "the blues."[56] Acceptance of these feelings as "normal" gives the woman permission to give extra attention to herself and to share her feelings with a significant other person. This can prevent loss of self-esteem and can promote a more positive attitude. Some women find counseling extremely valuable at this time to facilitate coping with new feelings and life issues.

Evidence suggests that reduced estrogen may cause the part of the brain in charge of recent memory to become sluggish.[34, 68] However, it is important to consider the effects of lifestyle changes and other concerns at midlife on both men and women that result in sensory overload and, thus, forgetfulness. Organizing according to priority and keeping a written schedule can aid memory. Eventually, the woman's body adjusts to lower hormonal levels.

Artificial Menopause. Women who have had their uterus removed (hysterectomy) no longer menstruate, but, because they have their ovaries, they may still experience the perimenopausal symptoms associated with gradual ovarian hormone decline. Women who have their ovaries removed (oophorectomy), whether or not they also have a hysterectomy, experience a sudden and complete loss of female hormones. Since their bodies have no time to make the normal, gradual transition, the symptoms discussed above are usually more pronounced in number and severity than during natural menopause. Providing no contraindications exist, hormonal replacement therapy (HRT) may be beneficial. It can lessen the severity of the symptoms and ease the passage through this span of change.

Hormonal Replacement Therapy

Many women receive small doses of estrogen to relieve the complications of reduced estrogen levels. It is well established that HRT can reduce osteoporosis. Sixty percent of osteoporotic fractures can be prevented with estrogen replacement, and the incidence and seriousness of rheumatoid arthritis is decreased.[46] Hormone replacement therapy also reduces the LDL ("bad") cholesterol and increases the HDL ("good") cholesterol, thereby reducing the risks of atherosclerosis, such as heart disease (reduced by about 50%) and strokes (reduced by about 20%).[24, 46, 56] However, HRT also has inherent health risks. The incidence of endometrial cancer, biliary disease, and breast cancer is increased (increase of 20% for 5 years use and 40% after 10 years use).[46] The incidence of endometrial cancer is reduced if progestin is added to the estrogen, but a slight increase in blood pressure occurs.[24, 46] Consequently, the benefits and risks of HRT must be balanced against each other. "*The benefits of estrogen therapy appear to far outweigh the risks when measured in terms of mortality.*"[46] More than 25% of female deaths due to heart disease before age 75 could be prevented through the use of HRT.[46] The symptoms of endometrial or breast cancer can be detected and treated early if good surveillance techniques are used.

Sexual Response and Expression

A woman's sexual response and expression do not have to be negatively affected by the climacteric. If a woman has positive sexual and social relations before her climacteric, she usually remains active and satisfied throughout the perimenopausal phase. With regular sexual stimulation, the lining of the vagina retains most of its natural elasticity and lubrication during middlescence.

After menopause is firmly established, the woman no longer has to use birth control, a factor she may find liberating and enhancing to her sex life. The higher levels of androgens can increase libido. The woman may feel less fatigue and more vigor if she had previously been anemic because of excessive bleeding during menses. Physical fitness is closely tied to self-image, an important factor in sexual response. Obesity, for example, can have an inhibiting effect on sexuality. The woman who believes she looks nice has a more positive self-image than the one who has ignored her level of health and appearance. During these years, a woman and her partner may have more time for each other and, thus, they may become both physically and psychosocially closer. The sexual partners should communicate their needs to each other to enhance their relationship.

Midlife Pregnancy

An increasing number of women are choosing to have their first baby after 35 years of age (see Chap. 30). The decreased fertility of women older than 35 years may make conception more difficult. However, some women become pregnant during middlescence by accident rather than by choice. Cessation of birth control before menopause is complete may result in an unexpected pregnancy.

Although middle-age women are often considered by the medical profession to be at increased risk during pregnancy, their risk is not appreciably higher than that of younger mothers unless they have preexisting medical conditions such as diabetes mellitus or hypertension.[64] The incidence of chromosomal abnormalities and spontaneous abortion does increase with maternal age, as does the incidence of cesarean birth.[41]

Benign Fibrocystic Breasts

A fibrocystic breast lump is the most common benign (noncancerous) breast condition in females. Although frequently referred to as **fibrocystic breast disease,** it is not a disease per se, but a variation of normal.[43, 45] By age 30, most women have some fibrocystic breast lumps that progress in number until a woman reaches menopause. After that, the symptoms may regress unless the woman takes HRT.[34, 74]

Fibrocystic breasts are caused by the cyclic hormonal stimulation of each menstrual cycle. The epithelial cells that line the mammary ducts of the breasts continuously secrete small amounts of colostrumlike fluid that escapes unnoticed through the nipple. Just as the hormones cause proliferation of the endometrium each month, they have a similar effect on these cells, causing swelling of these cells and partial occlusion of the ducts. Before the tissues can fully return to their previous state, the rising hormones of another menstrual cycle again stimulate proliferation of the tissues. Consequently, the cells gradually swell, become fibrotic, and eventually obstruct the duct. The fluid formed behind the obstructed ducts cannot escape, causing tiny fluid-filled sacs called cysts to develop. After years of repeated hormonal stimulation and regression, 90% of *all* female breasts develop some degree of fibrocystic tissue by their 50th year.[74] The breasts begin to feel lumpy instead of smooth. Some of the cysts may be large and movable, but most are small and merely create "bumpiness." This condition is self-limiting. When the cyclic hormonal changes cease at menopause, the tissues begin to decrease in size, allowing the cysts to drain and recede in size.

A woman may experience generalized discomfort in one or both breasts before the menstrual period when the swelling is at its peak; the tenderness is more typically felt in the upper, outer quadrant of the breast. Breast self-examination should be performed after the menstrual period when swelling is least pronounced. There is a very low, if any, correlation between fibrocystic breasts and breast cancer. However, any breast lump should be evaluated by a physician to rule out cancer. Breast cancer appears to have a much stronger relationship to lack of reproduction. Roman Catholic nuns have a 50% to 180% higher risk of breast cancer than the rest of the women in the United States.[75]

Treatment for fibrocystic breasts varies considerably, but

recommendations often include a caffeine-free, high-fiber, low-fat diet and intake of vitamin E and analgesics.[25] A complete breast health care plan includes: (1) monthly breast self-exams, (2) periodic professional breast exams, and (3) routine mammograms.

Mammogram. Mammography is an x-ray that creates an image of the breast on film. Carcinoma of the breast can exist in a preclinical state for up to 8 years before it is palpable.[56] Therefore, mammograms are essential because they can detect breast cancers in their earliest and most curable stages. Today's low-dose mammogram is considered safe and 85% to 95% accurate.[1]

Male

Testes decrease in size and firmness with age. This effect may be partially caused by the reduced ability of functioning Leydig's cells to produce sufficient testosterone.[76] A decline in testosterone during middlescence can lead to a decrease in muscle strength; it also affects sperm production. Although males produce sperm into late adulthood, the number of sperm and their motility decline around the 50th birthday.[77]

Climacteric

Many male climacteric symptoms parallel those of the middlescent female: loss of body hair, weight gain, headaches, decreased muscle strength, fatigue, digestive disturbances, insomnia, and wrinkles. Some men even experience hot flashes. (This could be due to the increased levels of LH secreted by the pituitary gland as it tries to stimulate the production of more testosterone).[34]

Men do not share a common time during midlife at the end of which they can no longer father offspring. They do, however, go through a transition that often begins in the 40s. The male climacteric, which occurs at a much slower rate and over a relatively longer span of time than the female climacteric, may include mood swings, irritability, decreased libido, alterations in concentration span, and memory lapses.[41,60] Like those associated with the female climacteric, these symptoms may be caused by other factors. The extent of male climacteric symptoms has been difficult to ascertain, probably because of the reluctance of men to discuss symptoms candidly.

Sexual Response and Expression

The penis undergoes some atrophy with age because of decreased blood supply.[77] Men with diabetes and those who smoke or drink or have arteriosclerotic disease experience earlier atrophy. The erectile tissue and blood vessel walls of the penis may begin to become less elastic after 55 years of age. The combination of these two factors may cause a delay in the attainment of an erection because an erection depends on the accumulation of blood within the penis. However, most men do not experience sufficient loss to prevent attaining an erection or participation in coitus during middlescence.

Some middlescent men may begin to experience a reduced force of ejaculation and a smaller volume of fluid ejaculated if they have an enlarged prostate.[53] However, most

of these changes occur so slowly that they go unnoticed until late adulthood. The man who engages in regular sexual activity that he finds pleasurable usually does not detect changes.[51]

Many middle-age men find that they require more time and stimulation to achieve an erection; those involved in meaningful relationships often report that this extra time enhances both psychosocial and sexual intimacy. Middlescent men usually require longer periods between erections than they did as young adults.[41,60] Once an erection is achieved, however, it can usually be maintained for longer periods of time than was possible in earlier years. The man should not lose his facility for erection at any time, presuming general good health and no psychogenic blocking, well into late adulthood. Masters and Johnson's research indicates that the male's loss of erectile prowess is not a natural component of aging but may be more related to lack of understanding, fear of performance, or disuse.[52]

As aging proceeds, males experience more noticeable changes in the frequency, strength, and duration of erection and sex drive, factors that may lead to concern for their "maleness."[53] Several health alterations may influence erectile power, including arteriosclerotic changes of the iliac and pelvic vessels, which can cause decreased blood supply or atrophy; pressure on pelvic nerves from intervertebral disc protrusions; diabetes; and tumor growth in the bowel, pelvis, or prostate.[7,53,76] Some medications, especially antihypertensives, muscle relaxants, and tranquilizers, may also cause impotence.[77]

Midlife Fatherhood

Most men remain fertile throughout life. Middlescent men who remarry may father a "second family." Some are concerned that men who are approaching late adulthood may father children with chromosomal abnormalities.[12] Like older mothers, some may find late adult fathering to be a rejuvenating experience, whereas others may be fatigued and unable to cope with the parenting energy a child needs to develop his or her potentials (see Chap. 31).

FACTORS THAT INFLUENCE HIGH-LEVEL WELLNESS

Stress

Life is full of factors that cause stress. A **stressor** is any demand on mind and body. **Stress** is the arousal of the mind and body in response to demands made on them.[69] These definitions embody three important points. First, stress is ever-present and universal. Whether a person is awake or asleep, some degree of arousal or response exists. Stress cannot be avoided, rather it must be identified, assessed, and managed. Second, stress is multi-faceted. Stress (arousal) effects essentially every system of the physical body as well as all five domains. Thoughts and feelings are intertwined with biophysical processes (Fig. 35-5). Third, stress in itself is simply a fact of life and therefore is neutral. It is how a person responds to it that makes it positive or negative.

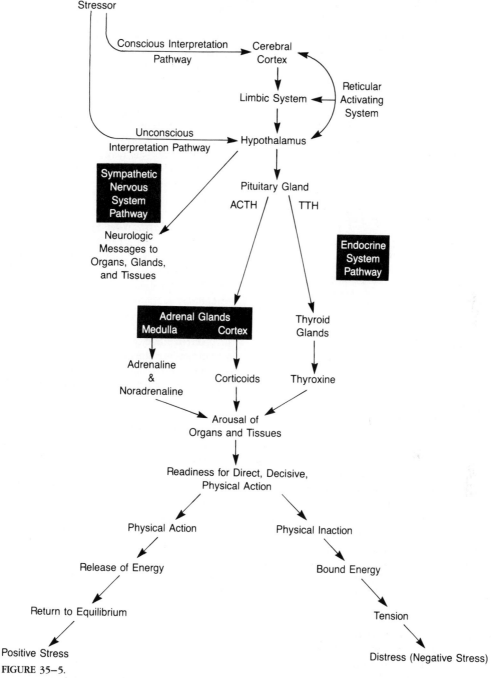

FIGURE 35–5.
Understanding stress. How an individual responds to a stressor results in either positive stress or negative stress. (Schaffer, W. (1987). Stress management for wellness. *New York: Holt, Rinehart and Winston. With permission.)*

Positive stress is arousal that contributes to health (high-level wellness), satisfaction, and productivity.[69] Positive stress is useful in many ways: it helps a person respond quickly and with increased physical strength (e.g., averting an auto collision, lifting a heavy fallen object off a child); it helps a person perform well (e.g., practicing a speech before giving it, proofreading a job application before submitting it); it helps a person prepare for deadlines (e.g., filing date for tax returns, finishing a costume before dress rehearsal); it helps a person realize potentials over a period of time (e.g., attending every meeting of a committee and actively participating, altering a recipe until the sauce is the right consistency). Positive

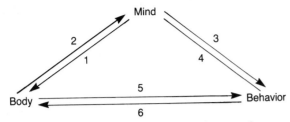

1. *Feeling of fear causes muscle tension (among other things).*
2. *Activation of the sympathetic nervous system leads to greater mental alertness.*
3. *Feeling of fear leads to avoidance behavior.*
4. *Avoidance behavior is followed by mental appraisal of the situation.*
5. *Physical arousal leads to stronger, faster behavior responses.*
6. *Persistent fighting-off of an attacker results in physical fatigue.*

(Schafer, W. (1987). Stress management for wellness. New York: Holt, Rinehart and Winston. With permission.)

FIGURE 35–6.
The stress response. A fundamental assumption of the holistic lifespan approach to stress is that mind, body, and behavior are closely intertwined.

stress can also add variety, a sense of adventure, and a sense of purpose to daily life. Attempting to avoid stress (if such a thing were possible) proves to be stagnating. *The challenge is to identify one's own zone of positive stress and to maintain a lifestyle that enables one to stay in that zone most of the time.*

Distress (or negative stress) occurs when too much or too little arousal, temporarily or chronically, results in harm to the body and mind (Fig. 35-6).[69] Negative stress symptoms (e.g., trembling hands, tight shoulders, poor concentration, irritability) serve as warning signs. They are messages that something is wrong and needs to be changed. Unfortunately, such symptoms often are ignored or remain undetected.

Then they can become chronic and may be converted to or replaced with physical illness. Any biophysical system of the body can malfunction because of negative stress. Headaches, psoriasis, ulcers, skin rashes, colitis, gastritis, chronic lower back pain, heart attack, vertigo (dizzy spells), and high blood pressure may result.[69]

Selye referred to these as "diseases of adaptation" (more appropriately, "maladaptation"). Some other diseases of adaptation as identified by Selye include rheumatoid arthritis, allergic conditions, and asthma.[70] It is important to point out that these symptoms may be caused by factors other than negative psychological stress. However, inadequate coping skills may aggravate or precipitate symptoms in a sensitive person.

General Adaptation Syndrome

Dr. Hans Selye, the "father" of stress syndrome theories, identified a universal pattern of physical stress known as the **general adaptation syndrome** (GAS), which helps explain how the body handles stress over time and how psychic stress sometimes is translated into physical stress. According to Selye, GAS consists of three stages (Fig. 35-7):[70]

1. **Alarm Stage**: When the person recognizes a stressor or threat, it triggers biophysical responses for facing the stressor. The autonomic nervous system and the adrenal medulla increase production of norepinephrine and epinephrine, which increase cardiac rate and output, increase blood pressure, increase the respiratory rate, decrease the blood supply to visceral organs, increase the blood supply to vital organs (heart, brain, liver, peripheral muscles), and dilate the pupils. These responses constitute a physiologic "call to arms"—the fight, flight, or fright responses to the stressor. This stage may last from a few minutes to more than 24 hours.

2. **Resistance Stage**: As the adrenal cortex produces anti-inflammatory or pro-inflammatory hormones, the body begins to adapt to or cope with the stressor. The purpose of adrenal cortical activity is an attempt to confine the

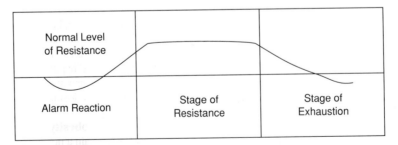

FIGURE 35–7.
The general adaptation syndrome. These stages can be seen easily in the body's reaction to physical trauma. The same sequence also occurs as one reacts to personal and social situations in daily life, such as verbal attack, prolonged isolation, or chronic overload. (Schafer, W. (1987). Stress management for wellness. New York: Holt, Rinehart and Winston. With permission.)

effects of the stressor to the smallest area of the biological system that is capable of overcoming the stressor. The resistance stage may last a short time, or it may last for months or even years (e.g., as in recovering from tuberculosis or living with a disabled family member).

3. **Exhaustion Stage**: In this stage, the "adaptation" energy of the biological system is exhausted and the person becomes ill. The body may make a "last ditch" effort to resolve the stressor. If the stressor is overcome, the adaptation energy is used to effect recovery, with return to healthier states. Repeated assaults from stressors and the stress responses required to cope with them may exhaust all adaptation energy, leading to severe physical illness (e.g., ulcer, heart attack). When the body functions can no longer be maintained, the person dies.

Each individual's stress responses tend to follow the pattern given above. A person's responses are mediated by his or her perception of the stressor. By learning what constitutes a personal threat, a person can modify responses to conserve adaptation energy. It also behooves each person to identify his or her characteristic responses: Does one act outwardly ("fight" response); act inwardly ("flight" response); or ride the fence, not knowing which way to turn ("fright" response)? Identification of stressors and individual responses is the first step in learning to predict and control both stressors and responses (see Chap. 36).

Selye also identified the **local adaptation syndrome** (LAS) as the body's response to a wound. It is an attempt by the body to keep the response in the smallest area possible. An example of LAS is the circumscribed area of inflammation around a cut on a finger; it is a localized response with no (or only slight) systemic involvement.

Post-traumatic Stress Disorder

At least 15% of Vietnam war veterans suffered, or continue to suffer, **post-traumatic stress disorder** (PTSD).[33] This is a syndrome that some people develop as a result of living through a traumatic experience. The stressor doesn't have to be war; PTSD is also common in those who have experienced an earthquake, kidnapping, death of a close family member, airplane crash, or some other tragedy-laden situation. The victims of PTSD can be any age. The chronic or periodically recurring symptoms of PTSD include digestive disturbances, insomnia, nightmares, sleepwalking, accident proneness, impaired memory, displaced anger, poor frustration management, avoidance of close interpersonal relationships, work inhibition, "flashbacks," and frequent physical illnesses.[33] These symptoms may not manifest themselves immediately after the stressor occurs, but months or years later. Victims of PTSD require psychotherapy.

Type-A Behavior

Research has recently identified type-A behavior pattern as a major contributing factor to cardiovascular disease.[7, 23] Type-A behavior pattern is not a personality trait but a continuum of life approach behaviors, including impatience with delay, excessive competitiveness, high goals, restlessness, extreme achievement striving, and inappropriate irritability.[23] Type-A people have such an intense sense of urgency for accomplishing their priorities that they often ignore warnings of cardiovascular problems. They abhor repetitious exercises, relaxation techniques, or other ways to reduce tension. In essence, they make no realistic effort toward positively controlling their stressors or their stress reactions. Eventually, unless they recognize the need for treatment, they may suffer one or more heart attacks. If they choose to become motivated to do so, type-A people can alter their lifestyle and response to stressors, thus reducing their risk for cardiovascular disease and increasing their level of wellness.[23]

Obesity

Obesity is not only a common stressor in industrialized nations but is also the result of stress. The definition of obesity has varied throughout medical history; it is no longer synonymous with just being overweight. **Obesity** is an abnormal increase in body fat, the result of which is a significant impairment to high-level wellness.[3, 6, 14, 67]

Although an individual can become obese anytime during the life span, the prevalence of obesity increases with age, reaching peaks in men aged 45 to 54 years and women aged 55 to 60 years.[3] Although people traditionally thought of obesity in terms of its esthetic and social effects, we are now becoming aware of its complex effects on biophysical health.

Increasing evidence suggests that obesity leads to or aggravates numerous illnesses, including heart disease, respiratory disorders, maturity-onset diabetes, gallstones, arthritis, cancer, and complications of pregnancy.[30, 59] Intracellular accumulations of fat have been shown to initiate progressive scarring and cellular death, leading to functional impairment of the involved organ.[7] Obesity also significantly lowers life expectancy.[73]

Types of Obesity

Researchers have identified two types of obesity: lifelong obesity and adult-onset obesity.[30] **Lifelong obesity** applies to those who are obese as infants, gain significant weight during pubescence, and continue to gain fat (and weight) as they age. These people have a tendency to deposit fat everywhere in their bodies. They have a greater than average number of fat cells ("hyperplastic obesity"), and their fat cells tend to be larger than average. People with lifelong obesity have a difficult time losing weight, and they tend to gain fat easily.[67]

Adult-onset obesity, which is more common, refers to people who maintain a normal weight until early adulthood. These people tend to deposit much of their visible fat in their abdomen (hence, the term "middle-age spread"). People with adult-onset obesity have a normal number of fat cells, but their fat cells are larger than normal ("hypertrophic obesity").[67] These people tend to be less obese than people who have been overweight all their lives. They also tend to have an easier time losing weight when they alter their diet and exercise patterns. They are more successful at keeping their weight down after reducing.

Causes

Genetic factors probably influence a person's chance of becoming fat more than any other factor. Within families, if one parent is obese, a child has a 40% chance of becoming obese. This chance becomes 80% if both parents are obese but is only 7% if neither parent is obese.[22] It is recognized that families also exert social pressure and teach children habits and attitudes toward food.

Other psychosocial factors cause individuals to overeat and to become overfat.[6] Among these are equating food with love and using food as a reward or to relieve boredom. However, it should be emphasized that psychosocial causes cannot be applied to all obese people. Obesity may be related to endocrine dysfunction. Two major theories of biophysical factors contribute to weight management problems, the fat cell theory and the set-point theory.[78]

Fat Cell Theory

This theory posits that the percentage of body fat an individual carries is determined by the number of fat cells in the body, which is partly determined by inheritance and partly by eating patterns developed during critical periods of biophysical development, including the gestational period, early infancy, and pubescence.[78] Once the body has added fat cells to accommodate extra calorie storage, these cells remain and in some unknown way (perhaps as chemical messengers) encourage the individual to overeat.

Set-Point Theory

This theory maintains that an internal mechanism, a **set-point,** regulates the amount of weight for which an individual's body is genetically "programmed" or "set."[35] The reason so many people lose weight only to "bounce back" is because their body weight is returning to its set-point. The only known way to lower the set-point is to raise the BMR. Raising the BMR is accomplished by increasing levels of physical activity, especially aerobic exercise. Those who wish to lose and then maintain weight at the lower level need to combine a program of aerobic exercise with a diet low in fat and high in complex carbohydrates.[83, 86] When their ideal goal is reached, they must maintain the same BMR to keep their new set-point and adjust their food intake to maintain their weight.

Substance Abuse

Middlescents abuse the same substances as young adults. Some abuse these substances for the first time when they are in their 40s or 50s, falsely hoping to recapture youth, escape current crises, or enhance their energy level. Other middle-age people have been abusing these substances for years, and their bodies are experiencing the negative, cumulative effects.

Tobacco Smoking

Each year 350,000 Americans die prematurely from the effects of smoking. Millions more live with a disability related to tobacco and the compounds released when it is smoked.[77] A person doesn't have to smoke for several years before the body experiences the negative stress of tobacco. Just a few puffs temporarily slow down the action of the bronchial cilia, tiny hairlike structures that help protect the lungs from germs and foreign particles.

Three of the most damaging compounds inhaled with cigarette smoking are nicotine, tars, and carbon monoxide. Tars damage the lung tissue of nonsmokers as well as smokers. When these billions of tiny hot particles cool inside the lungs, they form a brown, sticky mass that contains chemicals that eventually can produce cancer.[10] Smoke from an idling cigarette contains almost twice the tar and nicotine of an inhaled cigarette and thus may be twice as toxic to the nonsmoker as smoke inhaled by the smoker. An idling cigarette adds contaminates to the air for about 12 minutes while the average smoker is usually inhaling on the average for 24 seconds.[2] Since pipe and cigar smokers inhale less than cigarette smokers, they contribute even more relatively unfiltered smoke (and, therefore, more toxic compounds) into the air.

Inhaled carbon monoxide, in smokers and nonsmokers alike, decreases the oxygen-carrying capacity of the red blood cells, thereby reducing the amount of oxygen supplied to the brain, heart, and to the rest of the body.[77] Carbon monoxide commonly leads to headaches, dizziness, and lassitude. The deleterious effects of inhaled carbon monoxide are numerous, including impairment of the healing process any place in the human body, increased risk of complications from anesthesia, and increased risk of blood clot formation.[77]

Cigarette smoking, in general, can decrease the level of wellness in both smokers and nonsmokers who already have an alteration in health. For example, tobacco smoke in the air can trigger respiratory difficulty in a person plagued with chronic lung disease. Tobacco smoke should never be present around infants and young children (whether they are ill or not) because they already are prone to more respiratory infections. Smokers have more respiratory infections than nonsmokers.[5]

Several other harmful gases in tobacco smoke have also been identified: nitrogen dioxide, hydrogen cyanide, hydrogen sulfide, hydrocyanic acid, and arsenic.[10] These substances may also trigger allergic reactions. For an unknown reason, tobacco smoke decreases the levels of high density lipoproteins (HDLs), the "good" lipids that help protect against heart attacks (see Chap. 26).[67, 77]

Former smokers decrease their risk for illness with every day that they abstain from smoking.[10] Information on how to quit smoking and on "freedom from smoking" clinics can be obtained from a local chapter of the American Lung Association or American Cancer Society.

Ethyl Alcohol (ETOH)

Social Drinkers

Some middlescents begin drinking alcoholic products for the first time in midlife; others have been drinking alcoholic beverages for years. Chronic use produces tolerance, thereby necessitating a gradual increase in dose to achieve the same effects.[17] Chronic exposure to excessive ETOH can damage any tissue in the body. Immoderate use (the definition of which is relative for each individual and the way his or her body metabolizes ETOH) of alcohol increases the risk of developing cancer of the mouth, larynx, esophagus, liver, and lungs.[77]

Alcoholism

The difference between a person who abuses alcohol and one who becomes alcoholic is biophysical addiction. An **alcoholic** is a person who has lost control over ETOH drinking behaviors and who, after each use, suffers withdrawal symptoms when blood alcohol levels approach or reach zero.[17,77]

Repeated exposure to ETOH produces tolerance and addiction similar to that characteristic of opioid addiction. It is believed that chemical reactions between body amines (nitrogen compounds) and acetaldehyde, an intermediate metabolite of ETOH, form opioid-like substances that affect the brain.[77] Individuals who are alcoholics may have a genetic predisposition to addiction because their metabolism cannot break down acetaldehyde at normal rates.[77] Abrupt withdrawal produces potentially fatal symptoms.

Withdrawal symptoms include perspiration, muscle cramps, nausea, and anxiety.[77] These symptoms can also include withdrawal seizures and delirium tremens ("DTs"). Delirium tremens are characterized by profound confusion, vivid hallucinations, delusions, tremor, agitation, inability to sleep, dilated pupils, fever, and rapid heartbeat. They can be fatal if the alcoholic experiences cardiac arrest after an extended period of excitement.

Alcoholics also suffer many other physical changes that occur with chronic ETOH use, such as gastritis, peptic ulcers, heart disease, pancreatitis (inflammation of the pancreas), and cirrhosis (liver disease).[17,77] Alcoholics tend to develop either obesity from excess calorie consumption or malnutrition because of nutritional deficiencies. They may experience decreased libido. Their tolerance to ETOH produces cross-tolerance to most central nervous system depressants, including anesthetics.[77] Because they need such large doses of anesthetics for surgery, and because of the high incidence of malnutrition and poor resistance to infection, habitual users of ETOH tend to be poor surgical risks. Ethyl alcohol also interacts with many other drugs, decreasing the effectiveness of some (e.g., anticoagulants, thus increasing the possibility of blood clot formation) and enhancing the effects of others (e.g., tranquilizers, thus leading to life-threatening respiratory depression).[77]

Treatment consists of weaning from alcohol and, if necessary, psychological counseling. The need for treatment must first be accepted by the alcoholic. Support groups usually prove helpful both to the patient with alcoholism and to members of his or her family.

Drug Abuse

In addition to tobacco smoking and alcohol, many other chemical substances are abused by middlescents (and other age groups as well). Some middlescents smoked "pot" (marijuana), or "tripped" on lysergic acid diethylamide (LSD) once or twice during the 1960s and 1970s; others continue to use these drugs.

Long-term Use of Marijuana

The long-term effects of marijuana are not conclusive, but many middlescents are concerned about how their past abuse will affect their minds and bodies in the present and the future. Chronic heavy use may cause paranoia, decreased motivation, or other unpredictable adverse psychosocial effects.[67]

LSD

LSD is highly potent, with amounts as small as 1/700 millionth of a person's body weight producing a psychedelic experience (changes of perception, hallucinations, delusions of grandeur, feelings of omnipotence, sense of loss of control, distortions of time, space, and body-image, and mood changes). Psychoactive drug experiences vary greatly and are influenced by the user's personality and the social setting in which the drug is taken.[77] Flashbacks of the psychedelic experience may occur at any time, but most have occurred from 12 to 18 months later.

Cocaine

Cocaine is the strongest natural stimulant available.[77] Its action on the central nervous system initially affects the cerebral cortex. Cocaine has rapidly become a popular "recreational" drug, especially among middle-class Americans. Because the price of cocaine ("coke") is high, its use has become falsely synonymous with a lifestyle of wealth and glamour. Nevertheless, in the United States, more than 25 million people have tried cocaine, of whom 2 to 3 million have become compulsive users.[79]

When used nasally ("snorted"), it causes vasoconstriction, resulting in inflammation of the nasal mucosa and possible perforation of the nasal septum. Injected cocaine ("mainlined") produces increased heart rate, blood pressure, and body temperature.[77] Therapeutic use of cocaine is limited to euphoric analgesia during ear, nose, and throat surgery for cancer patients with intractable pain.[77]

An inexpensive variety of cocaine known as "crack" is found in small chips or "rocks" that are smoked. The popularity of "crack" is especially tragic because it quickly promotes addiction. Crack creates paranoia and anxiety. The cycle of intense "highs" and crashing depressions leads to the abuser's need to increase the frequency of use.

Drug Abuse Treatment

The needs are vast in treating the person who willfully or indiscriminately abuses drugs. Substance abuse affects all domains of the abuser and the people in the abuser's environment. It is a strength for substance abusers to admit they have a problem; it is also a strength for them to realize that they cannot medically treat themselves and that they need professional help.

Health Maintenance Activities

Most disability and deaths that occur during middlescence are preventable. Many of the illnesses are due to lifestyle and health care factors that can be changed (e.g., cirrhosis, alcoholism, and accidents, many of which can be avoided by abstinence from alcohol and other substances).

Nutrition

The concept of nutrition is such an integral part of health maintenance that a reference has been made to it under almost every body system discussed earlier in this chapter.

Calories

A person who is 50 years of age does not have the same energy needs that he or she did at 30 years of age because of decreased lean muscle mass, reduced BMR, probably a slower pace of lifestyle, and, in general, the normal aging process. Consuming fewer calories requires judicious planning. One still needs to eat breakfast, to avoid eating before going to sleep, and to select snacks carefully. It is important to obtain the appropriate percentage of proteins, carbohydrates, and fats within the reduced amount of calories. Adequate fluid intake and fiber in foods assist in the elimination of fecal wastes and reduce constipation problems (Fig. 35-8).

Fat

If a middlescent cannot maintain a blood cholesterol level below 200 mg, he or she may need to decrease saturated fat under doctor's supervision, from 10% to 7% of the total daily calories. This decrease means using more polyunsaturated fats in place of saturated fats.[31] However, too small an amount of fat in one's diet can result in a deficiency of the essential fatty acid linoleic acid.[86]

Vitamins and Minerals

The middlescent's goal should be to meet nutritional needs through a well-balanced dietary plan and, if desired, to use a daily multi-vitamin and mineral supplement to ensure adequate intake. Although calcium is supplied by green leafy vegetables, legumes, nuts, and whole grain, it is difficult to achieve adequate calcium intake without consuming milk in some form (e.g., cheese, ice cream, pudding). There are several reasons why many middlescents can't or won't drink milk: they are allergic or sensitive to it; they have lactose intolerance; it constipates them; it has too many calories; they don't like the taste. If one is not drinking milk, then a calcium

FIGURE 35–8.
Food continues to be a major attraction at social events. Middlescents need to choose food carefully to ensure adequate nutrition without excessive caloric intake.

citrate supplement can be substituted. Although the typical American diet contains 10 to 15 g of table salt (or 4–6 g of sodium daily), the estimated safe intake is only 2.8 to 8.3 g of salt (or 1.1–3.3 g of sodium).[20]

Sleep and Rest

The number of awakenings after sleep onset increases with age.[55] Middle-age adults normally spend less time in deep sleep and may need less sleep overall; however, this decrease does not negate their need for rest, which often balances the time lost in sleep. The need for sleep may be quantitatively greater for the person who is experiencing negative stress.

Exercise

Regular exercise promotes high-level wellness if it is individualized to the person's needs. No exercise regimen (even at a well-known gymnasium or health spa) should be initiated by a middlescent until a physician has been consulted. Most people who are older than 30 years of age or who are overweight should have a stress electrocardiogram (ECG or EKG) to assess the tolerance for an exercise program.

With appropriate exercise, bones are stronger, muscles are more firm and atrophy less, the skin is more resilient, bladder and bowel patterns of elimination are more regular, the lungs oxygenate the body better, the heart pumps more efficiently, energy is more apparent, and sleep is deeper.[44]

Most middlescents exercise to lose weight and to increase the efficiency of the cardiovascular system. Continuous rhythmic exercise maintained for a period long enough to positively stress the cardiovascular system is desired. Moderation, as defined by one's personal physician and how one's body responds to exercise, is the key, especially as one approaches late adulthood. Overexertion, evidenced by symptoms of dizziness, tightness in the chest, and breathlessness that doesn't resolve easily, should be avoided and reported to a physician.

Health Maintenance

Every middlescent should have a tentative health care calendar or individualized schedule for health-related examinations. The following suggestions are guidelines for the average middlescent.

Dental exams should occur every 6 months, more frequently for those who experience periodontal "pocketing" of gums around teeth. Dental x-rays are recommended every 2 years.

The eyes should be examined every 1 to 2 years by an ophthalmologist or optometrist. The adult older than age 40 is increasingly susceptible to glaucoma (an increase in intraocular pressure that can lead to blindness).

After age 40, each person should have an annual complete physical examination,[17] which includes a health history and assessment of blood pressure, pulse, temperature, weight, chest and lungs, neurological reflexes, breasts, rectum, skin, eyes, ears, mouth, and nose. Women should have a pelvic exam; men should have both a prostate and testicular exam at this time. Laboratory procedures that should be performed annually include a urinalysis check for glucose, protein, calcium, and renal plasma flow and a complete blood panel that includes measurement of blood fats, cholesterol, glucose, thyroid hormones, and hemoglobin.[17, 67]

A chest x-ray should be taken yearly if a person is, or has a history of being, a heavy smoker; otherwise, one should be taken every 2 years.[2] A skin test for tuberculosis should be performed every 2 years.

A stool slide test to check for hidden blood should be performed every year after age 50.[1] A proctoscopy should be performed to examine the rectum and colon. (After two initial exams that are negative and 1 year apart, a proctoscopy should occur every 3 to 5 years after a person is 50 years old).[1]

A middlescent woman should have a mammogram every 2 years when she is in her 40s; she should have a mammogram yearly thereafter. Pap tests should be performed at least every 3 years.[1] Women who have multiple sex partners should have an annual Pap test. If the woman is undergoing HRT (and still has her ovaries and uterus), is infertile or obese, or has ovulation failure or abnormal uterine bleeding, she should have a sample of endometrium tissue examined for endometrial cancer.[17]

Sexually active middle-age people, especially those with multiple sex partners, are at risk for sexually-transmitted diseases and may need to be screened for them.

Immunizations should be kept current (same as recommended for early adulthood). A middlescent should consult a health professional if he or she experiences any unusual symptoms.

Health Concerns

In spite of the health changes discussed, the middle-age years are usually highly productive years accompanied by high-level wellness. Some of the most common health concerns that serve as stressors (not mentioned previously in this chapter) are briefly discussed in this section.

Headaches

For some middlescents, migraine and tension headaches are replaced by even more serious headaches: temporal arteritis, trigeminal neuralgia, or cluster headaches. All cause excruciating pain on one side of the face or head. Temporal arteritis can even cause blindness.[58]

Temporal arteritis causes a persistent, burning pain in one temple where the affected artery is often visibly inflamed. Attacks occur at random. Trigeminal neuralgia and cluster headaches may occur in patterns of several per day, then vanish for months or years at a time. Cluster headache pain is usually described as a constant throbbing or pulsating; they are often triggered by drinking alcoholic beverages. Cluster headaches typically last half an hour or more, often waking their victims from sleep. The pain of trigeminal neuralgia is razor-sharp; it consists of jabs of pain lasting 20 to 30 seconds and rarely occurs during the night.

All three headaches can be relieved with medications or surgery. Cluster headaches may disappear when the person reaches late adulthood.

Arthritis

Arthritis simply means "inflammation of a joint." Although arthritic changes can occur any time during the life span, they are more common as a person ages. Pathological changes in the membranes that surround the joint, the cartilage that covers the ends of the bones that form the joint, or in the bones themselves may accompany the inflammation.[7] **Osteoarthritis** (degenerative joint disease) is the most common form of arthritis but usually does not become severe enough to cause symptoms until late adulthood.

Rheumatoid arthritis often appears before a person is 50 years old.[76] More common in females, it progresses slowly and causes disabling stiffness, pain, swelling, and tenderness in the small joints of the body (hands, feet, knees, ankles, elbows, wrists). Rheumatoid arthritis often resembles a disease of the immune system because it can cause inflammation of other parts of the body (e.g., blood vessels, heart, eye muscles, nerves, spleen, liver).[7] Increased physical or emotional stressors can precipitate "flare-ups" of rheumatoid arthritis. It can be treated with medication or surgery. Most persons with rheumatoid arthritis have some degree of disability all their lives.

Cardiovascular Disease

The most prevalent chronic disease that causes death during midlife is cardiovascular disease (CVD).[82] Cardiovascular disease is an inclusive term for diseases of the heart and blood vessels. An individual person can control many of the factors that aggravate CVD: diet (decrease saturated fats, cholesterol, sodium, and sometimes calories); tobacco smoking (quit smoking); negative stress (find individual zone of positive stress); alcohol and other abusive drugs (refrain from use or abuse); and exercise (get regular exercise according to one's abilities and limitations).[84,85] In addition, a person who has diabetes can help control blood vessel changes by controlling the diabetes.

The most common heart disorder in the United States is atherosclerosis; arteriosclerosis is the most common disease of the arteries (both are discussed in Chap. 26).

Angina Pectoris

Angina pectoris is a condition characterized by a feeling of tightness or fullness at the bottom of the breastbone. It may radiate down one or both arms or into the neck and jaws. This pain results from insufficient oxygen getting to the heart cells (especially when the body is under stress and the heart rate is increased). It is almost always related to atherosclerotic narrowing of the arteries that supply blood to the heart muscle itself.[76] The changes in the affected heart cells can be reversed with proper treatment.

Heart Attack

Middlescents probably fear a heart attack (also known as myocardial infarction, coronary thrombosis, coronary occlusion) more than any other event. A heart attack is caused by an arrest in or sudden insufficiency of blood flow to the heart.[76] Heart cells become damaged and die. The most common complaint of a person who is suffering from a heart attack is uncomfortable pressure, fullness, squeezing, or pain in the chest that lasts 2 minutes or more. A person prone to or who has already suffered a heart attack should be under medical treatment.

Hypertension (High Blood Pressure)

Hypertension in middlescence is defined as persistent levels of blood pressure in which the systolic pressure is above 140 mm Hg and the diastolic pressure is above 90 mm Hg.[7,32] Genetic factors play a role in the development of hypertension.

Hypertension is not restricted to older people, but its incidence tends to increase with age. It is not, however, an automatic consequence of aging. It has been estimated that about 30% of the population in industrialized societies suffer from hypertension by the age of 65 years.[76] The most common causes of hypertension in older people are atherosclerosis and arteriosclerosis. High blood pressure is serious because it can lead to heart attack, kidney damage, or rupture of blood vessels. In addition to controlling the factors that precipitate

cardiovascular disease, most people with hypertension require drug therapy.

CONCLUSION

Most middlescent persons experience high-level wellness, especially if a good foundation of health maintenance has been laid during the early adult years. It is interesting to note that scientists who work with the United States space program chose middlescent individuals to be the first astronauts on the moon. Ranging from 38 to 45 years, they were chosen because they were mentally alert, physically sound, and emotionally stable individuals.

Individuals born during the "baby boom" after World War II are now entering their middle years. Many of these "baby boomers" are unwilling to adopt old philosophies on how to "graciously" accept inevitable decline. They perceive midlife as a unique phase of adulthood that offers new challenges and opportunities, as a new chapter in the process of continued growth and well-being.

Aging should be viewed as a normal process marked by progressive changes. Since the physical body is demonstrating change in its response to stressors, the middlescent is charged with negotiating new boundaries for his or her individual zone of positive stress, which includes eating, sleeping, resting, exercising, recreating, learning, loving, and, in general, living to maximize all domains.

Regular physical checkups can help detect and contain chronic illnesses before permanent damage is done, especially in cases of glaucoma, diabetes mellitus, cardiovascular disease, and cancer, all of which could have their onset in middle age. Any person who is capable of correctly performing cardiopulmonary resuscitation (CPR) should learn to do so. Many productive lives could thus be saved.

It may be more difficult to maintain high-level wellness during middlescence, but it is possible to extend the vigor of youth to promote high-level productivity and feelings of personal satisfaction.

REFERENCES

1. American Cancer Society. (1989). *Good news that may save your life.* Costa Mesa, CA: American Cancer Society. (Report No. 6439.01)
2. American Lung Association of Orange County, CA. (1989, December). Tobacco smoke emissions. *Fact Sheet.*
3. Bernstein, R. S. (1986). Evaluating and treating obesity. In E. B. Feldman (Ed.), *Nutrition in the middle and later years.* New York: Warner.
4. Brincat, M., et al. (1987). A study of the decrease of skin collagen content, skin thickness, and bone mass in the postmenopausal woman. *Obstetrics and Gynecology, 70,* 840–845.
5. Brown, R., et al. (1987). Respiratory infections in smokers. *American Family Physician, 36*(5), 133–140.
6. Brownell, K. D. (1984). The psychology and physiology of obesity: Implications for screening and treatment. *Journal of the American Dietetic Association, 84,* 406.

7. Bullock, B. L., & Rosendahl, P. P. (1988). *Pathophysiology: Adaptations and alterations in function* (2nd ed.). Glenview, IL: Scott, Foresman.

8. Burnett, R. G. (1987). *Menopause*. Chicago: Contemporary Books.

9. Burnside, I. M. (1988). *Nursing and the aged* (3rd ed.). New York: McGraw-Hill.

10. Cigarette Smoking. (1989). *Facts about your lungs*. New York: American Lung Association. (No. 0171)

11. Clark, J. W. (1986). *Clinical dentistry* (Vol. 1, rev. ed.). Philadelphia: Harper and Row.

12. Cohen, F. (1984). *Clinical genetics in nursing practice*. Philadelphia: J. B. Lippincott.

13. Corso, J. F. (1981). *Aging sensory systems and perception*. New York: Praeger.

14. Cryer, A., & Van, R. L. R. (1985). *New perspectives in adipose tissue: Structure, function, and development*. London: Butterworths.

15. Davies, I., & Fotheringham, A. P. (1981). Lipofuscin—does it affect cellular performance? *Experimental Gerontology, 16,* 119–125.

16. Dustan, H. P. (1986). Systemic arterial hypertension. In J. W. Hurst, and Loque, R. B. (Eds.), *The heart arteries, and veins* (6th ed.). New York: McGraw-Hill.

17. Edelman, C., & Mandle, C. L. (1986). *Health promotion throughout the lifespan*. St. Louis: C. V. Mosby.

18. Eliopoulos, C. (1987). *Gerontological nursing* (2nd ed.). Philadelphia: J. B. Lippincott.

19. Engel, N. S. (1987). Menopausal stage, current life change, attitude toward women's roles, and perceived health status. *Nursing Research, 36,* 353–357.

20. Feldman, E. B. (1986). *Nutrition in the middle and later years*. New York: Warner Books.

21. Forbes, G. B. (1987). *Human body composition: Growth, aging, nutrition, and activity*. New York: Springer-Verlag.

22. Foreman, L. (1983). The fat fallacy. *Health, 15*(9), 23.

23. Friedman, M., & Ulmer, D. (1984). *Treating Type-A behavior — and your heart*. New York: Alfred A. Knopf.

24. Gillmer, M. D. G. (1989). Metabolic effects of combined oral contraception. In M. Filshie & J. Guillebaud (Eds.), *Contraception: Science and practice* (pp. 11–38). Boston: Butterworths.

25. Goodwin, P. J. (1988). Studies in women with cyclical mastopathy. *British Journal of Surgery, 75,* 839–844.

26. Hall, D. A. (1976). *The aging of connective tissue*. New York: Academic Press.

27. Hall, D. A. (1985). Biology of aging: Metabolic and structural aspects. In J. C. Brocklehurst (Ed.), *Textbook of geriatric medicine and gerontology* (2nd ed., pp. 46–61). New York: Churchill Livingstone.

28. Harmon, D. (1983). Free radicals and the origination, evolution, and present status of the free radical theory of aging. In D. Armstrong, et al. (Eds.), *Aging: V. 27. Free radicals in molecular biology, aging, and disease* (pp. 1–12). New York: Raven Press.

29. Hayflick, L. (1979). The cell biology of aging. *Journal of Investigative Dermatology, 73*(1), 8–14.

30. Hirsch, J. (1988). New light on obesity. *New England Journal of Medicine, 318,* 509.

31. Iacono, J. M. (1987). Recommendations of the fat and fiber groups from the workshop on new developments on fat and fiber in carcinogenesis. *Preventive Medicine, 16,* 592–595.

32. Joint National Committee on Detection, Evaluation, and Treatment of High Blood Pressure. (1984). The 1984 Report of the Joint National Committee on Detection, Evaluation, and Treatment of High Blood Pressure. *Archives of Internal Medicine, 144,* 1047.

33. Journal of the American Medical Association. (1988). Health status of Vietnam veterans. *Journal of the American Medical Association, 259,* 2701–2719.

34. Jovanovic, L., & Subak-Sharpe, G. J. (1987). *Hormones: The woman's answer book*. New York: Ballantine Books.

35. Keesey, R. E., & Corbett, S. W. (1984). Metabolic defense of the body weight setpoint. In A. J. Stunkard & E. Stellar (Eds.), *Eating and its disorders*. New York: Raven Press.

36. Kennedy, R. D., & Caird, F. I. (1981). Physiology of aging of the heart. *Cardiovascular Clinics, 12*(1), 1–8.

37. Kline, D. W., & Schieber, F. (1985). Vision and aging. In J. E. Birren & K. W. Schaie (Eds.), *Handbook of the psychology of aging* (2nd ed.). New York: Van Nostrand Reinhold.

38. Kneisl, C. R., & Ames, S. W. (1986). *Adult health nursing: A biopsychosocial approach*. Reading, MA: Addison-Wesley.

39. Kobasa, S. C., et al. (1985). Relative effectiveness of hardiness, exercise, and social support as resources against illness. *Journal of Psychosomatic Research, 29,* 525–553.

40. Koretz, J. F., & Handleman, G. H. (1988). How the human eye focuses. *Scientific American, 259*(1), 92–99.

41. Ladewig, P. W., London, M. L., & Olds, S. B. (1990). *Essentials of maternal-newborn nursing* (2nd ed.). Redwood City, CA: Addison-Wesley.

42. Lamb, M. (1977). *Biology of aging*. New York: John Wiley and Sons.

43. Leis, H. P., et al. (1983). Fibrocystic breast disease. *Female Patient, 8,* 56–77.

44. Lindsay, R. (1987). Prevention of osteoporosis. *Clinical Orthopaedics and Related Research, 222,* 44–59.

45. Love, S. M., Gellman, R. S., & Silen, W. (1982). Fibrocystic 'disease' of the breast—a nondisease? *New England Journal of Medicine, 307,* 1010–1014.

46. Mack, T. M., & Ross, R. K. (1989). Risks and benefits of long-term treatment with estrogens. *Schweizerische Medizinsche Wochenschrift, 119,* 1811–1820.

47. Maddi, S. (1986, August). *The great stress-illness controversy*. Paper presented at the meeting of the American Psychological Association, Washington, DC.

48. Maffly, R. H. (1981). The body fluids: Volume, composition and physical chemistry. In B. M. Brenner & F. Rector (Eds.), *The kidney*. Philadelphia: W. B. Saunders.

49. Marcus, R. (1982). The relationship of dietary calcium to the maintenance of skeletal integrity in man: An interface of endocrinology and nutrition. *Metabolism, 31*(1), 257.

50. Masiak, M. J., Naylor, M. D., & Hayman, L. L. (1985). *Fluids and electrolytes through the life cycle*. Norwalk, CT: Appleton-Century-Crofts.

51. Masters, W. H., & Johnson, V. E. (1966). *Human sexual response*. Boston: Little, Brown.

52. Masters, W. H., & Johnson, V. E. (1970). *Human sexual inadequacy*. Boston: Little, Brown.

53. Matteson, M. A., & McConnell, E. S. (1988). *Gerontological nursing: Concepts and practice*. Philadelphia: W. B. Saunders.

54. Mazzaferri, F. I. (1986). *Textbook of endocrinology* (3rd ed.). New Hyde Park, NY: Medical Examination.

55. Mendelson, W. B. (1980). *The use and misuse of sleeping pills*. New York: Plenum Medical Book.

56. Mishell, D. R., & Brenner, P. F. (1986). Menopause. In D. R. Mishell, Jr. & V. Davajan (Eds.), *Infertility, contraception, and reproductive endocrinology* (2nd ed., pp. 179–202). Oradell, NJ: Medical Economics Books.

57. Mjör, I. A. (1985). Frequency of secondary caries at various anatomical locations. *Operative Dentistry, 10*(3), 88–92.

58. Murphy, W. (1982). *Dealing with headaches.* Alexandria, VA: Time-Life Books.

59. National Institutes of Health. (1985). Health implications of obesity. *Annals of Internal Medicine, 103,* 147.

60. Pesmen, C. (1984). *How a man ages.* New York: Ballantine Books.

61. Porcino, J. (1983). *Growing older, getting better: A handbook for women in the second half of life.* Reading, MA: Addison-Wesley.

62. Reaven, G. M., & Reaven, E. P. (1985). Age, glucose intolerance, and non–insulin-dependent diabetes mellitus. *Journal of the American Geriatric Society, 33,* 286–290.

63. Recker, R. R. (1985). Calcium absorption and achlorhydria. *New England Journal of Medicine, 313,* 70–73.

64. Redwine, F. O. (1988). Pregnancy in women over 35. *Female Patient, 13*(5), 30.

65. Reese, D., & Sears, C. (1989). Tooth report: Boning up on gums. *American Health, 8*(7), 43.

66. Rockstein, M. (Ed.). (1974). *Theoretical aspects of aging.* New York: Academic Press.

67. Samuels, M., & Samuels, N. (1988). *The well adult.* New York: Summit.

68. Sarrel, P., & Cole, E. (1985, May). *Sexuality in the climacteric: Issues and answers.* Paper presented at the annual meeting of the American Association of Sex Educators, Counselors, and Therapists, Chicago, IL.

69. Schafer, W. (1987). *Stress management for wellness.* New York: Holt, Rinehart and Winston.

70. Selye, H. (1976). *The stress of life* (rev. ed.). New York: McGraw-Hill.

71. Severson, J. A. (1984). Neurotransmitter receptors and aging. *Journal of the American Geriatrics Society, 32,* 24.

72. Siiteri, P. K. (1987). Adipose tissue as a source of hormones. *American Journal of Clinical Nutrition, 45*(Suppl. 1), 277–282.

73. Simopolulos, A. P. (1984). Body weight, health, and longevity. *Annals of Internal Medicine, 100,* 285.

74. Sloane, E. (1985). *Biology of women* (2nd ed.). New York: John Wiley and Sons.

75. Snowdon, D. A., Gonzalez, N., & O'Leary, B. M. (1989). Making mammography a habit. *Journal of the American Medical Association, 262,* 207.

76. Spence, A. P. (1989). *Biology of human aging.* Englewood Cliffs, NJ: Prentice-Hall.

77. Spencer, R. T., et al. (1989). *Clinical pharmacology and nursing management* (3rd ed.). Philadelphia: J. B. Lippincott.

78. Stunkard, A. J., & Stellar, E. (1984). *Eating and its disorders.* New York: Raven Press.

79. Tarr, J., & Macklin, M. (1987). Cocaine. *Pediatric Clinics of North America, 34*(2), 319–331.

80. Troll, L. E. (1982). *Continuations: Adult development and aging.* Monterey, CA: Brooks/Cole.

81. Walford, R. I. (1980). Immunology and aging. *American Journal of Clinical Pathology, 74,* 247.

82. Wenger, N. K., Goodwin, J. F., & Roberts, W. C. (1986). Cardiomyopathy. In J. W. Hurst, and Loque, R. B. (Ed.), *The heart arteries, and veins* (6th ed.). New York: McGraw-Hill.

83. Whitney, E. N., Cataldo, C. B., & Rolfes, S. R. (1987). *Understanding normal and clinical nutrition.* St. Paul, MN: West Publishing.

84. Willett, W. C., et al. (1987). Relative and absolute excess risks of coronary heart disease among women who smoke cigarettes. *New England Journal of Medicine, 317,* 1303–1309.

85. Williams, P. T., et al. (1987). Associations of dietary fat, regional adiposity, and blood pressure in men. *Journal of the American Medical Association, 257,* 3151–3256.

86. Williams, S. R. (1990). *Essentials of nutrition and diet therapy* (5th ed.). St. Louis: Times Mirror/Mosby College Pub.

87. Wyatt, R. J. (1985). *After middle age.* New York: McGraw-Hill.

Psychosocial Development During Middle Adult Years

Lois G. Andreas

Historically, the 40th birthday has been seen as a personal landmark, the beginning of old age. When life is tenuous, many parents do not live to see their children into adulthood. As life spans have lengthened, people have developed an increased appreciation for both the quality of life and the changing relationships between generations. Today, neither grandparenthood nor "the big four-O" signals the end of life. A new era has emerged—middlescence—the generation in between the active years of parenthood, personal, and career development and those of retirement or formal old age.

During middlescence, arbitrarily the years between 40 and 60, most adults have passed the stage of youthful idealism, must acknowledge the reality of the passage of time, respond to present opportunities, and begin to make plans for the future. The individual who actively developed his or her value system and identity during the earlier years finds the changes that accompany middlescence merely one more step in the evolving understanding and expression of the self. This continuation of "identity homework" assists the middle-age adult to realistically assess expected and unexpected life events. Uncertainty, differences, tragedies, and other stressors are tolerated with greater equanimity (Fig. 36-1).

Past experiences and decisions have a cumulative effect on the quality of one's life. An adverse environment may result in unemployment, poverty, homelessness, and related health problems. Many of these negative environments are chosen (perhaps by default) during earlier years by failure to complete an education, premature assumptions of sexual, parental, and family responsibilities, or inadequate self-discipline. Other negative environments may be the result of changing technology, political issues, cultural upbringing, disasters, or national economy.

Because of environmental circumstances beyond their control, even emotionally mature people can be caught in the throes of physical survival and social stigma. Conversely, some miserable, immature individuals can be stuck in the throes of affluence and power. Financial or even social status does not equate with emotional maturity. *Internal issues of coping and adaptation,* not the external problems of poverty or oppression, *define successful middlescence.* When prior choices and identity resolution have been adequate and when a person has mastered previous developmental tasks, he or she arrives at middle age with abundant strengths.

The plus side is that middlescence is not too late to resolve one's identity homework. One has multiple opportunities to actively examine what has been and what is yet to be. As life is reevaluated, midcourse adjustments can be made. Consequently, these years can be a time of crisis, reversal, constriction, and disintegration, or one of stability, expansion, healing, renewal, and self-actualization, depending on the person's willingness and ability to face life's exigencies.

The transitions of the middlescent years become challenging and exciting as op-

FIGURE 36–1.
Some people find the physical changes that accompany middlescence to be uncomfortable reminders of escaping time. (Garfield. Copyright © United Features Syndicate, Inc., 1982. With permission.)

portunities for personal development and service to others are recognized. Depending on the person's assets, coping abilities, unique opportunities, and support systems, the individual can function at ever evolving higher levels of development. As an individual reevaluates family relationships, lifestyle, career goals, and personal interests, he or she often discovers new energy, insightfulness, attitudes, approaches, and even self-appreciation. Middle age offers more opportunities for creativity and generativity than any prior phase of development.

THEORETICAL PERSPECTIVES ON PSYCHOSOCIAL DEVELOPMENT OF MIDDLESCENCE

Many theorists believe that there is continued psychological scaffolding during adult life that is determined by past experiences and decisions. Others believe that progression toward a more complex self is based on crisis resolution. Some theorists describe changes as self-actualization or gradual evolving of the self, punctuated by temporary, stressful, and even regressive events. In actuality, these theorists are perhaps describing different aspects of the same experience.

The Psychodynamic Theorists

Freud

Sigmund Freud believed that an individual reached emotional maturity as the five stages of childhood (oral, anal, phallic, latency, and genital) were mastered successfully. Unresolved conflicts became a negative part of the person's adult personality structure, resulting in anxiety and symptomatic behaviors.[29]

Freud did not see adulthood as a period of further growth and development but rather as a time when unconscious conflicts of childhood could be resolved. He proffered that an adult could gain insight into neurotic behavior by exploring the meaning of thoughts, feelings, and actions as they relate to one's childhood experiences. He believed that successful psychoanalysis resulted in a "reasonably happy adult" who regained access to blocked potentials.

Jung's Psychoanalytical Theory

Carl Jung's main interest was the "second half of life." As a student of Freud, he agreed that many adults were still caught up in the emotional conflicts of childhood. However, he also observed that personal development could not be completed by the end of adolescence.

Jung was the first to become aware of a midlife crisis, or, as he termed it, "a critical turning point of life." He proposed that a major opportunity for change occurs around 40, the "noon of life," when a person can develop and integrate new or neglected aspects into one's personality.[44] He viewed this as a time of reversals, when a man takes on more traditionally feminine characteristics by becoming more affective and shifting to interpersonal commitment, and a woman assumes more traditionally masculine roles by becoming more instrumental or powerful and returning to work. Thus, a greater sense of balance between male and female characteristics (androgyny) emerges and permits men and women to express their true personalities and be less concerned about cultural stereotypes (Fig. 36-2).

Sullivan's Interpersonal Theory

After almost 20 years of clinical investigation, Harry Stack Sullivan concluded that early life experiences continued to influence mental health (as opposed to mental illness). The "self system" (personality and self-esteem) develops through the process of approval and disapproval in contacts with significant others. When tension is recurrent in interactions with others, serious problems of adult living are precipitated.[97]

Sullivan describes a series of tools and tasks relevant to each of his stages. The main tool of adulthood is *collaboration,* the ability to adjust one's own behavior and needs to another's needs or goals, thus gaining mutual gratification. Emphasis is on consensual validation through reciprocal

FIGURE 36–2.
Middlescence is a wonderful period in the life cycle. The person has enough experience to provide competence and confidence and enough physical energy to invest with enthusiasm.

communication. The main task of adulthood is *to achieve feelings of love and intimacy* through mutual acceptance of all aspects of the other. According to Sullivan, this highly developed intimacy is not the principle business of life but is, perhaps, the principal source of satisfaction in life.

Erikson's Epigenetic Theory

Erik Erikson bridges the gap between psychoanalytical models and the task-oriented theorists that follow. He also embraces a humanist philosophy in his impressive analysis of life-span biographical sketches of leaders such as Ghandi. Erikson popularized the idea of the life span as a continuum of developmental phases.[22] Ideally, as each is resolved, the individual gains an increased sense of unity. Aging per se does not ensure maturity; but maturity increases as each task is mastered. Potential for growth and further development always exists.

Erikson's seventh stage, **generativity versus stagnation,** is considered pivotal to successful negotiation of the middle years (see Appendix C for a listing of all stages). However, the identity homework, which assumed such great significance in adolescence (see Chap. 25), is ongoing. Through the processes of observation, reflection, self-discovery, and increasing differentiation, identity becomes more stable and unique as life experiences are integrated into a unified sense of self and expression. If identity is well founded, it eases the transitions of midlife and continues to strengthen one's self-concept and value system.

The primary focus of generativity is to accept responsibility for and offer leadership in establishing and guiding the next generation. It encompasses procreativity, produc-

tivity, and creativity.[23] Each individual and culture resolves this task differently. Some express generativity by nurturing their own or others' children or by supporting continued development of other adults, others by their unique creative involvement in social causes and organizations, still others by investing ideas and energy into new business ventures or the creative arts (Fig. 36-3).

When one fails to master the challenges of generativity, regression to stagnation and personal impoverishment oc-

FIGURE 36–3.
Erikson's task of generativity takes many forms as the individual tries to improve the quality of life for those around him or her or to leave something of value for future generations.

curs.[23] One has not found something higher than self to live for, and consequently one develops a sense of being "stuck in a rut" or bogged down and without self-fulfillment. The refreshing, renewing enrichment inherent in generativity is missed. The stagnating individual seems to be vegetating, doing nothing more than the required activities of daily living and work. This behavior results in a self-absorbed, preoccupied, egocentric, nonproductive person (the contemporary "couch potato"). Recognition of the emptiness and pain of stagnation may motivate some individuals toward generativity.

Recently, several developmentalists have attempted to investigate the predictive validity of Erikson's theory as a model for successful aging. An inventory has been developed to measure Erikson's eight stages of the life-span in adults.[18] Some results suggest that psychosocial crises have different implications based on gender.[98]

Task-Oriented Theorists

Peck's Developmental Tasks of Middle Age
Robert Peck concluded that reassessment of self is the prevailing theme of middle age.[72] He thought Erikson's stages of intimacy and generativity were more crucial to young adulthood, while Erikson's last stage, integrity, represented the major issue of life after age 30. Feeling that the latter half of life deserved as much attention as the earlier years, he looked for additional tasks faced during middle and old age.

Peck's first task of middle age is **valuing wisdom versus valuing physical powers.** Biological changes are inevitable, causing physical powers such as strength, stamina, and youthful attractiveness to decline. From his analysis of thousands of business people (mostly men), he observed that most reach a critical transition period somewhere between the late thirties and early forties where "middle age depression" can occur if physique continues to be a major source of identity. If, however, this source of identity is replaced by deeper values and judgment, the individuals gain the necessary wisdom (emotional stability, motivation, and intellectual ability) for solving life problems.

Mastery of Peck's second task, **socializing versus sexualizing** in human relationships, emphasizes redefining men and women as individual personalities rather than as sexual objects. Mastery provides the potential for added depth and understanding in interpersonal relationships.

As his third task, Peck defines **cathectic or emotional flexibility versus cathectic impoverishment** as the capacity to shift emotional investments from one person or activity to another. The potential for crisis exists because, as parents and friends begin to die and children grow up and leave home, they need to be replaced adaptively by investing in new interpersonal pursuits.

Peck's fourth task of middle age is **mental flexibility versus mental rigidity.** As the mature person faces new problems in life, he or she creatively seeks new solutions and actively explores options offered by others. Immature adults continue to face problems with the same solutions used in the past. They become rigid, inflexible, close-minded, and set in their ways. "But this is the way we've always done it."

Schuster's Tasks
Clara Schuster offers 10 developmental tasks (see unit introduction) for the middle adult years that build off the successful mastery of the tasks of the young adult years. These tasks address all five domains but focus primarily on the individual's continued identity refinement and its expression in relationships to others. The healthy middlescent continues to discover new strengths within one's self that provide a new confidence for facing life's exigencies, solving problems, exploring talents, and relating to others. Healthy development does not depend on physical integrity, financial comfort, marital status, or reproductive success but depends on the person's ability to find meaning in life and relationships. Healthy middlescents tap into and feel their own strength as they meet the needs of others; their creative energies are released as they let go of past goals and fears; they find freedom from fear as they face their own mortality; their energies are renewed as they expend themselves in serving others (Fig. 36-4).

Levinson's Theory of Individual Life Structure
Daniel Levinson postulates a concept of "individual life structure." Based on his biographical study of 40 men, he discovered age-linked "seasons" or "eras."[54] Middle adulthood, initiated by the midlife transition, starts around age 40. Transitional tasks include **reappraising one's life, integrating the polarities** (or opposing tendencies such as young/old, destruction/creation, and masculine/feminine), and **modifying one's life structure** to prepare for middle adulthood. Introspection occurs again near the "age 50 transition" (50–55). Be-

FIGURE 36–4.
Interests, talents, and skills continue to be influenced both by past experiences and by one's current associations to provide a basis for social relationships and for aesthetic expression.

tween transitions, the individual works on building his or her life structure and accomplishing major goals.

Levinson describes middle adulthood as a period of increased reflection, reduced irritation from self-conflicts and external demands, and increased compassion and loving of self and others. This "dominant generation" assumes responsibility for themselves as well as the development of children and young adults. (Note similarities to Erikson's generativity). Levinson's initial studies on women suggest that both men and women go through similar developmental periods, but there are significant differences in the issues they face and the ways they traverse the periods.[53] In one study, women whose lives were organized around work tended to fit Levinson's categorization better than women with traditionally feminine commitments to their partners and children.[40]

Other Stage Theorists

Gould and Sheehy both include women in their descriptions but rely on stage patterns developed mainly from study of men.[31] Gould indicates that the transformation or growth process at midlife differs and may even conflict for men and women if they have led traditional lifestyles. Women are recognizing options that expand their sense of independence and power, while men are becoming more sensitive to life and options outside the work world.[34]

Since adult development has been explored mainly from a masculine perspective, most theorists do not address the fact that women reach midlife with a different psychological history than men and face a different social reality and different possibilities for love and work.[33] Gilligan and some other theorists hypothesize that the complexity of women's roles requires a more abstract theory based on the multidimensional lives of women to appreciate the meshing and relativity of education, work, and family life.[32, 33, 40]

Bernice Neugarten theorizes that women tend to define their age status relative to the timing of events within the family cycle.[65] She observes that chronological age is an increasingly unreliable indicator of development and that the timing of these experiences is more pertinent.[67]

Humanist Theorists

Abraham Maslow concentrated on mental **health** (as opposed to mental illness) and factors that he felt psychoanalysts neglected: creativity, potential for freedom, happiness, and contentment. One of his most important concepts is **self-actualization,** the drive to develop potentials and to become a better person. Self-actualized adults view the self and others objectively and realistically, learn from others, admit what they don't know, and develop kinship with others regardless of differences. They are dedicated to something they feels is important, can face challenges, and can be creative, flexible, and spontaneous. From a humanist perspective, middlescence is the time when a person can fully blossom.

The needs that motivate self-actualization are presented in a hierarchical format (see Appendix C). As lower level needs are met, more mature needs emerge. Individuals motivated by deficiencies are concerned with meeting lower level needs: physical survival, safety, love, belonging, and esteem. In contrast, self-actualizing persons have met these needs and consequently are freed to develop their innate capacities. Maslow felt that fewer than 1% of people become truly self-actualized.[57] He recognized his theory as inadequate in explaining why so many fail to develop their potentials but theorized that many have difficulty moving toward self-actualization because of an inadequately supportive environment (see "life-span needs" in Epilogue).

Universality in theories of middle age is impossible, since each theorist proceeds from his or her own perspective. Placing these specific theories in a holistic framework, however, helps to explain the complexities of human development. This approach recognizes that an individual's behavior is a composite of physiological, affective, cognitive, social, and spiritual factors. The role of social, cultural, and historic change in individual development is also acknowledged.[52]

CHALLENGES OF MIDDLESCENCE

Middle age is a period of heightened sensitivity to one's relative position within a complex social environment and in the continuity of generations. It is a time for occupational, intrapersonal, and interpersonal fulfillment. Self-assessment is a prevailing theme as life is reconsidered in light of aging and death. Early signs of physical decline must be acknowledged, and roles that were formerly taken for granted are questioned. At the same time, career changes, second careers, reentry into the work force, resumption of educational pursuits, involvement in community and civic organizations, and planning for retirement and leisure time all provide opportunities for increased or continued productivity and creativity during the middle years.

Family Relationships

Family of Creation

Spouse

The most significant social system of interaction is one's family. This includes one's family of origin as well as one's family of creation. The person may be single or in a couple relationship. Children may or may not be present. The midyears frequently see renegotiation and renewal for marriages. Power and responsibility must be rebalanced as family membership and personal needs change. This struggle becomes most obvious as children leave the home and each partner is faced with examining the relationship. Separate interests and responsibilities, considered normative during young adulthood, are challenged as the couple is again faced with togetherness.

Men, traditionally immersed in careers, tend to base their self-concepts predominantly on career success and may consider themselves good husbands and fathers because they provide adequately.[6] Many midlife men become aware of overinvolvement at work and inadequate involvement with their families as their children begin to leave home.[54] They may sense occupational peaking, become weary of self-assertion, and regret that they have, to varying degrees, sacrificed interpersonal and family commitments.[25]

Women have assumed increasingly complex roles as educational levels increase and career patterns expand. New patterns have emerged for women and require coordination of family and work roles outside the home throughout adult life.[66] No single role guarantees a sense of satisfaction and self-esteem.[6] Satisfaction depends on the value attached to a role and whether it permits one to express competencies and interests.[31] Many women are still socialized to define their role in terms of the timing of events within the family cycle, middle age being the time when children are supposed to leave the home. Thus, even unmarried or childless women often discuss middle age in terms of a family they might have had. Some women may make a "last chance" effort to have children before it is biologically too late. Consequently, for many women, midlife issues relate to the ending or absence of child rearing and the increased need for new goals and outlets for energies.

A husband and wife may take developmentally divergent paths. If a wife is seeking more growth and diversity through work or other commitments and the husband is seeking more evidence of love and emotional support, the potential for conflict is heightened. Survival of the marriage after children leave the home, to a great extent, depends on the growth, maturity, and commitment attained by each over the years. If marital communication and common interests have been maintained, the potential to expand a rewarding relationship exists. If spouses have grown apart, the differing interests can lead to tension and resentment. The stress involved in the changes in roles and identity can lead to divorce.

The couple can react to the changes with role rigidity or role disequilibrium, by falling apart or by revitalizing development.[100] For many couples, middle and late adulthood are times to renew their companionship. They may go on second honeymoons, take time to revitalize their sensuality, and increase their intimacy through stronger bonds of friendship and companionship.

Many people are not involved in spousal relationships, being lifelong singles, divorced, or widowed. Lifelong singlehood may "just happen" for some, while it is a conscious choice for others. Nevertheless, strong and stable interpersonal relationships are just as critical to mental health and management of stress for singles as for married persons. Most singles have at least one *significant other* of the same or opposite gender or may be an "adopted" family member.[55, 95] Men become increasingly aware that they may be contributing to their single state and fear growing old alone.[103] Single men and women often wonder if they should have married, stayed married, remarried, or had children. Regardless of marital status, commitments to relationships must still be renewed and intimacy reestablished as identity homework continues.

Offspring

Midlife presents a wide variety of parenting possibilities. Many women today deliberately defer marriage or motherhood. Between 1972 and 1982, birth of first children for 35 to 39 year old women rose 83%.[38] Increasing numbers of women are having children with the intention of rearing them alone. In addition, single men and women are adopting children with greater frequency. Thus, at 40, some individuals or couples are preparing for their first child, some have young children, while others have adolescents. Still others have reared their children and are facing the empty-nest period or grandparenthood. This variety gives validity to Neugarten's idea that the occurrence and timing of life events are more pertinent than chronological age in determining development.[67]

Parenthood is *not* a prerequisite for happiness in middle age. Middle-age, childless couples do not differ from empty-nest couples in any area of life satisfaction except with regard to relationships with children.[4] Those without children are not necessarily unhappy about choosing to forgo child rearing, nor are they necessarily less fulfilled. However, some evidence suggests that parenting serves as a foundation for mastery of generativity in middle-age men.[93]

Ideally, individuals change and mature as they face the challenges of parenthood. Parenting provides opportunities for creativity and an avenue for sharing the joy of life with others. At each age, children require a new balance of authority, friendship, and releasing. A child's growth necessitates a change in the parents as new responsibilities emerge. Hopefully, mutually satisfying relationships are established beginning with teaching, learning, and playing together. As a child matures, support of growth and working together become more of a focus. Finally, as the child achieves independence, emotionally, socially, and financially, the relationship evolves into one of mutual support and involvement, adult to adult.

Empty Nest. Parents are described as experiencing the "empty-nest syndrome" when they feel depression specific to the absence of children to nurture. Research documents that women are more likely than men to be affected by the exodus of offspring (although fathers who missed much of their children's development are more likely to suffer empty-nest depression).[84] Mothers are more likely to anticipate the event and express concern or sadness, but they may also experience a sense of relief and look forward to increased freedom from child care and housekeeping responsibilities.[4, 17, 100] Women who cherish the increased time and independence do not experience stress over the departure of children, nor do they view the "empty nest" as a disaster. Instead, they turn their generativity toward new horizons in this new phase of life.

Parenting rarely ends with the departure of children from the home, and many nests are never truly empty. Though not residing in their parents' home, most offspring continue to need the emotional support and mentor qualities found in a warm parenting relationship. Parents remain significant to their children throughout—and beyond—their lifetimes.[60]

Some children may not leave home when expected or may return home for financial reasons. Thus, parents may be prevented from experiencing the freedom necessary to evaluate marital relationships, redevelop intimacy, and expand latent talents and interests.[16, 27]

The transition from active parenting to continuing parenthood presents adjustment problems. Roles need to be mutually redefined and restructured with grown children.[33, 71] If a woman's identity and time management have depended on the activities of her children or have focused on their demands and ignored her own needs, she may experience depression.[31] She is losing the sense of connection on which she relies and the activity of caring through which she judges her worth.[33] If, however, she is able to transplant the rich emotions and unique power of parenting to other generative endeavors—and feels a sense of competence and effectiveness—she is less likely to experience despair.

Grandparenthood. Grandparenting is a phenomenon of middle age that extends into late adulthood, owing to decreasing mortality rates and lengthening life spans. For the first time in history, most children get to know all of their grandparents.[36] Grandparenthood has been described as a roleless role, encompassing rich diversity.[5] The range extends from vigorous, youthful, involved adults to feeble elderly in need of care themselves. From a developmental perspective, it

would seem obvious that a 40-year-old grandparent would vary considerably from one who is 65 or 85.

Grandparents serve as models of aging and integrity to both parents and grandchildren.[47] Their presence serves to maintain the identity and sense of continuity of the family and to provide a buffer against its mortality.[5] Becoming a grandparent, however, means enlarging one's identity to include these new roles and to deal with the resulting changes in family relationships.[88] Grandparenthood provides opportunities to reface issues related to parenting and generativity.[23] With the perspective of greater wisdom and maturity, an individual might look forward to being a better grandparent than he or she was a parent.[68] This new role is facilitated by the removal of many of the constraints related to rearing one's own children.

Few grandparents wish to return to a parenting role with their grandchildren. Many grandparents are too involved in their own careers to repeat the parenting career. The absence of continuous, direct responsibility is a relief to them. Their relationship can concentrate on leisure and psychosocial and cultural transmission issues. Figure 36-5 identifies a range of activities that grandparents typically share with grandchildren. Even when grandchildren consume a good deal of their time, most grandparents do not think of their current lives as focusing primarily on their grandchildren.

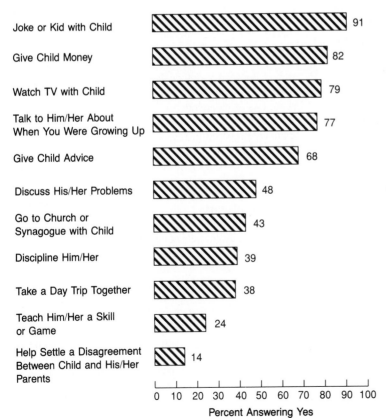

FIGURE 36–5.
Percentage of grandparents who engaged in various activities with their grandchildren during the previous 12 months. (Cherlin, A. J., & Furstenberg, F. F. (1986). The New American Grandparent *(p. 74). New York: Basic Books. With permission.)*

Five styles of grandparenting have been identified.[68] The **formal grandparent** maintains clearly demarcated lines between themselves and the parents, displaying interest in the children but not offering advice or seeking extra time with the grandchildren. A **fun-seeker** relationship is informal, leisure oriented, and mutually satisfying. These grandparents make opportunities for memory-filled experiences. A **surrogate parent** is usually a grandmother who assumes caregiving responsibility, while the parents work or pursue an education. The **reservoir of family wisdom** is often the grandfather, who assumes an authoritarian role, with parents taking subordinate positions. Lastly, the **distant figure** is the grandparent who is involved only in family functioning for ritualistic occasions.

Developmentally, grandparenthood may have multiple meanings to people. It may offer a sense of completion, a recognition of their role in the succession of generations, an affirmation of their value system, a hedge against death, and a source of great personal pleasure.[13] Many grandparents value being a teacher or resource person, appreciate the opportunity to play a new emotional role, and achieve vicarious satisfaction through their grandchildren's accomplishments (Fig. 36-6).[68]

FIGURE 36–6.
Grandparenthood adds a whole new dimension to one's life. Many grandparents say that they enjoy the privileges of parenthood without the responsibilities.

As in all developmental tasks, opportunities for growth are crossed with potential for developmental arrest or regression. Ambivalence in anticipating the new role of grandparenthood is normal.[56] One must deal with doubts regarding readiness to become a grandparent, perhaps feeling prematurely old. One must also come to terms with the new identity role and the changing family relationships. It is a challenge to balance intense interest and concern for grandchildren without usurping the parents' roles.

Understanding how grandparenting intersects with other life processes and aging tasks can have a positive impact on well-being in adulthood.[46] Facing retirement and anticipating the loss of career involvement can be replaced by grandchildren who positively value their grandparents' love and wisdom; coming to terms with growing old and facing mortality can be entwined with the security that generational continuity is ensured, and traditions, culture, folklore, and skills can be passed on. Generativity endeavors are enhanced and extended by willing, active involvement in grandparental relationships with one's kin or friends.

Family of Origin

Aging Parents

Although the developmental focus of middle age has traditionally been on generational relationships with the young, middlescents must also help older family members meet the transitions of later life. Three- and even four-generation families have become a common phenomenon. Consequently, filial responsibility has become a new role and major developmental task for adult children.[8] Adult children have become known as the "sandwich generation"; their needs are sandwiched between those of their children who are seeking increased independence and those of aging parents who are facing loss of independence.[24, 63]

Although parental aging is expected, most adults are not optimally prepared to respond to age-related transitions in the lives of their parents or to assume increased responsibility for them during illness, disability, or even the process of dying.[63] Dealing with personality changes or alternative living accommodations is less stressful and disruptive than the psychic adjustment required with role reversals in leadership and caregiving. Of all caregiving groups, adult children report the highest levels of emotional strain, especially children with the closest parental bonds.[37]

Adult daughters, and some daughters-in-law, usually become the primary filial caregivers, although sons also participate, especially if no females are available.[79] Since many middle-age women already work or are returning to work or school, their ability to provide care to elderly parents is seriously tested.[24] These women are identified as high-risk for stress-related health problems. A 50-year-old woman's responsibilities may include children, grandchildren, husband, home, career, and a 70- or 80-year-old dependent parent.

The intensity of family relationships and support may increase as the functional skills of elderly parents decrease.[13]

Ironically, middle-age adults are experiencing peak independence and career mobility. Nevertheless, most adult children act responsibly in helping parents and in ensuring or providing adequate care and support.[79] Although an elderly parent in the home can be mutually gratifying and helpful, most older adults prefer to maintain their independence and live near their children, not with them.[8] The primary support they desire is emotional. Middlescents indicate that they are comfortable adjusting family, but not work, schedules to help out. They share the financial burden but find it undesirable to share households.[63]

When problems exist or seem likely, both sides often avoid discussing issues so as not to worry one another. Parents seem to discuss funeral wishes more easily than their children. They feel a need to discuss what they want to happen if they become incapacitated or unable to live alone. Clear intergenerational communication is essential, focusing on mutual awareness and respect for one another's needs, limits, and abilities.[19] Contrary to popular belief, older people are not alienated from their families. Strong ties exist and most elderly people value relationships with their adult children. The issue for *both* middlescent adults and their parents centers around independence—achieving it, maintaining it, or losing it. The paradox is that independence is actually enhanced and personal growth is experienced by renewing one's bond to one's family of creation.

Sharp declines in birth rates since the 1950s will decrease available filial caregivers for the current generation of middle-age adults as they swell the ranks of older adulthood within the next 20 to 30 years. The potential impact of this fact on both the next generation of older adults (current middlescents) and middle-age adults (current young adults) is recognized but remains unresolved.

Siblings

Sibling relationships increase in importance with middle-age adults and are most often characterized by positive feelings rather than negative feelings or feelings of rivalry.[75] However, adult sibling interactional problems may surface again, especially when dividing an estate or assigning care responsibilities if rivalry was inadequately handled during earlier years.

When families include more than one living adult child, filial responsibility is often shared.[59] However, those geographically closer to parents usually assume more responsibility for parental care and may harbor feelings of anger or resentment toward more distant or less involved relatives. These feelings may be compounded if guilt and emotional distancing are felt by those who are less involved, and they in turn feel resentful and angry toward those living closer.[63] The result is often confusion over roles and care-providing needs. Thus, intergenerational communication must encompass the sibling relationships as well as the parent relationship. The obligations of caring for aging parents can renew bonding and commitment and bring parents, brothers, and sisters closer together.[100]

Generational Relationships

The middlescent adult serves as the bridge between generations, both within the family and in the wider context of the community.[72] Generativity involves being responsible for and caring for others and younger adults, serving as a mentor, providing leadership, and generally contributing to the strength and continuity of subsequent generations.[93] Since values and expectations shift as times change, life and world events impact generational relationships.[82] Middlescents now approaching age 60 were born during the Depression years and grew up during World War II. The "baby boomers," born after the war and now approaching their fifties, are products of a more affluent society, while those approaching middle age were born in the 1950s, an era of prosperity turned into upheaval and dropout by the Vietnam War and the drug subculture in the 1960s. Television, space exploration, desegregation, changing sex roles, drugs, and computer technology are but a few of the massive changes that have become a part of a 40 year old's cultural experience that were not a part of a 60 year old's experience at the same point in development.[69]

Peers

Midlife reassessment, children leaving the home, grandparenting, caring for elderly parents, career reentry, returning to education, and leisure choices all influence peer choices in middle age. When children leave the home, more time is provided for a person to enjoy an active social life with people of all ages. Middlescents generally have many acquaintances, but deep friendships are still limited by time availability, longevity of acquaintance, values, and interests. The healthy husband and wife encourage each other to develop peer relationships different from their "couple" friends or the spouse's work peers.

Nurturing friendships and having at least one confidante relationship is viewed as health-promoting for men and women, married or single. As extended families become less available, extended friendships become essential, especially to singles. Friends often become "close kin."[55, 74]

Community

Generativity includes extending a sense of caring, commitment, and responsibility beyond one's immediate family and peer group to the neighborhood, church organizations, and local or even extended communities. Middle age provides a time for expanding relationships and taking an interest in the welfare of others by finding a new balance of involvement with society. Society's rewards become less important and one's contributions and resources more important.[23, 54] In other words, the truly generative person finds intrinsic reward in involvement with others. Extrinsic rewards are unexpected "icing" on the cake (Fig. 36-7).

Men and women generally select areas of social or civic service that have special meaning to them. An adult whose parent died of cancer may choose to volunteer for a hospice, while another with teen-age children might be involved with

FIGURE 36–7.
Generativity is expressed by sharing one's skills and interests with the next generation.

FIGURE 36–8.
Community activities and traditions provide challenges for middlescents to continue to hone their talents and opportunities to share and model these skills and traditions for younger generations.

Mothers Against Drunk Driving (MADD). Young adults typically are involved on a smaller scale at the local level because their main energies, of necessity, are directed toward career and family development. Well-developing middle-age adults, however, assume increasingly responsible positions in occupational, social, and civic organizations. Even at local levels, middlescents are needed to volunteer in major service positions. As their skills, interest, and time increase, they assume leadership functions or shift to larger social systems. Although most adults are not involved on the national or international level, those who are typically come from the middle adult segment (Fig. 36–8).

Career

Changes and Choices

Traditionally, men focus on a narrow career track for 20 to 25 years until sometime after midlife. They tend to "take stock" during middle age, noting discrepancies between early career expectations and actual accomplishments.[15, 54, 69] A heightened awareness of age and the brevity of time left to live and work result in an emotional reaccounting. Some people renew efforts to realize their "dreams" before it is too late. Some scale down professional aspirations and become more

involved with family. Others, exhausted by the responsibility of trying to get ahead, decide to be content with life as it is.

Middlescent men are often surprised by the awareness of age in their work settings.[65] Being referred to as a "senior member" or "experienced employee" by a young colleague brings the difference sharply into focus. For some, these references offer a sense of accomplishment or prestige, for others, an uncomfortable awareness of aging. Although the man may experience the privilege of rank, there is a concomitant loss of older associates for support and guidance.[69] The man may also fear competition from or loss of job to a younger adult. Those who do lose their jobs usually experience a severe crisis. Men who are not able to find an acceptable job replacement continue to define this crisis as one of the most distressing events of their lives.[86]

Women, on the other hand, traditionally experience multiple role demands and a pattern of entries and exits from the labor force.[14, 66] Eventually, a women with children faces an empty nest and is released from daily responsibility for her children. She becomes free to pursue a new career, service, or educational opportunity, reenter a career left behind, or more fully invest in a career simultaneously pursued with child-rearing and family responsibilities.

Studies have shown that women who are lifelong singles

generally achieve higher educational and career status, are more assertive and goal-oriented, and have higher self-esteem than married women who have invested primarily in home and family.[74] High-achieving women may find it more difficult to identify true peers. They need to seek out other women who are like themselves, both as supportive friends and as appropriate comparison points.[6] Women's professional groups and networking organizations can serve this need.

Reentry into Paid Work Force

Presumed diminishing capacity and prejudice may pose employment dilemmas for a man who wishes to change careers or a woman who is entering the work force after an absence of many years. Flexibility, adaptability, and trainability are important factors in adjusting to new work situations.[3] Even when one has been out of the labor force for extended periods of time, specific skills, such as organizational talents, mature wisdom, and volunteer accomplishments, can be emphasized to relate to an employer's needs.[12] Retraining and continuing education programs are beginning to accommodate to the learning patterns of middlescents. Prior knowledge and experience, as well as initial anxiety and low self-confidence, are taken into account.

Education

Education is often the key to personally satisfying lives in middle age by opening new interests, opportunities, and skills.[74] College programs are reflecting an increased enrollment of adults. Many institutions and businesses are actively seeking older students as a way to increase revenues. Research indicates increasingly widespread participation of midlife women in formal education, many pursuing lifelong career goals.[61] Men, returning in smaller numbers, are usually changing careers or expanding educational credentials to ensure job competitiveness. Life experiences and joy in learning seem to facilitate their education.[3] Experiences from parenting, volunteering, and earlier jobs spark meaningful educational insights. Adult students often have to overcome obstacles such as a change in self-image, lack of confidence, fear of competition, and feeling out of place with younger students. Some may feel guilt when family and friends exert negative pressure that stems from anger over lack of free access to the person for support, fun, and comfort. Yet, once accommodated to the classroom, older students are empowered toward self-expression, creativity, and enhanced self-image.

Increasing Responsibility

As a person approaches midlife, he or she becomes less dependent on colleagues, supervisors, and mentors. This independence challenges the adult to find new ways to combine authority and leadership, while encouraging participation and fostering the growth of young adults toward greater independence and authority.[54] Being a mentor is one of the special contributions that individuals in middle adulthood can make to society. As people move toward senior positions,

they have the wisdom, skills, and life experience, plus a generation of separation, that distinguishes them from younger adult colleagues. Acting as a mentor offers new responsibilities, challenges, and opportunities that fall into the realm of true generativity. One may mentor formally or informally in a career, in the community, or even in a classroom as a fellow student.

One may have a sense of obligation when doing something for another. Yet, the greatest benefit may be in developing mutually supportive relationships with younger but capable adults.[95] Mentor relationships are focused toward helping younger adults to obtain valuable knowledge and skills and to become more independent, integrated human beings. Skills are sharpened as one concentrates on providing leadership to less-experienced persons. The reward comes in the vicarious experience of observing the independence or success of the other and knowing that you are a major contributor.

Leisure Time

Quality of Life

Modern leisure seems to be a mixed blessing, either being too scarce or too plentiful, depending on one's circumstances. It has the potential to enhance the quality of life and to be a stress-reducer, yet some people actually become more tense when faced with leisure or relaxation options.[20] Leisure activities can provide balance for work, fulfilling needs and providing outlets not met by jobs. In other cases, highly work-oriented individuals may carry their orientation into their leisure time.[99] Personality, more than situation, may determine leisure style.[39, 99]

Middlescent people may need to rediscover the significance of leisure activities. Later, these activities may be substituted for the work role.[81] Leisure activities may be home-centered, including gardening, canning, home repairs, sewing, or furniture refinishing. Some concentrate on travel, evenings out, or visiting friends. Others prefer more personally expressive leisure forms such as music, hobbies and crafts, writing, or painting, and still others devote their energies to community or church projects and welfare. Midlife reassessment of identity and values can expand leisure options that promote continued growth and development.

Development of Latent Talents and Interests

Freedom from child care responsibilities provides increased leisure time for men and women to pursue talents and interests that have, of necessity, remained dormant. These talents may open the doors to a new career or opportunity for community service, as well as to expanded peer networks and even new cultural horizons.

Service to Others

Many choose leisure activities with an eye to an extended sense of caring and responsibility typical of generativity. They feel that being of service to others is a productive way to spend leisure time, as well as another outlet for personal identity and creativity. Awareness of community resources and involvement in community activities can solidify a sense of commitment to others. The church or local community become "family" as they search for ways to improve life for others. Their choices may include volunteering, participating on community boards, running for an organizational or political office, or renovating a community landmark. Involvement profits other areas of life as well, enhancing self-esteem, channeling energy constructively, reducing stress, and serving as a bridge between preretirement and postretirement. The rewards of generativity far outweigh the energies expended.

Physical Changes

One of the major tasks of middlescence is to adapt to changes in the functioning of the physical domain.

Physical Appearance

The biophysical changes in middlescence often precipitate psychosocial responses. Living in a culture that emphasizes youthful appearance can make it frightening to be other than young.[54] At midlife it can be startling to realize suddenly that the body no longer fits the image. Overt changes such as graying and thinning hair, wrinkling faces, and drooping, drying skin accompany the maturing process. These biological changes frequently are more of an age marker for men than women, as they begin to be more aware of looking older and monitoring their own health.[65,91,103] Unattached men tend to be more concerned about changes in their physical appearance than their married counterparts.[70]

Some people try to compensate for aging by attempting to recreate a more youthful appearance or lifestyle, getting a younger wife or husband, having an extramarital affair, a new baby, hair transplants or cosmetic surgery, or frantically dieting and exercising. Alcohol or drugs may be used to enable one to avoid what one cannot face. Rather than facing and maturing with the changes and experiences of age, this person clings to the immature identities of adolescence. Focusing on oneself in this indulgent way leads to stagnation. One is in danger of missing the enrichments afforded by allocentric generativity.

Recognizing and accepting that the consequences of aging are inescapable encourage a shifting from physical values to mental values (Peck's "valuing wisdom versus valuing physical powers"). Individuals who have and continue to work on identity accept these changes as part of the normal aging process. Competency, complexity, and wisdom replace youthful attractiveness in self-definition as young–old polarities are integrated.

Strength and Stamina

The more covert signs of aging include a gradual decline in the ability to exercise strenuously, do hard physical labor, and respond to stress. Gradual decreases in physical power and stamina are normal through adulthood. Giving up youthful activities can be distressing to those who retain adolescent images of youth and age. Men and women who are comfort-able with their changing bodies and tolerant of imperfections stop striving to have "the perfect body." Diet and exercise are chosen to benefit individuals in a constructive health-centered rather than self-centered way. Individuals are able to make successful transitions when they accept physical limitations, assume prophylactic health maintenance habits, and value other middle age assets, such as maturity, wisdom, self-assurance, and cognitive skills.

Climacterium

Female Climacterium

The female climacterium, or "change of life," is shrouded in old wives' tales (e.g., severe depression, mental illness, physical traumas, and loss of attractiveness or sexual skills). Menopause does not produce a negative psychological state when one recognizes it for what it is: *a normal developmental stage in the lives of women.*[7,73,76,96] The traditional model falsely presumes that, until the moment of final menses, women are, want to be, and see themselves as potentially fertile. These assumptions are not necessarily compatible with patterns of reproduction in modern societies, in which the majority of women, by choice, have their last child before age 35.[45] The traditional model also attributes depression in middlescence to a woman's reaction to a household without children (assuming that children are leaving home as their mothers become menopausal). In actuality, no link exists between menopause and empty nest, nor does any evidence suggest that these two events occurring together cause depression.

To the contrary, one study identified that only 3% of women express regret during or after menopause about physical changes they have experienced.[77] Most women are relieved from the concerns of unwanted pregnancy and contraception. Although a significant event, the climacterium or menopause is relatively undramatic for most women. Even hot flashes have only minor effects on women's attitudes. Recent research on emotional responses to menopause reveals that social factors play a larger role than physical factors in a woman's response to the event.[96] Menopause per se is not a cause of depression, but rather it is reported by women who are already depressed because of factors related to work, home, or family.[73,77] Women who emphasize youthfulness and physical attractiveness, invest heavily in mothering roles, or experience excessive dependency needs or low self-esteem exhibit more menopausal symptomatology. Women with interests, education, or professions that potentiate their generativity are less apt to be negatively affected by menopause. If a woman perceives menopause as a loss of femininity, she may experience a grief reaction accompanied by depression. If, however, her self-concept is positive and she understands the physiology of what is happening, she is less likely to experience problematic emotional reactions.[92]

In nonindustrialized societies, many women actually experience an increase in status at climacterium. In modern societies, the same does not hold, possibly because Western cultures have encouraged more equality.[9] A period of increased freedom and self-concept seems to emerge as modern women come into their own in a different way. Changes in childbearing practices over the years also may affect how menopause is experienced. Women have fewer children and terminate childbearing 10 to 15 years before menopause. Since unpleasant physiological symptoms, such as hot flashes, sweating, and vaginitis, are more extreme in modern societies,[26] some hypothesize that lactational hormones may provide a modulating or preventive effect on menopausal symptomatology of women who bear children during the middlescent years.[49]

Male Climacterium

Men may also undergo a "climacterium," experiencing physical, constitutional, and psychological changes.[26, 92, 96] These changes are more gradual and usually less dramatic than those for women. Occurring between the ages of 40 and 60, it is associated in part with hormonal changes. Psychosocial adjustments men must make when faced with reexamining life goals, careers, accomplishments, value systems, and social relationships may also be causative. Men also experience the loss of children who leave the home, elderly parents who become ill or who die, or decreased status in the work place.[26] Symptoms exhibited by men are generally similar to those experienced by women (see Chap. 35). Anxiety, depression, loss of interest and self-confidence, fatigue, irritability, and moodiness are commonly voiced concerns. In some cases, the man may feel a decrease in sexual drive and may have difficulty sustaining an erection. Consequently, he may feel that his sexuality is threatened.

Sexuality

Sexuality in its broad interpretation includes self-image, self-esteem, and social–emotional intimacy with another. More than a physiological act, it includes social roles, the way one packages one's self, and the degree of sensitivity to the needs of another. In its narrow interpretation, it includes those behaviors and interpersonal skills, such as tenderness and warmth, that lead to intimate physical relationships with another. There is no reason why an individual in good health cannot enjoy full expression of sexuality throughout middle and late adulthood.

Menopausal changes do not arrest or even hamper a woman's ability to continue a sexual relationship. Despite popular myth to the contrary, sexual interest and capacity for gratification continue well beyond menopause.[31] Women show only slight declines in sexual capacity throughout life, although the physiological changes can affect some sexual activities (see Chap. 35).

Recognizing the effects of aging on male sexuality is also important. It takes men longer to reach orgasm, and the pleasure associated with it may decline. Fear and worry can result as a man becomes aware of a loss in rapidity of physical response.[92, 103] Providing information on these normal responses of aging may help alleviate anxiety over performance.

Preparation for the Later Years in Life

Facing One's Mortality

Personal mortality becomes a salient issue during middle age, partially prompted by the normal physical changes of the aging process. One also becomes increasingly aware that many peers are succumbing to heart attacks, cancer, and other diseases.[69] In one study, individuals who reported midlife crisis had significantly greater scores on death concern than did those who reported no crisis.[15] Middle-age adults become acutely aware that time and life are finite as they evaluate their lives and plan for the future. Life becomes restructured in terms of time left to live, rather than time since birth.[65] Despite this fact, few middlescents express a wish to be young again, noting that a difference exists between wanting to *feel* young and wanting to *be* young.

Widowhood is common in middle age because women tend to marry men older than themselves and men die at a comparatively younger age. The middlescent "single-again" person grieves for the loss of companionship but also for a lost future, the years of retirement and mutually enjoyed experiences planned for these later years of life, free from children, and with more financial security. Many men and women find that after divorce or widowhood they are unprepared to handle life on their own. Discovering and expressing uniqueness is part of generativity. Once singlehood is accepted, then being alone offers opportunities to creatively tap into that uniqueness.[64]

Reassessment of One's Value System

Middle age calls for reflection, self-evaluation, and recognition that one is moving toward death. Facing one's mortality forces reassessment of identity perhaps more than any other issue of middlescence. This introspection is likely to bring one to more basic and spiritual issues.[44] As beliefs and values are scrutinized and reprioritized, attempts to reorganize at newfound levels of security are made. These attempts entail recommitting one's life to meeting higher level needs (e.g., self-actualization and aesthetic pursuits). Solidifying values, expressing and mastering the self, contributing through productive and creative endeavors, and gaining spiritual integrity are positive outcomes. The challenge is to identify and integrate values that have given life meaning to strengthen the generativity potential inherent in each individual.

Planning for Retirement

Attitudes toward retirement are related to lifelong personality patterns and vary with goals, income status, financial concerns, age, health, occupation, job commitment, and cultural background.[99] Some retire willingly and early, usually with adequate income. Others retire unwillingly because of poor health or coercion and often without financial security. Many simply do not leave the work force. Homemakers, farmers, or others who are self-employed are more likely to continue working as long as they want or can. The trend in modern society is toward earlier retirement. Consequently, many retirees have a chance at a second career.

Single individuals may experience more difficulty in retirement.[74] Although they may have a wide variety of family relationships, they may feel alone. Lowered income can limit activities and be a source of strain.[89]

With the increase in life spans, the postjob years are longer than ever before. Labor force statistics continue to identify a trend toward early retirement of males in their later fifties and early sixties. At the same time, women age 55 to 64 have shown increasing labor force participation.[81] As people of retirement age move in and out of the labor force, work and leisure become less distinct as they seek an optimal mix of both.

Retirement is a process that should begin years before the event, yet studies indicate that few people actually make plans for this event.[89, 99] Each person should spend time defining what retirement means in his or her life and prepare for it.[95] When selected activities fail to provide continuity with the past while meeting current and future needs for retirement, a sense of alienation can result as one's life patterns are abruptly broken.[78] New and unaccustomed roles must also be learned. Discovering outlets for self-expression while relinquishing earlier sources of gratification without bitterness requires creativity.[58] Relationships change because of loss of work contacts. Adding to or replacing occupational social groups by expanding interests and participating in church, club, and civic organizations can help meet interactional and generativity needs simultaneously.[89]

MIDLIFE CRISIS

Crisis or Transition?

Exigencies of Life

After examining the challenges of middlescence, it becomes apparent that intrapersonal and interpersonal confrontations are inevitable. Confrontations imply the need for change, and change creates stress. Clearly, people differ in how they cope with challenges, change, and stress.[86] Whether or not the confrontations of midlife precipitate a full-blown crisis, discomfort, or a relatively orderly transition depends on personality, past experiences in dealing with stress, the number of choices available, the degree of control one has, and the amount of support received from others. A person can grow and learn from dealing with stress by using one's resources to good advantage.

Resolution of Previous Tasks

Every novel situation presents the potential for crisis.[11, 94] Previous experience provides us with prototypes for facing new experiences. According to Erikson, the strengths derived from earlier encounters affect current resolution but do not completely determine it.[22]

Erikson's tasks of identity and intimacy are reworked and expanded in midlife. Positive resolutions of earlier years facilitate positive resolution of the conflicts of middlescence. However, if the basic groundwork for "identity homework" was not solidly established, it is more difficult to initiate during middlescence because of strong affective coping patterns to avoid self-confrontation.

Dreams Versus Reality

As an individual faces the midlife transitional period, discomfort is experienced as the discrepancies between youthful expectations and actual achievements are realized.[69] Suddenly, the naïve or ambitious dreams of young adulthood face the test of reality. Some dreams have lost their meaning and are no longer worthy of pursuit. Sometimes the anticipated options have decreased or vanished altogether. People with marked potential are faced with measuring up. Even if great achievements were made, one may wonder what is next or may become bored. Modifying expectations of earlier years for a more realistic, attainable self is a part of the ongoing identity homework of midlife. Valuing competence over outstanding career achievements and strong friendship bonds or companionship over the dream of marital bliss are two ways mature adults bridge the gap.

Stress

Stress is the arousal the mind and body experience when a demand taxes a person's resources or coping abilities.[48, 85, 102] **Stressors** are the events and stimuli that cause stress, from major life changes, such as divorce or retirement to everyday annoyances, such as concerns about weight and physical appearance, home maintenance, misplacing or losing objects, and having too much to do.[37] Selye's stress adaptation theory can be used to explain the physiological effects of stress (see Chap. 35).

Individual interpretation of stressors determines psychosocial response. Stress is experienced when stressors are interpreted to be threatening.[85] Table 36-1 shows the role that interpretation plays in stress development.[21] Lazarus, recognized for his innovative study of chronic stress and coping among men and women in their fifties and sixties, poses that a person automatically and subjectively "appraises" the nature

TABLE 36–1. THE A-B-C'S OF STRESS AND DISTRESS

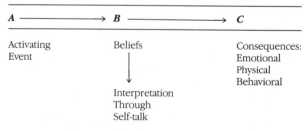

A	B	C
Activating Event	Beliefs	Consequences: Emotional Physical Behavioral
	↓	
	Interpretation Through Self-talk	

From Schafer, W. (1987). Stress management for wellness (p. 222). New York: Holt, Rinehart, and Winston, after a model by Albert Ellis and Robert Harper. With permission.

of a threat and assesses his or her resources for dealing with it.[50,51] Beck also recognizes the impact of a person's "cognitive set" in responding to stress.[2] The same stressor may be regarded as trivial, significant, or overwhelming, depending on the meaning ascribed to it.

Crisis Theories

Stress and crisis are not synonymous. A crisis is an acute emotional upset that arises from situational, developmental, or social sources. It results in a temporary inability to cope by one's usual problem-solving devices.[42] Three "balancing factors determine whether a person will enter a crisis state: perception of the event, situational supports, and coping mechanisms" (Fig. 36-9).[1]

Caplan observes that crisis occurs when a person perceives an obstacle to important life goals.[11] Customary methods of problem solving and usual coping mechanisms do not work to effect a solution; consequently, affective equilibrium is upset. The individual attempts to redefine and solve the problem or resigns to the inevitable. Either approach results in a new state of equilibrium, sometimes better and sometimes worse than before (Fig. 36-10).

Crisis Intervention

Two characters are used to write the Chinese word for crisis: one means "danger," the other, "opportunity."[1] With any crisis or new challenge, the opportunity for positive change and personal growth exists.[11,80] People are generally forced to try new approaches or to reevaluate priorities. They are also most open to new ideas to help face the crisis. Once the crisis is over, the individual negotiates new criteria for equilibrium and is less open to assistance. Therefore, acute crisis is more likely to have a positive outcome if outside intervention (counseling) is received before new survival patterns are established.

The goal of crisis intervention is psychological resolution of the problem. Since change occurs, new behaviors result. Crisis resolution occurs with or without the assistance of others. The person frequently advances to higher levels of functioning because new ways to solve problems have been learned. When an individual prepares for normal life events (e.g., birth of child, empty nest, retirement), he or she can often prevent the development of crisis.

Characteristics of Midlife Crisis

A review of the literature on midlife crisis indicates little consensus as to what extent such a crisis exists.[15,34,54,65,100] Some have called it an "artifact of the media," since crisis, transition, and change occur all through life.[86] As previously discussed, many people consider midlife a normal time for a person to reevaluate the total life situation.[92] One study revealed that, although 70% of men experience a midlife crisis, nearly two thirds of these were considered minor.[15] Twenty percent of the subjects in Levinson's study had worked out

satisfactory life structures by midlife and consequently experienced no midlife crisis.[54]

Whether or not midlife changes precipitate a crisis depends in part on the individual's perception of the events. Perceived as a challenge, something that can be handled, these confrontations may cause stress, but the energies can be harnessed and positively directed. Perceived negatively and handled ineffectively, stagnation, boredom, decreased self-image or self-confidence, depression, and anxiety may result. This individual becomes more vulnerable to additional stress because of decreased resistance.[35] The onset of midlife crisis is normally slow and subtle as feelings of discontent come and go. There is no single cause, rather various issues relevant to personal aging, family, and career are involved. Feelings of dissatisfaction with the way life has developed and ambivalence about the future are evident. These broad symptoms designate what has become known as "midlife crisis."[7,69,90]

Responses to Crises

Fight or Flight

When the stress response is activated, the anxiety generated becomes a potent source of energy. If constructively channeled, it can stimulate action necessary to alter a stressful situation. An individual has some choice and control in harnessing and directing the energy into positive avenues.

A perceived threat and the resultant anxiety can stimulate physiologically based "fight" or "flight" reactions.[10] In "fight reaction," an individual perceives the threat to be low in relation to available coping mechanisms. The threat is confronted head-on. In "flight reaction," the risk is judged to be high in relation to available coping mechanisms, so attempts are made to escape the threat by any means possible.[2] Regressed behavior, such as avoidance, emotional withdrawal, or increased dependency on others, is a manifestation. "Freezing" occurs when the individual is immobilized or unable to prepare any defense.

Approach–Avoidance Conflicts

Two classic methods of coping with conflict and stress are approach and avoidance. These tendencies refer to cognitive and emotional activity oriented either toward or away from a goal.[83] In a conflict situation, opposing desires, interests, feelings, and goals coexist. Generally, the approach tendency is strengthened as one nears a desirable goal, while the avoidance tendency is reinforced when one faces undesirable goals. Various combinations of approach–avoidance tendencies can occur. A single decision may have both approach and avoidance components, increasing conflict as the person makes a choice. For instance, should one top the meal off with a delicious chocolate dessert and suffer the consequences of weight gain or deny the craving and keep the weight under control? The situation is complicated if one's hostess shares that the dessert is her culinary magnum opus. One is forced to reassess priorities.

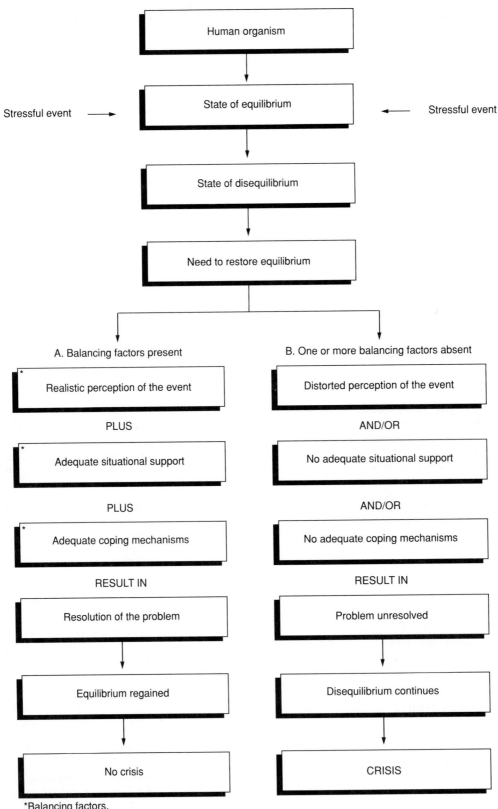

*Balancing factors.

FIGURE 36–9.
The effect of balancing factors in a stressful event. (Aguilera, D. C., & Messick, J. M. (1986). Crisis intervention: Theory and methodology (5th ed.). St. Louis, MO: C. V. Mosby. With permission.)

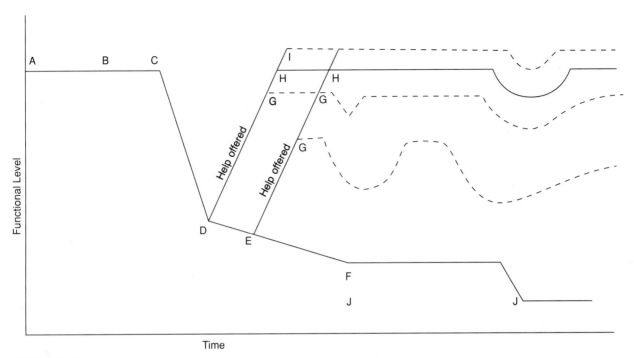

FIGURE 36–10.

Model of crisis response. (A) **Equilibrium:** *The person or family functions adaptively in the routines and demands of daily living. (B)* **Stressor:** *An unusual circumstance occurs and demands novel responses or greatly taxes skills previously used to face life's exigencies. (C)* **Disequilibrium:** *The person's or family's adaptive responses break down or are unable to meet the situational demands. (D)* **Crisis:** *The cumulative effect of disequilibrium results in anxiety and disorganization. This is the optimal time for crisis intervention. (E)* **Dysfunction:** *A crisis state continues and further depletes energy reserves. Crisis intervention can still be beneficial. (F)* **Chronic Dysfunction:** *People or families who do not receive help, or who are unreceptive to help, may develop a life style of chronic dysfunction. Each new stressor may lead to a lower level of functioning. (G)* **Outcome 1:** *The individual or family may be helped by the intervention but is unable to return to prestressor levels of functioning. Resiliency for facing future crises is reduced. (H)* **Outcome 2:** *The person or family returns to prestressor functional level. Newly learned skills may facilitate adaptation to future stressors and crises. (I)* **Outcome 3:** *This person or family exceeds the prestressor functional level. New insights, skills, and strengths are available to optimally facilitate adaptation to future stressors and creatively prevent future crises. (J)* **Future Stressors:** *New insights and coping skills provide a buffer against adopting dysfunctional behaviors or disintegrated behaviors. Resiliency is maintained and "crises" can be contained to shorter periods of time.*

Although individuals have been described as approachers or avoiders, these methods of coping are not mutually exclusive. In fact, flexibility in using both avoidance and approach strategies is adaptive.[83] Avoidance strategies, such as denial or acquiescence, may be valuable coping tools when emotional resources are known to be limited. Avoidance strategies reduce stress and prevent anxiety from becoming overwhelming. Approach strategies, on the other hand, allow one to take advantage of changes in a situation that might make it more controllable. In a working-through process, oscillating periods of denial and encroachment occur, becoming less intense until the problem is resolved. (See Table 36-2 for costs and benefits of these two approaches.)

Nonproductive Responses to Stress

Many courses of action seem to be constructive but are at best compensatory and at worst destructive. A solution is compensatory when, instead of resolving a problem, it offers a defensive substitute as a counterbalance.[69] It is destructive when it leads to lower levels of psychosocial functioning. In addition to several nonproductive responses already mentioned in the context of theory, the following can be considered problematic:[43]

1. **Compliant reactions** impart a sense of helplessness, sadness, depression, or lack of initiative. Other people are overwhelmingly and inappropriately relied on for support and resolution of problems. Compliance preserves the integrity and respect of others at the loss of one's own sense of identity.

2. **Aggressive responses** are expressed as hostility, anger, or resistance. These are used to protect oneself, but at the cost of alienating others.

3. **Moving away behaviors** are manifested by avoidance, withdrawal, apathy, silence, evasiveness, passivity, or inability to respond. These can virtually eliminate external sources of support.

TABLE 36–2. POTENTIAL COSTS AND BENEFITS OF APPROACH AND AVOIDANCE

Reaction	Benefits	Costs
Approach	Appropriate action Ventilation of affect Assimilation and resolution of trauma	Increased distress Nonproductive worry
Avoidance	Stress reduction Allows for dosing Increased hope and courage	Interference with appropriate action Emotional numbness Intrusions of threatening material Disruptive avoidance behaviors Lack of awareness of relationship of symptoms to trauma

Roth, S., & Cohen, L. J. (1986). Approach, avoidance and coping with stress. American Psychologist, 41, 817.

Long-Range Effects of Stress

Prolonged and intensive stress can result in illness and death.[11, 50, 87] However, life's obstacles, no matter how traumatic, when faced openly and realistically can be turned into opportunities for growth.[28]

Stress Management

Reevaluation of Values and Priorities

When healthy, mature adults encounter stress, they assume responsibility to clarify the problem and modify the situation. Their personhood is viewed as a separate issue from the problem. Therefore, they have the ability to be more objective and flexible in facing stressful events. When they realize that the problem can't be changed, they reassess their values and their priorities to alter their expectations or approaches to deal with it. Being able to defer need gratification or to seek substitutes are possible ways to accept and cope with stressful situations.

If an individual anticipates and recognizes that a change will be disruptive and allows a period of "moratorium" for self-repair, he or she is more likely to emerge stronger.[25] A sense of continuation can be found within oneself if given opportunities to rearrange and recenter commitments. Sullivan was convinced that faith and hope create strong thrusts toward health in most people.[97] Likewise, belief in and patience with one's inner resources, along with sufficient solitude to invest in identity homework, can help one to prepare for and manage anticipated changes and resulting stress.

Developing Coping Skills

It is neither possible nor desirable to eliminate all stressors, but it is important to bring stress to manageable levels. The uniqueness of stressful experiences and the variety of stress management techniques available suggest that interventions should be determined only after carefully evaluating individual stressors and needs.[41, 62]

Approaches to stress management generally involve reduction of the physical, psychological, and behavioral manifestations of anxiety inherent in stress reactions:[101]

1. Relaxation and exercise are powerful ways to reduce the physical signs of anxiety. Physical exercise can burn off some of the energy related to high levels of tension. Exercise increases the body's natural endorphin production, which, in turn, helps increase tolerance to pain and stress.

2. Deliberate identification and modification of thoughts and attitudes that increase anxiety can reduce the psychological aspects of stress. Careful identification of the specific stressors and potential solutions enables one to gain or maintain a sense of control over the situation, or at least of one's response to the situation. It may be difficult to change a feeling in response to a specific stressor, but one *can* choose and control one's appraisal of the situation.

3. Positive experiences in facing anxiety-provoking situations gradually help to increase the confidence in one's ability to deal with new situations. Therefore, in essence, identity homework has become a habit in one's approach to life's events and conflicts. It involves identifying values, establishing priorities, setting specific goals, developing plans for implementation, and following them through.

Constructive coping responses promote health, life satisfaction, productivity, and self-development.

Positive Problem-Solving Methodologies

By assessing the balance between an individual's strengths and deficits in the areas of situation, self, supports, and strategies, coping ability can be predicted and modified by building strengths where needed and cutting losses as necessary.[86] Problems too often are avoided or dwelt on rather than approached systematically and assertively as follows:[101]

1. Define the problem as clearly as possible.
2. Generate as many solutions as possible, and write them down.
3. Note the advantages and disadvantages of each.
4. Choose the best approach.

5. Specify how, when, and with whom you can put it into practice.
6. Do it!

The obvious result is a more defined problem. Just seeing the issue in writing often seems to help one feel a sense of control. The ideas generated may help to decrease the effects of anxiety. Even though one may have thought of these ideas before, they are now in the form of a concrete and practical plan. If an identified stressor is caring for an aging parent, for example, the pressure may be minimized by having other relatives assist on certain days, arranging for day care, and so forth. Self-help groups, support groups, or counselors can provide added ideas as well as support if assistance is needed in working through a problem.

The Opportunities of Middlescence

Flowering
The self-evaluation and self-discipline skills developed during adolescent years and strengthened through young adulthood continue to be significant through midlife. Deeper exploration of selfhood solidifies strengths, values, and convictions independent of material success. Improvements in judgment, increased tolerance, heightened self-understanding, and a better grasp of realities become reassuring aspects of middle adulthood.[65] Self-images are enhanced by feelings of security and self-reliance, resulting in relaxation of roles. Women often feel a firm sense of identity for the first time in their lives and delight in the self-discovery. Men can enjoy an increased sense of expressiveness and compassion. Although men and women may move in opposite directions in midlife, they move toward the same goal, wholeness or completion.[37] Like mellow fruit or wine, life experiences and development produce a full-flavored, matured individual: one who perceives self less seriously and more in context; one who is ready to take advantage of life's opportunities for dynamic productivity.

Productivity
Even when a middlescent recognizes that accomplishments have not matched expectations, one can still have a positive self-image and view oneself as successful. Human experience and relationships are appreciated more; prestige, power, physical appearance, and physique, less. Life may be valued more deeply because of an awareness of death, and life's potentials may be appreciated in a new way.

Lessening of earlier restrictions, increased free time, and newfound energy provide freedom and spontaneity to extend oneself to the larger community. Erikson proposes that a basic strength of generativity results in a widening commitment to *take care of* persons, products, and ideas.[23] All the basic strengths from earlier developmental phases (hope, will, purpose, skill, fidelity, and love) are essential as one redirects energies to being concerned about, caring for, and contributing to the welfare of the next generation. As one becomes a parent in the broader sense, the productive and creative opportunities for self-actualization and generativity increase.

Creativity
Creativity constantly renews marriage, friendship, and other significant relationships. It is essential for active participation in work and leisure-time activities and for flexible attitudes toward children and young people.[58] New interests or those left dormant during early struggles to establish a family and career now can be developed or expanded. Hobbies or talents can blossom into serious work. New energies are released with the development of creative abilities.

Creativity also includes satisfaction with life as it unfolds and a confident attitude toward the future.[58] Motivation no longer comes from the desire to please others, but to please oneself. The result is increased self-reliance. Spontaneity often complements creativity as one experiences the joy of life.

Expand Beyond Me and Mine
Although one becomes introspective in middle age and shows less concern for what others think, the need to be generative propels many into leadership and decision-making positions. Whether within the family or the larger community, healthy middlescents use their skills and experience to help and guide the younger generation. Competency, a feeling of being in control of one's life and actively involved in the larger world, is an obvious trademark of middle age.[82]

Patience and tolerance in interpersonal relationships enhance how others are viewed. Middlescence presents many couples with the opportunity for greater communication, creativity, commitment, and true companionship. As the major duties of parenting decline, it is often a surprise to find delightful companionship in grown children. Serving as a mentor for younger or new workers constructively channels valuable resources of wisdom and experience into productive avenues. Being self-disciplined, yet independent, confident, and committed, provides the security and impetus for "other-directed" involvement.

IMPLICATIONS

Preparing for Middlescence

As healthy people approach midlife, they reflect on choices made and their progress in attaining goals they have set for themselves. They also continue to confront and refine their own beliefs and inhibitions, thus providing opportunities for continued development. Viewing life as a continuum, rather than midlife as a last chance, opens one to the exciting benefits of change. Midlife need not be a calamity. In the process of facing life's exigencies head-on, one must recognize and anticipate the need to surrender temporarily the security of familiar patterns, unrewarding work, or values no longer meaningful for the long-range security of self-actualization and self-confidence. The real fear should be of stagnation, not developing.

Living Life More Fully

The new adult ideal is an ever-evolving but unified and integrated self, one who keeps alive the energy and adaptability of youth while cultivating the wisdom of age.[30] The ideal adult also blends traditional masculine and feminine traits and is capable of autonomous and assertive action as well as contemplative behavior. Realistic appreciation of accomplishments and successes provides the freedom for continued growth and development. Viewing life in its broader context encourages self-generation and continued identity development. At the same time, it fosters accountability and commitment to cultivating the next generation.

REFERENCES

1. Aguilera, D. C., & Messick, J. M. (1986). *Crisis intervention: Theory and methodology* (5th ed.). St. Louis, MO: C. V. Mosby.
2. Beck, A. T. (1984). Cognitive approaches to stress. In R. L. Woolfolk & P. M. Lehrer (Eds.), *Principles and practice of stress management*. New York: Guilford Press.
3. Belbin, E., & Belbin, R. M. (1968). New careers in middle age. In B. L. Neugarten (Ed.), *Middle age and aging*. Chicago: University of Chicago Press.
4. Bell, J. E., & Eisenberg, N. (1985). Life satisfaction in midlife childless and empty-nest men and women. *Lifestyles: A Journal of Changing Patterns, 7,* 146–155.
5. Bengtson, V. L. (1985). Diversity and symbolism in grandparental roles. In V. L. Bengtson & J. F. Robertson (Eds.), *Grandparenthood*. Beverly Hills, CA: Sage Publications.
6. Braiker, H. B. (1986). *The type E woman*. New York: Signet.
7. Brandes, S. (1985). *Forty: The age and the symbol*. Knoxville, TN: University of Tennessee Press.
8. Brody, E. M. (1985). Parent care as a normative family stress. *Gerontologist, 25,* 19–29.
9. Brown, J. K. (1985). Introduction. In J. K. Brown & V. Kerns (Eds.), *In her prime: a new view of middle-aged women*. South Hadley, MA: Bergin and Garvey Publishers.
10. Cannon, W. B. (1929). *Bodily changes in pain, hunger, fear, and rage*. New York: Appleton-Century-Crofts.
11. Caplan, G. (1964). *Principles of preventive psychiatry*. New York: Basic Books.
12. Catalyst Staff. (1980). *Marketing yourself*. New York: Bantam Books.
13. Cherlin, A. J., & Furstenberg, F. F. (1986). *The new American grandparent*. New York: Basic Books.
14. Chesney, M. A., & Hill, R. D. (1988). Work. In E. A. Blechman & K. D. Brownell (Eds.), *Handbook of behavioral medicine for women*. New York: Pergamon Press.
15. Ciernia, J. R. (1985). Death concern and businessmen's midlife crisis. *Psychological Reports, 56,* 83–87.
16. Clemens, A. W., & Axelson, L. J. (1985). The not-so-empty nest: The return of the fledging adult. *Family Relations, 34,* 259–264.
17. Cooper, K. L., & Gutmann, D. L. (1987). Gender identity and ego mastery style in middle aged, pre- and post- empty nest women. *Gerontologist, 27,* 347–352.
18. Darling-Fisher, C. S., & Leidy, N. K. (1988). Measuring Eriksonian development in the adult: The modified Erikson psychological stage inventory. *Psychological Reports, 62,* 747–754.
19. Edinberg, M. A. (1988). *Talking with your aging parents*. Boston: Shambhala Pub.
20. Editors of American Health Magazine. (1986). *The relaxed body book*. Garden City, NY: Doubleday.
21. Ellis, A., & Harper, R. (1979). *A new guide to rational living*. Englewood Cliffs, NJ: Prentice-Hall.
22. Erikson, E. H. (1963). *Childhood and society*. New York: W. W. Norton.
23. Erikson, E. H. (1982). *The life cycle completed*. New York: W. W. Norton.
24. Fischer, L. R. (1986). *Linked lives: Adult daughters and their mothers*. New York: Harper and Row.
25. Fiske, M. (1980). Changing hierarchies of commitment in adulthood. In N. J. Smelser & E. H. Erikson (Eds.), *Themes of work and love in adulthood*. Cambridge, MA: Harvard University Press.
26. Flint, M. (1982). Male and female menopause: A cultural put-on. In A. M. Voda, M. Dinnerstein, & S. R. O'Donnell (Eds.), *Changing perspectives on menopause*. Austin, TX: University of Texas Press.
27. Fox-Lefkowitz, A. B. (1985). Father's perception of the empty nest transition. *Dissertation Abstracts International, 45,* 3616-B.
28. Frese, M., Stewart, J., & Hannover, B. (1987). Goal orientation and playfulness: Action styles as personality concepts. *Journal of Personality and Social Psychology, 52,* 1182–1194.
29. Freud, S. (1965). *New introductory lectures in psychoanalysis* (J. Strachey, Ed.). New York: W. W. Norton.
30. Giele, J. Z. (1980). Adulthood as trancendence of age and sex. In N. J. Smelser & E. H. Erikson (Eds.), *Themes of work and love in adulthood*. Cambridge, MA: Harvard University Press.
31. Giele, J. Z. (1982). Women in adulthood: Unanswered questions. In J. Z. Giele (Ed.), *Women in the middle years*. New York: John Wiley and Sons.
32. Giele, J. Z. (1982). Women's work and family roles. In J. Z. Giele (Ed.), *Women in the middle years*. New York: John Wiley and Sons.
33. Gilligan, C. (1982). Adult development and women's development: Arrangements for a marriage. In J. Z. Giele (Ed.), *Women in the middle years*. New York: John Wiley and Sons.
34. Gould, R. L. (1980). Transformations during early and middle adult years. In N. J. Smelser & E. H. Erikson (Eds.), *Themes of work and love in adulthood*. Cambridge, MA: Harvard University Press.
35. Greenspoon, J., & Olson, J. (1986). Stress management and biofeedback. *Clinical Biofeedback and Health, 9,* 65–80.
36. Hagestad, G. O. (1985). Continuity and connectedness. In V. L. Bengtson & J. F. Robertson (Eds.), *Grandparenthood*. Beverly Hills, CA: Sage Publications.
37. Halpern, J. (1987). *Helping your aging parents*. New York: McGraw-Hill.
38. Hansen, J. P. (1986). Older maternal age and pregnancy outcome: A review of the literature. *Obstetrical and Gynecological Survey, 41,* 726–742.
39. Havighurst, R. J., & Feigenbaum, K. (1968). Leisure and life style. In B. L. Neugarten (Ed.), *Middle age and aging*. Chicago: University of Chicago Press.
40. Helson, R., Mitchell, V., & Hart, B. (1985). Lives of women who become autonomous. *Journal of Personality, 53,* 257–285.
41. Hillenberg, J. B., & DiLorenzo, T. M. (1987). Stress management training in health psychology practice: Critical clinical issues. *Professional Psychology: Research and Practice, 18,* 402–404.

42. Hoff, L. A. (1989). *People in crisis*. Redwood City, CA: Addison-Wesley.

43. Horney, K. (1972). *Our inner conflicts*. New York: W. W. Norton.

44. Jung, C. G. (1971). *The portable Jung* (J. Campbell, Ed.). New York: Viking Press.

45. Kaufert, P. A. (1985). Midlife in the Midwest. In J. K. Brown & V. Kerns (Eds.), *In her prime: A new view of middle-aged women*. South Hadley, MA: Bergin and Garvey.

46. Kivnick, H. Q. (1985). Personhood and the life course. In V. L. Bengtson & J. F. Robertson (Eds.), *Grandparenthood*. Beverly Hills, CA: Sage Publications.

47. Kivnick, H. Q. (1986). Grandparenthood and a life cycle. *Journal of Geriatric Psychiatry, 19*, 39–55.

48. Knapp, T. R. (1988). Stress versus strain: A methodological critique. *Nursing Research, 37*, 181–184.

49. Lancaster, J. B., & King, B. J. (1985). An evolutionary perspective on menopause. In J. K. Brown & V. Kerns (Eds.), *In her prime: A new view of middle-aged women*. South Hadley, MA: Bergin and Garvey.

50. Lazarus, R. S. (1966). *Psychological stress and the coping process*. New York: McGraw-Hill.

51. Lazarus, R. S., & Folkman, S. (1984). *Stress, appraisal and coping*. New York: Springer.

52. Lerner, R. M., & Kauffman, M. B. (1985). The concept of development in contextualism. *Developmental Review, 5*, 309–333.

53. Levinson, D. J. (1980). Toward a conception of the adult life course. In N. J. Smelser & E. H. Erikson (Eds.), *Themes of work and love in adulthood*. Cambridge, MA: Harvard University Press.

54. Levinson, D. J., Darrow, C. N., Klein, E. B., Levinson, M. H., & McKee, B. (1978). *The seasons of a man's life*. New York: Alfred A. Knopf.

55. Lindsey, K. (1982). *Friends or family*. Boston, MA: Beacon Press.

56. Maloni, J. A., McIndoe, J. E., & Rubenstein, G. (1987). Expectant grandparents class. *Journal of Obstetrics, Gynecologic, and Neonatal Nursing, 16*, 26–29.

57. Maslow, A. (1968). *Toward a psychology of being*. Cincinnati: Van Nostrand Reinhold.

58. Matilla, V., Joukamaa, M., & Salokangas, R. K. (1988). Mental health in the population approaching retirement age in relation to physical health, functional ability and creativity. *Acta Psychiatrica Scandinavica, 77*, 42–51.

59. Matthews, S. H. (1987). Provision of care to old parents: Division of responsibility among adult children. *Research on Aging, 9*, 45–60.

60. McCrae, R. R., & Costa, P. T. (1988). Recalled parent–child relations and adult personality. *Journal of Personality, 56*, 417–434.

61. Morgan, W. R. (1986). Returning to school in midlife: Mature women with educational careers. In L. B. Shaw (Ed.), *Midlife women at work (a fifteen year perspective)*. Lexington, MA: D. C. Health.

62. Murphy, L. R. (1986). A review of organizational stress management research: Methodological considerations. *Journal of Organizational Behavior Management, 8*, 215–227.

63. Myers, J. E. (1988). The mid/late life generation gap: Adult children with aging parents. *Journal of Counseling and Development, 66*, 331–335.

64. NCWRC. (1989). Alone . . . is sometimes a nice place to be. *National Center for Women and Retirement Research, 1*(Winter), 4.

65. Neugarten, B. L. (1968). The awareness of middle age. In B. L. Neugarten (Ed.), *Middle age and aging*. Chicago: University of Chicago Press.

66. Neugarten, B. L., & Hagestad, G. O. (1985). Age and the life course. In R. H. Binstock & E. Shanas (Eds.), *Handbook of aging and the social sciences*. New York: Van Nostrand Reinhold.

67. Neugarten, B. L., & Neugarten, D. A. (1987). The changing meaning of age. *Psychology Today, 21*, 29–33.

68. Neugarten, B. L., & Weinstein, K. K. (1968). The changing American grandparent. In B. L. Neugarten (Ed.), *Middle age and aging*. Chicago: University of Chicago Press.

69. Nichols, M. P. (1986). *Turning forty in the 80's: Personal crisis, time for change*. New York: W. W. Norton.

70. Nolen, W. A. (1984). *Crisis time: Love, marriage, and the male at midlife*. New York: Dodd, Mead.

71. Oliver, R. (1982). "Empty-nest" or relationship restructuring? A rational-emotive approach to a midlife transition. *Women and Therapy, 1*, 67–83.

72. Peck, R. C. (1968). Psychological developments in the second half of life. In B. L. Neugarten (Ed.), *Middle age and aging*. Chicago: University of Chicago Press.

73. Perlmutter, E., & Bart, P. B. (1982). Changing views of "the change": A critical review and suggestions for an attributional approach. In A. M. Voda, M. Dinnerstein, & S. R. O'Donnell (Eds.), *Changing perspectives on menopause*. Austin, TX: University of Texas Press.

74. Porcino, J. (1983). *Growing older, getting better: A handbook for women in the second half of life*. Reading, MA: Addison-Wesley.

75. Pulakos, J. (1987). Brothers and sisters: Nature and the importance of the adult bond. *Journal of Psychology, 121*, 521–522.

76. Ransohoff, R. M. (1987). *Venus after forty*. Far Hills, NJ: New Horizon Press.

77. Raymond, C. A. (1988). Studies question how much role menopause plays in some women's emotional distress. *Journal of the American Medical Association, 259*, 3522–3523.

78. Reichard, S., Livson, F., & Petersen, P. G. (1968). Adjustment to retirement. In B. L. Neugarten (Ed.), *Middle age and aging*. Chicago: University of Chicago Press.

79. Remnet, V. L. (1987). How adult children respond to role transitions in the lives of their aging parents. *Educational Gerontology, 13*, 341–355.

80. Riegel, K. F. (1979). *Foundations of dialectical psychology*. New York: Academic Press.

81. Robinson, P. K., Coberly, S., & Paul, C. E. (1985). Work and retirement. In R. H. Binstock & E. Shanas (Eds.), *Handbook of aging and the social sciences*. New York: Van Nostrand Reinhold.

82. Rosenfeld, A., & Stark, E. (1987). The prime of our lives. *Psychology Today, 21*, 62–72.

83. Roth, S., & Cohen, L. J. (1986). Approach, avoidance and coping with stress. *American Psychologist, 41*, 813–819.

84. Rubin, L. (1981). *Women of a certain age: The midlife search for self*. New York: Harper and Row.

85. Schafer, W. (1987). *Stress management for wellness*. New York: Holt, Rinehart, and Winston.

86. Schlossberg, N. K. (1987). Taking the mystery out of change. *Psychology Today, 21*, 74–75.

87. Selye, H. (1956). *The stress of life*. New York: McGraw-Hill.

88. Severino, S. K., Teusink, J. P., Pender, V. B., & Bernstein, A. E. (1986). Overview: The psychology of grandparenthood. *Journal of Geriatric Psychiatry, 19*, 3–17.

89. Shaughnessy, J. (1988). Pre-retirement planning and the role of the occupational health nurse. *AAOHN Journal, 36,* 70–77.

90. Sheehy, G. (1976). *Passages: Predictable crisis of adult life.* New York: E. P. Dutton.

91. Sheehy, G. (1981). *Pathfinders.* New York: William Morrow.

92. Smith, S. F., Karasik, D. A., & Meyer, B. J. (Eds.). (1984). *Review of psychiatric and psychosocial nursing.* Los Altos, CA: National Nursing Review.

93. Snarey, J., Son, L., Kuehne, V. S., Hauser, S., & Vaillant, G. (1987). The role of parenting in men's psychosocial development: A longitudinal study of early adulthood infertility and midlife generativity. *Developmental Psychology, 23,* 593–603.

94. Snyder, C. R., Ford, C. E., & Harris, R. N. (1987). The effects of theoretical perspective on the analysis of coping with negative life events. In C. R. Snyder & C. E. Ford (Eds.), *Coping with negative life events.* New York: Plenum Press.

95. Stevenson, J. S. (1977). *Issues and crises during middlescence.* New York: Appleton-Century-Crofts.

96. Strickland, B. R. (1988). Menopause. In E. A. Blechman & K. D. Brownell (Eds.), *Handbook of behavioral medicine for women.* New York: Pergamon Press.

97. Sullivan, H. S. (1953). *The interpersonal theory of psychiatry* (H. S. Perry & M. L. Gawal, Eds.). New York: W. W. Norton.

98. Tesch, S. (1985). Psychosocial development and subjective well-being in an age cross-section of adults. *International Journal of Aging and Human Development, 21,* 109–120.

99. Troll, L. E. (1982). *Continuations: Adult development and aging.* Monterey, CA: Brooks/Cole.

100. Troll, L. E. (1985). *Early and middle adulthood: The best is yet to be—maybe* (2nd ed.). Monterey, CA: Brooks/Cole.

101. Whitmore, B. (1987). *Living with stress and anxiety.* Manchester, UK: Manchester University Press.

102. Wilson, H. S., & Kneisl, C. R. (1988). *Psychiatric nursing.* Menlo Park, CA: Addison-Wesley.

103. Witkin-Lanoil, G. (1986). *The male stress syndrome.* New York: Berkeley.

XI THE LATE ADULT YEARS

The late adult years offer a period of continued development for the healthy individual. However, the quality of these years depends on many factors, including the choices made during earlier years and their cumulative effect on the individual's health and economic status.

The freedom from employment enjoyed by most people of this age group provides time for expanding the interests of earlier years. Many senior citizens find their time filled with "catching up" on hobbies, household chores, and social interests. Many retirees describe these years as "the best years of my life." Others seem to lose purpose and meaning to life when structure and responsibilities are no longer offered by a regular work day.

Many older persons extend the period of generativity by continuing to maintain vital involvement in family and community. Although there may need to be some slowing of the pace of activities, most elderly people remain active and independent until their death. Relatively few elderly people need nursing home or family assistance during the final years of life.

Developmental Tasks of Late Adulthood

*1. Find satisfaction in reduced or nonemployment activities:
- leisure time
- volunteer work
- family relationships
- continue to share job and career-related expertise

*2. Validate value, meaning, and responsibilities of life lived:
- take pleasure in memories of personal successes
- place contributions in context of history
- accept own humanness in the failures and disappointments of life
- share events and stories of earlier years with younger generation
- share observations, values, and wisdom learned from continuities of life

*3. Prepare for own death:
- adapt to death of peers, siblings, and spouse
- accept own mortality
- gradually transfer social and civic responsibilities to others
- arrange for distribution of personal possessions
- solidify concept of life after death

4. Pace activities with physical ability and endurance:
- seek assistance as necessary
- continue health maintenance practices
- separate self-worth from issues of forced dependency
- continue proactive, high-level involvement in life

5. Maintain maximal independence in activities of daily living:
- residence
- self-care
- decision making
- financial management

---

*Tasks marked with an asterisk are deemed most crucial to continued maturation.

Biophysical Development During Late Adulthood

Carol A. Miller

37 *For age is opportunity no less Than youth itself, though in another dress. And as the evening twilight fades away The sky is filled with stars, invisible by day.*

HENRY WADSWORTH
LONGFELLOW

Since early times, people have been curious about the universal phenomenon of aging. Both subjective and objective definitions of old age emerge as one seeks answers to the question: "When does late adulthood begin?" Sometimes, the answer lies in the chronological age of the persons offering the definition. Many persons in their sixties and seventies may not see themselves as "old." However, the adolescent or young adult may categorize anyone over 40 or 50 as "old." The question generally is addressed from three perspectives: One is to look at biological aging as it is defined by scientists and gerontologists; another is to look at subjective and objective definitions of aging; the third and most common approach is to look at arbitrary categories based on chronological definitions.

Biological theories of aging address questions such as how cells age, what triggers the process of aging, and what age-related changes occur independently of external or pathological influences. Some of the major biological theories have been reviewed in Chapter 35. Conclusions that can be drawn from biological theories of aging are the following:

1. Biological aging occurs in all living organisms.
2. Biological aging is natural, inevitable, irreversible, and progressive with time.
3. The course of aging varies from individual to individual.
4. The rate of aging for different organs and tissues varies among individuals.
5. Biological aging is influenced by nonbiological factors.
6. Biological aging processes are different from pathological processes.
7. Biological aging increases one's vulnerability to disease.

Definitions of Aging

Aging is defined objectively as a universal process that begins at birth; but, subjectively, aging is associated with chronological age or the older adult years. Children generally do not identify themselves as "aging," but they delight in announcing "how old" they are. They usually view birthdays as a positive experience that will admit them to additional opportunities, privileges, and responsibilities. Adolescents tend to perceive age as the criterion for legal participation in coveted activities like dating or driving. During adulthood, however, aging is negatively associated with "being old" (which may imply "no longer useful" or "infirm"). Thus "old age" is often defined as an age that is several years or a decade beyond one's current age. Consequently, it is not uncommon to hear people of 75 years or more refer to "old people" as if they were a species different from themselves.

People identify age as the length of time that has elapsed since one's birth. As such, chronological age often serves as an objective basis for social organization. For example, societies establish chronological age criteria for certain activities, such as education, driving, military service, and the collection of retirement benefits. To participate legally in these activities, individuals must provide documentation of chronological age.

Retirement is a life event that is closely associated with being "old." Thus American society has accepted the age of 65 (which was established in 1935 as the minimum age criterion for eligibility for full Social Security retirement benefits)[31] as the culturally designated age for becoming a "senior citizen." Until recently, gerontologists used this chronological standard to identify the population of "old" people. In the past two decades, however, there has been a growing trend to identify characteristics of subgroups, such as people who are older than 75 or 90 years. A common trend is to divide late adulthood into chronological subcategories such as "young-old" (60–74 years), "middle-old" (75–89 years), and "old-old" (90 years and older). This trend is caused by the increasing recognition that older adults are not a homogeneous group and, in fact, become more heterogeneous as they become older (Fig. 37-1). This text uses the age of 60 years as the arbitrary definition for the beginning of "late adulthood." Those who reached their 60th birthday in 1986

could expect to live approximately 20.4 more years (22.6 for white female; 20.3 for black female; 18.2 for white male; 16.1 for black male). Those who reached 85 could expect to live an average of 6 more years.[60]

Characteristics of the Older Adult Population

Increasing Diversity with Increasing Age

One of the most consistent findings in recent gerontological research is that, as people age, on virtually every measure, they become less and less like others of the same age.[2] This finding contradicts many beliefs that were popular before the late 1960s, particularly the belief that older adults are a homogenous group. Negative myths and stereotypes about older adults were so common several decades ago that the term *ageism* was coined by Robert Butler in 1968 to refer to "a process of systematic stereotyping and discrimination against people because they are old, just as racism and sexism accomplish this for skin color and gender."[11] Because of the rapid and recent growth of scientific research in the field of aging, many myths and stereotypes about older adults have

FIGURE 37–1.
All persons show the biophysical effects of aging. Nevertheless, genetic factors, socioeconomic status, nutrition, personal choices on lifestyle, and unpredictable events such as accidents and disease processes have a cumulative impact on health, outlook on life, and speed of biophysical aging—creating much individuality among persons of the same chronological age.

been dispelled. For example, the adage, "You can't teach an old dog new tricks," is now recognized as fallacious.

Number and Proportion

Although the proportion of old to young people in the United States and other industrialized societies is partially influenced by diminishing birth rates, the principal reasons for the recent surge in the growth of the proportion of persons in the older population are a rising life expectancy and a declining mortality rate. The average age of the whole population is gradually getting older. In 1987, the median age in the United States was 32.1 years, in 2000 it is expected to be 36.4 years, and 41.8 years by 2030.[59] In 1985, approximately 2,045,000 people in the United States entered the category of

"old age" by reaching age 65 years; by contrast, the number of people who exited this category (through death) was only 1,430,000.[65] In 1987 there were more than twice as many children as older people; by 2030, however, the two population groups are expected to be about equal, each constituting about one-fifth of the population.[59]

Health and Social Characteristics

Since 1957, the National Center for Health Statistics (NCHS) has continuously collected data about patterns of diseases for non-institutionalized people in the United States (Table 37-1). In looking at data about the health and functioning of older people, it is obvious that as people age, the incidence of chronic illness increases. Eighty percent of people over 65

TABLE 37–1. SELECTED HEALTH AND SOCIAL CHARACTERISTICS OF PEOPLE 65 YEARS AND OVER IN THE UNITED STATES

ACTIVITY LIMITATION DUE TO CHRONIC ILLNESS	*65–74 YEARS*	*75+ YEARS*
Limited, not in major activity	6%	7%
Limited in amount or kind of activity	20%	24%
Unable to carry on the major activity	25%	22%
Totals	41%	53%

ADDITIONAL HEALTH CHARACTERISTICS		
Number of disability days per year per person	15	
Percent who rate their health as excellent	70	
Percent who rate their health as poor	10	

Age = proportion of people aged 65 and older by decade

Age 65–74	59%
Age 75–85	32%
Age 85 +	9%

Gender = number of males per 100 females

65–69 years	83
70–74 years	74
75–79 years	64
80–84 years	53
85+ years	40

Race = people age 65 and over by race

White	90%
Black	8%
Other	3%

Marital Status	Women	Men
Married	40%	77%
Widowed/divorced	55%	18%
Single	5%	5%

Educational Level		
Less than high school	51%	
High school or over	49%	

Income Level		
Below poverty level		12%
Between poverty level and 1.5 times the poverty level		16%

(Adapted from U.S. Senate, Special Committee on Aging [1987–1988]. Aging America: Trends and Projections. Washington, DC: U.S. Department of Health and Human Services.)

report one or more chronic illnesses.[64] The NCHS data from the years 1961–62 and 1980–81 were compared to address the question of whether the increase in life expectancy had resulted in better health or more disability.[46] Although disabilities increased with age, "there has been a consistent and substantial trend toward better relative health among the aged between 1961 and 1981."[46] Possible explanations for this trend include (1) better life-long health practices of older adults, as well as higher incomes and levels of education; (2) improvements in health care due to Medicare and Medicaid; and (3) the increasing availability of social, economic, nutritional, and psychological programs for older adults.[46] Most older persons are able to function at home, perform activities of daily living, and interact with their environment.

A significant change in social characteristics of old people in the United States is the increased number of multigenerational families, which is a direct result of the greater number of people living beyond 75 or 85 years. Twenty-five percent of people over 65 still have at least one living parent; 10% have a "child" who is also over 65; and of the people over 65 who have children, 94% are grandparents, and 46% are great-grandparents.[62] The mid-1980s marked the beginning of an era when the average woman in the United States spends more time caring for parents than for children.

SOMATIC CHANGES

Skeletal System

During adulthood, a height loss of about 2 to 4 cm per decade is normal owing to osteoporosis and other age-related changes. Muscle atrophy and calcification of cartilage in the chest wall cause a stooped posture, with a slight bending forward of the head and neck and a flexion of the hips and knees. This posture changes the center of gravity and thus may interfere with the ability of older adults to maintain their balance.[58]

Bones

Bone growth reaches maturity in early adulthood, but bone remodeling continues throughout adulthood. In late adulthood, osteoporosis (increased porosity or "softening" of the bone structure) affects bone remodeling in both men and women. The effects of decreased estrogen associated with menopause accelerates the rate of bone loss in women.

Osteoporosis is characterized by a gradual loss of bone mass, which predisposes persons to fractures. Osteoporosis involves a two-phase pattern of bone loss affecting both cortical and trabecular bone. This pattern has "a protracted slow phase that occurs in both sexes and a transient accelerated phase that occurs in women after menopause."[50] Bed rest and immobility will increase trabecular bone loss.[28, 42, 43]

Joints and Connective Tissue

All joints show the effects of wear and tear, with degenerative changes beginning in young adulthood and continuing throughout one's lifetime. By late adulthood, the cumulative effect of these changes is a diminished range of motion in the upper arms, lower back, hips, knees, and feet. The impact of diminished joint functioning is that older people have more difficulty in their ability to respond to environmental stimuli and to perform activities of daily living.

Osteoarthritis

Approximately 30% of persons over 65 experience activity limitations because of arthritis or rheumatism.[60] Osteoarthritis (overgrowth of bone ends and destruction of the articular cartilage) is the most common type of arthritis and is considered a universal phenomenon of aging.[57] Symptoms generally begin during middlescence and become progressively more involved with age. Men and women are equally affected. It can be caused by either age-related or disease-related changes, affecting each person to a different degree. Symptoms of mild osteoarthritis include joint swelling, limited range of motion, stiffness (especially in the morning or after periods of inactivity), and pain or discomfort (especially after vigorous activity or with weather changes). More severe forms may include joint deformity, posture changes, and gross or fine motor impairments.

Foot Problems

Adults of all ages commonly experience foot problems. In fact, after the age of 65, three-fourths of all people complain of foot pain.[29] Some types of foot problems are due to chronic illnesses, such as diabetes and arthritis. Other types are primarily the result of factors such as wear and tear, poor-fitting shoes, prolonged standing or walking, and degenerative changes in the skeletal system. Bunions (enlargement of the great toe joint), calluses, hammer toes (flexed toes), and heel spurs (calcium deposits) are examples of foot problems that commonly affect healthy older adults. Foot ulcers and infections are examples of problems that may be secondary to chronic illnesses. Many of the problems can be corrected or alleviated with medical attention.

Muscular System

Lean Body Mass and Fat Tissue

Beginning in middlescence, the lean body mass begins to decrease, until a reduction of about 20% is reached in the eighth decade.[39] Between the ages of 20 and 80, body fat gradually increases by 50% in men and 33% in women.[39] Some areas of subcutaneous tissue *atrophy*, or waste away (such as sun-exposed areas), and other areas (such as the waist of men and the thighs of women), *hypertrophy* (enlarge), with the overall effect being a gradual increase in the proportion of body fat.

Muscles

Four major muscle changes occur in older adults: diminished number of motor neurons, a loss of muscle mass, deterioration of muscle fibrils, and deterioration of muscle cell membranes.[67] The result of these changes is a gradual decline in motor function and a loss of muscle strength and endurance. Around age 40, muscle strength begins to decline, resulting in an overall decrease of 30% to 50% by the age of 75 or 80.[67] Consequently, older adults experience muscle fatigue after a shorter duration of exercise (Fig. 37-2).

Weight Losses and Gains
Although weight gain is common during middlescence, weight loss is common during late adulthood. Weight loss is commonly associated with physical problems, such as diabetes or cancer, as well as with psychosocial impairments, such as dementia or depression. Weight gain is less common during late adulthood, and most of the older adults who are overweight were overweight before the late adult years.

Neurosensory Changes

Central Nervous System
As the brain ages, it gradually experiences a loss of neurons, diminished blood flow, accumulations of lipofuscin, reduction of weight, decline in synaptic functions, changes in neurotransmitter activity, decreased utilization of glucose and oxygen, and the presence of senile plaques and neurofibrillary tangles.[17] These changes, as well as changes in the peripheral nervous system, can interfere with the ability to receive, process, and respond to stimuli. As reaction times slows, there will be slower performance in walking and other activities of daily living. Additionally, decreased reaction time may interfere with perception and cognition. However, this is a very individualized age change with some older adults experiencing less slowing than others.

Gait and Balance
After age 75, the combined effects of skeletal, muscular and neurological changes often create gait changes. Women develop a waddling gait and a narrower base of walking and standing. Additionally, they have less muscular control and develop bowlegged-type changes that affect the lower extremities and alter the angle of the hip. These changes are thought to contribute to the increased susceptibility of women to both falls and fractures, particularly unexpected falls from low heights.[58] In contrast, the gait of older men becomes wider. The walking pattern of older men is characterized by less arm swing, a shorter stride, decreased steppage height, and a more flexed position of the head and trunk. The impact of these changes is that older men and women have a slower walking speed and spend more time in the support than the swing phase of the gait.[58]

Maintenance of balance in an upright position is a complex skill that is affected by age-related decreases in proprioception abilities and vibratory sensation. In addition, age-related changes in the vestibular system interfere with efficient functioning of the righting reflexes (see Chap. 6). These changes interfere with the ability of older adults to prevent a fall once they begin losing their balance.[58]

Pain and Tactile Sensitivity
Older adults experience a decrease in their tactile (touch) sensitivity. Also, beginning around age 50, there is a progressive decline in pain sensitivity.[34] One consequence of decreased tactile sensitivity is the increased susceptibility of older adults to scald burns because of their diminished ability to feel dangerously hot water temperatures—a factor that makes it a good idea to use a thermometer for measuring water temperature of hot water bottles and baths.

Gustatory and Olfactory Changes
Older adults experience declines in both olfactory (smell) and gustatory (taste) sensations. Degenerative changes in olfactory cells and in the nasal epithelium begin around the age of 30 and progress throughout adulthood. Older adults experience a diminished sensitivity to olfactory stimulation that may be even greater than decreases in their gustatory functioning.[4] Although there is disagreement about an age-related decline in the number of taste buds, there is agreement about a gradual and progressive age-related decline in gustatory ability. Explanations for reduced taste sensitivity include the following: effects of medication; alterations in saliva; the presence of dental, oral, and systemic diseases; occlusion of the upper palate by dentures; slowing of taste cell regeneration; or changes of the nervous system that influence the reception and processing of taste information. The result is a decreased appreciation for the subtle flavors of food and the increased use of spices and salt (which may be dangerous to cardiac functioning).

Vision
Nine percent of persons age 65 to 74, 15.9% of persons age 75 to 84, and 27.6% of persons over 85 years of age have significant visual impairment.[60] Age-related changes are found in all the structures of the eye. Some changes affect the appearance of the eye, but do not affect vision, (for example, a white or yellowish ring around the iris, dullness and increased opacity of the cornea, yellowing of the sclera, faded pigment in the iris, reduced orbital fat, accumulation of dark pigment around the eyes, drooping of eyelids, and the general appearance of sunken eyes).[67] Diminished tear production can lead to dry eyes. Although this condition may be uncomfortable, it does not affect visual abilities.

Changes that affect visual abilities include an increase in the lens size and density, alterations of the corneal curvature, increased sclerosis (hardening) and rigidity of the iris, smaller size of the pupils, atrophy of the ciliary muscle, shrinkage of gelatinous substance in the vitreous, atrophy of the photoreceptor cells, thinning and sclerosis of retinal blood vessels, and degeneration of neurons in the visual cortex.[36] *Presbyopia* is the earliest of these changes (see Chap. 35). As the lens ages, old cells are not shed. As a result, the yellowing of the lens tends to make blue-green and yellow-white colors more difficult to distinguish. The yellowing may also decrease clarity and increase glare, creating a need for better lighting (diffuse, to decrease glare) in order to see adequately. Other

FIGURE 37–2.
Many older adults are able to maintain muscle tone, joint flexibility, and physical stamina through regular exercise.

changes include a slower response to changes in illumination or distance, diminished depth perception, a narrowing of the visual field, and a slower processing of visual information.[36] Disease processes include an increased incidence of cataracts (clouding of the lens) and glaucoma (increased intraocular pressure).

Hearing

Twenty-three and two-tenths percent of persons age 65 to 74, 34.3% of persons 75 to 84, and 51.4% of persons over 85 have significant hearing impairment.[60] Degenerative changes affect all three compartments of the ear and the entire auditory nerve pathway. In the outer ear, the growth of longer and thicker hair (especially in men), thinning and drying of the skin lining of the canal, a higher concentration of keratin, and diminished sweat gland activity predispose the older adult to a build-up of wax. In the middle ear, the tympanic membrane becomes less resilient, the ossicles become calcified, and the muscles and ligaments become stiffer.[45] In the inner ear, one finds: fewer neurons and hair cells; diminished endolymph and blood supply; degeneration of the spiral ganglion and arterial blood vessels; decreased flexibility of the basilar membrane; and a narrowing of the auditory meatus. The result of these changes is *presbycusis* (sensorineural hearing loss).[45] Presbycusis interferes with the ability of the older adult to hear high-pitched sounds and sibilant consonants, such as *ch, f, g, s, sh, t, th,* and *z.*[45] When high-pitched sounds are filtered out, words become distorted and jumbled; sentences become incoherent. The presence of background noise intensifies this hearing problem.

Impact of Sensory Changes

Because of the decline in all sensory abilities, older adults experience difficulties in many areas of functioning that are important to their safety and quality of life. For example, food appeal may be significantly diminished, interfering with adequate nutrition and caloric intake. Age-related vision changes may influence driving a vehicle; shopping for groceries; going up and down stairs; maneuvering safely in public environments; reading watches, clocks, thermostats, thermometers, and appliances; watching television; and reading newspapers, directories, labels on food items, recipes, or reading for pleasure. Hearing deficits may lead to social isolation, boredom, feelings of low self-esteem, and a diminished ability to test reality. Individuals who are unable to discriminate words are afraid to respond to questions, and may choose not to answer rather than risk feeling foolish. Performance on cognitive assessments may be negatively influenced by a person's fear of not hearing the questions accurately, as well as by the actual reduction in the ability to receive and interpret sensory stimuli.

Cardiovascular System

Myocardium

Approximately 15% of persons over 65 have coronary heart disease.[60] Although anatomical changes have been identified in older hearts, many questions have been raised about whether the changes are attributable to aging, disease, or other risk factors. Some changes, which may be age- or disease-related, are amyloid deposits, lipofuscin accumulation, basophilic degeneration, valvular thickening and stiffening, and increased amounts of connective tissue.[33] Changes in heart size have shown atrophy as well as hypertrophy, but these changes are now thought to be primarily attributable to disease-related factors. The only identified age-related change in heart size is a slight left ventricular hypertrophy.[33, 66] Changes in the cardiac conduction system include increased amounts of myocardial fat, collagen, and elastic fibers; a decrease in the number of pacemaker cells and a greater irregularity in their shape; and decreased numbers of cells in the sinus node, the atrioventricular node, the bundle of His, and the right and left bundles. Other changes that are thought to be age-related include thickening of the atrial endocardium and atrial ventricular valves, and calcification of at least part of the mitral annulus of the aortic valve (Fig. 27-3).[66]

FIGURE 37–3.
Continued participation in physical activities and moderate exercise help to maintain healthy cardiac action and to reduce cardiovascular risk factors. Most tasks can still be accomplished by spreading the work over a longer period of time or using alternative tools.

Age-related changes that affect the middle layer of the arteries include an increase in collagen and a thinning and calcification of elastin fibers. The inner layer, or *tunica intima,* is most directly affected by age-related changes and most involved with the disease-related atherosclerotic processes. With increasing age, the tunica intima thickens because of fibrosis, cellular proliferation, and lipid and calcium accumulation. In addition, the endothelial cells become irregular in size and shape.[66] These changes make the arterial walls more vulnerable to atherosclerosis, as discussed in the next section.

Veins undergo changes similar to those affecting the arteries, but to a lesser degree. Veins become thicker, more dilated, and less elastic with increasing age. Valves in the large leg veins become less efficient in facilitating the return of blood to the heart; consequently, blood may pool in the lower extremities. Peripheral circulation is further influenced by an age-related reduction in muscle mass and a concurrent reduction in the demand for oxygen.[10]

Atherosclerosis

Atherosclerosis is the most common form of arteriosclerosis (which is the broad category of disorders that cause hardening and thickening of the arterial walls). The term comes from the Greek word *athera,* meaning "gruel." This is descriptive of the gruel-like material found in the central portion of atherosclerotic plaques.[1]

The *reaction to injury* theory is a widely accepted explanation for the development of atherosclerosis.[51] According to this theory, atherogenesis is a cyclical process involving the following steps: (1) the inner wall of the artery is injured as a result of repeated or continuing insults; (2) circulating platelets arrive; (3) smooth muscle cells from the middle layer move into the inner layer and multiply at the site of injury; and (4) lipids and connective tissue accumulate. The initial injury might be caused by chemicals (e.g., cholesterol), mechanical stress (as with high blood pressure or physical trauma), or immunological factors (as with kidney transplantation). With repeated or chronic injury, the intima thickens and blood flow over the injured site is altered. This sequence can cause further injury, eventually causing a stroke or heart attack. This process can be halted by addressing the source of the initial injury (such as by treating high blood pressure) or by decreasing the amount of low-density lipoproteins.

Impact of Cardiovascular Changes

Because of age-related cardiovascular changes, the maximum heart rate achieved during strenuous exercise is diminished, even in healthy older adults. In addition, the prevalence of *arrhythmias* (irregular heartbeat) increases because of the age-related changes that affect the cardiac conduction mechanism. Because of changes in the vasculature, there is a slight increase in systolic blood pressure and a concomitant widening of the pulse pressure. Between ages 40 and 80, the systolic pressure increases by approximately 25 mm Hg in men and 35 mm Hg in women.[22] Another consequence of cardiovascular changes is an increased susceptibility to postural hypotension (a drop in blood pressure caused by position change). Older adults who have postural hypotension will experience a drop in blood pressure on rising from a lying or sitting position. This may precipitate sufficient decrease in oxygen to the brain to experience transient light-headedness, or even fainting—factors leading to falls. This problem is likely to occur within 1 hour of eating a meal, or when arising during the night. It is sometimes exacerbated by medication effects.

Influence of Lifestyle

Adequate exercise and nutrition can significantly improve cardiovascular health in older adults. The incidence of atherosclerosis is increased with obesity, diabetes, hypertension, male gender, increased age, physical inactivity, cigarette smoking, specific hereditary and personality factors, and dietary habits that contribute to high blood lipids. Although some of these risk factors, such as gender and heredity, cannot be altered, many of these risk factors are lifestyle factors within the control of individuals (see Chap. 35).

Respiratory System

Upper Respiratory Structures

Age-related connective tissue changes cause the nose to have a retracted columella (septum) and a poorly supported, downwardly rotated tip. Although these are minor changes, they can result in mouth-breathing during sleep and snoring. The older adult with a combination of mouth-breathing and diminished saliva might awaken with a dry mouth and sore throat. Because cartilage in the epiglottis and upper airway structures becomes calcified, the trachea of the older adult is stiffened. The cough and laryngeal reflexes are blunted, and there is a concomitant decrease in coughing.[56] Age-related reductions in laryngeal nerve endings may contribute to diminished efficiency of the gag reflex.[12]

Chest Wall and Lungs

The rib cage and the vertebral skeletal structures become osteoporotic, the costal cartilage becomes calcified, and the respiratory muscles become weaker. Other structural changes affecting respiratory performance include kyphosis (hump back), shortened thorax, chest wall stiffness, and increased anteroposterior diameter of the chest. The overall impact on respiratory performance is diminished respiratory efficiency and reduced maximal inspiratory and expiratory force. To compensate for these changes, older adults depend increasingly on accessory muscles, particularly the diaphragm, and are, therefore, more sensitive to any changes in intra-abdominal pressure.

Even in healthy older adults, lungs become smaller and flabbier, and their weight diminishes by approximately 20%.[37] Around the age of 30, the alveoli progressively enlarge and their walls become thinner. This process continues throughout adulthood, resulting in a decreased surface area of the lungs. The pulmonary artery trunk becomes thickened, less extensible, and wider in diameter. Additionally, the number of capillaries diminishes, and there is a decrease in pulmonary capillary blood volume. Lastly, the mucosal bed, where diffusion takes place, thickens.[37] As a consequence of these changes, the effective alveolar surface is reduced.

Lung Volumes, Air Flow, and Gas Exchange

In older adults, air volumes are altered because of the age-related changes in the chest wall and in lung elastic recoil. Because various lung volumes are interrelated, however, the total lung capacity remains essentially the same owing to compensatory mechanisms. Because of early airway closure and other age-related changes, gas exchange is more likely to be compromised in the lower than the upper lung regions. Consequently, inspired air is preferentially distributed in the upper regions and a ventilation-to-perfusion mismatch results. The result of this mismatch is a gradual decrease in oxygenation of arterial blood of approximately 4 mm Hg per decade.[56]

Impact of Changes

Under conditions of physical stress, older adults may become fatigued and dyspneic (have difficulty breathing) because their respiratory system is less efficient in gas exchange. Even this effect may be compensated for, at least partially, through physical conditioning. The major consequence of age-related respiratory changes is increased susceptibility to lower respiratory infections. The combination of changes in respiratory functioning and immunity contributes to the increased risk of acquiring pneumonia and influenza in later adulthood. People age 65 and older have an excess yearly death rate from pneumonia or influenza of 9 per 100,000.[52] Older adults also are more susceptible to tuberculosis. The most common reason for this is the reactivation of long-dormant tuberculosis because of diminished resistance or debilitating illness.

Influence of Smoking and Other Lifestyle Factors

Active or passive (breathing the air contaminated by another's smoke) tobacco smoke has detrimental effects on the respiratory system, including (1) bronchoconstriction, (2) inflammation of the mucosa throughout the respiratory tract, (3) earlier airway closure, and (4) inhibited ciliary action leading to increased coughing and mucous secretions and diminished protection from harmful organisms. Risks for older adults are compounded by age-related changes and the cumulative effects of cigarette smoking. Even in otherwise healthy people, smokers have a double or triple rate of decline in the forced expiratory volume, compared to that in nonsmokers.[56]

Another environmental risk factor is the inhalation of air pollutants. Like cigarette smoking, the effects of air pollution are cumulative and, therefore, have a greater impact on older adults who have been exposed to these risks over much of their lifetime. Because hazards in the work place were largely unregulated prior to the 1970s, many older people never benefited from the protections enforced under the Occupational Safety and Health Act. Consequently, older adults may have been exposed to toxic substances with both cumulative

and long-term effects. Much of the information now available regarding the harmful effects of certain chemicals was not understood or known when these older adults were part of the work force. Therefore, older adults are more likely than younger adults to experience the long-term effects of occupational exposure to harmful substances.

Integumentary System

Skin

The three layers of the skin are the epidermis, dermis, and subcutaneous tissue. The epidermal layer consists of corneocytes, which continually migrate to the surface where they are shed, and melanocytes, which give the skin its color. With increasing age, corneocytes become larger and more irregularly shaped, and the rate of epidermal proliferation slows. The primary age-related factor affecting melanocytes is a decrease of 8% to 20% in the number of active cells each decade, particularly after the age of 30.[34] These changes cause the skin to look paler, thinner, and irregularly pigmented. Additional age-related changes in the epidermis are a diminished moisture content and a flattening of the dermal-epidermal junction. Consequently, the skin has less turgor and is injured more easily. Beginning in early adulthood, the dermal layer gradually becomes thinner, and circulation is gradually reduced. Sweat and sebaceous glands, which are located in the dermis, show a decrease in secretions.

Cosmetic indicators of these age-related changes include sagging, wrinkling, and various growths and lesions. Age-related signs that are evident around the eyes include increased pigmentation, "crow's feet" wrinkles, and fat and fluid accumulation in the upper lid and under the eye. In the neck, the skin sags and a "double chin" may be evident. Various skin lesions, most of which are harmless, begin to appear (Table 37-2).

Hair and Nails

In early adulthood, nail growth begins to slow, with a gradual decrease of 30% to 50% over the life span.[26] The nails tend to become increasingly soft, fragile, brittle, and likely to split. In appearance, the older nail is dull, opaque, longitudinally striated, and yellow or gray in color. Toenails may thicken because of frequent trauma or poor circulation.[26]

By age 50, about 50% of people have graying hair and about 60% of white men have a noticeable degree of baldness.[26] Body hair distribution also shows age-related changes, caused at least in part by hormonal changes of menopause. Patches of coarse terminal hair develop over the upper lip and lower face in older women, and in the ears, nares, and eyebrows of older men.[67] Beginning around the age of 40, both men and women experience progressive loss of body hair, initially in the trunk, then in the pubic area and axillae.[26]

Environmental Influences

Because the effects of ultraviolet radiation (UVR) are cumulative, they may not be noticed until 10 years after initial exposure. Characteristically, UVR-damaged skin has a thickened

TABLE 37–2. SKIN LESIONS COMMON IN OLDER ADULTS

Common Terms	Description
Age spots, liver spots, senile freckles	Flat, brown lesions, most common on exposed areas
Seborrheic keratosis	Raised, brown or black plaques with sharp edges and a waxy texture
Senile angiomas, cherry or ruby angiomas	Pinpoint, superficial elevations of blood vessels
Venous stars	Bluish, irregular, spider-shaped lesions, mainly on legs or chest
Venous lakes	Raised, bluish lesions with sharp borders, mainly on lips or ears
Skin tags (papillomas)	Flesh-colored, stalk-like lesions
Corns, calluses	Hard masses of keratin, caused by repeated pressure or irritation

(Adapted from Miller, C. A. [1990]. Nursing care of older adults: Theory and practice. *Glenview, IL: Scott, Foresman.)*

epidermis, enlarged sebaceous glands, and dilated and tortuous blood vessels.[35] Ultraviolet radiation increases the incidence of harmless as well as cancerous and precancerous skin lesions.[35] There is an increased incidence of skin cancers in older adults.

Impact of Changes

Dry skin is a very common complaint of older adults, caused by a combination of age-related changes and external factors, such as dry environments, adverse medication reactions, UVR exposure, and frequent bathing, especially with soap. Because the skin of older adults is less resistant to abrasive and shearing forces, it is more susceptible to bruising and blisters. Regeneration of healthy skin takes twice as long for the typical 80-year-old person as for a 30-year-old person, contributing to delayed wound healing.[34] Because age-related changes compromise the ability to defend against foreign materials, older adults are more susceptible to skin infections. Because of the epidermal changes (discussed above), older adults tan less deeply and more slowly, and the pigmentation may be mottled and irregular. Older adults also are more vulnerable to hypothermia and heat-related illness because of age-related skin changes and central nervous system responses that interfere with sweating, shivering, circulation, and insulation against adverse environmental temperatures (Fig. 37-4).

Gastrointestinal System

Digestive Tract

Because the first stage of digestion takes place in the mouth, all structures in the mouth are essential to digestion. With increasing age, the tooth enamel becomes harder and more brittle, and the dentin becomes more fibrous, leading to an increased incidence of tooth chipping.[69] With age, the tooth pulp and nerve shrink and the space gradually calcifies, factors that lead to decreased sensitivity to pain.

Decades of abrasive and erosive action may gradually wear down the chewing cusps to flatter surfaces. Inadequately treated gingivitis may become periodontitis (infection of the soft tissues surrounding the teeth). Periodontitis can lead to infection and destruction of the periodontal ligaments and then to bone infection. As bone tissue degenerates, the teeth can loosen and come out. Good dental hygiene throughout

FIGURE 37–4.
This 100-year-old woman shows many of the integumentary and visual changes typical of elderly persons. Despite her advanced age, she is obviously alert and vitally involved, enjoying life's events from the perspective of experience and new priorities.

life can prevent this scenario. Crooked teeth is another common cause of tooth loss in the elderly, and is preventable. Teeth need to impact on the long axis of the tooth when chewing. The cumulative effects of improper alignment is excessive bone stress with degeneration leading to loosening and loss of teeth. Tooth loss is not necessarily a consequence of aging.

Age-related changes of the oral mucosa include loss of elasticity, atrophy of epithelial cells, and diminished blood supply to the connective tissue. Saliva production is diminished in older adults owing to a combination of age-related changes, disease conditions, and medications. Dry mouth and vitamin deficiencies compound the changes, making the oral mucosa more susceptible to ulceration and infection, factors that increase the need for more intensive oral hygiene measures.[69] Chewing efficiency in older adults is affected by age-related changes in the neuromuscular structures involved in mastication (chewing). Consequently, older adults chew food for longer periods before swallowing, and they swallow larger food particles.[21]

The second phase of digestion occurs when food is propelled through the pharynx and esophagus into the stomach. In older adults, the intensity of esophageal propulsive waves decreases and the frequency of nonpropulsive waves increases. Another change affecting the second phase of digestion is a decrease in gastric juice secretion. This change begins around age 40, and by age 60 the volume of gastric juices is only 70% to 80% that of the young adult. Because of diminished gastric juices, the absorption of protein, iron, vitamin B_{12}, calcium, and folic acid is impaired.[7] Absorption of these nutrients is further compromised by factors that are not necessarily age-related, but are common in older adults, such as the use of antacids and other medications. Because of interference with the absorption of nutrients, age-related changes in the stomach increase the susceptibility to certain pathological conditions, such as pernicious anemia.

Research on age-related changes of the small intestine is scant, but there is evidence that many structures in the small intestine atrophy.[69] One effect of these changes is diminution of fat absorption with increased age. Changes in the small intestine and other structures also interfere with absorption of calcium and vitamin D. Absorption of these nutrients in older adults may be further compromised by inadequate intake of calcium, which is one of the most common dietary deficiencies of older adults.

Age-related changes in the large intestine include a reduction in mucous secretion and a decreased elasticity of the rectal wall.[67] Despite the emphasis on constipation as a common problem of older adulthood, the changes of the large intestine have little impact on motility of feces through the bowel. Although loss of elasticity of the intestinal wall might contribute, even this change is inconsequential if the urge to defecate is responded to promptly.

Impact of Changes on Eating Patterns

Impairment of cognition, balance, mobility, manual dexterity, or any of the five senses, may interfere with the procurement, preparation, consumption, or enjoyment of food. Changes in any of these skills, as well as any chronic illness, may influence one's eating habits. Some older adults experience difficulty getting to the grocery store, pushing a shopping cart, reaching for food items on high shelves, reading the small print on food packages, and coping with the glare of bright lights, especially in the white-coated frozen food sections. Food preparation activities that are likely to be more difficult for older adults include cutting food items, measuring ingredients accurately, carrying food and liquid without spilling, standing for long periods in the kitchen, safely using the oven or stove, and reading the temperature controls correctly.

Environmental conditions and transportation resources may have a detrimental effect on older adults who are unable to compensate for inclement weather conditions. People who depend on others for transportation or who have difficulty maneuvering in adverse weather conditions, may feel forced to shop for groceries less frequently or to purchase their groceries at the local convenience stores, where prices are higher and selection is limited. An older person who usually walks to the store or who depends on public transportation may be unable to obtain groceries when snow or slippery conditions create safety hazards. Likewise, in extremely hot or sultry conditions, the older adult may not be able to tolerate the temperature and humidity, especially if car transportation is not readily available. The environment in the grocery store may create additional difficulties for some older people. For example, the combined glare of fluorescent lights, highly polished floors, cellophane wrappers, and white freezer cases often make it extremely difficult, if not impossible, for the older adult with vision changes to read labels, especially when the print is small and faded.

Food appeal is significantly influenced by its odor, color, flavor, texture, temperature, and appearance. Because discernment of these qualities depends on sensory perception, age-related declines in gustatory and olfactory abilities may negatively affect food appeal. In addition, diminished gustatory and olfactory skills may lead to excessive use of condiments and seasonings, such as salt and sugar. Food choices are influenced by the condition of the oral cavity and teeth, as well as the quantity and quality of natural or replacement teeth. For example, dry mouth may interfere with comfort as well as digestion. With diminished saliva production, food is less enjoyable and more difficult to chew, and the teeth and tongue become increasingly susceptible to bacterial action.

Psychosocial factors also may affect an older person's appetite and eating habits. Changes in mealtime companionship, which may occur through loss or disability of a spouse, often have a negative impact on eating habits. Depression and loneliness, common psychosocial experiences, are typically accompanied by loss of interest in food. Any move from an independent living setting usually results in the older adult having less control over food selection and mealtime patterns. The older adult living in congregate housing or a long-term care facility may have trouble adjusting to new and sometimes undesired opportunities for mealtime socialization. A noisy or crowded dining environment may reduce food enjoyment and consumption. Such an environment may be particularly stressful for an older adult who uses a hearing aid or who is accustomed to eating alone. The potential outcomes of these changes include loss of interest in eating and poor nutrition (Fig. 37-5).

Urinary System

Urinary Tract

The kidney increases in weight and mass from birth until early adulthood, then the number of functioning nephrons begins to decline, particularly in the cortex.

This decline continues through the remainder of life, resulting in a decrease in kidney mass of approximately 25% by the age of 85. Many of the remaining glomeruli become sclerotic and inactive. Beginning in the forties, renal blood flow gradually diminishes, particularly in the cortex, at a rate of 10% per decade.[32] These age-related changes result in a reduction in the glomerular filtration rate (GFR) of one-third to two-thirds by the eighth or ninth decade.[32] The renal tubules also are affected by age-related changes; consequently, the kidney is less efficient in the tubular exchange of substances and the conservation of water and sodium. These changes may predispose a healthy older person to nocturia (excessive urination at night) and hyponatremia (low blood sodium). In the presence of many disease conditions, these changes will interfere with the kidney's ability to concentrate urine and excrete water, leading to potential for increased risk of fluid and electrolyte imbalance during illness.

The normal adult bladder can store about 200 mL of urine before the sensation to void is perceived. With the accumulation of 350 to 400 mL of urine, sensations of fullness and discomfort are perceived. With increasing age, hypertrophy of the bladder muscle and thickening of the bladder wall interfere with the bladder's ability to expand, decreasing the

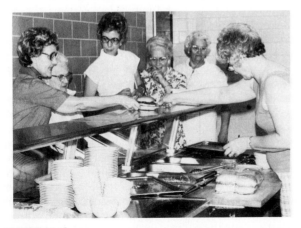

FIGURE 37–5.
It is difficult and discouraging for many older persons to try to cook for one. Many senior citizen centers offer highly nutritious meals at low cost—a factor that can improve the health status and increase the life span of the elderly.

amount of urine that can be stored comfortably to about 250 to 300 mL. Younger adults begin to feel the sensation of fullness when the bladder is about half full. Because of age-related changes, however, this sensation occurs at a later point for older adults, and may not occur at all.[67]

Male Genitourinary Problems

Almost half of all older men experience difficulties with urination because of benign prostatic hypertrophy (BPH). In its early stage, BPH obstructs the flow of urine, causing difficulty initiating voiding, intermittent flow during voiding, and incomplete emptying. With progressive hypertrophy, the bladder wall loses its ability to force the urine past the obstruction because of reduced elasticity and thinning of the bladder wall. Subsequently, urinary retention occurs, increasing the risk of infection. Eventually, serious kidney problems may develop. Other disease-related conditions that may cause or contribute to urinary incontinence include bladder calculi, prostatic cancer, surgery, and postirradiation damage.

Female Genitourinary Problems

Postmenopausal estrogen depletion leads to weakening of the pelvic floor muscles. Obesity and previous trauma secondary to childbirth are additional factors that contribute to weakening of the pelvic floor muscles for some older women. With relaxation of the pelvic muscles, any sudden increase in intra-abdominal pressure may cause the involuntary release of small amounts of urine ("stress incontinence"). A cystocele, rectocele, or urethrocele may develop as a result of extreme pelvic muscle stretching or relaxation, secondary to the combination of age-related changes and a history of childbirth trauma. Pelvic muscle weakness also interferes with complete emptying of the bladder, resulting in residual urine and increased risk of infection. Another effect of estrogen depletion is atrophy of the vaginal and trigonal tissues and a diminished resistance of those tissues to pathogens. Vaginitis and trigonitis may develop, and may be accompanied by urinary urgency, frequency, and incontinence.

Impact of Changes

One major consequence of the renal changes involves the excretion of water-soluble medications. The excretion of some medications, such as digoxin and antibodies, is heavily dependent on efficient renal functioning. Medication excretion may be delayed, causing an accumulation of toxic substances. It has been estimated that older adults require a 50% higher urine volume to excrete the same solute load as their younger counterparts.[49] Consequently, medication doses may need to be adjusted to account for age-related kidney changes. The aging kidney has diminished ability to compensate for conditions such as water deprivation or excessive fluid loss. Even with normal states of hydration, the age-related decrease in the glomerular filtration rate delays water excretion and may lead to hyponatremia. An example of a normal daily activity that can challenge the renal functioning of older adults is exercise. When older adults perspire during exercise, they may fatigue easily because of the age-related delay in the mechanism for water and sodium conservation.

Incontinence

The bladder of the older adult has a decreased capacity, empties incompletely, and experience increased irritability. These changes result in shorter intervals between voidings and less time between the perception of the signal to void and the actual need to empty the bladder. Consequently, urgency and frequency are often experienced during the day, and nocturia may occur 1 to 3 times per night. Additionally, chronic residual urine is likely to cause bacteriuria. These conditions predispose the older person to urinary **incontinence** (an involuntary loss of urine); which can become a social or hygienic problem.

Types of incontinence include:

1. **Urge incontinence** is the inability to hold urine long enough to get to the toilet, despite the perception of the urge to void.
2. **Stress incontinence** is the sudden leakage of small amounts of urine because of an activity that increases abdominal pressure, such as coughing, laughing, sneezing, lifting, or exercise (frequent in older women).
3. **Overflow incontinence** is the leakage of small amounts of urine, periodically or continually, without the urge to void or without being able to pass large amounts (frequent in men who have BPH).
4. **Total incontinence** is the complete absence of urinary control, resulting in the continual leakage of small amounts or the periodic expulsion of large amounts.

Urge, stress, and overflow incontinence are likely to occur in the presence of conditions that commonly affect older adults, such as prostatic hypertrophy in men and pelvic muscle weakness in women. When combined with environmental barriers or mobility limitations, even small degrees of incontinence may result in total incontinence for the older adult.

Environmental Factors

Environmental factors may create obstacles to reaching and using the toilet in home, public, and institutional settings. The combination of mobility limitations and age-related changes in the urinary tract may lead to incontinence. Examples include (1) stairs or long hallways which separate bedrooms or living areas from bathrooms; (2) distance between the toilet facilities and the older adult greater than 40 feet; (3) small bathrooms and narrow doors and halls that do not accommodate walkers or wheelchairs; and (4) restaurants, shopping malls, and other places with poorly visible or poorly color-contrasted signs designating gender-specific bathroom facilities.

Reproductive System

Female Reproductive Changes

Reproductive abilities generally decline during the fifth decade, when the frequency of ovulation diminishes under the influence of decreased estrogen production. Menopause, the cessation of menses that typically occurs around age 50, is usually an indicator that reproductive functions are terminated. Reproductive abilities are usually absent within 1 year of the last menstrual period. Endogenous estrogen declines in all postmenopausal women, but the extent and manifestations of estrogen deficiency vary. Some factors that may influence postmenopausal levels of endogenous estrogen include the interval since the onset of menopause; the production of hormones by the adrenal cortex; and body weight, with higher body fat being positively correlated with higher levels of estrogen.[30] Greatly diminished estrogen precipitates the following changes: (1) the cervix, uterus, and fallopian tubes atrophy; (2) the vaginal wall and mucosa become thinner; (3) the vagina diminishes in length and width; (4) Bartholin's glands secrete less fluid; (5) the amount of vaginal lubrication during sexual excitement is diminished; (6) the labia lose their fullness; and (7) pubic hair becomes sparse. Decreased estrogen also causes a gradual replacement of mammary gland tissue with fat tissue. Connective tissue changes cause the breasts of older women to become less firm and more pendulous. Hormonal (estrogen) replacement therapy can help to prevent or delay some of these changes (see Chap. 35).

Male Reproductive Changes

Male reproductive functioning is dependent on the production of hormones, the production and release of sperm, and the motility of sperm. Testosterone production as well as the number of normal viable sperm gradually diminish in older men. These changes, however, are not necessarily age-related and are more likely associated with pathological conditions and decreased sexual activity.[30, 67] Beginning around age 30, the penis undergoes age-related changes, such as hardening of the blood vessels.[30] Although these degenerative changes do not cause cessation of reproductive functioning, they may cause a reduction in fertility.

Sexual Interest and Activities

Sexual activity at any age is influenced by social circumstances, such as the response and availability of an acceptable and desirable partner. For older adults, particularly older women, social circumstances are often the strongest determinant of sexual activity. Studies consistently show that the level of sexual activity for older women is directly related to their marital status, whereas the level of sexual activity for older men is not as closely associated with marital status. Men at all ages report a higher frequency of extramarital sexual relationships, and older widowers have a higher likelihood of remarriage in comparison with older widows.[8]

Chronic illnesses have a negative impact on sexual performance and may precipitate impotence in men. Specifically, neurologic, endocrine, and cardiovascular illnesses are highly associated with sexual dysfunctioning. The chronic illnesses most commonly associated with erectile failure in men are diabetes mellitus and myocardial infarction. Any chronic illness that causes serious functional impairment, such as arthritis or respiratory disease, can interfere with sexual interest and performance. People with limited energy, agility, or respiratory capacity may use compensatory approaches to achieving mutually satisfying sexual relationships.[14] Problems with a sexual relationship may arise when a person is dependent on the sexual partner for assistance in activities of daily living. When a person is dependent on a sexual partner for assistance with very personal tasks, such as cleansing of the genitalia and rectal area, conflicts may arise because these activities are closely connected with sexual activities.

The role of medication as a cause of disorders of sexual functioning was brought to the public's attention in a 1983 *New York Times* article. It cited medications as the single largest cause of impotence in men, and listed more than 50 medications with potential adverse sexual effects.[9] Medications affect sexual functioning adversely through a variety of mechanisms, including their influence on the release of hormones and their actions on the autonomic and central nervous systems. Specific medication effects that interfere with sexual functioning in men include a decreased or absent libido, difficulties in obtaining or maintaining an erection, and premature or retrograde ejaculation. A less common adverse medication effect is priapism, or prolonged erection, which is associated with some psychotropic medications. Medications may cause women to experience diminished lubrication, decreased or absent libido, or inability to achieve an orgasm.[53]

Other observations on sexuality and aging include the following:[68]

1. Although the frequency of sexual activity gradually declines with increasing age, the level of sexual interest and competence of older adults does **not** decline.

2. Decrease in sexual activity with advancing age is not attributable to age-related physiological changes, but to social circumstances, pathological conditions, and other risk factors.

3. The social circumstances that most frequently lead to decreased sexual activity are spousal death or illness and lack of an available partner. The sexual activity of older women is more often affected by these conditions than is that of men.

4. Sexual interest, attitudes, and activity are a continuation of lifelong patterns, and do not change significantly with advanced age.

5. Throughout life, men are more sexually active than women.

Response to Sexual Stimulation

The Masters and Johnson investigation is recognized as the landmark study on physiological responses to sexual stimula-

tion.[41] An analysis of data on older subjects concluded that they maintain their ability to respond to sexual stimulation, but their response is slower and less intense. Masters and Johnson also concluded that older adults who engage in sexual activity experience fewer changes in their response to sexual stimulation than those who are sexually inactive. Changes in response to sexual stimulation, or in the ability to be sexually stimulated, are thought to be associated with health and sociological factors that commonly occur in older adults. Table 37-3 summarizes the age-related changes in the responses of men and women to sexual stimulation.

Additional Somatic Changes

Thermoregulation

Temperature regulation in older adults is impaired in several ways. First, older adults tend to have a lower normal body temperature and a diminished response to fever-producing illnesses.[54] Thus, they may not have an elevated temperature when they are acutely ill, and a slightly elevated temperature may easily be overlooked if their normal temperature is below the expected temperature of 98.6°F. Also, the lower body temperature may cause the older person to feel cool. Second, older adults are more vulnerable to hypothermia because they are less efficient in their response to cold. Age-related changes affect the response to cold temperatures beginning around age 70 to 75. Thus, older adults have a dulled perception of cold environments, and they may not initiate protective actions, such as adding more clothing or raising the environmental temperature.[67] The third area of altered temperature regulation in older adults is their diminished ability to respond to hot environments. The age-related changes that contribute to this problem include delayed and diminished sweating and inaccurate perception of environmental temperatures.[19] Thus, older adults are more likely to develop heat-related problems, and the incidence of illness and death in older adults is higher during heat waves (Fig. 37-6).

Sleep and Rest

Researchers agree that older adults spend increasing amounts of time in bed, with and without attempting to sleep, and a decreasing proportion of time in actual sleep. Disagreement arises, however, about changes in the total sleep time of older adults. One review of research on total sleep time in non-institutionalized older adults concluded that studies using polygraphs in sleep laboratories showed a reduction of total sleep time, whereas surveys using subjective data showed an age-related increase in total sleep time over a 24-hour period.[16] When daytime naps are included, the average daily sleep duration for both older and younger adults is 6.5 to 7.5 hours, but the mean duration of sleep **and** rest for older adults is 10 to 12 hours.[48]

One's sleep efficiency, or the percentage of time asleep during nocturnal time in bed, influences one's perception of

TABLE 37–3. AGE-RELATED CHANGES IN RESPONSE TO SEXUAL STIMULATION

Female Response	Male Response
EXCITEMENT PHASE	
Breasts not as engorged Sexual flush absent or diminished Delayed or diminished vaginal lubrication Decreased expansion of vaginal wall Decreased vasocongestion of labia	Twofold to threefold longer time required to attain erection Less firm erection Longer maintenance of erection before ejaculation Increased difficulty regaining an erection if lost Reduced or absent scrotal and testicular vasocongestion
PLATEAU PHASE	
Decreased areolar engorgement Less intense sexual flush Less intense myotonia Decreased degree of deepening of labial color Decreased vasocongestion of labia Reduced Bartholin secretions Slower/less marked uterine elevation	Diminished or absent nipple turgidity and sexual flush Less intense muscle tension Slower penile erectile pattern No color change in glans penis Delayed and diminished testicular elevation
ORGASM PHASE	
Decreased frequency of rectal sphincter contractions Decreased number and intensity of orgasmic contractions	Decreased frequency of rectal sphincter contractions Diminution of ejaculatory expulsion force by about 50% Absent or diminished sense of ejaculatory inevitability Fewer and less intense ejaculatory contractions
RESOLUTION PHASE	
Slower loss of nipple erection Quicker return to preexcitement stage	Slower loss of nipple erection Longer refractory period Very rapid penile detumescence Very rapid testicular descent

(Miller, C. A. [1990]. Nursing care of older adults: Theory and practice. Glenview, IL: Scott, Foresman.)

the quality of sleep. Sleep efficiency is greatly diminished in older adults, because of a prolonged sleep latency, or the time required to fall asleep, and an increased number of awakenings during the night. Beginning in the thirties, the number of awakenings during the night gradually increases to the point that, by later adulthood, one-fifth of the night may be spent in periods of wakefulness.[16] The quality of sleep is also affected by the amount of time spent in deep sleep and dream stages. In older adulthood, the dream stage of sleep diminishes in both length and intensity, and stage IV sleep periods become very short or may even be absent.[16] In summary, older adults have more difficulty falling asleep, awaken more readily and more frequently, and spend more time in the drowsiness stage and less time in the dream stage. Table 26-1 offers ideas on how to help promote healthy sleep patterns in persons of all ages.

Hematologic and Immunologic Systems

Blood production is not significantly altered in healthy older adults, but it may be altered by diseases, nutritional deficiencies, and minor life stresses.[55] With increased age, hemoglobin and hematocrit levels may decline slightly, but any significant decline is due to nutritional deficiencies or disease-related processes. Anemia, which commonly occurs in older adults, should not be considered an age-related change.[3] The erythrocyte sedimentation rate does increase in older adults, and immune responses are affected by age-related changes in T cells, leukocytes, and other cells that protect against harmful organisms. There is also a decline in antibodies and an increase in immunoglobins and some autoantibodies.[55] Because of age-related immunologic changes, older adults are more susceptible to pneumonia and other infections, and their response to infections is blunted.

FIGURE 37–6.
The elderly feel the cold more readily than younger persons and frequently need a sweater or shawl to maintain comfortable body temperature.

Endocrine and Metabolic Systems

With increased age, the basal metabolic rate diminishes slightly because of changes in the proportion of fat and lean tissue. Already discussed is the diminished ability to maintain fluid and electrolyte balance in the presence of conditions that cause physiological stress, such as diseases or dehydration. When fluid and electrolyte disturbances do occur, it is more difficult to correct these imbalances. Other age-related endocrine changes, besides those of the reproductive system, include diminished thyroid activity, decreased insulin production, diminished efficiency of glucose utilization, and a decline in adrenal gland size and output.

FACTORS INFLUENCING HIGH-LEVEL WELLNESS

Illness

Illnesses in older adults differ from illnesses in younger adults in several aspects. First, the manifestations of illness and chemical imbalances become less predictable and more subtle with increasing age. For example, many older people who have heart attacks do not feel any pain or experi-

ence other "typical" manifestations.[40] Older adults are much more likely to experience mental changes or vague physical complaints, rather than chest pain, when they have a heart attack. Older adults who develop pneumonia may not have any cough or elevated temperature, but they may simply feel fatigued or experience subtle difficulties in performing activities. Because of these more subtle and less predictable manifestations, illnesses may not be accurately identified and may progress to serious stages before they are treated. By the time illnesses or adverse medication effects are noted and attended to, additional complications or permanent impairments may have developed.

A second distinguishing feature of biophysical disturbances in older adults is the increased likelihood of developing mental changes because of illnesses, chemical imbalances, or medication effects. Because the older brain is less able to compensate for biophysical imbalances, elderly persons can easily develop confusion, depression, memory impairments, or other mental changes. Medications, even over-the-counter drugs, are more likely to cause confusion or depression, especially in the presence of disease processes.

A third unique aspect of illness in older adults is that any one symptom may have many possible explanations. Biophysical changes may be related to any one or a combination of (1) psychosocial factors, (2) environmental changes, (3) age-related changes, (4) acute illness, (5) a new chronic illness, (6) exacerbation of an existing chronic illness, or (7) an adverse effect of medication(s) or other treatments.[44] The following example of Mrs. Smith, a hypothetical, but typical older adult, illustrates how all seven of these potential causes of biophysical changes can affect one person.

> One month ago, Mrs. Smith, who is 84 years old, moved from her family home to an assisted living apartment after her husband died. She has had high blood pressure for 20 years and has been experiencing small strokes, which cause her to feel dizzy and confused for brief periods. She takes pills every day for high blood pressure. Three days ago, Mrs. Smith developed an upper respiratory infection and has been taking over-the-counter cold preparations to relieve her symptoms. Yesterday, Mrs. Smith fell when she got out of bed.

Potential causes of Mrs. Smith's new symptom (i.e., the fall) could be any of the following: (1) physiological reaction to the stressor of grief or the move from her family home; (2) an unfamiliar environment; (3) age-related changes that interfere with her ability to maintain balance or to see and respond to environmental barriers; (4) biophysical changes secondary to the upper respiratory infection; (5) impaired circulation to the brain because of the small strokes; (6) impaired circulation from her long-standing high blood pressure; or (7) adverse effects of her blood pressure medication, the over-the-counter cold medication, or the interaction between these two medications.

A fourth unique characteristic of illness in older adults, is that when illnesses occur they are likely to have seriously detrimental effects on the individual. In the example above, when Mrs. Smith falls she is likely to fracture a hip because of osteoporosis. If she does fracture her hip, Mrs. Smith is more likely than a younger person to become permanently impaired, and perhaps move to a more dependent level of care. Even if Mrs. Smith does not fracture a bone, she is likely to develop a fear of falling, or "fallaphobia," as a consequence of her fall. Thus, illness in older adults may combine with other factors to seriously impair biophysical functioning, psychological well-being, and quality of life.

Influence of the Environment

The Environment and Older Adults

During late adulthood, the environment has an increasingly significant impact of biophysical functioning. Because older adults experience vision, hearing, and mobility impairments, the environment can facilitate or impede adaptation to biophysical changes. The environment especially can affect the safety of older adults, particularly in regard to falls.

In recent years, gerontologists have recognized the importance of environmental influences on the ability of older adults to function safely and effectively in their daily activities. A noted gerontologist, M. Powell Lawton, proposed the "person-environment fit" theory to explain the interrelationship between older adults and their environment. Briefly, Lawton proposes that, for each person's level of competence, there is a level of environmental demand that is most advantageous to that person's functioning. The individual's level of competence, or functioning, is influenced by ego strength, motor skills, biological health, cognitive capacity, and sensory-perceptual capacity.[38] In brief, this means that the more impaired the individual, the greater the impact of the environment. Thus, the environment can cause older adults to limit their activities or to perform activities unsafely, or it can facilitate a higher level of functioning when it is adapted to meet their needs.

The Environment and Sensory Functioning

Auditory and visual impairments are two of the most common problems of older adults. These impairments can interfere with safety, performance of daily activities, and quality of life. Environmental factors often contribute to poor visual and auditory functioning. The presence of extraneous background noises may interfere with the accurate interpretation of sounds and words. Simple actions, such as closing doors or turning radios and televisions down or off, are often sufficient action to establish effective communication with an individual who is hard of hearing. Table 37-4 lists examples of environmental adaptations that can enhance visual abilities.

Health Promotion and Maintenance

The goal of *health promotion* activities is to assist individuals to optimize functioning; the goal of *health maintenance* activities is to detect disease early. Many activities, such as exercise, are essential both to health promotion and health maintenance. Older adults may express an "it's too

---

TABLE 37–4. ENVIRONMENTAL MODIFICATIONS TO ENHANCE VISUAL ABILITIES

ILLUMINATION

Older adults need 3 to 5 times as much light as younger people do.
Sources of illumination should be placed 1 to 2 feet away from the object to be viewed.
The amount of light decreases fourfold when the distance is doubled.
A gradual decrease in illumination from foreground to background is preferred over sharp contrasts.
Position light sources behind the shoulder that corresponds to the eye with the best vision.
Light bulbs should be changed when they become dim, rather than waiting for them to burn out.
Provide adequate lighting in stairways and hallways.

GLARE CONTROL AND DARK/LIGHT ADAPTATION

To reduce glare from reading material, place the light source to the left side for right-handed readers, and to the right side for left-handed readers.
Avoid glossy paper for reading materials.
Use a clear plastic shower curtain, rather than solid colors or printed curtains, for the tub or shower.
Use light-colored sheer curtains to eliminate glare from windows with direct sunlight.
Place night-lights in hallways and bathrooms, or keep a high-intensity flashlight at the bedside.
Use illuminated light switches.

COLOR CONTRAST

Use brightly colored tape or paint on the edges of stairs, especially on the top and bottom steps.
Use contrasting rather than matching colors for china, placemats, and napkins.
Use a toilet seat cover or toilet seat that contrasts with bathroom walls and floor.
Use utensils with brighly colored handles.
Place pillows of contrasting colors on stuffed furniture.
Use decorative or light plates over light switches and wall sockets; avoid light switch plates that blend in with the wallpaper.
Use black ink pens rather than blue ink or pencils.

(Miller, C. A. [1990]. Nursing care of older adults: Theory and practice. Glenview, IL: Scott, Foresman.)

---

late to bother" kind of attitude when it comes to changing habits such as smoking, exercise, or diet. However, with increasing age, health promotion and maintenance activities gain in importance because of the increasing number of risk factors that can compromise functioning. The cumulative effects of some risks, such as smoking and exposure to sunlight, begin to have more negative effects during middle and later adulthood. Thus, in later adulthood, a focus on health promotion and maintenance activities is crucial to high-level wellness.

Exercise

Exercise is one of the most important influences on high-level wellness in late adulthood. The many positive effects of exercise on the bones, muscles, heart, lungs, blood pressure, and

FIGURE 37–7.
Water exercises facilitate full range of motion without undue stress to the heart. Exercise groups provide socialization and motivation as well as guided supervision.

overall biophysical health are well documented. In addition to having beneficial effects on biophysical health, exercise has been associated with improved psychosocial health, reduced stress, lessened depression, improved intellectual functioning, and increased feelings of well-being. Aerobic exercise, which increases the heart rate and oxygen flow, is the most beneficial type of exercise for people who do not have mobility limitations or cardiopulmonary diseases. Walking at a pace that increases the heart rate is perhaps the most convenient way of performing aerobic exercise. Many senior centers or adult education programs offer group exercise classes specifically designed for older adults. These classes provide structure, socialization, and peer contact, all of which can serve as motivators for participation in a regular exercise program. Large indoor shopping malls provide a safe and comfortable environment for walking, and many malls allow group or individual walking in the early morning before the stores are open (Fig. 37-7).

Nutrition
Like exercise, nutrition exerts a crucial influence on high-level wellness for people of any age, young or old. In fact, the presence of age-related changes, disease processes, functional limitations, and medication effects can increase the importance of nutrition in later adulthood. For example, the age-related decrease in gastric secretions will interfere with the absorption of vitamin B_{12}, even in healthy older adults.[7] Except for a decreased caloric intake, the nutrient requirements of older adults do not differ significantly from those of middlescent adults. However, older adults must consume higher quality foods to obtain the same amount of vitamins and minerals with fewer calories. Another important aspect of nutrition in later adulthood is the inclusion of adequate

amounts of fluid and fiber in the daily diet. Older adults should drink 8 to 10 glasses of fluid daily to compensate for age-related changes and disease processes. Table 37-5 is a guide for the daily food intake for older adults.

Because the concept of stress has been discussed at length in the chapters on middlescence, only those aspects that are unique to later adulthood will be discussed here. There are many sources of stress in later adulthood ranging from daily hassles to major life events. The life events most likely to occur have several characteristics that distinguish them from the life events and adjustments associated with

---

TABLE 37–5. DAILY FOOD GUIDE FOR OLDER ADULTS

- The daily diet of older adults should include at least the minimal number of servings from each food group.
- The amount of each type of food will vary according to caloric needs of each older person.
- It is important to remember that nutrient requirements do not diminish with age, but caloric needs decrease gradually in older adulthood; therefore, the quality of foods must be improved to derive the same nutrients with fewer calories.
- To meet minimal nutrient requirements, the following basic guidelines should be followed for daily food intake:

Servings	Food Item
4	Fruits and vegetables
4	Breads and cereals
2–3	Meat, fish, poultry, or legumes (dried peas and beans, lentils, nut butters, soy products)
2	Milk and milk products, such as cheese
1–2	High-fiber foods (which should be included in the calories listed above)
10+	8-oz glasses of liquid

young adulthood: (1) they are viewed as losses, rather than gains; (2) they are more likely to occur close together, with less time available to adjust to each event; (3) they often are more intense, demanding greater energy for the coping process; (4) they are longer-lasting, and often become chronic problems; and (5) the inability to avoid them may evoke a feeling of powerlessness. Examples of events requiring major psychosocial adjustments in older adulthood are widowhood, retirement, chronic illness, death of friends, and relocation from the family home. Many of these life events are discussed in Chapter 38.

Coping abilities will significantly influence the impact of stress on an individual. Thus, a most important consideration regarding stress and aging is the coping responses of older adults. Older adults tend to use passive, emotion-focused coping styles. This is in contrast to younger adults, who generally use more active and problem-focused forms of coping. Coping mechanisms of older people include distancing, positive appraisal, and acceptance of responsibility. The coping patterns of older people are consistent with and appropriate for the less changeable types of problems with which they are faced.[23] Table 37-6 summarizes some of the coping strategies that can be helpful in meeting the challenges of late adulthood.

In addition to the coping strategies summarized in the table, stress management activities and group interventions are two coping strategies that can be quite helpful but are often overlooked. Stress management activities include physical activity, mental imagery, relaxation techniques, deep abdominal breathing, and social and recreational activities. Self-help and support groups are gaining in popularity, and these groups can address specific needs of older adults. For example, caregiver support groups assist older adults to cope with the overwhelming feelings and responsibilities related to the care of dependent and impaired relatives. Other examples of group interventions that might be helpful to older adults are bereavement groups and specific disease-related groups, such as Parkinson's support groups.

TABLE 37–6. COPING STRATEGIES FOR THE CHALLENGES OF OLDER ADULTHOOD

Psychosocial Adjustment	*Coping Strategy*
Ageist stereotypes	Develop a firm self-identity, challenge myths, and question any behaviors that are based on age-determined expectations.
Retirement	Develop new skills, use time for hobbies and personal pursuits, and become involved in meaningful volunteer activities.
Reduced income	Take advantage of discounts for seniors.
Declining physical health	Maintain good health practices (nutrition, exercise, rest).
Functional limitations	Adapt the environment to ensure optimal and safe functioning, take advantage of assistive devices and equipment, and accept help when necessary.
Changes in cognitive skills	Take advantage of educational opportunities, enroll in classes, keep mentally stimulated, join a discussion group, use the library, avoid dwelling on inabilities and focus on abilities, and take advantage of increased potential for wisdom and creativity.
Death of spouse, friends, and family members	Allow yourself to grieve appropriately, take advantage of opportunities for group and individual counseling and support, establish new relationships, renew old friendships, cherish the happy memories of the past, and realize new freedoms.
Relocation from family home	Look into the broad range of options for housing, appreciate the relief from the responsibilites of home ownership, and take advantage of new services and opportunities for socialization.
Other challenges to mental health	Maintain a sense of humor, use stress reduction techniques, learn assertiveness skills, and participate in support groups.

(Miller, C. A. [1990]. Nursing care of older adults: Theory and practice. Glenview, IL: Scott, Foresman.)

Sexual Activity

Problems with sexual functioning in older adults are often associated with acceptance of fallacious myths and attitudes, which can be alleviated by providing accurate information about sexual functioning. The negative side effects of medications and medical problems frequently can be diminished or eliminated through the provision of care and counseling by knowledgeable health professionals. This is not always easily accomplished, however, because of strong feelings about the privacy of this topic. Excellent leadership and communication skills are requisites for providing information about sexual functioning. Table 37-7 is a sample teaching tool that can be used as a basis for discussion.

Health Maintenance

Health maintenance includes screening tests and detection activities designed to identify illnesses and disabilities at an early stage. An annual physical examination is recommended for all older adults. For adults who are age 75 or older, or who are affected by a chronic illness, functional abilities should be assessed as part of the annual examination. Health examinations should include an assessment of all over-the-counter and prescription medications that are taken regularly or periodically. Lifestyle factors, such as diet, smoking, activity level, alcohol consumption, home safety, and use of seat belts, also should be addressed. Eye and dental examinations should be obtained annually.

With increasing age, the early detection of cancer becomes more important, since cancer is the second most frequent cause of death in older adults.[61] Annual mammography and stool tests for occult blood are two cancer detection tests that are highly recommended. The recommended frequency of some cancer screening tests, such as a Pap smear, is controversial. However, it is suggested that a battery of baseline screening tests for cancer should be done between 60 and 65 years of age.

Immunizations against tetanus, pneumonia, and influenza are important disease prevention measures in later adulthood. Tetanus immunization is frequently overlooked because it is considered a routine childhood immunization. However, many older adults never had a primary series because the practice of routine vaccinations did not begin in the United States until the 1940s. Some older adults may need an initial series of tetanus, and all adults will need a tetanus booster every 10 years. For people age 65 or older, a one-time pneumococcal vaccination is recommended. Annual influenza immunizations are recommended for people with chronic heart or respiratory problems and for all people age 65 or older.[5]

Community-Based Health Promotion Activities

Older adults are joining the ranks of people who are concerned about actively promoting optimal health and fitness. Organized group activities, such as "senior wellness" programs, are becoming more common. Many of these health promotion activities take place in or are sponsored by hospi-

TABLE 37-7. FACT SHEET ON SEXUAL FUNCTIONING FOR OLDER PEOPLE

- Older people remain fully capable of enjoying orgasm, but their response to sexual stimulation is usually slower, less intense, and of shorter duration. Increasing the amount and diversity of sexual stimulation, and experimenting with different positions can compensate for these changes and increase your sexual enjoyment.
- The "use it or lose it" principle applies to sexual activity.
- Sexual problems in older people occur for the same reasons they occur in younger people. That is, they may be related to illness or disability, medications or alcohol, or psychological and relationship factors. The only cause of sexual problems that is unique to older people is the self-fulfilling prophecy of the sexless senior stereotype.
- The following habits promote good sexual functioning: performing regular exercise, avoiding consumption of alcohol, maintaining optimal health and nutrition, using hearing aids and corrective lenses to improve sensory functioning, and engaging in sexual activities when you are relaxed and your energy level is at its peak.
- If you experience problems with sexual functioning, advice should be sought from a professional who is skilled in working with older individuals. Medical help can be obtained from a urologist or gynecologist. If there is no medical basis for the problem, a sex therapist or marriage counselor might be helpful.

FACTS SPECIFIC TO OLDER MEN

- Periodic difficulties with erection and ejaculation may occur, and do not necessarily indicate that you are impotent.
- After you have reached orgasm, it may be 1 or 2 days before you are able to reach full orgasm again.

FACTS SPECIFIC TO OLDER WOMEN

- A water-soluble lubricant (e.g., K-Y Jelly) will compensate for decreased vaginal lubrication. Do *not* use a petrolatum jelly, because it is not very effective and can predispose you to infection.
- Estrogen is beneficial in preventing some problems with sexual functioning, but the relative risks and benefits of such therapy should be considered and discussed thoroughly with a physician.
- Older women may develop vaginal irritation or urinary tract infections, especially after sexual intercourse, because of the thinning of the vaginal wall. Such problems may be avoided by the following interventions: use an estrogen cream or vaginal lubricant; have your partner thrust his penis downward, toward the back of your vagina; drink plenty of fluids; empty your bladder before and after intercourse; and maintain good hygiene of your vaginal area.

(Miller, C. A. [1990]. Nursing care of older adults: Theory and practice. Glenview, IL: Scott, Foresman.)

tals or senior centers. Community-based health promotion and maintenance activities include blood pressure checks, safe driving courses, stop-smoking classes, flu shots and other immunizations, health screenings (such as for vision and hearing), various types of exercise (such as walking, aerobics, or aquatics), classes (on topics such as nutrition, stress reduction, and general health care), education and screenings for early detection of cancer (such as breast or colorectal cancer), and classes about seasonal health issues, such as hypothermia, heat-related illness, and colds or flu (Fig. 37-8).

Safety

Safety in the Home

An unsafe environment is often a causative factor in falls and fractures. Most falls occur in the home, particularly in stairways, bedrooms, and living rooms. The following activities are associated with falling in home settings: slipping on wet surfaces (especially the bath tub); slipping while descending stairs, getting in and out of beds and chairs; and tripping over floor coverings (e.g., throw rugs) or objects on the floor.[58] Table 37-8 gives examples of environmental modifications that can be made to enhance safety for older adults and improve their level of functioning and well-being.

Driving

Decisions about driving a car represent one of the most emotionally charged issues older adults and their families face. Changes in visual abilities, musculoskeletal functioning, and central nervous system functioning can affect the older adult's ability to drive safely; yet to release the privileges (and responsibility) of driving places the person in a dependent position. It may be seen as the loss of adult status, autonomy, or even as imprisonment or infantilization. Consequently, some adults may continue to drive when decreased reflexes and judgment skills make it unsafe to do so. Most older persons can continue to drive safely if they are aware of their limitations and take appropriate compensatory actions,

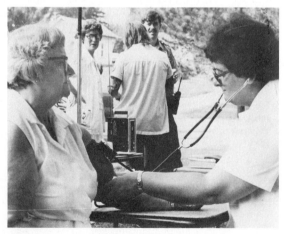

FIGURE 37–8.
Many communities provide free health screening for high blood pressure, glaucoma, and diabetes. Early detection and treatment can prevent the "domino effect" so common in elderly who fail to adequately attend to preventive health needs because of the high cost of health care and inadequate insurance coverage.

TABLE 37–8. ENVIRONMENTAL MODIFICATIONS TO PROMOTE SAFETY

ILLUMINATION

Provide lighting that is adequate but not glare-producing.
Assure that light switches are easy to reach and manipulate.
Place night-lights in appropriate places.

HAZARDS

Remove throw rugs and other hazardous floor coverings.
If area rugs are used, tack their edges to the floor and make sure they have a nonslip backing.
Keep cords, clutter, and other obstacles out of pathways.

FURNITURE

Chairs should be the right height and depth for the individual, and they should have arm rests.
Place small furniture away from the walking area.

STAIRWAYS

Make sure that lighting is adequate.
Have light switches at the top and bottom of the stairs.
Place securely fastened hand rails on both sides.
Have nonskid treads and use colored tape to mark the edges of the steps, particularly the top and bottom steps.
Never place objects on stairways.

BATHROOM

Use grab bars near the tub and toilet.
Place skidproof strips or a rubber mat in the tub.
Make sure the height of the toilet seat is appropriate.

BEDROOM

Use a mattress that is firm enough at the edges to provide enough support for sitting.
Keep the pathway between bedroom and bathroom clear of objects and adequately illuminated.

KITCHEN

Use storage areas to their best advantage (e.g., keep frequently used objects in the most accessible places).
Keep appliance cords out of the way.
Use nonslip mats in front of the sink.
Make sure the markings on stoves and other appliances are clearly visible.
Store food, medications, cleaning supplies, and poisonous substances, such as insect spray, in different locations.

OVERALL SAFETY

Maintain temperature high enough to prevent hypothermia in the winter, and cool enough to prevent heat-related problems in the summer.
Keep telephones accessible, and consider the use of a cordless portable phone, especially for emergencies.
Wear sturdy shoes with nonskid soles.

(Miller, C. A. [1990]. Nursing care of older adults: Theory and practice. Glenview, IL: Scott, Foresman.)

such as driving more slowly to allow for the delays experienced in reaction times.

Slower visual adaptation to dark and light creates problems when driving in and out of tunnels, and when driving at night on streets with inconsistent lighting. Decreased peripheral vision interferes with the wide visual field that is important in avoiding collisions. Decreased acuity may interfere with the perception of moving vehicles. Diminished accommodation and acuity create problems when the older adult tries to read the dashboard instruments after focusing on the road. Glare interferes with the perception of objects, and is heightened by rainy, snowy, or sunny conditions. Bright sunlight shortly after sunrise or before sunset may totally interfere with the perception of red and green stop lights because of the older adult's increased sensitivity to glare.[47]

Older adults are more likely to reduce the amount of driving rather than to stop driving altogether. People age 70 and older drive about one-third the distance of people age 35 to 39.[20] For the older adult, even this reduction in the amount of driving, however, has consequences, such as social isolation and dependency on others. Older adults can take advantage of transportation programs that are commonly offered by the community, churches, hospitals, and local senior centers. Those who continue to drive their own car can learn new or improved driving skills to compensate for functional limitations. The American Association of Retired Persons offers a driver retraining program, called "55 Alive/Mature Driving" (American Association of Retired Persons, 1909 K St., N.W., Washington, DC 20049), which is designed to meet the needs of older motorists. Many automobile insurance companies offer discounts for older adults who participate in this program, and in some states such discounts are mandatory for all companies.

Hypothermia and Hyperthermia

Hypothermia and hyperthermia are seasonal hazards frequently associated with cold spells and heat waves. These weather-related problems most often affect older adults who live in climates in which there are extremes of weather. Maintenance of an environmental temperature around 75°F. is the single most important intervention to prevent hypothermia or hyperthermia. Relative humidity can be altered to minimize the discomfort and detrimental effects associated with extremely cool or warm environments. The ideal humidity for indoors is between 40% and 50%, and an acceptable range is between 20% and 70%.[13] Older adults can be encouraged to humidify the air in their homes during the dry winter months by using humidifiers, either alone or with their heating system.

In cool environmental temperatures, hypothermia can be prevented through the use of proper clothing and covering and the avoidance of risk factors. Older adults should be encouraged to wear several layers of warm clothing during the daytime, and caps and warm socks while sleeping. Electric blankets used during the night are a relatively inexpensive form of protection in cool environments, but proper safety precautions must be taken.

During heat waves, it is important that older adults use measures to cool the environment. Older adults may be reluctant to use fans or air conditioners because of a desire to cut down on utility bills. However, if they understand the health risks associated with hyperthermia, they may be prompted to use these appliances judiciously. If the home setting cannot be cooled adequately during heat waves, older adults can be encouraged to spend time in air-conditioned public places. Nonenvironmental interventions to prevent hyperthermia during heat waves include adequate fluid intake and avoiding heavy meals and strenuous exercise. Frequent cool baths can also help to reduce body temperatures.

Medications

Specific age-related changes that affect medication action include alterations in kidney function, cardiac output, liver function, serum albumin, gastric acidity, body composition, and receptor sensitivity. The impact of these age-related changes on any particular medication is determined by the chemical characteristics of the medication, the extent of the age-related changes, and the presence of risk factors, particularly disease processes and chemicals from a variety of sources. Because of these factors, medications are less predictable in their effects and more likely to cause side effects in older adults. Table 37-9 summarizes the age-related changes that influence medication action.

Pathological processes as well as age-related changes may profoundly affect medication action. The consumption of more than one medication greatly increases the potential for adverse effects and altered therapeutic effect. Because older adults take more medications than do younger persons, they have an increased incidence of adverse or altered medication effects. Additional risks may arise from misunderstandings of the recommended medication dosage or consumption pattern. Other factors, unrelated to age, such as gender and smoking habits, when combined with age-related changes and risk factors, further increase the risk of adverse and altered effects.

Many factors can interfere with adequate medication monitoring, thus creating additional problems for older adults:

1. The use of several sources of medical care, usually with little or no communication about prescription medications.

2. The physician's lack of information about medications obtained from non-physician sources (i.e., over-the-counter medications and prescription medications offered by friends and relatives).

3. The physician's lack of information about the person's noncompliance with a treatment regimen or the use of folk remedies.

TABLE 37–9. AGE-RELATED CHANGES THAT MAY INFLUENCE MEDICATION ACTIONS

Age-Related Changes	Effect on Some Medications
Decreased body water, decreased lean tissue, increased body fat	Increased or decreased serum concentration
Decreased serum albumin	Higher proportion of unbound active molecules
Decreased cardiac output, decreased hepatic blood flow	Decreased tissue perfusion, increased serum concentration
Decreased renal blood flow	Decreased elimination, increased serum concentration
Decreased gastric acid, increased gastric pH	Altered absorption of medications that are sensitive to stomach pH
Altered thermoregulation, fluid regulation, and baroreceptor control	Increased potential for adverse effects
Altered receptor sensitivity	Increased or decreased therapeutic effects

(Miller, C. A. [1990]. Nursing care of older adults: Theory and practice. Glenview, IL: Scott, Foresman.)

4. The assumption that once a medication is started it should be continued indefinitely.
5. The assumption that once an appropriate medication dosage is established it will not need to be changed.
6. The assumption that a lack of adverse effects early in the course of treatment indicates that adverse effects will never occur.
7. Financial limitations that influence the person's medication consumption patterns.
8. Visual changes may make it difficult to distinguish between green-blue or yellow-white medications, causing the person to take too much or too little of the recommended medication, if the person uses vision alone to differentiate the pills.
9. Memory changes and the repetition of experience associated with taking medication may create problems in remembering whether or not a dose has been taken—again leading to overdosing or underdosing and their resultant problems.

Although adverse effects of medication are not unique to older adults, they occur more commonly with increasing age and are more likely to be attributed erroneously to pathological conditions or age-related changes and circumstances. When an older adult experiences an adverse medication reaction, two or three potential causes, other than the medication, can usually be identified. For example, when an older adult becomes depressed, a psychosocial factor such as widowhood may be identified as the source of the depression. Even if the person is taking a medication that is known to cause depression (such as reserpine), the medication effect may be overlooked, and the depression may be viewed as the primary problem. This incorrect assumption may lead to treatment with additional medications, rather than the direct and more

appropriate approach of evaluating for prescription side effects.

Substance Abuse

Nicotine

In recent years, much attention has been paid to the serious detrimental effects of nicotine and the beneficial effects of quitting smoking. In 1985, the United States Public Health Service identified the cessation of smoking as one of six areas where health promotion activities can make a difference for older adults. In the "Healthy Older People" public education campaign, older adults were advised that quitting smoking was "the single, biggest step toward better health."[63] The detrimental effects of both active and passive smoking that are discussed in Chapters 26 and 35 apply to later adulthood as well.

Alcohol

Alcoholism, a significant covert problem of later adulthood, includes two categories of drinkers. The largest category includes those individuals who drank excessively in younger years and continue to drink in later adulthood. The other category includes those who begin abusing alcohol during their later years. Alcoholism in older adults differs from alcoholism in other populations in several respects:[27]

1. Older people are more sensitive to the effects of alcohol because of age-related and disease-related changes.
2. Older people are more likely to experience alcohol-related complications because of their concomitant use of medications.
3. Alcoholism is more difficult to diagnose in older people because of the presence of medical problems.
4. Older adults tend to drink smaller quantities but more

frequently, in contrast to younger adults who tend to drink larger quantities but less frequently.

5. Alcoholism is more readily hidden and denied because older alcoholics tend to be more isolated and have fewer social responsibilities than younger alcoholics.

6. For younger people, alcoholism is more of a primary problem, but for older adults, alcoholism is secondary to stress.

Interrelationship Between Biophysical and Psychosocial Changes in Older Adults

As emphasized in Chapter 2 and throughout this text, the holistic approach considers the interdependent functioning of all five domains. In older adulthood, the aspect of interdependence that is particularly important is the relationship between biophysical and psychosocial changes. One reason for this increased significance is that the brain is less efficient and effective in its response to chemical imbalances. Thus, biophysical changes are likely to cause mental changes in older adults. For example, older adults who become dehydrated are more likely to become confused or disoriented, and they may not complain of thirst or have any notable physical complaints. The following section briefly discusses the relationship between biophysical changes and dementia and depression.

A discussion of the interrelationship between dementia and biophysical changes must begin with a discussion of the term *senility* because the term is most commonly, but inaccurately, used in reference to cognitively impaired older adults. Senility was originally was defined as "old age," and as such it was a neutral term. In recent centuries, the term has been applied to a state of being mentally and physically infirm because of old age, and it is now consistently associated with being old and feebleminded.[15] This association is unfortunate because it implies that cognitive impairments are a normal and inevitable consequence of being old. In reality, severe cognitive impairments are a consequence of disease processes that affect only a small percent of older adults. **Dementia** is the term that is most accurate in reference to impaired cognitive functioning. Although most older adults with dementia suffer from an irreversible disease such as Alzheimer's, about 10% to 20% of cognitively impaired older adults who have not been evaluated have a reversible disorder.[6] The most common causes of reversible dementia disorders include disease processes and medication effects. Like dementia, depression can be closely associated with impaired biophysical functioning in older adults. Alcohol, medications, and physical illnesses are some biophysical factors that can cause or contribute to depression in older adults. Thus, in older adulthood, the relationship between biophysical health and psychosocial functioning takes on a new significance (Fig. 37-9).

FIGURE 37–9.
Adequate sensory and social stimulation can help to prevent some forms of dementia in the elderly. Group projects can help them to extend Erikson's task of generativity through the retirement years when more time is available to pursue special projects.

IMPLICATIONS

Longer Life: In Sickness or Health?

Now that people are surviving illnesses that led to premature deaths in previous decades, multiple chronic illnesses have emerged. Ken Dychtwald, founder of "Age Wave," recently stated that, "When life expectancy was 45 years, the average American spent approximately 1% of his or her life in a state of ill health or morbidity. Today the average American, whose life expectancy is about 75 on the average, spends approximately 10 to 15% of his or her life in a state of illness, usually chronic illness."[18] Despite this high prevalence of chronic illness, most older adults view themselves as healthy and functional. There is a growing consensus among health care practitioners that health promotion activities and health care services aimed at maintaining and improving optimal levels of functioning can reduce the incidence and side effects of chronic illness in late adulthood. Some feel that although the onset of significant illness may be postponed, the life span cannot be extended to the same extent; change in lifestyle is a means of improving the quality of life, rather than merely prolonging the quantity of life.[24, 25] The health promotion and maintenance practices discussed earlier are examples of interventions directed at improving functioning and quality of life for older adults. By incorporating these activities into their daily lives, older adults can accomplish Schuster's fifth developmental task of late adulthood: maintaining maximal independence in activities of daily living.

New Options to Meet the Needs of Older Adults

Many of the interventions directed toward attaining and maintaining maximal level of functioning discussed in previous sections focus on the individual. A central concept of the holistic model is that individuals and their environments are interrelated. Thus, a final consideration regarding biophysical development in older adulthood is to focus on the increasing range of new programs and services to address unique needs of older adults. Many communities in the United States and other first-world nations today provide home-delivered meals, special transportation vehicles, chore and housecleaning services, and assistance with personal care. Lonely and socially isolated older adults can find companionship at senior centers and can take advantage of opportunities for group travel. Older adults who are seeking to maintain generativity activities can serve others through programs such as the Retired Senior Volunteer Program. Older adults seeking intellectual stimulation can participate in low-cost or free educational programs offered at local colleges, or enroll in programs such as Elderhostel (80 Boylston St., Boston, MA, 02116). More dependent or impaired older adults might receive services from adult day care programs, or their caregivers might find needed relief through in-home respite care.

Even nursing homes are changing dramatically from the image of "old folks homes." Today, nursing homes are likely to have a holistic approach in which all domains of functioning are addressed. The 1980s marked the first time in the United States that older adults who could not remain independent in their home could find assistance in places other than a family home or nursing home. New options in housing include assisted living, group homes, and a variety of so-called "life-care communities," where older people receive different types or levels of care as their needs change. There is an ever-broadening range of options for care, services, and facilities available to meet the needs of older adults no matter what their level of functioning.

Meeting the Challenges of Late Adulthood

Despite the many biophysical changes that occur, late adulthood does not have to be a time of inevitable decline. From a holistic perspective, this phase of life can be a time of great satisfaction and continued personal development. People can enter this phase of life with a great asset. That is, they bring a long history of overcoming obstacles and coping with life's challenges. In Chapter 2, we discussed the holistic perspective of viewing stress as a challenge, an opportunity for learning and personal development. If growth and development occur only when one is faced with a stressor that encourages stretching and change, then late adulthood is perhaps the phase that has the most potential for personal development. Thus, in late adulthood we can truly reach our full potential as human beings.

REFERENCES

1. Adelman, B. (1988). Peripheral vascular disease. In J. W. Rowe & R. W. Besdine (Eds.), *Geriatric medicine* (pp. 219–230). Boston: Little, Brown.
2. Ansello, E. F. (1988). A view of aging America and some implications. *Caring, 7*(3), 4–8, 62–63.
3. Baldwin, J. G. (1989). True anemia: Incidence and significance in the elderly. *Geriatrics, 44*(4), 33–36.
4. Bartoshuk, L. M., Rifkin, B., Marks, L. E., & Bars, P. (1986). Taste and aging. *Journal of Gerontology, 41*(1), 51–57.
5. Berk, S. L., & Alvarez, A. (1986). Vaccinating the elderly: Recommendations and rationale. *Geriatrics, 41*(1), 79–88.
6. Besdine, R. W. (1988). Dementia and delirium. In J. W. Rowe & R. W. Besdine (Eds.), *Geriatric medicine* (pp. 375-401). Boston: Little, Brown.
7. Bowman, B. B., & Rosenberg, I. H. (1983). Digestive functioning and aging. *Human Nutrition: Clinical Nutrition, 37C,* 75–89.
8. Brecher, E. M. (1984). *Love, sex, and aging: A Consumers Union report.* Boston: Little, Brown.
9. Brody, J. E. (1983, September 28). How many prescription drugs can cause decreased sexual activity. *New York Times,* (p. III, 1,1).
10. Buskirk, E. R. (1985). Health maintenance and longevity: exercise. In C. E. Finch & E. L. Schneider (Eds.), *Handbook of the biology of aging* (pp. 894–931). New York: Van Nostrand Reinhold.
11. Butler, R. N. (1987). Ageism. In G. L. Maddox (Ed.), *The encyclopedia of aging* (pp. 22–23). New York: Springer.

12. Close, L. G., & Woodson, G. E. (1989). Common upper airway disorders in the elderly and their management. *Geriatrics, 44*(1), 67–72.

13. Collins, K. J. (1986). Low indoor temperatures and morbidity in the elderly. *Age and Ageing, 15,* 212–220.

14. Cornelius, D. A., et al. (1982). *Who cares? A handbook on sex education and counseling services for disabled people* (2nd ed.). Baltimore: University Park Press.

15. Covey, H. (1988). Historical terminology used to represent older people. *The Gerontologist, 28,*291–297.

16. Dement, W., Richardson, G., Prinz, P., Carskadon, M., Kripke, D., & Czeisler, C. (1985). Changes of sleep and wakefulness with age. In C. E. Finch & E. L. Schneider (Eds.), *Handbook of the biology of aging* (2nd ed., pp. 692–717). New York: Van Nostrand Reinhold.

17. Duara, R., London, E. D., & Rapaport, S. I. (1985). Changes in structure and energy metabolism of the aging brain. In C. E. Finch & E. L. Schneider (Eds.), *Handbook of the biology of aging* (pp. 595–616). New York: Van Nostrand Reinhold.

18. Dychtwald, K. (1989). Conversations with . . . Ken Dychtwald, PhD: Where will the *Age Wave* carry physicians? *Geriatrics, 44* (3), 117–119.

19. Eisenman, P. A. (1986). Hot weather, exercise, old age, and the kidneys. *Geriatrics, 41*(5), 108–114.

20. Evans, R. (1988). Older driver involvement in fatal and severe traffic crashes. *Journal of Gerontology Social Sciences, 43*(6), 186–193.

21. Feldman, R. S., Kapur, K. K., Alman, J. E., & Chauncey, H. H. (1980). Aging and mastication: Changes in performance in the swallowing threshold with natural dentition. *Journal of the American Geriatrics Society, 28* (3), 97–103.

22. Fleg, J. L. (1985, June). How does aging affect the heart? Functional changes. *Drug Therapy,* pp. 52–70.

23. Folkman, S., Lazarus, R. S., Pimley, S., & Novacek, J. (1987). Age differences in stress and coping processes. *Psychology and Aging, 2,* 171–184.

24. Fries, J. F. (1980). Aging, natural death, and the compression of morbidity. *New England Journal of Medicine, 303,* 130–135.

25. Fries, J. F. (1984). The compression of morbidity: Miscellaneous comments about a theme. *The Gerontologist, 24*(4), 354–359.

26. Gilchrest, B. A. (1982). Skin. In J. W. Rowe & R. W. Besdine (Eds.), *Health and disease in old age* (pp. 381–392). Boston: Little, Brown.

27. Giordano, J. A., & Beckham, K. (1985). Alcohol use and abuse in old age: An examination of type II alcoholism. *Journal of Gerontological Social Work, 9* (1), 65–83.

28. Gordon, G. S., & Genant, H. K. (1985). The aging skeletal. *Clinics in Geriatric Medicine, 1*(1), 95–118.

29. Gudas, C. J. (1986). Common foot problems in the elderly. In E. Calkins, P. J. Davis, & A. B. Ford (Eds.), *The practice of geriatrics* (pp 441–450). Philadelphia: W. B. Saunders.

30. Harman, S. M., & Talbert, G. B. (1985). Reproductive aging. In C. E. Finch & E. L. Schneider, (Eds.), *Handbook of the biology of aging* (pp. 457–510). New York: Van Nostrand Reinhold.

31. Hendricks, J., & Hendricks, C. D. (1986). *Aging in mass society: Myths and realities.* Boston: Little, Brown.

32. Kaysen, G. A. & Myers, B. D. (1985). The aging kidney. In M. C. Geokas (Ed.), *Clinics in geriatric medicine: The aging process* (pp. 207–222). Philadelphia: W. B. Saunders.

33. Klausner, S. C., & Schwartz, A. B. (1985). The aging heart. *Clinics in Geriatric Medicine, 1*(1), 119–141.

34. Kligman, A. M. Grove, G. L., & Balin, A. K. (1985). Aging of human skin. In C. E. Finch & E. L. Schneider (Eds.), *Handbook of the biology of aging* (pp. 820–841). New York: Van Nostrand Reinhold.

35. Kligman, L. H. (1986). Photoaging: Manifestations, prevention, and treatment. *Dermatological Clinics, 4*(3), 517–528.

36. Kline, D. W., & Schieber, F. (1985). Vision and aging. In J. E. Birren & K. W. Schaie (Eds.), *Handbook of the psychology of aging* (pp. 296–331). New York: Van Nostrand Reinhold.

37. Krumpe, P. E., Knudson, R. J., Parson, G., & Reiser, K. (1985). The aging respiratory system. In M. C. Geokas (Ed.), *Clinics in geriatric medicine: The aging process* (pp. 143–175). Philadelphia: W. B. Saunders.

38. Lawton, M. P. (1982). Competence, environmental press, and the adaptation of older people. In M. P. Lawton, P. G. Windley, & T. O. Byerts (Eds.), *Aging and the environment: Theoretical approaches* (pp. 33–59). New York: Springer.

39. Lye, M. D. W. (1985). The milieu interieur and aging. In J. C. Brocklehurst (Ed.), *Textbook of geriatric medicine and gerontology* (pp. 201–209). New York: Churchill-Livingstone.

40. MacDonald, J. B. (1984). Presentation of acute myocardial infarction in the elderly: A review. *Age and Ageing, 13,* 196–200.

41. Masters, W. H., & Johnson, V. E. (1966). *Human sexual response.* Boston: Little, Brown.

42. Mazess, R. B. (1982). On aging bone loss. *Clinical Orthopaedics and Related Research, 165,* 239–252.

43. Meier, D. E. (1988). Skeletal aging. In B. Kent & R. N. Butler (Eds.), *Human aging research: Concepts and techniques* (mss. p. 9, pp. 221–244). New York: Raven Press.

44. Miller, C. A. (1990). *Nursing care of older adults: Theory and practice.* Glenview, IL: Scott, Foresman.

45. Olsho, L. W., Harkins, S. W., & Lenhardt, M. L. (1985). Aging and the auditory system. In J. E. Birren & K. W. Schaie (Eds.), *Handbook of the psychology of aging* (pp. 332–377). New York: Van Nostrand Reinhold.

46. Palmore, E. B. (1986). Trends in the health of the aged. *The Gerontologist, 26*(3), 298–302.

47. Panek, P. E., Barrett, G. V., Sterns, H. L., & Alexander, R. A. (1977). A review of age changes in perceptual information processing ability with regard to driving. *Experimental Aging Research, 3,* 387–449.

48. Quan, S. F., Bamford, C. R., & Beutler, L. E. (1984). Sleep disturbances in the elderly. *Geriatrics, 39*(9), 42–47.

49. Reiff, T. (1987). Water loss in aging and its clinical significance. *Geriatrics, 42*(6), 53–62.

50. Riggs, L. B., & Melton, L. J. (1986). Involutional osteoporosis. *The New England Journal of Medicine, 314*(26), 1676–1685.

51. Ross, R., & Glomset, J. (1976). The pathogenesis of atherosclerosis. *New England Journal of Medicine, 295,* 369, 420.

52. Schneider, E. L. (1983). Infectious diseases in the elderly. *Annals of Internal Medicine, 98,* 395–400.

53. Simonson, W. (1984). *Medications and the elderly.* Rockville, MD: Aspen.

54. Smith, I. M. (1986). Prevalence, diagnosis, and treatment of infectious diseases. In E. Calkins, P. L. Davis, & A. B. Ford (Eds.), *The practice of geriatrics* (pp. 540–554). Philadelphia: W. B. Saunders.

55. Snyder, C. S. (1990). Hematologic disorders. In A. Staab & M. Lyles (Eds.), *Manual of geriatric nursing* (pp. 357–388). Glenview, IL: Scott, Foresman.

56. Sparrow, D., & Weiss, S. T. (1988). Pulmonary system. In J. W. Rowe & R. W. Besdine (Eds.), *Geriatric medicine* (pp. 266–275). Boston: Little, Brown.

57. Staab, A. S. (1990). Musculoskeletal disorders. In A. S. Staab & M. Lyles (Eds.), *Manual of geriatric nursing*. Glenview, IL: Scott, Foresman.

58. Tideiksaar, R. (1989). *Falling in old age: Its prevention and treatment*. New York: Springer.

59. U. S. Bureau of the Census. (1989). *Population profile of the United States: 1989*. Washington, DC: U. S. Government Printing Office. (Current Population Reports, Series P-23, No. 159)

60. U. S. Bureau of the Census. (1990). *Statistical Abstract of the United States: 1990* (110th ed.). Washington, DC: Superintendent of Documents.

61. U. S. Department of Health and Human Services. (1980, Feb.). *Monthly Vital Statistics Report, 29*(2).

62. U. S. House of Representatives, Select Committee on Aging. (1987). *Exploding the myths: Caregiving in America* (Committee Publication No. 99–611). Washington, DC: U.S. Government Printing Office.

63. U. S. Public Health Service, Office of Disease Prevention and Health Promotion. (1985). *Healthy Older People*. Washington, DC: U.S. Department of Health and Human Services.

64. U. S. Senate, Special Committee on Aging. (1987–88). *Aging America: Trends and projections*. Washington, DC: U. S. Department of Health and Human Services.

65. Uhlenberg, P. (1987). A demographic perspective on aging. In P. Silverman (Ed.), *The elderly as modern pioneers* (pp. 183–204). Bloomington, IN: Indiana University Press.

66. Wei, J. Y. (1988). Cardiovascular system. In J. W. Rowe & R. W. Besdine (Eds.), *Geriatric medicine* (pp. 167–192). Boston: Little, Brown.

67. Whitbourne, S. K. (1985). *The aging body: Physiological changes and psychosocial consequences*. New York: Springer-Verlag.

68. White, C. B. (1982). Sexual interest, attitudes, knowledge, and sexual history in relation to sexual behaviors in the institutionalized aged. *Archives of Sexual Behavior, 11,* 11–21.

69. Young, E. A., & Urban, E. (1986). Aging, the aged, and the gastrointestinal tract. In E. A. Young (Ed.), *Nutrition, aging, and health* (pp. 91–131). New York: Alan R. Liss.

Psychosocial Development of the Older Adult

Robert Bornstein

Any attempt to understand and appreciate the adult in old age necessitates a life-span developmental perspective because the individual, at any given point of the life span, is a partial product of all of the developmental processes and forces, events, and determinants that constitute his or her life history. Previous events, experiences, and choices continue to exert an impact on the quality of life. Memories, habits, knowledge, expectancies, and self-concept provide a basic continuity in the lives of adults.

However, this continuity is not total because individuals are also a partial product of the developmental processes and forces, events, and determinants that *currently* impinge on them. To the extent that earlier development allows and current circumstances encourage, require, or dictate new adaptations, adjustments, and behaviors, individuals will, at any given point in the life span, be capable of marked change. In contrast to the stereotype about increasing rigidity in old age, many new and highly positive behaviors often appear for the first time during the latter years of life! Old age can continue to be a period of renewal and expansion, discovery and growth.

Any attempt to understand and appreciate the older adult will necessitate the use of a systems perspective (see Chap. 2). The phrase *developmental process(es)* is usually used to denote patterns of change that are intrinsically determined and universally found (i.e., patterns that are a part of the essential nature or constitution of the species). Terms like *forces, events,* and *determinants* are typically used to denote influences that are extrinsic or external; not necessarily universal nor part of the essential nature of the species. As such, these influences impinge on some but not others or impinge on individuals in the same culture in different forms or to different degrees. It should be noted that the interaction between the individual and external influences is not a "one-way street," in which external forces simply have their effect on the individual. Throughout life, the individual's reactions and responses also create changes in the environment.

STABILITY AND CHANGE IN THE PERSPECTIVES AND BEHAVIOR OF AGING INDIVIDUALS

The Stable Sense of Self-Identity

Despite all the changes that take place in individuals over a lifetime, people retain a very clear sense of being themselves. Most changes take place rather subtly over time and are fairly readily incorporated into the individual's self-image. Still other and perhaps somewhat more dramatic changes are, if and when noted, simply treated as part of the natural progression or extension of the individual's life. Even in the case of extremely sudden and dramatic changes, people continue to see themselves as basically the same persons they were before the transformation and the events that brought it about. The only difference is that they are now beset by "problems" they didn't have before, or they have finally "flowered" and become the person they always had the potential to be.

One interesting expression of this stable sense of self identity is the tendency to resist redefining oneself as "old."[11,67] As we grow older, we shift our definitions for middle and old age to later and later ages. When we can no longer deny that we are "middle-aged" or "old" by chronological standards, we often react by shifting our criteria, so that we still remain "as young as we look, think, feel, or act." For some individuals, this reaction may be "defensive"; an attempt to ward off the anxiety produced by the perception of any of a number of threatening elements commonly associated with aging in our society. For others, it may represent a perfectly rational and reasonable shift in the salience of self-defining characteristics—the real "me" is internal, how "I" think, feel, and act; not superficial external characteristics like gray hair, wrinkled skin, or chronological age. Research suggests that if and when we make the psychological transition into old age, it will most likely be the result of the perception that our health is significantly failing!

A second expression of stability of identity is the tendency to continue to refer to oneself by the major roles and activities that occupied time and energies during earlier periods of life. Thus, we describe ourselves as a *retired* or *ex*-school teacher, businessman or woman, or plumber rather than simply as *retirees*. This is especially true for those who based their identity on issues of profession, power or prestige—factors which have provided external structure and meaning to one's existence.

This stable sense of self-identity is not confined to our own self-perception; because of associations and activities, one's behavior patterns are observed by others and used by them as a guideline for relationships. Behavioral patterns tend to remain stable throughout adulthood.[62] "[The aging individual] continues to exercise choice and to select from the environment in accordance with his own long-established needs. He ages according to a pattern that has a long history and that maintains itself, with adaptation, to the end of life . . . There is considerable evidence that, in normal men and women, there is no sharp discontinuity of personality with age, but instead an increasing consistency. Those characteristics that have been central to the personality seem to become even more clearly delineated, and those values the individual has been cherishing become even more salient."[62]

This conclusion remains true for all personality types. Researchers have identified a minimum of eight different personality types or patterns in 70- to 79-year-old men and women.[62] The **reorganized, focused,** and **disengaged** personality types (collectively referred to as *integrated personalities*) are represented by well-functioning individuals who have intact cognitive and psychosocial skills and a high degree of life satisfaction. These three types differ from one another in terms of their respectively decreasing commitments to various activities and roles. Reorganizers are individuals who substitute new activities and roles for lost or diminished ones, thus maintaining high overall levels of activity. Focused adults compensate for lost activities and roles by concentrating on those that are still open and available to them. They maintain moderate overall levels of activity. Disengaged persons voluntarily move away from or give up roles and activities, with the result that their overall activity levels are lowered (Fig. 38-1).

The **holding on** and **constricted** types (collectively referred to as the *armored-defended personalities*) are represented by striving, ambitious, and achievement-oriented individuals who tend to defend themselves against the anxiety generated by the realization of their own aging. The former type does so by continuing to engage in the activities of their

FIGURE 38–1.
Some older adults remain actively involved (e.g., chicken roasts for the Lions' Club) as long as possible, thereby contributing to the welfare of the community and helping to maintain the traditions of the culture.

younger years, whereas the latter type tend to close themselves off from any and all experiences that verify their particular fears about growing older. For example, researchers have documented a number of age-related and physiological changes that take place in sexual functioning.[57] Although Masters and Johnson assure us that none of these normal age-related changes are a necessary cause for a decline in the satisfaction derived from sexual relations, the individual with a constricted personality may see them as evidence of a decrease in virility or sexual prowess. Rather than suffer the humility of what he or she believes to be a reduced sexual performance, this person may opt for not performing at all. Since all of the available evidence suggests that these age-related changes in sexual functioning are minimized in individuals who remain sexually active, this form of defensive adaptation is likely to actually impair this individual's ability to perform when and if he or she chooses to do so, thus completing the cycle! For both groups, satisfaction and morale remain high as long as their defenses work; if and when they fail, their life satisfaction and morale are reduced.

The **succor-seeking** and **apathetic types** are represented by *passive-dependent individuals;* the former are able to maintain themselves moderately well as long as someone responds to their covert appeals of emotional need. The latter are characterized by extreme passivity. "I'll take whatever is directed to me or left over." The life satisfaction and morale of these individuals is low unless they are cared for in stable and nurturant environments. The eighth personality type is labeled the **disorganized** type and represents those individuals who have gross losses or deficits in psychological functions. These eight personality types do not represent an exhaustive listing of possibilities. Other researchers have identified additional variations in the aging personality.

Stability of Adjustment as Outcome

A number of psychological theories describe the life span as a progressive series of stages each characterized by its own developmental task or tasks. Each stage represents another turning point or crisis in the sense that the individual's degree of success or failure in mastery of the task(s) will result in either positive or negative psychosocial movement.

Using Erik Erikson's theory as but one example, mastery of his developmental task for old age results in **ego integrity.**[17] Ego integrity denotes acceptance of the way one has lived and is still living one's life; it is the subjective realization that the choices and decisions made while in various life stages were the best ones that the individual was capable of making at those points in time. It is also the evaluation that one was, and still is, in control of one's life. As the infant learned to trust *life* as a result of the successful resolution of Erikson's first developmental task, so the successfully aging adult learns to trust *death* via the successful resolution of this final task. With ego integrity comes the experience of calmly accepting death as the natural conclusion to a life filled with dignity.

Adults who fail to master (successfully cope with) the developmental tasks central to old age will develop what

Erikson calls **ego despair.** Ego despair is a state of conflict about the way one has and continues to live one's life. It is the subjective experience of dissatisfaction, disappointment, or disgust about the course of one's life, together with the conviction that if given another chance it would be done differently. It also connotes anxiety about future events and a sense of helplessness or lack of control over them. The realization of the inevitability of death, for example, becomes a source of utter panic, terror, and fear.

Stage theories tend to make a second major assumption: that the ability to successfully resolve the developmental tasks (or crises) of one stage is, to a large degree, determined by how successful one has been in dealing with the tasks of previous stages. This assumption receives a great deal of empirical support. If and when individuals do "fall apart" in old age, they are likely to have had a history of difficulty in dealing with the tasks associated with earlier life stages. Conversely, elderly individuals who are successfully coping with their current developmental tasks tend to have a history of success in dealing with the tasks of earlier life stages. This relationship is not perfect, however. For a variety of reasons, some people who appeared to be successful in the past can and do falter at later times; and some people with a history of previous failures can and do become successful in later life, especially when they successfully undergo psychotherapy. The person may resolve some of the developmental tasks later in life as insights emerge. The relationship is certainly strong enough to conclude that there appears to be a basic continuity or stability across the life span in the capacity of individuals to adjust.

With the exception of organic brain syndrome (OBS), which clearly does increase in frequency as individuals age, the frequencies of other forms of mental illness (e.g., psychoneuroses, functional psychoses, personality disorders) appear to remain relatively stable throughout adulthood. However, a progressive accumulation of poor adjustments may lead to an increase in the kinds of stressors that contribute to progressively poorer adjustments, alcoholism and suicide.

Although adults age 65 and older comprise only slightly more than 11% of the United States population, they also account for 15% to 20% of first admissions to mental hospitals and 30% of the chronic patient population. The large majority of these individuals are admitted with a diagnosis of OBS. However, several prominent professionals argue that, for a variety of reasons, the reported incidence of OBS is a gross overestimate of its actual rate. It has also been noted that older adults are more likely to receive treatment in mental hospitals, whereas their younger counterparts are more often treated in local outpatient facilities, day-care programs, and community mental health centers.[45]

Stability of Adjustment as Process

Thus far, we have viewed adjustment as an outcome variable measured in terms of the degree of success or failure in adapting to, or coping with, stressors during old age. It can, however, also be viewed as a process or set of processes in which the focus is on the techniques or styles of adaptation and coping that individuals use when confronted by stressors. Five typical or generalized patterns of coping (and noncoping) are identified:[39] (1) the **instrumental,** in which individuals, alone or with the assistance of others, take action to correct problems; (2) the **intrapsychic** or **cognitive** in which individuals mentally work or restructure problem situations to achieve solutions; (3) the **affective** in which people release tension or express emotions; (4) the **escapist** in which people avoid or deny problems or engage in *displacement activities* such as increasing exercise or eating more; and (5) **resigned helplessness,** in which people feel impotent and unable to cope.

Some conclusions were drawn when a sample of nonseverely impaired older people who were entering special housing and a variety of homes for the aged were studied with regard to these coping styles: (1) the most frequently used coping styles were the instrumental and affective, while the escapist and resigned helplessness were relatively rare; (2) the use of both the instrumental and cognitive coping styles resulted in significantly higher reports of morale than did use of the affective style; and (3) coping strategies appeared to remain stable over the relatively brief duration of the study.

When the work of other researchers is considered, the overall impression is threefold.[29, 42, 46, 58] First, certain situations may, by nature, require or evoke specific coping styles. Second, most elderly adults demonstrate a considerable degree of flexibility in that they possess a broad range of coping strategies and tend to select those that appear to be appropriate to, or at least potentially effective in, any given situation. Since stressful situations tend to be variable, and since one must cope with the problem as well as the emotional distress produced by the problem, the selection of coping techniques or style ought to be quite situationally variable. Third, there is little or no change with age in either the range of available coping strategies or the appropriateness of those selected in given situations. Thus, there appears to be a good deal of stability across adulthood in terms of the range, flexibility, and appropriateness of coping styles (with the exception of the relatively small portion of the elderly population who experience significant cognitive impairment and whose range of coping styles does appear to become restricted).

The Stability of Quantitatively Measured Subjective Well-Being

One set of myths and inaccurate stereotypes portrays elderly people as relatively unhappy and dissatisfied individuals who suffer from poor self-concepts and lowered levels of self-esteem. In actuality, studies of self-esteem and self-concept in the older adult have yielded variable results.[3, 4, 6, 53, 60] Some have found increases in self-esteem with age, others indicate little or no change over time, and still others report slight declines. It therefore appears safe to conclude only that the self-esteem and the self-concepts of older adults are about as positive as those of their younger counterparts. Older adults appear to score about as high as do younger adults on these

self-reported measures of well-being, morale, happiness, and life-satisfaction.[15, 32, 49] When and if older adults do experience lowered levels of psychological well-being, its primary source is most likely to be poor or declining health.[20, 78]

It thus appears that these quantitative measures of well-being remain remarkably stable over the entire course of adulthood. This conclusion should not come as a surprise to the reader, given the previous discussion about the maintenance over time of both a broad range of coping strategies and the flexibility in selecting strategies that are appropriate to situations. Quite simply, we ought to expect these quantitative measures of subjective well-being to remain stable over time, since the capacity to cope or adjust also tends to remain stable over time for most older adults.

Change in the Evaluative Bases for Judgments

A second factor that contributes to the stability of quantitative measures of subjective well-being is, interestingly enough, the fact that the qualitative bases on which the judgments of quantity are made are themselves variable over time![7, 9, 66] Robert Peck's theory provides several useful examples of how this works.[65] Peck's developmental tasks of old age are (1) **ego differentiation versus work-role preoccupation**; (2) **body transcendence versus body preoccupation**; and (3) **ego transcendence versus ego preoccupation.**

During the middle adult years, a person's sense of identity and feelings of worth, morale, happiness, and life-satisfaction are strongly dependent on judgments of success or failure in his or her chosen work role or occupation. We need to remember that homemakers and mothers also have work roles and occupations; indeed, they probably constitute the sector of the work force that is the most overworked, underpaid, and least appreciated. For those elderly individuals whose sense of identity and worth is still totally bound up in their career (*work-role preoccupation),* the advent of retirement or the "empty nest" can usher in a period of declining well-being. On the other hand, elderly individuals who are *ego differentiated* possess a sense of self-identity and worth that is defined along several different dimensions. Retirement or the empty nest is likely to be less problematic for these individuals since other valued roles and activities can replace occupational work as the basis for self-definition and worth. Obviously, a qualitative shift from the work-role preoccupation typical of middle age to a state of ego differentiation in old age is likely to enable one to maintain a reasonable level of quantitatively measured well-being.

Body transcendence is the ability to "rise above" declining body functions; *body preoccupation,* on the other hand, denotes a dwelling on them. From about age 30 on, most age-related changes in the functioning of our bodies' systems are in the direction of loss or decline. Quantitative judgments of well-being that are based on preoccupation with bodily functions are therefore likely to decline with advancing age. Transcendence allows one to retain reasonable levels of life-satisfaction, happiness, and morale because one realizes that although he or she may be one of the 80% of elderly adults who have one or more chronic illnesses, he or she, along with the vast majority of others, is not disabled by these illnesses in terms of day-to-day living.[19] The inner self, not the body, is viewed as the "true me."

Ego transcendence denotes the acceptance, without undue fear and anxiety, of death as the inevitable conclusion of one's life. It is not a passive acceptance, but rather an active involvement with a future that extends beyond the boundaries of one's own mortality. *Ego preoccupation* denotes a refusal to let go on life, an immersion in a system of continued self-gratification. The former orientation is obviously more likely to free one to enjoy life while it lasts; therefore, a switch to it will allow one to maintain reasonable levels of subjective well-being. Presumably, those individuals who resolve Erikson's task in favor of ego integrity over despair will be the same individuals who resolve Peck's task in favor of ego transcendence over ego preoccupation.

A third factor that contributes to the stability of quantitative measures of subjective well-being is the relative variability over time of one's "reference groups." We rarely, if ever, simply generate an absolute value when asked questions like "how happy are you?" Instead, we generate relative values based on some standard of comparison. There is a tendency for our reference group to age as we age. For some individuals, the standard might be "how happy I was last month or last year." For others, the standard of comparison might be "the men's happiness" or "the happiness of fellow students in this nursing program." This produces a very interesting phenomenon in old age. This discussion is best deferred to later in the chapter. Be sure to look for it!

Stability and Change in Life Activities

In considering what happens to people's involvement in life activities as they age, three theories come immediately to mind: **disengagement, activity,** and **identity continuity.** Strikingly, each arrives at a different conclusion about the relationship between activity levels and successful aging (subjective well-being). Since the focus of this discussion is on what actually happens to activity levels, rather than what ought to happen theoretically, the description of these three theories will, of necessity, be quite brief and sketchy.

Disengagement theory contains three basic premises or assumptions.[16] The first is that since individuals inevitably die while the societies to which they belong are continuous, it is necessary for a given society to find ways of minimizing the social disruption that might result from the death of large numbers of its members. Thus, the likelihood of severe societal disruption can be minimized by removing (disengaging) large numbers of older adults (who are more likely to die than their younger counterparts) from the mainstream of society before their actual deaths. Compulsory retirement would appear to represent one such societally based disengagement mechanism.

The second premise is that individuals undergo a self-disengagement process during the middle and later years of life. This process is characterized by a general reduction in energy levels, a reduction in societal involvement in the form of both fewer relationships and changes in the quality of those relationships that are maintained, a change from active involvement to mentorships (preparing or helping others to assume full responsibility), and an increased preoccupation with one's own needs and desires.

The third and final premise is that the degree of well-being one experiences in old age is dependent on the form and amount of congruence between the individual's wants and expectations and those of the society. Thus, activity levels for most aging adults ought to decline over time (since this is what both they and their society want), and this pattern of congruence ought to be accompanied by high levels of morale, happiness, and life-satisfaction.

While disengagement theory predicts that (for the majority of older adults) happiness, satisfaction, and high morale will be associated with declines in activity, the **activity theory** argues that successful aging depends on the maintenance of relatively high activity levels in old age. The term *activity level* refers to more than just physical exertion; it also includes psychological as well as social activities and functions. Since activity theory is cognizant of the fact that some areas of activity and functioning may be lost or curtailed as a result of the normal vicissitudes of aging, it further assumes that successful aging can still occur through the substitution of new activities for the lost ones. For example, diminished physical activity resulting from declines in physical health can be compensated for by a concomitant increase in either psychological or social activities. Since activity theory says that some older individuals experience higher life-satisfaction and morale than others because they are able to maintain relatively high levels of activity, it probably serves as the most frequently cited theoretical argument for creating activity programming for older adults (Fig. 38–2).

The **identity continuity theory**[2] assumes that neither reducing activity levels (disengagement theory) nor maintaining high activity levels (activity theory) is essential for successful aging. It assumes that successful aging is associated with the ability of the individual to maintain those patterns of behavior that existed prior to old age. Life-satisfaction and morale are related to the degree of continuity maintained over time—a continuity in one's behavioral patterns and one's lifestyle, regardless of the actual level of activity represented in those patterns and styles.

What actually happens to activity levels over time? Empirical studies suggest that the identity continuity theory is most accurate. General behavior patterns tend to remain quite stable across adulthood (as well as across earlier portions of the life span). What about predictions of well-being? Once again those supporting the identity continuity theory seem best suited to the empirical evidence: It is the maintenance of activity patterns across adulthood that best predicts high levels of subjective well-being. Both the reorganized and disengaged personality types experience a high degree of life-satisfaction in spite of being very different from each other in terms of overall activity patterns.

FIGURE 38–2.
Older persons are reservoirs of cultural information. Culture-specific knowledge and skills survive because it is shared with younger generations. Such close contact breaks down "generation gaps" and dispels ageism myths.

The identity continuity theory uses two psychological mechanisms to explain how and why continuity in activity levels occurs over time. Nevertheless, it can still be argued that it becomes increasingly more difficult for relatively high activity level people to maintain these patterns over time. The *substitutions allowed* premise of activity theory offers a way out of this dilemma; relatively high overall levels of activity can be maintained in later life by substituting different roles and activities as one ages.

The Shift from External to Internal Orientation

Recall the second premise of the disengagement theory. Increasing age is associated with inevitable losses of energy, people, and roles, and a growing awareness and expectation of death. Personal disengagement can therefore be viewed as an adaptive process in which older people cope by decreasing their overall level of activity, interacting less frequently with others, assuming a more passive orientation, and be-

coming increasingly preoccupied with their own lives as a preparation for the next major transition—death itself. Regardless of the theory's validity (or lack of it), the conjecture about becoming increasingly internally oriented with age is an amazingly common thesis among theories of aging.

Buhler,[10,33] Gould,[27,28] Erikson,[17] Jung,[37] and Levinson,[50,51] suggest that the middle adulthood years are accompanied by a heightened awareness of personal mortality and increased introspection that then continues into and through old age. Neugarten speaks of the years 50 to 59 as a time of increased *interiority,* when individuals reorient their perception of time from number of years already lived to the number of years remaining, and when introspection, contemplation, reflection, and self-evaluation become increasingly salient components of the individual's mental life.[61] Neugarten and others have also suggested that this personality shift is internally manifested; it may or may not be accompanied by clearly observable shifts in the individual's interactions with the external world. One area in which the reorientation manifests itself externally is in interpersonal involvements. In agreement with disengagement theory, there is a considerable amount of empirical evidence pointing to age-related decreases in both the amount and variety of social interactions and contacts.[67] This shift may represent the termination of unproductive, unwanted, or unneeded relationships.[39,55] In any case, there is a consensus that this internal reorientation of the personality appears earlier and more consistently than does a reorientation in the external manifestations of personality.

It is a matter of conjecture whether or not this reorientation is a precursor to the **life review.** According to Butler, the life review is a universal process that occurs at any point in life when an individual confronts his or her mortality. Its occurrence in elderly adults, however, is a more leisurely process, accompanied by heightened intensity and vividness of past life events, and an emphasis on putting one's life in order. The process itself consists of a progressive return to consciousness of one's life-history experiences, especially those involving previously unresolved conflicts that can once again be examined in a final attempt at comprehension and resolution. There is continued identity homework, as one reviews values and priorities, decisions and accomplishments, accumulations and relationships, problems and opportunities.

To the degree that one is successful in the life review process (old wrongs are righted, the individual takes pride in the accomplishments of his or her life) a sense of serenity will exist, and fear and anxiety about death will be alleviated. This outcome appears to be synonymous with Erikson's concept of ego integrity and Peck's notion of ego transcendence. An unsuccessful life review (feelings that life was unfair, inability to find meaning, shame over wasted time, talents and opportunities, persistent clinging to immature forms of identity), can result in severe depression, terror, anxiety, panic, or feelings of guilt—an outcome strikingly similar to the concepts of ego despair and ego preoccupation. It is obvious that in passing through the life review, each individual experiences a final opportunity for the integration of his or her past life with the present personality. When this happens, dramatic shifts in personality can and sometimes do take place.

Shifting Motivations

Several shifts in motivation that begin in middle age and become increasingly exaggerated in old age dovetail nicely with, and can be considered supportive of, the external to internal reorientation. Kuhlen,[47] for example, suggests that there is a mid-life shift from an **expansion to a constriction orientation.** According to this view, the first half of life is characterized by a self-in-the-external-world orientation that is governed by personal needs (motives) for achievement, growth, and acquisition. In contrast, the second half of life is characterized by a more internal, person-centered orientation that is governed by self-preservation and self-satisfaction needs (motives). The general thrust of these needs is to compel the individual to "hold on to" that which he or she has already gained. Thus, adventuresomeness or risk-taking is likely to be stifled, since the risk of loss is a more salient feature than the possibility of gain.

Another example is the work of Gutmann, who proposes a shift from **active to passive mastery.**[30,31] Prior to about age 50, people retain an active mastery orientation toward their relationship with the environment (i.e., they are confident that personal goals can be achieved by means of their own energy, aggressiveness, and actions). They also believe that boldness and risk-taking will be rewarded. After age 50, however, the environment is increasingly perceived as being more complex, more dangerous, and less amenable to individual manipulations. This increasingly threatening view of the environment activates a number of defense mechanisms whose goal or aim is to conform, adapt, or accommodate to environmental demands. This, then, is the passive mastery orientation.

The overall picture derived from these shifts in motivation is that of an increased tendency among the aged to behave in ways that are more passive, cautious, and conforming. Although this picture receives support from some empirical research, other studies do not support this view, or find it only sporadically. Again, it may be the case that these internal reorientations in motivation are not directly or consistently expressed in external situations.

One shift that does exhibit behavior change is in the form of a "gender expansion." College students may begin to notice that their fathers seem to "mellow out"; or that younger siblings "get away with" things that they were not allowed to do. They may also notice that their mother is becoming less and less likely to do things for other family members when and if the activities interfere with her own wishes and desires. In fact, she tends to complain more often and more adamantly about such interferences, and she is likely to be far more direct in striving to get her own needs met. Men appear to become increasingly motivated by, or open to, their affiliative needs over time, while women become increasingly con-

cerned about securing satisfaction of their own personal needs as they grow older. It is not entirely clear, however, whether this expansion in gender-role behaviors is a purely intrinsic aspect of the aging process (as in Jung's theory) or is the joint product of intrinsic processes together with changes in socially defined roles and expectations. The latter interpretation suggests that once the children are "grown up" and retirement occurs, it becomes possible for the individual to relinquish certain restrictions on behavior and to become free to express one's truer nature.

Yet another picture of the normal ebb and flow of shifting motivations during the later adult years can be found in the work of Levinson and associates, who picture adulthood as a series of alternating periods of stability and instability or transition.[50,51] At the beginning of each stable period, an **individual life structure** (the overall pattern or design of that person's life) is put into place. It is formed out of the decisions that the individual has made in regard to the five domains, and it is subjectivity satisfying to the degree that it meets the needs, goals, and values of the individual and works in the real world. Toward the end of each stable period the individual tends to become increasingly dissatisfied with his or her current life structure because circumstances will have shifted as a function of accumulated real-life experiences and body aging (Fig. 38–3). A transitional period is about to begin. A major task of any transitional period is the reassessment of the individual's stances on what Levinson refers to as **life's basic polarities:** young-old, creation-destruction, masculinity-femininity, and attachment-separateness. As a single

FIGURE 38–3.
Pets provide company and contribute to life satisfaction for many persons. Research indicates that people with pets actually live longer!

example of this process, let's look at the young-old polarity. In young adulthood, being young tends to conjure up many positive associations such as being lively, growing, energetic, imaginative, idealistic, heroic, and full of possibilities, while being old tends to conjure up such images as being senile, tyrannical, impotent, and disengaged. As we age chronologically, our accumulated experiences and changing perspectives cause us to reexamine these earlier images. Youth is now associated with being somewhat impulsive, fragile, and lacking in experience, while maturity is associated with being realistic, wise, powerful, and accomplished. The resolutions of all four polarities becomes a means of reviewing and reevaluating one's previous life structure and considering possibilities for the next one. Decisions are then made about the form of the life structure to be implemented in the next stable period. This very brief description of Levinson's theory clearly suggests that motivations and the content areas they are channeled into will shift as one makes the transition from middle to old age.

ASPECTS OF THE ENVIRONMENT: THEIR INFLUENCE AND EFFECT

Age-Graded Social Systems and Norms

Societies assign people to social categories or strata on the basis of age, as well as socioeconomic class, caste, gender, race, or ethnicity.[12, 13] Thus, age is a powerful determinant of a group's roles, obligations, benefits, and privileges (factors that change as a result of movement from one strata to another). The effect can be relatively direct as in the case of an **age status system** that specifies the sequences of roles, obligations, benefits, and privileges available to group members, or it can be relatively indirect as in the case of socially defined **age norms** that communicate the degree of appropriateness of various age-behavior associations.

There appears to be a consensus among gerontologists that elderly people in first-world societies have fewer "guidelines" for behavior than do their younger counterparts. In terms of age status systems, most transitions to older strata are accompanied by uncompensated role losses in the sense that new roles are not clearly defined. Thus, retirement, "empty nest," and the loss of one's spouse all result in the loss of several obligatory adult roles together with concomitant losses of social identity, the means for structuring one's use of time, and sources of interpersonal interactions. Evidence exists to suggest that there are fewer explicit norms for old age than there are for younger ages; and those that do exist have been characterized as general, vague, and perhaps even inappropriate.[34, 48]

Since there is little or no behavioral guidance provided for the "elderly role," older adults may feel as if they are adrift in uncharted waters on which they will either sink or swim. Some evidence suggests that given the absence of normative guidelines, many of the elderly maintain the norms associated with middle age, a strategy that would seem likely to result in

more negative than positive outcomes.[15] On the other hand, there appears to be a bipotentiality here. The loss of obligatory roles together with the lack of well-defined age norms could, for some elderly individuals, usher in an unfettered and opportunistic time for exploring and satisfying new or previously prohibited patterns of behavior and motivations (Fig. 38-4).

Retirement

Retirement means vastly different things to different people. It may signify the abrupt and unsought termination of one's livelihood, a welcomed relief from the tedium of a boring job, or the natural conclusion of a successful career and job well done. It may provide more time to pursue already established and pleasurable activities, enough time to engage in activities that were previously "out of the question," or release unlimited amounts of unoccupied time. Retirement may be associated with a broadening or expansion of one's lifestyle or signal the beginning of severe "cutbacks." Whatever the specific, subjective and objective meanings of retirement, it involves "separation from a sphere of activity that has provided social order, economic remuneration, and some degree of personal identity and prestige for the greater part of the adult years."[68]

FIGURE 38–4.
Retirement provides more time and opportunities to pursue interests and hobbies, many of which can become another source of income.

The transition into and through retirement can be usefully divided into stages or phases that reflect and indicate the changing nature of the individual's concern about retirement.[1] In the **preretirement period,** the individual begins to consider retirement issues including time management and finances. In the early or *remote phase* of this period, both the notion of someday retiring and the thoughts about what it will be like are rather vague; but in the *near phase,* the individual begins to actually prepare for retirement by adopting new attitudes towards the work role and by entertaining fantasies about life in retirement. After the **retirement event,** there is a *honeymoon phase,* in which the individual begins to actualize these fantasies. A *disenchantment phase* then sets in for most retirees, its onset determined by the realization that personal fantasies and actual resources (reality) are incongruent. The true **postretirement period** begins with the *reorientation phase,* when more realistic routines for day-to-day living are established. The next phase is that of *stability,* which is characterized by the maintenance of work, decision-making strategies, and satisfying routines. The majority of the postretirement years are lived in this phase. Increases in illness, disability, and dependence on others make it increasingly difficult to continue carrying out the retirement role that had been established. Consequently, a final or *termination phase,* may emerge as the individual abruptly or gradually releases the postretirement routines and relationships.

The Decision to Retire

During the 20th century, the number and percentages of retired persons have increased dramatically. In 1900, approximately 70% of American men age 65 and over were still employed. The comparable figures for 1960, 1975, and 1986 were 35%, 22%, and 16%.[19] A concomitant trend over the past few decades has been for an increasingly larger proportion of these men to opt for early retirements, despite 1978 legislation that shifted the age of mandatory retirement from age 65 to age 70.[76] Brief discussions of several of the variables that influence the decision to retire and its timing are presented below.

Occupational Status and Personal Attitudes Toward Work

Satisfaction with work derives from both intrinsic and extrinsic sources. The former refers to pleasures inherent in the performance of the work itself; the latter, to a number of associated gains such as financial remuneration or social status based on occupation. It is generally assumed that dissatisfaction with work is more likely to be associated with positive attitudes toward retirement. However, this is not always the case; Some persons are dissatisfied with life, regardless of their employment status. Most adults have positive attitudes toward both work and retirement.[22, 26]

When occupational status is factored in as a mediating variable, workers in the highest status occupations tend to be more apprehensive and reluctant about retiring. This is presumed to be a reflection of the greater satisfactions with

work—both intrinsic and extrinsic—experienced by these individuals. These same individuals are generally also in the best position to enjoy their retirement because of their ability to maintain their previous lifestyles, thanks to their preretirement investments and relatively high retirement incomes. Many of these individuals continue to work in some part-time capacity and often do not completely retire. In contrast, workers in low status occupations (skilled, semi-skilled, and unskilled positions) are more likely to view retirement as relief from intrinsically unsatisfying jobs; but they are also likely to view retirement with concerns about their ability to maintain themselves and their family on inadequate retirement incomes. These workers typically retire as a result of mandatory retirement policies. Workers in the middle status occupations (lower-level executives and mid-level managers) fall somewhere between these two extremes in regard to attitudes toward work and retirement. They may opt for early retirement if (1) there is a decrease in work satisfaction because their career has reached a plateau with little or no likelihood of further advancement, (2) the availability of early retirement packages makes continued employment less financially attractive, or (3) they realize that they are young and healthy enough to enjoy extended leisure time. Obviously, the relationships between actual retirement, occupational status, and attitudes toward both work and retirement are very complex.

HEALTH STATUS. The most frequently stated reason for retiring for both men and women is "poor health."[32] Poor health obviously makes continued employment difficult. It is, therefore, both a major and a legitimate reason for retirement, especially for those who decide to retire early. Some may use it as a partial rationalization, since "ill health" would appear to be a more socially desirable justification than "simply not wanting to work any longer" (Fig. 38-5).

ECONOMIC AND FINANCIAL STATUS. When you exclude those cases where retirement is mandated by either institutional policies or ill health, decisions about and attitudes towards retirement appear to be significantly affected by financial considerations. Persons who anticipate an adequate income in retirement tend to have a more positive attitude and disposition toward it; those who anticipate financial insecurity are quite negative in attitude and reluctant to retire.

PRERETIREMENT PLANNING. Over the past two decades, an increasing number of agencies, companies, and corporations have instituted preretirement planning programs as part of their benefit (compensation) packages. Most of these programs provide information about financial planning, including company benefits, pensions, Social Security, tax-deferred annuities, and insurance. They also often provide advice and counseling on such diverse retirement-related topics as personal feelings and attitudes, possible changes in lifestyle, legal matters, health care, service for elderly adults, and leisure time. The research available to date suggests that although

FIGURE 38–5.
Although a spouse may be disabled, he or she can still be included in community events.

such programs are viewed quite positively by workers, and may increase financial stability, they do not necessarily enhance social and emotional satisfaction after retirement.[23, 24]

The Adjustment to Retirement

Until fairly recently, retirement was believed to cause a major identity crisis replete with personal disorganization and distress, familial disruption, and failing health. The assumption underlying the crisis view of retirement was that the work role constituted the single most salient and central defining feature of a person's self-concept and self-identity. The loss of that role on retirement thus left the individual in a state of personal disorganization until such time, if ever, that he or she could reestablish a sense of personal worth and meaningfulness on the basis of some other set of self-defining roles, activities, and characteristics. Research conducted over the past 20 or 30 years, however, makes it clear that the crisis view of retirement is overly pessimistic and exaggerated.[73] Nevertheless, retirement does bring into play several concomitant variables, any one of which may turn out to be problematic. However, research suggests that most retirees make quite adequate adjustments to these additional variables.[19, 59, 73]

HEALTH ADJUSTMENTS. A common myth associated with retirement, especially a mandatory one, is that it is bad for one's health. We have all heard tales about a happy and healthy individual who, when forced into retirement, began to deteriorate rapidly, both physically and psychologically. This brief scenario, however, is quite atypical and disconcordant with

known facts. Most people who deteriorate and die shortly after retirement do so from the worsening of an illness that predated retirement and served as a major determinant of their retirement decision.[21, 35] In still other cases, deteriorating health over the course of the retirement years, especially the later ones, is a direct expression of an age-related increase in susceptibility to diseases—an expression that is independent of retirement itself. Finally, there are a few cases in which the individual's health status actually improves on retirement.[73]

Here are some striking health care statistics for the elderly.[19] In 1986, older people accounted for 31% of all hospital stays and 42% of all hospital care days; they also visited doctors an average of 9 times per year, compared to only five for persons under age 65. While representing about 12% of the United States population, older adults accounted for approximately 31% of total health care expenditures in 1986. In contrast to the average $1,300 spent on younger persons, the figure for older persons was $4,200. Government benefit programs (Medicare and Medicaid) were projected to have covered about two-thirds of these expenses, whereas private plans absorbed some additional costs. Nevertheless, about $1,000 of health-related costs were projected to come from out-of-pocket payments.

These data are useful in making two points about the joint effects of poor health and retirement on well-being. First, although chronic medical conditions clearly increase in frequency with age, they rarely limit the individual's ability to conduct day-to-day activities. They may, however, adversely affect retirement in terms of interfering with specific forms of recreation as well as with plans for extended vacations and travel. Second, since the increased health problems of the elderly are costly, they add to the already increased financial difficulties brought about by retirement and its reduced income.

FINANCIAL ADJUSTMENTS. Generally speaking, the average retired individual can be expected to have an income that is reduced by one-third to one-half of its preretirement value. In 1986, the *median income* of older persons was $11,544 for males and $6,425 for females; for families headed by a person aged 65 or over, the median income was $19,932. For both older individuals and families, the major source of income in 1985 was Social Security benefits (35%), income from other assets (25%), earnings—not everyone aged 65 and over is completely retired—(23%), and public or private pension plans (14%).[19] Another way to look at the financial status of elderly persons is to examine the data on poverty.

The poverty level is an estimate of the amount of income needed for survival. This estimate is based on the assumption that less income is needed by families headed by elderly persons since there are fewer family members to care for (the empty nest), and since assets accumulated over the years will reduce the number of required or necessary expenditures (e.g., home ownership eliminates the need to pay rent). Adherents to the political economy of aging perspective (to be discussed later) are likely to question why certain known facts (in comparison to assumptions) are not also routinely considered; for example, the increased health costs previously mentioned, or the need to repair or replace depreciated items purchased long ago. The **near poverty level** is defined as an income somewhere between poverty and 125% of that value. Considered together, 21% of the elderly were poor or near poor in 1986.[19] Blacks, women, and other ethnic or minority group members fare worse than the average.

The types of day-to-day adjustments made necessary by declining income in retirement vary as a primary function of the amount of discretionary dollars available. For some individuals and families it requires finding less expensive forms of recreation, travel, or vacations and perhaps eating out less often. For those with few if any discretionary dollars, it entails living a "no frills" life of simply trying to meet one's essential financial obligations and hoping that no unforeseen and costly crises arise. For those who must live on inadequate retirement incomes, the adjustment may include delaying prophylactic, or even needed health care, postponing household repairs, finding cheaper (and often less nutritional) foods, or doing without other conveniences and necessities, such as telephone, heat, and clothing.

MARITAL ADJUSTMENTS. Most people are married and living with their spouses when retirement occurs. In 1986, 77% of all older men and 40% of all older women were still married.[19] The significantly lower figure for women reflects the fact that 50% of them are widowed, especially those at older ages. On retirement, women are likely to return to full-time status as homemakers. In contrast, most retired husbands do not have a readily available role to fall back on that provides for structured use of the increased leisure time. Many husbands apparently react or adjust by taking on a more active role (and often managerial attitudes) in the running of the household. Others simply make more work for their wives.

The type of adjustment made appears to be moderated by variables associated with socioeconomic class. In the upper and middle classes, a more androgynous approach to sex roles allows and encourages sharing of household activities before retirement. The increased involvement of retired husbands in home-based activities is therefore seen as desirable by both spouses. However, if the husband transfers his managerial skills to "snoopervising" the wife's activities, much tension may ensue. In the lower socioeconomic strata, sex roles tend to be more stringently defined along traditional masculine and feminine lines. Attempts on the part of this husband to "manage," participate in, or direct household affairs are likewise met with displeasure. Regardless of socioeconomic background, the most troublesome adjustment occurs when the husband simply spends his increased leisure time "lazying around the home," expecting his wife to cater to his every need, in addition to her other chores. Under these circumstances, the wife is more apt to resent and complain about her husband's intrusion into her domain.[44]

Simply stated, part of the adjustment of both spouses to retirement requires the renegotiation and reallocation of household responsibilities and activities. Although this aspect of retirement can further strain marriages, it can also serve as the impetus for achieving new heights of marital satisfaction. When both share the responsibilities, more time is available for leisure activities.

LEISURE-TIME ADJUSTMENTS. When defined simply as "free or unrestricted time," the amount of leisure increases considerably on retirement. Although virtually any activity used to occupy this free time is considered a legitimate leisure-time activity, most activities tend to fall into four basic but sometimes overlapping categories: (1) **physical activities** that include but are not limited to camping, fishing, golfing, hunting, aerobics, swimming, gardening, and chores around the home; (2) **social activities,** including visits with family, friends and neighbors, playing cards, and volunteer work; (3) **cultural activities** such as concerts, sporting events, club or church meetings, or community improvement; and (4) **solitary activities,** which include all avenues of reading (books, magazines), watching (television), and listening (radio, music), pursuing college courses, sewing, or other hobbies.

Since one's choice of leisure-time activities at any age is affected by many variables, including the amount of leisure time available, income level, health status, talents and abilities, interests, and personal needs, adults of any given age can be expected to vary widely in terms of their preferred leisure activities. Despite this variation, a general pattern of change can be detected across adulthood in preferred activities. Those of young adults tend to involve active participation and to be focused outside of the home, whereas elderly adults tend to engage in activities that are more passive, solitary, and home-based. Middle age appears to be a transitional period between these two orientations. Accompanying this shift in preferred leisure-time activities is an overall general tendency for active leisure-time activities (or participation in activities outside the home) to decline, reflecting declines in both health and financial status.[25,43]

The relationship between leisure activities and feelings of well-being appears to be fairly straightforward; those activities that are used for the sole purpose of occupying one's excess free time do not contribute to well-being, while those that are subjectively viewed as personally meaningful and worthwhile do increase one's sense of well-being.[64] Many retirees find more time to engage in activities that benefit the welfare of others, thus extending Erikson's task of *generativity* into the late adult years. Such personal investments are unlikely to develop "out of the blue" in the retirement years; the truly rewarding leisure activities of retirement are most likely to be rooted in interests and identities developed earlier in life.

Adjustment to Retirement in Summary

Although adjusting to retirement has many facets, an individual rarely experiences a devastatingly sudden loss, drop, or decline in any one aspect on retirement. Thus, for example, several adjustments to declining health will have already been made by most individuals whose decision to retire is based partially on considerations of health. Individuals with high preretirement incomes rarely move into poverty or near poverty on retirement. Those who do face near poverty tend to have had relatively low preretirement incomes. It can therefore be assumed that preretirement lifestyles already reflect anticipated financial adjustments. The same principle holds true for marital, residential, and leisure-time adjustments (Fig. 38-6).

The point is that adjustments necessitated by retirement are numerous, but not of overwhelming magnitude; rather, they tend to reflect the individual's preretirement status. Thus, adjustment as outcome is partially predicated on one's preretirement status. To the degree that one is enabled in retirement to reasonably maintain his or her previous lifestyle, feelings of well-being will be maintained. Furthermore, even real declines in lifestyle need not automatically result in a loss of well-being. Since any declines in lifestyle that are actually experienced by the individual are likely to pale by comparison to the negative myths associated with retirement, most retirees will still report relatively positive evaluations of life-satisfaction, happiness, and morale. In summary, the data collected to date suggest that most persons make very adequate adjustments to retirement.[21,59,73]

Attitudes Toward Aging and the Elderly

A rather extensive literature generated before the middle 1970s clearly demonstrated the existence of negative attitudes toward aging and the elderly across an extremely broad range of psychosocial attributes including the following: achievement, activity levels, adjustment, adaptability, autonomy, defensiveness, efficiency, energy levels, general knowledge and problem-solving capacity, happiness, illness, personal acceptability, productivity, self-pity, and withdrawal. This literature also showed that the most negative attitudes were held by young adults, and that the attitudes held by older adults about other old adults were only slightly more positive. Only when elderly people were questioned about their own attitudes toward themselves were truly favorable responses noted! These data can be interpreted in several different ways. First, young adults may be correct in the sense that aging is an essentially negative process, and old age a comparatively poor time of life. This, in turn, would suggest that the self-reported attitudes of the elderly are defensive in nature. On the other hand, it can be argued that accurate and reliable information

FIGURE 38–6.
Retirement years provide more time to participate in activities with the extended family. Many grandparents share activities with their grandchildren that they missed with their own children because of time constraints.

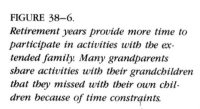

about the status and quality of life in old age can be generated only through the direct, self-knowledge reports of the elderly themselves. Thus, even the elderly's attitudes toward other elderly persons would be considered less valid. Together with younger adults, these two groups may be responding on the basis of stereotypes rather than actual knowledge. The third possibility is that both previous interpretations are partially correct. From this perspective, the most accurate picture is that presented in the attitudes held by elderly adults toward other elderly adults.

Which of the three interpretations is most correct is of more than theoretical interest. For example, it can be reasonably argued that society's attitudes toward the elderly will be reflected in the ways that others interact with them. Thus, if the elderly are viewed as withdrawn, then fewer individuals may choose to initiate social interactions with them. We already know that the attitudes held by both professionals and staff who work with the elderly have a pronounced effect on the quality of care and treatment provided. In this regard, stereotypical attitudes among service providers tend to be reflected in a preference for working with young people rather than the old, and engaging in more negative behavior when working with elderly people.[71, 75]

It can also be argued that society's attitudes toward aging and elderly people ought to be reflected in the self-perceptions of those elderly people themselves. Since these attitudes tend to be negative, the prediction is that elderly adults ought to experience lowered levels of both self-concept and self-esteem. As stated previously, however, this does not appear to be the case. But why isn't it? Perhaps the answer lies in the interesting phenomenon of the elderly's reference group alluded to earlier. If we assume that young and old alike come to believe in the negative myths about aging, then the picture of elderly adults as poor, unhappy, unproductive, incompetent, and so forth, becomes a reference group. When young people are asked questions about the elderly, they resort to this stereotype for answers. The same would hold true for older adults asked about the elderly. But when the elderly are asked questions about themselves, the effect produced by using this stereotyped reference group is quite different. Their own self-experience in comparison to the negative stereotypes leads them to the conclusion that they, as individuals, are faring much better than average. Hence, their feelings about themselves are elevated, and they experience heightened self-esteems and self-concepts. Thus, for many elderly adults whose status does not conform to the stereotype, the very existence of negative stereotypes may actually facilitate feelings of well-being!

We began this discussion of attitudes toward aging with a review of the literature prior to the middle 1970s. Since then, a general cultural shift appears to have generated more positive attitudes toward aging and the elderly.[38] This trend is certainly welcomed, but it is not entirely clear how much of this shift has influenced actual behavior directed toward the elderly. If maintained and enhanced, it ought to result in an improvement in the number and quality of interactions initiated with the elderly as well as in the type and quality of care

provided them. Its future effects on measures of self-esteem and self-concept in the elderly is entirely unknown.

The Political Economy of Aging

The political economy of aging represents a macro-analysis of the general social, economic, and political conditions that combine to influence or effect older people as a group.[18] This analysis begins with the core assumption that dominant groups or classes within a society attempt to perpetuate their own interests by maintaining or enhancing class inequities. Thus, **ageism** can cause biased treatment equivalent to that caused by **sexism** or **racism.** From this perspective, it is not aging per se that is problematic for the elderly, but discrimination against them resulting in inadequate income, poor health care, and substandard housing (to name just a few problems). It is further argued that these problems have been created by (or result from) social, economic, and political policies at the national level that are designed to maintain the marginality of the elderly in order to benefit the dominant class or classes. In this regard, several analysts have suggested that the already huge and rapidly expanding service industry of agencies, providers, and planners for the elderly—consisting of mostly middle- and upper-income group members—both helps to confirm the marginality of the elderly as a dependent class while it also increases its own social, economic, and political status. Again, systems like Social Security, Medicare, and Medicaid can be viewed from this perspective as methods or means of social control that are designed less to meet the real needs of the elderly than to serve the economic needs of the more dominant classes. In summary, the political economy of aging analysis argues that current "solutions" tend to maintain rather than solve the problems associated with aging. However, the current laws and social agencies are more likely the results of inadequate recognition of or anticipation of needs, coupled with a rapidly growing population of persons over 65 years of age, rather than deliberate attempts to maintain fiscal and physical marginality. Either way, true solutions will not be forthcoming until the magnitude of the needs are recognized and the underlying social, economic, and political issues are adequately resolved.

Age Concentration

To understand the effects of age concentration on the well-being of the elderly, three different levels of residential options available to older adults need to be considered: age segregation, age integration, and age homogeneity (where a large proportion, but not all of the residents are elderly). The general literature suggests that *age homogeneity* is positively associated with well-being in the elderly, while both age segregation and integration produce rather mixed results. These mixed results appear to be caused by additional contextual factors that are sometimes associated with specific segregated and integrated environments.

Age segregation, as in the case of retirement communities, is typically accompanied by high levels of morale and life-satisfaction. This effect is a partial reflection of the self-selection process in which elderly adults, who enjoy and gain satisfaction of their needs through similar age-related lifestyles, tend to congregate in geographic areas providing access to age-appropriate activities or in communities specially designed and restricted to older adults.[41] On the other hand, age segregation within institutionalized settings produces very mixed results when satisfaction is studied. Those institutions whose structure, policies, and services are designed for the least-able residents, but apply them equally to all residents, appear to produce deleterious effects on the activity levels and affective-cognitive functioning of their elderly clients (Fig. 38-7).

Age integration appears to produce quite positive effects in terms of improved community attitudes toward the elderly and a reduction in age-based stereotypes.[40] There may well be additional benefits to the elderly that accrue from this form of "mainstreaming." However, when age integration is considered within the context of low-income public housing, the effects are far more likely to be negative. This occurs because, by definition, the residents are already in need and they are also more likely to be exposed to higher crime rates and the possibility of victimization.

Ethnicity

An ethnic group is a collection of people whose members share one or more of the following origins or backgrounds: racial, national, tribal, religious, linguistic, or cultural. Such groups, when embedded within larger and differently constituted host populations, often become minority groups. For our purpose, minority groups are defined in a psychological and sociological sense rather than a numerical one; they are groups who are singled out by the larger society for differential and unequal treatment that includes reduced access to power and resources, and stigmatization based on the presumed possession of inferior traits and characteristics (see Chap. 17).

When an individual is elderly and also a member of an ethnic minority, he or she has to cope with the problems associated with both. It therefore comes as no surprise that ethnic minority elders represent segments of the United States population that are even more underprivileged than the general population of those age 65 and over in terms of income, employment, housing, transportation, recreation, and health care. On the other hand, ethnic minorities tend to create subcultures that provide their membership with the means for combating discrimination, prejudice, and the unfamiliarity of the dominant society's customs, languages, and institutions, in addition to providing a reference group through which self-worth is established.[74] The three most common sources of such support within these subcultures appear to be community-based institutions, the church, and the family system. While the nature of the expectations for and actual receipt of familial support of the elderly tends to vary from one ethnic group to another, it appears that the family system always functions as the primary source of support for its elderly members.

Institutionalization and Relocation

Despite the common belief that retirement is frequently associated with a relocation, older people are actually less likely to change residences than any other age group. The relatively low rate of relocation among the elderly should not be automatically interpreted as satisfaction with current residences. It might mean the inability to relocate because of limited economic, health, or relational circumstances.

Since the overwhelming majority of elderly people who are in need of day-to-day living assistance clearly prefer to receive it from other family members, there is a concomitant desire to be in close proximity to them. Those family members who provide such assistance also have a clear preference for proximity. Neither, however, appears to want to actually share the same household![38] Consequently, when elderly do relocate, the majority of them move to a residence in the same

FIGURE 38–7.
When elderly persons are of necessity segregated, most of them miss contact with children. They appreciate and "brighten" with the presence of the activities and enthusiasm of young people, who show respect and interest in them as people.

state or county. Those who do cross state lines are most likely to come from Northeast and Midwest regions and to relocate in the sunbelt states—Florida being the most frequent choice.[5]

Therefore, although most residential relocations are to settings other than institutions, the two topics are covered together because the dynamics involved appear to be essentially identical. In a nutshell, older adults are likely to experience declines in both physical and psychological well-being in cases when the relocation entails an already physically frail individual, a move to a less desirable setting, an involuntary move, or a move without adequate preparation.[36] Conversely, relatively healthy individuals who plan for and voluntarily move to more suitable settings tend to experience improvements in psychological and physical well-being.

Of the four factors mentioned as determinants of the outcome of relocation, the desirability or suitability of settings requires further discussion. Residential suitability or desirability is determined by both sociopsychological milieu and actual physical features. Therefore, both must be considered, and they ought to be judged in subjective terms related to the degree to which they provide for person–environment congruence. Objective measures of environmental settings do not consider the personal wants, needs, and desires of the individual, since they vary from person to person. (Some of these issues will be addressed under the heading of Physical Space and Design.)

Does the relocation provide for continuity with aspects of the previous environment, such as contact with significant others, access to familiar places, and retention of meaningful personal possessions? If it does, and these things are important to the individual, then the relocation will have a positive outcome. If it does not, and these things are important, the outcome will be negative. A neutral outcome occurs when these things do not represent meaningful or salient features for the individual. Discontinuity may produce a positive outcome when the relocation means escape from unwanted or undesirable relationships, places, and possessions! The same analysis is appropriate to all individual needs including those for privacy, socializing, recreation, personal care, and independence, to mention just a few.

Since some degree of stress is associated with any and all changes in one's normal routine, and since this is as true for pleasant changes as it is for unpleasant ones, relocation is bound to be stressful regardless of the setting. Therefore, the individual's preferred or dominant mode or style of coping also becomes a determinant of the outcome. No wonder that outcomes vary so much from circumstance to circumstance and individual to individual!

Physical Space and Design

The issues here are precisely those associated with the concept of creating barrier-free environments for disabled individuals. Given the nature of the age-related changes that take place in the body's subsystems (e.g., skeletal, circulatory, perceptual, nervous), as well as in general health, it can

reasonably be argued that elderly adults represent a special case of individuals who are "less able" than they once were (see Chap. 37). From this perspective, providing a totally barrier-free environment includes planning for increased illumination while toning down harshness or glare, increasing the discriminability of colors for aesthetic purposes, lowering cupboards for easier and less risky access to their contents, providing more legible print on all appliances (e.g., stoves, refrigerators, washers), installing safety guards in areas where slips and falls are very common (e.g., the bathroom), and safety-proofing stairways.

The community where the residence is located must also be considered in terms of the ease of access and transportation to and from stores, libraries, shopping centers, sources of recreation, and personal and professional services. The physical structures of community services may facilitate or hinder their use by the elderly. Sometimes space and design issues are quite subtle. For example, my dentist has recently moved into more spacious quarters that are lavishly decorated and filled with equipment representing the latest technology. Unfortunately, his four dental chairs are now separated by only partial partitions that remain open at the top and bottom ends. This means that I can sometimes see and continuously hear his exchanges with other patients; and I know that they, in turn, are privy to ours. This relative lack of privacy serves as an additional source of stress during my visits to his office; and quite frankly, I much preferred the reduced stress associated with the old set-up. Elderly adults in need of various types of social or professional services are likely to react similarly to the lack of privacy or loss of anonymity. Given our culture's comparative adoration of "independence" and relative disdain of "public welfare," the fear of lost anonymity may be great enough to dissuade elderly adults from seeking such assistance.

The organization of classrooms provides another example. Most of them are arranged so that the instructor and students have relatively unobstructed views of one another, an organization that facilitates the lecture method. But this same organization hinders group discussion since students are forced to turn around continually in their seats in order to establish face-to-face contact with each other. That is why instructors of discussion courses will ask that the chairs be rearranged into a circular pattern. The same principle holds true in any physical setting to be used as a social gathering place. Is a day-care or recreation room designed to satisfy the needs of relatively small groups of individuals who wish to engage in private, face-to-face interactions, or is it organized into rows of seats that are directed toward the large-screen television at the front of the room?

Formal Organizations

Formal organizations can be distinguished from other, more personal social groupings by the following characteristics: (1) relatively large and shifting membership; (2) clearly articulated and specialized goals or purposes (charters, mottos, credos), and (3) a relative lack of shared intimacy among members. In contrast, personal, intimate, or "primary group-ings" are characterized by relatively small but stable memberships, face-to-face interactions that are associated with shared intimacy, and no officially declared statement of purpose.

There are two aspects of participation in formal organizations that are important: the extent of opportunities afforded the elderly to participate, and the extent of the elderly's actual integration (involvement) in them. In comparison to other societies, the United States is said to isolate or restrict opportunities for the participation of the aged in important formal organizations and interests.[63] As social roles and memberships are lost, the social participation of the elderly becomes increasingly channeled away from formal organizations and into informal ones, with the net result of diminished social participation.[70] Social integration (social participation) tends to be positively correlated with several measures of psychological well-being. A word of caution is necessary, however. Objective measures of social integration, like the number and type of social activities engaged in, the amount of time spent in participation, or the number of social contacts and relationships maintained, do not appear to be important determinants of well-being. Instead, the best predictor of well-being turns out to be a subjective measure—the degree to which social integration satisfies or meets the personal needs of the individual.

Informal Organizations

Informal, intimate, or primary groups are better designed and used for meeting personal needs than are formal organizations. These groups can be divided into three levels that represent increasingly meaningful and intimate relationships. They also appear to serve somewhat different functions. All, however, exercise a great deal of influence on the well-being of aging individuals.

The Support Network or System
This group consists of all those individuals who may provide support during times of stress, whether out of a sense of obli-gation, affection, or both. It consists of providers of personal services, such as physicians, social workers, meals-on-wheels volunteers, neighbors, peers, friends, family members or kin, and confidant(e)s (Fig. 38-8).

Participation and integration into a support network or system has been repeatedly shown to be positively correlated with well-being.[74] Once again, however, subjective measures of participation and integration turn out to be far more predictive than objective ones.[52] Three examples of the latter are the size or number of people in the network, the frequency of contacts with them, and the amount of time spent in feeling that one's needs can and are being adequately satisfied. For some individuals, a few key family members, or even a single confidant(e), may suffice to bring about this feeling.

Friends, neighbors, and confidant(e)s tend to provide the major source of companionship for the elderly, followed by family members. On the other hand, assistance in day-to-day living activities such as shopping, cleaning, and preparing meals comes primarily from adult children—especially women—and other family members. Friends and neighbors are an additional source of such assistance and take on special importance for elderly adults without available family. Formal support agencies appear to be the least preferred option for most elderly persons in need of day-to-day help.[14, 72, 77]

Family and Kin
Most older adults live in a family unit consisting of an aged husband and wife. Given the difference in life expectancy between men and women and the fact that women are typically younger than men at the time of marriage, it is not surprising to note that more older men live with a spouse than do older women. When a spouse does die, older women are more likely to continue to live alone.

The fact that relatively few older adults live in multigenerational households is often cited as evidence to support the stereotype that old people are frequently lonely, destitute, and abandoned by their families. However, older adults tend to remain fiercely independent and self-reliant; while they welcome their children's concern and affection, they continue to feel that they want to take care of themselves and

FIGURE 38–8.
Peer networks and informal groups recognize and support individuality.

loathe "imposing" on their children. Simply stated, older adults prefer to maintain their own households if at all possible. Nevertheless, contact between family members are surprisingly frequent; in 1984, 66% of non-institutionalized older adults with children lived within 30 minutes of at least one child; 62% reported having at least weekly visits with one or more children; and 76% talked to one or more children on the phone at least weekly.[19] This pattern of living arrangement and ties to family has sometimes been called "intimacy at a distance." This arrangement appears to work well, providing maximal independence to all concerned, while simultaneously providing free access and needed emotional support in both directions.

The Confidant(e)

Family and kin are major sources of emotional support, second only to that provided by a confidant(e). A *confidant(e)* is any "significant other" with whom one can openly and honestly share the most intimate details of one's life—the hopes, dreams, and fantasies as well as the fears, anxieties, and dreads. He or she will be a good listener who can accept whatever is shared as a reflection of the human condition, rather than as evidence of the individual's lack of worth. This is what Carl Rogers refers to as "unconditional positive regard."[69] The confidant(e) also encourages the individual to use his or her coping skills to formulate possible solutions to current problems. Once solutions have been proposed, the confidant(e) continues to provide the loving support that enables the individual to take action to implement one or another solution. Assuming reasonably intact coping and decision-making skills, the particular solution chosen is probably less important than the actual act of implementation (taking action). One's self-concept and self-esteem are automatically enhanced by the feeling of still being in control of one's life. Taking action clearly serves to bolster feelings of being in control. The combination of unconditional positive regard together with encouragement and loving support in action-taking makes the confidant(e) a highly significant influence on well-being at any age.[54,56]

IMPLICATIONS

Our behavior is not the sole result of our personalities; it is also greatly influenced by forces that are external-situational determinants. In fact, when personality and situational determinants are pitted against each other in research, it is usually the situational determinants that are found to be the more influential. Even more influential than either taken alone is the combination or interaction of the two. Most behavioral scientists interpret this interaction to mean that people read or perceive the environment according to the dictates of their personalities; having done so, that reading establishes the situational determinants that will then drive behavior. This is why two or more individuals may respond quite differently in what appears, by all objective measures, to be the same environ-

ment. Simply stated, individual differences in personality can transform the same objective environment into subjectively different ones. On the other hand, some situational determinants appear so salient that they offer little or no choice of response. Additional differences in personality work to determine how the situational determinants within the environment will be responded to. The two factors then combine to determine the effectiveness of the individual's behavior.

Inter-Individual Differences

According to the best available evidence, individuals become increasingly differentiated from one another on most if not all psychological and social traits and characteristics as they grow older. A quick review of the second section of this chapter will suffice to point out the broad range of statuses that are possible within different personalities. It is not entirely clear whether or not this differentiation continues throughout the latter portions of the life span. It thus appears safer to say that the range of inter-individual differences reaches some maximum value sometime in young adulthood to middle age, and that it remains relatively constant thereafter.[8] The crucial point is that the extent of the differences among adults is so great as to preclude the validity of any stereotype. Hence, predictions about how adults will respond to any set of circumstances must take into consideration the highly idiosyncratic nature of their individual personalities.

The Range and Nature of Environmental Influences

The other half of the behavioral equation is represented by environmental influences or situational determinants. It is important to remember that some of the environmental influences discussed in this chapter appear to be universal or near universal in occurrence, while others may or may not be a constituent of any given individual's unique life history. Also recall that some environmental influences seem to "override" inter-individual differences in personality in the sense that they tend to elicit similar coping mechanisms in almost everyone; other environmental influences appear to be more amenable to individualistic styles of interpretation and response.

From a theoretical and academic perspective, we cannot hope to understand, nor predict with any accuracy, the behavior of elderly adults until we acquire a reasonably complete understanding of environmental contexts. There is also a practical side to this issue. Only when we have a complete catalog of environmental influences will we be able to make reasoned decisions about when, if, and how to best modify the entire system. Just as parents strive to provide children with an environment that is maximally conducive to the development of healthy, happy, and productive lives, as a society, we should strive to do the same for the ever-increasing number of elderly adults who live among us.

Subjectively Measured Person–Environment Congruence

Talking about the development of healthy, happy, and productive life is tantamount to talking about well-being. One's inner life or psychological status, taken in isolation, will not allow us to generate accurate predictions about that individual's well-being; nor will measures of environmental context taken in isolation. Even when both sets of factors are considered together, objective measures of the environment appear to add little to our understanding of well-being. Generally speaking, well-being appears to depend on the individual's subjective evaluation of the degree to which the environment allows or provides for the satisfaction of his or her wants, needs, and desires (i.e., the amount of person–environment congruence evaluated on a personal and subjective basis).

Because feelings of well-being are determined subjectively, they need not be directly proportional to the absolute amount of congruence. They are more likely to be proportional to the degree to which one's expectations about congruence, derived out of personal beliefs and past experience (recall the notion of the reference group), are currently being met. When these expectations are not met (when our wants, needs, and desires are no longer adequately satisfied), well-being declines. When we receive as much or greater satisfaction than anticipated, we still experience well-being; but its magnitude is not directly proportionate to the degree of abundance! Person–environment congruence in terms of our personal expectations for continuity over time appears to be the crucial determinant.

The Bipotentiality of Human Experience

Scattered throughout this chapter are examples of events and circumstances that, in combination with the responses to them, demonstrate the bipotentiality of human experience. By their very definition, the developmental tasks of old age can be handled in ways that are detrimental to well-being or in ways that enhance personal growth. For some adults, the loss of certain roles turns out to be devastating; for other adults, the loss becomes the opportunity for extending oneself by instituting new patterns of behavior that may prove to be equally or even more rewarding.

The crucial point is that the realistic appraisal of and attention to the problems of aging can reap benefits, whereas blindness to the more positive aspects of aging can be harmful. We do not wish to cover up the fact that some elderly adults live out their last years in social isolation, unhappiness, poor health, poverty, intellectual confusion, and terror at the thought of death. But to focus exclusively on this outcome and to assume that it is a valid description of all, or even most, old people is to perpetuate a myth of aging and to create fears surrounding our own inevitable aging process. The counter-realization that many, if not most, elderly adults live out their last years in happy and joyous homage to a life filled with

dignity, gives us hope and encouragement about our own futures. It allows us the freedom to "get on with it"!

REFERENCES

1. Atchley, R. C. (1976). *The sociology of retirement.* Cambridge, MA: Schenkman.
2. Atchley, R. C. (1980). *The social forces in later life* (3rd ed.). Belmont, CA: Wadsworth.
3. Bengston, V. L., Reedy, M. N., & Gordon, C. (1985). Aging and self-conception: Personality processes and social contexts. In J. E. Birren & K. W. Schaie (Eds.), *Handbook of the psychology of aging.* New York: Van Nostrand Reinhold.
4. Bennett, R., & Eckman, J. (1973). Attitudes toward aging: A critical examination of recent literature and implications for future research. In C. Eisdorfer & M. P. Lawton (Eds.), *The psychology of adult development and aging.* Washington, DC: American Psychological Association.
5. Biggar, J. C. (1984). *The graying of the sunbelt.* Washington, DC: Population Reference Bureau.
6. Birren, J. E. (1964). *The psychology of aging.* Englewood Cliffs, NJ: Prentice-Hall.
7. Black, K. W. (1971). Transition to aging and the self-image. *Aging and Human Development, 2,* 296–301.
8. Bornstein, R., & Smircina, M. T. (1982). The status of the empirical support for the hypothesis of increased variability in aging populations. *The Gerontologist, 22,* 258–260.
9. Breyspraak, L. (1984). *The development of the self in later life.* Boston: Little, Brown.
10. Buhler, C. (1982). Meaningfulness of the biographical approach. In L. R. Allman & D. I. Jaffe (Eds.), *Readings in adult psychology: Contemporary perspectives.* New York: Harper & Row.
11. Bultena, G. L., & Powers, E. A. (1978). Denial of aging: Age identification and reference group orientations. *Journal of Gerontology, 33,* 748–754.
12. Butler, R. N. (1969). Ageism: Another form of bigotry. *The Gerontologist, 9,* 243–246.
13. Butler, R. N. (1980). Ageism: A foreword. *Journal of Social Issues, 36,* 8–11.
14. Canter, M. K. (1979). Neighbors and friends—an overlooked resource in the informal support system. *Research on Aging, 1,* 434–463.
15. Clark, M. (1967). The anthropology of aging: A new area for studies of culture and personality. *Gerontologist, 7,* 55–64.
16. Cumming, E., & Henry, W. E. (1979). *Growing old: The process of disengagement.* New York: Arno Press.
17. Erikson, E. H. (1978). *Childhood and society* (rev. ed.). New York: W. W. Norton.
18. Estes, C. L., Swan, J. H., & Gerard, L. E. (1984). Dominant and competing paradigms in gerontology: Towards a political economy of aging. In M. Minkler & C. L. Estes (Eds.), *Readings in the political economy of aging.* Farmingdale, NY: Baywood.
19. Fowles, D. G. (1987). *A profile of older Americans.* Washington, DC: American Association of Retired Persons, and The Administration on Aging.
20. George, L., & Landerman, R. (1984). Health and subjective well-being: A replicated secondary data analysis. *International Journal of Aging and Human Development, 19,* 133–156.
21. George, L., & Maddox, G. (1977). Subjective adaptation to loss of

the work role: A longitudinal study. *Journal of Gerontology, 32,* 456–462.

22. Glamser, F. D. (1976). Determinants of a positive attitude towards retirement. *Journal of Gerontology, 31,* 104–107.

23. Glamser, F. D. (1981). The impact of preretirement programs on the retirement experience. *Journal of Gerontology, 36,* 244–250.

24. Glamser, F. D., & DeJong, G. F. (1975). The efficacy of pre-retirement preparation programs for industrial workers. *Journal of Gerontology, 30,* 595–600.

25. Glamser, F. D., & Hayslip, B. J. (1985). The impact of retirement on participation in leisure activities. *Therapeutic Recreation Journal,* 28–38.

26. Goudy, W. J., Powers, E. A., & Keith, P. (1975). Work and retirement: A test of attitudinal relationships. *Journal of Gerontology, 30,* 193–200.

27. Gould, R. (1978). *Transformations: Growth and change in adult life,* New York: Simon & Schuster.

28. Gould R. (1980). Transformational tasks in adulthood. In S. I. Greenspan & G. H. Pollock (Eds.), *The course of life: Psychoanalytic contributions toward understanding personality development.* Washington, DC: National Institute of Mental Health.

29. Griffith, J. W. (1983). Women's stress responses and coping: Patterns according to age groups. *Issues in Health Care of Women, 4,* 327–340.

30. Gutmann, D. L. (1964). An exploration of ego configurations in middle and later life. In B. L. Neugarten & Associates, *Personality in middle and late life.* New York: Atherton.

31. Gutmann, D. L. (1977). The cross-cultural perspective: Notes toward a comparative psychology of aging. In J. E. Birren & K. W. Schaie (Eds.), *Handbook of the psychology of aging.* New York: Van Nostrand Reinhold.

32. Harris, L., & Associates. (1981). *Aging in the eighties: America in transition.* Washington, DC: National Council on the Aging.

33. Havighurst, R. J. (1973). History of developmental psychology: Socialization and personality development through the life span. In P. B. Baltes & K. W. Schaie (Eds.), *Life-span developmental psychology: Personality and socialization.* New York: Academic Press.

34. Havighurst, R. J., & Albrecht, R. (1953). *Older people.* New York: Longmans, Green.

35. Haynes, S., McMichael, A., & Tyroler, H. (1978). Survival after early and normal retirement. *Journal of Gerontology, 33,* 269–278.

36. Hooyman, N. R., & Kiyak, H. A. (1988). *Social gerontology: A multidisciplinary perspective.* Boston: Allyn and Bacon.

37. Jung, C. (1960). *Collected works.* The stages of life. Princeton, NJ: Princeton University Press.

38. Kahana, B. (1982). Social behavior and aging. In B. B. Wolman (Ed.), *Handbook of developmental psychology.* Englewood Cliffs, NJ: Prentice-Hall.

39. Kahana, B., & Kahana, E. F. (1979). *Strategies of coping in institutional environments.* Bethesda, MD: National Institutes of Health. (NIH Grant No. 24959-04, Final Progress Report)

40. Kahana, B., Kahana, E. F., & Kiyak, A. (1979). Changing attitudes towards the aged. *National Journal,* pp. 1913–1919.

41. Kahana, B., Kahana, E. F., & McLenigan, P. (1980). *The adventurous aged: Voluntary relocation in the latter years.* (33rd Annual Scientific Meeting of the Gerontological Society). San Diego, CA: Gerontological Society.

42. Kahana, E. F., & Kahana, B. (1982). Environmental continuity, discontinuity, futurity and adaptation of the aged. In G. Rowles & R. Ohta (Eds.), *Aging and milieu: Environmental perspectives on growing old.* New York Academic Press.

43. Kelly, J. R., Steinkamp, M. W., & Kelly, J. R. (1986). Later life leisure: How they play in Peoria. *The Gerontologist, 26,* 531–537.

44. Kerckhoff, A. C. (1966). Husband-wife expectations and reactions to retirement. In I. H. Simpson & J. C. McKinney (Eds.), *Social aspects of aging.* Durham, NC: Duke University Press.

45. Kramer, M., Taube, C. A., & Redick, R. W. (1973). Patterns of use of psychiatric facilities by the aged: Past, present, and future. In C. Eisdorfer & M. P. Lawton (Eds.), *The psychology of adult development and aging.* Washington, DC: American Psychological Association.

46. Kübler-Ross, E. (1969). *On death and dying.* New York: Macmillan.

47. Kuhlen, R. G. (1964). Personality change with age. In P. Worchel & D. E. Byrne (Eds.), *Personality change.* New York: Wiley.

48. Kuypers, J. A., & Bengston, V. L. (1973). Social breakdown and competence: A model of normal aging. *Human Development, 16,* 181–201.

49. Larson, R. (1978). Thirty years of research on the subjective well-being of old Americans. *Journal of Gerontology, 33,* 109–125.

50. Levinson, D. J. (1978). *The seasons of a man's life.* New York: Knopf.

51. Levinson, D. J. (1986). A conception of adult development. *American Psychologist, 41,* 3–13.

52. Liang, J., Dvorkin, L., Kahana, E. F., & Mazian, F. (1980). Social integration and morale: a re-examination. *Journal of Gerontology, 35,* 726–757.

53. Lowenthal, M., & Chiriboga, D. (1973). Social stress and adaptation: Toward a life course perspective. In C. Eisdorfer & M. P. Lawton (Eds.), *The psychology of adult development and aging* Washington, DC: American Psychological Association.

54. Lowenthal, M., Haven, C. (1968). Interaction and isolation: Intimacy as a critical variable *American Sociological Review, 33,* 20–30.

55. Lowenthal, M., Thurnher, M., & Chiriboga, D. (1975). *Four stages of life.* San Francisco, CA: Jossey-Bass.

56. Mariwaki, S. Y. (1973). Self-disclosure, significant others and psychological well-being in old age. *Journal of Health and Social Behavior, 14,* 226–232.

57. Masters, W. H., & Johnson, V. E. (1966) *Human sexual response.* Boston: Little, Brown.

58. McCrae, R. R. (1982). Age differences in the use of coping mechanisms *Journal of Gerontology, 37,* 454–461.

59. Mutran, E., & Reitzes, D. C. (1981). Retirement, identity and well-being; Realignment of role relationships. *Journal of Gerontology, 36,* 733–740.

60. Nehrke, M., Hulicka, I., & Morganti, J. (1980). Age differences in life-satisfaction, locus of control and self-concept. *International Journal of Aging and Human Development, 11,* 25–33.

61. Neugarten, B. L. (1977). Personality and aging. In J. E. Birren & K. W. Schaie (Eds.), *Handbook of the psychology of aging.* New York: Van Nostrand Reinhold.

62. Neugarten, B. L., Havighurst, R. J., & Tobin, S. S. (1968). Personality and patterns of aging. In B. L. Neugarten (Ed.), *Middle age and aging.* Chicago: University of Chicago Press.

63. Parsons, T. (1949). Age and sex in the social structure of the United States. In T. Parsons (Ed.), *Essays in sociological theory, pure and applied.* Glencoe, IL: Free Press.

64. Peacock, E. W., & Talley, W. M. (1985). Developing leisure com-

petence: A goal for late adulthood. *Educational Gerontology, 11,* 261–276.

65. Peck, R. F. (1968). Psychological developments in the second half of life. In B. L. Neugarten (Ed.), *Middle age and aging.* Chicago: University of Chicago Press.

66. Pierce, B., & Chiriboga, D. (1979). Dimensions of adult self-concept. *Journal of Gerontology, 34,* 80–85.

67. Riley, M. W., & Foner, A. (1968). *Aging and society.* New York: Russell Sage Foundation.

68. Robinson, J. (1985). Retirement. In C. S. Schuster & S. S. Ashburn (Eds.), *The process of human development: A holistic life-span approach* (2nd ed., pp. 833–850). Boston: Little, Brown.

69. Rogers, C. (1961). *On becoming a person: A therapist's view of psychotherapy.* Boston: Houghton Mifflin.

70. Rosow, I. (1967). *Social integration of the aged.* Glencoe, IL: Free Press.

71. Schwartz, A. N. (1974). Staff development and morale building in nursing homes. *The Gerontologist, 14,* 50–55.

72. Shanas, E., & Associates. (1968). *Old people in three industrial societies.* New York: Atherton Press.

73. Streib, G. F., & Schneider, C. J. (1971). *Retirement in American society: Impact and progress.* Ithaca, NY: Cornell University Press.

74. Sussman, M. B. (1985). The family life of old people. In R. Binstock & E. Shanas (Eds.), *Handbook of aging and the social sciences.* New York: Van Nostrand Reinhold.

75. Troll, L. E., & Schlossberg, N. (1970). A preliminary investigation of "age bias" in the helping professions. *The Gerontologist, 10,* 14–20.

76. U. S. Senate Special Committee on Aging. (1985–86). *Aging America: Trends and projections.* Washington, DC: U.S. Department of Health and Human Services.

77. Veroff, J., Douvan, E., & Kulka, R. A. (1981). *Mental health in America: Patterns of help seeking from 1957 to 1976.* New York: Basic Books.

78. Zautra, A., & Hempel, A. (1984). Subjective well-being and physical health: A narrative literature review with suggestions for future research. *International Journal of Aging and Human Development, 19,* 95–110.

XII EPILOGUE

The quality of an individual's life is not directly related to issues of gender, ordinal position, talent, ability or disability, race, or any factor of genetic endowment. Success, or the ability of an individual to have sufficient energy or self-discipline to invest in self-development and maximization of potentials, depends heavily on the subtle interplay between the person and the environment. The specific experiences available to each person may depend on the era, geography, climate, culture, financial status, family complex, educational opportunities, raw materials, career options, community, prejudices, and other factors unique to the history of individuals and cultures. But these environmental factors do not in and of themselves determine an individual's life purpose, happiness, or satisfaction. Even under the most austere circumstances, if adequate personal support is offered, individuals can bud and blossom, and, in turn, serve the needs of those around them. The question becomes, "What can we as family members, friends, community members, and professionals do to facilitate the maximization of the potentials of those around us?" Yet such commitment to the needs of others is not all sacrifice, for service is not a one-way street. In the process of serving or meeting the needs of others, we each discover our own strengths, and contribute to our own life satisfaction and success.

Despite individual uniquenesses and needs that change in accordance with developmental levels and environmental stressors, there are some needs that remain constant throughout life span and cultural changes. The following five factors describe the mechanisms by which we are refueled and renewed to face the exigencies of life. When these factors are not provided by other persons in the environment, the quality of life and the ability to maximize innate potentials may be stunted.

Life verve, creativity, motivation, perseverance, curiosity, comprehension, physical and affective energy, the sense of adventure and daring, the sense of hope, the expectation of success, and the willingness to stand alone are all intricately tied to the input from the environment, especially during the formative years. Gradually, one becomes more independent of the environment's feedback. But to fully maximize our potentials, we always need some environmental support.

LIFE SPAN NEEDS

1. **Acceptance**
   unearned, unconditional love
   affirmation
      of individual uniquenesses
      of feelings, values, ideas, goals

2. **Companionship**
   true peers
   contingent, synchronized communication
   emotional intimacy
   continuity of close relationships over time
   model/mentor
   sharing of life's tasks and experiences

3. **Challenges and Goals**
   appropriate to developmental level
   to foster growth and realize potentials
   to think for self

to harness and focus energies
to self-evaluate and improve product/behaviors
to elicit one's commitment

4. **Support**
   as necessary for success
   to avoid destructive liability
   to buffer stress
   to realize potentials
   to actualize ideas

5. **Service Opportunities**
   to foster development of others
   to realize and develop talents
   to strengthen self-esteem
   to increase sense of value
   to provide source of genuine happiness

39

To Live—Not Somehow, but Triumphantly!*

Clara S. Schuster

In 1970 Alvin Toffler startled the world with his provocative treatise on the relationship between technology and the quality of life. In his book, *Future Shock,* he observed that as technological knowledge increases, the entire pace of life is accelerated.[53] Individuals experience more frequent changes in employment and places of residence. Consequently, they have to adapt to new places, people, and things; relationships become more transient; and the individual is forced to cope with an increasing number of novel experiences in a shorter period of time. Toffler expressed the following concern:

> As change accelerates in society, it forces a parallel acceleration within us. New information reaches us and we are forced to revise our image-file continuously at a faster and faster rate. Older images based on past reality must be replaced, for, unless we update them, our actions become divorced from reality and we become progressively less competent. We find it impossible to cope.[54]

To cope successfully with this rapid change, commitments to others and involvement in the life of the community may be decreased, factors that threaten the very core of interpersonal and intrapersonal relationships. The patterns of response and the skills learned in earlier years may become outdated; they may no longer be adequate to meet the demands of daily living.

In primitive, nomadic, and agrarian cultures, cultural change is slow. Children are able to use their parents as models for desirable and adaptive behaviors. Entire cultures and their mores are transmitted intact, generation after generation (Fig. 39-1).[54] The family is the core unit of society, and cooperation is essential to survival. The inventions that spurred the industrial revolution over a hundred years ago in first-world nations, created radical changes in types of employment, community size, educational needs, and family structure. The large, extended family, which thrived in a permanent location with all of its members involved in some way in family concerns, gave way to the smaller, mobile nuclear family that was free to move easily to various places of employment and survive financially in crowded tenements.[54]

Today, Western civilizations are immersed in another cultural revolution. Practitioners and lay persons alike face the startling reality that the present world is vastly

---

*Bertha Munro

FIGURE 39–1.
Cultural values, traditions, and skills can be passed on intact in segregated cultures.

different from the world in which they were reared, and that it promises even more changes in the future. We are on the crest of what Toffler terms the *third wave* of major cultural change.[54] Computerization has not only reduced our workload, but in some situations, has made human efforts obsolete. Our culture and the individuals within it are threatened by the very technology we have created. To question our ability to survive might seem to the reader to disregard the obvious lessons of history. We seem not only to have survived, but to have transcended what were earlier regarded as the fixed limits of our world. It would appear that our adaptive capabilities are infinite. However, we are concerned with more than just physical survival, more than the provision of safety, more than the protection of the physician self. Professional persons and political leaders must also address psychological and spiritual survival—in short, the **quality** of life. Can we continue to cope with the rapid pace of change and still maintain high-level wellness as societies, as families, and as individuals?

Although not everyone is caught up in the technological revolution, we are all, nevertheless, influenced by various technological advances, such as new modes of travel, new forms of entertainment, new banking systems, and new communication systems. The educational programs implemented in our schools and the health care services provided for our citizens influence the quality and philosophy of daily life as well as our future. These social changes precipitate concurrent changes in personal areas, such as hair and clothing styles, language usage, interpersonal relationships, leisure-time activities, and moral codes.

Change is especially stressful when (1) the pace of change is accelerating so rapidly that an individual is exposed to two or even more major cultures, or critical suprasystems, within a life span; (2) there is inadequate preparation in the skills needed to adapt to the new requirements; (3) there are inadequate or insufficient models with whom to identify who

exhibit the crucial personal skills necessary for adapting to change; or (4) change results in conflict with, questioning of, or rejection of, one's beliefs or value system.

From the first days of life, we attempt to organize information into meaningful units (schemata) that can be retrieved and used to understand, to predict, or to control the outcome of events. This organizational skill becomes even more crucial as more information comes to us and as events require rational decisions on our part. Information overload, in the form of too many novel experiences, taxes our ability to process the information, to organize it, and to make effective, rational decisions.[53] The existence of only one or two of the above conditions is sufficient to jeopardize effective coping; the presence of all of them creates an overwhelming sense of overload and may threaten one's ability to survive—socially, affectively, spiritually, cognitively, and even in some few cases, physically.

A number of eloquent voices from within the social sciences have expressed uneasiness about the individual's ability to live healthily in today's world.[36,38,44,54] People obviously do not possess endless plastic ability to adapt to life change.[25,49] It is important, therefore, that we have a better understanding of the specific nature of these threats to our survival to learn how to work with the environment[38,39] and with the new technologies[54] to create new, more vibrant and meaningful lifestyles. The question becomes: What have we learned from the past that can help us in the present to prepare for the future?

THREATS TO SURVIVAL: A PERSPECTIVE ON CONTEMPORARY STRESSORS

The very nature of technology breathes a threat to well-established coping responses. Technology requires change as a condition for improvement. Therefore, if society is dependent on technology, significant and frequent change will be the inevitable result. With the current rate of technological advance and its impact on lifestyle, we are forced to consider and to develop strategies for maintaining psychosocial and cognitive equilibrium. We must balance our responsibilities and needs against our skills and assets to cope with what appears to be the advent of perpetual change.

Increased stress is an inevitable response to perpetual change. Stress arises from three sources: pressure, frustration, and conflict. **Pressure** stems from both internal feelings and external circumstances when there is a demand to speed up or intensify efforts. **Frustration** occurs when the ability to achieve a desired goal is impeded or blocked. **Conflict** occurs not from a single obstacle, but when a choice must be made between two or more options, especially if both are seen as positive or as negative. All three types of stress are closely interrelated and are usually combined to form the total stress pattern of a person's life (Fig. 39-2).

Stress can occur on physiological or psychological levels (see Chaps. 35 and 36). It is often difficult, however, to make a clear-cut distinction between the two, since they interact and the human organism generally responds as a total unit. The severity of stress refers to the degree of disruption to the person-as-a-system and is determined primarily by the importance, duration, frequency, multiplicity, and complexity of the demands on the individual. The longer a stressor operates, the more severe it is likely to become. This is not to indicate that the stressor per se intensifies but, rather, the person's ability to cope with the stressor often begins to weaken, causing an increase in the amount of stress *felt* by the individual. Similarly, when a number of stressors are operating at the same time or in a rapid sequence, they are cumulatively more decompensating than if these events occur separately or over a longer period of time. Severe or multiple stressors lead to

FIGURE 39–2.
A paradox of today's society: "Hurry up and wait."

overloading, a situation that dramatically interferes with the ability of people to adapt to change. The four characteristics of technological societies that are most likely to produce feelings of stress are discussed below.

Too Much Change Too Soon

The hypothesis that rapidly changing lifestyles and environments threaten our coping abilities has been evaluated by Thomas Holmes and Richard Rahe.[23] After extensive clinical observations and research, they devised the Social Readjustment Rating Scale (SRRS), which assigns a Life Change Unit (LCU) to events that disrupt "everyday stability." The SRRS for persons living in the United States is shown in Table 39-1.

An analysis of the list indicates that most of the items concern concrete social events, many of which are desirable, such as going on vacation, achieving an outstanding personal goal, or completing one's education. Nevertheless, because of the disruption in daily patterns of living brought about by such events, the potential for confrontation with novel experiences and the need for making conscious decisions is increased, which in turn increases stress. Any stressor, whether real or perceived, external or internal, will elicit physiological responses (see Chap. 35). Once adaptation occurs, homeostasis will return. But prolonged or repeated stressors can lead to permanent alterations in body functioning, especially if a major body system is involved.[33] Therefore, the individual who is exposed to too many social changes in too short a time will experience an erosion of the system's recuperative powers, which may result in physiological illness.[34]

Holmes and Rahe define a *life crisis* as any clustering of life changes whose individual values add up to 150 or more LCUs in 1 year. In their studies, they found that 37% of individuals with 150 to 199 LCUs, 51% of individuals with 200 to 299 LCUs, and 79% of individuals with 300 or more LCUs became physically ill within 6 months.[22] Both the severity and the frequency of illness correlated with higher LCU ratings. Although the research of Holmes and Rahe was geared toward the relationship between life change and susceptibility to physical illness, their conclusions have significance for any kind of massive or frequent changes within the individual's external or internal environment.

The effect of an event may be contingent on context, perception, interpretation of the event, and what the individual expects the stress level to be, as well as previous coping skills. Perception of stress may be culturally mediated.[9] Stress is aggravated when the person feels out of control of changes or choices and feels subject to the whims of the environment; helplessness syndrome may develop.[46]

Erosion of Values without Adequate Replacement

One of the more profound consequences of the technological age with its radical and repeated change has been the relativation of once securely-grounded values. With biological

TABLE 39–1. SOCIAL READJUSTMENT RATING SCALE

Life Event	Life Change Unit (LCU) Value
Death of spouse	100
Divorce	73
Marital separation	65
Jail term	63
Death of close family member	63
Personal injury or illness	53
Marriage	50
Fired at work	47
Marital reconciliation	45
Retirement	45
Change in health of family member	44
Pregnancy	40
Sex difficulties	39
Gain of new family member	39
Change in financial state	38
Death of close friend	37
Change to different line of work	36
Change in number of arguments with spouse	35
Mortgage over $10,000	31
Foreclosure of mortgage or loan	30
Change in responsibilities at work	29
Son or daughter leaving home	29
Trouble with in-laws	29
Outstanding personal achievement	28
Wife beginning or stopping work	26
Beginning or ending school	26
Revision of personal habits	24
Trouble with boss	23
Change in work hours or conditions	20
Change in residence	20
Change in schools	19
Change in social activities	18
Mortgage or loan less than $10,000	17
Change in sleeping habits	16
Change in number of family get-togethers	15
Change in eating habits	15
Vacation	13
Minor violations of the law	11

(Holmes, T. H., and Rahe, R. H. [1967]. The social readjustment rating scale. Journal of Psychosomatic Research, 11, 216. Copyright © 1967, Pergamon Press. Used with permission.)

knowledge doubling every 5 years and genetic knowledge doubling every 2 years,[39] we face moral and ethical issues undreamed of even 10 years ago (Chap. 30). With rapid total world communication a reality, one begins to realize that a personal point of view might be conditioned and culture-specific. People appear to be stripped of any claim to ultimate truth. Traditional values frequently appear to lose validity under the scrutiny of contemporary problems and situations and may come to represent what a specific person at a particular time and place holds to be desirable. Yet, the acquisition of a healthy sense of identity involves a cohesive blending and acceptance of a wide range of internalized values, ideals, and role images as well as a sense of affirmation by one's environment. This internal and external acceptance leads to a sense of security about one's place in the world and a confidence about the future.[59]

Each of us must have a *raison d'être*. Life without a goal or a purpose gives rise to severe psychosocial disequilibrium.[59] Having a purpose to one's life is one of the main reasons why individuals who have the finances to remain unemployed (e.g., members of wealthy families, retirees, and many homemakers) may still seek gainful employment or may become deeply involved in the arts, community projects, politics, or volunteer services. When the work ethic is no longer essential to one's survival or even to one's self-esteem, new role expectancies must replace this value.

A cultural revolution is transforming the rules that once guided everyday life and personal decisions.[61] Work may lose its meaning for the individual unless it contributes to personal goals. As traditional values are relinquished, they tend to be replaced by the pursuit of self-fulfillment and affluence.[44,61] A hedonistic mentality encourages some individuals to "do their own thing"—a factor that can precipitate social chaos.[61] Respect for individuality actually begins to diminish, and conflict and confusion ensue. Yankelovich observes that a concentration on one's own perceived needs serves as a barrier to the achievement of meaningful interpersonal relationships or employment positions of responsibility, because these require one to balance self-needs with those of others to achieve mutuality and compatibility.[61]

Today we have the technology to set up the conditions for the creation of life (e.g., cloning of animals, gene construction, extrauterine conception, and pregnancy after menopause), to sustain life after clinical death, to transplant body organs, to maintain life with artificial blood, and to implant an artificial heart. Such technological advances present problems and ethical questions undreamed of in earlier generations. Arnold Toynbee warns that we need to "redirect our attention and energy from mastery of the biosphere . . . to the mastery of ourselves and of our relations with each other. This is what all the historical religions and philosophies have been telling us with one voice for a long time . . . We must somehow master ourselves—master ourselves in the sense in which the historic religions and philosophies all beseech us to master ourselves, and until we can do that and unless we can do that, we shall be under threat from the technosphere which is our own . . . creation."[56] Toffler agrees, stating that technology offers us the potential for improved personal and family life.[54]

Toynbee contends that we are social creatures—we would perish otherwise—but he expresses concern that we may not be social enough to hold our power in check: "Ethics and values maintain the checks and balances between science and politics."[6] However, "today, too many decisions appear to be made on the basis of expediency rather than integrity."[2] Watergate and the Iran–Contra affair are examples. Most people realize that a life without values, order, and goals is a meaningless one and attempt to find some structure and values to guide their behaviors.[7,54]

Rifkin challenges us to find enduring values to guide our ethical decisions.[39] We define a **value** as any philosophy, event, person, place, or object which, when freely chosen and acted upon, contributes to the meaning of an individual's life and enhances growth. By definition, then, a value assists one in finding meaning; this distinguishes a value from other objects or events that may motivate behavior. The act of valuing is to choose voluntarily to be influenced deeply by certain philosophies, theologies, objects, persons, or events in the environment. Values give strong meaning, direction, goals, order, and even roles to one's life.

Since thousands of beliefs cannot be equally important to an individual, a hierarchy or priority value tends to be assigned to each belief held by a person. Rokeach's research indicates that there are five levels of belief systems, arranged here in descending order according to their usual significance to the individual:[41]

1. **Primitive** beliefs, the most important, comprise of a core of values that a person holds because they are derived from cultural consensus. Consequently, they are the most resistant to any change, but when they do change, they greatly influence personal functioning.

2. **Deep personal experience** beliefs, which are based on subjective experiences, have inordinate value to the believer whether or not anyone else accepts them.

3. **Authority** beliefs are values that we hold because an authority figure whom we trust also holds them. They do not necessarily have to be grounded in reality to be viable to a person; they are based on the confidence one has in the authority figure.

4. **Peripheral** beliefs come from a variety of sources, and represent many opinions that can easily change as new data or experiences come into one's consciousness.

5. **Inconsequential** beliefs are superficial and largely untested ideas that do not necessarily influence the functioning of the total system.

Rokeach concludes that when a priority belief is challenged and rendered less viable, the individual will experience a high degree of disequilibrium and decreased adaptive functioning. The person is found to rework his or her identity. When deeply held values are challenged and rejected with an inadequate lead time to reformulate them, one's sense of identity and integrity is gravely threatened. The vacuum may be filled with a "pragmatic" code of conduct—right and wrong are based on expediency rather than issues of integrity. A situational ethic based on one's response to certain events rather than on adherence to an abiding principle creates its own stress, since a new decision must be created each time,

and subsequent decisions may violate the value upon which the former decision was made.

Maslow observes that "we need something 'bigger than we are' to be awed by and to commit ourselves to in a new, naturistic, empirical, non-churchly sense."[27] There are so many different systems of values wrapped up in the life of a society, challenging traditional belief systems, that people are profoundly affected, often becoming indecisive about which values or goals make sense to them. Consequently, some people will fill the vacuum by accepting the ready-made values of another person, usually a strong leader. This choice offers structure, safety, and security, since one does not have to extend efforts toward "identity homework," to "recreate the wheel," or find values to live by. However, to accept another's values without question or to strive for perfection as a value in itself, may be counterproductive or even destructive; leading to a "loss of humanness in experience."[7] One of the privileges of living in a Western culture is the responsibility to choose among alternatives. When one abdicates this choice to another, does it free the individual to pursue other interests, or does it restrict him or her? The Jonestown, Guyana, tragedy of 1978, in which more than 900 people committed suicide in obedience to their "leader," offers an extreme case in point. "The cult sells community, structure, and meaning at an extremely high price: The mindless surrender of self."[54]

In the face of a changing culture, individuals must address the question of meaning if they are to survive holistically. They must "rediscover and scrutinize the immutable and the permanent which constitute the dynamic, unifying aspect of life."[1] Perhaps a starting point for discovering these values is to explore religious traditions. Heath observes that "religious traditions agree in most of their basic assumptions about healthy adult growth . . . maturing involves persistent, disciplined commitment [stable values] that brings inner certitude, serenity, calm, repose, and self-confidence [stability of the self]; as a person matures, he becomes more alive, joyful, and spontaneous, and transcends [or becomes more autonomous of] the reality of his body and surrounding world."[21] Heath's definition of maturation is very supportive of Maslow's theory of human development. It should be noted that in this context, religion—"the feelings, aspirations and acts of man, as they relate to total reality"[1]—is not synonymous with a particular theory or doctrine.

Margaret Mead observed that "Most Americans—even though they acknowledge some slight connection with religion, accept the label of some denomination, and obey a certain set of ritualistic requirements—do not admit the existence of a significant connection between the lives they lead, the careers they pursue, the thoughts they think, and their relationship to God or their spiritual existence."[29] Most religions emphasize that "to **be** is more important than to **have** since **being** leads to transcendence and joy, while **having** only leads to apathy and despair."[1] One's values, then, facilitate the integration of an inner life with outer behaviors.

Stable core values can decrease the energy expended in decision-making processes, since the answer is often an integral part of the values held. An adherence to values can reduce conflicting decisions and enhance integration of one's identities.

Values can offer continuity from the past to present, and into the future. The values learned from the examples and explanations of parents can provide strength and affiliation or emptiness and alienation. Those who reach Kohlberg's highest levels of moral development—who risk their lives out of a deep-seated attachment to the welfare of others (for example, to rescue Jews in Nazi Europe or blacks in America's Civil War days) reflect the moral values held and acted upon by their parents and church.[32] Inner and outer behaviors maintain integrity. When one's value system no longer appears to offer an adequate frame for decision making, stress is increased unless a solid replacement is identifiable. Whatever the approach taken, the search for abiding values is essential to survival in a technological age.

The Inability to Meet Changing Demands with Existing Skills

Chapter 17 contained a discussion of the problems encountered when skill development is inadequate to meet the demands of the environment. Skill-building is an integral part of personality development. Mastery of specific skills, whether culturally, developmentally, or personally imposed, is crucial to the development of self-confidence and self-esteem. It is essential that a number of skills develop simultaneously in a holistic fashion for the individual to meet the demands of the environment. These skills fall into four general areas:[18]

1. **Systemic skills** are the skills essential for coping with the basic systems (e.g., the use of one's body, communication skills for interacting with family and social institutions, self-care).
2. **Instrumental skills** are task-oriented skills that one can rely on to complete jobs adequately, such as general skills (reading and writing), functional skills (the use of tools), and professional skills (practicing medicine or law).
3. **Interpersonal skills** enable one to enter into deeply satisfying, reciprocal human relationships.
4. **Imaginal skills** bring fantasy, emotions, and the reflective intellect into creative and productive thought.

The onset of rapidly changing social and technological demands for one category of skills can have implications for other areas. The individual may find that the interpersonal skills that facilitated rich relationships in a rural environment are inadequate in a fast-paced urban area where truncated relationships are common. When existing instrumental skills are inadequate to cope with changing demands, the individual who fails to update skills or is unable to do so may become unemployable (Fig. 39-3). The stress generated by the

FIGURE 39–3.
Computerization is forcing many persons of all ages back to school to acquire the skills essential to maintain employability.

change of lifestyle or a perceived personal inadequacy further jeopardizes systemic, interpersonal, and imaginative skills. Once efficient adaptation in one area is decreased, it becomes increasingly difficult for the individual to function effectively in other aspects of life.

The commonly held understandings, meanings, and rules of a culture increase internal and external predictability as well as control. Ethnic groups, which are comprised of individuals who are kept together by their regard for common symbols and skills, establish their own commonly understood, yet often unspoken, rules and rituals as cultural norms. This is as true for life in a New York City ghetto or wealthy Chicago suburb as it is for life on a Navajo reservation or in a mining town in Kentucky. Enmity between groups seems to be strongest when the group feels a need to protect their identity or individuality. Parents and adolescents sometimes find themselves belonging to two different cultures or ethnic groups. The parents' traditional, instrumental, skill-oriented culture may be rejected by the teenage culture, which is centered around interpersonal and imaginal skills.[26] When adolescents see the parents' culture fixated on an adherence to roles imposed by external sources, they fight the artificiality of such structured relationships and struggle to increase the interpersonal skills they feel their parents were unable to model for them. They sense that in an impersonal technological environment, their psychological survival may depend on achieving psychological intimacy, and therefore strip away the roles and social games that interfere with knowing and being known.[36]

The family system as well as the individual may be affected by changing demands. The interpersonal skills of chronically unemployed families are considerably retarded. However, it is not just the lack of adequate finances that precipitates depressed behaviors. Martin Seligman's research on the helplessness syndrome has relevance here as well as to childhood development (see Chap. 13). Learned helplessness is accompanied by a general sense of inadequacy caused by events that the individual or family member perceive are beyond their control. The adult discovers that his or her behavior no longer produces the desired responses from the environment (i.e., gainful employment). For an individual to maintain self-confidence and self-esteem, each new challenge of the environment requires that the individual develop skills to control the outcome adequately. When it becomes apparent that one cannot produce responses that will have a predictable effect on the environment, the feeling of helplessness can then become a self-perpetuating phenomenon. It sabotages the desire to respond to environmental demands, retards the ability to perceive success, and results in a greatly heightened sense of hopelessness and helplessness.[46] Seligman's theory may be as relevant to family system functioning as it is to individual system functioning.

The Feeling of Depersonalization in a Technological Age

One-to-one relationships facilitate psychological well-being, help to reduce the stress of minor problems, and decrease the sense of loneliness one can feel even when surrounded by people.[42] Superficial or role-regulated relationships contribute to a feeling that one's individuality is insignificant or undervalued. One of the by-products of the technological age is the loss of true community and the resultant loss of personal identity. Rapidly changing events tend to encourage people to relate and disengage quickly. Under such conditions, one may avoid intimacy with another individual because the nature of the relationship could change, and one may have invested too heavily to change these relationships effectively. The result is depersonalization, a sense of loneliness or isolation, the consciousness of being out of meaningful contact with one's environment. Feelings of stress increase as the population density of communities increases.[14] There is increased somatic and emotional distress and decreased persistence to task.

Abraham Maslow's theory of hierarchical needs has relevance here. Maslow believes that each person has a biologically based inner nature pushing towards self-actualization, but that is nevertheless weak and easily overcome by a rapidly changing or unsupportive environment. He believes that in an environment in which proper stimulation, justice, freedom, and orderliness exist, the basic hierarchy of survival and deficiency needs will be met. The individual will be allowed to expand horizons, to become more fully integrated; as a result, one is more likely to recognize and actualize poten-

tials.[27] Maslow's hierarchy of motivating concepts is illustrated in Figure 39-4.

While Maslow's theory explains some of the environmental conditions that are essential in allowing and encouraging people to actualize their potentials, it also indicates why some people never develop or meet the higher-order needs. Maslow indicates that only about 1% of individuals are able to actualize their potentials fully.[27] A rapidly changing, inadequately supportive, stressful environment forces many people to deal continually with threats of deprivation of lower-level needs. As a result, life is dominated by an overriding urgency to survive—if not physically, then psychologically. Brennecke contends that in this technological age, the dissolution of predictability threatens the need structure of the personality so massively that many people are still preoccupied with the basic survival needs of bodily comfort, security, and love and are doing little or nothing to fulfill their potentials. Under such stress, it is all they can do to maintain an appearance of self-confidence and a semblance of balance in their lives.[4]

Maslow observes that "Striving, the usual organizer of most activity, when lost, leaves the person unorganized and unintegrated."[27] Consequently, increased leisure time (whether resulting from unemployment or shorter working hours) can precipitate boredom and therefore stress in the individual.[47] For many people, the goal of work is leisure, but when too much unoccupied free time is available, it becomes a greater burden than too little free time.[40] Persons from widely varying backgrounds recommend that individuals develop specific, meaningful activities to occupy leisure time. Benjamin Spock recommends developing one's creative skills or engaging in activities that will enhance the community welfare.[51] Arnold Toynbee feels that if individuals are educated in the proper use of leisure time, our culture has the capability of becoming a second Renaissance instead of a parasitic society.[55]

The very advances that absorb our jobs and seem to make our humanness obsolete can actually allow us to become more human and can give us the freedom to spend

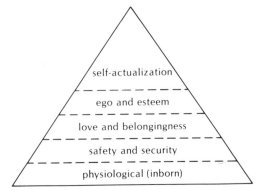

FIGURE 39–4.
Maslow's hierarchy of human needs.

more time in service to others—to actualize our own and the community's potentials. This will be accomplished, however, only by a reevaluation of values, goals, and roles.

COPING WITH EXTERNAL STRESS

When an external stimulus evokes stress, the individual usually attempts to eliminate either the stimulus or the unpleasant emotional state aroused by it. Some persons, however, like Theseus in Greek mythology, will attempt to control the stressor by "harnessing" the energy it elicits to capitalize on an otherwise difficult situation (for example, channeling stage fright into a brilliant piece of acting). Gail Sheehy observes that this skill is a trademark of persons of high well-being.[48] The route chosen will depend on past experience, the circumstances, and one's philosophical approach to life. We will explore four major theoretical positions explaining how individuals adapt to specific stressors (as opposed to the cumulative stressors discussed in the previous section) or the emotional state aroused by them.

Social Learning Theory

The principles of learning have emerged from the observation that individuals tend to repeat those behaviors that result in desirable effects. The ABCs of learning are as follows: (A) The individual becomes aware that the **antecedent** (stimulus or appropriate conditions) is present; and (B) **behaves** (gives a response or performs a skill) in a way that (C) has resulted in a desirable **consequence** in previous situations. Therefore, behaviors learned through personal experience are very tenacious. After several experiences, the behavior can be labeled a *habit,* that is, behavior repeated without much forethought. This basic paradigm is as valid for learning how to remain upright on a bicycle as it is for obtaining a desired object from the parent. Habits help to avoid stress by reducing the amount of energy one must expend in deciding how much to move a muscle to get the desired result or how to approach a social relationship.

Superstitious fears can result when an innocent stimulus is accidentally paired with a noxious stimulus. The child or individual may blame the wrong stimulus for the unpleasant experience and feel increased stress in the presence of the innocent party (e.g., a car may backfire loudly just as mother's friend comes through the door, resulting in a fear of that friend). If one's behavior appears to prevent recurrence of the stressful stimuli, then a continuing link between the stimulus and one's response is formed. Superstitions or conditioned responses can exact a high price if they are too defensive in nature, prevent meaningful interaction, or are inadequate to cope successfully with a changing environment.

Behaviors, once learned, can be either adaptive or maladaptive. Some behaviors may be highly useful in alleviating anxiety and dealing with life's stressors. For example, sensitivity to the environment creates a healthy vigilance, caution, and openness that leads to more effective coping behaviors. In

fact, a moderate amount of anticipatory fear about realistic threats is essential for the development of effective inner defenses for coping with the threat (avoidance). However, too many previously negative responses from the environment following efforts to cope with a situation may effectively extinguish the individual's attempts to take positive action to meet a problem situation. For example, when parents, teachers or employers comment only on a person's failures and inadequacies, the person may become discouraged and stop trying to please the other, resulting in a decrease in the quality of work.

Novel experiences generally produce stress because the individual (1) has not had sufficient experience to discriminate the relevant cues in the situation (and thus must depend on trial and error or over-generalization); and (2) is not sure of the environmental response to the behavior (i.e., whether it will be reinforced or punished). Individuals need models to imitate, assistance in discriminating cues, and information about the response system to allay anxiety in novel situations, especially during the earlier years.

B. F. Skinner expresses concern that Western cultures promote the *pleasing effects* of the consequences of behavior at the expense of the *strengthening effects* by reinforcing inadequate efforts and sensual or hedonistic interests rather than behaviors that promote high-level wellness of the individual or the culture.[50] Although opportunities for self-expression and individuality are greater today than in 1960, so are expectations for self-reliance and competence, a factor that can lead to dissatisfaction.[31]

Psychodynamic Theories

Like learning theories, psychodynamic approaches are difficult to summarize adequately in a few paragraphs. Whereas learning theory approaches stress from a conditioning standpoint, psychodynamic theories approach it from the perspective of developmental inadequacies. Defensive behaviors are employed to protect the ego from disintegrating trauma. The sense of "I" is protected at all costs.

It should be pointed out that the use of defense mechanisms is not necessarily maladaptive; everyone uses one or more of them regularly because they serve to reduce stress levels and the accompanying biophysical and psychic anxiety. However, when an individual uses defense mechanisms extensively, to the point where he or she is no longer assessing and dealing effectively with reality (reality distortion), then the integrity of the affective or cognitive domain (or both) is gravely threatened. Many therapists believe that the excessive use of defense mechanisms is the basic pathology of mental illness. Defensive behaviors can seriously interfere with reality functioning and essentially prevent adaptive functioning, thus leading to failure and tremendous frustration. Effective intervention can reverse the process by helping the person to develop more effective strategies for dealing with stress.

The basic ingredients for evoking stress, from the psychodynamic viewpoint, are the instincts and their insatiable need for gratification. The founding father of the movement, Sigmund Freud, believed that biological instincts are an inherent part of human nature. A certain amount of internal tension or stress always exists, simply because the organism experiences deprivation or inadequate satiation of these impulses as a normal process of biological functioning.[17]

Psychodynamic theorists believe that there are three basic instincts: self-preservation, sexual gratification, and actualization. (Later in his life, Freud postulated the existence of the death instinct, but this is of little concern to our presentation.) Most theorists say that gratification of instincts per se is ineffective in reducing stress; one must act intelligently. The ego, the part of the mind that comprises the thought and perceptual processes, aids the individual in finding satisfaction for instinctual needs in the external world. The superego, which becomes differentiated to represent the rules and regulations of society to the self, uses an experience of guilt to raise tension and thus to redirect the meeting of instinctual needs (or the reduction of stress induced by need deficit) by more appropriate means, through the ego. Freud calls this function *reality principle functioning.*[17]

Anxiety arises whenever an externally or internally motivated instinct becomes strong enough to arouse conflict. This anxiety recalls the anticipation of punishment and guilt and triggers the defensive process. According to psychodynamic thought, defense mechanisms are used to maintain homeostasis by balancing the two stress sources. A defense mechanism eases the conflict between the demands of the instincts and those of the environment by forging out a compromise between them. The defense behavior channels that energy into action that may or may not be acceptable to others and to one's own superego.

Psychodynamic thought tends to see most coping behavior as defensive—that is, reactive rather than proactive. Most defenses function outside of our conscious awareness. Some of the commonly found defense mechanisms are given in the following list:

Denial. Suppressing awareness of other things, people, events, or consequences that could arouse anxiety or threaten one's psychic integrity.

Repression. Involuntary denial of instinctual wishes, feelings, and experiences, so that associated anxiety will not be experienced.

Suppression. Conscious exclusion of events from memory or refusal to acknowledge instinctual needs.

Sublimation. Focusing attention and interest on a substitute for an unacceptable feeling; usually, consciously diverting energies into creative, constructive, socially acceptable activities.

Displacement. Shifting emotional energies from one object, idea, person, or situation to another that is less threatening and cannot retaliate.

Compensation. Overemphasizing a desirable attribute or skill to make up for a perceived or real disability or failure.

Projection. Attributing negative wishes, feelings, and impulses to other persons while denying that they originate in oneself.

Introjection. Crediting oneself with another's values, attributes, and behaviors to avoid conflicts, to enhance acceptance, or to avoid the threatening nature of one's own instincts.

Rationalization or intellectualization. Losing awareness of the significance of one's own wishes and impulses while offering a socially acceptable, fairly logical explanation for one's behaviors, feelings, or decisions.

Regression. Retreating to more primitive patterns of coping (associated with earlier developmental stages) to avoid the challenges of the higher forms of behavior.

Undoing. Emitting behaviors that seek to cancel out or atone for what are considered unacceptable thoughts of previous behaviors.

Ego restriction. Abandoning an activity because of inferiority feelings, thus restricting one's range of adaptability or the horizons of one's life.

Reaction formation. Going to the opposite extreme to avoid behaviors that would allow expression of one's impulses.

Systems Viewpoint

Herman Witkin was greatly interested in the relationship of defensive behavior to the individual's level of maturity and stress.[58] However, he saw the relationship in terms of psychological differentiation rather than psychosexual development. Like Werner (see Chap. 2), Witkin hypothesized that the individual begins life in a highly undifferentiated state. As the individual matures, the subsystems of psychological operations within the individual (e.g., feeling, perceiving, and thinking) become more heterogeneous and specialized. Highly differentiated psychological functioning enables the individual to differentiate between the self-system and others, and to make more specific responses to a specific stimulus instead of a diffuse response to many stimuli. Poorly differentiated persons tend to rely on, or are more likely to be influenced by, the behaviors, values, and decisions of others; whereas highly differentiated persons are able to identify their own ideas, feelings, and values.

Witkin's studies indicate that poorly differentiated or **field-dependent** individuals tend to be characterized by low self-esteem, difficulty with organization and priority setting, a tendency to deny or to repress their emotional responses, passivity, and an inability to function independently.[58] His research indicates that field-dependent individuals use the more primitive forms of defense mechanisms by turning away from their own perceptions through the use of repression and denial. Because of their inability to differentiate clearly between their own ideas and the ideas of others or between their emotional and intellectual domains, field-dependent persons exhibit more stress responses because they are unable to channel energies to pursue a specific goal.

Field-independent persons, on the other hand, because of their more highly-developed or differentiated affective domain, perceive events differently and are able to respond to specific elements or factors within a situation without undue influence from other events or other persons.[58] Field-independent individuals are more likely to use intellectualization or sublimation to cope with adverse, stress-producing stimuli, since they generally possess richer and more diversified resources for coping than the less differentiated person. As a result, according to Witkin, field-independent individuals think more clearly, respond more specifically, initiate actions, exhibit more control over external events as well as their own responses and behaviors, are highly organized, and exhibit high self-esteem.[58]

The internationalization of one's own values, standards, and goals guides perception and self-control (major characteristic of effective mastery of "identity homework"). Therefore, according to Witkin, the ability to identify and to internalize goals becomes a critical factor in determining one's level of maturity (the degree of differentiation and effectiveness of integration of the various subsystems of the affective, cognitive, social, and spiritual domains).[58] Classic psychodynamic thought, coupled with more contemporary research, such as that of Witkin, shows clearly the importance of reducing stress through accurate, realistic insight, mature, internalized values, and creative coping responses.

Cognitive Viewpoints

Despite the striking differences between social learning, psychodynamic, and systems theories, they share a basic assumption: The emotionally stressed person is victimized by forces over which he or she has little, if any, control. Learning theory regards the disturbance in terms of involuntary responses based on accidental conditionings that occurred previously in one's life. Since the individual cannot modify these conditioned reflexes merely by knowing about them and trying to will them away, the application of counterconditioning by a competent therapist is required. Psychodynamic thought attributes the individual's reaction to stress to unconscious psychological factors that are sealed off by defensive behavior. The systems view stresses system immaturity that affects the processing of input and, consequently, the output behaviors (see Werner's Continuums, Chap. 2). The inability to adequately separate the affective and cognitive domains prevents the effective functioning of either. While later psychodynamic theorists emphasized the role of an autonomous ego and the conscious mind,[19] it is the cognitivists who highlight proactive responses.

Cognitive theory assumes that each person has the potential for various rational techniques to deal with disturbing elements in the consciousness. Cognitive theorists hold that most stress problems stem directly from a person's magical, superstitious, empirically unvalidated thinking, and that "if disturbance-creating ideas are vigorously and persistently disputed by the rigorous application of logico-empirical thinking, they can almost invariably be eliminated."[11] Misconceptions that produce stress can be corrected with the same problem-solving apparatus that one has acquired through the various stages of development. In this approach, a person regards a disturbance as a misunderstanding or misinterpretation that can be resolved either through obtaining adequate and accurate information or by recognizing the logical fallacy of these misunderstandings.

Cognitive theorists are optimistic about the individual's ability to filter large amounts of information; they believe that one can label all external stimuli efficiently, monitor imagination, and distinguish between the real and imaginary elements of a situation. They believe that individuals are able to hypothesize and test accumulated inventories of formulas, equations, and axioms that enable them to make deductions when confronted with problems similar to those previously resolved.[3]

Cognitive psychologists feel that in the course of development, individuals acquire many techniques and generalizations that enable them to judge whether or not they are reacting realistically to situations. The individual processes, decodes, and interprets incoming messages using a self-regulating system that issues instructions and prohibitions, self-praise, or self-reproaches. According to the cognitive theorist, a person can respond effectively to the environment to the extent that the input of the environment is meshed with the individual's internal psychological system. If this system shuts out or twists around the signals from the outside, the individual will be completely out of phase with what is going on around him or her.[3]

Events are often controlled by factors beyond one's will. Nevertheless, individuals do have a uniquely rational dimension to their functionings and the possibility, difficult though it many be, of taking action that will change and control their futures. Since reaction to stress is often the result of irrational and illogical thinking and is thus determined not so much by external circumstances but by perceptions and attitudes toward those circumstances, a reorganization of these perceptions and thinking can help one to develop adequate coping behaviors to deal effectively with stressors.[12] In other words, one can choose his or her attitude or reaction to a stressor, becoming proactive instead of reactive to life.

The belief in the ability of the individual to determine personal behavior and emotional experience is expressed in Ellis's *A-B-C theory* of personality.[12] *A* is the existence of the fact, event, behavior, or attitude of another person; *C* is the reaction of the individual (e.g., emotional disturbance or unhappiness) that follows from *A*. However, it is not *A* that is the cause of *C,* but *B,* which is the self-verbalization by the individual about the meaning of *A*—the definition or interpretation of *A* as being awful, terrible, good, or solvable. It is, therefore, not so much the environmental cues as one's definition and interpretation of these cues that becomes the cause of maladaptive thinking and behavior. Thus the mind plays a unique role in coping successfully or unsuccessfully with a stressful environment (see Table 36-1).

Each of the major theoretical schools has touched on important ingredients of stress reactions. The learning theorists have shown us the power of environmental cues in disrupting and in shaping our lives. Psychodynamic theorists reveal to us how the needs and drives of the human personality can retard reality functioning and responses to stress from within. The systems viewpoint stresses the intrapersonal and interpersonal differentiation of the individual as a significant factor in stress perception and management. The cognitive theorists have stressed the inhibiting or liberating effect of one's own information-processing system. While all four views clarify the ways in which individuals react adversely to stress, it remains for us to suggest ways in which individuals can better cope with stress arising from the rapid and profound changes that people are experiencing in today's world. In these next sections we will discuss how one can build on this large theoretical base to provide concrete suggestions for coping with the stressors inherent in a technological society.

IMPLICATIONS FOR FOSTERING OPTIMAL DEVELOPMENT OF HUMAN POTENTIALS

Douglas Heath, in his cross-cultural research on maturity and competence, discovered that persons who were considered mature within their culture by their peers consistently differed from immature persons in similar ways.[21] He found that "mature persons are able to symbolize their experiences; they are also more allocentric [opposite of egocentric], integrated, stable, and autonomous in their cognitive skills, concepts of themselves, values, and personal relationships."[21] He hypothesized that successful adaptation or achievement of a new level of maturity releases affective energy that results in increased enthusiasm, joy, humor, and a sense of power, since such experiences foster identity integration that in turn encourages integrity and results in spontaneity.[21] After research in cultures as diverse as rural Turkey and urban America, Heath was able to identify a core set of traits possessed by matured persons: (1) ability to anticipate consequences; (2) calm and clear thinking; (3) potential fulfillment; (4) orderly, organized approaches to life's problems; (5) predictability; (6) purposefulness; (7) realisticness; (8) reflectiveness; (9) strong convictions; (10) implacability.

Heath's research blends well with the theories of Seligman, Maslow, Witkin, Sheehy, and many others in suggesting that previous successes foster sufficient self-confidence to risk initiating active efforts to cope when novel situations arise that force one to generalize from previous experiences or to create new solutions to problems. Heath observes, however, that a sense of competence does not mature in a vacuum. "Effectiveness is associated not only with a private sense of competence or self-esteem, but also with a belief that others also judge one's self to be able to cope successfully."[21] Thus we also are affected by the suprasystems, the family, and the culture in which we are reared—their support, the opportunities offered, and the competencies valued.

In the introduction to this final unit and chapter of the book, Schuster identifies five elements (acceptance, companionship, challenges, support, and service opportunities) that other persons in the environment need to provide to each of us as we travel through life to facilitate maximization of our potentials. Although the expression of each of these elements will differ with developmental and cultural needs and goals, mutuality in providing these elements strengthens both bonding and individuality, and recognizes and enhances our humanness.

In 1970 the White House Conference on Children and Youth observed that "We are experiencing a breakdown in the process of making human beings human."[5] Talbot observes that "Millions of children grow up in conditions that stunt their intellectual and emotional growth as well as their physical growth."[52] "To be fully human, one must be attached to, care for, and be interdependent with other human beings. To be totally self-absorbed, as we learn from the writings of the new narcissists, is finally to feel lonely, bored, and despairing in the face of the meaninglessness of life."[10]

With these remarks in mind, we shall review what research and child development experts indicate assists the child to develop a sense of competence and fosters high self-esteem during the developmental years. However, "being a person is not something we get set or that we construct, once and for all. It is a constant, evolving, changing thing. This focus on process, on the evolution of experience, is something that changes our expectancies of ourselves."[7]

Infancy

Selma Fraiberg notes that "our survival as a human community may depend as much upon our nurture of love in infancy and childhood as upon the protection of our society from external threats."[15] Such love, security, and the opportunity for healthy attachment are best realized in a family that plans for and eagerly anticipates the child's arrival. In such an environment, the potential for parental commitment and devotion and their ability and willingness to sacrifice personal goals temporarily for the needs of the infant are increased. The presence of caring adults is the most crucial component for healthy development during infancy.

Erikson speaks about the need to develop trust. Mahler emphasizes that primary narcissism, or autistic behavior, is characteristic of the early months. Thus regularity is required in meeting the child's basic physiological needs. This regularity of experiences helps the child to organize information into meaningful, useful, schemata. A regular but flexible schedule helps the child to begin to predict events, yet allows both the parents and the child to meet their individual needs.

The parents must be able to invest themselves in the child so fully that synchrony of interaction is established early. This means that the parent and young child take turns during periods of communication or play. Each plays an equal role in maintaining the interaction. Each responds specifically to the behaviors of the other and initiates new directions. Communication is not unidirectional with the adult initiating all contacts, toy uses, or communication topics. This early respect as *partners* in the communication dyad facilitates attending and engenders trust. Through brief interactions, the child begins to associate specific behaviors with predictable, pleasant events. This association is the beginning of competence—learning to control the outcome. Seligman's theory on learned helplessness is very significant at this stage of development.[46]

The infant needs a stable person to attach to or to "fall in love with." This factor more than any other is essential to the development of those most human qualities of sensitivity, caring, empathy, and giving. Inadequate physical as well as emotional contact during infancy hinders identification with a significant adult.[27] Lap games become an essential vehicle for early sharing of the culture (e.g., pat-a-cake) as well as exchanges of tenderness.

Selma Fraiberg, from her studies of child development, infants with failure-to-thrive, and family relationships, feels that there is a very close link between the love-respect relationships of adulthood and the love-acceptance relationship experienced during infancy. "In every act of love in mature life there is a prologue which originated in the first year of life. There are two people who arouse in each other sensual joy, feelings of longing, and the conviction that they are absolutely indispensable to each other—that life without the other is meaningless. Separation from the other is intolerable . . . To a very large extent the disease of non-attachment can be eradicated at the source, by ensuring stable human partnerships for each baby."[15]

Even the infant needs a change of pace and exposure to new experiences to prevent boredom and further withdrawal into his or her own world. However, new experiences or stimuli must be modified or presented gradually if they are to capture and maintain the infant's interest; otherwise they may cause withdrawal to avoid sensory overload or "flooding."[60] Mobiles can be used to capture visual interest; their slow movement allows practice in visual following. Parental conversation should generally be slower, restricted in word usage, and repeated often. Gentle tactile and kinesthetic stimulation, such as holding, patting, caressing, and changing position, is essential for neurophysical maturation as well as emotional well-being.[15] Repetitive body games, such as "creepy spider" and "peek-a-boo," provide variation, yet allow the infant to anticipate the end result. A gradual change of stimulus and the provision of a variety of social, sensorimotor language, and kinesthetic experiences help to prepare the infant for more active involvement with the environment during the toddler years.

The infant also needs opportunities to practice the skills already possessed—whether they are looking behaviors, manipulating an object, eating solid foods, or communicating. Since initial efforts are generally fleeting and weak, rein-

forcement of early skills is essential as a stepping stone to the development of stronger or more complex skills. It is here that the baby learns how to learn. The provision of toys that respond easily with only minimal effort on the infant's behalf is crucial during the early months. Thus reinforcement for one's efforts at control is "cost-effective." The behaviorists' concept of successive approximations, which emphasizes the reinforcement of rudimentary skills, is very appropriate for the development of competency that leads to initiative in later childhood.

Toddlers and Preschoolers

According to Erikson, the toddler and preschooler are developing autonomy and initiative. Once they learn that their actions can affect the environment, they become "drunk with their own power" and try to control the whole world. It is important, therefore, that parents help the child to develop appreciation for the limits of his or her power to maintain both physical and psychological safety. This need is often difficult to balance with the child's continuing need to practice emerging skills. However, the child who has parents who set consistent, reasonable limits, and who follow through with the guidance and limits they offer, gradually begins to internalize limits, learns to control impulses, and thus develops self-discipline. The child recognizes his or her own ability to tell the self "no." This recognition enhances the child's self-esteem and self-confidence (since the child can begin to trust the self), especially if the parents notice and reinforce efforts at self-control. As the child learns to harness and focus energies, learning and social relationships are enhanced.

The child's needs for physical affection, love, and acceptance do not diminish during the preschool years. Although the child may want the attention less frequently or in a different form (parents need to respect the child's pace and preferences), the toddler or preschooler still needs tangible and frequent evidence of the parents' love, which affirms his or her value to them. One of the best ways to offer this reassurance is to *spend time with the child*. Toys and other material possessions are secondary to the child when compared to social play time with the parents. Social play time offers an opportunity for synchronized, cooperative use of language, which is essential to the development of language and cognitive skills as well as social skills. The turntaking play and communication patterns established during infancy must continue during this period of life. The typical adult-directed conversation consists of a series of questions to help the child remember past events or "show off" knowledge to another adult. This is not turntaking, since the adult is initiating all the topics of interaction. The young child's tension level rises with increased behavior problems and decreased cooperativeness. The child may feel as if he or she is taking an examination! Many of the typical resistive behaviors of young children can be avoided through sensitive listening and responding and the offering of safe choices instead of ultimatums.

The child's exposure to adult language is just as important as the parents' ability to understand and respond specifically and sensitively to the child's attempts to communicate. From infancy and throughout life, "the more empathetically and accurately parents read their children's signals, and the more sensitively they respond to them from the heart, the more likely the child will be protected from erosions in mental health. Children who know they are operating from a firm base do not 'spoil'; instead they are able to draw on a well of security lasting a lifetime. Don't hold back on the instincts of love and caring."[45] The social play time offers an opportunity to develop this sensitivity on the part of the parent, while fostering the child's optimal development.

The toddler and especially the preschooler need exposure to models who possess both similar and valued characteristics with whom they can identify. Models serve to stimulate the desire to develop similar skills and provide the child with a feeling of power and virtue. The opportunity to play with peers helps the child to develop cooperative social skills, to practice language, and to compare self-competencies with more realistic performance levels (Fig. 39-5).

Stability of experiences is crucial during these early years when children are learning roles and relationships, and when cognitive organizational skills are still limited. Their ability to be flexible or to adapt to entirely new circumstances is limited. When a move to a new neighborhood, a hospitalization, or a separation from family members is unavoidable, every effort needs to be extended to continue as much stability in relationships and routines as possible. The practices of parents do affect and shape a child, but it is a dynamic relationship that is constantly changing; therefore, no **single** experience will ensure success or failure in later life. However, parents do need to attempt to ensure as much stability as possible to provide information that facilitates the child's ability to organize and to predict events and thus control outcomes. It is the continuity between the internal prediction and the external outcome that fosters the child's sense of competence and high self-esteem.

Young children need challenges to help stretch their burgeoning skills. Many parents try to spare their children "the necessity of overcoming any kind of obstacle, including, of course, any kind of contradiction from their parents. The result is intolerably aggressive and, at the same time, neurotic children. Quite apart from the fact that trying to raise unfrustrated human beings is one of the most cruel deprivation experiments possible, it puts its unfortunate victim in a position of tormenting insecurity . . . Small wonder their world breaks down and they become openly neurotic when they are suddenly exposed to the stress of public opinion."[26] Environmental and social challenges are essential for learning how to solve a problem, how to work, how to assess one's self against a standard. Rules and developmentally appropriate challenges give a child structure, security, motivation, and a valid source of self-esteem.

School-Age Children

Erikson feels that the development of industry—the ability to work—is crucial during the school-age years. Children need opportunities to master skills during the school years.[24] In fact, individuals at each age need opportunities not only for exposure to new, meaningful skills, but to practice them as an end in themselves until they are mastered sufficiently to be used as a tool to accomplish other, more complex skills. Both the school and the home can help children to discover and develop their unique potentials, while they also offer opportunities to gain those skills that are deemed crucial to successful adaptation in the culture (e.g., reading, computational skills, self-care skills).

The White House Conference of 1970 recognized that both the home and the school need to involve children in genuine responsibilities—not duties or busy work—so that they learn to "deal constructively with personal and social problems . . . to acquire the capacity to cope with difficult situations."[5] Such genuine involvement enhances self-esteem by offering respect for and confidence in the child's capabilities; it makes the child a genuine part of the team, an integral part of the system's functioning. At the same time, it helps to develop the skills of perseverance and cooperation, brings the pride of accomplishment, and leads to a feeling of competence—all integral parts of the task of industry. When a number of responsibilities are assigned, children can learn how to organize their time and to establish priorities. Some parents try to absorb all responsibilities from children—a

FIGURE 39–5.
Computer games familiarize preschoolers with the type of equipment they will be using in school and in later careers.

task that becomes increasingly easy in a technological society—because they feel that childhood is a time for fun, not for responsibility. They overlook the fact that childhood is also a time of preparation for adult responsibilities, and that it is much easier to learn those responsibilities through successive approximations. The assumption of responsibilities involves the development of the effective domain, or attitudes, as well as the acquisition of appropriate psychomotor skills. As an anonymous sage has observed, "One's greatest opportunities frequently come cleverly disguised as unsolvable problems." Affective growth can occur when problems are faced and mastered; one learns how to establish priorities and weigh outcomes. Such skills are learned gradually. Each choice or decision involves not only the attainment of one goal, but the relinquishing of an alternative.[7] Living with the results (successes and failures) of one's decisions in childhood can help to prepare one to make more astute decisions during the adolescent and adult years, when a single decision may in fact change the entire course of one's life.

Peers, an essential ingredient to the psychosocial development of children of all ages, become increasingly important to school-agers. Parents may help children to select their friends through the modeling of what they deem to be desirable behaviors, attitudes, and values. However, "mothers and fathers will serve children best if they accept the power of their children's friends, recognize their presence, and work with rather than against them . . . the child's indiscriminate choice of friends is most likely when family ties are weak and when the child's sense of belonging is fragmented."[45] Bronfenbrenner and many others observe that negative or unhealthy "attachment to age-mates appears to be influenced more by a lack of attention and concern at home than by any positive attraction of the peer group itself. In fact, these children have a rather negative view of their friends and of themselves as well. They are pessimistic about the future, rate lower in responsibility and leadership, and are more likely to engage in antisocial behavior, such as lying, teasing other children, 'playing hooky,' or 'doing something illegal.' "[5] Warm, readily available models in the form of parents, teachers, and peers who possess skills and characteristics that the child regards as culturally or personally desirable, offer the child stable relationships and goals toward which to focus energies while striving for mastery of tasks that lead to higher levels of competence and self-esteem (Fig. 39-6).

Although technology may be calling for different instrumental skills, alternative interpersonal skills, and the reassessment of priorities, some intrapersonal values remain stable and may indeed assume even greater salience in the new culture. These values are best taught in the home by the example of the parents as they deal with the exigencies of daily life. Five enduring values include **joy,** the habit of being pleased; **love,** the sense of identification with another person; **honesty,** the quality of being able to be trusted; **courage,** the ability to face crisis with optimism; **faith,** something to believe in.[57] Such values transcend cultural change.

Adolescence

The basic needs of adolescents are really not very different from those of younger children; they still need warm, caring parents who continue to serve as role models and continue to respect the need for turntaking and mutual responsibility in initiating ideas during conversations. However, they also need expanded opportunities to have contact with other adults who model characteristics, career skills or social competencies that the young person regards as desirable and compatible with his or her unique abilities and interests. They need opportunities to develop skills in preparation for assuming adult roles and responsibilities; this may involve part-time or volunteer work.

FIGURE 39–6.
Planting a tree often helps to give a child a sense of belonging to the community and a link to the future. (Photograph by Candy Shultz.)

The most critical tasks of adolescence involve the development of an independent, internal identity—one's own ideology, values, and roles. Benjamin Spock observes that children who are reared by parents who are sure of their own convictions and ethical standards and who share these values constructively with their children have children who are more considerate, easier to live with, and happier in themselves.[51] There comes a point, however, when individuals must identify their own values as separate from those of their parents (even though they may end up with an identical value system) if they are to become field-independent. What one believes is central to personal integrity. One must learn to acknowledge and to accept inner feelings as a natural, normal part of life experiences without denial or suppression. These feelings can be important signals to the individual's level of functioning and to areas that need attention.[7] It is through attending to one's real feelings and assessing conflicts, priorities, and goals that one's true values begin to be identified. Adolescents often experience conflict with the family as they attempt to prove to themselves and the world that what they believe is not a "warmed-over version borrowed from [the] family."[24]

Eisenberg observes that "At their best, the adolescent years are characterized by the development of idealism and concern for the general welfare. No educational task is more critical than the cultivation of these most human of all qualities by providing experiences to permit their fullest flowering."[11] Such opportunities can be offered through the Red Cross, scouting, and other organizations. Adolescents thrive on activities that allow them to give of themselves, such as helping younger children learn to read or play a game; helping disabled children or adults to learn a new skill; beautifying or improving the community; or assisting older persons with letter-writing, transportation, or self-help needs. Such activities reduce feelings of alienation, increase feelings of competence and involvement, and provide a constructive outlet for leisure time—all excellent preparations for living in a technologically advanced society (Fig. 39-7).[10] Talbot observes that "One of the basic issues today is the survival of a society in which people are useful to each other, glad to be alive, and of value to themselves."[52]

Young and Middle Adult Years

Happiness, personal peace, or lack of anxiety are often identified as goals during the adult years. But "most adults have lost . . . the ability to laugh from sheer happiness; perhaps they have lost happiness itself. Adulthood as we know it brings sobriety and seriousness along with its responsibilities." Most middlescents become "genuinely indifferent to the interesting experiences of life and consider that absorbing something new into the old patterns is simply too much trouble."[30] Like Heath, Montagu observes that the mature adult retains human traits associated with childhood (this tendency is called **neoteny**), such as: imaginativeness, playfulness, open-mindedness, willingness to experiment, flexibility, humor, energy,

FIGURE 39–7.
Leisure-time activities and attitudes learned during school years are likely to continue into the adult years.

eagerness to learn, honesty, spontaneity, and the need to love.[30]

One does not find happiness as an end in itself. True happiness is not the absence of stress but a by-product of contentment with oneself and of conquered challenges. Stress is an essential prerequisite. As a person identifies a challenge and overcomes it through personal efforts, a deep sense of confidence, contentment, and competence ensues—all components of self-esteem. Happiness appears to be the antithesis of helplessness. Happiness (or helplessness and overpowering stress) is most likely to evolve from four situations during the adult years: (1) general personal relationships, (2) employment, (3) personal time, or (4) specific personal relationships.

The potential for conflict is an integral part of any relationship. Differences, however, can be a "positive source of nourishment for the relationship,"[7] and can be used for the growth of the individuals involved when both partners of the interaction recognize that they are equally responsible for the outcome of the relationship. Any confrontation can be painful, but can lead to greater authenticity and genuine mutuality, which helps us to appreciate the humanity of each person with whom we have contact.[7] "Game playing" has no place in this type of relationship.

Stress evolves when employment conflicts with one's values, goals, or priorities. It is easy to get caught up in a "role" imposed by employment, status, or social conventions. A person can literally become a stranger to one's self because so much attention is focused on external constraints rather than internal guidelines. Reich notes that "As the individual is drawn into the meritocracy, his working life is split from his home life, and both suffer from a lack of wholeness."[36] Many individuals today are rejecting occupations with high financial remuneration and seeking those that provide dignity and allow them to be more fully human.[38,61] "Money, important as it is to comfortable survival in the modern world, is not an end in itself but a means to an end, and . . . vocational choices should be made on broader bases than just how much a job pays. Life satisfaction derives from doing something constructive that one likes to do and does well" (Fig. 39-8).[52]

In a harried world, one may sometimes feel like crying, "Stop the world—I want to get off." This attitude reveals a critical component of reducing stresses. Every individual needs some private time each day in which to reflect, to pursue a hobby, or to unwind in a personal way. Since we can predict the results of "flooding" by sensory or experiential overload, we can also prevent it.[29] Thirty minutes of watching a sunset or a sunrise; praying silently; watching a flight of birds or a snowfall; or listening to quiet music, rain, the muffled sounds of children playing, or the rustle of leaves can allow a person to slow down, to "regroup"—to restore adequate equilibrium to face life's responsibilities once again. Many religions stress the necessity of setting aside a Sabbath day for rest. "Quiet time" allows one to release instrumental values for sacred or expressive ones and to find a deeper meaning and purpose to life.[61]

Commitment to a specific personal relationship—to belong to someone—appears to be another significant component in reducing stress. The ability to love appears to be the most crucial and fundamental characteristic of happy individuals. Spock observes that an individual who genuinely loves at least one other person is more likely to have a stable, gratifying career, comfortable relationships with other persons, and a good marriage.[51] Maslow defines love based on mutuality as follows: "Two separate sets of needs become fused into a single set of needs for the new unit. Or love exists when the happiness of the other makes me happy, or when I enjoy the self-actualization of the other as much as I do my own, or when the differentiation between the word **other** and the words **my own** has disappeared."[28] This degree of commitment must not be confused with a fused ego identity. Quite the opposite is true. In a healthy relationship, each person recognizes and values the individuality of the self and the other, but each is so committed to the well-being of the other as well as the self that the concentration on selfish interests is obliterated by genuine concern and caring for the other with the same sensitivity and respect offered to the self.

Family Relationships

Virginia Satir depicts the family as a "factory" where people are made.[43] The quality of the product depends on the quality of relationships and communication within the family.[8,43] "Children's well-being has important life-cycle consequences. The productivity and attainments of adults rests on their well-being as children and on the investments of their parents—and society generally—have made them during their formative years."[20] Leaders in family development studies are concerned about the loosening of family relationships and parental commitment to systematic guidance of children.[35] They cite increases in juvenile delinquency, disruptive school behaviors, drug use, suicides, pregnancy, and runaways as symptoms of family stress. Yet in the technological society, both parents are frequently working and thus are spending less time with their children. Surrogate caregivers are becoming essential to provide child care during parental absence, potentially eroding family ties and presenting the child with alternative models and values. Families are changing residences, neighborhoods, schools, and friends at alarming rates.[5] This mobility attenuates ties to extended family members and friends, as well as neighborhood commitments. As a result, "the nuclear family has become almost the sole source of affective sustenance . . . With all our emotional eggs in the nuclear family basket, breakage is both more inevitable and more devastating when it does occur."[11] Thus, the family becomes even more important in a technological age as a refuge from the stressors of life, as a source of stability, as a builder of self-esteem, and the central focus of fulfillment (Fig. 39-9).[8,43]

As a society, therefore, we need to support the integrity of the family and to provide opportunities for meaningful relationships between parents and their children including: more flexible work hours (those who have tried it report reduced stress, increased work productivity, and improved family relationships); community family activity centers; easily accessible day-care programs that allow parents to visit during the day; opportunities for children to visit the parents' place of employment; and more part-time employment options for parents who wish to spend more time with the family.[5]

Alvin Toffler observes that the technological society offers the potential to improve the quality of family life.[54] With increased use of computers, many people will be able to have a terminal in their own home instead of going to a central office to work. This option translates into financial savings for the business (less office and parking space), and to the individual (transportation and clothing). Reduced transportation also means reduced air pollution. Terminals in the home will allow the adults to set their own working hours and to share the job with each other or even with the children. This can translate into reduced personal stress, increased family cooperation, better role modeling for the children, earlier development of positive work attitudes, and more leisure time.[54]

The community can also benefit from an increased com-

FIGURE 39–8.
An individual's attitudes and pace of life are strongly affected by the community in which he or she resides. The community of origin may differ greatly from the community of residence.

FIGURE 39–9.
Positive family relationships are essential in a "too hurried," "too technical," "too impersonal" world. The family can offer a well of strength, support and refueling.

munity stability. An individual no longer needs to move to the locale of a new job. The computer can hook up with any central location. With increased stability of residence, community commitment and participation will be increased. So while many decry the destructive impact of technology and the development of modular relationships that are frequently and easily fractured (increasing stress and the use of coping skills), Toffler heralds the generative potentials of technological advances.

Studies by Fraiberg and many others support the importance of the family to the developing child—the adult of tomorrow. However, the family is also important to the continued development of its adult members. Chapter 29 emphasized the necessity of choosing one's partner wisely. A good marriage does not just happen; the partners must work hard to maintain the spontaneity, joy, and love of the early months. Mutual respect must be maintained. All this requires commitment to the conjugal bond and to the other members of the family—commitment that can be eroded by rapid changes in other areas of one's life. One's values, priorities, and goals, again become crucial in influencing commitments and focusing one's energies. True interdependence and sharing become crucial elements in developing this "commitment and the sense of community which underpin love, generosity, and caring."[10] The family allows for mastery of Erikson's tasks of intimacy and generativity as well as satisfying Maslow's need to love and to belong.

Late Adult Years

Because of the separation of extended family members and the need for small, transportable families in a highly mobile society, elderly persons may be widely separated from their own siblings, their children, or both. Consequently, many

older adults may feel that they no longer belong; they have lost their value as a person; they no longer have anywhere to offer their assistance; they are not needed; and they will have no one to care for them should they need assistance. Some may even die for lack of someone who cares. In short, feelings of alienation may be very acute. When problems do arise, they may be forced to turn to government agencies for aid; this may increase their stress if they value self-reliance and independence and feel that such agencies are only for indigent, disabled, or incompetent persons.

Many communities are resolving this problem by establishing community centers for senior citizens where they can share skills with each other, or more important, actively involve themselves in the welfare of the community through part-time employment services and volunteer programs. Older citizens offer a large untapped source of stability and involvement for communities (Fig. 39-10). Many elderly persons assist with tutoring services in the schools or offer foster grandparent services for children in institutional settings or even to neighbors whose natural grandparents live too far away to maintain close contact. Others offer their expertise in constructing equipment for Head Start programs, recreational centers, church schools, or neighborhood child care centers.

FIGURE 39–10.
Older adults provide continuity with the past and models for our future.

Many older persons are merely waiting for someone to tell them that they are wanted and needed. **At each age, individuals need to feel wanted, needed, appreciated, and an integral part of the significant suprasystems to which they belong.** Elderly adults are a national treasure. In recognition of this, Presidential greeting cards are sent (if requested by friend or relative) to persons 80 years of age or more and to couples marking their fiftieth wedding anniversary. Those celebrating their 100th birthday are sent a personal presidential letter (write to Greeting Office, Room 39, The White House, Washington, DC, 20050).

CONCLUSION

We have been discussing fostering individual high-level wellness in light of rapidly changing technological advances. The survival of the individual is affected not only by the immediate system of which he or she is a part (the family), but also by the suprasystem in which the family is embedded (the society). It should be clear by now that if change is too severe and too frequent, one's adaptive efficiency is lowered, resulting in both psychological and physiological deterioration. Appropriate experiences during earlier developmental years can help an individual to develop skills in problem solving and value clarification that will lead to greater stability and flexibility. Appropriate challenges and experiences offered during developmental years can increase the coping resources of the individual and result in a firm self-confidence, which immunizes the individual against the helplessness syndrome (see Chap. 13).

Those who are preparing children to cope with a technological society should be aware that, throughout childhood, children need:

1. To be wanted and loved by warm, caring adults who provide a stable family system;
2. To be valued, accepted, and offered respect for personal interests, ideas, needs and talents;
3. Stable models with whom to identify;
4. Challenges to stimulate the desire to use higher-level skills;
5. Assistance in mastering age-appropriate skills that foster the development of competence and responsibility;
6. Opportunities to identify and to explore all their feelings—both positive and negative;
7. Opportunities to participate in a variety of experiences that develop flexibility and a wide continuum of skills;
8. Opportunities to organize responsibilities, to establish priorities, to solve problems, and then to live with the consequences;
9. Opportunity to belong to and to become involved in helping others in order to strengthen their own skills while developing a sense of commitment to others; and
10. Encouragement to think for themselves—guided assistance in developing their own standards, values, and goals (Fig. 39-11).

Individuals who are offered these experiences during the early developmental years are more likely to develop the characteristics of competence and maturity, as identified by Heath, and the characteristics of field-independent individuals as described by Witkin. They are also more likely to be able to integrate their various identities into a stable view of self, as proposed by Erikson. Since they have met lower-level needs, they are free to expend energies in actualizing their unique potentials, as described by Maslow. They will be prepared to function with relatively little guidance from others and to maintain their own direction despite the contradicting attitudes, judgments, and values of others—all of which is excellent preparation for the adult years in a rapidly changing society.

Every person faces challenges and even disasters at some point in life. Nevertheless, it is not the situation that creates a tragic life, but the individual's response to the circumstances. Gail Sheehy, in her book *Pathfinders,* documents life stories of persons both famous and unknown who have faced impossible situations, yet have survived not "somehow," but *triumphantly,* to become family, community, and even national

Dennis the Menace

" THE BEST THING YOU CAN DO IS TO GET VERY GOOD AT BEING YOU."

FIGURE 39–11.
Dennis the Menace. (Copyright used by permission of Hank Ketcham and © by News Group Chicago, Inc.)

leaders. The key to triumph was attitude—the ability, the desire, the commitment to find growth and challenge instead of failure in the most trying circumstances. Through the creative handling of past transitions, the identification of a specific meaning and direction in life, a commitment to work toward achievement of long-term goals, and a satisfaction with one's own growth and development, these individuals develop a sense of happiness and well-being that undergirds their lives through new transitions as well as life's most tragic accidents.[48] These persons have found a balance between their personal development and the development of others, which frees them to be more fully themselves. They have found a way to "bloom" where they are "planted," despite rocky soil or inadequate rain.

Arnold Toynbee observes that "The material side of life is not an end in itself. It is only a means to an end. I have already shown that I believe that the true purposes of human life are spiritual; surely we ought to try to make machinery our servant for helping us to carry out these spiritual purposes. It will be our master, perhaps, in the sense that we shall have to live in the uncongenial environment of factories and offices in great cities; but, in any environment, we can lead the spiritual life; and this is what man is for."[55] Victor Frankl made the same observation at the close of World War II: It is not the circumstances, but one's attitude toward them, that give meaning and value to one's life.[16] Humans possess remarkable resiliency. Even the most difficult of circumstances can have a positive outcome.[37] "Man's religion and ethics will once again express the true realities of his way of life: Solidarity with his fellow man, a genuine community representing a balanced moral-aesthetic order, and a continuing expansion of man's inner capacities."[36]

This is the purpose and the challenge of life: To help each person to maximize his or her potentials—to live life not somehow, but triumphantly. Such a goal, however, will be achieved only through self-respect and mutual respect. This means recognition of ourselves as a part of the universe rather than as an autonomous unit.[38] It means creating a niche for ourselves in the social environment, identifying a core value system by which to live, and finding a meaning to life through commitment to values higher than ourselves. "It is in serving others . . . that we discover ourselves and the purposes for which we were created."[13] Each of us must do our part to create a high-quality life for ourselves and for others, a life which is found by respecting the balance between the rights and the responsibilities of ourselves and others within our various suprasystems. Other then will each of us be afforded the opportunity to maximize our potentials, and only then will we be able to maximize the potentials of the society, nation, and world in which we live.

> Success is never final, failure is never fatal;
> it is courage that counts.
> —Winston Churchill

> May you live all the days of your life.
> —Jonathan Swift

REFERENCES

1. Anshen, R. N. (1972). Introduction. In M. Mead (Ed.), *Twentieth century faith: Hope and survival.* New York: Harper and Row.
2. Archer, J. (1977). *Personal communication.*
3. Beck, A. T. (1979). *Cognitive therapy and the emotional disorders.* New York: New American Library.
4. Brennecke, J. H., & Amick, R. G. (1980). *The struggle for significance* (3rd ed.). Encino, CA: Glencoe.
5. Bronfenbrenner, U. (1976). The roots of alienation. In N. B. Talbot (Ed.), *Raising children in modern America: What parents and society should be doing for their children.* Boston: Little, Brown.
6. Brown, B. S. (Ed.). (1973, July). Mental health in the future: Politics, science, ethics and values. *Annals of the American Academy of Political and Social Science, 408.*
7. Bugental, J. F. T. (1970). Changes in inner human experience and the future. In S. C. Wallia (Ed.), *Toward century 21: Technology, society, and human values.* New York: Basic Books.
8. Curran, D. (1985). *Stress and the healthy family.* Minneapolis, MN: Winston Press.
9. Dohrenwend, B. S., & Dohrenwend, B. P. (1984). Life stress and illness: Formulation of the issue. In B. S. Dohrenwend & B. P. Dohrenwend (Eds.), *Stressful life events and their contexts.* New Brunswick, NJ: Rutgers University Press.
10. Douvan, E. (1978). The caring society. *Educational Horizons, 57(1),* 3.
11. Eisenberg, L. (1976). Youth in a changing society. In V. C. Vaughan & T. B. Brazelton (Eds.), *The family—can it be saved?* Chicago: Year Book.
12. Ellis, A., & Harper, R. A. (1979). *A new guide to rational living.* N. Hollywood, CA: Wilshire.
13. Fairbanks, E. L. (1990). *Education for a life style of service* (Inaugural Address, March 2, 1990). Mt. Vernon, OH: Mt. Vernon Nazarene College.
14. Fleming, I., Baum, A., & Weiss, L. (1987). Social density and perceived control as mediators of crowding stress in high-density residential neighborhoods. *Journal of Personality and Social Psychology, 52,* 899–906.
15. Fraiberg, S. H. (1978). *Every child's birthright: In defense of mothering.* New York: Bantam Books.
16. Frankl, V. E. (1962). *Man's search for meaning: An introduction to logotherapy* (I. Lasch, Trans.). Boston: Beacon Press.
17. Freud, S. (1964). *New introductory lectures on psycho-analysis* (Standard Edition, Vol. 22). London: Hogarth Press.
18. Hall, B. P., & Smith, P. (1976). *Development of conscience: A confluent theory of values.* New York: Paulist Press.
19. Hartmann, H. (1958). *Ego psychology and the problem of adaptation* (D. Rappaport, Trans.). New York: International Universities Press.
20. Haveman, R., Wolfe, B. L., Finnie, R. E., & Wolff., E. N. (1988). *The vulnerable.* Washington, DC: Urban Institute Press.
21. Heath, D. C. (1977). *Maturity and competence: A transcultural view.* New York: Gardner Press.
22. Holmes, T. H., & Masuda, M. (1970). *Life change and illness susceptibility.* Chicago: American Association for the Advancement of Science. (Symposium on Separation and Depression: Clinical Research Aspects. American Association for the Advancement of Science, Annual Meeting, Dec. 26–30).
23. Holmes, T. H., & Rahe, R. R. (1967). The social readjustment rating scale. *Journal of Psychosomatic Research, 11,* 213.
24. Kagan, J. (1976). The psychological requirements for human

development. In N. B. Talbot (Ed.), *Raising children in modern America: What parents and society should be doing for their children*. Boston: Little, Brown.

25. Lerner, R. M. (1984). *On the nature of human plasticity*. Cambridge, UK: Cambridge University Press.

26. Lorenz, K. (1972). The enmity between generations and its probable ethological cause. In M. W. Piers (Ed.), *Play and development*. New York: Norton.

27. Maslow, A. H. (1968). *Toward a psychology of being* (2nd ed.). Princeton, NJ: Van Nostrand.

28. Maslow, A. H. (1973). A theory of human motivation: The goals of work. In F. Best (Ed.), *The future of work*. Englewood Cliffs, NJ: Prentice-Hall.

29. Mead, M. (1972). *Twentieth century faith: Hope and survival*. New York: Harper and Row.

30. Montagu, A. (1989). *Growing young* (2nd ed.). Granby, MA: Bergin and Garvey.

31. Nasar, S. (1987). Do we live as well as we used to? *Fortune, 116*(6), 32–46.

32. Oliner, S. P., & Oliner, P. M. (1988). *The altruistic personality: Rescue of the Jews in Nazi Europe*. New York: Free Press.

33. Rahe, R. H. (1984). Developments in life change measurement: Subjective life change unit scaling. In B. S. Dohrenwend & B. P. Dohrenwend (Eds.), *Stressful life events and their contexts*. New Brunswick, NJ: Rutgers University Press.

34. Rahe, R. H., & Arthur, R. (1968). Life change patterns surrounding illness experience. *Journal of Psychosomatic Research, 11,* 341.

35. Regier, G. (1986). *Cultural trends and the American Family*. Washington, DC: Family Research Council.

36. Reich, C. A. (1970). *The greening of America*. New York: Random House.

37. Richardson, G. A., & Kwiatkowski, B. M. (1981). Life-span developmental psychology: Non-normative life events. *Human Development, 24,* 425.

38. Rifkin, J. (1980). *Entropy*. New York: Viking Press.

39. Rifkin, J. (1983). *Algeny*. New York: Viking Press.

40. Robinson, J. P. (1977). *How Americans use time: A social-psychological analysis of everyday behavior*. New York: Praeger.

41. Rokeach, M. (1976). *Beliefs, attitudes, and values: A theory of organization and change*. San Francisco: Jossey-Bass.

42. Rook, K. S. (1987). Social support versus companionship: effects of life stress, loneliness, and evaluation by others. *Journal of Personality and Social Psychology, 52,* 1132–1147.

43. Satir, V. (1988). *Peoplemaking*. Palo Alto, CA: Science and Behavior Books.

44. Schaeffer, F. A. (1983). *How then should we live? The rise and decline of western thought and culture*. Westchester, IL: Crossway Books.

45. Segal, J., & Yahraes, H. (1978). Protecting children's mental health. *Children Today, 7*(5), 23.

46. Seligman, M. E. P. (1975). *Helplessness: On depression, development, and death*. San Francisco: Freeman.

47. Selye, H. (1974). *Stress without distress*. Philadelphia: J. B. Lippincott.

48. Sheehy, G. (1981). *Pathfinders*. New York: Morrow.

49. Skinner, B. F. (1980). *Beyond freedom and dignity*. New York: Knopf.

50. Skinner, B. F. (1986). What is wrong with daily life in the western world? *American Psychologist, 41,* 568–574.

51. Spock, B. M. (1985). *Raising children in a difficult time* (2nd ed.). New York: Pocket Books.

52. Talbot, N. B., & Wells, L. (1976). Implications for action. In N. B Talbot (Ed.), *Raising children in modern America: Problems and prospective solutions*. Boston: Little, Brown.

53. Toffler, A. (1970). *Future shock*. New York: Random House.

54. Toffler, A. (1980). *The third wave*. New York: William Morrow.

55. Toynbee, A. J. (1971). *Surviving the future*. New York: Oxford University Press.

56. Toynbee, A. J. (1971). Technical advance and the morality of power. In G. R. Urban (Ed.), *Can we survive our future? A symposium*. New York: St. Martin's Press.

57. Whitman, A. (1981). Five enduring values for your child. *Reader's Digest, 118*(710), 163.

58. Witkin, H. A. (1974). *Psychological differentiation: Studies of development*. New York: Wiley.

59. Wixen, B. N. (1973). *Children of the rich*. New York: Crown.

60. Wolfgang, C. H. (1977). *Helping aggressive and passive preschoolers through play*. Columbus, OH: Charles E. Merrill.

61. Yankelovich, D. (1981). New rules in American life: Searching for self-fulfillment in a world turned upside down. *Psychology Today, 15*(4), 35.

Glossary

Accommodation: According to Piaget, the creation of a new schema or the modification of an old one to differentiate more accurately a behavior or a stimulus from already categorized schemata. Cognitive *work*.

Adaptation: Process of adjusting comfortably to new and different conditions.

Adolescence: The period of transition between childhood and adulthood (with emphasis on the social and emotional components). Adolescent thought and behavior patterns may continue on into the 20s and 30s or later.

Affective domain: One's internal responses to events; one's intrapersonal relationships, self-concept, emotions.

Allocentric: Other-centered; concerned about the well-being of other persons (the opposite of egocentric).

Alveolus (pl. alveoli): A small, saclike dilation. Pulmonary alveoli are structures in the respiratory system through which gas exchange occurs between inspired air and pulmonary capillary blood. Mammary alveoli are the structures of the female breast that secrete milk.

Anomaly: Malformation; marked deviation from the expected standard.

Aspirate: To inhale a foreign substance into the lungs.

Assimilation: According to Piaget, the process whereby a stimulus or information is incorporated into an already existing schema, even though perception of it must be distorted or only partially acknowledged in order to do so. Cognitive *play*.

Attachment: The primary social bond that evolves between an infant and his or her principal caregiver. An orientation toward or sense of belonging to the other. Attachments evolve later in life toward other meaningful persons.

BMR (basal metabolic rate): The rate at which the body uses oxygen and sugar (energy expenditure) under conditions of absolute rest to maintain the essential life processes.

Behavior: Any reactive or proactive response that can be described, observed, and measured. Behavior may include changes in pupil dilatation, pulse rate, and galvanic skin responses as well as neuromuscular, verbal, or problem-solving activities.

Biophysical domain: The concrete, physical reality of the self system; the tool through which the other four domains express themselves.

Bonding: Emotional commitment to another person. Particularly used to identify the attachment of the parent to his or her infant.

Client: A person who engages the professional services of another to alleviate or solve a problem; in specific settings, is synonymous with patient, student, recipient, defendant, and so forth.

Cognition: The process of obtaining understanding about one's world; the internal manipulation of external or hypothetical events through the use of symbols.

Cognitive domain: The interpreter, processor, and organizer of stimuli; one's "knowing system"; the conscious problem solver and decision maker for the system.

Concept: A thought or abstract idea about a given phenomenon extracted from an individual's experiences and mediated by mental operations; one's comprehension of essential attributes or relationships.

Congenital: "Born with"; a condition existing at birth even though it may not manifest itself for several months or years.

Crisis: Any internal or external event that taxes the coping skills of the individual, requires a major adjustment in patterns of daily living, or creates acute emotional upset.

Dependency: The extent to which one individual relies on another for his or her existence or level of functioning.

Deprivation: The withholding of a need-satisfying stimulation, object, or relationship.

Development: The refinement, improvement, or expansion of an existing component or skill. In the biophysical domain, development means an increase in body size by enlargement of cells already present.

Developmental task: A skill associated with a particular phase of the life span, mastery of which is associated with healthy or successful growth, and on which continued growth and development is contingent.

Deviation: An unpredictable or pathological behavior or characteristic.

Disability: An inability to execute a specific skill or to perform some function expected of persons in the culture. Usually arises from an impairment.

Discipline: The processes and methods used by adults to teach and guide children toward desired behavior.

Domain: A subsystem or major sphere of functioning of the human system. Five interdependent domains are recognized: biophysical, cognitive, social, affective, and spiritual.

Drives: Energy structures which, by responding to needs, activate physiological processes in appropriate organ systems to alleviate the need and thus secure survival.[1]

Egocentrism: *Cognitive*—The belief that other persons see events from the same visual viewpoint, experience the

---

[1]Anthony, E. J. and Benedek, T. (Eds.), (1970). *Parenthood: Its psychology and psychopathology,* (p. 168). Boston: Little, Brown.

same feelings, and understand the same information. The *inability* to understand that others have a different view of an event (normal perception of the world during the toddler and preschool years). *Affective*—The belief that one's self-generated ideas and solutions to problems are superior. The *unwillingness* to entertain other people's viewpoints because of the emotional investment in one's own ideas (an ego-defensive approach typical of adolescence).

Electrolyte: A substance dissolved in water that possesses an electrical charge.

Enculturation: The process of teaching a child the values, stories, customs, traditions, and social skills central to the culture.

Ethnocentrism: The viewing and judging of life and life-styles through the eyes of one's own social, cultural, and national milieu and values. The tendency to denigrate "foreign" ways, foods, customs, values, and so forth.

Family: A unique social system comprised of two or more interdependent persons, that remains united over time, and serves as a mediator between the needs of its members and the forces, the demands, and the obligations of society.[2]

Fractionization: The severe disharmony or disunity of a family. May be expressed through affective alienation, aggression, separation, or divorce.

Gamete: A cell produced by the reproductive system for the purpose of procreation of the species (i.e., sperm, ovum).

Genotype: The genetic makeup of a person.

Grief: Feelings associated with the loss of a significant relationship. May be a material object, goal, person, pet, body part, and so forth.

Growth: The addition of new components, cells, or skills.

Health: The state of adaptation of a system to its suprasystems and subsystems (see Chap. 2).

Helplessness syndrome: According to Seligman, a psychological state that results when an individual believes or learns that he or she cannot control events; therefore, either no effort or ineffective effort is made to affect one's life events.

High-level wellness (high-level health): The ability of an individual to optimally use current potentials to meet the demands of the realities of everyday life.

Holistic approach: Assessment and therapeutic approaches which recognize the person as an indivisible totality, who is influenced by past experiences, current developmental level, situational contexts, family relationships, potentials, abilities, and personal goals.

Hyperplastic cell growth: *see* **Growth.**

Hypertropic cell growth: *see* **Development.**

Identification: The process that leads a child to think, feel, and behave as though the characteristics of another person belong to him or her.[3]

Identity homework: The process of exploring, accepting, and internalizing one's unique characteristics and value system. This is a difficult and often painful process beginning in adolescence and continuing throughout the rest of life as problems and conflicts arise and decisions must be made. Successful mastery results in stability, integrity, life direction, and self-appreciation (see Chap. 25).

Ideology: A systematic body of concepts that includes one's moral principles.

Individuation: According to Mahler, the recognition of one's separate will, goals, and identity from that one one's primary caregiver.

Intervention: Supportive or therapeutic strategies designed to compensate for or eliminate a specific problem.

Learning: The dynamic process by which changes occur in behavior as a result of new insights and understandings of environmental contingencies.

Loss: An acute awareness of being deprived of a desired relationship to a person, object, goal, state, or self.

Lunar month: 28 days, or 4 weeks.

Maturation: The process of achieving full or *optimal development* of a component or skill. In the biophysical domain, the final differentiation or refinement in the functioning of cells, tissues, and organs, and the establishment of cooperation among the components of the body.

Maturational crisis: The confrontation of an individual with the need to master a developmental task.

Maximization of potentials: Uninhibited, judicious use of one's innate talents, current abilities, and external resources. Minimal energy is expended in maintaining optimal functioning.

Need: A factor essential for an individual's continued growth and development; may arise from any domain. Failure of the environment to meet the need results in disequilibrium, failure to maximize potentials, or even death.

Neonate: The first month or 28 days of life.

Object constancy: *Piaget*—The cognitive awareness that an object or person is the same object or person regardless of the angle or location from which the person or object is viewed. This skill generally appears at about 5 months. *Mahler*—The affective and cognitive ability to retain an image of (or symbol for) mother (or other primary meaningful relationship) within memory to *refuel* from that image in the absence of the person.

Object permanence: The cognitive awareness that an object continues to exist even though one is not in direct contact with the object. In sighted infants, this skill usually appears at about 8 months.

Object relations: In psychoanalytic theory, the emotional

---

[2]Horton, T. E. (1977). Conceptual basis for nursing intervention with human systems: Families. In J. E. Hall & B. R. Weaver (Eds.), *Distributive nursing practice: A systems approach to community health.* Philadelphia: J. B. Lippincott.

[3]Mussen, P. H., et. al. (1990). *Child Development and Personality* (7th ed.) New York: Harper and Row.

investment in another person—particularly the primary relationship with the mother.

Ontogenetic: Referring to the developmental history of an individual.

Ordinal position: The birth order or hierarchical status held by a child within the family system.

Parameter: A particular value characterizing the limits of a specific function or population.

Peers: One's equals, companions, or counterparts.

Perception: Interpretation of sensory stimuli.

Perinatal: The period immediately surrounding birth.

Perineal: Pertaining to the pelvic floor and the associated structures occupying the pelvic outlet.

Personality: The integrated totality of the characteristic habits, attitudes, and ideas of an individual and the distinctive organization of his or her responses to social stimuli.[4]

Phenotype: The characteristics an individual displays for a particular trait based on genetic makeup.

Practitioner: A professional person who has been trained to develop intervention strategies designed to alleviate problems encountered in the processes of living.

Preadolescence (pubescence): The period between childhood and adolescence, marked by physical and emotional transition to adolescence.

Proactive: Growth-producing, adaptive behaviors guided by one's values and goals, allowing the individual to maintain control of personal responses or environmental events. Opposite of *reactive,* when the individual exhibits "knee jerk" reactions with little or no control over personal responses to environmental stimuli or events.

Prosocial: Behavior directed toward acquiring more mature social behaviors, meeting the needs of others, or facilitating more cooperative relationships.

Psychosocial: The joint reference to the affective and social domains. The intrapersonal and interpersonal responses of an individual to external events.

Pubertal period: The span of time surrounding puberty when the body undergoes primary and secondary sexual changes that prepare the individual for reproduction.

Puberty: That point in time when the individual is first capable of reproduction; the initial production of gametes.

Pubescence: *see* **Preadolescence.**

RBC: Red blood cells.

Reciprocity: Social give and take; a complementary interchange. A state of mutual dependence, requiring cooperation and respect.

Reflex: A naturally occurring, involuntary, unlearned neuromuscular response to a stimulus.

---

[4]Smith, W. C. (1953). *The stepchild,* (p. 202). Chicago: University of Chicago Press.

Refueling: The process of making contact with a significant person to obtain the emotional reassurance and affirmation that provides emotional energy to face the exigencies of life. Mahler uses this term to describe the young child's attempts to reestablish bodily contact with the primary caregiver in order to restore sufficient affective energy to allow for independent exploration and interaction with the environment.

Schema (pl. **schemata**)**:** According to Piaget, a unit or category of thought; a classification for a phenomenon, behavior, or event.

Sensorimotor: Those behaviors that involve the combined use of sensory skills and body movements to understand and bring about interaction with the environment.

Sibling: An individual sharing the same parents.

Situational crisis: Any event arising from the individual's interaction with the environment that constitutes a stressor. These events usually occur suddenly (e.g., confrontation with authority, illness, natural disaster, separation from significant others).

Social domain: One's external responses to events; one's interpersonal relationships and social skills.

Somatic: Pertaining to the body.

Sphincter: A ringlike band of muscle fibers that constricts a passage or closes a natural opening.

Spiritual domain: One's life force, soul, consciousness of existence; one's transcendental relationships.

State 4: The quiet, alert, awake state of consciousness found in the neonate and young infant. The child is most attentive to environmental stimuli in this state.

Stimulus (pl. **stimuli**)**:** An event, agent, or action that is perceived through the senses and elicits a response.

Stress: The arousal the mind and body experience when a demand taxes a person's resources or coping abilities.

Stressor: Events and stimuli that cause stress.

Subsystem: The components of the target unit of study.

Successive approximations: The gradual changing of behaviors toward a desired end behavior. At each step, a higher level of performance (incorporating more aspects of the terminal skill) is acquired until the end behavior is achieved.

Suprasystem: Any selected unit or group outside of the target system that impacts on the functioning of the unit.

Synthesize: To combine components to form a whole or an integrated entity.

System: The target unit of study.

Trimester: A 3-month period, usually connected with the pregnancy process.

Variable: A characteristic or value that is subject to change; an arbitrary factor that may or may not affect the functioning of the unit under study.

Variation: An alternative or predictable behavior. Not considered pathological.

APPENDICES

Appendix A
*Developmental Tasks of Life Phases**

CLARA S. SCHUSTER

The Beginning of Life (Pre-, Peri-, and Postnatal)

*1. Develop body systems sufficiently to maintain extra-uterine life
*2. Develop awareness of and contingently respond to environmental stimuli
*3. Adopt techniques for controlling the state of alertness

Infancy

*1. Establish a meaningful emotional/social relationship
*2. Learn how to learn
*3. Develop social communication skills
4. Develop voluntary control of neuromuscular systems
5. Establish rhythms for activities of daily living
6. Recognize self as a person, physically separate from attachment person

Toddler and Preschooler

*1. Recognize self as a person, psychologically separate from attachment person
*2. Learn how to harness and focus energies
*3. Learn prosocial behaviors (to be socialized)
*4. Adopt collective communication skills
*5. Develop basic self-control skills
*6. Learn to live with consequences of own choices
7. Coordinate body movements for skill mastery
8. Learn basic values and mores of the family and culture
9. Function independently in basic activities of daily living
10. Seek information and understanding

School-agers

*1. Derive a sense of belonging from associations with others
*2. Learn how to work
*3. Establish a conscience
4. Master the basic skills valued by the society
5. Develop competence in selected areas
6. Develop appreciation of socially/culturally generated roles
7. Participate in and identify with cultural traditions

8. Balance the issues of dependence, independence, and interdependence
9. Refine communication skills
10. Refine motor strength and coordination

Adolescence

*1. Appreciate own uniqueness
*2. Develop independent, internal identity
*3. Determine own value system
*4. Develop self-evaluation skills
*5. Assume increasing responsibility for own behavior
6. Find meaning in life
7. Acquire skills essential for adult living
8. Seek affiliations outside of family of origin
9. Adapt to adult body functioning

Early Adulthood

*1. Achieve independence from, or establish contributory interdependence with, family of origin
*2. Identify the basis of own personal worth
*3. Develop ability to share inner self with others to increase understanding and cooperation (emotional intimacy)
*4. Find something higher than self to live for
5. Develop satisfying social relationships
6. Balance expression of personal needs and interests with the expectations and opportunities of the culture
7. Assume responsibility for independent decision making
8. Develop expertise in career (includes parenting)

Middlescence

*1. Find self-confidence in inner identity, values
*2. Balance or come to grips with discrepancies among dreams, goals, and realities
*3. Develop a philosophy for dealing with own mortality
*4. Identify and share factors that give life meaning and continuity
*5. Extend sense of caring and responsibility beyond the immediate families of origin or creation
6. Develop wisdom
7. Establish new relationships with other people
8. Find satisfaction in career or job
9. Adapt to changes in physical domain
10. Assume active responsibility for maintaining high-level wellness in all five domains

---

*The tasks with their explanatory subtasks are presented at the beginning of each relevant unit throughout the text. The tasks marked with an asterisk are deemed most crucial to continued maturation and development.

Late Adulthood

*1. Find satisfaction in reduced or nonemployment activities
*2. Validate value, meaning, and responsibilities of life lived
*3. Prepare for own death
4. Pace activities with physical ability and endurance
5. Maintain maximal independence in activities of daily living

Family Tasks

*1. Clearly identify who does and who does not belong to the family system
*2. Develop deep commitment to the welfare of the family unit as well as to each of its members
*3. Maintain open communication for expression of needs, values, frustrations, disappointments, excitements, ideas, interests, etc.

*4. Appreciate and support the uniqueness of each family member
*5. Establish common philosophies, values, and goals
*6. Establish rules regulating conduct and relationships consistent with family philosophies, values, and goals
*7. Divide responsibilities for maintenance of the family as an effective functioning unit

Life-Span Needs

1. Acceptance
2. Companionship
3. Challenges and goals
4. Support
5. Service opportunities

Appendix B
Selected Theories of Development

SHIRLEY S. ASHBURN

Sigmund Freud

Alfred Adler

Harry Stack Sullivan

Erik H. Erikson

Abraham Maslow

B. F. Skinner

Robert J. Havighurst

Jean Piaget

Human behavior is complex, and the theories proposed to explain it are diverse and, at times, in conflict. It becomes evident in reading selected theorists that there is no ultimate answer that consistently or comprehensively describes human behavior. At best, the available theories give only a partial view of development—explaining only one domain or only a brief period of the life span. Consequently, to understand human development from a holistic view, one must use more than one theory to explain behavior. Each of the theorists is discussed in terms of his concept of human growth and development, the major concepts and terms, the techniques of inquiry, and the practical applications of the theory.

SIGMUND FREUD (1856–1939)

Sigmund Freud offered the first formal theory of personality. His ideas have probably influenced contemporary personality theory more than the thoughts of any other single individual. It is therefore logical to introduce Sigmund Freud and his subject matter first in this brief discussion of theorists and theories. His theory deals mainly with the affective domain and its influence on the social domain.

Freud's concept of personality development, like those of others to be studied, was heavily influenced by his own early childhood experiences. The confidence and pride expressed by Freud's mother is reflected in his lifelong characteristic of an extremely high degree of self-confidence.[21] Freud loved his mother dearly and worked hard to retain her favor. He originally chose medicine as a career because he thought that medical study would help him to attain the personal goal of scientific research. However, after receiving his medical degree at the University of Vienna, Freud lacked the independent income needed to expedite his goal. He therefore established a practice as a clinical neurologist and began to study the personalities of those experiencing emotional disturbances. It was during these years that Freud was greatly influenced by the process of hypnosis, as well as by Dr. Josef Breuner's "talking-cure" method. Using these methods, Freud worked very intensely with his patients and listened carefully as his patients described their childhood experiences. From these scenarios, he gradually developed a theory about the processes and functions of the personality.

As Freud's popularity grew, he attracted many followers (most of whom were physicians), who often met with him weekly. The Nazis considered Freud an "enemy of the state," but it was not until after the arrest of his daughter, Anna, that he fled from Vienna to London. He died in London in 1939, having continued his work almost until his death.[12]

Freud's Major Concepts and Terms

Freud defined *instinct* as the representation in the mind of energy that originates within the body. He viewed this stimulus as basic to the personality and as the force that drives and gives direction to behavior.[9] Freud hypothesized that an innate psychic structure organized the personality into the id, the ego, and the superego (see Chap. 16).

Freud viewed anxiety as the source of neurotic and psychotic behavior. He conceived of three types of anxiety, all differing in their potential threat to the individual. It was his daughter, Anna Freud, who described *defense mechanisms,* which are viewed as the response that an individual makes in an attempt to cope with and reduce anxiety (see Chap. 39).

Freud's Concept of Human Growth and Development

Freud believed that a person's unique character develops from the quality of the mother–child interaction. He explained behavior by analyzing the conflicts among instincts, reality, and society. He grouped instincts into two categories: life instincts and death instincts. Life instincts are oriented toward growth and development, trying to satisfy the individual's needs for food, water, air, and sex. Freud termed the form of psychic energy manifested by the life instincts as the *libido.* He postulated the *aggressive drive* as an important component of the death instinct—the wish to die turned against objects other than the self.[9]

Freud theorized that the development of these life forces follows certain stages, during which the foci or body sites of energy change as the concomitant tasks related to them are mastered. He concentrated on the mouth, anus, and sex organs as these foci. Freud stated that in each stage a conflict exists that must be resolved satisfactorily before the individual can progress to the next stage. He believed that people could become fixated at any stage or any part of these stages and that this fixation would be demonstrated in their adult behavior.[9]

Freud's Technique of Inquiry

Since Freud considered the major motivational forces to be in the unconscious, he devised free association and dream analysis as his two basic methods of acquiring data. He felt that relaxed individuals who said out loud everything that came to their minds might eventually purify problems from repressed experiences. Freud also believed that the analysis of dreams could unravel unpleasant memories that had long been repressed.[9]

Freud allowed no one else to observe or interpret the data his patients gave him, and this behavior led to much criticism of his theory. Many of his followers modified his theory and thus gave birth to new concepts—their theories follow in the next few pages.

Applicability of Freud's Theory

Experimental psychologists contend that psychoanalysis is not based on systematic, controlled research. It should be pointed out, however, that most experimental psychologists also disagree with other personality theorists and their subjective approaches to interpreting human behavior.

Some of Freud's critics feel that people are more strongly influenced by social experiences than by libidinal or sexual energies. Most believe that people have more control over their behavior than Freud acknowledges. The fact that Freud based his theory on observations of many emotionally crippled individuals is another reason his concepts are not always fully accepted. Another argument is based on the fact that Freud's basic assumptions (e.g., the Oedipal complex) do not appear to be applicable across cultures.

Despite all these criticisms, Freud presented a foundation for personality theory that has not been equaled. His theory can be used in implementing psychotherapy, guiding parent–child relations, and interpreting normal as well as abnormal behavior.

ALFRED ADLER (1870–1937)

Alfred Adler's concepts of the uniqueness of humans represented the first major departure from Freud's theory. Adler emphasized the conscious as the core of personality. Believing that personality is shaped by one's social environments and interactions, he proposed that individuals can actively guide and fashion their own growth and development.[1]

Adler was the second-born of six children of a Viennese merchant. It is easy to assume that Adler drew from the experiences of his own unhappy childhood when he proposed that a person can compensate for feelings of inferiority. (Adler was unable to run and play with other children because he had rickets. When he was 3 years old, he saw his younger brother die in the bed next to him.) Initially viewed as awkward and unattractive, Adler expended much energy to gain acceptance from his peers. He wanted to increase his sense of worth—a positive feeling he had not attained within his home and family. Adler rose from being considered a mediocre student who should not pursue an academic career to become the best student in the class.[21]

After studying medicine at the University of Vienna and several attempts in various fields of medicine, he entered neurology and psychiatry. Adler worked closely with Sigmund Freud for 9 years; however, their relationship was not a particularly friendly one. After World War I, Adler organized many government-sponsored child counseling clinics in Vienna. He was very busy in the following years, frequently visiting the United States to lecture. It was on a lecture tour that he succumbed to a heart attack in 1937.[21]

Adler's Concepts and Terms

Adler believed that inferiority feelings are ever-present in humans and are the stimulus for growth. He felt that a person could compensate for either imagined or real inferiorities. Adler proposed that a person could develop an *inferiority complex* or "an inability to solve life's problems" (1) by being organically inferior, (2) by being spoiled and then having to meet rejection, or (3) by being neglected. He believed that people strive for "superiority" or "perfection" and are always seeking improvement. This quest for superiority increases tension and thus calls forth more efforts. Adler also believed that the best situation for making these efforts was that of a self-reliant individual working cooperatively with others within his culture.[2]

Adler's Emphasis on Human Growth and Development

Adler believed that each individual cultivates a unique pattern of striving for superiority; that is, every person formulates a lifestyle or character. This lifestyle is learned from early parent-child interactions. Adler postulated that one's lifestyle is firmly set by early childhood.[1] Even the very young, he said, are free to interpret their experiences. An individual may choose to change in later years only if he or she realizes that inappropriate and disturbing responses are inadequate "holdovers" from childhood.[2] Adler believed that getting along with others is the first task one encounters in life; this way of coping becomes a basis for later behavior. He also proposed birth order as one of the major social factors in one's childhood that affects the type of lifestyle one chooses.

According to Adler, all individuals must solve three categories of problems during their lifetime—problems involving behavior toward others, problems of occupation, and problems of love. He spoke of four basic styles that people use in working through these problems: avoidance, expecting to get everything from others, dominating others, and cooperating with others by acting in accordance with their needs.[21]

Adler's Techniques of Inquiry

Adler developed his theory from information he gained in informal conversations with his patients. He paid particular attention to body language (the expression of feelings or thoughts by means of bodily movements). Adler also gained information by analyzing order of birth and dreams, and by asking clients to recall their first memories of childhood.[17]

Some criticize Adler's theory for its simplicity; others state that he was not always systematic and that he left many questions unanswered. There are also those who question how a child less than 5 years of age can choose his or her own lifestyle.

Alfred Adler's theory has become most applicable to school guidance counseling, penal reform, psychosomatic medicine, and individual psychology.

HARRY STACK SULLIVAN (1892–1949)

Harry Stack Sullivan's conception of personality is a unique blend of biology, sociology, psychiatry, and social psychology.

He believed that an individual should be studied only in terms of interactions with others. He did not believe that one's personality is firmly fixed during the preschool years; he believed that personality could change greatly until and during the adolescent years.

After Sullivan's family moved to a New York farm when he was 3 years old, his closest "friends" were the farm animals. The Sullivans were the only Roman Catholic family in a Yankee Protestant community, and he was the only surviving child in his immediate family—he apparently knew loneliness from early childhood. One of Sullivan's close friends claims that it was only in his adult years that Sullivan was finally able to establish a comfortable relationship with his father, and only after Sullivan's mother died.[16]

Sullivan is reported to have felt very "out of place" during his school years and to have had a traumatic adolescence. During his early 20s, when he was in medical school, he studied psychoanalysis and entered into it as a patient. Later, as an executive medical officer in a rehabilitation division of the Federal Board for Vocational Education, he became interested in working with individuals with neuropsychiatric conditions; he especially wanted to know what kept the neurotic from becoming schizophrenic. Sullivan believed that the cultural environment greatly shapes a person's personality. Studying patients' behavior as a psychiatrist both in hospital settings and in his private office, he focused on their interpersonal relations.

Sullivan's Major Concepts and Terms

Personification was Sullivan's term for a group of related attitudes, feelings, and concepts about oneself or another that have been acquired from extensive experience. He referred to *experience* as events that the individual participates in and that become more distinct and ordered during development.[20]

Sullivan identified three ways of experiencing the world around us—three levels of thinking by which a person relates to others, called the **prototaxic, parataxic,** and **syntaxic** experiences. These various perceptions range from simply perceiving sensations immediately as they occur, to learning logical relationships and being able to test one's perceptions against those possessed by others (see Chaps. 8 and 11).

Sullivan's Concept of Human Growth and Development

Sullivan focused on the individual as a product of the interpersonal environment. Like many other theorists, he believed that development of the self is sequential with the individual's accumulating significant experiences.[22] Sullivan thought that the juvenile era (see the list below) was the first developmental stage in which the limitations and peculiarities of the home as a socializing agent began to be opened for remedy. If the limitations of the home were not remedied during this time, he thought, subsequent development might be warped.[16] He stressed that tension and anxiety arise from a person's interaction with the environment. He also believed that the individual consists relatively equally of rational cognitive processes and irrational emotional processes.

Sullivan divided the life span as follows:[23]

1. *Infancy* lasts to the maturation of the capacity for language behavior.
2. *Childhood* lasts to the maturation of the capacity for getting along with peers (until about 5 or 6 years of age).
3. *The juvenile era* lasts to the maturation of the capacity for **isophilic intimacy** (Sullivan's term for affection or liking for others of the same gender, such affection is lacking the genital element characteristic of homosexuality), until about 9 or 10 years of age.
4. *Preadolescence* lasts to the maturation of the "genital lust dynamisms," i.e., "chumships" or the "first reciprocal love relationship" (from about 10 or 11 to 13 years of age).
5. *Early adolescence* lasts to the maturation of the patterning of lustful behavior (until the age of about 17 years).
6. *Late adolescence* lasts to maturity (until the early twenties).

Sullivan proposed that during a person's early twenties, if all positive components of his theory had been met by the individual, the individual was ready to take a place as a full-fledged member of society.[21]

Sullivan's Techniques of Inquiry

Although he used some dream analysis, Sullivan gained most of his data from his patients through interviews. His interviewing approach was unique in that he believed that as the therapist, he should be both a participant and an observer. This approach led to a lengthy series of interviews involving significant interpersonal interactions.

Applicability of Sullivan's Theory

Very little criticism of Sullivan's theory exists. Perhaps part of the reason for this is that most of his works were lectures and papers published posthumously; these unsystematic works have not led to much research or critique of his theory. Nevertheless, his emphasis on working with an individual's potentials and his methods of treatment of individuals experiencing schizophrenia are becoming widely admired. Areas in which Sullivan's theory can be of great value are psychotherapy, interpersonal communication, parent–child relations, and education.

Sullivan collaborated with many scientists and devoted much of his time and energy to international affairs in the pursuit of world peace. Dr. Charles S. Johnson, then President of Fisk University, made the following remark at memorial services for Sullivan: "[Sullivan was the] hope of understanding and controlling the group tensions and international conflicts by which our civilization is now so darkly endan-

gered."[23] Patrick Mullahy, a noted author and psychiatrist, has stated his belief that "in the history of modern psychiatry, Sullivan will be ranked second only to Freud."[16]

ERIK H. ERIKSON (1902–)

Erik Erikson was trained by Sigmund Freud's daughter, Anna Freud. He augmented Freud's theory by adding culture and society (in addition to biological forces) as factors that influence personality development. Erikson also believes, unlike Freud, that personality continues to develop through the life span. Unlike most other psychoanalysts, Erikson has made special efforts to have experiences with children who were not emotionally disturbed as well as with those who were.

Erikson's career has been most diverse. He was born of Danish parents in Frankfurt, Germany. His father died soon after his birth, and his mother later married a pediatrician who had cured young Erikson of a childhood illness. Because his stepfather adopted him, some of Erikson's early papers are written under the name Homberger. Later, when he became an American citizen in 1939, he chose to be known by his original name.[13]

Erikson, who coined the term **identity crisis,** apparently experienced several such crises during his younger years. For example, he was not told for several years that Homberger was not his biological father. Erikson later labeled this situation as one of *loving deceit.* Erikson was rejected by his peers both at school and at synagogue; his German classmates rejected him because he was Jewish, and his Jewish friends rejected him because his appearance, that of a tall, blond Dane, caused him to look very unlike the rest of them.[21]

After achieving only mediocre grades in school, Erikson "dropped out" of society. He made two attempts at attending art school during that period, but each time he chose to leave and resume his wandering throughout Germany and Italy (he says that he spent his time "neurotically" reading, recording his thoughts in a notebook, and observing life around him).[21]

At the age of 25, Erikson began his professional career. He accepted an invitation to teach at a small school in Vienna that had been established for the children of Sigmund Freud's patients and friends. At this time he received training in psychoanalysis that was conducted by Anna Freud, and her special interest in the psychoanalysis of children became his as well.

Erikson later settled in Boston and set up a private practice specializing in the treatment of children.[21] In 1936 Erikson accepted an invitation from the Institute of Human Relations at Yale University to teach. It was at Yale that he and an anthropologist focused their studies on the ways children were reared among the Sioux Indians of South Dakota. This study affected Erikson's thoughts on the influence of culture on childhood events. He noticed symptoms related to a feeling of being alienated from one's cultural customs that resulted in an unclear, confused self-image or identity; he noted similar symptoms when he observed emotionally disturbed World War II veterans who had experienced crisis-filled war situations. Erikson called this phenomenon *identity confusion,* a concept that could not be described or applied while using only Freudian theory.[10, 21]

Erikson taught both at the Institute of Child Welfare at the University of California at Berkeley and at Harvard University before he retired in 1970. Erikson continues to be involved in psychohistorical analyses that explain the lives of influential persons; and in writing about additional insights on his theory.[6]

Erikson's Major Concepts and Terms

Erikson is concerned with psychosocial development, or human development viewed in terms of its dependence on interaction with others. He views experience as feeding into *ego-identity,* the synthesis of accumulated experiences of the individual's view of self. He defines eight stages of growth for humans. Simultaneously, within each developmental phase, two opposing forces cause a crisis and demand a solution. Erikson defines successful resolution as giving one the opportunity to advance to the next of his "eight stages of man" (see Appendix C). He sees failure or delay as an obstacle to the optimal development of the individual. However, an unsuccessful resolution may be resolved later in life under positive circumstances.[5]

Erikson's Concept of Human Growth and Development

Unlike Freud, Erikson believes that an individual's social view of self is more important than libidinal urges. Erikson's relatively more optimistic outlook on human growth and development also speaks to new opportunities for particular strengths to develop at each stage. These "basic virtues" emerge only when each crisis is met and must be continuously upheld throughout a person's lifetime to be useful. The task of identity (adolescence) is seen as the major task of life. All previous tasks were foundational to self-discovery, and all adult tasks are predicated on comfortable resolution of "identity homework." The reader should refer to Appendix C to review Erikson's stages of the life span; they are discussed throughout the chapters in this text, especially in Chapter 25.

Erikson's Techniques of Inquiry

Erikson holds that no single technique of data collection can be applied in the same way to every subject. Instead, he believes the technique should be highly individualized. His techniques varied from watching children play with toys to being a participant–observer among Indian tribes. He is well-known for his psychohistorical approach to prominent people. Using what he calls "disciplined subjectivity," he attempts to incorporate other people's perceptions of their own lives and his own so that he can better explain how they dealt with various crises in their lives.

Erikson's works are sometimes criticized because he has not defined some of his concepts (e.g., fidelity, hope) well enough for further research. There are also those who disagree with Erikson's concept of "identity" as applied to women; these critics suggest that women find identity through affiliation, whereas men find identity through individualization.[8]

Applicability of Erikson's Theory

Erikson is a very influential theorist. His developmental framework offers a guide to rearing and understanding children. His theory is also applied in psychotherapy, psychiatry, education, and to the psychoanalytic meaning of moral responsibility.

ABRAHAM MASLOW (1908–1970)

Abraham Maslow is renowned for his contributions to humanistic psychology. Maslow believed that to determine the apex of human potential, he had to study what he considered to be the very best representatives of the species. He diligently studied a large group of personalities, some of whom were no longer living (e.g., case histories of Abraham Lincoln and Thomas Jefferson) to extract what he believed to be the salient factors for successful development.

Born of Russian Jewish immigrant parents who wanted their son to rise above their lot in life, Maslow unhappily maintained his minority group status throughout his childhood. Out of loneliness he began to read, projecting that learning would pave the way out of the Brooklyn ghetto into which he had been born. He said that he wanted to study "everything"! At the University of Wisconsin, he received training from Harry Harlow (working with behaviorism and experiments with monkeys). It was also during this time that he married his fiancée of 4 years. (He proclaimed that it was only with his marriage and entry to the University of Wisconsin that his life began.) He attributed the birth of his first child as the culminating force that pulled him away from behaviorism ("I was stunned by the mystery and by the sense of not really being in control") and thrust him toward the development of his humanistic theory. A deeply sensitive man, Maslow was so disturbed by World War II that he dedicated himself to improving the human condition. In addition to engaging in research at several institutions of higher learning, he also formulated a political, economic, and ethical philosophy (with an obvious humanistic psychology base) while working under a foundation grant at Brandeis University.[21]

Maslow's Major Concepts and Terms

Maslow proposed a hierarchy of needs that must be met by each individual in order to reach his or her potential. Those forces motivating development in the first stages must be satisfied before the forces of the next stage can become the focus. However, one stage (or need) does not have to be fully conquered before the next sequential one is undertaken. Partial satisfaction of needs will allow the person to work on the next stage, but with a decreasing percentage of satisfaction in each need as a person climbs the hierarchy. However, only one of these needs can be dominant at a time.

At the bottom of Maslow's hierarchy, the physiological needs assume priority. Once these needs have been satisfied, safety needs become the focus. Next in importance are the needs for "belongingness" and love, followed by the need for esteem. Potentials are realized when the final stage of self-actualization is reached. After reaching this stage, the individual must continue to "be" or to be actively engaged in "doing one's thing"; otherwise, that person's potentials will cease to be fully realized. Obviously, there are several prerequisites to attaining or maintaining a state of self-actualization; among these are freedom from either self-restraints or cultural restraints, realistic self-assessment, and an emotionally supportive environment (see Chap. 39).[14, 15]

Maslow estimated that only 1% or less of the population ever become self-actualizing individuals. He postulated that self-actualization, although an innate need, cannot be universal, because the other four needs in his hierarchy are hard to meet in a poverty-stricken, emotionally deprived environment. He also believed that the hierarchy does not apply to all individuals, because some people may become satisfied with meeting lower-level needs.[15]

Maslow's Concept of Human Growth and Development

Maslow stated that because an individual's "inner nature is good or neutral rather than bad, it is best to bring it out and to encourage it rather than to suppress it."[15] Although he emphasized the important influence of early childhood on later development, he did not believe that a person was a slave to his past. He felt, for example, that excessive freedom in childhood could lead to an insecure adulthood. What Maslow termed *freedom within limits* was the correct equation for laying the foundation for a potentially self-actualizing person. He also stressed that satisfaction of basic needs was crucial within the first 2 years of life if a child were to become a secure adult (the need for safety being strongest, he said, during the infant years). Maslow pointed out that most normal adults still require some degree of security.

Maslow also believed that the need to know and to understand begins in late infancy and in childhood. Inhibiting a child's curiosity could, he said, retard the child's development of a fully functioning personality. He made many statements about the tasks a healthy child must accomplish (although he did not arbitrarily attach these tasks to any age groups)—he said that a child "must give up being good out of fear" and rather should be good because he wants to be. He also said that the child "must become responsible rather than dependent, and hopefully must become able to enjoy this responsibility."[15]

Maslow's Techniques of Inquiry

Maslow concluded that self-actualizing people possess a common pattern of personal characteristics. In his search for these characteristics in others, he soon decided that college students in Western culture had not yet developed traits that could be labeled as self-actualizing. After studying middle-age and older individuals, he concluded that very few people attain that stage of his hierarchy. To study the subjects whom he thought self-actualized, Maslow explained that he used any available technique that appeared to be appropriate; the techniques ranged from analyzing biographical sketches of deceased individuals to administering the Rorschach ink blot test to persons still living.[21]

Applicability of Maslow's Theory

Maslow's concern for humanity was evident from his writings and from the dedication of his life. Maslow realized that critics would be skeptical of his lack of systematic research in forming his theory. His reply was that since the problem could not have been studied by rigorous scientific procedures, the only alternative would have been not to study it at all.[21] The goal of self-actualization as an innate need has also been questioned.

It goes without saying that Maslow's theory has prompted more research on the problems of realizing human potential. His theory has become immensely popular among the young, among psychologists, and among the educated public. Sensitivity-training group sessions make use of his ideas. There are even heads of business who incorporate Maslow's concepts as a way of increasing employee drive.

B. F. SKINNER (1904–1990)

The reader might wonder why B. F. Skinner, a controversial theorist who does not speculate on (or consider very important) the topic of personality, is included in this section of the text. The answer is that not only has his viewpoint been extremely productive of research, but his attempt to account for all human behavior strictly in terms of what can be observed remains a strong force in psychology today. Skinner did not believe that a person is controlled by any innate or inner conscious drive; he asserted that the only way to predict and control behavior is by correlating the person's behavior with what is occurring in the person's environment.

It would appear that many events in Skinner's adult life (as well as basic concepts in his theory) were grounded in his childhood experiences. He was born in Susquehanna, Pennsylvania, to a family that administered continuous admonitions about what God, other people, and the police might think about his actions. As a child he loved animals and the study of animal behavior. He later even taught pigeons to play Ping-Pong.[21]

Skinner enjoyed school so much that he was usually the first to arrive each day. Later, while majoring in English at

Hamilton College in New York, he became disenchanted with many different facets of the collegiate scene—sports (in which he did not excel), curriculum requirements (he did not feel that any were necessary), and his fellow students (he thought they lacked academic motivation). His discontent grew, as did his mischievous pranks. At one point he was cautioned that he would have to behave during his commencement exercises if he wished to graduate (it would appear that he had already established his pattern of not really caring if he was considered different by others). After graduation, his intention and desire were to become a writer. Although he constructed a study in his parents' attic, he soon found that he used his time in that room for everything, it seemed, except writing—listening to the radio, building ship models, and, eventually, wondering if he needed to see a psychiatrist. He moved to Greenwich Village in New York City and later toured Europe. During this time he decided that he himself had "nothing to write" but that he still wanted to understand human behavior. Inspired by the writing of Pavlov and Watson, he entered Harvard graduate school to study psychology. By adhering to an extremely rigid schedule, he completed his doctoral studies in 3 years.[21]

Skinner's Major Concepts and Terms

Skinner displayed little interest in the individual person; he was searching for general laws of human behavior in terms of stimulus and response. He accounted for differences in human behavior by saying that experiences evoke varying responses, or reinforcement value. He viewed the human being as a machine that always operates according to fixed laws. Very simply, he stated that all behavior can be controlled. It is the kind and the extent of reinforcement that follows a behavior that determines if that behavior will be repeated.

Skinner identified two kinds of behavior—respondent and operant. *Respondent behavior* occurs when a response is elicited by a known and specific stimulus. Respondent behaviors can be simple, as in the initiation of a reflex action, or learned, such as those behaviors involved in conditioning. *Operant behaviors* are those that are emitted to obtain a response or reinforcement from the environment or from other persons.[22]

Skinner's Concept of Human Growth and Development

Skinner believed that beginning in infancy, selected human behaviors become reinforced in such a way that they form patterns. These patterns of behavior are referred to as "personality" by Skinner (it must be noted that he discussed this concept infrequently, because he believed it is of no relative significance).[3]

Since Skinner believed that all aspects of behavior are controlled from without and that a person is a product of past reinforcements, it follows that his thoughts on child rearing deal with manipulating a child's environment so that certain behaviors will be reinforced at certain intervals over a period of time. He did believe that, later in life, people can control their futures by controlling their environments.[22]

Skinner's Techniques of Inquiry

Skinner's methods of research are extremely different from those of the other theorists mentioned in this section. First, he derived his theories from studies of animals. Rationalizing that all behavior follows the same laws, he reasoned that animals and humans are alike (the only difference being that humans can learn to control not only themselves but the environment as well). In addition, Skinner chose to study one subject at a time. He believed that since all behavior is guided by the same rules, any information gained can be applied to all animals (including humans). He made use of an operant conditioning apparatus that has come to be known as a *Skinner box*. Using this apparatus, the experimenter can control subject behavior by limiting stimuli and controlling the reinforcement schedule.

Applicability of Skinner's Theory

Although application of Skinner's theory is readily apparent in many areas, his approach has been censured, especially by humanistic critics. He is criticized especially for his generalization of animal research to human beings. However, one must note that his theory has been used effectively with members of every phylogenetic level, including humans (even gifted adults). Many find his concept of human behavior (being totally controlled by external forces) as dehumanizing and threatening. Nevertheless, Skinner remains an influential force in psychology. His principle of operant conditioning has led the way to effective use of behavior modification in classrooms, prisons, residential and mental institutions, and even in the home by parents. "Brain-washing" is an example of the systematic use of behaviorist principles.

Skinner maintained that he was not bothered by his critics (who, he said, did not understand him) and that his research proved that humans can make the world a better place in which to live through systematic alteration of the environment. He taught in several universities, and was Professor Emeritus of Psychology at Harvard University until his death.

ROBERT J. HAVIGHURST (1900–1991)

No text that discusses human growth and development would be complete without mention of Robert Havighurst's concept of developmental tasks. He did not originate the concept of developmental tasks, but rather identified those tasks he believed crucial to healthy development. Havighurst believed that "living in a modern society is a long series of tasks to learn, where effective learning will bring satisfaction and reward; while learning poorly brings unhappiness and social disapproval."[11] Havighurst said that he was greatly influenced by Erikson's theory of psychosocial development, and especially by his publications on adolescence and identity.[11]

Havighurst's Major Concepts and Terms

Havighurst defined a developmental task as "the task which arises at or about a certain period in the life of the individual, successful achievement of which leads to his happiness and to success with later tasks, while failure leads to unhappiness in the individual, disapproval by the society, and difficulty with later tasks."[11] He added that such a task represents a combination between an individual's need and society's demands.

Some developmental tasks arise primarily because of physical maturation (e.g., learning to walk). Others arise mainly from the cultural pressure of society (e.g., learning to read). Still another source of developmental tasks, according to Havighurst, is the personal values and goals of the individual. He believed that by age 3 or 4, the individual's personality is active in identifying and mastering developmental tasks.

Havighurst stated that there may be critical periods in the development of an individual when the organism is maximally receptive to specific stimuli, termed *teachable moments*. He also noted that some tasks are recurrent through life (e.g., "learning to get along with age-mates").

Havighurst's Concept of Human Growth and Development

Havighurst summarized and discussed the principal developmental tasks of six age periods, each period, in turn, containing six to ten developmental tasks. The reader will find his developmental tasks in Appendix C.

Havighurst's Techniques of Inquiry

Havighurst gained much of his insight and formed many of his concepts while studying growth and development in the academic world and while working under the auspices of the General Education Board at the Rockefeller Foundation. Havighurst's major approach to data gathering appears to be observation of naturalistic behaviors.

Applicability of Havighurst's Theory

Havighurst's developmental tasks concept "occupies middle ground between the two opposing theories of education: the theory of freedom—that the child will develop best if left as free as possible, and the theory of constraint—that the child must learn to become a worthy, responsible adult through restraints imposed by his society."[11]

There are those who criticize the way Havighurst divided the life span (especially his inclusion of so many significant developmental milestones in just one period—infancy and early childhood). His tasks are limited to what he called the American culture, and although at times he spoke to the different foci emphasized by various socioeconomic levels, he still adhered for the most part to middle-class norms and able-bodied persons. Some critics feel that his work is outdated in parts; for example, he described early adulthood as a time to marry and rear children (not everyone today has a similar goal), and he spoke of middle-age persons as strengthening their occupational associations (many "occupationally mobile" people in this age group today leave one job for another, and the type of work may be in completely different fields).

Regardless of these criticisms, Havighurst's ideas have proved useful to many people who seek a general understanding of development in American culture. They are especially valuable to educators. Havighurst maintained an active retirement as a professor of education and human development and a member of the Committee on Human Development from the University of Chicago.

JEAN PIAGET (1896–1980)

Jean Piaget was one of the most influential contemporary psychologists. The works written by Piaget and his associates (originally in French) focus on the cognitive development of childhood. Piaget is especially interested in **how** the mind works and organizes information, rather than in **what** or **how much** it remembers.[18]

Piaget was born in 1896 in Neuchâtel, Switzerland. He said that his intelligent parents influenced him in several ways to study both psychology and genetic epistemology (study of how knowledge is acquired). Piaget recalled that his scholarly father stirred him to ask questions and to explore at an early age. As a 10 year old, Piaget published his first scholarly paper, which described a partially albino sparrow he had observed in a public park.[24] By the age of 15, he had decided to study knowledge as an entity in itself and to explain it biologically. Piaget said that his mother's neurosis initially encouraged him to study psychoanalysis and pathological psychology, but that he preferred to pursue and study the ranges of normalcy and not to focus on the "tricks of the unconscious."[13]

At the age of 18, Piaget received his baccalaureate from the University of Neuchâtel. In 1918, three years later, he received his doctorate in the natural sciences from the same institution. During this time Piaget studied mollusks and their adjustment over time to a changing environment. It was from this long-term study that he became interested in the concept of interaction with the environment (which later became a cornerstone of his theory of mental development).[25]

As soon as Piaget had completed his doctorate, he became intrigued with psychology. This interest took him to Paris to work with Alfred Binet in a grade school, where his task was to aid in standardizing tests. Piaget soon became occupied in analyzing the *incorrect* answers that the children gave as responses to questions. From that time on, he used clinical observation and structured questioning of children to provide data for analyzing and understanding how intelligence developed.

By age 30, Piaget was famous for his work in psychology. Although he is often considered a child psychologist, he wished to be known as a person who was primarily concerned with describing and explaining, in a very systematic way, the growth and development of intellectual structures and knowledge.[24] In 1955, with the aid of a Rockefeller Foundation grant, the Centre International d'Epistémologie Génétique was established in Geneva. Under this program, three scholars were chosen every year to visit and to do research with Piaget and his associates.

Having published more than 80 books and hundreds of journal articles, Piaget remained a prolific author. Each year after the results of a year's research had been completed, Piaget traveled to an isolated farmhouse in the Alps to write for the summer.[25]

Piaget held several honorary degrees from prominent universities around the world. His works have generated more interest and research than those of any other person in psychology during the last 50 years.[24]

Piaget's Major Concepts and Terms

Piaget came to believe that intellectual acts are the evidence of *adaptation* to and *organization* of the perceived environment. To understand these processes of intellectual organization and adaptation, Piaget coined four basic concepts: *schema, assimilation, accommodation,* and *equilibration.*[7, 19]

1. SCHEMA (PLURAL, SCHEMATA). Schemata are the cognitive structures by which individuals intellectually adapt to and organize their environment. Schemata can be simplistically thought of as categories or units of information. A schema may consist of a motor movement, a sensory experience, an emotional memory, a fact, or any concrete or abstract association.

2. ASSIMILATION. Assimilation is the cognitive process by which the person integrates new perceptual matter, stimulus events, or information into **existing** schemata or patterns of behavior. One changes reality to fit into what is already known.

3. ACCOMMODATION. The establishment of a new schema or the modification of an old schema. This results in a change in, reorganization of, or development of cognitive structures (schemata). One changes the self to fit reality.

4. EQUILIBRATION. The balance between assimilation and accommodation. When disequilibration occurs, it provides motivation for the individual to assimilate or to accommodate further.

Piaget believed that mental development is a process that begins the day the infant is born (and possibly sooner). He also theorized that the path of cognitive development is the same for all people, although they progress at different rates. His stages of development are discussed throughout this book.

At each new level of cognitive development, previous levels are incorporated and integrated. Schemata are continually being modified through the life span. Although qualitative changes in cognitive structure cease after the development of formal operations, quantitative changes in content and function of intelligence continue.[7, 19]

Piaget's Techniques of Inquiry

Piaget's investigations were primarily clinical. His usual procedure was to observe a child's behavior in natural surroundings, and to formulate a hypothesis concerning the structure that underlies the child's response to, or interaction with, the material and events in the environment. He tested the hypothesis by altering the child's surroundings. This alteration was accomplished by rearranging the materials, by posing the problems in a different way, or by overtly suggesting to the subject a response different from the one predicted by the theory. Piaget made many detailed, longitudinal observations of his own three children. Although most of his early works were rather intuitive, some of his more recent endeavors employed rigid experimental strategies (using, for example, statistical findings and adequate sample sizes). Piaget said that the important thing is to "make contact with the child's thinking."[4]

Applicability of Piaget's Theory

The current interest in Piaget's efforts evolved as psychologists began to recognize the importance of what he had to say. His research has been criticized by some, however, because of the small sample size and its less rigid, "nonexperimental" mode. (Of course, if one accepts Piaget's assumption that the general course of development of intellectual structures is the same in all individuals, the small sample size poses no problem.)

In 1972 Piaget answered some of his critics who contested that his theory covered only the years from birth to about age 15. As a result, Piaget performed additional research and hypothesized that individual differences in cognitive processes among adults are influenced more by aptitudes and experiences, such as career and education, than by the general characteristics determining the individual's type of formal thinking. Not all adults use Piaget's highest level of intellectual functioning in all situations.

Piaget's works are frequently used by those who find themselves in daily contact with children. Teachers, counselors, school psychologists, and, lately, many parents are using the practical implications of Piaget's theory to aid in enhancing the individual cognitive potential of the children for whom they provide care.

REFERENCES

1. Adler, A. (1967). *The individual psychology of Alfred Adler* (Ansbacher, H. L., and Ansbacher, R.R. Eds.). New York: Harper and Row.

2. Beecher, W., & Beecher, M. (1973). Memorial to Dr. Alfred Adler. In H. H. Mosak (Ed.), *Alfred Adler: His influence on psychology today.* Park Ridge, NJ: Noyes Press.

3. Carpenter, F. (1974). *The Skinner primer: Behind freedom and dignity.* New York: Free Press.

4. Duckworth, E. (1973). Language and thought. In M. Schwebel & J. Ralph (Eds.), *Piaget in the classroom.* New York: Basic Books.

5. Erikson, E. H. (1963). *Childhood and society* (2nd ed.). New York: W. W. Norton.

6. Erikson, E. H., Erikson, J. M., & Kivnick, H. Q. (1986). *Vital involvement in old age.* New York: W. W. Norton.

7. Flavell, J. H. (1963). *The developmental psychology of Jean Piaget.* New York: Van Nostrand.

8. Franz, C. E., & White, K. M. (1985). Individuation and attachment in personality development: Extending Erikson's theory. *Journal of Personality, 53,* 224–256.

9. Freud, S. (1935). *A general introduction to psycho-analysis* (Authorized English translation of the revised edition by J. Rivière). New York: Liveright.

10. Hall, E. A. (1983). A conversation with Erik Erikson. *Psychology Today, 17*(6), 22.

11. Havighurst, R. J. (1972). *Developmental tasks and education* (3rd ed.). New York: McKay.

12. Jones, E. (1981). *The life and work of Sigmund Freud.* New York: Basic Books.

13. Maier, H. W. (1978). *Three theories of child development* (3rd ed.). New York: Harper and Row.

14. Maslow, A. H. (1943). A theory of human motivation. *Psychological Review, 50,* 370.

15. Maslow, A. H. (1982). *Toward a psychology of being* (2nd ed.). New York: Van Nostrand Reinhold.

16. Mullahy, P. (1970). *Psychoanalysis and interpersonal psychiatry; The contributions of Harry Stack Sullivan.* New York: Science House.

17. Orgler, H. (1973). *Alfred Adler: The man and his work* (4th ed.). London: Sidgwick and Jackson.

18. Phillips, J. L. (1975). *The origins of intellect: Piaget's theory.* San Francisco: Freeman.

19. Piaget, J. (1970). Piaget's theory. In P. H. Mussen (Ed.), *Carmichael's manual of child psychology* (3rd ed.). New York: Wiley.

20. Schell, R. E., & Hall, E. (1983). *Developmental psychology today* (4th ed.). New York: Random House.

21. Schultz, D. P. (1981). *Theories of personality* (2nd ed.). Monterey, CA: Brooks/Cole.

22. Skinner, B. F. (1983). Origins of a behaviorist. *Psychology Today, 17*(9), 22.

23. Sullivan, H. S. (1971). *The fusion of psychiatry and social science.* New York: Norton.

24. Wadsworth, B. J. (1984). *Piaget's theory of cognitive and affective development.* New York: Longman.

25. Wall, W. D. (1982). Jean Piaget: 1896–1979. *Journal of Child Psychology, Psychiatry and Allied Disciplines, 23*(2), 97.

Appendix C
Developmental Frameworks of Selected Stage Theorists

CLARA S. SCHUSTER

No one in the world can alter truth.
All we can do is seek it and live it.

—MAXIMILIAN KOLBE

Evelyn Millis Duvall
Development of the Family System

Jean Piaget
Levels of Cognitive Development

Erik H. Erikson
Psychosocial Developmental Levels

Robert J. Havighurst
Developmental Tasks of Life Phases

Abraham H. Maslow
Levels of Motivating Needs

Evelyn Millis Duvall

Development of the Family System*

A. Stages
    1. Married couple
    2. Childbearing family
    3. Family with preschool children
    4. Family with school-age children
    5. Family with teenagers
    6. Family as a launching center
    7. The "empty nest" family
    8. The aging family
B. Tasks of each stage
    1. Physical maintenance
    2. Allocation of resources
    3. Division of labor
    4. Socialization of family members
    5. Reproduction, recruitment, and release
    6. Maintenance of order
    7. Placement of members into the larger society
    8. Maintenance of motivation and morale

---

* From E. R. M. Duvall (1985). *Marriage and family development* (6th ed.). New York: Harper and Row.

JEAN PIAGET
LEVELS OF COGNITIVE DEVELOPMENT

Period	Age	Characteristics
Sensorimotor	0–2 years	Thought dominated by physical manipulation of objects and events
Substage 1	0–1 month	Pure reflex adaptations No differentiation between assimilation and accommodation
Substage 2	1–4 months	Primary circular reactions Slight differentiation between assimilation and accommodation Repetition of schemata and self-imitation, especially vocal and visual Reflex activities become modified with experience and coordinated with each other
Substage 3	4–8 months	Secondary circular reactions Differentiation between assimilation and accommodation, still overlap Repeat action on things to prolong an interesting spectacle Beginning to demonstrate intention or goal-directed activity
Substage 4	8–12 months	Coordination of secondary schemata Clear differentiation between assimilation and accommodation Application of known schemata to new situation Schemata follow each other without apparent aim Beginning of means-ends relationships
Substage 5	12–18 months	Tertiary circular reactions Ritualistic repetition of chance schema combinations Accentuation and elaboration of ritual Experimentation to see the result, find new ways to solve problems
Substage 6	18–24 months	Invention of new solutions through mental combinations Primitive symbolic representation Beginning of pretense by application of schema to inadequate object A symbol is mentally evoked and imitated in make-believe A symbolic schema is reproduced outside of context; thus, transition between practice play and symbolic play proper
Preoperational	2–7 years	Functions symbolically using language as major tool
Preconceptual	2–4 years	Uses representational thought to recall past, represent present, anticipate future Able to distinguish between signifier and signified Egocentric, uses self as standard for others Categorizes on basis of single characteristic
Intuitive	4–7 years	Increased symbolic functioning Subjective judgments still dominate perceptions Beginning to think in logical classes Able to see simple relationships Able to understand number concepts More exact imitations of reality
Concrete operations	7–11 years	Mental reasoning processes assume logical approaches to solving concrete problems Organizes objects, events into hierarchies of classes (classification) or along a continuum of increasing values (seriation) Reversibility, transitivity, and conservation skills attained
Formal operations	11–15 years	True logical thought and manipulation of abstract concepts emerge Hypothetical deductive thought Can plan and implement scientific approach to problem solving Handles all kinds of combinations in a systematic way

(From J. Piaget, The Psychology of Intelligence, *Transl. by M. Piercy and D. E. Berlyne [Totowa, NJ: Littlefield, Adams, 1973], and* Play, Dreams and Imitation in Childhood, *transl. by C. Gattengo and F. M. Hodgson [New York: Norton, 1951]. Also from J. H. Flavell,* The Developmental Psychology of Jean Piaget *[New York: Van Nostrand, 1963].)*

At each stage the family must successfully accomplish all eight tasks to function optimally. The tasks of the family support and complement the development of its individual members.

Each level incorporates and integrates processes from previous levels. Schemata are continually added and modified throughout life. Quantitative changes continue to occur throughout life, but qualitative changes cease after the development of formal operational thought.

ERIK H. ERIKSON
PSYCHOSOCIAL DEVELOPMENTAL LEVELS

Developmental Level	Basic Task	Negative Counterpart	Basic Virtues
1. Infant	Basic trust	Basic mistrust	Drive and hope
2. Toddler	Autonomy	Shame and doubt	Self-control and willpower
3. Preschooler	Initiative	Guilt	Direction and purpose
4. School-ager	Industry	Inferiority	Method and competence
5. Adolescent	Identity	Role confusion	Devotion and fidelity
6. Young adult	Intimacy	Isolation	Affiliation and love
7. Middlescent	Generativity	Stagnation	Production and care
8. Older adult	Ego-integrity	Despair	Renunciation and wisdom

(From E. H. Erikson, Childhood and Society *[2nd ed.] New York: Norton, 1963.)*

A specific age should not be attached to developmental levels, since each person progresses at his or her own rate. A child may be in several developmental levels simultaneously, may advance in spurts, or may regress to an earlier level in adverse circumstances. Both genetic and environmental factors can influence the rapidity with which one progresses through the stages. Failure to achieve positive growth will lead to the development of the negative counterpart and, according to Erikson, mental illness.

Robert J. Havighurst

Developmental Tasks of Life Phases*

1. Infancy and early childhood
    a. Learn to walk
    b. Learn to take solid food
    c. Learn to talk
    d. Control elimination of body wastes
    e. Learn sex differences and sexual modesty
    f. Form concepts and learning language to describe social and physical reality
    g. Get ready to read
    h. Learn to distinguish right and wrong and begin to develop a conscience
2. Middle childhood
    a. Learn physical skills necessary for ordinary games
    b. Build wholesome attitudes toward oneself as a growing organism
    c. Learn to get along with age-mates
    d. Learn an appropriate masculine or feminine social role
    e. Develop fundamental skills in reading, writing, and calculating
    f. Develop concepts necessary for everyday living

g. Develop conscience, morality, and a scale of values
    h. Achieve personal independence
    i. Develop attitudes toward social groups and institutions
3. Adolescence
    a. Achieve new and more mature relations with age-mates of both sexes
    b. Achieve a masculine or feminine social role
    c. Accept one's physique and use body effectively
    d. Achieve emotional independence of parents and other adults
    e. Prepare for marriage and family life
    f. Prepare for economic career
    g. Develop an ideology—a set of values and an ethical system as a guide to behavior
    h. Achieve socially responsible behavior
4. Early adulthood
    a. Select a mate
    b. Learn to live with a marriage partner
    c. Start a family
    d. Rear children
    e. Manage a home
    f. Start an occupation
    g. Assume civic responsibility
    h. Find a congenial social group
5. Middle age
    a. Assist children to become responsible and happy adults
    b. Achieve adult social and civic responsibility
    c. Attain and maintain satisfactory performance in occupation
    d. Develop adult leisure activities
    e. Relate to spouse as a person
    f. Accept and adjust to physiological changes
    g. Adjust to aging parents
6. Later maturity
    a. Adjust to decreasing physical strength and health

* From R. J. Havighurst, *Developmental Tasks and Education* (3rd ed.) New York: McKay, 1972.

b. Adjust to retirement and reduced income
c. Adjust to death of spouse
d. Establish affiliation with one's age group
e. Adopt and adapt to social roles in a flexible way
f. Establish satisfactory physical living arrangements

Havighurst feels that development is a cognitive learning process. Tasks develop out of a combination of pressures arising from physical development, cultural expectations, and individual values and goals. He postulates the occurrence of "teachable moments" when a special sensitivity or readiness to learn a task arises from the unique combination of physical, social, and psychic readiness.

Abraham H. Maslow

Levels of Motivating Needs*

A. Primary motives (basic needs): survival needs, vital for continuing existence
1. Oxygen
2. Water
3. Nutrition
4. Elimination
5. Physiological homeostasis
6. Rest and sleep
7. Avoidance of pain
8. Sex (basic motive, but not considered essential to survival)

---

* From A. H. Maslow, *Motivation and Personality* (2nd ed.) New York: Harper & Row, 1970; and *Toward a Psychology of Being* (2nd ed.) Princeton, NJ: Van Nostrand, 1968.

B. Secondary motives: social needs, learned or acquired
1. Security
2. Social approval
3. Affiliation
4. Status
5. Knowledge acquisition
6. Achievement
C. Hierarchy of motives
1. Physiological (inborn)
2. Safety and security
3. Belongingness and affection
4. Esteem and self-respect
5. Self-actualization
a. Self-fulfillment
b. Desire to know and understand
c. Aesthetic need

As lower-level needs are met and found to be satisfying, the individual moves on to the next level. Levels are not fixed. Lower-level needs are always present, but as need tension is reduced, the person is free to concentrate on higher-level needs. Adverse environmental circumstances can require increased attention to lower-level needs. Those who remain at a given level after the needs have been satisfied become bored, fatigued, and resentful. Satisfaction of higher-level needs produces more genuine happiness, serenity, and richness of inner life; therefore, the needs of that level are more highly valued by persons who have experienced gratification at that level. Pursuit of higher-level needs indicates a trend toward psychological health. However, Maslow believes that only about 1 percent of the adult population is actually in the process of true self-actualization, even though the people in this group may be involved in many creative endeavors.

Appendix D
Physical Growth:
NCHS Percentile Charts

**BOYS: BIRTH TO 36 MONTHS
PHYSICAL GROWTH
NCHS PERCENTILES**

NAME _____ RECORD # _____

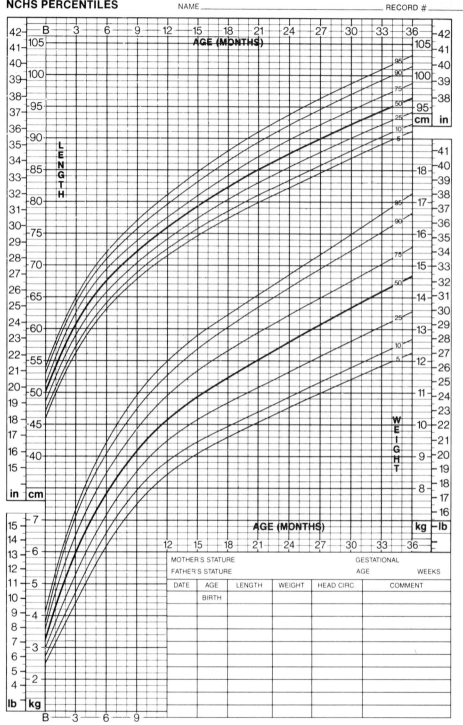

BOYS: BIRTH TO 36 MONTHS
PHYSICAL GROWTH
NCHS PERCENTILES

NAME_____ RECORD #_____

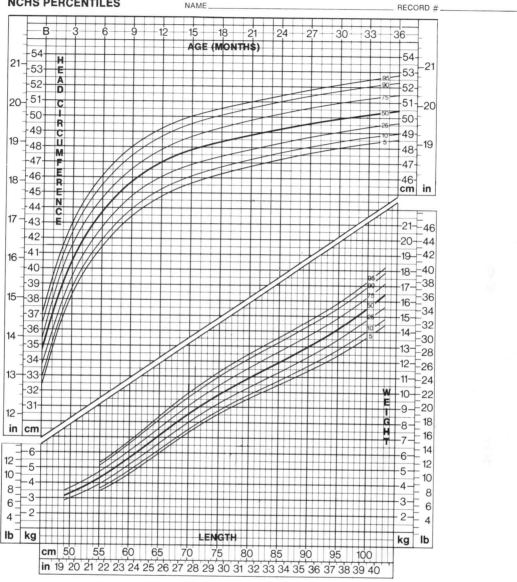

BOYS: 2 TO 18 YEARS
PHYSICAL GROWTH
NCHS PERCENTILES

NAME _____ RECORD # _____

BOYS: PREPUBESCENT
PHYSICAL GROWTH
NCHS PERCENTILES

NAME _____ RECORD # _____

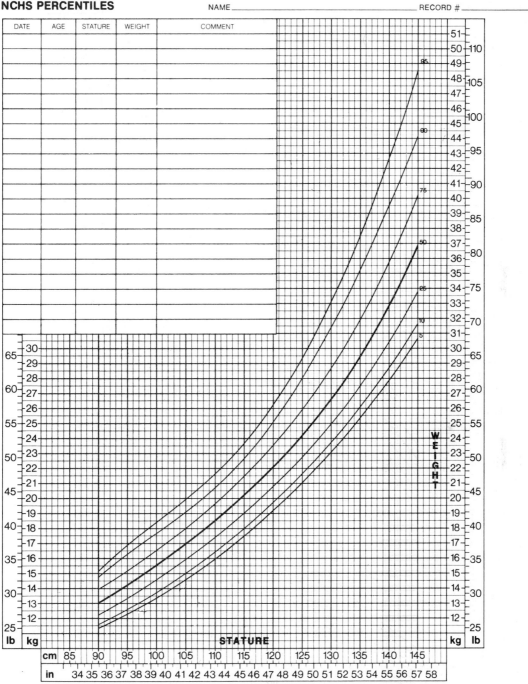

DATE	AGE	STATURE	WEIGHT	COMMENT

GIRLS: BIRTH TO 36 MONTHS
PHYSICAL GROWTH
NCHS PERCENTILES

NAME_____   RECORD # _____

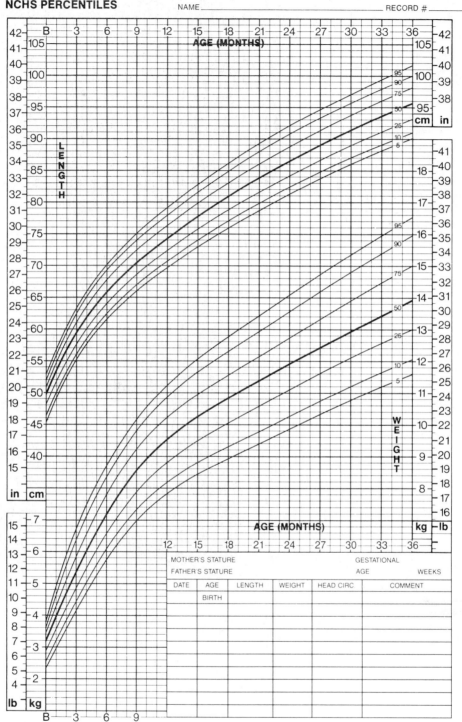

GIRLS: BIRTH TO 36 MONTHS
PHYSICAL GROWTH
NCHS PERCENTILES

NAME _____   RECORD # _____

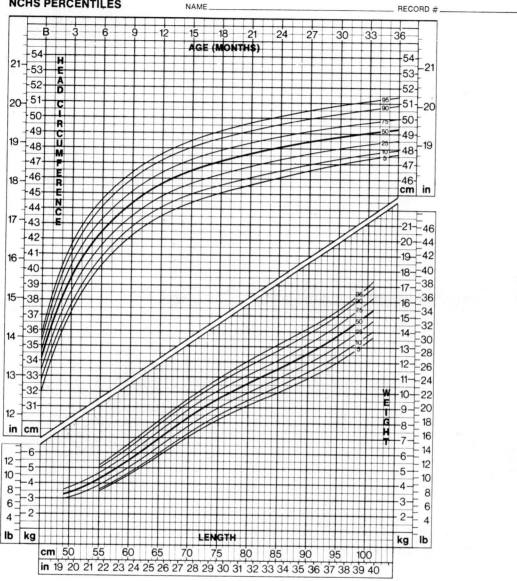

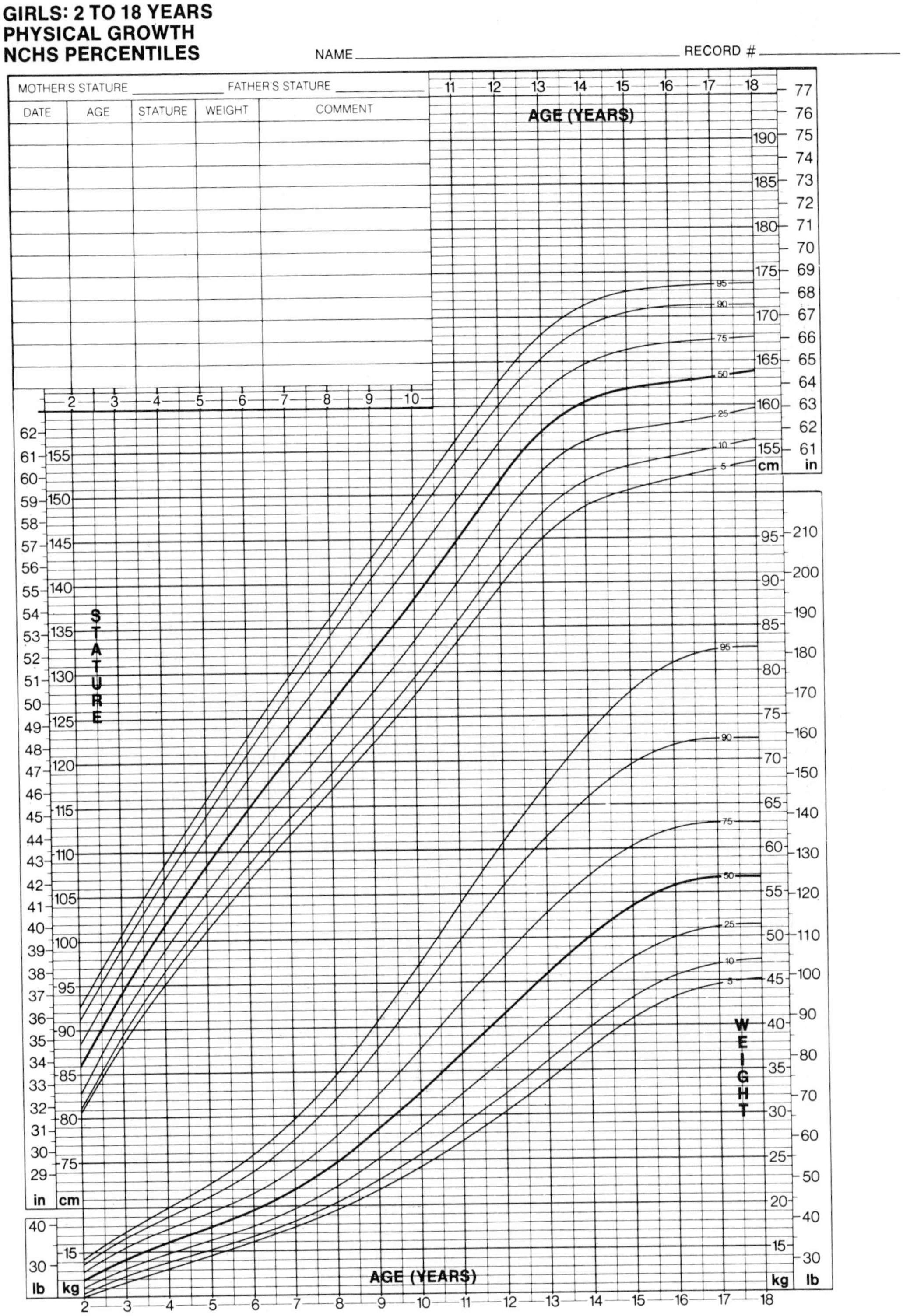

GIRLS: 2 TO 18 YEARS
PHYSICAL GROWTH
NCHS PERCENTILES
NAME
RECORD #
MOTHER'S STATURE
FATHER'S STATURE
DATE
AGE
STATURE
WEIGHT
COMMENT
AGE (YEARS)
STATURE
WEIGHT
in
cm
lb
kg
95
90
75
50
25
10
5

GIRLS: PREPUBESCENT
PHYSICAL GROWTH
NCHS PERCENTILES

NAME _____ RECORD # _____

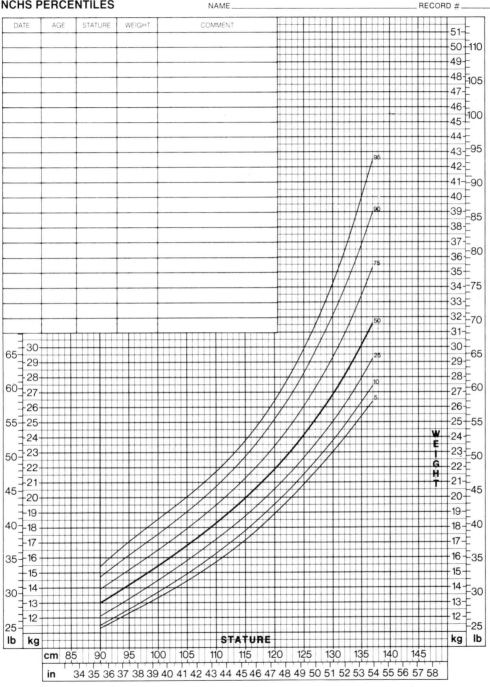

Appendix E
Normal Physiological Parameters Through the Life Span

CLARA S. SCHUSTER

TABLE 1

Age	Vital Signs			Height		Weight		Blood Values		
	Pulse	Resp.	BP	Cm	Inches	Kg	Pounds	Hgb (g/100 mL)	Hct (%)	WBC/mm³
Birth	140 ± 20	55 ± 25	$\frac{69}{55} \pm \frac{19}{13}$	50 ± 2	20 ± 1	$3.4 \pm .6$	7.5 ± 1	18 (14–24)	56 (44–69)	19,000 (9–30)
14 days	135 ± 15	40 ± 15	$\frac{77}{54} \pm \frac{15}{13}$					17 (12.5–20)	52 (42–60)	12,000 (5–21)
1 month	130 ± 20	35 ± 10	$\frac{85}{52} \pm \frac{16}{13}$	53 ± 2.5	21 ± 1	$4.4 \pm .8$	10 ± 1.5	14 (11–17)	43 (35–49)	10,800 (5–19.5)
3 months			$\frac{90}{50} \pm \frac{16}{13}$	60 ± 2	23.5 ± 1	$5.7 \pm .8$	12.5 ± 2	11 (10–14)	35 (28–42)	11,000 (5.5–18)
6 months	120 ± 20	31 ± 9	$\frac{91}{53} \pm \frac{15}{13}$	65.5 ± 3	26 ± 1	7.4 ± 1	16.5 ± 2.5	11.5 (10.5–14.5)	38 (30–40)	11,900 (6–17.5)
12 months	115 ± 20	30 ± 10	$\frac{91}{55} \pm \frac{15}{14}$	74.5 ± 3	29 ± 1.5	10 ± 1.5	22 ± 3	12.5 (11–15)	37 (33–42)	11,400 (6–17.5)
2 years	110 ± 20	28 ± 8	$\frac{91}{56} \pm \frac{15}{13}$	87 ± 4	34 ± 2	12.4 ± 2	27.5 ± 4	13 (12–15)	38 (33–42)	10,500 (6–17)
3 years	105 ± 15	25 ± 5	$\frac{92}{55} \pm \frac{16}{14}$	96 ± 5.5	38 ± 2	14.5 ± 2	32 ± 5	13.5 (12.5–15)		9,000 (5.5–15.5)
4 years	100 ± 20	23 ± 4	$\frac{93}{56} \pm \frac{15}{13}$	103 ± 6	40.5 ± 2.5	16.5 ± 3	36.5 ± 5			
5 years	95 ± 15	22 ± 3	$\frac{94}{56} \pm \frac{15}{13}$	109 ± 6	43 ± 2.5	18.4 ± 3	40.5 ± 6		40 (31–43)	8,500 (5–14.5)
6 years	90 ± 20	21 ± 3	$\frac{96}{57} \pm \frac{15}{13}$	117 ± 7	46 ± 2.5	21.5 ± 4	47.5 ± 8	14 (13–15.5)		
8 years	90 ± 10	20 ± 3	$\frac{99}{59} \pm \frac{15}{13}$	129 ± 7.5	50.5 ± 3	27 ± 5	59 ± 11			8000 (4.5–13.5)
10 years	85 ± 15	19 ± 3	$\frac{102}{62} \pm \frac{15}{13}$	139.5 ± 8	55 ± 3	32.5 ± 7	71 ± 14		42 (33–44)	

TABLE 2

Age	Vital Signs			Height		Weight		Blood Values			Calories 24 hr		Protein
Males	Pulse	Resp.	BP	Cm	Inches	Kg	Pounds	Hgb (g/100 mL)	Hct (%)	WBC/mm³	Per Pound	Total	gram/24 hr
12 years	85 ± 9	19 ± 2	$\frac{107}{64} \pm \frac{15}{13}$	150 ± 8	59 ± 3	39 ± 9	85 ± 12	13 (11–16)	38 (34–40)	8,000 (4.5–13.5)	30	2,400	35
14 years	80 ± 8	18 ± 3	$\frac{112}{69} \pm \frac{15}{14}$	163 ± 9	64 ± 4	49 ± 11	108 ± 20	14 (13–16)	41 (37–43)		31	2,800	54
16 years	75 ± 8	17 ± 3	$\frac{117}{67} \pm \frac{15}{14}$	172 ± 8	68 ± 4	59 ± 9	130 ± 20	15.5 (13–17)	45 (40–48)	7,800 (4.5–13)	31	3,000	56
18 years	70 ± 8	16 ± 3	$\frac{121}{70} \pm \frac{15}{14}$	174 ± 8	68.5 ± 4	63 ± 10	140 ± 20				25	3,200	60
19–22 years												3,000	
23–49 years	70 ± 10	18 ± 2	$\frac{124}{70} \pm \frac{16}{14}$	175 ± 8	69 ± 4	68 ± 12	150 ± 25	16 (13–18)	47 (39–49)	7,500 (4.3–10.8)	18–25	2,700	58
50–69 years												2,400	
70+ years												2,000	56

Age	Vital Signs			Height		Weight		Blood Values			Calories 24 hr		Protein
Females	Pulse	Resp.	BP	Cm	Inches	Kg	Pounds	Hgb (g/100 mL)	Hct (%)	WBC/mm³	Per Pound	Total	gram/24 hr
12 years	90 ± 9	19 ± 3	$\frac{107}{66} \pm \frac{15}{13}$	152 ± 8	60 ± 3	40 ± 10	88 ± 20	13 (11–16)	38 (34–40)	8,000 (4.5–13.5)	30	2,300	42
14 years	85 ± 8		$\frac{110}{67} \pm \frac{15}{14}$	160 ± 7	63 ± 3	50 ± 10	110 ± 18	13.5 (12–16)	40 (35–42)	7,800 (4.5–13.0)	24	2,400	46
16 years	80 ± 8	18 ± 3	$\frac{112}{67} \pm \frac{15}{14}$	162 ± 7	63.5 ± 3	53 ± 11	117 ± 17		41 (36–44)		21		48
18 years	75 ± 8		$\frac{112}{66} \pm \frac{15}{14}$			54 ± 11	120 ± 20				19	2,300	46
19–22 years		17 ± 3		163 ± 7	64 ± 3			14 (12–16)	42 (36–48)	7,500 (4.3–10.8)		2,000	
23–49 years	70 ± 10						120 ± 25				15–20		44
50–69 years			$\frac{120}{70} \pm \frac{16}{10}$			55 ± 12						1,800	
70+ years												1,600	48
Pregnant							+15–30	12 (11–15)	36 (34–40)			+300	+30
Lactating							+2–5					+800	+20

TABLE 3

Age	Calories /lb	Calories /kg	Calories Average total	Protein (g)	Water oz/lb	Water mL/kg	Water total	Output (urine/24 hr)	Sleep/24 hr	Head Circum. (cm)
Birth							45–90	15–60	22	
3 days	55	115	95–145	Kg × 2.2	2¼	80–100	250–300	40–400	16–22	34 ± 2.5
14 days						125–150	400–500			
1 month	50	110	500	Kg × 2.0	2¼	140—160	750–850	250–450	15–18	36.5 ± 2.5
3 months										40 ± 2.5
6 months		150	750	Kg × 1.7		130–155	950–1,100	400–550	15–16	43 ± 3
12 months			1,100	Kg × 1.4		120–135	1,100–1,300		13–15	46 ± 3
2 years	45	100	1,200	Kg × 1.2	2	115–125	1,300–1,500	500–600	12–14	49 ± 3
3 years			1,300	Kg × 1.15						50 ± 3
4 years	41	90	1,500	Kg × 1.10	1½	100–110	1,600–1,800	600–750		50.5 ± 3
5 years			1,600			90–100	1,800–2,000			51 ± 2.5
6 years			1,800	Kg × 1.05				650–1,000	11–12	51.5 ± 2.5
8 years	36	80	2,000	Kg × 1.00	1	70–85	2,000–2,500			52.5 ± 2.5
10 years			2,200						9–11	53 ± 3
10–12 years						60–75				53.5 ± 3
12–14 years						50–60	2,200–2,700	700–1,500		54 ± 3
14–16 years						40–50			8–9	54.5 ± 3
16–18 years										55 ± 3
18–22 years			see Table 2		¾				7–9	
23–50 years						40	2,000–3,000			
51+ years								1,000–2,000	5–7	55.5 ± 3
Pregnant women						30				
Lactating women							3,000–4,500		9–10	

Appendix F
Desirable Weights for Adults

1983 METROPOLITAN HEIGHT AND WEIGHT TABLES*

Men					Women				
Height		Small Frame	Medium Frame	Large Frame	Height		Small Frame	Medium Frame	Large Frame
Feet	Inches				Feet	Inches			
5	2	128–134	131–141	138–150	4	10	102–111	109–121	118–131
5	3	130–136	133–143	140–153	4	11	103–113	111–123	120–134
5	4	132–138	135–145	142–156	5	0	104–115	113–126	122–137
5	5	134–140	137–148	144–160	5	1	106–118	115–129	125–140
5	6	136–142	139–151	146–164	5	2	108–121	118–132	128–143
5	7	138–145	142–154	149–168	5	3	111–124	121–135	131–147
5	8	140–148	145–157	152–172	5	4	114–127	124–138	134–151
5	9	142–151	148–160	155–176	5	5	117–130	127–141	137–155
5	10	144–154	151–163	158–180	5	6	120–133	130–144	140–159
5	11	146–157	154–166	161–184	5	7	123–136	133–147	143–163
6	0	149–160	157–170	164–188	5	8	126–139	136–150	146–167
6	1	152–164	160–174	168–192	5	9	129–142	139–153	149–170
6	2	155–168	164–178	172–197	5	10	132–145	142–156	152–173
6	3	158–172	167–182	176–202	5	11	135–148	145–159	155–176
6	4	162–176	171–187	181–207	6	0	138–151	148–162	158–179

* Weights at ages 25–59 based on lowest mortality. Weight in pounds according to frame (indoor clothing weighing 5 lb for men and 3 lb for women; shoes with 1 in heels). Data from: 1979 Build Study, Society of Actuaries and Association of Life Insurance Medical Directors of America, 1980. Copyright 1983 Metropolitan Life Insurance Company. Reprinted with permission.

Appendix G
Resources for Disabled Individuals and Families

Able Child, 325 W. 11th St., New York, NY 10014 (adapted toys and games).

Accent on Living, P.O. Box 700, Gillum Rd. and High Dr., Bloomington, IL 61701.

Accessible Tours, 344 Main St., Mount Kisco, NY 10549, (914) 241-1700 (tour information for physically disabled persons).

Activating Children Through Technology (ACTT), 27 Horrabin Hall, College of Education, Western Illinois University, Macomb, IL 61455, (309) 298-1634 (software evaluation and toy modifications for severely disabled children).

Alexander Graham Bell Association for the Deaf, Inc., 3417 Volta Pl., NW, Washington, D.C. 20007, (202) 337-5220.

Allergy Foundation of America, 118-35 Queens Blvd., Forest Hills, NY 11375, (718) 261-3663.

American Academy for Cerebral Palsy, P. O. Box 11086, Richmond, VA 23230.

American Camping Association, Bradford Woods, 5040 State Road 67 North, Martinsville, IN 46151, (317) 342-8456.

American Diabetes Association, 1660 Duke St., Alexandria, VA 22314, (800) 232-3472.

American Foundation for the Blind, 15 W. 16th St., New York, NY 10011, (800) 232-5463. *Products for People with Vision Problems, International Guide to Aids and Appliances for Blind and Visually Impaired Persons* (Listings of jobs, computer adaptation information, etc.).

American Spinal Injury Association, Northwest Memorial Hospital, Room 619, 250 East Superior, Chicago, IL 60611.

Association for Children with Learning Disabilities, 4156 Library Rd., Pittsburgh, PA 15234.

Association for Persons with Severe Handicaps (TASH), 7010 Roosevelt Way NE, Seattle, WA 98115.

Association of Foot and Mouth Painters, 503 Brisband Building, Buffalo, NY 10403.

Autism Society of America, 1234 Massachusetts Ave., NW, Suite 1101, Washington, DC 20005.

Canadian Cerebral Palsy Association, 40 Duncas St. W, Suite 222, P.O. Box 110, Toronto, Ont., Canada M5G 2C2.

Care-Sew-Much Designs, 1920 Sheely Dr., Ft. Collins, CO 80526, (303) 482-6590 (adaptive clothing).

Christian Council on Persons with Disabilities, P.O. Box 458, Lake Geneva, WI 53147.

Clearinghouse on the Handicapped, Office of Special Education and Rehabilitative Services, Room 3106 Switzer Building, Washington, DC 20202, (202) 732-1245; *Directory of National Information Sources of Handicapping Conditions and Related Services.*

Coalition on Sexuality and Disability, 122 E. 23rd St., New York, NY 10010.

Council of State Administrators of Vocational Rehabilitation, 1055 Thomas Jefferson St. NW, Suite 401, Washington, DC 20006, (202) 638-4634.

Council for Exceptional Children, 1920 Association Dr., Reston, VA 22091, (800) 345-TECH (Center for Special Technology Information Exchange), (800) 336-3728 (Information Services); *Directory of Services and Facilities for Handicapped Children.*

Epilepsy Foundation of American, 1828 L St., NW, Suite 406, Washington, DC 20036.

Equipment for the Disabled, Mary Marlborough Lodge, Nuffield Orthopaedic Center, Headington, Oxford, England OX3 7LD, Oxford (0865) 750103; (excellent booklets with pictures and discussions of equipment, sources, and use of equipment for dealing with all types of disabilities).

Especially Grandparents, The Grandparents Program, ARC of King County, 2230 Eighth Ave., Seattle, WA 98121.

Exceptional Parent (magazine for parents), PSY-ED Corp., 296 Boylston St., Boston, MA 02116.

FashionAble, Rocky Hill, NJ 08553, (609) 921-2563 (self-help and adaptive clothing).

Federation of the Handicapped, 211 W. 14th St., New York, NY 10011.

God's Special People (magazine for parents), P.O. Box 729, Ocean Shores, WA 98569, (206) 289-2540.

Handi*Camp, 1881 Washington St., Braintree, MA 02184, (617) 848-8767.

Happy Canine Helpers, Inc., 16277 Montgomery Rd., Johnston, OH 43031, (614) 965-2204 (dogs for physically impaired individuals).

Help Yourself Aids, P.O. Box 289, Elmhurst, IL 60126 (wheelchair accessories and self-help aids).

I.B.M. National Support Center for Persons with Disabilities, P.O. Box 2150 HO6R1, Atlanta, GA 30055, (800) IBM-2133 (adaptive computer equipment for blind and physically disabled).

J. A. Preston Company, 60 Page Rd., Clifton, NJ 07012, (800) 631-7277 (adaptive equipment for multiply disabled, all ages).

Joni and Friends, P.O. Box 3333, Agoura Hills, CA 91301, (818) 707-5664 (spiritual help for disabled persons).

Keshet, Jewish Parents of Children with Special Needs, P.O. Box 59065, Chicago, IL 60645, (312) 588-0551.

Little People of America, Box 633, San Bruno, CA 94066, (415) 589-0695.

Multicultural Impact, Inc., University Affiliated Program, Children's Hospital of Los Angeles, P.O. Box 54700, Los Angeles, CA 90054, (213) 669-2300.

National Association for Gifted Children, 8080 Springvalley Dr., Cincinnati, OH 45236.

National Center for Stuttering, 200 E. 33rd St., New York, NY 10016, (800) 221-2483.

National Committee on Arts for the Handicapped, 1825 Connecticut Ave. NW, Suite 418, Washington, DC 20009, (202) 332-6960.

National Down Syndrome Society, 141 Fifth Ave., New York, NY 10010, (212) 460-9330.

National Easter Seal Society for Crippled Children and Adults, 2023 W. Ogden Ave., Chicago, IL 60612, (800) 221-6827.

National Head Injury Foundation, 333 Turnpike Rd., Southborough, MA 01772, (800) 444-6443.

National Information Center for Handicapped Children and Youth (NICHCY), 1555 Wilson Blvd., Suite 600, Rosslyn, VA 22209, (703) 522-0870.

National Odd Shoe Exchange, P.O. Box 56845, Phoenix, AZ 85079, (602) 246-8725.

National Rehabilitation Information Center (NARIC), Catholic University of America, 4407 Eighth St. NE, Washington, DC 20017, (800) 34N-ARIC. (ABLEDATA and REHABDATA computerized data bases provide the nation's most comprehensive, up-to-date listing of research, products, organizations, resources, and literature related to the needs of disabled persons and their families.)

National Wheelchair Athletic Association, Templeton Gap Rd., Suite C, Colorado Springs, CO 80907, (303) 632-0698.

Nationwide Flashing Signal Systems, 8120 Fenton St., Silver Spring, MD 20910, (301) 589-6671 (adaptive equipment for deaf individuals).

Parent Network, 1301 E. 38th St., Indianapolis, IN 46205.

Parents' Campaign for Handicapped Children and Youth, 1201 16th St., NW, Washington, DC 20036.

Parents of Chronically Ill Children, 29 Lovell Valley Dr., Springfield, IL 62702, (217) 522-6810.

People-to-People Committee for the Handicapped, 1522 K St., NW, Washington, DC 20005; *Directory of Organizations Interested in the Handicapped.*

Post-Polio Syndrome Association, 45-02 Maryland Ave., St Louis, MO (314) 361-0475.

PRIDE (Promoting Real Independence for the Disabled and Elderly), 1159 Poquonnock Rd., Groton, CT 06340, (203) 447-7433.

Sibling Information Network, Department of Educational Psychology, Box U-64, The University of Connecticut, Storrs, CT 06268, (203) 486-4034.

Special-Needs Parent Information Network (SPIN), P.O. Box 2067, Augusta, ME 04330, (800) 325-0220.

Spina Bifida Association of America, 343 S. Dearborn St., Chicago, IL 60604.

Tall Clubs International, (800) 521-2512.

The World Institute on Disability, 1720 Oregon St., Suite 4, Berkeley, CA 94703, (415) 486-8314.

Toys for Special Children, 101 Lefurgy Ave., Hastings-on-the-Hudson, NY 10706 (adapted toys and games).

United States Department of Housing and Urban Development, Office of Independent Living for the Disabled, 541 7th St., Room 9106, Washington, DC 20410, (202) 755-7366 (literature on adaptation of home environments).

Appendix H
Living Will

TO MY FAMILY, MY PHYSICIAN, MY LAWYER, MY CLERGYMAN
TO ANY MEDICAL FACILITY IN WHOSE CARE I HAPPEN TO BE
TO ANY INDIVIDUAL WHO MAY BECOME RESPONSIBLE FOR MY HEALTH, WELFARE OR AFFAIRS

Death is as much a reality as birth, growth, maturity and old age—it is the one certainty of life. If the time comes when I, _____, can no longer take part in decisions for my own future, let this statement stand as an expression of my wishes, while I am still of sound mind.

If the situation should arise in which there is no reasonable expectation of my recovery from physical or mental disability, I request that I be allowed to die and not be kept alive by artificial means or "heroic measures." I do not fear death itself as much as the indignities of deterioration, dependence and hopeless pain. I, therefore, ask that medication be mercifully administered to me to alleviate suffering even though this may hasten the moment of death.

This request is made after careful consideration. I hope you who care for me will feel morally bound to follow its mandate. I recognize that this appears to place a heavy responsibility upon you, but it is with the intention of relieving you of such responsibility and of placing it upon myself in accordance with my strong convictions, that this statement is made.

Signed _____

Date _____

Witness _____

Witness _____

Copies of this request have been given to _____

_____

_____

_____

To Make the Best Use of Your Living Will*

1. Sign and date the Living Will before two witnesses. (This is to ensure that you signed of your own free will and not under any pressure.)

2. If you have a physician, give him a copy for your medical file and discuss it with him to make sure he is in agreement. Give copies to those most likely to be concerned "if the time comes when you can no longer take part in decisions for your own future." Enter their names on the bottom line of the Living Will. Keep the original nearby, easily and readily available.

3. Above all, discuss your intentions with those closest to you, **now.**

4. It is a good idea to look over your Living Will once a year and then to redate it and initial the new date to make it clear that your wishes are unchanged.

* Reprinted with the permission of the Euthanasia Educational Council, 250 West Fifty-Seventh Street, New York, New York 10019. Copies available on request.

Appendix I
Suggested Interview Guides

CLARA S. SCHUSTER

I. **Parenting Interview**
  A. Data Gathering

   Identify a person between 28 and 40 years of age who has at least one child living in the home.

   Talk with the person at a time when at least one child is home so that you will have an opportunity to observe the child and parent interact.

   Ask questions that will elicit the person's perceptions of their own childhood, their parents, and themselves as a parent. This can provide insight into the parent's current attitudes and behaviors, as well as potential support and stress sources. Sample questions:

   1. Tell me about your life as a child.
   2. What is your best memory of childhood?
   3. What is your most painful memory of childhood?
   4. What was your relationship like with your siblings?
   5. What was your relationship like with your parents?
   6. Describe your parents as parents.
   7. How much did you feel that your parents were available to you (i.e., to sit and talk or to go on walks; did they stop their activities to listen)?
   8. How actively were your parents involved in teaching you about hygiene, cultural standards, table manners, sex, religion, values, and schoolwork?
   9. How did you feel about their involvement?
   10. What do you remember doing with your parents (hobbies, theme parks, table games, car washing, and so forth)?
   11. How and for what did your parents discipline you?
   12. Describe yourself as a person when you were a child and now.
   13. What is your relationship like with your parents now?
   14. How did you respond when you first learned that you were going to be a parent?
   15. How do you feel now about being a parent?
   16. How would you describe yourself as a parent?
   17. What has been your greatest disappointment in parenting?
   18. What has been your greatest satisfaction in parenting?
   19. How has your concept of parenting changed over the years?
   20. How much time do you spend talking with your child each day?
   21. What do you talk about?
   22. What rules do you have for your child?
   23. How do you enforce them?
   24. How has your concept of discipline changed over the years?
   25. How would you describe your relationship with your child?
   26. What do you feel are the goals of parenting (major responsibilities)?
   27. What would you like to change about your parent–child relationship?
   28. How do you see that your parents have influenced your parenting?
   29. How do you see that your parents have influenced you as a person?
   30. What advice would you offer a person who is having a first child?
   31. How actively are you involved in teaching your children the issues mentioned in question 8 above?
   32. What would you do differently if you had your life as a parent to start over again?
   33. Ask the parent to do three things with the child, and observe the interactions for:
     a. turntaking
     b. degree of mutual respect
     c. type of guidance
     d. balance of power, control
     e. emotional availability
     f. amount of joy each expresses in the relationship
     g. cooperation
     h. suggested activities include:
       1. a fun activity that requires the parent and child to work together to accom-

plish the task (read a book, assemble a puzzle, draw an etch-a-sketch picture).

2. asking the child to do a chore (set table for supper, pick up room, sort and put clothes into the washer, walk the dog).

3. asking the parent to do some activity with the child that the child chooses.

B. Data Analysis
 1. Sensitivity of the parent to the child's developmental level and needs
 2. Degree of synchrony between the parent and child
 3. Weighting on the control versus permissiveness continuum
 4. Emotional availability of the parent
 5. How did childhood experiences contribute to:
    a. the parent's current personality?
    b. the parent's parenting behaviors?
    c. the parent's discipline approach?
    d. the parent's understanding of child development?
 6. What are the parent's underlying values and goals, and how do these influence the parent–child relationship?
 7. What family resources are available for this person to tap when experiencing problems with the child(ren)?

C. Maximizing Potentials
 1. What ideas would you recommend to enhance the parent–child relationship?
 2. What alternative guidance or discipline approaches would you recommend?

II. Identity Interview

A. Data Gathering

Identify a person between 18 and 25 years of age who is willing to share with your his or her feelings about "life."

Elicit information from the person about the following:

views of self as a person
relationship to family members
relationship to peers
life goals
self-discipline
comparison of self to peers
ability to identify and deal with feelings
negotiation skills
concept of death
moral development
values identification
field dependence/independence

Sample questions:
 1. Describe yourself as a person.
 2. What is your relationship like with your parents?
 3. How has that relationship changed in the last 3 years?
 4. Describe your relationship with your brothers and sisters.
 5. What are things like at school or your job for you?
 6. What do you and your best friend do and talk about?
 7. What are your life or career goals?
 8. What are you doing now that will help you to achieve that kind of life?
 9. In what ways do you see yourself as similar to your peers?
 10. How are you different from your peers?
 11. How do you feel about those differences?
 12. How do you feel about the AIDS crisis?
 13. How do you feel about the abortion issue?
 14. How well do you feel you are prepared to face adult life and responsibilities?
 15. What is the most frightening aspect of life to you right now?
 16. What is the most exciting aspect of life to you right now?
 17. How did you feel about your parents' guidance and discipline?
 18. How do you feel about their guidance now?
 19. What will you do differently if you have children?
 20. Who do you talk to if you are upset or depressed?
 21. What do you do if you feel angry or if you have a difference of opinion about what to do?
 22. How do you feel about the death of yourself?
 23. What do you do in your leisure time?
 24. How do your attitudes, beliefs and values affect your behaviors?
 25. Who would you like to be like? Why? How does your model change your behavior?
 26. What is the most important aspect of life to you right now?
 27. How do you think *you* have changed in the last 3 years?
 28. What do you like most about yourself?
 29. What do you least like about yourself?
 30. What values do you hold in common with your parents?
 31. What is the most important meaning of life to you?
 32. What advice would you give to a 15 year-old to help him or her to face today's world?

33. Is there anything else you want me to know about you?
B. Data Analysis
   1. To what degree has this person mastered Erikson's first 6 levels of socioemotional development?
   2. What is this person's major source(s) of identity?
   3. How well is this person prepared to face the responsibilities and rigors of adult life?
   4. Where is this person on a continuum of external versus internal guidance?
   5. What degree of comfort does this person feel with him- or herself?
   6. What degree of comfort does this person feel with others?
   7. What level of concept of death has been achieved?
   8. To what degree has this person mastered each of Schuster's developmental tasks of adolescence?
C. Maximizing Potentials
   1. What recommendations would you make to this person to assist him or her toward a greater sense of personal control and direction?
   2. What could this person do to facilitate the process of "identity homework"?

III. Life-Review Interview
A. Data Gathering:
Choose a person age 65 or older who, in your opinion, is mentally alert enough to relate his or her life history, and is willing to share his or her life with you.

Since an older person's energy level may be limited, it may be necessary to spend two interviewing sessions to gather adequate data.

Use very open-ended questions such as the following:
What was life like when you were growing up?
What were you like?
Tell me about the most difficult time of life for you.
Elicit information about these aspects of the person's life:
   1. View and description of self as a person
   2. Relationship to family of origin—parents, siblings
    a. during developmental years
    b. during adult years
    c. currently
   3. Relationship to family of creation—spouse, children
    a. during adulthood
    b. currently

   4. Relationship to peers
    a. during childhood and adolescence
    b. during young and middle adult years
    c. currently
   5. Comparison of self to peers
    a. past
    b. present
   6. Life goals—as a young adult, and now
   7. Mentors and role models through life
   8. Anticipated changes in the next 5 years
   9. Feelings about career choice
   10. Feelings about marital partner and lifestyle choice
   11. Best time in life
   12. Response to physiological changes
   13. How values and priorities have changed over lifetime
   14. How values and priorities have changed over last 5 years
   15. Hobbies and leisure activities
   16. Community involvements—past and present
   17. Thoughts on death of self
   18. How he or she feels about the AIDS crisis
   19. How he or she feels about the abortion issue
   20. Role of religion in the person's life
   21. Greatest surprise about life
   22. Greatest disappointment about life
   23. Greatest experience in life
   24. Greatest burden in life
   25. Changes he or she would make if faced with the same life experiences
   26. Current life goals
   27. Effect of parents on current lifestyle, values, goals
   28. Preparation for retirement and adequacy of income
   29. Most significant aspect of life
   30. What advice would he or she give to a 20 to 25 year old
   31. Any other information the person feels free to offer
B. Data Analysis
   1. Effect of past life on current life
    a. family relationships
    b. involvement, social orientation
    c. attitudes
    d. career and retirement planning
    e. physical health
   2. How could this person have been better prepared by parents to face adult responsibilities?
   3. Summary of the degree of achievement of Erikson's developmental tasks of the life span—what evidence supports your analysis?
   4. Degree of achievement of Schuster's developmental tasks for the middle adult years

5. Degree of achievement of Schuster's developmental tasks for the late adult years
6. Developmental tasks yet to be achieved and variables that may affect successful achievement of the task(s).
7. Concept of death of self
8. Degree of satisfaction with life
9. What factors have affected this person's current health status?

C. Maximizing Potentials
   1. Identify specific activities, community agencies, family support systems, health measures, and other resources this person can use to maximize potentials.
      a. physiological
      b. cognitive
      c. affective
      d. sociocultural
      e. spiritual
   2. How can this person contribute to the lives of others at this stage of life?

Photo Credits

Figures 6–10, 7–12, 9–1C, 9–6, 9–10, 10–10, 11–2, 11–4, 11–7, 12–19, 13–8, 13–9, 13–10, 15–4, 15–6, 15–8, 16–2, 16–9, 16–10, 17–4, 17–11, 17–14, 17–17, 18–2, 18–6, 18–8, 19–2, 19–9, 19–8, 20–10B, 20–14, 20–15, 21–1, 21–3, 21–4, 21–8, 21–9, 21–10, 21–11, 21–12, 21–14, 21–15, 22–1, 22–2, 22–3, 22–5, 22–6, 22–8, 23–2, 23–3, 23–6, 23–7, 23–9, 24–1, 24–4, 24–5, 24–6, 24–9, 24–12, 24–13, 25–1, 25–2, 25–3, 25–4, 25–5, 25–6, 25–7, 25–8, 25–9, 25–10, 26–1, 26–2, 26–3, 26–6, 26–9, 27–1, 27–5, 27–6, 27–7, 27–8, 27–9, 27–11, 28–2, 28–4, 28–5, 28–6, 28–7, 28–8, 28–10A&B, 29–3, 30–2, 32–3, 32–6, 33–3, 33–6, 34–2, 34–6, 35–2, 35–3, 35–8, 36–2, 36–3, 36–4, 36–7, 37–1, 37–2, 37–4, 37–5, 37–7, 37–8, 37–9, 38–1, 38–2, 38–3, 38–4, 38–5, 38–7, 38–8, 39–2, 39–3, 39–5, 39–6, 39–10, Unit I, IV, and VI openers: Mt. Vernon News. Figures 5–1A, 6–6, 6–8, 7–3, 7–8, 8–9, 9–1B, 11–6, 31–13: © Ann West. Figure 4–8: Courtesy Mead-Johnson Laboratories. Figure 5–1B: Reprinted from Pillitteri, A. (1986) Child health nursing. (3rd ed.). Boston: Little, Brown. Figures 5–2 and 5–5: Bennett. Figure 5–3: Courtesy of the Department of Medical Photography, Children's Hospital, Buffalo, NY. Figure 6–9: Reprinted from Pillitteri, A. (1986) Child health nursing. (3rd ed.). Boston: Little, Brown. Figure 8–3: © David Powers/Stock, Boston. Figure 8–8: Columbus Dispatch. Figures 9–1D, 9–7: Candy Schultz. Figure 9–10: Glenn Jackson. Figure 10–1: © Laimute Druskis/Stock, Boston. Figure 10–4: © Elizabeth Crews/Stock, Boston. Figure 10–7: Glenn Jackson. Figure 11–8: © Elizabeth Hamlin/Stock, Boston. Figure 11–9: © Jennifer Bishop/Stock, Boston. Figure 12–4: © Karin Rosenthal/Stock, Boston. Figure 13–3: Columbus Dispatch. Figure 13–5: Glenn Jackson. Figure 13–6: Columbus Dispatch. Figure 13–7: Glenn Jackson. Figure 14–5: Frank Siteman MCMLXXIII/The Picture Cube. Figure 14–6: Glenn Jackson. Figure 15–1: © Jean-Claude Lejeune/Stock, Boston. Figure 15–7: © Peter Menzel/Stock, Boston. Figure 16–1: Lauren Green. Figure 16–3: Glenn Jackson. Figure 17–8: © Schuyler Photography/Stock, Boston. Figure 17–9: © Patricia Gross/Stock, Boston. Figures 18–3, 18–7: Glenn Jackson. Figure 19–1: Columbus, Ohio Dispatch. Figure 19–4: Sarah Putnam/The Picture Cube. Figure 19–5: Glenn Jackson. Figure 19–6: Eugene Richards/The Picture Cube. Figure 21–2: Glenn Jackson. Figure 21–13: © Elizabeth Crews/Stock, Boston. Figure 22–12: © Peter Menzel/Stock, Boston. Figure 22–13: © Gale Zucker/Stock, Boston. Figures 23–8, 24–3: Glenn Jackson. Figure 25–9: © Michael Weisbrot/Stock, Boston. Figure 25–12: © Gale Zucker/Stock, Boston. Figure 26–4: © Ed Slaman. Figure 26–7: © Spencer Grant/Stock, Boston. Figure 26–8: © Ann McQueen/Stock, Boston. Figure 26–10: Glenn Jackson. Figure 27–2: © Richard Pasley/Stock, Boston. Figure 27–3: Glenn Jackson. Figure 27–4: © Peter Menzel/Stock, Boston. Figure 28–1: Glenn Jackson. Figures 28–9, 29–2: © Frank Siteman/Stock, Boston. Figure 29–4: Athens News. Figure 29–6: Nancy A. Black/The Dixie Studio. Figure 29–7: © Ellis Herwig/Stock, Boston. Figure 29–8: © Ed Slaman. Figure 30–4: © Lionel Delevigne/Stock, Boston. Figure 31–1: American Red Cross. Figure 31–3: Reprinted from Pillitteri, A. (1986). Child Health Nursing (2nd ed.). Boston: Little, Brown. Figure 31–6: Reprinted from Pillitteri, A. (1992). Maternal-Child Health Nursing. Philadelphia: J.B. Lippincott Co. Figure 31–7: Reprinted from Pillitterri, A. (1992). Maternal-Child Health Nursing. Philadelphia: J.B. Lippincott Co. Figure 32–1: © Barbara Apel/Stock, Boston. Figure 32–2: © John Coletti/Stock, Boston. Figure 32–4: © Jean-Claude Lejeune/Stock, Boston. Figure 32–7: © Ed Slaman. Figure 32–8: Glenn Jackson. Figure 33–2: © Gale Zucker/Stock, Boston. Figure 33–4: © George Bellerose/Stock, Boston. Figure 33–5: © Olive R. Pierce/Stock, Boston. Figure 34–5: Glenn Jackson. Figure 35–4: Evelyn Maddox. Figure 36–6: © Ed Slaman. Figures 37–3, 37–6, 38–6: Glenn Jackson. Figure 39–1: Reprinted from Boyle, J. & Andrews, M. (1989). Transcultural nursing. Glenview, IL: Scott, Foresman, p. 153. Figure 39–6: Candy Schultz. Figure 39–7: © Michael Weisbrot/Stock, Boston. Unit II opener: Reprinted from Pillitteri, A. (1985). Maternal-Newborn Nursing (3rd ed.). Boston: Little, Brown, p. 599. Unit III opener: © Elizabeth Crews/Stock, Boston. Unit V opener: © Peter Vandermark/Stock, Boston. Unit VII opener: © Jean-Claude Lejeune/Stock, Boston. Unit VIII opener: © Owen Franken/Stock, Boston. Unit IX opener: Marth and Lynn Huenemann. Unit X opener: © Jean-Claude Lejeune/Stock, Boston. Unit XI opener: Glenn Jackson. Unit XIII opener: © Bob Daemmrich/Stock, Boston. Appendices opener: Columbus Dispatch.

INDEX

Names of contributing authors are italicized. Page numbers followed by f *indicate illustrations;* t *following a page number indicates tabular material;* n *following a page number indicates a note; numbers followed by* g *refer to the glossary.*

AARP (American Association of Retired Persons), driver retraining program of, 825
A-B-C theory of personality, 863–864
Abel, James, 439–442
Abortion, 653–654
Abrasion(s), due to birth trauma, 110
Abstinence, as contraceptive method, 650
Abstract reasoning, 515
Abuse. *See also* Child abuse; Sexual abuse
  elder, 728
  spouse, 727, 728
Academic skill(s), prerequisite for first grade, 278
Academic skills disorder(s), 455
Acceptance
  in anticipation of death, 402
  need for, 853
  in reaction to one's own uniqueness, 354, 355
  in response to death, 385–387
  in response to disability, 360–361, 741
Accident(s). *See also* Safety
  death of child due to, 406
  in early adulthood, 572–573, 572f
  in infancy, 162–163
  in school years, 435
Accommodation, in Piaget's theory, 19, 226–227, 312, 891
  defined, 875g
Accutane, 508
  teratogenic effects of, 75t, 77
Achievement pressure, on school-age child, 482–484
Acid–base balance, 563
Acne
  in adolescence, 508
  in early adulthood, 561
Acne cosmetica, 561
Acne rosacea, 561
Acquired immune deficiency syndrome (AIDS), congenital infection with, 78
Acrocyanosis, in newborn, 89

Acronym(s), as mnemonic device, 529
ACTH. *See* Adrenocorticotropic hormone
Action for Children's Television (ACT), 292
Action–space concept, 152
Active mastery, in Gutmann's theory, 837
Activity(-ies), stability and change in involvement in, in late adulthood, 835–836, 836f
Activity theory, 835
Actor-observer effect, 521
Adaptation
  to adulthood, 609–611
  defined, 875g
  to mainstream culture in early adulthood, 609
  in response to death, 384–387
  in response to disability, 360
Adaptive Behavior Scale, 455
Addiction. *See also* Substance abuse
  defined, 573
Adenoid(s), in school-age child, 432
ADH (antidiuretic hormone), 129
Adjustment, stability of, in late adulthood, 833–834
Adler, Alfred, 16–17, 884
  concepts and terms of, 884–885
  on development during school years, 468
  technique of inquiry of, 885
Adolescence, 491–551
  biophysical development in, 494–512
  characteristic play activities in, 328
  cognitive development in, 513–531
  concept of death in, 379t, 385–387
  conflict with parents in, cultural change and, 859–860
  defined, 494, 875g
  developmental tasks of
    Havighurst's, 895
    Schuster's, 493, 881
  growth spurt of, 501, 501f
  maximizing communication potentials in, 272

needs during, 867–868
  parenthood during, 723–724, 723f
  psychosocial development in, 532–551
  response to infant sibling during, 689, 689f
  self-direction in, 347–348
  sexuality during, 303–307
  somatic development in, 501–505
  substages of, 533–534
  in Sullivan's theory, 886
Adolescence of family, 717
  therapeutic approach in, 729f, 730
Adoption, 664–665
  bonding in, 686, 686f
  breast-feeding after, 678
  by single parent, 628
Adrenal function
  in infancy, 129
  in toddler and preschool years, 201
Adrenalin. *See* Epinephrine
Adrenocorticotropic hormone (ACTH), 129
  in initiation of labor, 672
Adult–adult relationship, in family, maintenance of, 696–698, 707–708
Adulthood. *See also* Early adulthood; Late adulthood; Middlescence
  children reaching, family relationships and, 706–707, 706f
  cognitive development during, 578–599
  defined, 601
  maximizing communication potentials in, 272–273
  moral development during, 347
  play in, 327–328
  self-direction in, 348
Adulthood of family, 717
  therapeutic approach in, 729f, 730
Advertisement(s), television, school-age child and, 479
Aesthetic anxiety, 353
Aesthetic intimacy, 607, 608
Affective approach to problems, 834